Great Soviet

Encyclopedia

Bol'shaia Sovetskaia

Entsiklopediia

A. M. Prokhorov, Editor in Chief

THIRD EDITION • VOLUME 11

Moscow, Sovetskaia Entsiklopediia Publishing House, 1973

Great Soviet

Encyclopedia

A TRANSLATION OF THE THIRD EDITION

VOLUME 11

MACMILLAN, INC.
New York
COLLIER MACMILLAN PUBLISHERS
London

Copyright © Macmillan Educational Corporation 1976

Library of Congress Catalogue Card Number 73-10680

Manufactured in the United States of America

Board of Advisors—Great Soviet Encyclopedia

Editorial and Translation Staff

Explanatory Notes

BIBLIOGRAPHIES

All bibliographies that appear in the Russian-language edition of the Encyclopedia are fully listed in the English edition. Bibliographic entries follow the same order and are listed in the same language in which they appear in the Russian work. Those works that are written in languages using the Latin alphabet are rendered as they are. Languages in other alphabets are given in the Library of Congress transliteration system for that language or, if there is no Library of Congress system, in the transliteration system used throughout the Encyclopedia.

Names of authors whose works are translated into Russian appear in the original language, not in Russian transliteration.

This method of presentation is such that all entries in the bibliographies can be checked through the National Union Catalog. Therefore, the spelling of an author's name may occasionally differ from text to bibliography; this is because in text the Russian-language edition spells the names of all peoples of the Soviet Union in Russian but in bibliographies sometimes lists their works in the original languages. Insofar as possible, the English edition transliterates names in the bibliographies from the original language into the Library of Congress system (or the system used throughout) and gives this variant transliteration in brackets.

The bibliographies are selective and serve as sources for the authority of the article and for additional information. They contain suggestions for further reading, sources for historical and current data, and sometimes further bibliographies.

Usually the structure of the bibliographies reflects the structure and content of the article. That is, general works are listed first, followed by more specialized references. In long bibliographies for articles dealing with Soviet views on broad subjects, a system is generally followed whereby the classic reference works of Marxism-Leninism are given first, followed by works in Russian or other languages of the Soviet Union, then foreign language publications, and, finally, reading lists. The entries may be arranged alphabetically by author or chronologically; they may also be listed under clearly defined subject fields. On Western subjects, foreign authors are sometimes listed first.

Bibliographies of articles on people are divided into two parts: WORKS—that is, works written by the subject; and REFERENCES—that is, works about the subject. Under REFERENCES, the publications in Russian are listed first, then foreign works in Russian translation, and then foreign works in all other languages. If a publication appears in several editions, either the first or most valuable edition (from a scholarly point of view) is presented.

ARTICLE NUMBER CODE

To assist those readers who wish to refer to the Russian edition, each article has been coded with a number for easy reference to the *Bol'shaia Sovetskaia Entsiklopediia*. For example, the article "Alexander Nevsky" has the number [1–1199–2]. This means that in the Russian edition the article may be found in Volume 1, column 1199, second article in the column.

ABBREVIATIONS

Following is a list of frequently used special abbreviations:

ACP(B)—All-Union Communist Party (Bolshevik)
ASSR—Autonomous Soviet Socialist Republic
CPSU—Communist Party of the Soviet Union
RCP(B)—Russian Communist Party (Bolshevik)
RSDLP—Russian Social Democratic Labor Party
RSDLP(B)—Russian Social Democratic Labor Party (Bolshevik)
RSFSR—Russian Soviet Federated Socialist Republic
SSR—Soviet Socialist Republic
Izbr. proizv. or *soch.*—selected works
Izbr. voen. proizv.—selected military writings
Poln. sobr. soch.—complete collected works
Sobr. soch.—collected works
Soch.—works

TRANSLITERATION

For the languages of the USSR we are using the Library of Congress transliteration system when available and modified to eliminate diacritical marks. Languages for which there is no Library of Congress system, for example, Tadzhik, are transliterated according to the system developed by Professor Edward Allworth in *Nationalities of the Soviet East* (Columbia University Press, 1971). The only exceptions are for proper names so familiar in English that to transliterate them otherwise would mislead the user. For works cited in text we have translated the titles so that the full sense of the article will be preserved. The transliteration table used throughout the work for Russian Cyrillic is given below.

Articles—Volume 11

The articles in the Russian-language Bol'shaia Sovetskaia Entsiklopediia *are alphabetized according to the Cyrillic alphabet; in our edition, they are translated and alphabetized within each volume according to the English alphabet. Thus, the articles in Volume 11 of the Russian edition are listed below; they run from A through Z in English because of the title changes that occur when they are translated. In this complete list of articles for Volume 11, the astericks indicate those titles that appear in the Russian edition only; these constitute only 1 percent of the total wordage of the volume.*

Abutilon
Advanced Capital
Aggravated Crime
Amplifier Stage
Anabasis Aphylla
Arenaria
Barn Swallow
Barracks
Barracks Communism
Beefwood
Beet Storage Rot
Black Beetles
Boar
*Board
Boxer Rebellion
Branchiura
Brants
Brassica
Bright-drawn Steel
Broadtail
Bulrush
Bureaucratisms
Burl
Ca
Caatinga
Cabala
Caballero
Caballero Calderón, Eduardo
Cabanatuan
Cabanis, Pierre-Jean-Georges
Cabaret
Cabbage Aphid
Cabbage Cutworm
Cabbage Palm
Cabernet
Cabet, Étienne
Cabeza de Vaca, Álvar Núñez
Cabimas
*Cabin
Cabinet
Cabinet Lands
Cabinet of His Imperial Majesty
Cabinet Schools
Cabiri
Cable
Cable, Electrical
Cable Box
Cable Conduit System
Cable Crane
Cable Finder
Cable Layer
*Cable Length
Cable Production
Cable Saw
Cable Ship
Cable Terminals
Cable Theory
Cable Transmission
Cableway
Cabo Branco

Cabochiens
Cabomba
Cabombaceae
Cabot (Italian navigators)
*Cabot (strait)
Cabotage
Cabral, Amilcar
Cabral, Luis
Cabral, Pedro Alvares
Cabrera y Griñó, Ramón
*Cabriolet
Cacao
Caccia
Caccini, Giulio
*Cáceres
*Cacheting
Cachexia
Cachin, Marcel
Cachucha
Cacique
Cacodyl
Cacomistle
Cacophony
Cactus
Cadaverine
Cadence
Cadet Corps
Cadets
Cádiz
Cádiz, Bay Of
Cádiz, Gulf of
Cádiz Constitution of 1812
Cádiz Cortes
Cadmium
Cadmium Plating
Cadorna, Luigi
Cadoudal, Georges
Cadres
Caen
Caetani, Leone
Caetano, Marcello
*C.A.F.
Caftan
Cagayan de Oro
Cagliari
Cagoulards
Caguas
Cahiers du Communisme
Cahors (city)
Cahors (wine)
Caibarién
Caid
Caillaux, Joseph Marie Auguste
Caiman
Cain
Cairo
Cairo, University of
Cairo Conference of 1943
Cairoli, Benedetto
Cajamarca

Cajuput Tree
Cakchiquel
Calabash
Calabria (region)
Calabria (peninsula)
Caladium
Calah
Calais
Calame, Alexandre
Calamian Islands
Calamine
Calamitales
Calanoida
Calatrava, Order Of
Calbayog
Calbe
Calceolaria
Calcex
Calcicoles
Calciferols
Calcifuges
Calcination Of Straw
Calcinosis
Calciphyre
Calcite
Calcium
Calcium Bromide
Calcium Carbide
Calcium Carbonate
Calcium Chloride
Calcium Fluoride
Calcium Hydroxide
Calcium Nitrate
Calcium Oxide
Calcium Sulfate
Calcium Sulfide
Calculation, Cost
Calcutta
Calcutta, University Of
Caldas
Calderas
Calderón de la Barca, Pedro
Calean
Caledonian Canal
Caledonian Folding
Calendar (accounts)
Calendar (dates)
Calendar Disturbances
Calendar Poetry
Calender
Calendering
Calends
Calendula
Calgary
Cali
Caliber
Calibration
Calibrator
California
California, Gulf of

California, University of
California Current
California Financial Groups
California Indians
California Oil-bearing Region
Californium
Caligula
Caliper
Caliper Logging
Callao
Callas, Maria
Callatis
Calles, Plutarco Elias
Callicrates
Calligraphy
Callimachus
Callimico
Callinus
Calliope
Callistephus
Callose
Callot, Jacques
Callus
Calmalloy
Calmette, Albert
Calmette, Joseph
Calomel
Calonne, Charles Alexandre de
Caloocan
Caloric Value of Food
Calorie
Calorimeter
Calorimeter, Ionization
Calorimetry
Calotes
Calpurnius Siculus, Titus
Calque
Caltanissetta
Caltha
Calvados
Calville Blanche
Calvin, John
Calvin, Melvin
Calvinism
Calvino, Italo
Calvo Doctrine
Calycanthaceae
Calypso
Calyptrogen
Calzabigi, Ranieri
Cam, Diogo
Camagüey (province)
Camagüey (city)
Camargue
Camarilla
Camassia
Camau
Cambay, Gulf of
Cambiform Cells
Cambium
Cambodia
Cambodian Inscriptions
Cambodian Plain
Cambrai
Cambyses II
Camden
Camélinat, Zephyrenne
Camellia
Cameralism

Camerarius, Rudolph Jacob
Cameron, Charles
Cameron, Julia Margaret
Cameron, Verney Lovett
Cameroon (republic)
Cameroon (estuary)
Cameroun
Camillus, Marcus Furius
Camisards
Camisole
Camões, Luís Vaz de
Camorra
Camotes
Camouflage Painting
Camouflet
Camouflet Blasting
Campaign
Campana, Dino
Campanella, Tommaso
Campanella
Campania
Campanian Stage
Campanile
Campeche (state)
Campeche (city)
Campeche, Bay of
Campen, Jacob van
Campert, Jan Remco Theodoor
Cam Pha
Camphausen, Ludolf
Camphene
Camphene Rearrangements
Camphor
Camphoraceous Plants
Camphorosma
Camphor Tree
Campignian Culture
Campin, Robert
Campina Grande
Campinas
Campo
Campo Formio, Treaty of (1797)
Campo Grande
Campolon
Campomanes, Pedro Rodriguez
Campos
Camptonite
Camus, Albert
Canada
Canadian Anticyclone
Canadian Arctic Archipelago
Canadian Basin
Canadian Broadcasting Corporation
Canadian Imperial Bank of Commerce
Canadian Labour Congress
Canadian Press
Canadian River
Canadians
Canadian Tribune
Canaigre
Canal
Canaletto
Canals, International
Cananea
Canaries Current
Canaris, Walter Wilhelm
Canary
Canary Islands
Canavalia

Canberra
Cancan
Cancioneiro
Cancrinite
Candau, Marcolino Gomes
Candela, Felix
*Candelabrum
Candeloro, Giorgio
Candia, Alberto
Candidate
Candidate Minimum Examinations
Candidate of Sciences
Candidiasis
Candilis, Georges
Canclones
Canga Argüelles, José
Canisius, Peter
Canister
Canna
Cannae
Cannes
Cannes Conference (1922)
Cannibalism
Canning, George
Cannizzaro, Stanislao
Cannizzaro Reaction
Cannoneer
Cannula
Cano, Alonso
Canoas
Canoe
Canon (art)
Canon (music)
Canon (religious literature)
Canonical Ensemble
Canonization
Canon Law
Canopic Jar
Canossa
Canova, Antonio
Cánovas del Castillo, Antonio
Canrobert, François
Cantabile
Cantabrian Mountains
Cantabrians
Cantacuzeni
Cantal (department)
Cantal (volcano)
Cantata
Canth, Minna
Cantharidin
Cantharophily
Can Tho
Cantilena
Cantillon, Richard
Canton (city)
Canton (political division)
Canton Administration in Bashkiria
Cantonists
Cantor, Georg
Cantor, Moritz
Cantor
Cantor's Axiom
Cantor Ternary Set
Cantus Firmus
Canudos Peasant Rebellion (1896–97)
Canuleius, Gaius
*Canvas
Can Vuong

Canyon
Canzone
Canzonet
Cao Bang
Capablanca, José Raúl
Capadocia, Guillermo
Cape Astronomical Observatory
Cape Basin
Cape Colony
Cape Folded Zone
*Capella
Cape Mountains
Cape of Good Hope Province
Cape Region
Capetians
Cap-Haïtien
Capillariases
Capillaries
Capillaroscopy
Capillary Circulation
Capillary Condensation
Capillary Phenomena
*Capillitium
Capital (architecture)
Capital (economics)
Capital Investments
Capitalism
Capitalist Cycle
Capitalization
Capital Script
Capitania
Capitano del Popolo
Capitol
Capitoline
Capitoline Triad
Capitularies
Capitulation
Capitulations
Capodimonte
Capo d'Istria, John
Caponier
Caporetto
Capote, Truman
Cappadocia
Capparaceae
Capparis
Capping
Capra, Frank
Capri
Capriccio
Caprification
Capri School
Caprivi, Leo von
Caprolactam
Capsian Culture
*Capstan
Capsulated Microorganisms
Capsule
Capsule Hydroelectric Generator Unit
Captain
Capua
Capuana, Luigi
Capuchin
Capuchins
Carabineers
Caracal (city)
Caracal (animal)
Caracalla
Caracara

Caracas
Caradocian Stage
Caragea, Boris
Caragiale, Ion Luca
Caramanlis, Constantine
Caramel
Carantania
Caraş-Severin
Carassius
Carat
Carathéodory, Constantin
Caravaggio, Michelangelo Merisi da
Caravaggism
*Caravan
Caravansary
Caravaque, Louis
Caravel
Carbamide Glue
Carbamide Resins
Carbanions
Carbazole
Carbenes
Carbides
Carbine
Carbinol Resins
*Carbo-
Carbocyclic Compounds
Carbohemoglobin
Carbolite
*Carbonado
Carbonari
Carbonates
Carbonates, Natural
*Carbonation
Carbonatites
Carbonatization
Carbonic Anhydrase
Carboniferous System (Period)
Carbonium Ions
Carboranes
Carbothermy
Carboxyhemoglobin
Carboxylases
Carboxylate Rubbers
Carboxylation
Carboxylic Acids
Carboxymethyl Cellulose
Carboxypeptidases
Carbromal
Carbuncle
Carburetor
Carburization Process for Scrap
Carcassonne
Carchemish
Carcinogens
Cardamon
Cardamon Hills
Cardan Mechanism
Cardano, Geronimo
Cardano's Formula
Cardan Shaft
Cardboard
Cardboard Machine
Cardboard Production
Card Clothing
Cárdenas, Lázaro
Cárdenas
Cardiff
*Cardigan (county)

Cardigan (bay)
Cardinal (church official)
Cardinal (bird)
Cardinal Points of an Optical System
Cardinal Veins
*Cardio-
Cardiocrinum
Cardiography
Cardiology
Cardiology, Institute of
Cardiosclerosis
Cardiospasm
Cardiotonsillar Syndrome
Cardoso, Onelio Jorge
Cardox
Cardozo, Benjamin Nathan
Carducci, Giosue
Carducho, Vicente
Career
Carême, Maurice
Caria
Cariban Languages
Caribbean Andes
Caribbean Current
Caribbean Sea
Cariboo
Caribou
Caribs
Caricature
Carics
Carinthia (region)
Carinthia (province)
Carleman, Tage Gillis Torsten
Carleton, William
Carletonville
Carlisle
Carlists
Carlist Wars
Carlota-Joaquina
Carlsbad
Carlsbad Caverns
Carlstadt, Andreas
Carludovica
Carlyle, Thomas
Carmagnole
Carman, William Bliss
*Carmarthenshire
Carmel, Mount
Carmelites
Carmine
Carmona, Antonio Oscar de Fragoso
Carnac
Carnallite
Carnap, Rudolf
*Carnarvonshire
Carnatic
*Carnation
Carné, Marcel
Carneades
Carnegie
Carnegiea
Carnian Stage
Carnic Alps
Carnitine
Carnival
Carnosauria
Carnosine
Carnot, Lazare Nicolas Marguerite
Carnot, Marie François Sadi

Catarrhal Fever of Sheep
Catarrh of the Respiratory Tract
Catastrophism, Theory of
Catatonia
Cateau-Cambrésis, Treaty of (1559)
Catechins
Catechism
Catecholamines
Catechu
Categorical Imperative
Categories
Category
Category Telegram
Catelectrotonus
*Catenoid
Catharobionts
Cathars
Catharsis
Cathelineau, Jacques
Cathepsins
Catheterization
Cathetometer
Cathode
Cathode Drop
Cathode Follower
Cathode Luminescence
Cathode Sputtering
Catholic Action
Catholicism
Catholic League (1576)
Catholic League (1609)
Catholicos
Catiline
Cationic Dyes
Cato
Cats, Jacob
Cattaneo, Carlo
Cattleya
Catullus, Gaius Valerius
Cauca (department)
Cauca (river)
Caucasian Bureau of the Central
    Committee of the RCP (Bolshevik)
Caucasian Bees
Caucasian Brown Cattle
Caucasian Cattle
Caucasian Committee
Caucasian Fine-wooled Sheep
Caucasian Languages
Caucasian Line Cossack Host
Caucasian Mineral Waters Region
Caucasian Preserve
Caucasian Race
Caucasian Regional Committee of the RCP
    (Bolshevik)
Caucasian Union Committee of the
    RSDLP
Caucasian War of 1817–64
Caucasus
Caudillo
Caudine Forks
Caulerpa
*Cauliflory
Caupolicán
Caura
Causalgia
Caustic Surface
Caustobioliths
Cauvery

Cavaignac, Godefroy Éléonore Louis
Cavaignac, Louis Eugène
Cavalcanti, Alberto
Cavalcanti, Guido
Cavalieri, Francesco Bonaventura
Cavalieri's Principle
Cavaliers
Cavalli, Francesco
Cavallini, Pietro
Cavalry
Cavatina
Cavendish, Henry
Cavendish Laboratory
Cavern
Cavernitis
Cavitation
Cavite
Cavos, Catterino
Cavour, Camillo Benso di
Caxias do Sul
Cayenne
Cayeux, Lucien
Cayman Islands
Cenotypal Rocks
Cenozoic Era
Central Valley
*Chamber (adjective)
*Chamber (noun)
Chamber (mining)
Chamber Collegium
Chamber Furnace
Chamberlain
Chamber Music
Chancellary of Secret Investigations
Chancellor
Channel (information)
Channel (information theory)
Channeling of Charged Particles in
    Crystals
Channel-type Reactor
Chapel
Chaplain
Chapter
Charlemagne
Charles (kings of England)
Charles (kings of France)
Charles (kings of the Holy Roman Empire)
Charles (kings of Sweden)
Charles (archduke of Austria)
Charles the Bold
Charles I (emperor of Austria)
Charles I (king of Hungary)
Charles I (king of Naples-Sicily)
Charles I (king of Portugal)
Charles II (Charles the Bald)
Charles III (Charles the Fat)
Charles Albert
Charles D'Orléans
Charles Emmanuel I
Charles Martel
Checkrow Planting
Chelydridae
Chestnut
Chestnut Soils
Cirque
Cist
Coal, Hard
Coal Tar
Cockatoo

Cock of the Rock
Cocoa Butter
Collation Map
Combustion Chamber
Commercial Bank of Italy
Communications Cable
Communications Cable Junction Box
Communications Channel
Compartment Furnaces
*Conductor
Constitutional Democrats
Contact
Contribution to the Critique of Political
    Economy, A
*Cornice
Corporal
Cossack
Cossacks
Cossack Schools
Costa Cabral, António Bernardo da
Costmary
Cottony-cushion Scale
Cough
Court Musician
Cowper, Edward Alfred
*Cowper Stove
Crambe
Crankcase
Crayon Manner
Cuando
Cuanza
Cuban Crisis (1962)
*Cumberland (county)
Cumberland (sound)
Cumberland Plateau
Cumbrian Mountains
Cunningham, Walter
Cuttack
Cutter
Cyma, Ionic
Cyprinidae
Cyprinodontidae
Defectoscopy, Capillary
Dental Caries
Diagrammatic Map
Diamondback Moth
Domesticated Carp
Don Carlos
Don Carlos Mayor
Don Carlos Menor
*Dried Apricots
Drop
Drops
Dwarfed Males
Dwarf Fruit Tree Cultivation
Dwarfism
Dwarf Plants
Dwarf Star
Dynamoelectric Stage
Eaton, Cyrus
Edge-punched Card
*Edging
Ejection Seat
Eland, Common
*Elm
Entroprocta
Erythronium
Eton
Falconets

Kabal'nye Kholopy
Kabanov, Viktor Aleksandrovich
Kabarda-Balkar Autonomous Soviet
  Socialist Republic
Kabarda-Balkar University
Kabarda-Cherkess
Kabardinian Horse
Kabardinian Plain
Kabardinka
Kabardino-Balkarskaia Pravda
Kabardins
Kab ibn Zuhayr
Kabir
Kableshkov, Todor Lulchov
Kablits, Iosif Ivanovich
Kablukov, Ivan Alekseevich
Kablukov, Nikolai Alekseevich
Kabuki
Kabul (city)
Kabul (river)
Kabulova, Saodat
Kabwe
Kabyles
Kabylia
Kachalov, Nikolai Nikolaevich
Kachalov, Vasilii Ivanovich
Kachanovka
Kachanovskii, Vladimir Vasil'evich
Kachari
Kachenovskii, Dmitrii Ivanovich
Kachenovskii, Mikhail Trofimovich
Kachin Language
Kachins
Kachinskaia Step'
*Kachin State
Kachiry
Kachkanar (city)
Kachkanar (mountains)
Kachug
Kachura, Iakov Dem'ianovich
Kacprzak, Marcin
Kaczawskie Góry
Kadada
Kadaia
Kádár, János
Kaden-Bandrowski, Juliusz
Kadesh
Kadi
Kadievka
Kadłubek, Wincenty
Kádner, Otakar
Kadnikov
Kadochnikov, Pavel Petrovich
Kadom
Kadoma
Kadomtsev, Boris Borisovich
Kadomtsev
Kadoshkino
Kadri, Fat'ma Kadyrovna
Kadui
Kaduna
Kadyi
Kadykchan
Kadyr-Guliam
Kadyri, Abdulla
Kadyrov, Gaptrakhman
  Faizurakhmanovich
Kadzharan
Kadzherom

Kadzhi-sai
Kaédi
Kafa
Kafan
Kafarov, Petr Ivanovich
Kafarov, Viktor Viacheslavovich
Kafedra
Kafengauz, Berngard Borisovich
Kaffa
Kaffir
Kaffir Wars
Kafirnigan
Kafka, Franz
Kafr al-Zayyat
Kafue (national park)
Kafue (river)
Kagal'nik
Kagame, Alexis
Kagamigahara
Kagan, Iurii Moiseevich
Kagan, Veniamin Fedorovich
Kagan (city)
Kagan (title)
Kagarlyk
Kagawa
Kagera (national park)
Kagera (river)
Kagoshima (prefecture)
Kagoshima (city)
Kagu
Kagul (city)
Kagul (lake)
Kagul (river)
Kahn, Louis
Kahun
Kai
Kaiakent
Kaiakent-Khorochoi Culture
Kaichen
Kaierkan
Kaieteur Falls
K'aifeng
Kaigorodov, Dmitrii Nikiforovich
Kailali
Kailas
*Kainan
Kainar, Josef
Kainazarova, Surakan
Kainda
Kaindy-Katta
Kainite
Kainuunselkä
Kainz, Josef
K'aip'ing
Kairak
Kairakkum
Kairakkum Reservoir
Kairakkum Sites
Kairakty
Kairouan
Kairov, Ivan Andreevich
Kaiser, Georg
*Kaiser
Kaiserslautern
Kaišiadoris
Kaitags
Kaitarma
Kaits
Kaitukov, Georgii Kharitonovich

Kaiumov, Malik Kaiumovich
Kajava, Viljo
Kakabadze, David Nestorovich
Kakabadze, Polikarp Malkhazovich
Kakaidy
Kakharov, Abdulakhad
Ka-khem
Kakhet
Kakhetia
Kakhetin Rebellion of 1659
Kakhi
Kakhkhar, Abdulla
Kakhovka
Kakhovka Base of Operations
Kakhovka Reservoir
Kakhovskii, Petr Grigor'evich
Kakinada
Kakogawa
Kaktynš, Adolf
Kakurin, Nikolai Evgen'evich
Kala
Kalaa Beni-hammad
Kalach
Kalachinsk
Kalachinskii, Mikhas' Ivanovich
Kalach-na-Donu
Kalachov, Nikolai Vasil'evich
Kalach Upland
Kaladze, Karlo Razhdenovich
Kalahari Desert
Kalahari Gemsbok National Park
Kalaidovich, Konstantin Fedorovich
Kalai-mir
Kalai-mor
Kalakan
Kalakhana
Kalakutskii, Nikolai Veniaminovich
Kalamai
Kalamazoo
Kalambo Falls (archaeological site)
Kalambo Falls (waterfall)
Kalamita
Kalamitskii Gulf
Kalanchak
Kalandarishvili, Nestor Aleksandrovich
Kalangui
Kalantar, Levan Aleksandrovich
Kalar (River)
Kalar (mountains)
Kalarash
Kalashnikov, Mikhail Timofeevich
Kalashnikov, Vasilii Ivanovich
Kalashnikovo
Kalata
Kalatozov, Mikhail Konstantinovich
Kalaus
Kalbinskii
Kalchev, Kamen
Kal-Do Process
Kaldor, Nicholas
Kalecki, Michał
Kaledin, Aleksei Maksimovich
Kaledin Revolt
Kaleidoscope
Kalesnik, Stanislav Vikent'evich
Kalevala (urban-type settlement)
Kalevala (epic)
Kalevipoeg
Kalf, Willem

Kal'gin, Anatolii Nikolaevich
Kalgoorlie
Kali
Kal'ia
Kaliaev, Ivan Platonovich
Kaliaev, Sandzhi Kaliaevich
Kaliakra
Kalian
Kaliazin
Kaliazin Petition
Kalibek
Kalidasa
Kalila and Dimna
Kalim
Kalima
Kalimantan
Kalinčiak, Jan
Kalinga
Kalinin, Anatolii Veniaminovich
Kalinin, Gennadii Pavlovich
Kalinin, Konstantin Alekseevich
Kalinin, Mikhail Ivanovich
Kalinin (city)
Kalinin (urban-type settlement)
Kalinin, University of
Kalininabad
Kalinin Children's Literature Printing
    Combine
Kalinin Cotton Textile Combine
Kalinin Dramatic Theater
Kalinin Glaciation
Kaliningrad (city, Kaliningrad Oblast)
Kaliningrad (city, Moscow Oblast)
Kaliningrad, University of
Kaliningrad Oblast
Kaliningrad Seaport
Kaliningrad Theater
Kalininkend
Kalinino (urban-type settlement, Armenian
    SSR)
Kalinino (urban-type settlement, RSFSR)
Kalinin Oblast
Kalinin Printing Combine
Kalininsk (city, RSFSR)
Kalininsk (city, Moldavian SSR)
Kalininskii
Kalininskoe
Kalinka, Walerian
Kalinkovichi
Kalinnikov, Vasilii Sergeevich
Kalino
Kalinovka (urban-type settlement, Vinnitsa
    Oblast, Ukrainian SSR)
Kalinovka (urban-type settlement, Kiev
    Oblast, Ukrainian SSR)
Kalinovo (urban-type settlement, Ukrainian
    SSR)
Kalinovo (urban-type settlement, RSFSR)
Kalinovskaia, Valentina Fedorovna
Kalinovskii, Konstantin Bronislavovich
Kalinovskii, Konstantin Semenovich
Kalisz
Kalisz Alliance Treaty of 1813
Kalita
Kalitin, Nikolai Nikolaevich
Kalitskii, Kazimir Petrovich
Kalitva
Kalix
Kalka

Kalkaman
Kalkan
Kalki
Kallai, Gyula
Kallaste
Kállay, Miklós
Kallikreins
Kallima
Kallio, Kyösti
Kálmán, Emmerich
Kalmar
Kalmar, Union of
Kalmarsund
Kalmar War of 1611–13
Kal'mius
Kal'mius Sakma
Kalmyk
Kalmyk Autonomous Soviet Socialist
    Republic
Kalmyk Cattle
Kalmykov, Betal Edykovich
Kalmykov, Valerii Dmitrievich
Kalmykova, Aleksandra Mikhailovna
Kalmyks
Kalmyk University
Kalnberzin, Ian Eduardovich
Kalnciems
Kalnin', Alfred Ianovich
Klanin', Arvid Ianovich
Kalnin, Oskar Iur'evich
Kal'ning, Otto Ivanovich
Kálnoky, Gustav
Kalnroze, Valdis
Kalnyn', Eduard Fridrikhovich
Kal'o, Rikhard Ianovich
Kaloian
Kalomiris, Manolis
Kalong
Kalos Limen
Kalousek, Josef
Kaltan
Kaluga (city)
Kaluga (fish)
Kaluga Oblast
Kalush
Kalvarija
Kama (deity)
Kama (urban-type settlement)
Kama (river)
Kama Hydroelectric System
Kamaishi
Kamakura
Kamal, Galiaskar
Kamal, Sharif
Kamalov, Foma Georgievich
Kamanin, Nikolai Petrovich
Kama Paper and Pulp Combine
Kama Reservoir
Kamarhati
Kamarovskii, Leonid Alekseevich
Kamasintsy
Kama Truck Plant
Kamban, Gudmundur Jónson
Kambarka
Kamberi
Kambuja
Kamchadaly
Kamchatka (peninsula)
Kamchatka (river)

Kamchatka Current
Kamchatka Gulf
Kamchatka Oblast
Kamchatka Sea
Kamchiia
Kamelik
Kamenets
Kamenetskii
Kamenets-Podol'skii
Kamenev, Lev L'vovich
Kamenev, Sergei Sergeevich
Kamenka (city, Ukrainian SSR)
Kamenka (urban-type settlement,
    Moldavian SSR)
Kamenka (urban-type settlement, Primor'e
    Krai, RSFSR)
Kamenka (urban-type settlement,
    Arkhangel'sk Oblast, RSFSR)
Kamenka (urban-type settlement, Ivanovo
    Oblast, RSFSR)
Kamenka (urban-type settlement, Voronezh
    Oblast, RSFSR)
Kamenka (city)
Kamenka (river)
Kamenka-Bugskaia
Kamenka-Dneprovskaia
Kamenka Gorodishche
Kamen'-Kashirskii
Kamennaia Mogila
Kamen'-na-Obi
Kamennoe
Kamennogorsk
Kamennomostskii
Kamennyi Brod
Kamenolomni
Kamenov, Evgeni Ganchev
Kamensk
Kamenskii, Fedor Fedorovich
Kamenskii, Grigorii Nikolaevich
Kamenskii, Valentin Aleksandrovich
Kamenskii, Vasilii Vasil'evich
Kamenskoe Plato
Kamensk-Shakhtinskii
Kamensk-Ural'skii
Kamer-Fur'erskii Zhurnal
Kamer-Iunker
Kamerlingh Onnes, Heike
Kamernyi Teatr
Kames
Kameshkovo
Kamieński, Henryk
Kamieński, Maciej
Kamikaze
Kamil, Mustafa
Kaminaljuyú
Kamiński, Kazimierz
Kaminskii, Anton Antonovich
Kaminskii, Grigorii Naumovich
Kaminskii
Kamkov, Boris Davidovich
Kamlanie
Kamleia
Kammari, Mikhail Davidovich
Kammerer, Paul
Kamno
Kamo (pseudonym)
Kamo (city)
Kamo (river)
Kamo Chomei

Kamov, Nikolai Il'ich
Kamozin, Pavel Mikhailovich
Kampala
Kampar
Kampen
Kampinos
Kampot
Kamskoe Ust'e
Kamunta
Kamyl'
Kamyshany
Kamyshevakha (urban-type settlement,
   Voroshilovgrad Oblast, Ukrainian
   SSR)
Kamyshevakha (urban-type settlement,
   Zaporozh'e Oblast, Ukrainian SSR)
Kamyshin
Kamyshlov
Kamyshovaia Bukhta
Kamyshovyi Range
Kamysh-Samar Lakes
Kamysh-Zaria
Kamyslybas
Kan, Sergei Borisovich
Kan
Kanagawa
Kan'ami
Kanamycin
Kanarese
Kanaris, Konstantinos
Kanash
Kanászduda
Kanatchikov, Semen Ivanovich
Kanazawa
Kanchalan
Kanchenjunga
Kanchipuram
Kandahar
Kandalaksha
Kandalaksha Bay
Kandalaksha Coast
Kandalaksha Preserve
Kandalov, Innokentii Ivanovich
Kandava
Kandeevka (Kandievka) Uprising of 1861
Kandelaki, Nikolai Porfir'evich
Kandelaki, Vladimir Arkad'evich
Kandev, Lambi Stanchev
Kandiba, Boris Nikolaevich
Kandil'-Kitaika
Kandil'-Sinap
Kadinskii, Viktor Khrisanfovich
Kandinsky, Wassily
Kandó, Kálmán
Kandry
Kandy
Kanem-Bornu Empire
Kanev
Kanev Reservoir
Kanevskii, Aminadav Moiseevich
Kan Forest-Steppe
Kangalassy
Kang Gam Chang
Kanggye
K'anghsi
Kanghwa, Treaty of
Kanghwa Man
Kangiui
Kangly

Kangting
Kangyu Culture
K'ang Yu-wei
Kanibadam
Kanimekh
Kanin, Aleksandr Ignat'evich
Kanin Nos
Kanin Peninsula
Kanishka
Kanitel'
Kankaev, Bakhtiar
Kankan
Kankles
Kankrin, Egor Frantsevich
Kankrin Reform
Kankunskii
Kanna, Ion
Kannabikh, Iurii Vladimirovich
Kannada
Kannada Literature
Kannel
Kano (city)
Kano (school of painting)
Kanonnikov, Innokentii Ivanovich
Kanpur
Kansai (economic region)
Kansai (urban-type settlement)
Kansan Uutiset
Kansas
Kansas City
Kansas-Nebraska Act of 1854
Kansas River
Kansk
Kansk-Achinsk Coal Basin
Kanskoe Belogor'e
Kant, Hermann
Kant, Immanuel
Kant (urban-type settlement)
Kant (song)
Kantegir
Kantele
Kantemir, Antiokh Dmitrievich
Kantemir, Dmitrii Konstantinovich
Kantemirov
Kanthal
Kantokuen
Kantonist Schools
Kantorovich, Leonid Vital'evich
Kant's Hypothesis
Kanun
Kanuri
Kanuri-Tubu
Kaoko Veld
Kaolack
Kaolin
Kaolinite
Kaolinization
Kapchagai
Kapchagai Reservoir
Kapchinskii, Anatolii Konstantinovich
Kapeliushnikov, Matvei Alkumovich
Kapelldiener
Kapel'meister
Kapfenberg
Kapiev, Effendi Mansurovich
Kapishche
Kapital, Das
Kapitonov, Ivan Vasil'evich
Kapitonov, Viktor Arsen'evich

Kapitsa, Andrei Petrovich
Kapitsa, Petr Leonidovich
Kapitsa's Law
Kapitsa's Temperature Jump
Kaplan, Viktor
Kaplanian, Rach'ia Nikitovich
Kapler, Aleksei Iakovlevich
Kaplun, Sergei Il'ich
Kaplunovskii, Vladimir Pavlovich
Kapnist, Vasilii Vasil'evich
Kapok
Kaposvár
Kapova Cave
Kapp, Artur Iosifovich
Kapp, Eugen
Kappel', Vladimir Oskarovich
Kappel, Wars of
Kapp Putsch of 1920
Kapsukas
*Kaptal
Kapterev, Petr Fedorovich
Kapteyn, Jacobus Cornelius
Kapuas
Kapur, Raj
Kapustin, Mikhail Nikolaevich
Kapustinskii, Anatolii Fedorovich
Kapustin Yar
Kapustnik
Kaputdzhukh
Kaputikian, Sil'va Barunakovna
Kara
Karabagi, Usta Gambar
Karabagliar
Karabair Horse
Karabakh
Karabakh Horse
Karabakh Khanate
Karabakh Upland
Kara-Balty
Karabanovo
Karabas
Karabash (city, RSFSR)
Karabash (urban-type settlement, Tatar
   ASSR)
Karabekaul
Karabi-Iaila
Karabil'
Kara-Bogaz-Gol
Karabudakhkent Burial Grounds
Karabük
Karabulak (urban-type settlement, Kazakh
   SSR)
Karabulak (urban-type settlement,
   Chechen-Ingush ASSR)
Kara Buran Kol
Karaburnu
Karachaevsk
Karachai-Balkar
Karachai-Cherkess Autonomous Oblast
Karachais
Karachala
Karachev
Karachi (city)
Karachi (health resort)
Karadag
Karadam
Karadar'ia
Karadzha, Stefan Todorov
Karadžić, Vuk Stefanović

Karaeri
Karaev, Kara Abul'faz ogly
Karagailinskii
Karagaily
Karaganda
Karaganda, University of
Karaganda Coal Basin
Karaganda Metallurgical Combine
Karaganda Oblast
Karaganov, Aleksandr Vasil'evich
Karageorge
Karageorgevich
Karagie
Karagin Gulf
Karagin Island
Karagodeuashkh
Karagöz
Karai
Karain
Karaiskakes, Georgios
Karaite
Karaites
Karajan, Herbert von
Kara-Kala
Kara-Kalpak
Kara-Kalpak Autonomous Soviet Socialist
    Republic
Kara-Kalpaks
Kara-Kalpak Steppe
Karakeev, Kurman-Gali
Karakhan, Lev Mikhailovich
Karakhanids
Karakhanid State
Karakitai (people)
Karakitai (state)
Karakoin
Karakol
Karakoram
Karakorum
Kara-Koyunlu
Karakozov, Dmitrii Vladimirovich
Kara-Kul' (urban-type settlement)
Karakul (oasis)
Kara-Kul' (lake)
Karakul Breed
Karakul Breeding, Institute of
Karakum
Karakum Canal
Karakurt
Karalaev, Saiakbai
Karaliichev, Angel
Karaman
Karami, Rashid Abd al'Hamid
Karamian, Artashes Ivanovich
Karamian, Erazm Aleksandrovich
Karamuran
Kara-Murza, Georgii Sergeevich
Karamysh
Karamzin, Nikolai Mikhailovich
Karandash
Karandeev, Konstantin Borisovich
Karanovo
Kara Penal Colony
Karas, Vjekoslav
Karas
Kara Sea
Karaslavov, Georgi
Karasor
Kara-su (city)

Kara-su (river)
Karasubazar
Karasuk (city)
Karasuk (river)
Karasuk Culture
Karataev, Mukhamedzhan Kozhaspaevich
Karatal
Karatau (city)
Karatau (urban-type settlement)
Karatau (mountain range, southern
    Kazakh SSR)
Karatau (mountain range, RSFSR)
Karatau (mountains, Gur'ev Oblast,
    Kazakh SSR)
Karatau Phosphorite-bearing Basin
Karate
Karateginskii Range
Karatepe
Karaton
Kara Tragedy
Karatsiupa, Nikita Fedorovich
Karatygin, Viacheslav Gavrilovich
Karatygin
Karaugom
Karaunkiur
Karavaev, Georgii Arkad'evich
Karavaev, Nikolai Mikhailovich
Karavaeva, Anna Aleksandrovna
Karavaevo
Karavelov, Liuben
Karavelov, Petko Stoichev
Karawanken
Karay, Refik Halid
Karazhal
Karazin, Vasilii Nazarovich
Karbuna Treasure
Karbyshev, Dmitrii Mikhailovich
Karcag
Kardashev, Nikolai Nikolaevich
Kardhitsa
Kardis, Treaty of
Kardovskii, Dmitrii Nikolaevich
Kareev, Nikolai Ivanovich
Kareli
Karelian
Karelian Autonomous Soviet Socialist
    Republic
Karelian Birch
Karelian Branch of the Academy of
    Sciences of the USSR
Karelian Coast
Karelian Culture
Karelian Folding
Karelian Isthmus
Karelian Labor Commune
Karelians
Karelin, Adrei Osipovich
Karelin, Grigorii Silych
Karelin, Vladimir Aleksandrovich
Karen
Karenga
Kargala
Kargala Treasure
Kargapol'e
Kargapolov, Mikhail Ivanovich
Kargasok
Kargat (city)
Kargat (river)
Karger, Mikhail Konstantinovich

Kargin, Valentin Alekseevich
Kargopol'
Kargopol' Culture
Kari Abdullah
Kari-Iakubov, Mukhitdin
Karikás, Frigyes
Karim, Fatykh
Karim, Khanif
Karim, Mustai
Karimata
Karinian, Artashes Balasievich
Karinskii, Mikhail Ivanovich
Karinskii, Nikolai Mikhailovich
Karinthy, Frigyes
Karintorf
Karitskii, Konstantin Dionisievich
Karjalainen, Ahti
Karjalanselkä
Karkaralinsk
Karkaralinsk Mountains
Karkaralinsk Settlements
Karkavitsas, Andreas
Karkhaneh
Karkinitskii
Karla Libknekhta Imeni
Karlgren, Bernhard
Karliev, Alty
*Karling
Karl Marx (A Brief Biographical Sketch
    With an Exposition of Marxism)
Karl Marx Peak
Karl-Marx-Stadt (administrative district)
Karl-Marx-Stadt (city)
Karlo-Libknekhtovsk
Karlo-Marksovo
Karlovac
Karlovka
Karlovo
Karlovy Vary
Karlovy Vary Upland
Karłowicz, Mieczysław
Karlowitz Congress of 1698–99
Karlsbad Salt
Karlsen, Genrikh Georgievich
Karlskoga
Karlskrona
Karlsruhe
Karlstad
Karlstad, Treaty of (1905)
Karlstein
Karluks
Karlygan
Karm, Kaarel Iukhanovich
Karma
Karmadon
Karmaliuk, Pavel Petrovich
Karmaliuk, Ustim Iakimovich
Kármán, Theodore von
Karmathians
Karmen, Roman Lazarevich
Karmir-Blur
Karnai, Ali Magometovich
Karnak
Karnaukhov, Mikhail Mikhailovich
Karnaukhovka
Karny, Alfons
Karogs
Károlyi, Mihály
Karonin, S

Karotamm, Nikolai Georgievich
Karpachev, Sergei Vasil'evich
Karpechenko, Georgii Dmitrievich
Karpenko-Karyi, Ivan Karpovich
Karpinsk
Karpínski, Franciszek
Karpinskii, Aleksandr Petrovich
Karpinskii, Viacheslav Alekseevich
Karpinskii (mountain)
Karpinskii (volcano)
Karpinskite
Karpov, Aleksandr Terent'evich
Karpov, Fedor Ivanovich
Karpov, Lev Iakovlevich
Karpov, Vladimir Borisovich
Karpovich, Petr Vladimirovich
Karpovka Reservoir
Karpuninskii
Karpushikha
Karranay
Karren
Karrer, Paul
Karroo
Karryev, Aga Karryevich
Karryev, Baimukhamed Atalievich
Kars
Kars, Treaty of (1921)
Karsakpai
Karsava
Karsavin, Lev Platonovich
Karsavina, Tamara Platonovna
Karshi
Karshi Steppe
Karskie Vorota
Karskii, Evfimii Fedorovich
Kars Kingdom
Karst (plateau)
Karst (geology)
Karstology
Karsun
Kart
Kartalin Range
Kartaly
Karting
Kartini, Raden Adjeng
Kartli (region)
Kartli (mountains)
Kartlians
Kartli Kingdom
Kartlis Tskhovreba
Kartodikromo, Marco
Kartofel' i Ovoshchi
Karts
Kartsevskii, Sergei Osipovich
Kartsganag
Kartuli
Kartveli
Kartvelian Languages
Kartvelishvili, Lavrentii Iosifovich
Karun
Karvaš, Peter
Karviná
Karymskaia Sopka
Karymskoe
Karyogamy
Karyogram
Karyology
Karyolysis
Karyoplasm

Karyopyknosis
Karyorrhexis
Karyosystematics
Karyotype
Kas
Kasack, Hermann
Kasai
Kasakh
Kasan
Kasansai (urban-type settlement)
Kasansai (river)
Kasatkin, Ivan Mikhailovich
Kasatkin, Nikolai Alekseevich
Kasatkin, Viktor Ivanovich
Kasatonov, Vladimir Afanas'evich
Kash
Kashan (city)
Kashan (river)
Kashchenko, Nikolai Feofanovich
Kashchenko, Petr Petrovich
Kashchenko, Vsevolod Petrovich
Kashevarov, Aleksandr Filippovich
Kashevarova-Rudneva, Varvara
    Aleksandrovna
Kashgar (city)
Kashgar (river)
Kashgar Mountains
Kashgar Plain
Kashgars
Kashi, Jamshid ibn Masud al-
Kashihn, Daniil Nikitich
Kashin
Kashira
Kashira Gorodishche
Kashira State Regional Electric Power
    Plant
Kashirin, Nikolai Dmitrievich
Kashiwa
Kashkadar'ia
Kashkadar'ia Oblast
Kashkarov, Daniil Nikolaevich
Kashkin, Ivan Aleksandrovich
Kashkin, Nikolai Dmitrievich
Kashkin, Nikolai Sergeevich
Kashlyk
Kashmir (historical region)
Kashmir, Vale of
Kashmiri
Kashmiri Literature
Kashmiris
Kashtan, William
Kashubs
Kas'ian, Sarkis Ivanovich
Kas'ianov, Aleksandr Aleksandrovich
Kasiian, Vasilii Il'ich
Kasim al-Anvar
Kasim Khan
Kasimov
Kasimov Kingdom
Kasimzade, Enver Ali ogly
Kaskelen
Kasli
Kasli Castings
Kašpárek
Kasparov, Vladislav Minasovich
Kasperle
Kaspi
Kaspiisk
Kaspiiskii

Kasplia
Kasprowicz, Jan
Kasprzak, Marcin
Kassa
Kassák, Lajos
Kassala
Kassandra (peninsula)
Kassandra (gulf)
Kassarskoe Gorge
Kassel
Kassem, Abdul Karim
Kasserine
Kassil', Lev Abramovich
Kassin, Nikolai Grigor'evich
Kassirskii, Iosif Abramovich
Kassite
Kassites
Kassner, Rudolf
Kasso, Lev Aristidovich
Kastal'skii, Aleksandr Dmitrievich
Kasteev, Abylkhan
Kastler, Alfred
Kastornoe
Kastorskii, Vladimir Ivanovich
Kasugai
Kasum-Ismailov
Kasumov, Mir Bashir Fattakh ogly
Kasur
Kasymov, Mukhammedzhan
Katabasis
Kataev, Ivan Ivanovich
Kataev, Semen Isidorovich
Kataev, Valentin Petrovich
Kataisk
Katamorphosis
Katangli
Katanov, Nikolai Fedorovich
*Katarovka
Katav-Ivanovsk
Katayama, Sen
Kateb Yacine
Katenin, Pavel Aleksandrovich
Katerini
Katerinopol'
Kathak
Kathakali
Katheder-Socialism
Kathiawar Peninsula
Katipunan
Katiusha
Katkov, Mikhail Nikiforovich
Katla
Katmai
Katmandu
Kato, Genichi
Kato, Kiyomasa
Katorga i Ssylka
Katowice
Katowice Województwo
Katsiev, Khabu Khadzhikurmanovich
Katsina
Katsman, Evgenii Aleksandrovich
Katsones, Lambros
Katsumata, Seiichi
Katsura, Taro
Kattakurgan
Kattegat
Katuar, Georgii L'vovich
Katukov, Mikhail Efimovich

Katulin, Aleksei Zakharovich
Katul'skaia, Elena Kliment'evna
Katun' (mountains)
Katun' (river)
Katun' (glacier)
Katunki
Katushev, Konstantin Fedorovich
Katushki
Katyrev-Rostovskii, Ivan Mikhailovich
Katz, Bernard
Kauchuk i Rezina
Kaudzit, Reinis Reinisovič and Matis
    Reinisovič
Kauffmann, Angelica
Kaufman, Aleksandr Arkad'evich
Kaufman, Illarion Ignat'evich
Kaufman, Konstantin Petrovich
Kaufman, Nikolai Nikolaevich
Kaunas
Kaunas Art Museum
Kaunas Medical Institute
Kaunas Polytechnical Institute
Kaunas Reservoir
Kaunchi Culture
Kaunda, Kenneth David
Kaundy
Kaunitz, Count Wenzel Anton
Kaushany
Kaushutov, Ata
Kautilya
Kautsky, Benedikt
Kautsky, Karl
Kautsky, Minna
Kautskyism
Kava
Kavadh I
Kavaja
Kaval
*Kavaler
Kavalergardy
Kavalerovo
Kavalla
Kavarskas
Kavat-Kala
Kavelin, Konstantin Dmitrievich
Kaverin, Veniamin Aleksandrovich
Kavkazskii Rabochii
Kavkazskii Rabochii Listok
Kavraiskii, Vladimir Vladimirovich
Kavraiskii Method
Kavtaradze, Sergei Ivanovich
Kawa
Kawabata, Yasunari
Kawagoe
Kawaguchi
Kawakami, Jotaro
Kawakibi, Abd al-Rahman al-
Kawalerowicz, Jerzy
Kawasaki (city)
Kawaski (boat)
Kawi
Kaya, Seiji
*Kayah
Kayahs
Kayak
Kaya Kum
Kayes
Kayibanda, Grégoire
Kayseri

Kaz
Kazach'ia Lopan'
Kazachok
Kazakievich, Emmanuil Genrikhovich
Kazakh (city)
Kazakh (language)
Kazakh Agricultural Institute
Kazakh Arkhar-Merino
Kazakh Art Gallery
Kazakh Drama Theater
Kazakhfil'm
Kazakh Fine-wooled Sheep
Kazakh Horse
Kazakh Melkosopochnik
Kazakh Pedagogical Institute
Kazakh Polytechnic Institute
Kazakh Railroad
Kazakhs
Kazakh Soviet Socialist Republic
Kazakhstan Economic Region
Kazakhstanskaia Pravda
Kazakh Theater of Opera and Ballet
Kazakh University
Kazakh White-faced Cattle
Kazakin
Kazakov, Aleksandr Vasil'evich
Kazakov, Aristarkh Andreevich
Kasakov, Iurii Pavlovich
Kazakov, Konstantin Petrovich
Kazakov, Matvei Fedorovich
Kazakov, Mikhail Il'ich
Kazakov, Nikolai (Miklai) Ivanovich
Kazakov, Vasilii Ivanovich
Kazakova, Rimma Fedorovna
Kazalinsk
Kazan, Elia
Kazan
Kazan, University of
Kazan Aviation Institute
Kazan Bol'shoi Dramatic Theater
Kazanbulak
Kazan Campaigns of 1545–52
Kazan Cathedral
Kazan Chemical-Technological Institute
Kazan Chronicler
Kazan Conspiracy of 1863
Kazan Demonstration of 1876
Kazandzhik
Kazane
Kazanets, Ivan Pavlovich
Kazanka (urban-type settlement)
Kazanka (river)
Kazan Khanate
Kazanluk
Kazanluk Basin
Kazanluk Rose
Kazanluk Tomb
Kazanoko, Dzhabagi
Kazan Operation of 1918
Kazanovka
Kazan Physics and Mathematics Society
Kazan School
Kazanskii, Boris Aleksandrovich
Kasanskii, Evgenii Sergeevich
Kazan Stage
Kazantsev, Florentii Pimenovich
Kazantsev, Nikolai Dmitrievich
Kazantsev Brake
Kazantzake, Galatea

Kazantzakis, Nikos
Kazarinova, Nina Nikolaevna
Kazarma
Kazarnovskii, Isaak Abramovich
Kazarskii, Aleksandr Ivanovich
Kazatin
Kazatskoe
Kazbegi, Aleksandr
Kazbegi
Kazbek
Kazbek Treasure
Kaz Daği
Kazei, Marat
Kazem-Bek, Mirza Mukhammed Ali
Kazemi, Mortaza Moshfeq
Kazerun
Kazhim
Kaziasker
Kaziiau Ali
Kazi-Magomed
Kazimierz Dolny
Kazimirova, Ekaterina Grigor'evna
Kazin, Vasilii Vasil'evich
Kazincbarcika
Kazinka
Kaziranga
Kazi Zadeh al-Rumi
Kazlu-Rūda
Kaz'min, Petr Mikhailovich
Kaznacheev, Sergei Konstantinovich
Kaznacheevskii
Kazreti
Kazym
Kazyr
Kelamayi
Keyserling, Hermann Alexander
Kham
Khond
King Crab
Kodiak (town)
Kodiak (island)
Kompong Cham
Kompong Som
Krasnorechenskoe
Kurnool
Kutch
Kutch, Rann of
Kvaisi
Kvant
Kvapilová, Hanna
Kvareli
Kvarkush
Kwajong Pop
Kwakiutl
Kwa Languages
Kwangju
Kwango
Kwanto (region)
Kevanto (plain)
Kwantung Army
Kwara
*Laboratory Work
Land Roller
Land Use Maps
Large White Butterfly
*Leg
Lepisosteus
Library Catalog
Library Cataloging

VOLUME 11

ABUTILON, a genus of annual or perennial plants of the family Malvaceae, including grasses, shrubs, and, more rarely, small trees, often slightly downy. The leaves are usually simple or lobed (other shapes only rarely). The blossoms are usually large, having axils but lacking a subcalyx. The corolla is usually yellow. The fruit consists of several (more than ten) separate pods, initially growing together, that contain several seeds each. *Abutilon* comprises more than 150 species (some sources give more than 400), growing in the tropics and subtropics of both hemispheres. There is only one species, piemarker (*A. theophrasti* or *A. avicennae*), in the USSR, growing in the southern European part, the Caucasus, and Middle Asia. It is most often cultivated as a fiber crop. There are approximately ten other species that are raised for fiber or for decorative purposes.

Piemarker is an annual grassy plant with a straight, slightly branched stem at the top, growing in cultured varieties to a height of 4 m. The root is rodlike with numerous side rootlets. The leaves are sequential and scaly, with lengths up to 15 cm. They are deeply lobed and crenulate at the edges. The yellow or orange flowers are separate or gathered into broomlike racemes. The fruit consists of 12–15 sharp pods. The seeds are bud-shaped and nearly black; 1,000 seeds weigh 14–18 g. The growing period for piemarker is 100–150 days. During the first month the foliage above ground develops very slowly, while the root system grows rapidly.

Abutilons are basically self-pollinating. They need light and moisture, particularly during blossoming and seed formation. Thick plantings slightly retard stem growth. The seeds begin to sprout at temperatures of 10°–12°C, and the sprouts can withstand cold down to 2°C. The optimal temperature for growth and development is 20°–22°C. The most suitable soils for cultivation are chernozems and marshland.

The dry stems of abutilons are up to 25 percent fiber, which is spun and then made into burlap, binder twine, string, and the like. The fiber is durable but brittle; it is frequently boiled in a weak solution of sodium hydroxide to improve it. By-products are made into paper and insulating plates. The seeds contain 16–20 percent semisiccative oil that is suitable for making soap or drying oil. The original source and ancient center of abutilon cultivation is China, where it is still grown extensively. Plantings may also be found in the Mongolian People's Republic, Japan, Egypt, and the USA. In the the USSR abutilons are grown for collections and in experimental research plantations.

REFERENCES:
Lubianye kul'tury: Sb. st. Edited by Ia. M. Tollochko. Moscow, 1950.
Lubianye kul'tury. Edited by Ia. M. Tollochko. Moscow, 1953.

[11–946–1]

ADVANCED CAPITAL, the amount of money invested by the capitalist in an enterprise for the purpose of receiving profit.

Advanced capital is spent for the acquisition of the means of production—constant capital *c*—and for the purchase of labor power—variable capital *v*. Constant and variable capital serve as the means to extract surplus value, which is created by the labor of hired workers in the process of production and is embodied in the produced commodities. Different elements of advanced capital have different kinds of turnover: one of them transfers its value to the newly created commodity by degrees and returns gradually to the capitalist in the form of money; the other transfers its value as a whole and returns in full to the capitalist in the form of money at the end of each completed cycle of the capital. Depending on this distinction, the advanced capital is divided into a fixed and a circulating component. The movement of the advanced capital can be expressed by the following formula, which Marx called the general formula for capital: $M—C—M'$, where M is the initially advanced sum of money, C is the commodity, and $M' = M + m$, the initially advanced sum of money plus the surplus value. The capital owner advances money; that is, as a buyer he invests it in the means of production and in labor power, with the goal of getting it back with a profit in his capacity as a seller of his commodities. His profit represents an increment on the advanced capital.

In the process of its transformations, from the money form to the commodity form and back again, advanced capital appears as a self-increasing, self-propelling substance, with money and commodities representing only forms of its being. Capital as a value is not advanced for the sake of receiving a single profit; the goal of the owner is the ever-growing increase in value. Therefore, the advanced value is constantly being recirculated. Initially the advanced capital represented a form of movement of merchant and usurer capital. With the advent of the capitalist mode of production, advanced capital now manifests itself as a form of movement of any capital, including industrial capital.

I. L. GRIGOR'EVA [11–1036–1]

AGGRAVATED CRIME, in criminal law, a crime having one or more elements stipulated by law (aggravating circumstances) indicating its greater social danger compared to nonaggravated (simple) forms of the same crime. For example, under Soviet criminal law intentional homicide motivated by hooliganism (Criminal Code of the RSFSR, art. 102, par. b) is an aggravated crime compared to homicide without aggravating circumstances (Criminal Code of the RSFSR, art. 103). In articles establishing punishment for various kinds of crimes, the law considers as aggravating circumstances such factors as recidivism, a criminal record, large inflicted damage, and commission of the crime by an organized group. A more severe punishment is prescribed for aggravated crimes. [11–1693–3]

AMPLIFIER STAGE (in Russian, *kaskad usileniia*), a radio-engineering device that contains an amplifier, a load circuit, and

1

a coupling circuit to the preceding or following amplifier stage. The amplifier may be either an electronic semiconductor device, such as a transistor or tunnel diode, or an electron vacuum tube (receiving amplifier tube, klystron, or traveling-wave tube). A signal fed to the input of an amplifier stage is reproduced with amplification at the output (in the load circuit). The ratio of the output voltage, current strength, or power to the input voltage is called the voltage, current, or power gain of the stage.

According to the frequency or spectrum width of the signals amplifier stages are classified as DC, audio-frequency, intermediate-frequency, or broad-band types; according to the type of connection of the amplifier they are classified as common-base, common-emitter, or common-collector stages for a transistor and as common-grid, common-cathode, and common-plate stages for a receiving amplifier tube. Amplifiers usually have several stages, which are connected in series. This is called a cascade connection—hence, the Russian name for the individual sections.   V. M. RODIONOV [11–1478–2]

ANABASIS APHYLLA (in Russian, *itsegek*), a plant of the family Chenopodiaceae. It is a low, branching semishrub with tiny, scalelike, opposite leaves; the flowers are spikelike inflorescences. The fruit is berry-shaped and has yellowish or pink winglike appendages. It grows in the saline and clayey deserts and semideserts of Southeast, Middle, and Central Asia and also in the southern European part of the USSR, the Caucasus, and Southern Siberia. The young, green branchlets of *A. aphylla* contain alkaloids, most importantly anabasine, an effective agent for control of insect pests in agriculture; anabasine is also the raw material for obtaining nicotinic acid, or niacin.   [11–147–1]

ARENARIA, a genus of birds of the family Charadridae. The body is approximately 25 cm long; the plumage is variegated (black with white and rust).

There are two species. The turnstone (*A. interpres*) is found in northern Europe, Asia, and North America; in the USSR it is found along the coasts of the Arctic Ocean, the Baltic Sea, and the Bering Sea. The turnstone winters in Africa, southern Asia, Australia, and South America. The black turnstone (*A. melanocephala*) is distinguished by darker plumage. It inhabits the coast of Alaska; in the USSR some migrating birds have reached Vrangel' Island and the Chukotka Peninsula.

Turnstones stay on seacoasts. The nest (a hole with scanty lining) is made on the ground. The clutch contains three or four variegated eggs; both parents sit on the nest for 21–23 days. The bird feeds on small invertebrates, which it finds by turning over stones (hence the name), and on algae tossed up by the sea.
[11–831–2]

BARN SWALLOW (*Hirundo rustica*), a bird of the order Passeriformes. The upper part of the body and a stripe on the breast are black with a blue sheen, the head and throat are reddish chestnut, and the abdomen is white or rust colored. The body measures 18–23 cm long. The tail feathers are in the form of thin, narrow sickles. The barn swallow is distributed in Europe, North Africa, Asia, and North America. In the USSR it is found everywhere south of the forest tundra. A migratory bird, it nests in structures near human habitation. The nest is cup-shaped and made of clumps of dirt mixed with saliva; it is fastened beneath eaves. There are two clutches per summer. The barn swallow is beneficial by destroying flies and other flying insects.

REFERENCE
Ptitsy Sovetskogo Soiuza, vol. 6. Edited by G. P. Dement'ev and N. A. Gladkov. Moscow, 1954.   [11–1472–1]

BARRACKS, a building with residential, service, and training premises for the permanent quartering of the personnel of military units. The first known specialized structures for the quartering of troops were in ancient Rome and Carthage. Barracks were built in Spain from the 16th century and in France from the 17th century. The first barracks in Russia were built in 1741 in St. Petersburg, for the quartering of the Semenovskii, Preobrazhenskii, Izmailovskii, and Cavalry Guards Regiments.

In the Soviet armed forces, in accordance with the Interior Service Regulations of the Armed Forces of the USSR (1960), each barrack must have special premises for the quartering of each company.   [11–415–1]

BARRACKS COMMUNISM, the concept used by Marx and Engels to denote the most vulgarized and primitive notions about communism as a system characterized by asceticism with regard to the satisfaction of human needs, by a despotic, thin stratum of "revolutionary leaders," by bureaucratization of the entire system of social relations, and by a view of man as a blind instrument for carrying out the will of higher authorities.

The introduction of this concept was occasioned by the publication of S. G. Nechaev's article "The Basic Principles of the Future Society" (1870). In this "future," cut to Nechaev's specifications, the ruling principle is to "produce as much as possible for society and to use as little as possible"; labor is obligatory on pain of death, and the discipline of the rod prevails. "What a fine model of barracks communism! Everything is here: common dining halls and sleeping quarters, price-fixers, and offices supervising education, production, and consumption, in a word, all social activity, and at the head of everything, as the supreme leader, stands, nameless and unknown, 'our committee' " (K. Marx and F. Engels, *Soch.*, 2nd ed., vol. 18, p. 414). The founders of scientific communism described the methods proposed for achieving this "barracks paradise" as an apologia for treachery, lies, intimidation, and force—as bourgeois immorality carried to an extreme.

This ruthless criticism of "barracks communism" and of Nechaev's views reflects the profound humanistic essence of Marxism. From his earliest works Marx opposed "crude and thoughtless communism," which for the sake of illusory rejection of private property negates the personality of man. "The thought of every piece of private property as such," wrote Marx, "is at least turned against wealthier private property in the form of envy and the urge to reduce things to a common level. . . . Crude communism is simply the culmination of this envy and of this leveling-down proceeding from the preconceived minimum. It has a definite, limited yardstick. That such an annulment of private property by no means represents the real assimilation of it is in fact proved by the abstract negation of the entire world of culture and civilization, by the regression to the *unnatural* simplicity of the poor and crude man who has few needs and who has not only failed to go beyond private property, but has not even reached it" (K. Marx and F. Engels, *Iz rannikh proizvedenii*, 1956, pp. 586–87).

This subtle and profound analysis of the roots of "barracks communism," with its leveling aspirations, has not lost its relevance to this day. Marxism-Leninism links the appearance of such tendencies to certain social and political phenomena, primarily the backwardness, underdevelopment, and petit bourgeois character of a social milieu shaped by centuries of exploitation, humiliation, subjugation, and arbitrary power, a milieu that may survive for a while even after the socialist revolution. The pressure of such an environment and the penetration of its attitudes and prejudices into the psychology of political leaders and into the ideology of political organizations create an opportunity for the rise of various manifestations of "barracks communism" in both theory and practice. An example of this may be seen in the theories and aspirations of certain ideologists in China from the late 1950's to the 1970's. In these theories patriarchal, petit bourgeois, and preproletarian perversions of communism were interwoven in a unique and grotesque manner.

The concept "barracks communism" stands in irreconcilable contradiction to the objective developmental tendencies in socialist society, and it is categorically refuted by the theory of scientific communism. Marxist-Leninist parties resolutely struggle against any manifestation of "barracks communism," both in the theory and the practice of socialist construction.
A. E. BOVIN [11–415–3]

BEEFWOOD (*Casuarina*), a genus of woody and bushy plants of the family Casuarinaceae. There are at least 60 species, found chiefly in Australia but also in Tasmania and from Fiji and New Caledonia to Burma. In the USSR, *C. equisetifolia,* whose jointed shoots resemble horsetails, is cultivated as an ornamental in the Caucasus.

The leaves are in verticils, squamiform, grown together in dentate sheaths. The blossoms are small, lacking a perianth, and unisexual. Male flowers have one stamen in delicate terminal racemes; female flowers have one pistil and are gathered into spherical, lignifying inflorescences. The fruit is in the form of a winged nutlet, which upon maturing opens into two flaps, like a pod. The seeds lack an endosperm. Beefwood is one of the oldest dicotyledons. [11–529–2]

BEET STORAGE ROT, a dangerous disease of the beet root during storage, caused by various fungi and bacteria. Most often the sick plants develop a white downy film that turns gray or pinkish (yellowish) white; on dried roots the film is often greenish black. The internal tissues grow soft and dark, although sometimes the color does not change. Infection by *Mucorales* and saprophytic fungi and bacteria causes alcohol fermentation and other types of fermentation, accompanied by unpleasant smells.

Storage rot affects small and old roots more strongly. The disease is intensified by such factors as unfavorable conditions in the beet's mineral intake during its vegetation period, weakening of the plants by disease and pests, freezing and drying, and mechanical damage to the roots. Infected roots usually become unfit for any use. Control measures include the use of beet types resistant to storage rot, high-level beet agrotechnology, correct storage, and prevention of freezing, drying, or mechanical damage. M. S. DUNIN [11–363–4]

BLACK BEETLES (Histeridae), a family of beetles. Body length, 0.8–20 mm. The body is thick, with a hard shell, clavate feelers, shortened wing covers, and digging legs. The larvae have short legs and two double-jointed appendages at the end of the abdomen. There are approximately 3,500 species, of which 280 are found in the USSR. Black beetles are predators, feeding on the larvae of other insects. They live in carrion, in dung, in burrows and nests of animals and birds, and under bark; some species live in anthills. A number of species are beneficial because they destroy harmful insects (such as fly larvae in dung, flea larvae in burrows, and bark beetles). [11–1169–5]

BOAR, wild boar (*Sus scrofa*), an artiodactylous mammal of the family Suidae. Body length, up to 2 m; height at the withers, up to 1.2 m; weight, up to 300 kg. The upper and lower tusks, particularly large on the males, are turned up and out. The body is covered with coarse bristles, and in the winter, with a soft undercoat. Adult boars are brown; the young have light lengthwise stripes. They inhabit North Africa, Europe, and Asia. In the USSR they live in the Baltic region, Byelorussia, the Ukraine, the Volga delta, Middle Asia, Kazakhstan, Southern Siberia, and Primor'e.

The wild boar prefers forests and reeds near reservoirs and mountain forests. It is omnivorous, feeding on rhizomes, tubers, grass, acorns, the fruit of wild apple and pear trees, worms, insect larvae, snails, and small rodents. Wild boars herd in small groups and are nocturnal animals. They mate from November through January, and three or four young are born from March to May. Boars are hunted for their meat, hide, and bristles. They sometimes damage crops. Domestic pigs derived from the wild boar.

REFERENCES
Sludskii, A. A. *Kaban.* Alma-Ata, 1956.
Sokolov, I. I. "Kopytnye zveri." Moscow-Leningrad, 1959. (*Fauna SSSR: Mlekopitaiuschie,* vol. 1, issue 3.)
Mlekopitaiushchie Sovetskogo Soiuza, vol. 1. Edited by V. G. Geptner and N. P. Naumov. Moscow, 1961. I. I. SOKOLOV [11–248–3]

BOXER REBELLION (Russian, I Ho T'uan Rebellion), an anti-imperialist uprising of peasants and urban poor in northern China between 1899 and 1901. The revolt was begun by the secret religious society I Ho Ch'uan (Righteous Harmony Fists), whose rebel units were later renamed I Ho T'uan (Righteous Harmony Bands), from which the rebellion took its name. Because the original name of the society included the word *ch'uan* (fist), the rebels were called boxers by foreigners, as a result of which the uprising has been given the inaccurate name Boxer Rebellion.

The revolt began in Shantung Province, where the presence of foreign imperialists was especially noticeable. Unrest had also grown as a result of a series of natural disasters in 1899. Early in 1900 the center of the rebellion shifted to the capital province of Chihli. The rebels destroyed railroad and telegraph lines, religious missions, and some government offices, gaining de facto control over a large area. Gradually, the rebellion spread to Shanshi Province and to Manchuria as well. Efforts of government troops to oppose the rebel forces proved fruitless, and the governor of Chihli, Yü Lu, was forced to negotiate with the leaders of the revolt, Li Lai-chung and Chang Te-ch'eng. On June 13–14, the rebels entered Peking and besieged the legation quarter for 56 days. During the attack, the German minister von Ketteler was killed.

Alarmed, the imperialist powers (Great Britain, Germany, Austria-Hungary, France, Japan, the United States, tsarist Russia, and Italy) organized an intervention in China. On June 17 their forces captured the Taku forts. Fearing the rebels, the Ch'ing government declared war on the powers but in fact did nothing to defend the country against the interventionists. Instead, it continued its punitive operations against the rebels outside the capital. The governors of the central and southern provinces harshly repressed participants in the antiforeign outbreaks that occurred in the latter part of the year. In mid-July, the foreign troops overcame the heroic resistance of the rebels and captured T'ientsin; shortly thereafter they began to march on Peking. By this time the interventionist forces numbered about 40,000. The Manchu government offered only weak resistance, and Peking was captured by mid-August. With the arrival of the foreign commander in chief, the German field marshal von Waldersee, punitive expeditions were begun against various areas of continuing unrest and against the peaceful population. The Ch'ing rulers fled from Peking to Hsian.

The rebellion was suppressed by 1901, although resistance continued in some areas until 1902. The imperialist powers imposed the coercive Boxer Protocol on China. Nonetheless, the I Ho T'uan Rebellion was an important stage in the spontaneous struggle of the Chinese peasantry and urban poor against imperialist intrusion into China.

REFERENCES
Lenin, V. I. "Kitaiskaia voina." *Poln. sobr. soch.,* 5th ed., vol. 4.
Vosstanie ikhetuanei: Dokumenty i materialy. Moscow, 1968. (Bibliography, pp. 250–53, 266–69.)
Giles, L. *The Siege of the Peking Legations.* [Nedlands, 1970.]
G. V. EFIMOV [11–164–2]

BRANCHIURA (carp lice), an order of crustaceans, comprising six genera with 130 species, including the genus *Argulus* with 109 species. The Branchiura parasitize the bodies and gills of fish and sometimes amphibians. Their body length measures up to 3 cm. They are dioecious. Nearly completely formed crustaceans hatch from eggs laid by the female. Branchiura are temporary parasites and bloodsuckers. Certain species, such as *Argulus foliaceus, A. coregoni,* and *A. japonicus,* cause significant damage to commercial pisciculture; their massive invasions bring about the death of fry and adult fish. Countermeasures include improving the oxygen content of bodies of water and using pesticides such as chlorophos. [11–1358–2]

BRANTS (*Branta*), a genus of birds of the order Anseriformes. The head is small, the bill short and black, and the feet black. Brants resemble other geese in general build and way of life. There are five species, four of which inhabit the USSR. The black brant (*B. bernicla*) weighs approximately 2 kg; it nests in the tundra and forest tundra of Siberia, from Iamal to Chukotka, on many islands of the arctic region, and in North America from Alaska to Greenland.

The barnacle goose (*B. leucopsis*) nests on the southern island of Novaia Zemlia, on the Lofoten Islands, Spitsbergen, and in the eastern part of Greenland. The Canada goose (*B. canadensis*) weighs from 1.5 to 8 kg (various subspecies); it inhabits northern and northwestern America, and on rare occasions flies into Anadyr'. The red-breasted goose (*B. rufficollis*) is sometimes classified in the genus *Rufibrenta*. It is distributed from the lower reaches of the Ob' River to the Khatanga. Its numbers are small and rapidly decreasing. The Hawaiian brant (*B. sandvicensis*) was common in the Hawaiian Islands; it has been almost exterminated (about 50 birds have been preserved). Brants, except for the Hawaiian and the red-breasted goose, are game birds.

The Russian word *kazarka* is also applied to two species of geese of the genus *Anser:* the white-fronted goose (*A. albifrons*) and the lesser white-fronted goose (*A. erythropus*).

REFERENCE
Ptitsy Sovetskogo Soiuza, vol. 4. Edited by G. P. Dement'ev and N. A. Gladkov. Moscow, 1952.   E. V. KOZLOVA   [11–414–2]

BRASSICA, a genus of plants of the family Cruciferae. They are annuals, biennials, or perennials. The roots are spindle-shaped and branched; the stems, erect or elevated and branching. The leaves are alternate with the lower ones often gathered into a rosette. The leaves and stems may be glabrous or downy. The flowers are gathered in racemes or corymbs, and the petals are most often yellow. The fruit is a pod. The seeds are spheroidal and slightly alveolate, and they vary in color from dark brown to brownish, ruddy, or yellow; their diameter is about 2 mm.

The genus *Brassica* contains more than 100 species, and wild species are found throughout Eurasia. Most species originated in the Mediterranean area or in China. The genus *Brassica* includes cultivated species used as vegetables and for feed, including various turnips (*B. napus rapifera, B. napus, B. rapa subsp. rapifera, B. campestris*), rapes, Indian mustard, Abyssinian cabbage, and black mustard, and a number of wild species. Species grown as vegetables and for feed include cabbage (*B. oleracea*), pakchoi (*B. chinensis*), and pe-tsai (*B. pekinensis*). Cabbage is a polymorphic species. According to the classification of P. M. Zhukovskii (1964), cabbage includes the following varieties: wild leaf cabbage (*B. var. oleracea*), or wild cabbage (*B. silvestris*), branching cabbage (var. *ramosa*), brussels sprouts (var. *gemmifera*), feed leaf cabbage (var. *viridis*), kohlrabi (convar. *gongylodes*), Portugal cabbage (var. *costata*), savoy cabbage (var *sabauda*), true head cabbage (var. *capitata*), broccoli (var. *italica*), and cauliflower (var. *botrytis*). Some researchers divide cabbage into several species. Thus, the Soviet botanist T. V. Lizgunova (1948) distinguishes six independent species: head cabbage (*B. capitata*), savoy cabbage (*B. sabauda*), brussels sprouts (*B. gemmifera*), kohlrabi (*B. caulorapa*), cauliflower (*B. cauliflora*), and leaf cabbage (*B. subspontanea*). These species, which developed as a result of centuries of cultivation (more than 4,000 years ago), differ greatly in their vegetative organs, but their reproductive organs are very similar. The leafy types were the first to be cultivated. Cauliflower, kohlrabi, pakchoi, and pe-tsai are also ancient forms. The varieties of head cabbage evolved from cultivated leafy cabbages.

Resistant to cold, cultivated brassicas are light-loving plants that grow well on highly fertile soils but will not thrive on marshy or acid soils. All species of *Brassica* are biennial plants except for cauliflower and pe-tsai. Brassicas are grown on all continents and everywhere in the USSR, where head cabbage is one of the chief vegetable crops, accounting for 30 percent of the land under vegetable crops and thereby holding first place. Brassicas also hold first place among vegetable crops in terms of planted area in Great Britain, France, the German Democratic Republic, Norway, and Czechoslovakia.

All species of *Brassica* may be eaten fresh, boiled, or braised, or they may be salted, marinated, dried, or frozen. They contain carbohydrates, proteins, minerals, and vitamins (such as vitamin C and the B group). The brassicas also have dietetic and therapeutic qualities.

Head cabbage has the greatest economic importance. The head, which is used for food, is the gigantic terminal bud that grows on a stem 15–20 cm long, which thickens in its central part to form a stump. The leaves are large (25–60 cm), entire, and lyrate. The heads are rounded, flat, or have other shapes. They range from very loose to very dense, have diameters measuring 10–45 cm, and weigh 0.3–16 kg. In the Soviet Union among the most common varieties of white cabbage are those that mature early (Gribovo Number One 147), moderately early (Zolotoi Gektar or Golden Hectare), in midseason (Gribovskaia Slava 231 and Slava 1305), and moderately late and late (Late Byelorusskaia 455 and Moscow 15, Amager 611, and others). The yield is 20–90 tons per hectare (ha). Red cabbage is grown far less frequently. Its head keeps well over the winter and is used in salads, as side dishes, and for marinating. Well-know varieties are Gako, Kamennaia Golovka (Little Stone Head), and Topas. The yield is up to 30 tons.

Savoy cabbage is characterized by a higher protein content and good taste when boiled (used as a side dish and for fillings). Its head is relatively loose, being composed of delicate crinkled leaves. Some varieties are Iubileinaia (Jubilee) 2170, Venskaia Ranniaia (Early Vienna grade) 1346, and Vertue 1340. The yield is 17–30 tons per ha. In brussels sprouts little heads the size of walnuts form in the axils along the main stem. They are used in boiled form in soups and as a side dish. The variety Hercules is widespread. The yield is 4–5 tons per ha.

Cauliflower is especially valued for its nutritional content, digestibility, and good taste. The part that is eaten is the head, which consists of numerous juicy, delicate shoots with the embryos of racemes. Two subspecies are distinguished—*simplex*, which includes the most primitive forms, and *abortiva,* which contains the more cultivated forms with thick white or yellowish heads. The subspecies *simplex* includes the varieties known as broccoli, or asparagus cabbage; it is widespread in the Mediterranean area and Western Europe but is seldom grown in the USSR. Cauliflower is grown from the extreme south to the extreme north, chiefly in the Mediterranean area, Western Europe, and the United States. In the USSR it is grown near major cities. The most common varieties cultivated in the USSR belong to the subspecies *abortiva:* Snezhinka (Snowflake), Skorospelka (Fast-maturing), Otechestvennaia (Homeland), Moskovskaia Konservnaia (Moscow Canning), and Urozhainaia (Productive). The heads are picked at the point of technical ripening when they reach a diameter of 8–10 cm (300–500 g). The yield on open terrain is up to 18 tons per ha.

The edible part of kohlrabi is the turnip-shaped thickening of the stem, which is eaten raw or in fried or braised form. Its taste is like that of the cabbage heart. Leaf cabbage is raised as a vegetable (like spinach), for feed, and sometimes as a decorative plant.

Pakchoi is widespread in China and Japan. In the USSR it is planted in the Far East. The leaves are used like spinach or for salads. Pe-tsai is raised as a vegetable (the leaves) and as an oil-producing plant (the seeds). It is common in East Asia and is cultivated to a limited degree in the United States and Western Europe; in the Soviet Union it is grown in the Far North and the Far East.

Brassicas are rotated with vegetable, vegetable and fodder, or fodder crops. Good predecessors are beans, cucumbers, onions, tomatoes, beets, and other row crops as well as perennial leguminous grasses. In preparing the soil for brassicas up to 80 tons per ha of organic fertilizer should be applied. The most common method of cultivating brassicas is by transplanting. The seedlings are grown in hothouses, cold or heated frames, and in the open in southern areas. The seedlings can be prepared in feeding pots or without them and with or without intermediate transplanting (thinning out). Care of brassicas consists of interrow tillage, weeding, hilling, fertilizing, watering, and pest and disease control. Owing to the growth of mechanization, brassica cultivation without transplanting—planting seeds directly in open fields—is being practiced on a wide scale. This method has become important in the Far East and in southern regions of the USSR. The winter method is used for growing white cabbage in the Abkhazian ASSR, Azerbaijan SSR, the Black Sea coast of Krasnodar Krai, and the southern shores of the Crimea. Seeds are sown in hothouses in September to obtain seedlings, and the seedlings are planted in open fields in November. The crop is harvested in the middle of May. The techniques of raising brassicas for seed are approximately the same as those of growing them for food. One brassica seed plant yields 40–50 g of seeds (0.5–0.6 tons per ha).

Pests and diseases of brassicas. The flea beetle, cabbage maggot, diamondback moth, cabbage butterfly, cabbage cutworm, cabbage aphid, cabbage bug, and blossom beetle are among the pests that do major damage to brassicas. The most common diseases are clubroot of crucifers, wire stem, alternaria blight, downy mildew, gray mold, and storage rot.

REFERENCES
[Popova, E. M.] "Kapusta." In *Semenovodstvo ovoshchnykn kul'tur: Dlia nechernozemnoi polosy SSSR.* Edited by E. I. Ushakova. Moscow, 1953.
Biokhimiia ovoshchnykh kul'tur. Edited by A. I. Ermakov and V. V. Arasimovich. Leningrad-Moscow, 1961.
Zhukovskii, P. M. *Kul'turnye rasteniia i ikh sorodichi,* 3rd ed. Leningrad, 1971.
Lizgunova, T. V. *Kapusta.* Leningrad, 1965.

I. E. KITAEVA and IU. I. MUKHANOVA [11–1089–2]

BRIGHT-DRAWN STEEL, hot-rolled structural steel that is subjected to additional treatment by cold drawing with small reductions in order to obtain more precise sectional sizes (third to fifth grades of fit), to improve surface quality, and for some steels, to upgrade physical and mechanical properties by cold hardening. Warm drawing (the metal is preheated up to 100° C) is used for the bright-drawing (sizing, gauging) of low-ductility steels. Bright-drawing is used mainly for round (3–100 mm), square, and hexagonal rods. The bright-drawn rods are 6–15 m long. The camber of the bright-drawn steel rods that develops during the drawing process is corrected on straightening machines. High-alloy bright-drawn steel is polished after sizing and straightening. [11–592–2]

BROADTAIL, the pelts of prematurely born lambs (abortions during the last stage of pregnancy) or fetuses (taken from the wombs of pregnant ewes slaughtered for meat) of the Karakul breed of sheep. Broadtail has short, silky hair that lies close to the flesh side of the hide and a moiré pattern with curl not yet formed. The color is the same as that of karakul—black or various shades of gray or brown. Despite a flesh side that is less tough than that of karakul and their small size, broadtail pelts with a distinct moiré pattern are highly valued (almost on a level with the highest grades of karakul) and are in great demand. Broadtail is used to manufacture jackets, collars, and hats. The pelts of prematurely born lambs aged 140–145 days are called Persian lamb. These pelts are larger than those of broadtail and have hair that approximates that of karakul. It is a little less valuable than broadtail. (See references under KARAKUL.)
[11–1151–1]

BULRUSH (*Scirpus*), a genus of perennial, rarely annual, plants of the family Cyperaceae. The flowers are bisexual, in spikelets, gathered into umbrelled paniculate or capitate inflorescences. There are usually six perianth bristles; however, sometimes they are absent. There are two or three stigmas. More than 250 species are found throughout the world. In the USSR there are approximately 20 species, growing in damp places and in water. The great bulrush (*Scirpus lacustris*), which often makes up vast thickets, forms peat. Its stalks, measuring up to 2.5 m in height, are used to weave various articles. They are also used as material for packing, heat insulation, and construction. The stalks are eaten by muskrats and water rats. The species *S. sylvaticus* is fed as hay to cattle; its young shoots are a favorite food of deer. The species *S. gracilis* (native to India) and *S. prolifer* (native to Africa and Australia) are cultivated as ornamentals. The genera *Holoschoenus* and *Dichostylis,* which are distributed in the moderately warm regions of Eurasia, are sometimes considered as the genus *Scirpus.* Plants of the genus *Phragmites* of the family Gramineae are often incorrectly called bulrush.

T. V. EGOROVA [11–858–3]

BUREAUCRATISMS, words and expressions characteristic of the style of official papers and documents. Documents, acts, declarations, applications, certificates, and warrants are written according to an established form. However, the official formulations and requisite stereotyped expressions (clichés) of official discourse should not be transferred to colloquial speech and the literary language. Examples of Russian bureaucratisms are the use of *lesnoi massif* ("forest tract") instead of *les* ("forest") and *proizvodit' polivku* ("to conduct an irrigation") instead of *polivat'* ("to irrigate"). Bureaucratisms may also differ grammatically from corresponding elements of the colloquial and literary languages—for example, Russian *imeet byt'* ("will have existence") rather than *budet* ("it will be"). The essential differences, however, are in vocabulary and syntax—for example, the words *sei* for *etot* ("this") and *kakovoi* for *kotoryi* ("which").
[11–1009–5]

BURL, a distinctive excrescence of the trunks, branches, and roots of leafy and, more rarely, coniferous trees. Burls apparently develop as a result of the damage done to trees by fires, fungi, and pasturing cattle. They appear where there is an overabundance of shoots and where dormant buds and adventitious buds grow closely together. In these areas of the tree there is also an intense development of cordate rays with the formation of tracheidal flexures and wood fibers (cross-grained wood). The wood in a burl grows 1½ to 3 times faster than the normal wood of a tree; it is also heavier and harder. The planes exposed after cutting have beautiful patterns. Burls are used by joiners, carvers, and turners as material for the production of small articles. The wood from burls is also used for veneers. Walnut burls, which reach a diameter of 1.5–2 m, are particularly valuable. In the USSR, walnut burls are found mainly in Middle Asia and, occasionally, in the Caucasus. Birch, linden, and alder burls are used in the production of particularly small items.
[11–1016–3]

CA (also, Song Ha), a river in the Democratic Republic of Vietnam (DRV), originating in Laos. Length, approximately 500 km. In its upper reaches, it cuts through spurs of the Truong Son, crosses a maritime plain, and then flows into the Gulf of Bac Bo (Tonkin) of the South China Sea. The water level is at its highest during the summer. In its lower course, its waters are used for irrigation. The city of Vinh (DRV) is situated on the river. [11–244–1]

CAATINGA, a tropical deciduous vegetation growing sparsely in the forests of northeastern Brazil. The constant arid conditions, interrupted by short rains, favor mainly the growth of scrubs, medium-height trees, and shrubs. The *caatinga* is characterized by bottle trees, thorny trees, and leaf succulents (sun spurges and cacti) and cauline succulents. [11–245–1]

CABALA (an ancient Hebrew word, literally meaning "traditional lore"), a mystical current in Judaism.

Cabala combined the pantheistic constructions of Neoplatonism and the mythologems of gnosticism with a Jewish belief in the Bible as a world of symbols. *The Book of Creation,* a treatise written between the third and the eighth century A.D. and the first attempt at abstract speculation in the Hebrew language, teaches about the 32 elements in the creation of the world. These elements included the ten fundamental numbers (as in Pythagoreanism in Greece) and the 22 letters of the Hebrew alphabet. The cabala in the proper sense of the word arose in the early 13th century among Jews of Spain and Provence and developed in a complex interrelationship of mutual influence and conflict with an Arabic Jewish philosophical movement in Andalusia.

The fundamental work of the cabala is the *Book of Splendor,* or *Zohar,* which was written in Aramaic in Castile at the end of the 13th century. The book was probably written by Moses de Leon (Moshe de Leon), who, however, preferred to attribute it to the second-century Talmudic sage Simeon ben Yokhai. The *Zohar* takes the typical form of allegorical interpretations of biblical texts. The cabala took god as an absolute, incorporeal, indefinable, and boundless entity (*Ein Sof*), a negation of everything objective. However, this nothingness is at the same time everything in the objects into which its essence flows, and it limits itself for this purpose. Thus, the cabala replaces the theory of the creation of the world with the concept of emanation. The indefinable god acquires definition in the ten *Sefirot*, or stages in the unfolding of its meaning, which are analogous to the spheres of gnosticism (Supreme Crown, Wisdom, Intelligence, Love, Power, Compassion, Lasting Endurance, Majesty, Foundation of the World, and Kingdom); the relation of these hypostasized attributes of god is represented in a "tree of *Sefirot*." In their totality, the *Sefirot* form the cosmic body of the perfect essence of the primeval man, the *Adam Kadmon,* in whom are concentrated the potentials of world being (compare the gnostic myth of the divine man who existed before the beginning of time). Strictly speaking, the cabala does not recognize anything besides or outside of god, and evil may therefore be presented, in this strictly monistic system, merely as a mode of the divine substance itself.

So-called practical cabala is a special aspect of cabala based on the faith that with the help of special rituals, prayers, and inner acts of will man can actively interfere in the divine cosmic process of history (for example, he can hasten the coming of the Messiah), since every "impulse from below" (from man) must necessarily be reciprocated by an "impulse from above" (from god). The major authority of practical cabala was Isaac Luria (Yitskhak ben-Shlomo Ashkenazi), or Ari (1534–72); his system of cabalistic theurgy had an influence on mystical currents in Judaism from the 17th to the 19th century, such as Shabbateanism and Hasidism.

Interest in cabala began spreading in the 15th century among Christian scholars of Europe, who tried to synthesize it with the dogmas of Christianity within the framework of a universal religion that would embrace all mankind (G. Pico della Mirandola, J. Reuchlin, C. Agrippa, Paracelsus). J. Boehme's theory that world conflict originates in the very nature of god was very similar to cabalistic theory. Certain practices of the Masons show a superficial assimilation of cabalistic symbolism. G. Hegel, V. Solov'ev, N. Berdiaev, C. G. Jung, and M. Buber were directly or indirectly influenced by cabalistic mysticism.

Marxism views cabala, like other currents of Western European mysticism of the period, as a fanciful reflection in the social consciousness of the crisis that accompanied the transition from the Middle Ages to modern times.

REFERENCES
Langer, G. *Liebesmystik der Kabbala.* Munich, 1956.
Scholem, G. *Major Trends in Jewish Mysticism,* 4th print. New York, 1969. Pages 119–286.　　　　S. S. AVERINTSEV [11–273–2]

CABALLERO, a knight in medieval Spain. In the early period of the Reconquista, the term referred to a mounted soldier who purchased weapons and a horse and its gear at his own expense, in order to participate in the wars. Since around the 12th century, the word *hidalgo* has been used in the same sense as caballero.　　　　[11–248–1]

CABALLERO CALDERÓN, EDUARDO. Born Mar. 6, 1910, in Bogotá. Colombian author and journalist.

Since 1939, Caballero Calderón has headed the literary section of the newspaper *El Tiempo.* From 1946 to 1948 he held diplomatic posts. He made his literary debut in 1936 with the book of essays *Underground Paths.* He later wrote historical and philosophical essays and books on the landscape and people of Colombia. His novel *The Art of Living Without Dreams* (1943) is about the Colombian intelligentsia. The novel *The Good Savage* (1966) deals with a Latin American student in Paris. In the novels *The Rejected Christopher* (1952) and *The Landless Slave* (1954), Caballero Calderón realistically described the life of the Colombian peasantry.

REFERENCES
Obras, vols. 1–3. Medellín, 1963–64.
Cain. Barcelona, 1969.

In Russian translation:
S'ervo bezzemel'nyi. Preface by Z. I. Plavskin. Moscow, 1963.
　　　　[11–247–1]

CABANATUAN, a city in the Philippines, in the central part of the island of Luzon, in the province of Nueva Ecija, on the Pampanga River. Population, 95,900 (1969). It is the commercial center of a rice-growing region on the Manila plain. This plain is known as the rice granary of the country. There are food-processing enterprises, primarily rice mills.　　[11–249–1]

CABANIS, PIERRE-JEAN-GEORGES. Born June 5, 1757, in Cosnac, Corrèze; died May 5, 1808, in Rueil. French materialist philosopher and physician, a student of Condillac.

Cabanis' political views were close to those of the Girondins, and he was a friend of Mirabeau and Condorcet. During the Great French Revolution he played a leading role in reorganizing the medical school and took part in the coup d'etat of 18 Brumaire.

Cabanis' materialist and atheist views were less consistent and militant than were those of the older generation of 18th-century French materialists. He maintained that the brain produced thought just as the pancreas or the liver produced secretions. Cabanis is thus considered a precursor of vulgar materialism. Together with A.-L.-C. Destutt de Tracy, Cabanis was a founder of the theory of "ideology" as the science of the general and immutable laws of the formation of ideas. He held that medicine was the chief means for perfecting mankind, since by acting on the body it would be possible to achieve mental transformations. Cabanis had an important influence on the development of medicine and physiology, particularly in 18th-century America. In his last years he tended toward vitalism.

WORKS
Oeuvres complètes, vols. 1–5. Paris, 1823–25.
Oeuvres philosophiques, parts 1–2. Paris, 1956.
In Russian translation:
Otnosheniia mezhdu fizicheskoiu i nravstvennoiu prirodoiu cheloveka, vols. 1–2. St. Petersburg, 1865–66.
REFERENCES
Zabludovskii, P. E. "Kabanis—vrach-materialist XVIII."*Klinicheskaia meditsina,* 1939, vol. 17, issue 5.
Dubois, E. F. *Examen des doctrines de Cabanis,* vols. 1–2, Paris, 1842.
Guillois, A. *Le Salon de Madame Helvétius, Cabanis et les idéologues.* Paris, 1894.
Vermeil de Conchard, P. P. *Trois Études sur Cabanis.* Brive, 1914.
　　　　M. KH. RABINOVICH [11–249–2]

CABARET, originally an improvised presentation given by poets, musicians, or actors in literary and artistic cafés. The performers read poetry, sang topical ditties, and staged short, satirical sketches. There was a master of ceremonies to help create an unconstrained and gay atmosphere. Cabarets became widespread in France (mostly Paris) in the 1880's but lost their improvisational character gradually, as the bourgeoisie began frequenting them and professional artists from variety shows began to appear on their stages.

In Russia two of the most popular cabarets were Letuchaia Mysh (The Bat) in Moscow and Krivoe Zerkalo (The Distorting Mirror) in St. Petersburg, both founded in 1908. In present-day bourgeois countries cabarets are restaurants with variety shows that are usually intended solely for entertainment and occasionally have erotic and vulgar overtones.　　　　[11–272–1]

CABBAGE APHID (*Brevicoryne brassicae*), an insect of the family Aphididae, of the order Homoptera. Adult aphids, which measure approximately 2 mm long, are green with a grayish white waxy film. The females are winged or wingless; the males are winged. Cabbage aphids are widespread. They cause damage to cultivated cruciferous plants, particularly cabbage and rutabaga. In the USSR they are especially harmful in the south. The eggs of the cabbage aphid winter (sometimes the females and larvae as well). In the spring the larvae hatch and develop into wingless fundatrices, which produce parthenogenetically up to

40 larvae. The latter turn into wingless fundatrigeniae, which reproduce similarly until fall, yielding between eight and 20 generations. Initially, cabbage aphids live on cruciferous weeds and on cabbage and rutabaga seeds. In midsummer, in addition to the fundatrigeniae, winged migrantes develop, which fly to cabbage and other cultivated cruciferous plants. The sexual generation appears in autumn; eggs, which will winter, are laid by the fertilized females on cabbage stumps and weeds.

The cabbage aphid, by feeding on plant juices, causes leaf decolorization and curl, arresting the development of the head. Measures taken to control this insect include destroying weeds, tilling after the harvest, using phosphorous and potash fertilizers, treating plants with insecticides, and placing crucifers near the seeds of plants, such as carrot, parsnip, and fennel, which attract beneficial insects. These insects, such as the hover fly, destroy the cabbage aphid.   L. G. Ter-Simonian [11–1094–2]

CABBAGE CUTWORM (*Barathra brassicae*), a butterfly of the family Noctuidae. The wingspread measures 50 mm. The front wings are gray-brown with dark crosswise stripes and a kidney-shaped spot in the center; the hind wings are lighter. The caterpillar is 50 mm long and greenish gray, green, or brown. The eggs are gray and hemispherical.

The cabbage cutworm is found in Europe, with the exception of the extreme north, and Asia (the Caucasus, Siberia, Middle Asia). It damages crucifers, especially cabbage, as well as tobacco, sunflowers, beets, peas, onions, lettuce, and many other plants. There are one to three generations a year. The chrysalides hibernate through the winter in the ground, and the butterflies fly out in May and June. The eggs are laid on the underside of leaves in groups of ten to 15. In eating, caterpillars leave irregularly-shaped holes in the leaves and inner passages in the cabbage heads, soiling them with their excrement. Measures taken to control the cabbage cutworm include deep autumn plowing; releasing a cabbage cutworm parasite, the *trichogramma* (as many as 50,000 per hectare), during the pest's egg-laying period; sowing plants of the family Umbelliferae (carrots, parsnips, fennel), which attract the cabbage cutworm parasite *Ernestia consobrina* Meig; and treating plants with insecticides. [11–1094–1]

CABBAGE PALM (*Roystonea oleracea,* formerly *Oreodoxa oleracea*), a palm (up to 40 m high) with pinnate leaves (up to 8 m long). It grows wild in the Antilles and in Honduras and is cultivated in the tropics. The cabbage palm's tender and juicy terminal bud is used for food. Some palm species of such genera as *Euterpe* and *Borassus,* whose terminal buds are also used for food, are sometimes called cabbage palms. [11–1093–2]

CABERNET, varieties of French wine grapes. In the USSR the varieties Cabernet Sauvignon and Cabernet Franc are grown in the Krasnodarsk and Stavropol krais of the RSFSR, in the Crimea and other regions of the Ukrainian SSR, in the Moldavian SSR, and in the Georgian SSR. They are used for producing high-quality dry red wines, fortified wines, and dessert wines. These grapes are also used in the production of champagne. [11–289–3]

CABET, ÉTIENNE. Born Jan. 1, 1788, in Dijon; died Nov. 8, 1856, in St. Louis, USA. French publicist, writer, lawyer, utopian communist.

Cabet, the son of an artisan, was a participant in the Carbonari movement and the Revolution of 1830. As a historian of revolution, he wrote the *Popular History of the French Revolution 1789–1830* (vols. 1–4, 1839–40). In 1833 he became the publisher of the journal *Le Populaire.* Because of repression he emigrated to Belgium. In 1834, Cabet went to live in Great Britain, where he became acquainted with R. Owen. In 1940 he wrote the book *How I Became a Communist* and the novel *Voyage to Icaria* (Russian translation, vols. 1–2, 1935). In the novel, Cabet depicted communism as an association founded on social equality, brotherhood, unity, and democracy in accordance with the principles of reason and the demands of nature.

Cabet's utopia had petit bourgeois features, such as the equali-

zation of consumption, the preservation of privately owned agricultural enterprises, and the preservation under communism of a pantheistic kind of religion. He believed that communism could be achieved through persuasion and peaceful reforms. As a whole his utopia has much in common with the views of 18th-century utopian communists. In comparison with the teachings of the most important socialist thinkers of the first half of the 19th century, Cabet's utopia represented a step backward. However, because of the undeveloped class consciousness of the proletariat at that time, his Icarian Communism was widely accepted by French artisans and workers. K. Marx characterized him as being France's "most popular, although the most superficial, representative of communism"(K. Marx and F. Engels, *Soch.,* 2nd ed., vol. 2, p. 146). In 1843, Cabet began publishing *The Icarian Almanac. . . .* With the assistance of R. Owen in 1848 he obtained a plot of land in Texas and organized a colony of Icarians there. Dissension among the members led to a crisis, which resulted in the exclusion of Cabet from the colony. In 1856, shortly before his death, he founded another community.

REFERENCES
Lux, H. E. *Kabe i ikariiskii kommunizm.* St. Petersburg, 1906. (Translated from German.)
Hepner, A. *Ikariitsy o Severnoi Amerike.* St. Petersburg, 1906. (Translated from German.)
Volgin, V. P. *Frantsuzskii utopicheskii kommunizm.* Moscow, 1960. Pages 207–38.
Istoriia frantsuzskoi literatury, vol. 2. Moscow, 1956.
Bonnaud, F. *Cabet et son oeuvre.* Paris, 1900.
Prudhommeaux, J. *Icarie et son fondateur, E. Cabet.* Paris, 1907.
Angrand, P. *E. Cabet et la République de 1848.* Paris, 1948.
Cretinon, J. F., and F. M. Lacour. *Voyage en Icarie. . . .* Paris, 1952.
    I. I. Zil'berfarb [11–275–1]

CABEZA DE VACA, ÁLVAR NÚÑEZ. Born in 1490; died in 1564 (according to some sources, 1507–59). Spanish conquistador.

In 1528, Cabeza de Vaca sailed from western Florida to Texas on one of the ships of P. Narváez' military expedition. He was shipwrecked off the coast of Texas. From 1529 to 1536, in wandering from one Indian tribe to another, he was the first to cross the Great Plains and the Rio Grande basin, finally reaching Mexico. In 1541–42, after being appointed governor of the province of Rio de la Plata, he landed on the coast of Brazil at 27°S lat. and crossed the southern part of the Brazilian plateau. He discovered the Iguaçu River, a left tributary of the Paraná, and traveled to its mouth. From there he marched west to the Paraguay River, sailing as far as 18°S lat. in search of silver. In 1544, Cabeza de Vaca was arrrested by a rival and deported to Spain in 1545. He described his travels in *Tales of Failures* (1555).

REFERENCES
Magidovich, I. P. *Istoriia otkrytiia i issledovaniia Severnoi Ameriki.* Moscow, 1962.
Magidovich, I. P. *Istoriia otkrytiia i issledovaniia Tsentral'noi i Iuzhnoi Ameriki.* Moscow, 1965.   I. P. Magidovich [11–320–1]

CABIMAS, a city in Venezuela, on the northeast shore of Lake Maracaibo, in the state of Zulia. Population, 141,300 (1969). It is a center for the extraction and refining of petroleum. A pipeline links Cabimas with the oil-exporting port of Punta Cardón. [11–290–3]

CABINET, the official designation for the government in several foreign countries, including Great Britain, India, Zambia, Kenya, the United States, Tanzania, and Japan. It is headed by either a prime minister (Great Britain, India, and Japan) or a head of state, such as a president (USA, Zambia, Kenya, and Tanzania). In some countries, such as Great Britain and India, the cabinet does not include every member of the government; it consists only of the prime minister and the ministers heading the most important governmental offices (for example, the ministers of defense, foreign affairs, finance, and domestic affairs).

[11–290–5]

CABINET LANDS, the property of the imperial family that was managed by the Cabinet of His Imperial Majesty, an office within the Imperial Court Ministry.

Cabinet lands were concentrated in the Altai (from 1747), Transbaikalia (from 1786), and Poland (Łowicz Principality, three districts with several dozen estates). In Siberia these lands covered 67.8 million hectares. Gold, silver, lead, and copper were mined, and factories produced iron, cast iron, and steel. In 1796 there were nearly 70,000 male serfs, convict settlers, and hired laborers on these lands. In the second half of the 18th century the mining industry on cabinet lands was highly developed. In the first half of the 19th century these enterprises could not compete with the developing capitalist industry and were closed down or leased. Beginning in 1861 there was intensified exploitation of forests and leasing of lands. Settlement on the estates was permitted after 1865, and by 1907 nearly 1 million peasants had migrated to them. In the period preceding the October Revolution, cabinet lands in the Altai produced yearly revenues of 3–4 million rubles. In 1917 cabinet lands were confiscated by the Soviet government.

REFERENCES
Agapova, T. I. "Vozniknovenie i razvitie kabinetskogo khoziaistva na Altae v XVIII v." In the collection *Sibir' perioda feodalizma,* issue 1. Novosibirsk, 1962.
Karpenko, Z. G. *Gornaia i metallurgicheskaia promyshlennost' Zapadnoi Sibiri v 1700–1860 gg.* Novosibirsk, 1963.   V. I. DULOV   [11–290–6]

CABINET OF HIS IMPERIAL MAJESTY, the office that managed the personal property of the royal family, among other matters, between 1704 and 1917. Established in 1704 by Peter I, it was the tsar's chancellery, managing his finances and property and conducting his correspondence. It was headed by a cabinet secretary, A. V. Makarov. Abolished on May 27, 1727, it was reestablished on Dec. 12, 1741, as the private chancellery of Empress Elizabeth Petrovna. When the Imperial Court Ministry was established in 1826, the cabinet was incorporated into it. It was abolished on Feb. 26, 1917.

REFERENCES
"200-letie Kabineta ego imperatorskogo velichestva, 1704–1904." *Istoricheskoe issledovanie.* St. Petersburg, 1911.
Obzor deiatel'nosti Kabineta ego imperatorskogo velichestva za 1906–1915. St. Petersburg, 1916.
Gosudarstvennye uchrezhdeniia Rossii v XVIII v. Moscow, 1960.
S. M. TROITSKII   [11–290–4]

CABINET SCHOOLS, schools that arose in Russia on cabinet lands during the second half of the 18th century. They were under the direct supervision of the office of the tsar, the Cabinet of His Imperial Majesty. The school at the silver smeltery in Nerchinsk, founded in 1761, was a school of this type. The principal function of the cabinet schools was the training of the children of workers and office employees for various lower-skilled positions at factories. The most experienced workmen at factories and mines joined the teaching staffs of these schools. Beginning in the late 19th century, cabinet schools were placed under the jurisdiction of the Ministry of Public Education.

[11–291–1]

CABIRI (also Cabeiri), in Greek mythology, deities originating in Asia Minor (probably Phrygia), who fulfilled the combined functions of chthonic deities and fertility demons. The Cabiri were also considered the protectors of seafarers and the saviors of the shipwrecked. Their cult was widespread along the coasts of Asia Minor, on the islands of the northern Aegean Sea, and partly in northern and central Greece. The most ancient and famous sanctuaries of the Cabiri were located in Thebes (Boeotia), on the island of Lemnos, and especially on the island of Samothrace. Here they were revered as "great gods," and the mysteries, which had been extremely popular beginning with Hellenic times, were performed in their honor.   [11–292–1]

CABLE (or rope), a flexible article manufactured from steel wire, filaments, yarn (hemp yarn), or vegetable, synthetic, or mineral fibers. Cables can be subdivided by their method of manufacture into twisted, nontwisted, and braided types.

Metal (steel) cables are manufactured from uncoated (bright), zinc-coated, or aluminum-coated wire of circular or shaped cross section, with tensile strength $\delta_r = 900$–$3,500$ meganewtons per sq m (MN/m^2), or 90–350 kilograms-force per sq mm (kgf/mm^2). The cross section of steel cables may be round, hexagonal, rectangular, or square. Twisted round cables may have various lays—for example, a single spiral lay, which may be open, semisheathed, or sheathed; double lay (hawser lay), made up of three to eight strands, which may be circular or shaped (trihedral or oval); or triple lay (cable lay), made up of hawser-laid cables (strands). According to the arrangement of wires in the strand layers, cables may have linear, point, or combination contact between the wires. Depending on the lay of the strands, cables may be of the untwisting, nonuntwisting, or low-twist types (there may be 18–31 strands, with opposite directions of lay in individual layers). The direction of lay for the strands of a cable can be right-hand (designation Z) and left-hand (designation S); the combination of directions of lay for the individual elements and for the cable as a whole can be crossed right-hand (SZ), crossed left-hand (ZS), one-way right-hand (ZZ), and one-way left-hand (SS). Twisted circular cables have a diameter of up to 100 mm. Combined twisted cables are made of hemp and steel. In this case the steel strands are covered by a layer of hemp yarn or plastic. Nontwisted cables consist of tightly packed groups of steel wires or spiral cables compressed from the outside by a spiral wrapping or by clamps. Such cables are usually assembled at the place of use; their diameter may be up to 1.5 m. The breaking load of nontwisted cables depends on their diameter and can be as high as 1,000 MN. Braided cables are produced by braiding an even number of strands (usually four), half of which have a right-hand braid and the other half a left-hand braid. Such cables have a square cross section. Flat cables consist of an even number of strands (four to twelve), with an alternating (right-hand and left-hand) lay, fastened together (stitched) with strands or pins; such cables have a rectangular cross section, and they are up to 250 mm wide.

Table 1. Characteristics of various types of cable

	Diameter (mm)	Breaking load (KN)[2]
Metallic cables		
Spiral open	0.65–34.4	0.44–965.0
Spiral sheathed		
supporting[1]	30–70	596–3,950
hoisting[1]	20–60	349–3,751
Hawser-laid (LC), with core		
fibrous core	2.2–63	2.62–2,230
metallic core	1.9–61.0	2.41–2,460
Trihedrally twisted	18–43.5	203.5–1,405
Nonuntwisting	3.5–68.0	7.08–3,255
Combined cables		
Hemp-steel	8–32	8.9–112.7
Nonmetallic cables		
Untarred hemp	9.6–111.5	6.3–497.5
Tarred hemp	9.6–111.5	6–472.5
Sisal	6.7–111.5	3.85–476
Manila	9.6–111.5	7.76–637
Cotton	3–8	0.4–3.0
Polypropylene	7.9–28.7	7–48
Capron	7.9–63.7	11.8–592.0

[1]Data for breaking load are based on total strength of wire [2]1 kN = 1,000 kgf

Nonmetallic (fiber) cables for ropes are spun from long bast fibers of Russian (soft), manila, and sisal (stiff) hemp, from seed fibers of coconut and cotton, and from synthetic fibers (polypropylene, capron, nylon, perlon, and others) and asbestos fibers. Short fibers (hemp and cotton) are used in the manufacture of cord, binder twine, and other articles. Nonmetallic cables are made in stranded lays (three- and four-strand), with right-hand hawser cable lay (three-strand), as ordinary braided round cables (halyards), or as high-flexibility (nautical) cables. The diameter of fiber cables made from tarred or untarred Russian hemp, manila hemp, or sisal hemp is 6.7–111.5 mm. Cables made from stiff hemp, as compared with those made of soft hemp, have the advantage of greater strength, better wear resistance, and lower weight. Cables made from synthetic fibers exhibit high-strength properties. The strength characteristics of various kinds of cables are given in Table 1.

Table 2. Uses of various types of cable

Metal

Spiral open	Guy ropes, reinforcement of structural members and engineering products, and lightning-protection cables of high-voltage power lines
Spiral sheathed	Cableways and mine hoists
Hawser type, crossed lay . . .	Hoisting and transportation mechanisms and machines, boring equipment, timber procurement
Hawser type, shaped strands	Funicular cableways and inclined mine hoists
Cable-laid, multistrand	Maritime and river transport (mooring and towing)
Combined	Trawling equipment
Nontwisted	Reinforcement of structural members and suspension bridges
Flat	Mine hoists (cage hoists), shaft-sinking equipment (hoists)
Braided	Load hoisting equipment (prevents rotation of the load)

Nonmetallic

Hawser type, untarred	Ship's tackle, binding of packaging material
Hawser type, tarred	Tackle and others (primarily for maritime and river transportation)
Cable-laid	Mooring and towing
Braided (halyards)	Rigging for sailing ships, equipment for towing a nautical log

Cables are widely used in many areas of economy, among them construction, transportation, fishing, mining, and metallurgy (see Table 2). M. A. BUKSHTEIN [11-939-4]

CABLE, electrical, one or more insulated wires enclosed in hermetic sheathing. As a rule, the sheathing is covered by protective coatings. Cables are used in the transmission of electric power or signals (high-voltage power lines; power supply for industrial enterprises and transportation and municipal institutions; communications trunk lines; urban telephone networks; radio and television communications links; power supply for mobile operating machines, such as excavators and coal-cutting and peat-digging machines, and electrical equipment of ships and aircraft). The design of a cable depends essentially on the operating conditions in the cable run (underground; in water, air, or chemically active mediums; at low or high temperatures; or under conditions of high humidity).

Cables of all types have some common design components: current-carrying strands, insulation, and sheathing. Current-carrying strands are made of copper or aluminum, which, with the exception of silver, have the lowest electrical resistance (the specific resistivity ρ of electrolytic copper is 1.7×10^{-8} ohm·m; that of aluminum, 2.9×10^{-8} ohm·m). Depending on operating conditions the current-carrying strands may have various degrees of flexibility and may consist of a single wire or many wires twisted together. In power cables the current-carrying strands have standard cross sections. The choice of cross section depends on the power to be transmitted. In the USSR the most commonly used cross sections are 10, 16, 25, 35, 50, 70, 95, 120, and 150 sq mm. In communications cables the current-carrying strands have standard diameters.

Cable insulation consists of a one-piece, laminated or frame-and-air dielectric separating the current-carrying strands from one another and from the sheath. In multistrand cables the twisted, insulated strands are covered with additional insulation (belted); as a rule, its material is the same as that of the primary insulation. The belted insulation serves as a binding that imparts a circular shape to the cable. Insulation materials must have high electrical resistance and provide the electrical strength needed for particular operating conditions, while maintaining minimum insulation thickness; dielectric losses (tan δ) must be low; and the dielectric constant (ϵ) must be minimized. The materials must have high resistance to aging. For certain operating conditions additional requirements may apply to insulation, such as incombustibility and increased flexibility and wet strength. The heat resistance of insulation—that is, the ability to withstand high temperatures without a significant reduction in operational reliability—is of particular importance, since an increase in the upper limit of operating temperatures makes possible a reduction in overall dimensions and weight of the cable. Materials most widely used as insulation are cable paper and telephone paper, rubbers based on natural and synthetic latex, and plastics (polyethylene in various modifications, polyvinyl chloride, and polystyrene). Mineral oils, oil-rosin compounds, and certain inert gases under pressure can also be used as components of insulating materials.

Sheaths in the form of continuous tubes covering the current-carrying strands protect the strands from mechanical damage and the effects of moisture, light, and chemicals. For cables with easily moistened (hygroscopic) insulation the preferred sheath materials are lead or aluminum (materials with a near-zero diffusion constant). Lead sheaths are easily molded at relatively low temperatures (180°–220°C). In spite of several disadvantages—high density (11.4 g/cm^3), danger to workers' health, and low vibration resistance and mechanical strength—lead sheaths are widely used in the manufacture of cables. Aluminum is more promising for this purpose, since its strength is 2.0–2.5 times that of lead, it is lighter by a factor of 3.3, its vibration resistance is higher, and it is in better supply than lead. However, the molding of aluminum requires more complicated equipment, because plastic deformation of aluminum requires considerable force even at temperatures of 450°–500°C. To increase flexibility, aluminum sheaths for large-diameter cables are corrugated. Cables with continuous plastic insulation usually have sheaths consisting of various polyvinyl chlorides and polyethylene pigmented with 1–2 percent carbon black (the moisture permeability of polyvinyl chlorides is 10 times higher than that of polyethylene). Cables with rubber insulation usually have a sheath made of materials with a synthetic latex base, which imparts to the insulation oil and gasoline resistance, noncombustibility, and high cold resistance, flexibility, and mechanical strength.

To protect cable sheaths against mechanical damage and corrosion, protective coverings, most of which contain an armored layer (armor), are applied to the sheaths. In most cases the armor consists of two steel strips 0.3–0.8 mm thick, sometimes galvanized or asphalt-covered. The strips protect the cable from damage during underground laying, as well as within buildings and in channels, blocks, and tunnels. To protect a cable from the effect of considerable tension forces, it is enclosed in an armor made from round (less frequently flat) galvanized steel wires with a diameter of 1.4–6.0 mm (such protection is mandatory for cables laid on the bottom of bodies of water and in boreholes). Soft covers or fillers consisting of several layers of asphalt-impregnated paper strips or of cable braid (jute) are placed above and below the armor. Cables laid in highly corrosive environments or in the ground where stray currents are present, as well as all cables with an aluminum sheath (independent of operating conditions), are protected by reinforced cover layers that contain layers of plastic, either in strips or continuous. Cables laid in mines or in buildings exposed to fire hazard are protected by noncombustible coverings, such as glass braid or coal-tar pitch. Protection of cables against minor mechanical damage is provided by armor shielding made from galvanized steel wires with a diameter up to 0.3 mm or by braiding with fibrous materials impregnated with nondecaying substances.

The USSR produces more than 1,000 types of cables, whose brands, types, usage, design, and characteristics are given in corresponding standards. A detailed classification of cables by groups, taking into account common technological processes, has been adopted for manufacturing planning and organization and is the basis for specialization of cable-producing factories

Table 1. Main types of cable produced in the USSR

	Design features	Areas of use
KShVGL 3 × 95 + 3 × 10 highly flexible (jacketed) high-voltage cable	Combination power cable (3 strands of 95 sq mm cross section and 3 grounding strands of 10 sq mm cross section) with rubber insulation in a double rubber sheath (jacket). Outside diameter, 69 mm; manufacturing length, 200 m.	For supplying power to earthmoving and mining machinery (excavators; spreaders, and others) under all weather conditions
MNSA and MSSA oil-filled cables with central channel	Single-strand with paper insulation in a lead sheath, reinforced by copper strips, with a corrosion-proof covering; channel consists of a spirally wound stainless-steel wire of 150–800 sq mm cross section. Voltage, 110–220 kV.	For connecting step-up transformers of large power plants to outside distribution equipment and for laying across water obstacles and in built-up areas; laid in trenches and tunnels and on the bottom of bodies of water (wire armor up to 6 mm thick is mandatory)
MVDT (high-pressure) oil-filled cable in steel tubing	Three-strand with paper insulation; laid in a steel tube with a diameter of up to 219 mm, filled with oil under pressure; enclosed in a corrosion-proof covering. Voltage, 220–500 kV; tubing is welded at the actual location of the cable run.	
SB, ASB, AB, and AAB armored power cables; SBG, ASBG, and AABG cables without protective covers	Three-strand, with paper insulation in a lead or aluminum sheath; protected by armor consisting of steel strips (2 layers) and by jute and asphalt coatings. Cross section, 25–240 sq mm; voltage, 1–10 kV; limiting temperature, 80°C; manufacturing length, more than 200 m.	For power and light installations; laid underground (in trenches) or along walls of buildings
KLShV-6 jacketed elevator cable with bearer cable	Highly flexible 6-strand cable; copper strands with rubber insulation; strands are twisted around a rubber-sheathed steel cable (breaking stress, 200 kgf or 2 kN); enclosed in a common rubber sheath. Outside diameter, 14 mm.	For elevator installations with a lift height of up to 40 m; free-hanging
GESK armored cable, filled with gas under pressure	Three-strand, with paper insulation, shielded with a metallized paper strip and a copper strip; gas is fed between strands. Cross section, 70–150 sq mm; voltage, 60–138 kV; limiting temperature, 70°C.	For high-voltage transmission lines. No limit on difference in laying levels.
KBM 8/6 armored communications trunk cable	Combination of 8 main and 6 small coaxial pairs, 1 quadruple, 8 paired, and 6 single conductors for service traffic and signaling; air insulation, lead sheath, steel-strip armor	For long-distance lines and for communication among points along cable run
TPP 100 × 2 × 0.5 telephone cable	Multipair cable (100 pairs of copper strands 0.5 mm in diameter) with polyethylene insulation in polyethylene sheathing; shielded by a smooth or corrugated aluminum strip. Electric resistance, 90 ohms/km; temperature, from −50° to 50°C; manufacturing length, 200–350 m.	For distribution and connecting telephone lines in city networks
KVRG 19 × 1.5 control cable	Multistrand cable (19 strands of solid wires, cross section 1.5 sq mm), with rubber insulation in polyvinyl chloride sheath. Voltage, up to 2 kV; temperature, from −40° to 50°C; manufacturing length, not less than 100 m.	For connecting electrical instruments and control, protective, and communications devices
KOBD-4 armored borehole cable	Single-strand (steel-copper) with rubber insulation (heat-resistant up to 80°C), in an oil- and gasoline-resistant rubber hose; armor consists of two braids of steel wire; manufacturing length, 3.0–3.5 km.	For electrical prospecting (core sampling) of petroleum, ore, and coal deposits and in sinking deep boreholes
RK-75-7-16 high-power, radio-frequency coaxial cable	Single-strand with solid polyethylene insulation in metal braiding; polyvinyl chloride sheath. Characteristic impedance, 75 ohms; diameter across insulation, 7 mm; temperature, 40°–70°C; manufacturing length, not less than 50 m.	For electric power supply to transmitting antennas and from receiving antennas in radio installations
KPT-41 television camera cable	Combination of three coaxial pairs, three quadruple and 19 single wires, one paired and five odd wires; with polyethylene insulation in a polyvinyl chloride sheath. Characteristic impedance, 75 ohms; manufacturing length, 50 m.	For connecting mobile television cameras to power sources and transmitting equipment

and workshops. Cables usually have a letter designation, with an indication of the number and cross section or diameter of the current-carrying strands (see Table 1). For some cables the value of the most important characteristic is also given (operating voltage or rated characteristic impedance), or a characteristic design feature is indicated (type and number of coaxial pairs, double or quadruple twist, and so on). The letters usually denote the metal of the conductor, sheath, and insulation, as well as the presence and type of protective covering and armor and frequently the area of usage (control, shipboard, signaling and block signaling, or installation work). For example, ASK 3 × 95-6 is a power cable that has three aluminum strands with a cross section of 95 sq mm enclosed in a lead sheath and an armor made of circular steel wires, with a reinforced protective cover-

ing on the outside, for a rated voltage of 6 kilovolts (kV); TPVBG 100 × 2 × 0.5 is a telephone cable with polyethylene insulation in a polyvinyl chloride sheath, armored with 100 pairs of steel strips with corrosion-proof coating; the diameter of the copper strands is 0.5 mm.

Data on the cables that are most widely used in various areas of technology are given in Table 1, along with an indication of the main brands for each type and a description of design characteristics, main parameters, cable-laying conditions, operating conditions, and main areas of use.

REFERENCES

Bragin, S. M. *Elektricheskii i teplovoi raschet kabelia.* Moscow-Leningrad, 1960.

Bachelis, D. S., N. I. Belorussov, and A. E. Saakian. *Elektricheskie kabeli, provoda i shnury,* 2nd ed. Moscow-Leningrad, 1963. (Handbook.)
Kabeli i provoda, vols. 1–3. Moscow-Leningrad, 1959–64.
Osnovy kabel'noi tekhniki. Moscow-Leningrad, 1967.
Privezentsev, V. A., and E. T. Larina. *Silovye kabeli i vysokovol'tnye kabel'nye linii.* Moscow, 1970.   V. M. TRET'IAKOV [11–279–1]

CABLE BOX, a device for mechanical and electrical connection of cables in a cable line; it is also used to connect a cable line to electrical installations and transmission lines. Cable boxes can be classified as connector, branch, and terminal (joining) types. The design and fittings of cable boxes depend on the intended uses operating conditions, and the type of cable.

The simplest kind of cable box is used for voltages up to 1 kilovolt (kV) and consists of a cast-iron housing or conical steel funnel filled with a bituminous substance that serves as insulation between the joined cables and the grounded walls of the box. Injection-molded cable boxes made from epoxy compounds are promising, since they simplify construction and installation significantly and reduce the weight and overall dimensions of the box.

Connector cable boxes for 6–35 kV are enclosed in watertight lead housings (up to 10 kV) or brass housings (up to 35 kV). For underground cable runs, cable boxes are placed in cast-iron casings. Plugged cable boxes (a variety of connector boxes) are used to prevent shifting of the impregnating compound in inclined sections of cable run. Connector, branch, and terminal boxes for voltages of 110–500 kV are very complex electrical units; they may be as long as 2.5 to 6 m and may have a diameter of up to 0.6 m.

REFERENCES
Branzburg, E. Z., and S. T. Sokhranskii. *Montazh kabel'nykh muft na napriazhenie do 35 kv.* Moscow-Leningrad, 1961.
Privezentsev, V. A., and E. T. Larina. *Silovye kabeli i vysokovol'tnye kabel'nye linii.* Moscow, 1970.   V. M. TRET'IAKOV [11–285–1].

CABLE CONDUIT SYSTEM, the aggregate of pipelines and inspection devices used in laying, installing, and servicing cables. Devices for concealed installation of cables in buildings are a variety of cable conduit systems. A complete cable conduit system includes shafts (in the basements of buildings) that contain central station equipment for electrical communications, and collecting mains and ducts, in which the cables run exposed, without pipes, and on special supports.

Underground cable conduit systems have span lengths of up to 125 m between inspection devices. Such systems are constructed using either single conduits or packs of several conduits arranged as a unit. They are buried in the earth, mainly under sidewalks, at a depth of 0.4–1.8 m. Conduits are made of concrete, ceramics, asbestos cement, polyethylene, plolyvinyl chloride, and tarred fibers. Their inside diameter is usually 100 mm (conduits with a diameter of 55 to 90 mm are in limited use); they are 1–6 m long. Conduits of each type are joined in such a way as to ensure maximum water-tightness and provide sufficient mechanical strength. To provide an adequate water runoff, the conduits and units of a system are laid with a slope, either from one inspection device to the next or from the midpoint of a span to both sides, with each side sloping toward an inspection device.

In a conduit system for communications cables, the underground inspection devices (manholes and chambers) are classified according to design, dimensions, and dimensional proportions (standard and special types); according to configuration, which depends on the direction and number of conduits or conduit units (straight-through, angular, branching, or station-type); according to material (brick or reinforced concrete; the latter type is subdivided into built-up and cast types); according to design load (for conduits installed under sidewalks, a truckload of 20 kilonewtons; for conduits installed under the roadway, a trailer load of 300 kilonewtons); according to standard dimensions, which depend on the number of channels entering from the station (large or small chambers; small, medium, or large manholes; or of a station type for 3,000, 6,000, 10,000, and 20,000 channels); and according to the shape (retangular, oval, polyhedral, or ellipsoidal).

An underground cable conduit system provides access to the cables at any time (through the inspection devices), thus eliminating the necessity of cutting the pavement and excavating. Such access is required for inspection, repair, and replacement, as well as for development of the cable system to the ultimate planned size.   G. SH. MIZHERITSKII [11–284–2]

CABLE CRANE (cableway crane), a structure used to raise and lower loads and to transport loads horizontally over distances of 100–1,500 m. Such cranes are used in open mine workings (strip pit rock, ore, block rubble, and so on) and at construction sites (earth or concrete).

A cable crane installation consists of two supports with a supporting cable stretched between them. A carriage equipped with a block-and-pulley hoist and a suspended scoop or car that can be raised or lowered moves along the cable on rollers. The carriage is driven by a traction cable, which passes through guide pulleys on the supports to the driving (traction) pulleys of a winch. The block hoist and the load are raised and lowered by the winch through a hoist cable. The supports are of the tower type. The tower containing the drive equipment and operating gear is the machine tower; the opposite tower is the support tower. The supports may be stationary or mobile. If stationary towers are used, additional transportation within the quarry (ditch) becomes necessary. Mobile towers usually move along rails, in parallel if both towers are mobile or radially if only one tower can move. The height of supports is up to 50 m. To increase the output of the installation, cable cranes may be equipped with two scoops, each of a capacity of up to 10 cu m.

Cable cranes have a load capacity of 5–50 tons, a span of 100–1,500 m, and a hoisting height of 50 m or more. For large spans the speed of movement of the carriage on the supporting cable is up to 8–10 m/sec, the speed of lowering is 1.3–1.5 m/sec, the speed of movement of the supports is 1.3–1.5 m/sec, the number of cycles per hour is up to 25–30, and the power consumption is 7–9 kilowatt-hours per ton-km.
      M. V. VASIL'EV [11–288–3]

CABLE FINDER, a set of instruments used in finding the location and depth of a cable run for underground or underwater cables; it is also used to locate damaged areas of the cable strands when they are completely grounded.

A cable finder consists of an audio-frequency amplifier, an antenna (at the input), and earphones (at the output). Its principle of operation is based on the possibility of determining the intensity (or tension) of a magnetic field at various points along the cable run. The magnetic field around the cable is generated by an alternating current of low (audio) frequency, which is supplied by a generator connected to one end of the cable. The cable finder is moved in such a way as to produce maximum volume of sound in the earphones. The layout of a cable run for underground or underwater cables can be determined in this way for depths up to 300 m. The magnetic field—and consequently the volume of the sound in the earphones—weakens sharply at the location of a fault in the conductors (if the fault results in complete grounding).   [11–275–2]

CABLE LAYER, a mechanism for laying underground and submerged cables. Cable layers in common use can be classified according to the design of their operational member as blade-type (loosening action), hydraulic, and rotor-type mechanisms.

A blade-type cable layer is intended to lay cables in thawed clayey or sandy soils or in previously loosened frozen and stony soils. This type of mechanism can also be used to lay cables across small rivers, canals, and other bodies of water (for cables buried in the bottom). If tractors cannot pass through a river or swamp because of depth greater than 1 m or slimy bottom, the tractive effort from the tractor or towing winch is applied to the cable layer through long cables. When a cable layer is towed by tractors, the blade loosens the soil to a depth of up to 1.5 m and forms a narrow slit between the loosening part and the surface of the soil. A hollow container is fastened by hinges to the rear side of the blade; one or more cables pass through it and are laid on the bottom of the slit. The forward blade loosens the top layer of soil and removes obstacles, such as stones or roots. The tractive effort required depends on the density of soil and on the desired depth of the cable run; it ranges from 150 to 500 kilonewtons (15–50 tons-force). The tractive effort can be provided by three to seven tractors. The output of blade-type cable layers is up to 5 km of cable run per shift (8 hr). There are also blade-type underwater cable layers, which are used to bury coastal sections of marine and ocean cables in the bottom to protect them against damage caused by trawling or dredging operations. An underwater cable layer is towed by a ship at a speed of 1–3 km/hr and slides along the bottom (at depths up to 200 m) on skids, digging a trench approximately 0.1 m wide and 0.6–0.7 m deep. Such a cable layer is equipped with a television camera, a hydrophone, and instruments to measure the speed and the distance covered. All data from the bottom are transmitted to the ship through a special connecting cable.

A hydraulic cable layer is intended for laying cables across large rivers. For this purpose a pump on the ship discharges water through a pipe at a head of 10 m. Water leaves the pipe through a nozzle at the desired depth and forms a strong jet that washes away the soil. Another pipe is mounted along the water pipe. The cable passes through this second pipe, corresponding to the movement of the ship, and unwinds from a cable drum mounted on the ship. The cable is laid in the trench formed by the action of the water jet. The output of a hydraulic cable layer is 10–30 m/hr.

A rotor-type cable layer is intended for laying cables in thawed and frozen soils. It consists of a self-propelled rotor excavator, of a trailer carriage, and of equipment for loading, transporting, and laying the cable. The main working member of the mechanism is a disk or wheel with cutting teeth. The output of a rotor-type cable layer is up to 1 km per shift (8 hr).

REFERENCES

Mazel', S. I., and L. I. Ustinov. *Mekhanizatsiia stroitel'stva i remonta kabel'nykh linii sviazi.* Moscow, 1962.
Spravochnik stroitelia kabel'nykh sooruzhenii sviazi. Moscow, 1968.

D. A. Baron   [11–276–1]

CABLE PRODUCTION, the manufacture of metal and nonmetallic (fiber) cables or ropes by means of appropriate technological equipment. The main operations of cable production are the rewinding of wire or yarn onto the spools of wire-drawing benches or reeling benches, the twisting of strands in a strand-twisting machine, and the twisting of cables in cable-twisting or braiding equipment.

Main technical parameters. Cable production technology is influenced by such parameters as the pitch of lay, the type of contact between wires in a strand and between strands in a cable, the direction and angle of lay, and the number of strands. The pitch of lay in strands for cables with point contact should not exceed 11 nominal diameters of circular or shaped strands; for cables with linear contact, it should not exceed 9 diameters; for six-strand cables, 6.5 diameters; for cables with shaped strands, 7.5 diameters; for cables with triple stranding, 7 diameters; and for the strands of a flat cable, 16 diameters.

The strands of cables with point contact are manufactured in one or more layers. There are not more than five wire layers in a strand; the total number of wires can be as high as 61 (and sometimes 91). Every layer in point-contact cables is laid at the same angle of lay; in linear-contact cables, various angles are used, usually in the same direction of lay. Spiral cables have alternating directions of lay for all or some of the layers (there may be as many as ten). The strands in cables with linear contact (not more than three layers) are made in a single production operation; the wires (not more than 48) are all laid in the same direction. The angles of lay relative to the axis of the strand are 12°–15° for point-contact cables and 16°–20° for linear-contact cables (for the outer layer). The angle of lay for the strands in a cable is chosen to approximate the angle of lay of the wires in a strand. To produce cables with one-way lay, cable-stranding machines are equipped with a planetary gear, which rotates the frames holding the loading spools and maintains tension on the strands to preserve the tightness of their lay.

For nonmetallic (fiber) cables, the strands are laid in a single operation, independent of the number of yarns. The pitch of lay

for the strands of three-strand cables is 0.65–0.75 of the circumference; for hawser cables it is 0.85–1.0; and for cords it is 0.9–1.2. The angle of lay is 27°–33°. The direction of lay of the strands and of the cable or cord may differ. An anticorrosion grease is applied to wires and strands before laying. Finished products are also greased and are wound on a reel before shipment to consumers.

Metal cables. Metal cables are manufactured on strand-twisting and cable-twisting machines, which have identical functional diagrams and differ only in their dimensions and the number of loading spools (from three to 48). A metal or fiber core is located on the frame (base) of the machine, and wires or strands are twisted around it. The twisting part of the machine has a template, which distributes wires or strands, and a preformer for producing strands or cables that will not untwist. The strands or cables are shaped into a cone and compressed in a squeezing mechanism with dies. A roller mechanism straightens the cable array, which is then wound on reels or drums by a tensioning mechanism.

There are two types of machines, distinguished by the design of the laying member. In the rotor (basket) type, the spools in the frames are located between individual disks and rotate with the laying member. In the tube (cigar) type, the loading spools are located one behind the other in unbalanced carriages within a cigar-shaped tube (along its axis) but do not rotate with the tube. In both cases the spools rotate around their own axes as a result of force arising from the pull exerted on wires, yarns, or strands by the tensioning mechanism. In rotor machines the core passes through a hollow rotor shaft; in tube machines it passes along the inside surface of the tube. The direction of lay is determined by changing the direction of rotation of the laying member; the pitch of lay is adjusted by a choice of the speed of rotation of the laying member and the peripheral speed of the tensioning mechanism. For cables up to 20 mm in diameter, tube machines have a higher output than rotor machines and some cable-twisting machines. Braided and flat cables are produced on special machines and bench-type carriages. Nontwisted cables are installed by consumers at the site of use.

Nonmetallic cables. Nonmetallic cables are manufactured on machines called ropeways and on stationary strand-twisting and cable-twisting machines. In ropeways the yarns are successively pulled and twisted into strands up to 350 m long. Then, after having passed through the stationary front part and the movable part of the machine, the strands are slightly twisted and divided into groups of three or four on a carriage equipped with a rammer (a device for twisting the cable). The strands are given a cable lay and then a hawser lay by means of hooks mounted in the front part and the movable part of the machine. Ropeways are used in the manufacture of cables or cords of various diameters and up to 250 m long, using two or three standard sizes.

In stationary machines cables and cords are produced in one or two operations. In fiber-twisting machines, as distinguished from machines producing strands of wire, spools with yarn are located in spool holders and the laying member is combined with pulling and receiving mechanisms located within it. In modern machines one turn of the laying member (strander) results in the production of two pitches of lay in the strand, because of special strand loading (with an extra turn). Cable-twisting machines for cables made of fibrous materials differ from wire-cable twisting machines of the rotor type in the number of loading frames and the design of the planetary gear.

Small-diameter rope and cord products are made in a single operation (simultaneous production of strands and twisting into a cable), using combined cording machines and devices that consist of two combined twisting members, one for producing the strand and the other for laying the rope or cord. Halyards are made on braiding machines; nautical braided ropes are produced on special braiding machines.

REFERENCES

Bukshtein, M. A. *Priadenie zhestkikh lubianykh volokon i proizvodstvo kruchenykh izdelii.* Moscow, 1945. (*Priadenie lubianykh volokon,* part 3.)
Glushko, M. F. *Stal'nye pod"emnye kanaty.* Kiev, 1966.

Sergeev, S. T. *Nadezhnost' i dolgovechnost' pod"emnykh kanatov.* Kiev, 1968.
Bukshtein, M. A. *Proizvodstvo i ispol'zovanie stal'nykh kanatov,* 2nd ed. Moscow, 1973.   M. A. BUKSHTEIN [11–947–1]

CABLE SAW, a device for cutting stone in which the cutter is a cable 3–6 mm in diameter. Cable saws are used in quarries to cut blocks from the rock of a mountain massif and in stone-working enterprises for the manufacture of facing blocks.

The stone is cut by a nonfraying steel cable up to 1,500 m long. A slurry of water and grains of an abrasive substance is fed continuously into the cut under the cable. The cable is driven by a pulley at the drive station; constant cable tension is maintained by a tensioning device. The cable moves at a speed of 7–11 m/sec. Among the abrasives used in cutting are quartz sand, for cutting rock of medium hardness (such as marble), and carborundum, for cutting very hard rock, such as granite (under workshop conditions only). The cable is supported over its entire length by a system of pulleys. Vertical operating motion of the cable (in the saw cut) can be produced by the use of stands. Such stands have provisions for moving the pulleys. A cable saw can produce a saw cut up to 50 m long. The depth of the saw cut is usually about 3 m; however, this depth can be increased by the use of higher saw stands. The speed at which the cable cuts a stone depends on the hardness of the stone, the degree of cable wear (as the cable wears, it entrains less abrasive), and the properties of abrasive materials. When quartz sand is used to cut marble, the cutting speed is 3–15 cm/hr; when carborundum is used to cut granite (under workshop conditions only) the speed is about 5 cm/hr.

A design aimed at future improvement of the cable-sawing process incorporates cutters made from a hard alloy or enclosed in diamond armor and attached to the cable. Cutters made of hard alloys are capable of cutting limestone with an ultimate strength of 15 meganewtons per sq m, or 150 kilograms-force per sq cm, as well as gypseous stone and other soft stones; diamond cutters are capable of cutting marble.

Cable saws are widely used in mining marble, travertine, and other rocks consisting of carbonaceous compounds, in areas with a warm climate. In areas with a long winter cable saws are less useful because of the freezing of recirculated water. A cable saw is capable of producing curved cuts because of the small diameter of the cable and therefore is frequently used for the construction of monuments and production of complex architectural components.   A. M. ORLOV [11–944–2]

CABLE SHIP, a ship to lay submarine communications cables and power lines; also used to raise such cables from the bottom and to repair them. The first cable ship was the small English steam tugboat *Goliath,* which on Aug. 28, 1850, was used to lay the first submarine telegraph cable across the Strait of Dover. The largest cable ship of the 19th century was the English steamship *Great Eastern,* with a displacement of 32,000 tons, designed by the English engineer I. Brunel. The *Great Eastern* was used in 1865–74 to lay the first series of transatlantic telegraph cables. During the 1960's the world fleet of cable ships consisted of more than 30 vessels, among them the British ships *Monarch* (displacement, 12,000 tons; built in 1946) and *Alert* (8,000 tons; 1961), the French ship *Marcel Bayard* (7,000 tons; 1961), the Soviet ships *Ingul* and *Iana* (each 6,900 tons; 1963), and the American ship *Long Lines* (17,000 tons; 1962).

The holds of a cable ship, which are cylindrical containers, are called tanks. As many as several thousand kilometers of submarine communications cable are coiled and placed in the tanks. During the cable-laying operation, electric signal repeaters are installed in the cable in special rooms on the deck of the ship, called hangars. The ends of each manufactured length of cable (10–50 km long) are carried onto the deck and are connected to the appropriate repeater. Thus, the assembled length can be either the total length of the main line or the part of the length that can be stored in the cable ship before the laying of the cable is begun. Electrically driven cable machines are used to lay the cable or to raise it for repairs; one such machine is located at the stern and two at the bow (port and starboard). A cable equipped with repeaters is laid from the stern; cables without repeaters are laid from the bow. Cables are also raised from the bow of the cable ship. A cable winch develops a force up to several hundred kilonewtons (tens of tons-force); it has tensioning equipment incorporating pulleys 2–3 m in diameter or of the caterpillar type. The latter type is preferred for laying a cable equipped with repeaters in rigid cylindrical housings. A cantilever (outrigger) protrudes from the bow of the ship; it is equipped with pulleys for the cable being laid and for the carrying cable used in raising. Cable-laying at depths of 5,000–6,000 m is conducted at speeds up to 8 knots (15 km/hr); when repeaters are passing through a cable machine the speed of laying is reduced to 1–2 knots. Cable ships are equipped with apparatus that provides continuous control of the characteristics of the cable being laid or repaired and of the condition of the repeaters. Cable ships are also equipped with apparatus for maintaining ship-to-shore communications through the cable being laid; equipment used in searching for the cable or in raising the cable, including grappling devices (grapnels); buoys for temporary marking of a damaged cable section; floats used in carrying a cable to the shore; and equipment for splicing cable ends.

Ordinary freighters and tugboats are used to lay cables in rivers, lakes, canals, coastal waters, and harbors. Such ships are temporarily equipped with winches used in laying or raising the cable and with large-diameter pulleys, which are located at the stern (for laying cable) or at the bow (for raising cable).

REFERENCE
Podvodnye kabel'nye magistrali sviazi. Edited by I. S. Ravich and D. L. Sharle. Moscow, 1971.   D. L. SHARLE [11–286–4]

CABLE TERMINALS, devices for terminating the strands of communications cables on contacts to which the appropriate circuits of communications apparatus are connected. Cable terminals consist of sets of contact clamps and pins mounted in terminal blocks made of an insulating material (moldings). Connecting or cross-connecting wires are fastened to the outside of the terminal blocks by screws or solder. In long-distance junction boxes, connections are made by special prongs or plug-and-socket units. Some cable terminal devices (protective strips or cable junction boxes) also provide protection of communication lines against lightning discharges and dangerous electric voltages.   [11–288–2]

CABLE THEORY, a theory used to describe the conduction of bioelectric potentials along a cylindrical cell. Cable theory proceeds from the idea that a nerve, muscle, or other cell may be represented as a section of a cable that is placed in a conducting medium and has a cell membrane that acts as an insulator. The cable model of the cylindrical cell and the theory of computation of the ratio of the magnitudes of current and voltage based on that model make possible experimental determination of the electrical parameters of the cell membrane and evaluation of the conditions of propagation of subliminal electric impulses.

REFERENCES
Katz, B. *Nerv, myshtsa i sinaps.* Moscow, 1968. (Translated from English.)
Khodorov, B. I. *Problema vozbudimosti.* Leningrad, 1969.
                                           [11–286–3]

CABLE TRANSMISSION, a device for transmitting rotary motion from one shaft to another shaft by means of a closed loop of cable that passes around pulleys attached to the drive and driven shafts. Under current manufacturing conditions cable transmissions have been replaced by the more convenient and economical electric drive. Cable transmissions were used for axis-to-axis distances of more than 12 m (for distances of up to 25 m, hemp ropes were used; for distances up to 125 m or more, steel cables were used). Cable transmissions made possible distribution of the torque from one drive shaft to several driven shafts.

REFERENCE
Rötscher, F. *Detali mashin,* vols. 1–2. Moscow-Leningrad, 1933–34. (Translated from German.)   [11–944–1]

CABLEWAY, a structure for transporting freight and passengers in which a cable stretched between supports is used to move gondolas or chairs. Cableways are usually built in mountainous or broken country or in other locations where surface travel is difficult, in locations where the shortest possible crossing of a highway, railroad, river, or lake must be provided, and in cities with well-developed surface transportation. A distinction is made among freight, passenger, and combined cableways and, according to design, between two-cable and single-cable cableways, with loop or shuttle movement of the cars.

Freight cableways are usually built with a two-cable loop design. The carriage of a gondola rolls on a stationary supporting cable. The gondolas are moved by a traction cable. The length of such cableways is virtually unlimited, since they are composed of consecutively connected independent sections (6–12 km). Some freight cableways in Switzerland are 200 km long, with an angle of elevation of up to 30°. A loop cableway is capable of transporting 30–500 tons (in a few cases, up to 1,000 tons) of freight per hour at car speeds of 1.5–3.3 m/sec. For shorter distances, two-cable shuttle cableways are built; they have one or two gondolas that carry up to 150 tons of freight per hour at a speed of up to 10 m/sec. The length of such a cableway is up to 3 km; the maximum angle of elevation is 45°. In single-cable cableways the cars are connected to and move with the cable at speeds of 1 to 2.5 m/sec. The cars usually move on a loop route. The capacity of single-cable cableways is 10–150 tons per hr, and the maximum angle of elevation is 25°. Freight cableways are used in many chemical industries and in ore mining.

Passenger cableways are usually of a two-cable design. Cableways built as a shuttle usually have one or two cars, each designed for 12 to 100 passengers. Cableways built as a loop usually have cars designed for four passengers. In passenger cableways the safety of operation is provided by a braking cable, a double traction cable, or the use of a braking device, which engages the supporting cable if the traction cable breaks. Passenger cableways can be up to 12 km long; lifting is possible up to a height of 3 km; and car speed is from 1.5 to 11 m/sec. There are also single-cable (usually loop-type) cableways with rigidly mounted one- or two-passenger seats, which the passengers can occupy or leave while the cableway is in motion. Such cableways are built mainly in mountainous resort areas (Austria, Switzerland, Italy, France, and Japan). In the USSR cableways are operated in the Crimea and the Caucasus (for example, in Priel' brus'e, Kabarda-Balkar ASSR), and in Iuzhno-Sakhalinsk. They transport 200–1,000 passengers per hour at speeds of 1 to 2.5 m/sec, over distances from 0.6 to 2 km and through level differences of 0.5 km. Single-cable ski tows are widely used. The skier is moved at a speed of 1.5 m/sec, while standing on skis and supported by a spring suspension attached to the traction cable. During the summer some ski tows are coverted to chair lifts. Cableways may be used for simultaneous transportation of freight and passengers. Such combined cableways are particularly efficient in logging and mining operations. In addition to suspension-type cableways, land cableways (cable hoists) are being introduced (1970). Such installations make possible, for example, the movement of loaded vehicles on steep inclines or the passage of ships through dams (instead of the usual method, through locks).

REFERENCES
Baramidze, K. M., and I. Ia. Kogan. *Passazhirskie podvesnye kanatnye dorogi.* Moscow, 1962.
Belaia, N. M., and A. G. Prokhorenko. *Kanatnye lesotransportnye ustanovki.* Moscow, 1964.
Dukel'skii, A. I. *Podvesnye kanatnye dorogi i kabel'nye krany,* 4th ed. Moscow-Leningrad, 1966.
Mashiny nepreryvnogo transporta. Edited by V. I. Plavinskii. Moscow, 1969.   V. S. KIREEV [11–942–1]

CABO BRANCO (Portuguese, "white cape"), a cape in eastern Brazil, the easternmost point of the South American continent (34° 46′ W long. and 7° 09′ S lat.).   [11–297–3]

CABOCHIENS, participants in the popular revolt of 1413 in Paris. One of the leaders of the uprising was Simon Le Coustel-lier (a skinner by trade), nicknamed Caboche ("pate," hence Cabochiens).

The revolt was provoked by an increase in taxes during the Hundred Years' War (1337–1453) and by the civil war between the Armagnacs and Burgundians, feudal factions fighting for power during the reign of the feebleminded Charles VI. The revolt was preceded by the convocation of the Estates General in Paris at the end of January 1413, at which the deputies demanded administrative and financial reforms and the arrest of crown officials who were guilty of abuses. There was a growing discontent among the artisans of Paris. The royal government made some concessions, replacing a number of high officials and establishing a commission to prepare administrative and financial reforms. At the same time, fearing unrest, it ordered a large garrison to be stationed in the Bastille. This action touched off the revolt on Apr. 27, 1413. Artisans (especially from the guilds of the butchers, skinners, and tanners), apprentices, and the urban poor played the major role. The leaders of the uprising were the owners of slaughterhouses, secretly bribed by the leader of the Burgundians, John the Fearless, who sought to use the movement in his struggle with the Armagnacs. Having seized weapons in the town hall, the insurgents besieged the royal palace, demanding a reduction of taxes, the regulation of tax collection, and the dismissal of crown officials.

The insurrection of the Cabochiens was exploited by the prosperous urban classes to obtain from the government moderate administrative and financial reforms, primarily the reorganization and improvement of the state apparatus. These reforms were embodied in the Cabochien Ordinance, adopted by the Estates General on May 26–27, 1413. The lower strata of the Parisian populace, whose interests had not been taken into consideration, continued the uprising, showing hostility not only toward the royal government but also toward the prosperous burghers. Frightened by the scope of the movement, the moderates dissociated themselves from the Cabochiens, and the Armagnacs and Burgundians joined together to crush the rebellion in late August 1413. At the beginning of September the Armagnacs occupied Paris, and the Cabochien Ordinance was abolished.

REFERENCES
Sebentsova, M. M. "Kabosh'eny i ordonans 1413 g." *Uch. zap. MGPI im. V. I. Lenina,* 1946, vol. 37, issue 3.
Sebentsova, M. M. "Vosstanie kabosh'enov." *Trudy Moskovskogo gos. istoriko-arkhivnogo instituta,* 1958, vol. 12.
Coville, A. *Les Cabochiens et l'ordonnance de 1413.* Paris, 1888.
[11–295–3]

CABOMBA, a genus of aquatic plants of the family Cabombaceae, formerly included in the Nymphaeaceae family. These plants are perennial grasses with creeping rootstock. The alternate, long-petioled leaves are submerged (finely dissected) and floating (entire, peltate, and leathery). The flowers are solitary and on long peduncles. There are three sepals, three petals, and three to six stamens. The fruit is three-seeded. Around seven species are found in tropical and subtropical America. Several species, including *C. aquatica* and *C. rosifolia,* are cultivated in aquariums. Plants of this genus are propagated with pieces of rhizome.   [11–294–2]

CABOMBACEAE, a family of dicotyledonous plants, closely related to the family Nymphaeaceae, with which it is frequently classified. They are perennial aquatic rhizomatous herbs with three sepals and petals and usually three to six or 12 to 18 stamens, although sometimes more, as in *Brasenia.* The family comprises two genera, *Cabomba* and *Brasenia,* the latter represented by one species growing in the tropical, subtropical, and temperate regions of Asia (in the USSR, in the Far East) and North and South America, as well as in eastern Australia and tropical Africa.

REFERENCE
Takhtadzhian, A. L. *Sistema i filogeniia tsvetkovykh rastenii.* Moscow-Leningrad, 1966.   [11–294–3]

CABOT (also Cabota, Caboto). Navigators.

John (Giovanni) Cabot. Born between 1450 and 1455, in Genoa; died 1499 (?). John Cabot moved to Venice on Mar. 28, 1476. In 1490 he entered the service of England. Sent by Bristol merchants in search of a western sea route to China, he reached at least the island of Newfoundland in 1497. While there, he discovered (perhaps for the second time) the Grand Banks. In 1498 he reached the American continent and explored a large section of its eastern coast.

Sebastian Cabot. Born circa 1475 in Venice; died 1557 in London. Son of John Cabot; accompanied his father on voyages in 1497 and 1498. After moving to Spain, Sebastian Cabot was appointed pilot major there (Feb. 5, 1518). From 1526 to 1530, at the head of a Spanish fleet, he explored the Río de la Plata and the lower course of the Paraná River and discovered the lower section of the Paraguay River. Returning to England, he became a royal adviser for maritime affairs and was one of the organizers of the expedition of H. Willoughby and R. Chancellor (1553–54) in search of the northeast passage. He was also one of the founders of the British Muscovy Company in 1554 or 1555.

REFERENCES

Magidovich, I. P. *Ocherki po istorii geograficheskikh otkrytii.* Moscow, 1967.

Harrisse, H. *John Cabot, the Discoverer of North America, and Sebastian His Son.* London, 1896.

Beazley, C. R. *John and Sebastian Cabot.* London, 1898.

Williamson, J. A. *Voyages of the Cabots . . . .* London, 1929.

Rubio y Esteban, J. M. *Exploración y conquista del Río de la Plata, siglos XVI y XVII.* Barcelona, 1942.   [11–294–4]

CABOTAGE, shipping between ports within a country. Two types may be distinguished: long sea trade, the transport of freight and passengers between ports on different seas, and short sea trade, transport between ports on the same sea. For purposes of cabotage, the following bodies of water in the USSR are considered as single seas: the Black Sea and the Sea of Azov; the White Sea and the Arctic Ocean; and the Sea of Japan, the Sea of Okhotsk, and the Bering Sea. In the USSR, cabotage is conducted exclusively by ships bearing the flag of the USSR.

[11–295–2]

CABRAL, AMILCAR (pseudonym, Abel Djassi). Born Sept. 12, 1924, in Guinea (Bissau); died Jan. 20, 1973, in Conakry. Leader in the national liberation movement of Guinea (Bissau) and the Cape Verde Islands.

Cabral graduated from a *lycée* in São Vicente (Cape Verde Islands) and an agronomy institute in Lisbon. He was one of the founders (1956) and general secretary of the African Party for the Independence of Guinea and the Cape Verde Islands, which since January 1963 has led the armed struggle against the Portuguese colonialists. He wrote many works on the national liberation movement. An honorary doctor of the African Institute of the Academy of Sciences of the USSR (1971), he was active in the movement for solidarity among the countries of Asia and Africa. He was treacherously murdered by agents of the colonialists.

WORKS

Djassi, Abel. *The Facts About Portugal's African Colonies.* London, 1960.

Cabral, A. *Revolution in Guinea.* London, 1969.

Sur la Situation de notre lutte armée de libération nationale. [No place] 1970.

Guinée "portugaise": Le Pouvoir des armes. Paris, 1970.

Rapport bref sur la situation de la lutte. [No place] 1971.

[11–296–1]

CABRAL, LUIS. Born May 11, 1931, in the city of Bissau. State leader in the Republic of Guinea-Bissau; brother of A. Cabral.

Cabral graduated from school in the city of Bissau in 1948. Since 1953 he has been active in the national liberation struggle of the people of Guinea-Bissau; he was one of the founders of the African Party of Independence for Guinea and the Cape Verde Islands (PAIGC). After 1961 he was secretary of the National Workers' Congress of Guinea-Bissau and occupied positions of responsibility in the PAIGC. In July 1973 he became deputy secretary-general of the PAIGC. Since the attainment of independence and proclamation of the Republic of Guinea-Bissau in September 1973 he has been chairman of the State Council.

[Article added by Soviet editors]

CABRAL, PEDRO ALVARES. Born circa 1467; died circa 1520. Portuguese navigator.

In 1500, Cabral was appointed commander of a fleet that was to sail to India following Vasco da Gama's route. Sailing south from the Cape Verde Islands, Cabral strayed far from his path toward the west and on Apr. 22, 1500, at 17° S lat., discovered a land that he mistook for islands and named it the Land of the True Cross. (That same year it was renamed Holy Cross, and a few years later the unofficial name of Brazil became firmly established.) Cabral sailed toward the Cape of Good Hope and in the middle of September 1500 reached India near the city of Calicut. He destroyed Calicut for its refusal to trade with the Portuguese and concluded agreements favorable to Portugal with the neighboring ports of Cochin and Cannanore. By January 1500 he had left the country, and at the end of July he returned to Portugal with a valuable load of Indian goods. The sale of these goods covered the expenses for the expedition more than twice over.

REFERENCE

Magidovich, I. P. *Ocherki po istorii geograficheskikh otkrytii.* Moscow, 1967.   [11–296–3]

CABRERA Y GRIÑÓ, RAMÓN (count of Morella). Born Dec. 27, 1806, in Tortosa; died May 24, 1877, in Wandsworth, near London. Spanish politician and one of the military leaders of the Carlists.

In the first Carlist War (1833–40) Cabrera y Griñó's troops fought in the southeastern part of Spain, in the district of Maestrazgo. In 1837 he took part in the campaign of Don Carlos the Elder against Madrid. Emigrating in 1840, he returned to lead an unsuccessful Carlist uprising in Catalonia in 1848–49, after which he again emigrated.   [11–297–1]

CACAO, (1) a plant of the genus *Theobroma* of the family Sterculiaceae and (2) the food product obtained from the seeds of that plant [in English, the term "cocoa" is more commonly used for the food product].

The seeds of cacao beans have a bitter astringent taste, which is caused by the presence of tanins and theobromine, and do not have the aroma and taste characteristic of chocolate products. The color of the beans ranges from violet to gray and white. In order to improve their flavor, freshly picked beans separated from the pulp are fermented for two to seven days. As a result of complex biochemical processes, the beans turn various shades of brown and acquire a pleasant aroma and taste. Next the beans are dried in the sun on plantations or are dried by heated air.

Cacao is a valuable food raw material. The average composition of the kernel (evaluation of the dry substance) is water, 4–6 percent; fat, cocoa butter, 51–54 percent; starch, 7–10 percent; glucose, fructose, 1–2 percent; protein, 10–12 percent; theobromine, caffeine, 1–1.5 percent; tannins, 4–7 percent; acids, 1–2 percent; and mineral substances, 2–3 percent.

After the beans are cleaned, sorted, and thermally treated, they are broken into nibs and finely ground to make ground cacao, which in turn is used to make cocoa butter and chocolate. Cocoa butter is made by pressing the ground cacao. The remaining cake is coarsely broken and pulverized to make cocoa powder, which is used to prepare the beverage cocoa.   [11–551–4]

CACCIA, a poetic and musical genre of 14th-century Italy. In *cacce* the words usually depict the hunt, although such subjects as fishing and fairs were also treated. The French term for the genre was *chasse.*

The music was intended to illustrate the text. *Cacce* were usually composed for two singing voices and one instrument; imitation and canon were widely used in the vocal parts (one voice chasing the other). Purely instrumental *cacce* developed later. Program instrumental pieces depicting the hunt were composed in subsequent periods, but they did not follow the old *caccia* patterns.   [11–1648–2]

CACCINI, GIULIO. Born circa 1550 in Rome; died Dec. 10, 1618, in Florence. Italian composer, singer, theorbo virtuoso, and theoretician of vocal art. Composer of one of the first operas (*Eurydice*, 1602).

Caccini was a member of the Florentine *camerata*, a group of poets, musicians, and philosophers who played a decisive role in the formation of Caccini's artistic views. He was one of the creators of the Italian bel canto, and his works are melodious and full of virtuoso passages. Caccini also composed a collection of madrigals and arias for voice with accompaniment (*New Music*, 1602), which contains complete directions on the methods of vocal execution.

REFERENCES
Livanova, T. *Istoriia zapadnoevropeiskoi muzyki do 1789 goda.* Moscow-Leningrad, 1940.
Kretzschmar, H. *Istoriia opery.* Leningrad, 1925. (Translation.)
Ehrichs, A. *Giulio Caccini.* Leipzig, 1908.   [11–1648–3]

CACHEXIA, a state of profound wasting and physical debility manifested by severe emaciation, weight loss, dry and flabby skin, loss of hair, disappearance of subcutaneous fat, atrophy of muscles and viscera, and low serum protein level. Edema, hemorrhages, and sometimes mental derangement can occur with cachexia. It results from prolonged malnutrition or starvation, severe metabolic disorders, chronic arsenic, lead, mercury, or fluorine poisoning, and severe lesions of the digestive tract (atrophy of the intestinal mucosa, condition after resection of the stomach and intestines). Cachexia may occur in severe cases of tuberculosis or other chronic infections, some lesions of the endocrine glands, (hypophysis, thyroid, adrenals, pancreas), large slow-healing wounds, abscesses, and malignant tumors (especially of the esophagus and stomach).   [11–1629–4]

CACHIN, MARCEL. Born Sept. 20, 1869, in Paimpol; died Feb. 12, 1958, in Paris. Figured in the French and international workers' movement.

Cachin graduated from the University of Bordeaux, where he subsequently taught philosophy. In 1891, Cachin joined the Workers' Party, led by J. Guesde and P. Lafargue, with whom he was personally acquainted. He headed the party organization in the department and edited the party newspaper, *La Socialiste de la Gironde*. He took part in the Amsterdam Congress of the Second International in 1904. Cachin was one of the leaders of the French Socialist Party (SFIO) from 1905 to 1920. He participated in the Stuttgart (1907) and Basel (1912) congresses of the Second International and was a supporter of the Marxist tendency in the French workers' movement. On the death of P. Lafargue, Cachin became editor of the newspaper *L'Humanité* in 1912 and was the director of the newspaper from October 1918 until his death. He served as a parliamentary deputy from 1914, except for an interval in 1933–35.

Under the influence of the revolutionary movement in France and Russia, especially the Great October Socialist Revolution (he visited Russia in the spring of 1917 and the summer of 1920), Cachin moved to a communist position. He attended the Second Congress of the Third International in Moscow in 1920, where he frequently met with Lenin. Supporting the recognition of Soviet Russia in parliament and the press and opposing anti-Soviet intervention, Cachin remained to the end of his life a true friend of the USSR. He played a leading role in the establishment of the French Communist Party (PCF). After many months of struggle (under the leadership of Cachin) for the affiliation of the SFIO with the Comintern, the Tours Congress of the SFIO in December 1920 adopted by majority vote Cachin's resolution to create a communist party. Cachin became a member of the Directing Committee, which functioned during the first three years of the existence of the PCF. He was then elected to the first Central Committee and Politburo of the PCF, of which he remained a member to the end of his life. He was repeatedly subjected to persecution and arrest.

From 1924 to 1943, Cachin was a member of the Executive Committee and later a member of the Presidium of the Executive Committee of the Comintern. He participated in the Fourth, Sixth, and Seventh Congresses of the Comintern.

Cachin played a significant part in the organization of the Popular Front in France (1934–38). He defended republican Spain against the fascist insurgents and interventionists (1936–39) and supported the strengthening of friendship with the USSR on the basis of the Franco-Soviet Treaty of Mutual Assistance of 1935. During World War II (1939–45) and the occupation of France by fascist German troops (1940–44), Cachin took part in the Resistance, working in the underground. After the war, he warned the French people against the anti-Soviet policy of the reactionary forces and opposed France's entry into NATO and other aggressive blocs. Cachin was a staunch fighter for peace and the security of peoples.

A true defender of the interests of the working people, a fighter for the cause of peace and democracy, a patriot and a proletarian internationalist, Cachin enjoyed great popularity among the peoples of France, the USSR, and other countries. He was awarded the Order of Lenin in 1957 for his many years of work for strengthening friendship between the peoples of the USSR and France.

WORKS
Écrits et portraits, recueillis par M. Hertzog-Cachin. Paris, 1964.
Marcel Cachin vous parle. Paris, 1959.
La Vie et les combats de Marcel Cachin. Paris, 1949.
In Russian translation:
Zamysly frantsuzskikh imperialistov protiv SSSR. Moscow-Leningrad, 1928.
Frantsiia—organizator interventsii. Moscow-Leningrad, 1931.
Kompartiia Frantsii vysoko derzhit boevoe znamia kommunizma. Moscow, 1935.
"Moi vstrechi s Leninym." *Novaia i noveishaia istoriia,* 1957, no. 4.
Nauka i religiia. Moscow, 1958.
REFERENCES
Thorez, M. *Marcel Cachin: La Leçon d'une vie.* Paris, 1958.
Antiukhina-Moskovchenko, V. I. "Marcel Cachin—revoliutsioner leninskoi shkoly" (biographical essay). *Novaia i noveishaia istoriia,* 1970, nos. 1, 2, 4.
Frevil', Zh. *Rozhdenie Frantsuzskoi kommunisticheskoi partii.* Moscow, 1951. (Translated from French.)
                    V. I. ANTIUKHINA-MOSKOVCHENKO [11–1652–2]

CACHUCHA, a Spanish (Andalusian) dance, performed in 3/8 time. It originated in southwestern Spain in the province of Cádiz. It is performed by men and women separately. One of its basic elements is the tapping out of the rhythm with the heels and castanets. In the 19th century the cachucha was a European stage dance.   [11–1648–1]

CACIQUE, an Indian chieftain in Mexico, the West Indies, and Central America before the Spanish conquest. The post of cacique was usually hereditary in a particular clan or family. The caciques and their descendants formed the aristocratic elite among the Aztecs, Mayans, and other tribes. Some of the caciques went over to the side of the Spanish colonialists and became feudal landowners and officials.

In Latin America and in Spain, influential politicians from among landowners, the bourgeoisie, and the military who have seized power in a particular region of the country are called caciques. The system of administration whereby the central government exercises its authority in localities with the help of caciques has come to be known as caciquism.

REFERENCE
Zorita, A. *Breve y sumaria relación de los señores de la nueva España.* Mexico City, 1942.   [11–1474–4]

CACODYL, a radical of dimethylarsine $(CH_3)_2As-$. Cacodyl enters into the composition of the so-called cacodyl compounds, which include dicacodyl (tetramethyldiarsine) $(CH_3)_2As-As(CH_3)_2$, cacodyl oxides (oxides of dimethylarsine) $(CH_3)_2AsO$, and cacodyl chlorides (dimethylchloroarsine) $(CH_3)_2AsCl$.   [11–552–6]

CACOMISTLE (*Bassariscus astutus*), a carnivorous mammal of the family Procyonidae. The body measures up to 38 cm long, the tail being somewhat longer. The animal weighs up to 1.1 kg.

The body is slender and elongated, with short legs and a pointed snout. The upper parts are yellowish brown with a black wash and the underparts are lighter. The head has light patches and black or dark brown rings around the eyes. The tail is bushy, with black and white rings. The cacomistle is distributed in North America, from Oregon to New Mexico, primarily inhabiting mountainous places. A nocturnal animal, it is a good climber. It feeds on small mammals, birds, invertebrates, and plants. Three to four young are born in May-June. Sometimes cacomistles are kept as domestic animals to catch harmful rodents. [11–552–7]

CACOPHONY, combinations of tones that convey the impression of being piled up in a disorderly and chaotic manner. It is usually created by an accidental combination of tones (for example, when an orchestra tunes up), but some representatives of contemporary music abroad intentionally employ cacophonic elements in their compositions. [11–553–1]

CACTUS (Cactaceae), a family of dicotyledonous perennial plants usually having thickened, succulent, fleshy stems covered with spines, hairs, or bristles. Cacti may be treelike, shrubby, or vinelike; some, such as those of Pereskioideae are small trees. The stem may be spherical, ovoid, cylindrical, columnar, or occasionally flattened and segmented. As a rule, the stem does not have developed leaves (normally developed leaves are found only in the subfamily Pereskioideae), but it is adapted for photosynthesis and transpiration, as well as for the accumulation of moisture. The cactus stem has a well-developed water-bearing parenchyma (large cacti can hold up to 2,000 liters of water), and the cells contain a mucous substance that impedes the loss of water. Many cacti have a waxy surface or a thick, sometimes woolly, covering. There are a few stomata below the surface, and almost all cacti have ribs or papillae (modified leaf bases). Cacti are distinguished by the presence on the stems of areoles, clearly defined areas with hair and a spine originating from the axillary buds and their scales.

The flowers are often large, sometimes with diameters of up to 25 cm, brightly colored, usually solitary (occasionally arranged in apical inflorescences), almost always bisexual, and usually regular. The perianth has many spirally arranged segments, the outermost of which are the sepals and the innermost, the staminal petals. In many genera the petals are fused at the base into a tube. There are many stamens, and the ovary is usually inferior. The fruit is usually polyspermous, fleshy, berrylike, and sometimes dry. Many cacti blossom only late in the evening or at night. They are pollinated by insects or birds (including hummingbirds), although sometimes by bats. The seedlings of many cacti have seed leaves.

There are about 85 genera (according to other sources 50–220), comprising more than 2,000 species, found almost exclusively in North and South America. Half of all the species are found in Mexico. Only one genus, *Rhipsalis,* occurs in tropical Africa (probably imported), on Madagascar and the Mascarene Islands, and in Sri Lanka. Cacti usually grow in tropical and subtropical deserts, extending in some areas up to 4,500 m into the mountains; they are rarely found in tropical rain forests, in savannas, or along seacoasts. Some cacti, such as various species of *Opuntia,* are naturalized in Australia, China, the Mediterranean region, and other countries; in the USSR they grow on the Southern Crimean Shore.

Cacti are used for food (the fruit and the flesh of the stems), fodder (particularly the spineless members of *Opuntia*), fuel, light building material (the woody stems of some species), and the making of hedgerows (especially prickly *Opuntia* and some members of the genus *Cereus*). Many cactus species are grown indoors and in greenhouses (*Mammillaria, Opuntia, Cereus, Cephalocereus,* and *Epiphyllum*). Cacti are propagated by seeds, cuttings, or graftings. Depending on the species, the seeds may retain their germinating potential for several years. The sprouts appear between three and 30 days after sowing. Grafting is done from May to August. For many cactus species, *Trichocereus Spachianus, Trichocereus pachanoi, Eriocereus Jusberta,* and *Pereskia aculeata* are used as stock.

Cacti are grown in a soil mixture composed of leaf mold, clay sod, large-grain sand (with an admixture of gravel), crushed charcoal, and lime, with the proportion depending on the species. Organic fertilizers are used only for epiphytes, such as *Zygocactus* and *Epiphyllum;* mineral fertilizers are used for others.

Cacti blossom from early spring to late autumn; species of *Zygocactus* and *Rhipsalis* flower in winter. When they are not flowering, most species are dormant. In winter most cacti grown indoors and in greenhouses are kept at a temperature of 8°–10°C, although some are maintained at 5°–6°C and epiphytes at 14°–16°C; they are watered infrequently. In summer cacti require a warm, sunny spot, fresh air, much watering, and regular spraying. During the budding period, some cacti should not be moved, as this may cause the buds to fall.

REFERENCES
D'iakonov, V. M., and N. I. Kurnakov. *Kaktusy i ikh kul'tura v komnatnykh usloviiakh.* Leningrad, 1953.
Pažout, F., Z. Valniček, and R. Šubik. *Kaktusy.* Prague, 1963. (Translated from Czech).
Takhtadzhian, A. L. *Sistema i filogeniia tsvetkovykh rastenii.* Moscow-Leningrad, 1966.
Backeberg, C. *Die Cactaceae,* vols. 1–6. Jena, 1958–62.
Backeberg, C. *Das Kakteenlexikon.* Jena, 1966.
R. A. UDALOVA and S. G. SAAKOV [11–553–2]

CADAVERINE, α,ϵ-pentamethylenediamine, $NH_2(CH_2)_5NH_2$. A colorless liquid with a boiling point of 178°–179°C. Cadaverine is readily soluble in water and alcohol and yields crystallizing salts. It is contained in the products of protein decay (putrefaction) and is formed from lysine during its fermentative decarboxylation. Previously, cadaverine was thought of as one of the ptomaines, but the toxicity of cadaverine is relatively low. Cadaverine is found in plants and can be obtained synthetically from trimethylenecyanide. [11–366–2]

CADENCE, a harmonic or melodic formula that occurs at the end of a section in a musical work and imparts a completeness and wholeness. In harmony the distinction is made between full (concluding with the tonic triad) and half cadences (concluding with the dominant or subdominant). In turn, full cadences are subdivided into authentic (tonic is preceded by the dominant) and plagal (tonic is preceded by the subdominant), perfect (tonic appears as last chord, with the tonic note in the soprano, and either the dominant or subdominant preceding it, both in root position) and imperfect (in which the conditions for forming the perfect cadence are not observed). Interrupted cadences replace the tonic in the authentic cadence with another chord. By dividing a musical composition into separate sections, cadences help to establish a definite logical and functional relationship among them.

Cadenza. A cadenza is a virtuoso solo episode in an instrumental concerto; it may be a free fantasia based on the theme of the concerto. The Viennese classical school left the composition or extemporization of cadenzas to the performer. Later composers (beginning with Beethoven), striving for a structural and stylistic compositional unity, wrote their own cadenzas.
IU. N. KHOLOPOV [11–368–4]

CADET CORPS (*kadetskii korpus*), in Russia, secondary military educational institutions restricted to children of the privileged classes. They originated in the second half of the 17th century, when cadet schools were set up in Prussia to prepare children of the nobility for military service.

In Russia the first cadet corps was founded in 1732 in St. Petersburg under the name Korpus Kadet, or Corps of Cadets. (After 1752, when the Naval Cadet Corps was founded, it was renamed the Land Forces Gentry Cadet Corps and later, the First Cadet Corps.) In setting up cadet corps the government of Anna Ivanovna appeased the nobility, who demanded among other privileges the right to serve in the army only as officers. But in the 18th century the cadet corps trained not only officers but also civilian officials, diplomats, judges, and others. In the first half of the 19th century they became strictly military educational institutions, in which students received general as well as specialized military education.

In 1863 the cadet corps were transformed into military *Gymnasiums* and became general educational institutions but retained the military uniform and a semimilitary regime. In 1882 these *Gymnasiums* were again reorganized into cadet corps, although the program of general educational instruction was essentially maintained. This reform amounted to a greater militarization; civilian teachers were replaced by officers, and military discipline was strengthened. As for military organization the cadet corps were divided into companies and the companies, into detachments. In the postreform period some cadet corps admitted children who were not of gentry origin, but children of the nobility, primarily of officers, remained in the majority.

The curriculum and the program changed many times throughout the history of the cadet corps. After 1900, when Prince Konstantin Konstantinovich was in charge of military education, the program was greatly expanded. Chemistry, mechanics, and some higher mathematics were added to the curriculum, and the number of class hours of natural history and physics were increased. Thus, the program of the cadet corps corresponded more or less to the curriculum of the *Realschulen*.

The cadet corps were administered by the Main Directorate of Military Educational Institutions. By 1917 there were 29 cadet corps in the Russian Empire (not counting the Naval Corps and the Corps of Pages, with a total of over 10,000 cadets). After the February Revolution of 1917 the cadet corps were renamed *Gymnasiums* of the military departments, but the program of instruction did not change at all. In 1918 the cadet corps were closed because of the liquidation of the old army.

REFERENCES
Lalaev, M. S. *Istoricheskii ocherk voenno-uchebnykh zavedenii, podvedomstvennykh Glavnomu ikh upravleniiu,* part 1. St. Petersburg, 1880.
Zaionchkovskii, P. A. *Voennye reformy 1860–1870 godov v Rossii.* [Moscow] 1952.
"Kadetskie korpusa." In *Voennaia entsiklopediia,* vol. 11. St. Petersburg, 1913.   P. A. ZAIONCHKOVSKII   [11–369–1]

CADETS. (1) In feudal France and Prussia young members of the nobility in military service with soldier ranks and children of the feudal aristocracy enlisted in military service prior to receiving their commission as officers.

(2) In prerevolutionary Russia and various other states from the 18th to early 20th century, the name given to those studying in the cadet corps.   [11–373–1]

CÁDIZ, a city and an important port in southwestern Spain, in Andalusia, on the coast of the Bay of Cádiz of the Atlantic Ocean. Capital of Cádiz Province. Population, 137,900 (1969).

Cádiz is a major transportation junction and industrial center in the south of the country. It handles more than 1 million tons of freight annually. Its principal industries are aviation and shipbuilding; large shipyards are located in the environs of the city. There are fish-canning, tobacco, textile, and other industrial enterprises. Cádiz is a military naval base.

In antiquity the city was known as Gades. It was founded by the Phoenicians in about 800 B.C. or, according to some data, in 1100 B.C. Circa 500 B.C., Cádiz fell under the rule of Carthage. In 206 B.C. it was seized by the Romans; in 49 B.C. it became a Roman municipium. In the fifth century Cádiz was seized by the Visigoths, and in the eighth century it was captured by the Arabs, from whom it was conquered in 1262 by the king of Castile, Alfonso X. During the Spanish revolution of 1808–14, Cádiz was the provisional residence of the central junta and of the Cortes. A rebellion of the troops and ship crews in Cádiz served as the start of revolutions in 1820 and 1868.

Cádiz basically has a regular city plan. Among the noteworthy sights are the 17th-century fortress walls, the Old Cathedral of Santa Cruz (13th century, reconstructed in the 17th century), the Church of Santa Cueva (end of the 18th century, architect Benjumeda; paintings by F. Goya, 1793–95), and numerous 18th- and 19th-century buildings done in the style of classicism. There is a provincial museum in Cádiz.   [11–375–1]

CÁDIZ, BAY OF, an inlet of the Atlantic Ocean at the southwestern coast of the Iberian Peninsula. The bay is separated from the ocean by the Island of León, or San Fernando. It is about 15 km long and measures 10 km wide at the entrance. The shores of the bay are low-lying. The depth ranges from 9 to 16.5 m. There are many shoals along the northern coast. High tide occurs twice a day and measures about 3 m. The speed of the tidal currents reaches 6 km/hr. The coastal area is densely populated. Cádiz, a large city and port, is situated on the bay.

[11–375–2]

CÁDIZ, GULF OF, an open gulf of the Atlantic Ocean at the southwestern coast of the Iberian Peninsula. It washes the low-lying, mildly jagged shores of Spain and Portugal. The gulf is up to 100 m deep. High tide occurs twice a day and measures up to 3 m. The Guadiana and Guadalquivir rivers empty into the gulf. The principal port on the gulf is Vila Real de Santo António (Portugal).   [11–376–2]

CÁDIZ CONSTITUTION OF 1812, a Spanish constitution, adopted by the constituent Cortes in Cádiz on Mar. 18, 1812, and made public on Mar. 19, 1812, during the Spanish Revolution of 1808–14.

The constitution declared that "sovereignty resides in the nation, which retains the exclusive right to establish its own fundamental laws" (art. 3). Spain was proclaimed a hereditary monarchy (art. 14), with legislative power vested in the Cortes and the monarch (art. 15) and executive power represented by the monarch (art. 16). The constitution proclaimed individual freedom and the inviolability of domicile (arts. 286 and 307) but declared Catholicism the official religion of Spain and prohibited the practice of any other religion (art. 12). The constitution proclaimed the equality of Spaniards of the mother country and those of the Spanish colonies (art. 18) and established a national militia in the provinces (art. 362). On his return to Spain, King Ferdinand VII revoked the constitution on May 4, 1814. Restored at the outbreak of the Spanish Revolution of 1820–1823 (it was proclaimed by Riego y Núñez on Jan. 1, 1820, and Ferdinand VII swore to uphold it on Mar. 9, 1820), it was again abolished on Oct. 1, 1823, by Ferdinand VII. On Aug. 12, 1836, the constitution went into effect for a third time in response to the demands of the masses and remained in force until the adoption of a new constitution on June 18, 1837.

REFERENCE
Constitution politique de la monarchie espagnole: Promulguée à Cadiz le 19 mars 1812. . . . Paris, 1820.   L. V. PONOMAREVA   [11–375–3]

CÁDIZ CORTES, a constituent assembly in Spain during the Spanish Revolution of 1808–14. Convened on Sept. 24, 1810, on the island of León, it was transferred to Cádiz on Feb. 20, 1811, and sat until Sept. 20, 1813.

The Cortes adopted a number of important resolutions aimed at strengthening the revolution. In October 1810 it enacted a law establishing equality between Spaniards and Latin Americans and guaranteed freedom of speech and the press. In August 1811 a law was promulgated abolishing seignorial rights and privileges; and in February 1813 the Inquisition was abolished and laws directed against the religious orders adopted. The Cortes began to confiscate and sell church lands and abolished a number of taxes that had been imposed for the benefit of the church. Guilds and corporations of artisans were abolished, and free trade between Spain and its American colonies was established.

On the whole the legislation of the Cádiz Cortes embodied the chief demands of the bourgeois revolution. However, the Cortes was unable to take the lead in the struggle of the masses against the French occupation forces, which had invaded Spain in 1808, or against the forces of domestic reaction. The Cortes' authority extended only to the small part of Spain free of foreign occupation. The Cortes could not bring itself to confiscate the land belonging to secular feudal owners and to distribute it among the peasants. The most important step taken by the Cádiz Cortes was the adoption of the Cádiz Constitution of 1812.

REFERENCES

Marx, K. *Revoliutsionnaia Ispaniia.* In K. Marx and F. Engels, *Soch.,* 2nd ed., vol. 10.
Maiskii, I. M. *Ispaniia, 1808–1917.* Moscow, 1957.
Trachevskii, A. S. *Ispaniia deviatnadtsatogo veka,* part 1. Moscow, 1872.

[11–376–1]

CADMIUM, Cd, a chemical element of Group II of the periodic system of Mendeleev. Atomic number, 48; atomic weight, 112.40. Cadmium is a white, shiny, heavy, soft, ductile metal. The element consists of a mixture of eight stable isotopes with the mass numbers 106 (1.215 percent), 108 (0.875 percent), 110 (12.39 percent), 111 (12.75 percent), 112 (24.07 percent), 113 (12.26 percent), 114 (28.86 percent), and 116 (7.58 percent).

Historical information. During inspection of a drugstore in 1817 the german chemist F. Strohmeyer found that the zinc carbonate there contained an unknown metal as an impurity, which was precipitated in the form of a yellow sulfide on treatment with hydrogen sulfide in an acid solution. Strohmeyer called the discovered metal cadmium (from the Greek *kadmeia,* impure zinc oxide, also zinc ore). Independently from him, the German scientists K. Hermann, K. Karsten, and W. Meissner discovered cadmium in Silesian zinc ores in 1818.

Distribution in nature. Cadmium is a rare, widely scattered element with a clarke value of 1.3×10^{-5} percent by weight in the lithosphere. Migration in hot underground waters with zinc and other chalcophilic elements is characteristic of cadmium as is its concentration in hydrothermal deposits. The mineral sphalerite, ZnS, contains up to 0.5–1 percent cadmium in some locations; the maximum content is 5 percent. Greenockite, CdS, is found less frequently. Cadmium is concentrated in marine sedimentary rocks—shales (Mansfeld, GDR)—as well as in sandstones, in which it is also combined with zinc and other chalcophilic elements. Three very rare well-identified cadmium minerals are known in the biosphere: the carbonate $CdCO_3$ (otavite), the oxide CdO, and the selenide CdSe.

Physical and chemical properties. The cadmium crystal lattice is hexagonal, $a = 2.97311$ Å, $c = 5.60694$ Å (at 25°C). The atomic radius measures 1.56 Å, and the ionic radius of Cd^{2+} measures 1.03 Å. The density is 8.65 g/cm^3 (at 20°C); the melting point, 320.9°C; the boiling point, 767°C; the coefficient of thermal expansion, 29.8×10^{-6} (at 25°C); thermal conductivity (at 0°C), 97.55 W/(m·°K), or 0.233 cal/(cm·sec·°C); specific heat (at 25°C), 225.02 joules per kilogram · degree Kelvin, or 0.055 cal/(g·°C); specific electrical resistivity (at 20°C), 7.4×10^{-8} ohm·m (7.4×10^{-6} ohm·cm); temperature coefficient of electrical resistivity, 4.3×10^{-3} (0°–100°C); tensile strength, 64 meganewtons per square meter (MN/m^2), or 6.4 kilograms-force per square millimeter (kgf/mm^2); relative elongation, 20 percent; and Brinell hardness, 160 MN/m^2, or 16 kgf/mm^2.

In accordance with the external electron configuration of the atom $4d^{10}5s^2$, the valence of cadmium in compounds is equal to 2 (there are, however, indications of the formation of Cd_2^{2+} ions during the solution of cadmium in molten $CdCl_2$). Cadmium loses its luster on exposure to air with formation of a thin coating of the oxide CdO, which protects the metal from further oxidation. Intense heating in air leads to the combustion of cadmium to give the oxide CdO, a crystalline powder of light brown to dark brown color and density of 8.15 g/cm^3; CdO sublimes without melting at 700°C. Cadmium combines directly with the halogens, and the resulting compounds are colorless. $CdCl_2$, $CdBr_2$, and CdI_2 are readily soluble in water (about one part anhydrous salt in one part water at 20°C), whereas CdF_2 is less soluble (one part in 25 parts water). Cadmium reacts with sulfur to yield the sulfide CdS, which is lemon-yellow to orange-red in color and insoluble in water and dilute acids. Cadmium readily dissolves in nitric acid with the evolution of nitrogen oxides and the formation of a nitrate, which gives the hydrate $Cd(NO_3)_2$ ·$4H_2O$). Cadmium slowly liberates hydrogen from hydrochloric and dilute sulfuric acids; upon evaporation of the solutions hydrates of chloride, $2CdCl_2 \cdot 5H_2O$, and sulfate, $3CdSO_4 \cdot 8H_2O$, crystallize out. Solutions of cadmium salts have acidic reactions owing to hydrolysis. Alkali hydroxides precipitate from these solutions the white hydroxide $Cd(OH)_2$, which is insoluble in an excess of reagent. However, the action of concentrated caustic solutions on $Cd(OH)_2$ yields hydroxocadmiates, for example, $Na_2[Cd(OH)_2]$. The Cd^{2+} cation readily forms complex ions with ammonia—$[Cd(NH_3)_4]^{2+}$—and with cyanide—$[Cd(CN)_4]^{2+}$ and $[Cd(CN)_6]^{4-}$. Numerous basic, double, and complex cadmium salts are known. Cadmium compounds are toxic; inhalation of its oxide vapors is particularly dangerous.

Preparation and uses. Cadmium is prepared from the by-products of the processing of zinc, lead-zinc, and copper-zinc ores. These products, containing 0.2–7 percent cadmium, are treated with dilute sulfuric acid, which dissolves the oxides of cadmium and zinc. Cadmium is precipitated from the solution by the addition of zinc dust. The spongy residue (mixture of cadmium and zinc) is dissolved in dilute sulfuric acid, and cadmium is separated by electrolysis of this solution. Electrolytic cadmium is remelted under a layer of sodium hydroxide and cast into sticks. The purity of the metal is not less than 99.98 percent.

Metallic cadmium is used in nuclear reactors, for anticorrosion and decorative coatings, and in storage batteries. Cadmium is the basis for some bearing alloys, and it is a component of low-melting alloys (for example, Wood's alloy). Low-melting alloys are used for joining glass to metal, in automatic fire extinguishing systems, for fine and complex castings in gypsum molds, and for other purposes. Cadmium sulfide (cadmium yellow) is a pigment used in art. Cadmium sulfate and amalgam are used in the Weston standard cell.

Cadmium in the organism. The cadmium content of plants is 10^{-4} percent (on a dry basis), whereas the cadmium content of some animals (sponges, coelenterates, worms, echinoderms, and tunicates) is 4×10^{-5}–3×10^{-3} percent (on a dry basis). Cadmium has been detected in all vertebrates. The liver is particularly rich in cadmium. The physiological importance of cadmium has not been adequately investigated, but it is known that cadmium affects carbohydrate metabolism, the synthesis of hippuric acid in the liver, and the activity of some enzymes.

REFERENCES

Pogodin, S. A. "Cadmium." In *Kratkaia khimicheskaia entsiklopediia,* vol. 2. Moscow, 1963.
Remy, H. *Kurs neorganicheskoi khimii,* vol. 2. Moscow, 1966. Pages 476–86. (Translated from German.)   S. A. POGODIN [11–377–2]

CADMIUM PLATING, the process by which cadmium is applied to the surface of steel articles by the method of electrodeposition to form protective coatings against atmospheric corrosion. The coating thickness usually varies from 15 to 25 μm. The most important parts of aircraft and ships, as well as products to be used under tropical conditions, are plated with cadmium. The presence of sulfur dioxide in the atmosphere (which is characteristic of industrial areas) lowers the corrosion protection properties of cadmium coatings. In this case, the desired resistance of articles to corrosion is achieved through zinc plating. The electrolytes used in cadmium plating usually contain simple salts of cadium with admixtures of colloids (gelatin or glue), which give quite satisfactory coatings. Complex cadmium salts, mostly cyanides, are used for coating objects having complex configurations.   [11–378–1]

CADORNA, LUIGI. Born Sept. 4, 1850, in Pallanza; died Dec. 23, 1928, in Bordighera. Italian marshal (1924) and count.

Cadorna entered military service in 1866. Subsequently, he commanded, in succession, a regiment, a division, and a corps and worked to reorganize the Italian Army. From 1914 to 1917 he was chief of the General Staff. After May 1915, when Italy entered the war on the side of the Entente, Cadorna was the de facto commander in chief of the Italian Army. His repeated attempts from 1915 to 1917 to defeat the Austro-Hungarian troops on the Isonzo River were unsuccessful. After the defeat of the Italian troops at Caporetto, Cadorna was removed from his post on Nov. 8, 1917. He wrote several works on Italy's participation in World War I.   [11–381–1]

CADOUDAL, GEORGES. Born Jan. 1, 1771, in Kerléano; died June 25, 1804, in Paris. A leader of counterrevolutionary royalist uprisings during the Great French Revolution. Son of a peasant.

In 1793 Cadoudal took part in the counterrevolutionary revolt in the Vendée and after its suppression became the leader of the Chouans, a counterrevolutionary movement in northwestern France. In June 1794 he was arrested by the Jacobin government but was freed after the Thermidorian coup of that year. From 1797 to 1803, with some interruptions, he was an émigré in Great Britain. In December 1800 and August 1803 he organized attempts to assassinate Napoleon Bonaparte. On Mar. 9, 1804, he was arrested in Paris, tried, and executed.

REFERENCES

Lenotre, G. *G. Cadoudal.* Paris, 1929.
Lachouque, H., and J. Arnna. *Cadoudal et les chouans.* Paris, 1951.

[11–387–1]

CADRES. (1) The basic (permanent) staff of trained, qualified workers in enterprises, institutions, party, trade union, and public organizations engaged in some area of work. Broadly all the permanent members of a staff. (2) In a state's armed forces, all the officers and enlisted men on active duty.

The main political and economic problems in socialist society can be solved only through the proper placement of cadres and their expedient use so that each worker contributes to the maximum extent that his education, work experience, and personal qualities allow. Lenin felt that no policy could be carried out unless it was expressed in the assignment and relocation of personnel, that is, in the distribution of party forces (see *Poln. sobr. soch.,* 5th ed., vol. 40, p. 237). Cadres are evaluated and placed according to their political and practical qualities. The policy of the CPSU and the Soviet government in regard to cadres is aimed at promoting talented, politically conscious, educated, and professionally trained personnel. While solicitous of older cadres and making maximum use of their experience and knowledge, party and state agencies also promote younger prospective cadres, which is necessary for the continuity of the political lines of the Communist Party and its revolutionary traditions.

In the process of eliminating the actual inequality in economy and culture among big and small nations, the Communist Party and the Soviet government, in the course of socialist construction, have trained highly qualified national cadres in the Union republics.

Table 1. Specialists with higher education employed in the USSR national economy (by Union-republic nationalities)

	1940	1960	1970
Russian	493,900	2,070,300	4,033,600
Ukrainian	128,800	517,700	1,031,200
Byelorussian	21,200	95,100	204,000
Uzbek	2,900	46,500	139,600
Kazakh	1,800	34,800	96,800
Georgian	23,300	88,600	149,300
Azerbaijani	8,000	47,900	98,100
Lithuanian	6,400	30,000	66,700
Moldavian	700	11,300	32,600
Latvian	7,300	24,900	43,200
Kirghiz	100	9,400	23,900
Tadzhik	300	10,900	29,600
Armenian	19,600	74,100	128,100
Turkmen	200	10,400	25,900
Estonian	4,100	19,300	35,700
Total	909,000	3,545,200	6,853,000

In the USSR women take an active part, on an equal footing with men, in economic, government, cultural, and sociopolitical life. Women predominate in some spheres of activity; for example, in 1970, 85 percent of the personnel in public health and social security and 72 percent in education and culture were women. The degree of need for specific cadres is determined by the planning agencies. The USSR has a system for training cadres that incorporates secondary general schools, vocational schools, technicums, higher educational institutions, military schools, academies, and graduate courses. There are other areas of specialized education as well—for example, pedagogy and agriculture. The number of specialists with higher education employed in the national economy grew from 136,000 in 1913 to 6,853,000 in 1970, and those with secondary education increased from 54,000 to 9,988,000.

In the years 1929–32 the average number of workers graduated yearly from factory schools and schools of that type was 113,000. In 1970, 1,781,000 graduated from vocational schools. The training of cadres in a socialist state is not only a question of acquiring professional knowledge but also of developing a Marxist-Leninist world outlook and a communist attitude toward labor. Thus, special educational institutions also exist for training administrative officials and party, trade union, and Komsomol personnel.

The creation of the material and technical base for communism within the context of the scientific and technical revolution has placed increased demands on cadre training. Technical progress has fundamentally altered the character of labor. The number of skilled cadres has grown rapidly, new professions have appeared, the tasks of managing the economy have grown more complex, and automatic control systems have been introduced. Economic education and the training of cadres in the new and long-range directions of science and technology have acquired primary importance.

The CPSU considers it necessary "to consistently extend and unceasingly *improve the system of training and retraining cadres* —the organizers of production at all levels, including the highest leadership cadres, and above all in the field of Marxist-Leninist economic theory, the theory and practice of management, and the scientific organization of labor and new methods of planning, economic incentive, and economic mathematics techniques and modern computer technology" (*Materialy XXIV s"ezda KPSS,* 1971, p. 298).

Cadres receive advanced training at institutes for the improvement of skills and in special departments and courses in all fields of education. Particularly great demands are made of the leadership cadres, who are expected to have a mastery of modern managerial methods, a feel for new developments and their long-term prospects, and an ability to use the most efficient means of problem-solving and to draw on the knowledge and experience of others. The Institute for the Management of the National Economy opened in February 1971 in Moscow. It perfects the training of leadership cadres, including ministers, in industry

The best training ground for cadres in all spheres of activity is the struggle to make all workers highly skilled and to raise significantly the cultural and technical level of the working class and kolkhoz peasantry. In kolkhozes in 1970, some 1.7 million people learned new professions or specialties or raised their skill levels.

Table 2. Training and improvement of skills in the USSR for industrial and office workers in enterprises, institutions, and organizations

	1950	1970
Total industrial and office workers trained in new professions or areas of specialization	2,600,000	5,000,000
industrial workers	2,300,000	4,500,000
Total industrial and office workers completing training in the improvement of skills	5,000,000	12,000,000
industrial workers	3,500,000	9,000,000

The growing demand for highly qualified specialists in all levels of the party and state apparatus and in all fields of the economy, science, culture, and the arts has created an increased responsibility of the cadres to society for the quality of the work they perform. An important means for training cadres and improving their work is self-criticism and criticism, particularly from below. The party works with cadres toward creating congenial conditions in an atmosphere of trust combined with highly exacting and close scrutiny to see that party and government decisions are implemented. A resolution of the Twenty-fourth Congress of the CPSU specifies: "We must raise the cadres' sense of responsibility in regard to tasks assigned to them and take the necessary measures in regard to those who violate discipline, who do not draw the necessary conclusions from criticism, and who conduct themselves incorrectly. Every functionary should remember that socialist discipline is equally obligatory for all" (*ibid.*, p. 210). The correct policies of the CPSU in educating, selecting, and placing cadres have assured the victory of socialism and the great successes of communist construction in the USSR. [11–384–2]

CAEN, a city and port in northern France (Normandy), on the Orne River, near the coast of the English Channel, with which it is linked by a ship canal. It is the administrative center of Calvados department. Population, 114,000 (1968). There is a metallurgical industry, as well as machine-building, textile, chemical, cement, ceramic, food, and woodworking enterprises. Coal is imported in large amounts to meet the needs of the lower Normandy iron-ore region, of which Caen is the center. Dairy products and wine are among the city's exports.

Caen was founded in the early 11th century, and its university was founded in 1432. Architectural monuments include the Romanesque churches of La Trinité (1059–66) and St. Nicholas (end of the 11th century), an 11th-century castle, the Church of St. Peter (13–14th centuries, rebuilt in the 16th century in Early Renaissance style), the late Gothic Church of St. John (15th century), the baroque Notre-Dame-de-la-Gloriette (17th century), the ruins of the Hôtel d'Escoville (1538), and the monastery with its Romanesque church of St. Etienne (1064–77) and buildings from the early 18th century (now a *lycée*). Caen was rebuilt after its destruction in 1944. New avenues were laid out in the center, and in 1957 the university campus was completed (architects, H. Bernard and E. Hur). A museum of fine arts is located here.

REFERENCE
Doré, R. *Caen et Bayeux.* Caen, 1950. [11–864–2]

CAETANI, LEONE. Born Sept. 12, 1869, in Rome; died Dec. 24, 1935, in Vancouver (Canada). Italian Islamic scholar.

Caetani graduated from the University of Rome with a degree in Oriental philology in 1891. He traveled extensively through the Middle East. From 1909 to 1913, Caetani was a deputy in the Italian parliament representing the Socialist Party; he opposed the Italian aggression in Libya in 1911–12. In 1930 he emigrated to Canada.

Caetani edited a number of sources on the history of early Islam. He proposed the migration theory of the origin of Islam: nomadic tribes, responding to changes in physiographical conditions in Arabia, periodically moved to Mesopotamia, Palestine, and Syria, founding cities and states. Caetani linked the origin of Islam with the last stage of the migratory movement of the population of Arabia.

WORKS
Annali dell'Islam, vols. 1–10. Milan, 1905–26.
Studi di storia orientale, vols. 1, 3. Milan, 1911–14.
Cronografia islamica. Paris-[Rome, 1912].
Onomasticon arabicum . . . , vols. 1–2. Rome, 1915.

REFERENCE
Beliaev, E. A. *Proiskhozhdenie islama: Khrestomatiia,* part 1. Moscow-Leningrad, 1931. [11–1669–3]

CAETANO, MARCELLO. Born Aug. 17, 1906, in Lisbon. Portuguese state figure. Son of a schoolteacher.

After graduating from the law faculty of the University of Lisbon in 1927, Caetano entered the Ministry of Finance, where he became a close associate of A. Salazar. He began to teach law at the University of Lisbon in 1933. Caetano was national commissar of the Union of Portuguese Youth from 1940 to 1944 and director and dean of the department of political economy and industrial production of the Higher Technical Institute from 1942 to 1944. He was minister of colonies from 1944 to 1947, becoming chairman of the executive committee of the National Union Party in 1947. Caetano was president of the Corporative Chamber of parliament from 1950 to 1955; in 1952 he was named lifetime member of the State Council. He was minister without portfolio subordinate to the premier from 1955 to 1958 and rector of the University of Lisbon from 1952 to 1967. As successor to the fascist dictator Salazar, Caetano assumed the post of chairman of the Council of Ministers of Portugal in 1968. On Apr. 25, 1974, Caetano was removed from this post and arrested during the antifascist coup d'etat. In May 1974 he was exiled to Brazil. [11–1670–1; updated]

CAFTAN, a man's and woman's double-breasted outer garment with a deep wrapover. The caftan was widely used as an article of clothing by various strata of the population in pre-Petrine Russia. It had long sleeves. The caftans of the rich were made of velvet, brocade, and better quality cloth; they were trimmed with expensive furs and had jeweled buttons and ornaments. The caftans of the poor were of simple cloth lined with inexpensive furs and had copper and tin buttons. The caftan was worn by the common people in various localities of Russia until the early 20th century and was sewn from simple cloth or homespun fabric. The latter included *sermiaga* (caftan of coarse, undyed cloth), *zipun* (outer peasant garment of homespun cloth), and *tiazhelko* (a simple *zipun*). A short caftan was known as a *polukaftan.* [11–1628–4]

CAGAYAN DE ORO, a city and port in the Philippines, on the northern part of the island of Mindanao, on the Bay of Macajalar. It is the administrative center of Misamis Oriental Province. Population, 92,600 (1969). It is a center of the fishing industry and also has food-processing enterprises and garment factories. [11–364–1]

CAGLIARI, a city and port in Italy, on the southern coast of Sardinia. It is the administrative center of Sardinia and of Cagliari Province. Population, 225,800 (1970). It is an important transport junction. The port's freight turnover is nearly 3 million tons (1970), with lead and zinc ores, salt, wine, and olive oil as the chief exports. It has shipbuilding, oil-refining, chemical and petrochemical, electrical engineering, and food industries. Wood products and building materials are also produced. [11–706–5]

CAGOULARDS, members of a French fascist organization in the 1930's called the Secret Committee of Revolutionary Action. They received the name Cagoulards from the French word *cagoule,* a hood with openings for the eyes, worn by members of the organization at secret meetings.

The Cagoulards were secretly supported by certain groups among the French bourgeoisie and the reactionary military. The organization maintained arms caches, was responsible for bombings and arson, and committed acts of terrorism against democratic political figures. In 1937 the Cagoulards assassinated the Rosselli brothers, well-known Italian antifascists, and raided the building of the Confederation of French Entrepreneurs. The Popular Front governments (1936–38) took action against the Cagoulards, and by 1940 the organization had virtually disintegrated. After the occupation of France by fascist Germany in 1940, many Cagoulards became active collaborationists and supporters of the Vichy regime. [11–366–1]

CAGUAS, a city in eastern Puerto Rico. Population, 95,000 (1970). A highway links it with the port of San Juan. Caguas is a commercial center of an agricultural region (sugarcane, tobacco, fruit, livestock). There is production of raw sugar, rum, and tobacco items and the processing of hides. [11–365–2]

CAHIERS DU COMMUNISME, the theoretical and political monthly journal of the Central Committee of the French Communist Party, published in Paris since 1924. It discusses the most important problems of party strategy and tactics and publishes articles on problems of Marxist-Leninist theory and on various aspects of international politics. Much attention is given to ideological problems. Circulation, 20,000 (1974). [11–537–2]

CAHORS, a city in southwestern France, on the Lot River (a tributary of the Garonne). Population, 21,000 (1968). Cahors is the administrative center of Lot Department. It is the center of a grape-growing and wine-making region. (A sweet red wine got its name from the city.) The Cathedral of Saint-Etienne (12th century) is located there. [11-1016-2]

CAHORS, a dessert wine made from red grapes (Cabernet, Saperavi), and named after the French city of Cahors, despite the fact that the region produces more white wines than red. A unique aspect of the processing is heating the pulp to 45°–50°C and higher or heating entire grape clusters to 80°–90°C by steam, dry air, or immersion for two to three minutes in boiling water or must. The better Cahors of the USSR, with an alcohol content of 16 percent by volume and a 16–20 percent sugar content, are made in the Crimea ("Iuzhnoberezhnyi"), Armenia ("Artashak"), Azerbaijan ("Shemakha"), and Uzbekistan ("Uzbekiston"). [11-364-5]

CAIBARIÉN, a city and port in Cuba, in northern Las Villas Province. Population, 26,400 (1967). Sugar is exported from the city, and metalworking, food, and building materials enterprises are located there. Caibarién is the center of a large agricultural region (sugarcane, fruits, livestock). There is also fishing. [11-536-5]

CAID, in Algeria, Tunisia, and Morocco, the representative of central power, the ruler of an individual city, region, tribe, or group of tribes. The caid was usually chosen from the powerful feudal nobility; the institution of the caid existed since the late Middle Ages. In Algeria and Tunisia it was abolished in the 1950's and early 1960's. [11-531-2]

CAILLAUX, JOSEPH MARIE AUGUSTE. Born Mar. 30, 1863, in Le Mans; died Nov. 21, 1944, in Mamers. French politician and state figure; a leader of the Radical Party.

Caillaux served as finance minister in 1899–1902, 1906–09, and 1911 and from December 1913 to March 1914. From 1911 to January 1912 he was prime minister and minister of internal affairs. Caillaux advocated the introduction of a progressive income tax. In foreign policy he favored rapprochement with Germany. During the Agadir Incident of 1911, he worked for a Franco-German compromise agreement. During World War I, Caillaux advocated finding a means of reconciliation with Germany. In December 1917, on the demand of G. Clemenceau, Caillaux was deprived of his immunity as a deputy; he was arrested the following month on a charge of treason. He was tried in 1920. After the amnesty of January 1925 he was elected senator, in which post he served until 1940. In 1925 and 1926, Caillaux was finance minister, and between 1932 and 1940 he was chairman of the financial commission of the Senate. [11-545-2]

CAIMAN, the common name for three genera of reptiles (*Caiman, Melanosuchus,* and *Paleosuchus*) of the family Alligatoridae. They are distinguished from true alligators by the absence of a bony septum in the olfactory cavity and the presence of a bony abdominal shell. There are five species, found in bodies of water in Central and South America.

The largest is the black caiman (*Melanosuchus niger*), which reaches a length of 4–5 m. It is found in the Amazon River basin. The female lays 30–40 eggs (each up to 9 cm) in a depression in moist soil near water. The black caiman feeds mainly on fish, but also eats waterfowl, marsh birds, and mammals. It will often attack small cattle, particularly during flash floods in semi-inundated pasture lands.

REFERENCE
Wermuth, H., and R. Mertens. *Schildkröten, Krokodile, Brückenechsen.* Jena, 1961. [11-540-1]

CAIN, according to the biblical myth, the oldest son of Adam and Eve, a farmer.

Out of envy Cain killed his brother Abel, a "shepherd of sheep," because Abel's offerings were accepted by the god Yahweh, whereas Cain's were rejected. God cursed him for the murder of his brother and marked him with a special sign (the "mark of Cain"). The legend of Cain also entered Islam (Kabil

and Khabil). In the myth about Cain's murder of Abel many investigators see a mythologized reflection of the struggle between agricultural and livestock-raising ethnic groups. [11-531-3]

CAIRO, capital of the Arab Republic of Egypt (ARE). The most important political, economic and cultural center of the country. It is situated to the south of the Nile Delta, primarily on the right bank of the Nile and on the islands of Zamalik (Gezira) and Roda. It has a tropical climate. The average temperature in January is 12°C and in July, 27°C. Annual precipitation totals approximately 34 mm. During April and May there is a hot dry wind called the *khamsin.* Cairo has airports, is a major junction of international communications and is the center of highway, railway, and river transport in the ARE. It is the largest city in Africa, with more than 5 million inhabitants (1970, estimate; 678,000 in 1907; 1.1 million in 1927; 2.1 million in 1947; 3.3 million in 1960). It accounts for about 15 percent of the ARE's population and about 34 percent of its urban population.

Administration. In administrative and territorial respects, Cairo is equivalent to a governorate (*muhafaza*). The city administration is headed by a governor appointed by the president of the ARE and by the People's Council (59 members) made up of members of the municipal committee of the Arab Socialist Union (ASU) and of representatives from the district organizations of the ASU and from women's and youth organizations. There is also the Executive Committee appointed by the prime minister from among representatives of the ministries of education, finance, internal affairs, health, and others. Branch agencies of the municipal administration (departments) handle diverse economic, social, and cultural problems, maintain law and order, see to civil defense, and so on.

History. Cairo was founded in 969 by the Fatimid military leader Jawhar (Goher) al-Sakali in the vicinity where the fortress of Babylon stood in antiquity, approximately 30 km from the ancient Egyptian city of Memphis. Jawhar called the city Misr al-Qahira, which means "Egypt the Victorious"; hence, the Arabic name of Cairo, al-Qahira. Gradually Cairo absorbed other fortress-cities built earlier in the same region by the Arabs, including Fustat, which under the Umayyads was the administrative center of Egypt, and Katai, built at the end of the ninth century under the Tulunids. From 973 to 1171, Cairo was the capital of the caliphate of the Fatimids. Under the Ayyubids (1171–1250) and the Mamelukes (1250–1517), it was a major commercial and artisan center. In 1517 it was seized by the Ottoman Turks, who plundered and destroyed the city. During the Egyptian Expedition of 1798–1801, Cairo was occupied by French troops. The population of the city repeatedly rose in rebellion against the French occupiers (1798, 1800). In 1795 and again in 1804–05, there were rebellions against the Mamelukes and Turks. In the 19th century, particularly in the first half, new sections and enterprises were built, the first Egyptian printing plant was established, and educational institutions were founded. In 1882, Cairo was occupied by British troops. From 1914 to 1922, it was the administrative center of a British protectorate. After 1922 it was the capital of the Kingdom of Egypt.

Cairo was the most important center of the anti-imperialist, national liberation movement in Egypt. There were uprisings in 1919 and 1921; major anti-British demonstrations and actions took place in the 1930's, in 1946, in 1951 and early 1952, and at other times. On July 23, 1952, a coup d'etat took place in Cairo, which marked the beginning of the revolution of national liberation in Egypt. From 1953 to 1958, Cairo was the capital of the Republic of Egypt and from 1958 to 1971, the capital of the United Arab Republic; since 1971 it has been the capital of the Arab Republic of Egypt. Since 1971, Cairo has also been the capital of the Federation of Arab Republics. Cairo is also the site of the headquarters of the League of Arab States (since 1945) and the residence of the permanent secretariat of the Afro-Asian People's Solidarity Organization (AAPSO, 1957).

N. G. KALININ

Economy. About one-quarter of the industrial production of the country is concentrated in Cairo and its suburbs. There are machine-building, metalworking, textile, chemical, food-processing (including oil presses), tobacco, cement, and printing enterprises. Plants for the production of railroad cars and for the assembly of trucks, tractors, and television and radio equipment were built after the revolution of 1952. The socialist countries play a significant role in the creation of industrial enterprises. With Soviet help the following plants were built in the 1960's: a forging plant, the first stages of a machine-tool building plant and a coking plant in the Cairo suburb of Helwan, and plants for the production of files, emery boards, and sandpaper. The Helwan Steel Plant has been expanding since 1968. With the help of the Czechoslovak Socialist Republic, bicycle and ceramics plants have been built. A cigarette factory was built with the help of the German Democratic Republic. Crafts industries have been considerably developed. There is a thermal power plant whose capacity is 643,000 kW (1967). In addition, Cairo is a major financial and commercial center.

Architecture and city planning. Cairo may be clearly divided into two parts, the old and the new. The old city, which occupies the eastern and southern districts, has numerous narrow streets and two- to four-story pisé and stone houses. It contains architectural monuments from the fourth century B.C. to the 19th century A.D. Among the buildings from Roman times (late first century B.C. to fourth century A.D.) is the tower in the fortress of Babylon by the architect Apollodorus. Among the Byzantine structures (fourth to seventh centuries) are the Coptic Church of St. Sergius and Bacchus, the Church of Our Lady, and the Church of St. Barbara, all in the fortress of Babylon.

The early Arab monuments that have survived include the Amir ibn-al-As Mosque (641–642, rebuilt in the ninth century) in Fustat, the ibn Tulun Mosque (876–879), and the Nilometer (715) on the island of Roda. Monuments preserved from the Fatimid period include the remains of the stone city walls and gates (11th century); the mosques of al-Azhar (970–972, repeatedly rebuilt), al-Hakim (990–1013), al-Juyushi (1085), al-Akmar (1125), and al-Salih Talai (1160); the mausoleums of Sab'a Banat ("The Seven Daughters," 11th century) in Fustat and Umm Kulthum (1122); and residential houses from the tenth and 11th centuries discovered during excavations in Fustat. A number of large structures from the time of the Ayyubid and Mameluke dynasties have survived. These include the citadel of Salah-al-Din (Saladin; 1176–83); the mausoleum, mosque, and hospital complex of Sultan Kala'un (1284–85); the mosque-madrasah of Sultan Hasan (1356–63); the mosque-madrasah of Sultan Barkuk (1384–86; architect, Shihab al-Din); the mausoleum and mosque of Sultan Qait Bey (1472–74); the mausoleums of Imam al-Shafi (1211), Sanjar al-Jawli (1303–1304), and the Mamelukes (15th century and early 16th century); and the al-Muayyad Mosque (1415–20). Among the buildings preserved from the period of the Ottoman Empire are the mosques of Sinan Pasha (1571) and Muhammad Ali (1830–48; architect, Yusuf Buhna) and houses from the 16th to 18th century.

The new city occupies the western and northwestern districts and also includes Heliopolis to the northeast, where quarters dating from the start of the 20th century are located on the site of the ancient Egyptian city. New Cairo has straight wide avenues, large squares, boulevards, and gardens. The streets are lined with multistory buildings constructed during the second half of the 19th century and the 20th century: government offices, the University of Cairo, the television center, the Egyptian Museum, banks, restaurants, and hotels. In accordance with the general plan of 1955, work is proceeding on the reconstruction and urban renewal of Cairo, in particular, of the embankments of the Nile. *Egypt Awakening,* a marble monument executed by the sculptor Mahmud Mukhtar between 1919 and 1928, was erected in Cairo. The city is the center of crafts industries that produce articles of leather, metal, wood, and other materials.

Educational, scientific, and cultural institutions. Located in Cairo are an Academy, the Institute of Egypt, the University of Cairo, the universities of Ayn Shams and al-Azhar, and other institutions of higher learning and scientific research. The city has ten museums, including the Egyptian Museum, the Coptic Museum, the Museum of Islamic Art, the Museum of Modern Art, and the Geological Museum. The largest of its libraries is the National Library, with about 1 million holdings.

Cairo has theaters and theatrical troupes, including al-Gumhuriyya, al-Uzbekiyya, the Theater of July 26, the National Theater (both musical and drama troupes), the World Theater, the Masrah al-Gayb Theater, the Tawfiq al-Hakim Theater, the Comedy Theater, the Opera Theater (being rebuilt after a fire), and the Puppet Theater.

REFERENCES
Khodzhash, S. *Kair.* Moscow, 1967.
Aldridge, J. *Kair.* Moscow, 1970. (Translated from English).
Abd al-Rahman Zaki. *Al Qahira,* vols. 1–2. Cairo, 1935.
Clerget, M. *Le Caire,* vols. 1–2. Cairo, 1937.
Schemeil, M. *Le Caire. . . .* Cairo, 1949.   [11–532–2]

CAIRO, UNIVERSITY OF, founded in 1908 with private funds; transformed in 1925 into a state university and placed under the Ministry of Public Education.

After the revolution of 1952, the University of Cairo received material support from the state and broadened its student body, both from Arab and other states. The number of students enrolled in the natural science faculty rose significantly, and an enormous amount of work was done to create textbooks in Arabic.

In 1938 a branch of the University of Cairo was created in Alexandria. Out of it grew the University of Alexandria, which opened in 1942. In 1955 a branch of the University of Cairo was opened in Khartoum (Sudan). In 1962 a branch (faculty of medicine) was opened in Al-Mansura. Taha Husayn, the Egyptian writer and scholar who subsequently created the chair of classical philology, was once a student at the university.

In the 1971–72 academic year, there were 12 faculties at the University of Cairo: philology, law, two faculties of commerce, socioeconomic and political sciences, natural sciences, medicine, dentistry, pharmacy, engineering, agriculture, and Arab philology (Dar al-Ulum). More than 64,000 students attended the university, and approximately 3,000 instructors worked there.

Instruction is conducted basically in Arabic, although English and French are also used in the natural sciences and technical faculties. Attached to the University of Cairo are the Oceanographic Institute in Suez, a biological station on the Red Sea (Al-Ghurdaqah), the Helwan Astronomical Observatory, the Institute of Statistical Studies and Research, and other scientific research institutes and laboratories. The university library, which was founded in 1932, has more than 500,000 volumes (1971).   O. K. DREIER   [11–536–3]

CAIRO CONFERENCE OF 1943, a meeting held in Cairo on Nov. 22–26, 1943, which was attended by USA president F. Roosevelt, Great Britain's prime minister W. Churchill, Chiang Kai-shek, the head of the Kuomintang government of China, and their military and political advisers.

The participants of the conference adopted a declaration, which was published on Dec. 1, 1943, after the Soviet government had become acquainted with it at the Tehran Conference of 1943. In this document the governments of the USA, Great Britain, and China solemnly declared that they "covet no gain for themselves and have no thought of territorial expansion." The declaration stated that the Allies intended to deprive Japan of all its conquered territories, including all the islands in the Pacific Ocean seized or occupied by it since the beginning of World War I (1914–18). The declaration advanced the demand that "all the territories Japan has stolen from the Chinese, such as Manchuria, Formosa, and the Pescadores [northeastern China, the island of Taiwan, and the P'eng-hu Lieh-tao Islands], shall be restored to the Republic of China."

The declaration also spoke of granting freedom and independence to Korea "in due course." Thus, the countries that signed the declaration put off the granting of independence to Korea for an indefinite period. The prospects of military action in the Pacific theater of the war were discussed at the Cairo Conference. (In the course of this discussion serious disagreements were revealed, chiefly between the British and American delegations.) Certain questions concerning Allied strategy in Europe were also discussed.

As later events showed, the decisions reached at the Cairo Conference were a screen behind which the imperialist circles of the USA and Great Britain could conceal their plans of aggression.

After the capitulation of Japan on Sept. 2, 1945, British troops were again introduced into Hsiang-kang (Hong Kong). In 1950, under the cover of the United Nations, the USA unleashed a war of aggression against the People's Democratic Republic of Korea. In the same year the USA virtually occupied the islands of P'eng-hu Lieh-tao and the island of Taiwan, which belong to the People's Republic of China. Thus, the decisions reached at the Cairo Conference were rudely violated.

PUBLICATIONS

"Soveshchanie Ruzvel'ta, Chan Kai-shi i Cherchillia v Severnoi Afrike." *Izvestiia,* Dec. 3, 1943.

REFERENCES

Boratyński, S. *Diplomatiia perioda vtoroi mirovoi voiny.* Moscow, 1959. (Translated from Polish.)

Israelian, V. L. *Antigitlerovskaia koalitsiia, [1941–1945].* Moscow, 1964. Chapter 15.

America, Britain and Russia: Their Co-operation and Conflict, 1941–1946. Edited by W. H. McNeill. Toronto [1953].   [11–535–1]

CAIROLI, BENEDETTO. Born Jan. 18, 1825, in Pavia; died Aug. 8, 1889, in Capodimonte, near Naples. Italian liberal politician and statesman.

With his four brothers, Cairoli was part of the national liberation movement during the 1840's through the 1860's. He helped organize Garibaldi's expedition of the Thousand and commanded its 7th Company. After the unification of Italy, Cairoli headed a faction of the leftist liberal group of industrial and trade circles. In 1878 and from 1879 to 1881 he was the prime minister.

Cairoli's government assisted the development of capitalism in Italy and encouraged the spirit of bourgeois enterprise. It supported the movement for the return to Italy of the Southern Tirol and other regions that remained in Austrian hands. Cairoli pursued a policy of nonparticipation in any alliances, hoping to take advantage of the disagreements among European powers. France's seizure in 1881 of Tunis, to which Italy also had pretensions, marked the failure of Cairoli's foreign policy and led to his resignation.   [11–546–6]

CAJAMARCA, a city in northern Peru. Population, approximately 40,000. Located on the slopes of the Cordillera Occidental mountain range, at an elevation of more than 2,800 m.

Cajamarca is a highway junction and the trading center of an agricultural region (sugarcane, cotton, tobacco, rice, dairy cattle-breeding). It has enterprises producing powdered milk, butter, cheese, and leather goods and is a center for the production of handmade straw hats.

Cajamarca was one of the important cities of the Inca empire until the beginning of the 16th century. It was under Spanish rule from the 16th to the 19th century. The architecture of Cajamarca flourished in the first half of the 18th century. The rich deep carvings, resembling a plush carpet, give a special magnificence to Cajamarca's churches (the cathedral of Santa Catalina, 1682–1762; San Antonio, 1699–1737; and El Belen, 1699–1746). The two-story clay houses have tile roofs that project outward a great distance and portals with carved pilasters and pediments.

REFERENCE

Gridilla, A. *Cajamarca y sus monumentos.* Cajamarca, 1939.
          [11–1629–2]

CAJUPUT TREE (*Melaleuca leucadendron*), an evergreen tree of the family Myrtaceae, with white bark and more or less vertical leaves. It grows in the forests of northern and northwestern Australia and in Asia (Indochina and Indonesia) and is often cultivated. Cajuput oil, which is an essential oil, is made from the leaves and young branches; it is used in dentistry and as an antiseptic. Cajuput oil is colorless or yellowish, smells of camphor, and contains cineole, α-terpineol and its esters, and other substances.   [11–389–1]

CAKCHIQUEL, an Indian people of Guatemala. The Cakchiquel live primarily in the departments of Chimaltenango and Guatemala. They number more than 300,000 persons (1970, estimate) and speak a language of the Quiché group of Mayan languages. Most of the Cakchiquels are Catholics, although they retain considerable vestiges of their pre-Christian religious beliefs. Early state formations, with the city of Iximché as the chief center, existed among the Cakchiquel before the Spanish conquest in the early 16th century. The principal occupation of the Cakchiquel is farming; the traditional handicrafts of weaving and pottery-making are well developed.   [11–556–3]

CALABASH, a vessel made from the fruit of the calabash tree or from gourds. The calabash, intended primarily to store beverages, has been used in Africa, South America, and New Guinea since ancient times. Calabashes are often decorated with plant or geometric designs done by burning, incising, or painting in bright natural colors.   [11–574–3]

CALABRIA, a region in southern Italy, primarily on the Calabrian Peninsula. Area, 15,100 sq km. Population, 2 million (1970). It comprises the provinces of Catanzaro, Cosenza, and Reggio di Calabria. Catanzaro is the main city.

The main economic activity in Calabria is agriculture, in which approximately half of the economically active population is engaged. Large landed estates are typical; land-starvation and poverty are prevalent among the peasants, causing large-scale emigration. Viticulture, truck farming, and floriculture (growing jasmine for essences) are important. Calabria produces 23 percent of the country's olives, 15 percent of its citrus fruits, and 12 percent of its figs. There are extensive pasture areas for the raising of livestock. In 1969 there were 369,000 sheep, 138,000 goats, 185,000 cattle, 264,000 hogs, and 51,000 horses, donkeys, and mules.

About a third of the economically active population is engaged in industry. Electric power is produced mainly at the Plateau la Sila hydroelectric power station; the output was 0.9 billion kilowatt-hours in 1969. Calabria has zinc-smelting and chemical plants (in Crotone), a plant producing railroad cars (in Reggio di Calabria), a cement plant, and a rolling mill. There are food, garment, and wood-products industries.

REFERENCE

Gambi, Lucio. "Calabria." Turin, 1965. (*Le regioni d'Italia,* vol. 16.)
          T. A. GALKINA   [11–557–4]

CALABRIA, a peninsula in southern Italy; the southern part of the Apennine Peninsula between the Ionian Sea, the Strait of Messina, and the Tyrrhenian Sea. Length, approximately 250 km. Width, from 40 to 100 km. Most of it is occupied by the Calabrian Apennines, which are composed mainly of limestone and flysch in the east and of granites and gneisses in the west. Elevation, up to 1,956 m (in the Aspromonte Massif). On the mountain slopes there is maquis, and in places beech and pine forests. Along the coasts there are narrow, very hilly tilled plains. Calabria is subject to earthquakes. The major cities are Reggio di Calabria, Catanzaro, and Cosenza.   [11–557–3]

CALADIUM, a genus of plants of the family Araceae. They are perennial herbs with a tuberous rhizome and sagittate or oblong leaves. The flowers are unisexual, without a perianth, and are gathered into a spadix (with pistillate flowers at the base, staminate flowers higher up, and a sterile part of the spadix above them), which is surrounded by a convolute white spathe. The fruit is a berry with several seeds. There are approximately 15 species, which grow in the rain forests of tropical America. Some species (for example, *C. bicolor, C. marmoratum,* and *C. picturatum*) are cultivated and have given rise to many horticultural varieties with different leaf shapes and colors.
          [11–558–1]

CALAH (also Kalhu), one of the largest cities of Assyria; founded by King Shalmaneser I in the first half of the 13th century B.C. Located on the left bank of the Tigris River (now the archaeological site of Nimrud, near the city of Nimrud in Iraq).

Calah was the capital of Assyria from the 13th to the 11th century B.C. and in the ninth and eighth centuries B.C. At the end of the seventh century B.C. it was destroyed by the Midianites and the Babylonians. The ruins of Calah were excavated by the British archaeologist A. H. Layard from 1845 to 1851 and by an expedition from the British School of Archaeology in Iraq from 1949 to 1963. A citadel was unearthed along with temples, a ziggurat, the obelisk of Shalmaneser III, and palaces (the palace of Ashurnasirpal II, which has reliefs and sculptures in the round, and the unfinished palace of Esarhaddon). Small ivory sculptures dating from about 715 B.C. have been found, as well as a large number of cuneiform documents. Some reliefs from the palace of King Ashurnasirpal are housed in the Hermitage.

REFERENCES
Golenishchev, V. S. *Opisanie assiriiskikh pamiatnikov.* St. Petersburg, 1897.
Mallowan, M. E. L. "The Excavations at Nimrud (Kalhu)."*Iraq*, 1958, vol. 20, part 2, pp. 101–08.
Mallowan, M. E. L. *Nimrud and Its Remains,* vols. 1–2. [London, 1966.]
[11–568–3]

CALAIS, a city and port in northern France, on the Strait of Dover. Administrative center of the department of Pas-de-Calais. Population, 75,000 (1968).

Calais is a transportation center of international importance, through which passes maritime passenger traffic to Dover in Great Britain. It is also a fishing and commercial center. There are metallurgical, ship-repair, electrotechnical, and chemical enterprises in the city. Calais also produces its traditional lace, tulle, and embroidery.

The city grew out of a fishing village in the late ninth and the tenth century. In the 13th century it was fortified by the Count of Boulogne. From the 13th century it played a significant role in the trade between France and England. In 1347, during the Hundred Years' War, Calais was captured by the English after a lengthy siege; it remained a stronghold of the English in their later struggle against France. In 1558, Calais was captured by the Duke of Guise and reunited with France. The Cateau-Cambrésis Peace of 1559 confirmed Calais as French.   [11–574–2]

CALAME, ALEXANDRE. Born May 28, 1810, in Vevey, Switzerland; died Mar. 17, 1864, in Menton, France. Swiss painter and graphic artist (etcher, lithographer).

Calame painted romantically theatrical, majestic mountain landscapes noted for precise rendering of details and perspective effects.

REFERENCE
Schreiber-Favre, A. *A. Calame.* Geneva, 1934.   [11–560–2]

CALAMIAN ISLANDS, a group of islands in the South China Sea, in the Philippine Islands archipelago; approximately 100 islands with a total area of about 1,800 sq km are included. The Calamians are situated between the islands of Mindoro and Palawan. The largest islands in the group are Busuanga, Culion, and Coron. The islands are hilly and are covered with dense tropical forests; many of them are fringed with coral reefs. The Calamian Islands are the site of rice, corn, and coconut palm plantations. There is fishing, lumber is exported, and there is a deposit of manganese ores.   [11–562–2]

CALAMINE, hemimorphite, a mineral from the group of zinc hydrosilicates; chemical composition, $Zn_4[Si_2O_7][OH]_2 \cdot H_2O$. Contains 67.5 percent ZnO.

Calamine crystallizes in the rhombic system. The crystals are usually small and found only in vacancies. Calamine is found most frequently in the form of crystalline crusts with a radiate-fibrous structure and in nodular and stalactite masses. The color is white, yellow, or greenish blue (from admixtures of iron and copper compounds). Hardness on the mineralogical scale, 4–5; density, 3,400–3,500 kg per cu m. The crystals show pyroelectric properties when heated. Calamine forms in the oxidation zone of lead and zinc deposits. Rich accumulations have been found

in the USSR (eastern Transbaikal and central Kazakhstan) and abroad (Upper Silesia in Poland). It is used as an ore for obtaining zinc.   [11–562–3]

CALAMITALES, an order of extinct plants with segmented stems, resembling giant horsetails.

Members of this order reached a height of 8–12 m and a diameter of 0.5–1 m. The stem consisted of nodes and internodes. The nodes of the shoots had whorls of branches or simple linear leaves with one vein (the genera *Annularia* and *Asterophyllites*). The spore-bearing cones of Calamitales were composed of alternating fruiting and sterile leaves (sporangiophores). Calamitales differed anatomically from horsetails in having highly developed secondary wood; however, like horsetails, they had in their trunks a large cavity in place of the pith, which was destroyed early in development. The basic genus of Calamitales, *Calamites,* had three subgenera (*Stylocalamites, Calamitina,* and *Eucalamites*). Primitive Calamitales (*Osterocalamites*), which appeared at the end of the Devonian period and became extinct in the middle of the Carboniferous period, were replaced by Calamitales proper, which in turn disappeared during the Permian period. Calamitales reached their greatest distribution and dimensions in the tropical zone (the Euramerican paleofloral region), where they grew in lowlands and, 5; in swampy places.   [11–562–5]

CALANOIDA, a suborder of planktonic invertebrate animals of the order Copepoda. Some zoologists consider Calanoida an independent order.

Calanoida are from 0.5 to 14 mm in size. The head is fused with the first thoracic segment, forming the cephalothorax, on which there are a nauplius eye and five pairs of appendages (antennae I and II, mandibles, and two pairs of maxillae). The thorax bears maxillipeds and five or four pairs of swimming legs. Respiration is effected by the entire body surface. The female deposits eggs in the water or carries them in an egg sac until giving birth. Calanoida feed on phytoplankton (only a few are predators) and are themselves the principal food of fish fry, plankton-feeding fish (such as herring, anchovies, sardines, and Pacific saury) and whalebone whales. More than 2,000 species are known, belonging to 200 genera united in 30 families. They are widely distributed in marine and fresh bodies of water and are very numerous. (In the surface waters of the ocean there are up to tens of thousands of individuals per cubic meter.) The majority of marine Calanoida are characterized by luminescence. A typical representative of Calanoida is *Calanus finmarchicus.*

REFERENCES
Zhizn' zhivotnykh, vol. 2. Moscow, 1968. Pages 406–10.
Brodskii, K. A. *Veslonogie rachki Calanoida Dal'nevostochnykh morei SSSR i Poliarnogo basseina.* Moscow-Leningrad, 1950.
K. A. BRODSKII [11–565–2]

CALATRAVA, ORDER OF, a religious order of knights in Spain, founded in Castile in 1158 during the Reconquista, sanctioned by Pope Alexander III in 1164. Its name was derived from the strategically important Calatrava Castle (now in Ciudad Real), which the order had seized from the Moors. Through grants from the Castilian kings, the order acquired great landholdings. It played an important political role in the country, intervening in questions concerning ascension to the throne. In 1489 the monarchy took over the administration of the order. King Ferdinand V was sanctioned by the pope as the grand master of the Order of Calatrava. The order was dissolved in 1873.   [11–568–1]

CALBAYOG, a city and port in the Philippines, on the western coast of the island of Samar. Population, 106,800 (1970). There is fishing, and the city is a trade center for agricultural products (rice and copra).   [11–683–1]

CALBE (also, Kalbe), a city in the German Democratic Republic, near Magdeburg, on the Saale River. Population, 16,300 (1970). The city is a river port and a railroad junction. In the early 1950's the "West" metallurgical enterprises were constructed (using the iron ore from the deposits in Harbke and the lignite coke produced in the city of Lauchhammer). Calbe is the site of a steam power plant and a cement factory. Brown coal is mined nearby.   [11–683–2]

CALCEOLARIA, a genus of plants of the family Scrophulariaceae (figwort). Included in this genus are herbs, semishrubs, and shrubs. The leaves are opposite or verticillate. The blossoms have a four-part calyx and a vividly labiate, bulging corolla (the lower lip is usually larger). There are two or three stamens. The fruit is a capsule. There are approximately 400 species, found primarily in the Peruvian and Chilean Andes. Several species are also native to Central America. Many species are ornamentals. Hybrids of the species *Calceolaria corymbosa, C. arachnoidea,* and *C. crenatiflora* were used in the creation of numerous garden varieties. The hybrids have yellow, orange, red, or violet flowers; they have either spotted or striped corollas. They are grown in cool conservatories and propagated by seeds or cuttings.   [11–697–7]

CALCEX, tablets containing a compound salt of hexamethylenetetramine (Urotropin) and calcium chloride, taken internally for catarrhal diseases.   [11–697–6]

CALCICOLES (also calciphiles), plants that grow predominantly in soils rich in calcium, and also on outcrops of limestones, marls, chalk, and other rocks. The confinement of calcicoles to soils that contain a considerable quantity of lime is a result of the alkaline reaction of the soil and some of the soil's physical properties (for example, easy permeability by water or rapid absorption of heat). Examples of calcicoles are the snowdrop anemone, six-petaled spiraea, European larch, and *Quercus calcarea.* Under certain conditions, some calcicoles can grow on noncalcareous soils.   [11–697–8]

CALCIFEROLS, vitamins of the D group, closely related to sterols in chemical structure.

Calciferols are found in the form of ergocalciferol (vitamin D_2) and cholecalciferol (vitamin D_3), which are produced by the irradiation with ultraviolet rays of ergosterol and dehydrocholesterol, respectively. Ergocalciferol has been found in very small quantities in plant products. Cholecalciferol is contained chiefly in products of animal origin (cheese, butter, egg yolk, beef liver, cod and halibut livers, herring, salmon, tuna). Calciferols regulate calcium and phosphorus metabolism in the body.
                                                          [11–704–1]

CALCIFUGES, plants that grow well on soils with an acid or neutral reaction and poorly on those rich in lime. If the action of calcium is in equilibrium with the concentration of hydrogen ions (pH no higher than 5.7), calcifuges may grow under conditions of high calcium content (for example, 300 mg per liter for sphagnum mosses). Examples of calcifuges are sphagnum mosses and many higher marsh plants (such as cotton grass, sundew, and butterbur).   [11–698–1]

CALCINATION OF STRAW, a method of treating straw with lime to increase its digestibility and nutritional value. The rigidity of straw, which makes it difficult to eat and digest, results from the fact that as the plant grows and develops the cellular tissue becomes impregnated with lignin, a substance that makes the straw strong and gives it woody properties. Calcination of straw is based on the ability of alkalis to break the bond between lignin and the cellular tissue. Straw that has been treated with a lime solution is fed to cattle and sheep together with silage and in concentrates.

REFERENCE
Kormshchikov, P. A. *Kal'tsinirovanie grubykh kormov.* Moscow, 1958.
                                                          [11–702–1]

CALCINOSIS, calcification, the deposit of calcium salts in tissues and organs that do not normally contain them in undissolved form.

In old persons, lime is deposited in the cartilage of the ribs and larynx. A normal phenomenon is the grains of lime found in the pineal gland and the vascular plexus of the brain (brain sand). Under pathological conditions, calcium salts are deposited both inside and outside the cells. Sometimes these salts take the form of grains or granules, and sometimes they form larger clumps. The process is called petrifaction, and the calcified area is called the petrifact. Calcium salts fall out of solution and are deposited in tissues because of the unstable state of protein colloids, changes in the pH toward greater alkalinity, and increases in calcium concentration in the blood. Several forms of calcinosis are distinguished, according to the mechanism of development.

Dystrophic calcification is a localized process in tissue areas with sharply lowered metabolism, as a result of which oxidative processes are decreased, the tissue becomes more alkaline, and lime falls out of solution. Dystrophic calcification occurs in dystrophic processes (dystrophy) and tissue necrosis.

Calcareous metastases are a manifestation of a general disruption of calcium metabolism in which the calcium concentration in the blood is elevated. Osteomyelitis, myeloma, and other diseases induce processes that destroy bone tissue and release lime from it.

The causes of calcium accumulation in the blood include diseases of the large intestine and kidneys and hypovitaminosis D. In contrast to dystrophic calcification, the sedimentation of lime in healthy, unchanged tissues and organs occurs only in those tissues that normally have an alkaline medium (lungs, stomach, kidneys, and arteries).

Interstitial calcinosis (calcium gout) is distinguished by the fact that there is no depletion of calcium in the bones and no excess concentration of calcium in the blood. The depositing of lime occurs in the skin and subcutaneous tissues or may spread to the muscles and other tissues. The cause of interstitial calcinosis has not yet been clearly shown. It is detected chiefly during X-ray examination. Treatment is both symptomatic and directed toward removing the primary causes of the condition.
                                                          [11–702–3]

CALCIPHYRE, a metamorphic rock composed of calcite or dolomite; it contains smaller quantities of garnet, pyroxene, forsterite, spinel, feldspar, and other minerals. Calciphyre is contrasted with marble, which contains few impurities.
                                                          [11–704–2]

CALCITE (calcareous spar), a mineral with chemical composition $CaCO_3$, containing 56 percent CaO and 44 percent CO_2 and frequently Mg, Fe, Mn (up to 8 percent) as well as Zn, Co, Sr, and Ba. Calcite crystallizes in the trigonal system. It exists in the form of crystals with various habits—rhombohedral, scalenohedral, prismatic, or tabular—as well as in the form of stalactites and solid, granular, and earthy masses (chalk). The Ca and C atoms in the calcite structure are arranged at the lattice points of the rhombohedral lattices as though pushed into one another. The O atoms are in groups of three around each C atom and lie in the same plane. Calcite is brittle and exhibits perfect cleavage on the rhombohedron [1011]. Twins are a characteristic feature. Calcite crystals exhibit a high birefringence, and many are strongly fluorescent. Calcite's hardness on the mineralogical scale is 3 and its density, 2,720–2,800 kg/m^3. When heated, calcite decomposes at a temperature of 825°C; it is readily soluble in acids.

Calcite is one of the most widely distributed minerals in the earth's crust, particularly among the hydrothermal formations in contact metasomatic deposits and in amygdaloids and geodes of igneous rocks. It is sometimes formed under magmatogenic conditions, producing carbonatites. Calcite precipitates from hot calcareous springs in the form of tufa (travertine). Enormous masses of calcite are formed as deposits in ocean basins, partly by biogenesis. Calcite appears as the main constituent of limestone, marble, and other sedimentary and metamorphic rocks widely used as construction and facing materials. Pure and transparent varieties of calcite—for example, Icelandic spar—are used in the optics industry.

REFERENCES

Opticheskie materialy dlia infrakrasnoi tekhniki. Moscow, 1965.
"Kal'tsit." In *Fizicheskii entsiklopedicheskii slovar'*, vol. 2. Moscow, 1962.
Kostov, I. *Mineralogiia.* Moscow, 1971. (Translated from English.)
      M. D. DORFMAN and M. O. KLIIA [11–703–1]

CALCIUM (Ca), a chemical element in group IIA of Mendeleev's periodic table. Atomic number, 20; atomic weight, 40.08; a silver-white, lightweight metal. The natural element consists of a mixture of six stable isotopes: ^{40}Ca, ^{42}Ca, ^{43}Ca, ^{44}Ca, ^{46}Ca, and ^{48}Ca, the most abundant of which is the first (96.97 percent).

Calcium compounds, such as limestone, marble, and gypsum (as well as lime, the product of limestone calcination), have been used in construction since antiquity. Chemists considered lime to be an element as recently as the end of the 18th century, but in 1789 A. Lavoisier suggested that lime, magnesia, baryta, alumina, and silica are compound materials. H. Davy electrolyzed a mixture of moist slaked lime and mercuric oxide in 1808 using a mercury cathode to prepare a calcium amalgam from which he removed the mercury by distillation and obtained a metal that he named calcium (from the genitive *calcis* of the Latin *calx,* "lime").

Occurrence in nature. Calcium is the fifth most abundant element in the earth's crust (after oxygen, silicon, aluminum, and iron): 2.96 percent by weight. It migrates vigorously and accumulates in various geochemical systems, forming 385 minerals (the fourth largest number of minerals formed by an element). The earth's mantle contains little calcium and the earth's core probably contains even less (iron meteorites contain 0.02 percent). Calcium predominates in the lower part of the earth's crust, accumulating in basic rocks. A large amount of calcium is found in the feldspar anorthite, $Ca[Al_2Si_2O_8]$; basic rocks contain 6.72 percent and acidic rocks, such as granites, contain 1.58 percent. An extremely sharp differentiation of calcium takes place in the biosphere, principally because of the "carbonate balance," by which the soluble bicarbonate $Ca(HCO_3)_2$ is formed from the reaction between carbon dioxide and calcium carbonate, $CaCO_3$: $CaCO_3 + H_2O + CO_2 \rightleftarrows Ca(HCO_3)_2 \rightleftarrows Ca^{2+} + 2HCO^-_3$. This reaction is reversible and the basis for the redistribution of the element. Calcium dissolves in water with a high CO_2 content, but at a low CO_2 content the mineral calcite ($CaCO_3$) precipitates to form large deposits of limestone, chalk, and marble.

Biogenic migration also plays a very large role in the history of the element. Calcium is chief among the metallic elements in living matter. Organisms are known that contain more than 10 percent calcium (more than carbon) and build their skeleton from calcium compounds (mainly $CaCO_3$); these include calciferous algae, many mollusks, echinoderms, corals, and rhizopods. Deposits of the skeletons of marine animals and plants lead to the accumulation of colossal masses of algal, coral, and other limestones, which, buried deep within the earth and mineralized, are transformed into various types of marble.

Large territories with damp climates (wooded zones, tundra) are characterized by a lack of calcium, which is readily leached out of the soils. This phenomenon is a cause of low soil fertility, low productivity and poor growth in domestic animals, and, frequently, of diseases of the skeleton. Liming of soils and supplemental feeding of domestic animals and birds are therefore of great importance. Conversely, $CaCO_3$ is poorly soluble in dry climates, and steppe and desert regions are therefore rich in calcium. Gypsum ($CaSO_4 \cdot 2H_2O$) is frequently enriched in solonchak and salt lakes.

Rivers carry large quantities of calcium to the oceans; however, the calcium does not remain in the ocean water (average content, 0.04 percent) but concentrates in the skeletons of organisms and settles to the bottom after their death (mostly in the form of $CaCO_3$). Limestone sediments are widely distributed over the bottom of all oceans at depths to 4,000 m ($CaCO_3$ dissolves at greater depths and organisms at those depths frequently suffer a calcium deficit).

Underground waters play an important role in the migration of calcium. In places they vigorously leach out $CaCO_3$ in masses of limestone, which results in the formation of karst and of caverns, stalactites, and stalagmites. Not only calcite but also calcium phosphates (for example, the Karatau phosphorite deposits in Kazakhstan) and dolomite ($CaCO_3 \cdot MgCO_3$) were widely deposited in the oceans of past geological epochs. Gypsum was deposited upon the evaporation of lagoons.

In the course of geologic history the biogenic formation of carbonate increased and the chemical precipitation of calcite decreased. The Precambrian oceans (more than 600 million years ago) contained no animals with limestone skeletons; these animals first became widespread in the Cambrian (corals, sponges). An explanation is found in the high CO_2 content of the Precambrian atmosphere.

Physical and chemical properties. The crystal lattice of the α-form of calcium (stable at ordinary temperatures) is face-centered cubic; $a = 5.56$ Å. Its atomic radius is 1.97 Å; the ionic radius of Ca^{2+}, 1.04 Å. Its density is 1.54 g per cm^3 (20°C). The hexagonal β-form is stable above 464°C; melting point, 851°C; boiling point, 1482°C; temperature coefficient of linear expansion, 22×10^{-6} (0°–300°C); thermal conductivity at 20°C, 125.6 watts per m·°K, or 0.3 calories per cm·sec·°C); specific heat capacity (0°–100°C), 623.9 joules per kg·°K), or 0.149 cal per g·°C); specific electrical resistivity at 20°C, 4.6×10^{-8} ohm·m, or 4.6×10^{-6} ohm·cm; temperature coefficient of electrical resistivity, 4.57×10^{-3} (20°C); modulus of elasticity, 26 giganewtons per m^2 (2,600 kilograms-force per mm^2); tensile strength, 60 meganewtons per m^2 (6 kgf/mm^2); elastic limit, 4 MN/m^2 (0.4 kgf/mm^2); yield point, 38 MN/m^2 (3.8 kgf/mm^2); relative elongation, 50 percent; Brinell hardness, 200–300 MN/m^2 (20–30 kgf/mm^2). Calcium of sufficiently high purity is ductile. It may be pressed, rolled, and cut.

The configuration of the outer electron shell of the calcium atom is $4s^2$, so that calcium is divalent in its compounds. Calcium is very active chemically. At ordinary temperatures it reacts very readily with atmospheric oxygen and moisture; it is therefore stored in hermetically sealed vessels or under mineral oil. When heated in air or in oxygen it ignites, resulting in the formation of the basic oxide CaO. The calcium peroxides CaO_2 and CaO_4 also occur. Calcium reacts with cold water rapidly at first, but the reaction is then retarded because of the formation of a film of $Ca(OH)_2$. Calcium reacts vigorously with hot water and with acids, giving off H_2 (this does not occur with concentrated HNO_3). Calcium reacts with flourine at lower temperatures and with chlorine and bromine above 400°C, yielding CaF_2, $CaCl_2$, and $CaBr_2$, respectively. In the molten state these halides react with calcium to form the so-called subcompounds CaF and CaCl, in which the calcium is formally univalent. Heating calcium with sulfur yields calcium sulfide (CaS), which adds additional sulfur to give polysulfides, such as CaS_2 and CaS_4. Calcium reacts with dry hydrogen at 300°–400°C to give the hydride CaH_2, an ionic compound in which hydrogen is the anion. Calcium and nitrogen react at 500°C to give the nitride Ca_3N_2. The reaction of calcium with ammonia at low temperatures gives the complex ammoniate $Ca[NH_3]_6$. Heating calcium with silicon, phosphorus, or graphite in the absence of air gives calcium silicides (Ca_2Si, CaSi, and $CaSi_2$), calcium phosphide (Ca_3P_2), and calcium carbide (CaC_2), respectively. Calcium forms intermetallic compounds with aluminum, silver, gold, copper, lithium, magnesium, lead, and tin.

Production and uses. Calcium is produced industrially by two methods: (1) by heating a briquetted mixture of CaO and powdered aluminum at 1200°C in a vacuum of 0.01–0.02 mm Hg; the calcium vapors, evolved according to the equation $6CaO + 2Al = 3CaO \cdot Al_2O_3 + 3Ca$, condense on a cold surface; or (2) by electrolyzing a melt of $CaCl_2$ and KCl, using a liquid copper-calcium cathode, to give a copper-calcium alloy (65 percent calcium) from which the calcium is distilled at 950°–1000°C in a vacuum of 0.1–0.001 mm Hg.

The pure metal calcium is used as an agent for reducing uranium, thorium, chromium, vanadium, zirconium, cesium, rubidium, and some rare-earths from their compounds. Metallic calcium is also used for deoxidizing steels, bronzes, and other alloys, removing sulfur from petroleum products, dehydrating organic liquids, removing nitrogenous impurities from argon, and as a gas absorber in electrovacuum instruments. Antifrictional materials based on a lead-sodium-calcium system and lead-calcium alloys for the fabrication of electric-cable sheaths are used widely in industry. A calcium-silicon-calcium alloy (silicocalcium) is used as a deoxidizing agent and degasifier in the production of high-quality steels. The uses of calcium compounds are described in separate articles.

A. IA. FISHER and I. A. PEREL'MAN

Calcium in the organism. Calcium is one of the biogenic elements, that is, elements that are necessary for the normal progress of the life processes. It is present in all tissues and fluids in animals and plants. Only rarely are organisms capable of developing in an environment lacking in calcium. In some organisms the calcium content is as high as 38 percent; in man, the content is 1.4–2 percent. The cells of plants and animals require strictly fixed proportions of Ca^{2+}, Na^+, and K^+ ions in the extracellular fluids. Plants obtain calcium from the soil. Plants are divided into the calcephiles and calcephobes, depending on their behavior toward the element. Animals obtain calcium from food and water.

Calcium is essential for the formation of a number of cell structures, for the maintenance of the normal permeability of the outer cell membranes, for the fertilization of the egg cells of fish and other animals, and for the activation of a number of enzymes. Ca^{2+} ions transmit stimuli to muscle fiber and bring about its contraction, they increase the strength of cardiac contractions, they increase the phagocytic function of leukocytes, they activate the immunoprotein system in blood, and they participate in blood coagulation. Almost all of the calcium in cells is present in the form of compounds with proteins, nucleic acids, phospholipids, and complexes with inorganic phosphates and organic acids. In the blood plasma of man and the higher animals as little as 20–40 percent of the calcium may be combined with proteins. In animals with skeletons as much as 97–99 percent of the calcium is used as structural material: in invertebrates, mainly in the form of $CaCO_3$ (the shells of mollusks and corals), and in vertebrates, mainly as phosphates. Many invertebrate animals store calcium for the construction of a new skeleton prior to shedding their shells or for providing for the vital functions in unfavorable conditions.

The calcium content of human blood and the blood of other higher animals is regulated by hormones of the parathyroid and thyroid glands. Vitamin D plays an important role in these processes. Calcium absorption takes place in the anterior section of the small intestine. Calcium assimilation decreases when the acidity of the intestinal tract is lowered and is a function of the calcium-phosphorus-fat ratio in the food. The optimum ratios of calcium to phosphorus are about 1.3 in cow's milk, 0.15 in potatoes, 0.13 in beans, and 0.016 in meat. In cases of excess phosphorus or oxalic acid in the food, calcium absorption decreases. Absorption is accelerated by the bile acids. For man, the optimum proportion of calcium to fat in food is 0.04–0.08 g Ca to 1 g fat.

The elimination of calcium takes place mainly through the intestinal tract. Mammals lose large quantities of the element with their milk during lactation. Upsets in phosphorus-calcium metabolism in young animals and children lead to rickets, and in adults, to changes in the composition and structure of the skeleton (osteomalacia). I. A. SKUL'SKII

In medicine. The use of calcium preparations eliminates disturbances related to a deficiency of Ca^{2+} ions in the body (for example, in tetanus, spasmophilia, and rickets). Calcium preparations reduce increased sensitivity to allergens and are used in the treatment of allergic conditions (serum allergy, nettle rash, angioneurotic edema, hay fever). They lower increased permeability of the blood vessels and have an anti-inflammatory effect. They are used for hemorrhaging vasculitis, radiation sickness, inflammatory and exudative processes (pneumonia, pleuritis, endometritis), and certain skin conditions. They are prescribed to control bleeding, improve the activity of heart muscle, and reinforce the action of digitalis preparations. They are used as weak diuretics and as antitoxins in cases of magnesium-salt poisoning. Jointly with other drugs, they are used to stimulate labor. Calcium chloride is prescribed orally and intravenously. Ossocalcinol (a 15-percent sterile suspension of a specially prepared bone meal in persic oil) is suggested for tissue therapy.

Calcium preparations also include gypsum ($CaSO_4$), which is used in surgery for casts, and chalk ($CaCO_3$), which is prescribed for internal use in cases of elevated gastric acidity and for the preparation of tooth powder.

REFERENCES

Kratkaia khimicheskaia entsiklopediia, vol. 2. Moscow, 1963. Pages 370–75.
Rodiakin, V. V. *Kal'tsii, ego soedineniia i splavy.* Moscow, 1967.
Kaplanskii, S. Ia. *Mineral'nyi obmen.* Moscow-Leningrad, 1938.
Vishniakov, S. I. *Obmen makroelementov u sel'skokhoziaistvennykh zhivotnykh.* Moscow, 1967. [11–698–3]

CALCIUM BROMIDE, $CaBr_2$, a salt; colorless crystals. Density, 3.35 g per cm³; melting point, 760°C.

Calcium bromide is readily soluble in water (594 g per 100 g H_2O at 0°C). The crystalline hydrate, $CaBr_2 \cdot 6H_2O$, melts at 38.2 °C. Calcium bromide is obtained by the interaction of bromine and milk of lime in the presence of ammonia. It is used in the preparation of sensitized photographic materials.

[11–704–3]

CALCIUM CARBIDE, CaC_2, a compound of calcium and carbon; one of the most important carbides used in technology. Chemically pure calcium carbide is colorless; industrial calcium carbide varies in color from light brown to black. Calcium carbide has a density of 2.2 g/cm³, and a melting point of 2300°C. Calcium carbide interacts with water to form acetylene: $CaC_2 + 2H_2O = C_2H_2 + Ca(OH)_2$; the process is carried out in an excess of water for withdrawal of the liberated heat (30.4 kcal/mole, that is, 127.3 kilojoules per mole). Upon heating, calcium carbide interacts with nitrogen to form calcium cyanamide: $CaC_2 + N_2 = CaCN_2 + C$.

Calcium carbide is prepared in electric furnaces at temperatures ranging from 1900° to 1950°C according to the reaction $CaO + 3C = CaC_2 + CO$, in which a large quantity of heat (450.5 kilojoules per mole) is absorbed. Lime and anthracite or coke serve as raw material for the process. Most of the operating carbide furnaces have an opening at the top; CO is burned down to CO_2 after its discharge from the furnace. Closed furnaces with CO extraction have also been constructed. Calcium carbide has found wide application in technology, primarily in the manufacture of acetylene and calcium cynamide and in the reduction of alkali metals.

REFERENCES

Kuznetsov, L. A. *Proizvodstvo karbida kal'tsiia.* Moscow-Leningrad, 1950.
Strizhevskii, I. I., S. G. Guzov, and V. A. koval'skii. *Atsetilenovye stantsii,* 2nd ed. Moscow, 1959. [11–1196–3]

CALCIUM CARBONATE, $CaCO_3$, a salt.

Calcium carbonate occurs in nature in two mineral forms with differing crystalline structures: aragonite and the widely distributed calcite. Calcium carbonate decomposes when heated above 900°C: $CaCO_3 = CaO + CO_2$ (a means of obtaining lime). It is sparingly soluble in water (14 mg calcite per liter at 18°C) and readily soluble in acids. Natural calcium carbonate (limestone, marble) is used as a construction material; chalk (powdered calcium carbonate) serves as a filler for rubber stock, paper, and linoleum. A softer and finer product, called precipitated calcium carbonate (obtained through the reaction of $CaCl_2$ and Na_2CO_3), is used in the manufacture of tooth powder and cosmetics. [11–705–1]

CALCIUM CHLORIDE, $CaCl_2$, a salt; colorless crystals with a density of 2.51 g/cm³ and melting point of 772°C. Calcium chloride easily absorbs water vapor, subsequently deliquescing. Its solubility per 100 g H_2O is 74 g at 20°C and 159 g at 100°C. Aqueous solutions of calcium chloride freeze at low temperatures (20-percent solution at −18.5°C and 30-percent solution at − 48°C). Calcium chloride forms the hydrate $CaCl_2 \cdot 6H_2O$, which remains stable up to 29.8°C; at high temperatures, crystalline hydrates are precipitated from the saturated solution with four, two, and one molecules of H_2O. When $CaCl_2 \cdot 6H_2O$

(58.8 percent) is mixed with snow or ice (41.2 percent), the temperature drops to $-55°C$ (cryohydric point).

Calcium chloride is obtained as a byproduct in the manufacture of soda and is used for the preparation of calcium metal, in the drying of gases and liquids, in refrigeration, and in medicine.

[11–705–8]

CALCIUM FLUORIDE, CaF_2, a salt; colorless crystals. Density, 3.18 g per cm^3; melting point, 1360°C.

Calcium fluoride is practically insoluble in water. It exists in nature in the form of the mineral fluorite (fluorspar) and is a component of apatite. Calcium fluoride serves as a source material in the preparation of hydrogen fluoride and other compounds and as a flux in metallurgy. [11–705–7]

CALCIUM HYDROXIDE, slaked lime, $Ca(OH)_2$, a strong base; colorless crystals. Density, 2.24 g per cm^3.

Commercial calcium hydroxide is a fluffy white powder. It dehydrates to CaO when heated. Calcium hydroxide is only slightly soluble in water: 0.165 g per 100 g H_2O at 20°C and 0.077 g at 100°C. Its solubility increases sharply in the presence of salts. An aqueous solution of calcium hydroxide is known as lime water; a suspension is known as milk of lime. Calcium hydroxide readily absorbs atmospheric carbon dioxide: $Ca(OH)_2 + CO_2 = CaCO_3 + H_2O$. The compound serves as an inexpensive alkali. It is also used in construction.

[11–704–4]

CALCIUM NITRATE (also called nitrocalcite, lime saltpeter, Norge niter), $Ca(NO_3)_2 \cdot 4H_2O$, a salt; colorless crystals that dissolve in water of crystallization at 42.7°C. Calcium nitrate crystallizes into an anhydrous salt at temperatures above 51.1°C. Its density is 2.36 g/cm^3. Because it is highly hygroscopic, it must be stored under moisture-free conditions. The solubility of anhydrous calcium nitrate is 127 g per 100 g H_2O at 20°C. Calcium nitrate is obtained by treating limestone with weak nitric acid; it is also formed during the absorption of nitrogen oxide by milk of lime.

Calcium nitrate is used as a nitrogen fertilizer in agriculture and is produced in granulated form. Commercial products contain no less than 15.5 percent nitrogen; furthermore, 4–7 percent ammonium nitrate is added during production in order to reduce the hygroscopicity of the fertilizer; the moisture content should not exceed 15 percent. Calcium nitrate is applied to the soil for all crops but is most effective in acidic soils, particularly for topdressing of winter crops in the spring. [11–698–2]

CALCIUM OXIDE (also quicklime), CaO, a compound of calcium and oxygen; colorless crystals with a density of 3.4 g/cm^3 and a melting point of 2585°C. The industrial product is a white porous substance. Calcium oxide reacts vigorously with water, liberating a considerable amount of heat and forming calcium hydroxide: $CaO + H_2O = Ca(OH)_2$ (slaking process). Calcium oxide is obtained by the calcination of limestone or chalk. It is widely used in construction, the chemical industry, metallurgy, agriculture, and water purification. [11–705–3]

CALCIUM SULFATE, $CaSO_4$, a salt, existing in nature as the dihydrate $CaSO_4 \cdot 2H_2O$ (gypsum, selenite) and in an anhydrous state (anhydrite). Anhydrous calcium sulfate occurs in the form of colorless crystals with a density of 2.96 g/cm^3 and a melting point of 1450°C. It combines very slowly with water, exhibiting a poor solubility of 0.2036 g per 100 g H_2O at 20°C and 0.067 g at 100°C. The half-hydrate $CaSO_4 \cdot 1/2 H_2O$ is known; when mixed with water, it hardens rapidly, converting into $CaSO_4 \cdot 2H_2O$. Calcium sulfate is used in the manufacture of figures and casts, as a construction material, and in medicine. [11–705–4]

CALCIUM SULFIDE, CaS, a salt; colorless crystals with a density of 2.58 g/cm^3 and a melting point of 2000°C. Calcium sulfide is obtained by the calcination of $CaSO_4$ with charcoal. It is used in the preparation of luminophors and in the tanning industry for the removal of hair from hides. Calcium hydrosulfide $Ca(SH)_2$ is used in the production of synthetic fibers. [11–705–5]

CALCULATION, COST, the calculation of the prime cost of a unit of output or job performed. Cost calculation is one of the basic indexes of the prime-cost plan and report. It reflects in monetary form the enterprise's expenditures for the production and sale of a unit of a particular type of output as well as expenditures for the performance of a unit of work (such as shipping or repair) in industry and other economic sectors.

Plan cost calculations are compiled for a period being planned using progressive input norms for labor and the means of production; the progressive norms reflect continued technical progress and improvement in the organization of production and labor. Report cost calculations are computed on the basis of accounting figures and characterize the actual level of expenditures. Normative cost calculations are a variety of current planning calculations; they are prepared in a number of sectors in connection with the normative method of recording expenditures. The current actual norms, characterizing basically the attained level of expenses, form the bases for these calculations. Projected cost calculations are a variation of long-range planning cost calculations; they are necessary, together with other indexes, to determine the efficiency of capital investments and new machinery.

Cost calculation is an important means of implementing ruble control and a system of economy measures. It permits comparison of the levels of prime costs and profitability for enterprises producing identical articles, and it makes possible the correct solution of problems in such areas as specialization, the allocation of production programs among enterprises, and material-technical supply. The preparation of planning cost calculations on the basis of progressive norms is an essential condition for establishing sound wholesale prices in industry and other sectors of the national economy. Calculations of the prime cost of agricultural products are used to plan state purchase prices.

Cost calculations are drawn up by types of output. In them the basic expenses are computed according to their purpose. At industrial enterprises the following are singled out: expenditures directly related to the technological process of manufacturing particular types of articles, that is, expenditures for raw and processed materials, fuel, and energy for production purposes; wage payments to production workers and deductions for social security; expenditures on preparation for and starting up of production; equipment maintenance and operating expenditures, including depreciation and current repair; general shop and plant expenditures, that is, systemwide (particularly administrative) expenditures; and other production expenditures, including those for scientific research and experimental work and for standardization. In report cost calculations, unproductive expenditures (losses from spoilage and rejects) are singled out. For an enterprise as a whole the cost calculation also includes nonproduction expenditures, including sales expenditures. A uniform classification of expenditures is separately determined in each sector, with due regard for its characteristics.

The magnitude of expenditures in the basic subheadings of cost calculations is determined by many factors. Expenditures for raw and processed materials, fuel, and energy depend on the expenditure per unit of output, the makeup of prices, and transportation and preparatory expenditures. The sum of wage payments in the cost calculation is determined by the level of labor productivity and the average wage of production workers. Expenditures for equipment maintenance and operation and general shop, plant, and nonproduction expenditures per unit of output depend on the substantiation of the sums of these expenditures for the primary subheadings provided for in estimates and also depend on the level of output.

Depending on how they are counted, expenditures included in the cost calculation are divided into direct and indirect. Direct expenditures include those determined per unit of output or for particular sectors of production on the basis of norms and direct record-keeping data; indirect expenditures include expenditures recorded and planned for production as a whole and distributed in some way or other among the production shops and sections, between finished products and incomplete production, and among types of articles.

REFERENCES
Bunimovich, V. *Kal'kulirovanie sebestoimosti promyshlennoi produktsii.* Moscow, 1967.
Shchenkov, S. *Bukhgalterskii uchet v promyshlennosti.* Moscow, 1969. Chapter 5.
V. A. BUNIMOVICH [11–689–1]

CALCUTTA, a city in India located in the Ganges River delta, on the Hooghly River, one of the Ganges' distributaries, at a distance of 140 km from the shore of the Bay of Bengal. It is one of the country's most important economic and cultural centers and also the administrative center of the state of West Bengal.

The historical center of Calcutta is its fortress, Fort William (constructed in the 18th century), on the eastern bank, in Maidan Park. The fortress divides the city into two parts: in one there are the European quarters, with mansions, government buildings, and a university; in the other there are industrial and commercial enterprises and the workers' quarters.

Calcutta proper (with a population of 3.1 million in 1971) is the core of a large conurbation that continues to grow rapidly. By 1971, Greater Calcutta, with an area of 425 sq km and a population of 7 million, had the largest population of any city in the country. This conurbation includes several dozen cities (among them Howrah, which is connected with Calcutta by a bridge, Behala, Bhatpara, Garden Reach, Kamarhati, and Baranagar) that are merging into a narrow belt for a distance of 100 km (3–4 to 15–20 km in width) along both banks of the Hooghly. Greater Calcutta is the most important center in India for migrants, who come pouring into the city in search of work. Native inhabitants are less than half of the population. More than one-third of Calcutta's population is non-Bengali—these people are mainly Bihari, but also Hindustani, Oriya, Rajasthani, Telugu, and Punjabi.

Calcutta was founded by the British East India Company in 1690; the city was built around the company's trading post and Fort William. From 1773 to 1911, Calcutta was the principal center of British colonial administration in India. (From December 1911 until 1947 the center was Delhi.) Calcutta was the chief port through which British colonial trade was carried on with India. In the mid-19th century, large factories (primarily jute factories) and plants were built. Calcutta became an important center of the workers' and left-wing democratic movement. The workers of Calcutta played a large role in the national liberation struggle, which led to India's winning independence in 1947.

Calcutta's exceptionally favorable economic-geographic location (as the focus of the territory of the Ganges basin) has fostered the overall economic growth of the city. Calcutta is a transportation terminus and the country's second largest seaport, after Bombay (in exports it occupies first place), with a cargo turnover of 9–10 million tons. The satellite port of Haldia was built in 1970 on the Hooghly River below Calcutta. There is an international airport at Dumdum.

The main branch of industry in Greater Calcutta is jute production (nine-tenths of the total Indian production and almost half of the world output). Metalworking and various kinds of machine building have also developed (approximately one-fourth of India's total output, including the production of industrial equipment, electrical instrument building, shipbuilding and ship repair, and the manufacture and assembly of automobiles, trucks, motorcycles, bicycles, and machine tools). There is also production of plastic and rubber articles, chemicals and pharmaceuticals, dyes, paints, cotton textiles, knitwear, glass, and leather footwear. There is a printing industry and a diverse food-processing industry. Calcutta is a major scientific and cultural center. It has numerous educational institutions, including a university and a number of other higher educational facilities. Scientific research institutions include the Indian Statistical Institute. The National Library (founded in 1902) has more than 1.2 million volumes; there is also the Indian Museum (1814) and the Victoria Museum (1906). On the bank of the Hooghly River in Howrah there is a botanical garden.

I. V. SAKHAROV [11–691–1]

CALCUTTA, UNIVERSITY OF, the oldest and largest university in India. It was established in 1857 on the basis of Hindu College (founded in 1827). The University of Calcutta also includes the following colleges: Presidency (founded in 1855), Sanskrit (1824), Bethune (1849), Doveton College (1823, for youths from Christian families), La Martiniere, the Muslim Madrasah College (1781), and the Armenian College (established in 1821 by wealthy members of the Armenian community). The University of Calcutta is an affiliating and teaching university: it works out programs for the colleges under its administration, conducts examinations and awards diplomas, and instructs students. In 1912 graduate work was established in the humanities, and in 1917 in the natural and exact sciences.

During the academic year 1971–72 the university had under its jurisdiction 212 colleges and schools in Calcutta and other cities in West Bengal. In the same year the university included the following faculties: humanities, science and mathematics, commerce, law, journalism, teacher training, fine arts and music, engineering, technology, medicine, agriculture, veterinary science, and home economics. At that time the university with its affiliated colleges and schools had an enrollment of about 200,000 students. In 1972 the university library contained approximately 430,000 volumes. The university also has an observatory (founded in 1875). [11–692–1]

CALDAS, a department in central Colombia, in the Cordillera Central and in the part of the Magdalena River valley that is adjacent to these mountains. Area, 7,300 sq km; population, 827,000 (1971). The city of Manizales is its administrative center. Caldas is a significant coffee-producing region (one-third of the national output). Bananas, sugarcane, tobacco, corn, wheat, and beans are also cultivated. Gold is mined here. It is also the site of food, textile, leather-footwear, pulp-and-paper, chemical, glass, cement, and machine-building industries. [11–686–2]

CALDERAS, large oval-shaped or round depressions of volcanic origin, with steep sides that are frequently stepped. Calderas are up to 10–20 km across and several hundred meters deep. A distinction is made between explosion calderas, which are formed during powerful explosions of gases escaping from volcanic vents, and collapse calderas, which occur when the roof of an underground volcanic focus sinks along circular fractures because material has been discharged from the focus during volcanic eruptions. Collapse calderas are more common and larger than explosion calderas. [11–686–3]

CALDERÓN DE LA BARCA, PEDRO (fully, Pedro Calderón de la Barca Henao de la Barreda y Riaño). Born Jan. 17, 1600, in Madrid; died there May 25, 1681. Spanish playwright. Member of an old gentry family.

Calderón studied civil and canon law at the universities of Alcalá and Salamanca. His first literary efforts date to the period 1619–23; after 1625 he devoted himself fully to literature. Ordained in 1651, Calderón was a favorite at the court of Philip IV. During his early period (approximately until the mid-1620's), influenced by Lope de Vega Carpio, Calderón wrote such "comedies of the cloak and sword" as *Love, Honor, and Power* (1623, published 1637) and *The Play of Love and Chance* (1625, published 1636) and the nationalistic patriotic drama *The Siege of Breda* (1625, published 1636).

Calderón's plays until the mid-1630's attempted broad generalizations, posed philosophical and ethical problems, and simultaneously developed several themes in one play—for example, *The Constant Prince* (1628–29, published 1636), the moral and philosophical drama *Life Is a Dream* (1631–32, published 1636), and *Under His Own Guard* (1636, published 1650). His "dramas of honor" (*Doctor of His Own Honor,* 1635, published 1637), were more deeply analytical, disclosing some important character trait of the hero. *The Mayor of Zalamea* (1640–45, published 1651) shows honor to be a moral prerogative that is not exclusively a characteristic of the gentry and provides a vivid picture of the lawlessness then prevalent in Spain. Social motifs also characterized his other plays.

In his late period Calderón wrote plays with music, singing, and ballets for court festivals. He also wrote such religious dramas as *The Devotion of the Cross* (1630–32, published 1636) and *The Purgatory of St. Patricio* (1634, published 1636) and *autos,* which are philosophical plays on mythological subjects with a theological interpretation, on themes from the Old Testament, and on legendary and historical subjects, inspired by sermons from the Gospels.

Most of Calderón's plays are "high comedy": their heroes are drawn solely from the aristocracy and strictly observe the code of gentry honor; the plays have moral underpinnings, complex versification, and refined language. Although he inherited the traditions of Spanish Renaissance literature, Calderón expressed disillusionment with the humanism of the Renaissance. Calderón saw the source of evil and cruelty in the very nature of man; the sole means of reconciliation with life was Christianity, which demands that pride be subdued. His work juxtaposed Renaissance and baroque motifs.

In Russia, Calderón's plays were known as early as the beginning of the 18th century and were first staged in the second half of the 19th century. The most interesting productions were *The Devotion of the Cross* (1910) and *The Constant Prince* (1915) directed by Vs. Meyerhold and *Life Is a Dream* (1914) directed by A. Ia. Tairov. Calderón's comedies have been produced by many Soviet theaters.

WORKS
Obras completas, vols. 1–3. Madrid, 1959.
In Russian translation:
Soch., fascicles 1–3. Translated with an introduction by K. D. Bal'mont. Moscow, 1900–12.
P'esy, vols. 1–2. Foreword by N. B. Tomashevskii. Moscow, 1961.

REFERENCES
Mering, F. "Sud'ia iz Zalamei." In his book *Literaturno-kriticheskie raboty,* vol. 1. Moscow-Leningrad, 1934.
Istoriia zapadnoevropeiskogo teatra, vol. 1. Moscow, 1956.
Balashov, N. I. "Slavianskaia tematika u Kal'derona i problema Renessans-Barokko v ispanskoi literature." *Izv. AN SSSR: Seriia literatury i iazyka,* 1967, vol. 26, issue 3.
Balashov, N. I. "Religiozno-filosofskaia drama Kal'derona i ideinye osnovy barokko v Ispanii." In the collection *XVII vek v mirovom literaturnom razvitii.* Moscow, 1969.
Frutos Cortés, E. *Calderón.* Barcelona, 1949.
Shergold, N. D., and J. E. Varey. *Los autos sacramentales en Madrid en la época de Calderón, 1637–1681: Estudio y documentos.* Madrid [1961].
Valbuena Briones, A. *Perspectiva crítica de los dramas de Calderón.* Madrid [1965].
Karczewska-Markiewicz, Z. *Calderón de la Barca.* Warsaw, 1970.
N. B. TOMASHEVSKII [11–686–4]

CALEAN, a pipe that was widely used in Turkey, Persia, India, China, Afghanistan, and Middle Asia (the *chilim*); at present it is going out of use.

The calean consists of a vessel filled with water, a pipe with tobacco secured in its neck (the lower end of the tube is submerged), and a leather hose or wooden tube placed in the vessel above the level of the water (the smoker draws the smoke, which has been filtered through the water, through the hose or tube). Caleans are made from the fruit of the pumpkin or coconut or from metal; expensive caleans are decorated with silver and ivory. [11–706–3]

CALEDONIAN CANAL, a waterway in Scotland, following the depression of the Great Glen of Scotland from Loch Linnhe to Moray Firth (at the city of Inverness). The Caledonian Canal links Loch Lochy and Loch Ness. It is 88 km long, of which 32 km is an artificial canal. There are 29 locks. The canal was built in the early 19th century; it now has limited importance as a transportation route. [11–580–1]

CALEDONIAN FOLDING, all the tectonic processes—folding, mountain building, and granitization—of the end of the early Paleozoic and beginning of the middle Paleozoic. These processes marked the end of the development of the geosynclinal systems that had existed since the end of the Proterozoic and beginning of the Paleozoic. The term was introduced by the French geologist M. Bertrand in 1887.

Regions of Caledonian folding in Europe include the Caledonides of Ireland, Scotland, Wales, northern England, the northwestern part of the Scandinavian Peninsula, and the islands of Spitsbergen and in Asia, the Caledonides of central Kazakhstan (the western part), Zapadnyi Saian, Gornyi Altai, Mongolian Altai, and southeastern China. Also included among the Caledonides are the folded structures of Tasmania and the Great Dividing Range of eastern Australia, northern and eastern Greenland, Newfoundland, and the northern Appalachians. In addition sections of Caledonian folding have been identified in the Urals, in the northeastern part of the Verkhoiano-Chukotka folded region, in eastern Alaska, in the central and northern Andes, and in certain other younger folded structures.

The earliest phases of Caledonian folding date back to the middle and end of the Cambrian (Salair, or Sardinian); the primary phases encompass the end of the Ordovician, the beginning of the Silurian (Taconian), the end of the Silurian, and the beginning of the Devonian (late Caledonian); and the concluding phases cover the middle of the Devonian (Acadia, or Svalbard). Formations from the period of geosynclinal subsidence are clay slate, graywacke, or sometimes flysch and carbonate, spilite-keratophyre, or diabase. There are intrusions of ultrabasic rocks in the interior zones of many Caledonian geosynclines. In the Silurian, and especially in the early and middle Devonian, thick reddish continental beds of Molasse formation (the ancient red sandstone of the British Isles) developed extensively in intermontane troughs. Incomplete development and the absence of foredeeps are considered to be characteristic of Caledonides. The Caledonides of Scotland, Scandinavia, eastern Greenland, and Newfoundland, where large tectonic sheets (overthrust blocks) are known, are the most complex in structure.

The young platforms that formed at the site of the Caledonides were distinguished by great mobility. After the cessation of vertical movements and leveling of the relief these platforms were tectonically activated in the late Paleozoic in connection with the Hercynian tectogenesis in adjacent geosynclines. New activity, leading to the restoration of mountain relief in most of the areas of Caledonian folding, occurred in Neocene and Anthropogenic times. Caledonian mountain building caused tectonic activity in certain areas of the Baikal folding, for example, on the southern margin of the Siberian platform.

REFERENCES
Tektonika Evropy: Ob'iasnitel'naia zapiska k Mezhdunarodnoi tektonicheskoi karte Evropy. Moscow, 1964.
Tektonika Evrazii. Moscow, 1966.
Bogdanov, N. A. *Paleozoi vostoka Avstralii i Melanezii.* Moscow, 1967.
Pronin, A. A. *Kaledonskii tsikl tektonicheskoi istorii Zemli.* Leningrad, 1969.
The British Caledonides. Edinburgh-London, 1963.
Rodgers, J. *Tectonics of the Appalachians.* New York, 1970.
V. E. KHAIN [11–579–1]

CALENDAR (from the Latin *calendarium,* meaning account book; such books showed the first day of each month, the *calendae,* on which debtors in ancient Rome paid interest), the system of reckoning prolonged intervals of time based on the periodic phenomena of nature related to the movements of celestial bodies. The development of the calendar reflects the conditions of the economic way of life of various peoples.

Astronomical foundations. The calendar reflects astronomical phenomena: the alternation of day and night, the change of lunar phases, and the alternation of seasons. The units of measurement for long intervals of time are established on the basis of these phenomena: the mean solar day (24 hours), the synodic month (29 days, 12 hours, 44 minutes, and 3 seconds of mean solar time), and the tropical year (365 days, 5 hours, 48 minutes, and 46 seconds of mean solar time). It is not possible to select an integral number of tropical years that would contain an integral number of synodic months and an integral number of mean solar days; these three magnitudes are incommensurable. This explains the difficulty in constructing calendars and the appearance, over several millennia, of numerous calendar systems that have attempted to overcome these difficulties. Attempts to coordinate the day, month, and year have led different peoples at different times to create three types of calendars: lunar calendars, based on the movements of the moon and constructed for the purpose of coordinating the course of the day and the lunar month; lunisolar calendars, which represent attempts to coordinate all three units of time; and solar calendars, in which the day and the year are approximately coordinated.

Calendar eras. In all calendar systems the sequential counting of years is begun from some historical or legendary event, the starting point of the era. Most countries of the world use the Christian chronology, which was first proposed in the sixth century by the Roman monk Dionysius Exiguus and in which the "birth of Christ" serves as the starting point. In the USSR this starting point is abbreviated "ne," which means "our era," or "new era."

Lunar calendars. In the lunar calendar the year is divided into 12 months, each of which alternately has 30 or 29 days. The lunar year has a total of 354 days. In order for the first day of each year to fall on a new moon (this is one of the requirements of the lunar calendar), additional days are added to the last month in certain years; the years having 355 days are leap years. Because the lunar calendar is shorter than the solar calendar by about 11 days, each year the beginning of the lunar year shifts to an earlier time and may fall in any month of the solar year. Thus, in 1973 the beginnning of the lunar year falls on February 4, while in 1974 it falls on January 25; in 1975, on January 14; in 1976, on January 3 and December 23; in 1977, on December 12; in 1978, on December 2; in 1979, on November 21; in 1980, on November 9; and so on. The seven-day week coincides by days with the days of the week in the solar calendar. The lunar calendar has become common in the Islamic countries, where it is called the Hegira (or hijra). The starting point of the chronology in this calendar is July 16, A.D. 622. At the present time lunar calendars are used in Algeria, Iraq, Kuwait, Lebanon, Libya, Mauritania, Morocco, Nigeria, Saudi Arabia, Syria, Somalia, Sudan, Tunisia, and a number of other countries.

Lunisolar calendars. Lunisolar calendars are the most complex because they coordinate the movement of the sun with the alternation of lunar phases. Lunisolar calendars are based on the ratio of 19 solar years to 235 lunar months (with an error of less than 1.5 hours). In the course of each 19 years, 12 years have 12 lunar months (of 29–30 days) and seven years have 13 lunar months. Additional months are added in the third, sixth, eighth, 11th, 14th, 17th, and 19th years of the 19-year cycle. In antiquity lunisolar calendar systems were used in Babylonia, China, Judea, Greece, Rome, and other countries. In the 20th century a lunisolar calendar is the official calendar in Israel, where the beginning of the year falls on one of the days between September 5 and October 5. In a number of Far Eastern countries (Vietnam, China, Korea, Mongolia, Japan), an unofficial 60-year cyclical calendar is used in everyday life in which the start of the year falls on one of the days between January 20 and February 20.

Solar calendars. One of the first solar calendars, the Egyptian calendar, was created in the fourth millennium B.C. The calendar consisted of 365 days and was divided into 12 months of 30 days each; five holidays not included in the months were added at the end of the year. Among the solar calendars are the Julian, the Gregorian, the French Republican calendar, the unified national calendar of India, and the proposed World calendar. At the present time the international calendar is the Gregorian calendar.

JULIAN CALENDAR. The modern calendar traces its origins to the ancient Roman solar calendar, which was introduced on Jan. 1, 45 B.C., as a result of a reform carried out in 46 B.C. by Julius Caesar (from whom the name is taken). January 1 also became the beginning of the new year (before this the new year in the Roman calendar had begun on March 1). The average length of the year in the Julian calendar was set equal to 365 1/4 days, which corresponded to the length of the tropical year known at that time. For convenience, three consecutive years numbered 365 days each and the fourth, the leap year, numbered 366. The year was divided into 12 months, for which the ancient names were preserved: Januarius, Februarius, Martius, Aprilis, Maius, Junius, Quintilis, Sextilis, September, October, November, and December. The number of days in the months was organized so that all odd-numbered months had 31 days and all even-

numbered months, 30. Only February in the common year had 29 days. In 44 B.C. the month of Quintilis (the fifth month) was renamed Julius in honor of Julius Caesar, and in 8 B.C. the month of Sextilis (the sixth month) was renamed Augustus in honor of the Roman emperor Augustus. In addition, the alternation of long and short months was changed: one day was added to August at the expense of February and at the same time one day was shifted from September to October and one day from November to December. The correct use of the Julian calendar began in A.D. 7; from this time, all years of the Julian calendar whose ordinal number is divisible by 4 are leap years. In A.D. 325, at the Council of Nicaea, the Julian calendar was adopted by the Christian Church.

GREGORIAN CALENDAR. Because the length of the Julian year was 11 minutes and 14 seconds greater than the tropical year, an error of one day accumulated each 128 years. Therefore, the vernal equinox, which had fallen on March 21 in A.D. 325 fell on March 11 at the end of the 16th century. The error was corrected in 1582 when a reform of the Julian calendar was proclaimed by a bull of Pope Gregory XIII. The correction lay in moving the sequence of ten days ahead, and it was ordered that the day after Thursday October 4 be considered Friday, but October 15, not October 5. In this way the vernal equinox was again returned to March 21. In order to prevent new errors, it was decided to discard three days every 400 years. In this way, instead of the 100 leap-year days each 400 years in the Julian calendar, the new calendar had only 97. Excluded from the group of leap years were the century years (years with two zeros on the end) whose number was not divisible by 4 without a remainder, specifically, 1700, 1800, and 1900. The corrected calendar was called the Gregorian calendar, or the New Style (distinguished from the Julian, which was called the Old Style). The average length of the year in this calendar is just 26 seconds more than the length of the tropical year, which results in an error of only one day in 3,280 years. The difference between the Old and New styles totals 11 days in the 18th century, 12 days in the 19th century, and 13 days in the 20th century.

The Gregorian calendar was introduced in different countries at different times. In the 1580's it was introduced in Italy, Spain, Portugal, Poland, France, Luxembourg, the southern Netherlands, Bavaria, Austria, the Catholic cantons of Switzerland, and Hungary. In other countries it began to be used in the early 17th century (Prussia), at the end of the 17th century (the Protestant part of Germany, Norway, and Denmark), in the 18th century (northern Netherlands, Great Britain, Sweden, and Finland), in the 19th century (Japan), and in the 20th century (China, Bulgaria, Rumania, Greece, Turkey, and Egypt). In Russia the Gregorian calendar was introduced after the Great October Socialist Revolution by a decree of the Council of People's Commissars of the RSFSR on Jan. 24, 1918 (published on Jan. 25 and 26, 1918). According to this decree a correction of 13 days was introduced and the day after Jan. 31, 1918, was considered to be February 14, not February 1. The days of the week of both calendars coincide and therefore the day of the week is preserved during the transfer from one to the other. Thus, Apr. 10, 1870, Old Style, and Apr. 22, 1870, New Style, both fall on Friday. By the mid-20th century the Gregorian calendar was used by virtually all countries of the world.

ANCIENT RUSSIAN CALENDAR. The ancient Slavs divided the year into 12 months whose names were closely related to observed natural phenomena. At the same time, depending on local climate, the same months received different names in different regions. The most firmly established names were *sechen* (January), wood cutting time; *liutyi* (February), time of bitter cold weather; *berezozol* (March), which has several interpretations: the beginning of birch blooming, tapping of birch trees, or burning birch wood for charcoal; *tsveten'* (April), time when orchards bloom; *traven'* (May), time when grass becomes green; *cherven'* (June), time when cherries ripen; *lipets* (July), time when linden trees bloom; *serpen'* (August), from the Russian word for sickle, harvest time; *veresen'* (September), time when heather blooms; *listopad* (October), time when leaves fall from trees; *gruden'* (November), from the Russian word *gruda* meaning a frozen wheel rut in a road; and *studen'* (December), which means chilly or cold. Many ancient Slavic names of months later passed into numerous Slavic languages and have been preserved to a significant degree in certain modern languages (in particular, Ukrainian, Byelorussian, and Polish).

In the tenth century, with the adoption of Christianity, ancient Rus' also adopted the system of chronology that had been used by the Romans: the Julian calendar, the Roman names of months, and the seven-day week. In this chronology the years were counted from the "creation of the world," which supposedly occurred in 5,508 B.C. The year began on March 1 when agricultural work began. This chronology continued to be used until the end of the 15th century, when the beginning of the year was moved to September 1. A ukase by Peter I (dated Dec. 15, 1699) introduced the Christian system of chronology in Russia in 1700 and moved the beginning of the year to January 1. The ukase ordered that the day after Dec. 31, 7208, from the "creation of the world," be considered Jan. 1, 1700, from the "birth of Christ."

FRENCH REPUBLICAN CALENDAR. The French Republican calendar was introduced by a decree of the National Convention dated Oct. 5, 1793. Sept. 22, 1792, the day the king was overthrown and the Republic was proclaimed, which in this year coincided with the autumnal equinox, was adopted as the beginning of the chronology. The year was divided into 12 months of 30 days each. The names of the months reflected phenomena of nature and the meteorological and agricultural conditions of the climatic zone of France. To reconcile the length of the calendar and tropical years, five more days were added at the end of each year and six days in leap years. Instead of the seven-day week, the month was divided into three ten-day periods. On Jan. 1, 1806, the Republican calendar was replaced by the Gregorian calendar.

WORLD CALENDAR. The Gregorian calendar has a number of shortcomings: the months are of unequal length (28, 29, 30, and 31 days), the quarter years are unequal (90, 91, or 92 days), the half-years are unequal (181, 182, or 184 days), and there is no regular correspondence between dates and days of the week. Therefore, as far back as the 19th century the question of reforming the calendar began to be discussed, that is, introducing a calendar that would not have the aforementioned shortcomings of the current calendar. Many plans for a new calendar were worked out in different countries. For example, one of them suggested that the calendar year contain 364 days (four quarter years of 91 days each and 13 full weeks in a quarter year), with each date always falling on the same day of the week. To coordinate it with the tropical year, one extra day must be added at the end of each year (World Day or Peace Day) and once every four years a second extra day must be added after June 30 (Leap-year Day).

However, the developed political and economic relations existing between the countries of the world make it possible to carry out calendar reform on a multinational scale only. The Economic and Social Council of the United Nations is studying the problem of calendar reform.

REFERENCES
Idel'son, N. I. *Istoriia kalendaria*. Leningrad, 1925.
Idel'son, N. I. "Kalendar'." In *Bol'shaia Sovetskaia Entsiklopediia*, 2nd ed., vol 19. Moscow, 1953.
Siuziumov, M. Ia. "Kalendar'." In *Sovetskaia istoricheskaia entsiklopediia*, vol. 6, Moscow, 1965.
Seleshnikov, S. I. *Istoriia kalendaria i khronologii*. Moscow, 1970. (With extensive bibliography.)
Tsybul'skii, V. V. *Sovremennye kalendari stran Blizhnego i Srednego Vostoka*. Moscow, 1964.
Ginzel, F. K. *Handbuch der mathematischen und technischen Chronologie*, vols. 1–3. Leipzig, 1906–14.   S. I. SELESHNIKOV [11–582–3]

CALENDAR, a printed table or booklet giving months and dates, days of the week, holidays, and often astronomical information.

Among the various kinds of calendars are tabular calendars, consisting of a table listing the days of the year; turnover calendars, whose sheets are turned on a special holder; tear-off calendars; table calendars, books giving detailed descriptions of anniversaries, important dates, and other information; business calendars for writing memorandums; and calendars with colored

illustrations. The last category includes calendars bound in book or album form and wall calendars, which have an advertising or gift-presentation format and consist of a series of monthly tables with reproductions, decorative drawings, or color photographs.

In ancient Rome the term "calendar" was first used to designate books in which creditors recorded the interest that was paid monthly on the calends (hence the name). Later the word came to be applied to the books listing religious holidays, the birthdays of emperors, and the days of Senate meetings. The oldest Roman calendar that has come down to us dates from A.D. 354.

There were many lists and compilations indicating holidays and giving legends of Christian saints, which were known as calendars, books of saints' days, martyrologies, or Menaias. The Orthodox Slavs called their calendars *mesiatseslovy* (books of months). In the Middle Ages the publication of calendars was controlled by the church. Calendars with a secular content began to appear in the 14th century. In Kievan Rus' the first attempt to specify what should or should not be done on certain days was undertaken in the *Izbornik* (collection) of Sviatoslav (1076). Western calendars began to appear in Russia in the 16th century, and Russian calendars modeled on them began to be produced, such as the *Godovoi razpis', ili mesiachilo* (Yearly Register, or Months) for 1670.

In Russia the regular publication of printed wall calendars began under Peter I. The most complete extant calendar is Bruce's calendar, compiled by the Moscow publisher V. A. Kipriianov. The calendar consisted of six tables and contained, in addition to useful astronomical information, a "prognostic" predicting the weather, harvests, wars, and illnesses according to the position of heavenly bodies. Characteristically, the "prognostic" was preceded by the words "war and peace cannot be foretold by stargazing alone."

After 1727 the St. Petersburg Academy of Sciences had the sole right to publish calendars. After 1770 calendars were called *mesiatseslovy*. They were printed in small editions (17,000–18,000 copies) and sold at extremely high prices. In the mid-19th century the *mesiatseslovy* contained much historical, astronomical, geographical, and meteorological information, as well as data on rail and ship transport. Private individuals began to publish calendars in 1865. One of the first private publishers of Russian calendars was the Czech A. A. Hatcuk.

In the early 20th century, the publisher I. D. Sytin initiated the publication of cheap, colorful calendars for the mass market. His widely distributed table calendars, the All-Purpose Calendar and the Universal Russian Calendar, contained much useful information. The printings of Sytin's table calendars reached the unprecedented figure of 6 million copies. Later, with the help of L. N. Tolstoy, Sytin arranged for the publication of a tear-off calendar with a printing of 8 million.

At the same time other publishing houses were producing expensive calendars, such as G. Goppe's The King of Bells: An Illustrated Calendar-Almanac and The Universal Calendar and A. S. Suvorin's Russian Calendar. Special calendars were published for different professions (military men, jurists, beekeepers); there were calendars for children, calendars for women, and household-management calendars. From 1899 to 1915, P. N. Arian published the First Women's Calendar. The Bolshevik publishing house Zerno issued a table calendar entitled the Calendar for Everyone for 1908, for which V. I. Lenin wrote his article "The International Socialist Congress in Stuttgart" in 1907.

The first calendar published after the October Revolution and the change (February 1918) from the Julian to the Gregorian calendar was the Soviet Calendar, a table calendar for 1919, which was published by the Sytin printing plant for the All-Russian Central Executive Committee of the RSFSR. Later, tear-off and turnover calendars were issued, as well as such table calendars as the Universal Table Calendar, the Worker's Table Calendar, the Peasant's Calendar, and Red Village.

The most widely used and popular calendars in the USSR are issued by Politizdat. These include general tear-off calendars with editions of about 16 million copies, the Calendar for Women (14 million copies), the Calendar for Schoolchildren (2.5 million copies), the Table Calendar, and the illustrated calendars Motherland, In the World of Beauty, Women's Calendar, Calendar for Youth, and Sport. Politizdat also issued the special illustrated Lenin Calendar commemorating the 100th anniversary of Lenin's birth, and the Karl Marx Calendar, in honor of the 150th anniversary of Marx' birth. In 1972, Politizdat printed a total of 40 million calendars. Other central publishing houses of the USSR issue the Soldier's Calendar, the Rural Calendar, the Theater Calendar, the Cinema Calendar, In the World of Music, One Hundred Memorable Dates, Little Star (for October children's groups), the Philatelist's Calendar, and the Calendar of Important and Memorable Dates. Moreover, several Union and autonomous republics publish tear-off and table calendars in the languages of the peoples of the USSR.

In foreign countries illustrated wall calendars in tabular form without texts are widely used. The reverse sides of the sheets of tear-off calendars usually bear messages, chiefly on religious and ethical themes.

A. V. TOLMACHEV [11–586–1]

CALENDAR DISTURBANCES (1584–89), a movement of the burgher opposition of Riga against the patrician elite of the magistracy and against the threat of complete subordination of the city to the Rzecz Pospolita (the Commonwealth of Poland and Lithuania).

The Calendar Disturbances were sparked by the order of the Polish king Stephen Báthory introducing the new (Gregorian) calendar in Riga and restoring the Jesuits to their former position. Since these proposals were initiated by Pope Gregory XIII, they were interpreted by the Protestants of Riga as an encroachment on the rights of the city's burghers and as interference in matters of faith. Merchants of the Great Guild and guild artisans of the Lesser Guild took part in the rebellion, which lasted from the end of 1584 to the summer of 1589. They demanded a restriction on the rights of the magistrate and the participation of both guilds in the administration of and control over the city treasury. They were supported by the plebeians, who were mostly Latvians. The movement was suppressed with the help of Polish-Lithuanian troops.

REFERENCE
Istoriia Latviiskoi SSR, vol. 1. Riga, 1951. Pages 186–90.

[11–581–2]

CALENDAR POETRY, works of oral folk poetry included in holiday rituals. Calendar rites, games, and songs are associated with natural phenomena, the sun's yearly cycle, and agricultural labor. Belief in the magical power of words, gestures, and actions to ensure a good harvest lay at the heart of these rituals. Christian festivals were later made to coincide with these essentially pagan calendar ceremonies and the poetry associated with them.

Russian calendar poetry combined magical incantations, Christian motifs, and everyday experiences. The winter and spring ceremonial cycles were poetically the richest. During the winter holidays people sang *koliadki* and *ovseni* (carols) and *podbliudnye pesni* (songs associated with fortune-telling games in the days after Christmas). The coming of spring was marked by Shrovetide folk songs and games, and summer rituals centered on the holiday of Ivan Kupala. Autumn ritual songs and games coincided with the gathering of the harvest and were characterized by vivid imagery and optimism. As education became widespread and as man acquired greater power over nature, calendar rituals gradually disappeared from the people's everyday life. Although much of calendar poetry lost its direct link with ritual, it was preserved in peasant songs in the form of songs accompanying games and lyric songs.

REFERENCES
Anichkov, E.V. *Vesenniaia obriadovaia pesnia na Zapade i u slavian,* parts 1–2. St. Petersburg, 1903–05.
Chicherov, V. I. *Zimnii period russkogo zemledel'cheskogo kalendaria XVI–XIX vv.* Moscow, 1957.
Propp, V. Ia. *Russkie agrarnye prazdniki.* (*Opyt istoriko-etnograficheskogo issledovaniia.*) Leningrad, 1963.

[11–581–1]

CALENDER, a press with two to 20 horizontal rollers between which material (fabric, paper, or rubber) in the form of rolls or sheets is passed to increase its density or smoothness or to apply an embossed pattern or design. Machine calenders, supercalen-

ders, embossing calenders, and gauging calenders are used in the paper industry. The rollers of calenders (except embossing calenders) have a smooth, polished surface and are usually made of metal. The required pressure between the rollers is produced by the weight of the rollers themselves; in some instances it may be supplemented by pneumatic or hydraulic clamping devices. Calenders are also used in the textile and chemical industries.

[11–564–3]

CALENDERING, the processing of materials (fabric, paper, or rubber) on a calender. In the production of paper, calendering is done on machine calenders installed at the end of the drying section of a paper machine or on separate supercalenders. Paper processed on a supercalender is called calendered or glossy paper; paper that has been passed through a machine calender and has a lower gloss is called machine-finished paper. The smoothness produced by calendering depends on the type of rollers (it is greater with the combined use of cast-iron and paper rollers), their temperature (smoothness increases under heating), the paper composition and moisture content (paper with greater kaolin content calenders better), and the pressure between the calender rollers. In the production of rubber, calendering is used for manufacturing sheet rubber in various thicknesses, for plasticizing and heating rubber stock, and for rubberizing fabric. In textile manufacturing, calendering is used for packing cotton, linen, and jute fabrics, adding luster to them, and applying embossed patterns.

[11–565–1]

CALENDS, the name of the first day of the month in the ancient Roman calendar. *Calends,* like *nones* and *ides,* were used to count the days of the month, which were reckoned backward from these days, for example, "the sixth day before the *calends* of March" or "the third day before the *nones* of January." The expression *ad Calendas Graecas* denotes a time that will never come, since *calends* were used only in the ancient Roman calendar.

[11–588–1]

CALENDULA, a genus of plants of the family Compositae. They are subshrubs and perennial or annual herbs with ramiform stems and entire leaves. The inflorescences are solitary calathide heads on long flower stalks. The numerous ligulate flowers are yellow, pistillate, and proliferous. The tubular flowers are bisexual but do not bear fruit. The achenes are incurved (annular); the exterior achenes are shaped differently from the middle and interior ones. There are more than 20 species of *Calendula,* distributed primarily from the Mediterranean region to Iran. Species are also found in Central Europe; there are four species in the USSR. They grow along seacoasts, in shrub thickets, and on cliffs. Some species, such as the marigold (*Calendula arvensis*), grow as weeds. Many varieties of the pot marigold (*C. officinalis*) have been cultivated for a long time. This species has mainly double yellow and orange flowers of all shades. It is also a medicinal plant, providing a gargle for inflamed mouth infections and an ointment for boils, wounds, and ulcers. The oily extract from the ligulate flowers is used as a food dye. In some countries, dried calathide heads are used as a seasoning for soups and sauces.

O. M. POLETIKO [11–587–1]

CALGARY, a city in southern Canada in Alberta Province, in the foothills of the Rocky Mountains. Population, 400,000 (1971). Calgary is a rail and highway junction and an important industrial, trade (grain, cattle), and transportation center. An important factor in Calgary's growth has been the development of the oil industry. Oil refineries and petrochemical, food (primarily meat-packing), machine-building, and chemical industries are there, as is a university.

[11–573–4]

CALI, a city in western Colombia. Cali is located in the foothills of the Cordillera Oriental, at an altitude of 1,000 m in the Cauca River valley; it is the administrative center of the Valle Del Cauca Department. Population, 898,000 (1971). Cali is linked with Bogotá by railroad and highway. It is the industrial and major cultural center of the Cauca valley. Cloth (cotton and artificial silk), footwear, rubber-engineering components, cardboard and paper, pharmaceuticals, paints, soap, tobacco and tobacco products, and bicycles are manufactured in Cali. It has two universities. The city was founded in 1536. Bituminous coal is mined near Cali. [11–589–3]

CALIBER, the diameter of the bore of a firearm and also the diameter of a shell (bullet); one of the basic measures of the power of a firearm. Caliber is determined by measuring the inside barrel diameter for a smoothbore gun, the distance between opposite ribs for a rifled gun, and the maximum cross section for shells (bullets). Tapered-bore guns have inlet and outlet calibers.

A scale with the diameters of stone and cast-iron (shot) balls was first developed in Nuremberg in 1540. In Russia, Peter I established his own unit of measurement—the artillery pound—a cast-iron ball with a diameter of 2 inches weighing 115 *zolotniks* (approximately 480 grams). On the basis of this artillery pound a scale was created for smoothbore artillery, in which a 3-pound ball corresponded to a caliber of 2.8 inches (70 mm) and a 12-pound ball corresponded to a caliber of 4.7 inches (120 mm). Caliber was first designated in linear measures (inches and lines) in Russia in 1877, including a 3-inch cannon, 6-inch cannon, and 3-line rifle.

The calibers of all types of modern weapons are usually designated in millimeters. The length of a gun barrel in artillery is more often expressed in caliber—the length of the gun barrel is equal to as many calibers as the number of times the bore diameter goes into the barrel length. The caliber of smoothbore hunting rifles is expressed by the quantity of round pellets, equal in mass and diameter, which are cast from 400 grams of pure lead and go into the gun bore without play. For example, if 12, 16, 20, or more pellets are cast, then the caliber of these guns will be expressed by the gauges 12, 16, 20, and so forth, respectively. [11–591–2]

CALIBRATION, verification of a measure or set of measures by taking a group of measurements.

Calibration consists in determining the error or correction of a group of gauges (such as a set of weights) or of a single multivalent gauge (such as a linear scale) for various combinations of the gauge or for various ranges of the scale. A comparison is made of the measures or of the sections of the scale in which one of the measures or scale values is taken as the basis of comparison.

REFERENCES
Malikov, M. F. *Osnovy metrologii,* part 1. Moscow, 1949.
Amatuni, A. N. "Kalibrovka podrazdelenii shtrikhovykh mer." In *Entsiklopediia izmerenii, kontrolia i avtomatiki (EIKA),* issue 6. Moscow-Leningrad, 1966. Page 33. [11–593–1]

CALIBRATOR, in electrical and radio engineering, a precision device for tuning and calibration of measuring instruments (determination of errors or correction of scale values). Its operation is based on comparison to a standard of the value being measured.

Calibration generators operating on several strictly defined frequencies from 100 hertz (Hz) to 100 megahertz (MHz) are usually used for frequency calibration of frequency meters, standard-signal generators, radio reception and transmission equipment, and other instruments with a continuously variable tuning range. Electrical oscillations are supplied by a piezoelectrically stabilized generator with a relative frequency error of up to $\pm 1 \times 10^{-5}$. In addition to the fundamental frequencies, harmonics of the fundamental frequencies in the range of 20–40 gigahertz (GHz) are also used. In a continuous frequency range heterodyne frequency meters are also used for this purpose. A calibrating generator usually consists of a reference crystal oscillator, a frequency converter, a mixer-detector, and an audiofrequency amplifier, which make possible calibration without any additional apparatus. The principle of operation of a calibrator is based on a comparison of the frequency being measured with the fundamental frequency (or one of its harmonics) of a crystal oscillator and separation of the difference frequency by the zero-beat method in a mixer-detector.

Frequency standards are calibrated by means of receiver comparators according to the signals of radio stations transmitting on superlong wavelengths. Under certain conditions of propagation of long waves ($\lambda = 10,000$ m), phase stability over a 24-hour period makes possible highly precise comparison of the frequency of the signals received to standard frequencies. In 1970 there were seven radio stations that regularly transmitted signals of great frequency precision. Their signals could be received throughout the world. Calibrators also exist for checking the voltage indicated by electron-tube voltmeters; they are called calibration voltage sources (for direct and alternating current).

Calibrators are also used for precision work in metrology, for measuring sets of standards, and for calibrating instrument scales. Calibration should not be confused with graduation, which is a metrological operation that consists in the division of an instrument scale into units established for it.

REFERENCES
Malikov, M. F. *Osnovy metrologii,* part 1. Moscow, 1949.
Izmereniia v elektrotekhnike: Spravochnik, vol. 1. Compiled by B.A. Dobrokhotov. Moscow-Leningrad, 1965.
Shkurin, G. P. *Spravochnik po elektroizmeritel'nym i radioizmeritel'nym priboram,* 3rd ed., vols. 1–2. Moscow, 1960.
V. V. BOGOMAZOV [11–592–1]

CALIFORNIA, a state on the Pacific coast of the USA, on the border with Mexico. Area, 411,000 sq km; population, 19.95 million (1970). The capital of the state is Sacramento; Los Angeles, San Francisco, and San Diego are the largest cities. In 1970, 90.9 percent of the population was urban.

The state is mountainous: the Coast Ranges extend longitudinally in the west, with elevations above 2,500 m (Mt. Pinos), and the mountains of the Sierra Nevada, including Mt. Whitney (4,418 m), are in the east. In the north and south these mountain ranges are connected by rather low mountains that enclose the Central Valley, which is watered by the Sacramento and San Joaquin rivers. The Mojave, a sand desert, and deep tectonic depressions, such as Death Valley and the Salton Sea, are located in the extreme east and southeast. California is subject to earthquakes. The climate on the coast is Mediterranean, with a warm summer and a damp winter. The vegetation consists of mountain pine forests and sclerophyllous evergreen shrubbery. The climate on the interior slopes of the mountains and in the Central Valley is hot and dry. Most of the valley is under cultivation, and the southern districts and the foothills are covered with annual grasses and bushes. Located in California are the Yosemite, Lassen Volcanic, and Sequoia and Kings Canyon national parks.

California is the most rapidly developing state of the USA, the first in number of incoming settlers, and one of the most important economically. The settlement of the state in the middle of the 19th century was linked with the "gold rush." California's population grew from 1.5 million in 1900 to 10.6 million in 1950 and to 19.7 million in 1967, when it became the most populous state in the USA. The population grew by 48 percent from 1950 to 1960 and by 27 percent from 1960 to 1970. More than 90 percent of the population is concentrated in the coastal plains of southern and central California and in the Central Valley. California is first among the states of the USA in commercial agriculture and in the number of automobiles and is second in employment in manufacturing (1.6 million in 1970).

Approximately 50 million tons of oil and much natural gas are extracted annually, mainly in the Los Angeles area. Gold, mercury, potassium salts, and iron ore are also mined. The output of electric power plants in 1969 was 22 million kilowatts. California is a highly important center of military production. A leading position is occupied by the aviation, space and rocket, and radio-electronic industries, which fill mainly defense orders and which are located in Los Angeles, San Diego, San Francisco, and San Jose. The oil-refining and chemical industries, shipbuilding, automobile assembly production, and other branches of machine building are also well developed. Ferrous metallurgy is located in Fontana, which is near Los Angeles, and in areas near San Francisco. California is first among the states in food processing, especially canning; this industry is based on local agricultural produce. The film industry is centered in southern California, in Hollywood and other suburbs of Los Angeles.

The agricultural economy is characterized by a combination of intensive agriculture, mainly on irrigated lands, and extensive cattle-raising. Approximately two-thirds of the commodity output is composed of agricultural products: various fruits and vegetables (mainly in the Central Valley), citrus fruits (in the Los Angeles area), and long-fiber cotton (in the Colorado River basin). There were approximately 4 million head of cattle and 1.5 million sheep in 1969. Fishing is also an important branch of the economy. In the north, logging (timber cutting) and the wood-products industry are of considerable importance. Tourism has great economic significance. There are approximately 13,000 km of railway lines (1968) and 10 million automobiles (1969). Sea transport plays an important role. The principal ports are San Francisco and Los Angeles. US military bases are located within California.

Europeans first visited the territory of California in the 16th century. The colonization of California by the Spaniards began in the 18th century and was accompanied by the extermination of the local Indian population. Russian settlers played an important role in the exploration and economic development of California. After the proclamation of the independence of Mexico in 1821, the territory of California became part of that newly independent country. As a result of the war of aggression of the USA against Mexico in 1846–48, California was seized from Mexico and annexed to the USA. The territory became a state in 1850.   [11–634–1]

CALIFORNIA, GULF OF, a gulf of the Pacific Ocean along the western coast of North America. It is separated from the ocean by the peninsula of Lower California and is in effect a semienclosed sea. Length, 1,240 km; maximum width, 220 km; area, 177,000 sq km; average depth, 818 m. Depths increase from the head (34 m) to the mouth (3,292 m, the greatest depth of the gulf). There are many islands, the largest of which are Tiburón and Angel de la Guarda. The climate is subtropical. Surface currents circulate counterclockwise. Winter temperatures vary from 15°C in the northwest to 21°C in the southeast, and in the summer they rise to 28°C. The salinity of the water is 35.1–35.5 parts per thousand in the north (near the mouth of the Colorado River), diminishing to 30 parts per thousand. Tides are irregular and occur twice daily (up to 2.9 m). Fish in the Gulf of California include tuna, flounder, mackerel, and sea bass. Accumulations of *Ciliata infusoria* cause tinting of the water in various shades of red. The principal port is Guaymas (Mexico).   [11–632–1]

CALIFORNIA, UNIVERSITY OF, one of the largest institutions of higher learning in the USA, opened in 1868 as the state educational institution of California; based on the College of California, founded in 1855 in Oakland, near San Francisco.

The University of California (as of the 1971–72 academic year) was made up of nine university campuses, each of which actually represents an independent educational institution, as well as six large scientific research institutions, nine experimental agricultural stations, and a great number of colleges and other divisions. The largest university campuses are at Berkeley, Davis, Los Angeles, and Santa Barbara. The campus at Berkeley, founded in 1872, includes a graduate division and colleges of agriculture, chemistry, engineering, and letters and science, as well as schools of business administration, criminology, forestry and forest preservation, law, librarianship, social relations, optometry, public health, and journalism. It also contains a scientific research center in atomic physics and a library with 3.7 million volumes. There are 28,000 students enrolled at the Berkeley campus.

The campus at Davis, founded in 1905, includes colleges of agriculture, environmental sciences, letters and science, and engineering, as well as schools of law, medicine, and veterinary science. The library contains 730,000 volumes. There are 13,000 students enrolled in the Davis branch.

The University of California at Los Angeles, founded in 1919, includes a graduate division, colleges of letters and science, engineering, and the fine arts, as well as schools of architecture and city planning, business administration, dentistry, education, law, librarianship, and public health. The library contains 2.8 million volumes. The university has approximately 28,000 students.

The Santa Barbara campus, founded in 1891, includes a graduate division, colleges of letters and science and of engineering, a college of creative studies for students showing ability for research in various fields, a school of education, and 12 scientific research institutes and centers, including the Bureau of Educational Research, the Center for the Study of Developing Nations, a computer center, an institute of oceanology, and the Quantum Institute. The library contains 630,000 volumes, and 14,000 students are enrolled.

There are also campuses of the University of California at Irvine (founded in 1965), Riverside (1907), San Diego (1912), San Francisco (1873), and Santa Cruz (1965). In the 1971–72 academic year, more than 100,000 students were receiving instruction at the University of California, from a faculty of over 6,000 instructors, including approximately 3,000 professors. The libraries of the university contained approximately 10 million volumes.   [11–632–4]

CALIFORNIA CURRENT, a cold current in the northeast Pacific Ocean, the eastern periphery of the northern subtropical clockwise circulation of surface waters. It moves from the north to the south along California as the southern branch of the North Pacific Drift. In the south it passes into the North Equatorial Current. Width, 550–650 km; velocity, 1–2 km/hr. The mean water temperature in February varies from 12°C in the north to 25°C in the south; in August the respective figures are 17°C to 26°C. The salinity in the north is 33–34 parts per thousand.   [11–633–1]

CALIFORNIA FINANCIAL GROUPS, a coalition of major West Coast financiers and industrialists in the United States, bringing together several separate monopoly groupings: the Bank of America (the Giannini group), the Western Bank Corporation (Los Angeles), and the San Francisco group. The coalition emerged in the early 20th century and was consolidated in the mid-1950's. The total assets jointly controlled by these groups was more than $70 billion in late 1970.

The most influential group within the coalition is the Bank of America group, whose assets are valued at about $25 billion. The Bank of America heads this group and either directly or indirectly, through the specially created holding company Transamerica Corporation, maintains close ties with the Kaiser industrial conglomerate. The latter consists of four major corporations: Kaiser Steel, Kaiser Aluminum, Kaiser Engineers, and Kaiser Aerospace and Electronics. The strengthening of this group after World War II is connected with the arms race produced by the Cold War, the Korean and Indochina wars, and the increased number of military contracts placed by the government. In the late 1960's the California financial groups accounted for 25 percent of all Pentagon contracts and nearly 50 percent of contracts related to US space research. Through personal alliances and holdings of controlling blocks of shares, the Giannini group is closely related to the largest military-industrial concerns in the United States, which belong to the Western Bank Corporation group: Lockheed Aircraft, McDonnell Douglas, and the Litton Industries industrial conglomerate; it is also associated with a number of air transport companies and oil monopolies. Representatives of this group occupy high posts in the US government.

Western Bank Corporation and the San Francisco group both have assets exceeding $20 billion. These groups do not have a very extensively developed system of credit institutions (controlling only a few commercial banks and insurance companies) and have weak links with Wall Street. The nucleus of the Western Bank Corporation consists of aviation and electronics concerns and oil companies. The San Francisco group consists basically of naval shipbuilding, petroleum refining, paper milling, and the production of power-system equipment, valuable minerals, and agricultural machinery.

REFERENCES

Perlo, V. *Imperiia finansovykh magnatov.* Moscow, 1958. (Translated from English.)
Men'shikov, S. M. *Millionery i menedzhery: Sovremennaia struktura finansovoi oligarkhii v SShA.* Moscow, 1965.

Zorin, Val. *Nekoronovannye koroli Ameriki,* 2nd ed. Moscow, 1967.
Tsagolov, G. N. *Milliardery iz provinstsii.* Moscow, 1968.
Zhukov, E. F. *Strakhovye monopolii v ekonomike SShA.* Moscow, 1971.
    Pages 140–45.   E. F. ZHUKOV   [11–631–2]

CALIFORNIA INDIANS, the aboriginal population of the state of California in the USA: a multiplicity of tribes (including the Karok, Yurok, Hupa, Mono, Pomo, Wintun, Maidu, Yokuts, and Miwok tribes) of various language families (such as the Athapascan, Algonquian, Hokan, Penutian, and Shoshonean groups). The California Indians were distinguished by particular features of their economies, the basis of which was gathering, combined with fishing and hunting. The colonization of California, first by the Spaniards and then by the Americans (especially in the second half of the 19th century), was accompanied by extermination of Indians and the disappearance of many tribes. The survivors were settled on reservations. According to official 1970 figures, the Indian population in California was 40,000. The California Indians live in poverty; they work as hired hands and engage in small-scale farming.

REFERENCE
Narody Ameriki, vol. 1. Moscow, 1959.   [11–631–1]

CALIFORNIA OIL-BEARING REGION, a petroleum-bearing region in the United States, located along the coast of southern California (including the continental shelf) and extending into the southern part of the Central Valley. Explored reserves in 1968 were 590 million tons of petroleum and 240 billion cu m of natural gas. The most significant extraction is in the Los Angeles area. The total petroleum extraction in the California oil-bearing region is about 50 million tons a year (1970), primarily from Miocene and Pleistocene deposits.   [11–630–2]

CALIFORNIUM, Cf, an artificial radioactive chemical element of the actinide series, atomic number 98. It has no stable isotopes. It was originally produced in 1950 by the American scientists S. Thompson, A. Ghiorso, K. Street, and G. Seaborg using the nuclear reaction ^{242}Cm(d,n)^{245}Cf. The element was named after the location of its discovery (the state of California).

The known isotopes of californium have mass numbers 242 to 256. The following isotopes are relatively stable and may be prepared in macroquantities by prolonged irradiation of uranium or plutonium with neutrons: ^{249}Cf ($T_{1/2} = 360$ years), ^{250}Cf (13.2 years), ^{251}Cf (more than 800 years), and ^{252}Cf (2.65 years). The first solid compounds of californium, ^{249}Cf$_2$O$_3$ and ^{249}CFOCl, were produced in 1958. The most typical state of oxidation of californium, like the other heavy actinides, is $+3$; a less typical state is $+2$. Californium may be separated from the other actinides using extraction and chromatographic methods. Compounds of ^{252}Cf may be used as powerful small-scale neutron sources.

REFERENCES
Gol'danskii, V. I., and S. M. Polikanov. *Tiazhelee urana.* Moscow, 1969.
Vdovenko, V. M. *Sovremennaia radiokhimiia.* Moscow, 1969.
                                    S. S. BERDONOSOV   [11–629–7]

CALIGULA (Gaius Julius Caesar Germanicus). Born A.D. 12 in Antium; died A.D. 41 in Rome. Roman emperor (from 37 A.D.) of the dynasty of Julius Claudius; son of Germanicus and successor to Tiberius.

Caligula received his sobriquet (Latin for "little boot") because of the little boots of the soldier type he wore in childhood. He strove to make his power unlimited and demanded that godly honors be shown him. Caligula's squandering of the state's resources on triumphal ceremonies, games, and spectacles and on awards to the praetorian guard led to an exorbitant increase in taxes and to the confiscation of wealth, especially that of the senators. Caligula's morbid suspiciousness, cruelty, and wild behavior aroused dissatisfaction in the Senate and in the praetorian command. He was murdered in the palace by the praetorian tribune Cassius Chaerea.   [11–595–1]

CALIPER, a device that is lowered into a bore hole on a cable to determine the diameter of the hole. Mechanical and ultrasonic calipers are used.

The most commonly used mechanical caliper consists of three or four lever feelers (probes), which are pressed against the walls of the bore hole by springs, and a rheostat whose sliding contact is connected to the feelers by means of pushrods. A change in the diameter of the borehole produces a proportional change in the resistance of the rheostat. This resistance is measured on the surface and, as a result, a curve is produced showing the change in the diameter of the borehole from the face to the mouth of the hole. Recent models are equipped with a controlled lever device that can be opened and closed repeatedly on command from the surface.

An ultrasonic caliper is a hydrolocating device with two directional electroacoustic transducers located on opposite sides of the borehole instrument. Each transducer operates alternately as an ultrasonic oscillation emitter and detector. The time interval between the moments of the transducer's emission and its reception of the ultrasonic pulse reflected from the wall of the borehole is measured on the surface. Since the interval is proportional to the distance from the device to the borehole wall, two longitudinal profiles of the borehole are produced, characterizing its diameter.

Since the cross section of a borehole is usually noncircular, instruments have been developed that permit measurement of the size and shape of the cross section.
                                    V. T. CHUKIN   [11–319–2]

CALIPER LOGGING, measurements taken to produce a caliper log (a graph of changes in the diameter of a borehole with depth). The measurement of borehole diameter was first proposed in 1935 by the Soviet scientist S. Ia. Litvinov.

The actual diameter of a borehole (the diameter of a circle equal in area to the cross section of the hole in a plane perpendicular to its axis) differs from the diameter of the boring bit with which it was drilled. An increase in diameter (formation of cavities) is observed in certain clayey rocks because of their crumbling as a result of swelling of particles; in rock salt and potassium salt, which dissolve in drilling fluid; in porous sands, which are washed away during drilling by the jet of drilling fluid; in cavernous and fissured rocks; and when a borehole is intersected by karst caverns. A reduction in the diameter of a borehole occurs in permeable rocks as a result of the formation of a clay crust because of seepage of the drilling fluid into the bed and swelling of some rock under the action of water.

Caliper logs are used in conjunction with data obtained by other geophysical methods for the precise determination of the geologic cross section of a borehole and, in particular, for the location of reservoir beds. In addition, caliper logs make possible monitoring of the condition of the borehole during drilling and the discovery of intervals that are favorable for the installation of sealing (packing) devices and determination of the amount of cement required for sealing the annular space when the casing string is run into the borehole.

REFERENCE
Spravochnik geofizika, vol. 2. Moscow, 1961.
                                    V. T. CHUKIN   [11–319–3]

CALLAO, a city in Peru, near Lima. Population, 335,400 (1970). Callao is a seaport on the Pacific Ocean. It is served by a railroad and several highways. Fishing vessels are produced there, and it has metalworking, chemical, textile, and food (fish-processing, meat) industries. It is a fishing center, the main catch being anchovies.   [11–706–4]

CALLAS, MARIA (real surname, Kalogeropoulou). Born Dec. 3, 1923, in New York. Opera singer (lyric-dramatic soprano).

Callas, a Greek by nationality, is an outstanding representative of contemporary vocal art. In 1937 she began to study singing under E. de Hidalgo at the Conservatory of Athens. In 1938 she made her debut at the Athens Opera. In the late 1940's, Callas sang in Italian theaters. Since the early 1950's she has sung in the world's most prominent theaters, including La Scala in Milan (1950), Covent Garden in London (1952), the Chicago Opera House (1954–55), and the Metropolitan Opera House in New York (1956–58). In 1960, Callas became a soloist at La Scala.

Her vocal technique is similar to that of the Italian romantic school of opera (mastery of bel canto). Her performances are characterized by a unity of vocal and dramatic imagery. Callas' most successful parts have included the title roles in Donizetti's *Lucia de Lammermoor* and *Anna Bolena*; Norma, Amina, and Imogena in Bellini's *Norma, La Sonnambula,* and *Il Pirata;* Violetta in Verdi's *La Traviata;* and the title role in Puccini's *Tosca.*

REFERENCE
Timokhin, V. "Mariia Kallas." In *Vydaiushchiesia ital'ianskie pevtsy: Ocherki.* Moscow, 1962.   [11–641–2]

CALLATIS (also Kallatis), an ancient Greek city-state on the western shore of the Black Sea (present-day Mangalia, Rumania).

Founded at the end of the sixth century B.C., Callatis quickly became a large city-state (polis) with a highly developed economy. From the early 330's B.C. to 281 B.C. it was subject to Macedonia. Between 313 and 305 B.C. the inhabitants of Callatis were in a state of rebellion, which was supressed by Lysimachus. More than 1,000 Callatian citizens fled to the Bosporan State. Under Mithridates VI, Callatis became part of Pontus. In 28 B.C. it became part of the Roman province of Moesia. In the first half of the seventh century A.D., Callatis was destroyed during the Avar and Slav invasions. Excavations (from 1901, O. Tafrali, T. Sauciuc-Săveanu, and R. Vulpe) have uncovered the remains of massive defensive walls, city blocks, temples, public and private buildings, and numerous works of art, inscriptions, and household objects. The necropolises have been investigated. In one of the burials dating from the fourth century B.C., the remains of a Greek manuscript on papyrus were found.

REFERENCES
Blavatskaia, T. V. *Zapadnopontiiskie goroda v. VII–I vv. do n. e.* Moscow, 1952.
Preda, K. *Kallatis.* Bucharest, 1963.   T. V. BLAVATSKAIA [11–641–4]

CALLES, PLUTARCO ELIAS. Born Sept. 25, 1877, in Guaymas, Sonora; died Oct. 19, 1945, in Mexico City. Mexican statesman and political figure. Teacher by profession.

Calles was one of the participants in the Revolution of 1910–17, and in 1914 he became a general. From 1918 to 1923 he occupied important ministerial posts. He was president from 1924 to 1928. At first he pursued a policy aimed at strengthening the national sovereignty of the country, defending Mexico's right to its own natural resources against the encroachments of American monopolies and supporting Nicaragua in its national liberation struggle against US imperialism. However, he eventually capitulated totally to native reaction and American capital, supporting a policy of concessions to US oil monopolies and suppressing democratic forces within the country. In 1930, under his immediate influence, Mexico severed diplomatic relations with the USSR. From 1933 to 1935 he was minister of finance. In 1936 he was expelled from the country for his antinational reactionary activity and interference in the affairs of the progressive government led by L. Cárdenas y del Río. Returning to Mexico in 1941, he abandoned politics.   [11–688–1]

CALLICRATES (Kallikrátēs), Greek architect of the mid-fifth century B.C.

Callicrates worked in Athens. He participated in the building of the so-called long walls and in the fortification of the eastern part of the Acropolis walls. He also built the Parthenon (447–438 B.C., together with Ictinus) and the small Ionic-style Temple of Athena Nike (planned 449 B.C., finished c. 420 B.C.) on the Acropolis.   [11–643–1]

CALLIGRAPHY, the art of beautiful and precise handwriting. The history of calligraphy is linked with the stylistic evolution of art and with the history of script and writing instruments (the reed pen, or *qalam,* used in ancient Greece and Rome, also used by Oriental peoples during the medieval period; the quill pen, used in Europe through the first half of the 19th century; and the brush, used in Far Eastern countries). Calligraphers strive not only to provide ease in reading but also to endow handwriting with emotional graphic expressiveness. Calligraphy tends to be either clear outlines that can be read from a distance; expressive, cursive italic script; or ornamental patterns that, at times, impede readability.

In China and other Far Eastern countries, calligraphy was highly valued as an art that communicated emotional and symbolic meanings through graphic signs. These signs do not only communicate the meaning of the word but also embody the thoughts and feelings of the artist. As a result, the calligraphy of China, Korea, and Japan is characterized by rhythmic freedom and vividly expressive brushwork. Well-known Chinese calligraphers include Wang Hsi-chih (fourth century), Hsüantsung (eighth century), and Mi Fei (11th century). In Islamic countries, where the pictorial arts were limited, calligraphy became extremely ornamental and rhythmic; geometric and floral designs were often combined with figurative elements. The most notable calligraphers included the masters of neskhi—Ibn Mukla (tenth century), Ibn Bawwab (11th century), and Yaqut Mustasimi (13th century), in Baghdad—as well as the masters of nastaliq—Mir Ali Tabrizi (14th century), Sultan Ali Meshkhedi (15th century), and Mir Ali Harawi, Shah Mahmud Nishapuri, and Ahmad al-Husayni (16th century) in Iran and Middle Asia.

In ancient Greece and Rome, Greek and Latin script was developed; this classical script was characterized by clarity and harmonious proportions. In medieval Europe scriptoria were the calligraphic centers. During this period, the classical regularity of Carolingian calligraphy was replaced by ornamental and fractured Gothic script. In Russia there are outstanding examples of calligraphy; the earliest was the *Gospel of Ostromir,* which was transcribed by Deacon Grigorii in 1057.

Since the 15th century, engravers, scribes, and artists have assumed the leading role in European calligraphy. They created fanciful calligraphic compositions, which subsequently became luxury items. Book printing sharply restricted the use of calligraphy. With the invention of the typewriter, this art basically became a subject of study in elementary schools (penmanship). Calligraphy is also used as an artistic device in book design, poster art, and commercial graphic art.

REFERENCES
Kazi Ahmad. *Traktat o kalligrafakh i khudozhnikakh.* Moscow-Leningrad, 1947.
Istrin, V. A. *Razvitie pis'ma.* Moscow, 1961.
Bonacini, C. *Bibliografia delle arti scrittorie e della calligrafia.* Florence, 1953.
L'art de l'écriture. Paris–Baden-Baden, 1965.   [11–642–1]

CALLIMACHUS. Born 310 B.C., in Cyrene, North Africa; died 240 B.C., in Alexandria. Poet of the Alexandrian school.

Callimachus was the creator of the genre of the short poem. His narrative poem *Hecale* is an epyllion, a small-scale epic. His four books of narrative elegies are called *Causes.* He also wrote the poetry collection *Iambs* and the first catalogue of Greek writers, *Tables.* Sixty-four of his epigrams are extant. Callimachus greatly influenced subsequent Greek and Roman poetry.

WORKS
In Russian translation:
Izbrannye gimny i epigrammy. Translated by V. Alekseev. St. Petersburg, 1899.
Grecheskaia epigramma. Edited by F. A. Petrovskii. Moscow, 1960.
REFERENCES
Istoriia grecheskoi literatury, vol. 3. Edited by S. I. Sobolevskii [et al.]. Moscow, 1960.
Cahen, E. *Callimaque et son œuvre poétique.* Paris, 1929.
                                                            [11–644–2]

CALLIMICO, a genus of New World monkeys. Body length, 18–25 cm; tail length, 25–32 cm. The animal dwells in the Amazon Basin. The genus has one species, *Callimico goeldii,* and occupies an intermediary place between the families Callithricidae (monkeys with claws on the fingers) and Cebidae (monkeys with prehensile tails). Members of the genus *Callimico* have claws on their extremities, as do members of the family Callithricidae. They have three molars, as do members of the family Cebidae (there are only two in Callithricidae). Some zoologists classify *Callimico* as an independent family.   [11–644–3]

CALLINUS. Dates of birth and death unknown. Greek poet; flourished in the first of the seventh century B.C.

Callinus, who was born in the city of Ephesus, invented the elegy. His elegies were predominantly political in nature. Only four fragments of Callinus's elegies have been preserved; the longest has 21 verses. Callinus also wrote a hymn to Zeus and several verses on themes from the folk legends of the Trojan mythological cycle.

EDITIONS
Diehl, E. *Anthologia lyrica graeca,* vol. 1. Leipzig, 1954.
In Russian translation:
In *Khrestomatiia po antichnoi literature,* vol. 1. Edited by N. F. Deratani. Moscow, 1958.
REFERENCE
Istoriia grecheskoi literatury, vol. 1. Moscow-Leningrad, 1946. Page 191.
[11–644–4]

CALLIOPE, in Greek mythology, one of the nine Muses, the patroness of epic poetry. She was the daughter of Zeus and Mnemosyne. According to several ancient Greek legends, she was the mother of the mythological poet and singer Orpheus. Calliope is usually portrayed holding waxed tablets and a style (small stick for writing).   [11–645–2]

CALLISTEPHUS, a genus of annual herbaceous plants of the family Compositae, with one species, China aster (*Callistephus chinensis*). In floriculture this species, which is also commonly known as the annual aster, is represented by numerous varieties. These varieties differ in height, form, structure, and color of the anthodium.   [11–645–3]

CALLOSE, a polysaccharide, insoluble in water, contained in plants and consisting of glucose-molecule residues joined in a spiral chain (as opposed to cellulose, in which the glucose molecules are joined in a straight chain).

Callose lines the tubules of the sievelike layers of phloem; as these tubules age, the amount of callose increases and the tubules become plugged and cease functioning. When a plant is injured, callose is deposited on the cell walls of the parenchyma, forming a callus. Callose is also found in the cell walls of some algae and fungi.   [11–645–6]

CALLOT, JACQUES. Born in 1592 or 1593, in Nancy; died there Mar. 24, 1635. French engraver and graphic artist.

Beginning in 1608, Callot studied in Rome. In 1611 he began working in Florence, where he became a masterful etcher. In 1622 he returned to France. Callot's etchings include large panoramic compositions (*The Siege of Breda,* 1627) and groups of small engravings (*Capricci,* 1617, 1623). In his work Callot reproduced reality with multiple images. He portrayed various, often bizarre, human types (the series *The Beggars,* 1622) and dramatically depicted contemporary events (the two series *The Disasters of War,* 1632–33). Callot also treated religious subjects (*The Martyrdom of St. Sebastian,* 1632–33), mythological subjects (primarily in his early work), and theatrical themes (the series *Balli,* 1622). He also is well known for his landscapes. Each of his plates (with sharp spatial jumps from the foreground to the background) depicts several episodes and crowds of active figures.

In Callot's work the realism of keenly observed and sharply delineated details combines with grotesque expressiveness, which includes fantastic elements, to form a whole. Callot used the technique of graduated biting, which gave him particular precision of drawing, flexibility and clearness of line, richness of shadows in the foreground, and subtlety and softness of tonal transitions.

REFERENCES
Glikman, A. S. *Zhak Kallo.* Leningrad-Moscow, 1959.
Lieure, J. *Jacques Callot,* 5 vols. Paris, 1924–29.
Bechtel, E. de T. *Jacques Callot.* New York, 1955.
IU. K. ZOLOTOV   [11–645–5]

CALLUS. (1) Tissue formed in plants on the surface of a wound (cracks, taps, the bases of cuttings, and areas of concrescence of stock and scion). A callus promotes the healing of wounds. Consisting of thin-walled parenchymal cells, a callus develops when there is cell division of any living tissue of the plant (cambium or phloem) in the peripheral zone of the pith, lying next to the protoxylem. Adventitious roots and buds, particularly with grafting, often develop in the callus. **(2)** Corpus callosum, an accumulation of callose that obstructs the sieve plate when the sieve tubes of the phloem age. Use of the term in this sense is obsolete.   [11–646–1]

CALMALLOY, a thermomagnetic nickel-based alloy containing 30 percent copper.

Calmalloy is characterized by linear magnetization dependence on temperature between 20° and 80°C. The temperature coefficient of magnetization is 0.8×10^{-4} tesla per °C; the saturation magnetization is 0.01 tesla at 20°C. Calmalloy is used in electric metering devices (galvanometers, energy meters) as permanent magnetic shunts for reducing the instrument temperature error.   [11–692–2]

CALMETTE, ALBERT. Born July 12, 1863, in Nice; died Oct. 29, 1933, in Paris. French microbiologist and hygienist. Member of the French Academy of Medicine (1919) and the Academy of Sciences in Paris (1927).

Calmette graduated from the University of Paris medical department in 1885. He was a student of L. Pasteur. From 1895 to 1919 he was director of the Pasteur Institute and simultaneously (1898–1917) professor of hygiene and bacteriology of the medical department at Lille; in 1917 he became vice-director of the Pasteur Institute in Paris. His principal works dealt with tuberculosis, smallpox, plague, the biological purification of sewage, microbiological and serological techniques, and the development of serotherapeutic methods of treating snakebites; he also proposed a diagnostic reaction to test for tuberculosis. Together with the French scientist C. Guérin he created an antituberculosis vaccine, known throughout the world as BCG, which was first used on newborns in 1921. From 1893 to 1897 he studied the epidemiology of plague in Saigon. Together with the French microbiologist A. Yersin, he was the first to apply the techniques of serotherapy.

WORKS
Predokhranitel'naia vaktsinatsiia protiv tuberkuleza pri pomoshchi BCG. Moscow-Leningrad, 1929. (Translated from French.)
Rukovodstvo po mikrobiologicheskoi i serologicheskoi tekhnike, 2nd ed. Moscow-Leningrad, 1937. (Translated from French.)
REFERENCES
Liubarskii, V. A. "Kal'mett." *Zhurnal mikrobiologii i immunobiologii,* 1934, vol. 12, issue 1, pp. 1–6.
Togunova, A. I. "Zhizn' i deiatel'nost' A. Kal'metta." *Vestnik Akademii meditsinskikh nauk SSSR,* 1964, no. 8.
R. S. RABINOVICH   [11–695–1]

CALMETTE, JOSEPH. Born Sept. 1, 1873, in Perpignan; died Aug. 16, 1952, in Toulouse. French historian. Professor at the University of Toulouse (from 1911). Author of numerous works on the history of medieval Europe (primarily of France). Calmette's main concern was political history and the history of law.

WORKS
Etudes médiévales. Toulouse, 1946. (Contains a list of Calmette's works.)
Les Rois de France. Paris, 1948.
Trilogie de l'histoire de France, vols. 1–3. Paris [1948–52].
Les Grands Ducs de Bourgogne. Paris [1949].
Le Reich allemand au Moyen âge. Paris, 1951.   [11–695–2]

CALOMEL (from the Greek *kalos,* "beautiful," and *melas,* "black"), mercurous chloride, Hg_2Cl_2; a colorless powder. When treated with caustic alkalies or ammonia, it turns black (hence the name). The darkening occurs as result of the precipitation of finely powdered mercury according to the reactions

$$Hg_2Cl_2 + 2NaOH = Hg + HgO + 2NaCl + H_2O$$

$$Hg_2Cl_2 + 2NH_4OH = HgNH_2Cl + Hg + NH_4Cl + 2H_2O$$

Calomel has a density of 7,160 kg/m^3 and evaporates without fusion. Its sublimation point is 383.7°C. It is poorly soluble in water.

Calomel is used in the preparation of calomel electrodes and as a catalyst in organic reactions. In medicine it serves as an antibacterial agent, applied externally in ointment form in cases of wart infections and gonorrheal conjunctivitis and as a safeguard against venereal diseases (locally). Calomel is sometimes used internally as a cholagogue.

In nature calomel exists as a rare mineral of the halide group. It crystallizes in the tetragonal system and has an adamantine luster. Its hardness on the mineralogical scale measures 1.5. Native calomel exhibits very high double refraction. It is formed in the oxidation zone of mercury deposits.   [11–665–2]

CALONNE, CHARLES ALEXANDRE DE. Born Jan. 20, 1734, in Douai; died Oct. 29, 1802, in Paris. French statesman.

From 1783 to 1787, Calonne was controller-general of finances. He attempted to replenish the exhausted state treasury by borrowing at high interest, reminting gold coins, and increasing taxes. Threatened with the financial failure of the government, Calonne in 1786 followed the example of A. R. J. Turgot and J. Necker in proposing reforms: an increase in the tax obligations of the privileged classes by instituting a uniform land tax, abolition of the royal highway service duties (*corvée*) and of the salt tax (excise), sale of part of the royal estates, and curtailment of expenses at the royal court. However, the Assembly of Notables, which had been summoned upon his initiative in 1787, rejected these proposals. Calonne was forced to retire (April 1787), and in that same year he moved to Great Britain. During the Great French Revolution he was one of the leaders of the émigré counterrevolutionaries. Calonne returned to France in 1802.

REFERENCES
Jolly, P. *Calonne: 1734–1802.* Paris [1949]
Lacour-Gayet, R. *Calonne: Financier, reformateur, contrerévolutionnaire, 1734–1802.* Paris, 1963.   [11–666–2]

CALOOCAN, a city in the Philippines, located in the southwestern part of the island of Luzon. Population, 274,500 (1970). It is part of the industrial complex of Greater Manila. Caloocan has traditional branches of industry, such as the production of rubber articles, food processing and the production of food specialty items, and textile and garment industries. The city also has metallurgical, machine-building, and chemical industries.   [11–666–3]

CALORIC VALUE OF FOOD, the energy accumulated in food substances (proteins, fat, and carbohydrates); the energy value of foodstuffs, expressed in calories (cal) or kilocalories (kcal). The concept is used, for example, in the comparative evaluation of food products and in planning diets.

The caloric value is determined by the presence of unoxidized atoms of carbon and hydrogen. A molecule of fat contains more unoxidized atoms of carbon and hydrogen than a carbohydrate molecule or a molecule of protein. One g of fat yields 9.3 kcal (1 kcal = 4.1868 $\times$ 10^3 joules); 1 g of carbohydrate, 4.1 kcal; and 1 g of protein, 4.1 kcal. The following gives the caloric value (in kcal) of some products (per 100 g): milk (kefir, sour milk), 62; butter, 734; first-grade beef, 154; first-grade mutton, 206; ham, 365; choice sausage, 290; eggs, 150; scallions, 21; fresh cucumbers, 15; potatoes 89; cabbage, 27; carrots, 36; apples, 48; lemons, 41; cepes, 32; walnuts, 612; rye bread, 204; and sugar, 390. The caloric value of foodstuffs must be known in order to work out rations, which are determined by the energy expenditures of persons of different occupations, sexes, and ages.

In animal husbandry, the caloric value is used in the comparative evaluation of the nutritional value of feeds, for establishing norms of feeding livestock, and for planning feed requirements. The caloric value of dry matter in most feeds is 4.0–4.5 Mcal per 1 kg. The useful caloric value of a feed for the animal depends on the digestibility of the feed and the absorbability of the digestible substances.   [11–667–2]

CALORIE, a unit of heat that is not part of a system of units. Designation, cal. In addition to the calorie, the kilocalorie (also known as the large calorie) is widely used; 1 kcal = 1,000 cal.

Originally, the calorie was defined as the quantity of heat necessary to raise the temperature of 1 g of water by 1°C. Neither the temperature interval within which the heating was performed nor its conditions had been defined prior to the late 19th century. Various calories have therefore been used: the 0°, 15°, 20°, and 25° calories as well as the average calorie and the thermochemical calorie. The 20° kilocalorie was used in the USSR from 1934 to 1957. This kilocalorie was equal to the quantity of heat (with an accuracy of up to 0.02 percent) required to heat 1 kg of water from 19.5° to 20.5°C.

The First International Steam Table Conference (London, 1929) introduced the international calorie, defined as 1/861.1 of the international kilowatt-hour (kW-hr). The International Steam Table Conferences in 1954 and 1956 accepted the decision on transition from the calorie to a new unit, the absolute joule (J), which subsequently was included in the International System of Units. The following relationship was established between the calorie and the joule: 1 cal = 4.1868 J (exactly). The 20° calorie is equal to 4.181 J. The calorie used widely in thermochemistry is equal to 4.1840 J.   [11–674–2]

CALORIMETER, an instrument for measuring the quantity of heat that is either evolved or absorbed in the course of a physical, chemical, or biological process. The term "calorimeter" was proposed by A. Lavoisier and P. Laplace (1780).

Modern calorimeters are used in the temperature range from 0.1° to 3500°K and make it possible to measure quantities of heat to an accuracy of 10^{-2} percent. Calorimeters vary in design, which is determined by the nature and duration of the process being studied, the temperature range in which the measurements are performed, the quantity of heat being determined, and the accuracy required.

A calorimeter designed for measuring the total quantity of heat Q evolved during a process from start to finish is called an integrating calorimeter. A calorimeter for measuring the heat output L and its changes during various stages of the process is called a heat flux meter, or "calorimetric oscillograph." In accordance with the design of the system and the method of measurement, the following calorimeter types are distinguished: liquid and aneroid calorimeters and single and twin (differential) calorimeters.

A liquid integrating calorimeter, of variable temperature with an isothermal jacket, is used to measure the heat of solution and the heat of chemical reactions. This calorimeter consists of a liquid-filled (usually water) vessel, which contains a chamber where the process under investigation is carried out ("bomb calorimeter"), a stirrer, a heater, and a thermometer. Heat evolved in the chamber is then distributed between the chamber, the liquid, and other parts of the calorimeter, which are collectively called the calorimetric system of the instrument. Changes of state (for example, of temperature) of the calorimetric system make it possible to measure the quantity of heat introduced into the device. The heating of the calorimetric system is measured with a thermometer. The actual measurements are preceded by the calibration of the calorimeter, which consists in the determination of the temperature change of the calorimetric system that results from supplying a known quantity of heat (by the heater or as a result of a chemical reaction occurring in the chamber involving a known quantity of standard material). Calibration yields the calorimeter's heat value, that is, the coefficient by which the calorimeter's temperature change measured with the thermometer is to be multiplied in order to determine the quantity of heat introduced into the system. The heat value of such a calorimeter is the heat capacity c of the calorimetric system.

Determination of the unknown heat of combustion or of another chemical reaction Q reduces to the measurement of the change in temperature Δt of the calorimetric system, caused by the process being studied: $Q = c \cdot \Delta t$. The value of Q is usually assigned to the mass of the material present in the calorimetric chamber.

Calorimetric measurements permit the direct determination of only the sum of the heats of the process under investigation and of various secondary processes, such as mixing, evaporation of water, and fracture of the ampul with material. The heat of the secondary processes must be determined experimentally or by calculation and must be omitted from the final result. One of the inevitable secondary processes is the heat exchange between the calorimeter and the surrounding medium through radiation and thermal conductivity. In order to take the secondary processes into account, primarily the heat exchange, the calorimetric system is surrounded by a jacket, the temperature of which is regulated.

The jacket temperature in liquid isothermal calorimeters is maintained at a constant level. The greatest difficulty in determining heats of chemical reactions is not due to problems related to consideration of secondary processes but to problems related to the determination of the completeness of the reaction and the necessity of taking several reactions into account.

In integrating calorimeters of another type, isothermal (constant temperature) calorimeters, the introduced heat does not change the temperature of the calorimetric system but causes changes in the aggregate state of a material that constitutes part of this system (for example, melting of ice in the Bunsen ice calorimeter). The quantity of introduced heat is calculated in this case from the mass of the material that has changed its state of aggregation (for example, the mass of melted ice, which can be measured from the change in volume of the ice-water mixture) and from the heat of phase transition.

Aneroid integrating calorimeters are most frequently used for determining the enthalpy of materials at high temperatures (up to 2500°C). The calorimetric system in calorimeters of this type consists of a block of metal (usually copper or aluminum) with wells for the reaction vessel, the thermometer, and the heater. The enthalpy of the material is calculated as the product of the heat value of the calorimeter and the difference between the increases in temperature of the block measured after dropping into its cavity an ampul with a known quantity of material and then another ampul without the material but heated to the same temperature.

The heat capacities of gases, and sometimes of liquids, are determined in the "labyrinth" flow calorimeters from the temperature difference between the inlet and outlet of a steady-state flow of liquid or gas, from the flow rate, and from the Joule heat emitted by the electric heater of the calorimeter.

In contrast to an integrating calorimeter, a calorimeter working in the heat flow measurement mode must be capable of significant heat exchange in order that the heat quantities introduced into the calorimeter may be rapidly removed and the state of the calorimeter may be determined by the instantaneous value of the thermal flux resulting from the process. The thermal flux of the process is determined from the heat exchange between the calorimeter and its jacket. Such calorimeters, developed by the French physicist E. Calvet (1895–1966), consist of a metal block with channels having cylindrical cells. The process under investigation is allowed to proceed in the cells, whereas the metal block performs the function of the jacket (its temperature is maintained at a constant level to an accuracy of $10^{-5°}$–$10^{-6°}$K). The temperature difference between the cell and the block is measured with a thermopile having up to 1,000 junctions. The heat exchange of the cell and the electromotive force of the thermopile are proportional to the small temperature difference arising between the block and the cell when heat is evolved or absorbed in it. Most often two cells are placed into the block functioning as a differential calorimeter: the thermopiles of each cell have the same number of junctions, and therefore the difference between their electromotive forces permits a direct determination of the difference between the strength of thermal fluxes entering the cells. This method of measurement makes it possible to eliminate the distortion of the quantity being determined by random temperature fluctuations of the block. Two thermopiles are usually mounted on each cell: one of these makes it possible to compensate for the thermal flux of the process under investigation on the basis of the Peltier effect, whereas the second one (indicator) measures the uncompensated part of the thermal flux. In this case, the instrument performs as a differential compensating calorimeter. Such calorimeters are capable of measuring the thermal flux of processes with an accuracy of up to 1 microwatt (μW) at room temperature.

The usual calorimeter names, such as "for chemical reactions," "bomb calorimeter," "isothermal," "ice calorimeter," or "low-temperature calorimeter," are historical in origin and indicate mainly the type and range of calorimetric applications, without being either a complete or relative characteristic of the instruments in question.

A general classification may be based on an analysis of three principal variables that determine the measurement methods: temperature of the calorimetric system T_c, temperature of the jacket T_j surrounding the calorimetric system, and the quantity of heat L evolved in the calorimeter per unit time (thermal flux).

Calorimeters with constant T_c and T_j are called isothermal, whereas those with $T_c = T_j$ are called adiabatic. Calorimeters operated at a constant temperature difference $T_c - T_j$ are called calorimeters with constant heat exchange. T_j is constant and T_c is a function of L in isoperibolic calorimeters.

An important factor affecting the final results of measurements is the reliable performance of automatic temperature regulators of the isothermal or adiabatic jackets. In adiabatic calorimeters, the jacket temperature is controlled in such a manner as always to be close to the changing temperature of the calorimetric system. The adiabatic jacket is a light metal screen, equipped with a heater, which decreases the heat exchange to such an extent that the temperature of the calorimeter varies only by several ten thousandths of a degree per minute. This frequently makes it possible to lower the heat exchange during the time span of the calorimetric experiment to an insignificant value, which can be neglected. When necessary, the results of the direct measurements may be corrected for heat exchange, the calculation method of which is based on Newton's law of heat transfer—the proportionality of the thermal flux between the calorimeter and the jacket to the difference between their temperatures, if this difference is not very large (up to 3°–4°C).

For calorimeters with isothermal jackets, the heat of chemical reactions may be determined with errors up to 0.01 percent. If the calorimeter's dimensions are small, its temperature varies by more than 2°–3°C, and if the process under study is extended, then the correction for heat exchange in the case of the isothermal jacket may comprise as much as 15–20 percent of the measured quantity, which may limit the accuracy of measurements. It is more appropriate in these cases to use the adiabatic jacket.

Adiabatic calorimeters are used for the determination of the heat capacity of solid and liquid materials in the range from 0.1° to 1000°K. At room temperature as well as at lower temperatures, adiabatic calorimeters, protected by vacuum jackets, are immersed into Dewar vessels, filled with liquid helium, hydrogen, or nitrogen. At elevated temperatures (above 100°C), calorimeters are placed into thermostated electric furnaces.

REFERENCES
Popov, M. M. *Termometriia i kolorimetriia*, 2nd ed. Moscow, 1954.
Skuratov, S. M., V. P. Kolesov, and A. F. Vorob'ev. *Termokhimiia*, parts 1–2. Moscow, 1964–66.
Calvet, E., and H. Prat. *Mikrokalorimetriia*. Moscow, 1963. (Translated from French.)
Experimental Thermochemistry, vols. 1–2. New York–London, 1956–62.   V. A. SOKOLOV [11–667–3]

CALORIMETER, IONIZATION, an instrument for determination of the particle energy of cosmic rays ($\sim 10^{11}$ electron volts [eV] and higher). In an ionization calorimeter the energy of a cosmic-ray particle is absorbed by a thick layer of material (in a fashion similar to the way in which heat is absorbed in an ordinary calorimeter). During interaction with matter, as a result of nuclear reactions, high-energy cosmic-ray particles generate a large number of secondary particles or photons, which in turn form new particles. The ultimate result of these events is the formation of an avalanche of charged particles, which moves within the material, ionizes its atoms, and thereby loses its energy. If the thickness of the layer of absorbent material is sufficiently great, and if the avalanche of charged particles is completely retained by the material, then the number of ions generated is proportional to the energy of the primary cosmic-ray particle. To measure the total number of ions, the absorber, which is made of a dense material (usually iron or lead), is divided into a number of layers several centimeters thick, and ionization chambers are placed between the layers.

The ionization calorimeter was invented in 1954 in the USSR, and it has come to be widely used, both in the USSR and abroad, in studies of the interaction of high-energy cosmic-ray particles (10^{11}–10^{13} eV) with atomic nuclei. In this case, the calorimeter is usually combined with instruments that make possible observation of the results of the interaction, such as cloud chambers, nuclear photographic emulsions, and spark chambers.

Typical dimensions of ionization calorimeters are as follows: height, 1.5–2.0 m; area of cross section, ~ 1 sq m; weight, 10–20 tons. A unique ionization calorimeter with an area of 10 sq m and a weight of 70 tons was constructed at the high-altitude station on Mount Aragats (Armenia, USSR) in 1964. Ionization calorimeters have also been used by the USSR in the large Proton space stations.

REFERENCES

Grigorov, N. L., V. S. Murzin, and I. D. Rapoport. "Metod izmereniia energii chastits v oblasti vyshe 10^{11} eV." *Zhurnal eksperimental'noi i teoreticheskoi fiziki,* 1958, vol. 34, fasc. 2, p. 506.
Bugakov, V. V. [et al.]. "Printsipy ustroistva nauchnoi apparatury dlia izucheniia kosmicheskikh luchei vysokoi energii na kosmicheskoi stantsii 'Proton-4.' " *Izv. AN SSSR: Seriia fizicheskaia,* 1970, vol. 34, p. 1818.
Grigorov, N. L. [et al.]. "Iadernaia laboratoriia v kosmose: Novyi etap v izuchenii chastits sverkhvysokikh energii." *Priroda,* 1965, no. 12, p. 7.   N. L. GRIGOROV   [11–671–1]

CALORIMETRY, the totality of methods for determining the heat effects (quantities of heat) accompanying various physical, chemical, and biological processes. Calorimetric methods are used to determine heat capacities of materials; heats of phase transitions (melting, boiling, and other transitions); heat effects of magnetization, electrification, solution, sorption, chemical reactions (for example, combustion), and metabolic processes in living organisms; and in a number of cases, the energy of electromagnetic radiation and that of nuclear processes.

The apparatus used in calorimetric measurements are called calorimeters. Their design is determined by the conditions of measurement (primarily by the temperature interval) and by the required accuracy. Calorimeters for use above 400°K (arbitrary limit) are called high-temperature calorimeters, whereas those for use in the temperature range corresponding to liquid nitrogen, hydrogen, and helium are called low-temperature calorimeters.

The results of calorimetric measurements are widely used in heat engineering, metallurgy, and chemical technology. They are used to calculate the quantities of heat required to heat, melt, or vaporize materials in various engineering processes and to calculate the time limits of chemical reactions and the conditions for carrying out these reactions. Thus, the temperature and pressure range in which synthetic diamonds are obtainable from graphite were determined by calculations based to a large extent on calorimetric determinations of heat capacities and heats of combustion of these materials. Calorimetric measurements make it possible to determine the regions of stability of various minerals and to elucidate the conditions for their simultaneous presence in rocks. Low-temperature calorimetric data are being widely used in studies of mechanical, magnetic, and electrical effects in solids and liquids at low temperatures as well as in calculations of thermodynamic functions (for example, the entropy of substances).   B. A. SOKOLOV

In biology, calorimeters are used for determining the heat effects accompanying the processes of life. Two types of chemical processes are continuously occurring in organisms: endothermic processes (with heat absorption) and exothermic processes (with heat evolution), the latter type predominating. Calorimetry has shown, for example, that a coliform bacterium evolves 4×10^{-9} joules (J) (10^{-9} cal) of heat per hour; a mouse evolves 420 J (100 cal); and a human evolves 2×10^5 J, or ~ 5×10^4 cal [specific heat evolution presents a completely different picture: 1,050 J/(g·hr), 21 J/(g·hr), and 4 J/(g·hr), respectively]. The organisms are usually placed into a calorimeter for measurement of their heat production. When direct calorimetry is difficult, indirect methods are used. Indirect determination of the heat production by an organism may be performed, for example, on the basis of the intensity of its gas metabolism. In this case, the quantities of oxygen (O_2) absorbed by the organism per unit time and the quantities of carbon dioxide (CO_2) liberated per unit time are measured. The ratio of these quantities (respiratory coefficient) yields the quantity of O_2 expended separately for the oxidation of proteins, fats, and carbohydrates. The heat content of these reactions is known, which makes it possible to calculate the total heat production of the organism.

V. A. BERNSHTEIN   [11–673–1]

CALOTES, a genus of lizards of the family Agamidae. The body length in most species does not exceed 40 cm, although in some it may attain 60 cm. The members of this genus have a serrated crest of enlarged scales along the spine. There are about 30 species, occurring in south Asia, including the Malay Archipelago. They are diurnal, spending most of their time in trees and shrubs. They feed chiefly on insects and are able to change color rapidly and sharply. Among the more common species is *C. versicolor;* during the reproductive period the head and neck of the male as he sits in the sun turn yellow, the trunk becomes red with black spots, and the legs and tail turn black, causing him to appear suffused with blood, hence the Russian common name *krovosos* (bloodsucker).

REFERENCE

Wermuth, H. *Agamidae.* Berlin, 1967. (*Das Tierreich,* issue 86.)
                                                               [11–674–4]

CALPURNIUS SICULUS, TITUS. Roman poet of the first century B.C. Biographical information about him has not been preserved.

The seven eclogues which are extant suggest that Calpurnius Siculus was a court poet of the Emperor Nero. His work is characterized by the combination of didacticism with the bucolic genre.

PUBLICATIONS

T. Calpurnii Siculi De laude Pisonis et Bucolica . . . , quae dicuntur carmina. Brussels, 1954.
REFERENCE
Istoriia rimskoi literatury, vol. 2. Edited by S. I. Sobolevskii [et al.]. Moscow, 1962. Pages 30–34.   [11–697–1]

CALQUE (in linguistics), semantic borrowing by means of the literal translation of the separate parts of a word or phrase. A lexical calque is a word created by full morphological substitution, that is, by the translation of each morpheme, for example, Russian *pred-met* (object) from Latin *ob-ject-um* or Russian *sushchestvitel'noe* (substantive) from Latin *substantivum.* In phraseological calques, whole expressions are modeled after foreign patterns, as in Russian *prisutstvie dukha* (composure) from French *présence d'esprit* or English *five-year plan* and French *plan cinquiennel* from Russian *piatiletnii plan.* A special type of calque is one in which a word is given a figurative meaning, modeled on a foreign word with the same literal meaning, for example, Russian *vkus* (taste) from French *goût* or Russian *cherta* (feature), from French *trait.* When the inappropriate meaning of a homonymous foreign word is used, an erroneous calque is formed, as in Russian *byt' ne v svoei tarelke* ("to be out of sorts"; literally, "not in one's plate") from the French *il n'est pas dans son assiette* (*assiette,* "plate," "position"). The calque is a very common linguistic phenomenon and is primarily literary in origin.   V. V. RASKIN   [11–688–3]

CALTANISSETTA, a city in Italy on the island of Sicily, administrative center of Caltanissetta Province. Population, 63,800 (1970). Caltanissetta is Italy's main center for sulfur mining. Natural gas is also extracted there. [11–697–2]

CALTHA, a genus of plants of the family Ranunculaceae (buttercup). These are perennial herbs with cordate or reniform leaves. The perianth is simple and corolliform; it is primarily golden-yellow. There are approximately 20 species, distributed in the temperate and arctic regions of the northern hemisphere. In the USSR there are eight or nine species. The most common is the marsh marigold (*Caltha palustris*), which grows in swamps, in damp areas, and near bodies of water. The marsh marigold (double-flowered varieties) and *C. polypetala* are cultivated as ornamentals. [11–677–2]

CALVADOS, a department in northern France, on the English Channel. Area, 5,700 sq km. Population, 545,000 (1972). The administrative center is Caen. Economic activities include livestock raising (dairy cattle and horses), the growing of grain and sugar beets, and horticulture. Most of the department's food industry (butter, cheese, apple cider) and its machine-building industry are concentrated in Caen. There is a fishing industry. Calvados has several sea resorts, including Deauville.

[11–683–3]

CALVILLE BLANCHE (in Russian, Calville white winter), variety of apple of French origin. The fruits are large, weighing (300–500 g); they are shaped like flattened ribbed spheres and are yellow with a slight blush. The flesh is yellow, juicy, tart, and aromatic. The fruits are eaten fresh. The variety requires special soil, climate, and care. It bears abundantly on dwarf stocks but poorly on ordinary ones. It is also used in tub gardening. This variety is distributed throughout Western Europe. In the USSR it is grown in the Ukrainian SSR, the Georgian SSR, and the southern RSFSR. [11–683–4]

CALVIN, JOHN. Born July 10, 1509, in Noyon, France; died May 27, 1564, in Geneva. A leader of the Reformation and the founder of Calvinism.

Calvin was the son of an important church official. He received a theological and legal education. Under the influence of Luther's preaching he began to lean toward Protestantism, and in 1533 he abandoned the Catholic Church. Because of the increasing persecution of Protestants in France he fled to Basel in 1534; his principal work, *Institutio Religionis Christianae,* was published here in 1536 (first in Latin, then in French). In it he set forth a systematic exposition of his new doctrine. In the same year Calvin arrived in Geneva, where the Reformation had already triumphed. His introduction (with the aid of the magistracy) of austere decrees on church discipline and moral principles for the burghers and his disputes with Reformation leaders in Bern (from which city Geneva had initially derived its Reformation ideas) caused him to be banished from Geneva and to move to Strasbourg (1538). In September 1541, Calvin returned to Geneva and remained there until the end of his life, having become the head of a new movement in Protestantism called Calvinism.

Under Calvin's influence the Genevan magistracy adopted a new form of church organization, which with certain variations was subsequently adopted by Calvinist congregations in other countries. Reflecting the interests of the bourgeoisie during the period of the primitive accumulation of capital, Calvin promulgated a series of reforms aimed at strengthening "secular asceticism." With the aid of the consistory, which headed the church and which had in effect subjected the secular authorities to itself, he abolished the pomp and splendor of Catholic rites; as an adviser to the government he succeeded in establishing a petty and captious supervision over the citizens, compulsory attendance at church services, and the banning of amusements, dancing, and brightly colored clothing. Calvin exhibited an extreme religious intolerance toward Catholicism and also to the popular Reformation movements (especially Anabaptism), whose followers he condemned as atheists. On Calvin's insistence the opponents of his doctrine were subjected to banishment, the death

penalty (in 1553, M. Servetus was burned at the stake), and other punishments.

WORKS
Opera quae supersunt omnia, vols. 1–59. Edited by G. Baum, E. Cunitz, and E. Reuss. Braunschweig, 1863–1900. (*Corpus reformatorum,* vols. 29–87.)
Opera selecta, vols. 1, 3, 4, 5. Edited by P. Barth. Munich, 1926–36.
S. D. SKAZKIN [11–683–5]

CALVIN, MELVIN. Born Apr. 7, 1911, in St. Paul, Minn. American biochemist. Member of the National Academy of Sciences in Washington, D. C.

Calvin graduated from the Michigan College of Mining and Technology in 1931. Beginning in 1937 he taught in the chemistry division of the University of California (Berkeley), where he became a professor in 1947. In the 1940's he began working on the problem of photosynthesis. By 1957, using CO_2 with a carbon tracer, he explained the chemical process by which plants assimilate CO_2 (the Calvin carbon reduction cycle) during photosynthesis. He was awarded the Nobel Prize for chemistry in 1961. Calvin is a foreign member of the London Royal Society and an honorary member of many foreign societies and academies of sciences.

WORKS
Chemical Evolution. Eugene, Ore., 1961.
The Path of Carbon in Photosynthesis. Englewood Cliffs, N.J., 1957. (With J. A. Bassham.)
The Photosynthesis of Carbon Compounds. New York, 1962. (With J. A. Bassham.) [11–573–1]

CALVINISM, a Protestant doctrine the founder of which was J. Calvin; it arose in the 16th century during the Reformation.

At the basis of Calvinist doctrine, which "was one fit for the boldest of the bourgeoisie of his time" (F. Engels, in K. Marx and F. Engels, *Soch.,* 2nd ed., vol. 22, p. 308), lie the doctrines of absolute predestination and of divine nonintervention in the orderly functioning of the world. According to the doctrine of absolute predestination, god, even before the creation of the world, predestined certain people to "salvation" and others to destruction, some to heaven and others to hell, and this judgment of god was absolutely immutable. The doctrine of predestination "was the religious expression of the fact that in the commercial world of competition success or failure does not depend upon a man's activity or cleverness, but upon circumstances uncontrollable by him. It is not of him that willeth or of him that runneth, but of the mercy of unknown economic powers" (*ibid.*). However, the teaching of predestination did not doom a man to a fatalistic submission to fate. According to Calvin, a man must be confident that he is "god's elect" and prove this by his life and actions. God, as Calvin asserted, does not directly disturb the orderly functioning of the world that he created, and the indication that a man is one of the elect is success in his professional activity. Thus, the bourgeoisie's entrepreneurial activity with its striving for accumulation and profit received a religious justification. The "secular asceticism" preached by Calvinism was expressed in simplicity of life and parsimony, in the elimination of numerous Catholic holidays, and in the increase of the number of working days. From Geneva (the homeland of Calvinism) this doctrine spread to England (the Puritans), Scotland, the Netherlands, certain regions of Germany, France, Hungary, and Poland. As the religious ideology of the bourgeois era of the primitive accumulation of capital, Calvinism played a major organizing role in two early bourgeois revolutions—that of the Netherlands (16th century) and especially the English Revolution of the 17th century.

The republican organization of a Calvinist church was radically different from the hierarchical structure of the Catholic Church. Standing at the head of the church communion were the elders (presbyters), elected from among the lay members of the communion, and the preachers, whose duties were not connected with priestly activity but only with ministerial service (from the Latin *ministerium;* hence their title, "ministers"). The presbyters and ministers made up the consistory. Such an organization of the church provided scope to the influence of the most powerful people in the communion and was extremely beneficial to the economically strong stratum of the bourgeoisie; it also fully embodied the bourgeois ideal of an "inexpensive church" (simplification of ritual, the elimination of luxury, etc.).

Calvinism was no less intolerant of those who held differing beliefs (especially of popular Reformation movements) than was Catholicism. In contrast to the popular "heretical" doctrines that denied the need for the church as a social institution, Calvinism preached that salvation was possible exclusively within the framework of the church. The ecclesiastical organization of Calvinism was built on the harshest discipline and absolute submission of the rank-and-file members of a congregation to its leaders. This Calvinist ecclesiastical organization was adopted not only by the bourgeoisie; it was also a convenient weapon for the struggle of the aristocratic strata of the gentry against royalist absolutism, for example, in France (the Huguenots).

Calvinism, together with Zwinglianism, which rapidly merged with Calvinism, in its various denominations (the Reformed Church, Presbyterianism, and Congregationalism) achieved its greatest dissemination in the USA, Great Britain and certain of its former dominions, the Netherlands, and Switzerland; by the end of the 1960's there were approximately 45 million adherents of Calvinism.

REFERENCES
Engels, F. "Liudvig Feierbakh i konets klassicheskoi nemetskoi filosofii." K. Marx and F. Engels, *Soch.*, 2nd ed., vol. 21.
Kapeliush, F. D. *Religiia rannego kapitalizma.* Moscow, 1931.
Porshnev, B. F. "Kal'vin i kal'vinizm." In the collection *Voprosy istorii religii i ateizma,* issue 6. Moscow, 1958.
Vipper, R. Iu. *Vliianie Kal'vina i kal'vinizma na politicheskie ucheniia i dvizheniia XVI veka.* Moscow, 1894.   S. D. SKAZKIN   [11–684–1]

CALVINO, ITALO. Born Oct. 15, 1923, in Santiago de las Vegas, Cuba. Italian writer; member of the Italian resistance during World War II.

Calvino's neorealistic works—the novella on partisan life *The Path to the Nest of Spiders* (1947) and his collection of short stories *The Raven Comes Last* (1949)—express antifascist, democratic ideas. During the 1950's, Calvino intensified his social criticism, unmasking the antihumanitarian quality of modern capitalist society in the novellas *A Building Speculation* (1957; Russian translation, 1965) and *The Cloud of Smog* (1958) and in the cycle of short story-parables about the poor man Marcovaldo (1953–56).

Calvino is the creator of an original philosophical and allegorical prose genre, in which he poses acute contemporary ethical problems: the novellas *The Cloven Viscount* (1952), *The Baron in the Trees* (1957; Russian translation, 1965), and *The Nonexistent Knight* (1959) and the satirical, imaginative short stories *Cosmicomics* (1965; Russian translation, 1968). Calvino collected and reworked folk tales (the collection *Italian Fables,* 1956; Russian translation, 1959).

WORKS
Ti con zero. Turin, 1967.
Il castello dei destini incrociati. Parma, 1970.
In Russian translation:
Kot i politseiskii: Izbrannoe. Moscow, 1964.
["Rasskazy."] In the collection *Ital'ianskaia novella XX veka.* Moscow, 1969.
REFERENCES
Potapova, Z. M. *Neorealizm v italianskoi literature.* Moscow, 1961.
Pescio Bottino, G. *Calvino.* Florence, 1967.
G. D. BOGEMSKII   [11–685–1]

CALVO DOCTRINE, the principle of the inadmissibility of armed or diplomatic intervention by one state in another for the purpose of exacting payment of debts. It was proclaimed for the first time by the Argentinian legal expert and diplomat C. Calvo (1824–1906) in 1868, when European powers were intervening in Latin American countries under the pretext of exacting from the governments of these countries payments on the debts owed to citizens of the European powers. The principle was incorporated in several treaties concluded by Latin American countries among themselves and with European powers (such as the Italian-Paraguayan Treaty of 1893 and the French-Mexican-Nicaraguan Treaty of 1894). Early in the 20th century the doctrine was developed and to some extent altered by Drago, the Argentinian minister of foreign affairs.   [11–685–2]

CALYCANTHACEAE, a family of dicotyledonous plants. They are shrubs with opposite, entire, pinnately veined, exstipulate leaves. The flowers are solitary and bisexual; they have a concave calyculate torus with spiral distribution of its parts. The perianth consists of many petaloid leaflets. There are five or more stamens. The fruit is a compound nutlet. There are two genera, *Calycanthus* and *Chimonanthus.* The three or four species of *Calycanthus* are native to North America; the three species of *Chimonanthus,* to China. The species of both genera are often cultivated for their fragrant flowers. Of particular value is the *Chimonanthus praecox,* which blossoms in the winter and in the early spring. In the USSR species of the family Calycanthaceae are grown on the Black Sea Shore of the Caucasus and, sometimes, in the Crimea and Middle Asia.

REFERENCE
Zemiatin, B. N. "Kalikantovye." In *Derev'ia i kustarniki SSSR,* vol. 3. Moscow-Leningrad, 1954.   [11–603–1]

CALYPSO, a French oceanographic vessel. Built in 1942, the *Calypso* operates under programs of the Ministry of National Education and the Geographic Society of France. The vessel is 47 m long, 7.7 m wide, and displaces 360 tons. Its free cruising range is 5,000 nautical miles (9,260 km); it has a crew of 12 and ten scientific workers. The vessel is equipped with oceanographic winches and has special gear for underwater research and television and motion-picture filming. In 1967, under the command of J.-Y. Cousteau, the *Calypso* began research operations in the tropical seas of the world.   [11–628–2]

CALYPTROGEN, the formative tissue found in the growing point of a root, giving rise to the rootcap. Calyptrogen, as a rule, is characteristic of monocotyledonous plants. In most dicotyledonous plants, instead of calyptrogen, there is a tissue that also gives rise to the root's absorbent external piliferous layer; this tissue is called dermatocalyptrogen.   [11–628–3]

CALZABIGI, RANIERI. Born Dec. 23, 1714, in Livorno; died July 1795, in Naples. Italian librettist.

From 1750 to 1760, Calzabigi resided in Paris. In 1760 he moved to Vienna, where he collaborated with the composer C. W. von Gluck and the choreographer G. Angiolini. He participated in the reform of opera and ballet. Calzabigi expressed ideas concerning the reform of opera as early as 1755 in the *Dissertation on the Dramatic Poetry of Signor Father P. Metastasio.* He wrote the librettos for Gluck's ballets and operas (*Orpheus and Eurydice, Alcestis,* and *Paris and Helen*). Many Italian composers wrote operas to Calzabigi's texts.

REFERENCE
Michel, H. "R. Calzabigi als Dichter von Musikdramen und als Kritiker." *Gluck-Jahrbuch,* 1918, fourth year of publication.   [11–697–5]

CAM, DIOGO (or Diogo Cão). Born circa 1440; date of death unknown. Portuguese navigator.

In 1482, Cam sailed along the west coast of Africa between 1° and 13°30′ S lat., discovering enroute the mouth of the Congo River. Between 1484 and 1486 he advanced along the western shores of Africa to 22° S lat., thus discovering the entire coastline of Angola and a large part of the uninhabited southwestern coast —from the mouth of the Kunene River to Cape Cross. According to one version, Cam died on the return voyage; according to another, he returned to Portugal in 1486.   [11–863–1]

CAMAGÜEY, a province in eastern Cuba. Area, 26,300 sq km; population, 813,200 (1970). The province produces 25 percent of Cuba's raw sugar. It is also an important irrigated agricultural center, producing rice and citrus fruits. Livestock is raised for meat and dairy products. There are food (mainly sugar and meat), textile, and leather footwear industries. Agricultural machinery and artificial fertilizers are also produced. The economic and administrative center of the province is the city of Camagüey. [11–709–2]

CAMAGÜEY, a city in eastern Cuba; administrative center of the province of Camagüey. Population, 197,000 (1970). The city, which is situated on the Central Highway, is an important economic center of Camagüey province. There are food, textile, chemical, and agricultural machine-building industries. Camagüey, which was founded in the 16th century, is the site of architectural monuments from the colonial period.
[11–709–3]

CAMARGUE, a group of adjacent wildlife sanctuaries in France, founded in 1928, in the department of Bouches-du-Rhône. Total area (1970), approximately 13,500 hectares. The topography of the Rhône's ancient delta and several bodies of water of varying salinity have been preserved. Pink flamingos and white herons are among the approximately 300 species of birds that nest in the area. There is a unique juniper forest (*Juniperus phoenicea*) with trees up to 7 m tall and up to 50 cm in diameter. The Tour-du-Valat biological station studies the fauna and flora of the national park.

REFERENCE
Weber, K., and L. Hoffmann. *Camargue: Seele einer Wildnis.* Bern, 1968. [11–712–1]

CAMARILLA, a group of influential courtiers. The term "camarilla" came into use at the time of King Ferdinand VII of Spain, who ruled in 1808 and again from 1814 to 1833. During his reign his retainers, who actually ruled the country, began to meet in a small anteroom to the more spacious royal apartments (camarilla). The court clique under Ferdinand VII and several other Spanish kings represented the interests of the reactionary nobility and clergy and used its position for personal gain. The word "camarilla" has become a generic term. [11–712–2]

CAMASSIA, a genus of herbaceous bulbous plants of the family Liliaceae. The bulbs are small, the leaves are linear, and the flowers are in long racemes. The flowers are rather large, with a pale blue-violet or white stellate perianth. There are five or six species in North America. These plants are ornamentals.
[11–713–1]

CAMAU, a peninsula in southern Indochina, between the South China Sea and the Gulf of Siam, in the western part of the Mekong Delta. The peninsula is covered with swamps, some of which have been drained, and its vegetation is typical of alluvial plains. Mangrove thickets are scattered along the shore. Rice is cultivated on the peninsula. [11–713–2]

CAMBAY, GULF OF, a gulf in the northern Arabian Sea, on the western coast of India. It extends 250 km inland, separating the Kathiawar Peninsula from the mainland. The gulf is up to 36 m deep. The Narbada and Tapti rivers flow into it. The tides are mixed, reaching a height of 11.9 m. Port cities on the gulf are Surat (on the Tapti River estuary) and Bhaunagar.
[11–715–3]

CAMBIFORM CELLS, the elongated, living, thin-walled, pointed or narrow-tipped cells in the phloem of plants.
Cambiform cells have no transverse septa; they correspond in function to the cells of parenchymatous phloem. They arise from the cells of the procambium or the fusiform cells of the cambium and maintain a shape characteristic of both (hence the name). Formerly, the term "cambiform" was applied to all thin-walled phloem elements of the conducting bundles. [11–717–2]

CAMBIUM, the formative tissue, or meristem, primarily in the roots and stems of dicotyledonous and gymnospermous plants. The cambium is in the shape of a monostichous concentric cylinder (in cross section, it appears annular). As a result of cambial activity, the axial organs grow in thickness. Secondary phloem is produced toward the outside of the axis, and secondary xylem

toward the inside. Cambium originates from the cells of the procambium, which lie between the primary phloem and primary xylem. The pericycle plays an important role in the formation of the cambium in roots. It appears that there is no cambium in leaves; however, if there is any, its activity terminates at an early stage in leaf development.

Cambial cells are prosenchymatous in form—elongated, pointed (with beveled ends), and flat. They extend the length of the plant. Cambial cell walls are soft and consist of cellulose; the primary pit fields contain plasmodesmata. Cambial cells divide, becoming phloem cells (toward the outside of the cambium) or xylem cells (toward the interior of the plant). Usually, much more xylem is formed than phloem. As a result of the division of some cambial cells, tiny cells are formed; these make up phloem-xylem rays. The phloem forms on one side of the ray; the xylem, on the other.

During the autumn and winter, cambial activity ceases (in temperate zones). The periodic activity of the cambium results in the formation of annual rings. Depending on the character of cell division, cambium is divided into storied and nonstoried types. In some dicotyledons (such as beets), additional cambial layers form consecutive rings toward the periphery (polycambium formation). O. N. CHISTIAKOVA [11–716–2]

CAMBODIA

GENERAL INFORMATION
NATURAL FEATURES
POPULATION
HISTORICAL SURVEY
NATIONAL UNITED FRONT OF CAMBODIA
ECONOMIC GEOGRAPHY
HEALTH AND SOCIAL WELFARE
EDUCATION AND CULTURAL AFFAIRS
LITERATURE AND ART

General information

Cambodia is a state in Southeast Asia, on the Indochinese Peninsula. In the west and northwest it is bounded by Thailand, in the north by Laos, in the east and southeast by Vietnam, and in the south and southwest by the Gulf of Siam. Area, 181,000 sq km. Population, 7 million (1970). The capital is Phnom Penh.

Administratively, Cambodia is divided into the provinces (khet) of Batdambang, Kampong Spoe, Kampong Thum, Kampong Cham, Kampong Chhnang, Kampot, Kandal, Kaoh Kong, Kracheh, Mondol Kiri, Otdar Meanchey, Prey Veng, Pouthisat, Preah Vihear, Rotanokiri, Svay Rieng, Siemreab, Stoeng Treng, and Takev. The cities of Bok Kou, Keb, Kampong Saom, and Phnom Penh form separate administrative units.

Natural features

A large part of the country is occupied by the low-lying Cambodian Plain, composed chiefly of alluvial and lacustrine deposits. The coast along the Gulf of Siam is about 300 km in length. In western Cambodia are the Kravanh (Cardamomes) Mountains, with a maximum elevation of 1,813 m (Mount Aoral), which are composed chiefly of sandstone. In the north are the southern spurs of the sandstone Dangrek Mountains, and in the east are found the western spurs of the Annamite Mountains, which are formed predominantly from crystalline rocks.

Cambodia has a subequatorial monsoonal climate, with humid summers and relatively dry winters. The hottest month is April (temperatures 29°–30°C on the plain) and the coolest month is December (25°–26°C). Annual precipitation varies from 700 to 1,500 mm on the plain to 2,000 mm in the mountains.

The country has a dense river system. The largest river is the Mekong, part of whose lower course flows through Cambodia. The Mekong's water level fluctuates sharply with the seasons (12–15 m in the mountains and 7–9 m in the lowlands), with maximum discharge occurring in early autumn. The size of Tonle Sap, a large shallow lake in western Cambodia, also varies greatly.

Forests and thinly wooded areas occupy about three-fourths of Cambodia. In the east are deciduous tropical forests, and the mountains are covered with evergreen forests of valuable wood (sal, teak, and varnish and camphor trees), growing on lateritic soils. In the remainder of the country the prevailing vegetation is savanna with sparsely wooded areas and dense thickets of bamboo and shrubs. Mangrove forests grow on the coast along the Gulf of Siam. A considerable part of the Cambodian Plain has fertile alluvial soils.

The fauna is abundant and varied. There are tigers, panthers, black bears, and elephants in the mountains. Crocodiles are found in the Mekong and its tributaries, and the numerous waterfowl include pelicans and flamingos. Lake Tonle Sap is rich in fish.   N. M. KAZAKOVA

Population

The Khmer, or Cambodians, who number about 6 million (1970, estimate) and constitute 85 percent of the total population, live mainly in the central lowland. In the cities, the Mekong Valley, and the regions around Lake Tonle Sap there are about 200,000 Vietnamese, about 400,000 Chinese, and about 150,000 Cham and Malays; about 100,000 Upland Khmer (Kui, Mnong, Stieng) live in the northeast and about 30,000 Lao in the east. About 3,000 French live for the most part in the cities. The official language is Khmer, but French is also widely spoken. The Khmer and the majority of the Upland Khmer are Theravada Buddhists (some of the Upland Khmer have preserved their traditional beliefs), the Chinese are Confucianists and Mahayana Buddhists, the Cham and Malays are Sunni Muslims, and the French and some of the Vietnamese are Catholics.

The Gregorian calendar is the official calendar, although a lunar-solar calendar is also widely used.

The annual population growth rate has been estimated at 2.5 percent. Males constitute 50.2 percent of the total population and females 49.8 percent. In 1970 about 76 percent of the economically active population was engaged in agriculture, fishing, and forestry. The average population density is about 40 per sq km, with the highest density occurring in the Mekong Valley, around Phnom Penh, on the shores of Lake Tonle Sap, and in the coastal lowlands (250 or more per sq km). Northern and western Cambodia is very sparsely populated (two per sq km). Urban dwellers account for more than 12 percent of the total population. The largest cities are Phnom Penh (over 1.2 million in 1972), Batdambang, and Kampong Cham.

REFERENCE
Narody Iugo-Vostochnoi Azii. Moscow, 1966.

Historical survey

To the mid-19th century. Information about the earliest settlement of Cambodia dates from the early Neolithic period (fifth millennium B.C.), by which time tribal organization had already arisen and the population had begun to farm, fish, and hunt. By the middle of the first millennium B.C. the ancestors of the Khmer had developed a distinctive Bronze Age culture. The working of iron began at the end of the first millennium B.C., when the tribal system had disintegrated among the people of the fertile valleys of Cambodia and the Mekong Delta and the formation of a class society had begun.

The first state known to have existed on the territory of Cambodia was Funan, which flourished in the Mekong Delta between the first and sixth centuries A.D. The economic base of this society was the commune; its principal occupation was wet rice cultivation. The cities were large craft and commercial centers, and Funan maintained trade and cultural relations with southern India and China. Funan was a monarchy. Ancient Cambodia was strongly influenced by Indian culture, including Hinduism and Buddhism. A class society developed in the central and northern parts of present-day Cambodia between the first and fifth centuries. The states that arose in these regions recognized Funan's suzerainty until the middle of the sixth century, after which they became independent.

In the seventh and eighth centuries the states of Land Chenla and Water Chenla were established in Cambodia. In this period the economic position of the landed aristocracy weakened, such new forms of exploitation as *corvée* and mortgage appeared, the sale of land became widespread, and a free peasantry arose. Middle-level landholders in the service of the state became a more important element in Cambodian society. The civil service gradually merged with the higher ranks of the Hindu priesthood and acquired a hierarchical structure. Indigenous elements began to dominate the culture, and a written Khmer language developed. The Kambuja empire began to form in the Mekong Delta and adjoining regions in the ninth century, becoming the largest state on the Indochinese Peninsula by the 11th century. From the 11th through the 13th centuries Khmer feudal lords several times conquered Champa, waged wars with Dai Viet (Vietnam), and reached the borders of Pagan. Cambodian territory was greatly expanded. Prolonged warfare and the construction of many temples, such as Angkor Wat, Angkor Thom, and Bayon, were accompanied by a further subjugation of the communal peasants. Class struggle, manifesting itself in peasant uprisings, intensified. By the late 13th century the Kambuja empire had disintegrated, and by the end of the 14th century the theocratic power of the monarch had disappeared. The core of the ruling class comprised feudal chiefs without landed estates, whose payment for services was a share of the taxes collected from the communal peasants. When land ownership by temples (which had arisen in the ninth century) was abolished in the late 14th century, the number of peasants directly dependent on the state increased. A temporary economic stabilization of feudalism led, especially in the first half of the 16th century, to a growth of the productive forces of society—improvements in the irrigation system and expansion of rice fields. The 16th century saw the development and growing importance of cities, including Phnom Penh (which had become the capital in 1443), Lovek, Pursat, and Oudong. The royal government promoted the dissemination of Buddhism, and enormous statues of Buddha were erected. In the late 16th century Thai armies ravaged the western part of the country.

In the 18th and 19th centuries Cambodia's social structure rested on peasant communes that were as a rule under direct state control. There were few large feudal landholdings or small manors. In the early 18th century Cambodia's growing weakness brought it under the domination of Siam and Vietnam.

French colonial rule (from the mid-19th century to 1953). In the mid-19th century France, which had embarked on a policy of conquest in Indochina, sought to extend its colonial rule to Cambodia. In 1863 it imposed a protectorate treaty on Cambodia, which in 1884 was superseded by a still more oppressive treaty making Cambodia virtually a French colony. The Khmer monarchy, placed under the control of a French governor-general, retained only executive power in local affairs. In 1887, Cambodia, Annam, Tonkin, and Cochin China became part of the Indochinese Union, which the French colonialists established in order to centralize the colonial administration; Laos was later incorporated into the union. The Khmer economy came under the control of the French, who abolished the king's ultimate ownership of land and created a "concessionary reserve" out of which agricultural land was allocated to French citizens and to members of the bureaucratic elite who collaborated with the colonialists. Cambodia's domestic market was opened to the unlimited and tariff-free import of French goods, which delayed national industrial development. In addition to retaining such long-standing feudal taxes as the head tax and the land tax, the colonialists also introduced a number of new taxes, including taxes on livestock, on peasant homes, and on sugar and coconut palms. Direct taxes accounted for 50 percent of the income of the state budget, the bulk of which was spent on maintaining the colonial administration and army and on subsidizing French planters and entrepreneurs. The people resisted the subjugation of Cambodia and waged an armed struggle for the restoration of independence. The largest uprisings took place in the 1860's under the leadership of Atiar Sua and Pu Kombo and in the 1880's and 1890's under the leadership of Prince Si Vattha. The 1890's saw the beginning of the systematic colonial exploitation of Cambodia by French capitalists. During World War I (1914–18) the French imperialists increased their export of raw materials, and Khmer soldiers fought in Europe. In the 1920's there was a still greater influx of French capital into the Cambodian economy and an increase in the cultivation of rubber (about 60 percent of all French investments in Cambodia), corn, rice, coffee, and pepper, which were produced for export. In the late 1920's and the 1930's from 15,000 to 20,000 tons of rubber, from 150,000 to 250,000 tons of rice, and from 300,000 to 400,000 tons of corn were exported annually. An extensive network of highways was built. Industry developed slowly and there were only a few small mining and light industrial enterprises. French capital dominated industry and trade.

The major forms of exploitation were the rent-tax and the state *corvée*. Usury flourished, and from 80 to 85 percent of the peasant households were almost permanently indebted to moneylenders. Except on plantations, only a small fraction of the agricultural output was produced for the market, and there was little stratification among the peasantry. Buddhism dominated the Cambodians' outlook. The independence struggle continued in the form of peasant uprisings, the largest of which, the uprising in Kampong Chhnang Province under Atiar So (1926), was cruelly suppressed by punitive expeditions. In the 1930's many progressive representatives of the Khmer working people and intelligentsia joined the Communist Party of Indochina, which was founded in 1930. The national liberation struggles of the Khmer and Vietnamese peoples were closely intertwined. The national liberation struggle gathered momentum in 1937 and 1938 under the favorable conditions created by the accession to power of the Popular Front government in France. In World War II (1939–45), the Japanese occupied Cambodia (1940). Although the country formally remained a French protectorate, the Japanese occupation forces turned Cambodia into a military base, forced the population to construct military installations, intensively exploited the country's natural resources, and exported agricultural raw materials. The Cambodian people rose up against the intensified imperialist oppression. The insurrections that began in 1943 against the foreign imperialists—the movement led by the priest Hem Chieu and the armed uprising in Phnom Penh—were cruelly suppressed. In March 1945 the Japanese military command announced the dissolution of the French protectorate and the restoration of Cambodia's "independence." The resistance movement against the Japanese imperialists arose under the leadership of the patriotic organization Free Khmer (Khmer Issarak). After 1945, when the French imperialists landed troops in Cambodia in an attempt to restore their rule, the resistance movement turned against the French. On Jan. 7, 1946, the French colonialists forced the royal government to accept an agreement (modus vivendi) restoring the French protectorate over Cambodia. Between 1946 and 1949 the Khmer Issarak movement spread to the southeastern, southwestern, and northwestern regions; partisan bases were created; and people's committees operated in some of these regions.

The upsurge of the patriotic movement in Cambodia and throughout Indochina, primarily resulting from the defeat of the Japanese imperialists, compelled the French colonial administration to grant the country "internal autonomy." Elections to a constituent assembly were held in Cambodia in September 1946. The assembly ratified a constitution, the first in Cambodia's history, which took effect on May 6, 1947. The constitution confirmed Cambodia's "autonomy" within the French Union and laid the foundation for a bourgeois democratic regime. Cambodia was proclaimed a constitutional monarchy, and bourgeois democratic freedoms were guaranteed. The supreme legislative body was a parliament (the National Assembly) elected for four years by universal, direct, and secret balloting. All Cambodian subjects who had reached the age of 20 were granted the right to vote, with the exception of monks and servicemen and their wives. The constitution provided for the Council of the Kingdom as the second house of the National Assembly. The supreme executive body was the Council of Ministers.

Under the Franco-Cambodian treaty signed in Paris on Nov. 8, 1949, France recognized de jure the independence of Cambodia as an "associated state" within the French Union. The Cambodian legislature, however, refused to ratify the treaty because France in actuality retained the entire administration of the country. The national liberation movement in Cambodia was growing in strength, and a congress of people's representatives of all strata of the population convened in April 1950 on the initiative of the Khmer Issarak leadership. The congress formally approved the creation of the National United Front (Nekhum Khmer Issarak) and its program and by-laws and elected the Central Executive Committee. The congress also formed the Central Liberation Committee and adopted the Declaration of Independence of Free Khmer. To rally anti-imperialist forces and to coordinate the struggle of the peoples of Cambodia, Vietnam, and Laos to drive out the French colonialists, their common enemy, the creation of a united liberation front of these three countries was formally approved in March 1951. In June 1953 the French government recognized Cambodia's sovereignty in foreign affairs, and in August of that year agreements were concluded for the transfer to the government of Cambodia of full control over foreign policy and the judiciary. On Nov. 9, 1953, an official ceremony was held in Phnom Penh marking the end of French rule and the withdrawal of French troops. This day was declared a national holiday, the Independence Day of Cambodia.

Independent Cambodia. At the Geneva Conference on Indochina in 1954 the Cambodian delegation announced that its country would not join any military alliances and would not permit any foreign bases on its soil. The following year Norodom Sihanouk, who had become king on Apr. 25, 1941, abdicated in favor of his father Norodom Suramarit in order to found and lead the political organization, the People's Socialist Community (Sangkum). The Sangkum was victorious in the general elections for the National Assembly held on Sept. 11, 1955. The National Assembly voted on September 25 to replace the phrase in the 1947 constitution "Cambodia is an autonomous state belonging to the French Union as an associated state." with the phrase "Cambodia is a sovereign and independent state." The first Sangkum government, formed in October 1955, carried out various social reforms, including granting women the right to vote and recognizing their social equality with men (law of Dec. 6, 1955); voters were given the right to recall deputies. The government adopted a policy of developing the national economy, eradicating the consequences of colonial rule, and reducing the country's dependence on foreign economic aid (*see below:* Economic geography). At the same time monarchical groups within the country attempted to restrict the role of the progressive forces.

Cambodia pursued a foreign policy of neutralism and peaceful coexistence, joining the UN in 1955 and establishing diplomatic relations with the USSR on May 13, 1956. In 1957 a neutralist foreign policy was provided for by law.

When King Norodom Suramarit died in 1960 the throne remained vacant. The position of head of state was established on June 12, 1960, and invested with great power under the constitution. Norodom Sihanouk became the head of state of Cambodia. In 1962 the government proposed that foreign powers recognize Cambodia's neutrality and territorial integrity and give it international guarantees. In view of the increased subversive activities of US imperialism, the Cambodian government rejected American aid in November 1963 and requested that all American missions and services in Cambodia connected with American aid programs be closed.

On Mar. 18, 1970, a coup d'etat took place in Cambodia, removing Norodom Sihanouk, who was abroad at the time, from his position as head of state. General Lon Nol became the leader of the Phnom Penh regime that resulted from the coup d'etat. The armed aggression of the USA in Cambodia began in late April 1970. Under the pretext of eliminating the "threat to the lives of American soldiers in South Vietnam," large units of American and Saigon troops (20,000 men) invaded Cambodia from the south. Their strength increased to 80,000 by late May.

Cambodian patriots responded to the aggression with efforts to consolidate the progressive national forces, and the National United Front of Cambodia (FUNK) was created in May 1970. The FUNK emphasized in its political program that it would coordinate its actions with the struggle of the Vietnamese and Laotian peoples against American aggression on the Indochinese Peninsula. The Royal Government of National Union of Cambodia, headed by Penn Nouth and Khieu Samphan, was established at the same time. The patriotic forces of Cambodia created the Cambodian People's National Liberation Armed Forces, which began an armed struggle against the American and Saigon interventionists and the troops of the Phnom Penh regime.

The pressure of public opinion in the USA and other countries forced the American government to withdraw its troops from

Cambodia on June 30, 1970, although tens of thousands of soldiers of the Saigon puppet regime remained in the country and the US Air Force carried out heavy bombings of Cambodian areas held by the patriotic forces. The USA increased military and financial aid to the Phnom Penh authorities.

On Oct. 9, 1970, the Lon Nol regime in Phnom Penh proclaimed the Khmer Republic. In March 1972 Lon Nol disbanded the parliament and government and declared himself president of the republic. A new constitution was adopted by a referendum held in Phnom Penh on Apr. 30, 1972. A presidential election was held on June 4, and members of the National Assembly were elected on September 3 and the Senate on September 17. The Central Committee of the FUNK declared all these measures to be illegal. While pursuing in Cambodia a policy of "Vietnamization" (the essence of which was to make Asians fight Asians), the USA continued its military and financial aid to the Phnom Penh regime, and the US Air Force actively supported the operations of the Saigon and Phnom Penh troops against the patriotic forces.

Led by the FUNK, the Cambodian national liberation forces, composed of regular and regional units of various sizes and partisan detachments, gained strength. In 1971 and 1972 they were victorious on all major strategic points of the Cambodian front and were able to paralyze the operations of the Phnom Penh troops. By late 1972 the patriotic forces of Cambodia had liberated a large part of the country.

By 1972 the FUNK comprised the Peasant Alliance, the Association of Patriotic Teachers and Intelligentsia, the Union of Khmer Writers, the Association of Democratic Youth, representatives of national minorities and of the Buddhist leadership, several student organizations outside Cambodia, and other organizations.

The struggle of the people of Cambodia against the aggression of American imperialism was supported by all progressive forces, above all by the socialist countries. The statements of the Supreme Soviet of the USSR and of the government of the USSR of May 4, May 10, and July 15, 1970, condemned the aggressive actions of the USA in Cambodia. The heads of government of the socialist countries (Bulgaria, Hungary, the German Democratic Republic, Mongolia, Poland, Rumania, the Soviet Union, and Czechoslovakia) declared on May 14, 1970, that their governments would continue to render all necessary aid to the peoples of Vietnam, Laos, and Cambodia. In the address of the Twenty-fourth Congress of the CPSU (1971) entitled "Freedom and Peace to the Peoples of Indochina!" it was stated that the Soviet Union "consistently and vigorously supported and supports the liberation movement of Laos and Cambodia, which makes an outstanding contribution to the cause of peace and the national independence of peoples." The statement of the Political Consultative Committee of the member states of the Warsaw Pact (January 1972) expressed support for the Cambodian patriots. In 1975 the Cambodian patriotic forces gained a decisive victory and liberated the country's entire territory.

REFERENCES
Hall, D. *Istoriia Iugo-Vostochnoi Azii.* Moscow, 1958. (Translated from English.)
Dement'ev, Iu. P. *Politika Frantsii v Kambodzhe i Laose, 1852–1907.* Moscow, 1960.
Sochevko, G. G. *Sovremennaia Kambodzha (1941–1965).* Moscow, 1967.
Verin, V. P. *Gosudarstvennyi stroi Kambodzhi.* Moscow, 1959.
Mikheev, Iu. Ia. *Amerikantsy v Indokitae.* Moscow, 1972.
Inscriptions du Cambodge, vols. 1–6. Edited and translated by G. Coedès. Paris, 1927–54.
Aymonier, E. *Chronique des anciens rois du Cambodge* (translation and commentary). Saigon, 1881.
Malleret, L. *L'archéologie du delta du Mékong,* vols. 1–2. Paris, 1960.
Groslier, B. *Angkor et le Cambodge au XVI siècle.* Paris, 1958.
Briggs, L. P. *The Ancient Khmer Empire.* Philadelphia, 1951.
Coedès, G. *Pour mieux comprendre Angkor.* Paris, 1947.
Leclére, A. *Histoire du Cambodge.* Paris, 1914.
Dauphin-Meunier, A. *Histoire du Cambodge.* Paris, 1961.
Migot, A. *Les Khmers.* Paris, 1960.
Le Cambodge. Saigon, 1960.
Bibliografiia Iugo-Vostochnoi Azii. Moscow, 1960. Pages 173–75.

D. V. DEOPIK and IU. IA. MIKHEEV

National United Front of Cambodia

The National United Front of Cambodia (FUNK) was founded in 1970.

Economic geography

During the protectorate period, Cambodia served as a source of agricultural raw material for France. Since 1953, during the years of independence, the country has been gradually overcoming the legacy of colonialism. A two-year plan (1956–57) and a five-year plan (1960–64) for developing the national economy were adopted and essentially fulfilled. The economy comprises a state sector (industrial enterprises, the power industry, irrigation, communications, transportation), a national private capitalist sector, and a mixed sector in which both national and foreign capital participate. The government bought up some of the assets of the French companies, nationalized foreign trade and commercial banks in 1963, and established the National Bank in 1965. But foreign capital remains important in the economy; French capital is especially significant in the rubber industry. After the events of 1970 (*see above:* Historical survey) the country's economy was in an extremely difficult situation, and the American and Saigon aggression caused great economic damage.

Agriculture is the mainstay of the economy. According to UN data for 1966, agriculture, forestry, and fishing accounted for about 41 percent of the gross national product; industry, power production, and construction for about 17 percent; and trade, transportation, and other branches for about 42 percent. Farms of small and middle landowners predominate. Between 1956 and 1959, in order to reduce capitalist exploitation of the peasants, the government encouraged the development of supply and marketing cooperatives and expanded government credit in the countryside. There were 1,200 tractors in 1970. In 1967 agricultural land covered 3.6 million hectares (ha), or 20 percent of Cambodia's total area, of which 2.8 million ha, or 78 percent, were under cultivation and about 0.6 million ha, or about 17 percent, were pasture.

Crop cultivation is the leading branch of agriculture; the principal crop is rice, covering 66 percent of the cultivated area. It was estimated in 1971 that 1.9 million ha were planted to rice, chiefly on the alluvial land along the Mekong River and Lake Tonle Sap, and that the total harvest reached 2.7 million tons. Corn (94,000 ha sown, 122,000 tons harvested in 1971), sweet potatoes and yams, and soybeans are important food crops. Cambodia also produces sugar palms, coconut palms, sugarcane, black pepper, peanuts (15,000 tons harvested in 1970), tobacco, cotton, jute, sesame seeds, cassava, ramie, and kapok (coarse plant fiber). Among important fruit crops are oranges and tangerines (40,000 tons), bananas (141,000 tons), and pineapples (41,000 tons). The growing of hevea has become very important, and 35,000 tons of natural rubber were produced in 1971. Livestock is raised primarily to provide draft animals. In 1969–70, Cambodia had 3.3 million head of cattle, including 0.9 million water buffaloes.

The annual production of commercial timber is about 400,000 cu m. Other forest products include cardamom, gutta-percha, and lacquer. Fishing is especially developed on Tonle Sap. In 1968, 171,000 tons of fish were caught in inland waters and the Gulf of Siam.

Industry for the most part utilizes local agricultural raw materials. Mineral resources have been inadequately studied. Phosphorite, magnesite, iron ore, nonferrous metal ores, precious stones, marble, and basalt are extracted on a small scale. Electricity is supplied mainly by thermal power plants; 133 million kW-hr were produced in 1970. The principal processing industries include flour milling, rice husking, sugar refining, tobacco curing, fish packing, and the making of alcoholic beverages. Rubber processing and woodworking are also significant. Between 1956 and 1968 relatively large metalworking, woodworking, paper, textile, cement, food, and petroleum-refining enterprises were built in the state sector. The output of building materials has increased. Several industries were built with the help of socialist countries, including textile and paper factories, a plywood plant, a cement plant, a tractor and automobile assembly plant, a tire plant, a brewery, and a sugar refinery. Industry is concentrated in Phnom Penh, Batdambang, and Kampong Saom. Small-scale industry is found throughout the country, mainly in the private sector, and supplies the population with consumer goods and food products.

In 1970 the country had 652 km of railroad and about 5,000 km of paved highways. Waterways, especially the lower Mekong, are important in transport. Phnom Penh is a major center of river and ocean transport and has a freight turnover of more than 0.5 million tons. The seaport of Sihanoukville (Kampong Saom) was built in 1960 on the coast of the Gulf of Siam. Pochentong international airport is near Phnom Penh. Cambodia exports rice, natural rubber, corn, lumber, sesame seeds, kapok, black pepper, fish, and fish products; its chief imports are machinery, equipment, textiles, metals, and metal products. Its leading trade partners are France, Japan, Singapore, Hong Kong, the USA, the Federal Republic of Germany, and Great Britain. The monetary unit is the riel.　　　G. G. SOCHEVKO

Health and social welfare

Exact demographic data for the birth rate, mortality, and infant mortality are not available. Infectious, primarily parasitic, diseases predominate. Cambodia has a high incidence of helminthiasis—ankylostomiasis, ascariasis, and trichocephalosis. About half of the population lives in regions in which malaria is endemic. Diseases that are found everywhere include trachoma, amebiasis, typhoid fever, paratyphoid, fungus diseases, and arbovirus infections (dengue and the chikungunya), and there are frequent cases of mite rickettsiosis (tsutsugamushi).

In the central lowland region there is a high incidence of ankylostomiasis (especially in the southwestern and northeastern parts of the region), ascariasis, and trichocephalosis; salmonellosis and cutaneous mycosis are widespread. Cases of fasciolopsiasis have also been recorded in the lowland area, as well as clonorchiasis and opisthorchiasis (in the northern part of the region). Malaria is endemic in the mountain regions surrounding the lowland; cases of Japanese encephalitis have been recorded here, and also of wuchereriasis (in the foothills of the Kravanh Range) and taeniasis (in the northeast). Between 1956 and 1960 the USSR built a 500-bed hospital with outpatient facilities in Phnom Penh as a gift to the Cambodian people. In 1965, Cambodia had 70 hospitals with 4,700 beds (0.7 beds per 1,000 population), 273 doctors (one per 25,000 population), 13 dentists, 31 pharmacists, and about 2,700 auxiliary medical personnel (more recent data are unavailable).

　　　I. B. PANINA and O. L. LOSEV

Veterinary services. Infectious, especially parasitic, diseases predominate among farm animals. Leptospirosis and tuberculosis are major diseases of water buffalo. Many cattle are afflicted each year, especially during the rainy season, by pasteurellosis. Rabies (14 cases in 1971) and foot-and-mouth disease (five outbreaks in 1971) have been recorded. Melioidosis is enzootic and most frequently encountered among pigs; it is transmitted by rodents. There were 40 veterinarians in the country in 1971.

　　　S. I. KARTUSHIN

Education and cultural affairs

The first secular schools arose in the mid-19th century with the coming of the French colonialists. In 1953 the country had only 980 state primary schools with 173,000 students, about 1,500 primary temple schools with about 100,000 students, seven secondary schools, and one institution of higher learning. By the end of the colonial period about 80 percent of the population was illiterate. After independence, the educational system was greatly expanded. In 1965 the proportion of illiterates among persons over the age of 15 had declined to 67 percent. In 1967 state allocations for education amounted to 1.4 billion riels, or 21.6 percent of the budget.

The public education system comprises the six-year free primary school (two levels, three years each), the *collège* (four years of instruction), and the *lycée* (seven years of instruction, divided into two levels of four and three years respectively). The curricula of the *collège* and of the first level of the *lycée* are identical;

at the second level of the *lycée* students may specialize either in the humanities or in the natural sciences and mathematics. Graduates of a *lycée* receive the "full baccalaureate," which carries the right to enter an institution of higher learning. In 1965–66 the public education system comprised 1,129 state schools, 1,531 temple schools, and 93 secondary schools (20 *lycées* and 73 *collèges*). In 1968–69 there were 998,000 pupils in the primary schools and 107,000 students in the secondary schools. Vocational and technical education is provided by vocational schools and technical *collèges,* which admit graduates of primary schools. Skilled workers are trained by vocational centers. In 1966 there were 23 vocational and technical schools, as against five in 1954, the largest of which were the National School of Art and Crafts in Phnom Penh and a technical *collège* in Kampong Cham. In 1967–68, 5,800 students were receiving vocational and technical training. Teacher training is provided by pedagogical centers and the National University. Cambodia had nine institutions of higher learning, with 14,500 students in 1968–69. The largest of these institutions are the National University, which was founded in 1960 and has departments of medicine, pedagogy, law, commerce, letters and humanities, and the social sciences, and the Royal Technical University in Phnom Penh. Between 1962 and 1964 the USSR built the Higher Technological Institute in Phnom Penh as a gift to the Cambodian people.

In Phnom Penh are the National Library (31,000 volumes), the National Museum (founded in 1917, with a collection of Khmer art from the sixth to the 20th centuries), and the museum of the royal palace.　　　E. S. CHESHKOVA

Literature and art

The earliest traces of Cambodian literature of the pre-Angkor period (second to ninth centuries) are the Sanskrit inscriptions on the walls of the Vo-canh temple in present-day Vietnam (third century) and of the Tonle-Bati temple (sixth century). The first inscriptions in ancient Khmer date from the early seventh century. During the Angkor period (802–1433) there was a flowering of Khmer culture, which developed under the influence of Brahmanism and Mahayana Buddhism. Important writers who used Sanskrit were Yasovarman II, Kavisvara, Eukindra, and Subhadra, and major authors who wrote in Khmer included Kaosathitpadey Kau, Duong, Tieu Non, Neakpang, Samphear, and Phokdey. Some literary works of the Angkor period were written in Pali. Among important works are the lyrical narrative poem *Indravedi* and the epic *Reamker,* both written in Khmer and using themes from the Indian *Ramayana.* The most significant event in the literature of the middle period (1434–1862) was the folk narrative poem *Tum and Teav* (15th century) about a boy and girl's tragic love. Under the French colonial regime (1863–1953) Sottan Preytya En, Saom Loth, and Nu Khan continued to create traditional works. One of the best works of this period is the narrative poem *Sratop Tyek* by Bamrae Utey Ngyng, using themes from ancient legends. The 1930's and 1940's saw the appearance of the first novels with a humanistic orientation: *The Rose of Paili* (1936) by Nyok Thaem, *Sophat* (1938) by Rim Kin, and *The Wilted Flower* (1947) by Nu Hat. The Union of Khmer Writers was established in 1955, soon after the country attained independence. The works of such writers as Tuy Ol, Hel Sumpha, Suon Soren, and Nop Savan raised important social and political problems. Folklore is being collected and published.　　　IU. A. GORGONIEV

The most ancient works of Cambodian art are decorated ceramics of the Neolithic period and bronze articles from the middle of the first millennium B.C. The shrines (*prasats*) built in the sixth century in Angkor Borei and in the seventh century in Sambor Prei Kuk are rectangular brick towers divided by pilasters and crowned with a pyramid of pseudostories: the walls are decorated with stucco ornamentation and pseudoportals. In the sixth century Indian influence produced statues having soft and generalized modelling. The statues of the seventh and eighth centuries—graceful, elegant, full of life, and at the same time majestic—are more distinctly Cambodian. In the ninth century Cambodian architecture developed the complex of shrines and auxiliary buildings, surrounded by an enclosure (with a *gopura* gateway) and later also by galleries and canals (the Preah Ko in Roluos, ninth century; the Banteay Srei, tenth century). At the same time there arose the temple mountain—a terraced pyramid surmounted by one or five shrines and surrounded by galleries and canals (the Bakong in Roluos, ninth century; the Prang in Koh Ker, tenth century). In the tenth century laterite and sandstone replaced brick, and there was a florescence of ornamental carving in which dense floral designs were interwoven with figures of deities, heavenly maidens, animals, and monsters. The frontal statues of the ninth to 13th centuries are monolithic, with powerful contours and graphic, stylized detail.

The immense Angkor complex, built between the ninth and 13th centuries, encompasses many richly ornamented temples and palaces. The most important of the Angkor structures are the mighty Angkor Wat temple mountain (c. 1113–50), architecturally the most perfect, and the capital of Angkor Thom (late 12th to 13th century), an integrated and majestic architectural ensemble with huge faces of deities on numerous towers. The endless rows of reliefs in the galleries of the Angkor temples are outstanding for their lively and expressive depiction of battles and scenes from everyday life and for their rhythmic quality and lithe contours.

In the 14th century stone architecture declined, and the ancient cities were abandoned. Wood was used for the construction of palaces and Buddhist temples (for example, the royal palace and the "Silver Pagoda" in Phnom Penh) with galleries, roofs ending in sharp points, carving, molding, and gold painting on lacquer. Bell-shaped stupas of stone were built. In sculpture, stone gave way to wood and bronze (Buddha statues; statuettes of dancing girls and epic heroes), and relief was superseded by paintings (with size paint) on themes from Buddhist legends.

The buildings erected in the cities since the second half of the 19th century are in the style of French eclectic architecture. In the murals and paintings of Okna Tep Nimit Tlaka (early 20th century) decorative stylization is combined with the realistic portrayal of faces. The proclamation of independence in 1953 was followed by the planned development of cities, such as Kampong Saom (built 1957–1960) and Bok Kou (built 1962). Concrete buildings have been erected in cities, some using indigenous traditions, such as galleries, towers, and steeply sloping roofs (architect, Vanmolivan), and others employing the modern style, with loggias and sunshades. Many frame houses, often with porches, are being built in the cities and countryside. Among the traditional folk crafts are manual silk weaving, *batik*, carving in wood and ivory, metal engraving, painting on pottery, embroidery, and leather cutting (openwork panels, figures for the shadow theater). Painting and the graphic arts are developing (Ngok Dim and Sam Yun).   IU. D. LEBEDEV

The musical culture, classical musical system, and instruments of the Khmer have their roots in antiquity. Orchestras and various instruments are represented on the bas-reliefs of the ancient Angkor temples. The Khmer classical musical system reached its culmination in the Angkor period and since then has remained almost unchanged.

Khmer music is based on a pentatonic scale. Its structure is determined by rhythm, and therefore the most important part of the orchestra is the percussion section, including drums (sampho, chkhayam), double kettledrums (skor-thom) defining the rhythm of the dances and songs, and cymbals and gongs "singing" the accompaniment. The melody is played by the oboe (pei o, pei-pok, pra pei) or the reed flute (khlui), and the tonic is performed by stringed instruments, which were introduced in the 12th century and which comprise lutes (sadieu, chapei, and takhe) and fiddle-like instruments (tro-che, tro-sao, tro-kmae).

Performances of the court ballet are accompanied by a large classical orchestra differing from the popular orchestra only in the number of instruments. The Institute of Fine Art, founded in Phnom Penh in 1966, trains professional actors, musicians, and dancers. The institute collects instrumental, song, dance, and literary folk art, and adaptations of these folk forms are presented in temporary open-air theaters. A concert hall has been built in Phnom Penh.   I. B. MARUNOVA

Inscriptions giving the names of women dancers, singers, and musicians, as well as wall representations of jesters and buffoons, have been preserved in the ancient temples. There are three main types of theatrical performances—the court ballet, the shadow theater, and the folk theater. The court ballet draws on the tradition of medieval Cambodian ballet from the Angkor period. It is known as Siamese ballet because the actors were formerly of Thai nationality and the dancers were accompanied by choral singing of ballads in Thai; since the early 20th century theatrical performances have been given in Khmer. The subjects of these dance-dramas are ancient legends and fairy tales. About 30 such subjects are known. The main roles are played by women, and the troupe has two male dancers who take the parts of demons, jesters, and animals. The men wear masks, and the women perform without masks but use stylized make-up.

The shadow theater is usually presented during religious holidays. The themes and silhouettes of the puppets must conform strictly to tradition. The performances are accompanied by the narration of an actor standing behind the screen. The folk theater enjoys great popularity. There are usually two actors, and no costumes or sets are used. The performances consist of short scenes similar to the farces of medieval Western Europe. The dialogue is improvised, and there is much singing. There are permanent troupes in Phnom Penh, Siem Reap, and other cities. In the early 1960's an attempt was made in Phnom Penh to create a modern theater offering adaptations of plays by Shakespeare and Racine, among other writers. The State Dramatic Theater, which was founded in Phnom Penh in late 1955, strives to create a modern national repertory. The Cambodian Court Ballet toured the USSR in 1964 and 1969.

REFERENCES

Kryzhitskii, G. *Ekzoticheskii teatr.* Leningrad, 1927.
Vseobshchaia istoriia arkhitektury, vol. 9. Leningrad-Moscow, 1971. Pages 196–241.
Kim Saet. *Pravoat aksarsastr khmaer.* Phnom Penh, 1960.
Li Theamteng. *Aksarsastr khmaer.* Phnom Penh, 1960.
"Liste des manuscrits khmers." *Bulletin de l'Ecole française d'Extrême-Orient,* 1902, vol. 2, no. 4.
Leclère, A. *Les Livres sacrés du Cambodge.* Paris, 1906.
Coedès, G. *Inscriptions du Cambodge,* vols. 1–6. Hanoi-Paris, 1937–54.
Coral-Remusat, G. de. *L'Art Khmer.* Paris, 1951.
Maspero, H. "Les Langues Mon-Khmere." In *Les Langues du monde* (new edition). Paris, 1952.
Thiounn, S. Ch. *Danses cambodgiennes,* 2nd ed., Phnom Penh, 1956.

[11–717–3; update]

CAMBODIAN INSCRIPTIONS, writings found in Cambodia carved on stone stelae, at the entrances of temples, and on slate slabs. Most of the inscriptions date from the sixth to the 12th centuries and are written in Sanskrit and in old Khmer. Some of the inscriptions are royal edicts, most frequently transferring property to the temples. A number of them concern the settlement of disputes over land or other property and describe judicial procedure. One inscription contains an oath of officials to King Suryavarman I (1002–50). The Ecole Française de l'Extrême-Orient translates and publishes Cambodian inscriptions.

REFERENCES

Barth, A. *Inscriptions sanscrites du Cambodge.* Paris, 1882.
Coedès, G. *Inscriptions du Cambodge,* vols. 1–8. Paris, 1926–66.

[11–736–2]

CAMBODIAN PLAIN, a low-lying plain in the southern part of the Indochinese Peninsula, with an area of 200,000 sq km. Altitudes of less than 200 m predominate. The plain is bounded by the Kravanh (Cardamomes) Mountains on the west, by the spurs of the Korat Plateau on the north, and by the Annamite Mountains on the east. It is composed mainly of light alluvial and lacustrine deposits of the Mekong River and its many tributaries. Lake Tonle Sap, the largest lake on the Indochinese Peninsula, is located on the plain. The area has a subequatorial monsoonal climate, with annual precipitation ranging from 700 to 1,500 mm. It is covered primarily by thinly wooded areas, by savannas that appeared after the forests were cut, and in places by meadows and swamps. The Cambodian Plain is densely populated, and rice cultivation is well developed.   [11–736–1]

CAMBRAI, a city in northern France, on the Schelde River in the department of Nord. Population, 40,000 (1968). Cambrai is a transportation junction. Its industry is represented by the production of lace, batiste, and knitted fabric and of goods made from them, primarily underwear; beer is brewed and sugar and confectionery produced there.

In antiquity a Roman city called Cameracum, Cambrai became part of the Frankish kingdom in the fifth century and was given to Lotharingia (Lorraine) by the Treaty of Verdun of 843. In 1076, Cambrai won the status of a commune in a struggle against its bishops, who were foreigners imposed by the emperor.

During the Italian wars of 1494–1559, the League of Cambrai against Venice was formed in Cambrai in 1508, and in 1529 a peace between France and the Holy Roman Empire was concluded in Cambrai. France acquired Cambrai in the Peace of Nijmegen of 1678.

In World War I, Cambrai was captured by German troops in August 1914. On Nov. 20–21, 1917, the British Third Army of sixth infantry and three cavalry divisions, supported by 378 tanks, struck two German divisions near Cambrai. The suddenness of the action and the great superiority in men and matériel led to a rapid breakthrough. But the British command failed to exploit the success: the infantry and the cavalry were left behind by the tanks, which suffered great losses. As a result the battle became positional on November 22, and from November 30 to December 6 the German Second Army of General Marwitz, 11 divisions strong, suddenly and powerfully counterattacked and recaptured a great part of the lost ground, capturing numerous prisoners.

The Battle of Cambrai marked the first mass use of tanks and the beginning of the antitank defense. [11–736–3]

CAMBYSES II. Date of birth unknown; died in 522 B.C. Ancient Persian king of the Achaemenid dynasty; ruled from 530 to 522. Son of Cyrus the Great.

In 525, Cambyses conquered Egypt, defeating the Egyptian army at Pelusium, and took Pharaoh Psamtik III prisoner. After seizing the throne of Egypt, Cambyses founded what was, according to the calculation of the ancient Egyptian historian Manetho, the 27th dynasty of pharaohs. In 524 he invaded Cush but was defeated. Upon learning of the outbreak of Gaumata the Magian's rebellion against him in 522, Cambyses left for Persia. He died en route under mysterious circumstances.

REFERENCES
Dandamaev, M. A. *Iran pri pervykh Akhemenidakh.* Moscow, 1963.
Olmstead, A. T. *History of the Persian Empire.* Chicago, 1948.
[11–717–1]

CAMDEN, a city in the USA, in the state of New Jersey. It is a suburb of Philadelphia, situated on the left bank of the Delaware River. Population, 102,600 (1970). Camden is a seaport and a railroad junction. More than 30,000 people are employed in industry, which includes shipbuilding, radio electronics, chemicals, and the manufacture of plastic items. Camden was founded in 1681. The museum of the American poet Walt Whitman is located there.
[11–738–3]

CAMÉLINAT, ZEPHYRENNE. Born Sept. 14, 1840, in Main la Ville; died Mar. 5, 1932, in Paris. Participant in the French labor movement; a leader of the Parisian federation of the First International. Worker in bronze.

Camélinat was director of the treasury during the Paris Commune of 1871. After the defeat of the Commune, he emigrated to Great Britain. He returned to France in 1880 after amnesty was declared. Camélinat participated in the socialist labor movement. From 1885 to 1889 he was a member of the Chamber of Deputies. In 1920 he became a member of the French Communist Party (FCP). In 1924, Camélinat was the presidential candidate of the FCP in the elections of the French Republic.
[11–738–7]

CAMELLIA, a genus of evergreen shrubs or trees of the family Theaceae. The simple, alternate leaves are on short leaf stalks. The large, solitary flowers are white or red. There are five or more petals and many stamens. The common camellia (*Camellia japonica*) and its hybrid forms have single or double odorless flowers and are raised outdoors in the Caucasus and southern Crimea and indoors (often in greenhouses). The plants of this genus are propagated by cuttings and seeds. Tea is made from the young shoots of the species *C. sinensis* and *C. assamica.* The leaves of the tea oil tree (*C. sasanqua*), which is native to Japan and China, yield an essential oil containing 97 percent eugenol, a valuable disinfectant used in dentistry. Species are grown in the Black Sea regions of the Caucasus.

REFERENCE
Sealy, J. R. *A Revision of the Genus Camellia.* London, 1958.
[11–738–8]

CAMERALISM, a special program of studies of administrative and economic disciplines taught in European universities in the Middle Ages and in the universities of Russia from the 1850's. In Germany, for example, this program included economic, geographic, and other subjects. Cameralism received its name from the cameral managements established in the Middle Ages by princes, dukes, and kings with extensive business activities. The so-called cameral disciplines were taught at special university departments and special schools (cameral schools) for the training of bureaucrats and administrators for the affairs of the high feudal lords; disciplines taught included mainly mining, forestry, and agricultural sciences. Marx characterized cameralism as "a medley of smatterings, through whose purgatory the hopeful candidate for the German bureaucracy has to pass" (K. Marx and F. Engels, *Soch.,* 2nd ed., vol. 23, p. 13). [11–795–2]

CAMERARIUS, RUDOLPH JACOB. Born Feb. 12, 1665, in Tübingen; died there Sept. 11, 1721. German botanist; professor and director of the botanical gardens at the University of Tübingen (1688).

Camerarius was the first to demonstrate the existence of male and female sexes in plants. He showed that seeds do not develop when the female plants (mulberry and hepatica) are isolated from the male plants and when the staminate flowers (corn and hemp) or the anthers (castor-oil plant) are removed. Comparing the sexual parts of plants and animals, Camerarius identified the stamens as the male sexual organs and the pistils as the female sexual organs. He also identified the pollen in the stamens as the source of fertilization.

WORKS
De sexu plantarum epistola. Tübingen, 1694.
In Russian translation:
"O pole u rastenii." In I. Kel'reiter, *Uchenie o pole i gibridizatsii rastenii.* Moscow-Leningrad, 1940. [11–796–3]

CAMERON, CHARLES. Born in the 1730's, in Scotland; died 1812, in St. Petersburg. Russian classicist architect. Scottish by birth.

Cameron studied in France and Italy. In 1779 he began working in St. Petersburg as Catherine II's court architect. From 1802 to 1805 he was the principal architect of the Admiralty College. His most important project was a complex of buildings at Tsarskoe Selo (now the town of Pushkin). In the Agate Pavilion (1780–85) with the Cold Baths, Cameron used architectural motifs that were characteristic of Roman baths. His other buildings at Tsarskoe Selo include the Hanging Garden (1783–86) and Cameron Gallery (1783–86; ramp, 1793). In the latter building, Cameron effectively contrasted the massive, monumental forms of the ground floor and the light, open gallery of the upper tier. He also built the palace and park pavilions at Pavlovsk (1780–1801), which form a harmonious architectural complex with the surrounding park. The palace is characterized by classical clarity and elegance; the architect's imagination and his distinctive interpretation of classical architectural elements and decorative motifs are clearly revealed.

Cameron's interiors, including the Arabesque Hall, the Snuff Box, and the Green Dining Hall of the Great Palace in Pushkin, as well as the Greek and Roman halls in Pavlovsk Palace, are distinguished by an extraordinary refinement and elegance of form and decor, as well as by a masterful coordination of different materials. These interiors were all created in the 1770's and 1780's; they were destroyed by the fascist Germans during the Great Patriotic War (restored, 1945–69). Cameron also constructed the Razumovskii Palace in Baturin, in the Ukraine (1799–1803).

REFERENCE
Taleporovskii, V. N. *Charl'z Kameron.* Moscow, 1939. [11–801–2]

CAMERON, JULIA MARGARET. Born June 11, 1815, in India; died Jan. 26, 1879, in Ceylon. English portrait photographer.

Cameron took up photography in 1863. As an amateur, she lacked the technical perfection of many professional photographers. However, she surpassed them in her depth of understanding of a subject's individuality. She was particularly successful in revealing strong, intense characters. Her subjects, most of whom were friends of her family, included C. Darwin, T. Carlyle, J. F. W. Herschel, H. W. Longfellow, R. Browning, and A. Tennyson. Cameron's photographs were characterized by soft focus, gentle facial modeling, and a sparse setting. Most of her negatives were destroyed in a fire.

[11–801–1]

CAMERON, VERNEY LOVETT. Born July 1, 1844, in Radipole, Dorsetshire; died Mar. 27, 1894, in Salisbury. British naval officer, explorer of Central Africa.

Sent to help D. Livingstone, Cameron in March 1873 traveled west from the shore of the Indian Ocean at 6° 30′ S lat. On the way from Zanzibar to Lake Tanganyika he met African companions of Livingstone carrying his remains to the sea. Cameron reached Lake Tanganyika in 1874, explored part of its shores, discovered its western outlet, the Lukuga River, and reached the Lualaba River, which he rightly considered as belonging to the Congo system. He followed the Lualaba southward to approximately 8° S lat., traced the watershed between the basins of the lower Congo and the upper Zambezi, and reached the Atlantic Ocean at 12°30′ S lat. in November 1875. While crossing Africa, Cameron made about 4,000 altitude measurements, thus initiating the precise study of the relief of Central Africa.

WORKS
Across Africa, vols. 1–2. London, 1885–88. [11–800–4]

CAMEROON (or Cameroun), United Republic of Cameroon (La République Unie du Cameroun).

GENERAL INFORMATION
CONSTITUTION AND GOVERNMENT
NATURAL FEATURES
POPULATION
HISTORICAL SURVEY
POLITICAL PARTIES AND TRADE UNIONS
ECONOMIC GEOGRAPHY
ARMED FORCES
HEALTH AND SOCIAL WELFARE
EDUCATION AND CULTURAL AFFAIRS
SCIENCE AND SCIENTIFIC INSTITUTIONS
PRESS AND RADIO
LITERATURE
ARCHITECTURE AND ART
THEATER

General information

Cameroon is a state in Central Africa. It is bordered on the northwest by Nigeria, on the north and northeast by Chad, on the east by the Central African Republic, and on the south by the People's Republic of the Congo, Gabon, and Equatorial Guinea; on the west coast is the Bight of Biafra in the Atlantic

Ocean. Area, 475,400 sq km. Population, 5.84 million (1970, estimate). The capital is the city of Yaoundé.

Cameroon was divided in 1972 into administrative provinces (see Table 1), which were in turn subdivided into departments, districts, and arrondissements.

Table 1. Administrative and territorial divisions

Province	Area (sq km)	Population (1970)	Administrative center
East	113,200	280,000	Bertoua
West	13,500	1,000,000	Bafoussam
Coastal	21,500	650,000	Douala
Northern	165,300	1,580,000	Garoua
South Central	119,000	1,130,000	Yaoundé
Northwestern Southwestern	42,900	1,200,000	Bamenda Buea

Constitution and government

Cameroon is a republic. The present constitution became effective on June 2, 1972. The head of state and government is the president, who is elected by the population for a term of five years through universal and direct elections. The president appoints and dismisses ministers and their deputies, is the supreme commander in chief of the armed forces, and has the right to proclaim a state of emergency. The supreme legislative body is a unicameral parliament (the National Assembly), composed of 120 deputies elected for a term of five years through universal, direct, and secret voting according to an established principle of representation. The constitution grants the right to vote to all citizens who have reached 21 years of age. The supreme executive body, the government, is not responsible to the parliament. The administration in the departments, districts, and arrondissements is headed by officials who are appointed by the central authority.

Natural features

Cameroon is located in the equatorial and northern subequatorial zones, within the natural regions of Central Africa and the Sudan. Most of the shoreline of the Bight of Biafra in the north is low, sandy, or swampy, with wide estuaries. Rocky shores without natural harbors predominate south of Kribi.

Terrain. A lowland up to 150 km wide stretches along the coast, which is dominated by isolated, volcanic Mount Cameroun (4,070 m). An internal plateau rises over the lowland in steep spurs. The plateau in the southern part of Cameroon, with an altitude of 600–900 m, has a rolling landscape. The Adamaoua Plateau in the central part of Cameroon is more uplifted and dissected (average altitude, 1,000–1,500 m; highest peak—Mount Bambuto, 2,740 m). The plateau is marked by young lava fields and cones of extinct volcanoes. The broad Bénoué River basin separates it from the Mandara Mountains to the North (altitudes of 1,000–1,100 m or more). The extreme north of the country is occupied by the flat alluvial plains of the Lake Chad basin (altitude, about 300 m).

Geological structure and mineral resources. A large part of Cameroon is an extension of the early Precambrian crystalline foundation of the African Platform, a foundation composed of dislocated gneiss, crystalline shales, and granites; in the southeastern part of Cameroon the foundation has a sloping, Upper Proterozoic sedimentary cover, which forms the northwestern border of the Congo Valley. At the beginning of the Cretaceous period the coast of the Gulf of Guinea was greatly submerged, and much of it became part of the system of perioceanic depressions of Africa's western periphery. The border zone between Cameroon, Nigeria, and the Republic of Chad belonged to the southeastern wall and spurs of the Bénoué graben depression, which is filled with a great amount of Cretaceous and Lower Paleogenic deposits. The Bénoué graben runs parallel to a zone of fractures (the Cameroon line), which from the end of the Cretaceous period was the site of repeated volcanic activity (the Mount Cameroun volcano); in the same zone intrusions of young granitoids were found (dating from the end of the Cretaceous to the beginning of the Paleogenic period).

The most important minerals are Precambrian iron ores (total reserves, 150 million tons), gold, young mantle bauxites (the biggest deposit is Minim-Martap; preliminary estimates place the total reserves at 1 billion tons), and natural gas in the region of the Logbaba perioceanic depression (total reserves, about 400 million cu m).   V. E. KHAIN

Climate. Southern Cameroon has an equatorial and continually humid climate. The average temperature of the warmest month (February or March) is 24°–28°C and of the coldest month (July or August), 22°–24°C. The annual precipitation is 1,500–2,000 mm in the interior regions, over 3,000 mm along the coast, and up to 10,000 mm on the western and southwestern slopes of Mount Cameroun. The rest of the country has an equatorial monsoon climate with a rainy summer (from April-May to September-October) and a dry winter (lasting from four to seven months). The average monthly temperatures are from 19°–21°C to 22°–24°C on the Adamaoua Plateau and from 26°C to 32°–33°C in the lower regions of the north. In the north annual precipitation is 500 mm or less.

Rivers and lakes. Cameroon has a dense river network with much water. The basins of the Sanaga, Nyong, Ntem, and other rivers that empty into the Bight of Biafra cover the southwestern and central part of the country. The rivers of southeastern Cameroon (the Kadeï and the Dja) belong to the system of the Sangha River of the Congo River basin. The Bénoué River, the chief tributary of the Niger, rises in the northern slopes of the Adamaoua Plateau. The extreme north and northeast of the country (with the Logone and Chari rivers) belongs to the Lake Chad basin, the southern extremity of which is in Cameroon. The rivers have many rapids, possess an abundance of hydroelectric power, and are mostly not suitable for navigation (except the Bénoué and the sections of the coastal rivers near their mouths).

Soil and flora. Forests cover from 15 million to 16 million hectares, or about one-third of the country. Humid evergreen equatorial forests grow on red-yellow ferrolite soils in the south of the country, and mangroves grow along the coast. The humid equatorial forests have many trees yielding valuable lumber, such as mahogany (cashew, sapelli, and sipo), Persian parrotia (azobe), ebony, *Atzelia bipindensis,* obeche, and *Picnanttas angolensis.* The central part of the country has many parklike deciduous-evergreen forests and high-grass savannas of the Guinea-Sudan type on red ferrolite soils, and the northern part has savannas of the Sudan type and desert savannas on red-brown or black tropical soils. The highest regions are covered with mountain evergreen forests or secondary savannas on brown humus-ferrolite soils; Mount Cameroun has mountain-meadow vegetation above the mountain-forest line.

Fauna. The fauna of Cameroon combines elements of the forest fauna of the West African subregion and the savanna fauna of the East African subregion of the Ethiopian zoogeographic region. The forests abound in animals living in trees, particularly monkeys; there are also elephants, hippopotamuses, crocodiles, many birds, snakes, and a great variety of insects. In the savannas there are ungulates (buffalo, rhinoceroses, antelope, and giraffes) and predatory animals (lions, cheetahs, and leopards). Large birds include ostriches, pelicans, marabous, crowned cranes, and bustards. The fauna of Cameroon is protected in the Bénoué, Bouba-Djida, and Waza national parks and the Bafia, Dja, Douala-Edéa, Campo, and Faro preserves.

Natural regions. The coastal region is a lowland with mangroves and swampy forests and volcanic Mount Cameroun, which is marked by vertical topographic zonality. The low mountains of southern Cameroon have humid equatorial forest topography. The upland of central Cameroon includes a mosaic of seasonally humid forests and high-grass savannas in the relatively low eastern part and mountain-forest and mountain-savanna topography in the higher western part. The plain of northern Cameroon has dry savanna topography.
                                                        I. N. OLEINIKOV

Population

The majority of the population belongs to three language families: Bantu in the south and east (about 2.2 million, 1969 estimate), Eastern Bantoid in the center and the west (about 1.7 million people), and Hausa in the north (0.9 million people). The Bantu people include the Douala, Balundu, Basa, and Batanga in the coastal regions; the Fang, including the Bulu, Eton, Yaoundé, Bene, and Bete around the city of Yaoundé; and the Maka, Ndzem, and Kaka in the east. The Babinga, Baka, and Bakola Pygmies (about 10,000 people) also speak Bantu languages. The eastern Bantoid group of peoples includes the Bamileke, Bamoum, Widekum, Tikar, and Tiv; and the Hausa peoples include the Bata, Mandara, Masa, and Kotoko. Peoples of Central Sudan live in the north and in the central regions; they number about 35,000 people and include the Chamba, Mbum, Gbaya, and Bute; about 500,000 Fulbe live in the north. The official languages are French and English. Slightly more than 40 percent of the population practice traditional beliefs and rites, about 40 percent are Christians (primarily in the central and southern part of the country), and about 20 percent are Muslims (chiefly in the northern part). The Gregorian calendar is official.

From 1960 to 1970 the average population increase was 2.1 percent per year. The economically active population amounts to 3,153,600 people (1970 estimate), or 54 percent of the total population. In Eastern Cameroon about 90 percent and in Western Cameroon almost all of the economically active population is engaged in agriculture. A considerable part of the working class of Eastern Cameroon is engaged in agriculture, and many workers are employed in construction, transportation, and trade; the number of industrial workers is small. Most of the workers in Western Cameroon are employed in large agricultural companies. The workers of Cameroon are mainly rural migrants who rarely manage to break their ties with agriculture.

The population distribution is uneven. The average density is 12.3 persons per sq km (1970). The greatest population density is in the coastal zone (50 to 100 people per sq km) and on the plateau in the west (over 300 people per sq km); on the Adamaoua Plateau the population density drops to two people per sq km. The urban population amounts to 20 percent (1970). The most important cities are Douala (250,000; 1970), Yaoundé (178,000), Bafoussam, Foumban, Maroua, Kumba, Victoria, Garoua, and Tiko.

Historical survey

Man inhabited what is now Cameroon in very ancient times. Excavations near Maroua, Bétaré Oya, Yaoundé, and Okola uncovered stone work implements of the Middle and Upper Paleolithic eras. The earliest inhabitants are considered to have been Pygmies. In the first millennium B.C. there were apparently two centers of ancient culture in Cameroon, one along the coast in the region of Mount Cameroun and the other in the regions adjoining Lake Chad. The tribes living there engaged in hunting, livestock raising, and primitive farming. They had contact with the countries of the Mediterranean through the Sahara and apparently by naval routes. From about the eighth to the 14th century A.D. northern Cameroon was part of the region of the Sao archaeological culture, which was widespread in Africa.

In the 15th and 16th centuries the Mandara sultanate arose in the region of the Mandara Mountains; it included the northwestern regions of northern Cameroon. The sultanate was apparently dependent on the Bornu state. Islam began spreading from there to Cameroon in the 18th century. In the early 19th century the Fulbe, a nomadic pastoral tribe, invaded Cameroon, conquered the Mandara sultanate, and founded several feudal Muslim principalities—called *lamidats*—in northern and central Cameroon. The strong, feudal, centralized Bamoum state played a great role in the history of the peoples of central Cameroon in the 18th and 19th centuries; this state provided protection for smaller principalities in the fight against the Fulbe.

Among most of the peoples of southern Cameroon the primitive communal system was at different stages of disintegration in the 18th and 19th centuries. The state arose there relatively late and only among the Douala people. The first information concerning this state dates from the early 19th century. The Douala state developed on the basis of middleman trade with Europeans. The trade articles were at first slaves and later ivory, palm oil, and pepper. The Europeans brought in salt, fabrics, dishware, copper bars, and alcohol. The first Europeans to penetrate Cameroon were Portuguese sailors, who landed in 1472 on the Cameroon coast at the mouth of the Wouri River. Seeing a great number of prawns in the river, they called it Rio dos Camarões, or river of prawns; subsequently the Europeans extended this name to the whole country (Kamerun in German, Cameroun in French, and Cameroon in English).

Dutch missionaries and traders began arriving in Cameroon in the late 16th century, as did British, French, and German missionaries and traders in the early 18th century. An American Presbyterian mission was founded in 1885 and a German Catholic mission in 1890. In 1884, G. Nachtigal, a German traveler and emissary of the German government, imposed on the rulers of Douala a 30-year treaty whereby it would be a protectorate of Germany. After consolidating itself on the coast from 1885 to 1895, Germany began to move into the interior regions of the country. The rulers of several states of central Cameroon (Bamoum, Tikar, and others), weakened by internal feudal strife and attacks by the Muslim *lamidats* of Fulbe, made an agreement with the German conquerors. In other regions the Germans had to overcome the resistance of the local population and the armed struggle of several peoples, such as the Bakwiri (1891–94), the Basa and Bakoko (1892–1905), and the Maka and Ndzem (1898–1907). The borders of the German colony of Cameroon were fixed in agreements between Germany and Great Britain of 1885, 1886, and 1893 and between Germany and France of 1885, 1894, and 1911. Cameroon became an important source of agricultural raw materials for Germany. Palm-nut kernels, palm oil, rubber, and lumber were exported from the country. German monopolies and individual groups of settlers seized from the local population the most fertile and conveniently located lands and founded on them plantations for the cultivation of cacao, coffee, tea, rubber trees, bananas, and oil palms. Highways and railroads were built using forced native labor.

The oppressive foreign rule caused a new wave of uprisings— around Bacho in 1904, in Bamenda in 1904–07, in the Dja-Nyong interfluve in 1905–07, and on the Adamaoua Plateau in 1907. These uprisings were suppressed by German punitive detachments.

At the beginning of World War I (1914–18), Cameroon became a theater of military operations between the Anglo-French and German armies. Cameroon was occupied by the British and French armies by February 1916 and divided between Great Britain and France in March. Some peoples (such as the Douala, Bamileke, and Tikar) were split up. In July 1922 the League of Nations sanctioned the division and gave France a mandate over Eastern Cameroon and Great Britain a mandate over Western Cameroon. The colonial legislation of French Equatorial Africa was introduced in Eastern Cameroon, and Western Cameroon was incorporated into Nigeria, which was a British colony. Great Britain ruled its possessions through indirect administration; the old historical forms of rule were formally retained, and representatives of the local traditional aristocracy became part of the colonial administration. The British founded in Western Cameroon a large plantation economy, which made large masses of the peasants landless. France ruled its colony mainly through direct administration. French capital exploited the population first of all through nonequivalent trade, a taxation policy, and the use of forced labor. The peasantry of Eastern Cameroon was drawn into the production of export crops (cacao, coffee, and bananas). Eastern Cameroon became a source of cheap agricultural raw materials.

The peoples of Eastern and Western Cameroon unleashed a struggle against the French and British colonialists; there were disturbances and uprisings at various times, including in 1922, 1928–29, and 1931. In World War II (1939–45), after the French government of Pétain capitulated before fascist Germany in 1940, Eastern Cameroon joined the forces of the French Resistance and virtually freed itself of the control of the Vichy government. The National Council of Nigeria and the Cameroons, a mass organization of the native population founded in 1944, set forth for the first time the goal of political independence.

After World War II (from Dec. 13, 1946) the status of mandate territory for both parts of Cameroon was replaced by the status of UN trusteeship; France retained administration of Eastern Cameroon and Great Britain that of Western Cameroon, which was divided into Northern and Southern Cameroon.

The plunder of the natural wealth and cruel exploitation of the peoples of Cameroon by foreign monopolies and the continuing artificial division of the country caused greater and greater indignation in the population. The Union of the Populations of Cameroon (UPC), a party founded in Eastern Cameroon in 1948, took the lead in the struggle for independence. The party rapidly grew into one of the largest mass political organizations. The French administration repeatedly repressed the UPC (the directing committee of the party was arrested in 1950, and its regular congress was prohibited in 1952). In May 1955 the UPC organized a demonstration for the unification and independence of the country in several cities of Eastern Cameroon. The French troops fired at the demonstrators, and the UPC and its affiliated youth and women's organizations were outlawed. In response to the police terror, the patriots of Cameroon opened a partisan struggle, which began in 1955 and in the course of which UPC leader Ruben Um Nyobé died (September 1958). Under the pressure of the liberation struggle the French government undertook several constitutional maneuvers: Eastern Cameroon was declared a trustee state on Apr. 16, 1957, and a Legislative Assembly and a government were formed, but with extremely limited powers. However, these reforms did not successfully stop the liberation movement. With the struggle of the Cameroon people increasing in fervor, the UN proclaimed the independence of Eastern Cameroon on Jan. 1, 1960. In March 1960 the first constitution of the new state was published, and Eastern Cameroon became the Republic of Cameroon. On Nov. 13, 1960, the Republic of Cameroon and France concluded agreements on cooperation and technical aid; the government of Cameroon pledged to coordinate its policy of economic development and its foreign policy with France. France retained the right to keep its armed forces in Cameroon (the French troops withdrew from Cameroon in 1964); French companies were given considerable privileges.

After the proclamation of the independence of Nigeria in October 1960, a plebiscite was held, upon decision of the UN, in February 1961 in the northern and southern parts of Western Cameroon. Following the plebiscite, Northern Cameroon became part of the Federation of Nigeria; the inhabitants of Southern Cameroon voted for union with the Republic of Cameroon. The Federal Republic of Cameroon (FRC) was formed on Oct. 1, 1961. The member states of the federation were named respectively West Cameroon (formerly Southern Cameroon) and East Cameroon (formerly the Republic of Cameroon). Ahmadou Ahidjo, president of the Republic of Cameroon and leader of the Cameroonian Union (UC, founded in 1958), the ruling party of Eastern Cameroon, became president and head of the federal government; John Ngu Foncha, until 1970 leader of the Kamerun National Democratic Party (KNDP; founded in 1955), the ruling party of Western Cameroon, became vice-president. After the formation of the FRC the 1960 agreement with France was extended to the whole federation.

The long period of rule by Great Britain in Western Cameroon and by France in Eastern Cameroon brought about different levels of socioeconomic and cultural development for the two regions, weak transportation links, and differences in foreign economic and political orientations. The government of the FRC undertook several steps to strengthen the state and to create a unified economy; the Nigerian pound sterling in Western Cameroon was replaced by the African franc in 1962; the construction of highways and railroads linking the two territories of the state was begun; and a unified metric system was introduced on Jan. 1, 1964. The Cameroon National Union (CNU), a single political party for the whole federation, was founded in 1966. In addition to the UC, the new party included the KNDP and the parties of the legal opposition—the Cameroon National Convention (founded in 1960) and the Cameroon Union Congress (created in 1965)—as well as the legal wing of the UPC. The first congress of the CNU, held in March 1969, set forth a program for the development of the FRC, including attaining economic independence, strengthening the unity of the country, and forming a Cameroon nation. A policy of planned liberalism (see the section on economic geography) was proclaimed as a basis for economic development. As a result of the referendum held in Cameroon on May 20, 1972, the FRC was transformed into the United Republic of Cameroon (URC). A new constitution proclaiming the formation of an indivisible URC was enacted on June 2, 1972. The extraordinary congress of the CNU held on June 2–3, 1972, set forth ways for further stepping up the activity of the CNU within the unified state.

Cameroon was admitted to the UN on Sept. 20, 1960. In 1961 it participated in the founding of the Afro-Malagasy Union. In July 1973, Cameroon left this organization. Cameroon became a member of the Organization of African Unity in 1963 and of the Central African Customs and Economic Union in 1966. In 1962 and 1963, Cameroon and the Soviet Union concluded trade agreements and agreements on cultural, economic, and technological cooperation, and the two countries established diplomatic relations on Feb. 20, 1964. The government of Cameroon works for strengthening African solidarity and unity, against the racist regimes in Africa, and for the liquidation of the vestiges of colonialism on the African continent.

REFERENCES

Orlova, A. S. "Uroven' obshchestvennogo razvitiia narodov Kameruna k nachalu evropeiskoi kolonizatsii Afriki." *Sovetskaia etnografiia,* 1959, no. 5.
Istoriia Afriki v XIX–nachale XX v. Moscow, 1967. Pages 331–34.
Noveishaia istoriia Afriki. Moscow, 1968.
Lebeuf, I. P. *Archéologie tchadienne: Les Sao du Cameroun et du Tchad.* Paris [1962].
Mveng, E. *Histoire du Cameroun.* Paris [1963].
Mohamadou, E. *L'Histoire de Tibati.* Yaoundé, 1965.
Annuaire national 1967, République Féderale du Cameroun, Partie Histoire. Yaoundé, 1968.
Le Vine, V. Th. *Le Cameroun,* vols. 1–2. Paris, 1970.   V. P. LOGINOVA

Political parties and trade unions

The Cameroon National Union, or NUC (Union Nationale Camerounaise), was founded in 1966. The National Union of Cameroon Workers was founded in 1972 through a merger of the Cameroon Federation of Unions (founded in 1963), the Union of Denominational Workers Organizations of Cameroon (founded in 1962), and the West Cameroon Trade Union Congress.

Economic geography

General state of the economy. The basis of the economy is agriculture, specializing in the production of export crops. Cameroon holds the fourth place in Africa, after Ghana, Nigeria, and the Ivory Coast, in the harvest of cacao beans. The processing of agricultural raw materials predominates in industry. Foreign trade plays a great role. As a result of the long domination of German and later of French monopolies in Eastern Cameroon and of British monopolies in Western Cameroon, the economy is extremely backward, produces mainly agricultural goods and raw materials, and is greatly dependent on the world capitalist market.

After the proclamation of independence, the government carried out measures to strengthen and develop the economy; among others, it set up the Railroad Administration of Cameroon; the National Investment Company, the Cameroon National Society for Commerce, Industry, and Development; and the Society of Producers of Oil Palm Goods of Mbongo and Eséka. But on the whole foreign capital has not only retained but expanded its position in the economy of Cameroon. The policy of promoting private capital investments and the great benefits and privileges granted by the Cameroon investment code open new opportunities for the penetration of foreign monopolies into the economy. During the 1960's the French, West German, and American monopolies strengthened their positions in Cameroon, and the International Bank for Reconstruction and Development, the European Economic Community (EEC), and other international capitalist organizations were very active.

While the development of a private national sector has been promoted since 1969, the government policy also provides for a greater role of the state in the economy, for an increase in partici-

pation by the state in foreign companies and the development of such companies, and for the establishment of state enterprises and companies. The agricultural cooperatives are mainly purchasing and marketing cooperatives. A program of economic and social development divided into five-year periods has been drawn up for 1960 through 1980. During the first two five-year programs (1960–61 to 1964–65 and 1965–66 to 1970–71) the gross national product increased from 113.6 billion African francs in 1960 to 269.4 billion African francs in 1970–71. The third five-year program, from 1971–72 to 1975–76, provides for the development of an infrastructure and of agricultural production, for an accelerated development of the industrial potential, and for security for about half of all the investments from domestic capital investments.

Agriculture. Although communal farming has continued in most of the regions, it is disintegrating. Commodity relations and private peasant farming are developing in regions specializing in export crops, and a differentiation of the peasantry is under way. The northern regions have retained semifeudal relations.

In 1970 cultivated lands planted with agricultural crops amounted to 2.2 million hectares, or 4.7 percent of the total territory of Cameroon; of these lands 56 to 57 percent were planted with food crops, 14 to 15 percent with food and export crops (coffee and cacao), and 29 to 30 percent with export crops alone. Slash-and-burn farming is almost universal, and the main production implement is the hoe (on small farms).

The chief export crops are cacao (112,000 tons in 1971–72), coffee (89,000 tons in 1971), bananas (125,000 tons in 1970), cotton (18,000 tons of cotton fiber in 1971), rubber (12,000 tons), peanuts (195,000 tons), and oil palms (47,000 tons of palm oil in 1971). In the eastern part of Cameroon the production of these crops is almost entirely in the hands of Africans; in the western part most of the plantations belong to a state company, the Cameroon Development Corporation. Export crops are grown mainly in the Yaoundé-Ebolowa region (cacao), in the Nkongsamba region (coffee), on the slopes of Mount Cameroun, in the region of the city of Bamenda, and on the coast of the Atlantic Ocean (bananas, cacao, rubber trees, oil palms, and tea). Cotton and peanuts are grown in the north. Crops grown for domestic consumption include cassava (930,000 tons in 1970); millet and sorghum (426,000 tons in 1971); rice (22,000 tons) and corn (355,000 tons), mainly in the northern part of Cameroon; and sweet potatoes and yams, mainly in the southern part. These crops are grown on small subsistence or semisubsistence peasant farms. New export and food crops are being introduced, including tropical fruit (especially pineapples), sugarcane, tobacco, and pepper.

Livestock raising, which is basically extensive, plays an important role in the economy of the northern and western regions. In 1970 meadows and pastures covered 8.3 million hectares. In 1970–71 there were 2.1 million head of cattle, 350,000 pigs, and 3.8 million sheep and goats.

Only 7.5 million hectares of the country's forests are accessible for exploitation and 3 million hectares are actually exploited. Cameroon has a monopoly in supplying to the world market azobe timber, a very valuable tropical timber used in the construction of dockyards and in making sleepers; ilomba, sapelli, and cashew timber are also exported. Lumber is obtained from regions convenient for export, in the coastal regions, and along the railroads. Lumber procurement amounts to about 400,000 tons a year.

Fishing is developed in the coastal regions, in the basins of the Logone and Chari rivers, and in the Bénoué River. The fish catch is 15,000 tons in the sea (1969) and 65,000 tons in the rivers and lakes. A considerable part of the fish is exported to neighboring countries. Prawns are also caught.

Industry. About 4 percent of the economically active population is engaged in industry (1970). The mining industry is poorly developed. Mining of mineral raw materials, which is almost completely controlled by French capital, yields small quantities of tin (35 tons in 1971) around Mayo Darlé, gold (3 kg) around Ndokayo and Batouri, cyanite (disthene) near Edéa, and building materials.

The hydroelectric resources are considerable but poorly utilized. A hydroelectric power plant on the Sanaga River, which had a capacity of 197,000 kilowatts (kW) in 1970, produces the bulk of the electric power (1.2 billion kW-hr in 1971); the power plant belongs to the mixed French-Cameroonian Enelcam Society. There are also hydroelectric power plants in Dschang (260 kW), Foumban (128 kW), Buea-Njoke (1,500 kW), Macalé (720 kW), and Luermannfall (300 kW); there are 20 steam power plants.

The most important branches of the manufacturing industry are lumber and wood processing and the preliminary processing of agricultural raw materials, which are dominated by French private capital in the eastern part and by British private capital in the western part of Cameroon. There were about 30 sawmill enterprises in 1969; part of the output (up to 70 percent) is used for domestic consumption. The eastern part of Cameroon has enterprises producing wood plates, about ten furniture enterprises, and match, plywood, and parquetry factories. The processing of agricultural raw materials includes cotton-cleaning, oil, and soap enterprises; factories processing cacao and coffee; rice-polishing and tobacco factories; beer breweries; tea factories; slaughterhouses; meat-canning and flour-milling plants; sugar refineries; and enterprises for preliminary rubber processing. In this part of the country there are also a spinning and weaving factory, a dyeing combine, plants for the assembly of bicycles and transistor radios and for producing small agricultural implements, and two cement plants. The western part of Cameroon is the site of several sawmill enterprises and factories for the production of palm oil, tea, and rubber. The main industrial centers are the cities of Douala and Yaoundé.

Cameroon's largest enterprise is the aluminum plant in Edéa, which belongs to the mixed French-Cameroonian Alucam Society; the plant receives alumina from the Republic of Guinea and electric power from the hydroelectric power plant on the Sanaga River, taking over 90 percent of the power plant's electric power output; in 1971 the aluminum plant produced 51,000 tons of aluminum in plates. The production of corrugated sheet aluminum was organized in 1962, and the production of rolled aluminum, in 1968.

Handicrafts, which are developed everywhere, include pottery, weaving, leatherwork, wood and bone carving, and jewelry.

Transportation. The automobile is the chief means of transportation. In 1970 the country had 32,700 km of roads, of which 1,300 km were covered with asphalt, and 1,014 km of railroads. The trans-Cameroon Yaoundé-Ngaoundere railroad, 705 km long, is under construction (1972); its construction is being financed by the USA, France, and the EEC. The first section of the railroad, the 296-km Yaoundé-Belabo section, was put into operation in 1969. Sea transportation is almost entirely in the hands of French companies. The main ports are Douala (freight turnover, 1.8 million tons in 1970), Kribi (70,000 tons), Victoria (90,000 tons), and Tiko (90,000 tons in 1970). River navigation is possible only in the high-water season (from July to October) on the Bénoué River; the river port of Garoua had a freight turnover of 20,000 tons in 1971. The largest airports are in Douala and Yaoundé.

Air-Cameroon, a national airline created in October 1971, has international flights.

Foreign trade. Cameroon's foreign trade is growing systematically. From 1961 to 1970 exports increased 2.6 times and imports 2.8 times. In 1965, 1967, and 1970, Cameroon had an unfavorable balance of trade because of a drop in world prices on some of Cameroon's agricultural export products and a great increase in the import of equipment, machines, and semifinished goods. The chief export articles are cacao and its products (accounting for 31 percent of the export value in 1970–71), coffee (23.4 percent), aluminum (9 percent), lumber (9.4 percent), cotton fabrics (7.8 percent), bananas (about 1 percent), rubber (over 2 percent), tobacco, oil and nut kernels of the oil palm, and peanuts. The chief import articles are equipment (26.8 percent of the import value in 1970–71), finished goods (42.1 percent), semifinished goods (12.4 percent), food products (9.4 percent), and mineral raw materials (4.9 percent). France, Cameroon's main trade partner, accounts for 50.4 percent of Cameroon's imports and 29.6 percent of its exports (1970); imports from and exports to the other states of the EEC account for 19.1 and 40.1 percent of the total, followed by the USA with 7.7 and 9.7

percent and Great Britain with 3.7 and 1.9 percent. Trade with the socialist countries is developing. In 1971 the trade turnover between Cameroon and the USSR amounted to 5.1 million rubles, including Cameroon's imports from the USSR totaling 1.4 million rubles. Cameroon exports to the USSR coffee, cacao beans, cacao oil, natural rubber, and logs of valuable trees and imports from the USSR various industrial goods and food products. The monetary unit is the African franc; 255.79 African francs are equal to US $1 (May 1972).

Internal differences. The Coastal Province accounts for 4.5 percent of the territory, about 10 percent of the population, and nine-tenths of the total industrial output (aluminum-casting, food, textile, and woodworking industries); there is banana, coffee, and cacao cultivation and fishing. The West Province, accounting for 2.8 percent of the territory and 16 percent of the population, is the main region of banana harvesting in the eastern part of Cameroon. The South Central Province, accounting for about 25 percent of the territory and 22 percent of the population, is the chief region of coffee and cacao bean harvesting. The East Province, accounting for 23.8 percent of the territory and 5 percent of the population, is a region of lumber procurement and the cultivation of coffee, cacao beans, and rubber trees. The Northern Province, accounting for about 35 percent of the territory and about 30 percent of the population, is a region of nomadic and seminomadic livestock raising and the chief region for the cultivation of rice, peanuts, and cotton and for the production of dried and cured fish. The Northwestern and Southwestern provinces account for 9 percent of the territory and 16 percent of the population. Bananas, cacao, coffee, oil palms, and tea are grown along the coast, and livestock is raised in the mountains. Food crops, primarily root crops, are cultivated everywhere, and lumber production is developing.

REFERENCES
Loginova, V. P. *Federativnaia Respublikia Kamerun.* Moscow, 1968.
Golubchik, M. M. *Federativnaia Respublika Kamerun.* Moscow, 1968.
Mel'nikov, I., and V. Korochantsev. *Kamerun.* Moscow, 1972.
Atlas du Cameroun. Yaoundé, 1959.
"Le Marché Camerounais 1971." *Marchés tropicaux et méditerranéens,* 1971, no. 1,325. (Special issue.)   V. P. LOGINOVA

Armed forces

The armed forces consist of ground troops, an air force, and a navy. The president is the supreme commander in chief, and the state minister of the armed forces provides the general leadership. The army is made up of volunteers. At the beginning of 1971 the total strength of the armed forces was about 3,400 men.

Health and social welfare

Medicine and public health. According to incomplete data, in 1965 the birthrate was 49.9 per 1,000 population and the deathrate, 25.7; infant mortality is very high—137.2 per 1,000 babies born alive (1967). Pathology is dominated by infectious and parasitic diseases and avitaminoses. Onchocersiasis and genitourinary schistosomiasis are prevalent everywhere. Trypanosomiasis, loaiasis, and ancylostomiasis are encountered in the southern forest regions; leprosy is found in the center and in the west of this region; frambesia and foci of wuchereriasis, intestinal schistosomiasis, and amebiasis are found in the southwest. In the mountain region there are foci of taeniasis and malaria is endemic. Wuchereriasis is endemic in the northern part of the savanna region. The largest focus of intestinal schistosomiasis is on the Adamaoua Plateau. Wuchereriasis is widespread in the northern region, where there are also outbreaks of skin leishmaniasis and taeniasis.

In 1967 there were 85 hospitals and medical centers with 11,200 hospital beds, of which 7,400 were located in 50 state medical institutions (only 2.1 beds per thousand population). Outpatient service is provided by outpatient departments of hospitals, one polyclinic, 473 public health centers, 210 dispensaries, 15 medical posts, and one mobile brigade. In 1968 there were also 39 prenatal, six pediatric, and eight dental centers.

In 1971 there were 160 doctors (one doctor per 37,000 population), of whom 146 were state employees, 446 assistant doctors, 11 dentists, 55 pharmacists, and more than 650 intermediate-level personnel. Nurses and midwives are trained at schools in Ayos, Yaoundé, and Douala.

In 1967 appropriations for public health amounted to 2.5 percent of the state budget. In the same year the USSR presented to the Cameroonian people 700,000 doses of antitetanus vaccine and a medical library, and in 1971 it gave 100,000 doses of anticholera vaccine.

T. A. KOBAKHIDZE and O. L. LOSEV

Veterinary services. The tsetse fly causes widespread trypanosomiasis of farm animals (844 new outbreaks; all figures for 1973), which causes great damage to livestock raising. There are frequent outbreaks of emphysematous carbuncle (656) and hemorrhagic septicemia of cattle (121), caused by the large amount of precipitation and the swamps in many regions of Cameroon. Streptothricosis and babesiasis are noted in the savanna regions. Cattle plague and cattle pulmonary pneumonia (11) are enzootic on the Adamaoua Plateau, and there are cases of malignant anthrax (28) and foot-and-mouth disease (11). There are also incidences of rabies (seven new outbreaks among farm animals), rickettsiosis and brucellosis. Farm animals are widely affected by helminthiasis (dicroceliasis, fascioliasis, paramphistomasis, cysticercosis).

There were 19 veterinarians in Cameroon in 1973. French specialists from the Fort Lamy laboratory of the Republic of Chad conduct scientific research and practice to some extent preventive veterinary medicine.

M. G. TARSHIS

Education and cultural affairs

Since Western Cameroon was ruled by Britain and Eastern Cameroon by France before independence, the two parts of the country have different public education systems. The education system in Eastern Cameroon is similar to the French system, and instruction is in French. At six years of age children enter elementary school, which is composed of three two-year cycles—the preparatory, elementary, and intermediate cycles. At the age of 11 or 12 students take competitive examinations for admission to general educational or vocational secondary schools. Complete secondary education is provided by seven-year general educational and technical lycées. At the end of the lycée students take examinations to obtain the *baccalauréat*, which is necessary to enter a higher school. Incomplete secondary education is provided by four-year general educational and technical colleges. The education system of Western Cameroon is composed of the eight-year elementary school, broken down into two cycles of four years each, and a five-year secondary school. Instruction is in English. Both French and English are compulsory subjects in all the schools of the country.

The public education system included 60 percent of the children in 1970. In the 1969–70 academic year there were about 900,000 students in the elementary schools and over 64,000 students in the secondary schools. The church is influential in the public education system; more than 50 percent of the elementary school students attend missionary schools, and about 70 percent of the secondary school students attend missionary educational institutions.

Vocational and technical education is poorly developed. In the 1969–70 academic year there were 15,500 students in vocational and technical schools. The only school that provides a complete secondary technical education is the technical lycée in Douala. Elementary school teachers are trained by the normal school in the city of Nkongsamba and by pedagogical courses (more than 3,000 students in the 1967–68 academic year).

The largest higher educational institution is the university, which opened in Yaoundé in 1962. The university has three faculties—philosophy and humanities, law and economics, and natural science. The university has several specialized educational institutions. Yaoundé is also the site of the Higher Normal School, which trains secondary-school teachers, as well as the Advanced School of Agriculture and the National School of Administration. The higher educational institutions had 2,690 students in the 1969–70 academic year. The National Agricultural College and a forestry school are under construction in Cameroon (1972); the construction is financed by credit granted by the Soviet Union according to an agreement signed in April 1966. The largest library in Cameroon is the National Library of Cameroon in Yaoundé (10,000 volumes). V. P. BORISENKOV

Science and scientific institutions

The Council of Scientific and Applied Research, a government body, was set up in 1962; the National Office of Scientific and Technological Research was created in May 1965; and the Cameroon Association for Assisting the Development of Science was founded in 1972. The chief center of scientific research is the University of Yaoundé, where research is conducted by about 150 professors, of whom over 70 are Cameroonians. The main orientations are medicine, the geography of Cameroon, and the agricultural sciences. The university has a chemical laboratory for medicinal plants and a medical research center.

The Pasteur Institute in Yaoundé conducts research in virology, and the institute in Kumba carries on helminthology research. The Research Institute of Cameroon, jointly with the French National Institute of Geography and the French Office of Scientific and Technical Research Overseas, studies hydrology, hydrogeology, and oceanography and is working on the cartography of the country; a national atlas of Cameroon has been composed.

State centers of agronomic research engage in the selection of new crops and work in contact with French scientific institutions. (The French Institute of Cacao and Coffee, for instance, directs centers in Nkolbissong and Nkoemvone.) There are also agronomical centers in Guétale and Maroua (food crops and cotton), in Dschang (food crops, coffee, tea, and cinchona tree), and in other cities. French scientific research institutes for studying oil and oil plants, fruit and citrus fruit, cotton, and other crops have experimental farms and plantations in Cameroon.

A laboratory in Douala and a botanical research station conduct research in forestry; Victoria has a botanical garden.

REFERENCE
Le Deuxième Plan quinquennal du Cameroun. Paris, 1966.

V. P. LOGINOVA

Press and radio

French-language publications (1973) include the *Journal officiel de la République Unie du Cameroun,* an official publication published twice a month, also published in English; *La Presse du Cameroun,* a daily newspaper founded in 1927, with a circulation of 10,000 copies (all figures for 1970); *L'Unité,* the organ of the UNC, a weekly newspaper founded in 1959, with a circulation of 10,000 copies; *L'Effort Camerounais,* a Catholic weekly newspaper founded in 1955, with a circulation of 5,000 copies; and *La Semaine Camerounaise,* a Protestant weekly journal, with a circulation of 4,000 copies.

The Cameroon Press Agency, the official news agency founded in 1960, publishes a daily bulletin. Radio broadcasting started in 1955. There are radio-broadcasting centers in Yaoundé, Garoua, and Buea. Programs are broadcast in English, French, and the local languages.

Literature

Oral folk art, including legends, tales, and songs, plays a great role in the life of the peoples of Cameroon. In the early 20th century the Bamoum people had a native writing system (created by the ruler of the Bamoum state, the sultan Njoya). Three books had been written by 1921—a history of the Bamoum state (French translation, 1952) and medical and religious treatises. But this writing did not develop further. From the 1930's works in the local languages (Bulu and Douala), mainly folkloric, began to appear sporadically. The modern literature of Cameroon is written mainly in French and to a lesser extent in English (by writers who are natives of Western Cameroon).

The first works in French (transcriptions of folklore and ethnographic essays) appeared in the 1920's. The best-known writer of this period was I. Moumie-Etia (1889–1939). Literature began to develop in the 1950's, in the period of the armed struggle against the colonialists. The tense political situation and the national character of the movement lent a civic spirit to poetry and prose. This period produced the brilliant poet E. Yondo (born 1930), author of the collection *Kamerun! Kamerun!* (1960;

Russian translation, 1963), whose work is rooted in folk-song traditions. The social novel held the most prominent place in prose in the 1950's. Writers portrayed various strata of society and elucidated important problems of life in Cameroon. Their criticism was directed against colonialism in all its manifestations and against obsolescent elements of the patriarchal society. The most prominent writers of the 1950's were Mongo Beti (pseudonym of A. Biyidi; also wrote under the pseudonym Eza Boto; born 1932), author of the novels *Cruel City* (1955), *The Poor Christ of Bomba* (1956; Russian translation, 1962), *Mission to Rala* (1957; Russian translation, 1961), and *King Lazarus* (1958; Russian translation, 1966); F. Oyono (born 1929), author of the novels *Houseboy* (1956; Russian translation, 1964), *The Old Man and the Medal* (1956; Russian translation, 1962), and *The Road From Europe* (1960); B. Matip (born 1932), author of the novella *Africa, We Don't Pay Attention to You* (1956) and the fairy-tale collection *To the Beautiful Star* (1962); and the poet F. Sengat-Kuo.

The proclamation of independence in 1960 was followed by a movement for the unification of the country's cultural forces; the Cameroon Cultural Society, a local section of the African Society of Culture, was founded in 1962; the Association of Cameroonian Poets and Writers was formed in 1966; and *Abbia*, a journal devoted to cultural questions published in English and French, was first published in February 1963. The editor in chief of *Abbia* is the cultural figure, poet, and publicist B. Fonlon. The prose of the 1960's essentially develops the tradition of the social novel of mores. R. Philombe (pseudonym of P. L. Ombede; born in 1930), author of the novel *Sola, My Darling* (1966) and of the collection of novellas *Letters From My Storeroom* (1964); F. Bebey (born in 1929), author of the novel *Agatha Mudio's Son* (1968); and F. B. M. Evembe, author of the novel *Temporarily on Earth* (1966), all expose the conflict between the traditional way of life and modern times and denounce such survivals of the past as polygamy and the purchase of brides. J. M. Nzouan Keu (born in 1933) draws mainly on mythological materials for his novellas (the collection *The Breath of the Ancestors*, 1965).

REFERENCES
Gal'perina, E. L. "Literaturnye problemy v stranakh Afriki." In the collection *Sovremennaia literatura za rubezhom*. Moscow, 1962.
Ivasheva, V. V. *Literatura stran Zapadnoi Afriki*. Moscow, 1967.
Potekhina, G. I. *Ocherki sovremennoi literatury Zapadnoi Afriki*. Moscow, 1968.
Korochantsev, V. "Pod zvezdami nezavisimosti." *Literaturnaia gazeta*, Oct. 28, 1970, no. 44.   G. I. POTEKHINA

Architecture and art

In addition to traditional African round and rectangular huts (made of clay, stone, wood, or bamboo) on a wooden frame and with a conical straw roof, there are found in Cameroon (among the Musgo, a people belonging to the Mandara group) original cone-shaped dwellings (6–8 m high), entirely molded of clay like a large vessel. Triangular grooves creating an interesting plastic pattern are made on the walls of the hut as protection against erosion. The entrance and the walls inside the hut are decorated with incised or painted polychromatic geometric patterns.

In the late 19th century big cities (Yaoundé and Douala), built in eclectic Arabic and European styles, arose in Cameroon. In the 1950's and 1960's large modern public buildings (some of them designed by local architects such as Ngode and Collins) were built in the central regions and standard houses and barracks in the outlying regions.

Wood carving is common among all the peoples of Cameroon. Numerous household articles (chairs, benches, and armchairs) include complex carved compositions of small human, animal, and bird figures. Ritual statuettes in the shape of poles are carved of wood. To make these statuettes more picturesque, they are painted in bright colors, ornamented with shiny shells, bracelets, and beads, and small pieces of metal and glass are placed in the eyes. Cameroonians make a great variety of masks (most of them frightening) carved from one piece of wood, covered with leather, and brightly colored. Greatly distorted and exaggerated features and forceful and lush carving make these masks extremely effective. Various kinds of crafts are developed.

Cameroonians make clay vessels, pipes, and ashtrays; bronze jars, vases, and pipes are cast by the lost-wax method. Other arts include embroidery and the making of calabashes and various ritual objects of beads on a wire frame. A national art school is now developing; the painters and sculptors Abossolo, Kenfak, and Mpando have made great contributions to it.

REFERENCES
Ol'derogge, D. *Iskusstvo narodov Zapadnoi Afriki v muzeiakh SSSR.* Leningrad-Moscow, 1958.
L'Habitat au Cameroun. Paris, 1952.
Germann, P., and F. Herrmann. *Beiträge zur afrikanischen Kunst.* Berlin, 1958.

Theater

Dance and music game spectacles have been common among the peoples of Cameroon from very ancient times. Since the proclamation of independence, a national theatrical art has been developing and dance collectives and amateur theaters have been organized. The People's Theater of Cameroon opened with a play on a biblical theme, *Games About Adam* (1960), and then staged plays by the theater's director Boé A-Amang, *The Chase After Money* (1965) and *Lovers From Nowhere* (1968). The Avant-garde of Africa, directed by Dikongue Pipa, staged his plays *Legend of a Sorcerer* (1967) and *The Inevitable Compromise* (1969). Guillaume Oyônô Mbia's comedies of morals *Three Suitors: One Husband, Until Further Notice* and *Our Daughter Will Not Marry* are staged not only in Cameroon but also in many other African countries. In 1969 the Cameroonian Federation of Amateur Theater (founded in 1968) organized the first festival of dramatic art with the participation of 12 of the best amateur theater companies of Cameroon. In 1970–71 the federation held the First Theater Season, a nine-month festival, in the cities of Yaoundé and Douala.

N. I. L'VOV [11–803–2]

CAMEROON, an estuary in the Atlantic Ocean (part of the Bight of Biafra), on the western coast of Africa, near the country of Cameroon. It is formed by the common mouth of the Cameroon, Wouri, and Mungo rivers. The coasts of the estuary are low-lying, covered with mangrove vegetation, and indented by small bays (bights). The depth of the estuary ranges from 11 to 24 m, but decreases to 6 m in the sandbars at the entrances to the rivers. The tides are semidiurnal, with a height of 1.6 m. The speed of the tidal currents during ebb tide reaches 10 km per hr. The port of Douala is located on the Cameroon estuary.

[11–802–2]

CAMEROUN, a volcanic massif (mountain mass) in Africa, by the shores of the Gulf of Guinea. Elevation, 4,070 m. It is a trachybasaltic stratovolcano, with a dome-shaped form, gentle slopes, and numerous lateral cones and craters. The main peak is the active cone Fako, which last erupted in 1959. The greatest amount of precipitation in Africa (approximately 10,000 mm a year) falls on the western and southwestern slopes of the Cameroun massif. There are equatorial rainforests (partially replaced by plantations) along the lower sections of the slopes. There are mountain forests higher up and mountain meadows in the highest zone.   [11–803–1]

CAMILLUS, MARCUS FURIUS. Lived from circa 447 to 365 B.C. Roman general and politician of patrician descent.

Camillus was a censor, dictator five times, and tribune with consular power six times. According to Roman legends, Camillus captured the Etruscan city of Veii after a siege that lasted ten years (406–396). Accused by plebeian tribunes of appropriating the booty, Camillus went voluntarily into exile. After Rome was defeated by the Gauls (390 or 387), he returned from exile and defeated the Gauls; this earned him the honorary title of *pater patriae*, father of his country. In the 380's Camillus fought successful wars against the Aequi, Volscians, and Etruscans, and he repulsed a new attack of the Gauls in 367.   [11–822–2]

CAMISARDS (French word, derived from *camiso*, "shirt" in the Languedoc dialect), the participants in the antifeudal peasant and plebeian uprising of 1702–05 in the province of Languedoc in southern France. They became known as Camisards because they wore white shirts over their usual clothing.

The insurrection was caused by the violent measures taken by the government and the Catholic clergy against the Calvinists after the revocation of the Edict of Nantes of 1598 and by increased taxes resulting from the War of the Spanish Succession. The center of the movement was in the Cévennes Mountains, where the Camisards, under such leaders as J. Cavalier and Roland (Pierre Laporte), occupied villages and cities, burned Catholic churches, the homes of the clergy, and chateaux, and seized tithes and taxes from the tax farmers and tax collectors. The Camisards demanded freedom of worship and the abolition of taxes. The ideological banner of the insurgents was Calvinism with elements of a revolutionary peasant-plebeian heresy and an egalitarian program. The Camisards believed themselves chosen to establish a millennial "reign of equality and brotherhood." In 1703–04 the uprising spread to the regions of Vivarais, Le Puy, Velay, Rouergue, and Orange. Pope Clement XI proclaimed a crusade against the Camisards. Royal troops, led by Marshal de Montrevel, were sent to Languedoc at the beginning of 1703. After its troops suffered several defeats the French government was compelled to concede an agreement in May 1704 whereby the Calvinists of Languedoc were promised freedom of worship. The principal insurgent forces, demoralized by the betrayal of Cavalier (who was bribed by the government) and by the death of Roland, were defeated in the autumn of 1704. Nevertheless, the government succeeded in suppressing the uprising only in the spring of 1705, when it made concessions on tax matters. Outbreaks of the rebellion continued until 1715. The movement was especially strong in 1709 in the Cévennes and Vivarais.

REFERENCES
Korobochko, A. I. "Vosstanie kamizarov (1702–1705)." In the collection *Srednie veka*, issue 3. Moscow, 1951.
Engel'gardt, R. Iu. "Novye istochniki po istorii vosstaniia kamizarov." *Uchenye zapiski Kishinevskogo universiteta*, 1963, vol. 64.
Chabrol, J. P. *Bozh'i bezumtsy*. Moscow, 1963. (Translated from French.)
Ducasse, A. *La Guerre des camisards*. Paris, 1962.

A. I. KOROBOCHKO [11–821–4]

CAMISOLE (Russian, *kamzol*), a man's garment, fitted at the waist, knee length, sometimes sleeveless, and worn under a caftan. The camisole was introduced in France in the first half of the 17th century; in the 18th century it became widespread in other Western European countries and in Russia, with the introduction of Western European dress among noblemen. The camisole was made from broadcloth, silk, or velvet and decorated with embroidery, lace, or buttons. In the national costume of the Bashkirs, Tatars, and Kazakhs a sleeveless garment fitted at the waist that is worn by both men and women is called a *kamzol*. [11–821–3]

CAMÕES, LUÍS VAZ DE. Born December 1524 or January 1525, in Lisbon; died there June 10, 1580. Portuguese poet; the most important representative of the Portuguese Renaissance. Son of a nobleman.

Camões served as a soldier in Morocco (1549–51) and India (1553–70). His lyrical poems are filled with a sense of the disharmony of the world. The theme of most of his sonnets is unhappy love, and some are critical of courtly life. In his comedies, written approximately between 1544 and 1549, Camões adhered to the principles of the Italian humanist drama, glorified the Renaissance ideal of exalted love (*Filodemo*, published in 1547), and denounced despotic power (*El-Rei Seleuco*, published in 1645). Camões achieved world renown with his epic poem *Os Lusíadas* (1572; first Russian translation by A. Dmitriev, 1788), which takes its name from the mythological Lusus, from whom, according to legend, the Portuguese are descended. The poem relates the voyage of Vasco da Gama to India and its colonization by the Portuguese. Many pages of *Os Lusíadas* describe the courage, heroism, and fortitude of the people. Glorifying the history of Portugal and extolling his people's striving to expand their knowledge of the world and their practical activity, Camões overlooked the tragic consequences of the conquests for the subjugated peoples. His faith in the unlimited possibilities of reason and his exposure of universal venality and of the power of gold make *Os Lusíadas* one of the outstanding works of Renaissance humanism. Establishing the standards of the Portuguese literary language, this work was significant in shaping the realist school in poetry.

WORKS
Obras completas, vols. 1–5. Lisbon, 1946–54.
In Russian translation:
Luziady (excerpts). In *Khrestomatiia po zarubezhnoi literature: Epokha Vozrozhdeniia*, vol. 1. Compiled by B. I. Purishev. Moscow, 1959.
Sonety. Translated from the Portuguese, with a preface, by V. Levik. Moscow, 1964.

REFERENCES
Braga, T. *Camões: A obra lírica e épica*. Porto, 1911.
Cidade, H. *Luís de Camões*, vols. 1–3. Lisbon, 1952–56.
Nogueira, J. *Os Lusíadas de Luís de Camões*. Rio de Janeiro, 1960.
Nogueira, J. *Dicionário e gramática de "Os Lusíadas."* Rio de Janeiro, 1960.
Domingues, M. *Camões: A sua vida e a sua época*. [Lisbon, 1968.]
Bismut, R. *La lirique de Camões*. [Paris, 1970.]

Z. I. PLAVSKIN [11–834–4]

CAMORRA, a secret society of bandits in southern Italy, similar to the Mafia. It became particularly widespread in the 18th century on the mainland part of the Kingdom of the Two Sicilies. It drew its members from among the *déclassés* of the towns and villages. It had an extensive network and its own hierarchy, laws, and jargon.

During the Bourbon Restoration (1815–60) it was used by the monarchy to suppress antifeudal movements. After the unification of Italy, it became a tool of separatist groups in the south, which brought on governmental persecution and led to its decline at the turn of the century. Remnants of the *camorristi* formed gangs of extortioners, and the word has become synonymous in Italian with extortion and violence. [11–834–2]

CAMOTES, an interisland sea in the Philippine archipelago, between the islands of Leyte, Bohol, and Cebu.

The Camotes Sea joins the Visayan Sea to the north and the Mindanao Sea to the south, through the Canigao Channel and the Bohol Strait. The shores are low-lying in some places and steep in others. The depth of the sea reaches 323 m. The Camotes Islands are located toward the central part of the sea. The climate is tropical monsoon; typhoons are common from June through October. The water temperature in winter is 24°–27°C; in summer, 28°–29°C. The salinity is approximately 34.5 parts per thousand. The tides are irregular semidiurnal (1–2 m). Fishing is of local importance. The ports include San Isidro and Palompon (Leyte), Cebu (Cebu), and Talibon (Bohol Island). [11–834–3]

CAMOUFLAGE PAINTING one of the types of concealment painting used to make it difficult to recognize various objects by visual-optic and photographic means of reconnaissance. Camouflage painting most often involves the use of two or three colors in large spots in order to distort the external appearance of the object (for example, the tank, building, airfield, or ship). The color of particular spots and strips of paint are merged with the surrounding background. The spots and strips are usually different in shape and size, at an angle of 30°–60° to the contours of the object, and overlap from one surface of the object to another. [11–847–5]

CAMOUFLET. (1) The explosion of an artillery shell, mine, or aerial bomb underground without forming a crater; it is sometimes detected by the underground sound of the explosion, by the slight swelling of the ground above the point of the explosion, or by smoke escaping to the surface through cracks.

(2) An underground explosion especially arranged to destroy enemy underground structures.

(3) In a metaphorical sense—an unexpected unpleasantness, a dirty trick, a failure. [11–847–3]

CAMOUFLET BLASTING, the explosion of deep-lying explosive charges, which destroys or deforms the surrounding medium but does not cause residual deformation of the surface. Camouflet blasting is used to form underground cavities as storage areas for liquids and gases, to break up solid mineral products at great depths for the purpose of extracting them by mining or leaching, to reduce the stability of a coal mass and give it the necessary pliability when seams being worked are dangerous in terms of sudden blowouts of coal and gas, and to discharge rock pressure and degas such seams (camouflet-squall blasting with charges set in an area of stress concentration in front of the working face). [11–847–4]

CAMPAIGN (Russian *kampaniia,* from the French *campagne*). **(1)** Specially organized work for a certain period, activities aimed at implementing important recurring social and political, economic, or cultural measures (for example, election campaigns, sowing campaigns).

(2) In Russian a word referring to a period of uninterrupted operation of a unit, mechanism, or machine; the duration of its work from the moment it is started until it is stopped for a major overhaul (for example, the *kampaniia* of a blast furnace).

(3) A military campaign. [11–837–3]

CAMPANA, DINO. Born Aug. 20, 1885, in Marradi, Tuscany; died Mar. 1, 1932, in Castel Pucci, Tuscany. Italian poet.

Campana led a wandering life, attempting many professions. In *Orphic Songs* (1914), the only collection of his poetry and rhythmic prose published during his lifetime, he expressed the spiritual crisis in which Italian culture found itself prior to World War I. Anxiety, escape from the commonplace, and futile flights toward the unattainable are his main poetic themes. He often sacrifices logical construction for melodiousness. His poetry has a powerfully morbid, irrational basis, and the images take on symbolic meanings. He spent the last 14 years of his life in a mental hospital.

WORKS
Canti orfici e altri scritti, new ed. Florence, 1952.
In Russian translation:
["Stikhi."] In *Ital'ianskaia lirika, XX vek.* Moscow, 1968.
REFERENCES
Gerola, G. *Dino Campana.* Florence, 1955.
Galimberti, C. *Dino Campana.* [Milan, 1967.] [11–835–2]

CAMPANELLA, TOMMASO. Born Sept. 5, 1568, in Stilo, Italy; died May 21, 1639, in Paris. Italian philosopher, poet, and political figure; creator of a communist utopia. Son of a shoemaker; Dominican friar from 1582.

In 1591, Campanella published his *Philosophia sensibus demonstrata* in defense of the philosophy of nature of B. Telesio and against Scholastic Aristotelianism. He was prosecuted by an ecclesiastical court on charges of heresy. In 1598–99 he led a conspiracy in Calabria against Spanish rule; captured, he was sentenced to life imprisonment. During nearly 27 years of confinement in Neapolitan prisons he wrote dozens of works on philosophy, politics, astronomy, and medicine, of which some were published in Germany and others circulated in manuscript. In 1626, through the intervention of Pope Urban VIII, who had become interested in his astrological prophecies, Campanella was put under the supervision of the Roman Inquisition; in May 1629 he was freed and acquitted. In 1634 he escaped to France, where, under the protection of Cardinal Richelieu, he was able to publish some of his writings.

In philosophy Campanella propounded the necessity of empirical knowledge and developed a doctrine of dual revelation (nature and Scripture). He defended Galileo but did not accept the idea of the infinity of the universe, although he did acknowledge the existence of a plurality of worlds.

His communist utopia is a program for general social transformation on the basis of communal property (*City of the Sun,* written in the form of a mariner's tale in 1602; published 1623; Russian translation, 1906) under a universal theocracy (*The Messiah's Monarchy*). In his ideal communist community, private property and the family have been abolished and children are raised by the state; labor is honored and is equally obligatory for all; the workday has been shortened to four hours, owing to a high level of productivity and the use of machines; and much attention is given to the development of science ("magical knowledge") and to education and vocational training. The leadership of the communist community is exercised by a caste of scholar-priests. After the collapse of the Calabrian conspiracy, Campanella rested his hopes for the realization of his program on European sovereigns (at first the Spanish king and later the French) and the pope. He strove for the spiritual unity of mankind within a Catholicism reformed in accordance with his ideals.

Campanella's nature philosophy was one of the prerequisites for the new natural science, and his communist utopia makes him an early precursor of scientific socialism.

His poetry (*canzoni,* madrigals, sonnets) affirms with great power his faith in human reason and exposes the contradictions between the individual's unhappy fate and the perfection of the universe, as well as the tragedy of the man who has lighted the torch of knowledge in darkness.

WORKS
Poesie filosofiche. Lugano, 1834.
Tutte le opere, vol. 1. Milan–Verona, 1954.
Lettere. Bari, 1927.
Opuscoli inediti. Florence, 1951.
Cosmologia. Rome, 1964.
I sacri segni, vols. 1–6. Rome, 1965–68.
In Russian translation:
In *Antologiia mirovoi filosofii,* vol. 2. Moscow, 1970. Pages 180–92.
REFERENCES
Rutenburg, V. I. *Kampanella.* Leningrad, 1956.
Shtekli, A. E. *Kampanella.* Moscow, 1966.
Gorfunkel', A. Kh. *Tommazo Kampanella.* Moscow, 1969. (With bibliography.)
De Sanctis, F. *Istoriia ital'ianskoi literatury,* vol. 2. Moscow, 1964. (Translated from Italian.)
Storia della letteratura italiana, vol. 5: *Il seicento.* Milan, 1967.
Bonansea, B. M. *T. Campanella.* Washington, 1969.
Badaloni, N. *Tommaso Campanella.* Milan, 1965.
Corsano, A. *Tommaso Campanella.* Bari, 1961.
Firpo, L. *Bibliografia degli scritti di Tommaso Campanella.* Turin, 1940.
Firpo, L. *Ricerche Campanelliane.* Florence, 1947.
A. Kh. Gorfunkel' [11–836–1]

CAMPANELLA, a musical piece imitating the sound of small bells. The Italian violinist and composer N. Paganini called the rondo of his Concerto in B Minor for Violin and Orchestra *La Campanella.* The piano transcription of the rondo by F. Liszt is extremely popular. [11–837–1]

CAMPANIA, an administrative region in southern Italy, with an area of 13,600 sq km and a population of 5.2 million (1970). It comprises the provinces of Avellino, Benevento, Caserta, Naples, and Salerno, and its capital is Naples, a leading Italian port.

The coastline of the Tyrrhenian Sea is strongly indented. The Apennine mountain system extends through the entire region. There is much volcanic and seismic activity (the active volcano Vesuvius). The climate is Mediterranean on the coast (with an annual precipitation of more than 650 mm) and colder in the mountains, with snowfall in winter. The soil on the volcanic rock is fertile.

Campania is the most economically developed region of southern Italy. Nearly 36 percent of the economically active population is engaged in agriculture. Early vegetables and fruit, including citrus fruit, are grown on the coastal plains, and wheat and corn are the principal crops in other areas. Campania produces 98 percent of Italy's hemp, a third of its tomato and tobacco harvests, and a fourth of its potato crop. On the hillsides are vineyards and olive groves. Animal husbandry is of secondary importance, with sheep raising predominating (452,000 head in 1970).

The chief industries (employing more than a third of the labor force) are metallurgy, shipbuilding, the production of railroad equipment, electrical engineering, radio electronics, oil refining, cement production, and armaments. There are also large flour mills, macaroni factories, and canneries. The region accounts for nearly a twentieth of the national output of electric power (in 1970, 5 billion kW-hr, primarily by steam power plants). Industry is concentrated along the coast of the Bay of Naples, where the industrial enterprises of Naples and nearby towns form the only large industrial complex in southern Italy (Greater Naples), with which the district of Caserta (radio electronics) is closely connected.

The region has a well-developed tourist industry. Its seaside resorts, such as Sorrento, Pozzuoli, Capri, and Ischia, are widely known.

At the beginning of the first millennium B.C., Campania was inhabited by Oscan tribes. From the eighth century B.C., Cumae and other Greek colonies were established here. The region was conquered by the Etruscans in the sixth century B.C., by the Samnites after the mid-fifth century B.C., and by the Romans after the mid-fourth century B.C. As a result of the administrative reforms of Augustus (27 B.C.), Campania formed a single district with Latium and Picenum. One of the region's important centers was the city of Capua. Campania's importance in antiquity resulted from its advantageous geographic position, its fertile land, and its important trade routes (Via Appia, Via Latina). Picturesque coasts and the presence of curative springs made it a favorite country retreat of the Roman aristocracy; the luxurious villas in Baiae (modern Baia), Puteoli (Pozzuoli), and Nuceria (Nocera Inferiore) were especially renowned. In the Middle Ages the name Campania largely went out of use. During the 12th and 13th centuries its territory became at first a part of the Kingdom of Sicily and later of the Kingdom of Naples; from 1504 to 1860 it was part of the Kingdom of the Two Sicilies. The name Campania reappeared with the creation of a united Italy.
[11–838–1]

CAMPANIAN STAGE, a stage of the Upper Cretaceous, identified in France by the French geologist H. Coquand in 1857. A typical cross section contains light blue, gray, and whitish clayey limestones and marls with numerous ammonites and sea urchins. The Campanian stage corresponds in time to the greatest transgression of the seas over former land in the Cretaceous period. It is extensively developed both on platforms and in geosynclinal areas. The Campanian stage may be identified in Upper Cretaceous deposits in Europe, Africa, Asia, and North America by the presence of a group of typical fossils, including Foraminifera, belemnites, mollusks, and sea urchins.
[11–839–3]

CAMPANILE, the bell tower in medieval and Renaissance Italian architecture. The tower was four-sided or circular and, as a rule, was detached from the church. The prototype of the campanile was the city watchtower. The structure appeared well-proportioned and light as a result of an increase in the number or dimensions of the openings near the top. The lower floors, for the most part, did not have any apertures. An example of the campanile is the bell tower (known as Giotto's Tower) of the Cathedral of Florence. The construction of this campanile was begun by Giotto in 1334 and was continued by Andrea Pisano from 1337 to 1343. It was completed by F. Talenti around 1359.
[11–837–2]

CAMPECHE, a state in Mexico, on the Yucatán Peninsula. Area, 56,100 sq km; population, 251,600 (1970). The city of Campeche is its administrative center. The state is a plain, covered primarily by a tropical forest. Chicle, the sap of the sapodilla, is extracted here. There is apiculture and slash-and-burn agriculture. Henequen plantations are located along the coast. The henequen is processed in the city of Campeche, which is also the site of food industry.
[11–841–4]

CAMPECHE, a city in Mexico, administrative center of Campeche state. Population, 70,000 (1969). Campeche is a port on the Bay of Campeche (export of henequen and timber) and an important transport junction for the Yucatán Peninsula. Henequen fiber is processed here. There are also food and fishing industries. The city was founded in 1540.
[11–842–1]

CAMPECHE, BAY OF, a bay in the southern part of the Gulf of Mexico, west of the Yucatán Peninsula. It extends more than 300 km inland. Its breadth at the mouth is nearly 750 km. Its offshore depth reaches 3,286 m; the depth near the eastern shore (Campeche Bank) is 34 m. The tides are predominantly diurnal and range in height from 0.6 to 1.2 m. The bay's main ports are Campeche, Coatzacoalcos, and Veracruz.
[11–842–2]

CAMPEN, JACOB VAN. Born Feb. 2, 1595, in Haarlem; died Sept. 13, 1657, in Randenbroek, near Amersfoort. Dutch architect.

Van Campen, the son of a landowner, apparently received artistic training in Italy (1615–21), where he studied the work of Palladio. From 1621 to 1630 he worked in Haarlem. His work is representative of 17th-century Dutch classicism. Van Campen developed an imposing, restrained, and somewhat cold style. His major works included the small Mauritshuis in The Hague (in collaboration with P. Post, 1633–35) and the Town Hall in Amsterdam (now the Royal Palace, 1648–55). The Town Hall is characterized by clearly delineated architectural elements. It has a domed rotunda and a four-story vaulted Burgher Hall.

REFERENCE
Swillens, P. T. A. *Jacob van Campen.* Assen, 1961.   [11–841–1]

CAMPERT, JAN REMCO THEODOOR. Born Aug. 15, 1902, in Spijkenisse; died Jan. 12, 1943, in Neuengamme, Germany. Dutch writer. Son of a physician.

A participant in the resistance movement during the occupation of the Netherlands by Hitlerite Germany (1940–45), Campert was imprisoned in 1942 in a concentration camp, where he perished. Most popular are his patriotic poems "Home and Shelter" (1941), "Sonnets for Cynara" (1942), and, especially, his rebellious "Song of the Eighteen Doomed Prisoners" (1941). In the novel *Life in Darkness* (1935, new edition 1962), he portrays the déclassé of Amsterdam society.

WORKS
Verzamelde gedichten, 1922–1943. The Hague, 1947.
REFERENCE
Hoekstra, H. G. *Over J. Campert.* Amsterdam, 1946.   [11–841–3]

CAM PHA, a city and port in northeast Vietnam, in the Democratic Republic of Vietnam, on the coast of the Gulf of Tonkin in the South China Sea. Population, approximately 8,000. Coal is mined nearby and exported from Cam Pha; mining equipment is repaired and wood products are made there.   [11–847–6]

CAMPHAUSEN, LUDOLF. Born Jan. 10, 1803, in Hünshoven; died Dec. 3, 1890, in Cologne. German political figure, bourgeois liberal, and banker. One of the leaders of the big bourgeoisie in the Rhineland.

Camphausen became a deputy of the Rhineland provincial *Landtag* in 1843 and of the United Landtag in 1847. From Mar. 29, 1848, to June 20, 1848, during the Revolution of 1848–49, he was prime minister of Prussia. Camphausen's government was sympathetic to reactionary monarchist circles, clothing "counterrevolution in its bourgeois liberal attire" (K. Marx and F. Engels, *Soch.,* 2nd ed., vol. 5, p. 99). Camphausen was a representative of Prussia in the provisional central German government in Frankfurt am Main from June 1848 to April 1849. He became a member of the Prussian House of Lords in 1850.

REFERENCES
Marx, K., and F. Engels. *Soch.,* 2nd ed., vols. 6–7. (See Index of Names.)
Schwann, M. *Ludolf Camphausen als Wirtschaftspolitiker,* vols. 1–3. Berlin, 1915.   [11–840–3]

CAMPHENE   (3,3-dimethyl-2-methylenebicyclo-[1,2,2]-heptane), a hydrocarbon of the terpene series; colorless crystals with a characteristic camphor odor; melting point, 51°–52°C and boiling point, 160°–161°C.

Camphene is volatile, highly soluble in ether and benzene, less soluble in alcohol, and insoluble in water. It occurs in small quantities in turpentines and in essential pine oils, from which it may be isolated by distillation and freezing out. It is also found in lavender and fennel oils as well as in other essential oils. Camphene is produced industrially by the catalytic isomerization of pinene. Widely used in industry, it is an intermediate product in the synthesis of camphor. Chlorination of camphene yields very effective insecticides. [11–847–9]

CAMPHENE REARRANGEMENTS, intramolecular rearrangements of compounds of the terpene series. Camphene rearrangements of the first and second types are known. Mutual transformations of terpenes during the camphene rearrangements are analogous to the retrograde pinacol-pinacoline rearrangement in the aliphatic series. Thus, dehydration of borneol in the presence of acids leads not to the expected unsaturated hydrocarbon (bornylene) but rather to its structural isomer (camphene) as a result of a camphene rearrangement of the first type. The industrial synthesis of camphor from alpha-pinene also includes a camphene rearrangement of the first type.

Camphene rearrangements of the first type were discovered by E. Vagner (1899), and H. Meerwein subsequently studied their mechanism. Camphene rearrangements of the second type were discovered in 1927 by S. Nametkin. For this reason, camphene rearrangements of the first type are frequently called Vagner or Vagner-Meerwein rearrangements, and rearrangements of the second type are known as Nametkin rearrangements.

REFERENCES
Reutov, O. A. *Teoreticheskie osnovy organicheskoi khimii.* Moscow, 1964.
Nesmeianov, A. N., and N. A. Nesmeianov. *Nachala organicheskoi khimii,* vol. 2. Moscow, 1970. V. N. FROSIN [11–848–1]

CAMPHOR, 1,7,7-trimethylbicyclo-(1,2,2)-heptanone-2, a ketone of the terpene series; colorless crystals with a characteristic odor. Camphor is highly volatile; it is slightly soluble in water but readily soluble in organic solvents. It exists in the form of two optically active isomers, the (+)- and (−)-forms (melting points, 178.5°–179°C), and in the form of a racemic mixture, the (±)-form (melting points, 178°–178.5°C).

Camphor is widespread in nature; it is a component of many essential oils, such as basil oil, oil of wormwood, and oils of coniferous trees and the camphor tree. Camphor-tree oil is a source of (+)-camphor, or so-called natural camphor. Industrial camphor, in the (±)-form, is produced by processing of turpentine or its basic component, pinene. Camphor is used mainly as a plasticizer of cellulose nitrate and acetate (in the production of celluloid and motion-picture film), as an inhibitor (an additive that increases the storage stability) for smokeless powder, and as a moth repellent.

Camphor is a medicinal substance of the group of nerve stimulants. It stimulates respiration and blood circulation and strengthens the metabolic processes in the heart muscle. It is injected subcutaneously in the form of "camphor oil" (camphor solution in peach oil) or taken internally in powders (ground camphor) and in gelatin capsules in cases of cardiac weakness or collapse, to stimulate respiration, and in cases of infectious diseases and cases of narcotic and barbiturate poisoning. Bromocamphor (in powder or tablet form) and *Kamfotal* tablets (containing bromocamphor and phenobarbital) are prescribed as sedatives for the central nervous sytem in cases of high nervous excitability, neurasthenia, and heart neurosis. Camphor is used in the form of camphor oil, camphor ointment, camphor spirits, and *Denta* drops (dental drops containing camphor, chloral hydrate, and alcohol) as irritants and analgesics, and partly as antiseptics. These preparations are applied as salves in cases of inflammations and rheumatism; the dental drops are introduced into tooth defects.

REFERENCES
Rudakov, G. A. *Khimiia i tekhnologiia kamfory.* Moscow-Leningrad, 1961. [11–848–2]

CAMPHORACEOUS PLANTS, plants that contain essential camphor oil, the main component of which is camphor. The most important camphoraceous plants include the garden basil, which is a tropical shrub of the family Labiatae native to southern Africa, and the camphor tree. The garden basil is grown in the USSR as an annual plant. The camphoraceous Siberian fir is native to the USSR. Its needles are the source of borneol, from which camphor is obtained. [11–849–2]

CAMPHOROSMA, a genus of plants of the family Chenopodiaceae. They are annual or perennial herbs and low undershrubs with alternating linear or subulate leaves and a camphoraceous odor. The tiny flowers are mostly monoecious, with a tetramerous or pentamerous perianth. The plant has four or five stamens. There are approximately ten species, distributed from the Mediterranean to Central Asia (Dzungaria). They grow in solonetzic steppes, semideserts, salt marshes, takyrs, and rocky slopes. There are four species in the USSR. The most common are *C. monspeliaca* and *C. lessingiana.* Their grass stalks contain essential oils. These plants can be used as fodder for camels, goats, and sheep. [11–849–3]

CAMPHOR TREE (*Cinnamomum camphora*), an evergreen tree of the family Lauraceae. Height, 20–50 m. It has leathery, aromatic leaves. Its small flowers are plain and whitish. All parts of the tree contain essential camphor oil; the camphor is obtained from the oil by oxidation. The wood of this tree is not damaged by insects. It grows wild in South China (primarily on the islands of Taiwan and Hainan) and in southern Japan; it is also grown in these regions for commercial purposes. In the USSR the camphor tree is grown on the Black Sea Shore of the Caucasus, but only on a small scale; camphor is obtained primarily from synthetic sources. [11–849–1]

CAMPIGNIAN CULTURE, an archaeological culture of the early Neolithic period (sixth millennium to fourth millennium B.C.) in France, named after the Campigny site in the department of Seine-Maritime. The concept of the Campignian culture was introduced in 1886 by the French archaeologist F. Salmon.

The population of the culture engaged in fishing and hunting for deer, wild horses, and oxen. Much importance was also attached to the gathering of cereal grasses (grain mortars and barley grain impressions in pottery have been discovered), which paved the way for the development of agriculture. The dog was the only domestic animal. Dwellings were round pit houses measuring 6 m in diameter. Typical stone implements included the tranchet (a triangular chopping tool with a broad cutting edge and a handle attached to the narrow end) and the pick (axmattock, an oval tool with lateral working edges). The tools were used for woodworking (making boats, rafts, weirs). The ax-mattock was also used for digging. Polished axes appeared in later Campignian culture sites. Pottery—flat-bottomed and pointed-bottomed vessels made of clay mixed with sand and crushed shells—was made for the first time in the Campignian culture.

REFERENCES
Vsemirnaia istoriia, vol. 1. Moscow, 1955.
Nougier, L.-R. *Les Civilisations campigniennes en Europe occidentale.* Le Mans, 1950. [11–842–6]

CAMPIN, ROBERT. Born circa 1378; died Apr. 26, 1444, in Tournai. Flemish painter.

Campin, who worked in Tournai, has been identified as the Master of Flémalle. His works reflected the 14th-century Flemish tradition of miniature painting and sculpture. Campin was the first Flemish painter to apply the artistic principles of the Renaissance. His works are more archaic than those of his younger contemporary J. van Eyck. However, they are distinguished by unaffectedness, simplicity, and, at times, earthy treatment of religious subjects. Campin's works include the Merode altarpiece (Metropolitan Museum of Art, New York) and the Werl altarpiece (1438, Prado, Madrid). He greatly influenced his Flemish successors, including his pupil Rogier van der Weyden. Campin was one of the first European portraitists.

REFERENCE
Frinta, M. S. *The Genius of Robert Campin*. Paris, 1966.
[11-840-4]

CAMPINA GRANDE, a city in northeastern Brazil, in the state of Paraíba. Population, 196,000 (1970). It has a railroad station. Campina Grande is a center for textile and food industries. There are also ferrous metallurgical, chemical, furniture, and leather enterprises. [11-842-4]

CAMPINAS, a city in southeastern Brazil, in the state of São Paulo. Population, 376,500 (1970). A railroad and highway junction, Campinas is the center of an important agricultural region (coffee, cotton, sugarcane, grains). It has textile, machine-building (electric locomotives, sewing machines), metallurgical, chemical, leather, and food industries. [11-842-5]

CAMPO (Portuguese, "plain"), savanna-type vegetation in Brazil.

Campos cerrados consist of sparse, low-growing (2–3 m) trees and shrubs and stiff matted grasses; campos limpos are treeless and consist of grassy herbs. [11-843-6]

CAMPO FORMIO, TREATY OF (1797), the treaty ending the victorious war of the French Republic against Austria. The treaty was signed on Oct. 17, 1797, near the Italian village of Campoformio by Count L. Cobenzl for Austria and by General Bonaparte for France. With the Treaty of Campo Formio, Austria dropped out of the first anti-French coalition. Austria recognized the French conquests, conceded the Belgian province of the Austrian Netherlands to France, recognized the formation of the Cisalpine Republic (including Lombardy), and agreed to assist in the allotment of the lands on the left bank of the Rhine to France. In compensation, Austria received Salzburg, part of Bavaria, and most of the territories of the Venetian Republic, which was eliminated by the treaty. The Ionian Islands and territory in Albania, which had formerly been Venetian, were transferred to France.

PUBLICATION
Martens, C., and F. Cussy. *Recueil manuel et pratique de traités* . . . , vol. 2. Leipzig, 1846. Pages 148–51.
REFERENCE
Manfred, A. Z. "Ital'ianskii pokhod Bonaparta v 1796–1797 gg." *Novaia i noveishaia istoriia*, 1969, nos. 5–6. [11-844-2]

CAMPO GRANDE, a city in western Brazil, in the state of Mato Grosso. Population, 140,400 (1970). Metallurgy is an important activity. Campo Grande is a center of the food industry, particularly of combined slaughterhouses–refrigeration plants. The cattle trade is also important. [11-845-2]

CAMPOLON, a medicinal preparation, a concentrated aqueous extract of the livers of cattle or marine animals (whales and dolphins), containing vitamin B_{12} and folic acid. It stimulates bone-marrow function and normalizes blood formation. Campolon is used intramuscularly in various forms of anemia, liver diseases, and gastric diseases (atrophic gastritis). [11-843-2]

CAMPOMANES, PEDRO RODRIGUEZ. Born July 1, 1723, in Santa Eulalia de Sorribas, Asturias Province, Spain; died Feb. 3, 1803, in Madrid. Count, Spanish statesman, economist, historian, one of the leading advocates of the policy of enlightened absolutism in Spain. Son of an Asturian peasant.

Campomanes studied with Dominican monks. He was a lawyer and director of the postal department. From 1763 to 1789 he was minister of finance, from 1789 to 1791 chairman of the Royal Council of Castile, and from 1791 to 1798 state secretary. As a supporter of the teachings of the Physiocrats, he sought to free the Spanish economy from feudal restrictions, introducing free trade in grain, facilitating trade with the colonies, and attempting to impede the accumulation of property through mortmain. He helped regularize state finance, encouraged the creation of manufactories and technical schools, and contributed to the improvement of roads and means of communication. A staunch Catholic, he nevertheless sought to limit the privileges of the church to the benefit of the crown. He favored expelling the Jesuits from Spain (achieved in 1767) and laid the foundation for the work of "economic societies," which discussed the problems of the economic development of Spain. From 1764 he headed the Royal Academy of History. Campomanes wrote several economic, legal, and historical works.

WORKS
Tratado de la regalia de amortización. Madrid, 1765.
Discurso sobre el fomento de la industria popular. Madrid, 1774.
Discurso sobre la educación popular de los artesanos y su fomento. Madrid, 1775.
Memoria sobre los abusos de la Mesta. Madrid, 1791.
N. N. KOSOREZ [11-843-3]

CAMPOS, a city in southeastern Brazil, in the state of Rio de Janeiro. Population, 319,100 (1970). Campos is a railroad and highway junction and the commercial and industrial center of a developed agricultural region in the Paraíba River valley, where coffee, sugarcane, and tobacco are raised. The city has food enterprises (mainly sugar), as well as textile, cement, and tobacco industries. [11-845-3]

CAMPTONITE, magmatic dike rock consisting of plagioclase (usually labrador) and brown amphibole (barkevikite); it also contains pyroxene (titanaugite), biotite, and olivine. All varieties (amphibole camptonite, biotite camptonite, and others) usually contain a good deal of secondary calcite and zeolite, which either fill amygdules or form irregular secretions. [11-845-1]

CAMUS, ALBERT. Born Nov. 7, 1913, in Mondovi, Algeria; died Jan. 4, 1960, in Villebleven, France. French writer, publicist, and philosopher.

The son of a worker, Camus studied in the department of philosophy at the University of Algiers, worked in the theater, participated in public activities, and wrote for the left-wing press. He published two collections of lyrical essays—*Betwixt and Between* (1937) and *Marriage* (1939). From 1934 to 1937 he was a member of the Communist Party. Camus moved to France in 1938, where he worked on the underground newspaper *Combat*, which he headed after the liberation from German occupation. The novella *The Stranger* (1942), the philosophical work *The Myth of Sisyphus* (1942), and production of the plays *Cross Purpose* (1944) and *Caligula* (1944) brought Camus fame. He belonged to J.-P. Sartre's circle until their break in 1951. His social and political journalism (collected in three books, *Tropical Notes*, 1950–58), the philosophical and ideological essay *The Rebel* (1951), the novel-parable *The Plague* (1947), which was inspired by the Resistance Movement, the mystery *State of Siege* (1948), and a play about Russian Socialist Revolutionary terrorists, *The Just Assassins* (1950), made Camus one of the "rulers of men's minds" among the petit bourgeois intelligentsia of the West—a philosopher who dreamed of an intermediate "third path" during the Cold War. His agonizing attempts to remain a "free spirit" by not joining either of the struggling camps, although he was in the thick of their social and ideological battles, affected Camus deeply, as is apparent in the novella *The Fall* (1956), the book of stories *Exile and the Kingdom* (1957), and *The Swedish Speeches* (1958; given on the occasion of his receiving the Nobel Prize for literature in 1957).

Camus's philosophical views were not strictly systematic but had much in common with the existentialist frame of mind, despite his openly expressed disagreement with the leading existentialist thinkers. Starting with the idea of the failure in the 20th century of the past claims of reason—whether worldly common sense, the rationalist theology of divine providence, or science—Camus proceeded to a perception of the order and ultimate metaphysical meaning of existence. According to him, the experience of human existence, which inevitably culminates in death, leads the thinking individual to the discovery of the "absurd" as his "eternal lot" on earth. However, this truth should not disarm the individual; on the contrary, it should awaken in him a higher courage to continue to live in spite of "chaos" and to get along without any arguments in favor of this decision.

Camus proclaimed the completeness of corporeal communication with nature to be the only value in principle and exposed civic, spiritual, and moral values as not genuine. However, during the Resistance, he reexamined the slogan "nothing is forbidden" in the light of the concept of the duty of every person toward "others" (*Letters to a German Friend,* 1943–44). Subsequently, he arrived at a moralistic humanism based on the teachings of Christian charity and opposed to the morality that rests on social-historical aims. Thus, while he avoided Nietzscheanism, Camus also openly disagreed with revolutionary morality, preferring to it the righteousness of those who "do not make history but who suffer" its misfortunes.

Camus believed that in creating literary works the writer's task was to clothe the chaotic world in ordered and complete forms. In this respect, he was a follower of 17th- and 18th-century French writers and moralists, whose work was characterized by strict, sharp clarity. Camus's books gravitate to the parable, to the "tragic myth" of spiritual revelation, when man suddenly discovers his metaphysical fate as a mortal grain of sand and, guided by this truth, builds his path. From the demonic rebellion against fate in *Caligula* and the "pagan" immorality in *The Stranger,* through the stoic resistance in *The Plague* and the refined variant of the teaching "Thou shalt not kill" in *The Just Assassins,* to the bitter feeling of alienation from happiness in *Exile and the Kingdom* and *The Fall*—this is the path of Camus's heroes, who are tormented by their quest for life's truth. Their wanderings between willfulness and duty, loneliness and solidarity, and rebelliousness and withdrawal, are evidence of the unstable intellectual atmosphere in the West in the mid-20th century. Marxist philosophers in France and abroad have criticized Camus's views as the expression of the ideological ambiguity of split petit bourgeois consciousness.

WORKS

Théâtre, récits, nouvelles. Paris, 1962.
Essais. Paris, 1965. In Russian translation: *Izbrannoe.* [Introductory article by S. Velikovskii.] Moscow, 1969.

REFERENCES

Shkunaeva, I. D. *Sovremennaia frantsuzskaia literatura.* Moscow, 1961.
Evnina, E. M. *Sovremennyi frantsuzskii roman, 1940–1960.* Moscow, 1962.
Mikhailova, L. "Nekotorye aspekty gumanizma v filosofii A. Kamiu." *Trudy Moskovskogo instituta narodnogo khoziaistva,* 1967, no. 47.
Karpushin, V. A. "Kontseptsiia lichnosti u A. Kamiu." *Voprosy filosofii,* 1967, no. 2.
Nicolas, A. *A. Camus.* Paris, 1966.
Quillot, R. *La Mer et les prisons, essai sur A. Camus.* Paris, 1956.

BIBLIOGRAPHY

Crepin, A. *A. Camus: Essai de bibliographie.* Brussels, 1960.

S. I. VELIKOVSKII [11–861–3]

CANADA

General information

Canada is a state in North America and a member of the British Commonwealth. The country occupies the northern part of the continent of North America and numerous islands adjacent to it: along the western shores, Vancouver and the Queen Charlotte Islands; in the north, the Canadian Arctic Ar-

chipelago; and along the eastern coastline, Newfoundland, Cape Breton, Île d'Anticosti, and Prince Edward. Canada borders on the USA on the south and northwest (the state of Alaska). On the north it is bordered by the Arctic Ocean, on the west by the Pacific Ocean, and on the east by the Atlantic Ocean. Its area is 9,976,100 sq km. As of 1971, the population was 21.8 million. The capital is the city of Ottawa.

Canada is divided into ten provinces, which are subdivided into counties and districts. There are also two territories. (See Table 1.)

Constitution and government

Canada is a parliamentary monarchy whose nominal head of state is the king (or queen) of England. The country became one of the first dominions of Great Britain in 1867. Its constitution consists of a large number of laws and constitutional customs. The fundamental operative constitutional law—the British North America Act of 1867, which has been amended several times—was adopted by the British Parliament. Civil rights and liberties are regulated by a law adopted in 1960. The Statute of Westminster (1931) established the complete independence of Canada and the other dominions.

Canada has a federal structure of government. The functions of the head of state are carried out by a governor-general, who is appointed by the king (or queen) of England upon the advice of the prime minister of Canada. The role of the governor-general in political life is not great. Although the governor-general is formally the chief executive power who approves bills passed by Parliament, he does not play an important role in Canadian politics. In addition to the governor-general, there is the Privy Council with 130 members, including members of the royal family, the ministers, and representatives (the speakers) of the houses of Parliament.

Table 1. Provinces and territories of Canada

	Area (sq km)	Population (1971)	Administrative centers
Provinces			
Newfoundland	404,600	522,000	St. John's
Prince Edward Island .	5,600	112,000	Charlottetown
Nova Scotia	54,600	789,000	Halifax
New Brunswick	72,500	635,000	Fredricton
Quebec	1,540,700	6,028,000	Quebec
Ontario	1,068,600	7,703,000	Toronto
Manitoba	650,100	988,000	Winnipeg
Saskatchewan	651,900	926,000	Regina
Alberta	661,200	1,628,000	Edmonton
British Columbia . . .	948,700	2,185,000	Victoria
Territories			
Northwest Territories .	3,379,600	35,000	Yellowknife
Yukon Territory	536,400	18,000	Whitehorse

The highest legislative body—the Parliament—consists of two houses. The members of the House of Commons are elected by the people for a term not exceeding five years. (Representation is proportional to the population of each province. Thus, for example, there are 88 deputies from Ontario, 74 from Quebec, and 19 from Alberta.) The House of Commons elected in 1972 was made up of 109 Liberals, 107 representatives from the Progressive Conservative Party, 31 New Democrats, 15 representatives from the Social Credit Party, and two independents. Members of the Senate, who are appointed by the governor-general upon the advice of the prime minister, remain in power until age 75. (Until 1965 they were senators for life.) The Senate has 102 members (24 each from Ontario and Quebec, and from four to ten from each of the other provinces). The right to vote is granted to all citizens who have reached age 21.

The government of Canada is the cabinet, which is made up of the prime minister and the ministers who head the most important departments (defense, foreign affairs, finances, and trade and commerce). As a rule, the ministers are deputies in the House of Commons. The prime minister possesses very broad powers and is the commander in chief of the armed forces.

Royal power is represented in the provinces by lieutenant-governors, who are appointed by the governor-general upon the recommendation of the Canadian government. The provinces have legislative assemblies, most of which are unicameral and are elected by the people for terms not exceeding five years. The assemblies form the provincial governments. Local government bodies—county, district, and municipal councils—are in fact subordinate to provincial government bodies.

The highest judicial body is the Supreme Court, whose nine members are appointed by the governor-general. (The judges may hold office until they reach age 75.) The same method is used to form the Exchequer Court (seven members), which tries suits in instances where one of the parties is the state treasury. Superior and local courts have also been established in the provinces. M. V. BAGLAI

Natural features

Canada lies in the arctic, subarctic, and temperate zones. The smaller, western part of Canada is mountainous, but its climate is made milder by the influence of the Pacific Ocean. Most of the larger, eastern part of the country is level, with an extreme continental climate. It is strongly affected by the arctic region.

The coasts of the north and, in part, of the northeast are low and weakly dissected (the northern part of Hudson Bay). In the east they are steep and primarily of the fjord type (for example, Baffin Island, the Labrador Peninsula, and the island of Newfoundland). In the west the coasts are very high and deeply dissected by fjords.

Terrain. The central part of the continent and the adjacent parts of the Canadian Arctic Archipelago are occupied by plains (including lowlands) and plateaus, including the Hudson Bay Lowland, which is exceptionally flat, and the Laurentian Upland (maximum elevation 1,000 m), which is characterized by a lacustrine, hilly terrain. On the Central Plains—the lowlands of the Mackenzie River, the Manitoba Lowland, the plains of Alberta and Saskatchewan, the area surrounded by Lakes Erie, Huron, and Ontario, the Ontario Peninsula, and the lowland of the St. Lawrence Valley—glacial-accumulation forms of terrain prevail. The piedmont plateau of the Great Plains (elevations, 500–1,500 m) is characterized by dissection caused by erosion, as well as by glacial-accumulation forms of terrain. The western extreme of Canada is occupied by the Cordillera mountain system (elevations between 3,000 and 3,500 m; greatest elevation, Mt. Logan, 6,050 m). In the northeast along the coasts of the Canadian Arctic Archipelago and in the northern part of the Labrador Peninsula there is a band of mountains with elevations of 1,500–2,000 m. Located in the extreme southeast is the region of the Appalachian Uplands, which have a low-mountain terrain.

Geological structure and minerals. The country's central and largest part is occupied by the Canadian Shield, which is part of the North American (Canadian) Platform. The Precambrian formations of the shield include gneisses, crystalline schists, and volcanic (primarily basal) and, to a lesser degree, sedimentary rocks, interspersed with granites of various ages. After the completion of geosynclinal development Precambrian rocks were widespread in a number of major regions: Lake Superior (2.48 billion years ago), Great Slave Lake (2.48 billion years ago), Great Bear Lake (1.7–1.78 billion), and the Churchill (1.65–1.85 billion), South (1.7–1.9 billion), and Nain rivers (1.5 billion), as well as the Grenville Folded Zone (950 million), which extends along the eastern edges of the shield. The rocks of the first two regions are Archean massifs, whereas the others belong to the Archean and Proterozoic periods. In the west the Canadian Shield is buried under the Interior Canadian Platform, which is composed of sedimentary formations from the Upper Precambrian and more recent periods. Farther west the Interior Canadian Platform gives way first to the Mesozoic folded region of the Rocky Mountains and then to the Cenozoic folded zone of the Cordillera. In the east the shield is framed by the Caledonian folded system of the Appalachians, and in the north, in the region of the Canadian Arctic Archipelago, by the Caledonian Franklin Arctic Folded Region.

Canada is rich in various minerals. The Precambrian rocks of the shield are known to contain major deposits of uranium, iron, nickel, copper, zinc, lead, gold, and silver of various origins. On the Interior Platform and in the Mesozoic areas there are exten-

sive deposits of coal, petroleum, and natural gas from the Paleozoic and Mesozoic eras. Most characteristic of the Appalachian Region are deposits of copper, lead, zinc, and asbestos, as well as iron, coal, and rock salt.

Climate. Most of Canada has an arctic or subarctic climate, but in the south the climate is moderate and primarily continental. The average January temperature ranges from −35°C and −30°C in the far north and from −18°C and −20°C in the south-central regions to −5°C and −7°C on the Atlantic coast and 1°–4°C on the Pacific coast. The average July temperature ranges from 4°–7°C in the north to 16°–18°C in most of the southern regions, and may go as high as 21°C in the extreme southern part of the Ontario Peninsula. The total annual precipitation on the west coast is more then 2,500 mm; on the east coast, as much as 1,250 mm; in the central regions, 400–250 mm; and in the north, less than 150 mm. Almost all of Canada has a long-lasting snow cover, whose maximum thickness is 150 cm (on the Labrador Peninsula). In the northern half of the country there is a continuous as well as discontinuous distribution of perennially frozen rocks. There is glaciation in the extreme northeastern part of the Canadian Arctic Archipelago as well as in the Cordillera.

Rivers and lakes. The river network is dense. It is fed primarily by snow and rain. On the plains the high-water period occurs during the spring, whereas the Cordillera system has summer floods. The rivers remain frozen from three months in the south to nine months in the north. The plains regions, which cover about two-thirds of Canada, belong to the Atlantic and Arctic basins. On them complex lake and river systems have developed, which drain huge areas. The largest of the river and lake systems are the 3,000-km-long St. Lawrence and Great Lakes system (Canada owns only one-third of the water area of the lakes), the Finlay-Peace-Slave-Mackenzie rivers and Lesser Slave, Athabasca, Great Slave, and Great Bear lakes, and the Bow-Saskatchewan-Nelson rivers and Bow, Cedar, Winnipeg, Winnipegosis, Manitoba, and Cross lakes.

Most of the rivers of the mountainous west, which belong to the Pacific basin, are short and have narrow, deeply indented valleys. The most important of them are the Fraser River and the Yukon and Columbia rivers, whose upper reaches belong to Canada. The mountain and plains rivers of Canada are ill-suited for navigation, but they do possess great waterpower reserves. The country's total hydroelectric power potential has been estimated at approximately 60 million kW (kilowatts), of which more than 25 million kW are now being used. The annual discharge of all the rivers totals 1,207 cu km. Because of the numerous lakes (more than 200 large ones), the flow of the rivers is well regulated. Most of the plains lakes are of relict, glacial, or glacial-tectonic origin, whereas the mountain rivers are primarily of tectonic and glacial-tectonic origin.

Soils and flora. The flat eastern part of the extreme north (the northern islands of the Canadian Arctic Archipelago) is occupied by the zone of arctic wastelands, with a sparse cover of lichens and a few varieties of grass. To the south the wastelands give way to the tundra zone, covered with moss-lichens and moss-shrubbery and located on the southern islands of the Canadian Arctic Archipelago as well as on the coast of the continent. Farther south, extending in a band from the foothills of the Cordillera to the Atlantic coast, lies the forest tundra zone and the sparse forests on the near side of the tundra, which grow on mostly rocky, permafrost-taiga soils; there is also the zone of taiga forests, which is composed primarily of white and black spruce, American larches, Banks pines, and balsam firs, growing on podzol and, in places, swampy soils.

In the southern part of the central region the taiga gives way to forest-prairie and prairie zones with characteristic, park-like aspen forests in the north and primarily arid-prairie vegetation (feather grass and grama grass) in the south. The fertile gray forest, meadow-chernozem, chernozem, and chestnut soils of these regions are cultivated. More than half of the prairie zone is tilled. Located south of the taiga in the extreme southeastern part of the country is a zone of coniferous and broad-leaved forests on podzol and brown forest soils. Forests have been preserved primarily in relatively inaccessible regions such as the Appalachian Uplands. However, the fertile soils of the plains territories (for example, the lowlands of the St. Lawrence Valley and the Ontario Peninsula) have been cultivated, and some areas have been completely built up.

In the Cordillera there is a zone of high elevations. In the north the mountain-taiga forests of the valleys on the slopes give way to sparse mountain-taiga forests, which, in turn, give way to the mountain tundra. The valleys of the intramontane regions to the south are occupied by mountain prairies, which give way at higher altitudes to belts of mountain forest prairies (park-like forests), mountain coniferous forests, subalpine coniferous forests, and alpine meadows. From the foothills to the peaks, the Pacific slopes of the Cordillera are occupied by tall coastal forests of western red cedar, western hemlock, Douglas fir, Sitka spruce, giant fir, and other highly productive species. The average annual increase of timber is 10 cu m per ha (hectare), and the long-term reserve is 900–940 cu m per ha (as compared to a 5–6 cu m increase per ha and 500–550 cu m reserve per ha in coniferous-broad-leaved forests and a 1–3 cu m increase per hectare and 100–300 cu m reserve per ha on the taiga). The total forest area of Canada is more than 440 million ha (more than one-third of Canada's territory). Commercial forests occupy 240 million ha and include a timber reserve of approximately 21–22 billion cu m.

Fauna. Canada belongs to the Neoarctic Zoogeographic Region. On the islands of the Canadian Arctic Archipelago and in the tundra zone of the continent, reindeer, musk oxen, polar bears, arctic foxes, lemmings, arctic hares, tundra ptarmigans, and snowy owls are found. Inhabiting the taiga zone and parts of the forest tundra are elk, forest deer, bisons, red squirrels, northern flying squirrels, porcupines, hares, martens, bears, lynx, red foxes, wolves, and beavers. Characteristic of the coniferous and deciduous forests of eastern Canada are white-tailed deer, wapiti, marmots, hares, raccoons, gray squirrels, and red lynx. The southern deforested regions are inhabited by mule deer, pronghorn, pocket gophers, susliks, prairie dogs, skunks, corsacs, badgers, and coyotes. Among the specifically high-mountain species prevalent in the Cordillera are the mountain goat, mountain sheep, grizzly bear, and puma. The rivers and lakes as well as the coastal waters have abundant fish. Of the greatest commercial importance in the Atlantic waters are cod, herring, haddock, flounder, and crabs. In the Pacific the catch consists primarily of blueback, humpback, and chum salmon, as well as halibut. The principal commercial fish in the lakes are whitefish and lake trout.

Preserves. Canada has a system of national and provincial parks. The largest national parks, which preserve the entire complex of landforms, are Banff, Wood Buffalo, Glacier, Jasper, Yoho, Cape Breton Highlands, Kootenay, Prince Albert, and Riding Mountain. Among the provincial parks are Algonquin, Garibaldi, Laurentian, and Strathcona.

Natural regions The arctic region includes the Canadian Arctic Archipelago, Boothia and Melville peninsulas, and the far north of Labrador. The climate is very harsh, and the seaways are packed with ice almost the entire year round. The North Laurentian Upland, a region of tundra wastelands, has a harsh climate, an unbroken expanse of perennial permafrost, and an abundance of lakes and swamps. A gently rolling forest region with numerous rivers, lakes, and swamps, the South Laurentian Upland has a cold climate, and only parts of the ancient lake plains are suitable for agriculture. The Mackenzie Basin is primarily a plains region with extensive, extremely swampy lowlands. It is covered in the north by sparse woods and in the south by dense taiga forests. The climate is sharply continental. The Maritime Region (the region of the Appalachian Uplands and the island of Newfoundland) has a cold climate. The uplands with their rocky soils are covered by taiga and mixed forests. The Lake Region (the lowlands of the St. Lawrence Valley and the Ontario Peninsula), primarily a flat region, has a moderate climate. The virgin forests (mixed and broad-leaved) have been cut down.

The South Great Plains is a piedmont and prairie region with an extreme continental climate. The fertile chernozems and gray forest soils have been intensively tilled. The Northern Cordillera is a high-mountain region where compact mountain massifs prevail (the Canadian part of the Yukon Plateau). It is covered with mountain tundra and taiga. The climate is subarctic. The Southern Cordillera includes the Rocky Mountains and interior plateau. In parts of the high plateaus the climate is moderate; in the valleys it is dry. Considerable areas of land have been prepared for use as pasture and for growing a variety of crops. The mountain ranges are covered with forests and are glaciated. The Pacific Region includes the western slope of the Coastal Mountains and the offshore islands. The climate is maritime, warm and moist, and favorable for the growth of tall coniferous forests.

REFERENCES
Antipova, A. V. *Kanada: Priroda i estestvennye resursy.* Moscow, 1965.
Ignat'ev, G. M. *Severnaia Amerika: Fizicheskaia geografiia.* Moscow, 1965.
Canada: A Geographical Interpretation. Toronto, 1967.
Geology and Economic Minerals of Canada, 4th ed. Ottawa, 1957.

A. V. ANTIPOVA and N. A. SHTREIS
(geological structure and minerals)

Population

Approximately two-thirds of the Canadian population (1970, estimate) is made up of English Canadians (about 9 million) and French Canadians (about 6 million). Included in the English group are Canadians of English, Irish, Scottish, and Welsh as well as German, Dutch, and other origins. Certain differences among them continue to be preserved. About one-fourth of the population consists of national minorities—for the most part, relatively recent (20th-century) immigrants and their descendants. According to the census of 1961, the largest national minorities (in thousands) are Germans (1,050), Ukrainians (473), Italians (450), Dutch (430), Poles (324), Jews (173), Norwegians (149), Hungarians (126), Russians (119), Chinese, and Japanese. As of 1969, there were more than 240,000 Indians in Canada, including Algonquins, Cree, Iroquois, Athapaskan, Salish, Sioux, Wakashan, Tsimshian, Haida, Kutenai, and Tlingit. Most of the Indians live on reservations. About 17,000 Eskimos have settled on the arctic coast.

Canada has two official languages: English and French. The French Canadians, as well as most of the English Canadians of Irish descent, are Catholics. The majority of the English Canadians are Protestants of various denominations (for example, United Church of Canada and Anglican Church of Canada). The official calendar is the Gregorian.

Between 1963 and 1970 the population increased by an average of 1.7 percent per year. From 1951 to 1961 the population grew by 30 percent and from 1961 to 1971, by 18.1 percent (an average of 1.8 percent per year). During this period it was concentrated basically in the major urban centers. Most of the population increase is attributable to natural growth, which between 1951 and 1971 accounted for about four-fifths of the total growth in the population. During the same period 3.2 million immigrants came to Canada. The population increase was particularly great in the most rapidly developing central (Quebec and Ontario) and western provinces (Alberta and British Columbia). On the whole, however, Canada is still sparsely settled. The average population density is 2.2 persons per sq km. More than nine-tenths of the population is concentrated in a relatively narrow band along the border with the USA. About half of the population lives in three regions whose area is small: the Oshtoham conurbation (Oshawa-Toronto-Hamilton; 4 million persons on 10,000 sq km), the southeastern part of the province of Quebec, with its center in the city of Montreal (4 million persons on 7,000 sq km), and the valley of the lower Fraser, with the city of Vancouver (1.6 million persons on 130,000 sq km). At the same time, in the northern regions (the Northwest Territory, the Yukon Territory, and the northern parts of the provinces of Manitoba, Alberta, and Saskatchewan) the density does not, as a rule, exceed 0.2 persons per sq km.

In 1970, 76 percent of the population was living in cities. Moreover, according to the census of 1971, about half the population inhabited the largest cities (figures include the suburbs): Montreal (2.72 million), Toronto (2.61 million), Vancouver (1,-071,000), Winnipeg (535,000), Hamilton (496,000), Edmonton (491,000), Quebec (476,000), Ottawa (448,000), and Calgary (400,000). The rural population makes up 24 percent of the total population, but only 10 percent of the inhabitants of rural Canada actually live and work on farms.

In 1968 there were 7,919,000 persons in the labor force, of whom 23.3 percent worked in the manufacturing industries, 7.2 percent in agriculture, 2.9 percent in mining, fishing, lumbering, and hunting, 6.2 percent in construction, 8.9 percent in transportation, communications, and electric power engineering, 16.7 percent in trade, 4.3 percent in finance and insurance, and 30.5 percent in the service industries (including state civil servants). According to a 1968 estimate, approximately 80 percent of the labor force is made up of hired workers. About 5 percent were owners of large industrial and commercial enterprises and capitalist farms, who essentially had at their disposal most of Canada's national wealth.

Historical survey

Precolonial. The oldest population of Canada was composed of Eskimo and Indian tribes of the Algonquin and Athapaskan groups, which preserved clan-tribal relations until the coming of the Europeans. Only among the Indians of the Pacific coast were there the beginnings of a class society. The principal occupations of the people were hunting, fishing, and food gathering. The Iroquois tribes farmed the St. Lawrence Valley.

French and British domination (until 1867). Reliable information about the first European settlers in Canada dates from the end of the 15th century. In 1497 the expedition of Giovanni Caboto (John Cabot), a Venetian seafarer in the service of England, reached the shores of Newfoundland. Jacques Cartier's French expedition entered the Gulf of St. Lawrence in 1534, and in 1535 another expedition led by Cartier sailed up the St. Lawrence River to the region of present-day Montreal. In 1605 the French founded the settlement of Port Royal in Acadia (now Nova Scotia), and in 1608, Quebec, which became the center of the colony of New France. Prior to the establishment of a royal administration in 1663, the colony was run by a series of trading companies, each of which had a monopoly on the fur trade and robbed the Indians.

The settlement of the territory of Canada, which was accompanied by the extinction of Indian tribes, proceeded slowly. In 1663 there were only 2,500 settlers still living in French Canada (New France). The colony was administered by a governor and a council made up of feudal aristocrats and clergy. Under French rule Canada developed a feudal system with seignorial ownership of the land, which hindered the expansion of peasant tillage and peasant settlement of areas beyond the boundaries of the seignorial lands. The Catholic Church was a major landowner. The second half of the 17th century was marked by the emergence of capitalist relations and the beginning of the formation of the French-Canadian nation.

Canada was colonized in an atmosphere of fierce struggle between France and England for the domination of North America. Nova Scotia—the first English colony in Canada—was founded in the 1620's; still earlier (1583) the island of Newfoundland was declared an English possession. The English Hudson's Bay Company, which operated on the northern coast of Canada, was founded in 1670. The initial Anglo-French military encounters in Canada took place at the end of the 1680's and the beginning of the 1690's. Under the Treaty of Utrecht, which was signed in 1713 after the War of the Spanish Succession, France yielded Hudson Bay to the British, as well as the French part of Newfoundland, which had been seized in the 17th century, and Acadia. In 1758 the Pacific coast of Canada was declared a British possession. (In 1858 it received the status of a colony under the name of British Columbia.) As a result of the Seven Years' War (1756–63), Great Britain took possession of all of New France, the population of which had reached 63,000 by that time.

The Quebec Act, which was passed by the British Parliament in 1774, preserved in the colony (which came to be called Quebec) the seignorial regime and the church's right to collect tithes. It also guaranteed religious tolerance. During the American Revolution (1775–83), Canada became a refuge for 40,000 Loyalists, who received generous land grants there. By a constitutional act of 1791, Great Britian finally established the borders and the structure of its colonial possessions in North America. Quebec was divided along the Ottawa River into two provinces —Lower Canada (with a predominantly French population) and Upper Canada (with a predominantly British population). Bicameral parliaments were created in both provinces. Nevertheless, all power in the colony belonged to the governor. The ruling upper classes were composed of the landowning aristocracy, the big commercial bourgeoisie of British descent, the higher clergy, and officials. Nationalist conflicts interwoven with social conflicts increased sharply because of the British conquest and the intention of the mother country and the colonial upper classes to assimilate the French-Canadian population.

The 1820's and 1830's were characterized by significant shifts in the way in which capitalist relations developed. In particular, these shifts were promoted by immigration to Canada from the mother country and the USA. (In 1836 the white population of British North America totaled 1 million.) Great Britain's colonial policy, which was directed at preserving feudal institutions and large-scale landowning, came increasingly into conflict with the aspiration of the settlers to gain ownership of lands on the basis of the principle of free bourgeois property ownership. Dissatisfaction with the regime gradually seized all strata of society.

The War of 1812 (1812–14) promoted the consolidation of Canadian society, since the country was confronted with the threat of capture by the USA. After the war there was an upswing in the movement for democratic reforms and self-government. In the provinces parties of reform advocates ("patriots") were formed under the leadership of representatives of the local bourgeoisie. Prominent leaders of the patriots were W. L. Mackenzie (Upper Canada), L. J. Papineau (Lower Canada), and J. Howe (Nova Scotia and New Brunswick). By 1834 the advocates of reform were in control of the parliaments in Lower and Upper Canada. Because of the economic crisis of 1836–37 and the stubborn refusal of the authorities to make concessions to the colonists, an armed uprising broke out in Lower Canada on Nov. 6, 1837, and in Upper Canada on December 4. The insurgents' lack of coordination and their leaders' indecisiveness led to the suppression of the uprising. Many patriots fled to the USA. However, an armed conflict on the American-Canadian border lasted for about two years. Only with difficulty did Great Britain succeed in maintaining control over Canada, using force of arms and making concessions and compromises when unavoidable.

In 1838, Lord Durham was sent to Canada on a special mission. Subsequently, he presented the British government with a report proposing the partial introduction of self-government in Canada. Upper and Lower Canada were united into the province of Canada in 1841. New governments responsible to their parliaments were formed in the provinces of Canada and Nova Scotia in 1848, and in 1854 the seignorial system, which had outlived its prime, was eliminated, and limitations on trade were abolished. Reforms promoted the capitalist development of Canada, which occurred more rapidly from the mid-19th century. An industrial revolution took place in Canada, characterized by the construction of transcontinental railroad lines, the development of steamship lines, and the settlement of the western regions. With the accelerated growth of industry, a proletariat took shape, and the workers' movement was born. (The first trade union—the printers'—was founded in Quebec as early as 1827.) During the winter of 1843, 1,300 workers on the construction site of the Lachine Canal went on strike. The movement to unite all the British colonies in North America grew stronger during the 1850's. Out of the movement emerged the principal political parties of Canada—the Conservatives and the Liberals.

In 1867 the British Parliament adopted the British North America Act, under which a federation was created—the Dominion of Canada. In addition to Canada itself, which was divided into the provinces of Quebec (Lower Canada) and Ontario (Upper Canada), the federation included Nova Scotia and New Brunswick. The dominion's Parliament, which was modeled on the British, consisted of two houses—a lower one elected by the people, and a higher one appointed by the governor-general. An important step toward Canada's complete independence from the mother country, the formation of the dominion completed the period of reforms that had been evoked by the uprising of 1837–38.

Development of capitalism after the formation of the federation (1867–99). The Conservative government headed by J. Macdonald completed the unification of the former British colonies in North America within the Dominion of Canada. In 1870, with the consent of the British government, the Hudson's Bay Company ceded to the Dominion of Canada extensive territories in the northwest, from the Great Lakes to the Rocky Mountains. In the same year the province of Manitoba was formed on these territories. British Columbia became a part of Canada in 1871 and Prince Edward Island, in 1873. The creation of a centralized state eliminated the customs barriers between the various regions of Canada and laid the foundation for the formation of a national market. The colonization of the Canadian west was accompanied by the expropriation of the lands held by the Indians, who were forced to live on reservations. The Land Law of 1872 defined the conditions for surveying the extensive prairie region. Enormous tracts of land were acquired by the Hudson's Bay Company, as well as by railroad companies and speculators in colonial associations. Failure to pay attention to the interests of the people who lived on the prairies (Indians and halfbreeds [*métis*]) provoked the insurrections of 1869–70 and 1885, which were led by Louis Riel.

At the time that the federation was formed Canada was an agrarian country, whose various regions were poorly connected economically. The Macdonald government attracted British capital for building railroads, which required an acceleration in the development of heavy industry. (From 1867 to 1900 the Canadian railroad network increased from 3,700 km to 28,400 km, and in 1885 the construction of the Canadian transcontinental railroad was completed.) However, during the last third of the 19th century the Canadian economy had some backward characteristics, which were to a large degree caused by the efforts of British capital to keep Canada in the position of a supplier of raw materials. From 1871 through 1901 the population of Canada did not increase significantly. (During this period it rose from 3.7 million to 4.8 million, and about 2 million persons emigrated to the USA.)

In the elections of 1873 the Conservatives were defeated. The administration of A. Mackenzie's Liberal cabinet (1873–78) coincided with a severe economic crisis. When the Macdonald government returned to power, it adopted the "national policy," the main point of which was the introduction of protectionism aimed at protecting the interests of the Canadian bourgeoisie and the domestic market from US trade expansion. The 1870's and 1880's were characterized by the growth of the workers' movement. In June 1872 a law legalizing trade-union activity was adopted, and in 1873 the National Canadian Workers' Union, which was active for four years, was established. The Canadian Congress of Trade Unions was founded in 1886.

The epoch of imperialism (to the end of World War I). At the end of the 19th century and the beginning of the 20th the rate of Canada's economic growth accelerated—a phenomenon promoted by conditions in the world market (increased demand for raw materials and decreased costs of maritime freight), the diversion of the flow of European immigrants from the USA in favor of Canada, and increased input of foreign capital (more than $2.5 billion between 1900 and 1913). The growth of the economy was also promoted by a state policy of investments and subsidies to the magnates of heavy industry and by a protectionist policy, which in 1897 the government of the Liberal W. Laurier (1896–1911) supplemented with a preferential tariff system for British imports.

By the beginning of World War I (1914–18) the value of the output of the manufacturing industry had increased fourfold. Between 1900 and 1918 the population of Canada increased by 64 percent: moreover, the population of the three prairie provinces quadrupled. With their highly commercial wheat production, the prairies became a principal exporting region between 1900 and 1911. Canada's entry into the epoch of imperialism was characterized by the acceleration of the concentration of capital and of industrial production. As a result of mergers, the number of banks fell from 36 to 21 between 1900 and 1917. Furthermore, three banks (the Bank of Montreal, the Royal Canadian Bank, and the Commercial Bank of Canada) had at their disposal 70 percent of the nation's banking resources. In the same period the number of industrial enterprises rose by 130 percent, but their capital increased by 520 percent. The steel, textile, and cement industries as well as railroad transportation were characterized by particularly high growth rates. Banking and industrial capital merged.

Between 1900 and 1917 monopoly capitalism in Canada was characterized by dependence on British and American capital, with the latter continuously expanding its hold over the economy. Raw materials dominated Canadian exports. The Laurier government and subsequently, the government of the Conservative R. Borden (1911–17) suppressed the workers' struggle for their rights. (There were 1,500 strikes between 1900 and 1915.) Antilabor laws were adopted, and a system of mandatory arbitration was introduced. Persistent struggle by the workers led to the adoption of a law providing for compensation for on-the-job injuries and to the establishment of the Ministry of Labor, as well as agencies to investigate working conditions in industry.

In 1904 the Socialist Party of Canada was founded. However, the Socialists were not successful in gaining influence over the masses of workers or in joining with the trade unions. They did not master the principles of Marxism in sufficient depth, and their ranks were permeated with the spirit of sectarianism. In 1911 several groups that had broken away from the Socialist Party formed the Social Democratic Party of Canada. Since the beginning of the 20th century the farmers' movement, which is directed against the dominance of the monopolies, has been important in Canadian politics.

World War I, in which Canada participated on the side of Great Britain, stimulated the further growth of monopoly capitalism, which was accompanied by a strengthening of the economic position of the USA in Canada. At the same time, the war sharpened the contradictions in capitalism, as well as the social and national antagonisms in the country. The movement against the government, which intended to introduce compulsory military service, confronted the ruling class with the threat of a national crisis and compelled the bourgeoisie to form a coalition government in October 1917—the "Unionist" government, which consisted of Conservatives and those Liberals who advocated that the war be pursued "to a victorious conclusion."

Period of the general crisis of capitalism (after 1918). PRIOR TO 1945. The beginning of the general crisis of capitalism was marked by an upswing in the workers' and farmers' movements. The toiling people hailed the victory of the October Revolution in Russia, and a campaign of protest was provoked by the decision of the Borden government (1917–20) to send Canadian troops to participate in the intervention against Soviet Russia and to introduce compulsory military service (1918). The strike struggle intensified sharply. Between 1911 and 1914, 244 strikes occurred and in 1919, 336. The most important of them was the Winnipeg Strike of 1919. The Communist Party of Canada was founded in 1921.

The strengthening of the position of the Canadian bourgeoisie during World War I and the rapid growth of American capital investments led to the weakening of British influence in Canada. (At the end of 1922, US investments totaled $2,593 million and British investments, US$2,464 million.) At the Paris Peace Conference of 1919–20, Canada was an independent party to the peace treaties. Like the other British dominions it received the right to be represented in the League of Nations. In 1920 an agreement was reached on the establishment of Canadian diplomatic representation in the USA. (The agreement went into effect in 1927.) The Statute of Westminster, which was adopted by the British Parliament in 1931, implemented the resolution of the imperial conferences of 1926 and 1930 on the legal equality of the dominions and the mother country with respect to all rights and laws.

Because of the dependence of the national economy on foreign trade and the predominance of raw materials among the nation's exports, the world economic crisis of 1929–33 hit Canada with particular severity. The level of industrial production fell by more than 50 percent between 1929 and 1933, and at the beginning of 1933 the number of unemployed, including the members of their families, was more than 1.3 million (12 percent of the entire population). The catastrophic decline of farm commodity prices led to the ruin of 240,000 farms. Endeavoring to promote sales of Canadian goods in the British Empire, R. Bennett's Conservative government (1930–35) supported the initial agreements in 1932 on imperial preferences.

The Bennett government repeatedly used armed force to disperse demonstrators and suppress strikes. Declared illegal in 1931, the Communist Party continued to operate illegally until 1936. Its leaders, including T. Buck, who were thrown into prison in 1931, were freed in 1934. Under Bennett's administration approximately 10,000 people were arrested. The Liberals regained power in 1935 under the leadership of W. L. M. King (prime minister during 1921–26, 1926–30, and 1935–48), and they remained in power until 1957.

The ruling circles of Canada fully supported the policy pursued by Great Britain, France, and the USA, which encouraged fascist agressors. On Sept. 10, 1939, Canada entered World War II (1939–45) on the side of Great Britain. Canada supplied the countries of the antifascist coalition—primarily Great Britain—with raw materials, foodstuffs, and weapons. As the result of a plebiscite held in April 1942, the government obtained the right to send to overseas theaters of military action against the forces of the fascist bloc not only recruited troops (volunteers) but also conscripted troops. A powerful war industry developed in the country, and new branches of industry were established, including the machine-tool and synthetic rubber industries. Between 1939 and 1945 industrial production increased by 250 percent, and there was a further concentration of production and capital. The Canadian bourgeoisie had great opportunities to make profits on military orders. Wages were "frozen," signifying greater exploitation of the working class, especially when one considers the rapid rise of the speed-up during the period. The strike struggle grew more acute. The number of trade-union members almost doubled (359,000 in 1939; 711,000 in 1945). In June 1940 the Communist Party was outlawed again, and hundreds of Communists and other progressive leaders were imprisoned. The Communists reestablished a legal party in August 1943 under the title of the Labor Progressive Party (since 1959, the Communist Party of Canada). On June 12, 1942, diplomatic relations were established between Canada and the USSR, and on Feb. 11, 1944, a Canadian-Soviet agreement on military supplies was concluded.

AFTER WORLD WAR II (1939–45). After the war the British position in Canada continued to grow weaker. In particular, the remnants of Canada's formal dependence on the mother country were eliminated (for example, the law on Canadian citizenship, 1947). In 1949, Canada annexed Newfoundland, the last British possession in North America. At the same time the influence of US ruling circles on the policy of Canada grew stronger. Canada assisted in the implementation of the Marshall Plan. Although it was economically a highly developed imperialist country, Canada was an object of the expansion of US monopoly capital. Crowding out their British competitors in a fierce struggle, US monopolies seized the key positions in the Canadian economy. By the end of 1969 almost half of the largest industrial companies of Canada were under the control or in the direct possession of American capital, and even Canada's foreign trade was linked with the USA.

The postwar period was marked by the further growth of the workers' movement. In 1956 the two largest trade-union centers merged to form the Canadian Labour Congress. Between 1960 and 1970 the number of strikes doubled (274 in 1960, 595 in 1969, and 540 in 1970), and the number of strikers increased by five to six times (49,400 in 1960, 306,800 in 1969, 261,200 in 1970). As a result of strikes an estimated 4 million workdays were lost in 1971. The demands of the strikers have been basically economic—that is, they have been directed against increases in the cost of living (expenses for apartment rent and community services account for one-fourth to one-third of a working-class family's budget) and the increasing gap between the growth rates of monopoly profits and workers' wages. (In 1968 the latter increased by only 7.5 percent, whereas profits rose 20 percent.) At the same time, strikes have often been struggles against the policy of wage "freezes," which was adopted by the government at the end of the 1960's, and struggles for the right to participate in the consideration of questions related to the organization of production (for example, the introduction of new equipment and the protection of workers from the negative consequences of automation). There has been a growing tendency to diminish and even to eliminate the dependence of the Canadian trade-union movement on US trade-union leaders.

In Quebec the strike struggle against the yoke of the monopolies merged with the struggle against the economic and national inequality of the French-Canadian population. (During the 1960's the wages of French Canadians were, on the average, 40 percent lower than the wages of English Canadians.) The movement of the French Canadians for complete and equal rights with English Canadians in all fields of economic and political life is supported by all progressive forces in Canada. At the same time the bourgeois separatist movement, which called for the secession of Quebec from the Canadian federation, became active. However, in the elections to the Parliament of the province of Quebec in October 1973 the separatists suffered a heavy defeat. Candidates of the ruling Liberal Party won 99 of the 110 seats.

The ruling circles of Canada were active in the unleashing of the cold war. The Liberal government and the Conservative one that replaced it (1957–63) concluded a number of agreements with the USA, which American monopolies took advantage of to control the economy, foreign policy, and defense of Canada. In February 1947 an American-Canadian agreement was announced concerning the extension of military cooperation during the postwar period. Canada was among the initial proponents of the creation of the aggressive NATO bloc (1949). In 1958 a united antiaircraft defense command for North America was established (NORAD). US military bases were established on Canadian territory. Beginning in the mid-1960's, cabinets formed by the Liberals, who had come into power again in 1963, adopted a more constructive approach to domestic and foreign policy problems, taking national interests into consideration. The government of P. E. Trudeau (prime minister since 1968) declared its intention to ensure Canada's "political self-preservation" and independence and, in particular, to control the further development of relations with the USA, a nation that presents a constant threat to the sovereignty, independence, and cultural identity of Canada. Although it advocates the continued existence of NATO, the Canadian government has curtailed its military participation in the bloc. The government has declared its intention to develop relations with the countries of Latin America, Asia, and Europe, including the socialist countries. A delegation from Canada participated in the work of the Congress on Security and Cooperation in Europe. In May 1971, Trudeau paid an official visit to the USSR, during which a Soviet-Canadian protocol on consultations was signed. In October 1971, A. N. Kosygin paid a return visit to Canada, concluding a general agreement on exchanges.

In the struggle of the Canadian people for peace and social progress the unity of democratic forces has assumed increasing importance.

REFERENCES
Mizhuev, P. G. *Krest'ianskoe tsartsvo: Ocherk istorii i sovremennogo sostoianiia Kanady*. St. Petersburg, 1905.
Sosenskii, I. *Voina i ekonomika Kanady*. [Moscow] 1947.
Sushchenko, V. V. *Anglo-Amerikanskie protivorechiia v Kanade posle vtoroi mirovoi voiny*. Moscow, 1956.
Mileikovskii, A. G. *Kanada i anglo-amerikanskie protivorechiia*. Moscow, 1958.
Altaev, B., and K. Lomov. *Novoe v rabochem dvizhenii Kanady*. [Moscow] 1960.
Natsional'nye problemy Kanady. Moscow, 1972.
Buck, T. *Izbrannye proizvedeniia*. Moscow, 1972. (Translated from English.)
Buck, T. *Nasha bor'ba za Kanadu*. Moscow, 1961. (Translated from English.)
Ryerson, S. B. *Osnovanie Kanady: Kanada s drevneishikh vremen do 1815 g.* Moscow, 1963. (Translated from English.)
Ryerson, S. B. *Neravnyi souiz: Istoriia Kanady, 1815–1873*. Moscow, 1970. (Translated from English.)

70 CANADA

Lanctot, G. *A History of Canada,* vols. 1–3. Toronto, 1963–65.
Clark, S. D. *Movements of Political Protest in Canada.* Toronto, 1959.
Canada and Its Provinces: A History of the Canadian People . . . , vols. 1–23. Toronto, 1914–17.
Garneau, F. H. *Histoire du Canada,* 8th ed., vols. 1–9. Montreal, 1944–46.

V. A. TISHKOV (prior to 1867),
O. S. SOROKA-TSIUPA (1867–1918),
and S. F. MOLOCHKOV (from 1918)

Political parties, trade unions, and other social organizations

Political parties. The Liberal Party, which was founded in the 19th century, received its organizational form in 1873. In power since 1963, it expresses the interests of the big monopolistic bourgeoisie. The Progressive Conservative Party, founded in 1854, expresses the interests of the big monopolistic bourgeoisie and the well-to-do farmers. Founded in 1961, the New Democratic Party, an outgrowth of the Social Democratic Cooperative Commonwealth Federation and some of the trade unions, belongs to the Canadian Labour Congress. The Social Credit Party was founded in 1935. The party leadership, which is linked with US oil monopolies and their Canadian partners, advocates sharply anti-Soviet and anti-Communist positions. The Communist Party of Canada was founded in 1921. In 1965 the Communist Party of Quebec, part of the Communist Party of Canada, was established at a congress of Communists of the province of Quebec.

Trade unions and other social organizations. The first trade unions in Canada were formed during the 1820's. By 1973 the trade unions had more than 2 million members. The largest trade-union associations are the Canadian Labour Congress (founded in 1956; more than 1.75 million members) and the Confederation of National Trade Unions (founded in 1921), which operates mainly in the province of Quebec. Characteristic of the Canadian trade-union movement are close ties with US trade unions: two-thirds of Canada's trade-union members belong to international American-Canadian trade-union organizations, and more than half belong to the American Federation of Labor–Congress of Industrial Organizations (AFL-CIO).

Among Canada's other social organizations are the Canada-USSR Association, founded in 1960, the Quebec-USSR Society, founded in 1960, and the Canadian Peace Congress, founded in 1949. The Women's Voice, a bourgeois-liberal pacifist organization, was founded in 1960.

B. V. ALEKSASHKIN

Economic geography

General state of the economy. Canada is an industrial-agrarian country with a high level of capitalist development. However, its economy has an ambivalent character. On the one hand, Canada is the object of exploitation by the monopolies of the USA and other imperialist states. Raw materials and semifinished goods prevail among its exports. Many of Canada's leading companies are multinational, with the country's national capital closely interwoven with foreign capital. On the other hand, Canada is a major capitalist power that exports capital and exploits the less developed countries of the capitalist system. Large-scale capitalist production prevails in both industry and agriculture. As of 1971, Canada occupied seventh place among the industrial producers of the capitalist world (3.2 percent of the world's industrial output). In national per capita income and average level of labor productivity it is behind only the USA and Switzerland.

In the capitalist world (as of 1970), Canada ranked first in the mining of nickel, zinc, and silver ores, potash, and asbestos, as well as in the production of newsprint. The country was second in the mining of gold, platinum, niobium, and molybdenum ores, natural gas, and sulfur, as well as in the production of aluminum, cellulose, and sawn lumber, and third in mining lead, cobalt, magnesium, cadmium, uranium, and titanium ores. On the whole, Canada produces about 7 percent of the capitalist world's raw materials and semifinished products, all of which are derived from minerals or timber. The country also produces up to one-sixth of the capitalist world's exports in the same categories. At the same time, Canada is a major purchaser of machinery, equipment, and other finished products from industrially developed countries.

Foreign capital plays an important role in the Canadian economy. As of 1968, foreign monopolies controlled 70 percent of Canada's mining and 57 percent of its processing industry. The USA holds 81 percent of the foreign investments in Canada. At the end of 1968 the country's long-term foreign debt totaled Can$38 billion, of which four-fifths was owed to the USA. As of 1968, the nation's investments abroad totaled approximately Can$19 billion, of which $11 billion was allotted to long-term investments in the economies of Brazil and of countries in the Caribbean basin, for example. Approximately 43 percent of Canada's investments abroad are controlled not by Canadian capital but by foreign capital, of which 31 percent comes from the US. In penetrating Canada's economy, foreign monopolies (primarily American ones) compete with Canadian capital, sharpening the struggle to "Canadianize" the country's economy. Foreign penetration is particularly noticeable in the new regions of intensive exploitation of natural resources—for example, in the Canadian North.

The relatively high rate of growth of the Canadian economy since World War II (4.5 percent per year) is closely associated with the large volume of capital investment in the economy. From 1939 to 1969 approximately Can$250 billion was invested in the economy, processing enterprises and mining installations were built, and farming became more mechanized. In the postwar period significant structural and regional shifts have occurred in the Canadian economy. (See Table 2.)

Table 2. Branch structure of the economy

	1939	1949	1959	1968
All branches (conventionally computed net cost of production, millions of dollars)	3.2	9.7	18.1	31.8
Breakdown of total (in percent)				
Agriculture	26.2	20.8	9.9	9.0
Lumbering	8.4	3.6	3.2	2.3
Fishing and hunting	1.3	0.9	0.7	0.6
Mining	12.2	5.9	7.7	9.9
Electric power	4.7	2.8	4.0	4.3
Construction	5.7	11.0	19.9	16.5
Manufacturing industry	41.5	55.0	54.6	57.4

The growth of industrial production was directly connected to the renewal of fixed capital and the creation of new branches of the manufacturing and processing industries (aviation, electrical engineering, and petroleum refining), as well as of the extracting industries (mining of iron ore, petroleum, natural gas, potash, and uranium and molybdenum ores). The high demand for Canadian raw materials resulted in the accelerated development of the raw materials branches of the economy (that is, branches that are linked, to one degree or another, with the exploitation of lumber, mineral, or energy resources). On the one hand, this has brought into economic circulation the resources of a number of poorly developed regions in western and northern Canada. On the other hand, however, it has led to the plundering of the country's natural wealth and to great currency losses, resulting from the difference in the value of raw materials and finished products.

Even with its relatively high rate of economic growth, Canada still has a perennial army of unemployed (3 percent of the total number employed in 1953, 3.9 percent in 1965, 4.7 percent in 1969, 5.9 percent in 1970, and 6.4 percent in 1971 [552,000 persons]).

Industry. Between 1939 and 1969 the volume of industrial output grew sixfold, primarily because of the mining and lumber and paper industries, as well as transportation machine building, ferrous and nonferrous metallurgy, electrical engineering, and the chemicals industry.

During the postwar period the role of mining in the economy increased considerably, although its relative weight in the overall structure of the economy declined. The intensified development of mining has been the decisive factor in the economy's shift of emphasis toward the northern and western parts of the country. In terms of production Canada's mining industry was second only to the USA in the capitalist world in 1970 (value of output, approximately $5 billion). The per capita output of mineral raw materials and semifinished goods is higher in Canada than in any other developed capitalist country. Specifically, it is one-third higher than that of the USA. (See Table 3 for information on the extraction of the principal minerals.)

Table 3. Output of principal minerals

	1939	1949	1959	1971
Coal (million tons)	14.2	17.4	9.6	17.6
Petroleum (million tons)[1] . . .	1.0	2.9	24.8	72.0
Natural gas (billion cu m) . . .	1.0	1.7	11.7	77.0
Iron ore (million tons)	0.1	3.3	22.2	43.3
Copper (thousand tons)[2] . . .	286.0	239.0	358.9	648.0
Nickel (thousand tons)[2] . . .	103.0	117.0	169.2	267.0
Zinc (thousand tons)[2]	239.0	262.0	385.6	1,270.0
Lead (thousand tons)[2]	204.0	145.0	169.2	395.0
Molybdenum (tons)[2]	1.0	—	339.8	12,000.0
Tungsten (WO_3) (tons)[2]	4.0	191.0	—	1,395.0
Uranium (U_3O_8) (thousand tons)[2]	—	—	14.4	3.6
Gold (tons)	158.0	128.0	139.4	69.5
Silver (tons)	721.0	549.0	993.0	1,393.0
Asbestos (million tons)	0.3	0.5	1.0	1.5
Potash (million tons)	—	—	0.04	3.6
Sulfur (million tons)	0.2	0.2	0.8	5.7

[1]Crude [2]By metal content of the ore

With respect to the total volume of all types of energy (calculated on the basis of conventional fuel) Canada held fifth place among the capitalist countries in 1970, whereas in volume of per capita energy requirements it was only slightly behind the USA. In the fuel-energy balance, petroleum accounted for 47 percent, coal 11 percent, natural gas 19 percent, hydroelectric power 23 percent, and firewood less than 1 percent. Waterpower is used to produce most of the country's electric power. As of Jan 1, 1971, the rated capacity of hydroelectric power plants was 28.3 million kW—that is, two-thirds of the capacity of all Canadian electric power plants. The principal hydroelectric power plants are in the provinces of Quebec (47 percent of the capacity), Ontario (24 percent), and British Columbia (14 percent.) The most powerful plants are situated on the St. Lawrence, Betsiamites, Manicouagan-Outardes, Peace, Nelson, and Churchill rivers. A number of large thermoelectric and atomic power plants have been built near Toronto and Vancouver. In 1970 the Pickering Atomic Power Plant was put into operation. (Located east of Toronto, it has a projected capacity of 2.2 million kW.) The Bruce Atomic Power Plant (capacity, 3.2 million kW) was under construction in the province of Ontario in 1973.

The manufacturing industry developed significantly in connection with the demand for armaments during World War II. Between 1939 and 1944 alone the volume of production increased by 2.5 times. In 1966, 22 percent of the labor force in the manufacturing industries was employed in machine building and metalworking, 16 percent in woodworking, 14 percent in food processing, 7 percent in ferrous and nonferrous metallurgy, 7 percent in electrical engineering, and 6 percent in the chemicals industry.

As of 1970, the total output of the manufacturing industries was divided among transportation machine building (12.3 percent), general machine building (3.7 percent), ferrous and nonferrous metallurgy and metalworking (15.9 percent), the cellulose and paper industry (8.5 percent), woodworking (4.2 percent), electrical engineering (6 percent), the chemicals industry (5.8 percent), petroleum refining and coal processing (4 percent), food processing and tobacco curing (19.8 percent), textiles (3.4 percent), the garment industry (2.8 percent), and miscellaneous industries (13.6 percent).

Machine building provides about one-fourth of the value of the output of the manufacturing industries. Its principal branch is transportation machine building (the manufacture of motor vehicles, ships, airplanes, railroad cars, and locomotives). Well developed among the other branches are the manufacture of farm machinery and the production of power equipment and equipment for mining and lumbering. Machine-tool manufacture is poorly developed: many of the leading branches of the

industry depend on equipment imported from the USA, Great Britain, the Federal Republic of Germany (FRG), and Japan. Transportation machine building has been concentrated primarily in subsidiary enterprises of American or British machine-building companies. The principal centers for machine building are Toronto, Montreal, Windsor, Hamilton, Brantford, Oshawa, Halifax, and Vancouver.

Ferrous metallurgy is concentrated in the cities of Hamilton (49 percent), Sault Ste. Marie (18 percent), and Welland in the Lake Region, and Sydney (8 percent) on the Atlantic coast. Aluminum is produced in the cities of Arvida (40 percent), Kitimat (25 percent), Baie Comeau (20 percent), and Île Maline (10 percent) and polymetals, in Trail, Valleyfield, and Beeledune Puene. Copper and nickel are produced in Sudbury, Noranda, Montreal, Port Colborne, Thompson, and Fort Saskatchewan.

In terms of capacity Canada's petroleum refineries hold one of the foremost places in the capitalist world. The principal refineries are located in the chief centers of petroleum consumption (Montreal, 30 percent of Canada's petroleum production, and Vancouver, 5 percent) or at transportation terminals (Sarnia, 12 percent, and Edmonton, 7 percent). The chemicals industry is represented by a number of large plants that turn out basic chemical products as well as high-polymer compounds. The production of chemical fertilizers, synthetic rubber, and plastics is increasing rapidly. The principal centers of the chemicals industry are Sarnia, Montreal, Toronto, Niagara Falls, and Kitchener.

In lumbering, sawmilling, and woodworking, as well as cellulose and paper production, Canada is second in the capitalist world after the USA. Cellulose and paper production has undergone the greatest development. About two-thirds of the capacity of this branch is located in eastern Canada near the large hydroelectric power plants on the St. Lawrence River and its tributaries. After World War II new plants were built in the taiga zone of Manitoba, Saskatchewan, and Alberta and especially in the Canadian Far West on the Pacific coast, where cellulose and paper production is closely coordinated with sawmilling. Located in the Far West is two-thirds of the capacity of the sawmilling industry, whose principal centers are Trois-Rivières, Corner Brook, Powell River, Hull, Port Alberni, Prince George, The Pas, and Prince Rupert.

The chief branches of the food-processing industry are flour milling, meatpacking, fish canning, and distilling of alcoholic beverages, all of which are very important for export. The largest mills are located in ports from which grain is exported (Port Arthur, Montreal, and Vancouver). Among the branches of light industry, textiles, leather and footwear, and garments are relatively well developed. About half of the output of light industry comes from Montreal. Other important centers include Toronto, Vancouver, and Winnipeg. (See Table 4.)

Table 4. Output of major industrial products

	1950	1960	1971
Electric power (billion kW-hrs)	55.0	114.5	215.1
Cast iron and ferrous alloys (million tons)	2.3	4.0	8.0
Steel (million tons)	3.1	5.3	11.0
Copper (thousand tons)	218.0	378.0	478.0
Lead (thousand tons)[1]	155.0	144.0	168.0
Zinc (thousand tons)[1]	185.0	236.0	372.0
Nickel (thousand tons)[1]	112.0	195.0	267.0
Aluminum (thousand tons)[1]	377.0	691.0	980.0
Petroleum products (million tons)	13.1	34.7	68.5
Synthetic rubber (thousand tons)	59.4	162.2	196.1
Paper pulp (million tons)	7.6	10.2	15.8
Newsprint (million tons)	4.8	6.1	7.5
Sawed lumber (million cu m)	9.4	18.5	30.0
Passenger automobiles (thousands) . . .	284.0	326.0	1,096.0
Trucks (thousands)	106.0	71.0	279.0
Radios (thousands)	821.0	676.0	1,995.0
Televisions (thousands)	355.0	339.0	541.0
Cotton fabric (million sq m)	297.0	240.0	221.0
Woolen fabric (million m)	23.0	13.8	22[2]

[1]Obtained by smelting [2]Million sq m

Table 5. Sown area and harvest of principal agricultural crops

	Sown area (million ha)			Harvest (million tons)		
	1935–39[1]	1955–59[1]	1971	1935–39[1]	1955–59[1]	1971
Wheat	10.4	9.2	7.8	8.5	12.7	14.3
Oats	5.4	3.9	3.3	5.2	5.8	5.9
Barley	1.7	3.6	6.2	1.9	5.2	14.3
Corn	0.07[2]	0.2	0.5	0.2[2]	0.8	2.7
Flaxseed	0.1[2]	1.1	0.8	0.03[2]	0.6	0.7
Fodder grasses	3.8	4.6	5.6	14.2	17.6	32.0

[1]Annual average [2]1934–38

Approximately seven-tenths of the manufacturing industry's production capacity is located in the industrial zone of the central provinces of Ontario and Quebec, about one-eighth each in the Far West and the prairie region, and one-twentieth in the maritime region.

Agriculture. Canadian agriculture is characterized by high levels of commodity production, mechanization, and specialization. Approximately three-fourths of the agricultural lands are held by large-scale capitalist farmers who own areas of more than 40 ha each. The competitive struggle against the large mechanized farms has led to the ruin of small farms. Between 1951 and 1966 the number of farms fell by 30 percent. Farmlands total 70 million ha (7.6 percent of Canada's territory), 44 million ha of which are tilled or used as pasture. In addition to cereal crops, sown grasses, industrial crops (flax, rape, and tobacco), and fodder crops (potatoes and corn) hold prominent places in the breakdown of the sown area. (See Table 5.)

During the postwar period important changes have taken place in the structure of agriculture. In 1971, three-fifths of the goods produced came from animal husbandry (see Table 6) and only two-fifths from cultivated crops. (In 1939 these proportions were the reverse.) The structure of each branch of agriculture has also changed. Intensive branches of animal husbandry and crop cultivation (gardening, horticulture, vegetable and fruit growing) have increased their share in the total output. In 1970 there were 700,000 tractors in operation, as well as 200,000 combines and 400,000 trucks, and nine-tenths of the farms had been electrified.

Table 6. Livestock
(thousands)

	1947/48–1951/52[1]	1970
Cattle	7,945	13,069
Dairy cows	2,936	2,551
Pigs	4,792	7,086
Sheep	1,176	1,012
Horses	1,580	324

[1]Annual average

Grain is grown chiefly in the prairie provinces, especially Saskatchewan and Manitoba. Dairy livestock raising and poultry raising are found primarily in the southern parts of the provinces of Ontario and Quebec and in southwestern British Columbia, whereas meat-and-wool animal husbandry is important in British Columbia and Alberta. Truck gardens and orchards are cultivated in British Columbia, Nova Scotia, and Ontario. A number of branches of agriculture tend to cater to exports: more than half the wheat and flaxseed as well as one-third of the barley are exported.

Lumbering is most highly developed in the provinces of British Columbia, Quebec, and Ontario. Canada provides about one-tenth of the wooden goods produced in the world and one-third of the world's lumber exports. There are approximately 90,000 persons employed in fishing. The annual catch is more than 1 million tons of fish, two-thirds of which is exported. Half of the catch is made in the coastal waters off the Atlantic maritime provinces, primarily on the Newfoundland Banks (cod, herring, and crabs), and two-fifths in the Pacific coastal waters and rivers (salmon and halibut).

Transportation. Before World War II more than 90 percent of all Canadian freight was hauled by railroad. During the postwar period the role of rail transportation began to decline (to 60 percent in 1969), as truck transportation, pipelines (99,000 km in 1968), and aviation gained importance. Certain changes have been made in the configuration of the transportation network. To the east-west transcontinental roads were added a number of railroads and highways running north-south (including the Alaskan [Alcan] Highway, 2,500 km long, the Mackenzie Highway, and the Vancouver–Fort Nelson, Sept-Îles–Schefferville, and Grimshaw–Pine Point railroads). As of 1971, there were 71,000 km of railroads and 800,000 km of highways. In 1971 the country had 8.1 million motor vehicles, including 6.3 million passenger cars. In the north and in mountainous regions snowmobiles are used. (In 1969 there were more than 800,000 of them.) Of great importance are maritime and river transportation, as well as haulage on the waterway through the Great Lakes. Since the completion in 1959 of the deepwater seaway along the St. Lawrence River, ocean-going vessels weighing as much as 26,000 tons can reach ports on the Great Lakes. As of 1969, the tonnage of Canada's merchant marine fleet (including lake and river vessels) was 3.7 million gross registered tons. The principal ports (based on cargo turnover in millions of tons in 1969) are Vancouver (21.5), Sept-Îles (17.2), Montreal (15.9), and Thunder Bay (12.5). The role of aviation is great, especially in the northern areas. The principal airports are Montreal, Toronto, Vancouver, Winnipeg, and Ottawa.

Foreign trade. In terms of the turnover of foreign trade in 1969, Canada occupied sixth place in the capitalist world (6 percent). Approximately one-fourth of the goods produced by Canada are exported. More than two-thirds of the value of Canadian exports is in raw materials, semifinished products, and foodstuffs. Canada's exports are newsprint, wheat, sawed lumber, paper pulp, nickel, aluminum, petroleum and petroleum products, iron ore, copper, asbestos, uranium, and potash. Most of the value of the nation's imports is accounted for by finished industrial products, as well as coal and tropical products such as coffee, rubber, bananas, and cacao. (See Table 7.)

The geography of Canada's foreign trade has usually been characterized by the strong predominance of the USA and Great Britain. Because US monopolies took advantage of Great Britain's weakened position during and after World War II, Britain's share in Canada's foreign trade was reduced from 32

Table 7. Exports and imports by groups of goods
(percent of total)

	Exports			Imports		
	1948	1959	1970	1948	1959	1970
Livestock	2.8	1.1	0.4	0.1	0.2	0.2
Foodstuffs, beverages, and tobacco	27.6	20.3	10.9	10.6	10.2	7.8
Raw materials	10.1	21.6	18.2	26.1	13.2	8.4
Semifinished goods	45.8	49.0	35.2	28.3	25.3	20.7
Finished goods	13.6	7.7	35.1	33.7	49.7	61.7
Miscellaneous items	0.1	0.3	0.2	1.2	1.4	1.2

percent in 1939 to 8 percent in 1969, whereas the US share of trade with Canada during the same period increased from 50 to 70 percent. The USA, which needs Canadian industrial raw materials and semifinished goods, became the principal market for Canadian goods.

The value of Canadian exports in 1971 was Can-$17,847,000,000 and of imports Can$15,608,000,000. Major trading partners, in percents, were the USA, 68.1 (exports) and 70.1 (imports); Great Britain, 7.6 and 5.3; Japan, 4.4 and 5.1; the FRG, 1.8 and 2.8; the Netherlands, 1.3 and 0.5; and Italy, 1.2 and 1. Canada has established economic ties with the USSR and other socialist countries. The monetary unit is the Canadian dollar. As of February 1973 the Gosbank (State Bank of the USSR) set the exchange rate at Can$1 = 0.83 rubles.

Internal differences. The central region (the southern parts of the provinces of Ontario and Quebec) is well developed industrially. Inhabited by two-thirds of the country's population, it accounts for more than two-thirds of the country's industrial output. Most of the region's territory is located on the Canadian Shield, which is rich in minerals. There are also great reserves of hydroelectric power (30 million kW) and timber (half of Canada's reserves). The southern part of the shield is framed by the fertile lands of the St. Lawrence Valley and the agricultural regions of southern Ontario. The central region's economic development was promoted by its rich natural resources and its advantageous geographic position in the center of the country, adjacent to the industrially developed US northeast on convenient transportation routes (the Great Lakes and the St. Lawrence River).

The shore belt from Windsor to Toronto and from there to Montreal has an almost unbroken chain of industrial cities, sporadically interrupted by regions of intensive agriculture. Located in the region is nine-tenths of Canada's production capacity for motor vehicles, airplanes, farm machinery, electric power equipment, and electrical equipment, four-fifths of the capacity of the chemicals and light industries, and two-thirds of the capacity of the cellulose and paper industries and nonferrous and ferrous metallurgy. The region also accounts for half the output of mining and agriculture. The region's agriculture specializes in animal husbandry as well as the cultivation of vegetables, tobacco, and fruit. The largest industrial centers are Montreal and Toronto, where one-third of Canada's industrial output is produced.

The prairie region (most of the provinces of Manitoba, Saskatchewan, and Alberta) encompasses the Canadian part of the Great Plains. The region has one-sixth of the country's population and accounts for one-tenth of its industrial output. Since the beginning of the 20th century the prairie region has been an important agricultural region. Before the end of the 1950's extensive agriculture prevailed, specializing in the production of grain, meat, and wool. With the discovery in 1947 of a major petroleum deposit (Leduc, in Alberta), as well as new deposits of polymetals, potash, uranium, and coal, the mining, petroleum, and gas chemicals industries developed. In 1969 the value of the region's industrial production was three times the value of its agricultural production. The chemicals industry (Edmonton and Calgary), food processing (Calgary and Winnipeg), and nonferrous metallurgy (Thompson and Fort Sakatchewan) have been developed.

The Far West (the province of British Columbia) accounts for one-tenth of the nation's population and one-tenth of its industrial output. A region of new industries, it specializes particularly in the production of raw materials and semifinished products for export. In 1971 the region provided four-fifths of the plywood produced in the country, two-thirds of the sawed lumber, one-fourth of the paper pulp, and one-fifth of the paper. Great quantities of polymetals, copper, and molybdenum ores are mined. About half of the capacity of the region's processing industries is concentrated in Vancouver. Other important industrial centers are Victoria (shipbuilding and aircraft construction), Kitimat (aluminum), and Trail (lead and zinc).

The maritime region (basically the provinces of Newfoundland, Prince Edward Island, New Brunswick, and Nova Scotia) lags considerably behind the other regions of Canada in its level of development. Although about one-tenth of the country's population lives in the region, it accounts for only approximately one-sixteenth of Canada's industrial output. During the postwar period the maritime region has been characterized by the country's lowest population growth rates as well as the lowest growth in output and in volume of capital investments. Relatively poor in natural resources, the region has a narrow energy base (only coal). It is far away from the country's principal industrial centers. Most of the population is engaged in fishing, agriculture, and coal mining. The principal industrial centers are St. John (petroleum refining) and Halifax (shipbuilding and automotive assembly).

The Canadian North consists of the Yukon Territory, the Northwest Territories, and the northern parts of the provinces of Alberta, Saskatchewan, Manitoba, Ontario, and Quebec. During the postwar period there has been accelerated exploitation of mineral, hydroelectric power, and timber resources, and a network of new industrial cities and settlements has been created. Despite the smallness of the newly created centers, they occupy a prominent place in the total Canadian output (for example, Pine Point—polymetals, Knob Lake—iron ore, Tungsten—tungsten, and Clinton Creek—asbestos).

REFERENCES

Antipova, A. V., and I. F. Antonova. *Kanada.* Moscow, 1972.
Mileikovskii, A. *Kanada i anglo-amerikanskie protivorechiia.* Moscow, 1958.
Borodaevskii, A. D. *Kanada i mezhimperialisticheskaia bor'ba za istochniki syr'ia.* Moscow, 1968.
Sushchenko, V. V. *Monopolisticheskii kapital Kanady.* Moscow, 1964.
Canada Yearbook: 1960–1970. Ottawa, 1960–70.
Canada: One Hundred, 1867–1967. Ottawa, 1967.   L. N. KARPOV

Armed forces

The armed forces consist of the army, air force, and navy. The supreme commander in chief is the prime minister, and the highest military leadership is exercised by the Council of Defense and directly by the minister of defense. The Council of Defense includes the minister of defense (chairman), three civilians, including the deputy minister of defense and the chairman of the military scientific research committee, and the chief of staff for defense and his deputy. The army is made up of recruited volunteers. As of 1972 the total number of men in the armed forces was approximately 90,000, of whom more than 5,000 were included in the joint armed forces of NATO on the territory of the FRG.

Organizationally, the armed forces are united into seven commands: mobile, antiaircraft defense, naval, training, air transport, communications, and European. In addition, there is a separate air division that has been transferred to the joint armed forces of NATO. Subordinate to the mobile command are four mechanized brigade groups, two airborne landing brigade groups, a parachute regiment, and four squadrons of tactical fighter airplanes (including one training group), several aviation transport squadrons, and helicopters. Their armaments include up-to-date types of combat matériel and weapons of Canadian as well as American and British manufacture. Subordinate to the antiaircraft defense are three squadrons of fighter aircraft and two squadrons of antiaircraft guided missiles. The air transport command is in charge of strategic aviation transfers. There are about 300 airplanes in the mobile antiaircraft defense and air transport commands.

Subordinate to the naval command are the Atlantic and Pacific fleets as well as the naval air force. There are four submarines, several destroyers, six base minesweepers, 22 patrol vessels, and several auxiliary vessels of domestic and foreign manufacture. The naval air force has four squadrons of antisubmarine defense and one squadron of deck-based helicopters.

Health and social welfare

Medicine and public health. In 1969 the birthrate was 17.6 per 1,000 inhabitants, the total mortality rate was 7.3, and infant mortality was 19.3 per 1,000 live births. The principal causes of death are diseases of the cardiovascular system, malignant growths, diseases of the vessels of the central nervous system, and pneumonia. The chief causes of infant mortality are premature births and birth defects. The level of on-the-job injuries is high: in 1972 there were about 12,000 accidents, of which more than 5,000 were fatal. Infectious diseases such as tuberculosis, syphilis, and meningococcal meningitis are especially widespread among the Indians and Eskimo. Since the 1950's the rising incidence of mental illness, alcoholism, and drug addiction has presented serious public-health problems. In the Canadian North, a region with a harsh climate and a sparse population (basically Indians and Eskimo), an increase in the incidence of tuberculosis, infectious diseases, and mental illness has been noted. Pneumonia, scurvy, and keratosis are frequently encountered there, as well as echinococcosis (especially in the west), alveolysis (encountered also on the islands of the Canadian Arctic Archipelago), trichinosis, and diphyllobothriasis. In the south cardiovascular diseases and malignant tumors prevail. Salmonellosis is widespread. Cases of toxoplasmosis have been recorded in the central provinces and cases of Q-fever, in Quebec Province.

In 1970 there were 210,600 hospital beds (ten beds per 1,000 inhabitants). There were 30,000 physicians (one physician per 717 inhabitants), 6,500 oral surgeons, 9,000 pharmacists, and 114,600 nurses working in Canada in 1969.

Canada has a system of old-age pension insurance. The pension fund is made up of contributions from workers (1.8 percent of their wages) and entrepreneurs. The minimum age at which a worker is entitled to receive a pension is very high—65 (prior to 1965 it was 70). Moreover, pensions are paid only to persons who have lived in Canada for at least ten years (the "residence qualification," which was 20 years until 1965). As a result of persistent class struggle, the workers have gained some improvements in pension insurance conditions. Those who have completely lost their capacity to work are paid pensions according to the degree of their disability.

Medical personnel are trained at 15 medical schools, which are generally part of various universities.

Canada's sulfur springs are well known (Hot Springs in the province of Alberta—a well-equipped mountain-balneological health resort at an elevation of 1,450 m). Among the nation's tuberculosis sanatoriums are Ste. Agathe in Montreal and a number of others on Lake Muskoka near Toronto, in Manitoba, and in Nova Scotia. There are summer camps on the islands of Newfoundland and Cape Breton and in the province of New Brunswick.   O. L. LOSEV and A. A. ROZOV

Veterinary services. Farm animals are relatively free of infectious and parasitic diseases. Rabies is the most widespread disease (283 new foci in 1971), and in the Canadian North a special form of the disease has been observed among wild animals and dogs (arctic dog disease). Sporadic cases of malignant anthrax, tuberculosis, brucellosis, and classic hog cholera have been recorded. More frequently encountered diseases are helminthiases and skin and metabolic diseases.

As of 1971, there were more than 2,000 veterinarians in Canada. Specialists are trained in three colleges in the provinces of Ontario, Quebec, and Saskatchewan. The state veterinary service is administered by the Department of Agriculture. Scientific research is conducted at the Eastern Institute (in Ottawa, Ontario) and the Western Institute (in Lethbridge, Alberta), as well as in a number of laboratories.   I. A. BAKULOV

Education and cultural affairs

Problems of elementary and secondary education are under the jurisdiction of the provincial authorities. Each province has a department (ministry) of education. To coordinate the work of the provincial departments the Committee of Canadian Ministers of Education was established in 1960. In 1967 it became the Council of Canadian Ministers of Education, with a secretariat in Toronto. The federal government is responsible for organizing the education of the Indians and Eskimo. However, schooling is received by only an insignificant number of the children of the native peoples of Canada (in the academic year 1968–69, only 38,000). Because schools are locally financed, there are disparities in the material potentials of the schools of different regions. In addition to the state schools there is a network of private basically denominational schools (for example, Catholic and Protestant). Education is compulsory for all children between the ages of six and 14–16 (depending on the province).

Among Canada's preschool institutions are nurseries for children between ages 1½ and three, toddlers, schools for children

age three and four, and kindergartens for children age five to six. Although they are attached to the state elementary schools, the kindergartens are usually private. During the academic year 1969–70 more than 350,000 children, or 75 percent of the children of preschool age, were enrolled in preschool institutions.

Historically, two school systems developed in Canada: the French and the English. The former, which is encountered primarily in the province of Quebec, is organized in accordance with the reform of 1964 into a six-year elementary school and a five-year secondary school (two cycles of two and three years of instruction). During the second cycle the students are placed in general educational or vocational divisions. After completing their secondary educations, students may enroll in colleges of general and occupational education, where they receive either three years of vocational training or two years of academic education that prepares them for enrollment in a university.

The English school system closely resembles that of the US: a six-year elementary school, a three-year junior high school, and a three-year senior high school, or an eight-year elementary school and a four-year secondary school. The students in the senior high school are sharply differentiated. Like their US counterparts, Canadian schools give intelligence tests, with the aid of which secondary school students are assigned to academic or practical study plans—a distribution that coincides with the children's social status. As a rule, the academic curriculum is closed to the children from low-income families. Graduation from senior high school grants students the right to enroll in a university.

During the academic year 1969–70 there was a total enrollment of 3.8 million pupils in all elementary schools and 1.5 million in the secondary schools.

Vocational training is given at the vocational divisions of secondary schools and in vocational high schools (state and private), as well as at enterprises in training centers. Junior colleges have been established for those who have graduated from secondary schools. They offer terms of instruction ranging from one to three years and train specialists with middle-level qualifications. During the academic year 1968–69 there were 263,100 students enrolled in institutions offering vocational training.

The system of higher education includes universities, colleges (many of which are attached to universities), and technical institutes. Tuition, which has been raised repeatedly, is charged for instruction at higher educational institutions. About 15 percent of the students are granted small stipends. The largest institutions of higher learning are the universities of Toronto, Ottawa, and Manitoba (Winnipeg), Alberta (Edmonton), and British Columbia (Vancouver), as well as McGill (Montreal), Laval (Quebec), Western Ontario (London), and Queen's (Kingston) universities. During the academic year 1969–70 there were 479,000 students enrolled in higher educational institutions, including 298,000 at universities.

The largest libraries are the University of Toronto Library (founded in 1842; more than 3.6 million volumes), the Laval University Library in Quebec (founded in 1852; 885,000 volumes), the Montreal Public Library (founded in 1902; 912,000 volumes), the Toronto Public Library (750,000 volumes), and the National Library of Science in Ottawa (more than 760,000 volumes).

The principal museums are the National Museum of Canada (founded in 1842) and the National Gallery of Canada in Ottawa (founded in 1880), the Royal Ontario Museum (founded in 1912) and the Art Gallery of Ontario in Toronto (founded in 1900), and the Museum of Fine Arts in Montreal (founded in 1860).
                                                Z. A. MAL'KOVA

Science and scientific institutions

Natural and technical sciences. The development of the sciences in Canada was based on the work of European scholars, chiefly émigrés from France and Great Britain. In the 17th century, the Frenchman J. Cornut wrote the first geographical, botanical, and zoological descriptions of the Canadian territories, and S. de Champlain made the first geological investigations. A description of the flora of eastern Canada was included in a work by J. P. de Tournefort. The Swedish naturalist P. Kalm, who left a description of his journey through Canada in 1749, is known as the father of Canadian botany.

During the first half of the 19th century a systematic study of the Canadian territory was begun by scientists, fur traders such as A. Mackenzie, and seafarers (J. Franklin, W. Parry, and J. Ross). The work of J. Bigsby, who drew up one of the first geological maps of North America, provided a basis for the assumption that there were large reserves of valuable minerals in Canada. From 1836 to 1846, A. Gesner investigated the geological structure and mineral resources of Nova Scotia, New Brunswick, and Prince Edward Island. In 1842 the Canadian Geological Service was founded. Its first director, W. Logan, established the existence of the Canadian Shield and was the first (1863) to identify specifically a group of Precambrian deposits. From 1841 to 1869 he directed the geological survey of Canada, in 1863 he and T. Hunt published the *Geology of Canada*, and in 1869 he drew up one of the most complete maps of the country.

Research in chemistry was initially limited to narrowly practical problems connected with the needs of medicine, agriculture, metallurgy, glassmaking, and various industries. In 1852, A. Gesner invented a method of obtaining kerosene from petroleum and founded a kerosene company.

During the second half of the 19th century Canadians began to form their own schools of science. The country's economic and political condition stimulated progress primarily in applied biological disciplines such as botany, breeding, dendrology, forestry, zoology, entomology, and ichthyology. In 1862, L. Provancher published his fundamental work, *Canadian Flora.* Taxonomy began to develop in the 1880's with the work of such scientists as John and James Macoun and J. Fletcher. O. Brunet established the first herbarium at Laval University (Quebec) in 1860. From 1883 to 1902, John Macoun published the *Catalogue of Canadian Plants* (vols. 1–7) and assembled a collection of Canadian plants that became the basis of the National Herbarium in Ottawa. After the founding in 1886 of experimental farms and laboratories under the Department of Agriculture, with the participation of scientific groups in the provincial universities, systematic research was begun in applied botany and agriculture under the direction of W. Saunders, a botanist and specialist in breeding, who laid the foundation for the introduction into Canada of specific varieties of wheat, several of which he brought from Russia. The founder of ornithology in Canada was T. McIlwraith, the author of the book *Birds of Ontario Province* (1886). G. Dawson founded the national school of paleobotany, and J. Whiteaves was the founder of Canadian paleontology.

J. Fields, who established the first Canadian school of mathematics at the University of Toronto, played an important role in stimulating research in mathematics. The development of Canadian mathematics was considerably influenced by J. Sylvester, who had worked in the USA.

At the end of the 19th century and the beginning of the 20th, little work was done in applied chemistry and physics because Canada did not have a chemicals or electrical engineering industry. Outstanding among Canadian scientists were W. Gibbs, who worked out a new electrochemical method for obtaining phosphorus, and T. Willson, who proposed a new method for producing calcium carbide (1892).

The expansion of production to fill orders from Great Britain and the USA during World War I gave considerable impetus to the development of Canadian science. In order to coordinate scientific research, the National Research Council was founded in 1916. Originally, it had three departments: physics, chemistry, and biology (including medicine).

Prior to World War II most scientific research was done in the universities, and very few scientific studies were undertaken by Canadian industry. Thus, in the leading branch of machine building—transportation machine building—research was conducted by US firms. In 1932 the National Research Council established its own laboratories for experimental biology, applied physics, general chemistry, and research on construction, radio engineering, and medicine.

Research in chemistry developed during the period between the two world wars and after World War II. Cheap electric power promoted the growth of energy-consuming industries. Considerable work was conducted on chemicals production technology, especially on explosives. Research was done on the chemistry of binding substances and cements (T. Thorvaldson), organic chemistry, and forest chemistry (P. Gagnon, C. Allen, and R. Ruttan), and the chemistry of the cellulose-paper industry (C. Thorne, J. Bates, and G. Tomlinson). L. Pilden developed a technique for producing sodium metal. A great deal of work was done in biochemistry by such scientists as J. Anderson and R. Larmour. An outstanding discovery in pharmaceutical chemistry and the chemistry of hormones was made in 1921–22, when F. Banting, whose work was directed by J. Macleod, discovered and obtained insulin. (Both men were awarded a Nobel Prize in 1923.) Well known in theoretical chemistry are the works of H. Thode (physical chemistry, the chemistry of isotopes), A. Campbell (physical chemistry), and F. Beamish (analytical chemistry). For his research in physics and analytical chemistry G. Herzberg was awarded a Nobel Prize in 1971.

Scientific research in physics was begun even prior to World War I by H. Callendar, who worked in Canada between 1893 and 1898, and E. Rutherford, who worked there from 1898 to 1907. H. Barnes' studies of water and ice achieved worldwide recognition. Working with F. Soddy, Rutherford established the characteristics of X rays, having determined the ratio of the charge to the mass of X particles, and he founded the theory of radioactivity. J. McLennan at the University of Toronto proved the existence of cosmic rays, investigated the spectra of the Northern Lights, and was the first on the American continent to obtain liquid helium. He founded the Canadian school of low-temperature physics, whose members still do productive research. Geophysics was developed considerably by D. Keys and A. Eve. During the prewar and postwar years a school of human geography developed in French Canada under scientists such as R. Blanchard and B. Brouillette, but in the rest of Canada, Anglo-American geographic concepts prevailed (for example, D. Putnam and T. Lloyd).

From the beginning of World War II work in nuclear physics expanded. A nuclear laboratory was established at the University of Montreal in 1942, with the aid of scientists from Great Britain and the USA. In 1945 the first Canadian research reactor was put into operation and in 1947, a research reactor which, at that time, was the largest in the world. A scientific research center on atomic energy was established at Chalk River in 1944, and in the early 1960's one was built at Whiteshell. The first atomic power plant in Canada was put into operation in 1962. Research in atomic energy focuses on the development and introduction of systems for the production of cheap electric energy. A significant contribution to the development of nuclear physics in Canada was made by J. Mackenzie.

The Canadian school of mathematics was strengthened by the German émigrés P. Scherk and H. Zassenhaus. It also included a significant number of scholars who were working temporarily in Canada (for example, S. Newcomb, R. C. Archibald, R. Richardson, G. Pall, A. Tucker, and I. Kaplansky). Mathematical statistics underwent intensive development in the work of A. Warren at the University of Manitoba in Winnipeg and M. Mackenzie at the University of Toronto. Canada has modern computer centers, the largest of which is located at the University of Toronto. It serves the National Research Council as well as the scientific research institutions of the Canadian Department of Defense. At the University of Alberta (Edmonton), studies are being conducted on general systems theory by L. von Bertalanffy and his colleagues.

During the postwar years Canada began to develop its own research in the technical sciences (radar apparatus and electrical engineering), as well as in mining and the cellulose-paper industry. Research in biology has increased (for example, studies on genetics and breeding at McGill University under the direction of J. Boyce, as well as work on photosynthesis). There has also been an increase in research on petroleum geology. Complex research is also being done on the arctic.

The Scientific Research Center for Communications, which was known as the Military Scientific Institute of Long-Distance

Communication until 1968, has its own program that focuses on the study of the cosmos. A Canadian artificial earth satellite of the Alouette-Isis type, which is designed to investigate the ionosphere, was launched jointly by Canada and the USA. The satellite Isis I was launched in 1969. Subsequently, Alouette I and Alouette II were launched. With the aid of the USA and France, Canada is working on a system of satellite communications.

The development of scientific research at the end of the 1960's and during the 1970's demanded the perfection of a system of administering and coordinating the sciences. Appropriations for the National Research Council increased sharply. In 1964 the Scientific Secretariat was established under the office of the prime minister and in 1966, the Science Council of Canada, a consultative body under the government. The largest scientific institutes are the Canadian Aeronautics and Space Institute, the Canadian Institute of Mining and Metallurgy, the Chemical Institute of Canada, the Biological Institute for Cell Research, the Institute for Animal Research, the Institute for Plant Research, the Canadian Forestry Institute, and various research institutions attached to the universities (for example, the Institute of Experimental Medicine and Surgery at the University of Montreal and numerous oncologic-institutes.   Z. E. GEL'MAN

Social sciences. PHILOSOPHY. During the 19th century philosophical trends in Canada developed under the influence of French and Anglo-American sources. Moreover, the fundamental source of the French influence remained the Catholic philosophy of neo-Thomism.

At the end of the 19th century and the beginning of the 20th J. Watson and his disciples played an important role in disseminating philosophy in Canada. The views of the school of speculative philosophy, which were formed under the influence of Anglo-American neo-Hegelianism, facilitated the assimilation of the doctrines of classical German idealism (primarily the ideas of Kant and Hegel). The idealism of this trend in Canadian philosophy was close in spirit to right-wing Hegelianism. Opposed to speculative philosophy was the realism of G. S. Brett, who became very influential during the first quarter of the 20th century. Unlike Anglo-American neorealism and critical realism, Brett's philosophy was not dominated by epistemological problems. Its fundamental category was "integralness," understood pluralistically as something not reducible to an abstract uniform "essence"—that is, as a qualitative diversity of being, a "many-colored garden of life." The adherents of Brett's "integral realism" were F. H. Anderson and T. A. Goudge in Toronto and A. H. Johnson at Western Ontario University (London). R. C. Lodge attempted to create an "equalizing philosophy"— that is, an essentially eclectic doctrine combining idealism, realism, and pragmatism. The contemporary works of Canadian philosophers have been noticeably influenced by neopositivism, and the nation's few Protestant philosophers have been influenced by Christian existentialism.

The teaching of philosophy in the universities has been affected by a policy of attracting foreign professors into the faculties. Attention is focused on the history of philosophy, particularly on the ancient and medieval periods. The largest centers, which are of international importance for the development and teaching of neo-Thomist philosophy, are the School of Higher Philosophy at Laval University in Quebec (founded by M. and L. Paquet and headed by C. de Koninck), the Albertus Magnus Institute of Medieval Research (founded by the Dominican Order in Ottawa; located in Montreal since 1942; faculty of philosophy headed by L. M. Régis), and the influential Catholic center for the study of medieval philosophy at the Papal Institute for Medieval Research in Toronto. (Founded in 1929, it has attracted the most important Thomist philosophers from various countries, including E. Gilson—the director of the institute— and J. Maritain.)

Founded in 1958, the Canadian Philosophical Association unites philosophers of both English and French backgrounds. Located in Montreal are the French Canadian Association and the Philosophical Association, which is attached to McGill University. Propaganda for the Marxist-Leninist world view is conducted by the Communist Party of Canada. Philosophical journals published in Canada are *Dialogue* (since 1962; the organ of the Canadian Philosophical Association), *Etudes mediévales*

(since 1939; the organ of the Papal Institute for Medieval Research in Toronto), *Laval théologique et philosophique* (since 1945; the organ of Laval University in Quebec).

B. E. BYKHOVSKII

HISTORICAL SCHOLARSHIP. In Canada there are English-Canadian and French-Canadian trends in historiography. Their appearance during the first half of the 19th century reflected the emergence and the development of two nations within the country.

The principal themes of French-Canadian historiography include the history of Canada prior to 1763, the problem of the historical fate of the French Canadians after the British conquest of Canada, and their place and role in modern Canada. The foundations of French-Canadian historiography were laid in the mid-19th century by the works of F.-X. Garneau. In the 20th century, French-Canadian historiography has been represented by the works of T. Chapais, A. Maheux, L. Groulx, and G. Lanctot.

In the English-Canadian historiography of the second half of the 19th and the beginning of the 20th centuries the British, or imperial, school of constitutional history prevailed. Its representatives (for example, W. Kingsford, R. Christie, G. Parkin, J. Dent, A. Bradley, and J. Hannay) were oriented toward the Conservative Party. They regarded the history of Canada as a model of the "transplanting" of British institutions, and they substantiated the idea of the imperial unity and preservation of Canada, faced with the threat of American expansionism, within the framework of the British Empire. The biographical genre prevailed in their works.

With the onset of the general crisis of capitalism, the imperial school was subjected to frontal criticism. Canada's evolution from colonial status to national independence became the leading theme of constitutional historiography (R. Trotter, R. Langstone, and R. M. Dawson). Liberal historiography, which during this period became the principal trend in bourgeois historical scholarship, relied on the study of historical phenomena specific to the Canadian experience (R. Lower and F. Underhill). The liberal historians even went so far as to show why Canada's complete separation from Great Britain was necessary (J. Dafoe). Under the influence of the concepts of the American historian F. J. Turner, the treatment of Canadian history in the spirit of the idea of "North American exclusiveness" became widespread. At the same time, historians became more interested in socioeconomic problems and an economic trend was established for the first time in Canadian historiography (H. A. Innis and W. Macintosh). The works of Innis laid the foundations for the Laurentian School (D. Creighton), which defended the thesis that the trade capital of the St. Lawrence valley had had a determining role in creating a centralized Canadian state.

In 1922 the Canadian Historical Association, which united the principal groups of historians, was founded. After World War II the economic trend in Canadian historiography declined. The proportion of historical biographies among historical publications began to rise again. Social democratic historiography, which originated in the 1930's, limited itself basically to investigating the history of the social democratic movement in Canada (for example, C. McNaught and W. Young). Marxist historiography made a contribution to the study of the general problems of the country's historical development (S. Ryerson) as well as to the study of important, narrower problems (M. Fairley's work on the uprising of 1837–38). In addition, Marxist historians such as T. Buck and L. Morris worked on the history of the workers' and communist movements.

Almost all research in history is done at the universities of Toronto, Montreal, and Quebec. The University of Toronto has published the journal *Canadian Historical Review* since 1920. The activity of Marxist historians is coordinated by the Center for Marxist Studies (founded in 1959).   O. S. SOROKO-TSIUPA

ECONOMIC SCHOLARSHIP. Written primarily by Englishmen, the first works on economics appeared in Canada during the 1820's and 1830's and were associated with the problems of the efficacy of colonizing the country (R. Gourley and E. G. Wakefield). The first representative of theoretical political economy was also an Englishman, J. Rae, who lived in Canada from 1822 to 1850. He criticized the system of free trade in Canada and some of A. Smith's theoretical positions, and he demonstrated the necessity for state intervention to accelerate the development of the economy. Many of Rae's ideas were ahead of his time, and they have been reechoed in present-day bourgeois theories, such as theories of economic growth.

The formation of the Dominion of Canada and the rise of new economic problems stimulated the growth of economic scholarship. During the 1880's the leading universities in Toronto, Montreal, Kingston, and Fredricton began to establish departments of political economy. A number of British professors were invited to direct the new university departments (E. J. Urwick, a follower of A. Marshall, and W. J. Ashley, a proponent of the historical school of thought, who laid the foundations for the Toronto school of political economy, which took shape during the 1920's). The first political economist of Canadian origin was A. Shortt, who studied the problems of the domestic economy at the beginning of the 20th century. The 1920's and 1930's saw the emergence of a trend that studies the concrete problems of Canadian economic policy (for example, J. Deutsch, H. S. Gordon, W. Mackintosh, and D. Slater). The founder of Canadian economic history was H. A. Innis. The theoretical positions advanced by him—especially the "raw materials theory"— have been developed by contemporary Canadian economic historians such as D. Creighton, C. Barber, H. Aitken, and W. Easterbrook.

During the 1960's work was begun on problems of public consumption, labor relations, unemployment and its causes, and economic programming. A new progressive trend, which was opposed to Canada's growing economic dependence on the USA, began to develop in the works of economists such as H. Maccollum, J. Minifie, L. Lameteri, and D. Porter. In the universities of the French-speaking province of Quebec the influence of the Catholic Church remains powerful, and the principal economic doctrine of class peace between labor and capital has taken on a clerical-nationalist tone.

The development of Marxist economic theory finds expression in the programs of the Communist Party of Canada, the works of the Center for Marxist Studies, and the works of Marxist economists.

The centers of economic scholarship are the universities of Toronto and Western Ontario and Queen's University (Kingston). The leading organization concerned with economic problems is the Department of Economics and Accounting (founded in 1967). Journals on economics include the *Canadian Journal of Economics* (since 1935), *Queen's Quarterly* (since 1893), *L'Actualité économique* (since 1925), and *Relations industrielles* (since 1945).   T. K. PAZHITNOVA

Press, radio, and television

In 1973 more than 1,500 newspapers, journals, and other periodicals were published in Canada. Among the English periodical publications are the *Toronto Daily Star* (since 1892; circulation, about 365,000), which reflects the point of view of the Liberal Party, *The Globe and Mail* (since 1844; circulation, 262,000), and the *Ottawa Journal* (since 1885; circulation, 78,300). Other English publications are the *Montreal Star* (since 1869; circulation more than 190,000), which is close to the leadership of the Progressive Conservative Party; the *Gazette* (since 1778; circulation, 140,000); and *The Ottawa Citizen* (since 1844; circulation, about 140,000). The most important French newspapers are the Catholic *Le Devoir* (since 1910; circulation, more than 40,000), *La Presse* (since 1884; circulation, 194,000), *Le Soleil* (since 1896; circulation, more than 150,000), and *Le Droit* (since 1913; circulation, approximately 50,000). The principal journals are *Maclean's Magazine* (since 1905; circulation, 625,000) and *Weekend Magazine* (since 1951; circulation, more than 2 million). Publications of the Communist Party of Canada include the newspaper *Canadian Tribune* (since 1940) and the theoretical journal *Communist Viewpoint* (since 1969).

The Canadian news agency—the Canadian Press—was founded in 1917.

Radio and television broadcasting is done by the Canadian Broadcasting Corporation (CBC), which was founded in 1936.

There are more than 360 radio stations and more than 300 television stations in operation.   B. V. ALEKSASHKIN

Literature

Canadian literature has developed primarily in English and French. Literary works are also published in Russian, Ukrainian, and other languages. Some of the creative oral art of the native population—the Indians and Eskimo—has been collected by 20th-century English-Canadian writers. In defense of the rights of the Indians, the poetess Pauline Johnson (1862–1913) devoted her life to a literary reworking of their legends. The tragic lot of the Eskimo is narrated in the books *People of the Deer* (1952) and *The Desperate People* (1959) by F. Mowat (born 1921), the author of books on the settlement and mastery of the Canadian North.

Literature in French. In the literature of the period of French colonization, works on religious topics and diaries of the first settlers prevailed. After the establishment of British rule in Canada (1763), French literature reflected the resistance of French Canadians to assimilation. The shaping of a French-Canadian literature was considerably influenced by French culture, as well as by religious, patriotic, and patriarchical ideas. The quickening of Canadian social and cultural life in the mid-19th century promoted the rise of a patriotic school of romantic poets, which included L. Fréchette (1839–1908) and P. Lemay (1837–1918). Its leader was O. Crémazie (1827–79)—the first major French-Canadian poet and the publisher of the first literary journal, *Les Soirées canadiennes* (1861–65). The romantic prose of the 19th century (the novels of A. Gérin-Lajoie, 1824–82, and P. de Gaspé *père,* 1786–1871) celebrated the historical past. The Montreal school of poets, which came into being in 1895 and consisted chiefly of writers who had remained true to romanticism (C. Gill, 1871–1918, and E. Nelligan, 1879–1941), sought new poetic means and endeavored to free itself from the influence of Catholic ideology.

At the beginning of the 20th century regional literature, which idealized the patriarchal way of life and piety of the peasants, became widespread. The novel *Marie Chapdelaine* (1916) by L. Hémon (1880–1913) influenced literature about the colonial period, enriching it with realistic elements. During the period between the two world wars the Canadian adherents of the French Parnassians came to the fore. S.-D. Garneau (1912–43) was one of the first Canadian poets to attempt to convey a tragic sense of the world.

During the 1930's realism developed, becoming the principal trend in French-Canadian literature by the mid-1940's. Writers addressed themselves to social problems. R. Lemelin (born 1919) wrote satiric descriptions of church officials and scourged hypocrisy and philistinism (the novel *At the Foot of a Gentle Slope,* 1944). In the novel *Secondhand Luck* (1945), Gabrielle Roy (born 1909) described life in the workingmen's quarter of a large capitalist city, revealing the inner world of the heroes with psychological depth. The novels of Ringuet (pseudonym of P. Panneton, 1895–1960) showed the decline of the patriarchal way of life.

Since the 1950's prose has increasingly tended toward psychologism, depicting man's alienation in capitalist society. This trend is evident, for example, in the works of Y. Thériault (born 1915) and E. Cloutier (born 1921). Protest against religious asceticism is encountered in the creative work of A. Langevin (born 1927) and A. Giroux (born 1916). In the novel *The Asbestos Fire* (1956), J.-J. Richard (born 1911) showed the clash between workers and the American capitalists who own the enterprises. H. Aquin (born 1929) summons French Canadians to struggle for their national worth in the novel *The Next Episode* (1965). Characteristic of the novels of C. Jasmin (born 1930) is an abstract humanism. Marie Claire Blais (born 1940) drew a realistic picture of the life of French Canadians in the novel *A Season in the Life of Emmanuel* (1966).

From the late 1940's through the 1960's poets have attempted to reflect the intellectual and emotional life of their contemporaries. A. Grandbois (born 1900) turned to topics of love, life, and death, and in the poetry of Anne Hébert (born 1916) motifs of despair alternate with a consciousness of the greatness and beauty of the surrounding world. The poems of Rina Lasnier (born 1915) are characterized by a religious, mystical mood. Political ideas permeate the poetry of R. Giguère (born 1929), J.-G. Pilon (born 1930), P. Chamberland (born 1939), and J. Brault (born 1932). Reflected in their creative work is the theme of the French Canadians' struggle against economic and political inequality. The prose writer L. Groulx (1878–1967) and some of his followers have adopted nationalist attitudes toward English Canadians.

Literature in English. To a large degree, early English-Canadian literature was limited by the traditions of English romanticism; frequently, it was imitative. The difficulties of mastering new lands were narrated by the prose writers Frances Brooke (1724–89), Catherine Traill (1802–99), and Susanna Moodie (1803–85), and by the poets O. Goldsmith (1787–1861) and A. McLachlan (1818–96). A clever, dishonorable Yankee is the hero of the satiric book by T. Haliburton (1796–1865), *The Clockmaker, or the Sayings and Doings of Samuel Slick of Slickville,* which was published in installments. The Confederation poets were romantics who wrote about the beauties of nature and called for the unification of Canadians of different nationalities. The creative work of such Confederation poets as C. Roberts (1860–1943) and W. B. Carman (1861–1929) was noticeably influenced by the poets R. W. Emerson, J. Keats, and A. Swinburne. The poetry of D. C. Scott (1862–1947), however, was more original.

The historical novel was a widespread prose genre during the second half of the 19th century. At the beginning of the 20th century, prose was characterized by regionalism, and a favorite genre was the "local idyll." Worldwide recognition was won by the creative art of S. Leacock (1869–1944), who described the mores of the inhabitants of small Canadian towns, the power of money, and the inadaptability of the "little" man.

Literary journals began to appear, as well as the first histories and anthologies of Canadian literature. In 1921 the Canadian Association of Writers was created, which brought together primarily English-Canadian writers. Among the poets who won fame during the 1920's were W. MacDonald (born 1880), a passionate opponent of war, an internationalist, and a democrat, and E. J. Pratt (1883–1964), who glorified the power of nature and man. Many poets of the 1930's and 1940's addressed themselves to social problems: Patricia Page (born 1917), L. Dudek (born 1918), and the poets associated with the journals *Preview* (1942–45) and *First Statement* (1942–45). The Communist poet D. Wallace (born 1890) has written about the struggle of the working class and about the USSR. The traditions of the English family were celebrated in idyllic tones by Mazo de la Roche (1879–1961) in the multivolume chronicle of the Whiteoak family. An important place is occupied by the theme of animals, particularly in the works of C. Roberts, E. Thompson Seton (1860–1946), who combined artistic conceptions with a scientific quality, and Grey Owl (pseudonym of G. S. Belaney, 1888–1938).

Since the mid-20th century, Canadian literature in English has begun to exhibit Canadian national traits. Critical realism has developed since the 1940's. The heroes of realistic novels by F. P. Grove (1872–1948) are working people. The creative art of the realistic writer M. Callaghan (born 1903) is permeated with humanism and sympathy for the oppressed. In works such as the novel *Two Solitudes* (1945), H. MacLennan (born 1907) calls for unity between Canadians of English and French descent. The lack of communication among people in modern capitalist society was the theme of MacLennan's novel *The Return of the Sphinx* (1967). A profound understanding of Canadian psychology characterizes H. Garner's (born 1913) realistic novels and short stories (for example, the collection *Men and Women,* 1966). The theme of many works written during the 1960's is the chaos of contemporary capitalist reality: for example, *Where the High Winds Blow* (1960) by D. Walker (born 1911), *The Emperor of Ice Cream* (1965) by B. Moore (born 1921), *Words of My Roaring* (1966) by R. Kroetsch (born 1927), and *Erubus* (1968) by R. Hunter. Faith in the working class and an understanding of the necessity for unity among workers of different nationalities in the struggle for their rights characterize H. Buller's novels *One Man Alone* (1963) and *Quebec in Revolt* (1965).

D. Carter (born 1910), a propagandist for the ideas of Marxism and editor of *Northern Neighbors,* a journal about the USSR, is the author of the novels *The Future Is Ours* (1950) and *Sons Without Fathers* (1955).

The attention of progressive Canadian writers has been drawn to such problems as the threat of Canada's subordination to the USA, the sharpening of the nationalist discord between French Canadians and English Canadians, the problems of the Canadian North, and the status of the Indians and the Eskimo. On the other hand, the Canadian book market is being flooded with American hack works that are saturated with sex and murder. They have influenced the creative work of Canadian writers (the novels of G. Bowering, P. West, and S. Symons).

Works on the history of Canadian literature have begun to appear. The English-language journal *Canadian Literature,* which elucidates problems in English-Canadian and French-Canadian literature, has been published since 1959. It also prints articles in French.

REFERENCES

Vannikova, N. I. *Kanadskaia literatura na frantsuzskom iazyke (1945–1965).* Moscow, 1969.
Vannikova, N. I. "Dve storony odnoi problemy." *Inostrannaia literatura,* 1970, no. 7.
Zateriannaia ulitsa: Sovremennaia kanadskaia novella. [With a foreword by L. Orel.] Moscow, 1971.
Tougas, G. *Histoire de la littérature canadienne-française.* Paris, 1960.
Literary History of Canada. Toronto, 1965.
Grandpré, P. *Dix ans de vie littéraire au Canada français.* Montreal, 1966.
Sylvestre, G. *Canadian Writers.* Toronto [1966].
Story, N. *The Oxford Companion to Canadian History and Literature.* Toronto, 1967.
Europe, 1969, Feb.–March, nos. 478–79.

L. S. OREL

Architecture and art

By the time of the European colonization the Canadian Indians were living in earth huts (the hunters of the Saskatchewan Mountains), hut-wigwams (forest hunters), tepees covered with hides (the prairie Indians), and communal frame houses covered with bark (forest farmers) or made of hewn wood (the fishermen of the west coast). The art of the Indians included very rich polychrome wood carvings (the west coast Indians' totem and grave-marking poles, masks, and implements that combined real and imaginary motifs), carving and engraving on stone, bone, and horn, ornaments made of feathers and shells, fabrics with bright designs and embroidery that used porcupine quills as well as hair from deer and elk, and paintings (symbolic motifs and depictions of animals and war and hunting scenes). The Eskimo lived in dome-shaped igloos made of snow, as well as in wood, stone, and bone structures built half underground. They did carving and engraving in stone, bone, and horn.

Between the 17th century and the beginning of the 19th, French émigrés brought their own architectural traditions to eastern Canada—houses with massive, thick walls and steep roofs, hall churches with one or two small towers above their facades, and public buildings in the French style (architects J. Demers and T. Baillairgé). They also brought their own style of wood carving (F. Baillairgé and L. Quevillon), silversmithing in the spirit of the baroque and classic styles (F. Ranvoizé), and religious and portrait painting (F. Beaucourt and A. Plamondon). During the second half of the 18th century and the beginning of the 19th the part of Canada colonized by the British was characterized by efficient wood frame and stone architecture in the spirit of classicism (architect J. Merrick). Landscape graphic art also developed there (T. Davies).

Cities began to grow rapidly in the mid-19th century. In western Canada new cities were characterized by rectangular grids of streets and by low buildings. An eclectic style is typical of the churches, administrative buildings, and private homes in Ottawa, Montreal, Toronto, and Quebec (architects E. Lennox and J. Lyle). From the end of the 19th century the influence of US architecture increased (for example, high-rise office buildings and hotels by the architects F. Darling and J. Pearson).

In addition to the imitators of French and American art, original masters of landscape and scenes of peasant, provincial, or Indian life achieved distinction beginning in the mid-19th century (P. Kane and C. Krieghoff; and at the turn of the 20th century, H. Watson, J. H. Walker, M. Cullen). The flowering of a national, realistic art in the 20th century is associated with lyric urban and rural landscapes (J. W. Morrice and C. Gagnon) and epically broad, brightly decorative, romantic images of untouched Canadian nature (T. Thomson and the Group of Seven, including J. MacDonald, A. Lismer, F. Varley, and A. Jackson), as well as with the folk images of the sculptor Frances Loring and the animistic graphic art of E. Thompson Seton.

In the mid-20th century the old cities underwent intensive growth and reconstruction, and the construction of housing (including wooden buildings) was expanded. Large industrial and public complexes of reinforced concrete and steel have been built in the contemporary style (the Annacis Island complex, the Toronto City Hall, and the Ville Marie Plaza and the World's Fair [Expo '67] in Montreal). Under standardized plans that apply the principles of zoning and microregions, cities have been built near industrial enterprises (for example, Kitimat and Elliot Lake). Among these new cities is one located above the arctic circle (Inuvik). Social contradictions are manifested in the contrasts between the splendid administrative and business complexes and the great number of obsolete residential structures.

In contemporary art modernist trends prevail (for example, the painter J.-P. Riopelle and the sculptor L. Archambault). However, realistic traditions have been maintained by F. Taylor and T. Macdonald, members of the Workers' Art League. Design and a number of types of decorative art have also developed (the working of metal, rug-making, and ceramics). Outstanding among the creative folk arts are Ukrainian wood carving and embroidery and Eskimo stone sculpture. Applied graphic arts have basically followed the models of US "mass culture."

REFERENCES
Gowans, A. W. *Looking at Architecture in Canada.* Toronto, 1958.
Ross, M., ed. *The Arts in Canada.* [Toronto, 1958.]
Hubbard, R. H., ed. *An Anthology of Canadian Art.* Toronto, 1960.
Harper, J. R. *Painting in Canada.* [Toronto, 1966.]

Music

From ancient times music was an important part of the daily life of the country's native inhabitants and of the settlers. Because of Canada's historical development, the shaping of its music was connected with English and French culture from the 17th century. Before the end of the 18th century church music prevailed. The growth of secular music was promoted by British military bands. Amateurs and music lovers arranged concerts beginning in the late 18th century and operas beginning in the early 19th century. Among the first Canadian composers were the Frenchman J. Quesnel, the composer of the first Canadian opera, *Colas et Colinette* (1790, Montreal); the German F. Glackemeyer; and the Englishman T. Molt.

During the second half of the 19th century more musical activities developed in the large cities. Amateur musical societies were established (for example, quartets and philharmonic societies) and European musicians and opera troupes and symphony orchestras from the USA appeared in Canada. In addition, genuine Canadian folk music emerged (for example, songs of everyday life, romantic ballads, and fishermen's songs). One of the first active musical figures was the composer C. Lavallée, the author of the popular patriotic song "O Canada," which became the national anthem.

At the end of the 19th century and the beginning of the 20th, Canada produced its first professional composers and performers, who had received their musical education in Europe. The singer E. Albani and the violinist K. Parlow (a student of L. S. Auer) won worldwide fame. Professional orchestras and choral groups were founded.

Canadian music began to develop intensively in the mid-1940's, particularly under the impetus of the composers H. Willan and A. Laliberté, the composer, organist, and teacher W. Pelletier, the composer and musical figure C. Champagne, and the composer and folklorist H. Gratton.

The most important centers of Canadian musical culture are Montreal, Toronto, Quebec, Ottawa, and Winnipeg, all of which have orchestras and theater groups, most of them privately supported. Established in 1949 were two state music groups—the Canadian Opera Company in Toronto, which tours throughout the country, and the National Youth Orchestra. The National Center for the Arts, which was opened in Ottawa in 1969, includes opera and drama theaters, an experimental studio, and a concert hall for chamber music. Canada has eight higher music education institutions (conservatories and academies), and in a number of cities, music schools and departments of music have been opened at universities. Since 1965 international music festivals have been held annually in Montreal, as well as competitions for performing musicians.

Among contemporary musicians are the composers M. Blackburn, J. Weinzweig, P. Mercure, F. Morel, C. Pépin, G. Ridout, M. Surdin, and H. Freedman; the conductors J. Beaudry, A. Brott, P. Dervaux, and V. Feldbrill; the pianists G. Gould, A. Cuerti, and J. Heller; the violinist I. Haendel; the women singers L. Marshall, T. Stratas, and M. Forrester; and the male singers R. Verreau, E. Johnson, L. Quilico, and L. Simmoneau. Canadian composers belong to the professional organization the Canadian Association of Composers, Authors, and Publishers. Other music organizations include the Canadian League of Composers, the Canadian Music Council, and a division of Musical Youth, an international society. The *Canadian Music Journal* has been published since 1965 in Toronto.

REFERENCES
MacMillan, E. *Music in Canada.* Toronto, 1955.
Kallmann, H. *A History of Music in Canada: 1534–1914.* Toronto, 1960.
L. G. GRIGOR'EV

Dance and ballet

The dance traditions of the native population, which are associated primarily with folk and religious rituals such as worship of the sun, had no influence on the development of choreography in Canada. The European settlers who came to Canada in the 17th century performed their own national dances. Instruction in ballet has been provided since the early 18th century in Quebec and other cities. At the end of the 18th century ballet artists from the USA toured Canada and in the mid-19th century, dancers from France and Austria. The formation of a Canadian national school of ballet was influenced by A. P. Pavlova's tours as well as by the Canadian tours of the Ballet Russe de Monte Carlo and other troupes during the 1930's. The first Canadian troupe—the Winnipeg Ballet—was an outgrowth of the ballet school founded in 1938 by the British ballet mistress G. Lloyd and the ballerina B. Farally. (It became professional in 1949 and in 1953 became known as the Royal Winnipeg Ballet.) The repertoire of the Winnipeg Ballet has included productions staged by G. Lloyd, B. MacDonald, M. Conte, and A. Spohr.

A significant role in the subsequent development of ballet was played by the Canadian Ballet Festivals. (First held in 1948, they took place in various cities until 1954.) In 1951 the National Ballet Company was created in Toronto under the direction of the ballerina and ballet mistress C. Franca; its repertoire has included classical ballets as well as works by modern British choreographers. In 1952, Les Grands Ballets Canadiens was established in Montreal under the direction of the ballerina L. S. Chiriaeff. It was the outgrowth of a television ballet group. In 1967 the country had four troupes (companies).

Among Canada's leading ballet performers are L. Smith, D. Adams, S. Taverner, A. M. and D. Holmes, and C. Hennessy. There are several ballet schools, the most important of which is the National Ballet School, which was founded in 1959 in Toronto. The bulletin *Nouvelles chorégraphiques* has been published since 1964.

REFERENCES
Thistle, L. "Ballet in Canada: 1962–1963." In *Ballet Annual and Yearbook, 1964.* London [1963].
Guillemette, P. "Histoire de la Danse-Théâtre au Canada." *Art et danse,* 1970, nos. 102–11.
E. IA. SURITS

Theater

The Canadian theater began to develop in the 17th century in the French provinces of Quebec and Acadia. Plays by Corneille,

Racine, and Molière were produced. In 1774 the first known Canadian play (in English), *Acadius, or Love in a Calm,* was produced in the city of Halifax. The first permanent theater opened in Montreal in 1825. During the 18th and 19th centuries theatrical productions were staged in Montreal, Quebec, and Halifax by French, English, American, and local actors. Included in the repertoires of theater troupes were works by the Canadian playwrights J. Quesnel, C. Heavysege, and C. Mair. From the end of the 1880's until World War I the professional theatrical touring system known as the "road" flourished. Troupes traveled continuously around the country. During the 1920's and the 1930's amateur theater became the basic form of theatrical art, and numerous troupes were organized at universities, schools, churches, and clubs. The most important ones performed in Montreal, Ottawa, St. Boniface, Vancouver, London, Toronto, and Regina.

At the end of the 1940's professional theaters were founded in the large cities. The oldest of them is the Rideau Vert (Montreal, founded in 1949 by Y. Brind'Amour). Among its productions have been plays by Shakespeare, Molière, P. Calderón de la Barca, P. Claudel, I. S. Turgenev, and A. P. Chekhov. Other troupes that became well known include the New Play Society and Theater Toronto (Toronto), Neptune Theater (Halifax), Citadel Theater (Edmonton), Globe Theater (Regina), Manitoba Theater Center (Winnipeg), Canadian Repertory (Ottawa), and Nouveau Monde and Comédie Canadien (Montreal). Their repertoires have included plays by the Canadian dramatists R. Davies, M. Dubé, J. Coulter, G. Pharis Ringwood, S. Fowke, L. Sinclair, M. Callaghan, and N. Williams, as well as world classics and contemporary foreign plays.

In the French-Canadian theaters (particularly in Quebec), a national theater culture is being created. English-Canadian theater groups are greatly influenced by the US theater. Among the leaders in the theater arts are J. Colicos, Y. Brind'Amour, F. Hyland, D. Pelletier, W. Hutt, C. Plummer, and J. Gascon. Annual festivals of the dramatic arts have been organized in such cities as Charlottetown, Vancouver, Montreal, and Ottawa. Since 1953 a Shakespeare Festival has been held at Stratford, Ontario, in which the best Canadian troupes and actors participate. At the National Theater School classes are conducted in both English and French. (The school meets during the winter in Montreal and during the summer in Stratford.) The journal *Théâtre canadien* is published in English and in French.

A. P. MAKAROV

Motion pictures

Regular production of Canadian films began in 1914, after the organization of a film division under the Department of Trade and Commerce. (Later, this film division became the Canadian Government Motion Picture Bureau.) Canadian film-makers produced primarily brief documentaries and advertising films, as well as newsreels. An important role in the emergence of a national film art of Canada was played by the British director J. Grierson, whose work in Canada (1939–46) had a decisive influence on the documentary motion picture. Under his guidance a number of Canadian directors began their work: S. Legg, S. Hawes, R. Spottiswoode, J. Beveridge, and N. McLaren, who since the 1940's has been among the prominent experimenters in cartoons.

The National Film Council was organized in Ottawa in 1939 to direct the state production of documentary films. During World War II the film series *The World in Combat* became well known. It reflected actual wartime events (for example, the films *In Embattled Russia,* 1942, and *The Goal Is Berlin,* 1944). During the late 1940's a number of directors achieved distinction: C. Low, R. Kroitor, J. Feeney, P. Patry, and G. Côté.

In 1956 the National Film Board was established in Montreal, which became the center of Canadian motion-picture production. However, the output of feature films depends upon the initiative of individual directors and producers, since the state does not provide sufficient support for the motion-picture industry. Competition from television has led to a sharp decline in attendance at motion-picture theaters. (In 1953, the total motion-picture audience was 241 million, but by 1963 it had fallen to 88 million.) Among the best films are *The Racketeers* (1958, directed by M. Brault and G. Groux), *City of Gold* (1957, directed by C. Low), and *So That Life Might Continue* (1963) and *Between the Sea and Fresh Water* (1970, both directed by Brault). A significant place is also occupied by popular-science and educational films on problems of technology, agriculture, medicine, urban construction, and art. Among the leaders in motion pictures are C. Jutra, G. Carle, R. Garceau, J.-P. Lefèbre, G. Munro, and K. Pindall. International film festivals are held in Stratford, Montreal, and Vancouver (for the first time in 1957), and annual prizes have been established to encourage the production of better films. As of 1969 there were about 700 documentary and popular-science films in production. More than 30 feature films in English and French are made each year. There are 1,400 motion-picture theaters (including drive-in theaters). The Canadian Film Archives was founded in 1958 and the Canadian Film Library, in 1960.   [11–867–1]

CANADIAN ANTICYCLONE (North American anticyclone), a region of high atmospheric pressure over North America; one of the seasonal centers of atmospheric activity that show up on mean climatic maps of the winter months over a period of several years. The Canadian anticyclone is conditioned by the predominance of anticyclones over cyclones in the winter atmospheric circulation over the northern and central parts of the continent.   [11–916–4]

CANADIAN ARCTIC ARCHIPELAGO, a group of islands belonging to Canada and located off the northern coast of North America. Area, 1.3 million sq km. The largest islands are Baffin, Ellesmere, Victoria, Banks, and Devon. The archipelago is located within the continental shelf. On the north and the east it is washed by the Arctic Ocean (Beaufort Sea, Lincoln Sea, Robson and Kennedy channels, Kane Basin, Smith Sound, and Baffin Bay) and on the southeast and south, by the Atlantic Ocean (Davis Strait, Hudson Strait, and Foxe Basin). The depth of the straits ranges from 150 to 300 m.

In the east the terrain is high-mountainous. The eastern shores of Ellesmere, Devon, and Baffin islands, which are made up of ancient crystalline rocks, are deeply indented by fjords, have rocky cliffs, and are difficult to reach. The plateau-like summits, which are up to 1,500–3,000 m high, are covered with ice caps. The central and southern portions of the archipelago are occupied by low-mountain ridges, hilly uplands, and benched plateaus from 200–500 m high, which consist primarily of sedimentary rocks of the Paleozoic era. The coasts of Victoria, Banks, and Prince of Wales islands are, for the most part, perpendicular and deeply dissected by valleys. The northwestern part of the archipelago (Prince Patrick, Mackenzie King, Borden, and Ellef Ringnes islands) is a low-lying area made up of friable marine deposits and characterized by extensive permafrost forms of terrain. The most important minerals are petroleum and natural gas (Melville, Bathurst, and Cornwallis islands) and iron ores (the northern part of Baffin Island).

The climate is arctic and extremely harsh. In the east it is moister and in the west, sharply continental. The average January temperature ranges from −23°C in the southeast to −35°C in the northwest, and the average July temperature varies from 7°C in the south to 4°C in the north. The absolute minimum temperatures go as low as −50°C. The total annual precipitation ranges from 400–450 mm in the southeast to 100 mm and less in the north. Perennially frozen soils are prevalent everywhere.

Today, glaciation is widely developed in the north and northeast (total area, 154,000 sq km). At the northern tip of Ellesmere Island there is a region of shelf ice up to 20 km wide that gives rise to arctic ice islands. The boundary of the perennial pack ice runs along the northwestern edge of the archipelago. The northwest maritime route is difficult to reach. During the summers the eastern straits (Hudson, Davis, and Lancaster), as well as the bodies of water along the continental coastline (Amundsen Gulf, Dolphin and Union Strait, and Queen Maud Gulf), are the most free of ice.

The flora of the Canadian Arctic Archipelago includes 340 species of higher plants. In the extreme north the vegetation of the arctic wastelands prevails. The south is characterized by mossy-lichen and mossy-scrub tundras on typical tundra soils, for the most part rocky. The fauna of the archipelago consists chiefly of polar species—reindeer, polar bears, arctic foxes, lemmings, and alpine partridges. The most typical indigenous species is the musk ox. The coastal waters are inhabited by seals, whales, and Atlantic walruses.

The population of the Canadian Arctic Archipelago (several thousand persons, primarily Eskimo) is engaged in sea hunting, hunting, and fishing. The most important populated points are Frobisher Bay (population, 1,631 in 1966), which is the site of an international airport, Cambridge Bay, with its trading post and large airport, and Resolute, which has a scientific observatory.

REFERENCES

Agranat, G. A., A. B. Kupriianov, and V. F. Puzanova. *Naselenie i resursy Amerikanskogo Severa.* Moscow, 1963.
Antipova, A. V. *Kanada: Priroda i estestvennye resursy.* Moscow, 1965.
Dunbar, M., and K. Greenaway. *Arctic Canada From the Air.* Ottawa, 1956.
Swithinbank, C. *Ice Atlas of Arctic Canada.* Ottawa, 1960.
Thompson, H. A. *The Climate of the Canadian Arctic.* Ottawa, 1967.

A. V. ANTIPOVA [11–867–5]

CANADIAN BASIN, a depression of the floor of the western part of the Arctic Ocean. To the south the Canadian Basin is bounded by the continental slope of North America, on the north by the Mendeleev Range, and to the west and east by the Chukchi and Alpha rises. It is up to 3,810 m deep. The bottom of the Canadian Basin is an abyssal plain covered with clayey silt.

[11–916–2]

CANADIAN BROADCASTING CORPORATION (CBC), the Canadian radio broadcasting corporation; established in 1936. The CBC is financed by the government as well as by income from advertising. As of 1973, it united more than 300 television stations and 360 radio stations. The principal centers of the CBC are Montreal (domestic broadcasts in French and broadcasting to other countries) and Toronto (domestic broadcasts in English).

[11–966–4]

CANADIAN IMPERIAL BANK OF COMMERCE, one of Canada's largest commercial banks. In 1971 the Canadian Imperial Bank of Commerce occupied second place among the nine Canadian chartered banks, which are licensed to operate under charters issued in accordance with the Banking Act of 1871.

Founded in 1867 under the name of the Canadian Commercial Bank, the Canadian Imperial Bank of Commerce acquired its present name in June 1961 after its merger with the Imperial Bank of Canada. The bank's principal operations are attracting funds, advancing credit, and buying up securities. Although the Canadian Imperial Bank of Commerce conducts extensive operations abroad, the volume of its foreign operations is not equal to that of the Royal Bank of Canada or the Bank of Montreal. In terms of the number of branches in Canada (1,500), the Canadian Imperial Bank of Commerce held first place in 1971. There are 19 branches in the USA (including one in New York), as well as two branches in London and 47 branches in Caribbean countries (Jamaica, Barbados, and Trinidad). In addition, there are several subsidiary banks that specialize in managing their clients' estates—for example, the Canadian Bank of Commerce Trust Company in New York and banks with the same name in Jamaica, Barbados, and Trinidad. On Oct. 31, 1971, the basic balance sheets showed (in Canadian currency) a total balance of $11.4 billion, deposits of $10.419 billion, loans of $5.711 billion, securities investments worth $2.864 billion, and a paid-in capital of $69.7 million.

V. I. RYZHYKOVA [11–917–1]

CANADIAN LABOUR CONGRESS, the largest trade-union association in Canada.

Created in 1956 by the merger of the Trades and Labour Congress of Canada and the Canadian Congress of Labour, as of 1973 the Canadian Labour Congress had more than 1.75 million members (75 percent of the total trade-union membership in Canada). Most of the trade unions belonging to the congress are branches of corresponding US trade unions and are referred to as "international." The biennial congress is considered the highest body of the Canadian Labour Congress. De facto leadership of the congress is exercised by the Executive Council. The Canadian Labour Congress belongs to the International Congress of Free Trade Unions. Its official organ is *Canadian Labour.*

[11–918–2]

CANADIAN PRESS, the Canadian news agency. A cooperative association of newspaper owners founded in 1917, the Canadian Press is the principal channel of official information for the press, radio, and television. As of 1973, it served more than 100 Canadian newspapers, as well as radio and television stations. Foreign news is received primarily from the Associated Press, Reuters, and France Presse.

[11–967–1]

CANADIAN RIVER, a river in the USA; a right tributary of the Arkansas River. Length, approximately 1,500 km. Basin area, 124,000 sq km. It rises in the Sangre de Cristo Mountains (in the Rocky Mountains) and flows through the Great Plains and the Central Plains. There are sharp fluctuations in the flow; high water occurs in spring. The average annual discharge is 177 cu m per sec. The Canadian River is used for irrigation.

[11–966–3]

CANADIANS, the present-day population of Canada, which totals 21.8 million (1971 estimate).

The Canadian population consists of two nations (*natsii;* nations in the historical sense)—French Canadians and English Canadians—a number of other nationality groups, and the Indian and Eskimo national minorities.

French Canadians make up about 30 percent of the entire population of the country and more than 80 percent of the population of the province of Quebec. The nucleus of the French-Canadian nation, which developed at the end of the 18th century and the beginning of the 19th, consisted of the first European settlers in Canada (Frenchmen and Bretons), who founded the colony of New France during the first half of the 17th century. In 1763, New France became a British colony. In the struggle against British colonialism the French Canadians defended their language (French), which in 1968 became one of the country's two official languages. In addition, they have preserved their national culture. The French Canadians have raised the issue of national self-determination. The majority of French Canadians are Catholics.

After Canada became a British colony, it was rapidly settled by emigrants from Great Britain and its colonies in America. The influx of new settlers created a numerical imbalance in which the English-speaking population outnumbered the French-speaking. The English Canadians occupied a dominant position in the country. The economic growth of the country, the struggle for independence from Great Britain, and the armed struggle against several attempts by the USA to annex Canada, as well as against economic domination by US monopoly capital, contributed to the growth of a sense of national identity among the English Canadians. At the end of the 19th century and the beginning of the 20th the English-Canadian nation took shape. Representing about 44 percent of Canada's present population, the English Canadians have created their own national culture. They include several ethnic groups: English, Scots, Irish, and assimilated settlers from continental Europe. Their language is English, with certain unique traits. The majority of religious English Canadians are Protestants of various denominations. Most of the Irish, however, are Catholic.

In addition to the two principal nations, the Canadian population includes numerous nonassimilated groups of recent (20th-century) settlers (about 25 percent of the population). The most important of them are Germans, Ukrainians, Italians, Jews, Poles, and Dutch. The Indians (more than 240,000) and Eskimo (about 17,000) are oppressed national minorities.

REFERENCES

Narody Ameriki, vol. 1. Moscow, 1959. (Contains bibliographies, pp. 621, 625.)

Berzina, M. Ia. *Formirovanie etnicheskogo sostava naseleniia Kanady (Etnostatisticheskoe issledovanie).* Moscow, 1971.
Ryerson, S. B. *Unequal Union.* [Toronto] 1968.

Iu. P. Averkieva   [11–918–5]

CANADIAN TRIBUNE, a weekly newspaper; the organ of the Communist Party of Canada. The *Canadian Tribune* has been published in Toronto since 1940. (From May through November 1947 it was known as the *Daily Tribune.*) It features articles on Canada's international and domestic position and on the activities of the Communist Party of Canada and other progressive organizations. In addition, the *Canadian Tribune* elucidates the problems of the struggle of the working class and of all laborers for their rights and against the yoke of monopoly capital.

[11–967–2]

CANAIGRE (*Rumex hymenosepalus*), a perennial plant of the genus *Rumex*, approximately 1 m in height. It grows wild in the southern United States and in Mexico. The radical tubers contain tannides, which are used to tan soft leather.   [11–966–2]

CANAL, in hydraulic engineering, a regularly shaped man-made channel (waterway) built in the earth, with nonpressured movement of the water. Canals are built in open excavations or in embankments (when crossing gorges or ravines) and sometimes half in excavations and half in embankments (a canal on a slope). According to purpose, a distinction is made among navigation canals (man-made waterways), power-engineering canals (diversion channels), irrigation canals, water-supply canals, drainage canals, lumber-flotation canals, fish-ladder canals, and general-purpose canals.

Connecting navigation canals join navigable rivers, lakes, and seas (for example, the V. I. Lenin Volga-Don Ship Canal, the Moscow Canal, the Dnieper-Bug Canal, and the Panama Canal). Bypass canals are built to improve navigation conditions and to avoid rapids in rivers and turbulent sections of large lakes and seas (the Ladoga canals, the Onega Canal, and the Gulf Intracoastal Canal). Straightening canals eliminate meandering of a navigation route and reduce the length of the waterway (the Khoroshevo Canal on the Moscow River and the canal on the Don River below the Tsimliansk Hydroelectric Power Plant). Approach canals provide an approach to large cities, inland port areas, and industrial enterprises from a sea, lake, or river (the Leningrad and Astrakhan sea canals and the Manchester Ship Canal).

Navigation canals are also divided into open and lock canals. Open canals are built by joining waterways whose water levels are almost the same; canals with locks are used when there is a difference in levels or when the route of the canal crosses a high water divide. Lock canals usually consist of several sections, called races, on different levels; locks or ship hoisters are installed between them. Bypass and approach canals are generally open; connecting canals have locks. The water in navigation (lock) canals may move by gravity flow (free-flowing canals), or it may be pumped by pumping stations (machine canals). Navigation canals are characterized by great length (for example, the coastal canal from New York to Florida in the USA is about 1,800 km long, the Baltic–White Sea Canal is 227 km long, and the Dnieper-Bug Canal is 196 km long; among sea canals, the Suez Canal is 171 km long and the Panama Canal is 81.6 km long) and by broad transverse dimensions (the Suez Canal is 120–150 m wide across the top and 12–13 m deep).

Diversion channels take water from a river, reservoir, or lake to a hydroelectric power plant or draw off water that has passed through the turbine. Such canals are typically very short; delivery canals are usually not more than 5–10 km long (maximum of 30 km), and return canals are seldom more than a few kilometers long. The water flow (carrying capacity) of diversion channels varies; in some cases it is more than 1,000 m^3/sec (for example, the carrying capacity of the diversion channel of the Montélimar Hydroelectric Power Plant in France is 1,860 m^3/sec). In the USSR the Zemo-Avchala, Rioni, and Kondopoga hydroelectric power plants and the Sevan grid have diversion channels.

Irrigation canals are designed to supply water to irrigated lands. They usually form a system of main canals, distribution canals, the irrigation canals themselves, and drainage canals. Water enters irrigation canals by gravity flow or is fed by pumps. In large irrigation systems the length of the main canals may be several hundred kilometers (the Karakum Canal's first section, up to the city of Ashkhabad, is more than 800 km long, the North Crimean Canal is more than 400 km long, and the Bol'-shoi Fergana Canal is about 300 km long). The water flow at the head of these canals is 250–500 m^3/sec.

Agricultural water-supply canals deliver water to waterless and arid regions for the needs of agriculture (primarily for livestock raising). Examples are the agricultural water-supply canals in the lower regions of the Volga and the canals of the Terek-Kuma Water-Supply System. Since small, oasis-like irrigated areas are usually formed when water is supplied to arid lands, agricultural water-supply canals are often at the same time irrigation canals (for example, the Nevinnomyssk and Kuban'-Kalaus canals).

Drainage canals collect water that comes from a drainage network (on swampy or overly moist terrain) and conduct it to a river, lake, or sea by gravity flow or through the use of pumping stations. Drainage canals are usually routed along the lowest points of the territory being drained (along thalwegs).

Water-supply canals deliver water from the source of supply to the place of consumption (an industrial region, city, or community). Among the large water-supply canals in the USSR are the Irtysh-Karaganda Canal, with a total length of about 460 km and a carrying capacity of 75 m^3/sec at its head, and the Severskii Donets–Donbas Canal, which is about 130 km long, with a water flow of 25 m^3/sec at its head. Operating conditions and public-health requirements sometimes necessitate the covering of water-supply canals (for example, the canal—about 30 km long—that delivers water from the Ucha Reservoir to Moscow).

Timber-flotation canals are built to float timber (as individual logs or in rafts), usually from the place where it is cut to a river that is suitable for flotation or to a sawmill. Flotation canals are also built in the area of hydraulic-engineering complexes to direct floating timber around hydraulic-engineering structures.

Fish-ladder canals supply water to man-made breeding grounds, provide a connection between rivers and isolated bodies of water (lakes) in which fish are found, and supply fresh water to estuaries (for example, in the lower course of the Kuban' River).

General-purpose canals are built to accomplish several water-management tasks simultaneously. Such canals have been developed on a particularly large scale in the USSR in connection with multiple use of river resources. For example, the Moscow Canal delivers water for navigation and water supply for the city of Moscow, the V. I. Lenin Volga-Don Canal (together with the Tsimliansk Hydroelectric Power Plant) is a navigation–irrigation–water-supply and power complex, and the Irtysh-Karaganda Canal solves irrigation problems in Central Kazakhstan, in addition to its primary task of water supply.

The cross section of a canal depends on the purpose of the canal, the structural features of the ground, and the conditions for earthwork. The most common shapes of canal cross sections built in soft soils are trapezoidal and polygonal. The latter is usually used in building large navigational canals. A rectangular profile is advisable when canals are built in rock excavations. Sometimes (for example, when a canal route passes through populated areas or in sloping sectors) the rectangular cross section in soft soils is reinforced by constructing vertical retaining walls.

The dimensions of a canal's cross section are determined by hydraulic calculations for a given water flow and the current velocity that is permissible for the particular conditions; for navigation and timber-flotation canals the size of ships and rafts that will be passing through must also be taken into account. The ratio between the area of the clear section of navigation canals and the area of the midship section of the hypothetical ship should not be greater than 4:1 for canals on first-category waterways, 3.5:1 for second-category waterways, and 3:1 for the third and fourth categories. If the ratio is smaller, resistance to the movement of ships increases substantially.

The slope of canal walls is determined by the nature of the soil. Where excavations are very deep, and also under difficult geological conditions, the strength of the walls is checked through calculations.

The velocity of water current in canals has maximum and minimum values: the maximum, to avoid erosion of the bed of the canal, and the minimum, so that the bed does not become silted or overgrown with vegetation. For example, for canals in soft ground (sand and sandy loam), with a water depth of more than 3 m, current velocities of 0.4–1.5 m/sec present no danger of erosion; in hard rock (marl or sandstones), the velocities may be 3.1–5.6 m/sec. Formulas based on the principle of the so-called alluvium-transporting capability of a current are used to determine silt-free water velocities. Minimum canal velocities for preventing overgrowth with vegetation are 0.3 m/sec for small canals and 0.5 for large canals.

The bed of the canal is lined to protect it against erosion by the current and waves, to reduce water losses from seepage into the soil, and to decrease the roughness of the bottom and walls (to increase the carrying capacity of the canal). Lining that serves only to protect the walls of the canal against erosion is made of rock paving, fill, and laying and of concrete and reinforced-concrete slabs. This kind of lining is usually used on navigation canals. For irrigation, agricultural water-supply, and drainage canals, sod-brushwood, wicker, and other types of reinforcements are sometimes used. Antiseepage lining (screens) is usually made of clay, sandy loam, and well-decomposed peat. The screens are covered with a layer of sand or gravel to protect them against mechanical damage and the effects of temperature. Concrete, reinforced-concrete, and asphalt-concrete linings are the most versatile; they provide reliable protection against erosion for the canal bed, ensure its watertightness, increase its carrying capacity and, at the same time, make possible complete mechanization of construction work. In addition to installing lining or screens, silt deposition, mechanical packing of the soil, and films made of synthetic materials are used to combat seepage in canals.

Structures on canals. In addition to special structures related to the operation of canals, such as locks (on navigation canals), pumping stations (on machine canals), and flood gates, many other hydraulic-engineering structures for various purposes are also erected along all canals. Among them are structures in places where the canal intersects streams (pipes, inverted siphons, and aqueducts), at intersections with transportation routes (viaducts, tunnels, bridges, and ferry crossings), and in places where there is a sharp break in the relief of the terrain (knickpoints and races).

Historical survey. Long before the Common Era, in the ancient states of the Southeast and East, the development of irrigation and water-supply canals became necessary as farming developed. For example, irrigation was known in the valley of the Nile River in Egypt in 4400 B.C. and in China (on the Yangtze River) in the third millennium B.C. The construction of navigation canals—for example, the canal from the Nile to the Red Sea, sixth century B.C., and the Chinese Grand Canal—also began in ancient times.

In the Middle Ages navigation canals were constructed primarily in Holland, France, and England. The invention of the chamber lock in Holland in the 15th century was of great importance for the construction of navigation canals. In the 16th and 17th centuries the development of trade and early industrial manufacture required an improvement in transportation routes and the design of navigation canals. In the 17th and 18th centuries and the first half of the 19th century, waterways were the primary and most economical transportation arteries. Among the most important structures of that period are the navigation canals in France (the Seine-Loire, Languedoc and Central canals), Germany (Vinow, Oder-Spree, Oder-Vistula, and Elbe-Havel), and England (Bridgewater and Caledonian). Sea canals (Suez, Kiel, and Panama) were built in the second half of the 19th century and in the 20th century in connection with the extensive development of world trade and for strategic purposes.

Canals for irrigation were built on the territory of the USSR as early as the eighth to sixth centuries B.C., in the ancient states of Khwarizm and Urartu. Irrigation canals were built in the 12th and 13th centuries A.D. in Georgia (Alazani and Samgori). Later canal building developed primarily for purposes of improving river navigation (for example, the navigation canal on the Sukhona River, 13th century), for hydraulic-engineering purposes (for supplying water to water-powered mills), and sometimes for drainage of land. Intensive construction of canals developed during the reign of Peter I. The Oka River was linked to the headwaters of the Don by the Ivanovskii Canal, the Vyshnii Volochek Water System was built to connect the Volga with the Msta River and the Baltic Sea, the Ladoga canals were built, and later, various connecting navigation canals, such as the Mariinskii, Tikhvin, Oginskii, and Severnaia Dvina, were added.

A new stage in the construction of navigation and irrigation canals and diversion channels in the USSR began after the Great October Socialist Revolution. Surveying for the Volga-Don Canal was under way as early as 1918. In the period of reconstruction—and especially during the prewar five-year plans—extensive construction of canals that were of great general importance to the national economy of the USSR was carried on. The plan of GOELRO (State Commission for the Electrification of Russia) played a large role in the construction of power-engineering canals; a number of hydroelectric power plants with diversion channels (for example, the Zemo-Avchala and Kondopoga plants) were built on the basis of this plan. The largest irrigation complex of the prewar five-year plans was the Bol'shoi Fergana Canal. The Baltic–White Sea and Moscow canals, as well as a number of irrigation canals in Middle Asia and the Caucasus, were built during the 1930's.

After the Great Patriotic War (1941–45) canal construction was even more extensive. The following canals were built and put into operation: the V. I. Lenin Volga-Don Canal, the Karakum Canal (up to Ashkhabad), the Golodnaia Step' Canal, the Don Main Canal, the Northern Crimean Canal, the Severskii Donets–Donbas Canal, the Dnieper–Krivoi Rog Canal, and the Amu-Bukhara Canal.

REFERENCES
Uginchus, A. A. *Kanaly i sooruzheniia na nikh.* Moscow, 1953.
Askochenskii, A. N. *Oroshenie i obvodnenie v SSSR.* Moscow, 1967.
Grishin, M. M. *Gidrotekhnicheskie sooruzheniia.* Moscow, 1968.
P. N. KORABLINOV [11–919–1]

CANALETTO (real name Giovanni Antonio Canale). Born Oct. 18, 1697, in Venice; died there Apr. 20, 1768. Italian painter, master of the architectural landscape.

Canaletto studied under his father, the theatrical artist Bernardo Canale. Working primarily in Venice, he also worked in Rome (1719–20 and c. 1740) and London (1745–55). He was influenced by the Venetian landscape painters L. Carlevaris and M. Ricci. Canaletto painted panoramic landscapes, depicting primarily architectural landmarks of Venice and colorful episodes from urban life. He also painted views of England.

Canaletto's works are characterized by objective precision of drawing and perfection of perspective. These elements are combined with an elegant, vibrant color scheme; airy effects; and ceremonial, pageant-like composition. Canaletto made many landscape etchings, which are distinguished by spontaneous observations and gentle chiaroscuro gradations (series *Views,* 1740–44). B. Bellotto, who was Canaletto's nephew and pupil, inherited his sobriquet.

REFERENCES
Constable, W. G. *Canaletto,* vols. 1–2. Oxford, 1962.
[Berto, G., and L. Puppi.] *L'opera completa del Canaletto.* Milan [1968].
Links, J. G. *Views in Venice by Canaletto.* New York, 1971.
O. D. NIKITIUK [11–930–1]

CANALS, INTERNATIONAL, in international law, manmade waterways that connect various seas and are used for international navigation. By shortening the seaways of the world, international canals play a major role in maritime navigation and world trade. They also are of great strategic military significance (for example, the Kiel Canal, the Suez Canal, and the Panama Canal). From the legal standpoint, international canals must be distinguished from straits, which are natural seaways, and from national (inland) canals, which are not used for international shipping and are under the exclusive sovereignty of the given state.

International canals, as man-made structures located in the territory of a state, are an integral part of its territory and are subject to its jurisdiction, taking international legal regulations into account. International canals may be leased to another state.

The navigational conditions for passage through international canals are regulated by international conventions. These conditions are based on the principle of free passage for the vessels of all countries through the international canal, respect by the states using the canals for the sovereign rights of the state through whose territory the canal passes, the removal of the canal from the sphere of military operations in the event of an armed conflict, and the obligation to pay the stipulated fees for passage.

REFERENCE
Barabolia, P. D., L. A. Ivanashchenko, and D. N. Kolesnik. *Mezhdunarodno-pravovoi rezhim vazhneishikh prolivov i kanalov.* Moscow, 1965. [11–935–1]

CANANEA, a city in northwest Mexico, in the state of Sonora. It is situated at an altitude of more than 1,500 m. Population, 21,000 (1960). A railroad branch links it with US railroads. It is a center for copper mining and has a copper-smelting plant (40,000 tons of crude copper annually) belonging to Anaconda, a US company. [11–937–1]

CANARIES CURRENT, a cold current in the northeastern part of the Atlantic Ocean. It constitutes the eastern periphery of the northern subtropical clockwise circulation of the surface waters. It runs from north to south along the Iberian Peninsula and northwest Africa as a branch of the North Atlantic Drift. In the south it merges into the North Equatorial Current and swerves partially into the Gulf of Guinea. The current's width is 400–600 km, and its velocity reaches 2 km/hr. The water temperature in February ranges from 12°C to 23°C, and in August from 19°C to 26°C. Its salinity varies from 36.0 to 36.8 parts per thousand. [11–939–1]

CANARIS, WALTER WILHELM. Born Jan. 1, 1887, in Aplerbeck, near Dortmund; died Apr. 9, 1945, in the Flossenbürg concentration camp. Fascist German military figure, admiral (1940). The son of the director of a steel mill.

Canaris joined the navy in 1905. During World War I he served on the cruiser *Drezden* and in 1915 was interned in Chile after the *Drezden* was sunk. In 1916, Canaris was sent to Spain by the German secret service; there he was involved in espionage activities and arranged for German submarines to be provisioned from Spain and Portugal. After the November Revolution of 1918 in Germany, he was an aide to G. Noske, the war minister; he helped organize the assassination of K. Liebknecht and R. Luxemburg and then headed the "investigation" of this incident. He also took part in the so-called Kapp putsch of 1920. In the following years, he served in the German Navy, establishing close bonds with the National Socialists. After 1935, Canaris directed the secret service and counterespionage service (Abwehr), under the War Ministry and then in 1938 subordinated to the supreme command of the armed forces.

Canaris organized international military provocations and diversions (in the seizure of Austria in 1938 and of Czechoslovakia in 1939 and in the assault on Poland in 1939). He set up a broad espionage and diversionary network in Europe, Asia, Africa, and America. In February of 1944 he was discharged. With the approaching defeat of fascist Germany, Canaris in 1944 took part in the generals' conspiracy against Hitler and was arrested and hanged. [11–938–2]

CANARY (*Serinus canaria*), a bird of the family Fringillidae of the order Passeriformes. The canary has a body length measuring 12–14 cm. The male has a yellowish green back with dark streaks and a yellow breast and throat; the female's plumage is greenish. The bird is widely distributed on the Madeira Islands, the Azores, and the Canary Islands (hence the name). It was brought to Europe and domesticated in the 16th century; it multiplies readily in captivity. Many varieties have been bred, differing in appearance and song; for this reason the birds are popular as pets, kept in cages.

Similar to the canary is the serin (*S. serinus*), which is sometimes considered to be only a subspecies of canary. The serin is distributed in northwest Africa, in Asia Minor, on the Arabian Peninsula, and in Europe (except northern Europe). It lives in the USSR in the western European areas.

The canary settles in gardens and parks, nesting in trees. The female lays three to five eggs and incubates them for 13 days. The bird feeds mainly on seeds.

REFERENCE
Lukina, E. V. *Pevchie i tsvetnye kanareiki.* Moscow, 1966.
[11–937–5]

CANARY ISLANDS, a group of islands in the Atlantic Ocean 100–120 km off the northwestern coast of Africa. They are part of the territory of Spain and administratively have been divided by Spain into two provinces: Las Palmas and Santa Cruz de Tenerife. The most important islands are Gran Canaria, Tenerife, and Fuerteventura. Area of the islands, 7,300 sq km; total population, 1.2 million (1970 census). The basic population consists of Spaniards, into whom have merged groups of the local population, the Guanches. The language spoken is Spanish, and the religion is Catholicism.

The islands were formed by basalt; there are many extinct and active volcanoes (on Tenerife, Palma, and Lanzarote). The maximum elevation is 3,718 m (the active volcano Teide on the island of Tenerife). The climate is tropical and characterized by trade winds; it is moderately hot and dry. Annual precipitation amounts to 300–500 mm. Growing on the slopes of the volcanoes are evergreen shrubs and forests. The flora includes many indigenous species (the dragon tree, Canary fig palm, Canary pine). Bananas, grains, potatoes, citrus fruits, tobacco, grapes, and beans are cultivated. Livestock raised includes goats, sheep, and cattle. Fishing is also important, and there are climatic resorts. The Canary Islands constitute an important transit base in the Atlantic Ocean. The principal cities and major ports are Las Palmas and Santa Cruz de Tenerife. [11–938–4]

CANAVALIA, a genus of perennial prostrate trailing, climbing, or, sometimes, woody plants of the family Leguminosae. The leaves are ternate. The flowers are large, up to 6 cm long; they are usually purple or violet, in racemose inflorescences. The fruit, or bean, is 6–40 mm long, hard, swordlike, with 4–15 large seeds. Approximately 50 species exist in the tropics and subtropics, mainly of America and Africa. The sword bean (*Canavalia gladiata*) and the jack bean (*C. ensiformis*) are widely cultivated as annual vegetable plants in India, Indochina, Japan, and southeastern North America. The seeds and unripe beans are edible. In the southern regions of North America, the jack bean is sometimes used as green manure. Some species are ornamentals. [11–865–2]

CANBERRA, the capital of the Commonwealth of Australia and an important administrative, cultural, scientific, and business center. The city has been the site of the Australian Parliament and government since 1927.

Canberra is located in southeastern Australia, on a hilly plain at an elevation of 500–600 m, and has a subtropical continental climate. The city's average temperature is 5.9°C in July and 20.7°C in January. Total annual precipitation is 620 mm. Area, 298 sq km; population, 141,200 (1971). The city, together with its suburbs, forms an independent administrative unit, the Australian Capital Territory, with an area of 2,369.5 sq km and a population of 143,500 (1971). Canberra is linked by railroad lines with Sydney and Melbourne and is a junction of highway and airline routes. An airport is located near the city. Food and light industries play a leading role in the city's economy. Farms near Canberra supply the city with meat, milk, fruit, and vegetables. Tourism plays a considerable role in Canberra's economy, with more than 1 million tourists a year.

The founding of Canberra dates from the 1908–09 decision of the Australian Parliament establishing it as the site for the federal capital. Construction began in 1913 and followed the plans of an American architect, W. B. Griffin, who had won an international competition held by the Australian government in 1911–12. A garden city on the shores of Lake Burley Griffin, Canberra is divided into commercial, administrative, and educational zones. The plan is based on a system of squares, with commercial centers and streets radiating from and encircling the squares. The districts are separated from each other by park zones and are linked by a well-developed network of highways and bridges. The city's buildings are in a restrained, neoclassical style: for example, the Parliament building, built in 1927. The construction of buildings higher than ten or 11 stories is prohibited. The Australian National University, built in 1952 and designed by the architect B. B. Lewis, is among the city's structures built in contemporary style.

The Australian National University, the National Library, and the Australian Academy of Sciences are located in Canberra. An important astronomical observatory is situated near the city, on Mount Stromlo. Canberra has a cultural center, with two auditoriums, several amateur theater troupes (companies), and the Albert Hall for concerts. There are also racecourses in the city.

REFERENCE
Canberra: A Nation's Capital. Edited by N. L. White. Sydney-London [1954]. [11–951–2]

CANCAN, a French dance that emerged in Paris in the 1830's at public balls. It is in 2/4 time, with an energetic, lively tempo. Characteristic steps are kicking out the legs and jumps. The dance was widely used in French classical operettas, especially those by the composer J. Offenbach (*Orpheus in Hades*, finale). Later, the cancan appeared on the stage of cafés chantants, where it acquired an extremely vulgar character. The French painter Toulouse-Lautrec often depicted women dancing the cancan. [11–972–2]

CANCIONEIRO, a collection of love poems and satirical poems of Spain and Portugal. Compiled in the 12th to 14th centuries in the Portuguese Galician dialect.

The oldest preserved *cancioneiros* are *Cancioneiro da Ajuda; Cancioneiro da Vaticana* (late 13th century); and the most complete compilation, *Cancioneiro da Biblioteca Nacional* (or *da Colocci Brancuti*), 16th-century copies of 14th-century originals. The collections brought together approximately 200 poets, whose verses paradoxically combine the traditions of Portuguese folk poetry with the influence of Provençal chivalrous lyric poetry.

Cancioneiros of poets writing in Spanish were first compiled in the 15th century: *El cancionero de Baena* (published 1851), compiled by Juan Alfonso Baena circa 1445; *Cancionero de Stúñiga,* published 1872; and *Cancionero general,* 1511, collected by Hernando del Castillo. In 1516 the Portuguese poet and humanist Garcia de Resende published an anthology of lyric and satiric works from the mid-15th century to the early 16th century in Portuguese and Spanish called *Cancioneiro Geral.*

REFERENCES
Menéndez Pidal, R. "Drevneishaia ispanskaia liricheskaia poeziia: Arabskaia poeziia i poeziia evropeiskaia." In his book *Izbrannye proizvedeniia: Ispanskaia literatura Srednikh vekov i epokhi Vozrozhdeniia.* Moscow, 1961. (Translated from Spanish.)
Smirnov, A. A. *Srednevekovaia literatura Ispanii.* Leningrad, 1969.
Menéndez y Pelayo, M. *Antología de poetas líricos castellanos . . . ,* vols. 1–13. Madrid, 1890–1908.
Rodrigues Lapa, M. *Liçoes de literatura portuguesa: Época medieval,* 3rd ed. Coimbra, 1952.
A. I. DROBINSKII and Z. I. PLAVSKIN [11–991–2]

CANCRINITE (named after the Russian statesman E. F. Cancrin [Kankrin]), the group name of minerals representing a perfect isomorphic series of mixed crystals with the composition $nNa_6Ca_2[AlSiO_4]_6(CO_3)_2\cdot2$—$3H_2O$ (carbonate cancrinite) + $mNa_6Ca_2[AlSiO_4]_6(SO_4)_2\cdot2$—$3H_2O$ (sulfate cancrinite, or

vishnevite). The Na:Ca ratio varies; often an impurity of K_2O (up to 5 percent) is detected. Cancrinite belongs to the aluminosilicates, with a framework of hexagonal SiO_4 rings and AlO_4 tetrahedrons connected in vertical six-membered groups. In the ring cavities lie large ions of $[SO_4]^{2-}$ or $[CO_3]^{2-}$, forming molecular intrusive groups with the Ca or 2Na. The mineral crystallizes in the hexagonal system (crystals are very rare); granular or fine-grained aggregates are common. Cancrinite is colorless, gray, or pink; sometimes it is light blue (sulfate cancrinite). The prismatic cleavage is perfect. The mineral has a hardness of 5–5.5 on the mineralogical scale and a density of 2,420–2,500 kg/m^3. In nature it forms from nepheline under the action of sulfate or carbonate postmagmatic solutions. It is found in nepheline syenites and other basic rocks as well as in alkaline pegmatites as a rock-forming mineral. [11–973–1]

CANDAU, MARCOLINO GOMES. Born May 30, 1911, in Rio de Janeiro. Brazilian physician and public health leader; foreign member of the Academy of Medical Sciences of the USSR (1968); doctor of medicine (1963) and doctor of juridical sciences (1963).

Candau studied medicine at the school of medicine of the state of Rio de Janeiro, at the University of Brazil, and at Johns Hopkins University, USA. He worked in the Brazilian public health service from 1934 to 1950, when he joined the World Health Organization (WHO); he became its director general in 1953. Candau has written on the problems of malaria, parasitology, biostatistics, and rural hygiene and on questions of public health administration. He is an honorary member and honorary doctor of numerous academies, universities, and medical associations throughout the world. [11 956–2]

CANDELA, FELIX. Born Jan. 27, 1910, in Madrid. Mexican architect and engineer.

In 1935, Candela graduated from the Higher School of Architecture in Madrid. He participated in the Spanish Civil War of 1936–39 and emigrated to Mexico in 1939. Candela designed thin-shell reinforced-concrete roofs of various shapes, some of which are particularly unusual; for example, he developed thin-walled coverings in the form of hyperbolic paraboloids. His roof designs made possible the use of low-cost sheathing made out of straight boards. In collaboration with other architects, Candela constructed a number of industrial and commercial buildings, as well as several laboratories and churches. In 1954 he built the Church of the Virgin of the Miraculous Medal in Mexico, which is distinguished by its complex and irrational spatial structure.

REFERENCE
Faber, S. *Candela. . . .* New York, 1963. [11–957–1]

CANDELORO, GIORGIO. Born Mar. 20, 1909, in Bologna. Italian Marxist historian. The son of an office worker.

Candeloro studied at the University of Rome. During World War II he was a member of the Party of Action and was active in the anti-Fascist struggle: he fought in the ranks of the Italian resistance movement in 1943–44 against the Hitlerite occupiers. Candeloro joined the Italian Communist Party in 1947 and was among the leadership of the Roman federation of the Italian Communist Party from 1956 to 1961. Candeloro is a *privatdocent* in the history of political doctrines. He taught history and philosophy in Roman secondary schools for many years and became a professor at the University of Pisa in 1972.

WORKS
Storia dell'Italia moderna, vols. 1–6. Milan, 1956–70.
In Russian translation:
Profsoiuznoe dvizhenie v Italii. Moscow, 1953.
Katolicheskoe dvizhenie v Italii. Moscow, 1955.
Istoriia sovremennoi Italii, vols. 1–5. Moscow, 1958–71. [11–958–3]

CANDIA, ALBERTO. Born 1918; died 1948. Figure in the working-class movement of Paraguay.

Candia played an active role in the student movement of the late 1930's and early 1940's. Later he headed the union of dock workers and joined the Paraguayan Confederation of Workers. After joining the Paraguayan Communist Party (PCP), he enjoyed much authority in the working-class movement. Beginning in 1945 he occupied a number of leading posts in the PCP, becoming general secretary of its Central Committee in 1947. In 1948 he was arrested and after brutal torture was murdered in prison. [11–964–2]

CANDIDATE. (1) An individual contending or being considered for a governmental or public post (such as a presidential candidate or legislative candidate) or any position.

(2) In prerevolutionary Russia, individuals who completed with distinction studies in a university or in any equivalent higher education establishment (lyceum, academy), and presented written work on their chosen theme. The degree of *kandidat* was introduced in 1804; although it was abolished by the 1884 statutes, it was retained up until 1917 in Warsaw and Iur'ev (Tartu) universities, Demidov Lyceum (Iaroslavl'), and ecclesiastical academies, which were not affected by the statutes. The degree was used in combination with the name of the education establishment or branch of learning (for instance, *kandidat* Moskovskogo Universiteta or *kandidat slovesnosti* [candidate in philology]); on entering governmental service the holder of the degree was entitled to a rank of the tenth class (*kollezhskii sekretar'*, collegiate secretary). Another title was *kandidat kommertsii* (candidate in commerce), which was awarded to individuals who completed with distinction studies at the St. Petersburg or Kharkov commercial schools. [11–960–1]

CANDIDATE MINIMUM EXAMINATIONS, examinations taken by graduate students and applicants for the candidate of sciences degree in the USSR for the purpose of receiving the right to defend a candidate's dissertation.

Candidate minimum examinations (the number and scope of which are established by the Ministry of Higher and Specialized Secondary Education of the USSR) are given in dialectical and historical materialism, a foreign language, and a specialized discipline, the scope of the requirements in the latter being determined in accordance with the dissertation topic by the subdepartment (section, laboratory) of the higher educational or scientific research institution. When defending a dissertation on a topic that does not correspond to his principal specialization, the student or applicant takes supplementary candidate minimum examinations in the general scientific discipline to which the topic of his dissertation belongs. Preparation for the candidate minimum examinations presupposes independent study by the graduate student or applicant of scientific literature and the carrying out of scientific research. In order to take the candidate minimum examinations and fulfill the work for the dissertation, graduate students who are taking correspondence courses are given extra leave with full pay. Individuals who pass the candidate minimum examinations receive a certificate that gives them the right to defend a dissertation and the right to enter graduate study without entrance examinations, but it cannot serve as a legal document about education. There is no time limit for taking the candidate minimum examinations and no time limit on the period of validity of the certification.

The list of higher educational and scientific research institutions that are entitled to give candidate minimum examinations is approved by the Ministry of Higher and Specialized Secondary Education of the USSR. Individuals confirmed in the academic rank of docent are exempted from taking the candidate minimum examinations. In exceptional cases the Supreme Certifying Commission partially or completely exempts some individuals from taking the candidate minimum examinations. These individuals (mainly workers in production) have prepared a dissertation or, in place of a dissertation, have permission to defend published works or inventions and discoveries that have been registered with the Committee for Inventions and Discoveries of the Council of Ministers of the USSR. Persons who have completed work on the creation of new machines, control systems, instruments, structures, and technological processes are also exempt or partially exempt. Any of these published works, inventions, discoveries, or various completed work may have been accomplished or developed either by an individual or by a group.

M. N. VOLKOV and B. G. PANOV [11–961–1]

CANDIDATE OF SCIENCES (or candidate), the first advanced degree in the USSR, awarded to individuals with higher education who pass the candidate minimum examinations and who publicly defend a dissertation for the candidate's degree. The degree was established by a decree of the Council of Peoples' Commissars of the USSR on Jan. 13, 1934. The candidate of sciences degree is conferred by academic councils of higher educational institutions (departments) or of scientific research institutions, and as a check, dissertations for the candidate's degree are examined by the Supreme Certifying Commission. In 1972 the right to accept candidates' dissertations for defense was granted to the councils of approximately 1,000 higher educational and scientific research institutions. A total of 249,200 scientific associates possessed the candidate of sciences degree in 1971.

The holder of the candidate of sciences degree has the right to participate in competitions for appointments to the positions of docent, senior research associate, and head of a subdepartment, laboratory, or other section in a higher educational or scientific research institution and has the right to defend a dissertation for the advanced degree of doctor of sciences. The candidate of sciences degree corresponds to the doctor of philosophy degree which exists in the USA, Great Britain, and other countries. M. N. VOLKOV [11–960–2]

CANDIDIASIS (also, blastodendriosis or candidosis), a disease caused by yeastlike fungi of the genus *Candida*. These fungi, which are widely distributed in nature, thrive on seeds, vegetables, and fruits (particularly those that are rotten). Under certain conditions, they become pathogens and cause superficial diseases of the skin (which usually run a mild course) or infections of the mucous membranes. The fungi can also cause deep infections, even in the internal organs. In particular, confectioners, workers in the fruit and vegetable industry, and employees of bath and shower facilities are exposed to candidiasis. Infection occurs through contact with someone carrying the disease or with objects that have been contaminated by the fungi.

Superficial candidiasis is primarily localized in cutaneous folds, including interdigital spaces (particularly between the fingers). The fungi cause red exzemalike lesions of various sizes, with white flaking epidermis along the edges. Candidiasis of the mucous membranes is manifested as thrush, or mycotic stomatitis. Thrush is characterized by the formation of a white, readily removed film on the mucous membranes of the oral cavity and cracks in the corners of the mouth that heal with difficulty and frequently recur. Infection of female sexual organs is accompanied by itching and leukorrhea. The disease frequently appears on nails and cuticles. Sometimes candidiasis becomes chronic and generalized. Of the internal organs, candidiasis most often infects the gastrointestinal tract (esophagitis, gastritis, enteritis, and colitis), the respiratory organs (bronchitis, pneumonia, pleuropneumonia that sometimes resemble tuberculous infiltrates), and the urinary system. Treatment of the disease includes local disinfection and the application of antiphlogistics. Antifungal antibiotics, such as nystatin or levorin, and vitamins B_2, PP, B_6, and C are also prescribed. Prevention can be accomplished by eliminating the conditions allowing the fungi to grow.

A. L. MASHKILLEISON

Candidiasis in animals. Infections occur in domestic fowl, cattle, swine, sheep, and dogs (usually occurring in the young). Sick animals are the source of infection. Damage resulting from candidiasis is significant, particularly if care and feeding is poor. The incubation period is 3–15 days; the most usual clinical sign is the formation of white deposits on mucous membranes. The most frequent form of the disease in animals is intestinal, causing diarrhea. For young animals the disease is acute, causing plague in 3–8 days; it is a chronic disease for adults. In cattle, candidiasis usually is manifested as mastitis. Laboratory work is crucially important in the diagnosis of the disease in animals. Treatment is successful only in minor cases (using iodine preparations and certain antibiotics). Preventive measures include the isolation of infected animals and disinfection. [11–959–4]

CANDILIS, GEORGES. Born Apr. 11, 1913, in Baku. French architect.

Candilis studied at the Athens Polytechnic Institute. From 1946 to 1951 he worked with Le Corbusier in Paris. In 1951 he began designing housing in Morocco, Algeria and Iran. In 1963, Candilis became a professor at the Ecole Nationale Supérieure des Beaux-Arts. Since 1955, in collaboration with A. Josic and S. Woods, he has designed university buildings (Free University of Berlin, West Berlin, 1963) and new cities, including Bagnols-sur-Cèze (in Languedoc, under construction since 1956) and Le Mirail (the twin city of Toulouse, constructed during the 1960's). In his city planning, Candilis strives to meet fully the demands of the residents' social and private activities. He also seeks to reduce the adverse effects of traffic on the life of a city through the design of malls, houses on piles, and "internal streets."

WORKS

Candilis, G., S. Woods, and A. Josic. *Building for People.* Washington, D.C., 1968.   [11–962–2]

CANELONES, a city in southern Uruguay, administrative center of Canelones Department. Population, 14,000 (1963). Canelones has a railroad station and chemical and paper industries.   [11–967–3]

CANGA ARGÜELLES, JOSÉ. Born 1770; died 1843. Spanish count, political figure, and economist.

During the Spanish revolution of 1808–14, Canga Argüelles helped organize resistance to the French occupation. He was a deputy to the Cádiz Cortes and minister of finance during the Regency, and he helped prepare the Cádiz Constitution of 1812. In 1814, after the restoration of absolutism in Spain, he was exiled. He took part in the Spanish revolution of 1820–23 and occupied the post of minister of finance in 1820–21; he belonged to the party of moderates (*moderados*). An émigré from 1823 to 1829, he was not active in political life after returning to Spain. He was the author of several studies in economics. His five-volume work *Financial Dictionary for Directors of Finance* (1826–27), written from a bourgeois-liberal viewpoint, is rich in material on the economic life of Spain in the late 18th and early 19th centuries.   [11–952–3]

CANISIUS, PETER (Pieter de Hondt). Born May 8, 1521, in Nijmegen, Holland; died Dec. 21, 1597, in Freiburg, Switzerland. Catholic theologian with whose name is linked the beginning of the Jesuit order in Germany and the implementation of the Counter-Reformation.

Canisius entered the Jesuit order in 1543 in Mainz. In 1549 he settled down at the University of Ingolstadt; in 1552 he was in Vienna. In 1556 he was placed at the head of the Jesuit order in the German Province. He founded many Jesuit colleges and compiled three catechisms—the *Summa Doctrinae Christianae* (1555), a short catechism (1556), and *Catechismus Minor seu parvus Catechismus Catholicorum* (1558).   [11–970–1]

CANISTER (in Russian, *kartech';* from Polish *kartecza,* from Italian *cartoccio,* literally "bundle" or "cartridge"), a type of artillery shell used by the artillery to strike at enemy personnel at close distance. (The Russian word *kartech'* also refers to large buckshot, 5 mm or more in diameter.)

In the 14th through 16th centuries canisters had different sizes and shapes and consisted of pieces of stone or iron, which were loaded into the bore above an explosive charge and fastened with a plug. Later, canisters were placed in a bag to protect the bore. In the 17th through 19th centuries canisters were shells with spherical cast-iron or lead bullets placed in a metal container or cardboard packing. Canister bullets were lethal at a distance of up to 300 m and spread up to 50 m along the front. In the early 19th century canisters gradually lost their value after the invention of shrapnel; they are no longer used in modern artillery.   [11–1388–4]

CANNA, the only genus of the family Cannaceae. The plants are large perennial herbs with strong stalks; they often have tuberous thickened rhizomes. The leaves are large, broad, pinnately veined, and sheathed. The flowers are irregular, monoecious, large, and usually brightly colored; they are gathered into a paniculate terminal racemose or inflorescence. The perianth is binate. Only half of the anther of one stamen is fertile; the remaining half and the other stamens are petaloid and are staminodia. The stigma has a petal-like style. The ovary is inferior and trilocular. The fruit is a capsule. There are approximately 50 species, found in tropical and subtropical America. There are approximately 1,000 garden varieties (for example, *Canna* × *generalis* and *C.* × *hortensis*), which are used in cultivation. They differ in color, leaf color, size, height of stalk, and form of the staminodia. The species Indian shot (*C. indica*) is cultivated in Europe as a greenhouse ornamental; *C. edulis* is grown in the Americas and Australia for its rhizomes, which contain starch from which the queensland arrowroot is obtained.   [11–975–1]

CANNAE, village in southeastern Italy on the Aufidus River (modern Ofanto River) near which, on Aug. 2, 216 B.C., occurred the largest battle of the Second Punic War, between the Roman Army commanded on the day of battle by Consul Terentius Varro and Hannibal's Carthaginian Army. The Roman Army comprised 80,000 infantry and 6,000 cavalry, of which 63,000 infantry and all the cavalry participated in the battle; the Carthaginian Army comprised 40,000 infantry and 10,000 cavalry. The Roman infantry, in a deep and dense battle formation, attacked the center of the Carthaginian forces and pushed them back. But the Carthaginian cavalry crushed the Roman cavalry on the flanks, whereupon the Roman infantry was surrounded and virtually wiped out. The Roman losses were 48,000 killed and 10,000 taken prisoner; the Carthaginians lost 6,000.

After the defeat of the Roman Army, many southern Italian and Sicilian cities defected to Hannibal's side. However, owing to the lack of forces, Hannibal was unable to take advantage of the victory and move against Rome. The battle of Cannae is an outstanding example of the art of warfare. "Never before had an entire army been so completely crushed" (F. Engels, *Izbr. voen. proizvedeniia,* 1956, p. 211).

REFERENCES

Razin, E. A. *Istoriia voennogo iskusstva,* vol. 1. Moscow, 1955.
Strokov, A. A. *Istoriia voennogo iskusstva,* vol. 1. Moscow, 1955.
Del'briuk, G. *Istoriia voennogo iskusstva v ramkakh politicheskoi istorii,* vol. 1. Moscow, 1936.
Shliffen, A. *Kanny,* 2nd ed. Moscow, 1938.   [11–980–1]

CANNES, a resort city in southern France, on the Mediterranean coast in the Alpes-Maritimes Department. Population, 68,000 (1968). A port and transportation junction. Cannes is the site of the International Film Festival (since 1946; in the Palais des Festivals). It has an extensive hotel industry; other industries (textiles, garments, food) are primarily concerned with serving the resort population. There is an aircraft plant. The city is picturesquely situated along a gulf; the old city is west of the port.

Cannes is part of the group of famous resorts that make up the French Riviera, located on the Côte d'Azur. It is a major tourist center. The climate is subtropical Mediterranean; summers are very warm and dry (average July temperature, 22.6°C), and winters very mild and sunny (average January temperature, 9.3°C). Annual precipitation is 580 mm.

The resort offers sunbathing, fresh air, and sea bathing (June to mid-October) and treats patients with fundamental disorders of the nervous system, overweight problems, chronic diseases of the respiratory organs, and some diseases of the cardiovascular system and the kidneys. Cannes has sanatoriums, solariums, hydrotherapy and physiotherapy clinics, boardinghouses, hotels, and an excellent sandy beach. There are also theaters and concert halls, sports arenas, and swimming pools in the city.   [11–973–4]

CANNES CONFERENCE (1922), a conference of the supreme council of the Entente that was attended by representatives of Belgium, Great Britain, Italy, France, Japan, and Germany; members of the Reparations Commission (created in 1919 to determine the amount of reparations to be imposed on Germany and its allies and the ways of collecting the money); and an observer from the USA. The conference took place on January 6–13, in Cannes, France; it was a preparatory stage of the Genoa Conference of 1922.

On Jan. 6, 1922, the Cannes Conference unanimously adopted the resolution offered by British prime minister Lloyd George calling for the convocation of an economic and financial conference of all European states in Genoa. The Soviet government, which had repeatedly stated that it favored economic cooperation with other powers, accepted the invitation to attend the Genoa Conference as soon as it was received (it was extended by the government of Italy on January 7). The Cannes Conference prepared the way for the Genoa Conference by approving an outline agenda and a six-article statement on the "basic terms necessary for fruitful work." The first article of "conditions" recognized that each nation has "the right to choose for itself the system it prefers." Lenin remarked that in this article the Cannes Conference, "by recognizing the *equality* of the two *property systems* (capitalist or private property, and communist, *so far* accepted only in the RSFSR), is thus compelled to recognize, even if only indirectly, the collapse, the bankruptcy of the first property system and the inevitability of its coming to an *agreement* with the second, on terms of equality" (*Poln. sobr. soch.,* 5th ed., vol. 45, pp. 192–93). The remaining articles envisaged guaranties for foreign capital and property in Russia and the recognition by Russia of all private debts and obligations of the former governments. It was especially indicated that the Western powers would recognize the Soviet government only upon the satisfaction of the enumerated conditions. These conditions were a hopeless attempt to force the Soviet government by diplomatic pressure to make serious concessions of principle to the capitalist countries.

The Cannes Conference granted to Germany a delay in making upcoming reparations payments. In the course of the conference the French and the British conducted negotiations on a prospective pact that would guarantee British assistance to France in case of an attack by Germany; however, no agreement was reached.

PUBLICATIONS

Dokumenty vneshnei politiki SSSR [vol. 5]. Moscow, 1961.
Materialy Genuezskoi konferentsii. Moscow, 1922. Pages 3–10.
A. I. STEPANOV   [11–979–2]

CANNIBALISM. (1) The practice of eating human flesh, widespread in the past among certain tribes and peoples. There were two basic forms of cannibalism: as a source of food and as a religious and magical ritual. Cannibalism as a source of food, as shown by excavated bones that had been burned and split open for extracting the marrow, probably was practiced in the early Stone Age. Later on, with the development of the primitive communal system, the improvement in production, and the increase in food resources, cannibalism as a source of food survived only as an exceptional phenomenon caused by famines. Numerous tribes and peoples practiced religious and magical cannibalism: they ate various parts of slaughtered enemies, prisoners of war, and deceased kinsmen (endocannibalism). The custom was based on the conviction that the victim's strength and other properties would be transmitted to the eater. Vestiges of religious and magical cannibalism have survived in certain rites of modern world religions—for example, communion (the eating of bread and wine symbolizing the body and blood of Christ) in Christianity.   A. I. PERSHITS

(2) The eating by animals of members of the same species. Cannibalism is one of the manifestations of intraspecific competition and a factor in natural selection. It is most often observed with unfavorable environmental conditions: an overconcentration of population and a shortage of food or water. Thus, in harsh winters when small mammals have died off, wolves, lynxes, and other large carnivores sometimes eat one another. A lack of food or other bad conditions will cause females to eat their young. Mealworm beetles (*Tenebrio*) feed on their own eggs when their population density becomes high, thereby preventing an increase in the population. Those species that have a more expressed inclination for cannibalism are more likely to survive than other species under unfavorable conditions. Instances are also known of permanent, or obligate, cannibalism that develops in evolution as a useful adaptation. Thus, female karakurts and praying mantises eat the males after mating.

The male American salamander satisfies its hunger by consuming a portion of the eggs from the clutch it is guarding. The parasitic larvae of certain ichneumon flies (*Galesus*) attempt to destroy their colarvae since the host can sustain only one specimen of the parasite. Certain predatory fishes (for example, the Balkhash perch) consume their young and thus can subsist in a body of water when there is no other food for them.

REFERENCE

Mekhanizmy biologicheskoi konkurentsii: Sb. st. Moscow, 1964. (Translated from English.)   I. KH. SHAROVA [11–977–2]

CANNING, GEORGE. Born Apr. 11, 1770, in London; died Aug. 8, 1827, in Chiswick. British statesman, Tory.

Canning graduated from Oxford University in 1791. He was elected to Parliament in 1793. From 1796 to 1799 he was undersecretary of state for foreign affairs in the cabinet of W. Pitt the Younger. He was foreign secretary from 1807 to 1809. A strong opponent of Napoleonic France, he conducted a policy of actively supporting Spain with financial, diplomatic, and military aid. From 1814 to 1816 he was ambassador to Portugal. He supported the repressive measures of the Liverpool government against the democratic movement in Britain; at the same time he headed the so-called Left Tories, who came out for certain concessions to the industrial bourgeoisie. In 1822 he became an influential member of Liverpool's cabinet, in which he was foreign secretary. He succeeded in carrying through certain reforms (lowering the duties on grain and raw materials, facilitating the export of industrial goods, easing some criminal laws). In 1823 he condemned the French intervention in Spain and supported the British government's recognition of the independence of the former Spanish colonies in Latin America. He supported the autonomy of Greece, where in 1821 an uprising had broken out against the Turkish yoke. In April 1827 he became prime minister.

Canning was an energetic and flexible director of British foreign policy. Expressing the aspirations of the English bourgeoisie for the establishment of hegemony in Europe and in world markets, he adopted a policy of opposition to the policies of the continental powers of the Holy Alliance.

WORKS

Speeches, vols. 1–6. London, 1828.

REFERENCES

Tarle, E. V. "Angliiskaia godovshchina: 1827–1902." *Soch.,* vol. 1. Moscow, 1957.
Petrie, C. *George Canning,* 2nd ed. London, 1946.   [11–977–3]

CANNIZZARO, STANISLAO. Born July 13, 1826, in Palermo; died May 10, 1910, in Rome. Italian chemist. One of the originators of the atom-molecular theory.

Cannizzaro studied medicine at the universities of Palermo and Pisa. In 1845 he began working with the Italian chemist R. Piria (1814–65). Cannizzaro participated in a national uprising in Sicily, emigrating to France (1849) after its suppression. In Paris he collaborated with the French chemist F. Cloëz (1817–83); in 1851 they successfully prepared cyanamide by the reaction $CNCl + NH_3 = CNNH_2 + HCl$. Upon his return to Italy, Cannizzaro was appointed professor of chemistry at the National College in Alessandria (1851), where he discovered the Cannizzaro reaction. He was a professor at the universities of Genoa (from 1856), Palermo (from 1861), and Rome (1871–1910); it was in Rome that he began studying santonin and its derivatives (from 1873).

Cannizzaro's historical contributions to science include the refinement of atomic weight values for certain elements (metals in particular) on the basis of Dulong and Petit's law and the demonstration of the universal application of Avogadro's principle to determining the molecular weights of simple and complex substances in the vaporous state. He rigorously differentiated the concepts of "atom," "equivalent" (combining weight), and "molecule." Cannizzaro's views were reflected in his published works (1858) and expounded in his address to the International Congress of Chemists held at Karlsruhe in 1860. They received universal recognition in subsequent years.

WORKS
Scritti vari e lettere inedite. Rome, 1926.
In Russian translation:
Obzor razvitiia poniatiia ob atome, chastitse i ekvivalente i razlichnykh sistem formul. Kiev, 1873.
O predelakh i o forme teoreticheskogo prepodavaniia khimii. Kiev, 1873.

REFERENCES
Mendeleev, D. I. "Khimicheskii kongress v Karlsrue." *Soch.,* vol. 15. Moscow-Leningrad, 1949.
Giua, M. *Istoriia khimii.* Moscow, 1966. (Translated from Italian.)
Bykov, G. V., and V. A. Kritsman. *Stanislao Kannitstsaro. Ocherk zhizni i deiatel'nosti.* Moscow, 1972. (Includes a bibliography of Cannizzaro's works.) S. A. POGODIN [11–978–2]

CANNIZZARO REACTION, the conversion of aldehyde into a mixture containing equal molar quantities of alcohol and acid in an aqueous or water-alcohol solution of alkali; for example,

$$2C_6H_5CHO + KOH \rightarrow C_6H_5COOK + C_6H_5CH_2OH$$

The Cannizzaro reaction is a redox process characteristic of aromatic and heterocyclic aldehydes as well as of aldehydes in the aliphatic series that do not contain any hydrogen atoms near the carbon, bonded with the aldehyde group. This reaction can be carried out successfully in the case of two unlike aldehydes ("crossed" Cannizzaro reaction). Thus, benzyl alcohol $C_6H_5CH_2OH$ and formic acid $HCOOH$ are produced from a mixture of benzaldehyde C_6H_5CHO and formaldehyde $HCHO$. This version of the Cannizzaro reaction is widely used for the reduction of inaccessible aldehydes into the corresponding alcohols. S. Cannizzaro discovered the reaction in 1853.

[11–979–1]

CANNONEER, in pre-Revolutionary Russia, a private in the artillery. [11–985–3]

CANNULA, a hollow tube with a blunt end designed for introducing into the human (or animal) body drugs or X-ray contrast media, restoring the patency of the respiratory tract, or withdrawing fluids from the body cavities. It is also used for anatomical, pathologicoanatomic, and laboratory studies. Cannulas are made of metal, glass, or plastic. [11–1014–2]

CANO, ALONSO. Baptized Mar. 19, 1601, in Granada; died there Sept. 3, 1667. Spanish sculptor and painter, representative of the baroque style.

Cano began studying under J. Montañés and F. Pacheco in Sevilla in 1616. He worked there until 1637. He subsequently worked in Madrid, Valencia, and Granada (from 1652). Maintaining the traditions of painted wooden sculpture, Cano's polychromatic sculptures are imposing and are characterized by subtle spirituality and eloquent expressiveness. Examples of his sculpture are the retables of the Church of Santa Maria in Lebrija (near Sevilla, 1628–38) and the statues and busts of saints in the Granada Cathedral (1658–60). Cano's paintings, which are characterized by idealization of forms, external prettiness, and Italian artistic influences, are less distinctive than his sculptures. His paintings include *The Virgin Presenting the Infant Christ to St. Anthony* (1645–52, Prado, Madrid) and the series *Seven Joys of the Virgin* (1652–64, Granada Cathedral). In 1703, Cano's design for the western facade of the Granada Cathedral was carried out by the architect J. Granados.

REFERENCE
Wethey, N. E. *Alonso Cano.* Princeton, 1955. [11–980–2]

CANOAS, a city in southern Brazil, in the state of Rio Grande do Sul. Population, 122,000 (1968). Canoas has a railroad station and is a highway junction. Building materials (glass, cement) are produced in Canoas, which also has metallurgical, transportation machine-building, electrotechnical, chemical, furniture, pulp and paper, and slaughtering-refrigerating industries.

Nearby is an oil-refining plant (of the state-owned Petrobraz company). [11–982–1]

CANOE. (1) A boat used by many Indian tribes of North America. Canoes were made from an entire tree trunk (hollowed out by fire and chopping), or else a frame was first constructed and later covered with bark. Canoes had symmetrically pointed bows and sterns and were of various sizes, with seating capacities ranging from two to 100 persons.

(2) A modern canoe is a paddle boat without oarlocks that is typified by a dugout-shaped hull and a paddling method using one single-bladed shovel-shaped paddle. Steering is done by twisting the paddle in the water and changing its trajectory at the end of the stroke. There are domestic general purpose canoes (for carrying loads and passengers, for hunting and fishing), touring canoes, and sport canoes (for "flat" racing on calm water and for water slalom on rough mountain streams). Canoes are classed according to production method as those hollowed out of whole tree-trunk pieces and those made by covering a frame with waterproof materials (special plywoods, skins, rubberized fabrics, synthetic coatings, and plastics).

The finest canoes are the sport canoes, which are made of polished plywood (the best being made of mahogany) or plastic material. Touring canoes are usually built for two or three persons and have collapsible frames or are inflatable. Water slalom canoes are made of fiberglass with unsinkable, airtight compartments in the bow and stern. The paddlers sit on the bottom of the canoe or on bench-type seats; in sport canoes the paddlers kneel on one knee. The number of paddlers in a canoe ranges from one to several dozen persons (from one to six in sport canoes). The dimensions, weight, and shape of sport canoes are limited by regulations. The cross-section and longitudinal lines of the hulls of these canoes must be convex and continuous. One-man canoes have a maximum length of 520 cm, a minimum width of 75 cm, and a minimum weight of 16 kg; for two-man canoes these specifications are 650 cm, 75 cm, and 20 kg, respectively; for six-man canoes they are 1,100 cm, 85 cm, and 50 kg, respectively. E. L. KABANOV [11–987–3]

CANON, in the fine arts, an aggregate of firmly established rules, defining for works of art the compositional and coloristic norms, the system of proportions, and the iconography that is suitable for a particular representation. The word "canon" also refers to a work that serves as a normative model. Canonical systems, the result of religious prescriptions, prevailed in ancient Oriental and medieval art (for example, the dogmatic ecclesiastical canonical patterns in icon painting). Ancient Greek, ancient Roman, and Renaissance artists attempted rationally to find ideal laws governing the proportions of the human body; they wanted to discover immutable, mathematically substantiated rules governing the creation of the human figure. [11–983–3]

CANON, a form in polyphonic music based on each voice presenting the same melody, which is taken up by the next voice before the preceding one has stated it completely (the principle of strict imitation). Two- and three-part canons are most common, although four- and five-part ones are encountered. The melody in a canon can begin in each of the successive voices on the same tone as the lead voice or at any given interval.

There are various types of canon—for example, the melody in the successive voices can be augmented or diminished in all values or given in another temporal formulation, in inversion (direction of the intervals is changed), or in retrograde motion (from the last tone to the first). The double canon has two melody themes being imitated simultaneously. Circular, or infinite, canon leads back to the beginning; thus it can be repeated any number of times. Riddle canon only notes the melody and leaves the solution of its imitation to the performer.

Canon arose around the 12th century and came into extensive use in the 14th century, an era marked by the domination of polyphony; in the 15th century major works of sacred music (canonic Mass) were often built on a canonic basis. Later canon was more often an element of another form, particularly the fugue. It reached its highest level of development in the works of J. S. Bach.

Remarkable examples of canon are also found in works by Russian composers—for example the quartet "What a Wonderful Moment" from Act 1 of *Ruslan and Ludmila* by Glinka and the duet "The Enemies" from Act 2, Scene 2 of *Eugene Onegin* by Tchaikovsky.

REFERENCES
Taneev, S. *Uchenie o kanone.* Moscow, 1929.
Bogatyrev, S. *Dvoinoi kanon.* Moscow-Leningrad, 1947.
T. F. MIULLER   [11–983–4]

CANON, a collection of dogmatic precepts.

(1) The biblical canon—all the books of the Bible considered by the church to be "divinely inspired" (as distinct from the Apocrypha) and used during the divine services as the "holy scriptures." The Old Testament canon, written in Hebrew, was put together early in the second century A.D. The canon of the Old Testament in Greek translation (put together later) differs in the list of the books and their wording. The New Testament canon was determined by Athanasius of Alexandria in A.D. 367, but the disputes (especially with regard to the inclusion of the Book of Revelation) continued up to the ninth century. The canons of the Orthodox, Catholic, and Protestant churches differ with regard to the list of included books.

(2) The church canons—rules established by the church on doctrine, worship, and church organization given the force of "law" by the highest level of church authority (church councils, mainly ecumenical councils, and papal decrees).   [11–983–2]

CANONICAL ENSEMBLE, a statistical ensemble for macroscopic systems (such as a crystal or a gas in a vessel) that are in thermal contact with an environment whose temperature is constant. Such systems may be considered as small parts (subsystems) of a large closed system in a state of thermal equilibrium. In canonical ensembles the interaction of a subsystem with the remainder of the closed system (the "thermostat") is characteristically assumed to be weak, so that the energy of the interaction is negligible in comparison with the energy of the subsystem. Therefore it is possible to speak of the energy of the subsystem as a definite quantity. However, interaction between the subsystem and the thermostat leads to exchange of energy between them, as a result of which the subsystem may exist in different energy states. The distribution of the probability of different microscopic states of the subsystem (that is, states defined by the values of the coordinates and velocities of all particles of the subsystem) is given by a canonical Gibbs distribution.

The concept of the canonical ensemble was introduced by J. W. Gibbs; it makes it possible easily to obtain the basic results of statistical physics and, in particular, to derive the laws of thermodynamics.   G. IA. MIAKISHEV   [11–985–4]

CANONIZATION, in the Catholic and Orthodox churches the inclusion of some person in the list of saints. In Catholicism it is an act that has been strictly defined with respect to law and public worship. The church-wide method of canonization was introduced by Pope Alexander III during the second half of the 12th century and was fixed in 1200 by Innocent III; the right to canonize became the exclusive prerogative of the Roman popes. In implementing canonization the church always pursues political aims.

Orthodoxy does not have as strict a system of canonization as Catholicism. In Russia church-wide canonization was introduced in the 16th century and was placed under the tsar's control; from the time of Peter I it was implemented by imperial decree upon the recommendation of the synod.   [11–985–1]

CANON LAW, the totality of decisions of church councils and papal decrees.

Canon law reflected the fact "that the church was the all-embracing synthesis and the most general sanction of the existing feudal domination" (K. Marx and F. Engels, *Soch.,* 2nd ed., vol. 7, p. 361). The first codification of canon law was undertaken in the 12th century by the Bolognan monk Gratian, who wrote the treatise *Concordia discordantium canonum,* which became significant as a source of law. In 1582, during the rule of Pope Gregory XIII, an enlarged and revised edition of Gratian's treatise called the *Corpus juris canonici* was published. The jurisdiction of church courts was especially broad in the Middle Ages, which was a period marked by the strengthening of the bond between church and state. A significant number of nonreligious (chiefly civil) legal matters were within clerical jurisdiction, including marriage and family affairs, property questions, and even criminal cases. Correspondingly, the norms of canon law were not limited to the organization and relations within the church, but they embraced various branches of law.

As absolutism developed and secular courts increased in importance, the sphere of activity of canon law gradually became more restricted until it was finally fixed under the bourgeois social structure. Thus the *Code of Canon Law of 1917* published by Pope Benedict XV regulates only matters within the church. The norms contained in this code can be considered legal only to the extent that they are recognized as compulsory by any given state.

In the Orthodox Church, canon law is considered to be the totality of canon rules established chiefly at church councils. A significant part of these rules was included in the ecclesiastical law that was in effect in tsarist Russia.

P. S. GRATSIANSKII   [11–985–5]

CANOPIC JAR. (1) In ancient Egypt, four tall vessels (made of alabaster, faience, or other material), in which the viscera of the deceased—which had been removed during the process of mummification—were placed. The lids of the canopic jars were made in the shape of the heads of the sons of the god Horus (the baboon-headed Hapi, the human-headed Imset, the hawk-headed Qebhsnuf, and the jackal-headed Duamutef). The jars were placed in a special box having reliefs of the goddess-protectresses of the canopic jars: Isis, Nephthys, Mut, and Neith.

(2) In ancient Etruria (Italy), an urn in which the ashes were stored after cremation of the corpse. The Etruscan canopic jar was rounded or oval and had two handles, sometimes a high pedestal, and a lid in the form of a human head.   [11–986–3]

CANOSSA, a castle in northern Italy, 18 km from the city of Reggio nell'Emilia. The castle was the scene of a famous incident that occurred during the investiture struggle: the meeting in January 1077 between Pope Gregory VII (a guest of Countess Matilda of Tuscany, the owner of the castle) and Henry IV, the excommunicated and deposed German emperor. According to some chronicles, Henry IV, dressed as a penitent sinner, stood for three days at the walls of the castle awaiting reception by the pope. The expression "to go to Canossa" came to mean a humiliating capitulation (although the "going" to Canossa of Henry IV was actually only a political maneuver).   [11–987–2]

CANOVA, ANTONIO. Born Nov. 1, 1757, in Possagno, Veneto region; died Oct. 13, 1822, in Venice. Italian neoclassical sculptor.

Canova studied in Venice (1768–74) under the sculptor Toretti. He worked primarily in Venice and Rome. His early works followed the traditions of baroque art, but he subsequently embarked on formal imitation of classical sculpture.

His effective tombs (of Clement XIII, 1792, St. Peter's Basilica, Rome), statues of mythological heroes (*Cupid and Psyche,* 1793 version, Louvre, Paris; 1800 version, Hermitage, Leningrad), and idealized portraits (Pauline Borghese as *Venus Victrix,* 1805–07, Borghese Gallery, Rome) combine serene composition, clarity, and elegant proportions with cold abstract images, features of saccharine sentimentality and salon prettiness, and the lifeless smoothness of polished marble. Canova's work served as a model for 19th-century European academic sculpture.

REFERENCES
Kosareva, N. K. *Kanova i ego proizvedeniia v Ermitazhe,* 2nd ed. Leningrad, 1963.
Coletti, L., ed. *Mostra Canoviana* (Catalog). Treviso, 1957.

[11–982–2]

CÁNOVAS DEL CASTILLO, ANTONIO. Born Feb. 8, 1828, in Málaga; died Aug. 8, 1897, in Santa Agueda. Spanish government figure, writer, and historian.

Cánovas del Castillo was a liberal in his youth, helping to develop the Manzanares program of 1854, which called for convening a constituent cortes, lowering taxes, and creating a popular militia. In 1857 he was governor of Cádiz and in 1864 minister of finance. During the revolution of 1868–74 he came out against a republic and for the Bourbon monarchy. One of the chief architects of the 1874 restoration, he was the founder (1875) and leader of the Conservative Party. From 1875 to 1881 (with brief intervals), 1884 to 1885, 1890 to 1892, and 1895 to 1897 he was prime minister. He contributed to the strengthening of the country's system of constitutional monarchy. He was assassinated by an Italian anarchist.

WORKS

Historia de la decadencia de España . . . , 2nd ed. Madrid, 1910.
Estudios del reinado de Felipe IV, vols. 1–2. Madrid, 1888.
Obras poeticas. Madrid, 1887.   [11–983–1]

CANROBERT, FRANÇOIS. Born June 27, 1809, in St. Céré; died Jan. 28, 1895, in Paris. Marshal of France (1856).

Between 1835 and 1849, Canrobert participated in colonial wars in North Africa. In 1850 he became an adjutant to Louis Napoleon Bonaparte and took part in his coup d'etat of Dec. 2, 1851. During the Crimean War of 1853–56, Canrobert first commanded a division and then (from Sept. 14 [26], 1854, to May 4 [16], 1855) all French troops in the Crimea, after which he resumed divisional command. From 1859 he commanded a corps. During the Franco-Prussian War of 1870–71, Canrobert's corps was thrown back to the fortress of Metz after the battle at Saint-Privat; there the entire corps was captured when the army of A. Bazaine capitulated. From 1871 to 1876, Canrobert was the leader of the Bonapartists in the French National Assembly; later he was a senator.   [11–988–2]

CANTABILE, a songful or lyrical quality of a melody or a musical performance. Since the mid-18th century the direction "cantabile" is often placed at the beginning of a piece of music with the indication of tempo to specify the character of the music (*andante cantabile* in Tchaikovsky's String Quartet, Opus 11). Occasionally the term is used alone as a title (Cui's Cantabile for Cello and Piano).   [11–997–4]

CANTABRIAN MOUNTAINS (Cordillera Cantabrica), mountains in northern Spain. They extend along the southern shore of the Bay of Biscay. Length, about 500 km; maximum elevation, 2,648 m (Torre de Serredo).

The northern slopes are steep, precipitously sheer in places, and deeply dissected by river valleys and canyons; in the south they are flat, turned toward the meseta. The highest, western part (with an average elevation of about 2,000 m) is formed of Paleozoic quartzite, marble, and limestone; the eastern part (the Basque Mountains) is lower (with elevations of 1,000–1,500 m) and consists primarily of ridges whose peaks and slopes have softer outlines; it is formed of Mesozoic limestone, sandstone, and dolomite. Karst is widespread. There are deposits of coal, iron, and polymetallic ores. The climate is moist, especially on the northern slopes; annual precipitation amounts to more than 1,000 mm. There is a dense network of fast-flowing rivers. The northern slopes have broad-leaved and mixed forests (oak, beech, chestnut, and pine); predominant in the south are evergreen and deciduous shrubs. Above 1,600–1,800 m are subalpine scrub and alpine meadows.   [11–997–5]

CANTABRIANS, one of the Iberian tribes in northern Spain. According to ancient authors, they were characterized by austere customs and great bravery. They stubbornly fought the Romans during the second and first centuries B.C. and were finally subdued during the reign of Augustus in 29–19 B.C. The territory that had been settled by the Cantabrians became part of the Roman province of Hispania Citerior (or Tarraconia).
                    [11–998–1]

CANTACUZENI. (1) An aristocratic Byzantine family (Kantakuzenoi) that rose to eminence at the end of the 11th century. The Cantacuzeni acquired particular influence at the beginning of the 14th century. They owned estates in Thrace and in the Peloponnesus. One of the Cantacuzeni was viceroy of the Peloponnesus, and his son became emperor (John VI Cantacuzene). Of the sons of John VI, Manuel received the Peloponnesus (Morea) as an appanage, and Matthew received Thrace. After Manuel's death (1380) the Cantacuzeni held on to Morea for a brief time, but in 1381 (or 1382) they were compelled to yield it to the Palaeologi.

(2) An aristocratic Walachian family (Cantacuzino), which traced its origin back to the Byzantine family of Cantacuzeni, some of whose members entered the service of the Turks after the fall of Byzantium (mid-15th century). Serban Cantacuzino (1640–88) was hospodar of Walachia from 1678. In the early 18th century many members of the Cantacuzino family moved from Walachia to Russia. During the 19th and early 20th centuries the Cantacuzinos occupied prominent political posts in Rumania.

REFERENCE

Nicol, D. M. *The Byzantine Family of Kantakouzenos (Cantacuzenus), ca. 1100–1460.* Washington, D.C., 1968.   [11–998–2]

CANTAL, a department in France, located in the Massif Central. Area, 5,800 sq km; population, 168,000 (1971). Its capital is Aurillac. The main sector of the economy is agriculture. The principal crops are rye, wheat, buckwheat, oats, and potatoes. Dairy farming is prevalent on mountain pastures. There is cheese production (cantal and blue cheese). Cantal has leather and wood-products industries.   [11–998–4]

CANTAL, an old cone-shaped volcano in the Massif Central in France. Elevation, 1,858 m. The base has a diameter of 60 to 80 km. Cantal was formed by Neocene eruptions during which andesites and basalts were discharged. The peak is collapsed, and the slopes are broken up into individual plateau-like sections. Vegetation is of the mountain-meadow type.   [11–998–3]

CANTATA, a large work for voices and instruments, usually soloists, chorus, and orchestra. There are solemn, joyful, lyrical, sorrowful, and narrative cantatas in two basic types: secular and church (sacred). A cantata is usually made up of an orchestral introduction, arias, recitatives, and choruses. It is related to the oratorio but is written on a smaller scale, without dramatic plot development, and primarily in chamber style.

The cantata developed in Italy in the first half of the 17th century. Initially the Italian cantata was monodic; later it grew closer to opera. It flourished in the mid-17th century with the work of such composers as G. Carissimi, A. Stradella, and A. Scarlatti. The Italian cantatas were secular; the church cantata took shape in Germany, giving the chorus added importance in relation to the orchestra and soloists. J. S. Bach's church and secular cantatas are among the greatest examples of the genre.

The first Russian cantatas were written in the 18th century. In the second half of the 19th century a number of significant cantatas were written by Russian composers of the classical school, including Tchaikovsky (*Moscow*), Rimsky-Korsakov (*From Homer*), S. I. Taneev, and S. Rachmaninoff. The Soviet cantata is distinguished by the heightened role of the chorus and the use of intonations from folk and popular songs. The most prominent themes are historical-heroic (*Alexander Nevsky* by Prokofiev and the symphony-cantata *In Kulikovo Field* by Iu. A. Shaporin) and patriotic (*Cantata About the Motherland* by A. G. Arutiunian and the symphony-cantata *My Ukraine* by A. Ia. Shtogarenko).

REFERENCES

Khokhlovkina, A. *Sovetskaia oratoriia i kantata.* Moscow, 1955.
Shirinian, R. *Oratoriia i kantata.* Moscow, 1960.
Schmitz, E. *Geschichte der Kantate und des geistlichen Konzerts,* vol. 1: *Geschichte der weltlichen Solokantate,* [3rd ed.]. Hildesheim, 1965.
                    B. V. LEVIK   [11–999–2]

CANTH, MINNA (pseudonym of Ulrika Vilhelmina Canth, née Johnsson). Born Mar. 19, 1844, in Tampere; died May 12, 1897, in Kuopio. Finnish writer. Daughter of a merchant.

Canth's first works, which describe life in the Finnish countryside, include *Short Stories* (1878) and the plays *Burglary* (1882) and *In Roinilan's House* (1883). In her play *The Laborer's Wife* (1885; translated into Russian as *Khomsantu,* 1960) and short stories (such as "Poor Folk," 1886), the disfranchisement and misery of Finnish workers and their growing discontent with exploitation were portrayed realistically. In the drama *Children of a Cruel Lot* (1888), a hero who is a rebel was presented for the first time in Finnish literature. In short stories (such as "Hanna," 1886) and the play *Sylvi* (1893; Russian translation, 1960), Canth exposed bourgeois morality and rearing and defended equal rights for women. In the 1890's the urgency of social problems in Canth's works gave way to a moralizing, conciliatory tendency (*The Preacher's Family,* 1891; *Anna Liisa,* 1895).

WORKS

Kootut teokset, vols. 1–4. Helsinki, 1925–28.
Valitut teokset. Helsinki, 1957.

REFERENCES

["Dramaturgiia M. Kant."] In Karkhu, E. G. *Finliandskaia literatura i Rossiia, 1850–1900.* Moscow-Leningrad, 1964.
Frenckell-Theslleff, G. *Minna Canth.* Helsinki, 1944.
Tarkiainen, V., and E. Kauppinen. *Suomalaisen kirjallisuuden historia.* Helsinki, 1961.
Kannila, H. *Minna Canthin kirjallinen tuotanto: Henkilöbibliografia.* [Helsinki, 1967.]   I. Iu. MARTSINA [11–996–1]

CANTHARIDIN, the active principle of Spanish flies and other bugs of the family Meloidae (blister beetles); a terpenoid anhydride of cantharidic acid. Cantharidin is poorly soluble in water and readily soluble in fats and organic solvents. It severely blisters the skin and mucous membranes. It causes pain, a burning sensation, and formation of blisters. Ingestion causes poisoning, accompanied by catarrh of the urinary tract, salivation, vomiting, diarrhea, abdominal pain, and excitation of the central nervous system.   [11–998–6]

CANTHAROPHILY, the cross-pollination of flowers by beetles that feed on the pollen or on some of the juicy tissues of the flower. Special suitability for cantharophily is generally not observed among flowers and beetles. Full, or true, cantharophily is inherent in only a few plants (for example, cycads and calycanths).   [11–999–1]

CAN THO, a city in southern Vietnam, in the Mekong Delta on the Bassac River; administrative center of Can Tho Autonomous Municipality (Nam Phan Region). Population, 110,000 (1969). Can Tho is the center of a rice-growing area. Rice is processed and coconut oil is manufactured in the city; a soap-making factory and tobacco enterprises are also there. Can Tho has an experimental agricultural station. It is a river port.
                    [11–1008–2]

CANTILENA. (1) A melody, either vocal or instrumental, of a lyrical character.

(2) The lyrical quality of music or its execution; a vocalist's ability to lyrically execute a melody.

(3) In the 13th–15th centuries in Western Europe the term for small, secular homophonic and polyphonic vocal works of a lyrical and epic cast and for dance songs.

(4) From the end of the 17th century, a song or musical piece with a lyrical melody.   [11–1001–2]

CANTILLON, RICHARD. Born 1680; died 1734. Banker, economist, and demographer. One of the first to study the capitalist mode of production.

An Irishman by origin, Cantillon was a businessman in Great Britain and France. His book *Essay on the Nature of Commerce* was published posthumously in French in 1755. Cantillon was the first to try to depict the circulation of industrial capital in the form of a diagram (this was done later by F. Quesnay in a more developed and logically consistent form). Many propositions developed by Cantillon (such as the differentiation between profit and entrepreneurial income, the analysis of the effect of currency devaluation on commerce, and the relationship between the amount of money in circulation and the mass of goods) were subsequently accepted in bourgeois political economy.

REFERENCE

Eidel'nant, A. B. "Kantil'on i ego mesto v teorii vosproizvodstva (K istorii *Ekonomicheskoi tablitsy* Kene)." *Vestnik Komakakademii,* 1927, book 23, pp. 120–48.   [11–1001–3]

CANTON, a city in the northeastern United States, in the state of Ohio. Population, 110,000 (1970; with suburban population, 372,000). Railroad junction. In 1969 approximately 50 percent of the economically active population was engaged in industry. Canton is one of the leading centers for the production of electric steel and roller bearings in the United States. Other manufactures include industrial equipment, engines, electrical appliances, rubber and plastic products, and building materials. Coal is mined near Canton.   [11–1004–3]

CANTON. (1) In Switzerland, the name for federal territorial units. Each canton has its own constitution and legislative and executive organs. Each canton is represented by two deputies in the upper chamber of the federal parliament.

(2) The name for administrative territorial units in Belgium and France. Cantons in France are also electoral districts for the general-council elections of a department.   [11–1004–1]

CANTON ADMINISTRATION IN BASHKIRIA, a system of administration established by the tsar's ukase of Apr. 10, 1798. Canton administration converted the indigenous population (Bashkirs, Teptiars, and Mishars) into a military cossack class that provided recruits for an irregular army (for example, the Bashkir-Meshcheriak Host) that was divided into cantons (or districts).

In introducing canton administration, tsarism placed on the local population the entire burden of military patrol service on the eastern borders, used this population in wars in the west (such as the Patriotic War of 1812 and the Crimean War of 1853–56), and fragmented the multinational population by attracting the Bashkir feudal lords to its side and granting them great benefits for their service. The introduction of this system of administration did away with the remnants of Bashkir self-government; as a result the way of life and economic activity of the indigenous population came to be regulated by military commanders; military tribunals were established. The Muslim clergy became completely subordinate to the military authorities. Canton administration remained in effect with minor changes until 1865.

REFERENCE

Ocherki po istorii Bashkirskoi ASSR, vol. 1, part 2. Ufa, 1959. Pages 33–64.   A. N. USMANOV [11–1005–3]

CANTONISTS. (1) In Prussia from 1733 to 1813, military recruits subject to conscription from one district (*Kanton*), each of which recruited its own regiment.

(2) In Russia from 1805, the term "cantonist" was applied to soldiers' sons who were registered at the military department from the day of their birth. To train soldiers' children for military service, garrison schools were opened as early as 1721; in 1798 they were renamed military orphans divisions, and in 1805 their wards began to be called cantonists. In 1824 the cantonists were placed under the authority of the department of military settlements. The category of cantonists was abolished in 1856.
                    [11–1005–2]

CANTOR, GEORG. Born Mar. 3, 1845, in St. Petersburg; died Jan. 6, 1918, in Halle. German mathematician.

Cantor graduated from the University of Berlin in 1867. He developed the theory of infinite sets and the theory of transfinite numbers. In 1874 he proved the uncountability of the set of all real numbers, thus establishing the existence of inequivalent (that is, having different powers) infinite sets; he formulated

(1878) the general concept of the power of a set. Between 1879 and 1884, Cantor systematically set forth the principles of his study of infinity. He introduced the concepts of limit point and derived set, constructed an example of a perfect set, developed one of the theories of irrational numbers, and formulated one of the axioms of continuity. In 1897 he retired from scientific work. Cantor's ideas encountered intense opposition from his contemporaries, in particular from L. Kronecker, but they subsequently exerted great influence on the development of mathematics.

WORKS

Gesammelte Abhandlungen mathematischen und philosophischen Inhalts. Berlin, 1932.
In Russian translation:
"Uchenie o mnozhestvakh." In the collection *Novye idei v matematike,* no. 6. St. Petersburg, 1914. [11–1006–3]

CANTOR, MORITZ. Born Aug. 23, 1829, in Mannheim; died Apr. 10, 1920, in Heidelberg. German historian of mathematics.

Cantor worked at the University of Heidelberg from 1853 to 1913. His work (*Lectures on the History of Mathematics,* vols. 1–4, 1880–1908) contains reference material on the history of mathematics and covers the period from the most ancient times to 1799 (the fourth volume was written by a group of authors under Cantor's editorship).

WORKS

Vorlesungen über Geschichte der Mathematik, 1st–3rd eds., vols. 1–4. Leipzig, 1893–1924. [11–1006–4]

CANTOR, in the Catholic Church, a singer; in Protestant churches, a singing teacher, choir conductor, and organist, whose duties also often included the composition of music for the church (for example, J. S. Bach at St. Thomas in Leipzig). In a Jewish synagogue, the main singer, or hazan. [11–1006–5]

CANTOR'S AXIOM, one of the axioms characterizing the continuity of a line. It states that a nested sequence of closed intervals whose lengths tend to zero has a single common point. It was formulated by G. Cantor in 1872. [11–1006–6]

CANTOR TERNARY SET, a perfect set of points on a line that does not contain a single interval; it was constructed by G. Cantor in 1883. It is obtained by first removing the middle third (1/3, 2/3) from the closed interval [0, 1], then removing the middle thirds (1/9, 2/9) and (7/9, 8/9) of the remaining closed intervals [0, 1/3] and [2/3, 1], and so on. The Cantor ternary set has the power of the continuum. The set may be defined arithmetically as the totality of ternary fractions $0.a_1a_2 \ldots a_n \ldots$, where each of the digits $a_1, a_2, \ldots, a_n, \ldots$ is 0 or 2. The Cantor ternary set plays an important role in various problems of mathematics (in topology and in the theory of functions of a real variable). [11–1007–1]

CANTUS FIRMUS, a melody borrowed from any secular or religious work or specially created and used as the basis for a polyphonic musical composition. The method of cantus firmus developed in Western European music in the 12th century, became particularly widespread in the 16th, and began losing its importance in the 17th. [11–1008–1]

CANUDOS PEASANT REBELLION (1896–97), an uprising that centered on Canudos in the state of Bahia in Brazil.

After Negro slavery was abolished in Brazil in 1888, large groups of former slaves and fugitive landless peasants came to settle around Canudos. The area became the center of a unique peasant community, where land, forests, pastures, and water were considered communal property. In 1896, Canudos had a population of 25,000–30,000. The main principles of the community were joint labor, common ownership of land, and equality of all its members. Private property was declared illegal and criminal. The government sent troops against Canudos, but the peasants built fortifications and repulsed and routed several punitive expeditions. However, the peasants were powerless against the artillery, which destroyed their primitive fortifications. Government represssions were cruel and almost all the rebels were killed. The government did not permit any mention of Canudos in the press for five years. The Canudos peasant rebellion is a heroic page in the history of the Brazilian peasants' struggle for land and freedom.

REFERENCE

Fako, R. "Krest'ianskaia voina v Kanudose." *Novaia i noveishaia istoriia,* 1959, no. 1. [11–1008–3]

CANULEIUS, GAIUS. Flourished in the fifth century B.C. Tribune in 445 B.C. in ancient Rome.

Gaius Canuleius passed a law in the Senate that abolished the ancient prohibition of marriages between patricians and plebeians. His second bill, which provided for the election of consuls from both patricians and plebeians, was not adopted. [11–1008–4]

CAN VUONG ("in defense of the emperor"), a liberation movement in northern and central Vietnam from 1885 to 1896. It was a response to the treaty of 1884 between France and Vietnam establishing a French protectorate. Participants in the movement fought for national independence, supporting the monarchy and the traditional feudal order.

The *can vuong* movement was led by representatives of the class of feudal lords and of the feudal intelligentsia (*van than*). The movement began with a rebellion in Hué (Quang Tri Province) led by Ton That Thuet and supported by numerous popular actions. The major centers of rebellion formed in the provinces of Huu Nguyen, Thanh Hoa, and Nghe An. All the demonstrations were suppressed by French punitive forces. However, the struggle of the Vietnamese people continued and became a broad anti-French peasant movement, under the leadership of De Tham, which lasted until 1913.

REFERENCES

Shiltova, A. P., and V. F. Mordvinov. *Natsional'no-osvoboditel'noe dvizhenie vo V'etname (1858–1945).* Moscow, 1958. Pages 90–92.
Mkhitarian, S. A. *Rabochii klass i natsional'no-osvoboditel'noe dvizhenie vo V'etname (1885–1930).* Moscow, 1967. Pages 61–64.

S. A. MKHITARIAN [11–952–2]

CANYON, a deep river valley with very steep, often perpendicular, walls and a narrow floor, usually completely occupied by the riverbed. One of the largest canyons in the world is the Grand Canyon of the Colorado River in the USA (length, over 320 km; depth, to 1,800 m). [11–1013–1]

CANZONE, a lyric poem of the medieval Provençal troubadours about knightly love; originally developed in Italy in the 13th to 17th centuries. The canonical canzoni had strophic construction (five or six strophes); the last strophe was short and addressed the person to whom the canzone was dedicated. The classical models of canzoni were created by Dante and Petrarch.

The canzone was always closely associated with music; polyphonic vocal canzoni were related to the frottola and villanelle. In the 16th and 17th centuries in Italy, instrumental canzoni appeared, originally as adaptations of the French *chanson* and later as original compositions in the *chanson* style. Composers of canzoni included A. Gabrieli, C. Merulo, and G. Frescobaldi in Italy and D. Buxtehude and J. S. Bach in Germany.

The 17th-century development of canzoni for instrumental ensembles led to the formation of the *concerto grosso;* canzoni for keyboard instruments evolved into the fugue; and canzoni for solo instrument with accompaniment became the sonata. In the 18th and 19th centuries "canzone" was sometimes used for vocal and instrumental lyrical musical pieces ("The Heart Is Stirred by Ardent Blood," from Mozart's *The Marriage of Figaro,* or the slow movement of Tchaikovsky's Symphony No. 4). Canzoni appear as stylized pieces in the work of such 20th-century poets as V. Ia. Briusov and M. A. Kuzmin. [11–1011–2]

CANZONET, in the 16th and 17th centuries, a short polyphonic song; in the 18th century, also a solo strophic song, often with dance elements. The *canzonet* genre began in Italy. Nineteenth-century composers sometimes called instrumental pieces "canzonets" (for example, the middle movement of Tchaikovsky's Concerto for Violin). [11–1012–1]

CAO BANG, a city in the northern part of the Democratic Republic of Vietnam. Administrative center of Cao Bang Province (Bac Bo District, Viet Bac Autonomous Region). Near Cao Bang, in Tinhtuc, are tin deposits and mines and an ore-dressing combine. The city is the trade center for an agricultural region (livestock raising and vegetable growing). [11–1014–3]

CAPABLANCA, JOSÉ RAÚL (full name, José Raúl Capablanca y Graupera). Born Nov. 19, 1888, in Havana; died Mar. 8, 1942, in New York. Cuban chess player, world champion from 1921 to 1927.

Capablanca's greatest successes were the victory over world champion E. Lasker and the first prize at international tournaments in San Sebastian (1911), London (1922), New York (1927), Moscow (1936), and Nottingham (1936), the last a tie with M. M. Botvinnik. Cuba has conducted international tournaments in Capablanca's memory since 1962.

WORKS
In Russian translation:
Moia shakhmatnaia kar'era. Moscow, 1926.
Osnovy shakhmatnoi igry. Moscow-Leningrad, 1930.
Uchebnik shakhmatnoi igry. Leningrad-Moscow, 1936.
REFERENCE
Panov, V. N. *Kapablanka (Biografiia i 64 izbrannye partii).* Moscow, 1960. [11–1016–4]

CAPADOCIA, GUILLERMO. Born circa 1909; died Sept. 29, 1951. Figure in the working-class movement of the Philippines.

A cook by profession, Capadocia in the late 1920's became one of the leaders of the Union of Proletarians, a revolutionary trade union organization; in 1930 he was among the founders of the Communist Party of the Philippines. Capadocia spent the years 1931–37 in prison and exile. From 1937 to 1941 he was general secretary of the Communist Party, and from 1938 to 1941 he was executive secretary of the largest trade union confederation in the country, the Collective Labor Movement. From 1945 to 1950 he was vice-president of the Philippine Congress of Labor Organizations. In 1950 he fled Manila under threat of arrest and became a commander of the National Liberation Army units in the Visayan archipelago. Capadocia was killed in battle on Panay Island.

REFERENCE
Levinson, G. I. *Filippiny na puti k nezavisimosti.* Moscow, 1972. [11–1016–5]

CAPE ASTRONOMICAL OBSERVATORY (Royal Observatory at the Cape of Good Hope), a scientific establishment of Great Britain, located 5 km from Cape Town (Republic of South Africa). It was founded in 1820 and modeled on the Greenwich Observatory, with which it has been formally united since 1960.

Between 1879 and 1907, the observatory was expanded and reequipped. Its instruments include a triple equatorial telescope with a 61-cm photographic and 46-cm and 20-cm visual objectives, a 33-cm astrograph with a 25-cm guider, a 15-cm visual refractor, 102-cm and 46-cm reflectors, a 10-cm heliograph, a 13-cm chromospheric flare patrol, a transit circle, an impersonal prismatic astrolabe, and a cinetheodolite. The observatory is primarily involved in the determination of the precise coordinates, parallaxes, proper motions, and radial velocities of stars; stellar photometry and colorimetry; time service; and solar service. It publishes *Annales* (since 1886). [11–1080–4]

CAPE BASIN, a drop in the ocean bottom in the southeast Atlantic, situated between the continental slope of Africa and the Mid-Atlantic and Walvis ridges.

The Cape Basin extends from north to south for about 1,500 km and from west to east for 1,000 km. Its maximum depth is 5,000 m. The surface of the bottom is hilly, with underwater volcanoes that reach 3,000 m in height. The sediments are red ooze. [11–1081–1]

CAPE COLONY (Dutch Kaapkolonie, from Kaap de Goede Hoop), a Dutch and later an English possession in Southern Africa.

Cape Colony was founded in 1652 on the Cape of Good Hope by the Dutch East India Company. In 1795 it was seized by Great Britain; from 1803 to 1806 it again came under the control of the Dutch, but in 1806 it was again captured by Great Britain. The Cape Colony territory continued to expand at the expense of the Africans' lands (Bushmen, Hottentots, and Bantu). By 1894, after a number of aggressive wars waged by Boer and English colonizers (Kaffrarian wars), the Cape Colony's eastern border had reached the Umtamvuna River. In 1895 the southern part of Bechuanaland, annexed in 1884–85, was included in the colony. Cape Colony was made a part of the Union of South Africa after the creation of the latter in 1910 (Republic of South Africa after 1961).

REFERENCE
Walker, E. A. *A History of Southern Africa,* 3rd ed. London, 1959. [11–1080–5]

CAPE FOLDED ZONE, a belt of middle Upper Paleozoic and Lower Triassic folded deposits in the extreme south of Africa (Republic of South Africa).

The course of the Cape Folded Zone is westward in the east and northwest in the west. An older Upper Proterozoic metamorphic foundation is exposed at the core of some of the uplifts. The folding is Middle Triassic. Some researchers suggest that the Cape Folded Zone constitutes the eastern continuation of the displacement of the sierras in Argentina. [11–1083–1]

CAPE MOUNTAINS, mountains in southern Africa, located in the Republic of South Africa between Port Elizabeth on the east and the mouth of the Olifants River on the west.

The Cape Mountains are approximately 800 km long and consist of several parallel ranges. The average elevation is 1,500 m, with a maximum elevation of 2,326 m. The Cape Mountains are composed of sandstones and quartzites. They run east to west for 600 km, from Port Elizabeth to Worcester, and they frame a longitudinal valley (the Little Karroo) from the north (the Swartberge) and south (the Langeberge and Outeniquaberge). From Worcester they turn west-northwest (the Olifantsrivierberge and the Sederberge).

The climate in the west is Mediterranean, with winter precipitation (more than 600 mm on the windward slopes). Precipitation is more uniform to the east (more than 800 mm a year). There is snow on the peaks in winter. The leeward slopes and the inner valleys are semidesert. Mainly secondary thickets of evergreen shrubs grow on the windward slopes to the west; mixed coniferous and deciduous forests grow on brown and mountain-forest-brown soils in the east. [11–1083–2]

CAPE OF GOOD HOPE PROVINCE (Dutch, Kaapland), a province in the Republic of South Africa. Area, 721,000 sq km; population, 7,111,000 (1970), including 4,235,000 Black Africans (Bantu), 1,752,000 Cape Coloureds (mulattoes), 1,102,000 Europeans, and 21,600 Asians. The Bantu and Coloureds are subjected to racial discrimination. The administrative center of the province is the city of Cape Town.

The coastal lowland and the Cape Mountains (elevation, to 2,000 m) in the south are separated from the inland Great Karroo high plateau by the Great Escarpment (altitude to 2,500 m) and the Great Karroo basin. The climate of the inner regions is tropical, arid to the east and semidesert to the west. The climate of the maritime coastal plains is subtropical, Mediterranean to the southwest and monsoonal to the southeast. The largest rivers are the Orange, the Sundays, and the Great Fish. The vegetation is evergreen shrub to the southwest and savanna, shrubby semidesert, and desert on the plateau.

There are 1,635,000 people (including 865,000 Bantu; 1960) active in the economy of the Cape Province: 43 percent in agriculture, 15 percent in industry, 6 percent in construction, 10 percent in commerce, 4 percent in transportation, and 22 percent in the services. Most of the agricultural lands belong to large capitalist farms and plantations. Extensive livestock raising, particularly the raising of sheep for wool, has been greatly developed; in 1961 there were 24.5 million sheep in the Cape Province, accounting for 60 percent of the country's wool clip. Wheat is among the predominant cultivated crops. Viticulture and horticulture are also developed. More than 90 percent of the manganese ore mined in the republic (the principal deposit is in Postmasburg) and more than 40 percent of the diamonds (Kimberly and Namaqualand) are concentrated in the Cape Province; deposits of copper and iron ores, barites, and asbestos are also being worked. Manufacturing has been developing in the province since World War II. The large enterprises include machine building (automobile assembly and coach building, electro-technical, ship repair) and the chemical and cement industries. Light industry (textiles, garments, and leather footwear), glassmaking, woodworking, and the food industry (flour milling, tobacco, dairy, wine-making) have also been developed. Railroads cover 8,700 km, of which 1,300 km have been electrified (1964). The most important ports are Cape Town (second in the country in freight turnover), East London, and Port Elizabeth. The republic's main naval base is in Simonstown.

V. F. KHUDOLEI [11–1082–1]

CAPE REGION, a floral region in extreme southwestern Africa, mainly in the coastal area. Width, approximately 100 km. In terms of physical geographical conditions and the general nature of the vegetation, the Cape Region differs sharply from adjacent territories. The Cape Region is similar to the Mediterranean region in its moderate temperatures, wet winters (700 mm a year, with a winter maximum of 70 percent), and comparatively hot summers. Therefore, the vegetation of these two regions is also similar: thickets of sclerophyllous evergreen shrubs and undersized trees resembling maquis. More than 6,000 species of higher plants grow in the Cape Region, of which more than half are endemic (from the families Amaryllidaceae, Iridaceae, Proteaceae, Bruniaceae, Grubbiaceae, and Penaeaceae). Most typical of the Cape Region are the families Compositae, Ericaceae, Leguminosae, Iridaceae, and Proteaceae. The flora in this area has genetic ties with tropical Africa (via the flora in the Karroo and Namib regions, which is intermediate in composition); the Mediterranean area; and a number of southern hemisphere regions, particularly the Australian region. This indicates the probability of ancient land links between these areas. Many cultivated plants of European and other origins are grown in the Cape Region. The indigenous flora of the region is the richest source of ornamental plants, many of which have become well known in Soviet floriculture (for example, the amaryllis and Kaffir lily).

REFERENCES
Il'inskii, A. P. *Rastitel'nost' zemnogo shara.* Moscow-Leningrad, 1938.
Vul'f, E. V. *Istoricheskaia geografiia rastenii: Istoriia flor zemnogo shara.* Moscow-Leningrad, 1944.
Alekhin, V. V., L. V. Kudriashov, and V. S. Govorukhin. *Geografiia rastenii s osnovami botaniki,* 2nd ed. Moscow, 1961.
Hutchinson, J. *A Botanist in Southern Africa.* London, 1946.

V. S. GOVORUKHIN and A. I. TOLMACHEV [11–1081–2]

CAPETIANS, a dynasty of French kings (from 987 to 1328). The founder of the dynasty was Hugh Capet, who was elected king after the death of the last king of the Carolingian dynasty. Under the Capetians, the monarchy became hereditary rather than elective (this was at first a de facto development but became de jure after the 12th century). The Capetians succeeded in expanding the territory of the royal domain and were able to consolidate three-fourths of the territory of modern France by the beginning of the 14th century. Capetian policies promoted the establishment of a centralized state. After the death of Charles IV, who left no sons, the French crown passed to the Valois dynasty (a branch of the Capetians).

The Capetian dynasty consisted of Hugh Capet (who ruled from 987 to 996), Robert II (996–1031), Henry I (1031–60), Philip I (1060–1108), Louis VI the Fat (1108–37), Louis VII (1137–80), Philip II Augustus (1180–1223), Louis VIII (1223–26), Louix IX (Saint Louis; 1226–70), Philip III the Bold (1270–85), Philip IV the Fair (1285–1314), Louis X (1314–16), Philip

V (second son of Philip IV; 1316–22), and Charles IV (third son of Philip IV; 1322–28).

REFERENCES
Petit-Dutaillis, C. *Feodal'naia monarkhiia vo Frantsii i v Anglii X—XIII vv.* Moscow, 1938. (Translated from French.)
Fawtier, R. *Les Capétiens et la France.* Paris, 1942.
Calmette, J., *Le Réveil capétien.* [Paris, 1948.]
Bailly, A. *Les Grands Capétiens.* Paris [1952]. [11–1020–2]

CAP-HAÏTIEN, a city and port in the north of Haiti. Population, 37,000 (1967).
Cap-Haïtien is the commercial center of an agricultural region. Coffee, sugar, and fruit are exported. [11–1017–1]

CAPILLARIASES, helminthic diseases of animals caused by nematodes of the genus *Capillaria.* Various species of these helminths are intestinal parasites of chickens, turkeys, guinea hens, mink, sable, foxes, and cattle.
Capillaria are thin, filamentous parasites 5 to 50 mm long. They develop outside the host, most species requiring intermediate hosts (earthworms). The nematodes cause inflammation (generally chronic) of the intestine or urinary bladder (depending on the site of infestation) in the host. Phenothiazine is used in treatment. To prevent capillariases in poultry, chicken coops should be cleaned regularly and the litter subjected to biothermal disinfection. Fur-bearing animals should be kept on a screened floor that is raised above the ground.

REFERENCE
Skriabin, K. I., and A. M. Petrov. *Osnovy veterinarnoi nematologii.* Moscow, 1964. [11–1021–4]

CAPILLARIES, the minute blood vessels that run through all human and animal tissues and form a network between the arterioles transporting blood to the tissues and the venules carrying blood from the tissues. Gases and other substances are exchanged between the blood and adjacent tissues through the capillary walls.
The capillaries were first described by the Italian naturalist M. Malpighi (1661) as the missing link (whose existence had been predicted by W. Harvey) between the venules and the arterioles. Capillaries usually vary in diameter from 2.5 to 30 μm. Wide capillaries are also called sinusoids.
A capillary wall consists of three layers: an inner, or endothelial, layer; a middle layer, or basement membrane; and an outer layer, or tunica adventitia. The endothelial layer consists of flat polygonal cells that change according to their condition. The endothelial cells are characterized by the presence in the cytoplasm of a large number of micropinocytotic vesicles, 300–1,500 Å in diameter, which move between the edge of the cell facing the lumen and the edge facing the tissues. They transport portions of the substances needed to bring about an exchange between blood and tissues. Between the endothelial cells are slit-like spaces, 100–150 Å across, and two types of intercellular compounds, with and without areas of obliteration. The basement membrane, 200–1,500 Å wide, is made up both of a cellular component and of a noncellular component that consists of intertwined fibrils embedded in a homogeneous substance rich in mucopolysaccharides. The cellular component (pericytes, or Rouget cells) is completely enveloped by the noncellular component. The adventitial tunic consists of fibroblasts, histiocytes, and other cellular and fibrous structures, and the interstitial substance of connective tissue. The layer passes into the connective tissue that surrounds the capillaries and forms the pericapillary zone.
The ultrastructure of the wall of an arterial capillary differs from that of a venous capillary in the size of the lumen (the arterial and venous lumens are generally about 8 μm and 7–12 μm, respectively) and in the orientation of the nuclei of the endothelial cells (in an arterial capillary the long axis of the nucleus runs along the course of the capillary; in a venous capillary, it runs perpendicularly). The endothelial layer is smooth and thick in an arterial capillary but attenuated, with numerous cytoplasmic processes, in a venous capillary. In an arterial capillary the swelling of the nuclei and cytoplasm of the endothelial

cells usually results in closure of the lumen, but in the cells of a venous capillary the same process only constricts the lumen. The permeability of the capillary wall is due mainly to the permeability of the endothelium. The noncellular component of the basement membrane also plays a part in the permeability of the capillary wall.

Some investigators believe that the pericyte is a contractile cell capable, like a muscular cell, of actively changing the size of the capillary lumen. Others maintain that the pericyte is a special cell involved in the motor innervation of the capillary: in response to a nerve impulse transmitted from the central nervous system through the pericyte to the endothelial cells, the latter instantly accumulate fluid (swell) or release it (shrink), causing the size of the capillary lumen to change. The ultrastructure of the capillary wall varies from organ to organ. For example, in muscular organs the capillaries have a wide endothelial layer and a narrow basement layer. In kidney capillaries the basement layer is wide but the endothelial cells are attenuated and in places have membrane-covered openings, or fenestrae. Both the endothelial layer and the basement layer are thin in the lungs. The capillaries of bone marrow have no basement layer at all, and the capillaries of the liver and spleen have pores. Capillaries are classified according to the ultrastructure of the endothelial and basement layers in the various organs.

One of the principal biological properties of the capillary wall is its reactivity: the capacity for prompt and adequate change in the activity of all components of the wall in response to environmental influences. Changes in the reactivity of the capillary wall may underlie the pathogenesis of several diseases.

Lymph capillaries, unlike capillaries of the blood circulatory system, have only an endothelial layer, which lies against the surrounding connective tissue and is attached to it by collagen fibrils with special filaments. Lymph capillaries run through almost all human and animal organs and tissues except the brain, splenic parenchyma, lymph nodes, cartilage, sclera, crystalline lens, and certain other tissues. The shape and outlines of the lymphatic network vary with the structure and function of the organ and with the properties of the connective tissue in which the capillaries are found. The lymph capillaries perform the function of drainage, helping colloidal solutions of protein substances not reaching the blood-bearing capillaries to flow out of the tissues and removing foreign particles and bacteria from the body. The wall of a lymph capillary is permeable to small and large molecules passing both through the endothelial cells, aided by the micropinocytotic vesicles, and through the intercellular spaces, which are wider than in the blood-bearing capillaries and are not closed by areas of obliteration. Lymph from the intercellular spaces collects in the lymph capillaries, which merge to form lymphatic vessels.

REFERENCES

Zhdanov, D. A. *Obshchaia anatomiia i fiziologiia limfaticheskoi sistemy.* Moscow, 1952.
Shakhlamov, V. A. *Kapilliary.* Moscow, 1971.
Krogh, A. *Anatomiia i fiziologiia kapilliarov.* Moscow, 1927. (Translated from German.) V. A. SHAKHLAMOV [11–1025–2]

CAPILLAROSCOPY, an intravitam method of study involving the examination, under magnification, of capillaries of the epithelial or endothelial integuments of animals and man (skin, mucous membranes).

In man, the capillaries are examined in the skin fold of the nail bed, where they can be viewed most conveniently. A microscope or a special instrument, the capillaroscope, is used for this purpose. The use of the microscope (20–100 power magnification) after the application of a drop of clarifying oil to the skin and good oblique illumination provide good visibility. Changes are observed in the capillaries with disturbances of the peripheral blood circulation of a variety of etiologies (in vascular neuroses, the early stages of cardiac insufficiency, endarteritis obliterans). The changes observed during capillaroscopy are not strictly specific to a given pathological condition; they arise as an adaptive mechanism to any disturbance of the general blood flow. Therefore, capillaroscopy is used only as a supplementary diagnostic method in general clinical examinations. [11–1025–1]

CAPILLARY CIRCULATION, the movement of blood through the smallest blood vessels, or capillaries, providing for the exchange of substances between the blood and tissues.

Capillary circulation is made possible by the difference between the hydrostatic pressures of the venous and arterial ends of capillaries. The pressure in the arterial end is 30–35 mm Hg, or 8–10 mm higher than the osmotic pressure of blood plasma. As a result of this difference in pressures, water and many of the substances dissolved in it (except macromolecular proteins) pass from the blood plasma into the interstitial fluid, transporting vitally needed substances to the tissues. As the blood flows through a capillary, hydrostatic pressure drops in the venous end to 12–17 mm Hg, or approximately 10 mm below the osmotic pressure of the blood. As a result, water and the substances dissolved in it pass from the interstitial fluid into the plasma, helping thereby to remove metabolic products from the tissues. The rate of capillary circulation corresponds to the rate of metabolism. For example, in a body at rest, there are 30–50 functioning capillaries per sq mm of cross section of skeletal muscle; during intensive muscular activity the number may increase 50–100 times. I. N. D'IAKONOVA [11–1022–3]

CAPILLARY CONDENSATION, the condensation of vapor in the capillaries and microcracks of porous bodies or in the interstices between closely packed particles.

A necessary condition for capillary condensation is the wetting of the surface of the material (particles) by the liquid. Capillary condensation starts with the adsorption of vapor molecules by the condensation surface and the formation of liquid menisci. The pressure of the saturated vapor over concave menisci is, according to Kelvin's equation, lower than the saturated vapor pressure p_0 over a flat surface. Capillary condensation proceeds, therefore, at lower vapor pressures than the saturation pressure p_0. The volume of liquid condensed in pores attains its limiting value at external vapor pressure $p = p_0$, where the liquid-gas interface has zero curvature (plane, catenoid).

The complex capillary structure of a porous body may be the cause of capillary hysteresis, that is, the dependence of the quantity of liquid condensed in the pores not only on vapor pressure but also on the prehistory of the process, that is, how the given state was attained—by the condensation or by the evaporation of the liquid.

Capillary condensation increases the absorption (sorption) of vapors by porous bodies, particularly near the point of vapor saturation. The phenomenon of capillary condensation is used industrially in trapping liquids by finely porous materials (sorbents). Capillary condensation also has an important role in the processes of drying and moisture retention in soils, construction materials, and other porous materials.

REFERENCE

Kurs fizicheskoi khimii, 2nd ed., vol. 1. Edited by Ia. I. Gerasimov. Moscow, 1969. N. V. CHURAEV [11–1021–6]

CAPILLARY PHENOMENA, physical phenomena caused by the surface tension at the interface of immiscible media. Capillary phenomena usually include those phenomena in liquid media caused by the curvature of their surface at their boundary with another liquid or gas or with their own vapors.

Surface curvature leads to the appearance of the additional capillary pressure Δp in the liquid, the magnitude of Δp being related to the average curvature r of the surface by Laplace's equation, or $\Delta p = p_1 - p_2 = 2\sigma_{12}/r$, where σ_{12} is the surface tension at the boundary between the media and p_1 and p_2 are the pressures in liquid 1 and in medium (phase) 2 in contact with the liquid. In the case of a concave liquid surface ($r < 0$), the pressure in the liquid is lowered with respect to the neighboring phase: $p_1 < p_2$ and $\Delta p < 0$. The sign of Δp changes to the opposite sign for convex ($r > 0$) surfaces.

Capillary pressure is created by forces of surface tension acting in the direction of the tangent to the interface. Curvature of the interface leads to the appearance of a component directed into the volume of one of the contacting phases. For a flat interface ($r = \infty$) this component is nonexistent and $\Delta p = 0$.

Capillary phenomena include various cases of equilibrium and motion of the liquid surface under the action of both intermolecular forces and external forces (mainly gravity).

In the simplest case, when external forces are either absent or compensated, the liquid surface is always curved. Thus, under the conditions of weightlessness, a limited volume of liquid that is not in contact with other bodies assumes the form of a sphere under the influence of surface tension. This form corresponds to the stable equilibrium of the liquid, since the sphere has the minimum surface for the given volume, and the surface energy of the liquid is therefore also minimal.

The liquid assumes the form of a sphere even if it is surrounded by another liquid of equal density (the effect of gravity is compensated by Archimedes' principle, the force of buoyancy). The picture changes substantially when the force of gravity remains uncompensated. A low-viscosity liquid (for example, water) assumes the form of the vessel into which it is poured, provided that a sufficient amount of the liquid is used. The free surface of the liquid turns out to be practically flat, since the forces of gravity overcome the effect of surface tension, which tends to produce curvature and reduce the liquid surface. With decreasing liquid mass, however, the role of surface tension again becomes a determining factor: dispersion of a liquid in a gaseous medium or of a gas in liquid leads to the formation of small drops or bubbles that are practically spherical in shape.

The properties of systems consisting of many small droplets or bubbles (emulsions, liquid aerosols, and foams) and the conditions of their formation are to a large extent determined by the surface curvature of particles, that is, by capillary phenomena. Capillary phenomena are of equal importance in the formation of a new phase—of liquid droplets in steam condensation, of vapor bubbles in boiling liquids, and of solid-phase nuclei in crystallization.

The form of the contact surface between liquids and solids is substantially influenced by wetting phenomena, which are caused by molecular interactions between liquid and solid. Figure 1 shows a profile of the surface of a liquid wetting the wall of a vessel (see Figure 1). Wetting implies that a liquid interacts more strongly with the surface of a solid than does a gas over the liquid. The forces of attraction acting between the molecules of the solid and the liquid cause the latter to climb along the wall of the vessel, which leads to curvature of the surface region adjacent to the wall. This creates negative (capillary) pressure, which at each point of the curved surface precisely balances the pressure generated by the rise of the level of the liquid. The hydrostatic pressure within the volume of liquid remains unchanged in this case.

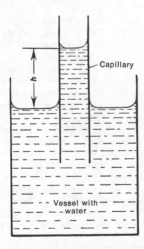

Figure 1. Capillary rise of a wetting liquid (water in a glass vessel and capillary)

If the flat walls of the vessel are moved toward one another in such a way as to lead to superposition of the curved areas, a concave meniscus (a fully curved surface) is formed. The capillary pressure in a liquid is negative under the meniscus and causes the liquid to be sucked up into the slit to the point where

the weight of the column of liquid (of height h) balances the active capillary pressure Δp. At equilibrium,

$$(\rho_1 - \rho_2)gh = \Delta p = 2\sigma_{12}/r$$

where ρ_1 and ρ_2 are the densities of the liquid 1 and gas 2, respectively, and g is gravitational acceleration. This expression, known as Jurin's equation (J. Jurin, 1684–1750), determines the height h of the capillary rise of a liquid that completely wets the walls of a capillary. A liquid that does not wet the surface forms a convex meniscus, which results in its drop in the capillary below the free surface level of the liquid ($h < 0$).

The capillary imbibition of liquids by porous bodies plays an essential role in supplying water to plants and in the propagation of moisture in soils and other porous bodies. Capillary impregnation of various materials is widely used in chemical engineering.

Curvature of the free surface of a liquid under the influence of external forces accounts for the existence of capillary waves (ripples on the surface of a liquid). The field of physicochemical hydrodynamics is concerned with the capillary phenomena observed during the movement of liquid interfaces.

The movement of a liquid in capillaries may be caused by differences in capillary pressure arising from differences in curvature of the liquid surface. The flow of liquid is in the direction of lower pressure. For wetting fluids the flow is in the direction of the meniscus with the shorter radius of curvature (Figure 2, a).

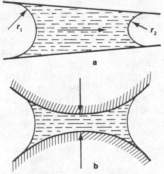

Figure 2. (a) Movement of a liquid in a capillary through the influence of differences in capillary pressures ($r_1 > r_2$), (b) contracting effect of capillary pressure

The vapor pressure (reduced according to Kelvin's equation) over the wetting menisci is the cause of capillary condensation (of liquids) in fine pores.

Negative capillary pressure pulls together the walls that are restraining the liquid (Figure 2, b). This may lead to the considerable volume deformation of highly disperse systems and porous bodies, or capillary contraction. Thus, for example, the rise in capillary pressure that takes place during drying leads to considerable shrinkage in materials.

Many of the properties of disperse systems (permeability, strength, sorption of liquids) are determined to a large extent by capillary phenomena, since high capillary pressures are generated in the fine pores of these materials.

Capillary phenomena were discovered and studied by Leonardo da Vinci (15th century), B. Pascal (17th century), and J. Jurin (18th century) in experiments with capillary tubes. The theory of capillary phenomena was developed in the works of T. Young (1805), P. Laplace (1806), S. Poisson (1831), J. Gibbs (1875), and I. S. Gromeka (1879, 1886).

REFERENCES
Adam, N. K. *Fizika i khimiia poverkhnostei.* Moscow, 1947. (Translated from English.)
Gromeka, I. S. *Sobranie sochinenii.* Moscow, 1952.
N. V. CHURAEV [11–1023–1]

CAPITAL, in architecture, the prominent crowning part of a vertical support (pillar or column). The capital transmits the weight from the architrave and superstructure to the support (or to an architectural element, such as a pilaster, that figuratively expresses this supportive function). Various types of capitals appear in the wood and stone architecture of different peoples. The earliest appearance of capitals was in the architecture of ancient Oriental countries. In ancient Greece and Rome, three types of columns were developed—the Doric, the Ionic, and the Corinthian. A combination of elements of the Ionic and Corinthian types resulted in the Composite capital. The use of these classical types of capitals was widespread in European architecture. In China, Japan, and Mexico distinctive capitals were created. New forms also evolved in Byzantine, Romanesque, Gothic, Armenian, Georgian, Middle Asian, and ancient Russian architecture. Since the Renaissance, there have been numerous variations of classical Greek and Roman capitals; classical forms have been combined with local ornamental motifs.

V. F. MARKUZON [11–1061–2]

CAPITAL, an economic category expressing the exploitation of hired labor by the capitalists; it is the value that returns surplus value. Capital concentrated in the hands of the capitalists is the means of appropriating surplus value. It represents a historical category; that is, it is characteristic of a certain socioeconomic formation.

Capital comes into existence at that stage of commodity-production development when labor power becomes a commodity. In the process of the primitive accumulation of capital the direct producers became separated from the means of production, which became concentrated in the hands of the capitalist entrepreneurs. Deprived of the means of production, the worker was forced to sell his labor power to the capitalists. This process meant a conversion from simple commodity production into capitalist production. In the production process the capitalist combines the commodities that he has acquired on the market: labor power and the means of production. As a result of the productive consumption of labor power and the means of production in the production process after the capitalist completes the sale of the newly produced commodity, he receives a greater value than the one he invested. The general formula for capital was advanced by Karl Marx: $M—C—M'$, in which M is money, C is the commodity, and M' is the amount of money plus the increase. This increase, which is the surplus over the advanced amount, represents the surplus value, which comes from the appropriation by the capitalist of the excess value created by the unpaid labor of the hired workers over and above the price of their labor. The production and appropriation of surplus value in ever-growing proportions constitute the goal of capitalist production. In the era of imperialism, the acquisition of monopoly profit becomes the moving force of capitalist production. As capitalism develops and the domination of capital increases, the degree of the exploitation of workers grows.

Bourgeois political economy ignores capital as a social relation and usually considers it as an aggregate of things (the means of production). Such an interpretation of capital is required to prove that the profit of the capitalists is engendered by capital itself and is supposedly not the result of the exploitation of hired labor. The true scientific analysis of the category of capital was given by Marx: "Capital," he emphasized, "is not a thing, but rather a definite social production relation, belonging to a definite historical formation of society, which is manifested in a thing and lends this thing a specific social character" (K. Marx and F. Engels, *Soch.,* 2nd ed, vol. 25, part 2, pp. 380–81).

Marx revealed the qualitative difference between constant and variable capital, that is, between that part of the initially advanced capital earmarked for the acquisition of the means of production and the part used to buy labor power. Marx showed that the means of production do not create new value by themselves. In the process of production their value is only transferred to a newly created product (commodity) without any surplus. The new value is created by a specific commodity—labor power in the process of its consumption, that is, as a result of the labor of hired workers. Thus, the value of the means of production (constant capital c) remains unchanged in the process of production, but the value of labor power (variable capital v) increases by the amount of the surplus value (s). Constant capital serves only as a precondition for the creation of surplus value, which is in fact created by variable capital. The division of capital into constant and variable components was originated by Marx. It shows that only the hired labor creates the surplus value, which is appropriated without compensation by the capitalist; the

source of capitalist profit and of the income of all exploiter classes is the unpaid labor of hired workers.

A prerequisite for the functioning of capital is its constant movement, capital turnover. According to the character of the turnover, that is, the means by which the value is transferred to the created product, the capital can be fixed or working. Marx scientifically substantiated the division of the capital into fixed and working capital, and at the same time he showed the untenability of the identification of fixed and working capital with constant and variable capital, a generalization put forward by bourgeois economists. Marx revealed the role of productive capital, which functions in the process of production.

In the process of capital turnover a part of the capital remains permanently in the form of commodities and money. Isolating these parts of the capital results in the creation of commercial and loan capital, from which the owners of the capital derive that part of surplus value which takes the form of commercial profits and interest. As capitalists strive to derive ever-greater profits, they are compelled to use part of the surplus value for accumulation, which leads to a growing concentration and centralization of capital and to a higher level of concentration of production and the emergence of capitalist monopolies. In this process, capitalism shifts from free competition to monopolistic capitalism.

The teachings of Marx on capital and surplus value constitute the basis of the teachings of Marxist-Leninist political economy on capitalism. Lenin developed Marxist-Leninist political economy by thoroughly analyzing the movement of capital during the era of imperialism and revealing for the first time the essence of an important category of political economy—finance capital.

In a socialist society the means of production are owned by the people and constitute the fixed assets and stocks of socialist enterprises. Therefore, the means of production, goods, and money cannot be transformed into capital.

REFERENCES
Marx, K. *Das Kapital,* vol. 1. K. Marx and F. Engels, *Soch.,* 2nd ed, vol. 23.
Marx, K. *Teorii pribavochnoi stoimosti* (vol. 4 of *Das Kapital*). *Ibid.,* vol. 26, chs. 1, 3, 4.
Engels, F. "Konspekt pervogo toma *Kapitala* K. Marksa." *Ibid.,* vol. 16.
Lenin, V. I. "Tri istochnika i tri sostavnykh chasti marksizma." *Poln. sobr. soch.,* 5th ed., vol. 23.
Lenin, V. I. "Karl Marks." *Ibid.,* vol. 26.

V. G. SHEMIATENKOV [11–1028–1]

CAPITAL INVESTMENTS, the input of labor, material and technical resources, and monetary means for the reproduction of fixed assets.

In capitalist countries, capital investments are one of the most important forms of capital accumulation. The dynamics and the structure of capital investments in these countries determine the rate of growth and the course of the economic cycle.

In the USSR, capital investments are an integral part of capital construction, as are design and site exploration and the development of corresponding project organizations; construction work and installation of equipment; and the development of the output capacities of construction and installation organizations. According to the methodology adopted in the USSR, capital investments do not include the expenses of geological prospecting unconnected with the construction of specific projects; planning and projects of construction of cities and urban-type settlements or of standard building designs; afforestation and the planting of trees and forest strips; the acquisition and formation of basic livestock herds; or the acquisition of equipment for existing state agencies, schools, hospitals, and establishments for the care of children. Capital investments also do not include major repairs of fixed capital.

The expense of capital investments is charged to the accumulation fund of the national income and partly to the depreciation allowance (more than 40 percent of the total); planning and accounting of capital investments is done using accounting prices (1969 prices). In developing the plans for the national economy, the total volume of capital investment includes all sources of finance: from state and cooperative enterprises and organizations, kolkhozes, the population (construction of privately owned houses and apartments), the state budget, and credit institutions. Important sources of financing capital investments are the fund for production development and the fund for social and cultural development and housing construction. The major result of capital investment is that fixed assets are completed at the proper time. A characteristic trait, as well as an important advantage, of the socialist economy is that the completions of fixed assets and the capital investments are constantly growing (see Table 1).

Table 1. Fixed assets put into operation and capital investments
(in comparable prices; billions of rubles)

	Fixed assets completed	Capital investments
1918–28 (excluding fourth quarter of 1928)	3.9	4.4
First five-year plan (1929–32, including fourth quarter of 1928)	9.4	8.8
Second five-year plan (1933–37)	17.4	19.9
Third five-year plan (1938–first half of 1941; interrupted by war)	18.6	20.6
July 1, 1941–Jan. 1, 1946	19.1	20.8
Fourth five-year plan (1946–50)	42.8	48.1
Fifth five-year plan (1951–55)	81.1	91.1
Sixth five year plan (1956–60)	158.0	170.5
Seventh five-year plan (1961–65)	231.9	247.6
Eighth five-year plan (1966–70)	324.4	353.8
1971	82.6	88.0
1972	93.1 (plan)	94.3
Total for 1918–72	1,082.3	1,167.9

Completions of fixed assets increased 34 times from the introduction of the first five-year plan to 1966–70. The yearly average growth rate of capital investments in the USSR amounted to 9.7 percent in the period 1951–70 (compared to the US rate of 2.6 percent; in 1950 the capital investments in the USSR were 30 percent of the capital investments of the USA, whereas by 1970 they were approximately at the same level). The implementation of construction programs ensured a rapid rate of growth for the Soviet economy and the qualitative improvement in the proportions between the sectors, the growth of the economic potential of the country, the raising of the technological level of all sectors, an improvement in the distribution of productive forces, and the rise in the material well-being of the people.

A systematic growth of capital investments is characteristic for other socialist countries as well. The yearly average growth rates of capital investments for the period from 1961 to 1965 amounted to 7.9 percent in Bulgaria, 4.7 percent in Hungary, 5 percent in the German Democratic Republic, 7 percent in Poland, 11.2 percent in Rumania, and 2 percent in Czechoslovakia. From 1966 to 1970 the growth was 12.5 percent in Bulgaria, 10.5 percent in Hungary, 9.9 percent in the German Democratic Republic, 8.5 percent in Poland, 11.2 percent in Rumania, and 7.3 percent in Czechoslovakia.

Of great significance for the national economy has been the shortening of the period needed for the creation of new productive capacity, which raises the efficiency of capital investments. In their physical and material form, capital investments consist of the output of the machine-building industry (equipment, tools), of the construction industry (including buildings and other construction, as well as assembly and placing of equipment), and of agriculture (that part of the livestock herd intended for reproduction). In the USSR, the sector principle is adopted as a basis for planning capital investments; that is, capital investments are planned according to the sectors of material production and the sectors of the nonproductive sphere, with sectorial and territorial planning being combined. Capital investments are distributed according to sectors, based on the rates and proportions of development outlined in the national economic plans. More than one-third of all capital investments are directed to the development of industry and especially to those sectors that ensure technological progress and increased labor produc-

tivity (power industry, machine construction, chemical and petrochemical industry) and the sectors processing agricultural raw materials and producing consumer goods. In 1966–70, the share of capital investments in agriculture was 18 percent of the total. More than one-fourth of all capital investments go to housing construction and to development of public education, science, culture, and the arts. The economic efficiency of capital investments has increased because of the increased share of equipment, tools, and inventory, which amounted to 34 percent of all capital in 1946–50 and to 41 percent in 1966–70.

Capital investments and the completions of fixed assets ensure the maintenance of working capacities and the replacement (simple reproduction) and increase (extended reproduction) of fixed assets. Extended reproduction (net investment) of production fixed assets is realized through the construction of new and the reconstruction and expansion of existing enterprises and the replacement of old equipment with modern machines and devices. In 1960, 55 percent, and in 1970, 58 percent of total capital investments consisted of reconstruction, expansion, and reequipment of existing enterprises. In the USSR, 89 percent of all capital investments were made by state and cooperative (excluding kolkhoz) enterprises, agencies, and organizations and 9 percent by kolkhozes. The capital investments of the population in privately owned houses and apartments in 1970 accounted for the remaining 2 percent.

The basic form of planning capital investments is the five-year plan, broken down by years. The targets of the five-year plan are clearly defined and specified in the annual plans, which take into account the course of the economic development and the change in resource availability. The plan includes targets for completions of fixed assets; for the volume of capital investments, including construction work and installation of equipment; and for the level of unfinished construction. The plans are drawn in terms of sectors, ministries, and departments of the USSR and the Union republics. For the substantiation of capital investments, diagrams of the development of sectors of the national economy and industry are used, as are diagrams of the placement of productive forces in the economic regions and the Union republics, balances of production capacities and material resources, and technical and economic calculations and standards (such as specific capital investments, the length of the construction period, and any work done in anticipation). A calculation of the efficiency of the capital investments is made at the same time as the basic indexes of these investments are developed.

The Communist Party and the socialist state pursue a policy aimed at increasing capital investments, particularly investments in progressive sectors of the economy. At the same time, steps are taken to make significant improvements in the efficiency of capital investments, to ensure the most rational use of material and financial resources earmarked for construction, to provide for the necessary concentration of capital investments, and to reduce the number of enterprises and projects being built simultaneously and to take measures against the accumulation of unfinished construction above the permissible norm. Construction of industrial projects, houses, and child care establishments and other nonproductive units is coordinated.

REFERENCES
Materialy XXIV s"ezda KPSS. Moscow. 1971.
Gosudarstvennii piatiletnii plan razvitiia narodnogo khoziaistva SSSR na 1971–1975 gody. Moscow, 1972.
Krasovskii, V. P. *Problemy ekonomiki kapital'nykh vlozhenii.* Moscow, 1967.　　　　　　　　　　　　　　　M. S. GUREVICH [11–1057–3]

CAPITALISM, social and economic structure based on private property in the means of production and the exploitation of wage labor by capital; capitalism replaces feudalism and precedes socialism, the first phase of communism.

The main attributes of capitalism are the dominance of commodity-money relations and private property in the means of production, developed social division of labor, the increasing socialization of production, the transformation of labor power into a commodity, and the exploitation of wage laborers by capitalists. The aim of capitalist production is the appropriation of the surplus value created by the labor of wage workers. As the relations of capitalist exploitation become the dominant type of productive relations and bourgeois political, legal, ideological, and other social institutions come to replace precapitalist forms of the superstructure, capitalism becomes a social and economic structure that includes the capitalist mode of production and the corresponding superstructure. Capitalism passes through several stages in its development, but its most characteristic features remain essentially unchanged. Antagonistic contradictions are inherent in capitalism. Its main contradiction, that between the social nature of production and the private capitalist form of appropriation of the result of production, engenders anarchy of production, unemployment, economic crises, and an implacable struggle between the basic classes of capitalist society, the proletariat and the bourgeoisie; this basic contradiction predetermines the historical doom of the capitalist system

The emergence of capitalism was prepared by the social division of labor and the development of a commodity economy within the womb of feudalism. As capitalism emerges, the class of capitalists, which concentrates money capital and the means of production in its own hands, forms at one pole of society, and the mass of people deprived of the means of production and thus forced to sell their labor power to the capitalists forms at the other pole. Advanced capitalism is preceded by a period of the so-called primitive accumulation of capital, the essence of which is the robbery of peasants and small artisans and the seizing of colonies. The transformation of labor power into a commodity and of the means of production into capital signified the transition from simple commodity production to capitalist production. Simultaneously, the initial accumulation of capital was a process of rapid expansion of the internal market. Peasants and craftsmen who had previously lived on the proceeds of their own entrprises were turned into wage workers and forced to live by selling their labor power and to buy the essential articles of consumption. The means of production, which were concentrated in the hands of the minority, were turned into capital. An internal market was created for the means of production essential to the renewal and expansion of production. The great geographical discoveries (mid-15th to mid-17th centuries) and the seizing of colonies (15th to 18th centuries) secured for the nascent European bourgeoisie new sources of capital accumulation (the export of precious metals from the seized countries, the robbery of peoples, income from trade with other countries, and the slave trade) and led to the growth of international economic ties. The development of commodity production and exchange, accompanied by the differentiation of commodity producers, served as the basis for the further development of capitalism. Scattered commodity production could no longer meet a growing demand for goods.

Simple capitalist cooperation—that is, the joint labor of many people carrying out separate production operations under the control of capitalists—became the point of departure for capitalist production. The source of cheap labor power for the first capitalist entrepreneurs was the mass ruination of craftsmen and peasants as a result of property differentiation, "enclosures" of land, the adoption of laws concerning the poor, devastating taxes, and other measures of extraeconomic constraint. The gradual strengthening of the economic and political positions of the bourgeoisie prepared the way in a number of countries of Western Europe for bourgeois revolutions (the Netherlands in the late 16th century, Great Britain in the mid-17th century, France in the late 18th century, and a number of other European countries in the mid-19th century). Having made radical changes in the political superstructure, the bourgeois revolutions accelerated the replacement of feudal productive relations by capitalist relations; they cleared the ground for the capitalist system, which had ripened in the womb of feudalism, and for the replacement of feudal property by capitalist property. The development of the productive forces of bourgeois society took a major step with the appearance of the manufactory (mid-16th century). However, by the mid-18th century, the further development of capitalism in the advanced bourgeois countries of Western Europe had run up against the narrowness of the manufactory's technical base. The need developed to shift to large-scale factory production involving the use of machines. The transition from the manufactory to the factory system was

achieved in the course of the industrial revolution, which began in Great Britain in the second half of the 18th century and was completed around the mid-19th century.The invention of the steam engine led to the appearance of a multitude of machines. The growing need for machines and machinery resulted in the modification of the technical base of machine-building and the transition to the production of machines by machines. The emergence of the factory system signified the establishment of capitalism as the dominant mode of production and the creation of the material and technical base corresponding to capitalism. The transition to the machine stage of production promoted the development of productive forces; the emergence of new branches and the incorporation of new resources into economic circulation; the rapid increase in the population of cities; and increasingly lively external economic ties. It was accompanied by a further increase in the exploitation of wage laborers: that is, the broader use of the labor of women and children, the lengthening of the work day, the intensification of labor, transformation of the worker into an appendage of the machine, the growth of unemployment, and the sharpening of the opposition between mental and physical labor and between the city and the countryside. The basic laws of development of capitalism are identical in all countries. However, the genesis of capitalism has different features in different countries, features that are determined by the concrete historical conditions in each one.

The classical path of capitalist development—primitive accumulation of capital, simple cooperation, manufactory production, and the capitalist factory—is characteristic of a small number of Western European countries, chiefly Great Britain and the Netherlands. The industrial revolution was completed, the factory system of production emerged, and the advantages and contradictions of the new, capitalist mode of production were fully manifested earlier in Great Britain than in other countries. The growth of industrial production was extraordinarily rapid in comparison with other European countries and was accompanied by the proletarianization of a substantial portion of the population, the deepening of social conflicts, and cyclical crises of overproduction that have been repeated regularly since 1825. Great Britain became the classical country of bourgeois parliamentarism, and at the same time the birthplace of the contemporary workers' movement. By the mid-19th century, Great Britain had achieved world industrial, commercial, and financial hegemony and was the country where capitalism had attained its highest development. It was no accident that the theoretical analysis of the capitalist mode of production provided by K. Marx was based primarily on the British situation. V. I. Lenin noted that the major distinguishing features of British capitalism of the second half of the 19th century were "vast colonial possessions and a monopolist position on the world market" (*Poln. sobr. soch.*, 5th ed., vol. 27, p. 405).

The formation of capitalist relations in France, the strongest Western European power of the era of absolutism, was slower than the process in Great Britain and the Netherlands, primarily because of the stability of the absolutist state and the comparative strength of the nobility's social position and the strength of the small peasant economy. The dispossession of the peasants proceeded not by means of "enclosures," but by the tax system. The system of farming out taxes and state debts and later the protectionist policies of the government with respect to incipient manufactory production both played a large role in the formation of the bourgeois class. The bourgeois revolution occurred nearly a century and a half later in France than in Great Britain, and the process of primitive accumulation stretched out over three centuries. The Great French Revolution, which radically eliminated the feudal absolutist system that had hindered the growth of capitalism, simultaneously led to the emergence of a stable system of small peasant ownership of land that put its stamp on the entire subsequent development of capitalist productive relations in France. The extensive introduction of machinery did not begin there until the 1830's. During the 1850's and 1860's, France became an industrially developed state. The distinctive feature of French capitalism was its usurious character. The growth of loan capital based on the exploitation of the colonies and on profitable credit operations abroad turned France into a rentier country.

In other countries, the genesis of capitalist relations was accelerated by the influence of the existing seats of developed capitalism. Thus, the USA and Germany set out on the path of capitalist development later than Great Britain, but by the end of the 19th century they had already joined the ranks of the capitalist countries. Feudalism had not existed in the USA as an all-embracing economic system. The displacement of the native population into reservations and the development by farmers of lands that had been opened up in the western part of the country played a major role in the development of American capitalism. This process established what is known as the American path of capitalist development in agriculture, a path based on the growth of capitalist farming. As a result of the rapid growth of American capitalism after the Civil War, as early as 1894 the USA was first in the world in terms of volume of industrial production.

In Germany, the liquidation of the system of serfdom was carried out "from above." The redemption of feudal obligation on the one hand led to the mass proletarianization of the population and on the other hand put into the landlords' hands the capital necessary to turn Junker estates into large-scale capitalist farms using hired labor. It was thus that the preconditions for the Prussian path of development of capitalism in agriculture were created. The unification of the German states into a single customs union and the bourgeois revolution of 1848–49 accelerated the development of industrial capital. The railroads played an exceptional role in the industrial upsurge of the mid-19th century in Germany, promoting the economic and political unification of the country and contributing to the rapid development of heavy industry. The political unification of Germany and the war indemnities it received after the Franco-Prussian War of 1870–71 became powerful stimuli to the further development of capitalism. During the 1870's there was a process of rapid establishment of new branches of the economy and re-equipping of old ones on the basis of the most recent achievements of science and technology. Utilizing the technological achievements of Great Britain and other countries, Germany was able to overtake France in terms of its level of economic development as early as 1870, and by the end of the 19th century it was approaching the level of Great Britain. In the East, capitalism developed most fully in Japan, where, as in the Western European countries, it arose on the foundation of disintegrating feudalism. In the three decades after the bourgeois revolution of 1867–68, Japan developed into one of the industrialized capitalist powers.

By the beginning of the 20th century, as a result of the evolution of capitalism, a number of advanced capitalist states existed in the world and had achieved a high level of economic and military might. A fierce struggle unfolded among these powers for colonies in Africa and Asia, and as a result of this struggle, virtually all of the unoccupied territories on the earth were divided up. A world system of capitalism arose. Capitalist productive relations also began to appear in the countries of Asia, Africa, and Latin America, which had been drawn into the system of the world capitalist economy as markets and sources of raw materials and foodstuffs. The development of capitalism in the colonial and dependent countries was accompanied by cruel exploitation, oppression, and violence on the part of the imperialist states.

Premonopoly capitalism. An all-around analysis of capitalism and the concrete forms of its economic structure in the premonopoly stage was provided by K. Marx and F. Engels in a number of works, primarily *Das Kapital,* in which they revealed the economic law of movement of capitalism. The doctrine of surplus value—the cornerstone of Marxist political economy—exposed the secret of capitalist exploitation. The appropriation of surplus value by the capitalists occurs as a consequence of the fact that the means of production and the means of livelihood are the property of the small class of capitalists. In order to live, the worker is forced to sell his labor power. With his labor he creates more value than his labor power costs. Surplus value is appropriated by the capitalists; it serves as the source of their enrichment and of the further growth of capital. The reproduction of capital is simultaneously the reproduction of capitalist productive relations, based on the exploitation of the labor of another person.

The pursuit of profit, which is a modified form of surplus value, determines the entire movement of the capitalist mode of production, including the expansion of production, the development of technology, and the increase in the exploitation of workers. In the stage of premonopoly capitalism, the competition of noncooperating, scattered commodity producers is replaced by capitalist competition, which leads to the formation of an average rate of profit—that is, equal profit for equal capital. The value of goods produced assumes a modified form of the price of production, which includes the cost of production and the average profit. The process of averaging out profit takes place in the course of intrabranch and interbranch competition, through the mechanism of market prices and the infusion of capital from one branch to another and through the sharpening of the competitive struggle between capitalists.

In perfecting the technology in various enterprises, using the achievements of science, developing the means of transportation and communication, and improving the organization of production and commodity exchange, the capitalists automatically develop social productive forces. The concentration and centralization of capital promote the emergence of large-scale enterprises, in which thousands of workers are concentrated, and lead to the growing socialization of production. However, the enormous, constantly increasing wealth is appropriated by individual capitalists, which leads to a deepening of the basic contradiction of the system. The greater the degree of socialization in capitalist production, the wider the gap between the actual producers and the means of production, which are private capitalist property. The contradiction between the social nature of production and capitalist appropriation assumes the form of antagonism between the proletariat and the bourgeoisie. It is also manifested in the contradiction between production and consumption. The contradictions of the capitalist mode of production are revealed most acutely in periodic economic crises. These crises, which are the objective form of the forcible overcoming of the contradictions of capitalism, do not resolve the contradictions but further deepen and aggravate them—evidence of the inevitability of the downfall of capitalism. Thus, capitalism itself creates the objective preconditions for a new system based on social ownership of the means of production.

The antagonistic contradictions and historically foredoomed nature of capitalism are reflected in the superstructure of bourgeois society. The bourgeois state, in whatever form it takes, always remains the instrument of the class rule of the bourgeoisie, the organ for suppressing the toiling masses. Bourgeois democracy is restricted and formal in nature. In addition to the two main classes of bourgeois society (the bourgeoisie and the proletariat), the classes inherited from feudalism, that is, the peasantry and the owners of landed estates, are preserved under capitalism. With the development of industry, science and technology, and culture in capitalist society, the social stratum of the intelligentsia grows—that is, the people performing mental labor. The main tendency of development of the class structure of capitalist society is the polarization of society into two main classes as a result of the erosion of the peasantry and intermediate strata. The main class contradiction of capitalism is that between the workers and the bourgeoisie, which is expressed in the sharp class struggle between them. In the course of this struggle, revolutionary ideology is worked out, political parties of the working class are created, and the objective preconditions of socialist revolution are prepared.

Monopoly capitalism. In the late 19th century and early 20th century, capitalism entered a higher, final stage of its development—imperialism, that is, monopoly capitalism. At a certain stage, free competition resulted in such a high level of concentration and centralization of capital that it naturally entailed the emergence of monopolies. It is these monopolies that determine the essence of imperialism. Rejecting free competition in individual branches, the monopolies do not eliminate competition as such, "but exist above it and alongside it, and thereby give rise to a number of very acute, intense antagonisms, frictions, and conflicts" (Lenin, *Poln. sobr. soch.,* 5th ed., vol. 27, p. 386). Lenin worked out the scientific theory of monopoly capitalism in his work *Imperialism, the Highest Stage of Capitalism.* He defined imperialism as "capitalism at the stage of development at which the dominance of the monopolies and finance capital is established, in which the export of capital has acquired pronounced importance, in which the division of the world among the international trusts has begun, in which the division of all territories of the globe among the biggest capitalist powers has been completed" (*ibid.*, p. 387). In the monopoly stage of capitalism, the exploitation of labor by finance capital leads to the redistribution, to the benefit of the monopolies, of the portion of the total surplus value falling to the share of the nonmonopolistic bourgeoisie and of a part of the necessary product of wage laborers, through the mechanism of monopoly pricing. Certain displacements in the class structure of society occur. The rule of finance capital is personified in the financial oligarchy—the big monopoly bourgeoisie, which subordinates most of the national wealth of the capitalist countries to its own control. Under the conditions of state-monopoly capitalism, the leading circles of the big bourgeoisie are substantially strengthened; they exert a definite influence on the economic policies of the bourgeois state. The economic and political weight of the nonmonopoly middle and petite bourgeoisie decreases. Fundamental changes in the composition and size of the working class take place. In the advanced capitalist countries taken together, while the growth of the total gainfully employed population was 91 percent from 1900 to the 1970's, the number of people working for wages increased by nearly 200 percent, and the proportion of them in relation to the total number of employed people grew during this period from 53.3 to 79.5 percent. Under the conditions of modern technological progress, with the expansion of the service sphere and the growth of the bureaucratic state apparatus, the numbers and relative weight of office employees have increased. The social position of these workers approaches that of the industrial proletariat. Under the leadership of the working class, the most revolutionary forces in capitalist society and all toiling classes and social strata are waging the struggle against their oppression by the monopolies.

In its process of development, monopoly capitalism evolves into state monopoly capitalism, which is characterized by the interlocking of the financial oligarchy with the upper echelons of the bureaucracy, the increased role of the state in all spheres of social life, the growth of the state sector in the economy, and increasingly active policies aimed at mitigating the socioeconomic contradictions of capitalism. Imperialism, particularly in the state-monopoly stage, signifies a profound crisis of bourgeois democracy, an intensification of reactionary tendencies, and the increased role of force in domestic and foreign policy. It is inseparable from the growth of militarism and of military expenditures, the arms race, and tendencies toward the unleashing of aggressive wars.

Imperialism sharply aggravates the basic contradiction of capitalism and all other contradictions of the bourgeois system that follow from it, contradictions that can be resolved only by socialist revolution. Lenin made a profound analysis of the law of the uneven economic and political development of capitalism in the era of imperialism and reached the conclusion that the victory of the socialist revolution, initially in a single capitalist country, was inevitable.

World War I and the victory of the Great October Socialist Revolution, which abolished capitalism in Russia, inaugurated the general crisis of capitalism, which decisively influenced the internal contradictions of imperialism on the one hand and the course of the world revolutionary process on the other. The general crisis of capitalism is characterized primarily by the formation of two opposite socioeconomic systems (the capitalist and socialist systems) and by the struggle between them, in the course of which the forces of socialism steadily gain strength and the positions of capitalism steadily weaken; the disintegration of the colonial system of imperialism takes place. The internal contradictions of the imperialist states and of the world capitalist economy become aggravated, the crisis of bourgeois politics and ideology is intensified, and the struggle between labor and capital grows, as does the struggle between the toiling and exploited classes and the monopoly bourgeoisie.

The general crisis of capitalism accelerates the development of state-monopoly capitalism and a further increase in the socialization of production. Such new phenomena as state regulation of the economy, programming, capitalist integration, and the shift from the old colonial rule to neocolonialism signify a certain modification of the basic characteristics of imperialism without the alteration of its essence. Free competition capitalism, imperialism, and state-monopoly capitalism all represent different stages of a single socioeconomic structure. During this historical development, the structure of production and the mechanism of appropriating surplus value change, but the basic features of capitalism—commodity production, private property in the means of production, and the exploitation of wage labor by capital—remain unchanged.

The characteristic feature of contemporary capitalism is that it has been forced to adapt to new circumstances in the world. With a contemporary condition of economic competition and the struggle between two opposite systems, the ruling circles of the capitalist countries fear the development of the class struggle into a mass revolutionary movement; thus, the bourgeoisie strives to employ more disguised forms of exploiting and oppressing workers, and often readily carries out partial reforms to keep the masses under their ideological influence and political control. The monopolies use the achievements of scientific and technological progress to strengthen their own positions and increase exploitation of the toiling masses. But the adaptation to new conditions and processes, which has been prompted by the general laws of development of productive forces and by the scientific and technological revolution, does not mean the stabilization of capitalism as a system. The general crisis is deepening. Even the most developed capitalist countries experience serious economic shocks, accompanied by growing inflation and unemployment and the crisis of the currency and financial system. At the beginning of the 1970's, there were about 8 million unemployed people in the advanced capitalist countries. None of the attempts of contemporary capitalism to adapt to the new conditions eliminate the contradictions between the imperialist states. The economic and political struggle unfolds among the main centers of imperialist rivalry: the USA, Western Europe, and Japan.

Historical place of capitalism. In its time, capitalism played a progressive role as a natural stage in historical development. It destroyed the patriarchal and feudal relations among people based on personal dependence and replaced them with money relations. Capitalism created large cities, sharply increased the urban population at the expense of the rural population, did away with feudal fragmentation, which led to the formation of bourgeois nations and centralized states, and raised the productivity of social labor to a higher level.

As early as the mid-19th century, Marx and Engels wrote: "The bourgeoisie, during its rule of scarce one hundred years, has created more massive and more colossal productive forces than have all preceding generations together. Subjection of Nature's forces to man, machinery, the application of chemistry to industry and agriculture, steam navigation, railroad, the electric telegraphs, clearing of whole continents for cultivation, the canalization of rivers, whole populations conjured out of the ground—what earlier century had even a presentiment that such productive forces slumbered in the lap of social labor?" (*Soch.*, 2nd ed., vol. 4, p. 429). From that time on, the development of productive forces, despite unevenness and periodic crises, continued at an even more highly accelerated rate. By the 20th century, capitalism was able to place at its service many achievements of the modern scientific and technological revolution: atomic energy, electronics, automation, jet technology, and chemical synthesis, to name a few. But under the conditions of capitalism, social progress is continued at the price of a marked aggravation of social contradictions, the wasting of productive forces, and the suffering of the masses of people of the whole world. The era of primitive accumulation and capitalist "development" of the outlying areas of the world was accompanied by the annihilation of entire tribes and nationalities. Colonialism, which served as the source of enrichment of the imperialist bourgeoisie and the so-called worker aristocracy in the parent countries, resulted in protracted stagnation of the productive forces in the countries of Asia, Africa, and Latin America and was conducive to the preservation of precapitalist productive relations in these countries. Capitalism used the progress of science and technology to create means of mass destruction and annihilation. It bears responsibility for the enormous human and material losses in the increasingly frequent destructive wars. Solely in the two world wars unleashed by imperialism, more than 60 million people died and 110 million were wounded or became invalids. In the stage of imperialism, economic crises became more acute in character. In the context of the general crisis of capitalism, there is a steady narrowing of the sphere of capitalist domination: the worldwide socialist economic system is developing rapidly, and its share in world production is growing steadily, while the share of the capitalist world economic system is decreasing.

Capitalism cannot cope with the productive forces it has created, forces that have outgrown capitalist productive relations, which are like fetters on their further development. The objective material preconditions for the transition to socialism are created within the womb of bourgeois society in the process of the development of capitalist production. Under capitalism, the working class grows, unites, and organizes; in alliance with the peasantry, at the forefront of all toiling people, it makes up a mighty social force capable of overthrowing the obsolete capitalist system and replacing it by socialism.

In the struggle against imperialism, the embodiment of capitalism under contemporary conditions, three revolutionary streams are united—world socialism, the antimonopoly forces in the advanced capitalist countries, headed by the working class, and the world national liberation movement. "Imperialism is powerless to regain the historical initiative it has lost, to reverse the development of the modern world. The main path of development for humanity is determined by the world socialist system, the international working class, and all revolutionary forces" (*Mezhdunarodnoe soveshchanie kommunisticheskikh i rabochikh partii*, Moscow, 1969, p. 289).

By means of apologist theories, bourgeois ideologists attempt to prove that contemporary capitalism is a system devoid of class antagonism and that in highly developed capitalist countries factors giving rise to social revolution are generally absent. However, such theories are defeated by reality, which exposes more and more the irreconcilable contradictions of capitalism.

V. G. SHEMIATENKOV

Russia. The development of capitalism in Russia was accomplished essentially on the basis of the same socioeconomic laws as in other countries, but it had distinctive features of its own. The history of capitalism in Russia is divided into two main periods: the genesis of capitalist relations (second quarter of the 17th century to 1861) and the consolidation and dominance of the capitalist mode of production (1861–1917). The period of the genesis of capitalism consists of two stages: the origin and formation of the capitalist structure (second quarter of the 17th century through the 1760's) and the development of the capitalist structure (1770's to 1861). The period of capitalist dominance is also divided into two stages: the stage of progressive, ascendant development (1861 to the end of the 19th century) and the stage of imperialism (the beginning of the 20th century to 1917). (The question of the genesis of capitalist relations is a complex and controversial one in the history of Russian capitalism. Certain historians adhere to the periodization given above, and others see the genesis of capitalism beginning earlier, in the 16th century; still others date the beginning of capitalism at a later period, the 1760's.) It is an important characteristic of the development of capitalism in Russia that the genesis of capitalist relations was a slow process, stretching out for more than two centuries in the context of the dominance of feudal relations in the economy.

Simple capitalist cooperation developed increasingly in industry beginning in the second quarter of the 17th century. At the same time, the manufactory was becoming a stable and ever-growing form of production. In contrast to the Western European countries where the capitalist manufactory prevailed, Russian manufactories were divided into three types in terms of their social nature: capitalist manufactories, in which hired labor was utilized; serf manufactories, based on forced labor; and mixed manufactories, which employed both forms of labor. At the end of the 17th century, there were more than 40 metallurgical, textile, and other manufactories of all types in the country. Capitalist relations developed a great deal in the area of river transport. In the first half of the 18th century, simple capitalist cooperation developed and the number of manufactories grew. At the end of the 1760's, there were 663 manufactories, including 481 in manufacturing industry and 182 in mining and metallurgy.

During this period, the nature of social relations and industrial production underwent important and contradictory changes. In the first two decades of the 18th century, it was primarily enterprises of the capitalist type that formed in the manufacturing industry. However, the narrow market in labor power and the rapid growth of industry gave rise to a shortage of free hands. For this reason, the government began to attach state peasants to mills on a broad scale. The edict of 1721 allowed merchants to purchase peasant serfs to work in their enterprises. This edict was applied particularly extensively in the 1730's and 1740's. At the same time, laws were promulgated registering hired workers to the enterprises in which they were working, and the attachment of state peasants increased. The industrial activities of peasants and *posadskie liudi* (merchants and artisans) were restricted. As a result, the serf manufactory held the leading position in the mining industry right up until 1861. The use of unfree labor also increased in the manufacturing industry during the 1730's and 1740's. However, in this branch, the feudal serf system retarded the development of capitalist relations only briefly. From the early 1750's, the use of hired labor in manufacturing again began to grow rapidly, particularly in newly built enterprises. The attachment of peasants to manufactories came to an end after 1760. In 1762, the edict of 1721 was revoked. Restrictions on the industrial activity of peasants and *posadskie liudi* were gradually removed, and so by 1767, by official statistics, of the 43,600 workers employed in manufacturing industry, 17,900 (41 percent) were hired laborers and 25,700 were forced laborers (59 percent). The use of hired labor in river transport continued to increase. In the 1760's, there were 120,000 hired workers on ships. In industry as a whole, the number of hired workers, including those employed in small industry and in water transport, amounted to about 220,000 in the 1760's. Capitalist relations arose in agriculture in the second half of the 17th century, and the process of stratification of the peasantry began in Russia. There emerged among the rural population a small group of rich peasants who organized commodity production in agriculture, employing the hired labor of impoverished peasants. Another indicator of stratification was the appearance of migratory workers among the peasantry, that is, peasants who went to work for wages in industrial enterprises and in river transport. During this period, the capitalist stratification of the peasantry was most noticeable in the northern coastal areas and the Urals. The substantial weight of wage labor in industry, the new tendencies in government economic policy of the 1750's and 1760's, the increased stratification of the peasantry, and changes in the sphere of ideology that were expressed in progressive circles' realization that serfdom had to be ameliorated or even abolished —all these factors make it possible to assert that by the 1760's capitalist elements had already formed a system of social relations and that the capitalist structure was forming in the womb of the feudal serf system.

The dominant serf order hindered the formation of new capitalist relations but could not halt the process completely. By the end of the 18th century, there were as many as 2,294 manufactories—2,094 in manufacturing and 200 in mining and metallurgy. Between the 1770's and the 1790's, there was intensive development of the economy from small-scale commodity production to the capitalist manufactory. The number of industrial villages increased, particularly in the central provinces of the country. The newly rich peasant became a noticeable figure among capitalist entrepreneurs. By official data, 81,747 workers were employed in the manufacturing industry in 1799; of this figure, 33,567 were hired workers (41.1 percent) and 48,180 were forced laborers (58.9 percent). By the end of the 18th century, the total number of hired workers in industrial production in the country had nearly doubled since the 1760's, reaching 420,000. In certain industrial provinces, the departure of peasants for industrial and agricultural employment involved as much as 20 percent of the male population.

Capitalist relations developed still more intensively in the first half of the 19th century. An important feature in the development of large-scale manufacturing was the further increase in the numbers and relative proportion of hired workers: in 1799—33,600 (41.1 percent), in 1825—114,600 (54.4 percent), and in 1860—462,000 (81.8 percent). The cotton industry became a leading capitalist branch: hired workers made up 92.1 percent of the total. Capitalist relations were becoming consolidated in the linen, silk, and broadcloth industries. In this area, hired workers numbered about 65 percent of the total. Forced labor remained dominant in the sugar-beet industry and the mining and metallurgy industry. Hired labor was also employed in the gold fields of Siberia, which were developed precisely in this period.

The industrial revolution began in Russia in the mid-1830's. The manufactory based on manual labor was replaced by the factory. The development of capitalist relations continued in agriculture. By approximate calculations, there were about 4 million hired workers in industry and agriculture on the eve of the reform of 1861. The formation of the basic classes of capitalist society, the proletariat and the bourgeoisie, proceeded along with the development of capitalist relations; a national Russian market took shape. At the same time, the feudal serf system gradually disintegrated, and in the 1830's it entered a period of profound crisis.

The victory of capitalism as a system occurred in Russia as a result of the implementation of the peasant reform of 1861 and not by revolutionary means. Consequently, vestiges of serfdom were preserved in the economic and political areas (estate land ownership, autocracy, and so forth), and these determined a number of features in the subsequent development of capitalism.

The development of industry accelerated after the abolition of serfdom. Enterprises using forced labor shifted to hired labor or closed down. New, purely capitalist branches of heavy industry appeared: in the Donbas, coal mining and metal smelting; in Baku, oil drilling; and in St. Petersburg, machine building. Railroad construction assumed enormous dimensions. A capitalist credit system was created. During the 1880's and 1890's, the influx of foreign capital into Russia increased. Crises arose in the Russian capitalist economy in 1867 and 1873. A sharp increase in industry began in the 1890's and continued to the end of the century: coal mining increased more than three times and oil drilling and iron smelting by nearly three times, the length of railroads almost doubled, and so forth. During these years, Russia's industry developed more rapidly than that of Germany or the USA. The process of the formation of the proletariat was accelerated. At the end of the 19th century, there were about 10 million hired workers in the country, including about 3.5 million agricultural workers. Including their families, the proletariat numbered no less than 22 million people, that is, 18 percent of the entire population of the country.

The development of agriculture from 1861 to the end of the 19th century was characterized primarily by an increase in commodity production and the growth of domestic and foreign markets. With respect to social relations, the most important phenomenon in the countryside was the disintegration of the peasantry into the rural bourgeoisie and rural proletariat. At the end of the 19th century, the rural bourgeoisie amounted to about 20 percent of all peasant households in a number of regions. Economically, however, it was dominant in the countryside. Between 34 and 50 percent of peasant land belonged to the rural bourgeoisie, including half or more of the rented land; this class owned 38 to 62 percent of the draft animals and 70 to 80 percent of the improved implements of production. The rural poor made up about 50 percent of peasant households, but they owned only 18 to 32 percent of the land, 10 to 30 percent of the draft animals, and 1 to 3.6 percent of the improved implements of production. The middle peasantry made up about 30 percent of the peasant households; their position was very unstable, and their disintegration was proceeding. The landlords deprived of the free labor of peasants by the reform of 1861 were forced to reorganize their farms in conformity with capitalist conditions. In the late 19th century, the capitalist system of agriculture predominated in 19 provinces of European Russia. The economy of these provinces (the Baltic coast, western and central Byelorussia, the Right-bank and Steppe Ukraine, Bessarabia, the Don, and the Lower Volga Region) was more closely bound up with the domestic and foreign market and was marked by more highly developed capitalist relations than that of other areas. In 17 provinces of the central chernozem region, the nonchernozem belt, and the Middle Volga Region, areas in which large landlord latifundia survived and which were remote from markets, the corvée system predominated. In seven provinces of the Left-bank Ukraine, eastern Byelorussia, and neighboring Russian regions, a mixed system of estate farming was prevalent.

The most typical feature of the history of capitalism in the postreform period was the contradiction between bourgeois productive relations, which had become dominant and were conducive to the development of productive forces, and vestiges of serfdom in the form of *dvorianstvo* (nobility) land ownership and autocracy, which hindered this process. The most advanced industrial and finance capitalism were combined in Russia with the most backward agriculture. The second feature was the development of capitalism not only in depth (that is, the further growth of capitalist agriculture and capitalist industry in a given territory), but also in breadth (that is, the spread of capitalist relations to new territories and regions, such as the Caucasus, Middle Asia, and Siberia). The development of capitalism in breadth proceeded by various routes, and the degree of its penetration into the economy of the national borderlands was not uniform. But as capitalism grew, the economic ties and all the other ties of the national borderlands with the center of the country and among each other constantly expanded and became stronger; these areas became organic parts of the capitalist economy of Russia. The rapid development of capitalism in breadth slowed its development in depth in the older areas. As a consequence, the sharpness of the contradictions inherent in capitalism and engendered by it was lessened and their resolution was retarded. On the whole, the development of capitalism was uneven: capitalist industry was concentrated primarily in the central part of European Russia, in the south, and in the Baltic region. The third important characteristic of Russian capitalism was the extremely high level of concentration of production in the main areas of industry. This preordained a comparatively brief term of development along progressive lines and its rapid growth into monopoly capitalism.

At the turn of the 20th century, capitalism in Russia entered the monopoly stage, the stage of imperialism. In the course of its development, the necessary preconditions for socialist revolution were created. The concentration and centralization of production and capital reached such a level that their socialization and shift into the hands of the people became an urgent social necessity. Imperialism exacerbated the contradictions inherent in capitalism to the extreme. The force capable of resolving these contradictions also grew—the Russian proletariat, which, under the leadership of the Bolshevik Party, united all the toiling people and oppressed masses of Russia around itself and in October 1917 overthrew capitalism, opening a new, socialist era in the history of humanity.

I. A. BULYGIN

REFERENCES

Marx, K., and F. Engels. "Manifest Kommunisticheskoi partii." *Soch.*, 2nd ed., vol. 4.
Marx, K., and F. Engels. "Nemetskaia ideologiia." *Ibid.*, vol. 3.
Marx, K. "K kritike politicheskoi ekonomii." *Ibid.*, vol. 13.
Marx, K. "Zarabotnaia plata, tsena i pribyl'." *Ibid.*, vol. 16.
Marx, K. "Kritika Gotskoi programmy." *Ibid.*, vol. 19.
Marx, K. *Kapital*, vols. 1–3. *Ibid.*, vols. 23–25, parts 1 and 2.
Marx, K. "Teorii pribavochnoi stoimosti" (vol. 4 of *Kapital*). *Ibid.*, vol. 26, parts 1–3.
Engels, F. "Polozhenie rabochego klassa v Anglii." *Ibid.*, vol. 2.
Engels, F. "Anti-Dühring." *Ibid.*, vol. 20.
Lenin, V. I. "Po povodu tak nazyvaemogo voprosa o rynkakh." *Poln. sobr. soch.*, 5th ed., vol. 1.
Lenin, V. I. "Chto takoe 'druz'ia naroda' i kak oni voiuiut protiv sotsial-demokratov?" *Ibid.*, vol. 1.
Lenin, V. I. "K kharakteristike ekonomicheskogo romantizma." *Ibid.*, vol. 2.
Lenin, V. I. "Razvitie kapitalizma v Rossii." *Ibid.*, vol. 3.
Lenin, V. I. "Kapitalizm v sel'skom khoziaistve (O knige Kautskogo i o stat'e g. Bulgakova)." *Ibid.*, vol. 4.

Lenin, V. I. "Karl Marks." *Ibid*, vol. 26.
Lenin, V. I. "O lozunge Soedinennykh Shtatov Evropy." *Ibid.*, vol. 26.
Lenin, V. I. "Imperializm, kak vysshaia stadiia kapitalizma." *Ibid.*, vol. 27.
Lenin, V. I. "Gosudarstvo i revoliutsiia." *Ibid.*, vol. 33.
Mezhdunarodnoe soveshchanie kommunisticheskikh i rabochikh partii: Dokumenty i materialy: Moskva, 5–17 iiunia. Moscow, 1969.
Programma KPSS. Moscow, 1971.
Materialy XXIV s"ezda KPSS. Moscow, 1971. Pages 3–31.
Novye iavleniia v nakoplenii kapitala v imperialisticheskikh stranakh. Moscow, 1967.
Ekonomicheskaia teoriia Marksa-Lenina i sovremennyi kapitalizm. Moscow, 1967.
"Kapital" K. Marksa i problemy sovremennogo kapitalizma. Edited by N. A. Tsagolov and V. A. Kirov. Moscow, 1968.
Inozemtsev, N. N. *Problemy ekonomiki i politiki sovremennogo imperializma.* Moscow, 1969.
Inozemtsev, N. N. *Sovremennyi kapitalizm: Novye iavleniia i protivorechiia.* Moscow, 1972.
Politicheskaia ekonomiia sovremennogo monopolisticheskogo kapitalizma, vols. 1–2. Moscow, 1970.
Plekhanov, G. V. "Nashi raznoglasiia." In his book *Izbr. filosofskie proizvedeniia,* vol. 1. Moscow, 1956.
Khromov, P. A. *Ekonomicheskoe razvitie Rossii v XIX–XX vv, 1800–1917.* Moscow, 1950.
Iatsunskii, V. K. "Osnovnye etapy genezisa kapitalizma v Rossii." *Istoriia SSSR,* 1958, no. 5.
Strumilin, S. G. "Istoriia chernoi metallurgii v SSSR." In his book *Izbr. proizv.* Moscow, 1967.
Rubinshtein, N. L. "Nekotorye voprosy formirovaniia rynka rabochei sily v Rossii XVIII v." *Voprosy istorii,* 1952, no. 2.
Ustiugov, N. V. *Solevarennaia promyshlennost' Soli Kamskoi v XVII veke.* Moscow, 1957.
Perekhod ot feodalizma k kapitalizmu v Rossii: Materialy Vsesoiuznoi diskussii. Moscow, 1969.
Bulygin, I. A. [et al.]. "Nachal'nyi etap genezisa kapitalizma v Rossii." *Voprosy istorii,* 1966, no. 1.
Pavlenko, N. I. "Spornye voprosy genezisa kapitalizma v Rossii." *Voprosy istorii,* 1966, no. 11.
Zaozerskaia, E. I. *U istokov krupnogo proizvodstva v russkoi promyshlennosti XVI–XVII vv.* Moscow, 1970.
Druzhinin, N. M. "Osobennosti genezisa kapitalizma v Rossii v sravnenii so stranami Zapadnoi Evropy i SShA." *Novaia i noveishaia istoriia,* 1972, no. 4. [11–1037–1]

CAPITALIST CYCLE, the continually repeating movement of capitalist production from one economic crisis to another. It includes the phases of crisis, depression, revival, and boom. In the development of each phase, the conditions are created for the transition to the next phase of the cycle. "As the heavenly bodies, once thrown into a certain definite motion, always repeat this," wrote Marx, "so is it with social production, as soon as it is once thrown into this movement of alternate expansion and contraction. Effects, in their turn, become causes, and the varying accidents of the whole process, which always reproduces its own conditions, take on the form of periodicity" (K. Marx and F. Engels, *Soch.*, 2nd ed., vol. 23, p. 647–48). The cyclical course of reproduction of social capital is conditioned by the basic contradiction of capitalism—the contradiction between the social nature of production and the private capitalist form of appropriation.

The decisive phase of the capitalist cycle is the crisis of overproduction. In it the cycle reaches its culmination and ends, and the prerequisites for the development of a new cycle take shape. The material basis for movement through the cycle is the massive renewal of fixed capital. Although the periods of intensive capital investment are different and do not by any means coincide with each other, as Marx noted, a crisis always creates a starting point for a new large-scale investment of capital. In this connection, ever since large-scale industry became consolidated, the average period over which machinery is renewed has been one of the important features in explaining the long-term cycle through which industrial development passes" (*ibid.*, vol. 29, p. 237).

The first crisis of general overproduction, which initiated the first capitalist cycle, broke out in Great Britain in 1825. By the mid-19th century, the triumph of large-scale machine industry

in a number of countries, the deepening of the international division of labor, and the development of worldwide economic ties created conditions under which the capitalist cycle became international in nature. At about that time, the approximate ten-year duration of the capitalist cycle was distinctly manifested. Subsequently, in the 1870's, the development of productive forces and the associated exacerbation of the antagonistic contradictions of capitalism resulted in a decrease in the duration of the capitalist cycle to seven or eight years; the destructive force of the cyclical crises of overproduction increased.

Under the conditions of the general crisis of capitalism—in the context of the struggle between two social systems, the growth of state-monopoly capitalism, and the militarization of the economy—certain changes in the mechanism of the capitalist cycle take place. The financial oligarchy uses a far-reaching system of state-monopoly anticrisis measures. The effects of the sharply increased economic might of the largest monopolies and their attempts to regulate production and sales in order to obtain higher profits are seen in the manifested forms of the capitalist cycle. At the same time, the intensification of the struggle of the working people against the oppression of monopoly capital exerts an increasingly substantial influence on the course of the capitalist cycle.

As early as the 19th century, Marx, analyzing the development of the capitalist cycle, noted that in the course of accumulation the periodic phases of the cycle are interrupted by irregular fluctuations that follow one another with increasing frequency. The development of the scientific and technical revolution and the processes of structural reorganization of the economy under the conditions of contemporary capitalism inevitably lead to the more frequent appearance of partial, intermediate and supplementary crises. The subsequent period of economic stagnation and a gradual "slipping" into crisis becomes the constant concomitant of the cyclical boom.

As a result of changed conditions in the development of the capitalist cycle, the phases of revival and boom in many capitalist countries have been more intensive and the crisis drops in production have been less profound since World War II. However, the operation of capitalism's characteristic laws of cyclical development of production can be clearly traced in the course of the postwar economic development of the imperialist countries.

After World War II, international economic ties were weakened; as a result, the "synchronization" of the cycle's phases in the various capitalist countries was disrupted. Thus, the schedule of phases in the USA differed substantially, for example, from those in Japan or France. Nonetheless, the entire course of development of the processes of reproduction makes it possible to trace in an increasingly exact manner the general laws of development of the international capitalist cycle. Thus, the world economic crisis of 1957–58, which initiated the second postwar cycle, brought a decline in production not only in the USA, but also in Great Britain, Sweden, Belgium, the Netherlands, and Norway. The rate of growth of industrial production abruptly slowed down in the Federal Republic of Germany, Italy, and France.

The cyclical fluctuations of capitalist production increase the instability of the material situation of working people. During crisis years, the industrial reserve army grows constantly, and a large number of industrial and office workers find themselves unemployed. Invariably, capitalism seeks the way out of the crisis by further increasing the exploitation of the workers. One characteristic of the development of the contemporary capitalist cycle is the reduction of the role of cyclical factors in the behavior of prices, especially prices on consumer commodities: if previously crises of overproduction were always accompanied by substantial decreases in prices, in the 1950's and 1960's the increase in the high cost of living in most cases did not stop even under crisis conditions. These processes inevitably lead to the further aggravation of the contradictions of bourgeois society. The capitalist cycle and particularly the economic crises serve as an expression of the historical limitations of the capitalist mode of production; they show the inability of the bourgeois system to cope with the productive forces that have been called into being.

REFERENCES

Marx, K. *Kapital*, vol. 1. In K. Marx and F. Engels, *Soch.*, 2nd ed., vol. 23, chs. 3, 6, 23, 24.
Marx, K. *Kapital*, vol. 2. *Ibid.*, vol. 24, chs. 2–6, 12–16, 20–21.
Marx, K. *Kapital*, vol. 3. *Ibid.*, vol. 25, chs. 6, 14–18, 27, 48, 51.
Marx, K. "Teorii pribavochnoi stoimosti" (vol. 4 of *Kapital*). *Ibid.*, vol. 26, part 2.
Engels, F. *Anti-Dühring. Ibid.*, vol. 20, sec. 3, ch. 1.
Lenin, V.I. "K kharakteristike ekonomicheskogo romantizma." *Poln. sobr. soch.*, 5th ed., vol. 2.
Lenin, V.I. "Razvitie kapitalizma v Rossii." *Ibid.*, vol. 3.
Lenin, V.I. "Uroki krizisa." *Ibid.*, vol. 5.
Lenin, V.I. "Marksizm i revizionizm." *Ibid.*, vol. 17.
Programma KPSS. Moscow, 1971.
Materialy XXIV s"ezda KPSS. Moscow, 1971.
Mirovye ekonomicheskie krizisy, 1848–1935, vol. 1. Moscow, 1937.
Iakovlev, A. *Ekonomicheskie krizisy v Rossii.* Moscow, 1955.
Sovremennoe ekonomicheskoe polozhenie kapitalisticheskikh stran. Moscow, 1959.
Trakhtenberg, I. *Kapitalisticheskoe vosproizvodstvo i ekonomicheskie krizisy.* Moscow, 1959.
Varga, E. *Sovremennyi kapitalizm i ekonomicheskie krizisy.* Moscow, 1962.
Kuz'minov, I. *Poslevoennyi kapitalisticheskii tsikl.* Moscow, 1962.
Mendel'son, L. *Teoriia i istoriia ekonomicheskikh krizisov i tsiklov,* vols. 1–3. Moscow, 1959–64.
Sovremennye tsikly i krizisy. Moscow, 1967.

R. M. ENTOV [11-1055-1]

CAPITALIZATION. (1) The conversion of surplus value into capital, that is, the utilization of surplus value for the expansion of capitalist production. The capitalized surplus value forms a fund of capital accumulation that, like capital, is divided in two parts: the additional constant capital, used for the acquisition of additional means of production, and the additional variable capital, used for buying additional labor power.

(2) The process of the formation of fictitious capital. In bourgeois society, each regularly recurrent income (such as ground rent or dividends) is capitalized: it is calculated at the average loan interest rate as if it were income from capital in the form of a loan at this interest rate. Each unearned income received by virtue of the ownership of securities is considered as interest from a certain capital, which in reality does not exist (imaginary capital). The securities issued (shares, bonds of corporations or the state) become capital and bear interest. The increase in the rates of the shares (capitalized dividends), particularly in the period of cyclic upsurge, leads to the accumulation of fictitious capital, which qualitatively and quantitatively differs from the accumulation of real capital and which is determined by its own laws. At the same time, the excessive expansion of fictitious capital and the subsequent stock exchange collapse may seriously affect the process of capital accumulation. Since the whole mass of fictional capital represents a capitalized income, the change of its value does not depend on the value movement of the actual (real) capital that it represents. Capitalization means the further development of the fetishist character of capitalist relations of production, that is, a further development of the treatment of money and things as if they had a kind of magic power over men.

REFERENCES

Marx, K. *Kapital,* vol. 3. K. Marx and F. Engels, *Soch.*, 2nd ed., vol. 25, chs. 1–2, secs. 5–7.
Novye iavleniia v nakopenii kapitala v imperialisticheskikh stranakh. Moscow, 1967.

I. L. GRIGOR'EVA [11-1036-6]

CAPITAL SCRIPT (also called monumental script), the most ancient variety of the Latin alphabet. Inscriptions have been found dating from the sixth to the fourth century B.C. It attained its final form by the first century A.D.

Capital script is majuscule, with no spaces between words; the spaces are sometimes replaced by dots. Book capital script is characterized by rounded lines. Rustic capital script (fourth to seventh century A.D.) was less strict in form and had a number of variations (Roman ornamental or book rustic script). In the early second century A.D., book capital script was superseded by the uncial and cursive. The outlines of capital Latin letters form the basis of the capital letters of the Latin typeface.

REFERENCES

Diringer, D. *Alfavit.* Moscow, 1963. Pages 612–18. (Translated from English.)
Friedrich, J. *Geschichte der Schrift,* Heidelberg, 1966.
Jensen, N. *Die Schrift,* 3rd ed. Berlin, 1969. [11-1057-1]

CAPITANIA, from the 16th through early 19th century an administrative and territorial unit in Brazil (it originally was a hereditary feudal estate that representatives of the Portuguese feudal aristocracy received from the king). *Capitanias* also existed in other Portuguese colonies—the island of Madeira, the Azores, and the Cape Verde Islands. [11-1061-1]

CAPITANO DEL POPOLO, an official in an Italian urban commune (from the middle of the 13th century through the 15th). He headed the small commune, which consisted of *popolani* (townspeople) and excluded the *nòbili* (noblemen residing in the city). Within the all-city commune, the small commune had its own army (people's militia), administrative bodies (two councils), and legal system. The *capitano del popolo* in the small commune was analogous to the *podestà* (mayor) in the all-city commune. Gradually, with the strengthening of the merchants and guilds, the *capitano del popolo* began to play a decisive role in the political life of the city. [11-1060-2]

CAPITOL, a building in Washington, D.C., the capital of the USA, where the US Congress meets. It was built in the classical style during the years 1793–1865 (architects W. Thornton, B. Latrobe, and T. Walter). The buildings in the US state capitals where the legislative assemblies meet are also called capitols. [11-1062-2]

CAPITOLINE, one of the hills on which ancient Rome stood. From very ancient times the Capitoline was the center of a religious cult. The Capitoline Temple was located here. Senate sessions were sometimes held in the temple, and meetings of the people occasionally took place on the square in front of it. Criminals were thrown from the steep southwestern slope of the Capitoline (the Tarpeian rock). [11-1062-1]

CAPITOLINE TRIAD, in ancient Rome the group of three major gods held sacred in the Capitoline Temple, on the Capitoline Hill. The triad consisted of Jupiter, Juno, and Minerva. Worship of the triad ceased when the temple was destroyed by the Vandals in 455. [11-1062-3]

CAPITULARIES, laws and directives of the Frankish kings in the Carolingian dynasty; the texts were divided into short articles (in Latin, *capitula*).

The only extant capitularies are in collections of copies; these date from as early as 827. Capitularies regulated many matters, such as military duty, the administration of conquered lands, coinage, and tariffs. Directives legalizing the feudal dependence of peasants were among the most significant capitularies. One important historical source is the capitulary *De villis*, which was Charlemagne's instructions concerning the economic organization of royal domains issued circa 800.

REFERENCES

Danilov, A.I. "Kapituliarii o pomest'iakh . . . ." *Trudy Tomskogo gos. un-ta,* 1953, vol. 121, issue 2.
Ganshof, F.L. *Was waren die Kapitularien?* Weimar, 1961.

[11-1063-2]

CAPITULATION. (1) The cessation of resistance by ground, air, and naval forces or part of them in theaters or other regions of military operations, fortresses, or fortified regions and inhabited localities or at sea or on naval bases and elsewhere upon conditions presented by the victor or agreed upon in negotiations between the commanders. Capitulation is, as a rule, accompanied by the surrender of all armament, military ships and aircraft, fortresses, fortified areas, and matériel to the enemy, while personnel become prisoners of the victor.

(2) In international law, the cessation of armed struggle and the surrender of the armed forces of a belligerent state. Capitulation, as a rule, involves the imposition of political, economic, military, and other obligations on the state that has capitulated.

An unconditional capitulation is usually signed if the armed forces have been completely routed and includes recognition of this fact by the defeated state and the surrender of all armed forces. The victorious state may temporarily assume supreme power and establish an occupation regime in the defeated state.

After the unconditional capitulation of Hitlerite Germany and Japan at the end of World War II (1939–45) the Allies, in accordance with special agreements such as the Potsdam Declaration of July 26, 1945, carried out measures toward a democratization of the political regime in these countries, outlawed and disbanded criminal state organizations and political parties, and imposed economic, political, military, and other obligations on Germany and Japan. [11–1064–1]

CAPITULATIONS, a special type of unequal treaty that specified the privileges accorded foreigners by the host state. The content of the capitulations reflected the relative power positions of the parties to the treaty.

Originally, capitulations were a privilege that a government could extend to the citizens of another country and could abolish as it saw fit. Such relations existed, for example, between the Italian cities and Byzantium and between Christian principalities in Palestine and the Egyptian Mameluke sultans. In the middle of the 15th century the sultans of the Ottoman Empire granted capitulations to the citizens of Genoa and Venice. In 1535 or 1536 the Turkish sultan Suleiman I Kanuni ("the Lawgiver") granted the first capitulation to France. This capitulation, dating from the period of the greatest might of the Ottoman Empire, as well as earlier capitulations, was not unequal. As the Ottoman Empire became weaker the content of the capitulations changed. For example, in 1740, France's privileges in the Ottoman Empire were broadened and confirmed "in perpetuity." From the end of the 18th century, the capitulations were included in treaties concluded by the Ottoman Empire with foreign states. From voluntarily granted privileges, capitulations became terms of bondage that fixed the privileges of the foreign states and their subjects.

During the 18th and 19th centuries, the system of capitulations was spread by the European states and the USA to many countries of Asia and Africa, including China, Japan, Iran, Egypt, Algeria, Tunisia, and Morocco. As a rule the capitulations provided for the complete freedom (immunity) of foreigners from local jurisdiction. Moreover, foreigners were granted extensive privileges in trade, navigation, and local self-administration, and they were freed from many taxes and levies. The capitalist powers used the system of capitulations to further enslave the dependent countries.

In the late 19th century, Japan succeeded in abolishing the capitulations it had granted. In the majority of Balkan countries that had been part of the Ottoman Empire, capitulations were abolished after the liberation of these countries from the Ottoman yoke. In those parts of the Ottoman Empire which were virtually turned into colonies of the European powers, the capitulations were abolished in order to establish undivided European rule. Such was the case in 1830 in Algeria, in 1883–84 in Tunisia, and in 1912 in Tripolitania.

With the rising national liberation movements in Asia and Africa, the system of capitulations began to crumble. The decline was furthered by the Soviet state, which resolutely opposed all capitulation privileges and renounced the capitulation rights that had been granted to Tsarist Russia: the Soviet policy was reflected in the treaties with Turkey and Iran in 1921 and with China in 1924. Turkey finally freed itself from the system of capitulations in 1923 under the terms of the Treaty of Lausanne. The system was abolished in 1928 in Iran, between 1937 and 1949 in Egypt, and between 1943 and 1947 in China. [11–1063–3]

CAPODIMONTE (Capodimonte National Museum and Galleries), in Naples, one of the largest art museums of Italy, founded in 1738. It is located in the former Royal Palace of Capodimonte (1738, architect G. A. Medrano; reconstructed, 1952–57). It includes mainly the art collections of the Farnese princes and the Neapolitan kings. The museum houses European art from the 13th to the 19th century. There are paintings by Simone Martini, Masaccio, Giovanni Bellini, Parmigianino, Titian, P. Brueghel, and El Greco, as well as sculptures by A. Pollaiuolo and Bologna. The museum houses Italy's best collections of 17th-century Italian paintings, European and Oriental ceramics, weapons, furniture, and decorative fabrics.

REFERENCE
Molajoli, B. *Notizie su Capodimonte: Catalogo delle Gallerie e del Museo.* Naples, 1960. [11–1071–2]

CAPO D'ISTRIA, JOHN (also Ioannis Kapodistrias). Born Feb. 11, 1776, on the island of Corfu; died Oct. 9, 1831, in Navplion. Count, Greek statesman.

Capo d'Istria was trained in medicine in Italy. From 1803 to 1806, he was secretary of state in the Septinsular Republic, which was created in the Ionian Islands pursuant to the Russo-Turkish convention of 1800. At the invitation of Alexander I, he moved to Russia in 1809 and worked in the Russian diplomatic service until 1827. From 1815 to 1822, he was second secretary of state; after 1822 he was virtually in retirement and lived in Switzerland. Capo d'Istria belonged to the moderate wing of the Greek national liberation movement. During the Greek War of Independence (1821–29), he was elected president of Greece by the national assembly at Troezen (April 1827). Capo d'Istria favored friendly relations with Russia; this aroused domestic opposition, which the French and British supported. He died the victim of a plot.

REFERENCE
Teplov, Vl. A. *Graf Ioann Kapodistriia, prezident Gretsii.* St. Petersburg, 1893. [11–1072–1]

CAPONIER (in French, *caponnière*), a structure for defensive firing designed for conducting flanking or oblique fire.

There are machine-gun, gun, and combined gun and machine-gun caponiers. In the old fortresses caponiers were designed to enfilade the moats of the fort and were placed against the inner (scarp) wall of the moat. Since World War I (1914–18) caponiers have been installed in field position systems and fortified areas. Caponiers are usually placed on rear slopes or behind a local object of the terrain for conducting artillery or machine-gun fire flanking the obstacle zone and the approaches to neighboring weapon emplacements. [11–1072–3]

CAPORETTO, a population center in northern Italy, on the Isonzo River, where the Austro-Hungarian forces (the German Fourteenth Army, supported by the Austro-Hungarian Tenth and Second armies) inflicted a crushing defeat on the Italian Second and Third armies during World War I (Oct. 24–Nov. 9, 1917).

The Austro-Hungarian forces began their attack on October 24 and immediately broke through the Italian front, driving the Italian forces into chaotic retreat. Only when 11 Anglo-French divisions were thrown into battle was the front stabilized by November 9 along the Piave River. As a result of the breakthrough, the Italian Army lost more than 130,000 soldiers killed and wounded, 355,000 taken prisoner (according to Italian figures, 40,000 killed and wounded and 215,000 captured), 3,152 artillery pieces, 1,732 mortars, 3,000 machine guns, huge supplies of provisions, and about 14,000 sq km of territory. About 300,000 soldiers, unable to continue fighting, fled into the country's heartland. Despite its successes, the Austro-German advance on the Italian front did not alter the general strategic position of the Entente. The defeat of the Italian forces at Caporetto greatly aggravated the internal situation in Italy and promoted the growth of a revolutionary crisis there.

REFERENCES
Kaporetto: Razgrom ital'ianskoi armii na r. Izontso v oktiabre 1917. Moscow, 1938.
Conquet, A. *Srazhenie pod Kaporetto (1917).* Moscow, 1940. (Translated from French.) [11–1073–1]

CAPOTE, TRUMAN. Born Sept. 30, 1924, in New Orleans. American writer.

Capote began his literary career writing screenplays and short stories. The theme of his novel *Other Voices, Other Rooms* (1948) is man's loneliness in the modern bourgeois world. Capote further developed this theme in his later works: the collections *A Tree of Night* (1949; some stories translated into Russian, 1967) and *Breakfast at Tiffany's* (1958; some stories translated into Russian, 1965) and the short novel *The Grass Harp* (1953; Russian translation, 1966). These works are characterized by lyricism, stylistic mastery, and close psychological insight. In 1965, Capote published the journalistic novel *In Cold Blood* (Russian translation, 1966), which sought to reflect the burning issues of reality by uncovering the social and psychological roots of crime. He received an O. Henry Award in 1946, 1948, and 1951.

WORKS

The Thanksgiving Visitor. New York, 1968.
In Russian translation:
Odin iz putei v rai. Moscow, 1967.
Golosa travy. Moscow, 1971.

REFERENCES

Lidskii, Iu. Ia. *Ocherki ob amerikanskikh pisateliakh XX v.* Kiev, 1968.
Truman Capote's "In Cold Blood": A Critical Handbook. Belmont, Calif., 1968. (Bibliography, pp. 239–69.)   [11–1073–3]

CAPPADOCIA, an ancient region in the central part of Asia Minor. The ancient inhabitants called themselves the Hatti (Hattians). In the middle of the third millennium B.C., Indo-European tribes began invading Cappadocia from the northwest, and by the 18th–17th centuries B.C., their merging with part of the Hatti was complete (the nationality that formed as a result was known as the Hittite). In the 20th–19th centuries B.C., there were Assyrian trade colonies in Cappadocia. In the 1880's the so-called Cappadocian Tablets were found in Cappadocia in the archives of the ancient Assyrian colony of Kanesh, or Kanes (at Kültepe, Turkey). The center of the Hittite kingdom was located in Cappadocia in the second millennium B.C.

In the early sixth century B.C., Cappadocia was captured by Media, and during the late sixth century, it was part of the Persian Kingdom of the Achaemenids. During this time, Cappadocia was divided into two satrapies: Greater Cappadocia, which occupied the inner part (main city, Mazaca), and Pontic Cappadocia (or Pontus), along the coast of the Black Sea (main city, Sinope). The name Cappadocia was subsequently kept only for the former. In the fourth century B.C., Cappadocia was nominally part of the state of Alexander the Great. At the end of the fourth century B.C. it was subordinate to the Seleucids, but in the middle of the third century B.C. it became an independent kingdom. In the first century B.C. it became a dependency of Rome, and in A.D. 17 a Roman province. Cappadocia subsequently became part of the Byzantine Empire. In 1074 it was seized by the Seljuks. In the 15th century it became part of the Ottoman Empire.

REFERENCES

Ranovich, A. *Vostochnye provintsii Rimskoi imperii v I–III vv.* Moscow-Leningrad, 1949.
Golubtsova, E. S. *Ocherki sotsial'no-politicheskoi istorii Maloi Azii v I–III vv.* Moscow, 1962.
Göetze, A. *Kleinasien,* 2nd ed. Munich, 1957.
T. M. SHEPUNOVA   [11–1075–1]

CAPPARACEAE, a family of dicotyledonous plants. It includes herbs, shrubs, lianas, and sometimes trees, with simple or palmately compound alternate leaves that often have small stipules. The flowers are bisexual, rarely unisexual and regular, and most often more or less irregular. There are usually four each of sepals, petals, and stamens. The ovary is sessile, or, more often, on a long gynophore. The fruit may be a capsule, or pod-like, or berry-like.

There are approximately 45 genera (more than 800 species) in the family, growing in tropical, subtropical, and less frequently in temperate countries, often in regions with an arid climate, particularly in Africa. Two genera are found in the USSR—*Capparis* and *Cleome,* with 13 species. The *Cleome* genus and related genera are sometimes separated into a special family, Cleomaceae.

REFERENCES

Flora SSSR, vol. 8. Moscow-Leningrad, 1939.
Takhtadzhian, A. L. *Sistema i filogeniia tsvetkovykh rastenii.* Moscow-Leningrad, 1966.   [11–1019–2]

CAPPARIS, a genus of plants of the family Capparidaceae. It includes trees, bushes, or perennial grasses, sometimes with thorns (modified stipules). There are between 250 and 300 known species, primarily tropical and subtropical varieties; they often grow in arid regions.

In the USSR there are two species. The most economically important species in Eurasia is the caperbush (*C. spinosa*), a perennial subshrub. Its leaves are rounded, with spiny stipules. The flowers are large, white or pale rose, with numerous stamens; the ovary is on a gynophore. The fruit is a pod-shaped berry with a reddish pulp. This species is found primarily in the Mediterranean region, the Middle East, and India. In the Soviet Union it grows in the southern Crimea, the Caucasus (except for the mountainous and damp areas), and Middle Asia. The caperbush is cultivated in Western and Southern Europe, India, the Philippines, North Africa (Morocco), and North America. In the USSR, wild caperbushes are used commercially in the Dagestan ASSR. In Western Europe the variety *C. spinosa var. genuina* (without thorns) produces between 500 g and 3 kg of fruit from a single plant. The flower buds, young fruits, and the tips of shoots are marinated in vinegar and pickled; they are then used as a condiment for sauces and soups. Ripe fruits are also used in dry form. They contain approximately 18 percent protein. The seeds have up to 30 percent fat, while the buds have 0.32 percent rutin. These plants contain the alkaloid capparidin. They are also nectar-bearing.   [11–1020–1]

CAPPING, a complex of engineering and technological measures that provide for drilling in subterranean waters, oil, and gas, raising them to the surface, and the possibility of exploitation under optimum conditions (yield, chemical composition, and temperature) that remain stable over a period of time. The term "water intake" is also used as a synonym for the interception of subterranean fresh water, thermal springs, and industrial effluents.

Capping, which has been known since the early days of civilization, was highly developed in ancient Rome (the thermal baths of Emperor Caracalla; water-supply works), Mesopotamia, Portugal (Aquae Flaviae), and the Caucasus (*karez,* or underground irrigation canals).

Modern capping structures for subterranean waters are characterized by great diversity of types and designs, which take into consideration the special features of the hydrogeologic conditions of an area, composition of the water, and technical and sanitary requirements, which are determined by preset conditions of water consumption and the specific purpose for which the water is to be used. The simplest type of capping structure is the shaft well, which intercepts the subterranean waters of shallow-lying water tables; the walls of the well are reinforced with masonry or cast concrete to prevent cave-ins. For drilling in several water-bearing beds, the table designated for recovery is isolated from the underlying and overlying beds (strata) by plugging them. Drifts, which are extended horizontal or gently sloping mine tunnels built in highly broken areas, are used in addition to wells. The drifts are sometimes accompanied by a system of sloping, horizontal, or rising holes drilled into the side walls and face section of an underground gallery to increase the influx of water. In the USSR drift capping has been performed in Piatigorsk; abroad, it has been done in Bagnères-de-Luchon (France) and Ben-Haroun (Algeria). A nonpressured source can be capped by means of a chamber.

Boreholes (singly or in groups) are the most commonly used type of capping structure. Mechanized drilling permits the opening of water-bearing horizons and zones under rather difficult mining and geologic conditions at depths of 2 km or more. This makes possible reliable separation of the water-bearing horizons in well holes (pipe casing or cementing of the annular space), prevention of cave-ins of the walls and the breakthrough of water into the annular space, and installation of pumping equipment that provides withdrawal at constant yield rates. Steel piping is usually used for casing such wells. For the recovery of aggressive subterranean waters (waters containing carbonic acid and hydrogen sulfide, as well as waters with a low pH), capping wells are cased with pipes made of corrosion-resistant materials, such as alloy steels, vinyl plastic, polyethylene, and asbestos cement. Capping structures of underground mineral water deposits are made in the form of pump rooms, pavilions, and galleries.

Capping of oil and gas deposits consists in sealing and separating the interpipe space of wells and control of their operating conditions and the supply of gas or fluid to the well (or withdrawal from it). This is accomplished by special equipment built over the heads of oil or gas wells. Capping differs according to the recovery methods used (flow wells, air-lift wells, gas-lift wells, and pumping wells).

REFERENCES

Abramov, S. K., M. P. Semenov, and A. M. Chalishchev. *Vodozabory podzemnykh vod,* 2nd ed. Moscow, 1956.
Lavrushko, P. N., and V. M. Murav'ev. *Ekspluatatsiia neftianykh i gazovykh skvazhin.* Moscow, 1964.
Poiski i razvedka podzemnykh vod dlia krupnogo vodosnabzheniia. Moscow, 1969.
Vartanian, G. S., and L. A. Iarotskii. *Metodicheskie ukazaniia po poiskam, razvedke i otsenke ekspluatatsionnykh zapasov mestorozhdenii mineral'nykh vod.* Moscow, 1970.
                    V. G. AFONIN and G. S. VARTANIAN [11–1085–2]

CAPRA, FRANK. Born May 18, 1897, in Palermo. American motion-picture director.

Capra graduated from the California Institute of Technology. He began to work in motion pictures in 1921 and turned to directing in 1926–27. He was a leading figure in American cinematography of the 1930's, directing such films as *Lady for a Day* (1933), *It Happened One Night* (1934), *Mr. Deeds Goes to Town* (1936), *You Can't Take It With You* (1938), and *Mr. Smith Goes to Washington* (1939). These films dealt with the urgent social problems of American life—the critical plight of farmers and the venality and corruption of the ruling circles—without actually revealing their root causes.

Capra's films were very popular because of their realistic background, the high literary quality of the screenplays (R. Riskin was the screenwriter for most of the films), and the charm and shrewd characterizations of the protagonists.

REFERENCE

Kolodiazhnaia, V., and I. Trutko. *Istoriia zarubezhnogo kino,* vol. 2. Moscow, 1970. Pages 94–125. [11–1076–2]

CAPRI, an island in the Tyrrhenian Sea, in the southern part of the Bay of Naples. Italian territory. Area, 10.4 sq km; maximum elevation, 589 m.

Capri is composed primarily of limestone. Its shores are steep and have numerous picturesque caves and natural arches (for example, the Blue Grotto). Subtropical agriculture, horticulture, and fishing are Capri's major industries, along with tourism (Capri, Anacapri). Maxim Gorky lived on Capri between 1906 and 1913 and was visited there by V. I. Lenin in 1908 and 1910 [11–1077–2]

CAPRICCIO, a brilliant virtuoso instrumental piece with a free form, often implying whimsical alternation of episodes and moods.

Originally capricci were vocal pieces of the madrigal type, but at the turn of the 17th-century there appeared instrumental capricci that had a polyphonic texture and were close to the ricercar, canzone, fantasia, and toccata. The 18th-century solo capricci were seemingly improvised cadences that gave the performer an opportunity to demonstrate the fertility of his imagination. Later the form moved closer to the étude in violin music (24 capricci by N. Paganini for violin solo, also known in piano adaptations by F. Liszt and R. Schumann); it also approached the "characteristic" piece for the clavier and the piano.

The 19th-century orchestral capricci usually had a strong national flavor (Tchaikovsky's *Capriccio italien* and Rimsky-Korsakov's *Capriccio espagnol*). [11–1079–1]

CAPRIFICATION, pollination of the flowers of the fig tree with the participation of small (up to 2.5 mm) fig wasps, the succession of whose generations in the course of a year is connected with the development of different forms of inflorescences.

Some fig plants have inflorescences, caprifigs, with male (staminate) flowers and female short-styled flowers; others, figs, have female long-styled flowers and under-developed male flowers. In the spring the fig wasp enters the ovarie of female short-styled flowers to deposit its eggs. The larvae that hatch from the eggs feed on the contents of the ovules and develop into adult insects who mate here. When the fertilized female flies out of the inflorescence, she becomes covered with pollen from the staminate flowers. Then, in searching for short-styled flowers into which to deposit her eggs (she cannot deposit eggs in long-styled flowers, because she has a short ovipositor), the female wasp crawls into inflorescences with female long-stemmed flowers and pollinates them. Normal achenes develop from the pollinated flowers, and the fleshy floral receptacle grows to form the fig.

In early spring in the subtropics, the fig develops inflorescences, profichi (chiefly caprifigs), in which wasps emerging from overwintering inflorescences deposit their eggs. The summer inflorescences, mammoni (chiefly figs), develop in August; the flowers in these inflorescences are pollinated and fruits are formed. Autumn inflorescences, mamme, are sterile (caprifigs), and they appear at the end of September; the larvae of the fig wasps hibernate in them. [11–1077–6]

CAPRI SCHOOL, a school founded on the island of Capri (Italy) by persons who broke away from the Bolshevik Party; it was active from August to December 1909.

In June 1909 a conference of the enlarged editorial board of the newspaper *Proletarii* determined that the initiators of the Capri school were following "their own special ideological and political group goals" (*KPSS v rezoliutsiiakh . . . ,* 8th ed., vol. 1, 1970, p. 283). In December 1909, some lecturers at the Capri school (including A. A. Bogdanov and G. A. Aleksinskii) and a number of pupils organized the anti-Bolshevik group Vpered.

REFERENCE

Istoriia KPSS, vol. 2, ch. 4. Moscow, 1966. [11–1077–4]

CAPRIVI, LEO VON. Born Feb. 24, 1831, in Charlottenburg; died Feb. 6, 1899, in Skyren, near Krosno, Poland. German statesman, general, and count (1891).

Caprivi was head of the Admiralty from 1883 to 1888 and commanded the X Army Corps from 1888 to 1890. From 1890 to 1894 he was imperial chancellor, and from 1890 to 1892 he also held the post of prime minister of Prussia. The period of the tenure of Caprivi, who replaced Bismarck as chancellor, was called "the new course." Attempting to reach a rapprochement with Great Britain, Caprivi declined in 1890 to renew the Reinsurance Treaty of 1887 with Russia. In the same year he concluded a treaty with Great Britain on the exchange of the island of Zanzibar for the island of Heligoland. Some of Caprivi's reforms, such as the social legislation of 1891, aimed at weakening the growth of the labor movement. He concluded a number of trade treaties, including one with Russia in 1894, which aided the export of German manufactured goods and lowered the tariffs on imported agricultural products. These treaties aroused strong dissatisfaction among the Junker landowners and led to Caprivi's dismissal. [11–1077–3]

CAPROLACTAM, a lactam of ϵ-aminocaproic acid; a white crystalline substance. Melting point, 68°–69°C; boiling point, 262.5°C; index of refraction n_D^{20}, 1.4768.

Caprolactam is highly soluble in water and organic solvents, such as alcohol, ether, and benzene, and is hydrolyzed in aqueous acid and alkaline solutions to ϵ-aminocaproic acid, $H_2N-(CH_2)_5COOH$. An important property of caprolactam is its ability to polymerize, forming the vaulable polymer polycaproamide.

All of the commercial methods of preparing caprolactam include preparation of an intermediate—cyclohexanon oxime—and its conversion (Beckmann rearrangement) into caprolactam under the action of fuming sulfuric acid or concentrated H_2SO_4 at 60°–120°C. One of the main methods of preparing caprolactam from cyclohexane (I) involves the catalytic oxidation of cyclohexane (by atmospheric oxygen) into cyclohexanone (II). Upon interaction with hydroxylamine, the latter is converted into cyclohexanon oxime (III):

The most efficient and economical method is direct photochemical nitrosation of (I) into cyclohexanon oxime chlorhydrate. The procedure is simple: upon continuous saturation with gaseous HCl, a solution of nitrosylchloride, NOC1, in (I) is irradiated using a 10-kilowatt mercury lamp. The oxime (III) can also be obtained from other available raw material, such as benzoic acid, C_6H_5COOH; it is hydrogenated to cyclohexanocarboxylic acid, $C_6H_{11}COOH$, which is subsequently treated with nitrosylsulfuric acid. The original commercial method of preparation of caprolactam from phenol is still widely used.

In all methods, the caprolactam produced is isolated rectification (redistillation) or extraction (for example, by benzene), with subsequent rectification.

Caprolactam is used primarily in the preparation of polyamide plastics, films, and fibers. In 1970 the world production of caprolactam reached 1.6 million tons.

REFERENCE
Sovremennye metody sinteza monomerov dlia geterotsepnykh voloknoobrazuiushchikh polimerov. Sb. statei. Edited by I. L. Knuniants. Moscow, 1961. [11–1079–2]

CAPSIAN CULTURE, an archaeological culture of the late Upper Paleolithic and of the Mesolithic (ninth to fifth millennia B.C.) widespread in North Africa and Mediterranean countries. It was named after a site near the city of Gafsa (Capsa) in Tunisia. The people of the Capsian culture engaged in hunting and gathering. A distinctive feature of their settlements is huge heaps of shells mixed with animal bones. The most typical flint tools were geometric microliths, which served as inserts for composite tools, and arrowheads (bows and arrows appeared here somewhat earlier than in northern Europe). Fragments of vessels made from ostrich eggshells, often decorated, have also been found. The Capsians may have been the actual creators of the ancient rock paintings in North Africa and eastern Spain. The common cultural features of the Upper Paleolithic and Mesolithic populations of the Mediterranean countries are explained, evidently, not only by the similarity of geographic conditions, but also by the ties between the populations of these regions.

REFERENCES
Aliman, A. *Doistoricheskaia Afrika.* (Translated from French.) Moscow, 1960.
Zamiatnin, S. N. "O vozniknovenii lokal 'nykh razlichii v kul 'ture paleoliticheskogo perioda." In *Proiskhozhdenie cheloveka i drevnee rasselenie chelovechestva.* Moscow, 1951.
Wulsin, F. R. *The Prehistoric Archaeology of Northwest Africa.* Cambridge, 1941. [11–1080–2]

CAPSULATED MICROORGANISMS, bacteria, yeasts, and mold fungi whose cells are surrounded by a gelatinous capsule consisting chiefly of polysaccharides and protecting the cell against unfavorable external influences. *Azotobacter, Leuconostoc,* pneumococcus, and some kinds of asporogenous yeasts (such as *Torulopsis*) have thick capsules. The existence of capsules is determined by staining specimens or placing them in an india ink preparation; a light zone corresponding to the capsule can then be seen around capsulated microorganisms. Pathogenic capsulated microorganisms become avirulent when they lose their capacity to form capsules. [11–1084–2]

CAPSULE, in biology:
(1) In animals and man, the membrane surrounding various organs and their parts (for example, the kidney, liver, or joint capsules) and also pathological formations (parasites that have implanted themselves in tissue, necrotic masses, foreign bodies). A capsule is composed primarily of fibrous connective tissue and sometimes of adipose cellular tissue.
(2) The gelatinous layer around a cell characteristic of the capsulated bacteria, formed from macromolecular substances produced by these microorganisms [11–1083–4]

CAPSULE HYDROELECTRIC GENERATOR UNIT, a horizontal axial hydraulic generator unit with a rotary-blade hydroturbine, enclosed in a metal capsule housing. The first two capsule hydroelectric generator units, each with a rating of 195 kilowatts (kW), were made by the Swiss firm Escher Wyss in 1936 for the small Rózdzień Hydroelectric Power Plant in Poland.

The high efficiency of capsule hydroelectric generator units (greater capacity and smaller size in comparison with conventional vertical units; high power factors) results from the absence of any significant turns and twists of the flow and from the smoothness of the contours of the flow section of the generator unit. The capsule of such generator units may be on top, in the supply chamber, or on the bottom, in the suction pipe. The first type of arrangement is most commonly used. The generator of a capsule hydroelectric generator unit is sometimes connected to turbines through a step-up gear (usually a planetary booster) to increase its speed of rotation.

Capsule hydroelectric generator units are used in low-head hydroelectric power plants (with heads of 15–20 m), as reversible hydroelectric generator units at low-head pumped-storage hydroelectric power plants and at tidal electric power plants. In the USSR, for example, there are 20 17.5-MW capsule generator units in operation at the Kiev Hydroelectric Power-Plant. Capsule hydroelectric generator units are built with capacities up to 45 MW. Abroad, French firms have made the greatest progress in the development of capsule hydroelectric generator units.

REFERENCE
Bernshtein, L. B. *Opyt ekspluatatsii gorizontal'nykh osevykh gidroagregatov (kapsul'nykh i shakhtnykh).* Moscow-Leningrad, 1966.
M. F. KRASIL'NIKOV [11–1084–3]

CAPTAIN, an officer rank in the army of most states.
The rank (title) of captain appeared for the first time in France, where in the Middle Ages commanders of individual military districts were called captains. After 1558 company commanders were called captains, and higher commanders were called captain generals. In Russia the rank of captain appeared first in the 16th century as a title for foreign officers; in the 17th century it was applied to company commanders in the new type of regiments; in the early 18th century it was introduced throughout the whole regular Russian Army; in the cavalry (except in the dragoons) the rank of *rotmistr* corresponded to the rank of captain. From 1705 to 1798, there existed also the rank of lieutenant captain, which was later replaced by the rank of staff captain. In 1882 the rank of captain in the dragoon regiments and in the gendarmerie corps was replaced by the rank of *rotmistr*.

Captain is also an officer rank in the navies of most countries; some countries have the ranks of corvette captain, frigate captain, and captain of the ship. From the early 18th century the

Russian Navy had the following captain's ranks: commander (1707–32, 1751–64, and 1798–1827), captain of the ship (1701–13 and 1732–51), captain first and second class (1713–32 and 1751–1917), captain third class (1713–32), captain fourth class (1713–17), and lieutenant captain (1713–1884 and 1909–11).

In the Soviet armed forces in 1935 the military rank of captain was introduced in the ground forces and in the air force; in the same year the ranks of captain first, second, and third class and lieutenant captain were introduced in the navy.   [11–1060–1]

CAPUA, an ancient city in Campania, 4 km southeast of modern Capua.

Capua was founded in the sixth century B.C. by the Etruscans. After the Latin War of 340–338 B.C., it received from Rome the right to govern itself. At this time it occupied an important place in Italy in terms of wealth and prominence. In the first century B.C., the schools of gladiators at Capua were famous; Spartacus was a gladiator in one of them. In A.D. 456, the city was laid waste by the Vandals. From the beginning of the seventh century it was the center of one of the Lombard principalities making up Benevento. In 842 it was destroyed by the Arabs. A new city was built in 856. The modern city of Santa Maria Capua Vetere is located on the site of ancient Capua.   [11–1098–1]

CAPUANA, LUIGI. Born May 28, 1839, in Mineo, Catania Province, Sicily; died Nov. 29, 1915, in Catania. Italian critic and writer.

Capuana was a professor of Italian literature at the Pedagogic Institute in Rome and, from 1902, at the University of Catania. An adherent of the *verismo* literary movement, he expounded its theoretical program in *Essays on Modern Literature* (1879–82) and *On Art* (1885). Strongly influenced by French naturalism, Capuana insisted that Italian literature have a national character and originality. Capuana depicted Italian provincial life in his literary works: the collection of short stories *The Peasant Women* (1894) and the novel *The Marquis of Roccaverdina* (1901).

WORKS
In Russian translation:
[*Novelly.*] In the collection *Ital'ianskie novelly, 1860–1914.* Introduction by B. G. Reizov. Moscow-Leningrad, 1960.
REFERENCES
Madrignani, C. A. *Capuana e il naturalismo,* Bari, 1970.
Raya, G. *Bibliografia di L. Capuana (1839–1968).* Rome, 1969.
   [11–1088–1]

CAPUCHIN (*Cebus*), a genus of American prehensile-tailed monkey of the Cebidae family.

Capuchins have relatively large, round skulls, with a shortened facial section, moderately long limbs, and a well-developed thumb. The tail is long and covered with hair, and the final third is prehensile. Capuchins inhabit the lush tropical forests of Central and South America, living in trees, chiefly in groups of eight to 30 individuals. They feed on leaves, fruits, nuts, insects, bird eggs, and fledglings. There are several species. The white-throated capuchin (*C. capucinus*) has black fur on most of its body but yellowish-white fur on the forehead or throat and chest and shoulders, a body length of about 45 cm, and a tail of 40–50 cm. The brown capuchin (*C. apella*) has a black crest, a body length of 35–45 cm, and a tail of 38–48 cm. Capuchins are often kept in zoos, where they usually reproduce successfully.

REFERENCES
Weber, M. *Primaty.* Moscow-Leningrad, 1936. (Translated from German.)
Zhizn' zhivotnykh, vol. 6:*Mlekopitaiushchie.* Moscow, 1971.
   M. F. NESTURKH [11–1097–3]

CAPUCHINS, Catholic monastic order founded as a branch of the Franciscan order in 1525 in Italy.

The order received its name because of the pointed hood (*capuccio*) sewn to the cassock of coarse cloth that the monks wore. The founder of the Capuchins was the Franciscan monk Matteo da Bascio, who strove to restore the ascetic character of the early Franciscan communities. The rule of the Capuchins

was approved by Pope Clement VII in 1528 or 1529. They were confirmed as an independent order by Pope Paul V in 1619. During the 16th and 17th centuries the order spread throughout a number of countries in Western Europe. The Capuchins played a large role in the Counter-Reformation. Their primary goal was to strengthen the influence of Catholicism on the popular masses.

Even today the Capuchins remain a bastion of clericalism. By 1972 there were approximately 14,000 Capuchin monks; the order of Capuchinesses, founded in the 16th century, numbered about 2,500 nuns.   [11–1097–2]

CARABINEERS, select riflemen in the infantry and cavalry.

From the 15th century the light infantry and cavalry of the Basques and Gascons in Spain were called carabineers; the term was also used in France from the 16th century. From the 17th century carabineers were select riflemen. In the late 17th century in France and in the middle of the 18th century in Austria detachments and companies of carabineers were brought together into privileged military units, which existed until the 19th century. There were also carabineer units in Prussia in the 18th century. In Russia from 1763 to 1796 there were at various times from nine to nineteen cavalry regiments of carabineers, and from 1815 to 1857 there were from four to eight infantry carabineer regiments (analogous to the Jaegers). In Italy the carabineer troops (formed in 1814) fulfill the function of a gendarmerie.   [11–1102–4]

CARACAL, a city in Rumania, in Oltenia district. Population, 24,300 (1970). Railroad junction. The major industry is food-processing, chiefly fruit and vegetable canning.   [11–1126–1]

CARACAL (*Felis caracal*), a predatory mammal of the Felidae (cat) family. The body length reaches 85 cm, and the tail is about 25 cm; height at the shoulder is about 45 cm.

The caracal has tufts of hair on the tips of its ears and short fur that is sandy yellow on top and whitish underneath; the tufts and outer sides of the ears are black. It resembles the lynx in appearance. Caracals are distributed in the deserts and piedmonts of Africa and Asia. They are not common in the USSR, where they are found only in southern Turkmenia and occasionally in Uzbekistan. They feed on small mammals, such as pikas, susliks, jerboas, and rabbits, and birds; occasionally they will attack Persian gazelles. The caracal is a protected species in the USSR.

REFERENCE
Mlekopitaiushchie Sovetskogo Soiuza, vol. 2, part 2. Moscow, 1972.
   [11–1125–5]

CARACALLA (also Septimius Bassianus Caracalla; imperial name, Marcus Aurelius Antoninus). Born 186, in Lugdunum; died 217, near Edessa. Roman emperor from 211.

At first Caracalla ruled jointly with his brother Geta, but after murdering his brother in 212, he ruled alone. Gaining the loyalty of the soldiers by raising their pay and giving them rewards, he exerted pressure on the senatorial and municipal leaders. He instituted a reign of terror, during which there took place the execution of aristocrats and the famous jurist Papinian and the massacre of the inhabitants of Alexandria, who opposed a supplementary conscription into the army. In 212 he issued the *Constitutio Antoniniana,* an edict which granted citizenship to almost all the inhabitants of the provinces, making them equal to the Romans as subjects and taxpayers. In 213 he undertook a campaign against the Germanic tribes of the Chatti and Alamanni on the Rhine and then moved against the Iazyges and Carpi on the Danube. These were followed by a successful campaign into Parthia in 215. During a new Parthian campaign, in 217, he was killed by conspirators led by the Praetorian prefect Opellius Macrinus.   [11–1126–3]

CARACARA, the common name for birds of the subfamily Daptriinae, family Falconidae, order of diurnal birds of prey. In contrast to the true falcon, the caracara lacks a tooth on the upper beak and has naked cheeks and throat (sometimes sparsely covered with feathers). It has blunt wings, a long crop, and weak claws. It flies rather poorly but runs well; therefore it tends to stay on the ground.

Caracaras are insectivorous or omnivorous and frequently feed on carrion. They are found in America from the southern USA to Tierra del Fuego. There are four genera with nine species. The common caracara, or carancha (*Polyborus plancus*), is about 70 cm long; its back is dark brown with lighter cross stripes, and its head is crested. It lives in open level terrain and nests in bushes. It lays two to three eggs in a clutch, which are incubated for 28 days.   [11–1140–1]

CARACAS, the capital of Venezuela; an important political, commercial, financial, industrial, transportation, and cultural center of the country. It is situated in a mountain valley of the Caribbean Andes, 13–14 km from the coast of the Caribbean Sea, at an elevation 900–1,000 m. The climate is subequatorial and humid: Average January temperature is 18.6°C; average July temperature, 21.2°C; annual precipitation, 820 mm. In 1812 and 1900 the city was almost completely destroyed by earthquakes. Caracas and the adjacent area are set apart as the federal (capital) district. Area, 1,900 sq km. Population (including the suburbs within and outside the boundaries of the federal district), 2.2 million (1970). The city is administered by a governor appointed by the president; there is also a municipal council elected by the population.

The city was founded on St. Jacob's Day (July 25) in 1567 by the Spanish conquistador Diego de Losada, on the site of a burned-out settlement of the Caracas Indians. He named the city Santiago de Léon de Caracas. During the 16th and 17th centuries, it suffered attacks by pirates. In 1577 it became the residence of the Spanish governor; and in 1777, the capital of the captaincy general of Venezuela. The uprising in Caracas in April 1810 marked the beginning of the War of Independence of the Spanish-American Colonies (1810–26). During the war, Caracas was the site of the most fierce fighting between the patriots and the Spanish. Caracas became the capital of Venezuela after the disintegration of Gran Colombia in 1830 and the formation of the republic of Venezuela. After World War II (1939–45), Caracas was Venezuela's most important center for the worker and student movement.

Among Caracas' industries are those engaged in the production of processed foods, textiles, clothing, leather footwear, chemicals, petrochemicals, pharmaceuticals, rubber goods, glassware, paper, cement, and metal goods. Motor vehicles and other types of machinery are assembled. Offices of the major national and foreign banks, industrial concerns, and commercial companies are located in Caracas. The city is linked by railroads and highways to the port of La Guaira, the Maiquetía International Airport, and the cities of Maracay and Valencia. The Pan American Highway connects Caracas with Bogotá (Colombia); in the southeast, there is a highway leading to Ciudad Bolívar.

Since colonial times, the city has had a regular street plan. A cathedral (original structure, 1664–74, architect P. de Medina) stands in the central square, Plaza Bolívar. In 1936 the reconstruction of old thoroughfares and the building of new ones was undertaken. Imposing complexes of public and commercial buildings have also been constructed; these include the Centro Social Simon Bolívar (1938, architect S. Domínguez), university city (begun in 1944, architect C. R. Villanueva), Avenue Bolívar with the two skyscrapers, Torres del Silensio, and the Plaza Venezuela with the skyscraper Edificio Polar (1952–54, architects J. M. Galia and M. Vegas Pacheco). Residential complexes include Cerro Grande, El Paraiso, and Cerro Belen. The Museum of Fine Arts (architect O. Niemeyer), the National Pantheon, and the Capitolia are among the public buildings constructed in the mid-20th century. Sections of slums remain.

Caracas is the site of the Central University of Venezuela, two private universities (Santa Maria University and the Catholic University of Andrés Bello), eight colleges of music and art, the National Pedagogical Institute, and the Higher School of Medicine. Its academies include the Academy of Venezuela, the National Academy of History, the National Academy of Medicine, the Academy of Political and Social Sciences, and the Academy of Physical, Mathematical, and Natural Science. There are other scientific research institutions and several international societies, including the Institute of Experimental Medicine. The city is also the site of the National Library, the Central University Library, and various academy libraries. Museums include the Bolívar Museum, Bolivar's House, the Museum of Fine Arts, the Collection of Venezuelan Birds, the Museum of Natural Sciences, and the Museum of Colonial Art.

Among the city's theaters and theatrical concert halls (used also to show films) are Aténeo, Teatro Alberto de Paz, Tilingo, Florida, Urdaneta, Caribe, Lido, Aula Manga, Teatro Nacional, Teatro Municipal, Concha Acústica (an open amphitheater), and the Puppet Theater. The companies performing in these theaters include Universitario, Compás, Mascaras, Teatro del Duende, Leonsio Martínez, Teatro de Bolsillo, and the troupe directed by R. Antilano. Music schools include the Padre Sojo Academy of Music and the Fischer Academy of Music.

REFERENCES
Venesuela: Ekonomika, politika, kul'tura. Moscow, 1967.
Stolitsy stranmira. Moscow, 1966.
Villanueva, C. R. *Caracas de ayer y de hoy.* Caracas [1943].
                                                            [11–1140–2]

CARADOCIAN STAGE (named after the Silurian king Caradoc), the fifth stage (of six) from the bottom of the Ordovician system. Established by the British scientist R. Murchison in Wales (1839).

The Caradocian stage is represented by sandstones and argillites with limestone lenses. According to present-day divisioning, the Caradocian stage includes five graptolite zones from *Nemagraptus gracilis* to *Pleurograptus linearis*, which constitute the middle and upper divisions of the Ordovician system. The deposits of the Caradocian stage are widely distributed in the northwestern part of the Eastern European Platform, in Kazakhstan, Middle Siberia, and the northeastern part of the USSR. They have been found everywhere in the countries of Western Europe, in Burma, the Chinese People's Republic, Australia, North Africa, and America. In the Estonian SSR and Leningrad Oblast, oil shale deposits are found in the lower part of the Caradocian stage.   [11–1123–1]

CARAGEA, BORIS. Born Jan. 11, 1906, in Balchik, Bulgaria. Rumanian sculptor. Honored Artist of the Socialist Republic of Rumania, or SRR (1951). Corresponding member of the Academy of the SRR.

Caragea graduated from the School of Fine Arts in Bucharest in 1932. He is a professor at the Institute of Fine Arts in Bucharest. He created monuments to the Soviet soldier-liberator in Iași (1947) and to V. I. Lenin in Bucharest (1960)—both in bronze. He also created easel sculptures (*The Meeting,* 1950; *Victory,* 1957; both in bronze, Museum of Arts of the SRR, Bucharest). Caragea has been awarded the State Prize of the SRR (1950 and 1953).   [11–1121–3]

CARAGIALE, ION LUCA. Born Jan. 30, 1852, in Haimanale, now Caragiale; died June 9, 1912, in Berlin. Rumanian writer and playwright. Academician of the Academy of the Rumanian Socialist Republic (elected posthumously). Son of a minor official.

Caragiale studied at the Ploești *Gymnasium* but left in the fourth year and enrolled in courses of mime and recitation at the Bucharest conservatory (1868–70). During the 1880's he had close ties with representatives of the incipient socialist movement, C. Dobrogeanu-Gherea and A. Bacalbaşa. A democratic *raznochinets* (member of a class other than the nobility), Caragiale denounced contemporary society. In the comedy *Stormy Night* (1878), he satirized the successful bourgeoisie, with its proprietary attitudes and sham liberalism and patriotism. The one-act comedy *Mr. Leonida Face to Face With Reaction* (1879) was directed against political philistinism. The comedy *The Lost Letter* (1884) was a biting satire on the political system of bourgeois-landowner Rumania. The comedy *Carnival* (1885) ridiculed the triviality of the petite bourgeoisie. In Caragiale's essays, short stories, and satirical articles which appeared in the collections *Notes and Stories* (1892), *Light Stories* (1896), *Short*

Stories (1897), and *Moments* (1901), he condemned the reality of Rumanian politics with caustic irony. A campaign of persecution and slander was organized against Caragiale by reactionary circles, and in 1904 he moved to Berlin. In 1907 he responded to the peasant uprising enveloping Rumania with the article "1907: From the Spring to the Fall," in which he supported the just demands of the insurgents, stigmatized the ruling parties who were responsible for the tragic situation of the people, and insisted on the implementation of fundamental democratic reforms. Caragiale's work served the progressive forces of Rumania in their struggle for freedom and exerted considerable influence on the development of Rumanian literature. The Bucharest National Theater was named after Caragiale.

WORKS

Teatru. Bucharest, 1889.
Opere, vols. 1–7. Bucharest, 1930–42.
Opere, vols. 1–3—. Bucharest, 1959–62—.
In Russian translation:
Izbrannoe. Preface by I. Konstantinovskii. Moscow, 1953.
Momenty i ocherki. Bucharest, 1962.
Komedii, iumoreski, rasskazy. Moscow, 1963.

REFERENCES

Chezza, L. *Tvorchestvo I. Karadzhale.* Kishinev, 1961.
Sadovnik, Sh. P. *I. L. Karadzhale.* Leningrad-Moscow, 1964.
Konstantinovskii, I. *Karadzhale.* Moscow, 1970.
Ion Luka Karadzhale (bio-bibliografiia). Moscow, 1952.
Studii și conferințe cu prilejul centenarului I. L. Caragiale. Bucharest, 1952.
Alexandrescu, Ș. *Caragiale în timpul nostru.* [Bucharest, 1963.]
Cazimir, Ș. *Caragiale: Universul comic.* [Bucharest] 1967.
Elvin, B. *Modernitatea clasicului I. L. Caragiale.* [Bucharest] 1967.

SH. P. SADOVNIK [11–1121–5]

CARAMANLIS, CONSTANTINE (Konstantinos Karamanlis). Born Feb. 23, 1907, in the city of Proti. Greek statesman and politician.

By training, Caramanlis is a lawyer. In 1935–36 and again in 1946, he was elected to parliament from the Populist (monarchist) Party. Between 1946 and 1955 he occupied a number of ministerial posts. In August 1951 he joined the Greek Rally, the party of the big industrial and financial bourgeoisie. In January 1956 he reorganized the National Rally as the National Radical Union. During the years 1955–58, 1958–61, and 1961–63, Caramanlis was prime minister of Greece. The domestic policy of his government was noted for the suppression of democratic freedoms and the persecution of progressive forces. Under his rule Greece became more dependent economically and politically on the USA and further subordinated to the interests of NATO. Under pressure from the masses, Caramanlis resigned in June 1963 and emigrated to France.

When the military dictatorship collapsed in July 1974, Caramanlis became prime minister in the interim government. In September 1974 he reconstituted the National Radical Union as the New Democracy Party, with himself as leader of the party. On Nov. 21, 1974, Caramanlis became prime minister of the reorganized Greek government. [11–1156–5]

CARAMEL, a confectionery product of sugar. Caramel is a concentrated nutritional food product that contains a complex of sugars (sucrose, maltose, and glucose) and fruits, berries, nut kernels, cocoa, and other ingredients.

There are hard and filled caramels. The hard caramel consists of a caramel mass obtained by boiling down a sugar solution with starch syrup or invert syrup to a dry-matter content of 97–99 percent. In contrast to sugar, from which it is prepared, the cooled caramel mass has an amorphous structure, is transparent, and is light yellow in color. Within a certain temperature range (75°–90°C) the caramel mass has a plastic texture. To impart flavor properties to the hard caramel, food acids (citric and tartaric), essences, and colorings are added and evenly distributed throughout the plastic caramel mass before it is shaped. Transparent caramel is shaped in the form of rectangular bars (such as Teatral'naia and Vzletnaia) or in the form of small figures of various shapes (sour drops). In manufacturing nontransparent caramel (lemon and orange slices), the caramel mass

is processed on pulling machines to saturate it with air. After shaping, the caramel is cooled, whereupon it hardens and acquires the brittleness and firmness necessary for subsequent wrapping and packing or finishing. In preparing filled caramel, the caramel mass is used to make only the outer casing, and before shaping a filling is introduced (such as fruit or berry, liqueur, honey, and milk).

Caramel is hygroscopic and to maintain its stability during storage it is covered with a protective layer of finely granulated sugar, cocoa powder, chocolate glaze, or a moisture-resistant high-fat mixture and wrapped or packaged in tins or waxed cardboard boxes. Caramel manufacture in the USSR is completely mechanized. [11–1157–1]

CARANTANIA (Karantanija), early feudal state of the Slovenes in the Mura River basin and upper reaches of the Drava River during the seventh to 11th centuries.

Carantania was formed as an independent state after the collapse of the state of Samo (658). In about the year 745, it came under the protection of the duke of Bavaria. Between 788 and 820, it was a vassal principality of the Frankish state. After 820, Carantania became part of the Frankish state. With the collapse of the latter, Carantania was incorporated into the East Frankish kingdom. In 976, Emperor Otto II created the duchy of Greater Carantania out of Carantania and a number of marches or feudal principalities where the Slavic population was predominant, including the Carantanian and Podravian. In the early 11th century, Greater Carantania broke up into a number of feudal possessions, including Carinthia, Carniola, and the Carinthian march (later called Styria).

REFERENCE

Grafenauer, B. *Ustoličevanje koroških vojvod in država karantanskih Slovencev.* Ljubljana, 1952. [11–1164–2]

CARAȘ-SEVERIN, an administrative district in southwest Rumania, in the Banat Mountains. Area, 8,500 sq km. Population, 366,300 (1970). Administrative center, Reșița. The district accounts for 2.7 percent of the total industrial production and 1.1 percent of the agricultural output of the country. Industry includes heavy metallurgy and machine building (Reșița, Oțelul-Roșu, Bocșa), woodworking (Caransebeș), and food processing. Iron ore (Ocna-de-Fier and copper ore (Moldova-Nouă) are also mined. The leading agricultural crops include corn, wheat, potatoes, and curly flax. There are numerous orchards in the foothills of the mountains. Livestock in Caraș-Severin numbered (1971) approximately 84,000 cattle, 35,000 hogs, and 269,000 sheep. The balneological health resort of Băile-Herculane, whose springs were used by the ancient Romans, is located 40 km north of Turnu-Severin. [11–1192–2]

CARASSIUS, a genus of fish of the family Cyprinidae. There are two species—the golden, or common, crucian carp (*Carassius carassius*) and the silver crucian carp (*C. auratus*). The golden crucian carp is found in Eastern and Western Europe, as well as in Asia (as far east as the Lena River). The dorsal fin is long, and the pharyngeal teeth are uniserial. The body, which is vertically compressed, is dark brown with golden tones on the sides. The paired fins and anal fins are usually reddish. Species of this genus reach a length of 45 cm and a weight of 3 kg. The golden crucian carp lives in bodies of water that are overgrown with marshes, in enclosed lakes, and, less frequently, in rivers with sluggish currents. When the water freezes over or dries up, the fish burrow into the mud to depths reaching 70 cm. Thus, they survive cold winters and hot summers. Golden and silver crucian carps reach sexual maturity at three or four years of age. Spawning occurs in the spring; fecundity reaches 300,000 eggs. The eggs are deposited in clusters on benthic vegetation. The golden crucian carp feeds on vegetation, zooplankton, zoobenthos, and detritus.

The silver crucian carp is found in the basin of the Pacific Ocean, throughout Siberia, and in the lower reaches of the rivers in the Aral Basin in the European USSR. It has two subspecies: *C. auratus auratus* and *C. a. gibelio.* Their silver body measures up to 45 cm long and weighs more than 1 kg. A domesticated variety of the genus *Carassius* is the goldfish.

Female silver crucian carps sometimes live in bodies of water without their male counterparts. Under these conditions, they crossbreed with other fishes, such as golden crucian carps and domesticated carps. The fishes of the genus *Carassius* are commercially valuable and are raised and bred in ponds.

A. A. SVETOVIDOVA [11–1170–3]

CARAT, a unit of weight, abbreviated *kar.* in Russian and ct internationally, which is used in the jewelry trade for measuring the weight of precious stones and pearls. The carat is used in a number of countries to indicate the purity of precious metal alloys. The metric carat, which was established by the fourth General Conference on Weights and Measures (Paris, 1907) and adopted in the USSR in 1922, is equivalent to 200 mg (exactly) or 2×10^{-4} kg.

[11–1172–2]

CARATHÉODORY, CONSTANTIN. Born Sept. 13, 1873, in Berlin; died Feb. 2, 1950, in Munich. German mathematician.

Carathéodory graduated from the Belgian Military Academy in 1895 and studied mathematics in Berlin and Göttingen. He became a professor of the university in Munich in 1924. Carathéodory is the author of works on the theory of conformal mappings, the general theory of set measure, and a new formulation of the theory of the field of extremals (in the calculus of variations). In 1909 he gave a logically precise axiomatic formulation of the laws of thermodynamics.

WORKS

Gesammelte mathematische Schriften, vol. 2. Munich [1955].
Funktionentheorie, vols. 1–2. Basel, 1950.
In Russian translation:
Konformnoe otobrazhenie. Moscow-Leningrad, 1934.   [11–1174–2]

CARAVAGGIO, MICHELANGELO MERISI DA. Born Sept. 28, 1573, in Caravaggio, in Lombardy; died July 18, 1610, in Port' Ercole, in Tuscany. Italian painter.

Caravaggio initiated the realist direction in 17th-century European painting. He studied under S. Peterzano in Milan from 1584 to 1588. He went to Rome between 1589 and 1593 and worked there until 1606. Caravaggio subsequently worked in Naples (1607 and 1609–10), on the island of Malta, and in Sicily (1608–09). His work, which does not belong to any definite artistic school, was a reaction against the dominant directions in Italian art during the late 16th and the early 17th centuries—mannerism and academicism.

Caravaggio's early works (1592–98) are characterized by resonant color and subtle chiaroscuro. They reflect the traditions of 16th-century Northern Italian painting (for example, the work of G. Savoldo, L. Lotto, and A. Moretto). At the same time, these early works exhibited a number of essentially new elements. Caravaggio rejected idealized images and allegorical interpretations of themes, turning to individualistically expressive images (*Sick Bacchus,* Borghese Gallery, Rome) and a straightforward study of nature in simple surroundings (*Boy With a Basket of Fruit,* Borghese Gallery, Rome).

Disputing the artistic conceptions of mannerism and academicism, Caravaggio introduced playful and festive folk elements into a classical framework (*Bacchus,* 1592–93, Uffizi Gallery, Florence). He repudiated the prevailing systems of genres and contributed to the creation of new kinds of painting—the still life (*Basket of Fruit,* c. 1596, Pinacoteca Ambrosiana, Milan) and the genre painting (*Fortune Teller,* Louvre, Paris). Caravaggio interpreted religious themes in an innovative intimately psychological manner (*Rest on the Flight Into Egypt,* Galleria Doria-Pamphili, Rome).

In the late 1590's, Caravaggio developed an original stylistic device. He illuminated the painting's foreground with a bright shaft of light, setting it off against a background submerged in profound shadow. The figures in the foreground appear salient, and an impression of intimacy between the picture and the viewer is created (*The Lute Player,* Hermitage, Leningrad).

Caravaggio's mature works (1599–1606) are compositionally complex and exceptionally dramatic. They are characterized by powerful contrasts of light and shadow, an expressive simplicity of gesture, energetic modeling, and resonant, rich colors. These elements reflect the emotional tension that arises during unexpected lofty and ideal occurrences in the ordinary life of people and during moments of man's intellectual opposition to a hostile environment. Among Caravaggio's mature works are *The Calling of St. Matthew* and *The Martyrdom of St. Matthew* (1599–1600, Church of San Luigi dei Francesi, Rome), *The Crucifixion of St. Peter* and *The Conversion of St. Paul* (1600–01, Santa Maria del Popolo, Rome), *Madonna di Loreto* (c. 1603–06, Church of Sant' Agostino, Rome), *The Deposition of Christ* (1602–04, Pinacoteca, Vatican), and *Death of the Virgin* (c. 1605–06, Louvre, Paris). The artist's portrayal of earthy human types and his resolute affirmation of democratic ideals in painting aroused the bitter opposition of the supporters of official art. A number of his works were rejected by his clients.

From 1606 to 1610, Caravaggio wandered throughout Southern Italy. His late works, which date from this period, reflect the artist's further development of realist tendencies and his broadening grasp of life's phenomena (*Seven Works of Mercy,* 1607, Church of Pio Monte della Misericordia, Naples). Caravaggio also expressed a deepened sense of the tragedy of life in his late works. Along with notes of sorrowful estrangement, these paintings reflect a spirit of lofty stoicism (*The Beheading of John the Baptist,* 1609, Cathedral of San Giovanni, Valletta; *The Burial of St. Lucy,* 1608, Church of Santa Lucia, Syracuse). Caravaggio dealt with the theme of man's loneliness in a vast world. He was attracted to the image of a closely knit human collective, united by an atmosphere of kinship and spiritual warmth. In Caravaggio's late works, the light is soft and flickering, and the color palette tends toward tonal unity (*The Adoration of the Shepherds,* 1609, National Museum, Messina). Caravaggio's technique in these works is characterized by free improvisation.

The innovative art of Caravaggio was imitated by artists in Italy and other European countries. It greatly influenced the development of realist currents in many European schools of art.

REFERENCES

Znamerovskaia, T. *Mikel'andzhelo da Karavadzho.* Moscow, 1955.
[Vsevolozhskaia, S.] *Mikel'andzhelo da Karavadzho.* Moscow, 1960.
Vipper, B. R. *Problema realizma v ital'ianskoi zhivopisi XVII–XVIII vekov.* Moscow, 1966. Pages 34–54.
Venturi, L. *Il Caravaggio.* Novara, 1951.
Joffroy, B. *Le Dossier Caravage.* [Paris, 1959.]
Jullian, R. *Le Caravage.* Lyon-Paris, 1961.
L'opera completa del Caravaggio. Milan, 1967.
Longhi, R. *Caravaggio.* Dresden [1968].
Friedlaender, W. *Caravaggio Studies,* 2nd ed. New York [1969].

M. I. SVIDERSKAIA [11–1104–3]

CARAVAGGISM. (1) A group of artistic devices, characteristic of 17th-century European realist painting, during its initial stage. These devices were particularly expressed in the work of the Italian painter Caravaggio, who championed democratic artistic ideals and was interested in the direct reproduction of nature in painting. He was particularly sensitive to the objective reality of a representation. In his works, Caravaggio emphasized contrasts of light and shadow and sought to impart grandeur to genre motifs. The adoption of Caravaggio's methods was an important step in the creative development of many of the prominent artists of the 17th century, including P. P. Rubens and Rembrandt. However, in many cases, this development was not a direct result of the influence of Caravaggio and his followers F. Ribalta, D. Velasquez, and Georges de La Tour.

(2) A trend in 17th-century European painting, represented by the followers of Caravaggio. In Italy, Caravaggio continued to be influential until the end of the 17th century. Caravaggism penetrated every important artistic center and was particularly evident in the painting in Rome, Genoa, and Naples. The legacy of Caravaggio received its most original and independent interpretation in the work of O. Borgianni, O. Gentileschi, C. Saraceni, and G. B. Caracciolo. Caravaggism was expressed as a superficial borrowing of formal methods and devices in the work of a number of painters, including L. Spada and B. Manfredi.

The most important representatives of Caravaggism outside of Italy included H. Terbrugghen, G. van Honthorst, and D. van Baburen in Holland; T. Rombouts and A. Janssens in Flanders; Valentin de Boullogne and S. Vouet in France; J. Ribera in Spain; and A. Elsheimer in Germany.

REFERENCES

Vipper, B. R. *Problema realizma v ital'ianskoi zhivopisi XVII–XVIII vekov.* Moscow, 1966. Pages 55–81.

Schneider, A. von. *Caravaggio und die Niederlander.* Marburg, 1933.

Catalogo della mostra del Caravaggio e dei caravaggeschi. Milan, 1951.

Moir, A. *The Italian Followers of Caravaggio.* Cambridge (Mass.), 1967.

M. I. SVIDERSKAIA [11–1104–3]

CARAVANSARY, an inn and trading post for caravans along the roads in the cities of Southwest Asia, Middle Asia, and Transcaucasia. Caravansaries, which have been known since antiquity, were widespread during the ninth through 18th centuries as cities grew and the caravan trade intensified.

Two types are most common: the hall caravansary and the caravansary with an inner court. The hall caravansaries, seen in Armenia, are retangular buildings divided into naves. The middle nave is designed for men and goods; the animals are kept in the side naves. The other type has small buildings of one or a few stories, where travelers stay with their merchandise; the buildings open on an enclosed court, where the animals are kept. Roadside caravansaries were fortified with protective walls or else were attached to inns or fortresses (*rabats* and *khans*). The development of railroads and other modern type of transport have brought about a decline in the importance of caravansaries on transit roads. [11–1109–1]

CARAVAQUE, LOUIS. Born at the end of the 17th century; died June 9 (20) or 15 (26), 1754, in St. Petersburg. French painter.

From 1716, Caravaque lived in Russia. He worked from 1718 in the government Bureau of Construction, where he had Russian pupils. He painted decorated ceilings and panels (not preserved), battle scenes (*The Battle of Poltava,* 1717, Hermitage, Leningrad), and numerous portraits in the baroque style, which were uninspiredly drawn but bright in color (*Portrait of Empress Anna Ivanovna,* 1730, Tret'iakov Gallery, Moscow). Caravaque's works had some influence on Russian portrait painting of the mid-18th century. [11–1108–1]

CARAVEL, a sailing ship with high sides, one deck, three or four masts, and high superstructures at the bow and stern.

Caravels were widely used by Mediterranean countries from the 13th through the 17th century (first by Italy and then by Spain and Portugal). From the 15th century caravels were used for ocean voyages; in 1492 a caravel flotilla under the command of Columbus crossed the Atlantic Ocean, and in 1498, Vasco da Gama sailed from Europe to India in a caravel. [11–1109–2]

CARBAMIDE GLUE, a glue based on urea-formaldehyde and melamine-formaldehyde resins ("carbamide resins") and their mixtures. Large quantities of carbamide glue are used in the wood-product industry, primarily for the manufacture of plywood and furniture; it is also used to join porcelain and metal.

Carbamide glue is an aqueous solution of carbamide resin. It frequently contains a hardener (oxalic, phthalic, or hydrochloric acids or certain salts) and a filler (soybean or cereal flour, starch, wood flour, or gypsum). For example, K-17 glue consists of 100 parts MF-17 resin, 7–22 parts 10-percent aqueous oxalic acid solution, and 6–8 parts wood flour (by weight).

Carbamide glue is prepared by mixing a resin solution with other glue ingredients to form a composition. The glue is sometimes produced in the form of a foamed mass. The shelf life of carbamide glue varies from 0.5 to 48 hr, depending on type. Carbamide glue without a hardener has a shelf life largely dependent on the temperature conditions. MMF glue can be stored for 12 months at 10°C and for only 0.5 months at 40°C. The addition of ammonia liquor, urotropin, urea, or melamine doubles the shelf life of carbamide glue.

Carbamide glue can harden upon heating, as well as during storage at ordinary temperatures (only in the presence of a hardener). The surface to be glued is prepared according to general procedure before application of carbamide glue. The glue is usually applied with a brush, whereas low-viscosity compositions are sprayed on; the glue is allowed to dry slightly (sometimes the drying is omitted), and then the components to be glued are joined at a pressure of 0.15–1.7 meganewtons per sq m (MN/m^2), or 1.5–17.0 kilograms-force per sq cm (kgf/cm^2). During application of hot-setting carbamide glue, the components are heated in a press.

Carbamide glue forms adhesive compounds with good mechanical strength (10–13 MN/m^2, or 100–130 kgf/cm^2) and satisfactory moisture resistance. Glues based on melamine-formaldehyde resin have better properties than those based on urea-formaldehyde resin; however, the latter is considerably less expensive. As a result, urea-formaldehyde resin is frequently mixed with a small quantity of melamine-formaldehyde resin to significantly improve the quality of the glue. [11–1194–5]

CARBAMIDE RESINS, the polycondensation products of formaldehyde and urea (carbamide) and its derivatives—thiourea, dicyandiamide, and melamine.

Carbamide resins—urea-formaldehyde resin and melamine-formaldehyde resin, in particular—are important in the manufacture of thermosetting plastics and glues. [11–1194–4]

CARBANIONS, molecular particles that contain a negatively charged tricovalent carbon atom:

$$>\!C^-$$

Carbanions are highly reactive and are therefore unstable; they occur as intermediate particles in many organic reactions. For example, they form upon action of strong bases B: (the dots indicate an unshared electron pair) on hydrocarbons, from which any hydrogen atom is readily liberated as a proton:

$$>\!C\!-\!H \ + \ :B \ \rightleftharpoons \ >\!C^- \ + \ H\!:\!B$$

Thus, sodium trityl, a bright red compound of ionic structure that contains a trityl anion, is formed upon the action of sodium amide on triphenyl methane:

$$(C_6H_5)_3CH \ + \ Na^+NH_2^- \longrightarrow (C_6H_5)_3C^-Na^+ \ + \ NH_3$$

This carbanion is stable because of the distribution of the negative charge among several carbon atoms.

Most organometallic compounds have a covalent structure; however, because of polarization of the metal-carbon bond, excess electron density appears in the carbon atom bonded to the metal:

$$\overset{\delta^-}{H_3C}\!\frown\!\overset{\delta^+}{MgBr}$$

This atom is partially carbanionic; therefore, organometallic compounds serve as carbanion donors.

Ylides, which are bipolar ions that contain a positively charged heteroatom (N, P, As, O, or S) and a negatively charged carbon atom, are a special type of carbanion. An example is pyridine fluorenylylide:

The existence of carbanions as kinetically independent particles has been rigorously proved in a few cases, but the concept of their intermediate formation is frequently used to interpret the mechanism of organic reactions, many of which have great theoretical and practical value (for example, anionic polymerization).

REFERENCES

Cram, D. *Osnovy khimii karbanionov.* Moscow, 1967. (Translated from English.)

Breslow, R. *Mekhanizmy organicheskikh reaktsii.* Moscow, 1968. (Translated from English.) B. L. DIATKIN [11-1195-1]

CARBAZOLE, dibenzopyrrole, a heterocyclic compound; colorless crystals that are insoluble in water and soluble in organic solvents. Melting point, 245°–247°C; boiling point, 354°–355°C. It is a weak base, forming unstable salts and acids.

Carbazole is extracted from coal tar (from anthracene oil) and is also prepared synthetically from aminodiphenyl and phenanthrene. It is used in the manufacture of dyes, pharmaceuticals, and insecticides. [11-1194-1]

CARBENES, unstable organic compounds containing an electrically neutral divalent carbon atom $R'R''C$: (the dots denote two electrons); they are intermediate particles in many organic reactions. The simplest carbene, methylene, $:CH_2$, is formed in thermal or photochemical dissociation of diazomethane or ketene:

$$CH_2N_2 \longrightarrow :CH_2 + N_2$$

Other carbenes may be produced analogously. Dihalocarbenes form during thermal dissociation of alkali salts of trihaloacetic acids:

$$CCl_3COONa \longrightarrow :CCl_2 + NaCl + CO_2$$

Various methods are used for stabilizing carbenes, depending on the conditions of generation and the nature of the compounds interacting with the carbenes. For example, the following can occur: (1) dimerization of carbenes, $:CH_2 + :CH_2 \longrightarrow CH_2=CH_2$; (2) intrusion of carbenes through the carbon-hydrogen bond (for example, into hydrocarbons), $R—H + :CH_2 \longrightarrow R—CH_3$; or (3) combination of carbenes by a multiple bond (for example, ethylene), with the formation of a three-member ring,

$$CH_2=CH_2 + :CH_2 \longrightarrow \begin{array}{c} CH_2—CH_2 \\ \diagdown \diagup \\ CH_2 \end{array}$$

The last reaction is widely used in the synthesis of various three-member cyclic compounds.

REFERENCE

Knuniants, I. L., N. P. Gambarian, and E. M. Rokhlin. "Karbeny." *Uspekhi khimii,* 1958, vol. 27, issue 12, p. 1361.

B. L. DIATKIN [11-1196-1]

CARBIDES, compounds of carbon and electropositive elements, primarily metals and certain nonmetals. Carbides can be subdivided into three main groups according to the type of chemical bond: ionic (or saltlike), covalent, and metallic. Certain carbides belong to the group of nonstoichiometric compounds, which are solid substances of variable composition that do not conform to the laws of stoichiometry.

Ionic carbides. Ionic carbides are formed by strongly electropositive metals; they contain metal cations and carbon anions. The group includes acetylenides with $[C\equiv C]^{2-}$ anions, which can be represented as products of the substitution of metals for hydrogen in acetylene, C_2H_2, and as methanides (products of the substitution of metals for hydrogen in methane, CH_4). The carbides of alkaline metals (LiC_2 and Na_2C_2), magnesium (MgC_2), and alkaline-earth metals (CaC_2 and SrC_2), and higher carbides of rare earths (YC_2 and LaC_2) and actinides (ThC_2) are acetylenides. As the ionization potential of the metal in this group decreases, there is an increase in the tendency to form "polycarbides" with complex anions from carbon atoms

Table 1. Properties of some ionic carbides

	Crystal structure	Density (g/cm³)	Melting point (°C)	Heat of formation (kcal/mole)*	Specific volume resistance (μohm·cm)
Li_2C_2 ...	rhombic	1.30	—	14.2	—
Na_2C_2 ...	hexagonal	1.60	800 (decomposition)	−4.1	—
K_2C_2 ...	hexagonal	1.62	—	—	—
MgC_2 ...	tetragonal	2.07	—	21 ± 5	—
CaC_2 ...	tetragonal	2.21	2300	14.1 ± 2.0	—
BaC_2 ...	tetragonal	3.72	2000 (decomposition)	12.1 ± 4.0	—
LaC_2 ...	tetragonal	5.25	2360	38.0	45
CeC_2 ...	tetragonal	5.56	2290	—	60
Be_2C ...	cubic	2.44	2400	28.0	1.1×10^6
Al_4C_3 ...	rhombohedral	2.95	2100	49.5	—

*1 kcal/mole = 4.19 kJ/mole

(MeC_8, MeC_{16}, and MeC_{24}). These carbides have a graphite-like lattice, in which the metal atoms are arranged between layers of carbon atoms. Upon reaction with water or dilute acids, ionic carbides of the acetylenide type—such as calcium carbide—decompose with evolution of acetylene (or acetylene mixed with other hydrocarbons and sometimes with hydrogen). The carbides Cu_2C_2 and Ag_2C_2 explode on impact, have low chemical stability, decompose readily, and oxidize upon heating. The carbides Be_2C and Al_4C_3, which hydrolyze readily, with liberation of methane (see Table 1), belong to the methanide group.

Covalent carbides. Covalent carbides, typical examples of which are silicon carbide, SiC, and boron carbide, B_4C (more correctly $B_{12}C_3$), are distinguished by the strength of their interatomic bonds. They exhibit a high degree of hardness, chemical inertness, and heat resistance and are semiconductors. The structure of certain covalent carbides, such as SiC, is similar to that of diamond. Their crystal lattices are giant molecules.

Metallic carbides. Metallic carbides are usually constructed as interstitial phases of carbon atoms in cavities of the crystal lattices of transition metals. The nature of these carbides, as interstitial phases, determines their great hardness and wear resistance, the near absence of plasticity at ordinary temperatures, their brittleness, and the low level of other similar mechanical properties. The carbides of this group are good electric conductors (hence the name "metallic"). Many of them are superconductors (the temperatures of transition into the superconductor state are as follows: Nb_2C, 9.18°K; NbC, 8°–10°K; Mo_2C, 12.2°K; MoC, 6.5°K). The cross alloys of carbides TiC, ZrC, HfC, NbC, and TaC have properties that are valuable in technology. For example, compositions of 25 percent HfC and 75 percent TaC have the highest melting point (approximately 4000°C) of all refractory metals and substances. Metallic carbides have high chemical stability in acids and lower stability in alkalies. They form hydrocarbides, oxycarbides, and carbonitrides upon interaction with H_2, O_2, and N_2, which are also interstitial phases and have properties similar to those of carbides. Compounds of more complex structure, such as Mn_3C, Fe_3C, Co_3C, and Ni_3C (see Table 2), also belong to the metallic carbides.

Preparation and use. The most common methods used in the preparation of carbides include heating of mixtures of metal and carbon powders in an inert gas or reduced gas medium and fusion of metals, with simultaneous carbidization (MeO + C $\longrightarrow$ MeC + CO) at temperatures of 1500°–2000°C. Methods used to manufacture products from carbide powders include powder metallurgy, decanting of molten carbides (usually under pressure in a gaseous medium to prevent decomposition at high temperatures), diffusion carburizing of products previously prepared from metals and nonmetals, precipitation as a result of a reaction in the gaseous phase (in particular during the production of carbide fibers), and plasma metallurgy. The mechanical methods generally used to process products made of metallic carbides and high-strength carbide-metal alloys have proved unsuitable and are being replaced by abrasive and ultrasonic processing and electric-spark techniques.

Among the ionic carbides, calcium carbide is important in technology as a valuable source of acetylene. Covalent and me-

Table 2. Properties of some metallic and covalent carbides

	Boundaries of region of homogeneity (atomic % C)	Crystal structure	Density (g/cm^3)	Melting point $(°C)$	Heat of formation $(kcal/mole)^a$	Coefficient of thermal expansion $(20°–1800°C)$ $(1/1°C) \times 10^6$	Thermal conductivity $(cal/cm \cdot sec \cdot °C)^b$	Specific volume resistance $(\mu ohm \cdot cm)$	Electron work function^c ϕ_{eff} (eV)	Microhardness (GN/m^2)	Elastic modulus (GN/m^2)
TiC	37–50	cubic face-centered	4.94	3150	43.9	8.5	0.069	52.5	4.20	31	460
ZrC	38–50	same	6.60	3420	47.7	6.95	0.09	50	4.02	29	550
HfC	36–50	same	12.65	3700	55.0	6.06	0.07	45	3.95	28.5	359
VC	40–47	same	5.50	2850	24.1	7.2	0.094	76	4.07	25.5	431
NbC	41.2–50	same	7.80	3600	33.7	6.5	0.044	42	3.93	20.5	540
TaC	42.2–49	same	14.5	3880	34.0	8.29	0.053	24	3.82	16	500
Cr_3C_2	—	rhombic	6.74	1895	8.1	11.7	0.046	75	—	13.3	380
Mo_2C	31.2–33.3	hexagonal densely packed	9.06	2580	11.0	7.8	0.076	71	—	15	544
W_2C	29.5–33.3	same	17.13	2795	7.9	—	0.072	75.5	4.58	14.5	428
WC	—	hexagonal	15.70	2785	9.1	5.2	0.083	19.2	—	18	722
Fe_3C	—	rhombic	7.69	1650	−5.4	—	—	—	—	10.8	—
SiC	—	hexagonal	3.22	2827^e	15.8	4.7^f	0.24	0.13×10^6	—	33.4	386
B_4C	$17.6–29.5^d$	rhombohedral	2.52	2250^e	13.8	4.5^f	0.29	9×10^5	—	49.5	480

^{a}1 kcal/mole = 4.19 kJ/mole ^{b}1 cal/cm·sec·°C = 419W/(m·°K) ^{c}at 1800°K ^{d}Percent by weight ^{e}Decomposes

tallic carbides have also come to be widely used. For example, refractory carbides are used in the manufacture of heating elements for resistance furnaces and protective casings for thermocouples and crucibles. Superhard and wear-resistant carbides serve as the base material for hard powdered metal alloys (tungsten-cobalt and titanium-tungsten) and for abrasives in grinding and finishing processes (in particular SiC and B_4C). Carbides are a component of heat-resistant high-temperature alloys, (cermets), in which hard but brittle carbides are casehardened by viscous yet sufficiently refractory metals. Ferric carbide, Fe_3C, forms a "cementite phase" in iron-carbon alloys (cast iron and steel) that is hard but extremely brittle and nonplastic. Because of their high chemical stability, carbides are used in chemical engineering and the chemical industry for the manufacture of pipelines, nozzles, and reactor linings. Because of their metallic or semiconductor conductance, good thermal emission properties, and the ability to be transformed into a superconducting state, they are used in the manufacture of resistors and various elements of semiconductor devices and in the construction of electric contacts, magnetic materials, and hot cathodes in electronics. (See Table 3 for mechanical properties of carbides.)

REFERENCES

Samsonov, G. V. *Tugoplavkie soedineniia: Spravochnik po svoistvam i primeneniiu.* Moscow, 1963.
Kosolapova, T. Ia. *Karbidy.* Moscow, 1968.
Tugoplavkie materialy v mashinostroenii: Spravochnik. Edited by A. T. Tumanov and K. I. Portnoi. Moscow, 1967.
Osobo tugoplavkie elementy i soedineniia: Spravochnik. Moscow, 1969.
Tugoplavkie karbidy. Edited by G. V. Samsonov. Kiev, 1970. [Collection.]   G. V. SAMSONOV and K. I. PORTNOI [11–1197–3]

CARBINE, a short, lightweight rifle. The precursor of the carbine was invented at the end of the 15th century. From the 18th century through the first half of the 20th century it was included in the armament of the cavalry and artillery. After World War II (1939–45) the improved automatic carbine became part of the armament of most armies. Certain hunting rifles are also called carbines.   [11–1102–3]

CARBINOL RESINS, synthetic polymers, copolymerization products of dimethylvinylethynyl carbinol $CH_2{=}CH{-}C{\equiv}C{-}$ $C(CH_3)_2{-}OH$ with butyl and/or methyl methacrylate in particular. Carbinol resins serve as the base for the preparation of carbinol varnishes and glues.

Carbinol varnishes are colorless or colored solutions of carbinol resins in ethyl Cellosolve and/or ethyl alcohol. The dry varnish residue constitutes 23–45 percent, and the drying time at 20°C is 30–90 minutes. Colorless varnishes are used for varnishing polychromatic printing products to improve their external appearance, durability, and water resistance. Colored varnishes (basic blue K dye) are used in noncopying paper reproduction (photocopying) for lacquering pencil drawings on tracing paper.

Carbinol glues are prepared from a carbinol resin base containing a filler (Portland cement) and a solvent (acetone). The shelf life of carbinol glue is 1–2.5 hr at a temperature of 5°–10°C and without exposure to direct sunlight. It is used to glue together metals, ceramics, and plastics at room temperature (aging 20–24 hr) or at 60°–70°C (aging 6–8 hr); the excess pressure during the gluing process is not less than 50 kilonewtons per square meter, or 0.5 kilogram force per square centimeter. The adhesive compound exhibits good shear strength.

REFERENCES

Dmitriev, P. I. "Tekhniko-ekonomicheskaia effektivnost' vnedreniia laka sinego KS-229 dlia zashchity chertezhei." *Lakokrasochnye materialy i ikh primenenie,* 1967 no. 2.
Kardashov, D. A. *Sinteticheskie klei,* 2nd ed. Moscow, 1968.
[11–1201–4]

CARBOCYCLIC COMPOUNDS, isocyclic organic compounds in which the molecules contain rings of carbon atoms.

Carbocyclic compounds differ from heterocyclic compounds, in which the rings contain in addition to carbon, atoms of other elements, such as (usually) oxygen, nitrogen, or sulfur; they differ also from acyclic compounds, which have no rings at all. Carbocyclic compounds form one of the basic classes of organic compounds; they are subdivided into the alicyclic compounds and the aromatic compounds (benzenoid and nonbenzenoid). Carbocyclic compounds are extremely widespread, and many of them are of great practical importance. For example, most petroleum hydrocarbons and terpenes, a number of antibiotics, and many dyes, pharmaceuticals, and insecticides are included

Table 3. Mechanical properties of carbides

	Hardness H			Tensile strength (MN/m^2)			Compressive strength (MN/m^2)			Elastic modulus (GN/m^2)		
	20°C	1230°C	1730°C	20°C	1230°C	1730°C	20°C	1230°C	1730°C	20°C	730°C	1230°C
TiC	31.0	1.6	0.3	560	200	90	1,350	470	260	460	420	400
ZC	29.0	2.0	1.3	300	100	—	1,700	300	—	550	520	500
NbC	20.5	0.75	0.28	—	—	—	1,400	400	200	540	500	470
WC	18.0	0.9	0.45	—	—	—	2,700	600	100	722	690	600
SiC	33.4	2.2	0.9	180	230	—	800	400	160	386	373	350

among the carbocyclic compounds. Carbocyclic compounds are also used in the preparation of synthetic resins and plastics.

[11–1213–6]

CARBOHEMOGLOBIN, $HbCO_2$, hemoglobin (Hb) compounded with carbon dioxide (CO_2).

The bond between hemoglobin and carbon dioxide is easily formed and easily broken. The CO_2 that evolves in the course of the metabolic activities of tissues diffuses into the capillaries, where part of it combines with Hb (which had previously given off oxygen to the tissues). In the lungs, CO_2 splits off from the carbohemoglobin present in the erythrocytes. About one-third of the CO_2 released through the lungs (most of the CO_2 is transported as carbonates in plasma and erythrocytes) is transported in the form of carbohemoglobin.

[11–1195–2]

CARBOLITE, a type of synthetic phenolaldehyde resin obtained by the polycondensation of phenol (cresol) with formaldehyde in the presence of petroleum sulfoacids, a process known as G. S. Petrov's catalysis. Carbolite was first produced in Russia in 1914.

[11–1204–2]

CARBONARI, members of a secret political society that arose in southern Italy at the beginning of the 19th century during the period of Napoleonic rule. The term is connected with the legend that traces the origins of the Carbonari to medieval charcoal burners.

After 1815 the Carbonari movement spread to all the Italian states and was especially active in the Kingdom of the Two Sicilies. Various social groups took part in the movement, from liberal nobility to lower clergy, peasants, and artisans. The bourgeoisie was the guiding force of the Carbonari, along with members of the free professions and officers. The main goals of the movement were national liberation (first from the French and then from the Austrian oppression which manifested itself in some degree in all of Italy) and a constitution. The majority of the Carbonari favored a constitutional monarchy, but a radical minority advanced republican demands. In the main features of its structure, the society repeated Masonic organizational structure with its hierarchy, complex rituals, and symbolism. At first there were two main stages of initiation: "pupil" and "master." Later the number of stages rose to nine. The lower Carbonari cells or "daughter *vendite*" were subordinate to "maternal *vendite*," which in their turn were directed by the high *vendite* located in the larger cities of Italy. A session of a *vendita* was accompanied by a great number of symbolic rituals. For example, when new members were accepted into the society the colorful and emotional drama of the crucifixion of Christ, who was considered the protector of the Carbonari, was acted out.

The Carbonari led the bourgeois revolutions of 1820–21 in the Kingdom of the Two Sicilies and in Piedmont. After these revolutions were suppressed by Austrian troops, the Carbonari were cruelly repressed. However, soon afterward a neo-Carbonari movement was reborn in the Kingdom of the Two Sicilies and continued to exist until the end of the 1840's. The Carbonari took part in the revolutionary uprisings of 1831 in Romagna, Parma, and Modena.

Under the Italian influence, Carbonari movements arose in France, Switzerland, and the Balkans in 1820–21. The main goal of the French Carbonari was the overthrow of the Bourbon dynasty; all their attempts to stir up a rebellion ended in failure. Carbonari took part in the July Revolution of 1830 and the revolutionary movement of the 1830's; later they merged with secret republican societies.

REFERENCES

Koval'skaia, M. I. *Dvizhenie karbonariev v Italii, 1808–1821.* Moscow, 1971.
Candeloro, G. *Istoriia sovremennoi Italii,* vols 1–2. Moscow, 1958-61. (Translated from Italian.)
Berti, G. *Demokraty i sotsialisty v period Risordzhimento.* Moscow, 1965. (Translated from Italian.)
Lepre, A. *La rivoluzione napoletana del 1820–1821.* Rome, 1967.
Witt, J. *Les Sociétés secrètes de France et d'Italie. . . .* Paris, 1830.
Calmette, A. "Les Carbonari en France sous la Réstauration." *La Révolution de 1848.* Paris, 1912–14. Volume 9, pp. 402–17, vol. 10, pp. 52–73.   M. I. KOVAL'SKAIA [11–1204–6]

CARBONATES, salts of carbonic acid H_2CO_3. There exist normal carbonates with a CO_3^{2-} anion (for example, K_2CO_3), acid carbonates (hydrocarbonates or bicarbonates) with an HCO_3^- anion (for example, $KHCO_3$), and basic carbonates [for example, $Cu_2(OH)_2CO_3$, the mineral malachite]. Only the normal carbonates of alkali metals, ammonium, and thallium are soluble in water. These solutions exhibit an alkaline reaction owing to the considerable degree of hydrolysis that occurs. Calcium, strontium, barium, and lead (divalent) normal carbonates are poorly soluble. Acid carbonates dissolve readily in water. As a rule, carbonates decompose upon heating ($CaCO_3 = CaO + CO_2$), even before reaching the melting point; carbonates of alkali metals and thallium are exceptions. Hydrocarbonates are converted into normal carbonates ($2NaHCO_3 = Na_2CO_3 + H_2O + CO_2$) upon heating. Strong acids effect the decomposition of normal and acid carbonates with the liberation of CO_2 ($K_2CO_3 + H_2SO_4 = K_2SO_4 + H_2O + CO_2$).

Normal carbonates are widely distributed in nature and constitute one of the groups of minerals. Certain natural, normal, and basic carbonates are extremely valuable metallic ores, for example, carbonates of zinc, lead, copper, iron, and manganese. Nonmetallic raw materials, such as limestone $CaCO_3$, magnesite $MgCO_3$, and witherite $BaCO_3$, are used in construction, in the manufacture of refractory materials, in the chemical industry, and for other purposes. Soda (Na_2CO_3 and $NaHCO_3$) and, to a lesser degree, potash K_2CO_3 prepared from synthetic carbonates are widely used in technology. Hydrocarbonates fulfill a very important physiological role as buffers.   [11–1200–1]

CARBONATES, NATURAL, a group of widely distributed minerals composed of salts of carbonic acid (H_2CO_3). Natural carbonates form more than 80 natural compounds (minerals) with the lithophilic (Na, Ca, Mg, Sr, Ba, TR) and chalcophilic (Zn, Cu, Pb, Bi) elements. One or two main cations with or without additional anions are included in the composition of natural carbonates.

The basic structure of natural carbonates is a plane triangle $[CO_3]^{2-}$, where the carbon atoms are arranged in a triple coordination in relationship to the oxygen atoms. The $[CO_3]^{2-}$ groups are isolated and are joined together by cations or by the supplementary anions $(OH)^-$, F^-, and Cl^-. Natural carbonates exhibit a lamellar structure owing to the foliate arrangement of the $[CO_3]^{2-}$ groups (calcite type) or a chain formation [bastnaesite $Ce(CO_3)F$ type] when the $[CO_3]^{2-}$ group dissociates along the axis. Planar $[CO_3]^{2-}$ groups are arranged either in parallel layers and chains or according to a different symmetry. Most of the natural carbonates crystallize in the orthorhombic, monoclinic, or hexagonal (trigonal) system. These carbonates possess a hardness of 3–5 on the mineralogical scale, increased solubility in water (aqueous carbonates of alkali metals, in particular), rapid solubility in hydrochloric acid, and high birefringence. They dissociate upon heating. The color of carbonate minerals depends on the presence of chromophore ions. Copper carbonates are green and blue; uranium carbonates yellow; carbonates of iron and rare earth metals, cinnamon; and cobalt and manganese carbonates, pink. The remaining carbonates are either colorless or of very pale color.

Natural carbonates are formed under diverse conditions: in sedimentary marine deposits (in marine deposits, calcium carbonates form thick strata of limestone, partly of biogenic origin, and dolomite), in hydrothermal ore deposits (calcite, siderite, ankerite), in the erosion crust (magnesite), in metasomatic formations (magnesite, siderite), and in the oxidation zone of polymetallic deposits (malachite, azurite, smithsonite, cerussite). Carbonatites are produced by the magmatogenic process, which is related to the formation of apatite and rare earths. Many natural carbonates (for example, smithsonite, malachite, cerussite, strontianite, and siderite) are used as ores for Zn, Pb, Bi, Ba, Sr, Cu, Fe, Mn, rare earths, and other metals; as raw materials in the cement and chemical industries (dolomite, magnesite); and as building materials (limestone, marble).   [11–1207–1]

CARBONATITES, rocks of magmatic or metasomatic origin, composed primarily of carbonates (calcite, dolomite, ankerite) and spatially related to complexes of ultrabasic-alkalic composition. The term "carbonatite" was introduced by the Norwegian petrographer W. Brøgger (1921). He also proposed that calcite carbonatites be called sövites, dolomite carbonatites be called rauhaugites, biotite-dolomite veined carbonatites be called beforsites, and red-colored carbonatites (in which the carbonate is partially replaced by iron oxides, primarily hematite) be called redbergites.

The complexes of ultrabasic-alkalic rock in which carbonatites are found are generally located along major faults on the platforms. They may be "blind," that is, not reach the earth's surface, or "open," reaching the surface in the form of volcanoes that erupt carbonatite lava (the Oldoinyo Lengai volcano in Tanzania). Geophysical data show that the complexes are dozens of kilometers deep. Carbonatites make up the central parts of the complexes, forming stocks and chimney deposits measuring from 0.1 to 15–20 km and more in area as well as irregularly shaped deposits, branching zones, stockworks, and circular, conical, and radial dikes. In open-type complexes they fill volcanic vents, frequently cementing brecciated volcanic rocks. Where carbonatites develop on ultrabasites and ijolites, in some complexes there occur forsterite-apatite-magnetite rocks with small amounts of calcite (phoscorites, kamaphorites); these rocks are sometimes high-quality magnetite ores (for example, Kovdor on the Kola Peninsula in the USSR) or are rich in apatite (the Palabora Massif in the Republic of South Africa). When carbonatites develop on nepheline syenites, aureoles of albitites with tantalum-niobium mineralization often form.

Carbonatites are multistage formations that form in the temperature interval between 600° and 300°C. Early-stage carbonatites consist of calcite, diopside or forsterite, biotite or phlogopite, apatite, and magnetite. They are enriched with Ti, Zr, Ta, Nb, and U.

Carbonatites of the late stages consist of 80–95 percent dolomite or ankerite and calcite, and, more rarely, siderite and strontianite. They contain alkaline amphiboles, serpentine, ferroferriphlogopite, aegirite, chlorite, and epidote. Sulfides typically appear (pyrite, pyrrhotite), as well as fluorite, barite, magnetite, rutile, pyrochlore, lueshite, columbite, fersmite, burbankite, bastnaesite, parisite, carbocernaite, and ancylite. Carbonatites are characterized by high concentrations of Sr, Ba, F, Nb, Ce, Th, Pb, Zn, and Mo.

Carbonatites and their associated rocks are an important form of mineral deposit. Related to them are large deposits of phlogopite and vermiculite (Kovdor and Gulinskoe in the USSR), iron (Kovdor in the USSR, Palabora in the Republic of South Africa), phosphorus (Palabora in the Republic of South Africa, Sukulu in Uganda), and rich deposits of niobium ore (Araxá in Brazil, Lueshe in Zaïre, Oka in Canada), well as deposits of tantalum (Nqombwa, Zambia), zirconium (Palabora, Republic of South Africa), rare earths (Mrima, Kenya), copper (Palabora, Republic of South Africa), fluorite (Tagna, USSR), and raw materials for cement and lime (Tororo and Sukulu in Uganda). In addition, it is possible to extract barite and strontianite from some of the deposits. Under conditions of hypergenesis a weathering mantle develops on carbonatites; the content of useful components (apatite, pyrochlore, bastnaesite) in it is three to five times greater than in bedrock.

REFERENCES
Ginzburg, A. I. [et al.] "Redkometal'nye karbonatity." In *Geologiia mestorozhdenii redkikh elementov,* fasc. 1. Moscow, 1958.
Ginzburg, A. I., and E. M. Epshtein. "Karbonatitovye mestorozhdeniia." In *Genezis endogennykh rudnykh mestorozhdenii.* Moscow, 1968.
Smirnov, V. I. *Geologiia poleznykh iskopaemykh,* 2nd ed. Moscow, 1969.
Karbonatity. Edited by O. Tuttle and J. Gittins. Moscow, 1969. (Translated from English.)
Heinrich, E. W. *The Geology of Carbonatites.* Chicago, 1966.

A. I. GINZBURG [11–1205–2]

CARBONATIZATION, a process of change occurring in rocks leading to the formation of carbonates of calcium, magnesium, iron, and other metals. Basic intrusive and particularly extrusive rocks most frequently undergo carbonatization under the action of hydrothermal solutions rich in carbon dioxide. Cases of strong carbonatization of granodiorites are known to occur in connection with processes causing the formation of gold and lead-zinc ore deposits. The changes that take place in the carbonate rocks themselves should also be included in the carbonatization processes, both in the diagenetic stage and in the subsequent stages of transformation, particularly in cases of hydrothermal metamorphism of carbonate rocks related to magmatic intrusions. Sometimes carbonatization of ultrabasic rocks is accompanied by the formation of talc and fuchsite (chrome mica) and is therefore referred to as platy venitization. In some regions, carbonatization serves as a prospecting indicator of certain mineral deposits.   [11–1205–1]

CARBONIC ANHYDRASE, carboanhydrase, carbonate hydrolyase, an enzyme of the lyase class that catalyzes the reversible formation of carbonic acid from carbon dioxide and water: $CO_2 + H_2O \rightleftarrows H_2CO_3$. Carbonicanhydrase is a metalloprotein containing zinc. Molecular weight, about 30,000.

Carbonic anhydrase is found in erythrocytes and in cells of the kidneys, the gastric mucosa, and the retina of the eye. Erythrocytic carbonic anhydrase provides for the bonding of CO_2 with blood in the tissues and for its rapid release in the lungs or branchia. Carbonic anhydrase makes for the formation of acid urine in the kidney, hydrochloric acid in the gastric mucosa, bicarbonates of pancreatic juice in the pancreas, and eggshells (containing $CaCO_3$) in the oviducts of birds. Carbonic anhydrase is specifically and strongly inhibited by sulfonamides, which contain an aromatic group. Diamox (acetazolamide), Pentazane (methazolamide), and other agents used in the treatment of glaucoma and diseases of the retina and nervous system are examples of especially active carbonic anhydrase inhibitors. Carbonic anhydrase also occurs in the leaves of certain plants.

E. IU. CHENYKAEVA [11–1201–7]

CARBONIFEROUS SYSTEM (PERIOD), the fifth system of the Paleozoic group, corresponding to the fifth period of the Paleozoic era of earth history.

It has been established by radio geological methods that the Carboniferous period began 350 million years ago; it was 65–75 million years long. The Carboniferous period followed the Devonian and preceded the Permian period. The Carboniferous system was distinguished in 1822 by W. Conybeare and W. Phillips in Great Britain. In Russia the Carboniferous system and its fossil flora and fauna were studied by such scientists as V. I. Meller, S. N. Nikitin, and F. N. Chernyshev and in the Soviet period by M. D. Zalesskii, A. P. Ivanov, E. A. Ivanov, D. V. Nalivkin, M. S. Shvetsov, M. E. Ianishevskii, L. S. Librovich, S. V. Semikhatova, D. M. Rauzer-Chernousova, A. P. Rotai, V. E. Ruzhentsev, and O. L. Einor. In Western Europe the most important research has been done by the English scientist A. Vaudhan and the German paleobotanist W. Gothan. In North America the principal investigators include C. Schuchert and C. Dunbar.

Subdivisions. In the USSR and certain other countries (China, Japan) the Carboniferous system is divided into three parts. In Western Europe a two-part division is customary; in this case the upper division corresponds not only to the middle and upper divisions accepted in the USSR but also to the top part of the lower division (the Namurian stage). In the United States the lower division of the Carboniferous system in its Western European definition (including the lower part of the Namurian stage) is considered an independent system, the Mississippian, while the upper division is termed the Pennsylvanian system. (See Figure 1.)

There is no international breakdown of the stages of the Carboniferous system into zones. A breakdown into zones is used only for the lower division in Western Europe and the marine deposits of the USSR.

General description. The deposits of the Carboniferous system are found on all continents. The classical sections are in Western Europe (Great Britain, Belgium, and the Federal Republic of Germany), Eastern Europe (the Donbas, the Moscow syneclise), and North America (the Appalachians and the Mississippi River basin, for example). The mutual arrangement of platforms and geosynclines in the Carboniferous period remained the same as it had been during the Devonian period.

On the platforms of the northern hemisphere the Carboniferous period is represented by marine deposits (limestone, sand-clay sediments that are often coal-bearing). In the southern hemisphere, continental deposits—detrital and glacial (fre-

Figure 1. Chart of the stratigraphy of the Carboniferous system

Divisions[1]	Stages[1]	Eastern European Platform (suprahorizons, horizons, zones)		Donets Basin (suites, horizons)	Western Europe			North America
					Divisions	Stages	Substages	Systems
Upper C_3	Orenburgian C^o_3		*Daixina sokensis*	$P(C^3_3)$	Upper Carboniferous	Stephanian		Pennsylvanian
			Triticites jigulensis					
			Triticites stuckenbergii	$O(C^2_3)$				
	Gzhelian C^g_3		*Triticites arcticus, T. acutus Triticites montiparus Obsoletes obsoletes*	$N(C^1_3)$				
Middle C_2	Moscovian C^m_2		Miachkovo Podol'sk Kashira Vereia	$M(C^7_2)$ $L(C^6_2)$ $K_{4-8}(C^5_2)$		Westphalian	D	
							C	
	Bashkirian C^b_2		Melekess Cheremshan Kama Region	$J(C^4_2) + K_{1-3}(C^5_2)$ $G(C^2_2) + H(C^3_2)$ $F(C^1_2)$			B A	
			Severnaia Kel'tma	$E_{1-9}(C^5_1)$			C	
Lower C_1	Namurian C^n_1		Krasnaia Poliana	$E_{1-3}(C^5_1)$	Lower Carboniferous (Dinantian)	Namurian	B	Mississippian
			Protva	C^n_1a—d			A	
		Serpukhov	Steshevo					
			Tarusa	C^v_1g				
	Viséan C^v_1	Oka	Venev Mikhailovka Aleksin	C^v_1f		Viséan	Zones: D₃ D₂ D₁ S₂ S₁ C₂	
		Iasnaia Poliana	Tula Bobriki	C^v_1e				
		Malin	Radaevka Elkhovka	C^v_1a—d				
	Tournaisian C^t_1	Chernyshino	Kizel Cherepet'	C^t_1d C^t_1c		Tournaisian	L	
		Likhvin	Upa Malevka Trans-Volga	C^t_1b C^t_1a		Etroeungtian		

[1] Accepted in the USSR

quently tillites)—are most common. Lava sheets, tuffs and tuffites, siliceous coarse-fragmented sediments, and flysch are also found in the geosynclines.

By the nature of geological processes and the paleogeographic situation the Carboniferous period is divided into two stages almost everywhere in the world; the first of them covers the early Carboniferous, while the second covers the middle and late parts. After the early Carboniferous, as a result of the Hercynian folding; marine conditions over vast areas of the middle Paleozoic geosynclines were replaced by continental conditions. In some places in Southeast Asia and the Eastern European and North American platforms, seas engulfed land sectors that had only recently risen. The Carboniferous is one of the thalassocratic periods; vast areas within the boundaries of the present continents were covered by the sea. Subsidences and the transgressions caused by them occurred more than once during the Carboniferous period. The greatest transgressions occurred in the first half of the period. During the early Carboniferous the sea covered Europe (with the exception of Scandinavia and the adjacent regions), a large part of Asia, North America, the extreme western part of South America, northwestern Africa, and the eastern part of Australia. The seas were shallow for the most part and had many islands. The largest single land mass was Gondwana. A markedly smaller land mass stretched from Scandinavia through the northern part of the Atlantic, Greenland, and North America. The central part of Siberia between the Lena and Enisei rivers and Mongolia and the Laptev Sea was also land. By the middle Carboniferous the sea had receded from almost all of Western Europe, the Western Siberian Lowland, Kazakhstan, Central Siberia, and other regions.

In the second half of the Carboniferous period mountain ranges were uplifted in the zones of Hercynian orogenesis (the Tien-Shan, Kazakhstan, the Urals, the northernwestern part of Europe, eastern Asia, and North America).

The climate of the continents was varied and changed from stage to stage. A common feature was the high humidity of the tropical, subtropical, and temperate belts, which promoted the spread of forest and swamp vegetation on all the continents. The accumulation of plant remains, primarily in peat bogs, led to the formation of numerous coal basins and deposits.

It is conventional to distinguish the following phytogeographic regions: Euramerican or Westphalian (tropical and subtropical), Angara or Tunguska (nontropical), and Gondwanian (temperate climate). The climate of the Euramerican region became drier and subarid in places toward the end of the Carboniferous period. Other regions preserved their high humidity not only until the end of the Carboniferous but also during the Permian period. The greatest humidity and optimal conditions for peat accumulation (coal accumulation) in the Euramerican region were as follows: in the Greater Donbas at the end of the early Carboniferous and in the middle Carboniferous, in Western Europe in the Namurian and Westphalian, in North America in the middle and upper Carboniferous, and in Kazakhstan in the late Viséan and the middle Carboniferous. In the southern part of the Angara region (the Kuznetsk Basin and other basins) the peat bogs grew intensively beginning the middle Carboniferous; in Gondwana this growth occurred from the late Carboniferous until the end of the Permian period. Only a limited territory had a dry climate during the Carboniferous. For example, during the Tournaisian age one of the arid climate zones stretched from southern Kazakhstan through the Tien-Shan to the Tarim massif. The basins distinguished by dry climate in this age stretched from Kazakhstan to the Siberian highlands and lower reaches of the Lena River. Marked and long-lasting aridization of the climate came in the Bashkirian age and continued until the Permian and Triassic in Kazakhstan, in the region from the Turgai to the Teniz and Dzhezkazgan basins; copper ores formed in these areas.

In the Tournaisian age the equator ran (according to the paleomagnetic data of A. N. Khramov) through the Black Sea and the Scandinavian peninsula; from the Viséan age until the late Carboniferous it extended from the Balkan peninsula toward northwestern Europe. In the middle and late Carboniferous the north pole was evidently located north of the mouth of the Lena River. Marked climatic contrasts among different belts developed beginning in the middle and late Carboniferous. Beginning in the middle Carboniferous the part of USSR territory east of a line from Lake Balkhash to the mouth of the Enisei River differed from the part west of the line by its temperate climate. This is indicated by the nature of the flora and marine fauna. Only the Sikhote-Alin', like virtually all non-Soviet Asia (with the exception of Mongolia), belonged to the belt of tropical and subtropical climates. On the continent of Gondwana (in Australia and Antarctica), during the middle and late Carboniferous, a climate that promoted glaciation occurred periodically.

Magmatic activity manifested itself in the form of eruptions and intrusions in the Uralian, Tien-Shan, Kazakhstan, and Mongolian-Okhotsk geosynclines, as well as in many others in Western Europe, non-Soviet Asia, North and South America, and eastern Australia. The Carboniferous period was one of the periods of greatest magmatic (especially intrusive) activity, which was closely related to the apogee of Hercynian orogenesis.

The organic world. At the very beginning of the period the predominant flora included small-leaved Lycopsida (*Lepidodendropsis* and *Sublepidodendron,* for example), fern-like gymnosperms (pteridosperms), primitive articulated stem plants, and Pteropsida (primarily protoferns). Even in the early Carboniferous the primitive Lycopsida were replaced by large treelike *Lepidodendron* and *Sigillaria,* which were especially common in the middle Carboniferous. In the tropics (the Euramerican region) during the middle Carboniferous there prevailed forests consisting of high-trunked Lycopsida with large numbers of pteridosperms (*Neuropteris, Mariopteris, Alethopteris*) and other ferns, calamites, and Sphenopsida. To the north (the Angara region) during the early Carboniferous the Lycopsida predominated, and in the middle and late Carboniferous the cordaites and pteridophytes prevailed. It appears that at this time the glossopterian flora especially characteristic of the Permian had already developed in the Gondwana region. In phytogeographic regions with temperate climates there was a comparatively gradual development of flora from the middle Carboniferous to the early Permian. In the tropics during the late Carboniferous, on the contrary, there was a radical change in the vegetation of swampy lowlands in some places owing to aridization of the climate. The principal plant groups became the pteridosperms and treelike ferns. Conifers spread in the elevated areas.

The seas of the Carboniferous abounded in blue-green algae (*Beresella, Ungarella, Donezella*), while fresh waters had green coal-forming algae (*Pila, Reinschia*).

The animal world of the Carboniferous was extremely varied. In the seas the foraminifera were very common and underwent rapid evolutionary changes during the Carboniferous, producing dozens of genera and thousands of species. For stratigraphy the most important are the superfamily Fusulinidae: *Eostaffela* in the Lower Carboniferous; the genera *Fusulina, Fusulinella,* and others in the Middle Carboniferous; and *Triticites* and others in the Upper Carboniferous. Among the coelenterates the tetracorals continued to dominate (*Caninia, Dibunophyllum, Lithostrotion*) along with the tabulate corals (*Syringopora,* for example) and the stromatoporoids. There were various mollusks (bivalves, gastropods), rapidly evolved ammonoid cephalopods (various species of *Goniatites* and *Eumorphoceras* in the lower Carboniferous, *Gastrioceras* in the Middle Carboniferous, *Uddenites* and others in the Upper Carboniferous), which are especially important for comparing sections from places that are far away from each other, and nautiloids. Some bivalves (*Carbonicola* and *An-*

thracomya, for example) inhabited strongly freshened lagoons and deltas, which permits them to be used for the stratigraphy of coal-bearing strata. Brachiopods, especially the orders Productida and Spiriferida, were common in the shallow seas. In the early Carboniferous (the Viséan age) in the Moscow region, the Urals, and the Tien-Shan there were abundant large thick-shelled *Gigantoproductus,* strongly variable *Striatifera* that lived in banks, and others; in the middle and late Carboniferous numerous species of the *Choristites* genus were widespread. Some sectors of the sea floor were especially favorable for the development of bryozoans; representatives of the Fenestellidae family (genera *Polypora, Fenestella,* and *Archimedes*) were prevalent. There were various arthropods. Trilobites continued to exist, although in small numbers. There were many different groups of ostracods. Among the Echinodermata the crinoids developed abundantly; their segments make up whole layers in the limestone beds. Fossils of sea urchin are common in some places, while blastoids are rare.

Various classes of vertebrates, especially fish (marine and freshwater) underwent significant evolutionary changes. Bony fish and sharklike fish (*Cladodus* and *Stenacanthus,* for example) developed. On land the amphibians (stegocephalians) were dominant; reptiles were still rare. Fossils of numerous insects have been found (mayflies, dragon flies, Dictyoptera), some of them of gigantic size.

Biogeographic regionalization. The phytogeographic areas of Angara or Tunguska (Siberia, eastern Kazakhstan, and Mongolia) and the Euramerican (North America, Europe, North Africa, Anatolia, the Caucasus, central Kazakhstan, Middle Asia, China, and Southeast Asia) began to differentiate in the early Carboniferous; separation of the Gondwana region (South America, southern Africa, India, Australia, and Antarctica) took place at the end of the early Carboniferous, and during the late Carboniferous the formation of the Catasian region (China and Southeast Asia) from the Euramerican region took place. All charts of zoogeographic regionalization show a northern nontropical region (northern Asia and part of the arctic), a southern nontropical region (Australia and part of South America), and the tropical region lying between them, which included Tethys. Several provinces are identified within these regions (which are given different names).

Deposits in the USSR. Among the widespread Carboniferous deposits in the USSR two basic types of sections and formations are distinguished: platform and geosynclinal. The platform type is found on the Eastern European Platform and in the Tunguska Basin in Eastern Siberia. The geosynclinal type is found in the Donbas, the Caucasus, the Urals, the Tien-Shan, and Kazakhstan.

The section of the Carboniferous in the Donbas is classical in completeness, excellent exposure, and abundance and variety of paleontological remains. The Lower Carboniferous there is represented by limestones, while the Middle and Upper Carboniferous are represented by a thick (6–12 km) coal-bearing stratum: alternating layers of clay rock, sandstones, limestones, and coal beds. The shallow Carboniferous sections on the Eastern European Platform and the varied types of strata of all three subdivisions of the Carboniferous in the Urals, Tien-Shan, Kazakhstan, the Altai, the Kuznetsk Basin, the Tunguska Basin, the Verkhoiansk Range, and the Transbaikal region are interesting. Overlaid by younger deposits, Carboniferous deposits cover the entire central and eastern parts of the Eastern European Platform (and the Dnieper-Donets basin), a significant part of the Western Siberian and Turanian plates (*plity*), large areas in the Tunguska Basin, and territory east of the Lena River. Stratotypes of the Moscovian and Gzhelian stages are found in the Moscow syneclise, and the stratotype of the Bashkirian stage is found in the Urals.

Minerals. Hard and brown coals form a series of basins and deposits on all continents and are limited to Hercynian foredeeps and internal basins. Basins in the USSR include the Donets (hard coals), Moscow (brown coals), Karaganda (hard coals), and Kuznetsk and Tunguska (coals of the Carboniferous and Permian systems). In addition there are deposits in the Ukraine, the Urals, central Caucasus, and elsewhere. In Central and Western Europe there are basins and deposits in Poland (Silesia), the

German Democratic Republic and Federal Republic of Germany (Ruhr), Belgium, the Netherlands, France, and Great Britain. In the United States there are the Pennsylvanian and other basins. Many petroleum and gas deposits date to the Carboniferous (Volga-Ural region, the Dnieper-Donets basin). Also known are numerous deposits of iron ore, manganese, copper (the largest is Dzhezkazgan), lead, zinc, aluminum (bauxite), and refractory and ceramic clays.

REFERENCES

Ivanova, E. A., and I. V. Khvorova. "Stratigrafiia srednego i verkhnego karbona zapadnoi chasti Moskovskoi sinklizy." *Tr. Paleontologicheskogo in-ta AN SSSR,* 1955, vol. 53, book 1.
Atlas litologo-paleogeograficheskikh kart Russkoi platformy i ee geosinklinal'nogo obrameleniia (and an explanatory note), part 1. Moscow, 1960.
Miklukho-Maklai, A. D. *Verkhnii paleozoi Srednei Azii.* Leningrad, 1963.
Atlas paleogeograficheskikh kart SSSR: Kamennougol'nyi period. Moscow, 1965. (Maps and an explanatory note.)
Geologiia uglenosnykh formatsii i stratigrafiia karbona v SSSR. Moscow, 1965. (International Congress on Stratigraphy and Carboniferous Geology, Session 5, Paris, 1963.)
Atlas litologo-paleogeograficheskikh kart SSSR, vol. 2. Moscow, 1969.
Geologicheskoe stroenie SSSR, vol. 1. Moscow, 1968.
Problemy stratigrafii karbona. (Trudy Mezhvedomstvennogo stratigraficheskogo komiteta SSSR, vol. 4.) Moscow, 1970.

O. L. EINOR [11–747–3]

CARBONIUM IONS, molecular particles containing a trivalent positively charged carbon atom. Carbonium ions are highly reactive and therefore unstable. They form on heterolytic cleavage of the C—X bond (the electron pair which effects this bond is removed with the X group):

$$\geqslant C \overset{\frown}{} X \longrightarrow \geqslant C^+ + X^-$$

For example, the action of strong acids on triphenyl carbinol yields a triphenylmethyl cation salt:

$$(C_6H_5)_3C\text{—}OH + H_2SO_4 \rightleftharpoons (C_6H_5)_3C^+ + HSO_4^- + H_2O$$

This carbonium ion is stable due to the distribution of the positive charge among several carbon atoms. Carbonium ions also form during the action of aprotic acids on halogen derivatives, for example,

$$CCl_4 + AlCl_3 \rightleftharpoons CCl_3^+ + AlCl_4^-$$

They also form during the addition of a proton or other cation to the multiple bond:

$$(CH_3)_2C = CH_2 + H^+ \rightleftharpoons (CH_3)_3C^+$$

Carbonium ions readily interact with anions, with molecules containing an unshared electron pair or a multiple bond, and with other compounds, attacking areas with increased electron density. Carbonium ions are intermediate particles in many organic reactions of both theoretical and practical value (for example, alkylation and acylation according to the Friedel-Crafts reaction, reactions of electrophilic combination with olefins, isomerization and cation polymerization of olefins, and pinacolic and retropinacolic, Dem'ianov, and Wagner-Meerwein rearrangements).

REFERENCES

Breslow, R. *Mekhanizmy organicheskikh reaktsii.* Moscow, 1968. (Translated from English.)
Roberts, J., and M. Caserio. *Osnovy organicheskoi khimii,* parts 1–2. Moscow, 1968.(Translated from English.)

B. L. DIATKIN [11–1209–1]

CARBORANES, chemical compounds composed of boron, carbon, and hydrogen atoms and having the general formula $B_nC_mH_{n+m}$. In carboranes, the B and C atoms are arranged at the vertices of the more or less regular polyhedron; every atom of B or C is bonded to one H atom. One of the B or C atoms in carboranes can be replaced by one atom of another element, such as phosphorus, arsenic, tin, or aluminum. The state of aggregation for carboranes changes from gaseous to solid as n

increases. Carboranes and their derivatives are noted for their high thermal and chemical stability. Their properties are in many ways similar to those of aromatic hydrocarbons. Carboranes are therefore capable of undergoing various transformations related to the substitution of the H atoms located at the C or B atom.Carboranes are primarily formed by the interaction of acetylene derivatives with the corresponding boranes.

The carborane $B_{10}C_2H_{12}$ is used in the preparation of different types of polymers used in solid rocket fuels and as a thermostable coating.

REFERENCES

Mikhailov, B. M. *Khimiia borovodorodov.* Moscow, 1967.
Zhigach, A. F., and D. S. Stasinevich. *Khimiia gidridov.* Leningrad, 1969.

N. I. BEKASOVA [11–1212–1]

CARBOTHERMY, metallurgical processes based on the reduction of metals from their compounds using carbon and carbon-containing materials at high temperatures. Metallurgical coke is the most abundant carbon-containing material. Two types of reduction are known: direct (using solid carbon) and indirect (using carbon monoxide). Carbothermic reduction is the basis of ferrous metallurgy. Lead, tin, and a considerable quantity of zinc and certain other metals are produced by the carbothermic process in nonferrous metallurgy.

REFERENCE

Esin, O. A., and P. V. Gel'd. *Fizicheskaia khimiia metallurgicheskikh protesessov,* part 1. Sverdlovsk, 1962. [11–1213–2]

CARBOXYHEMOGLOBIN, HbCO, a compound formed by the binding of carbon monoxide (CO) to hemoglobin (Hb).

Carboxyhemoglobin solutions are bright red. Their absorption spectrum has maximums at wavelengths of 570 and 539 mμ. Carboxyhemoglobin breaks down to Hb and CO 10,000 times more slowly than does oxyhemoglobin to Hb and O_2. Therefore, when CO is present in inhaled air the oxygen is gradually displaced from the hemoglobin. Even at an atmospheric CO concentration of 0.1 percent, more than half the hemoglobin in the blood is converted to carboxyhemoglobin, interfering with the transfer of O_2 from the lungs to the tissues and causing carbon monoxide poisoning. [11–1202–1]

CARBOXYLASES, a group of enzymes of the lyase class, catalyzing decarboxylation (CO_2 separation) of keto and amino acids. Cocarboxylase acts as a coenzyme of carboxylases that decarboxylize keto acids, pyridoxal phosphate serves as a coenzyme of carboxylases that catalyze the decarboxylation of amino acids. [11–1202–3]

CARBOXYLATE RUBBERS, synthetic rubber whose macromolecule contains a small number of —COOH carboxyl groups. The carboxylate rubbers that have been studied most thoroughly are copolymers of butadiene (or a mixture of butadiene with styrene or acrylonitrile) and 1–5 percent methacrylic acid. The main method of preparing carboxylate rubbers is emulsion polymerization.

A feature of carboxylate rubbers is the ability to be vulcanized by the oxides and hydroxides of divalent metals, particularly ZnO, MgO, and Ca(OH)$_2$ because of the presence of carboxyl groups. The partial reaction of carboxyl groups with these vulcanizing agents during the preparation of rubber mixes or at other stages of the production process preceding vulcanization hinders the processing of carboxylate rubber in apparatus and limits its potential for practical use.

Vulcanized rubber specially prepared from raw carboxylate rubbers using systems composed of metal oxides and sulfur-containing vulcanizing agents, such as thiuram, are characterized by good mechanical properties and high thermal stability. For example, the tensile strength of black-filled vulcanized rubber prepared from butadiene-styrene carboxylate rubber (type SKS-30-1) is about 40 meganewtons per sq m (about 400 kilograms-force per sq cm), its relative elongation is about 800 percent, and its wearability is about 140 cu cm per kilowatt-hr. After aging for 480 hr at 100°C, the vulcanized rubber retains about 90 percent of its original tensile strength and relative elongation.

Aqueous dispersions (latexes) of carboxylate rubbers are used for the impregnation of tire cord to increase the strength of its bond with vulcanized rubber, as well as for dressing leather and finishing paper. Carboxylate rubbers are used in the manufacture of some industrial products and of glues for joining rubber and metal. [11–1202–2]

CARBOXYLATION,

the direct introduction of the carboxyl group —COOH to organic compounds by the action of CO_2. For example, carboxylation of organometallic compounds occurs during the passage of CO_2 through a solution of the compound; subsequent hydrolysis yields carboxylic acid:

$$CH_3MgBr + CO_2 \longrightarrow CH_3 COOMgBr \xrightarrow{H_2O} CH_3COOH$$

Salicylic acid and n-aminosalicylic acid (PASA), used in medicine, are obtained through a singular carboxylation process involving the corresponding phenolates, for example,

$$C_6H_5ONa + CO_2 \longrightarrow$$

[benzene ring with OH and COONa substituents]

Carboxylation in an organism is effected by specific enzymes, for example, pyruvate carboxylase catalyzes the carboxylation of pyruvic acid. Carboxylation plays an important role in the oxidation of intermediate products of the decomposition of carbohydrates, fats, and proteins in the organism. [11–1203–1]

CARBOXYLIC ACIDS,

a class of organic compounds that contain a carboxyl group:

[structure of carboxyl group: —C with double-bonded O and OH]

Carboxylic acids can belong to the aliphatic (fatty), alicyclic, aromatic or heterocyclic series, depending on the nature of the radical bonded to the —COOH group. A distinction is made among monobasic, dibasic, and polybasic acids (monocarboxylic, dicarboxylic, and polycarboxylic, respectively) according to the number of carboxyl groups in the molecule. Carboxylic acids may be saturated or unsaturated and may contain double or triple molecular bonds.

Most carboxylic acids have trivial names, many of which are related to their origin in nature—for example, formic, malic, valeric, and citric acids. According to the Geneva nomenclature, the names of carboxylic acids are derived from the designations of hydrocarbons with the same number of carbon atoms, with addition of the ending "-ic" and the word "acid"—for example, methanoic (formic) acid and ethanoic (acetic) acid. Carboxylic acids are frequently regarded as hydrocarbon derivatives. For example, the acid used in the construction of HC≡C—COOH is called acetylene carboxylic acid.

Acidic properties are determined by the ability of carboxylic acids to dissociate in an aqueous solution:

$$RCOOH \rightleftharpoons RCOO^- + H^+$$

As a rule, carboxylic acids are weaker than mineral acids. The dissociation constants of monobasic saturated fatty acids range from 1.7×10^{-4} (formic acid) to 1.3×10^{-5} (higher homologues) at 25°C. The strength of carboxylic acids is also largely dependent on the electrophilic activity of the radical bonded to the carboxyl. The addition of an electronegative substituent such as NO_2, CN, or Cl in a position adjacent to the carboxyl group markedly increases the acidity— for example, cyanoacetic acid, $CNCH_2COOH$, is approximately 200 times as strong as acetic acid, CH_3COOH. The effect of substituents decreases in proportion to the distance from the carboxyl. Dicarbonic acids are more powerful than monocarbonic acids, since the effect of one carboxyl on the other increases as they become closer together. For example, in the acid series, oxalic acid, HOOC—COOH, is stronger than malonic acid, $HOOCCH_2COOH$, which in turn is stronger than succinic acid, $HOOC(CH_2)_2COOH$. The acidity of unsaturated acids is higher than that of saturated acids; the nearer the double bond to the carbonyl, the greater its effect. For example, acrylic acid, $CH_2=CH—COOH$, is four times as strong as propionic acid, $CH_3—CH_2—COOH$. Aromatic acids are stronger than saturated aliphatic acids (the dissociation constant of benzoic acid is 6.5×10^{-5}).

Carboxylic acids are liquids (the lower fatty acids) or solids (the higher fatty acids and aromatic acids). (See Table 1.) The lower members of the unsaturated carboxylic acids in the fatty series are highly soluble in water, the middle members (C_4–C_{10}) and the aromatic acids are soluble to a limited extent in organic solvents, and the higher fatty acids are insoluble in water; like the aromatic acids, they dissolve readily in alcohol, ether, and benzene.

The most important chemical property of carboxylic acids is the capacity to become derivatives. Upon reaction with bases, carboxylic acids yield salts: $RCOOH + NaOH \rightarrow RCOONa + H_2O$. Esters are readily formed upon treatment of carboxylic acids with alcohols in the presence of mineral acids: $RCOOH + R'OH \rightarrow RCOOR' + H_2O$. Acid halides of carboxylic acids RCOX (X is a halogen atom) are formed upon the action of acid halides of mineral acids on carboxylic acids (for example, $PCl_3, POCl_3$, and $SOCl_2$). Carboxylic acid anhydrides, $(RCO)_2O$, are produced by heating the acids with dehydrating agents. Acid halides and anhydrides of carboxylic acids are used as acylating agents. The dehydration of ammonia salts of carboxy-

Table 1. Some representative carboxylic acids and their properties

	Formula	Melting point (°C)	Boiling point (°C)	Density* (g/cm³)
Aliphatic (fatty) acids				
Formic acid	HCOOH	8.4	100.5	1.220 (20)
Acetic acid	CH_3COOH	16.6	118.2	1.049 (20)
Pelargonic	$CH_3(CH_2)_7COOH$	12.3	255.6	0.906 (20)
Palmitic acid	$CH_3(CH_2)_{14}COOH$	62.8	390	0.841 (80)
Stearic acid	$CH_3(CH_2)_{16}COOH$	69.6	360 (with decomposition)	0.839 (80)
Adipic acid	$HOOC(CH_2)_4COOH$	153.5	265 (100 mm Hg)**	1.366 (20)
Acrylic acid	$CH_2=CHCOOH$	12.3	140.0	1.062 (16)
Methacrylic acid	$CH_2=C(CH_3)COOH$	16	163	1.105 (20)
Oleic acid	$CH_3(CH_2)_7CH=CH(CH_2)_7$ COOH	16	223 (10 mm Hg)	0.895 (18)
Aromatic acids				
Benzoic acid	C_6H_5COOH	121.7	249.2	1.322 (20)
Cinnamic acid	$C_6H_5CH=CHCOOH$	136	300	1.245 (20)
Terephthalic acid	$p=HOOCC_6H_4COOH$	—	300 (sublimates)	—

*Figures in parentheses are temperature (°C) **1 mm Hg = 133.322 N/m²

lic acids (1) and the reaction of acid halides with ammonia (2) yield acid amides:

$$RCOONH_4 \longrightarrow RCONH_2 + H_2O$$

$$RCOCl + 2NH_3 \longrightarrow RCONH_2 + NH_4Cl$$

Various methods are used to produce carboxylic acids. The oxidation of primary alcohols and aldehydes yields carboxylic acids containing the same number of carbon atoms. Ketone oxidation is accompanied by rupture of the C—C bond. Dicarbonic acids are formed from cyclic ketones—for example, adipic acid from cyclohexanone:

Saturated hydrocarbons can undergo destructive oxidation to form a mixture of products, among which are carboxylic acids. Approximately 350 kg of carboxylic acid are obtained from 1 ton of paraffin using this method. Oxidation of the side chain of fatty aromatic hydrocarbons or polynuclear aromatic hydrocarbons yields aromatic carboxylic acids—for example, phthalic acid is formed by the oxidation of *o*-xylol or naphthalene:

Unsaturated hydrocarbons are oxidized at the double bond:

$$CH_3-CH=CH-CH_3 \xrightarrow{[O]} 2CH_3COOH$$

An important method of synthesizing carboxylic acids is the hydrolysis of their nitriles, which are readily produced by the reaction of halide derivatives of hydrocarbons with sodium cyanide:

$$RCl + NaCN \longrightarrow RCN \longrightarrow RCOOH$$

At the present time, the synthesis of carboxylic acids by carbonization (that is, addition of a CO group to organic compounds) is widely used in industry:

$$RCH_2OH \xrightarrow{CO} RCH_2COOH$$

$$RCH=CH_2 \xrightarrow[H_2SO_4]{CO, H_2O} RCH(CH_3)COOH$$

Certain carboxylic acids are obtained from natural products. For example, salts of higher fatty acids (soaps) and glycerol are prepared by alkaline hydrolysis (saponification) of fats and oils. Citric acid is produced from the haulm of the cotton plant and from the stems of common tobacco plants (after the extraction of nicotine from them). Many carboxylic acids are prepared by the fermentation of carbohydrates in the presence of a certain species of bacteria (butyric-acid, lactic, citric-acid, and other types of fermentation).

Carboxylic acids are widespread in nature; they exist in the free state and as derivatives (primarily esters). For example, pelargonic acid is contained in volatile geranium oil, and citric acid is found in lemons. Glycerides of higher normal carboxylic acids of the fatty series are constituents of animal and vegetable fats and oils, among which palmitic, stearic, and oleic acids predominate.

Carboxylic acids and their derivatives, as well as numerous compounds that contain other functional groups in addition to the carboxyl (such as amino acids and hydroxy acids), are of considerable biological importance and have found various practical applications. Formic and acetic acids, for example, are used in the dyeing and printing of textiles; acetic acid and acetic anhydride are used in the manufacture of cellulose acetate. Amino acids are a component of proteins. Salicylic acid, p-aminosalicylic acid, and others are used in medicine.

Higher fatty carboxylic acids are widely used as raw material for the manufacture of soap, lacquers and paints, and surface-active agents, as emulsifiers in the production of rubber, and as plasticizers in the manufacture of vulcanized rubber. Adipic acid is one of the base products in the manufacture of polyamide fiber (nylon), terephthalic acid is used in the production of polyester fiber (*lavsan* and terylene), and the polymer nitrile of acrylic acid (Orlon) is used as a synthetic fiber whose properties are similar to those of natural wool. The polymers and copolymers of methacrylic acid esters are used as organic glass.

REFERENCES

Nenitescu, C. D. *Organicheskaia khimiia*, vols. 1–2. Moscow, 1962–63. (Translated from Rumanian.)
Nesmeianov, A. N., and N. A. Nesmeianov. *Nachala organicheskoi khimii*, books 1–2. Moscow, 1969–70.   [11–1209–2]

CARBOXYLMETHYL CELLULOSE, a simple ether of cellulose having the general formula $[C_6H_7O_2(OH)_{3-x}(OCH_2-COOH)_x]_n$. The sodium salt of carboxylmethyl cellulose (sodium carboxylmethyl cellulose) is of great practical value. Like carboxylmethyl cellulose, it is a solid white substance with a bulk weight of 400–800kg/m^3; the density of the salt is 1.59 g/cm^3. Its solubility in alkali or in water is determined by the degree of etherification of the cellulose as well as by the conditions of solution. Carboxylmethyl cellulose is obtained during the interaction of cellulose with chloroacetic acid or (during the preparation of sodium carboxylmethyl cellulose) with its sodium salt in the presence of NaOH.

Sodium carboxylmethyl cellulose is used (1) to stabilize clay suspensions used in the drilling of petroleum and gas boreholes, (2) as an additive in detergents to inhibit the resorption by the fabric of impurities from the washing solution, (3) to size warp threads and as a thickener in printer's ink, (4) as a flotation reagent, (5) to increase the plasticity of ceramic materials and the durability of the unfinished product (article), and (6) to control the rheological properties of cement suspensions.

REFERENCE

Khimiia i tekhnologiia proizvodnykh tselliulozy. Edited by L. P. Perepechkin and Iu. L. Pogosov. Vladimir, 1968.   [11–1203–3]

CARBOXYPEPTIDASES, an enzyme group of the hydrolase class (carboxypeptidase-A, carboxypeptidase-B, and yeast carboxypeptidase) that catalyze the stepped hydrolysis of polypeptides from the C-end, that is, from the amino acid that contains a free carboxyl group (—COOH). The molecular weight of carboxypeptidases exceeds 34,000. Carboxypeptidase-A is most active on aromatic amino acids; carboxypeptidase-B, on lysine or arginene; and yeast carboxypeptidase, on glycine or lysine. In addition, carboxypeptidases have esterase activity (the ability to split ether bonds). Carboxypeptidase-A enters the duodenum from the pancreas where it is produced in the form of inactive procarboxypeptidase-A, which becomes carboxypeptidase-A, primarily under the influence of trypsin.

REFERENCES

Dixon, M., and E. Webb. *Fermenty.* Moscow, 1966. (Translated from English.)
Mosolov, V. V. *Proteoliticheskie fermenty.* Moscow, 1971.

[11–1203–4]

CARBROMAL, Adalin, a soporific drug used in powder or tablet form as a sedative in neurasthenia hysteria, various neurological diseases, insomnia, and light sleep. Carbromal is contraindicated for patients who are unusually sensitive to bromine.   [11–1213–7]

CARBUNCLE, an acute, suppurative, necrotizing inflammation of the skin and subcutaneous tissue that tends to spread rapidly around a cluster of hair follicles and sebaceous glands.

Carbuncles are usually found on the back of the neck, on the face, and on the back. They generally appear when the skin becomes contaminated in places where it has been rubbed by clothing, the result of invasion by pyogenic microbes (staphylococci and streptococci). Exhaustion, diabetes mellitus, and gastrointestinal, liver, and kidney disorders are conducive to the appearance and development of carbuncles. The skin is inflamed and purple-blue at the site of the lesion, and the process is accompanied by suppuration. After the dead portions are sloughed off, multiple funnel-shaped openings form in the skin; this stage is followed by a wound with a dirty gray base and undermined margins. Carbuncles are accompanied by general intoxication, high temperature, and, in severe cases, vomiting and loss of consciousness. Treatment involves rest, local injection of novacain and antibiotics, X-ray therapy, ultrahigh-frequency sound therapy, blood transfusion, high-calorie diet, and, in the necrotic stage, surgery. Carbuncles are prevented through hygienic care of the skin and underclothes.

A. B. GALITSKII [11–1213–8]

CARBURETOR, a device used to meter the flow of fuel and to prepare a combustible mixture of liquid fuel and air for internal combustion engines with external mixing layouts. The process of preparing a combustible mixture is called carburetion. In order to achieve complete and rapid combustion and maximum heat release in the cylinder, the fuel must be mixed with air in a certain way. Preparation of the mixture consists of breaking down the liquid fuel into small droplets (atomizing), intensively mixing the fuel and air, and vaporizing the mixture. Atomization of fuel in a carburetor occurs when a thin jet of fuel is allowed to flow from an atomizer into a rapidly moving air stream. The air stream breaks up the fuel into small droplets which mix with the air and are conveyed through the intake manifold into the cylinders of the engine.

Carburetors can be classified into three groups with differing directions of air flow: downdraft (descending stream), updraft, and horizontal. Downdraft carburetors are used primarily in motor-vehicle engines. Carburetors with horizontal flow are used primarily in motorcycle, boat, and supercharged motor-vehicle engines.

A carburetor is connected to the intake manifold of an engine. During the intake stroke the piston moves away from the cylinder head, creating a vacuum within the cylinder that outside air rushes to fill. The air passes with great velocity through the mixing chamber, where it picks up the fuel. The amount of combustible mixture fed into the cylinder is regulated by the throttle valve. The simplest types of carburetors are not equipped to change the composition of the combustible mixture, although changes are required if the operating conditions of the engine are changed. To adapt to changes in operating conditions, carburetors are equipped with automatically controlled metering devices. The graph of the compositional changes of the combustible mixture fed to the engine as a function of air comsumption or as a function of engine load shows the operating characteristics of the carburetor. The adjustment and working condition of the carburetor greatly influence engine operation. Carburetors that are out of adjustment cause a deterioration of operating economy and engine performance and an increase in the toxicity of exhaust gases.

REFERENCES
Gribanov, V. I., and V. A. Orlov. *Karbiuratory dvigatelei vnutrennego sgoraniia,* 2nd ed. Leningrad, 1967.
Bleiz, N. G. *Avtomobil'nye karbiuratory, benzonasosy, fil'try.* Moscow, 1967.
B. A. KUROV [11–1215–1]

CARBURIZATION PROCESS FOR SCRAP, a process for producing steel in open-hearth furnaces or in electric furnaces. In this process carbon is introduced into the charge not by cast iron but by high-carbon-content materials (carburizing materials), such as coke, anthracite, coal, or charcoal. When this process is used for producing steel, the metallic part of the charge consists entirely of steel scrap, in contrast to other versions of the open-hearth process, where the charge contains 30–80 percent cast iron. In the semicarburization process the metallic charge contains a small quantity of cast iron (3–5 percent); the balance is steel scrap. Both of these processes are used only when cast iron is not available or is in short supply within a given economic district. Some of the disadvantages of the carburization process for scrap are a lower output than that of other versions of the open-hearth process; a shortened period of furnace trouble-free operation (because of the increased heat consumption and the

increased time required to smelt the charge); an increased consumption of fuel and of deoxidizers; and usually a higher sulfur content of steel (since the sulfur contained in the carburizing materials ends up in the steel). [11–1216–1]

CARCASSONNE, a city in southern France, capital of the department of Aude (historically, the region of Languedoc). It is situated on the Aude River near a canal linking the Mediterranean Sea with the Garonne River. Population, 46,000 (1968). The city is an important transportation junction. Industry includes the production of wine, spirits, rubber products, clothing, headwear, and footwear.

On the right bank of the Aude is the upper (old) city, containing a double line of ramparts with gates and 52 towers. The inner ring was built at the end of the fifth century, and the outer, in the 13th. Also located there are a citadel built in the second third of the 12th century, the Romanesque-Gothic cathedral of St. Nazaire, and a medieval bridge over the Aude. On the left bank is the lower city (Ville Basse), founded in 1247, with the Gothic churches of St. Michael and St. Vincent (13th and 14th centuries); it has straight streets. A museum of fine arts is also located in Carcassonne.

REFERENCES
Poux, J. *La Cité de Carcassonne,* vols. 1–3. Toulouse, 1931–38.
Morel, P. *Carcassonne.* Grenoble-Paris, 1962. [11–1283–1]

CARCHEMISH, an important ancient artisan and trade city on the right bank of the Euphrates River in northern Syria, near modern Jarablus. The city was founded about 3000 B.C. and existed until Roman times. The first written mention of the city dates from the 18th century B.C., when Carchemish was under the cultural influence of Mesopotamia. For a short time in the 15th century B.C., Carchemish was a vassalage of Egypt, and later, up to the 12th century B.C., of the Hittite empire. From the 12th to the eighth centuries B.C., Carchemish was the center of an independent kingdom. Sargon II conquered the city in 717 B.C. In 605 B.C., a battle took place there in which the Babylonian emperor Nebuchadnezzar II defeated the Egyptian pharaoh Necho II and the Assyrian emperor Ashur-uballit II; this led to the ruin of the Assyrian state. Excavations conducted in 1876, 1878–1881, and 1908–19 have revealed fortifications; foundations and architectural details of palaces, temples, and other buildings; various sculptures; and cuneiform and hieroglyphic inscriptions.

REFERENCE
Klengel, H. *Geschichte Syriens im 2. Jahrtausend vor unserer Zeit.* Part 1: *Nordsyrien.* Berlin. 1965. [11–1459–1]

CARCINOGENS (blastomogens, cancerigens), chemical compounds capable of causing cancer and other malignant tumors, as well as benign neoplasms, when the body is exposed to them. Several hundred such substances, belonging to various classes of chemical compounds, are known. For example, certain polycyclic hydrocarbons with a phenanthrene group in the molecule, azo dyes, aromatic amines, nitrosamines, and other alkylating compounds show marked carcinogenic activity. Carcinogens are found in certain industrial products, in air polluted by industrial waste, and in tobacco smoke.

The earliest notions of the existence of cancer-producing substances date from the 18th century, when cases of skin cancer in English chimney sweeps were connected with systematic contamination of the skin with coal tar and soot. In the early part of the 20th century skin cancer was induced in animals by smearing coal tar on their skin for a number of months. The carcinogens 3,4-benzpyrene and other polycyclic hydrocarbons were subsequently isolated from the tar. Urinary bladder cancer frequently developed in workers in the aniline dye industry, who were exposed to the carcinogens β-naphthylamine, benzidine, and 4-aminodiphenyl before the introduction of appropriate preventive measures. Lung cancer afflicts smokers more often than it does nonsmokers, and it afflicts those living in cities, where air pollution levels are high, more often than those living in rural areas.

The same carcinogen can give rise to tumors of different kinds and locations, depending on the site of application, and a given type of tumor can be caused by different substances. All carcinogens can be divided into three groups, according to the nature of their action: (1) locally active, (2) organotropic, that is, causing tumors not at the site of application but in certain organs, and (3) multiple, that is, producing different tumors in various organs.

The effect of carcinogens depends both on the amount of the substance and on the duration of its action; accumulation (deposition) in a tissue or organ intensifies the effect. Neoplasms do not develop immediately after exposure to a carcinogen. They do so only after a long period of time—one-fifth to one-seventh of the maximum lifetime of the given organism (this period might be 15–20 years for man and four to six months for mice). A neoplasm is preceded by precancerous changes.

The similarity of the chemical structure of carcinogenic hydrocarbons and many biologically active substances, such as sex hormones, biliary acids, and other steroids, suggested that the impairment of steroid metabolism could lead to carginogen formation in the body itself; this assumption was later confirmed experimentally. Such carcinogens, in addition to products of impaired steroid metabolism, include certain amino acid metabolites, such as tryptophan. Carcinogenic action is related to the chemical activity and electronic structure of the part of the carginogenic molecule responsible for the formation of complexes with certain cell components (apparently, nucleic acids and some proteins). It should be taken into account in considering the mechanisms of carcinogenesis that many carcinogens show pronounced mutagenic action.

Prevention of the action of carcinogens is based on a study of their distribution in man's environment and on the use of prophylactic measures in occupational, public, and personal hygiene. It is important, therefore, to control pollution of the air, water, and soil by industrial wastes and to keep carcinogenic impurities out of food and drinking water. An effective way to prevent tumors is to discover which compounds have carcinogenic properties and remove them from the sphere of man's activities.

REFERENCES

Modeli i metody eksperimental'noi onkologii. Edited by A. D. Timofeevskii. Moscow, 1960.
Neiman, I. M. *Osnovy teoreticheskoi onkologii.* Moscow, 1961.
Rukovodstvo po obshchei onkologii, 2nd ed. Edited by N. N. Petrov. Leningrad, 1961.
Shabad, L. M. *Endogennye blastomogennye veschestva.* Moscow, 1969.
Shabad, L. M. *Metody izucheniia blastomogennosti khimicheskikh veshchestv.* Moscow, 1970.   L. M. SHABAD [11–1010–2]

CARDAMOM (*Elettaria cardamomum*), a perennial herbaceous plant of the family Zingiberaceae. It has creeping rootstock. The leaves are lanceolate and are arranged in two rows along the vegetative shoots; they measure 2–4 m tall. The flower stalks, measuring up to 60 cm long, end in panicles with pale green blossoms. The fruit is a trilobate capsule with reddish-brown seeds of irregular shape. The seeds are used as a spice in cooking. They contain 3.5–7 percent oil, which is used in food and tobacco products. The oil is also used in medicine. Cardamom grows wild in the rain forests on the mountains of southern India. The plant is cultivated primarily in India, Sri-Lanka (Ceylon), Indochina, and South China.   [11–1220–2]

CARDAMOM HILLS, hills in the extreme south of India, in the southern part of the Western Ghats. Maximum altitude, 2,019 m. The terrain is characterized by a sharply outlined crest, steep slopes, and deep gorges. The hills are composed primarily of gneiss, crystalline schist, and charnockite and are covered with tropical rain forests. There are many tea and rubber plantations in the region, and the production of spices is also important.   [11–1221–1]

CARDAN MECHANISM (also universal joint or universal coupling), a mechanism that permits rotation of two shafts at a varying angle to each other by means of a movable connection

of the links (rigid Cardan mechanism) or the flexible properties of special elements (flexible Cardan mechanism). The Cardan mechanism is named for G. Cardano, who proposed a suspension for the preservation of a constant position of a body upon any rotation of its mounting.

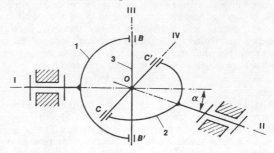

Figure 1. Diagram of Hooke's joint: (1) and (2) jaws; (3) spider; (*B*), (*B'*) and (*C*), (*C'*) joints; (I), (II), (III), and (IV) axes of rotation

The simple rigid Cardan mechanism is called Hooke's joint (Figure 1). The axes of rotation (I) and (II) intersect at an angle α with the fixed point O at the center of a circle of radius $OB = OB' = OC = OC'$. Thus, for any value of angle α when $0° \leq \alpha < 90°$, joints B, B' and C, C' in pairs describe the circumference of the same radius in planes perpendicular to axes (I) and (II). When these two conditions are met, the transmission of rotation with various angles α is possible. This property of a Cardan mechanism has brought about its widespread use in various machines—such as aircraft, instruments, lathes (articulated coupling), motor vehicles (Cardan drive), and agricultural machinery—that require a change in the relative position of the shafts transmitting rotation. A drawback of the single universal coupling is the nonuniformity of the speed of rotation of the driven shaft at a constant rate of the driving shaft. The change in the rate of the driven shaft increases with an increase in the angle α.

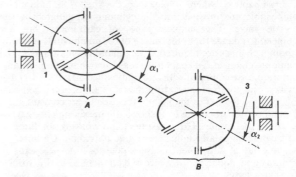

Figure 2. Diagram of double Hooke's joint: (1) driving shaft, (2) transmission shaft, (3) driven shaft, (*A*) and (*B*) universal joints

For $\alpha = 90°$, transmission of rotation using a single universal coupling becomes impossible. In such cases, as well as in cases requiring uniform rotation of the driven shaft, a double universal coupling (Figure 2), in which angles α_1 and α_2 are equal and the jaws on shaft (2) are in the same plane, should be used. If there is insufficient space for a double universal coupling, a Cardan is used whose design is based on division of the angle between the shafts by a bisecting plane (Figure 3). The angle of inclination of the shafts of a rigid double universal coupling may reach 38°. Flexible Cardan mechanisms, with flexible elements made of a durable elastic material (Figure 4), are used for shaft angles of inclination of 3°–5°.

REFERENCES

Mertsalov, N. I. *Teoriia prostranstvennykh mekhanizmov.* Moscow, 1951.
Zinov'ev, V. A. *Prostranstvennye mekhanizmy s nizshimi parami.* Moscow-Leningrad, 1952.
Artobolevskii, I. I. *Teoriia mashin i mekhanizmov,* 2nd ed. Moscow, 1967.   E. M. STARIKOV [11–1222–1]

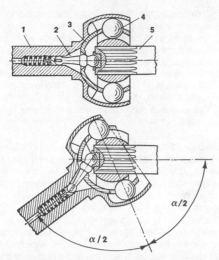

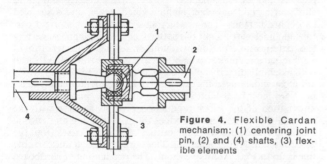

Figure 3. Cardan mechanism whose operation is based on the principle of division of the angle between the shafts by a bisecting plane: (1) and (5) shafts located in the same plane and intersecting at an angle; (2) guide pin, which sets the separator upon a change in the angle between the shaft axes; (3) separator; (4) ball bearings lying in the bisecting plane

Figure 4. Flexible Cardan mechanism: (1) centering joint pin, (2) and (4) shafts, (3) flexible elements

CARDANO, GERONIMO

CARDANO, GERONIMO (Girolamo Cardano; Hieronymus Cardanus). Born Sept. 24, 1501 (1506 by other accounts), in Pavia; died Sept. 21, 1576, in Rome. Italian philosopher, physician, and mathematician.

Cardano elaborated a cosmological system in *De subtilitate rerum* (1550) and *De rerum varietate* (1557) that was close to other formulations by the Renaissance natural philosophers (B. Telesio, G. Bruno). Although materialist features are noticeable—eternal matter is assumed to be the fundamental substance—a mystical Neoplatonism predominates. According to Cardano, the world is constructed out of three elements, earth, water, and air; matter has two properties, warmth and humidity. Fire is only a form of existence of the all-pervading and omnipresent celestial warmth, that is, of matter, which thus resembles the light of the Neoplatonists. The becoming of a thing is due to the world soul. The mind, identical in all men, is passive, and only a divine principle, which is placed in it, makes possible the knowledge of god in mystical exaltation. Cardano makes a distinction between the mind and the intellect, the active element of human consciousness; man understands the essence of things only where the object, as in mathematics, which is highest form of knowledge, is formed by the intellect and is assimilated to it.

Cardano's natural philosophy is both the foundation and the final synthesis of his most diverse scholarly activity in astrology and alchemy, medicine and physics, mathematics, engineering, and psychology. His works played an important role in the development of algebra; he was one of the first in Europe to admit negative roots of equations. His name is linked with the formula for the solution of the reduced cubic equation (Cardano's formula). Cardano also studied the transmission of motion and the theory of levers.

WORKS

Opera omnia, vols. 1–10. Lyon, 1663.

In Russian translation:
O moei zhizni. Moscow, 1938.

REFERENCES

Struik, D. J. *Kratkii ocherk istorii matematiki*, 2nd ed. Moscow, 1969. (Translated from German.)
Rivari, E. *La mente di G. Cardano.* Bologna, 1906.
Simili, A. *G. Cardano nella luce e nell'ombra del suo tempo.* Milan, 1941.
Bellini, A. *G. Cardano e il suo tempo.* Milan, 1947.

N. V. KOTRELEV [11–1223–1]

CARDANO'S FORMULA, a formula for finding the roots of the reduced cubic equation

$$x^3 + px + q = 0$$

The formula has the following form:

$$x = \sqrt[3]{-\frac{q}{2} + \sqrt{\frac{q^2}{4} + \frac{p^3}{27}}}$$
$$+ \sqrt[3]{-\frac{q}{2} - \sqrt{\frac{q^2}{4} + \frac{p^3}{27}}}$$

Any cube root has three values, among which only one is real. The values of the cube roots in Cardano's formula should be taken such that their product be equal to $-p/3$; it is precisely these values that must be summed to obtain the root of the equation. In this way it is possible to find the three roots of the equation. Cardano's formula is named for G. Cardano and was first published by him in 1545, although the question of whether it was found by Cardano himself or copied by him from N. Tartaglia, or discovered even earlier (c. 1515) by S. dal Ferro, is impossible to answer with complete certainty.   [11–1224–1]

CARDAN SHAFT (named for G. Cardano), a device in motor vehicles for the transmission of rotation from a driving shaft to a driven shaft when the shafts are at an angle to one another. The angle and distance between the shafts often change continuously during operation.

In motor vehicles, a Cardan shaft is used to connect the motor and transmission (at an angle of up to 5°), the transmission and transfer case (at an angle of up to 5°), and the transmission or transfer case and the rear-axle drive (at an angle of up to 15°), as well as in steering gear or winch drive.

A Cardan shaft consists of a propeller shaft with two (less frequently one) Cardans. If the propeller shaft is connecting mechanisms between which the angle and distance vary (for example, the transmission and rear-axle drive of a motor vehicle), overhang balance is provided in the form of a slip splined joint, which makes possible a change in the length of the shaft within set limits. Depending on the angle between the propeller shafts in a Cardan shaft, rigid or flexible semi-Cardan joints, full Cardans of unequal angular velocity, or Cardans of equal angular velocity may be used. Full Cardans, which have two jaws, needle bearings, a spider, mounts for the spider journals, and a tightening mechanism, are the most commonly used type. The efficiency of a single Cardan is 0.985–0.99.

REFERENCE

Malakhovskii, Ia. E., A. A. Lapin, and N. K. Vedeneev. *Kardannye peredachi.* Moscow, 1962.   M. I. LUR'E [11–1221–2]

CARDBOARD, a variety of paper that differs from ordinary paper in its greater quantity of paper pulp per unit area. There is no uniform international classification that makes a sharp distinction between paper and cardboard. For example, in the USSR, cardboard is the term for paper matter with more than 250 g of pulp per sq m; in the German Democratic Republic, more than 150 g/m²; and in Poland, more than 180 g/m².

The operations in the production of cardboard are beating, molding, pressing, and drying; they do not differ in principle from similar operations for making paper, although material with coarser and stiffer fibers (such as brown wood pulp, hemicellulose, sulfate pulp, and waste paper) is more frequently used as raw material to make cardboard.

Types of cardboard include packing, printing, footwear, electric-insulation, and millboard. Packing cardboard is used to make boxes and cartons. Types of printing cardboard are binder's board (for making book bindings and clean products), matrix board (for making matrices for molding stereotypes), and ticket cardboard. Types of millboard include facing board (for facing dry gypsum plaster) and wallboard (for covering building walls). Types of industrial cardboard are fitting board (for making sealing gaskets), sound-deadening and thermal-insulation cardboard, and waterproof and filter board.

Cardboard is made on cardboard machines. A distinction is made between single-ply and multi-ply cardboard. The layers of multi-ply cardboard are usually prepared from fibers. The inner layers are molded from cheaper compositions; the outer layers are molded from more durable and expensive fiber (for example, the inner layers of most types of box cardboard are molded from white pulp with a small amount of cellulose added, from waste paper, or from other cheap fibrous materials; the outer layers are made of bleached or unbleached sulfate pulp).

The properties of cardboard are evaluated by a series of general and special technical parameters. The general parameters include mass per square meter, thickness, and moisture content. The special parameters include absorbent capacity, electric-insulation properties, and deformation upon moistening and drying. The required properties for each type of cardboard are provided by the selection of the proper intermediate products, by their treatment, and by the introduction of adhesives, binders, fillers, and dyes into the cardboard, and by the application of polymer films and metal foil to the surface of the cardboard.

REFERENCES
Lapiński, J. *Kartonodelatel'nye mashiny.* Moscow, 1966. (Translated from Polish.)
Legman, G. *Osnovy tekhnologii pererabotki bumagi i kartona.* Moscow, 1968. (Translated from German.) M. M. KOTIK [11–1426–2]

CARDBOARD MACHINE, a machine that produces cardboard in a continuous sheet. Cardboard machines are divided according to function and design into four main types, fourdrinier (flat-screen), multicylinder, combination, and multicylinder with horizontal molding.

Single-ply cardboard weighing up to 500 g/m^2 is produced on fourdrinier cardboard machines, which are virtually identical to paper machines, although they have a larger drying section because of their higher output (up to 850 tons per day). Such cardboard machines weigh about 4,000 tons and are about 170 m long; the power of the motors that drive all their mechanisms is about 13 megawatts. A staff of five to six is required to operate such machines.

Multicylinder cardboard machines produce multi-ply cardboard weighing 600 g/m^2 and more. The fourdrinier section of such machines consists of five to eight hollow cylinders 0.9–1.5 m in diameter (the cylinder walls are made from a fine metal screen). The cylinders are located in baths, into which the pulp is introduced continuously. Upon rotation of the cylinder, water passes through the screen within the cylinder and the matted fiber remains on the screen in the form of a layer weighing 40–100 g/m^2. The individual layers are removed in succession by a conveyor belt and are joined into a continuous cardboard sheet. Machines have been constructed in which the pulp is introduced into the cylinder from an inlet device and reduced pressure is maintained within the cylinder.

The press section of the cylinder machines is divided into a preliminary section, with three to five pairs of roller presses, and a main section, with two to four pairs. The drying and cutting sections are similar to the fourdrinier machine. It is possible to produce cardboard made up of layers of different fibrous materials on such machines. For example, the outer layers may be of bleached fiber and the inner layers may be of waste paper or wood pulp. The output of cylinder cardboard machines is as high as 500 tons per day.

Combination cardboard machines are used mainly for preparing one-sided or two-sided lithographic cardboard (chrome-substitute type) weighing up to 500 g/m^2. The fourdrinier section of the machine consists of flat screens in conjunction with four to six cylinders. The cardboard sheet in such machines is joined together on the flat screen before final drawing-off by a box or

couch spindle. The width of combination machines is up to 4.2 m, and their output is up to 300 tons per day.

The screen section of cardboard machines with horizontal molding with a number of screens (Inverform type) consists of one lower screen and a number of upper screens located one on top of the other, with the number of upper screens equal to the number of cardboard layers. The pulp is introduced between the lower and upper screens, through which the dehydrated sheet is produced. The width of such machines is 6 m, and their output is up to 350 tons per day. M. M. KOTIK [11–1428–1]

CARDBOARD PRODUCTION, the manufacture of various items from paper and cardboard, mainly packaging products such as boxes, drums, packets, cartons, and bags, as well as household items and toys. Cardboard and paper packaging is significantly cheaper and more convenient than wood, metal, or glass. The various types of packaging are soft, semirigid, rigid, combined, and outer packaging (boxes).

The production of soft paper packages (packets, envelopes, and bags) is completely automated. The automatic machines perform all the production processes, including printing, gluing, and shaping. For example, various types of packets—such as flat packets, packets with side folds, and square-bottom and hexagonal-bottom packets—may be produced automatically. The output of such automatic machines may be as high as 120,000 packets per hour. Types of semirigid packages include folding packets and cartons made of paper with a density similar to cardboard; rigid packages include glued, sewn, and assembled cardboard cartons. The production of semirigid and rigid cartons includes cutting out the pattern and folding and converting the pattern into a carton by gluing or sewing. The structure of folding cartons makes possible their transport in folded form, with assembly directly before use. Corrugated cardboard cartons are most widely used for external packaging. Automatic assembly lines have been built for their production, making possible automation of the entire production process, starting with the entry of the intermediate product into the printing and cutting machine and ending with the output of finished boxes from the assembly and gluing machine. The output of such an assembly line is up to 15,000 units per hour. The production of cardboard boxes from intermediate products of complex shape without glue or brackets is promising. Such intermediate products are punched on flat-die or rotation presses.

In the production of combination packages, metal tops and bottoms are attached to paper bodies made on winding machines. A special branch of cardboard production is the production from paper pulp of cast products such as bottles, cans, pails, and cartons.

REFERENCES
Babitskii, S. L. *Izgotovlenie bumazhnoi i kartonnoi tary sypuchikh produktov i upakovka.* Moscow, 1967.
Danilevskii, V. A. *Proizvodstvo transportnoi kartonnoi tary.* Moscow, 1968. M. M. KOTIK [11–1427–2]

CARD CLOTHING, material with a uniform spiny surface, which is used to cover the carding elements of carding machines in the textile industry. Card clothing consists of a flexible foundation in which steel wire staples with pointed ends, usually bent near the foundations, are mounted at an angle. The card clothing foundation consists of several layers of glued cotton material, sometimes with an additional layer of rubber or felting. Card clothing is made in various sizes, expressed by an arbitrary number, according to the fineness of the wire and the number of staples per square centimeter. For example, No. 100 consists of 39 staples per sq cm made of wire 0.34 mm in diameter. Card clothing is being replaced by all-metal serrated clothing.

G. N. KUKIN [11–1237–3]

CÁRDENAS, LÁZARO (full name, Lázaro Cárdenas y del Río). Born May 21, 1895, in the state of Michoacán; died Oct. 19, 1970, in Mexico City. Statesman and military and political figure of Mexico.

The son of an artisan weaver, Cárdenas in 1913 became involved in the Mexican Revolution of 1910–17. In 1928 he received the rank of division general. From 1928 to 1932 he was governor of Michoacán. He became minister of the interior in 1931 and minister of war in 1933. From 1934 to 1940, Cárdenas was the president of Mexico. He opposed the predominance of British and American capital in the country. During his tenure, railroads (1937) and petroleum enterprises (1938) belonging to foreign companies were partially nationalized. Cárdenas initiated an agrarian reform and fought against the interference of the Catholic Church in the political life of the country. The peasant and labor union movements were developed, and progressive organizations, including the Communist Party, became very active while he was in office. From 1943 to 1945 he was minister of national defense. After 1949 he was active in the peace movement. He was a laureate of the International Lenin Prize for Strengthening Peace Between Nations (1955). In 1969 he became honorary president of the World Peace Council.

[11–1225–1]

CÁRDENAS, a city and port on the northern coast of Cuba, in Mantanzas Province. Population, 55,200 (1970). Its industry includes sugar refining and food processing. There is also a shipyard. Sugar and henequen (fiber made from the leaves of the agave plant) are exported. The city is a fishing center; sea salt is extracted commercially east of Cárdenas. [11–1224–3]

CARDIFF, a city in Great Britain; capital of Wales. Situated on Bristol Bay, at the mouth of the Taff River. Population, 278,200 (1971). It is part of the conurbation of southeast Wales. An important industrial center and transportation hub.

In the late 19th and early 20th centuries, Cardiff's advantageous position made it a major port in Britain for the export of bunker coal from the coalfields of South Wales, peaking in 1913, when it exported 36 million tons, or two-fifths of the total British export. Today, coal shipments are nonexistent for all practical purposes, and Cardiff now serves as a port for importing iron ore, other raw materials, and food supplies. Its industry includes ferrous metallurgy and various forms of machine building (including auto manufacture and ship repair); food processing and printing are highly developed.

Several colleges of the University of Wales are located in Cardiff. The castle (c. 1090), Llandaff Cathedral (12th–15th centuries), and the Church of St. John (15th century) are of historical and architectural interest. The city has grown intensely since the 19th century; new industrial and port structures and workers' residential areas with characteristically clustered houses have been built. The Civic Center in Cathays Park (planned 1924–46) creates a large verdant area; the city hall (1904; architect, H. Lanchester) and the National Temple of Peace (1938; architect, P. Thomas) are part of the complex. The National Museum of Wales and the Welsh Folk Museum, with collections of folk art, are also located in Cardiff. Cumbran, a companion city designed by the architect J. West, was built in the 1950's.

[11–1235–1]

CARDIGAN, a bay of the Irish Sea, on the western coast of Great Britain (Wales). Length, 56 km; width, approximately 102 km; depth, up to 56 m. The shores are rocky. Many rivers drain into Cardigan Bay. Tides are semidiurnal and reach a height of 8 m. Ports include Fishguard and Portmadoc. [11–1225–2]

CARDINAL, in the Catholic Church the highest member of the clergy after the pope.

Cardinals are the closest advisers and assistants to the pope in matters of church administration; they form the College of Cardinals, headed by a dean. Cardinals are appointed by the pope. The pope himself is elected exclusively by the College of Cardinals according to a decree of the Lateran Council of 1179. In 1586, Pope Sixtus V established that the number of the cardinals should not exceed 70. Up to the middle of the 20th century, Italians predominated in the College of Cardinals. The number of cardinals in the college was increased by Pope John XXIII and Pope Paul VI, and by October 1969 the College of Cardinals consisted of 131 members, as well as bishops from Asian and African countries.

The cardinals living in Rome (cardinals of the Curia) head the central organs of the Vatican, including the congregations and the tribunals. The cardinals are divided hierarchically into three groups—cardinal bishops, cardinal priests, and cardinal deacons. According to the decision of Pope Paul VI in 1970, cardinals who reach the age of 75 retire but retain their cloth; when they reach the age of 80, they remain members of the college but lose the right to belong to the Roman Curia and to participate in the election of a new pope. [11–1225–4]

CARDINAL (*Cardinalis cardinalis*), a bird of the family Fringillidae, order Passeriformes. Body length, approximately 20 cm. The male's feathers are bright red (the color of a cardinal's mantle). The base of the bill is black. The female is brown.

The cardinal is found in the USA (naturally in the east; introduced to California and the Hawaiian Islands), Mexico, and northern Central America. It dwells in forests, gardens, and parks, feeding on seeds and insects. It lays a clutch of three to four eggs, which the female alone incubates for 12–13 days.

[11–1225–5]

CARDINAL POINTS OF AN OPTICAL SYSTEM, the points on the optical axis OO' (see Figure 1) of a centered optical system that can be used to construct the image of an arbitrary point in space for objects in the paraxial region, which is the region around the axis of symmetry of the system where a point is represented by a point, a straight line by a straight line, and a plane by a plane.

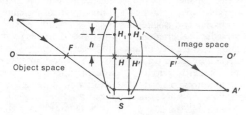

Figure 1. Position of the image A' of an arbitrary point A projected by an optical system S can be found if the cardinal points F, F', H, and H' of the system are known: a ray passing through the front focus F is directed by the system parallel to its optical axis OO', and a ray that is incident upon the system parallel to the axis OO' is directed through the back focus F' after refraction

There are four cardinal points in an optical system: the front and back foci F and F' and the front and back principal points H and H'. The back focus is the image of an infinitely remote point located on the optical axis in the object space, and the front focus is the image in the object space of an infinitely remote point in the image space. The principal points are the points of intersection with the optical axis of the principal planes, which are the planes for which the optical system S produces full-size mutual images (every point H_1 located in the principal plane HH_1 at a distance h from the axis OO' appears in the other principal plane $H'H'_1$ as the point H'_1 at the same distance h from the axis as point H_1).

The distance from point H to point F is called the front focal distance (negative in the figure), and the distance from point H' to point F' is called the back focal distance (positive in the figure).

The construction of an image A' of an arbitrary point A for a centered optical system using the points F, H, H', and F' is shown in Figure 1.

REFERENCE

Tudorovskii, A. I. *Teoriia opticheskikh priborov*, 2nd ed. [part] 1. Moscow-Leningrad, 1948. Page 265.   G. G. SLIUSAREV [11–1226–3]

CARDINAL VEINS, the main paired anteroposterior veins carrying blood to the heart, well developed in the embryos of all vertebrates and man. In adults, the cardinal veins are completely developed only in rotifers, fish, and caudate amphibians.

The anterior cardinal veins, or jugular veins, collect blood from the head, while the posterior cardinal veins collect blood from the kidneys and walls of the trunk. The anterior and posterior cardinal veins merge on each side of the body to form the ducts of Cuvier. In lungfish and terrestrial vertebrates the function of the posterior cardinal veins is performed by the posterior (inferior) vena cava, which in part develops from them. The vestiges of the posterior cardinal veins are reduced in acaudate amphibians but form the vertebral and azygos veins in terrestrial vertebrates. The anterior cardinal veins are part of the anterior (superior) vena cava. [11–1226–2]

CARDIOCRINUM, a genus of bulbous plants of the lily family.

Cardiocrina are monocarpous plants that bloom in the fourth or fifth year and form a massive stem, about 2.5 m in height and covered with heart-shaped leaves. The leaves closest to the roots are about 30 cm long. The flowers are white, brownish inside; they are aromatic and up to 15 cm in length. There are 20–25 flowers in an inflorescence. The three known species of *Cardiocrinum* grow in the damp forests of the Himalayas, central and eastern China, Japan, Sakhalin Island, and the Kuril Islands. All species of *Cardiocrinum* are ornamental. They are propagated both by seed, which germinate a year after sowing, and by daughter bulbs. [11–1228–2]

CARDIOGRAPHY, the recording of the heart's contractions; in the broader sense, all methods of registering the heart's contractile functions.

The first cardiogram (more precisely, a mechanocardiogram) was taken by the French physiologist E. Marey in 1863 by recording the cardiac impulse at the fifth intercostal space. An impulse results when the heart contracts from an ellipsoid, becoming rounder and thicker, its apex rising and pressing against the chest wall. The irregularity of individual waves on the cardiogram and the difficulty of interpretation led to the replacement of the method by more refined ones: ultrasound impulse cardiography, ballistocardiography, dynamocardiography, kinetocardiography, seismokymography, roentgenokymography, electrokymography, and phonocardiography.

I. N. D'IAKONOVA [11–1227–3]

CARDIOLOGY, a branch of medicine concerned with the structure, function, and diseases of the heart and blood vessels, the causes, mechanisms of development, clinical symptoms, and diagnosis of the diseases, and the development of methods of treatment (including surgical), prevention, and rehabilitation of individuals with injuries to the cardiovascular system.

Before the appearance of the field of cardiology proper, questions of the cardiovascular system were taken up necessarily by internal medicine, surgery, pediatrics, neuropathology, physiology, normal and pathological anatomy, and pharmacology. The findings of these studies had created a body of knowledge of the cardiovascular system when, because of the increasing incidence of cardiovascular diseases, cardiology evolved into an independent medical discipline in the 19th and 20th centuries. The evolution of cardiology as an independent study was also the result of the development and perfection of techniques for studying the blood vessels and heart, the accumulation of data on the causes and mechanisms of development of cardiovascular diseases, and the development of techniques for preventing and treating these diseases. While retaining its connection with many medical sciences, cardiology makes use of certain methods of investigation unique to itself.

Fragmentary information on the structure of the human cardiovascular system can be found in the oldest sources. The Greek physician Galen (second century A.D.) developed the first diagram of blood circulation. This scheme lasted until the 17th century, when it was challenged by the English scientist W. Harvey in his *Exercitatio anatomica de motu cordis et sanguinis in animalibus* (1628). Harvey's discovery of the circulation of the blood marked the beginning of a rapid accumulation of both anatomicophysiological and clinical data on the cardiovascular system. Coronary circulation, certain heart defects, and angina pectoris were described between the 17th and the 19th centuries. The diagnosis of many heart diseases was facilitated by the introduction in 1819 of mediate auscultation (using a stethoscope) by the French physician R. Laennec.

Great contributions to the knowledge of the anatomy and physiology of the cardiovascular system were made in the 19th century by the Czech physiologist J. Purkinje (1839), who studied the cellular structure of the myocardium, the German physician W. His (1890–94), the German pathologist L. Aschoff, the Japanese pathologist S. Tawara (1906), and the Englishmen A. Keith and M. Flack (1907), who discovered and described the elements of the system of nervous excitation in the heart. The German physiologist K. Ludwig discovered the general vasomotor center in the medulla oblongata. He also suggested methods of recording blood pressure and determining the rate of blood flow. A substantial contribution to cardiology was made in Russia by S. P. Botkin, who found the place for the most effective auscultation of diastolic murmurs in aortic insufficiency (third and fourth intercostal spaces, or points of Botkin).

The blossoming of physiology at the turn of the 20th century, particularly the work of the Russian scientists I. M. Sechenov, I. F. Tsion, and A. B. Fokht, the Russian physiologists I. P. Pavlov, V. Ia. Danilevskii, L. A. Orbeli, K. M. Bykov, and V. N. Chernigovskii, the French physiologist C. Bernard, and the English scientist E. H. Starling, encouraged the development of a functional approach in cardiology. New methods of examination were introduced. In 1903 the Dutch scientist W. Einthoven recorded the electric currents generated by the human heart (electrocardiography); this method was subsequently improved and developed as a result of the work of the Russian physiologist A. F. Samoilov and the Soviet internists V. F. Zelenin and L. I. Fogel'son, the English physician T. Lewis, and the German physician R. F. Wenckebach. In 1905 the Russian physician N. S. Korotkov proposed the acoustic method of determining blood pressure. The introduction into clinical practice of cardiac fluoroscopy and roentgenography, contrast angiocardiography, roentgenkymography and electrokymography, phase roentgenocardiography, cardiac and vascular catheterization, radiocardiography, phonocardiography and ballistocardiography, a dye-dilution technique to study hemodynamics, ultrasound cardiography, and immunology were of great value in diagnosing cardiovascular diseases. The Soviet physiologist E. B. Babskii proposed an original method of studying cardiac activity called dynamocardiography.

The founder of clinical cardiography is considered to be the English physician J. Mackenzie, who published the first scientific work devoted to a comprehensive study of arrhythmias (1902), a work on the nature, diagnosis, and treatment of heart diseases (1908), and a study of angina pectoris (1923). The works of the French physician H. Huchard, known for his manual of cardiology (1893), the English physicians T. Lewis and G. Pickering, the German physician E. Romberg, and the American physician W. Osler played a major role in elucidating the pathology of blood circulation. One of the greatest contemporary cardiologists was the American physician P. D. White, who carried out major clinical and epidemiological studies on atherosclerosis and coronary insufficiency, malignant endocarditis, syphilis of the cardiovascular system, and arrhythmia. The American scientists C. Wiggers and L. Katz investigated the dynamics of blood circulation. V. P. Obraztsov and N. D. Strazhesko described in detail the clinical picture of coronary thrombosis and myocardial infarction (1909). G. F. Lang proposed and elaborated a neurogenic concept of hypertension that was further developed by A. L. Miasnikov and his co-workers. G. F. Lang developed a classification of cardiovascular diseases, approved by the 12th All-Union Congress of Internists in 1935, according to which every disease must be characterized from a variety of aspects—etiological, pathologicoanatomical, pathologicophysiological, functional, and symptomatological. The same congress also adopted a classification system for circulatory insufficiency proposed by Strazhesko and V. Kh. Vasilenko. The studies of N. N. Anichkov and S. S. Khalatov on the creation of experimental cholesterol atherosclerosis enabled them to formulate a cholesterol theory of atherosclerosis, which won wide acceptance and made it possible to reveal the main pathogenetic mechanisms of this disease.

The research of Soviet cardiologists showed that disturbances of nervous regulation with subsequent humoral disorders play a leading role in the appearance and progress of hypertension, atherosclerosis, and coronary insufficiency. A. L. Miasnikov successfully elaborated these ideas. The studies of P. E. Lukomskii and B. V. Il'inskii on atherosclerosis and coronary insufficiency are widely known. The role of neurologic factors in the mechanism of development of atherosclerosis was demonstrated by I. V. Davydovskii and E. M. Tareev. Various aspects of angina pectoris and myocardial infarction were explored by G. F. Lang, M. S. Vovsi, M. M. Gubergrits, V. F. Zelenin, and M. N. Tumanovskii. D. D. Pletnev and V. Kh. Vasilenko studied the complications connected with myocardial infarction (for example, thromboembolism).

Rheumatic heart disease is a major problem in cardiology; it has been studied by both pathologists (V. T. Talalaev, M. A. Skvortsov, N. A. Kraevskii, and A. I. Strukov) and clinicians (M. P. Konchalovskii, M. V. Chernorutskii, N. D. Strazhesko, A. I. Nesterov, E. M. Gel'shtein, and I. A. Kassirskii). The clinical aspects of malignant endocarditis were studied by G. F. Lang, N. D. Strazhesko, N. A. Kurshakov, N. S. Molchanov, and E. M. Tareev. Various functional disturbances of the myocardium were also studied by Ia. G. Etinger, V. Kh. Vasilenko, and A. A. Kedrov. Many aspects of pulmonary heart were worked out in detail by the Soviet scientists B. E. Votchal, V. F. Zelenin, V. Kh. Vasilenko, B. E. Kogan, B. I. Kushelevskii, P. E. Lukomskii, V. V. Parin, and N. N. Savitskii.

Radioactive isotopes have been used to investigate the cardiovascular system since the middle of the 20th century. Certain older methods (phlebography, oscillography) found application in clinical practice in conjunction with improved electronic apparatus.

V. N. Vinogradov, P. E. Lukomskii, E. I. Chazov, and Z. I. Ianushkevichius were awarded state prizes for organizing the care of patients with myocardial infarction and introducing new methods of treatment (anticoagulants, fibrinolysin). V. V. Zakusov and others worked out certain problems in the pharmacotherapy of cardiovascular diseases.

A high level of technical development, as well as modern diagnostic methods, has made surgical intervention feasible in cardiovascular diseases. The development of surgical treatment of heart defects helped to stimulate extensive study of the diagnosis and clinical aspects of these diseases. Operations were performed for coronary insufficiency and removal of thrombi. In 1967 a Cape Town surgeon, C. Barnard, performed history's first transplant of a heart from one man to another. By 1972 more than 200 such operations had been performed (USA, France, USSR).

Surgery of the heart and blood vessels has been progressing successfully in the USSR through the work of A. N. Bakulev, B. V. Petrovskii, P. A. Kupriianov, A. A. Vishnevskii, V. I. Kolesov, N. M. Amosov, and E. N. Meshalkin, all of whom were awarded the Lenin Prize. The State Prize was awarded to A. A. Vishnevskii, N. L. Gurvich, V. A. Negovskii, and B. M. Tsukerman for developing electroimpulse therapy and introducing it into clinical practice.

Important contributions to heart surgery have been made abroad by C. S. Beck, C. P. Bailey, A. Blalock, L. O'Shaughnessy, P. D. White, A. Dogliotti, W. B. Cannon, M. de Bakey, D. Cooley, and R. C. Lillehei.

Experimental cardiology, a complex of physiological, pathophysiological, biochemical, and morphological studies conducted for the purpose of studying the circulatory system, both healthy and diseased, is an independent branch of cardiology. The main concerns of modern experimental cardiology are the clinical physiology of circulation; the regulation of vascular tone in health and in sickness; the physiology and pathology of coronary circulation (specifically, myocardial infarction), the contractile function, automatism, and excitability of the heart, normal and pathological; compensatory hyperfunction, hypertrophy, and insufficiency of the hypertrophic heart; the physiology and pathology of pulmonary circulation; the physiology and pathology of regional and capillary circulation; and the pathogenesis of atherosclerosis. These objectives are being pursued successfully both in the USSR and abroad.

The All-Union Scientific Medical Society of Cardiologists (affiliated with the International Society of Cardiology and the European Society of Cardiology) and republic societies of cardiologists were organized in 1963. The International Association of Cardiologists was established in 1950. It includes European, Asian, Pacific, and inter-American associations of cardiologists.

Cardiological care in the USSR is provided in the cardiology departments of hospitals and in the cardiorheumatological offices of polyclinics, in which patients are treated and given advice and efforts are made to control cardiovascular diseases. Specialized service for patients of acute myocardial infarction includes specialized first aid teams, infarct departments, and intensive care units in hospitals.

The journal *Kardiologiia* has been published in Moscow since 1961. Articles on cardiology are published in other medical periodicals as well. The international cardiological journal *Cor et vasa* (Prague) was founded in 1959.

The following journals are published abroad: *Kardiologia polska* (Lodz, since 1957), *Archiv für Kreislaufforschung* (Dresden-Leipzig-Darmstadt, since 1937), *Zeitschrift für Kreislaufforschung* (Dresden-Leipzig-Darmstadt, since 1909), *Circulation* (New York, since 1949), *American Journal of Cardiology* (New York, since 1958), *American Heart Journal* (St. Louis, since 1925), *British Heart Journal* (London, since 1939), *Japanese Heart Journal* (Tokyo, since 1960), *Acta cardiologica* (Brussels, since 1946), *Cardiovascular Diseases and Cardiovascular Surgery* (Amsterdam, since 1957), *Minerva Cardioangiologica* (Turin, since 1953), and *Journal of Cardiovascular Surgery* (Turin, since 1960).

Cardiological research in the USSR is carried out by the A. L. Miasnikov Institute of Cardiology of the Academy of Medical Sciences of the USSR, the Institute of Rheumatism of the Academy of Medical Sciences of the USSR, the A. N. Bakulev Institute of Cardiovascular Surgery of the Academy of Medical Sciences of the USSR, the Institute of Experimental and Clinical Surgery of the Ministry of Public Health of the USSR, the A. V. Vishnevskii Institute of Surgery of the Academy of Medical Sciences of the USSR, the Institute of Circulatory Pathology of the Ministry of Public Health of the RSFSR (Novosibirsk), the Institute of Pharmacology and Chemotherapy, the M. D. Tsinamzgvrishvili Institute of Clinical and Experimental Cardiology (Tbilisi), and the Institute of Cardiology and Heart Surgery (Yerevan). Aspects of the physiology and pathology of blood circulation are also concerns of the Institute of Normal and Pathological Physiology of the Academy of Medical Sciences of the USSR, several institutes of the Academy of Sciences of the USSR, and a number of clinics of medical colleges and institutes of advanced training for physicians.

Major scientific cardiological centers abroad include the Institute of Blood Circulation (Prague), the Cardiological Center (East Berlin), the National Heart and Lung Institute (Bethesda), the Cardiovascular Institute (San Francisco), the Cardiovascular Institute of the Michael Reese Hospital (Chicago), and the National Cardiological Institute (Mexico City).

REFERENCES

Botkin, S. P. *Kurs kliniki vnutrennykh boleznei i klinicheskie lektsii,* vols. 1–2. Moscow, 1950.
Zelenin, V. F. *Bolezni serdechno-sosudistoi sistemy.* Moscow, 1956.
Lang, G. F. *Bolezni sistemy krovoobrashcheniia.* Moscow, 1958.
Parin, V. V., and F. Z. Meerson. "Rol' i zadachi eksperimental'noi kardiologii." *Vestn. AMN SSSR,* 1961, no. 5.
Mnogotomnoe rukovodstvo po vnutrennim bolezniam, vols. 1–2. Moscow, 1962–64.
Samoilova, S. V. *Anatomiia krovenosnykh sosudov serdtsa.* [Atlas.] Moscow, 1970.
Brugsch, T. *Kardiologie,* 4th ed. Leipzig, 1955.

I. K. SHKHVATSABAIA   [11–1228–4]

CARDIOLOGY, INSTITUTE OF (full name, A. L. Miasnikov Institute of Cardiology of the Academy of Medical Sciences of the USSR), a scientific organization that engages in research on the origin, development, treatment, and prevention of diseases of the human cardiovascular system.

The Institute of Cardiology was founded in 1945 in Moscow as the Institute of Internal Medicine; in 1948 it was incorporated into the Academy of Medical Sciences of the USSR. In 1967 it was reorganized as the A. L. Miasnikov Institute of Cardiology, named in honor of the Soviet internist A. L. Miasnikov, who was its founder and the director of the institute between 1948 and 1967. In 1972 the institute consisted of eight clinical departments (including heart surgery), a department of functional examination methods, an X-ray and radiology department, a scientific and medical information section, and laboratories—clinical and biochemical, X-ray–phonodiagnostic, pathophysiological (two), pathologicoanatomic, and cardiovascular epidemiological. The Institute of Cardiology is the leading research organization in the USSR concerned with arterial hypertension, atherosclerosis, coronary disease, heart failure, and circulatory insufficiency.

The Institute of Cardiology has residents in clinical medicine and graduate research students in full-time and correspondence programs. The institute has the right to hear defenses of dissertations for the candidate degree. It periodically publishes the results of scientific meetings and conferences, as well as monographs and collections of articles.

I. K. SHKHVATSABAIA [11–1228–3]

CARDIOSCLEROSIS, a pathological condition of the heart muscle caused by the growth therein of connective tissue in place of functional muscular tissue.

Cardiosclerosis as a rule is the result of a chronic or acute heart disease (coronary insufficiency, myocarditis). The condition may be either diffuse or focal. For example, myocardial infarction may result in focal sclerosis. One of the chief and earliest symptoms of cardiosclerosis is shortness of breath (only during physical exertion at the onset of the condition, and later on at rest). As the condition progresses the signs of cardiac insufficiency appear: rapid pulse, edema in the legs, enlargement of the liver, pulmonary congestion, and dyspneic attacks. Irregular heart beat is a frequent manifestation of cardiosclerosis (extrasystole, auricular fibrillation). The heart enlarges. The proliferation of connective tissue in the heart valves may result in heart defects.

Treatment is aimed at improving the blood supply to the heart muscle (administration of vasodilators and anticoagulants), correcting cardiac insufficiency (administration of strophanthin, digitalis, diuretics), and eliminating arrhythmia (quinidine, novocainamide).

REFERENCES
Lang, G. F. *Bolezni sistemy krovoobrashcheniia,* 2nd ed. Moscow, 1958.
Miasnikov, A. L. *Gipertonicheskaia bolezn' i ateroskleroz.* Moscow, 1965.
Wenckebach, K. F. *Herz- und Kreislauf-Insuffizienz,* 4th ed. Dresden-Leipzig, 1942.
White, P. D. *Heart Disease,* 3rd ed. New York, 1945.

N. R. PALEEV [11–1223–1]

CARDIOSPASM, a condition manifested by spasm of the esophagus at its point of passage into the stomach.

The causes of cardiospasm are unknown. Functional disturbance of the vagus nerve, which maintains the peristaltic activity of the esophagus, and expansion of the cardia play a major role in its origin. The condition may occur at any age, but it occurs most often between 20 and 40. It sets in with difficulty in swallowing (dysphagia), which may develop suddenly or gradually. Warm liquid food passes most easily through the esophagus of most patients, although in some cases solids are more easily swallowed. When dysphagia occurs, patients try to help the food pass through the esophagus by eating while standing or walking around or by pressing the rib cage with their hands. The retention of swallowed food dilates the esophagus above the site of constriction. Generally there are constant or intermittent pains near the xyphoid process that irradiate to the neck or heart region. If regurgitated, the stagnant food mass may flow into the respiratory tract and cause aspiration pneumonia and pulmonary abscesses. A decrease in the amount of water and food reaching the stomach may result in severe emaciation.

Cardiospasm should be treated with a hygienic regime and special diet. At night the esophagus should be freed from its contents by irrigating it with warm water or camomile infusion. Antispasmodics (atropine, papaverine) and ganglioplegics are prescribed. Surgery is indicated if more conservative treatment proves ineffective.

N. R. PALEEV [11–1233–2]

CARDIOTONSILLAR SYNDROME, a group of changes in the heart (mostly subjective) manifested by frequent exacerbations of chronic tonsillitis.

Cardiotonsillar syndrome is usually found in children and adolescents, generally in girls and sometimes in young women. The patients complain of throbbing and pain in the region of the heart, irregular heartbeat, shortness of breath, and general malaise. The body temperature may rise slightly, and transitory pains in the joints appear at night. These symptoms are reminiscent of those of rheumatic endocarditis, but unlike the latter cardiotonsillar syndrome does not lead to heart defects or serious lesions of the heart muscle (myocardium). All symptoms of cardiotonsillar syndrome disappear as soon as the tonsils are removed (tonsillectomy) and antibiotics are administered. The syndrome was first described in the 1930's as a chiefly reflex process, with the diseased tonsils affecting the heart muscle. The possibility of the reflex origin of changes in the heart was demonstrated experimentally. It was found in the 1960's that the cardiac symptoms associated with focal infection of the nasopharynx may also be related to intoxication with more severe injury to the heart muscle (myocardial degeneration or focal myocarditis).

V. A. NASONOVA [11–1234–1]

CARDOSO, ONELIO JORGE. Born May 11, 1914, in Calabazar de Sagua, Las Villas province. Cuban writer.

Cardoso writes short stories distinguished by a colloquial idiom, humorous style, and affection for the working man—for example, "The Coal Miners" (1945) and "Old Iron" (1952). Many of his stories have antiwar and anti-imperialist themes and reflect the basic conflicts in the prerevolutionary Cuban countryside. Cardoso is a leader of the Union of Writers and Artists of Cuba. In 1962 he published a collection of articles, *Men Among the People.*

WORKS
Cuentos completos. [Havana, 1969].
Iba caminando. Havana, 1966.
In Russian translation:
Korallovyi kon'. Moscow, 1962.
[*Rasskazy.*] In *Kubinskaia novella XX veka.* Moscow-Leningrad, 1965.
REFERENCE
Portuondo, J. A. *Bosquejo histórico de las letras cubanas.* Havana, 1962.

S. P. MAMONTOV [11–1237–5]

CARDOX, a means of flameless explosion based on the instantaneous conversion of the liquid carbon dioxide in a steel cartridge to a gas by the heat emitted upon igniting a combustible compound contained in its heating element. [11–1237–2]

CARDOZO, BENJAMIN NATHAN. Born May 24, 1870, in New York, N.Y.; died July 19, 1938, in Port Chester, N.Y. An American jurist, a representative of the school of sociological jurisprudence.

Cardozo graduated from Columbia University in 1889. After 1913 he was a judge in various high courts of the state of New York and then a justice of the US Supreme Court. He was known for his writings, which emphasized the role of the judge in originating law. Noting the necessity of a definite compromise between the stability of the law and social dynamics, Cardozo considered that such a situation gave a judge the right to decide which law or legal precedent should be applied. The pragmatic views of Cardozo led to the unlimited broadening of the rights of the court, the judicial abuse of power, and the impairment of the role of law and justice in the hearing of specific cases in court.

WORKS
The Nature of the Judicial Process. New York, 1921.
The Growth of the Law. New York, 1924. [11–1237–1]

CARDUCCI, GIOSUE. Born July 27, 1835, in Val di Castello, Tuscany; died Feb. 16, 1907, in Bologna. Italian poet.

The son of a doctor who was a Carbonarist, Carducci graduated from the secondary school in Pisa. In the 1860's he supported G. Mazzini and G. Garibaldi. Later, when Italy was united, Carducci accepted the bourgeois monarchy. In the 1890's he held the post of senator. As a poet, Carducci opposed the sentimental, religious works of the romantics and favored courageous and joyous poetry in the spirit of classicism. His narrative poem *Hymn to Satan* (published 1865) praises freedom, worldly pleasures, and the victory of human reason over religion. In his most significant collection, *Iambs and Epodes* (1867–79), Carducci grieves for the heroes who died for Italy and castigates the bourgeois opportunists who used the victory of the people for their own selfish ends. In his lyrical collection *New Rhymes* (1861–87), romantic motifs and a tendency to realism are evident. His poems in the collection *Barbarian Odes* (1877–89) are based on ancient metrics. Carducci is also famous as a critic; he wrote articles on Dante, Petrarch, and Boccaccio. He was awarded the Nobel Prize in 1906.

WORKS

Edizione nazionale delle opere di G. Carducci, vols. 1–30. [Bologna, 1935–40].
In Russian translation:
Izbrannoe: [*Stikhi*]. Moscow, 1958.

REFERENCES

Lunacharskii, A. "Poet i meshchanstvo." *Sobr. soch. v 8 tomakh,* vol. 5. Moscow, 1965. Pages 136–42.
Poluiakhtova, I. K. *Istoriia ital'ianskoi literatury XIX v. (epokha Risordzhimento*). Moscow, 1970. Pages 188–92.
Flora, F. *La poesia e la prosa di Giosuè Carducci.* Pisa [1959].
Natali, G. *Giosuè Carducci.* Florence, 1961. (With bibliography.)
N. G. ELINA   [11–1238–3]

CARDUCHO, VICENTE (also V. Carducci). Born 1578, in Florence, Italy; died 1638, in Madrid. Spanish painter and art theorist. Of Italian origin.

Together with Bartolomé Carducho, his brother and teacher, V. Carducho arrived in Spain in 1585, where he was a court painter from 1609 on. His work belongs to the transitional style between late Renaissance and baroque. It is marked by cold theatricality and eclecticism (the cycle of paintings on subjects from the history of the Cartesian Order, 1626–32; some of which are in the Prado in Madrid). Carducho's more valuable legacy was as an important historian and theorist of the aesthetics of mannerism.

WORKS

Diálogos de la pintura. Madrid, 1633. (New edition, Madrid, 1865.)
[11–1238–2]

CAREER, rapid and successful advancement in various fields, including public, scientific, and office work; the attainment of recognition, honor, or material rewards. The word "career" is also used to define a type of occupation or profession, such as a career artist or a career doctor. Careerism is the pursuit of personal success in office, scientific, or other work. It is mercenary in its aims and a detriment to the public interest.
[11–1462–1]

CARÊME, MAURICE. Born May 12, 1899, in Wavre. Belgian poet; writes in French.

Carême began publishing in the mid-1920's with the collection of verses *The Mansion* (1926). Originally a teacher, he has devoted himself to literature since 1943. Pastoral scenes of his homeland, philosophical meditations, opposition to war, and love are Carême's favorite themes. He also writes poetry and tales for children, fables, and parables and translates poetry. Several of his poems have links with folk songs and ballads. Carême has a life-affirming world view.

WORKS

Pierres de lune: Poèmes. Paris, 1968.
Le sablier. Brussels, 1969.
In Russian translation:
["Stikhi."] In the collection *Stikhi bel'giiskikh poetov.* Moscow, 1959.
["Stikhi."] In the collection *Iz sovremennoi bel'giiskoi poezii.* Moscow, 1965.
Stikhi dlia detei. Moscow, 1967.

REFERENCE

Charles, J. *M. Carême . . . Choix de textes: Poèmes inédits. Bibliographie, portrait, fac-similé.* [Paris, 1965].
M. N. VAKSMAKHER   [11–1259–2]

CARIA, an ancient region in southwestern Asia Minor (in modern Turkey). It was named for the Carian tribe, which settled in the region at the end of the second millennium B.C. The studies of the Soviet scholar V. V. Shevoroshkin have established that the language of the Carians belongs to the Hittite-Luwian (Luvian) group of Indo-European languages. At the end of the second millennium B.C., the coast of Caria and the offshore islands were colonized by the Greeks, who founded the cities of Halicarnassus, Cnidus, Miletus, and Magnesia. In the sixth to the fourth century B.C., Caria was subordinate to the Achaemenids but retained its local rulers and satraps. At the end of the fourth century B.C., it was conquered by Alexander the Great. Later, the region was a dependency of the Seleucids. In 129 B.C., Caria was incorporated into the Roman province of Asia.

REFERENCES

Shevoroshkin, V. V. *Issledovaniia po deshifrovke kariiskikh nadpisei.* Moscow, 1965.
Robert, L., and J. Robert. *La Carie: Histoire et géographie historique. . . .* Paris, 1955.   T. M. SHEPUNOVA   [11–1279–3]

CARIBAN LANGUAGES, a family of languages that at the time of the European conquest was used in much of Guiana and part of present-day Venezuela and northern Brazil. Pockets of the Cariban languages are interspersed throughout western Colombia and the interior regions of Brazil. The so-called Island Carib in the Lesser Antilles (and now also in Central America) is a language of the Arawakan family with a Carib superstrate (that is, elements borrowed from the languages of newcomers). According to rough figures, Cariban languages are spoken by approximately 100,000–150,000 people. More than 100 Cariban languages are known, although their genetic classification remains to be worked out.

The Cariban languages are characterized by disyllabic and trisyllabic roots and by primarily open syllables. Verbs are inflected for subject and object, type (causative, passive, and so on), aspect, tense and mood. These grammatical meanings are expressed by prefixes and suffixes, which are primarily agglutinative. In the personal conjugation of the verb and in the personal possessive prefixal inflection of the noun five persons are distinguished: first person, second person, third person, third-person reflexive ("oneself"), and the dual person ("I and thou").

REFERENCE

Hoff, B. J. *The Carib Language.* The Hague, 1968.
A. B. DOLGOPOL'SKII   [11–1261–1]

CARIBBEAN ANDES, mountains in Venezuela along the Caribbean coast; approximately 800 km long. The Caribbean Andes consist of a coastal and an interior range: the Cordillera de la Costa rises to an altitude of 2,765 m and is broken up by a series of eroded tectonic valleys, including the Tuy River and Lake Valencia valley; the interrupted Serrania del Interior rises to 2,600 m.

The coastal range is composed chiefly of metamorphic rock of the Mesozoic period, with granite intrusions along its axis; the southern range is made up of igneous and sedimentary rock of the middle Cenozoic. Earthquakes are common. There are deposits of oil and natural gas at the southern foot of the range. The vegetation is of a succulent scrub type on the lower part of the slopes, and there are mixed deciduous and evergreen mountain forests and scrub meadows above 900–1,000 m.
[11–1260–6]

CARIBBEAN CURRENT, a current in the Caribbean Sea, an extension of the North Equatorial Current of the Atlantic Ocean. It flows to the west and northwest along the Great Antilles Islands and then south at speeds of 1–2.8 km/hr and higher. The water temperature is 25°–28°C; salinity is approximately 36.0 parts per thousand.   [11–1263–1]

CARIBBEAN SEA (named after the Carib Indians), a partially enclosed sea of the Atlantic Ocean, between Central and South America on the west and south and the Greater and Lesser Antilles on the north and east. In the northwest the Yucatán

Channel connects it to the Gulf of Mexico; in the northeast and east it is joined to the Atlantic Ocean by passages through the Antilles; and in the southwest it is joined to the Pacific Ocean by the man-made Panama Canal. Area, 2,754,000 sq km. Average depth, 2,491 m. Average water volume, 6,860,000 cu km. The coasts are mountainous in some places and low-lying in others. In the west and near the Antilles the coasts are ringed with coral reefs. The coastline has many indentations; among the gulfs in the west and south are the Gulf of Honduras, the Gulf of Darien, and the Gulf of Venezuela (Maracaibo).

The Caribbean is one of the largest seas of the transition zone. It is separated from the ocean by a system of island arcs of different ages, the youngest being the Lesser Antilles arc, which has volcanoes that are still active. The large islands of Cuba, Hispaniola, Jamaica, and Puerto Rico with already formed continental crust (the northern part of Cuba) or subcontinental crust make up the older island arcs. The Cayman–Sierra Maestra island arc is also young; it is formed for the most part by the underwater Cayman Ridge, along which runs a deepwater trench (7,680 m) with the same name. The other underwater mountain ridges (Aves Ridge, Beata Ridge, and the Marcelino sill) are apparently submerged island arcs. They divide the floor of the Caribbean Sea into a number of basins: the Grenada Basin (4,120 m), Venezuelan Basin (5,420 m), Colombian Basin (4,532 m), Bartlett Deep with the Cayman Trench, and the Yucatán Basin (5,055 m). The floors of the basins have suboceanic type crusts. The bottom deposits are calcareous foraminiferal ooze; in the southwestern part there is weakly manganous calcareous mud; and in the shallow waters there are various types of coral deposits, including numerous reef structures.

The climate is tropical, is influenced by trade-wind circulation, and is characterized by great uniformity. Mean monthly air temperatures vary from 23° to 27°C. Cloud cover is 40–50 percent. The amount of precipitation ranges from 500 mm in the east to 2,000 mm in the west. Between June and October tropical hurricanes occur in the northern part of the sea. Hydrological conditions are distinguished by great uniformity. Under the influence of the trade winds the surface current moves from the east to the west. Near the coast of Central America it turns northwest and passes through the Yucatán Channel into the Gulf of Mexico. The speed of the current is 1–3 km/hr and up to 6 km/hr near the Yucatán Channel. The Caribbean Sea is an intermediate basin for waters entering from the Atlantic Ocean, which give rise to the Gulf Stream when they leave the Gulf of Mexico and return to the ocean. Mean monthly water temperatures on the surface vary from 25° to 28°C; annual fluctuations are less than 3°C. Salinity is about 36.0 parts per thousand. Water density is 1,023.5–1,024.0 kg per cu m. The color of the water varies from light bluish green to green. Tides are primarily irregular and semidiurnal; their height is less than 1 meter. Vertical changes in the hydrological characteristics occur down to depths of 1,500, m; below this the sea is filled with uniform water entering from the Atlantic Ocean. Its temperature is 4.2°–4.3°C, and the salinity is 34.95–34.97 parts per thousand. The Caribbean Sea is inhabited by sharks, flying fish, sea turtles, and other types of tropical fauna. Sperm and humpback whales are found, and near the island of Jamaica there are seals and manatees.

The Caribbean Sea is very important economically and strategically as the shortest sea route connecting ports of the Atlantic and Pacific oceans through the Panama Canal. Among the most important ports are Maracaibo and La Guaira (Venezuela), Cartagena (Colombia), Limón (Costa Rica), Santo Domingo (Dominican Republic), Colón (Panama), and Santiago de Cuba (Cuba).

O. K. Leont'ev and A. M. Muromtsev [11–1262–1]

CARIBOO, a mountain massif in the Canadian Rockies, in British Columbia. Length, about 300 km; average elevation, 3,000 m (the highest elevation is Mount Sir Wilfrid Laurier, 3,581 m). The range is composed of Precambrian crystalline rocks, with some Miocene basalts and andesites, and is sharply dissected by trough valleys. There are glaciers. The mountains are covered with sparse coniferous forests; above 2,000 m, by alpine meadows. Wells Gray Provincial Park is in the southern part of the range. [11–1263–3]

CARIBOU, the common name for the North American species of the wild reindeer. There are forest and tundra caribou. The forest caribou are larger and are distributed in the taiga; the tundra caribou are smaller and inhabit the open tundra, coming to the taiga only in winter. [11–1263–2]

CARIBS (incorrectly, Caraibs), a group of Indian tribes in South America (the Motilón, Macushi, Arecuna, Waiwai, Carijona, Bacairí, and others) who speak Cariban languages and have common origins. According to rough estimates, there are approximately 100,000–150,000 Caribs. Their religion consists of tribal cults.

The Caribs live primarily in the tropical forest and savanna zone north of the Amazon River (in Venezuela, Colombia, Brazil, Honduras, and other countries). They engage in seminomadic slash-and-fallow agriculture, fishing, hunting, and foodgathering. Their main form of social organization is the neighbor community, with considerable vestiges of maternal kinship relations.

REFERENCE
Narody Ameriki, vol. 2. Moscow, 1959. [11–1264–1]

CARICATURE, an artistic method of typification, the use of a cartoon or grotesque for the purpose of deliberate, tendentious, critical exaggeration and emphasis of the negative side of life or people. In caricature, which is a specific manifestation of the comic, satire and humor are used to expose, criticize, and deride various social and political phenomena, as well as everyday occurrences.

In the broad sense of the word, a caricature is any representation that deliberately creates a comic effect; combines the real and the fantastic; exaggerates and emphasizes the figures, faces, clothing, or manners of people; and alters the relationship between people and their surroundings. Unexpected comparisons and juxtapositions are also properties of a caricature. In this sense, caricature can be applied to an extremely wide range of subjects and can be compared to carnivals, theatrical buffoonery, burlesque, and epigrams. This type of caricature originated in antiquity. It later appeared in medieval reliefs and folk art, particularly popular prints. Caricature can be used in various kinds of art, for example, poster art.

In a more narrow sense of the word, caricature is a distinctive kind of pictorial art. Usually an element of the graphic arts, it is rarely used in painting and sculpture. Caricature is the main form of graphic satire and is clearly ideological and socially critical in content. The art usually flourishes during periods of large-scale social conflicts and intense activities of the masses. It serves as a powerful and effective weapon in the struggle of democratic forces.

The origins of the genre of caricature are tied to the Peasants' War of 1524–26 in Germany, the Reformation, and the first bourgeois revolutions of the 16th through 18th centuries in the Netherlands, England, and France. During this period, the influence of inexpensive popular prints, folk morals, and the aesthetic principles of folklore was clearly discernible in caricatures. This influence was typical during later stages of the development of caricature—for example, in Russian caricature of 1812, Mexican political graphic art between 1910 and 1920, and Chinese caricature of the 1920's.

Text plays an important role in caricature. The active social role of this art is reflected by its popularity—it is the most widespread of all the various forms of pictorial art. Caricatures are executed in the media that provide the greatest circulation —wood engraving, etching, and lithography. They are also reproduced by the printing press. Caricatures are distributed in the form of leaflets, magazine and newspaper illustrations, and easily accessible anthologies.

Maintaining its critical purposes and its distinctive form, the art of caricature also reflects the stylistic elements of the art of its time. Classical principles are expressed in many caricatures of the late 18th and early 19th centuries. The influence of modernism is evident in magazine caricatures of the early 20th century. Elements of expressionism are reflected in the work of a number of German caricaturists between 1910 and 1930. Of all the artistic genres of an epoch, caricature most directly focuses on the social events of the day. By bringing art closer to urgent social problems, it affects artistic development as a whole.

At the beginning of the 19th century, the romanticists, who allotted a prominent place to irony and the grotesque in their art, theoretically substantiated the aesthetic significance of caricature for the first time. However, as early as the first half of the 18th century, W. Hogarth satirized the customs and manners of contemporary English society in his paintings and engravings. His work marked the beginning of the systematic development of caricature as an important branch of the representational arts. Hogarth was followed by J. Gillray, T. Rowlandson, and G. Cruikshank, professional English graphic artists and caricaturists of the second half of the 18th century and the early 19th. These three artists developed their own type of caricature; transforming genre scenes into a distinctive type of dramatized spectacle, they exposed the ugly and ludicrous sides of life. The fervor of the social criticism in English caricature never went beyond expressions of parliamentary opposition or derision of morals and manners. However, the English caricaturists did help establish many of the artistic devices of subsequent European caricature.

Caricaturists began to execute works that responded to and commented upon all of the major social, state, and international events—for example, caricatures that appeared during the Great French Revolution, British anti-Napoleonic leaflets, and Russian satirical popular prints by I. I. Terebenev, A. G. Venetsianov, and I. A. Ivanov. Russian caricatures were directed against the expansionist intentions of Napoleon and the Gallomania of the Russian nobility. A. O. Orlovskii created incisive caricatures of serf owners. In the satirical etchings of F. Goya, which castigated Spanish reactionism and obscurantism, unprecedented force and artistic depth were imparted to the grotesque language of caricature.

In the 19th and 20th centuries, the development of caricature was closely related to journalism. Caricatures ranged in content from political pamphlets to topical satire. The art became particularly associated with progressive journalism and its social and political orientation. Daily contributions to journals and newspapers became the caricaturists' usual form of creative expression. Nineteenth-century progressive caricaturists, participating in class struggles, devoted a great deal of attention to the central theme of critical realism—the defense of the rights and dignity of the individual in a money-oriented society. The work of the most prominent caricaturist, H. Daumier, which was permeated by antibourgeois zeal, was also characterized by its broad scope of expression that ranged from incisive criticism to sad humor. This antibourgeois attitude was also reflected in the caricatures by G. Pilotell and Molock that were devoted to the Paris Commune of 1871.

As a result of restrictions imposed by censorship, incisive social criticism often took the form of caricatures ridiculing the customs and manners of a society. These customs and manners symbolized the vices of the political order and social life. The text accompanying the illustration helped the reader to grasp the hidden satirical meaning. This type of illustration was characteristic of the artists N. A. Stepanov, N. V. Ievlev, and P. M. Shmel'nikov, who contributed to mid-19th-century Russian satirical journals, such as *Iskra* (The Spark) and *Gudok* (The Whistle). These journals supported the revolutionary and democratic struggle against autocracy and serfdom.

The art of caricature borrows the allegorical and symbolic techniques of the popular print, which personify such abstract concepts as labor, capital, and freedom. One of the most effective and capacious satirical devices is the social mask, a grotesque generalized image. This device is either an individual portrait or a generalized representation that epitomizes the essential characteristics of the ruling classes. It was used by the French artists C. Philipon, Grandville, and Daumier to create denunciatory portraits of the bourgeois king Louis Philippe and the rogue Robert Macaire. Satirical portraits of the tsar and his high officials, which evolved into social masks, appeared in political graphic art in Russia. They were particularly prevalent during the Revolution of 1905–07 (V. A. Serov, B. M. Kustodiev, and E. E. Lansere). Artists who were affiliated with the German journal *Simplizissimus* (founded in 1896) and the Russian journals *Satirikon* (1908–14) and *Novyi Satirikon* (1913–18) furthered the development of a terse, grotesque, graphic vocabulary for caricature.

Twentieth-century caricature reflects the growing complexity of the relationships of various social forces. In the caricatures of the Revolution of 1905–07 in Russia the ideas of the general democratic struggle for freedom and socialist ideas were expressed. The latter were further developed in the political illustrations of the pre-October Bolshevik newspaper *Pravda*. Antimilitaristic caricature, protesting the expansionist policies of imperialism that impart suffering and pain to mankind, was particularly intense and emotionally incisive. The political drawings of F. Mazereel, in which elements of the grotesque, the tragic, and the romantically pathetic are combined, greatly influenced the development of caricature.

As the class struggle of the proletariat became more critical between 1910 and 1920, progressive caricaturists were affiliated more frequently with the workers' and communist press. These progressive artists included R. Maynor, W. Gropper, F. Ellis, and J. Burk in the USA; George Grosz, O. Dix, H. Zille, and R. Schlichter in Germany; L. Laforge, R. Dubosc, and R. Cabrol in France; and J. Lada in Czechoslovakia. Since the 1930's, antifascist satirical drawings have played important roles (I. Beshkov in Bulgaria and D. Low in Great Britain). After World War II, the progressive caricaturists Jean Effel (France), L. Mittelber (France), and H. Bidstrup (Denmark) became extremely popular.

In the USSR, during the early years of Soviet power, caricature became an integral element of various types of mass propagandist art. The ideological and stylistic principles of Soviet caricature were developed in revolutionary satirical posters (including the *Okna ROSTA* [ROSTA placards]) by V. V. Mayakovsky, M. M. Cheremnykh, D. S. Moor, V. N. Deni, and V. V. Lebedev. Its political role as a direct appeal to the widest masses of people and the fervor of its criticism of the external and internal enemies of the revolution also grew. In the 1920's and 1930's, numerous satirical journals that were central to the development of professional caricature appeared in the RSFSR and other republics. Notable Soviet caricaturists include I. A. Maliutin, M. M. Cheremnykh, A. A. Radakov, L. G. Brodaty, B. E. Efimov, N. E. Radlov, Iu. A. Ganf, K. P. Rotov, B. I. Antonovskii, Kukryniksy, A. M. Kanevskii, V. N. Goriaev, K. S. Eliseev, B. I. Prorokov, L. V. Soifertis, I. M. Semenov, A. Azimzade, and V. G. Litvinenko. Caricatures that attack the reactionary, imperialist, and colonialist forces in the world are published regularly in newspapers and have acquired great political significance.

During the Great Patriotic War of 1941–45, caricature, being among the most widely circulated forms of art, played an important role in the patriotic instruction of the people in the struggle against fascist aggression. Cartoons appeared regularly in journals, newspapers (including the newspapers at the front), and propaganda leaflets; it also was a principal element in poster art (for example, the *Okna TASS* [TASS placards]).

Since the end of the war, caricaturists have expanded their range of subjects. They address their work to the various aspects of daily life, history, and international and domestic affairs, as well as to the struggle against vestiges of capitalism. Soviet caricaturists and their counterparts in other socialist countries (A. Beier-Red and H. S. Zandberg in the German Democratic Republic; B. Linke and E. Lipiński in Poland; S. Venev in Bulgaria; and Cik Damadian in Rumania) are active in the struggle for communist ideals.

REFERENCES

Shvyrov, A. V., and S. S. Trubachev. *Illustrirovannaia istoriia karikatury s drevneishikh vremen do nashikh dnei.* St. Petersburg, 1903 [date on title page is 1904].

Atsarkina, E. N. *Revolutsionnaia karikatura Germanii 1848–1870 godov.* Moscow-Leningrad, 1931.

Iavorskaia, N. *Sovremennaia revolutsionnaia politicheskaia satira na Zapade.* Moscow-Leningrad, 1932.

Nekrasova, E. *Ocherki po istorii angliiskoi karikatury kontsa XVIII i nachala XIX vekov.* [Leningrad] 1935.

Varshavskii, L. R. *Russkaia karikatura 40–50-kh godov XIX veka*. Moscow, 1937.

Kalitina, N. N. *Politicheskaia karikatura Frantsii 30-kh godov XIX stoletiia*. Leningrad, 1955.

Efimov, B. E. *Osnovy ponimaniia karikatury*. Moscow, 1961.

Stykalin, S., and I. Kremenskaia. *Sovetskaia satiricheskaia pechat', 1917–1963*. Moscow, 1963.

Sternin, G. *Ocherki russkoi satiricheskoi grafiki*. Moscow, 1964.

Vipper, B. R. *Stat'i ob iskusstve*. [Moscow, 1970.] Pages 129–36.

Champfleury [Fleury-Husson, J.] *Histoire de la caricature . . .* [books] 1–5. Paris, 1865–80.

Fuchs, E. *Die Karikatur der europäischen Völker vom Altertum bis zur Neuzeit*, 2nd ed., vols. 1–2. Berlin, 1902; 3rd ed., vols. 1–2. Berlin, 1904.

Hofmann, W. *Die Karikatur von Leonardo bis Picasso*. Vienna, 1956.

G. IU. STERNIN [11–1266–2]

CARIES, a pathological process involving the gradual destruction of bony tissue or teeth.

Caries of bony tissue is caused by degeneration or infection of bone or periosteum that results in necrosis of portions of bone followed by absorption or disengagement of the dead tissues and formation of a bone ulcer. Caries may also be accompanied by specific inflammatory processes (for example, tuberculosis or syphilis). The mechanism of development and clinical symptoms of caries vary with the cause, location of the focus, and so forth. In acute inflammations (for example, osteomyelitis), when a focus of suppuration arises in bone and sometimes spreads to the surrounding tissues, caries is manifested by systemic intoxication, and bone destruction progresses rapidly. In chronic and especially specific processes, caries develops slowly without severely pronounced symptoms. Treatment consists in medication (antibiotics, sulfanilamides) and specific treatment (antisyphilitic, antituberculotic). Surgery is frequently effective.

[11–1264–2]

CARINTHIA, a historical region in Central Europe, in the Drava River basin.

The territory of Carinthia was settled toward the end of the sixth century by the Slovenes, a Slavic people. In the first half of the seventh century, it was part of Samo's state; next, it became part of Carantania; and with the disintegration of the latter at the beginning of the 11th century, Carinthia was made a separate duchy. Beginning in the 12th century Carinthia was subjected to vigorous germanization as a result of which the northern part became German. After 1282 it was part of the holdings of the Count of Tirol. In 1335 it became a possession of the Hapsburgs. In 1849 it was made an independent administrative unit (crown land) of the Austrian Empire. In the second half of the 19th century the ethnic boundary of the Slovenes moved to the south. According to the terms of the Treaty of St. Germain (1919), the greater part of Carinthia was made into one of the provinces of Austria (the Klagenfurt region was given to Austria following a plebiscite in 1920); the Mežica River valley, along with Dravograd and Jezersko, went to the Kingdom of Serbs, Croats, and Slovenes (which became Yugoslavia in 1929); and the Kanal Valley and Trbiž (Treviso) went to Italy. These territorial arrangements were confirmed by the Italian Peace Treaty of 1947 and the Austrian State Treaty of 1955.

[11–1273–1]

CARINTHIA (Kärnten), a province in southern Austria. Area, 9,500 sq km. Population, 519,000 (1968), one-fifth of whom are Slovenes and Croatians. The administrative center is Klagenfurt.

Located in Carinthia are the northern slopes of the Carnic Alps, the Karawanken, the southern spurs of the Hohe Tauern, and other ranges of the Eastern Alps. The peaks range in height from 3,300 to 3,700 m. The mountains in the southern part are composed mostly of limestones; the northern mountains, predominantly of crystalline rocks. The mountains are divided by intermontane basins such as the Klagenfurt Basin. Approximately half of the territory is covered with forests. Out of the total working population, 30 percent are engaged in industry and crafts, 19 percent in agriculture and forestry, and 12 percent in trade and transport. Magnesite is mined at Radenthein and lead-zinc ores at Bleiberg-Kreuth. Lumbering and the wood-products industry are well developed, as is the pulp and paper industry. Gailitz is an important center for nonferrous metallurgy. Dairy and meat livestock farming predominate in agriculture. Half the arable land is given over to feed crops, including grasses. There is shipping on the Drau River. The mountains attract tourists.

[11–1273–2]

CARLEMAN, TAGE GILLIS TORSTEN. Born July 8, 1892, in Visseltofta; died Jan. 11, 1949, in Jursholm. Swedish mathematician. Professor at the University of Stockholm from 1924.

Carleman's principal works dealt with the theory of functions (quasi-analytic classes, functional approximation, trigonometric series), integral equations, and spectral theory.

WORKS
Sur Les Équations intégrales singulières à noyau réel et symétrique. Uppsala, 1923.
Les Fonctions quasi analytiques. Paris, 1926.
"Über die asymptotische Verteilung der Eigenwerte partieller Differentialgleichungen." *Berichte über die Verhandlungen Sächsischen Akademie der Wissenschaften zu Leipzig. Matematisch-physikalische Klasse*, 1936, vol. 88.

[11–1297–1]

CARLETON, WILLIAM. Born 1794 in Prillisk, County Tyrone; died Jan. 30, 1869, in Dublin. Irish writer and journalist.

Carleton became famous with the publication of *Traits and Stories of the Irish Peasantry* (vols. 1–2, 1830). In the 1840's he joined a group of revolutionary democratic writers associated with the journal *Nation*. His realistic novels, *Valentine McClutchy, the Irish Agent, or Chronicles of the Castle Camber Property* (1845) and *The Black Prophet, A Tale of the Famine* (1847), portrayed the tragic struggle of the peasants against hunger and disease.

WORKS
Autobiography. London, 1968.

REFERENCES
Kiely, B. *Poor Scholar: A Study of the Works and Days of W. Carleton (1794–1869)*. London, 1947.
Flanagan, T. *The Irish Novelists, 1800–1850*. New York, 1959.

[11–1310–1]

CARLETONVILLE, a city in the Republic of South Africa, in Transvaal Province. Population, 103,500 (1968), of whom 80,000 are Bantu. It is one of the centers of the gold-mining Witwatersrand region. Carletonville has food processing and light industries.

[11–1310–2]

CARLISLE, a city in Great Britain, on the Eden River, near where it empties into Solway Firth (Irish Sea). Population, 71,500 (1971). The city has railroad repair shops and metalworking, textile, and food industries.

[11–1296–4]

CARLISTS, representatives of the absolutist, clerical political current in Spain that relies on the reactionary clergy, the titled aristocracy, and the top army officers.

The movement received its name from the pretender to the Spanish throne, Don Carlos the Elder. In the 1830's and 1870's the Carlists unleashed major rebellions in Spain, known as the Carlist Wars. Later on, as the traditionalist movement, the Carlists supported the most reactionary forces in the country. Carlists were active in the military fascist rebellion of July 18–19, 1936, and collaborated with the Franco regime. Many of them supported Juan Carlos, who was confirmed in 1969 at Franco's direction as the future king of Spain after Franco's death. Many Carlists opposed several aspects of Franco's policies from an absolutist and clerical viewpoint.

[11–1304–1]

CARLIST WARS, dynastic wars from 1833 to 1840 and from 1872 to 1876 between two branches of the Spanish Bourbons.

The First Carlist War began on Oct. 4, 1833, in the city of Talavera after the death of King Ferdinand II, when the gentry that favored absolutism (Carlists) stirred up a rebellion. Led by the son of Carlos IV, Don Carlos the Elder (who took the name Carlos V), they rose up against María Cristina, the regent in the early years of the reign of Isabella II. In the ensuing struggle for power, the Carlists used the peasantry of the Basque Provinces, Navarre, Valencia, Aragon, and Catalonia, where the influence of the local aristocracy and the Catholic clergy was strong. Relying on the desire of the people of these regions for autonomy, Don Carlos promised to restore their ancient freedoms. María Cristina found support among the bourgeoisie and liberal gentry, who compelled her to agree to a number of liberal bourgeois reforms from 1834 to 1843. The Carlists basically held to a policy of guerrilla warfare. The Carlist detachments in Catalonia and the Basque Provinces headed by T. Zumalacárregui and R. Cabrera y Griño were especially active. In 1837 a Carlist army of 14,000 men led by Don Carlos tried to take Madrid. After this attempt failed, the Carlist movement rapidly waned. In 1839, Don Carlos was forced to cross the French frontier, and in 1840, Cabrera's army ceased its resistance.

The Carlists unleashed a new war in 1872, hoping to place on the throne the grandson of Carlos V, Don Carlos the Younger (who took the name Carlos VII). With the help of the Vatican and of reactionary circles in several European states, the Carlists succeeded initially in seizing a significant part of Catalonia and Valencia. However, the Carlists suffered a number of shattering defeats and were compelled to lay down their arms in 1876.

REFERENCES
Maiskii, I. M. *Ispaniia (1808–1917).* Moscow, 1957.
Lafuente, M. *Historia general de España,* vol. 24. Barcelona, 1930.
B. M. MERIN [11–1303–2]

CARLOTA-JOAQUINA. Born Apr. 25, 1775, in Aranjuez, Spain; died Jan. 7, 1830, in Queluz, near Lisbon. Wife of the Portuguese king João VI and head of the clericalist and absolutist party.

With her son Miguel, Carlota-Joaquina organized a number of unsuccessful plots and rebellions to overthrow João VI, nullify the gains of the bourgeois revolution of 1820, and restore an absolutist regime in Portugal. [11–1308–6]

CARLSBAD, a city in the western United States, in New Mexico. Population, 21,300 (1970). Carlsbad is the center of a mining region with large reserves of potash; it is the leading American city in potash mining. [11–1308–7]

CARLSBAD CAVERNS, karst caverns in the USA, in the Guadalupe Mountains of New Mexico, southwest of the city of Carlsbad. They are noted for having the largest chambers, or grottoes, in the world. The caverns reach a depth of 339 m, and the overall length of their halls and passages is approximately 12 km. The largest hall, which is in the shape of the letter T, is 610 m long, 335 m wide, and up to 87 m high. It covers an area of 5.7 hectares. Carlsbad is the habitat and hibernation place for a large number of bats. Because of the enormous stalagmites, the remarkable size of the halls, and the beauty of the grottoes, great numbers of tourists are drawn to the caverns. In 1930 the Carlsbad Caverns were designated as a national park. [11–1308–8]

CARLSTADT, ANDREAS (Andreas Bodenstein; the name Carlstadt came from his birthplace, the city of Carlstadt in Lower Franconia). Born circa 1480; died Dec. 24, 1541, in Basel. A leader of the Reformation in Germany.

Carlstadt became a professor at the University of Wittenberg in 1518. He had already sided with Luther in 1517. Reflecting the mood of the more radical burgher circles, be began to speak more resolutely than Luther in favor of the reform of religious life. In 1521 and 1522, Carlstadt and his followers made far-reaching changes in the church in Wittenberg: among other steps, they removed icons and other cult objects from the churches and abolished clerical celibacy. Persecuted by Luther, Carlstadt from 1523 continued his radical Reformationist preaching in Orlamünde. He spoke out against attempts to limit the Reformation to the religious sphere. At the same time he opposed the ideas of social revolution propagandized by T. Müntzer. After the Peasant War of 1524–26, Carlstadt was accused of sympathizing with the rebels. However, because of the intercession of Luther, he was not persecuted. From 1534, he was a professor at the University of Basel, in Switzerland.

REFERENCES
Barge, H. *Andreas Bodenstein von Karlstadt,* vols. 1–2. Leipzig, 1905.
Hertzsch, E. *Karlstadt. . . .* Gotha, 1932.
M. M. SMIRIN [11–1311–3]

CARLUDOVICA, a genus of plants of the family Cyclanthaceae. The plants resemble small palms with shortened trunks. The flowers are unisexual and are on a spadix. Every pistillate flower is surrounded by four staminate flowers. The baccate fruits form an aggregate fruit. There are three species in Central America and northwestern South America. The leaves of the jipijapa (*Carludovica palmata*) provide the material used in the production of panama hats and other articles. [11–1313–1]

CARLYLE, THOMAS. Born Dec. 4, 1795, in Ecclefechan; died Feb. 5, 1881, in London. British essayist, historian, and philosopher.

Carlyle graduated from the University of Edinburgh in 1814. His world view was formed under the influence of German romanticism and classical idealism, as expressed by such representatives as J. G. Fichte and F. W. von Schelling. These ideas infuse the philosophical novel *Sartor Resartus* (literally, "the tailor mended"), written by Carlyle in 1833–34 (Russian translation published in 1902). According to the "philosophy of clothing" developed in the book, the whole world and all history are external transient garments or emblems, behind which there is an eternal divine essence, the sole reality.

A number of Carlyle's works from the 1830's and early 1840's show sympathy for the working masses and at times combine a radical critique of capitalism with an idealization of the Middle Ages and appeals for a restoration of hierarchical feudal social relations; the latter tendency brought him close to feudal socialism. His work *The French Revolution* (1837; Russian translation, 1907) justified the overthrow of the absolutist structure by the masses, but it also contained the extremely subjective idealistic conception of the "cult of the hero." This concept was further developed by Carlyle in a series of lectures between 1837 and 1840, which was published in 1842 as *On Heroes, Hero Worship, and the Heroic in History* (Russian translation, 3rd ed., 1908). According to Carlyle, the laws of the world set down by providence are revealed only to "the elect," to "heroes," who are the only real creators in history: "The history of the world is but the biography of great men." In his view, the masses are only a crowd, a tool in their hands. He noted that the heroic principle periodically weakens in society and then the blind destructive forces hidden in the crowd burst forth; but this lasts only until society again finds its "true heroes," for example, Cromwell or Napoleon. Such, according to Carlyle, is the closed circle of history. The idea of a "cult of the hero" was widely accepted by bourgeois historiography. With the development of the class struggle of the proletariat, the petit bourgeois historical and philosophical ideas of Carlyle became more reactionary.

WORKS
The Works, vols. 1–30. London, 1896–1905.
Letters, vols. 1–2. London–New York, 1888.
REFERENCES
Marx, K., and F. Engels. *Soch.,* 2nd ed., vols. 1, 7. (See index of names.)
Nemanov, I. N. "Sub'ektivistsko-idealisticheskaia sushchnost' vozzrenii T. Karleilia na istoriiu obshchestva." *Voprosy istorii,* 1956, no. 4.
I. N. NEMANOV [11–1296–7]

CARMAGNOLE (from Carmagnola, a city in Piedmont, Italy), a French revolutionary folk song and dance.

The carmagnole was first sung in Paris shortly after the taking of the Tuileries on Aug. 10, 1792. The original lyrics, which were composed by citizens of Marseille, were set to a traditional folk tune that accompanied round dances of southern France. Later, various lyrics were improvised. The carmagnole was banned by Napoleon I when he was first consul; however, the song reappeared during the revolutions of 1830 and 1848 and during the heroic days of the Paris Commune of 1871 (words by G. B. Clémant and others). Until the appearance of the "Internationale," the carmagnole was the most popular song of French workers. In the early 1920's, it became popular among Soviet youth in a version with lyrics by V. M. Kirshon.

REFERENCES
T'erso, Zh. *Pesni i prazdnestva frantsuzskoi revolutsii.* Moscow, 1933. Pages 95–100. (Translated from French.)
Khokhlovkina, A. "Iz istorii pesen frantsuzskoi revoliutsii." *Sovetskaia muzyka,* 1961, no. 12.   [11–1316–1]

CARMAN, WILLIAM BLISS. Born Apr. 15, 1861, in Fredericton; died June 8, 1929, in New Canaan, Conn. Canadian poet. Wrote in English.

Carman graduated from the University of Edinburgh in 1883. He lived in the USA from 1908 to 1925. Carman's collections *Low Tide on Grand Pré* (1893) and *Songs From Vagabondia* (1894–1901) are marked by an elegiac mood. More interesting are the collections *From the Book of Myths* (1902), *Sappho* (1903), and *Songs of the Children of the Sea* (1904). Carman is also the author of collections entitled *Poems* (1904) and *Last Poems* (1921). He saw the ideal of human existence in unity with nature ("White Gull"). Carman belonged to the Confederation group of romantic poets.

WORKS
Selected Poems. New York, 1954.
REFERENCES
Rashley, R. *Poetry in Canada.* Toronto, 1958.
The Oxford Book of Canadian Verse. Toronto–London–New York, 1960.
Literary History of Canada. Toronto, 1965.   [11–1318–2]

CARMEL, MOUNT, a mountain in the northern part of Palestine (on the territory of the state of Israel). In 1929–34 human skeletal remains together with Levalloisian-type stone implements and the bones of fossil animals were discovered in the caves of Tabun and Skhul on Mount Carmel's western slope. In the Tabun cave, an almost complete skeleton of a Neanderthal woman and the lower jaw of a male skull with a distinct chin prominence were found. In the Skhul cave, the bones of ten skeletons in varying states of preservation were found, characterized by great individual differences and by a combination of Neanderthal and modern features in the structure of the skull and other parts of the skeleton. The Tabun and Skhul populations lived 40,000–45,000 years ago. Some scholars consider the population of the Mount Carmel caves to be the result of the hybridization between Neanderthal man and the populations of modern type; others see them as an evolutionary transition from ancient man to modern man.

REFERENCES
Roginskii, Ia. Ia., and M. G. Levin. *Antropologiia.* Moscow, 1963.
McCown, T. D., and A. Keith. *The Stone Age of Mount Carmel,* vol. 2. Oxford, 1939.   [11–1317–3]

CARMELITES, members of a Catholic mendicant monastic order, founded in the second half of the 12th century in Palestine by the Italian crusader Berthold.

The Carmelites' first monastic community was located on Mount Carmel (hence the name). Their rule was approved by Pope Honorius III in 1226. After the failure of the Crusades, the Carmelites moved to Western Europe (13th century), where under Pope Innocent IV they were turned into a mendicant order in 1245 or 1247. In the 16th century the order was again reformed, after which it split into two branches (the Carmelites and the Discalced, or Barefoot, Carmelites). In 1972 the order numbered about 8,000 monks; the women's order of Carmelites (established in the 15th century) numbered more than 12,000 nuns.   [11–1317–2]

CARMINE, a red dye extracted from the bodies of wingless female cochineal insects. Carmine, a complex organic carminic acid, is extracted from the insects with hot water and acetic acid. It is soluble in water and alkalies. One gram of carmine is obtained from 150–175 insects. Carmine is used as a food coloring and a cosmetic dye. It is also used to stain microscopic specimens.   [11–1319–1]

CARMONA, ANTONIO OSCAR DE FRAGOSO. Born Nov. 24, 1869, in Lisbon; died there Apr. 18, 1951. Portuguese statesman, marshal.

After graduating from the Royal Military College, Carmona served in the army in Portugal and in the colonies. From 1923 to 1926 he was minister of war. In May 1926 he joined General Gomes da Costa in a coup d'etat that established a military dictatorship. In July 1926 he ousted Gomes da Costa and became prime minister and chief of state; in 1928 he took the title of president. Carmona began to reform the state structure along fascist lines. In 1928 he brought A. Salazar into the government as minister of finance with extraordinary powers. He paved the way for Salazar's takeover; Salazar, on becoming prime minister in 1932, established a fascist dictatorship in the country.   [11–1319–3]

CARNAC, a village in southern Brittany, in the department of Morbihan, in France. Located in the vicinity of Carnac are megalithic monuments dating from the late Neolithic and early Bronze ages (end of the third through the first half of the second millennium B.C.). The monuments include cromlechs, avenues of menhirs, and oval and elongated mounds, some with chambers beneath them. Among the items found in the chambers were stone axes, arrowheads, beads, and clay dishes. Most of the avenues of menhirs fall into one of three groups, located along one line at a set distance from the others. Various images are carved on a number of the menhirs.

REFERENCES
Le Rouzic, Z. *Carnac.* [Rennes] 1955.
Niel, F. "Dolmens et menhirs." In the collection *Que sais-je?,* 1958, no. 764.
"Carnac." In *The Concise Encyclopedia of Archaeology,* 2nd ed. London, 1970.   [11–1320–4]

CARNALLITE (named after the German geologist R. von Carnall, 1804–74), a mineral, a complex hydrated chloride of magnesium and potassium with composition $KCl \cdot MgCl_2 \cdot 6H_2O$. It usually also has insignificant amounts of Br, Li, Rb, Cs, and mechanical particles of clay minerals, hematite, and hydrated oxides of iron. Carnallite crystallizes in the orthorhombic system and usually forms granular aggregates with halite, sylvite, and other salt deposit minerals. It is colorless or tinted murky brown, reddish pink, and other colors as a result of impurities contained in it. Carnallite is hygroscopic and characterized by a bitter salty burning taste. Its hardness on the mineralogical scale is 2–3; it has a density of $1,600 \text{ kg/m}^3$. It is one of the principal minerals in potassium salt deposits. The largest deposit in the USSR is at Solikamsk in the Urals. Major deposits abroad are found in the German Democratic Republic (Stassfurt, Aschersleben), the Federal Republic of Germany, the United States, and Tunisia.   [11–1322–2]

CARNAP, RUDOLF. Born May 18, 1891, in Wuppertal; died Sept. 16, 1970, in Santa Maria, Calif. German-American philosopher and logician; a leading logical positivist and philosopher of science.

Carnap taught at the University of Vienna from 1926 to 1931 and was a professor of philosophy at the German University in Prague from 1931 to 1935. In 1935 he emigrated to the USA, where he was a professor at the University of Chicago from 1936 to 1952 and at the University of California from 1954 until his death. He was a member of the American Academy of Sciences.

Influenced by L. Wittgenstein and B. Russell, Carnap considered the task of the philosophy of science to be the analysis of the structure of knowledge in the natural sciences so that, with the help of mathematical logic, the fundamental concepts of science would be made more precise. Three stages may be discerned in the evolution of Carnap's work. In the first period, which lasted until the early 1930's, Carnap was a member of the Vienna Circle and elaborated the ideas of logical empiricism. He advanced several radical neopositivist views, such as physicalism, and denied the character of philosophy as a world view. In the second period Carnap advanced the thesis that the logic of science is the analysis of purely syntactical connections between propositions, concepts, and theories; he denied the possibility of scientific discussion of questions concerning the nature of real objects and their relation to the propositions of the language of science. Carnap developed the theory of logical syntax, constructing a language for the extended predicate calculus with equality and with a rule of infinite induction as an instrument for the logical analysis of scientific language.

In the third period, after 1936, Carnap was occupied with the construction of a "unified language of science." He came to the conclusion that a purely syntactical approach was inadequate and that it was necessary to consider semantics as well, that is, the relation between language and the field of objects described by it. On the basis of his semantic theory, Carnap constructed inductive logic as a logic of probability. He also developed a formalized theory of inductive conclusions (in particular, conclusions by analogy) and elaborated a theory of semantic information. He also wrote about semantic interpretation and the quantification of modal logic. Several of his results were used in research on cybernetics by MacCulloch, Peets, and Warren. In his final years Carnap rejected many of the views he had held in the first stage of his career and stated more resolutely his belief in the existence of "unobserved material objects" as the basis for constructing logical systems. However, failure to understand the dialectics of knowledge prevented Carnap from developing this natural-scientific, materialist tendency.

In the area of social issues in the USA, Carnap was a resolute opponent of racial discrimination and American aggression in Vietnam.

WORKS

Der logische Aufbau der Welt. Berlin-Schlachtensee, 1928.
Scheinprobleme in der Philosophie. Berlin-Schlachtensee, 1928.
Abriss der Logistik. Vienna, 1929.
Der logische Syntax der Sprache. Vienna, 1934.
Studies in Semantics, vols. 1–2. Cambridge, Mass., 1942–43.
Testability and Meaning, 2nd ed. New Haven, Conn., 1954.
The Continuum of Inductive Methods. Chicago, 1952.
Logical Foundations of Probability, 2nd ed. Chicago, 1962.
In Russian translation:
Znachenie i neobkhodimost'. Moscow, 1959.
Filosofskie osnovaniia fiziki: Vvedenie v filosofiiu nauki. Moscow, 1971. (Contains bibliography.)

REFERENCES

Narskii, I. S. *Sovremennyi pozitivizm.* Moscow, 1961.
Smirnov, V. A. "O dostoinstvakh i oshibkakh odnoi logiko-filosofskoi kontseptsii." In *Filosofiia marksizma i neopozitivizm.* Moscow, 1963.
Hill, T. *Sovremennye teorii poznaniia.* Moscow, 1965. (Translated from English.)
P. A. Schilpp, ed. *The Philosophy of Rudolph Carnap.* La Salle (Ill.)–London, 1963. (Contains a bibliography.)
I. S. Dobronravov, D. Lakhuti, and V. K. Finn [11–1322–3]

CARNATIC, a region in India between the Eastern Ghats and the Coromandel Coast; the area is populated by Tamils. In the first half of the 18th century, the principality (or nawabship) of the Carnatic was formed with its capital at Arcot; the principality played an important role in the political life of southern India. From 1746 to 1754, the Carnatic became the arena for a struggle between the French and British East India companies, ending with the victory of the British. The British protégé Muhammad Ali became the ruler of the principality. In 1801 the territory of the Carnatic was included in the Indian province of Madras. After India gained independence in 1947, the Carnatic became part of the state of Madras, which was formed in 1950; in 1969, Madras was renamed Tamil Nadu. [11–1323–2]

CARNÉ, MARCEL. Born Aug. 18, 1909, in Paris. French film director.

Carné has been working in motion pictures since 1928, beginning as an assistant director. He was also a journalist. In 1936 he made his first full-length film, the psychological drama *Jenny.* His next film was the grotesque satirical comedy *The Strange Drama of Dr. Molyneux* (1937), depicting the insecurity and instability of modern bourgeois life. He developed the same themes, but in their anxiety-laden and tragic aspects, in the films *Port of Shadows* (*Quai de Brumes;* 1938) and *Daybreak* (*Le Jour Se Lève;* 1939), which won Carné recognition as a master of poetic realism in the French cinema. The characteristic features of Carné's artistic technique are a poetic mood (lyrical suburban landscapes), melancholic anxiety, and the theme of man's fatal predestination to tragic loneliness in a hostile world. *Les Visiteurs du Soir,* a film made by Carné in 1942 based on a medieval legend, is an allegorical portrayal of the resistance to the violence of the fascist occupation forces. The film *Les Enfants du Paradis* (1945) draws on the tradition of French romantic art. The film is of a brilliantly spectacular nature and gives full play to the director's fantasy.

The greatest French movie actors, including J. Gabin, Arletty, P. Brasseur, and J.-L. Barrault, have played in Carné's films. His later films include *Juliette, ou la Clef des Songes* (1951), *Thérèse Raquin* (1953; based on a novel by E. Zola), *L'Air de Paris* (1954), *Les Tricheurs* (1958), *Three Weeks in Manhattan* (1965), and *Murderers in the Name of Order* (1971).

WORKS

Obmanshchiki. In *Stsenarii frantsuzskogo kino.* Moscow, 1961. (Translated from French.)

REFERENCES

Leproon, P. *Sovremennye frantsuzskie kinorezhissery.* Moscow, 1960.
Iurenev, R. "Marsel' Karne." In *Frantsuzskoe kinoiskusstvo.* Moscow, 1960. (Collection of articles.)
Sokol'skaia, A. *Marsel' karne.* [Leningrad] 1970. (Contains a list of his films, pp. 209–15.) V. I. Bozhovich [11–1324–5]

CARNEADES. Born in 214 B.C.; died in 129 B.C. Native of Cyrene. Ancient Greek philosopher; head of Plato's Academy and founder of the so-called New, or Third, Academy.

An adherent of skepticism, Carneades developed a theory of probability. He left no written works. Carneades was a member of the delegation of philosophers sent to Rome in 156–155 B.C.

REFERENCES

Rikhter, R. *Skeptitsizm v filosofii,* vol. 1. St. Petersburg, 1910. Pages 80–83.
Credaro, L. *Lo scetticismo degli accademici,* vols. 1–2. Milan, 1889–93. [11–1325–1]

CARNEGIE, a nonmagnetic sailing ship (brigantine) built in the USA in 1909. Displacement, 568 tons. From 1909 through 1921, geomagnetic observations were made from the *Carnegie* in the Atlantic, Pacific, and Indian oceans; in 1928 and 1929, oceanographic research was conducted in the Pacific. The *Carnegie* sank in November 1929 off Samoa. [11–1325–2]

CARNEGIEA, a genus of treelike cacti. Its solitary species is the saguaro, or the giant cactus (*Carnegiea gigantea*). It has a tall columnar trunk (height, up to 10–12 m; diameter, up to 30–65 cm). It has numerous branches in the central part of the trunk that resemble candelabra. The flowers, which are white and funnelform, open at night. Each flower has approximately 3,500 stamens and 2,000 ovules. The fruits are juicy and edible. This cactus grows very slowly, no more than 1 m every 20–30 years; the plant lives 100–200 years. It is the dominant species in the deserts of Sonora, Arizona, and southeastern California, growing in isolation on hills and frequently along riverbanks. [11–1325–3]

CARNIAN STAGE (name derived from the Carnic Alps), a lower stage of the Upper Triassic system (period). It was first identified in Austria in 1895 by the geologist E. Mojsisovics von Mojsvar; here the stage is represented by fine-grained reddish limestones containing ammonites (*Arcestes, Tropites*). In the USSR, Carnian beds have been identified in the Caucasus, in the Verkhoiansk Mountains, and on the Novosibirskie Islands, and they are extensively developed in the Crimean-Caucasian geosynclinal region and in the northeastern part of the USSR. [11–1326–3]

CARNIC ALPS, a mountain range in the eastern Alps, on the border between Austria and Italy. Length, 120 km; maximum altitude, 2,780 m (Mt. Hohe Warte). It is composed primarily of crystalline schists and limestone and has a narrow crest and steep slopes. There are broad-leaved (oak and beech) and coniferous (fir, spruce, and pine) forests. [11–1326–2]

CARNITINE, betaine-γ-amino-β-oxybutyric acid, $(CH_3)_3\overset{+}{N}$-$CH_2CH(OH)CH_2CO_2^-$, a crystalline compound with basic properties; dissolves readily in water and alcohol. Its molecular mass is 161.21, and its melting point, $195°$–$197°C$ (with decomposition).

Carnitine is primarily found in animal muscle, from which it was first extracted by V. S. Gulevich (1905); it is also found in bacteria and plants. It takes part in fatty exchange within an organism by acting as a carrier of fatty acid radicals through the membranes of the mitochondria. These membranes are impermeable to activated fatty acids (compounds with coenzyme A). With the aid of carnitine, therefore, fatty acids enter the scope of activity of the oxidizing enzymes localized within the mitochondria. Carnitine apparently also participates in the reverse transport of fatty acids. It is an essential dietary constituent and a growth factor in certain insects; therefore it is considered to be a vitamin (vitamin B_T). [11–1326–4]

CARNIVAL, a form of popular festivity with street parades and theatricalized games; primarily an open-air event.

The origins of the carnival lie in pagan rites commemorating the change in seasons and in the spring agricultural festivities and fairs. The name "carnival" originated in Italy in the late 13th century. *Commedia dell'arte,* the most popular national form of theater in 16th-century Italy, developed with the carnival. The Russian form of carnival, called *maslenitsa,* was a unique national celebration held during the Shrovetide winter festivities. In the 18th century, carnival was particularly popular in Italy (Venice and Rome), Germany, and France (Nice); it is now celebrated in Latin America and Spain.

In the USSR, carnival celebrations are held on youth, student, and sports holidays. [11–1320–1]

CARNOSAURIA, a superfamily of extinct carnivorous dinosaurs—theropods. The carnosaurs were very large bipedal reptiles. They were the principal terrestrial predators of the Mesozoic: *Teratosaurus* was the most characteristic of the Triassic; *Megalosaurus,* of the end of the Jurassic and beginning of the Cretaceous; and *Tyrannosaurus,* of the end of the Cretaceous. The carnosaurs had a high massive skull, powerful daggerlike teeth, a relatively short neck, and small forelimbs, especially in the later forms. There were several families comprising many species and genera. Carnosaur remains are found on all the continents. [11–1329–1]

CARNOSINE, $C_9H_{14}O_3N_4$, a dipeptide (β-alanyl histidine), composed of the amino acids of β-alanine and L-histidine. Discovered by G. S. Gulevich in 1900 in a meat extract. Molecular weight, 226. It crystallizes into colorless needles that are readily soluble in water but insoluble in alcohol. It is found in the skeletal musculature of most vertebrates.

Carnosine and its constituent amino acids are absent in certain species of fish (only L-histidine or β-alanine is present); it does not occur in the muscle of invertebrates. The carnosine content in the muscle of vertebrates usually varies from 200 to 400 mg percent raw muscle weight, depending on the muscular structure and function; in the human body it ranges between 100 and 150 mg percent.

Carnosine has diverse effects on the biochemical processes that occur in skeletal muscles; however, its biological role has not been definitively established. The addition of carnosine to a solution bathing the muscle of the isolated neuromyal specimen causes restoration of contractions of the fatigued muscle.

S. E. SEVERIN [11–1330–1]

CARNOT, LAZARE NICOLAS MARGUERITE. Born May 13, 1753, in Nolay; died Aug. 2, 1823, in Magdeburg. French statesman and military figure, mathematician. Member of the Institut de France (1796). Member of the Legislative Assembly of 1791–92 and of the Convention of 1792–95.

During the Jacobin dictatorship, Carnot was a member of the Committee of Public Safety (from 1793). He emerged as a major military organizer of the struggle against the interventionists and royalists; contemporaries called him the "organizer of victory." During the Thermidorian reaction, in July 1794, he opposed M. Robespierre. From 1795 to 1797, Carnot was a member of the Directory. After the coup of 18 Fructidor, he fled abroad. In 1800 he returned to France. From April to August 1800, he was minister of war. In March 1802 he became a member of the Tribunate. Carnot voted against the Empire, although he remained a supporter of Napoleon. During the Hundred Days in 1815, he was minister of the interior in Napoleon's government; he received the title of count. After the second restoration of the Bourbons, he was exiled from France in 1815.

Carnot's mathematical works deal with analysis and geometry. In his *Reflections on the Metaphysics of the Calculus of Infinitely Small Numbers* (1797), Carnot argued in favor of the correctness of the results of this calculus. Carnot's study of various means of substantiating analysis, including the methods of exhaustion, prime numbers, and limits, as well as his critique of Lagrange's theory of analytic functions, partially prepared the way for the reform of analysis in the early 19th century. In his works *On the Correlation of Geometric Figures* (1801), *Position Geometry* (1803), and *Theory of Transversals* (1806), Carnot appeared as the forerunner of J. Poncelet and the other creators of projective geometry. Carnot also wrote a number of works on applied mechanics (*Experiments on Machines in General,* 1783) and on fortification (*On the Defense of Fortresses,* vols. 1–3, 1810).

WORKS
In Russian translation:
Razmyshleniia o metafizike ischisleniia beskonechno malykh, 2nd ed. Moscow-Leningrad, 1936. (Contains bibliography.)

REFERENCE
Reinhard, M. *Le Grand Carnot,* vols. 1–2. Paris, 1950–52

[11–1326–5]

CARNOT, MARIE FRANÇOIS SADI. Born Aug. 11, 1837, in Limoges; died June 24, 1894, in Lyon. French statesman. The grandson of L. N. Carnot.

From 1878 to 1887, Carnot was in the Freycinet, Brisson, and other governments. In 1887 he became president of the French Republic. Carnot supported the creation of the Franco-Russian alliance which was concluded in 1891–93. He was killed by the anarchist S. Caserio. [11–1327–1]

CARNOT, NICOLAS LÉONARD SADI. Born June 1, 1796, in Paris; died there Aug. 24, 1832. French physicist. One of the founders of thermodynamics. Son of L. N. Carnot.

In 1814, Carnot graduated from the Ecole Polytechnique in Paris and won appointment to the engineering corps. He left military service in 1828. In his only published work, *Reflections on the Motive Power of Fire and on the Machines Capable of Developing This Power* (1824), he considered in general form the question of "producing motion from heat." In his analysis of the ideal cyclic process (Carnot cycle), he was the first to reach the conclusion that useful work is produced only when heat moves from a heated body to a colder body. Carnot also advanced the hypothesis that the amount of work is due to the temperature difference between the heater and the cooler and does not depend on the nature of the substance used in the heat engine. Carnot adhered in his reasoning to the caloric (thermogen) theory, but subsequently, as can be seen from his notes, which were published posthumously, he rejected this theory, recognizing the interconvertibility of heat and mechanical work. Carnot gave an approximate definition of the mechanical equivalent of heat and set forth, in general form, the law of the conservation of energy. Carnot's work was appreciated only in 1834, when B. P. E. Clapeyron, following Carnot's reasoning, introduced a graphic method of describing the processes. Later, by developing Carnot's doctrine, R. Clausius and W. Thompson (Lord Kelvin) derived the second law of thermodynamics.

WORKS

Réflexions sur la puissance motrice du feu et sur les machines propres à développer cette puissance, new ed. Paris [1953.]
In Russian translation:
Razmyshleniia o dvizhushchei sile ognia i o mashinakh sposobnykh razvivat' etu silu. Moscow, 1923.
"Razmyshleniia o dvizhushchei sile ognia i o mashinakh sposobnykh razvivat' etu silu." In the collection *Vtoroe nachalo termodinamiki.* Moscow, 1934. Pages 17–61.

REFERENCES
Radtsig, A. A. "Sadi Karno i ego 'Razmyshleniia o dvizhushchei sile ognia.'" In *Arkhiv istorii nauki i tekhniki,* fasc. 3. Leningrad, 1934.
Fradkin, L. Z. *Sadi Karno: Ego zhizn' i tvorchestvo: K 100-letiiu so dnia smerti, 1832–1932 gg.* Moscow-Leningrad, 1932.
La Mer, V. C. "Some Current Misinterpretations of N. L. Sadi Carnot's Memoir and Cycle." *American Journal of Physics,* 1954, vol. 22, no. 1.   [11–1327–2]

CARNOT CYCLE, a reversible cyclic process in which heat is converted into work, or vice versa. It consists of two isothermal and two adiabatic processes that alternate.

The Carnot cycle was first examined by the French scientist N. L. S. Carnot (1824) as the ideal operating cycle of a heat engine. The conversion of heat into work is accompanied by the transfer of a certain amount of heat by the engine's working substance from the hotter body (the heater) to the cooler.

The Carnot cycle proceeds as follows: at a temperature T_1 the working substance (such as steam in a cylinder under a piston) is brought into contact with a heater that has a constant temperature T_1 and isothermically acquires from it an amount of heat δQ_1 (here the steam expands and performs work). In Figure 1 this process is represented by the segment AB of the isotherm. The working substance, expanding adiabatically (along the adiabatic curve BC), then cools to temperature T_2. At this temperature, as it becomes isothermically compressed (segment CD), it gives off a quantity of heat δQ_2 to the cooler with temperature T_2. The cycle ends with an adiabatic process (DA in Figure 1) that returns the working substance to its initial thermodynamic state. When the temperature difference ($T_1 - T_2$) between the heater and cooler is constant, the working substance performs the following amount of work in one cycle:

$$A = \delta Q_1 - \delta Q_2 = \frac{T_1 - T_2}{T_1} \delta Q_1$$

This work is numerically equal to the area $ABCD$ (Figure 1) bounded by the segments of the isotherms and adiabatic curves forming Carnot's cycle.

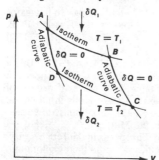

Figure 1. The Carnot cycle in a (p, V) diagram: (δQ_1) quantity of heat received by the working substance from the heater, (δQ_2) quantity of heat released by the working substance to the cooler. The area $ABCD$ is numerically equal to the work performed in the cycle.

The Carnot cycle is reversible and can be carried out in the reverse sequence (in the direction $ADCBA$). Here the quantity of heat δQ_2 is collected from the cooler and, together with the lost work δA (which has been converted into heat), is transferred to the heater. A heat engine operates in this mode as an ideal cooler.

The Carnot cycle has the highest efficiency $\eta = \delta A/\delta Q_1 = (T_1 - T_2)/T_1$ of all possible cycles accomplished in the same temperature interval ($T_1 - T_2$). In this sense the efficiency of the Carnot cycle serves as a measure of the efficiency of other working cycles.

Historically, the Carnot cycle played an important role in the development of thermodynamics and heat engineering. It was used to prove the equivalence of the formulations of the second law of thermodynamics given by R. Clausius and W. Thomson (Lord Kelvin), to determine the absolute temperature scale, and frequently also to derive various thermodynamic relations (such as the Clausius-Clapeyron equation)

REFERENCES
Fermi, E. *Termodinamika.* Kharkov, 1969. (Translated from English.)
Putilov, K. A. *Termodinamika.* Moscow, 1971.   [11–1328–2]

CARNOTITE (named after the French chemist M.-A. Carnot, 1838–1920), a mineral, a complex vanadate of potassium and uranium from the group of uran-micas. Its composition is $K_2(UO_2)_2[V_2O_8] \cdot 3H_2O$. Carnotite contains admixtures of Ca (up to 3.3 percent) and insignificant amounts of Cu, Pb, and other elements. The structure is complex and lamellar, which is evident from its good mica-like cleavage. Monoclinic-system crystals are rare; granular and powdery aggregates, which are bright yellow and greenish yellow in color, are common. The mineral has a hardness of 2–3 on the mineralogical scale and a density of 4,460 kg/m^3. It is highly radioactive, containing up to 63.42 percent UO_3.

Carnotite is ordinarily found in zones of weathering of sedimentary rocks rich in organic remains. It was first discovered in vanadium-bearing sandstones of Jurassic age in the states of Utah and Colorado in the United States. It has also been found in calcareous sandstones in the province of Shaba in the Republic of Zaire, at Radium Hill in Australia, and elsewhere. It is a valuable ore of uranium and vanadium.   [11–1330–2]

CARNOT'S THEOREM. (1) The theorem of the efficiency of heat engines that was established by N. L. S. Carnot in 1824. According to the theorem, the efficiency of the Carnot cycle does not depend on the nature of the working substance or the design of the heat engine but is determined only by the temperatures of the heater and cooler. Carnot's theorem played an important role in the establishment of the second law of thermodynamics.

(2) In impact theory, the theorem of the loss of kinetic energy during an absolutely inelastic impact. It is named for L. N. Carnot. The kinetic energy lost by a system upon impact is equal to the kinetic energy that the system would have had if its points had moved at the velocities lost, that is,

$$T_0 - T_1 = \frac{1}{2} \sum_i m_i (v_{0i} - v_{1i})^2$$

where

$$T_0 = \frac{1}{2} \sum_i m_i v_{0i}{}^2 \quad \text{and} \quad T_1 = \frac{1}{2} \sum_i m_i v_{1i}{}^2$$

are the values of the kinetic energy of the system before and after impact, respectively; m_i is the mass of the i-th point; v_{0i} and v_{1i} are the velocities of the i-th point before and after impact; and ($v_{0i} - v_{1i}$) is the lost velocity of the point. Carnot's theorem is a direct consequence of the application of the laws of conservation of momentum and energy for an isolated mechanical system to the phenomenon of inelastic impact. In many cases Carnot's theorem makes possible the determination of the velocities of bodies after inelastic impact.   [11–1328–1]

CARNUNTUM, an ancient Celtic habitation site on the right bank of the Danube, near Hainburg, Austria. Under the emperor Augustus, Carnuntum was used as a camp during the war with Maroboduus (A.D. 6). Later, it acquired the significance of an important fortification on the Danube frontier of the Roman Empire. In 73 it was enclosed with a stone wall and became an outpost for Roman legions. During the Roman wars with the frontier tribes, Carnuntum was destroyed and then reconstructed several times (the last time in 375); it was razed once and for all circa 400. The site was excavated in the 1920's and 1930's. Two amphitheaters, a praetorium, a forum, thermae, a mithraeum, and other buildings were discovered.

REFERENCES
Swoboda, E. *Carnuntum,* 2nd ed. Vienna, 1953.

Schober, A. *Römerzeit in Österreich* [2nd ed.]. Vienna, 1955.
[11–1330–4]

CARO, HEINRICH. Born Feb. 13, 1834, in Poznań; died Sept. 11, 1910, in Dresden. German chemist.

Caro graduated from the University of Berlin in 1855. Between 1868 and 1889 he was director of the Baden Aniline and Soda Factory. He synthesized the dyes induline (1863), chrysoidine (1873), eosin (1873), methylene blue (1876), and auramine (1883), among others. He collaborated with A. Baeyer on the preparation of indole (1877) and later with C. Graebe and K. Liebermann on the development of a production process for the preparation of alizarin. In 1890, Caro obtained permonosulfuric acid H_2SO_5 (Caro's acid).

REFERENCE
Bernthsen, A. "Heinrich Caro." *Berichte der Deutschen chemischen Gesellschaft*, 1912, vol. 45. pp. 1987–2042. [11–1331–2]

CAROL (Hohenzollern-Sigmaringen), rulers of Rumania.

Carol I. Born Apr. 20, 1839, in Sigmaringen, Germany; died Oct. 10, 1914, in Sinaia, Rumania. Prince of Rumania from 1866 to 1881 and then king. A relative of the Prussian king William I, he was elected prince by a reactionary coalition of landowners and bourgeoisie known as the "monstrous coalition." His foreign policy was favorable to Germany and Austria-Hungary. In 1883 he concluded a secret treaty of Rumanian adherence to the Triple Alliance of 1882.

Carol II. Born Oct. 15, 1893, in Sinaia, Rumania; died Apr. 4, 1953, in Estoril, Portugal. King from 1930 to 1940. In February 1938 he established a royal dictatorship, abolished political parties and trade unions, and formed the National Renaissance Front, a reactionary, fascist-type organization. In March 1939 he concluded an economic treaty with Germany that was highly unfavorable to Rumania. He also submitted to the Vienna Arbitration of 1940, which took northern Transylvania away from Rumania and granted it to Hungary. In September of that year, however, as the result of growing internal and external opposition, he abdicated and went abroad.

REFERENCE
Țuțui, G., and M. Popa. *Hohenzollernii în Romînia*. Bucharest, 1962.
[11–1337–1]

CAROLINA, a national German criminal code compiled in 1532.

The *Carolina* was named after Emperor Charles V. In addition to German customary law, in particular the penal code of Bamberg of 1507, the sources used by the compilers of the *Carolina* were statutes borrowed from Roman law and several Italian legal forms. Striving to unify German law, the code took into consideration the particularist tendencies of the various German lands. Its significance as a national German code was reduced by the qualification that the age-old, inherited, and lawful customs, that is, the privileges of the princes and feudal estates, were to be preserved.

Like the "bloody legislation" in Great Britain, which allowed the persecution of the peasant paupers, the *Carolina* was harsh toward the poor: malicious vagrants, it said, "should be executed as soon as they are taken to prison regardless of whether they have committed any other deed" (*Karolina*, Alma-Ata, 1967, pp. 191–92). Legal procedures made up the basic content of the *Carolina*. The code also defined a broad range of punishable deeds, including state, religious, and purely criminal offenses. It defined such concepts of criminal law as complicity, attempted murder, and aiding and abetting.

Published seven years after the Peasants' War in Germany, the *Carolina* placed almost unlimited severity at the basis of criminal justice. For state, religious, property, and many other crimes, it provided for burning at the stake, quartering, breaking on the wheel, hanging, drowning, burying alive, dragging to the place of execution, torture with red-hot tongs, and the cutting off of hands, among other punishments. Judicial discretion was not restricted in any essential way. Questioning under torture was recognized as the normal form of investigation

The *Carolina* exerted a great influence on German particularist legislation: in some areas it simply was reissued as the locally valid law; in others, it was supplemented and revised. The code was in effect until the end of the 18th century.

REFERENCES
Karolina. Translated from Middle German, with an introduction and commentary by S. Ia. Bulatov. Alma-Ata, 1967.
Z. M. Chernilovskii [11–1332–4]

CAROLINE ISLANDS, an archipelago in the western part of the Pacific Ocean in Micronesia, named for the queen of the Spanish king Charles II. It is now a United Nations trust territory, under the administration of the United States since 1947. It consists of 936 individual islands or clusters of volcanic islands and atolls situated between 1° and 10° N lat. and 131° and 163° E long. The islands themselves have a total land area of 1,320 sq km. The major groups and islands include the Palau group (Babelthuap Island, 397 sq km) and Yap (100 sq km) in the west and the Senyavin group (Ponape Island, 334 sq km), Truk (100 sq km), and Kusaie (110 sq km) in the east.

All of the larger islands (maximum altitude, 791 m) are volcanic in origin and are ringed with coral reefs. The islands of the western group are part of an arching group of islands on a ridge that is rising slowly but steadily; those of the eastern group rise directly from the ocean floor. There are deposits of organic phosphates. The climate is equatorial or subequatorial. Precipitation ranges from 2,250 mm to 3,000–4,500 mm and even 6,000 mm (in the mountains of Kusaie Island) a year. The Carolines lie in a region where an average of 25 typhoons form annually. Such storms take place at all times of the year but are most common from July to November, with a maximum in September. The volcanic islands have tropical evergreen forests of screw pines. On the mountain slopes are evergreen rain forests with tree-ferns, and bamboo at the upper borders. The drier slopes are covered with savannas. On the coral islands, coconut palms and screw pines predominate.

The native population of the Carolines consists of small ethnic groups of Micronesians, speaking various languages of the Malay-Polynesian family. Altogether, they number about 67,000 (1969, estimate). The larger groups include Truk Islanders (26,000) on Truk, Nomoi, and other islands; Ponapeans (15,000) on Ponape, Pingelap, and other islands; and Palauans (12,000) on Palau. Most of the islanders are Christians (Catholic and Protestant). English is the official language. The major occupations of the population are agriculture (coconut palm, sugarcane, taro, sweet potato), fishing, and livestock breeding.

The islands were discovered in 1528 by the Spanish navigator Saavedra. Some of them were explored by the Russian F. P. Litke in 1828. [11–1336–2]

CAROLINE, MARSHALL, AND MARIANA ISLANDS, a United Nations trust territory in the Pacific Ocean, under the administration of the United States. It consists of groups of islands in the western Pacific, about 1,400 islands in all. Area, 1,800 sq km. Population, 107,000 (1971). Its administrative center is on the island of Saipan in the Marianas.

The islands were discovered by Europeans in the 16th century. Russian navigators played a significant part in their exploration. In the late 19th and early 20th centuries they were possessions of Germany. In 1914 they were seized by Japan, which received a League of Nations mandate for their administration in 1920. During World War II, after a series of pitched battles in 1944, American armed forces were able to occupy the Marshalls (February), the Marianas (July and August), and the western part of the Carolines (September and October). In 1947 they were constituted as a United Nations trust territory under US administration. Several American military bases are located there.
[11–1336–1]

CAROLINGIAN RENAISSANCE, the cultural flowering in the empire of Charlemagne and the kingdoms of the Carolingian dynasty in the eighth and ninth centuries, chiefly on the territory of modern France and Germany.

The Carolingian renaissance expressed itself in the organization of new schools, the gathering of a number of educated persons at the royal court, a new interest in classical literature and secular disciplines in general, and the development of the fine arts and architecture. The renaissance was closely connected with the military, political, and economic efforts of the Carolingians to affirm their authority throughout their empire. Such an aim demanded trained administrators and an educated clergy. For this reason new schools were founded in Tours, Corbie, Fulda, Rheims, Reichenau, and elsewhere. The center of the movement was the unique circle known as the Academy, which was headed by Alcuin at the court of Charlemagne. Among its members were Charlemagne himself, his biographer Einhard, and the poet Angilbert.

During the Carolingian renaissance, interest in secular disciplines grew considerably. Alcuin, Rabanus Maurus (the abbot of Fulda), and others attempted to give a new, medieval interpretation to the "seven liberal arts," an interpretation that would correspond more closely to the demands of feudal ecclesiastical culture. A special role in the cultural revival was played by immigrants from Ireland like Sedulius Scottus, a student of Greek and a poet and scholar, and Johannes Scotus Erigena, the first original philosopher of the Middle Ages, who developed a pantheistic cosmology.

The period also saw significant developments in historiography. At the court of Charlemagne, an apologetic history, the Royal Annals, was composed, and local chronicles like the Annals of Fulda and the Annals of St. Bertin appeared (c. 830–60). The outstanding historical work of the Carolingian renaissance, however, was the History of the Langobards, written by Paul the Deacon. Political tracts and biographies like Einhard's life of Charlemagne and Bishop Thegan's life of Louis the Pious were also written. Literature developed considerably, national (Romance and Germanic) languages were formed, and a new, more easily read style of writing, the Carolingian minuscule, was worked out. In the scriptoria of monasteries, numerous books were copied, forming the basis for the collection of valuable Carolingian manuscripts that have survived.

With Carolingian art, which drew on the impressive heritage of late classical and Byzantine art as well as on local barbarian traditions, the bases of European medieval feudal art were laid. The extensive building carried out during this epoch is known to modern scholars largely through literary sources, which describe great complexes of monasteries and imperial residences (*Pfalzen*), consisting of palaces and chapels, fortified "burgs," and basilica churches with a developed overall composition and dynamic outlines. Among the few surviving structures of the period are the central octagonal chapel at the imperial residence in Aachen (before 798), the rotunda chapel of St. Michael at Fulda (c. 820–22), the three-naved church with *Westwerk,* transept, and tower at Corvey (822–85), and the chapel built over the gates in Lorsch (c. 774).

Churches and palaces were extensively decorated with mosaics, as in the oratory at Germigny-les-Prés (after 806), and frescoes, of which fragments have been preserved in the churches of Munster (c. 800) and Auxerre (841–58). The monumental painting of the ninth century combined Early Christian tradition, reminiscent of classical antiquity in its treatment of space and volume, with elements of dynamism and distinctive expression. These elements appeared even more clearly in manuscript miniatures (representations of evangelists, biblical scenes, Carolingian monarchs). In some miniatures, like those in the Gottschalk Gospel (c. 781–83; National Library, Paris) and the Ada Gospel (early ninth century; City Library, Trier), classical style is blended with medieval symbolism and ornamentation. In others, like the Ebbo Gospel (c. 816–35; City Library, Epernay) and the Utrecht Psalter (ninth century, University Library, Utrecht), an impassioned agitation, directness of observation, and freedom and dynamism of composition and line are displayed. A number of local schools of miniature painting can be distinguished (the palace school at Aachen and schools at such centers as Rheims and Tours). The sculpture of the period consisted largely of carving in ivory (such as book covers, miniature diptychs, combs, and caskets). Casting, coinage, and engraving in metal were also developed, as were decoration with enamel and jewels and carving in stone and alabaster. The primitive form of the statue of Ste.-Foy (tenth century; treasury of the monastery at Conques), covered with gold leaf and richly decorated with jewels, is witness to the continuing vitality of barbarian tradition.

REFERENCES
Ramm, B. Ia. " 'Karolingskoe vozrozhdenie' i problemy shkol'noi obrazovannosti v rannem srednevekov'e." *Uchenye zapiski Leningradskogo gosudarstvennogo pedagogicheskogo instituta im. M. N. Pokrovskogo,* 1940. Vol. 5, history department, no. 1.
Ramm, B. Ia. "K voprosu ob istochnikakh po istorii shkoly v karolingskuiu epokhu." *Uchenye zapiski Leningradskogo gosudarstvennogo pedagogicheskogo instituta im. Gertsena,* 1948, vol. 68.
Köhler, W. *Die karolingischen Miniaturen,* vols. 1–3. Berlin, 1930–60.
Otto, W. *Die karolingische Bilderwelt.* Munich, 1957.
Karl der Grosse: Werk und Wirkung. Aachen, 1969.
Hubert, I. J., J. Porcher, and W. F. Volbach. *Carolingian Art.* London, 1970.   B. IA. RAMM and TS. G. NESSEL'SHTRAUS   [11–1333–2]

CAROLINGIANS, a royal and imperial dynasty of the Frankish state, named for Charlemagne.

The Carolingians replaced the Merovingians in 751 and ceased to exist in the tenth century. The early development of the Carolingian (Pepinid) line began in the seventh century, when their ancestor, Pepin of Landen, became chief of Austrasia. His grandson, Pepin of Herstal (died in 714), ruled as chief of the whole Frankish state, and his great-grandson, Charles Martel (chief, 715–41), strengthened the position of the family even more by his energetic activity. He laid the ground for the dynastic coup which his son, Pepin the Short, carried out in 751 to establish himself as the first Frankish king of the Carolingian line. The dynasty reached its apogee under Charlemagne (ruled 768–814, emperor from 800), who subordinated almost all of Western Europe to his authority. On Charlemagne's death, the imperial crown passed to his son Louis the Pious (ruled 814–40). By the Treaty of Verdun in 843, the empire was divided among the sons of Louis: Lothair, Louis the German, and Charles the Bald. Charles III the Fat (emperor 881–87) restored the unity of the empire for a short time. After its final breakup, the Carolingians ruled in Italy until 905, in the East Frankish kingdom (Germany) until 911, and in the West Frankish kingdom (France) until 987.   [11–1333–1]

CARONÍ, a river in Venezuela, a right-bank tributary of the Orinoco. Length, 892 km; basin area, about 85,000 sq km. It originates on and flows across the Guiana Highlands, forming waterfalls and cataracts along its entire course. Floods are common from April to October. The average annual rate of flow is about 4,600 cu m per sec. The river is navigable to a point 100 km from its mouth. As of 1972, a system of hydroelectric power stations was under construction; the first, at Guri, producing 525 megawatts, was opened in 1968. The projected output of the entire system is about 6 gigawatts.   [11–1337–2]

CAROSSA, HANS. Born Dec. 15, 1878, in Tölz; died Sept. 12, 1956, near Passau. German writer (Federal Republic of Germany). A physician by profession.

Carossa's poetry (published in collections in 1910, 1916, 1946, 1948) strove for clarity, euphony, and precision of style and was characterized by Christian and apolitical themes. His prose was basically autobiographical and similarly avoided major social issues. His works include *A Childhood* (1922), *A Rumanian Diary* (1924; published in 1934 as *War Diary*), *Doctor Gion* (1931), *The Year of Sweet Illusions* (1941), and *Different Worlds* (1951). In 1941 he was elected president of the profascist European Writers' Union. Carossa's other works included travel notes (*Italian Sketches,* 1946, and *Rome in Winter,* 1947) and literary criticism, written from the standpoint of the Christian Democratic Party.

WORKS
Sämtliche Werke, vols. 1–2. [Zürich] 1963.
REFERENCES
Mel'nikov, D. "V gushche bor'by." *Novyi mir,* 1955, no. 4.
Braun, F. *Zeitgefährten.* Munich, 1963. Pages 103–16.   [11–1338–2]

CAROTENE, $C_{40}H_{56}$, an orange-yellow pigment of the carotenoid group; a precursor of vitamin A. It is synthesized by plants; it is particularly abundant in leaves as the plants begin to bloom. Carrot roots are rich in carotene (hence the name; it was first isolated from them, and in some varieties it constitutes 31 mg percent of raw substance). The pigment is also present in the fruit of the dog rose (2–16 mg percent), currant, mountain ash, sea buckthorn, and vines of the genus *Actinidia.*

Plants contain mainly β-carotene, which as a precursor of vitamin A is twice as active as its isomers, α- and γ-carotene. Vitamin A is biosynthesized only in animals. The liver of whales and some fish is particularly rich in this vitamin (100 kg of whale liver contains about 100 g of vitamin A, the daily dose for 50,000 persons). Carotene increases the fertility of animals, accelerates the growth and development of young animals, and prevents xerophthalmia in animals.

The role of carotene in plants is rather obscure. It appears to play an important part in photosynthesis, respiration, and growth. Carotene readily forms peroxides in which a molecule of oxygen is bound at a double bond and can then participate in the oxidation of various compounds.

K. E. OVCHAROV [11–1342–1]

CAROTENOIDS, yellow, orange, or red pigments (cyclic or acyclic isoprenoids) synthesized by bacteria, fungi, and higher plants.

Animals do not ordinarily form carotenoids, although they use them to synthesize vitamin A. The carotenoids include carotene and xanthophylls, which are widely found in plants; lycopene ($C_{40}H_{56}$), found in the fruits of the tomato, dog rose, and nightshade; zeaxanthin ($C_{40}H_{56}O_2$), found in corn kernels; violaxanthin and flavoxanthin, found in squashes and gourds; cryptoxanthin ($C_{40}H_{56}O$), found in papaya; physalin ($C_{72}H_{116}O_4$), found in the flowers and fruits of *Physalis;* fucoxanthin ($C_{40}H_{56}O_6$), found in brown algae; crocetin ($C_{20}H_{24}O4$), found in the stigmata of saffron; and taraxanthin ($C_{40}H_{56}O_4$), found in the flowers of snapdragon and coltsfoot. The relative content of the various carotenoids changes in the course of development of the plant and under the influence of environmental conditions. The concentration of carotenoids is highest in the plastids of the cells.

Carotenoids promote the fertilization of plants by stimulating the germination of pollen and the growth of the pollen tubes. They play a part in the absorption of light by plants and in the perception of light by animals. They are also a major factor in the processes of photosynthesis and oxygen transport in plants. The number and position of the double bonds in the molecules of the carotenoids determine their color; over 150 carotenoids (pigments) are known. Carotenoids with a larger number of double bonds absorb in the long-wave part of the spectrum, and their color is bright orange or red.

REFERENCES
Goodwin, T. *Sravnitel'naia biokhimiia karotinoidov.* Moscow, 1954. (Translated from English.)
Kretovich, V. L. *Osnovy biokhimii rastenii,* 5th ed. Moscow, 1971.

K. E. OVCHAROV [11–1342–2]

CAROTHERS, WALLACE HUME. Born Apr. 27, 1896, in Burlington, Iowa; died Apr. 29, 1937, in Wilmington, Del. American scientist in the field of polymer chemistry and technology. Member of the National Academy of Sciences of the USA (1936).

Carothers graduated from the University of Illinois in 1921, then taught organic chemistry at several American universities (1921–28). He became chief chemist at the research laboratory of E. I. du Pont de Nemours and Company in 1928. In 1931, together with J. A. Nieuwland, Carothers synthesized a chloroprene rubber—neoprene. He produced synthetic musk for the perfume industry in 1932. Carothers formulated a method of preparing polyamide for the production of synthetic nylon fiber in 1937. He aided the transformation of polymer chemistry into an independent field of organic chemistry. Carothers also proposed a theoretical substantiation for polycondensation and introduced the concepts of monomer functionality and linear and three-dimensional polycondensation into the chemistry of polymers.

WORKS
High Polymers, vol. 1: *Collected Papers of W. H. Carothers on High Polymeric Substances.* Edited by H. Mark and G. S. Whitby. New York, 1940. [11–1332–1]

CAROTID SINUS (*bulbus caroticus, sinus caroticus*), the dilated area of the common carotid artery before bifurcation into its external and internal branches.

The carotid sinus is an important reflexogenic zone that plays a part in maintaining the constancy of arterial pressure, heart action, and blood gases content; it is the site of baroreceptors, which react to changes in blood pressure, and chemoreceptors, which react to changes in the chemical composition of the blood and in oxygen tension. The carotid sinus is innervated by the sensory branch of the glossopharyngeal nerve (sinus nerve, Hering's nerve). Excitation of the nerve endings in the carotid sinus is the first link in the chain of the carotid reflexes.

I. N. D'IAKONOVA [11–1341–3]

CAROTID SINUS REFLEXES, reflexes that bring about changes in arterial pressure, heart action, and respiration in response to the stimulation of nerve endings (baroreceptors or chemoreceptors) in the carotid sinus.

The carotid sinus reflexes are among the mechanisms that regulate by reflex action the constancy of arterial pressure and maintain the level of gas exchange required by the body. For example, an elevation in blood pressure stimulates the baroreceptors; then, by reflex action (through the vasomotor center and the cardioinhibitory center), it dilates the blood vessels, lowers arterial pressure, and reduces the rate of heart contractions. Changes in the gas content (a decrease in oxygen tension or increase in carbon dioxide tension) or pH of the blood excite the chemoreceptors of the carotid sinus, altering arterial pressure and the level of gas exchange. The carotid sinus reflexes are always adaptive in character, maintaining the constancy of the body's internal environment (homeostasis).

REFERENCES
Smirnov, A. A. *Karotidnaia refleksogennaia zona.* Leningrad, 1945.
Chernigovskii, V. N. *Interotseptory.* Moscow, 1960.

I. N. D'IAKONOVA [11–1341–2]

CAROUSEL. (1) A special machine designed to give circular rides at amusement parks and fairs. The carousel is an apparatus that turns about a fixed axis and has wooden seats in the form of figures (horses, elephants, or boats). The gay, colorful carousels are decorated with glass beads, spangles, and multicolored lamps. Carousels have been known in Russia since the early 18th century.

(2) An equestrian competition that replaced the medieval tournaments of knights. It was fashionable in 17th-century Italy and France. Carousels were held in Russia in the 18th century. The display was usually accompanied by allegorical dances and scenic representations based on mythological and historical subjects. The riders sometimes wore costumes. [11–1453–2]

CARPACCIO, VITTORE. Born circa 1455 or 1465, in Venice; died circa 1526, in Capodistria (?), present-day Koper, Slovenia. Italian painter of the early Renaissance; representative of the Venetian school.

Carpaccio, a student of Gentile Bellini, was influenced by Antonello da Messina and Giovanni Bellini. He painted series from the lives of St. Ursula (1490–95, Academy, Venice) and of St. George and St. Jerome (1502–07, Scuola di San Giorgio degli Schiavoni, Venice). In these paintings, legendary holy events are treated like real scenes contemporaneous with the artist's life. Carpaccio depicted interiors and urban landscapes in these works. He combined his fascination with narration and the poetic freshness of everyday details with his aspiration to create an integral and colorful picture of the world. He subtly re-created the ambience of space, light, and air to soften the sonority of local color. Thus, Carpaccio anticipated the painting discoveries of the 16th-century Venetian masters.

REFERENCES
Lauts, J. *Carpaccio: Painting and Drawings.* New York, 1962.
Zampetti, P. *Vittore Carpaccio: Catalogo della mostra.* Venice, 1963.
L'opera completa del Carpaccio. Milan [1967].

O. D. NIKITIUK [11–1350–1]

CARPATHIAN OPERATION OF 1915, an offensive of the Russian armies of the southwestern front in World War I (1914–18) from January to April 1915.

The objective of the Russian command was to reach the Hungarian plains and put Austria-Hungary out of the war. The German command, anticipating the impending Russian offensive, transferred the six divisions that formed the Southern Army from the Carpathians to help Austria-Hungary. On January 10 the German command itself opened an offensive with the forces of the German Southern Army and the Austro-Hungarian Third and Fifth armies, striking blows at Sambor and Stryi.

Almost simultaneously General A. A. Brusilov's Russian Eighth Army, reinforced by the XXII Corps of the Tenth Army, moved to the offensive but did not advance to any significant extent. The enemy tried to closely envelop the flank of the Eighth Army and to break through the rear of the Russian troops toward the Austro-Hungarian fortress of Przemyśl, which was blockaded by the Russian Eleventh Army. After fierce battles the left flank of the Eighth Army retreated toward the Dnestr. The further offensive of the enemy was stopped by troops that were transferred from the right flank of the Eighth Army (eight and a half infantry divisions and five cavalry divisions, making up the newly formed Ninth Army). On March 9 (22) the Austro-Hungarian garrison of 120,000 men defending Przemyśl surrendered. The troops of the Russian Eleventh Army released by the surrender were distributed among the Eighth and Third armies.

In March the Russian troops opened a new offensive against the German Southern Army and the Austro-Hungarian Third Army and advanced in the direction of Ungvár (Uzhgorod) but stopped about 30 km short of the city. To repel this offensive the enemy introduced the newly formed German Beskid Corps into action. The bloody battles in the Carpathians lasted until April. The Carpathian Operation did not attain its objectives, because the Russian troops were short of reserves, artillery, and ammunition. The enemy lost 800,000 men and the Russian forces, about 1 million men.

A. V. KUDRITSKII [11–1344–1]

CARPATHIANS, a mountain system in the eastern part of Central Europe, in Hungary, Czechoslovakia, Poland, the USSR, and Rumania. The Carpathians stretch 1,500 km from the Devin Gates west of Bratislava to the Iron Gates on the Danube, forming an arc that protrudes to the northeast and east. The width in the northwest is about 250 km; in the central region (the narrowest) it is about 120 km, and in the southeast as much as 430 km.

Terrain. The Carpathians are a complex system of mountain massifs and ranges arranged in belts and separated by longitudinal and transverse valleys. The mountains are divided into the Western Carpathians, the Eastern Carpathians (a portion of which is formed by the Ukrainian Carpathians), and the Southern Carpathians. The Carpathians also include the Western Rumanian Mountains, which adjoin the Southern Carpathians on the north, and the broad Transylvanian Plateau. The highest point in the Carpathians is Mount Gerlachovka (2,655 m), and prevailing elevations are 800–1,200 m. The Transylvanian Plateau lies at an altitude of 600–800 m.

Along the entire outer side of the Carpathian arc there stretches a zone of foothills (40–60 km) composed chiefly of loose Neocene deposits (sandstones, clays, gypsums). The Western Carpathian foothills are dissected by the valleys of the Morava, Oder, and Vistula rivers and their tributaries and by the Oświęcim and Sandomierz basins, the bottoms of which lie at an altitude of 200–300 m. Within the Eastern Carpathians, the foothills are hilly and ridgy in relief, with elevations of 400–500 m. In the south and southeast the relief of the foothills becomes low-mountain, with elevations of 800–1,000 m, and there are areas of clay and salt karst and active mud volcanoes. The entire outer edge of the Carpathians from the Morava River to the Dîmboviţa River is composed chiefly of flysch. On the northern

and eastern slopes this causes a predominance of rounded peaks and gentle slopes. More rugged topography is usually confined to the outcrops of dense sandstone massifs (Gorgany and Bieszczady). The central zone of the Carpathians is formed by a broken chain of rock massifs composed primarily of crystalline rock (granites and gneisses) and limestones. The highest massifs are the Tatra, the Low Tatra, the Rodnei, Făgăraş, Parîng, and Retezat (more than 2,000 m). The crests of the ranges often bear traces of Pleistocene glaciation. Alpine landforms are most evident in the Tatra and Făgăraş massifs. Owing to the rather extensive distribution of limestones and dolomites, many regions of the Carpathians have karst relief, especially in the massifs of the Slovakian Karst, Hăghimaş, and Anina.

Along the inner side of the Carpathian arc stretches a band of volcanic massifs. In the west their elevation usually does not exceed 1,000 m (Kremnické Pohoří, Štiavnické Pohoří, Vihorlat Massif). Sometimes these massifs have the appearance of table mountains, and in places they form rugged contours. In the east the volcanic mountains increase in altitude, and in the Caliman Massif attain an altitude of 2,102 m (Mt. Pietros).

The Western Rumanian Mountains (up to 1,848 m) consist of rugged massifs and karst. Many of the intramontane basins in the Carpathians are of tectonic origin. The Transylvanian Plateau lies between the Southern and Eastern Carpathians and the Western Rumanian Mountains. It is composed predominantly of loose Neocene deposits and in places is covered by loess. The plateau's terrain is characterized by a complex combination of hilly elevations, flat surfaces, and river valleys. In places along the edges of the plateau there are mud volcanoes.

Because of relatively low elevations, the Carpathians are comparatively easily crossed, particularly in the central portion. The major passes through which railways and highways have been built for the most part lie at elevations of 500–1,000 m (Dukla, Jablonitsa, Predeal).

Geological structure and minerals. The Carpathians are part of the northern branch of the alpide geosynclinal (folded) region. The major portion of the Carpathian arc is composed of thick Cretaceous and Paleogene flysch series that frequently form disrupted folds and sheets tilted toward the Ciscarpathian Foredeep. A series of tectonic (structural facies) zones have been identified, separated by major overthrusts with amplitudes sometimes exceeding 40 km. The basic fold phases are pre-Neocene and Pliocene. In the Eastern Carpathians there stretches the extensive Maramureş Massif consisting of several complexes and sheets of crystalline schists and gneisses and of a Mesozoic sedimentary cover. The Southern Carpathians are composed chiefly of ancient crystalline schists and granites with a sedimentary Upper Paleozoic and Mesozoic cover; an overlapping structure is characteristic. The folded flysch region of the Western and part of the Eastern Carpathians is rimmed on the inner side by the narrow Pieniny Cliff Zone—a belt of Jurassic limestone cliffs and tectonic detached masses among the flysch. In the Western Carpathians, behind the cliff zone stretches a band of slightly dislocated Paleogene Podhale flysch, and then there rises the Central Zone of the ancient cores of the Western Carpathians, which has an overlapping structure. The Central Zone consists of numerous crystalline massifs (Tatra, Low Tatra) with a sedimentary cover from the Upper Paleozoic and Mesozoic. The formation of these sediments ended in the Cretaceous period, and there is very little post-Cretaceous folding. In the east, along the major faults, this entire system has subsided and serves as the basement on which the Transcarpathian Interior Trough has developed. This trough extends across the Ukrainian SSR and is composed of a slightly dislocated Neocene series (Burdigalian-Pliocene). To the south the trough adjoins the Pannonian Central Massif, which is buried beneath a thick series of chiefly Neocene deposits from the Hungarian Depression. Along the inner portion of the Carpathian arc, Neocene volcanic rock is widely found (andesites, basalts). On the outer side the Carpathians are rimmed by the Ciscarpathian Foredeep, which is composed of a thick series of Neocene molasses. The foredeep is divided into an interior zone with a flysch base and with a complete series of folded molasses and an external zone with a platform base and only the upper, very slightly dislocated molasses. Along their border stretches a buried folded ridge, which is a continuation of the Świętokrzyskie Mountains in Poland. Regional marginal faults separate the foredeep from the flysch Carpathians and from the platform and also separate the various zones. During the period of sedimentation in the flysch trough, the interior cordilleras margined the facies zones, and during folding they served as resistant blocks and caused the development of regional thrusts.

The chief minerals associated with the Ciscarpathian Foredeep are oil and gas (also in the Carpathians), ozocerite, and common and potassium salt. In the Carpathians there are various building materials, including marble (Maramureş), and mineral springs of diverse composition. In the Transcarpathian Trough rock salt is mined. There are mercury deposits in Transcarpathia, and the Slovak Ore Mountains contain ore deposits. In Rumania there are deposits of bituminous coal and lignite, iron and manganese ores, and deposits of nonferrous and rare metals (Baia Mare, Munţii Metalici).

Climate. The climate of the Carpathians is temperate and transitional from marine to continental. Because of their areal extent and altitude differences, the mean January temperature is from $-5°$ to $-4°C$ in the north and east and from $-3°$ to $-2°C$ in the south. On the highest peaks it drops to $-9°$ or $-10°C$, and in places even lower. In some intramontane depressions winter temperature inversions have been noted. The mean July temperature in the foothills is $17°-18°C$ in the north and east and $19°-20°C$ in the south; in the upper mountain zone it drops to $5°-4°C$, and in places lower. The annual precipitation in the foothills varies from 600–800 mm on the outer side of the Eastern and Southern Carpathian arc to 900–1,000 mm in the Western Rumanian Mountains and the Western Carpathians. In the alpine zone, total precipitation increases to 1,200–1,400 mm in the south and 1,800–2,000 mm in the northeast. Maximum precipitation occurs in the summer. Most precipitation is in the form of rainfall. In the foothills the snow cover may last from two to three months (in some areas forming only sporadically), from five to seven months in the mountains, and in places even longer. In the Carpathians there are no contemporary glaciers or perpetual snow.

Rivers and lakes. The Carpathians form one of Europe's main divides. The rivers of the Vistula and Oder basins, encompassing a large portion of the northern Carpathian slopes, flow into the Baltic Sea. Most of the Carpathian rivers are part of the Danube Basin; the rivers on the northeastern slopes are in the Dnestr Basin. Annual drainage fluctuates from 50–100 mm in the Carpathian foothills to 800–1,000 mm and more in the alpine areas. The rivers are fed by snow and rain. Their regime is characterized by sharp annual fluctuations in discharge, with the greatest discharge occurring in the spring (owing to the melting of snow) and in the first half of summer (torrential rains). The Carpathian rivers are an important potential source of electric power, and many of them are used for irrigation. The few lakes in the Carpathians are found chiefly in the alpine areas, where they fill the bottoms of ancient cirques.

Types of landscapes. In the Carpathians, landscapes are distributed according to the principles of altitude zonation. In the past the foothills were covered with forest steppe and oak and beech-oak forests, which are now almost completely cut down. In their place are found orchards, vineyards, and arable land. In the mountains the natural landscapes have survived better. The lower zone of the mountains is occupied by oak forests rising to an altitude of 550–600 m in the north and 700–800 m in the south. Above these elevations they are gradually replaced by beech forests extending to an altitude of 1,100–1,250 m in the north and 1,300–1,350 m in the south. The soil cover consists mainly of mountain-forest brown soils, and rendzinas have developed on the calcareous soils. Beech forests occur most widely in the Southern Carpathians and the Western Rumanian Mountains; elsewhere they are found along the inner side of the mountain arc. Above the beech forests grow mixed forests of beech, fir, and spruce, which are especially well developed along the outer side of the Carpathian arc, where they often descend to the foothills and frequently replace the beech forests. The mixed forests rise to an altitude of 1,200–1,300 m in the north and 1,500–1,550 m in the south. The upper limit of forest vegetation is formed by coniferous forests, chiefly spruce but sometimes larch and pine. These forests end at an altitude of 1,500–1,600 m in the north and 1,700–1,800 m in the south. Coniferous forests are best developed in the Eastern Carpathians, usually growing on mountain-forest brown and mountain-podzolic soils. In many places the coniferous forests have been significantly reduced by cutting, and their upper boundary has descended to 100–200 m below the natural tree line. The forests give way to a zone of subalpine shrubs and meadows extending to an altitude of 1,700–2,000 m in the north and 2,100–2,200 m in the south. This zone is represented primarily by *Krummholz,* consisting of thickets of dwarf pine, juniper, and alder, interspersed with grassy mountain meadows (balds). Above this region, to an altitude of 2,300–2,400 m, lies a zone of alpine meadows and shrubs; it occurs only sporadically, chiefly in the Western and Southern Carpathians, where it alternates with talus and rock. The vegetation is represented by formations of alpine grasses and sedges with an admixture of alpine motley grass and by thickets of rhododendron and dwarf willow. Mountain peat-meadow soils predominate. On some peaks rising above 2,300–2,400 m there are fragments of a subnival zone, with a predominance of barren or lichen-covered rock.

The animal world is represented for the most part by forest fauna. Squirrels and rabbits are widespread; predators include bears, wolves, lynx, and marten; and ungulates are represented by deer, roe deer, chamois, and wild boar. Birds include capercaillies, owls, woodpeckers, and cuckoos. An extensive network of preserves and parks has helped to maintain the natural landscapes. These include Babia Góra and Pieniny (Poland), Tatra (Poland and Czechoslovakia), Aggtelek (Hungary), Retezat (Rumania), and Carpathian (USSR).

Population is unevenly distributed. The most heavily populated areas are the foothills and intramontane basins, where field crops, grapes, and fruit are cultivated. The mountains are comparatively sparsely settled, and here the chief occupations are herding and forestry. Among the many resorts in the Carpathians are Krynica, Zakopane, and Szczawnica in Poland; Bükkszek and Parádfüred in Hungary; Pieštany, Sliač, and Tatranská Lomnica in Czechoslovakia; Băille-Herculane, Vatra Dornei, and Sinaia in Rumania; and Truskavets and Morshin in the USSR. Tourism is well developed, as well as mountain climbing and winter sports, primarily in the Tatra, Făgăraş, Retezat, and the Ukrainian Carpathians.

REFERENCES

Anuchin, V. A., and A. I. Spiridonov. *Zakarpatskaia oblast'.* Moscow, 1947.

Armand, D. L. *Rumyniia.* Moscow-Leningrad, 1946.

Vlasova, T. V. *Vengriia.* Moscow, 1948.

Gerenchuk, K. I., M. M. Koinov, and P. M. Tsys'. *Pryrodno-geografichnyi podil L'vivs'kogo ta Podil's'kogo ekonomichnikh raioniv.* L'vov, 1964.

Lencewicz, S. *Fizicheskaia geografiia Pol'shi.* Moscow, 1959. (Translated from Polish.)

Pecsi, M., and B. Sarfalvi. *Vengriia.* Moscow, 1962. (Translated from Hungarian.)

Pryroda Ukrains'kykh Karpat. L'vov, 1968.

Fiziko-geograficheskoe raionirovanie Ukrainskoi SSR. Kiev, 1968.

Bulla, B. *Magyarország természéti földrajza.* Budapest, 1964.

Kondracki, J. *Geografia fizyczna Polski,* 2nd ed. Warsaw, 1967.

Mihăilescu, V. *Carpaţii Sud-Estici de pe teritoriul R. P. Romîne.* Bucharest, 1963.

N. N. RYBIN (physical geography) and O. S. VIALOV
(geological structure and minerals) [11–1344–2]

CARPEAUX, JEAN BAPTISTE. Born May 11, 1827, in Valenciennes; died Oct. 11, 1875, in Counbevoie. French sculptor, painter, and graphic artist.

In 1844, Carpeaux began studying at F. Rude's studio in Paris. In 1848 he became a student under J. Duret at the École des Beaux-Arts. His works include the spiritually tragic sculptural group *Ugolino* (bronze, 1857–60, the Louvre, Paris), the decorative and festive high reliefs *The Triumph of Flora* (plaster of paris, 1863–66, facade of the Pavilon de Flore, Tuileries, Paris) and *The Dance* (stone, 1865–69, facade of the Paris Opera, Paris), and the sculptural group *Four Parts of the World* (bronze, 1867–72, in the fountain in the Luxembourg Gardens, Paris).

Carpeaux's works, such as *Fisher-girl* (terra-cotta, 1871, Push-kin Museum of Fine Arts, Moscow), are distinguished by dynamic forms, influenced by 18th-century sculpture. There is a fanciful play of light and shade, and the figures are sensual and graceful; at the same time, they occasionally display some of the pretentiousness of *salon* art. Carpeaux is also well known as a sculptor of numerous portrait busts.

REFERENCE
Clément-Carpeaux, L. *La Vérité sur l'oeuvre et la vie de Jean-Baptiste Carpeaux (1827–1875),* vols. 1–2. Paris, 1935.   [11–1355–4]

CARPENTARIA, GULF OF, a bay of the Arafura Sea on the northern shore of Australia, between Cape York Peninsula and Arnhem Land. It cuts inland for 600 km. The maximum depth of the gulf is 69 m. The average monthly temperature of the water on the surface in the greater part of the gulf is 23°C to 25°C in winter and 29°C in summer. The gulf's salinity is 34.8 parts per thousand. The tides are irregular and semidiurnal; their heights reach 3.2 m. There are strong tidal currents near the shore.   [11–1351–1]

CARPENTER, MALCOLM SCOTT. Born May 1, 1925, in Boulder, Colo. US pilot and astronaut. Navy lieutenant commander.

In 1949 Carpenter graduated from the University of Colorado (with a major in aviation technology). After graduating from the navy's test-pilot school (1954), he worked in the electronic systems department of the navy's aviation test center. From 1959 he was in the National Aeronautics and Space Administration's group of astronauts. On May 24, 1962, he completed a five-hour flight around the earth (three orbits) in the Mercury spaceship (MA-7, also called *Aurora 7*).   [11–1351–2]

CARPENTIER, ALEJO. Born Dec. 26, 1904, in Havana. Cuban writer.

Carpentier began his literary activity in the 1920's and belonged to the Group of the Minority. He also edited the progressive journal *Revista de avance.* He lived as an émigré in Paris (1928–39) and in Venezuela (1945–59). After the victory of the revolution of 1959, Carpentier participated in Cuba's social and cultural life.

His early writing is connected with "Afro-Cubism," a literary movement that drew on the dual (European and African) sources of Cuba's culture. Carpentier's first novel was Afro-Cubist: *Ecue Jamba-o* (1933) naturalistically depicted the religious rites of the Negroes. In the 1940's he made comparisons between Latin America and Western Europe in his works, noting common features of historical and cultural development. The historical novella *Earthly Kingdom* (1949; Russian translation, 1962) deals with the revolution in Haiti at the turn of the 19th century and the mythological element of the Negro collective consciousness.

Carpentier's novel *Lost Traces* (1953; Russian translation, 1964) demonstrates the simultaneous existence of different stages of history in Latin America. His multilevel historical novel *The Age of Enlightenment* (1962; Russian translation, 1968) raises the problem of the special character of the history of Latin America's development.

WORKS
In Russian translation:
Muzyka Kuby. Moscow, 1962.
REFERENCES
Dashkevich, Iu. "Alekho Karpent'er: romanist i ego mir." *Inostrannaia literatura,* 1970, no. 7.
Márques Rodríguez, A. *La obra narrativa de A. Carpentier.* [Caracas, 1970.]   N. S. ZIUKOVA [11–1351–3]

CARPOGONIUM, the female sexual organ in red seaweed. It is bottle-shaped and consists of a broad lower (abdominal) section and a narrow upper section, the trichogyne. After fertilization of the egg cell, the trichogyne dies off. Carpospores form in the lower part; they are sometimes located at the ends of the cellular threads growing from either the egg cells or special cells that are connected to the egg cells by threads.   [11–1358–1]

CARPOLOGY, the division of plant morphology studying the form and structure of fruits and seeds. Since the propagation of plants is made possible by various agents (wind, water, birds, mammals, and man) it is not sufficient to study only the morphological character of fruits and seeds (for example, the origin of the fruit from a specific part of the flower or the structure of seed and fruit coats). Ecological factors must also be taken into account. Carpology is basically the study of the morphogenesis and ontogenesis of fruits and seeds. A primary function of carpology is the establishment of a classification system. A morphological classification of fruits based on the consistency of the pericarp (dry and succulent fruits) and on the number of seeds in the fruit (single-seed or multiple-seed fruits) was worked out by the German botanist J. Gaertner. Russian scientists, including Kh. Ia. Gobi, developed his system further. Their classification takes several ecological factors into account, such as the method by which the fruit is opened. The most urgent tasks of carpology are the establishment of a convenient and detailed applied scientific classification of fruits and the categorization of the fruits and seeds of weeds. These classifications will greatly aid agronomists, seed developers, and workers in quarantine and seed quality-control laboratories.

REFERENCES
Kaden, N. N. "O nekotorykh osnovnykh voprosakh klassifikatsii, tipologii i nomenklatury plodov." *Botanicheskii zhurnal,* vol. 46, no. 4, 1961.
Takhtadzhian, A. L. *Osnovy evoliutsionnoi morfologii pokrytosemennykh.* Moscow-Leningrad, 1964.   L. V. KUDRIASHOV [11–1359–2]

CARRACCI, a family of Italian artists of the Bolognese school, representatives of academism. Lodovico Carracci (baptized Apr. 21, 1555, in Bologna; died there Nov. 13, 1619) and his cousins Agostino Carracci (born Aug. 15, 1557, in Bologna; died Mar. 22, 1602, in Parma) and Annibale Carracci (born Nov. 3, 1560, in Bologna; died July 15, 1609, in Rome) received their artistic training in Bologna. Their early works show the influences of Correggio, Michelangelo, and Tintoretto. Eclectically combining the devices of these masters, the Carraccis created their own style, which was a reaction against mannerism. They founded the Accademia degli Incamminate (Academy of Those Who Have Entered Upon the Correct Path) in Bologna circa 1585, which played an important role in the development of the principles of academic art. The academy's methodology included painting from life. At the same time, following the formal traditions of the masters of the High Renaissance, the academy stressed the idealization of reality.

The Carraccis created a new type of altar painting, characterized by monumental compositions, bright colors, and effective foreshortening and representation of gestures. Their altarpieces include the *Madonna of Bargellini* (Lodovico Carracci, 1588), *The Last Communion of St. Jerome* (Agostino Carracci, 1591–93)—both are in the National Picture Gallery in Bologna—and the *Assumption of the Virgin* (Annibale Carracci, 1592) in the Church of Santa Maria del Popolo in Rome. The Carraccis collaborated in the painting of frescoes in several Bolognese palaces, including the Palazzo Fava (1580–85) and the Palazzo Magnani (1588–90).

Annibale Carracci was more talented than Agostino and Lodovico. He worked in Bologna, Parma, Venice, and Rome. Annibale's genre paintings and portraits are noted for their keen and spontaneous observations (*Self-portrait,* 1590's, the Hermitage, Leningrad). His landscape paintings, which are imbued with a sense of the grandeur and harmony of nature, played an important role in the development of the ideal landscape. The frescoes by Annibale and Agostino in the Palazzo Farnese in Rome (1597–1604) anticipated the decorative artistic complexes of the baroque period. In many ways, the two major schools of 17th-century European art—baroque and classical—were based on various elements in the art of the Carraccis.

REFERENCES
Catalogo critico della mostra dei Carracci. Bologna, 1956.
Posner, D. *Annibale Carracci.* London, 1971.
V. E. MARKOVA [11–1360–5]

CARRAGEEN (also, Irish moss), the commercial name for the red seaweeds *Gigartina mamillosa* and *Chindrus crispus,* which occur along the coasts of the North Atlantic (*C. crispus* is also found along the Kola Penninsula and in the Far East). The principal component is slime (56–79 percent), which is composed of polysaccharides and swells considerably in water. After it has been boiled and subsequently cooled, carrageen congeals into a gelatinous mass. This seaweed, which is dried during processing, is used in the textile industry for sizing material, in the food industry for clarifying beer, and in the paper industry for preparing suspensions and solutions. It is also used to prevent the settling of suspensions. [11–1360–2]

CARRANZA, VENUSTIANO. Born Dec. 29, 1859, in Cuatro Ciénegas; died May 21, 1920, in the state of Puebla. Statesman and military and political figure of Mexico.

Carranza was an important landowner. During the Mexican Revolution of 1910–17, he was one of the leaders of the national bourgeoisie and the landowners who had become bourgeois in their outlook. In 1914 he was proclaimed provisional president. Carranza became president in 1917. His government accepted a constitution (which is still in force) that was bourgeois, democratic, and, to a significant degree, anti-imperialistic. However, Carranza, as a spokesman of the interests of the ruling classes, brutally suppressed the peasant and workers' movement. He was overthrown as a result of a revolt and murdered during his flight from the capital. [11–1360–3]

CARRARA, a city in central Italy in Tuscany, in the province of Massa-Carrara, 6 km from the Ligurian Sea. Marina di Carrara is the outer harbor of the city. Population, 66,800 (1969). Carrara is known for its quarries of white marble. Approximately half of those occupied in the industry of the city work in the quarrying and processing of marble, most of which is exported. There are small chemical, metalworking, and oil-refining enterprises. There is an academy of fine arts and an art *lycée* in the city. [11–1360–4]

CARRÉ, a combat formation of troops in the shape of one or several squares or rectangles.

It was used in several European armies from the 17th through the 19th centuries in offensive and defensive operations, primarily to repulse cavalry attacks. In the Russian Army of the 18th century, especially in the wars with Turkey, the combat formation of the troops was constructed of several carrés. In the first half of the 18th century the Russian troops used large carrés; in the second half of the 18th century P. A. Rumiantsev in the Battle of Kagul (1770) deployed his troops in several small carrés, each with 3,000 to 4,000 men, which facilitated the implementation of maneuvers. A. V. Suvorov used company carrés in the battle of Tutrakan (1773). In the early 19th century, with the development of the extended formation, the carré lost its significance. [11–1238–4]

CARREL, ALEXIS. Born June 28, 1873, near Lyon; died Nov. 5, 1944, in Paris. French experimental surgeon and pathophysiologist.

In 1896, Carrel graduated from the medical faculty in Lyon. From 1904 he worked at the Hull Physiological Laboratory in Chicago, and from 1906 at the Rockefeller Institute in New York. In 1912 he received the Nobel Prize for working out original methods of suturing blood vessels "end to end," keeping blood vessels and organs viable in a liquid medium, and treating and healing wounds; for designing a perfusion pump that supplies blood and oxygen to an organ while it is outside the body; and for working out the technique of growing tissue culture.

WORKS
"Neue Untersuchungen über das selbständige Leben der Gewebe und Organe." *Berliner klinische Wochenschrift,* 1913, no. 24, pp. 1097–1101.
The Treatment of Infected Wounds. New York, 1917. (With G. Dehelly.)
The Culture of Organs. New York, 1938. (With C. A. Lindbergh.)

REFERENCE
Smith, R. B. "Alexis Carrel." *Investigative Urology,* 1967, vol. 5, no. 1, pp. 102–05. [11–1361–1]

CARRERA, JOSÉ MIGUEL. Born Oct. 15, 1785, in Santiago; died Sept. 4, 1821, in Mendoza, Argentina. Political and military figure in Chile. Born into a wealthy family.

Beginning in 1806, Carrera lived in Spain, where he studied commerce; he also was involved in the struggle of the Spanish people against the French occupation. Carrera returned to Chile in 1810, at the outbreak of the war for independence of the Spanish colonies in America. In 1811 he led a military coup d'etat that dissolved congress and established a dictatorship; he considered this to be the only means of effectively rebuffing the royalists and the "moderate" elements, who did not share his belief in the need for radical action. Carrera carried out a number of measures directed at strengthening the position of the patriotic liberation movement: he introduced a constitution in 1812, opened a national institute and national libraries, and began the publication of the first Chilean newspaper, *Aurora.* Carrera's dictatorship, however, aroused bitter resistance from the "moderates," which weakened the camp of the patriots. After the defeat of the patriots at the battle of Rancagua (1814), Carrera left the country. [11–1362–3]

CARRERA, RAFAEL. Born Oct. 24, 1814, in Guatemala City; died there Apr. 4, 1865. Statesman and military figure of Guatemala. The son of an Indian father and a black mother.

Carrera came into prominence during the years of struggle between the liberals and conservatives in the United Provinces of Central America (1823–38). In 1838, Carrera led a reactionary mutiny of the conservatives and brought about the disintegration of the federation in 1839. In the same year he became the virtual dictator of Guatemala. Carrera frequently organized interventions into Honduras and El Salvador. In 1844, with the support of the army, the landowners, and the church, he was elected president (until 1848). He abolished the reforms that had been introduced by the liberals. In 1851, Carrera was again elected president, and in 1854 he was named to the post for life. Under Carrera, the economic dependence of Guatemala on Great Britain increased. [11–1362–2]

CARRERA ANDRADE, JORGE. Born Sept. 28, 1903, in Quito. Ecuadorian poet.

Carrera Andrade served in the diplomatic corps from 1929 to 1949. He is the author of the books of verse *The Unspoken Pond* (1922), *Garland of Silence* (1926), *News From Sea and Land* (1930), *Period of Labor* (1935), *Verses Like Life* (1962), *Man of the Planet* (1963), and *Chronicle of the Indies* (1965). His favorite theme is philosophical reflections on nature. Carrera Andrade also wrote travel sketches, literary essays, and works on the history of Ecuador: *A Gallery of Mystics and Rebels* (1959) and *The Fairy-tale Kingdom of Quito* (1963).

WORKS
Edades poéticas. Quito, 1958.
In Russian translation:
["Stikhi."] *Inostrannaia literatura,* 1965, no. 2.
REFERENCE
Benitez Vinueza, L. "Jorge Carrera Andrade: el sensualismo poético." *Revista nacional de cultura,* 1963, nos. 156–57. [11–1362–4]

CARRHAE, an ancient city in northwestern Mesopotamia (the modern city of Harran in Turkey), near which a battle occurred on May 9, 53 B.C., between the Roman forces of M. Crassus (more than 40,000 men) and the Parthian troops of Surenas. The Parthian superiority in cavalry resulted in the rout of the Roman advance guard and the disorderly retreat of the Romans toward Carrhae. On May 10, Crassus was killed during negotiations and the remnants of the demoralized Roman army (12,000–14,000) withdrew beyond the Euphrates River. [11–1364–2]

CARRIAGE, a subassembly of a mechanism or machine that supports a number of parts and moves along guides or, less frequently, rotates in bearings. In metalworking machines the carriage is the lower (supporting) part of a slide, which moves along the guides of a bed (in lathes) or traverse (in planers and vertical lathes), or it is a part of a machine table that moves in the guides of a console (in shapers and milling machines). In looms the carriage is a shed-forming mechanism used in the production of finely patterned fabrics and for complex weaving. In typewriters the carriage is a frame with a cylinder for the paper. In bicycles the entire pedal mechanism is called the carriage. [11–1260–1]

CARRILLO, SANTIAGO. Born Jan. 18, 1915, in Gijón, in Asturias, Spain. Figure of the Spanish and international workers' movement. The son of a worker.

Carrillo joined the Federation of Socialist Youth in 1928. At the same time, he began to work as an apprentice in the printing shop of the newspaper *El Socialista* and subsequently became a member of the editorial board. Carrillo was elected to the committee of the Madrid organization of the Federation of Socialist Youth in 1930 and was a member of the executive committee of the federation from 1932 to 1936. He was the director of the central organ of the federation, *Renovación*, from 1932 to 1934 and was general secretary of the federation from 1934 to 1936. Carrillo joined the Revolutionary Committee in October 1934 during the armed uprising and was arrested for his role on this committee. He actively participated in the creation of the United Socialist Youth of Spain in April 1936. Both communist and socialist youth joined this new organization, of which Carrillo was elected general secretary. He joined the Communist Party of Spain in 1936. During the National Revolutionary War of the Spanish People (1936–39) against the Italian and German interventionists and the fascist rebels, he became a member of the junta for the defense of Madrid.

Carrillo emigrated after the defeat of the Spanish republic. He became a member of the Central Committee of the Communist Party of Spain in March 1937. He was a candidate member of its politburo from 1937 to 1945 and has been a member of the politburo since 1945. In 1960 he became a member of the executive committee. He was secretary of the Communist Youth International in 1940. Carrillo became a member of the secretariat of the Spanish party's Central Committee in 1954 and has been general secretary since 1960. [11–1363–1]

CARRIÓN, BENJAMIN. Born Apr. 20, 1898, in Loja. Ecuadorian writer, historian of literature, and public figure.

Carrión graduated from the Central University of Ecuador in Quito in 1922. In 1932–33 he was minister of public education. From 1939 to 1949, Carrión was a professor of literature at the Central University. In the early 1950's he served as president of the House of Ecuadorian Culture, an organization uniting the progressive creative forces of the country. Carrión wrote the novels *The Disillusionment of Miguel Garcia* (1929) and *Why Christ Does Not Return* (1963) and the collections of journalistic and philosophical essays *The Creators of a New America* (1928), *Map of America* (1930), *Letters to Ecuador* (1943), and *Saint Gabriela Mistral* (1956). He also produced works on the history of his native literature: *A Survey of Modern Ecuadorian Poetry* (1937) and *New Ecuadorian Prose* (vols. 1–2, 1951–52).

WORKS
Atahuallpa. Quito, 1956.

REFERENCES
Mamontov, S. P. "Literatura Ekvadora." In *Ekvador: Istoriko-etnograficheskie ocherki*. Moscow, 1963.
Barrera Isaak, J. *Historia de la literatura ecuatoriana*, vol. 4. Quito, 1955.
Moreira, D. "B. Carrión." *Cuadernos americanos*, Sept.-Oct., 1969, no. 5. L. S. OSPOVAT [11–1363–2]

CARSHUNI (also Karshuni), a Syriac script. It was used by Arabic-speaking Christians in Syria in the fifth and sixth centuries, both in everyday life and for the copying of Nestorian liturgical books. Together with Nestorianism, Carshuni spread to central and southeast Asia as far as China and India. [11–1460–3]

CARSON, EDWARD HENRY. Born Feb. 9, 1854, in Dublin; died Oct. 22, 1935, in Minster, Kent. Baron (from 1921), British politician, member of the Conservative Party.

Carson was a lawyer by education and a leader of the Irish Unionists. He created armed detachments, the so-called Ulster Volunteers, in Ulster in 1912 to oppose the national liberation movement in Ireland. He was naval minister of Great Britain in 1915 and minister without portfolio in 1917–18. He strongly supported the partition of Ireland in 1921 and the preservation of British rule in Ulster. [11–1370–1]

CARTAGENA, a city and important port and industrial center in Spain on the Mediterranean coast, in the province of Murcia. Population, 147,400 (1969). The port has an annual turnover of goods of over 10 million tons. Nonferrous metals and fruit are exported, and oil is imported. Oil refining (the capacity of the plant is approximately 8 million tons) and the petrochemical industry are located in a suburb, the port city of Escombera; the production of lead, zinc, and cadmium is located in another suburb, La Unión. Other industries include shipbuilding and chemicals (in particular, sulfuric acid). There is also a steam power plant, with a capacity of 250 megawatts.

Cartagena, known in ancient times as Carthago Nova, was founded around 228 B.C. by the military leader Hasdrubal as the Carthaginian military base for the conquest of Spain. The city was under Roman rule from 209 B.C. to the fifth century A.D. It was conquered by the Vandals in 425, by Byzantium in 534, by the Visigoths in the seventh century, and by the Arabs in 711. In the course of the Reconquista, Cartagena was annexed by Castile in 1243.

Cartagena was one of the ports of the Republican fleet during the National Revolutionary War of the Spanish People of 1936–39. [11–1377–1]

CARTAGENA, a city in northern Colombia, on the coast of the Caribbean Sea, the administrative center of Bolívar Department. Population, 323,000 (1971).

Cartagena is an important Colombian port, with a goods turnover of half a million tons in 1969. The city is linked by highway with Bogotá. It is the economic and commercial distribution center of northern Colombia. The production of crocheted and knitted wear, shoes, vegetable oils, flour, and sugar are important branches of Cartagena's economy. An oil refinery and chemical enterprises are located near the city. Exports include oil and coffee.

Cartagena was founded in 1533 by the Spanish conquistador Pedro de Heredia on the site of an Indian settlement. Cartagena was the largest port and fortress during the flourishing of the Spanish colonial empire.

Many monuments from the colonial period remain intact, including the strong city walls and fortifications (1532–1796, engineers J. B. Antonelli, A. de Arevalo, and others), the cathedral (1538–1796, architects, J. C. Chacon and others), and monasteries, churches, and houses of the 16th to 18th centuries, all mainly in the baroque style. Modern structures include the baseball stadium (1947, architects G. A. Ortega and M. G. Solano), with a reinforced concrete roof projecting far over the stands.

REFERENCE
Porto del Portillo, R. *Plazas y calles de Cartagena*. Bogotá, 1945. [11–1377–2]

CARTAGO, a city in western Colombia, in Valle del Cauca Department. Population, 64,800 (1968). Cartago is a station on the Medellín-Cali railroad line and is the commercial and transport center of an agricultural region in the Cauca River valley (coffee, sugarcane, tobacco, bananas, corn, and cattle raising). The city was founded in 1540. [11–1376–1]

CARTAN, ÉLIE JOSEPH. Born Apr. 9, 1869, in Dolomieu; died May 6, 1951, in Paris. French mathematician. Member of the Paris Academy of Sciences (1931).

Cartan graduated from the École Normale Supérieure in 1891. In 1912 he became a professor at the University of Paris. His principal works were on the theory of continuous groups, the theory of differential equations, and differential geometry. In 1894 he laid the foundations of the algebraic theory of Lie groups, and in 1913 he constructed the theory of representations of semisimple Lie groups. Furthermore, he connected Lie groups with differential geometry and topology. In 1899–1902 he created the method of exterior differential forms, which enabled him to solve the problem of the compatibility of the Pfaff equations. In differential geometry of multidimensional spaces he constructed generalized spaces of affine, projective, and conformal connectedness; he also proposed the general method of moving frames, which, in conjunction with the method of exterior differential forms, is an efficient means of solving geometric problems. The Kazan Physics and Mathematics Society in 1937 awarded the N. I. Lobachevskii Prize to Cartan for his studies in geometry and group theory.

WORKS

Selecta. Paris, 1939.
In Russian translation:
Metod podvizhnogo repera, teoriia nepreryvnykh grupp i obobshchennye prostranstva. Moscow-Leningrad, 1933.
Geometriia rimanovykh prostranstv. Moscow-Leningrad, 1936.
Integral'nye invarianty. Moscow-Leningrad, 1940.
Teoriia spinorov. Moscow, 1947.
Geometriia grupp Li i simmetricheskie prostranstva. Moscow, 1949.

REFERENCE

Chern, S. S., and G. Chevalley. "Elie Cartan and His Mathematical Work." *Bulletin of the American Mathematical Society*, 1952, vol. 58, no. 2. (Contains a bibliography.)   [11–1376–5]

CARTAN, HENRI PAUL. Born July 8, 1904, in Nancy. French mathematician. Son of E. J. Cartan.

Cartan graduated from the Ecole Normal Supérieure in 1926. In 1940 he became a professor at the University of Paris. His principal works deal with the theory of analytic functions of many variables, topology, and homological algebra. Cantan's annual seminar at the Ecole Normale Supérieure, devoted to the exposition of the newest results in these branches of mathematics as well as in algebraic geometry and the theory of automorphic functions, helped to spread the latest findings in these fields and also to spread the language and style of thinking characteristic of the French school of mathematics.

WORKS

In Russian translation:
Gomologicheskaia algebra. Moscow, 1960. (With S. Eilenberg.)
Elementarnaia teoriia analiticheskikh funktsii odnogo i neskol'kikh kompleksnykh peremennykh. Moscow, 1963.

REFERENCE

Seminaire H. Cartan, 1948–1964, vols. 1–6. New York, 1969.
                                                        [11–1376–4]

CARTEL, a form of monopolistic agreement among companies, usually belonging to one economic sector, for the purpose of extracting monopolistic profits through quotas regulating the volume of production and of products marketed for all its basic participants. One of the forms of cartel agreements is the syndicate. The development of cartel agreements has also involved partial exchange of commercial information, standardization of accounting, and the organizing of patent pools for joint purchase and use of patents. In the cartel, as in any form of monopolistic practice, capitalist efficiency and technical progress are intertwined with elements of stagnation and decay. In the present-day scientific and technical revolution, however, the cartel is the most flexible form of monopoly concentration, and this fact has determined certain characteristics of its development.

Cartels arose at the end of the 19th century as a result of the concentration of production and the centralization of capital. In the first half of the 20th century they became particularly widespread in Germany. The American antitrust laws prohibited the monopolization of particular spheres of business activity, above all the formation of cartels. This legislation accelerated the process of mergers and absorption and the formation of holding companies and other developed forms of monopolistic concentration. In those sectors lacking an appropriate level of production concentration for the appearance of monoplies, cartels continued to exist in disguised form.

In the mid-1950's and early 1960's domestic cartels developed in the Western European countries. During these years laws were passed making the registration of cartels compulsory. The purpose of such legislation was to foster monoplization on the basis of more rapid concentration of production. Although state registration does impose a number of limitations on the preservation of old cartels and the formation of new ones, this form of monopolization became widespread in Western Europe. In Great Britain, where registration of cartels was made compulsory in 1956, 2,240 applications had been submitted by the end of 1958. In the Netherlands the new law went into effect in 1958, and 1,133 cartels were registered by the beginning of 1960. In 1960 there were 925 cartels in Sweden; in 1958, Denmark had 925. In West Germany and Japan, where more rigid restrictions have been instituted, the number of officially registered cartels is much smaller. Along with the domestic cartels many international ones have arisen in the 20th century, especially in the world capitalist markets for raw materials and intermediate goods.

Under present conditions, with a high level of concentration of production and capital, most of the developed capitalist countries are witnessing the rise of various forms of agreements among large companies, based on such factors as "mutual understanding," knowledge of the market, mutual observance of unstated quotas, and hidden agreements on price changes. These agreements are more effective than the old cartels in ensuring a monopoly in the market; unlike the old cartels, which regulated the marketing practices of numerous medium-size and small companies, the new arrangements guarantee a monopoly for a few large sellers. Cartels are now being supplanted by combinations known as conglomerates, which are built on a production and scientific-technical basis and incidentally perform cartel functions.   IU. B. KOCHEVRIN [11–1380–1]

CARTEL, INTERNATIONAL, an agreement (alliance) among monopolies or firms from different countries (but operating primarily in one economic sector) to divide up markets and sources of raw materials, establish monopoly prices, exploit patents, and take other steps to obtain maximum profits. International cartels also include domestic cartels and other forms of domestic monopolistic associations.

The appearance of international cartels is related to capitalism's transition to the stage of imperialism. This was pointed out by V. I. Lenin: "Under capitalism the home market is inevitably bound up with the foreign market. Capitalism long ago created a world market. As the export of capital increased and as the foreign and colonial connections and 'spheres of influence' of the big monopolist associations expanded in all ways, things 'naturally' gravitated toward an international agreement among these associations and toward the formation of international cartels" (V. I. Lenin, *Poln. sobr. soch.*, 5th ed., vol. 27, p. 364). The international cartel is a new stage in the world concentration of capital and production.

The growth in the number and economic strength of international cartels accelerated especially after World War I, during the general crisis of capitalism. In this period the sphere of influence of capital was growing increasingly narrow and the problem of markets was becoming more acute. Whereas there were about 100 international cartels before World War I, by the start of World War II there were about 1,200. International cartels helped prepare and unleash World War II.

After the war, with the appearance and development of the world socialist economic system and with the heightened competitive struggle among the Western European capitalists and the capitalists of the United States and Japan, the process of cartelization became more intense. In the 1950's there were tens of thousands of international cartels. They operate as international (most often secret) agreements among capitalists directed against the working people of their own countries and the peoples of other countries.

With the growth of state-monopoly capitalism international cartels often appear as agreements among particular capitalist countries directed primarily against the world socialistic economic system. Such organizations as the European Coal and Steel Community and the European Atomic Energy Community have become the military-economic base of NATO. Their development is linked with the intensified process of capitalist integration.

The most important international cartels are in maritime shipping, machinery and equipment, fertilizers, chemical products, ferrous and nonferrous metals, and petroleum.

Maritime shipping. The cartels in maritime shipping exist primarily in the form of conferences and pools. A conference is an agreement among shipowners on general conditions for shipping, distribution of work by region, and prices for maritime shipments. The pool is a higher form of the cartel. In the pool the participants agree on how to distribute cargoes and passengers, incomes, and so on.

The maritime shipping cartels have various names. Usually the names indicate the service region (for example, the United Kingdom–Australia Conference, the Association of West India Transatlantic Steamship Lines).

Most of the maritime shipping cartels operate on international waterways. One shipping company may be a member of several international cartels that operate in different areas.

Maritime shipping cartels appeared in the last quarter of the 19th century. The first cartel agreement in route shipping was the Calcutta Conference, which was formed in 1875 for shipping cargo between India and Great Britain. Between the two world wars, separate cartels covering different shipping regions concluded agreements for the first time. Before the world economic crisis of 1929–33 the international maritime shipping cartels controlled more than 50 percent of the passenger traffic and about 80 percent of cargo shipping.

After World War II the number of cartel agreements on route shipping increased. In 1972 there were about 370 agreements covering a large majority of the shipping routes between the ports of the capitalist countries. The power of the shipowning cartels grew substantially, and the practice of concluding agreements among separate cartels in route shipping expanded. With the development of container vessels in the late 1960's and early 1970's, consortiums appeared whose purpose was to monopolize this shipping. By monopolizing shipping on certain routes and establishing increased rates for cargo and passenger shipping, the maritime shipping cartels receive high profits. Shipping rates are rising steadily. The cartel agreements are unable to eliminate competition in capitalist maritime shipping. It exists among shipowning companies that belong to the cartels, among individual cartels, and between cartels and outsiders. The policies of the maritime shipping cartels and the high prices they set for shipping have a negative effect on the development of international trade and particularly on the trade of the developing countries. E. M. KRAMAROV

Machinery and equipment. Cartels in machinery and equipment are typically found in electrical engineering and in transportation machine building, that is, the sectors with a high level of production concentration.

The largest cartel is the electrical equipment cartel. It was formed in 1930, closed down in 1942, and was restored in 1945. By the early 1970's it included 40 companies: 17 in Great Britain, five in Switzerland, four apiece in France, Italy, and the Federal Republic of Germany (FRG), three in Sweden, and one apiece in Belgium, Austria, and Finland. There are 16 trade sections for particular types of equipment (for example, generators and electrical engines, hydroturbines, steam turbines, and transformers). The activity of the cartel is based on agreements concerning prices, compensations, and notification (all members of the cartel inform each other of requests for information, orders received, and so on); these agreements enable them to sell equipment at high monopoly prices. The British companies have the strongest position in the cartel. US companies do not participate in the cartel formally, but in fact they exercise great influence because the largest American electrical engineering monopolies are closely linked with the West German and French members of the cartel.

The radio-equipment cartel was formed in 1925 and reestablished after World War II. It includes a number of companies from the USA, the FRG, Great Britain, France, and other coun-

tries, including General Electric, Westinghouse, Siemens, AEG-Telefunken, and General Electric–English Electric. In the postwar period major changes have taken place in the radio and electronics industry; many new types of products have appeared, above all electronic computers. American monopolies have captured a dominant position in the computer market.

In 1969 a cartel agreement was concluded between two large motor vehicle monopolies, the American-owned Chrysler Corporation and the Japanese company Mitsubishi Heavy Industries. The agreement envisions cooperation in the production and assembly of motor vehicles and in technical, trade, and financial matters (in the USA, Japan, and third countries). In 1968 an agreement with similar cartel features was concluded between two other motor vehicle monopolies, Italian-owned Fiat and the French company Citroën.

International cartels in machinery often take the form of international associations, federations, bureaus, or committees. The associations unite large numbers of companies. An example is the International Association of Rolling Stock Builders, which includes more than 80 railroad-car companies in Western European countries and controls the railroad car market in Western Europe. Large West German, British, French, Belgian, and Italian companies are the leaders of the association. A similar role in the Western European market for diesel locomotives is played by the European Builders of Internal Combustion Engine and Electric Locomotives. A. A. ZMEEV

Fertilizers. Before World War II the international fertilizer market was dominated by the international potash cartel (formed in 1926), the nitrogen cartel (1928), and the phosphate cartel (1933). The fertilizer exporters were included in these cartels. After the war the American monopolies gained a much stronger position and began to force West German, French, and Italian monopolies out of the principal markets. In 1962 a new international nitrogen cartel was formed in Zürich (Switzerland). It includes nitrogen fertilizer producers from the continental countries of Western Europe only. The cartel's coordinating center is the joint-stock company Nitrex AG; it has a share capital of 1 million Swiss francs, which is divided equally among members of the cartel. As in the prewar cartel, West German monopolies have 30 percent of the shares. When the cartel was formed, its members handled 83.5 percent of nitrogen production in Western Europe and 35 percent of all production in the capitalist countries. Nitrex collects all orders for deliveries of nitrogen fertilizer and distributes them among members of the cartel.

The international potash cartel, which operated until World War II, included monopolies in France, Germany, Spain, Poland, Great Britain, the USA, and other countries; since the war its functions have been performed by the International Potash Institute in Bern (Switzerland), which represents primarily the interests of the Western European countries, and by two American organizations, the Potash Institute of North America and the Foundation for International Potash Research.

The international cartel for phosphates, which until World War II included phosphate exporters in the USA, North Africa, Germany, the Netherlands, and other countries, has been broken up into a number of regional cartels. They coordinate their activity at the world-market level. As under the conditions of the prewar agreement, 50 percent of the phosphates exported from the United States are shipped to the Western European countries, 20 percent go to Japan, and 30 percent to Canada and the Latin American countries; about 90 percent of the export of phosphates from North African countries is directed to Western Europe, with none of the exporters delivering phosphates to the USA. I. I. L'VOVSKAIA

Chemical products. Cartels in chemical products appeared at the end of the 19th century and spread especially widely between World War I and World War II.

The soda cartel appeared in 1872. Its activity before World War II was regulated by agreements concluded in 1924, 1929, and 1938. The members of the cartel were the Belgian Solvay monopoly, the American national soda export cartel Alkasso, the English chemical trust Imperial Chemical Industries (ICI), and the German chemical trust I. G. Farbenindustrie. The cartel regulated the export of soda products to the entire capitalist world. The domestic markets of the cartel members were their exclusive territories.

The cartel for aniline dyes (1927) controlled more than 90 percent of all production of organic synthetic dyes in the capitalist world. The I. G. Farbenindustrie trust played the leading part in this cartel, which also included companies in France, Switzerland, Italy, Great Britain, Poland, the USA, and Japan.

The intensified competition in markets for chemical products after World War II impelled the largest monopolies to restore prewar cartels or establish new ones. In particular, cartel agreements for soda products, dyes, and quinine have been reestablished.

In the postwar period the cartel regulation of markets for a number of chemical products has been carried on under the banner of various international associations, scientific research centers, standards bureaus, and business alliances (such as the International Group of National Pesticide Manufacturers' Associations, the European Committee of Paint, Printing Ink, and Artists' Colors Manufacturers Associations, and the International Rayon and Synthetic Fibers Committee). Patent and license agreements, especially for new types of chemicals, are increasingly being used to regulate markets and production.

I. I. L'VOVSKAIA

Nonferrous metals. The best-known nonferrous metals cartels are the aluminum and copper cartels. Before the start of World War I two international cartels functioned in the aluminum market, the first in 1901–08 and the second in 1913–14. After the war the principal aluminum monopolies concluded a new agreement on prices (1923), and in 1926 they formed the third international cartel, whose activity was disrupted by the world economic crisis of 1929–33. The fourth international aluminum cartel, the most powerful one, was formed in 1931 as a joint-stock company under the name Alliance Aluminum Company, with a 99-year period of operation. The cartel was formed by the largest aluminum companies in Great Britain, Germany, Canada, France, and Switzerland. Stock was distributed among the members in proportion to their production capacity. A share of stock gave the right to produce a certain amount of aluminum. The start of World War II disrupted the operation of the cartel, but it was not formally disbanded until after the war. By the early 1960's the world capitalist aluminum market faced a real threat of oversupply for an extended period. Under these conditions the aluminum monopolies returned again to the idea of coordinated influence on the market, which is seen in particular by their uniform price policy.

The international copper cartel, Copper Exporters Incorporated (1926), controlled 86 percent of copper production in the capitalist countries and virtually directed the London metals exchange. The cartel included leading American and Western European copper monopolies, including American Metal Climax Incorporated and the American Smelting and Refining Company. The cartel broke up during the economic crisis of 1929–33. In 1935 a new copper cartel was formed for three years; it controlled about 75 percent of the production in the capitalist countries. The cartel included the largest copper companies, which were run by American, English, and Belgian capital. During the crisis of 1957–58, the reduction in copper consumption and sharply increased production led to the accumulation of a substantial surplus and a drop in prices. For this reason the leading companies agreed on a simultaneous and uniform reduction in copper production. Later (1962–63) they achieved even greater control over copper prices than had been the case with the 1926 cartel. The growth in demand for copper led to the breakup of this agreement in 1966. V. G. ELIZAROV

Ferrous metals. The international steel cartel, which operated before World War II, was formed in 1937 on the basis of a 1933 agreement dividing up markets among Germany, France, the Saar, Belgium, and Luxembourg. Czechoslovakia and Austria joined the agreement in 1934, Hungary, Poland, and the British steel federation in 1935, and the US steel monopolies in 1937. The cartel controlled virtually the entire capitalist steel market. In 1938 about 85 percent of steel production in the capitalist countries came from countries whose companies were members of the cartel. Cartels dealing in ferrous-metal products were closely allied to the steel cartel, although they existed independ-

ently of it. After World War II attempts were made to reestablish the steel cartel. In 1953 the metallurgical monopolies of France, Belgium, and Luxembourg signed an agreement, which came to be known as the Brussels convention, to organize a steel cartel. West German and Dutch companies joined the organization in the same year, and Italy and Austria subsequently joined.

The worsening situation in the ferrous metals market led to the formation of the International Iron and Steel Institute (IISI), a cartel-type organization, in 1967. Unlike the prewar cartel it does not divide up foreign markets. The IISI was officially formed to strengthen contacts among steel-industry people of various capitalist countries and to further the exchange of information concerning the ferrous metals market. In 1970 the IISI included more than 100 metallurgical companies in 24 capitalist countries, producing about 95 percent of the steel in the capitalist world. The number of votes for each country depended on its volume of steel production. Therefore the institute's work is actually controlled by the USA.

In addition to the general cartels there are cartels for particular types of rolled products. Companies in Germany, France, Belgium, Czechoslovakia, Luxembourg, the Saar, Poland, the USA, Great Britain, and Canada were members of the pipe cartel formed in the mid-1920's; they were later joined by Japanese and Italian producers and Swedish importers. In 1935 the pipe cartel broke up. In 1950 a few of the members of the pipe cartel concluded a gentlemen's agreement. The members of this group are French, West German, Belgian, Dutch, and Italian industrialists. In addition to the pipe cartel, the rail cartel has continued to function in the postwar years. Because rail production in the capitalist countries is concentrated in a relatively small number of companies, the companies have been able to control the market. Before World War II tin producers concluded several agreements to divide up the market, with British and US monopolies dominating the market. In the postwar period a new cartel has been in operation; this is the tin "club," which includes producers in Great Britain, the FRG, France, Italy, Belgium, Luxembourg, the Netherlands, Canada, and Japan. The cartel establishes control over the market by concluding agreements that limit mutual trade and provide for division of the markets of the nonmember countries. The cartel has been able to involve American companies unofficially in its activity.

L. M. RAITSIN

Petroleum. The petroleum cartel includes seven major oil trusts in the United States, Great Britain, and the Netherlands. These are Standard Oil Company of New Jersey, Standard Oil Company of California, Mobil Oil, Gulf Oil, and Texaco in the United States, British Petroleum in Great Britain, and Royal Dutch–Shell in Great Britain and the Netherlands. In a number of situations these companies cooperate closely with the French monopoly Compagnie Française des Petroles. The cartel was formed in the late 1920's and early 1930's and spread to all the capitalist countries and all sectors of the petroleum industry, from the exploration for and extraction of petroleum to the production and marketing of petroleum products.

The US oil monopolies that belong to the cartel are the property of private American capital. Private capital in Great Britain and the Netherlands controls Royal Dutch–Shell. With British Petroleum, 49 percent of the shares issued belong to the state. In Compagnie Française des Petroles, 35 percent of the shares in terms of value and 40 percent in terms of voting rights belong to the state. Therefore, the oil cartel represents an alliance of private and state-owned monopoly capital, one that follows a particularly aggressive policy in relation to the developing countries that own the oil. This policy is executed with the direct support of those countries' governments.

The intensified competitive struggle between cartel members and outside monopolies after World War II, the trend toward state monopolies in the industrially developed countries, which are the principal users of oil and petroleum products, and the strengthening of the anti-imperialist movement in the petroleum-producing developing countries and nationalization of the property of cartel members in some of them have led to a reduction in the cartel's share in petroleum. Between 1963 and 1969 the cartel's share of petroleum extraction (outside US borders) dropped from 82.1 percent to 76.8 percent, its share of petroleum refining dropped from 65.3 percent to 56.1 percent, and its share in the marketing of petroleum products went from 62.6 percent to 54.1 percent.   I. M. REZNIKOVA [11–1381–1]

CARTEL PRICE, a uniform monopoly price fixed by members of a domestic cartel by mutual agreement; once the price is set, individual companies belonging to the cartel are not permitted to undercut it. In cases where many different products are produced by cartel members, the cartel price may take the form of a uniform scale of prices for all products that are subject to cartel regulation.

Cartel prices ordinarily are much higher than the prices that preceded the cartel agreement. Since they are intended to ensure an average profit to the least efficient company among the cartel members, the other cartel members receive a monopoly profit whose size is determined by the difference between their production costs and the production costs of the least efficient member. Cartel price regulation is possible only through combined limitation of production and sales. The cartel price is determined by a number of factors, including the possibility of eliminating outsiders or including them in the cartel; the lack of competition from substitute products that consumers could switch to; and the absence of forces that would undermine the cartel from within (for example, through secret discounts below the established price). The cartel price is one of the most obvious forms of the monopoly price; in many cases, it leads to prolonged retardation of technical progress in the cartel-controlled sector.

IU. B. KOCHEVRIN [11–1387–1]

CARTER, HERBERT DAYSON. Born Feb. 2, 1910, in St. John, New Brunswick. Canadian writer and public figure. Writes in English.

Carter became editor in 1956 of the progressive monthly *Northern Neighbors,* which sheds light on life in the Soviet Union. His book *Russia's Secret Weapon* (1942) deals with the future of Soviet science. In 1950 he published the antifascist novel *The Future for Us* (Russian translation, 1952). Carter's *Sons Without Fathers* (1955; Russian translation, 1958) was the first Canadian novel to depict a workers' collective. Author of *We Saw Socialism* (1951–52; with Charlotte Carter), a book about the USSR, Carter also describes life in the Soviet Union in *The Great Lie* (1958), written in answer to a slanderous campaign against the USSR, and *Hope of the World.* His other books include *Science and Revolution* (1966) and *The Power of the Workers* (1970).

REFERENCE
Sozonova, I. "Bol'shaia pravda." *Inostrannaia literatura,* 1958, no. 11.
L. S. OREL [11–1387–2]

CARTER, HOWARD. Born May 9, 1873, in Swaffham, Norfolk; died Mar. 2, 1939, in London. British archaeologist.

Carter did his first excavations in Egypt in 1891 in the vicinity of Tell el-Amarna and at other sites of Upper Egypt. In 1902 he began conducting excavations in the Valley of the Kings. In 1922 he discovered the tomb of Tutankhamen, a pharaoh of the 18th Dynasty (15th century B.C.), in which many art remains were found.

WORKS
Carter, H., and A. Mace. *The Tomb of Tut-ankh-Amen Discovered by the Late Earl of Carnarvon and H. Carter,* vols. 1–3. London–New York, 1923–33.
Grobnitsa Tutankhamona. Moscow, 1959. (Translated from English.)
[11–1388–1]

CARTESIANISM, a school in philosophy and natural science during the 17th and 18th centuries whose theoretical source was the ideas of the French philosopher R. Descartes (whose Latin name is Cartesius—hence the term).

Cartesianism is characterized by a consistent dualism—an extremely sharp division of the world into two independent substances—extended substance (*res extensa*) and the thinking substance (*res cogitans*). However, the problem of their mutual interaction within a thinking being remained fundamentally unresolved. Also characteristic of Cartesianism was the develop-

ment of a rationalistic mathematical (geometrical) method. The self-evidence of consciousness (Descartes' "I think, therefore I am"), as well as the theory of innate ideas, forms the starting point for Cartesian epistemology. Cartesian physics, in contrast to that of Newton, considered everything extended to be corporeal, thus rejecting the idea of empty space; it described motion with the aid of the concept "vortex." Cartesian physics subsequently found its expression in the theory of short-range action. The development of Cartesianism was marked by two opposing trends, one toward materialistic monism, as in H. de Roi (Regius) and B. Spinoza, and the other toward occasionalism, as in A. Geulincx and N. de Malebranche.

REFERENCES
Bykhovskii, B. *Filosofiia Dekarta.* Moscow-Leningrad, 1940. Chapter 10.
Istoriia filosofii, vol. 1. Moscow, 1957. Pages 382–408.
Liozzi, M. *Istoriia fiziki.* Moscow, 1970. (Translated from Italian.)
Brockdorff, C. *Descartes und die Fortbildung der kartesianischen Lehre.* Munich, 1923.
Mouy, P. *Le Développement de la physique cartésienne (1646–1712).* Paris, 1934.
Dibon, P. *Sur l'Histoire de la philosophie cartésienne.* Groningue, 1955.
L. A. LIAKHOVETSKII [11–1379–1]

CARTHAGE (Phoenician *Qart hadasht,* literally "new town"), a slave-owning city-state in North Africa, which subjugated a significant part of coastal North Africa, the southern part of Spain, and a number of islands in the Mediterranean Sea from the seventh to the fourth century B.C. Phoenician colonists from the city of Tyre founded Carthage in 825 B.C. Owing to its convenient geographic location, Carthage soon became a major trade center. The city also maintained close contacts with the countries of the eastern Mediterranean and the Aegean Sea, Italy, and Tartessus.

Carthage was an oligarchical state, with power in the hands of groups of the commercial-agricultural aristocracy, who continually fought with each other for superiority and influence. Legislative power belonged to the council of ten (which was changed to the council of 30 in the middle of the fifth century B.C.) and the council of elders (which was expanded in the middle of the fifth century B.C. from 100 to 300 members). Supreme executive power was held by two elected suffetes (magistrates). The council of 104 was created to control the magistrates and particularly the military leaders. The magistrates were elected on the principle of "nobility and wealth." The popular assembly did not play a significant role; it assumed power only in the case of disagreement between the magistrates, having the right in such a case not only to discuss the proposals introduced by the magistrates but also to introduce its own measures. Sources mention bribery and corruption as characteristic features of political life in Carthage.

Large-scale agriculture based on the use of slaves was widely developed. In handicraft production, half-slave producers were exploited along with the slaves. Besides the private workshops, there were state facilities where the labor of state slaves was exploited. The agricultural population of the territories subject to Carthage were obligated to pay a tax of one-tenth of the grain harvest. The exploitation of the subject peoples provoked frequent uprisings. The Phoenician colonies (Utica, Hippo, Leptis Magna, Leptis Minor) that were part of Carthage's empire had a social and political structure resembling that of Carthage and, apparently, enjoyed internal autonomy. They were obligated to pay a duty tax on their trade.

In 534 B.C., Carthage, in alliance with the Etruscans, defeated the Phocaean Greeks at the battle of Alalia. Later, Carthage destroyed Tartessus. As a result of these victories, Carthage consolidated its supremacy in the western Mediterranean and its monopolistic position in the area's trade. However, after suffering a defeat at the hands of the Greeks in the battle of Himera (c. 480 B.C.), Carthage was forced to halt its offensive against the Greeks for a long time. In the middle of the fifth century B.C., Carthage subjugated the Libyan agricultural population of North Africa. By this time, the empire that Carthage had created included North Africa, western Sicily, southern Spain, and Sardinia.

At the end of the fifth century B.C., Carthage renewed the struggle for Sicily, which it conducted with varying success against Syracuse for about 100 years. By the third century B.C. almost all of Sicily except Syracuse was under its power. Sicily was the main objective of the struggle between Carthage and Rome during the First Punic War (264–241 B.C.). After suffering defeat both in Sicily itself and on the sea, Carthage was forced to relinquish Sicily to Rome as well as pay Rome a considerable indemnity. Riots among the mercenaries, from whom the Carthaginian government had withheld payment after the conclusion of the war, triggered a major uprising of the Libyan peasantry (241–238 B.C.), in which runaway slaves also took part. Carthage suppressed this revolt with great difficulty.

In the 230's and 220's B.C., power in Carthage passed into the hands of a democratic group led by Hamilcar Barca, who advocated renewing the war with Rome. Between 237 and 219 B.C., the Carthaginians not only reestablished their economic and military power but also significantly extended their domains in Spain (up to the Iberus River) under the command of Hamilcar Barca (until 229 B.C.), Hasdrubal (until 221 B.C.), and Hannibal. The siege and capture of the city of Saguntum, a Roman ally, led to the Second Punic War (218–201 B.C.). In the war, the Romans and the Carthaginians waged a struggle for supremacy in the western Mediterranean and for dominance in trade and navigation. By invading Italy and inflicting a series of crushing defeats on the Romans (the most important of which was the battle at Cannae in 216 B.C.), Hannibal created an immediate threat to Rome's existence. However, he was unable to retain the initiative. The Romans massed their forces for a retaliatory strike and carried the war to Africa. After the defeat at Zama (202 B.C.), the Carthaginians were compelled to conclude a peace treaty with Rome, which deprived Carthage of its possessions in Spain and also prohibited Carthage from waging war without Rome's consent.

In 149 B.C. the Romans, fearful of the growth of Carthage's economic power, began the Third Punic War (149–146 B.C.), as a result of which Carthage, after a three-year siege, was completely destroyed and its inhabitants sold into slavery. Part of the Carthaginian territory was transferred to the Numidians, and the rest became the Roman province of Africa. Excavations have been conducted in North Africa since the 1850's.

The art of Carthage, Phoenician in origin, was influenced by the art of ancient Egypt and Greece. Majestic buildings were constructed in the city (multistoried houses, temples, mausoleums), mostly of stone and sun-dried brick. One of the few surviving buildings is the mausoleum of Ateban in Dougga (Thugga—200 B.C.; architect, Abarish), a towerlike structure topped by a pyramid. The art of Punic Carthage can be judged from items found in burials near the city; jewelry, clay lamps, vessels, statuettes, grimacing masks, and sarcophagi with relief depictions of human figures.

REFERENCES
Mashkin, N. A. "Karfagenskaia derzhava do Punicheskikh voin." *Vestnik drevnei istorii,* 1948. no. 4.
Mashkin, N. A. "Poslednii vek punicheskogo Karfagena." *Vestnik drevnei istorii,* 1949 [no.] 2.
Shifman, I. Sh. *Vozniknovenie Karfagenskoi derzhavy.* Moscow-Leningrad, 1963.
Meltzer, O. *Geschichte der Karthager,* vols. 1–3. Berlin, 1879–1913.
Gsell, St. *Histoire ancienne de l'Afrique du Nord,* vols. 1–4, 3rd and 4th eds. Paris, 1920–29.
Picard, G. *Le Monde de Carthage.* Paris [1956].
Picard, G., and C. Picard. *The Life and Death of Carthage.* . . . London, 1968.
Warmington, B. H. *Carthage.* London [1960].
Cagnat, R. *Carthage, Timgad, Tébessa et les villes antiques de l'Afrique du Nord,* 3rd ed. Paris, 1927.
Cintas, P. *Céramique punique.* Paris, 1950.

I. SH. SHIFMAN [11–1455–1]

CARTIER-BRESSON, HENRI. Born Aug. 22, 1908, in Chanteloup, Ile-de-France. Major French photographer.

Cartier-Bresson studied painting under A. Lhote (1929) and turned to photography in 1931. He is one of the founders of Magnum Photos (1947), the international agency of photojournalists. Using a Leica with a standard 50-mm lens, Cartier-Bresson avoids complex and cumbersome technical equipment. He depicts the familiar events of the world around him and the manners and customs of people of different lands. The seeming simplicity of his images is combined with humanistic pathos and social criticism.

Cartier-Bresson's antifascist position first appeared in photographs taken in the late 1930's in Spain; he was also a member of the French Resistance. Many of his photographs have an antiwar cast. Cartier-Bresson traveled throughout Europe, America, and Asia in the late 1940's and 1950's. His travels in the USSR resulted in the collection *The People of Moscow* (1957). *Vive La France!* was published in 1971.

REFERENCE
Photographies de Henri Cartier-Bresson. Paris, 1963.   [11–1451–4]

CARTOGRAM, a map that shows the average intensity of a phenomenon for individual regions (units) of the territorial division shown on the map.

For example, a cartogram may characterize the average population density or the extent of plowed land (average hectares of arable land per hundred hectares of total land area) according to country, region, or district. To make the map easier to read, each territorial unit is colored or hachured according to the computed intensity of the phenomenon in it, so that the density of the coloring or hachures reflects this intensity.

Cartograms are especially widely used for graphic reproduction of statistical data on population and agriculture. A shortcoming of cartograms is that they do not show differences in the intensity of the phenomena within each territorial unit; this problem is lessened by a further territorial division.

[11–1391–2]

CARTOGRAM, AGROCHEMICAL, a map that shows the extent to which soil is supplied with nutrient elements that can be assimilated by plants—phosphorus, potassium, nitrogen, magnesium, and trace elements—or the need for lime and gypsum. There are large-scale, medium-scale, and small-scale agrochemical cartograms. In the USSR, large-scale cartograms are used to determine the total fertilizer requirements in the economy and to establish the correct amounts and types of fertilizers for individual fields. They are also used in developing plans for the liming and gypsuming of soils in kolkhozes and sovkhozes. Cartograms showing the supply of available phosphorus and potassium are the most common; those showing the supply of nitrogen, magnesium, and the trace elements are less common.

Medium-scale agrochemical cartograms have been prepared for certain oblasts and agricultural zones of the USSR and small-scale ones for some republics and economic regions. The V. V. Dokuchaev Soil Institute has compiled an agrochemical cartogram for the entire USSR. The cartogram identifies the soil-agrochemical zones and regions with similar agronomic, soil, and climatic conditions, which determine the effectiveness of fertilizers and the lime and gypsum requirements of the soil. Small- and medium-scale agrochemical cartograms are needed for preparing scientifically based plans for the production of mineral fertilizers and their distribution among the various regions of the USSR.

Abroad, agrochemical cartograms are called agrochemical maps. They are classified and compiled by methods similar to those used in the USSR.

REFERENCES
Agrokhimicheskoe kartografirovanie pochv. Moscow, 1962.
Rukovodstvo po sostavleniiu pochvennykh i agrokhimicheskikh kart. Moscow, 1964.
Obshchesoiuznaia instruktsiia po krupno-masshtabnym pochvennym i agrokhimicheskim issledovaniiam territorii kolkhozov i sovkhozov. Moscow, 1964.
Posobie po provedeniiu analizov pochv i sostavleniiu agrokhimicheskikh kartogramm. Moscow, 1965.
Sokolov, A. V., N. N. Rozov, and E. N. Rudneva. "Pochvennoagrokhimicheskaia karta SSSR." *Agrokhimiia,* 1966, no. 1.

A. V. SOKOLOV [11–1391–3]

CARTOGRAPHIC CONVERTER, a device for converting cartographic projections. In a mechanical cartographic converter an elastic film on which a projection of the initial material has been inscribed is stretched until the cartographic grids of the material and the original coincide. The converted image is then photographed or copied by hand.

Opticomechanical cartographic converters are used for complex transformations of cartographic projections (an example is the photo converter with a slit device; see Figure 1). The image of the initial material placed on the object surface is projected by a lens onto the picture surface. The image on the picture surface is shifted in direction XX by moving the lens. The initial projection is converted by fixing the scan of the image on photographic paper through the slit. The photographic paper is also shifted in direction YY along the flexible curve.

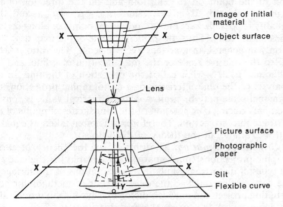

Figure 1. Photographic converter with slit device

Electronic cartographic converters are being developed. In such devices the image produced on the screen of a cathode-ray tube changes when there is a change in the voltage on the deflector plates. A. G. IVANOV [11–1413–1]

CARTOGRAPHIC GRID, a graphic representation of the geographic meridians and parallels on a plane (map). In the compilation of geographic maps a cartographic grid is used to construct the cartographic representation; when the map is used, the cartographic grid makes possible determination of the coordinates of any point (geographic or rectangular, depending on the type of cartographic grid) and the azimuths of lines and estimates of the magnitude of the distortions caused by the cartographic projection on various parts of the map. [11–1392–3]

CARTOGRAPHIC INSTRUMENTS, instruments used for the compilation and preparation of maps for publication. Coordinate plotters, beam compasses with base-line rulers, curves, Drobyshev rules (for drawing arcs of circumference using holes with tapered edges), and normal (Geneva) rules (for measuring lines with a precision of as much as 0.2 mm by means of two moving magnifying glasses) are used to construct the mathematical base (the cartographic grid and reference points). To transfer the cartographic image from the source to the map being drawn instruments are used that make possible reduction or magnification of the image without changing the cartographic projection of the source (pantographs, reproduction devices, and projectors), as well as transformation of the cartographic projection of the original material (cartographic converters). Drawing and engraving instruments are used in making manuscript and smooth-delineation originals of maps.
A. G. IVANOV [11–1394–1]

CARTOGRAPHIC METHOD OF RESEARCH, the use of geographic maps for the analysis, recognition, and prediction of phenomena. The cartographic method is used to study the rules of spatial arrangement of phenomena and their interrelationships, dependence, and development. The many procedures for analyzing and processing maps that are typical of the cartographic method can be grouped in the following basic methods.

(1) Visual analysis, which involves direct visual study from maps of the spatial arrangement, combinations, relationships, and changes in phenomena.

(2) Graphic methods of analysis, which involve the construction of profiles and cross sections (which give a graphic representation of the vertical structure of the phenomena), relief diagrams (which combine perspective representation of the terrain with vertical cross sections of it), and various kinds of charts and diagrams (for example, hypsographic curves) on the basis of maps.

(3) Cartometric work, which involves using maps to determine the coordinates, distances, lengths, elevations, areas, volumes, angles, and other quantitative characteristics of objects shown on the map (with an estimation of the accuracy of the results obtained).

(4) Mathematical and statistical analysis, in which maps are used to study any homogeneous phenomena (air temperatures, density of rural settlement, and crop yield), and their location and changes with time as determined by numerous factors with unknown functional relationships, and to learn the type and closeness of relationships among various phenomena (by computing correlation relationships, such as correlation coefficients and ratios).

(5) Mathematical simulations, the purpose of which is the construction of spatial mathematical models—that is, a mathematical description of the phenomena or processes on the basis of raw data taken from the map—and subsequent study of the models to interpret and explain the phenomena; in particular, a methodology has been developed for composing approximating equations for surfaces, both real (for example, the terrain of the earth's surface) and abstract (the annual precipitation).

(6) Transforming maps to obtain derivative maps specially designed and convenient for specific research (for example, using a hypsometric map to make a derivative map of the steepness of slopes to study and forecast erosion processes).

The cartographic method of research usually uses various combinations of the procedures mentioned above. Many of them now involve the use of electronic computers for automatic processing of the data taken from the map "manually." At the same time, methods are coming into use for automatic generation of the necessary data from the map and for automatic interlinked processing of the data (for example, for automatic determination of areas according to maps).

REFERENCES
Berliant, A. M. "Kartograficheskii metod issledovaniia." In *Itogi nauki: Kartografiia, 1967–69,* fasc. 4. Moscow, 1970.
Salishchev, K. A. *Kartografiia,* 2nd ed. Moscow, 1971.
K. A. SALISHCHEV [11–1412–1]

CARTOGRAPHIC METHODS OF PRESENTATION, graphic methods used on maps to show the spatial arrangement of phenomena and their combinations, relationships, and development. A special system of characters—the cartographic symbols, which are summarized and systematized in a relatively small number of cartographic methods of presentation—is used in cartography for this purpose. The primary methods include those of signs, line symbols, isolines, and the qualitative background; angle diagrams; the point method; area patterns; signs of motion; and collation and choropleth maps.

The sign method (nonscale signs) is used for objects that are not expressed in the scale of the map and are usually used to represent phenomena that are localized at points. The signs indicate the location and type of the objects and may also describe their size, importance, or change over time (for example, symbols for populated points that indicate the type of settlement, population, and administrative significance). The shape, size, and color of the signs are used to represent the characteristics of the objects being mapped. The symbol may have a geometric shape, it may be a letter of the alphabet, or it may resemble in outline the object being represented. Geometrically shaped signs whose area is proportional to the numerical index of the objects being shown are often used—for example, proportional to the number of workers when mapping industrial enterprises or centers.

Line symbols are used to show political and administrative borders and power lines and for linear objects whose width is not expressed in the scale of the map (for example, roads and rivers). The qualitative and quantitative characteristics of linear objects are shown by the type of lines (for example, various dotted lines) and the color and the width of the symbols.

The isoline method is used to convey the quantitative characteristics of phenomena that are continuous and change gradually in space (for example, terrain and climatic phenomena).

The qualitative background method shows the breakdown of a territory (its regionalization) according to some particular natural, economic, or political and administrative features. It is used for qualitative description of phenomena that are continuous over the earth's surface (for example, soil cover) or have a large-scale scattered distribution (for example, population). The first step is the development of a classification of the phenomenon being mapped; the territory then is divided according to the classification into qualitatively homogeneous parts (districts, regions, and so on). Finally, areas belonging to the same class are given the color assigned to the particular type or hachured accordingly.

Angle diagrams (that is, diagrams related to definite points) are used to describe seasonal and other periodic phenomena (the annual course of temperatures and precipitation; changes in snow cover), the frequency and velocity of winds from various directions (in the form of wind roses), and the frequency and velocity of ocean currents.

The point method is used to map large-scale scattered phenomena (rural population, croplands, and livestock farming). For this purpose a definite number of objects (units) is symbolized by a point (more precisely, a small circle) located at the place on the map where the objects actually exist. As a result a certain number of points of equal magnitude and identical significance are written on the map; their grouping (density) gives a graphic picture of the location of the phenomenon, and their number makes possible determination of its dimensions or the number of objects.

Area patterns, or areas of distribution of some particular phenomena (various species of plants and animals; various types of farmland) are shown on maps by contouring a section with a solid or dotted line of definite design or by coloring or hachure. The diversity of methods for representing ranges makes possible the combination of a number of ranges on the same map, even if they overlap.

Signs of motion are used for natural and social phenomena (ocean currents, migration of birds or population, shipping, and directions of military strikes).

Graphic methods are widespread, above all vectors (arrows), which may be used to characterize the speed, stability, power, and other features of the phenomena by differences in their shape, size, and color. A second common method is bands (strips) for passenger and cargo flows, which are laid out along the routes of movement; their width usually indicates the size of the flow.

Collation and choropleth maps are used for a graphic spatial representation of statistical data (for example, population data) that are being processed or published in summary form, as applied to administrative or other territorial divisions rather than individual points or objects. Collation maps show the distribution of a phenomenon by means of diagrams that are located within units of the territorial grid and express the total magnitude of the phenomenon (for example, the amount of arable land) within the borders of each territorial unit. The choropleth map is a method of showing the average intensity of a particular phenomenon (average population density, percentage of land under cultivation, and so on) within definite territorial units, most often administrative units. In this case each territorial unit is colored or hachured so that the intensity of the color or hachure indicates the intensity of the phenomenon.

K. A. SALISHCHEV [11–1410–1]

CARTOGRAPHIC PROJECTIONS, representations of the entire surface of the earth's ellipsoid or some part of it on a plane; produced mainly for the construction of a map.

Scale. Cartographic projections are made on a definite scale. By hypothetically reducing the earth's ellipsoid by a factor of M—for example, 10,000,000—we obtain a geometric model of it, a globe, the representation of which on a plane in actual size gives a map of the surfaces of the ellipsoid. The quantity $1:M$ (in this case, 1:10,000,000) defines the principal, or general, scale of the map. Because the surfaces of the ellipsoid and sphere cannot be shown on a plane without breaks and folds (they do not belong to the class of developable surfaces), any cartographic projection inherently contains distortions of the length of lines and of angles typical of any map. The basic characteristic of any cartographic projection at any point on it is the particular scale μ. This is a quantity that is the inverse of the ratio of an infinitely small segment ds on the earth's ellipsoid to its representation $d\sigma$ on the plane: $1/\mu = ds/d\sigma$, where μ depends on the position of the point on the ellipsoid and on the direction of the segment selected. It is clear that $\mu_{min} \leq \mu \leq \mu_{max}$ and that equality is possible here only at individual points or along certain lines on the map. Thus, the principal scale of the map describes it only in general, in a certain average sense. The ratio μ/M is called the relative scale or the magnification of a line, and the difference $\mu/M - 1$ is called the distortion of the line. In the analysis of the characteristics of a cartographic projection, the principal scale may be neglected; its numerical value is considered only during computation of the coordinates of points of the cartographic projection. Therefore, M is often taken as equal to 1 (for example, in the theory of distortions).

General information. The purpose of the theory of cartographic projections (mathematical cartography) is the study of all types of distortions of plane representations of the surface of the earth's ellipsoid and the development of methods for constructing projections in which distortions have a minimum value (in some sense) or a predetermined distribution.

Proceeding from the needs of cartography, the theory of cartographic projections deals with representations of the surface of the earth's ellipsoid on a plane. Since the earth's ellipsoid is slightly compressed and its surface deviates slightly from that of a sphere, and also because cartographic projections are needed to draw maps in medium and small scales ($M > 1,000,000$), consideration is often limited to representations on a plane of a sphere with radius R whose deviations from the ellipsoid can be neglected or somehow taken into account. Therefore, we then have in mind representations on the plane xOy of a sphere relative to the geographic coordinates ϕ (latitude) and λ (longitude).

The equations of any cartographic projection have the form

$$(1) \qquad x = f_1(\phi,\lambda) \qquad y = f_2(\phi,\lambda)$$

where f_1 and f_2 are functions that satisfy certain general conditions. The representations of the meridians $\lambda =$ const. and the parallels $\phi -$ const. in the given cartographic projection form the cartographic grid. The projection may also be defined by two equations that use some coordinates other than the rectangular x and y coordinates of the plane. Some projections—for example, perspective projections (in particular, orthographic projections; see Figure 2) and perspective-cylindrical projections (Figure 7)—may be defined by geometric constructions. A cartographic projection is also defined by the rule of construction of a corresponding cartographic grid or by such characteristic properties as can be used to obtain equations of the form of (1) that fully define the projection.

Brief historical survey. The development of the theory of cartographic projections, like that of cartography as a whole, is closely associated with the development of geodesy, geography, astronomy, and mathematics.

The scientific foundations of cartography were laid in ancient Greece (sixth to first centuries B.C.). The gnomonic projection used by Thales in making star maps is considered to be the oldest cartographic projection. The development and use of cartographic projections in the compilation of geographic maps (by Hipparchus, Ptolemy, and others) began after the earth was found to be spheroidal (third century B.C.).

The significant upsurge of cartography in the 16th century brought about by the great geographical discoveries led to the creation of a number of new projections; one of them, proposed by

G. Mercator, is still used today. In the 17th and 18th centuries, when the widespread organization of topographic surveying began to provide reliable material for the compilation of maps of significant territories, cartographic projections were developed as the basis for topographic maps (the French cartographer R. Bonne; G. D. Cassini) and the most important groups of cartographic projections were studied (J. Lambert, L. Euler, and J. Lagrange).

The development of military cartography and a further increase in the scope of topographic work in the 19th century required a secure mathematical foundation for large-scale maps and the institution of a system of retangular coordinates based on a more suitable cartographic projection. This requirement led to the development by K. Gauss of the fundamental geodetic projection. Finally, in the mid-19th century A. Tissot (France) produced a general theory of distortions of cartographic projections.

The development of the theory of cartographic projections in Russia was closely tied to practical needs and produced many original results (L. Euler, F. I. Shubert, P. L. Chebyshev, and D. A. Grave). New groups of cartographic projections and specific variations of them (to the stage of practical use) were developed and important questions of the general theory of projections and their classification were treated in the works of Soviet cartographers V. V. Kavraiskii and N. A. Urmaev.

Theory of distortions. Distortions in the infinitely small area around any point of a cartographic projection follow certain general rules. At any point on a map in a projection that is not conformal, there are two perpendicular directions that correspond to two perpendicular directions on the surface being represented; these are the cardinal directions of representation. The scales in these directions (cardinal scales) have extreme values: $\mu_{max} = a$ and $\mu_{min} = b$. If the meridians and parallels on a map in any projection intersect at right angles, their directions are the cardinal directions for that projection. The distortion of length at the given point of the projection graphically represents the ellipse of distortion, which resembles (and is located similarly to) the representation of an infinitely small circle inscribed around the corresponding point of the surface being depicted. The radii of the ellipse are numerically equal to the particular scales at the given point in the corresponding directions; the semiaxes of the ellipse are equal to the extreme scales, and their directions are cardinal.

The relationship among elements of the ellipse of distortion, the distortions of the cartographic projection, and the partial derivatives of functions (1) is established by the basic formulas of the theory of distortions.

Classification according to position of the pole of the spherical coordinates. The poles of a sphere are special points of geographic coordination, although the sphere does not have any special characteristics at these points. Thus, when mapping areas that have geographic poles, the use of coordinates in which the poles are ordinary points of coordination, rather than geographic coordinates, is sometimes desirable. Therefore, spherical coordinates whose coordinate lines—the verticals (on which the conventional longitude $a = $ const.) and altitude circles (almucantars), where the polar distances $z = $ const.—are similar to the geographic meridians and parallels, except that their pole Z_0 does not coincide with the geographic pole P_0 (Figure 1), are used on a sphere. The conversion from the geographic coordinates ϕ and λ of any point on a sphere to its spherical coordinates z and a for a given position of the pole Z_0 (ϕ_0, λ_0) is carried out according to the formulas of spherical trigonometry. Any cartographic projection given by equations (1) is called normal $(\phi_0 = \pi/2)$. If the same projection of a sphere is computed according to the same formulas (1) but with z and a in place of ϕ and λ, the projection is called transverse for $\phi_0 = 0$ and oblique for $0 < \phi_0 < \pi/2$. The use of oblique and transverse projections reduces distortion. Normal (A), transverse (B), and oblique (C) orthographic projections of a sphere (surface of a globe) are shown in Figure 2.

Classification according to nature of distortions. In conformal cartographic projections the scale depends only on the position of a point, not on its direction. The ellipses of distortion degenerate into circles. Examples are the Mercator and stereographic projections.

In equal-area (equivalent) projections, areas are preserved; more precisely, the areas of figures on maps made in such projections are proportional to the areas of the corresponding actual figures, and the proportionality constant is inverse to the square of the principal scale of the map. The ellipses of distortion always have the same area but differ in shape and orientation.

Conventional cartographic projections are neither conformal nor equal-area. The most important projections of this type are the equidistant projections, in which one of the principal scales is equal to 1, and the orthodromic projections, in which the great circles (orthodromes) are represented by straight lines.

When a sphere is represented on a plane the features of conformality, equal area, equal distance, and orthodromes are incompatible. The following are used to show distortions at different places in the area represented: (1) ellipses of distortion constructed in various places on the grid or sketch of the map (Figure 3); (2) isokols, or lines of equal distortion value (in Figure 8,C, see the isokols of greatest distortion of angles ω and the isokols of the scale of areas p); (3) the representation of certain spherical lines, usually orthodromes (O) and loxodromes (L), at certain places on the map (see Figures 3,A and 3,B).

Classification of normal projections according to type of representation of meridians and parallels. Classification according to type of representation of meridians and parallels results from the historical development of the theory of cartographic projections and covers most known projections. It has preserved the names related to the geometric method of producing projections, but the groups considered are now defined analytically.

The cylindrical projections (Figure 3) are projections in which the meridians are shown by equidistant parallel straight lines and the parallels are straight lines perpendicular to the meridians. Such projections are advantageous for showing territories that extend along the equator or a parallel. The Mercator projection, a conformal cylindrical projection, is used in navigation. The Gauss-Krueger projection, a conformal transverse cylindrical projection, is used in the compilation of topographic maps and in triangulation.

The conic projections (Figure 4) are projections in which the parallels are shown by concentric circles and the meridians by straight lines orthogonal to them. In these projections distortion does not depend on longitude. They are especially suitable for territories that extend along parallels. Maps of the entire territory of the USSR are often made in conic orthomorphic and conic equidistant projections. They are also used as geodetic projections.

Azimuthal projections (Figure 5) are projections in which the parallels are concentric circles and the meridians are their radii, with the angles between the meridians equal to the corresponding differences in longitude. Perspective projections are a particular case of azimuthal projections.

Pseudoconic projections (Figure 6) are projections in which the parallels are represented by concentric circles, the central meridian is a straight line, and the other meridians are curves. The Bonne equal-area pseudoconic projection is common; it was used for a 3-*verst* (1:126,000) map of the European part of Russia in 1847 (1 *verst* = 1.07 km).

Pseudocylindrical projections (Figure 8) are projections in which the parallels are represented by parallel straight lines and the central meridian is a straight line perpendicular to these straight lines and serves as the axis of symmetry of the projections, whereas the other meridians are curves.

In polyconic projections (Figure 9), the parallels are represented by circles whose centers are located on one straight line that represents the central meridian. Additional conditions are imposed in the construction of any given polyconic projections. One of the polyconic projections has been recommended for the international (1:1,000,000) map.

There are many projections that are not classified with the types mentioned above. Cylindrical, conic, and azimuthal projections, called simple projections, are often classified as circular projections in the broad sense, separating the circular projections in the narrow sense (projections in which all meridians and

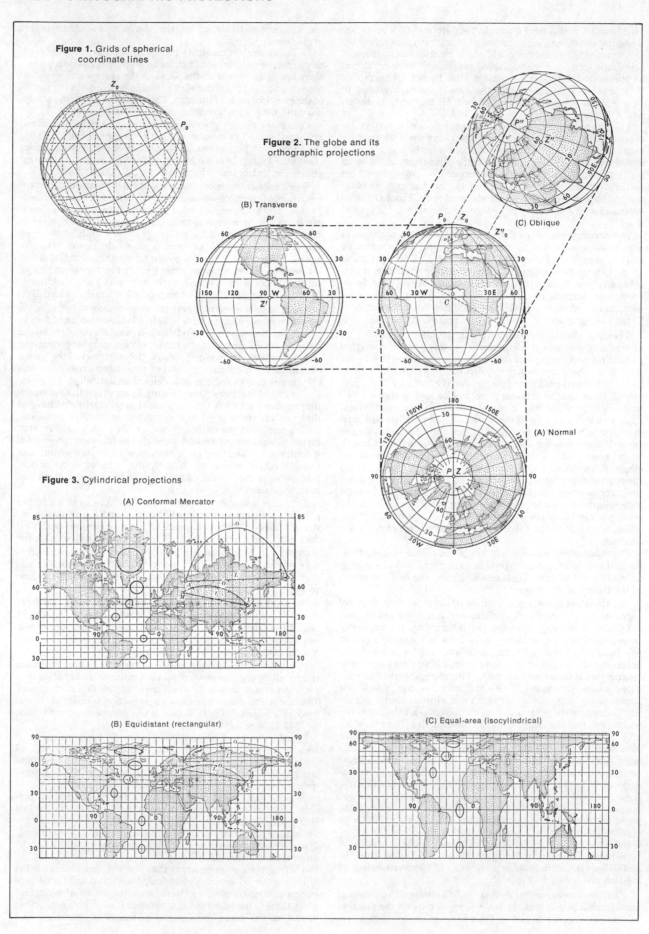

Figure 1. Grids of spherical coordinate lines

Figure 2. The globe and its orthographic projections

(B) Transverse

(C) Oblique

(A) Normal

Figure 3. Cylindrical projections

(A) Conformal Mercator

(B) Equidistant (rectangular)

(C) Equal-area (isocylindrical)

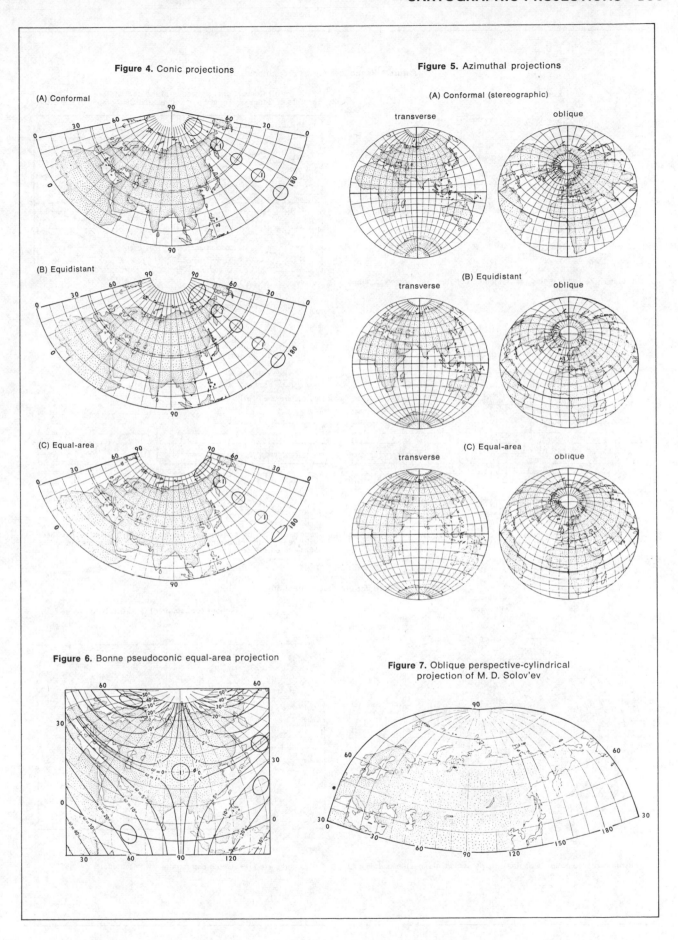

Figure 4. Conic projections

(A) Conformal

(B) Equidistant

(C) Equal-area

Figure 5. Azimuthal projections

(A) Conformal (stereographic)

transverse   oblique

(B) Equidistant

transverse   oblique

(C) Equal-area

transverse   oblique

Figure 6. Bonne pseudoconic equal-area projection

Figure 7. Oblique perspective-cylindrical projection of M. D. Solov'ev

Figure 8. Pseudocylindrical projections

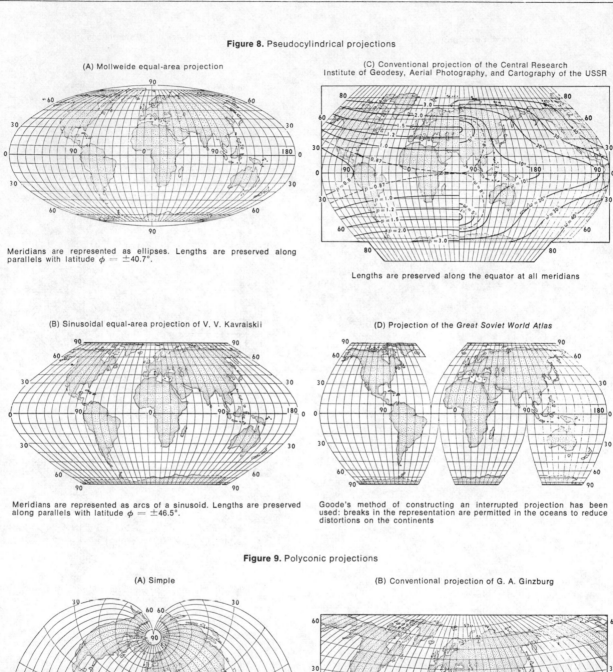

(A) Mollweide equal-area projection

Meridians are represented as ellipses. Lengths are preserved along parallels with latitude $\phi = \pm 40.7°$.

(C) Conventional projection of the Central Research Institute of Geodesy, Aerial Photography, and Cartography of the USSR

Lengths are preserved along the equator at all meridians

(B) Sinusoidal equal-area projection of V. V. Kavraiskii

Meridians are represented as arcs of a sinusoid. Lengths are preserved along parallels with latitude $\phi = \pm 46.5°$.

(D) Projection of the *Great Soviet World Atlas*

Goode's method of constructing an interrupted projection has been used: breaks in the representation are permitted in the oceans to reduce distortions on the continents

Figure 9. Polyconic projections

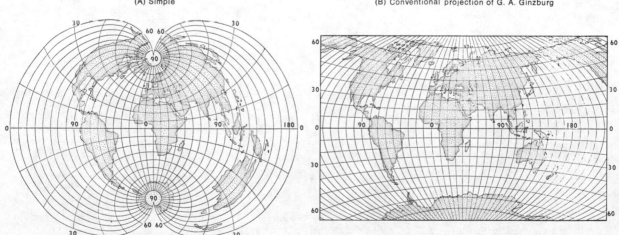

(A) Simple

Conventional projection. Lengths are preserved along all parallels and on the central meridian.

(B) Conventional projection of G. A. Ginzburg

Lengths are preserved along parallels with latitude $\phi = \pm 45°$

parallels are represented by circles—for example, the conformal Lagrange projections and the Grinten projection).

Use and selection. The use and selection of cartographic projections depend primarily on the purpose and scale of the map, which determine the nature of permissible distortions in the cartographic projection chosen. Large-scale and medium-scale maps intended for measurement are usually made in conformal projections; small-scale maps to be used for general surveys and to determine the ratio of the areas of certain territories are made in equal-area projections. In this case there may be some violation of the determining conditions of the projections ($\omega \equiv 0$ or $p \equiv 1$) without causing tangible error; in other words, the selection of conventional projections is permissible. Projections with equal intervals along the meridians are most often used in this case, as well as when the purpose of the map does not entail any preservation of angles or areas. When selecting a cartographic projection, one begins with the simplest types and then proceeds to the more complex projections, possibly even modifying them. If none of the known cartographic projections meets the requirements made of the map being drawn in relation to its purpose, then a new, most appropriate cartographic projection is sought. Distortion is minimized. The problem of constructing optimal projections, in which all types of distortions have been reduced to a minimum, has not yet been fully resolved.

Cartographic projections are also used in navigation, astronomy, and crystallography. Projections for mapping the moon, the planets, and other celestial bodies are being sought.

Conversion. When considering two cartographic projections given by the corresponding systems of equations $x = f_1(\phi,\lambda)$, $y = f_2(\phi,\lambda)$ and $X = g_1(\phi,\lambda)$, $Y = g_2(\phi,\lambda)$, one may establish the conversion from one projection to the other by removing ϕ and λ from these equations:

$$X = F_1(x, y) \qquad Y = F_2(x, y)$$

When the type of functions F_1 and F_2 is concretely determined, these formulas give a general method for obtaining the derivatives of the projections and make up the theoretical basis for all possible methods and technical procedures of map-making. For example, affine and linear fractional transformations are performed by means of cartographic converters. However, more general conversions require the use of new technology, particularly electronic equipment. The problem of building improved converters of cartographic projections is a pressing problem of modern cartography.

REFERENCES
Vitkovskii, V. *Kartografiia (Teoriia kartograficheskikh proektsii).* St. Petersburg, 1907.
Kavraiskii, V. V. *Matematicheskaia kartografiia.* Moscow-Leningrad, 1934.
Kavraiskii, V. V. *Izbr. trudy,* vol. 2, issues 1–3. [Moscow] 1958–60.
Urmaev, N. A. *Matematicheskaia kartografiia.* Moscow, 1941.
Urmaev, N. A. *Metody izyskaniia novykh kartograficheskikh proektsii.* Moscow, 1947.
Graur, A. V. *Matematicheskaia kartografiia,* 2nd ed. Leningrad, 1956.
Ginzburg, G. A. *Kartograficheskie proektsii.* Moscow, 1951.
Meshcheriakov, G. A. *Teoreticheskie osnovy matematicheskoi kartografii.* Moscow, 1968.   G. A. MESHCHERIAKOV [11–1394–2]

CARTOGRAPHIC REFERENCE SERVICE, the aggregate of work to provide cartographers and users of maps with the information necessary for the compilation, updating, and use of maps. It involves the collection, systematization, analysis, and processing of the information and its delivery to users. The sources of information are maps, atlases, and various printed, manuscript, digital, and graphic documents that can be used for the compilation of new maps and the verification, evaluation, and updating of existing maps.

All sources of information are divided into two groups according to content and use. Some sources are used for finding maps, describing them, and evaluating their quality (maps and the textual material on them; catalogs and prospectuses of maps; reports on cartographic, topographic, and geodetic work; descriptions of maps; and articles on and reviews of cartographic works). Materials from this group are used to find new cartographic sources and to prepare catalogs, descriptions of maps, charts of the coverage of different territories by particular maps, and charts of cartographic materials recommended for the compilation of maps.

Other sources are designed for the collection of specific data on the state of and changes in the objects being mapped (new, more accurate, and more detailed maps, catalogs of the coordinates of reference points, census data, the latest geographic and special descriptions, and reference works on administrative and territorial divisions).

The second group of sources is used for observation of changes that take place in the objects shown on maps; such changes are regularly entered in current reference documents, the most important of which is the current reference map. Work with this group of sources produces various documents required for the drafting, compilation, and updating of maps and for working with them (lists of collected sources, bulletins on cartographic and geographic changes, lists of the coordinates of reference points, reference dictionaries and lists of geographic names, and maps of the road network and maps of administrative borders). Depending on requirements, the documents prepared by the cartographic reference service are published or duplicated in a limited number of copies and distributed to users.

Centralized cartographic reference work is done by special cartographic institutions. In the Soviet Union cartographic reference service is organized by the Central Administration of Geodesy and Cartography (GUGK) and by the Military Topography and Hydrographic Directorate of the Ministry of Defense of the USSR. The principal organization that supplies information on cartographic work being done in the USSR is the Central Cartographic and Geodetic Collection of the GUGK. The cartographic divisions of the V. I. Lenin State Library in Moscow, the M. E. Saltykov-Shchedrin State Public Library in Leningrad, and the libraries of the Academy of Sciences of the USSR provide information on cartographic publications stored in their collections. Information on sectorial cartographic work (geological, soil, and other types) is concentrated at institutes of the Academy of Sciences of the USSR and at the corresponding departments. Cartographic enterprises (factories) organize their own internal reference services, which supply the production subdivisions of the particular enterprises. In foreign countries cartographic reference service is conducted by state topographical services and by private map publishers. The UN Department of Economic and Social Affairs regularly publishes collections of materials on the current state of world cartography.

REFERENCES
Salishchev, K. A. *Osnovy kartovedeniia,* 3rd ed., vol. 2. Moscow, 1962.
Salishchev, K. A. *Kartografiia,* 2nd ed. Moscow, 1971.
Tr. Tsentral'nogo nauchno-issledovatel'skogo in-ta geodezii, aeros''emki i kartografii, 1957, issue 116; 1962, issue 156.
        V. N. CHENTSOV [11–1423–2]

CARTOGRAPHIC SOURCES, graphic, photographic, digital, and textual data used for the compilation of geographic maps. A distinction is made among astronomical and geodetic sources, including the results of astronomical, triangulation, polygonometric, and leveling work to establish planimetric and altitudinal geodetic positions (represented primarily in digital form); photographic and surveying sources, including various kinds of surveying materials, such as aerial photographs, photographs produced by ground-based photogrammetric surveying, photographs taken from artificial earth satellites and spacecraft, photomaps, materials produced by topographical surveying methods, and various kinds of maps; and textual and tabular sources, including the results of geographic, economic-statistical, and other kinds of research and generalizations from it.

The recording of the content of cartographic sources in code (usually digital) on punched cards, punched tape, and similar carriers is becoming increasingly common; thus, the required information can be processed, stored, and retrieved by computers. Microfilm and microfiche are also coming into wide use.

Many countries have already begun to establish "banks" of geodetic, topographic, cartographic, and topical cartographic data. The banks are expected to replace most traditional cartographic sources by accumulating information in a form that makes possible the automatic processing, storage, and retrieval of particular data, as well as various combinations of data. The banks are an element in the overall system for the automation of cartographic processes.

In the compilation of a particular map the cartographic sources are tentatively divided into the following categories according to importance: (1) primary sources, from which the basic content of the map is taken; (2) supplementary sources, which aid in the precise determination of individual elements; and (3) auxiliary sources, which are used for general orientation and familiarization with the territory being mapped and with the types of maps and atlases that are similar to the ones being drafted or drawn.

Various criteria are used to evaluate cartographic sources. For example, when evaluating the quality of astronomical and geodetic sources, attention is devoted to their precision and the correspondence between the initial data and the system of coordinates being used in the map being drawn; when evaluating the suitability of aerial photographs, their stereo photogrammetric and photographic qualities and up-to-dateness are considered. The main criteria for the evaluation of general geographic maps are their scale, purpose, authorship, geometric precision, up-to-dateness, and completeness of content and quality of cartographic generalization, as well as the technical and economic feasibility of using the source. Another important criterion in evaluating general geographic and many topical maps—in many cases the decisive criterion—is their ideological and political orientation. The study and analysis of textual and tabular sources belong to special divisions of cartography (population, economic, historical, and soil cartography).

REFERENCES
Biushgens, L. M. *Analiz i otsenka inostrannykh obshchegeograficheskikh kart kak materialov dlia sostavleniia.* Moscow, 1957.
Salishchev, K. A. *Osnovy kartovedeniia,* 3rd ed., vol. 2. Moscow, 1962.

L. M. BIUSHGENS [11–1393–1]

CARTOGRAPHY, the science of geographic maps and methods for their compilation and use. This definition of cartography, the most widespread one, reflects its technical aspects. At the same time, the modern view of geographic maps as graphic figurative-symbolic models of space leads to a stricter definition of the subject and method of cartography: the science of the representation and study of the spatial arrangements, combinations, and interrelationships of the phenomena of nature and society (and their changes over time) by means of cartographic pictures, which reproduce particular aspects of reality. This definition includes within cartography maps of celestial bodies and of the heavens, globes, relief maps, and other spatial models that use cartographic symbols. The subject of cartography (the spatial arrangement, combinations, and relationships of phenomena) and the development of topical maps are increasingly allying it with the natural sciences. The term "cartography" is also applied to scientific and industrial cartographic activity and to its results —for example, state cartography. It is in this sense that the term is included in the name of the cartographic and geodetic service of the USSR (the Central Administration for Geodesy and Cartography of the Council of Ministers of the USSR).

Present-day cartography includes the following branches:
(1) The theoretical foundations of the science, including the teaching of the subject and methods of cartography and map theory (or, more completely, the theory of the cartographic representation of reality). The latter includes the theory of cartographic projections and the theory of generalization and methods of representation (the system of symbols). It considers types and kinds of maps and their classification and analysis.
(2) The history of cartographic science and map-making.
(3) The study of cartographic sources (systematic survey and analysis of cartographic sources and relevant questions of scientific information theory).
(4) The theory and technology of drafting and preparing maps.
(5) The theory and methods of using maps.

The problems of cartography arose during various periods of history and are in different stages of development. This has been reflected in the breakdown of cartography into separate disciplines: map studies, mathematical cartography, the compilation and design (or drafting) of maps, and the production of finished maps; cartometry is sometimes treated as a special discipline. In its present state, map studies includes the theoretical foundations of the science, its history, study of sources, and methods of using maps. Mathematical cartography, or the theory of cartographic projections, was the first to be established as a special discipline. Cartometry—the teaching of the use of maps to measure and compute coordinates, distances, lengths, elevations, and areas—has a long history; obviously, it constitutes just one method of using maps, but it is often used independently because of its practical importance and the antiquity and abundance of research. The theory and technology of drafting and making original maps has developed vigorously in the USSR under the name "compilation and design of maps." The task of map-making includes the study and development of the means of representation in cartography, using data from semiotics, color studies, and engineering psychology, as well as methods of the graphic arts, and taking into account printing requirements.

The uniqueness of particular types of maps—for example, geologic, soil, economic, and other maps based on the data of the corresponding sciences (geology, soil science, economic geography, and so on)—and the particular features of the compilation of such maps led to the development and separation of topical divisions of cartography: geologic cartography, soil cartography, economic cartography, and so on. These borderline disciplines belong to cartography according to method, but according to the content of the maps they belong to other sciences.

Special training for cartographers also includes map publication (study of the development of methods for reproducing and duplicating maps) and the economics and organization of map-making. However, the former, which is based primarily on the physicochemical and technical sciences, belongs to typography, whereas the latter belongs to the economics of various fields of science and engineering.

The oldest surviving cartographic pictures were made in Babylon and Egypt in the third to first millennia B.C. The first scientific foundations of cartography were laid in ancient Greece, where geographic maps were made that took into account the spherical shape of the earth. Ptolemy's famous *Geography* (second century A.D.) was essentially a manual for the compilation of geographic maps. It included a map of the world and 16 maps of large subdivisions of the earth.

The development of trade, navigation, and colonization in the age of the Renaissance and great geographic discoveries (15th and 16th centuries) aroused great demand for geographic maps, particularly world maps, which required the development of new cartographic projections and led to a general advancement of cartography. Medieval cartography attained its greatest development in the works of G. Mercator, whose atlas of 1595 is well known.

The establishment of scientific cartography in Russia dates to the 18th century and is related primarily to the activity of the Geography Department of the Academy of Sciences, where the first complete *Atlas Rossiiskoi* (Russian Atlas) was prepared and published in 1745.

In the 19th century military interests led to the need for detailed maps of terrain. In this period cartography was either considered to be a branch of geodesy or was restricted in its scientific interest to cartographic projections and, partially, to methods of measurement from maps—that is, to specific and relatively narrow mathematical problems. At the same time, the differentiation of sciences and practical needs in the second half of the 19th century brought about the development of many different topical maps (geologic, climatic, soil, and economic). The purely geometric treatment of cartography at this time hindered its development.

New views of cartography took root earliest in the USSR, where the planned economy required multifaceted mapping of the country. As early as the 1930's cartography came to be understood as the science of the methods and processes of compilation and reproduction of maps, which was a progressive idea in comparison with the previous concept of cartography. However, the study of the essence of maps and developing methods for their use remained in the shadow. The creation of major cartographic works in the USSR (among them the *Great Soviet World Atlas*) required that this gap be filled and that corresponding areas of cartography be developed. This led to the definition of the science that was cited at the beginning of this article.

Letters written in 1920–21 by V. I. Lenin concerning preparation of the first Soviet geographic atlases, as well as other documents written by Lenin on questions of cartography, were of great value to the development of the ideological and scientific foundations of Soviet cartography. Specifically, they emphasize the importance of a complete, reliable, and graphic representation of phenomena in all their aspects, interrelations, historical development, and contradictions.

Cartography is closely associated with geodesy and the geographic sciences. Geodesy provides exact data on the shape and dimensions of the earth, and topography and aerial photographic topography provide the primary cartographic sources—the large-scale topographical maps that are the initial basis for all geographic maps. The geographic sciences give the cartographer the knowledge necessary for making sound choices of the quantitative and qualitative characteristics of the phenomena being mapped and for their correct depiction, with due regard for regional features. In turn, the maps are an effective tool in geography, as in other sciences, for the study of the spatial arrangement, combinations, and interrelationships of all natural and social phenomena.

The practical importance of cartography is determined by the value and uniqueness of geographic maps as graphic and exact spatial models that are widely used in the national economy, in culture and education, and for defense.

Maps are produced either as the result of field surveys and the processing of data from them or in offices and laboratories by the use and revising of various sources, such as cartographic, geographic, economic, and statistical data.

The methods of field surveying and data processing are the subject of topography and aerial photographic topography. Topical surveying, such as geologic and soil surveying, is a task of the particular kind of cartography (geologic or soil). The office and laboratory methods of drafting and making maps are developed in cartography proper. During office work a preliminary program is outlined on the basis of the purpose of the map being drafted: scale, cartographic projection, content (a list of the elements of the content, their classification, and the completeness and detail with which each element is shown), and methods of representation. Next, the necessary sources are selected and the phenomena being mapped are studied in the sources to determine the typical features and characteristics that should be shown on the map. The final program for the map is prepared by considering the results of this work.

Work on graphic preparation of the original of the map (the compilation processes) follows. These processes include construction of the cartographic grid, complete or selective transfer of the content of the sources to it, generalization, and drawing of the original in the cartographic symbols established by the program. In the compilation of topical maps, the content of the sources is transferred to previously prepared or selected geographic positions.

In the process of preparing a map for publication the base sheet of the map is often used to make (by lining or engraving on plastic) secondary smooth-delineation maps as fair copies to ensure the production of high-quality press plates. Preparation of the map ends with the publishing processes, as a result of which the map is printed in the required number of copies.

In modern cartographic production, a group of specialists with various qualifications usually participates in the production of a map. Therefore, standardized scientific and technical supervision is needed in all stages of preparation of the map, including publication. This supervision is customarily called the editing of the map.

International scientific ties in cartography first formed and developed within the framework of the international geographic congresses. Specifically, it was on their initiative that the Washington conference to select a uniform prime meridian was convened (the 1871 congress in Antwerp) and that the *International 1:1,000,000 Map* and the *International Bathymetric Map of the Oceans* were compiled (the 1891 congress in Bern and the 1899 congress in Berlin, respectively). The formation in 1922 of the International Geographical Union, which, in addition to geographic congresses, organizes international commissions to work on the most important scientific problems, also promoted expanded research on cartography (national and regional comprehensive atlases, population mapping, land use maps, and international geomorphological maps). Finally, the formation in 1961 of the International Cartographic Association ensured systematic study of the problems of cartography based on cooperation among interested countries (convening scientific and technical conferences every two years and regular work by special commissions). The UN cartographic conferences that have met once every three years for the countries of Asia and the Far East (since 1955) and for the countries of Africa (since 1963) are important for the improvement of cartography in the developing countries. A particularly important recent international initiative is the *International Map of the World,* on a scale of 1:2,500,000, which has hypsometric representation of relief and gives a comparable picture of the continents and the world ocean (the map is being prepared by the cartographic and geodetic services of Bulgaria, Hungary, the German Democratic Republic, Poland, Rumania, the USSR, and Czechoslovakia).

The current development of cartography is reflected in the rapid rise in the number of scientific journals and collections of periodicals dealing with cartography.

REFERENCES
"Pis'ma V. I. Lenina o kartografii." *Geodeziia i kartografiia,* 1969, no. 3.
Salishchev, K. A. *Osnovy kartovedeniia,* 3rd ed., vol. 2. Moscow, 1962.
Salishchev, K. A. "Predmet i metod kartografii (nekotorye sovremennye vzgliady)." *Vestn. MGU: Geografiia,* 1970, No. 2.
50 let sovetskoi geodezii i kartografii. Moscow, 1967. (Collection of articles.)
Kostrits, I. B. "V. I. Lenin i razvitie sovetskoi kartografii." In *Itogi nauki: Kartografiia, 1967–1969,* issue 4. Moscow, 1970.

K. A. SALISHCHEV [11–1414–1]

CARTOMETRY, the division of cartography in which methods of measurement of various geographic objects on maps to find their area, length, volume, and other quantitative characteristics are studied. Direct measurement of the length and area of actual objects using geodetic methods can only be done when the objects have very small dimensions. Cartometry is concerned with the computation of larger quantities, such as the areas of states and oceans, the lengths of coastlines and rivers, and the areas of river drainage basins. It also includes methods for the computation of various quantitative characteristics of terrain (average elevation, average angle of slope, volume, and density of the river network) by measurement on maps.

REFERENCE
Volkov, N. M. *Printsipy i metody kartometrii.* Moscow-Leningrad, 1950.
[11–1426–1]

CARTOON, in art, a large preliminary drawing (not always black and white) with the dimensions of a projected work of art, such as a fresco, mosaic, stained glass, or Gobelin tapestry. By piercing the outlines of the cartoon, the composition of a projected fresco was transferred onto the wall. European artists used cartoons extensively during the Renaissance and during the 17th and 18th centuries. [11–1427–1]

CARTOUCHE, an ornament in the shape of a shield or a partially unrolled scroll, on which a coat of arms, emblem, or inscription was placed. Carved or stucco cartouches decorated the main entrances of palaces. Cartouches also appeared on geographic maps, tombstones, and ancient documents. The ornament was widely used in the 16th, 17th, and 18th centuries.

REFERENCE
Hadergott, B. *Die Kartusche.* . . . Göttingen, 1955.   [11–1445–1]

CARTULARIES, collections of copies of the documents legally registering gifts, primarily of land, for the use of the church in medieval Western Europe. Copies of royal grants and sometimes copies of agreements between secular persons were also included in the cartularies. The copies did not always agree with the originals. The earliest examples of cartularies date to the late seventh and the eighth centuries; they ceased to be compiled in the late 13th and the 14th centuries. The cartularies of the large monasteries often contain thousands of documents. Cartularies are one of the most important sources for the investigation of the social and economic processes of the feudal countryside. Such data as the size and structure of the landholdings of the various social strata, the duties of the peasants, and the means by which the feudal dependence of the peasants was formed can be determined from the cartularies.

In the broadest sense, cartularies were understood in the Middle Ages to be collections of any sort of documents.

[11–1444–5]

CARTWRIGHT, EDMUND. Born Apr. 24, 1743, in Marnham, Nottinghamshire; died Oct. 30, 1823, in Hastings, Sussex. English inventor of the power loom. After graduating from Oxford University (1764), he became a country clergyman. In 1785, Cartwright took out a patent for the treadle-operated loom, which he had invented; the shuttle was driven by hand. He was able to combine in this loom, which was improved in 1786, all the basic operations of hand weaving. In 1785, Cartwright built a mill with 20 looms in Doncaster, Yorkshire, and in 1789 installed a steam engine to drive them. Cartwright's loom was widely used after improvements made by other inventors (1813 and 1822).

REFERENCE
Tseitlin, E. A. *Ocherki istorii tekstil'noi tekhniki.* Moscow-Leningrad, 1940.   [11–1444–3]

CARUARU, a city in northeastern Brazil in Pernambuco state, on the Recife-Salgueiro railroad line. Population, 142,800 (1970). Caruaru is an important trade and distribution center of the state. It is the site of food, textile, leather, and other industries.   [11–1451–5]

CARÚPANO, a city in Venezuela, in Sucre state, on the Caribbean coast. Population, 45,100 (1969). Carúpano is a trading center and fishing port, serving the agricultural regions and fishing industries on the Península de Paria. Coffee and cacao are exported.   [11–1452–2]

CARUS, CARL GUSTAV. Born Jan. 3, 1789, in Leipzig; died July 28, 1869, in Dresden. German biologist and physician.

Carus was a professor at the Saxon Academy of Medicine and Surgery in Dresden. From 1862 to 1863 he was president of the Leopoldina, the German Academy of Natural Sciences in Halle. His main works dealt with the comparative anatomy of the nervous system, blood circulation in insects, and the development of muscles. Carus was the author of textbooks on anatomy, zoology, physiology, and gynecology.

WORKS
Lehrbuch der Zootomie. Leipzig, 1818.
Grundzüge der vergleichenden Anatomie und Physiologie, vols. 1–3. Dresden, 1828.
In Russian translation:
Osnovaniia kranioskopii. St. Petersburg, 1844.   [11–1453–1]

CARUSO, ENRICO. Born Feb. 24 (other sources give 25 or 27), 1873, in Naples; died there Aug. 2, 1921. Italian singer (tenor).

In his youth Caruso sang in a church choir and from 1891 studied under G. Vergine. He made his debut in 1894 at the Teatro Nuovo in Naples. He toured Italy between 1895 and 1898 and in 1900–01 sang at La Scala in Milan. Caruso was a leading soloist at the Metropolitan Opera House in New York (1903–20), toured triumphantly from 1898 in many countries (Russia, 1898 and 1900), and performed yearly in Italy.

Caruso was one of the most admired opera singers in the world; his voice, with an extraordinary range, beautiful timbre, and unusual strength, abounded in warmth of feeling. His brilliant acting and strength and passion in singing enabled Caruso to perform a range of tenor roles from lyric to tragic. His best parts were the Duke, Manrico, and Radamès in Verdi's *Rigoletto, Il Trovatore,* and *Aida;* Nemorino in Donizetti's *L'Elisir d'Amore;* Faust in Boito's *Mefistofele;* Canio in Leoncavallo's *Pagliacci;* Turiddu in Mascagni's *Cavalleria Rusticana;* Rudolfo, Cavaradossi, and Des Grieux in Puccini's *La Bohème, Tosca,* and *Manon Lescaut;* Don José in Bizet's *Carmen;* Eleazar in Halévy's *La Juive;* and Lionel in Flotow's *Martha.* Caruso performed Neapolitan songs with exceptional fervor.

WORKS
"Kak nuzhno pet'." *Teatral'naia gazeta,* 1914, nos. 16–18.
REFERENCES
L'vov, M. "E. Karuzo." *Sovetskaia muzyka,* 1955, no. 1, pp. 98–100.
Tortorelli, V. *E. Karuzo.* Moscow, 1965. (Translated from Italian.)
Fucito, S., and B. J. Beyer. *Iskusstvo peniia i vokal'naia metodika E. Karuzo,* 2nd ed. Leningrad, 1967. (Translated from German.)
Daspuro, N. *E. Caruso.* [Milan] 1938.
Mouchon, J.-P. *Enrico Caruso: Sa Vie et sa voix.* Langres, 1966.
Lauri-Volpi, G. *Voci parallele.* Milan, 1955. (In Russian translation: *Vokal'nye paralleli.* Leningrad, 1972. Pages 158–169.)
                                          S. M. GRISHCHENKO   [11–1451–6]

CARVER, THOMAS NIXON. Born Mar. 25, 1865, in Kirkville, Iowa; died in 1961, in Santa Monica, Calif. American economist. Exponent of vulgar bourgeois political economy. Graduated from the University of Southern California in 1891. Doctor of philosophy (1894). Professor of economics at Harvard University (from 1902).

Carver was an adherent of J. B. Clark's theory of marginal productivity, which he attempted to make more concrete through the use of mathematics. He asserted that the USA had entered an era of continual prosperity and that differences between workers and entrepreneurs were being erased. He called upon workers to reject the struggle against capital and to engage in cooperation with entrepreneurs. His antiscientific conceptions became basic to the theory of "people's" capitalism.

WORKS
The Distribution of Wealth. New York, 1904.
Principles of Political Economy. Boston, 1919.
The Present Economic Revolution in the United States. Boston, 1925.
Recollections of an Unplanned Life. Los Angeles, 1949.
                                          V. G. SARYCHEV   [11–1217–2]

CARYA (hickory), a genus of deciduous trees of the family Junglandaceae. Height, up to 60–65 m. The leaves are alternate and odd-pinnate. The flowers are unisexual. The staminate flowers are in pendulous catkins, and the pistillate flowers are in two- to ten-flowered spikelets. The fruit is a false drupe, which splits at ripening into four woody valves. There are approximately 20 species, distributed in the southeastern United States and in China. In the USSR, five species have been cultivated, including the pecan (*Carya pecan*) and the shagbark (*C. alba*); these species should be cultivated in rows. The nuts of some species are used for food. They contain up to 60–70 percent oil, which is used in confectioneries.

REFERENCES
Derev'ya i kustarniki SSSR, vol. 2. Moscow-Leningrad, 1951.
Kul'tura orekhoplodnykh. Moscow, 1957.   [11–1279–2]

CARYATID (from the Greek *karyatides,* literally, the priestesses of the Temple of Artemis at Caryae, in Laconia, ancient Greece), in architecture, the sculptural representation of a standing female figure, serving as the support of a beam. Sometimes the figure only gives the impression of fulfilling a supportive function and simply serves as a decoration of the actual support. Caryatids were widely used in ancient Greek and Roman architecture, as well as in European architecture of the 17th, 18th, and 19th centuries.   [11–1260–5]

CARYOPHANON (also *Simonsiella*), a genus of microorganisms of the family Oscillospiraceae. They are long, rod-shaped or filamentous (15–30 nanometers × 3 nanometers), slightly curved mobile organisms with numerous flagella. They are divided by septa into short cells. They do not form spores and are weakly gram-positive. These organisms reproduce by segmentation into two or three parts or more called hormogonia. They are found in water, rotting organic matter, intestines of insects, cattle manure, and human feces.   [11–1278–1]

CARYOTA, a genus of plants of the family Palmae. They are tall palms (up to 25 m) that die after fruitage. The leaves are bipinnate, approximately 6.5 m long, with small cuneate segments. The flowers are in very large racemose inflorescences (approximately 3.5 m long). The fruit is berry-like. There are approximately 12 species, growing in India, Sri Lanka, Indochina, China (in Yunan), the Malay Archipelago, the Solomon Islands, and tropical Australia. Sugar is obtained from the juice of the inflorescences of several species, including the jaggery palm (*Caryota urens*) and the species *C. mitis;* the juice is made into wine. Starch is obtained from the heartwood of the trunks. The wood of many species is used in construction. Fiber from the leaves is used to make rope and other articles.   [11–1277–1]

CASABLANCA (Arabic, Dar-el-Beida), a city and port on the western coast of Morocco, a city prefecture. Population, 1.4 million (1970).

Casablanca is one of the largest cities and ports of Africa; in 1970 it had a freight turnover of 12 million tons, three-fourths of which was phosphorite exports. The city is a major highway and railroad junction and has an international airport. Casablanca is the chief economic center of Morocco; of all Moroccans employed in the manufacturing industry, 55 percent work in Casablanca in such industries as metalworking (including motor-vehicle assembly), the food industry (fish packing, flour milling, and sugar refining), and the textile, chemical, cement, and printing industries. The major national and international financial and trade institutions of Morocco are located in Casablanca, and an international fair is held there every year.

The date of the founding of Casablanca has not been precisely established. According to some data, the city of Anfa arose on the site of present-day Casablanca in the seventh century. In 1468, Anfa was captured by the Portuguese and destroyed. In the second half of the 18th century the city was rebuilt under the Moroccan sultan Sidi Muhammad ibn Abd Allah (reigned 1757–90) and named Dar-el-Beida (Arabic, white house; in Spanish, Casablanca). In 1907, Casablanca was occupied by France and remained part of the French zone of the protectorate until the proclamation of the independence of Morocco on Mar. 2, 1956. Since the 1930's the city has been rapidly growing, its population increasing from 20,000–25,000 in the early 1920's to 160,000 in 1931 and to 682,000 in 1952; this growth was due to the leading role of the port in the export of raw minerals. From the 1930's through the 1950's, Casablanca was a major center for the formation of the Moroccan working class and the core of the national liberation movement.

The modern city has grown in a semicircle around the old city, the *medina,* which dates from the 16th century. The central part of Casablanca has multistory residential and office buildings (the Liberté Building, 78 m high, 1950, architect L. Morandi). The architectural monuments include the magnificent five-nave Cathedral of the Sacré Coeur (reinforced concrete, 1930–52, architect P. Tournon) with stained glass. The suburban areas have one-story traditional homes with inner enclosed courtyards bordered by galleries; there are also markets and mosques.
                                                             [11–1466–3]

CASABLANCA CONFERENCE OF 1943, a British-American conference between F. D. Roosevelt, president of the USA, and W. Churchill, prime minister of Great Britain, and including high military officials of these two countries.

The Casablanca Conference was held between January 14 and January 24 in a suburb of Casablanca in Morocco. The Casablanca Conference discussed prospective Allied military operations for 1943. An accord was reached on the landing of Allied troops in Sicily after the completion of the campaign in North Africa. The participants in the conference believed that this would not only help drive fascist Italy out of the war but also prepare a springboard for the landing of British and American troops in the Balkans. The Casablanca Conference put off the question of a second front in northern France to strike a blow at the vital centers of fascist Germany, despite pledges of action by the US and British governments to the Soviet government. Such a policy corresponded to the plan of the British and US statesmen, who hoped that the USSR and Germany would exhaust each other in a protracted war. The Casablanca Conference also confirmed a plan of operation in northern Burma which envisioned driving the Japanese troops out of Rangoon. The participants in the conference discussed the French administration in North Africa (Generals de Gaulle and H. Giraud were invited for this purpose), the position of Turkey in the war, and the fate of the colonies in the postwar period.

An important development of the conference was Roosevelt's statement at a press conference in Casablanca on Jan. 24, 1943, that the Allies would seek the unconditional surrender of Germany, Italy, and Japan.

PUBLICATION
War and Peace Aims of the United Nations, vol. 2. Boston, 1948. Pages 1–4.
REFERENCES
Israelian, V. L. *Antigitlerovskaia Koalitsiia.* Moscow, 1964.
Istoriia mezhdunarodnykh otnoshenii i vneshnei politiki SSSR. Vol. 2: *1939–1945.* Moscow, 1962.
Sherwood, R. *Ruzvel't i Gopkins glazami ochevidtsa,* vol. 2. Moscow, 1958. (Translated from English.)   [11–1467–1]

CASADESUS, ROBERT MARCEL. Born Apr. 7, 1899, in Paris; died there Sept. 18, 1972. French pianist.

Casadesus studied with his father, Francis, and with L. Diemer. He began touring Western Europe and the USA in 1920 and toured the USSR in 1929. He became the director of the American Conservatory at Fontainebleau near Paris in 1947.

Casadesus was the major modern performer in the tradition of Romantic pianists. His enormous and varied repertoire ranged from such keyboard masters of the 17th and 18th centuries as J. P. Rameau and D. Scarlatti to such impressionists of the 19th and 20th as C. Debussy and M. de Falla. But his most important works were the concertos of Mozart and Beethoven, for which he wrote cadenzas, and Beethoven's sonatas. He often performed duets with his wife, Gaby. Casadesus composed three symphonies, two piano concertos, and many other works for the piano.

REFERENCE
Kogan, G. "Rober Kazadezius." In his book *Voprosy pianizma.* Moscow, 1968. Pages 392–94.   [11–389–5]

CASAL, JULIÁN DEL. Born Nov. 7, 1863, in Havana; died there Oct. 21, 1893. Cuban poet. Son of a landowner; an official.

The influence of Spanish romanticism noticeable in Casal's early poetry had already given way to the influence of the French Parnassians by the time of his first book, *Leaves in the Wind* (1890); this influence in turn gave way to that of the French symbolists, as shown in the collection *Snow* (1892). *Busts and Rhymes* (1893) included both poetry and prose. Casal's poetry is characterized by pessimism and an escape from reality into an exotic world but at the same time by harmoniousness of form and musicality of verse.

WORKS
Poesías completas. Havana, 1945.
In Russian translation:
In the collection *Kubinskaia poeziia.* Moscow, 1959.
In the collection *Soldaty svobody.* Moscow, 1963.

REFERENCES
Portuondo, J. A. *Istoricheskii ocherk kubinskoi literatury.* Moscow, 1961. (Translated from Spanish.)
Monner Sans, J. M. *J. del Casal y el modernismo hispano-americano.* Mexico City, 1952. [11–1468–3]

CASALS, PABLO. Born Dec. 29, 1876, in Vendrell, near Barcelona; died Oct. 22, 1973, in Rio Piedras, Puerto Rico. Spanish cellist, conductor, composer, and public figure. Pupil of J. García (cello) and T. Bretón and J. de Monasterio (composition).

Casals made his debut as a virtuoso soloist in Paris in 1899. In 1901 he began touring with great success in many countries, performing in Russia between 1905 and 1913 both as a soloist and in groups with Rachmaninoff, A. I. Siloti, and A. B. Gol'denveizer. A. K. Glazunov dedicated his *Concerto-ballata* to Casals.

Casals formed a celebrated trio with A. Cortot and J. Thibaud. He performed in concert for approximately 75 years, and his work spanned an entire epoch in the art of cello interpretation. His playing was profound and rich, blending emotion and reflection; a virtuoso, Casals combined brilliant technique with subtle phrasing. One of his greatest contributions was his modern interpretation of J. S. Bach. Casals' compositions include symphonic poems, an oratorio, and chamber music for cello ensemble and for cello, violin, and piano.

Casals founded a symphony orchestra in Barcelona in 1920 and a workers' concert association in 1924, which he headed until 1936. In 1939 he was forced to leave Spain. He settled in Prades (French Pyrénées), where he instituted a festival of chamber music in 1950 (D. F. Oistrakh and other Soviet musicians participated). Casals moved to Puerto Rico and organized the annual Casals Festival there, which has continued after his death. Casals cello competitions have been held since 1957 in various countries (the first was in Paris). Casals was an antifascist and a fighter for peace.

REFERENCE
Ginzburg, L. *Pablo Kazal's,* 2nd ed. Moscow, 1966.
L. S. GINZBURG [11–1469–1]

CASANOVA, DANIELLE. Born Jan. 9, 1909, in Ajaccio, Corsica; died May 9, 1943, in Oświęcim. Heroine of the French Resistance Movement.

The daughter of a Corsican teacher, Casanova went to Paris in 1927 to study medicine. She was active in the student movement and the Communist Youth Organization and joined the French Communist Party in 1933. In 1932, Casanova was elected a member of the Central Committee of the Communist Youth Organization and became chairman of the French Girls' Union in 1936. In 1935 she came to Moscow to attend the congress of the Communist Youth International and was elected a member of the Executive Committee. During the occupation of France by fascist Germany (1940–44), Casanova was one of the organizers of French youth and women for the struggle to liberate her country. She was arrested by the Gestapo in February 1942 and died of typhus in a fascist concentration camp in May 1943. A street in Paris is named after Casanova.

REFERENCE
Téry, S. *Serdtse, polnoe solntsa.* [Moscow] 1958. (Translated from French.) [11–399–2]

CASANOVA, GIOVANNI GIACOMO. Born Apr. 2, 1725, in Venice; died June 4, 1798, in Dux Castle, in Bohemia. Italian writer and memoirist.

Casanova led a stormy life, traveling all over Europe and often being imprisoned. He is the author of several historical works and a fantasy novel, *Icosameron* (1788). *The History of My Flight* (1788) was part of his posthumously published *Memoirs* (1st ed., in German, translated from the original French; parts 1–12, 1822–28). Casanova's memoirs are extraordinarily candid about his intimate life and present penetrating observations on the social mores of his time and a sober evaluation of historical events.

WORKS
In Russian translation:
Memuary. St. Petersburg, 1887.
REFERENCES
Zweig, S. "Tri pevtsa svoei zhizni: Kazanova—Stendal'— Tolstoi." *Sobr. soch.,* vol. 6. Leningrad [1929].
Lucas-Dubreton, J. *Le Don Juan de Venise: Casanova.* Paris [1955]. [11–399–3]

CASARÈS, MARIA (real surname, Casarès Quiroga). Born Nov. 21, 1922, in La Coruña, Spain. French actress.

Casarès graduated from the department of dramatic arts of the Paris Conservatory and began her stage career in 1942. She has played in many of the theaters of Paris, including the Atelier, the Marigny, the Comédie-Française, and the Théâtre National Populaire; since 1960 she has been with the troupe of the Athénée. Her best roles have included Victoria in *State of Siege* by Camus, Grushen'ka in *The Brothers Karamazov,* adapted from Dostoevsky, Périchole in *The Carriage of the Holy Sacrament* by Mérimée, the title roles in Hugo's *Marie Tudor* and Racine's *Phèdre,* and Mrs. Patrick Campbell in *Dear Liar* by J. Kilty. Intellect and great technical skill are combined with a strongly spirited performance in the artistry of Casarès. Casarès made her film debut in 1945 and has appeared in *The Charterhouse of Parma* and *Orpheus.* [11–413–1]

CASCADE, in landscaping, a natural or artificial waterfall descending over terraced steps. In park architecture cascades are created by building at various levels of bodies of water and of steps and terraces over which the water descends. Examples of famous cascades are those in Italy, in the Villa d'Este in Tivoli (1550–72, architect P. Ligorio) and the Villa Aldobrandini in Frascati (1598–1604, architects G. della Porta and C. Maderna), as well as those in the park in Petrodvorets.

In the figurative sense a cascade is a rapid irrepressible flow of something—for example, words or sounds. [11–477–3]

CASCADE GENERATOR (also Cockcroft-Walton generator), a high-voltage generator that operates on the principle of voltage multiplication. The first such generator was built in 1932 by J. Cockcroft and E. Walton and was used to accelerate ions to high energies. Such generators usually have four to ten stages. A special connection circuit using rectifiers and capacitors makes possible an increase of the voltage in each stage with respect to the preceding stage by twice the voltage amplitude of the high-voltage transformer (by several hundred kilovolts) that is connected to the first stage.

Cascade generators are widely used in high-voltage technology, to test high-voltage equipment, and also in acceleration technology to produce ions with energies of 3–4 million electron volts and higher.

REFERENCE
Komar, E. G. *Uskoriteli zariazhennykh chastits.* Moscow, 1964.
B. M. GOKHBERG [11–1479–3]

CASCADE RANGE, a mountain range of the North American Cordillerra, located in the USA and Canada. Length, about 1,000 km; maximum altitude, 4,392 m (Mount Rainier, a volcano).

The Cascade Range gets its name from the abundance of terrace-like waterfalls (cascades) on the Columbia, Fraser, Klamath, and other rivers that cut through the range. The range is formed by Mesozoic crystalline rocks covered by huge layers of Paleogene and Neocene lavas. Above this strongly dissected volcanic plateau, which is from 1,800 to 2,500 m high, rise isolated cones of volcanoes, such as Mount Baker, Mount Rainier, Mount Hood, and Lassen Peak, with altitudes of 3,000 to 4,000 m and more. Most of the volcanoes are extinct, although their slopes abound in fumaroles and hot springs. In the late 19th and early 20th centuries Mount Rainier and Lassen Peak showed their greatest volcanic activity. The volcanic peaks are covered with vast snow fields and glaciers. Dark coniferous forests grow on the humid western slopes of the range and pine trees on the dry eastern slopes; above 2,800–3,000 m, the forests give way to subalpine and alpine meadows. There are copper and gold deposits in the mountains. Crater Lake, Mount Rainier, and Lassen Volcanic national parks are located in the Cascade Range.

A. V. ANTIPOVA [11–1479–2]

CASCADE TRANSFORMER, two or more electrical transformers connected in series to transform or use high voltage alternating current.

The principle of cascade excitation of transformers, particularly those connected in a circuit in which each transformer in turn is excited from a part of the step-up winding of the preceding transformer, is usually used. Cascade transformers for voltages up to 1.5 or 2 megavolts with a total of four to eight transformers in the cascade may be constructed according to this principle. The drawbacks of such a cascade transformer (the installed transformer capacity far exceeds the power of the cascade, there is considerable inductance, the distribution of the pulse voltages along the individual links of the cascade is nonuniform, and the design is cumbersome) are partially eliminated in the capacitor type of design. The windings are wound in a single layer on insulating cylinders; the number of cylinders and their length and diameter are chosen such that when the windings are connected in series the potential buildup on the turns corresponds to the potential distribution over the capacitance of the concentric layers of the winding. This design does not require large insulators, reduces the dimensions and weight of the transformer, and simplifies its installation and operation. Cascade connection of current- and voltage-measuring transformers is sometimes used for voltages of more than 110 kilovolts.

REFERENCE
Petrov, G. N. *Elektricheskie mashiny,* parts 1–3. Moscow-Leningrad, 1956–68. [11–1480–2]

CASCARA SAGRADA, the bark of the North American species of the cascara buckthorn (*Rhamnus purshiana*). It is used in dried form or in the form of a processed medicinal preparation as a mild laxative. Cascara sagrada is not used in medicine in the USSR. [11–1481–1]

CASEIN, a complex phosphoprotein that is formed from its precursor caseinogen as a result of the splitting of peptide bonds in the process of milk curdling. Casein is readily soluble in saline solutions in neutral or alkaline media, and it precipitates when acidified. Its molecular weight is 75,000–100,000.

Casein is a heterogeneous protein; by physical and chemical methods it can be divided into three fractions that are similar to one another in amino-acid composition, (α-casein β-casein, and γ-casein). Dried casein is a tasteless and odorless white powder. Casein is the principal protein component of milk and milk products. Cow's milk contains 2.8–3.5 percent casein; human milk, 0.3–0.9 percent. This most important dietary protein contains a complete complement of the essential amino acids; it contains especially high percentages of methionine (~ 3.5 percent), lysine (~ 6.9 percent), tryptophan (~ 1.8 percent), leucine (~ 12.1 percent), and valine (7.0 percent). The stomachs of mammals shortly after birth contain the enzyme chymosin, or rennin, which curdles milk (this can also be catalyzed by other proteolytic enzymes). In industry casein is used in the manufacture of paints, glues, synthetic fibers, and plastics.

I. B. ZBARSKII [11–521–5]

CASELLA, ALFREDO. Born July 25, 1883, in Turin; died Mar. 5, 1947, in Rome. Italian composer, pianist, conductor, and musicologist.

Casella was a professor at the Conservatory of St. Cecilia in Rome in 1915. As a conductor and pianist (a member of the Trio Italiano in the 1930's) he performed in many countries (Russia in 1907 and 1909; the USSR in 1926 and 1935). In 1917 he founded the National Music Society in Rome (since 1923, the Corporation for New Music, a branch of the International Society for Contemporary Music). He is an exponent of modernism and neoclassicism in music.

His operas (*The Snake Woman* and *Tale of Orpheus,* both staged in 1932), ballets, symphonies, and piano transcriptions contributed to a revival of interest in classical Italian music. Casella also wrote on musicology, including an essay on the evolution of the cadence, and monographs on I. F. Stravinsky and J. S. Bach. He has prepared editions of many classical piano works.

The Casella International Piano Competition has been held in Naples since 1952.

REFERENCES
Glebov, I. [Asaf'ev, B. V.] *A. Kazella.* Leningrad, 1927.
A. Casella. Edited by F. d'Amico and G. M. Gatti. Milan [1958].
[11–522–3]

CASEMATE. (1) An area in a fortification for the protection of personnel from direct hits by artillery shells and aerial bombs. Prototypes of casemates were known in ancient times. The perfection of artillery and the appearance of aviation provided the impetus for the widespread development of casemates. Depending on its purpose, a casemate is called a combat, observation, living, or ammunition casemate. It is customary to call all those modern fortifications with casemates as casemated, distinguished from open fortifications.

(2) An armored enclosed area on ships for the installation of guns, the storage of shells, and the protection of personnel from enemy fire. Casemates were widely used on artillery ships in the second half of the 19th century and the first half of the 20th century. Because of changes in warship design (in particular armor plating), casemates have almost completely lost their importance.

(3) Before the 20th century, an isolation cell in a prison located in a former fortress, primarily for the detention of political prisoners. [11–522–4]

CASERTA, a city in southern Italy, in the region of Campania; the capital of the province of Caserta. Population, 61,700 (1970). Railroad junction. There are flour mills and plants for the production of tobacco. Wine and olive oil are also produced. There are electronics, chemical, and glass industries. Caserta is the site of a Romanesque cathedral (1113–53; Gothic bell tower, 1234) and the Palazzo Reale (from 1752, architect L. Vanvitelli).
[11–524–3]

CASHBOOK, a bookkeeping register for the accounting of cash movements. All cash operations immediately after they are made are registered in the cashbook, with the number designation of the cash document backing the cash receipt or payment, the name of the person who turned in or received the money, and the amount of the operation. Cashbook accuracy is supervised by the chief (senior) bookkeeper of the economic organization.
[11–1509–2]

CASH FUND. (1) The cash balance of an enterprise (organization) for payments of wages, annuities, scholarships, and other disbursements, as well as for petty cash payments. In the USSR the amount of the cash balance and the procedure for cash disbursements are determined by the Regulation on Cash Operations of Enterprises, Institutions, and Organizations, which was approved by the Council of Ministers on Jan. 15, 1949.

(2) Bookkeeping accounts in which the movement of the cash funds of an enterprise is reflected. [11–1494–2]

CASHIER'S OFFICE (cash desk), a structural subdivision of some enterprises and organizations, in particular banks entrusted with operations relating to cash and other valuables.
[11–1494–2]

CASHMERE, a light woolen, wool mixture, or cotton fabric with a twill interweaving. Cashmere is usually solid colored and made of carded wool yarn; it is used in making women's and children's dresses and other items of clothing. Its name comes from cashmere shawls (whose fabric it resembles), which are made from fine goat's wool in Kashmir. [11–1652–1]

CASH OPERATIONS, operations connected with the cash receipts and payments of enterprises, institutions, and organizations. In the USSR, cash operations are performed in accordance with the Regulations for Conducting Cash Operations by Enterprises, Institutions, and Organizations (approved by the Council of Ministers of the USSR on Jan. 15, 1949) and apply mainly to monetary settlements with the population and credit institutions. Cash operations are registered in a cashbook.

[11–1510–1]

CASH PLANNING, in the USSR and other socialist countries the planning and regulating procedures dealing with cash turnover passing through the branches of the state bank of issue and with changes in the amount of money in circulation that serves as means of exchange, payment, and saving for the working people. Along with the planning of the money income and expenditure of the population, cash planning is a basic form of planning money circulation in the country. Cash planning is possible only in socialist countries, whose planned economies allow a clear differentiation between ready-cash money turnover and noncash payments and the centralization of all accounting and cash operations in one single state bank of issue.

In the USSR, cash planning is implemented in close connection with credit planning through the drawing up of cash plans of the Gosbank (State Bank) of the USSR; these plans are based on indexes of the national economic plan, the state budget, the balance of money income and expenditure of the population, and the economic and financial plans and estimates of enterprises, institutions, and organizations. Before the credit reform in 1930, the turnover of cash funds was not planned directly. The amount of money in circulation was indirectly defined in credit plans through coordination of the size of credit operations of Gosbank and the volume of free funds attracted in accounts and deposits. The cash plan for Gosbank was first drawn up for August 1930. Cash planning developed with the development of the socialist economy and the improvement of national economic planning. Today, cash turnover is planned both for the country as a whole and for each republic, krai, oblast, raion, and city; the planning is done not only according to the volume and direction of the flow of money but also according to the economic content, that is, by the income sources and the intended function of payment. The accounting of the actual money turnover is implemented in the same way. Thus, any deviation in the course of carrying out the national economic plan can be rapidly and effectively exposed and can be overcome through use of internal reserves found in the economy; also, money issue and withdrawal from circulation based on territorial considerations can be regulated in a centralized manner. Cash planning is also done in other socialist countries.

REFERENCES

Batyrev, V. *Organizatsia i planirovanie denezhnogo obrashcheniia v SSSR.* Moscow, 1952.
Batyrev, V., and G. Kaganov. *Organizatsiia i planirovanie denezhnogo obrashcheniia v SSSR* (textbook). Moscow, 1964.
Atlas, Z. V. *Sotsialisticheskaia denezhnaia sistema.* Moscow, 1969. Pages 276–84.
Kaganov, G. V. *Organizatsiia i planirovanie denezhnogo obrashcheniia v SSSR.* Moscow, 1971.   P. P. ROSLIAKOV [11–1509–3]

CASH PLAN OF GOSBANK, a basic form of planning and regulating money circulation in the country; a document defining the main trends of cash movement, the amounts and sources of cash receipts by Gosbank (State Bank), the amounts and intended purposes of cash payments by Gosbank, and changes in the amount of money in circulation. This document is based on the planned volumes and economic significance of the flows of cash in the national economy, which move mainly from socialist enterprises and organizations to the population (income payments to the population) and from the population to the enterprises and organizations (use by the population of its income for buying goods and services).

The cash plan is prepared yearly and quarterly (with a breakdown for each month) according to the nomenclature shown in Table 1.

All sections of the Gosbank system as well as all enterprises, institutions, and organizations that have accounts of payment or

Table 1. The cash plan of the USSR Gosbank

Income	Expenditure
Sales	Wages
Railroad, water, and air transportation revenues	Costs of agricultural state procurements and purchases
Taxes and fees	Payments from kolkhoz accounts
Rent and payments for municipal utilities	Payments from deposits for nonagricultural procurements and other purposes
Local transportation revenues	Loans for individual housing construction, household acquisitions, and pawnbrokers' operations
Revenues to be passed on to kolkhozes	Assistance to enterprises of the Ministry of Communications
Revenues of postal enterprises of the Ministry of Communications	Assistance to savings banks
Savings bank revenues	Pensions, allowances, and insurance indemnities
Revenues of places of entertainment	Allowances for business trips and management-operational expenses
Domestic service revenues	
Revenues to be passed on to housing cooperatives	
Other revenues	
Total	Total
Excess of expenditure over income	Excess of income over expenditure

current accounts with the bank participate in the preparation and execution of the cash plan. The plan is approved by the Council of Ministers of the USSR.

P. P. ROSLIAKOV [11–1510–2]

CASIMIR (Kazimierz). In Poland:

Casimir I the Restorer. Born July 25, 1016; died Oct. 24 (or Nov. 28), 1058. Prince of the Piast dynasty; ruled from 1038 or 1039. Aided by the German emperor Henry III, Casimir I ascended the throne at a time of declining central authority and of a widespread antifeudal peasant movement (1037–38). He pursued a policy of unifying the Polish lands. With the support of Kievan Rus', with which he concluded an alliance about 1039, he obtained the return of Mazovia in 1047; in 1054 he acquired Silesia. Casimir helped to consolidate in Poland a church hierarchy independent of the higher German clergy.

Casimir II the Just. Born 1138; died May 5, 1194. Prince from 1177.

Casimir III the Great. Born Apr. 30, 1310, in the village Kowal, now in Bydgoszcz Województwo; died Nov. 5, 1370, in Kraków. King from 1333; last king of the Piast dynasty.

Casimir III promulgated the Wiślica and Piotrków Statutes in 1346–47, establishing in Poland a limited monarchy. He introduced independent higher courts of German law and forbade Polish cities to carry their judicial appeals to foreign countries. He carried out a monetary reform between 1337 and 1346 that brought about price stabilization and promoted the development of trade. Casimir III ended the struggle with the Teutonic Order by ceding Eastern Pomerania to it. He regained Kujawy for Poland in 1343. With the assistance of Hungary and Bohemia he seized Galician Rus' between 1349 and 1352 and subsequently annexed part of Volynia. Under Casimir III, the University of Kraków was founded (1364).

REFERENCES

Borawska, D. *Kryzys monarchii wczesnopiastowskiej w latach trzydziestych XI w.* Warsaw, 1964.
Sieradzki, J. *Polska wieku XIV: Stadium z czasów Kazimierza Wielkiego.* Warsaw, 1959.   [11–525–5]

CASIQUIARE, a river in southern Venezuela. It measures 410 km long and drains an area of about 45,000 sq km. In its upper course the Casiquiare accepts about one-third of the runoff of the Orinoco River and near the city of San Carlos joins with the Negro River of the Amazon system. The linking of the two largest rivers of South America is a classic example of the bifurcation of rivers. The Casiquiare is joined with the Orinoco through a "canal," a natural channel about 30 km long and with a gradient of up to 5 m, which serves to divert the water from the Orinoco to the Negro River basin. [11–1474–5]

CASONA, ALEJANDRO
(pseudonym of Alejandro Rodríguez Álvarez). Born Mar. 23, 1903, in Besullo, Asturias; died Sept. 24, 1965, in Madrid. Spanish dramatist.

In 1931, Casona organized the National Theater in Madrid and in 1933, founded the Theater of Teaching Missions. From 1939 to 1963 he lived as an émigré in Argentina, where he participated in the Movement of Defenders of Peace. Casona's first plays, *The Siren Who Turned Up on Land* (1934) and *Our Natasha* (1935), are devoted to student life. His plays, imbued with humanism, have close ties with the traditions of popular theater—for example, the lyrical dramas and comedies *Suicide Is Forbidden in Springtime* (1937), *Trees Die Standing* (1949; Russian translation, 1959), *Seven Screams in the Ocean* (1952; Russian translation, 1957), *The Third Word* (1954), and *The Caballero of the Golden Spur* (1965).

WORKS
Obras completas, vols. 1–2. [Madrid; 2nd ed., 1966–67].

REFERENCES
Rodríguez Richart, J. *Vida y teatro de Alejandro Casona*. Oviedo, 1963.
Gurza, E. *La realidad caleidoscópica de Alejandro Casona*. Oviedo, 1968.
[11–1483–4]

CASO Y ANDRADE, ALFONSO.
Born Feb. 1, 1896, in Mexico City; died there Dec. 1, 1970. Mexican archaeologist and ethnologist. Specialist in the history of pre-Columbian cultures and the ethnology of the modern Indian population of Mexico.

From 1949 to 1968, Caso served as director of the Instituto Nacional Indigenista. He conducted excavations of archaeological remains in the state of Oaxaca (Monte Albán, 1931–32 and 1934–35; Mitla, 1934–35) and at other sites.

WORKS
Indigenismo. [Mexico City] 1958. [11–1483–2]

CASPIAN NAVAL FLOTILLA,
the oldest Russian naval flotilla.

It was created by order of Peter I in November 1722 in Astrakhan; it participated in the Persian campaign of 1722–23 and assisted the Russian troops in the capture of Derbent and Baku in 1796 and during Russia's war with Iran of 1804–13. According to the Treaty of Gulistan of 1813, the Caspian Naval Flotilla was to be the only naval flotilla in the Caspian Sea. In 1867, Baku became its main base. As the situation in the Caspian Sea stabilized, the strength of the flotilla was gradually reduced, and by the early 20th century it had two gunboats and several armed steamships.

The sailors of the Caspian Naval Flotilla actively participated in the revolutionary movement in Baku in 1903–05 and in the establishment of Soviet power there in 1917. In April–June 1918 the Astrakhan Krai Military Fleet was formed in Astrakhan to support the troops of the Red Army; in the autumn of 1918 the fleet was reinforced by torpedo boats and submarines sent from the Baltic Sea; on Oct. 13, 1918, it was renamed the Astrakhan-Caspian Naval Flotilla. In August 1918 the ships of the Caspian Naval Flotilla in Baku were seized by the Socialist Revolutionaries' and Mensheviks' counterrevolutionary government formed in August 1918.

In July 1919 the Astrakhan-Caspian Flotilla was combined with the Volga Naval Flotilla and renamed the Volga-Caspian Naval Flotilla. On May 1, 1920, the ships of the flotilla entered Baku, where the Caspian Military Fleet was formed; the fleet was composed of three auxillary cruisers, ten torpedo boats, four submarines, and other vessels. The Red Fleet of Soviet Azerbaijan was at Baku at the same time as the Caspian Fleet. In 1920 both fleets liberated the Caspian Sea from the White Guards.

In July 1920 the Caspian and Azerbaijan fleets were combined into the Naval Forces of the Caspian Sea, which was renamed the Caspian Naval Flotilla on June 27, 1931. In the Great Patriotic War (1941–45) the Caspian Naval Flotilla covered important naval troop transports and the transportation of war matériel and freight, especially during the battle of Stalingrad of 1942–43 and the battle for the Caucasus of 1942–43. The flotilla was awarded the Order of the Red Banner in 1945.

REFERENCES
Boevoi put' Sovetskogo Voenno-Morskogo flota, 2nd ed. Moscow, 1967.
Makovskii, A., and B. Radchenko. *Kaspiiskaia krasnoznamennaia.* Moscow, 1961. V. I. SHLOMA [11–1484–4]

CASPIANS,
tribes of the Ibero-Caucasian group who inhabited the steppe regions of eastern Azerbaijan. They were first mentioned by Herodotus in the fifth century B.C. Their chief occupation was nomadic stock raising. Later (before the first century B.C.), the Caspians merged with the Medes, Albani, and other tribes. The tribes' name was given to the Caspian Sea as well as to one of the regions of ancient Azerbaijan—Caspiana.
[11–1484–2]

CASPIAN SEA
(from the Greek *Kaspion pelagos,* the Latin *Caspium Mare*), the world's largest inland body of water, located on the territory of the USSR (RSFSR, Kazakh SSR, Turkmen SSR, and Azerbaijan SSR) and Iran. The Caspian is frequently considered the largest lake in the world; this is inaccurate, however, since by its size, the nature of its processes, and its developmental history the Caspian is a sea. It received its name from the ancient Caspi tribes who inhabited the eastern part of the Caucasus. Among its other historical names are the Hyrcanian, Khvalyn (Khvaliss), and Khazar seas—also derived from the names of ancient peoples who inhabited its shores.

Physical geographic survey. GENERAL INFORMATION. The Caspian Sea extends almost 1,200 km from north to south, and it has an average width of 320 km and a shoreline of about 7,000 km (including more than 6,000 km within the USSR). Its area is about 371,000 sq km, and its level is 28.5 m below the level of the world ocean (1969). The maximum depth is 1,025 m. In 1929, prior to the considerable drop in the level of the Caspian Sea, its area was 422,000 sq km. The largest gulfs are Kizliar and Komsomolets in the north, Mangyshlak, Kenderli, Kazakh, Kara-Bogaz-Gol, and Krasnovodsk in the east, and Agrakhan and Baku in the west. In the south there are shallow lagoons. The Caspian has up to 50 islands, predominantly small ones (with a total area of about 350 sq km). The most important are Kulaly, Tiulenii, Chechen', Artem, Zhiloi, and Ogurchinskii.

The most important rivers—the Volga, Emba, Ural, and Terek—flow into the northern part of the sea. Their combined annual flow accounts for about 88 percent of all river water entering the Caspian. Large rivers—the Sulak, Samur, and Kura—and a number of smaller ones flow into the sea on the western shore (contributing 7 percent of the inflow). The remaining 5 percent of the inflow comes from the rivers of the Iranian shore (Gorgan, Aras, and Safid). On the eastern shore, including the coast of the Kara-Bogaz-Gol, there is not a single permanent stream.

SHORELINE. The shores of the northern Caspian are low and gently sloping and are characterized by the extensive development of low coastal areas that form as a result of sediments brought in by wind-driven waves. Delta shores have also developed here (the deltas of the Volga, Ural, and Terek). As a whole, the shores of the northern Caspian are growing intensively as a result of the drop in the level of the sea, the rapid growth of the deltas, and the abundant influx of terrigenous material. The western shores of the Caspian are also largely shores of accumulation (with numerous bars and spits), while some areas on the coasts of Dagestan and the Apsheron Peninsula are abrasion shores. The eastern coast consists predominantly of abrasion shores resulting from the cutting away of the limestone of the adjacent semidesert and desert plateaus by the sea. There are also accumulation forms such as the Kara-Bogaz Spit, which separates the largest gulf on the Caspian, Kara-Bogaz-Gol, from the sea, as well as the Krasnovodsk and Kenderli spits. South of the Krasnovodsk Peninsula accumulation shores prevail.

RELIEF. In terms of the character of the relief and the hydrological features, the Caspian Sea is usually divided into the North Caspian, Middle Caspian, and South Caspian. The North Caspian (about 80,000 sq km in area) is the shallowest part of the sea, with depths of 4–8 m. The bottom is formed by a slightly undulating accumulation plain and a series of shoals and accumulation islands, which are known as the Mangyshlak Bank. This bank separates the North Caspian from the Middle Caspian. The Middle Caspian (about 138,000 sq km in area) is divided into the Derbent Basin (maximum depth, 788 m), the shelf, and the continental slope, which is complicated by underwater landslips and canyons. On the gentle northern slope remains of ancient river valleys have been discovered. In the south the basin of the Middle Caspian is separated from the basin of the South Caspian by the Apsheron Bank, on which lie a number of shoals and islands. The South Caspian basin (maximum depth, 1,025 m), which covers about one-third of the area of the sea, has a narrow shelf along the western and southern (Iranian) shores; along the eastern shore the shelf is considerably wider. The bottom of the basin forms a flat abyssal plain. In the northern part of the basin there are several underwater ranges with a northwestern and southeastern strike.

GEOLOGICAL STRUCTURE AND MINERALS. The northern section of the Caspian Sea forms the edge of the Caspian tectonic depression, which is a part of the Eastern European Platform. The Mangyshlak Bank is structurally linked to the underwater Karpinskii swell (which was uplifted during the Hercynian orogeny) on the western shore and the Mangyshlak mountains on the eastern. The bottom of the Middle Caspian has a heterogeneous structure. Its eastern part is a submerged section of the Epihercynian Turan Platform. The Derbent Basin and the western parts of the shelf and the continental slope are the foredeep of the Greater Caucasus Geosyncline. The Apsheron Bank corresponds to one of the branches of recent structures that formed on the subsided folded structures of the Greater Caucasus; it connects the folded structures of the Greater Caucasus with the folded structures of the Kopetdag. The South Caspian is characterized by a suboceanic-type crustal structure, and the granite layer is absent here. Beneath the sedimentary layer, which is up to 25 km thick (this indicates, obviously, the great age of the South Caspian basin), lies a basalt layer up to 15 km thick.

Until the upper Miocene, the Caspian Sea basin was closely connected with the Black Sea in its geological history. After the upper Miocene folding, this link was broken, and the Caspian became a landlocked body of water. The connection with the ocean was reestablished during the upper Pliocene, in the Akchagyl age. During Anthropogenic times, owing to the alternation of glacial and postglacial ages on the East European Plain, the Caspian Sea repeatedly underwent transgressions (Baku, Khazar, and Khvalyn) and regressions. Traces of the transgressions and regressions have survived in the form of terrraces on the seashore as well as in the stratigraphy of the ancient Caspian deposits.

On the shelf there are terrigenous shell sands, coquina, and oolitic sands. The deepwater sections of the floor are covered by aleurite and silt sediments with a high content of calcium carbonate. In certain sections of the floor, bedrock of Neocene age has been exposed. The floor of the Caspian Sea has rich deposits of oil and gas. The Apsheron Bank is oil- and gas-bearing, as are the Dagestan and Turkmen regions of the sea. The areas of the sea floor adjacent to Mangyshlak and the Mangyshlak Bank are promising for oil and gas. The gulf of Kara-Bogaz-Gol contains the richest deposits of chemical raw materials (in particular, mirabilite).

CLIMATE. The chief baric centers that determine atmospheric circulation in the Caspian Sea region are the spur of the Asiatic high-pressure center in the winter and the spurs of the Azores high-pressure and the South Asian low-pressure centers in the summer. The characteristic climatic features are considerable continentality, predominance of anti-cyclonic weather conditions, dry winds, severe frosty winters (particularly in the northern part), sharp temperature fluctuations during the year, and little precipitation (excluding the southwestern part of the sea). Cyclonic activity develops on the atmospheric fronts and is also an important element in the climate and weather on the Caspian. In the northern and middle parts of the Caspian Sea, easterly winds prevail from October through April, and northwesterly winds prevail from May through September. In the southern part of the sea, the monsoon character of the winds is most sharply expressed. The strongest winds are found near the Apsheron Peninsula (the Baku northerly, which blows primarily in the autumn), the eastern shore of the middle section, and the northwestern part of the northern section. Here there are frequent storms during which the wind velocity reaches more than 24 m per sec.

The mean air temperature over many years during the warm months (July and August) over the entire sea is 24°–26°C, with an absolute maximum (up to 44°C) on the eastern coast. During the winter months temperatures range from −10°C in the north to 12°C in the south. Over the sea average annual precipitation is 200 mm, with up to 400 mm on the western coast, 90–100 mm on the arid eastern coast, and up to 1,700 mm on the subtropical southwestern coast. Evaporation from the greater part of the sea surface is very high, reaching 1,000 mm a year; in the eastern part of the South Caspian and near the Apsheron Peninsula it is up to 1,400 mm a year.

HYDROLOGICAL REGIME. A cyclonic circulation of water prevails in the Caspian Sea, and it is caused chiefly by the inflow of rivers and the prevailing winds. Masses of water move from north to south along the western coast toward the Apsheron Peninsula, where the current splits. One branch continues along the western coast; the other branch crosses the Caspian near the Apsheron Bank, and off the eastern coast it joins the waters moving north along that coast from the South Caspian. The circulation in the South Caspian is also cyclonic but is less clearly expressed, and between Baku and the mouth of the Kura River it is complicated by a local anticyclonic circulation. In the North Caspian unstable wind-driven currents of different directions prevail. Their speed is usually 10–15 cm per sec, and during strong winds that coincide with the direction of the currents, the speed can reach 30–40 and even 100 cm per sec. Owing to the frequent occurrence of moderate and strong winds, there is a large number of days with heavy seas. The maximum observed wave height is 11 m near the Apsheron Bank.

During the summer, average water temperature on the surface is 24°–26°C; it is up to 29°C in the south and up to 32°C in Krasnovodsk Gulf. Along the eastern shores the temperature sometimes drops to 10°–12°C in July and August. This phenomenon is due to the driving influence of the winds and the upwelling of deep water. In winter significant temperature contrasts are observed. In the north there are negative temperatures (down to −0.5°C), in the Middle Caspian the temperature is 3°–7°C, and in the South Caspian it is 8°–10°C. The northern part of the sea usually freezes for two or three months, with ice thickness reaching 2 m. In the Middle Caspian individual shallow bays freeze during severe winters. The ice is frequently broken up by the wind and then drifts from the North Caspian south along the western shore. In some years floating ice reaches the Apsheron Peninsula region and is capable of causing significant damage to hydraulic engineering structures in the sea.

The average salinity of the water is 12.7–12.8 ‰ (parts per thousand), with a maximum (excluding Kara-Bogaz-Gol) of up to 13.2 ‰ along the eastern shores and a minimum of 1–2 ‰ in the northwest. Salinity fluctuations over the area of the sea, on the vertical, and in time are insignificant, and only in the north are they more noticeable due to fluctuations in the Volga's drainage. The composition of the salts differs from ordinary sea salt by a greater content of sulfates, calcium carbonate, and magnesium carbonate and by a lower chloride content. This is caused by the influence of the inflow of rivers.

A vertical mixing of the water in the winter takes place throughout the entire vertical section in the North Caspian and a layer of 200–300 m in the deepwater regions; in the summer and autumn the mixing is limited to an upper layer of 15–30 m. During these seasons an intensive thermocline is formed (several degrees per meter) on the lower edge of the upper well-warmed and mixed layer (15–30 m), and this obstructs the spread of heat into the deep layers of the sea.

FLUCTUATIONS IN LEVEL. Brief nonperiodic fluctuations in the level of the Caspian Sea are caused by the winds, and in the north the winds can cause a temporary rise in the level by 2.5–2 m or a drop of up to 2 m. Seiches are observed with a period of from 10 minutes to 12 hours and an amplitude of up to 0.7 m.

Small seasonal fluctuations in the level also occur (about 30 cm).

Over the years and centuries, the level of the Caspian Sea has undergone significant fluctuations which have been caused primarily by changes in the sea's water balance. According to geological, archaeological, historical, and geomorphological data, it has been established that the Caspian Sea had a high level (up to 22 m below sea level) about 4,000 to 6,000 years ago, at the start of the Common Era, and at the beginning of the 19th century (the Neocaspian transgression). It is also known that there was a low level from the seventh through the 11th centuries A.D.(possibly 2–4 m below the present one). The last major drop in the level occurred between 1929 (when the level was at about −26 m) and 1956–57. At present the level fluctuates around the −28.5 m level by not more than several centimeters. The reasons for the latest drop in the level, aside from climatic changes that caused a reduction in the river inflow to the Caspian Sea and an increase in evaporation from its surface, were the hydraulic engineering construction on the Volga (the creation of large man-made reservoirs) and the use of river water for irrigating arid lands and for industrial needs. Another negative factor in the water balance is the flow of Caspian Sea water into Kara-Bogaz-Gol, which is 4 m lower than the Caspian. As a whole, the components of the water balance in 1970 were as follows. The input consisted of 66.8 cu km of precipitation, 266.4 cu km of river inflow, and 5 cu km of subterranean water. The consumption consisted of 357.3 cu km in evaporation, 4 cu km of flow into Kara-Bogaz-Gol, and 1 cu km of seawater used by man. Since the consumption exceeds the input, the water level has dropped by an average of 7 cm a year (over the 1966–67 period). A number of measures have been worked out for preventing a further drop in the sea level. (The level could decline another 2 m by the year 2000.) There are plans to divert the water of northern rivers such as the Vychegda and Pechora into the Volga Basin, which would give the Volga and the Caspian Sea about 32 cu km of water a year more. A plan has also been worked out (1972) for regulating the flow of Caspian waters into Kara-Bogaz-Gol.

FLORA AND FAUNA. The Caspian Sea is poor in terms of the species composition of the flora and fauna, but the biomass is large. The Caspian is inhabited by more than 500 plant and 854 fish and animal species, which are diverse in their origin. Among the plants in the Caspian the blue-green algae and diatoms (for example, *Rhizosolenia*) predominate. Among the recent arrivals are many red and brown algae. *Zostera* and *Ruppia* are the most widely distributed of the flowering marine plants. The algae Charophyta have the greatest biomass (up to 30 kg per sq m of bottom). Most of the fauna originated in Neocene times, and it has undergone great changes owing to the frequent and considerable fluctuations in salinity. This group includes sturgeons, herring, sprats, gobies, and "pugolovka" (*Benthophilus*) of the fish, zebra mussels and cockles of the mollusks, and gammarids, polychaetes, sponges, and one species of jellyfish from the other invertebrates. The Caspian is also inhabited by 15 species that migrated from the arctic and Mediterranean basins. An important group is made up of freshwater organisms (the pike perch of the fish). As a whole, a high degree of endemism is typical. Some organisms have settled in the Caspian quite recently either as a result of being carried in on the bottoms of seagoing vessels (chiefly various growths, for example, mytilaster, the *Rhizosolenia* algae, and barnacles and crabs) or of deliberate acclimatization by man (for example, the gray mullet of the fish and *Nereis* and *Syndesmya* of the invertebrates).

History of exploration. Documentary evidence concerning the acquaintance of Russians with the Caspian Sea and their voyages across it dates to the ninth and tenth centuries (ancient Arabic, Armenian, and Iranian manuscripts). Regular exploration of the Caspian Sea was begun by Peter I, upon whose initiative an expedition under the leadership of A. Bekovich-Cherkasskii was organized in 1714–15. In particular, Bekovich-Cherkasskii studied the eastern coast of the Caspian. In the 1720's, I. F. Soimonov began to conduct hydrographic research in the Caspian, and, during the second half of the 18th century, this research was continued by I. V. Tokmachev and M. I. Voinovich. At the beginning of the 19th century further research was carried out by Kolodkin, who was the first to make an instrumental compass

survey of the shores. In the middle of the 19th century a detailed hydrographic instrumental survey of the Caspian Sea was made under the leadership of N. A. Ivashintsev. The maps made as a result of these surveys served as the basis for the subsequent publications of maritime charts for the Caspian up to the 1930's.

In the 19th century major contributions to studying the natural conditions of the Caspian Sea were made by the scientists P. S. Pallas, S. G. Gmelin, G. S. Karelin, K. M. Baer, G. V. Abich, O. A. Grim, N. I. Andrusov, and I. B. Shpindler. In 1897 the Astrakhan Scientific Research Station (presently the Institute of Caspian Fisheries) was founded. In 1866, 1904, 1912–13, and 1914–15 expeditionary research on the hydrology and hydrobiology of the Caspian was carried out under the leadership of N. M. Knipovich. This work was continued after 1917 by the Caspian Expedition of the Academy of Sciences of the USSR, which was also led by Knipovich.

In the first decade after the October Revolution, the research of the Soviet geologists I. M. Gubkin, D. V. Golubiatnikov, V. D. Golubiatnikov, P. A. Pravoslavlev, V. P. Baturin, and S. A. Kovalevskii played an important role in the study of the geological structure of and presence of oil on the Apsheron Peninsula as well as the geological history of the Caspian Sea. At this time, B. A. Appolov, V. V. Valedinskii, K. P. Voskresenskii, and L. S. Berg made significant contributions to studying the water balance of and the fluctuations in the level of the Caspian.

After the Great Patriotic War of 1941–45 comprehensive systematic research was started on the Caspian Sea. It aimed at studying the hydrometeorological regime, biological conditions, and the geological structure of the sea. Among the institutions taking part in this research were Moscow State University, the Institute of Geography of the Academy of Sciences of the Azerbaijan SSR, the State Institute of Oceanography, the observatories of the Hydrometeorological Service, the Institute for Geology and Exploitation of Combustible Minerals (IGIRGI) of the Academy of Sciences of the USSR, the Institute of Geophysics of the Academy of Sciences of the USSR, the Aeromethods Laboratory and the All-Union Geophysics Scientific Research Institute of the Ministry of Geology of the USSR, the Caspian Institute for Sturgeon Fisheries, and other scientific institutions of the republic academies of sciences and ministries.

Economic and geographic survey. The Caspian Sea has long been famous as a region where valuable types of fish can be caught—in particular sturgeons (82 percent of the world catch) and herring, as well as freshwater fish (bream, pike perch, Caspian roach, and wild carp). As a result of the drop in the sea level (which has led to the disappearance of valuable spawning grounds) and the controlling of the flow of the Volga, Kura, and Araks rivers (which has worsened conditions for the breeding of diadromous and semidiadromous fish), the quantity and the catch primarily of the valuable types of fish (herring and sturgeons) have sharply declined. In 1936 the gross catch was about 500,000 tons, and in 1956 it was 461,000 tons (21,500 and 15,000 tons of sturgeons, 197,000 and 18,000 for the roach, and 55,000 and 8,400 for the pike perch, respectively). The comparatively slight decline in the gross catch can be explained by a sharp increase in the catch of less valuable fish, mainly sprats. Owing to the decline in the number of sturgeons, work is being done to breed and replenish the valuable types of fish. In the North Caspian, seals are also hunted.

In 1924 oil began to be produced in Il'ich Bay (near Baku) for the first time, but output increased particularly after the Great Patriotic War of 1941–45. Petroleum is produced offshore from derricks (Neftianye Kamni) and man-made islands. The main regions are Apsheron and Sangachaly Raion on the western coast and Cheleken on the eastern. The offshore oil fields produce more than 50 percent of the total oil produced in the Azerbaijan SSR. The mining of sodium sulfate, mirabilite, and epsomite in the Kara-Bogaz-Gol region is also of great economic significance.

Owing to the ever increasing need for fresh water, units for desalinizing seawater have appeared on the Caspian Sea. The largest of them (for obtaining fresh water for industry and everyday needs in nearby desert and semidesert regions) are being built (1972) in the towns of Shevchenko and Krasnovodsk.

The Caspian Sea is of great importance for transportation, both domestically and in commerce with foreign countries. The main cargoes transported over the Caspian are oil, lumber, grain, cotton, rice, and sulfate. The most important ports are Astrakhan, Baku, Makhachkala, Krasnovodsk, and Shevchenko. They are also connected by regular passenger runs. Sea-rail ferries operate between Baku and Krasnovodsk. A ferry service is also planned (1972) between Makhachkala and Shevchenko. In Iran the main ports are Bandar-e Pahlavi and Bandar-e Shah.

REFERENCES

Kolebaniia urovnia Kaspiiskogo moria. Moscow, 1956.
Fedorov, P. V. *Stratigrafiia chetvertichnykh otlozhenii i istoriia razvitiia Kaspiiskogo moria.* Moscow, 1957.
Geologicheskoe stroenie podvodnogo sklona Kaspiiskogo moria. Moscow, 1962.
Materialy Vsesoiuznogo soveshchaniia po probleme Kaspiiskogo moria. Baku, 1963.
Zenkevich, L. A. *Biologiia morei SSSR.* Moscow, 1963.
Leont'ev, O. K., and A. I. Khalilov. *Prirodnye usloviia formirovaniia beregov Kaspiiskogo moria.* Baku, 1965.
Pakhomova, A. S., and B. M. Zatuchnaia. *Gidrokhimiia Kaspiiskogo moria.* Leningrad, 1966.
Geologiia neftianykh i gazovykh mestorozhdenii Azerbaidzhana. Moscow, 1966.
Kaspiiskoe more. Moscow, 1969.
Kompleksnye issledovaniia Kaspiiskogo moria: Sb. statei, fasc. 1. Moscow, 1970.
Giul', K. K., T. N. Lappalainen, and V. A. Polushkin. *Kaspiiskoe more.* Moscow, 1970.
Giul', K. K., P. V. Zhilo, and V. M. Zhirnov. *Bibliograficheskii annotirovannyi spravochnik po Kaspiiskomu moriu.* Baku, 1970.

K. K. GIUL' and O. K. LEONT'EV [11-1485-3]

CASPIAN SEAL (*Phoca caspica*), a mammal of the family Phocidae of the order Pinnipedia. It measures 120–148 cm long and weighs 30–60 kg. The color of the body varies highly with each individual and changes with age: from white in the newborn to yellow and grayish brown with brown and dark spots in the adults. The Caspian seal lives only in the Caspian Sea. In the fall it migrates to the northern part of the sea where it gathers in large numbers on ice (breeding ground), gives birth, and molts. In the spring it returns to the south. It feeds primarily on trash fish. The Caspian seal is important in the seal-hunting industry (its fur, hide, and fat are used). Because of unrestrained trapping (about 100,000 animals per year), its numbers have declined. There are an estimated 600,000 seals remaining (1970).

[11-1485-2]

CASSADÓ, GASPAR. Born Sept. 30, 1897, in Barcelona; died Dec. 24, 1966, in Madrid. Spanish cellist and composer.

Cassadó first studied with his father, Joaquín Cassadó, the organist, conductor, and composer. At the age of seven he began to learn the cello under D. March in Barcelona, and he gave his first public performance at the age of nine. Between 1908 and 1914, Cassadó lived in Paris; in 1910 he became a pupil of P. Casals. He was influenced by Debussy, Ravel, and de Falla.

Cassadó began his successful tours of the musical capitals of the world in 1918 and continued giving concerts until his death. He settled in Florence in 1934; in 1947 he began giving master classes at the Chigiana Academy in Siena (Italy) and in 1958 at the school of music in Cologne. In 1962 and in 1966 he was a jury member at the International Tchaikovsky Competition. He toured the USSR in 1963 and 1965.

Cassadó composed a number of works, chiefly for cello solo, for cello and piano, and for string ensemble. Among his many transcriptions is a cello concerto based on piano pieces by Tchaikovsky. [11-1468-1]

CASSANDER. Born circa 355 B.C.; died circa 298 B.C. Macedonian general and statesman. King of Macedonia from 306 until his death. Son of Antipater.

After his father's death in 319, Cassander rebelled against Polyperchon, who had been appointed regent by Antipater. In 317, Cassander restored the oligarchy in Athens. In 316 he and the other *diadochi* waged war against Antigonus I. The mother (316) and later the widow and son (309) of Alexander the Great were murdered on Cassander's orders. By the terms of the peace treaty among the *diadochi* in 311, Cassander was recognized as the ruler of Macedonia, and in 306 he took the royal title.

[11-1495-4]

CASSANDRA, in ancient Greek mythology, the daughter of the Trojan king Priam and Hecuba.

Captivated by Cassandra's beauty, the god Apollo endowed her with the gift of prophecy. But after she rejected him, Apollo decreed that no one would believe her prophecies. The Trojans, in particular, did not heed the words of Cassandra, who cautioned Paris against abducting Helen, an act that triggered the Trojan War. After the capture of Troy by the Greeks, Agamemnon took Cassandra captive; she died with him at the hands of his wife, Clytemnestra.

Figuratively, the term "Cassandra's prophecies" means gloomy predictions that are mistrusted by listeners.

[11-1495-5]

CASSATION, the appeal or protest to a higher court of court judgments and sentences that have not taken legal effect, and the consideration by the higher court of appeals and protests with the aim of verifying the legality and grounds of judgments and sentences.

In the USSR, the courts of cassation above raion (city) people's courts are oblast courts and other courts of equal standing, supreme courts of ASSR's and, in Union republics not subdivided into oblasts, the supreme courts of Union republics. Judgments of the supreme court of an ASSR or of oblast courts and other courts of equal standing in their capacity as courts of original jurisdiction are appealed to the Supreme Court of the Union republic. Sentences of military tribunals are appealed to military tribunals of the various armed services, military districts, army groups, fleets, and separate armies; the judgments of military tribunals of this higher category are appealed to the Military Collegium of the Supreme Court of the USSR.

In criminal cases, the prisoner, his defense counsel and legal representative, and the victim and his representative have the right of cassation complaint. A person acquitted by a court may bring a complaint against a sentence with respect to the reasons and grounds for acquittal. A civil plaintiff, a civil defendant, and their representatives may bring a complaint against a judgment with respect to the part of the judgment that relates to civil claims. In civil cases the plaintiff, the defendant, and other persons involved in the case have the right to bring a complaint. The public procurator is obliged to lodge a protest against any illegal unjustified judgment or decision. The judgments and sentences of all courts may be appealed, except judgments and sentences of the Supreme Court of the USSR and of the Supreme Court of a Union republic. Cases in courts of cassation are considered by panels consisting of three members of the court.

In considering a case, the court of cassation is not bound by the limits of the complaint or protest and must verify the case in full with respect to all the persons convicted (all the parties in a civil case), including those who have not brought a complaint against the sentence or the judgment or those with respect to whom no protest has been entered.

The court of cassation may uphold a sentence or judgment without any change, may vacate a sentence or judgment (in full or in part) and refer the case for a new investigation or a new court hearing, may vacate a sentence or judgment (in full or in part) and terminate the case, or may change a sentence or judgment. In civil cases a court of cassation may render a new decision without referring the case for a new hearing if the circumstances of the case were fully and correctly established by the court of original jurisdiction but an error was committed in the application of the norms of the law. A sentence may be vacated on the grounds that a law for a more serious crime ought to have been applied or because too lenient a sentence has been imposed only in those instances when the public procurator has entered a complaint or the victim submitted an appeal on these grounds. A judgment of acquittal may be vacated only on complaint of a procurator or on appeal of a victim or of a person acquitted by the court.

The instructions of the court of cassation, insofar as they relate to ensuring the completeness of investigation of the circumstances of a case, are binding during supplementary investigation and the reexamination of the case in court. However, the court of cassation has no right to consider as proved facts that were not established in the sentence or judgment or were rejected by the sentence or judgment. It has no right to predetermine questions of whether the criminal charge or claim has been proved, questions of the authenticity of evidence, questions of the superiority of some evidence over other, or questions of the extent of punishment or the amount of recovery.

In foreign socialist countries the functions of the courts of cassation are performed by regional courts (Czechoslovakia, Hungary, and Rumania), district courts (Bulgaria and the German Democratic Republic), and *województwo* courts (Poland). The supreme courts of these countries function as courts of cassation with respect to sentences and judgments of the courts given above in those instances when the latter consider cases in their capacity as trial courts.

The institution of cassation originated in France at the end of the 18th century, during the bourgeois revolution. Cassation in bourgeois law differs fundamentally from the cassation in the USSR. The bourgeois process is characterized by pure cassation, that is, the challenge of a sentence solely on formal grounds (violations of substantive and procedural law). The reviewing court may not consider the merits of the case; it may vacate a judgment but may not change it.

In most bourgeois countries, appeals from decisions of lower courts are taken to courts of appeal. In Great Britain the court of criminal appeal is the Court of Queen's Bench, but appeal is permitted only on grounds of an incorrect application of the law. In France, the Court of Cassation is the highest judicial instance for criminal and civil cases. I. D. PERLOV [11–1495–8]

CASSATION, a multipart entertaining musical work for instrumental ensemble, performed during various ceremonial festivities (usually outdoors). It frequently begins and ends with a march. Related to the serenade, divertimento, and nocturne, the cassation was popular in 18th-century Austria and Germany. Haydn and Mozart composed several cassations. [11–1497–1]

CASSEGRAIN ANTENNA (named for the 17th-century French physicist N. Cassegrain), a reflecting antenna that consists of a radiator and primary and secondary (auxiliary) electromagnetic energy reflectors (mirrors) assembled according to the scheme of a Cassegrain telescope. The Cassegrain antenna is widely used in radio communications, radar, and radio astronomy in the centimeter wavelength band.

The primary reflector, which is a paraboloid of revolution, determines the width of the directivity pattern of the Cassegrain antenna and forms a plane front of the radiated electromagnetic wave. A radiator, usually a horn, dielectric, helical, or dipole antenna, is located at the vertex of the primary reflector; such an arrangement significantly reduces the length of the lines feeding energy from the transmitter to the radiator. The auxiliary reflector, of smaller diameter, is a hyperboloid of revolution, one focus of which coincides with the focus of the primary reflector, and the second with the phase center of the radiator. A radiator with a directivity pattern of special shape and a low level of fringe radiation is used to reduce the dissipation of electromagnetic energy beyond the edges of the auxiliary reflector.
O. N. TERESHIN and G. K. GALIMOV [11–1498–1]

CASSEGRAIN REFLECTOR SYSTEM, a type of reflector. In the Cassegrain system the image of a heavenly body is formed behind the primary parabolic mirror by the rays of light directed through an opening in it by means of a secondary convex hyperbolic mirror. The system was proposed by the French physicist N. Cassegrain in 1672. [11–1498–2]

CASSEL, GUSTAV. Born Oct. 20, 1866; died Jan. 15, 1945. Swedish economist, belonging to the mathematical school of bourgeois political economy.

Cassel received a mathematics degree at the University of Uppsala in 1895 and was a professor of political economy and finance at the University of Stockholm from 1904 to 1933. Cassel's views were eclectic. In opposition to the labor theory of value, Cassel proposed a distorted and oversimplified conception of price based on the principle of scarcity of utilities, interpreting money circulation, wages, and economic crises in the light of this conception.

WORKS
Theoretische Sozialökonomie. Leipzig, 1918.
The Theory of Social Economy. London, 1932.
On Quantitative Thinking in Economics. Oxford, 1935.
In Russian translation:
Mirovaia denezhnaia problema. Moscow, 1922.
Osnovnye idei teoreticheskoi ekonomii. Moscow, 1929. [11–1498–3]

CASSEL, a city in the medieval county of Flanders, now in France. During the Flemish Uprising of 1323–28, near Cassel on Aug. 23, 1328, the rebellious Flemish burghers and peasants fought a decisive battle with the French king Philip VI of Valois and the Flemish count Louis of Nevers. The rebel troops were crushed, ending the rebellion and unleashing cruel reprisals by the victorious feudal lords. [11–1498–5]

CASSETTE, TAPE, a device in the form of a sealed flat box containing a magnetic tape.

The tape cassette is inserted into a tape recorder and the tape transport mechanism puts the tape in motion. The cassette is coupled with the other functional parts of the tape recorder through small windows in the housing. The device protects the tape from accidental damage, and it is simple to use and convenient to store.

The cassettes in use contain either one or two rolls of closed-loop or free-loop tape. Wide-tape cassettes are used in video tape machines. [11–1499–2]

CASSETTE MOTION PICTURES, various systems for showing motion pictures on the screen of an ordinary television receiver by means of an attachment in which a cassette or disk with a recording of the motion-picture film is placed. Cassette films are promising for educational purposes, for individual rentals, and for the making of various motion pictures in the home (in any place where there is a television receiver).

Cassette motion-picture apparatus is arranged as follows: The image and sound are recorded on a disk or on a tape (motion-picture film, magnetic tape, and so on) that is wound in a special cassette. The cassette or disk is then placed in special apparatus (the attachment for the television receiver) that converts the image and sound into video signals and the associated audio signals, respectively. Several cassette systems are known at the present time (1973).

Super 8 system. The initial material in the Super 8 system is motion pictures made on Super 8 film or obtained by printing on it from 35-mm or 16-mm film. The film, with silent or sound movies, is wound in a standard cassette with a capacity of 20 to 120 m, which is then placed in the television receiver attachment (a television film scanner). The video signals produced by the attachment are fed to the input of the television receiver, and the viewer sees the images on its screen. This system also makes it possible to show the films by means of a motion-picture projector on an ordinary reflecting or transparent screen.

Electronic Video Recorder system (EVR). The essence of the EVR system is the production by means of an electron beam in a vacuum of a recording on special 8.75-mm motion picture film from positive images on 35-mm or 16-mm film, from a video recording on magnetic tape, or from a video camera. After the negative has been developed, a positive copy is obtained from the negative by a special contact printing method. The image of black-and-white film is arranged in two lines; the image of color film is in a single line. The sound is recorded on a magnetic track. A cassette loaded with black-and-white film is designed to be shown by means of the attachment for a period of 60 min (2 × 30 min); a cassette loaded with color film, 30 min. This system is intended only for the reproduction of professionally produced motion-picture films.

Selectavision. In the Selectavision system the original black-and-white or color image is recorded by means of a laser in the form of holograms on a special film. A nickel matrix that contains the hologram's pattern is made for each hologram by the electrolytic method. About 1,000 copies may be produced on a thin, transparent 16-mm vinyl tape from one matrix film. The tape is then wound into a cassette, and its images are reproduced by means of a laser and transformed into a video signal in the television receiver attachment. The maximum showing time of the film (from one cassette) is 60 min. The system is intended only for the reproduction of professionally produced programs.

Video and audio recording and reproduction with magnetic tape. A system for video and audio recording and reproduction with magnetic tape consists of a portable video tape recorder, a small television camera, and a special unit for recording television programs, which makes possible simultaneous viewing of one program and recording of another. The image and sound are recorded on magnetic tape 19.05, 12.7, or 6.25 mm wide and can be used repeatedly (up to 30 times). To reproduce the video recording, the video tape recorder is connected to the input of any television receiver. Playback lasts 25–60 min. This system cannot only reproduce a purchased or rented television program but also record it under amateur (semiprofessional) conditions.

Video and audio recording and reproduction with a flexible plastic disk. In one system using a flexible plastic disk the television receiver is connected to special apparatus, similar to a phonograph, that uses a thin foil disk 210 or 300 mm in diameter with a mechanical recording (like the recording on a phonograph record) of the image and sound. The duration of a film showing is 5 or 12 min. The image and sound are reproduced from the video disk, which rotates at 1,500 rpm, by an electromechanical method in the special phonograph when it is connected to any television receiver. The motion pictures may be reproduced from a disk as many as 1,000 times.

Another system, proposed by the Philips company, is based on a contactless optical reading method. The recording is done on a plate resembling a phonograph record with a succession of microscopic elongated depressions of identical depth and width but differing in length and spacing from one another. These differences encode the data on the sound and on the brightness and chromaticity of the image. A laser beam plays the role of the needle in the video phonograph. On one such video record, which is the same size as the ordinary long-playing phonograph record, there are no less than 45,000 motion-picture frames. A showing of such a motion picture lasts 30–45 min. Such systems cannot be used to make image recordings independently.

REFERENCES

Tel'nov, N. I. "Novye metody zapisi-vosproizvedeniia tsvetnykh televizionnykh izobrazhenii." *Tekhnika kino i televideniia,* 1971, no. 5.
Sakmari, L. "Novoe v oblasti audiovizual'noi tekhniki." *Tekhnika kino i televideniia,* 1971, no. 9.
Rot, V. "Novaia sistema mekhanicheskoi zapisi izobrazhenii na videoplastinkakh." *Tekhnika kino i televideniia,* 1971, no. 9.

V. I. USHAGINA [11–1500–1]

CASSIA (also known as senna), a genus of perennial herbs, shrubs, or small trees of the family Leguminosae. The leaves are compound, even-pinnate, with five to ten pairs of narrow leaflets. The flowers are yellow (more rarely, white or reddish) and are gathered into racemes. Although they are irregular, their petals are almost identical in size. There are ten stamens—three are often reduced. There are approximately 500–600 species, distributed primarily in the tropics and subtropics of both hemispheres (particularly in America).

Several species are used in medicine, including *Cassia angustifolia* (native to western Arabia), *C. acutifolia* (native to mountainous regions of the Sudan, cultivated in the USSR in Middle Asia and Kazakhstan), and *C. obovata* (native to Sudan; cultivated in Transcaucasia, Krasnodar Krai, and the southern Ukraine). They are the source of Alexandrian leaf. Senna leaves, the leaves of *C. acutifolia,* contain anthraglycosides, which act as a cathartic when taken internally. They are used in the form of an infusion, as a cathartic tea (black draft). Senna leaves are

a component of the complex powder of licorice root. In the USSR, *C. angustifolia* and *C. acutifolia* are cultivated as annuals on irrigated lands in southern Kazakhstan and Middle Asia.

In order to develop normally, cassia needs a sunny exposure and warmth. It grows best in loose nonsaline, loamy soils with deep ground water. Cassia should be planted in soil from which pasture crops have been harvested. Before planting, immediate fall plowing is done, with preliminary irrigation. During plowing, manure (20–30 tons per hectare) or compost with superphosphate (3 centners/ha) is applied. Early in spring the field is harrowed, and the soil is leveled. The field is sown (8 kg/ha); the width between the rows of seeds is 60–70 cm. During the period of growth and development (the phase of blooming and branching), the plants are fed ammonium sulfate and superphosphate and irrigated five or six times. When a yellowish tint appears on the lower leaves, harvesting is begun. The second, or principal, gathering of leaves occurs after 20–25 days. The leaves are dried in shade or sun. The yield of air-dried leaves and fruits is 8–10 centners/ha.

[11–1508–3]

CASSINI, GIOVANNI DOMENICO (Jean Dominique Cassini). Born June 8, 1625, in Perinaldo; died Sept. 14, 1712, in Paris. Astronomer. An Italian by birth. Member of the Paris Academy of Sciences (1669). Director of the Paris Observatory (from 1669).

Cassini discovered the rotation of Jupiter (1665) and Mars (1666), four new satillites of Saturn (1671–84), and the division of Saturn's rings into an inner ring and an outer ring by a dark gap (the Cassini division). He also investigated the optical liberation of the moon. Cassini made the first reliable determination of the sun's parallax from joint observations of Mars with the French astronomer J. Richer (9.5″–10.0″; modern value, 8.8″).

[11–1505–1]

CASSINI, JACQUES. Born Feb. 18, 1677, in Paris; died Apr. 15, 1756, in Thury, near Clermont. French astronomer and geodesist. Member of the Paris Academy of Sciences (1694). Director of the Paris Observatory (from 1712). Son of G. D. Cassini.

Cassini was one of the participants in the measurement of the great arc of the Paris meridian (at the end of the 17th century and beginning of the 18th century). He was the first to carry out measurement of the angle of a parallel (1734). In the controversy about the shape of the earth, he supported for a long time the erroneous viewpoint that the earth is elongated along its axis of rotation.

[11–1505–2]

CASSIODORUS (Flavius Magnus Aurelius Cassiodorus Senator). Born circa 487 at Scyllacium, in Calabria; died circa 578 at Vivarium. Writer and statesman of the Ostrogothic state.

Cassiodorus was a retainer of Theodoric and his successors. He favored rapprochement between the Ostrogoths and the Romans. In his old age he became a monk and founded the monastery of Vivarium, which became one of the centers of early medieval culture, on his estate on the western shore of the Gulf of Taranto. He wrote the 12-book *History of the Goths,* which has survived in Jordanes' abridged version. Cassiodorus also composed several works on the history of the church and the *Variae* —collections of letters, rescripts, and the like—which are an important source for the history of the Goths.

WORKS

In *Monumenta Germaniae historica: Auctorum antiquissimorum,* vols. 11–12. Berlin, 1894.
In *Patrologiae latina,* vol. 69. Paris, 1865.

[11–1505–4]

CASSIOPEIA, a constellation of the northern sky. Its brightest stars ϵ, δ, γ, α, and β, which form a figure W, have brightnesses of 3.4, 2.7, 2.4, 2.2, and 2.3 visual stellar magnitudes, respectively. In 1572 a supernova flared up in the constellation. The most powerful known source of radio emission originates from the constellation, which is located in the Milky Way. The best conditions for observing it are from September to November. It is visible the year round everywhere in the USSR. It is named for Cassiopeia, in ancient Greek mythology the wife of the Ethiopian king Cepheus and the mother of Andromeda.

[11–1505–6]

CASSIRER, ERNST. Born July, 28, 1874, in Breslau, now Wrocław; died Apr. 13, 1945, in New York. German idealist philosopher, representative of the Marburg school of neo-Kantianism.

Cassirer was a professor (1919–33) and rector (1930–33) at the University of Hamburg. After 1933, Cassirer lived in exile: in Oxford (Great Britain), in Göteborg (Sweden) from 1935 to 1941, and in the USA from 1941 until his death.

At the start of his career Cassirer studied the philosophical problems of natural science and elaborated a theory of concepts, or "functions"; after 1920 he created an original philosophy of culture. Following the lead of H. Cohen and P. Natorp, Cassirer eliminated from the Kantian system the concept of the "thing-in-itself" as one of the two factors (the other being the subject of cognition) that create the world of "experience"; material for the construction of experience ("multiformity") is created in Cassirer's system by thought itself. Accordingly, space and time cease to be perceptions (as they were in Kant) and are transformed into concepts. Instead of the two Kantian worlds, there exists a single world, the "world of culture"; ideas of reason, like categories, become constitutive instead of regulative, that is, they are the principles that create the world. Cassirer terms these principles "symbolic functions," inasmuch as they represent the highest values and are connected with the "divine" in man.

The diverse fields of culture, termed "symbolic forms" (language, myth, religion, art, science) are regarded by Cassirer as independent formations, irreducible to each other. Cassirer's philosophy of culture also determined his idealistic conception of man as a "symbol-creating animal." He is the author of several books on the history of philosophy, on G. von Leibniz, I. Kant, R. Descartes, and the philosophies of the Renaissance and the Enlightenment. Cassirer's ideas, especially his theory of "symbolic forms," was a decisive influence on the Warburg school's studies of cultural history.

WORKS

Das Erkenntnisproblem in der Philosophie und Wissenschaft der neueren Zeit, vols. 1–4. Berlin, 1906–57.
Freiheit und Form. Berlin, 1916.
Philosophie der symbolischen Formen, vols. 1–3. Berlin, 1923–29.
An Essay on Man. New Haven, Conn.–London [1945.]
The Myth of the State. London, 1946.
Zur modernen Physik. Oxford, 1957.
In Russian translation:
Poznanie i deistvitel'nost'. St. Petersburg, 1912.
Teoriia otnositel'nosti Einshteina. Petrograd, 1922.

REFERENCES

Buczyńska, H.*Cassirer.* Warsaw, 1963.
Ernst Cassirer. Edited by P. A. Schilpp. Berlin, 1966. (Contains a bibliography.)   A. A. KRAVCHENKO   [11–1506–1]

CASSITERITE (or tinstone), a mineral with the chemical composition SnO_2. Theoretically it contains 78.62 percent Sn but usually includes impurities of Nb, Ta, Zr, Sc, W, and Fe; thus, the Sn content varies within 68–78 percent.

Cassiterite crystallizes in the tetragonal system, forming prismatic or dipyramidal crystals. Geniculated twins are characteristic. The crystalline structure is analogous to that of rutile. Cassiterite is usually encountered in the form of small and large crystals, drusoid aggregates, or compact granular masses as well as in the form of cryptocrystalline, colloform segregations, concretions, and sinter formations. The color is dark brown, almost black, yellow with a reddish brown cast; nearly colorless varieties are also known. Cassiterite has an adamantine luster, a hardness of 6–7 on the mineralogical scale, and a density of 6,040–7,120 kg/m³ (lowest in light-colored cassiterite).

The deposits are usually genetically linked with granitic rocks. The most interesting commercial accumulations of the mineral are characteristic for hydrothermal quartz-cassiterite and sulfide-cassiterite veins. Cassiterite is stable in zones of oxidation and surface weathering; with the destruction of primary deposits, it accumulates in placers. In the USSR, cassiterite deposits

are found in the northeast in Primor'e, in Middle Asia, and in the Kazakh SSR. Abroad, it is found in Malaysia, Thailand, Indonesia, the People's Republic of China, Bolivia, Nigeria, and elsewhere. Cassiterite is the chief ore for obtaining tin.

A. B. PAVLOVSKII   [11–1507–2]

CASSIUS LONGINUS, GAIUS. Year of birth unknown; died 42 B.C. in Philippi. Roman military and political figure. From the plebeian Cassius family. Tribune of the plebeians in 49, praetor in 44.

Cassius fought in the Parthian campaign of M. Licinius Crassus in 53. In the civil war of 49–45 he joined the side of Pomey, but after the battle of Pharsalus (48) he left this side and was pardoned by Caesar. In 44 he was one of the organizers of the assassination of Caesar. On orders of the Senate, Cassius fought a war against Dolabella, Caesar's proconsul in Syria. After the formation of the second triumvirate in 43, Cassius allied himself with M. Brutus against the triumvirs. He committed suicide after being defeated in the battle of Philippi (42).

[11–1503–2]

CASSOLA, CARLO. Born Mar. 17, 1917, in Rome. Italian writer.

Cassola's first collections of stories were published in 1941 and 1942. The resistance movement, to which he belonged, is the subject of his novel *Fausto and Anna* (1952). His most famous novellas are *Old Comrades* (1953; Russian translation, 1965), depicting the life and struggle of a group of Communist members of the underground during the years of fascism and the resistance, and *The Felling of the Forest* (published 1953; Russian translation, 1958), in which Cassola shows his hero at his work and in unity with nature. The novel *Bubo's Girl* looks at the resistance in the light of postwar problems. Cassola moved away from sociopolitical themes to focus on the feelings of his characters in his more recent works (*The Arid Heart,* 1961; *Memorable Times,* 1966; and *Fear and Sadness,* 1970).

WORKS

Un matrimonio del dopoguerra. Turin, 1957.
Una relazione. Turin, 1969.
In Russian translation:
"Babá." In *Ital'ianskaia novella XX veka.* Moscow, 1969.

REFERENCES

Potapova, Z. M. *Neorealizm v ital'ianskoi literature.* Moscow, 1961.
Macchioni, Jodi R. *Cassola.* Florence, 1967. (Bibliography, pp. 117–26.)
    G. D. BOGEMSKII   [11–1511–1]

CASSONE, a type of wooden chest popular in Italy during the Middle Ages and the Renaissance. Its front and side walls were decorated with gilded and red stucco, carvings, and paintings (usually of a secular character). Such eminent artists as Botticelli and Uccello worked on cassoni. In the late 15th century architectural influence in its trimming increased: the sides were often divided into panels with carving and intarsia.

REFERENCES

Faenson, L. "Ital'ianskie svadebnye sunduki."*Dekorativnoe iskusstvo SSSR,* 1967, no.1.
Schubring, P. *Cassone.* Leipzig, 1923.   [11–1511–2]

CASSOU, JEAN. Born July 9, 1897, in Deusto near Bilbao, Spain. French writer. Son of an engineer.

Cassou received a literature degree in Paris. He has published research in music, literature, and fine art, particularly Spanish. In his novel *The Bloody Days of Paris* (1935; Russian translation, 1937), which deals with the Paris Commune of 1871, Cassou focused on the revolutionary proletarian struggle from a historical perspective. A member of the French Resistance, Cassou wrote *Thirty-Three Sonnets, Written in Prison* (1944), filled with both anguish and hope. His novel *The Center of the World* (1939; published 1945) depicts the period from the eve of World War I to World War II. Cassou is a steadfast opponent of imperialism and reaction.

WORKS
Grandeur et infamie de Tolstoï. Paris [1932].
Le Livre de Lazare. Paris, 1955.
La Clef des songes. Lausanne [1964].
Le Voisinage des cavernes. Paris [1971].
In Russian translation:
"Zh. Kassu o povesti V. Poznera 'Ispaniia—pervaia liubov'.' " *Inno-strannaia literatura,* 1967, no. 11.
REFERENCES
Istoriia frantsuzskoi literatury, vol. 4. Moscow, 1963.
Georgel, P. *J. Cassou . . . Choix de textes: Bibliographie portrait, fac-similé.* Paris, 1967. (*Poètes d'aujourd'hui.*)

L. T. BELUGINA [11–1511–3]

CASTAGNINO, JUAN CARLOS. Born Nov. 18, 1908, in Mar del Plata; died Apr. 21, 1972, in Buenos Aires. Argentine painter and graphic artist.

Castagnino studied at the National College of Art in Buenos Aires (1929–34) and worked in Italy, France, and Spain (1938–40). He was a neorealist; in the 1930's and 1940's he worked with such artists as D. Siqueiros and A. Berni on monumental murals depicting contemporary life and the history of the Argentine people. He did murals for the Gallery of Peace (1945), the Paris Gallery (*Man—Cosmos—Hope,* 1959), the Obelisk Gallery (*As the Street Comes to Life,* 1961) and other public buildings in Buenos Aires. Castagnino's works depict the people's struggle for their rights.   [11–1513–2]

CASTAGNO, ANDREA DEL. Born circa 1421, in Castagno, Tuscany; died Aug. 19, 1457, in Florence. Early Renaissance Italian painter. Representative of the democratic tendency in Florentine art during the mid-15th century.

Castagno was initially influenced by Masaccio, Donatello, and Paolo Uccello. He worked primarily in Florence. In 1442 he worked in Venice, and there is some evidence that in 1454 he worked in Rome. Between 1445 and 1457, Castagno painted the series of frescoes *Famous Men and Women,* which included portraits of Dante, Boccaccio, Petrarch, and the *condottiere* Pippo Spano, in the monastery of Santa Apollonia in Florence (now in the Castagno Museum). His work is characterized by resounding colors and fluid, energetic modeling of forms. An intense expressiveness of pose and foreshortening imparts dramatic poignancy to his works. Castagno painted the frescoes *The Trinity* (Church of the Annunciation, Florence, 1454–55) and *The Last Supper* (Castagno Museum, 1445–57). His male figures are endowed with energetic vitality and embody all the distinctive features of the Renaissance idea of man.

REFERENCES
Richter, G. M. *Andrea del Castagno.* Chicago, 1943.
Russoli, F. *Andrea del Castagno.* Milan, 1957.

V. E. MARKOVA [11–1513–3]

CASTALIAN SPRING, a spring on Mount Parnassus near Delphi (in Central Greece). In ancient Greece the Castalian Spring was revered as the sacred spring of the god Apollo and the Muses, granting inspiration to poets and musicians. Waters from the spring also served as a purifying ablution for the many pilgrims who journeyed to Delphi.   [11–1512–2]

CASTE (Portuguese *casta,* "clan," "generation," "descent"; Sanskrit equivalent *jati*), an endogamous hereditary group of people that occupies a fixed place in the social hierarchy that is connected with a traditional occupation. A caste is limited in its social intercourse with other castes.

In one form or another there were elements of caste division in the social structures of many ancient and medieval states (for example, the privileged caste of priests in ancient Egypt and Iran and the samurai caste in Japan), but only in India did the caste system become an all-encompassing social system. Here it originated in ancient and early medieval society, primarily within the framework of four classes or varnas, in the process of forming a feudal class structure and ethnic communities from clan-tribal groups. The formation of new castes (mostly centered on crafts and trades) was linked to the further social division of labor. "The crude form in which the division of labor appears with the Indians and Egyptians calls forth the caste system in their State and religion" wrote K. Marx and F. Engels (*Soch.,* 2nd ed., vol. 3, p. 38). The caste system is an important element of the entire religious system of Hinduism. The latter facilitated the development of a universal caste structure. Once it had been established, a caste could include any kind of group—class, occupational, ethnic, or religious. Therefore, along with the basic group of castes, which expressed the class and occupational division of Indian feudal society, castes based on religious sects came into being (Gosain, Jogi, and Lingayats), as well as castes based on assimilated large ethnic communities of tribes. Hindus regard all non-Hindus as "extra-caste," but groups of "nonbelievers" living in a Hindu environment (for example, Christians, Sikhs, and Muslims) are accorded the de facto status of castes. Remnants of the caste system have also been preserved within the Christian, Sikh, and especially Muslim communities in India; they retain the division into hierarchically arranged, endogamous groups.

Within the boundaries of settlement of each Indian nationality, the castes form a hierarchical structure. Already in early medieval society, the upper stratum of the caste hierarchy was composed of the Brahman and warrior-landowner castes (the "twice-born"). These were the castes from which the class of feudal lords was created, as well as the class of village community members with complete rights (the Rajputs, Kunbi, Nayars, Reddi, Vellala, and Jats). A high place in the hierarchy was also occupied by the urban trading and moneylending castes, such as the Baniya and Chetty. Standing somewhat lower were the lessees and craftsmen in certain specialties (weavers, jewelers, potters, carpenters, blacksmiths, and so forth). The lowest level of the class-caste hierarchy was occupied by castes whose members did not enjoy the rights of communal possession and use of lands. Most of them belonged to a stratum of semislaves, semiserfs who were exploited by the feudal upper classes of the community. This group included castes that performed jobs that, according to Hindu tradition, were considered "unclean," such as sweepers, leatherworkers, and laundrywomen. Widespread and numerous social restrictions were imposed on these castes; contact with them was considered defiling for persons belonging to higher castes. Hence they acquired the term "untouchables" (*achju* in Hindi).

In modern times such untouchables became one of the principal bases for India's agricultural proletariat, forming within it a layer of enslaved farm laborers; in the exploitation of these workers the vestiges of precapitalist relations are still strong.

Castes function within fixed territorial boundaries (a village, groups of villages, an urban quarter, or an entire city). Councils, or panchayats, control the economic and social activity of caste members, supervise the execution of caste regulations, and carry out legal actions. In traditional Indian society, which was represented by a system of communities based on a caste hierarchy, membership in a particular caste in principle assured a person of corresponding conditions of existence, and at the same time predestined him forever to the type of life that he had inherited by birth. Over the course of a long period the socioeconomic status of certain castes changed, and there was a corresponding change in their position within the caste hierarchy.

The development of capitalism led to a disruption of the traditional connections of caste members with particular occupations and particular permanent regions of settlement. The restrictions on social intercourse between the members of different castes weakened, mainly in cities, which were outside the traditional way of life. The most persistent features of the caste system have been endogamy and the hereditary transfer of caste membership.

Castes were influential in the formation of classes in modern Indian society. Thus, most members of the Indian bourgeoisie derive from the tradesman and moneylender caste, and most of the upper strata of farmers, officials, and intellectuals derive from the warrior-landowner and Brahman castes. During the period of British colonial domination (from the middle of the 18th century to 1947) the British authorities retained the caste system, using it to break up the national liberation movement. M. K. Gandhi, the leader of the national liberation movement, opposed caste discrimination and favored the unification of all castes and religious groups in the liberation struggle.

In accordance with the 1950 Indian constitution, all castes have equal rights. Caste discrimination has been prohibited by law (1955), and special measures have been undertaken to improve the economic and social status of the untouchables and "backward tribes." Nevertheless, caste differences are still used, primarily in villages, to intensify the exploitation of laborers, especially those who belong to the lowest castes. Caste restrictions have been preserved to the greatest degree in southern India. They are used in the political struggle because modern India's political structure has adapted itself to castes as the most universal form of traditional social organization in the country. In elections to local and the central legislative organs, all political parties take into consideration the caste composition of the voters. In the Indian republic, changes in the socioeconomic position of castes led to sharp caste conflicts during the 1950's and 1960's and to the efforts of a number of castes to raise their status in the caste hierarchy. At the same time, there was massive attempts to eliminate the category of untouchability. The Communist Party of India and other progressive forces are fighting for de facto caste equality and against caste discrimination.

REFERENCES

Kasty v Indii. Moscow, 1965.
Kudriavtsev, M. K. *Obshchina in kasta v Khindustane.* Moscow, 1971.
Senart, E. *Les Castes dans l'Inde.* Paris, 1927.
Hutton, J. H. *Caste in India,* 3rd ed. London, 1961.
Ghurye, G. S. *Caste, Class, and Occupation,* 4th ed. Bombay, 1961.
Karve, I. *Hindu Society—An Interpretation.* Poona, 1961.
Srinivas, M. N. *Caste in Modern India.* Bombay, 1962.
Dumont, L. *Homo hierarchicus.* Paris, 1966.

G. G. KOTOVSKII   [11–1523–1]

CASTELAR Y RIPOLL, EMILIO. Born Sept. 8, 1832, in Cádiz; died May 25, 1899, in San Pedro del Pinatar. Spanish politician, leader of the right-wing republicans, writer, and historian.

In 1853, Castelar y Ripoll graduated from the University of Madrid. From 1858 to 1866 he was the director of the university's faculty of Spanish history. After the unsuccessful Republican rising of 1866, he emigrated to France, where he lived until the beginning of the Spanish Revolution of 1868–74. He opposed the monarchy and advocated the establishment of a republic in Spain.

Upon his return to his homeland, Castelar y Ripoll became a deputy to the constituent cortes. He was the minister of foreign affairs from February to June 1873, the chairman of the cortes from August to September 1873, and the president of the republic from Sept. 7, 1873, to Jan. 3, 1874. After the restoration of the monarchy in 1874, Castelar y Ripoll was elected a deputy to the cortes. He opposed the monarchist constitution of 1876. In 1888 he retired from political life. Castelar y Ripoll wrote a great number of historical works, novels, memoirs, and travel chronicles.

WORKS

Historia de Europa en el siglo XIX, vols. 1–6. Madrid, 1895–1901.
Cuestiones politicas y sociales, vols. 1–3. Madrid, 1870.
Historia del movimiento republicano en Europa, vols. 1–2. Madrid, 1873–74.
Historia del descubrimiento de America. Madrid, 1892.
La Rusia contemporánea. . . . Madrid, 1881.
Obras escogidas, vols. 1–12. Madrid, 1922–23.

J. GARCÍA   [11–1514–3]

CASTELLAMMARE DI STABIA, a port city and resort in southern Italy, in the Campania region, Naples Province, located on the shore of the Bay of Naples of the Tyrrhenian Sea. Population, 70,300 (1969). The city has a shipyard. It produces cast and rolled steel, transportation equipment, railroad cars, cement, fruit preserves, olive oil, and cheese. A large American oil refinery is nearby.   [11–1515–1]

CASTELLÓN DE LA PLANA, a city in Spain in the region of Valencia. Administrative center of Castellón Province. Population, 85,000 (1970). The city is the center of an irrigated agricultural region, well known for its citrus fruits. There are also fruit and vegetable canneries and textile, cement, and chemical indus-

tries. The city is a new center for petroleum refining and petrochemistry.   [11–1516–2]

CASTELLUCCIO, an archaeological culture of the early Bronze Age (the end of the third millennium to the first half of the second millennium B.C.) widespread in southern and southeastern Sicily. The culture is characterized by small settlements (sometimes fortified), with elliptical dwellings partially dug into the ground, and by burials in catacombs, abandoned flint mines, or natural caverns. The pottery— amphorae and other vessels— is decorated with painted brown or black crisscrossed bands on a yellow or red background. The implements include flint tools with bifacial blades, axes made of basalt and greenstone, and grain mortars. Typical ornaments are pendants and beads made of stone, bone, and copper. Especially interesting are the bone plates, decorated with a series of small cones and delicate designs (possibly, schematized idols), which resemble those found on the island of Malta and in southeastern Italy, southern Greece, and Troy. The Castelluccio culture also displays ancient ties with the middle stage of the Helladic culture and with the culture of northwestern Anatolia of the end of the third millennium B.C.

REFERENCES

Childe, V. G. *U istokov evropeiskoi tsivilizatsii.* Moscow, 1952. (Translated from English.)
Bernabó Brea, L. *Sicily Before the Greeks.* New York, 1966.

V. S. TITOV   [11–1515–2]

CASTELNAU, ÉDOUARD (Viscount de Curières). Born Dec. 24, 1851, in St. Affrique; died Mar. 18, 1944, in Montastruc-la-Conseillèra, Haute-Garonne. French general.

Castelnau participated in the Franco-Prussian War of 1870–71. He became first deputy to the chief of the General Staff in 1911. Appointed to the Supreme War Council in 1913, Castelnau assisted in the formulation of a plan for the strategic deployment of a war against Germany. During World War I (1914–18) he commanded an army and an army group in France. From December 1915 to the middle of 1916, he was the chief of staff to the commander in chief of the French armies, J. Joffre. From 1919 to 1923, Castelnau served as a deputy to the French National Assembly and the chairman of a military committee.

[11–1516–1]

CASTELNAU, FRANCIS. Born 1812 in London; died Feb. 4, 1880, in Melbourne. French traveler.

Castelnau headed French government scientific expeditions for the study of the Brazilian Highlands and the Amazon Basin. He crossed South America twice. From 1843 to 1845, starting from Rio de Janeiro, Castelnau followed the entire valley of the Araguaia River in the Brazilian Highlands. He ascended the river from its mouth to the valley of the Tocantins River (a tributary of the Araguaia). He continued to the Tocantins' upper course. Turning westward, Castelnau explored the Mato Grosso plateau, where he established the exact source of the Paraguay River. He then crossed the Chaco Boreal and the Altiplano. After crossing the Andes, he reached the city of Lima. The entire journey, on horse and on foot, covered over 10,000 km. In 1846 and 1847, Castelnau traveled eastward from Lima, crossed the Andes, and descended the valleys of the Urubamba and Ucayali rivers to 8° S lat. He then descended the Ucayali and Amazon rivers to the sea. This expedition covered approximately 8,000 km.

WORKS

Expédition dans les parties centrales de l'Amérique du Sud, parts 1–7. Paris, 1950–61.

REFERENCE

Magidovich, I. P. *Istoriia otkrytiia i issledovaniia Tsentral'noi i Iuzhnoi Ameriki.* Moscow, 1965.   [11–1515–3]

CASTELO BRANCO, CAMILO (full name, Camilo Ferreira Botelho Castelo Branco). Born Mar. 16, 1825, in Lisbon; died June 1, 1890, in San Miguel de Seide. Portuguese author.

Castelo Branco's early romantic works were *Agostinho de Ceuta* (1851); the play *Thorns and Flowers* (1857); the novels *Anathema* (1851), *Lisbon Secrets* (1854), and *The Black Book of*

Father Dennis (1855), all of which portray the life of the urban lower class; and the autobiographical novel *Doomed Love* (1862). Realistic tendencies appear in the novella, *A Worthy Man* (1856) and his comedy of everyday life *Fafe the Firstborn in Lisbon* (1861) and are more clearly evident in *Stories of the Minho* (1875–77).

WORKS

Obras, vols. 1–3. Rio de Janeiro, 1953–54.

REFERENCES

Lacape, H. *Camilo Castelo Branco.* Paris, 1941.
Prado Coelho, J. do. *Introducão ao estuda da novela camiliana.* Lisbon, 1946.   [11–1667–1]

CASTEX, RAOUL VICTOR PATRICE. Born Oct. 27, 1878, in St. Omer; died Jan. 11, 1968. French naval theoretician, admiral (1935).

Castex joined the navy in 1898. He taught at a naval school, being its director in the 1930's, and then at the Institute of Advanced Studies of National Defense. He retired in 1939.

Castex wrote many theoretical works on military questions. In the most important, on strategic theory, he denies the advisability of big naval engagements and argues that the main task of the navy is to defend its own sea communications, to disrupt the communications of the enemy, and to participate in landing operations in cooperation with other services in the armed forces; he emphasized the special importance of naval forces in protracted wars.

WORKS

Théories stratégiques, vols. 1–5. Paris, 1929–35.   [11–1514–2]

CASTIGLIONE, BALDASSARE. Born Dec. 6, 1478, in Casatico, near Mantua; died Feb. 2, 1529, in Toledo, Spain. Italian writer.

Castiglione's best-known work is *The Courtier* (books 1–4, 1528), a treatise in dialogue form. In the spirit of late humanism, Castiglione enumerated the qualities of the ideal courtier, or, in a broader sense, of the well-brought-up, broadly educated man with a developed personality. This ideal was current throughout Europe in the 16th and early 17th centuries and was reflected in literature.

WORKS

Opere, a cura di C. Cordie. Milan-Naples [1960].
In Russian translation:
"Iz 'Knigi o pridvornom.' " In *Khrestomatiia po zarubezhnoi literature. Epokha Vozrozhdeniia,* vol. 1. Compiled by B. I. Purishev. Moscow, 1959.

REFERENCES

De Sanctis, F. *Istoriia ital'ianskoi literatury,* vol. 2. Moscow, 1964.
Rossi, M. *B. Castiglione.* Bari, 1946.   [11–1516–6]

CASTIGLIONE DELLE STIVIERE, a city in Northern Italy, Lombardy, Mantua Province. During Napoleon's Italian Campaign of 1796–97, his troops defeated the Austrian army of Field Marshal D. Wurmser near Castiglione (Aug. 5, 1796). In late July the Austrian forces left Tirol in order to raise the blockade of the fortress of Mantua, which was besieged by the French troops. The offensive was conducted by two columns. The column of General P. Quasdanovich (Kvaždanović), consisting of approximately 18,000 men, advanced west of Lake Garda toward Brescia. Wurmser advanced with more than 24,000 men east of Lake Garda toward the Mincio River. Napoleon lifted the seige of Mantua and concentrated his troops, about 30,000 men, west of the Mincio River. Between July 31 and Aug. 3, he defeated Quasdanovich's troops east of Brescia, and on August 5 he defeated the main force of the Austrians, who were advancing towards Castiglione. Wurmser reinforced the Mantua garrison and retreated toward Trent.   [11–1516–7]

CASTILE, a feudal state in the center of the Iberian Peninsula from the 11th through the 15th century. In 932, Castile became a county in the kingdom of Leon. In 1035 it was declared a kingdom, with Burgos as its capital. In subsequent years Castile was united with Leon several times (1037–65, 1072–1157, and

1230). After its reunification with Leon in 1230, Castile became the most powerful state of the Iberian Peninsula. The capital of the united kingdom was the city of Toledo.

Castile played a leading role in the Reconquista and extended its territory to the southern coast of the peninsula during the war against the Arabs (conquest of Cádiz in 1262). Castile's victories were consolidated by the large-scale population movement from the north to the south in the 11th, 12th, and 13th centuries. In order to induce the peasants to participate in the Reconquista, rural communities were granted the rights of the *behetría* (free communes). The serfs' personal freedom and right to change feudal lords was recognized almost universally. The rights and liberties of urban and rural communities were stipulated in *fueros,* or charters. In the mid-13th century, townsmen were represented in the cortes. The attempts of the feudal lords to bind the peasantry to the land led to several peasant uprisings during the 15th century. The dynastic union of Castile and Aragon in 1479 marked the beginning of the unification of Spain into a single state.   S. V. FRIAZINOV [11–1516–3]

CASTILHO, ANTÓNIO FELICIANO DE. Born Jan. 28, 1800, in Lisbon; died there June 18, 1875. Portuguese poet.

Castilho's first collections of idyllic poetry were *Letters of Echo to Narcissus* (1821) and *Spring* (1822). The narrative poems *Night in the Castle* (1836) and *Jealousy of the Bard* (1838) and the collection *Autumn* (1863) reflect romantic trends. Elegiac motifs and descriptions of nature are characteristic of Castilho's poems. Late in life, Castilho took part in the "Coimbra question," a polemic on Portuguese literature, he defended the outmoded principles of romantic art against realism.

WORKS

Obras completas, vols. 1–80. Lisbon, 1903–10.

REFERENCE

Castelo Branco, C. *Castilho-Alguns, aspectos vivos da sua obra.* Lisbon, 1935.   [11–1667–2]

CASTLEREAGH, ROBERT STEWART, VISCOUNT (Marquis of Londonderry). Born June 18, 1769, in Dublin; died Aug. 12, 1822, in North Cray, Kent. British statesman.

A member of the Tory Party, he was a leader of the Real Tories, a Tory group that represented mainly the interests of the land-owning aristocracy. He was a graduate of Cambridge University. Chief secretary for Ireland from 1798 to 1801, Castlereagh was instrumental in establishing the colonialist Anglo-Irish union of 1801, which deprived Ireland of parliamentary autonomy. Secretary of state for war from 1807 to 1809, he was one of the organizers of the British attack on Denmark in 1807. Castlereagh was foreign secretary from 1812 to 1822 and exerted a decisive influence on the policy of Liverpool's Tory cabinet. During Napoleon's invasion of Russia in 1812 he opposed any aid to Russia. In 1813 he helped to create the Sixth Coalition, trying to use Prussia and Austria against Napoleonic France while at the same time setting them against Russia. One of his major tasks was the strengthening and considerable territorial expansion of militarist Prussia. At the Congress of Vienna (1814–15), on Jan. 3, 1815, he concluded a secret treaty with Austria and France directed mainly against Russia. He supported the Holy Alliance.

Castlereagh's policy contributed to the triumph of the feudal and absolutist reaction in Europe.

REFERENCES

Webster, C. K. *The Foreign Policy of Castlereagh, 1812–1815.* London, 1931.
Webster, C. K. *The Foreign Policy of Castlereagh, 1815–1822.* London, 1925.   L. A. ZAK [11–1482–2]

CASTOR OIL, a fatty vegetable oil obtained from the seeds of the castor-oil plant. It is one of the nondrying liquid oils; it contains 3–9 percent oleic acid, 3–5 percent linoleic acid, and at least 80 percent ricinoleic acid. The high content of the ricinoleic acid is responsible for the properties of castor oil: high kinematic viscosity (more than $110 \times 10^{-6} \ m^2/sec$ at 50°C) and density (950–974 kg/m^3 at 15°C). Unlike other fatty vegetable oils, it is readily soluble in alcohol but poorly soluble in benzine.

Castor oil is widely known for its medicinal properties. The ancient Egyptians used it to make all kinds of ointments and balms. It is best known for its use as a laxative. Combined with quinine, Pituitrin, pachycarpinum, and other substances, it is used to induce labor. Ointments and balms containing castor oil are used in the treatment of burns and ulcers, softening of the skin, and so forth. Castor oil has also found application in some branches of industry—for example, soap manufacture and oil boiling. Castor oil is a high-grade lubricant.   [11–1517–8]

CASTRATI, a special kind of Italian singer of the 16th through 18th centuries (also called *sopranisto*). Castration in early childhood left their voices with a boy's pitch (soprano or mezzo-soprano) and timbre but with an adult's power. The *castrati* sang high parts (including female parts), difficult virtuoso passages, and sustained notes. In the 16th century *castrati* performed widely in Catholic church choirs, from which women were banned, but in the 17th and 18th centuries they became central to Italian opera.   [11–1518–3]

CASTRATION, the artificial removal of the gonads in animals and man. In many invertebrates, castration does not bring about significant changes because their gonads are unrelated to internal secretion.

Experiments with fish, amphibians, birds, and mammals show that castration causes the secondary sex characteristics to disappear or remain underdeveloped. For example, castration causes the disappearance of the sex drive and changes the external appearance of birds: sexual dimorphism is lost, and castrated males and females come to resemble one another. Castration causes profound changes in mammals: stunted growth of bones (especially in the limbs), disappearance or underdevelopment of secondary sex characteristics, and obesity.

In humans, castration is performed therapeutically as an unavoidable operation in several diseases of the sex glands (malignant tumor, trauma, and so forth) and some other organs (for example, breast cancer in women). It is done either by total surgical removal of the gonads from males or females or by blocking their functioning with ionizing radiation or by introducing hormones (or substitutes) that inhibit the gonadotropic function of the pituitary gland.

The earlier castration is performed, the more pronounced the resultant changes. For example, castration before puberty causes eunuchoidism; in adults, it causes metabolic disturbances, mental disorders, and impairment of sexual potency, although interest in sex and capacity for a sex life persist, sometimes for a long period.

Animals are castrated primarily for economic reasons and less commonly for therapeutic ones (neoplasm of the gonads, trauma of the testes). Surgery is the most common method: the testes are removed through incisions in the scrotum; a bloodless method disrupts the blood supply of the testes by crushing or compressing the spermatic cords.

A castrated stallion is called a gelding; a castrated bull, an ox; a boar, a barrow; a ram, a wether; a rooster, a capon; and a hen, a poulard. Castrated animals are calmer and fatten better. Their flesh lacks a disagreeable specific odor and is tastier and more nutritious. Stallions are gelded at three or four years; bulls to be used as work animals at one year and those to be fattened at six months; sheep and goats at four to six months; and boars at seven to nine weeks. A metabolic change takes place in castrated animals causing their fat to be deposited more quickly.   [11–1519–1]

CASTRATION OF PLANTS, the removal of immature anthers from a monoecious flower in order to prevent possible self-pollination; an essential technique for hybridizing plants capable of self-pollination.

The anthers are usually removed with tweezers, sometimes with special needles or small scissors. Plants are castrated, as a rule, in the bud stage one or two days before the pollen and stigma of the pistil are ready for pollination. In cereal grasses, only some of the flowers are castrated because of the uneven development of the flowers in the ear (or head). In wheat, the flowers in the center of the ear are castrated and all the others are removed; in the awned varieties, the awns are also removed.

When a plant is castrated, the ear is held in the left hand while the flowering glumes are drawn apart with tweezers and the anthers cut out. A special effort is made to avoid harming the stigma of the pistil or leaving individual anthers or parts of them (if there are only a few anthers, they should be tabulated as a control).

Gauze or parchment bags (insulators) are immediately placed over the castrated flowers or racemes and tied below the flower or raceme on the stem after first wrapping it in cotton. The gauze insulators prevent the castrated flowers from coming into contact with pollen carried by insects, and the parchment insulators provide protection against wind-born pollen. The insulators are left on the flowers or racemes for some time after pollination. To check the quality of castration, some of the castrated flowers are left in the bags without pollination. Castrated flowers are not insulated when there is free pollination of the plants.

Cereal grasses with small flowers (millet, foxtail millet) are castrated thermally: the heads are immersed in hot water (45°–50°C) for four to five minutes to render the pollen inviable.   [11–1519–2]

CASTRÉN, MATTHIAS ALEXANDER. Born Dec. 2, 1813, in Tervola; died May 7, 1852, in Helsinki. Finnish philologist and ethnologist. Doctor of sciences (1839).

Castrén graduated from the University of Helsinki in 1838 and was appointed a professor there in 1851. He was the first to translate the entire *Kalevala* into Swedish. From 1838 to 1849, on commission of the St. Petersburg Academy of Sciences, Castrén traveled through Finland, Karelia, Arkhangel'sk Province, and Siberia (the Ob' and Enisei basins, from the mouth to the Saians and Transbaikalia). He made a major contribution to the study of the languages and ethnography of the Finno-Ugric, Samoyedic, Tungusic-Manchurian, and Paleo-Asiatic peoples. Castrén compiled grammars and dictionaries for 20 languages. He advanced the theory of the kinship of the Finno-Ugric, Samoyedic, Turkic, Mongolian, and Tungusic-Manchurian languages, which he classified in the Altaic linguistic family. He considered the homeland of these peoples to be the Altai-Saian mountain region.

WORKS

Puteshestviia Aleksandra Kastrena po Laplandii, Severnoi Rossii i Sibiri. Moscow, 1860.

REFERENCES

Pamiati M. A. Kastrena: K 75-letiiu so dnia smerti. Leningrad, 1927.
Murav'ev, V. B. *Vekhi zabytykh putei.* Moscow, 1961.
Ravila, P. "M. A. Castrén—philologist." *Journal de la Société Finno-Ougrienne,* 1952, vol. 56.

R. A. AGEEVA   [11–1520–1]

CASTRO, JOSUÉ APOLONIO DE. Born Sept. 5, 1908, in Recife, state of Pernambuco. Progressive Brazilian scientist, physiologist, anthropologist, and hygienist; foreign member of the Academy of Medical Sciences of the USSR (1963).

Castro graduated from the faculties of medicine (1929) and of philosophy (1938) of the Brazilian University and became a professor of anthropology there in 1936, a professor of philosophy in 1939, and director of the institute of nutrition in 1946. He was made chairman of the Executive Council of the Food and Agriculture Organization of the UN in 1951. Castro is president of the World Association of Struggle against Hunger and president of the International Medical Association for the Study of Living Conditions and Health. He was a member of the Brazilian Parliament from 1955 to 1963.

Castro is the author of works on anthropology, physiology, and problems of consumption, including the world-famous book *The Geography of Hunger* (1946; Russian translation, 1954), in which he sharply criticizes the modern Malthusians and concludes that the basic reason for widespread starvation is "the imperialistic exploitation of man and the earth." He shows the necessity of an essential solution to the problem of starvation through radical changes in agricultural relations in the capitalist countries and the destruction of the remnants of feudalism and the consequences of neocolonialism in the developing countries. Castro received the International Peace Prize in 1955.

G. G. ABRAMISHVILI [11–1520–2]

CASTRO ALVES, ANTONIO DE. Born Mar. 14, 1847, on the Sabeceiras estate near Curralinho; died July 6, 1871 in Bahia. Brazilian poet.

Castro Alves was the foremost revolutionary romantic poet of Brazil. His drama *Gonzaga, or the Revolution in Minas* (performed, 1867; published, 1875) lauded the heroes of the revolutionary conspiracy of the late 18th century. Freedom is the major theme of his verse collections *Floating Foam* (1870) and *Slaves* (published posthumously, 1883) and his narrative poems *The Groans of Africa* (1868), and *The Slave Ship* (1869). He was an ardent defender of the Negroes. In such verse cycles as *Paulo Alfonso's Waterfall* (published, 1876), Castro Alves re-created the majestic landscapes of Brazil. His works were paeans to the power of love.

WORKS
Obras completas, 2nd ed., vols. 1–2. Rio de Janeiro, 1944.
In Russian translation:
Stikhi. Introductory essay by I. Tynianova. Moscow, 1958.

REFERENCES
Amadu, Zh. *Kastro Alves.* Afterword by I. Terterian. Moscow, 1963.
Calmon, P. *A vida de Castro Alves,* 3rd. ed. Rio de Janeiro, 1961.
Horch, H. J. *Bibliografia de Castro Alves.* Rio de Janeiro, 1960.

[11–1522–2]

CASTROP-RAUXEL, a city in the Federal Republic of Germany, in North Rhine–Westphalia, near Dortmund. Population, 84,000 (1970). River port on the Rhine-Herne Canal (freight turnover, 1.4 million tons). It is one of the coal-mining centers of the Ruhr. In addition to coal mining, there is chemical (nitrogen), petrochemical, and cement industry and the manufacture of pipe and metal items. [11–1522–1]

CASTRO RUZ, FIDEL. Born Aug. 13, 1927, in Birán, Oriente Province. Statesman, politician, and military figure of Cuba, with the title of commander in chief of the Revolutionary Armed Forces of Cuba. The son of an affluent landowner.

Castro graduated from the law department of the University of Havana, receiving a doctorate in law in 1949, after which he practiced law for a time. In the early 1950's he joined the Party of the Cuban People (the Ortodoxo). In 1952 the party nominated him for deputy to the National Congress of Cuba, but the elections were never held because in March 1952 the reactionary pro-American military headed by General Batista y Zaldívar staged a coup d'etat and established a dictatorship. The Ortodoxo Party gradually disintegrated in the struggle against the dictatorship. Castro succeeded in rallying a small group of former members of the party and began to prepare the overthrow of the Batista dictatorship. On July 26, 1953, members of the group made an armed attack on the Moncada Barracks in Santiago de Cuba. The action was cruelly suppressed, and Castro was tried by a military tribunal. At the trial he delivered the speech *History Will Absolve Me,* which was a devastating critique of Batista's bloody dictatorship and a program for the national liberation struggle and revolutionary transformation of Cuba. The tribunal sentenced Castro to 15 years in prison, but he was amnestied in May 1955 under the pressure of public opinion. He emigrated in the same year to Mexico.

In December 1956 a group of revolutionaries headed by Castro landed in Oriente Province on the *Granma,* a small yacht. The group, which over time became the rebel army, initiated a partisan struggle against the dictatorial regime. After the victory of the revolution and the overthrow of the Batista dictatorship on Jan. 1, 1959, power in Cuba was assumed by the democratic forces rallied around the rebel army headed by Castro. In February 1959, Castro became prime minister of the revolutionary government of the Republic of Cuba. On Apr. 16, 1961, he declared that the Cuban revolution was a socialist revolution. During the April 1961 invasion of Cuba by hirelings of US imperialists at Playa Girón (Bay of Pigs), Castro directed the operations that routed the interventionists. Initially secretary of

the national leadership of the Integrated Revolutionary Organizations and then secretary of the United Party of the Socialist Revolution, Castro was elected first secretary of the Central Committee of the Communist Party of Cuba in October 1965. Castro received an honorary degree of doctor of law from the M. V. Lomonosov Moscow State University in 1963, the International Lenin Prize for Strengthening Peace Between Nations in 1961, the title Hero of the Soviet Union in 1963, and the Order of Lenin in 1972. He has been awarded the Joliot-Curie Gold Peace Medal and has received a number of awards from many countries.

WORKS
[*Discursos pronuciados . . . , 1965–1968.*] Havana, 1968.
In Russian translation:
Rechi i vystupleniia. Moscow, 1960.
Rechi i vystupleniia, 1961–1963. Moscow, 1963.
Nashe delo pobezhdaet: Rechi i vystupleniia, 1963–1964. Moscow, 1965.
Pust' vechno zhivet bessmertnyi Lenin! Moscow, 1970.
Sila revoliutsii—v edinstve. Moscow, 1972.
Budushchee prinadlezhit internatsionalizmu. Moscow, 1973.

[11–1521–2]

CASTRO RUZ, RAÚL. Born June 3, 1931, in Birán, Oriente Province. Statesman, politician, and military figure of Cuba. Lieutenant general of the Revolutionary Armed Forces of Cuba. Brother of Fidel Castro.

Castro became active in the youth movement at an early age. On July 26, 1953, he participated in the armed attack on the Moncada Barracks in Santiago de Cuba. Arrested and imprisoned, he was amnestied in 1955 and emigrated to Mexico. On Dec. 2, 1956, Castro was among the 82 young patriots who landed in Oriente Province on the *Granma,* a small yacht. During the struggle against the Batista dictatorship he commanded the second partisan column. After the victory of the revolution in January 1959, Castro headed the military and civil administration in Oriente Province and in the same year became minister of the Revolutionary Armed Forces of Cuba. He was a leader of the Integrated Revolutionary Organizations and a leader of the United Party of the Socialist Revolution from its inception. A member of the Politburo and second secretary of the Central Committee of the Communist Party of Cuba since October 1965, Castro has been first deputy prime minister of the revolutionary government of the Republic of Cuba since 1962. [11–1521–1]

CASTRUCCIO CASTRACANI DEGLI ANTELMINELLI. Born Mar. 29, 1281, in Castruccio, near Lucca; died Sept. 3, 1328, in Lucca. Italian *condottiere;* Luccan *signore.*

Castruccio, the son of a merchant, was banished from Lucca in 1300 because he was a Ghibelline. He became a *condottiere* for France and, later, for the Visconti and Scaliger families. Having returned to Lucca in 1314, Castruccio was proclaimed the captain-general and *signore* of Lucca in 1316; the latter position was for life. He was given the title of vicar-imperial in 1320. Castruccio changed the Guelph constitution and ruled tyrannically. He waged war in order to expand the domain of Lucca and to create a Tuscan Ghibelline state. He gained control of Pistoia in 1325 and Pisa in 1328; he defeated the Florentines at Altopascio in 1325. Pope John XXII excommunicated him in 1324 and 1328. The German king Louis IV the Bavarian, who supported the Ghibellines, granted Castruccio the title of duke in 1327. Castruccio is the subject of N. Machiavelli's *The Life of Castruccio Castracani of Lucca.* [11–1518–2]

CASUARIIFORMES, an order of ratite birds comprising two families, the emu and the cassowary (Casuariidae). The cassowaries have a laterally compressed bill, a crown casque that protects them from thorns and burs, and naked, brightly colored areas on the neck. The plumage is black and hairlike, and the reduced wing feathers have been transformed into long, bare shafts that protect the body as the cassowary, neck extended, moves through dense thickets. Their legs are strong and tridactyl, and the inner toe has a long sharp claw with which the birds can inflict serious wounds. There are three species in the cassowary family, inhabiting the dense tropical forests of New

Guinea, the islands of Aru, Ceram, and New Britain, and the northeastern coast of Australia. They feed on seeds, berries, and fallen fruit. The nest is a shallow depression on the floor of a forest glade. After the female has laid from three to five green eggs they are incubated and later reared by the male.

[11–529–3]

CASUS BELLI, a term used in diplomacy to designate an event or fact serving as a direct formal ground or pretext for the declaration of a state of war. For example, the casus belli for World War I was the murder in Sarajevo of the Austrian archduke Ferdinand.

[11–530–1]

CASUS FOEDERIS, a term used in diplomacy to indicate the situation or fact that will activate a treaty alliance to render mutual assistance. Contemporary international law gives every state the right to individual or collective self-defense (collective self-defense is understood to be assistance rendered by one state to another to resist armed aggression or the threat of aggression). Collective self-defense can be exercised by states without any preliminary formal agreement, or it can be based on special treaties of alliance that usually give the exact terms of the obligation to render mutual help and also specify the casus foederis.

[11–530–2]

CATABOLISM, a set of chemical processes constituting the reverse of anabolism.

Catabolic processes are directed toward splitting the complex compounds that form the structural elements of organs and tissues (proteins, nucleic acids, phospholipids) or that are deposited in the organs and tissues as reserve material (fat, glycogen). As a result of catabolism, complex compounds lose their specific properties and are converted to substances that are partly utilized for biosynthesis and partly eliminated from the body (intermediate and final products of metabolism).

[11–1527–2]

CATACHRESIS, in stylistics, a combination of lexically incompatible words that form a unique and meaningful whole (compare with oxymoron, a combination of words with contrasting and opposite meanings, such as in "a living corpse.")

There are two types of catachresis: (1) that which comes into being naturally, through the development of the nominative means of a language, and which may be perceived at first as incorrect word usage ("white brownstone," "to sail a steamship"); and (2) that which is created deliberately, for an intended effect ("black gold," "when the crab whistles"). Catachresis can be either a verbal blunder ("let not the arms of the sharks of imperialism extend to us"), where the tropes are joined mechanically, or an illustration of great artistic skill:

But through the listless night the serpents of remorse
More shrewdly burn within me . . .

A. S. Pushkin
[11–1564–2]

CATACLASIS, the deformation and crushing of minerals within rock during tectonic movements. Cataclasis occurs chiefly along and near tectonic ruptures (faults, displacements, overthrusts), where the relative shifts of rock sections have caused the grinding of minerals. Weak cataclasis can be ascertained only by examining a thin section of a crystal under polarized light and is shown by an "undulating decline," notably in quartz crystals. Under the same conditions, stronger cataclasis results in a "mosaic decline," indicating that various sections of the crystal have acquired through deformation a different orientation of the optic axes. Still stronger cataclasis is exhibited in the crushing of individual granules (granulation), which results in a "concrete" structure (larger angular or circular granules remain among the finely crushed material). The rock is transformed into mylonite, a compact, frequently silicified mass consisting of minute fusiform, lenticular, and flaky mineral fragments difficult to distinguish under a microscope.

In soft rocks, cataclasis may be seen in the formation of "clays of crushing" and "rock flour." In the process of cataclasis, feldspars, micas, calcite, and certain other minerals are bent and split along the cleavage planes.

The zones that have undergone cataclasis are permeable to the movement of mineral aqueous solutions, including ore-bearing ones, and this causes the accumulation of various ores. The structure of rock that has undergone cataclasis is termed cataclastic.

REFERENCE
Eliseev, N. A. *Metamorfizm.* Leningrad, 1959.
V. V. BELOUSOV [11–1530–5]

CATACOMB CULTURE, an archaeological culture of the early Bronze Age widespread in the first half and third quarter of the second millennium B.C. in the area north of the Black Sea and in the Lower Volga Region. The culture was differentiated in the early 20th century by V. A. Gorodtsov. The bearers of the Catacomb culture were a group of related tribes, in origin related to the tribes of the Pit-Grave (Iamnaia) culture, which inhabited the same territory in the third millennium B.C. Clan settlements and mound burials are typical of the Catacomb culture. The dead were buried in catacombs beneath mounds; they were interred in a flexed position on their sides and were sprinkled with red coloring symbolizing fire. Items found in the graves include decorated clay ware, marked with cord stamps (the nature of the designs makes it possible to include the Catacomb culture in the broader range of the Corded-ware culture), stone and bronze implements and weapons, and bone and bronze ornaments. The tribes of the Catacomb culture engaged in stock-raising and agriculture and knew the metallurgy of copper and bronze. They bartered with the surrounding tribes, particularly with those of the Caucasus, and through them were linked with Southwest Asia, Iran, and Egypt. In the tribes of the Catacomb culture, the matriarchal family was replaced by the patriarchal and the prerequisites for property differentiation arose (the burials of chieftans and tribal elders are distinguished by a richer inventory). By the end of the third quarter of the second millennium B.C., the tribes of the Catacomb culture had been supplanted by the tribes of the Timberframe (Srubnaia) culture which had moved up from the Middle Volga Region.

REFERENCES
Popova, T. B. "Plemena katakombnoi kul'tury." In the collection *Tr. Gosudarstvennogo istoricheskogo muzeia,* issue 24. Moscow, 1955.
Klein, L. S. "Novye dannye o khronologicheskikh vzaimootnosheniiakh iamnoi i katakombnoi kul'tur." *Vestnik LGU: Seriia istorii iazyka i literatury,* 1960, issue 4, no. 20. T. B. POPOVA [11–1531–1]

CATACOMBS, subterranean passages of artificial or natural origin, used in antiquity for the fulfillment of religious rites and for the burial of the dead. They were known in the vicinity of Rome, in Naples, on the islands of Sicily and Malta, in Egypt (Alexandria), and in North Africa, Southwest Asia, Asia Minor, the Balkans, and other locations. The most extensive catacombs are the Roman ones. The catacombs were widely used by early Christian communities in the second to the fourth centuries. They consist of branched labyrinths of narrow galleries and small halls; some of them are decorated with rich murals from the late classical and from the early medieval period. Structures similar to the catacombs have been preserved from the ancient Rus' period in the Kiev-Pecherskaia Laura (monastery). The term catacombs is sometimes used for large, abandoned subterranean excavations—large quarries and so forth.

The catacombs of Odessa and Adzhimushkai, which were used during the partisan struggle, are famous. [11–1532–1]

CATAGENESIS (in geology), the natural processes that alter sedimentary rock after it has developed from sediments by diagenesis and before it has become metamorphic rock. Some geologists, such as N. M. Strakhov, distinguish metagenesis, a stage between catagenesis and metamorphism. The term "catagenesis" was introduced in 1922 by A. E. Fersman to designate the chemical transformations in rock after it has been covered by layers of new sediment. Since then it has gradually come to replace other names for postdiagenetic processes, for example, epigenesis.

The chief factors in catagenesis (including the stage of metagenesis as interpreted by M. N. Strakhov) are temperatures rising to 300°–350°C at a depth of 8–12 km, at the border of the metamorphic zone; pressure increasing to 180–290 meganewtons per sq m (1,800–2,900 atmospheres) at these depths; and pore water (solutions), which interacts with the rock saturated with it.

An important result of catagenesis is rock consolidation, which initially occurs without the destruction of its structure and later with its destruction. By the end of the stage the porosity of sandstones, aleurolites, and argillites usually does not exceed 1–2 percent. Initially free, and later bound, water is squeezed out and removed. The mineral composition of terrigenous rock undergoes changes that intensify with depth and age. Some minerals are dissolved, while others precipitate. There is extensive regenerative growth of quartz granules, chloritization, albitization, and zeolitization. New structures arise, such as microstylolitic seams, and the forcing of some sandstone granules into others also occurs. Organic matter, losing CO_2 and hydrocarbons, is transformed until it reaches the semianthracite stages.

A knowledge of the principles of catagenesis is of great practical significance, for example, in evaluating the probability of discovering petroleum in sedimentary strata and in forecasting the properties (grades) of fossil coal and building materials.

REFERENCES
Fersman, A. E. *Geokhimiia Rossii.* Petrograd, 1922.
Diagenez i katagenez osadochnykh obrazovanii. Moscow, 1971. (Translated from English.) N. B. VASSOEVICH [11–1528–1]

CATALAN, the language of the Catalans, which belongs to the Romance group of languages.

Catalan is spoken by more than 5 million people (1967, estimate) in Spain, Andorra, France, and the Balearic Islands. The dialects of modern Catalan are divided into two groups—oriental (the Central dialect, including the city of Barcelona, as well as the Balearic, Roussillon, and Alghero dialects) and occidental (the Lérida and Valencia dialects). The Central dialect is the basis of the literary language. The founder of the modern literary language and the most prominent writer of the 19th century was J. Verdaguer.

Catalan has much in common with both Spanish and Provençal. One of the distinctive features of its grammatical structure is the periphrastic preterite (the verb *anar,* "to go," plus infinitive), which replaces the simple past. The pronominal system is characterized by an abundance of adverbal forms which generate groups made up of two or three units.

REFERENCES
Shishmarev, V. F. *Ocherki po istorii iazykov Ispanii.* Moscow-Leningrad, 1941.
Vasil'eva-Shvede, O. K. "O meste katalanskogo sredi romanskikh iazykov." *Uch. zap. LGU,* 1961, no. 299, issue 59.
Badia Margaret, A. *Gramática catalana,* vols. 1–2. Madrid, 1962.
Fabra, P. *Diccionari general de la llengua catalana.* Barcelona, 1954.
 E. M. VOL'F [11–1533–1]

CATALANI, ANGELICA. Born May 10, 1780, in Sinigaglia, Ancona Province; died June 12, 1849, in Paris. Italian singer (soprano).

Catalani made her opera debut in 1797 in Venice singing *Lodoïska* by S. Mayr. She began performing in Europe, including Russia, in 1804. She was endowed with perfect vocal gifts and had an extraordinary mastery of coloratura. Her roles included Semiramide in *The Death of Semiramide* by Portugal, the title role in Zingarelli's *Clitennestra,* Camilla in *The Orazi and Curiazi* by Cimarosa, and Susanna in *The Marriage of Figaro* by Mozart. Catalani directed the Théâtre Italien in Paris between 1814 and 1817. She retired in 1828.

REFERENCES
Timokhin, V. *Vydaiushchiesia ital'ianskie pevtsy.* Moscow, 1962.
Della Corte, A. *Satire e grotteschi.* Turin, 1946. [11–1532–3]

CATALANS, a nationality living in eastern Spain, primarily in Catalonia but also in Aragon and Valencia and on the Balearic and Pine islands. The population in Spain is more than 5.3 million (1970, estimate). Catalans also live in France (approxi-

mately 200,000), Italy (approximately 15,000, mainly on the island of Sardinia), Andorra (approximately 7,000), and the USA and Latin America (approximately 200,000). They speak Catalan and Spanish, and their religion is Catholicism.

The ancestors of the Catalans were Iberian tribes who came under the influence of the Celts, Carthaginian and Greek colonists, and, after the third century B.C., the Romans. The Alani, and later the Visigoths, ruled the territory of the Catalans for a short time in the fifth century. In the early eighth century the Catalans were conquered by the Arabs, who were driven out of northern Catalonia by the Franks in the late eighth century. The ethnic distinctiveness of the Catalans among the peoples of Spain was determined to a great extent by their prolonged contacts with the Franks. From the formation of a unified Spanish kingdom in the late 15th century until the mid-20th century, the Catalans have fought against the centralizing policies of the Spanish rulers and struggled for regional autonomy. During this struggle the Catalan nationality gradually took shape. The Catalans are engaged in industry (especially textiles), agriculture, and, along the coast, fishing. The distinctive culture of the Catalans is clearly expressed in their dances (the *sardana* and *contrapás*), choral singing, and crafts (artistic smithing, majolica). The Catalans possess a rich literature in their own language.

REFERENCE
Narody zarubezhnoi Evropy, vol. 2. Moscow, 1965.
 N. N. SADOMSKAIA [11–1551–1]

CATALAN SCHOOL, the most progressive branch of 14th- and 15th-century Spanish painting. The distinctive historical development of Catalonia, its local artistic traditions, and its close commercial contacts with France, Italy, and the Low Countries lay behind the flourishing of the Catalan school of painting. The school had its origins in the unrefined but vitally expressive Romanesque frescoes of the 11th, 12th, and 13th centuries. The founder of the Catalan school was Ferrer Bassa. He uniquely combined Romanesque traditions with elements of Sienese and Florentine painting in his frescoes in the chapel of San Miguel at the monastery of Pedralbes near Barcelona (1346).

Catalan painters were principally involved in the decoration of *retablos.* Elements anticipating the Renaissance were combined with firmly established principles of late Gothic art. The Catalan masters never painted with oils. Figures were painted in tempera; the saints' halos (represented as concentric circles), various parts of their drapery, and their attributes, as well as the decorative background, were made out of gilded stucco. This form of flat relief served as a natural transition from the planar representation of the fresco to the statuary and other sculptural elements on the *retablo.* Painting was organically included in the total decorative architectural composition.

The painting of the Catalan school reflected the medieval attitude toward a painted surface as an important element in and of itself. Catalan artists were able to combine this attitude with a vivid sense of the realness of their paintings. They sought to create images that were individualistic and close to life and to represent the environment in which their heroes lived. Catalan artists tended to depict colorful and cheerful narratives. Daily scenes of contemporary Catholic society were represented within the framework of Christian legend.

In the 14th and early 15th centuries, the Catalan school was influenced by Italian painting. This influence was reflected in the art of the Serra brothers, L. Borrasá, and B. Martorell, who attempted to give their figures three-dimensionality and to impart a sense of spatial depth, retaining a general planarity of composition. In the mid-15th century, the influence of Dutch painting was particularly strong. J. Huguet organically transformed Dutch traditions, endowing them with depth of feeling and intense passion. In his portraits of saints, Huguet attained poignancy and reality of expression in his figures.

The unification of Spain in 1479 undermined the independence of Catalonia and impeded further development of the Catalan school of painting, which, at that time, stood on the threshold of the Renaissance. The distinctive features of the Catalan school eventually became common properties of Spanish art.

REFERENCES
Sanpere y Miquel, S. *Los cuatrocentistas catalanes,* vol. 1. Barcelona, 1906.
Gudiol Ricart, J. *Historia de la pintura en Cataluña.* Madrid [195—].
Folchi Torres, J. *L'art català.* Barcelona, 1957.
Durliat, M. *L'art catalan.* Paris-Grenoble, 1963.

T. P. KAPTEREVA [11–1549–1]

CATALASE, an enzyme of the hydroperoxidase group that catalyzes the oxidation-reduction reaction during which water and oxygen are formed from two molecules of hydrogen peroxide:

$$2H_2O_2 \xrightarrow{\text{catalase}} 2H_2O + O_2$$

Catalase is obtained in crystalline form; its molecular mass is 250,000. The enzyme is widely distributed in the cells of animals, plants, and microorganisms. It is a chromoprotein having an oxidized heme as a prosthetic (nonprotein) group. Since the specificity of catalase for a substrate–reducing agent is low, it can catalyze not only the decomposition of H_2O_2 but also the oxidation of the lower alcohols. The function of catalase is to destroy the toxic hydrogen peroxide that forms in the body during various oxidative processes. [11–1532–2]

CATALAUNIAN FIELDS (in Latin, Campi Catalaunici), a plain in northeastern France, named for the city of Catalaunum, present-day Châlons-sur-Marne. In the second half of June, A.D. 451, the "battle of the peoples" was fought west of the present-day city of Troyes. In the battle the Roman troops (under the command of Aetius) and their Germanic allies, the Visigoths, Burgundians, Franks, Alani, and other tribes, defeated the Huns, led by Attila. This stopped the advance of the Huns into Europe and led to the collapse of their "empire." [11–1533–2]

CATALEPSY, the phenomenon of "waxy rigidity," observed in catatonia or hypnotic sleep (hypnosis). With an increase in muscle tonus, there is an onset of rigidity (flexible rigidity), so that either the entire body or the extremities remain in any position in which they are placed. [11–1533–4]

CATALEXIS. (1) The type of verse meter at the rhythmic end of a line (clausula), that is, at the last stressed syllable and any unstressed syllables following it. The number of unstressed syllables can vary; in Russian verse there are usually from none to two (rarely three or more).

(2) In the narrow sense of the word: in discussing feet in old prosody, catalexis described a line ending a foot shorter than other lines by one or two unstressed syllables; for example, "Mútno nébo, nóch, mutná" ($— \cup / — \cup / — \cup / —$). The ear distinguishes the clausula irrespective of the character of the foot, so that contemporary Russian poetics tends not to classify lines of verse as catalectic (with a shortened foot at the end), acatalectic (full), or hypercatalectic (extended).

REFERENCE
Zhirmunskii, V. M. *Vvedenie v metriku.* Leningrad, 1925. Pages 131–38.

[11–1533–3]

CATALONIA (Cataluña), a historical region in northeastern Spain, including the provinces of Barcelona, Tarragona, Gerona, and Lérida. Area, 31,900 sq km; population, 5 million (1970), mainly Catalans. Barcelona is the administrative, economic, and cultural center and main port of Catalonia. Much of the region is occupied by the Catalan Mountains, which reach 1,712 m; a narrow band of coastal plain stretches along the Mediterranean Sea. Maquis and oak and pine forests grow on the slopes.

Catalonia is one of the most important industrial regions of Spain, accounting for almost one-third of the total value of the country's output in manufacturing. About 70 percent of the region's population and about 80 percent of all the people employed in industry live in Barcelona and its industrial suburbs and satellite cities. The main branches of industry are metalworking and machine building (30.4 percent of all those employed in the industries in Spain in 1969), the textile industry (72.2 percent), and the chemical industry (35 percent). Catalonia contains about 80 percent of the production capacities of Spain's cotton and wool industry, whose development has for the most part been dependent on imported raw materials. The synthetic fiber and the petrochemical industries are developing. The most developed branches of machine building are the production of textile machines (over 80 percent of the national output), metalworking machine tools (about one-sixth), and automobiles and tractors; 218,300 passenger cars, or 59 percent of the total Spanish output, were produced in Barcelona in 1969. Catalonia is also the site of an electrical and electronics industry, the production of railroad equipment, motor building, paper and cement industries, and the mining of potassium-rich minerals and brown coal.

In 1969 the electric power output was 7.27 billion kilowatt-hours, produced mainly by hydroelectric power plants.

Agriculture produces for the market, with large mechanized capitalist farms dominating production. Less than 36 percent of the total area is cultivated, and orchards cover about two-fifths of the cultivated lands. Poultry raising and swine raising are developed.

S. V. ODESSER

The name "Catalonia" first appeared in official documents in the early 12th century as a designation for the county of Barcelona and the adjoining lands. Previously the region had been in close contact with the Franks, who conquered it from the Arabs between 785 and 811; this fact contributed to the development of the Catalans as a separate ethnic group. In 1137 the county of Barcelona was united with the Kingdom of Aragon through a personal union; in 1164 it became part of Aragon, the counts of Barcelona becoming kings of Aragon. However, Catalonia retained a large degree of political independence; it retained its Cortes, legislative rights and administration, and commercial and tax privileges. Catalonia was economically the most developed part of the Kingdom of Aragon. Catalonian cities conducted large-scale trade, which was promoted by Aragon's conquest of the Balearic Islands, Sicily, Sardinia, and Naples in the 13th through the 15th centuries. In the 13th and 14th centuries an oppressive serfdom was established in Catalonia. Peasant uprisings in 1462–72 and 1484–86 compelled the king of Aragon to abolish serfdom in Catalonia in 1486. When Spain was united in 1479, Catalonia became one of the provinces but retained many of its liberties (*fueros*) until the 18th century. The population of Catalonia, which gradually developed into a separate nation, defended its *fueros* against infringements by the royal power in the uprisings of 1640–42 (the Segador uprising) and of 1705–14.

In 1714 the Spanish government, after having suppressed an uprising of the Catalans, abolished the fundamental Catalonian liberties. When a new administrative division was introduced in Spain in 1833, Catalonia ceased to exist as a separate administrative unit. The national movement became stronger in Catalonia beginning in the 1840's. In 1914, as a concession to the national demands of the Catalans, the Spanish government created a body of local self-government for all of Catalonia, the Mancomunidad, which was abolished in 1925 by the dictator M. Primo de Rivera. The establishment of the Spanish Republic in 1931 was followed by a new upsurge of the national movement in Catalonia. On Sept. 9, 1932, the Spanish Constituent Cortes adopted a law on the autonomous status of Catalonia, and on Nov. 20, 1932, in accordance with the statute, a Catalan parliament was elected and a local government was formed. After the suppression of the October revolutionary uprising of 1934, the Catalan autonomous administration was virtually abolished. The victory of the Popular Front in 1936 brought to the Catalans the restoration of their autonomous rights, which they enjoyed until the capture of Catalonia by the Francoists in February 1939. In the 1950's and 1960's the national movement in Catalonia achieved some successes in the development of the national culture, such as the publication of books in Catalan.

REFERENCES
Soldevila, F. *Història de Catalunya,* 3rd ed. [Barcelona] 1937.
Valls-Taberner, F., and F. Soldevila. *Historia de Cataluña,* vols. 1–2. Madrid-Barcelona, 1955–57.
Garcia Venero, M. *Historia del nacionalismo catalán (1793–1936).* [Madrid] 1944.

L. V. Ponomareva [11–1547–1]

CATALONIAN MOUNTAINS, mountains in northeastern Spain, stretching about 250 km from northeast to southwest along the coast of the Mediterranean Sea, from the Pyrenees to the lower course of the Ebro River. They consist of two parallel chains, a maritime chain with elevations of 400–600 m, and an interior chain with elevations to 1,712 m (Mount Montseny), divided by a longitudinal tectonic basin. The mountains are composed of Paleozoic crystalline rock (granites, quartzites, and others, mainly in the northern part), as well as of Mesozoic and Cenozoic limestones, sandstones, and clay. There is karst. The climate is Mediterranean. The mountains are covered by forests of several species of oak, chestnut, beech, Aleppo pine, stone pine, and maquis. The foothills and foothill plains are sites of olive plantations, vineyards, orchards, and corn and wheat fields.
[11–1550–1]

CATALPA, a genus of plants of the family Bignoniaceae, consisting of deciduous trees with broad leaves. The flowers, which are white with spotted insides, are gathered into large racemes or panicles. The corolla is campanulate and two-lipped. The fruit is an elongated pod, measuring up to 40 cm long; it has numerous seeds bearing tufts of soft hair at each end. Eleven species are distributed from East Asia to North America. In the southern European region of the USSR, the southern catalpa, or Indian bean (*Catalpa bignonioides*), is the most frequently cultivated plant of this genus. The species *C. Bungei, C. speciosa,* and *C. ovata* are also grown there. Catalpa is propagated from seeds, cuttings, and roots. It grows well in moist soils. It is a photophilic plant. The wood of these trees is light, soft, and durable. The oil obtained from the seeds of the southern catalpa contains eleostearic acids (approximately 30 percent); when it is placed in the light, it dries quickly and hardens. All species of catalpa are ornamentals.
[11–1551–2]

CATALYSIS, a change in the rate of a chemical reaction owing to the presence of substances (catalysts) that enter into the intermediate interactions with the reactants yet regain their original chemical composition after each intermediate interaction cycle. Reactions involving catalysts are known as catalytic reactions. The quantity of reactant that can undergo the transformation in the presence of the specified quantity of catalyst is not limited by any stoichiometric relations and may be quite large. Catalytic reactions differ from induced, or conjugate, reactions, in which one reaction is caused or accelerated (induced) by another and an irreversible transformation of the inductor-substance occurs. Possible changes that take place in the catalyst during catalytic reactions are due to side processes that do not determine the course of catalytic action in any way.

The action of the catalyst opens up a new reaction path, usually involving a larger number of steps, in which the catalyst enters the active complex (activated complex) during at least one stage. If during this process the reaction rate becomes greater than the rate in the absence of the catalyst, the catalysis is positive (frequently identified with the concept of catalysis in general). The reverse is also possible, when negative catalysis occurs: one of the possible reaction paths is excluded in the presence of the catalyst and only the slower ones remain, thereby retarding or even almost completely suppressing the reaction. A special case of catalysis involves the acceleration of a reaction under the effect of the reaction product or of an intermediate substance formed during the reaction (autocatalysis).

Catalysis is not connected with the change in free energy of the catalyst, and therefore the catalytic action cannot shift the equilibrium position of the chemical reaction. Catalysts accelerate both the forward and the reverse reactions when approaching the state of equilibrium.

The activation energy (E), that is, the difference between the energy of the active complex and that of the original reacting molecules, is a basic factor in determining the rate of chemical transformation. If it is assumed that the reaction does not disturb the equilibrium distribution of energy between the molecules, then the possible formation of the active complex and, consequently, the reaction rate in the first approximation, is proportional to $\exp(-E/RT)$, where R is the gas constant and T is the absolute temperature. From here it follows that the reaction rate increases as E decreases and, owing to the exponential dependence, grows considerably even during a small reduction of E.

Figure 1 shows the change in energy during a reaction without a catalyst (curve 1) and in the presence of a catalyst (curves 2 and 3). Curve 2 with two maxima corresponds to the formation of one intermediate product.

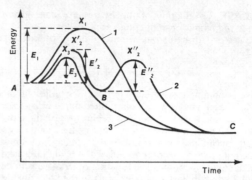

Figure 1. Change in energy of reaction system during reaction process. (*A*) initial state, (*B*) intermediate compound, (*C*) end products, (*X₁*), (*X′₂*), (*X″₂*), and (*X₃*) active complexes.

The number of steps and intermediate products is often much larger. The interaction of the reactants with the catalyst may not even result in the formation of a stable intermediate product (curve 3). Even in this case, however, the catalyst is included in the active complex, and the interaction of the reactants with the catalyst determines the course of the reaction. If the energy of the active complexes in all stages of the reaction process with a catalyst is lower than the energy of the active complex without a catalyst (that is, $E′_2$, $E″_2$, and E_3 are lower than E_1), then participation of the catalyst leads to an increase in reaction rate (positive catalysis). In many cases of catalysis, acceleration of the reaction is achieved as a result of the appearance of energy-rich particles during the course of this very reaction; the concentration of these particles may exceed that at equilibrium. For example, the catalytic effect of water on the oxidation of carbon monoxide is related to the development of the reaction paths involving hydroxyl radicals and hydrogen atoms. Negative catalysis is frequently connected with disruptions of the chain reaction owing to chain breaking as a result of the interaction of the negative catalyst with the active particles. The retarding effect of oxygen on the union of hydrogen and chlorine may serve as an example.

The nature of the intermediate chemical interaction that occurs during catalysis is extremely diverse. Two groups of catalytic processes are generally distinguished: acid-base (heterolytic) and oxidation-reduction (homolytic). An intermediate acid-base interaction between the reactants and the catalysts (for example, proton transfer from the catalyst to the reactants and vice versa) occurs in processes of the first group. In the final stage the proton is shifted in the reverse direction and the catalyst regains its original composition. In catalysis by aprotic acids the interaction is carried out by way of the free electron pair of the reactant. Examples of acid-base catalysis include (1) hydrolysis of esters, which is accelerated by acids; (2) hydration of olefins in the presence of phosphorus-acidic catalysts; (3) isomerization and cracking of hydrocarbons using aluminosilicate catalysts; (4) alkylation; and (5) polymerization. During the course of oxidation-reduction catalysis reactions, the intermediate interaction is associated with the electron transfers between the catalyst and the reactants. This group includes (1) oxidation of sulfur dioxide into trioxide during the preparation of sulfuric acid; (2) oxidation of ammonia into nitric oxide during the preparation of nitric acid; (3) numerous processes involving the partial oxidation of organic compounds, for example, ethylene into ethylene oxide and naphthalene into phthalic anhydride; (4) hydrogenation; (5) dehydrogenation; (6) cyclization and aromatization of hydrocarbons; and (7) decomposition of hydrogen peroxide. Primarily metals of periods IV, V, and VI of the D. I. Mendeleev system, which have an incomplete *d* electron shell, exhibit oxidation-reduction catalytic activity, as do the compounds of these metals and, to a lesser degree, the compounds of elements with an f shell that is being filled (lanthanides and actinides).

The groups discussed above by no means include all the various catalytic reactions known to occur. The nature of the intermediate interaction during catalysis is much more complex and is dependent on all the details of the electron structure of both the reactants and the catalyst. The specific mechanisms of catalytic reactions are diverse and have been firmly established in only a few cases.

Catalysis is classified as homogeneous or heterogeneous according to the phase condition of the reactants and the catalyst. Microheterogeneous catalysis, occurring in colloidal systems (for example, enzyme catalysis), occupies the intermediate position. During homogeneous catalysis, the catalyst and reactants form one homogeneous system, with no phase boundaries existing between the catalyst and the reactants. In heterogeneous catalysis, however, the catalyst and reactants are found in different phases and are divided by a phase boundary. The most important case is the one where the catalyst is a solid and the reaction system forms a liquid or gaseous phase. The intermediate interaction occurs primarily on the surface of the solid catalyst during this process.

Selection of the composition of the catalyst in a specified reaction is a very complex problem and is still primarily resolved empirically. A number of theoretical approaches based on the correlation of individual specific properties of catalysts with their activity have been proposed and developed in the USSR. For example, the multiplet theory of catalysis (first published in 1929) assumes the intermediate interaction of reactants with several atoms on the surface of solid catalysts and gives a controlling importance to the matching of the distances between the atoms in reactant molecules and the parameters for the crystalline structure of the catalyst. Later, this theory was extended by the concept of the necessity of a definite correspondence between the bond energies that split and form in the course of the reaction and the energies of reactant-catalyst bonds, which occur during intermediate interaction. A very widespread concept in the 1950's pertained to the dependence of catalytic activity of solid catalysts having semiconductor properties on their electrical characteristics, that is, the electron theory of catalysis. According to this theory, it is assumed that the intermediate interaction of the reactants with the catalyst is realized during the participation of conductivity electrons from the solid catalyst and therefore depends on its total electron properties—for example, the destruction of energy zones and local electron levels, the release of electrons, and current carrier concentration. In the case of heterogeneous catalysis, it was generally assumed (first in 1939) that active centers, in the form of edges, angles, or different structural deformations (dislocations) in a standard crystalline structure exist on the surface of solid catalysts. It was also proposed that individually arranged atoms or aggregates of several atoms (ensembles) exhibit specific catalytic properties during application of the catalytically active substance on the inert carrier.

The development of accurate methods of determining the catalyst surface has made it possible to establish that the activity related to the unit surface (specific catalytic activity) is determined by the chemical composition and depends very little on the structural dislocations. The specific catalytic activity of various crystal faces is differentiated several times in certain cases. Deviations in chemical composition (stoichiometric deviation, introduction of impurities, local chemical formations) have a substantial effect on activity.

During the 1960's the intermediate chemical interaction in heterogeneous catalysis was primarily thought of as local, and as determined by the electron structure of individual atoms or ions of a catalytically active constituent on the catalyst surface, taking into account the effect of the immediate environment. The development of this approach was aided by the discovery (by way of experiment) of a similar effect produced by solid catalysts containing a particular metal during heterogeneous catalysis and by soluble complexes containing the same metal during homogeneous catalysis in solutions. Furthermore, the theories of crystalline and ligand fields, which were applied even earlier in the chemistry of complex compounds, were successfully used. Correlations between the catalytic activity and bond energies of reactants in the presence of a catalyst during intermediate interaction have been established for many classes of catalysts and catalytic reactions, thereby simplifying the selection of catalysts for individual cases.

The first scientific reference to catalysis appeared early in the 19th century. In 1806 the French chemists N. Clément-Desormes and C. Desormes discovered the catalytic action of nitric oxides on the oxidation of sulfurous gas in a chamber process for the preparation of sulfuric acid. In 1811 the Russian chemist K. S. Kirkhgof noticed that dilute acids can induce the conversion of starch into sugar (glucose); in 1814 he established that this reaction can be catalyzed by diastase from barley malt. This was the beginning of research on biological catalysts, that is, enzymes. In 1818 the French chemist L. Thénard determined that many solids exhibit an accelerating effect on the decomposition of hydrogen peroxide solutions, and the British chemist H. Davy discovered the oxidability (on platinum) of alcohol and ether vapors. The German chemist J. Dobereiner established (1822) that hydrogen and oxygen combine on platinum at ordinary temperatures. It was subsequently discovered that a number of other substances also exhibit a markedly high effect on the rate or occurrence of chemical reactions. This led to the isolation of a group of phenomena named by the German chemist E. Micherlich as contact (1833) and by the Swedish chemist J. Berzelius as catalytic (1835).

In later years a considerable number of catalytic reactions were discovered; over the last 50 years catalysis has become the leading method of conducting chemical reactions in industry. The use of catalysts enables chemical transformations to be realized at high rates and low temperatures. Most of the industrial catalytic processes would not be realized without catalysts. Selection of catalysts makes it possible to direct the chemical transformation toward the formation of a specified product from a number of possible ones. The application of stereospecific catalysts makes it possible to control the structure of the end products, such as polymers. In the early 20th century the problem of fixation of nitrogen in the air was resolved with the aid of catalysis. Promoted iron and other catalysts have made it possible to surmount the chemical inertness of elemental nitrogen and to effect the synthesis of ammonia. At the same time, a catalytic method was developed for preparing nitric acid by the oxidation of ammonia on platinum wires. Modern techniques used in the production of hydrogen from natural gas are based on catalytic reactions. Catalytic methods also occupy an important position in petroleum refining technology. Hundreds of millions of tons of high-grade motor fuel are produced by way of such catalytic reactions as cracking, hydrocracking, reforming, cyclization, and isomerization of petroleum hydrocarbons. Catalytic methods play a particularly large role in the realization of processes of organic synthesis. The USSR was the first country in the world to develop and effect the production of synthetic rubber based on the conversion of ethyl alcohol into divinyl in the presence of the multicomponent Lebedev oxide catalyst. Catalytic methods are used in the preparation of most of the products of petrochemical synthesis: solvents, aromatic hydrocarbons, monomers for the manufacture of synthetic rubber, synthetic fibers, and other polymer materials. Catalysts are also widely used in polymerization.

Catalysis plays a leading role in the chemical transformations that occur in living systems. The entire complex system of regulation of life processes in organisms is based on catalytic reactions. Biological catalysts, called enzymes, are substances of protein origin containing chemically active groups, often including atoms of transition elements. Enzymes surpass industrial catalysts in certain properties. In the USSR and other countries, extensive research is being carried out on new types of complex synthetic catalysts—complex compounds, organic semiconductors, and polymers characterized by a simpler composition than enzymes but simulating their effect to a certain degree. The science of catalysis has played a fundamental role both in the advancement of the chemical industry and in the discovery of the most important biological mechanisms.

REFERENCES

Balandin, A. A. *Mul'tipletnaia teoriia kataliza,* parts 1–2. Moscow, 1963–64.

Vol'kenshtein, F. F. *Elektronnaia teoriia kataliza na poluprovodnikakh.* Moscow, 1960.

Catalysis, vols. 1–7. Edited by P. H. Emmett. New York, 1954–60.

Ashmore, P. *Kataliz i ingibirovanie khimicheskikh reaktsii.* Moscow, 1966. (Translated from English.)

Thomas, J., and W. Thomas. *Geterogennyi kataliz.* Moscow, 1969. (Translated from English.)

Kiperman, S. L. *Vvedenie v kinetiku geterogennykh kataliticheskikh reaktsii.* Moscow, 1964.

Boreskov, G. K. *Kataliz v proizvodstve sernoi kisloty.* Moscow-Leningrad, 1954.

Krylov, O. V. *Kataliz nemetallami.* Leningrad, 1967.

"Osnovy predvideniia kataliticheskogo deistviia." *Trudy IV Mezhdunarodnogo kongressa po katalizu,* vols. 1–2. Moscow, 1970.

G. K. Boreskov   [11–1534–1]

CATALYST POISONS, substances that induce the "poisoning" of catalysts (usually heterogeneous catalysts), that is, reduce their catalytic activity or completely stop the catalytic effect. The poisoning of heterogeneous catalysts occurs as a result of the adsorption of the poison or the product of its chemical transformation on the surface of the catalyst. The poisoning may be temporary or permanent. For example, during the synthesis of ammonia on an iron catalyst, oxygen and its derivatives temporarily poison Fe. In this case, the surface of the catalyst is freed of oxygen under the action of a pure $N_2 + H_2$ mixture and the degree of poisoning is reduced. Sulfur compounds permanently poison Fe, since the activity of the catalyst is not successfully reduced by the action of the pure mixture. Thorough purification is required to prevent poisoning of the reacting mixture that passes onto the catalyst.

The most widespread catalyst poisons for metal catalysts include substances containing oxygen (H_2O, CO, CO_2), sulfur (H_2S, CS_2, C_2H_5SH), selenium, tellurium, nitrogen, phosphorus, arsenic, and antimony, as well as unsaturated hydrocarbons (C_2H_4, C_2H_2) and metal ions (Cu^{2+}, Sn^{2+}, Hg^{2+}, Fe^{2+}, Co^{2+}, Ni^{2+}). Acidic catalysts are usually poisoned by basic admixtures and basic catalysts, by acidic admixtures.

[11–1545–2]

CATALYSTS, substances that change the rate of chemical reactions by repeated intermediate chemical interaction with the reactants but are not part of the composition of the end products. Catalysts are universally distributed in living nature and are widely used in industry. More than 70 percent of all chemical

Table 1. Industrial catalysts

Processes and their features	Catalysts and selected properties
(1) Cracking of petroleum products	Synthetic amorphous and crystalline (zeolites) aluminosilicates, including additions of oxides of rare-earth elements
systems with compact moving bed	Catalyst in the form of beads, 3–6 mm diameter
systems with fluidized bed	Microspherical catalyst, particle size, 0.08–0.2 mm
(2) Reforming—preparation of high-octane gasolines and aromatic hydrocarbons	Platinum (0.2–0.6 percent) on aluminum oxide with additions of chlorine, fluorine, rare-earth metals; cylindrical granules or beads, 2–3 mm in size
(3) Conversion of natural gas and other hydrocarbons with water vapor to obtain hydrogen	Nickel (5–25 percent) on thermostable carrier (usually on an aluminum oxide base); cylindrical granules, rings, or beads, 10–20 mm in size
(4) Preparation of hydrogen from carbon monoxide and water vapor	Iron chromium oxide catalysts (6–9 percent Cr_2O_3); working temperature 350°–500°C, relatively stable to action of sulfur compounds. Mixtures of oxides of copper, zinc, aluminum, iron; working temperature 200°–250°C, residual carbon monoxide content as compared to iron chromium catalysts decreases from 1.5–2.5 to 0.2–0.3 percent; readily poisoned by sulfur and require thorough gas purification.
(5) Synthesis of ammonia	Metallic iron promoted by oxides of alumnium, calcium, potassium
(6) Oxidation of sulfur dioxide in production of sulfuric acid	Vanadium catalysts on carriers (usually silicate) active substance has composition $V_2O_5 \cdot m\, Me_2O \cdot nSO_3$ (Me—alkali metal); cylindrical and spherical granules, tablets, or rings, 5–12 mm in size
(7) Oxidation of ammonia in production of nitric acid	Metallic platinum (wire), alloys of platinum with certain metals, less common catalysts on oxide base (cobalt, bismuth, iron)
(8) Oxidation of ethylene into ethylene oxide	Silver, porous metallic or on inert carriers
(9) Oxidation of naphthalene into phthalic anhydride	Vanadium pentoxide, fused or on carriers (promoted by sulfates of alkali metals)
(10) Synthesis of methyl alcohol from carbon monoxide and hydrogen	Zinc-chromium oxide catalysts; working temperature 375°–400°C, pressure 20–30 MN/m² (200–300 kgf/cm²). Catalysts containing copper; working temperature 250°C, pressure 5 MN/m² (50 kgf/cm²).
(11) Synthesis of ethyl alcohol by direct hydration of ethylene	Phosphoric acid on siliceous carrier
(12) Synthesis of acetaldehyde from acetylene	
homogeneous Kucherov process	Aqueous solution of mercury sulfate
heterogeneous process	Phosphates of calcium and cadmium
synthesis of acetaldehyde from ethylene, homogeneous process	Aqueous solution of paladium and copper chlorides
(13) Dehydrogenation of butane, isobutane, isopentane into olefins and diolefins (production nonomers for synthetic rubber)	Aluminum chromium oxide and iron chromium oxide; calcium-nickel phosphates and other catalysts; often used in fluidized bed
(14) Hydrogenation of benzene into cyclohexane (phenol into cyclohexanol) in production of caprolactam	Nickel (35–50 percent) on carriers. For benzene from coking byproduct—sulfide of nickel, cobalt, molybdenum, tungsten; sulfide catalysts are not poisoned by sulfur-containing compounds.
(15) Hydrogenation of fats	
suspended catalysts	Nickel and nickel-copper catalysts in the form of highly dispersed powder (black) or on carriers
fixed catalyst bed	Nickel on carriers, fused or caked nickel catalysts
(16) Synthesis of vinyl chloride from acetylene	Mercuric chloride on activated carbon

transformations of substances (more than 90 percent in new productions) are realized with the aid of catalysts. The various catalysts produced by industry are classified according to (1) the type of catalyzed reaction (acid-base, oxidation-reduction), (2) the groups of catalytic processes or the specific features of their industrial use (for example, catalysts for the synthesis of ammonia and cracking of petroleum products, catalysts used in fluidized beds), (3) the nature of the active center (metallic, oxide, sulfide, organometallic, complex), and (4) the method of preparation. Some types of catalysts used in industry are given in Table 1. Protein catalysts, that is, enzymes, assist in effecting metabolic processes in all living organisms.

The most important property of catalysts is specificity of action; that is, each chemical reaction or group of uniform reactions can be accelerated only by very specific catalysts. Catalyst specificity is most clearly manifested in that catalysts can determine the course of the reaction, that is, various products are formed from the same original substances depending on the type of catalyst used. For example, from a mixture of carbon monoxide and hydrogen, using different catalysts it is possible to obtain methane, a mixture of liquid hydrocarbons, high-molecular-weight solid hydrocarbons, mixtures of oxygen-containing compounds of various composition, and methyl or isobutyl alcohols. Selectivity serves as the measure of specificity of catalysts and is estimated by the the ratio of the specific reaction rate to the general transformation rate of the initial substances in the presence of a given catalyst. Catalytic activity is another important indicator of catalytic properties exhibited by substances. It is expressed as the difference in the rates of one particular reaction, measured both in the presence and in the absence of a catalyst, other conditions being equal. Catalytic activity is related to the unit of weight, volume, concentration, or surface of the catalyst. Activity relative to 1 m^2 of catalyst surface is known as specific catalytic activity. If without a catalyst the reaction practically does not occur, then the measure of activity is taken to be the reaction rate under specific conditions, relative to the unit quantity of the given catalyst. Owing to the specificity of catalysts, it is possible to compare the catalytic activity of substances with respect to only one particular reaction. In applied research, catalyst activity is often expressed as conversion, that is, the quantity of product (or reacted substance) obtained in a unit of time per unit volume of catalyst, and as selectivity, that is, the yield of the specific product in relation to the theoretically possible product.

In addition to activity and selectivity, another operational characteristic of catalysts is stability, which often determines the advisability of using catalysts for one or another industrial process. Industrial catalysts change in the course of time; their activity and selectivity decrease as a result of various side processes—for example, as a result of (1) interaction with impurities during the introduction of the raw material ("poisoning"), (2) the sintering and recrystallization of the catalyst at elevated temperatures or by the effect of the reaction medium (aging), (3) the precipitation of tarry matter and coke on the surface of the catalyst, and (4) the adsorptive reduction of strength (Roebinder effect). Therefore, after a certain period of time catalysts are subjected to special treatment (regeneration) or, if possible, are replaced by new ones. The life of industrial catalysts during continuous processes in equipment with a fixed catalyst bed averages six to 36 months. The most stable catalysts can operate continuously for more than ten years (for example, vanadium catalysts for SO_2 oxidation). Catalysts with a service life of less than one to two months are generally not used in fixed-bed reactors. In the case of such catalysts and those that operate in short cycles with frequent regeneration (for example, aluminosilicate catalysts for cracking, catalysts for hydrocarbon dehydrogenation), it is sometimes advisable to use moving-bed reactors, in particular, reactors with fluidized catalyst beds.

Specific chemical compounds or their mixtures serve as catalysts in homogeneous catalytic processes. In this case, the catalytic properties of the catalysts are wholly determined by their chemical composition and structure. Heterogeneous catalytic processes using solid catalysts in the form of porous grains with a highly developed inner surface are primarily used in industry. The catalytic properties of solid catalysts are dependent on the size of their inner surface and the porous structure as well as on composition and structure. The essential stages of catalytic processes with solid catalysts are the transfer of reactants, products, and heat between the reaction mixture and the external surface of the catalyst grains (external transfer) and the transfer of substances and heat within the porous catalyst grains (internal transfer). The influence of internal mass transfer by diffusion is most frequent in the use of industrial catalysts. When this rate is insufficient, the efficiency of the catalyst decreases and the overall intensity of the process drops. Furthermore, this can lead to a reduction in the yield of unstable intermediate products capable of further transformation on the surface of the catalysts, which in many cases are specific (for example, during partial oxidation of hydrocarbons). The rate of transfer by diffusion within the grains of the catalyst is determined by its porous structure. If the reactants are in the gaseous phase, it is advisable to use catalysts with a maximum developed inner surface and pores measuring approximately 1×10^{-7} m in diameter for slow reactions to ensure the necessary rate of molecular counterdiffusion of the reactants and products. For reactions proceeding at an average rate (2–10 kmol/hr per 1 m^3 of catalyst), the optimum diameter of pores in the case of a uniform porous structure corresponds to the mean free path of molecules, equaling 1×10^{-7} m at atmospheric pressure and decreasing with increasing pressure. The branched nonuniform porous grain structure is most beneficial in many cases; here fine pores, creating a large inner surface, adjoin the large transfer pores. At atmospheric pressure the transfer from grains of uniform porous structure to those with a branched nonuniform porous structure increases the activity of the unit catalyst volume by a factor of 3–9. Increased understanding of the effect of a porous structure on the activity and selectivity of catalysts, the elaboration of methods of investigating specific catalytic activity and porous structure, and the use of computers for the mathematical modeling of complex processes have created the prerequisites for the transition from empirical to scientifically based methods of developing industrial catalysts.

Various methods are used in the preparation of catalysts: precipitation from solutions, impregnation, mixing (for example, mixed catalysts), and fusion with subsequent washing out of the inactive part (skeletal catalysts). Many catalysts undergo special treatment prior to use, for example, activation, during which the active substance (for example, a metal in a highly dispersed state as a result of the reduction of oxides) is formed and the porous structure is created. The active substance (such as platinum) is supported on the surface of the carrier to stabilize its highly dispersed state or to minimize expense. Different substances that exhibit stability under process conditions, for example, aluminum oxide, silica gel, synthetic and natural silicates, or activated carbon, act as carriers. Carriers can affect catalytic properties and therefore must be selected with care for use with industrial catalysts.

A tendency to pass from single-component catalysts of simple composition to complex multicomponent and polyfunctional catalysts has been observed. The latter reveal surface areas differing according to the nature of the catalytic action. A number of successive chemical transformations are effected on polyfunctional catalysts in one apparatus during a single passage of the reaction mixture. Very often, particularly when the intermediate substance is unstable, a higher yield of the desired product is obtained as compared to separate individual processes in the presence of monofunctional catalysts. Some examples of polyfunctional catalysts are the Lebedev catalyst for the preparation of divinyl from ethyl alcohol and the aluminoplatinum catalyst for the manufacture of high-octane gasoline. Promoted catalysts are being used more frequently and for various purposes. Their activity is significantly improved by the addition of substances (promoters) which, when taken separately, may not exhibit catalytic properties.

Every industrial process requires a specific catalyst with an optimum combination of properties. Therefore a large number of different catalysts are produced, differing in chemical composition, porous structure, and granule size and shape.

World catalyst production totals 500,000–800,000 tons per year; approximately 250 basic types of catalysts are manufactured, each type having several varieties. Particular differences are found between catalysts designed for one specific purpose and produced in different countries or by different firms, especially between catalysts used in new processes. A concentration of catalyst production is observed everywhere. Large catalyst plants and workshops are being constructed, which makes it possible to improve the quality of production and to mechanize and automate production; catalysts previously prepared for use within an enterprise have now been put on sale on both the domestic and international markets.

REFERENCES

Kataliticheskie svoistva veshchestv. Spravochnik. Edited by V. A. Roiter. Kiev, 1968.
"Poristaia struktura katalizatorov i protsessy perenosa v geterogennom katalize" (Fourth International Congress on Catalysis. Symposium III). Novosibirsk, 1970.
Nauchnye osnovy podbora katalizatorov geterogennykh kataliticheskikh reaktsii. Sbornik. Edited by S. Z. Roginskii. Moscow, 1966.
Nauchnye osnovy podbora i proizvodstva katalizatorov. Sbornik. Edited by G. K. Boreskov. Novosibirsk, 1964.
Polifunktsional'nye katalizatory i slozhnye reaktsii. Moscow, 1965. (Translated from English.)
Kataliz. Voprosy izbiratel'nosti i stereospetsifichnosti katalizatorov. Moscow, 1963. (Translated from English.)
Metody issledovaniia katalizatorov i kataliticheskikh reaktsii, vols. 1–3. Novosibirsk, 1965.

G. K. BORESKOV and A. A. SAMAKHOV   [11–1539–1]

CATALYSTS, BIOLOGICAL, biocatalysts, substances formed in living cells that accelerate (positive catalysis) or slow down (negative catalysis) the chemical processes in the body. Biological catalysts include primarily catalysts of a protein nature, the enzymes.   [11–1545–1]

CATAMARAN (from Tamil *kattumaram,* literally "logs bound together").

(1) A raft for short trips and fishing among peoples along the Asiatic coast of the Indian Ocean and neighboring islands, propelled by paddles or sail. Similar rafts were used by the native inhabitants of the islands of the Pacific Ocean and South America. The term "catamaran" also referred to a small paddle boat or sailing vessel consisting of several logs, hollowed out and pointed on both ends, interconnected by cross bars.

(2) A modern twin-hulled vessel (with two parallel hulls connected on the top side by trusses or a continuous deck) or single-hulled sailing vessel with one or two outlying balance floats on the side. It is exceptionally swift and stable. There are various kinds of catamarans: for sea and river fishing, carrying passengers and cargo, towing and rescue work, sports and tourism, and scientific research.   [11–1552–1]

CATAMARCA, a province in northwestern Argentina. Area, 99,800 sq km. Population, 172,000 (1970). Administrative center, the city of Catamarca. Most of the territory is occupied by mountains (reaching a height of 6,880 m). Livestock is pastured (sheep, goats, llamas, alpacas, and vicuñas). There is viticulture on the irrigated lands in the foothills. Industry (for the most part, the processing of agricultural products and leather) is represented basically by cottage enterprises.   [11–1552–2]

CATAMARCA, a city in northwestern Argentina, located in the foothills of the Andes. Administrative center of Catamarca Province. Population, 46,000 (1960). Railroad station. The economy is basically agricultural and includes processing grapes for wine and home processing of wool and vicuña to make textiles and ponchos, the national costume.   [11–1552–3]

CATAMNESIS, a summary of all information about a patient obtained on a single or several occasions after the end of his initial period under observation.

A catamnesis is prepared after a patient's discharge from a hospital or after his last examination or treatment. The physician obtains data concerning the patient from a variety of sources: the results of a medical examination, excerpts from the case history, the patient's answers to questions, and information imparted by

the patient's relatives and persons who know him well. A catamnesis is very important in all branches of medicine, especially in psychiatry. Certain mental disorders have been identified as independent diseases with the help of the catamnesis, such as schizophrenia and manic-depressive psychosis. The catamnesis is helpful in following the progress of psychiatric patients after various methods of treatment and in tracing the history of persons who have had mental diseases in childhood.   [11–1552–4]

CATANDUANES, an island in the Philippine Archipelago; part of the Republic of the Philippines. Area, 1,448 sq km; elevation, up to 814 m. A coral reef extends along the northern coast. There are evergreen forests. Catanduanes has tropical agriculture.

[11–1553–5]

CATANIA, a city and port in Italy, located on the eastern coast of the island of Sicily, in the foothills of Mount Etna. Administrative center of Catania Province. Population, 414,600 (1970). The city is an important transportation junction. It has dry docks for repairing ships, workshops for repairing steam locomotives and railroad cars, plants that manufacture farm machinery and electronics parts, oil refineries, and chemical enterprises. The city also processes food and wood and manufactures silk, cotton, and ceramics. Deposits of natural gas are located near Catania.

Catania has a university (15th century), an astrophysics observatory, a volcanologic institute, and a botanical garden. There are ruins of ancient Greek and Roman structures, a castle (1329–50), and a cathedral (11th–18th centuries).

Catania (Latin, Catana) was founded in the eighth century B.C.   [11–1553–6]

CATANZARO, a city in southern Italy, in Calabria, capital of Catanzaro Province. Population, 83,000 (1970). Catanzaro is a railroad junction with a port (Marina di Catanzaro) on the coast of the Gulf of Squillace in the Ionian Sea. It has food, woodworking, metalworking, and textile industries; pottery is also produced.   [11–1553–4]

CATAPHYLAXIS, lowered resistance of animal and human tissues to pathogenic microbes, as a result of which the microorganisms that have penetrated the body or that are circulating in the blood settle more readily and reproduce in the tissues.

The term "cataphylaxis" was coined in 1919 by the English scientists W. Bullock and W. Cranmer. Lowered tissue resistance after mechanical, thermal, or biological injury depends neither on the absence of phagocytes at the site of injury nor on a decrease in the phagocytic activity of the leukocytes. Cataphylaxis is the result of impairment by injury of the normal physiological and biochemical properties of tissues.

[11–1563–2]

CATAPULT. (1) In military terminology a throwing machine activated by the elastic force of twisted cords made from sinews, hair, and so forth. Catapults were used in ancient Greece and Rome up to the end of the fifth century mainly for besieging fortresses; lightweight versions (from the fourth century B.C.) were also used in field combat. Catapults hurled stones, logs, barrels with burning tar, and other objects over distances of a few hundred meters and lances up to 185 cm long and weighing up to 1.5 kg over distances up to 150 m.

(2) A device for imparting initial (launch) velocity to airplanes, gliders, and so forth on a short runway. A catapult consists of a driving apparatus (trolley, "shuttle", hook, etc.), a guiding device (usually rails), and a launching mechanism. The driving apparatus with the aircraft attached to it is accelerated either by a jet engine or by employing the energy of steam, gunpowder, compressed air, springs, or rubber bands. Toward the end of the takeoff run, the driving mechanism is abruptly halted, and the aircraft separates from the driving apparatus with the necessary velocity for independent flight.

Catapults with horizontal guiding devices are employed mainly on aircraft carriers, where steam catapults are usually employed that provide an airplane acceleration on a runway of 60–80 m up to a velocity of 200–300 km/hr. Catapults with vertical guiding devices are used for practicing ejection from airplanes on the ground, training flight crews, and studying the effects of great strains on man over short time periods.

REFERENCE
Korotkin, I. M., Z. F. Slepenkov, and B. A. Kolyzaev. *Avianostsy.* Moscow. 1964.   G. M. Badaev and E. P. Golubkov [11–1554–2]

CATARACT, an opacity of the crystalline lens of the eye that prevents light from penetrating into the eye and that results in decreased visual acuity. The term "cataract" reflects the mistaken conception of the ancient Greeks that a cataract is caused by the effusion of a turbid fluid between the iris and the lens. Cataracts are distinguished according to the location of the opacity in the lens: capsular (in the capsule covering the lens), cortical (in the peripheral layers of the lens), and nuclear (in its central layers).

Cataracts may be congenital or acquired. Congenital cataracts develop in the intrauterine period, and the opacity generally does not enlarge or change with age. In congenital cataracts, parts of the lens almost invariably remain transparent, and visual acuity is not completely impaired. Depending on the site of the opacities, cataracts may be anterior or posterior polar (limited opacities of the capsule of the lens), lamellar, and so forth.

Senile cataracts constitute most of the acquired cataracts, and they are characterized by progression of the opacities of the lens. In senile cataracts, opacities appear first in the periphery of the lens (incipient senile cataract), and vision remains unimpaired. The number of opacities then increases and they coalesce, resulting in a marked decrease in visual acuity (immature cataract). As the condition develops, all the layers of the lens become cloudy and it turns grayish white or mother-of-pearl; visual acuity decreases to photoperception—that is, the eye becomes virtually blind (mature senile cataract). Also acquired are complicated cataracts that arise in some systemic diseases (diabetes, cholera, digestive disorders) or result from diseases of the eye itself (inflammation of the uveal tract, progressive myopia). Cataracts resulting from eye injuries, effects of radiation, and so forth constitute a large group of acquired cataracts.

Treatment is generally surgical. In some cases it involves transplanting an artificial lens.

REFERENCE
Dymshits, L. A. "Bolezni khrustalika." In *Mnogotomnoe rukovodstvo po glaznym bolezniam,* vol. 2, book 2. Moscow, 1960.
L. A. Katsnel'son [11–1559–4]

CATARRH, or catarrhal inflammation, an inflammation of the mucous membranes; they become red, swollen, edematous and form and exude a fluid (exudate). The exudate may be transparent (serous catarrh) or admixed with mucus (mucous catarrh) or pus (suppurative catarrh).

Catarrh may be caused by a bacterial or viral infection—for example, catarrh (inflammation) of the upper respiratory tract: bronchitis, laryngitis, and head cold; or it may be caused by pathogenic fungi—for example, colitis. Catarrh of the stomach (obsolete name, gastritis) develops from improper diet, abuse of alcohol, and smoking.

In acute forms of catarrh, the matter exuded by the mucous membranes gradually decreases and full recovery ensues. Delayed treatment may cause an acute form to develop into a chronic inflammation, which may produce severe irreversible changes in the mucous membranes, including attenuation (atrophy) or disorderly proliferation (hypertrophy) with deterioration or complete loss of function of the affected organ. Chronic catarrh is prevented by prompt and comprehensive treatment of the acute forms.   [11–1559–1]

CATARRHAL FEVER OF SHEEP, a noncontagious, viral, transmissible disease of sheep characterized by infection of the mucous membranes of the mouth, swelling of the tongue, and fever. The disease was first detected in Africa in 1876; it is also found in the USA, the Near East, and on the Iberian Peninsula. It has not been reported in the USSR. In view of the danger that it presents, catarrhal fever of sheep is included by the International Bureau of Epizootics in the convention for mandatory notification.

Under natural conditions, sheep, especially lambs, are susceptible, as are cattle, goats, and antelopes to a lesser extent. The source of the infection is sick and convalescent sheep, whose blood may retain the virus up to four months. Blood-sucking insects from the genus *Culicoides* are carriers of the causative agent of the disease. In Africa, wild animals (antelopes) are a natural reservoir of the causative agent. Catarrhal fever of sheep is a seasonal disease that occurs chiefly in low-lying areas in warm and very rainy weather. No specific treatment has as yet been devised. Animals that recover from the disease acquire permanent immunity. Prevention and control calls for quarantine and vaccination of sheep in a threatened zone.

REFERENCE
Maloizuchennye zabolevaniia sel'skokhoziaistvennykh zhivotnykh. Edited by Ia. R. Kovalenko [et al.]. Moscow, 1967.   [11–1560–1]

CATARRH OF THE RESPIRATORY TRACT, an acute inflammatory disease involving the mucous membranes of the respiratory tract (rhinitis, pharyngitis, laryngotracheitis, bronchitis). Respiratory catarrh may be combined with inflammation of the conjunctiva (conjunctivitis) or lungs (pneumonia).
[11–1559–2]

CATASTROPHISM, THEORY OF, an early 19th-century hypothesis that viewed the geological history of the earth as the alternation of long periods of relative calm with comparatively brief, catastrophic events that greatly changed the face of the planet.

The idea of catastrophes, which had its origin in remote antiquity, began to be used in the 17th and 18th centuries for interpreting geological history. Since until the early 19th century the age of the earth was estimated to be not more than 100,000 years, it was difficult to explain as the result of ordinary causes the enormous changes undergone in the past by the earth and the organic world and recorded in beds of rock. In an effort to find a way out of this difficulty the French naturalist G. Cuvier in 1812 advanced the hypothesis of catastrophes (revolutions), during which all living things perished over large areas of the planet; later these desolate places were settled by other species of organisms that had survived the catastrophe in remote areas. The hypothesis was an attempt not only to explain the vastness of past transformations of the earth but also to resolve the contradiction between the prevailing belief that species were immutable and the fact, already firmly established, that geological sections showed numerous differences in plant and animal fossils.

Cuvier's ideas were elaborated by the French paleontologist A. d'Orbigny, the Swiss geologist J. Agassiz, and the English geologist A. Sedgewick, who counted 27 catastrophes in the history of the earth, during which the entire organic world presumably perished. According to these scientists, after each catastrophe new plants and animals, unrelated to those that had previously existed, were "created by a divine act"; each time the plants and animals were more complex and perfectly organized than before. In the periods between catastrophes the newly created living things presumably neither developed nor changed. The concept of catastrophism and of numerous acts of creation was in accord with the biblical version of the creation of the world. In accepting this concept it was possible to explain the contemporary state of the earth's surface as the result of the most recent act of creation.

Nonetheless, the catastrophism of the early 19th century played an important role in the development of biostratigraphy because its doctrine of the sharp boundaries between rock beds of different ages and its belief in the uniqueness of the organic world in each period (epoch, age) promoted the concept of dominant fossils. Catastrophism also had a positive influence in disseminating the idea of progress in the organic world and the concept of sporadic events that disrupt the uniformity of the earth's history. This promoted the subsequent development of ideas that combined evolutionary change with rapid, discontinuous development. By the mid-19th century, with the ascendancy of the idea that existing geological forces are sufficient to bring about over a long period of time all the changes recorded in the earth (C. Lyell), the theory of catastrophism lost its significance. Later, catastrophism was also superseded in biology by the development of the evolutionary ideas of C. Darwin and others.

The rejection of catastrophism was not final, however. In the first half of the 20th century it was partially revived in the form of "neocatastrophism"—the idea that phases of folding and mountain building occurred simultaneously throughout the world, interrupting long periods of relative calm and the slow evolution of the crust (H. Stille and his followers). Theories have also arisen holding that catastrophic events occur in the universe, causing intensified radiation that leads to the death of some groups of organisms and to rapid mutational changes in others, resulting in the appearance of new species and genera of living organisms (the German paleontologist O. Schindewolf). The ideas of neocatastrophism have been convincingly criticized by N. S. Shatskii in tectonics and by L. Sh. Davitashvili in paleontology.　　　　　　　　V. V. TIKHOMIROV [11–1562–1]

CATATONIA, or catatonic syndrome, a mental disorder dominated by impairment of motor activity.

Catatonia is a syndrome in schizophrenia and in psychoses resulting from poisoning, infection, or organic brain lesions. There are two alternating phases: stupor and excitement. In catatonic stupor, the tone of the skeletal muscles increases to the point where the patient remains frozen in any position, however uncomfortable, in which he is placed (catalepsy). The rigidity may reach the extremes of muscular tension: stupor with the extremities drawn close to the abdomen and the head bent, that is, the fetal position. The facial expression is frozen and the patient remains completely mute. External stimuli (for example, pain) or even extraordinary circumstances (fire, earthquake) do not prompt the patient to protect himself. Any attempt to change the position of a person in a deep stupor will induce muscular resistance.

Catatonic excitement may be bizarre and pathetic (the patients behave foolishly, ranting, singing, and striking affected poses) or impulsive, frantic, and aggressive. The mind of catatonics may stay clear or become clouded. Catatonia is relieved through the treatment of the causative disease.　　[11–1563–1]

CATEAU-CAMBRÉSIS, TREATY OF (1559), two peace treaties that concluded the Italian Wars (1494–1559). The treaties were signed in the city of Cateau-Cambrésis (France) in 1559, the first on April 2 between France and England and the second on April 3 between France and Spain. According to the first treaty, England returned Calais to France for a ransom of 500,000 ecus to be paid over eight years. According to the second treaty, France gave up its claims to Italy, returned Corsica to Genoa, and withdrew its troops from Piedmont and Savoy, which it had been occupying from 1536 and which were now returned to the duke of Savoy. French garrisons remained in only five Piedmontese fortresses: Turin, Chieri, Pinerolo, Chivasso, and Villanova d'Asti. The Treaty of Cateau-Cambrésis consolidated the dominance of Spain in the Duchy of Milan, the Kingdom of Naples, and Sicily and Sardinia.

REFERENCES
Ruble, A. de. *Le Traité de Cateau-Cambrésis.* Paris, 1889.
Romier, L. "Les Guerres d'Henri II et le traité du Cateau-Cambrésis." In *Mélanges d'archéologie et d'histoire de l'Ecole française de Rome,* [1910] 30th year, pp. 3–50.　　　　　　　[11–1586–1]

CATECHINS, phenols of vegetable origin. Characteristic representatives of catechins are the stereoisomers catechin and epicatechin.

Catechins are colorless crystalline substances, often with a bitter, astringent taste. They are easily soluble in water and alcohol. Tannins are formed upon their polymerization. Catechins have been found in a number of edible fruits (apples, peaches, apricots, quinces, plums, and cherries) and berries (strawberries, currants, raspberries, gooseberries, and red bilberries). A large amount is present in the young shoots of the tea plant (as much as 20–25 percent of the dry weight), in catechu acacias, in grapes (primarily in the pits and skin), and in cocoa beans. The compounds are extracted from tea leaves on an industrial scale.

Catechins are highly active biologically. They regulate capillary permeability, increase the elasticity of capillary walls, and promote more efficient use of ascorbic acid by the organism. Therefore, catechins are among the substances that have vitamin-P activity, and they are used in the treatment of diseases connected with functional disorders of the capillaries and of edemas of vascular origin. Tea catechins have antimicrobial properties and are used in the treatment of dysentery. Oxidative conversions of catechins play an important role in food production technology, including the fermentation of tea, wine-making, and the preparation of cocoa.

REFERENCES
Zaprometov, M. N. *Biokhimiia katekhinov.* Moscow, 1964.
Biokhimiia fenol'nykh soedinenii. Edited by G. Harborne. Moscow, 1968. (Translated from English.)
　　　　　　　　　　　　M. N. ZAPROMETOV [11–1574–1]

CATECHISM. (1) A handbook containing the basic principles of Christian doctrine. During the first centuries of Christianity, the catechism was the oral instruction of those about to be baptized as Christians. Beginning with the 16th century the catechism became a book, a manual of instruction, which popularly set forth (usually in the form of questions and answers) the teachings of the Christian church. The Orthodox, Catholic, and Protestant churches each have their own catechism.

(2) In the figurative sense, a catechism is a work written in the form of questions and answers.　　　　　[11–1573–2]

CATECHOLAMINES, pyrocatechin derivatives that participate in physiological and biochemical processes in animals and man. The catecholamines include epinephrine, norepinephrine, and dopamine.

Being hormones from the medullary layer of the adrenals and mediators of the nervous system, catecholamines reflect and determine the condition of the sympathetic division of the autonomic nervous system. They play an important role in neurohumoral regulation and neurotrophic functions and take part in the body's metabolism and adaptive reactions to ensure the constancy of the internal environment and physiological functions (homeostasis). The effects of the catecholamines are the result of their reaction with adrenoreceptors, reactive cellular systems that react specifically with catecholamines. The α-adrenoreceptors are associated mainly with excitation; the β-adrenoreceptors, with the inhibition of smooth muscles and with the acceleration and intensification of cardiac contractions. Catecholamines are present in blood, organs, tissues, and urine. During physical and mental exertion and in certain diseases (for example, in tumors of the adrenal medulla), the catecholamine content of the blood and urine increases sharply. Catecholamines undergo metabolic conversions (oxidative deamination, O-methylation, quinoid oxidation) that lead to their inactivation or alter their physiological and biochemical properties. When functioning as mediators, the catecholamines are deposited in special granules at the nerve endings.

A number of pharmaceutical agents act on the different stages of catecholamine synthesis, release, deposition, and metabolism. For example, reserpine depletes the catecholamine reserve; pargyline and iproniazid suppress the oxidative deamination, and Aldomet the synthesis and deposition, of catecholamines; and guanethidine and bretylium prevent the transmission of nervous impulses. These substances are used to intensify or to moderate the activity of the sympathetic nervous system.

REFERENCES
Adrenalin i noradrenalin. (Conference reports). Moscow, 1964.
Matlina, E. Sh., and V. V. Men'shikov. *Klinicheskaia biokhimiia katekholaminov.* Moscow, 1967.
Manukhin, B. N. *Fiziologiia adrenoretseptorov.* Moscow, 1968.
　　　　　　　　G. N. KASSIL' and E. SH. MATLINA [11–1574–2]

CATECHU, a substance obtained from the wood of the East Indian acacia (*Acacia catechu*) of the family Leguminosae (the plant is native to India and Sri Lanka). By boiling small pieces of the wood, an extract is obtained. After evaporation, the extract becomes a thick reddish brown mass. Catechu contains 25–55 percent tannin. It dissolves in acetic acid and is precipitated from solution by sulfuric acid or gelatin. Catechu is used to tan hides and, when oxidized by potassium bichromate, it is used as a dye for cotton and silk fabrics.   [11–1575–1]

CATEGORICAL IMPERATIVE, a term introduced by the German philosopher I. Kant to designate the basic law, or rule, of his ethics. It has two formulations: "So act that you can will the maxim of your conduct to be a universal law" (*Soch.*, vol. 4, part 1, Moscow, 1965, p. 260) and "So act as to treat humanity, whether in your own person or in another, always as an end and never only as a means" (*ibid.*, p. 270). The first of these expresses the formal conception of ethics that is characteristic of Kant, and the second places limitations on this formalism. According to Kant, the categorical imperative is a universal principle obligatory for all men, which must guide everyone, regardless of origin or social position. The abstract and formal nature of the categorical imperative was criticized by Hegel.

In discussing the postulates of Kant's ethics, K. Marx and F. Engels wrote that Kant "made the materially motivated determinations of will of the French bourgeois into pure self-determinations of the 'free will', of the will in and for itself, of the human will, and so converted it into purely ideological conceptual determinations and moral postulates" (*Soch.*, 2nd ed., vol. 3, p. 184).

REFERENCE
Williams, T. C. *The Concept of the Categorical Imperative.* Oxford, 1968.
                [11–1568–3]

CATEGORIES, in philosophy, the most general and fundamental concepts, reflecting essential, universal properties and relations of the phenomena of reality and cognition. Categories originated and developed as the result of generalizing from the historical development of cognition and social practice.

In the early forms of philosophical thought, categories emerged as principles of departure, as the world's "first principles": water, air, earth, fire, ether, and other primal elements. When the distinction was made between being and thinking, between consciousness and cognition, the categories took on a logical aspect. For example, Plato recognized five basic categories: essence (being), motion, rest, identity, and difference. Aristotle wrote a special treatise entitled *Categories,* in which categories are treated as a reflection and the highest generalization of objective reality. He distinguished ten categories: essence (substance), quantity, quality, relation, place, time, position, state, action, and affection. However, Aristotle did not reveal the dialectical interrelationships among the categories. His system of categories was the predominant one for many centuries.

In the modern period thinkers advanced various systems of categories, treating them either materialistically or idealistically. Thus, I. Kant regarded categories as the a priori forms of understanding. In his view they are merely the forms into which, as it were, is cast the diverse content of the material of cognition, which is furnished to them from the outside by the senses. The categories do not define objects in themselves (the "things-in-themselves") but rather the cognizing subject, the structures of his thought. Kant distinguished the following categories: quality (reality, negation, and limitation), quantity (unity, plurality, and totality), relation (substance and property, cause and effect, and community, or reciprocity), and modality (possibility and impossibility, existence and nonexistence, necessity and contingency). This system encompasses the most important categories of human thought and, to a large degree, still retains its significance.

Enormous progress was made by the system of categories set forth by G. Hegel, for whom philosophy is nothing else but a dialectical system of categories—in thought, nature, spirit, and history. The purely logical categories are these: being (quality, quantity, and measure), essence (ground, appearance, and actuality—this last, moreover, includes substance, cause, and reciprocity, or mutual interaction), and the Concept, or *Begriff* (subject, object, and absolute idea). Although he demonstrated

the dialectics of categories, their interconnection and reciprocal transitions, he treated categories as the production of a thinking world spirit.

Certain contemporary bourgeois philosophers regard the categories as a special autonomous world of ideas, torn away from both the material, objective world and the subjective world of man. Subjective idealists assert that categories have no objective content. Thus, for example, the existentialists assume that any category that man uses in his thought bears his own unique and profoundly personal coloration. Emphasis on the intimately personal sphere of inner life and the forms of its expression in concepts and symbols, which are full of psychologism, is fundamental to existentialism. In contrast to existentialism, which strives to "humanize" categorial concepts, to deprive them of objective content, and to accord them an emotionally subjective sense, neo-positivism attempts to reduce philosophical categories to the terms of formal logic and to the concepts of specialized spheres of scientific knowledge. Neo-Thomists have imbued the categories with a religious sense, asserting that they have existed since the beginning in the divine reason as archetypes of real things, properties, and relations.

By using the attainments of world philosophical thought, Marxism has developed the categories on the basis of dialectical materialism. The categories of the materialistic dialectic are a generalization of the experience and practice of the previous history of mankind. They include the singular, particular, general, part, whole, form, content, essence, phenomenon, law, necessity, contingency, possibility, reality, quality, quantity, and measure, among others. They reflect the entire world (insofar as it is known) but not everything in the world. They reflect it only on the plane of universal properties, relationships, and regularities of development. Categories form the basic intellectual means for the philosophical cognition of being and of the results of its concrete scientific and artistic reflection. The concepts of specialized fields of knowledge have arisen through studies that have generalized from a certain separate sphere of being. However, no system of analytical concepts has exhausted the entire richness of mankind's intellectual experience as embodied in global philosophical categories.

Categories are focal points of cognition, "stages," moments of thought's penetration into the essence of things.

In characterizing the cognitive significance of categories, V. I. Lenin wrote: "Man is confronted with a *web* of natural phenomena. Instinctive man, the savage, does not distinguish himself from nature. Conscious man does distinguish, categories are stages of distinguishing, i.e., of cognizing the world, focal points in the web, which assist in cognizing and mastering it" (*Poln. sobr. soch.*, 5th ed., vol. 29, p. 85). In expressing, as it were, the world's framework, the categorial structure of thought is relatively stable. Nevertheless, it is also changeable and historical. The content of the categories is especially mobile. During the course of history the role and place of individual categories have changed. The materialistic dialectic has been enriched by new categories (for example, structure and system), and already existing categories have been deepened.

Categories are an ideal analogy of the material world, its general properties, connections, and relationships; from this are derived their methodological value and the need to apply them to the study of phenomena in nature, society, and thought. The categories of dialectic, as distinct from general concepts in specific fields of knowledge, which play a methodological role only within a delimited sphere of thought, penetrate the entire fabric of scientific thought. In addition to reflecting reality, categories are a necessary intellectual means of transforming it. The theoretical reproduction of reality and its creative transformation in thought are possible only within a system of categories. Categories play the role of "yardsticks" of the intellectually grasped object, the logical means of its comprehension and fixation. They are the organizing principles of thought, the focal points of the connection between subject and object, the standards, as it were, with the aid of which we make sense of all the richness of sensory immediacy.

Philosophical categories, by continuously accumulating within themselves the results of individual specialized disciplines, have facilitated the separation and the synthesis of world-view and general methodological moments in the content of scientific thought. It is precisely the categories of human thought that present an index of the level of mankind's general intellectual development during a given historical period. It was not in vain that Hegel called philosophy an epoch seized in thought. Thanks to categories, particular objects are perceived and conceived as particular manifestations of the general, as included within a system of generalized relations. The mastery of categories during a person's individual development is a necessary condition for the formation of the capacity for theoretical thought.

The categories of materialist dialectics are in a definite relationship among themselves, and they represent a system. In discussions being conducted on the composition of categories in this system and their hierarchy, the following principles concerning its structure have been generally accepted as points of departure. In objective reality everything is interconnected and is in a state of univeral reciprocal interaction. Hence even the categories reflecting the world have a definite interconnectedness. Each category reflects a certain aspect of the objective world, while taken together they "embrace conditionally, approximately, the universal law-governed character of eternally moving and developing nature" (*ibid.*, p. 164). Each of the categories, by reflecting the universal connection among things, thereby expresses something absolute. Therefore, none of the categories can be replaced, "overcome," or changed into another. The system of categories is constructed on the basis of a unity between the logical and the historical. A logically consistent elaboration of categories within the system of Marxist philosophy must in an abbreviated form reflect the history of the formation and development of the categorical structure of human thought, proceeding from the simple to the complex. Categories are interconnected in such a way that each of them can be understood only as an element of the entire system of categories. The process of the development of phenomena consists in their passing through a step-by-step transition from simple things to complex ones, from lower to higher forms of being. Knowledge too advances in just such a regular sequence.

REFERENCES
Kategorrii materialisticheskoi dialektiki. Moscow, 1956.
Georgiev, F. I. *Kategorii materialisticheskoi dialektiki.* Moscow, 1960.
Sheptulin, A. P. *Sistema kategorii dialektiki.* Moscow, 1967.

A. G. SPIRKIN [11–1565–2]

CATEGORY, in linguistics, linguistic meanings that are correlated and interrelated on the basis of a common semantic feature and represent a closed system of subdivisions of this feature. Examples are the category of person in the Russian language (encompassing three meanings, based on the feature of participation in the act of speech), the category of gender in Russian adjectives, and the lexical category of color designation.

Categories are distinguished according to the nature of their semantics (denotative, semantic-syntactical), the degree of their obligatory use in a given language (grammatical, nongrammatical), and the means of expression (morphological, lexical, syntactical). Categories that are semantically close may be obligatory in some languages and optional in others. Thus, the category of locative relationships among nouns is expressed in the Lak language by a category comprising a series of locative cases (*k'atluin,* "to the house"; *k'atluinmai,* "in the direction of the house"; *k'atluikh,* "above the house and past it"), whereas in Russian the corresponding meanings are expressed by separate lexical units. The grammatical (obligatory) categories in a language form rigid hierarchical systems. For example, categories expressed by the noun in Hungarian include number, possession, the person and number of the possessor, the relative, the number of the relative, and case.

B. IU. GORODETSKII [11–1569–2]

CATEGORY TELEGRAM, the general designation for a telegraphic communication of importance and priority. In the USSR telegrams are divided into categories and dispatched in the sequence extra-category, priority (including SOS telegrams and storm telegrams warning of dangerous weather or natural disas-

ters), high governmental, governmental, express, and ordinary. Telegraph offices are required to dispatch extra-category and SOS telegrams immediately, priority telegrams within three to six minutes, high-governmental, governmental, and express telegrams within 20 minutes, and ordinary telegrams within 40 minutes (with delivery to the addressee within one hour).

[11–1568–2]

CATELECTROTONUS, altered state of a nerve or other excitable tissue that develops in the region of the cathode when a constant current passes through the tissue. The permeability of the cell membrane and the bioelectric potential change, and the irritability of the tissue is increased. Opposite changes occur in the region of the anode (anelectrotonus).   [11–1603–2]

CATHAROBIONTS, catharobia organisms that inhabit unpolluted cold waters with a large quantity of dissolved oxygen (for example, the trout). Saprobionts are organisms that inhabit polluted waters.   [11–1561–1]

CATHARS, adherents of a heresy that was widespread in Western Europe (chiefly in Italy, Flanders, and southern France) from the 11th to 13th centuries and which served as a vehicle of protest against feudal oppression for broad strata of the burghers (particularly artisans) and some of the peasants.

Their doctrine, borrowed to a great extent from the Bogomils, was dualistic: an opposition between good (the unseen, spiritual, and only true world, created by God) and evil (the earthly, material world created by Satan). The Cathars' condemnation of everything earthly and carnal led to extreme asceticism; they rejected marriage, forbade the use of animals for food, and permitted suicide. They did not recognize the church sacraments, veneration of saints, or indulgences, and they exposed the vices of the Catholic clergy. (They considered the pope of Rome Satan's deputy.) They demanded the liquidation of the church's landholdings and refused to pay the church tithe. They created their own religious organization at the head of which stood preceptors, the perfect (*perfecti*), who were bound to lead an ascetic life.

The church, supported by secular power, waged a bitter struggle against the Cathars. The Cathar doctrine was the foundation for the Albigensian heretical movement. The Cathar heresy was almost completely eradicated during the period from 1300 to 1350 as a result of merciless persecution.

REFERENCE
Borst, A. *Die Katharer.* Stuttgart, 1953.

S. M. STAM [11–1561–4]

CATHARSIS, a term used in ancient Greek philosophy and aesthetics to designate the essence of aesthetic experience. The concept dates back to Pythagorean philosophy, which urged the use of music for the purification of the soul. According to the Stoics, Heraclitus spoke of purgation by fire. Plato taught that catharsis was the freeing of the soul from the body and from passions or pleasures. Aristotle spoke of the educative and purifying significance of music, through which man gains relief and is purged of his emotions and desires, experiencing an "innocent joy." In the absence of further clarification, Aristotle's famous definition of tragedy as the purging of emotions (*Poetics,* ch. 6) has given rise to controversy over what is meant by catharsis. G. E. Lessing interpreted it ethically; the 19th-century German scholar J. Bernays defined it in medical terms as something that brings relief; and the German E. Zeller saw it as a purely aesthetic phenomenon. Science has been unable to definitively resolve the problem of the essence of Aristotelian catharsis, since it is unclear whether catharsis ought to be understood simply as the elimination of particular emotions or as their harmonization. The Austrian doctor and psychologist S. Freud used the term to designate a method of psychotherapy.

REFERENCES
Losev, A. F. *Ocherki antichnogo simvolizma i mifologii,* vol. 1. Moscow, 1930. Pages 728–34. (Contains bibliography.)
Akhmanov, A. S., and F. A. Petrovskii. Introductory essay in Aristotle, *Ob iskusstve poezii.* Moscow, 1957.

Boekel, C. W. van. *Katharsis*. Utrecht, 1957. (Bibliography.)
A. F. Losev [11–1561–3]

CATHELINEAU, JACQUES. Born Jan. 5, 1759, in Pin-en-Mauges; died July 14, 1793, in St. Florent. One of the military leaders of the Vendée insurrection during the Great French Revolution; a peasant by birth.

Cathelineau took command of peasant detachments of rebels in March 1793; under his leadership they captured the cities of Cholet and Saumur. In June 1793 he was chosen commander in chief of the Vendean Catholic and royal army. In July 1793 he led his army in the storming of Nantes and was fatally wounded in battle nearby. [11–1570–1]

CATHEPSINS, intracellular proteinases of the hydrolase class that catalyze the hydrolysis of the peptide bond in peptides and proteins.

Cathepsins are widely distributed in animal and plant tissues and in microorganisms. Cathepsins are divided according to the character and specificity of enzymic action into endopeptidases, which are capable of hydrolyzing internal peptide bonds in the molecules of proteins and peptides, and exopeptidases, which act solely on compounds with one or more free terminal carboxyl or amino groups. Cathepsins can also catalyze reactions that may result in lengthening the peptide chain. Almost all cathepsins are activated by compounds containing sulfhydryl groups (cysteine, glutathione). [11–1571–1]

CATHETERIZATION, the introduction of a special device (catheter) into the natural ducts and cavities of the human body in order to irrigate them and evacuate their contents.

All the requirements of asepsis (sterilization of the catheters, treatment of the hands and of the inlets) must be observed in catheterization. In treating ear diseases, physicians use metal catheters with a knoblike end to ventilate the tympanic cavity through the eustachian tube. In cardiology, a special catheter is inserted into the heart to establish a diagnosis and, if required, to determine the nature and scope of surgical intervention. The cardiac catheter is a thin tube 100–125 cm long made of a specially treated silk material that is impermeable to X rays; an attached movable tip ensures the proper passage of the device through the vessel. In cardiac catheterization, blood specimens can be taken from the heart's cavities, a contrast medium can be introduced into the cavities for subsequent X-ray examination, and blood pressure can be measured in the cavities at the various phases of cardiac activity. In urology, the ureters can be catheterized with a special catheterization cystoscope. The procedure is used to determine the patency of the ureters, to collect urine separately from each kidney, and to inject a contrast medium into the renal pelvis for subsequent X-ray examination (pyelography).

Catheterization is performed with a tubelike device made of rubber, silk cloth impregnated with varnish, or metal. Catheters differ in shape and thickness; these values are measured by numbers on a special scale. Urologists ordinarily use catheters of rubber or metal that are 24–36 cm long for the male and 14–16 cm long for the female. Catheters with a small balloon at the end are also used. When inflated with air or filled with fluid, the balloon prevents the device from slipping out. Ureteral catheters are made of a silk material impregnated with varnish; they are 40–45 cm long. The length of a catheter is usually marked off in centimeters so that it can be inserted to a precise distance.

REFERENCES
Mnogotomnoe rukovodstvo po khirurgii, vol. 9. Moscow, 1959. Pages 62–64.
Rukovodstvo po klinicheskoi urologii. Moscow, 1969. Pages 150–51.
V. G. Tsomyk [11–1572–5]

CATHETOMETER, an instrument for measuring a vertical distance between two points, which need not be situated along the same vertical. A cathetometer consists of a rod mounted vertically with the aid of a level and three leveling screws; a horizontally placed telescopic tube, which can be moved along the rod while remaining perpendicular to it; and a device for the accurate aiming of the tube. The eyepiece of the cathetometer tube is equipped with crosshairs. In using a cathetometer the crosshairs are successively aimed at each of the selected points, and the unknown distance is determined by the displacement shown on a scale on the cathetometer's rod. The cathetometer was invented by the French physicists P. Dulong and A. Petit (1816); various improvements in its construction were contributed by D. I. Mendeleev. [11–1573–1]

CATHODE. (1) In an electron tube or a gas-discharge tube, the electrode that is the source of electrons that ensure the conductivity of interelectrode space in a vacuum or maintain the steadiness of the passage of an electric current through the gas. Depending on the mechanism of emission of electrons, there exist thermionic cathodes, photocathodes, and cold cathodes.

(2) The negatively charged electrode (pole) of a source of current (galvanic cell, storage battery).

(3) The electrode of an electrolytic cell, an electric arc, and other similar devices that are connected to the negative pole of a source of current. [11–1580–1]

CATHODE DROP, a relatively rapid potential drop near the cathode in an electrical discharge in a gas. It is usually brought about by an excess of positive ions at the cathode created by a positive space charge, which shields the cathode. However, in some forms of non-self-sustained electrical current in a gas where there is intense electron emission from the cathode, a cathode drop is developed by the negative space charge (an excess of electrons); such a cathode drop limits emission and inhibits further increase of the space charge.

The main processes that make possible the flow of electric current in a gas operate in the zone of cathode drop and its immediate vicinity. The essential differences among the various forms of gas discharge result from the particular features and differences of these cathode processes. The qualitative feature of the processes in the zone of cathode drop is manifested quantitatively in the value of the cathode drop that is specific for the particular form of discharge. For example, a low cathode drop, of the order of the ionization potential of the gas and lower (1–10 volts), is the most typical feature of an arc discharge, and a high cathode drop (many hundreds of volts) distinguishes a glow discharge from the other types of current in a gas. (As seen from opposite the cathode, the zone of cathode drop adjoins the quasineutral plasma interval called a positive column in the arc discharge and the area of the "negative glow" in a glow discharge.) The specific value of cathode drop is a function of the kind of gas, the cathode material, and the condition of the cathode surface. It is independent of the distance between the electrodes and the magnitude of the discharge current over a wide range of values. However, at sufficiently high currents it increases sharply (anomalous cathode drop), to many dozens of volts in an arc discharge and to several thousand volts in a glow discharge.
A. K. Musin [11–1580–2]

CATHODE FOLLOWER, an amplifier of electric power in which, as a result of strong negative feedback, the output voltage across the load in the cathode circuit of an electron tube is approximately equal to the voltage at the input (it follows the voltage). [11–1583–1]

CATHODE LUMINESCENCE, luminescence that occurs when a phosphor is excited by an electron beam; a type of radioluminescence. The original term designating a beam of electrons was "cathode ray"; hence the term "cathode luminescence." The phenomenon occurs in gases, molecular crystals, and organic and crystal phosphors, but only crystal phosphors are resistant to the electron beam and provide a sufficiently bright glow. These are used as cathode phosphors.

To excite cathode luminescence the energy of the exciting electrons needs to be only about 1.5 times the ionization potential of the crystal phosphor. However, when such low-velocity electrons are used, steady luminescence cannot be achieved: the electrons very quickly charge the surface of the phosphor negatively, so that exciting electrons slow down and lose energy when they are repelled from it. If the electron energies are high, secondary electron emission occurs at the surface of the phosphor and the charge on the phosphor is carried off by the secondary electrons. Consequently, the electron beams used in practice have energies of 100 electron volts (eV) to 25 keV, and in some cases—such as lasers—up to 1 MeV.

As the high-energy electrons interact with the atoms of the phosphor's lattice, they ionize them, thus creating a second generation of electrons that, in turn, ionize other atoms. This process continues until the energy of the knock-on electrons is sufficient for ionization. The electrons are decelerated in a thin layer of the phosphor (less than 10^{-4} cm thick), so that the density of excitation is very high. The electron holes and electrons created as a result of the ionization migrate along the lattice and may be captured by centers of luminescence. Cathode luminescence occurs when the electrons and electron holes recombine at the centers of luminescence. The centers of cathode luminescence are the same as for photoexcitation, and consequently the spectra are similar. The efficiency of cathode luminescence is 1–10 percent; most of the energy of the electron beam is converted into heat.

The phenomenon of cathode luminescence is used extensively in technology, particularly vacuum electronics. It is cathode luminescence that causes the screens to glow in black-and-white and color television receivers, all oscillographs, and image converters. The phenomenon is the basis for AsGa, CdS, and ZnS lasers that are excited by an electron beam.

REFERENCES

Moskvin, A. V. *Katodoliuminestsentsiia*, parts 1–2. Moscow-Leningrad, 1948–49.
Elektronno-luchevye trubki i indikatory, parts 1–2. Moscow, 1949–50. (Translated from English.)   E. A. SVIRIDENKOV [11–1583–2]

CATHODE SPUTTERING, the destruction of the negative electrode (cathode) in a gas discharge as a result of the impact of positive ions. In a broader sense it is the destruction of a solid through bombardment by charged or neutral particles.

On the one hand, cathode sputtering is an undesirable phenomenon that shortens the life of electronic devices; on the other hand, it is of practical use for cleaning surfaces, revealing the structure of a substance (ionic etching), depositing thin films, and producing directional molecular beams. The bombarding ions that penetrate the target produce displacement of its atoms. These displaced atoms in turn can produce new displacements. Some of the atoms reach the surface and pass out of it. Under certain conditions particles may leave the target's surface in the form of ions. In single crystals conditions are most favorable for particle emission in directions in which the atomic packing density is greatest. Collision chains (focusons), by means of which the energy and momentum of displaced particles are transmitted with the lowest losses, are formed in these directions. The process of ion channeling, which determines the depth of penetration of ions into a target, plays an important role in cathode sputtering.

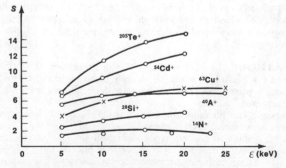

Figure 1. Dependence of sputtering coefficient S for a copper target on energy $\mathcal{E}$ of bombarding ions

Cathode sputtering occurs when the energy of the ions $\mathcal{E}$ is higher than a value $\mathcal{E}_0$, called the cathode sputtering threshold. The value of $\mathcal{E}_0$ ranges from a few to several dozen electron volts

(eV). It is characterized quantitatively by the sputtering coefficient S, which is equal to the number of atoms dislodged by one ion. Near the threshold S is very small (10^{-5} atoms per ion), but under optimum conditions it may be as high as several dozen. Its value is independent of gas pressure at pressures $p < 13.3$ newtons per sq m (N/m^2), or 0.1 mm of mercury, but when $p > 13.3$ N/m^2, S decreases because of the greater number of particles that settle back onto the surface. The value of S is affected both by the characteristics of the bombarding ions, such as their energy $\mathcal{E}$ (see Figure 1), their mass M (see Figure 2), and

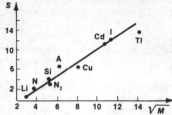

Figure 2. Dependence of sputtering coefficient S on mass M of the bombarding ions ($\mathcal{E} = 400$ eV)

their angle of incidence α on the target (see Figure 3), and by the properties of the substance being sputtered, such as the cleanliness of the surface, the temperature, the crystal structure, and the mass of the target's atoms.

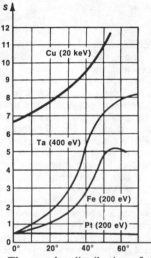

Figure 3. Dependence of sputtering coefficient S on angle of incidence α of ions bombarding the surface of Cu, Ta, Fe, and Pt (the numbers indicate the energy of the ions)

The angular distribution of the particles escaping from the sputtered surface is anisotropic. It is a function of the energy of the ions, and for single crystals it also depends on the type of crystal lattice and the structure of the facet being sputtered. The substance being sputtered is deposited on the screen in the form of individual spots with a symmetry pattern identical to that of the facet being sputtered and of the etch figures formed on the sputtered face as a result of the cathode sputtering. The energy of the sputtered particles varies from fractions of an electron volt up to values of the order of the energy in the primary ions. The average energy of the sputtered particles is usually dozens of electron volts and depends on the properties of the target material and the characteristics of the ion beam.

REFERENCES

Morgulis, N. D. "Katodnoe raspylenie." *Uspekhi fizicheskikh nauk*, 1946, vol. 28, nos. 2–3, p. 202.
Pleshivtsev, N. V. *Katodnoe raspylenie*. Moscow, 1968.
Kaminsky, M. *Atomnye i ionnye stolknoveniia na poverkhnosti metalla.* Moscow, 1967. (Translated from English.)
Thompson, M. *Defekty i radiatsionnye povrezhdeniia v metallakh.* Moscow, 1971. (Translated from English.)

V. E. IURASOVA [11–1581–1]

CATHOLIC ACTION, a general term for the Catholic apostolate—organizations of laymen functioning under the direct administration of the church hierarchy.

Secular Catholic organizations first originated in Europe in the mid-19th century. Catholic Action organizations operate in

Europe (they are especially active in Italy, Spain, France, and the Federal Republic of Germany), Asia, Africa, and North and South America. Catholic Action is a mass, multimillion-member organization that permits the church to effect a penetration into various segments of the population and to subordinate them to its influence owing to the establishment of an extensive network of various types of associations. These latter are at the level of the parish and bishopric and on the national and international level, and they are specialized according to age, sex, and occupation. The largest international associations are the World Union of Catholic Women's Organizations, the International Federation of Catholic Young Women and Girls, and the World Federation of Catholic Youth.

After World War I (1914–18), despite the church's constant declarations concerning the apolitical nature of Catholic Action, it became a part of the political struggle. The purpose of Catholic Action is the propagation and dissemination of Catholicism, especially in the developing countries, and the struggle against ideologies and forces that are hostile to Catholicism—above all, communism—as well as against workers' and democratic movements. Their methods of influence are participation in the process of electoral struggle and the support of Catholic parties; publication of periodicals; engaging in public education and entertainment; training of staffs of activists; missionary work; charities; and individual influence upon believers.

During the 1960's changes in the church's position, brought about by the strengthening of the forces of peace, socialism, and democracy, caused the strengthening within Catholic Action of progressive elements that have been advocating a rapprochement with left-wing organizations.

REFERENCES

Koval'skii, N. A. *Mezhdunarodnye katolicheskie organizatsii.* Moscow, 1962.
Falconi, C. *La Chiesa e le organizzazioni cattoliche in Europa.* Milan, 1960.
Mohr, H. *Das Katholische Apostolat: Zur Strategie und Taktik des politischen Katholizismus.* Berlin, 1962.

N. K. KISOVSKAIA [11–1593–4]

CATHOLICISM, one of the principal branches (along with Orthodoxy and Protestantism) of Christianity. According to the official data of the Catholic Church (obviously exaggerated) there were 614 million Catholics in the world in 1970 (including 250 million in Europe, 226 million in Latin America, 55 million in the USA, 47.8 million in Asia, and 32 million in Africa). There is an especially large number of practicing Catholics (in proportion to the total population) in Italy, Spain, Portugal, France, Belgium, Austria, and the Latin American countries. Within the socialist countries among the believing part of the population Catholics predominate in Poland, Hungary, Czechoslovakia, and Cuba. In the USSR there are Catholics in the Baltic area, mainly in Lithuania, as well as the western regions of Byelorussia and of the Ukraine.

The emergence of the Catholic Church as a distinct entity within Christianity began in the third to the fifth centuries with the increase in economic, political, and cultural differences between the western and eastern parts of the Roman Empire, especially after its division into the Western Roman and Eastern Roman Empires in 395. The principal cause of the splitting up of the universal Christian church into a western (Roman Catholic) and an eastern (Eastern Catholic or Greek Orthodox) group was the rivalry between the Roman popes and the Constantinople patriarchs for leadership within the Christian world. The first split took place around 867 (it was repaired at the turn of the tenth century); a second occurred in 1054 and became final with the capture of Constantinople by the Crusaders in 1204 (when the patriarch of Constantinople was forced to leave the city).

Since it is one form of the Christian religion, Catholicism does acknowledge the basic dogmas and rituals of Christianity, at the same time it has a number of unique features in its doctrine, worship, and organization.

The Catholic Church's organization is marked by strict centralization and a monarchical and hierarchical character. According to Catholic doctrine, the pope (who is also the primate of Rome) is the visible head of the church, the successor of the apostle Peter, and the true representative of Christ on earth; his authority is above that of the ecumenical councils. These tenets, which were especially clearly formulated at the turn of the 13th century during the reign of Pope Innocent III, were confirmed by the First Vatican Council (1869–70). This same council proclaimed the dogma of the pope's infallibility (an idea first set forth during the 11th century by Pope Gregory VII) when he acts in the role of supreme pontiff, performing the duties of the pastor and teacher of all Christians (speaking ex cathedra); thus it is he who determines what will become doctrine in questions of faith and morals.

The Catholic Church (in contrast to Protestantism) acknowledges not only the "holy scriptures"—that is, the Bible—as the source of its doctrine but also "sacred tradition." Moreover, within this tradition Catholicism includes, in addition to ancient oral tradition, the decrees passed by the seven ecumenical councils (as do also the Orthodox), the resolutions of succeeding church councils, and papal messages. This has facilitated the exaltation of the papacy, and it has also permitted the Catholic Church to adapt itself more flexibly to changing historical conditions.

In the Catholic dogma concerning the trinity the "holy spirit" proceeds not only from god the father (as in the "Creed," which is acknowledged by Orthodoxy) but also from the son (*filioque*).

Catholicism makes a sharp distinction between clergy and laity. This is expressed in a number of institutions that are absent from the Orthodox Church, including celibacy, or the obligation of the clergy not to marry (within Orthodoxy only monks vow not to marry), and communion in bread and wine only by the clergy and in bread alone by the laity (now in certain instances they are also allowed to partake of wine). The Catholic Church forbids a person to leave his spiritual vocation. The privileges of the Catholic clergy are based to a considerable degree on the church doctrine of the superabundant treasure-house of grace (which does not exist in Orthodoxy): the acts of Christ, the apostles, the mother of god, and the saints, as well as the heroic exploits of pious Christians above what was required of them, have created a "reserve" of good deeds and "grace," on account of which the church has the right to remit sins, granting pardon to the sinners. (This was used by the Catholic Church as the basis for the trade in indulgences that began in the 12th century.)

Only in Catholicism is there a dogma concerning purgatory—an intermediate stage between hell and paradise, where the souls of those who have died and are awaiting their final judgment can be purged of sins that were not redeemed by them during their lifetime by proceeding through various kinds of trials, as well as with the aid of prayers on their behalf and "good deeds" by their friends and relatives on earth; the clergy has the power to cut short the time that a person must spend in purgatory. This was finally confirmed by the Council of Trent during the 16th century.

The Catholic as well as the Orthodox Church recognizes the seven sacraments, but in dispensing them there are certain differences. Thus, the Catholics do not baptize by immersion but by sprinkling; anointing (confirmation) is carried out not at the same time as baptism but on children who are at least eight years old and, as a rule, by a bishop. The bread used for communion among Catholics is unleavened rather than leavened (as among the Orthodox). Marriage between lay people is indissoluble, even if one of the spouses is found guilty of adultery.

A particular characteristic of Catholicism is a widespread, exalted worship of the mother of god (the madonna). In 1854, Pope Pius IX proclaimed the dogma of the immaculate conception of the Virgin Mary (rejected by the Orthodox Church); in 1950 the Catholic Church proclaimed the dogma of her bodily ascension into heaven.

The service of worship in Catholicism is characterized by a particularly showy, theatrical divine liturgy, which is supposed to have an effect upon the imagination and the senses of the believers. In addition to singing, use is made of instrumental music (the organ) and churches are decorated with sculptures and paintings. The worship of all kinds of relics has been developed to an extreme degree, as has the cult of martyrs, saints, and the blessed. The Catholic divine service of worship used to be conducted only in Latin. However, the Second Vatican Council of 1962–65 authorized services to be held in the modern national languages as well. Many holy days in Catholicism appeared after the schism of the churches, including the holy days of Corpus Christi, the Sacred Heart, and the Immaculate Conception of the Virgin Mary.

Prior to the 13th century Catholic theology was based to a considerable extent upon the teaching of Augustine (fourth and fifth centuries). Subsequently in Catholic philosophy there occurred a departure from Augustinian Platonism. During the 13th century Thomas Aquinas revised the theological system of Catholicism; he made use of Aristotle's philosophy, adapting it to Catholic dogmas. In 1879 an encyclical of Pope Leo XIII ("Aeterni patris") proclaimed the doctrine of Thomas Aquinas to be the official philosophical doctrine of Catholicism; the conceptions of this medieval theologian were subjected to a unique kind of renovation and adaptation to the modern level of civilization.

Over many centuries Catholicism was the predominant ideology in the countries of Western Europe. The role of the Catholic Church was especially great during the epoch of feudalism. "By means of its feudal organization," wrote F. Engels, "the church provided a religious sanctification to the secular state structure, which was based on feudal principles. . . . Church dogma was the point of departure and the basis of all thought" (K. Marx and F. Engels, *Soch.*, 2nd ed., vol. 21, p. 495). During the Middle Ages, because the Catholic Church was a large landowner, it managed to exert considerable political influence in the feudal world. The papacy strove to subordinate the secular authority to itself (especially from the 11th through the 13th century); it came out with claims to worldwide domination, and in order to extend the sphere of its influence (beyond the borders of Western Europe), it organized the Crusades. The anticlerical movements that had come into being and the heresies that began to multiply in the 11th century were harshly suppressed by the Catholic Church; the church resorted to excommunications and interdicts, waged wars (for example, the Albigensian Wars), and established the Inquisition.

With the formation of centralized states, tendencies arose within the Catholic Church toward the autonomy of national churches (the doctrine of Wycliffe, Gallicanism, and so forth). From the 14th and 15th centuries there was constantly increasing resistance to the autocratic power of the popes; the council movement came into being, which demanded the supremacy of the ecumenical councils over the popes.

During the period of the formation of bourgeois society the Catholic Church, which was marked by extreme conservatism and reaction, was dealt a very serious blow. As a result of the Reformation (16th century) in a number of European countries Catholicism was supplanted by Protestantism. The position of Catholicism was somewhat strengthened by the Counter-Reformation (16th and 17th centuries), which was headed by the papacy. In struggling for domination over minds the Catholic Church cruelly persecuted progressive scholarly thought (the trials of G. Bruno, G. C. Vanini, Galileo, for example). Up to the middle of the 19th century the Catholic Church continued to be a bulwark of feudal-monarchical forces.

With the establishment of the political supremacy of the bourgeoisie, however, there began a process of rapprochement between the Catholic Church and reactionary bourgeois circles, based for the most part on the joint struggle against the workers' movement and Marxism. This process culminated in the period of imperialism, when the Catholic Church itself became a major owner of capital. The principal social purpose of Catholicism has become the sanctification of the capitalist order by the authority of the church. This defense of the basic foundations of capitalism is constantly waged under the plausible mask of protecting "higher Christian values" and "natural law." Moreover, illusions are being demagogically disseminated concerning the possibility of "Christianizing" capitalism and improving it.

The Catholic Church of today is a major religious, political, and ideological organization, the center of which is the papal state of the Vatican (the permanent residential seat of the church's head—the pope). The central organs for the administration of the Catholic Church are the institutions that make up the Roman Curia, which are subordinate to the pope. In bourgeois countries where Catholicism is widespread the pope has diplomatic representatives, including nuncios and internuncios. After the pope the highest ecclesiastical figures are the cardinals, his closest advisers and aides in administering the church. Also belonging to the higher levels in the church hierarchy are the archbishops (who administer the church provinces, which are divided into dioceses) and bishops (who administer these dioceses). Subordinate to the bishops are the parish priests. In bourgeois states the Catholic Church has a developed network of mass organizations. The entire church apparatus, with its enormous army of priests (in 1970, more than 400,000) subject to strict discipline, with numerous monastic orders (about 1,400,000 monks and nuns) and missionary organizations, and with its charitable and other kinds of institutions, is utilized for religious influence on the popular masses. In its social work the Catholic Church uses the press, films, radio, and television; it has its own Catholic universities as well as other educational institutions. To a considerable degree the Catholic Church relies on Catholic parties (the Christian Democratic Party in Italy, the People's Party in Austria, the Social Christian Party in Belgium, etc.), Catholic trade unions, and rural, youth, women's, and many other kinds of organizations. Most of the secular Catholic social organizations are combined into the system called Catholic Action.

However, the change in the balance of power in the world after World War II (1939–45) in favor of socialism, the national liberation movement, and scientific progress have led to a crisis in Catholicism. The Catholic Church at the beginning of the 20th century officially condemned the advocates of modernism (a trend that came into being at the end of the 19th century and proposed as its goal the adaptation of the doctrines of the faith to modern times); however, during the second half of the 20th century, when threatened by loss of its control over the diminishing flock, the church was itself compelled to take the path of modernizing its ideology and politics. Such are the reasons for the process of changing the dogma, worship, organization, and politics of the Catholic Church that began to take place in the 1960's. Such a renewal, which was clearly manifested at the Second Vatican Council of 1962–65 and in the subsequent resolutions of the church, was expressed in an attempt to simplify the church canons and the rituals of worship, to achieve the maximum mobility of all parts of the church, and to "democratize" their administration. A policy of ecumenism has been actively promoted. Questions concerning the church hierarchy and the prerogatives of the bishops have been raised anew within Catholicism. Dissatisfied with the overzealous supervision by the bureaucratic institutions of the Vatican, the bishops have been increasingly insistent in their demands for more independence. Pope Paul VI created a synod of bishops, which is convoked periodically by the pope in Rome. (It has purely advisory and informational functions.) A break with the historical tradition of the Catholic Church, the reform has been carried out for the purpose of attracting a larger number of people into the administration of church organizations, and the reorganization of the structure of the church apparatus has proceeded on all levels. Within the dioceses, councils of clergymen have been organized to assist the bishops in the administration of the diocese, as well as councils of the lay apostolate, in which not only the clergy are represented but also the laity. In many countries conferences of bishops are regularly convened; they are empowered to resolve a number of problems connected with the implementation of decrees by the council and the Vatican leadership.

The essence of the most important changes in the Catholic Church's social policy amounts to the church's sanction of those concessions to the workers that have already been "recognized" in the developed capitalist countries by bourgeois democracy and that have been achieved by the workers through intense class conflicts. Thus, the "Pastoral Constitution on the Church in the Modern World," which was adopted at the Second Vatican Council, recognizes the right of workers to join together as well as the legality (to be sure, with a number of reservations) of the strike as a means of defending rights, and it emphasizes the value of labor. Although the Catholic Church remains an opponent of socialism, nonetheless, in attempting to adapt itself to the modern situation, to "survive" through all political changes in a given country, and to "root itself" in any system, including the socialist systems that have been established in one-third of the world, the church has declared the social universality of Catholicism. In the same constitution of the Second Vatican Council it is stated that the church does not link itself "with any sort of special form of human culture or political, economic, or social system."

The social reform movement evoked a bitter struggle of trends and opinions in various units and at various levels of Catholic lay and ecclesiastical organizations.

The philosophical doctrine of Catholicism has also been subjected to a reevaluation, and discussions have been held between "traditionalists," who insist upon their unchanging preference for the philosophy of Thomas Aquinas, and "innovators," who consider it impossible in our time to be limited by the positions of Neo-Thomism. The innovators are turning more frequently to the philosophical system of P. Teilhard de Chardin (1881–1955), who attempted to replace the dogmatic medieval positions, which do not correspond to the psychological and intellectual makeup of modern man, with religious principles based on the humanistic ideas and data of 20th-century science.

There has been a considerable increase in the participation of practicing Catholics in class and general democratic movements. There is a deepening stratification among the members of Catholic organizations; left-wing groups have begun to appear that oppose reactionary clericalism and demand the implementation of democratic social reforms and a deepening of the dialogue with the Marxists and that call for unity of action among all anti-imperialist forces. This, in essence, is a revision both of the official ideology and of the social practice of the Catholic Church.

The Marxist-Leninist parties operating in capitalist countries, while defending their scientific atheistic position, are at the same time establishing contact by all the means at their disposal with Catholic workers and advocate unity of action among the entire working class and all antimonopolistic forces. They do so in order both to defend social progress and to oppose the antipopular policies of the monopolies and the threats of war and fascism.

REFERENCES
Mchedlov, M. P. *Katolitsizm.* Moscow, 1970.
Sheinman, M. M. *Vatikan i katolitsizm v kontse XIX–nachale XX v.* Moscow, 1958.
Berzin, E. O. *Katolicheskaia tserkov' v Iugo-Vostochnoi Azii.* Moscow, 1966.
Babosov, E. M. *Nauchno-tekhnicheskaia revoliutsiia i modernizatsiia katolitsizma.* Minsk, 1971.
Adam, K. *Das Wesen des Katholizismus,* 13th ed. Düsseldorf, 1957.
Pelikan, J. *The Riddle of Roman Catholicism.* New York [1959].
Landis, B. J. *The Roman Catholic Church in the United States.* New York, 1966.
Aranguren, J. L. L. *La crisis del catolicismo,* 2nd ed. Madrid, 1970.
S. D. SKAZKIN and M. P. MCHEDLOV [11-1587-3]

CATHOLIC LEAGUE (1576), a union of part of the French Catholic clergy and gentry during the religious wars. The head of the Catholic League was Henry, Duke of Guise. It was established in May 1576 supposedly to combat the Huguenots. The real purpose of the league was the limitation of the royal power by the feudal aristocracy (which had seized the dominant position in the league) and the weakening of centralization. Late in 1576 the Catholic League in effect disintegrated. It was reestablished in 1585. [11-1592-1]

CATHOLIC LEAGUE (1609), a union of the Catholic ecclesiastical and secular feudal lords of Germany, created on July 10, 1609, in order to combat the Protestant Union of 1608. The initiator and head of the Catholic League was Maximilian of Bavaria.

The Catholic League became one of the principal forces of Catholic reaction not only in Germany but throughout all of Western Europe as well. Material support from Spain permitted the league to create a large army, led by J. Tilly. With the beginning of the Thirty Years' War (1618–48) the Catholic League concluded an alliance with the Emperor Ferdinand II. Its troops won a number of victories during the Czech and Danish periods of the war. With the creation of the Imperial Army under the command of A. von Wallenstein the influence of the league decreased. But after the publication of the Edict of Restitution in 1629 the league succeeded in forcing Wallenstein to retire (1630). Tilly became commander in chief of the league's army as well as that of the emperor. However, after the defeats inflicted upon the troops of the Catholic League in 1631–32 by the Swedish king Gustavus II Adolphus, it was dissolved in accordance with the Peace of Prague (1635). [11-1592-2]

CATHOLICOS, the title of the head of the Armenian (since 363), Georgian (since 475), and Caucasian Albanian (since 552) churches.

The Armenian catholicos became the primate of the merged Albanian and Armenian churches; he now bears the title of supreme patriarch and catholicos of all the Armenians and has his residence in Echmiadzin (in the Armenian SSR). Subordinate to him is the Armenian catholicos of Cilicia, as well as the Armenian patriarchs of Jerusalem and Constantinople. Beginning in 475 the head of the Georgian church bore the title of catholicos of Kartli; later (beginning in the 17th century) he was called catholicos of all Georgia. Between 1811 and 1917 there was no catholicos in Georgia; the office was restored in 1917, with the residence in Tbilisi. The title of catholicos is also borne by the head of the Monophysite Church; in addition there is a catholicos of the Armenian Catholics (residence in Beirut). [11-1587-1]

CATILINE (Lucius Sergius Catilina). Born circa 108 B.C.; died 62 B.C., near Pistoria (present-day Pistoia), northern Etruria. Roman politician.

In the civil wars of 88–82 B.C., Catiline was a follower of Sulla, and later he participated in the proscriptions. He became praetor in 68 and served as propraetor in the province of Africa in 67–66. Upon his return, he was accused of extortions but was acquitted by the court. The trial prevented Catiline from participating in elections for the consulship. Apparently during that time Catiline plotted his first conspiracy, a plan for a coup d'etat that was not carried out (66). In 64, Catiline was defeated in the consular elections (Cicero was elected), but in 63 he stood for election again, trying to attract all the dissatisfied by promising debt cancellation. After his second defeat Catiline organized a conspiracy for the forceful seizure of power, but he could not carry out his intentions because the consul Cicero learned of the plot. Having received extraordinary powers from the Senate, Cicero demanded (on Nov. 7, 63) that Catiline leave Rome immediately. Catiline went to Etruria, where his followers gathered an army. In December 63, Catiline's followers in Rome were arrested, after being exposed, and were later executed. Catiline fell in a battle with the consular army. The vivid portrayal of Catiline given by his ambitious enemy Cicero (orations against Catiline) and the historian Sallust gave rise in modern times to a romantic view of Catiline and an exaggerated notion of the importance of his conspiracy. V. M. SMIRIN [11-1575-2]

CATIONIC DYES, organic dyes whose molecules contain the grouping $\overset{+}{N}R_3$ (where R is an alkyl or aryl radical) and the Cl^- or $CH_3SO_4^-$ anion in an aliphatic chain or in a heterocycle. Cationic dyes, usually azo, anthraquinone, or polymethine dyes, are used for dyeing polyacrylonitrile fibers. [11-1576-1]

CATO, a branch of the Porcius family of ancient Rome. The most famous representatives of the family are Cato the Elder and Cato the Younger.

Cato the Elder (or Cato the Censor; Marcus Porcius Cato Major). Born 234 B.C., in Tusculum; died 149 B.C. in Rome. Roman writer, founder of Roman prose literature, and statesman.

Cato the Elder served in the Second Punic War and was a praetor in Sardinia in 198 B.C. While serving as consul in Spain in 195, he suppressed an uprising of the local tribes. Cato was the first Roman historian who wrote in Latin. He is the author of *Origins,* a work that elucidates the history of Rome from the founding of the city to the Second Punic War, a great number of speeches and letters, a collection of sayings of famous people, and other works that have survived only in fragments. Cato compiled a kind of encyclopedia written in the form of precepts to his son Marcus (it has not survived). His treatise *On Agriculture,* which has survived in full (written about 160 B.C.; Russian translation, 1950), contains information on the organization of slaveholding estates, the development of wine-making, horticulture, and olive growing in Italy, and ancient customs and superstitions.

An implacable enemy of Carthage, Cato ended every speech in the Senate with a phrase that has become proverbial: "And yet I believe that Carthage must be destroyed" (*"Ceterum censeo Carthaginem esse delendam"*).

WORKS

In *Oratorum romanorum fragmenta,* 2nd ed., vol. 1. Edited by E. Malcovati. Turin, 1955.
De agricultura. Edited by Z. Mazzarino. Leipzig, 1962.
In Russian translation:
"Iz rechi za rodostsev." In *Rimskaia literatura v izbr. perevodakh.* Compiled by S. P. Kondrat'ev. Moscow, 1939.

REFERENCES

Kienast, D. *Cato der Censor.* Heidelberg, 1954.
De Regibus, L. *Il Censore e l'Africano.* Genoa, 1959.
Łos, Z. *Rzym na rozdozu: Studium monograficzne o Katone Starszem.* Warsaw, 1960.

Cato the Younger (or Cato of Utica; Marcus Porcius Cato Minor). Born 95 B.C.; died 46 B.C., in Utica. Roman politician. Great-grandson of Cato the Elder.

Cato the Younger was people's tribune in 62 B.C. and praetor in 54. He demanded the execution of Catiline's followers. During the first triumvirate (60–53) Cato opposed the triumvirs, especially Caesar. In the civil war of 49–45, Cato supported Pompey. After Pompey's defeat at Pharsalus in 48, Cato led the forces of the Pompeians in Africa. He committed suicide after Caesar's victory at Thapsus (46 B.C.). [11–1593–5]

CATS, JACOB. Born Nov. 10, 1577, in Brouwershaven; died Sept. 12, 1660, in Zorgh-vliet, near The Hague. Dutch poet; lawyer by profession.

Cats' literary career began at the age of 40. His principal works—*Marriage* (1625), *Mirror of Old and New Times* (1632), *Betrothal Ring* (1637), *Old Age, Rural Life, and Thoughts on Farming in Zorgh-vliet* (1656), and the autobiographical *Eighty Years of My Life* (1657)—are didactic and reflect a strict Calvinist morality. Cats depicts manners and customs within the framework of everyday concerns and bourgeois virtues and vices.

WORK

Alle de werken van Jacob Cats, vols. 1–2. Dordrecht, 1880.

REFERENCES

Korsakov, P. *Iakov Kats, poet, myslitel' i muzh soveta.* St. Petersburg, 1839.
Duinkerken, A. van. *Het tweede plan, Jacob Cats.* Amsterdam, 1945.
Brachin, P. *La Littérature néerlandaise.* Paris, 1962.   [11–1597–1]

CATTANEO, CARLO. Born June 15, 1801, in Milan; died Feb. 6, 1869, in Castagnola, near Lugano. Italian politician, scholar, and bourgeois democrat.

In the 1830's and 1840's, Cattaneo contributed to scientific-technical journals in Milan and engaged in science education. He felt that dissemination of technical and scientific knowledge was required for successful economic development. During the Risorgimento, the struggle for the liberation and unification of Italy, Cattaneo emerged as one of the leaders of the revolutionary republican camp. His political program was to make Italy an independent federal republic. During the Revolution of 1848–49, Cattaneo was one of the leaders of the anti-Austrian uprising in Milan and a member of the military council and later the military committee. After the defeat of the revolution in Lombardy, Cattaneo emigrated in August 1848 and did not return until 1859. In 1860, along with G. Mazzini, he attempted to help G. Garibaldi in his struggle against the monarchists in southern Italy.

As a scholar, Cattaneo made contributions to economics, Italian philosophy, history, geography, and literary criticism.

WORKS

Scritti politici, vols. 1–4. Florence, 1964–65.
Scritti letterari, artistici, linguistici e vari, new ed., vol. 1. Florence, 1968.   [11–1598–1]

CATTLEYA, a genus of plants of the family Orchidaceae. There are approximately 60 species, growing on trees and cliffs in the forests of Central and South America. The thickened stems, or pseudobulbs, are either ovoid, fusiform, or cylindric. The pseudobulbs hold reserves of water and nutrients during droughts. They bear one to three leaves and a peduncle with one or several flowers. The perianth has six petal-like structures, arranged in two circles. The interior three are usually larger; the lowest, or the lip, which is often the brightest, is curled into a tube around the column. The lip has a spreading, emarginate lobe with an undulate border. The flowers are usually various shades of violet, pink, and lilac. They are aromatic and measure up to 20–25 cm in diameter. Many species, including autumn cattleya (*Cattleya labiata*), *C. dowiana,* and *C. Warscewiczii,* are cultivated in greenhouses. Many garden varieties have been created.   [11–1598–6]

CATULLUS, GAIUS VALERIUS. Born circa 87 B.C.; died circa 54 B.C. Roman lyric poet. Native of Verona.

Catullus belonged to the Neoterics, a literary group that derived its inspiration from Alexandrian poetry. Writing during the final crisis of the Roman Republic, Catullus turned from the world he could not accept to an ideal world of poetry, friendship, and love. His literary legacy consists of 116 works, including lyric verse, epigrams, epyllia, epistles, and epithalamiums. His work influenced the development of Roman and, much later, European lyric poetry.

WORKS

Catullus. Edited by M. Schuster and W. Eisenhut. Leipzig, 1958.
In Russian translation:
Kniga liriki. Translated and with an introduction by A. Piotrovskii. Leningrad, 1929.
Valerii Katull. Moscow, 1963.

REFERENCE

Tronskii, I. M. *Istoriia antichnoi literatury,* 3rd ed. Leningrad, 1957.   [11–1600–2]

CAUCA, a department in southwestern Colombia. To the west is the Pacific Ocean, and in the east lie the Cordillera Occidental and the Cordillera Central. Area, 30,500 sq km. Population, 711,000 (1971). The administrative center is Popayán. The economy is based on livestock raising and tropical farming (coffee, cacao, sugarcane, rice, cotton). Ceramics, leather goods, and textiles are produced, and there is also lumbering and sulfur extraction.   [11–1605–3]

CAUCA, a river in Colombia, a left tributary of the Magdalena River. It is 1,350 km long (according to other data, 1,050 km long) and drains an area of about 80,000 sq km. The Cauca rises in the southern part of the Cordillera Central and then quickly descends into a broad (up to 46 km) and deep rift valley between the Cordillera Central and the Cordillera Occidental. Rapids alternate with quietly flowing stretches. On leaving the mountains, the Cauca spreads out over the Caribbean lowlands, forming branches and lakes. Flooding occurs in the spring and autumn, and the average annual discharge is about 2,000 cu m per sec. The river is navigable for about 600 km, from Cali to Cartago and from Antioquia to the mouth.   [11–1605–2]

CAUCASIAN BEES, a group of honeybee species, including Northern Caucasian, Gray Mountain Georgian, and Valley bees, found in the Caucasus. The bees are distinguished by an ability to fly from the hives when the temperature is relatively low (8–9°C) and sometimes during bad weather. They differ from Central Russian bees by their somewhat smaller body measurements, a longer proboscis, and larger extremities.   [11–354–1]

CAUCASIAN BROWN CATTLE, a breed of dairy-and-meat cattle. The breed was developed by crossing the local Caucasian cattle with the Brown Swiss breed; it was approved in 1960. Compared to Caucasian cattle, the animals of the new breed have an improved constitution and productive qualities, retaining good adaptability to local conditions. The skeleton is slight but stronger than than of Caucasian cattle. The coat is reddish brown. Cows weigh 400–450 kg, with a 600 kg maximum; bulls weigh 800–900 kg, The yields are 2,000–2,500 kg of milk per lactation and 3,500–4,000 kg on cattle breeding farms. The milk has a butterfat content of 3.8–3.9 percent. The dressed weight is 50–55 percent. The animals are being bred to improve their body form and productivity. They are raised in the Armenian SSR, the Georgian SSR, the Azerbaijan SSR, and the Dagestan ASSR.

REFERENCE
Manucharov, A.B., Sh. A. Rasi-Zade, and V. E. Bystritskii. *Kachestvennoe uluchshenie skotovodstva i sozdanie kavkazskoi buroi porody skota v Azerbaidzhane.* Baku, 1962.

E. A. ARZUMANIAN [11–344–1]

CAUCASIAN BUREAU OF THE CENTRAL COMMITTEE OF THE RCP (BOLSHEVIK), also Kavbiuro, a regional body authorized to represent the Central Committee of the RCP (Bolshevik) in the Caucasus.

The Caucasian Bureau was founded by a decision of a Central Committee plenum of Apr. 8, 1920. Its purpose was to direct all the organizational work of the party organizations in the Soviet areas of the Northern Caucasus. The Central Committee assigned the bureau the task of establishing contacts with the party organizations of Transcaucasia and of rendering assistance to them in directing the struggle of the working masses for Soviet power in the region. After the dissolution of the Caucasus Regional Committee of the RCP (Bolshevik) the Caucasian Bureau directly headed the work of the Transcaucasian party organizations. After the summer of 1920 it directed the party organizations of the Northern Caucasus, Sevastopol,' Kuban'–Black Sea Oblast, the Don region, and Transcaucasia.

For greater effectiveness in directing the local organizations, two so-called troikas (triumvirates) were established within the bureau—the Baku Troika and the Armavir Troika (later the Rostov Troika). The first was concerned with the party organizations of Transcaucasia, and the second with those of the Northern Caucasus, the Don region, and Kuban'–Black Sea Oblast. On Mar. 23, 1921, the Southwestern Bureau was separated from the Caucasian Bureau. The Azerbaijani, Armenian, and Georgian party organizations were under the bureau, as were those of the Gortsy Republic and Dagestan until their transferal to the Southwestern Bureau in October 1921.

The organ of the bureau was at first the newspaper *Sovetskii Kavkaz,* and after October 1920, *Sovetskii iug.* From 1920 to 1922 it published the magazine *Izvestiia Kavbiuro TsK RKP(b).*

The bureau existed until the First Congress of the Communist Organizations of Transcaucasia in February 1922, which elected a Transcaucasian Regional Committee of the RCP (Bolshevik). Among the members of the bureau at various times were S. M. Kirov, P. G. Mdivani, A. F. Miasnikov, F. I. Makharadze, A. M. Nazaretian, N. N. Narimanov, I. D. Orakhelashvili, G. K. Ordzhonikidze, Ia. I. Poluian, M. G. Pleshakov, E. D. Stasova, Iu. P. Figatner, and Sh. Z. Eliava.

REFERENCES
Ocherki istorii kommunisticheskikh organizatsii Zakavkaz'ia, part 1 (1883–1921). Tbilisi, 1967.
Zhvaniia, G. K. *Velikii Oktiabr' i bor'ba bol'shevikov Zakavaz'ia za Sovetskuiu vlast'.* Tbilisi, 1967. A. R. GUKASIAN [11–358–3]

CAUCASIAN CATTLE, native dairy cattle of the Caucasus. Caucasian cattle are descended from the old dwarf cattle of Egypt; they were brought to southern Europe and then to Asia Minor. They are divided into Greater and Lesser Caucasian cattle. Within the Greater Caucasian group are Dagestan, Khevsur, Osetin, and Karachevo local breeds; the Lesser Caucasian group includes Kazakh, Karabakh, and Megrelian local breeds.

The differences in productivity among these local breeds are insignificant. The coat of Greater Caucasian cattle is black or dark red, of Lesser Caucasian cattle red or light red. Greater Caucasian cows weigh 200–250 kg, the bulls 350–400 kg; Lesser Caucasian cows weigh 250–300 kg, and the bulls 450–550 kg. Milk productivity is 800–1,000 kg of milk per year, sometimes as much as 4,000 kg. Butterfat content of the milk is 3.7–5.7 percent. These cattle have low-quality meat.

Caucasian cattle are also used as work animals. They are being improved through cross breeding with Brown Swiss Simmental cattle. By crossing them with the Brown Swiss, the Caucasian Brown breed has been produced. Greater Caucasian cattle are raised in the mountains of the Greater Caucasus and in the lowland along the left bank of the Kura River; Lesser Caucasian cattle are raised in the uplands of the Lesser Caucasus and in the lowland along the right bank of the Kura up to its confluence with the Araks River. E. A. ARZUMANIAN [11–356–3]

CAUCASIAN COMMITTEE, a special interdepartmental body established in 1845 by the Russian government in connection with the introduction of the all-Russian administrative system into the Caucasus.

The Caucasian Committee was preceded by a series of temporary committees on the elaboration and introduction of civilian government in the Caucasus (1833–45). The Caucasian Committee subsequently became a permanent body, directing the civilian activity of the imperial administration in the Caucasus. The committee consisted of the ministers of war, finance, state properties, justice, and internal affairs, as well as the heir to the throne, the head of the gendarmes, and other high officials appointed by the tsar. In 1882, after the elimination of the Caucasian vicegerency and the establishment of a new administrative system for the Caucasus, the Caucasian Committee was abolished. [11–355–1]

CAUCASIAN FINE-WOOLED SHEEP (formerly called the Caucasian Rambouillet), a breed of sheep raised for wool and meat. The breed was developed between 1921 and 1936 at the Bolshevik Breeding Sovkhoz (breeding plant since 1960), Ipatovo Raion, Stavropol' Krai, by crossing New Caucasian Fine-Wooled sheep with rams of the American Rambouillet and Ascanian breeds.

Caucasian Fine-Wooled sheep are large, with regular conformation and a strong constitution. The head is thin, with a straight profile (rarely hook-nosed); the neck is short and broad, with 1–3 folds of skin; the backline is even; the body is deep, wide and long; the legs are thin and strong; the skin is thick, with small folds along the entire body. The fleece is tightly curled. The wool clip is 10–12 kg from the rams (sometimes as much as 25 kg) and 5.8–6.5 kg from the ewes (sometimes as much as 13 kg). The wool is 7.5–8.5 cm long and is mostly 64 quality. Yield of clean fleece is 38–43 percent. Caucasian Fine-Wooled rams weigh 90–100 kg, ewes 50–60 kg. Fertility in the ewes is up to 150 percent. The animals are hardy and well adapted to the arid steppe climate. The rams were used in breeding Altai sheep and the Azerbaijan Mountain Merino and also to improve several fine-wooled and coarse-wooled breeds. Caucasian Fine-Wooled sheep are raised in the Stavropol' and Krasnodar krais; in Rostov, Volgograd, Saratov, and Kuibyshev oblasts of the RSFSR; and in the Kazakh SSR, Georgian SSR, and Armenian SSR.

REFERENCE
Sannikov, M. I. *Porody ovets stavropol'ia i plemennaia rabota s nimi.* Stavropol', 1960. I. D. KRAINOV [11–350–3]

CAUCASIAN LANGUAGES (Ibero-Caucasian languages), the indigenous languages of the Caucasus, which are represented by three groups: Kartvelian, Abkhazo-Adyg and Nakho-Dagestan. Although there is no doubt concerning the genetic relationship of the Nakh and Dagestan languages, they are sometimes regarded as two different groups. The Abkhazo-Adyg and Nakho-Dagestan groups are often conventionally referred to as the Mountain Caucasian or North Caucasian languages. There are approximately 40 Caucasian languages, which are spoken by more than 4.5 million persons. Only Georgian has an ancient literary tradition (dating back to the fifth century). The Udi also apparently had a writing system between the fifth and eighth centuries. The Abkhaz, Abaza, Adygei, Kabardin-Cherkess, Chechen, Ingush, Avar, Lak, Darghin, Lezgin, and Tabasaran languages have only recently been put into writing, although individual records in some of them date as far back as the Middle Ages.

The Caucasian languages are characterized by substantial divergences, in addition to the existence of structural parallelisms. Phonetically, they share complex consonant systems, which include stops (voiced and voiceless aspirates, glottalized stops, and voiceless unaspirated stops) and uvular and pharyngeal consonants. Harmonic consonant clusters (complexes) are frequent, although poorly represented in the Nakho-Dagestan languages. There are sharp differences in the vowel systems of the Caucasian languages, which include from two or three phonemes in the Abkhazo-Adyg languages to 15 to 20 or more phonemes in a number of Nakho-Dagestan languages (in which long and short, phafyngealized, nasalized, and umlauted vowels occur). There is also considerable variation in the phonological structure of roots. Stress in the Caucasian languages is dynamic and, in general, weakly expressed.

Morphologically, the Caucasian languages tend to be agglutinative, although elements of fusion and, in particular, ablaut are to be found in them. The Abkhazo-Adyg languages have very complex conjugations and rather elementary declensions, whereas the reverse is true for the Nakho-Dagestan languages. Subject-object prefixation is typical for the verb. Syntactically, the Caucasian languages distinguish absolute (usually with intransitive verbs), ergative (with transitive verbs), and affective (with verbs of perception) sentence constructions. Sentences have free word order.

The vocabulary of the Caucasian languages is rich in onomatopoetic words. There are many common lexical borrowings from the Arabic, Persian, and Turkic languages.

The Kartvelian linguistic group is intermediate between the Abkhazo-Adyg and Nakho-Dagestan languages with respect to a whole range of features. The Abkhazo-Adyg and Kartvelian languages display more features in common, such as the following interesting lexical parallelisms: Kartvelian *mz_1e "sun" ~ Abkhazo-Adyg *maza "moon"; Kartvelian *$g^w\!\!\!/$ "heart" ~ Abkhazo-Adyg *$g^w\!\!\ni$ "heart"; and Kartvelian *pxa "framework" ~ Abkhazo-Adyg *pqa "framework."

There is no unanimity among linguists on the question of Caucasian linguistic interrelationships. Their genetic unity is often postulated on the basis of the presence of a number of structural and typological parallelisms and a certain number of common material features. This supposition, however, cannot be regarded as proved, which allows some linguists to maintain that a linguistic union exists here. The problem of external Caucasian linguistic relationships is even less clear.

REFERENCES

Klimov, G. A. *Kavkazskie iazyki.* Moscow, 1965.
Iazyki narodov SSSR. Volume 4: *Iberiisko-kavkazskie iazyki.* Moscow, 1967.
Dirr, A. *Einführung in das Studium der kaukasischen Sprachen.* Leipzig, 1928.
Deeters, G. "Die kaukasischen Sprachen." In *Handbuch der Orientalistik,* vol. 7. Leiden-Cologne, 1963.
Javaxishvili, I. V. *K'art'uli da kavkasiuri enebis t'avdapirveli buneba da nat'esaoba.* Tiflis, 1937.
Ch'ik'obava, A. R. N. *Iberiulkavkasiur enat'a shescavlis istoria.* Tbilisi, 1965.   G. A. KLIMOV [11–351–1]

CAUCASIAN LINE COSSACK HOST, a cossack host formed in 1832 from five old cossack regiments, the Kizliar, Terek Family, Grebenskoi, Mozdok, and Gortsy regiments, which were stationed from the mouth of the Terek River to Mozdok, and five cossack regiments from the Azov-Mozdok line, the Volgskii, Caucasian, Stavropol', Khoper, and Kuban'; the host also incorporated the Sunzha Regiment, which was formed in 1817, and the 1st and 2nd Vladikavkaz regiments, which were formed in 1831 under the name of the Malorossiiskii Regiments.

With the Black Sea Host, the Caucasian Line Cossack Host held the Caucasian defensive line from the mouth of the Terek to the mouth of the Kuban' and acted jointly with the Separate Caucasian Corps against the mountaineers of the Northern

Caucasus. The Kizliar and Terek Family regiments were merged in 1838, and the Laba and Urup regiments were formed in 1840 and 1850 respectively. With the growth of the host population, which exceeded 300,000 in the mid-19th century, the majority of the regiments were deployed in brigades in 1846; in 1860 the host was composed of nine brigades and four separate regiments. In 1860 the Terek Cossack Host was formed out of one part of the Caucasian Line Cossack Host; the other part, together with the Black Sea Cossack Host, formed the newly founded Kuban' Cossack Host.   [11–358–4]

CAUCASIAN MINERAL WATERS REGION, the region containing a group of balneological health resorts, at the juncture of the Stavropol' Highland and the northern slopes of the Greater Caucasus (Stavropol' Krai). The mineral springs in the region are varied and abundant. The main health resorts, of importance for the whole Soviet Union, are Piatigorsk, Kislovodsk, Essentuki, and Zheleznovodsk. The region as a whole is characterized by a temperate mountain-steppe climate. The average temperature ranges from 7.8°C to 8.6°C, and annual precipitation is around 600 mm (with a maximum in the early summer).

The presence of mineral springs is linked to the monoclinal complex of Mesocenozoic sedimentary formations, which gradually submerge from south to north, from the Greater Caucasus to the Stavropol' Highland.

South of the region, in the area of highly elevated mountain ranges, Paleozoic and Precambrian highly metamorphosed schist is exposed; to the north these formations are gradually replaced by sedimentary Silurian, Jurassic, Cretaceous, Paleogene, and Neocene strata. The rocks of monoclinal formations are broken by a system of numerous fractures and fissures running predominantly northeast and northwest. Two cuestas are clearly seen in the region: the Southern one is formed of Upper Jurassic limestone (Skalistyi Range), the northern of Upper Cretaceous limestone (the Dzhinal and Borgustan ridges). Post-Neocene intrusions of the granite-syenite-porphyry series also play a substantial part in the geological structure of the region. They form unique cupola-like mountains, or laccoliths, including Beshtau, Mashuk, Zheleznaia, Razvalka, Byk, and Zmeika.

The complexity of geological structure determines the specific hydrogeological conditions of the Caucasion Mineral Waters region. From the point of view of the possibilities for accumulation and movement of subterranean waters, the Mesocenozoic rocks that submerge in a monoclinal fashion toward the north form a great artesian slope, whose main region of alimentation coincides with an area in which ancient metamorphic rock comes to the surface. The primary water-bearing complexes are of Tithonian-Valanginian, Aptian-Albian, and Upper Cretaceous age. Water-bearing complexes of Jurassic and Paleogene deposits have secondary importance. The subterranean springs are predominantly fresh water; however, in the area of deeply settled crushed rock, carbon-dioxide and, less frequently, hydrogen-sulfide mineral waters of various ionic composition and temperature have developed. Areas of tectonic intrusions, as well as contact intrusions and sedimentary rock, give rise to individual sources of carbon-dioxide mineral waters (springs at Kislovodsk, Essentuki, Piatigorsk, Zheleznovodsk, Nagut, Berezov, Kuma) and a large number of mineral springs of various compositions.

The subterranean waters of the region (fresh and mineral) are formed primarily by the infiltration of atmospheric precipitation. Part of the subterranean waters are enriched by gases (carbon dioxide) formed under high temperatures deep in the earth—a result of recent volcanism. The composition of mineral waters is significantly affected by the leaching of the containing rocks and cation exchange and displacement. This last process is especially widespread in the upper parts of the profile, since this area is the destination of waters highly saturated with gas, which rise from deep in the earth through breaks in the rock. By pushing out less mineralized springs and partially mixing with them, these rising waters form the final chemical and temperature characteristics of the region's mineral springs.

The Caucasian Mineral Waters region is one of the oldest Russian health resort areas. The first testimony about its mineral springs was given by the physician G. Shober (1717), who was sent by Peter I to investigate the mineral springs of the Northern Caucasus. Health resorts date from 1803. The physician S. A. Smirnov, director of the Water Authority (1860's), played a large part in the development of the region. He founded a chemistry laboratory for water analysis and organized in 1863 in Piatigorsk the first Russian balneological society. The development of the health resorts and their wide use began only after the establishment of Soviet power. In 1972 the region had about 130 mineral springs, 90 of which were in operation. Near Piatigorsk is Lake Tambukan, rich in therapeutic mud. The region's scientific center is the Balneological Institute (Piatigorsk), established in 1920, which studies the therapeutic methods of the resorts and develops more effective methods for using the mineral springs.

The region is the most popular health resort region of the USSR. In 1914, 41,200 people visited the area; in 1940 there were more than 200,000; and in 1971, 416,000 people stayed at the labor union sanatoriums alone. All the resorts are linked by asphalt roads and an electric railroad system. There is a large passenger airport in the city of Mineral'nye Vody.

REFERENCES
Ovchinnikov, A. M. *Mineral'nye vody,* 2nd ed. Moscow, 1963.
Panteleev, I. Ia. *Essentukskie soliano-shchelochnye vody v sisteme Kavkazskikh Mineral'nykh vod.* Moscow, 1963.
Panteleev, I. Ia. *Ocherk istorii izucheniia i razvitiia Kavkazskikh Mineral'nykh vod.* Moscow, 1955.   G. S. VARTANIAN   [11–352–1]

CAUCASIAN PRESERVE, a preserve situated between the cities of Sochi and Maikop (Krasnodar Krai) mostly on the northern slopes of the Glarnyi Range in the upper reaches of the Bol'shaia Laba and Belaia rivers; part of it extends to the southern slopes in the upper reaches of the Mzymta, Sochi, and Shakhe rivers. Area, 262,500 hectares (1970).

The preserve was established in 1924 to maintain the typical nature complexes of the northwestern Caucasus. Fir forests predominate, thriving at elevations of 1,000 to 1,900 m; beech forests are widely found at 900–1,200 m. The southern slopes to 900 m are covered with oak forests, with some hornbeam, pear and apple, wild myrobalan, common and Norway maple, linden, and ash. The upper margin of the forests zone contains elfin woodland, including birch, mountain ash, redwood maple, and beech. At 1,900–2,500 m there are luxuriant subalpine and short-grass alpine meadows. Above 2,800–2,900 m, in the subnival zone, individual herbaceous plants are found among the bare rocks; yet higher, in the nival zone, the mountains are covered with perennial snow and ice. Among the particularly interesting animals are the tur, chamois, deer, wild boar, bear, pine and stone marten, long-clawed mole-vole, Caucasian blackcock, and Caucasian snow pheasant.

Work is being done in the Caucasian Preserve to reestablish the Caucasian wisent, which had been destroyed earlier. In 1940 wisent-bisons were introduced—hybrids resulting from the crossing of the wisent and the bison. Later, by replacing wisent-bison males with pure-blooded wisent, a herd of wisent was obtained (more than 600 head in 1970) with an insignificant amount of bison blood. Included in the Caucasian Preserve is a relict yew and box grove (301 hectares, near the city of Khosta).

REFERENCES
Bannikov, A. G., K. Iu. Golgofskaia, and V. A. Kotov. *Kavkazskii zapovednik.* Moscow, 1967.
Zapovedniki Sovetskogo Soiuza. Edited by A. G. Bannikov. Moscow, 1969.   L. K. SHAPOSHNIKOV   [11–354–2]

CAUCASIAN RACE, in the classification of the German anatomist and anthropologist J. Blumenbach (1776), a large race corresponding to the Europeoid race. In contemporary anthropological literature the term "Caucasian race" is used relatively infrequently.   [11–350–2]

CAUCASIAN REGIONAL COMMITTEE OF THE RCP (BOLSHEVIK), the highest party body of the Caucasian region, founded at the First Congress of Bolshevik Organizations of the Caucasian Region, held in Tbilisi on Oct. 2–7 (15–20), 1917.

The Caucasian Regional Committee directed the Communist organizations of Transcaucasia, the Northern Caucasus, Dagestan, and the southern Black Sea coastal region. Its permanent location was in Tbilisi; from June 1918 to February 1919 it was located in Vladikavkaz. The committee had two bureaus, the Tiflis Bureau and the Baku Bureau. At various times it published official organs in Russian, Georgian, and Armenian, including *Kavkazskii rabochii, Kavkazskaia pravda, Volna, Brdzola,* and *Banvori kriv.* In 1918 and 1919 the committee held a congress of the party organizations of the RCP (Bolshevik) of the Northern Caucasus in Vladikavkaz (in January 1919) and conferences of the Communist organizations of Transcaucasia in Tbilisi (in November 1918) and in Baku (in May 1919). The Committee met in plenary session no less than once a month.

Under difficult conditions the Caucasian Regional Committee performed substantial political, organizational, and agitational and explanatory work in winning over the masses and creating a political army of the revolution for the victory of Soviet power in the Caucasus. It exposed the traitorous policies conducted against the interests of the people by the Georgian Mensheviks, Armenian Dashnaks, Azerbaijani Musavatists, and other conciliationist parties and bourgeois nationalists, and it educated the toiling masses in the spirit of proletarian internationalism and of close unity with the Russian proletariat. The committee maintained close contact and regular correspondence with the party's Central Committee and with Lenin personally.

Among those who at various times were members of the committee were A. M. Akopian, N. N. Aladzhalova, I. I. Anaskhin, A. N. Atabekov, A. A. Bekzadian, S. G. Buachidze, D. Kh. Buniatzade, N. F. Gikalo, L. D. Gogoberidze, M. D. Guseinov, P. A. Dzhaparidze, I. I. Dovlatov, V. E. Dumbadze, S. I. Kavtaradze, F. V. Kalandadze, S. I. Kas'ian, E. A. Kvantaliani, G. N. Korganov, D. S. Korkmasov, N. M. Kuznetsov, V. V. Lominadze, F. P. Makharadze, A. I. Mikoian, A. A. Mravian, A. M. Nazaretian, V. I. Naneishvili, M. A. Orakhelashvili, M. P. Orakhelashvili, M. S. Okudzhava, G. F. Sturua, G. G. Sultanov, M. G. Toroshelidze, S. I. Todriia, A. L. Tumanov, Iu. P. Figatner, K. M. Tsintsadze, M. G. Tskhakaia, G. Chkheidze, D. A. Shaverdov, S. G. Shaumian, B. P. Sheboldaev, and E. I. Eshba.

With the formation of the independent Communist parties of Azerbaijan, Armenia, and Georgia, the committee terminated its activities on May 20, 1920, on the basis of the directives of the Central Committee of the RCP (Bolshevik).

REFERENCES
Ocherki istorii kommunisticheskikh organizatsii Zakavkaz'ia, part 1 (1883–1921). Tbilisi, 1967.
Zhvaniia, G. *Velikii Oktiabr' i bor'ba bol'shevikov Zakavkaz'ia za Sovetskuiu vlast'.* Tbilisi, 1967.
Ivanidze, K. *Pervyi Kraevoi s"ezd bol'shevistskikh organizatsii Kavkaza (2–7 okt. 1917).* Tbilisi, 1969.   K.M. IVANIDZE   [11–355–2]

CAUCASIAN UNION COMMITTEE OF THE RSDLP (KSK), the directing body of the Caucasian Union of the RSDLP from 1903 to 1906.

The committee was founded at the First Congress of the Social Democratic Organizations of the Caucasus in March 1903 in Tbilisi, which was attended by 15 delegates from the Tiflis, Baku, and Batum committees; the Kutaisi, Chiatura, Ozurgety, Gori, and Mikhailov (Khashuri) groups of the RSDLP; and the editorial boards of the newspapers *Brdzola* and *Proletariat.* The congress proclaimed the Caucasian Union an inseparable part of the RSDLP, acknowledged the Leninist *Iskra* as the leading organ of the party, and adopted the draft program and draft of the party rules worked out by the editorial board of *Iskra.* Among those elected by the congress as members of the committee were M. Z. Bochoridze, B. M. Knuniants, F. I. Makharadze, A. G. Tsulukidze, and M. G. Tskhakaia, as well as four who later joined the Mensheviks, S. V. Dzhibladze, N. N. Zhordaniia, A. G. Zurabov, and D. A. Topuridze. At various times the committee included N. N. Aladzhalova, V. S. Bobrovskii, M. N. Davitashvili, P. A. Dzhaparidze, D. S. Postolovskii, J. V. Stalin, S. M. Khanoian, A. Kh. Khumarian, and S. G. Shaumian.

The committee recommended the delegates to the Second Congress of the RSDLP in 1903. In September 1903 the Central Committee of the RSDLP confirmed the Caucasian Union as a regional organization of the party. According to the rules adopted at the Second Congress of the Caucasian Union in October 1903, the committee's task was to coordinate the activity of local party committees on the basis of proletarian internationalist principles and to expand the publication of Marxist literature in the national languages. At the committee's congresses and conferences there was discussion on the reports of the Central Committee of the RSDLP, as well as on the accounts of the committee itself and of local party committees. Among other issues discussed were the problem of obtaining arms and of preparing for armed insurrection. The committee published the illegal newpaper *Bor'ba proletariata* and its supplement *Listok "Bor'by proletariata"* in three languages—Georgian, Armenian, and Russian—and maintained the underground Avlabar press.

The Caucasian Union was a militant detachment of Russian Social Democracy, closely tied with Lenin and with the editorial boards of the newspapers *Vpered* and *Proletarii;* it gave direction to political demonstrations and strikes of the Transcaucasian proletariat, fought against Menshevism, and took part in the struggle for convening the Third Congress of the Party and for the implementation of its resolutions. Lenin rendered regular assistance to the committee. With the merger of the Bolshevik and Menshevik committees on the eve of the Fourth Congress of the RSDLP in 1906 the Caucasian Union Committee ceased its activities.

REFERENCES

Lenin, V. I. "Kavkazskomu Soiuznomu komitetu RSDRP." *Poln. sobr. soch.,* 5th ed., vol. 46, pp. 310–11.
Lenin, V. I. "Tsentral'nomu Komitetu RSDRP." *Ibid.,* vol. 47, pp. 63–65.
Listovki Kavkazskogo Soiuza RSDRP, 1903–1905 gg. Moscow, 1955.
Ocherki istorii kommunisticheskikh organizatsii Zakavkaz'ia, 1883–1921, vol. 1. Tbilisi, 1967.
Zhvaniia, G. K. *V. I. Lenin i Kavkazskii Soiuz RSDRP.* Tbilisi, 1956.

S. I. ELKINA [11–357–1]

CAUCASIAN WAR OF 1817–64, the military actions involved in tsarist Russia's annexation of Chechnia, Gornyi Dagestan, and the northwestern Caucasus. After the annexation of Georgia (1801–10) and Azerbaijan (1803–13), these two areas were cut off from Russia by the lands of Chechnia, Gornyi Dagestan, and the northwestern Caucasus (although juridically Dagestan had been annexed in 1813). These lands were inhabited by martial mountain nationalities who raided the Caucasian fortified line and interfered with relations with Transcaucasia.

After the end of the war with Napoleonic France, tsarism was able to increase its actions in this region. General A. P. Ermolov, who was appointed commander in chief in the Caucasus in 1816, moved from isolated punitive expeditions to a regular advance into the heart of Chechnia and Gornyi Dagestan by surrounding the mountain regions with a solid ring of fortifications; he cut trails through dense forests, built roads, and razed "unruly" *auls* (villages). These actions forced the population either to settle in the plains and thus live under the surveillance of the Russian garrisons or to retreat deep into the mountains. In 1817–18 the left flank of the Caucasian line was transferred from the Terek to the Sunzha River; the Pregradnyi Stan fortification was established on the middle course of the Sunzha in October, 1817. This was the first step in the regular advance deep into the territory of the mountain peoples and in effect marked the beginning of the Caucasian War.

The fortress of Groznaia was founded in 1818 on the lower course of the Sunzha, and the Sunzha line was extended by the fortresses of Vnezapnaia (1819) and Burnaia (1821). In 1819 the Separate Georgian Corps was renamed the Separate Caucasian Corps and was brought up to 50,000 men; Ermolov was also placed in command of the Black Sea Cossack Host (up to 40,000 men) in the northwestern Caucasus. In 1818 several Dagestani feudal chiefs and tribes formed an alliance and in 1819 opened a campaign on the Sunzha line, but they suffered a series of defeats between 1819 and 1821. The domains of some of these feudal chiefs were given to vassals of Russia, who were placed under the authority of a Russian commandant; for instance the lands of the Kazikumukh khan went to the Kiurin khan and the lands of the Avar khan to the Tarki *shamkhal* (title of local feudal ruler). Other domains became dependent on Russia, as with the lands of the Karakaitag *utsmii* (local title), or were abolished and placed under Russian administration, as was done with the Mekhtulla khanate and with the Azerbaijani khanates of Shekino, Shirvan, and Karabakh. Between 1822 and 1826 several punitive expeditions were launched against the Circassians (Cherkess) in the region beyond the Kuban'.

Persia and Turkey tried to take advantage of the anticolonialist movement in the Caucasus for their own ends, but after the Russo-Persian War of 1826–28, Russia annexed the Erivan and Nakhichevan khanates, and after the Russo-Turkish War of 1828–29, the entire Black Sea coast from the mouth of the Kuban' to the northern border of Adzharia (St. Nikolas Fortress), as well as the Akhaltsikhe and Akhalkalaki fortresses. Ermolov's actions led to the subjugation of almost all of Dagestan, Chechnia, and the region beyond the Kuban'. General I. F. Paskevich, who replaced Ermolov in March 1827, gave up the regular advance and the consolidation of occupied territories and essentially returned to the tactics of individual punitive expeditions, although the Lezghin line was built under his command in 1830. The construction of the Sukhumi Military Road led to the annexation of the Karachai region in 1828.

The increasing scale of colonization in the Northern Caucasus and the cruelty of the policy of conquest pursued by Russian tsarism caused large-scale spontaneous uprisings of the mountaineers. The first of them took place in Chechnia in 1825: mountaineers headed by Bey-Bulat captured the Amiradzhiiurt post, but their attempts to take Gerzel' and Groznaia failed, and the uprising was suppressed in 1826.

In the late 1820's a movement of mountaineers arose in Chechnia and Dagestan under the religious banner of Muridism, which included among its dogmas the *ghazava,* or holy war against the infidels, that is, the Russians. In this movement the liberation struggle against tsarism's colonial expansion was combined with the fight against oppression by local feudal chiefs. This movement had its reactionary aspect, namely the struggle of the leading Muslim clergy to create an imamate, or feudal theocratic state. This isolated the Murids from the other peoples, fanned fanatical hatred against the non-Muslims, and, most important, preserved the backward feudal social structure.

The movement of the mountaineers under the banner of Muridism widened the scale of the Caucasian War, although several peoples of the Northern Caucasus and Dagestan, such as the Kumyks, Ossetians, Ingush, and Kabardins, remained aloof from this movement. There were several reasons for this. First, Muridism did not appeal to some of these peoples, either because they had been Christianized, like some of the Ossetians, or because Islam had no deep roots among them, for instance, the Kabardins. Second, tsarism succeeded in winning over to its side some feudal chiefs and their subjects with carrot-and-stick policies. Although these peoples did not openly oppose Russian rule, their situation was very difficult: they lived under a double yoke, the yoke of tsarism and of the local feudal chiefs.

The first to call for a *ghazava* was Gazi Muhammad (Kazi Mullah), who proclaimed himself imam in December 1828 and proposed the unification of the peoples of Chechnia and Dagestan. However, several feudal chiefs, among them the Avar khan and the Tarki *shamkhal,* were pro-Russian and refused to recognize the imam's authority. Gazi Muhammad's attempt in February 1830 to take Khunzakh, the capital of Avaria, failed, although the expedition of the tsarist troops of the same year in Gimry also failed and merely strengthened the imam's influence. In 1831 the Murids took Tarki and Kizliar and besieged Burnaia and Vnezapnaia; their detachments also operated in Chechnia, near Vladikavkaz and Groznaia, and, supported by rebellious Tabasarans, besieged Derbent. The imam's power extended over a large area—Chechnia and much of Dagestan.

After late 1831 the uprising began to ebb because the Murids were losing the support of the peasants, who were dissatisfied with the imam's failure to fulfill his promise to do away with the inequality between the estates. After General G. V. Rozen was appointed commander in chief in the Caucasus in September 1831, the Russian troops launched several large expeditions in Chechnia and pushed Gazi Muhammad's detachments into Gornyi Dagestan. The imam took refuge in Gimry with a handful of Murids; he died there on Oct. 17, 1832, when the Russian troops took the *aul*. Gamzat Bek was proclaimed second imam; his military successes won over almost all the peoples of Gornyi Dagestan, including some of the Avars, but the ruler of Avaria, Khansha (female khan) Pakhu-Bike, refused to come out against Russia. In August 1834, Gamzat Bek captured Khunzakh and exterminated the family of the Avar khans, but he was killed on Sept. 19, 1834 in a plot by the khans' supporters. To cut off the relations of the Circassians with Turkey the Russian troops launched an expedition into the region beyond the Kuban' in 1834 and established the fortifications of Abinskoe and Nikolaevskoe.

Shamil was proclaimed the third imam in 1834. A large detachment sent against him by the Russian command destroyed the *aul* of Gotsatl', the chief residence of the Murids, and forced Shamil's troops to abandon Avaria. Assuming that the uprising had been essentially suppressed, Rozen did not conduct any combat actions for two years. During this time Shamil, selecting the *aul* of Akhul'go as his base, brought many of the elders and feudal chiefs of Chechnia and Dagestan under his control, conducted violent reprisals against feudal chiefs who did not submit to him, and won wide support among the masses. In 1837, General K. K. Fezi's detachment captured Khunzakh, Untsukul', and part of the *aul* of Tilitl', where Shamil's detachments had retreated; but great losses and a shortage of food placed the tsarist troops in a precarious situation, and on July 3, 1837, Fezi concluded a truce with Shamil. This truce and the withdrawal of the tsarist troops were in effect Russian defeats and heightened Shamil's authority. In the same year Russian troops established the fortifications of St. Dukha, Novotroitskoe, and Mikhailovskoe in the northwestern Caucasus. General E. A. Golovin replaced Rozen in March 1838 and in the same year founded the fortifications of Navaginskoe, Vel'iaminovskoe, Tenginskoe, and Novorossiskoe in the northwestern Caucasus. The truce with Shamil proved temporary and military actions were resumed in 1839. On August 22, 1839, General P. Kh. Grabbe's detachment captured Akhul'go, Shamil's residence, after an 80-day siege. Shamil was wounded but with the Murids broke through into Chechnia.

On the Black Sea coast the fortifications of Golovinskoe and Lazarevskoe were established in 1839, and the Black Sea shore line, running from the mouth of the Kuban' River to the borders of Megrelia, was created in the same year. The next year the Laba line was created, but the tsarist troops soon suffered several defeats between February and April 1840 when rebellious Circassians captured the fortifications of the Black Sea shore line— Lazarevskoe, Vel'iaminovskoe, Mikhailovskoe, and Nikolaevskoe.

In the eastern Caucasus the Russian administration's attempt to disarm the Chechens caused an uprising that enveloped all of Chechnia and then spread to Gornyi Dagestan. After fierce battles in the region of Gekhinskii forest and on the Valerik River (July 11, 1840) the Russian troops occupied Chechnia. The Chechens joined Shamil's troops, which were operating in northwestern Dagestan. From 1840 to 1843, although the Caucasian Corps was reinforced by an infantry division, Shamil won several major victories, occupied Avaria, and established his rule over much of Dagestan, thereby more than doubling the territory of the imamate and increasing his troops to 20,000 men. In October 1842, General A. I. Neigardt replaced Golovin, and two more infantry divisions were transferred to the Caucasus, which made it possible to press back Shamil's troops to some extent. However, Shamil regained the initiative, captured Gergebil' on Nov. 8, 1843, and drove the Russian troops out of Avaria. In December 1844, Neigardt was replaced by General M. S. Vorontsov. The following year he captured and destroyed Shamil's residence, the *aul* of Dargo, but the mountaineers surrounded Vorontsov's detachment, which escaped with great difficulties, losing a third of its personnel and all the guns and supply trains.

In 1846, Vorontsov returned to Ermolov's tactics for subjugating the Caucasus. Shamil's attempts to thwart the enemy's offensive failed (the failure of the breakthrough into Kabarda in 1846, the fall of Gergebil' in 1848, and the failure of the storm of Temir-Khan-Shura and of the breakthrough into Kakheti in 1849). Shamil succeeded in occupying Kazikumukh from 1849 to 1852, but by the spring of 1853 his detachments had been definitively pushed from Chechnia into Gornyi Dagestan, where the situation of the mountaineers had also become precarious. In the northwestern Caucasus the Urup line was created in 1850 and the following year an uprising of Circassian tribes headed by Shamil's vicegerent Muhammad Emin was suppressed.

On the eve of the Crimean War, Shamil, counting on aid from Great Britain and Turkey, stepped up his actions; in August 1853 he made an unsuccessful attempt to break through the Lezghin line at Zakataly. In November 1853 the Turkish troops were defeated at Bashkadyklar and the attempts of the Circassians to seize the Black Sea and Laba lines were repulsed. In the summer of 1854 the Turkish troops passed to the offensive, with Tiflis as their objective; at the same time Shamil's detachments, breaking through the Lezghin line, entered Kakheti and captured Tsinandali, but were stopped by the Georgian militia and then routed by the Russian troops.

The defeat of the Turkish army in 1854–55 definitively dashed Shamil's hope for outside help. By that time the internal crisis of the imamate, which had begun back in the late 1840's, had become more serious. Shamil's vicegerents, the *naibs*, had become in effect greedy feudal lords whose cruel practices aroused the indignation of the mountaineers and intensified social contradictions, and the peasants gradually abandoned Shamil's movement. In 1858 an uprising even broke out against Shamil's rule in Chechnia, in the region of Vedeno. The imamate was also weakened by the ravages of war and by great human losses in a long and unequal struggle where ammunition and food supplies were in short supply. After the conclusion of the Treaty of Paris in 1856, tsarism was able to concentrate large forces against Shamil: the Caucasian Corps was transformed into an army and brought to a strength of 200,000 men. The new commanders in chief, General N. N. Murav'ev (1854–56) and General A. I. Bariatinskii (1856–60), continued to close the blockade ring around the imamate and firmly consolidated the occupied territories. After his residence, the *aul* of Vedeno, fell in April 1859, Shamil fled to the *aul* of Gunib with 400 Murids. Executing converging movements, three detachments of Russian troops encircled Gunib and took it by storm on Aug. 25, 1859; almost all the Murids died in combat, and Shamil was forced to surrender.

The actions of the tsarist command in the northwestern Caucasus were facilitated by the disunity of the Circassian and Abkhazian tribes. The tsarist command took fertile lands from the mountaineers and gave them to cossacks and Russian colonists and carried out a mass expulsion of the mountain peoples. In November 1859 the main forces of the Circassians (up to 2,000 men) led by Muhammad Emin capitulated and the land of the Circassians was cut by the Belaia River line with the fortress of Maikop. Between 1859 and 1861 trails were made in the forests, roads were built, and the lands seized from the mountaineers were colonized. The resistance to the colonialists intensified in mid-1862.

To capture the remaining territories held by the mountaineers, with a population of about 200,000, up to 60,000 soldiers were deployed in 1862 under the command of General N. I. Evdokimov. The tsarist troops began an advance along the coast and into the heart of the mountains and captured the territory between the Belaia and Pshish rivers in 1863; by mid-April 1864 they had captured the entire coast as far as Navaginskoe and the inland area up to the Laba River (along the northern slopes of the Caucasus range). Only the mountaineers of the Akhchipsu society and the small Khakucha tribe in the Mzymta River valley were not subdued. The Circassians and Abkhazians, forced to the sea or driven into the mountains, were compelled either to resettle in the plain or, under the influence of the Muslim clergy, to emigrate to Turkey. The unpreparedness of the Turkish government to receive, house, and feed masses of people (up to 500,000 persons), the arbitrary behavior and violence of local Turkish authorities, and difficult living conditions caused a high mortality among the émigrés, and a few returned to the Caucasus. In 1864, Russian administration was established in Abkhazia, and on May 21, 1864, tsarist troops captured the last center of resistance of the Circassian tribe of the Ubykhs, the point of Kbaadu (now Krasnaia Poliana). This day is considered the end of the Caucasian War, although in fact military actions continued until the end of 1864 and anticolonial uprisings took place in Chechnia and Dagestan in the 1860's and 1870's.

The Caucasian War brought Chechnia, Gornyi Dagestan, and the northwestern Caucasus definitively under Russian rule. The annexation was conducted with the violent military feudal methods typical of the colonial policy of tsarism. At the same time the incorporation of these peoples into Russia, which had started on the path of capitalism, was objectively progressive, since ultimately it promoted their economic, political, and cultural development. The Russian people and their vanguard, the revolutionary Russian proletariat, became these peoples' protector and leader in the struggle for social and national liberation.

REFERENCES
Dubrovin, N. F. "Kavkazskaia voina v tsarstvovanie imp. Nikolaia I i Aleksandra II (1825–1864)." In *Obzor voin Rossii ot Petra Velikogo do nashikh dnei*, part 4, book 2. St. Petersburg, 1896.
Istoriia russkoi armii i flota, vol. 6. Moscow, 1911.
Khronika Mukhammeda-Takhira-al-Karakhi. Moscow, 1946.
Dvizhenie gortsev Severo-Vostochnogo Kavkaza v 20–50 gg. XIX v.: Sb. dokumentov. Makhachkala, 1959.
Smirnov, N. A. *Miuridizm na Kavkaze*. Moscow, 1963.
Gizetti, A. *Bibliograficheskii ukazatel' pechatannym na russkom iazyke sochineniiam i stat'iam o voennykh deistviiakh russkikh voisk na Kavkaze*. St. Petersburg, 1901.   A. G. KAVTARADZE [11–344–2]

CAUCASUS (the origin of the word has not been exactly determined—it may be connected with the Hittite *kaz-kaz*, the name of a people who lived on the southern coast of the Black Sea; the term is first encountered in the tragedy *Prometheus Bound* by Aeschylus, the ancient Greek dramatist), the territory between the Black Sea, the Sea of Azov, and the Caspian Sea, stretching from the Kuma-Manych depression in the north to the Soviet border with Turkey and Iran in the south. Area, 440,000 sq km.

The Caucasus is often divided into the Northern Caucasus and Transcaucasia, the boundary between which passes along the Glavnyi, or Vodorazdel'nyi, Range of the Greater Caucasus; the western extremity of the Greater Caucasus is considered part of the Northern Caucasus. These areas are not considered units of territorial division in physical geography.

Terrain. A mountainous relief predominates in the Caucasus; the Greater Caucasus mountain system stretches from the Taman' Peninsula to the Apsheron Peninsula. Ciscaucasia (Predkavkaz'e) with its broad plains and plateaus extends from the northern foothills of the Greater Caucasus to the Kuma-Manych depression. Two depressions lie south of the Greater Caucasus: the Colchis Lowland in the west, and the Kura-Araks Lowland in the east. The folded Talysh Mountains (with heights up to 2,477 m) and the coastal Lenkoran' Lowland are located in the southeast. In the central and western parts of the southern Caucasus lies the extensive Transcaucasian Highland, which consists of the marginal folded ranges of the Lesser Caucasus (Malyi Kavkaz) and the volcanic Armenian (Dzhavakhet-Armenian) Highland farther south.

Western Ciscaucasia is level for the most part (the Kuban'-Azov Lowland north of the Kuban' River and the Kuban' sloping plain south of it). Bordering on the Kuban' delta is the Taman' Peninsula with its low, broad ridges and mud volcanoes. The Stavropol' Highland (with heights up to 831 m) is located in the center of Ciscaucasia; this highland is characterized by plateaus that are trapeziform in cross section and whose surface is formed by limestone and sandstone, as well as by deep, usually asymmetrical valleys. A group of laccoliths is located to the southeast, rising above the plains to heights of 1,402 m (Mount Beshtau). South of the Terek River lies the Terek-Sunzha Highland with its two anticlinal ranges, the Terek and the Sunzha (with heights up to 926 m), separated by the synclinal Alkhanchurt Valley. From the west and south, the Kabardan, Ossetian, and Chechen sloping plains border on the Terek-Sunzha Highland. Eastern Ciscaucasia is occupied by the Terek-Kuma

depression (the southwestern margin of the Caspian depression), formed by sediment from marine transgressions and delta accumulations (both ancient and modern). An extensive land mass (formed by sands from the Terek-Kuma depression) with eolian relief forms is located north of the Terek River.

The Greater Caucasus mountain system is divided along its length into the western (up to Elbrus), central (between Elbrus and Kazbek), and eastern Caucasus (east of Kazbek). In the central part the mountain system is strongly compressed; it is wider in the west and east. The southern slope is steeper than the northern. The highest ranges, which correspond to the axial zone of the Greater Caucasus, are the Glavnyi, or Vodorazdel'nyi, and the Bokovoi; peaks of more than 4,000–5,000 m include, in the western Caucasus, Dombai-Ul'gen (4,046 m); in the central Caucasus, Elbrus (5,642 m), Shkhara (5,068 m), Dykhtau (5,203 m), and Kazbek (5,033 m); and in the eastern Caucasus, Tebulosmta (4,493 m) and Bazardiuziu (4,466 m). The frontal ranges and ridges on the northern side of the western and central Caucasus have a cuesta character. In places, karst is strongly developed in limestone.

The lowlands located south of the Greater Caucasus are primarily alluvial. Bordering on the Kura-Araks Lowland are southeastern Kobustan, the Apsheron Peninsula with its hills and mud volcanoes, the Iori-Adzhinouri highland region, and the Kura sloping plain (in the foothills of the Lesser Caucasus). Also belonging to this territory are the Vnutrenniaia Kartli (Gori) plain and the Alazani-Agrichai longitudinal valley (the Alazani-Avtoran intermountain area). The Lesser Caucasus reaches its greatest height in the Murovdag Range (Mount Giamysh, 3,724 m; east of Lake Sevan). Characteristic features of the Armenian Highland (highest point: Mount Aragats, 4,090 m) are extinct volcanoes, lava plateaus and plains, uplifts formed by lava and tufa, and in the south folded ranges (Aiotsdzor) and large intrusive massifs—for example, the southern part of the Zangezur Range with Mount Kaputdzhukh (Kapydzhik; 3,904 m). A tectonic depression, the Middle Araks trough, extends along the USSR border.

Goelogical structure and minerals. The territory of the Caucasus belongs to the Mediterranean geosyncline belt. In its structure, according to the principal orographic units, the following are distinguished: the young platform (plate) of Ciscaucasia, the mega-anticlinorium of the Greater Caucasus, the Rioni-Kura zone of intermontane depressions, and the mega-anticlinorium of the Lesser Caucasus.

In the foundation of the Ciscaucasian platform, the northwestern section (the Rostov prominence) represents the southeastern submersion of the Precambrian Ukrainian crystalline massif, which passes here into a central massif of the Paleozoic geosynclinal region. In the other parts of Ciscaucasia, a Middle Paleozoic folded foundation is developed. The accumulation of a sedimentary mantle in Ciscaucasia began in the Middle Jurassic and continued through the Miocene. At the end of the Miocene, the Stavropol' Highland was uplifted, separating the Azov-Kuban' and Terek-Kuma depressions. At the end of the Pliocene, the anticlinal zones of the Terek and Sunzha ranges rose.

The northern slope of the central part of the Greater Caucasus represents the margin of the Ciscaucasian platform, which was drawn in during the most recent volcanism. Farther south, separated by the Pshekish-Tyrnyauz fault zone, stretches the zone of intensive Hercynian folding of the Bokovoi Range. Still farther south, a Baikalian–early Hercynian metamorphic complex, replete with Hercynian intrusions of granite, protrudes in the zone of the Glavnyi Range. In the interstream belt, the ancient granitic and metamorphic formations of the Glavnyi Range were overthrust over the Mesozoic southern slope. West of the upper reaches of the Pshekha and east of the Terek River valley, the Baikalian-Hercynian foundation is submerged under a thick shale formation of the Lias-Dogger, which forms axial anticlines in the western and eastern sections of the Greater Caucasus. This formation is overlapped by flysch from the late Jurassic through Eocene. The flysch is crumpled into isoclinal folds and, in a number of sections, forms nappes with an amplitude of displacement southward of up to 20–25 km. On the northern slope the flysch is replaced by limestone.

The foundation of the Rioni-Kura zone of intermontane troughs and the mega-anticlinorium of the Lesser Caucasus is a metamorphic complex from the Upper Precambrian–Lower Cambrian. The complex is broken by Hercynian granitoids; it protrudes to the surface in the Dziruli, Khrami, Loksi, Arzakan, and Megri massifs. The area between the mountains is divided by the Dziruli massif (the Suram Range) into two depressions (or intermontane troughs)—the Rioni depression in the west and the Kura depression in the east. Thick deposits of the molasse type (from the end of the Paleogenic through the Anthropogenic) are widespread in these two depressions.

The Lesser Caucasus and the Armenian Highland are notable for their great structural heterogeneity. In the northwest the Adzhar-Trialeti zone, shaped by Cretaceous and Paleogenic formations, may be distinguished. Continuing this zone southeast of Tbilisi is the Somkhito-Karabakh zone of gently folded volcanogenic carbonaceous strata from the Jurassic and Cretaceous. Within the axial Sevan-Akera zone intrusions of ultrabasic magmatic rock are extensively developed. Farther south, extensive sheets of young lava are prevalent in the Akhalkalaki, Gegamskii, and Vardenis volcanic plateaus.

The Caucasus is rich in deposits of various minerals. Deposits of nonferrous metals are associated with the Devonian volcanogenic series of the Bokovoi Range, with the Jurassic schistose-diabase formation of the Glavnyi Range and the southern slope of the Greater Caucasus, and with the Jurassic and Cretaceous volcanogenic series of the Lesser Caucasus. Deposits of lead and zinc ores are found in northern Ossetia and on the southern slopes of the Greater Caucasus, in Georgia; deposits of copper and molybdenum are located in Kabarda-Balkaria (Tyrnyauz) and in Zangezur (Armenia); iron ore (magnetite) is found in Azerbaijan (Dashkesan); an important deposit of alunites is located in Zaglik in Azerbaijan. The deposit of manganese ores at Chiatura has worldwide significance. There are beds of coal at Tkibuli and Tkvarcheli. Petroleum is exploited in eastern Azerbaijan, Chechen-Ingushia, Krasnodar and Stavropol' krais, and the Dagestan ASSR. The gas deposits of Krasnodar Krai and central Stavropol' Krai have acquired great importance. The Caucasus is also rich in various mineral waters, building materials, and other minerals.

Climate. The Caucasus is located on the border of the temperate and subtropical climatic zones. The Greater Caucasus mountain system sharply delimits the boundary between them by impeding the flow of cold air masses from north to south into Transcaucasia and of a warm air masses from south to north into Ciscaucasia. The mountain barrier formed by the Greater Caucasus is particularly appreciable in winter when Ciscaucasia is filled with cold air masses arriving from the north and northeast, while Transcaucasia is protected from their intrusion. The average temperatures for January are −2° to −5°C in Ciscaucasia; 4.5°C to 6°C in western Transcaucasia (Colchis Lowland); and 1° to 3.3°C in eastern Transcaucasia (Kura-Araks and Lenkoran' lowlands). In summer the temperature differences between the northern and southern parts of the Caucasus diminish; the disparity is more noticeable between the temperatures of the western (with a more maritime climate) and the eastern (continental) parts of the Caucasus. The average July temperatures are 23°–24°C in the west and 25°–29°C in the east. The climate of western Ciscaucasia is temperate, continental, and steppelike; eastern Ciscaucasia has a more continental and dry, semidesert climate. The Colchis Lowland is distinguished by its humid subtropical climate with mild winters and a large amount of precipitation (1,200–1,800 mm or more a year). The Lenkoran' Lowland also has a humid, subtropical climate (the annual precipitation is about 1,200 mm), but with a dry season at the beginning of the summer. The dry, subtropical climate of the Kura-Araks Lowland (the annual precipitation is 200–400 mm; in the east less than 200 mm), with mild winters and an abundance of solar heat in the summer, is favorable for the cultivation of cotton. The climate of the Middle Araks Trough in the Armenian Highland is similar.

The mountainous relief of the Greater Caucasus gives rise to a high-altitude climatic zone, manifested by a lowering of the temperature and a shortening of the growing season as altitudes increase. More precipitation falls on its mountain slopes than on the neighboring plains. Above about 2,000 m, there is a prevailing westerly wind, in connection with which the influence of the Atlantic Ocean and the Mediterranean Sea is intensified. Owing to the position of the Greater Caucasus at an angle to the westerly air flows, the slope of the western and central Caucasus, which is turned toward the south-southwest, receives the greatest amount of precipitation (up to 2,500 mm, and at times 4,000 mm). This is the most humid region both in the Caucasus and in the USSR. The average air temperature for the Greater Caucasus at an altitude of 2,000 m is about −8°C in January and 13°C in August (the warmest month). Higher, a cold, alpine climate with high humidity and a nival climate on high crests predominate. In the northern part of the Black Sea coast of the Caucasus (the region of Novorossiisk to Gelendzhik) the climate is Mediterranean with a humid winter and a dry summer.

The Lesser Caucasus on its outer slopes (in relation to the Transcaucasian plateau) has a climate similar to that of the opposite slopes of the Greater Caucasus at the corresponding altitudes. There is much more precipitation in the west than in the east. On the slopes of the Talysh Mountains, the climate is humid with an annual precipitation of up to 1,700 mm. In the interior region of the Transcaucasian plateau (the Armenian Highland), the climate is much more continental (at an altitude of 2,000 m, the average temperature for January is −12°C, and for July, 18°C) than at the corresponding altitudes of the Greater Caucasus. The snow cover lasts for four to five months. The annual precipitation is 450–550 mm, with the maximum occurring in the spring. The moderately cold continental climate of the upland steppe plateaus gives way in the high ranges and massifs to a more humid alpine climate with a cool summer and a long, cold winter.

Glaciation. In the Greater Caucasus region glaciation is extensive. The total number of glaciers reaches 2,200; they occupy 1,430 sq km. About 70 percent of all glaciers and glaciated areas are on the northern slope and about 30 percent on the southern. The prevalence of glaciation on the northern slope is explained by its special orographic features and by the greater snow cover connected with the snow storms carried beyond the Vodorazdel'nyi Range by westerly winds. In the western and central Caucasus, glaciation is more significant than in the eastern Caucasus, where the climate is more continental. The largest glacier area is in the highest part of the Central Caucasus, where the length of some glaciers is more than 12 km (Dykhsu, Bezengi, and Karaugom on the northern slope and Lekziri and Tsaneri on the southern slope). Elbrus is a thick glacial node; Kazbek's glaciation is similar but less thick. Present-day glaciation is insignificant in the Transcaucasian Highland: small glaciers are encountered only on the summit of Aragats and in the highest part of the Zangezur Range.

Rivers and lakes. The rivers of the Caucasus belong to the basins of the Caspian Sea (the Kura and Araks, Sulak, Terek, and Kuma), the Black Sea (the Rioni and Inguri), and the Sea of Azov (the Kuban'). The distribution of the flow and the regime of the rivers depend for the most part on climatic conditions and relief.

Rivers with a prolonged high-water level (about six months) during the warm months are characteristic of the Greater Caucasus. Perennial snows and ice, as well as late-melting seasonal snow in the high-mountain regions, feed the rivers. Similar to this type is the regime of the rivers that rise in the highest ranges and massifs of the Transcaucasian Highland (Aragats, the Zangezur Range, and the Murovdag) and in the sections of the southern slope of the Greater Caucasus where there are no glaciers. Spring flooding is typical of the remaining rivers of the Transcaucasian Highland. Spring freshets and summer flash floods are typical of the rivers on the southern slope of the Greater Caucasus. The rivers of Ciscaucasia, with the exception of those flowing from the Greater Caucasus, flood in spring and become icebound in winter; in summer, however, they become very shallow and at times dry up. The Stavropol' area is irrigated from the Kuban' River.

The rivers of the Caucasus that do not rise in areas with stable snow cover typically have flash floods from heavy rains or rapidly melting snow; groundwater serves as an additional source. Flash floods occur throughout the year (on the Black Sea coast south of Sochi and in the Colchis Lowland), during the warm season (in the frontal ranges of the northern slopes of the Greater Caucasus and in the Terek River basin), and in the coldest six months (in the western extremity of the Greater Caucasus and on the northern Black Sea coast). *Seli*, violent streams of mud and stone after heavy rains or the melting of snow, are typical of many rivers in the eastern Caucasus and part of the central Caucasus. The frontal limestone ranges of the Greater Caucasus have karst rivers, which disappear underground in places and reappear on the surface. The regimes of these rivers, as well as of the rivers in the volcanic region of the Armenian Highland, are regulated only by sacrificing the substantial contribution they make to the feeding of groundwaters. The major rivers, which receive tributaries from different areas, have mixed regimes. Most important rivers of the Caucasus have a mountain character and flow in trough valleys and gorges in their upper reaches but flow peacefully in broad valleys in their lower reaches.

The lower reaches of the Kura, Kuban', and Rioni are navigable. The waters of many rivers are used for irrigation of the arid regions of Ciscaucasia, the Kura depression, and the Middle Araks Trough. Many hydroelectric power plants have been constructed on the rivers of the Caucasus, including the Mingechaur and Zemo-Avchala hydroelectric power plants on the Kura, the Khrami and Rioni plants, and many plants on the rivers of the Greater Caucasus.

Lake Sevan is the largest lake in the Caucasus. Its waters feed the Razdan River and are used for energy production (at the Sevan Cascade Hydroelectric Power Plant), as well as for irrigation in the southern Armenian SSR. There are many cirque lakes in the alpine region of the Greater Caucasus; there are also avalanche and karst lakes. On the sea coasts there are lagoonal lakes. Most of the lakes are fresh water, but in the arid regions of the eastern Caucasus the lakes are saline.

Principal types of landscapes. An exceptionally great diversity of landscapes is typical of the Caucasus because of the complexity of its orography and its climatic contrasts, as well as the individual features of the history of the formation of the different parts of the Caucasus and the influence of the neighboring territories. Both flat and mountainous landscapes are widely represented.

The flat landscapes of Ciscaucasia belong to the temperate zone; those in Transcaucasia belong to the subtropical zone. In western and central Ciscaucasia, steppe landscapes predominate. These give way to forest-steppe landscapes in the highest sections of the Stavropol' Highlands, in the Mineral Waters region, in the western Sunzha Range, and on the sloping plains near the foothills of the Greater Caucasus. The steppes with their fertile Ciscaucasian carbonaceous chernozems and leached chernozems (in forest-steppe regions) are almost completely under field and garden cultivation. The forest steppe and the slopes of the laccoliths of the Mineral Waters region are covered with broad-leaved forests of beech, hornbeam, oak, and ash. In eastern Ciscaucasia, there is a zonal landscape of wormwood semidesert with chestnut soils, which gives way to saltwort semidesert on saline soils. The landscape of the Terek-Kuma sands with their eolian relief is more steppelike. In the delta of the Terek and Sulak rivers, there are *plavni* (low parts of downstream valleys covered with reed and trees) and marsh and meadow landscapes, which, in the process of evolution, are turning into semidesert. The fauna of Ciscaucasia is related to that of the steppes of the southern part of the Eastern European plain and (in the east) to that of the semideserts and deserts of Middle Asia.

Semidesert landscapes (wormwood, saltwort, and, occasionally, ephemeral semideserts) of the subtropical type are prevalent in the most arid regions of the Kura depression: the Kura-Araks Lowland, the Apsheron-Kobustan region, and the Kura sloping plain. The soils (sierozems, meadow sierozems, and gray-brown soils) in many areas are cultivated with the aid of irrigation, producing cotton and other crops. Untilled areas serve as winter pastures. Amid the semideserts of the Kura-Araks Lowland, there are sections of solonchak desert. The fauna of the Kura-Araks Lowland resembles that of Middle Asia: Persian gazelles, long-eared hedgehogs, jerboas, and reed cats are encountered.

In the Colchis and Lenkoran' lowlands humid, subtropical landscapes predominate: in place of the former lowland forests, today there are plantations of various subtropical crops and rice fields (in the Lenkoran' Lowland). Swamp alder forests and marshy subtropical landscapes have been preserved. Large areas of marsh have been drained and opened up for subtropical agriculture.

The mountainous landscapes of the Caucasus form three regions: the Greater Caucasus, with a predominance of mountain-forest, mountain-meadow, and glacial-nival landscapes; the Lesser Caucasus, with mountain-forest and mountain-meadow landscapes; and the Armenian Highland, with a prevalence of mountain-steppe and mountain-meadow volcanic landscapes. The Talysh Mountains with their humid subtropical landscapes are part of the Girkan region, most of which lies in northern Iran.

The distribution of landscapes in the mountains is subject to the natural laws of high altitude zones. Subtropical-forest landscapes are prevalent in the lower layer of the southern slope of the Greater Caucasus and the northern slopes of the Lesser Caucasus and the Talysh Mountains. In the western regions of the Caucasus and in the Talysh Mountains, low-mountain humid subtropical landscapes have developed, with terra rossa and yellow soils, broad-leaved forests of a varied floral composition, evergreen shrubs in the undergrowth, and lianas. The fauna of the Talysh Mountains is connected with that of the Kopetdag and more southerly regions (leopard, porcupine). In eastern Transcaucasia (the mountainous rim of the Kura depression) subtropical forests have a xerophytic character and grow on mountain brown soils.

Mountain-forest landscapes predominate in the mountains of the Greater and Lesser Caucasus. The lower part of the mountain-forest belt in Transcaucasia above the subtropical forest landscapes forms oak forests with hornbeam, above which are found beech forests with hornbeam (which also occupy the mid-mountain areas of the Talysh Mountains). Above these belts, in the western parts of the Greater and Lesser Caucasus, dark coniferous forests are prevalent (Caucasus spruce and fir). On the northern slope of the central Caucasus and partly in the eastern Caucasus, there are pine forests. Mountain-forest brown soils predominate in the mountain forests of the Caucasus. The mountain forests serve as a source of valuable wood and play a major role in protecting the soil and conserving water. Mountain-steppe landscapes with mountain chernozems predominate in the midmountain regions of the northern slope of the eastern Caucasus (Dagestan) and, partly, of the central Caucasus, as well as on the lava plateaus and plains of the Armenian Highland. The high-mountain area of the Greater and Lesser Caucasus and the Armenian Highland is occupied by mountain-meadow landscapes (in the most continental regions by meadow-steppe landscapes). The high-grass meadows of the subalpine belt on typical mountain-meadow soils are used for raising hay and for periodic pasture for livestock; the low-grass meadows and carpet-like meadows of the alpine belt on mountain-meadow peat soils serve as summer pastures. The upper, subnival part of the mountain-meadow belt has a fragmentary soil-vegetation cover. On the highest crests of the Greater Caucasus and partially in the Armenian Highland (Aragats and the Zangezur Range) a glacial-nival landscape is prevalent. The mountain regions of the Greater and Lesser Caucasus are inhabited by forest and high-mountain fauna, including endemic species (the West Caucasian and Dagestani tur, Caucasian black grouse, and Caucasian ular) and even genera (the long-clawed mole-vole), as well as forms common to Western Europe (the chamois, red deer) and widely distributed forms (bear, lynx, and fox). The mountain fauna of the Armenian Highland is related to that of Asia Minor (the Asia Minor suslik, William's jerboa).

Preserves. Within the Caucasus are many preserves, in which complexes of various landscapes are maintained in their natural state. The best known are the Adzhameti Preserve in western Georgia, in the Rioni River basin; the Babaneurskii Preserve in Kakhetia, on the southern slope of the Greater Caucasus; the Batsara Preserve in Georgia, on the southern slope of the Greater Caucasus, on the left bank of the Batsara River; the Borzhomi Preserve near the city of Borzhomi, in the spurs of the

Meskheta Range; the Vashlovan Preserve in eastern Georgia, in the El'dar steppe; the Dilizhan Preserve in Armenia, in the basin of the upper course of the Agstev River; the Zakataly Preserve in the extreme northwest of Azerbaijan, on the southern slope of the Greater Caucasus; the Lagodekhi Preserve in Georgia, near the city of Lagodekhi; the Caucasus and Teberda preserves on the northern slope of the Greater Caucasus; the Ritsa Preserve in the Lake Ritsa region, on the southern slope of the Greater Caucasus; the Pitsunda Preserve on the Black Sea coast; and the subtropical S. M. Kirov Kyzylagach Preserve on the southwestern coast of the Caspian Sea.

Favorable natural conditions—the combination of the Black Sea coast and high mountain ranges located nearby—furthered the transformation of the Caucasus into one of the USSR's principal health resort regions and one of the main centers of Soviet tourism and mountain climbing. Within the Caucasus is the Caucasian Mineral Waters region, a large group of health resorts on the Black Sea coast from Anapa to Batumi, including Kabardinka, Gelendzhik, Dzhubga, Novomikhailovskoe, Nebug, Golovinka, Sochi, Leselidze, Gagra, Miussera, Pitsunda, Gudauta, Novyi Afon, Sukhumi, Gul'ripshi, Zelenyi Mys, Kobuleti, and Teberda. The principal centers of tourism and mountain climbing are found in the Georgian SSR and the Kabarda-Balkar ASSR.

REFERENCES
Gvozdetskii, N. A. *Kavkaz.* Moscow, 1963.
Kavkaz. Moscow, 1966.
Geologiia SSSR. Volume 9: *Severnyi Kavkaz.* Moscow-Leningrad, 1968. Volume 10: *Gruzinskaia SSR.* Moscow-Leningrad, 1964. Volume 48: *Armianskaia SSR.* Moscow-Leningrad, 1970. Volume 47: *Azerbaidzhanskaia SSR.* Moscow-Leningrad, 1972.
Milanovskii, E. E., and V. E. Khain. *Geologicheskoe stroenie Kavkaza.* Moscow, 1963.
Paffengol'ts, K. N. *Ocherk magmatizma i metallogenii Kavkaza.* Yerevan, 1970.
Safronov, I. N. *Geomorfologiia Severnogo Kavkaza.* Rostov-on-Don, 1969.
Zanina, A. A. *Kavkaz.* Leningrad, 1961. (*Klimat SSSR*, issue 2.)
Vazhnov, A. N. *Analiz i prognozy stoka rek Kavkaza.* Moscow, 1966.
Grossgeim, A. A. *Rastitel'nyi pokrov Kavkaza.* Moscow, 1948.
Gulisashvili, V. Z. *Prirodnye zony i estestvenno-istoricheskie oblasti Kavkaza.* Moscow, 1964.
Lotyshev, I. P. *Lazurnyi bereg Kavkaza* [*Putevoditel'*, 2nd ed.]. Krasnodar, 1962.
Azerbaidzhan. Moscow, 1971. (In the series *Sovetskii Soiuz.*)
Armeniia. Moscow, 1966. (In the series *Sovetskii Soiuz.*)
Gruziia. Moscow, 1967. (In the series *Sovetskii Soiuz.*)
Rossiiskaia Federatsiia: Evropeiskii Iugo-Vostok, Povolzh'e, Severnyi Kavkaz. Moscow, 1968. (In the series *Sovetskii Soiuz.*)
Atlas Azerbaidzhanskoi SSR. Baku-Moscow, 1963.
Atlas Armianskoi SSR. Yerevan-Moscow, 1961.
Atlas Gruzinskoi SSR. Tbilisi-Moscow, 1964.

N. A. GVOZDETSKII (physical geography) and
V. E. KHAIN (geological structure and useful minerals)

Population. The Caucasus has a complex ethnic and linguistic composition. More than 50 peoples live there, speaking languages from three linguistic families: Caucasian proper (or Ibero-Caucasian), Indo-European, and Altaic. The Caucasian family consists of the Kartvelian, the Abkhazo-Adyg, and the Nakho-Dagestan groups. The most numerous people of the Caucasian family (and of the Kartvelian group) are the Georgians (3,245,000; 1970 census), who live in the central Caucasus, south of the Greater Caucasus. (All the remaining peoples of this family, except the Abkhazians, are settled north of this range.) In Georgia, the Georgians constitute 66.8 percent of the total population. The Abkhazo-Adyg group comprises the following peoples, who are closely connected in origin: the Adygeians (100,000 in the Adygei Autonomous Oblast and the neighboring regions of Krasnodar Krai), the Cherkess (or Circassians; 40,000 in the Karachai-Cherkess Autonomous Oblast), and the Kabardins (280,000 in the plains region of the Kabarda-Balkar ASSR and in the Mozdok region, Severnaia Osetiia ASSR), as well as the Abkhazians (83,000 in the Abkhazian ASSR and the neighboring regions of the Adzhar ASSR) and the Abazas (25,000 in the northern Karachai-Cherkess Autonomous Oblast). The Nakh group consists of the Chechen (613,000 in the eastern and

central Chechen-Ingush ASSR and in Khasav"iurt Raion, Dagestan ASSR), the Ingush (150,000 in the western Chechen-Ingush ASSR and the adjacent regions of the Severnaia Osetiia ASSR), and small groups of the Batsbi, or Tsova-Tushians (Akhmeta Raion, Georgian SSR), whose language has been subject to strong influence from Georgian.

The overwhelming majority of the peoples of Dagestan—one of the most ethnically complex regions not only in the USSR but also in the world—are part of the Dagestan group, which is divided into the Avar, Darghin, Lak, and Lezghin subgroups. The Avar subgroup (396,000 in the western mountains of Dagestan and the northwestern Azerbaijan SSR) includes, besides the Avars, the numerically small Andi-Tsez peoples, who have almost merged with the Avars: the Andi, Botlikh, Godoberi, Chamalal, Kvanda, Tindal, Karata, Akhvakh, Tsez, Ginukh, Khvarshi, Bezhita, and Gunzib. The Avar subgroup also includes the Archi. The Darghin subgroup (231,000 in the mountains and foothills of middle Dagestan) is composed of the Darghin, Kaitag, and Kubachi. The Lak (86,000) live in the mountains of central Dagestan. The Lezghin subgroup includes the Lezghin (324,000 in southeastern Dagestan and the northern Azerbaijan SSR), the Tabasaran (55,000 in southeast Dagestan, west of Derbent), the Agul (8,800 in the high-mountain regions of southeastern Dagestan), the Rutul (12,000 in the upper reaches of the Samur River, in southern Dagestan), and the Tsakhur (11,000 west of the Rutul'). Included in this group are the numerically small nationalities of northern Azerbaijan: the Udi, Budukh, Kryz, and Khinalug.

The Russians, Ukrainians, Armenians, and the peoples of the Iranian group are members of the Indo-European family. The Russians (about 8 million) live in Stavropol' and Krasnodar krais and the cities of all the Union and autonomous republics of the Caucasus. The Ukrainians (more than 300,000) live in Krasnodar Krai (the Kuban' and Terek cossacks constitute a significant part of the Russian and Ukrainian population in the Northern Caucasus). The Armenians (3,559,000) are a special group in the Indo-European family. They make up the principal population of the Armenian SSR (88.6 percent), the Nagorno-Karabakh Autonomous Oblast, and Akhaltsikhe and Akhalkalaki raions of the Georgian SSR; many Armenians also live in the cities of the Caucasus. The Iranian group includes the Ossetians (488,000 in the Severnaia Osetiia ASSR and the Iuzhnaia Osetiia Autonomous Oblast), the Kurds (60,000 in Armenia, Georgia, and Azerbaijan), the Tats (17,000 in the northeastern Azerbaijan SSR and the southern Dagestan ASSR), the Mountain Jews, who speak the Tat language (in the Dagestan ASSR and the Azerbaijan SSR), and the Talysh (in the southeastern Azerbaijan SSR).

There are several groups speaking Turkic languages of the Altaic family. The 4.38 million Azerbaijanis live in the Azerbaijan SSR, where they constitute 73.8 percent of the population, as well as in the adjacent regions of the Georgian SSR, the Armenian SSR, and the Dagestan ASSR. Two closely related groups are the Karachai (113,000 in the southern mountains of the Karachai-Cherkess Autonomous Oblast) and the Balkars (60,000 in the southern and southwestern Kabarda-Balkar ASSR). Other groups include the Kumyk (189,000 in the northern plains section of the Dagestan ASSR and—in small numbers—in the Chechen-Ingush ASSR and Severnaia Osetiia ASSR); the Nogai (52,000 in Stavropol' Krai and the Dagestan ASSR); the Tatars (about 32,000 in the cities of the Azerbaijan SSR); and the Caucasian Turkmen (or Trukhmen—about 5,000 in eastern and northeastern Stavropol' Krai).

Also living in the Caucasus are small groups of Greeks, Assyrians, Moldavians, Estonians, Mordvinians, Koreans, and Gypsies. For all Caucasian peoples the language of communication between different nationalities is Russian.

Anthropologically, most of the population of the Caucasus is comparatively homogeneous and belongs to the southern branch of the Europeoid race. Only the Nogai and Trukhmen have predominately Mongoloid traits; the Russians have features of the northern branch of the Europeoid race.

The greater part of the population of the Caucasus professed Christianity in the past. The Russians, Ukrainians, most Ossetians, a large number of Georgians and Abkhazians (the last two peoples belonged to a separate Georgian church), and the Mozdok Kabardins were Orthodox; the Armenians were Monophysites and belonged to the Armenian Apostolic Church. Shiite Muslims in the Caucasus included the Azerbaijanis, Talysh, Tats, and a small number of the Lezghin. Some Georgians (the Adzhars and Enghilo), Abkhazians, and Ossetians were Sunni Muslims.

REFERENCE
Narody Kavkaza, vols. 1–2. Moscow, 1960–62. S. I. BRUK

Historical survey. The Caucasus is one of the regions of the earliest settlement by man in the USSR: in Armenia, sites of primitive settlement have been discovered that date to the early Stone Age. In the first half of the first millennium B.C. in Transcaucasia the first slaveholding state on the territory of what is now the USSR was formed—Urartu. Later states to emerge were the Colchian Kingdom (sixth century B.C.), the Ayratian Kingdom (fourth century B.C.), and Iberia (fourth and third centuries B.C.). In the second century B.C. two important states were formed: Caucasian Albania and Greater Armenia; the latter conducted a stubborn struggle against Rome. The Caucasus was frequently subjected to invasions by nomads (Scythians, Sarmatians, and Alani). In the first millennium A.D. the Caucasus became a center of the struggle between Byzantium and Sassanid Persia.

In the middle of the first millennium A.D. feudal relations were firmly established in much of the Caucasus, and Christianity became widespread. In the seventh and eighth centuries, the Arabs conquered Transcaucasia. Further development of feudal relations occurred during the struggle against foreign invaders, the Arabs and later the Seljuk Turks and the Byzantines; this situation led to the formation of large states in Armenia, headed by the Bagratids, and in Georgia, centered around the Tao-Klardzheti Principality. During the 12th and 13th centuries Georgia grew stronger. In the 13th century the Caucasus was subjected to the devastating invasion of the Mongol Tatars. In the 14th and 15th centuries Armenia and Georgia were the victims of destructive campaigns by foreign invaders. In Azerbaijan, Turkic state formations arose in the 15th century. The Northern Caucasus remained under the authority of the Mongol Tatars and their successors for a considerable time; as a result, the area's development lagged significantly, and patriarchal-feudal features were preserved until the 19th century. In the 16th century Armenia and Georgia became the object of a fierce struggle between Turkey and Persia.

Russian settlements appeared in the Northern Caucasus in the 16th century. After the fall of the Astrakhan Khanate in 1556, Russia's southern frontier was advanced to the Terek River, on which two fortresses were founded: Terek (at the mouth of the Sunzha River; 1567) and Terskii Gorodok (in the Terek delta; 1588). During their internecine struggle some of the feudal lords sought the support of Russia (for example, Kabarda had already accepted Russian sovereignty in 1557); others occupied positions inimical to Russia—for example, a Tarki *shamkhal* (feudal ruler) in Dagestan, against whom expeditions of Russian troops were sent in 1594 and 1604–05).

In the early 18th century Russian tsarism, seeking to strengthen its strategic position on the southern frontiers and to occupy the trade routes to Middle Asia and the Middle East, maintained a colonial policy in the Caucasus. As a result of the Persian campaign of 1722–23, Russian forces occupied the entire western coast of the Caspian Sea, as well as Derbent and Baku, but because of the aggravation of Russo-Turkish relations the Russian government became interested in alliance with Persia and, by the treaties of Resht (1732) and Gandzha (1735), restored the Caspian shore provinces to Persia. The southern border of the Russian Empire in the northeastern Caucasus was again moved to the Terek, where the fortresses of Kizliar (1735) and Mozdok (1763) were built, marking the beginning of the construction of the Caucasian fortified lines.

As a result of the Russo-Turkish War of 1768–74, it was confirmed that Kabarda would remain an integral part of Russia; northern Ossetia was annexed to Russia; and the Eia and Kuban' rivers became the Russian border in the northwestern Caucasus. Between 1777 and 1780 the Azov-Mozdok line

(through Stavropol') was established, but by 1778 its right flank had already been moved to the Kuban' River. As a result of the Treaty of Georgievsk in 1783 between Russia and the Kartli-Kakhetian Kingdom, a Russian protectorate was established over eastern Georgia, which was threatened by Turkey. In that year, the construction of the Georgian Military Road was begun; along this road several fortifications were built, including the fortress of Vladikavkaz (1784). The distribution of lands to Russian landlords began in the steppe area of Ciscaucasia.

The advance of the Caucasian fortified line southward strained relations with the peoples of the Kuban' area, Kabarda, and Chechnia. In 1778 the stubborn resistance of the Nogai was crushed, and the Kabardins who had risen in rebellion were defeated. In 1785 tsarist expansionism aroused a movement of mountain people in Chechnia headed by a Muslim priest—the Chechen Ushurma, who took the name Sheikh Mansur. In July 1785 he routed the strong Russian detachment sent against him. The movement spread to the neighboring provinces, but some of the Dagestan feudal lords did not support Mansur, thus facilitating the suppression of the revolt. Mansur crossed to Anapa to join the Turks in the struggle against Russia. During the Russo-Turkish War of 1787–91, Russian troops conducted military actions against the Circassians, and in September 1790, in the upper reaches of the Kuban', they routed both the Turkish forces of Batal Pasha, which had invaded Kabarda, and Mansur's Circassian detachments. According to the conditions of the Peace of Jassy of 1791, Turkey recognized the independence of Georgia and the tribes beyond the Kuban'. Between 1792 and 1798 the Black Sea and Kuban' cordon lines were created along the Kuban' River. In 1785 a Caucasian vicegerency (*namestnichestvo*) was established as part of the Astrakhan and Caucasian provinces, with its center at Ekaterinograd (now the *stanitsa* [large cossack village] of Ekaterinogradskaia). The territory of the vicegerency included the steppes between the lower courses of the Volga and Don and a part of the Northern Caucasus, to the Kuban' and Terek. The Caucasian Province was abolished in 1790 and the vicegerency in 1796.

The invasion of Georgia in 1795 by the Persian troops of Agha Muhammad Khan and their destruction of Tbilisi prompted Russia to undertake the Persian campaign of 1796. Russian troops advanced into Georgia and occupied Derbent, Kuba, and Baku, but after Pavel I's accession to the throne in 1796, the troops were recalled (except for two battalions that remained in Tbilisi). Eastern Georgia's attempt to find in Russia a protector against Turkish and Persian aggression led to that area's voluntary affiliation with Russia in 1801. In the 19th century Azerbaijan and part of Armenia were joined to Russia as a result of the Russo-Persian wars; later, as a result of the Russo-Turkish wars, western Georgia and the rest of Armenia were incorporated.

The first Russian administrative territories in Transcaucasia were the Georgian Province (1801) and the Imereti Oblast (1811), which were united in 1840 to form the Georgian-Imereti Oblast and divided in 1846 into Tiflis and Kutaisi provinces. In 1828 the Armenian Oblast was formed; it was renamed Erivan Province in 1849. An okrug, which was given the name Zakatal Okrug in 1860, was formed from Dzharo-Belokany Oblast (which had been set up in 1830). In 1840 the Caspian Oblast was formed; it was renamed Shemakha Province in 1846 and Baku Province in 1859. In the Northern Caucasus, in 1802, the Caucasian Province was again formed (with its center at the city of Georgievsk); it was renamed the Caucasian Oblast in 1822 (center, Stavropol'), and Stavropol' Province in 1847. In 1846, Derbent Province was created; in 1860 it was renamed Dagestan Oblast (with its center at Temir-Khan-Shura, now Buinaksk). From 1844 to 1882, a Caucasian vicegerency with its center at Tiflis was in existence. The vicegerent was commander in chief of the troops in the Caucasus and enjoyed unlimited powers. In 1845, with the introduction into the Caucasus of the all-Russian administrative system, the Caucasian Committee was established.

Tsarism's colonial policy led to the Caucasian War of 1817–64, the aim of which was to conquer Chechnia, Gornyi Dagestan, and the northwestern Caucasus. The Russian troops succeeded in crushing the stubborn resistance of the mountain peoples only in the second half of the 19th century. Despite the colonial oppression, incorporation in Russia was the sole means of deliverance of the Transcaucasian peoples from the heavy yoke of the backward Turkish and Persian feudal regimes. The incorporation of the entire Caucasus by Russia resulted in its inclusion in the all-Russian process of the development of capitalism and in the establishment of links between the progressive public and cultural figures of the Caucasus and Russia, as well as in the involvement of Caucasian workers in the revolutionary struggle against tsarism.

In 1861, Terek Oblast (with its center at Vladikavkaz) and Kuban' Oblast (center, Ekaterinodar; now Krasnodar) were formed. In 1867 the Black Sea Okrug of Kuban' Oblast (center, Novorossiisk) was established; in 1896 it was reorganized as the Black Sea Province. In 1866 the Sukhumi Military Section was created as part of Kutaisi Province; it was detached as an independent okrug in 1903. In 1868, Elizavetpol' Province was formed from parts of Tiflis and Baku provinces. In 1878, Kars and Batumi oblasts were set up on formerly Turkish territories (Batumi Oblast was an okrug of Kutaisi Province from 1883 to 1903). After the abolition of the vicegerency in 1882, the chief official of the civilian section in the Caucasus headed the administration of the Caucasus; he was simultaneously commander of the troops of the Caucasian Military District and head ataman of the cossack forces in the Northern Caucasus. Subordinate to him were six provinces—Black Sea, Kutaisi, Tiflis, Erivan, Baku, and Elizavetpol' (Stavropol' Province had been separated administratively from the Caucasus); five oblasts—Terek, Kuban', Dagestan, Kars, and Batumi (and, temporarily, from 1882 to 1890, Transcaspian Oblast); and two okrugs—Zakataly and Sukhumi.

From 1864 to 1883, after the abolition of serfdom in the Caucasus, the growth of capitalist relations gathered momentum. The construction of railroads expanded in the Caucasus after 1867; by 1883 the Batumi-Tbilisi-Baku main Transcaucasian line had been completed; branch lines were built to Yerevan, Batumi, Kars, Dzhul'fa, and other points in the 1890's. In 1900 the Transcaucasian line was joined to the all-Russian rail network by the Rostov-Baku line. The oil industry emerged in the Baku region in the second half of the 19th century; in 1901, it produced about half of the world oil output. The extraction of manganese and coal in Georgia, the production of cement in the Novorossiisk region, and other industries were begun. Capitalist relations in agriculture developed more slowly because of the preservation of feudal serfdom and tribal patriarchal vestiges.

In the 1890's, with the growth of the workers' movement, the first social democratic organizations came into existence, such as the Mesame Dasi, or Third Group, formed in Georgia in 1892; in 1901 the Baku committee was established. In the early 20th century the workers' movement grew, particularly in Baku. In 1903, at the First Congress of Caucasian Social Democratic Organizations, the Bolshevik Caucasian Union Committee of the RSDLP was elected. The proletariat of the Caucasus took part in the Revolution of 1905–07, during which a turbulent peasant movement spread. A new upsurge in the workers' movement in the Caucasus occurred in 1912–13.

During World War I the Caucasus became a theater of military operations. The Caucasian front was formed against the German-Turkish alliance. In 1914 the troops on the Caucasian front repelled the Turkish offensive and in 1915 and 1916 inflicted on them a series of major defeats. During the war Bolshevik organizations in the Caucasus were seriously weakened. In a majority of the soviets that arose after the February Revolution of 1917, the Mensheviks, Social Revolutionaries (SR's), and bourgeois nationalists seized the leadership. In March 1917 the bourgeois Special Transcaucasian Committee (OZAKKOM) came into existence in Tbilisi—the regional body of the bourgeois Provisional Government.

The victory of the Great October Socialist Revolution marked the beginning of the liberation of the Caucasian peoples from social and colonial oppression. The first Caucasian regional congress of Bolsheviks in October 1917 consolidated the Bolshevik organizations and established the Caucasian Regional Committee of the party. On Nov. 15 (28), 1917, a bloc of counterrevolutionary forces, in place of the OZAKKOM, established the Transcaucasian Commissariat, which declared the "independ-ence" of Transcaucasia. Soviet power in Transcaucasia was established only in Baku and adjoining districts.

On Apr. 22, 1918, the Transcaucasian Diet established a bourgeois federal republic. By May 1918, however, this entity had been broken up into separate "independent" bourgeois republics—Georgia, Armenia, and Azerbaijan—in which the Georgian Mensheviks, the Armenian Dashnaks, and the Azerbaijani Musavatists seized power. In April in Baku the Baku Commune of 1918 was formed; it heroically fought against internal and external counterrevolution, but as a result of the treachery of the SR's, Dashnaks, and Musavatists, Soviet power in Baku fell on July 31, 1918. The bourgeois-nationalist governments in Transcaucasia were puppets in the hands of the Germans and Turks, and later of the British interventionists, who carried out organized plunder of the land. In the Northern Caucasus, the Bolsheviks, supported by the broad masses of the people, succeeded in overcoming the resistance of the cossack and nationalist counterrevolutions; by early 1918, Soviet power was victorious there. A number of Soviet republics arose (the Kuban'–Black Sea Soviet Republic, the Terek Soviet Republic, and the Stavropol' Soviet Republic), which were consolidated in July 1918 as the Northern Caucasian Soviet Republic of the RSFSR.

In the Northern Caucasus, Soviet troops conducted a struggle against the White Guard army of General A. I. Denikin, diverting its forces from the central regions of Russia, but in early 1919 they were compelled to withdraw to Astrakhan, and a reign of terror was instituted by the White Guard. In early 1920 the Red Army crushed the remnants of Denikin's forces and restored Soviet power. In April 1920 the Red Army came to the aid of the working people of Azerbaijan, who had risen in rebellion, and on April 28 the Azerbaijan Soviet Socialist Republic was proclaimed, composed of the former Baku Province, a large part of Giandzha (renamed Elizavetpol') Province, and Zakataly Okrug. In July 1920 the Nakhichevan SSR was created as part of the Azerbaijan SSR. In February 1923 it was named the Nakhichevan Autonomous Krai, and in February 1924 it became the Nakhichevan Autonomous Soviet Socialist Republic. In July 1923 the Nagorno-Karabakh Autonomous Oblast was established as part of the Azerbaijan SSR.

In November 1920 the working people of Armenia rebelled and with the support of the Red Army overthrew the Dashnak government; on November 29 the Armenian SSR was formed from the territory of Erivan Province and part of Giandzha (Elizavetpol') Province. By the terms of the Treaty of Moscow of Mar. 16, 1921, the so-called Kars pashalic (Kars Oblast and parts of Batumi Oblast and Erivan Province) went to Turkey.

In February 1921 there was an uprising of the working people in Georgia, who turned for help to Soviet Russia. Soviet troops and the rebels drove out the Mensheviks, and, on February 25, the Georgian SSR was established. Tbilisi and Kutaisi provinces and part of Batumi Oblast formed the new republic. On the territory of Batumi Oblast, in July 1921 the Adzhar ASSR was formed as part of the Georgian SSR. On the territory of Sukhumi Okrug, the Abkhazian SSR came into existence in March 1921; in December 1921 it joined the Georgian SSR on the basis of a treaty, and in February 1931 it was reorganized as the Abkhazian ASSR. In April 1922 the Iuzhnaia Osetiia Autonomous Oblast was formed as part of the Georgian SSR.

On Mar. 12, 1922, the peoples of Transcaucasia united in the Transcaucasian Federation (ZSFSR), which, on Dec. 30, 1922, joined the USSR. In 1936 the federation was dissolved, and Georgia, Armenia, and Azerbaijan immediately entered the USSR with the rights of Union republics. In the Northern Caucasus, in 1921, the Gortzy ASSR, the Dagestan ASSR, Terek Province, and Kuban'–Black Sea Oblast were formed as part of the RSFSR. Adygei Autonomous Oblast was formed on part of the territory of Kuban'–Black Sea Oblast in 1922. The Gortzy ASSR (which was abolished in 1924) was divided to form several autonomous oblasts (AO): Kabarda AO (1921), reorganized in 1922 as Kabarda-Balkar AO; Karachai-Cherkess AO (1922), which was divided in 1922 into the Karachai AO and the Cherkess National Okrug (reorganized in 1928 as the Cherkess AO); Chechen AO (1922) and Ingush AO (1924), which were consolidated in 1934 to form Chechen-Ingush AO; and Severnaia Osetiia AO (1924).

In 1924, in accordance with the plan for dividing the USSR into raions, the Northern Caucasus, except for the Dagestan ASSR, entered Iugovostochnaia Oblast, RSFSR, which that year was renamed the North Caucasian Krai. The krai (with the exception of the seven autonomous oblasts) was divided into 14 okrugs (of them, ten were in the northern Caucasus: Armavir, Kuban', Maikop, Sal'sk, Stavropol', Sunzha, Terek, Black Sea, and the cities of Groznyi and Vladikavkaz with okrug status; the other okrugs were on the Don); in 1930 the okrugs were eliminated. In 1934 the Azov–Black Sea Krai was detached from the North Caucasian Krai and in 1937 was divided into Krasnodar Krai and Rostov Oblast. According to the Constitution of the USSR of 1936, three of the autonomous oblasts were transformed into the Kabarda-Balkar ASSR, the Severnaia Osetiia ASSR, and the Chechen-Ingush ASSR. In 1937, North Caucasian Krai was renamed Ordzhonikidze Krai and in 1943 Stavropol' Krai.

During the prewar five-year plans (1929–40), the peoples of the Caucasus, with the fraternal assistance of the other peoples of the USSR, achieved a high level of development in various branches of industry: oil, chemical, metallurgical, machine-tool, coal, mining, cement, food, and other industries. They constructed major electric power plants as well. Agriculture achieved substantial development, an important role in its rise being played by large-scale land-reclamation and irrigation works. The cultural revolution proceeded successfully. Socialist industrialization, the collectivization of agriculture, and the cultural revolution have changed the life of the peoples of the Caucasus. Most of them have been consolidated into the socialist nations and nationalities.

During the Great Patriotic War of 1941–45 major battles with the fascist German troops took place in the Caucasus, during which the Red Army defeated the enemy. In 1944 the Kabarda-Balkar ASSR was reorganized as the Kabarda ASSR. In place of the abolished Chechen-Ingush ASSR, Groznyi Oblast was created. Part of the abolished Karachai Autonomous Oblast entered the Cherkess Autonomous Oblast; the other part was transferred to the Abkhazian ASSR. In 1957 the Kabarda-Balkar ASSR was recreated, and the Chechen-Ingush ASSR was reestablished; the Cherkess Autonomous Oblast was transformed into the Karachai-Cherkess Autonomous Oblast. Since the Great Patriotic War the peoples of the Caucasus have progressed in the development of their economy and culture and in the creation of an advanced socialist society.

The Battle for the Caucasus, 1942–43. One of the most important battles of the Great Patriotic War of 1941–45 took place in the Caucasus. It includes a series of defensive and offensive operations by Soviet forces from July 25, 1942, through Oct. 9, 1943, between the Don River and the foothills of the Greater Caucasus. The battle is divided into two periods: the defensive (from July 1942 to early January 1943) and the offensive (from early January to October, 1943).

The fascist German command, in undertaking an offensive on the Caucasian operational axis (with the code name "Edelweiss"), expected to surround and destroy the troops of the Southern Front south and southeast of Rostov, who had withdrawn beyond the Don, and to seize the Northern Caucasus. The Germans then proposed to turn the flank of the Greater Caucasus with one group from the west, capturing Novorossiisk and Tuapse, and with another group from the east, seizing the oil-producing districts of Groznyi and Baku. Simultaneously with this flanking maneuver, the Germans planned to cross the Vodorazdel'nyi Range through its central passes and come out in the region of Tbilisi, Kutaisi, and Sukhumi. With this penetration into Transcaucasia, the enemy hoped to establish a direct link with the Turkish army, 26 divisions of which were deployed on the frontiers of the Soviet Union, as well as to create the prerequisites for an invasion of the Middle East. The enemy formed Army Group A (under Field Marshal W. List) to carry out these plans. This group outnumbered the Soviet forces on the Southern front 1.5 times in personnel (167,000 as opposed to 112,000); 9.4 times in tanks (1,130 against 121); twice in artillery (4,540 guns and mortars to 2,160); and 7.7 times in airplanes (1,000 to 130).

The fascist German offensive began on July 25, 1942. Under the onslaught of the adversary's superior numbers, the Soviet troops were compelled to withdraw south and southeast. On July 28 the Supreme Command Headquarters consolidated the Southern and Northern Caucasian fronts into a single Northern Caucasian front (under Marshal of the Soviet Union S. M. Budennyi); the Black Sea Fleet (under Vice Admiral F. S. Oktiabr'skii) and the Azov Flotilla (under Rear Admiral S. G. Gorshkov) were put under the command of the Northern Caucasian Front. Shortly afterward, two strategic groups were formed at the front: the Don Group (under Lieutenant General R. Ia. Malinovskii) on the Stavropol' axis and the Primor'e Group (under Colonel General Ia. T. Cherevichenko) on the Krasnodar axis. The Transcaucasian Front (under General of the Army I. V. Tiulenev) was assigned the preparation of the defense along the Terek River line and along the passes across the Vodorazdel'-nyi Range of the Greater Caucasus.

The rapid advance of the fascist German troops and the threat of encirclement forced the Soviet command to withdraw its forces first to the Kuban' River and then to a line passing along the foothills of the western part of the Greater Caucasus. The Supreme Command Headquarters reinforced the front with their reserves and ordered the Groznyi line to be protected by troops of the Northern Group of the Transcaucasian Front (under Lieutenant General I. I. Maslennikov). In August and September fierce fighting continued on the Maikop-Tuapse and Krasnodar-Novorossiisk lines. On August 11 the troops of the German Seventeenth Army (under General of the Infantry R. Ruof) succeeded in taking Maikop and Krasnodar and, on August 31, Anapa. On September 7 they reached the northern outskirts of Novorossiisk, but despite desperate efforts the enemy failed to break through to Tuapse. The fascist German forces also failed to break through to Sukhumi across the passes of the Greater Caucasus, although they introduced special mountain units that were able to seize some of the passes. From August to October the enemy persistently pushed forward on the Groznyi axis. On August 25 the troops of the First Panzer Army (under Colonel General E. Kleist) took Mozdok and on September 12 Malgobek. After meeting stiff resistance on the Groznyi line, the enemy regrouped his forces and, on October 25, broke through to Nal'chik and Ordzhonikidze. Near Ordzhonikidze, from November 6 to 12, the main attack force of the fascist German troops was routed and thrown back 40–50 km to the north. In November and December the enemy, under attack by the Soviet forces everywhere, went on the defensive.

The plans of the enemy were foiled by the heroic resistance of the defenders of the Caucasus—the troops of the Northern Caucasian Front (on September 1, reorganized as the Black Sea Group of the forces of the Transcaucasian Front), the Northern Group of the Transcaucasian Front, the Black Sea Fleet, and the Azov Flotilla. During the defense of the Caucasus Soviet troops paralyzed significant enemy forces and inflicted great losses, thus preventing the enemy from transferring forces to Stalingrad, where the Soviet counteroffensive began.

The crushing defeat of the fascist German troops at Stalingrad and the expanding general offensive of the troops of the Southern Front on the Rostov axis forced the enemy to begin withdrawing his forces from the Mozdok area to the northwest. On Jan. 3, 1943, the Northern Group of troops (after January 24, the Northern Caucasian Front, under the command of Lieutenant General I. I. Maslennikov) expanded the pursuit of the enemy and by January 24 had liberated Malgobek, Mozdok, Prokhladnyi, Mineral'nye Vody, Piatigorsk, Essentuki, Kislovodsk, Stavropol', and Armavir. The enemy's efforts to consolidate his position on the Kuban' River line were frustrated by the attacks of the Soviet forces. By January 30, Soviet troops had liberated Kropotkin and Tikhoretsk after having advanced 650 km in the month of January. The troops of the Black Sea Group (which, after February 9, were included in the Northern Caucasian Front) moved to the offensive on January 16 and by February 4 had freed Neftegorsk and Maikop. On February 9 they began the Krasnodar Operation, during which they liberated Krasnodar on February 12. The fascist German command succeeded in withdrawing part of the forces of Army Group A through Rostov and the other part to Taman'; they managed to consolidate their position on the "Blue Line," which had been prepared beforehand. Efforts to break through the enemy's defense, undertaken in the spring of 1943 by Soviet forces who had been extremely weakened in battle, were unsuccessful. In the fall, during the Novorossiisk-Taman' Operation of 1943 (September 9 to October 9), the troops of the Northern Caucasian Front (commanded after May 1943 by Colonel General I. E. Petrov), in cooperation with the Black Sea Fleet, liberated Novorossiisk and all of Taman' Peninsula.

Victory in the Battle for the Caucasus consolidated the southern flank of the Soviet-German front, and close coordination between the land forces and the air force, the navy, and the partisans was attained. Thousands of soldiers were awarded the medal "For the Defense of the Caucasus," which was instituted by a decree of the Presidium of the Supreme Soviet of the USSR on May 1, 1944.

REFERENCES
Velikaia Otechestvennaia voina Sovetskogo Soiuza 1941–1945: Kratkaia istoriia. Moscow, 1965.
Grechko, A. A. *Bitva za Kavkaz.* Moscow, 1967.

S. A. ZALESSKII (historical survey) and D. Z. MURIEV
(the Battle for the Caucasus, 1942–43) [11–326–1]

CAUDILLO. (1) The official title of Generalissimo F. Franco, the former head of state of Spain. The caudillo is invested with virtually unlimited powers of supreme governmental, political, and military leadership ("the caudillo is responsible before god and history").

(2) In several Latin American countries, the caudillo is the head of state, ruling as a personal dictator. [11–1604–3]

CAUDINE FORKS, a mountain pass in Samnium, near Caudia in central Italy; the site of a Samnite victory over the Romans during the Second Samnite War in 321 B.C. The Roman legions fell into the ambush laid by Gavius Pontius and surrendered. The disarmed Roman soldiers were forced to pass underneath a yoke made of two spears driven into the ground and joined at the top by a third. The Romans abandoned the Samnite cities they had already occupied and turned over 600 hostages. The expression "to pass beneath a Caudine yoke" has come to mean a great degradation or humiliation. [11–315–4]

CAULERPA, a genus of green algae of the order Siphonales. There are about 60 species inhabiting tropical and subtropical seas. The thallus of *Caulerpa* is a single polynuclear diploid cell, interlaced with trabeculae (siphon structure). A *Caulerpa* alga consists of a spreading, branching portion up to 1 m long and rhizoids and vertical shoots up to 30 cm tall. Reproduction is both sexual (isogamy) and vegetative (parts of the body break away). [11–1605–4]

CAUPOLICÁN. Date of birth unknown; died 1558 in Cañete. A military leader of the Araucanians.

In 1552, Caupolicán united separate groups of Indians in southern Chile in the struggle against the Spanish colonizers. The Araucanians, under the leadership of their chiefs, Caupolicán and Lautaro, staunchly resisted the colonialists. In 1558, Caupolicán was taken captive in the battle of Cañete and brutally killed. The Spanish poet Alonso de Ercilla y Zuñiga (1533–94), a participant in the subjugation of Chile, immortalized the heroic exploits and courage of Caupolicán in the epic poem *La Araucana.*

REFERENCE
Ercilla y Zuñiga, Alonso de. *La Araucana.* New York, 1902.
[11–1611–2]

CAURA, a river in Venezuela, a right tributary of the Orinoco. Length, 745 km; basin area, 52,000 sq. km. It originates in the south-central part of the Guiana Highlands, cutting through it to form rapids and waterfalls. There is considerable variation in the water discharge (with the maximum in the summer). The average annual discharge is 2,720 cu m per sec. The Caura River is navigable for 150 km from its mouth. [11–1611–3]

CAUSALGIA, a painful condition that develops after injury to the extremities, characterized by excruciating, unendurable, intermittently intensifying pains, mostly of a burning nature.

Causalgia results from injury to a nerve trunk (when it is not completely severed) that has an abundance of sympathetic nerve fibers such as the sciatic and tibial nerves in the leg and the median and (less commonly) ulnar nerves in the arm. Between five and ten days after injury, pain arises in the extremity along with marked autonomic disturbances—vascular, secretory and trophic. These changes, like the burning pains, sometimes involve the neck and upper part of the chest, when an arm is affected, and the lower part of the abdomen when a leg is affected. The pains intensify at the slightest movement or light contact with the skin (especially stroking) and are affected by emotional stress, noise, and light. Cooling and constantly wetting the skin usually diminishes the pains.

Causalgia occurs in two forms—ischemic (coldness and pallor of the extremity, trophic disorders) and hyperemic; the latter is milder and its disorders are less pronounced, and it tends to disappear spontaneously after four or five months. Treatment involves the injection of novocain or alcohol into the area of the affected nerve trunk or of the ganglion-blocking substances into the sympathetic ganglia. Physical therapy may be helpful (electrophoresis with novocain, X-ray therapy). Surgery is indicated (freeing the nerve from scars) if more conservative treatment fails. [11–1604–4]

CAUSTIC SURFACE, a surface that is an envelope of a system of light rays emitted by a luminous point and passing through an optical system. A caustic surface can also be defined as a surface at each of whose points there is an intersection of two rays diverging at an infinitesimal angle from a luminous point and converging after refraction at the boundaries of the system's optical mediums. The concentration of light energy takes place on a caustic surface and can be seen well in a hazy medium.

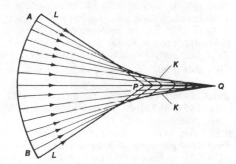

Figure 1. Form of caustic surface for an optical system that has spherical aberration. (AB) light wave front after passing through optical system, (L) light rays, (K) caustic, (PQ) line segment, along which image of point light source is distended in presence of spherical aberration (in a nonaberrational system a point source is represented by a point).

The aberrations of optical systems may be classified on the basis of the symmetry properties of caustic surfaces. The axial symmetry of a caustic surface (see Figure 1) corresponds to spherical aberration, and symmetry with respect to the meridional plane (for example, the plane of the figure) corresponds to the coma. In nonaberrational optical systems the caustic surface becomes a point—the image of a point source. [11–1611–7]

CAUSTOBIOLITHS, combustible fossils of organic origin, products of the transformation of plant, and more rarely animal, remains affected by geological factors. The term "caustobioliths" was proposed in 1888 by the German scientist H. Potonié, who divided caustobioliths into three groups according to origin: sapropelites, occurring as a result of the burial of lower organisms, primarily plankton algae, on the bottom of bodies of water (kerogen of oil shales, boghead coal); humites, formed from the remains of higher plants, primarily marsh plants (lignite, coal); and liptobioliths, which are coals enriched with the components of plant matter that are most resistant to decay, such as pitches, waxes, and cuticles. Mixed types of caustobioliths are also found (saprohumites, liptosapropelites [cannel coal]).

Potonié also included petroleum (as a product of the underground distillation of sapropelites) and combustible natural gases among the caustobioliths.

REFERENCES

Potonié, H. *Proiskhozhdenie kamennogo uglia i drugikh kaustobiolitov.* Leningrad-Moscow, Groznyi-Novosibirsk, 1934.
Muratov, V. N. *Geologiia kaustobiolitov.* Moscow, 1970.

N. B. VASSOEVICH [11–1612–1]

CAUVERY, a river in southern India. The Cauvery is approximately 800 km long, with a basin area of approximately 80,000 sq km. It originates on the slopes of the Western Ghats, crossing the southern part of the Deccan plateau, where in places it flows in narrow rocky gorges with waterfalls up to 91 m high. At the point of its influx into the Bay of Bengal it forms a delta with an area of approximately 10,000 sq km. The Cauvery is fed by rain. Monsoon conditions prevail, with two flood times—in summer, from the southwestern monsoon, and in winter (in the lower course), from the northeastern monsoon. The water discharge in an average flow at Mettur fluctuates between 300 and 12,800 cubic meters per second. At the waterfalls there are a number of hydroelectric power stations with a total capacity of more than 800,000 kilowatts. Two large reservoirs are located on the river, and more than 1 million hectares are irrigated with water from the Cauvery River. The river is navigable at the mouth and in small sections in an average current.

[11–317–4]

CAVAIGNAC, GODEFROY ÉLÉONORE LOUIS. Born 1801 in Paris; died there May 5, 1845. French politician. Bourgeois republican. Brother of General L.-E. Cavaignac.

Cavaignac participated in the July Revolution of 1830. During the July monarchy he was a leader of the republican Society of Friends of the People and participated in the republican uprising in Paris in April 1834. He was imprisoned in Paris. He escaped in July 1835 and lived in Great Britain until 1841. Back in France, Cavaignac contributed to the opposition newspaper *La Réforme* in 1843. [11–317–2]

CAVAIGNAC, LOUIS EUGÈNE. Born Oct. 15, 1802, in Paris; died Oct. 28, 1857, at Ourne. French statesman and general. Bourgeois republican.

Cavaignac served in the conquest of Algeria from 1832; he was appointed military governor of Algeria after the Revolution of February 1848. Upon becoming French minister of war in May 1848, he led the suppression of the June uprising in Paris. Cavaignac's epithet became the "butcher of the workers." He was chief executive of the French republic until mid-December 1848. [11–317–3]

CAVALCANTI, ALBERTO. Born Feb. 6, 1897, in Rio de Janeiro. Brazilian motion-picture director.

Cavalcanti graduated in 1917 from the University of Genoa. In the 1920's he joined an avant-garde film group in Paris, worked as an art director, and began directing in 1926 (his first film was *Train Without Eyes*). Cavalcanti's documentary films *Nothing but Hours* (1926) and *On Assignment* (1927) differed from avant-garde films in their tendency toward social commentary and their portrayal of everyday life.

He moved to Britain in 1934 and joined J. Grierson's group, becoming one of England's leading documentary film-makers. (He also directed features in the 1940's.) In 1949, Cavalcanti moved to Brazil, where he became a producer and founded the Cinefilmes Studio, which produced *Song of the Sea* (1954), a depiction of the hard life of simple people. Since the mid-1950's he has worked in Austria, Rumania, Italy, Great Britain, and Spain.

REFERENCES

Alberto Cavalcanti. Berlin, 1962. V. A. UTILOV [11–313–3]

CAVALCANTI, GUIDO. Born 1255 or 1259 in Florence; died there in 1300. Italian poet.

After G. Guinizelli, Cavalcanti became the major poet of the *dolce stil nuovo.* His canzones and sonnets celebrated sublime love for an idealized woman and attempted to reveal the philosophical meaning of this love. He also composed verses on earthly love, characterized by freshness and spontaneity (for example, his ballad "I Met a Shepherdess in the Woods").

WORKS

Le rime . . . edite e inedite. Florence, 1813.
In Russian translation:
"Sonety." In *Khrestomatiia po zarubezhnoi literature: Literatura srednikh vekov.* Compiled by B. I. Purishev and R. O. Shor. Moscow, 1953.

REFERENCES

De Sanctis, F. *Istoriia ital'ianskoi literatury,* vol. 1. Moscow, 1963.
Storia della letteratura italiana, vol. 1. Milan, 1965. [11–313–4]

CAVALIERI, FRANCESCO BONAVENTURA. Born 1598 in Milan; died Nov. 30, 1647, in Bologna. Italian mathematician. Monk of the Hieronymite order.

Beginning in 1629, on the recommendation of Galileo, Cavalieri occupied the chair of mathematics at the University of Bologna. In his work *Geometry* (1635) he developed a new method of determining areas and volumes, the method of indivisibles. The indivisibles are parallel chords of a plane figure and parallel plane sections of a solid. He introduced the concept of the "sum total" of the indivisibles drawn within the outline of a figure. The ratio of two "sum totals" of indivisibles was an embryonic form of the ratio of two definite integrals. The works of Cavalieri played a large role in the formation of the calculus of infinitesimals.

REFERENCE

Struik, D. J. *Kratkii ocherk istorii matematiki,* 2nd ed. Moscow, 1969. (Translated from German.) [11–313–1]

CAVALIERI'S PRINCIPLE. If the areas of the cross sections of two solids by any plane parallel to a given plane are invariably equal, then the two solids have the same volume. This proposition (and the analogous one for plane figures), which was already well-known to ancient Greek mathematicians, is usually called Cavalieri's principle, although the Italian mathematician F. B. Cavalieri in his *Geometry* (1635) does not take it as a principle but proves it. [11–313–2]

CAVALIERS, during the English Revolution of the 17th century, a derisive name given by supporters of the Parliament to their opponents, the Royalists; it came to be used in late 1641. The name emphasized the gentry nature of the royal army, in which the cavalry had primary significance. [11–312–3]

CAVALLI, FRANCESCO (real name, Pietro Francesco Caletti). Born Feb. 14, 1602, in Crema; died Jan. 14, 1676, in Venice. Italian composer. Son and pupil of a cathedral choirmaster in Crema.

Cavalli completed his musical education in Venice, where he lived from 1616. In 1617 he became a singer (tenor), at St. Mark's Basilica, and then its organist and conductor. He wrote church music (notably his *Requiem*), but basically he composed operas and was a leading master of the Venetian school. He wrote 42 operas, including *The Marriage of Teti and Peleo* (1639), *Didone* (1641), *Jason* (1649), *Xerxes* (1654), and *Mutio Scevola* (1665). Almost all his operas were commissioned by Venetian theaters.

REFERENCES

Kretzschmar, H. *Istoriia opery.* Leningrad, 1925. (Translated from German.)
Rolland, R. *Opera v XVII veke v Italii, Germanii, Anglii.* Moscow, 1931. (Translated from French.)
Prunières, H. *Cavalli et l'opéra italien au XVII siècle.* Paris, 1931.

[11–312–4]

CAVALLINI, PIETRO (actually Pietro dei Cerroni). Born circa 1240–50 in Rome; died there circa 1330. Italian painter, representative of proto-Renaissance art.

Cavallini created mosaics on the themes from the life of Mary in the church of Santa Maria in Trastevere, Rome (1291). He painted frescoes in the church of Santa Cecilia in Trastevere (c. 1293; fragments of the *Last Judgment* remain), and in the church of Santa Maria Donna Regina in Naples (1316–20; with assistants). While basing his work on the tradition of ancient painting, Cavallini was the first to move from the canons of Byzantine art. He gave his subjects corporeality and volume, modeling the forms with chiaroscuro and color. His work exerted a great influence on early 14th-century Italian artists, including his contemporary Giotto.

REFERENCES
Skvortsov, A. "Freski Kavallini." *Sofia* 1914, no. 3.
[Toesca, P.] *Pietro Cavallini.* Milan, 1959.　　　　[11–312–5]

CAVALRY, a combat arm that uses riding horses for movement and combat action.

The cavalry originated in the countries of the ancient world, in the regions where horses were raised on a large scale. Before the appearance of the cavalry in the armies of Egypt, China, and India, horse-drawn war chariots were used. The cavalry was used for the first time as a combat arm by the Assyrian Army in the ninth century B.C. and then spread to other slaveholding states. In the Persian Army it was the main combat arm from the sixth century B.C; it was divided into heavy cavalry (*clibanarii*), armed with swords and pikes, and light cavalry, armed with bows and arrows, javelins, and spears. A cavalry battle began with the shooting of arrows and the throwing of javelins to break up the combat formation of the enemy and ended with an attack by the heavy cavalry supported by mounted archers.

The Parthian cavalry in the third to first century B.C. was organized and used in combat in roughly the same way. The cavalry of the ancient Greek states (Sparta and Athens) was small. But since there were many horses in northern Greece (in Thessaly and Boeotia), Thebes could form a larger cavalry. In the first half of the fourth century B.C. the Theban general Epaminondas deployed cavalry for the first time in cooperation with infantry and skillfully used it to accomplish the defeat of the enemy in the battles of Leuctra and Mantinea. In the second half of the fourth century B.C. a regular cavalry was created in Macedonia as an independent combat arm along with the infantry. The cavalry of Alexander the Great was well trained and had great maneuverability and striking power; it was divided into heavy, medium, and light cavalry. The medium cavalry was the most numerous, but the heavy cavalry, which had mighty weapons and good means of defense, struck the decisive blow. In the campaigns of Alexander the Great the regular cavalry began playing a decisive role in combat (the battles of Granicus, Issus, and Gaugamela [Arbela]). In the Roman Army the cavalry was an auxiliary combat arm. In the Second Punic War (218–201 B.C.), Hannibal widely used the first-class cavalry of the Carthaginian Army to strike blows at the flanks of the enemy with a complete envelopment of his battle formation; Hannibal's cavalry played a decisive role in defeating the Roman Army on the Trebbia River and at Cannae.

After the establishment of feudalism in Western Europe in the eighth and ninth centuries, the knightly cavalry became the chief military force of the feudal army. The knights were armed with swords and heavy lances and protected by shields, helmets, and armor, which covered the entire body; from the second half of the 12th century the war horses were also covered with armor. The heavily armed knights could attack only at a short distance and at a slow gait; combat was reduced to duels between individual horsemen. The lowest organizational and tactical unit of the knightly army was the "lance," which consisted of one knight and the men serving him, including the weapon bearer, archers mounted and on foot, lancers, and servants—a total of from four to ten men; between 20 and 50 or more lances formed a "standard" (*khorugv'*), which consisted of vassals of an important feudal lord. Several standards formed the knightly army (usually not more than 800–1,000 knights). In comparison with the cavalry of the ancient world the knightly cavalry had lost its mobility and could not pursue the enemy.

In the army of the ancient Russian state (ninth and tenth centuries) the cavalry was represented by the prince's retinue, which was numerically smaller than the unmounted city and village militia. In the 11th and 12th centuries the size of the cavalry was increased to fight the nomads. The Russian cavalry exhibited a high level of mastery in the Battle on the Ice of 1242, when Alexander Nevsky led the cavalry in the rout of the German knightly forces. The battle of Kulikovo of 1380 was decided by Dmitrii Donskoi's ambush cavalry regiment. In the war of the Asian feudal states the Mongol-Tatar light cavalry of Genghis Khan and his successors (13th and 14th centuries) displayed a remarkable degree of organization and combat efficiency. The Mongols were excellent horsemen and perfect masters in the use of the bow and arrow, the saber, and the lasso. They skillfully maneuvered on the battlefield, used faked retreats and ambushes, and kept strong reserves for the final thrust.

With the invention and development of firearms (in the 14th century) and the increasing role of the infantry in the late 15th century, the knightly cavalry finally lost its importance. The defensive weapons of the horsemen were gradually made lighter, and in the 16th century light cavalry carrying firearms moved to the forefront. At the same time the tactics of cavalry combat changed; the depth of the deployed cavalry formation increased to eight, ten, or more ranks, and the attack in mounted formation and with silent weapons was abandoned; instead the ranks fired from the horse and moved up in turns from the depth of the battle formation. All this deprived the cavalry of maneuverability and capability for rapid strikes.

In the late 16th century a new and lighter type of heavy cavalry was created, the cuirassiers, who carried broad swords and pistols and wore cuirasses and helmets. The dragoons, which appeared at the same time, were armed with muskets and were originally a mounted infantry. In the Thirty Years' War (1618–48), Gustavus II Adolphus reduced the depth of the deployed cavalry formation in the Swedish Army to three ranks and revived shock tactics. The Swedish cavalry once more attacked on horse at a rapid gait and maneuvered on the battlefield, and the dragoons, trained for action on horse and on foot, became the main type of cavalry. In the 17th and 18th centuries the Western European states had three types of cavalry, including heavy cavalry—the cuirassiers; medium cavalry—the dragoons, carabineers, and mounted grenadiers; and light cavalry—the hussars, uhlans, and light cavalry regiments. In most states the cavalry made up one-half of the army; in France the cavalry was even 1½ times larger than the infantry. Until the 18th century the cavalry of Western European armies (except for the Swedish Army) continued to fire from horseback and move at a slow gait.

With the formation of the centralized Russian state in the second half of the 15th century, a large cavalry composed of landed gentry was created; in the second half of the 16th century this cavalry numbered between 150,000 and 200,000 men. In the 1630's the gentry cavalry began to be gradually replaced by cavalry regiments organized in the new way, of which there were 25 in 1681 (reiter and dragoon regiments). The cossack cavalry began to play an important role in the Russian Army in the 16th century. In the course of the military reforms of Peter I in the early 18th century a regular dragoon-type cavalry was created (40 dragoon regiments, including five garrison regiments); for the first time in history the cavalry was armed with horse artillery (two three-pound guns per regiment). The chief combat technique of the Russian cavalry was the mounted attack followed by a strike with silent weapons. Peter I used the cavalry widely for independent action (the battle at Kalisz in 1706 and the employment of the flying corps—the *corps volant*—in 1708). The battle at Lesnaia (1708) and the battle at Poltava (1709) set high standards for the combat application of the cavalry. A. D. Menshikov, an associate of Peter I who was appointed commander of the Russian cavalry in 1706, was a talented leader of the cavalry.

In the 1730's imitation of the Austro-Prussian systems and excessive enthusiasm for firing from horseback made the cavalry lose its ability for organized mounted action and for strikes with silent weapons. In this period in the Russian Army a heavy cavalry was created (ten cuirassier regiments). The new cavalry regulations introduced in 1755 restored to a large extent the Petrine traditions of the combat use of the cavalry. In the Seven Years' War (1756–63) the Russian cavalry proved a worthy opponent of the strong Prussian cavalry, which had been reorganized by Frederick II. In his reign the cavalry, which had a privileged status, was recruited only from Prussian landholders and constituted from 25 to 35 percent of the Prussian Army. All types of cavalry were equally trained for action on horse and on foot; to increase the speed of the attack the three-rank-formation was replaced by the two-rank deployed formation. The Prussian cavalry attained high combat qualities under the leadership of the prominent cavalry generals F. W. von Seydlitz and H. J. von Zieten.

Between 1760 and 1790 the number of heavy cuirassier regiments in the Russian Army was reduced, the number of medium and light cavalry regiments (carabineer, mounted grenadier, hussar, and light horse regiments) was increased, and combat training was improved. The combat application of the cavalry was improved under the leadership of P. A. Rumiantsev and A. V. Suvorov. In 1774, Rumiantsev introduced the two-rank deployed formation and prohibited firing in mounted formation. Under Paul I (1796–1801) the size of the heavy cavalry was increased in the Russian cavalry. The regulations of 1796 officially introduced the two-rank deployed formation and the march column "by four," which had actually been used already in the Russian cavalry.

The French cavalry of the Napoleonic wars was a formidable fighting force. It was divided into the heavy cavalry (cuirassiers), medium cavalry (dragoons), and light cavalry (hussars, mounted chasseurs, and uhlans). The large tactical units were the brigades, divisions (composed of two brigades), and, from 1804, cavalry corps. Napoleon divided the cavalry into strategic (reserve) cavalry and tactical cavalry, which carried out missions for the infantry. In 1812 four cavalry corps (about 40,000 men) of the reserve (strategic) cavalry were formed. The two-rank deployed formation and the column were used in combat. Big columns were employed for the decisive strike. During massed attacks the cavalry usually suffered enormous losses and was not always successful (Borodino, Leipzig, Waterloo).

In the Russian Army in 1806 combined infantry and cavalry divisions were created, and in 1812 there were introduced cavalry divisions composed of three brigades each and cavalry corps composed of two divisions each. Besides the regular cavalry there was also the cossack cavalry. The new cavalry regulations of 1812 introduced cavalry march formations that later became traditional: "by six" "by three," "by rows" (by two), and "by one"; the combat formation was based on two or more lines, and the squadrons of each line were placed in a two-rank deployed formation. In 1812 the whole cavalry, including the dragoons, fought only on horse. In the Patriotic War of 1812 the Russian cavalry furnished many outstanding examples of effective action and played a great role in the defeat of Napoleon's army. After 1812 the Russian cavalry received only a drill field and parade training, and its combat efficiency declined.

In the Crimean War (1853–56) and in the war of Austria, Italy, and France of 1859 the cavalry of all the armies was used without taking into consideration the use of rifled weapons and new combat conditions; it was ineffective and suffered great losses, giving rise to doubts concerning the value of the cavalry as an independent combat arm. But the Civil War in the USA (1861–65) convincingly demonstrated that large masses of cavalry could be effectively used for strategic action in deep raids at the rear and over the communication lines of the enemy. In the subsequent wars of the second half of the 19th century the cavalry was ineffective because no place had been found for it in modern combat.

By the beginning of World War I (1914–18) the cavalry made up from 8 to 10 percent of the armies in the European states; it was considered very important, but there were different views on the combat application of the cavalry; in Germany it was assigned an operational role and in France and other states, a merely tactical role. In Russia the cavalry was envisioned as having operational and tactical applications. In all armies the mounted formation was considered the chief method of the cav-

alry. The cavalry was divided into strategic (army) and tactical (divisional) cavalry. Strategic cavalry was composed of large cavalry units on a division level (divisions and detached brigades); a cavalry division had two or three brigades (with two regiments per brigade and from four to six squadrons per regiment); it was armed with artillery and machine guns. In the beginning of the war many German and French cavalry divisions were merged into cavalry corps. In Russia seven cavalry corps were formed only in 1916; before that time cavalry units were merged into temporary detachments. In the new conditions of World War I, with the great development of various types of military technology, mounted attacks became very ineffective and entailed enormous losses of men and horses. In the maneuvering period of the war (on the Western Front until late 1914, on the Eastern Front until October 1915) the cavalry was used mainly to fulfill operational missions. In the positional period of the war the cavalry units of the belligerent parties were withdrawn to the rear and used essentially as infantry. Although the Russian cavalry was numerically large and well trained, it did not play any substantial role in the war because the Russian command refused to concentrate large cavalry masses on the major operational axes and because it had no gifted cavalry commanders. After World War I mechanization and motorization led to a numerical decline of the cavalry in foreign armies, and by the late 1930's in most of the big capitalist states it was virtually abolished. By World War II (1939–45) only a few countries retained the cavalry (Poland, Hungary, Rumania, and Yugoslavia).

The formation of the Soviet cavalry began with the establishment of the regular Red Army in January 1918. The Workers' and Peasants' Red Army took over only three cavalry regiments from the demobilized old Russian Army. The formation of the cavalry was a very difficult matter. The majority of the cossacks were in the White Guard camp; the Ukraine and the southern and southeastern regions of Russia, which had supplied the bulk of cavalrymen and riding horses, were occupied by the interventionists or held by the White Guard; and there was a shortage of horse cavalry equipment, weapons, and experienced commanders.

The first large regular cavalry unit of the Red Army was the Moscow Cavalry Division; formed in August 1918 in the Moscow Military District, it was named the First Cavalry Division in March 1919. In addition, cavalry units on a division level and individual horse cavalry regiments and detachments were created at the front from partisan detachments and units of tactical cavalry. The 1st Composite Cavalry Division was formed in the Don District in November 1918 (renamed the 4th Cavalry Division in March 1919). In January 1919 the regular cavalry incorporated the 1st Cavalry Division of the Stavropol' partisans, which was formed in December 1918 (renamed the 6th Cavalry Division in March 1919). By the middle of 1919 the Red Army had five cavalry divisions (the 1st, 4th, 6th, 3rd Turkestan, and the 7th divisions); each division had six regiments with four squadrons in each. In the latter half of the 1919 individual cavalry divisions began to be consolidated into cavalry corps, thereby creating conditions for a concentrated employment of the strategic (army) cavalry. In June 1919 the 4th and 6th Cavalry divisions were consolidated into the First Horse Cavalry Corps under the command of S. M. Budennyi, and in September 1919 the Composite Cavalry Corps was formed under the command of B. M. Dumenko, composed of the 1st Partisan, the 2nd Mountaineer, and the 3rd Don Cavalry brigades.

The combat action in 1919 on the Southern Front against Denikin, who had large masses of horse cavalry, made it necessary to create a more powerful strategic formation and operational organization of the cavalry that would not be inferior to the enemy's. In November 1919 the First Horse Cavalry Corps was expanded into the First Horse Cavalry Army under the command of S. M. Budennyi; the army included the 4th, 6th, and 11th and from April 1920 also the 14th Cavalry divisions. By late 1919 the effective strength for combat of the Red Army included a total of 15 cavalry divisions. By this time the Soviet cavalry equaled the enemy's cavalry in strength. The Red Army cavalry units on division level and higher played a prominent role in the operations to defeat Denikin's and Kolchak's armies from late 1919 to early 1920, as well as in those against the troops of bourgeois and landlord Poland.

As the White Guard and interventionists were being driven out of the country, the possibility of forming a strategic cavalry greatly increased, and in 1920 ten cavalry divisions were again formed and established on the basis of cavalry brigades; these divisions became part of corps under the command of G. D. Gai, N. D. Kashirin, V. M. Primakov, and others. The Second Horse Cavalry Army was formed in July 1920 under the command of O. I. Gorodovikov (from September, F. K. Mironov), and was composed of the 2nd Blinov, 16th, 20th, and 21st Cavalry divisions; it played a great role in defeating Wrangel's troops in Northern Tavriia and the Crimea. The horse cavalry armies, composed of cavalry divisions, had machine guns mounted on horse-drawn vehicles (*tachanka*), artillery, armored car detachments, aviation, and armored trains; two or three rifle divisions were temporarily attached to them. By late 1920 the strategic cavalry was made up of 27 cavalry divisions, not counting detached cavalry brigades.

The combat importance of the cavalry greatly increased during the Civil War and military intervention (1918–20). This was brought about because of the amount of maneuvering necessary in the war and because the theaters of operation were vast with long fronts where the density of troops was insufficient. Under these conditions the cavalry took full advantage of its mobility and the element of surprise. The main method of fulfilling tactical combat missions was cavalry action in mounted formation. In the operations in the Northern Caucasus in February and March 1920 the size of the Soviet cavalry was 50 percent of the size of the infantry, and the cavalry of the Whites reached 110 percent of the size of the infantry. In the operations against Wrangel's troops in October and November 1920 the cavalry made up 33 percent of Soviet troops and 50 percent of Wrangel's troops. On the axis of the main thrusts the cavalry forces were equal. The concentration of large cavalry forces on the major operational axes by the two belligerent sides turned some operations of the Civil War into battles of masses of cavalry supported by the infantry. Once again in history mass mounted attacks by cavalry would be used (the battles at Egorlykskaia in February 1920, at Nikopol' in August, and at Genichesk in October 1920), as well as deep raids along the enemy rear. After the Civil War the Soviet cavalry played a great role in the struggle against the Basmachi in Middle Asia and against banditry in the Ukraine and the Northern Caucasus.

In the period of socialist construction the Soviet cavalry was armed with new combat matériel. The cavalry was designed as a mobile combat arm for mass action at the disposal of the front command. But the combat experience of early World War II (1939–45) and the use of large tank forces and aviation made the Soviet command change its opinions concerning the combat use of the cavalry and reduce it numerically. The number of cavalry divisions was reduced from 32 in 1939 to 13 in 1941 (including four mountain cavalry divisions).

At the beginning of the Great Patriotic War (1941–45) large cavalry units deployed at the southwestern and western borders (a total of seven divisions) waged combat while covering the retreat of the combined arms units. The Soviet command began forming new cavalry divisions in the summer of 1941, and 83 light cavalry divisions were additionally set up in late 1941. In the first few months of the war serious shortcomings became apparent in the combat use of the cavalry: the principle of its employment in mass was violated, and the cavalry was often used for attacks on strongly fortified lines and populated areas. In December 1941 a directive of the Supreme Headquarters ordered the consolidation of cavalry divisions into cavalry corps and prohibited the breaking up of cavalry corps that were subordinate to a front command and not an army command, as well as those that were given the mission (jointly with tank and mechanized troops) to exploit the success of a breakthrough of the defense, to pursue a retreating enemy, and to combat its operational reserves. In defensive operations the cavalry formed the maneuverable reserve of the fronts.

Fifteen cavalry divisions fought in the battle of Moscow of 1941–42; in the fierce battles at Moscow General P. A. Belov's First Guards Cavalry Corps and General L. M. Dovator's Sec-

ond Guards Cavalry Corps won special distinction. Among the units that fought in the battle of Stalingrad of 1942–43 were III Guards Cavalry Corps of General I. A. Pliev (from Dec. 17, 1942, General N. S. Oslikovskii), General Borisov's VIII (later the VII Guards) Cavalry Corps, and General T. T. Shapkin's IV Cavalry Corps.

When the Soviet Army passed to broad offensive actions in 1943, the cavalry was reorganized; a commander of the cavalry was appointed (Marshal of the Soviet Union S. M. Budennyi), a cavalry staff was formed (Chief of Staff General V. T. Obukhov, then General P. S. Karpachev); light divisions were abolished, divisions were enlarged and their firepower increased, and the antitank weapons of the cavalry corps were reinforced. After the reorganization the Soviet Army had eight cavalry corps, three divisions to a corps, including seven guards corps in the army in the field, and three detached cavalry divisions (in Transbaikalia and in the Far East). One cavalry corps was stationed in Iran.

In 1943 the cavalry played an important role in the battle for the Caucasus (General N. Ia. Kirichenko's IV Guards Kuban Cavalry Corps and General A. G. Selivanov's V Guards Don Cavalry Corps), in the battle of Kursk of 1943, and in the liberation of the Left-bank Ukraine (General V. V. Kriukov's II Guards Cavalry Corps). The VII Guards Cavalry Corps fought in the battle for the Dnieper in late September; it crossed the Dnieper River in force near Chernigov and seized a base of operations on the opposite bank.

While the reinforced cavalry corps were used in offensives for the exploitation of a success in the breakthrough of a defense, in 1943 cavalry corps began to be consolidated into temporary horse cavalry–mechanized groups (KMG) composed of one or two cavalry corps and one tank or mechanized corps; they were used for the same purposes. Highly effective actions of the KMG include that of General Kirichenko in the Donbas Offensive Operation of 1943, of General Pliev in the Bereznegovatoe-Snigirevka operation of 1944 and in the Odessa Operation of 1944, of Generals Oslikovskii and Pliev in the exploitation of success in the Byelorussian Operation of 1944, of General V. K. Baranov in the L'vov-Sandomir Operation of 1944, and of General S. I. Gorshkov in the Iaşy-Kishenev Operation of 1944. An organic KMG formed in late 1944 under the command of General Pliev (subsequently the 1st Guard KMG) served in combat for the liberation of Rumania and Hungary. The combat action of the Soviet-Mongolian KMG on the Transbaikal Front in August 1945 contributed to the defeat of the Japanese Kwantung Army in the Far East.

The firepower of the troops, which increased during the Great Patriotic War, limited the tactical use of the cavalry to infantry combat. The cavalry usually made contact with the enemy in mounted formation; upon reaching the previously planned line, the cavalry unit would dismount and deploy in battle formation. When conditons were favorable the cavalry sometimes used mounted attacks, especially if the enemy had not managed to consolidate its position or organize a system of fire.

To reduce the danger of attack by enemy aviation, cavalry units marched at night, in snowstorms or in fog, and maneuvered off the roads. The rank of guards unit was conferred on all cavalry corps of the army in the field for their high level of combat skill, bravery, and daring. The title of Hero of the Soviet Union was conferred on many cavalrymen, and orders and medals were awarded to tens of thousands of them.

After the Great Patriotic War the cavalry was greatly reduced in size. In the mid-1950's, because of the development of weapons of mass destruction and of the total motorization of the army, the cavalry ceased to exist as a combat arm and the cavalry units were disbanded.

REFERENCES

Engels, F. "Armiia." *Soch.*, 2nd ed., vol. 14.
Engels, F. "Kavaleriia." *Soch.*, 2nd ed., vol. 14.
Ivanov. P. A. *Obozrenie sostava i ustroistva reguliarnoi russkoi kavalerii ot Petra Velikogo do nashikh dnei.* St. Petersburg, 1864.
Pleve, P. A. *Ocherki po istorii konnitsy.* St. Petersburg, 1889.
Markov, M. I. *Istoriia konnitsy,* parts 1–5. Tver', 1888–96.

Griaznov, F. F. *Konnitsa.* St. Petersburg, 1903.
Svechin, M. *Kavaleriia na voine.* [No place] 1909.
Krasnaia konnitsa: Sb. trudov. Moscow, 1923.
Svechin, A. A. *Evoliutsiia voennogo iskusstva,* vols. 1–2. Moscow-Leningrad, 1927–28.
Shaposhnikov, B. M. *Konnitsa (Kavaleriiskie ocherki),* 2nd ed. Moscow, 1923.
Batorskii, M. *Sluzhba konnitsy.* Moscow, 1925.
Gatovskii, V. N. *Konnitsa,* books 1–2, 4. Moscow, 1925–28.
Budennyi, S. M. *Proidennyi put',* books 1–2. Moscow, 1959–65.
Dushen'kin, V. V. *Vtoraia konnaia.* Moscow, 1968.
Belov, P. A. *Za nami Moskva.* Moscow, 1963.
Pliev, I. A. *Razgrom "armii mstitelei."* Ordzhonikidze, 1967.
Pliev, I. A. *Cherez Gobi i Khingan.* Moscow, 1965.

V. A. ZAIONCHKOVSKII [11–304–1]

CAVATINA, a lyrical solo in opera and oratorio. In the 18th century it usually was contemplative and pensive and was distinguished from the aria by its greater simplicity, songlike melody, and modest scale. In the first half of the 19th century the exit aria of the prima donna or lead was called a cavatina—for example, Antonida's cavatina in *Ivan Susanin* by Glinka—but in the second half of the 19th century the term reverted to its 18th-century meaning. Short lyrical instrumental pieces have sometimes been called cavatinas. [11–315–1]

CAVENDISH, HENRY. Born Oct. 10, 1731, in Nice; died Feb. 24, 1810, in London. English physicist and chemist. Member of the Royal Society of London (from 1760).

Cavendish graduated from Cambridge University in 1753. His main works were devoted to the chemistry of gases and various branches of experimental physics. He developed a method of collecting, purifying, and investigating gases, which he used in 1766 to obtain hydrogen and carbon dioxide in pure form and to determine their specific gravities and other properties. He determined the composition of air (1781) and established the chemical composition of water (1784) by burning hydrogen. Cavendish obtained nitrogen oxides using an electric spark and investigated their properties (1785). Most of his works on heat and electricity were only published many years after his death (works on electricity in 1879, a collection of works in 1921). Cavendish introduced the concept of electric potential, investigated the relationship between the capacity of an electric condenser and the medium, and studied the interaction of electric charges (anticipating Coulomb's third law). He was the first to formulate the concept of specific heat. In 1798 he determined the average density of the earth using the method of torsional balance. Cavendish was extremely wealthy and worked in his own laboratory to the end of his life. The physics laboratory at Cambridge University, which was founded in 1871, was named in his honor.

WORKS
The Scientific Papers, vols. 1–2. Cambridge, 1921.

REFERENCES
Wilson, G. *The Life of Honourable Henry Cavendish.* London, 1851.
Berry, A. J. *Henry Cavendish: His Life and Scientific Work.* London, 1960. [11–316–1]

CAVENDISH LABORATORY, a physics laboratory at Cambridge Univeristy (Great Britain). It was founded in 1871 by the Duke of Devonshire, a relative of Cavendish, after whom it was named. The laboratory was initially used only as a training center for experimental physicists. Later (chiefly under the supervision of J. J. Thomson and E. Rutherford), it became one of the foremost scientific research laboratories in the world. The directors of the Cavendish Laboratory have been J. C. Maxwell (1871–75), J. W. Strutt (Baron Rayleigh) (1879–84), Thomson (1884–1919), Rutherford (1919–37), W. L. Bragg (1938–53), N. F. Mott (1945–71), and A. B. Pippard (since 1971). The world's foremost physicists have worked at the laboratory, including Rutherford, C. T. R. Wilson, J. S. E. Townsend, O. W. Richardson, M. L. E. Oliphant, F. W. Aston, P. M. S. Blackett, J. Chadwick, J. D. Cockroft, J. D. Bernal, P. Langevin, P. L. Kapitsa, F. Crick, and J. Watson.

The scientific problems that have been dealt with at the Cavendish Laboratory over the years include the electric discharge in gases, nuclear physics research, crystallography, X-ray structure analysis, molecular biology, and radio astronomy. Discoveries made at the laboratory include the discovery of the electron (1897), artificial nuclear spallation (1919), and the neutron (1932). A model structure of deoxyribonucleic acid (DNA) was proposed (1953) at the laboratory, and the Wilson cloud chamber (1912), the mass spectrograph (1913), and the linear accelerator (1932) were created there.

REFERENCES
Wood, A. *The Cavendish Laboratory.* Cambridge, 1946.
Larsen, E. *The Cavendish Laboratory, Nursery of Genius.* London, 1962.
Thomson, G. P. *J. J. Thomson and the Cavendish Laboratory in His Day.* London, 1964. I. D. ROZHANSKII [11–317–1]

CAVERN, a cavity that develops in body organs where there is destruction and death (necrosis) of tissues and subsequent liquefaction of the necrotic masses.

Caverns may be closed, not communicating with the external environment, or open, when contents of the cavern empty to the outside through natural channels. Caverns appear most often at the site of a purulent necrotic process or specific inflammation in the lungs (cavernous tuberculosis), kidneys (an abscess that opens into the renal pelvis), or liver (a suppurative node of *Echinococcus* that empties into the biliary tract). The presence of a cavern fosters the spread of the pathological process and the development of complications (hemorrhage, perforation).

[11–318–2]

CAVERNITIS, an inflammation of the corpora cavernosa of the penis.

Cavernitis is manifested by high body temperature and pain, redness, and swelling of the penis; an abscess may form relatively rapidly. Cavernitis arises acutely as a complication of local (urethritis) or systemic (sepsis) infectious processes. Cavernitis is treated with antibiotics, local heat, and surgery (lancing of abscesses). [11–319–1]

CAVITATION, the formation in a liquid of cavities (cavitation bubbles, or caverns), filled with gas, vapor, or a mixture of them. Cavitation bubbles are formed in locations where the pressure in the liquid becomes lower than a certain critical value p_{cr} (in a real liquid, p_{cr} is approximately equal to the saturated vapor pressure of the liquid at the given temperature). If the pressure drop occurs because of high local velocities in the flow of a liquid, then the cavitation is called hydrodynamic, whereas if it is the result of the passage of acoustic waves, it is called acoustic.

Hydrodynamic cavitation. Since tiny gas or vapor bubbles are always present in a real liquid, they become unstable and acquire the capacity for unlimited growth as they move with the flow and enter the pressure region where $p < p_{cr}$. After a bubble passes into the zone of higher pressure and the kinetic energy of the expanding liquid is exhausted, it stops growing and begins to contract. If the bubble contains a sufficient quantity of gas, then upon attaining a minimum radius it is regenerated and undergoes several cycles of damped oscillation; however, if it contains insufficient gas, then it collapses completely during its initial period of existence. Thus, a fairly sharply outlined "cavitation zone" forms in the vicinity of a streamlined body (for example, a pipe with a local constriction).

Collapse of a cavitational bubble occurs with great speed and is accompanied by a sonic pulse (a type of hydraulic shock); the smaller the quantity of gas in the bubble, the stronger the pulse. If the degree of development of cavitation is such that many bubbles are generated and collapse at random times, the phenomenon is accompanied by loud noise, with a continuous spectrum from several hundred hertz to several hundred or thousand kilohertz. If the cavitational cavern collapses near the body, the multiple impacts lead to the destruction (cavitational erosion) of the surface of the body (the blades of hydraulic turbines, ship's screws, and other hydraulic-engineering devices).

If the liquid were ideally uniform, and if the surface of the solid body with which it forms an interface were ideally wettable, then the rupture would occur at a pressure considerably lower than the saturated vapor pressure of the liquid. The tensile strength of water, with thermal fluctuations taken into account, is 150 meganewtons per sq m (MN/m^2), or 1,500 kilograms-force per sq cm (kgf/cm^2). Real liquids are less strong. The maximum tensile strength of thoroughly purified water at 10°C is 28 MN/m^2 (280 kgf/cm^2). However, rupture usually occurs at pressures that are only slightly lower than the saturated vapor pressure. The low strength of real liquids is associatd with the presence in them of cavitation nuclei, which are poorly wettable regions of solids, solid particles with gas-filled cracks, microscopic gas bubbles preserved from dissolution by monomolecular organic layers, and ionic formations generated by cosmic rays.

For a particular shape of the streamlined body, cavitation arises at a certain definite value of the dimensionless parameter

$$\kappa = 2(p - p_s)/\rho v_\infty^2$$

that is completely defined for a particular point in the flow, where p is the hydrostatic pressure of the flow against the body, p_s is the saturated vapor pressure, ρ is the density of the liquid, and v_∞ is the velocity of the liquid at a sufficient distance from the body. This parameter is called the cavitation number, which is a similarity criterion in the simulation of hydrodynamic flows. An increase in the flow velocity after the start of cavitation leads to a rapid increase in the number of cavitational bubbles, which is followed by their combination into a single cavitation cavern, whereupon the flow becomes a jet flow. In this case the flow retains its nonstationary nature only in the region of cavern collapse. Jet flow is formed particularly rapidly in the case of bluff bodies.

If atmospheric air or another gas is introduced into the cavern through a body in the vicinity of which cavitation is generated, the dimensions of the cavern increase. In this case a flow that corresponds to the cavitation number, found from the gas pressure p_c within the cavern—that is, $\kappa = 2(p_\infty - p_c)/\rho v_\infty^2$ —rather than from the saturation pressure p_s, will be established. The emergence of such a cavitational cavern will be described by the Froude number $Fr = v_\infty^2/gd$, where g is gravitational acceleration and d is a certain characteristic linear dimension. Since p_c may be much larger than p_s, it is possible under such conditions, but at low velocities of the incident flow, to obtain fluxes corresponding to very low values of κ—that is, to high degrees of development of cavitation. Thus, motion of a body through water with velocity of 6–10 m/sec may lead to flows around the body corresponding to velocities of up to 100 m/sec. Cavitation flows resulting from the supply of gas into the interior of the cavern are called artifical cavitation.

Hydrodynamic cavitation may be accompanied by a number of physicochemical effects, such as sparking and luminescence. The influence of electric currents and magnetic fields on cavitation that arises during flow around a cylinder in a water tunnel has been observed in a number of studies.

The study and prevention of cavitation are of great importance, since it has an adverse effect on the performance of hydraulic turbines, liquid pumps, ships' screws, underwater sonic emitters, hydraulic systems of high-altitude aircraft, and other devices, decreases their efficiency, and produces damage. Cavitation may be reduced by increasing the hydrostatic pressure—for example, by placement of the device at a sufficient depth below the free surface of the liquid—as well as by appropriate choice of the corresponding design elements to decrease the harmful effects of cavitation. To reduce erosion of turbine blades, they are made from stainless steels and polished.

Experimental studies of cavitation are performed in cavitation tubes, which are ordinary water tunnels equipped with devices for static pressure control.

REFERENCES
Kornfel'd, M. *Uprugost' i prochnost' zhidkostei.* Moscow-Leningrad, 1951.
Birkhoff, G., and E. Sarantonello. *Strui, sledy i kaverny.* Moscow, 1964. (Translated from English.)
Pernik, A. D. *Problemy kavitatsii,* 2nd ed. Leningrad, 1966.
Osherovskii, S. Kh. "Kavitatsiia v generatorakh," *Energetika i elektrifikatsiia,* 1970, no. 1.　　　　　　　　　　　A. D. PERNIK

Acoustic cavitation. Irradiation of a liquid with sound having a sonic pressure amplitude in excess of a certain threshold value leads during the half-periods of rarefaction to the formation of cavitation bubbles on the cavitation nuclei, which consist most frequently of gaseous inclusions in the liquid, and on the oscillating surface of the acoustic emitter. For this reason, the cavitational threshold increases with decreasing gas content of the liquid, with increasing hydrostatic pressure, upon compression of the liquid by high hydrostatic pressure (of the order of 10^3 $kgf/cm^2 \cong 10^2$ MN/m^2), with cooling of the liquid, and with increasing frequency of the sound and decreasing duration of exposure. The threshold is higher for a traveling wave than for a standing wave. The bubbles collapse during the half-periods of compression, thus generating short-lived pulses (of the order of 10^{-6} sec) of pressure (up to 10^3 $MN/m^2 \cong 10^4$ kgf/cm^2 and higher), which are capable of destroying very strong materials. Such destruction is observed at the surfaces of powerful acoustic emitters that are immersed in liquids. The pressure during the collapse of cavitational bubbles increases with decreasing sound frequency and increasing hydrostatic pressure; it is higher in liquids with low saturated vapor pressures. The collapse of bubbles is accompanied by adiabatic heating of the gas in the bubbles to temperatures of the order of 10^4 °C, which apparently leads to the luminescence of bubbles during cavitation (sonic luminescence).

Cavitation is accompanied by the ionization of gas in the bubbles. Cavitational bubbles group together to form cavitational regions of complex and variable shapes. The intensity of cavitation may be easily estimated from the destruction of thin aluminum foil in which holes are punched by the cavitating bubbles. The quantity and position of the holes formed during a fixed time interval make possible estimation of the intensity of cavitation and the configuration of the cavitation zone.

If the liquid is saturated with a gas, then the gas diffuses into the bubbles and prevents their complete collapse. The bubbles rise to the surface and thus reduce the gas content of the liquid. Intense oscillations of the gas-filled bubbles in the free liquid, as well as in the vicinity of solids, lead to microflows of the liquid.

The occurrence of cavitation limits the possibility of further increase in the intensity of sound radiated into the liquid as a result of a decrease in its wave drag and the corresponding decrease in the load on the emitter. Acoustic cavitation and the physical phenomena connected with it generate a number of effects. Some of them, such as the breakdown and dispersion of solids, emulsification of liquids, and cleaning of surfaces and parts, are due to the impacts accompanying the collapse of bubbles and the microflows in the vicinity of them. Other effects—for example, the initiation and acceleration of chemical reactions—are related to the ionization of gas in the bubbles. Because of these effects, cavitation is being used more widely in the development of new industrial processes and the advancement of existing processes. Many practical applications of ultrasound are based on the cavitation effect.

Acoustic cavitation is of great importance in biology and medicine. The pressure pulses that arise in cavitational bubbles lead to instantaneous disintegration of microorganisms and protozoa in aqueous mediums subjected to the action of ultrasound. Cavitation is used for the extraction of enzymes, hormones, and other biologically active substances from animal and plant cells.

REFERENCES
Bergmann, L. *Ul'trazvuk i ego primenenie v nauke i tekhnike.* Moscow, 1956. (Translated from German.)
Roi, N. A. "Vozniknovenie i protekanie ul'trazvukovoi kavitatsii." *Akusticheskii zhurnal,* 1957, vol. 3, issue 1, p. 3.
Sirotiuk, M. G. "Eksperimental'nye issledovaniia ul'trazvukovoi kavitatsii." In *Fizika i tekhnika moshchnogo ul'trazvuka,* vol. 2. Moscow, 1968.
Ul'trazvuk v gidrometallurgii. Moscow, 1969.
　　　　　　　　　　　　　　　　　N. A. ROI　[11–321–1]

CAVITE, city and port in the Philippines, in the southwest of the island of Luzon, on Manila Bay, Cavite Province. Population, 75,300 (1969). The city has food-processing enterprises and coffee factories. It is also a center of the fishing industry.

[11–325–1]

CAVOS, CATTERINO (Katerino Al'bertovich Kavos). Born Oct. 30, 1775, in Venice; died Apr. 28 (May 10), 1840, in St. Petersburg. Russian composer, conductor, and teacher. Italian by birth.

A student of F. Bianchi, Cavos was a conductor and composer of ballets in Padua. Beginning in 1799 he worked in St. Petersburg, initially at the Italian Opera, then from 1806 to 1821 at the Russian Opera. In 1832 he became music director of the imperial theaters. He composed many operas, among them *The Invisible Prince* (1805), *Il'ia the Bogatyr'* (1807), and *Ivan Susanin* (1815). He also composed ballets, whose themes he took from classical mythology, medieval poetry, and the works of Pushkin and which were staged by the choreographer C. Didelot. These included *Zéphyre et Flore* (1808), *Laura and Henry, or the Troubadour* (1819), and *The Prisoner of the Caucasus* (1823). Cavos' activities furthered the development of the Russian opera and ballet theater. Many outstanding singers were his students.

REFERENCE
Grachev, P. V. "K. A. Kavos." In *Ocherki po istorii russkoi muzyki, 1790–1825.* Leningrad, 1956. [11–359–1]

CAVOUR, CAMILLO BENSO DI. Born Aug. 10, 1810, in Turin; died there June 6, 1861. Count; statesman and diplomat of Piedmont (Kingdom of Sardinia) and of Italy during its unification; ideologist and leader of the moderate liberal monarchist bourgeoisie and of the part of the nobility that was becoming bourgeois in its outlook. His family belonged to the aristocracy.

Cavour graduated in 1829 from the Turin military academy. In 1847, together with C. Balbo, he founded the newspaper *Il Risorgimento,* which became the voice of the moderate liberal movement. During the Revolution of 1848–49 he became a deputy to parliament. From 1850 to 1852 he was minister of agriculture and commerce and in 1851–52 was also minister of finance. From 1852 to 1861 (with a break in 1859) he was prime minister of Piedmont and also headed several ministries, including foreign affairs and finance. Cavour's domestic policy was aimed at transforming the economic and political structure of Piedmont along bourgeois lines and included promotion of free trade, tariff reforms, and encouragement of railroad construction and banking. His government carried out a number of anticlerical measures, such as changes in the laws dealing with the church, abolition of religious orders, and government expropriation of church lands. Cavour's policies promoted the development of capitalist enterprises in Piedmont and the expansion of the new ruling group, the liberal bourgeoisie.

Cavour's ultimate aim was the unification of Italy under the Savoy dynasty. However, in the 1850's his plans were limited to the creation of the Kingdom of North Italy. Fearing revolution, Cavour sought to carry out this task by means of dynastic combinations and diplomatic deals; in this he relied on an alliance with the France of Napoleon III, a relationship cemented by the verbal agreement made at Plombières in 1858. In 1859, as a result of clever diplomatic maneuvers, Cavour succeeded in provoking Austria into a war with Piedmont, during which Cavour hoped to liberate Lombardy and Venetia with military support from Napoleon. However, the separate peace between France and Austria, the Peace of Villafranca of 1859, upset Cavour's plans and forced him to resign.

As the Revolution of 1859–60 neared, Cavour was returned to power, in January 1860. As a result of popular movements, absolutist regimes had been overthrown in Parma, Modena, Tuscany, and the Romagna. Taking advantage of this situation, Cavour brought about the unification of these states with Piedmont. At this time and during G. Garibaldi's southern expedition (which began in May 1860), Cavour's tactic was to assimilate into Piedmont "one after another of those parts of Italian territory that could be won by the sword of Garibaldi or torn out of age-old dependency by popular uprisings" (K. Marx and F. Engels, *Soch.,* 2nd ed., vol. 15, p. 94). Seeking to avert any further spread of revolution, Cavour sent Piedmontese troops in September 1860 into the papal territory and subsequently into the Kingdom of the Two Sicilies, which had been liberated by Garibaldi's army. With the proclamation of the united Kingdom of Italy in March 1861, Cavour became the first prime minister of Italy.

WORKS
Discorsi parlamentari, vols. 1–14. Florence, 1932–69.
Il carteggio Cavour-Nigra dal 1858 al 1861, vols. 1–4. Bologna, 1926–29.
La liberazione del Mezzogiorno e la formazione del Regno d'Italia: Carteggi di Cavour . . . , vols. 1–5. Bologna, 1949–54.
Lettere edite ed inedite, 2nd ed., vols. 1–7. Turin, 1883–87.
REFERENCES
Marx, K., and F. Engels. *Soch.,* 2nd ed., vols. 13, 15. (See index of names.)
Dobroliubov, N. A. *Poln. sobr. soch.,* vol. 5. Moscow, 1941. Pages 131–75.
Chernyshevskii, N. G. *Poln. sobr. soch.,* vols. 6, 8. Moscow, 1949–50.
Gramsci, A. *Izbr. proizv.,* vols. 1, 3. Moscow, 1957–59. (See index of names.)
Skazkin, S. D. "Kavur i vossoedinenie Italii." *Istorik-marksist,* nos. 5–6, 1935.
Omodeo, A. *L'opera politica del conte di Cavour,* vols. 1–2. Florence, 1940.
Mack Smith, D. *Cavour and Garibaldi, 1860.* Cambridge, 1954.
Romeo, R. *Cavour e il suo tempo,* vol. 1. Bari, 1969.

V. S. BONDARCHUK [11–360–2]

CAXIAS DO SUL, a city in southern Brazil, in the state of Rio Grande do Sul. Population, 144,300 (1970). Railroad station and highway junction. Caxias do Sul is a principal center of viticulture in the state. It also has metallurgical, textile, and food (meat-canning) enterprises. [11–1653–3]

CAYENNE, a city, the administrative center of French Guiana. Population, 24,500 (1967). Cayenne is the country's chief port, located at the mouth of the Cayenne River. Rum, wood, fish, raw leather, and other products are exported. Cayenne was founded in the first half of the 17th century. [11–537–4]

CAYEUX, LUCIEN. Born Mar. 26, 1864, in Semousies; died Nov. 1, 1944, in Mauves-sur-Loire. French geologist and lithologist. Member of the French Academy of Sciences (1928).

Cayeux became a professor at the École des Mines in Paris in 1907 and at the Collège de France in 1912. His principal works were devoted to studying the material composition and origin of sedimentary rocks (calcareous, siliceous, iron-ore, and phosphate rocks). Cayeux gave a monographic description of detrital and carbonate rocks of Cretaceous age in France.

WORKS
Introduction à l'étude pétrographique des roches sédimentaires, vols. 1–2. Paris, 1916.
Les Minérais de fer oolithiques de France, vols. 1–2. Paris, 1909–22.
Les Roches sédimentaires de France, roches siliceuses. Paris, 1929.
Causes anciennes et causes actuelles en géologie. Paris, 1941.

[11–537–1]

CAYMAN ISLANDS, a British possession in the West Indies, in the Caribbean Sea. The territory consists of the Grand Cayman, Little Cayman, and Cayman Brac islands. Area, 259 sq km. Population, 10,600 (1970 census). The inhabitants are Creoles, Negroes, and mulattoes; more than 80 percent live on Grand Cayman. Administrative center, Georgetown.

The islands are governed by a representative of the British crown. The main industries are agriculture, catching caimans and turtles, salt mining, and tourism. The Caymans were discovered by Christopher Columbus in 1503. [11–539–4]

CENOTYPAL ROCKS, magmatic rocks that preserve a fresh appearance despite their age. Cenotypal rocks are distinguished from paleotypal rocks, which are much decayed and therefore appear ancient. This terminology arose in the second half of the 19th century (W. C. Brögger, F. J. Levinson-Lessing) in connection with the refutation of the previously held but mistaken idea that fresh-looking cenotypal rocks are young and decayed (paleotypal) rocks are ancient. [11–544–1]

CENOZOIC ERA, the youngest group of strata of the earth's crust on the stratigraphic scale and the era corresponding to it, the most recent in the earth's geological history, encompassing the present epoch as well. The name was proposed by the English geologist J. Phillips in 1841. The Cenozoic era is subdivided into the Paleogene, Neocene, and Anthropogenic (Quaternary) systems or periods. Until 1960 the first two were classified in the Tertiary system or period. The span of the Cenozoic era is estimated at 60–70 million years, of which 40–45 million years are allotted to the Paleogene and 20–25 million to the Neocene; the duration of the Anthropogenic period is estimated by some at between 0.6 and 1.7 million years and by others at as much as 3.5 million.

General description. During the Cenozoic the present distribution of continents and oceans occurred. The very beginning of the era saw the completion of the breakup of the formerly unified southern continental mass, Gondwana, into the separate continental blocks of South America, Africa, the Indian subcontinent, Australia, and Antarctica, divided by the newly formed basins of the Indian Ocean and the southern part of the Atlantic Ocean —a process that had been under way since the Mesozoic. By the middle of the Cenozoic, Eurasia and Africa formed the continental mass of the Old World, joined by the mountain structures of the Mediterranean geosynclinal belt. In the Paleogene the vast Tethys Sea, stretching from Gibraltar to the Himalayas and Indonesia, occupied this geosynclinal belt. In the middle of the Paleogene the Tethys Sea spread to the neighboring platforms, flooding vast areas of present-day Western Europe, the southern part of the European USSR, Western Siberia, Middle Asia, North Africa, and the Arabian Peninsula. Beginning in the late Paleogene the seas gradually receded from these areas. By the end of the Neocene, as a result of Alpine tectogenesis, there had developed in the Mediterranean belt a system of young folded mountains, including the Atlas and Andalusian mountains, the Pyrenees, Alps, Apennines, Dinaric Alps, Stara Planina (Balkan Mountains), Carpathians, Caucasus, Hindu Kush, Pamirs, Himalayas, and the mountains of Asia Minor, Iran, Burma, and Indonesia. The Tethys gradually began to break up, forming in the course of long evolution the basins of the Mediterranean, Black, and Caspian seas.

Young folded mountain systems also formed on the periphery of the Pacific Ocean. Among them are the chains of mountainous island arcs, unique in structure and development, along the western edge of the Pacific (the Aleutian, Kamchatka-Kuril, Japan, Philippine, and New Zealand arcs), as well as the mountains along the coast of Antarctica and the Andes of South America. Arcs of mountainous islands also formed in the Atlantic (the Antilles and the southern Antilles arc between Cape Horn and Antarctica). Together with the adjacent deep-water ocean trenches, the island arcs form geosynclinal systems that continue to develop today. Most of them are separated from neighboring continents by the basins of marginal seas (the Bering, Okhotsk, Japan, South China, Tasman, and Caribbean seas and the Gulf of Mexico) that also developed during the Cenozoic.

In the northern half of the Pacific geosynclinal belt, vast areas consisting of Mesozoic folded structures (the Sikhote-Alin' and Verkhoiano-Chukotka folded regions and most of the Cordilleras of North America) experienced periodically intensified general uplifts with relative displacement of large blocks along fractures. In North America these uplifts were sometimes accompanied by massive lava discharges (the basalt sheets of the Columbia Plateau in the United States and the Meseta Central in Mexico). Here, block movements also encompassed the edge of the adjacent ancient North American (Canadian) Platform, thus creating a chain of block mountains, the Rocky Mountains, parallel to the Cordilleras.

In Eurasia arched uplifts and block displacements along fractures encompassed even larger areas of folded structures of various ages, causing the development of mountainous relief in areas that had earlier been leveled by prolonged denudation. Thus, there originated the mountain belt that includes the Tien-Shan, Altai, Saian, Iablonovyi, and Stanovoi ranges and the mountains of Central Asia, Tibet, the Scandinavian Peninsula, and the Urals. At the same time fracture systems of great length developed on the continents of the Old World, accompanied by linear rifts expressed in the relief as deep valley-like depressions often containing large bodies of water. The largest rift system, the East African rift zone, stretches in a north-south direction from the graben of the Jordan Valley and Dead Sea to the lower reaches of the Zambezi River in Africa. The development of this rift system was accompanied by intensive volcanic activity in East Africa, which continues to the present. The smaller Baikal rift system includes the basin of Lake Baikal and the graben-type depressions extending from it.

During the Paleogene the climate was significantly warmer than it is today. Even in the arctic region there were mixed forests, and the vegetation over most of Europe, northern Asia, and North America was tropical or subtropical.

The vast uplifts of continents in the second half of the Cenozoic caused most of the shelf of northern Eurasia and North America to dry up, partially isolated the Arctic Ocean, and created large mountainous areas on land. As a result, contrasts between the climatic belts appeared, and a general cooling of the earth's climate occurred. This cooling process, which had already begun at the end of the Paleogene, culminated in several periods of vast continental glaciation in the middle latitudes of the northern hemisphere during the Anthropogenic period. The terrestrial animals and plants that are now typical of the subpolar region migrated south as far as the Crimea and Northern Caucasus. Vast ice sheets developed in North America, Europe, and northern Asia. In the southern hemisphere the glaciers of the Andes and New Zealand increased greatly in size, and Tasmania was subjected to glaciation. The last ice sheet in North America and Europe disappeared between 10,000 and 12,000 years ago.

Cenozoic life. Terrestrial vegetation was altered in the middle of the Cretaceous period, when angiosperms (flowering plants) became dominant. By the beginning of the Cenozoic there had appeared most of the families and many of the genera of angiosperms existing today; as the climate changed they formed the communities typical of the different climatic belts. Beginning in the mid-Paleogene, grass formations of the savanna and steppe type appeared, and at the end of the Neocene there developed taiga-type coniferous forest formations and, later, forest-tundras and tundras. At the end of the Mesozoic and beginning of the Cenozoic the reptiles that had predominated during the Mesozoic became extinct and were replaced by mammals that, with birds, constituted the nucleus of the terrestrial vertebrates of the Cenozoic era. On most continents the higher placental mammals became dominant, and only in Australia (which became isolated before these mammals appeared on a large scale) did unique marsupials and, to some extent, monotremes develop. During the early Paleogene, mammals were represented almost exclusively by small primitive forms. By the middle Paleogene almost all the orders existing today had appeared, as well as several groups that subsequently became extinct. A great variety of mammals evolved and flourished. At the end of the Paleogene there were both very small mammals and large ones, including some larger than modern elephants. Mammalian fauna was particularly rich during the Neocene. Some mammals returned to the sea—earliest of all the cetaceans, which may have appeared prior to the Cenozoic and which by the beginning of the Eocene occupied about the same position among marine fauna as today. Much later, probably toward the end of the Paleogene, there appeared the pinnipeds (walruses, seals), which were descended from predatory mammals. The order Chiroptera is known to have existed from at least the middle of the Paleogene. A very ancient order, existing from the beginning of the Cenozoic, is that of the primates. Their long evolution culminated in the appearance of higher hominoid apes in the Neocene and the emergence of primitive man at the beginning of the Anthropogenic Period.

Invertebrate fauna differed less sharply from that of the Mesozoic. Beginning in the mid-Cretaceous period the appearance of flowering plants resulted in a great increase in the number and variety of insects, and their rapid development continued into later times. It is also possible that the change in vegetation during the Cenozoic caused a sharp increase in the number and variety of terrestrial air-breathing gastropods. Among marine invertebrates the major occurrence at the end of the Mesozoic and beginning of the Cenozoic was the complete extinction of the formerly widespread ammonites and belemnites, which had been dominant among Mesozoic invertebrates. Subsequently the composition of invertebrate fauna resembled that of the present day in that the dominant groups were bivalves, gastropods, sea urchins, hexacorals, and other groups similar to modern forms. An exception was the appearance and rapid development in the Paleogene of nummulites, a distinct group of large benthic foraminifers whose shells formed entire layers of Paleogene limestone in the Tethys zone and adjacent regions. By the beginning of the Neocene the nummulites were almost completely extinct, and only a few of their descendants, much smaller in size, have survived to the present in the tropical seas.

Minerals. There are comparatively few ore deposits of endogenic origin among Cenozoic minerals because the deep-lying interiors of the young folded mountain ranges with which they are associated have not as yet been fully uncovered by denudation. Most important are petroleum and natural gas, deposits of which are concentrated primarily in the foredeeps framing the alpine folded mountain systems (Mesopotamia, Ciscarpathia, Ciscaucasia). Cenozoic sedimentary strata also contain large deposits of brown coal, oolitic brown iron ore, manganese ore (Chiatura, Nikopol'), rock and potassium salts (Ciscarpathia, Transcarpathia), bauxites, phosphorites (Tunisia, Algeria, Morocco), and various building materials.

REFERENCES
Strakhov, N. M. *Osnovy istoricheskoi geologii,* part 2. Moscow-Leningrad, 1948.
Gignoux, M. *Stratigraficheskaia geologiia.* Moscow, 1952. (Translated from French.)
Krishtofovich, A. N. *Paleobotanika,* 4th ed. Leningrad, 1957.

E. V. SHANTSER [11–541–2]

CENTRAL VALLEY (the California Trough in Russian cartography), a valley in the southwestern United States, in the state of California. Bounded on the east by the Sierra Nevada and on the west by the Coast Ranges. Elevation, 20–160 m; length, 800 km; width, up to 80 km. It originated as a tectonic trough filled in with a thick stratum of sedimentary rock from the Cretaceous, Paleogene-Neocene, and Quaternary periods. The surface is level with gentle hills formed by ancient ridges along river beds and by detrital cones (in the east and south).

It has a Mediterranean-type subtropical continental climate. Precipitation ranges from 1,000 mm a year in the north to 150 mm in the south. The main rivers are the Sacramento in the north and the San Joaquin in the south. There is a dense network of irrigation canals. The northern part belongs with the zone of subtropical steppes with reddish chestnut soil, and the southern is semidesert. The Central Valley is an important region for farms (with artificial irrigation), orchards, and vineyards. Livestock is raised in the south. There are petroleum deposits (the California petroleum region). The principal cities are Sacramento, Stockton, and Fresno.   G. M. IGNAT'EV [11–630–1]

CHAMBER (or breast), in mining, a relatively short mine working with a large cross section. The dimensions and the characteristics of location, construction, and operation of chambers are determined by their purpose.

The term "chamber" includes workings used for the placement of equipment and special shaft or mine services (an underground electric power substation, pumphouse, catch basin, electric locomotive depot, control room, medical station, or waiting room), excavations for the mining of minerals by the underground method, and special-purpose underground structures (underground engine rooms of hydroelectric power plants; subway concourses). [11–794–2]

CHAMBER COLLEGIUM, a central state institution in 18th-century Russia created by Peter I in 1721. It was in charge of state revenues; state contracts; farming out revenues; the sale of state goods; state distilleries; fish and tallow production; the construction of state buildings, roads, and bridges; and customs. The organs of the Chamber Collegium were the local chamber offices until 1727, and later provincial and *voevodstvo* (territories

under military governors) offices. With the reform of the provinces in 1775, the collection of many state revenues was transferred to provincial revenue departments; this led to the closing of the Chamber Collegium and other collegiums in 1784. The Chamber Collegium was revived in 1797 and abolished once and for all in 1801.

REFERENCE
Gosudarstvennye uchrezhdeniia Rossii v XVIII v. (Zakonodatel'nye materialy.) Prepared for printing by A. V. Chernov. Moscow, 1960. [11–796–5]

CHAMBER FURNACE, the furnace of a steam boiler; usually a rectangular prismatic chamber in which fuel is burned in an air jet (fuel spray). Such furnaces burn pulverized solid fuel under boilers with steam capacities of 50–2,500 tons per hour or more and gaseous and liquid fuel under boilers with the same or lower capacities. Chamber furnaces are also installed on large hot-water boilers.

A chamber furnace consists of vertical walls, cover, and a cold hopper or hearth that are lined with refractory materials. Furnace baffles (pipes 32–76 mm in diameter through which the boiler water circulates) and an overhead or wall-mounted radiation superheater (in steam boilers) are installed on the interior surfaces of the chamber furnace. Fuel is fed into the chamber furnace, together with the air necessary for combustion, through jets mounted on the walls of the furnace and in its corners. During combustion of the powdered fuel, some of the ash is carried off by the flue gases from the furnace to the boiler-gas flues; the rest of it falls from the jet in the form of drops of slag, which are removed from the furnace as a granulated solid or a molten liquid, discharging from the furnace hearth through a tapping hole into a slag catcher filled with water. Semienclosed chamber furnaces, which have a narrow section separating the furnace into two parts (a combustion chamber and a cooling chamber), are also made in large boiler units that operate on pulverized fuel.   R. G. ZAKH [11–798–1]

CHAMBERLAIN (German, *Kammerherr*), a court title in Western European monarchies. It was first introduced in medieval Spain and was then established by Charles V in Germany in the 16th century and by Catherine II in Russia in the 18th century. Originally, the chamberlain was an official of the court in charge of some definite branch of court administration. Linked with these functions were the regalia of the chamberlain adopted in many countries—a golden key on a blue ribbon. In Russia, a ukase of Alexander I of Apr. 3, 1809, reduced the court staff of the chamberlains (*kamergery*), and the title subsequently became honorary. In Russia beginning in 1836, only members of the *dvorianstvo* (nobility or gentry) in state service with a rank not lower than *deistvitel'nyi statskii sovetnik* (actual state councillor, the fourth highest rank in the Table of Ranks), were recommended for the title of *kamerger*. [11–796–4]

CHAMBER MUSIC, a specific type of music differing from that performed in theaters and concert halls; chamber works are designed to be performed in small halls and for domestic or "room" use (hence the name). Compositions of this type are written for small instrumental groups (from a single soloist to a chamber ensemble). The music is characterized by economy and subtle and detailed expressive effects; it has great potential for conveying lyrical emotions and spiritual nuances. Chamber music originated in the Middle Ages. Until the end of the 16th century the term was applied only to vocal genres; in the 17th century it was extended to instrumental music as well. In the 16th–18th centuries the term "chamber music" gradually came to mean secular music as opposed to church music (chamber sonata versus church sonata).

The modern forms of the instrumental chamber ensemble—sonata, trio, quartet, quintet, and so on—developed in the works of the Viennese classicists Haydn, Mozart, and Beethoven, who created profound and perfectly formed models. With its rich expressive possibilities, the instrumental ensemble (especially the string quartet) attracted the attention of nearly every composer; it reflected all the basic trends of music of the 18th–20th centuries. The romantics (Schubert, Mendelssohn, Schumann) and later composers (Brahms, Dvořák) paid tribute to it. High artistry distinguishes the chamber music of such Russian composers as Tchaikovsky, Borodin, and Glazunov, whose traditions have been carried on by the Soviet composers N. Ia. Miaskovskii, Prokofiev, and Shostakovich.

Vocal chamber music was prominent in the late 18th century and particularly in the 19th. Schubert, Schumann, and other romantic composers created the art song, a new genre with great expressive possibilities. The art song was richly developed in Russia by M. I. Glinka, A. S. Dargomyzhskii, Tchaikovsky, Borodin, Mussorgsky, Rimsky-Korsakov, and Rachmaninoff. The genre of instrumental miniatures (character pieces, pieces in dance forms) also acquired great importance in that period.

Chamber-music concerts were given, mostly in small concert halls, in the 19th century, leading to the formation of societies of lovers of chamber music and numerous performing chamber ensembles.

REFERENCES
Vasina-Grossman, V. A. *Russkii klassicheskii romans.* Moscow, 1956.
Vasina-Grossman, V. A. *Romanticheskaia pesnia XIX veka.* Moscow, 1967.
Vasina-Grossman, V. A. *Mastera sovetskogo romansa.* Moscow, 1968.
Raaben, L. *Instrumental'nyi ansambl' v russkoi muzyke.* Moscow, 1961.
Raaben, L. *Sovetskaia kamerno-instrumental'naia muzyka.* Leningrad, 1963.
Walthew, R. H. *The Development of Chamber Music.* London–New York [1909].
Mersmann, H. *Die Kammermusik,* vols. 1–4. Leipzig, 1930–33.
Kilburn, N. *Chamber Music and Its Masters.* London, 1932.
Ulrich, H. *Chamber Music,* 2nd ed. New York–London, 1966.
Coeuray, A. *La Musique de chambre.* Paris, 1953.
Richter, J. Fr. *Kammermusik-Katalog.* Leipzig, 1960.
Cobbett, W. W. *Cyclopedic Survey of Chamber Music,* 2nd ed., vols. 1–3. London, 1963.
L. N. RAABEN [11–797–3]

CHANCELLERY OF SECRET INVESTIGATIONS, a central state institution in Russia from 1731 to 1762 for the investigation of political crimes. This institution is sometimes mistakenly identified with the Secret Chancellery, which existed from 1718 to 1726.

[11–1010–1]

CHANCELLOR (Russian, *kantsler;* from German *Kanzler).*
(1) In the feudal states of medieval Europe, the highest official, whose duties included directing the royal chancellery and archive and keeping the state seal.
(2) In tsarist Russia, state chancellor (*gosudarstvennyi kantsler*) was the highest civil rank. According to the table of ranks of 1722, it corresponded to the military rank of field marshal (*general-fel'dmarshal*).
(3) In Germany from 1871 to 1945, the *Reichskanzler* was the head of the government; from 1934 he also exercised the powers of head of state.
(4) In the Federal Republic of Germany and in Austria, the federal chancellor is the head of the government.
(5) In Great Britain, the chancellor of the exchequer is the minister of finance; the lord high chancellor is the chairman of the House of Lords.
(6) In Switzerland, the chancellor of the Federation is the leader in the secretariat to the highest federal executive and administrative bodies (Federal Council and Federal Assembly).

[11–1011–1]

CHANNEL (information channel). **(1)** The set of devices connecting communications lines, for receiving, transmitting, converting, and recording information. The initial and terminal devices may be telephones or telegraphs, tape recorders, punchers, computers, lasers, or acoustical devices. In communications, use is ordinarily made of radio channels, acoustical and optical communications lines, signal cable, wires, and telephone, telegraph, and radio relay lines. The technical characteristics of a channel are determined by the operating principle of the devices included in it, the type of signal, the properties and composition of the physical media in which the electrical, acoustic, and light signals are propagated, and the properties of the code or language being used. The effectiveness of channels is characterized by the speed and reliability of information transmission, the reliability of operation of the devices, and the time delay of signals.
(2) The aggregate of digital computer devices directly involved in the reception, storage, processing, and readout of information.

REFERENCES
Goldman, S. *Teoriia informatsii.* Moscow, 1957. (Translated from English.)
Shannon, C. *Raboty po teorii informatsii i kibernetiki.* Moscow, 1963. (Translated from English.)
E. IA. DASHEVSKII [11–928–1]

CHANNEL, in information theory, any device for transmitting information. Unlike engineering, information theory abstracts from the concrete nature of these devices, much as geometry studies the volumes of bodies in abstraction from the material of which they are made. In information theory specific communications systems are considered only from the point of view of the amount of information that can be transmitted reliably using them.

The concept of the channel is approached in the following way: the channel is defined by the set of "permissible" messages (or signals) x at the input, the set of messages (signals) y at the output, and the set of conditional probabilities $p(y|x)$ of receiving signal y at the output with input signal x. The conditional probabilities $p(y|x)$ describe the statistical property of the "noise" (interference) that distorts signals during the transmission process. If $p(y|x) = 1$ for $y = x$ and $p(y|x) = 0$ for $y \neq x$, the channel is called a channel without noise.

A distinction is made between discrete and continuous channels in accordance with the structure of input and output signals. In discrete channels signals at the input and output are sequences of "letters" from one and the same or different "alphabets" (codes). In continuous channels the input and output signals are functions of the continuous parameter t—time. Mixed cases are also possible, but it is usually preferred to consider one of the two cases as an idealization.

The ability of a channel to transmit information is characterized by a certain number—the carrying capacity, or simply capacity, of the channel. It is defined as the maximum amount of information relative to a signal at the input contained in a signal at the output (calculated per unit of time).

To be more precise, suppose that input signal ξ assumes several values x with probabilities $p(x)$. Then according to probability theory, the probabilities $q(y)$ that signal η will assume the value y at the output can be calculated by the formula

$$q(y) = \sum_x p(x)p(y|x)$$

just as probabilities $p(x,y)$ that events $\xi = x$ and $\eta = y$ will coincide can be determined by

$$p(x,y) = p(x)p(y|x)$$

The last formula is used to compute the amount of information (in binary units) $I(\eta, \xi) = I(\xi, \eta)$ and its average value

$$R = \lim_{T \to \infty} \frac{1}{T} I(\eta, \xi)$$

where T is the duration of ξ. The upper limit C of magnitudes R, taken for all permissible signals at the input, is called the channel capacity. Computing capacity, like computing entropy, is easier in the discrete case and significantly more complex in the continuous case, where it is based on the theory of stationary random processes.

Simplest of all is the case of a discrete channel without noise. Information theory establishes that in this case the general definition of capacity C is equivalent to the following:

$$C = \lim_{T \to \infty} \frac{\log_2 N(T)}{T}$$

where $N(T)$ is the number of permissible signals of duration T.
Example 1. Suppose the "alphabet" of the channel without noise consists of two "letters," 0 and 1, with a duration of τ seconds each. Permissible signals of duration $T = n\tau$ are repre-

sented by a sequence of the symbols 0 and 1. Their number is $N(T) = 2^n$. Accordingly,

$$C = \lim_{T \to \infty} \frac{\log_2 N(T)}{T} = \lim_{n \to \infty} \frac{n}{n\tau}$$

$$= \frac{1}{\tau} \text{ binary units (bits)/sec}$$

Example 2. Suppose that symbols 0 and 1 have durations of τ and 2τ seconds, respectively. In this case there will be fewer permissible signals of duration $T = n\tau$ than in Example 1. For example, where $n = 3$ there will be only three (instead of eight). Now we may calculate

$$C = \frac{1}{\tau} \log_2 \left(\frac{\sqrt{5} + 1}{2} \right) \approx \frac{0.7}{\tau} \text{ bits/sec}$$

When it is necessary to transmit on a given channel messages written using a certain code, these messages must be converted into permissible signals in the channel, that is, the appropriate encoding must be carried out. After transmission the decoding operation must be performed, that is, the inverse operation of converting the signal back into the message. Naturally it is advisable to do the encoding so that the average time spent on transmission is minimal. Where the duration of symbols at the channel input is identical, this means that one must select the most economical code with an "alphabet" that coincides with the input "alphabet" of the channel.

When the procedure for matching the source with the channel as described above is used, the phenomenon of delay occurs. This may be clarified by Example 3.

Example 3. Suppose that a message source sends independent symbols that assume the values x_1, x_2, x_3, and x_4 with probabilities equal to, respectively, 1/2, 1/4, 1/8, and 1/8 at time intervals of $1/\nu$ (that is, with a speed of ν). Assume that the channel is without noise, as in Example 1, and that coding is done instantaneously. The signal received is either transmitted on the channel if it is free or it waits (is placed in "memory") until the channel is free. Now if, for example, we have selected the code $x_1 = 00$, $x_2 = 01$, $x_3 = 10$, $x_4 = 11$ and $\nu \leq (1/2)\tau$ (that is, $1/\nu \geq 2\tau$), then in the time between the appearance of two sequential values of x it will be possible to transmit the coded notation, and the channel will be free. Thus, in this case the time interval 2τ passes between the appearance of some message "letter" and transmission of its coded notation along the channel. Where $\nu > (1/2)\tau$, a different result is observed: the nth "letter" of the message appears at the moment $(n-1)/\nu$ and its coded notation will be transmitted along the channel at moment $2n\tau$. Therefore, the time interval between the appearance of the nth "letter" of the message and the moment of its appearance after decoding of the transmitted signal will be greater than $n(2\tau - 1/\nu)$, which approaches infinity as $n \to \infty$. Thus, in this case the transmission will be carried on with unlimited delay. Therefore, to be able to transmit without unlimited delay for the given code, satisfaction of the inequality is necessary and sufficient. Selection of a better code can increase transmission speed by making it as close as one wants to the capacity of the channel, but this limit cannot be exceeded (needless to say, while preserving the requirement that delay is limited). This statement is completely general and is called the fundamental theorem of channels without noise.

It is relevant to add the following note in special relation to Example 3. For the messages considered, the binary code $x_1 = 0$, $x_2 = 10$, $x_3 = 110$, and $x_4 = 111$ is optimal. Because of the different lengths of the coded notations, delay time w_n for the nth "letter" of the initial message will be a random variable. When $\nu < 1/\tau$ ($1/\tau$—channel capacity) and $n \to \infty$, its average value approaches a certain limit $m(\nu)$, which depends on ν. As ν approaches the critical value $1/\tau$, the value of $m(\nu)$ increases in proportion to $(\tau^{-1} - \nu)^{-1}$. This once again reflects the general proposition that the endeavor to make transmission speed as close to maximal as possible involves an increase in delay time and in the necessary size of the "memory" of the coding device.

The assertion of the fundamental theorem (substituting "almost error-free" for error-free transmission) also applies to channels with noise. This fact, which is truly fundamental for the entire theory of information transmission, is called Shannon's theorem. The possibility of reducing the probability of erroneous transmission through channels with noise is achieved by using so-called noise-combating codes.

Example 4. Suppose that the input "alphabet" of the channel consists of two symbols 0 and 1 and the noise effect is expressed as follows: during transmission each of the symbols may with a slight (for example, equal to 1/10) probability p change into the other or, with a probability of $q = 1 - p$, remain undistorted. The use of a noise-combating code essentially amounts to selecting a new "alphabet" at the input of the channel. Its "letters" are n-element chains of the symbols 0 and 1 that differ from one another by a sufficient number of characters D. Thus, where $n = 5$ and $nD = 3$ the new "letters" can be 00000, 01110, 10101, and 11011. If the probability of more than one error for a group of five characters is small, then even when distorted these new "letters" can hardly be confused. For example, if the signal 10001 is received, it almost certainly came from 10101.

It turns out that with a proper selection of sufficiently large n and D this method is significantly more effective than simple repetition (that is, using "alphabets" of the 000, 111 type). However, possible improvement of the transmission process in this way inevitably involves greatly increasing the complexity of the coding and decoding devices. For example, it has been calculated that if $p = 10^{-2}$ initially and this value must be decreased to $p_1 = 10^{-4}$, then the length of the code chain n must be selected not less than 25 (or 380) depending on whether the channel capacity to be used is 53 percent (or 80 percent).

Iu. V. Prokhorov [11–925–1]

CHANNELING OF CHARGED PARTICLES IN CRYSTALS,

the movement of particles through the "channels" formed by parallel rows of atoms. In this case the particles undergo glancing collisions (the momentum is almost unchanged) with the rows of atoms confining them to the channels. If the particle's trajectory is contained between two atomic planes, it is called plane channeling in contrast to axial channeling, where the particles move between adjacent rows of atoms.

The channeling of charged particles was predicted by the American physicists M. T. Robinson and O. S. Oen in 1961 and was observed by several groups of experimenters in 1963–65. The channeling of heavy particles (protons and ions) occurs at energies of more than several keV, corresponding to the length of a de Broglie wave, which is small compared to the constant of a crystal lattice. Under these circumstances the channeling can be described by the laws of classical mechanics. In order for it to take place, the angle formed by the particles' velocity and the axis of the atomic row (or plane for plane channeling) should not exceed a certain critical value Ψ_{cr}. The larger the atomic numbers of the particles and the atom of the crystal and the smaller the separation between the atoms in the row along which channeling is taking place, the larger the angle Ψ_{cr}. For axial channeling, in some directions $\Psi_{cr} = 0.1°$–5° (for plane channeling it is several times smaller).

Channeled particles move along a trajectory that is further from the nuclei of the atoms of the crystal lattice than the trajectory of unchanneled particles. This has two results. (1) The path length of particles in a channel is substantially longer than that of unchanneled particles because the electron density in the channels is lower than the average in the crystal; the resulting increased path length of the ions is used in the ion implanting of semiconductors. (2) Inasmuch as channeled particles are moving relatively far from the nuclei and their inner electron shells (the K and L shells), the probability of nuclear reactions and the excitation of X rays by such particles is much less.

Particles may leave a channel as a result of scattering by defects in the crystal, and this is used to investigate such defects. The shadow effect is closely associated with channeling.

The channeling of electrons differs from the channeling of heavy particles. The features of the former are due to their wave properties and their negative charge.

REFERENCES

Tulinov, A. F. "Vliianie kristallicheskoi reshetki na nekotorye atomnye i iadernye protsessy." *Uspekhi fizicheskikh nauk*, 1965, vol. 87, issue 4, p. 585.

Lindhard, J. "Vliianie kristallicheskoi reshetki na dvizhenie bystrykh zariazhennykh chastits." *Uspekhi fizicheskikh nauk,* 1969, vol. 99, issue 2, p. 249.

Thompson, M. "Kanalirovanie chastits v kristallakh." *Uspekhi fizicheskikh nauk,* 1969, vol. 99, issue 2, p. 297.

Kagan, Iu. M., and Iu. V. Kononets. "Teoriia effekta kanalirovaniia." *Zhurnal eksperimental'noi i teoreticheskoi fiziki,* 1970, vol. 58, issue 1, p. 226.   IU. V. MARTYNENKO [11–934–1]

CHANNEL-TYPE REACTOR, a nuclear reactor consisting of a system of separate channels constructed such that the space between the channels is filled with a neutron moderator. The fuel elements along with the nuclear fuel are located within each channel and are cooled by an individual flow of the coolant. The flow to and from the coolant is realized through a piping system.

In principle the size of the core of a channel-type reactor is not limited because of the design features. In view of the tendency to increase unit reactor outputs, it is the core that favorably distinguishes channel-type reactors from shell-type reactors for which an increase in output and, correspondingly, an increase in the size of the core involve difficulties in the manufacture, transport, and installation of large shells. The separation of the coolant and moderator in channel-type reactors allows good neutron balance and effective heat removal in the core. This is achieved by the proper selection of the materials for the moderator and coolant. Channel-type reactors in which graphite serves as the moderator and industrial water serves as the coolant have been intensively developed, since graphite has satisfactory nuclear characteristics and the industrial water has good thermophysical properties.

Using special systems, it is possible to refuel channel-type reactors during operation, that is, without stopping and cooling the reactor. This improves the economic features of the power installation and allows a steady output of electricity. A core consisting of separate channels permits individual control of the state of each fuel assembly and in the case of damage, immediate replacement. However, in view of the considerable size of the core of channel-type reactors, the specific load is a number of times less than, for example, in shell-type reactors and usually does not exceed, on the average, 15 kW per 1 l of the core. The branched piping system for the coolant inlet and outlet complicates installation and servicing and increases the probability of leakage.

Various types of channel-type reactors have gained wide distribution in many countries. For example, the SGHWR reactor with a heavy-water moderator and boiling-light-water coolant (Great Britain), the NPR carbon-uranium reactor with a water coolant (USA), the AGR carbon-uranium gas-cooled reactor (Great Britain), the CANDU channel-type reactor with a heavy-water moderator and coolant (Canada), and the KC-150 gas-cooled reactor with heavy-water moderator (Czechoslovakia). The USSR has accumulated experience in the construction and use of channel-type reactors, including research reactors, power reactors, breeder reactors, and their combinations (dual-purpose reactors). Graphite, heavy water, and beryllium are used as neutron moderators in channel-type reactors and industrial water, steam-water mixture, superheated steam, and carbon dioxide are used as coolants.

The good economic features and absence of limitations in increasing the unit output of channel-type reactors favor further development despite the low power intensity of their cores. The construction of a number of atomic power plants with lot-produced carbon-uranium water-boiler RBM-K channel-type reactors in series with a power output of 1,000 MW is planned in the USSR. The first of these two-reactor atomic electric power plants—in Leningrad—is in the assembly stage.

V. P. VASILEVSKII [11–935–2]

CHAPEL. (1) In church architecture (Catholic and Anglican), a small room for preservation of relics, accommodation of choristers, and worship by the members of a notable family. Chapels were located in churches (in the aisles or around the choir), castles, and palaces. They were also built as separate structures (for example, the Sistine Chapel).

(2) A choir of singers. The word initially was used to designate the room in which the choir was originally placed. At first chapels were purely vocal. With the development of instrumental music, they usually became ensembles, including singers and instrumentalists. Prominent composers, such as J. S. Bach and F. J. Haydn, directed chapels. These types of choirs were introduced to Russia in the 18th century and became widespread, primarily on country estates. The composers S. A. Degtiarev, S. I. Davydov, and D. N. Kashin wrote for chapels. The most outstanding was the Imperial Chapel (now the M. I. Glinka Leningrad State Academic Chapel), with which D. S. Bortnianskii, M. I. Glinka, N. A. Rimsky-Korsakov, M. A. Balakirev, A. S. Arenskii, and S. M. Liapunov were affiliated.

In the past many court, theater, and civic orchestras were referred to as chapels. In the USSR this term is used for some instrumental groups (for example, bandore players).

[11–1017–3]

CHAPLAIN, in the Catholic and Anglican churches:
(1) A clergyman in charge of a chapel or home church and also an assistant parish priest.
(2) A clergyman in the army; in bourgeois states, as a rule, the chaplain has the rank of an officer or general. In addition to his religious functions, the chaplain is also responsible for the political convictions and morale of the soldiers and officers.

[11–1018–1]

CHAPTER. (1) In the Catholic and Anglican churches, the college of canons of the cathedral, making up a council working under the bishop to govern the diocese, or eparchy. Upon the death of the bishop, the diocese is governed by individuals who have been selected by the cathedral chapter from among its own membership. These individuals govern until the arrival of the new bishop.
(2) In Catholic monastic orders, as well as in religious orders of knights, the board of leaders. [11–1063–1]

CHARLEMAGNE (Latin, Carolus Magnus). Born Apr. 2, 742; died Jan. 28, 814, in Aachen. Became king of the Franks in 768 and emperor in 800. The Carolingian dynasty is named after Charlemagne.

After the death of Pepin the Short (768), Charlemagne began to rule part of the Frankish state (his brother Carloman held the other part). In 771 he became the sole ruler of the reunified state. Charlemagne expanded the boundaries of his kingdom through numerous campaigns (against the Lombards in 773–74 and 776–77; against the Bavarian duke Tassilo in 788; intermittently against the Saxons from 772 to 804; against the Arabs in Spain in 778–79 and 796–810; against the Avars from 791 to 799; and against the western Slavic tribes from 789 to 806). He was crowned emperor in Rome in 800 by Pope Leo III. Charlemagne's empire included various tribes and nationalities at different levels of social development. He undertook a number of measures to strengthen his borders (including the formation of marches) and strove to centralize power in the empire. The royal court became the center of state life.

Charlemagne attempted to organize systematic control over the counts (in whose hands local military and administrative power was concentrated) by means of "state envoys" (*missi dominici*). In order to bring the vast state under a single set of laws, he published numerous capitularies. He saw the Catholic Church as a source of support for the royal power: he awarded high posts and various privileges to its representatives, intervened in the appointment of bishops, and encouraged the compulsory conversion of conquered peoples. The feudalization of Frankish society was promoted by his internal policies: the establishment of the feudal land dependence of the peasantry, the growth of large-scale land ownership, and the increasing independence of the land-owning aristocracy. Charlemagne's distribution of deeds of immunity to the aristocracy created, in spite of his own aspirations, the social and economic prerequisites of feudal fragmentation. The empire of the Franks disintegrated under Charlemagne's successors. An upsurge in culture, the Carolingian Renaissance, was evident under Charlemagne.

REFERENCES

Halphen, L. *Charlemagne et l'Empire Carolingien.* Paris, 1947.
Calmette, J. *Charlemagne.* Paris, 1951.
Serejski, M. H. *Karol Wielki na tle swoich czasów.* [Warsaw] 1959.
Karl der Grosse . . . , vol. 1. Düsseldorf, 1965.
Tessier, G. *Charlemagne.* Paris, 1967.
Epperlein, S. *Karl der Grosse.* Berlin, 1971.

B. IA. RAMM [11–1291–4]

CHARLES. In England:

Charles I. Born Nov. 19, 1600, in London; died there Jan. 30, 1649. King (1625–49) of the Stuart dynasty. Son of James I.

Charles I adhered to a reactionary policy of feudal absolutism that ran counter to the interests of the bourgeoisie and the "new gentry" and evoked protest among the masses of the people in England. The English Bourgeois Revolution of the 17th century broke out in 1640. Charles I suffered defeat in the civil wars of 1642–46 and 1648. He was executed by a sentence of the High Court of the Tribunal that the Long Parliament had created.

Charles II. Born May 29, 1630, in London; died there Feb. 6, 1685. King of the Stuart dynasty.

After the execution of his father, Charles I (1649), Charles II was proclaimed king of Scotland by the Scottish Presbyterian parliament. In 1660 he was proclaimed king of England, his return to London marking the restoration of the Stuarts in England. Despite the constitutional guarantees established in the Declaration of Breda and his promises to rule jointly with Parliament, Charles II's reign was characterized by feudal reaction and attempts to restore absolutism.   [11–1284–2]

CHARLES. In France. The best known were as follows.

Charles III the Simple. Born Sept. 17, 879; died Oct. 7, 929, in Péronne. King from 898 to 923. Member of the Carolingian dynasty.

Charles III was forced to cede the territory of Normandy to the Normans (the treaty of 911 with the Norman leader Rollo). Taking advantage of the feudal discord in Germany after the death of the last Carolingian reigning there, Charles seized Lorraine in 911. In 922–23, the aristocracy rose up in rebellion against Charles. The rebels, who elected Rudolf of Burgundy king (July 923), took Charles III captive by treachery. He was imprisoned in the castle in Péronne until his death.

Charles V the Wise. Born Jan. 21, 1338, in Vincennes; died Sept. 16, 1380, in Nogent-sur-Marne. King from 1364. Member of the Valois dynasty.

Charles V was regent of France from 1356 to 1360 and in early 1364 (while his father, King John II the Good, was held prisoner by the English). During his regency, while searching for funds with which to wage war and ransom his father from captivity, he resorted to debasement of coinage. When the Paris uprising of 1357–58 broke out, he fled from Paris and tried to organize a blockade to starve the capital. The smashing of the Jacquerie and the betrayal of the uprising by the ruling circles of Paris made it possible for Charles to capture the city in the summer of 1358. Upon his accession to the throne, he substantially increased royal power, regulated the system of taxation, and reorganized the army, partially replacing the feudal militia by mercenaries. In 1369 he renewed military operations against the English. By the end of the 1370's these operations resulted in virtually the complete expulsion of the English from France.

REFERENCE

Calmette, J. *Charles V.* Paris [1945].

Charles VI the Mad. Born Dec. 3, 1368, in Paris; died there Oct. 21, 1422. King from 1380. Member of the Valois dynasty.

Being mentally ill, Charles VI ruled only in name. His reign was marked by a bitter struggle for power between two feudal aristocratic groups, the Armagnacs and the Burgundians. In 1420 the English forced Charles, who had been taken prisoner by the Burgundians (the allies of the English in the Hundred Years' War [1337–1453]), to sign a treaty in Troyes, by which the English king Henry V became heir to the French throne rather than the dauphin Charles.

Charles VII. Born Feb. 22, 1403, in Paris; died July 22, 1461, in Mehun-sur-Yèvre. King from 1422.

After the death of his father (Charles VI), Charles VII proclaimed himself king of France despite the treaty of Troyes of 1420 which Charles VI had signed. However, his power extended only to the lands south of the Loire (with his residence at Bourges); the rest of France was in the hands of the English and their allies, the Burgundians. With the aid of Joan of Arc, who led the struggle for the liberation of the French people, Charles was crowned in Reims in 1429, and in 1437 he entered Paris. He carried out a number of reforms that served to strengthen royal power. A standing army was established in 1439, and a permanent direct tax, the taille, was instituted. After 1435, he ended the regular convocation of the Estates General. He issued the Pragmatic Sanction of 1438, which legally formalized the independence of the Gallican Church from the pope and subordinated it, to a certain extent, to royal authority. He put down the Praguerie, a revolt of the feudal aristocracy (1440).

REFERENCES

Beaucourt, G. du Fresne. *Histoire de Charles VII,* vols. 1–6. Paris, 1881–91.
Erlanger, P. *Charles VII et son mystère.* [Paris, 1945.]

Charles IX. Born June 27, 1550, in St. Germain-en-Laye; died May 30, 1574, in Vincennes. King from 1560. Member of the Valois dynasty.

Until 1570, Charles' mother Catherine de Médicis was the actual ruler. Only after the peace of St. Germain of 1570, which temporarily ended the religious wars, did Charles IX manifest a certain degree of independence in his policies. He brought in a Huguenot leader, Admiral Coligny, and, influenced by him, Charles protected the Calvinists and leaned toward war against Spain. However, Catherine de Médicis was frightened by Coligny's influence and got Charles to consent to the Massacre of St. Bartholomew (1572).

Charles X. Born Oct. 9, 1757, in Versailles; died Nov. 6, 1836, in Gorizia. King from 1824 to 1830. Member of the Bourbon dynasty. Younger brother of Louis XVI.

Prior to his accession to the throne, Charles X held the title Comte d'Artois. On July 17, 1789, after the revolution had broken out, he fled abroad. He was one of the organizers of intervention against revolutionary France. During the Restoration (in the reign of his second brother, Louis XVIII, in 1814 and 1815–24), he was one of the leaders (along with J. B. Villèle and others) of the Ultraroyalists. Upon becoming king, Charles implemented extremely reactionary domestic and foreign policies, placing A. J. de Polignac at the head of the government in 1829 (for example, the July Ordinances of 1830 that restricted suffrage and freedom of the press and the expansion into Algeria in the summer of 1830). He was overthrown by the July Revolution of 1830. He went to Great Britain and from there, to Austria.

REFERENCE

Vivent, J. *Charles X.* Paris, 1958.   [11–1286–1]

CHARLES. Kings and emperors of the Holy Roman Empire.

Charles IV. Born May 14, 1316, in Prague; died there Nov. 29, 1378. Emperor and German king from 1347. King of Bohemia (as Charles I) from 1346 (Luxemburg dynasty). Son of John of Luxemburg and Elizabeth, sister of the Bohemian king Wenceslas III.

In Bohemia Charles IV implemented policies that strengthened the royal domain, enriched the royal treasury, restricted the rights of the Bohemian magnates, and encouraged handicraft industry, mining, and domestic and foreign trade. The growth in the importance of Prague was particularly marked under Charles IV: extensive construction was carried out and the University of Prague was founded (1348). The creation of the archbishopric of Prague (1344) helped to reinforce the independence of the Bohemian church. In carrying out his centralizing policies in Bohemia, Charles IV relied on trade and handicraft circles in the cities, the middle and petty gentry, and the clergy. The great feudal magnates, however, resisted the policy of centralization, which was made evident by the Bohemian sejms of 1348 and 1359 and by their rejection of the draft for a new Bohemian code of laws, the Majestas Carolina of 1355. Charles IV sought to create a vast hereditary monarchy in Central Europe. By buying up land, through marriage, and other methods, he acquired part of the Upper Palatinate, land in Thuringia and Saxony, Lower Lusatia, and in 1373, Brandenburg. (These lands were lost by the Luxemburgs after the death of Charles IV.) The imperial policies of Charles IV, who legitimized and expanded the privileges of the electors through the Golden Bull, helped to consolidate the political decentralization of Germany.

REFERENCES
Friedjung, H. *Kaiser Karl IV.* Vienna, 1876.
Šusta, Y. *Karel IV: Otec a syn.* Prague, 1946.
Šusta, Y. *Karel IV za císařskou korunou.* Prague, 1948.
Čtení o Karlu IV: A jeho době. Prague, 1958.
Kalista, Z. *Karel IV: Jeho duchovní tvář.* Prague, 1971.

G. E. SANCHUK

Charles V. Born Feb. 24, 1500, in Ghent; died Sept. 21, 1558, at the St. Yuste monastery in Spain. Emperor from 1519 to 1556. Spanish king (Charles I) from 1516 to 1556. Of the Hapsburg dynasty.

In 1506, Charles V inherited Burgundy and the Netherlands from his father, Philip the Handsome (the son of Maximilian I), and in 1516 he inherited the Spanish throne from his grandfather Ferdinand the Catholic. In 1519 he was elected emperor. Charles V subordinated all his policies to the realization of a reactionary program of creating a "worldwide Christian monarchy" and made militant Catholicism his banner. His absolutist policies in Spain and the Netherlands provoked a number of uprisings (the uprising of the Comuneros of 1520–22 and others in Spain and the Ghent uprising of 1539–40 in the Netherlands). He waged numerous wars against France, the Hapsburgs' main rival in Europe, and also against the Ottoman Empire. In the war of 1532–33 he halted the advance of Turkish forces into Hapsburg holdings, and in 1535 he captured Tunis from a vassal of the Ottoman Empire, but he was defeated in Algiers (1541). Spanish possessions in America also expanded considerably under Charles V. In fighting the Reformation in Germany, he issued the Edict of Worms (1521) against Luther. He defeated the German Protestant princes in the Schmalkaldic war of 1546–48, but in the new war that began in 1552, he suffered a bitter defeat and was forced to sign the religious Peace of Augsburg (1555). He then renounced the Spanish crown (he transferred the Spanish throne and the Netherlands to his son Philip II) and the imperial throne (in favor of his brother Ferdinand I).

In a period that constituted a turning point in the history of Western Europe, the policies of Charles V were historically reactionary in nature; they were aimed at supporting obsolescent, reactionary feudal forces and outdated state forms hostile to the national states that were forming.

REFERENCES
Baumgarten, H. *Geschichte Karls V,* vols. 1–3. Stuttgart, 1885–92.
Morel-Fatio, A. *Historiographie de Charles-Quint.* Paris, 1913.
Drion du Chapois, F. *Charles-Quint et l'Europe.* Brussels, 1962.
Correspondenz des Kaisers Karl V, vols. 1–3. Frankfurt am Main, 1966.

Charles VI. Born Oct. 1, 1685, in Vienna; died there Oct. 20, 1740. Emperor from 1711. Son of emperor Leopold I.

Charles VI sought unsuccessfully to obtain the Spanish crown. He waged wars against the Ottoman Empire (1716–18 and 1737–39) and also the War of the Polish Succession (1733–35). The territory of the Hapsburgs expanded considerably under Charles VI. He issued the Pragmatic Sanction of 1713, which regulated succession in the Hapsburg lands.

Charles VII (also Charles Albert). Born Aug. 6, 1697, in Brussels; died Jan. 20, 1745, in Munich. Emperor from 1742 to 1745. Elector of Bavaria from 1726 to 1745.

Charles VII was elevated to the imperial throne by the rivals of the Hapsburgs in the course of the War of the Austrian Succession. [11–1284–3]

CHARLES. In Sweden. The most important were as follows.

Charles VIII (Karl Knutsson). Born in 1409; died in 1470. King (with interruptions) from 1448 to 1470. Came from a wealthy noble family.

In the course of a popular uprising against Danish rule (1434–36), Charles VIII was elected one of the rulers of the Swedish state, becoming its sole ruler after the nobles murdered Engelbrekt Engelbrektsson, the leader of the uprising (1436). Charles suppressed the peasant movement in 1436–37. After the death of Christopher of Bavaria, who was the king of Denmark, Sweden, and Norway, he succeeded in getting himself elected to the Swedish throne. (This in effect marked the dissolution of the Union of Kalmar.) However, Charles VIII spent his entire reign struggling against the Danish king Christian I, who was attempting to reestablish the union.

Charles IX. Born Oct. 4, 1550, in Stockholm; died Oct. 30, 1611, in Nyköping. King from 1604. Youngest son of Gustavus I Vasa.

After the establishment of the Swedish-Polish union (1592), Charles IX led a popular movement against Sigismund, the king of Sweden and Poland (a nephew of Charles IX), who was attempting to reestablish Catholicism in Sweden. Charles was elected ruler of the government in 1595. In 1598 at Stångebro, he routed the troops of Sigismund, who had landed in Sweden, and had Sigismund dethroned (1599). In 1604, Charles was officially elected king of Sweden. He began an intervention against the Russian state under the guise of military aid to tsar Vasilii Ivanovich Shuiskii. (In 1611, Charles captured Novgorod.)

Charles X Gustavus. Born Nov. 8, 1622; died Feb. 13, 1660, in Göteborg. King from 1654.

Charles X came to the throne after the abdication of Christina (his first cousin). He relied on the support of the lesser nobility and prosperous peasantry. He instituted a decree on partial Reduction (which required nobles to give up crown lands) at the Riksdag of 1655. His aggressive foreign policy led to war with Poland, Denmark, and Russia and resulted in the expansion of Swedish holdings and the consolidation of Swedish rule in the Baltic (the Northern War of 1655–60 and the Russo-Swedish War of 1656–58).

Charles XI. Born Nov. 24, 1655, in Stockholm; died there Apr. 5, 1697. King from 1660 (ruled independently from 1672). Son of Charles X Gustavus.

In 1680, Charles XI established absolutism in Sweden with the support of the taxpaying estates; he began extensive Reduction at that time. Under his rule, Sweden participated in European wars (as an ally of France against Holland [1672–78] and on the side of Holland against France [1688–97]).

Charles XII. Born June 17, 1682, in Stockholm; died Nov. 30, 1718, in Fredrikshald, Norway. King from 1697. Military leader.

A son of Charles XI, Charles XII continued his father's absolutist great power policies, deriving strength from the economic and political might of Sweden and having at his disposal the best army and navy in Europe. His primary concern was in leading Swedish military operations in the Great Northern War of 1700–21. At the beginning of the war, the Swedish Army under the command of Charles XII was victorious over Denmark, forcing it to leave the Northern Alliance (Russia, Saxony, Poland, and Denmark) in 1700. Charles then moved his forces to the Baltic coast and routed Russia's forces at Narva on Nov. 19 (30), 1700. In 1701 he began military operations against Poland and Saxony. In the protracted struggle that lasted from 1701 to 1706, he smashed the Polish-Saxon forces and forced Augustus II, king of Poland (and also an elector of Saxony), to sign the Altranstädt peace treaty of 1706, renounce the Polish crown, and leave the Northern Alliance.

Charles' troops invaded Russia in the summer of 1708. Efforts to force his way toward Moscow from the directions of Smolensk and Briansk were repelled by Russian troops. Temporarily abandoning the attack against the heartland of Russia, in October 1708, Charles turned from the Kostenichi and Starodub area toward the Ukraine, hoping to receive aid from the traitor I. Mazepa, hetman of the Ukraine. After suffering a crushing defeat in the battle of Poltava (1709), Charles fled to Turkey, where he attempted without success to organize an attack against Russia by the Turkish Army from the south and the Swedish Army from the north. Although Turkey attacked Russia in 1711, the war ended swiftly, and Charles was unable to aid the Turks by sending the Swedish Army through Poland. In 1715 he returned to Sweden to create a new army. He carried out a number of domestic reforms aimed at mobilizing forces for war. Charles XII was killed in the siege of the Norwegian fortress of Fredrikshald. As a result of his defeat in Russia, Sweden was reduced to the status of a second-rate power.

Historical literature contains extremely contradictory evaluations of Charles XII's skill as a military leader. Nationalist Swedish and German historiography greatly exaggerates his role as a commander; it calls attention to his extraordinary bravery, the surprise and speed of his operations, and his achievement of victory with forces smaller than those of his enemy. The majority of military historians, however, believe that Charles XII introduced nothing new into military art, that he merely skillfully used the forms of troop organization and the tactics of his talented predecessor Gustavus II Adolphus; they characterize him as an exponent of adventurist strategies and policies. The victories of Charles XII were fruitless. His absence of more than 15 years from Sweden disorganized the administration of the state and complicated to an extreme degree direction of military operations in the vast area from Lake Ladoga to Pomerania. Long victorious over the weak and untrained forces of his enemies, Charles XII began to disregard the fundamental requirements of military art. This resulted in attacks by inadequate forces with insecure lines of communication (for example, in Russia in 1708–09), underestimation of the enemy, poor reconnaissance, the lack of a battle plan, and unrealistic expectations of aid from his allies.

REFERENCES

Engels, F. "Vneshniaia politika russkogo tsarizma." In K. Marx and F. Engels, *Soch.*, 2nd ed., vol. 22.

Tarle, E. V. *Severnaia voina i shvedskoe nashestvie na Rossiiu.* Moscow, 1958.

Munthe, A. *Karl XII och den ryska sjömakten,* [vols.] 1–3. Stockholm, 1924–27.

Karl XII på slagfältet, parts 1–4. Stockholm, 1918–19.

Hatton, R. M. *Charles XII of Sweden.* London, 1968.

Charles XIV John. King of Sweden and Norway from 1818 to 1844. His original name was Jean Baptiste Bernadotte.
[11–1288–1]

CHARLES (Karl). Archduke of Austria. Born Sept. 5, 1771, in Florence; died Apr. 30, 1847, in Vienna. Austrian general and military theoretician; duke of Teschen; field marshal. Third son of Emperor Leopold II.

From 1792 through 1809, Archduke Charles fought in the wars against France. Between 1796 and 1799, while commanding the Austrian Army on the Rhine, he defeated the French generals J. Moreau and J. Jourdan several times. In 1805, after Austria's forces were routed at Ulm and Austerlitz, he was appointed minister of war, reorganizing the Austrian Army from 1806 to 1808. He worked out new regulations and war manuals reflecting the lessons learned from the wars of revolutionary France, and he organized supply and retraining for the war against France. As a result of these measures, the fighting capacity of the Austrian troops increased substantially. In the Austro-French War of 1809, Charles, who was appointed commander in chief, was defeated at the battle of Regensburg on April 19–23. He was subsequently victorious at Aspern and Essling on May 21–22, but in the decisive battle at Wagram the Austrian Army was defeated. Charles was able, however, to withdraw the main force to Bohemia, thus avoiding a complete rout. He retired after the signing of the Treaty of Vienna in 1809.

In his theoretical works, Charles noted the advantage of swift actions and all-out attacks against the enemy in order to bring a war to a speedy and successful conclusion. However, in directing his forces, he was indecisive, striving to achieve victory without risk. He exaggerated the importance of the geographical factor.

WORKS

Ausgewählte Schriften, vols. 1–6. Vienna, 1893–94.

REFERENCE

Strategiia v trudakh voennykh klassikov, vol. 2. Moscow, 1926.
[11–1290–1]

CHARLES THE BOLD (Charles Le Téméraire). Born Nov. 10, 1433, in Dijon; died Jan. 5, 1477, near Nancy. Count of Charolais, duke of Burgundy (from 1467). Son of Philip the Good.

Charles the Bold strove to unify his fragmented holdings and turn Burgundy into a large and powerful state. On a number of occasions (1452–53, 1465, 1467, 1468) he suppressed with merciless cruelty the uprisings of the Dutch cities that had become part of the Burgundian state. He was the most dangerous and powerful enemy of Louis XI, who was energetically carrying out the centralization and territorial unification of France. The struggle between the two sovereigns was almost continual. Even while Charles' father was still alive, he was the actual leader of the coalition against Louis XI (the League of the Public Weal). He forced the French king to cede him cities on the Somme (the treaties of 1465 of Conflans and St. Maur). To secure the support of King Edward IV of England, he married Edward's sister Margaret. He attempted to seize Alsace (part of which he had received from Sigismund of Tirol, a Hapsburg, in 1469 as a guarantee) and Lorraine (a number of fortresses were transferred to him from Duke René II in 1473). However, he lost his allies (including the English king) and was left isolated through the adroitness of Louis XI, who relied on diplomatic negotiations and bribes. In the Burgundian Wars of 1474–77 (waged against Charles by Switzerland and Lorraine, secretly supported and subsidized by France), Charles was betrayed by mercenaries bribed by Louis XI and died in battle at Nancy.

REFERENCE

Néret, J. A. *Le Téméraire: Charles de Bourgogne.* Paris, 1952.
N. A. DENISOVA-KHACHATURIAN [11–1295–2]

CHARLES I. Born Aug. 17, 1887, in Persenberg, Lower Austria; died Apr. 1, 1922, in Funchal, Madeira Island. Emperor of Austria, king of Hungary as Charles IV (1916–18).

Charles I belonged to the Hapsburg dynasty. During the revolution of 1918, he was forced to renounce the Austrian throne on Nov. 11, 1918, and the Hungarian throne on Nov. 13, 1918.

REFERENCES

Turok, V. M. *Ocherki istorii Avstrii 1918–29.* Moscow, 1955.

Polzer-Hoditz, A. *Kaiser Karl.* Zürich, 1929. [11–1290–2]

CHARLES I (Károly Róbert, Charles Robert). Born 1288; died July 16, 1342, in Visegrád. Hungarian king from 1308 to 1342. Founder of the Anjou dynasty in Hungary.

During Charles' reign, the central regime, which was supported by the church, petty nobility, and city dwellers, was strengthened. Cities grew, and mining and trade expanded. In 1335, Charles signed the Visegrád trade agreement with Bohemia and Poland. He waged unsuccessful wars against Venice, Serbia, and Walachia. [11–1295–1]

CHARLES I (Charles d'Anjou). Born in March 1226; died Jan. 7, 1285, in Foggia. King of Sicily (1268–82; in name, from 1266) and Naples (1282–85). Count of Anjou, Maine, and Provence.

Charles I was the son of the French king Louis VIII. Proposed for the Sicilian throne by the papacy, he was crowned by Pope Clement IV in 1266. He took over the kingdom of Sicily in 1268, having triumphed over the kings of the Hohenstaufen dynasty (over Manfred at Benevento in 1266 and over his successor Conradin at Tagliacozzo in 1268). In 1270, Charles took part in Louis IX's crusade to Tunis. He sought to subjugate Northern and Central Italy, the Balkan Peninsula (where he captured a number of cities), all of Byzantium, and the Levant States. His extensive disbursements of land and privileges in Southern Italy and Sicily to the numerous French knights who accompanied him, as well as the sharp increase in feudal exploitation and oppressive taxation, resulted in a popular uprising in Sicily, known as the Sicilian Vespers, in 1282. Having lost his control of the island, Charles' possessions were limited to Southern Italy, known as the Neapolitan kingdom. [11–1290–3]

CHARLES I (Carlos I). Born Sept. 28, 1863, in Lisbon; died there Feb. 1, 1908. Portuguese king from 1889.

Charles I supported the most reactionary circles of the absolutist clerical party. He suppressed the republican uprising of 1891 and increased the economic and political dependence of Portugal on Great Britain. He was killed by a republican. [11–1311–2]

CHARLES II (known as Charles the Bald). Born June 13, 823, in Frankfurt-am-Main; died Oct. 6, 877, in Avrieux, the Alps. Ruler of the Western Frankish kingdom from 840. Western emperor from 875.

Charles II, the son of Louis the Pious, belonged to the Carolingian dynasty. By the Treaty of Verdun of 843, he secured the Western Frankish kingdom. In 870 he annexed a portion of Lorraine to his kingdom (Treaty of Mersen). Charles strove unsuccessfully to halt the breakup of the kingdom into independent feudal seigneuries. After the death of emperor Louis II in 875, Charles secured the title of emperor and king of Italy from the Roman pope. In 876, he made a futile attempt to seize the Eastern Frankish kingdom. [11–1291–1]

CHARLES III (known as Charles the Fat). Born in 839; died Jan. 13, 888, in Neidingen. Ruler of the East Frankish and West Frankish kingdoms (876–887 and December 884–887, respectively); king of all the East Franks (881–887).

Charles III was the son of Louis the German. He temporarily unified under his rule the territory of the former empire of Charlemagne. In 887 he was deposed by insurgent feudal lords. [11–1291–2]

CHARLES ALBERT. Born Oct. 2, 1798, in Turin; died July 28, 1849, in Oporto. King of Sardinia-Piedmont (1831–49).

Charles Albert belonged to the Savoy dynasty. During the Revolution of 1848–49, he introduced a moderately liberal constitution (Albertine Statute, 1848). As a result of his adherence to a policy of compromise and his concessions to the embattled camps, the Italians called him the "king of vacillation." Under pressure from the national liberation movement, he declared war on Austria. After Italy's defeat in the Austro-Italian War of 1848–49, Charles Albert abdicated the throne (Mar. 23, 1849) and fled to Portugal. [11–1291–3]

CHARLES D'ORLÉANS. Born Nov. 24, 1394, in Paris; died Jan. 5, 1465, in Amboise. French poet. Participant in the Hundred Years' War (1337–1453).

D'Orléans spent 25 years as an English prisoner. His ballades, rondeaux, and chansons, written in the traditional form of medieval lyrics, contain reflections on the transient nature of life and convey the poet's yearning for his homeland. Gentle lyricism adorns the poems devoted to his wife and those celebrating spring and the natural beauty of his native country. In his castle of Blois, Charles d'Orléans collected a large library; many poets, including F. Villon, took part in the poetic competitions here.

WORKS
Poésies, [vols.] 1–2. Paris, 1923–27.
In Russian translation:
[Selections.] In S. Pinus, *Frantsuzskie poety,* vol. 1. St. Petersburg, 1914.
REFERENCES
Istoriia frantsuzskoi literatury, vol. 1. Moscow-Leningrad, 1946. Page 179.
Champion, P. *La Vie de Charles d'Orléans.* Paris, 1911.
Charpier, J. *Charles d'Orléans.* Paris, 1958. (With bibliography.)
Choffel, J. *Le Duc Charles d'Orléans (1394–1465).* Paris [1968].
[11–1294–2]

CHARLES EMMANUEL I (Carlo Emanuele). Born Jan. 12, 1562, in Rivoli; died July 26, 1630, in Savigliano. Duke of Savoy from 1580.

Charles Emmanuel drew Savoy into numerous destructive wars, primarily against France (including the wars for the marquessate of Saluzzo, 1588–1601, and for the succession of Mantua, 1628–31). These wars undermined the country's economy and resulted in the loss of a number of territories. [11–1296–1]

CHARLES MARTEL (Carolus Martellus). Born c. 688; died Oct. 22, 741, at Quierzy. Mayor of the palace of the Merovingian Frankish state (715–41). Son of Pepin of Herstal of the Pepinid clan (later called the Carolingians).

In defeating the nobility of Neustria and Aquitaine and reestablishing the political unity of the Frankish kingdom, Charles Martel in effect concentrated supreme power in his own hands under the last kings of the Merovingian dynasty. In order to continue the centralization of the state and militarily strengthen it, he did away with the previous system of giving land holdings as outright property and began extensively granting land, called benefices, on the basis of conditional tenure; he created a land fund for distribution to the beneficiaries by confiscating the holdings of insubordinate magnates and extensively secularizing church lands. His reforms were an important phase in the development of feudal relations in the Frankish state. Victorious over the Muslims in the battle near Poitiers (732), he subjugated the Frisians and Alemanni. His successes ensured the transition of royal power to the Carolingians (under his son Pepin the Short). [11–1294–1]

CHECKROW PLANTING, a method of sowing agricultural crops in which a few seeds are distributed in each corner of a square (rectangle).

With checkrow planting, plants are more evenly distributed in the field and make better use of the soil and air nutrition and of the sunlight, expenditure of seed is minimized, mechanized work between rows both longitudinally and laterally is facilitated (permitting maintenance of the friability of the soil and eliminating weeds), and manual labor is significantly reduced. Checkrow planting is used for sowing corn, sunflowers, cotton, castor-oil plants, some vegetables, and other crops. In the USSR checkrow planting was first used in 1932–35 for corn (in the Ukrainian SSR). The spacing of clusters and the number of seeds in the cluster is established according to the biological characteristics of the crop, the soil conditions, and the moisture content in the soil. For example, in most regions the cultivation of corn for grain and of sunflower for seed brings best results when the spacing of clusters is 70 cm in each direction and there are two plants per cluster. Tractor-mounted SKNK-4, SKNK-6, SKNK-8, STKh-4A, STKh-4B, and other checkrow seeders are used for planting. Seeds are graded by size and their field germinating capacity is calculated to ensure accurate sowing of the necessary number of plants in a cluster.

S. A. VOROB'EV [11–1676–1]

CHELYDRIDAE, a family of reptiles of the suborder Cryptodira. The turtle's abdominal shell is small and cruciform; the back shell is massive and slightly protuberant. The jaws are powerful and hooked at the ends. The legs are strong, with developed membranes between the toes. There are two genera, each with one species.

The common American snapping turtle (*Chelydra serpentina*) can reach lengths of 90 cm (shell, approximately 40 cm) and weights of 20 kg. It is common in many rivers, lakes, and swamps of America (from southern Canada to Ecuador). It feeds mainly on fish, but sometimes attacks young ducks and geese. It is hunted commercially for its meat. When caught, the turtle defends itself and can inflict tearing wounds with its sharp jaws (hence the name).

The alligator snapper (*Macroclemys temminckii*) is the largest freshwater turtle: it reaches a length of 140 cm (shell, 80 cm) and a weight of 60 kg. It is found in the southern part of the USA. Its meat is valued highly. [11–539–6]

CHESTNUT, an arboreal plant of the genus *Castanea* of the family Fagaceae. There are 14 known species, distributed in North America, Japan, China, and the Mediterranean region. In the USSR, one species is found on the Black Sea Shore of the Caucasus and in Transcaucasia. The European, or Spanish, chestnut (*Castanea sativa*) is cultivated. The chestnut tree is large (height, up to 35 m; diameter, 2 m) and long-lived (500 and more years). It has a large, spreading crown and a strong, deep root system. The flowers, which are gathered into catkins, are small, unisexual or bisexual, and cross-pollinating. The fruits are nuts (length and width, 1.5–3 cm), with a delicate grayish brown woody pericarp. Three nuts are usually found in each involucre.

The tree begins to fruit after 5–10 years. When the tree is 50 years old, it produces at least 70 kg of nuts (up to 1 ton per hectare).

The chestnut is demanding in terms of light, warmth, and moisture. The tree grows best on brown semihumid acid soils. Chestnut trees are cultivated in Italy, Spain, France, and the USA. In the USSR, they are grown in the Caucasus, the Crimea, Transcaucasia, and Moldavia. The nuts are edible in fresh and cooked form. They are used as an ersatz coffee and as an ingredient in candy. The chestnut kernel contains more than 60 percent starch, up to 17 percent sugar, 8–11 percent nitrogen compounds, and over 2 percent fat. Chestnut wood, which is of very high quality is valued in wood-working industries and is also used in construction. It is resistant to rot. The wood, the bark, and the nutshells, which are rich in tanning and dyeing substances, are used in the production of textile dyes. There are several types of chestnut trees; they differ in size, taste of the nut, and rate of growth. In the USSR, there are several varieties, including the large-fruited and small-fruited types. Foreign varieties include the Lyon and the Neapolitan; both have very large and tasty fruits.

Usually chestnuts are propagated by seeds. However, the best varieties are propagated by grafts and cuttings. The seeds are stratified in the autumn and planted in a nursery in the spring. The seedling stocks are then grafted with a fistula or bud. Chestnut trees are grown on slopes in deep, well moistened, fertile soils. Each seedling is planted in an area measuring 18 m × 18 m or 20 m × 20 m. The spaces between the rows are used for temporary plantings (for example, filbert trees). The crown of the chestnut tree is formed by 8–10 boughs and by a trunk measuring 70–80 cm high. The tending of the soil, including its fertilization and irrigation, is very similar to the care of apple orchards. The most dangerous insect pests are the moth and weevil. Chestnut trees are susceptible to several diseases, including root and trunk cancer and core brown rot. Besides the species of the family Fagaceae, there are species of the family Hippocastanaceae that are also called chestnuts, for example, the horse chestnut (*Aesculus hippocastanum*).

REFERENCES
Rikhter, A. A., and V. A. Kolesnikov. *Orekhoplodnye kul'tury.* Simferopol', 1952.
Krotkevich, P. G. *Kul'tury orekhoplodnykh.* Kiev, 1954.
V. A. KOLESNIKOV [11–1665–1]

CHESTNUT SOILS, a soil type occurring in arid steppes. The soils cover large areas of Turkey, Mongolia, northern China, the United States, and Argentina. In the USSR chestnut soils are widely found in the Kazakh SSR, in the southern part of the Ukrainian and Moldavian SSR's, in the Northern Caucasus, in the southern part of Western Siberia (Kulunda), and the arid parts of the Volga Region. Isolated pockets of chestnut soils are encountered in central Siberia (the Minusinsk Depression and the Tuva Basin) and in Transbaikalia. In all, chestnut soils cover about 107 million hectares in the USSR.

The climate in the chestnut soil zone is continental and arid. The genetic and zonal properties of chestnut soils include deficient drainage, a shortage of productive moisture, alkalinity, and soil heterogeneity. The parent material consists chiefly of calcareous deposits with a predominance of loesslike loams, calcareous sandy loams, loesses, calcareous sands, sandy loams, and alluvium. Chestnut soils contain carbonates and, in most cases, gypsum in the lower part of the profile. The presence of readily soluble salts causes the alkalinity of chestnut soils. The upper (humus) horizon has a chestnut color to a depth of 13–25 cm, and its structure is cloddy-granular or cloddy-silty. The absorbing complex is largely saturated with calcium (as much as 70–80 percent) and magnesium (15–30 percent). Nonsolonetzic chestnut soils contain up to 0.2–0.3 percent water-soluble salts, and solonetzic soils contain 0.2–0.3 percent in the upper portion and 0.5–2 percent at a depth of 120–170 cm.

Chestnut soils are divided into three subtypes: dark chestnut, chestnut, and light chestnut, based on differences in the salt profile, humus content and composition, and depth of occurrence of calcareous deposits, gypsum, and readily soluble salts.

The humus content depends on mechanical composition. The dark chestnut clayey and loamy soils contain 3.5–4.5 percent humus and the light loamy and sandy loamy soils 2.5–3 percent; in the chestnut soils, the humus content is 2.5–3.5 and 2.0–2.5 percent, respectively; and in the light chestnut soils it is 1.5–2.5 and 1.2–1.8 percent, respectively.

In their mechanical composition, chestnut soils are subdivided into clayey, heavy loamy, medium loamy, light loamy, sandy loamy, and sandy soils. The solonetzic chestnut soils are distinguished by poor physical properties, such as a rapidly decomposing structure and low porosity and permeability. The reaction of chestnut soils is usually neutral or slightly base (pH 7.0–7.5). Such crops as wheat, barley, oats, millet, corn, and sunflowers are grown on dark chestnut and chestnut soils. On light chestnut soils, used chiefly for pastures and hayfields, farming is possible with irrigation.

REFERENCES
Prasolov, L. I., and I. N. Antipov-Karataev. "Kashtanovye pochvy." *Pochvy SSSR,* vol 1. Moscow-Leningrad, 1939.
Gerasimov, I. P., and M. A. Glazovskaia. *Osnovy pochvovedeniia i geografiia pochv.* Moscow, 1960.
Pochvovedenie. Edited by I. S. Kaurichev and I. P. Grechin. Moscow, 1969.
M. N. PERSHINA [11–1666–1]

CIRQUE, a natural bowl-shaped depression near the summit of a mountain, with steep rocky walls and a sloping concave bottom. It is formed by the action of small glaciers, snow fields, and subsequent frost weathering. Some cirques have permanent glaciers or firn accumulation; others have seasonal accumulations of snow, and very often the cirque bottom is filled with water (high-mountain lakes). [11–1098–6]

CIST (stone chest), a rectangular burial structure consisting of upright stone slabs supporting several roofing slabs. Cists were widely used during the Bronze Age and were associated with different archaeological cultures. They were used for individual and group burials. Barrows were sometimes constructed over the cists. In the USSR, the burial tradition in cists is evident in almost all regions of the Caucasus (until the 19th century in the northern Caucasus) and also in the Crimea, where it was most characteristic of the Tauri. The cists of the Tauri (second half of the first millennium B.C.) contain flexed collective burials; bronze ornaments and beads were found in the burials.

REFERENCES
Krupnov, E. I. *Drevniaia istoriia Severnogo Kavkaza.* Moscow, 1960.
Leskov, A. M. "Rannetavrskie mogil'niki gornogo Kryma." In the collection *Skifo-sarmatskoe vremia.* Leningrad, 1961. Pages 104–13.
[11–769–1]

COAL, HARD, a solid combustible mineral of plant origin; a type of mineral coal with a higher carbon content and greater density than brown coal (lignite). Hard coal is a dense rock of black and sometimes gray-black color with a shiny mat or semimat surface. It contains 75–97 percent and more carbon, 1.5–5.7 percent hydrogen, 1.5–15 percent oxygen, 0.5–4 percent sulfur, up to 1.5 percent nitrogen, and 45–2 percent volatile matter; the amount of moisture varies between 4 percent and 14 percent; ash constitutes usually between 2–4 percent and 45 percent. The highest heat of combustion figured for a moist ashless mass of hard coal is 23.8 megajoules per kg (5,700 kilocalories per kg).

Hard coals are formed from products of the decay of the organic remains of higher plants; these products have undergone changes (metamorphism) under the pressure of surrounding rocks in the earth's crust at comparatively high temperatures. With an increase in the degree of metamorphism in the combustible mass of hard coal the carbon content increases consistently and, at the same time, the amount of oxygen, hydrogen, and volatile matter decreases; there are also changes in the heat of combustion and clinkering capacity. The industrial classification of hard coals by ranks that has been adopted in the USSR is based on changes in these qualities as determined by the results of the thermal decomposition of coal (the discharge of volatile matter and the characteristics of the nonvolatile remainder). The ranks are long flame, or candle (LF); gas, or bottle (G); gas-metabituminous (GF); metabituminous, or fat (F), coking metabituminous (CF); coking (C); lean clinkering (LC); lean (L); weak clinkering (WC); subanthracite (S); and anthracite (A). Anthracite coals are sometimes singled out as a separate group. Coals of ranks G, F, C, LC, and, to some extent, LF and L are generally used for coking. Between coal of rank LF and coal of ranks L–A there is a gradual decrease in moisture in the working fuel from 14 percent in LF coal to 4.5–5.0 percent in ranks L–A; at the same time the oxygen content (in the combustible mass) decreases from 15 percent to 1.5 percent and the hydrogen content drops from percent 5.7 to 1.5 percent. The content of sulfur, nitrogen, and ash does not depend on the rank to which the particular coal belongs. The heat of combustion of the combustible mass of coal rises steadily from 32.4 megajoules (MJ) per kg, or 7,750 kilocalories (kcal) per kg, for rank LF to 36.2–36.6 MJ/kg (8,650–8,750 kcal/kg) for rank C and then decreases to 35.4–33.5 MJ/kg (8,450–8,000 cal/kg) for ranks S and A.

Hard coals are also classified by the size of the pieces obtained during extraction. The categories are slab (S) for more than 100 mm, macrofragmental (M) for 50–100 mm, nut (N) for 26–50 mm, fine (F) for 13–25 mm, seed (S) for 6–13 mm, chip (C) for less than 6 mm, and run-of-mine (R), which is not limited by size. Combinations of letters, such as LM, are used to indicate the rank and size of pieces for the coals.

The classifications of hard coals in a number of western European countries are based on approximately the same principles as those used in the USSR. The United States has the most extensive classification of hard coals, which is based on the release of volatile matter and the heat of combustion. The coals are divided into subbituminous, with a high discharge of volatile matter (corresponding to Soviet ranks LF and G); bituminous with moderate discharge of volatile matter (corresponding Soviet ranks F and C); bituminous with a low discharge of volatile matter (LC and L); and anthracite coals, which are divided into semianthracites (some L and A) and anthracites proper and meta-anthracites (A). In addition, there is an international classification of hard coals based on the content of volatile matter, the clinkering capacity, the coking capacity, and the industrial properties of the coals.

The formation of coal typifies all geological systems since the Silurian and Devonian; coal is very common in the deposits of the Carboniferous, Permian, and Jurassic systems. Coal occurs in the form of seams of varying thickness (from fractions of a meter to several dozen meters and more). The depth at which coals occur may vary; in some cases it emerges on the surface and in others it may occur as deep as 2,000–2,500 m and lower. With the present level of mining technology, coal may be extracted by the open-pit method at depths to 350 m. The total geological reserves of hard coal in the USSR come to about 4,700 billion tons (1968 estimate), which breaks down by rank (in billions of tons) to 1,719 LF, 331 LF–G, 475 G, 69.4 GF, 156 F, 21.5 CF, 105 C, 88.2 LC, 634 WC, 205 L, 540 L–A, and 139 S and A. The largest reserves of hard coal in the USSR are found in the Tunguska Basin. The largest developed coal basins in the USSR are the Donets, Kuznetsk, Pechora, and Karaganda basins. Major basins in other countries include the Appalachian and Pennsylvania Anthracite in the USA; Upper Silesia in Poland and its continuation into Czechoslovakia, the Ostrava-Karvina; the Ruhr in the Federal Republic of Germany; the Greater Hwang Ho Basin in China; South Wales in Great Britain; Valenciennes in France; and Brabant in Belgium. Coal has many uses: as home-heating and power fuel, as raw material for the metal and chemical industries, and for the extraction from the coal itself of rare and dispersed elements.

REFERENCES

Gapeev, A. A. *Tverdye goriuchie iskopaemye.* Moscow, 1949.
Zhemchuzhnikov, Iu. A., and A. I. Ginzburg. *Osnovy petrologii uglei.* Moscow, 1960.
Energeticheskoe toplivo SSSR: Spravochnik. Edited by T. A. Zikeev. Moscow, 1968.   A. K. MATVEEV [11–787–2]

COAL TAR, one of the products of coal coking; a viscous black liquid with a characteristic phenol odor, a density of 1,120–1,250 kg per cu m, and a yield of ~ 3 percent of the coal bulk after coking. Coal tar was originally (in the first half of the 19th century) a waste product of gas production. Numerous aromatic hydrocarbons and their derivatives were later discovered in coal tar and have been used since the second half of the 19th century as raw material in the synthesis of dyes, medicines, and other products.

Coal tar is a complex mixture of heterocyclic aromatic compounds and their derivatives. These compounds boil off over a broad range of temperatures (see Table 1). The composition of coal tar from different plants is uniform, depending less on the coal composition than on the coking conditions. More than 400 individual compounds have been extracted from coal tar, and some of them are produced on an industrial scale. The primary processing of coal tar is carried out at coke by-product plants. The tar is distilled in units that include a tube furnace for heating and evaporation and rectifying columns for separating the distillate into fractions. The individual substances are extracted from the coal tar fractions (see Table 1) either by crystallization or by treatment with reagents (for example, an alkali solution in the extraction of phenols). Among the residues left after extraction are process oils, which are used as the absorbers of benzene products from coking gas, for preserving wood, and in producing lamp black. Pitch (the residue after separating the coal tar into fractions) is used for manufacturing electrode coke and coatings. Coal tar production in the USSR has been growing steadily; the USSR has the highest output and the most complete processing of coal tar in the world.

REFERENCES

Koliandr, L. Ia. *Ulavlivanie i pererabotka khimicheskikh produktov koksovaniia,* 2nd ed. Kharkov, 1962.
Litvinenko, M. S., and I. M. Nosalevich. *Khimicheskie produkty koksovaniia dlia proizvodstva polimernykh materialov.* Kharkov, 1962.
                                        D. D. ZYKOV [11–760–1]

COCKATOO, a bird of the subfamily Kakatoeinae of the family Psittacidae. The body measures 60–95 cm long. A characteristic feature is the crest on the head. Cockatoos are found from the islands of Kalimantan and Flores, the Philippines, and New Guinea to the Solomon Islands, Australia, and Tasmania. There are five genera: *Prosciger, Calyptorhynchus, Callocephalon, Kakatoe,* and *Nymphicus.* These genera comprise 17 species. The birds live in forests, often near fields, and stay in flocks. They eat fruits and seeds, and their powerful beaks are capable of cracking even the very hard fruits of palm trees. In some places cockatoos seriously damage crops. They build their nest in tree hollows or in fissures of cliffs. The large cockatoos lay two or three white

Table 1. Composition of coal tar

Fraction	Output (% of tar bulk)	Boiling point (°C)	Density at 20°C (kg per cu m)	Recoverable substances
Light	0.2–0.8	To 170	900–960	Benzene and its homologues
Phenol	1.7–2.0	170–210	1,000–1,010	Phenols, pyridine bases
Naphthalene	8.0–10.0	210–230	1,010–1,020	Naphthalene, thionaphthene
Heavy (absorbing)	8.0–10.0	230–270	1,050–1,070	Methyl naphthalenes, acenaphthene
Anthracene	20.0–25.0	270–360 (and to 400)	1,080–1,130	Anthracene, phenanthrene, carbazole, others
Pitch	50.0–65.0	Over 360	1,200–1,300	Pyrene and other highly condensed aromatic compounds

eggs; the small birds of the genus *Nymphicus* lay five or six eggs. Cockatoos are often kept in cages. [11–551–2]

COCK OF THE ROCK (*Rupicola rupicola*), a bird of the family Cotingidae of the order Passeriformes. It is up to 30 cm long. The males have bright orange plumage, with black wing and tail feathers, and a crest of feathers on the head. The plumage of the females and young is brownish, and the crest is smaller. The cock of the rock is found in the mountain forests of South America, from Colombia and Guyana to Bolivia. In april, the mating period, the males gather in groups and give the mating call. The nest is built in crevices in cliffs, and the clutch contains two eggs. The bird feeds on fruit. [11–787–1]

COCOA BUTTER, a fatty pale yellow oil with a weak aromatic smell of cocoa; obtained from the beans of the cacao tree. The beans contain up to 50 percent cocoa butter. Cocoa butter contains tristearine and thus has a solid consistency at room temperature. It melts at a temperature of 30°–34°C. Cocoa butter is used in the confectionery industry as well as in the preparation of medicinal suppositories, ointments, and lipstick. Cocoa butter may be replaced by mixtures of hydrogenated fats.

[11–552–1]

COLLATION MAP, a map in which a diagrammatic figure is used to show the total magnitude (and sometimes also the structure and dynamics) of a certain statistical index within each unit of the territorial division shown on the map. For example, a collation map may show the size of the population and its structure for countries, regions, and districts, the gross output of industry and its growth in a certain period, the area of farm land, or the area of forests and differentiation by species. It is important to remember that a collation map does not represent the true location of the phenomenon (population, forests, and so on) within individual territorial units. [11–1424–1]

COMBUSTION CHAMBER, a space for the combustion of gaseous, liquid, or solid fuel. Combustion chambers may be of the intermittent-operation type for two-cycle and four-cycle reciprocating internal-combustion engines or of the continuous-operation type for gas-turbine engines, turbojet engines, air-breathing engines, and liquid-propellant rocket engines.

In reciprocating internal-combustion engines the combustion chamber is usually formed by the interior surface of the cylinder head and the piston head. The combustion chamber of a gas-turbine engine is most often part of the engine; it may be annular, cannular, or tubular. A distinction is made between direct-flow and reverse-flow combustion chambers, depending on the direction of the flow of air and combustion products; reverse-flow combustion chambers are seldom used because of strong hydraulic resistance. The products of combustion pass from the combustion chamber into the gas turbine, but in some engines (augmented turbojet engines, liquid-propellant rocket engines) the products of combustion generate jet thrust as they accelerate in the nozzle behind the combustion chamber.

The basic requirements for all continuous-operation combustion chambers include stability of the combustion process, high thermal stress, maximum completeness of combustion, minimum heat loss, and reliable operation during the rated service life of the engine. The structural materials used in the manufacture of continuous-operation combustion chambers depend on the temperatures to be developed in them: for temperatures up to 500°C, chrome-nickel steels are used; for temperatures up to 900°C, chrome-nickel steels with an admixture of titanium; and for temperatures above 950°C, special materials. Continuous-operation combustion chambers are major elements in aerospace engines and specialized and transportation gas-turbine assemblies, which are widely used in power engineering, the chemical industry, railroad transportation, and river- and oceangoing vessels. I. I. AKOPOV [11–795–1]

COMMERCIAL BANK OF ITALY (Banca Commerciale Italiana), one of the largest joint-stock banks in Italy. Together with the Bank of Rome and the Italian Credit Bank, it is a bank of national significance.

The Commercial Bank of Italy was founded in 1894 in Milan with an initial capital of 20 million lire. German capital owned 75 percent of the shares. During the world economic crisis of 1929–33 the bank was on the verge of bankruptcy but was saved by a governmental subsidy of 5 billion lire, granted on the condition that the government be sold 95 percent of its shares. Since the 1960's these shares have belonged to the state-owned Institute for the Reconstruction of Industry (IRI). By law the bank has the right to give only short-term credit; in giving medium-term credit it acts through Mediobanca, the bank of medium-term credit founded in 1946 by the three banks of national significance. It acts as a go-between in the floating of securities of joint-stock companies, finances foreign trade, and assists in the export of capital. It is closely connected with West German banks.

By 1972 the Commercial Bank of Italy had 283 branches and offices in Italy, one branch in the USA, one in Great Britain, one in Singapore, and two in Turkey and representatives in Paris, Tokyo, Frankfurt am Main, Sydney, Cairo, and Mexico City. It owns a subsidiary bank in Paris with ten branches (1972). Its balance total as of 1972 amounted to 6.73 trillion lire, deposits were 5.733 trillion lire, loans were 3.108 trillion lire, and capital and reserves were 80 billion lire. M. IU. BORTNIK [11–136–1]

COMMUNICATIONS CABLE, a cable used to transmit information by currents of various frequencies. Telegrams, photographs, telephone conversations, sound and television broadcasts, statistical data for computer centers, and signals of telemechanical systems are transmitted through communications cables.

The history of communications cables began almost 150 years ago, soon after the invention of the electric telegraph by the Russian scientist P. L. Shilling in 1832. The current-carrying conductors or telegraph cables were insulated at first with gutta-percha and later with cotton fabric impregnated with an insulating compound; the conductors were twisted together, forming a core. The core was pulled into steel or lead tubing to provide protection against moisture. The use of cores enclosed in a continuous lead sheath began in the late 1870's. Telegraph cables were operated in a single-wire system; the ground was the second conductor.

The manufacture of symmetrical cables for urban telephone exchanges began after the invention of the telephone in 1876. The telephone cables differed from telegraph cables in that they had twisted pair lay-up. To improve signal transmission characteristics, cotton insulation was gradually replaced by dry air-and-paper insulation. The first underground cable conduit systems appeared in cities in 1882. The conduits consisted of concrete-covered steel pipes in which lead-sheathed cables were laid. In the 19th century the number of circuits (pairs) in a telephone cable did not exceed 200. However, the growth of telephone traffic in the cities was accompanied by an increase in the number of circuits per cable. In 1901 a 400-pair cable was manufactured. In 1910 the number of pairs per cable reached 900; in 1932, 2,400; and in 1961, 3,600.

The construction of long-distance telephone lines began in the early 20th century. At that time inventions made by the American engineer M. Pupin and the introduction of electron-tube line repeaters made feasible an increase in the distance of signal transmission by cable. Beginning in 1930, multiplexing and high frequencies were used to increase the traffic rate of communications cables. Coaxial cables, which were capable of transmitting television broadcasts, appeared in the 1930's and 1940's. Until World War II (1939–45), paper was the primary insulation material for communications cables. After the war polymeric materials, such as polyethylene and polystyrene, became predominant. As a rule, the current-carrying conductors of symmetrical cables are single copper wires with a diameter of 0.3–1.6 mm. The insulated conductors of symmetrical cables are twisted into pairs (one circuit) or into quads (two circuits). The number of pairs in symmetrical low-frequency cables ranges from one to 3,600 (in experimental cables, up to 4,800); in coaxial cables, from two to 20 (each pair can transmit up to 3,600 telephone conversations).

Communications cables are made with six types of sheathing. Metal sheaths are made of lead, smooth or corrugated aluminum, or corrugated steel. Plastic sheaths are made of polyethylene or polyvinyl chloride; metal-plastic sheaths are made of alumopolyethylene. Adjacent sections of communications cables are joined in cable junction boxes; cables are connected to communications equipment through cable distribution boxes.

Communications cables are classified according to design (symmetrical and coaxial), the range of transmission frequencies f (low-frequency, where $f < 10$ kHz, or high-frequency, where $f > 10$ kHz), sphere of use (for long-distance lines or for local urban and rural exchanges, for radio broadcasting, and for communications in mines), and the properties of the cable run (underground cables, cables laid in trenches or conduit systems; overhead, or suspension, cables; and underwater cables, which are divided into two groups—cables laid on the bottom of rivers, canals, and lakes and cables laid in seas or oceans at a great depth by a cable ship for long-distance, overseas, or intercontinental communications lines).

REFERENCES
Kuleshov, V. N. *Teoriia kabelei sviazi.* Moscow, 1950.
Grodnev, I. I., P. M. Lakernik, and D. L. Sharle. *Osnovy teorii i proizvodstvo kabelei sviazi.* Moscow-Leningrad, 1959.
Konstruktivnye i elektricheskie kharakteristiki kabelei sviazi. Moscow, 1959.
Grodnev, I. I., and K. Ia. Sergeichuk. *Ekranirovanie apparatury i kabelei sviazi.* Moscow-Leningrad, 1960.
Gordnev, I. I. *Kabeli sviazi.* Moscow-Leningrad, 1965.
Inzhenerno-tekhnicheskii spravochnik po elektrosviazi: Kabel'nye i vozdushnye linii sviazi, 3rd ed. Moscow, 1966.
Shvartsman, V. O. *Vzaimnye vliianiia v kabeliakh sviazi.* Moscow, 1966.
Mikhailov, M. I., and L. D. Razumov. *Zashchita kabel'nykh linii sviazi ot vliianiia vneshnikh elektromagnitnykh polei.* Moscow, 1967.

D. L. SHARLE [11–282–1]

COMMUNICATIONS CABLE JUNCTION BOX, a device used to connect adjoining sections of communications cables. Among the specialized types of junction boxes are balancing boxes, in which special measures are taken to increase the protection of the cable circuits against mutual influence; coil-loaded boxes, in which all or some of the spliced conductors are connected by inductance coils, gas-tight boxes, which keep the cable under a constant excess pressure, thus monitoring the integrity of sheating; and insulating boxes, which, at the required points, provide a break in the circuit formed by the metal sheathing of a cable to protect the cable line against dangerous external currents and voltages. [11–286–1]

COMMUNICATIONS CHANNEL, the engineering devices and communications circuit in which signals containing data propagate from a transmitter to a receiver. The engineering devices (electrical signal amplifiers and devices for encoding and decoding the signals) are located at intermediate (repeater) stations and the terminal stations of the channel. The communications circuit may be various kinds of lines such as aerial and cable wires, radio and radio-relay links, and wave guides. The transmitter converts the messages into signals, which are fed to the input of the communications circuit; from the signal received at the channel's output, the receiver reproduces the transmitted messages. The transmitter, communications circuit, and receiver constitute a communications system, or a data-transmission system.

A distinction is made among telephone, sound-broadcasting, television, facsimile, telegraph, telemetry, remote-control, and digital data-transmission channels, depending on the purpose of the system of which the communications channel is a part; depending on the type of signals transmitted by the channels, they may be classified as continuous or discrete with respect to both values and time. A communications channel usually has a large number of inputs and outputs and is called a multiplexed channel; it can provide two-way signal transmission.

REFERENCE
Nazarov, M. V., B. I. Kuvshinov, and O. V. Popov. *Teoriia peredachi signalov.* Moscow, 1970. [11–929–2]

COMPARTMENT FURNACES, the general name for a group of industrial furnaces in which the products remain stationary relative to the furnace during the heating period. Compartment furnaces are used for heating metal stock before rolling and forging, for heat treatment of metal and glass articles, and for baking ceramic and enamel ware. They are classified according to design and construction as updraft furnaces, cover furnaces, heat-treatment furnaces, car furnaces, and pit furnaces. If several articles are placed in a compartment furnace at the same time but are loaded and unloaded one by one, the temperature of the furnace is constant. Under complex treatment conditions, when the articles must be heated or cooled at a specific rate, the temperature of the furnace is controlled accordingly.

Compartment furnaces are heated by gas or liquid fuel. Heat-treatment furnaces, which operate with a controlled atmosphere, are heated by electric resistance heaters or radiant piping. Electric heating is often suitable for ensuring precise operating conditions and for heating with an uncontrolled atmospheric composition. Fixed hearth compartment furnaces, which are used in forge shops, are the most common type. The melting chamber of such furnaces is in the shape of a parallelepiped 0.6–2.0 m long, 0.6–1.5 m wide, and up to 1 m high. Furnace capacity is 70–600 kg/hr, with a heat consumption of 5,000–7,000 kilojoules per kg.

REFERENCE
Grissik, A. M. "Osnovnye napravleniia razvitiia plamennykh nagrevatel'nykh i termicheskikh pechei mashinostroitel'noi promyshlennosti i raboty instituta 'Teploproekt' v etoi oblasti." In the collection *Plamennye pechi i sushila mashinostroitel'noi promyshlennosti.* Moscow, 1966. Pages 3–13. [11–799–1]

CONSTITUTIONAL DEMOCRATS (Cadets), members of the Constitutional Democratic Party. The party's official name was People's Freedom Party.

The Cadets were the chief party of the counterrevolutionary liberal-monarchist bourgeoisie in Russia. The party was formed during the course of the 1905–07 revolution in Russia. The founding congress of the Cadets, which adopted a program and a set of party rules, was held in Moscow, Oct. 12–18, 1905. The formation of the party followed the activity of the liberal bourgeois Union of Liberation and Union of Zemstvo Constitutionalists; these two groups provided the central core for the new party. The party was definitively established at its second congress in St. Petersburg, Jan. 5–11, 1906, at which its program was made more precise and a permanent Central Committee was elected. (The first congress, because of its small attendance, had only elected a temporary Central Committee.) Among the chief figures in the Cadet leadership were P. N. Miliukov, A. M. Koliubakin, V. A. Maklakov, A. I. Shingarev, P. B. Struve, F. I. Rodichev, I. V. Gessen, A. I. Kaminka, V. D. Nabokov, Prince Pavel D. Dolgorukii, Prince Petr D. Dolgorukii, M. M. Vinaver, A. A. Kornilov, Prince D. I. Shakhovskoi, and I. I. Petrunkevich. In 1906 the party had 70,000–100,000 members. Representatives of the bourgeois intelligentsia predominated on the Central Committee—lawyers, professors, literary figures, *zemstvo* (local government) activists, and liberal landowners. The newspaper *Rech',* which in fact became the central organ of the party, began publication in February 1906. The third and fourth congresses of the party were also held in 1906, the third in St. Petersburg, April 21–25, and the fourth at Helsinki, September 23–28. The fifth congress was held in Helsinki, Oct. 23–25, 1907. No further congresses were called until 1916.

The Cadet program adopted in October 1905 left open the question of what form the state should take. (Paragraph 13 stated: "The constitutional structure of the Russian state is determined by its basic laws.") But three months later, when the situation had changed and the defeat of the revolution was under way, the second Cadet congress made this formula more precise: "Russia should be a constitutional and parliamentary monarchy," with ministers responsible to the "representatives of the people," that is, a one-chamber or two-chamber parliament elected on the basis of universal suffrage. The program included demands for bourgeois freedoms, such as freedom of speech, freedom of conscience, freedom of assembly, freedom of movement, and the inviolability of one's home and person. The agrarian part of the program provided for the distribution of state lands, crown lands (*udel'nye* and *kabinetnye*), and church and monastery lands to peasants with little or no land, and for the partial alienation of privately owned land through purchase at "equitable, not market, prices." On labor matters, the program called for the extension of labor legislation to all forms of wage labor, the gradual introduction ("insofar as is possible") of the eight-hour day, the right of workers to strike and form unions, and compulsory government insurance, "with the costs to be carried by the employers." Special attention was paid to enlarging the rights of the *zemstvos*, extending such units of local self-government throughout the country, and creating smaller units of self-government. On the national question, the Cadets demanded the right for non-Russians to use their own languages in public life, as well as autonomy for Poland and Finland within the empire. The relatively radical character of the program is explained by the fact that the party was formed at the culminating phase of the revolution, when the revolutionary spirit of the masses was at its height, and the Cadets aimed at influencing these masses and drawing them along behind them. The Cadets' aspiration to fill the role of "leader of the nationwide opposition" was based on their mistaken assumption of the peasantry's political backwardness and a conviction peculiar to liberal bourgeois intellectuals in general that they represent the interests of the nation as a whole, "above classes."

The Cadets' chief thesis was the categorical rejection of revolution, to which they counterposed the path of "peaceful" and "constitutional" development for Russia. Their aim was to "bring the revolutionary chaos under control" and guide it into the channels of "normal social reform." Until the Manifesto of October 17, 1905, the liberal bourgeoisie in part regarded the revolutionary movement as justified, with certain reservations, and even sympathized with it, attempting to frighten the tsarist regime by revolution and hoping to make a deal with it in order to win a "constitution" at the expense of the people. The Manifesto of October 17, in the Cadets' opinion, signified the realization of the revolution's goals and the beginning of "an era of creative parliamentary work." After the armed insurrections of December 1905 the Cadets made a sharp turn to the right. They protested against the "tyranny of the revolution" and condemned the "madness of armed insurrection" and tactics of "extremists," especially of the revolutionary Social Democrats.

The Cadets used the State Duma as the arena for their political activity. The victory of the Cadets in the elections to the First State Duma in 1906 was assured by the constitutional illusions of the broad layers of the democratically minded voters (especially the peasants), who, because of the boycott of the Duma elections by the Social Democrats and the Socialist Revolutionaries (SR's), gave their votes to the Cadets as the only opposition party. Of the 478 deputies, the Cadet Duma group numbered 179 and became the directing center of the Duma. The Cadet S. A. Muromtsev became president of the Duma. In the spring of 1906 the Cadets entered into secret negotiations with the government in regard to assuming ministerial offices. Speculating on the fear of the Trudoviks (the Toilers group of deputies in the Duma) that the Duma would be dispersed, the Cadets demanded that the former pursue a moderate policy and repudiate any conflicts with the government. The Cadets tried to win over the Trudoviks through a draft agrarian law (the draft of the 42). However, the Trudoviks rejected it, introducing their own draft law (that of the 104). The Cadets' policies in the Duma brought about a sharp decline in their influence among the masses. In an attempt to shore up their prestige and to avert a call by the left-wing parties for revolutionary action in response to the dissolution of the Duma, a group of the Cadet deputies signed the Vyborg Appeal in July 1906. This called on the population to offer passive resistance to the government. But two months later the Fourth Congress of the Constitutional Democratic Party opposed any attempt to implement the appeal.

In the Second Duma the Cadet representation was reduced by almost half (98 deputies out of 518), but as a result of the waverings of the Trudoviks, the Cadets maintained their position as the "center." The right-wing Cadet F. A. Golovin was elected president of the Duma. Under the conditions of the further decline of the revolution, the Cadets' politics took on a more and more moderate and counterrevolutionary character. "There is no longer any of last year's vacillation between reaction and the struggle of the people," wrote Lenin in characterizing the rightward evolution of the Cadets. "This has yielded to frank hatred for this struggle, a cynically outspoken ambition to put a stop to the revolution" (*Poln. sobr. soch.,* 5th ed., vol. 15, p. 20). The Cadets' capitulatory policies made it easier for the government to dissolve the Second Duma and carry out the June 3, 1907, coup d'etat. This betrayal of the people's interests exposed the Cadets conclusively in the eyes of the masses. Any elements whatsoever of a democratic tendency at that point abandoned the party.

In the period of reaction after June 3 the Cadet party went through a state of crisis and collapse. As Miliukov acknowledges, the Cadets ceased to exist as an organizational unit. At the fifth congress they decided against any independent drafting of legislation and took the road of "seriously criticizing" the draft legislation of the government and "introducing improvements in it." Their fifth congress resolved that the Cadets should enter into a bloc with the Octobrists in the Third Duma and "decisively rebuff" the leftists should they try to undermine the work of the Duma. The Cadets described their role in the Third Duma, in which they were a minority (54 deputies), as that of the "responsible" opposition, as distinct from the "irresponsible" opposition of the Social Democrats, who used the Duma for propaganda purposes. In 1909 the Cadets took part in the ideological offensive of the reaction against revolution and democracy, contributing to the renegade collection *Vekhi.* In the summer of 1909, at a luncheon given by the lord mayor of London, Miliukov declared: "so long as there is a legislative chamber in Russia controlling the budget, the Russian opposition will remain His Majesty's opposition, and not an opposition to His Majesty." This declaration was approved by a Cadet conference in November 1909.

The new revolutionary upsurge, the deepening crisis of the ruling circles, the legislative paralysis of the Duma, and the fear of becoming completely isolated from the masses in the event of a new revolution—all these things together forced the Cadets to adopt a more "leftist" tone in the Fourth Duma. They introduced legislation for universal suffrage, reform of the State Council, and bourgeois freedoms, condemned the policies of the Ministry of Domestic Affairs, and carried out other similar activities. In 1913 the Cadet leaders were forced to acknowledge that the solution to political problems lay not in the Duma but in "rapprochement with the masses." However, as before, the liberal bourgeoisie feared the revolutionary movement of the masses more than they did the reaction. Thus, the Cadets continued to place their main hopes in the Duma on a bloc with the Octobrists.

World War I set aside for the moment the contradictions between the liberal bourgeoisie and the autocracy. The Cadets solemnly declared their "unity" with the government and proclaimed the need to set aside all "differences" until the war had been victoriously concluded. The defeats on the battlefront, the corruption of the tsarist regime, the prospect of total military collapse, and the deepening of the revolutionary situation in the country revived and strengthened the oppositional mood not only among the bourgeoisie but also among the landlords. In 1915 the Cadets played a decisive role in the formation of the so-called Progressive Bloc in the Duma (consisting of Cadets, Octobrists, Progressives, and others). The Bloc's program (calling for a "government of public confidence" and a minimum of liberal reforms) was aimed at warding off the imminent revolution and carrying the war "to a victorious conclusion."

The February Revolution of 1917 abruptly changed the Cadets' situation. They began to play a leading role in the first bourgeois Provisional Government, in which the Cadets Miliukov, Shingarev, N. V. Nekrasov, and A. A. Manuilov were ministers. "The Cadet party," Lenin noted, "the chief capitalist party, held pride of place as the ruling and government party of the bourgeoisie" (*Poln. sobr. soch.,* 5th ed., vol. 34, p. 58). Having come to power, the Cadets did everything they could to prevent the resolution of the agrarian and national questions or any other fundamental question of the revolution. They favored continuation of the war. Their seventh congress, held in Petrograd, Mar. 25–28 (Apr. 7–10), 1917, taking the antimonarchist mood of the masses into account, declared that "Russia must be a democratic republic." In 1917 the Constitutional Democratic Party had no more than 50,000 members.

The imperialist foreign policy of Miliukov's ministry aroused sharp protests on the part of the revolutionary masses during the April Crisis of 1917. The leaders of the bourgeoisie saw their way out of the crisis by forming a coalition government with the SR's and Mensheviks on May 5 (18). The Cadet ministers in the government were Shingarev, Nekrasov, Manuilov, and Shakhovskoi. The eighth congress of the Constitutional Democratic Party, held in Petrograd, May 9–12 (22–25), declared "full support for the new Provisional Government." However, on July 2 (15), as the political situation reached a point of extreme tension, the Cadets left the government, calculating that by the threat of destroying the coalition they could force the SR-Menshevik leadership of the soviets to take the road of openly suppressing the mass movement and establishing a "strong authority." Having eliminated dual power and established, with the aid of the compromisers, the single rule of the bourgeoisie, the Cadets entered the newly formed coalition government on July 24 (August 6) with F. F. Kokoshkin, S. F. Ol'denburg, P. P. Iurenev, and A. V. Kartashev as ministers. The ninth congress of the Cadets (Moscow-Petrograd, July 23–28 [August 5–10]) steered a course toward a counterrevolutionary coup and establishment of a military dictatorship. The Cadets demanded the dissolution of the Bolshevik Party and organized a new slander campaign against the Bolsheviks and Lenin.

The collapse of the Kornilov revolt laid bare the counterrevolutionary nature of the Cadets as the "main Kornilovite party" (Lenin, *op. cit.,* p. 217) and greatly weakened their position. The SR-Menshevik leaders arrived at a new agreement with the Cadets, with the result that the last Provisional Government (formed on September 25 [October 8]) had the following Cadet ministers: A. I. Konovalov, N. M. Kishkin, S. A. Smirnov, and A. V. Kartashev. In the face of the oncoming revolution, the Cadets intensified their activities in mobilizing counterrevolutionary forces and began to prepare for a new attempt at a Kornilov-type coup. This political line was confirmed by the decisions of the tenth congress of the Constitutional Democratic Party in Moscow, October 14–16 (27–29). The October Socialist Revolution frustrated the Cadets' plans. On Nov. 28 (Dec. 11), 1917, the Soviet government issued a decree declaring the Cadets to be a "party of enemies of the people." Members of the leading bodies of the party were subject to arrest and trial before a revolutionary tribunal. The Cadets went underground and continued their bitter struggle against Soviet power. Cadet leaders led a number of underground anti-Soviet centers, such as the National Center and the League of Restoration. They collaborated with the White Guard generals Kaledin, Kolchak, Denikin, and Wrangel and took part in a number of White Guard governments.

After the defeat of the White Guards and interventionists, most of the leading Cadet elements fled abroad. At a conference of Central Committee members of the party, held in Paris in May 1921, a split occurred. Miliukov appeared at the head of the so-called democratic group, which held that the essence of a "new tactic" should be that of undermining the proletarian dictatorship from within. In 1924, Miliukov's group formed the Republican-Democratic Association. The other Cadet group, headed by Gessen and Kaminka, which continued to support the "invading from outside" stand, centered on the newspaper *Rul'.* The Cadet party as a unified political organization had definitively ceased to exist.

REFERENCES

Lenin, V. I. *Poln. sobr. soch.,* 5th ed. (See Index vol., part 1, pp. 212–17.)
V. I. Lenin i istoriia klassovykh politicheskikh partii v Rossii. Moscow, 1970.
Chermenskii, E. D. *Burzhuaziia i tsarizm v pervoi russkoi revoliutsii,* 2nd ed. Moscow, 1970.
Komin, V. V. *Bankrotstvo burzhuaznykh i melkoburzhuaznykh partii Rossii v period podgotovki i pobedy Velikoi Oktiabr'skoi sotsialisticheskoi revoliutsii.* Moscow, 1965.
Oktiabr'skoe vooruzhennoe vosstanie: Semnadtsatyi god v Petrograde, books 1–2. Leningrad, 1967.
Spirin, L. M. *Klassy i partii v grazhdanskoi voine v Rossii (1917–1920 gg.).* Moscow, 1968.   A. IA. AVREKH and N. F. SLAVIN [11–369–2]

CONTACT, the geometric concept signifying that at a certain point, two curves (or a curve and a surface) have a common tangent line or two surfaces have a common tangent plane. The order of contact is a characteristic of the proximity of two curves (a curve and a surface, or two surfaces) in the neighborhood of their common point.   [11–1469–5]

CONTRIBUTION TO THE CRITIQUE OF POLITICAL ECONOMY, A, the work by K. Marx that, along with the first volume of *Das Kapital* (1867), marked a revolutionary turn in political economy. It was published in 1859. The writing of the work followed the economic research that Marx did from 1850 to 1858. Among his economic manuscripts of 1857–59, there are fragments of the initial text of the first installment of *A Contribution to the Critique of Political Economy,* as well as a draft plan for the projected third chapter (see K. Marx and F. Engels, *Soch.,* 2nd ed., vol. 46, part 2, pp. 407–96, 513–21). In the second Russian edition of the works of Marx and Engels, *A Contribution to the Critique of Political Economy* was included in Volume 13.

In the preface of *A Contribution to the Critique of Political Economy,* Marx gave a classic characterization of the materialist conception of history. He pointed out that in social production, people enter into specific relations of production, relations that do not depend upon their will and that correspond to a particular phase of development of the productive forces. "The totality of these relations of production constitutes the economic structure of society, the real foundation, upon which the legal and political superstructure is erected and to which correspond definite forms of social consciousness. . . . It is not the consciousness of men that determines their existence, but their social existence that determines their consciousness. At a certain stage of development of society, the material productive forces of society come into conflict with the existing relationships of production or—this merely expresses the same thing in legal terms—with the property relations within the framework of which they have operated hitherto. From forms of development of the productive forces these relations turn into their fetters. Then begins an era of social revolution" (*ibid.,* vol. 13, pp. 6–7). Bourgeois relations of production are the last antagonistic form of the social process of production. But at the same time, the productive forces developing in the womb of bourgeois society create the material conditions for resolving this antagonism. "The prehistory of human society accordingly closes with this social formation" (*ibid.,* p. 8). Looking primarily at capitalism, Marx wrote that "no social order is ever destroyed before all the productive forces for which it is sufficient have been developed" (*ibid.,* p. 7).

In a review of *A Contribution to the Critique of Political Economy,* Engels noted that "to the highest degree, revolutionary conclusions not only for theory, but for practice as well," follow from the materialist conception of history (*ibid.,* p. 491). In this work by Marx, the foundations for the analysis of the capitalist mode of production were laid. Marx regarded the exploration of the commodity cell of capitalism and its further development in the form of money as a prerequisite for the analysis of capital and surplus value, the analysis of the relations of production of capitalism in their entirety.

The analysis of the two aspects of a commodity, use value and value, requires the examination of the dual nature of the labor that creates the commodity. Marx showed that one of the features of labor under the conditions of private property is that the social relations between people present themselves as relationships among things. Value emerges as a relationship among commodity owners, a relationship hidden under a material shell.

In the preface to the first volume of *Das Kapital,* Marx noted that he had summarized the content of *A Contribution to the*

Critique of Political Economy in the first section of *Das Kapital:* "many points only hinted at in the earlier book are here worked out more fully, whilst, conversely, points worked out fully there are only touched upon in this volume" (*ibid.*, vol. 23, p. 5). Thus, in *A Contribution to the Critique of Political Economy,* Marx did not yet trace the development of forms of value from simple value to cash value. Generally, he used the same term, "exchange value," to express both value and exchange value. The analysis of the two extremes of the expression of value—the comparative form of value and equivalent value—is also lacking here. On the other hand, the information contained in *A Contribution to the Critique of Political Economy* on the theory of money is more extensive than the corresponding sections of the first volume of *Das Kapital.* In the former, Marx shows that money is of necessity engendered by circulation itself. In the role that money plays, there begins to function a special commodity whose natural characteristics enable it to serve as an adequate entity of value and to act as the embodiment of social labor in the exchange process among private commodity producers. Gold and silver are used as money and have value not because they fulfill a particular function, but because they are products of labor. Money is the most developed expression of value, the result of the contradiction between concrete and abstract labor and between use value and value that is inherent in a commodity. In this form, private labor appears as social labor.

Having analyzed the various functions of money (as a measure of value, a means of circulation, a means of forming treasuries, a means of payment, and an international measure of value), Marx showed that all of them develop along with the development of the capitalist mode of production. Thus, the function of money as a means of payment expands with the development of bourgeois production, at the expense of its function as a means of purchase (means of circulation); and as the boundaries of domestic circulation are broken through, with the formation of the world market, money increasingly plays the role of an international measure of value, a universal means of exchange. Marx formulated the law that determines the quantity of money essential for normal circulation and established the dependence of a mass of circulating money on commodity prices, on the rates of circulation, and on the sum of reciprocally canceled payments.

In this work, Marx completed the critical analysis of the petit bourgeois, utopian theories of "workers' money" developed by J. Gray, J. F. Bray, and other English socialists, as well as by P. J. Proudhon and his followers. Marx showed that the abstract possibility of crisis is contained in the very form of money. For this possibility to become a reality, a transition from simple commodity production to capitalist production is necessary. With this transition, the contradiction between private and social labor that is inherent in the commodity develops into a more developed form—the contradiction between the social nature of production and the private capitalist mode of appropriation. Only under the conditions of the capitalist mode of production does the abstract possibility of crises become a reality. The economic theories of Marx, published in their mature form for the first time in *A Contribution to the Critique of Political Economy,* ideologically armed and rallied the working class in its struggle against the bourgeoisie and against the foundations of the capitalist system.

REFERENCES

Leont'ev, L. A. *O rabote K. Marksa "K kritike politicheskoi ekonomii" (1859–1959)*. Moscow, 1959.
Malysh, A. I. *Formirovanie marksistskoi politicheskoi ekonomii.* Moscow, 1966. Pages 331–49.   V. S. Vygodskii [11–241–2]

CORPORAL, military rank of noncommissioned officers in various foreign armies (the US, Great Britain, France, Italy, and others). In the Russian Army, the rank of corporal is referred to as early as 1647; it was officially introduced by the Military Regulations of Peter I. In the first half of the 19th century it was replaced by the military rank of noncommissioned officer.

[11–1077–1]

COSSACK (Turkic, "a daring, free man"), a person who broke with his social environment (14th to 17th century); at the end of

the 15th century the term "cossack" was applied to the free people living at the edges of the Russian state.   [11–390–1]

COSSACKS, a military estate in prerevolutionary Russia from the 18th to the early 20th century.

From the 14th to the 17th century the cossacks were free people, exempt from taxes and working for hire, primarily in various trades; also called cossacks were people who performed military service in outlying areas of the country and the so-called free cossacks. Military-service cossacks were divided into city, or regimental, and *stanitsa* (large cossack village), or outpost, cossacks and were utilized for the defense of cities and outposts respectively, in return for which they received lands from the government on the condition of service tenure, as well as a salary. As a social group, the cossacks were similar to the *strel'tsy* (semiprofessional musketeers) and artillerymen. During the 18th and 19th centuries a large proportion of these cossacks were transferred into a tax-paying estate and entered the category of *odnodvortsy;* others entered the cossack hosts (the Siberian, Orenburg, and other hosts).

The growth of feudal exploitation and serfdom in the Russian and Polish-Lithuanian states during the 15th and 16th centuries and the redoubled national-religious oppression in the Ukraine, which has been seized by Poland, resulted in the mass flight of peasants and *posadskie liudi* (merchants and artisans) beyond the boundaries of these states—primarily to the unoccupied lands in the south. As a result, from the second half of the 15th century fugitive peasants and *posadskie liudi* who called themselves free people—cossacks—settled beyond the line of fortified outposts on the southern and southeastern outskirts of Russia and the Ukraine, essentially along the Dnieper, Don, and Iaik rivers and their tributaries.

The necessity of waging a constant struggle against the neighboring feudal states and seminomadic peoples required that all these people unite into military communities. In the 15th and early 16th centuries, communities of Don, Volga, Dnieper (Cherkassy), Greben', and Iaik cossacks emerged. The Zaporozh'e Sech arose in the first half of the 16th century, and the communities of Terek Cossacks and the military-service Siberian Cossacks originated in the second half of the 16th century. In the second half of the 16th century the Polish government, seeking to utilize the upper elements of the Ukrainian cossacks in its own interests, created the category of registered cossacks, who were on salary, and attempted to transfer the remaining cossacks into tax-paying estates and enserf them. The rapidly increasing Ukrainian cossacks constituted the leading force in the popular uprisings against Polish rule in the Ukraine in the late 16th century and first half of the 17th century and especially in the War of Liberation of the Ukrainian People of 1648–54, which was led by Bogdan Khmel'nitskii. In the mid-17th century the *Sloboda* (tax-exempt settlement) Cossacks were formed in the eastern part of the Ukraine, which was ceded to Russia.

Initially, hunting, fishing, and honey gathering made up the foundation of the economic life of the cossacks. Livestock raising appeared comparatively early; farming, as a rule, began to spread later, roughly from the second half of the 17th century. During the 16th and 17th centuries war booty and state stipends were important sources of the livelihood of the cossacks. The cossacks rapidly brought under cultivation vast expanses of the fertile lands of the Dikoe Pole and other borderlands of Russia and the Ukraine.

During the 16th and 17th centuries under the leadership of Ermak, V. V. Atlasov, S. I. Dezhnev, V. D. Poiarkov, E. P. Khabarov, and others, the cossacks participated actively in opening up Siberia and the Far East to Russians. In the 16th century and the first half of the 17th century the tsarist government did not have sufficient forces to subjugate the "free" cossacks, but it strove to utilize them to defend the boundaries of the state, sending them stipends, ammunition, and grain. This policy facilitated the gradual transformation of the cossacks into a special privileged military estate (a process that became finalized in the 19th century) whose position was determined by the fact that in exchange for service to the state, each cossack host was allotted land, which it occupied and which was turned over for the use of the cossack *stanitsy*. This feudal form of land tenure was retained up to the October Revolution.

From the very beginning the cossacks were heterogeneous. In the process of social differentiation the number of poor cossacks (*golyt'ba*, *netiagi*, and others) increased, and these cossacks participated actively in the peasant wars and uprisings of the 17th and 18th centuries. At the same time, a wealthy upper element emerged from the midst of the "thrifty" cossacks. This upper element captured the leadership position in the cossack communities, forming the group of elders (*starshina*). By the beginning of the 19th century the elders had become part of the *dvorianstvo* (nobility or gentry) of Russia.

During the 16th and 17th centuries the cossacks enjoyed autonomy in the spheres of law, administration, and foreign relations. All the most important matters were discussed by general assemblies of the cossacks (the *rada* and the *krug*), whose decisions were influenced to a certain degree by the masses of the rank and file. The tsarist government, drawing its support from the prosperous cossacks and elders, gradually (particularly from the early 18th century) began to restrict the autonomy of the cossack regions, seeking to subjugate the cossacks completely to the central authorities.

In the 17th and 18th centuries broad strata of cossacks persistently defended their freedom against the encroachments of the tsarist government. The freedom-loving cossacks were one of the primary moving forces behind the peasant wars and uprisings of the 17th and 18th centuries. Their ranks produced such outstanding leaders in the struggle against feudalism as S. T. Razin, K. A. Bulavin, and E. I. Pugachev.

At the beginning of the 18th century cossack communities were transformed into irregular cossack hosts. In 1721 they came under the jurisdiction of the war department. Elections for the atamans and elders of the hosts were gradually eliminated; the government began to appoint them. After the Peasant War of 1773–75 led by E. I. Pugachev, the Zaporozh'e Sech was eliminated, and the Don, Ural (formerly the Iaik), and other hosts were once and for all subordinated to the war department. In the second half of the 18th and the 19th century a number of cossack hosts were eliminated and new ones, completely subordinated to the government, were created (the Astrakhan Host in 1750; Orenburg Host in 1755; Black Sea Host in 1787; Siberian Host in 1808; Caucasus Border Host in 1832, divided in 1860 along with the Black Sea Host into the Kuban' and Terek hosts; the Transbaikal Host in 1851; Amur Host in 1858; Semirech'e Host in 1867; and Ussuri Host in 1889). These hosts played a significant role in colonizing the sparsely settled outlying areas (Siberia, the Far East, Semirech'e, and parts of the Northern Caucasus) and in spreading farming.

By the early 20th century there were 11 cossack hosts in Russia (the Don, Kuban', Terek, Astrakhan, Ural, Orenburg, Semirech'e, Siberian, Transbaikal, Amur, and Ussuri hosts). In addition, there were a small number of Krasnoiarsk and Irkutsk cossacks, who in 1917 formed the Enisei Cossack Host and the Yakut Cossack Regiment of the Ministry of Internal Affairs.

Table 1. Total cossack population and cossacks in military service in 1916

Cossack host	Population	In military service
Don	1,495,000	about 100,000
Kuban'	1,367,000	about 90,000
Orenburg	533,000	27,000
Transbaikal	265,000	14,500
Terek	255,000	18,000
Siberian	172,000	11,500
Ural (in 1917, Iaik)	166,000	11,500
Amur	49,000	3,500
Semirech'e	45,000	3,500
Astrakhan	40,000	2,500
Ussuri	34,000	2,500
Enisei Cossacks (Irkutsk and Krasnoiarsk)	about 10,000	600
Yakut Regiment	about 3,000	300
Total	about 4,434,000	about 285,400

All cossack hosts and regions settled by the cossacks were militarily and administratively subordinated to the Main Directorate of Cossack Hosts; from 1910 they were subordinate to the Cossack Section of the Main Headquarters of the War Ministry, headed by the ataman of all cossack hosts, who was the heir to the throne from 1827. At the head of each host stood the appointed ataman; under him there was a host staff, which managed the affairs of the host through appointed atamans of sections or district atamans (the latter in the Don and Amur hosts). *Stanitsa* and *khutor* (smaller settlement) atamans were elected at assemblies.

The male cossack population 18 years of age and over was obligated to perform military service for 20 years (by the statute of 1875 for the Don Host, later extended to other hosts), including three years in the "preparatory" ranks; 12 years in the "combat" ranks, of which four years were spent in active service (first line) and eight years on "privilege" (second and third line) with periodic summer encampments; and five years in the reserves. In 1909 the period of service was reduced to 18 years by decreasing the "preparatory" ranks to one year. A cossack was obliged to appear for military service with his own uniform, equipment, silent weapons, and saddle horse.

On the eve of World War I (1914–18) in peacetime the cossacks put forward 54 horse cavalry regiments, 23 batteries, six infantry reconnaissance battalions, 11 detached troops, four detached squadrons, and the imperial escort (a total of 68,500 men). In wartime (by 1917) the cossacks presented 164 horse cavalry regiments, 54 batteries, 30 dismounted battalions, 179 detached troops, 78 half-troops, nine horse cavalry and infantry squadrons, 63 reserve troops and three and a half reserve batteries, and the imperial escort (a total of more than 200,000 men).

Because of their fine combat training and military traditions, cossack forces played an important role in Russia's wars of the 18th and 19th centuries, particularly in the Seven Years' War of 1756–63, the Patriotic War of 1812, the Caucasian War of 1817–64, the Crimean War of 1853–56, and the Russo-Turkish War of 1877–78. In the late 19th and early 20th centuries, relying on the economic prosperity of the cossacks, their privileged status as a military estate, and their political backwardness, tsarism employed them extensively to perform police service and suppress the national liberation and revolutionary movement, particularly in the period of the Revolution of 1905–07.

The basis for the enlistment of cossacks into military service and police functions was the system of land tenure that took its final shape in the cossack regions in the 19th century. A statute of 1869 consolidated communal ownership of the *stanitsa* (yurt) lands, from which each cossack was allotted one "share" of 30 *desiatiny* (one *desiatina* equals 1.09 hectares; in practice, plots averaged between 9 and 23 *desiatiny*). The remaining land constituted a reserve for the host, intended primarily to replenish the parcels of the *stanitsa* as the cossack population grew. In 1916, 63 million *desiatiny* were at the disposal of the cossacks for 474,000 men in military service. (The total cossack population was more than 4.4 million.) The lands of the cossack *dvoriantsvo* were declared hereditary property in 1848. Through all these measures tsarism strove to maintain the economic and sociopolitical structure of the cossacks, which caused the retention of many feudal features in their economy and daily lives.

At the same time, the development of capitalism drew the cossacks into commodity-money relations, undermining the foundations of its isolation as an estate. Because landlord ownership of land was weak in cossack regions, capitalist relations began to penetrate the enconomy of the cossack *stanitsy* fairly rapidly, a process which was aided by the influx of newcomers (*inogorodnie*) after the abolition of serfdom. The Don, Kuban,' and other regions became areas of commercial farming; leasing of the lands of the hosts became widespread, and antagonism arose between the cossacks and the *inogorodnie*. Class stratification occurred among the cossacks themselves. The economy of the prosperous upper elements acquired a capitalist character. At the same time, the number of poor cossack peasant farms increased, although on the whole, the cossacks' supply of land remained considerably higher than that of the peasants, particularly in European Russia. By the beginning of the 20th century industry was developing in certain cossack regions (the Don,

Kuban', and Siberia), and impoverished cossacks joined the ranks of the working class.

Class struggle became exacerbated among the Cossacks by the beginning of the 20th century. During 1906–07 there were revolutionary actions and disturbances in a number of cossack units (the 2nd Urup Regiment, infantry reconnaissance battalions, etc.). But because of the peculiarities of the military-estate organization of the cossacks, class struggle did not yet assume a broad scope. The majority of cossacks remained "as monarchist as ever" (V. I. Lenin, *Poln. sobr. soch.*, 5th ed., vol. 38, p. 277). However, the rapidly developing differences "in the size of holdings, amount of taxes paid, and terms of medieval land tenure as a reward for service, and so forth" (*ibid.*, vol. 16, p. 315), as well as the influence of impoverishment and the general revolutionizing of the masses during World War I (1914–18), resulted in class, and not estate, antagonism becoming the chief contradiction in cossack regions by 1917.

During the February Revolution of 1917 cossack units went over to the side of the insurgent people. Soviets of cossacks' deputies arose on the Don, Kuban', and Terek and in Siberia. With the support of the Provisional Government, the Soviet of the Union of Cossack Hosts was established; its leadership supported General L. G. Kornilov. During March–May 1917 host *krugi* were held (in the Kuban', *rada*), and counterrevolutionary host governments headed by atamans were established. However, the cossack masses did not support Kornilovism.

During the October Revolution the Communist Party was able to carry along with it the cossack poor and the masses of the cossacks of the front. This, in particular, was the reason for the rapid rout of the Kerensky-Krasnov revolt. The working cossacks took part in smashing the counterrevolutionary revolts in the cossack regions and helped establish Soviet power there. In March through May 1918 the Don, Kuban'–Black Sea, and Terek soviet republics were formed as parts of the RSFSR.

The development of the socialist revolution in the countryside in 1918 sharpened the class struggle and caused serious vacillations among the cossacks. The kulak stratum and middle cossacks stood on the side of counterrevolution. A significant portion of the cossacks wound up in the ranks of the White Guard armies.

The organization of the cossack poor by the Communist Party, the victories of the Red Army, and the contradictions between the cossacks and the landlord-bourgeois counterrevolution brought about a shift of the masses of working cossacks to the side of Soviet power in late 1919. Cossack units under the command of P. V. Bakhturov, M. F. Blinov, S. M. Budennyi, B. M. Dumenko, N. D. Kashirin, F. K. Mironov, and others fought in the ranks of the Red Army. The shift of the cossacks to the side of Soviet power was consolidated at the First All-Russian Congress of Working Cossacks (February-March 1920). On the basis of the decisions of the congress on Mar. 25, 1920, a decree on the establishment in the cossack regions of the local bodies of government specified by the Constitution of the RSFSR was promulgated. In 1920, by a resolution of the All-Russian Central Executive Committee, all general statutes concerning land tenure and land use which were in effect in the RSFSR were extended to the cossack regions. These enactments put an end to the existence of the cossacks as a special military estate.

The working cossacks embarked upon the path of socialist construction. In April 1925 the plenum of the Central Committee of the ACP (Bolshevik) worked out measures to strengthen and develop the economy in the former cossack regions, pointing out the need for extensive enlistments of the leaders of the Red cossacks in party and soviet work and underscoring that the characteristic features of cossack life were not to be ignored. During collectivization the fierce resistance of the kulaks was broken in the cossack regions, and the differences between the cossacks and the *inogorodnie* disappeared. On Apr. 20, 1936, the Central Executive Committee of the USSR abolished the restrictions concerning service in the Red Army that had existed for cossacks. In addition to the existing cossack cavalry divisions, new ones were created. During the Great Patriotic War of 1941–45 large Cossack units commanded by P. A. Belov, L. M. Dovator, N. Ia. Kirichenko, I. A. Pliev, A. G. Selivanov, and others fought heroically at the fronts.

REFERENCES
Lenin, V. I. *Poln. sobr. soch.*, 5th ed., vol. 16, pp. 314–16; vol. 34, pp. 219–20; vol. 35, pp. 296–97; vol. 39, pp. 244, 302; vol. 40, pp. 166–87.
Stoletie voennogo ministerstva, vol. 11, parts 1–4. St. Petersburg, 1902–11.
Golobutskii, V. A. *Chernomorskoe kazachestvo*. Kiev, 1956.
Golobutskii, V. A. *Zaporozhskoe kazachestvo*. Kiev, 1957.
Istoriia Dona: S drevneishikh vremen do Velikoi Oktiabr'skoi sotsialisticheskoi revoliutsii. Rostov-on-Don, 1965.
Istoriia Dona: Ot Velikoi Oktiabr'skoi sotsialisticheskoi revoliutsii do nashikh dnei. Rostov-on-Don, 1967.
Khoroshkhin, M. *Kazach'i voiska*. St. Petersburg, 1881.
　　　　　　A. P. Pronshtein and K. A. Khmelevskii [11–511–5]

COSSACK SCHOOLS, *stanitsa* (large cossack village) and settlement educational institutions for the cossack estate in Russia (the Don, Orenburg, Ural, and other cossack hosts).

Cossack schools appeared in the 19th century. By 1910 they numbered 5,510, including 73 secondary schools and one higher educational institution (the Aleksei Don Polytechnic Institute). A great deal of attention was devoted to the military training of the pupils. Until 1916 the cossack schools were under the jurisdiction of the Administrative Directorate of the Host and of the atamans of the military sections of the corresponding cossack host. In 1916 the cossack schools were placed under the jurisdiction of the Ministry of Public Education with regard to administrative and educational matters.　　　　[11–518–2]

COSTA CABRAL, ANTÓNIO BERNARDO DA, Marquis of Tomar (from 1878). Born May 9, 1803, in Fornos de Algodres; died Sept. 1, 1889, in São João da Foz do Douro. Portuguese statesman, leader of the Chartists, who supported a limited constitutional monarchy based on the Charter of 1826. From 1842 to 1846 he was the head of the government and the de facto dictator of Portugal. He was forced into retirement by growing popular discontent, but from 1848 to 1851 he again headed the government.　　　　[11–296–2]

COSTMARY (*Chrysanthemum balsamita*), a perennial herbaceous plant of the family Compositae. The leaves are entire. The numerous small calathide heads with yellow disc flowers and white ray flowers are gathered into a common corymbose inflorescence. This species grows primarily on the arid mountain slopes in the Caucusus. It is also found in Asia Minor and Southeast Asia. Costmary is cultivated as a condiment in kitchen gardens. It often grows wild. It is used to destroy moths, fleas, and other insects.　　　　[11–681–1]

COTTONY-CUSHION SCALE (*Icerya purchasi*), an insect of the family of giant coccids of the suborder Coccidae of the order Homoptera, a dangerous pest of citrus crops. The reddish brown body, which measures 5–7 mm long, is oval or nearly round. In mature females there is a large (sometimes 25 mm long), white, fluted ovisac. The cottony-cushion scale is native to Australia. As a result of the exportation of seedlings, the insect appeared in all countries in which citruses are cultivated. In the USSR it is found in the Abkhazian ASSR, the Adzhar ASSR, and Krasnodar Krai. The insect harms citrus crops, silver acacia, fig, pomegranate, cypress, and several other plants. There are two or three parthenogenetic generations each year. The larvae winter, and adult females appear in early May. The females soon deposit more than 2,000 eggs in the ovisac. The larvae hatch in the ovisac and emerge within a few hours. Cottony-cushion scales sometimes congregate in large colonies on shoots, branches, trunks, leaves, and fruits. They suck out the juices of the plant. As a result, plant growth is inhibited and fruit yield is decreased.

The most widely applied control measure is the use of the predatory Australian lady beetle (*Rodolia cardinalis*), an example of a biological control measure for plant protection. When there is a large population of cottony-cushion scale, insecticides are used (a chemical control measure).

REFERENCES
Borkhsenius, N. S. *Chervetsy i shchitovki SSSR*. Moscow-Leningrad, 1950.

Rubtsov, I. A. *Vrediteli tsitrusovykh i ikh estestvennye vragi.* Moscow-Leningrad, 1954.   P. I. MITROFANOV   [11–166–1]

COUGH, a reflex act usually occurring as a result of the irritation of the mucous membrane in the respiratory tract during an inflammatory process caused by pathological products (for example, sputum) or foreign bodies. A cough is one of the principal indications of disease in the respiratory organs (larynx, trachea, bronchi, and lungs). The cough center in the brain can sometimes be stimulated without irritation of the respiratory tracts. This is the so-called nervous cough that occurs in cases of fear and embarrassment. A distinction is made between a dry cough (without the formation and secretion of sputum) and a wet cough (with sputum).

The cough stimulus begins by deep inhalation, followed by a tensing of the bronchial and all the respiratory muscles resulting in forced expulsion. In so doing, the rima glottidis is closed, and intrathoracic pressure rises sharply. With the opening of the rima glottidis, the air bursts forth from the respiratory tract, carrying with it the sputum that has accumulated in the bronchi and pulmonary alveoli, dust particles, and so forth. Thus, a cough can be beneficial in helping to cleanse the respiratory tract. However, a protracted and severe cough that occurs with infections of the pleura, liver, and some other organs is harmful to the organism, since a systematic elevation of the intrathoracic and intrabronchial pressure leads to the gradual formation of pulmonary emphysema and impedes the flow of blood through the veins to the heart. This can lead to cardiopulmonary insufficiency.

Treatment is directed at the affliction that has caused the cough. With a wet cough, particularly if it is difficult to bring up the sputum, expectorants are used; with a dry, persistent cough, cough suppressants are administered.   [11–1651–2]

COURT MUSICIAN, a composer or performer in the service of a prince, duke, king, emperor, or tsar. In Russia the position of court musician existed from the 18th to the beginning of the 19th century.   [11–797–2]

COWPER, EDWARD ALFRED. Born Dec. 10, 1819; died May 9, 1893. British engineer and inventor.

Beginning in 1834, Cowper was a mechanic's apprentice in London. From 1846 he worked in Birmingham. In 1857 he invented an air-heating device for blast furnaces that was named the Cowper stove. He also designed and patented a steam compound generator (1857), a wheel with steel spokes and rubber tires (1868), and a printing electromagnetic telegraph (1879). Cowper was a member of the Iron and Steel Institute (Great Britain).   [11–1610–4]

CRAMBE, a genus of annual or perennial plants of the family Cruciferae. They are generally densely branched herbs with large succulent leaves. The flowers are usually white. The fruit is two-sectioned, with an infertile lower section and a fertile monospermous upper section. There are between 20 and 25 species in Eurasia and Africa. In the USSR there are between 18 and 20 species, distributed on steppes, semideserts, and arid mountain slopes and sometimes along seacoasts (Baltic Region, southern European USSR, the Caucasus, Middle Asia, and the southern part of Western Siberia). The best-known species is sea kale (*C. maritima*). The stalks of its vernal leaves are used as a vegetable, which is smilar to asparagus. Sometimes sea kale is cultivated. The young shoots of *C. tatarica* and the raw leaves of *C. orientalis* are also used for food. The species *C. Kotschyana* is a valuable fodder, nectar-bearing, and starch-yielding plant; it is suitable for cultivation. The seeds of *C. abyssinica,* which grows in the Abyssinian Highlands, contain up to 53 percent nutrient oil.   [11–1596–1]

CRANKCASE, a nonmoving part of a machine or mechanism, usually box-shaped; it supports parts and protects them against contamination. For example, the crankcase of a piston engine supports the crankshaft, cylinders, and other parts. The lower part of the crankcase is used to hold lubricating oil. Crankcases are made of cast iron, steel that has not been heat-treated, and alloys of light metals.   [11–1388–2]

CRAYON MANNER, a variant of the stipple method of intaglio engraving on metal, which imitates pencil, charcoal, red chalk, or pastel lines. The effects of the crayon manner are achieved by applying small strokes or dots on a grounded plate with a roulette or a mattoir. The plate is then immersed in acid. The crayon manner was a popular reproduction technique in the 18th century (G. Demarteau and L. M. Bonnet in France). The technique has been rarely used in the 20th century.   [11–1163–1]

CUANDO (also, Kwando; known as Linyanti in the lower course), a river in Namibia, Botswana, and Angola (in its middle course it forms the border between Angola and Zambia); right tributary of the Zambezi. Length, approximately 800 km. Originating on the Bié plateau, the Cuando flows through savannah forests as a series of rapids; in its lower reaches, it flows through a marshy plain and receives a branch of the Okavango River on the right. High water occurs during the rainy season (October and November).   [11–1694–2]

CUANZA (also, Kwanza), a river in Angola. Length, 960 km; basin area, 147,700 sq km. Originating on the Bié plateau, it flows through a deep valley to the north and then to the northwest and west. The river has numerous rapids and waterfalls. In the lower course it flows through a coastal lowland and becomes navigable (for 258 km from the mouth). The Cuanza discharges into the Atlantic Ocean, south of the city of Luanda. The river is deep during the rainy season. The Cambambe hydroelectric power plant is located on the river's middle course.   [11–1694–3]

CUBAN CRISIS (1962), a crisis produced by the aggressive actions of American imperialism directed against Cuba.

The victory of the Cuban Revolution of 1959 and the revolutionary government's implementation of radical measures infringing upon the interests of the American monopolies met with acute hostility from the ruling circles of the USA. From the first months of 1959, these circles exerted political and economic pressure on Cuba, including an economic blockade, the infiltration of saboteurs, and the bombing of Cuban cities, in order to wipe out Cuba as a revolutionary center in the western hemisphere. In April 1961 the Playa Girón region was invaded by mercenaries, who were quickly routed by Cuba's armed forces. Nevertheless, the ruling circles of the USA did not renounce their plans of smothering the revolution. In February 1962, Cuba was expelled from the Organization of American States. Incursions into the air space and territorial waters of Cuba became more frequent during 1961–62.

In view of the obvious threat of renewed intervention, the Cuban government began to strengthen the country's defense potential; in particular, it concluded an agreement with the USSR to place strategic weapons in Cuba. Citing this fact, the government of the USA established a naval blockade of Cuba late in October 1962 and concentrated powerful naval, air, and marine forces in the Caribbean region for an invasion of Cuba. Through a number of political and diplomatic measures the Soviet government worked to alleviate the grave international crisis and eliminate the threat of an invasion of Cuba. It condemned the aggressive actions of the government of the USA, called upon the peoples of the world to bar the way to the aggressors (see the "Declaration of the Soviet Government," *Pravda,* Oct. 24, 1962, p. 1), and at the same time adopted a decision to carry out some measures of a military nature in the USSR.

The steps taken by the Soviet Union and the firm resolve of the Cuban people, reflected in the program for ensuring security in the Caribbean region proposed by the Cuban government, forced the government of the USA to evaluate the emerging situation more soberly. In late October and early November 1962, Soviet-American negotiations on the conditions for settling the crisis were conducted with the participation of representatives of Cuba and the secretary-general of the UN. As a result of the negotiations, Soviet strategic weapons were removed from

Cuba and the government of the USA lifted the blockade of Cuba, withdrew from Guantánamo (an American military base on the territory of Cuba) the additional troops brought there during the crisis, demobilized reservists, canceled military preparations in Florida, and took upon itself commitments of nonaggression against Cuba.

REFERENCE
Gromyko, Anat. "Karibskii krizis." *Voprosy istorii,* 1971, nos. 7–8.
[11–1261–2]

CUMBERLAND, a sound in the Atlantic Ocean, off the southeastern coast of Baffin Island. It cuts inland for 259 km and measures approximately 74 km wide and 360–550 m deep at the entrance. The shores are high and mostly rocky. Cumberland Sound is covered with ice from late September through June. Tides are semidiurnal and at syzygy measure 7 m.
[11–715–4]

CUMBERLAND PLATEAU, plateau in southeastern United States, the southwestern foothills of the Appalachians. Elevations range from 1,200 m in the east to 500 m in the west. The plateau is composed of layers of sandstone and limestone, gently sloping to the west. The eastern edge, washed by the Tennessee and Clinch rivers, forms a steep precipice above the Great Appalachian Valley, at 300 m relative elevation. The Cumberland Plateau is cut by the deep valleys of the rivers of the Cumberland and Tennessee systems; karst is widespread. Deciduous forests (mostly cleared) grow on the plateau. Coal is mined (the Appalachian Coal Basin).
[11–715–5]

CUMBRIAN MOUNTAINS (in Russian, Cumberland Mountains), a mountain massif in the west of Great Britain. It is composed primarily of Paleozoic shales and quartzites, with large intrusions of granite. The Cumbrian Mountains have picturesque rocky peaks with elevations to 978 m (Scafell Pike) and well-expressed forms of glacial relief. There are also glacier lakes coinciding with the lines of tectonic faults. The mountains have a humid maritime climate. On the slopes are heaths, meadows, and peat bogs. Oak-ash and birch forests grow in the valleys. The Lake District National Park has been in the Cumbrian Mountains since 1951.
[11–715–7]

CUNNINGHAM, WALTER. Born Mar. 16, 1932, in Creston, Iowa. Astronaut of the USA.

In 1951, Cunningham began his service in the US Navy, where he was trained as a pilot. He later left active military service but remained in the Marine Corps reserves with the rank of major. In 1960 he graduated from the University of California at Los Angeles with a major in physics. In 1961 he received a master's degree in physics at UCLA and subsequently a doctorate. He worked for an industrial corporation, where he studied the problem of defense against ballistic rockets launched from submarines and also problems of the earth's magnetism. In 1963, Cunningham became an astronaut for the National Aeronautics and Space Administration (NASA). Together with W. Schirra, Jr. and D. Eisele he completed a space flight from Oct. 11 to Oct. 22, 1968, on the Apollo 7, which made 163 revolutions around the earth. This was the first test flight of the command module of the Apollo spacecraft.
[11–978–1]

CUTTACK, a city in India, located in the state of Orissa in the delta of the Mahanadi River. Population 194,000 (1971). The city is a transportation junction and the state's trade and industrial center. It has textile, food-processing, metal-working, and wood-processing industries. Cuttack is well known for its production of artistic modeled articles of silver and gold. It is also the site of Utkal University and the Central Rice Research Institute.
[11–1530–3]

CUTTER, a small boat or combat ship. Cutters range in length from 1.5 to 40 m and are up to 7 m in width, with displacements from a few dozen kilograms to 150 metric tons. Cruising speeds are from 3 to 70 knots (5.5–130 km/hr). The underwater body of a cutter may be of a keel type or a flat-bottom type with or without planing steps. Cutters may have displacement, hydroplane, or hover propulsion and may be powered by steam, internal combustion, or gas turbine engines or by sails and oars. Screw, airscrew, or water jet propellers may be employed.

In navies, cutters are used as combat ships, auxiliary vessels, and base floating facilities. Combat cutters of modern navies include rocket, gun, and torpedo boats, antisubmarine vessels, minesweepers, patrol boats, and landing craft. Cutters are equipped with rockets, cannon, and torpedoes, depending on their function. Cutters employed as auxiliary vessels or base floating facilities include tugboats and hydrographic, diving, ambulance, rescue, and passenger boats. Passenger and rescue craft can be part of the equipment of large warships and of auxiliary commercial and industrial boats. In commerce, cutters are used for transporting passengers, carrying small cargoes, towing small barges, and fishing, as well as for scientific investigation, pilot transit, and patrol duty. In motorboating, racing and pleasure boats with stationary or removable motors are used. Cutters equipped with sails and oars have ten to 14 oars, double masts, and a transom stern.
B. F. BALEV [11–1571–2]

CYMA, IONIC, an architectural detail, a molding that is formed by the combination of two conjugate curves (convex and concave). The convex arc has larger radius of curvature than the convex arc of a Doric cyma. According to where the convex arc is located (above or below), two types are distinguished: the cyma recta (used in capitals and cornices) and the cyma reversa (often used in the bases of columns and in socles).
[11–294–1]

CYPRINIDAE, a family of fishes of the order Cypriniformes. The body is scaleless or covered with cycloid scales. There are approximately 200 genera and more than 1,000 species. In the USSR there are more than 50 genera. Cyprinids are freshwater migratory fishes; they are found throughout the world, except for South America, Australia, and Madagascar. They are the most abundant fauna in the USSR, Southern Asia, and tropical Africa. In the USSR, cyprinids are found in the Amur River and in the basins of the Black, Azov, and Caspian seas. They dwell in cold rapid waters and also in very warm waters that are poorly oxygenated. Their eggs are usually deposited on vegetation. Some species lay eggs on sand and rocks; others simply deposit them in deep water. The Amur false gudgeon (*Pseudogobio rivularis*) and the Chinese chebachok (*Pseudorasbora parva*) guard their eggs.

Many cyprinids have commercial importance, such as the North Caspian roach (*Rutilus rutilus caspicus*), the European bream (*Abramis brama*), and the carp (*Cyprinus carpio*). Some species, including the carp and the crucian carp (*Carassius carassius*) are raised and bred in ponds. The domesticated carp, grasscarp (*Ctenopharyngodon idella*), black carp (*Mylopharyngodon piceus*), bighead carp (*Aristichthys nobilis*), and the silver carp (*Hypophthalmichthys molitrix*) have been adapted to waters in the European USSR, Middle Asia, Rumania, Poland, Cuba, and the German Democratic Republic.
A. A. SVETOVIDOVA [11–1357–4]

CYPRINODONTIDAE, a family of small freshwater fish of the order Microcyprini. The body, which measures 3–10 cm long, is spindle-shaped or round, with a vertically compressed caudal peduncle. The fins are spineless, the head is usually somewhat flattened, and the mouth is small, finite, and directed upward. The jaw usually protrudes; the teeth are small and well developed. There are approximately 430 species in fresh waters of the tropical and temperate zones of America, as well as in Africa and South and Southeast Asia. There are three species in Southern Europe; none are found in the USSR. Cyprinodonts lay their eggs on benthic vegetation; some species bury them in the mud. Several species are extremely hardy, inhabiting hot springs at temperatures of 40°–50°C (fish or the genus *Cyprinodon*). Many cyprinodonts are found in areas where there are dry and rainy spells. When bodies of water dry up, the fish die but the eggs buried in the mud survive. When the rains begin, masses of fish develop.

Many species of the family Cyprinodontidae are extremely beautiful (particularly the males) and easily adapt to aquariums. In the USSR, various species of the genera *Epiplatys, Aplochelius, Aphyosemion, Notobranchus, Rivulus, Fundulus,* and *Oryzias* are among the fishes that are bred for aquariums. Some cyprinodonts are used in ecological and genetic experiments; these include the species *Fundulus heteroclitus* and representatives of the genera *Oryzias, Cyprinodon,* and *Aphanius.*

T. S. Rass [11–1358–3]

DEFECTOSCOPY, CAPILLARY, a method of flaw detection based on the penetration of the defects by certain substances through the phenomenon of capillary pressure, as a result of which there is an artificial increase in the light and color contrast of the flaws relative to the intact areas. [11–1021–5]

DENTAL CARIES, an affection of the solid tissues of the teeth manifested by their gradual destruction (enamel, dentin, cementum) and the formation of cavities.

The causes of dental caries are varied and have not been completely determined. According to the chemical-parasitic theory, it results from the mineral part of the teeth being dissolved by acids formed in the mouth during the breakdown of the carbohydrates in food; the organic portion of the teeth is subsequently decomposed by microbes. Dental caries may also develop without the action of microbes as a result of metabolic disturbances in the dental tissues. Diet is an important factor in the origin of dental caries. Dental caries was induced experimentally by giving animals food containing a large quantity of sugar. In localities where the drinking water is low in fluorine, the incidence of dental caries is particularly high. The individual enzyme peculiarities of the body, diseases, a mother's diet during pregnancy, improper artificial feeding of infants, and rickets also affect the incidence of dental caries.

Caries generally affects the teeth of the upper jaw, especially the fifth milk and first molar teeth. The carious process is usually concentrated near natural depressions on the tooth surface and on the contiguous surfaces in the neck of a tooth (region next to the gum). The disease starts with the formation of a defect in the enamel or neck part of the cementum projecting freely into the mouth. On reaching the dentin, the process spreads wide and deep, forming a carious cavity. Once started, the process does not stop but gradually progresses. The enamel loses its luster and transparency at the site of dental caries, and pigmentation and roughness appear. When the integrity of the enamel is impaired, pain is felt on eating sweet, acid, salty, hot, or cold food. Dental caries is usually chronic. Acute dental caries is generally found in young people, and it is often due to a disturbance of internal secretion.

Treatment consists in restoration of the anatomical structure and function of the tooth by filling it. The procedure involves removal of the soft dentin and formation of a suitable cavity to hold the filling.

Prevention consists in taking action to increase tooth resistance to caries (providing the body with the essential salts, chiefly calcium and phosphorus, and vitamin D) during formation and mineralization of the teeth (from the fourth to fifth month of intrauterine development to age 11 years). After the teeth erupt prevention consists in proper diet and oral hygiene.

REFERENCES

Rukovodstvo po terapevticheskoi stomatologii. Moscow, 1967.
Pilz, W., C. Plathner, and H. Taatz. *Grundlagen der Kariologie und Endodontie.* Leipzig, 1969.
V. N. Isaev [11–1264–3]

DIAGRAMMATIC MAP, a simplified map, usually without a grid. The schematic representation makes it possible to form a general idea of the phenomenon or event shown in graphic form on the map and to emphasize its fundamental characteristics. The content of a diagrammatic map is strictly limited to elements that are important for an understanding of the subject. Previously published geographic maps are sometimes used as the basis for a diagrammatic map; the content of the diagrammatic map is drawn onto them in a generalized, schematic form and made very clear. [11–1431–1]

DIAMONDBACK MOTH (*Plutella maculipennis*), a butterfly of the family Plutellidae, injurious to cruciferous plants. Wingspan, 14–17 mm. The anterior wings are grayish or blackish brown with a wavy white stripe on the interior edge; the posterior wings are gray with a long fringe. The caterpillar is 9–12 mm long, spindle-shaped, and green. The eggs are pale yellow. The diamondback moth is distributed throughout the world. It does most damage to cabbage and rutabaga plants. There are between one and eight generations each year; the chrysalides winter on cruciferous weeds, stumps, and leaves. The moths emerge between April and June. One to three eggs are laid on the underside of leaves or on stems. The caterpillars first penetrate into the leaf tissue. They subsequently appear on the leaf surface, eating "little windows" in the leaves. Measures taken against the diamondback moth include destruction of weeds, tillage of harvest remains, and treatment of plants with insecticides and the microbiological preparation entobacterin. [11–1093–1]

DOMESTICATED CARP, a form of carp reared in ponds. The domesticated carp breeds differ in scaly covering: there are scaly, mirror, and leather carp. The Ukrainian mirror and Ukrainian scaly carp are bred in the USSR. The carp is thermophilic (it tolerates a temperature of up to 35°C) and hardy, lives in ponds with little oxygen, and tolerates considerable pollution. It reaches sexual maturity in three–five years. It spawns in spring on freshly flooded vegetation and produces 700,000–800,000 eggs. The fry feed at first on zooplankton and then on zoobenthos (mainly chironomid larvae). Toward fall the fish begin to feed on vegetation.

Domesticated carp is the main fish raised in warm-water pond fish farms in most countries. Its growth rate is greatest when the water temperature ranges from 20° to 28°C and the oxygen content of the water is 5–7 mg per liter in summer and no less than 4 mg per liter in winter. When the water temperature drops below 14°C, the carp consumes much less food, and at 1°–2°C it becomes torpid, ceases to feed, and loses weight. Insufficient food and poor maintenance result in degeneration. The fish productivity of the ponds is increased by concentrated stocking and feeding (introduction of feed into a pond in addition to natural carp food). When a pond is stocked normally in terms of solely the natural food already present, the carp usually are not fed. When the stocking is done at twofold, threefold, fourfold, or fivefold concentrations, special feed mixtures are added in the form of a doughy mass or granules. The mixtures include oil cakes, groats, seeds of legumes (lupine, vetch, peas, lentils, soybeans, beans), grain, flour, and grain bran (from corn, rye, barley, and sorghum), horse chestnuts, malt sprouts, brewers' grains, and feed of animal origin (fish, meat, blood meal, slaughterhouse and meat-packing wastes). In specialized state carp fish farms, the fish are fed mixed feed of industrial origin. Feeding domestic carp increases the fish yield per hectare of pond area by five to six times or more.

In the USSR, domestic carp is raised in the RSFSR, Ukraine, Byelorussia, and elsewhere. Fish-breeding ponds and a great variety of bodies of water, including rice paddies, are used for this purpose. The following breeds are raised: scaly, mirror (with scales scattered over the body), linear (with scales arranged along the lateral line), leather (without scales), Ukrainian mirror, and Ukrainian scaly carp. In the pond fish farms of the European USSR, fingerlings weigh 25–30 g, commercial two-year-olds weigh 500–800 g, and three-year-olds weigh 1,200–2,000 g. In 1971, the state fish farms of the USSR and fish farms of kolkhozes and sovkhozes produced 646,700 and 160,000 centners of domesticated carp, respectively. Efforts are under way to develop breeds that withstand cold and to introduce them into the northern regions of the country.

REFERENCE

Martyshev, F. G. *Kratkii kurs prudovogo rybovodstva.* Moscow, 1964.
A. A. Svetovidova and A. S. Vavilkin [11–1343–1]

DON CARLOS. Born July 8, 1545, in Valladolid; died July 14, 1568, in Madrid. Heir to the Spanish throne, son of Philip II.

On bad terms with his father, Don Carlos planned to flee Spain but was arrested in 1568 by Philip. He died while in prison.

His fate has served as the subject for a number of legends and works of literature, including V. Alfieri's tragedy *Philip* and F. von Schiller's *Don Carlos*. In the 19th century the opera *Don Carlos* was composed by G. Verdi on the theme. [11–1308–3]

DON CARLOS MAYOR. Born Mar. 29, 1788, in Madrid; died Mar. 10, 1855, in Trieste. Leader of the Spanish Carlists, brother of King Ferdinand VII.

After the death of his brother, Don Carlos Mayor was a pretender to the Spanish throne under the name Charles V. He unleashed the First Carlist War (1833–40). Defeated in 1839, he fled to France. In 1854 (according to some authorities, 1845), he renounced his claims to the throne in favor of his son, Carlos Luis. [11–1308–4]

DON CARLOS MENOR. Born Mar. 30, 1848, in Laibach, Austria (now Ljubljana, Yugoslavia); died July 18, 1909, in Varese, Italy. Leader of the Spanish Carlists, grandson of Don Carlos Mayor.

Pretender to the Spanish throne under the name Charles VII, Don Carlos Menor unleashed the Second Carlist War (1872–76). Defeated, he fled to France. [11–1308–5]

DROP, a small volume of liquid that is bounded in a state of equilibrium by a surface of rotation.

Drops form when a liquid flows slowly out of a small opening or runs off the edge of a surface, as well as when a liquid is atomized or emulsified. Drops also form when vapors condense on solid nonwettable surfaces and on condensation nuclei (ions, dust particles) in gaseous media; water droplets in the atmosphere arise in this way in the formation of dew, fog, and clouds.

The form of a drop is determined by the effect of surface tension (tending to decrease the surface of the drop) and external forces (above all, gravity). Microscopic drops for which gravity is not a decisive factor, and drops under the conditions of weightlessness have the form of a sphere, which is a body with minimum surface for a given volume. Large drops under earth conditions take a spherical form only when the densities of the drop and of the surrounding medium are equal. Falling raindrops, affected by gravity, the pressure of the opposing air current, and surface tension, assume the shape of a bun (broader across than vertically). Drops assume the shape of a flattened sphere on nonwettable surfaces, and they spread out on wettable surfaces.

The form and size of drops breaking away from the end of a capillary tube (pipette) depend on the diameter of the tube, the surface tension σ, and the density of the liquid. This relationship forms the basis for the determination of the surface tension of liquids from the weight of the drops leaving a vertical cylindrical tube (stalagmometer) and from the shape of the drops suspended from the end of a tube or resting on a flat surface.

Iu. N. Drozhzhin [11–1070–1]

DWARFED MALES, males that differ strikingly from females of the same species in size and, as a rule, in greater simplicity of organization.

Dwarfed males are an extreme manifestation of sexual dimorphism, which has been described in a number of species of rotifers, roundworms, segmented worms, mollusks, crustaceans, spiders, and insects. In some animals the dwarfed males differ from the females only in significantly lesser size. In some segmented worms the dwarfed males have a simplified organization as well. In *Bonellia* the males are 1–3 mm in length and live in the body of the female, which may be 7 cm in length, not counting the proboscis. Dwarfed male barnacles have a greatly reduced skeleton, legs, and internal organs (with the exception of the testes), and several live on the body of each female. Dwarfed males among certain rotifers have reduced intestines and excretory organs. After fertilization of the female the males die. Other species of rotifer with dwarfed males have females that are capable of parthenogenesis. The transition from dioecism to hermaphroditism brings with it the disappearance of the male. However, some species of barnacles that have made an incomplete transition to hermaphroditism have "complemental males," which were described by C. Darwin (for example, *Scal-*

pellum vulgare). An extreme form of reduction in the male is observed among gastropod parasites of Holothurioidea, such as in the male of *Entocolax ludwigi* (about 0.5 mm in diameter), which in structure and position in the female's body (which is up to 2 cm in length) is similar to a testis and has lost the nature of an independent organism.

REFERENCES
Darwin, C. *Zooligicheskie raboty. Sochineniia,* vol. 2. Moscow-Leningrad, 1936. Pages 56–64, 82–87, 90–94, 641–47.
Kovalevskii, A. O. "O planarieobraznom samtse bonellii." In *Izbrannye raboty.* Moscow, 1951. Pages 423–28.
Rukovodstvo po zoologii, vol. 2. Moscow-Leningrad, 1940.
[11–1300–2]

DWARF FRUIT TREE CULTIVATION, growing low fruit trees, chiefly apple and pear.

In the USSR, dwarf fruit tree cultivation is widespread in the southern regions (where the soil temperature does not drop below −11°C even in winter). Trees grafted on slow-growing (dwarfing) stock begin to bear fruit sooner than those grafted on fast-growing stock, have higher yields (30 tons per hectare or more), and produce larger, sweeter, and better colored fruits. The small size of the trees in a dwarf orchard eases the task of caring for them and gathering the harvest. Low-growing fruit trees are obtained by grafting ordinary varieties on special slow-growing (dwarfing) stock, by propagating varieties of natural dwarf plants, by limiting the growth of fast-growing trees using surgical methods or chemical agents, or by growing plants in a limited amount of soil (pots, tubs, boxes).

Grafting is the principal method used to grow dwarf trees. Paradise apple is used as dwarfing stock for apple in the southern regions of the European USSR, and red-leaved paradise apple and other stock obtained by Soviet breeders is used in the chernozem zone. With grafting upon such stock, the trees are only 2.5–3 m tall (dwarf plants). Stock from the doucin group is used to grow semidwarf trees. Forms from the semidwarf group bred in the I. V. Michurin Fruit and Vegetable Institute are being tested in the central regions of the European USSR where the stock from the doucin group is not winter hardy. The main dwarfing stock for pear is quince of various kinds. (Amateur fruit growers sometimes use Juneberry or hawthorn as dwarfing stock for pear.) Fruit trees grafted on dwarfing stock have shallow-growing roots and therefore require highly fertile soil and an ample water supply.

Dwarf fruit trees are used to create uniform tracts of orchards to permit the use of standard cultivation practices; as fillers for orchards of fast-growing trees; to recondition fruit plantations; in reclaiming mountain slopes (where it is easier to care for small trees); in decumbent cultivation of fruit trees, since the small size of the plants makes it easy to cover them for the winter; for tub and forcing culture; and to create shaped trees and espaliers, where the ornamental properties of plants are combined with the presence of fruits. A stepped crown is formed in dwarf trees and a sparse stepped flat crown (green wall) in semidwarf trees.

The artificial shapes of dwarf fruit trees on espaliers—in the form of palmettes, cordons, and so forth—have not become very popular because of the difficulty in breeding them. Other techniques of growing slow-growing trees are rarely used because of their awkwardness (in tubs or boxes) or because they have not been sufficiently worked out (use of chemical agents).

REFERENCES
Budagovskii, V. I. *Karlikovye podvoi dlia iabloni.* Moscow, 1959.
Smirnov, V. F. *Kul'tura karlikovykh plodovykh derev'ev,* 4th ed. Moscow, 1960.
Andriushchenko, D. P. *Kul'tura karlikovoi iabloni i grushi v Moldavii.* Kishinev, 1962.
Budagovskii, V. I. *Promyshlennaia kul'tura karlikovykh plodovykh derev'ev.* Moscow, 1963.   V. I. Budagovskii [11–1298–2]

DWARFISM, nanism, abnormal shortness (less than 130 cm for males and less than 120 cm for females).

The commonest cause of dwarfism is endocrine pathology. Dwarfism can be divided arbitrarily into proportional and disproportional (normal and achondroplastic) types. The former group includes pituitary, thyrogenic (cretin), and infantile dwarfism and dwarfism caused by brain disease, such as encephalitis and hydrocephaly. In pituitary dwarfism, which is caused by affection of the anterior lobe of the hypophysis (or the parts of the hypothalamus that regulate pituitary function) by tumor, infection, poisoning, or injury, the dwarf is almost normal mentally but the bodily proportions and size are those of a child, the gonads are underdeveloped, obesity is common, and the facial skin is wrinkled and senile. Thyrogenic (cretin) dwarfism, caused by affection of the thyroid gland, is accompanied by impairment of ossification, metabolic disturbances, dryness of skin, and mental retardation. Types of the disproportional category include rachitic dwarfism, caused by marked skeletal deformity, dwarfism in chondrodystrophy (congenital abnormality in cartilage formation), and dwarfism in systemic bone diseases.

Treatment (before body growth ceases) is aimed at eliminating the causes of the dwarfism; this sometimes involves substitution therapy. Dwarfism is characteristic of certain tribes in Africa (Pygmies), Asia, and Oceania.   [11–1302–6]

DWARF PLANTS, plants that are abnormally small for a given species or genus. Dwarf varieties of birch, pine, willow, and fir develop as a result of poor soil or adverse climatic conditions in the arctic and the antarctic, as well as on high mountains. Dwarf fruit trees and ornamentals are produced by artificial grafting on stocks with poorly developed root systems or by cultivating seedlings in pots filled with tightly packed soil. Artificial dwarfs include oak, gingko, maple, cherry, and plum trees. In a lifetime of 100 years, dwarfs barely reach the height of 1 m. Dwarf plants are widely cultivated in Japan.   [11–1300–1]

DWARF STAR, a star of relatively small size and low luminosity. Most dwarf stars form the lower part of the main sequence of the Hertzsprung-Russell diagram. Their average density ranges from 1 to 60 g/cm^3. Evidently, all stars of average and small mass are dwarf stars at a certain stage in their evolution, which is characterized by the start of nuclear reactions and the burning of hydrogen in the star's nucleus. In addition, dwarfs include stars existing in a state of gravitational contraction for a long time because of their very small mass. Dwarf stars have well-developed convection zones and extended chromospheres; therefore, emission lines are encountered in their spectra. A typical dwarf star is our sun. Among dwarfs there are a considerable number of stars with variable characteristics. A large part of the spherical subsystem of the Milky Way Galaxy and of the planar subsystem excluding the spiral arms consists of dwarf stars. The white dwarfs considerably differ in their structure from ordinary (or red) dwarfs.   V. S. AVEDISOVA [11–1298–1]

DYNAMOELECTRIC STAGE, a device consisting of two or more electric machines that are interconnected mechanically and electrically, or only electrically. It is used to provide smooth and economical control of the speed of rotation of an electric motor (usually an induction motor) in medium- and high-power nonreversible electric drives. The speed is controlled by altering the booster electromotive force in the rotor circuit of the induction motor that is developed by one or more DC or AC commutator machines. In a constant-power dynamoelectric stage (P = const.) one of the auxiliary machines is connected mechanically to the shaft of the main motor. In constant-torque stages (T = const.) there is no mechanical connection and, instead of a single auxiliary machine, two are used, one of which may be an AC or DC commutator machine or a converter (rotary converter, ionic converter, and so on). The latter converts the slip energy of the induction motor into DC electric power, which is then converted into mechanical energy by the DC machine and returned to the shaft of the stage.   [11–1479–1]

EATON, CYRUS. Born Dec. 27, 1883, in Pugwash, Nova Scotia, Canada. Public figure of the USA, industrialist.

Eaton graduated from McMaster University in Toronto in 1905. In 1913 he adopted American citizenship and became an entrepreneur. After World War II he was one of the leaders of the Cleveland financial group. In the early 1950's he became active in American public life. He has repeatedly spoken out in favor of lessening international tension and implementing the principles of peaceful coexistence. He initiated the Pugwash Conferences, attended by outstanding scientists and public figures of the world. In 1960 he received the International Lenin Prize for Strengthening Peace Between Nations.   [11–146–7]

EDGE-PUNCHED CARD, an information carrier in the form of a card made of heavy paper, light cardboard, or sheet plastic, with standard shape and dimensions and one or several rows of holes (perforations) along the edges. Information is written in the middle of the card, and its characteristic features are coded by a system of notchings from the holes to the edges of the card. The document is searched and retrieved from a set of cards by means of needles that pass through the holes corresponding to the assigned characteristics, thus establishing the identity of the sought-for and available information. Cards in which the needles pass through notchings are mechanically separated from the cards that do not have the notchings, that is, that have characteristics differing from the assigned ones. Edge-punched cards are used in information systems as a small-scale means of mechanization that significantly speeds up and simplifies the information retrieval process.   [11–1375–2]

EJECTION SEAT, a seat designed for cosmonauts; it is equipped with a device for catapult ejection from the cabin and subsequent descent by parachute. Cosmonaut ejection before landing (at a height of a few km) is used in several spacecraft landing systems, such as that of the Vostok. Ejection seats are also employed in case of accident during the spacecraft launch and entry into orbit. Ejection seats have a number of systems and devices, including mortar-deployed parachute systems, oxygen supply, ventilation devices for the spacesuit, a transceiving radio, food supply, and survival equipment to be used by the cosmonaut upon landing. The cockpits of modern aircraft are equipped with catapult ejection devices.   [11–1555–1]

ELAND, COMMON (*Taurotragus oryx*), an artiodactylous mammal of the family Bovidae. Body length is up to 3.5 m; height at the withers, up to 1.8 m; and weight, up to 900 kg. The tail may be up to 60 cm long and has a tuft of hair on the end. Males and females have long, spirally twisted horns. Under the neck is a fold of skin (dewlap). The animal is light grayish yellow in color.

The common eland is found in eastern and southern Africa. It inhabits savannas, living in herds and feeding on grass, tree leaves, and shrub foliage. In its natural habitat it reproduces in all seasons. Gestation lasts eight-and-a-half to nine months, and the female gives birth to one calf. The common eland is killed for its meat and hide. In some places it is being extensively destroyed. It can be tamed easily. In the USSR the common eland has been acclimatized in Askaniia-Nova, where work is being done to domesticate it. The female gives up to 7 liters of milk in a 24-hour period; the milk has a high fat content (up to 13 percent). Work to domesticate the common eland is also being done in Africa.

REFERENCE
Zoopark 'Askaniia-Nova.' Kiev, 1963.   I. I. SOKOLOV [11–974–2]

ENTOPROCTA (or Kamptozoa), a phylum of invertebrate animals. Entoprocts are small, primarily colonial, animals (measuring from 1 mm to 1 cm) that lead a sessile way of life. The body consists of a calyx containing all the organs, which is attached by a flexible stalk to the substrate (in colonial forms, to the branching trunk of the colony—the stolon). The calyx is rimmed with a circlet of tentacles. The mouth and anus open on a recessed space (atrium) between the bases of the tentacles. There is no coelom. Most entoprocts are dioecious; some are hermaphroditic. In the recess between the tentacles, the female has a brood cavity, where the eggs are fertilized and develop to the stage of trochophore-like larva. Development is accompanied by metamorphosis. In addition to sexual reproduction, there is asexual reproduction by means of budding.

All entoprocts are marine, except for one freshwater species, *Urnatella gracilis*. Entoprocts feed on detritus and microscopic algae. They live in shallow waters, which are rich in algae, but some descend to a depth of up to 300 m. In the USSR, 16 species are found in the northern seas and two in the Black Sea and Sea of Azov, one of which has found its way into the Caspian Sea.

REFERENCES
Rukovodstvo po zoologii, vol. 1. Edited by L. A. Zenkevich. Moscow-Leningrad, 1937.
Zhizn' zhivotnykh, vol. 1. Moscow, 1968.   G. A. KLIUGE   [11–844–3]

ERYTHRONIUM, a genus of herbaceous bulbous plants of the family Liliaceae. The bulb is ovoid and cylindrical; the stalk is usually short (10–30 cm, rarely up to 60 cm) with two unmottled or mottled basal leaves and one or several nodding flowers. The perianth segments, which are pinkish purple, yellow, or white, are recurved. There are approximately 25 species, found primarily in the mountainous regions of North America. Some species are also found in the mountains of Western Europe (*Erythronium dens canis*), the Caucasus (*E. caucasicum*), Southern Siberia (*E. sibiricum*), and Japan. Some species are used as ornamentals in gardens and parks. They are often grown in special gardens of alpine vegetation.   [11–965–1]

ETON, a town in Great Britain in the south of the county of Buckinghamshire, on the left bank of the Thames opposite the city of Windsor. Population, approximately 5,000 (1970). Eton is famous for the school founded there in 1440, Eton College, which takes most of its students from aristocratic families.
[11–146–8]

FALCONETS (*Microhierax*), a genus of birds of the family Falconidae. The body is 18–20 cm long. The beak is strong and has two teeth on the culmen. The wings are relatively long but blunted, and the claws are disproportionately large. There are five species. Falconets are found in an area stretching from northern India and southeastern China to the Philippines. They live on the edge of forests or in cut areas. The prey of the falconet includes large beetles, butterflies, dragonflies, and small birds, which it spots while sitting on isolated dead trees. They swallow small prey on the wing. The falconet nests in hollows and lays white eggs.   [11–1302–1]

FAREBOX, a special device for collection of fares in urban transportation that makes it unnecessary to have a conductor make the collection.   [11–1494–2]

FAT-LIQUORING, in the leather industry the impregnation of dry leather with a hot mixture of high-melting fat-liquoring and impregnating substances. Fat-liquoring is used in the maufacture of industrial-grade leather, chrome tanning leather (soles of shoes), and Russia pigskin to increase water resistance and improve other properties. Leather that has been dried to a 4–6 percent moisture content level and heated is immersed for 2–5 min in a molten mixture of 50–70°C. The mixture is composed primarily of beef fat, stearin, ceresin, paraffin, and, in certain cases, synthetic rubber.   [11–640–1]

FELSENMEER, vast placers of blocks of rock on the flat surfaces of mountain peaks, located above the treeline. They form as the result of the processes of frost weathering together with the phenomena of solifluction under conditions of a severe continental climate and the development of permafrost rock.
[11–766–2]

FILM HOLDER, a lightproof device that contains photographic film or a photographic plate. Film holders (cartridges) for compact cameras consist of a cylindrical housing containing a spool, with the film wound around its core, and a cover for the housing. The film is drawn out of the holder through a slit in the housing. Such film holders are made of plastic or metal. To provide more rapid loading of the camera, special film holders are used, including the rapid (spoolless) and the Kodapak, which has both supply and take-up parts (with a spool only in the take-up part). Film holders also exist that are loaded with wide,

rolled film or film units for cameras in which the photographic image is produced by the one-step (diffusion) process.

Plate holders (magazines), which are flat and rectangular, have a movable shutter (sliding plate) in front of the photosensitive layer on the plate. The housings for such film holders are made of metal, plastic, wood, or cardboard. Plate holders are either inserted into the camera's housing or are fastened to its rear portion. They are classified as single, double, or magazine types, depending on the number of photographic plates they contain. A variety of the plate holder is the adapter, which is usually loaded with film packs.   S. V. KULAGIN   [11–1499–3]

FINANCIAL BOARD (*kazennaia palata*), a body of the Ministry of Finance, established in 1775 in the provinces of Russia. At first, the financial boards administered state property and the construction departments. From the second half of the 19th century they directed bookkeeping and accounting in the province and district treasuries. After the Great October Socialist Revolution, the financial boards were abolished.   [11–523–3]

FLYING-SPOT SCANNER, a television device in which the image transmitted is scanned by a light spot traveling along the screen of a projection kinescope.

The flying-spot scanner is most widely used in color-television broadcasting to transmit motion picture films and transparencies. Its principle of operation is explained in Figure 1. A television raster with unmodulated luminance (constant intensity) is formed on the kinescope screen by line-scanning and frame-scanning generators. This raster is projected onto a film frame or transparency by an objective lens. During the scanning a light spot consecutively transilluminates the entire film frame or transparency line by line, affecting the brightness of the light flux according to the optical density (transparency) of the image. The modulated light flux is then picked up by a condensing lens and directed to a device that splits the light flux into its spectral components. After color separation for light fluxes pass through photomultipliers for linear conversion to videosignals of red, green, and blue. The amplitudes are determined by the luminance and chrominance of the area of the image being transmitted at the moment. In motion-picture transmission the movement of the film is coordinated with the interlaced scanning of the image by a device in the motion picture projector.

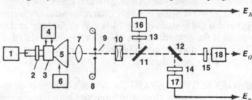

Figure 1. Diagram of flying-spot scanner: (1) pulse amplifier for blanking retrace of kinescope electron beam; (2) focusing system; (3) deflecting system; (4) line-scanning and frame-scanning generators; (5) projection kinescope; (6) high-voltage source; (7) objective lens; (8) film transport device; (9) frame window; (10) condensing lens; (11) and (12) semitransparent dichroic mirrors; (13), (14), and (15) light filters; (16), (17), and (18) photomultipliers; (E_R) video signals corresponding to red, (E_G) green, and (E_B) blue

The flying-spot scanner is also used as an episcope for transmitting opaque images (cards, photographs, maps) and, occasionally, action scenes from a television studio; in these cases the light flux from the kinescope is projected onto an opaque image. The studio must be darkened when using the scanner. The object is illuminated by light pulses during the vertical retrace.

REFERENCE
Teoriia i praktika tsvetnogo televideniia. Edited by P. V. Shmakov. Moscow, 1962.   N. G. DERIUGIN   [11–794–3]

FRAME (or skeleton), in engineering, the shell of any product, structural element, building, or installation; it consists of separate beams that are attached to each other. Frames are made of wood, metal, or reinforced concrete. The frame determines the strength, stability, durability, and shape of a product or installation. Strength and stability are provided by rigid attachment of the beams in interlocking connections or hinged joints and by special stiffening elements, which give the product or installation a geometrically invariant shape. The rigidity of frames is often increased by sheathing, casing, or walls on the product or installation.

The skeleton of a building consists mainly of columns and of crossbeams, girders, and trusses, which rest on the columns and on which the ceiling and roof are laid. Depending on the type of building in which they are used, frames may be single-stage or multistage; one-bay, two-bay, or multiple-bay; and with the main load-bearing structures placed transversely, longitudinally, or in both directions. The skeletons of buildings may be complete or incomplete: a complete skeleton absorbs all vertical stresses of the building, and the elements of the skeleton are found throughout the building layout; an incomplete skeleton is placed only within a building in which the outer walls are load-bearing and, together with the skeleton, support the building.

According to the way in which overall rigidity and stability of buildings are provided, a distinction is made between frame-type skeletons, in which the interlocking connections of the columns and crossbeams are rigidly constructed as frames capable of absorbing deformation moments and transverse forces from wind load and dead load, and skeletons with ties having articulated or partially binding joints, in which wind loads are absorbed by rigid horizontal and vertical stiffeners.

REFERENCE
Drozdov, P. F., and I. M. Sebekin. *Proektirovanie krupnopanel'nykh zdanii (karkasnykh i beskarkasnykh).* Moscow, 1967.
N. V. MOROZOV [11–1281–1]

FRAME. (1) A photograph on film with the image of a phase of motion or the static position of the objects being photographed. The linear and spatial design, the brightness and color values, and the nature of the optical image in a frame, as well as the boundaries of the space depicted in the frame, are all dominated by the development of the idea and by the content of the scene being photographed. The design of a frame takes into account the qualities of dynamic composition that are influenced by the motion within a frame of the objects being photographed. When a moving camera is used, such motion is often combined with the motion of the frame itself. The format of a frame and its relative location on the film are determined by the dimensions and location of the film gate of the camera. The dimensions of frames with a sound track produced on standard 35-mm motion-picture film are as follows: height, 16 mm; width, 22 mm; aspect ratio, 1:1.375. For frames on wide, 70-mm film the aspect ratio is as high as 1:2.2; for the frames of a wide-screen film the ratio is 1:2.35.

(2) A sequence frame (sequential section) is a component part of a film that contains a moment of the action as photographed by a moving or stationary camera. Each sequence frame must be organically and compositionally linked with adjacent frames in terms of the content, continuity of subject, and choice of composition, rhythm, and color values.

(3) A scene frame (in screenplays used in producing films) is a narrative of contents and a detailed description of the frame being filmed, the action taking place in the frame, the dialogue, and also the sound track and the acting and staging decisions.
A. V. GAL'PERIN

(4) A photographic frame is a single image of an object being photographed, with boundaries limited by certain dimensions. The boundaries of a frame are determined during photography during printing on photographic paper, or in the production of slides.

(5) A television frame is a complete single television image. It is composed of two partial images, the half-frames or fields. The odd-numbered lines of the picture being scanned are swept consecutively by the first field; the even-numbered lines (located between the odd-numbered lines) are swept by the second field. The number of lines in a frame varies; it is determined by the parameters of the television system (525, 625, 819 lines, and so on). Video signals modulate the electron beam in a picture tube only during forward sweep of the beam in scanning; during the return sweep the beam is extinguished and returns to the starting point of the next field. The field frequency is chosen to equal the nominal frequency of the power-supply line. For a frequency of 50 hertz (Hz) the frame is transmitted for a period of 1/25 sec; for a frequency of 60 Hz, for a period of 1/30 sec (or, one field for 1/50 or 1/60 sec, respectively). The number of frame changes per second n, the nominal number of lines z, and the line frequency f_c exhibit the following relationship: $n = f_c/z$. The ratio of frame width to frame height (aspect ratio) is usually 4:3.
N. G. DERIUGIN [11–381–4]

FRAME-PANEL MEMBERS, structural elements that consist of supporting members of the frame and enclosing structures (walls, ceilings, and roofing) made from panels. Wood, metal, and reinforced-concrete frame-panel members are widely used in modern low- and high-rise construction of residential, public, and industrial buildings. Reinforced-concrete connecting frames that transmit the loads to vertical and horizontal stiffeners are most widely used in multistory buildings, which receive great wind stresses. Frame-panel members with a wood frame consisting of columns, crossbars, and cross stays are used in low-rise construction. The enclosing structures of the members (outer walls and coverings) consist of wood shielding panels with thermal insulation.

Frame-panel members consisting of concrete and reinforced-concrete elements have been most widely used in the USSR in the development of industrial construction. Frame-panel members with steel elements are appropriate mainly for high-rise public buildings (30 stories or more). In residential and public buildings, frame-panel members are planned with or without supports; in industrial buildings with boom loads, they are planned with supports. The outer walls of a building with a complete scheme consist of columns and panels made of light or heavy concrete or sheet materials (asbestos cement, stainless steel, aluminum, or plastics) with a thermal insulator. Such frame-panel members are usually used in multistory buildings (more than nine stories). In low-rise buildings and buildings with supporting outer walls, incomplete frame-panel members are used and the supporting walls are made of single-layer light concrete panels or reinforced-concrete or insulated concrete panels.

In frame-panel buildings with room-size ceiling panels, the frames may be planned without crossbeams (the beamless plan), with the roofing panels resting directly on the columns. The beamless plan is also used when greater space is required—for example, in public and industrial buildings.

In interlinked frame systems, the vertical stiffeners are located between the columns and are made of reinforced-concrete or concrete panels; in multistory buildings (25–40 stories), they are made as a cast reinforced-concrete wall. The panels of the stiffener are joined to each other vertically and horizontally, as well as with roofing panels or crossbeams located in the plane of the stiffener by welding steel inserts; the seams are sealed with cement mortar. The inserts are also used for attaching the stiffener panels to the columns. The linking structures of the frame elements in junctions and joints are determined on the basis of a calculated plan, with transmission of strains through the inserts or through reinforced concrete by casting the junctions and joints at the construction site; a combination of the two methods is also used.

REFERENCES
Kuznetsov, G. F., N. V. Morozov, and T. P. Antipov. *Konstruktsii mnogoetazhnykh karkasno-panel'nykh i panel'nykh zhilykh domov.* Moscow, 1956. [Album.]
Dykhovichnyi, Iu. A. *Konstruirovanie i raschet zhilykh i obshchestvennykh zdanii povyshennoi etazhnosti.* Moscow, 1970.
N. V. MOROZOV [11–1282–1]

GALINGALE (*Alpinia officinarum*), a perennial plant of the family Zingiberaceae. It is also known as the Galanga minor, as distinguished from the Galanga major (*Alpinia galanga*). It grows in East Asia.

REFERENCE
Atlas lekarstvenykh rastenii SSSR. Moscow, 1962.   [11–573–2]

GALLINULE (*Gallinula*), a genus of birds in the order Gruiformes. There are four species: the common gallinule (*Gallinula chloropus*) is found in the USSR. Length, approximately 35 cm. Its legs are long, and the beak and tail are short. The back is brownish olive, and the belly gray; there are white lengthwise stripes along the sides. The head is black, with a red spot on the forehead, and the beak is red with a yellow top. Birds of the *Gallinula* genus are found throughout the world, except Australia.

In the USSR, the common gallinule is found as far north as Leningrad and Omsk and as far east as the Altai. It also nests in Primor'e Krai, Sakhalin Island, and the southern Kuril Islands.

Gallinules are migratory birds and only rarely stay the winter in their nesting grounds. They settle in freshwater, overgrown, grassy bodies of water and build nests in the middle of the water in rushes or bushes. The female lays six to 12 eggs twice a year. They feed mainly on aquatic invertebrates.   [11–859–7]

GATLING GUN, a multibarreled firearm mounted on a wheeled carriage or tripod and designed for rapid fire. The first Gatling gun, built by the American inventor R. Gatling in the 1860's, had from six to ten barrels of 13 or 25.4 mm caliber and fired up to 200 rounds per minute. Many armies, including the Russian, used Gatling guns. The more refined Gatling gun designed by the French inventors J.-B. Verchère de Reffye and Montigny had 37 barrels and was called a *mitrailleuse*. In the 1880's, Russian inventors, among them A. P. Gorlov, invented a still more refined gun that had from five to ten barrels and that fired standard rifle cartridges. In the late 19th century Gatling guns lost their value because shrapnel fired by artillery guns proved more effective. Further searches for the technological solution to the problem of rapid fire led to the construction of the machine gun.   [11–1388–3]

GAUGE, a scaleless measuring device designed for checking the dimensions, shape, and relative positions of the parts of articles. The checking consists in a comparison of the dimensions of a product with a measuring gauge in terms of the fit or degree of contact of their surfaces. This comparison makes possible classification of products as acceptable (if the dimensions lie within tolerance limits), defective (with repair possible), or irreparable.

The most widely used limit (go–no go) gauges are go gauges, which are made according to the minimum limiting size of an opening or the maximum size of a shaft and fit into acceptable products, and no-go gauges, which are made for the maximum size of an opening or the minimum size of a shaft and will not fit into acceptable products. Gauges are also classified according to purposes: working gauges, used for testing products at the manufacturing plant; acceptance gauges, used by the consumer for rechecking products; and reference gauges, which are used for testing or regulation of working and acceptance gauges. The advantages of gauges are simplicity of design and the possibility of integrated checking of products of complex shape; disadvantages include low versatility and the inability to determine actual size deviations. The use of these gauges in machine building is decreasing because of the introduction of universal measuring methods and mechanized and automatic devices.

M. A. PALEI   [11–590–2]

GIDE, a river in Sweden. The Gide River flows into the Gulf of Bothnia in the Baltic Sea. Length, 204 km; basin area, approximately 3,500 sq km. There are ten waterfalls along its course (the largest, 25 m high). The Gide is used for timber rafting. There is a hydroelectric power plant on the river.   [11–217–3]

GJÖA, a wooden single-masted vessel with a displacement of 47 tons and powered by motor and sail. From 1903 to 1906, R. Amundsen's expedition sailed aboard the *Gjöa* through the Northwest Passage for the first time from east to west (via the Lancaster and Peel sounds, along the coast of the Boothia Peninsula, and west along the mainland). The expedition conducted magnetic observations and gathered ethnological data on the Eskimo.   [11–218–1]

GOLDEN NEMATODE (*Heterodera rostochiensis*), a roundworm of the family Heteroderidae. Body length, about 1 mm.

The golden nematode is a parasite of the roots (less often, of the tubers) of potatoes, tomatoes, and, occasionally, deadly nightshade. It is found in Europe, Asia, North and South America, Africa, and Australia. It is also found in several republics of the USSR. Development from the larval stage to maturity takes place in the tissues of the roots or tuber of the host plant. The transparent wormlike male crawls out of the root into the soil; the anterior end of the female remains attached to the root or tuber, its swollen body covered by a thick cuticle, protruding outside the plant. The male dies after fertilization. The female forms more than 1,000 eggs; these remain inside her body, which turns into a cyst after her death. In the spring the larvae emerge from the cyst and embed themselves in the plant roots.

The golden nematode retards the development of the host plant, significantly reducing yield; when infestation is extreme the potato plants form either no tubers at all or from one to three tiny tubers. A kilogram of soil in heavily infested fields may contain as many as 2,500 cysts of golden nematode. Countermeasures include quarantine, planting resistant varieties of potatoes, crop rotation and removal of the infested roots and tubers from the fields, and disinfection of the soil with chloropicrin, Carbathion, or Nemagon.

REFERENCE
Kir'yanova, E. S., and E. L. Krall'. *Paraziticheskie nematody rastenii i mery bor'by s nimi,* vols. 1–2. Leningrad, 1969–71.   [11–1442–3]

GOVERNMENT FACTORIES, in prerevolutionary Russia, state industrial enterprises under the jurisdiction of various government departments, such as war, navy, and mines.

The primary purpose of the government factories and works was to meet the government's needs for military matériel; as a result, most of them were military, mining, or metallurgical works. Throughout their existence, the government factories were centers for the spread of technological innovations. In their own way they were schools at which workers and skilled craftsmen from private factories could learn. The government factories originated in the 17th century but became widespread only in the early 18th. State peasants were assigned to work in them. As far back as the early 18th century the government began to transfer these factories to private individuals. These transfers became common from the 1730's through the 1750's, but in the late 18th century the state bought back most of the former government factories, which had been ruined by their noble owners. In the 19th century the factories fell into decline and were not able to meet the needs of the state. This became especially apparent during the Crimean War of 1853–56 and in the 1860's and 1870's, when the factories were unable to reequip the Russian Army.

In the early 20th century the major government factories and works included several arsenals and the Tula Works, the Izhevsk Works, the Sestroretsk Armaments Works, the Okhta Powder Works, and the St. Petersburg Cartridge Works, all under the war department; the Obukhov and Izhora works and a number of shipyards, under the navy department; and the works at Perm', Zlatoust, and Votkinsk, under the department of mines. On the eve of World War I, the government factories and works were the basic military suppliers for the Russian Army. During the war they increased their productivity but were still unable to provide the front with all the necessary matériel.

The workers in the government factories throughout their history were active in the class struggle. Among the largest revolutionary actions by workers in these factories, the most famous were the "Obukhov defense" in 1901, the struggle of the workers at the Zlatoust works in 1905–07, and a number of major strikes at the Perm' Works in 1915–16.

REFERENCES
Strumilin, S. G. *Istoriia chernoi metallurgii v SSSR,* vol. 1. Moscow, 1954.

Pavlenko, N. I. *Istoriia metallurgii v Rossii XVIII v.* Moscow, 1962.

Sigov, S. P. *Ocherki po istorii gornozavodcheskoi promyshlennosti Urala.* Sverdlovsk, 1936.

Sidorov, A. L. "K voprosu o stroitel'stve kazennykh voennykh zavodov v Rossii v gody pervoi mirovoi voiny." In the collection *Istoricheskie zapiski,* [vol.] 54. [Moscow] 1955. [11–524–2]

GRADING OF FRUIT, grouping fruit by size; one of the operations in the market processing of fruit.

Depending on the biological characteristics of the variety, fruit is divided into four, five, or more grades. Grading is done by hand (comparing to standard samples) or on grading machines (according to weight or size). Hand grading is usually combined with sorting or packing; machine grading is done after sorting. [11–593–3]

GRADING OF SEEDS, in a seeder, the division of seeds, according to size, into groups corresponding to the sizes of the compartments in the seeding mechanism.

Seed is sorted so that seeds can be sown one by one or in sets of a predetermined number, decreasing waste of the sowing material and cutting down sharply on the labor needed to tend the plantings. Corn, sugar beet, cotton, and other crop seeds are graded after preliminary machine-cleaning. Agricultural grading machines or seed cleaners with the necessary gratings are used for the process.

Large-scale seed grading was first used in the USSR with corn after construction in 1956–57 of grading plants, which supply seeds (packed according to grade in sacks) to kolkhozes and sovkhozes. Corn kernels fall into six grades, according to thickness and width (see Table 1).

Table 1

Grade number	Size of seeds (mm)	
	Width	Thickness
1	9.0–10.5 (11.0)	3.75–5.5
2	8.0–9.0	3.75–5.25
3	7.0–8.0	3.75–5.0
4	6.5–7.0	3.75–4.75
5	8.0–10.5 (11.0)	5.25–7.0
6	6.5–8.0	4.75–7.0

Sugar beet seeds are graded (using screens with round openings) into two groups (diameter, 4.5–5.5 and 3.5–4.5 mm). Cotton seeds are graded in cotton ginning plants, according to width, thickness, and length, into two groups, after first removing the linters from their surface. [11–593–4]

GREAT HORNBILL (*Buceros bicornis*), a bird of the Buceroti-dae family, order Coraciiformes.

The plumage of the great hornbill is black and white. There are two horny protuberances on the bill. The bird may reach about 120 cm in length. The great hornbill is found in forests of the lower belt of the mountains of Hindustan, eastern Indochina, and Malacca. It nests in hollow trees at a height of 3–30 m. The clutch usually contains two white eggs. When brooding, the female seals herself up in the hollow tree, closing the entrance with her own droppings and leaving a narrow opening through which the male can give her food. After the nestlings have hatched, the female abandons the nest and rebuilds the broken wall. Both she and the male feed the young birds. The great hornbill feeds mainly on fruits (sometimes damaging orchards), in addition to reptiles, rodents, and large insects. [11–566–3]

GUARD, an armed detachment appointed to protect and defend military objectives or to render military honors.

In the Soviet armed forces there are garrison (camp) and interior (ship) guards and honor guards. Garrison and interior guards are composed of the commander of the guard, who may be an officer or a sergeant, depending on the importance of the object and the number of posts; privates of the guard, their number depending on the number of posts and shifts; and if necesssary a deputy commander and corporals of the guard. For the protection and defense of the military objects, sentries are assigned—armed soldiers (privates of the guard) directly in charge of the protection and defense of the posts entrusted to them.

Honor guards are appointed for the welcome at the garrison of the chairman of the Presidium of the Supreme Soviet of the USSR, the chairman of the Council of Ministers of the USSR, the generalissimo of the Soviet Union, the minister of defense of the USSR, marshals of the Soviet Union, and admirals of the Fleet of the Soviet Union. Moreover, an honor guard may also be assigned to banners carried at formal sessions, the unveiling of state monuments, the welcome and escorting of representatives of foreign states, and the funerals of servicemen and of civilians who have rendered special services to the state. An honor guard is composed of infantry units from platoon to company level and a band. An honor guard may also be composed only of officers and sergeants.   I. I. ANDRONOV [11–1178–3]

GUARD DUTY, a troop duty designed for the protection and defense of armaments and combat equipment warehouses and for the guarding of personnel confined to the guardhouse. In the Soviet armed forces the organization of guard duty is determined by the Garrison and Guard Duty Regulations of the Armed Forces of the USSR. The performance of guard duty is considered a fulfillment of combat tasks. In a garrison, guard duty is under the direction of the garrison commander; in a military unit, under the commander of the unit. Men are assigned to perform guard duty for military units in accordance with the lists of details for the guards; these men are formed into guards for the duration of the guard duty. The personnel of the guards are removed from subordination to the direct commanders and placed under the command of persons designated by the Garrison and Guard Duty Regulations of the Armed Forces of the USSR. [11–1179–1]

GUMS, the macromolecular carbohydrates that are the basic constituents of the plant exudates produced by disease or mechanical damage to the cortex.

Gums are polymers of monosaccharides, such as glucose, galactose, arabinose (pectinose), rhamnose, and glucuronic acid, that either dissolve or swell in water. Also included in the category are certain polysaccharides of microorganisms (in particular, those accumulated in culture fluids) and derivatives obtained by the modification of natural polysaccharides, such as cellulose and starch.

Gums are used in the food and paper industries as adhesives, stabilizing agents in emulsions and suspensions, and high-viscosity solutions. In medicine they serve as mucilage, which reduces the irritation caused by certain medicinal substances and lowers absorption. They are also used in the preparation of pills and emulsions. Gum arabic, agar-agar, dextrans, alginic acids, and guaran are among the gums that have found a broad range of uses. [11–738–5]

GUNBOAT (in Russian, *kanonerskaia logka;* from French *canonnière,* from *canon,* "gun"), a combat artillery ship designed for combat operations in coastal waters, in shallow waters, and in rivers. Gunboats are divided into sea and river types.

Gunboats may be specially designed, but in wartime the number is usually increased by reequipping shallow-draft vessels from the commercial, fishing, and industrial fleets. Gunboats are used to deliver artillery strikes at coastal objectives and the men and matériel of the enemy, to destroy small coastal ships and vessels, and for artillery support of the coastal flanks of the ground troops. In addition they may be used in landing operations and in operations against landing forces, to lay mines and transport troops, and for convoy service and patrol duty. The displacement of gunboats does not exceed 2,500 tons, and their speed is from nine to 20 knots (17 to 37 km per hour). Their main armament consists of between two and five 76-mm to 152-mm artillery mounts. For defense against enemy aircraft, gunboats may have small-caliber (20–37 mm) automatic antiaircraft guns and large-caliber antiaircraft machine guns. Since World War II the development of coastal rocket artillery has reduced the role of gunboats as naval artillery ships for coastal action, according to foreign data, but they still retain their value in wartime for actions in lakes and rivers.   B. F. BALEV [11–984–2]

GYPSOPHILA, a genus of plants of the family Caryophyllaceae. They are perennial or annual, often branched herbs (rarely small semishrubs) with small flowers. There are about 120 species in the temperate zone of the Old World and in Australia (one species). In the USSR there are about 70 species, growing mainly in the Caucasus and in Middle Asia. A widespread species, *G. paniculata,* forms spherical shrubs (tumbleweed). The roots of this and several other species, contain up to 20 percent of saponins and are known as white soap root. They are used for washing wool and silk. The species *G. elegans* and *G. paniculata* are cultivated as ornamentals. The species *G. aretioides,* growing in southern Transcaucasia, Turkmenia, and Iran, forms firm cushions up to 2 m in diameter and weighing up to 150 kg.   [11–1645–1]

HACKBERRY (*Celtis*), a genus of deciduous or more rarely evergreen trees of the family Ulmaceae. The leaves are asymmetrical and serrated, with three veins at the base. The blossoms are opaque and polygamous, with a simple five-membered perianth. The fruit is a drupe. There are about 50 species in tropical and arid regions of the temperate zones in the western and eastern hemispheres. In the USSR there are two species. Caucasian hackberry (*C. caucasica*) is a tree up to 20 m tall with grayish green downy leaves that grows in the Caucasus and Middle Asia. Smooth hackberry (*C. glabrata*) is 4–6 m tall and grows on dry rocky slopes of the Crimea and Caucasus.

Hackberry is widely used for greenery and for protective forestation, especially in arid regions. The fruit is edible; the leaves are used for animal fodder and the bark in tanning hides. The wood is hard and durable; it is used in cabinetry, woodworking, and carving.   I. A. GRUDZINSKAIA [11–1281–2]

HARD LABOR (Russian *katorga;* from Late Greek *katerga,* "galley"), a type of punishment in states based on exploitation; this punishment involves the use of convicts for hard physical labor.

The term "hard labor" arose in the Middle Ages to designate punishment involving the use of convicts as oarsmen on galleys, where they were chained to benches in the hold. In the 16th and 17th centuries in Western Europe (for instance, in France and Great Britain), convict labor was used to do the most arduous jobs in prisons, large ports, mines, and other installations. Branding and chaining of convicts and putting them in the pillory was a routine procedure. In 18th- and 19th-century France, hard labor was usually combined with banishment to overseas territories, mainly as a measure of political repression—for instance, participants in the Paris Commune were transported to New Caledonia. In Great Britain, members of the Chartist movement, Irish revolutionaries, participants in the Dublin uprising of 1916, and other dissenters sentenced to prison terms made up the convict labor force.

In Russia hard labor was instituted in the late 17th century, when the tsar's ukase of 1691 replaced capital punishment with transportation (exile) to penal colonies for certain types of crime. Hard labor for life and for shorter terms was established by the military regulations of 1716 as a form of punishment. In the 18th century convict labor was used to build St. Petersburg, ports, canals, and roads. Convicts also worked in state mines and plants in the Urals and Siberia (for instance, the Nerchinsk hard labor zone). Participants in the popular movements led by K. A. Bulavin and E. I. Pugachev served hard labor terms. In 1765 noblemen were granted the right to banish their peasant serfs to penal colonies. In 1797 the following three categories of hard labor were established: in the Nerchinsk and Ekaterinburg mines, at the Irkutsk cloth factory, and in the construction and maintenance of fortresses. The Statute on Exiles, which was confirmed by Emperor Alexander I in 1822, instituted hard labor for terms of up to 20 years and for life. Beginning in the first half of the 19th century the number of political prisoners (for instance, Decembrists and the Petrashevtsy) among hard labor convicts began to increase. In the 18th century and in the first half of the

19th, hard labor was invariably accompanied by cruel tortures.

By the early 20th century the following hard labor institutions existed in Russia: the Shlissel'burg Fortress; the Nerchinsk prisons; the Aleksandrovskoe Central Prison; the Iletsk and Tobol'sk prisons; the Novoborisoglebsk and Novobelgorod prisons in Kharkov Province; the Ust'-Kamenogorsk prison in Semipalatinsk Province; and the Ust'-Kut saltworks, the Irkutsk saltworks, and the Nikolaevskii ironworks in Irkutsk Province. Beginning in the 1890's convict labor was used in the construction of the Siberian railroad and later, of the Amur railroad. In the early 1880's most hard labor convicts were *raznochintsy* (intellectuals of no definite class) and peasants; workers began appearing in the 1880's, and at the turn of the 20th century the bulk of political prisoners were workers and social democrats. The prisoners responded to the cruel treatment by organizing escapes, hunger strikes, and revolts (for instance, the Kara tragedy of 1889). During the Stolypin reaction there existed hard labor central prisons in Tobol'sk, Moscow (Butyrka prison), Shlissel'burg, Pskov, Novonikolaevsk (Kherson Province), Smolensk, Vladimir, Yaroslavl, and Vologda. The Orel central prison, which was set up in 1908 and where 20 percent of the inmates were political prisoners, was notorious for its severe conditions. The prominent Bolsheviks F. E. Dzerzhinskii, G. K. Ordzhonikidze, M. F. Frunze, and F. A. Artem-Sergeev served hard labor terms in central prisons. The rigorous detention system in the hard labor prisons caused mass revolts of political prisoners—for instance, in the Orel central prison in 1910 and 1912, in Gornyi Zerentui in 1910, and in the Shlissel'burg Fortress in 1912. Members of the Bolshevik faction in the Fourth Imperial Duma repeatedly protested against the mistreatment of political prisoners in hard labor prisons. Hard labor was abolished in March 1917, after the overthrow of the autocracy.

REFERENCES
Maksimov, S. V. *Sibir' i katorga,* 2nd ed., parts 1–3. St. Petersburg, 1891.
Gernet, M. N. *Istoriia tsarskoi tiur'my,* 3rd ed., vols. 1–5. Moscow, 1960–63.
Dvorianov, V. N. *V sibirskoi dal'nei storone (Ocherki istorii tsarskoi katorgi i ssylki, 60-e gody XVIII v.–1917 g.).* Minsk, 1971.
Spravochniki po istorii dorevoliutsionnoi Rossii: Bibliografiia. Moscow, 1971. Pages 204–08.   N. P. EROSHKIN [11–1594–2]

HARLEQUIN DUCK (*Histrionicus histrionicus*), a bird of the family Anatidae. Length, approximately 45 cm; weight, 500–800 g. The bill is short, the tail is pointed and gradated, and there is a large paddle on the hind digit. The plumage is slate black, with a brightly colored head. The harlequin duck is found in the mountains of Asia (Eastern Siberia) and North America (northwest), as well as along the Atlantic coast of North America and the Greenland and Iceland coasts. It nests near mountain rivers, and winters near rocky sea coasts. The clutch contains four to eight eggs. The harlequin duck feeds on crustaceans, mollusks, and aquatic insects. It is of little commercial significance.   [11–792–4]

HARTEBEEST (*Alcelaphus caama*), an artiodactyl mammal of the family Cavicornia, a member of the group of bubaline antelopes. Body length, up to 230 cm; height at withers, up to 150 cm; weight, up to 180 kg. The hartebeest has a well-proportioned body with slender legs. Both the male and the female have short horns with two sharp curves. The tail is approximately 30 cm long and is covered with long hairs; there is no tuft at its tip. The hartebeest is reddish in color, with a white patch, or "mirror", on the haunches; its head, legs, tail, and thighs are partially black. The hartebeest is found on the savannas of southern Africa. It stays in small groups of five to ten individuals and feeds on grass and leaves. It is hunted for its meat and skin. In many regions the hartebeest is in danger of extinction.   [11–244–3]

HEATER, a device for heating air in air heating and ventilation systems and in dryers. Heaters may be ribbed and made of smooth pipe or of the finned-coil or lobed types. The most common types of heaters are radiators—ribbed heaters in which the heat carrier (steam or hot water) flows through pipes with ribs on the outside, heating the air passing through them. Electric and flame heaters are also used. [11–674–1]

HELMET (in Russian, *kaska*), a leather or metal headgear, usually capped by a metal point or crest, used to protect the head in armies, fire departments, and various paramilitary organizations. Metal helmets appeared in early antiquity (the Bronze Age). In the 18th and 19th centuries helmets were often adorned with feather or horsehair plumes. In World War I all armies used steel helmets as a protection against shrapnel bullets, stones, and small fragments of projectiles, including mines and grenades. The Soviet Army used pointed helmets (*kaski*) until 1939, when they were replaced by plain steel helmets (in Russian, *shlew*). [11–1477–2]

HERPESTES, mongooses, a genus of mammals of the family Viverridae.

The body of the mongoose is low and elongate, from 23 to 64 cm in length; the tail is an additional 23–51 cm. Weight ranges from 0.5 to 3.2 kg. The fur is short, in some, an olive-gray or yellowish-brown monotone, and in others, variegated (with white markings). The inguinal glands produce a strong-smelling secretion. There are eight species of *Herpestes,* distributed in southern Europe, Africa, southern Asia, and neighboring islands. The animals live in forests and brush and among the reeds around bodies of water. They hunt day and night, usually singly, although small groups may form. They live in burrows or natural crevices in the ground. They feed on small rodents, birds, reptiles, fish, crustaceans, and insects. Some species are known for their ability to kill and eat large venomous snakes. There are between two and four offspring in a litter. The animals were imported to the West Indies and the Hawaiian Islands for the purpose of ridding them of rats and snakes, but they reproduced intensively and became harmful to poultry farming. A typical representative of the genus is the ichneumon, or African mongoose. O. L. Rossolimo [11–157–2]

HOLM OAK (*Quercus ilex*), an evergreen tree of the family Fagaceae. It grows to 25 m and has a smooth bark. The leaves are elliptical, leathery, shiny, tomentose beneath, and entire or serrate. The acorns are 2 to 3.5 cm long.

The tree is native to the Mediterranean region, where it is found both in mixed groves and separate stands. In the USSR it is cultivated in the southern Crimea and in the Caucasus along the Black Sea coast (south of Sochi), where it bears abundant fruit every year. The holm oak is ornamental and grows rapidly, attaining a height of 22–25 m in 40–45 years. It is drought resistant, does not require good soil, and can withstand short temperature drops to as low as −20°C. The wood is very hard and durable, with a density of 1.14 g per cu cm, and has a brown core. It is valuable for building underwater structures, and the wood of the roots is used in woodworking. The bark contains up to 7.25 percent of tannins. The holm oak is also suitable for landscaping and forestation. T. G. Leonova [11–786–2]

HOT-BULB ENGINE, an obsolete type of internal-combustion engine in which the gas mixture is ignited by a hot bulb (ignition bulb). Structurally, the hot bulb is the removable noncooled part of the combustion chamber of a hot-bulb engine. [11–667–1]

HOWARD, GEORGE WILLIAM FREDERICK (the seventh earl of Carlisle). Born Apr. 18, 1802, in London; died there Dec. 5, 1864. British political figure; a Whig.

Howard was an active supporter of the parlimentary reform of 1832. He was secretary for Ireland from 1835 to 1841, becoming a member of the cabinet in 1839. Howard was the first among the Whig aristocrats occupying an official post to come out in support of the Anti-Corn Law League. [11–1296–6]

HUNTING (electrical machinery), any periodic deviation in operating performance from the established state.

The most typical form of hunting is variation in the rate of rotation of the shaft in synchronous electrical machines brought about by a sudden change in the load on the shaft or in the parameters in the external electrical network (the disconnection or connection of parts of the network, short circuits in the line, improper connection of a generator to the network during its synchronization). For example, when a rapid change in torque occurs on the shaft of a motor, the rotor alters its angular position, with a certain angular acceleration, in order to reestablish the disturbed equilibrium. When synchronism has been achieved, the rotor, with its extra accumulation of kinetic energy, continues to increase its angular velocity, so that synchronism is again disturbed. As a result of the hunting, the shaft of the electrical machine oscillates mechanically, leading possibly to a disruption of the normal operation of the equipment.

REFERENCE
Petrov, G. N. *Elektricheskie mashiny,* parts 1–3. Moscow-Leningrad, 1956–68. [11–1637–2]

HYDROELECTRIC SYSTEM, a group of hydroelectric power plants located in series along a watercourse and interconnected to form a common water-use system. The construction of a hydroelectric system makes possible more complete use of the energy resources of a river, increases discharge control (which results in increased power and capacity of the hydroelectric plants), and improves the power switching capabilities of individual plants. It is also the most promising course for reconstruction of river transportation.

On the Volga and Kama rivers the construction of hydroelectric systems led to the creation of a waterway with a standard guaranteed depth of 3.65 m for a distance of 3,000 km along the Volga and 1,200 km along the Kama; the Volga-Kama and Dnieper hydroelectric systems are the basis of a standard deepwater transportation system that will link the ports of the Caspian, Black, Baltic, and White seas and the Sea of Azov. The largest systems in the USSR are the Enisei Hydroelectric System (eight plants), the Angara Hydroelectric System (six plants), the Volga Hydroelectric System (eight plants), the Dnieper Hydroelectric System (six plants), and the Kama Hydroelectric System (four plants). [11–1478–1]

HYÈRES, a city in southern France near the Mediterranean coast (Rade d'Hyères), in the Var Department. Population, 38,000 (1968). Hyères is a winter resort and a tourist center. Early vegetables are grown, and salt is extracted from seawater. Hyères was a port in the Middle Ages. [11–216–2]

HYLIDAE, a family of tailless amphibians, ranging from 2.5 to 13.5 cm in length. There are 31 genera, distributed throughout the world, chiefly in the tropical regions of North and South America and in Australia. Many Hylidae are arboreal. Some species reproduce in trees, depositing their eggs in the rainwater that accumulates in the axils of leaves, and others, such as the species of *Phyllomedusa,* lay their eggs in curled leaves overhanging water. The females of the marsupial frogs that inhabit the tropical regions of the New World have a cutaneous sac (pouch) on the back, where the fertilized eggs are deposited. In some species the eggs are carried in the sac only during the first stages, and in others they remain there until fully formed. The most widespread genus is *Hyla,* comprising 350 species, of which two species, *H. arborea* and *H. japonica,* are encountered in the USSR. The species *H. arborea* is found in the Ukraine, including the Crimea, and in the Caucasus. It is up to 5 cm long, and its color may change, depending on surroundings. Males have a voice pouch under the skin on the throat that inflates when they croak. In the spring the female deposits as many as 1,000 eggs in the water. P. V. Terent'ev [11–1691–3]

ICH'ANG, a city in China, in Hupeh Province, on the middle course of the Yangtze River, below Sanhsia Gorge. It is known as the "gateway" to the Szechwan Basin. Population, 90,000 (1956). It is an important river port, transshipment point, and industrial center. The city has chemical, paper, textile, machine-building, food-processing, and pharmaceutical industries.
[11–167–3]

ICHIGI, a type of footwear worn by both men and women. Ichigi are high boots, sewn with soft leather or colored morocco.

Sometimes they have a soft sole and are worn with leather overshoes. Ichigi are worn by some Russians in Siberia, by Tatars and Bashkirs, by most of the peoples of Middle Asia, and by some peoples of the Caucasus, for example, the "archita" worn by the Ossets.   [11–167–4]

ICHIHARA, a city in Japan, on the island of Honshu, on the shore of Tokyo Bay, in the prefecture of Chiba. Population, 156,000 (1970). It has electrical-engineering, petrochemical, and glass industries.   [11–146–5]

ICHIKAWA, SHOICHI. Born Mar. 20, 1892; died Mar. 15, 1945. Activist in the working-class movement of Japan.

Ichikawa graduated from the department of literature at Waseda University in 1916 and became involved in the working-class movement. When the Communist Party of Japan was established in 1922, he joined it and edited the journal *Musan kaikyu* (The Indigent Class). In 1923 he was imprisoned. In 1928 he represented the Communist Party of Japan at the sixth congress of the Comintern in Moscow, where he was elected a member of the organization's Executive Committee. Upon returning to Japan he headed the party's Central Committee. He was arrested in April 1929. At his trial in 1931 he defended the program and tactics of the party. He was sentenced to life imprisonment. In his absence the seventh congress of the Comintern (1935) elected him a member of its Executive Committee. He was tortured to death in Miyagi prison.   [11–145–2]

ICHIKAWA, a city in Japan, on Honshu, in Chiba Prefecture; suburb of Tokyo. Population, 261,000 (1970). Major industries include the building of transport machinery and airplanes, metallurgy, wool textiles, and food processing.   [11–146–1]

ICHIKAWA, one of the oldest actors' dynasties in the Japanese kabuki theater. In Japan an actor's dramatic name traditionally is passed on to his son or adopted pupil. In the 1940's and 1950's, the best-known members of the Ichikawa dynasty were Danjuro XI, Ennosuke II, Sadanji III, Dansiro III, and Yaozo IX. In the 1960's and early 1970's, the Ichikawa dynasty included Ebizo X, Monnosuke VII, and Ennosuke III.

Danjuro Ichikawa is one of the branches of the Ichikawa dynasty of actors. It numbers 11 generations. One of its most outstanding members was Danjuro I (born May 1660; died Feb. 19, 1704). In 1673 he created a new stage makeup, which subsequently became the traditional makeup for the *aragoto* roles (war heroes). Another notable representative was Danjuro Ichikawa XI (born Jan. 6, 1909; died Nov. 10, 1965). He was among the most popular contemporary actors of the kabuki theater. He usually portrayed romantic, heroic masculine characters (*tachiyaku* roles).

Another branch of the dynasty, the Sadanji Ichikawa, numbers three generations. The most outstanding member of this branch was Sadanji Ichikawa II (born Oct. 19, 1880; died Feb. 23, 1940). He contributed to the development of the modern drama, the *shingeki,* in Japanese theater. One of the most progressive actors of his time, Sadanji II sought to revitalize the art of the kabuki. In 1928 he headed a company which performed in Moscow.

Ennosuke Ichikawa is a third branch of the Ichikawa dynasty. The most prominent representative of this branch was Ennosuke Ichikawa II (born May 10, 1888; died June 12, 1963). In 1919 he went abroad to become acquainted with the dramatic arts of Western Europe and North America. In 1944 he became the head of the four most important kabuki theatrical companies. From 1955 to 1963, Ennosuke II was a member of the Academy of Arts of Japan. In 1961 he and his company toured the USSR.

REFERENCES
Kabuki. Moscow, 1965. [Translated from English. Introductory article and notes by L. D. Grisheleva.]
Gundzi, M. *Iaponskii teatr kabuki.* Moscow, 1969.
                                    L. D. GRISHELEVA [11–145–1]

I CHING (Book of Changes), ancient Chinese literary classic, originally used in the process of divination and later incorporated into the Confucian canon (the Five Books). The oldest section of the *I Ching* consists of 64 graphic figures (hexagrams), with an aphorism attached to each and explaining its significance. This section appears to date back to the eighth or seventh century B.C. In the fourth and third centuries B.C., a number of interpretations of the hexagrams and aphorisms were written, known as the Ten Wings. These laid the basis for a specific trend in ancient Chinese thought that proceeded from the conception of changeability of all reality and the cyclical transformation of various phenomena into others as the result of the interrelation of yin and yang, the forces of darkness and light. According to this view, the hexagrams were symbols that illustrated the universal revolution of the cosmos and also provided norms of behavior for people. Within this framework, various natural philosophical conceptions were elaborated that later played a significant role in the emergence of neo-Confucianism. A large number of Chinese and Japanese philosophical works of medieval and modern times have also sought to interpret the *I Ching*.

REFERENCES
Shutskii, Iu. K. *Kitaiskaia klassicheskaia 'Kniga peremen'.* Moscow, 1960.
Wilhelm, R. *I. ging: Das Buch der Wandlungen,* vols. 1–2. Jena, 1924. (Translated from Chinese into German and illustrated.)
                                                      [11–167–1]

ICHINOMIYA, a city in Japan, in the southern part of Honshu, in Aichi Prefecture. Part of the Nagoya conurbation. Population, 219,000 (1970). It is a center of the textile industry and has garment factories and dyeing enterprises. Rubber goods are also produced.   [11–146–4]

ICHINSKAIA SOPKA (Hoashen), the highest and only active volcano in the Sredinnyi Range of Kamchatka, situated on the range's first western chain. It has an altitude of 3,621 m and is composed chiefly of andesite and dacite lava. The three peaks of the cone are covered with snow and glaciers the year round. At an altitude of about 3,000 m, there are active outflows of hot gases (fumaroles and solfataras). There are many minor domes and slag cones.   [11–167–5]

ICHKO, TREATY OF, an agreement between the leaders of the First Serbian Uprising (1804–13) and the Turkish government of Selim III, concluded in December 1806. It is named for the representative of the rebels, Petar Ichko. According to the terms of the treaty, the numerous taxes levied on the Serbs were henceforth to be paid as a single tribute, collected by the Serbian authorities and turned over to a Turkish finance official; Turks would be permitted to live only in the cities of Serbia; the janissaries were to be removed from the country; and the Serbs were to take over the defense of their own borders. The agreement established the basis for the de facto autonomy of Serbia. In December 1806, with the outbreak of the Russo-Turkish War of 1806–12, it was repudiated by the Serbs, who renewed the struggle against the Turks in alliance with Russia.

SOURCE
Novaković, St. "Ičkov mir." *Glasnik Srpske kraljevske akademije,* 1903, book 66.   [11–167–6]

ICHNIA, a city (since 1957), administrative center of Ichnia Raion, Chernigov Oblast, Ukrainian SSR. It has a railroad station on the Odessa-Bakhmach line. Population, 13,700 (1971). A distillery, a powdered milk plant, a cannery, a packaging plant, and a brickyard are located there.   [11–168–1]

ICHTHYOFAUNA, the aggregate of fishes of any body of water or basin of a zoogeographic region and the aggregate of fishes inhabiting the earth at any given period of its history. The ichthyofauna of most basins is not uniform in origin; it is composed of species differing in their geographic origin and grouped in different faunal complexes. For example, the ichthyofauna of the Aral basin is composed of the highland-Asiatic faunal complex and of the Ponto-Caspian, the Turkestan, and other complexes. The diversity of the ichthyofauna is determined by the initial faunal complexes that formed a given ichthyofauna, by the history of the basin, and by present-day life conditions of the various species of fishes. As a rule, in the number of species the ichthyofauna of tropical waters is the more diverse, and most diverse is the ichthyofauna of the equatorial waters of the western Pacific Ocean. The poorest ichthyofauna is that of the arctic waters. [11–163–1]

ICHTHYOL, an anti-inflammatory, locally analgesic, and, to some extent, antiseptic agent; an ammonium salt of the sulfonic acids of shale oil.

Ichthyol is applied externally for skin conditions (burns, erysipelas, eczema); for neuralgia and arthritides, in the form of ointments or aqueous-alcoholic lotions; and for diseases of the pelvic organs (metritis, parametritis, salpingitis, prostatitis), in the form of suppositories. Ichthyol ointment, ichthyol-naphthalane ointment, ichthyol-naphthalane paste, and ichthyol suppositories are manufactured. [11–159–1]

ICHTHYOLOGY, a branch of vertebrate zoology that studies fish and their structure, the functioning of their organs, their life habits in all stages of development, and their distribution in time and space, classification, and evolution. Ichthyological research encourages the efficient management of the fishing industry, promoting the development of fishing and fish culture. The many-sided study of fish has led to a number of important biological generalizations on the question of species, variation and evolution, distribution of fishes (bipolar and amphiboreal distribution, theory of faunal complexes), the theory of development (stages in development, for example) and migrations, and population dynamics. These generalizations are also important for the development of bionics (primarily biohydroacoustics) and some other problems.

The oldest generalizations in ichthyology date back to Hindu scholars (Susruta, sixth century B.C.). The first book on fish culture, one also containing information on fish habits, was published in China in the middle of the first millennium B.C. The first systematization of fish is found in Aristotle (fourth century B.C.), who in his *History of Animals* treated fish as a separate group of aquatic vertebrates and included many facts on their anatomy, reproduction, and habits. Knowledge of fish in Europe did not increase significantly until the 15th century. It was not until the second half of the 15th century that economic development and the expansion of trade created more favorable conditions for the development of all branches of natural science, including the study of fish mainly as a valuable economic object. A great deal of information was gathered in 450 years (15th–19th centuries) on the fauna of marine and freshwater fish (the works of the French scientists P. Belon and G. Rondelet, the Italian scientist I. Salviani, the Swedish scientists P. Artedi and C. Linnaeus, and the German scientists M. Bloch and J. Müller). Later, fish fauna was studied by the French scientist A. Valenciennes; the American scientists D. Jordan and C. Hubbs; the British scientists A. Günther; H. Boulanger, C. Regan, and J. Norman; and the Swedish scientist E. A. Stensio. The scientists who investigated the fish fauna of Russia, including S. P. Krasheninnikov, P. S. Pallas, J. A. Güldenstaedt, I. I. Lepekhin, E. I. Eikhval'd (C. E. Eichwald), K. F. Kessler, and N. A. Varpakhovskiy, made particularly important contributions.

In the 19th century, ichthyology separated from zoology and became an independent discipline. A new stage in its development was begun, directly connected with the rapid increase in fishing and characterized by research on the population dynamics of commercial fish, the effect of fishing on fish reserves, and the conditions of propagation of fish reserves. In Russia, the scientific and commercial research undertaken by K. M. Baer and N. Ia. Danilevskii in the Caspian Sea, the Sea of Azov, the Black and North seas, and Lake Pskov was very important.

Scientific and commercial research was carried out in the late 19th century and in the early 20th century by the German scientist F. Heinke (on herring), the Danish scientist C. Petersen (on cod and flounder), and the Norwegian scientist J. Jort (on herring and cod). In Russia, research at this time was concerned with the development of fish culture (V. P. Vrasskii, O. A. Grimm, I. N. Arnol'd, N. A. Borodin) and with the study of the

country's natural fish resources in connection with the opening up of new commercial regions and maintenance of an efficient fishing industry (the studies of V. K. Brazhnikov, V. K. Soldatov, and P. Iu. Shmidt on the Far Eastern seas, those of V. I. Meisner, A. N. Derzhavin, K. A. Kiselevich, and N. L. Chugunov on the Caspian). The work of N. M. Knipovich, who was director of the Murmansk (1898–1901), Caspian (1904, 1912–13, 1914–15), and Azov–Black Sea (1922–27) expeditions, was particularly important. Other important contributions were made by L. S. Berg (classification, distribution, paleontology of fishes), V. V. Vasnetsov and S. G. Kryzhanovskii (morphology and embryology of fish), I. F. Pravdin (classification of fish), A. N. Severtsov (anatomy of fish), and E. K. Suvorov (commercial ichthyology).

Beginning in the middle of the 20th century, ichthyologists developed better methods of studying the age and growth of fish, feeding habits, reproduction, population dynamics, and the distribution and migration of fish. Recent advances in physics and chemistry were incorporated into the methods of ichthyological research and into the fishing industry: for example, the use of sonar for locating fish, electric lights to attract and catch fish, and radioisotopes to study the nutrition of fish and to label them. Extensive underwater observations are made at various depths using bathyscaphes, bathyplanes, and underwater television. As a result, it has become possible to make a detailed study of the reaction of fish to sound waves of different frequencies, to light, and to the effects of the electric and magnetic fields. Research in these directions in the USSR is carried out at several institutes of the Academy of Sciences of the USSR and at certain universities and institutes of the fishing industry. Ichthyologists are studying fish ecology, classification and zoogeography (handbooks and surveys of all the principal faunas and groups of fish have been prepared), morphology, embryology, physiology and biochemistry (also the physiology of metabolism and fish behavior), genetics, and paleoichthyology.

The chief concerns of modern ichthyology are the dynamics of fish schools, the development of fish (both individual and historical), and the behavior and migration of fish. These matters must be studied in order to promote active marine fishing, propagation of commercial fish reserves, particularly in rivers where the flow has been regulated, and pond fish culture. The urgent tasks of modern ichthyology include the development of a scientific foundation for increasing the extraction of food resources from oceanic waters and the intensification of their exploitation and the creation of an efficient fishing industry in marine and continental waters. A major objective is to elaborate the principles and methods of increasing the productivity of aquatic ecosystems by stimulating the reproduction of schools of commercial fish and exploiting them efficiently, reconstructing the ichthyofauna of bodies of water, and initiating meliorative measures.

There are international associations that promote the development of ichthyological research. The largest are the International Council for the Exploration of the Sea (founded in 1902), the International Commission for the North Atlantic Fisheries, and the Soviet-Japanese Fishing Commission. Soviet ichthyologists take part in their work. The fishing division of the Food and Agriculture Organization of the United Nations with its regional councils and commissions plays a major role in organizing international measures in the fishing industry.

Ichthyological research is conducted in most countries by many scientific organizations. It is especially well developed in the USSR, Japan, the United States, Canada, Great Britain, France, Poland, the German Democratic Republic, the Federal Republic of Germany, Norway, Sweden, Denmark, Iceland, India, and Australia.

In the USSR ichthyological research is conducted at the All-Union Scientific Research Institute of Marine Fisheries and Oceanography (VNIRO) and at such marine institutes as the Polar Scientific Research Institute of Marine Fisheries and Oceanography (PINRO) with a branch in Arkhangel'sk, the Pacific Institute (TINRO) with branches (Kamchatka, Okhotsk, Sakhalin, Amur), the Atlantic Institute (AtlantNIRO), the Azov–Black Sea Institute (AzcherNIRO) with a branch in Odessa, and the Azov, Caspian, and Baltic institutes. In addition there are the Institute of Sturgeon Culture with branches and the Estonian and Azerbaijan laboratories; the State Institute of Lake and River Fisheries (Gos. NIORKh) with branches; the Siberian Institute of the Fishing Industry (Sib. NIRKh) with branches; the All-Union Institute of Pond Fisheries (VNIIPRKh) with branches; the Ukrainian Institute of Lake, River, and Pond Fisheries; the Byelorussian Institute of the Fishing Industry; the Kazakh Institute of the Fishing Industry with branches; and institutes of the Academy of Sciences of the USSR (Institute of Zoology, Institute of Evolutionary Morphology and Ecology of Animals, Institute of Oceanography, Institute of Biology of Inland Waters, Murmansk Institute of Marine Biology, Far Eastern Institute of the Biology of the Sea). There are also institutes of the republic academies, notably, the Institute of the Biology of the Southern Seas of the Ukrainian Academy of Sciences, the Institute of Hydrobiology of the Ukrainian Academy of Sciences, the Sevan Hydrobiological Station of the Armenian Academy of Sciences, and Moscow State University, Leningrad State Universty, Tomsk State University, Irkutsk State University, and the Kaliningrad Higher Fish Technical Educational Institution.

Specialists in ichthyology are trained at various universities (Moscow, Leningrad, Tomsk, Perm', Odessa, Kazan, Kishinev) and in technical institutes and technicums of the fishing industry. All ichthyological research is coordinated by the Ichthyological Commission of the Ministry of the Fishing Industry of the USSR and the Scientific Council for Ichthyology and Hydrobiology of the Academy of Sciences of the USSR.

The results of ichthyological research are published in the *Trudy* of the various institutes and in such journals as *Voprosy ikhtiologii* (since 1953), *Zoologicheskii zhurnal* (since 1916), and *Rybnoe khoziaistvo* (since 1920). Among the ichthyological journals published abroad are *Copeia* (New York, since 1930), *Journal of Fisheries Research Board of Canada* (Ottawa, since 1934), and *Japanese Journal of Ichthyology* (Tokyo, since 1950).

REFERENCES
Ocherki po obshchim voprosam ikhtiologii. Edited by E. N. Pavlovskii. Moscow-Leningrad, 1953.
Berg, L. S. *Sistema ryboobraznykh i ryb, nyne zhivushchikh i iskopaemykh,* 2nd ed. Moscow-Leningrad, 1955.
Suvorov, E. K. *Osnovy ikhtiologii,* 2nd ed. Moscow, 1948.
Soldatov, V. K. *Promyslovaia ikhtiologiia,* parts 1–2. Moscow-Leningrad, 1934–38.
Nikol'skii, G. V. *Ekologiia ryb.* Moscow, 1963.
Nikol'skii, G. V. *Teoriia dinamiki stada ryb kak biologicheskaia osnova ratsional'noi ekspluatatsii i vosproizvodstva rybnykh resursov.* Moscow, 1965.
Nikol'skii, G. V. *Chastnaia ikhtiologiia,* 3rd ed. Moscow, 1971.
Iudkin, I. *Ikhtiologiia,* 5th ed. Moscow, 1970.
G. V. NIKOL'SKII [11–159–2]

ICHTHYOPHTHIRIOSIS, an invasive disease of many species of fish caused by the ciliate *Ichthyophthirius.*

Ichthyophthyriosis is often found on fish farms in eastern and western Europe, Canada, and the USA. All age groups of fish are susceptible to the disease, but the most severe ichthyophthiriosis occurs in fry and in breeders older than three years. The source of infestation is other fish affected by the disease. The parasites produce inflammation of the skin, fins, gills, and eyes. The affected fish become less active, keep to the shore, and hardly react to external stimulation. Farms affected with ichthyophthiriosis are subject to quarantine restrictions and their ponds and fish stock are disinfected. The diseased fish are treated in saline and other baths. [11–163–2]

ICHTHYOPHTHIRIUS, a genus of protozoa of the order Holotricha comprising the one species (*Ichthyophthirius multifiliis*). It parasitizes fish that live in fresh and slightly saline waters, under the epithelium of the skin and gills, under the cornea of the eye, and often the fins; it produces whitish swellings of the skin—pustules. At 28°C the growth of *Ichthyophthirius* in the fish lasts about one day and at 20°C, seven days. Mature infusorians (up to 1 mm in size)—trophonts—emerge from the pustules into the water and, upon falling to the bottom of the water, become encysted. In the cyst, division occurs eight to 12 times

and 500 to 1,000 (sometimes up to 2,000) tiny forms (20–30 microns in diameter) develop, which are covered with cilia. Known as tomites, these forms emerge from the cyst into the water and infect other fish. *Ichthyophthirius* often cause mass destruction of fish, particularly of fry. Their control is effected with chemical agents. [11–163–3]

ICHTHYOPTERYGIA, a subclass of extinct Mesozoic reptiles, which attained their widest distribution in the Jurassic Period. The sole order is Ichthyosauria. The Ichthyopterygia were large (up to 12 m long) predators, the descendants of terrestrial animals that adapted to life in the open sea and underwent a number of changes in structure: the body acquired a fish-like form, the snout became elongated, the neck disappeared, the extremities were converted into paddle-like organs, cutaneous fins developed on the end of the tail and on the back, the vertebrae became biconcave (as in fish), sclerotic plates counteracting water pressure appeared in the eye sockets, and the skin lost its scaly covering.

Owing to the fact that the Ichthyopterygia were exclusively acquatic and the structure of their extremities was such that they were unable to emerge on dry land, they became viviparous. Their principal food was fish and cephalopods. Remains of ichthyopterygia are distributed in Mesozoic marine deposits of the northern hemisphere, including the USSR; the most numerous finds are in Central Europe. The resemblance of these reptiles to sharks and dolphins (animals of different classes of vertebrates), which developed in the process of evolution as a result of similar ways of life, is a classic example of morphological convergence.

REFERENCE
Osnovy paleontologii: Zemnovodnye, presmykaiushchiesia i ptitsy. Moscow, 1964.   A. K. ROZHDESTVENSKII [11–158–4]

ICHTHYORNITHES, an order of extinct toothed birds widespread in the Cretaceous period. There were two genera. The birds, known from North America, measure up to 1 m high. In contrast to birds that lived in the Cenozoic, the Ichthyornithes had biconcave vertebrae, and their jaws were studded with tiny sharp teeth that bent backward and were set in separate sockets. The left and right rami of the lower jaw were not joined. The Ichthyornithes had a well-developed sternum with a keel and wings and flew well. They fed on fish. [11–162–1]

ICHTHYOSIS, fish skin disease, xeroderma, a skin disease characterized by sharply increased keratogenesis and retarded keratolysis.

Incidence of ichthyosis is a familial condition in half the cases and hereditary in 25 percent. It appears in early childhood (most often around age three), intensifies at puberty, and lasts throughout life. It is expressed in dryness of the skin and the accumulation of horny masses on the skin's surface, in the form of scales or of massive horny plates that resemble fish scales. The excretion of oil and perspiration decreases sharply. The affection spreads over the entire skin surface, except at joint folds, axillae, and inguinal folds. On the face and scalp, ichthyosis appears in the form of furfuraceous desquamation. The condition of the skin improves in the summertime as a result of increased excretion of oil and sweat. Ichthyosis is treated with hot baths containing soda or table salt, followed by lubrication of the skin with emollient creams. Cod-liver oil and vitamins may be taken internally (in particular vitamin A). In the summer, prolonged sojourns in the south can be helpful (sea bathing).
I. N. VEDROVA [11–158–3]

ICHTHYOSTEGA, the most ancient and primitive genus of extinct amphibians. *Ichthyostega* measured approximately 1 m long. The structure of its skull as a whole was that of most labyrinthodonts, but there were characteristics typical of crossopterygians (short snout with a rostral element, vestiges of bones of the gill cover, lateral organs enclosed in bony canals). The extremities and girdles were constructed like those of terrestrial animals, but the tail bore a fin with bony rays. Apparently *Ichthyostega* lived in water and never abandoned it for long. It is an important connecting link between terrestrial vertebrates and fish, and proves the origin of amphibians from crossopterygians. Remains of *Ichthyostega* and closely related forms have been discovered in Upper Devonian deposits of Greenland.

REFERENCE
Shmal'gauzen, I. I. *Proiskhozhdenie nazemnykh pozvonochnykh.* Moscow, 1964. Chapter 8.   [11–162–2]

ICH'UN, a city in Northeast China, in Heilungkiang Province, at the confluence of the T'angwangho and Ich'unho (Sungari basin), on the slope of the Lesser Khingan Range. It is a center of the lumber industry and has wood-products and chemical enterprises.   [11–168–2]

ICTERIDAE, a family of birds of the order Passeriformes. The body is 16.5–53 cm long. The bill is conical, slender in some species, and massive and sometimes enlarged at the base in others. The tail is graduate, and the plumage black or brownish, sometimes with red or yellow patches. There are 88 species, distributed throughout North and South America. They inhabit deserts, prairies, swamps, and forests, biologically replacing skylarks, starlings, orioles, and other Old World birds. Many species are polygamous and form colonies. Their nests vary from small open ones on the ground to large (1.8 m long) "purses" in trees. The number of eggs in a clutch varies from two or three (in the tropics) to five or six; only the female sits on them. Some species are parasites, depositing their eggs in the nests of other birds. They feed on insects, seeds, nectar, and the juice of fruits, and certain species, for example, *Icterus galbula,* injure fruit trees.
                                                                   [11–1503–3]

IFE, a city in Nigeria, in the Western State. Population, 154,600 (1970). Highway junction and center of the cocoa industry. It is the site of a university, founded in 1961, and of the Ife Museum. Gold is mined near the city.

Ife is one of the most important centers of ancient civilization in West Africa. From the 12th century to the 19th, Ife was the city-state of the Yoruba people. The Yorubas still revere Ife as their ancestral homeland. The city has been studied since 1908, and systematic excavation began in 1953.

The flowering of Ife's artistic culture, apparently related to the earlier Nok culture, occurred between the 12th and 14th centuries. The bronze and terra-cotta sculpture found in the city has become famous throughout the world. The terra-cotta heads, which were placed on sacrificial altars, are outstanding for the perfection and beauty of their forms. The softly modeled faces have an unusual delicacy of textural nuances. The bronze heads depicting gods and rulers are executed on a relatively large scale and employ a simplified stylization. The elaborate headdresses and facial markings impart a certain decorative quality. Equally striking are the bronze half-figures, apparently of the kings of Ife, in which elastic plasticity and harmonious proportions combine with a wealth of ornamental decoration. The rich and varied plastic forms (gods of the Yoruba pantheon and deified kings, called *oni*) created by the anonymous artists of Ife, were apparently used in sacrificial ceremonies in honor of the Yorubas' ancestors. Ife's bronze sculpture greatly influenced the development of Benin's artistic culture. Certain stone relics date from an earlier period, such as the 5.16-m granite pillar called Opa Oranyan (Staff of Oranyan, a mighty warrior and the son of the founder of Ife, Oduduwa).

REFERENCES
Ol'derogge, D. A. *Iskusstvo narodov Zapadnoi Afriki v muzeiakh SSSR.* Leningrad-Moscow, 1958.
Frobenius, L. *The Voice of Africa,* vols. 1–2. London, 1913.
An Introduction to the Art of Ife. Lagos, 1955.
Willett, F. "Ife and Its Archaeology." *Journal of African History,* 1960, vol. 1, no. 2, pp. 231–48.
Willett, F. *Ife in the History of West African Sculpture.* [London, 1967.]
                                                                   [11–154–3]

IFFLAND, AUGUST WILHELM. Born Apr. 19, 1759, in Hannover; died Sept. 22, 1814, in Berlin. German actor, playwright, and director.

Iffland, the son of a pastor, received a religious education. From 1777 to 1779 he was an actor in the theater of Gotha. From 1779 to 1796 he performed in Mannheim Theater, becoming its principal director in 1792. Iffland began working in the Berlin Royal Theater in 1796. He portrayed Franz Moor and Phillip in Schiller's *The Robbers* and *Don Carlos,* Shylock in Shakespeare's *The Merchant of Venice,* and the title role in Lessing's *Nathan the Wise.* His best performances were in his own plays or in plays written by A. von Kotzebue.

Iffland's plays are representative of the genre known as bourgeois drama. In his plays *Crime From Vainglory* (1784) and *The Hunters* (1785; Russian translation, 1802) the virtuous little world of the burgher, into which evil intrudes in the person of the nobleman, is depicted. His only political drama, *The Cockades* (1791), reflects the events of the Great French Revolution and ends with the revolutionaries' abandonment of their struggle. As a director, Iffland devoted a great deal of attention to the staging of a performance. His memoirs, *My Career in Theater* (1798; Russian translation, 1816), reflect his experiences.

WORKS
Dramatische Werke, vols. 1–16. Leipzig, 1798–1802.
REFERENCES
Troitskii, Z. "Avgust-Vil'gel'm Iffland." In *Karl Zeidel'man i formirovanie stsenicheskogo realizma v Germanii.* Moscow-Leningrad, 1940.
Klingenberg, K. H. *Iffland und Kotzebue als Dramatiker.* Weimar, 1962.
                                                                   [11–156–4]

IFNI, a region in Morocco. Seized by Spain in 1860, the region was included in the Spanish zone of Morocco under the Franco-Spanish agreements of 1904 and 1912 for the division of spheres of influence in that country. In 1958, Spain proclaimed it a Spanish province. Its people long resisted the Spanish colonialists, and after many years of negotiations between the governments of Spain and Morocco, a treaty was concluded on Jan. 4, 1969, returning Ifni to Morocco. In June 1969 the region was reunited with Morocco, becoming part of Tarfaya Province.
                                                                   [11–156–1]

IFUGAO, a people living in central Luzon (Philippines). Population, 100,000 (1970, estimate). Their language is related to the Indonesian languages. Most of the Ifugao have retained their ancient religious beliefs (headhunting was part of their rites until the early 20th century), although some have been converted to Christianity. The chief occupation is hoe cultivation. On the mountain slopes is found one of the most extensive systems of rice terraces in the world. Corn, taro, sweet potatoes, yams, and cotton are also cultivated, and the most important domestic animals are chickens and pigs. Handicrafts such as weaving, plaiting, and blacksmithing are well developed.

REFERENCES
Barton, R. F. "Ifugao, malaiskoe plemia nagornoi chasti Filippin." In the collection *Sovetskaia etnografiia,* nos. 1–2. Moscow, 1931.
Narody Iugo-Vostochnoi Azii. Moscow, 1966.
Conklin, H. C. *Ifugao Bibliography.* New Haven, 1968.   [11–156–3]

IHARA SAIKAKU (also Ibara Saikaku; pseudonym of Togo Hirayama). Born in 1642; died in 1693. Japanese writer.

Saikaku was the son of a merchant. He published several collections of verse in the genre of humorous *renga* ("linked verse") and became famous for the speed of his poetic improvisation. Saikaku's first novel, *The Life of an Amorous Man* (1682), which depicted the life of the merchant class, enjoyed enormous success. Among his other works are the novel *The Life of an Amorous Woman* (1686), the collection of novellas *Five Women Who Loved Love* (1686), and the collection of short stories *Saikaku's Tales of the Provinces* (1685). In the last years of his life, Saikaku wrote in the didactic genre (*Eitaigura,* 1688), warning townspeople against prodigality and imitating the aristocracy. He was the first Japanese writer to reflect the life of the modern city and to support the third estate in its demand for equality. Saikaku is called the Japanese Boccaccio. He influenced the development of the national literature not only by the new content of his works but also by his style.

WORKS
In Russian translation:
Novelly. [Commentary by E. Pinus and V. Markova and introductory article by E. Pinus.] Moscow, 1959.
REFERENCE
Ivanenko, N. G. "Ikhara Saikaku i ego sbornik novell 'Eitaigura'." In the collection *Kitai, Iaponiia.* Moscow, 1961.

N. G. IVANENKO [11–157–1]

I HO CH'UAN (Righteous Harmony Fists), the secret religious society in China that led the Boxer (I Ho T'uan) Rebellion (1899–1901). It became widespread after 1898. Those who joined the society vowed "not to be greedy, not to indulge in debauchery, not to disobey parents, not to violate existing laws, and to destroy foreigners and kill corrupt officials." The society's teachings were dominated by medieval backwardness, completely rejecting Western science and culture. The group was especially active in Shantung and Chihli provinces and drew its chief support from peasants, who naïvely believed that if they trained their bodies and learned certain magical incantations they would achieve immortality in fighting the enemy. Their anti-imperialist struggle was accompanied by attacks on the feudal nobility and the Ch'ing authorities. After the suppression of the revolt, I Ho Ch'uan disbanded.   [11–165–1]

IIA, a river in Irkutsk Oblast, RSFSR. Length, 486 km; basin area, 18,100 sq km. Arising on the northern slopes of the Vostochnyi Saian, it is a mountain river in its upper reaches. Farther down, its valley widens and its flow becomes calmer. Eventually it flows into Oka Gulf of the Bratsk Reservoir, which extends for 320 km. The river is fed chiefly by rain. The average annual rate of flow at the city of Tulun, 119 km from the mouth, is 149 cu m per sec. The river freezes over in late October or early November and thaws in late April or early May. Its chief tributaries include the Kirei, from the right, and the Ikei and Ilir, from the left.   [11–186–2]

IIUS, BELYI AND CHERNYI (White and Black Iius), two rivers in Khakass Autonomous Oblast, Krasnoiarsk Krai, RSFSR. The Belyi Iius (Pikhterek) is 224 km long and has a basin area of 5,370 sq km, and the Chernyi Iius is 178 km long and has a basin area of 4,290 sq km. Both rivers originate on the eastern slopes of the Kuznetsk Alatau. On their upper reaches, both are swift mountain rivers; lower down, they flow across the hilly steppes on the western edge of the Chulym-Enisei basin. They are fed chiefly by melting snow. The average annual rate of flow on the Belyi Iius, 55 km from its mouth, is 41 cu m per sec. Both rivers are used to float logs. The two rivers eventually flow together to form the Chulym River, a right tributary of the Ob'.   [11–186–1]

IKHSANOVA, LIABIBA FAIZOVNA. Born Aug. 23, 1923, in the village of Srednie Shuni, Viatskie Poliany Raion, Kirov Oblast. Soviet Tatar children's writer. Member of the CPSU since 1945.

The daughter of a village school teacher, Ikhsanova graduated from the geography department of the University of Kazan in 1948. Her first book, *On the Serebrianka River,* appeared in 1948 (Russian translation, 1953). Other significant works include the science fiction novella *Seven Days in the Earth* (1949; Russian translation, 1959); the collections of stories *Bright Dreams* (1952) and *Street of the Cosmonauts* (1963); and the novellas *Niiaz* (1959), *Niiaz in School* (1961), *The Willows Are Bending* (1964), *A Mother's Diary* (1968), and *Little Spark* (1969).

WORKS
In Russian translation:
Rebiata iz Sary Alan. Moscow, 1970.   [11–158–1]

IOKUBONIS, GEDIMINAS AL'BINO. Born Mar. 8, 1927, in Kupishkis. Soviet sculptor. Honored Art Worker of the Lithuanian SSR (1965). Corresponding member of the Academy of Arts of the USSR (1967).

Iokubonis studied at the Kaunas Institute of Applied and Decorative Art (1946–51) and at the Art Institute of the Lithuanian SSR in Vilnius (1952) under I. I. Mikenas. An audacious generalization of forms and an energetic manifestation of the plastic structure of the volume typify his monuments and sculptures, which display national-romantic spirit. Iokubonis' works include *The Chairman of the Kolkhoz* (bronze, 1957), and a portrait of I. Ianulenis (granite, 1962), both in the Art Museum of the Lithuanian SSR, Vilnius; a monument to the victims of fascism in the village of Pirchiupis (granite, 1960; Lenin Prize, 1963; architect V. P. Gabriunas); a portrait of I. Venozhinskis (granite, 1964); and a monument to Lenin in Il'ich square in Moscow (bronze and granite, 1967; architect V. A. Chekanauskas).

REFERENCE
Budrys, St. *Gediminas Jokūbonis.* Vilnius, 1963.   [11–224–1]

IORDAN, IORGU. Born Sept. 29 (Oct. 11), 1888, in Tecuci. Rumanian linguist and academician of the Academy of the Socialist Republic of Rumania (1945). Specialist in comparative Romance philology, Rumanian language and toponomy, and French and Italian literary history.

After graduating from the University of Iaşi, Iordan completed his studies in Western Europe. He was a professor at the University of Iaşi (1911–46) and of Bucharest (1946–58) and served as director of the Institute of Linguistics (1949–52 and from 1958). Between 1945 and 1947 he was Rumanian ambassador to the USSR, and in 1955 he was appointed chairman of the Commission for the Study of the Development of the Rumanian Language and People under the auspices of the Academy of the Socialist Republic of Rumania. He founded the bulletin *Alexandru Philippide* (1934–48), published by the Institute of Rumanian Philology, and has served as editor in chief of the journals *Limba romînă* (from 1952) and *Revue de linguistique* (1956–63), renamed *Revue roumaine de linguistique* in 1964.

WORKS
Lingvistica romanică: Evoluţie, Curente, Metode. Bucharest, 1962.
Limba romînă contemporană, 2nd ed. Bucharest, 1956.
Toponimia romînească. Bucharest, 1963.
In Russian translation:
Grammatika rumynskogo iazyka. Moscow, 1950.
Romanskoe iazykoznanie. Moscow, 1971.   R. A. AGEEVA [11–229–1]

IORGA, NICOLAE. Born June 18, 1871, in Botoşani; died Nov. 28, 1940, near Bucharest. Rumanian political figure, historian, and literary scholar; academician of the Rumanian Academy (1910).

In 1906, Iorga was one of the founders of the reactionary National Democratic Party. From 1918 to 1920 he served as chairman of the National Assembly and from 1931 to 1932 as prime minister and minister of public education. Iorga wrote numerous works on the history of Rumania, Turkey, and the Balkan countries; he also studied Rumanian literature of various periods and wrote the *History of Romance Literatures.* He founded the literary movement known as Sămănătorism (from the name of the journal, *Sămănătorul* [The Sower]), which emerged as a result of the intensification of the peasant question in Rumania. As leader of the movement, Iorga called for the creation of a literature that could be understood equally by "lord and peasant." In foreign policy, he supported an Anglo-French orientation. During the last years of his life, he denounced the aggressive policy of fascist Germany. He was killed in 1940 by fascists belonging to the Iron Guard.

WORKS
Geschichte des rumänischen Volkes in Rahmen seiner Staatsbildungen, vols. 1–2. Gotha, 1905.
Geschichte des osmanischen Reiches, vols. 1–5. Gotha, 1908–13.
La Place des roumains dans l'histoire universelle, vols. 1–3. Bucharest, 1935.
Istoria Românilor, vols. 1–10. Bucharest, 1936–39.
Istoria literaturii romîne din veacul XIX, vols. 1–3. Bucharest, 1907–09.
Istoria presei romîneşti [De la primele începuturi pănă la 1916 . . .]. Bucharest, 1922.
Istoria literaturii romîneşti, 2nd ed., vols. 1–3. Bucharest, 1925–33.
Istoria literaturii contemporane, vols. 1–2. Bucharest, 1934.

REFERENCE

Dradoiescu, P. "N. Iorga, date biografice." *Cuvîntul romînesc,* 1920–21.
vol. 2.   Iu. A. Kozhevnikov and A. I. Telefus   [11–228–1]

IOSHKAR-OLA (Tsarevokokshaisk until 1919, Krasnokokshaisk from 1919 to 1927), a city, the capital of Mari ASSR. Located 50 km north of the Volga, on its left tributary, the Malaia Kokshaga. The city has a railroad station on a branch of the Kazan-Moscow line, and it is a highway junction. Population, 180,000 (1972; it was 1,700 in 1897, 4,300 in 1926, and 27,000 in 1939).

Ioshkar-Ola was founded in 1584 on the orders of Tsar Fedor Ivanovich after the incorporation of the Mari lands into the Russian state. It became part of Kazan Province in 1708 and became a district center in 1781. Soviet power was established there on Dec. 23, 1917 (Jan. 5, 1918). An anti-Soviet mutiny of Socialist Revolutionaries and bourgeois nationalists broke out in the city on Aug. 14, 1918, but was suppressed on August 28 by the 1st Nizhny Novgorod Workers' Detachment and the 1st Lettish Revolutionary Detachment.

In the years of Soviet power Ioshkar-Ola has become a big industrial center. The leading branches are machine building and metalworking, with the Elektroavtomatika Plant (which produces electrical automatic equipment), a plant producing semiconductor instruments, the Kontakt Plant, and plants producing commercial equipment, lumber machinery, and tools. The food industry is represented by a vitamin factory, a dairy, a canning plant, a meat-packing combine, and a confectionary factory; light industry is represented by an artificial leather plant and knitted goods, clothing, and footwear factories. Furniture and building materials are also produced. The educational institutions of Ioshkar-Ola include a university, a polytechnical institute, a pedagogical institute, a technological technicum, a construction technicum, a sovkhoz-technicum, a medical school, a music school, a cultural and educational school, and a research institute of language, literature, and history. The museum of local lore, which was founded in 1924, has archaeological collections and a collection of Soviet art. The city is the site of the Mari-language M. Shketan Theater of Music and Drama (1960, architects P. A. Samsonov and M. F. Ni), a Russian-language drama theater, a puppet theater, and a television station.

The Voznesenskaia Church (1756) and 19th-century stone and wood houses ornamented with carvings have been preserved. Several industrial buildings have been erected in the Soviet period. The university (1936, architect A. Z. Grinberg), the Sovetskaia Hotel (1960, architect I. I. Vinogradov), and a monument to V. I. Lenin (1966, sculptor M. G. Manizer) are located on Lenin Square, and the building of the oblast party committee of the CPSU and of the republic Council of Ministers (1971, architect S. A. Kleimenov) is on Lenin Prospect. Housing is being expanded on a large scale, and a plan for the further reconstruction of the city was drawn up in 1968.

REFERENCES

Samsonov, P. A. *Ioshkar-Ola–stolitsa Mariiskoi ASSR.* Ioshkar-Ola, 1960.
Samsonov, P. A. *Gorod na Kokshage.* Ioshkar-Ola, 1970.
[11–238–1]

IOVKOV, IORDAN (pseudonym of Iordan Stefanov). Born Nov. 9, 1880, in the village of Zheravna, in Sliven District; died Oct. 15, 1937, in Plovdiv; buried in Sofia. Bulgarian writer.

After graduating from secondary school, Iovkov taught in villages in Dobrudzha. He made his literary debut in 1905 with some imitative verses in the spirit of the symbolists. His *Stories* (vols. 1–2, 1917–18) made Iovkov well known. In his later short stories, his principal hero is the Bulgarian peasant (the collection *The Last Joy,* 1926). Iovkov also wrote the novella *The Reaper* (1920), the novel *An Estate Near the Border* (1934), and several plays. His short stories, which give a realistic picture of village life, are filled with admiration for the humanity of the Bulgarian peasant.

WORKS

Subrani suchineniia, vols. 1–7. Sofia, 1956.

In Russian translation:
Rasskazy. Moscow, 1957.

REFERENCES

Il'ina, G. Ia. "Iordan Iovkov." In *Ocherki istorii bolgarskoi literatury XIX–XX vv.* Moscow, 1959.
Sultanov, S. *Iovkov i negoviiat sviat: Literaturni etiudi.* [Sofia, 1968.]
Minev, D. *Iordan Iovkov: Spomeni i dokumenti,* 2nd ed. Varna [1969].
[11–219–2]

IPHICRATES. Late fifth century to first half of the fourth century B.C. Athenian military commander of mercenary troops known for his skillful use of peltasts, a medium-armed infantry.

Iphicrates lengthened the spears and swords of the peltasts and created an army that could carry out the missions of light and heavy infantry, that is, use throwing weapons and engage in hand to hand fighting and also move easily and rapidly. He was several times chosen strategos of Athens. Iphicrates won several victories during the Corinthian War (395–387 B.C.). In the 380's he fought in Thrace on the side of the local ruler Cotys, and in 374–373 he participated in the Persian campaign against Egypt. During the War of the Allies (357–355 B.C.), he was accused of treason but was acquitted. Iphicrates was a typical commander of mercenary units that were increasingly losing touch with the polis.   [11–155–2]

IPHIGENIA, in ancient Greek mythology, the daughter of Agamemnon, the king of Mycenae (or Argos). Agamemnon offered Iphigenia as a sacrifice to the goddess Artemis to ensure the safe sailing of the Greek forces headed for Troy. However, the goddess substituted a deer on the altar for the king's daughter. She transported Iphigenia from Aulis (a harbor in Boeotia) to Tauris (Crimea). In Tauris, Iphigenia served as Artemis' priestess.

The myth of Iphigenia is the subject of several tragedies, including Euripides' *Iphigenia at Aulis* and *Iphigenia in Tauris,* Racine's *Iphigenia,* Goethe's *Iphigenia in Tauris,* and Hauptmann's *Iphigenia in Aulis* and *Iphigenia at Delphi.* Several operas have been devoted to Iphigenia, for example, Gluck's *Iphigenia in Aulis* and *Iphigenia in Tauris.*   [11–155–1]

IRIDACEAE (Iris), a family of monocotyledonous plants, including perennial herbs with rhizomes, corms, or bulbs. There are some subshrubs. The leaves are ensiform or linear. The flowers are bisexual, with a petaloid perianth. There are three stamens. The style is usually composed of three lobes (sometimes expanded and petal-like). The ovary is inferior and is almost always triloculate; the fruit is a capsule. There are approximately 60 genera (1,400 species), found primarily in tropical and subtropical regions (particularly in South Africa and in tropical and subtropical America). Some species are found in temperate regions. In the USSR there are approximately 120 species (eight genera). There are many ornamentals among the Iridaceae, including species of the genera *Iris, Gladiolus,* and *Crocus.* Some species of the genus *Iris* are used in cosmetics. Saffron crocus (*Crocus sativus*) yields the seasoning saffron.

REFERENCE

Flora SSSR, vol. 4. Leningrad, 1935.   [11–1471–3]

IRIS, a genus of plants of the family Iridaceae. They are perennial rhizomatous herbs with sword-shaped or linear leaves. The flowers are large, with a brightly colored corolliform perianth; the ovary is three-celled and inferior; and the fruit is a trihedral, many-seeded pod.

There are about 200 species, distributed throughout the northern hemisphere; in the USSR there are about 60 species. The iris species that form tubers and bulbs are often subdivided into the genera *Junona, Xiphium, Iridodictum,* and *Gynandriris.* Irises are widely used for ornament, especially varieties of the species *I. kaempferi, I. hybrida, I. spuria,* and *I. iberica.* They grow best in sunny places with well-drained soil. The orrisroot is obtained from the rootstocks of some irises, and a coarse fiber for making brushes is produced from the leaves of the species *I. songarica.*

REFERENCES
Rodionenko, G. I. *Rod Iris.* Moscow-Leningrad, 1961.
Rodionenko, G. I. *Irisy.* Moscow, 1961.

G. I. RODIONENKO [11–1471–2]

ISCHEMIA, a local deficiency of blood; insufficient blood in an organ or tissue because of the narrowing or complete occlusion of the lumen of an afferent artery.

Transitory ischemia (like hyperemia) may result from physiological regulation of the blood supply, such as in reflex spasm of an artery caused by a mental factor (fright); the influence of pain, cold, chemical substances (epinephrine, ergotin), and biological stimuli (bacteria, toxins); the obstruction of an artery by a thrombus or embolus; constriction of the lumen of a blood vessel in connection with an atherosclerotic or inflammatory process in the wall; or compression of an artery by a tumor, scar, or foreign body. The aftereffects of ischemia depend on the degree of disruption of the blood flow, the rate of development and duration of the ischemia, the sensitivity of the tissue to oxygen deficiency, and the general condition of the body. Ischemia may end in complete restoration of the structure and function of the affected organ or tissue, but it also may lead to necrosis (infarct). The central nervous system and heart muscle are particularly sensitive to ischemia.   N. R. PALEEV [11–169–3]

ISHAN, the head and teacher of a Muslim community, usually belonging to one of the mystical sects (Dervish or Sufi); also, the head of the religious community in the Ishmaelite sect.

The word *ishan* means "they" in Persian; as early as the Middle Ages, it was used instead of a name when addressing the leaders and elders of the Sufi community. Exploiting the backwardness of the population, *ishans* played the role of sorcerers, medicine men, and soothsayers. In Soviet Middle Asia, communities headed by an *ishan* are few in number, isolated from one another, and anachronistic.

REFERENCES
Klimovich, L. *Islam v tsarskoi Rossii.* Moscow, 1936. Pages 41–44, 121–25, 357–61, 380.
Klimovich, L. *Islam,* 2nd ed. Moscow, 1965. Pages 147–54, 172–95.

[11–168–3]

ISHANTURAEVA, SARA ABDURAKHMANOVNA. Born Oct. 26 (Nov. 8), 1911, in Beshbulak, Iangi-Kurgan Raion, Namangan Oblast. Soviet Uzbek actress. People's Artist of the USSR (1951). Member of the CPSU since 1942.

In 1927, Ishanturaeva graduated from the Uzbek drama studio affiliated with the Moscow House of Culture. The studio formed the nucleus of the Khamza Uzbek Drama Theater in Tashkent. Among her best roles in plays by Uzbek playwrights are Dil'bar and Onakhon in Iashen's *Two Communists* and *Honor and Love* and Dzhamilia in Khamza's *Landowner and Farmhand.* Her outstanding roles in classical drama and contemporary Soviet and foreign plays include Katerina in *Thunderstorm* by Ostrovskii, Ophelia and Desdemona in *Hamlet* and *Othello* by Shakespeare, Jocasta in *Oedipus Rex* by Sophocles, Guli in *Alisher Navoi* by Uigun and Sultanov, Aini in *Algeria, My Homeland!* based on the novel by M. Dib, and Hurriiat in *Flight* by Uigun.

Ishanturaeva is one of the most important representatives of the dramatic art of Soviet Uzbekistan. Her acting is characterized by warmth, and a striving for verisimilitude and dramatically profound character portrayal. Ishanturaeva was a deputy to the second, third, and fourth convocations of the Supreme Soviet of the USSR, and she received the State Prize of the USSR in 1949. She has been awarded two Orders of Lenin, five other orders, and several medals.

REFERENCES
Uvarov, G. *Sara Ishanturaeva.* Moscow, 1951.
Avdeeva, L. *Sara Ishanturaeva.* Tashkent, 1960.   [11–168–4]

ISHEEVKA, an urban-type settlement in Ul'ianovsk Raion, Ul'ianovsk Oblast, RSFSR. It is situated on the Sviiaga River, a tributary of the Volga, 13 km north of Ul'ianovsk. It has a textile combine.   [11–169–1]

ISHEMGULOV, BULAT ZAKIROVICH. Born Feb. 16 (29), 1900, in the village of Chebenli, present-day Zianchurinskii Raion, Bashkir ASSR; died in 1938. Soviet Bashkir writer. Member of the CPSU from 1920.

Ishemgulov began to publish in 1917. He wrote poems, stories, and sketches about the struggle of young people for a new life (the collection *Komsomol Songs,* 1925), satirical dramatizations, feuilletons, and *chastushkas* (rhymed verse on topical themes), attacking vestiges of the past and condemning the reactionary essence of Islam. Outstanding among his works are the stories "Mullah Sabir's Letter From the Grave" (1924), "Prayer on Contract" (1926), and "The Atheists' Decree" (1927) and the collection *Godless Laughter* (1930). In the 1930's, Ishemgulov published the poems *Tractor Operator Aikhylu* (1933), *Roads* (1933), and *Zianchura* (1934).

WORKS
Äthärdhär yïyïlmahï. With an Introduction by Sh. Shähäretdinov. Ufa, 1934.
Haylanma äthärdhär. Ufa, 1959.
Haylanma äsärdhär. With an Introduction by G. Ramazanov. Ufa, 1969.
In Russian translation:
Izbrannoe. Moscow, 1957.   [11–169–2]

ISHIM, a city in Tiumen' Oblast, RSFSR. Located on the left bank of the Ishim River (a tributary of the Irtysh), where the Ishim River is crossed by the Sverdlovsk-Omsk railroad. Population, 57,000 (1972). Ishim arose in about 1670 as the village of Korkino. In the first quarter of the 18th century the village became the Korkino *sloboda* (tax-exempt settlement), and in 1782 the *sloboda* became a city under the name Ishim. The enterprises of the city serve mainly agriculture and transportation, with a truck trailer plant, Ishimsel'mash (which makes farm machinery), and a machine works. Other enterprises in the city include clothing, rugs, furniture, and footwear factories; flour milling, meat, and cream-and-cheese combines; and a confectionery factory, a liqueur and vodka plant, and a brewery. Ishim has a pedagogical institute, an agricultural technicum, and a medical school.   [11–170–2]

ISHIM, a river in the Kazakh SSR and the RSFSR, a left tributary of the Irtysh River. Length, 2,450 km; basin area, 177,000 sq km, including 36,000 sq km forming an interior drainage basin.

The Ishim rises in the Niiaz mountains on the northern edge of the Kazakh hillocks. In its upper reaches it flows mainly through a narrow valley with rocky banks. Below the city of Tselinograd the valley widens. Bending around the Kokchetav Upland, the Ishim makes a big loop and forms many small rapids. It then enters the West Siberian Plain and flows through the low-lying Ishim Steppe in a broad floodland with many oxbow lakes; in its lower reaches it flows through swamps. The Ishim is fed by snow. The period of spring high water is short and pronounced, occurring in May and June (in the lower reaches the overflowing Ishim becomes up to 15 km wide), alternating with a long period of low water in the summer, fall, and winter. The average discharge near the village of Vikulovo, 215 km from the mouth, is 56.3 cu m per sec; the maximum discharge is 686 cu m per sec. The Ishim freezes over in early November, and the ice breaks in April and May. The main tributaries are from the right: the Koluton, Zhabai, and Akkanburluk. The Viacheslavka and Sergeevka reservoirs are located on the Ishim. The waters of the Ishim are widely used for watering and irrigation. The river is navigable upward from Petropavlovsk over a stretch of 270 km and from Vikulovo to the mouth. The cities of Tselinograd, Derzhavinsk, Esil', Petropavlovsk, and Ishim are located on the Ishim.   [11–170–1]

ISHIMBAI, a city (a settlement until 1940) in the Bashkir ASSR. It is situated on both banks of the Belaia River, a tributary of the Kama. Its railroad station, Ishimbaevo, is located 166 km south of Ufa. Population, 55,000 (1972). It is a major center for the oil industry. The Ishimbai oil fields, opened in 1932, were the first major fields in the Volga-Ural Oil and Gas Region.

Industry includes an oil refinery, a plant manufacturing oil-drilling machinery, hosiery and underwear-knitting factories, and a heat and electric power plant. There is also a petroleum industry technicum.   [11–170–3]

ISHIMKA TREASURE, a group of ancient articles found in 1911 (near the village of Ishimka, 50 km north of Achinsk) on a small island amid the bogs in the taiga. The site was a sacrificial ground (similar to the Gliadenovo Kostishche) frequented by the population in the course of a millennium, beginning in the first centuries B.C. The treasure contained articles that were gifts to the gods and were connected with the ancient shamanistic ritual. They included such weapons as iron swords, daggers, spears, and arrowheads (including very ancient bronze arrowheads); metal mirrors of local and Chinese craftsmanship; and amulet-ornaments executed in the animal style. Among the latter are items of southern origin, typical of the Tagarskoe and the Tashtyk cultures, but most are characteristic of the forest belt of Siberia and the Ural Region (for example, the P'ianyi Bor culture). The existence of various imported items in the treasure testifies to the far-reaching trade relations of the native taiga hunters, who were suppliers of furs.

The Ishimka treasure is housed in the Krasnoiarsk Museum of Local Lore.

REFERENCES
Ermolaev, A. *Ishimskaia kollektsiia*. Krasnoiarsk, 1914. (*Opisanie kollektsii krasnoiarskogo muzeia. Otdel arkheologicheskii*, issue 1.)
Kiselev, S. V. *Drevniaia istoriia Iuzhnoi Sibiri* [2nd ed.]. Moscow, 1951.
                                                        [11–171–3]

ISHIMOVA, ALEKSANDRA OSIPOVNA. Born Dec. 25, 1804 (Jan. 6, 1805), in Kostroma; died June 4 (16), 1881, in St. Petersburg. Russian writer.

Ishimova's work was first published in 1831. Her short stories for children are for the most part adaptations of historical works, including those of N. M. Karamzin. The revolutionary democrats thought highly of her literary craftsmanship. Nevertheless, N. A. Dobroliubov deplored the religious and monarchical tendencies of the children's journals she published, *Zvezdochka* (Little Star) and *Luchi* (Rays).

WORKS
Istoriia Rossii v rasskazakh dlia detei, parts 1–6. St. Petersburg, 1837–40.
REFERENCE
Fomina, Iu. V. "A. O. Ishimova." In *Materialy po istorii detskoi literatury*, vol. 1, issue 1. Moscow, 1927.   [11–171–1]

ISHIM STEPPE, a plain in the southern part of Western Siberia, between the Irtysh and Tobol rivers, in Kurgan, Tiumen', and Omsk oblasts, RSFSR, and Severnyi Kazakhstan Oblast, Kazakh SSR. The plain, which varies in altitude from 120 to 140 m, is composed chiefly of sand and clay deposits of the Neocene era, covered with loess-like loams. The terrain is characterized by a series of crests and hollows, with the ridges extending from the northeast to the southwest. In the lowlands and valleys there are many fresh, bitter, and salt lakes, including Saltaim, Ik, and Sazykul'. The smaller lakes and rivers dry up in the summer. The vegetation is chiefly of a meadow-steppe and birch forest (*kolki*) type, growing on leached and normal chernozem and gray forest soils. In the south the plain is entirely under cultivation.   [11–171–2]

ISHKASHIM, a mountain range in the southwestern part of the Pamirs, in Tadzhik SSR. It stretches for about 90 km along the right bank of the Piandzh River. The highest point is Maiakovskii Peak, with an elevation of 6,096 m. There is an ice cover of recent origin. The mountains are composed chiefly of gneiss, amphibolite, and other Pre-Cambrian metamorphic rock. The slopes are covered with mountain steppe and desert, and in the deep river valleys there are sparse stands of juniper. The region has hot mineral springs, at one of which, Garm-Chashma, there is a health resort.   [11–172–1]

ISHKOV, ALEKSANDR AKIMOVICH. Born Aug. 16 (29), 1905, in Stavropol'. Soviet statesman and economic official. Became a member of the CPSU in 1927. The son of a worker.

Ishkov began work in 1919 as a foreman's helper in an electromechanical shop. He graduated from the Rostov Pedagogical Institute in 1957. Ishkov has held high positions in the fishing industry since 1930. From 1940 to 1946 he was people's commissar and from 1946 to 1948 minister of the fishing industry of the western regions of the USSR. Minister of the fishing industry of the USSR from 1948 to 1950, Ishkov was first deputy minister of the food products industry of the USSR (1953–54), minister of the fishing industry of the USSR (1954–57), minister of the USSR and a member of the State Planning Committee of the USSR (1957–62), and chairman of the State Committee for the Fishing Industry (1962–65). Ishkov has been minister of the fishing industry of the USSR since October 1965. Elected a candidate member of the Central Committee of the CPSU at the Twentieth through Twenty-fourth Congresses of the party, Ishkov was a deputy to the second, seventh, and eighth convocations of the Supreme Soviet of the USSR and has been awarded four Orders of Lenin, two other orders, and medals.
                                                        [11–172–3]

ISHLINSKII, ALEKSANDR IUL'EVICH. Born July 24 (Aug. 6), 1913, in Moscow. Soviet scientist in mechanics; academician of the Academy of Sciences of the USSR (1960) and the Academy of Sciences of the Ukrainian SSR (1948), Hero of Socialist Labor (1961). Member of the Communist Party since 1940. Graduated from Moscow University in 1935 and became a professor there in 1944. He was the director of the Institute of Mathematics of the Academy of Sciences of the Ukrainian SSR from 1948 to 1955 and since 1964 has been director of the Institute of Problems of Mechanics.

Ishlinskii's main work has been concerned with the theories of elasticity, plasticity, vibrations, and gyroscopes. He studied the principles of rolling friction on a deformable base (1938), developed an original theory of dynamic stability (1949) and a general theory of plasticity with linear hardening (1954), and proposed a new concept of deformation of the ground during an explosion (1954). He also studied the problems of shock absorption for instruments during sudden deceleration (1957), developed the theory of the space gyrocompass and other gyroscopic instruments (1952–63), and conducted important research on the general theory of inertial navigation and autonomous control (1957–68). He has been chairman of the All-Union Council of Scientific and Technical Societies (1970) and vice-president of the World Federation of Engineering Organizations (1971). He has received the Lenin Prize (1960) and has been awarded two Orders of Lenin, two other orders, and medals.

WORKS
Mekhanika giroskopicheskikh sistem. Moscow, 1963.
Inertsial'noe upravlenie ballisticheskimi raketami. Moscow, 1968.
REFERENCES
"A. Iu. Ishlinskii (K 50-letiiu so dnia rozhdeniia)." *Izv. AN SSSR: Mekhanika i mashinostroenie*, (1963), no. 5. (Contains a bibliography of Ishlinskii's works.)
A. Iu. Ishlinskii. Kiev, 1970. (*Bibliografiia uchenykh UkrSSR*.)
                                                        [11–172–4]

ISHMURAT, RIZA FAKHRUTDINOVICH (also Ishmuratov). Born Nov. 1, 1903, in the village of Badriash, present-day Ianaul Raion, Bashkir ASSR. Soviet Tatar playwright and public figure. Honored Art Worker of the Tatar ASSR (1953). Member of the CPSU since 1927. Son of a peasant. Fought in the Great Patriotic War (1941–45).

After graduating from a dramatic technicum in 1926, Ishmurat was a director in the Tatar Academic Theater. In 1926 he wrote his first comedies, *In the Realm of Sleep* and *Good-for-Nothing Philosopher*. Notable among his many dramatic works are the play *To Meet the Storm* (1952) about Lenin's student days and the tragedy *Immortal Song* about Musa Dzhalil' (1956). He also translated D. I. Fonvizin's *The Minor* into Tatar. Ishmurat has been awarded four orders.

WORKS
Saylanma äsärlär, vols. 1–2. Kazan, 1966–67.
REFERENCE
Istoriia tatarskoi sovetskoi literatury. Moscow, 1965.   [11–173–1]

ISHRAQ (Arabic, literally "radiance"), a term in medieval Muslim philosophy signifying intuitive attainment of truth through the "illumination" of a soul freed from ties with the material world. The doctrine of *ishraq,* which synthesizes ideas of Zoroastrianism and Neoplatonism, was regarded in the medieval Islamic world as a typically eastern doctrine and was contrasted to the western (Aristotelian) theory of knowledge based upon a discursive (conceptual) method of thought. The concept of *ishraq* shared the Neoplatonic idea of the world and its existence, movement, and beauty as an emanation of divine light. A detailed exposition of the philosophy of *ishraq* is contained in a treatise of the same name by the medieval Middle Eastern thinker Shihab al-Din Suhravardi (12th century).

REFERENCE
Nasr, S. H. *Three Muslim Sages: Avicenna, Suhrawardi, Ibn Aravi.* Cambridge, 1964.   A. V. SAGADEEV [11–173–2]

ISHTAR (Sumerian, Inanna), in Akkadian (Assyro-Babylonian) mythology and religion, the central female deity. Ishtar was at first revered as a local deity in Mesopotamia (in Akkad, Arbela, Uruk, and Nineveh). In the second millennium B.C. the cult of Ishtar spread among the Hurrites, Hittites, Mitanni, and Phoenicians. Three main functions of Ishtar are discerned: she is the goddess of fertility and carnal love; the goddess of war and strife; and an astral deity, the personification of the planet Venus.   V. K. AFANAS'EVA [11–174–1]

ISHUTIN, NIKOLAI ANDREEVICH. Born Apr. 3 (15), 1840, in Serdobsk, in present-day Penza Oblast; died Jan. 5 (17), 1879, in Kara. One of the first Russian professional revolutionaries and utopian socialists to combine the idea of propagandizing socialism among the people with conspiratorial and terrorist tactics. He was "a hereditarily honored citizen" of the city of Serdobsk.

Ishutin was brought up in Penza by the family of a cousin, D. V. Karakozov. In 1863 he became an auditor at Moscow University, where he carried on propaganda among the students. In Moscow he created the secret revolutionary organization known as the Ishutin Circle, which functioned from 1863 to 1866. On Apr. 8, 1866, he was arrested in connection with Karakozov's attempt on the life of Tsar Alexander II. He was condemned to death by the Supreme Criminal Court, a sentence which at the last moment was commuted to forced labor for life. Until May 1868, he was in solitary confinement at the Shlissel'burg Fortress; from here, mentally ill, he was taken to Eastern Siberia (Algach) and then to Aleksandrovskii Zavod (Nerchinsk Mines) in 1871 and to the forced-labor prison at Nizhniaia Kara in 1875.   E. S. VILENSKAIA [11–174–3]

ISHUTIN CIRCLE, a secret revolutionary organization founded in Moscow by N. A. Ishutin and set up to prepare a peasant revolution by means of a conspiracy of groups from the intelligentsia.

The Ishutin Circle emerged in September 1863, as a group aligned with the first Land and Liberty group. After the self-liquidation of the latter, the circle, having developed an independent existence, to some extent brought together the uncoordinated groups of the Moscow underground. In 1865 it established ties with the St. Petersburg underground (through I. A. Khudiakov), as well as with Polish revolutionaries, Russian political émigrés, and provincial circles in Saratov, Nizhny Novgorod, Kaluga Province, and elsewhere; it also attracted some semiliberal elements. The nucleus of the organization was composed mostly of natives of Penza Province, including Ishutin, P. D. Ermolov, M. N. Zagibalov, N. P. Stranden, D. A. Iurasov, D. V. Karakozov, P. F. Nikolaev, V. N. Shaganov, and O. A. Motkov. In December 1864 the circle's members helped arrange the escape from prison of J. Dąbrowski, a Polish revolutionary. In Moscow they founded a tuition-free school (September 1865), a bookbinding workshop (autumn of 1864) and a sewing workshop (February 1865). In Mozhaisk District they established a cotton wadding factory in October 1865 on a cooperative basis. Also in 1865 they conducted negotiations with the workers from the ironworking plant at Liudinovo in Kaluga Province, hoping to restructure that enterprise as a cooperative of the workers. Around the beginning of 1866 a steering committee (Organization and, within it, Hell, a tight controlling group) and the Society for Mutual Assistance were created. A program (Regulations) was drawn up that contained elements of subsequent Narodnik (Populist) programs of various tendencies (including propagation of socialism among the people, terrorist tactics, and conspiracy) and that projected the creation of a network of secret circles in the provinces. The circle's members attempted to organize N. G. Chernyshevskii's escape from penal servitude (1865–66) but were unsuccessful. After Karakozov's attempt upon the life of Tsar Alexander II (Apr. 4, 1866), the organization was partially exposed. The Supreme Criminal Court gave out various sentences to 32 members, and many members were subjected to administrative repression.

The period in which the Ishutin Circle was active was marked by a lull in the peasant movement and the onset of reaction in the country. Many of its members became involved in the revolutionary and social movement of subsequent decades.

REFERENCES
Pokushenie Karakozova. Stenograficheskii otchet . . . , vols. 1–2. Moscow, 1928.
Filippov, R. V. *Revoliutsionnaia narodnicheskaia organizatsiia N. A. Ishutina–I. A. Khudiakova (1863–1866).* Petrozavodsk, 1964.
Vilenskaia, E. S. *Revoliutsionnoe podpol'e v Rossii (1860-e gody XIX v.).* Moscow, 1965.
Vilenskaia, E. S. *Khudiakov (1842–1876).* Moscow, 1969.
    E. S. VILENSKAIA [11–174–4]

ITALIA, a semirigid dirigible built in 1927 in Italy. It had a volume of 18,500 m^3, a cruising speed of 90 km/hr, a range of 5,500 km, and a payload of 9.5 tons. Power was provided by three motors of 185 kW each (250 horsepower each). In 1928 a 16-man Italian expedition on the *Italia,* under the command of U. Nobile, made a flight from the Spitsbergen archipelago to the North Pole, but on the return flight it crashed north of Spitsbergen. Of the eight survivors, seven were rescued by the Soviet expedition on the icebreaker *Krasin* and one, by the Swedish pilot Lundborg.

REFERENCES
Běhounek, F. *Tragediia v Ledovitom okeane.* Moscow, 1962. (Translated from Czechoslovakian.)
Samoilovich, R. L. *Na spasenie ekspeditsii Nobile,* 4th ed. Leningrad, 1967.   B. A. KREMER [11–119–1]

ITALIAN, a language of the Romance group of the Indo-European languages. Italian is spoken in Italy (about 54 million people; 1971, estimate), in San Marino, in the Swiss canton of Ticino (Tessin), on the islands of Corsica and Malta, and among Italian emigrants (more than 7 million people), most of whom reside in the USA, Canada, Australia, and the Somali Republic (where Italian is one of the official languages).

Italian developed from Vulgar Latin after the fall of the Roman Empire. The first written records, in various dialects, date from the tenth to 12th centuries; the first literary documents date from the 13th century (the "Sicilian School" of poets). Italian dialects are divided into three groups: northern Italian (Gallo-Italian dialects of the Piedmont, Lombardy, Emilia-Romagna, Venice, and Istria), central-southern (Marche, Umbria, Latian, Campanian, Apulian, Abruzzese, Molise, Basilicata, and Sicilian dialects), and Tuscan (dialects of Florence, Siena, Arezzo, and Pisa). Some northern and central-southern dialects (the dialects of Venice, Milan, Naples, and Sicily) have written literary versions in addition to the spoken differences.

Common Italian was formed from the 14th-century Florentine dialect made popular by the Florentine writers Dante, Petrarch, and Boccaccio. In view of the fact that Italy lacked a single cultural and administrative center until 1871, Common Italian existed outside of Tuscany almost exclusively in written form as late as the 20th century and was accessible only to the literate segment of the population. In the 20th century, under the influence of radio and television, the oral literary norm is supplanting the dialects, adopting in turn a different dialect coloration in each region (*italiano regionale*).

The phonetic and morphological features of the Italian literary language (and the Tuscan dialects) include the following. All words in absolute final form end in a vowel sound. Seven stressed vowels (*i, e, ɛ, a, ɔ, o,* and *u*) and a number of stressed diphthongs (*uo, ie, io, ia, iu,* and *au*) are distinguished. Vowel clusters occur frequently (*lei,* "she"; *io,* "I"; *aiuola,* "flower bed"; *ghiaia,* "gravel"). There is a characteristic opposition between single and double consonants (*dita,* "fingers"; *ditta,* "firm"; *buco,* "hole"; *bocca,* "mouth"). Articulation of the sounds is sharp and tense. Gender and number of nouns are expressed by inflection (*rosa,* "rose"; *rose,* "roses"; and *capo,* "head"; *capi,* "heads"), and definite and indefinite categories are expressed by articles (*il/la,* "the"; *uno/una,* "a"). There are no cases; their meanings are expressed by the use of prepositions (*di,* "of"; *a,* "to"; *da,* "from"). The grammatical meanings of person, number, tense, and mood are expressed by inflection of the verb. The indicative tense system consists of four simple and four compound forms. Word order is free.

REFERENCES

Boursier, E. *Osnovy romanskogo iazykoznaniia.* Moscow, 1952. (Translated from French.)

Migliorini, B. *Storia della lingua italiana* [2nd ed.]. Florence, 1960.

Mauro, T. de. *Storia linguistica dell'Italia unita.* Bari, 1963.

Rohlfs, G. *Grammatica storica della lingua italiana e dei suoi dialetti,* vols. 1–3. Turin, 1966–68.

Camilli, A. *Pronuncia e grafia dell'italiano,* 3rd ed. Florence, 1965.

Battaglia, S., and V. Pernicone. *La grammatica italiana,* 2nd ed. Turin, 1968.

Cappuccini, G., and B. Migliorini. *Vocabolario della lingua italiana.* Turin, 1955.

Palazzi, F. *Novissimo dizionario della lingua italiana,* 2nd ed. Milan [1964].

Prati, A. *Vocabolario etimologico italiano.* [Turin, 1951.]

Battisti, G., and G. Alessio. *Dizionario etimologico italiano* [vols.] 1–5. Florence, 1968.   T. B. ALISOVA [11–141–3]

ITALIAN CAMPAIGN OF 1943–45, hostilities conducted by the combined forces of Great Britain and the USA against fascist German and Italian troops in Italy during World War II. At various times Algerian, Australian, Brazilian, Canadian, Greek, Indian, Italian, Moroccan, New Zealand, Palestinian, Polish, and Senegalese units of various sizes were included in the Allied forces.

Major defeats suffered by the fascist German and Italian troops in the winter and spring of 1943 on the Soviet-German front and in North Africa led to a sharp deterioration in the combat capacity of the Italian Army and to the rapid growth of the Resistance. Italy's forces included 82 divisions and eight brigades, 825 operational combat planes, and 263 combat vessels (including six battleships, ten cruisers, and 93 submarines). Of these, only 44 divisions of low combat capacity, six brigades, 600 operational planes, and 183 vessels were allotted for the defense of the home country; the remaining forces were serving in occupied countries and were fighting partisans in the Balkans and in southern France. The fascist German command was able to dispatch to Italy only seven German divisions, one brigade, about 500 planes, and 60 combat vessels.

On July 10 the Anglo-American troops (General H. Alexander's Fifteenth Army Group, with the support of large naval and air forces) under the overall command of General D. Eisenhower landed in Sicily (the Sicilian Operation of 1943), capturing it on August 17. Italy's ruling circles, attempting to retain power, engineered a palace coup. On July 25, on orders of the king, the head of the fascist government, B. Mussolini, was arrested and replaced by Marshal P. Badoglio. The loss of Sicily, the growth of the Italian people's struggle against the war, and the Soviet Army's rout of fascist German troops in the battle of Kursk (1943) forced the Badoglio government on September 3 to sign surrender terms.

On September 3 the British Eighth Army landed in southern Italy in the area of Reggio di Calabria and began to advance northward. On September 8 the Allied command announced the surrender agreement. The fascist German command, hastily transferring ten more divisions to Italy, disarmed almost the entire Italian Army and occupied a larger part of the country. The Italian government and the supreme command fled to the Allies. The Hitlerites in the occupied territory formed a fascist government headed by Mussolini, whom they had succeeded in freeing from imprisonment. On September 9, the American Fifth Army landed at Salerno, and together with the British Eighth Army began a slow advance northward. By the beginning of November fascist German troops of Army Group South (Tenth and Fourteenth armies) under Field Marshal A. Kesselring had pulled back to a prepared line along the Garigliano and Sangro rivers. Between November 1943 and March 1944 the Allied troops made several attempts to break through the enemy defenses. On January 22 seaborne force was landed at Anzio, and by February 6 the entire American VI Corps had landed. However, despite a superiority in forces and equipment, the Allies failed to break through the enemy defenses, and VI Corps was stalemated by the fascist Germans.

By early May 1944, Allied forces (under the supreme command of General H. M. Wilson) had been increased to 25 divisions (including five armored divisions), eight brigades (four armored and one commando), 9,400 guns and mortars, and 3,960 planes. The German Army Group South had 19 divisions (including one panzer division), 2,450 guns and motars, and 320 planes. In the German-occupied territory a partisan movement arose, led by the Communist Party and including Socialists, Catholics, the Action Party, and other groups. The partisans (about 80,000 in May) controlled a considerable part of Lombardy, Marches, and other regions, diverting sizable enemy forces. On May 11, Allied troops launched an offensive south of Cassino. After fierce fighting Allied troops advanced 30 to 60 km by May 26 and joined up with the American VI Corps. On June 4, American troops entered Rome, abandoned by the enemy, and by August 15 the Allied Fifteenth Army Group, supported by the partisans, had reached a line southeast of Rimini, Florence, and the Arno River. On August 28 the Allies resumed the offensive. By September 5 they had broken through the field fortification belt, and on September 15 they attacked the Gothic Line (north of Pisa, Florence, and Pesaro). Encountering stiff resistance, they were held up until the end of the year, penetrating the defense only in a narrow sector. A push into the Po Valley failed.

Only on Apr. 9, 1945, did Allied troops (under the supreme command of now Field Marshal Alexander) once again resume the offensive. With a 30-percent superiority in divisions (27 to 21), 650 percent in tanks and assault guns (3,100 to 396), 200 percent in field artillery (3,000 to 1,087), and 30-fold in aircraft (4,000 to 130), the Anglo-American command created a threefold superiority in divisions, sixfold in artillery, and 14-fold in tanks in the area of the main drive. By April 21 the Allies had broken through the entire German defense zone, advanced 40 km and, with the decisive assistance of the partisans, liberated Bologna. On April 24 they crossed the Po River. On the night of April 24–25 in Genoa, Milan, Venice, and elsewhere, a general uprising was ordered by the Communist Party, the Socialist Party, and other leftist forces. Led mainly by the Italian Communist Party, the revolt on April 26 enveloped northern Italy, which was almost entirely liberated by the Resistance. Using the success of the revolt, Anglo-American troops terminated the Italian campaign, accepting on May 2 the surrender of Army Group South.

In the Italian campaign the Germans lost 536,000 men (300,-000 prisoners) to the Allies and partisans; the Allies lost 320,-000. The Italian Campaign of 1943–45 is of theoretical military interest from the standpoint of the organization of large-scale landing operations from the sea and the conduct of offensive and defensive operations in mountainous conditions.

REFERENCES

Istoriia Velikoi Otechestvennoi voiny Sovetskogo Soiuza 1941–1945 gg., vols. 3–5. Moscow, 1963–64.

Kulish, V. M. *Vtoroi front.* Moscow, 1960.
Strel'nikov, V. S., and N. M. Cherepanov. *Voina bez riska.* Moscow, 1965.   N. M. CHEREPANOV [11–121–1]

ITALIAN CAMPAIGN OF NAPOLEON (1796–97), military operations of the French troops of General Napoleon Bonaparte against Austro-Sardinian troops in northern Italy during the war of 1792–97 between France and the First Coalition (including Austria, Great Britain, Prussia [up to 1795], Russia, Sardinia, and the Kingdom of the Two Sicilies).

In 1796 the French command prepared to move against Austria with the armies of Generals J. B. Jourdan and J. V. Moreau (155,000 men) on the Rhine River. The secondary task of seizing northern Italy was assigned to Bonaparte's Army of Italy (about 42,000 men). As the campaigns developed, however, Italy became the decisive theater. In early April 1796, the main forces of the Army of Italy (35,000) held the coast of the Gulf of Genoa, facing the Sardinian Army of General Colli (22,000) and the Austrian Army of Field Marshal J.-P. Beaulieu (30,-000). The mountain passes from Piedmont to France were secured by the French Army of the Alps, commanded by General F. C. Kellermann (20,000), which was opposed by the Duke of Aosta's Sardinian troops (20,000). On April 11 the French troops took the offensive. Concentrating superior forces in succession against the separate enemy forces stretched out along a broad front, Bonaparte defeated them one by one at Montenotte (April 12) and at Ceva and Mondovì (April 22). On April 28, Sardinia concluded an armistice with France, followed on May 5 by a peace treaty.

Bonaparte then forced Austrian withdrawals first from the Po River, then from the Adda. The French troops were victorious at Lodi on May 10, occupied Milan on May 15, and blockaded Mantua on June 4. Other French forces advanced on Tuscany and on June 29 occupied Livorno, a British naval base. The battle for Mantua, the chief strong point in Italy, began at the end of July. The Austrian command (under General Wurmser from May to October and then under Field Marshal Alvinczy) made four attempts to relieve the fortress but was frustrated in battles at Castiglione (August 5), Rovereto (September 5), Bassano (September 8), Arcole (November 15–17), and Rivoli (Jan. 13–15, 1797). On February 2, Mantua capitulated. In March the French invaded Austria and began an assault on Vienna. On April 18 the Leoben Armistice was signed, followed on October 17 by the Treaty of Campo Formio of 1797.

In the course of the campaigns, several republics were formed and bourgeois reforms instituted. However, the French Army, while destroying the feudal order, at the same time pillaged conquered territories, cruelly suppressing popular discontent. The new strategy employed by the French troops, combining columns with extended order, and Bonaparte's skill as a military leader were the main factors in the French success. Boldly maneuvering his limited forces, he was able to attain a numerical supremacy in the decisive areas, while the Austrians blindly followed the canons of cordon strategy and line tactics.

REFERENCES
Engels, F. *Izbrannye voennye proizvedeniia.* Moscow, 1958.
Bogdanovich, M. I. *Pokhod 1796 g. Bonaparta v Italii.* St. Petersburg, 1860.
Clausewitz, K. *Ital'ianskii pokhod Napoleona Bonaparta 1796 g.* Moscow, 1939.
Levitskii, N. A. *Polkovodcheskoe iskusstvo Napoleona.* Moscow, 1938.
      I. I. ROSTUNOV [11–137–1]

ITALIAN CAMPAIGN OF SUVOROV (1799), military operations of the Russo-Austrian troops of Field Marshal A. V. Suvorov against the French troops in northern Italy during the war of 1798–1802 between France and the Second Coalition (Great Britain, Austria, Russia, Turkey, and the Kingdom of the Two Sicilies). Russia's contributions to the coalition were the squadron of Vice Admiral F. F. Ushakov, dispatched to the Mediterranean from the Black Sea, two corps (about 33,000 men) sent to northern Italy, and the corps of General A. M. Rimskii-Korsakov (27,000) sent to Switzerland.

The French forces included the Army of Italy of General B. Schérer (58,000) in northern Italy and the Army of Naples of General J. Macdonald (34,000) in southern and central Italy. Opposing the French troops in northern Italy were the Austrian Army of 86,000 commanded by Field Marshal M. Melas and a Russian corps of 22,000 led by General A. G. Rozenberg (joined in June 1799 by another Russian corps, of 11,000). At the request of the Austrian Government, Suvorov was named supreme commander of the allied troops in northern Italy, taking command in Valeggio on April 4 (15). After blockading the fortresses of Peschiera and Mantua with part of his forces, Suvorov and 48,500 men left Valeggio on April 8 (19). On April 15–17 (26–28) in a battle near the Adda River he defeated a French army which since April 15 (26) had been headed by General J. V. Moreau. On April 17–18 (28–29) allied troops entered Milan. Moreau's army retreated to Genoa. On May 15 (26) the allied army occupied Turin.

The French command decided to strike Suvorov from two directions: from the south with Moreau's troops (14,000) in the Genoa area and from the east with those of Macdonald (36,000), which began advancing toward northern Italy on May 24 (June 4). Leaving a force at Alessandria to block Moreau, Suvorov with his remaining 22,000 men on June 4 (15) advanced against Macdonald, defeating him on June 6–8 (17–19) in a meeting engagement on the banks of the Trebbia River. Moreau's army hurriedly retreated to Genoa, where it was joined by the remainder of Macdonald's army. At the end of July a French army of 35,000 under the command of General B. C. Joubert advanced from the Genoa area to Alessandria, where the main allied forces were located. Suvorov, whose army had grown to 50,000 after the fall of Mantua on July 17 (28), was victorious at Novi on August 4 (15). The success of the Russian troops in northern Italy and of the Russian fleet in Ushakov's Mediterranean campaign of 1798–1800 led to the almost complete liquidation of French dominance in this area. Great Britain and Austria, fearing an increase in Russia's influence, decided to remove the Russian troops from Italy. On August 16 (27), Suvorov was ordered by the Austrian Court War Council, to unite his Russian troops with Rimskii-Korsakov's corps in Switzerland.

The allied victories in northern Italy were mainly the result of the fighting qualities of the Russian troops and of Suvorov's skill as a military leader, as well as the support of the Italians, who viewed the Russian troops as their liberators from the burdens of French occupation. At the same time the counterrevolution, which liquidated the republican regimes, profited by Suvorov's campaign.

REFERENCES
A. V. Suvorov: Dokumenty. Vol. 4: *Dokumenty, 1799–1800.* Moscow, 1953.
Bogdanovich, M. I. *Pokhody Suvorova v Italii i Shveitsarii.* St. Petersburg, 1846.
Miliutin, D. A. *Istoriia voiny 1799 g. mezhdu Rossiei i Frantsiei . . . ,* 2nd ed., vols. 1–3. St. Petersburg, 1857.
Clausewitz, K. *1799 g.,* part 1. Moscow, 1938.
Bogoliubov, A. N. *Polkovodcheskoe iskusstvo A. V. Suvorova.* Moscow, 1939.   I. I. ROSTUNOV [11–139–1]

ITALIAN COMMUNIST PARTY (ICP; Partito Comunista Italiano), founded Jan. 21, 1921, at a congress in Livorno by leftist revolutionary groups of the Italian Socialist Party (ISP). Until 1943 it was called the Communist Party of Italy and was the Italian section of the Communist International.

Ideologically, the most mature group in the ICP was the *Ordine nuovo,* which was led by A. Gramsci and which had its base in the city of Turin. However, a sectarian current headed by A. Bordiga played the dominant role in the ICP during the first years of its existence. The positions held by Bordiga's followers prevented the party from winning broad influence over the masses and hampered cooperation with other leftist forces in the struggle against advancing fascism. With the aid of the Comintern, the leadership of the ICP was changed in 1923–24. The new leadership nucleus, which included Gramsci, P. Togliatti, M. Scoccimarro, and U. Terraccini, held a debate on the tasks and tactics of the ICP, thus helping the party to overcome the sectarian views of Bordiga's followers. The Third Congress of the ICP (1926), which was a turning point in the Italian Communist movement, proposed tactics based on the mobilization of all strata of the working people for the struggle against fascism. The party's principal slogan became a call for unity addressed to the working class, the workers and peasants, the north and south, and the entire Italian people.

After all political parties had been disbanded during the period of overt fascist dictatorship (1926–43), the ICP was the only party in Italy to continue antifascist activities not only abroad but also at home, relying on an illegal press and a network of underground organizations. The Communists restored trade-union organizations abroad and established underground trade unions in Italy. Many of the party's leaders were victims of the Italian government's repressive measures. After the arrest of Gramsci in 1926, Togliatti became the leader of the party. In 1934 a pact calling for united action by the ICP and the ISP was signed in Paris. Later, it was renewed, and it remained in force until 1956. The ICP fought for the implementation of the Seventh Comintern Congress policy, which aimed for the creation of a united front of the working class and other toiling people against fascism and the threat of a world war. During the antifascist war in Spain (1936–39) thousands of Italian Communists fought in the International Brigades against the Spanish fascists and the Italo-German fascist interventionists. During that period the Communists began to cooperate not only with the Italian Socialists but also with the democratic *Giustizia e Libertà* (Justice and Liberty) groups.

In 1937–38 the ICP drew up a new program of struggle for socialism—a struggle for progressive democracy that was supported by the working class and that aimed at eliminating the dominance of monopolies and landowners, nationalizing large-scale industry, and turning over land to the peasants. This program was the basis for the programs of the parties of the left wing of the antifascist Resistance front that took shape during World War II.

During the war the ICP intensified its activity in the antifascist underground. In late 1942 the party participated in the establishment of the first Committee of National Liberation in Turin, which was the model for committees that were subsequently formed in other Italian cities. After the collapse of Italian fascism (July 1943) and the occupation of Italy by fascist German troops, the Communists were the most active leading force in the partisan movement that developed between 1943 and 1945. The Communists' policy helped to unify all the Italian antifascist forces. Communists and Socialists were brought into the Badoglio government, which was formed in 1944 on liberated territory.

After the liberation of Italy in 1945, the ICP decided to transform itself into a mass party firmly associated with all strata of the toiling people. Its membership soared from 15,000 at the beginning of 1943 to 1.7 million at the end of 1945.

The Fifth Congress of the ICP (December 1945–January 1946) advanced a concrete program of struggle for a democratic rebirth (nationalization of monopolies, agrarian reform, development of cooperatives, establishment of a democratic republic), which was to be accompanied by the preservation of antifascist unity and the leadership of the working class.

In 1946 the ICP and other leftist forces achieved the establishment in Italy of a republic based on a relatively broad bourgeois democracy. In particular, the party was successful in its campaign for the inclusion in the Constitution of 1947 of the democratic program provisions of the Resistance parties. This provided the ICP with an opportunity to struggle for profound democratic transformations on the basis of the Constitution. When the monopolistic bourgeoisie launched an offensive against the toiling people's democratic gains, the Communists and Socialists were ousted from the government in May 1947. The efforts of reactionaries to directly coerce the ICP were repulsed. In the wake of an attempt on Togliatti's life on July 14, 1948, a general strike gripped Italy (July 14–16), demonstrating the high degree of authority of the ICP among the popular masses.

As members of the opposition, the ICP and the ISP led a mass movement of workers against unemployment and for an improvement in the standard of living. They demanded more land for the peasants and the elimination of semifeudal relations in the countryside. The two parties also led all the toiling people in a movement for peace and for the preservation and broadening of the position of democratic forces in the country.

As a result of improved economic conditions and some rise in the standard of living of Italy's toiling people in the 1950's, opportunist illusions and revisionist attitudes became widespread in the workers' movement, chiefly in the ISP. In September 1956 the ISP dissolved the pact on unity of action with the ICP. Some manifestations of revisionism also appeared in the ICP. However, the new socioeconomic conditions also created favorable opportunities for the working class to take the offensive. This situation was noted by the Eighth Congress of the ICP (1956), which drew up a strategic line for a struggle by the Communists for socialism in Italy. The congress pointed out that in generating a mass movement for fundamental democratic and socialist transformations, the ICP was seeking to recruit increasingly broad strata of the population into an alliance with the working class. Wresting more and more positions of economic and political power from the ruling class, the democratic forces prepared through a bitter struggle to tip the scales for the final removal from power of the monopolistic bourgeoisie. Any of the acute political crises that arose during the struggle could have engendered attempts by the ruling circles to resort to armed force. Nonetheless, the broader the alliance of popular forces, the more confidently they could foil these attempts.

The basic line of the Eighth Congress was developed and specified in the party's subsequent theoretical and practical work. Adhering to this line, the Communists, in alliance with other leftist forces, foiled an attempt by the Tambroni government to stage a reactionary coup in July 1960. After the formation in 1962 of a left-center government coalition, in which the Socialists participated beginning in 1963, the ICP endeavored to support all the positive aspects of the activities of the coalition government. At the same time, however, the party sharply criticized the bourgeois-reformist narrowness of left centrism. From the end of 1964, when the government's program was essentially stripped of its democratic content, the ICP waged a direct struggle against the government. The party's influence grew steadily: in the parliamentary elections of 1963 it won more than 25 percent of the vote; in the 1968 elections, 26.9 percent; and in the 1972 elections, 27.2 percent.

The ICP continued to develop its tactical positions at the Eleventh (1966) and Twelfth (1969) Congresses. It put forth the slogan of creating a new democratic majority that would embrace all democratic forces, from Communists to leftist Catholic circles. The Twelfth Congress of the ICP stressed the possibility of developing through the class struggle new forms of democracy and self-government by the masses that would reinforce the toiling people's gains and contribute to further progress.

ICP delegations participated in the International Conferences of Communist and Workers' Parties in Moscow in 1957, 1960, and 1969. The ICP approved the work of these conferences.

The Thirteenth Congress of the ICP (1972) defined the party's task as a struggle for a democratic turnabout in the government and against the policies of the monopolies and attempt by extreme rightist forces to consolidate their position. The party resolutely opposed the right-center government formed in 1972. When this government fell, the ICP resumed its policy of constructive opposition and endeavored to rally the masses around an antifascist, democratic platform. During the preparations for its Fourteenth Congress, the ICP worked out a line of historical compromise which provided for the alliance of the three principal mass forces in Italy—the Communists, the socialists, and the Catholics—in a struggle for profound democratic and socialist reforms.

At its Eighth through Twelfth Congresses the ICP adopted the Theses—programs of action for the party in the immediate future. The Thirteenth Congress of the ICP adopted a detailed political resolution and preelection program. A political resolution was also adopted by the Fourteenth Congress (1975). In 1972 the ranks of the ICP were bolstered by members of the Italian Socialist Party of Proletarian Unity, which had been disbanded. The organizational principle of the ICP is democratic centralism. The party rules have been altered somewhat by every congress. Party cards are renewed once a year. The party chairman is L. Longo, and the secretary-general is E. Berlinguer. In 1969 the ICP had 1,503,000 members and in December 1974, 1,658,000 members. The central organ of the ICP is the newspaper *L'Unità*.

Table 1. Party Congresses of the ICP

Congress	Place	Date
First	Livorno	Jan. 21, 1921
Second	Rome	Mar. 20–24, 1922
Third	Lyon	Jan. 21, 1926
Fourth	Cologne-Düsseldorf	Mar.–Apr., 1931
Fifth	Rome	Dec. 29, 1945– Jan. 6, 1946
Sixth	Milan	Jan. 5–10, 1948
Seventh	Rome	Apr. 3–8, 1951
Eighth	Rome	Dec. 8–14, 1956
Ninth	Rome	Jan. 30–Feb. 4, 1960
Tenth	Rome	Dec. 2–8, 1962
Eleventh	Rome	Jan. 25–31, 1966
Twelfth	Bologna	Feb. 8–15, 1969
Thirteenth	Milan	Mar. 13–17, 1972
Fourteenth	Rome	Mar. 18–23, 1975

REFERENCES

Materialy VIII s''ezda Ital'ianskoi kommunisticheskoi partii. Moscow, 1957. (Translated from Italian.)
IX s''ezd Ital'ianskoi kommunisticheskoi partii. Moscow, 1960. (Translated from Italian.)
X s''ezd Ital'ianskoi kommunisticheskoi partii. Moscow, 1963. (Translated from Italian.)
XI s''ezd Ital'ianskoi kommunisticheskoi partii. Moscow, 1966. (Translated from Italian.)
Gramsci, A. *Izbr. proizv.*, vols. 1–3. Moscow, 1957–59. (Translated from Italian.)
Togliatti, P. *Izbr. stat'i i rechi*, vols. 1–2. Moscow, 1965. (Translated from Italian.)
Togliatti, P. *Rechi v Uchreditel'nom sobranii.* Moscow, 1959. (Translated from Italian.)
Togliatti, P. *Opere*, vols. 1–3. Rome, 1967–73.
30 let Ital'ianskoi kommunisticheskoi partii. Moscow, 1963. (Translated from Italian.)
40 let Ital'ianskoi kommunisticheskoi partii. Moscow, 1961.
50 let Ital'ianskoi kommunisticheskoi partii. Moscow, 1971.
XIII s''ezd Ital'ianskoi kommunisticheskoi partii. Moscow, 1972.
Ferrara, M., and M. Ferrara. *Beseduia s Tol'iatti.* Moscow, 1965. (Translated from Italian.)
Naumov, V. K. *Kommunisty Italii.* Moscow, 1972.
Boevoi avangard trudiashchikhsia Italii. Moscow, 1971.
Istoriia Italii, vol. 3. Moscow, 1971.
Komolova, N. P. *Noveishaia istoriia Italii.* Moscow, 1970.
Dorofeev, S. I. *Ekonomicheskia programma klassovoi bor'by.* Moscow, 1974.
Spriano, P. *Storia del Partito Comunista Italiano*, vols. 1–4. Rome-Turin, 1967–74.
S. I. DOROFEEV [11–124–1; updated]

ITALIAN CONFEDERATION OF WORKERS' TRADE UNIONS (ICWTU; Confederazione Italiana Sindicati Lavoratori), a national trade-union center of Italy, second in influence and membership to the Italian General Confederation of Labor. Founded in 1950 by the merger of the Free Italian General Confederation of Labor and the Italian Federation of Labor, which had been formed after a split in the Italian General Confederation of Labor in 1948, the ICWTU is influenced primarily by the Christian Democratic Party. According to data published by the organization, it had 2.2 million members in 1974. Although it was founded on a platform of reformism and class cooperation, since the end of the 1960's the ICWTU has turned increasingly to unity of action with the Italian General Confederation of Labor in a struggle to improve the condition of the working people and defend the rights and freedoms of trade unions. It joined the federation of three Italian trade-union centers, which was formed in 1972, and it belongs to the International Confederation of Free Trade Unions. The organ of the ICWTU is *Conquiste del lavoro.* [11–128–1]

ITALIAN CREDIT BANK (Credito Italiano), one of the three most important joint-stock commercial banks in Italy, which together make up the group of "banks of national significance." The Institute for the Reconstruction of Industry owns 81 percent of its shares. Its board of directors includes representatives from the major Italian monopolies Fiat and Montecatini Edison.

The Italian Credit Bank was founded in 1870 in Genoa with the backing of German capital. It received its present name in 1895. Originally it was an all-purpose deposit and investment bank. In 1930 it merged with the National Credit Bank and received aid from the government in return for part of its stock and the transfer of long-term investments in industrial enterprises to special state institutes. Since then it has been functioning as a deposit bank, carrying out all types of short-term credit operations. In 1946 it founded, together with the two other banks of national significance (the Bank of Rome and the Italian Commercial Bank), a special institution for medium-term credit, Mediobanca, in Milan. The Italian Credit Bank has shares in other Italian medium-term credit institutions, as well as in several Swiss and international investing companies. As of 1971 it had 299 branches. It has representatives in Great Britain, France, the Federal Republic of Germany, Switzerland, the USA, Argentina, and Brazil. As of 1971 it had a balance total of 4,790 billion lire, deposits of 4,148 billion lire, discount-loan operations amounting to 2,326 billion lire, securities of 615 billion lire, and capital and reserves of 58.2 billion lire.

K. A. SHTROM [11–136–2]

ITALIAN ENCYCLOPEDIA OF SCIENCES, LITERATURE, AND ART (*Enciclopedia italiana di scienze, lettere ed arti*), *Italiana*; the largest comprehensive Italian encyclopedia. It was published from 1929 to 1939 in 36 volumes, the last of which was an index to the entire publication and to the first supplement (*Appendice I*), which came out in 1938. Each of two subsequent two-volume supplements, which were issued in 1948–49 and 1961, covered more than ten years (1938–48 and 1949–60).

Most of *Italiana* clearly shows a preference for the humanities: special attention is paid to history, art, literature, geography, and biography. Extensive survey articles, with lists of recommended literature in a number of European languages, are predominant. Terms are accompanied by references to their French, Spanish, German, and English equivalents. The encyclopedia is richly illustrated, and its reproductions of works of art, geographic maps, and portraits are of utmost value.

Italiana was conceived as a monumental, luxury publication that would attest to the "grandeur" of fascist Italy. Many articles on current affairs are permeated by fascist ideology (even Mussolini was recruited as one of the contributors to the encyclopedia). This sharply diminishes the quality of the encyclopedia, despite the abundance of valuable information in it. The supplementary volumes devote more space to the natural sciences and technology. I. V. GUDOVSHCHIKOVA [11–131–1]

ITALIAN LOCUST (*Calliptamus italicus*), an insect of the family Acrididae (grasshoppers), a dangerous agricultural pest. The body, which measures 1.5–41 mm, is brown or gray with a brown tinge. The wings are pink at their base. The Italian locust is widely distributed in Southern Europe, North Africa, Southwest Asia, Middle Asia, northwestern Mongolia, and China. It is also found in southern European USSR, the Caucusus, southwestern Siberia, Altai Krai, Kazakhstan, and Middle Asia. It dwells primarily in grassy wormwood steppes. In the north it grows predominantly in open places with coarse soils; in the south, in river valleys and oases. The Italian locust damages cotton, sunflowers, legumes, melons, potatoes, cereal grains, and many other crops. There is one generation each year. The eggs winter in clusters in the upper layer of soil. The larvae hatch in the spring, and the adults appear in June and July. In the gregarious stage, Italian locusts form swarms and flocks, resembling those of the migratory locust *Schistocerca gregaria*. In the solitary phase, Italian locusts do not congregate.

REFERENCE
Vasil'ev, K. A. "Ital'ianskaia sarancha (*Calliptamus italicus L.*) v Tsentral'nom Kazakhstane." *Trudy nauchnoissledovatel'skogo instituta zashchity rastenii,* 1962, vol. 7.   E. P. Tsyplenkov   [11–128–2]

ITALIAN RYEGRASS (*Lolium multiflorum*), an annual or biennial plant of the family Gramineae. It is distributed in Europe, Asia Minor, Southeast Asia, and North Africa. Italian ryegrass is found in southern European USSR and in western Transcaucasia. It is a high-yield fodder grass, which is easily destroyed by frost. The most commonly cultivated variety is the annual *Lolium multiflorum* var. *westerwoldicum,* which is grown in many countries. In the USSR this variety is occasionally raised on the Black Sea Shore of the Caucasus, in the forest-steppe zone of the Ukraine, and in Byelorussia.   [11–141–1]

ITALIANS, a nation (*natsiia,* nation in the historical sense); the basic population of Italy. In Italy there are about 54 million Italians (1971, estimate). Large groups of Italians live in other European countries (more than 2.5 million), North and South America (about 7 million), North Africa (about 200,000), and Australia (more than 200,000). A small number of them live in Asia. The language of the Italian people is Italian. The overwhelming majority of believers among them are Catholic.

In the first millennium B.C., Italic tribes made up a significant part of the population of the Apennine Peninsula. Between the sixth and second centuries B.C. the Latins, an Italic tribe that inhabited the region of Latium and founded Rome, subjugated the remaining Italic tribes and the Etruscans, Ligurians, Veneti, and Celts, who inhabited the northern part of the peninsula, as well as the Greeks, Carthaginians, and Siculi, who lived in the south and on the islands of Sardinia, Sicily, and Corsica. The entire population of the peninsula was speaking vulgar Latin by the first and second centuries A.D. However, the languages of the tribes of Italy provided the foundation for the development of local dialectal characteristics, which subsequently influenced the formation of the dialects of the Italian language. From the first centuries of the Common Era many of the Romanized people of the Apennine Peninsula intermarried with slaves of diverse origins and from the fifth century, with Germanic tribes (Visigoths, Vandals, Ostrogoths, and Lombards). The Byzantines, Franks, Arabs, Hungarians, and Normans conquered parts of Italy during the sixth through the tenth century. Large numbers of the Italic population intermingled with the conquerors, giving rise to the Italian nationality and popular language. Literary Latin, however, remained the official language.

During the 11th to 13th centuries the formation of the Italian nationality was completed. The gradual establishment of a single literary language was very important for the shaping of the Italian nation. In the 13th and 14th centuries the Tuscan dialect began to acquire this significance. However, the prolonged political fragmentation of the country prevented the consolidation into a single nation of the population of the various regions of Italy, each of which had its own dialect and material and spiritual culture. The consolidation of the regions of Italy was completed only in the second half of the 19th century, with the development of capitalism and the establishment of a unified state.

Even today some differences persist in the material and spiritual culture of the various regions. (For example, village settlements and dwellings differ in northern, central, and southern Italy.) Oral folklore varies from region to region. Epic poems are characteristic of northern Italy, whereas short lyrical poems (*strambotti*) are typical of central and southern Italy. Folk songs, the rhythms and melodies of which vary from region to region, are widely enjoyed. (In Campania, for example, lyrical songs prevail. They are called "Neapolitan songs" after Campania's chief city, Naples.) Italy's folk dances—the tarantella, saltarello, *lombarda,* and *bergamasca*—are distinguished by their great variety. In the folk decorative and applied arts there are age-old traditions. The Italians have made a major contribution to the music and fine arts of the world.

REFERENCES
Narody zarubezhnoi Evropy, vol. 2. Moscow, 1965. (Bibliography, p. 610.)
Candeloro, G. *Istoriia sovremennoi Italii,* vols. 1–4, 1958–66. (Translated from Italian.)
Istoriia Italii, vols. 1–3. Moscow, 1970–71.
Iro-Volkskunde. Munich [1963].
Le regioni d'Italia, vols. 1–2, 13–16, 18. Turin, 1960–66.
    N. A. Krasnovskaia   [11–142–2]

ITALIAN SOCIALIST PARTY (ISP; Partito Socialista Italiano), founded in August 1892 at a congress in Genoa. From 1892 it was called the Italian Workers' Party, from 1893, the Socialist Party of Italian Workers' and from 1895, the Italian Socialist Party. In 1930 the party's name was changed to the Italian Socialist Party of Proletarian Unity, and in 1947, to the Italian Socialist Party. The party was known as the Unified Socialist Party from 1966 to 1968, when its name was changed to the Italian Socialist Party. The ISP is a section of the Socialist International.

In 1893 the Second Congress of the ISP adopted a program that proclaimed as the party's purpose a struggle to gain power for the working class and to socialize the means of production. The complexity of the situation in Italy, including the incompleteness of bourgeois-democratic reforms and the difference in the levels of development of the north and south, accounted for the specific characteristics of the ISP. The party expressed diverse and contradictory opposition sentiments—the revolutionary socialist aspirations of the progressive proletariat, the radical democratic sentiments of the masses, and the reformist tendencies of a segment of the intelligentsia and some strata of the working class. From the very beginning two basic currents took shape in the party: a left-wing current (the Implacables, then the Anarchosyndicalists, and still later, the Maximalists) and a right-wing current (reformist). The predominance of the reformists under F. Turati began in 1902 and ended in 1912, after the expulsion from the party of their extremist wing (for example, L. Bissolati and I. Bonomi), which had adopted chauvinist positions. From that time the ISP usually took more left-wing positions than the other social democratic parties in Western Europe.

Under the leadership of the Maximalists (G. M. Serrati and C. Lazzari) the ISP opposed the world imperialist war of 1914–18, but its opposition stemmed from a social-pacifist point of view. The party was among the initiators of and participants in the international socialist conferences in Zimmerwald (1915) and Kiental (1916). It actively supported a movement in defense of Soviet Russia, and in 1919 it announced that it was joining the Comintern. In the parliamentary elections of 1919 the ISP received 30 percent of the vote. During the postwar revolutionary crisis the party called for revolution, but its leaders failed to give purposeful, practical guidance to the mounting mass movement and were unable to devise specific means of attaining the victory of socialist revolution in Italy. In 1921 the revolutionary wing of the ISP withdrew from the party, forming the Communist Party of Italy. Under attack by fascism, which took power in Italy in 1922, the ISP had essentially ceased its activities in the country by 1926.

The lessons of the postwar revolutionary crisis and the struggle against fascism promoted a rapprochement between ISP émigré organizations and the Communist Party and the conclusion on Aug. 17, 1934, in Paris of a pact calling for unity of action between them. (The pact was renewed several times.) The Socialists participated actively in the struggle of the International Brigades in Spain (1936–39) and in the Resistance Movement in Italy during the occupation of the country by fascist German troops between 1943 and 1945.

Between 1944 and 1947 the ISP, which was under the leadership of P. Nenni at that time, joined antifascist coalition governments in Italy, aligning itself with their left wings. It cooperated with the Communist Party in the struggle for progressive democracy that developed after the liberation of Italy. In 1947, G. Saragat's right-wing grouping left the ISP, as did G. Romita's group in 1949. In 1951 these two groups formed the Italian Social Democratic Party (ISDP).

In 1955 the ISP had 700,000 members. Despite its militant class policy, the ideological level of the ISP was low. In the changed atmosphere of the mid-1950's—a time marked by an economic upsurge, some improvement in the standard of living of the masses, and a concomitant increase in reformist illusions among a segment of the working people—the ISP leadership group, which was headed by Nenni, began to evolve toward the right. After dissolving the pact on unity of action with the Communist Party in 1956, the ISP drew closer to the ruling Christian Democratic Party (CDP). From 1962 the Socialists supported the policy of the "left center," and in 1963 they joined the left-center government of A. Moro. In 1964 the left wing of the ISP seceded from the party and formed the Italian Socialist Party of Proletarian Unity. The ISP merged with the ISDP in 1966, essentially adopting the latter's platform.

The participation of a unified Socialist party in a coalition government demonstrated the impossibility of carrying out democratic reforms without relying on the masses. A new upsurge of the mass movement beginning in 1968 raised the danger that the party would be isolated from the broad strata of the toiling people. In the parliamentary elections of 1968 the ISP suffered a defeat, winning 1.5 million fewer votes than in the previous elections. Substantial forces in the party (the "new majority") called for a policy change toward more vigorous support of the working people's demands and toward cooperation with the Communist Party on certain issues. In 1969 the opponents of a turn toward the left in the party's course—former Social Democrats and a segment of extreme right-wing socialists —left the party and formed the Unitary Socialist Party, which became the Socialist Unity Party in 1971. In the parliamentary elections of May 7, 1972, the ISP garnered 3.9 million votes (9.6 percent of the vote). The 39th congress of the ISP (1972) came out against the right-center government that had been formed that year and in favor of restoring the left-center coalition. Until November 1974 the ISP was part of the new left-center government. Subsequently, it supported the two-party government of Moro. In general, the ISP favors cooperation with the Communist Party.

The ISP's program of action for the immediate future is formulated in the secretary's report to the party congress. The most recent party rules were adopted in 1968. The party is dominated by urban strata of the working people. In 1974 the ISP had about 640,000 members. The party chairman is P. Nenni, and the political secretary is F. de Martino. The daily newspaper *Avanti!* is the ISP's central organ. S. I. DOROFEEV [11–129–1; updated]

ITALIAN SOCIALIST PARTY OF PROLETARIAN UNITY (ISPPU; Partito Socialista Italiano di Unità Proletaria), existed from 1964 to 1972. The ISPPU was formed in January 1964 by representatives of a leftist trend who had seceded from the Italian Socialist Party in protest against the reformist policy of its leaders. The ISPPU adopted a policy of cooperation with the Italian Communist Party and other leftist forces in Italy in the struggle for the vital rights of the Italian working people and for socialism. In foreign policy the party supported active neutrality on the part of Italy, withdrawal from NATO, and friendship and cooperation with the USSR and other socialist countries. The ISPPU had 182,000 members in 1971. In 1972 an extraordinary congress of the ISPPU decided to disband the party and have its members join the Italian Communist Party.

[11–130–1]

ITALIAN UNION OF LABOR (Unione Italiana del Lavoro), a national trade-union center of Italy. Founded in 1950, the Italian Union of Labor is dominated by the Italian Socialist Party, the Social Democratic Party (Unitary Socialists), and the Republican Party. According to its own data, the organization had about 800,000 members in 1974. At the time of its founding the Italian Union of Labor adopted a platform of reformism and class cooperation. Beginning in the late 1960's it cooperated more frequently with the country's other trade-union centers in the strike movement, and eventually it joined the federation of three Italian trade-union centers, which was formed in 1972. The Italian Union of Labor belongs to the International Confederation of Free Trade Unions. Its press organ is *Il lavoro Italiano.*

[11–141–2]

ITALIAN WARS OF 1494–1559, wars between France, Spain, and the Holy Roman Empire (with the intervention of other states) for control of Italy, as well as for hegemony in Europe. The Italian Wars were fought primarily on the territory of Italy.

The political fragmentation of Italy and quarrels between the Italian states made it easier for the major powers to realize their aggressive designs. After the death of the king of Naples, Ferdinand I, in January 1494, the French king Charles VIII asserted his claim as heir of the house of Anjou (a collateral line of the French royal house) to the Kingdom of Naples, which had been taken from the Angevins by the house of Aragon in the mid-15th century. In the autumn of 1494, Charles VIII crossed the Alps with a powerful army that included a large detachment of Swiss mercenaries. He moved toward Naples, having enlisted the active support of Ludovico il Moro, duke of Milan. (Ludovico, who was quarreling with the house of Aragon in Naples, hoped to consolidate his position as ruler of Milan with the help of the French troops.) Venice and Pope Alexander VI maintained a position of friendly neutrality toward France.

Encountering no serious opposition from the northern and central Italian states, the French king passed through Rome and, having been invested by the pope in the Kingdom of Naples (January 1495), he seized Naples in February 1495. The pillage of the city by the French army and the institution of new requisitions aroused the indignation of the Neapolitans, and Charles VIII found himself threatened by a general uprising. In addition, the Italian states, which were frightened by the success of the French, changed their policies. To expel the French from Italy the Holy League (or League of Venice), which consisted of Venice, Milan, and the papacy, was created in March 1495. Emperor Maximilian I and the Spanish king Ferdinand II of Aragon aligned themselves with the league. Fearing that he would be cut off from France, Charles VIII abandoned Naples in May 1495 and retreated to the north with most of his troops. A battle against the army of the Holy League took place on July 6, 1495, near Fornovo. The French troops managed to break through and return to their homeland (October 1495). After the remaining French garrisons in Italy had been defeated several times by Spanish troops, France signed a surrender and removed all her troops from the territory of the Kingdom of Naples (December 1496).

However, peace did not come to Italy: the invasion by the French king had aroused the expansionist tendencies of some of the Italian states—above all, the papacy. A series of internal wars flared up, the biggest of which was the war between Pisa and Florence, which broke out in 1494. Besides, France had not renounced its aggressive plans. Louis XII, successor to Charles VIII, who had died in 1498, undertook a campaign in Italy in 1499, hoping to conquer the Duchy of Milan. (Louis XII based his claim to the duchy on his being the grandson of Valentina Visconti, whose family had ruled Milan until 1447.) Before invading Italy the French king reached an agreement on military aid with Venice and Florence and one on neutrality with the emperor and the pope. (The latter considered France a source of support in his struggle with the Italian states.) Having defeated the Milanese troops in a number of battles between 1499 and 1500, Louis XII seized the Duchy of Milan and took possession of all of Lombardy.

Meeting in 1500 in Granada, representatives of France and Spain concluded a secret treaty on the partition of the Kingdom of Naples. Between 1501 and 1502, French and Spanish troops conquered the kingdom; however, in the spring of 1503 a conflict broke out between France and Spain over disputed areas. In a battle at the Garigliano River (Dec. 29, 1503), Spanish troops routed the French. France was forced to renounce her claim to the Kingdom of Naples, which became a possession of the Spanish crown under the Treaty of Blois (1504). Thus, in the initial period of the Italian Wars two of the biggest states in Italy—the Duchy of Milan and the Kingdom of Naples—were seized.

The only Italian state that profited from the wars was Venice, which received substantial territory in Lombardy and Naples, as well as a number of Apulian ports after the fall of Milan. However, Venetian pretensions to hegemony in Italy began to threaten the interests of not only France and Spain but also the other Italian states. In December 1508 the anti-Venetian League of Cambrai was formed by the pope, the Holy Roman Empire, France, and Spain. A number of Italian states, including Florence, Ferrara, and Mantua, joined the league. In April 1509 the pope imposed an interdict on the Venetian Republic, and in the spring of 1509, France began military operations against Venice. Shortly thereafter, having scored a major victory over Venice at Agnadello on May 14, 1509, France seized Venetian possessions in Lombardy. In June 1509 the emperor's troops occupied Verona, Vicenza, and Padua. (The Venetians soon managed to reconquer Padua.) Venice managed to destroy the coalition by making treaties with Spain and with the papacy, satisfying the former by renouncing all claims to southern Italy and the latter, by returning the towns in Romagna that had been taken by Venetian forces. At the cost of a great effort, Venice recovered a significant part of its possessions. But its strength proved to have been sapped. After the war with the League of Cambrai, Venetian policy was primarily concerned with defending the territorial integrity of the state.

The strengthening of France's positions in northwestern Italy led to a reorientation among the warring powers. Under the aegis of Pope Julius II a new Holy League was formed in October 1511, with the aim of expelling the French from Italy. Venice, Spain, England, and the Swiss cantons became allies of the pope. A number of Italian states, such as Modena and Ferrara, took the side of France, but Florence maintained strict neutrality. Despite their victory in the battle of Ravenna (Apr. 11, 1512) the French, having sustained tremendous losses, were forced to give up Lombardy during 1512. (Anti-French uprisings in the towns of Lombardy and in Genoa also prompted this move.) The authority of the Sforzas was restored in Milan, and the Medicis returned to power in Florence. In November 1512, Emperor Maximilian I joined the Holy League. In the spring of 1513, Venice, having changed its orientation, concluded in Blois a treaty with France on the conquest and partition of northern Italy. Military operations were again launched on Italian territory in May 1513. At the end of 1513, France signed a truce with Spain and in August 1514 in London, a peace with England.

Francis I, who ascended the French throne in 1515, reopened the Italian Wars. French troops supported by Venetians defeated the Swiss mercenaries of the duke of Milan at Marignano on Sept. 13–14, 1515. France recovered Milan and Pavia, and Venice reestablished control over Bergamo and Brescia. In November 1516 the French king signed a treaty (the Perpetual Peace) with the Swiss cantons. By the Treaty of Noyon, which was signed by the French and Spanish kings in August 1516, France's right to Milan and Spain's right to Naples were recognized.

After the election of the Spanish king Charles I as emperor of the Holy Roman Empire (Charles V) in 1519, a new phase in the Italian Wars opened. The Holy Roman Empire, which incorporated a large part of Europe, formed a ring around France, endangering its territorial integrity. Territories in northern Italy that were controlled by France were the only gap in communications between Charles V's northern and southern possessions. Thus, possession of Milan became extremely important for France, whereas Charles V had to expel the French from northern Italy in order to unite his possessions. In 1521, Charles V concluded a secret treaty with Pope Leo X concerning the restoration of the Sforzas in Milan. In the same year military operations were reopened in Italy. The French army, which included Swiss mercenaries, suffered a major defeat at the hands of imperial troops in April 1522 at Bicocca. On Feb. 24, 1525, the French army was routed at Pavia, and the king of France was captured and sent to Madrid. Under the Treaty of Madrid (1526), Francis I yielded the duchies of Milan and Burgundy to Charles V. However, upon his return to France, the French king renounced the treaty, even though his sons were still being held as hostages in Italy. For the purpose of expelling the imperial troops from northern Italy, France, Pope Clement VII, Venice, Florence, and the Duke of Milan, supported by England, formed the League of Cognac in May 1526. The military operations of the league were extremely indecisive. In 1527 the imperial army (one of whose commanders was Charles, duke of Bourbon and constable of France, a French traitor) advanced through Milan toward Rome, pillaging and devastating everything along its route. In May imperial troops seized and sacked Rome and took the pope prisoner.

France tried to continue the war. In the summer of 1527, French troops took Milan and Pavia, and in 1528 they conquered a substantial part of the Kingdom of Naples. However, France failed to consolidate its successes. The pope entered into separate negotiations with the emperor, in whose favor he renounced claim to the towns of Piacenza, Parma, and Modena, and to whom he was obliged to pay a ransom. The Treaty of Barcelona was concluded by the pope and the emperor in June 1529. Abandoned by its Italian allies, France concluded a peace with the emperor at Cambrai in August 1529, under which France retained Burgundy but gave up Flanders and Artois and renounced its Italian claims. Francis I agreed to marry the sister of Charles V, and the emperor returned the French king's sons to their father in return for a ransom. The Kingdom of Naples was declared a Spanish possession, and the other Italian states were subjugated in one way or another to the emperor. In February 1530, Charles V was solemnly crowned king of Italy and Holy Roman Emperor in Bologna.

The Italian Wars reopened in 1536 after the occupation of Milan by imperial troops upon the death of Duke F. Sforza. French troops occupied Piedmont and Savoy. In 1538, with Pope Paul III playing the role of mediator, a ten-year truce was concluded between France and the Holy Roman Empire at Nice. The murder on the territory of the Duchy of Milan of two French envoys who were on their way to see the sultan became the pretext for the next war (1542–44). Francis I formed an alliance with the duke of Cleves, the kings of Denmark and Sweden, and the Turkish sultan; the king of England sided with the emperor. In 1543 a Franco-Turkish force took Nice, and in April 1544, French troops scored a brilliant victory over imperial forces at Ceresole. At the same time, imperial and English troops encroached upon the territory of France. The Peace of Crépy (September 1544), which was signed by the emperor and the French king, reiterated the terms of the Treaty of Cambrai (1529) regarding the territorial claims of both sovereigns. In addition, both sides promised to free the territories seized by them since 1536, and they reached an agreement on joint operations against the "infidels" (Turks). Peace between France and England was concluded in 1546 at Ardres.

The French kings, however, had not renounced their expansionist plans. Wars between France and the Holy Roman Empire broke out again in Italy. In 1547 the duke of Parma (son of Pope Paul III) was murdered, and the Duchy of Parma was occupied by imperial forces. The pope, attempting to establish on the ducal throne his nephew, a member of the Farnese family, appealed to the French king for assistance. This action served as the cause for military operations between French and imperial troops in 1551 at the walls of Parma and Mirandola. In 1553, with the assistance of the Turkish fleet, France seized Corsica from Genoa, which was a dependency of the Spanish Hapsburgs. With military support from France, Siena won its independence in 1552, expelling the Spanish from the city's territory. In 1554 B. Monluc's French garrison defended Siena, which was besieged by Spanish-Florentine forces. However, the French were forced to surrender the city in April 1555. In March 1555, French troops occupied Casale Monferrato in Piedmont. In February 1556 the king of France and the emperor concluded a truce at the Abbey of Vaucelles. (Under the truce, France was to retain Piedmont and Corsica.)

In the same year, however, Pope Paul IV, who was on hostile terms with Charles V, received from the French king the promise of troops for the purpose of expelling the Spanish from Italy. A French army led by Francis, the duke of Guise, advanced toward Naples in 1557. To counterbalance the French intervention in Italy, the Spanish king Philip II (in whose favor Charles V had renounced Spain, the Netherlands, and his Italian possessions) dispatched from the southern Netherlands to French territory a Spanish army under the Duke of Savoy, whose possessions had been occupied by the French. Paris was in danger. Routed in a battle at St. Quentin in August 1557, the French were compelled to abandon their Italian campaign. The French reconquest of Calais from the English (allies of Philip II) did not change the situation. Their finances exhausted, France and Spain were compelled to conclude the Treaty of Cateau-Cambrésis in 1559, which marked the end of French expansion in Italy, strengthened Spanish rule over the northern and southern parts of the peninsula, and reinforced the political fragmentation of Italy.

To some extent, the Italian Wars played a role in the development of the art of war: for the first time, manual firearms and artillery were widely used.

SOURCES
Dokumenty po istorii vneshnei politiki Frantsii, 1547–1548. Moscow-Leningrad, 1963.
REFERENCES
Istoriia Italii, vol. 1, chapter 10. Moscow, 1970.
Lemonnier, H. *Les Guerres d'Italie.* Paris, 1903.
Romier, L. *Les Origines politiques des guerres de religion,* vols. 1–2. Paris, 1913–14.
Fueter, E. *Geschichte des europäischen Staatensystem von 1492 bis 1559.* Munich, 1919.
Ercole, F. *Da Carlo VIII a Carlo V.* Florence, 1932.
L. G. KATUSHKINA [11–131–2]

ITALO-ETHIOPIAN WARS, colonial expansionist wars launched by Italy against Ethiopia.

The war of 1895–96 began with the capture of the province of Tigré by Italian troops under the command of General Baratieri in late 1895. Hoping to repulse the colonialists, Emperor Menelik II formed a 120,000-man army. On Dec. 7, 1895, Ethiopian troops under the command of Ras Makonnen dealt the first major defeat to Italian units in a battle at Amba-Alagi, and on Mar. 1, 1896, a 20,000-man Italian army was routed in a battle at the city of Adwa. Under a treaty signed on Oct. 26, 1896, in Addis Ababa, Italy was forced to recognize Ethiopia's full sovereignty.

The war of 1935–36 had its origins in the early 1930's, when Italy concentrated large contingents of troops in its colonies of Eritrea and Somaliland. In 1934–35, Italy provoked several border clashes with Ethiopia, and on Oct. 3, 1935, an Italian army commanded by Marshal P. Badoglio and armed with tanks, aircraft, and artillery invaded Ethiopia. The Italians were opposed by an Ethiopian army led by Haile Selassie I and made up of poorly armed and untrained detachments of civil guardsmen. (There were only 10,000 men in the regular units of the Ethiopian Army.) The Ethiopians put up heroic resistance to the Italian aggressors, but they were forced to retreat.

Only the Soviet Union, acting both in the League of Nations and outside it, called for an end to the aggression and for the provision of aid to Ethiopia. The Western powers essentially pursued a policy of encouraging the aggressor. In August 1935 the US Congress passed a law on neutrality, which deprived Ethiopia of the opportunity to buy armaments from the USA in the future. As late as January 1935, under a pact concluded between the French foreign minister, Laval, and Mussolini, France granted Italy freedom of action in Ethiopia. In December 1935, Great Britain and France concluded an accord providing for the de facto partition of Ethiopia (the Hoare-Laval plan). At the same time, Great Britain, France, and the USA were supplying Italy with weapons and strategic raw materials.

On May 5, 1936, Italian troops occupied Addis Ababa. On June 1, 1936, the Italian government announced the formation of the colony of Italian East Africa, which included Ethiopia, Eritrea, and Italian Somaliland. However, guerrilla war continued in Ethiopia until the country's liberation in May 1941.

REFERENCES
Popov, V. T. *Razgrom ital'iantsev pod Adua.* Moscow, 1938.
Lisovskii, P. A. *Abissinskaia avantiura ital'ianskogo fashizma.* Moscow-Leningrad, 1936.
Voblikov, D. R. *Efiopiia v bor'be za sokhranenie nezavisimosti, 1860–1960.* Moscow, 1961.
Berkeley, G. F.-H. *The Campaign of Adowa and the Rise of Menelik.* New York [1969].
Battaglia, R. *La prima guerra d'Africa.* [Turin] 1958.
Pignatelli, L. *La guerra dei sette mesi.* Milan [1965].
Barker, A. *The Civilizing Mission: The Italo-Ethiopian War, 1935–1936.* London, 1968.
G. V. TSYPKIN [11–120–2]

ITALO-GREEK WAR OF 1940–41, military operations by fascist Italy against Greece during World War II. On Oct. 28, 1940, Mussolini's fascist Italian government, seeking to establish its dominance in the Mediterranean, declared war on Greece. The Italian Ninth Army (eight divisions, including one tank division; up to 200,000 men; and 250 tanks, 700 guns, and 400 airplanes) under the command of General Visconti Prasca was dispatched against Greece from Albania, which Italy had occupied in 1939. In addition to border units, Greece had on its frontier two infantry divisions and two infantry brigades of the Epirus Army of General Papagos, which consisted of 27,000 men, 20 tanks, 70 guns, and 36 airplanes.

The Italian command, confident of a swift defeat of the Greek Army, launched an offensive against Kastoria and Florina, planning to capture Epirus and occupy all of Greece. However, the Greek Army, skillfully taking advantage of the mountainous terrain, put up stiff resistance, stopped the Italian offensive on November 14, and subsequently, increasing its forces to 12 infantry divisions, two cavalry divisions, and three infantry brigades, went over to a counteroffensive. On November 21, Greek troops, pursuing the retreating enemy, entered Albanian territory, where they were supported by Albanian partisans. The Italian command hastily brought in reinforcements and created the Eleventh Army, which was united with the Ninth Army to form the Albania Group of Armies (27 divisions commanded by General Soddu). Despite the enemy's superiority in forces, Greek troops advanced 25–60 km into Albanian territory, after which the struggle took on a positional character. Only after fascist German troops entered the war in April 1941 was the Greek Army defeated. On April 23, 1941, in Thessalonika General Tsolakoglu signed an act of surrender and armistice with Germany and Italy.

REFERENCES
Istoriia Velikoi Otechestvennoi voiny Sovetskogo Soiuza, 1941–1945, vol. 1. Moscow, 1963.
Kaval'ero, U. *Zapiski o voine.* Moscow, 1968.
Kir'iakidis, G. D. *Gretsiia vo vtoroi mirovoi voine.* Moscow, 1967.
N. M. CHEREPANOV [11–119–2]

ITALO-TURKISH WAR OF 1911–12 (the Tripolitan, or Libyan, War), an expansionist war undertaken by imperialist Italy with the connivance of other European powers, with the objective of wresting from the Ottoman Empire its North African provinces (Tripolitania and Cyrenaica) and turning them into an Italian colony.

Italy opened hostilities on Sept. 29, 1911. On Oct. 5, 1911, an Italian landing force occupied Tripoli and Homs. After the landing of an expeditionary corps of about 35,000 men under General C. Caneva, Italian troops overcame the resistance of small garrisons (about 5,000 men in Tripolitania and about 2,000 in Cyrenaica) and detachments of the local population and occupied the cities of Tobruk (October 14), Derna (October 17), and Benghazi (October 21), as well as a number of coastal oases. Turkish troops withdrew to the south.

However, despite military and technical superiority and brutal punitive measures, attempts by Italian troops to penetrate inland failed because of armed resistance from partisan detachments of the local population and from volunteer detachments that had arrived from Tunisia, Algeria, Egypt, and other Arab countries. By the end of 1911, Italian troops held only a strip of territory along the coast of North Africa. The strength of Italian troops in Tripolitania and Cyrenaica had risen to 100,000 by May 1912. In addition to launching new operations in North Africa, between April and October 1912, Italy began to bombard the Dardanelles (April and July)—a tactic that yielded no results—and occupied the Dodecanese Islands (May). However, during this period Italian troops never succeeded in capturing the interior areas of Tripolitania and Cyrenaica. Aircraft were used for reconnaissance and bombing for the first time in the Italo-Turkish War.

The intensified crisis in the ruling circles of the Ottoman Empire and the Balkan War that began in October 1912 forced the Turkish government to give up Tripolitania and Cyrenaica. On Oct. 15, 1912, a preliminary, secret treaty was signed in Ouchy, Switzerland, and on October 18 a public peace treaty was signed in Lausanne. The sultan promised to "grant" autonomy to the people of Tripolitania and Cyrenaica and to pull his troops out of these regions. However, at this time Tripolitania and Cyrenaica were in fact transformed into an Italian colony, which later became known as Libya. Italy promised to evacuate its troops from the Dodecanese Islands. (Nevertheless, the islands remained under Italian rule until the end of World War II, when they passed to Greece.) Turkey's renunciation of its rights to Libya and the Dodecanese was formalized in the Treaty of Lausanne (1923). A people's liberation struggle against the Italian colonialists in Libya continued until the Italian troops were driven out in 1943.

REFERENCES

Lenin, V.I. "Konets voiny Italii s Turtsiei." *Poln. sobr. soch.*, 5th ed., vol. 22.
Kiseleva, V. I. "Diplomaticheskaia podgotovka Ushi-Lozannskogo mira 1912 g." *Trudy Moskovskogo Gos. istoriko-arkhivnogo instituta*, 1958, vol. 12.
Iakhimovich, Z. P. *Italo-Turetskaia voina 1911–1912 gg.* Moscow, 1967. (Contains a bibliography.)
Maltese, P. *La terra promessa.* Milan, 1968.

Z. P. IAKHIMOVICH [11–120–1]

ITALY (Italia; the Italian Republic [La Repubblica Italiana]).

GENERAL INFORMATION
CONSTITUTION AND GOVERNMENT
NATURAL FEATURES
POPULATION
HISTORICAL SURVEY
POLITICAL PARTIES, TRADE UNIONS, AND
    OTHER SOCIAL ORGANIZATIONS
ECONOMIC GEOGRAPHY
ARMED FORCES
HEALTH AND SOCIAL WELFARE
EDUCATION AND CULTURAL AFFAIRS
SCIENCE AND SCIENTIFIC INSTITUTIONS
PRESS, RADIO, AND TELEVISION
LITERATURE
ARCHITECTURE AND ART
MUSIC
DANCE AND BALLET
THEATER
MOTION PICTURES

General information

Italy is a state in southern Europe and the central Mediterranean region. The country is bordered on the west by the Ligurian and Tyrrhenian seas, on the south by the Ionian Sea, and on the east by the Adriatic. About 20 percent of the border is a land boundary, most of which passes through various parts of the Alps. Italy is bounded on the north by France, Switzerland, and Austria and on the northeast by Yugoslavia. Italy's territory covers the southern slopes of the Alps, the Po Basin, the Apennine Peninsula, the islands of Sicily and Sardinia, and numerous tiny islands.

The area of Italy is 301,200 sq km. In 1971 the population was 54.7 million. The capital is Rome. Administratively, Italy consists of 20 regions (including two islands), which are divided into provinces that are, in turn, divided into communes. (See Table 1.)

Constitution and government

Italy is a republic, the present-day constitution of which came into force on Jan. 1, 1948. The head of state is the president, who is elected to a seven-year term by secret ballot at a joint session of both chambers of Parliament. Three delegates from each region, elected by the regional councils, also take part in presidential elections. (The Valle d'Aosta region elects only one delegate.) The president has broad powers, including the right to promulgate laws, issue executive orders with the force of law, dissolve Parliament, and appoint the premier and the ministers nominated by him. As commander in chief of the armed forces, the president of the republic presides over the Supreme Council of Defense.

The supreme legislative body is Parliament, which consists of two chambers: the Chamber of Deputies (630 members as of Aug. 1, 1972) and the Senate of the Republic (315 members as of Aug. 1, 1972). The Chamber of Deputies is elected in direct, general elections under a proportional system of representation, with voting for party lists. The Senate of the Republic is also elected in direct, general elections. Five senators are appointed

Table 1. Administrative divisions

Region	Provinces	Area (sq km)	Population (1970)	Capital
Piedmont	Alessandria, Asti, Cuneo, Novara, Turin, Vercelli	25,400	4,433,600	Turin
Valle d'Aosta	Valle d'Aosta	3,300	110,000	Aosta
Lombardy	Bergamo, Brescia, Como, Cremona, Mantua, Milan, Pavia, Sondrio, Varese	23,800	8,442,700	Milan
Trentino–Alto Adige	Bolzano, Trento	13,600	844,900	Trento
Veneto	Belluno, Padua, Rovigo, Treviso, Venice, Verona, Vicenza	18,400	4,122,200	Venice
Friuli–Venezia Giulia	Gorizia, Pordenone, Trieste, Udine	7,800	1,232,400	Trieste
Liguria	Genoa, Imperia, La Spezia, Savona	5,400	1,882,000	Genoa
Emilia-Romagna	Bologna, Ferrara, Forlì, Modena, Parma, Piacenza, Ravenna, Reggio nell'Emilia	22,100	3,858,800	Bologna
Tuscany	Arezzo, Florence, Grosseto, Livorno, Lucca, Massa-Carrara, Pisa, Pistoia, Siena	23,000	3,479,600	Florence
Umbria	Perugia, Terni	8,500	782,600	Perugia
Marchés	Ancona, Ascoli Piceno, Macerata, Pesaro e Urbino	9,700	1,368,800	Ancona
Latium	Frosinone, Latina, Rieti, Rome, Viterbo	17,200	4,705,100	Rome
Abruzzi	Chieti, L'Aquila, Pescara, Teramo	10,800	1,201,500	Pescara
Molise	Campobasso, Isernia	4,400	331,200	Campobasso
Campania	Avellino, Benevento, Caserta, Naples, Salerno	13,600	5,191,400	Naples
Apulia	Bari, Brindisi, Foggia, Lecce, Taranto	19,300	3,642,500	Bari
Basilicata	Matera, Potenza	10,000	620,900	Potenza
Calabria	Catanzaro, Cosenza, Reggio di Calabria	15,100	2,048,600	Catanzaro
Sicily	Agrigento, Caltanissetta, Catania, Enna, Messina, Palermo, Ragusa, Siracusa, Trapani	25,700	4,882,700	Palermo
Sardinia	Cagliari, Nuoro, Sassari	24,100	1,501,700	Cagliari

for life by the president of the republic, usually in recognition of special services. In addition, former presidents of the republic become life members of the Senate. In the 1972 elections to the Chamber of Deputies the Christian Democratic Party won 267 seats; the Italian Communist Party, 179; the Italian Socialist Party, 61; the Italian Social Movement (together with the monarchists), 56; the Liberal Party, 20; the Italian Social Democrats, 29; the Republican Party, 15; and all other parties, three. In the Senate, the Christian Democratic Party won 136 seats; the Italian Communist Party, 92; the Italian Socialist Party, 34; the Italian Social Democrats, 11; the Republican Party, five; the Italian Social Movement (together with the monarchists), 26; the Liberal Party, eight; and all other parties, three. The term of office of both chambers does not exceed five years. Suffrage is granted to all citizens who have reached 21 years of age.

Executive power is exercised by the government—the Council of Ministers, which is made up of the premier and ministers (including ministers without portfolio). The government is responsible to Parliament.

Under the constitution (art. 116), five regions (Sicily, Sardinia, Valle d'Aosta, Trentino–Alto Adige, and Friuli–Venezia Giulia) have special statutes granting them their own parliaments—regional councils—and governments (*giuntas*), which have limited legislative powers in matters of local government. Commissioners appointed by the central government coordinate the activities of these bodies. In the 15 remaining regions, which are governed under ordinary statutes, councils were elected only in 1970.

There are also elected bodies in the provinces and communes —the provincial and communal councils. In addition, the provinces have administrative bodies appointed by the president: prefects and councils of the prefecture.

The judicial system consists of the Court of Cassation (the highest court), civil courts (justices of the peace, *pretori* [career judges with jurisdiction in minor cases], and *tribunali* [courts with original and appellate jurisdiction]), criminal courts (*pretori, tribunali,* and courts of assizes), and appeals courts. Judges may not be removed from office. They are appointed and transferred by the Superior Council of the Judiciary, the chairman of which is the president of the republic. A special place in the judicial system is held by the Constitutional Court, which is made up of 15 judges appointed (one-third at a time) by the president, a joint session of Parliament, and the supreme general and administrative judicial bodies, which consist of the highest officials of the judiciary.

Natural features

Northern Italy is located in a forest region in the temperate zone, and southern Italy lies in the subtropical zone. The country's natural features are greatly influenced by the Mediterranean Sea, in whose basin Italy is situated. The coast is highly indented, and there are few good harbors. The southern coast of the Apennine Peninsula is the most heavily dissected. On the western coast there are several shallow, arcuate bays. The shores of the Ligurian Sea are, for the most part, eroded, abounding in small harbors. On the Tyrrhenian coast elevated sections alternate with accumulation plains. In the southeast, steep shores with signs of recent uplift prevail. Most of the eastern shore is flat. In the northeast there are many lagoons, and the shoreline is sinking (for example, near Venice). Italy's shoreline is about 7,500 km long.

Terrain. In Italy mountains and uplands prevail, making up about four-fifths of the territory. Northern Italy is occupied by the Alps, the highest of which are the Western Alps. (Mont Blanc, with an elevation of 4,807 m, is the highest point in Italy.) The steep slopes of the Western Alps are dissected by narrow, deep transverse ravines, and there are as many as 15 large valley glaciers. The Eastern Alps, with altitudes as high as 3,899 m (Mount Ortles), are also glaciated (primarily in the Bernina, Adamello, and Ortles massifs), and they are dissected by glacial troughs, some of which are occupied by lakes. There is a wide piedmont zone. In the northeast the Eastern Alps consist primarily of precipitous calcareous and karst massifs and ranges that run into the Karst Plateau in the east.

South of the Alps is the Po Basin, whose gently rolling or flat surface gradually descends eastward to the Adriatic Sea. High plains (200–500 m) composed primarily of friable, porous rock, are found at the foot of the Alps and the Apennines. Along the Po River there are clayey, swampy low plains (50–100 m high) that sink as much as 3 mm per year. South of the Po Basin, the medium-elevation Apennines extend almost 1,200 km along the Apennine Peninsula. In the north they consist of a series of parallel or echelon-like ranges and massifs, the highest of which are the Central Apennines (Mount Corno, 2,914 m). In the western part of the Apennine Peninsula medium-elevation mountains alternate with hills and small lowlands. There are a number of extinct and active volcanoes (Amiata, 1,734 m, and Vesuvius, 1,277 m) and lava fields. In the southeast, the Gargano and Murgian karst limestone plateaus run along the shores of the Adriatic Sea. The Calabrian Apennines (up to 1,956 m high) occupy the southern part of the Apennine Peninsula. The islands of Italy have mostly mountainous terrain. There are several well-known volcanoes on the islands: Etna (3,340 m), Stromboli, and Vulcano. Frequent, strong earthquakes are characteristic of central and southern Italy (Messina, 1908; Sicily, 1968).

Geological structure and mineral resources. Italy's territory belongs to the Alpine Geosynclinal (Folded) Region. A large part of its territory is made up of the Cenozoic folded mountain structures of the Alps and the Apennines, which are divided by the piedmont downwarp of the Po Basin. Parts of Hercynian and Precambrian gneiss-granite massifs emerge on Sardinia, the Calabrian Peninsula, and northeastern Sicily. A similar massif makes up the base of the Adriatic coast of Italy, where it is covered with a mantle of Mesozoic-Cenozoic limestones (the Murgian and Gargano plateaus).

The Italian Alps are located in the central crystalline, southern limestone, and graywacke (sandy-clayey) zones of the Alps. In the west the structure of the Alps includes autochthonous crystalline massifs such as Mercantour and Mont Blanc and the Pennine covers, which consist of crystalline schists and gneisses. In the Eastern Alps limestone rocks form a system of eastern-alpine sheets that override toward the north. The Northern Apennines also have a sheet structure. There are three systems of sheets, all of which override toward the northeast: the Lower Tuscan System (Paleozoic shales and Carrara marble), the Upper Tuscan System (Eocene sandstones), and the Ligurian System (flaky clays and shales with inclusions of ophiolite rocks). The Central and Southern Apennines are autochthonous mountains composed of Mesozoic Paleocene and Neocene limestones and Cretaceous flysch. In addition to sedimentary and metamorphic rocks, the structure of the western foothills of the Apennines near Rome includes thick volcanic strata of lava and tuff (trachyte and liparite), which make up a number of extinct volcanoes with enormous calderas that have become lakes (Bracciano, Bolsena, and Vico). Near Naples, volcanic tuff and lava make up the Phlegraean Fields, the site of various volcanic phenomena, including extinct volcanoes and fumaroles that expel vapors and gases. Situated in southern Italy are some of the world's largest active volcanoes (Etna and Vesuvius), whose location is related to deep fractures in the earth's crust. The Po downwarp is filled by a thick stratum (up to 8,000 m) of marine and continental sand and clay deposits of the Neocene and Anthropogenic eras.

Among the known deposits of combustible minerals in Italy are anthracite coal in southwestern Sardinia and the Alps (Aosta) and brown coal, lignites, and bituminous shales, which are confined to the Paleocene-Neocene deposits of the Central Apennines. Oil and fuel gases are extracted from the Neocene deposits of the Po downwarp and the foothills of the Apennines, Emilia, and the Mesozoic and Cenozoic deposits of Sicily (Ragusa). The main ore deposits—lead, zinc, and iron-ore complexes in Sardinia (Iglesiente) and iron-ore complexes on Elba and in the Colline Metallifere—are related to ancient metamorphic complexes. The karst depressions of Abruzzi, Apulia, and the Gargano Peninsula contain bauxites. Italy is second in the world (after Spain) in reserves of cinnabar (mercury ore). In addition to gypsum, the Neocene limestone-clay stratum of Sicily contains large deposits of sulfur. In the Northern Apennines there is a famous deposit of beautiful facing and sculptural

Carrara marbles (Tuscany). From the Miocene deposits in Sicily and Calabria, rock salt is mined. There are numerous mineral and hot springs. In Tuscany natural hot springs (100°–120°C) and steam emanating from underground are used to produce electric power. They are also a source of boric acid.

N. A. Sysoeva and M. V. Muratov

Climate. To a considerable extent, the climate of Italy is subject to the influence of the warm Mediterranean Sea, whose effect is reinforced by the Alps, which act as a barrier, protecting Italy from cold winds from the north. Over most of Italy the climate is subtropical Mediterranean, but in the Po Basin the climate is transitional from subtropical to temperate. In the mountains, altitudinal zonality is an important phenomenon. The summer is hot and dry, with July temperatures at the foot of the Alps averaging 20°–22°C, in the Po Basin, 22°–24°C, and on the Apennine Peninsula and the islands, 23°–28°C. During the passage of the sirocco the temperature rises to 40°–45°C. In the Alps at altitudes of more than 3,500 m the July temperature drops to 0°C. The average January temperature at the foot of the Alps and in the Po Basin is about 0°C and on the Apennine Peninsula and the islands, 1°–12°C. In the Alps, frosts of −15°C and −20°C occur frequently. In some valleys of the Alps (Aosta and Susa) sharp temperature rises in the winter and spring cause foehns. The climate of the Tyrrhenian coast is 1°–2°C warmer than that of the Adriatic coast. The coast of the Ligurian Sea, which is protected from the intrusion of cold air masses by the mountains in the north, also has warm winters. In the winter (in the autumn and spring in the central and northern regions) cyclones cause torrential precipitation and frequent weather changes.

The wettest regions are the Eastern Alps and the Northern Apennines (more than 3,000 mm a year), as well as all of the western mountain slopes. On the eastern slopes and in the interior regions of Italy the annual precipitation is 600–800 mm, and in the interior regions of Sicily and Sardinia it is less than 500 mm. In the Alps the greatest precipitation occurs in the summer. Spring and autumn are the seasons of greatest precipitation in the Po Basin and the northern Apennine Peninsula, whereas in the south, winter brings the heaviest precipitation. The snow line in the mountains is at an altitude of 2,800–3,200 m. Of the more than 800 glaciers in the Italian Alps, the largest is Miagge (10 km long), which is located in the Mont Blanc massif.

Rivers and lakes. The densest river network is in the north, where Italy's largest river, the Po (652 km long), forms a large navigable system that includes tributaries and canals. In the eastern part of the Po Basin are a number of rivers, including the Adige, Brenta, Piave, Tagliamento, and Reno. Sedimentation often raises the riverbeds above the surface of the plain in their lower course. They are held back by levees, ruptures of which cause great floods. (The most recent occurred in 1951, 1953, and 1966.) The rivers of the north are fed not only by rain but also by snow and glacial melt. The high-water periods occur in spring, summer, and autumn. The northern rivers are used for irrigation and in the Alps as sources of hydroelectric power.

There are fewer rivers on the Apennine Peninsula and the islands. Replenished by rain, they have autumnal or winter high-water periods, but in the summer they often dry up. The longest rivers of the Apennine Peninsula are the Arno and the Tiber.

Many of Italy's large lakes are situated in the foothills of the Lombard Alps in tectonic basins that were further deepened by ancient glaciers (for example, Lakes Garda, Como, and Maggiore). The lakes are navigable, and there are many resorts on their shores. On the Apennine Peninsula large lakes occupy the craters of extinct volcanoes (for example, Bolsena and Bracciano).

Soils and flora. Mountain broad-leaved forests made up primarily of oaks, with some chestnut, ash, and maple, are well developed in the Alps at altitudes of up to 800 m. At 800–1,800 m there are beech and coniferous forests on brown forest mountain soils, humus mountain soils, and rendzinas. Shrubs and subalpine and alpine meadows are found on mountain-meadow soils at higher altitudes. In the ridge section of the mountains, outcropped rocks and talus prevail.

Oak forests, flood-plain meadows, and shrubs on alluvial and brown forest soils were once common in the Po Basin, but today cultivated vegetation prevails. In the Apennines and on the islands of Sicily and Sardinia, at altitudes of up to 500–600 m, natural vegetation includes groves of evergreen holm and cork oaks, stone pine, Aleppo pine, and shrub formations on cinnamonic, volcanic, and some dark soils (smolnitz). At altitudes as high as 1,000–1,500 m broad-leaved mountain forests of oak, beech, and chestnut on cinnamonic and brown mountain soils and rendzinas prevail. Above 2,000 m, coniferous broad-leaved mountain forests of beech, spruce, fir, and pine are widespread. With the felling of forests, soil erosion has become a major problem. The upper sections of the highest massifs are occupied by subalpine meadows on mountain-meadow soils.

Fauna. Animals are found primarily in the mountains. The chamois, wildcat, stone and wood martens, and polecat inhabit the Alps and Apennines. The brown bear may be found in the Central Apennines. Hares, squirrels, and about 400 species of birds are common. There are many reptiles and fish. Tuna, mackerel, sardines, and flounder are commercially important.

National parks and preserves. A number of national parks have been established in Italy, including Gran Paradiso and Stelvio in the Alps and Abruzzo in the Apennines (for the preservation of mountainous landscapes, glaciers, unique geological sites, and alpine flora and fauna). Circeo on the Tyrrhenian coast was founded to preserve the natural oak and pine forests, dunes, and areas where dwarf palms grow. In 1969 the total area of national parks was about 200,000 hectares (ha).

Natural regions. The Alps are characterized by a high-mountain relief with recent glaciation and traces of ancient glaciation and by a pronounced altitudinal zonality of landscapes. The Po Basin, with landscapes that are transitional from Central European to Mediterranean, has become a densely populated industrial and agricultural region. In the Apennine Peninsula, Sicily, and Sardinia, mid-mountain relief prevails, the climate is subtropical, and the vegetation is evergreen.

REFERENCES

Birot, P., and J. Dresch. *Sredizemnomor'e,* vol. 1. Moscow, 1960. (Translated from French.)
Gratsianskii, A. N. *Priroda Sredizemnomor'ia.* Moscow, 1971.
Galkina, T., and N. Sysoeva. *Italiia.* Moscow, 1972.
Almagia, R. *L'Italia,* vols. 1–2. Turin, 1959.

Population

Italians make up more than 98 percent of the population. Living in the northern border regions of the country are 350,000 Rhaeto-Romanic speakers (mostly Friulians), 210,000 southern Tiroleans (Austrians), about 70,000 Frenchmen, and about 50,000 Slovenians and Croats. The population of southern Italy and Sicily includes approximately 80,000 Albanians and 30,000 Greeks, and there are 10,000 Catalonians in Sardinia. Approximately 50,000 Jews live in Italy. The official language is Italian. The dominant religion is Catholicism. The official calendar is the Gregorian.

In population, Italy ranks third in Western Europe (after the Federal Republic of Germany [FRG] and Great Britain). Between 1963 and 1970 the average annual population increase was 0.8 percent. Characteristic of the population of Italy has been a long, uninterrupted process of "aging"—that is, the proportion of persons older than 65 increased from 6.5 percent in 1911 to 10.4 percent in 1969, and the proportion of children under 15 declined during the same period from 33.9 percent to 24.4 percent. Between 1967 and 1969 the average number of emigrants per year was about 270,000—72,000 more than the average annual immigration. The emigrants go to European countries, especially the FRG, and to North America and Australia. Seasonal migration (agricultural workers in northern border regions) and internal migration have been increasing. (Every year, 1.5 million Italians change their place of residence within Italy, most of them moving from south to north.)

Of the entire work force (19.4 million people in 1970), 42 percent is employed in industry, 19 percent in agriculture, fishing, and forestry, and 30 percent in the service industries, including 13 percent in trade, 5 percent in transportation and communications, and about 2.5 percent in the hotel business. More than two-thirds of the work force is made up of wage workers. The dominant position in the economy is held by a relatively small stratum of big landowners, industrial and commercial bourgeoisie, and high officials.

Italy is one of the most densely populated European countries, with an average of 180 inhabitants per sq km. The population density of northern Italy (300–380 per sq km) exceeds the average. About 60 percent of the inhabitants of Italy are concentrated in cities with populations of more than 10,000. There are 45 cities with populations of more than 100,000. In 1970 the largest of them were Rome (2,779,000), Milan (1,714,000), Naples (1,278,000), Turin (1,191,000), Genoa (842,000), and Palermo (664,000). In recent years an intensified growth of large cities has been characteristic of Italy. Some of the cities, such as Milan, Genoa, Naples, and Palermo, are the nuclei of large urban agglomerations.

Historical survey

Primitive communal and slaveholding systems (*to the second half of the fifth century A.D.*). The territory of Italy was settled in the Paleolithic age. (This assertion is based on a number of archaeological finds, such as those in the Romanelli grotto near the town of Castro in Apulia, in the Barma Grande cave near the village of Grimaldi in Liguria, and at the Savignano dig in Emilia-Romagna.) The Bronze Age (second millennium B.C.) was widely represented in northern Italy by the archaeological culture known as terramara and in central Italy, by a number of cultures related to it and often referred to collectively as the Apennine culture. A number of cultures that arose on the territory of Italy during the Iron Age (from the beginning of the first millennium B.C.) left substantial archaeological traces. Of these cultures the leading one was the Villanovan.

The oldest tribes to populate the territory of Italy were the Ligurians, the Etruscans, and the Sicani (in Sicily). In the second and first millennia B.C. the Indo-European Italic tribes spread gradually over the greater part of the Apennine Peninsula. Among the Italic tribes the Latins achieved the highest degree of development. (In the sixth century B.C. they were at the stage of early class states.) According to tradition, in 754–753 B.C. the Latins and the Sabines (another Italic tribe) founded Rome. Between the fifth and third centuries B.C. the Apennine Peninsula was conquered by Rome. Until the fifth century A.D., the territory of Italy belonged to the Roman state, and a slaveholding system developed there.

In the third century A.D. the Roman Empire, the largest part of which was Italy, underwent a crisis of the slaveholding system. The elements of feudalism were conceived within the slaveholding society: a combination of large-scale ownership of land with small-scale farming, a predominantly natural economy (although urban life in Italy had not completely died out since the earlier Roman period), the binding of the peasants to the land, and the growth of the landowners' political power. German and other barbarian tribes that invaded Italy in the fourth and fifth centuries dealt heavy blows to the Roman Empire. In the early fifth century the Visigoths came to Italy, capturing Rome in 410. Rome was defeated by the Vandals in 455.

Period of feudalism (*second half of the fifth century to the first half of the 18th century*). In 476 the Western Roman Empire ceased to exist. The last Roman emperor, Romulus Augustulus, was overthrown by Odoacer, who established a barbarian kingdom (476–93) in Italy. His soldiers received one-third of the land of the Roman property owners; thus, the old order, in substance, remained almost unchanged. In 488 the Ostrogoths invaded Italy, founding their own kingdom (493–554). Their leader, Theodoric, was proclaimed king of the Goths and the Italic peoples. Under the Ostrogoths no fundamental changes took place in the socioeconomic system in Italy, but the proportion of land owned by free peasants increased somewhat. At the same time, the Ostrogothic aristocracy, which had acquired large landed properties, began to draw closer to the Roman-Italic aristocracy. In 535, Italy's territory was invaded by Byzantium's troops. The Ostrogothic king Totila succeeded in uniting all of the forces hostile to the Byzantines by taking advantage of discontent throughout the country with Byzantine policy, which aimed at restoring and strengthening slaveholding relations. However,

Byzantium conquered most of Italy in 554. The Byzantine emperor Justinian I issued the Pragmatic Sanction of 554, which was designed to restore the socioeconomic relations of the Roman Empire.

In 568 the Lombards came to northern Italy. Their conquest dealt the final blow to the slaveholding order. The Lombards expelled and killed a substantial number of the slaveholders. Confiscated lands were divided among the conquering farmers, and for a while the free peasants were the main producers. However, some of the large-scale Roman landowners, who controlled both slaves and coloni, had not been eliminated. Under the influence of Roman private ownership, the breakdown of the Lombard community and the formation of a class of dependent peasants and a class of feudal lords were accelerated. An early feudal state was being born. Part of Italy remained under Byzantine rule (the Exarchate of Ravenna, the Pentapolis, the Duchy of Rome, and the lands of southern Italy). In 751 the Exarchate of Ravenna was captured by the Lombards; subsequently, it was wrested from them by the Franks. In 756 a papal theocracy—the Papal States—was formed when the Frankish king Pepin the Short gave the territories of the Exarchate of Ravenna, the Duchy of Rome, and the Pentapolis to the pope. The Lombard state was conquered by Charlemagne in 774.

The subjugation of Italy by the Franks accelerated the development of feudal relations. In 781 the Kingdom of Italy was formed, with Charlemagne's son Pepin as king. The Carolingians held the Italian throne until the deposition of Charles the Fat in 887. To a large degree the king's power was nominal. Italy was fragmented into feudal possessions. Taking advantage of the weakness of royal power, secular and ecclesiastical feudal lords increased their prerogatives. The bishops became the real masters of the cities.

In the late ninth century a bitter struggle for the throne of Italy broke out among the feudal lords of Italy, Provence, and Burgundy. (From 900 to 905 the king of Provence, Ludwig III, the last member of the Italian branch of the Carolingians, was king of Italy.) As a result of the expansionist campaigns of the German king Otto I (951 and 961–62), Italy was incorporated into the Holy Roman Empire, which was formed by Otto in 962. Internecine feudal conflicts and forays by the Arabs beginning in the mid-ninth century (primarily in southern and central Italy) and by the Hungarians in the late ninth century (in northern Italy) contributed to the ruin of the free landowners and to their transformation into dependent peasant landholders: *libellarii* (long-term or hereditary tenants), those who held precaria, and those who held land on terms of emphyteusis (a perpetual hereditary lease that granted the tenant considerable freedom of control over a plot of land). Although the enserfment of the peasants began in the ninth century, the process had not yet been completed in the 11th century, and a large number of peasants remained free.

A distinctive feature of feudalism in Italy was the preservation of commodity and money relations and the existence of numerous cities that traced their origin to the Roman era. Even in the early Middle Ages domestic production and trade had not died out in some of the cities (Amalfi, Naples, Lucca, Ravenna, and Milan). To a certain extent, villages were also drawn into commodity and money relations. In Italy, handicrafts became separate from agriculture in the ninth and tenth centuries, earlier than in the other European countries. As a result, feudal towns —centers of handicrafts and trade—developed, chiefly on the basis of the surviving centers of Roman urban civilization.

In the tenth century the townspeople began a struggle against the seignior-bishops. In the 11th century Asti, Lucca, Pisa, Milan, and a number of other cities were freed from the power of the seigniors and formed communes. Corporations, or guilds, of craftsmen and merchants developed in the Italian cities in the 11th and 12th centuries. With the triumph of the communes, power passed from the seignior to a collegium of consuls, which included representatives of the urban aristocracy and wealthy merchants. Craftsmen and small-scale merchants were not given any power, nor did the popular assembly play an important role in governing the cities. The transition to a commune with political and economic rights undermined the power of the feudal lords and gave impetus to the development of Italy's economy and to the formation of republican city-states by the subjugation of neighboring small towns and rural territories. The republic, a new form of state, was the most progressive of that era.

The city-communes became powerful centers for the development of commodity and money relations. The Italian port cities (Venice, Genoa, Pisa, and Ancona) also flourished because of the Crusades, which transformed them into the chief commercial intermediaries between Europe and the East. The economic dominance of the cities of northern and central Italy led to changes in the agrarian system in that area of Italy. In the late 11th and 12th centuries, large-scale feudal lords reduced the manorial demesne and began to lease land to peasants, knights, merchants, and frequently even to members of the urban elite (the *popolo grasso,* or "fat people"). With the support of the cities, rural communes (outgrowths of the early feudal communes) were established in Italy in the 12th and 13th centuries and began to seek the right to self-government. This development contributed to the preservation of small-scale peasant farming. The rural communes, having been freed from the power of the feudal lords, generally fell under the authority of nearby cities.

The political history of the Italian cities in the 12th and 13th centuries was characterized by an exacerbation of the class struggle: in such cities as Pavia and Milan craftsmen, merchants, and low-ranking knights waged a struggle against the high nobility, and in late 13th-century Florence clashes began to occur between the *popolo minuto,* or "gaunt people" (the urban poor), and the *popolo grasso.* In foreign policy, the history of the cities during the same period was dominated by their heroic struggle against the German feudal lords, who invaded Italy under the leadership of Frederick I Barbarossa (five campaigns, 1154–76). In 1158 the emperor issued the decrees of Roncaglia, under which the Italian communes lost their political autonomy. During the struggle against the German feudal lords, the Guelph and Ghibelline parties emerged in the cities of Italy. Milan, the main center of resistance to the German invaders, was destroyed in 1162. Hoping to repulse the Holy Roman emperor, the cities of northern Italy united in the Lombard League in 1167. The struggle against the German feudal lords contributed to the appearance of elements of a sense of national identity among the Italian people. Under the Peace of Constance of 1183, the Italian cities regained de facto independence from the emperor.

In southern Italy and Sicily, both of which had been captured in the 11th century by the Normans, who founded the Kingdom of Sicily in the 12th century, the development of feudal relations proceeded more slowly than in northern and central Italy. As late as the 13th century there was still a large stratum of semifree peasantry. Frederick II Hohenstaufen, the king of Sicily and the Holy Roman emperor, turned the Kingdom of Sicily into a centralized bureaucratic monarchy and tried in vain to extend his rule over all of Italy. In the 1260's the house of Anjou subjugated southern Italy. The popular revolt of 1282 (the Sicilian Vespers) led to the disintegration of the Kingdom of Sicily. The house of Aragon took over in Sicily in the late 13th century and the early 14th and in southern Italy in the mid-15th century. Thus, southern Italy fell under Spanish rule.

Because of the early development of cities, the preconditions for early capitalist relations were created in the advanced city-states of northern and central Italy: banking was conducted on a large scale (Siena and Florence), as were overseas commerce (Venice, Genoa, and Pisa) and cloth-finishing (Perugia, Bologna, Siena, Florence, and Milan). Banking and commercial capital were used to develop industry. The expansion of handicraft production contributed to the decisions of a number of city-states (Bologna in 1256 and Florence in 1289) to free from servitude (serfdom) the peasants living on territories that were under the authority of the city-states. The elimination of servitude led to the separation of the direct producer from the means of production. The former servitors lost their plots of land and became sharecroppers (*mezzadri*) —semicapitalist tenants. A sizable segment of the peasantry moved to the cities, swelling the ranks of wage laborers in the workshops of wool-makers and cloth finishers. The abolition of serfdom undermined the economic and political influence of the class of feudal lords. As a result of a bitter struggle in the cities of northern and central Italy between the merchant-craftsmen strata (*popolo*) and the feudal lords, the lords were stripped legislatively of their political rights (for example, in Florence in 1293). By the end of the 13th century, feudalism in Italy, in contrast to feudalism in the other countries of Europe, had been substantially undermined and to some degree "broken up by the exceptional development of the cities, which politically dominated the countryside" (K. Marx in K. Marx and F. Engels, *Soch.,* 2nd ed., vol. 25, part 2, p. 365).

The great upsurge of productive forces in the cities and countryside of northern and central Italy led in the 14th to 16th centuries to the birth and development of early capitalist relations, which engendered a preproletariat: "In Italy, where capitalist production developed earliest of all, the relations of serfdom broke up earliest of all as well. The serf there was emancipated before he was able to ensure himself of any prescriptive right to land. Hence, emancipation immediately turned him into a proletarian placed outside the law, who, in addition, at once found new lords in the cities" (K. Marx, *ibid.,* vol. 23, p. 728, footnote).

In certain large cities of northern and central Italy, the number of hired workers receiving weekly wages reached tens of thousands. In the 14th century, capitalist factories emerged (mainly in cloth finishing), which were a combination of the centralized and dispersed forms of manufacturing. At the same time, ordinary medieval artisan workshops continued their production operations. The incipient breakdown of the guilds was manifested by their division into "senior" and "junior" guilds, by the deepening of social inequality within them, and by the intensified exploitation of pupils and apprentices, who were increasingly deprived of the opportunity to become independent craftsmen and who were, in fact, being transformed into permanent wage laborers. The guild system impeded the development of capitalist manufacturing, which, however, continued to exist until the end of the 16th century and contributed to Italy's economic prosperity.

Greater exploitation in the workshops caused many revolts by the preproletariat, including a strike in 1345 in Florence, revolts in 1371 in Perugia and Siena, and the revolt of the *ciompi* in 1378 in Florence. In the 14th century the increasing oppression of peasants in regions with poorly developed cities provoked major antifeudal revolts—for example, Dolcino's revolt in Piedmont, 1304–07, and the revolt of the *tuchini* in Savoy, 1382–87—and this led to some easing of exploitation. As a result of the exacerbation of the class struggle in the 14th and 15th centuries and of the *popolo grasso*'s fear of popular revolts, the republican form of rule in the city-states was replaced by tyranny, or seigniory. By the 15th century tyrannies had become firmly established in a number of city-states, including Florence, Milan, Bologna, Ferrara, and Urbino.

Early capitalist relations were the source of the new, basically antifeudal culture of the Renaissance, which was born in Italy, where it developed its most consummate features. (The Italian Renaissance is dated from the 14th to the 16th century.)

The economic achievements of the Italian cities in the 14th and 15th centuries did not lead to the country's unification or to the creation of a single national market. Despite its political dominance in certain city-states, where an embryonic form of caitalist production appeared, the urban stratum of the disunited Italian states did not develop into a national bourgeoisie. The political disunity of Italy, the relatively narrow base for capitalist development, which had left agriculture virtually untouched, the primarily export-oriented character of production, the shift of trade routes from the Mediterranean Sea to the Atlantic Ocean, and Turkish expansion, which interrupted Italy's trade relations with the Middle East, brought about the decline in the 16th century of industry and trade and the rechanneling of monetary capital from industry into usury and the acquisition of real estate. Feudal reaction set in, feudal dependence became stronger in the countryside, and the peasant was, in effect, bound to the land.

France and Spain took advantage of Italy's weakness by waging the Italian Wars of 1494–1559 on Italian territory. The papacy, maneuvering between France and Spain, facilitated their capture of Italian territories. In many cities the popular masses took action against the foreign invaders and the Italian nobility (for example, in Genoa in 1506–07 and in Palermo in 1516). The Treaty of Cateau-Cambrésis reinforced Italy's fragmentation. Spain took over the Duchy of Milan, Sicily, Sardinia, and southern Italy, and many other Italian states (except Venice, the Papal States, and the Duchy of Savoy) became its dependencies. Spain's restriction of the export of goods from Italy, as well as its imposition of numerous requisitions, contributed to a further decline of Italian industry and trade. In the 17th century the Italian economy began to decline sharply. The country's economy became primarily agricultural. Once an exporter of finished industrial products, Italy was transformed into an exporter of raw materials. Basically, industrial production in workshops survived only in the major centers of northern Italy.

The Catholic reaction began as early as the 16th century: for example, the Jesuit Order was established in 1534, and the Inquisition was reorganized. (In 1542 the Congregation of the Inquisition, a supreme tribunal for heresy cases, was established in Rome.) The desperate condition of the popular masses, foreign oppression, and the Catholic reaction promoted the growth of heretical movements, radical forms of Protestantism, and popular revolts. (In 1599 a conspiracy headed by Campanella was uncovered in southern Italy; revolts broke out in Palermo in 1647, in Salerno in 1647–48, and in Naples in 1647, led by Masaniello and Gennaro Annese.) The papal Curia and the Inquisition persecuted and condemned to death popular leaders and progressive thinkers such as G. Bruno and G. C. Vanini.

The economic and political decline of Italy grew still deeper in the first half of the 18th century. Cloth production in Florence and silk output in Venice dropped sharply. Foreign and domestic trade declined. As the amount of uncultivated land increased, crop yields decreased. The rural and urban masses became impoverished. The economic decline was exacerbated by wars fought in Italy: between 1701 and 1714, the War of the Spanish Succession; from 1733 to 1735, the War of the Polish Succession; and from 1740 to 1748, the War of the Austrian Succession. Under the Treaty of Rastatt (1714), Spanish lands were ceded to Austria, which was later forced to give up Sicily and the Kingdom of Naples to members of the Spanish branch of the Bourbons (1735). Venice, exhausted by wars with Turkey, lost its possessions in the eastern Mediterranean in 1718. Savoy pursued a maneuvering policy: in 1720 it received Sardinia from Austria, after which the Kingdom of Sardinia (1720–1861) was formed.

Period of the development and establishment of capitalism. RISORGIMENTO—THE STRUGGLE FOR LIBERATION AND UNIFICATION (SECOND HALF OF THE 18TH CENTURY TO 1870). The cessation of continual wars on Italian territory for several decades in the second half of the 18th century promoted the revival of the Italian economy. The rise and strengthening of capitalist relations, whose development had been interrupted in the 16th century, resumed. The crisis of feudal relations and the development of capitalist relations created the preconditions for the appearance in the second half of the 18th century of the Italian Enlightenment, represented by Beccaria, Filangieri, and Verri. In addition, in some Italian lands (for example, Lombardy, Tuscany, and Piedmont) reforms in the spirit of enlightened absolutism were carried out in the 1770's and 1780's.

The end of the 18th century saw the development of a movement called the Risorgimento (Italian for "revival"), which was aimed at liberating the country from foreign oppression and at transforming the fragmented Italian states into a single, unified state or a federation. Objectively, the Risorgimento was a struggle against the feudal-absolutist order and for the establishment of a bourgeois system. In the 1790's news of the bourgeois revolution in France stimulated the growth of revolutionary and opposition elements in Italy. Among the petite and middle bourgeoisie and the liberal (bourgeoisified) gentry an antifeudal, anti-Austrian, republican movement developed—Italian Jacobinism, which was an outgrowth of the ideas of the Italian and French Enlightenment. Seeking to unify Italy into a federation of republics or even into a single republic, Italian patriots pinned their hopes on assistance from revolutionary France. After Bonaparte's Italian campaign in 1796–97, republics were established in Italy. Until the collapse of the Napoleonic empire in 1814 a large part of Italy was in fact united under French rule. After 1804 the republics became kingdoms, and part of Italian territory was incorporated into the French Empire. Under French rule, bourgeois reforms were carried out in Italy (repeal of internal customs duties, abolition of feudal privileges, introduction of progressive Napoleonic codes, and secularization and sale of church lands). At the same time, the Napoleonic administration sent food and money, as well as works of art, out of Italy. The development of Italian industry was retarded by competition from French goods, which were imported duty-free, and after 1806, by the Continental Blockade.

Discontent and a yearning for national independence grew steadily in the country. After 1815 a network of secret anti-French societies of Carbonari sprang up throughout Italy. Peasants had initially welcomed the French as liberators from feudal oppression. However, disillusioned in their hopes of receiving land and crushed by the intolerable taxes and conscription introduced by the French authorities, most of the peasants soon became a reserve for reactionary forces. As early as 1799, when Napoleon's army in Italy was retreating under the onslaught of A. V. Suvorov's troops, a wave of anti-French and antirepublican peasant revolts swept over Italy. In 1813–14 anti-French revolts flared up in southern Italy and in Milan.

The Congress of Vienna of 1814–15 restored the feudal-absolutist monarchies in Italy. The Kingdom of the Two Sicilies, the Papal States, the duchies of Modena, Parma, Lucca, and Tuscany, and the Kingdom of Sardinia (Piedmont) were restored. Lombardy and Venice were reincorporated into the Austrian Empire. Piedmont retained a certain degree of autonomy. In the remaining Italian states Austria held almost complete dominion. Internal duties and certain feudal laws were restored, but the lands that had been confiscated from feudal nobles and the Catholic Church and sold to the bourgeoisie and to bourgeoisified noblemen remained under their new owners. Between 1815 and 1831 the Carbonari continued to guide the struggle against foreign (Austrian) oppression, feudal reaction, and political fragmentation.

The defeat of the bourgeois revolutions led by the Carbonari in the Kingdom of the Two Sicilies in 1820–21 and in Piedmont in 1821 and of the Revolution of 1831 in central Italy (Modena, Parma, and the Papal States) prompted Italian democrats to seek a new solution to the problems of the national liberation movement in Italy. A new concept of Italian revolution formulated between 1831 and 1833 by G. Mazzini proposed the unification of Italy into a single, independent democratic republic "from below"—that is, by means of a popular revolution. Afraid to encroach on the interests of the liberal gentry and the landed interests of the bourgeoisie, Mazzini did not raise the slogan of turning over manorial land to the peasants. As a result, Young Italy, the underground organization founded by him in 1831, was aloof from the masses, which at that time consisted mainly of peasants. The conspiracies and attempts at revolts prepared by Young Italy in the 1830's and 1840's invariably failed.

The ideology of the liberal wing of the Italian national liberation camp, which expressed the interests of the big bourgeoisie and the big bourgeoisified gentry, took shape during the 1840's. Italian liberals such as Gioberti entrusted the mission of unifying Italy to the papacy, while d'Azeglio and Balbo rested their hopes on the Kingdom of Sardinia. The liberals wanted to see Italy liberated "from above" as a confederation of several Italian monarchies.

The industrial revolution began in northern Italy in the 1840's, but it was hampered by the country's feudal fragmentation. It became increasingly clear that political unity was an indispensable precondition for the development of capitalism in Italy. The bourgeois Revolution of 1848–49 in Italy was basically a struggle for the country's liberation from Austrian oppression and from the absolutist regimes that were ruling the Italian states. During the revolution the Italian bourgeoisie was closely allied with the liberal gentry. Fear of the peasant masses prodded the liberals into a compromise with the feudal classes. Although they called on the peasants for a national liberation struggle, revolutionary democrats such as Mazzini were afraid to unleash and lead the revolutionary actitivity of the peasants. All of these factors, as well as the counterrevolutionary intervention of European powers such as France and Austria, led to the defeat of the Revolution of 1848–49.

In the 1850's the prerevolutionary order was restored in the Italian states. The constitutions introduced in 1848 remained in force only in Piedmont, where liberal cabinets led by d'Azeglio and Cavour held power. With government assistance, industry developed and railroads were built in Piedmont. Hoping that the Piedmont monarchy under King Victor Emmanuel II and Premier Cavour would unify Italy, liberal circles in the Italian states oriented themselves toward Piedmont, which endeavored to expand its possessions and pursued an anti-Austrian policy. Italian democrats were unable to work out a united program. The democrats who adopted the farthest left position demanded the limitation of manorial lands, a measure that would have helped to rally the peasants to the struggle, and C. Pisacane even demanded the transfer of manorial land to the peasants. Most republicans, seeing the weakness of the Italian democrats, who were out of touch with the masses, were inclined to drop the demand for a republic as the form of state for a future unified Italy, so that they might join with the liberals in the struggle for the unification of the country.

The Revolution of 1859–60 was the decisive stage of the Risorgimento. During the Austro-Italo-French War of 1859, which promoted the development of a revolutionary situation in central Italy, Lombardy was liberated from Austrian oppression. In the incipient revolution popular revolts triumphed in the duchies of Modena, Parma, and Tuscany, whose monarchs were expelled, and Romagna was liberated from papal authority. A revolutionary expedition organized in May 1860 by the democrats under G. Garibaldi in the southern part of Italy, where a peasant revolt had broken out in April, played a determining role in the unification of Italy. In July 1860, Sicily was liberated; and in September, Garibaldi's revolutionary army entered Naples, the capital of the Kingdom of the Two Sicilies. The liberation of southern Italy from Bourbon rule predetermined the triumph of the Revolution of 1859–60. The territories that had been liberated from Austrian oppression and from the oppression of semifeudal Italian sovereigns were incorporated into the Kingdom of Sardinia (Piedmont) in 1860. In 1861 the Kingdom of Sardinia became the unified Kingdom of Italy. As a result of the Austro-Italian War of 1866, Venice was liberated from Austrian oppression and incorporated into the Kingdom of Italy. The unification of Italy was completed in 1870 with the incorporation into Italy of Rome and the elimination of the secular power of the pope. Refusing to accept his loss of power, Pope Pius IX withdrew into the Vatican and declared himself a "moral prisoner." Relations between the Italian state and the Catholic Church were fully normalized only in 1929.

The Risorgimento, which occurred chiefly as a result of the struggle of the popular masses, was led by the liberal bourgeoisie and the gentry, the bloc that assumed the leadership of the Kingdom of Italy. Unified Italy became a constitutional monarchy whose constitution was based on Piedmont's Constitution of 1848. The peasant revolution that had broken out in the southern part of the country in 1860–61 was suppressed, and feudal vestiges in agriculture, which were especially numerous in southern Italy, were preserved.

The unified state from 1870 to 1900. In the last third of the 19th century the industrial revolution in Italy was completed. Industry became distinct from farming. The poverty of the countryside, where progress was hampered by feudal vestiges, deprived Italian industry of a sizable domestic market. The state intervened in economic life, generously subsidizing railroad construction and assisting the development of the most important national industries, especially metallurgy. A few large-scale enterprises established in Italy at the end of the 19th century were shielded by a protective tariff and relied heavily on orders and subsidies from the state and often on foreign capital as well. Italy's largest banks (the Commercial Bank and the Bank of Credit) were founded with foreign capital but given Italian names.

However, the pace of Italy's industrial development was still much slower than that of advanced capitalist countries such as the USA and Great Britain. The semifeudal agrarian south, which suffered from intolerable taxes and lagged behind the advanced areas of nothern Italy, where even the organization of agriculture was increasingly capitalist, became a domestic colony of the northern Italian bourgeoisie. An antidemocratic regime was established in the country. Strikes were virtually prohibited, and freedom of the press and of assembly and the right to organize unions were given only nominal recognition. Even after the electoral reform of 1882, which expanded the number of eligible voters from 600,000 to 2 million, only 6.9 percent of the population participated in the parliamentary elections. Enormous expenditures for the creation of an army and a unified state apparatus and for the financing of industry imposed a heavy tax burden on the popular masses. Every year hundreds of thousands of peasants (mostly southerners) emigrated from Italy. The wages of the urban proletariat were much lower than the subsistence minimum, and the workday was 12 and even 16 hours.

The consequences of the incomplete bourgeois revolutions and of the onerous yoke of the machinery of state gave the Italian people's struggle against poverty and oppression an antigovernmental, political character and attracted to it broad strata of workers, peasants, and the petite bourgeoisie. There were turbulent and "explosive" popular demonstrations. The economic and political immaturity of the Italian proletariat, most of whom worked at home or in small or tiny enterprises, hindered the development of the workers' movement, which also experienced difficulty in overcoming the influence of the petit bourgeois theories of Mazzini and Bakunin in the 1860's and 1870's. The ideology of the socialist groups, leagues, and circles that sprang up in the late 1870's and 1880's showed the influence of utopian socialism, economism, and anarchism.

Nonetheless, the penetration of Marxist ideas into Italy increased in the 1880's and 1890's. The most prominent Marxist propagandist was Antonio Labriola. With the formation in 1892 of the Italian Socialist Party (ISP) the workers' movement embarked on the path of an independent political struggle. Reformist ideas held by some of its members and its initial organizational weakness prevented the ISP from leading the popular uprisings of the 1890's (for example, the uprising in Sicily in 1893–94 and the popular discontent with high prices that swept over Italy in 1898).

The Italian state had hardly been formed when it launched colonial wars. In the 1880's and 1890's, Italian expansionism was directed at northeast Africa. The Depretis government concluded the Triple Alliance of 1882 with Germany and Austria-Hungary. Under the Crispi government Italy captured Somalia in 1889 and Eritrea in 1890. In 1895, Italian troops invaded Ethiopia, but they were routed.

Initial period of imperialism (from the early 20th century to the end of World War I). Between 1900 and 1914 the Italian economy developed rapidly, for the most part. Modern, large-scale industry was established, and Italian capitalism began to evolve into imperialism—a process that was essentially completed by 1914. An imperialist "pool" of interests took shape (major banks, metallurgy, shipbuilding, and shipping), and monopoly-like associations emerged in automobile production (Fiat), the food-processing industry (a sugar trust), and a number of other industries. Italy adopted a policy of imperialist aggression, capturing Libya in 1912 as a result of a war with Turkey. However, even in 1914, Italy was still primarily an agrarian country. Feudal vestiges in agriculture, the extreme poverty of the peasants, and a narrow domestic market (which industrialists tried in vain to offset through increased exploitation of the workers) accounted for Italian imperialism's economic and political weakness and for the extremely sharp class contradictions in Italian society. The ruling elite failed in its attempts to alleviate these contradictions by means of liberal reforms implemented by the Giolitti government (legalization of workers' organizations and strikes, labor protection laws, and substantital expansion of the suffrage—the number of eligible voters was increased to 8.7 million).

With the appearance of the first detachments of an industrial proletariat, the Italian workers' movement became more organized and more mature. In the early 20th century the ISP was dominated by a reformist wing whose leaders included F. Turati. However, a sharp struggle between various currents in the party was already under way. In 1908 the anarchosyndicalists were expelled from the ISP. The banishment from the ISP in 1912 of overt social chauvinists led by Bissolati, who had exposed themselves by supporting the colonial war against Turkey, made the ISP an "exception" among the Western European parties of the Second International. Leadership of the ISP passed to the party's left wing, signifying the failure of Giolitti's attempts to split and corrupt the Italian workers' movement by pursuing a policy of partial reforms. After Giolitti's resignation in the spring of 1914, the failure of his policy was again demonstrated by the revolutionary explosion of Red Week in June 1914 (a nationwide general strike and barricade fighting in a number of cities, including Ancona, Ravenna, Rome, Milan, and Florence).

World War I, which began on Aug. 1, 1914, caught Italy at a moment when the nation's internal social contradictions were very acute. Italy was not ready to take part in the war. Imperialist contradictions with Germany and Austria-Hungary over Italian markets, the Balkans, the Adriatic, and Asia Minor prevented Italy from coming out on the side of its official allies. On Aug. 2, 1914, the government of A. Salandra declared Italy's neutrality but busied itself with feverish preparations for war and with diplomatic bargaining with both belligerent groupings. The ISP, which demanded the preservation of neutrality, emerged as the organizer of the antiwar movement of the popular masses. Giolitti led the bourgeois neutralist movement. However, the expansionist aspirations of the monopolists took the upper hand over the demands of the poorly organized and internally divided neutralist camp. On May 23, 1915, having managed to obtain a promise of sizable territorial compensations from the Entente governments under the Treaty of London of 1915, Italy declared war on Austria-Hungary, and on Aug. 27, 1916, on Germany.

The economic, political, and military weakness of Italian imperalism caused an extremely acute economic and political crisis to envelop the country during the war years and led to the rapid development of a revolutionary situation. By the spring of 1917 the damage done to the nation's economy had reached a catastrophic level. Because it aroused enthusiasm among the Italian workers, the news of the overthrow of the autocracy in Russia in February 1917 made the situation in Italy even more tense. Within the ISP, the only Western European party of the Second International to adopt an antiwar position between 1914 and 1918, the struggle between various currents grew more intense. The party's right wing, headed by Turati and Treves, favored a "civil peace." The party leadership crept steadily toward centrism, while the ISP's new left wing, which had crystallized during the war and was headed by Serrati, agreed with the party as a whole that the task of struggling for peace was not linked with the proletariat's struggle for power. In the summer of 1917, Italy was swept by food riots, antiwar demonstrations, and political strikes. In August the antiwar, armed Uprising of Turin broke out. The acuteness of class contradictions and the paralysis of the government apparatus in the first days after the rout of the Italian Army in October 1917 at Caporetto created an objective opportunity for the Italian proletariat's struggle for power. However, the proletariat made no move in this direction. The Italian working people and their party were not ready for revolution.

The period of the general crisis of capitalism. 1918–22: REVOLUTIONARY UPSURGE AND THE ADVENT OF FASCISM. In the war almost 700,000 Italian soldiers were killed, and more than 1 million were crippled. The northeastern part of the country was devastated. The merchant fleet lost 60 percent of its vessels.

The development during the war of machine building, metallurgy, and a chemicals industry transformed Italy from an agrarian country into an agrarian-industrial country. However, the industries that had developed during the war years could not find markets, and a decline in production led to an economic crisis in 1920. Despite Italy's participation in World War I, Italian imperialism failed to realize its territorial claims completely. Under the Treaty of St. Germain of 1919 and the Treaty of Rapallo of 1920, Italy received Trentino and the southern Tirol, almost all of Istria, and a number of other lands, but Italian imperialism considered itself cheated by its war allies and claimed Dalmatia, Albania, and a number of other territories.

In 1919 and 1920 a violent revolutionary upsurge occurred in Italy. The revolutionizing of the Italian popular masses was greatly influenced by the victory of the Great October Socialist Revolution in Russia. Strikes in Italy took on a political character. The membership of the ISP grew, reaching more than 216,000 in 1920. The General Confederation of Labor (GCL), which had been founded in 1906, became a major force. In the first postwar parliamentary elections (November 1919) the Socialists received three times as many votes as in 1913, becoming the strongest faction in Parliament. The Popular Party, a Catholic group founded in January 1919 under the leadership of the clergyman L. Sturzo, was very successful. The ruling Liberal Party lost its absolute majority in Parliament. Between 1919 and 1922, Italy had five premiers (the Liberals V. Orlando, F. Nitti, G. Giolitti, I. Bonomi, and L. Facta).

In 1920 the class struggle became even more acute—the number of strikes exceeded 2,000, as compared with 1,800 in 1919. On the initiative of Ordine Nuovo, a group of left-wing Socialists led by A. Gramsci, the workers of Turin organized factory and plant councils as early as 1919. In August and September 1920 workers in the industrial cities of the north, reacting to a lockout declared by the entrepreneurs, began to occupy the closed enterprises. Virtually every metalworking, machine-building, and metallurgical plant and factory fell into the hands of 600,000 metalworkers. At a number of enterprises (chiefly in Turin and Milan) the workers began to organize production and create a Red Guard. The movement, which had initially been on the defensive, went over to the offensive. However, it did not grow into a struggle for power. The ISP turned over the leadership of the struggle to the GCL, whose leader, the reformist D'Aragona, was satisfied by a promise of concessions (a wage increase and worker control at enterprises) and therefore signed an agreement with the government to end the occupation of the enterprises. Subsequently, the workers' movement entered a period of decline.

In January 1921 there was a split in the ISP. In response to the refusal of the "maximalist" majority (led by Serrati and C. Lazzari) to break with the reformists (led by Turati), the left wing quit the party and on Jan. 21, 1921, formed the Italian Communist Party (ICP).

The big bourgeoisie launched a counteroffensive against the workers' movement. Industrialists and owners of farms supported the fascist movement, which was led in 1919 by B. Mussolini. The fascists formed armed detachments which adopted a tactic of raiding workers' and democratic organizations. By engaging in social demagoguery, using chauvinistic slogans, and making demands for "strong authority," the fascists, who essentially represented the interests of the most reactionary circles of finance capital and large-scale landowners, attracted relatively broad strata of the bourgeoisie, including small-scale property owners who were frightened by the scope of the revolutionary movement. The ruling circles of the bourgeoisie were ready to repudiate the Liberals, who had compromised themselves, and to move toward dictatorship. On Oct. 24, 1922, Mussolini demanded the inclusion of the Fascists in the government, and on October 30 columns of fascist Blackshirts entered Rome (the march on Rome). On October 31, Mussolini was made premier. In Parliament a majority of the deputies of the bourgeois parties gave a vote of confidence to the new government.

THE PERIOD OF THE FASCIST DICTATORSHIP (TO THE BEGINNING OF WORLD WAR II. From 1922 to 1924, Mussolini's government carried out a number of measures in the interests of the big bourgeoisie, including the dissolution of a commission investigating war profits, the reduction of direct taxes and raising of indirect taxes, and the reduction of the working people's wages. Increasingly, terrorism was used against opposition forces. In early 1923 many active members of the Communist Party were arrested. After the Fascists assassinated the Socialist G. Matteotti (June 10, 1924), the deputies of the opposition parties (the ISP, the Popular and Republican parties, some of the Liberals, and several other parties) withdrew from Parliament and formed the Aventine Bloc. The Communists, who had been led since late 1923 by Gramsci, also joined the bloc, proposing that the masses be called to a general political strike. However, the other parties did not accept this proposal, and the Fascists managed to stabilize the situation. The Fascists' foreign policy during this period was, by necessity, moderate, for the party's domestic position was unstable. In January 1924 a friendship treaty was concluded with Yugoslavia. On Feb. 7, 1924, Italy officially recognized the USSR, and diplomatic relations were established with the Soviet Union.

In 1925, Mussolini formed a one-party Fascist government. The final touches were put on the totalitarian Fascist dictatorship in November 1926 after the issuance of so-called emergency laws, under which all political parties and organizations except the Fascist Party were outlawed, a secret police was created, the death penalty was introduced, and the Special Tribunal was instituted to deal with anti-Fascists. The Grand Council of the Fascist Party, which controlled Parliament, began to pay a prominent role in the country's life. The shock force of the Fascist Party was the National Security Volunteer Milita. The Fascists dealt brutally with the opposition: the arrested leaders of the Communist Party, including Gramsci, and leaders of anti-Fascist organizations were sentenced by the Special Tribunal to long terms in prison. With the exception of the Communists, all the opposition parties essentially stopped fighting against fascism within the country. In 1927 the GCL's reformist leaders announced the organization's dissolution.

In 1929 the Fascist government and the Vatican signed the Lateran Agreements, which did away with the Italian state's long-standing conflict with the Catholic Church and assured Mussolini of the papacy's support.

The Fascists formed a centralized system of state-monopoly capitalism. In 1927 they began to organize a corporate state, which supposedly had as its objective the establishment of "cooperation between classes." The National Council of Corporations, which was founded in 1930, included representatives of wage laborers' trade unions, unions of entrepreneurs, and the Fascist Party. The council had authority over 22 corporations (formed in 1934), which corresponded to the basic branches of production. Each of the corporations was made up of entrepreneurs and working people. The corporations were supposed to establish working conditions. The deciding vote in them belonged to the capitalist representatives. Under the parliamentary reform of 1939, the Chamber of Fasces and Corporations, whose members were appointed by the Fascist Party and by the corporations, replaced the Chamber of Deputies. Thus, having eliminated the opposition parties, class trade unions, and Parliament, the Fascist Party established totalitarian forms of rule by monopoly capital.

While it actively prepared for aggressive wars, the Fascist government of Italy energetically implemented autarkic measures to reduce the Italian economy's dependence on imported raw materials and foodstuffs. The measures aimed at self-sufficiency included the *battaglia del grano* ("battle" to increase the production of wheat), the production of substitutes, the restriction of the consumption of scarce raw materials, and the accelerated construction of hydroelectric power plants. A highly important role was played in the implementation of these measures by state-monopoly associations headed by the Industrial Reconstruction Institute (IRI; founded in 1933). The campaigns for self-sufficiency required huge expenditures but failed to promote an overall growth of industry. From 1929 to 1939 production increased by only 15 percent, even though Italian industry had developed quite rapidly between 1921 and the world economic crisis of 1929–33.

Fascist imperialist plans were aimed at establishing Italian dominance in the Mediterranean region and at expansion in Africa. On Oct. 3, 1935, Italy attacked Ethiopia, which was occupied by Italian troops during eight months of military operations. On May 9, 1936, Mussolini declared Italy an empire. After the outbreak of the fascist revolt in Spain in July 1936, Mussolini sent an expeditionary corps to help the insurgents. The joint intervention of Italy and fascist Germany in Spain (1936–39) hastened Italy's rapprochement with Germany. In October 1936 the two countries signed an agreement on political cooperation—the Rome-Berlin Axis. Under the accord, the Mediterranean Sea was defined as Italy's sphere of influence, and Italy recognized Germany's right to establish a "new order" in Central Europe. In 1937, Italy joined the Anti-Comintern Pact. Italy participated in the 1938 Munich Agreement and on May 22, 1939, signed with Germany the Pact of Steel, which formalized the aggressive Italo-German military alliance. In April 1939, Italy occupied Albania.

Popular resistance to fascism began to grow more intense in the late 1920's and early 1930's, when strikes and demonstrations broke out in a number of places. In 1934 the Communist Party and the Socialist Party concluded an agreement on unity of action. The alliance of the two parties promoted the consolidation of all the anti-Fascist forces in Italy. Several thousand Italian volunteers fought in the International Brigades during the Spanish people's war against the German and Italian fascist intervention (1936–39). The anti-Fascist movement in Italy became substantial in the second half of the 1930's.

WORLD WAR II: THE COLLAPSE OF FASCISM, THE NATIONAL LIBERATION WAR OF 1943–45. At the beginning of World War II, which was unleashed by fascist Germany, fascist Italy declared itself a nonbelligerent (Sept. 1, 1939). The country was not yet ready for a major war. Italy entered the world war on June 10, 1940, at the time of the fall of France, when a German victory seemed imminent. Italian hostilities against France lasted for only a few days. On June 24 the two countries signed an armistice. Hoping to steal a march on Germany in the Balkans, Italy attacked Greece on Oct. 28, 1940. However, Italian troops suffered a number of defeats, and Greece did not surrender until after it was invaded by fascist German troops in April 1941. An Italian army corps also participated in the occupation of Yugoslavia (1941–44). In June 1941 fascist Italy and fascist Germany launched a war against the Soviet Union. Italy sent a corps and later, an army to the Soviet front. In the winter of 1942–43 the Italian Eighth Army was routed by Soviet troops in the middle reaches of the Don.

The Italian Army also suffered a series of defeats in Africa. Between January and May 1941, British troops drove Italian troops out of British Somaliland, Kenya, the Sudan, Ethiopia, Italian Somaliland, and Eritrea. By May 1943, Italian troops and the German troops that had been sent to their aid in the spring of 1941 had been defeated once and for all in Africa. In July 1943, Anglo-American troops landed in Sicily.

Continual military defeats and the deterioration of living conditions caused anti-Fascist sentiment to grow in Italy. The first to come out openly against fascism was Italy's working class. On the initiative of the Communists a general strike was held in northern Italy in March 1943. The impending military collapse and the threat of an anti-Fascist revolution forced the Italian ruling class to move rapidly to abandon the war. On July 25, 1943, Mussolini was ousted as premier and arrested. Monarchical circles, generals, and the elite of the Fascist Party took part in the plot against him. The king appointed Marshal Badoglio premier. On September 3 the Badoglio government secretly signed an armistice agreement with the Anglo-American command on terms of unconditional surrender. When the armistice was disclosed on September 8, fascist German troops occupied most of Italy. Defended by German bayonets, the fascist puppet Salo Republic was established on occupied territory. (It was headed by Mussolini, who had escaped from custody. He was executed by partisans in April 1945.)

On Sept. 3 and 9, 1943, Anglo-American troops landed in southern Italy. A new stage of the anti-Fascist liberation struggle —the Resistance Movement—began in the autumn of 1943. Shortly thereafter, the Resistance attained the scale of a national liberation war and became an anti-Fascist democratic revolution. It was headed by the Committees of National Liberation, which consisted of representatives of the anti-Fascist parties: the Communist and Socialist parties, the petit bourgeois Action Party, the Christian Democratic Party (CDP; a Catholic group founded in 1943), and the Liberal Party. The leading force in the Committees of National Liberation was the Communists, who had been led by P. Togliatti since 1926. In March 1944 the USSR became the first country in the anti-Hitler coalition to establish direct relations with the Badoglio government. (Full diplomatic relations were established between the USSR and Italy in October 1944.) In April 1944, Badoglio formed a new government made up of representatives of all the anti-Fascist parties, including the Communists. In June 1944, after Anglo-American troops entered Rome, Bonomi became the head of the government. In April 1945, under the leadership of the Committees of National Liberation, a liberation uprising began in northern Italy, and most of the cities were liberated by forces of Italian patriots (the April Uprising of 1945). The uprising was the final stage in the national liberation war.

AFTER WORLD WAR II. The armed struggle of the Italian people against fascism led to an enormous strengthening of democratic forces in the country. Under the leadership of the Communist Party, the most progressive segment of the alliance of anti-Fascist forces fought for as profound a democratization as possible of Italy's social system and struggled to undermine the power of the monopolies. Until 1956 the Communist Party was linked with the Socialist Party by a pact that called for unity of action. Even before the end of the war, mass democratic organizations were re-created and underwent considerable development. Among them were the Italian General Confederation of Labor, a youth organization, women's unions, and a cooperative movement. All the mass organizations united such diverse groups as the Communists, Socialists, Catholics, and supporters of the Action Party. After Italy's liberation the CDP, which became the center of attraction for conservative forces, achieved prominence in Italian politics. Relying on the support of the Vatican and the ruling classes, the CDP gradually became the party of monopoly capital and the main stronghold of bourgeois rule in Italy.

By the time the war had ended, Italy's economy was in total disarray: enterprises had stopped production, communications between the cities and the countryside had broken down, inflation was rampant, speculation flourished, and there were more than 2 million unemployed. The anti-Fascist unity governments led by F. Parri (1945) and A. De Gasperi (1945–47) included Communists and Socialists and implemented a number of measures designed to rebuild the economy. A sliding wage scale was introduced, and the rights of trade unions were expanded. "Management councils," which had originated during the war, continued to operate at a number of enterprises, where they became agencies of workers' control. (Subsequently, the bourgeoisie succeeded in gradually curtailing the activities of the councils, which were ultimately abolished.)

In the referendum of June 2, 1946, which offered a choice between the republican and monarchical forms of government, about 55 percent of the voters favored the elimination of the monarchy. On Dec. 22, 1947, a constitution for the Italian Republic was adopted. Leftist parties took part in drawing it up, managing to win the inclusion of a number of democratic provisions in it (for example, recognition of the need for the nationalization of a number of branches of the economy, for democratic control over the activity of monopolies, and for introduction of regional self-government, as well as recognition of the right to work, the right to social security, and the right to an education).

The countries of the antifascist coalition signed a peace treaty with Italy on Feb. 10, 1947, under which Italy renounced its colonies and recognized the independence of Albania and Ethiopia. The region of Trieste was set apart as the Free Territory of Trieste. (Under the Italo-Yugoslav treaty of 1954, a large part of the free territory, including the city of Trieste, reverted to Italy.)

By early 1947 the issue of the direction of the country's further development had arisen. The ICP and ISP insisted that new, profound democratic reforms be carried out and that restoration of the power of monopoly capital be prohibited. Subsequently, Italian bourgeois reactionaries, supported by the USA, attempted to deal a direct blow to the democratic forces. In May 1947, De Gasperi provoked a government crisis and ousted the Communists and Socialists from the government. In January 1947 the right wing of the ISP, led by Saragat, had left the ISP and created a new party that had adopted an anti-Communist platform. (Shortly thereafter, the Italian Social Democratic Party, an outgrowth of Saragat's party, was formed.) The CDP and the right-wing Socialists broke with all the mass organizations (for example, the trade unions, youth groups, and women's organizations) and created separate organizations. The government coalition parties (the CDP, the Italian Social Democratic Party, the Liberal Party, and the Republican Party) campaigned for election to the first postwar Parliament (1948), using anti-Communist slogans. The CDP won an absolute majority of seats in Parliament. On July 14, 1948, an attempt was made on Togliatti's life. Italy's working people responded with a general strike that was joined by more than 7 million people. The strike was evidence of the failure of the reactionaries' offensive and of the determination of the masses of the working people to continue the struggle for democratic ideals. The new De Gasperi governments (1947–53) enjoyed the support of the USA. In 1948, Italy accepted US assistance under the Marshall Plan, and in 1949, Italy joined NATO. NATO and US military bases were established in Italy.

In 1948, Italy regained its prewar level in industrial production and in 1950, in agriculture. The leading Italian monopolies (for example, Fiat and Falck) used funds received under the Marshall Plan to modernize their equipment completely. State industrial associations such as the IRI and later the National Hydrocarbons Board (founded in 1953) were very active. Substantial domestic and foreign demand for industrial and agricultural output, as well as cheap manpower and a continuous increase in the intensiveness of labor, promoted the rapid growth of the economy. (Even during the postwar upswing in the economy, Italy maintained the lowest wages of any Western European country.)

Mass actions by the working people—above all, a movement to occupy fallow private land—compelled the government to pass laws in 1950 concerning a partial land reform and to create a fund for the development of the South (the Southern Fund). At the same time, the government called out the police against strikers and demonstrators, trying to intimidate the democratic forces. In 1949 a conference of bishops adopted a resolution calling for the excommunication of anyone who voted for or supported the Communists or Socialists. The CDP leadership attempted a legal coup in 1953, proposing a new electoral law under which a party that received more than 50 percent of the vote would have a two-thirds majority in Parliament (that is, enough seats to change the constitution). However, in the 1953 elections the CDP lost its absolute majority of seats in Parliament, and the number of votes cast for the Communists and Socialists increased. The bourgeoisie's five-year concerted drive against the country's democratic forces had failed.

In the 1950's, Italy was transformed from an agrarian-industrial country into an industrial-agrarian one. There was a sharp increase in state intervention in the economy in the interests of the monopolies (state-monopoly capitalism). In 1951, Italy signed the European Coal and Steel Association agreement and in 1957, the European Economic Community (Common Market) treaty. At the same time, Italy began to strengthen its trade relations with the USSR and other socialist countries in the second half of the 1950's, and in the 1960's economic, cultural, and political contacts between Italy and the USSR increased.

The monopolies, which were making tremendous excess profits, pursued a policy of paternalism aimed at destroying the unity of the working class—that is, they bought off certain working class groups with various sops and social measures. This policy was pursued most intensively in northern Italy at plants owned by companies such as Fiat and Olivetti. The working class repulsed the reactionaries' attempt to govern the country through a rightist government supported by neo-Fascists in Parliament (the Tambroni government, March–July 1960) and thwarted a stunt pulled by the neo-Fascists, who in July 1960 tried with government permission to hold their congress in Genoa, one of the centers of the Resistance Movement.

After a long internal struggle in the CDP, in 1962 the party congress came out for a switch to a left-center policy, which presupposed cooperation with the ISP, the Social Democrats, and the Republicans on the basis of a program of reforms. The first left-center government, which was headed by A. Fanfani (1962–63) and which was supported but not joined by the Socialists, carried out a number of important reforms: the electric power industry was nationalized, pensions were increased, and the condition of the peasantry was somewhat improved. However, this effort to weaken the mass movement of the working people and isolate the Communist Party failed because the Communists applied the tactics of "constructive opposition" and supported all the positive aspects of the government program, while at the same time organizing a struggle against inconsistency and delays in the implementation of the reforms. The reactionaries tried unsuccessfully to change the situation in the country by force. (In the summer of 1964 the military intelligence agency SIFAR attempted to prepare a coup d'etat.) Subsequently, governments headed by A. Moro (1963–64, 1964–69) pursued a more moderate policy, even though they included Socialists. In January 1964 the left wing of the ISP formed an independent party (the Italian Socialist Party of Proletarian Unity). The ISP merged with the Social Democrats in 1966, forming the Unified Socialist Party. The results of the parliamentary elections of 1968 showed a new increase in the number of votes cast for the Communist Party and other leftist forces. The failure of the left-center course became obvious, since its main goal—the creation in the country of political stability based on a sharp weakening of the influence of democratic forces—had not been achieved.

By the end of the 1960's, the tendency to review some aspects of Italian foreign policy had grown noticeably stronger. For instance, although Italy remained an active participant in NATO, it argued that its Atlantic-bloc obligations did not extend to Southeast Asia (1966) and the Middle East (1970). Relations between Italy and the USSR—particularly economic ties—continued to become stronger. During a visit to Moscow by the Italian head of state G. Andreotti in October 1972, a Soviet-Italian protocol on consultations was signed.

By the 1970's the problem of relations between the government majority and the Communist Party had become the main issue in domestic politics. Leftist currents in the CDP, as well as the majority of the leadership of the ISP, were inclined to support tactics of cooperation with the Communist Party. In view of this, in 1969 rightists in the Socialist Party, influenced by US ruling circles, organized a split in the ISP and formed the Socialist Unity Party (since 1971, the Social Democratic Party). This party attempted to lead a new anti-Communist campaign and create an atmosphere of tension and unrest in the country. At the same time, a broad strike movement unfolded, led jointly by three trade-union centers (the Italian General Confederation of Labor, the Italian Confederation of Working People's Trade Unions, and the Italian Union of Labor). The events of the "hot autumn" of 1969, during which up to 20 million workers participated in several strikes, forced the government to satisfy many of the working people's demands (for example, by improving material conditions and expanding workers' rights at industrial enterprises). The reactionaries tried a new maneuver in early 1970, causing a protracted government crisis in order to have Parliament dissolved before its five-year term was up, thereby thwarting the adoption of a number of democratic bills. However, the threat of reactionary adventurism was repulsed by the democratic forces. Municipal elections and elections to 15 of the 20 regional councils (June 7–8, 1970) confirmed the increase in the influence of leftist forces. In three regions—Emilia-Romagna, Tuscany, and Umbria—representatives of leftist parties won a majority in local government bodies. In many city and provincial government bodies representatives of the ICP, the Italian Socialist Party of Proletarian Unity, and the ISP won a majority of seats. Unity of action by the major trade-union centers created concrete prospects for eliminating the split in the trade-union movement, and in 1972 a federation of the three trade-union centers was founded.

The upsurge in the workers' and democratic movement encountered a fierce counteroffensive by reactionary forces, including a move to the right in the policy of the CDP leadership and fascist provocations in a number of regions, including Calabria and Abruzzi. Because the policy of the "left center"—the government coalition of the CDP, the ISP, the Social Democratic Party and the Republican Party—had come to a dead end in early 1971, Parliament was dissolved before the completion of its five-year term. In extraordinary parliamentary elections in May 1972 rightist forces failed to improve their position, and the leftist parties received 40 percent of the vote (the ICP won 27.2 percent of the vote). Nevertheless, Andreotti's government, which was formed in the summer of 1972, included only representatives of the CDP, the Social Democratic Party, and the Liberal Party. The formation of this right-center government signified an attempt by Italy's ruling circles to alter the balance of forces in the country. In view of the obvious political failure of this attempt, a new left-center government was formed in 1973 under M. Rumor. Although it somewhat accelerated the drive against fascism, it proved unable to cope with the incipient inflation. In May 1974 the right wing of the CDP pushed through a national referendum on a divorce law, hoping to strengthen the conservatives' position. However, contrary to their expectations, about 60 percent of the voters supported a divorce law. In the fall of 1974 a two-party government (the CDP and the Republicans) was formed under A. Moro. A number of important government positions were given to right-wing members of the CDP.

In the struggle against reaction and neo-Fascism the unity of Italy's leftists and democratic forces is being strengthened for the implementation of social reforms and democratic transformations.

REFERENCES

Marx, K. *Kapital,* vols. 1, 3. In K. Marx and F. Engels, *Soch.,* 2nd ed., vol. 23, pp. 727–28; vol. 25, part 2, pp. 365, 367.
Marx, K. Engel' su, 25 sent. 1857. (Letter). *Ibid.,* vol. 29, pp. 153–55.
Engels, F. "Zametki o Germanii." *Ibid.,* vol. 18, pp. 571–72.
Engels, F. "K ital'ianskomu chitateliu." *Ibid.,* vol. 22, p. 382.
Engels, F. "Dialektika prirody." *Ibid.,* vol. 20, pp. 345–63.
Marx, K., and F. Engels. "Revoliutsionnoe dvizhenie v Italii." *Ibid.,* vol. 6.
Marx, K., and F. Engels. "Voina v Italii i Vengrii." *Ibid.*
Marx, K., and F. Engels. "Porazhenie p'emonttsev." *Ibid.*
Engels, F. "Savoiia, Nitstsa i Rein." *Ibid.,* vol. 13.
Engels, F. "Budushchaia ital'ianskaia revoliutsiia i sotsialisticheskaia partiia." *Ibid.,* vol. 22.
Engels, F. "Sotsializm mezhdunarodnyi i sotsializm ital'ianskii." *Ibid.*
Lenin, V. I. "Imperializm i sotsializm v Italii." *Poln. sobr. soch.,* 5th ed., vol. 27.
Lenin, V. I. *Detskaia bolezn' 'levizny' v kommunizme. Ibid.,* vol. 41.
Lenin, V. I. "O bor'be vnutri Ital'ianskoi sotsialisticheskoi partii." *Ibid.*
Gramsci, A. *Izbr. proizv.,* vols. 1–3. Moscow, 1957–59. (Translated from Italian.)
Togliatti, P. *Izbr. stat'i i rechi,* vols. 1–2. Moscow, 1965. (Translated from Italian.)
Istoriia Italii, vols. 1–3. Moscow, 1970–71.
Ocherki istorii Italii, 476–1918 gg.: Posobie dlia uchitelia. Moscow, 1959.
Komolova, N. P. *Noveishaia istoriia Itallii.* Moscow, 1970.
Iz istorii trudiashchikhsia mass Italii: Sbornik statei. Moscow, 1959.
Revoliutsii 1848–1849, [vols.] 1–2. Moscow, 1952.
Udal'tsova, Z. V. *Italiia v Vizantiia v VI v.* Moscow, 1959.
Vinogradov, P. G. *Proiskhozhdenie feodal'nykh otnoshenii v lungobard-skoi Italii.* St. Petersburg, 1880.
Kotel'nikova, L. A. *Ital'ianskoe krest'ianstvo i gorod v XI–XIV vv: Po materialam Srednei i Severnoi Italii.* Moscow, 1967.
Rutenburg, V. I. *Ocherk iz istorii rannego kapitalizma v Italii.* Moscow-Leningrad, 1951.
Rutenburg, V. I. *Narodnye dvizheniia v gorodakh Italii XIV–nach. XV v.* Moscow-Leningrad, 1958.
Gukovskii, M. A. *Ital'ianskoe Vozrozhdenie,* vols. 1–2. Leningrad, 1947–61.
Tarle, E. V. *Istoriia Italii v novoe vremia.* St. Petersburg, 1901.
Miziano, K. F. *Nekotorye problemy istorii vossoedineniia Italii.* Moscow, 1955.
Lur'e, A. Ia. *Garibal'di (1807–1882).* Moscow, 1957.
Nevler, V. E. *Dzhuzeppe Garibal'di.* Moscow, 1961.
Grigor'eva, I. V. *Rabochee i sotsialisticheskoe dvizhenie v Italii v epokhu I Internatsionala.* Moscow, 1966.
Kirova, K. E. *Revoliutsionnoe dvizhenie v Italii 1914–1917 gg.* Moscow, 1962.
Kobylianskii, K. V. *Velikii Oktiabr' i revoliutsionnoe dvizhenie v Italii (1917–1921).* Moscow, 1968.
Slobodskoi, S. M. *Ital'ianskii fashizm i ego krakh.* [Moscow] 1946.
Lopukhov, B. R. *Fashizm i rabochee dvizhenie v Italii, 1919–1929.* Moscow, 1968.
Lopukhov, B. R. *Bor'ba rabochego klassa Italii protiv fashizma, 1920–1922.* Moscow, 1959.
Lopukhov, B. R. *Obrazovanie Ital'ianskoi kommunisticheskoi partii.* Moscow, 1962.
Koval'skii, N. A. *Ital'ianskii narod protiv fashizma.* Moscow, 1957.
Filatov, G. S. *Ital'ianskie kommunisty v dvizhenii Soprotivleniia.* Moscow, 1964.

Filatov, G. S. *Vostochnyi pokhod Mussolini.* Moscow, 1968.

Komolova, N. P. *Dvizhenie Soprotivleniia i politicheskaia bor'ba v Italii, 1943–1947.* Moscow, 1972.

Petranovich, I. M. *Polozhenie rabochego klassa Italii.* Moscow, 1969.

Kholodkovskii, K. *Rabochee dvizhenie v Italii (1959–1963).* Moscow, 1969.

Komolova, N. P. *Klassovye boi v ital'ianskoi derevne.* Moscow, 1963.

Luzzato, G. *Ekonomicheskaia istoriia Italii: Antichnost' srednie veka.* Moscow, 1954. (Translated from Italian.)

Candeloro, G. *Istoriia sovremennoi Italii,* vols. 1–5. Moscow, 1958–71. (Translated from Italian.)

Candeloro, G. *Katolicheskoe dvizhenie v Italii.* Moscow, 1955. (Translated from Italian.)

Candeloro, G. *Profsoiuznoe dvizhenie v Italii.* Moscow, 1953. (Translated from Italian.)

Berti, G. *Demokraty i sotsialisty v period Risordzhimento.* Moscow, 1965. (Translated from Italian.)

Alatri, P. *Proiskhozhdenie fashizma.* Moscow, 1961. (Translated from Italian.)

Tridtsat' let zhizni i bor'by Ital'ianskoi kommunisticheskoi partii. Moscow, 1953. (Translated from Italian.)

Longo, L. *Narod italii v bor'be.* Moscow, 1952. (Translated from Italian).

Battaglia, R. *Istoriia ital'ianskogo dvizheniia Soprotivleniia (8 sentiabria 1943–25 aprelia 1945).* Moscow, 1954. (Translated from Italian.)

Hartmann, L. *Geschichte Italiens im Mittelalter,* vols. 1–4. Leipzig, 1897–1915.

Rodolico, N. *Storia degli Italiani.* Florence, 1954.

Doren, A. *Italienische Wirtschaftsgeschichte.* Jena, 1934.

Pernoud, R. *Les Villes marchandes aux XIV et XV siècles.* Paris, 1948.

Sapori, A. *Studi di storia economica, Secoli XIII–XVI,* vols. 1–3. Milan, 1955—.

Spini, G. *Storia dell'età moderna dall'impero di Carlo V all'illuminismo.* Rome [1960].

Fanfani, A. *Storia del lavoro in Italia dalla fine del secolo XV agli inizi del XVIII.* Milan, 1943.

Croce, B. *Storia del regno di Napoli,* 4th ed. Bari, 1953.

Omodeo, A. *L'età del Risorgimento italiano,* 9th ed. Naples [1960].

Spellanzon, C. *Storia del Risorgimento e dell'unità d'Italia,* vols. 1–7. Milan, 1933–60.

Croce, B. *Storia d'Italia, dal 1871 al 1915.* Bari, 1956.

Chabod, F. *L'Italia contemporanea 1918–1948.* Turin [1961].

Catalano, F. *L'Italia dalla dittatura alla democrazia, 1919–1948.* Milan, 1962.

Salvatorelli, L., and G. Mira. *Storia d'Italia nel periodo fascista.* Turin, 1961.

Romano, A. *Storia del movimento socialista in Italia,* vols. 1–3. Rome, 1954–55.

Spriano, P. *Storia del Partito comunista italiano,* vols. 1–4. Rome-Turin, 1967–74.

> V. I. RUTENBURG (to the mid-18th century), K. E. KIROVA (mid-18th century to 1918), G. S. FILATOV (1918–45), and S. I. DOROFEEV (from 1945)

Political parties, trade unions, and other social organizations

Political parties. The Christian Democratic Party (Partito della Democrazia Cristiana), which was founded in 1943, had 1.83 million members in 1974. It represents primarily the interests of monopoly capital, although it is also supported by a substantial number of Catholic working people. The CDP is associated with the Vatican, whose support it enjoys. Founded on Jan. 21, 1921, the Italian Communist Party (Partito Comunista Italiano) had 1,658,000 members in 1974. It has a prevailing influence in the Italian General Confederation of Labor, the Union of Italian Women, and the National League of Cooperatives. In 1972 the membership of the ICP increased, owing to the admission of former members of the Italian Socialist Party of Proletarian Unity, which had disbanded itself and asked its members to join the Communist Party. The Italian Socialist Party (Partito Socialista Italiano) was founded in 1892. It had 640,000 members in 1974. In 1947 the Social Democrats left the ISP. The rightist leadership of the ISP, headed by P. Nenni, merged with the Social Democrats in 1966, forming the Unified Socialist Party. In 1968 the previous name of the party—the ISP—was restored. However, in 1969 a new split occurred: a rightist, social-reformist grouping quit the party and created the Socialist Unity Party, which in 1971 renamed itself the Social Democratic Party (Partito Social-Democratico Italiano). The latter has about 250,000 members.

Founded in 1832, the Republican party (Partito Repubblicano) had 60,000 members in 1974. The Liberal Party (Partito Liberale), which was organized in the early 20th century, represents the interests of the middle bourgeoisie and landlords. The party had about 150,000 members in 1974. The Italian Social Movement (Movimento Sociale Italiano), a neo-fascist party and an outgrowth of the Fascist Party and fascist organizations, was founded in 1947. In 1972 it merged with the Democratic Monarchist Unity Party (founded in 1959). It had 300,000 members in 1974.

Trade unions and other social organizations. The Italian General Confederation of Labor (IGCL), which was founded in 1944, had 4 million members in 1974. It belongs to the World Federation of Trade Unions. Founded in 1950, the Italian Confederation of Workers' Trade Unions (ICWT), which is under the influence of the CDP, had 200,000 members in 1974. It belongs to the International Confederation of Free Trade Unions. The Italian Union of Labor (IUL), founded in 1950, had about 800,000 members in 1974. It belongs to the International Confederation of Free Trade Unions. In 1972 the IGCL, ICWT, and IUL formed a federation.

The Italian Communist Youth Federation, which was founded in 1921, had about 120,000 members in 1974. The Union of Italian Women, founded in 1945, had about 1 million members in 1972. Founded in 1886, the National League of Cooperatives incorporates 7,920 cooperatives and about 2 million members (1972). It belongs to the International Cooperative Alliance. The National Association of Italian Partisans, whose members took part in the Resistance Movement, was founded in 1947 and had about 300,000 members in 1972. The Italy-USSR Society, founded in 1945, has about 80,000 members (1972). The Italian Catholic Action, a secular organization of Catholics that is subordinate to the church, was founded in 1874 and had about 3 million members in 1972. The organization supports the CDP. The Christian Association of Italian Workers, a Catholic quasi-trade-union organization created by the Vatican in 1945, has about 700,000 members (1972).

> A. L. ADAMISHIN

Economic geography

General state of the economy. Italy is an industrial-agrarian country. As of 1970, 42 percent of the national income was provided by industry, 10.2 percent by agriculture, 38.42 percent by service industries (including 12 percent by commerce), 6.5 percent by transportation and communications, and 2 percent by the hotel business. The value of Italy's industrial output is almost four times as high as that of its agricultural output (1970). Each year 2.5 times as much capital is invested in industry as in agriculture. Most of Italy's exports—that is, about 95 percent in 1970—are produced by its manufacturing industries. In 1970, Italy was sixth in the capitalist world (behind the USA, the Federal Republic of Germany [FRG], Japan, Great Britain, and France) in the volume of industrial output (3.7 percent) and the extent of foreign trade. (Italy accounted for 4.8 percent of the exports of the capitalist countries in 1970.)

Since World War II the country's economy has been developing at a relatively rapid rate. Capitalist centralization and concentration have accelerated. Large-scale monopoly capital dominates most spheres of the economy. More than half of the chemicals industry belongs to the monopolistic Montedison group (Montecatini Edison), more than five-sixths of automobile manufacturing is connected with the Fiat concern, and a considerable portion of the rubber industry is monopolized by the Pirelli trust.

The state owns a large number of enterprises. There are state associations in the oil and gas industry (the National Hydrocarbons Board) and in metallurgy and machine building (the Industrial Reconstruction Institute, a state group that also controls the air and maritime fleets and the telephone network). The most widespread form of state intervention in the economy is the participation of specialized state bodies in joint-stock companies as holders of controlling shares. Various economic programs provide for the establishment of enterprises whose operation is ultimately subordinate to the interests of the monopolies. The state finances an average of 35–37 percent of the total investments in the economy. In addition to the large private and state monopoly associations, there are many small and tiny firms and enterprises, more than half of which are engaged in the distribution and service industries, as well as in the fishing, garment, woodworking, publishing, and food-processing industries.

Foreign capital has a prominent place in the economy. Between 1956 and 1970 the total volume of foreign investments was 652 billion lire, of which 86 percent came from the USA, Great Britain, Switzerland, and the FRG. Foreign investment is attracted chiefly by the oil-extracting, oil-refining, chemicals, machine-building (especially electrical and electronics equipment), and metallurgical industries. Participating in the operation of these industries are such American companies as Gulf Oil Corporation, Standard Oil of New Jersey, Westinghouse, General Electric, and the Ford Motor Company, the West German concerns AEG and Siemens, the British Petroleum Company, the Shell Oil Company (an Anglo-Dutch company), and Phillips Petroleum, a Dutch concern. A number of Italy's industrial companies have agreements with foreign monopolies (for example, Fiat and Citroen, the French firm).

Monopoly capital has also penetrated into branches of agriculture. However, particularly in southern Italy and on the islands, feudal vestiges retard the development of agriculture and limit the domestic market for industry. The age-old problem of the uneven development of the North and South has not been solved: the South is still a market and agrarian and raw-materials appendage of the industrial North. The Italian government has taken measures to stimulate the economic development of the South, including the Southern Italy Development Program and its financing, as well as a favorable tax policy calculated to attract investments in the industry of the southern regions of the country. Despite the creation of a few important industrial centers, fundamental changes have not occurred in the structure of the economy of southern Italy. Meanwhile, the share of the northern regions in the country's economy continues to grow. Italy's per capita gross national product (an average of US $1,710 in 1970) is very unevenly distributed: in the northern

rate slowed, and between 1970 and 1971 total industrial output dropped by 3 percent. In the period of the general crisis of capitalism the Italian economy has underutilized the machinery of production and suffered continuously from high unemployment. For example, in 1970 the machinery of production in industry was used to only 81.5 percent of its capacity, and in 1971 the figure fell to 77 percent (according to data for the second quarter). The average number of officially registered unemployed was 961,000 in 1970 and exceeded 1 million in 1971.

Unemployment is one of the country's most serious problems. Between 1960 and 1969 the number of people employed in agriculture decreased by 2.2 million, whereas the number of people employed in other branches of the economy increased by only 1 million. Italy is a source of cheap manpower for the other industrially developed countries of Western Europe. The cost of living is rising rapidly: for instance, between 1959 and 1970 it rose by 48 percent, with prices for food rising by 47 percent; clothing prices, 39 percent; apartment rent, 94 percent; and service costs, 62 percent.

Italy is a country of low wages. Only a very limited category of workers is paid more than 100,000 lire a month. Most workers are paid 60,000–70,000 lire, and especially in the south, a rather substantial group of working people receive a maximum of 40,000–60,000 lire a month (1972). Among the social hardships borne by the Italian working class are high apartment rent, which sometimes absorbs up to 40 percent of a worker's earnings, considerable expenses for transportation, expensive medical services, an inadequate number of health and children's institutions, and low pensions.

Industry. In Italy heavy industry prevails, and machine building plays the leading role among the branches of industry. After World War II the metallurgical, electric-power, chemicals, and petrochemicals industries underwent considerable development. There have been sharp increases in the volume of production of machine tools and motor vehicles and tractors (more than one-third of which go to the foreign market), as well as in the production of precision tools, plastics, and artificial fibers, two-thirds of the output of which is exported. Italian industry has become competitive in the international market. (See Table 2 on the structure of industry.)

Table 2. Structure of industry by number of employed persons

	1938		1961 (census)		1970	
	Total	Percent	Total	Percent	Total	Percent
Mining	137,400	3.2	104,200	1.9	116,700	1.4
Manufacturing industries	3,517,800	82.7	4,495,600	80.1	5,957,300	72.7
metallurgical	103,600	2.4	191,800	3.4	233,500	2.8
machine building	823,000	19.3	1,377,500	24.5	1,927,000	23.4
chemicals and petrochemicals	127,900	3.0	290,600	5.2	473,600	5.7
food and condiments	574,500	13.5	423,500	7.5	517,000	6.3
textiles	628,600	14.8	598,600	10.7	565,800	6.9
leather	215,500	5.1	49,900	0.9	56,400	0.7
clothing and footwear	308,700	7.2	513,400	9.1	969,300	12.5
woodworking and furniture	283,600	6.7	381,200	6.8	509,600	6.2
processing of nonmetallic minerals . .	206,800	4.9	318,700	5.7	348,000	4.2
paper and publishing	126,200	3.0	194,400	3.5	232,000	2.8
other branches	119,400	2.8	156,000	2.8	105,100	1.3
Building	558,500	13.1	894,400	15.9	1,976,000	24.0
Production and distribution of electric power and water	42,200	1.0	116,100	2.1	159,000	1.9

regions it is close to that of the most developed European countries, whereas in the southern regions it approaches that of the most underdeveloped European countries, such as Greece. Italy as a whole has one of the lowest per capita gross national products in the Common Market. (Specifically, it is one-third lower than that of France.)

Although its rate of growth has been relatively higher than that of other capitalist countries, Italy's economy has developed spasmodically. (For example, industrial output expanded by 11.5 percent between 1965 and 1966 but by only 2.9 percent between 1968 and 1969.) Periods of heightened activity and economic boom alternate with crises of overproduction. The crisis of 1970–71 was especially clear-cut—in 1970 the growth

MINING. Italy has an unevenly distributed and very small supply of raw materials and energy resources. Coal mining satisfies about 10 percent of the country's demand for solid fuel. Coal is mined in Sardinia and lignites (brown coal), in Tuscany and Umbria. In the postwar years the extraction of oil and natural gas was begun, primarily in Sicily and in the Po Basin. The domestic mining of iron ore does not meet the country's needs. In addition, it is beginning to decline—a trend that is also observable in the mining of complex-metal ores, about two-thirds of which are extracted in Sardinia. Italy is second to Spain in the production of mercury, providing about one-fourth of the world's output, and third in the capitalist world behind Japan and Spain in the large-scale mining of pyrites. Bauxites are mined on the Gargano Peninsula and in northwestern Sardinia, and manganese ore is mined in Liguria and Tuscany. Sulfur mining—a traditional branch of the Italian mining industry which is concentrated in Sicily—has declined sharply. Potassic salts are mined. Italy is famous for its natural building and finishing materials—marble and granite. (See Table 3.)

Table 3. Mining

	1938	1958	1970
Coal (tons)	1,348,000	680,200	295,500
Lignites (tons)	873,000	830,900	1,393,300
Petroleum (tons extracted) .	13,200	1,545,700	1,408,100
Natural gas (cubic meters) .	17,100,000	5,175,200,000	13,171,000,000
Bauxites (tons)	360,800	299,000	224,700
Iron ore (tons)	990,000	1,292,500	756,700
Cinnabar (tons)	195,500	294,100	305,900
Lead (tons)	39,500	56,000	55,300
Zinc (tons)	84,000	117,000	179,300
Manganese ore (tons)	48,300	44,100	50,100
Pyrites (tons)	930,300	1,514,300	1,518,400
Sulfur (tons)	2,363,900	1,497,500	354,200

ENERGY. The intensive industrialization of the postwar period has included a reorganization of the country's energy base. The proportion of solid fuel consumed has plummeted. In 1969 petroleum and gas accounted for 78.4 percent of Italy's energy balance, electric power, 11.9 percent, and solid fuel, 9.7 percent. The petroleum-refining industry has become the basis of the energy branch of the economy. (In 1970 there were 38 refineries with a total capacity of 154 million tons. They rely on imported petroleum. Locally extracted raw materials provide only 1.2 percent of the petroleum consumed in Italy.)

The electric-power industry is being developed primarily through the construction of new thermoelectric power plants and through the improvement of the capacities of already existing plants. The importance of hydroelectric power is declining: hydroelectric power plants, most of which are located in the Alps, produce about 40 percent of the total output of electric power. Several electric plants in the region of Larderello in Tuscany operate on hot springs. In the 1960's atomic power plants began to be established, including Foce Verde (210 megawatts; located near Latina), Garigliano (160 megawatts; in Punta Fiume in the province of Caserta), and Enrico Fermi (272 megawatts; located in Trino-Vercellise). They produce more than 3 billion kilowatt-hours of electric power. In 1972 the Caorso Atomic Power Plant in Lombardy went into operation. There are also experimental nuclear reactors located in Ispra, Frascati, Bracciano, Pisa, Saluggia, and Vallegrande.

The power plants are linked by electrical transmission lines (about 40,000 km), and 20 high-voltage lines connect Italy with France, Switzerland, and Yugoslavia. Since the nationalization of the power plants (1962–66), ENEL, a state association, has accounted for about 70 percent of Italy's output of electric power.

MANUFACTURING INDUSTRIES. The metallurgical industry depends on imported raw materials and fuel: 90 percent of the iron ore consumed in Italy, more than 75 percent of the scrap metal, about 70 percent of the manganese ore, and all of the coking coal are imported. Characteristic of Italian metallurgy are the sharp predominance of steel over pig-iron production and a high proportion of electrometallurgy. Most of the metallurgical plants are small and do not have a full cycle. Many of them are narrowly specialized. However, the foundation of the metallurgical industry is made up of four large metallurgical combines in the cities of Cornigliano (greater Geona), Bagnoli (greater Naples), Piombino, and Taranto. Much of the iron and steel industry, including the most important combines, is controlled by Finsider, a state company which accounts for 94 percent of Italy's production of pig iron and 60 percent of its steel and rolled steel output.

Important centers of electrometallurgy (the cities of Domodossola, Bolzano, and Brescia) are located in the foothills of the Alps and in Alpine valleys near hydroelectric power plants.

The production of aluminum, lead, zinc, and mercury are the most highly developed branches of nonferrous metallurgy. Most aluminum plants (specifically, all those producing primary aluminum) and alumina plants are located in the northeast (Venice, Bolzano, and Mori), and the main center for the production of secondary aluminum is Milan. The most important lead-smelting plants are located near the Sardinian deposits of complex-metal ores (the cities of San Gavino Monreale, Sant'Antioco, and Monteponi). Zinc-smelting plants are located in northern Italy near Alpine hydroelectric power plants (Brescia, Domodossola, and Ponte Nossa). Lead and zinc are also produced in large industrial centers, such as Milan, Turin, and Venice. Mercury is produced in Tuscany (for example, in Grosseto and Siena). Compared to that of other capitalist countries, Italy's output of magnesium is large (6,400 tons in 1969; plant in Bolzano).

MACHINE BUILDING. The leading role in the country's industry is played by machine building. Transportation machine building, especially the manufacture of motor vehicles, is an outstanding branch of this industry. Almost all the output is produced by five major enterprises. The largest motor vehicle plant operated by the Fiat concern is located in Turin. In addition, there are motor vehicle plants in Milan (the Alfa Romeo Company), near Naples (the town of Pomigliano d'Arco), and in Modena. A large number of motor scooters, motorcycles, motorcycle vans, and bicycles are produced. Shipbuilding is well developed. The largest shipyards are located near Genoa, as well as at the ports of Livorno, Naples, Venice, Trieste, Monfalcone, and Taranto.

The electrical equipment industry produces power equipment, electrical equipment, radio electronics equipment, household electrical appliances, medical equipment, and lighting devices. A few large enterprises produce two-thirds of the industry's total output. Most of them are located in Milan and the cities surrounding it. Smaller electrical equipment firms are located in Varese, Bergamo, Como, Turin, and Genoa. Industries that developed in the 1960's (specifically, electronics) are located both in the old industrial centers of the north (chiefly near Milan) and in the south (the regions of Latium and Campania).

Instrument-making and the production of precision machines and optical instruments have attained a high level, primarily in the industrial centers of the north. Italy is one of the leading countries in the world in the production of typewriters and calculators. In this industry, 80 percent of the output is supplied by enterprises of the Olivetti Company (linked to American capital), which are located in Ivrea.

Machine-tool building is an old industry. In the 1960's, Italy sharply increased both the output and the variety of machine-tool production, which is concentrated chiefly in Lombardy and Piedmont (Milan, Brescia, and Turin), as well as in Genoa, Bologna, and Naples. The production of ball bearings, which is monopolized by the Fiat subsidiary Riv, is well developed. In farm-machine building, tractor manufacturing is outstanding for the large scale of its operations.

CHEMICALS. The chemicals industry has a ramified structure. Locally extracted pyrites, natural gas, sulfur, and potassic salts are among the chemical raw materials used by the industry, as are imported petroleum, coal, phosphorites, and cellulose. The output of the chemicals industry is diversified, and the level of technology is high. The industry specializes in the production of nitrogen, sulfuric acid, chemical fibers, plastics, lacquers, organic dyes, soda ash, caustic soda, pharmaceuticals, and fertilizers (nitrate fertilizers, 805,000 tons by nitrogen content; complex fertilizers, 1,762,000 tons in 1970). The structure of the industry is becoming more complicated, and the output of products created by delicate organic syntheses is acquiring greater importance. (Inorganic chemicals constitute about one-fifth of the output of the industry.) An old and highly developed industry—the production of sulfuric acid—is monopolized by the Montedison concern.

Plastics and artificial fibers enterprises are located near centers of the textile industry in Lombardy and Piedmont. The highly developed lacquer and dye industry is concentrated primarily around Milan. The petroleum-refining industry is located mainly on the coast (for example, in Genoa, Naples, Venice, La Spezia,

Augusta, Milazzo, and Priolo), where imported petroleum is unloaded, and in areas where the consumption of petroleum products is highest (Lombardy), to which oil is brought in pipelines. A comparatively new, developing industry is petrochemicals. Some of its combines operate on locally extracted natural gas (Porto Marghera and Ferrandina), and others use the products of petroleum refineries (Priolo, Porto Torres, Gela, Cagliari, and Brindisi). Petrochemicals combines in Ravenna, Ferrara, and Mantua use both natural gas and refined petroleum products. The rubber and synthetic rubber industries are well developed.

TEXTILES. Textiles is one of the oldest industries. The highest output is produced by the cotton industry, which is centered primarily in Lombardy and Piedmont. The principal areas for the wool industry are Piedmont (Biella), Veneto, and Tuscany. Most of the fabrics made from artificial and synthetic fibers are exported. The production of natural silk has begun to decline as a result of the popularization of fabrics made from artificial fibers. (The chief center of the silk industry is Como.)

FOODS. The most highly developed food-processing industries are milling, the production of macaroni, and sugar refining. Traditional products are canned fruits, vegetables, meats and fish, juices, olive oil (first in output in the world), cheese, and grape wines. With France, Italy has outdistanced all other countries in wine-making. (See Table 4.)

Table 4. Output of main industrial products

	1938	1958	1970
Electric power (billion kW-hr)	15.5	45.5	117.4
Coke (thousand tons)	1,739.4	4,188.1	7,171.2
Pig iron (thousand tons)	862.8	2,059.8	8,331.6
Steel (thousand tons)	2,322.8	6,271.1	17,277.4
Ferroalloys (thousand tons)	65.8	107.3	197.0
Rolled metal (thousand tons)	1,734.6	4,635.2	13,928.8
Aluminum, primary (thousand tons) .	25.8	64.1	146.5
Lead, primary (thousand tons)	44.0	48.0	54.3
Zinc (thousand tons)	33.6	71.4	142.1
Mercury (thousand tons)	2.3	2.0	1.5
Passenger cars (thousands)	59.0	369.4	1,719.7
Other motor vehicles (thousands) . .	11.8	34.4	134.5
Tractors (thousands)	—	25.6	83.8
Bicycles (thousands)	—	352.9	370.2
Motorcycles, motor scooters, motor bikes (thousands)	—	488.6	698.2
Maritime vessels launched (gross reg. tons)	106.2	528.5	622.0
Typewriters (thousands)	—	396.9	521.2
Calculators (thousands)	—	230.7	972.5
Sewing machines (thousands)	—	441.8	1,004.9
Machine tools (thousand tons) . . .	18.0	23.5[1]	134.0[2]
Antifriction bearings (millions)	—	47.8	132.1
Cement (million tons)	4.6	22.0	33.1
Sulfuric acid (thousand tons)	1,721.2	2,031.3	3,324.2
Synthetic ammonia (thousand tons) .	113.2	609.2	1,548.3
Plastics (thousand tons)	7.7	174.0	1,629.7
Artificial fibers (thousand tons) . . .	—	141.3	182.7
Synthetic fibers (thousand tons) . . .	—	19.0	241.2
Cotton fabrics (thousand tons)	—	157.2	175.4
Silk fabrics (thousand tons)	—	—	17.1[2]
Woolen fabrics (thousand tons) . . .	—	—	34.0[2]
Sugar (thousand tons)	369.8	1,026.8	1,273.7
Wine (million hectoliters)	38.2	67.4	68.9
Tobacco products (billion cigarettes)	31.9	54.4	64.7[3]
Olive oil (thousand tons)	175.3	260.3	424.4

[1] 1956 [2] 1968 [3] 1969

Agriculture. Agriculture is characterized by large-scale capitalist landowning and small-scale land use. There are still large latifundia in the south. About a third of all landed wealth is concentrated in the hands of 20,000 major landowners (0.5 percent of the total number of landowners), whereas 2.7 million peasants (63.2 percent of the country's landowners), whose plots do not exceed 3 hectares (ha), own only 12 percent of the agricultural lands. Sharecropping is widespread. Many peasant farm laborers have no land. One of the acute contradictions in agriculture is the growing contrast between the levels of the social and productive development of the north and south.

In the 1960's and early 1970's a powerful upsurge was observed in the peasant movement, which is developing in close alliance with the working-class movement. Farm laborers have expressed their anger very forcefully: often, hundreds of thousands of them have gone on strike simultaneously throughout the country, seeking wage increases, equal pay for women, and the establishment of a guaranteed minimum wage. The center of the peasant movement was once the Po Valley, particularly the region of Emilia-Romagna. However, in the early 1970's the peasantry of southern Italy, who in the past had been politically the most passive part of the population, began to participate in the peasant movement.

Capitalist farms in the north produce most of the commodity output. With the increase in investments in agriculture after World War II, there was some improvement in the degree of mechanization. More fertilizers were used, crop and livestock yields rose, and new areas were developed. However, in terms of efficiency, agricultural production in Italy lags behind that of the other developed capitalist countries. (Wheat yield, for instance, is much lower in Italy than in France—23.3 and 34.4 centners per ha, respectively.) About 70 percent of Italy's territory is used for agriculture; of this area, plowed land occupies more than 40.5 percent, orchards and vineyards, 9.3 percent, meadows and pastures, 17.3 percent, and forests and shrubbery, 20.6 percent. The predominantly mountainous, hilly terrain hinders the cultivation of land by the usual method. Slopes are terraced and reinforced to protect the soil from erosion. In 1970, 631,000 tractors, 12,000 threshers, and 18,000 grain combines were in use, and about 3 million tons of various fertilizers were used.

The diversity of the natural environment affects specialization in agriculture. Italy raises a larger proportion of cereal crops—especially wheat, corn, and rice—than any other European country. (See Table 5.)

Table 5. Cultivated area and harvest of basic crops

	Area (thousand hectares)			Harvest (thousand tons)		
	1938	1956	1970	1938	1956	1970
Grains	7,448	7,003	5,864	10,310	13,644	16,070
wheat	5,116	4,877	4,138	8,184	8,684	9,630
corn	1,458	1,254	1,026	2,940	3,410	4,729
rice	149	138	173	817	663	819
Legumes	1,447	1,277	760	1,125	847	1,269
Potatoes	402	387	286	2,942	3,414	3,668
Garden crops	174	279	576	2,444	4,100	11,565
tomatoes	57	101	130	940	1,717	3,618
cabbage (heads cabbage and cauliflower)	58	83	81	781	1,272	1,571
muskmelons and watermelons . . .	24	26	42	398	427	1,039
artichokes	13	28	63	76	110	667
onions and garlic . .	12	23	33	145	312	577
Sugar beets	135	226	282	3,280	7,034	9,557
Tobacco	33	49	43	42	71	74
Cotton fiber	27	45	5	5	8	1.1
Cottonseed				10	13	1.6

The country's chief granary is the Po Valley, which produces almost half of the total wheat harvest. Hard wheat, which is especially suited to manufacturing macaroni, is raised chiefly in Sicily, Apulia, and Basilicata. Corn is grown primarily in

Veneto, Lombardy, and Piedmont. The chief rice-growing areas are the provinces of Vercelli and Novara in Piedmont. Orchards, viticulture, and olive cultivation are widespread. The region of Emilia-Romagna leads in the production of fruit, followed by the regions of Veneto, Campania, and Trentino-Alto Adige. In 1970 about 2 million tons of apples, about 2 million tons of pears, and 1 million tons of peaches were picked, as well as considerable quantities of almonds, cherries, plums, and walnuts. Vineyards occupy 1.1 million ha, not counting the areas where grapes are grown together with other crops. (In 1970, 10.7 million tons of grapes were harvested.) Viticulture is carried on primarily in the region of Apulia, which produces more than 18 percent of the country's total output of grapes, and there are large yields of grapes in Sicily and the regions of Veneto, Emilia-Romagna, Piedmont, and Latium.

Italy is one of the world's leaders in the cultivated area and yield of olives (1 million ha, excluding lands with mixed crops; a yield of 2.1 million tons of olives in 1970, mainly from Apulia, Calabria, and Sicily). Like the USA and Spain, Italy is a major producer of citrus fruits (1,362,000 tons of oranges, 279,000 tons of mandarin oranges, and 770,000 tons of lemons in 1970). Sicily produces three-fourths of the total yield of citrus fruits. Among the other crops grown in Italy, potatoes, melons, tomatoes, and cabbage are important. The country's mild climate makes it possible for Italy to deliver early vegetables to the European market. Among the regions of Italy, Campania is notable for its harvests of potatoes and tomatoes. Sugar beets (Emilia-Romagna and Veneto), tobacco (Apulia and Campania), and hemp (Campania) are widely cultivated.

Animal husbandry is a secondary branch of agriculture in Italy, mainly because of the inadequacy of the feed supply. (See Tables 6 and 7.) The chief cattle-raising areas are the regions of Lombardy, Emilia-Romagna, Piedmont, and Veneto. Sheep raising is most highly developed in Sardinia and Apulia and swine raising, in Emilia-Romagna, where the animals are fed the by-products of sugar refining. Animal husbandry is intensive only in the country's northern areas. Silkworm breeding is still important in a number of areas.

Table 6. Livestock

	1938	1970
Cattle	7,667,000	9,563,000
cows	3,828,000	4,472,000
Sheep	9,467,000	8,138,000
Goats	1,828,000	1,031,000
Pigs	2,940,000	9,224,000
Horses	791,000	296,000
Donkeys	796,000	293,000
Mules	431,000	188,000

Fishing is done primarily in the Adriatic Sea. In 1970, 186,000 tons of fish were caught, including herring, sardines, mackerel, and tuna, as well as 44,800 tons of shellfish and 10,700 tons of crustaceans. Oysters are bred in some man-made bodies of water in the south.

Transportation. Trucks carry most of the land freight shipments in Italy. There are 285,000 km of roads, including 3,900 km of superhighways. As of 1970, there were more than 11 million motor vehicles, including 10 million passenger cars. Italy has 20,200 km of railroad tracks, of which 9,300 km are electrified. (In electrified railroads Italy is third in the capitalist world, after Switzerland and Sweden.) Maritime transportation plays an important role in the Italian economy. In 1970 the total tonnage of the merchant marine fleet was 7,450,000 gross registered tons. (This figure includes only vessels weighing more than 100 gross registered tons.) The most important ports are Genoa (cargo turnover, 52.6 million tons), Venice, and Naples, and

Augusta, Taranto, and La Spezia, which handle only freight. The length of inland waterways, including canals, rivers, and lakes, is 2,400 km. The maximum length of the network of gas pipelines was 8,000 km in early 1970. There were 1,900 km of oil pipelines in 1969. Most of the pipelines are in the north. The largest airport of international importance is Fiumicino (Rome).

Table 7. Output of animal husbandry, poultry breeding, and silkworm breeding
(tons)

	1938	1970
Meat	679,000	1,240,000
Milk	1,639,000	10,397,000
Butter	58,000	67,000
Cheese	257,000	466,000
Eggs	308,000	584,000
Wool (unwashed)	—	12,000
Silk cocoons	20,000	2,000

Foreign trade. Italy's economy depends heavily on foreign trade. The country imports oil, coal, raw materials for the metallurgical and textile industries, tools and machinery, lumber, paper, and foodstuffs (for example, grain, meat, fish and coffee). The major exports are machines (transportation vehicles, various equipment, typewriters, and calculators), agricultural goods and foodstuffs (fruits, vegetables, canned tomatoes, and cheeses), textiles, the products of the garment, footwear, and chemicals industries, and petroleum products. The Common Market countries (especially the FRG, France, and Great Britain) and the USA play the leading role in Italy's foreign trade.

Foreign capital is invested in Italy's economy, and some Italian capital is invested abroad. (The amount of capital exported rose from US $81 million in 1959 to to US $498 million in 1968.) Capital is exported in the form of state and private credits and investments. The shipment of goods, fulfillment of work contracted for by other countries on credit terms, and technical assistance also involve the export of capital. Italy provides subsidies to a number of developing countries. The largest shipments of goods on credit go to Latin American countries and the next largest, to the developing countries of Asia and Africa. Italy provides technical assistance primarily to African countries such as Tunisia, Algeria, Morocco, Ghana, and Tanzania for the exploration of oil fields and hydroelectric resources and the construction of petroleum refineries, hydroelectric power plants, highways, and railroads. In Latin America, Italian capital is attracted by the most developed countries—Brazil, Argentina, Mexico, Chile, and Venezuela—where private Italian monopolies transmit technical experience and investors put capital directly into the construction of industrial enterprises. The activities of the Italian monopolies in developing Asian countries (India, Iran, and Pakistan) are aimed chiefly at developing the infrastructure (electric power, transportation, and communications). Italian capital is also becoming more active in the developed states of Western Europe.

Italy has substantial foreign-trade and economic relations with the socialist countries. The share of socialist countries in Italy's imports (1970) is 8.0 percent; in its exports, 8.8 percent. The Soviet Union supplies about 2.0 percent of all Italy's imports and buys 2.3 percent of its exports. Since 1957 trade between the USSR and Italy has been conducted through long-term agreements. In 1969 the USSR and the National Hydrocarbons Board (a state company) signed an agreement for the delivery to Italy of more than 100 billion cu m of gas and for the construction of a gas pipeline. An accord was concluded between the USSR and the Fiat firm in 1966 on cooperation in the construction of the Volga Automobile Plant in the city of Tol'iatti. Imports from socialist countries include corn, cotton, oilseeds, cattle, meat, lumber, coal, petroleum and refined petroleum products, pig iron, steel, and rolled metal. Italy supplies the socialist countries with citrus fruits, artificial and synthetic yarn and fabrics, clothing, paper, rolled metal, machinery for the textile and clothing industries, and chemical products.

The balance-of-payments deficit that is characteristic of Italy's foreign trade is covered by remittances from Italians living abroad (307 billion lire in 1970) and by revenues from foreign tourism (1,024 billion lire). In some years as many as 20 million foreign tourists visit Italy, and serving them has become a specialized branch of the economy. The chief centers of foreign tourism (in terms of the number of visitors) are Rome, Milan, Venice, Florence, Naples, Genoa, and Palermo.

The monetary unit is the lira. According to the Gosbank (State Bank) exchange rate in July 1972, 1,000 lire = 1 ruble, 42 kopeks.

Internal differences. The North (the regions of Piedmont, Valle d'Aosta, Lombardy, Trentino–Alto Adige, Veneto, Friuli–Venezia Giulia, Liguria, and Emilia-Romagna) occupies about 40 percent of the country and contains 45 percent of its population, including 69 percent of the population employed in industry. The North is the most industrially developed region of Italy. Its advantageous geographic location on the routes from Western and Central Europe to the east, its dense network of roads and convenient water routes, its favorable natural conditions, and its dense population have contributed to the region's rapid economic and cultural development. A preponderant proportion of Italy's industry is concentrated in the North, where labor- and energy-consuming industries and branches of industry that require skilled manpower prevail. The machine-building, power, metallurgical, and chemicals industries are especially well developed. The power plants of the North, most of which are located on Alpine mountain rivers, produce two-thirds of the country's electric power. (Three-fourths of Italy's total hydroelectric resources are concentrated in the North.) There are considerable deposits of natural gas in the region.

The agriculture of the North (particularly its eastern region), in which large capitalist farms predominate, produces half of the country's agricultural output, including about 80 percent of the corn yield, the entire rice harvest, a large portion of the sugar beet yield, and about 40 percent of the country's wheat yield. Animal husbandry is well developed. Viticulture, orchards, and truck farming are very important. On the Ligurian coast floriculture is well developed. Of the country's total fleet of tractors and combines, two-thirds are used in the fields of the North. The main industrial area of the North and of all Italy is the western region—Lombardy, Piedmont, and Liguria, which include such major industrial centers as Milan, Turin, and Genoa.

The Center (the regions of Tuscany, Umbria, the Marches, and Latium) occupies 19 percent of the country and contains more than 18 percent of its population. Capitalist industrial development of the region began later than in the North and was not as intensive, although the mining industry has long been established in the region. The economically most developed region is Tuscany, which is second to Sardinia in the scale of its mining industry. It also has a machine-building industry (Florence), a substantial metallurgical industry (Piombino), a chemicals industry (Rosignano Solvay), petroleum refining (Livorno), and glass and wool industries (Prato and Lucca). There are many branches of agriculture in the region. The chief agricultural crops are wheat, corn, potatoes, vegetables, grapes, and olives. Sharecropping is characteristic of agrarian relations in central Italy.

The region of Umbria (center at Terni), where metallurgy, machine building, and the chemicals and military industries are well developed, is the industrial base of central Italy. There is a hydroelectric power plant on the Velino River. Large-scale industry (for example, machine building and chemicals) was not established until the postwar years in Latium, where Rome is located. The Marches, where the only important industrial center is the port of Ancona (shipbuilding and petroleum refining), is a backward agricultural region.

The South (the regions of Campania, Abruzzi, Molise, Apulia, Basilicata, Calabria, the islands of Sicily and Sardinia, and a number of small islands) occupies 41 percent of Italy and contains 36 percent of its population. The South is economically the least developed part of the country. For many decades it has served as an agrarian and raw-materials appendage for the industrial North. After World War II the situation changed somewhat when, as a result of government economic policies aimed at developing the region, new industries were established (for example, metallurgy and petrochemicals). However, the appearance of "nuclei" of industrialization has not yet brought about fundamental advances in the structure of the economy of the South. The development of the mining industry in the South laid the foundation for the industrialization of that region of Italy. The economically most developed region of the South is Campania, whose basic industrial nucleus took shape around Naples. Apulia's industrial development is concentrated in the port cities of Taranto (metallurgy and shipbuilding), Bari, and Brindisi (petroleum refining and petrochemicals). Because of the proximity of natural gas deposits, the petrochemicals industry has developed in one of the poorest regions, Basilicata (Ferrandina and Pisticci), and in Sicily. In addition to the mining industry and nonferrous metallurgy, petroleum refining and the petrochemicals industry were established in the 1960's on the island of Sardinia.

Agriculture, which is primarily extensive in the South, is the basis of the region's economy. Campania, where agriculture is more intensive than in other parts of the South, supplies the market with vegetables and fruits, a considerable portion of which is exported after processing. About a fourth of the country's total potato harvest and more than a fourth of its tomato harvest come from Campania. Apulia is outstanding among the regions of the South and of all of Italy for its vineyards, tobacco plantations, and olive and almond groves. Sicily surpasses all other regions in harvests of hard wheat, citrus fruits, and beans.

REFERENCES

Kulagin, G. D. *Geografiia promyshlennosti Italii.* Moscow, 1954.
Puchik, E. P. *Italiia: Ekonomika i vneshniaia torgovlia.* Moscow, 1957.
Kolosov, L. S., and N. I. Timofeev. *Ekonomika Italii.* Moscow, 1960.
Kulagin, G. D. *Italiia.* Moscow, 1960.
Tendentsii razvitiia kapitalizma v Italii. Moscow, 1964. (Translated from Italian.)
Lisovskii, Iu. P. *Sel'skoe khoziaistvo i krest'ianskoe dvizhenie v sovremennoi Italii.* Moscow, 1966.
Vasil'kov, N. P. *Ekonomika sovremennoi Italii.* Moscow, 1969.
Galkina, T., and N. Sysoeva. *Italiia.* Moscow, 1972.
Almagia, R. *L'Italia,* vols. 1–2. Turin, 1959.
Pozzani, S. *L'economia italiana.* Milan, 1961.
Censimento generale dell'industria e del commercio, 1961, vols. 1–8. Rome, 1962–69.
Daneo, C. *Agricoltura e sviluppo capitalistico in Italia.* Milan, 1964.
Luzzatto, G. *Per una storia economica d'Italia.* Bari, 1967.
Saville, L. *Regional Economic Development in Italy.* Durham, N.C., 1967.
Lenti, L. *L'inventario dell'economia italiana.* Milan, 1969.
Annuario statistico italiano. Rome. (Yearbook.)
Calendario Atlante De Agostini. Novara. (Yearbook.)
Compendio statistico italiano. Rome. (Yearbook.)　　T. A. GALKINA

Armed forces

The armed forces consist of ground forces, an air force, and a navy. At the beginning of 1972 there were about 415,000 persons in the armed forces. In addition, there are about 80,000 *carabinieri.* The president is the commander in chief; the Supreme Council of Defense and the military cabinet (an agency under the president) exercise supreme military leadership. The immediate direction of the armed forces is the responsibility of the minister of defense, who has authority over the General Staff and the staffs of the ground forces, air force, and navy. The armed forces are manned in accordance with a law on universal military obligation and through the recruitment of volunteers. The period of active military service in the ground forces and the air force is 15 months and in the navy, 24 months.

The ground forces (about 295,000 men) include one army directorate and four army corps. There are seven divisions (five infantry and two armored tank), 11 detached brigades (four infantry, five Alpine, one armored cavalry, and one paratroop), and several divisions of missile and antiaircraft missile artillery, as well as detached infantry, artillery, antiaircraft, and engineering regiments and service and support units. Many of the units of the ground forces (for example, four divisions, five Alpine brigades, and a tank brigade) have been turned over to the united armed forces of NATO.

The air force (about 75,000 men) has been reduced organizationally to air wings and air brigades. There are about 300 combat planes, of which as many as 50 percent are up-to-date models. Divided territorially into four naval districts and two detached naval commands, the navy (more than 45,000 men) consists of a squadron of coastal forces (four divisions of ships and several submarine groups), landing forces, minesweeping forces, a marine battalion, and several groups of patrol planes and helicopters. There are more than 200 ships and cutters, including four light cruisers, 11 destroyers, and nine submarines. Naval bases, excluding deployment points, district headquarters, and commands, are Ancona, Brindisi, Livorno, and Augusta.

Health and social welfare

Medicine and public health. In 1971 the birthrate was 16.8 per 1,000 inhabitants, the death rate 9.6, and infant mortality 29.0 per 1,000 live births. Between 1964 and 1967 the average life expectancy was 71. Noninfectious diseases such as cardiovascular disorders and malignant neoplasms prevail in the pathology of the population. The highest mortality from diseases of the circulatory organs has been recorded in the regions of Piedmont, Valle d'Aosta (342 per 100,000 inhabitants between 1950 and 1952), and Fruili–Venezia Giulia (299.7). The lowest mortality from circulatory diseases has been recorded on Sardinia (146.8) and in the region of Calabria (169.1). Among malignant neoplasms, cancer of the respiratory organs is widespread, especially among men. (In 1959 the mortality rate was 16.5 per 100,000 inhabitants—27.9 among men and 5.5 among women). A sharp increase in the mortality rate from lung cancer and a high level of incidence of the disease have been noted in Liguria, Lombardy, Veneto, Emilia-Romagna, Tuscany, and Latium. In industrial centers (Milan, Turin, and Genoa) the death rate from cancer is higher than in agricultural areas. In Lombardy, Emilia-Romagna, and Tuscany, a high mortality rate from cancer of the digestive organs has been noted. The incidence of and mortality rate from diabetes mellitus are increasing continuously: in 1900 the death rate from the disease was 3.6 per 100,000 inhabitants, whereas in 1964 it was 17.2. The incidence of viral hepatitis is increasing (0.30 per 100,000 in 1955, as compared with 7.14 in 1966).

Between 1946 and 1970 the incidence of typhoid fever and paratyphoids declined from 113.8 to 24.1 per 100,000 inhabitants. (This trend was particularly noticeable in northern Italy.) In the country as a whole the incidence of tuberculosis is declining (between 1956 and 1958, 142.3–145.3 per 100,000 inhabitants, in 1964, 90.5, and in 1965, 83.0). The incidence of tuberculosis and the mortality rate from it are highest in Piedmont, Liguria, and Lombardy and lowest in Calabria, the Marches, Abruzzi, and Molise. A decline has been noted in the incidence of children's infectious diseases (diphtheria, poliomyelitis, scarlet fever, and whooping cough). In 1970 the incidence of brucellosis was 6.2 per 100,000. The chief sources of the infection for man are sheep and goats. The regions most affected by brucellosis are Valle d'Aosta, Tuscany, Basilicata, the islands of Sicily and Sardinia, and Emilia-Romagna, Abruzzi, and Molise. Cases of Q fever, leptospirosis, and tetanus have been recorded.

Italy has a private capitalist system of public health with a well-developed system of health insurance. Support of the aged and disabled is one of the sharpest socioeconomic issues of the class struggle of Italy's working people. As a result of nationwide strikes in 1968–69, in which the workers demanded pension reforms, the government was forced to make several concessions. For example, pensions were increased, but only for those who applied for them after 1968. Despite the reform, two-thirds of Italian pensioners continue to receive the minimum or a little more than the minimum pension. Although the government introduced some reform measures, it also restricted the rights of pensioners. Specifically, the law deprived citizens of the right to receive a pension if they continued to work after reaching retire-

ment age and abolished pensions granted for long and meritorious service. A law passed in 1969 established very high insurance premiums to be paid by working people (6.35 percent of their wages) and a long period of employment (40 years) during which workers and office employees must pay the premiums in order to receive pensions. The age of eligibility for pensions is 60 for men and 55 for women. Allowances for illness and temporary disability resulting from a job-related accident equal only about half of the worker's wages. Unemployment allowances are paid out for only six months. They are very small and do not even provide the officially recognized subsistence income. According to official data, the number of industrial accidents increased by 15 percent between 1965 and 1968. In 1969, 1.3 million occupational injuries and illnesses were recorded and in 1970, 1.4 million. At 85 percent of the enterprises and projects under construction in Italy the level of accident-prevention technology is extremely low.

In 1969 there were 2,200 hospital institutions with 511,000 beds (9.6 beds per 1,000 inhabitants). A total of 160 departments to combat cardiovascular and rheumatic diseases and 80 specialized centers to combat diabetes have been created. The chief centers in the fight against cancer are located in Milan, Rome, and Naples.

In 1969 there were 95,200 physicians (one per 559 inhabitants). There were 34,200 pharmacists and 69,100 nurses and midwives in 1965. Members of the medical profession are trained at 21 medical institutes, the medical-surgical faculty of the university in Rome, 11 dental schools, 22 pharmaceutical schools, 31 schools of obstetrics, and 68 nursing schools.

Located on the Ligurian coast, which has an especially favorable climate, is the Italian Riviera, the site of many climatic resorts (for example, Viareggio, Nervi, Lido, and San Remo). The mountain climatic resorts of Bolzano and Merano (northern Italy) and the balneological springs of Ciangano, Roncegno, and Salsomaggiore are also popular.

Expenditures on public health in 1966 totaled 360 million lire, or 3 percent of the state's entire budget.

E. V. GALAKHOV and L. N. ZAKHAROVA

Veterinary services. Cases of foot-and-mouth disease, tuberculosis of cattle and poultry, leptospirosis, and salmonellosis are recorded most often in northern and northwestern Italy, especially in Lombardy and Emilia, where the density of the animal population is higher than in other regions of Italy. Classic swine fever, Newcastle disease, pox and leukosis of fowl, colibacillosis of calves, enzootic mastitis of cattle, and diseases of fowl and swine associated with a shortage of trace elements, minerals, and vitamins are widespread. Southern Italy and the islands of the Mediterranean suffer continuously from outbreaks of brucellosis in sheep and goats and helminthiases of sheep. (In Sardinia and Sicily, cases of echinococcosis in cattle have been recorded.) Contagious agalactia and pleuropneumonia of sheep and goats have not been eliminated. Since 1945 viral diarrhea has been diagnosed among cattle. Many areas (chiefly the mountainous ones) have trouble with piroplasmoses (anaplasmosis of cattle and babesiasis). Outbreaks of anthrax (74 in 1973) and rabies in animals (including wild ones) have been recorded.

The veterinary services belong to the Ministry of Health system and conform structurally to the administrative division of Italy. Since 1957 a specialized veterinary police agency has been in operation. Italy has 7,000 veterinarians (1973), who are trained by the veterinary faculties of ten universities. The centers of scientific research are the Higher Institute of Health (Rome) and zonal institutes of zooprophylactic medicine in Brescia, Turin, Padua, Perugia, Rome, Teramo, Naples, Palermo, Foggia, and Sassari.

V. A. VEDERNIKOV

Education and cultural affairs

In Italy, the system of public education began to take shape in the second half of the 19th century. The first law on compulsory education, which required two years of primary education for children six to nine years old, was issued in 1859. Subsequently, the period of compulsory education was gradually increased to eight years (1923). The Constitution of 1947 established eight-year compulsory education for children age six to 14. However, in the academic year 1966–67 more than the 40 percent of the children in that age group were not receiving a full eight-year education. In addition to state schools, there are a large number of schools belonging to religious organizations. The teaching of religion is compulsory in all schools. The present-day system of public education in Italy includes preschool institutions (for example, maternal schools, kindergartens, and nursery schools for children age three to five). Most of them are private. In 1970 more than 1.6 million children (more than 50 percent of all children of that age) were being trained in preschool institutions, including about 1.5 million children enrolled in private preschool institutions.

Compulsory eight-year education consists of five years of primary school and three years of lower secondary school. In the academic year 1969–70 more than 4.4 million pupils were studying in 35,382 state primary schools, and about 345,000 pupils were enrolled in 2,610 private primary schools. About 2 million pupils were enrolled in 7,771 state lower secondary schools, and there were about 103,000 pupils in 1,000 private ones. Many children, especially in southern Italy, on the islands, and in rural areas, study in ill-equipped schools. Lower secondary schools are established only in communities with at least 3,000 inhabitants.

Various types of secondary general-education and vocational-technical institutions are open to those who have completed the compulsory eight-year curriculum. Complete secondary general-education schools are the classical *lycée* (*Gymnasium-lycée*) and the technical *lycée*, which have a five-year curriculum. To graduate from a classical *lycée*, a student must pass an examination for a matriculation certificate, which gives him the right to enter any university faculty, whereas the technical *lycée* certificate gives the student the right to enroll in any university faculty except philology and philosophy. In the academic year 1969–70, 174,-000 pupils were studying in 454 state classical *lycées*, and more than 30,000 pupils were enrolled in 269 private ones. More than 203,000 pupils were studying in 490 state technical *lycées*, and 15,400 in 106 private ones.

Vocational-technical education is conducted in three- to five-year vocational institutes that train skilled workers and in two-year technical schools, most of which are private. In the academic year 1968–69, 208,500 pupils were studying in 1,746 state vocational institutes, and 6,400 pupils were enrolled in 108 private vocational institutes and technical schools.

Technical institutes with five-year curricula provide a specialized secondary education. In the academic year 1969–70 there were 65 state agricultural technical institutes (14,400 pupils) and five private ones (about 1,000 pupils), 407 state industrial technical institutes (223,400 pupils) and 60 private ones (18,000 pupils), and 522 state commercial technical institutes (207,700 pupils) and 160 private ones (20,700 pupils). In addition, there were 38 state maritime technical institutes (12,800 pupils) and two private ones (110 pupils) and 547 state and private technical institutes training guides and service personnel for hotels (about 130,000 pupils). Certification that he has graduated from a technical institute gives the student the right to enter some faculties of the universities and other higher educational institutions.

In the academic year 1968–69, 43,000 pupils were studying in 176 state secondary arts and music schools and *lycées*, and 514 pupils in 33 private ones. Secondary pedagogical educational institutions include four-year teachers institutes that train teachers for the primary schools. (In the academic year 1969–70 more than 160,000 pupils were studying in 281 state teachers institutes, and about 49,000 pupils in 357 private ones. There are also three-year pedagogical schools that train educators for preschool institutions. (In the academic year 1969–70, 3,100 pupils were studying in 11 state pedagogical schools, and 22,500 pupils in 141 private ones.) Secondary-school teachers are trained at universities and higher normal schools.

Most of Italy's higher educational institutions are universities, both state and private. There are also higher arts schools, academies, and conservatories. The period of study in various faculties of the university ranges from four to six years. The oldest universities in Europe are the University of Bologna and the university in Parma (founded in the 11th century). Among Italy's major universities are the University of Rome, the University of Naples, and the universities in Bari, Florence, Genoa, Milan, Padua, Palermo, and Turin. The polytechnic institutes in Turin

and Milan, the Institute of Oriental Studies in Naples, and the university-type pedagogical institute in Pisa are also significant state higher educational institutions. In the academic year 1969–70 more than 486,500 students were attending Italy's higher educational institutions.

Italy has many important libraries. Among those located in Rome are the National Central Library (founded in 1876; 2.2 million volumes, 1,893 incunabula), the university library (founded in 1661; 886,000 volumes, 659 incunabula), the Angelica Library (founded in 1605; about 169,000 volumes, 1,086 incunabula), and the library of the National Academy of Lincei (founded in 1730; 412,000 volumes, 2,293 incunabula). Major libraries in Naples are the National Library (founded in 1804; more than 1.5 million volumes, 4,546 incunabula) and the university library (founded in 1615; 750,000 volumes). Located in Turin is the National Library (founded in 1720; 750,000 volumes, 1,600 incunabula) and in Milan, the National Library (founded in 1763; more than 807,000 volumes, 2,349 incunabula) and the Ambrosiana Library (founded in 1609; 850,000 volumes, 2,100 incunabula). There are national and university libraries in a number of other cities, including Bologna, Bari, Modena, Palermo, and Pisa.

Italy has more than 150 museums, of which many of the largest are located in Rome: the National Museum (founded in 1889), the Museum of Villa Giulia (founded in 1889), the Borghese Gallery (founded in 1616), the National Gallery of Ancient Art (founded in 1895), and the National Gallery of Modern Art (founded in 1883). There are national museums and art galleries in Florence, Messina, Naples, Palermo, Perugia, Ravenna, and Taranto. Other major museums include the Palace of the Doges in Venice and the Uffizi Gallery in Florence.

G. A. KASVIN

Science and scientific institutions

Natural and technical sciences. THE MIDDLE AGES AND THE RENAISSANCE (TO THE END OF THE 16TH CENTURY). Among the scholars who emerged at the juncture of ancient science in Italy and medieval science in Europe in the fifth and sixth centuries were A. Boethius, whose works in mathematics and music theory laid the groundwork for medieval monastic education, and Cassiodorus, the author of an encyclopedic compilation of the knowledge of his time in the natural sciences. In the Middle Ages monasteries were the centers of scholarship. With the development of urban communes, the role of the monasteries in the preservation and dissemination of knowledge diminished considerably. A secular medical school was founded at Salerno in the ninth century. In addition to applied work, scholars at Salerno worked on theoretical principles to link prescriptions (the *Antidotary*) with diagnostic methods (the *Passionarius*). Arabic works in medicine were also translated there by Constantine the African. In the 12th and 13th centuries a great deal of translating was done in southern Italy and Sicily: Gerard of Cremona and J. Campanus translated the *Elements* of Euclid, and works by Ptolemy and Aristotle were also translated into Latin. The sources for the translations were not the Greek originals but their Arabic interpretations, which were associated to a greater extent with the natural sciences. Arab treatises on zoology, pharmacy, and other subjects were also translated. In the 11th to 13th centuries the first universities were founded (for example, in the 11th century in Parma and Bologna, in 1222 in Padua, and in 1224 in Naples). Established by the rulers of states, the Italian universities were less dependent on the clergy than the universities of other European states.

The universities were centers for the accumulation of practical knowledge as well as for the study of scientific theory. Construction mechanics, navigation, commerce, and handicrafts confronted science with new problems. In 1202 the monk Leonardo Fibonacci of Pisa wrote the *Book of the Abacus,* an unusual encyclopedia of practical computation supplemented with an original contribution to arithmetic and algebra. In the 13th century eyeglasses were invented in Italy. The needs of commercial navigation led to the dissemination in the 13th to 16th centuries of navigational charts called portolanos. Between 1271 and 1295, Marco Polo traveled in China. In the first half of the 14th century botanical gardens were founded in Salerno and Venice.

The great geographic discoveries of the Renaissance stimulated the development of all the sciences. P. Toscanelli, a cosmographer, was the first to voice the idea that it was possible to reach India without going around Africa, by traveling west across the Atlantic Ocean. This idea, which was put into practice by C. Columbus, a Genoan, led to the discovery of America. In the mid-16th century G. Ramusio generalized the results of various voyages and discoveries in the three-volume work *Collected Travels.*

From the 15th century men in the applied arts and sciences played a greater role in the development of science. The artists P. Uccello and Masaccio elaborated a theory of perspective, and the architect and engineer F. Brunelleschi wrote treatises on applied optics, mechanics, and mathematics. Characteristic of science in Italy during this epoch was its association with art. The unity of science and art was strikingly embodied in the work of Leonardo da Vinci—scientist, engineer, artist, and author of a great deal of research in mechanics, optics, anatomy, botany, and other branches of science.

The needs of construction, military affairs, hydraulic engineering, and various production lines, including textiles (Florence), glass (Venice), and metalworking (Milan), promoted the development of the applied sciences in the latter half of the 15th century and in the 16th. In 1540, V. Biringuccio's *Concerning Pyrotechnics,* one of the first works on applied chemistry, appeared. C. Piccolpasso's *Three Books About the Potter's Art* was published in 1548 and G. della Porta's *Natural Magic,* an unusual encyclopedia of the knowledge of that time in chemistry, optics, and magnetism, in 1558. Applied mathematics and mechanics began to flourish. The author of a treatise on architecture and fortification. F. di Giorgio Martini, as well as the painter and mathematician P. della Francesca and the mathematician L. Pacioli, the author of *The Foundations of Arithmetic* (1494), worked in the city of Urbino, which was also the home of F. Commandino, who translated Archimedes, Pappus, and other Greek authors and did research on the centers of gravity of bodies. His pupil Guidubaldo dal Monte and the mathematician B. Baldi also lived in Urbino. S. del Ferro, who was a professor at the University of Bologna from 1496, surpassed the achievements of his predecessors in algebra, investigating particular cases of cubic equations. However, he did not publish his results, and some time later, N. Tartaglia and G. Cardano arrived at the same conclusions. In the work *Algebra* (1572), R. Bombelli provided the first basis for the simplest operations with complex numbers.

Translations done by the bridge builder and hydraulic engineer G. Giocondo, who published works by Vitruvius and Frontinus, and by the engineer, cosmographer, and optician F. Maurolico, who translated such authors as Archimedes, Apollonius, and Theodosius, played an important role in the development of science during this period in Italy. J. Scaliger published the works of Aristotle on zoology and Theophrastus' works on botany.

In many ways the birth of the science of geology is associated with the Italian Renaissance. Leonardo da Vinci, whose work included the designing and construction of canals, established the organic origin of mineral remnants that had been deposited when the seas receded from the land. In the 16th century similar conclusions were reached by G. Fracastoro, Cardano, and A. Cesalpino. Geology as the science of the earth figured in the works of U. Aldrovandi in the late 16th century. Subsequently, geology was dominated for two centuries by diluvianist views, according to which fossils had originated as a result of a universal flood. Fracastoro was virtually the first to oppose these views.

Anatomy, physiology, and medicine underwent substantial development. Not confining themselves to disseminating the works of the classical authors, researchers introduced into practice precise experimentation, in particular, the dissection of cadavers. The founder of this school of experimentation was Mundinus of Bologna (early 14th century), whose *Anatomy* long remained the only guide for students sanctioned by the church. Leonardo da Vinci played a great role in the development of biology. In his study of the human body detailed anatomical and physiological observations were inextricably intertwined, and he applied many of the principles of mechanics to them. The versatile scientist Fracastoro became famous as the author of *On Contagion* (1546), which rejected the view that "infections" caused contagious diseases and proposed instead that they were transmitted by invisible particles.

The founder of scientific anatomy, the Fleming A. Vesalius, compiled during his years in Italy (1537–43) the famous work *On the Structure of the Human Body.* Vesalius laid the foundation for the revision of Galen's ideas. He also introduced a new method of instruction that used anatomical specimens. J. Berengario da Carpi, G. Fallopius, B. Eustachio (Rome), and G. Aselli (Pavia) contributed a great deal to the development of the science of anatomy. M. Severinus (Naples) was among the founders of the science of the comparative anatomy of animals. A pupil of Fallopius, H. Fabricius of Aquapendente, began to work on anatomical problems and went on to do research on the functions of organs. He also worked in embryology.

The geographic discoveries of the late 15th and early 16th centuries played an enormous role in the development of biology. In addition to descriptions of plants, the first scientific classifications appeared. Cesalpino, who was a direct predecessor of Linnaeus, based his system of classification on an objective criterion —the structure and character of a plant's reproductive organs. Aldrovandi founded a botanical garden and established the largest archaeological and natural history museum of his time.

THE PERIOD OF THE CREATION OF THE FOUNDATIONS OF MODERN SCIENCE (LATE 16TH CENTURY TO THE LATE 18TH). Beginning in the late 16th century, Italian science was the most advanced in Europe. The philosopher and scientist G. Bruno, who developed Copernicus' heliocentric theory, fought against Scholasticism. The works of the Italian scientist Galileo were of enormous importance for all the natural sciences and especially for the affirmation of the heliocentric theory. The telescope designed by Galileo opened a new era in astronomy, and his work promoted the development of a trend toward experimentation in the natural sciences. Academies (created in Italy in the 16th and 17th centuries), which operated independently of the universities, promoted the development of new views in the natural sciences. The Telesian Academy (Naples), which was named for the philosopher and scientist B. Telesio, contributed a great deal to the struggle against scholastic Aristotelianism. Founded in 1603 in Rome, the Academy of Lincei (today the National Academy of Lincei) brought together outstanding experimenters, including Galileo, who participated in its work. The traditions established by Galileo were also supported by Florence's Academy del Cimento, which was founded in 1657. Its members included F. Redi, who proved the untenability of the idea of the spontaneous generation of life, the Dane N. Steno, one of the founders of crystallography and geology, the astronomer G. Cassini, and Galileo's pupil Viviani. Other pupils of Galileo who rendered considerable services to the development of science include B. Castelli, who did work in hydraulic engineering, F. B. Cavalieri, who developed Archimedes' methods of integration, and E. Torricelli, who discovered atmospheric pressure, invented a mercury barometer and an improved microscope, and elaborated an infinitesimal calculus.

In the 17th century iatrophysics (or iatromechanics), a current in biology, took shape in Italy. S. Sanctorius, a native of the Balkan Peninsula who worked in Italy as a physician, attempted to bring into medicine physical methods of studying metabolism and respiration (for example, weighing). G. Borelli published the two-volume work *On the Movement of Animals* (1680–81) and worked out problems in anatomy and physiology from the standpoint of mechanics and mathematics. His pupil L. Bellini discovered the role of the diaphragm in breathing and attempted to explain the function of the kidneys in terms of mechanics. M. Malpighi, an anatomist, used new methods, including microscopy, to study the structure of the organs of plants and animals. He was the first to describe the capillaries as the components of the circulatory system that link the veins and arteries.

In the 17th and 18th centuries, with the political fragmentation and economic decline of the Italian states and later, with the imposition of Austrian rule, Italian science lost its leading position in Europe. After the trials of Galileo, Catholic reactionaries encouraged attempts to interpret new discoveries from the standpoint of traditional Aristotelianism. Thus, for example,

F. Grimaldi's discovery of the diffraction of light did not receive an adequate interpretation. The results of an experimental verification of Galileo's laws of falling bodies, which was conducted by G. Riccioli, were not correctly evaluated. The developing biological sciences were basically descriptive. The works of G. Morgagni, the founder of pathological anatomy, G. Baglivi, who established the difference between smooth and striated muscles, A. Cocchi, the founder of the Florentine Botanical Society, and F. Fontana, a well-known pneumochemist, were of outstanding importance. Following up on Redi's work, L. Spallanzani conducted a series of experiments involving the heating of sealed containers and refuted the theory of the spontaneous generation of even microscopic organisms. The first to succeed in artificially fertilizing mammals, Spallanzani also investigated fertilization among amphibians, experimentally proving the role of sperm in this process.

In the early 18th century, A. Vallisneri advanced a criticism of the theological interpretations of the history of the earth (specifically, the diluvianist notions of English authors), compiling a general survey of sedimentary stratifications in Italy. A. L. Moro, a follower of Vallisneri, studied volcanic activity and earthquakes. His *Theory of the Earth* was commented on by C. Generelli, who developed the concept of continual mountain formation. Marine geology originated in the 18th century with the work of Marsigli and V. Donati. River erosion as the cause of the origin of valleys was investigated by Targioni. In 1759, G. Arduino subdivided all of Italy's geologic formations into Primary, Secondary, Tertiary, and Quaternary, thus laying the basis for a stratigraphic scale for the whole world. The first attempts to make use of paleontological remains to establish the relative age of the strata containing them date to the late 18th century (the work of Soldani).

In the first half of the 18th century the mathematician J. Riccati worked on the theory of differential equations. G. Gugliemini, who was trying to prove that the earth rotated, continued to do experiments on free-falling bodies in the late 18th century. From the 1740's to the 1760's, R. Bošković, a Croat, did scientific work in Italy, measuring the force of gravity and explaining gravitational anomalies. The classic works on electricity by L. Galvani and A. Volta date to the end of the 18th century. However, during this period Italian science failed to develop applied research sufficiently.

19TH CENTURY. In the first half of the 19th century a trend toward the unification of scientific forces emerged in Italy. The first congress of Italian naturalists, which was held in Pisa in 1839, was interpreted as a call for the unification of the country. In the same year the Italian Society to Promote Progress in the Sciences was founded in Rome. Between 1839 and 1847 congresses of naturalists were convened annually. After 1847 the congresses were not resumed until 1862, and until 1907, when the National Academic Association for Progress in Science was founded, they were not held regularly.

After Italy was unified, regular meteorological observations were undertaken for the first time. Many institutions of nationwide importance were organized. An observatory on Vesuvius that had been founded in 1841 was already operating at the time of Italy's unification. (It was headed by the physicist M. Melloni and later, by L. Palmieri.) In 1872 the Topographic Military Institute (later, the Geographic Military Institute) was established, in 1867, the Italian Geographical Society, and in 1876 in Rome, the Medical Academy. The Geological Society was founded in 1881 and in 1893, the Italian Anthropological Institute.

In the first half of the 19th century the works of only a few Italian scientists were outstanding. A. Avogadro, who in 1811 established the law that is named after him, made contributions that were extremely important for the elaboration of the theoretical foundations of chemistry as well as physics. Important research on fermentation was done by G. Fabroni. L. Brugnatelli, the publisher of the first Italian chemistry journals, was a versatile chemist. Giovanni Battista Amici perfected the microscope, and P. Ruffini, a mathematician, advanced new ideas that influenced the development of algebra. Earlier, G. Saccheri had published works in which he tried to substantiate Euclid's postulate on parallel lines. S. Breislak, a prominent Italian geolo-

gist of the first quarter of the 19th century, conducted regional research, primarily on Italy's volcanic areas. The works of the geologist and paleontologist G. Brocchi, who, in opposition to the theory of catastrophism, put forth the idea that species and genera of organisms of the past had "aged" and "died" naturally, were of great significance.

In the second half of the 19th century, Italian scientists made major achievements in chemistry and electrical engineering. A number of them won international fame. The chemist S. Cannizzaro introduced a clear concept of the molecule and revised the system of atomic weights. The research of the astronomers Schiaparelli and A. Secchi was substantial. Outstanding among Italian organic chemists were R. Nasini, L. L. Chiozza, C. Bertagnini, R. Piria, A. Sobrero, and I. Guareschi. A pupil of Wöhler, M. Schiff—the author of numerous chemical syntheses—worked in Florence. G. Pellizzari, a pupil of Schiff, discovered urazole. Among Italy's major physicists and electrical engineers during the period were R. Felici, A. Pacinotti, one of the inventors of the dynamo, and G. Ferraris, who discovered the revolving magnetic field. Palmieri built an "earth-electrical circle"—a prototype of an alternating-current generator (1845). A. Meucci obtained a patent for the invention of the telephone, and A. Righi created a generator for centimetric waves. In 1896, G. Marconi started work on radiotelegraphy, for which he received the Nobel Prize in 1909. The spread of Darwinism promoted the development in the late 19th century of research on the taxonomy and phylogeny of all known groups of animals. Outstanding work was done by the zoologists O. and A. Costa, G. B. Grassi, D. Rosa, P. Panceri, A. Della Valle, and A. Andres. In 1873 the Naples Hydrobiological (Zoological) Station, which attracted scientists from other countries, was founded. The science of anatomy continued to develop. A. Corti investigated the structure and function of the hearing apparatus of mammals, discovering the organ that was named for him. F. Pacini studied the retina of the eye and exteroceptors.

20TH CENTURY. In the period of imperialism, particularly under fascism, Italian science was influenced by the militarization of the country. Mathematical research has become more important in the 20th century. G. Veronese contributed a great deal to the development of geometry, and V. Volterra elaborated a theory of integral equations and laid the foundation for functional analysis. Curbastro G. Ricci and his pupils, especially T. Levi-Civita, elaborated tensor calculus. The works of L. Bianchi, F. Brioschi, E. Beltrami, and F. Casorati are well known. Also among Italy's distinguished mathematicians of the 20th century are L. Cremona, who published works in algebraic geometry, graphostatics, and descriptive geometry, and G. Peano, who worked on differential equations, the logical foundations of mathematics, and the axiomatic method, which is important in modern mathematics. The works of G. Fubini (1907) supplemented the first results on multiple integrals achieved by H. Lebesgue.

One of the modern schools of the theory of differential equations was inspired by a monograph by C. Carathéodory (1918) on the theory of the functions of a real variable. (Among the members of this school were R. Cacciopoli, Levi-Civita, G. Sansone, G. Scorza-Dragoni, and F. Tricomi.) Characteristic of this school is an interest in nonlinear problems. Algebraic geometry developed from other modern currents. Systematic research on the geometric properties of algebraic manifolds was done by a number of Italian mathematicians, including B. Segre, C. Severi, and A. Andreotti. In the 1960's new works oriented toward applied mathematics appeared, especially in the solution of problems of aerodynamics (L. Napolitano, 1966) and the theory of optimum management (L. Cesari). In the 1920's, U. Nobile built the airships *Norge* (1923) and *Italia* (1927).

In physics the most significant achievements have been in research on cosmic radiation and on quantum and nuclear physics. D. Pacini discovered the extraterrestrial origin of cosmic rays, and in 1933, B. Rossi established the complex character of cosmic radiation. E. Fermi made a major contribution to quantum theory. In 1934 he elaborated a quantitative theory of beta decay, and between 1934 and 1938 he and his pupils E. Amaldi, O. d'Agostino, B. Pontecorvo, and F. Rasetti made major experimental and theoretical discoveries in neutron physics, for which Fermi received the Nobel Prize in 1938. Fermi emigrated to the USA in 1938, and in 1942 he achieved the first self-sustaining nuclear chain reaction. After World War II, Amaldi and his colleagues did a variety of research projects in high-energy physics. G. Natta, who discovered stereoregular polymers, shared the Nobel Prize in 1963 with the German chemist K. Ziegler.

In the early 20th century the study of the anatomy and physiology of the nervous system developed a great deal. Progress in neurohistology is associated with C. Golgi, who laid the foundation of neuron theory (Nobel Prize, 1906) and discovered the intracellular organoid named for him (the Golgi complex). D. Bovet synthesized curare (Nobel Prize, 1957). Great contributions to the development of medicine were made by the pathologic anatomists E. Bizzozero and G. Banti, the microbiologists and epidemiologists D. Grassi and A. Ascoli, the surgeons G. C. Dogliotti and P. Valdoni, and the medical historians A. Castiglioni and Pacini.

In regional geology, Italian scientists attach great importance to the problem of the structure of the Alps and the Apennines. Volcanology is developing along traditional lines. In the study of minerals, works on the geology of mercury deposits have been outstanding. Geographic research aims at the integrated study of the Mediterranean. Italy's meteorology and geophysics hold a notable place in world science.

I. V. KRUT' (earth sciences), V. I. NAZAROV (biology), VASCO RONCHI ([Italy;] physics; science of the Middle Ages and the Renaissance), N. I. SIMONOV (mathematics), and A. N. SHAMIN (chemistry)

Social sciences. PHILOSOPHY. Until the late Middle Ages, Italian philosophy developed within the general framework of European medieval thought. Such major representatives of medieval philosophy as Peter Damian, Lanfranc, Anselm of Canterbury, Peter Lombard, and Thomas Aquinas were born in Italy, but they did most of their work outside their native land. The mystical doctrines of Arnold of Brescia and Joachim of Fiore reveal how strongly these thinkers were tied to Italy. Essentially, Italian philosophy began to take shape in the 13th and 14th centuries. An important role in its development was played by the universities of Bologna and Padua. The latter became the center of Averroist Aristotelianism (represented by Peter of Abano, for example), which is associated with the development of the doctrine of dual truth—philosophical and religious (Marsiglio of Padua).

During the Renaissance, Italian philosophy played a leading role in the development of European philosophy. Renaissance thought as a whole was imbued with ideas of humanism (in the broad sense of the word), which was initially pitted against late Scholasticism by such writers as Petrarch and Boccaccio. The philosophy of the Renaissance was still poorly defined within the culture of the period, and it lacked a clear-cut awareness of its specific subject matter and methods. In most instances, philosophy failed to set itself apart from theology, magic, the new experimental sciences, and the theory of art. The overall humanist fascination with the wisdom of the classics embraced tendencies to revive doctrines that were incompatible with the Christian world view, in particular, Epicureanism. Although materialistic and atheistic ideas had a powerful effect on the Renaissance (for example, in the works of G. C. Vanini), they were, on the whole, merely tendencies and aspects of various idealistic concepts. In the shaping of new moral and political principles a special place is held by Machiavelli, who affirmed the autonomous significance of "reasons of state" and their independence from any moral and religious foundation, and who put forth the ideal of the strong man who is called upon to triumph over blind "fate" by means of his "virtue." Machiavelli's ideas had a great deal of influence not only on the thinkers of his age but also on the sociological concepts of modern times.

In their philosophical constructions the humanists were somewhat influenced by Augustine and Eastern patrology, but they relied on the traditions of Platonism, attempting to synthesize them with Christian dogma (M. Ficino, Pico della Mirandola, and the work of the Platonic Academy in Florence). A turn toward Neoplatonism and esoteric doctrines such as the Cabala led to the propagation of occult sciences, including astrology and alchemy. This fascination with "magical sciences" gave birth to Italian natural philosophy (philosophy of nature) of the Renaissance, which reached its high point in G. Bruno. (Among its other representatives were G. Cardano, B. Telesio, F. Patrizi, and T. Campanella.) Imbued with pantheistic attitudes and hylozoism, the natural philosophy of the Renaissance affirmed the unity and hierarchical order of the world, where everything—from the sphere of the spirit to the sphere of the lowest creatures and matter itself—is permeated with "sympathetic" ties of substantive affinity. The ideal of the human magus who discovers the lawlike regularity of hidden forces and therefore controls the elements grew out of the idea of the unity of man (the microcosm) and nature (the macrocosm). The natural philosophers' aspirations to magical powers promoted the development of experimental knowledge and experimental natural science. Materialistic tendencies in the Italian philosophy of the Renaissance reached their highest development with P. Pomponazzi, who was, on the whole, an Aristotelian.

During the second half of the 17th century and the 18th, Italian philosophical thought declined—there were neither schools of philosophy nor influential philosophical currents. G. Vico, one of the founders of historicism in modern European philosophy and a precursor of Herder and Hegel, was an exception. He set forth a theory of a historical cycle—a cyclical development of nations—and provided philosophy with an example of the integral interpretation of various forms of spiritual culture and social life as a definite historical unity.

Various currents in Catholic thought—particularly, the doctrines of A. Rosmini-Serbati and V. Gioberti—prevailed in early 19th-century Italian philosophy. Influenced to a certain extent by Kant, Rosmini-Serbati and Gioberti argued against the Hegelian dialectic. Many of the progressive thinkers who emerged between the 1830's and the 1860's, including C. Pisacane, C. Cattaneo, and G. Ferrari, belonged to the democratic wing of the national liberation movement. Between the 1850's and the 1870's the most significant philosophical current was Neapolitan Hegelianism. A. Vera belonged to its right wing and B. Spaventa and F. De Sanctis, to its left wing. Characteristic of the left-wing Neapolitan Hegelians were an enlightened, humanistic, anticlerical orientation and a striving to overcome a dogmatic interpretation of Hegel. Because of its ambiguous quality, Neapolitan Hegelianism became one of the ideological sources of both Italian Marxism and Italian neo-Hegelianism. In the last decades of the 19th century Italian thought was dominated by positivism, a motley, basically unoriginal phenomenon whose most famous spokesman was R. Ardigò. Highly influential in the subsequent development of bourgeois sociological thought were a number of V. Pareto's concepts, such as the functionalist doctrine of "social equilibrium" and the theory of the circulation of elites.

In the early 20th century the subjective-idealist and objective-idealist forms of neo-Hegelian idealism, whose most important representatives were G. Gentile and B. Croce, respectively, achieved the dominant positions in Italian thought. The Italian neo-Hegelians developed the conservative aspects of Neapolitan Hegelianism. Considering Hegel's idealism insufficiently consistent, they saw as their task the liberation of Hegel's theory from "an erroneous idea of nature" and its transformation into "a pure philosophy of the spirit." Italian neo-Hegelianism, which took shape through a continuous struggle with Marxism, developed in the direction of Catholic spiritualism. From the mid-1920's Italy's official state ideology was fascism. However, fascism failed to create a philosophical system, although it borrowed from numerous sources, including religious-mystical, irrationalist, positivist, neo-Hegelian, and syndicalist thought. Neo-Hegelianism ceased to be the leading current in Italian philosophy in the 1940's. Croce did not establish a philosophical school. The influence of Gentile, who had supported fascism, continued to be highly significant. His followers split into two groups: the left-wing Gentilians (Ugo Spirito and G. Calogero), who put forth the principle of the "problematic" quality of the relativity of any philosophical solution, and the right-wing Gentilians, a more numerous and influential group whose members included, in particular, representatives of Christian spiritualism (for example, M. F. Sciacca and A. Carlini), which linked elements of Gentile's system with the ideas of Plato, Augustine, and Rosmini. In contrast to Thomism—the official philosophy of the Catholic Church—Christian spiritualism focuses on self-consciousness and its discovery on the path to god. Thomism is a very widely held philosophy in Italy. (Among the country's most distinguished Thomists are F. Olgiati, C. Giacon, U. Padovani, and G. Bontadini.) Representatives of the basic currents of Italian religious philosophy are united in the Gallarate Movement, which was founded in 1945. Congresses of its members are held annually.

After World War II existentialism developed considerably in Italy. E. Castelli is the chief representative of Christian existentialism. The founder of positive existentialism, N. Abbagnano, tried to overcome the pessimism and negativism of classic existentialism by connecting it with neopositivism and ethical formalism. A number of thinkers have been seeking paths from abstract humanism to Marxism. In this context the concepts of E. Paci and especially E. Garin, a prominent historian of philosophy, are of interest.

In the last third of the 19th century the ideas of Marx and Engels spread through Italy. Beginning with A. Labriola, an original Marxist thinker of the late 19th century, Italian Marxist philosophical thought was oriented chiefly toward elaborating the problems of historical materialism and the theory of scientific socialism. The ideological legacy of A. Gramsci, the founder of the Italian Communist Party, who consistently upheld and developed Marxist-Leninist theory, had a great influence on all of Italian culture and philosophical thought in the postwar period. Gramsci's followers—P. Togliatti and many modern Marxist researchers—have paid special attention to problems associated with the concept of "the Italian path to socialism." The works of A. Banfi, G. Della Volpe, and L. Lombardo-Radice focus on dialectical materialism, the theory of knowledge, logic, and the philosophy of natural science. Italian Marxists have done research on aesthetics, including criticism of bourgeois aesthetics, problems of the artistic method, and the history of aesthetic ideas. The Gramsci Institute (founded in 1949) is the center of Marxist thought.

The main centers of philosophical inquiry are the Institute of Philosophy at the University of Rome (founded in 1939), the Italian Society of Philosophical and Religious Research, and the Italian Society of Sociology (founded in 1937). Among the journals of philosophy published in Italy are *Archivio di filosofia* (since 1931), *De Homine* (since 1961), *Critica* (1903–44; called *Quaderni della critica* since 1945), *Filosofia* (since 1950), and *Giornale di metafisica* (since 1946). Other Italian philosophy journals are *Giornale critico della filosofia italiano* (since 1920), *Il Pensiero* (since 1956), *Rivista critica di storia della filosofia* (since 1946), *Rivista di filosofia* (since 1909), *Rivista di filosofia neo-scolastica* (since 1909), *Sophia* (since 1933), and *Sapienza* (since 1948). Published since 1963, the journal *Critica Marxista* focuses on questions of Marxist philosophy.

N. V. KOTRELEV (to the 19th century) and
S. A. EFIROV (from the 19th century)

HISTORY. The principal historical works of the early Middle Ages in Italy were the *Historia Gothica* by Cassiodorus (sixth century), which survived in a retelling by Jordanes, the *History of the Lombards* by Paul the Deacon (eighth century), and the historical works of Liutprand. With the growth of cities, medieval historical scholarship began to flourish in Italy. From the 11th to the 13th century numerous city chronicles were written: in Milan, by Arnulf and Landulph, in Genoa, by Caffaro, and in Modena, Parma, and other cities, by Salimbene. Among the many monastery chronicles of the period was the chronicle of Monte Cassino, which was written by many scholars, including Leo Marsicanus. Historical works by such scholars as Godfrey of Viterbo, Hugo Falcandus, and Landulph also date to this period. Chronicles on all of Italy were written by the Florentines Dino Compagni and Giovanni Villani in the 14th century.

Italian historical scholarship of the Renaissance abandoned theological historical concepts, began to criticize historical sources scientifically, and adopted a realistic approach to the analysis of historical events. Prominent representatives of the humanistic historiography of 15th-century Italy were Leonardo Bruni, G. F. Poggio Bracciolini, and Flavio Biondo. Lorenzo

Valla, who exposed the spurious Donation of Constantine, is considered the founder of the critical method. The principles of humanist historiography were most fully developed in the works of the major historians of the 16th century—Machiavelli, who was the first to emphasize the connection between the history of a state's foreign and domestic policies, and Guicciardini, who described the economic and political crisis in Italy around the beginning of the 16th century.

In the 17th century, Italian historiography entered a period of decline associated with the feudal and Catholic reaction. The main trend in 18th-century historiography was the collection, criticism, and publication of sources. L. A. Muratori's publications were the most significant of the period.

The shaping of bourgeois historical scholarship in Italy was associated with the ideas of the Enlightenment as well as with the ideological needs of the developing national movement. In the first decades of the 19th century a number of encyclopedic works were written by historians such as C. Troya, G. Capponi, and C. Cantù. The neo-Guelphs, a liberal Catholic school, prevailed. Their main spokesmen—Troya, Capponi, and Cesare Balbo—investigated primarily the problems of Italian medieval history. In the struggle of the communes and the papacy against foreign emperors they saw the prototype of the modern national movement. The neo-Guelphs were opposed by the Ghibelline school (G. B. Niccolini, A. Ranieri, A. Vannucci, and G. La Farina), which based its thought on Machiavelli's political and anticlerical ideas. Both schools disappeared after the Revolution of 1848.

The mid-19th century was characterized by a growing interest in socioeconomic history (works by L. Cibrario, L. Bianchini, and E. Poggi). In 1842 the first issue of the first Italian historical journal, *Archivio storico italiano,* was published in Florence. (In 1844 it was also issued in Naples.)

The unification of Italy opened a new stage in the development of historical scholarship. In the 1860's and 1870's numerous societies for the study of domestic history and many general and specialized historical journals were founded. In 1883 the Italian Historical Institute was organized. A great deal of documentary material was published for the first time, and the level of historical research improved. In the late 19th century the leading role was played by the philological school (for example, P. Villari), which had adopted the principles of positivism. Many Italian historians achieved world fame in the late 19th century and the 20th: E. E. Pais, a historian of classical culture, G. Ferrero, a specialist in the history of ancient Rome, and L. Caetani, a specialist in the history of Arabic peoples.

In the early 20th century the legal-economic school (for example, L. Salvemini and G. Volpe), which tried to synthesize historical, legal, and economic scholarship, achieved wide popularity in historiography. Its representatives made a substantial contribution to the study of the history of the Middle Ages. In the same period the ethical-political school, which was founded by B. Croce, began to take shape. It strongly influenced the development of world bourgeois as well as Italian historiography. In opposition to the false claims for the historian's impartiality and the metaphysical and sociological quality of the philological school, Croce presented the thesis of the historical character of everything in existence. However, his historicism was idealistic. Allotting a secondary role to socioeconomic history, Croce contended that the historian's main task was to study the spiritual and religious life of mankind—that is, to elaborate an ethical-political history.

Italy's entry into the epoch of imperialism and the development of an imperialist ideology engendered extremely reactionary tendencies in bourgeois historiography. For example, works by such historians as A. Oriani and E. Corradini were written in the spirit of nationalism and chauvinism. In the early 20th century a certain degree of progress was made by scholars such as G. Prato, L. Einaudi, A. Anzilotti, N. Rodolico, and G. Salvemini in the study of the political, economic, and ideological preconditions for the unification of Italy—the Risorgimento. Under fascist rule (1922–43) a segment of the Italian intelligentsia chose to give their support to fascism. Gentile and Volpe became the official ideologists of the Fascist regime. Because of its interest in developing an ideological justification for its expansionist program, the regime encouraged research in international politics. A number of specialized institutes were established: the Institute of the Middle and Far East, the Institute of Eastern Europe, and the Institute of International Politics.

The history of the Risorgimento and the liberal state to which it gave birth remained one of the main objects of historical study. Fascist historiography was represented by the works of scholars such as Volpe; antifascist historiography, by the works of historians of various political and historiographic backgrounds, including Salvemini and P. Gobetti; and liberal historiography, by Croce, A. Omodeo, and F. Chabod. Historians of an antifascist frame of mind rallied around Croce's journal *Critica* (Naples).

The groundwork for Marxist historiography in Italy was laid by the works of Gramsci and Togliatti. After the defeat of fascism and the end of World War II a strong Marxist current developed in Italian historiography and made a substantial contribution to elaborating, above all, the problems of modern and recent history. As the problems of research became broader and more numerous, many new historical institutes were founded.

After Italy's liberation from the fascist yoke, the reinterpretation of both its recent and its more remote past in the light of new historical experience became a pressing social need. Socioeconomic history and the history of the masses of the working people are well-covered themes in Italy's modern and recent history (for example, works by G. Luzzatto, E. Sereni, L. Dal Pane, L. Bulferetti, R. Villari, and P. Villari). The history of the workers' and socialist movement became an important separate field of scholarly research in the postwar years (for example, the works of Togliatti, A. Colombo, G. Berti, G. Trevisani, G. Manacorda, P. Spriano, G. Procacci, and A. Romano). In the 1950's Catholic historiography became more important in Italy through the work of such scholars as G. Spadolini, G. De Rosa, and A. Jemolo.

The publication of a number of synthesizing works on the history of the country is evidence of the achievements of present-day Italian historiography (for example, *The History of Italy*, vols. 1–5, 1959–60, edited by N. Valeri, and *The History of Modern Italy*, by G. Candeloro, vols. 1–6, 1956–70; Russian translation, vols. 1–5, 1958–71). In the postwar period the most thoroughly studied historical problems have been in the economic history of the Middle Ages, the Renaissance, the Risorgimento, the history of the workers' and socialist movement, and fascism and the antifascist movement. Italy's economy in the epoch of feudalism has been the subject of extensive research by A. Sapori, F. Melis, G. Luzzatto, R. Lopez and C. Cipolla. Questions on the ideology of the Renaissance were thoroughly elaborated in works by E. Garin, P. Rossi, N. Badaloni, and L. Firpo. In the postwar period the most significant works on the history of the Risorgimento were written by F. Della Peruta, G. Quazza, D. De Marco, and R. Romeo. Research on Italian fascism was presented in the works of Marxist historians such as P. Alatri and E. Santarelli, as well as in works by historians of other political and historiographic backgrounds, such as L. Salvatorelli, G. Mira, and R. De Felice. Problems of the Resistance were elaborated by the Marxist scholars and political figures L. Longo and R. Battaglia, the socialist historians F. Catalano, L. Basso, and R. Carli-Ballola, Catholic historians, and historians of other backgrounds.

The most important centers for the study of history are the Italian Institute of Medieval History (founded in 1883), the Institute of the History of the Risorgimento (founded in 1906), the Italian Institute of Classical History (founded in 1930), the Italian Institute of Modern and Recent History (founded in 1934), the Gramsci Institute (founded in 1949), and the G. Feltrinelli Institute (founded in 1949). In addition, the universities and numerous historical societies are important centers for the study of history. The chief history periodicals include *Archivio storico italiano* (since 1842), *Nuova antologia* (since 1866), *Archivio storico lombardo* (since 1874), *Archivio storico per le provincie napoletane* (since 1876), and *Rivista storica italiana* (since 1884). Among the other Italian journals of history are *Rassegna storica del Risorgimento* (since 1914), *Nuova rivista storica* (since 1917), *Civiltà moderna* (since 1929), *Studi storici* (since 1959), and *Critica Marxista* (since 1963).

V. I. Rutenburg, L. M. Bragina, and G. S. Filatov

ECONOMICS. In Italy the shaping of economics as an independent branch of knowledge dates to the mid-18th century. The mercantilists, the most prominent of whom were A. Serra and G. Montanari, attached special importance to the development of the circulation of goods and money, which, in their opinion, had made the greatest contribution to the growth of productive forces under the conditions peculiar to Italy. In their works Enlightenment figures of the late 18th century and the early 19th, including G. Vico, A. Genovesi, L. A. Muratori, and G. R. Carli, developed the ideas of the French encyclopedists, making them applicable to the needs of Italy's socioeconomic and sociopolitical development. An important role in the shaping of Italian economics was played by the founding of Europe's first faculty of political economy at the University of Naples in 1754. Established by Genovesi, it united scholars who made profound contributions to research in economics. The Genovesi school included F. Galiani, an outstanding Italian economist of the second half of the 18th century, who, among other Physiocrats, as Marx noted, approached in more or less apt statements "a correct analysis of commodity" (K. Marx and F. Engels, *Soch.*, 2nd ed., vol. 13, p. 44).

In the second half of the 19th century the development of Italian economics continued to be considerably influenced by the ideas and theories of foreign economists, most of whom were British or French. The doctrines and concepts of economic liberalism and positivism, which agreed most closely with the interests of the growing industrial bourgeoisie, were the prevailing trend. Among its representatives, C. Cattaneo, F. Ferrara, and A. Messedaglia were very successful in elaborating concrete economic problems in statistics, monetary circulation, and demography.

In the 1870's and 1880's the economic theory of Marx became known in Italy. Labriola's works marked the beginning of the development of the Marxist line in Italian economics, and capitalist relations were criticized by a number of writers, including G. Romagnosi, G. Mazzini, and C. Pisacane, who laid the foundation for theories of petit bourgeois socialism in Italy. The works of V. Pareto, who was one of the first to begin devising mathematical methods of analyzing economic processes and phenomena, were an important contribution to the development of economics in the late 19th century. Economic theories that prepared the way for state intervention in economic life (*dirigisme*) became popular in Italy in the late 19th and early 20th centuries. With the establishment of a fascist dictatorship in the country, this trend, whose representatives included C. Ferri and U. Spirito, reached its apogee in corporatist theories that became the official socioeconomic doctrine of the fascist state.

After World War II the development of economics in Italy took on a number of new features. Marxist economic thought, which became one of the most important currents, made an important contribution to the study of the structure and trends of development of the Italian economy and state-monopoly capitalism. (Among the most important representatives of Marxist economic thought are P. Togliatti, L. Longo, R. Grieco, G. Amendola, E. Sereni, and A. Pesenti.) National and international theoretical conferences of Marxist economists held by the Italian Communist Party were particularly important (a national conference on the trends of development of Italian capitalism, Rome, 1965, and a conference on the Italian and world economies, Rome, 1969). The economic thought of the postwar period has also been characterized by the continued influence of *dirigisme*, or the statolist school (from the Italian *stato*, "state"). Its most distinguished representatives include P. Sylos-Labini, N. Andreatta, and S. Lombardini. In addition, bourgeois economics has been using theoretical concepts and methods elaborated by the economic schools of other developed capitalist countries, endeavoring to adapt them to concrete conditions in Italy. The problems of finding means of overcoming interindustrial and regional imbalances in the national economy and of improving efficiency hold an important place in the works of Italian economists of various backgrounds.

Research in economics is done by state institutions, including the National Research Center (founded in the early 1960's), which coordinates research throughout the country, the Central Institute of Statistics (founded in 1926), the Institute for the

Study of Market Conditions (founded in 1957), and the National Institute of Agrarian Economics (founded in 1946). In addition, research is conducted by private institutions such as the Bureau for Study and Research (founded in 1946), which is associated with the Confederation of Italian Industry, and the Association for the Development of Industry in the South (founded in 1946). The university faculties of economics and research centers of the Bank of Italy, the Italian Commercial Bank, and some other state institutions also engage in scientific research.

Economic journals published in Italy are the weekly *Mondo economico* (since 1946), the monthly *Rivista di politica economica* (since 1911), *Moneta e credito* (since 1947), and *Rassegna economica* (since 1946). Articles on economics are also published in the theoretical journals of the Italian Communist Party—*Critica Marxista* (since 1963) and *Politica ed economia* (since 1970).

N. P. VASIL'KOV

JURISPRUDENCE. In the sixth century Justinian's Code became the principal object of study for Italian jurists. The most significant work on international law was a collection of diplomatic documents compiled by Cassiodorus (sixth century), which commented on certain legal norms. Some attention was paid to law in the Scholastic system of education. In the tenth century a school for the teaching of Lombard law was founded in Pavia. (Its most prominent members were Bonifilius, Lanfranc, Valcauso, Wilhelm, and Ugo.) Around the 11th century the Ravenna school of jurists, which studied Roman law, took shape. On the basis of commentaries on such legal documents as Justinian's Code and Institutes, a new school of law developed in Bologna in the late 11th century—the Bolognese school, or the school of glossators, of which Irnerius is considered the founder. His pupils Bulgarus, Martinus, Jacobus and Hugo became well known. The glossators played an important role in the revival of interest in Roman law and the development of juridical knowledge in Europe. Their successors—the commentators, or postglossators—wrote commentaries on the glosses and on Roman law. The most famous of the postglossators were Odofredus, Bartolus, and Baldus. The legists wrote subsequent commentaries on Roman law.

In the Middle Ages the study of ecclesiastical (canon) law underwent considerable development. A collection of canon law was compiled by the Bolognese monk Gratian in 1151 (Gratian's Decree, or Code). The most famous of his followers (the canonists or decretists) was Duranti, a teacher of law in Bologna and Modena who compiled an encyclopedia of law in 1275 (*Speculum iudiciale*). Thomas Aquinas had a substantial influence on the development of legal thought in Italy. (One of the most important parts of his system of thought was the doctrine of the state and society.) The earliest surviving Italian work on criminal law is a 13th-century book by Albertus Gandinus, which was printed in 1491. Works by Giulio Claro and Prosper Farinaccius were also devoted to criminal law. These scholars tried to justify the cruelty of medieval criminal law.

The turn toward antiquity and toward classical models in law and legal thought, which was characteristic of the Renaissance, developed into a revival of Roman law and Roman legal culture. In the 15th and 16th centuries the philological school of jurists, or "the elegant school of jurisprudence" (for example, Budaeus, A. Alciatus, and Cujas) took shape. Its adherents sought to turn from the writing of commentaries on glosses to a direct study of Roman law and Roman history and culture. As a result, Roman law became a substantial component of the overall culture of the Renaissance. Not only legal scholars but also prominent spokesmen for Italian humanism, such as L. Valla and A. Politian, studied Roman law. The first history of Roman law—*On Roman Magistrates, Priests, Legal Scholars, and Law*—was written by Valla's pupil Letus Pomponius.

Machiavelli and Guicciardini left a profound mark on Italian scholarship on the state and law. The utopian socialist Campanella stated a number of progressive ideas on questions of the state and law. In the second half of the 18th century the Italian Enlighteners sharply criticized feudal customs. The jurist G. Filangieri published the book *The Science of Legislation*, which gained fame throughout Europe and exerted some influence on the views of the Russian Decembrists. C. Beccaria, an Italian Enlightenment figure, set forth progressive principles of criminal law.

Among the jurists of the 19th century, P. S. Mancini, the founder of an Italian school of international law, holds a prominent place. His doctrine, which evolved at the time of the movement to unify Italy, influenced the science of international private law.

In the 1870's the anthropological school of criminal law, which is sometimes called Lombrosianism after its founder, the Italian scholar C. Lombroso, emerged. Lombroso's closest followers were R. Garofalo and E. Ferri.

In 19th- and 20th-century Italy, as in other countries, there has been a noticeable effort in all branches of bourgeois jurisprudence to escape from the framework of formal dogmatic methodology, which was characteristic of legal science in the 18th century and the early 19th. The trend away from formal dogmatic methodology emerged first and most clearly in Italy. In state law the juridical school was revamped and modernized with the aid of the institutionalist ideas of such jurists as S. Romano and S. Lessora. (The chief spokesman of the juridical school was V. Orlando, whose major work was *The Principles of Constitutional Law*. It was translated into Russian in 1907.) In the philosophy of law, neo-Kantianism, which had prevailed in the early 20th century, gave way to neo-Hegelianism, whose representatives included G. Del Vecchio. Under fascism, neo-Hegelian jurisprudence appeared in a great variety of forms, such as the political-legal doctrine of G. Gentile, one of the theorists of the fascist regime. The ideas of corporatism spread. After World War II a revived theory of natural law became popular among Italian jurists (for example, A. Passerin d'Entrèves, C. Passarelli, and G. Balladore Pallieri), in both neo-Thomist and secular variations (for example, A. Baratta and S. Cotta). Positivist (N. Bobbio) and neopositivist (U. Scarnelli) currents in law, as well as the sociological school (R. Treves), developed.

In 1945 a center for the study of social defense was founded in Italy on the initative of F. Gramatica. The theory of a "new social defense," which was taught both in Italy and abroad, attracted adherents among jurists of different political orientations. Within the framework of the theory Gramatica led a group of extremists whose members contended that the character of public-safety measures applied by a court should depend not on the character of a criminal act but on the degree to which the behavior of the suspect was antisocial. (In essence, this point of view signifies a total renunciation of the principle of legality in criminal law.)

Some Italian jurists view questions of state science and legal science from a Marxist position. Many important legal problems have been solved in the works of Gramsci, Togliatti, Longo, and other leaders of the Communist Party of Italy, as well as in the party's programmatic documents.

Centers for scientific research in law include the Institute of the History of Italian Law, the Institute of Roman Law, the Institute of Public Law and Political Doctrine (all in Rome), the Juridical Institute (Turin), and the Institute of the History of Law and Roman Law (Milan), as well as the universities, including those in Rome, Turin, and Milan. The most important law journals are *Bollettino dell'Istituto di Diritto Romano* (since 1888), *Giurisprudenza Costituzionale* (since 1956), *Giurisprudenza Italiana* (since 1848), *Rassegna di Diritto Romano* (since 1955), and *Rivista di Scienza Giuridiche* (since 1950).

P. S. GRATSIANSKII

LINGUISTICS. In Italy, linguistic problems such as the classification of languages, the causes of changes within languages, and the relationship between the general literary language and dialects were first touched on in Dante's treatise "Of the Vernacular" (1305). Until the mid-19th century, works about language had a general philological character: dictionaries, grammars, and commentaries on Latin and Italian texts were compiled. In 1582 the Academy of Crusca was established in Florence, and work was begun there on a standard dictionary of the Italian language (1612; 5th ed., 1863–1923). Linguistics took shape as a separate scientific discipline in the late 19th century in connection with the development of the comparative historical description of languages in general and Italian dialects in particular.

The founder of Italian linguistics was G. I. Ascoli, whose works on the classical languages and on Italian dialectology, including "Romansh Dialects" (1873), developed the methods of the Young Grammarians, a German school. Ascoli's followers were the Italian dialectologists C. Salvioni, P. G. Goidànich, and C. Merlo.

Linguistic geography, represented by G. Bertoni's *The Dialects of Italy* (1916) and M. Bartoli's *An Introduction to the New Linguistics* (1925) and *Essays on Areal Linguistics* (1945), was initally influenced by Croce's aesthetic concept of language as an act of individual creativity and was known as neolinguistics. G. Nencioni's book *Idealism and Realism in the Science of Language* (1946) includes criticism of Crocean linguistics from the standpoint of precise methods of research.

Until the mid-20th century, Italian linguistics avoided structural (precise) methods of language study and emphasized instead the description of language as a social phenomenon. In connection with this trend, dialectology, onomasiology, and linguistic geography developed through the work of B. Terracini, Merlo, G. Vidossi, and C. Battisti. Linguistic atlases (G. Bottiglioni and Vidossi) and etymological dictionaries (C. Battisti and G. Alessio) were compiled, general manuals of Indo-European and Romance linguistics were written (V. Pisani, G. Devoto, and C. Tagliavini), and problems of the substratum, lingual shifts, and ethnolinguistics were studied. Works devoted to the language and style of individual writers are also important in contemporary Italian linguistics (G. Folena, F. Mazzoni, and G. Contini). The study of Dante's language, which was begun in the 16th century, is conducted at the Italian Dante Society in Florence. Italian linguists and philologists are focusing attention on problems associated with the standardization of the Italian language, the relationship between the literary language and dialects, and the interaction of functional styles (B. Migliorini, Devoto, T. De Mauro, A. Schiaffini, and Terracini). Migliorini's *The History of the Italian Language* (1960) is a research work that makes generalizations on the history of the Italian language. The Academy of Crusca, which consists of three sectors—Italian philology, grammer, and lexicography—is the research center for the study of the Italian language. The journals of linguistics published in Italy are *Archivio glottologico italiano* (since 1873), *L'Italia dialettale* (since 1924), *Archivium romanicum* (1917–41), *Cultura neolatina* (since 1941), *Studi di filologia italiana* (since 1927), *Lingua nostra* (since 1939), and *Lingua e stile* (since 1966).

T. B. ALISOVA

Scientific institutions. The principal state institution that is responsible for the organization and supervision of research work in all the natural and technical sciences (except problems in atomic energy research) is the National Research Council. Established in 1923, the council has authority over 70 institutes and laboratories (of which 36 conduct fundamental research and 34, applied research) and 108 research centers (of which 78 conduct fundamental research and the rest, applied research). The council also organizes information services and supervises Italy's international scientific ties.

The conduct of research in atomic energy is supervised by the National Committee for Nuclear Energy, which was founded in 1960. It has authority over the National Laboratory at Frascati (a synchrotron and an ionized-gas laboratory), which was founded in 1953, and the Center for Nuclear Studies in Casaccia. The committee is directed by the Ministry of Industry, Commerce, and Artisan Enterprise, which also has authority over the State Electric Power Association, the mining industry's Geological Service and Chemical Service, and nine experimental stations for research on materials such as fuel and cellulose. The universities have many small research institutes with staffs of up to 20, which conduct primarily fundamental research.

The largest center for fundamental research is the National Institute of Nuclear Physics, which integrates the work of all of Italy's research institutions in this field.

Research in the agricultural sciences (for example, agricultural chemistry and bacteriology, soil science, genetics, and plant pathology) is conducted in 22 institutes, which are under the Ministry of Agriculture and Timber. The latter is also in charge of the Central Meteorological Administration, oceanographic institutes, and observatories. The Ministry of Health super-vises the work of laboratories in a number of fields, including biochemistry, pharmacology, biology, microbiology and parasitology, and hygiene and directs the activity of the Higher Institute of Health.

Italian firms have about 700 research institutions that do primarily applied work in metallurgy, chemistry, electronics, aircraft and automobile making, nuclear energy, and aerospace. In 1963 Italy's largest firms (the state association IRI) established the Experimental Metallurgical Center in Rome. With the aid of the IRI group, a research center and laboratory in tele-communications and a center for the study of marine engineering were founded. In 1969 more than 4,000 people were working in centers operating under IRI firms. Fundamental and applied research on petroleum and gas is conducted in the state petroleum and gas association, ENI, whose main centers are unified laboratories near Milan and one near Rome.

Scientific work in organic synthesis based on petrochemistry is also done in the research centers of the Montecatini Edison Company. Substantial work is done in the scientific institutions of the Fiat and SNIA Viscosa companies. However, many firms in Italy do not conduct scientific research, preferring to acquire patents and licenses abroad.

Italy's academies of sciences, scientific societies, and associations do not engage directly in scientific research. Of the science academies, the most significant is the National Academy of Lincei (1603). There are also a number of international research centers in Italy—the Institute of Genetics and Biophysics in Naples, the Center of Theoretical Physics in Trieste, the Center for Mechanics in Udine, and the Center for Nuclear Research in Ispra. Between 1960 and 1969 expenditures for research work in Italy increased from 55 billion to 422,470,000,000 lire—that is, an increase of more than eightfold. Nevertheless, in terms of expenditures for scientific research Italy holds one of the lowest ranks among the European countries.

E. D. TABAKEEV

REFERENCES
Italy. Edited by M. Millet. [Rome, 1970.]
Guareschi, I. *La chemica in Italia dal 1750 al 1800, Suppl. annuale, all'enciclopedia di chimica scientifica tecnologica e industriale,* vol. 25. Turin, 1909. Page 413.
Storia delle scienze, vols. 1–3. Turin, 1965.
Istoriia filosofii, vols. 1–2. Moscow, 1940–41.
Istoriia filosofii, vols. 1, 3, 5. Moscow, 1957–61.
Garin, E. *Khronika ital'ianskoi filosofii 20 v. (1900–1943).* Moscow, 1965. (Translated from Italian.)
Efirov, S. A. *Ital'ianskaia burzhuaznaia filosofiia 20 v.* Moscow, 1968.
Gentile, G. *Le origini della filosofia contemporanea in Italia,* vols. 1–4. Messina, 1917–23.
Sciacca, M. F. *La philosophie italienne contemporaine.* Paris [1953].
Saitta, G. *Il pensiero italiano nell'umanesimo e nel Rinascimento,* vols. 1–3. Bologna, 1949–51.
La filosofia contemporanea in Italia, vols. 1–2. Rome, 1958.
Garin, E. *L'umanesimo italiano,* 2nd ed. Bari, 1965.
Garin, E. *La cultura filosofica del Rinascimento italiano.* Florence, 1961.
Garin, E. *Storia della filosofia italiana* [2nd ed.], vols. 1–3. Turin, 1966.
Garin, E. *Cronache di filosofia italiana. 1900–1943.* [Bari] 1966. (*Quindici anni dopo 1945–1960,* vols. 1–2.)
Lombardi, F. *La filosofia italiana negli ultimi cento anni.* Rome [1959].
Marciano, F. E. *Storia della filosofia italiana.* Rome, 1959.
Vainshtein, O. L. *Zapadnoevropeiskaia srednevekovaia istoriografiia.* Moscow-Leningrad, 1964.
Istoriografiia novogo vremeni stran Evropy i Ameriki. Moscow, 1967.
Istoriografiia novoi i noveishei istorii stran Evropy i Ameriki. Moscow, 1968.
Croce, B. *Storia della storiografia italiana . . . ,* 2nd ed., vols. 1–2. Bari, 1930.
Maturi, W. *Interpretazioni del Risorgimento.* Turin, 1962.
La storiografia italiana negli ultimi vent'anni, vols. 1–2. Milan, 1970.
Fanfani, A. *Le origini dello spirito capitalistico in Italia.* Milan, 1933.
Un secolo di progresso scientifico italiano, 1839–1939, vols. 1–6. Rome [1939].

Press, radio, and television

As of 1974, the most influential bourgeois newspapers included *Corriere della Sera,* the newspaper of Lombard industrialists (published in Milan since 1876; circulation, 600,000), *La Stampa,* which is owned by the Fiat concern (published since

1866 in Turin; circulation, 404,000), and *Il Messaggero* (published in Rome since 1878; circulation, 350,000 on weekdays and up to 1 million on holidays or in connection with major political events). Other major bourgeois newspapers are *Il Giorno,* which is connected with the ENI (published since 1956 in Milan; circulation, 230,000), and *La Nazione* (published in Florence since 1859; circulation, 250,000).

Since 1924 the Communist Party has published both Rome and Milan editions of *L'Unità* (circulation, about 600,000), as well as the journals *Rinascita* (since 1944) and *Critica Marxista.* Local federations of the Communist Party publish weekly or biweekly newspapers.

The organ of the Italian Socialist Party is *L'Avanti,* which has been published in Rome and Milan since 1896 (circulation, about 190,000). The newspaper *Il Popolo* (circulation, 106,000), which has been published in Rome since 1944, is the organ of the Christian Democratic Party. *Paese Sera,* a progressive evening newspaper, enjoys wide popularity in Rome. Published since 1949, it has a circulation of about 180,500.

Radio broadcasts have been transmitted in Italy since Oct. 6, 1924, when a radio station went into operation in Rome. Television broadcasting began on a national channel in 1954 and on a second channel in 1961. Broadcasts are in Italian. There are four radio and television centers in Italy, located in Rome, Milan, Naples, and Turin.

Most domestic broadcasts are in Italian. (There are three main channels and numerous local ones.) In addition, there are broadcasts in German for the minority living in the Trentino–Alto Adige region (the Southern Tirol) and in Slovenian (for the regions adjoining Trieste). Broadcasts are beamed abroad in 22 languages. Radio and television are under the authority of the joint-stock company Radiotelevisione Italiana (RAI-TV), which is controlled by the state.   A. L. ADAMISHIN

Literature

Examples of early Italian folklore have not been preserved. Italian medieval literature developed after the fall of the Roman Empire. Between the sixth and 12th centuries it consisted chiefly of religious hymns, legends, and chronicles, all of them written in Latin. The rapid growth of cities promoted the appearance of literary works in national dialects in the late 12th century and the early 13th (narrative religious poetry and secular and religious lyric poetry). In the first half of the 13th century a Sicilian school of poetry took shape, which imitated the Provençal troubadours (Jacopo da Lentini, died 1233). Associated with a struggle among the cities of Tuscany was the rise of lyric political poetry (for example, Guittone d'Arezzo, c. 1230–c. 1294) and allegorical-didactic poetry (Brunetto Latini, c. 1220–c. 1294). The best example of 13th-century prose is an anonymous collection of short stories in the Tuscan dialect, *Il Novellino.*

At the end of the 13th century a new type of philosophical poetry developed—the *dolce stil nuovo* (sweet new style), which sang the praises of courtly love and illuminated the psychology of the lover—for example, in the works of the Bolognese poet G. Guinizelli (born 1230–40; died 1276) and the Florentine poets G. Cavalcanti (born 1255 or 1259; died 1300) and the young Dante. With its questioning of the estate system and glorification of human emotion, *dolce stil nuovo* poetry belongs to the pre-Renaissance.

The creator of a unified literary language in Italy was Dante Alighieri (1265–1321)—"the last poet of the Middle Ages and . . . the first poet of modern times" (F. Engels, in K. Marx and F. Engels, *Soch.,* 2nd ed., vol. 22, p. 382). His principal works were the novella "The New Life" (1292), which extolled his love for Beatrice, and the poem *The Comedy* (completed in 1321; called *The Divine Comedy* by the end of the 14th century), one of the greatest works of world literature, which posed problems of the author's time—moral, theological, and political—and portrayed human feelings and sufferings with enormous artistic power.

In Italy, the cradle of the Renaissance (14th–16th centuries), the ground for the literature of the period was prepared by the economic development of cities, by lively commercial ties with other countries, and by the overall growth of secular culture.

Characteristic of the literature of the Renaissance were a humanist world view, questioning of the estate system, buoyant free-thinking, a lofty notion of the potential of the human personality, and a fascination with antiquity. F. Petrarch (1304–74), the first lyric poet of the Renaissance, wrote the collection of verses *Canzoniere* (1470), which sang of his earthly love for Laura and delicately brought out the nuances of the emotion of love. In his poetry and prose—particularly the *Decameron* (published in 1471), a collection of short stories pervaded by anticlericalism, and the novella *Fiammetta* (published in 1472)—Boccaccio affirmed a new humanistic morality, praised the free active person, and rejected asceticism.

In the 15th century Renaissance ideas were developed in the works of the humanist scholars—philologists and philosopher-writers who studied antiquity and wrote in Latin, including G. F. P. Bracciolini (1380–1459), who wrote facetiae, L. B. Alberti (1404–72), and L. Valla (1407–57). An attempt to bring "scholarly humanism" closer to folk poetry was made by Florentine poets of the Medici circle: Lorenzo de' Medici (1449–92), the ruler of Florence; A. Poliziano (1454–94), who created the lyric drama *The Story of Orpheus* (staged in 1480); and especially L. Pulci (1432–84), author of the comic poem *Morgante Maggiore* (1480). A humanist world view permeates *Orlando in Love* (published in 1495), an unfinished chivalrous poem by M. Boiardo (1441–94), and the pastoral novel *Arcadia* (1504) by the Neapolitan J. Sannazaro (1455–1530), who influenced the development of the European pastoral of the 16th and 17th centuries.

In the first half of the 16th century the Italian Renaissance flowered. A unified literary language was established. At the end of the 16th century the incipient economic and political decline and the general feudal and Catholic reaction led to a crisis in humanism that affected the content of literature.

A number of genres developed. L. Ariosto (1474–1533), a native of Ferrara, wrote the poem *Orlando Enraged* (1516), a continuation of Boiardo's *Orlando in Love.* Imbued with love for earthly life, it ridiculed medieval notions and intertwined fantastic motifs with irony. In such works as *The Case,* Ariosto created the Italian comedy of manners. The development of comedy took a satiric turn in works by Machiavelli (1469–1527; *La Mandragola*), P. Aretino (1492–1556), and the philosopher G. Bruno (1548–1600; *The Candlestick,* 1582). The pastoral drama, a new genre that idealized reality, was originated by T. Tasso (1544–95; the *Aminta,* 1573) and G. B. Guarini (1538–1612; *The Faithful Shepherd,* staged in 1590).

Among the works of 16th-century prose fiction, which was gradually losing its anti-estate and anticlerical character, were *The Courtier* (1528) by B. Castiglione (1478–1529), the memoirs of Benvenuto Cellini (1500–71), and short stories by such writers as A. Firenzuola (1493–1543) and M. Bandello (c. 1485–1561). Lyric poetry was dominated by the epigones of Petrarch, who were led by the philologist and poet P. Bembo (1470–1547). The traditions of epic poetry were continued by Tasso, who had a sense of the tragic contradictions between the humanist ideals he cherished and religious ascetic ideology. The humanist principles that pervade a number of episodes in his poem *Jerusalem Delivered* (1575) clash with the preaching of asceticism, and the concept of public duty takes on a religious tone.

In the 17th century the Counter-Reformation, feudal reaction, and Spanish rule over a substantial area of Italian territory led to stagnation in the country's spiritual life and a crisis in its literature. Characteristic of the baroque poetry of G. B. Marini (1569–1625; the poem *Adonis,* 1623) and his followers were a bizarre quality and a striving to achieve formal novelty. The poet and dramatist G. Chiabrera (1552–1638) and the poet A. Tassoni (1565–1635), the author of the mock-epic *The Rape of the Bucket* (1622), fought against Marinismo. Noteworthy among 17th-century prose works is *A Fairy Tale About Fairy Tales,* or the *Pentameron* (1634–36), a collection of Italian fairy tales in the Neapolitan dialect, interpreted by G. Basile (1575–1632). Founded in the late 17th century, the Academy of Arcadia, which proclaimed a struggle against Marinismo, contributed to the development in the 18th century of classicism (tragedies by P. J. Martello, 1665–1727, and S. Maffei, 1675–1755) and rococo gallant poetry (for example, P. Rolli, 1687–1765). Both styles were interwoven in the work of the lyric poet and dramatist P. Metastasio (1698–1782), the creator of numerous melodramas, including *Dido Abandoned* (1724) and *Cato in Utica* (1728).

The Enlightenment began in the mid-18th century in Italy, where it promoted the development of a sense of national identity. Milan journals such as *La Frusta letteraria* (1763–65) and *Il Caffè* (1764–66) played an important role in spreading Enlightenment ideas. Abandoning the improvised *commedia dell'arte,* the playwright C. Goldoni (1707–93) created the realistic comedy of personalities (for example, *The Tavern Maid,* 1753, and *The Tyrants,* 1760), which expressed the democratic ideas of the third estate. In his dramatic fairy tales Goldoni's ideological opponent C. Gozzi (1720–1806) revived elements of the *commedia dell'arte* (for example, *Princess Turandot,* 1762) and ridiculed Enlightenment rationalism. Civic inspiration pervades tragedies by V. Alfieri (1749–1803; for example, *Saul*), which are directed against tyranny and in which revolutionary classicism gives way to preromanticism. The satiric poem *The Day* (parts 1–4, 1763–1804) by G. Parini (1729–99) is imbued with Enlightenment ideas.

Characteristic of the literature of the Risorgimento (late 18th century through 1870) are civic-mindedness and patriotism, which are encountered even in the work of V. Monti (1754–1828), despite its many ideological inconsistencies. The works of U. Foscolo (1778–1827), which interweave classicism with sentimentalism, reflect the growth of a sense of national identity as well as anger against the oppressed condition of the homeland (the novel *Last Letters of Jacopo Ortis,* 1798, and the poem "The Graves," 1807). C. Porta (1775–1821) wrote realistic verses in the Milanese dialect.

Around 1815–25 romanticism became the prevailing trend in Italian literature, establishing its own aesthetic principles (for example, articles, pamphlets, and messages by G. Berchet, 1783–1851, L. di Breme, 1780–1820, and A. Manzoni, 1785–1873). Berchet's lyric poetry, as well as *My Prisons* (1832), the memoirs of S. Pellico (1789–1854), were among the works reflecting the ideas of the national liberation movement. The lyric poetry of G. Leopardi (1798–1837) expresses a patriot's grief at the sight of his humiliated homeland, romantic despair, and a lack of faith in progress. Also originating in this period was the genre of the historical novel, whose creator, A. Manzoni, wrote *The Betrothed* (1827), in which the heroes are Italian peasants who oppose high-handed feudal rule. In this work a realistic portrayal of life is combined with romantic motifs, and Catholic religiosity comes into conflict with a genuinely historical approach. Among the works published in the 1830's and 1840's were historical novels by F. D. Guerrazzi (1804–73), tragedies by G. Niccolini (1782–1861), and lyric poetry by G. Mameli (1827–49) and A. Poerio (1802–48), which were permeated by the revolutionary ideas of Mazzini (1805–72). Historical novels of everyday life by M. d'Azeglio (1798–1866) and other followers of Manzoni showed the influence of liberalism and Catholicism. At the same time, satiric poetry written in the various dialects flourished, including pieces by the Florentine G. Giusti (1809–50) and the Roman G. Belli (1791–1863).

Among the noteworthy works written after the Revolution of 1848–49 was the poetry of A. Aleardi (1812–78) and L. Mercantini (1821–72), followers of Garibaldi. The transition from romanticism to realism is evident in *The Confessions of an Italian* (1858), a historical novel by I. Nievo (1831–61) that describes the development of the national liberation movement up to the Revolution of 1848–49. The same transition may be observed in *Spartacus* (1874), a novel by R. Giovagnoli (1838–1915). The political poetry of G. Carducci (1835–1907) is pervaded by the ideas of the Risorgimento and by a protest against the ease with which they were forgotten in unified Italy. In addition to developing both romantic and realistic motifs, his lyric poetry, which affirmed the joy of living, revived classicism (for example, the collections *New Rhymes,* 1861–87, and *Iambs and Epodes,* 1867–79).

After 1870, *verismo,* which depicted contemporary social reality and the everyday life of "ordinary people," became the leading trend in Italian prose. In his short stories (for example, the collection *The Life of the Fields,* 1880, and *Rustic Short Stories,* 1883), novels (for example, *The House by the Medlar Tree,* 1881), and plays G. Verga (1840–1922) sympathetically portrayed fishermen and peasants and ridiculed the clergy and the rural rich. Other outstanding proponents of *verismo* were the critic and novelist L. Capuana (1839–1915) and Grazia Deledda (1871–1936), an author of psychological novels. Similarly, Verga, Capuana, G. Giacosa (1847–1906), and M. Praga (1862–1929) created slice-of-life dramas. *Verismo* influenced the social poetry of G. Cena (1870–1917) and the populist poetry of Ada Negri (1870–1945). In the novel *The Heart of a Boy* (1886) the socialist writer E. De Amicis (1846–1908), who was close to the proponents of *verismo,* affirmed democratic and humanistic ideals, which also pervade the fairy tale *The Adventures of Pinocchio* (1880) by Collodi (pseudonym of C. Lorenzini, 1826–90).

At the end of the 19th century neoromantic and symbolist tendencies emerged in Italian literature. The chief representative of neoromanticism, which had a religous tone, was A. Fogazzaro (1842–1911), author of the novel *The Patriot* (1895). The poet G. Pascoli (1855–1912), who celebrated nature, rural life, and simple human emotions in collections such as *Tamarisks* (1891), gravitated toward symbolism. The most characteristic manifestations of decadence and Nietzscheanism were the aesthetic and hedonistic verses, plays, and novels of G. D'Annunzio (1863–1938), who in his later career wrote in praise of Italian imperialism and turned to fascism. At the end of the first decade of the 20th century *crepuluscolarismo*—twilight poetry, a trend that depicted ordinary life in melancholy tones—took shape in reaction to D'Annunzio's rhetoric. (Among the most outstanding representatives of twilight poetry was G. Gozzano, 1883–1916.) In 1909 the futurist school emerged under the leadership of F. T. Marinetti (1876–1944), whose creative work, permeated with hysterical antihumanism and militarism, laid the ideological foundation for fascism. The crisis of traditional morality and the tragedy of "little people" in the bourgeois world were most sharply described by L. Pirandello (1867–1936). Despite their paradoxical plots, his best short stories, novels (*The Late Mattia Pascal,* 1904), and plays (*Six Characters in Search of an Author,* 1921, and *Henry IV,* 1922) were humanistic and concerned with social problems.

Italy's participation in World War I (1915–18) and the upsurge in the workers' movement and growth of the fascist menace in the postwar years caused a sharp demarcation of literary forces. The journal *La Ronda* (1919–22) preached that the artist should be locked within "individual freedom of thought." In *The Confessions of Zeno* (1923), a novel by I. Svevo (1861–1928), self-analysis is substituted for a picture of the real world. Under the leadership of Gramsci (1891–1937) and the antifascist publicist P. Gobetti (1901–26), the left wing of the Italian intelligentsia fought for a democratic culture and literature under the difficult conditions created by fascism, which did away with all freedom of the press in Italy in 1926.

Twenty years of fascist dictatorship led some Italian writers to depart from social themes and realistic traditions. The "magical realism" of M. Bontempelli (1878–1960) and the Catholic fatalism of the historical novels of R. Bacchelli (born 1891; the trilogy *The Mill on the Po,* 1938–40) were an illusory escape from reality. In the poetry of the 1920's and 1930's, hermeticism prevailed, with its motifs of loneliness and its tragic sensations of the world expressed in a refined poetic form (G. Ungaretti, 1888–1970, E. Montale, born 1896, and U. Saba, 1883–1957). During the same decades a striving to depict reality critically was embodied in the work of C. Alvaro (1895–1956), who described the life of the peasantry of the south (*People from Aspromonte,* 1930), and A. Moravia (born 1907), who exposed the desolate spiritual world of the bourgeois intelligentsia (for example, the novel *The Indifferent Ones,* 1929). The realistic tradition survived in the work of antifascist writers who emigrated, such as G. Germanetto (1885–1959), author of *Memoirs of a Barber* (1930), and A. Ugolini (1896–1954), author of the collection *The Lantern* (1934). The intensification of antifascist sentiments in Italy in the late 1930's was reflected in short stories and novels written between 1936 and 1940 by C. Pavese (1908–1950) and in Moravia's satirical novel *Masquerade* (1941). *Conversations in Sicily,* published in 1941 by E. Vittorini (1908–66), expressed allegorically a protest against the military adventures of fascism.

The nationwide Resistance Movement against fascism and the fascist German invaders (1943–45) genuinely revived Italy's literature. In the mid-1940's, neorealism, which was imbued with an antifascist spirit, faith in the man of the people, and a desire to give a truthful picture of national life, became the leading realistic trend of the first postwar decade. Themes of the antifascist partisan struggle hold a significant place in the prose and poetry of the period—Vittorini's novel *Men and Nonmen* (1945); the novel *Agnese Goes to Die* (1949), by R. Viganò; *Old Comrades* (1953), a novel by C. Cassola (born 1917); and a number of poetry collections by S. Quasimodo (1901–68), including *A Foreigner's Heel on the Heart* (1946) and *Life Is Not a Dream* (1949). The memoir and documentary literature of the Resistance Movement is diverse. Among the members of the neorealistic movement in Italy was V. Pratolini (born 1913), who portrayed the fate and struggle of the Italian people from a historical perspective (the novels *A Tale of Poor Lovers*, 1947, and *Metello*, 1955). Characteristic of neorealistic literature is the interweaving of a lyrical theme with exposure of social injustice, as in *The Lands of Sacramento* (1950), a novel by F. Jovine; *Christ Stopped at Eboli* (1945) and *Words Are Stones*, two books by C. Levi (1902–75); *The Lie With Long Legs* (1948) and *My Family* (1956), comedies by E. De Filippo; and *Gramsci's Remains* (1957), a cycle of poems by P. P. Pasolini (1922–75). Neorealistic film drama flourished during the postwar years (for example, the work of C. Zavattini, born 1902, Pasolini, and G. Bassani, born 1916). The poet and story writer G. Rodari (born 1920) created progressive literature for children based on folk traditions, including *The Adventures of Cipollino* (1951) and children's verses written in the 1950's. Nonetheless, in the late 1950's neorealism began to show certain limitations—ideological obscurity, empiricism, and an inability to portray the complexity of man's spiritual world. Confused by the increasingly complex social conflicts in Italy, a number of neorealist writers yielded to modernist influences.

Applying the lessons of neorealism, Italian literature of the 1960's took on new ideological and artistic features. It deepened its portrayal of contemporary man, expanded the depiction of man's social environment and psychology, and sought new means of expression. In particular, the social-psychological novel was developed further. After *Roman Tales* (1953) and the novel *Two Women* (1957), in which the influence of neorealism is felt, Moravia turned to the problem of alienation, castigating timeserving and the loss of ideals by heroes from the bourgeois milieu (the novel *The Empty Canvas*, 1960, and the collection *The Automaton*, 1963). The novel *The Cloud of Smog* (1958) by I. Calvino (born 1923) and the grotesque satirical novel by G. Parise (born 1929), *The Boss* (1965), reveal the hostility of "neocapitalism" to man's spiritual world. In the philosophical allegorical novels *The Nonexistent Knight* (1959) and *Cosmicomics* (1965), Calvino poses contemporary problems of morals and ethics. The themes of war and the Resistance Movement interpreted as a problem of moral responsibility were dealt with more profoundly during the 1960's (Cassola's *Bubo's Girl*, 1960, and *The White Flag Over Cephalonia* 1963, a novel by M. Venturi [born 1925]). A number of works raised the theme of the working class and the formation of the human personality in labor and in sociopolitical activity (Pratolini, *The Permanence of Reason*, 1963).

In the same period an avant garde trend developed—Group 63, which combined an anarchic, antibourgeois orientation and leftism with a rejection of the realistic tradition and with purely formal experimentation that did not produce any serious artistic results. (A major representative of the group is E. Sanguineti [born 1930], who created theatrical "quartets" in the form of a conversation among four persons—*Traumdeutung* [its German title], or *The Interpretation of Dreams* [1965]. He is also the author of *Protocols* [1969].)

With the upsurge of the workers' and youth movement in Italy as the 1970's opened, the struggle of progressive Italian literature against bourgeois "mass culture" grew sharper. Taking advantage of the media, bourgeois society propagandizes philistine, consumerist ideals and a cult of sex and psychopathology. This campaign by reactionary ideology evoked a sharp rebuff from progressive Italian culture, which exposed moral and psychological injuries to the personality and the degeneration of spiritual values as a social calamity of modern Italian capitalism (M. Soldati's novel *The Actor*, 1970, and L. Orsini's collection of short stories *Anesthesia*, 1971).

The Marxist intelligentsia of Italy and the Italian Communist Party devote a great deal of attention to elaborating the principles of realism as an artistic method and to struggling against mass culture. The main trends in contemporary Italian literature are a sharply critical attitude toward bourgeois reality and an understanding of the writer's moral responsibility to society. Contemporary Italian literature occupies a prominent place in world culture.

Literary criticism. In the Middle Ages literary criticism was confined to Latin rhetoric and poetics, including the second part of Dante's treatise "Of the Vernacular" (early 14th century). Based on Neoplatonic and Aristotelian aesthetics, the literary criticism of the Renaissance (16th century) is represented by treatises by Bembo, L. Castelvetro (1505–71), G. Giraldi Cinzio (1504–73), and Tasso. In the 18th century G. Vico (1668–1744) laid the foundation for a new science of literature, permeated by elements of the historical approach, in the essay "Principles of a New Science of the General Nature of Nations" (1726). Literary criticism of the Enlightenment was represented by G. Tiraboschi (1731–94), the author of a history of Italian literature, S. Bettinelli (1718–1808), and G. Baretti (1719–89).

Romantic criticism rested on the aesthetic principles of Berchet's "Half Serious Letter of Chrysostom" (1816) and on Manzoni's theoretical works—"Letter to Signor Sc." (written in 1820 and published in 1823) and "On Romanticism: A Letter to Marquis C. D'Azeglio" (written in 1823 and published in 1846). The outstanding literary critic of the 19th century was F. De Sanctis (1817–83), who expressed the ideas of the Risorgimento in his major works—*Critical Essays* (1866), *The History of Italian Literature* (1870), and the lecture series "Italian Literature in the 19th Century" (published in 1897). In De Sanctis' works the development of literature is linked with the ideas of the age and with the historical development of the people, and in his aesthetics, materialist and realistic tendencies are prominent. The philosopher-critic Croce (1866–1952) held an idealistic, neo-Hegelian point of view. Proclaiming that art as a creative process was an end in itself, he viewed literature as a form of timeless beauty. This aesthetic principle espoused by Croce leads to the detachment of literature from national history. Nonetheless, a historical approach is characteristic of some of Croce's works of literary criticism. Between 1918 and 1939 most Italian bourgeois literary criticism (including the work of F. Flora, 1891–1962) was influenced by Croce's ideas.

L. Russo (1892–1961), who consistently adhered to anticlerical positions, was a notable progressive critic and literary historian. The works of Gramsci, the founder of Italian Marxist aesthetics and literary criticism, subjected Croce's ideas to thorough criticism. In articles published in the Communist press in the 1920's and in later works written while he was in prison in the 1930's (*Literature and National Life*, a volume from the *Prison Notebooks*), Gramsci examined national culture and literature from the standpoint of the Marxist view of history. He developed the concept of a national people's literature that would express the deep-seated aspirations of the masses at a given moment in national history. Gramsci's works were extremely important to the development of contemporary progressive Italian literary criticism. Today, the school of literary criticism that writes from the standpoint of Marxist aesthetics occupies a prominent place in Italian culture (for example, works by C. Salinari, N. Sapegno, and G. Ferrata). The recently founded Gramsci Institute is doing productive work on problems in aesthetics, artistic methodology, literary history, and criticism.

REFERENCES

Veselovskii, A. N. *Sobr. soch.*, vols. 3–4. St. Petersburg, 1908–09.
Dzhivelegov, A. K. *Ocherki ital'ianskogo Vozrozhdeniia*, vols. 1–2. Moscow, 1929.
Dzhivelegov, A. K. *Ital'ianskaia narodnaia komediia*, 2nd ed. Moscow, 1962.

Rubtsova, G. V. *Sovremennaia ital'ianskaia literatura.* Leningrad, 1929.

Gramsci, A. *Izbr. proizv.,* vols. 1–3. Moscow, 1957–59.

Potapova, Z. M. *Neorealizm v ital'ianskoi literature.* Moscow, 1961.

De Sanctis, F. *Istoriia ital'ianskoi literatury,* vols. 1–2. Edited by D. E. Mikhal'chi. Moscow, 1963–1964. (Translated from Italian.)

Mokul'skii, S. S. *Ital'ianskaia literatura: Vozrozhdenie i Prosveshchenie.* Moscow, 1966.

Reizov, B. G. *Ital'ianskaia literatura XVIII v.* Leningrad, 1966.

Kin, Ts. *Mif, real'nost', literatura.* Moscow, 1968.

Poluiakhtova, I. K. *Istoriia ital'ianskoi literatury XIX veka (epokha Risordzhimento).* Moscow, 1970.

Arrighi, P. *Le Vérisme dans la prose narrative italienne.* Paris, 1937.

Binni, W. *La poetica del decadentismo italiano.* Florence, 1949.

Garin, E. *L'umanesimo italiano.* Bari, 1952.

Rossi, V. *Il Quattrocento.* Milan, 1953.

Paoluzi, A. *La letteratura della Resistenza.* Florence, 1956.

Croce, B. *Poesia popolare e poesia d'arte.* Bari, 1957.

Croce, B. *Storia dell'età barocca in Italia.* Bari, 1957.

Salinari, C. *La questione del realismo: Poeti e narratori del novecento.* Florence, 1960.

Sapegno, N. *Il Trecento.* [2nd ed.] Milan, 1960.

Pullini, G. *Il romanzo italiano del dopoguerra.* Milan, 1961.

Storia della letteratura italiana, vols. 1–9. Milan, 1965–69.

Fubini, M. *Romanticismo italiano.* Bari, 1968.

Letteratura italiana: I critici, vols. 1–5. Milan [1969].

N. G. ELINA (literary criticism up to 1918) and
Z. M. POTAPOVA (literary criticism after 1918)

Architecture and art

The oldest artistic monuments in Italy date from the Paleolithic and Aeneolithic periods. These include Apulian cave paintings, Ligurian and Emilian stone statuettes of females with exaggerated forms, and ceramic ware with incised or painted designs (similar to the meander design in southern European ceramics). During the Bronze Age (second half of the second millennium B.C.), richly ornamented ceramic articles and geometricized bronze figurines were created depicting deities and warriors. These artistic works reflect the influence of Minoan-Mycenaean civilization. In Sardinia a distinctive megalithic structure evolved, the nuraghe, which was a truncated conical stone structure. At the same time, a terramara culture was developing in northern Italy. From the ninth to the fifth century B.C., Villanovan settlements were established. The monuments of the Etruscans, whose culture was related to that of the Villanovans, date from the period of the eighth to the second century B.C. Sculpture, craftwork, and ruins of temples have been preserved on the sites of Greek trading settlements that sprang up on the Italian coast (Syracuse, Selinus, and Paestum) in the eighth, seventh, and sixth centuries B.C. Ancient Greek, Etruscan, and local artistic traditions were the foundations of the art of ancient Rome, which thrived from the fifth century B.C. to the fifth century A.D.

The fall of Rome and the establishment of Christianity in Italy led to the development of medieval art. Based on late classical traditions, Italian medieval art was also influenced by Byzantine art and by the art of the various barbarian people who invaded Italy, such as the Goths, Lombards, and Franks. In the fourth, fifth, and sixth centuries, basilican churches that were as splendid as the palaces of the Roman emperors were built in Rome and several other cities (for example, San Giovanni in Laterano and San Paola Fuori le Mura, both in Rome). Centrally-planned houses of worship were also built, for example, San Vitale in Ravenna. Initially, classical buoyancy and three-dimensionality of images were retained in the multicolored mosaics that decorated the interiors of the temples (for example, the mosaics in Santa Costanza, Rome, fourth century). However, the mosaics gradually became more stylized and ascetic. Chiaroscuro modeling was abandoned and replaced by linear, two-dimensional treatment of forms. Refined coloristic combinations gave way to solemn, abstracted color schemes, as seen in the mosaics of San Vitale (sixth century) and the frescoes of Santa Maria Antiqua (Rome, eighth century). Late classical traditions were preserved for a long time in carved fretwork (column capitals and altar rails).

From the eighth to the tenth century, the architecture of Lombardy flourished. The basilicas, in which crypts were placed under the altar, were characterized by exterior walls that were divided by lesenes, blind arcades, and arched friezes. In Lombardy the free-standing bell tower, the campanile, evolved (for example, the southern tower of the Basilica of Sant' Ambrogio, Milan, ninth century). During the eighth, ninth, and tenth centuries, artistic influences of barbarian peoples increased in sculpture and in the decorative and applied arts. Ornamental bas-relief carving and jewelry-making, primarily inlaid work, developed.

During the 11th, 12th, and 13th centuries, the Romanesque style, which was developing throughout Europe, became prevalent in Italy. As a result of the country's feudal fragmentation, the style acquired manifold local characteristics. The general features of Italian Romanesque architecture were determined by the continued link with classical architectural principles. These features included a striving for clarity, balanced proportions, and festive decoration. In Northern and Central Italy, basilicas with three aisles were built; frequently they had an atrium (for example, the Basilica of Sant' Ambrogio, Milan, 11th and 12th centuries). The western facades of the churches were divided by arcades and dwarf galleries or were decorated by marble portals with canopies on columns, supported by stylized figures of lions (San Zeno Maggiore, Verona, 12th century). In Tuscany, structures built in the incrustation style, with patterned polychromatic marble facing on the interior walls, were widespread (San Miniato al Monte, Florence, begun in 1014). The cathedral complex in Pisa (baptistery, begun in 1153; cathedral, 1063–1160; campanile, 1174–1372) is characterized by its harmonious proportions and elegant decor. In Sicily elements of Byzantine, Arabic, and Norman architecture were uniquely combined. Examples of Sicilian architecture of this period include Cefalù Cathedral, with two towers flanking its western facade, and the Cathedral of Monreale, with interior ogive arches and magnificent and bizarre apsidal decoration. The massive, five-domed St. Mark's Basilica in Venice (ninth century, rebuilt from the 11th to the 15th centuries), which is notable for its splendorous interior (mosaics and marble inlay), is a distinctive variation of the Byzantine cross-of-domes plan.

The prosperity of cities of Italy during the 11th, 12th, and 13th centuries generated extensive urban construction. Italian cities took on their characteristic appearance at this time. Urban fortifications corresponding to the local terrain were built, resembling the fortified stone turreted dwellings in Bologna and San Gimignano. Town halls and cathedrals with well-proportioned campaniles were built in several cities, including Bergamo and Brescia. Most Italian cities were densely built up. In Florence, Bologna, and Verona the buildings were grouped around a central, usually cathedral, square according to a regular plan inherited from classical times. In Siena and Venice, structures were arranged irregularly. The cities had closely adjoining stone or brick buildings with three or four stories, austere blind facades interrupted by narrow window openings, and overhanging tiled gable roofs.

The traditions of ornamental barbarian carving were replaced by a striving for greater clarity and distinct rhythms of representation. This trend is evident in the Romanesque sculpture that covered the walls, porches, pillars, columns, and altar rails of cathedrals. Romanesque sculpture was highly developed in Emilia and Lombardy (the reliefs by the master sculptor Wiligelmo on the cathedral in Modena, circa 1106; the reliefs on the bronze doors of San Zeno Maggiore, Verona, 12th century; and the reliefs by the master sculptor Antelami on the cathedral and baptistery in Parma, 1178 and late 12th–early 13th centuries, respectively). In Tuscany, the pictorial and nonrepresentational carving on the facades and interior walls of cathedrals is organically combined with the polychromatic marble incrustation. In Rome during the 12th and 13th centuries the marble work of the Cosmati family was particularly outstanding. The Cosmati work in Roman churches included the intricate patterns on the columns and floors, as well as the episcopal thrones and altars.

In the 11th and 12th centuries, frescoes and mosaics were frequently characterized by the combination of Byzantine compositional schemes with naïve and somewhat crudely expressed narrative representations (the frescoes in the lower church of San Clemente, Rome, c. 1100; the frescoes in Sant' Angelo in Formis, near Capua, second half of the 11th century; the mosaics in Cefalù Cathedral, second half of the 12th century; and the mosaics in St. Mark's Basilica, Venice, 12th–14th centuries). In the 13th century, icon painting developed in Central Italy. The traditions of developed Byzantine art, characterized by a finished quality, emotionally expressive linear rhythm, and refined color combinations, enabled Italian painters to overcome the simplicity of Romanesque artistic language. However, in 13th-century Italian icon painting, the laws of Byzantine iconography conflicted with an elemental striving for greater animation, clarity, and humanization (for example, the altar figures by Cimabue).

In the middle of the 13th century, pre-Renaissance tendencies began to take shape in Italian art, particularly in Tuscany. Representatives included the sculptor Nicola Pisano and his followers Arnolfo di Cambio and Giovanni Pisano. Nicola Pisano achieved effective three-dimensional modeling and imparted corporeal strength to his figures in the reliefs on the pulpit of the Pisan baptistery (1260). The major representatives of pre-Renaissance painting were P. Cavallini (Rome), who used chiaroscuro modeling based on a study of late classical painting for the first time, and Giotto (Florence), the great reformer of Italian art. Breaking with the canons of Byzantine iconography, Giotto endowed traditional evangelical scenes with greater fidelity to the real world and achieved effective compositional solutions and dramatic expressiveness of images. In the 13th- and 14th century Sienese altar paintings of Duccio, the Lorenzetti brothers, and Simone Martini, several pre-Renaissance elements appeared within the framework of the traditions of Italian Byzantine art and French Gothic miniatures. In Sienese frescoes the use of certain archaic artistic devices was combined with a desire to represent the environment and with the introduction of landscape painting and portraiture (for example, Simone Martini's and A. Lorenzetti's frescoes in the Palazzo Pubblico). The paintings of the Bolognese masters were characterized by Gothic images and by the bold introduction of concrete details from life (for example, the frescoes in Campo Santo in Pisa and the frescoes by Altichiero and Avanzo in Padua).

In the late 13th and early 14th centuries, elements of the Gothic style became prevalent in Italian architecture. This style, however, did not become established as a strict architectural system in Italy. Specific Gothic motifs, such as ornate lancet windows, machicolations in the upper part of the towers, and crenellated summits, gave a distinctive decorative elegance and dynamic intensity to urban structures that were still Romanesque in spirit—for example, the Palazzo Pubblico in Siena (1297–1310) and the Palazzo Vecchio in Florence (begun in 1298). The verticality of the architectural elements and the sculptural decoration of the churches was balanced by the horizontality of the western facades (Siena Cathedral, 1284–1376; Orvieto Cathedral, 1290–1569). The interiors of Gothic churches, such as San Petronio in Bologna (begun in 1390) and Santa Maria Novella in Florence (c. 1278–c. 1360), were characterized by the clarity and symmetry of their spatial solution. In Venetian palaces the traceried lancet galleries and the richly decorated windows combined with the polychromatic marble facing of the facades to suggest a feeling of secular festiveness.

The Renaissance (15th and 16th centuries) was a pivotal stage in Europe's cultural development. Renaissance art blossomed most fully in Italy. Italian Renaissance artists combined their sensual apprehension of the vigor and poetry of earthly existence with a search for a clear, scientifically based means of representing the world around them. The creation of a well-structured system of artistic devices in Renaissance art was principally the result of the study and creative reinterpretation of the traditions of classical art. In Early Renaissance architecture (15th century) the classical system of orders was perceived in a new manner and became one of the primary elements of a rhythmical and structural organization of buildings based on the visual balance of their supported and supporting parts, as well as on their commensurate scale with man (for example, the urban patriciate's palazzi and country villas with gardens and parks; buildings of guilds and religious fraternities; and the basilican-planned churches and centrally-planned chapels built in Florence, Rimini, Rome, and Urbino by the architects Filippo Brunelles-

chi, Michelozzo, Leon Battista Alberti, Bernardo Rossellino, and Luciano Laurana). The articulation of the different orders on the facades and the various arrangements of the porticoes, loggias, and inner courtyards with arcade galleries created a sense of spatial freedom and lightness, as well as a feeling of joyful existence. Fifteenth-century buildings, which were sometimes majestic and sometimes graceful, often retained the graphically subtle treatment of architectural details characteristic of the Gothic style. The first experiments of city planning of the Renaissance belong to the 15th century. In 1459 the construction of a group of buildings was undertaken in the city of Pienza, according to a plan by the architect B. Rossellino. The buildings were arranged symmetrically around a central square.

Early Renaissance sculptors included Lorenzo Ghiberti, Donatello, Jacopo dell Quercia, Desiderio da Settignano, Andrea del Verrocchio, and the della Robbia family. They perfected the three-dimensional modeling of forms and understood the laws governing the structure of the human body. Their statues, equestrian monuments, and monumental decorative sculptures embodied the Renaissance heroic ideal of the perfect, harmoniously developed human form. During this period tombs decorated in the classical style, endowed with sublime tranquillity, were created. A knowledge of perspective was demonstrated in Early Renaissance reliefs, depicting crowded scenes with articulately modeled, three-dimensional figures. Busts dating from the 15th century are extremely descriptive portraits.

Early Renaissance painting, which is distinguished by its poetic, integral perception of the world, developed within the framework of numerous artistic schools (for example, the Florentine, Venetian, and Umbrian). The figures in the works of Masaccio, Andrea del Castagno, Andrea Mantegna, and Antonello da Messina were characterized by austerity and monumentality. At the same time, the works of Paolo Uccello and Benozzo Gozzoli had a poetic fairy-tale quality and colorful decorativeness. The images in the paintings of Fra Angelico, Filippo Lippi, and Sandro Botticelli were characterized by a subtle, lyrical meditativeness. Fifteenth-century Italian painters were attracted to detailed narratives. They enthusiastically included everyday details and elements from urban life in their representations of holy, evangelical scenes (Ghirlandaio, Gentile Bellini, and Vittore Carpaccio).

Florentine painters paid primary attention to the sculptural modeling of forms and the mathematically-based construction of perspective. Painters of the Umbrian school were concerned principally with the re-creation of space and of the ambience of light and air (Piero della Francesca). Venetian painters explored the expressive possibilities of color (Giovanni Bellini). Painters of the Ferrarese school (Cossa and Tura) expressed a love for the colorful diversity of the real world; at the same time, their paintings were characterized by the intensely expressive linear rhythms of the Gothic style. During the Renaissance, engraving, the medallic arts, and stage design flourished. Various types of decorative and applied art also developed (furniture, majolica, and glass).

During the High Renaissance (late 15th and the first quarter of the 16th century), the struggle for the affirmation of humanist ideals became intense. This struggle occurred at a time when the feudalization of the bourgeoisie had begun and foreign invasions had intensified. Art, having become an expression of national patriotic ideas, was distinguished by its exceptional power as a social agent. Architects sought consummate forms of central-domed construction, which best represented the harmonious structure of the world. The architecture of the High Renaissance was characterized by an exceptional diversity of spatial solutions, striking proportionality, and intricate modeling of architectural details (for example, the palaces and churches in Florence, Rome, and Venice that were built by Bramante, Raphael, Antonio da Sangallo the Elder, and J. Sansovino). Michelangelo's buildings are noted for their internal tension. The High Renaissance marked the first attempts to relate buildings to their surroundings.

The humanist concept of man as the center of the world found expression in High Renaissance art, which was characterized by the attempt to create lofty, ideal, classical images. The realistic achievements of the preceding period evolved into a distinctive artistic system. The great number of eminent artists during the High Renaissance resulted in extraordinary artistic diversity. Raphael's work was distinguished by lofty emotional harmony, clear classical drawing, and ordered composition. Giorgione and Titian, who were contemporaries of Raphael, painted sensual, lush images filled with vital dynamism. Leonardo da Vinci, through the extremely subtle play of aerial chiaroscuro, imparted a psychological atmosphere and gentle spirituality to his paintings. His images contrasted with those of Michelangelo, which were characterized by a dramatic power derived from the torsion of forms.

As a result of the advent of feudal reaction in the second third of the 16th century, Renaissance humanist ideals were abandoned. A subjective and exquisite mannerist style developed, permeated by dramatic alienation. Mannerist artists included the painters Pontormo, Parmigianino, and Bronzino, as well as the sculptors B. Cellini and Giovanni da Bologna. During the Late Renaissance (second half of the 16th century), the latent dramatic conflicts of the epoch were interpreted humanistically by Titian, Michelangelo, Veronese, and Tintoretto. The late works of Michelangelo and Titian were marked by profoundly dramatic images and more intensely expressive artistic language. The Late Renaissance works of the Venetian masters expressed an infatuation with the colorful vibrant world and with the consummate rhythmic plasticity of the human body. In addition, Venetians attempted to uncover man's complex relationship with his social and daily environment (Veronese and J. Bassano) and to express a sense of the dynamics and vastness of nature, filled with cosmic forces hostile to man (J. Tintoretto).

In the second half of the 16th century, the classical structures of Andrea Palladio reflected humanist Renaissance ideals. Mannerist tendencies, such as the use of sharply contrasting illogical forms and a bizarre manner of execution, were evident in the architecture of Giulio Romano, G. Vasari, and B. Ammanati. The interest of Late Renaissance architects, such as G. Alessi, in the spatial development of composition, the diversity of unusual elements, and the dynamic relationship with the environment developed further in architecture of the baroque period. The type of church created by Giacomo da Vignola was the prototype for many baroque churches in Western and Central Europe.

At the turn of the 17th century the baroque style took shape in Italian art. This style flourished in the second third of the century. Baroque art reflected the evolving concepts of the dynamic unity and changeability of the world, as well as of the dramatic paradoxes of man's relationship to his environment. During the period of Catholic feudal reaction, the new expressive possibilities of baroque art were used to celebrate the might of the church and secular magnates and to arouse religious passion in believers.

In the baroque period there arose a new synthesis of the arts; elements from various forms of the plastic arts were combined. Italian baroque architecture was characterized by magnificent theatrical devices, extremely large structures, and dynamic organization of internal space. The churches in Rome, Venice, and Turin built by G. L. Bernini, F. Borromini, G. della Porta, C. Maderno, Pietro da Cortona, and B. Longhena were noted for their complex geometric construction (including the domes). These structures were optically enlarged through the use of picturesque illusionistic effects, including undulating curvilinear facades and colonnades, as well as broken entablatures and cornices that suggested dynamic forms. An aristocratic type of villa evolved, with a spectacular, expressively modeled facade; the vestibules were flanked by curving staircases leading to suites of rooms of various shapes and layouts (G. L. Bernini and C. Maderno in Rome; G. Guarini and F. Juvarra in Turin).

In the 17th and 18th centuries, baroque principles influenced Italian city planning. In Rome interconnected streets and squares were constructed with spectacular vistas to accentuate a multiplicity of aspects in compositional terms (for example, the three streets that diverge from the Piazza del Popolo). Monumental sculptures—for example, fountains and obelisks—were integral elements of urban planning. In the mid-18th century, classicist tendencies began to appear in Italian architecture, for example, in the work of L. Vanvitelli, A. Galilei, and G. Pier-

marini. In the Italian art of the baroque period (17th and 18th centuries), baroque, realist, and classicist tendencies, which initially opposed one another, were joined together to form a single artistic phenomenon.

The 16th century marked the inception of academic art, whose formal and abstract principles were formulated by the Carracci brothers. In the early 17th century, academicism was renounced by Caravaggio, who preferred down-to-earth subjects and imparted tangibility and heroism to his simple folk figures and genre scenes. Caravaggio greatly influenced Italian painters and contributed to the development of realism in many 17th-century artistic schools in Europe. His influence was also reflected in the works of many baroque artists.

Italian baroque sculpture reached the peak of its development in the work of G. L. Bernini. In his monumental decorative works he organically combined sculpture and architecture. Bernini's works are distinguished by impetuous movement and fluidity of form.

The masters of baroque monumental painting were Pietro da Cortona, A. Pozzo, and L. Giordano. Their paintings were marked by virtuoso illusionistic effects, including bold dizzying foreshortenings and perspective constructions. Baroque art developed most fully in Central and Southern Italy. In Northern Italy, where Flemish and Dutch influences were felt, baroque art was more restrained and intimate; at times it was characterized by idyllic meditation. (Genoese paintings by B. Castiglione and V. Castello). In addition to baroque decorative monumental painting, genre painting held a notable place in 17th- and 18th-century Italian painting. The genre paintings by D. Fetti, B. Strozzi, and G. Crespi are characterized by poetic exhilaration and dramatic intensity. In Naples a distinctive type of seascape developed, pervaded by a sense of the richness and dynamics of nature.

In the 17th and early 18th centuries, Italian landscape painting was often imbued with a spirit of romantic rebellion. S. Rosa painted thieves, soldiers, and hermits in dusky landscapes. A. Magnasco's landscapes are distinguished by the subjectiveness and dramatic expressiveness of the painting technique.

During the 18th century, Venetian painting held a special place. It retained a festive life-affirming character. G. B. Piazzetta's genre compositions are characterized by a poetic, fresh outlook. G. B. Tiepolo combined the plasticity of figures with a sunny palette and a virtuosity of baroque spatial construction. P. Longhi's playfully grotesque genre scenes resemble rococo paintings. The topographically accurate urban landscapes, or *vedute*, predominated in 18th-century Venetian painting (G. A. Canaletto and B. Bellotto). F. Guardi's landscapes, which are distinguished by intimate motifs and the re-creation of the movements of light and air, foreshadowed the plein air experiments of 19th-century painters.

Beginning in the mid-18th century, late baroque architectural landscape painting and engraving in Italy revealed stronger classicist tendencies. This increase is evident in G. P. Pannini's paintings and G. B. Piranesi's etchings. Napoleon's Italian campaign of 1796–97 resulted in the spread of antifeudal sentiments in Italy and the establishment of classicist principles in art during the early 19th century. In several cities, such as Milan, Turin, Rome, and Florence, a number of streets and squares were rebuilt in a classicist spirit (Piazza del Popolo, Rome). In connection with the development of capitalism in the second half of the 19th century, extensive construction was undertaken in industrial and port cities, including Turin, Milan, and Naples. After Italy's reunification, city-planning projects were expanded in Rome, where a radial-ring system was introduced that permitted the preservation of historical structures. The city was built up predominantly with apartment houses of four or five stories, civic buildings, and monuments that were eclectic in spirit and frequently marked by pompousness of form. The grandiosity of the monument of Victor Emmanuel II (1885–1911, architect G. Sacconi) almost seems to overwhelm the structural groups of the Capitoline and the Roman Forum. Innovative materials and designs were used in a number of Italian buildings; for example, the Galleria Vittorio Emanuele II in Milan (1865, architect G. Mengoni) has a reinforced glass roof.

In the early 19th century the main current in the Italian pictorial arts was classicism. Italian art no longer played a leading role in the European artistic world. In backward feudal Italy, classicism lacked civic enthusiasm and acquired an academic character. Canova's marble statues, which are notable for the virtuosity of the sculpting technique, are cold and impersonal.

As a result of the upsurge in the national liberation movement, a romantic school in painting evolved. The portraits and historical paintings by F. Hayez reflect a romantic spirit. The Induno brothers' genre compositions are characterized by free brushwork. Various aspects of the plein air technique became prevalent in the works of the Neapolitan masters of the Posillipan school. By the 1860's a realist school developed in Tuscan painting. The painters of the *macchiaioli* group, such as T. Signorini and G. Fattori, created portraits, landscapes, and scenes of the national liberation struggle, which were distinguished by a bright palette and keen observation. S. Leghi depicted idyllic and meditative genre scenes. The works of the painter G. de Nittis and the sculptor M. Rosso displayed the influence of impressionism.

At the end of the 19th century, the *verismo* style in art reflected disappointment in the results of the national liberation movement and discontentment with the capitalist social system. Artists of *verismo* combined social criticism (which had been expressed in the works of the sculptor V. Vela) with naturalistic tendencies. In the 1890's several Italian painters adopted the technique of divisionism; G. Segantini used this technique in his genre landscape compositions.

In the 20th century, progressive tendencies appeared in Italian art, struggling against the dominant official and formalistic currents. At the outset of the century, characteristics of modernism, such as unusual compositions and whimsical bizarre decor, were reflected in architecture (structures by E. Basile and R. D'Aronco). In 1914, A. Sant'Elia formulated the principles of futurist architecture, which were, on the whole, utopian; however, they did include some practical ideas for city planning.

During the fascist dictatorship (1922–43), elements of historical stylization and unimaginative showiness, which had largely determined the characteristics of Italian neoclassicism, became more prevalent in architecture (structures of M. Piacentini). In the 1920's and 1930's, there were conflicts with the officially supported trends in architecture. The concept of rationalism in architecture appeared, with the aims of expressing humanist ideas and using innovative materials and designs that were functionally justified (the apartment houses and civic buildings by the architects G. Michelucci and G. Terragni).

During the democratization of society after the overthrow of fascism, Italian architecture experienced creative resurgence (particularly in the 1950's and 1960's). Modern building materials, such as reinforced concrete, reinforced cement, glass blocks, and plastics, were introduced. Italian architecture from this period is distinguished by bold constructional and spatial solutions, as well as by a keen sense of the functional expediency, engineering logic, and aesthetic expressiveness of modern architectural forms. These qualities are expressed in the Termini Station (Rome, 1950, principal architect E. Mantuori); the Little Sports Palace, or Palazzetto (Rome, 1957); and the Pirelli Building (Milan, 1956–60, architect G. Ponti, engineer P. L. Nervi, with assistants). The architects of the firm of Belgiojoso, Peressutti, and Rogers strive to combine modern architectural forms with national traditions (Torre Velasca, Milan). Construction in Italian cities, as a rule, is carried out in conformance with the distinctive, historical features of the already-existing buildings. New residential developments are built on the cities' outskirts. Traditional national architectural elements (inner courtyards, loggias, open stairwells, and awnings) are used in contemporary Italian housing (multistory clustered, low-rise galleried, and low-rise modular apartments).

Housing construction in Italy is not meeting the needs of the population. Different types of housing are available for the bourgeoisie and the poor. Insufficient attention is paid to the provision of modern conveniences and to the landscaping of new areas. In the 1960's private villas were built according to the principles of organic architecture; volumes flow into one another, and there is free play in the juxtaposition of masses.

The Italian pictorial arts of the 20th century have reflected the crises that are characteristic of a bourgeois culture during its imperialistic stage. At the beginning of the century, Italian painters of the Parisian school, such as A. Modigliani, executed portraits, including nude portraits, that lack three-dimensional modeling. These works are distinguished by expressive, flexible, curved lines; elongated proportions; and subdued yet emotionally charged color combinations. They express a subjective and melancholy view of the world.

Shortly after 1910 the representatives of futurism, a movement which had been founded in Italy, sought the abstract representation in art of the dynamics of the industrial age (the painters C. Carrà and G. Severini; the painter and sculptor U. Boccioni). Neoclassical tendencies began to appear around 1910 in the works of the metaphysical painters, such as G. Morandi, G. de Chirico, and the portraitist F. Casorati. G. Morandi's still lifes are clear and logically ordered. The landscapes of G. de Chirico are imbued with a sense of the tragic spiritual bankruptcy and starkness of the world. A number of artists returned to the traditions of Etruscan and archaic Greek art; their work was characterized by decorative stylization (M. Campigli's paintings and M. Marini's sculptures).

Fascist ideology was expressed in the monumental paintings of the artists of the Novecento group, such as M. Sironi, who combined academic tendencies and certain elements from the latest artistic trends with bombastic allegorical rhetoric. In the late 1920's and early 1930's, the official line in art was opposed by artists belonging to a number of groups (the Roman school and the Corrente group). These artists called for artistic freedom and expressed their social protests in dramatically expressive forms (the painters Scipione and R. Guttuso). During World War II (1939–45), a progressive realist trend evolved. Having grown in strength during its struggle against fascism, it reached the height of its development in the late 1940's. The realist painters and graphic artists included R. Guttuso, G. Mucchi, A. Pizzinato, C. Levi, G. Meloni, R. Vespignani, and G. Zigaina. In their work the realists strove for a broad depiction of reality with its acute paradoxes. Their works are characterized by the life-affirming democratic quality and heroic elation of the figures, as well as by the vivid emotional expressiveness of the artistic language. G. Manzù's realist sculptures are noted for the intensely dramatic and picturesque modeling of forms. The sculptures of E. Greco are distinguished by plastic unity and expressively sharp silhouettes.

In Italy, modernist trends, including the numerous variations of abstract art (paintings by R. Birolli, E. Morlotti, M. Reggiani, and A. Burri; sculptures by A. Viani and P. Consagra) and pop art (since the mid-1960's), have received official support. Despite realism's struggle against these officially backed modernist trends, it has continued to develop in Italy.

REFERENCES

Vseobshchaia istoriia iskusstv, vol. 2, book 1; vols. 3–6, book 1. Moscow, 1960–65.
Vseobshchaia istoriia arkhitektury, vols. 4–5. Moscow, 1966–67. Vol. 7: Moscow, 1969.
Alpatov, M. V. *Ital'ianskoe iskusstvo epokhi Dante i Dzhotto.* Moscow-Leningrad, 1939.
Lazarev, V. N. *Proiskhozhdenie ital'ianskogo Vozrozhdeniia,* vols. 1–2. Moscow, 1956–59.
Vipper, B. R. *Bor'ba techenii v ital'ianskom iskusstve XVI veka (1520–1590).* Moscow, 1956.
Vipper, B. R. *Problema realizma v ital'ianskoi zhivopisi XVII–XVIII vekov.* Moscow, 1966.
Rotenberg, E. I. *Iskusstvo Italii XVI veka.* [Moscow, 1967.]
Goriainov, V. V. *Sovremennoe iskusstvo Italii.* Moscow, 1967.
Katsnel'son, R. A. *Noveishaia arkhitektura Italii.* Moscow, 1963.
Berenson, B. *Zhivopistsy ital'ianskogo Vozrozhdeniia.* Moscow, 1965.
Danilova, I. E. *Ital'ianskaia monumental'naia zhivopis'.* Moscow, 1970.
Venturi, A. *Storia dell'arte italiana,* vols. 1–11. Milan, 1901–40.
D'Ancona, P. (et al.). *Storia dell'arte italiana,* vols. 1–3. Florence [1953–56].
Chastel, A. *L'art italien,* vols. 1–2. Paris [1956].
Delogu, G. *Italienische Baukunst.* Zürich [1947].
Kidder-Smith, G. E. *Italy Builds.* London [1955]. (In English and Italian.)

Briggs, M. S. *Architecture in Italy.* London–New York, 1961.

Marle, R. van. *The Development of the Italian Schools of Painting,* vols. 1–19. The Hague, 1923–38.

Galetti, U., and E. Camesasca. *Enciclopedia della pittura italiana,* [vols. 1–3.] Milan [1951].

Pittura italiana: Testi di E. Carli, C. Gnudi, R. Salvini, F. Bellonzi, vols. 1–4. Milan, 1959–60.

Pope-Hennessy, J. *An Introduction to Italian Sculpture,* parts 1–3. London, 1955–62.

Music

The music of Italy played a substantial role in the development of world music. Characteristic of Italian folk music are melodiousness, liveliness, and fiery rhythms. Folk dancing is characterized by 6/8 and 12/8 measures and a fast—often very fast—tempo. Among the traditional Italian dances are the tarantella, a southern Italian dance that became a national dance, the saltarella, about which written observations from the 13th and 14th centuries have been preserved, and dances related to the saltarella—the *lombarda* (a dance of Lombardy) and the forlana or furlana (a Venetian-Friulian dance). In addition to the tarantella, the siciliano is popular. Related to it are the barcarole (a Venetian gondoliers' song) and the Tuscan rispetto (a song of praise and a declaration of love). Plaintive songs called laments (a type of elegy) are well known. A flowing, singing melody, lyricism, and frequently, an emphasis on feeling are typical of Neapolitan songs, which are popular in Italy. Italian folk melodies nurtured opera and ballet music and penetrated the religious tradition of the Mass. Many Italian composers, as well as composers from other countries, including M. I. Glinka, A. S. Dargomyzhskii, and P. I. Tchaikovsky, turned to folk music in their creative work.

The music of ancient Rome had a substantial influence on the development of Italian music. As a result of the collection and reworking by the Roman Church of many local Christian hymns, in the sixth and seventh centuries church melodies were systematized and canonized, and the creation of a canonical Gregorian chant, which became the basis of the liturgical music of Western Europe, was completed. In eradicating from church music the lively folk melodies that had filtered into it, the Catholic Church encountered resistance from the urban communities, which endeavored to preserve the local characteristics of the melodies. For example, Milan defended its own, less ascetic melodies—the Ambrosian chant, which had evolved as early as the fourth century.

In the late tenth century Tuscany became a major center of Italian music. The theoretician Guido d'Arezzo, a reformer of musical notation whose work laid the foundation for modern notation, did some of his work in Tuscany. In Florence in the 14th century, *ars nova* (new art) developed—a progressive trend in early Renaissance musical creativity and theory that prepared the way for the flowering of secular two- and three-voice lyric songs (the madrigal and the ballad), genre songs (*caccia*), and instrumental music. Among the outstanding musicians of the period were the Florentine composer and organist F. Landini and the musical theorist Marchetto of Padua. A widely used form in the 13th and 14th centuries was the laud—a spiritually edifying monophonic or polyphonic song of praise with melodies modeled after the folk song. Lauds were sung at meetings of urban fraternities in many parts of Italy, including Tuscany and Venice.

During the Renaissance secular art developed, the influence of folk music became stronger, and theoreticians achieved significant successes. (For example, the Venetian composer and theorist G. Zarlino devised a theory of harmony.) In addition, new centers were founded where musicians could gather—the conservatories (educational institutions for professional musicians) and music academies. (An academy of music was organized in 1470 at the Medici court in Florence. In 1566 the St. Cecilia Academy was founded in Rome, and in 1666 a philharmonic academy was established in Bologna. O. dei Petrucci invented a new method of printing notes (patented in 1498). Secular vocal genres flourished—frottolas and villanellas, which, in contrast to the complex polyphony of Italian liturgical music, established a new type of polyphony in which chords prevailed (homophony) and a simple, easily remembered melody was isolated in the highest voice. These genres of songs, which were similar to folk songs, were popular among democratic strata of the urban population. In the 16th and 17th centuries the central place in secular music was held by the madrigal, which had achieved popularity during the early Renaissance and which had become a four- or five-voiced vocal poem, usually on amatory and lyric themes. The new type of madrigal was created by A. Willaert, L. Marenzio, Don Carlo Gesualdo, prince of Venosa, and C. Monteverdi.

In the 15th and 16th centuries Italian music assimilated the achievements of European polyphonists and at the same time influenced the masters of the Dutch school. Major schools of polyphonic music—the Roman, which emerged during the Counter-Reformation, and the Venetian—took shape in the 16th century. Centered in St. Peter's Basilica, the Roman school was headed by Palestrina, who created the classic models of Catholic a cappella choral polyphony. He clarified polyphony, and in some of his works he came close to the chord structure that was later established in the secular music of the Renaissance. (Palestrina also composed secular music—madrigals.) In contrast to the rigid, transparently chordal, a cappella style of the Roman school, the Venetian school, whose center was St. Mark's Basilica, created a spectacular, monumental-decorative style of vocal and instrumental polyphony in liturgical and secular music, using two or more choirs supported by the organ and instrumental ensembles. The major Venetian masters were Willaert (founder of the school), A. Gabrieli, and G. Gabrieli.

At the turn of the 17th century the transition from polyphony to homophony was completed in new types of vocal and instrumental music that developed in Italy—the opera, oratorio, cantata, and canzona (a solo with instrumental accompaniment). G. Carissimi and A. Stradella created highly artistic models of oratorios and cantatas. The foundation for the emergence of opera at the end of the 16th century was laid by the development of all genres of Italian music: secular music and dramatic musical presentations, including May presentations in villages, religious presentations, madrigal comedies, interludes, and pastoral ballets. In the evolution of opera a substantial role was played by music and poetry associations whose members endeavored to revive the classical tragedies and advocated a synthesis of poetry and music. The first opera composers—J. Peri and G. Caccini—belonged to a Florentine circle, the Camerata, which was founded in 1580. In 1597 the first opera—*Dafne* (music by J. Peri, words by O. Rinuccini)—was staged in Florence. In the 17th century the opera form spread throughout Italy. At the same time, the new musical stage genre that was developing in several cities took on various features. An academic aloofness on the part of the aristocratic artistic circle affected Florentine opera. In Mantua, opera assumed the character of a court spectacle, whereas in Rome it was influenced by clerical circles, and the opera of manners, a religious didactic form, appeared for the first time. During its development the opera found audiences outside the aristocratic milieu, although at first, private performances were staged for the elite. Public opera theaters charging admission began to open in Venice in 1637. (The first of them was San Cassiano.) The founder of the operatic school was Monteverdi—a classic opera composer and the author of musical tragedies, who created a new, "agitated" musical dramatic style (*concitato*). Among the major composers of the 17th-century Venetian opera school were F. Cavalli and M. A. Cesti.

At the turn of the 18th century the center of the art of opera shifted from Venice to Naples. The Neapolitan operatic school, which was headed by A. Scarlatti, cultivated the genre of the *opera seria* (the serious opera, which took its final shape in the early 18th century). Operas of this genre were written on standard heroic subjects drawn primarily from classical mythology. The most outstanding librettists were A. Zeno and P. Metastasio. *Opera seria* was characterized by a prevalence of solos (typically, the three-part *da capo* aria), without chorus or ballet. In it the art of solo singing—*bel canto*—approached perfection. However, in time the superficial virtuosic quality of the performance, which had advanced to the foreground, obscured the dramatic and musical content of the presentation. Opera became "a concert in costumes." Later representatives of the Neapolitan operatic school, especially N. Jommelli and T. Traetta, endeavored to avoid clichés by following the principles of Gluck's operatic reform.

In the mid-18th century in Naples and almost concurrently in Venice a new genre took shape—the *opera buffa* (comic opera, which initially tended toward buffoonery and later, toward sentimentalism). The forerunners of *opera buffa* were pieces of music played during comedies and comic musical intermezzos performed during the *opera seria*. The intermezzo was popular in the early 18th century (Pergolesi's *opera buffa La serva padrona* was staged in 1733 as an intermezzo between the acts of his own *opera seria Il prigionier superbo*.) A realistic genre grounded in folklore, imbued with social content, and close in its subject matter to urban and rural everyday life, the *opera buffa* introduced into opera vivid characterization and a fresh stream of social satire (abundant comic situations and parodies) and promoted the dissemination of democratic ideas. The most outstanding masters of the *opera buffa* were N. Piccinni, G. Paisiello, D. Cimarosa (Neapolitan school), and B. Galuppi (Venetian school). C. Goldoni, the author of many librettos, most of them for Galuppi's operas, played a significant role in the development of *opera buffa*.

The best Italian singers of the 18th century were trained by N. Porpora in Naples, by F. Pistocchi in Bologna, and by A. Lotti and M. Gasparini in Venice. Among the well-known performers of the 18th century were the castrati A. Bernacchi, G. Carestini, Caffarelli, and Farinelli. (In the late 18th century and the early 19th the castrati were gradually replaced by tenors.) Outstanding 18th-century female singers were L. Aguiari, A. de Amicis, F. Bordoni, C. Gabrielli, F. Cuzzoni, V. Tesi, and A. Tonelli. Among the most distinguished Italian male singers of the period were M. Allegranti, M. Babbini, F. Bussani, and G. David. In the 18th century new opera theaters opened, including the San Carlo in Naples (1737), La Scala in Milan (1778), and La Fenice in Venice (1792).

Instrumental music also flourished. Beginning in the 16th century and especially in the 17th and 18th centuries, the art of the lute (Francesco da Milano and V. Galilei) and music for the organ (G. Frescobaldi) and the harpsichord (D. Scarlatti) attained a high level of development. Music for bow instruments, especially the violin, became very important. Composer-performers, among whom the most outstanding were A. Corelli, A. Vivaldi, and G. Tartini, laid the foundation for new cyclical forms: the concerto for orchestral ensemble (the *concerto grosso*) and for solo instrument and the sonata for ensemble (the trio sonata) and for solo instrument. One of the early outstanding models of the program symphony (the concerto "The Four Seasons" for violin, string quintet, organ, and harpsichord) was composed by Vivaldi. G. Sammartini was among the creators of the symphony. The cellist and composer L. Boccherini was a master of 18th-century symphonic and chamber music.

The development of first-class musical instruments promoted the growth of instrumental music. The art of making string instruments had developed as early as the 15th century in Brescia and later in Cremona. In the 16th through the 18th centuries prominent masters—the Amati and Guarneri families and A. Stradivari—worked in Italy. Between 1709 and 1711, B. Cristofori invented the piano (a hammer-action clavier).

In the 18th century and the early 19th many Italian musicians worked in other European countries, including the composers A. Sacchini, L. Cherubini, and G. Spontini. F. Araja, B. Galuppi, G. Paisiello, G. Sarti, and D. Cimarosa worked in Russia. At the same time, Italy attracted many foreign composers, musicians, and singers, who completed their musical education there. Among the country's outstanding academic music centers was the Philharmonic Academy of Bologna, where the theorist G. Martini played the leading role in the 18th century. The academy's members included Mozart, the Czech composer J. Mysliveček, and the Russian musicians M. S. Berezovskii and E. I. Fomin.

At the turn of the 19th century, N. Paganini, a composer and violinist and one of the first romantic musicians, achieved prominence, as did M. Clementi, one of the creators of the classical piano sonata and the founder of the London school of pianists.

The operatic art of the 19th century developed under the direct influence of sociopolitical conditions. During the Risorgimento many composers responded sensitively to their compatriots' freedom-loving aspirations. In a number of G. Rossini's operas—particularly the heroic historical opera *William Tell* (1829, Paris)—a passionate call to struggle for freedom was sounded. The realistic *opera buffa* reached its summit in the work of Rossini (*The Barber of Seville*, 1816). The romantic trend in 19th-century Italian opera was represented by the work of V. Bellini and G. Donizetti. In his music the romantic, lyric composer Bellini expressed the anguish and aspirations of the Italian people and the dream of the liberation of the homeland. (The choruses from his opera *Norma* evoked outbursts of patriotic feelings from the public during the performance.) A high point of realism in 19th-century operatic art was the work of G. Verdi. Like such revolutionary patriotic songs as "Hymn to Garibaldi" (music by A. Olivieri, words by L. Mercantini, 1858) and "The Red Banner," the choruses and arias of Verdi's historical patriotic operas, including *Nabucco, I Lombardi, Ernani,* and *La battaglia di Legnano*, inspired the Italian people in their struggle with their enslavers. Performances of these operas were often accompanied by political demonstrations. A protest against social inequality is sounded in Verdi's operas *Luisa Miller, Rigoletto, Il Trovatore,* and *La Traviata*. The operas *Aïda* and *Otello* are masterpieces of operatic realism.

Other 19th-century Italian opera composers included S. Mercadante, G. Pacini, and A. Ponchielli. In the 19th century many Italian singers—representatives of the art of *bel canto*—won fame, including M. Alboni, A. Bosio, Giulia Grisi, Giuditta Grisi, A. Catalani, B. Marchisio, C. Marchisio, G. Pasta, A. Patti, G. Strepponi, E. Frezzolini, M. Battistini, A. Cotogni, L. Lablache, G. Mario, G. Ronconi, G. Rubini, F. Tamagno, E. Tamberlik, and A. Tamburini. A number of Italian musicians of the late 19th century and the 20th (A. Boito, F. Faccio, A. Catalani, and A. Franchetti) endeavored to transfer the principles of Wagner's music drama to opera.

At the end of the 19th century a new trend—*verismo*—developed in Italian opera. Among its representatives were R. Leoncavallo, P. Mascagni, U. Giordano, and G. Puccini. Permeated with deep psychological content, Puccini's work transcended the framework of *verismo*. The verists' operas were distinguished by true-to-life subjects and an accurate portrayal of the spiritual world of simple people and were characterized by accentuated emotionalism, sharply dramatic situations, and theatrical effects. Among the most outstanding Italian performers of the 20th century have been the female singers A. Barbi, G. Bellincioni, A. Galli-Curci, T. Dal Monte, E. Tetrazzini, and L. Tetrazzini and the male singers G. Anselmi, G. De Luca, B. Gigli, E. Caruso, A. Masini, T. Schipa, Titta Ruffo, and F. P. Tosti.

A revival of Italian instrumental music took place in the early 20th century, promoted by the composer and conductor G. Martucci and the composer and pianist G. Sgambati. The conductor A. Toscanini and the pianist and composer F. Busoni played an important role in world musical culture. Features of impressionism and neoclassicism emerged in the work of a number of Italian composers, including O. Respighi and A. Casella. G. F. Malipiero and I. Pizzetti tried to revive the traditions of old Italian music, and the work of F. Alfano, E. Wolf-Ferrari, and L. Rocchi also developed along more traditional lines. (Rocchi's work reflected the influence of the Russian school.) In the 1950's the influence of avant-garde music grew stronger in Italy. The works of a number of contemporary composers are characterized by an internal contradiction: a turn to themes of grand social scale and lofty ideological resonance is combined with more complicated and farfetched means of expression (for example, L. Nono's *Interrupted Song* [1956], which is based on letters from fighters in the Resistance Movement who were condemned to death, and a number of works by L. Dallapiccola and L. Berio). Among Italy's other contemporary composers are R. Vlad, G. F. Ghedini, I. Montemezzi, and G. Petrassi. The names of many musicians and singers have won recognition outside Italy, including the conductors P. Argento, V. De Sàbata, G. Cantelli, F. Previtali, T. Serafin, R. Fasano, V. Ferrero, and C. Zecchi. Also well known abroad are the pianist A. Benedetti Michelangeli, the violinist G. De Vito, the cellist

E. Mainardi, the female singers G. Simionato, R. Scotto, A. Stella, R. Tebaldi, and M. Freni, and the male singers G. Bechi, T. Gobbi, M. del Monaco, and F. Corelli. A contribution to the development of musical culture has been made by the Italian music critics L. Torchi, A. Bonaventura, A. Della Corte, G. Pannain, F. Torrefranca, and G. Barblan (president of the Society of Music Critics) and by the critic and composer M. Zafred.

Vocal art has attained a high level in Italy. Permanent opera troupes perform in many cities, and the leading companies—La Scala (Milan), San Carlo (Naples), La Fenice (Venice), and the Rome Opera—enjoy world renown. At the same time, many theaters experience constant financial difficulties, despite a law passed by the parliament in 1967 to provide partial subsidies to the major music groups. Most opera presentations and concerts are inaccessible to the broad public because of high ticket prices.

Numerous annual music festivals and competitions are held in Italy, including the International Contemporary Music Festival (since 1930), the Musical May (held in Florence since 1933), the Festival of the Two Worlds in Spoleto (since 1958; founded by the Italian composer G. C. Menotti, who lives in the USA), and the New Music Week in Palermo (since 1960). The Busoni pianists' competition is held in Bolzano (since 1949, annually), the G. B. Viotti music and dance competition, in Vercelli (since 1950, annually), the Casella competition, in Naples (since 1952, every two years; pianists participated until 1960, but since 1962 composers have also participated), and the Paganini violinists' competition in Genoa (since 1954, annually). An orchestra conductors' competition instituted by the St. Cecilia National Academy has been held every three years in Rome since 1956, the E. Pozzoli pianists' competition has been held in Seregno every two years since 1959, and the G. Cantelli young conductors' competition has been held every two years in Novara since 1961. The Verdian Voices vocalists' competition is held every year in Busseto. Founded in 1952 as a national competition and reorganized as an international one in 1953, the Guido d'Arezzo competition for choral groups (also known as the Polifonico) is held annually. Commercial popular music, which is promoted by large music publishing and record firms as well as by television, enjoys a wide following, and there are a number of popular-song festivals, including San Remo and Canzonissima.

Music societies include the Corporation of New Music (since 1923), the Association of Music Libraries, and the Society of Music Critics. Italy has many music education institutions (14 conservatories, as well as music *lycées* and schools) and scholarly institutes, including the Institute of Verdi Studies. The music publisher and commercial firm Ricordi and Company, which has branches in many countries, has been in business since 1808.

Among the music journals published in Italy are *La rassegna musicale* (since 1928) and *Il convegno musicale* (since 1964), both of which are issued in Turin, and *Musica e dischi* (since 1945), *Musica jazz* (since 1945), and *Scala* (since 1949), all of which are issued in Milan.

REFERENCES

Rolland, R. *Opera v XVII veke v Italii, Germanii, Anglii.* Moscow, 1931. (Translated from French.)
Rolland, R. *Opera do opery: Sobr. muzykal'no-istoricheskikh soch.,* vol. 4. Moscow, 1938. (Translated from French.)
Ivanov-Boretskii, M. V. *Muzykal'no-istoricheskaia khrestomatiia,* 2nd ed., vols. 1–2. Moscow, 1933–36.
Kuznetsov, K. A. *Muzykal'no-istoricheskie portrety.* Moscow, 1937.
Livanova, T. N. *Istoriia zapadnoevropeiskoi muzyki do 1789 goda.* Moscow-Leningrad, 1940.
Levik, B. *Istoriia zarubezhnoi muzyki,* issue 2, Moscow, 1961.
Rozenshil'd, K. *Istoriia zarubezhnoi muzyki do serediny XVIII veka,* fasc. 1. Moscow, 1963.
Martynov, I. I. *Istoriia zarubezhnoi muzyki pervoi poloviny XX veka.* Moscow, 1963.
Konen, V. D. *Istoriia zarubezhnoi muzyki,* fasc. 3, 2nd ed. Moscow, 1965.
Istoriia evropeiskogo iskusstvoznaniia ot antichnosti do kontsa 18 veka. Moscow, 1965.
Istoriia evropeiskogo iskusstvoznaniia: Vtoraia polovina 19 veka. Moscow, 1965.
Druskin, M. S. *Istoriia zarubezhnoi muzyki,* fasc. 4, 3rd ed. Moscow, 1967.
Della Corte, A. *L'opera comica italiana nel' 700,* vols. 1–2. Bari, 1923.
Bonaventura, A. *L'opera italiana.* Florence, 1929.
Convaglios, C. *Il folklore musicale in Italia.* Naples, 1936.
Abbiati, F. *Storia della musica,* vols. 1–5. Milan, 1939–46.
Sartori, C. *Bibliografia della musica strumentale italiana stampato in Italia fino al 1700.* Florence, 1952.
De Paoli, D. *L'opera italiana dalle origini all'opera verista.* Rome [1954].
Confalonieri, G. *Storia della musica,* vols. 1–2. Milan, 1958.

(Based on materials from the article by K. A. KUZNETSOV in the second edition of the *Great Soviet Encyclopedia*)

Dance and ballet

The European ballet was born in Italy, which offered traditions of the classical and medieval art of dancing as well as a rich folk dance culture. Theatrical dance evolved from ballroom dancing and dance processionals in court presentations (14th century) into allegorical and mythological pantomimes (15th and 16th centuries). Dance was also important in the *commedia dell'arte.* In the late 16th century the work of Italian masters such as the ballet master B. Baltazarini contributed to the shaping of ballet as a theater genre in France, and in the second half of the 17th century ballet became established in Italy as well, in court performances. During the 18th century almost all of Italy's music theaters staged ballets. The leading Italian ballet masters and dancers (for example, G. Angiolini and V. Galeotti) worked in France, Denmark, Russia, and other countries.

A new phase in the development of Italian ballet was associated with the beginning of the Italian people's struggle for the country's independence and unity in the late 18th century. This phase was reflected in the work of the ballet master S. Vigano, who staged heroic choreodramas (Beethoven's *The Creatures of Prometheus,* 1801, 1813; and *Othello,* set to collected music, 1818), and in productions by G. Gioia. Pupils of C. Blasis, who taught at the ballet school founded in 1813 at La Scala, appeared in the theaters of many countries. In the 1880's the works of the ballet master L. Manzotti, which were based on fairy tales, enjoyed success. Italian ballet masters devised a special virtuosic style of performance, which was adopted in the late 19th century by the dancing schools of other countries. Dancers mastered toe technique, executed more complicated turns and leaps, and achieved greater elevation. The Italian ballet artists E. Cecchetti, C. Brianza, P. Legnani, and V. Zucchi appeared on the Russian stage.

In the early 20th century Italian ballet entered a period of decline, undergoing only a small degree of revival in the 1920's and 1930's thanks to the work of B. G. Romanov and A. Milloss. In the mid-1940's the work of the La Scala ballet troupe and school increased substantially. Its repertoire included ballets by Tchaikovsky and Prokofiev and productions by G. Balanchine and J. Cranko. On the initiative of the director B. Menzotti, experimental productions were done by the La Scala troupe in the late 1960's for the female dancer C. Fracci (R. Vlad's *The Seagull,* based on A. P. Chekhov's play, and *Egyptian Nights,* set to music by Prokofiev). Ballet troupes at opera houses in Rome, Florence, Naples, Venice, and Palermo periodically give performances, including productions by Balanchine, L. F. Miasin, and B. F. Nijinska, and new works by Milloss. In the late 1960's the ballet *The Macbeths,* which castigated fascism, was performed to the music of R. Strauss in the San Carlo opera house in Naples. Between 1930 and 1960, Italy's leading ballet artists and ballet masters were A. Radice, O. Amati, V. Colombo, M. Pistoni, and U. Dell'Ara. In the early 1970's the dancers A. Aragno, E. Terabust, and L. Cosi became well known. Ballets are regularly staged for the Florentine Musical May, an international festival held annually since 1933, and for the festival in Spoleto (since 1958).

REFERENCES

Khudekov, S. N. *Istoriia tantsev,* vols. 1–4. St. Petersburg, 1913–17.
Klassiki khoreografii. Leningrad-Moscow, 1937.
Reyna, F. *Des Origines du ballet.* Paris, 1955.
Tani, G. "Il balletto in Italia." In *Cinquanta anni di opera e balletto in Italia.* Rome, 1954.

L. IA. SURITS

Theater

The Italian theater originated in folk agricultural rites and games. By persecuting the vestiges of pagan spectacles, the Catholic Church destroyed the remnants of the classical theater in Italy by the fifth or sixth century. The beginnings of the professional art of theater appeared in the cities by the ninth or tenth century in performances by mimes. Elements of the theater were also found in Shrovetide carnival games. (Venetian carnivals became especially famous later, in the 13th to 15th centuries, when they became city-wide holidays.) Although it fought against folk theater, the church used theatrical devices to create spectacles with religious content (liturgical drama and mystery plays). Lauds on themes drawn primarily from the Gospels were a popular form of religious presentation in the 14th century. However, the influence of folk theater penetrated even into these ceremonial acts, injecting them with secular and occasionally comic satiric motifs. The mystery play remained the principal type of theatrical presentation until the 15th century, when its Christian content gave way to a mythological content, and it became essentially secular. Poliziano's play in verse, *Fable of Orpheus,* the first example of Renaissance secular drama in Italian, was written in the mystery-play form.

The development of a new theater culture began in Italy during the Renaissance. At the turn of the 16th century the comedy of learning (*commedia erudita*) was created by such writers as Ariosto, Machiavelli, Aretino, Bruno, and Bibbiena and performed by amateur students or courtiers. The founders of the genre of tragedy, G. Trissino and G. Rucellai, imitated Greek models in their works. A genre characteristic of 16th-century Italian theater was the "tragedy of horrors" (for example, works by G. Giraldi Cinzio, S. Speroni, and L. Dolce), which was similar to the works of Seneca. A stylized pastoral held an important place in the repertoire of court theaters. Typical works in this genre were created by Tasso and Guarini. The most significant stage in the development of the semiprofessional theater in the first half of the 16th century was associated with the work of the dramatist and actor A. Beolco, the author of folklore-saturated comedies in the Paduan dialect and the creator of the character of Ruzzante, a merry peasant from Padua.

The most striking phenomenon of the Renaissance was the *commedia dell'arte* (comedy of masks), which originated in the 16th century under the influence of folk theater forms and which was closely connected with farcical theatrical spectacles held in public squares. The chief distinguishing feature of the *commedia dell'arte* was improvisation on the stage. Endowed with conventional traits, the masked characters created by the actors passed from one scenario to another, changing only in details. With the exception of the lyric characters of the lovers, the characters spoke in folk dialects, and the actors played in masks. In addition to promoting the development of stage art as a special type of professional activity, the improvisational presentations of the *commedia dell'arte* became a school of virtuoso acting skills and stage techniques that were adopted by the major dramatists and theater people of modern times. Well-known actors of the *commedia dell'arte* included A. Ganassa, the brothers T. Martinelli and D. Martinelli, I. Andreini (16th century), T. Fiorillo, D. Biancolleli (17th century), and A. Sacchi (18th century).

The Italian humanists' turn toward antiquity gave impetus to the development of the theory of drama. Italian theorists of drama such as Trissino and Castelvetro elaborated a dramaturgical canon that required a sharp separation of tragedy and comedy, strict observance of the unities of place, time, and action, and the use of lofty poetic speech in tragedy. The norms established by Italian theorists influenced the shaping of the aesthetics of classicism in France in the 16th and 17th centuries.

A new stage in the development of the national theater was associated with a reform by the dramatist Goldoni, who created the comedy of manners, which presented individualized characters and eschewed the traditional masks and improvisation. Working in Venice in the San Samuele, Sant'Angelo (with troupes under the direction of G. Imer and G. Medebac), and San Luca theaters, he devoted a great deal of attention to educating actors, instilling in them an understanding of the theater's tasks of enlightenment. Goldoni's closest followers among his pupils were the actor A. Matteucci, called "il Collalto," and the actress C. Bresciani. An opponent of Goldoni's comedy of manners, the dramatist Gozzi sought to revive fairy-tale themes combined with the improvisation and masked buffoonery of the *commedia dell'arte*. He created the genre of theatrical fairy tales —*fiabe*—which were first staged in the San Samuele theater between 1761 and 1765.

In the 18th century the Italian theater was marked by great diversity. Venice and Rome were major centers for the theater. Numerous dramatic troupes performed in special buildings, built, as a rule, for opera performances, in Milan, Naples, Florence, Genoa, and other cities, as well as in the homes of aristocrats and wealthy merchants. In addition to the literary theater, genres such as the puppet theater, performances by street acrobats and tightrope walkers, and all kinds of presentations at fairs and carnivals enjoyed great popularity.

The revolutionary events of the late 18th century stirred interest in the genre of heroic tragedy, whose most prominent representative was the dramatist V. Alfieri, whose works were initially staged in amateurs' circles. The theater went through a period that was characterized by the staging of freedom-proclaiming tragedies by Voltaire and M. J. Chénier, as well as by I. Pindemonte, V. Monti, and U. Foscolo. The national-liberation movement—the Risorgimento—laid the foundation for the appearance and establishment of the romantic trend in theater and dramaturgy (A. Manzoni, S. Pellico, G. Niccolini, and C. Marenco). In the early 19th century Alfieri's works were brilliantly performed by such actors as A. Morrochesi, P. Blanes (Florence), and C. Marchionni (Milan).

Revolutionary romantic drama created the prerequisites for the development of a new Italian school of acting, which was founded by the actor G. Modena, a participant in the revolutionary events of the 1830's and 1840's. Modena's artistic and social ideals were embodied most fully in the work of his pupils A. Ristori, E. Rossi, and T. Salvini. Characteristic of Modena's school were ideological purposefulness and political ardor in the portrayal of strong, resolute characters and the abandonment of elements of routine, everyday life, which diminished the heroic orientation of the art. The work of Rossi and especially Salvini displayed realistic tendencies and an effort to combine a heroic foundation with sincere feeling. The acting of that time—the summit of Italian theater—enriched European culture with its achievements.

After the unification of Italy (1870) and the establishment of a constitutional monarchy, Italian society and culture went through a period of disillusionment over the results of the Risorgimento. Heroic tragedy degenerated into historical drama with elements of melodrama. The bourgeois-philistine drama of A. Dumas *fils,* V. Sardou, and their Italian imitators became established in the actors' repertoires. There were no permanent dramatic theaters in Italy, and the government failed to concern itself with developing a national theater art. Financial difficulties forced the best representatives of the Italian theater to tour other countries. The leaders of troupes created for the duration of tours, and even outstanding actors, failed to set themselves the goal of creating a stage ensemble. The high level of art of individual actors did not have a positive effect on the general condition of Italian theater.

The increasing influence of *verismo,* which developed primarily naturalist tendencies in the theater, deprived the art of the stage of its heroic orientation. The most striking representative of Italian naturalism in acting was E. Zacconi. The dramatic actor E. Novelli enjoyed great popularity, and E. Duse, an actress of high dramatic quality and deep humanity, continued the traditions of Salvini. Other outstanding theater people of the second half of the 19th century and the early 20th included L. Belloti-Bon, F. Ando, E. Grammatica, I. Grammatica, T. di Lorenzo, A. Magi, C. Rossi, and R. Ruggieri. The work of such actors as A. Petito, G. Grasso, and E. Scarpetta took shape in the dialect theater (performances in local dialects). In the early 20th century the theater repertoire consisted to a large degree of dramas by D'Annunzio and other representatives of decadent playwriting. Somewhat later, the comedies of manners and especially the philosophical-psychological dramas of

Pirandello, who was highly esteemed by Gramsci, became very important.

Under the fascist dictatorship (1922–43), Italian theater and playwriting went through a profound crisis. The repertoire included escapist plays and cheap dramas, and modernist tendencies became widespread. Only the work of a number of theaters in Rome—the Art Theater under Pirandello, the Theater of Independents, and the Theater of Art under the actor and playwright A. G. Bragaglia—was of artistic interest. Through the pedagogical work of T. Pavlova and P. Sharov the Italian theater became familiar with the theater aesthetics of Stanislavsky. This led to the organization of the Academy of Dramatic Art in 1935 in Rome by the prominent man of the theater and historian S. D'Amico.

The heroic struggle of the Resistance Movement, the defeat of fascism, and the upsurge of democratic forces created the preconditions for the development of a progressive realistic theater. Under the influence of neorealist cinema, stage figures endeavored to present socially sharp, true-to-life productions and tried to renew the repertoire and artistic devices of the theater.

The progressive development of the theater was promoted by the work of the director L. Visconti, who, working chiefly with a troupe headed by the prominent actors R. Morelli and P. Stoppa, created productions that were notable for their humanism. The dialect theater of Naples, which was organized by the dramatist, director, and actor E. De Filippo, has occupied a special place in the postwar development of Italian theater. It has two troupes: a city troupe, which performs in the San Ferdinando theater, and a touring one, which travels around the country. The group stages primarily plays by De Filippo. Many of the productions, which are devoted to contemporary themes, are distinguished by a democratic and humanist orientation. The artistic practice of the Naples dialect theater is characterized by a synthesis of the traditions of the "improvised comedy" of the commedia dell'arte and a truthful depiction of everyday life of the times and by the fusion of tragic and sharply comic principles. Characteristic of the postwar development of the Italian theater was the appearance in the second half of the 1940's of teatri stabili—that is, permanent theaters. In 1947 the permanent Piccolo Teatro of Milan, under G. Strehler and P. Grassi, opened with a production of Gorky's Lower Depths. Subsequently, the Piccolo Teatro in Rome was organized under the director O. Costa and the Teatro Stabile in Turin, under G. De Bosio, as well as theaters in Genoa, Trieste, Padua, Venice, and Florence. Among the theaters of the early 1950's, the Theater of Italian Art (1952–54), which was organized by the director and dramatist L. Squarzina and the outstanding actor V. Gassman, became well known. Interest in Russian drama increased in the 1940's and 1950's, and plays by Gogol, Chekhov, and Gorky and adaptations of novels by Dostoevsky were incorporated into the repertoire.

By the mid-1960's the teatri stabili, which were subsidized by the state and the municipalities, had consolidated their position. As noncommercial enterprises, these theaters distribute discount subscriptions among workers, students, and office employees and organize debates. However, in the second half of the 1960's some teatri stabili entered a period of crisis. Pursuing only narrow educational objectives, they occasionally became conservative in their ideology and aesthetics. The best Italian private theater groups include a troupe headed by the director G. De Lullo and the actors R. Falk, A. Valli, and R. Albani. The repertoire of theaters consists chiefly of plays with progressive content and dramas and satirical comedies aimed against the reactionary policies of the ruling circles, the social vices of contemporary bourgeois society, and neofascism. In addition to the national and world classics (for example, Machiavelli, Alfieri, Goldoni, Shakespeare, Molière, and Chekhov), Italian theaters stage plays by Italian playwrights such as Pirandello, R. Viviani, U. Betti, De Filippo, P. Griffi, B. Griffi, B. Rondi, Squarzina, C. G. Viola, S. Cappelli, V. Faggi, M. Dursi, G. Sbragia, P. Levi, and A. Nicolai, as well as works by foreign authors, including Brecht, Williams, and Anouilh. In the Italian theater today, progressive tendencies coexist with reactionary ones. Based on biblical themes and shrouded in mysticism, many productions of Catholic plays by such playwrights as D. Fabbri instill in the audience ideas of nonresistance to evil and submissiveness to the existing law and order. The experimentation of some directors and dramatists who gravitate toward the theater of the absurd is highly formalistic. In the late 1960's political theaters began to put on productions, coming out against religious hypocrisy, bourgeois bureaucracy, and neofascism, but some of them occasionally lapse into anarchism, and leftist pseudorevolutionary slogans are sounded from their stages. Well-known Italian actors include G. Albertazzi, M. Benassi, A. M. Guarnieri, L. Brignóne, A. Proclemer, and P. Stoppa.

Plays presented on the sites of ancient theaters in Syracuse and Ostia are important in the Italian theater.

In 1962 the Cultural Center was organized in Milan under the dramatist and critic C. Terron with the purpose of bringing the art of the theater closer to the mass audience.

Numerous theatrical journals are published, including Il dramma (since 1925) and Sipario (since 1946).

REFERENCES

Miklashevskii, K. La Commedia dell'arte, ili Teatr ital'ianskikh comediantov XVI, XVII, XVIII stoletii, part 1. St. Petersburg, 1914–[1917].
Ovett, A. Ital'ianskaia literatura. Moscow, 1922.
Ignatov, S. Istoriia zapadnoevropeiskogo teatra novogo vremeni. Moscow-Leningrad, 1940.
Dzhivelegov, A., and G. Boiadzhiev. Istoriia zapadnoevropeiskogo teatra: Ot vozniknoveniia do 1789 g. Moscow-Leningrad, 1941.
Istoriia zapadnoevropeiskogo teatra. vols. 1–3. Moscow, 1956–63.
Dzhivelegov, A. K. Ital'ianskaia narodnaia komediia: Commedia dell'arte. Moscow, 1962.
Sanesi, I. La commedia, vols. 1–2. Milan, 1911–35.
Ruberti, G. Storia del teatro contemporaneo, 3rd ed. Bologna, 1931.
Apollonio, M. Storia del teatro italiano, vols. 1–2. Florence, 1954–58.
Pandolfi, V. Teatro italiano contemporaneo. Milan, 1959.
La commedia dell'arte, a cura V. Pandolfi, vols. 1–6. Florence, 1957–61.
　　　　　　　　　　　　　　　　　　G. N. BOIADZHIEV

Circus

Circus families who gave performances at city fairs have been known in Italy since time immemorial. The oldest Italian circus family, the Chiarinis, began its work in the 1580's. (Its most prominent members were Francesco, Angelica, Adelaida, and Giuseppe.) Among the well-known circus families of the 18th and 19th centuries were the Franconis, Tournaires, Guerras, Chiesis, Cinisellis, Sidolis, and Truzzis. Some Italian family troupes were also popular in other countries, where they frequently became the founders of circuses. The biggest Italian circus enterprises in the 20th century are those owned by D. Togni and O. Orfei.

Motion pictures

The first Italian film was made in 1896. Small motion-picture firms that specialized in feature films were organized in 1905–06 in Turin, Rome, and Milan. The rise of the Italian cinema dates to 1912–13, when pseudohistorical films and pictures on literary subjects achieved success. They were outstanding for their magnificent scenery, mass scenes, and shots of Italy's architectural monuments and landscapes. Among the "colossus" films issued in 1913 that gained wide renown were Quo vadis? (directed by E. Guazzoni), The Last Days of Pompeii (directed by L. Maggi), and especially Cabiria (directed by G. Pastrone). Comedies and drawing-room melodramas were also made.

By organizing wide publicity for popular actors, the motion-picture firms promoted the phenomenon of the movie star—F. Bertini, L. Cavalieri, and Hesperia for example. Several films produced between 1914 and 1915 under the influence of verismo tried to show accurately the life of the Italian people, who were suffering great privations (Lost in the Darkness, directed by N. Martoglio, and Assunta Spina, directed by G. Serena).

World War I deprived Italy of foreign film markets, and competition with the German and American motion-picture industries grew more intense. With the establishment of a fascist regime (1922) a crisis began in the Italian motion-picture industry. The appearance in the early 1930's of sound films somewhat revived the industry. At first, most of the sound films were musicals in which well-known singers played the principal roles. In the mid-1930's the fascist government attempted to use motion pictures as a propaganda medium. Control was established over film production and distribution, and in 1937 a complex of film studios was built in Rome, and a film institute—the Experimental Film Center (Centro Sperimentale del Cinematografo)—was established. However, few overtly facist, militarist films were produced. For the most part, costume spectaculars and drawing-room melodramas continued to come out. The works of many film-makers reflected a passive opposition to official fascist art. Among the motion pictures of this period, the lyric comedies of M. Camerini and some of A. Blasetti's films are outstanding for their humanity.

In the history of Italian motion pictures, the refined filmings of 18th- and 19th-century literary works were a unique phenomenon. They were produced by the "calligraphers," directors who were close to the literary trend of *prosa d'arte*—M. Soldati, R. Castellani, A. Lattuada, and F. Poggioli. The documentary—a film shot from real life without professional performers—was born (R. Rossellini, F. De Robertis). In spite of official propaganda, which demanded glorification of the "grandeur of the empire," a number of films of the 1940's did not entirely conform with official specifications, including L. Visconti's *Obsession* (1942), Blasetti's *A Walk in the Clouds* (1942; distributed in the Soviet Union under the title *Four Steps in the Clouds*), and V. de Sica's *The Children Are Watching Us* (1943). Profoundly human, these motion pictures showed the disintegration of Italian society, the instability of its foundations, and the cruelty and injustice that held sway in it. The activity of young, antifascist-minded film critics, who grouped around the Experimental Film Center and the journals *Cinema* and *Bianco e nero* during World War II, was very important in preparing the way for a new democratic cinema. Among the critics were G. De Santis, C. Lizzani, G. Puccini, A. Pietrangeli, M. Antonioni, Visconti, M. Alicata, G. Aristarco, and U. Casiraghi, who subsequently became prominent directors and film scholars, and the heads of the Experimental Film Center, L. Chiarini and U. Barbaro. After Italy was liberated from fascism and the Hitlerian occupation, a progressive trend emerged in the Italian motion-picture industry—neorealism. Its birth was influenced in particular by the theoretical works of V. I. Pudovkin and S. M. Eisenstein and by Soviet films of the 1920's and 1930's. The most significant representatives of Italian neorealism were the directors Rossellini, Visconti, De Sica, De Santis, P. Germi, Lizzani, L. Zampa, and Lattuada. Rossellini's film *Open City* (1945), which portrayed the Italian people's unity in the struggle against fascism, became the manifesto of neorealism. In 1945–46 the Resistance Movement became one of the main themes of the new Italian motion pictures (Rossellini's *Paisan*, A. Vergano's *The Sun Is Still Rising*, and Lizzani's *Danger, Bandits!*). The best neorealist films were devoted to themes drawn from postwar Italy—unemployment, homeless children, the growth of banditry, and the struggle against the Mafia. Among these outstanding films were De Sica's *Shoe Shine* (1946), *Bicycle Thief* (1948), and *Umberto D* (1951), Visconti's *La Terra Trema* (The Earth Trembles) (1948), De Santis' *Tragic Hunt* (1947), *Bitter Rice* (1949), *No Peace Among the Olives* (1950), and *Rome, Eleven O'Clock* (1952), and Lattuada's *Without Pity* (1948). Other distinguished neorealist films on postwar themes were Germi's *In the Name of the Law* (distributed in the Soviet Union as *Under the Sky of Sicily*, 1949) and *Road of Hope* (1950), E. De Filippo's *Naples, City of Millionaires* (1950), and Steno and M. Monicelli's comedy *Cops and Robbers*. However, progressive tendencies and social protest in motion pictures and a historical and critical approach to reality encountered serious obstacles—in particular, financial difficulties and oppressive censorship by the Christian Democratic government and the Vatican. Neorealist films were declared harmful and antinational. At the same time a great deal of American capital was filtering into Italian cinematography, and Hollywood monopolies gradually subjugated Italian motion-picture companies and studios. The rebuilding of the devastated Italian motion-picture industry was impeded. As a result, toward the mid-1950's neorealism, which had shown itself to be, for the most part, ideologically inconsistent, entered a period of crisis, and the advances that had been made in Italy's society and in the organized struggle of the working people were not sufficiently reflected in neorealist films. By this time a number of

films were using only purely external attributes of neorealism (*Bread, Love, and Dreams*, 1953, directed by L. Comencini), and some directors strayed away from progressive cinema. The film *La Strada* (1954; distributed in the Soviet Union under the title *They Wandered Along the Roads*), directed by F. Fellini, sounded the themes of loneliness, disunity, and religious-mystical motifs for the first time.

The growth of the democratic movement in the country in the late 1950's and early 1960's promoted for a short time the return of some Italian film-makers to antifascist and social themes. Among the films produced were Rossellini's *General Della Rovere* (1959) and *It Was Night in Rome* (1960), Monicelli's *The Great War* (1959), De Sica's *Two Women* (1960) and *The Condemned of Altona* (1962), Comencini's *Everybody Go Home!* (1961), and N. Loy's *Four Days of Naples* (1962). A number of films depicted from various ideological positions the present condition of Italian bourgeois society: a period of temporary stabilization, the semblance of prosperity, and the so-called economic miracle. Among them were Visconti's multilevel social film-novel *Rocco and His Brothers* (1960), Fellini's *La Dolce Vita* (1959) and *8½* (1962), and Antonioni's *L'Avventura* (1959), *La Notte* (1960), *Eclipse* (1962), and *Red Desert* (1964). Despite the contrasts in their work, Fellini and Antonioni, directors who have gained worldwide fame, showed in their films the profound isolation of people, the rupture of internal ties and the lack of spiritual content in bourgeois society, and the tragic fate of the artist in the capitalist world.

In the 1960's the writer P. P. Pasolini began to work as a director. At first, his contradictory work was permeated by furious social protest—*The Beggar* (1961), *Mamma Roma* (1962), and *The Gospel According to St. Matthew* (1964). However, in the 1970's it has become increasingly clear that openly erotic and crudely naturalistic motifs have gained the upper hand in Pasolini's work (*The Decameron* and *The Pigsty*, for example). Social commentary is extremely important in the work of the director F. Rosi (the harshly satirical films *Salvatore Giuliano*, 1961, and *Hands Over the City*, 1963). Monicelli directed the film *The Organizer* (1963), which is about the first Italian strike. Significant works of modern Italian literature have been made into films, including *Family Chronicle*, after V. Pratolini (1961, directed by V. Zurlini), *Bubo's Girl*, after C. Cassola (1963, directed by Comencini), and *The Indifferent Ones*, after A. Moravia (1965, directed by F. Maselli).

In the mid-1960's a considerable decline in the art of film in Italy could be readily discerned. The proportion of commercial films (Westerns, sentimental-erotic pictures, and detective comedies) increased sharply, and militarist pictures modeled on American films appeared. The most viable genre in the progressive cinema proved to be the social satirical comedy, which preserved some of the best traditions of postwar Italian films. Among those working in this genre were De Sica (*Boom*, 1963, and *Marriage Italian Style*, 1964), Germi, who created a series of satirical tragicomedies, including *Divorce Italian Style* (1961) and *Seduced and Abandoned* (1963), and E. Petri, Zampa, and the actor A. Sordi, who turned to directing.

Among Italian motion pictures of the second half of the 1960's, a rather important place is held by films made by young directors (for example, *Fists in His Pocket*, by M. Bellocchio, 1965, and motion pictures made by S. Samperi and F. Frezza), which reflected the anarchic protest of youth. However, these directors subsequently turned to making commercial motion pictures. At the beginning of the 1970's a progressive trend evolved in the Italian motion-picture industry—the "new" or "leftist political" cinema, which pitted its works, imbued with an antifascist, anticolonialist, democratic spirit, against the commercial output of the bourgeois cinema. The most prominent representatives of Italian "political cinema" include the directors Petri (*Investigation of a Citizen Above Suspicion*, 1969, and *The Working Class Goes to Heaven*, 1971), Rosi (*People Opposed*, 1970, and *The Mattei Affair*, 1972), and G. Montaldo (*God Is With Us*, 1969, and *Sacco and Vanzetti*, 1971). Other outstanding adherents of this trend are G. Pontecorvo (*Battle of Algiers*, 1966, and *Burn!*, 1971), B. Bertolucci (*The Conformist* and *The Spider's Strategem*, both in 1969), Zurlini (*The One Sitting on the Right*, 1969), Puccini (*The Seven Cervi Brothers*, 1967), and

D. Damiani, whose film *The Police Commissioner's Confession to the Prosecutor of the Republic* (1970) received one of the main prizes at the Seventh International Film Festival in Moscow in 1971.

M. Bolognini directed a significant film about the working class based on Pratolini's novel *Metello* (1970). The "leftist political cinema" has the support of members of the older generation (for example, Visconti's *Götterdämmerung* [in English, *The Damned,* 1968] and De Sica's *The Garden of the Finzi-Continis,* 1971). While Fellini produced the film *Satyricon* (1969; based on Petronius' novel), which was pervaded by a sense of the collapse of civilization and world catastrophe, Antonioni managed to move away from his main theme of human isolation. Working in the USA, he made the film *Zabriskie Point* (1970), which angrily castigated the brutal reality of American society and reflected the attitudes of rebellious American youth. This picture rightfully holds a prominent place both in Italian political cinema and in progressive American cinema.

Progressive documentary motion pictures, almost all of which are produced by amateur film-makers, have developed successfully in the postwar years. A democratic movement of amateur film-makers emerged and was formally organized on the initiative of the prominent film theorist C. Zavattini. Issued in 1970–71 were full-length documentary films about the strike struggle of the working class (*The Contract* and *Apollo,* directed by U. Gregoretti) and a film about the living conditions of Italian working people (*The Poor Die Sooner,* directed by Bertolucci). The film *The Tent on the Square,* which was shot by the actor G. M. Volentè in 1972, dealt with the struggle of strikers in Rome.

The most famous actors of the postwar Italian cinema include A. Magnani, G. Masina, S. Loren, G. Lollobrigida, C. Cardinale, M. Mastroianni, G. M. Volentè, A. Sordi, Totò, and U. Tognazzi. Soviet and Italian film-makers are beginning to collaborate in creative work, making a number of films together: *They Were Moving East* (in the US, *Attack and Retreat*), directed by G. De Santis (1964); *The Red Tent,* directed by M. K. Kalatozov (1970); *Sunflower,* directed by De Sica (1971); and *Waterloo,* directed by S. F. Bondarchuk (1971). Among the film festivals held in Italy are the International Film Festival in Venice (in 1932 and 1934–38 and since 1946) and festivals of documentary, scientific, and popular-education films in Padua, of travelogues in Trento, of comic films in Bordighera, of science-fiction films in Trieste, and of children's films in Palermo.

There are more than 40 film companies in Italy, and all of the largest film studios are located in Rome (including C. Ponti's and D. De Laurentis' firms). The Italian motion-picture industry produces more than 200 films a year. There are about 20,000 film projectors, of which about one-third belong to parishes. The Vatican and the Catholic Church influence the cinema through the Catholic press and the Catholic Film Center, as well as the parishes. The Communist Party and Italy's leftist forces give broad support to progressive figures in the motion-picture industry and struggle to preserve the national and democratic character of the Italian art of film. Among the specialized film journals are *Cinema nuovo, Bianco e nero, Filmcritica,* and *Cinema e film.* Many television movies are produced.

REFERENCES
Lizzani, C. *Ital'ianskoe kino.* Moscow, 1956. (Translated from Italian.)
Chiarini, L. *Sila kino.* Moscow, 1955. (Translated from Italian.)
Sadoul, G. *Vseobshchaia istoriia kino,* vols. 2, 3, 6. Moscow, 1958–63. (Translated from French.)
Solov'eva, I. *Kino Italii (1945–60): Ocherki.* Moscow, 1961.
Bogemskii, B. *Vittorio De Sica.* Moscow, 1963.
Shitova, V. *Lukino Visconti.* [Moscow, 1965.]
Katsev, I. *Dzhuzeppe De Santis.* [Moscow, 1965.]
Muratov, L. G. *Ital'ianskii ekran.* Leningrad, 1971.

G. D. BOGEMSKII [11–1–1]

ITAMI, a city in Japan on Honshu, in Hyogo Prefecture; northwest suburb of Osaka. Population, 154,000 (1970). It has enterprises of the pharmaceutical, rubber, textile, and food and condiment industries. [11–143–1]

ITAPECURÚ, a river in northeastern Brazil. The Itapecurú is about 650 km long and drains an area of about 40,000 sq km. The river rises in the Serra do Itapecurú on the northern rim of the Brazilian Plateau and flows into the São José Bay of the Atlantic. The Itapecurú is fed by rainwater, and high water occurs between March and May. The average discharge is less than 100 cu m per sec. The city of Codó lies on the river.

[11–143–2]

ITATKA, an urban-type settlement in Tomsk Raion, Tomsk Oblast, RSFSR. It is a railroad station on the Tomsk-Asino line, 54 km northeast of Tomsk. It has a logging and timber distribution enterprise. [11–144–1]

ITATSKII, an urban-type settlement in the Tiazhin Raion, Kemerovo Oblast, RSFSR. Railroad station (Itat) on the Novosibirsk-Achinsk line. It has a dairy and vegetable-drying plant. [11–144–2]

ITEL'MEN LANGUAGE, the language of the Itel'meny, one of the Paleo-Siberian languages of the Chukchi-Kamchatka family. It is spoken by 464 persons (1970 census) in Tigil' Raion, Koriak National Okrug, Kamchatka Oblast (on the western coast of Kamchatka). Of the three Itel'men dialects—the southern, eastern (Kamchatoretskii), and western—still spoken in the early 19th century, only two subdialects of the western dialect have survived. Itel'men does not have a script.

The phonetic system shows a high degree of consonant saturation, and the morphology is agglutinative. Grammatical formants and certain roots reveal a kinship to the Chukchi and Koriak languages, although the sound relationships between these languages have been little studied.

REFERENCES
Moll, T. A. "Ocherk fonetiki i morfologii sedankinskogo dialekta itel'-menskogo iazyka." *Uch. zap. Leningradskogo gos. ped. in-ta,* 1960, vol. 167.
Volodin, A. P., and A. N. Zhukova. "Itel'menskii iazyk." In the collection *Iazyki narodov SSSR,* vol. 5. Leningrad-Moscow, 1968.
Bogoras, W. "Chukchee." In F. Boas, *Handbook of American Indian Languages,* part 2. Washington, 1922.

A. P. VOLODIN [11–144–3]

ITEL'MENY, a people living in Tigil' Raion, Koriak National Okrug, Kamchatka Oblast. Numbering 1,300 (1970 census) persons, they speak the Itel'men language and Russian. The time of their appearance on the Kamchatka Peninsula has not been established. At the end of the 17th century, when Kamchatka was annexed to Russia, the Itel'meny inhabited almost the entire peninsula. They lived in a primitive communal system and engaged in fishing and hunting using Neolithic-type stone and bone implements. In the middle of the 18th century, under the influence of Russian settlers, the Itel'meny began to master vegetable gardening and stock raising. At the same time, the process of the merging of the Itel'meny and the Russians was under way. (This mixed population as well as the Itel'meny proper was called the Kamchadaly.) Fundamental changes have occurred in the Itel'-men economy and culture in the Soviet period. Most of the population is engaged in kolkhoz production (fishing, hunting, vegetable gardening, and stock raising). Illiteracy has been eradicated, and a national intelligentsia has emerged.

REFERENCE
Narody Sibiri. Moscow-Leningrad, 1956. (Bibliography.)

V. V. ANTROPOVA [11–144–4]

ITERATION, in mathematics, the result of a repeated application of some mathematical operation. Thus, if $y = f(x) \equiv f_1(x)$ is some function of x, then the functions $f_2(x) = f[f_1(x)]$, $f_3(x) = f[f_2(x)]$, . . . , $f_n(x) = f[f_{n-1}(x)]$ are called, respectively, the second, third, . . . , nth iterations of the function $f(x)$. For example, letting $f(x) = x^\alpha$, we obtain $f_2(x) = (x^\alpha)^\alpha = x^{\alpha^2}$, $f_3(x) = (x^{\alpha^2})^\alpha = x^{\alpha^3}$, and $f_n(x) = (x^{\alpha^{n-1}})^\alpha = x^{\alpha^n}$. The index n is termed the iteration index, and the transition from the function $f(x)$ to the functions $f_2(x)$, $f_3(x)$ . . . is called iteration. For certain classes of functions one may define iteration with an arbitrary real or even a complex index. Iterative methods are used in the solution of various types of equations and systems of equations.

REFERENCE
Collatz, L. *Funktsional'nyi analiz i vychislitel'naia matematika.* Moscow, 1969. (Translated from German.) [11–144–6]

ITERATIVUS, in biology, the capacity of certain tissues (for example, sympathetic-nerve plexuses and smooth muscles) to react to stimuli only when the stimuli follow one another with sufficient frequency. The explanation of iterativus is that each stimulus, while individually subliminal, increases the excitability of the tissue until the successive stimulation becomes supraliminal and produces excitation. [11–144–5]

ITIL', the capital of the Khazar state from the eighth to the tenth century, located 15 km above present-day Astrakhan on the banks of the Itil' River (Volga) and on a small island. Its inhabitants included Khazars, Turks, Slavs, and Jews. The population engaged in livestock raising, agriculture, fishing, handicrafts, and trade. The palace of the *kagan* was located in Itil', and the city also had temples, schools, baths, and bazaars. Dwellings consisted of wooden tents, felt yurts, and pit houses. In 965 the Kievan prince Sviatoslav Igorevich destroyed Itil'.

REFERENCES
Artamonov, M. I. *Istoriia khazar.* Leningrad, 1962. [11–146–3]

ITIL', in medieval Arabic and Persian literature, the Volga River. Tatars, Bashkirs, Chuvashes, and several other Turkic-speaking peoples still refer to the Volga as the Itil' River. [11–146–2]

ITO, MARQUIS HIROBUMI. Born Sept. 2, 1841, in the village of Toka, Suo Province; died Oct. 26, 1909, in Harbin. Japanese statesman and diplomat.

Ito directed the drafting of the reactionary Japanese constitution of 1889 (operative until 1946). He was the prime minister four times, 1885–88, 1892–96, 1898, and 1900–01. As one of the genro, he greatly influenced the policies of the Japanese monarchy during the last third of the 19th century and the first decade of the 20th. In 1900, Ito organized the bourgeois-landowner party Seiyukai. From 1906 to 1909 he was a general resident in Korea. During his residence there, he prepared for its annexation. Ito was assassinated by a Korean patriot. [11–146–6]

ITSENKO-CUSHING'S DISEASE (from the names of the Soviet neuropathologist N. M. Itsenko, 1889–1954, and the American neurosurgeon H. W. Cushing, 1869–1939), a disorder caused by excessive secretion of the pituitary adrenocorticotropic hormone (ACTH) with a consequent increase in adrenal function.

Excessive pituitary function may be caused by a tumor (basophilic adenoma) or by injury to the hypothalamic region of the brain, the site of production of a special substance (corticotropin releasing factor) that intensifies the synthesis and liberation of adrenocorticotropic hormone (ACTH). The symptom complex of Itsenko-Cushing's disease is brought about by the elevated level of secretion of adrenocortical hormones (glucocorticoids, mineralocorticoids, and ketosteroids); manifestations include adiposis (mainly in the region of the pectoral girdle, trunk, abdomen, and face), hypertension, hirsutism (in females), osteoporosis, diabetes mellitus, lowered sexual function, and dryness of the cutaneous integuments. Treatment involves X-irradiation of the pituitary region. Symptomatic treatment includes the administration of agents that lower blood pressure, antidiabetic preparations, and substances that inhibit adrenal function (amphenone, metopyrone). Subtotal or total adrenalectomy may be performed and followed by the administration of adrenal hormones.

M. I. BALABOLKIN [11–165–2]

ITÚRBIDE, AGUSTÍN DE. Born Sept. 27, 1783, in Valladolid, now Morelia; died July 19, 1824, in Padilla. Mexican statesman and military figure. Son of a Spanish nobleman.

Itúrbide joined the Spanish Army in 1798 and was promoted to the rank of colonel. He participated in the suppression of the national liberation movement that broke out in Mexico in 1810 and conducted cruel reprisals against Mexican patriots. During the Spanish revolution of 1820–23, Itúrbide, reflecting the interests of Mexican landowners, clergy, and military, headed a military action for separation from Spain. On May 19, 1822, Itúrbide proclaimed himself emperor under the name Agustín I and established a terrorist regime. The complete financial bankruptcy of the Itúrbide government and the siding of the army with the republicans led to the fall of the Itúrbide empire, and in March 1823, Itúrbide abdicated and fled to Europe. In 1824 he returned illegally to Mexico and was captured and shot.

REFERENCES
Al'perovich, M. S. *Voina za nezavisimost' Meksiki (1810–1824).* Moscow, 1964. Pages 268–338. [11–148–1]

ITURUP, the largest of the Kuril Islands (Sakhalin Oblast, RSFSR). Area, 6,725 sq km; length, 200 km; width, from 7 to 27 km. Iturup, which is in the southern part of the chain, consists of volcanic massifs and mountain ranges. The island has heights up to 1,634 m. Its coasts are high and precipitous. Alder shrubs are located in the northeastern part of the island; copses of Kuril larch are in the central part. In the southwest, there are mixed forests with lianas. Thickets of Kuril bamboo grow in the underbrush. Erman's birch and Japanese stone pines are found in the upper mountain belt. The city of Kuril'sk is located on Iturup. [11–148–2]

IUL'TIN, an urban-type settlement in Iul'tin Raion, Chukchi National Okrug, Magadan Oblast, RSFSR. Situated in the spurs of the Ekvyvatapskii range, Iul'tin is linked by highway with the port of Egvekinot (on Zaliv Kresta in the Bering Sea). Iul'tin is the site of an ore-dressing combine. [11–154–2]

IYVAN, KYRLIA (Kirill Ivanovich Ivanov). Born Mar. 4 (17), 1909; died 1943. Soviet Mari poet and film actor.

Iyvan was born in the village of Kupsola, in present-day Sernur Raion, Mari ASSR. He played the role of Mustafa in the first Soviet sound film, *The Road to Life* (1931). Iyvan first appeared in print in 1929. In 1931, he published (with Olyk Ipai) the verse collection *We Are Shock Workers.* In 1932 he published the collection *The Voice of Revolution, I Sing,* and in 1935, *Birthday.*

WORKS
In Russian translation:
Ot radosti poiu. (Introductory article by P. Zheleznov and reminiscences by M. Zharov and M. Kazakov.) Moscow, 1968.
REFERENCES
Mariiskie pisateli: Biobibliograficheskii spravochnik. Ioshkar-Ola, 1958.
Ocherki istorii mariiskoi literatury, part 1. Ioshkar-Ola, 1963. [11–240–3]

JAEGER, HANS HENRIK. Born Sept. 2, 1854, in Drammen; died Feb. 8, 1910, in Oslo. Norwegian writer.

Jaeger was trained in philosophy. His best-known dramatic work is the didactic play *Olga* (1883). In his naturalistic novel *From the Christiania Bohème* (1885), he contrasted anarchic personal freedom with bourgeois morality. The later novels *Diseased Love* (1893) and *Prison and Despair* (1895) reveal the decline of his creative powers.

WORKS
Faengsel og fortvilelse. [Christiania, 1902.]
REFERENCES
Shiller, F. P. *Istoriia zapadnoevropeiskoi literatury,* vol. 2. Moscow, 1937.
Storstein, O. *Hans Jaeger.* Oslo, 1935. [11–187–2]

JEDLIK, ÁNYOS ISTVÁN. Born Jan. 11, 1800, in Simö, now Zemno, Slovakia; died Dec. 13, 1895, in Győr. Hungarian scientist and inventor in electrical engineering. Member of the Hungarian Academy of Sciences (1858). Son of a peasant.

After graduating from a Benedictine lycée in Győr, Jedlik became a teacher in a *Gymnasium.* In 1840 he became a professor of physics at the University of Pest. He constructed the first model of a rotating electric motor (1827–28) and was the first to discover the principle of self-excitation, which he used in the multidisk unipolar generator he built in 1861. He invented a device that was the prototype of the capacitance voltage multiplier; the invention received a medal at the Vienna World's Fair in 1873, but it was never produced. Jedlik improved the design of voltaic cells and storage batteries, and he built a precision dividing machine. A number of his works dealt with optics and other areas of physics.

REFERENCES
Tsverava, G. K. *An'osh Iedlik.* Leningrad, 1972.
Ferenczy, V. *Jedlik Ányos István élete és alkotásai,* parts 1–4. Győr, 1936–39.   G. K. TSVERAVA [11–187–3]

JENA, a city in the German Democratic Republic, in the district of Gera, on the Saale River. Population, 88,300 (1970). Railroad junction. Jena is a center of the optical instrument industry. It is the site of the Carl Zeiss–Jena Plant, which employs 18,000 people and is one of the world's biggest enterprises. The plant produces various optical instruments, astronomical equipment, light and electron microscopes, medical equipment, camera lenses, and binoculars. These products, as well as optical glass and medicines, are manufactured primarily for export. Jena is the site of the Friedrich Schiller University, a planetarium, a seismological institute, an observatory, a botanical garden, and a school for preparing specialists in the fields of precision mechanics, optics, and medicine.   [11–213–1]

JENA, UNIVERSITY OF (also, Friedrich Schiller University), one of the major universities in the German Democratic Republic. It was founded in 1558 from an academy in Jena. At the time of its founding, the university had faculties of theology, law, and medicine, as well as a preparatory faculty of the fine arts. Until the end of the Thirty Years' War (1618–48), it was a stronghold of orthodox Lutheranism.

The university's first significant period of development occurred in the second half of the 17th century. In 1663, G. von Leibniz became a student there. In the 1690's the university began to experience a period of declining importance that lasted until the end of the 18th century. It subsequently became a center of 19th-century German romanticism, which embodied the ideas of the revolutionary bourgeoisie, and of classical bourgeois philosophy. Among those associated with the University of Jena at that time were J. W. von Goethe, J. G. Fichte, F. von Schelling, and F. von Schiller. From 1801 to 1807, G. Hegel taught a philosophy course at Jena. The well-known scientist and physiophilosopher L. Oken also played a major role at the university in the early 19th century. In 1841, Karl Marx defended his doctoral dissertation at the University of Jena. During the second half of the 19th century, the significance of natural science specializations became particularly great. The physicist E. Abbe and the biologist E. Haeckel did their work at the university. In the late 19th and early 20th centuries the University of Jena was the focus of extremely reactionary national-chauvinistic and aggressive imperialist ideology. In 1933 it became a center of fascist ideology.

Although it was heavily damaged during World War II, the university was reopened in 1945. It was the first university in the German Democratic Republic to be reopened after the war. A faculty for workers and peasants, which offered secondary school level courses, was organized there. As of the academic year 1971–72, there were 15 faculties: Marxism-Leninism, philosophy and history, philology, economics and cybernetics, pedagogy, literature and art, medicine, biology, chemistry, physics, mathematics, technology, law, theology, and physical education. Approximately 5,000 students were enrolled at the university; the teaching staff numbered more than 500. The university library, which was founded in 1558, housed more than 2 million volumes in 1971.   [11–215–3]

JENA-AUERSTÄDT, BATTLE OF (1806), two related battles fought on October 14 between the French and the Prussian-Saxon armies during the Russian-Prussian-French War of 1806–07.

In early October 1806, the Duke of Brunswick's Prussian-Saxon army of more than 100,000 men held defensive positions in the Jena-Weimar region. Napoleon's army of over 150,000 men moved from the Bamberg-Bayreuth region through the Frankenwald (Franconian Forest), trying to reach the flank and rear of the enemy. The main Prussian forces, over 50,000 men, began to retreat toward Auerstädt, leaving Prince F. von Hohenlohe's corps of 38,000 men at Jena and Rüchel's corps of 15,000 men at Weimar. Napoleon, taking Hohenlohe's corps for the main forces, turned the bulk of his troops toward Jena and Apolda; only L. Davout's corps of 27,000 men advanced toward Auerstädt. At Jena, Napoleon easily routed the Prussians, who lost 27,000 men and 200 guns. Davout's corps, despite the numerical superiority of the enemy, also defeated the Prussian troops, who lost 18,000 men and 115 guns in the engagement and fled from the field in panic.

Prussia was defeated because of the poor fighting capacity of its army, which relied on brutal discipline, continued to use the obsolete linear tactics, and was led by unimaginative generals. Napoleon's victory at Jena-Auerstädt led to the complete defeat of feudal Prussia and demonstrated the superiority of the military system of bourgeois France.   [11–213–2]

JENSEN, FRITZ. Born Dec. 26, 1903, in Prague; died Apr. 11, 1955, in Sawarak, northeastern Singapore. Austrian writer and journalist. Member of the Communist Party of Austria from 1929. A doctor by education.

Jensen was a doctor in the People's Liberation Army of China from 1939 to 1947. He was the founder, director, and an actor of the agitation troupe in Vienna. Jensen began publishing revolutionary poems in the early 1930's. In February 1934 he participated in the armed struggle of the Viennese workers against government troops and was thrown into a concentration camp. In 1936 he became chief doctor of the International Brigades, which fought in republican Spain. From 1950 to 1953, Jensen was editor of *Volksstimme,* the central organ of the Communist Party of Austria. His book *Reminiscences About Vietnam,* which was published in 1955, described the establishment of the Democratic Republic of Vietnam.

WORKS
China siegt, 2nd ed. Berlin, 1950.
Opfer und Sieger. Berlin, 1955.   [11–215–2]

JENSEN, JOHANNES HANS DANIEL. Born June 25, 1907, in Hamburg. German physicist.

Jensen studied first at the University of Freiburg and then at the University of Hamburg. From 1937 to 1941 he was a docent at the latter, and from 1941 to 1949 he was a professor at the Technische Hochschule in Hanover. In 1949 he became a professor at the University of Heidelberg. His principal works are concerned with the theory of atomic nuclei. He substantiated a number of features of atomic nuclei, in particular, the existence of the "magic" nuclei, which have high stability. With his coworkers (but independently of M. Göppert-Mayer) Jensen developed the shell model of the nucleus. He received a Nobel Prize in 1963.

WORKS
Elementary Theory of Nuclear Shell Structure. New York, 1955. (With M. Göppert-Mayer.)
In Russian translation:
Elementarnaia teoriia iadernykh obolochek. Moscow, 1958.
REFERENCE
Bagge, E. *Die Nobelpreisträger der Physik.* Munich, 1964.
                    [11–215–1]

JENSEN, JOHANNES VILHELM. Born Jan. 20, 1873, in Farsø, Jutland; died Nov. 25, 1950, in Copenhagen. Danish writer.

Jensen studied medicine and worked as a journalist. His first novels were *The Danes* (1896) and *Einar Elkjaer* (1898). In his collections of stories *Himmerland Tales* (1898–1910), Jensen describes the natural beauty of northern Jutland and the everyday life of its people. His historical novel *The Fall of the King* (parts 1–3, 1900–01) portrays the struggle of the Danish peasantry against the feudal lords in the Middle Ages. He propounded a theory of the rebirth of the "Gothic race" in such works as his collection of essays *Gothic Renaissance* (1901). Jensen's predilection for racial and biological theories is shown in his novel cycle *The Long Journey* (parts 1–6, 1908–22; Nobel Prize, 1944). In the novels *Madame d'Ora* (1904) and *The Wheel* (1905), he realistically depicted life in capitalist America. Jensen also published the collections *Poems* (1906), *Myths* (1907–44), *Seasons* (1923), and *Jutland Wind* (1931). Realism and modernistic tendencies are combined in his art.

WORKS
Samlede skrifter, vols. 1–8. Copenhagen, 1916.
In Russian translation:
Sobr. soch., vols. 1–9. Moscow, 1911–12.

REFERENCES
Gelsted, O. *Johannes Vilhelm Jensen.* Copenhagen, 1938.
Elbek, J. *J. V. Jensen.* [Copenhagen, 1966.]
Nedergaard, L. *J. V. Jensen.* Copenhagen, 1968.

A. A. KITLOV   [11–214–3]

JENSEN, WILHELM. Born Feb. 15, 1837, in Heiligenhafen, Schleswig-Holstein; died Nov. 24, 1911, in Munich. German writer.

Jensen was the son of a bureaucrat. He studied medicine, history, and philosophy at the universities of Breslau and Munich. His lyric poetry is imbued with an elegiac mood (the collection *Verses,* 1869). Jensen is the author of realistic novels and short stories based on contemporary themes, such as *Dark Erika* (1868) and *From an Old Family* (1884). His most interesting novels are *Around the Imperial Throne* (1878) and *Lost Worlds* (1882). Jensen's later works contain elements of fantasy (the novel *Gradiva,* 1903; Russian translation, 1912).

WORKS
Ausgewählte Gedichte. Leipzig, 1912.

REFERENCE
Schorn, K. *W. Jensen, der Mensch, seine Weltanschauung und seine Kunst.* Bonn [1924]. (Dissertation.)   [11–214–2]

JEWISH WAR (A. D. 66–73), an anti-Roman uprising in the Roman province of Judea sparked by abuses on the part of the Roman procurator Florus.

The uprising was headed by the Zealots and the Sicarii, who expressed the interests of the peasants and artisans. In the beginning they captured Jerusalem, and a Roman punitive expedition was completely defeated in November 66. In response the Romans sent a strong army under the command of the general Vespasian Flavius against the rebels, and in 67 and 68 the Roman army subjugated a large part of Judea. After the fall of Galilee, Johanan (John) of Giscala, the leader of the Galilean Zealots, broke through with his detachment to Jerusalem and assumed the leadership of the uprising. The general Joseph ben Mattathias (Flavius Josephus) defected to the Romans. When Vespasian was proclaimed emperor in 69 his son Titus was put in command of the Roman army, and he proceeded to lay siege to Jerusalem. An internecine struggle broke out in the besieged city. At first the struggle was between the Zealots and partisans of the Sanhedrin, the latter composed of representatives of the higher priesthood who wanted to surrender the city to the Romans; later, conflict developed between groups of Zealots and Sicarii, the latter led by Simeon bar Giora, who advocated a more resolute struggle. After a five-month siege the Romans captured Jerusalem, destroyed the city and the Temple (August 70), and made slaves of the prisoners, including Johanan. Simeon bar Giora was executed in Rome. The resistance of the Sicarii lasted until 73, when their last stronghold, the fortress of Masada, fell. The chief source for the history of the Jewish War is Flavius Josephus' *The Jewish War.*

REFERENCE
Ranovich, A. "Sotsial'naia revoliutsiia v Iudee v 66–73 gg." *Vestnik drevnei istorii,* 1937, no. 1.   I. L. MAIAK   [11–153–1]

JIHLAVA, a city in Czechoslovakia, in the southeastern part of the Czech Socialist Republic; located in the district of South

Moravia, on the Jihlava River. Population, 40,000 (1970). It is an important transportation junction and the site of machine-building, textile, woodworking, and food-processing industries. A number of examples of the architecture of the 13th through 16th centuries have been preserved there.   [11–217–1]

JIHLAVA, a river in Czechoslovakia (Danube basin). Length, 184 km. Basin area, about 3,000 sq km. It rises in the Jihlava Hills of the Bohemian-Moravian Highlands. At first it flows through a deep valley (up to 160 m), and in its lower reaches it crosses a plain. The water level is at flood stage in March. The cities of Jihlava and Třebíč are situated on the river.
[11–216–5]

JIHLAVA HILLS, mountains in Czechoslovakia; the southwest part of the Bohemian-Moravian Highlands. They rise to an altitude of 837 m (Mount Javořice). The hills are composed chiefly of granite and gneiss and have deposits of nonferrous and precious metals. The quarrying of granite is well developed. The hills are crisscrossed by numerous rivers belonging to the Morava and Vltava river systems (the Danube and Elbe basins, respectively). Fir forests and meadows prevail, with cultivated lands on the lower slopes.   [11–217–2]

JIZERA, the northwestern part of the Sudetes Mountains in Poland and Czechoslovakia. Length, about 40 km; maximum altitude, 1,127 m. In appearance, it is a mass of folded stone blocks, with steep, fault-like slopes and a flat top. The range is composed primarily of granite and crystalline schist. Coniferous forests cover the mountainsides.   [11–217–5]

JIZERA, a river in Czechoslovakia; its headwaters are on the border between Poland and Czechoslovakia. Rising in the Jizera Mountains, the river flows primarily over the hilly plains of North Bohemia until it joins the Labe (Elbe) River, entering it from the right. Length, 163 km. Basin area, 2,200 sq km. The average rate of flow in its lower reaches is about 25 cu m per sec. Its waters are used for timber rafting, as well as to drive a hydroelectric power plant. The cities of Turnov and Mladá Boleslav are located on the river.   [11–217–4]

JODL, ALFRED. Born May 10, 1890, in Würzburg; died Oct. 16, 1946, in Nuremberg. Colonel general (1944) of the fascist German Army.

Jodl fought in World War I and later served in staff positions of the Reichswehr and was chief of the Home Defense Department. From August 1939 to May 1945, Jodl was chief of operations of fascist Germany's armed forces and Hitler's chief adviser on operations and strategy. In the last days of the war his responsibilities were limited to the western theaters of operation. In Reims on May 7, 1945, on the instructions of Admiral K. Doenitz, Jodl signed the unconditional surrender of the German armed forces to the Western Allies. Tried as a war criminal, he was sentenced to death by the International Military Tribunal in Nuremberg on Oct. 1, 1946, and was hanged.   [11–221–3]

JOENPELTO, EEVA. Born June 17, 1921, in Sammatti. Finnish writer.

Joenpelto studied at the University of Helsinki. Her first novel, *The City of Kaakerholm* (1950), portrays the hard life of peasant women. The novel *Burning Rock* (1953) describes workers in a quarry. In *The Girl Walking Above the Waters* (1955) and its sequel *Sparkling Years* (1961), the lives of "little people" are shown against a broad social background. Psychological problems are explored in the novella *Brother's Shadow* (1951) and in the novels *Where the Birds Sing* (1957), *Late Summer* (1960), *Wise Men Sit in the Shade* (1964), *The Knight From the Depth of the Woods* (1966), and *Whether He Wanted To or Not* (1969).

REFERENCE
Tarkka, P. *Suomalaisia nykykirjailijoita.* Helsinki, 1968.   [11–240–1]

JOENSUU, a city in eastern Finland, on Lake Pyhäselkä (in the Saimaa system of lakes). Population, 36,600 (1970). Joensuu is the administrative center of the province of Pohjois-Karjala. The city is a commercial and transportation center and a timber-rafting lake port. Sawed lumber and plywood are produced in the city. [11–240–2]

JÕGEVA, a city (since 1938); the center of Jõgeva Raion, Estonian SSR. It is located on the Pedja River (in the basin of Lake Chudskoe). Jõgeva has a railroad station on the Tallinn-Tartu line, 50 km northwest of Tartu. The city has a creamery. The State Selection Station of the Estonian Scientific Research Institute for Agriculture and Land Reclamation is located near Jõgeva. [11–240–4]

JOHANI, ANDRUS. Born Aug. 19 (Sept. 1), 1906, in Tallinn; died Aug. 18, 1941. Estonian painter and draftsman.

Johani studied at the Tallinn State School of Industrial Arts (1922–26) and in Tartu under A. Vabbe at the "Pallas" Higher School of Art (1926–33). He was an outstanding master of the democratic trend in Estonian fine arts of the 1930's and one of the founders of Soviet Estonian art. He created a number of genre compositions, portraits, and landscapes, which are imbued with a strongly optimistic attitude. His works include *Women Ironing Linen* (1932), *The Workers' Uprising of June 21, 1940, in Tartu* (1941; both in the Tartu Museum of Art), and *Portrait of the Artist's Father* (1940; Tallinn Museum of Art). Johani was executed by the fascists near Tartu.

REFERENCES
Andrus Johani, 1906–1941 [Näituse kataloog]. Tartu, 1956. (In Estonian and Russian.)
Erm, V. *A. Johani [Albums].* Tallinn, 1968. [11–235–4]

JOHANNESBURG, the largest city in the Republic of South Africa, in Transvaal Province. Population, 1,364,500 (1968), including 773,400 Africans, 76,300 Coloureds, 476,700 persons of European origin, and 38,100 persons of Asian origin.

Johannesburg arose in 1886 in the center of the extremely rich Witwatersrand goldfields. It was seized by British troops during the Boer War of 1899–1902 and was incorporated into the Union of South Africa in 1910, along with the entire Transvaal. The largest demonstrations of the proletariat and other progressive forces against exploitation, racism, and reaction in all southern Africa have taken place in Johannesburg. There have been many big strikes in Johannesburg and in the surrounding region, including those of 1914, 1918, 1920, 1922, 1946, and 1961. The Congress of Peoples, held in Johannesburg in 1955, adopted the Charter of Freedom, which has become the program of action of all the progressive forces of the Republic of South Africa.
I. A. NIKITINA

Johannesburg is the biggest commercial and industrial center of the Republic of South Africa. Numerous enterprises of the mining, metalworking, machine-building, chemical, printing, textile, leather, and food industries are concentrated in the Johannesburg region. The headquarters of the major mining and financial concerns that control the extraction of gold and other minerals in the Republic of South Africa are located in the city. Johannesburg is a major railroad center.

Under the rule of the racist government of the Republic, the African population is forced to live in settlements lacking running water and electricity and located on the outskirts of the city. The non-Europeans, who constitute the majority of the labor force in all enterprises, are cruelly exploited and used only in low-paid jobs. Discriminatory laws deprive them of elementary political and civil rights.

Johannesburg has a university and an astronomical observatory.
A. S. POKROVSKII

Johannesburg is divided by railroads into two parts. The northern part contains the administrative and European quarters, the southern part the industrial and workers' quarters. The center of the administrative part of the city is the site of a neoclassic city hall building (built in 1915), a Masonic lodge, a cathedral (built in 1926), a public library (an example of modern architecture), a theater (built in 1962), the railroad station, the air terminal, banks, hotels, private residences, and villas. [11–236–1]

JOHNSON, EYVIND. Born July 29, 1900, near Boden. Swedish writer. Member of the Swedish Academy (1957); co-recipient of the Nobel Prize with H. Martinson (1974).

Johnson's first collection of short stories, *Four Strangers* (1924), was followed by the novel *Timans and Justice* (1925), in which he denounces Christianity as hostile to the emancipation of the working class. The influence of psychoanalysis may be seen in his novel *Remembered* (1928). A factory owner is depicted with caustic irony in the novel *Commentary on a Falling Star* (1929), and the cycle of novels about Olof (1934–37) portrays the lives of working-class youth. Johnson's novel *Night Maneuvers* (1938) and the trilogy *Krilon: A Novel About the Possible* (1941–43) attack fascism. His novellas *Pan Against Sparta* (1946) and *Surf* (1946) and his historical novels *Dreams About Roses and Fire* (1949) and *Storm Clouds Over Metapontion* (1957) show the influence of symbolism. Another notable historical work is *The Age of His Greatness* (1960), a novel about the reign of Charlemagne.

WORKS
Spår förbi kolonos. [Stockholm, 1961.]
In Russian translation:
["Rasskazy."] In the collection *Shvedskaia novella XIX–XX vv.* Moscow, 1964.
REFERENCE
Svensk litteratur 1900–1950. Stockholm [1958].
Andersson, U. "Eyvind Johnson i Grekland." *Ny Dag,* Jan. 2, 1962.
A. V. MAMONTOV [11–227–4]

JOHO, WOLFGANG. Born Mar. 6, 1908, in Karlsruhe. German writer (German Democratic Republic [GDR]).

Joho joined the German Communist Party in 1929 and was subjected to repression by the Nazis between 1937 and 1945. In 1960 he became editor of the journal *Neue Deutsche Literatur.* He is the author of the short story *The Shepherd's Pipe* (1947), which describes the experiences of a young man called up into Hitler's army. His short stories "The End of Captivity" (1949) and "The Transformation of Dr. Brad" (1949), his collection of short stories *Changes* (1957), and his novels *Jeanne Peyrouton* (1949), *The Twelve and the Two* (1950), and *The Path Out of Solitude* (1953) deal with the bourgeois intelligentsia, the best of whom achieve an understanding of the workers. The novel *No Compassion* (1962) tells the story of an intellectual of the GDR who flees to West Germany and finds that he is unable to survive. Joho is the author of the historical novel *The Dreamer's Rebellion* (1966). He was awarded the T. Fontane Prize in 1958 and the National Prize of the GDR in 1962.

WORKS
Traum von der Gerechtigkeit. Berlin, 1956.
Die Nacht der Erinnerung. Berlin, 1957.
Die Wendemarke. Berlin, 1962.
Ich bin hier Arzt. Berlin, 1964.
Das Klassentreffen: Geschichte einer Reise. Berlin-Weimar, 1968.
In Russian translation:
"Tak bylo 9 maia." In the collection *Na perelome.* Moscow, 1951.
"Predatel'stvo." In the collection *Sovremennye nemetskie rasskazy.* Moscow, 1959.
"Reportazh iz masterskoi." *Voprosy literatury,* 1964, no. 5.
REFERENCES
Mlechina, I. "Drugogo puti net." *Inostrannaia literatura,* 1963, no. 8.
"Das Klassentreffen." (Review.) *Neue Deutsche Literatur,* 1969, no. 4.
S. V. ROZHNOVSKII [11–237–1]

JÓKAI, MÓR. Born Feb. 18, 1825, in Komárom; died May 5, 1904, in Budapest. Hungarian author from a minor gentry family. His first novel, *Weekdays* (1846), is written in the traditions of romanticism, with which his subsequent work is also associated.

Beginning in 1847, Jókai edited the progressive journal *Életképek.* In 1848, he and S. Petőfi took part in the revolution, but Jókai soon returned to a position of reconciliation with the Hapsburgs. He celebrated the national liberation struggle in his novels *The Golden Age of Transylvania* (1852) and *The Sons of the Man With a Heart of Stone* (1869; Russian translation, 1959; film of the same name, 1965). His enthusiasm for the idea of gradual reform is reflected in the novels *A Hungarian Nabob* (1853; film of the same name, 1966), *Zoltán Kárpáthy* (1854), and *The New Squire* (1863).

Jókai placed his hopes in the development of a capitalist economy (the novels *Black Diamonds,* 1870, and *A Man of Gold,* 1873; Russian translations, 1882). Elements of entertainment occupy an important place in Jókai's later work, but the novel *The Prisoner Rabi* (1879) and the novella *Yellow Rose* (1893; Russian translation, 1956) contain realistic features.

WORKS
Válogatott művei [vols. 1–32]. Budapest, 1954–62.
REFERENCES
Klaniczai, T., J. Szauder, and M. Szabolcsi. *Kratkaia istoriia vengerskoi literatury XI–XX vv.* Budapest, 1962. (Translated from Hungarian.)
Sőtér, I. *Romantika és realizmus.* Budapest, 1956.
Dely, Zs. *A fiatal Jókai nyelve és stilusa.* Budapest, 1969.

E. I. MALYKHINA   [11–222–4]

JOMMELLI, NICCOLÓ. Born Sept. 10, 1714, in Aversa, near Naples; died Aug. 25, 1774, in Naples. Italian composer, representative of the Neapolitan school of opera.

Jommelli became a member of the Bologna Philharmonic Academy in 1741. He composed more than 70 operas; among his most outstanding were *Merope* (1741), *Artaxerxes* (1749), and *Phaëthon* (1753; 2nd version, 1768). Jommelli also wrote church music (for example, the famous *Miserere*) and intermezzi (for example, *Don Falcone,* which was performed in St. Petersburg in 1779). Anticipating the operatic reforms of C. W. Gluck, he assigned an important place to the accompanied recitative and intensified the dramatic role of the chorus and the orchestra in his operas.

REFERENCES
Livanova, T. N. *Istoriia zapadno-evropeiskoi muzyki do 1789 goda.* Moscow-Leningrad, 1940.
Abert, N. *Niccoló Jommelli als Opernkomponist.* Halle, 1908.

[11–225–3]

JONAS, FRANZ. Born Oct. 4, 1899, in Vienna; died there Apr. 24, 1974. Austrian statesman.

Jonas graduated from a printing school in 1917, got a job in the printing industry in 1919, and joined the socialist youth movement and later the Social Democratic Party. From 1932 to 1934, Jonas directed a district organization of the party in Vienna and was arrested several times for participation in the Social Democratic movement. After the liberation of Austria from the fascist German troops (1945), Jonas worked in the municipality of Floridsdorf (a district of Vienna), helped found the Socialist Party of Austria (SPA), and was chairman of the Vienna organization of the SPA from 1949 to 1965 and a member of the board and vice-chairman of the SPA from 1950 to 1965. Mayor of Vienna from 1951 to 1965 and deputy to the Austrian Parliament from 1952 to 1965, Jonas became federal president of the Austrian Republic in June 1965.   [11–226–2]

JÓNASSON ÚR KÖTLUM, JÓHANNES. Born Nov. 4, 1899, in Dalir. Icelandic poet. Member of the Communist Party of Iceland from 1932 and of the United Socialist Party of Iceland since 1938.

The son of a poor peasant, Jónasson úr Kötlum was a teacher for many years. In 1926 he published *Lullaby* and in 1929 *The Swans Sing,* collections of romantic and patriotic poems. The collections of poems *I Feign Sleep* (1932) and *I Awoke Nevertheless* (1935) are devoted to the workers' struggle for their rights, and the collection *The Sun Darkens* (1945) is an antifascist work glorifying the heroism of the Soviet people in the Great Patriotic War (1941–45). In the collection *Seven-Day Journey* (1955) the poet attempts to renew the poetic language. He also wrote the novels *Guardian Angels* (1943) and *The Mountains Have Split* (1943), depicting the Icelandic people during World War II (1939–45), and between 1949 and 1952 he published a trilogy about the emigration of Icelanders to America in the late 19th century. Notable among his later works are the collections *Nonpoems* (1962) and *The Son of Man* (1966).

REFERENCES
Andresson, K. E. *Sovremennaia islandskaia literatura, 1918–1948.* Moscow, 1957.
Einarsson, S. *A History of Icelandic Literature.* New York, 1957.

A. BERGMAN   [11–235–3]

JONG, ADRIANUS MICHAEL DE. Born Mar. 28, 1888, in Niewe-Vossmeer; died Oct. 18, 1943, in Blaricum. Dutch writer.

The son of a worker, Jong earned his living as a teacher. He first appeared in print in 1916. From 1919 to 1925 he edited the newspaper *Net volk,* the organ of the Social Democratic Workers' Party of the Netherlands, and in 1927–28, he was one of the editors of the journal *Nu.* A participant in the Resistance Movement, he was shot by the SS.

In his two cycles of novels *The Youth of Merijntje Gijzen* (parts 1–4, 1925–28) and *The Early Manhood of Merijntje Gijzen* (parts 1–4, 1935–38), Jong criticized bourgeois society from the standpoint of abstract humanism. He wrote books for children and memoirs, notably *The Glorious Years of Frank van Wezel* (1928). In 1942–43, Jong wrote a biographical novel about G. A. Bredero, *Reckless Ensign,* published in 1947.

WORKS
Merijntje Gijzen's jeugd, vols. 1–4. Amsterdam, 1941.
De martelgang van kromme Lindert, 14th ed. Amsterdam, 1951.
REFERENCE
Kelk, C. J. *Rondom tien gestalten.* Utrecht, 1938.

IU. F. SIDORIN   [11–226–3]

JONGKIND, JOHAN BARTHOLD. Born June 3, 1819, in Lattrop, Overijssel; died Feb. 9, 1891, in Côte-Saint-André, France. Dutch painter and graphic artist.

Beginning in 1837, Jongkind studied in The Hague, in the Academy of Arts and with A. Schelfhout. From 1846 to 1849 he studied in Paris under E. Isabey and F. E. Picot. He worked in Holland (1855–60), Belgium (1866–69), and France. A realist, Jongkind influenced the first of the impressionists. In his landscapes he carefully depicted the characteristics of the villages and cities of each country and the working life of the inhabitants. His work is noted for the spontaneity of his impressions; a free, loose, sometimes sketchy painting style; and a light, subtle range of colors. Jongkind worked extensively in watercolors and etching.

REFERENCE
Bakker-Hefting, V. *J. B. Jongkind.* Amsterdam [1962].   [11–226–4]

JÖNKÖPING, a city in Sweden, on the south shore of Lake Vättern; the administrative center of Jönköping County (Län). Population, 55,400 (1970). Machine-building, paper, and match industries are there.   [11–216–1]

JOOS VAN WASSENHOVE (also called Justus of Ghent). Born circa 1435 in Antwerp or Ghent; died after 1475 in Italy. Flemish painter.

Joos van Wassenhove worked in Ghent and in Urbino, Italy, during the 1470's. He made use of the generalized imagery, monumental quality, and harmony of composition of Italian painting but retained the sharp articulation of detail typical of Flemish art (*Communion of the Apostles,* 1473–74, the National Gallery of the Marches, Urbino).

REFERENCE
Lavalleye, J. *Juste de Gand.* Louvain, 1936.   [11–234–1]

JORDAENS, JACOB. Born May 19, 1593, in Antwerp; died there Oct. 18, 1678. Flemish painter.

Jordaens, the son of a cloth merchant, began his artistic training under A. van Noort in 1607. He organized a large studio, where his many commissioned works were executed. Jordaens' work, which is noted for its keen sensory perception of life, its powerful brushwork, and its inexhaustible optimism, strongly reflects folk elements and the realist tendencies characteristic of the Flemish school of art. Early Dutch traditions and elements of Carravagism are also evident. In his early paintings, such as *Family Portrait* (c. 1615, Hermitage, Leningrad) and *The Adora-*

tion of the Shepherds (1618, National Museum, Stockholm), Jordaens uses many of Carravagio's devices. These devices include the crowded arrangement of common people in the foreground of the picture, the emphasis on the materiality of objects, and the contrasts of light and shade.

Among Jordaens' best works, which were painted in the 1620's and 1630's, are *The Education of Jupiter* (1620, Picture Gallery, Kassel), *Family Portrait* (c. 1622–25, Prado, Madrid), *The Allegory of Fertility* (c. 1625–28, Museum of Ancient Art, Brussels), and *Boonenfeest* (1638, Hermitage). These paintings reflect the distinctive characteristics of Jordaens' realism—a predilection for sanguine peasant and burgher types, strong heavy figures, and lavish details; a preference for genre scenes and secular treatment of religious and mythological themes; and the use of warm colors and a strong, energetic, impasto painting technique.

Beginning in the 1640's, Jordaens painted overly crowded ceremonial compositions, which were characterized by a sense of pompousness and false enthusiasm (for example, the panel *The Triumph of Prince Frederik Hendrik of Orange,* 1652, Huis ten Bosch, The Hague).

REFERENCES
[Smol'skaia, N.] *Iakob Iordans.* Moscow, 1959. [Album.]
Puyvelde, L. van. *Jordaens.* Paris-Brussels, 1953. [11–229–2]

JORDAN MEASURABLE REGION, a region having a definite area or, what is the same thing, a definite plane measure in the sense of Jordan. The distinguishing property of a (Jordan) measurable region D is the possibility of including it "between" two polygons such that one of them is contained within the given region; the other, on the contrary, contains it; and the difference between their areas can be made arbitrarily small. In this case there exists only one number confined between the areas of all containing and contained polygons; and it is called the area of the (Jordan) measurable region D.

Some properties of measurable regions are (1) if a measurable region D is contained within a measurable region D_1, then the area of D does not exceed the area of D_1; (2) a region D consisting of two nonintersecting measurable regions D_1 and D_2 is measurable, and its area is equal to the sum of the regions D_1 and D_2; and (3) the common part of two measurable regions D_1 and D_2 is again a measurable region. In order that a region D be measurable, it is necessary and sufficient that its boundary have an area equal to zero; there exist regions that do not satisfy this condition and consequently are nonmeasurable (in the Jordan sense). [11–1678–5]

JORIS, DAVID (Jorisz; pseudonym, Johann van Brugge). Born 1501 in Bruges; died Aug. 25, 1556, in Basel. One of the leaders of the Dutch Anabaptists.

Joris was a burgher from the city of Delft. In 1535 he became an Anabaptist leader. His greatest influence came after the crushing of the popular movement in 1534–35 in the northern Netherlands, which had been led by revolutionary Anabaptists. At a conference of Anabaptist leaders in Bocholt, Westphalia, in 1536, he sought to reconcile the revolutionary elements with the "nonresisters." His movement, known as Davidiorism or Davidism, rapidly declined after his death in 1556. [11–230–1]

JOTUNI, MARIA. Born Apr. 9, 1880, in Kuopio; died Sept. 30, 1943, in Helsinki. Finnish author.

Jotuni created a "portrait gallery" of different social groups of the city and countryside in the collections of short stories *Relationships* (1905), *Love* (1907), and *When There Are Feelings* (1913) and in the novella *Humdrum Life* (1909). Her comedies contrast the world of the well-to-do and their deceitful ethics with the world of honest laborers (*Man's Rib,* 1914). In the comedies *Golden Calf* (1918) and *Under His Wife's Thumb* (1924) she sharply criticizes social relations. The tragedy *Klaus, the Master of Louhikko* (1942, published 1946) was written on a folkloric subject, and the tragedy *I Am Guilty* (1929), which is devoted to the theme of war and peace, deals with a biblical topic. Jotuni raises problems of love and marriage in the novel *A Shaky House* (published 1963).

WORKS
Kootut teokset, [vols.] 1–4. Helsinki, 1930.
Valitut teokset. Helsinki, 1956.
REFERENCE
Tarkiainen, V., and E. Kauppinen. *Suomalaisen kirjallisuuden historia.* Helsinki [1961]. [11–235–2]

JOVANOVIĆ, SLOBODAN. Born Nov. 21, 1869, in Novi Sad; died Dec. 12, 1958, in London. Serbian and Yugoslav historian, statesman, and ideologist of the Great Serbian bourgeoisie.

Jovanović took his degree in law in Geneva in 1890. From 1897 to 1941 he was a professor at the Great School in Belgrade (the school became the University of Belgrade in 1905). From Mar. 27 through Apr. 6, 1941, he served as deputy prime minister in the government of D. Simović. From January 1942 through June 1943, Jovanović headed the royal government-in-exile in London. In May 1946 he became chairman of a reactionary organization of Yugoslav émigrés, the Yugoslav National Committee. Jovanović is the author of a series of works on the history of Serbia from 1838 through 1903.

WORKS
Sabrana dela [vols.] 1–17. Belgrade, 1932–40. [11–218–3]

JOVINE, FRANCESCO. Born Oct. 9, 1902, in Guardialfiera, in the province of Campobasso; died Apr. 30, 1950, in Rome. Italian writer.

Jovine participated in the Italian resistance movement during World War II (1939–45). In the collection of satirical short stories *Empire in the Provinces* (1945), he unmasks fascist demagogy. Jovine's best work is the novel *Lands of Sacramento* (1950), in which he describes the struggle of the Italian peasantry for land during fascism's accession to power in the 1920's. An outstanding phenomenon of neorealist literature, Jovine's novel influenced the development of that literature.

WORKS
In Russian translation:
Zemli Sakramento. Moscow, 1955.
REFERENCE
Potapova, Z. M. *Neorealizm v ital'ianskoi literature.* Moscow, 1961. [11–219–1]

JÓZSA, BÉLA. Born 1898, in the village of Hadiş, former district of Odorhei; died Nov. 22, 1943, in Someş. Active member of the Rumanian labor movement.

From 1919 to 1924, Józsa was the leader of a trade union of lumberjacks in Cluj and then of a trade union at a shipyard in Galaţi. After that he worked in Red Aid, an organization for aid to political prisoners, in Bucharest from 1924 to 1927. From 1927 to 1940 he headed the workers' solidarity organization in Cluj and was a member of the committee of the Transylvania and Banat organization of the Communist Party of Rumania. He was arrested repeatedly. He was secretary of the provincial party organization in Someş from 1940 to 1943. He was betrayed by an agent provocateur and brutally tortured to death by the Horthy political police. [11–222–1]

JÓZSEF, ATTILA. Born Apr. 11, 1905, in Budapest; died Dec. 3, 1937, in the village of Balatonszárszó. Hungarian poet; became a member of the Hungarian Communist Party in 1930.

József was the son of a worker. He studied at the universities of Szeged and Vienna and at the Sorbonne. Imitation of E. Ady, G. Juhász, and W. Whitman is noticeable in his first collection, *Beggar of Beauty* (1922). However, in his collections *It Is Not I Who Shouts* (1924) and *No Father or Mother* (1929), despite the well-known influence of expressionism and surrealism, he was already asserting his own defiantly grotesque, but at times sincere, lyric manner. József's poetry, in which an intense dramatism appears, reflects the unfortunate condition of working people and their will for revolutionary struggle (the collections *Root Out the Stumps and Don't Whine,* 1931; *Night on the Outskirts,* 1932; and *Bear's Dance,* 1934). In his last collection, *Very Painful* (1936), bitter protest is interwoven with depression and despair.

WORKS

Összes versei. [Budapest] 1966.
Összes művei, vols. 1–4. Budapest, 1952–67.
Irodalom és szocializmus. [Budapest] 1967.
In Russian translation:
Stikhotvoreniia. Moscow, 1958.
Stikhi. Moscow [1962].

REFERENCES

Shargina, L. "Attila Iozhef." In the collection *Pisateli stran narodnoi demokratii.* Moscow, 1959.
Rossiianov, O. "Poeticheskii obraz u Attily Iozhefa." In the collection *Poeziia sotsializma.* Moscow, 1969.
Szabolcsi, M. *Fiatal életek indulója.* Budapest, 1963.
Forgács, L. *József Attila esztétikája.* Budapest, 1965.
Tötök, G. *A lira: Logika.* Budapest, 1968.
Balogh, L. *József Attila,* 2nd ed. Budapest, 1970.

O. K. ROSSIIANOV   [11–222–2]

JUDAH, KINGDOM OF, an ancient state in southern Palestine (from about 928 B.C. to 586 B.C.).

The Kingdom of Judah was formed after the fall of the Kingdom of Israel and Judah (which had arisen in the late 11th century B.C.) and was ruled by a dynasty of David's descendants. Its capital was Jerusalem. The kingdom was essentially characterized by the same social and economic processes as those of the Kingdom of Israel. Judah was greatly weakened by an invasion of the Egyptians during the reign of Rehoboam (928–911 B.C.) and protracted wars with the Kingdom of Israel. During the reign of Uzziah (785–733 B.C.) the Kingdom of Judah regained control over Idumaea and gained access to the Red Sea. King Hezekiah (who reigned from 727 to 698 B.C.) carried out, under the influence of the prophet Isaiah, a number of military, economic, social, religious, and ritual reforms aimed at strengthening the country against the possibility of war with Assyria. Hezekiah's foreign policy was at first cautious; later he joined an anti-Assyrian coalition but suffered defeat and became a tributary of Assyria.

The reign of King Josiah from 639 to 609 B.C. was a landmark in the history of the kingdom: Judah threw off the Assyrian yoke and even annexed a considerable part of the territory of the former Kingdom of Israel. The conditions of debtor slaves were eased and the worship of Yahweh was centralized in Jerusalem. The last kings of Judah abandoned the pro-Babylonian orientation and tried unsuccessfully to ally themselves with Egypt. In 587 B.C. the Kingdom of Judah was conquered by the Babylonian king Nebuchadnezzar II, Jerusalem and the Temple were burned, and many inhabitants were driven into captivity (the Babylonian Exile).   I. D. AMUSIN [11–153–3]

JUDAISM, a religion that arose in Palestine during the first millennium B.C.; it is practiced among Jews. (There are no reliable statistical data on the number of practicing Jews; the majority live in Israel and the USA.)

According to biblical legend, certain Western Semitic (Hebrew) nomadic tribes fled from the Egyptian pharaoh into the desert in the 13th century B.C. At the time of their invasion of Palestine they were united by the common worship of Yahweh, a god of the tribal federation. The tribal federation, which took the name of Israel ("god strives"), took final shape by the 11th century B.C. The worship of Yahweh (the pronunciation of his name later became taboo and was replaced by the word "Lord") did not exclude the worship of other deities, both of the Hebrews' own tribes and of the local Canaanites. There were no images made of Yahweh and no temples built to him; a tabernacle, or tent, with a coffer, or ark, inside, devoted to Yahweh, was considered the earthly dwelling-place of the god, who was invisibly present throughout the world. The official rites were performed by a special tribal group, or caste, called Levites. After the establishment of the Kingdom of Israel and Judah in the late 11th century B.C., King Solomon (King David's son) built a temple to Yahweh in Jerusalem. The worship of Yahweh thus became the basis of the official ideology of the state, which defended the interests of the slaveholders. When the kingdom was divided in the tenth century B.C. into the northern Kingdom of Israel proper and the southern Kingdom of Judah, centered on Jerusalem, the Temple retained its importance primarily for the southern kingdom; the northern kingdom had temples of its own. But even the southern kingdom officially retained other places of worship, both of Yahweh and of other gods.

The prophetic movement, which arose in the ninth and eighth centuries B.C., played the most important role in the gradual development of Judaism into a dogmatic religion. Sermons of the prophets were recorded beginning in the eighth century B.C. In the beginning the prophets did not insist on the universality of Yahweh but declared him a "jealous god" who did not permit his "chosen people" to worship other gods. There arose the concept of the "covenant," or "testament," between the tribes of Israel and Yahweh, according to which the former allegedly pledged not to worship other gods and to carry out Yahweh's wishes while Yahweh promised to give them authority over Palestine. Circumcision was declared the external sign of the covenant; actually circumcision was a rite practiced by many other peoples of the ancient East and a survival of the initiation rite that accepted a boy into the community of warriors. Some prophets protested against various manifestations of social injustice while continuing to defend the slaveholder ideology, which was universal at the time.

The destruction of the northern Kingdom of Israel in 722 B.C. and the deliverance of Jerusalem from the Assyrian siege in 700 B.C. were used by the prophets to spread their ideas among the inhabitants of the Kingdom of Judah.

The books of Genesis, Exodus, Leviticus, and Numbers, which were ascribed to Moses, who, according to legend, led the Israelites during their nomadic period, were essentially composed in the ninth, eighth, and seventh centuries B.C. These books expounded the mythical past of the Israelites, in addition to their legal and ethical norms, in the spirit of the concepts of the covenant and the jealous god; the rituals and many elements of the mythological world view were taken from earlier religious traditions. The books interpreting the history of the kingdoms of Israel and Judah from the point of view of the fulfillment or nonfulfillment of Yahweh's conditions by the kings and the population also date from the eigthth, seventh, and sixth centuries B.C. By the eighth and seventh centuries B.C. the prophets already began to deny the existence of other gods except Yahweh, but there is evidence that the population continued to worship other gods as late as the fifth century B.C. A manuscript of Deuteronomy, which sums up the teachings of the prophets, was "discovered" when King Josiah rebuilt the Temple in Jerusalem in 622 B.C. In the early fourth century B.C., Deuteronomy, together with the other four books of Moses, became known as the Pentateuch, or Torah (Law), the part of the Holy Scripture, or Bible, most revered in Judaism. Subsequently all social ills that befell the ethnic groups practicing the Judaic religion were explained by deviations from the letter of the Torah. This made for the dogmatic character of Judaism and the great importance attached to the literally exact fulfillment of the rituals prescribed by the Torah.

In 587 B.C. the Babylonian king Nebuchadnezzar II resettled a large part of the Judahites in Babylonia and the Temple of Jerusalem was destroyed. Among the resettled Judahites the prophet Ezekiel preached the restoration of Israel, but this time as a theocratic state with a new Temple in Jerusalem as its center. The state was to be founded by a descendant of King David, or the Messiah. The Iranian religion influenced the development of Judaism during the period of Babylonian captivity.

Under the Persian dynasty of the Achaemenids the Judahites were returned to Jerusalem, which had become a self-governing Temple city (sixth and fifth centuries B.C.), and a new "Second Temple" of Yahweh was built. But the leaders of the new religious community, Ezra and Nehemiah, did not accept into this community the Judahites who had not gone into captivity and the Israelites who had remained in Palestine, under the pretext that they had mixed with people who worshiped other gods. The rejected groups created a separate community, the Samaritans, who live in Palestine to this day. After Ezra, the isolation of the practicing Jews—under the pretext that they are the chosen people—became one of the most important dogmas of Judaism; later, however, circumcision and the fulfillment of the demands of the Torah were recognized as sufficient conditions for entering into the covenant with god, regardless of the convert's origin.

In the third and second centuries B.C., a large number of Judahites were resettled by their Hellenic conquerors in Egypt, Syria, and Armenia. Judah itself, the site of a bitter class struggle, saw the rise of various currents within Judaism—for example, the Essenes, who condemned the official orientation of Judaism (the Pharisees) and preached asceticism and primitive social equality. Christianity too was originally a Judaic sect and only later became a separate religion, distinct from Judaism. However, the Christian Bible incorporated the Judaic holy books in their entirety (the Old Testament, or the ancient covenant, as distinct from the New Testament, or the Gospel).

The canon of the Holy Scriptures of Judaism was definitively established in about 100 B.C. The canon included the Torah, the Prophets (written records of religious and political speeches and historical books of a prophetic nature), and the Writings (books of a different nature recognized as conforming to the dogmas of Judaism, including the books of Ruth, Esther, and Job, Ecclesiastes, and the Song of Songs). When the written canon was introduced, literacy became mandatory for all males of the Judaic religious community; this rule was retained throughout the Middle Ages.

After two uprisings against Roman rule (the Jewish War of A.D. 66–73 and the Bar Kochba uprising of A.D. 132–135), the Jews were banished from Jerusalem.

The most important ritual innovation of the Diaspora was the replacement of worship in the Temple, which, according to dogma, could be done only in Jerusalem, by prayer assemblies in synagogues under the leadership of rabbis, or teachers of the religious law, instead of priests; the rabbis also usually governed the civil and legal life of the members of the religious community. The religious teachings of Judaism were further elaborated by commentaries on the Bible (the Mishnah; completed by the third century A.D.) and the Gemara, a collection of legal (halakah) and folkloric (agadah) interpretations of biblical texts, often incredibly lapidary, nebulous in form, subjective, and contradictory; the Gemara and the Mishnah together form the Talmud (completed by the fifth century A.D.). The development of the religious and philosophical foundation of Judaism (especially monotheism) was influenced by Hellenistic idealist philosophy and early medieval (including Arabic) Neoplatonism and Aristotelianism. In the 12th century Maimonides generalized the teachings of early medieval Judaism: the unity of an incorporeal and eternal god who is the creator of all things and who has revealed to man through Moses and the prophets the eternity of the Torah, the expectation of the Messiah, retribution after death for one's deeds, and resurrection of the dead.

Jews who lived in areas dominated by other dogmatic religions were subjected to legal restrictions and sometimes even to the cruelest persecution; this was true especially in the Christian countries, since Christianity blamed the Jewish religious community of the first century A.D. for the death of Jesus. At the same time the dogma of Judaism, which called for isolation of the Jews from those of other religions, made it easier for the authorities of the Christian states to create Jewish ghettos. Despite the artificial seclusion of adherents of Judaism, several medieval kingdoms, in an attempt to escape the political influence of the great Christian powers, adopted the religion (for example, the Khazar kingdom in the Volga region in the late eighth and early ninth centuries). The Karaite sect, which arose during the eighth century in Iraq, Syria, and Palestine, rejected the rabbinate and all rabbinical commentaries on the Bible. Mystical teachings spread among Jews, such as cabala, of which the most important work was the *Zohar* of Moses de Léon in the 13th century. The cabala also influenced later religious and philosophical Judaic literature, such as Joseph Caro's *Shulkhan Arukh* in the 16th century, a code of ethics that regulated the life of believers down to the smallest detail.

In the 17th century a movement arose around the mystic and adventurer Sabbatai Zebi of Turkey, who had declared himself the Messiah; his movement found numerous followers among Jews of many countries, who mistakenly sought in Zebi's teachings salvation from social oppression. The collapse of this movement and deterioration in the conditions of the Jews both in the ghettos of Europe and in Asia and Africa produced, on the one hand, still greater isolation from other peoples, and, on the other hand, Hasidism, a movement founded by the Ba'al Shem Tov in the middle of the 18th century that rejected the authority of the rabbis and preached the personal communion of the believer with god through the most pious, or zaddikim. Both movements contributed to the deprivation of civil rights of the Jews and their alienation from general democratic movements.

In the second half of the 19th century a movement for the reform of Judaism arose among Jews in Germany, the USA, and other countries. The reformers wanted to bring Judaism closer to Protestantism, in an attempt to adapt Judaism to the established bourgeois system and to place it in the service of capitalism. According to the reformers, messianism, the expectation of the restoration of the Temple, and the creation of a theocratic state in Jerusalem should be understood figuratively, as a future realization of the ethical ideals of mankind that are supposedly contained in Judaism. However, orthodox Judaism remained the dominant current among Jews, especially in the USA and in Eastern Europe.

Judaism does not recognize temples and has no ecclesiastical hierarchy; synagogues are maintained by contributions from believers (capitalists make large contributions to their maintenance). The Synagogue Council of America in the USA manages several educational institutions.

Judaism is the official religion of the state of Israel. The synagogues, like the organizations of other religions, are financed by the Ministry of Religious Affairs; the rabbinate has judicial functions in family matters, marriage, and other affairs concerning Jews.

The major holidays of Judaism are the Sabbath, when all work is prohibited, including the cooking of food and traveling; the tenth day after the lunar New Year (the day of purification, or Yom Kippur), a time of fasting and atonement; Pesach, or Passover, in the spring; Pentecost; the Festival of Booths in the fall, followed in seven or eight days by a holiday of "rejoicing in the Torah." At the age of 13 a boy professing Judaism passes through the rite of bar mitzvah, which introduces him into the community of believers; at that time he must show his knowledge of the Holy Scriptures and make an appropriate speech in Hebrew. The life of people practicing Judaism is burdened by a multiplicity of archaic restrictions, rituals, and dietary taboos.

Judaism, as a religion, as well as Talmudic ritualism, prevents the Jewish working masses from understanding the true causes of social oppression. Judaism, like other religions, has always been a tool in the hands of the ruling and exploiting classes for the spiritual oppression of the working masses. Judaism has been taken over by Zionism, which is at present the official ideology of the state of Israel. Attempting to win over the masses of working Jews and to divert them from the world revolutionary labor and national liberation movements as well as to justify Israel's expansionist policies, Zionism began to use the tenets of Judaism for its political aims (for example, messianism, which proposes the creation of a new, "ideal" Israel, with Jerusalem as its center, that would include the whole of Palestine). Since the second quarter of the 20th century Zionism has found support among the most reactionary Jews, especially in the USA. In its chauvinist and annexationist policy Zionism makes use of the Judaic dogma that the Jews are god's chosen people and employs Judaism to substantiate the concept of a "worldwide Jewish nation" and other reactionary positions.

REFERENCES

Marx, K., and F. Engels. *O religii.* (Collection of articles.) Moscow, 1955.
Lenin, V. I. *O religii.* (Collection of articles; 2nd ed.) Moscow [1966].
Lunacharskii, A. V. *Ob ateizme i religii.* (Collection of articles, letters, and other materials.) Moscow, 1972.
Kritika iudeiskoi religii. (Collection of articles.) Moscow, 1962.
Wellhausen, J. *Vvedenie v istoriiu Izrailia.* St. Petersburg, 1909. (Translated from German.)
Ranovich, A. *Ocherk istorii drevneevreiskoi religii.* Moscow, 1937.
Kosidovskii, Z. *Bibleiskie skazaniia,* 2nd ed. Moscow, 1969.
Albright, W. F. *Archaeology and the Religion of Israel* [4th ed.]. Baltimore, 1956.

Eissfeldt, O. *Einleitung in das Alte Testament,* 3rd ed. Tübingen, 1964.
Noth, M. *Geschichte Israels,* 2nd ed. Göttingen, 1954.
The Old Testament and Modern Study. [London] 1961.
Vaux, R. de. *Les Institutions de l'Ancien Testament.* Paris, 1958–60.
Bousset, W. *Die Religion des Judentums im Späthellenistischen Zeitalter,* 3rd ed. Tübingen, 1926.
Judentum im Mittelalter. Berlin, 1966.
Kaufmann, J. *The Religion of Israel.* [Chicago, 1960.]
Schechter, S. *Studies in Judaism.* New York [1958].
Baron, S. W. *A Social and Religious History of the Jews,* 2nd ed., vols. 1–12, 14. New York, 1957–69.
Fohrer, G. *Geschichte der israelitischen Religion.* Berlin, 1969.

[11–148–4]

JUDAS ISCARIOT (also Scariot—"a man from the city of Kerioth"), according to biblical mythology, one of the 12 disciples (apostles) of Jesus Christ, the one who betrayed his teacher to the Jerusalem authorities for 30 pieces of silver.

In the Gospels and the Acts of the Apostles various versions of Judas Iscariot's betrayal and death are given. The story of Judas was developed in apocryphal literature and in medieval mysteries. The image of Judas Iscariot, who has become a symbol of betrayal, found its reflection in medieval and Renaissance art (usually portraying the Last Supper or Judas as he identified Jesus Christ to the guards with a kiss—hence the expression "the kiss of Judas") and literature (Dante).   [11–148–3]

JUDAS TREE (*Cercis siliquastrum*), a tree of the family Leguminosae. It attains a height of 7 to 15 m. Its leaves are deciduous, round, blunt, entire, and deeply cordate at the base. The flowers are bisexual and bright pink in color, and grow in clusters of three to six on the stem, on old branches, and in leaf axils. The fruit is a flat, many-seeded pod. The tree blossoms in the spring, before leafing, and reproduces by seeds.

The Judas tree grows wild on rocky slopes and calcareous rocks in southern Europe and southwestern Asia. In the USSR it is found in the wild state in the Crimea, the Caucasus, and Middle Asia. It is cultivated chiefly as an ornamental, but its lumber is sometimes used in woodworking and its buds as a pungent seasoning in sauces.   [11–154–1]

JULY DAYS OF 1917, the July political crisis, the third such crisis in Russia (after the April crisis and the June crisis) during the period from the February bourgeois-democratic revolution to the Great October Socialist Revolution; a new and very important stage in the development of a nationwide crisis.

The immediate cause of the July Days lay in the events of late June and early July: the unsuccessful offensive at the front and the disbandment of revolutionary military units. On July 2 (15) the Cadets walked out of the bourgeois Provisional Government, threatening the Mensheviks and the Socialist Revolutionaries (SR's) with the destruction of the government coalition. A government crisis was the result. The political situation in the country became increasingly strained. On July 3 (16) spontaneous demonstrations broke out in Petrograd. They were started by the soldiers of the 1st Machine-gun Regiment, who were strongly influenced by the anarchists. At a secret conference on July 2 (15) the anarchists had decided to call the Petrograd workers and soldiers out to an armed antigovernment demonstration. The Bolsheviks, who favored the peaceful development of the revolution, were opposed to an armed demonstration: the political crisis had not yet matured in the army and in the provinces, and Petrograd would not receive support.

However, on the evening of July 3 (16) the machine gunners' appeal met with a favorable response from soldiers of the Moscow, Grenadiers, Pavlovskii, 180th, and 1st Reserve regiments and the 6th Engineers Battalion. These units marched out in an armed demonstration under the slogans "Down with the Ten Capitalist Ministers" and "All Power to the Soviet of Workers' and Soldiers' Deputies." Workers from the Putilov Works and other Petrograd factories joined them. The compromiser leadership of the All-Russian Central Executive Committee forbade the demonstration, but it was impossible to stop the workers from demonstrating. In the predawn hours of July 4 (17), the Central Committee of the RSDLP (Bolshevik), jointly with the

Petrograd Committee and the Military Organization of the Party, decided to provide leadership to the movement in order to give it an organized and peaceful character. At about 12 o'clock on July 4 (17) a demonstration of 500,000 workers, soldiers, and sailors from the Baltic fleet began, under the slogan "All Power to the Soviets." At the headquarters of the Bolshevik Central Committee in the palace of Kshesinskaia the demonstrators were greeted by Lenin, who called upon the masses to show self-control and expressed his assurance that the slogan "All Power to the Soviets" would prevail. Ninety representatives from 54 major factories suggested that the joint session of the All-Russian Central Executive Committee of the Soviets should assume complete power, but the SR-Menshevik executive committees declared the demonstration to be a "Bolshevik plot," and rejected the demands of the masses. The military authorities sent troops against the peaceful demonstration. Clashes with armed counterrevolutionaries of such organizations as the Military League occurred at the Liteinyi Bridge, at the corner of Nevsky Prospect, in Sadovaia Street, and in other places. There were 56 dead and 650 wounded. Antigovernment demonstrations were held also in Moscow, Ivanovo-Voznesensk, Orekhovo-Zuevo, Nizhny Novgorod, Krasnoiarsk, Tomsk, and other cities. The will of the people had been made clear.

On July 5 (18) the Central Committee of the RSDLP (Bolshevik) published an appeal for the demonstrations to be ended. The SR-Menshevik leadership of the Central Executive Committee actively supported punitive measures by the government against the revolutionary people. They began to disarm the workers, disband the revolutionary military units, and make arrests. On July 5–6 (18–19) the editorial offices and printing plant of *Pravda* and the headquarters of the Central Committee of the RSDLP (Bolshevik) were destroyed. On July 6 (19) the Provisional Government issued an order for the arrest of Lenin, who was forced to go underground. On July 7 (20) troops loyal to the government arrived in Petrograd from the front. The government crisis was intensified by the resignation of Prime Minister G. E. Lvov. On July 8 (21), A. F. Kerensky became prime minister. The All-Russian Central Executive Committee of the Soviets proclaimed the Provisional Government to be a "government of the salvation of the Revolution" and acknowledged it to have "unlimited powers and unlimited authority." The SR-Menshevik soviets became a powerless appendage to the bourgeois government. The July Days marked the end of dual power. On Lenin's proposal, the slogan "All Power to the Soviets" was temporarily dropped by the Sixth Congress of the RSDLP (Bolshevik). "The counterrevolution has become organized and consolidated, and has actually taken state power into its hands," wrote Lenin (*Poln. sobr. soch.,* 5th ed., vol. 34, p. 1). The peaceful development of the revolution became impossible. The July Days intensified the contradictions in the country more than ever. The armed struggle of the workers for power was placed on the agenda.

REFERENCES
Lenin, V. I. *Poln. sobr. soch.,* 5th ed. (See index vol., part 1, p. 210.)
Shestoi s"ezd RSDRP (bol'shevikov): Protokoly. Moscow, 1958.
Revoliutsionnoe dvizhenie v Rossii v iiule 1917 g.: Iiul'skii krizis. Moscow, 1959. (In the series *Velikaia Oktiabr'skaia sotsialisticheskaia revoliutsiia.*)
Znamenskii, O. N. *Iiul'skii krizis 1917 g.* Moscow-Leningrad, 1964.

Iu. S. TOKAREV   [11–178–2]

JULY MANIFESTO (1944), the first act of state of People's Poland, adopted in Chełm on July 22, 1944, by the Polish Committee of National Liberation (PCNL).

The July Manifesto proclaimed that state power was passing into the hands of the working people, represented by the Krajowa Rada Narodowa (National Home Council), the council's executive body, the PCNL, and local agencies of authority. The manifesto abrogated the reactionary constitution of 1935 and all the laws promulgated by the fascist German occupation forces, declared that the Polish state was restored on the foundation of democratic freedoms and the equality of all citizens, enacted new labor legislation and social security for the working people, and promised the immediate implementation of agrarian reform. The July Manifesto appealed to the Polish people to fight for complete liberation from the fascist German invaders and to cooperate closely with the Soviet army. The manifesto emphasized that the settlement of the Soviet-Polish border question must be governed by the principle that Polish lands remain with Poland and that the Ukrainian, Byelorussian, and Lithuanian lands be restored to the Soviet Ukraine, Soviet Byelorussia, and Soviet Lithuania.

PUBLICATION

Konstytucja i podstawowe akty ustawodawcze Polskiej Rzeczypospolitej Ludowej, 5th ed. Warsaw, 1966.   IU. V. BERNOV. [11–180–2]

JULY MONARCHY, the period in French history from the July Revolution (1830), which put an end to the regime of the Restoration, to the February Revolution of 1848, which established the Second Republic. During the July Monarchy, "it was not the French bourgeoisie that prevailed" in the person of King Louis Philippe "but only one faction of it, the so-called finance aristocracy" (K. Marx; see K. Marx and F. Engels, *Soch.*, 2nd ed., vol. 7, p. 8).   [11–176–2]

JULY REVOLUTION (1830), in France, the bourgeois revolution that put an end to the Bourbon monarchy.

The regime of the Restoration, based on the nobility and clergy, was retarding the country's economic development. The industrial crisis and depression of 1827–30 and the crop failures of 1828 and 1829 worsened the already grave situation of the toiling masses and hastened the growth of revolutionary consciousness. Discontent was also increasing among the liberal bourgeoisie, who sought economic and political reforms to accelerate the capitalist development of the country. The immediate cause of the revolution was the ordinances, signed by the king on July 25 and published on July 26, 1830, that dissolved the Chamber of Deputies (which had been dominated by the liberal bourgeoisie), limited the franchise through imposition of a landed-property qualification, and increased the repression of the progressive press.

In Paris on July 27 an armed mass uprising broke out, calling for defense of the Charter of 1814 and dismissal of the Polignac cabinet; the workers and artisans, supported by the petite and middle bourgeoisie and the progressive segment of the intelligentsia, were the chief driving force of the uprising. On July 29 the insurgents gained control of the Tuileries Palace and other governmental buildings. The royal troops, defeated, left Paris, some regiments joining forces with the people. Revolutionary outbursts in provincial towns also ended in defeat for the defenders of the *ancien régime*. Power in the capital passed into the hands of the Municipal Commission, headed by influential figures from the moderate liberal wing of the big bourgeoisie (including the bankers J. Laffitte and C. Périer and General M. J. P. La Fayette). The weakness of petit bourgeois democracy and the lack of organization among the working class allowed the upper bourgeoisie to appropriate all the gains of the people's triumph and prevent the further development of the revolutionary process. Despite protests from republican groups the Chamber of Deputies, in which the Orleanists held a dominant position, decided to transfer the crown to the Duke of Orléans, Louis Philippe, who was closely connected with the big bankers. On Aug. 2, 1830, Charles X renounced the throne, and Louis Philippe was proclaimed King of the French on August 7.

The revolution had rather limited political results. A new constitution, the Charter of 1830, brought about a certain lowering (in comparison with the Charter of 1814) of the property and age qualifications for voters; extreme reactionary government bureaucrats and army officers were purged; regional and local self-government was introduced; and the authority of the crown was somewhat reduced. However, the working masses and small proprietors did not receive the right to vote, and laws against trade unions and workers' strikes remained in force, as did the heavy indirect taxes. The police and bureaucratic apparatus that had evolved during the Napoleonic empire was preserved; it merely passed into other hands.

Despite the limited character of the July Revolution, it had great progressive significance: it overthrew the political domination of the aristocracy and put an end to attempts at restoring in any form whatever the feudal-absolutist order. Power conclusively passed from the nobility to the bourgeoisie, although not to the entire bourgeoisie but only to one segment, the financial aristocracy (that is, the upper circle of the commercial, industrial, and banking bourgeoisie). In 1830 bourgeois monarchy was established in France. The July Revolution, which was greeted ardently by the progressive people of many countries, dealt a serious blow to the reactionary Holy Alliance. The attempts of the ruling circles of Russia, Austria, and Prussia to organize military intervention against France with the aim of restoring its old dynasty proved futile because of the contradictions among the European states and because of revolutionary outbursts in many countries on the continent. Eventually all the European states came to recognize the July Monarchy.

REFERENCES

Marx, K. "Klassovaia bor'ba vo Frantsii s 1848 po 1850." K. Marx and F. Engels, *Soch.*, 2nd ed., vol. 7.
Lenin, V. I. "Zametki publitsista." *Poln. sobr. soch.*, 5th ed., vol. 19.
Molok, A. I. "Iiul'skie dni 1830 g. v Parizhe." In the collection *Istoricheskie zapiski* [vol.] 20. Moscow, 1946.
Molok, A. I. "Bor'ba napravlenii vo frantsuzskoi istoriografii po voprosam restavratsii Burbonov i iiul'skoi revoliutsii 1830." In the collection *Frantsuzskii ezhegodnik 1959.* Moscow, 1961.
Orlik, O. V. *Rossiia i frantsuzskaia revoliutsiia 1830 g.* Moscow, 1968.
          A. I. MOLOK   [11–176–3]

JULY REVOLUTION IN EGYPT (1952), a common name for the revolutionary coup in Egypt in July 1952 that inaugurated the national liberation revolution.

The July Revolution took place against the background of the rise of the national liberation movement of the Arab peoples after World War II and the weakening of British imperialism in the Middle East. Its causes were feudal and colonial oppression and the unwillingness of Egypt's ruling circles to push on with the immediate tasks of national liberation and regeneration and to relieve the hopeless misery of the toiling masses. Another driving force of the revolution was the hatred of the people toward the corrupt palace camarilla and the venal "traditional" bourgeois political parties, who expressed the interests of the ruling elite and of British imperialism. The July Revolution was hastened by Egypt's defeat in the Arab-Israeli War of 1948–49 and the intensification of the mass movement against the tyranny of the feudal pashas and the British colonialists, a movement that developed into guerrilla warfare against the British troops in the Suez Canal Zone.

On the night of July 23 a group of patriotic military members of the secret Society of Free Officers, headed by Gamal Abdel Nasser, staged a revolutionary coup and overthrew the feudal-monarchist regime of King Farouk. On July 26 the deposed monarch abdicated and left the country and the Revolutionary Command Council (RCC) assumed power.

The young officers who assumed power after the military coup relied mainly on the army. Their aims were the complete national liberation of Egypt and the creation of the conditions for its independent development. The nature and the program of the July Revolution were expressed in the "six principles" set forth by Nasser: liberation of the country from colonialism and its network of agents; liquidation of feudalism; elimination of the rule of capital over state power; establishment of social justice; creation of a national army; and democratization of Egypt's internal life.

The first important steps of the revolutionary government included an agrarian reform, announced in September 1952, which limited big feudal landholding, and the opening of negotiations with Great Britain on the evacuation of British troops from Egypt. The program and measures of the RCC were supported by the overwhelming majority of the Egyptian people and by the Soviet Union and other socialist countries.

The July Revolution swept away the monarchy, led to the political liberation of Egypt from imperialism, and opened the path for the profound antifeudal and anticapitalist social and economic transformations that followed. It stimulated the development of revolutionary movements in other Arab countries.

V. P. Rumiantsev [11–178–1]

JUNE CRISIS OF 1917, the second political crisis in Russia (after the April crisis) during the period from February to October; one of the stages in the development of a nationwide crisis.

The crisis was caused by the irreconcilable contradictions between the masses of the people and the imperialist bourgeoisie on questions of peace and land and of the struggle against economic dislocation. The First All-Russian Congress of Soviets of Workers' and Soldiers' Deputies of June 3–24 (June 16 to July 7), at which the Socialist Revolutionaries (SR's) and Mensheviks predominated, gave support to the bourgeois Provisional Government and refused the Bolshevik demand for an end to the war and the transfer of power to the soviets. These actions heightened the anger of the masses. Certain antidemocratic actions by the Provisional Government, in particular a decree of June 7 (20) ordering the confiscation of the dacha of the former tsarist minister, P. N. Durnovo, in which a workers' club and the offices of the Vyborg district trade unions had been established, led to a strike by the workers of 29 factories in Petrograd on June 8 (21). The same day, in order to give the protest an organized character, the Central Committee and the Petrograd Committee of the RSDLP (Bolshevik) announced a peaceful demonstration of workers and soldiers on June 10 (23). At the insistence of the compromisers, on June 9 (22) the Congress of Soviets banned the demonstration. The compromisers accused the Bolsheviks of a "military conspiracy." During the night of June 9 (22) and the early hours of June 10 (23), the Central Committee of the RSDLP (Bolshevik), not wishing to oppose itself to the congress, ordered the demonstration to be canceled. With some difficulty, the Bolsheviks restrained the revolutionary enthusiasm of the workers and soldiers. The Cadets, SR's, and Mensheviks violently denounced the Bolsheviks, the workers, and the revolutionary soldiers. Fearing that they might lose the confidence of the people, the SR-Menshevik leaders were forced to pass a resolution at the congress in favor of holding a general political demonstration of confidence in the Provisional Government on June 18 (July 1). Against the expectations of the compromisers, and as a result of the Bolshevik efforts, the demonstration was held, with some 500,000 participants, under the slogans of "All Power to the Soviets," "Down with the Ten Capitalist Ministers," and "Bread, Peace, and Freedom." Demonstrations under the same slogans were held in Moscow, Minsk, Ivanovo-Voznesensk, Tver', Nizhny Novgorod, Kharkov, and elsewhere.

The June demonstration showed that, as Lenin said, "a crisis of unprecedented scale had descended upon Russia" (*Poln. sobr. soch.*, 5th ed., vol. 32, p. 362). The June crisis did not develop into a crisis of bourgeois power, but it did show that unity in the demands and actions of the workers and soldiers was growing stronger and that the influence of the Bolshevik Party was rising among the masses. The original causes of the crisis were not eliminated, and as a consequence the July Days soon followed.

REFERENCES.

Lenin, V. I. *Poln. sobr. soch.*, 5th ed. (See index vol., part 1, p. 210.)
Velikaia Oktiabr'skaia sotsialisticheskaia revoliutsiia: Dokumenty i materialy, vol. 4. Moscow, 1959.
Istoriia Velikoi Oktiabr'skoi sotsialisticheskoi revoliutsii. Moscow, 1962. Pages 72–78.
Istoriia KPSS, vol. 3, book 1. Moscow, 1967. Pages 140–47.
Prokhvatilov, Iu. A. *Iiun'skaia demonstratsiia.* [Leningrad, 1967.]

[11–181–3]

JUNE DAYS OF 1848, an armed mass uprising of Parisian workers (June 23–26, 1848), "the first great civil war between the proletariat and the bourgeoisie" (V. I. Lenin, *Poln. sobr. soch.*, 5th ed. vol. 38, p. 305). It was a response to the attack of a bourgeois reaction seeking to deprive the workers of the democratic rights and liberties they had won as a result of the February Revolution of 1848.

Uprisings at the end of April in Rouen, Elbeuf, and Limoges, the May 15 demonstration in Paris, the rebellion of June 22–23 in Marseille, and other expressions of popular unrest preceded the June Days. The immediate cause of the uprising was the governmental order to close the national workshops (in which more than 100,000 men were employed at the time), send into the army unmarried men between the ages of 18 and 25, who would be put out of work as a result, and dispatch the other men to agricultural work in the provinces. The government's provocative policy aroused the workers' indignation. On June 23 the Parisian workers went out on the barricades. The rebellion embraced the working-class districts of the eastern and northeastern parts of Paris and of its suburbs, including Montmartre, La Chapelle, La Villette, Belleville, Menilmontant, and Ivry. The number of insurgents was 40,000–45,000 (60,000, according to another source). The leadership of the armed struggle was provided by "brigadiers" and "delegates" of the national workshops, participants of political clubs, and commanders of detachments of the national guard from working-class suburbs and faubourgs (J. L. Defer, P. de Flotte, L. Pujol, and A. Legénissel). The lack of a common coordinating center and the poor communications between the detachments of insurgents from the various districts hindered realization of a general plan for offensive operations worked out by the officer J. Kersausie, who was a participant in the July Revolution of 1830. The insurgents demanded the arrest of members of the government, a fight against unemployment, and preservation of the national workshops, and they advanced the proletarian slogans "Long Live the Democratic and Social Republic," "Down With the Republic of Capital and Privilege," and the "Right to Work." A list of members of the future government was compiled that included L. A. Blanqui, F. V. Raspail, A. Barbês, A. Albert [Albert l'Ouvrier], and several other prominent revolutionaries. (At that time the majority of them were in prison.) Frightened by the scale of the rebellion, the National Assembly on June 24 invested the minister of war, General L. E. Cavaignac, with dictatorial powers. From the provinces troops were summoned to Paris, the arrival of which gave the government a tremendous advantage over the insurgent workers. On June 26 the rebellion was suppressed with extreme severity. One of the most important reasons for its failure was that the peasantry and petite bourgeoisie did not support the Parisian workers, believing to be true the slanderous statements of the counterrevolutionaries that the workers of Paris were the initiators of new financial burdens, in particular the introduction of the 45-centime tax. Workers' demonstrations of solidarity with the insurgents occurred only in some big industrial cities, such as Amiens, Dijon, and Bordeaux. K. Marx and F. Engels, in the *Neue Rheinische Zeitung*, exposed the slanderous fabrications of the reactionary press regarding the insurgents, emphasizing the great historical significance of the uprising. The June Days were the highest point of development of the Revolution of 1848–49 in Europe. They contributed to the growth of class consciousness among the proletariat. The suppression of the upsurge strengthened the bourgeois counterrevolution in France and in several other countries.

REFERENCES

Marx, K. "Iiun'skaia revoliutsiia," in K. Marx and F. Engels, *Soch.*, 2nd ed., vol. 5.
Marx, K. "Klassovaia bor'ba vo Frantsii s 1848 po 1850 g." *Ibid.*, vol. 7.
Engels, F. "Podrobnosti sobytii 23 iiunia." *Ibid.*, vol. 5.
Engels, F. "23 iiunia." *Ibid.*, vol. 5.
Engels, F. "Iiun'skaia revoliutsiia." *Ibid.*, vol. 5.
Lenin, V. I. "Iz kakogo klassovogo istochnika prikhodiat i 'pridut' Kaven'iaki?" *Poln. sobr. soch.*, 5th ed., vol. 32.
Molok, A. I. *Iiun'skie dni 1848 g. v Parizhe.* Moscow, 1948.
Tersen, E. "Juin 48." *La Pensée*, 1948, no. 19.

A. I. Molok [11–182–1]

JUNE OFFENSIVE (1917), an offensive operation by the Russian troops of the Southwestern Front under the command of General A. E. Gutor during World War I.

The June offensive was undertaken by the bourgeois Provisional Government, supported by the Socialist Revolutionaries and the Mensheviks, in order to consolidate its position and satisfy the Allied demand for more vigorous action by the Russian Army. If the offensive succeeded, the bourgeoisie hoped to take all the power in its hands and to crush the revolutionary forces in the country and the army; in the case of failure it hoped to put the blame for the disintegration of the army on the Bolsheviks. On June 18 (July 1) the Eleventh and Seventh armies launched an offensive, delivering the main attack toward L'vov from the regions of Złoczów (Zolochev) and Brzeżany (Berezhany); despite a considerable superiority in men and matériel, the offensive was unsuccessful and was stopped on June 20 (July 3). On June 23 (July 6) the Eighth Army, under the command of General L. G. Kornilov, assumed the offensive, delivering a secondary attack in the Halicz and Stanisławów (Galich and Stanislav) sector toward Kałusz (Kalush) and Bolechów (Bolekhov). The army broke through the enemy defenses and captured more than 7,000 prisoners and 48 guns; developing its success, it occupied Halicz and Kałusz and reached the Łomnica (Lomnitsa) River on June 30 (July 13). On July 6 (19) the Austrian-German troops counterattacked from the Złoczów region toward Tarnopol (Ternopol') and broke through the front of the Eleventh Army, forcing the Seventh and Eighth armies to retreat. On July 8 (21), Gutor was replaced by Kornilov. On July 15 (28) the Russian troops halted on the line Brody, Zbaraż (Zbarazh), and the Zbrucz (Zbruch) River.

The general plan linked the June offensive with an offensive on the Rumanian Front and secondary attacks on the Northern and Western fronts. The Rumanian Front offensive of the Rumanian Second Army and the Russian Fourth Army, which began on July 9 (22), developed successfully but was stopped on July 14 (27) upon the order of A. F. Kerensky, the supreme commander in chief. The July 9 (22) offensive of the Fifth Army of the Northern Front from the region of Molodečno in the direction of Vilno (Vilnius) and the July 10 (23) offensive of the Tenth Army of the Western Front from Jakobstadt (Jekabpils) toward Kovno (Kaunas) ended in a complete failure.

As a result of the bloody venture of the Provisional Government, Galicia was abandoned; the total losses of the Russian Army on all fronts exceeded 150,000 men. The June offensive drew 13 German and three Austro-Hungarian divisions to the Eastern Front. The June offensive and its failure revealed the counterrevolutionary policy of the Provisional Government and of the Socialist Revolutionaries and the Mensheviks, provoked the violent protest of the working masses and the soldiers that culminated in the July Days of 1917, and raised the prestige of the Bolsheviks, who demanded an immediate end to the war.

REFERENCES
Zaionchkovskii, A. M. *Strategicheskii ocherk voiny 1914–1918 gg.* Part 7: "Kampaniia 1917 g." Moscow, 1923.
Talenskii, N. A. *Kampaniia 1917 g.* Moscow, 1938.

A. G. KAVTARADZE   [11–184–1]

JUNE STRIKE (1918), in Rumania, a strike of the Rumanian revolutionary proletariat on June 7–14, 1918, that seized the major areas of the country not under German occupation. The strike was started by railroad workers of Paşcani, Bacău, and other centers of Moldavia. The strike was a manifestation of the workers' opposition to the war and the monarchy. The strike ended with the satisfaction of the major demands of the workers: restoration of the workers' trade unions, recognition of strike committees, and the abolition of the military regime on the railroads.

SOURCE
Documente din istoria mişcării muncitoreşti din România 1916–1921. Bucharest, 1966.   [11–181–2]

JUNGLE CAT (*Felis chaus*), a predatory mammal of the family Felidae. The body is up to 80 cm long; the tail, up to 30 cm. Jungle cats live in dense thickets along the river valleys of northeastern Africa and southwestern and southeastern Asia. In the USSR they are found in the Volga delta, on the western coast of the Caspian Sea, and in the river valleys of Middle Asia. They live in dense thickets of rushes, sedges, and cattails. Because it kills game animals and game birds, the jungle cat does damage in some places to hunting.   [11–860–3]

KAABA (from Arabic *ka'aba al-qubba*), Muslim shrine in Mecca. The Kaaba has the shape of a cube and is located in the center of a rectangular courtyard. The eastern corner of its outer wall contains a niche with the Black Stone (an ancient fetish). The spring of Zamzam flows beside it. In pre-Islamic times it was a sacred place to the pagan tribes of the Hijaz; according to tradition, 300 idols, to which different tribes paid homage, stood around it. Islam recognized the Kaaba's sanctity. After the year 630 the idols were destroyed, and the Kaaba became a major shrine and place of pilgrimmage exclusively for Muslims.

[11–244–2]

KAAKHKA, an urban-type settlement, administrative center of Kaakhka Raion, Ashkhabad Oblast, Turkmen SSR. Located at the foot of the Kopetdag range. It has a railroad station on the Ashkhabad-Mary line, 129 km southeast of Ashkhabad. Population, 9,000 (1970). A plant for ginning cotton is located there. Kaakhka also has a people's amateur theater.   [11–245–3]

KAATRA, KÖSSI. Born Nov. 6, 1882, in the small town of Lohja; died Nov. 15, 1928, in the small town of Huddinge, Sweden. Finnish author.

From 1903 to 1910, Kaatra worked as a journalist and as the director of the Workers' Theater in the city of Tampere. He participated in the general strike of 1905 and the Revolution of 1918 in Finland. He wrote the collections of verses *On the Threshold* (1903), *Sketches of Life* (1904), *Poems* (1905), *Scenes of the Great Strike and Other Workers' Songs* (1906), and *At the Turning Point* (1906). In the novella *The Reds and the Whites* (1919), Kaatra depicts the civil war of 1918 in Finland. He describes life in the workers' quarter in the novel *Mother and Son* (1924).

WORKS
Alhaisolauluja. Helsinki, 1922.
In Russian translation:
["Stikhotvoreniia."] In the anthology *Poeziia Finliandii.* Moscow, 1962.
REFERENCES
Karkhu, E. G. *Ocherki finskoi literatury nachala XX veka.* Leningrad, 1972.
Käy eespäin: Valikoima suomalaista työväenrunoutta. Helsinki, 1957.
Äikiä, A. *Laulaja tulivuoren juurella.* Helsinki, 1962.   [11–245–2]

KABACHNIK, MARTIN IZRAILEVICH. Born Aug. 27 (Sept. 9), 1908, in Ekaterinburg, now Sverdlovsk. Soviet organic chemist. Academician of the Academy of Sciences of the USSR (1958; corresponding member, 1953). Member of the CPSU since 1957.

Kabachnik graduated from the Second Moscow Chemical Engineering Institue in 1931. In 1954 he became head of the laboratory of organophosphorus compounds at the Institute of Heteroorganic Compounds of the Academy of Sciences of the USSR. His principal works are primarily devoted to the development of the chemistry of organophosphorus compounds and to the theoretical problems of organic chemistry. He has conducted research on the tautomerism, structure, and reactivity of organophosphorus compounds; has studied conjugation in systems with a tetrahedral phosphorus atom; and has developed new complexing reagents—organophosphorus complexones. A recipient of the State Prize of the USSR (1946), Kabachnik has been awarded the Order of Lenin, two other orders, and various medals.

WORKS
"Tautomeriia nekotorykh fosfororganicheskikh soedinenii." In the collection *Khimiia i primenenie fosfororganicheskikh soedinenii.* Moscow, 1957.
"Nekotorye voprosy stroeniia i reaktsionnoi sposobnosti fosfororganicheskikh soedinenii." In the collection *Khimiia i primenenie fosfororganicheskikh soedinenii.* Moscow, 1962.
"Fosfororganicheskie kompleksony," *Uspekhi khimii,* 1968, vol. 37, issue 7. (Jointly with others.)
REFERENCE
M. I. Kabachnik. Moscow, 1967. (*Materialy k biobibliografii uchenykh SSSR: Seriia khimicheskikh nauk,* issue 39.)   [11–273–1]

KABAK, public house in tsarist Russia in the 16th and the 17th centuries where alcoholic beverages were sold, either by the government or by tax farmers.

The first *kabak* appeared in Moscow in the 1550's. Ivan IV Vasil'evich forbade the sale of vodka in Moscow but opened a *kabak* for the use of members of the *oprichnina* there. All proceeds from sales in these public houses went to the treasury. After 1555, *kabaki* began to appear in other cities, replacing an earlier form of public house known as the *korchma*. In the 17th century, about a thousand *kabaki* were in existence. In 1746 the name was changed to "drinking establishment" (*piteinoe zavedenie*), but the earlier term continued to be used, gradually acquiring a pejorative connotation. After 1863, with the establishment of a state monopoly for sale of wine, *kabaki* began to be known as state wine shops (*kazennye vinnye lavki*).   [11–245–4]

KABAKCHIEV, KHRISTO STEFANOV. Born Jan. 2, 1878, in Galaţi, Rumania; died Oct. 6, 1940, in Moscow. A Bulgarian and international labor leader, a publicist. The son of a teacher.

Kabakchiev participated in student demonstrations against the government while he was at the *Gymnasium* in Varna in 1894 and helped organize student socialist circles in Gabrovo in 1896. He joined the Bulgarian Workers' Social Democratic Party (BWSDP) in 1897. He studied in the medical department of the University of Montepellier in France in 1897 and in the law department of the University of Geneva in 1898–99 and 1901, graduating from the law department of the University of Sofia in 1904. From 1905 to 1928 he was a member first of the Central Committee of the BWSDP(Narrow Socialists) and then, from 1919, of the Central Committee of the Bulgarian Communist Party (BCP). Editor in chief from 1910 to 1923 of the newspaper *Rabotnicheski vestnik,* the central organ of the party, Kabakchiev was a delegate of the BWSDP(NS) to congresses of the Second International in Stuttgart (1907), Copenhagen (1910), and Basel (1912). He was a deputy to the National Assembly from 1914 to 1923 and attended the Second (1920), Third (1921), Fourth (1922), and Sixth (1928) Congresses of the Comintern.

Kabakchiev translated several works of V. I. Lenin into Bulgarian and became acquainted with Lenin personally in 1920. After becoming political secretary of the BCP in 1923, Kabakchiev helped prepare the September Antifascist Uprising of 1923 and was in prison from September 1923 to February 1926. He emigrated to Vienna in late 1926 and to the USSR in May 1927. Kabakchiev worked in the Bulgarian section of the Comintern and in the Internation Control Commission, to which he was elected in absentia at the Fifth Congress (1924), and taught at the International Lenin School and at the Communist University.

Joining the ACP(Bolshevik) in 1928, Kabakchiev was a research associate of the Marx-Engels-Lenin Institute. He became a member of the History Institute of the Academy of Sciences of the USSR in 1935. Kabakchiev studied and wrote on the history of the BCP, of Bulgaria and other Balkan countries, and of the international labor movement. He became a doctor of historical sciences in 1935.

WORKS
Izbrani proizvedeniia. Sofia, 1953.
Spomeni. Sofia, 1955.
REFERENCE
Koleva, T. *Khristo Kabakchiev: Bio-bibliografiia.* Sofia, 1958.
                                             M. A. BIRMAN   [11–246–1]

KABAKOV, IVAN DMITRIEVICH. Born Nov. 10 (22), 1891, in the village of Kniazh Pavlovo, in present-day Buturlino Raion, Gorky Oblast; died Oct. 3, 1937. Soviet state and party figure. Became a member of the Communist Party in 1914. The son of an unskilled laborer.

Kabakov began work as a metalworker. Becoming a member of the Sormovo committee of the RSDLP in 1916, he was elected to the Nizhny Novgorod and Sormovo soviets in March 1917 and organized Bolshevik cells in business enterprises. He fought for the establishment of Soviet rule in Novgorod, engaged in party and soviet work in the city and the province, and was a member of the province party committee and of the province executive committee of the soviet. Kabakov became chairman of the Voronezh soviet in late 1918, secretary of the Iaroslavl' Province Party Committee in 1922, and first secretary of the

Tula Province Party Committee in 1924 (until 1927). He became chairman of the Urals Oblast Control Commission of the ACP (Bolshevik) in 1928, first secretary of the Urals Oblast Committee of the ACP(B) in 1929, and first secretary of the Sverdlovsk Oblast Committee of the ACP(B) in 1934. A delegate to the Eleventh through Seventeenth Congresses of the party, Kobakov was elected a candidate member of the Central Committee of the ACP(B) at the Thirteenth Congress and a member of the Central Committee at the Fourteenth through Seventeenth Congresses.
                                                          [11–245–5]

KABALA (Kabalaka, Kabalak), an ancient city, capital of Caucasian Albania until the sixth century and a major commercial center until the 15th century. In the 16th century it was destroyed by the Safavids. Its ruins are east of the village of Chukhurkabaly in Azerbaijan SSR. The remains of the citadel cover an area of more than 25 hectares (ha). East of the citadel lie the ruins of the temple and city quarters, occupying more than 50 ha.   [11–246–3]

KABALA (from Arabic *qabala,* "receipt," "bond").**(1)** A severe form of personal bondage, usually in connection with a loan. As such, the term first appeared in use in Rus' at the turn of the 15th century. It also applied to the juridical acts that outlined the obligations of the debtor.

(2) A thorough, extremely difficult position of servitude of an oppressed, exploited person, established against his will.
                                                          [11–246–2]

KABALEVSKII, DMITRII BORISOVICH. Born Dec. 17 (30), 1904, in St. Petersburg. Soviet composer, teacher, and public figure. People's Artist of the USSR since 1963, doctor of the arts since 1965, and full member of the Academy of Pedagogical Sciences of the USSR since 1971. Member of the CPSU since 1940.

Kabalevskii completed N. Ia. Miaskovskii's course in composition (1929) and A. B. Goldenweiser's course in piano (1930) at the Moscow Conservatory. He has been a professor there since 1939. Between 1940 and 1946 he was editor in chief of the journal *Sovetskaia Muzyka.* Since 1954 he has been a member of the collegium of the Ministry of Culture of the USSR. In 1952 he became secretary of the Union of Soviet Composers, in which he also heads the commission on the musical and aesthetic education of children and young people. Since 1969 he has headed the Council on Aesthetic Education under the Presidium of the Academy of Pedagogical Sciences of the USSR. Kabalevskii has been a member of the Council of Directors of the International Society for Music Education since 1961 and its honorary president since 1972. Since 1953 he has been a member of the Soviet Committee for the Defense of Peace. In performances of his own works, he appears both as a pianist and as a conductor.

Most of Kabalevskii's work draws upon contemporary socially significant themes. He frequently turns for inspiration to Soviet youth and children, as in three of his concerti—the Concerto for Violin (1948; State Prize of the USSR, 1949), the Concerto for Cello No. 1 (1949), and the Concerto for Piano No. 3 (1952), as well as cantatas, children's songs, and piano pieces. His work is strongly lyrical, with cheerful tones, a clear, songlike quality, joyous vitality, fervor, and humor. At the same time he captured in music the tragic events of the Great Patriotic War (1941–45) in such works as the opera *Taras' Family* (1950; State Prize of the USSR, 1951), based on B. Gorbatov's novella *The Unvanquished* and depicting the struggle of the Soviet people against the fascist invaders. In the opera *Colas Breugnon* (1937; revised version 1968, Lenin Prize, 1972), based on R. Rolland's novella, a lyrical theme blends with an unfolding of social conflict. Kabalevskii also composed the operas *In the Fire* (formerly *Near Moscow,* 1943), *Nikita Vershinin* (1955), and *The Sisters* (1969).

Kabalevskii has done much work in symphonic and cantata-oratorio music. He has written four symphonies (1932, 1933, 1934, 1956), a number of concerti—three for piano (1929, 1936, 1952), one for violin (1948), and two for cello (1949, 1964)—the suite for chorus and orchestra *People's Avengers* (1942), the cantata *The Leninists* (1959), and the *Requiem* for soloists, two choruses, and orchestra, with words by R. Rozhdestvenskii (1963; Glinka State Prize of the RSFSR, 1966). His chamber works include two string quartets (No. 2, 1945; State Prize of the USSR, 1946) and 24 preludes for piano. He has also written music for a number of films and plays. Kabalevskii was a deputy to the seventh and eighth convocations of the Supreme Soviet of the USSR. He is a corresponding member of the Academy of Arts of the German Democratic Republic (1970), honorary professor at the Conservatory in Mexico City (1959), and vice-president of the British Workers' Choral Society (1950). He has been awarded two Orders of Lenin and two other orders, as well as medals.

WORKS

Izbrannye stat'i o muzyke. Moscow, 1963.
Pro trekh kitov i mnogoe drugoe: Knizhka o muzyke. Moscow, 1970.

REFERENCES

Grosheva, E. D. *Kabalevskii.* Moscow, 1956.
Abramovskii, G. *D. Kabalevskii.* Moscow, 1960.
Danilevich, L. *Tvorchestvo D. B. Kabalevskogo.* Moscow, 1963.
Glezer, R. V. *D. B. Kabalevskii.* Moscow, 1969.
Nazarevskii, P. *D. B. Kabalevskii: Notograficheskii i bibliograficheskii spravochnik.* Moscow, 1969.
Pozhidaev, G. A. *D. B. Kabalevskii: Rasskazy o zhizni i tvorchestve.* Moscow, 1970.   L. V. DANILEVICH   [11–246–4; updated]

KABAL'NYE KHOLOPY, a category of serfs in Russia that first appeared in the 15th century and was most numerous in the 16th and 17th centuries.

The *kabal'nye kholopy* were bound in return for a money loan and were indentured to their creditor until they had worked off the debt in full. Until the end of the 16th century, only the origin of the bond distinguished *kabal'nye kholopy* from other groups of serfs, since their legal position was regulated by the norms and laws applying to serfs in general, including the Law Code of 1550 —the first legal document to refer to debt slavery.

The rapid growth of the group in the mid-16th century eventually forced the government to limit it. The Decree of Feb. 1, 1597, later included in the Law Code of 1649, significantly altered the legal position of the *kabal'nye kholopy*. The possibility of paying off the debt was abolished. Servitude lasted for the entire lifetime of the creditor, after whose death the men and their families were to be freed, even if the loan was not repaid.

Debt slavery was considered preferable to other forms of servitude. Thus, traditional serfs whose position was not regulated by any documents and voluntary serfs who were serving no less than six months gradually came to be grouped with the *kabal'nye kholopy*.

The convergence of the legal and economic status of the debt serfs with the status of the new class of serfs (*krepostnye krest'iane*) that emerged at the turn of 17th century accelerated in the second half of the 17th century; they were combined into a single group with the establishment of the poll tax (*podushnaia podat'*) in 1724. The transactions by which an individual became a *kabal'nyi kholop* were recorded in *kabala* charters. After 1586 the charters were kept in *kabala* registers. In addition, special registers were used in 1597–98.

REFERENCES

Kliuchevskii, V. O. "Podushnaia podat' i otmena kholopstva v Rossii." *Soch.,* vol. 7. Moscow, 1959.
Paneiakh, V. M. *Kabal'noe kholopstvo na Rusi v 16 v.* Leningrad, 1967.
Koretskii, V. I. *Zakreposhchenie krest'ian i klassovaia bor'ba v Rossii vo vtoroi polovine XVI v.* Moscow, 1970.
                                        V. D. NAZAROV   [11–248–2]

KABANOV, VIKTOR ALEKSANDROVICH. Born Jan. 15, 1934, in Moscow. Soviet chemist. Corresponding member of the Academy of Sciences of the USSR (1968).

A student of V. A. Kargin, Kabanov graduated from Moscow University in 1956. Since 1970 he has been head of the subdepartment of high-molecular-weight compounds at Moscow University. Kabanov has discovered and explained the phenomenon of rapid low-temperature polymerization of solid monomers during phase transformations. He has formulated and substantiated the principles of controlling polymerization by us-

ing complexing agents that alter the reactivity of monomers and the active intermediate products of the reaction. Kabanov has also achieved the synthesis of macromolecules on matrices from synthetic polymers that simulate matrix biosynthesis.

[11–250–1]

KABARDA-BALKAR AUTONOMOUS SOVIET SOCIALIST REPUBLIC, also Kabarda-Balkaria. Part of the RSFSR. The Kabarda-Balkar Autonomous Oblast was formed on Jan. 16, 1922, and transformed into an autonomous soviet socialist republic on Dec. 5, 1936. Its area is 12,500 sq km. Population, 614,000 (1972). The Kabarda-Balkar ASSR has eight raions, seven cities, and seven urban-type settlements. The capital is the city of Nal'chik.

Constitution and government

The Kabarda-Balkar ASSR is a socialist workers' and peasants' state and an autonomous soviet socialist republic. The present constitution was adopted on June 24, 1937, by the Extraordinary Tenth Oblast Congress of the Soviets of Kabarda-Balkaria. The highest bodies of state power are the unicameral Supreme Soviet of the Kabarda-Balkar ASSR (which is elected by the people for a term of four years, on the basis of one deputy per 4,000 people) and its presidium. The Supreme Soviet appoints the government of the republic—the Council of Ministers. The Kabarda-Balkar ASSR is represented in the Soviet of Nationalities of the Supreme Soviet of the USSR by 11 deputies. The local organs of state authority are city, raion, settlement, and village soviets of working people's deputies, which are elected by the people for two-year terms.

The Supreme Soviet of the Kabarda-Balkar ASSR elects the Supreme Court and the presidium of the Supreme Court for a term of five years. The Supreme Court is composed of two court collegiums, one for criminal and one for civil cases. The attorney of the Kabarda-Balkar ASSR is appointed by the Attorney-General of the USSR for a term of five years.

Natural features

Kabarda-Balkaria is located in the central part of the northern slope of the Greater Caucasus and the adjoining Kabardin Plain. The highest peaks are in the southwest and the south, where some mountains of the Bokovoi Range and the Glavnyi, or Vodorazdel'nyi, Range rise above 5,000 m (Elbrus, 5,642 m; Dykhtau, 5,203 m; and Shkhara, 5,068 m). To the northwest the terrain descends, dropping to below 200 m at the confluence of the Malka and Terek rivers. The Glavnyi and Bokovoi ranges have an alpine landscape; further northeast a band of cuesta-type foreranges stretches from west-northwest to east-southeast; the fore ranges exhibit Karst phenomena, such as craters, sinkholes, lakes, and springs. Descending toward the northeast, the terrain of the northern cuesta merges with the aggradational Kabardin Plain.

The mineral resources of the Kabarda-Balkar ASSR include molybdenum, tungsten (in Tyrnyauz), and polymetal ores, gold, coal, mineral building materials, and mineral-water springs.

Climatic conditions are governed by the laws of vertical zonality. In the Kabardin Plain the average January temperature is −4°C, the average July temperature 23°C, and the annual precipitation less than 500 mm. The length of the frost-free period in the plains is under 190 days. In the mountains the average temperature in January and February descends to −12°C or below, the temperature in July and August is 4°C or below, and the precipitation is 2,000 mm a year or more. Kabarda-Balkaria is one of the major centers of the modern glaciation of the Greater Caucasus. Several big glaciers descend from the Bezengi wall and from the mountains of the Bokovoi range; the most important glaciers are the Bezengi and Dykhsu.

The rivers are in the Terek River basin. The largest of them —the Terek, Malka, Baksan, Chegem, and Cherek—rise in high mountain glaciers. The thawing of seasonal and permanent snow and of the glaciers causes a high water level in spring and early summer. The small rivers in the band of foreranges have summer flooding caused by rain. The hydroelectric power reserves are estimated at 1.6 million kilowatts.

The Kabardin Plain has well-developed chernozem, meadow chernozem, and dark chestnut soils, with the latter in the far northeast. There is cultivated vegetation on the site of the formerly dominant low-lying steppe, and flood meadows, brushwood, and forests in the valleys of the Terek and of the lower course of the Malka. The low- and medium-mountain cuesta band has leached and mountain chernozem and brown mountain-forest soils covered with broad-leaved forests and cultivated vegetation (on the site of the broad-leaved forests and postforest meadows). Subalpine and alpine meadows are encountered on the mountain-meadow soils on the crest of the Skalistyi range and the Bokovoi and Glavnyi ranges, and upland xerophytes and pine forests grow in the valleys. Forests cover more than 180,000 hectares; the most common species are the beech, hornbeam, oak, birch, alder, and pine. The mountains are inhabited by the lynx, stone and pine marten, brown bear, boar, roe deer, chamois, and wisent; the most commonly found birds are the pheasant, the common and mountain partridge, the quail, and in the high mountains the snow partridge and the red grouse.

Steppe landscapes with agricultural lands dominate the Kabardin Plain. The cuesta zone is distinguished by forest-steppe, mountain-forest, and mountain-meadow landscapes (the latter with subalpine and alpine zones). The Bokovoi and Glavnyi ranges are an area of mountain-meadow landscapes with subalpine, alpine, and subnival zones and landscapes of the glacial-nival zone. The latter are the sites of glaciers, permanent snow, bare rock, and talus slopes.

N. A. GVOZDETSKII

Population

Kabardins and Balkars are the native population of the Kabarda-Balkar ASSR. According to the 1970 census, the population is composed of 265,000 Kabardins, 51,000 Balkars, 219,000 Russians, 10,000 Ukrainians, 9,000 Ossetians, and some other nationalities. The population increased 2.7 times between 1926 and 1972. The average population density is 49.1 persons per sq km (1972). The piedmont plain is most densely populated. The proportion of the urban population rose from 7 percent in 1926 to 53 percent in 1972. The cities of Nal'chik (171,000), Prokhladnyi (43,000), Maiskii (20,000), Baksan (19,000), Nartkala (19,000), Tyrnyauz (18,000), and Terek were founded during the Soviet period. (All city population figures are from 1972.)

Historical survey

The territory of Kabarda-Balkar has been settled since antiquity. Artifacts of the Mesolithic (eighth to fifth millennium B.C.) are represented by the Sosruko and Sos grottoes in the Baksan gorge and by the Kala-Tebe grotto in the Chegem gorge, and artifacts of the Neolithic have been discovered in the Agubek settlement and at the nomadic campsite on the Kenzhe River. The Bronze Age is represented by artifacts of the Maikop culture, including the Dolinskoe settlement and burial mounds in Nal'chik, by the North Caucasus culture, and by the Koban culture, which is represented by the Kamennomostskii burial mound and the Zhemtala treasure. Elements of the Scythian and Sarmatian cultures began spreading in Kabarda-Balkaria in the early Iron Age. Subsequently the Scythians, Sarmatians, and Alani had a great influence on the distant ancestors of the Kabardins: the Sinds, Maeonians, Zikhi, and Kerkety. These tribes were ancestors of the Adygeian, Kabardin, and Circassian peoples who lived on the Azov-Black Sea coast and were known by the collective name of Adygs. In the middle of the first millennium B.C. the Sinds on the Taman Peninsula had their own state, which later became part of the Bosporan state. The Sinds were farmers, artisans, and navigators. The invasion of the Huns in the fourth century A.D. led to an economic and cultural decline of all the Adyg tribes.

The Balkars were formed by the merging of northern Caucasian and Alani tribes with Bulgars and Kipchaks who had settled in the foothills of the Caucasus. The Kabardin-Circassian language belongs to the Abkhazo-Adyg group of the Ibero-Caucasian language family. The language of the Balkars belongs to the Kipchak group of the Turkic language family. In the early 13th century the Mongol-Tartar invasions forced the ancestors of the Balkars to resettle into the mountains after a long and bitter

struggle. In the 13th and 14th centuries some of the Adygs came to be known as Kabardins and settled in their present habitat. The territory of present-day Kabarda and Balkaria was devastated by the Mongol-Tartar invasions and part of the population was exterminated. In the 17th century the development of feudal relations, which had already arisen before the Mongol-Tartar invasion, led to the further feudal fragmentation of Kabarda into Greater and Lesser Kabarda and to a complex class and estate social heirarchy. The peasants were enserfed by princes and noblemen. The Balkars living in the mountain gorges divided into five mountaineer societies. The raids of the Crimean khans constantly threatened the lands of Kabarda-Balkaria with enslavement and the population with complete extermination. In 1557, Kabarda, then ruled by Temriuk, voluntarily joined the Russian state. The marriage of Ivan IV (the Terrible) to the Kabardin princess Maria Temriukovna further cemented the relations between Kabarda and Russia. From the middle of the 16th century on, the Kabardin people actively participated in the struggle of the Russian state for access to the Black Sea, and Kabardin aristocrats held prominent positions at the tsarist court and in the army. The strong points built on the Terek and Sunzha rivers for the defense of the Northern Caucasus from Crimean and Turkish invaders also promoted the establishment of Russian relations with Georgia, Armenia, and Azerbaijan.

The 1739 Treaty of Belgrade, which was signed after the war of 1735–39 between Russia and Turkey, declared Kabarda neutral, and in the Treaty of Kuchuk Kainarji in 1774, Turkey recognized that Kabarda was part of Russia. The union of Balkaria and Russia was completed in 1827. This union was progressive for Kabarda and Balkaria. It provided them with defense from the Crimean khanate and the Turkish empire, which had both introduced the most backward forms of feudal exploitation and driven the local population into slavery.

The feudal relations of the 19th century had a special character, because they were complicated by vestiges of the patriarchal clan systems. The peasants were dependent on the feudal lords to varying degrees. The growth of feudal exploitation led to peasant uprisings in 1804, 1824–25, 1837, and 1854. In the 1860's, Kabarda and Balkaria were made part of Terek Region. Sh. Nogmov, the first educator of the Kabardin people, made a great contribution to the development of cultural relations with Russia.

Serfdom was abolished in Kabarda and Balkaria in 1867, in connection with the bourgeois reform in Russia. The agrarian reform undermined but did not completely destroy patriarchal feudal relations. Capitalist relations were only embryonic. Development was accelerated in the late 19th and early 20th century in Kabarda by increased economic relations with Central Russia and construction of the Vladikavkaz railroad in the 1870's (Rostov-Vladikavkaz). The economic and class differentiation of the peasantry was under way. By 1916, landlords and kulaks owned more that 50 percent of the land, and about 40 percent of the peasant households had no horses. The process of capitalist development had not been completed by 1917.

The Russian Revolution of 1905–07 aroused the working masses to revolutionary struggle. The fighting *druzhinas* of 1905–07 were formed with the assistance of the Caucasian Union Committee of the RSDLP, the strike bureau of the Vladikavkaz railroad, and the social democratic organization of Mineral'nye Vody. In December 1905, demonstrations, meetings, and armed actions took place in Nal'chik, the *stanitsa* of Ekaterinogradskaia, and elswhere; peasants set fire to landlords' and kulaks' estates, drove out the local authorities, and siezed landlords' and state land. From December 26 to December 28, 1905, power in Nal'chik was in the hands of the rebels. In December 1905, martial law was proclaimed in Kabarda. The slogan of the agrarian movement of 1906 was "Land to the Peasants!" The authorities brutally suppressed the actions of the working people.

During Stolypin's agrarian reform landlords and kulaks seized a considerable part of the peasant lands and forests. This led to new agrarian disturbances, one of which took place in the Chegem gorge in 1910. In May and June 1913 these disturbances developed into the Zol'skoe, Chegem, and Cherek peasant uprisings, which were suppressed by punitive troops. The struggle of the poor peasants became more organized under the influence of the Bolsheviks, who were led in the Northern Caucasus by S. M. Kirov. These events served as a school of revolutionary education for the peasant organizers B. Kalmykov, T. Akhokhov, T. Kashezhev, M. Fanziev, Kh. Karashaev, and other leaders of Karakhalk (Poor Peasants), a revolutionary democratic organization of poor peasants (1913–16), as well as others, such as Iu. Nastuev and M. Eneev.

After the February Revolution of 1917 the authority of the bourgeois Provisional Government was represented by the counterrevolutionary Nal'chik District Civilian Committee, which was formed on March 27 (April 9). The first organization of the RSDLP was established in Nal'chik in late March 1917, and soviets of workers' and soldiers' deputies arose in Nal'chik and at Prokhladnaia station in April. Soviet power was established in Kabarda and Balkaria after Terek Oblast was proclaimed a Soviet republic on Mar. 4, 1918. In March, revolutionary detachments headed by delegates to the Terek People's Soviet occupied Nal'chik. The First People's Congress of Soviets, which was held in Nal'chik, Mar. 18–23, 1918, proclaimed soviet power in Kabarda and Balkaria. In implementing the Decree on Land, the Soviet government transferred all privately owned lands, orchards, forests, and pastures to members of the small peasantry. In June 1918 the anti-Soviet rebellion of G. Bicherakhov broke out, and the white Guards seized Nal'chik in October. The rebellion was routed in November 1918 by units of the Red Army with the participation of Kabardin and Balkar revolutionary detachments. In January 1919, General A. I. Denikin's White Guard troops occupied Kabarda and Balkaria. A rebellious movement unfolded under Bolshevik leadership, and on Mar. 24, 1920, partisan detachments, supported by the 11th Red Army, liberated all of Kabarda and Balkaria from the White Guards and nationalist gangs and restored Soviet power. In January 1921, Kabarda and Balkaria joined the Gortsy ASSR as administrative okrugs. The Fourth Congress of Soviets of the Kabardin Okrug proposed on June 10, 1921, the formation of an autonomous oblast. On Sept. 1, 1921, the All-Russian Central Executive Committee (CEC) of the RSFSR affirmed a decree on the formation of the Kabarda Autonomous Oblast as part of the RSFSR. On September 2 the Council of People's Commissars adopted a resolution signed by V. I. Lenin on extending material aid to the Kabarda AO. The Constituent Congress of Soviets of Kabarda was held Nov. 25–30, 1921. Satisfying the wishes of the working people of Kabarda and Balkaria, the All-Russian CEC of the RSFSR resolved on Jan. 16, 1922, that the Balkar Okrug should be separated from the Gortsy ASSR and united with the Kabarda Autonomous Oblast, thus forming the Kabarda-Balkar Autonomous Oblast.

In the period of the prewar five-year plans (1929–40) the Kabardin and Balkar peoples, because of the help of the Russian and other peoples of the USSR, passed from a patriarchal feudal economy to socialism, bypassing the stage of capitalism. More than 70 big industrial projects were built and industrial output increased 152 times from 1913 to 1940. In 1934, kolkhozes united 99.5 percent of the peasant farms, and from 1913 to 1932 the sowing areas increased by 68 percent. On Jan. 3, 1934, Kabarda-Balkaria was awarded the Order of Lenin for its successes in agriculture. Kabarda-Balkaria was transformed from an agrarian colonial borderland into an industrial-agrarian republic. A cultural revolution was carried out, and by 1940 the written language had been created and illiteracy basically eradicated and many of the formerly strong clan and feudal vestiges had disappeared. National cadres of the working class and intelligentsia had come forward, and higher educational institutions, scientific and scientific research institutions, and clubs had been established. The socialist transformations radically changed family and social life. The emancipated woman mountaineer had become an active builder of a new life. According to the Constitution of the USSR of 1936, the Kabarda-Balkar Autonomous Oblast was transformed into the Kabarda-Balkar ASSR. The Extraordinary Tenth Oblast Congress of Soviets of Kabarda-Balkaria adopted a republic constitution on June 24, 1937.

During the Great Patriotic War (1941–45) the territory of the republic became the scene of bitter battles. Soldiers of Kabarda-Balkaria fought on the fronts and the working people worked selflessly in the rear. At the price of great losses, the enemy occupied Kabarda-Balkaria in October 1942, but in January 1943 the republic was cleared of the invaders. More than 15,000 soldiers received government awards, 20 people were honored with the title of Hero of the Soviet Union, and more than 12,000 people were awarded orders and medals for labor in the Great Patriotic War. The Central Committee of the CPSU, the Soviet government, and the Russian and all the fraternal peoples of the USSR helped a great deal in the restoration of the republic economy. In 1943 a total of 11.35 million roubles were assigned to construction and restoration.

In March 1944, as a result of violations of socialist legality, the Balkars were resettled in regions of Middle Asia and Kazakhstan. The Kabarda-Balkar ASSR was renamed the Kabarda ASSR. On Jan. 9, 1957, the Presidium of the Supreme Soviet of the USSR issued a decree on the restoration of the national autonomy of the Balkar people and the transformation of the Kabarda ASSR into the Kabarda-Balkar ASSR.

In the postwar period Kabarda-Balkaria made remarkable strides in economic and cultural development. On July 4, 1957, the Kabarda-Balkar ASSR was awarded a second Order of Lenin to mark the 400th anniversary of Kabarda's unification with Russia and for successes of the working people in economic and cultural development. By 1972 the title of Hero of Socialist Labor had been conferred on 24 people and 27,253 people had been awarded orders and medals of the USSR. On Aug. 31, 1971, the republic was awarded the Order of the October Revolution on the 50th anniversary of the formation of the Kabarda-Balkar ASSR and for successes in communist construction. To mark the 50th anniversary of the USSR the republic was awarded the Order of Friendship of Peoples on Dec. 29, 1972.

Kh. G. Beriketov

Economy

In the Soviet period Kabarda-Balkaria has become a republic with a developed and diversified industry and a highly intensive agriculture. An industrial economic structure has been created. In 1970 industrial output accounted for 78 percent of the economy. Resorts are becoming increasingly important in the economy of Kabarda-Balkaria, and tourism and alpinism are developing.

Table 1. Output of basic types of industrial goods

Type of goods	1940	1950	1960	1971
Electric power (million kW-hr)*	93	114	219	179
Cable products in copperweight (thousand tons)	—	—	1.6	9.4
Instruments and means of automation and their spare parts (thousand rubles; wholesale prices for July 1, 1967)	—	—	5,131	29,843
Woodworking machine tools (units)	—	—	1,076	1,701
Building bricks (million units) . . .	15.7	10.0	68.1	121
Precast concrete structures and parts (thousand cu m)	—	—	49	183
Outdoor knitwear (thousand units)	65	59	126	1,627
Leather footwear (thousand pairs)	221	103	250	837
Meat (thousand tons)	5.6	6.3	14.8	18.3
Vegetable oil (thousand tons) . .	7.6	5.7	13.7	9.6
Cheese (tons)	343	334	618	2,496
Canned goods (million standard cans)	6.9	12.8	50.0	101
Grape wine (thousand decaliters)	75	22	168	1,406

* While output of electric power dropped in 1971, its consumption in the national economy increased through the reception of power on electric networks from other regions.

Industrial output increased 15.9 times from 1940 to 1971. In the prewar and the first postwar five-year plans the branches processing agricultural raw materials, such as light industry and the food industry, had a predominant share in the structure of industry. But in the late 1950's heavy industry took a leading role in the industrial complex. While light industry and the food industry continue to increase in absolute numbers, instrument making, machine building, and nonferrous metallurgy have taken the lead in industrial development. In 1971 the extracting industry accounted for 10.5 percent of the gross product and the manufacturing industry for 89.5 percent. Table 1 shows the major types of industrial output.

Electric power is produced by hydroelectric power plants. The biggest of them is the Baksan Hydroelectric Power Plant, which was built in accordance with Lenin's GOELRO plan.

The leading branches of heavy industry are machine building and metalworking, which account for 25.6 percent of the gross product, 25.9 percent of the value of fixed capital, and 40.9 percent of the industrial production personnel (1971). The output of machine building and metalworking increased 133.2 times from 1940 to 1970. The republic has enterprises producing electrical engineering equipment, machine tools, instruments, and tools. The largest of them are the Northern Caucasus Electrical Apparatus Plant and plants producing remote control equipment, machines, machine tools, and high-voltage equipment, all located in Nal'chik; a diamond tool plant in Terek; cable and repair plants in Prokhladnyi; an X-ray equipment plant in Maiskii; and a low-voltage equipment plant in Tyrnyauz.

On the eve of the Great Patriotic War (1941–45) a ferrous metallurgy has been created on the basis of the rich tungsten and molybdenum ores. This industry is represented by the Tyrnyauz mining and metallurgical combine, with a hydrometallurgical plant in Nal'chik.

The output of the building materials industry increased 23.5 times from 1940 to 1970. This industry produces reinforced-concrete structures, construction ceramics products, wall materials, nonore materials, and porous fillers. There are reinforced concrete plants in Nal'chik, Tyrnyauz, Prokhladnyi, and Nartkala; brick plants in Prokhladnyi and Baksan; and a cement plant in Nal'chik. The chemical industry, which is developing, includes lacquer and paint factories and tire repair plants. Commercial beech lumber is processed by local furniture enterprises, such as the Elbrus Furniture and Woodworking Firm in Nal'chik, the Baksan and Prokhladnyi furniture factories, and the Nal'chik, Maiskii, and Sovietskii woodworking plants. This wood is also shipped to other furniture enterprises in the Soviet Union as semifinished products.

Light industry and the food industry, which use local raw materials, account for 52.3 percent of the gross output, 23.2 percent of the value of the fixed capital, and 34.5 percent of the industrial production personnel (1971). The gross output of the food industry increased 5.3 times from 1940 to 1970, and that of light industry, 17.8 times. The food industry has 15 branches, the best developed of which are meat, butter and cheese, confectionery, fruit and vegetable canning, vegetable-oil extraction, starch and molasses, and winery. The leading enterprises are a meat combine, a confectionery factory, a dairy, and a creamery in Nal'chik; a cannery and a winery in Nartkala; and a butter and cheese dairy and a winery in Prokhladnyi. Light industry produces, among other things, textiles, clothing, footwear, and leather haberdashery. Nal'chik is the site of the Iskozh Combine, a large enterprise that includes an imitation leather plant and clothing fabrics and shoe-and-cardboard factories. Also located in Nal'chik are the Druzhba Knitwear Combine and clothing, shoe, and leather haberdashery factories. A knitwear factory is located in Baksan.

Grain farming and livestock raising are the leading branches of agriculture. In 1971 arable land covered 42.6 percent, hayfields 9.8 percent, and pastures 45.1 percent of the agricultural fields. There were 75 kolkhozes and 36 sovkhozes in early 1972. The republic used 8,600 tractors (in terms of standard 15 horsepower units), 766 grain-harvesting combines, and 3,900 trucks for agriculture in 1972. Table 2 shows the structure of the sowing areas.

Grain farming in the Kabarda-Balkar ASSR produces mainly wheat and corn. In 1971 the gross harvest of these two crops reached 196,800 tons and 99,500 tons respectively, an increase from 64,400 tons and 79,000 tons in 1940. Kabarda-Balkaria is one of the biggest corn-growing regions of the country and a major supplier of hybrid corn seeds for many regions of the USSR. With a well-developed fruit cultivation and viticulture, fruit and berry plantings cover 21,100 hectares (ha) and vineyards 3,000 ha (1971). The same year, the harvest of fruit and berries was 41,700 tons and of grapes, 9,300 tons. Irrigated farming, which increased from 19,000 ha in 1945 to 94,000 ha in late 1971, receives water from the Malo-Kabardin, Terek-Kuma, Baksan, and Cherek-Chegem irrigation systems.

Table 2. Crop areas
(in hectares)

	1913	1940	1971
Total cultivated area	173,000	270,500	332,000
Grain crops	155,300	167,500	144,700
Winter wheat	39,800	68,700	67,500
Corn	28,400	64,400	42,300
Millet	45,900	8,700	9,700
Industrial crops	4,100	42,900	39,600
Sunflowers	1,700	27,400	28,700
Southern hemp	—	11,400	9,000
Potatoes, vegetable and melon crops	4,500	15,100	15,500
Fodder crops	1,100	45,000	132,200

The major animals raised are dairy cattle, dairy-and-meat cattle, sheep, swine, fowl, horses (Kabardin breed), bees, and silkworms. In late 1971 the herd of livestock consisted of 270,000 head of cattle (161,000 in 1940), including 100,000 cows (66,000); 106,000 swine (42,000); and 384,000 sheep (410,000). Cattle, sheep, and horses are driven to the Zol'skoe subalpine pastures from May to August.

The output in livestock raising increased as follows from 1940 to 1971: meat (in slaughter weight), from 11,700 tons to 31,100 tons; milk, from 54,800 tons to 200,400 tons; eggs, from 30.4 million to 130.7 million; and wool, from 690 tons to 1,247 tons.

The following figures represent the increase of state purchases from 1940 to 1971: grain crops, from 98,500 tons to 166,000 tons; sunflowers from 16,200 tons to 22,100 tons; hemp (stems), from 16,800 tons to 28,500 tons; vegetables, from 7,100 tons to 60,200 tons; livestock and poultry, in liveweight of livestock and fowl, from 5,800 tons to 29,200 tons; milk, from 10,500 tons to 89,300 tons; eggs, from 19.5 million eggs to 67.6 million eggs; wool, in test weight, from 639 tons to 1,420 tons.

There were 133 km of operating railroads in Kabarda-Balkaria in 1971. Its territory is traversed by the North Caucasian railroad, with a 41-km branch from Kotliarevskaia station to Nal'chik and two lines from Prokhladnaia station to Gudermes via Mozdok and via Groznyi. Automobile transport is the major means of transport, and it plays an important role in the freight and passenger turnover within the republic. In 1971 the republic had 1,633 km of roads, including 1,386 km of hard-top roads. Highways connect Nal'chik with Ordzhonikidze, Stavropol', Groznyi, Makhachkala, Piatigorsk, Mineral'nye Vody, and Krasnodar. The Moscow-Tbilisi major highway passes through Kabarda-Balkaria. Airlines connect Nal'chik with Moscow, Rostov-on-Don, Ordzhonikidze, Groznyi, and other cities.

Kabarda-Balkaria exports nonferrous metals, instruments, means of automation and spare parts to them, centrifugal pumps, electrical technical and cable products, woodworking machine tools, motor and tractor trailers, and many products of light industry and the food industry. It imports mineral coal, petroleum products, ferrous and nonferrous metals and products made of them, chemical and mineral fertilizers, apparatus and instruments, machines, and engines.

There are several economic regions in the Kabarda-Balkar ASSR. The steppe region has a highly intensive agriculture composed of both farming and animal husbandry, as well as a developed industry. Grain farming based on artificial irrigation predominates. Almost all the commodity viticulture is concentrated here. There is dairy and dairy-and-meat livestock raising, and the raising of fine-wool sheep is a rapidly developing branch. Fur farming is also important. Industry (machine building, food, and building materials) is located mainly in the cities of Prokhladnyi, Nartkala, Maiskii, and Terek.

The piedmont region has a developed, diversified industry and intensive agricultural production. Industry includes machine building, metalworking, metallurgy, the chemical industry, woodworking, light industry, food, and building materials. Land farming is dominated by cultivation of maize, wheat, barley, and millet. Horticulture (apples and pears) and vegetable cultivation are also found here. Industrial crops, including sunflowers and southern hemp, play an important role. Animal husbandry specializes in dairy, meat-and-dairy, and meat-and-wool production. Natural pastures account for 33 percent of the agricultural lands. Poultry breeding is well-developed.

In the mountain region there is a highly developed mining industry, as well as electrical engineering, metallurgy, and forestry. There is specialization in the manufacture of animal husbandry products. Mountain horticulture is developing in the lowlands and river valleys. Grain crops (maize and wheat) and industrial crops (sunflowers) represent a considerable proportion of cultivated crops, and potatoes are also grown. The region is a major center of tourism, mountaineering, and mountain skiing.

The living standards of the people of the republic are constantly rising. From 1961 to 1971 the wages of workers and white-collar employees increased by 64 percent, and the compensation for labor on kolkhozes increased 2.6 times. Pension insurance funds have increased. From 1940 to 1971 the retail goods turnover of state and cooperative trade increased 13.1 times in comparable prices.

The housing fund in cities and urban-type settlements increased 6.9 times between 1940 and 1971. In 1971, 134,500 sq m of housing were opened for tenancy by state and cooperative enterprises and organizations and by housing construction cooperatives. Workers and white-collar employees built 47,300 sq m of housing with their own money and with the help of state credit; and kolkhozes, kolkhoz members, and the rural intelligentsia built 41,200 sq m by the same means.

T. KH. KHASHKHOZHEVA and V. KH. TEMIRZHANOV

Public health

In 1913, Kabarda-Balkaria had two hospitals with 20 beds, one dispensary, nine first-aid stations, two private pharmacies, and a total of 11 doctors. On Jan. 1, 1972, the republic had 49 hospital institutions with 5,300 hospital beds, or 8.6 beds for every thousand people; 79 polyclinics and dispensaries; 46 gynecologic consultation centers; and 45 children's nurseries with space for 2,600 children. There were 1,700 doctors, or one doctor for every 367 people, and more than 5,000 paraprofessional medical personnel. Medical personnel are trained by the Nal'chik Medical School. Nal'chik is a resort that uses the Belorech'e mineral springs. Dolinsk, the "Valley of Narzans" mineral spring, Adylsu, and Dzhilysu are resort areas. There are also sanatoriums and rest homes. Kabarda-Balkaria is a center of tourism and mountain skiing in the USSR. A complex of sports installations have been built in the Elbrus area, especially on the upper course of the Baksan River. There are cable cars on Cheget mountain and around Mount Elbrus. Popular tourist trails are found along the valley of the Malka River (the Valley of Narzans), along the valley of the Baksan toward Mount Elbrus (the Adyrsu and Adylsu gorges), across passes to the shore of the Black Sea, and along the Chegem and Cherek gorges. Mountaineering is common in the Elbrus area and the central part of the Greater Caucasus.

Education and cultural affairs

In the 1914–15 academic year there were 112 schools with 6,700 pupils and no higher or secondary specialized schools in what is now the Kabarda-Balkar ASSR. In the 1971–72 academic year there were 299 schools of general education with 146,100 students, 22 vocational and technical schools with 6,700 students, and ten specialized secondary schools with 10,300 students. The Kabarda-Balkar University in Nal'chik has a student body of 9,500. In 1969 there were 189 preschool institutions with 18,800 children attending them.

On Jan. 1, 1972, the republic had 230 mass libraries with 3.321 million books and magazines; a museum of local lore and an art museum in Nal'chik; 231 club institutions; 216 motion picture projectors; 11 Young Pioneers' houses and palaces and young

technicians' and naturalists' stations; and nine children's sports schools.

In 1972 the republic had eight scientific institutions, which had all been established during the Soviet period. The first research institute, founded in Nal'chik in 1926, is now the Kabarda-Balkar Research Institute of Economics, History, Language, and Literature under the Council of Ministers of the Kabarda-Balkar ASSR. Nal'chik is the site of the High-Mountain Geophysical Institute of the Chief Administration of Hydrometeorological Service under the Council of Ministers of the USSR; the institute works out the methodology and means of fighting hailstorms and snow avalanches. The Kabarda-Balkar State Agricultural Experimental Station, established in 1937, deals with the selection of grain, fruit, and vegetable crops regionalized for Kabarda-Balkaria. The Kabarda-Balkar Experimental Station of Horticulture was established in 1935. Scientific research is also conducted in departments of Kabarda-Balkar University. In 1972 the republic had more than 870 scientific personnel, including 32 doctors of science and about 400 candidates of science.

KH. G. BERIKETOV

Press, radio, and television

In 1971, publishing houses in Kabarda-Balkaria produced 123 books and pamphlets with a total of 625,000 copies; six periodicals and serial journals with a total annual circulation of 175,000, and 11 newspapers with a total annual circulation of 31.001 million copies. There are four republic newspapers: the Kabardin-Circassian-language *Lenin guegu* (Leninist Path, since 1921), the Karachai-Balkar-language *Kommunizmge zhol* (Path to Communism, 1921), and the Russian-language *Kabardino-Balkarskaia pravda* (1921) and *Sovetskaia molodezh'* (1939). *Oshkhamakho* (Elbrus, 1958) is a Kabardin-Circassian magazine devoted to literary, social, and political topics. The almanac *Shuiokhluk* (Friendship) has been published since 1958 in Karachai-Balkar. *Bloknot agitatora* has been published since 1951 in Russian, since 1952 in Kabardin-Circassian, and since 1958 in Karachai-Balkar. The Kabardin-Circassian-language almanac *Vachu enur* (The Light of the Stars, 1961) is published for children.

The republic radio and television broadcast one radio and one television program in Kabardin-Circassian, Karachai-Balkar, and Russian and receive a television program via the Orbita satellite system. The television center is located in the city of Nal'chik.

Literature

Although the Kabardins and Balkars speak different languages, their common history gave rise to an identical development of literatures. A Kabardin-Circassian alphabet was introduced in 1923 and a Karachai-Balkar alphabet in 1924.

An important source of the literature of Kabarda and Balkaria was folklore, which is richly represented by songs, fairy tales, proverbs, historical and heroic tales, and lyrical poetry. The Kabardins and Balkars created the heroic mythological epic poem *Narty*. This epic expresses with great artistic power the energy of labor, military valor, and world view of the people and their ethical, aesthetic, and other kinds of values. As early as the 19th century, the Kabardin poet and philologist Sh. B. Nogmov (1794–1844) created a Kabardin-Circassian alphabet and grammar and wrote the *History of the Adygeian People* (1861). The essays and short stories of S. Kazy-Girei (1801–43), written in Russian, were favorably reviewed by V. G. Belinskii and A. S. Pushkin. Some other prerevolutionary Kabardin and Balkar writers who wrote in Russian were S. Khan-Girei, the author of ethnographic essays; Kazi Atazhukin, an educator who published the first book in Kabardin-Circassian (1864); Iurii Akhmetukov (Kazi-Bek), the author of novellas, short stories, and essays; and the Balkar ethnographer and folklorist S. Urusbiev. The beginnings of enlightenment and literature could not be disseminated among the people in prerevolutionary conditions.

B. M. Pachev (1854–1936) was a pioneer of literature in Kabarda, as was K. B. Mechiev (1859–1945) in Balkaria. At the turn of the 20th century they wrote down the first poems and songs about the difficult lot of the working people, in an alphabet they created themselves. The Kabardins A. A. Khavpachev (1882–1972) and P. D. Shekikhachev (1879–1937) came to the fore later.

The development and flowering of literature began after the Great October Socialist Revolution. Pachev's voice resounded with heightened energy in his poems and songs—for example, in *Lenin's Strength Is Like the Sea*. In terms of its ideological and aesthetic level, Mechiev's poetry was the most significant phenomenon in the Balkar literature of the first postrevolutionary years.

Poetry predominated in the Kabardin-Balkar literature of the 1920's and 1930's. The democratic traditions of folklore, enriched by the study of Russian literature, were developing, and works were created in a variety of genres. The Balkar S. Shakhmurzaev (born 1886) wrote the songs *We Have Been Fighting for Hundreds of Years* and *V. I. Lenin* (1924), Pachev wrote the poems *Kabarda* (1925) and *My Word On Moscow* (1935), Mechiev composed the song *Lenin* (1924), and the Kabardin P. Keshokov (1871–1937) wrote the poem *Narty* (1920) and *Song About Kalmykov* (1930). Other works of this period include the songs and poems of the Kabardins Shekikhachev and T. Borukaev (1888–1937) and the Balkars B. I. Gurtuev (born 1910) and A. Budaev (1915–42). Ali Shogentsukov (1900–41), the founder of Soviet Kabardin literature, wrote revolutionary poems and the novel in verse *Kambot and Liatsa* (1934–36), the first long epic work depicting the mores and customs of old Kabarda. The bitter past of the people and the tragedy of the woman mountaineer are revealed in Ali Shogentsukov's poem *Madina* (1928) and in the work of Budaev and A. P. Keshokov (born 1914). The latter is the author of the poems *At the Foothill of the Mountains* (1934) and *The Fisherman's Daughter* (1939–40). The dramaturgy and prose of the 1930's portray social relations in the past, the oppressed condition of women, the awakening of national consciousness, and the people's movement toward revolution and socialism. Acutely social works were created at this time—for instance, *The Past Days of Gisa* (1935) by the Kabardin Z. Maksidov, *A Pood of Flour* (1936) by the Kabardin Ali Shogentsukov, and the collections of short stories by the Balkars S. Khochuev (1910–42) and Kh. Katsiev (born 1916). The Kabardin Z. Aksirov (born 1919) created the dramatic poem *Dakhanago Song*, on the folklore theme of the search for the people's happiness. Heroic popular themes inspire a number of dramas, such as *Korigot* (1936) by Shekikhachev, *Kanshoubi and Goshagag* (1939) by Z. Kardangushev (born 1918) and *Mazhid and Mar'iat* by M. Tubaev (born 1919). (All these authors are Kabardins.) *The Bloody Bride Purchase* (1940) by the Balkar R. Geliaev is similar in theme.

In the 1930's the problem of the modern positive hero was worked out in the novellas and plays of Dzh. Naloev (1906–37), S. Kozhaev, M. Afaunov, A. Shortanov, and B. Gurtuev.

The years of the Great Patriotic War saw the publication of anthologies of poems, essays and short stories: *All Take up Arms!* (1941), *In the Name of the Motherland* (1942), *On the Fronts of the War* (1943), and *Laughter Kills the Enemy* (1944). B. Bekulov's collection of poems *We Shall Win!* (1942) and the poems *My Motherland* (1941) by Ali Shogentsukov and *The Father* (1944–45) by A. P. Keshokov also appeared. Poems and short stories by Keshokov and K. Kuliev (born 1917) were regularly published in the army press at the front. Ali Shogentsukov, I. Kazharov, M. Kanukoev, B. Taov, B. Kushkhov, R. Geliaev, S. Khochuev, A. Budaev, and other writers died in the struggle against fascism. In the post war period the lyrical poetry of the Kabardins A. Keshokov, Adam Shogentsukov (born 1916), and B. Kuashev (1920–57) and the Balkars K. Kuliev and K. Otarov (born 1912) became a part of generally recognized Soviet literature. The books by popular poets of the Kabardin-Balkar ASSR are especially remarkable. Among these are A. Keshokov's *The Path of the Horseman* (1946), *The Land of Youth* (1948), *The Yew Tree* (1954), *The Heated Stones* (1964), and *The Brand* (1969) and K. Kuliev's *The Mountains* (1957), *The Bread and the Rose* (1957), *Fire on the Mountain* (1962), and *The Wounded Stone* (1964). More recently, new poets have come to prominence, for example, S. Makitov (born 1920), N. Shogentsukov (born 1924), F. Balkarova (born 1926),

Z. Naloev (born 1928), Z. Tkhagazitov (born 1934), T. Zumakulov (born 1934), and K. El'garov (born 1935).

Kabardin-Balkar prose developed only in the postwar period. The first novel in Kabardin literature, *The Mountaineers* by A. Shortanov (born 1916), published in 1954, is a narration about the people's fate in the first quarter of the 19th century. A. Keshokov's work in two parts, *The Mountain Peaks Do Not Sleep*, published 1958–65, describes the victory of the revolution in the Northern Caucasus and the first steps toward socialism. Other prose works include Kh. Teunov's (born 1912) novel *The Shogemokov Clan* (1969, revised edition), A. Shomakhov's (born 1910) novel *Dawn over the Terek* (1970), B. Gurtuev's *The New Talisman* (1969), Zh. Zalikhanov's *The Mountain Eagles* (1962), O. Etezov's *The Stones Remember* (1958) and *In the Ravine* (1954), M. Shavaeva's *Murat* (1964), and Kh. Katsiev's *Tamata* (1972).

Prose deals in an increasingly bold fashion with contemporary themes. Adam Shogentsukov's novella *The Spring of the Sofiiats* (1955) has become known all over the Soviet Union. It describes bitter conflicts in a poetic way, and it presents a profound analysis of characters. His novella *It'll Bear Your Name* (1970) depicts the moral quests of today's youth. Kh. Kashirgov (born 1912) created brilliant portraits of communists in *The Source of Happiness* (1955), a novella about a Kabardin village in the postwar period. Kh. Khavpachev (born 1926) published the collection of short stories *Good Morning*, and A. Naloev (born 1921) published the collections of short stories *Wind From the Urukh* (1960), *Humorous Dictionary* (1963), and *The Roads* (1969). Naloev's novella *The Changing of the Guards* (1967) is one of the best Kabardin late prose works about the war. The publication of the novella *Kinsfolk* and the short stories *Farizat*, *Two Jumpers*, and *The Mechanic* by the Kabardin S. Kushkhov (1930–60) constitute a significant phenomenon in contemporary prose. E. Gurtuev (born 1935) and B. Kardanov (born 1919) are writers who have recently come to light.

The postwar years have produced dramas devoted to history in general and revolutionary history in particular. A. Shortanov's *The Party's Envoy* and Z. Aksirov's *Kyzbrun* are about the life of the working people in feudal Kabarda, I. Botashev's (born 1925) *Dawn in the Mountains* is about the Civil war, and I. Mammeev's (born 1919) *The Wounded Wisent* is about the life of K. Mechiev. A. Shortanov's *When the Light Breaks* and *In One Family*, M. Shkhagaspsoev's *Tamashi Family*, A. Keshokov's *Al'kho* and *The Last Verst*, and the comedies of P. Misakov (born 1930) are noteworthy plays on contemporary themes. The almanac *Kabarda*, published in Russian and Kabardin-Circassian from 1945 to 1957; the almanac *Shuiokhluk* (Friendship), published in Karachai-Balkar since 1958; and the bimonthly magazine *Oshkhamakho* (Elbrus), published in Kabardin-Circassian since 1958, have been very important for the development of literature. The theme of friendship of peoples is widely reflected in the literature of the Kabardin-Balkar ASSR.

Literary scholarship and criticism are developing. Monographs about writers and poets, articles on special problems, and surveys have been published, including *Essays on the History of Kabardin Literature* (1968) and *A Collection of Articles on Kabardin Literature* (1957). The scholars Kh. Teunov, Z. Naloev, A. Khakuashev, L. Kashezheva, and M. Sokurov are engaged in active work on the literature of the republic. M. Sokurov

Architecture and art

Archaeologists have found in Kabarda and Balkaria remnants of wattle dwellings and pottery dating from the Neolithic period and early Bronze Age (Nal'chik burial mounds) and pottery and metal ornaments from the Koban culture and the culture of the Scythians and Sarmatians. Many burial mounds, family sepulchers, and crypts have been preserved, such as the tomb under a burial mound near the city of Nal'chik (third millennium B.C.), as well as unfortified settlements and fortified towns. The latter include the fortified town of Nizhnii Dzhulat near the city of Maiskii, which existed from the beginning of the Common Era through the 14th century, with remnants of a large mosque from the early 14th century, and the early medieval fortified town of Lygyt, near the village of Verkhnii Chegem, with a complex of defense installations from the late Middle Ages. In the high-mountain regions, ruins of late medieval fortress complexes built in inaccessible places (on slopes, in recesses, and on mountain peaks) have been preserved; the architecture is severe and laconic. These ruins include the Totur-Kala Fortress and the Dzhaboev Castle on the right bank of the Cherek River, the Bolat-Kala and Malkar-Kala fortresses in the Cherek gorge, a castle on Kurnoiat-Bashi Mountain and the three-tier Zylga Complex (also called the Borziev Castle), in the Balkar gorge. Majestic fortified towers have been found: the Abai tower near the former *aul* (village) of Kunnium from the late 16th and early 17th century; the Balkarukov Tower in the village of Verkhnii Chegem of the second half of the 17th century, which was built by masters from Svaneti; and the Ak-Kala Tower south of the village of Bezengi, dating from the 17th and 18th centuries.

There are many above-ground stone mausoleum crypts dating from the 14th to the 19th century. Some are rectangular with a high gabled roof, others are round or polygonal with a cone-shaped roof. The triumphal gate in the *stanitsa* (village) of Ekaterinogradskaia was built in 1785 and restored in 1847 and 1962.

In the Soviet period, mainly in the 1950's and 1960's, Nal'chik has been almost completely rebuilt and has become a modern garden city with a regular plan. The modern buildings are represented by the House of Soviets (1956, architects S. A. Maslikh and S. E. Vakhtangov), the N. K. Krupskaia Library (1959, architects I. V. and A. G. Lysiakov), the museum of local lore (1964, architect L. M. Timonina), a recreation and concert hall (1964, architect O. K. Shiriaeva), and the music and drama theater building (1967, architects E. M. Landau and others). In Dolinsk, modern sanatoriums, polyclinics, and boarding houses, and a public recreation center have been built; modern buildings in the Elbrus area include hotels in Itkol and Azau and on the Chegem River (all built by the architect V. M. Morgulis).

The folk art of Kabarda-Balkaria is represented by carving on wood (furniture, dishes, trunks), on stone (epitaphs), and on bone. Little caps and the hems and sleeves of women's festive dresses were covered with embroidery of gold thread in combination with cords and galloons, forming large patterns of plant and corniform motifs, rhombic figures, circles, and trefoils. Granulation, filigree, etching, and sometimes decorative stones ornamented metal articles, such as earrings, rings, buckles, clasps, and parts of horse harnesses. Patterns were laid on leather articles (pouches, purses, etuis) by stamping, appliqué, and embroidery. The Balkars made heavy felt rugs with geometric relief patterns or patterns of large corniform figures and sun designs by means of appliqué and mosaic techniques. (For the latter, pieces of heavy felt of different colors were sewn together.) The Kabardins made woven mats with geometric patterns.

Representational art appeared in the Soviet period and has been developing, especially since the 1950's. Landscape painting is very popular (N. N. Gusachenko, M. A. Vannakh, N. Z. Tryndyk, A. A. Zhereshtiev, M. A. Aksirov, Iu. S. Mushailov, and R. M. Khazhuev), as well as portrait and topical painting (N. N. Gusachenko, N. M. Tret'iakov, N. P. Tatarchenko, and N I. Dorofeev). Monumental painting and mosaic art have been developing since the second half of the 1960's (A. M. Sundukov, V. Kh. Temirkanov, and N. I. Efimenko). A. E. Glukhovtsev, V. S. Orlenko, P. G. Ponomarenko, and G. S. Pashtov represent easel painting and book illustration; Kh. B. Krymshamkhalov and M. Kh. Tkhakumashev, monumental sculpture; and V. P. Slavnikov, A. P. Durnev, and G. Kh. Bzheumykhov, small-scale sculpture. Rug-making is a developing craft. Rugs are made of fleece with traditional large corniform figures and topical representations and portraits (Gorianka factory in Nal'chik). Kabardin-Balkar divisions of the Union of Architects of the USSR and of the Union of Artists of the RSFSR were established in 1957; in 1968 the latter became the Union of Artists of the Kabarda-Balkar ASSR.   N. M. LEVITSKAIA

Music

Songs and dances are the prevailing genres in folk music, which is based on diatonic natural modes; the rhythm is characterized by an abundance of syncopation and triplets. The *Kafa,*

udzh, and *islamei* are popular Kabardin folk dances, and the *tyuz-tepseu, tyogerek-tepseu,* and *abzekh* are Balkar dances. The following are Kabardin and Balkar folk music instruments: *shyke-pshyne, zhiia-kobuz* (string instruments played with bows); *pshyne-dykuakue, kyngyr-kobuz* (harp-like instruments); *ape-pshyne, kyl-kobuz* (pizzicato instruments); *nakyre, syryna (zurna*-like wind instruments); *bzhemii, sybyzgy* (flute-like instruments); *pkh''achych, kars* (percussion instruments; *kars* are a kind of cymbals); and *pshyne* and *kobuz* (reeds; the *kobuz* is a diatonic harmonica). Sultan-Bek Abaev, Kiazim Mechiev, Bekmurza Pachev, and Kilchuka Sizhazhev are famous poets, folk musicians, and singer-narrators. The wealth of Kabardin-Balkar music has repeatedly attracted the attention of both prerevolutionary Russian and Soviet composers (M. A. Balakirev, S. I. Taneev, S. S. Prokofiev, and N. Ia. Miaskovskii).

Professionally composed music arose in Kabarda-Balkaria after the October Revolution, along with polyphonic choral singing. The work of A. M. Avraamov and T. K. Sheibler is closely linked with Kabardin-Balkar music. Avraamov composed the cantata *People's Happiness* (1936), *Kabardin Symphonic Dances* (1936), and the overture *Aul Batyr* (1940), and Sheibler wrote a rhapsody for piano and orchestra on Kabardin themes (1951) and the ballet opera *Narty,* which was produced in 1957 by the Bolshoi Theater. Recent works include the national opera *Madina* by M. F. Balov and Kh. Ia. Kardanov (produced in 1970 in Nal'chik); the ballets *Lialiutsa* (1964), *Dakhanago* (1966), and *Aminat* (1968) by L. L. Kogan; the cantata-oratorio-style *Requiem* (1965), the symphonic vocal suite *We Shall Live Under Communism* (1963), and the oratorio *Songs of My Motherland* (1967) by Balov; *The Immortal Lenin* (1969) by Kardanov; and cantatas by Kardonov and V. L. Molov. Balov, Kardonov, N. S. Osmanov, Molov, and D. K. Khaupa are symphonic composers, and A. G. Shakhgaldian, Balov, Osmanov, Kardanov, Molov, Khaupa, M. Zhetteev, I. Kh. Sherieva, and B. Pshenokov have written songs.

The folk singers and musicians I. Kazharov, B. Kaziev, O. Otarov, L. Aloev, A. Khavpachev, B. Ivanova, K. Kashirgova, and L. Tesheva have been famous since the 1930's. The 1950's and 1960's saw the rise of a number of professional performers: the singers and Honored Artists of the RSFSR I. Kh. Sherieva and V. T. Kuasheva; the Honored Artists of the Kabardin-Balkar ASSR V. K. Kodzokov, Kh. M. Beppaev, and B. A. Kuzhev; the Honored Artists of the Chechen-Ingush ASSR A. M. Pachev and L. K. Kul'baeva; the pianist and Honored Artist of the Kabardin-Balkar ASSR E. Kh. Borsokova; the choirmasters and Honored Artists of the RSFSR B. Zh. Blenaova, Iu. M. Betsuev, and M. M. Kunyzhev; and the conductors Kh. B. Afaunov, Iu. Iu. Aliev, Iu. Kh. Temirkanov, and I. Shcherbakov. In 1972 the musical institutions of the Kabardin-Balkar ASSR were the Musical Theater (1968), the Philharmonic Society (1943), the symphony orchestra (1943), the choir of the Kabardin-Balkar Radio and Television (1965), the folk dance ensemble *Kabar-dinka* (1965), the School of Music (1956), the school of cultural education (1960), and 13 children's music schools.

The Kabardin-Balkar division of the Union of Composers of the USSR was established in 1959.   KH. KH. KHAVPACHEV

Theater

The theater art of the Kabardin and Balkar peoples has its roots in everyday ritual spectacles and performances of folk singers (called *dzheguako*). After the establishment of Soviet power, clubs were opened and drama circles organized in Nal'-chik and the villages. The authors of the plays were members of amateur theater circles. Their plays dealt with the struggle against ignorance, with religious prejudices, and with survivals of feudalism in attitudes toward women. S. Gonov, A. Shortanov, A. Berezgov, T. Kimov, and M. Etezov were among the first playwrights. The 1930's saw the establishment in Nal'chik of the Theater of Working Youth, the Theater Studio, the Russian Drama Theater, and the Kabardin-Balkar traveling kolkhoz and sovkhoz theater, which contributed to the development of national art. The Kabardin-Balkar Theater of Drama was founded in 1940; its troupe was composed of graduates of the

Kabardin and Balkar studios of the State Institute of Theater and Arts (GITIS). The theater's repertoire included Vs. Ivanov's *Armored Train 14–69,* Z. Kardangushev's *Kanshaubi and Goshagak,* and plays by Shortanov, M. M. Tubaev, R. Giliaev, I. Zh. Botashev, and Z. A. Aksirov.

The theater's building in Nal'chik was destroyed during the Great Patriotic War (1941–45), and the theater reopened in 1948, uniting Russian and national troupes. In 1958 the Kabardin studio, composed of GITIS graduates, joined the collective, and the Balkar studio, composed of graduates of the Shchepkin Theater School, joined it in 1963. In 1961 the theater was named after Ali Shogentsukov, the founder of Kabardin literature.

The development of Kabardin-Balkar theater art and dramaturgy was greatly influenced by the culture and art of the Russian people and by classical Russian and world dramaturgy. Theaters staged the works of Shakespeare, Lope de Vega, Beaumarchais, Voltaire, N. V. Gogol, A. N. Ostrovskii, and other writers. The theater's productions include *Kambot and Liastsa* (1950) and *The Party's Envoy* (1960) by Shortanov; *Batyr, the Son of the Bear* by M. M. Shkhagapsoev (1957); *Dakhanago* (1957) and *Adiiukh* (1969) by Aksirov; *The Bloody Toi* by O. Etezov (1959); *Dawn in the Mountains* (1958) and *Eagles Love Heights* (1965) by Botashev; *Madina,* based on the work by Ali Shogentsukov (1960); *The Wounded Wisent* by I. Mammeev and *The Power of Love* by K. Erkenova (both 1965); *The Last Verst* by A. Keshokov (1968); and *The Black Trunk,* based on a work by Kh. Appaev (1969). The theater has staged plays in which V. I. Lenin is in the spotlight, including N. F. Pogodin's *Kremlin Chimes* (1958), *The Year of Dread* by A. Ia. Kapler and T. S. Zlatogorova (1965), and M. F. Shatrov's *In the Name of the Revolution* (1969). In 1972 figures in the theatrical arts included People's Artists of the RSFSR K. Kh. Dyshekov, M. K. Sonov, and A. M. Tukhuzhev; Honored Artists of the RSFSR T. T. Zhigunov, Kh. Kh. Tovkuev, and A. M. Sheriev; People's Artists of the Kabarda-Balkar ASSR K. I. Balkarova, M. Kh. Bolov, Kh. Kh. Kumakhova, M. Sh. Kuchukov, B. N. Sibekova, and M. I. Tubaev; Honored Art Worker of the RSFSR L. Kh. Erkenov; and Honored Art Workers of the Kabarda-Balkar ASSR S. A. Mal'tsev and S. A. Teuvazhev.

REFERENCES

Istoriia Kabardino-Balkarskoi ASSR, vols. 1–2. Moscow, 1967.
Kabardino-russkie otnosheniia v XVI–XVIII vv.: Dokumenty i materialy, vols. 1–2. Moscow, 1957.
Nogmov, Sh. *Istoriia adygeiskogo naroda, sostavlennaia po predaniiam kabardintsev.* Nal'chik, 1958.
Kumykov, T. Kh. *Prisoedinenie Kabardy k Rossii i ego progressivnye posledstviia.* Nal'chik, 1957.
Kardanov, Ch. E. *Agrarnoe dvizhenie v Kabarde i Balkarii.* Nal'chik, 1963.
Berbekov, Kh. M. *Perekhod k sotsializmu narodov Kabardino-Balkarii.* Nal'chik, 1963.
Kalmykov, B. E. *Revoliutsionnoe dvizhenie v. Kabarde.* Nal'chik, 1957.
45 let sovetskoi avtonomii Kabardino-Balkarii. [Nal'chik, 1966.]
Narody Kavkaza, vol. 1. Moscow, 1960.
Kusheva, E. N. *Narody Severnogo Kavkaza i ikh sviazi s Rossiei: Vtoraia polovina XVI–30-e gody XVII v.* Moscow, 1963.
Kumykov, T. Kh. *Ekonomicheskoe i kul'turnoe razvitie Kabardy i Balkarii v XIX v.* Nal'chik, 1965.
Gugov, R. Kh., and U. A. Uligov. *Ocherki revoliutsionnogo dvizheniia v Kabardino-Balkarii.* Nal'chik, 1967.
Ocherki istorii Kabardino-Balkarskoi organizatsii KPSS. Nal'chik, 1971.
Beriketov, Kh. G. *Lenin i Kavkaz.* Nal'chik, 1970.
Maslov, E. P., and K. N. Kerefov. *Ocherki ekonomicheskoi geografii Kabardino-Balkarskoi ASSR.* Nal'chik, 1964.
Rossiiskaia Federatsiia: Evropeiskii Iugo-Vostok, Povolzh'e, Severnyi Kavkaz. Moscow, 1968. (In the series *Sovetskii Soiuz.)*
50 let sovetskoi avtonomii Kabardino-Balkarii: Sb. st. Nal'chik, 1971.
50 let Kabardino-Balkarskoi ASSR: Stat. sb. Nal'chik, 1971.
Pod"iapol' skii, G. N., O. L. Opryshko, and S. M. Nakova. *Putevoditel' po Kabardino-Balkarii.* [Nal'chik, 1971.]
Kharenko, A. A. *Gornymi tropami Kabardino-Balkarii.* [Nal'chik, 1972.]
Ocherki istorii kabardinskoi literatury. Nal'chik, 1968.
Teunov, Kh. *Literatura i pisateli Kabardy,* 2nd ed. Moscow, 1958.
Kashezheva, L. *Kabardinskaia sovetskaia proza.* Nal'chik, 1962.
Khakuashev, A. Kh. *Ali Shogentsukov.* Nal'chik, 1958.
Naloev, Z. M. *Poslevoennaia kabardinskaia poeziia.* Nal'chik, 1970.
Sokurov, M. G. *Lirika Alima Keshokova.* Nal'chik, 1969.
Bychkov, D., and V. Pipinis. *Kabardinskie sovetskie pisateli.* Nal'chik, 1958.
Pisateli Kabardino-Balkarii. (Biobibliograficheskii ukazatel'). Nal'chik, 1965.
K"ëbërdey literaturëm i tkhidëm teukhua ocherkkhër. Nal'chik, 1965.
Krupnov, E. I. *Drevniaia istoriia i kul'tura Kabardy.* Moscow, 1957.
Shlykov, V. A. *Izobrazitel'noe iskusstvo Kabardino-Balkarii.* Nal'chik, 1963.
[Gorchakov, V. A.] *Khudozhniki Kabardino-Balkarii* (album of works). Leningrad, 1964.
Chechenov, I. M. *Drevnosti Kabardino-Balkarii.* Nal'chik, 1969.
Kh'ëkh"upaschchsë, Kh. *K"vëbërdey-Bal"k"ër muzïkë.* Nal'chik, 1963.
Shortanov, A. *Teatral'noe iskusstvo Kabardino-Balkarii.* Nal'chik, 1961.

[11–251–1]

KABARDA-BALKAR UNIVERSITY, founded in 1957 in Nal'chik (on the basis of the pedagogical institute created in 1932 in Piatigorsk and moved in 1937 to Nal'chik). As of 1972 it included the departments of history and philology, engineering, medicine, agriculture, chemistry and biology, and physics and mathematics. It had evening, correspondence, and preparatory divisions; a graduate curriculum; 43 subdepartments; 13 scientific research laboratories, a training and experimental station, a training and scholarly base in the El'brus region, an agrobiological station, an astronomical pavilion, a station for the observation of artificial earth satellites; and a botanical garden. Its library has nearly 500,000 titles. In the 1971–72 academic year, 9,600 students (35 nationalities, including young people from Syria and Jordan) were enrolled at the university. There were 550 teachers; 26 of them were holders of the doctor of sciences degree and professors, and more than 250 of them were holders of the candidate's degree and docents. Since 1957 the university has been publishing *Uchenye zapiski.* Over the years it has trained nearly 9,000 specialists.   K. N. KEREFOV [11–270–2]

KABARDA-CHERKESS, the language of the Kabardins and Cherkess who live in the Kabarda-Balkar ASSR, the Karachai-Cherkess Autonomous Oblast, and the city of Mozdok and some of the *khutors* (farmsteads) of Stavropol' Krai adjacent to it. Kabarda-Cherkess is also spoken by the Besleneevtsy, who live in four *auls* (villages) in the Karachai-Cherkess Autonomous Oblast and Krasnoiarsk Krai, and by the inhabitants of a number of *auls* in the Adygei Atonomous Oblast. Kabarda-Cherkess speakers number approximately 274,500 (1970 census). Kabarda-Cherkess is related to the Abkhaz-Adyg group of the Ibero-Caucasian languages. It is divided into four main dialects: Bol'shaia Kabarda, Mozdok, Beslenei, and Kuban'. An orthography for Kabarda-Cherkess was created after the Great October Revolution based at first on the Roman alphabet (1923–24) and later (from 1936) on Russian orthography.

Kabarda-Cherkess is characterized by an abundance of consonants. There are only three vowels: *a, e,* and *y.* Its morphology is characterized by strongly pronounced polysynthesism of verb forms. The verb has categories of person, number, tense, mood, transitive-intransitive, static-dynamic, version, causative, and potential. There are three cases: nominative, ergative-oblique, and instrumental. The usual sentence word order is: subject-object-predicate. A relative attribute always precedes the attributed word, and a qualitative attribute follows the attributed word. Participial and adverbial-participial phrase constructions function mostly as subordinate clauses.

REFERENCES

Turchaninov, G., and M. Tsagov. *Grammatika kabardinskogo iazyka.* Moscow-Leningrad, 1940.
Iakovlev, N. F. *Grammatika literaturnogo kabardino-cherkesskogo iazyka.* Moscow-Leningrad, 1948.
Grammatika kabardino-cherkesskogo literaturnogo iazyka. Moscow, 1957.
Ocherki kabardino-cherkesskoi dialektologii. Nal'chik, 1969.

A. K. SHAGIROV [11–270–3]

KABARDINIAN HORSE, one of the old saddle and packhorse breeds, first produced in the mountains of the northern Caucasus by the Kabardin people. The horses descended from native mountain horses of the Caucasus and steppe horses brought into the mountains, which were improved with Arabian and other Eastern breeds. In the 16th century Kabardinian horses were already extremely widespread. The modern-day Kabardinian is of average height, usually with a hook-nosed head, developed thorax, straight back, strong dry legs, and durable hooves. The coat is bay, dark bay, or black.

The average measurements of the stallions are: height at the withers, 155 cm; chest girth, 180 cm; and girth of metacarpus, 19.5 cm. Crossbreeds of the Kabardinian with the Thoroughbred —horses of the Anglo-Kabardinian group—surpass purebred Kabardinians in size and speed. The speed record for Kabardinian horses at 1,600 m is 1:53:4 and at 2,400 m is 2:44:2. Breeding of the Kabardinian is done by the Malka and Malokarachaev horse farms in the Stavropol'Krai and by kolkhozes in Kabarda-Balkar ASSR. Kabardinians and Anglo-Kabardinian crossbreeds are exported to many countries.

REFERENCES
"Kabardinskaia porda loshadei." In *Kniga o loshadi,* vol 1. Edited by S. M. Budennyi. Moscow, 1952, pp. 461–73.
Krasnikov, A.S. "Puti ulucsheniia kabardinskikh i karachaevskikh loshadei." *Konevodstovo i konnyi sport,* 1963, no. 2.

A. S. KRASNIKOV [11–270–5]

KABARDINIAN PLAIN, a plain in Ciscaucasia, situated in the Terek River basin, south of the lower reaches of the Malka River, in the northeastern part of the Kabarda-Balkar ASSR. The Kabardinian Plain slopes from the foot of the Greater Caucasus mountains to the northeast. (Absolute altitude decreases in this direction from 500 to 200 m.) It is composed of coarse gravel covered with loesslike loams. Soils are chernozem and prairie chernozem; where steppes once were there are now cultivated lands. (Corn crops, industrial crops, and melon crops are raised.) [11–271–1]

KABARDINKA, an urban-type settlement in Krasnodar Krai, RSFSR, a climatic seaside health resort. It is on the shore of Tsemes Bay on the Black Sea, 21 km southeast of the city of Novorossiisk, with which it has bus connections. It has very warm summers (mean temperature in August of 24°C) and mild winters (−3°C in January). Annual precipitation is 280 mm. In winter and fall, northeasterly winds often blow. Treatments at Kabardinka include climatic therapy, sea bathing (from June to the beginning of October), and the grape cure. It also has a well-equipped pebble beach, with a sandy, gradually sinking bottom. Nontubercular diseases of organs of breathing and functional disorders of the nervous system are treated there. Kabardinka also has a sanatorium for children suffering from pulmonary tuberculosis, as well as regular sanatoriums for children and juveniles, a resort hotel, and tourist centers. [11–250–4]

KABARDINO-BALKARSKAIA PRAVDA, a Russian-language republic newspaper of the Kabardinian-Balkar ASSR. Founded in 1921, it is published five times a week in Nal'chik and has a circulation of 63,000 (1970). [11–270–1]

KABARDINS (self-designation, Adyge), a people living mainly in the northern and northeastern parts of the Kabarda-Balkar ASSR. Small numbers of Kabardins live in several countries of the Near East. Their total population in the USSR is 280,000 (1970 census). Their language (Kabarda-Cherkess) belongs to the Abkhaz-Adyg group of the Ibero-Caucasian languages. Religious Kabardins are Muslims (Christianity and remnants of pagan beliefs existed among the Kabardins until the 18th century). The Kabardins and other Adyg peoples have a common ethnogenesis.

The formation of the Kabardins as a separate people dates to the 12th to 14th centuries and was associated with their movement from the west into the territory of their present homeland and with the development of feudal relations among them. The ancient ties between the Adygs, including the Kabardins, and the

Russians resulted in the incorporation of the Kabardins into Russia in 1557. The chief occupations of the Kabardins before the October Revolution were farming, livestock breeding, and handicrafts (woodworking, gunmaking, forging, saddle-making, weaving, felt- and jewelry-making, and gold embroidery).

During the years of Soviet power the backward farming of the Kabardins was transformed into large-scale, diversified, highly mechanized kolkhoz and sovkhoz production. Machine building, metallurgy, mining, electrical engineering, and the food industry were created in the republic. Great achievements were made in culture, science, literature and art; a national intelligentsia emerged.

REFERENCES
Narody Kavkaza, vol. 1. Moscow, 1960. (Bibliography.)
Istoriia Kabardino-Balkarskoi ASSR, vol. 1–2. Moscow, 1967.
[11–271–2]

KAB IBN ZUHAYR. Date of birth unknown; died 662. Arab poet. Kab ibn Zuhayr belonged to a nomadic Arabian tribe, the Ghatafan, and was the son of the famous pre-Islamic poet Zuhayr ibn Abi Sulma. At first he wrote mocking verses about the prophet Muhammad but later dedicated to him the verbose and bombastic *qasida* (ode) "Suad has left me . . . ." According to legend, Muhammad made the poet a gift of his cloak for this, whereupon the *qasida* came to be called the "Qasida of the Cloak"; it became Kab ibn Zuhayr's most famous work, inspiring many commentaries.

WORKS
Qasidat al-burda. Beirut, 1931.
La Bânat So'àd. Translated by R. Basset. Algiers, 1910.
REFERENCE
Fakhuri, Hanna al-. *Istoriia arabskoi literatury,* vol. 1. Moscow, 1959.
[11–189–5]

KABIR. Born circa 1440; died circa 1518. Indian poet who wrote in Hindi. About 80 works are ascribed to Kabir; those included in the Adi Granth, the sacred book of the Sikhs, constitute the most authentic part of his literary legacy. Kabir's poetic activity, which was connected with the Bhakti religious reform movement, opened a new stage in the history of Hindu literature. His poetry blends the opposing religious-mystical currents of Hinduism and Islam and the artistic traditions of the Hindu and Tajik-Persian classics.

WORKS
In Russian translation:
Poemy. In R. Tagore, *Sobr. soch.,* book 6. Petrograd, 1916.
Lirika. Moscow, 1965.
REFERENCES
Serebriakov, I. "Kabir." In the collection *Vostochnyi al'manakh,* vol. 2. Moscow, 1958.
Istoriia indiiskikh literatur. Moscow, 1964. (Translated from English.)
Dvivedi, Hazariprasad. *Kabir,* 5th ed. Bombay, 1955. [11–291–3]

KABLESHKOV, TODOR LULCHOV. Born Jan. 1, 1851, in Koprivshtitsa; died circa June 3, 1876, in Gabrovo. Bulgarian revolutionary, one of the leaders of the April Uprising of 1876. The son of a tax collector.

Kableshkov received his elementary education in his home town and continued his studies in Plovdiv (1864–67) and the Constantinople Lycée (1868–71). In 1876 he headed the secret revolutionary committee that prepared the anti-Turk uprising in the town of Koprivshtitsa. With the suppression of the uprising, he was taken prisoner; unwilling to endure humiliation by the Turks, he committed suicide.

REFERENCE
Todor Kableshkov. Biografichen ocherk. Sofia, 1956. [11–292–2]

KABLITS, IOSIF IVANOVICH (literary pseudonym, Iuzov). Born June 30 (July 12), 1848, in Trebiškis, in present-day Radviliškis Raion, Lithuanian SSR; died Oct. 4 (16), 1893, in St. Petersburg. Russian publicist; Narodnik (Populist). Descended from the *dvorianstvo* (nobility).

In the first half of the 1870's, Kablits was active in populist circles and participated in the movement "to the people." In St. Petersburg in 1874 he organized a circle of *vspyshkopuskateli* (incendiaries), whose goal it was to stir up local peasant uprisings in order to revolutionize the masses. Beginning in the late 1870's he contributed to the journals *Nedelia, Slovo,* and *Mysl'.* In the 1880's he renounced his revolutionary past. Kablits' main works were *The Principles of Populism* (1882; 2nd ed., 1888) and *The Intelligentsia and the People in the Social Life of Russia* (1885; 2nd ed., expanded and revised, published in 1883 as the second volume of the first work). Joining ranks with outright reactionaries in a number of his conclusions, Kablits held an extreme right-wing position in the Populist movement that was not shared by the movement's majority.　　　　　[11–292–3]

KABLUKOV, IVAN ALEKSEEVICH. Born Aug. 21 (Sept. 2), 1857, in the village of Prussy, Moscow Province; died May 5, 1942, in Tashkent. Soviet physical chemist. Honorary member of the Academy of Sciences of the USSR (1932; corresponding member, 1928). Honored Scientist of the RSFSR (1929); honored professor of Moscow University from 1910.

In 1880, Kablukov graduated from Moscow University, where he studied chemistry with V. V. Markovnikov. In 1881, under A. M. Butlerov, he completed the study *A New Method of Obtaining Oxymethylene* at the University of St. Petersburg. In 1885 he became a privatdocent at Moscow University. In 1889 he worked in Leipzig under W. Ostwald and in 1891 defended his doctoral dissertation, *Contemporary Theories of Solutions (Van't Hoff's and Arrhenius') in Connection With Studies on Chemical Equilibrium.* Kablukov was elected professor of chemistry at the Moscow Institute of Agriculture and Moscow University in 1903. At the same time he was acting as consultant at the Institute for Fertilizers and Insectofungicides and the Institute of Applied Mineralogy. He conducted fundamental research on the electrochemistry of nonaqueous solutions. Kablukov introduced the concept of ion solvation (at the same time but independently of V. A. Kistiakovskii), which served as the basis for combining the chemical and physical theories on solutions. He was the first to demonstrate (1887) that the heat of formation for molecules of isomeric organic compounds is not identical. Between 1904 and 1907, Kablukov used thermoanalysis to study the reciprocal systems of fused salts. He developed a method of obtaining bromine from the brine of Lake Saki in the Crimea.

The author of a number of works on the history of chemistry, Kablukov was an active participant in the work of scientific societies, for example, the Russian Physicochemical Society. He was awarded the Order of Lenin and the Order of the Red Banner of Labor.

WORKS
Osnovnye hachala neorganicheskoi khimii. Moscow, 1900; 13th ed., Moscow, 1936.
Osnovnye nachala fizicheskoi khimii, fascicles 1–3. Moscow. 1900–10.
Pravilo faz v primenenii k nasyshchennym rastvoram solei. Leningrad, 1933.
Termokhimiia, 2nd ed. Moscow-Leningrad, 1934.
Fizicheskaia i kolloidnaia khimiia, 4th ed. Moscow, 1949. (Coauthor.)
O mede, voske, pchelinom klee i ikh podmesiakh, 2nd ed. Moscow, 1941.

REFERENCE
Solov'ev, Iu. N., M. I. Kablukova, and E. V. Kolesnikov. *Ivan Alekseevich Kablukov.* Moscow, 1957. (Contains a list of works by Kablukov.)　　　　　[11–293–1]

KABLUKOV, NIKOLAI ALEKSEEVICH. Born Oct. 5 (17), 1849, in the village of Marfino, in present-day Mytishchi Raion, Moscow Oblast; died Oct. 17, 1919, in Moscow, Russian economist, statistician, and public figure. Kablukov became a doctor of political economy and statistics in 1895 and a professor in 1903.

In 1871, Kablukov graduated from Moscow University. From 1874 to 1879 he worked in the Statistics Division of the Zemstvo Board (*zemstvos* were bodies of local self-government). From 1879 to 1881 he traveled abroad. In London he met K. Marx, F. Engels, and A. Bebel. From 1882 to 1885 he was involved in many joint statistical investigations and contributed to such

journals as *Iuridicheskii vestnik* (Juridical Herald) and *Russkaia mysl'* (Russian Thought) and such newspapers as *Zemstvo, Moskovskii telegraf,* and *Russkii kur'er.* From 1885 to 1907 he was the head of the Statistics Division of the Moscow Province Zemstvo Board. From 1894 to 1919 he taught at Moscow University, becoming the head of the statistics subdepartment in 1903. After the Great October Revolution, Kablukov was elected chairman of the Executive Commission of the All-Russian Congresses of Statisticians and chairman of the Council on Statistical Affairs of the Central Statistical Board (1918).

In his views, Kablukov was a Narodnik (Populist) economist. He defended the idea of the "stability" of small peasant farming in Russia. His views were sharply criticized by Lenin, especially in *The Development of Capitalism in Russia* (see *Poln. sobr. soch.,* 5th ed., vol. 3, pp. 206–09, 247–52, 495–506, 536–41).

WORKS
Sbornik statisticheskikh svedenii po Moskovskoi gub., vols. 2, 3, 5, fasc. 1. Moscow, 1878–79. (Introductory articles, commentary, and some of the tables by Kablukov.)
Vopros o rabochikh v sel'skom khoziaistve. Moscow, 1884.
Lektsii po ekonomii sel'skogo khoziaistva. Moscow, 1897.
Ob usloviiakh razvitiia krest'ianskogo khoziaistva v Rossii, 2nd ed. Moscow, 1908. (Doctoral dissertation.)
Statistika, 5th ed. Moscow, 1922.
Melkoe khoziaistvo i kooperatsiia. Moscow, 1917.
Politicheskaia ekonomiia. Moscow, 1918.
Zadachi i sposoby sobiraniia statisticheskikh svedenii. Moscow, 1920.

REFERENCES
Pamiati N. A. Kablukova, vols. 1–2. Moscow, 1925–27. (Collection of articles.)
Svavitskaia, Z. M. "Moskovskii universitet i zemskaia statistika." In *Ocherki po istorii statistiki SSSR:* Sbornik 2. Moscow, 1957.
　　　　　F. D. LIVSHITS [11–293–2]

KABUKI, a form of classical Japanese theater, originally consisting of folk songs and dances performed by wandering actors. O-Kuni, who is considered the founder of Kabuki, organized a troupe of women in 1603. Although love songs and dances were the main features of the scenes in which O-Kuni appeared, there were also elements of dramaturgic composition. These elements subsequently became more prevalent. In 1629 the women's troupe was banned on the pretext of having violated the laws of morality. Since 1652 only men have appeared in Kabuki performances (*yaro*-Kabuki). As a result, a specific role involving the impersonation of women was established (*onnagata,* or *oyama*).

In the late 17th and early 18th centuries, Kabuki theater reached the height of its development, with the rise of an urban culture during the Genroku period (1688–1703). At this time, Kabuki made a major step forward from imitation (*monomane*) to a more natural manner of acting. Stage movements and speech acquired greater significance; they were influenced by the masterful work of the actor Sakata Tojuro and the playwright Chikamatsu Monzaemon.

The crisis of the feudal order brought about strict regimentation in all areas of Japanese life. This regimentation was reflected in Kabuki plays by the use of conventions, such as dance plays, ritualistic plays (*sho'sagoto*), and pantomime. The musical accompaniment, the stage design, the traditional poses (*mie*), the canons of acting (*kata*), the wigs, and the *kumadori* makeup (red symbolized justice, passion, and bravery; blue represented sangfroid, evil, and immorality) became extremely conventional. The tradition of the succession of stage names was established, and actors' dynasties with hereditary roles were formed.

During the first half of the 18th century, Ichikawa Danjuro II and Savamura Sojuro were two of the most highly praised Kabuki actors. In 1758 the dramatist Namiki Shozo introduced the revolving stage. This stage and the "flower path," or the *hanamiti* (a platform extending from the stage to the rear of the audience), were important achievements in the development of the Kabuki theater.

Toward the end of the 18th century, the center of the Kabuki arts moved from Kyoto and Osaka to Edo (now Tokyo). In addition to the performances of the traditional historical drama (*jidaimono*), a domestic play devoted to urban life (*sevamono*) was introduced in Edo. This new genre was established in Kabuki theater by the work of the well-known dramatist Tsuruya Namboku and by the realistic performances of Matsumoto Koshiro V.

After the bourgeois revolution of 1867–68 (the Meiji revolution), Japan embarked upon the path of capitalist development. This development was expressed in Kabuki dramaturgy. Plays reflected the new morality, and historical dramas (*katsurekimono*) were staged. Among the most famous Kabuki actors of the late 19th century were Ichikawa Danjuro IX, Onoe Kikugoro V, and Ichikawa Sadanji I. New Kabuki plays appeared that revived traditional stage devices.

In 1966 the state theater Kokuritsu gekijo was opened in Tokyo with the aim of preserving classical Kabuki theater. Kabuki actors are also affiliated with the Setiku and Toho, two prominent film companies, as well as with the only independent theatrical troupe, the Zenshinza.

During its tours in the USSR in 1928 and 1961, the Kabuki theater acquainted Soviet audiences with its popular actors Ichikawa Sadanji II, Ichikawa Ennosuke II, and Utaemon VI.

REFERENCES
Konrad, N. I. "Teatr Kabuki." In the collection *Teatral'nyi Oktiabr'* Leningrad-Moscow, 1926.
Konrad, N. I. *Teatr Kabuki.* Leningrad-Moscow, 1928.
Kabuki. Moscow, 1965. (Translated from English.)
Teatr i dramaturgiia Iaponii: Sb. Moscow, 1965.
Gunji, Masakatsu. *Iaponskii teatr Kabuki.* Moscow, 1969. (Translated from Japanese.)   B. V. RASKIN [11–297–4]

KABUL, the capital of Afghanistan; the political, economic, and cultural center of the country, as well as the administrative center of Kabul Province.

Kabul is located in the valley of the Kabul River (altitude, 1,820 m) in an oasis where the Asmai and Sherdar-waza mountains rise. The climate is subtropical and continental; the average temperature in January is 1°C, and in July, 26°C. Yearly precipitation averages 317 mm. Population of Greater Kabul, 480,400 (1969). The mayor, who is appointed by the government, directs the administration of the city.

Historical survey. The city is first mentioned, under the name "Kabura" or "Karur," by Ptolemy in the second century A.D. Kabul was part of the Kushan empire and later of the Ephthalite tribal union. After the disintegration of this union in the sixth century A.D. local rulers, the shahs of Kabul, governed the city. During the period of the Arab conquests Kabul was nominally subordinate to the caliph Muawiyah I (who ruled from 661 to 680). In the ninth century the Saffarids conquered Kabul; after their fall in 900, the city was successively ruled by the Samanids, the Ghaznavids, and the Timurids. Genghiz Khan destroyed the city in the 13th century. Under Baber, who conquered the city in 1504, Kabul became the capital of the Mogul Empire. Nadir Shah captured the city in 1738. In 1747 the city became part of the Durrani State and was named its capital in 1773. After the collapse of the Durrani state in 1818, Kabul became the center around which Afghanistan subsequently took shape. British forces seized the city in 1839 during the first Anglo-Afghan war (1838–42). At the end of 1841 a massive anti-British insurrection rose in Kabul and British troops were forced to abandon the city at the beginning of 1842. Kabul was again subjected to British occupation during the second Anglo-Afghan war (1878–80). At the end of the war the emir Abdur Rahman made Kabul the capital of the Afghan state. In February 1919, Emir Amanullah Khan proclaimed Afghanistan's independence in Kabul.

Economic survey. Even in the most ancient times caravan routes passed along the valley of the Kabul River. Today, Kabul lies at the junction of highways connecting it with Pakistan and India (through Jalalabad and further on through the Khyber Pass), Iran (through Kandahar and Herat), and the Soviet Union, the city is also the site of an international airport. Kabul is an important commercial center: the bulk of Afghanistan's foreign trade passes through it. The country's principal banks, the offices of foreign firms, and the boards of directors of the most important commercial joint-stock companies are located in Kabul. The city's major industries are metalworking, wood-

working, leather and footwear, food processing, and building materials. An automobile plant and a factory making prefabricated houses have been constructed with the cooperation of the USSR.

Architecture. The old part of the city has been significantly reconstructed (according to a master plan worked out in 1965 by the architect Seraj with the participation of Soviet specialists), but narrow, crooked streets, built with clay and lined with wooden frame houses, still remain. The fortress of Bala Hissar sits on a hill (its walls probably date from the fifth century but have been frequently rebuilt). Structures in Kabul's new areas include the royal residence (20th century), the Ministry of Foreign Affairs, the mausoleum of Mohammed Nadir Shah (20th century), the Hotel Intercontinental (1960's), Zarnegar Park, and residential areas with precast large-panel houses. Kabul's monuments include Independence Column (Monar-i Esteqlal) the Column of Deliverance (MonariNejat, 1929), and a monument in honor of the victory near Maiwand in 1880 (Abidaii Maiwand, 1950's; architect, Seraj). The airport is located in the north-northeastern section of the city (1962; designed by Soviet specialists).

Educational, scientific, and cultural institutions. Kabul is the site of the University of Kabul, the Polytechnic Institute (built with Soviet assistance), the Afghan Academy of History and Philology (Pashto Tolyna), the National Academy of Sciences, the Kabul Archaeological Museum, the Public Library (120,000 volumes), and four dramatic theaters (De Pohini Nindara, De Kabul Nindara, Arub Nindara, and Zeinab Nindara).

REFERENCES
Mohammed Ali. *A New Guide to Afghanistan,* 3rd ed. Lahore, 1958.
Mohammed Naser. *Kabul segodnia.* Kabul, 1970. (Written in Pashto.)
Dupree, N. H. *An Historical Guide to Afghanistan.* Kabul, 1971.
[11–299–1]

KABUL, a river in Afghanistan and Pakistan; the largest right tributary of the Indus.

The Kabul is 460 km long. Its sources are on the slopes of the Koh-i Baba Range. At its upper reaches the river is mountainous; downstream it crosses the Jalalabad intermontane depression and, beginning at the city of Peshawar, it flows through a hilly plain. The water level begins to rise in March, reaching its maximum discharge in June and July from the melting mountain snows. Rains cause flooding in autumn. At the middle course of the river the average water discharge is approximately 200 cu m per sec (maximum, 1,500–1,600 cu m per sec). The Kabul is used for irrigation and timber rafting. It is navigated in a section 120 km from its mouth (in Pakistan). The cities of Kabul and Jalalabad (Afghanistan) are located on the river, and the city of Peshawar (Pakistan), in the basin.   [11–298–1]

KABULOVA, SAODAT. Born Dec. 15, 1925, in Margilan, in present-day Fergana Oblast. Soviet Uzbek singer (lyric coloratura soprano). People's Artist of the USSR (1959).

Kabulova graduated from D. B. Beliavskaia's class at the Moscow Conservatory in 1954. Between 1941 and 1948 she worked in the Mukimi Uzbek Theater and since 1954 has been a soloist with the Uzbek Theater of Opera and Ballet in Tashkent. Kabulova has appeared in national Uzbek operas as Zukhra in *Takhir and Zukhra* by Dzhalilov and Brovtsyn, Dilorom in the opera of the same name by Ashrafi, and Leili in *Leili and Medzhnun* by Glière and Sadykov. She also performs in the classical repertoire, she has appeared as Gilda in Verdi's *Rigoletto,* Iolantha in Tchaikovsky's opera of the same name, and Mimi in Puccini's *La Bohème.* She has given concerts and has frequently performed on tour abroad. In 1969, Kabulova began teaching at the Tashkent Conservatory.   [11–301–1]

KABWE (until 1965, Broken Hill), a city in Zambia. Population, 67,200 (including suburbs; 1969). It is connected by rail with the Republic of Zaïre and Rhodesia. Lead, zinc, and vanadium are mined and smelted in the area. The skull of a Palaeoanthropus, the Rhodesian man, was discovered here in a mine in 1921.

    [11–274–1]

KABYLES, a Berber people inhabiting the mountainous areas of northern Algeria. They number about 1,300,000 (1970, estimate). Their language is related to the Berber languages, and the majority of the Kabyles also speak Arabic. They are Sunni Muslims. Their principal occupations are agriculture and livestock raising.

REFERENCES
Narody Afriki. Moscow-Leningrad, 1954.
Morizot, J. *L'Algérie kabylisée.* Paris, 1962.   [11–290–2]

KABYLIA, the general name for the strongly dissected mountain massifs on the Mediterranean coast in Algeria, between Algiers and Annaba. The massifs are composed chiefly of Paleozoic deposits and metamorphosed granite intrusions and have an average elevation of 800–1,200 m. The region comprises the massifs (from west to east) Grande Kabylie, including the Djurdjura chain in the south (highest point, 2,308 m); Petite Kabylie, including the Babor massifs (highest point 2,004 m); Kabylie de Collo; and Edough.

Kabylia, with an annual precipitation of 800–1,700 mm, is the most humid region in Algeria. The subtropical evergreen forests have been preserved only at elevations of more than 1,200 m. The inhabitants of the region, a Berber people called Kabyles, are chiefly engaged in agriculture (grain and fruit) and in livestock raising.   [11–290–1]

KACHALOV, NIKOLAI NIKOLAEVICH. Born June 20, 1883, in Dresden, Germany; died June 19, 1961, in Leningrad. Soviet scientist, expert in silicate technology, corresponding member of the Academy of Sciences of the USSR (1933).

Kachalov graduated from the St. Petersburg Mining Institute in 1911. Between 1930 and 1961 he was head of the subdepartment of glass technology at the Leningrad Institute of Technology. Beginning in 1948 he also worked at the Institute of Silicate Chemistry of the Academy of Sciences of the USSR. Kachalov's works were devoted to the processes of making optical glass and to glass grinding and polishing. Kachalov gave the first detailed account of the physical and chemical principles behind the most important technological processes in making glass. He also worked on refractory materials, porcelain technology, and the production of decorative glass. He was awarded the State Prize of the USSR (1947), the Order of Lenin, three other orders, and various medals.

WORKS
Farfor i ego izgotovlenie. Moscow-Leningrad, 1927.
Osnovy proizvodstva opticheskogo stekla. Leningrad, 1936. (Jointly with V. G. Voano.)
Osnovy protsessov shlifovki i polirovki stekla. Moscow-Leningrad, 1946.
Steklo. Moscow, 1959.

REFERENCES
Bakhrakh, A. M. *Iz istorii opticheskogo priborostroeniia: Ocherki,* vol. 1. Moscow, 1951.
Nikolai Nikolaevich Kachalov. Moscow, 1953. (*An SSSR. Materialy k biobibliografii uchenykh SSSR. Seriia khimicheskikh nauk,* issue 18.)   [11–1637–1]

KACHALOV, VASILII IVANOVICH (real surname, Shverubovich). Born Jan. 30 (Feb. 11), 1875, in Vilnius; died Sept. 30, 1948, in Moscow. Soviet Russian actor. People's Artist of the USSR (1936.)

Kachalov was the son of a priest. While a student at the law department of the University of St. Petersburg he was a member of the drama group directed by V. N. Davydov. He worked with the A. S. Suvorin Theater in St. Petersburg in 1896–97 and with the M. M. Borodai Company in Kazan and Saratov between 1897 and 1900. In 1900 he joined the troupe of the Moscow Art Theater.

Kachalov possessed exceptional artistry, enormous stage charm, and a voice rare in its musicality. As a man and artist he was distinguished by keen powers of analysis and a philosophical approach to life. He based his art on the force of both emotion and intellect and on his ability to reflect in drama the psychological and moral conflicts within his heroes. He played 55 roles with the Moscow Art Theater. His performances in the plays of A. P.

Chekhov and M. Gorky made him the favorite actor of the Russian democratic intelligentsia. Tuzenbakh, who dreams of a bright future, Petia Trofimov, who longs to meet life and struggle, and Ivanov, who despairs but rejects compromise (in Chekhov's plays *Three Sisters,* 1902; *The Cherry Orchard,* 1904; and *Ivanov,* 1904), all expressed the expectation of social change that seized Russian society at the beginning of the century. As the baron in Gorky's *The Lower Depths,* (1902), Kachalov revealed the social nature of the psychology in the gentleman's change into a tramp and pimp, providing a remarkable example of the art of dramatic transformation. He offered an acute portrayal of the problem of "the intelligentsia and revolution" in his role as Protasov in Gorky's *Children of the Sun* (1905).

Kachalov's best prerevolutionary roles included Berendei in *The Snow Maiden* by Ostrovskii (1900), Johannes Vockerat in *Lonely Lives* by Hauptmann (1903), the title roles in Shakespeare's *Julius Caesar* (1903) and Ibsen's *Brandt* (1906), Glumov in *Even a Wise Man Stumbles* by Ostrovskii (1910), Karenin in *The Living Corpse* by L. N. Tolstoy (1911) and Gorskii in *No Stronger Than Its Weakest Link* by Turgenev (1912). The brilliance of Kachalov's intellectual force was apparent in his portrayal of Chatskii in *Woe From Wit* by Griboedov (1906, revived in 1914 and 1938) and Hamlet in Shakespeare's *Hamlet* (1911). His protrayal of Ivan Karamazov in *The Brothers Karamozov* (adapted from Dostoevsky, 1910) was imbued with a passionate belief in the power of reason.

Between 1922 and 1924 Kachalov toured Europe and America with the Moscow Art Theater. In the Soviet era his art, along with its courageous and passionate humanism and its reassertion of the heroic principles in man, leaned toward particularly sharp satiric exposé. In 1926 in the role of Nicholas I in *Nicholas I and the Decembrists* (Kugel'), Kachalov achieved vivid stage presence in his psychological portrayal of the tsarprovocateur. In his role as Zakhar Bardin in Gorky's *Enemies* (1935) he continued in the direction of social satire and blended it with Gorky's dramatic art. His dramatic portrayal of the partisan leader Nikita Vershinin in *Armored Train 14–69* by Vs. Ivanov (1927) has taken a notable place in the history of Soviet theater. In the adaptation of Tolstoy's *Resurrection* (1930), Kachalov created, in his role as the author, what K. S. Stanislavsky called "a new genre—the voice of the author, his soul" (*Sobr. soch.,* vol. 8, 1961, p. 411).

Kachalov appeared on stage in recitations of verse and prose, as well as in literary-musical and dramatic works of his own composition. At times he played scenes with more than one character—from *Julius Caesar, Hamlet,* and *The Lower Depths,* for example. Kachalov was awarded the State Prize of the USSR (1943), two Orders of Lenin, and the Order of the Red Banner of Labor.

REFERENCES
Efros, N. E. *V. I. Kachalov.* Petrograd, 1920.
Kugel', A. R. *V. I. Kachalov.* Moscow-Leningrad, 1927.
Markov, P. A. *Teatral'nye portrety.* Moscow-Leningrad, 1939.
Ezhegodnik MKhT za 1948 g., vol. 2 ("Pamiati V. I. Kachalova"). Moscow-Leningrad, 1951. (Bibliography.)
V. I. Kachalov. Sb. statei, vospominanii, pisem. Moscow, 1954. (Bibliography.)
Vilenkin, V. Ia. *Kachalov.* Moscow, 1962.
Volkov, N. D. *Teatral'nye vechera.* Moscow, 1966.
                                T. M. RODINA [11–1635–6]

KACHANOVKA, a climatic health resort in the Ukrainian SSR, in the environs of the city of Ichnia Chernigov Oblast.

Summers are warm at Kachanovka, with an average July temperature of 18°–19°C, winters are moderately mild, with an average January temperature of −7°C. The total annual precipitation is 600 mm. There is a sanatorium for patients with active forms of pulmonary tuberculosis.   [11–1637–3]

KACHANOVSKII, VLADIMIR VASIL'EVICH. Born Mar. 1 (13), 1853, in the village of Velikii Les, Grodno Province; died Apr. 11 (24), 1901, in Nezhin. Russian Slavicist.

Upon graduating from the University of Warsaw in 1876, he traveled through the Slavic countries, Greece, Italy, and France to gather research material. In 1886 he obtained a teaching post at the University of Kazan, and between 1888 and 1896 he published the journal *Vestnik Slavianstva*. He was appointed professor of Slavic philology, history, and literature in the Institute of History and Philology at Nezhin in 1896. Kachanovskii is known for his work in Slavic philology and for his publication of monuments of Slavic literature.

WORKS
"Serbskie zhitiia i letopisi, kak istochnik dlia istorii iuzhnykh slavian." In *Slavianskii sbornik*, vol. 3. St. Petersburg. 1876.
Pamiatniki bolgarskogo narodnogo tvorchestva, issue 1. St. Petersburg, 1882.
Ob istoricheskom izuchenii russokogo iazyka. Kazan, 1887.
REFERENCE
Speranskii, M. N. *Pamiati V. V. Kachanovskogo.* Nezhin, 1901.

[11–1637–4]

KACHARI, a people living in the northern part of Assam State in India. Their population is more than 200,000 (1967, estimate). Their language belongs to the Bodo subgroup of the Tibeto-Burman languages. Their religion is Hinduism; vestiges of ancient animist beliefs are still preserved. The Kachari are divided into the mountain Kachari (Dimasa) and the lowland Kachari (Burraor Burra-Mech). The lowland Kachari have settled among the Assamese and Bengali and are gradually being assimilated by them. Their chief occupation is slash-and-burn agriculture; some Kachari work on tea plantations.

[11–1638–1]

KACHENOVSKII, DMITRII IVANOVICH. Born Dec. 8 (20), 1827, in Karachev in present-day Briansk Oblast; died Dec. 21, 1872 (Jan. 2, 1873), in Kharkov. Russian lawyer. Authority on international and state law, and on the history of political theories.

Kachenovskii was appointed a professor at the University of Kharkov in 1849. His work dealt primarily with international maritime law and the history of international law. He proposed the codification of international law by scholars from various countries and recommended the creation of an international organization for the elaboration and codification of international law.

Kachenovskii's outlook was close to that of the Westernizers. His defense of bourgeois-liberal ideas is put forward in *A View of the History of Political Science in Europe* (1859) and *On the Contemporary State of Political Science in Western Europe and in Russia* (1862).

[11–1638–4]

KACHENOVSKII, MIKHAIL TROFIMOVICH. Born Nov. 1 (12), 1775, in Kharkov; died Apr. 19 (May 1), 1842, in Moscow. Russian historian and literary critic. Academician of the St. Petersburg Academy of Sciences (1841).

Kachenovskii was appointed a professor at Moscow University in 1810 and became rector of the university in 1837. He began his literary activity in 1799 in the journal *Ippokrena* as a proponent of classicism. From 1805 to 1830 (with interruptions) he edited *Vestnik Evropy*, and it was in that journal that he began his criticism of N. M. Karamzin's *History of the Russian State* in 1818–19. In historical science, Kachenovskii is known as a founder and important representative of the "skeptical school." He advanced the groundless thesis that the oldest written sources of Russian history were spurious and rejected Karamzin's view that Kievan Rus' had attained a high level of development.

Kachenovskii's work, with its critical approach to the sources, played a positive role in stimulating criticism of noble and nascent bourgeois historiography. His conclusion that ancient Rus' remained at a generally low level of development was erroneous. Nevertheless, his criticism of Karamzin's views became significant as a protest against official ideology and attracted student sympathy, although Kachenovskii himself was far from espousing any revolutionary political views.

REFERENCES
Ikonnikov, V. S. *Skepticheskaia shkola v russkoi istoriografii i ee protivniki.* Kiev, 1871.
Rubinshtein, N. L. *Russkaia istoriografiia.* Moscow, 1941.

Ocherki istorii istoricheskoi nauki v SSSR, vol. 1. Moscow, 1955.
A. M. SAKHAROV [11–1638–5]

KACHIN LANGUAGE (Chingpaw, or Jinghpaw, language), the language of the Kachins, who live in the national states of Kachin and Shan in Burma and in the northwestern part of Yünnan Province in the People's Republic of China. Kachin is related to the Tibeto-Burman group of Sino-Tibetan languages. There are about 500,000 speakers of Kachin (1967, estimate), a language related to Burmese but differing from the latter in its numerous prefixes and well-developed system of suffixal forms of the predicate verb denoting the person and number of the subject and object. A script based on the Roman alphabet was created in the late 19th century.

REFERENCES
Puzitskii, E. V. *Kachinskii iazyk (Iazyk Chzhingpkho).* Moscow, 1968.
Hertz, H. F. *A Practical Handbook of the Kachin or Chingpaw Language.* Rangoon, 1911.
Hanson, O. *A Dictionary of the Kachin Language.* Rangoon, 1954.
E. V. PUZITSKII [11–1645–4]

KACHINS (self-designation, Jingphaw, or Chingpaw), a people inhabiting the forested mountain regions of northern Burma (the national states of Kachin and Shan). Population, about 400,000 (1967, estimate). About 100,000 Kachins also live in southwestern China, and there are small groups in northeastern India, Thailand, and Laos. The Kachins are divided into a number of ethnic groups speaking the Kachin language. They have preserved their traditional religious beliefs, ancestor worship and animism; a small number are Christians or Buddhists.

The ancestors of the Kachins inhabited eastern Tibet. They apparently first appeared on the territory of present-day Burma in the eighth century, although the main migration occurred later, between the 13th and 17th centuries. Early feudal relations combined with vestiges of primitive communal relations survived among the Kachins until the mid-20th century. Their chief occupation is slash-and-burn farming, with hill rice as the main crop. Their autonomous status within the Union of Burma has contributed to their ethnic solidarity and economic and cultural development.

REFERENCE
Narody Iugo-Vostochnoi Azii. Moscow, 1966. [11–1646–1]

KACHINSKAIA STEP', a steppe in the basin of the lower reaches of the Abakan River, in the southwestern part of the Minusinsk Depression (Krasnoiarsk Krai, RSFSR). Its surface forms a hilly plain. The soils are chernozem and chestnut with patches of solonetz. The steppe is covered with feather grass and fescue, and it is used for pasture. [11–1645–3]

KACHIRY, an urban-type settlement and the administrative center of Kachiry Raion, Pavlodar Oblast, Kazakh SSR. It is a landing on the right bank of the Irtysh River, 112 km below Pavlodar. Population, 11,000 (1970). There is a combine producing construction materials and structural components.

[11–1646–2]

KACHKANAR, a city (settlement prior to 1968) in Sverdlovsk Oblast, RSFSR, lying 106 km north of Nizhnii Tagil, and southeast of the Kachkanar mountain massif. It is the terminus of a branch of the Perm'-Goroblagodatskaia railroad line. Population, 33,000 (1970). There is an ore-dressing combine (mining and dressing of iron ore), using raw materials from large local deposits of titanium and magnetite ores. The annual output of the combine is 33 million tons of iron ore. The combine has been in operation since 1963. [11–1647–2]

KACHKANAR, a mountain massif in the northern Central Urals, in Sverdlovsk Oblast, RSFSR, with an elevation of 878 m. It is composed of igneous rock (gabbro, peridotites, pyroxenites), with which are associated large deposits of titanium and magnetite ores. The city of Kachkanar lies southeast of the massif.

[11–1647–1]

KACHUG, an urban-type settlement, center of Kachug Raion, Irkutsk Oblast, RSFSR. Kachug is situated on both banks of the Lena River, 257 km northeast of Irkutsk, with which it is linked by a motor road (the former Yakutsk Road). A landing on the Lena River, it has a shipyard (river tankers). It also has enterprises for the production of furniture, a logging and timber distribution establishment, and livestock-raising sovkhozes.

[11–1647–4]

KACHURA, IAKOV DEM'IANOVICH. Born Oct. 28 (Nov. 9), 1897, in the village of Iurkovka, in present-day Tul'chin Raion, Vinnitsa Oblast; died in 1943. Soviet Ukrainian writer. Participant in World War I and the Great Patriotic War.

Upon graduating from the Kiev Institute of Public Education in 1925, Kachura became a village schoolteacher. His first work was published in 1923. The collections of stories *Chronicle of a Collective* (1925) and *Without Bread* (1927) were followed by the novels *The Broken Oath* and *Intoxication* (both 1928), dealing with the Civil War, and *Ol'ga* (1931), depicting the life of miners. The historical novella *Ivan Bogun* (1940; Russian translation, 1941) is devoted to the Ukrainian people's war of liberation of 1648–54. His last collection, *Happiness* (1940), describes life on a collective farm. Kachura was taken prisoner in May 1942 and died in a fascist concentration camp.

WORK
Vybrani tvory, vols. 1–2. Kiev, 1958.
REFERENCES
Istoriia Ukrainskoi sovetskoi literatury. Kiev, 1965.
Buriak, B. S. *Iakiv Kachura: Zhyttia i tvorchist'.* Kiev, 1962.

[11–1647–5]

KACPRZAK, MARCIN. Born Nov. 6, 1888, in the village of Podol'shin, present-day Warsaw Województwo; died July 14, 1968, in Warsaw. Polish hygienist. Corresponding member of the Polish Academy of Sciences (1962). Foreign member of the Academy of Medical Sciences of the USSR (1961).

Kacprzak received his medical education and specialized training in hygiene in France and the USA; later, in 1915, he graduated from the Faculty of Medicine at tht University of Kharkov. During the first years of Soviet power he was active in the struggle against epidemics in Pskov Province. Between 1931 and 1939, Kacprzak served as head of the public health section of the Institute of Social Problems in Warsaw. In 1945 he became a professor in the Subdepartment of Preventive Medicine in the Department of Medicine at the University of Łódź. Subsequently, in 1947, he was appointed head of the Hygiene Department of the Warsaw Medical Academy, serving as rector of the academy from 1953 to 1962. Kacprzak was the first director of the Institute for Advanced Training and Specialization of Physicians. After World War II (1939–45) he became chairman of the State Council of Public Health and a director of the Polish Red Cross. Kacprzak is the author of many scientific works, including monographs, manuals, and textbooks, devoted to problems of epidemiology, general and school hygiene, work safety, and the organization of public health. He was awarded the Leon Bernard Medal. [11–1634–2]

KACZAWSKIE GÓRY, mountains in southwestern Poland, constituting the northern spurs of the Sudetes. The range is about 30 km long and attains a maximum elevation of 724 m. The mountains are composed of limestones, quartzites, schists and volcanic rocks. There are cuesta ridges. Iron ore deposits and quarries are worked. The slopes are covered with spruce forests; there is logging. [11–1635–4]

KADADA (known in its upper course as the Elan'-Kadada), a river in Penza Oblast, RSFSR, a left-bank tributary of the Sura. The Kadada River is 150 km long and drains an area of about 3,620 sq km. It flows through the Volga Upland. The mean annual flow at the mouth is about 9.41 cu m/per sec.

[11–367–1]

KADAIA, an urban-type settlement in Kalga Raion, Chita Oblast, RSFSR. It is situated on the Sredniaia Borzia River (tributary of the Argun' River), 262 km southeast of the Borzia railroad station, on the Karymskaia-Zabaikal'sk line. Lead and zinc ore are mined there. [11–368–1]

KÁDÁR, JÁNOS. Born May 26, 1912, in Rijeka. Statesman and political leader of the Hungarian People's Republic; prominent figure in the Hungarian and international workers' movement. Son of an agricultural worker. He was a helper and then a mechanic. He joined the labor movement at the age of 17 and became a member of the Hungarian Communist Youth League in 1931. In 1931 he became a member of the Communist Party of Hungary (CPH) and of the Secretariat of the Central Committee of the Hungarian Communist Youth League.

Under the fascist Horthy regime (1919–44), Kádár was active in the illegal work of the Communist Party. In 1941 and 1942 he was a member of the Pest Regional Committee of the CPH. In 1942 he was elected to the Central Committee and in 1943 became a secretary of the Central Committee of the CPH. He was repeatedly arrested for his revolutionary activity. He played a leading role in the organization of the antifascist movement in Hungary. In April 1944 he was arrested; he escaped from prison in November of that year.

After the country was liberated from fascist Horthy rule in April 1945, Kádár was elected deputy to the Provisional National Assembly and became a member of the Politburo of the Central Committee of the HCP. From April 1945 to August 1948 he was secretary of the Budapest City Committee of the party. From 1946 to 1948 he served as deputy general secretary of the Central Committee of the HCP, and from June 1948 to 1950 he was deputy general secretary of the Central Committee of the Hungarian Workers' Party (HWP). From August 1948 to June 1950 he was also minister of internal affairs. From June 1950 to April 1951 he was in charge of the department of party organizations and mass organizations of the Central Committee of the HWP.

In 1951, Kádár was arrested on false charges. After being rehabilitated in 1954, he was initially elected first secretary of the party district committee in the 13th district of Budapest and then, in 1955, first secretary of the Pest Regional Committee of the party. The July 1956 plenary session of the Central Committee of the HWP placed him on the Central Committee and elected him a member of the Politburo and a secretary of the Central Committee.

During the counterrevolutionary revolt in Hungary in October and November 1956, Kádár took the initiative in forming the Hungarian Revolutionary Workers' and Peasants' Government and in restoring and strengthening the party of the Hungarian working class. From November 1956 to June 1957 he was chairman of an interim central committee, and in June 1957 he became first secretary of the Central Committee of the Hungarian Socialist Workers' Party (HSWP). From November 1956 to January 1958 he was chairman of the Hungarian Revolutionary Workers' and Peasants' Government. From January 1958 to September 1961 he was a minister without portfolio and from September 1961 to June 1965 chairman of the Council of Ministers of the Hungarian People's Republic. In 1965 he became a member of the Presidium of the Hungarian People's Republic. Since 1957 he has been a member of the All-Hungarian Council of the People's Patriotic Front. Kádár was made a Hero of Socialist Labor of the Hungarian People's Republic in May 1962 and a Hero of the Soviet Union in April 1964. He was awarded the Order of Lenin in 1972.

WORKS
Izbrannye stat'i i rechi 1957–60, vols. 1–2. Moscow, 1960. (Translated from Hungarian.)
Izbrannye stat'i i rechi 1960–64. Moscow, 1964. (Translated from Hungarian.)
Szilárd népi hatalom: független magyarország. [Budapest] 1962.
A szocializmus teljes győzelméért. [Budapest] 1962.
Tovább a lenini útou. [Budapest] 1964.
Hazafiság és internacionalizmus. [Budapest] 1968.
A szocialista Magyarországért. [Budapest] 1972. [11–367–3]

KADEN-BANDROWSKI, JULIUSZ. Born Feb. 24, 1885, in Rzeszów; died Aug. 8, 1944, in Warsaw. Polish writer.

From 1905 to 1913, Kaden-Bandrowski lived in Germany and Belgium, where he completed his university studies and became associated with nationalist émigré circles close to J. Piłsudski. His novel *General Barcz* (1923; Russian translation, 1926) describes the events leading to the assumption of power by Piłsudski, who served as the prototype for Barcz. Kaden-Bandrowski's most important work is the cycle of novels *Black Wings* (1925–26; Russian translation, 1931), depicting the poverty of miners in bourgeois Poland. During the 1920's and 1930's Kaden-Bandrowski wrote the last two volumes of the cycle: *Mateusz Bigda,* published in 1933, and *The Silken Knot,* the manuscript of which was completed but destroyed during the Warsaw Uprising of 1944, in which the author perished.

REFERENCE
Sprusiński, M. J. *Kaden-Bandrowski. Życie i Twórczość.* Kraków, 1971.
[11–368–3]

KADESH, an ancient city in Syria on the Orontes River (near the modern city of Homs). It is known from hieroglyphic (Egyptian) and cuneiform sources from the 16th century B.C. Kadesh was inhabited by Semites. In the 15th century B.C. it was conquered by Egypt, and from the beginning of the 14th century to about 1200 B.C. it was subordinate to the Hittite empire. In the late 14th or early 13th century B.C., a battle between the Egyptian forces of Rameses II and the Hittites under the leadership of King Muwatallis occurred at Kadesh's walls. The city was apparently destroyed at the beginning of the 12th century B.C. by the Sea People. Kadesh is again mentioned in a document from 565 B.C. as the center of a district bearing the same name in the Neo-Babylonian Kingdom.

REFERENCES
Pézard, M. *Qadesh . . .* Paris, 1931.
Gardiner, A. *The Kadesh Inscriptions of Rameses II.* Oxford, 1960.
[11–373–2]

KADI, a lake in Khabarovsk Krai, RSFSR, located on the right bank of the Amur River on the northern spurs of the Sikhote-Alin' Range. The area of the lake is 67 sq km; the lake is joined by a channel with the Amur. The Kada River empties into Lake Kadi from the east. The shores of the lake are mostly low-lying and marshy.
[11–374–6]

KADIEVKA, a city in Voroshilovgrad Oblast, Ukrainian SSR, located 53 km west of Voroshilovgrad on the Kamyshevakha River (of the Severskii Donets River basin). The Kadievka railroad station is on the Popasnaia-Debal'tsevo line. Population, 139,000 (1972; 123,000 in 1959).

Kadievka arose in the 1840's in connection with the mining of coal. Its peopling and the start of its economic development date from the turn of the 20th century. It became a city in 1932. During the years of Soviet power, Kadievka has become one of the largest industrial centers of the Donbas, with highly developed coal, metallurgical, chemical, and machine-building industries. Coal mines are located nearby (including the Tsentral'naia-Irmino Mine, where the Stakhanovite movement began). Kadievka has plants for the production of coal byproducts, railroad cars, ferroalloys, carbon black, and hydraulic equipment, as well as chemical and metallurgical plants and coal washeries. The machine-building plants manufacture traveling cranes, escalators, and other equipment. Kadievka also has a branch of the Kommunarsk Mining and Metallurgical Institute, a mining technicum, and medical and pedagogical schools. There is also the Museum of the History of the City. Large-scale industrial and housing construction is under way. New residential communities have appeared; 100,000 sq m of living space was built between 1966 and 1970. In the postwar period (1946–70) the center and principal districts of Kadievka were virtually created anew.
[11–374–7]

KADŁUBEK, WINCENTY. Born circa 1150, near Stobnicy; died Mar. 8, 1223, at Jędrzejów. Polish chronicler.

From 1207 to 1218, Kadłubek was bishop of Kraków. His *Chronicle of the Poles,* covering the period to 1202, recounts legends about the ancient history of Poland and is a valuable source for Polish history of the 12th century. Besides glorifying the role of the Catholic Church, Kadłubek advocated the unity of the Polish lands and exalted the ancient history of the Polish people, whom he naïvely numbered among the peoples of classical antiquity.

PUBLICATION
Monumenta Poloniae historica, vol. 2. Lwów, 1872. Pages 191–455.
[11–376–3]

KÁDNER, OTAKAR. Born May 11, 1870, in Uhonice; died May 6, 1936, in Poděbrady. Czech democratic educator. Became an assistant professor of pedagogy at Charles University in Prague in 1907 and a full professor in 1911. He did research primarily in the history of pedagogy, general pedagogy, and organization of schools. His main works are *The History of Pedagogy* (vols. 1–3, 1909–23), *Fundamentals of General Pedagogy* (vols. 1–3, 1925–26), and *The Development of the School and the Contemporary School System* (vols. 1–4, 1929–38).

Kádner understood general pedagogy as the philosophy of education and as the sum of the theoretical propositions about the content, aims, and methods of education. The great interest he took in the experimental method and factual accounts was a reflection of the influence of positivist philosophy on him. Emphasizing the social role of education and the dependence of educational institutions on the level of development of society, Kádner regarded the goal of education as the harmonious development of all the physical and inner capabilities of the individual. He called for the democratization of education, holding that each person should receive education to the extent of his natural abilities and therefore that all class and social barriers in the school system should be abolished and the schools should become national in both content and organization. Kádner actively opposed clericalism and bureaucracy in the schools.

Kádner attributed great importance to teacher training and helped to found higher pedagogical institutions in Prague and Brno in 1921. They were organized by the teachers themselves, and the school in Prague was headed by Kádner from the day of its founding until his death.

REFERENCES
Otakar Kádner, jeho osobnost a dilo: Sbornik vzpominek a stati. Edited by J. V. Klimy. Prague, 1920.
Chlup, O. *Vývoj i pedagogických idei v novem věcu.* Brno, 1925.
A. I. PISKUNOV [11–379–1]

KADNIKOV, a city in Sokol Raion, Vologda Oblast, RSFSR, 19 km northeast of the Sukhona railroad station (on the Vologda-Arkhangel'sk line). It has a flax-processing mill and a dairy. Kadnikov became a city in 1780.
[11–379–2]

KADOCHNIKOV, PAVEL PETROVICH. Born July 29, 1915, in Petrograd. Soviet Russian film actor. People's Artist of the RSFSR (1965).

Kadochnikov graduated from the Leningrad Theatrical Institute in 1935 and worked until 1944 in the New Young People's Theater of Leningrad. He made his film debut in 1935 as Mikhas' in *Coming of Age.* He played the role of M. Gorky in the films *Iakov Sverdlov* (where he also played Lenia Sukhov, 1940), *A Teacher's Epic* (*Pedagogical Poem,* 1955), and *Prologue* (1956). Kadochnikov has also successfully appeared in lyrical comedies. These roles include Mukhin in *Anton Ivanovich Is Angry* (1941) and Rybal'chenko in *Honeymoon* (1956). His best roles were Major Fedotov in *A Reconnaissance Scout's Feat* (1947), Aleksei Meres'ev in *The Story of a Real Man* (1948), and Vladimir Staritskii in S. M. Eisenstein's film *Ivan the Terrible* (parts 1 and 2, 1945 and 1958). In this same film Kadochnikov also played Khaldei and the tsar's confessor, Evstafii.

Kadochnikov's directorial debut was the 1965 film *The Musicians of a Regiment* (together with G. S. Kazanskii), in which he also played the role of Chulkovskii. In 1970 he directed the film version of A. N. Ostrovskii's play *The Snow Maiden,* in which he also played Tsar Berendei and for which he wrote the scenario. He received the State Prize of the USSR in 1948, 1949, and 1951 and has been awarded the Order of the Red Banner of Labor and a medal.

REFERENCE
Rozina, V., and I. Solov'eva. *P. P. Kadochnikov.* Moscow, 1951.
[11–381–2]

KADOM, an urban-type settlement, center of Kadom Raion, Riazan' Oblast, RSFSR. Landing on the right bank of the Moksha River (a tributary of the Oka), 61 km northeast of the Sasovo railroad station on the Riazan'-Ruzaevka line. Kadom has a wood-products combine, starch and alcohol plants, and other enterprises. There is also a technicum for sewing.   [11–379–3]

KADOMA, a city in Japan on Honshu Island, Osaka Prefecture; part of the Osaka conurbation. Population, 141,000 (1970). It has electric machine-building and electronic industries.

[11–379–4]

KADOMTSEV, BORIS BORISOVICH. Born Nov. 9, 1928, in Penza. Soviet physicist. Academician of the Academy of Sciences of the USSR (1970; corresponding member, 1962).

Upon graduating from Moscow University (1951), Kadomtsev worked at the Institute of Physics and Energetics in Obninsk. In 1956, he began working at the Institute of Atomic Energy. His principal works are devoted to plasma physics and to the problem of controlled thermonuclear fusion. He has predicted some types of transient plasma and laid the foundations for the theory of transport phenomena (diffusion and thermal conduction) in turbulent plasma. He has provided a quantitative explanation of the phenomenon of anomalous behavior of plasma in a magnetic field. A number of his studies have been devoted to the problem of the thermal insulation of plasma in toroidal chambers. In 1966 he discovered the instability of plasma involving the so-called trapped particles. Kadomtsev received the State Prize of the USSR in 1970.

WORKS
"Gidromagnitnaia ustoichivost plazmy." In *Voprosy teorii plasmy,* fasc. 2. Moscow, 1963.
"Turbulentnost plasmy." *Ibid.,* fasc. 4. Moscow, 1964.
"Turbulentnye protsessy v toroidal'nykh sistemakh." *Ibid.,* fasc. 5. Moscow, 1967. (With O. P. Pogutse.)   [11–379–5]

KADOMTSEV, brothers active in the revolutionary movement in Russia. Their father, Samuil Evmen'evich, was a government treasury official of progressive views; political exiles frequented his home, including N. K. Krupskaia, who served her term of exile in Ufa, and Lenin, who visited S. E. Kadomtsev in 1900.

Ivan Samuilovich Kadomtsev. Born Dec. 4 (16), 1884, in Ufa; died there Jan. 14 (27), 1918. Joined the revolutionary movement in 1900. Member of the Communist Party from 1902. Completed secondary school.

During the Revolution of 1905–07, I. S. Kadomtsev was a member of the Ufa committee of Bolsheviks and led fighting *druzhinas* in the Urals. He also organized technical groups for making bombs and bringing weapons in from abroad. He was a delegate to the first conference of military and fighting organizations of the RSDLP (November-December 1906 in Tammerfors). He lived as an émigré from 1908; during this time he helped to send Bolshevik literature into Russia. From 1914 he was engaged in revolutionary work in the army and among workers in the Urals. During the October days in Moscow 1917 he took part in the battle for the Kremlin and was a member of the Moscow soviet. Subsequently he helped to organize the Red Guards in the Urals.

Mikhail Samuilovich Kadomtsev. Born No. 8 (20), 1886, in Ufa; died June 3, 1918. Member of the Communist Party from 1905.

In 1905, M. S. Kadomtsev was expelled from the Simbirsk Cadet Corps for having organized revolutionary demonstrations. During the revolution of 1905–07 he was an instructor in fighting *druzhinas* under the Urals district Bolshevik committee. He was arrested and condemned to permanent hard labor. In 1917–18

he helped to organize the Red Guards in the Urals and took part in the struggle against the White Guard troops of Ataman A. I. Dutov. He was in charge of the defense of Samara during the Czechoslovak revolt and was killed in battle near Samara.

Erazm Samuilovich Kadomtsev. Born Feb. 24 (Mar. 8), 1881, in Birsk; died Mar. 6, 1965, in Moscow. Member of the Communist Party from 1901.

E. S. Kadomtsev graduated from the cadet corps in Orenburg and the Pavel Military School in St. Petersburg. He fought in the Russo-Japanese War of 1904–05 and engaged in revolutionary work among the soldiers. Beginning in November 1905 he was an organizer and leader of fighting organizations in the Urals and chief of staff of the fighting *druzhinas* under the Bolshevik district committee. In March 1906 he became a member of the military combat center of the Bolshevik Central Committee in St. Petersburg and organizer of the central school for instructors of fighting *druzhinas.* He was a delegate to the first conference of military and fighting organizations of the RSDLP in 1906, at which he was elected a member of the Provisional Bureau of the military and fighting organizations. In 1908 he was arrested and sent into penal exile. He escaped from exile and went abroad in late 1909. Returning to Russia in 1914, he engaged in revolutionary work in the Urals and in St. Petersburg. He took part in the February and October revolutions of 1917 in the Urals. During the Civil War of 1918–20 he held command posts in the Red Army and subsequently was engaged in party and economic work. He was awarded the Order of Lenin.

REFERENCE
Khvostov, L. A. *Brat'ia Kadomtsevy.* Ufa, 1970.
P. A. VENGERSKAIA   [11–380–1]

KADOSHKINO, an urban-type settlement in Insar Raion, Mordovian ASSR. Railroad station on the Ruzaevka-Riazan' line. It is the site of an electrical engineering plant and a creamery.   [11–381–3]

KADRI, FAT'MA KADYROVNA. Born Apr. 1 (14), 1907, in Odessa; died Feb. 29, 1968, in Baku. Soviet Azerbaijani actress. People's Artist of the Azerbaijan SSR (1943). Member of the CPSU from 1943.

In 1926, Kadri graduated from the pedagogical and theatrical technicums in Baku and began performing in the Turkic Workers' Theater. Between 1932 and 1935 she worked in the Baku Russian Theater. Beginning in 1935 she was one of the leading actresses of the M. Azizbekov Azerbaijan Theater in Baku. The characters she created have gone down in the history of Azerbaijani theatrical art. They included Giul'tekin, Solmaz, and Sona in Dzhabarly's *Aidyn, The Bride of the Fire,* and *In 1905;* Mukhabbet in Ibragimov's play of the same name; Khuraman in Samed Vurgun's *Vagif;* Larisa and Katerina in Ostrovskii's *The Poor Bride* and *The Storm;* and Juliet in Shakespeare's play. Kadri taught in the theatrical technicum and later in the M. A. Aliev Azerbaijan Theatrical Institute. Her work has played an important role in the development of theatrical art in Azerbaijan and in the training of actors and directors. She was awarded two orders and various medals.

REFERENCE
Fat'ma Kadri: Narodnaia artistka Azerbaidzhanskoi SSR. Baku, 1958.
[11–382–1]

KADUI, an urban-type settlement, center of Kadui Raion, Vologda Oblast, RSFSR. It is situated on the Voron River, 4 km from its confluence with the Suda River (Volga River basin). Railroad station 170 km west of Vologda. Kadui has a logging and timber-distribution enterprise, a butter factory, a plant for the production of wine and extracts, and a wood-products enterprise. The Cherepovets State Regional Power Plant is under construction (1972).   [11–387–2]

KADUNA, a city in Nigeria, on the Kaduna River (tributary of the Niger); administrative center of the North-Central state. Population, 173,800 (1969). It is an important railroad junction. Kaduna is the site of textile mills, garment and shoe factories, a brewery, and a tobacco plant. Furniture, paper, and other clerical supplies are produced. There are also railroad repair shops. [11–387–3]

KADYI, an urban-type settlement, center of Kadyi Raion, Kostroma Oblast, RSFSR. It is situated on the Votgat' River (Volga River basin) on the Kostroma-Manturovo highway, 96 km east of the Sudislavl' railroad station on the Yaroslavl-Galich line. Kadyi has a logging and timber distribution enterprise and a butter factory. [11–387–4]

KADYKCHAN, an urban-type settlement in Susuman Raion, Magadan Oblast, RSFSR. It is located along the Magadan–Ust'-Nera highway. Coal is mined. [11–387–6]

KADYR-GULIAM (pseudonym of Vladislav Konstantinovich Ianushevskii). Born Dec. 28, 1866, in Vilnius; died Jan. 6, 1970, in Moscow. Acrobat, athlete, and founder and director of the Kadyr-Guliam group of acrobatic camel riders.

Kadyr-Guliam began his circus career at six years of age. In 1910 he went to Middle Asia and performed as an athlete and a wrestler. It was there in 1913 that he organized a springboard act and later a group of acrobatic camel riders, one of the most unusual acts in the Soviet circus and the world. The games, the everyday customs, and athletic competitions characteristic of Middle Asia are made use of in the act. After Kadyr-Guliam's death, his student F. M. Poludiablik took over the group.

WORKS
Ianushevskii, V. K. "10 Kadyr-Guliam." In the collection *Sovetskii tsirk, 1918–1938.* Leningrad-Moscow, 1938. [11–387–7]

KADYRI, ABDULLA (pseudonym, Dzhulkunbai). Born 1894; died 1940. Soviet Uzbek author.

Kadyri was born in Tashkent. His first works depict features of the old Uzbek way of life (the short story "The Profligate" and the play *The Unfortunate Fiancé;* both 1915). In his prerevolutionary work, the influence of the ideas of Jadidism (a bourgeois-liberal, nationalistic movement) was perceptible. After the Great October Socialist Revolution, Kadyri worked for the satirical journal *Mushtum* (The Fist). His ironic short stories and topical satires enjoyed success. In his novels *Days Past* (1925) and *Scorpion From the Altar* (1929), Kadyri wrote about the life of the Uzbek people in the mid-19th century. However, his realism is not always consistent: realistic pictures give way to naturalistic sketches. Kadyri's last novella, *Abid-Ketmen'* (1935), is devoted to the collectivization of agriculture in Uzbekistan.

WORKS
[Qadiriy, Äbdullä.] *Kichik äsärlär.* Tashkent, 1969.
In Russian translation:
Minuvshie dni. With a foreword by I. Sultanov. Tashkent, 1961.
Skorpion iz altaria. Moscow, 1964.
REFERENCES
Koshchanov, M. "O masterstve A. Kadyri . . . ." In his book *Zhizn', Kharactery, Masterstvo.* Tashkent, 1963.
Äliev, Ä. *Äbdullä Qadiriy.* Tashkent, 1967.
A. S. MIRBADALEVA [11–388–1]

KADYROV, GAPTRAKHMAN FAIZURAKHMANOVICH. Born Jan. 27, 1941, in Shatura, Moscow Oblast. Soviet athlete, motor racer, Honored Master of Sport (1965), and trainer. Champion of the USSR (1964, 1969–70), Europe (1964), and the world (1966, 1968–69, 1971–72) in motor races on an ice track. He has been awarded the Order of the Badge of Honor. [11–388–2]

KADZHARAN, a city (until 1958, a settlement) in Kafan Raion, Armenian SSR, on the eastern slopes of the Zangezurskii Range. Elevation, 2,000 m. Kadzharan is located 32 km west of the Kafan railroad station; it is linked to the station by highway. Population, 11,000 (1970). Kadzharan is a mining center. There are copper-molybdenum and building-materials combines in the city. Kadzharan has a construction technicum. [11–374–1]

KADZHEROM, an urban-type settlement in Komi ASSR, on the Isakova River (Pechora basin). Railroad station, 86 km southwest of the city of Pechora. There is a logging and timber distribution establishment. [11–374–3]

KADZHI-SAI, an urban-type settlement in Tonskii Raion, Issyk-Kul' Oblast, Kirghiz SSR. It is situated on the southern shore of Lake Issyk-Kul', on the Rybach'e-Przheval'sk highway, 115 km southeast of the Rybach'e railroad station. Population, 7,000 (1970). There is an experimental electrical engineering plant. Brown coal is mined in the region. [11–374–4]

KAÉDI, a city in southern Mauritania, on the Sénégal River; administrative center of Region IV. Population, approximately 10,000 (1969). It is the commercial and handicrafts center of a region in which agriculture (millet, corn, sweet potato) is combined with pasture cattle breeding and the production of gum arabic. [11–1669–2]

KAFA, an ancient Kabardinian group folk dance. The tempo is moderate; the musical measure is 6/8 or 2/4. The *kafa* is performed in pairs. A woman accompanies the dancers with an accordion. As she plays, she participates in the dance. The *kafa* begins and ends as a round dance; the middle part is performed in individual pairs. Variations of this dance are performed in Adygeia and Ossetia. [11–1624–4]

KAFAN, a city (a settlement until 1938) in the Armenian SSR. It is located on the southeastern slopes of the Zangezur Mountain Range at an elevation of 800 m, in the valley of the Vokhcha River, a tributary of the Araks River. Kafan is the terminal station on a branch of the Baku-Yerevan railroad line. Population, 31,000 (1971).

Kafan is the center of a mining industry. Copper ores are extracted nearby, and there is a copper-ore combine, an ore-dressing plant, and a furniture factory in the city. Enterprises of the food industry include a meat-packing plant, a cannery, and a milk plant. Kafan's educational institutions include a mining and metallurgical technicum, a medical school, and a music school. There is also a dramatic theater in the city.

[11–1625–1]

KAFAROV, PETR IVANOVICH (monastic name, Palladii). Born Sept. 17 (29), 1817, in Chistopol', present-day Tatar ASSR; died Dec. 6 (18), 1878, in Marseille. Russian sinologue. He studied at the Kazan Seminary and the St. Petersburg Religious Academy. In September 1840 he visited Peking as a member of a religious mission; he lived there intermittently for 38 years.

Kafarov had a wide range of scholarly interests. He compiled the large *Chinese-Russian Dictionary* (parts 1–2, 1888, finished by P. S. Popov). He translated the Chinese works *Journey of the Taoist Monk Ch'ang Ch'un to the West, The Old Mongolian Legend of Genghis Kahn* (1866), and *The Old Chinese Legend of Genghis Khan* (1877). A number of his works were devoted to the study of the history of religions in China (Buddhism, Christianity, and Islam) and the history of Chinese relations with other peoples, particularly Russian-Chinese relations. He took part in the Russian Geographical Society's 1870–71 archaeological and ethnographic expedition to Ussuri Krai.

WORKS
"Istoricheskii ocherk drevnego buddizma." In the collection *Trudy chlenov Rossiiskoi dukhovnoi missii v Pekine,* vol. 2. St. Petersburg, 1853.
"Vypiski iz dnevnika, vedennogo v Pekine v 1858 g." *Morskoi sbornik,* 1860, nos. 9–10.
"Istoricheskii ocherk Ussuriiskogo kraia. . . ." *Zapiski Imp. Russkogo geograficheskogo obshchestva,* 1879, vol. 8, fasc. 2.
Kitaiskaia literatura magometan. St. Petersburg, 1887.
Dorozhnye zametki na puti po Mongolii v 1847 i 1859 gg. St. Petersburg, 1892.
E. A. BELOV [11–1625–3]

KAFAROV, VIKTOR VIACHESLAVOVICH. Born June 18, 1914, in Šiauliai, now in the Lithuanian SSR. Soviet chemical engineer. Corresponding member of the Academy of Sciences of the USSR (1966). Member of the CPSU since 1952.

Kafarov graduated from the Kirov Institute of Chemical Engineering in Kazan in 1938. In 1944 he began working at the Mendeleev Institute of Chemical Engineering in Moscow, becoming head of a subdepartment in 1960. His research is devoted to the processes of and equipment used in chemical engineering as well as to the cybernetics of chemical engineering processes. Kafarov has been awarded the Order of the Red Banner of Labor twice and several medals.

WORKS

Osnovy massoperedachi. Moscow, 1962.
Ravnovesie mezhdu zhidkost'iu i parom, books 1–2. Moscow, 1966. (With others.)
Metody kibernetiki v khimii i khimicheskoi tekhnologii. Moscow, 1969.
Metody optimizatsii v khimicheskoi tekhnologii. Moscow, 1969. (With A. I. Boiarinov.)
Spravochnik po rastvorimosti vols. 1–3. Moscow, 1961–70. (With others.)
Programmirovanie i vychislitel'nye metody v khimii i khimicheskoi tekhnologii. Moscow, 1972. (With others.)   [11–1625–2]

KAFEDRA (in Russian). **(1)** [In English, "rostrum."] In ancient Greece and Rome, a place where rhetoricians and philosophers made their speeches.

(2) [In English, "pulpit."] An elevated platform from which sermons are delivered in the Christian church. Many pulpits are richly ornamented with carvings, statues, and reliefs. Examples include the pulpit for the baptistery of Pisa (1260, the work of Nicola Pisano) and the pulpit of St. Peter's Church in Rome (1657–66, the work of L. Bernini).

(3) [In English, "cathedra."] The chair used by a bishop (or other member of the higher clergy) during the divine liturgy and, in a figurative sense, a diocese (an episcopal district).

(4) [In English, "rostrum."] In educational institutions, lecture rooms, and assembly halls, the place where the lecturer or speaker delivers his talk.

(5) A *kafedra* (subdepartment) at an institution of higher learning (or in a *fakul'tet,* a "department") is the basic educational and scholarly subdivision. It carries out the educational, methodological, and scientific research work in one or several related disciplines and the teaching work among the undergraduate students, as well as the training of scientific and teaching personnel and the improvement of the qualifications of specialists. As a rule, *kafedras* are headed by a professor or a doctor of sciences. A *kafedra* has professors, *dotsents,* assistants, senior lecturers, senior and junior research associates, and graduate students. *Kafedras* also have their own training laboratories and offices. *Kafedras* are charged with conducting lectures, laboratory work, fieldwork, seminars, and other kinds of classes; directing student teaching and on-the-job training, research studies, and course and diploma projects (theses); and conducting course examinations and tests. A distinction is made between general institute-wide (university-wide) *kafedras,* which encompass the general scholarly disciplines that are studied in all or most of the departments of a higher educational institution, and departmental *kafedras,* which encompass the specialized disciplines taught in a given department.   [11–1625–4]

KAFENGAUZ, BERNGARD BORISOVICH (also Boris Borisovich Kafengauz). Born July 1 (13), 1894, in the city of Proskurov, now Khmel'nitskii; died June 27, 1969, in Moscow. Soviet historian. Doctor of historical sciences (1947). Professor in the department of history at Moscow State University (from 1948).

Kafengauz graduated from the department of history and philology of Moscow University in 1920 and then pursued a life of scholarship and teaching. He was senior research fellow at the Institute of History of the Academy of Sciences of the USSR from 1940 to 1965. Kafengauz was a specialist in Russian history of the 12th through 19th centuries. He was a coauthor of *History of the USSR From Ancient Times to Our Day, Essays on the History of the USSR, History of Moscow,* and *World History.* Kafengauz was awarded the Red Banner of Labor.

WORKS

Severnaia voina i Nishtadtskii mir (1700–1721). Moscow-Leningrad, 1944.

Istoriia khoziaistva Demidovykh v XVIII–XIX vv.: Opyt issledovaniia po istorii ural'skoi metallurgii, vol. 1. Moscow-Leningrad, 1949.
I. T. Pososhkov: *Zhizn' i deiatel'nost',* 2nd ed. Moscow, 1951.
Ocherki vnutrennego rynka Rossii pervoi poloviny XVIII v. (Po materialam vnutrennykh tamozhen). Moscow, 1958.
Drevnii Pskov: Ocherki po istorii feodal'noi respubliki. Moscow, 1969.

REFERENCES

Pavlenko, N. I. "Tvorcheskii put' B. B. Kafengauza." In the collection *Absoliutizm v Rossii (XVII–XVIII vv.).* Moscow, 1964.
Cherepnin, L. V. "B. B. Kafengauz—istorik i istochnikoved." In *Arkheografich. ezhegodnik za 1970.* Moscow, 1971.   [11–1626–2]

KAFFA, the name of the city of Feodosiia from the 13th through 18th centuries, when it was ruled by Genoese merchants.
                                                                                            [11–1624–5]

KAFFIR (from Arabic *kafir,* "infidel," "unbeliever"—that is, not a Muslim), a name used in the past (until the late 19th century) by neighboring Muslim peoples for the population of Nuristan (formerly Kafiristan), a high-mountain region of northeastern Afghanistan.   [11–1627–3]

KAFFIR WARS, the name given in bourgeois literature to the wars between the Xhosa (Kaffirs), a South African people, and the Anglo-Boer conquerors in the 18th and 19th centuries.

The armed resistance of the Xhosa to the colonizers lasted from the late 1770's to the early 1880's. The largest military clashes took place in the years 1779–81, 1789–93, 1799–1803, 1811–12, 1818–19, 1834–35, 1846–47, 1850–53, 1858, and 1877–79. As a result of these wars, the borders of Cape Colony were constantly moved to the east. By the early 1880's all the territory inhabited by the Xhosa had been seized by the colonizers. During the Kaffir Wars the colonizers took advantage of the lack of unity among the Xhosa and instigated conflicts among the tribes.

REFERENCES

Potekhin, I. I. *Formirovanie natsional'noi obshchnosti iuzhno-afrikanskikh bantu.* Moscow, 1955.
Walker, E. A. *A History of Southern Africa,* 3rd ed. London, 1959.
                                                                                            [11–1628–1]

KAFIRNIGAN, a river in the Tadzhik SSR; a right tributary of the Amu Darya. Length, 387 km. Basin area, 11,600 sq km. It rises in two branches from the southern slopes (partly from glaciers) of the Gissar Range and flows through the Gissar valley. The river is fed primarily by snow. The average annual discharge at the mouth is 156 cu m per sec. The average annual turbidity is more than 1,500 per cu m (in the lower reaches). The tributaries of the Kafirnigan are the Varzob and Khanaka from the right and the Iliak from the left. Its waters are used for irrigation. In the river's lower reaches the banks are covered with reeds and *tugai* forests. The city of Ordzhonikidzeabad is located on the river.   [11–1627–2]

KAFKA, FRANZ. Born July 3, 1883, in Prague; died June 3, 1924, in Kierling, near Vienna. Austrian author.

Kafka was the son of bourgeois Jewish parents. He studied at the law faculty at the University of Prague from 1901 to 1906 and worked for an insurance company from 1908 to 1922. Kafka's stories first appeared in magazines in 1909. The collection *Reflection* (1913) and the stories "The Judgment" and "The Stoker" (1913) and "The Metamorphosis" (1916) were published separately. After World War 1 Kafka published the story "In the Penal Colony" (1919) and the collections *A Country Doctor* (1919) and *A Hunger-Artist* (1924). His friend M. Brod, the executor of his will, published three novels by Kafka in 1925 and 1926—*Amerika* (unfinished), *The Trial,* and *The Castle*—as well as the collection of stories *The Great Wall of China* (1931).

Kafka's writing is characterized by verisimilitude of details, events, and the thoughts and behavior of individual people, presented in unusual, often absurd interrelationships and in nightmarish or fantastic fairy-tale-like situations. Embodied in the images and conflicts of Kafka's works are the tragic powerlessness of the doomed "little man," and at the same time the merciless cruelty and absurdity of the bourgeois social system and its laws, customs, and morals. The alogism of thought frequently makes it difficult to understand Kafka's prose.

Kafka's creative method, characteristic of 20th-century modernist literature, influenced, to varying degrees and in various forms, many German and Austrian writers, the Swiss authors M. Frisch and F. Dürrenmatt, the French writers J. P. Sartre and A. Camus, such representatives of the "literature of the absurd" as E. Ionesco and S. Beckett, and some literary figures of the USA and other countries of the Americas. Soviet literary criticism views Kafka's creative work as an artistically brilliant expression of the deep crisis of bourgeois society, seen as a hopeless impasse from which the writer saw no escape.

WORKS
Gesammelte Werke, vols. 1–8. Frankfurt am Main, 1951–58.
Tagebücher. [Frankfurt am Main, 1967.]
Briefe. Frankfurt am Main, 1958.
Briefe an Milena. Frankfurt am Main, 1952.
In Russian translation:
Roman, Novelly, Pritchi. [Preface by B. Suchkov.] Moscow, 1965.
"Iz dnevnikov." *Voprosy literatury*, 1968, no 2.
"Pis'mo k ottsu." *Zvezda*, 1968, no. 8.

REFERENCES
Zatonskii, D. V. *Frants Kafka i problemy modernizma*. Moscow, 1965.
Knipovich, E. "F. Kafka." In *Sila pravdy*. Moscow, 1965.
Dneprov, V. *Cherty romana XX v.* Moscow-Leningrad, 1965. Pages 117–71, 199–207.
Suchkov, B. "F. Kafka." In *Liki vremeni*. Moscow, 1969.
Janouch, G. *Gespräche mit Kafka*. Frankfurt am Main, 1951.
Richter, H. *Franz Kafka*. Berlin, 1962.
Brod, M. *Über Franz Kafka*. [Frankfurt am Main–Hamburg, 1966.]
L. Z. KOPELEV   [11–1627–4]

KAFR AL-ZAYYAT (also Kafr el-Zaiyat), a city in Egypt in the Nile Delta, on the Rosetta (Rashid), the western branch of the Nile. Population, 34,100 (1966). Railroad station. There are cotton- and woolen-spinning enterprises in the city. Cottonseed oil, soap, cigarettes, and superphosphate fertilizers are also produced.   [11–1628–3]

KAFUE, a national park in Zambia. It is located along the middle course of the Kafue River between its right tributaries, the Lunga and Nanzila, in the Northwest, Central, and Southern provinces. It is the largest national park in Africa, with an area of 2.25 million hectares. It was established in 1950 to protect the fauna of the grassy savannas and the savanna forests—black rhinoceros, hippopotamus, buffalo, zebra, elephant, lion, leopard, and antelope (roan, common eland, koodoo, bubaline, gnu, common waterbuck, wild goat, and duiker).   [11–1629–1]

KAFUE, a river in Zambia, left tributary of the Zambezi River. Length, approximately 1,000 km. The Kafue River rises on the Congo-Zambezi watershed plateau. It flows generally through low-lying, marshy areas. In its middle course, the river traverses outcrops of hard rocks in a deep gorge for a distance of 26 km. Its maximum discharge occurs during the summer rains. The river is navigable for a distance of 240 km from its mouth. The national park of Kafue is located in the middle of the Kafue basin.   [11–1628–5]

KAGAL'NIK (known as the Kagal'nichek in its upper course), a river in Rostov Oblast, RSFSR. Length, 162 km; basin area, approximately 5,040 sq km. It flows across the Kuban-Azov (Kuban) lowlands, into the Gulf of Taganrog of the Sea of Azov. It is fed primarily by melted snow. During the summer, its upper reaches dry up. Dams have been constructed along the river's course, dividing it into separate pools.   [11–362–1]

KAGAME, ALEXIS. Born May 15, 1912, in Nyanza, Kigali Prefecture. Rwandan historian and philologist; the father of written Rwandan literature. Professor at the National University and the National Pedagogical Institute of Rwanda; doctor of philosophy.

Kagame graduated from the higher theological seminary in Astrida in 1941 (he was ordained and made an abbot); he then graduated from the university in Rome (1955). In 1941–47 and

1950–52 he directed the publication of the newspaper *Kinyamateka* (published in Kinyarwanda). Kagame is the author of works on the history and standards of the common law of Rwanda in the precolonial period. He has also written poems in Kinyarwanda, based principally on themes from folklore. Kagame compiled a Kinyarwanda-French dictionary.

WORKS
Le Code des institutions politiques du Rwanda précolonial. [Brussels, 1952.]
La Philosophie Bantu-Rwandaise de l'Etre. Brussels, 1956.
Histoire du Rwanda, 2nd ed. [Leverville, 1958.]
Introduction aux grands genres lyriques de l'ancien Rwanda. Butaré, 1969.   [11–362–2]

KAGAMIGAHARA, a city in Japan; located on the island of Honshu, in the prefecture of Gifu. It is an eastern suburb of Gifu. Population, 78,100 (1970). Industry includes the manufacture of aircraft and automobiles.   [11–362–3]

KAGAN, IURII MOISEEVICH. Born July 6, 1928, in Moscow. Soviet physicist. Corresponding Member of the Academy of Sciences of the USSR (1970). Member of the Communist Party since 1955.

Kagan graduated from the Moscow Physical Engineering Institute in 1950. In 1956 he began working at the Institute of Atomic Energy, and in 1962 he became a professor at the Moscow Physical Engineering Institute. His principal scientific works are devoted to the kinetic theory of gases (he created the theory of transport phenomena in gases with rotational degrees of freedom), problems in molecular physics, solid-state theory, the theories of metals and imperfection systems (he predicted the existence of quasi-localized levels in the phonon spectrum), the theory of the Mössbauer effect, and the study of the interaction of nuclear radiation with matter (he predicted the suppression of a nuclear reaction and the change in nuclear parameters in crystals). Kagan has been awarded the Order of the Red Banner of Labor.   [11–362–5]

KAGAN, VENIAMIN FEDOROVICH. Born Feb. 25 (Mar. 9), 1869, in Šiauliai, Lithuanian SSR; died May 8, 1953, in Moscow. Soviet mathematician.

Kagan graduated from the University of Kiev in 1892. In 1923 he became a professor at Moscow University. Beginning in the 1890's he popularized the works of N. I. Lobachevskii. In *Foundations of Geometry* (vols. 1–2, 1905–07) he provided the axiomatics of Euclidean space with a thorough analysis of the consistency and independence of the axioms. He created the theory of subprojective spaces, which are the broad generalization of Lobachevskian space. Kagan was the founder of the school of tensor differential geometry in the USSR. He received the State Prize of the USSR in 1943.

WORKS
Osnovy teorii poverkhnostei v tenzornom izlozhenii, parts 1–2. Moscow-Leningrad, 1947–48.
Osnovaniia geometrii, part 1. Moscow-Leningrad, 1949.
Lobachevskii, 2nd ed. Moscow-Leningrad, 1948.

REFERENCES
"Veniamin Fedorovich Kagan" (obituary). *Trudy Seminara po vektoromu i tenzornomu analizu,* 1956, issue 10, pp. 3–14. (Contains a bibliography.)
Lopshits, A. M., and P. K. Rashevskii. *Kagan.* Moscow, 1969 (Contains a bibliography.)   [11–362–4]

KAGAN (until 1935, Novaia Bukhara), a city in Bukhara Oblast, Uzbek SSR. Situated in the Bukhara Oasis, it is a junction for railroad lines to Tashkent, Krasnovodsk, and Dushanbe, as well as for a branch line to Bukhara. Population, 34,000 (1970). It has a cotton ginning plant, an oil mill, a flour milling combine, a building materials combine, and railroad shops. It developed as a settlement around a railroad station at the end of the 19th century and became a city in 1929. Natural gas is produced nearby.   [11–363–2]

KAGAN (Turkic), title of the ruler of many Turkic-speaking peoples during the early Middle Ages. The term first appears in Chinese chronicles under the year 312. It was first used by the leaders of the Juan-juan, and in the middle of the sixth century, by the rulers of the Turkic Kaganate, from where it passed on to other Turkic-speaking peoples and states that were related to them in origin (or example, the Avars, Enisei Kirghiz, Pechenegs, and Khazars). After the Polianians freed themselves from the domination of the Khazars in the late eighth and early ninth century, the princes of Kiev took the title (it continued to exist in Rus' until the end of the 12th century) for themselves, thereby emphasizing the independence of Kievan Rus' from the Khazar Kaganate. In the Mongol empire, the title was used in the sense of emperor, while the rulers who were subordinate to the empire were known as khans. [11–363–1]

KAGARLYK, a city (since 1971), center of Kagarlyk Raion, Kiev Oblast, Ukrainian SSR, situated on the Rosava River (Dnieper River basin). Railroad station. Population, 10,900 (1970). Kagarlyk has a sugar combine, a butter factory, a brickyard, an asphalt plant, and a factory producing art objects. [11–363–3]

KAGAWA, a prefecture in Japan, on the northern part of the island of Shikoku. It also includes the island of Shodo. Area, 1,864.7 sq km. Population, 908,000 (1970), about 50 percent of which is urban. The major city and administrative center is Takamatsu. Most of the area (about 70 percent) is covered by mountains and highlands; but in the north there is a narrow strip of lowlands.

Kagawa is an agricultural region, with rice (the chief crop) accounting for about 77 percent of the cultivated area. Fruit growing (tangerines and peaches) is also important. The prefecture is a center for fishing and the maritime industries, as well as for the production of salt (accounting for up to 40 percent of total Japanese salt output). Manufacturing consists chiefly of light industry and food-processing (57.1 percent of the prefecture's industrial production). Nonferrous metallurgy, mainly copper smelting and gold refining (at the city of Naoshima), based on the mining of copper and complex ores, is also well developed. Another growing industry is heavy chemicals. Tourism is also important. [11–361–2]

KAGERA, a national park in Rwanda. It is located on the left bank of the Kagera River, on the border with Tanzania. Area, 251,000 hectares. The park was created in 1934 to preserve the fauna of the grassy savannas: lion, leopard, buffalo, zebra, hippopotamus, warthog, crocodile, antelopes (impala, common eland, topi, oribi, and others), and water and marsh birds. Since 1958 the black rhinoceros has been reacclimatized in Kagera. [11–364–3]

KAGERA, a river in eastern Africa, flowing through Rwanda, Tanzania, and Uganda and partially along the borders between them. It is considered to be a headstream of the Nile. Its length, from the confluence of the Nyawarongo and Ruvubu rivers, is 420 km, but from the source of the Rukarara (the point in the Kagera system farthest from the mouth) it is about 800 km. For the most part, the river flows across a broad, marshy plain, drawing water from many small lakes. It empties into Lake Victoria. The average annual rate of flow is 1,500 cu m per sec. The Kagera is navigable in its lower reaches. It was discovered by H. Stanley (1876) and explored by the Austrian O. Baumann (1892–93) and others. [11–364–2]

KAGOSHIMA, a prefecture in Japan, on the southernmost part of Kyushy Island. The prefecture includes other islands, such as Koshiki-retto and Osumi. Area, 9,141.6 sq km; population, 1.7 million (1970, 50 percent urban). Its major city and administrative center is Kagoshima. The primary branch of the prefecture's economy is agriculture, which is of national significance. Livestock raising predominates; the growing of fruits (tangerines), vegetables, and tobacco is being developed. Kagoshima ranks first in Japan in the yield of sweet potatoes and in the number of cattle (240,700 head in 1968). Industries include fishing, maritime trade, and forestry. The prefecture also has food-flavoring (53 percent of the industrial manufacturing, 1968), woodworking (15 percent), and textile (7 percent) enterprises. [11–364–6]

KAGOSHIMA, a city and port in Japan, on the southern part of Kyushu Island on Satsuma peninsula; administrative center of Kagoshima Prefecture. Population, 403,400 (1970). Transportation junction. Textile (cotton and silk mills), chemical, metallurgical, and food-flavoring industries are located in Kagoshima. Porcelain (Satsuma ware) is also manufactured. There is fishing in the southern Japanese waters. Kagoshima is the site of a university, and there is a center for space research in the region. [11–364–7]

KAGU (Rhynochetos jubatus), a bird of the order Gruiformes; the sole representative of the suborder Rhynocheti. The kagu is somewhat larger than a chicken. Its plumage is light gray with dark stripes; the bill and legs are bright red. It is found in the mountain forests of the island of New Caledonia in an area not greater than 40 sq km. The bird nests on the ground; it lays one speckled egg. The incubation period is 36 days. The chick, which is covered with dark brown speckled down, remains in the nest quite long. The kagu feeds on earthworms, terrestrial mollusks, and insects. It gets worms by plunging its bill into the ground (the nostrils are protected against the entry of earth by opercula). The few remaining kagu are on the brink of extinction owing to capture for zoos, chopping down of forests, and burning of grasses. Pigs and rats brought to the island cause great harm to the kagu. [11–364–8]

KAGUL, a city in Moldavian SSR, 5 km from the Prut River. Railroad station. Population, 26,500 (1970). Wineries are located in Kagul. There are plants for the production of smoked fish and dried fruits and a brewery; building materials are also manufactured. The Kagul experimental station for irrigated agriculture and a zonal agrochemical laboratory are located there. The city is the site of medical and pedagogical schools, as well as a sovkhoz-technicum for land improvement. There is also a museum of history and local lore. Kagul was founded in 1835. [11–365–5]

KAGUL, a lake in southwestern Odessa Oblast, Ukrainian SSR. Area, 103 sq km; length, 13 km; width, 6–11 km; maximum depth, 7 m. Its northern reach is narrow and funnel-shaped; its southern reach is wider. The lake is fed by rain and melted snow. The water level varies considerably, but during the low-water period it usually ranges from 1.5 m to 2 m. The bottom is composed of fine gray mire; the banks are sandy. The Kagul River flows into the lake. The Vekita Channel links the lake with the Danube River and with the lakes in its delta, Kugurkui and Ialpug. [11–365–3]

KAGUL, a left-bank tributary of the Danube. On July 21 (Aug. 1), 1770, during the Russo-Turkish War of 1768–74, a battle took place along the river near the village of Vulkaneşti (in present-day Moldavian SSR). The battle was between the Russian First Army of General P. A. Rumiantsev and the main Turkish forces under the grand vizier Khalil Pasha. According to clearly exaggerated estimates, the Turks had 150,000 men and 130–180 guns. Furthermore, the Russian rear was threatened by Crimean Tatar cavalry, numbering approximately 80,000. Rumiantsev assigned an 11,000-man contingent to guard the rear. He then used his remaining forces (27,000 men and 118 guns), grouped in five units in a square formation to attack the Turks from the front, flanks, and rear. After a hard battle, the Turkish forces were driven to flight. On July 23 (August 3), the Russians caught up with the retreating Turks as they were crossing the Danube at Kartal and scattered them, capturing 30 guns and the baggage train. The Turks lost about 20,000 men and 130 guns, while the Russians lost 1,500 men. The battle of the Kagul has become an important example of the destruction of the superior forces of an enemy. Rumiantsev used the most advanced maneuvering tactic of his day—an assault by separate but mutually supportive units. [11–365–4]

KAHN, LOUIS. Born Feb. 20, 1901, on the island of Saaremaa, Estonia; died Mar. 17, 1974, in New York. American architect.

In 1915, Kahn became a citizen of the United States. In 1924 he graduated from the University of Pennsylvania in Philadelphia. He was a professor at Yale University from 1948 to 1957. He became a professor at the University of Pennsylvania in 1957. Kahn's works from his mature period include the Richards Laboratories at the University of Pennsylvania (1957–61), the Salk Institute for Biological Studies in La Jolla, Calif. (1959–66), the Indian Institute of Management in Ahmadabad, India (1963), and administrative and school buildings in Dacca, Bangladesh (under construction since 1963).

His buildings are characterized by a harsh monumentality that is accentuated by weighty forms and geometrical clarity. The three-dimensionality of the structures is emphasized by the color and rough texture of the building materials. Kahn's style is similar to brutalism. The major and auxiliary spatial units are differentiated and exposed. Kahn ingeniously controlled the light and the movement of air (in countries with hot climates, he used additional walls and roofs).

Kahn was also a specialist in urban planning; he designed the general plan of Dacca in 1962. As a theorist, he considered architecture to be a harmonious space created by form and light.

REFERENCES
Sovremennaia arkhitektura, 1969, no. 2.
Arkhitektura zapada: Mastera i techeniia, book 1. [Moscow] 1972.
[11–863–2]

KAHUN (or Illahun; ancient Egyptian, Het-hotep-Senusert), a city dating from the 20th–19th century B.C., located near the pyramid of Sesostris II (Senusert II) and the Faiyum (Fayyum) Oasis in Egypt.

The city was built according to a common plan. It existed for about 100 years, whereupon it was abandoned and became buried by sand. Kahun was excavated in 1888–90 by the British archaeologist W. Flinders Petrie. The ruins of the buildings and fortifications were investigated, and the city's plan was traced out. Brick walls surrounded Kahun and divided it into two parts. Located in the eastern part was the palace complex (surrounded by a separate wall; certain chambers had columns and wall paintings) and the houses of the nobility. Situated in the western part were small houses (made of mud brick), which belonged to the artisans. The population was engaged in farming and handicraft production (pottery-making, weaving). Bronze and flint implements were discovered as well as pottery and a considerable number of papyri containing private correspondence and medical and other information.

REFERENCE
Vandier, J. *Manuel d'archéologie egyptienne,* vols. 1–3. Paris, 1952–58.
[11–1632–2]

KAI, a group of islands in the northwestern part of the Arafura Sea, south of New Guinea. They belong to the Moluccas of the Malay Archipelago and are part of Indonesia. The island group consists of two large islands (Kai Besar and Kai Ketjil) and several small ones. Total area, approximately 1,500 sq km. Kai Besar, a volcanic island with an elevation of up to 800 m, is covered with dense tropical forest; Kai Ketjil is a low coral island with coconut palm groves. Sweet potatoes, corn, rice, and tobacco are cultivated, and there is fishing. [11–536–4]

KAIAKENT, a balneological and mud-bath health resort in the Dagestan ASSR, located 80 km from Makhachkala, 4.5 km from the Kaiakent station, and 3 km from the Caspian Sea. Summers are warm (with average July temperatures of about 25°C) and winters are mild (with average January temperatures of 1°C). Therapeutic remedies include peat and silt muds from Lake Dipsus (the mud-bath therapy consists of immersion in the lake for periods of 15 minutes) and hydrosulfide and hydrogen sulfide thermal 38°–43°C) bicarbonate-chloride-sulfate waters, which are used for baths. Patients with diseases of the organs of motion and support, gynecological ailments, and skin diseases are treated here as well as those with disorders of the peripheral nervous system. [11–1672–1]

KAIAKENT-KHOROCHOI CULTURE, a late Bronze Age (late second millennium to early first millennium B.C.) archaeological culture of tribes in Dagestan and eastern Chechnia. The first remains were excavated near the Kaiakent Station (Dagestan ASSR) and near the village of Khorochoi (Chechen-Ingush ASSR).

The burial complexes are characterized by stone tombs with the dead in a sitting or flexed position, a small number of bronze objects, and modeled pottery decorated with small stuccoed cylinders or strokes in a herringbone pattern. Typical ornaments include bronze temporal pendants, antimony beads, small copper tubes, and cone-shaped pendants, all belonging to a headdress. Farming and livestock breeding formed the basis of the economy of the tribes of the Kaiakent-Khorochoi culture. Metalworking and pottery-making were well developed. Patriarchal tribal kinship relations became firmly established.

REFERENCES
Kruglov, A. P. "Severo-Vostochnyi Kavkaz vo II–I tys. do n.e.." In *Materialy i issledovaniia po arkheologii SSSR,* vol. 68. Moscow, 1958.
Munchaev, R. M. "Arkheologicheskie issledovaniia v Nagornom Dagestane v 1954 g.." In the collection *Kratkie soobshcheniia o dokladakh i polevykh issledovaniiakh Instituta istorii material'noi kul'tury AN SSSR,* vol. 71. Moscow, 1958.
Krupnov, E. I. "Kaiakentskii mogil'nik—pamiatnik drevnei Albanii." In the collection *Tr. Gosudarstvennogo istoricheskogo muzeia,* fasc. 11. Moscow, 1940. R. M. MUNCHAEV [11–1672–2]

KAICHEN (Japanese, "heavenly change"), a torpedo guided by a volunteer suicide pilot.

Kaichens were used in World War II by the Japanese armed forces to attack enemy surface ships. Work on the *kaichens* began in the second half of 1942 based on ordinary torpedoes. A *kaichen* was up to 16.5 m long, carried an explosive charge of over 1,360 kg, could go up to 74 km/hr (40 knots), and had a range of up to 74 km (40 miles). Piloted by one man, *kaichens* were classified as naval ammunition. In 1944, Japan began producing *kaichens* carrying between 4 and 8 tons of explosives. Japan also built the wooden *Shine* cutters, which had a similar mission, were driven by an automobile engine, and had an explosive charge of up to 2 tons; the midget *Kairyu* submarines, with a crew of two men and an explosive charge of up to 20 tons; and the *Koryu* submarines, with a crew of five men and an explosive charge of up to 50 tons. *Kaichens* were used for the first time in November 1944 against US ships in the Pacific Ocean.

After spotting an enemy ship, the submarine armed with *kaichens* took up a position on the ship's intended route and the suicide pilots took their place in the torpedo. The submarine commander launched the torpedo after instructing the pilot on the necessary course and speed. After traveling some distance, the torpedo pilot surfaced and directed the torpedo at the enemy ship. A total of 80 *kaichen* pilots died in combat operations.
N. V. ERONIN [11–549–2]

KAIERKAN, an urban-type settlement in Krasnoiarsk Krai, RSFSR, located south of Lake Piasino. Railroad station on the Dudinka-Noril'sk line, 20 km west of Noril'sk. Coal is mined.
[11–537–6]

KAIETEUR FALLS, a waterfall in Guyana (South America), on the Potaro River (Essequibo basin). Height, 225 m. The falls were discovered in 1870 by the British geologist C. Barrington Brown. The Kaieteur National Park was established in the area in 1929. [11–537–7]

K'AIFENG, a city in eastern China, in the province of Honan on the Great China Plain just south of the Huangho. Population, 289,000 (1959). The city is a transportation junction. Its industries include machine-building, chemicals, textiles (cotton), and food. There are numerous institutions of higher learning. K'aifeng is one of the oldest cities in the country; from 960 to 1127 it was the imperial capital. The city is laid out in a rectangle, enclosed by a fortified wall with four gates. There are remains of a 12th-century palace and the 13-tier T'ieh-Ta Pagoda (the "Iron Pagoda," 1041), as well as the Honan provincial museum. [11–549–4]

KAIGORODOV, DMITRII NIKIFOROVICH. Born Aug. 31 (Sept. 12), 1846, in Polotsk, present-day Vitebsk Oblast; died Feb. 11, 1924, in Leningrad. Russian natural scientist and natural-science propagandist.

In 1871, Kaigorodov graduated from the St. Petersburg Agricultural Institute (now the Lumber Industry Academy in Leningrad), and in 1875 he became head of the department of lumber technology and engineering there. He became a professor in 1882. Materials collected by the phenological network he organized in the European part of the USSR provided the basis for a bioclimatic regionalization of this area. Kaigorodov compiled a series of phenological maps of the spring migration of birds. He was the author of popular science books, including *Conversations About the Russian Forest* (two series, 1880–81), *From the Green Kingdom* (1888), and *From the Feathered Kingdom* (1892).

REFERENCES
Pamiati Dmitriia Nikiforovicha Kaigorodova. Leningrad, 1925. (Contains list of works.)
Remizov, G. A. "Otets russkoi fenologii." In *Zemlia i liudi: Geograficheskii kalendar' 1959.* Moscow, 1958. [11–536–6]

KAILALI, a town in southwestern Nepal, on the border with India. Population, approximately 5,000. Because of its location near the terminus of an Indian railroad branch, Kailali is a center of the rice trade with India. [11 539 1]

KAILAS, a mountain range in China, in the south of the Plateau of Tibet; it extends from northwest to southeast, running parallel to the Himalayas for 300 km. Elevations range up to 6,714 m (Mount Kailas); relative altitude above the plateau is 1,000–1,500 m. The range is composed primarily of granite. The southern slope is strongly dissected by erosion; the northern slope is gentle. The snow line is at an altitude of 5,700–5,900 m, and there are glaciers. Mountain dry steppes with sparse dwarf vegetation predominate. The sources of the Indus and Brahmaputra rivers are in the Kailas Range. [11–539–2]

KAINAR, JOSEF. Born June 29, 1917, in Přerov; died Nov. 16, 1971, in Dobříš. Czech poet.

The son of a railroad worker, Kainar studied in the faculty of philosophy at the University of Prague from 1937 to 1939. From 1969 he headed the Preparatory Committee of the Czechoslovak Writers' Union. In the verses from the time of World War II (1939–45), which were published in the collections *Incidents and Miniatures* (1940), *New Myths* (1946), and *Fates* (1947), Kainar expressed a tragic attitude that came from the years of German occupation and from the absurdity of bourgeois relations. In the postwar period Kainar participated actively in socialist reorganization. The verses contained in the collections *Great Love* (1950), *The Czech Dream* (1953), *I Love Man With a Bitter Love* (1959), and *Lazarus and the Song* (1960) reveal the poetry of everyday working life while exposing philistinism and platitude. Kainar is the author of witty feuilletons written in verse, songs, and topical songs: the collections *My Blues* (1966) and *The Latest News* (1971). He also wrote plays such as *Ubu Returns, or The Scars Will Not Remain* (1949) and *The Late Nasredin* (1959). Moreover, he wrote verses and tales for children. He translated the works of V. V. Mayakovsky and R. M. Rilke. Kainar received the K. Gottwald State Prize in 1953.

REFERENCES
Hájek, J. ["J. Kainar."] In his book *Osudy a cíle.* Prague, 1961. Pages 94–107.
Opelík, J. ["J. Kainar."] In his book *Jak číst poesie.* Prague, 1963. Pages 148–65. L. N. BUDAGOVA [11–541–1]

KAINAZAROVA, SURAKAN. Born June 5 (18), 1902, in the village of Dzhalamysh, present-day Sokuluk Raion, Kirghiz SSR. Innovator in agricultural production; field team leader of the Druzhba Kolkhoz of Sokuluk Raion, Kirghiz SSR. Twice Hero of Socialist Labor (1948, 1957). Member of the CPSU since 1939.

In 1947, Kainazarova's field team produced 971.5 centners of sugar beets per hectare in an area of 15 hectares. On her own plot she produced 1,000–1,100 centners per hectare. She was a delegate to the Third through Twelfth Congresses of the Communist Party of Kirghizia and was elected a member of the Central Committee of the party. She was a deputy of the Supreme Soviet of the USSR of the first and third convocations and a deputy and vice-chairman of the Supreme Soviet of the Kirghiz SSR. She retired in 1958. Kainazarova has been awarded three Orders of Lenin, the Order of the Red Banner of Labor, a medal, and the large gold medal of the All-Union Agricultural Exhibition. [11–540–2]

KAINDA, an urban-type settlement in Kalininskoe Raion, Kirghiz SSR; situated in the Chu valley. It has a railroad station 77 km west of the city of Frunze. Population, 8,000 (1970). A sugar refinery and a cable factory are located there. [11–531–4]

KAINDY-KATTA (also Kaindy or Kaindinskii), a mountain range in the Central Tien-Shan, in the Sarydzhaz basin, stretching southward from the Kainda valley, Kirghiz SSR. Elevation, more than 5,000 m; length, approximately 65 km. The mountains, which are composed of schists and limestones, are covered with perpetual snows and glaciers, (particularly in the east). Cliffs and taluses predominate. At the foot of the mountains, to the west, is mountainous semidesert. [11–531–5]

KAINITE, a mineral of the group of complex sulfates. Its chemical composition is $RMg(SO_4)Cl \cdot 3H_2O$. It crystallizes in a monoclinic system. It usually forms dense grainy masses; less frequently, tabular or prismatic crystals. The color is yellowish or whitish gray, sometimes reddish. Its hardness on the mineralogical scale is 2.5–3.0, and its density is 2,150 kg/m³. It dissolves readily in water and has a bitter salty taste.

Kainite is formed in salt-bearing beds when marine lagoons and enclosed salty continental lakes rich in soluble sulfates dry up. Together with other potassium salts, it is found in the USSR (Kalush and Stebnik, Ukrainian SSR) and abroad (Stassfurt, GDR). It is used as a chemical potassium-sulfate fertilizer and in the production of mixed fertilizers. [11–531–6]

KAINUUNSELKÄ, mountains in eastern Finland. Length, 125 km; maximum altitude, 384 m (Mount Paljakka). The mountains are composed primarily of gneisses and crystalline schists. There are dark coniferous forests and numerous lakes and swamps. [11–544–2]

KAINZ, JOSEF. Born Jan. 2, 1858, in Wieselburg, present-day Mosonmagyaróvár, Hungary; died Sept. 20, 1910, in Vienna. Austrian actor.

In 1875, Kainz made his professional theatrical debut. From 1883 to 1889 and from 1892 to 1899 he performed in the German Theater in Berlin. From 1899 to 1910, Kainz appeared in the Burgtheater in Vienna. His performances were characterized by subtle psychological analysis, emotional spirituality, elegant movements, and poetic qualities. Kainz became well known for his portrayals of young tragic heroes, for example, in Schiller's *Intrigue and Love* and *Don Carlos* and in Shakespeare's *Romeo and Juliet.* He portrayed characters searching for life's meaning and struggling for high ideals against evil and violence. Among Kainz' best parts were the title role in Shakespeare's *Hamlet,* Oswald in Ibsen's *Ghosts,* and Johannes in Hauptmann's *The Lonely People.* In J. N. Nestroy's *The Evil Spirit of Lumpazivagabundus* (role of Zwirn) and Molière's comedy *Tartuffe* (leading role), he created brilliant comic and satirical portraits. Kainz toured the USA, Denmark, and Russia.

REFERENCES
Khrestomatiia po istorii zapadnogo teatra na rubezhe XIX i XX vekov. Moscow-Leningrad, 1939.
Brahm, O. *Kainz: Gesehenes und Gelebtes,* 2nd ed. Berlin, 1910.
I. IA. NOVODVORSKAIA [11–545–1]

K'AIP'ING, a city in China, in Hupeh Province. It is one of China's main coal-mining centers. [11–545–3]

KAIRAK (in Uzbek and Tadzhik, *kairok*), stone castanets, four flat, oblong stones measuring 120–150 mm long and 50–70 mm wide. The stones are ground naturally, for example, in mountain streams. These instruments served as accompaniment to dances and performances by tightrope walkers and walkers on stilts. Their use was rather widespread. In the early 20th century, *Kairaki* were used in Bukhara, Tashkent, and Fergana Oblast. They are among the instruments in the Orchestra of Folk Instruments of the Uzbek SSR. *Kairaki* are seldom used among the people.   [11–546–1]

KAIRAKKUM, a city (settlement until 1963) in Leninabad Oblast, Tadzhik SSR; situated on the bank of the Kairakkum Reservoir, 8 km from the Leninabad railroad station on the Khavast-Kokand line. Population, 10,000 (1970). It is the site of the Kairakkum Hydroelectric Power Plant. Kairakkum has carpet, flour milling, and house-building combines, a reinforced-concrete structural components plant, and a fishing industry. A house of rest and a tourist center are also located there.

[11–546–2]

KAIRAKKUM RESERVOIR, a reservoir formed by the dam of the Kairakkum Hydraulic Engineering Complex on the Syr Darya River in the western part of the Fergana Valley (in the Tadzhik and Uzbek SSR's). The reservoir was filled during 1956–58. Area, 513 sq km; volume, 4.2 cu km; length, 55 km; maximum width, 20 km; average depth, 8.1 m; greatest depth, 25 m.

The water level of the Kairakkum Reservoir varies within a range of 7 m; it regulates the seasonal and, to some extent, long-term water discharge. It was built to ensure stable irrigation of existing irrigated fields and to irrigate more than 300,000 hectares of new lands. There is fishing in the reservoir (carp, members of the genus *Varicorhinus,* bream, and pike). The city of Kairakkum is on the bank of the reservoir.   [11–546–4]

KAIRAKKUM SITES, a group of scattered primitive settlement sites in the Kairakkum sands on the right bank of the Syr Darya River, in Leninabad Oblast, Tadzhik SSR. The sites were discovered in 1954 by A. P. Okladnikov and investigated in 1955–56 by B. A. Litvinskii. Certain investigators differentiate the Kairakkum sites into a separate archaeological culture, forming part of the Andronovo complex.

The sites date from the Bronze Age and Early Iron Age (from the middle of the second millennium to the beginning of the first millennium B.C.). The settlements (whose area did not exceed 3 hectares) consisted of rectangular dwellings up to 20 m long with stone hearths. The dead were buried in stone boxes in flexed positions on their sides and with the heads pointing toward the west. The population engaged in the stock raising (the bones of small livestock, cows, and horses were found) and metalworking (copper ore, slag, and molds for picks and perforated axes were discovered). The inhabitants used bronze knives, arrowheads, and hooks. The pottery was modeled: the vessels were flat-bottomed, had swollen sides, sometimes with a projection, and were rarely decorated (herringbone, zigzag, or triangular designs). The population maintained relations with the agricultural tribes of the Chust culture and with the stock raisers of Semirech'e and eastern Kazakhstan, which were part of the Andronovo complex.

REFERENCES
Litvinskii, B. A., A. P. Okladnikov, and V. A. Ranov. *Drevnosti Kairak-kumov.* Dushanbe, 1962.   E. E. KUZ'MINA [11–546–3]

KAIRAKTY, an urban-type settlement in Shetskii Raion, Dzhezkazgan Oblast, Kazakh SSR. Located 40 km northeast of the Agadyr' railroad station on the Karaganda-Mointy line. Lead ores and barytes are mined there.   [11–546–5]

KAIROUAN, a city in eastern Tunisia; administrative center of Kairouan *wilayat.* Population, 46,000 (1966). Railroad station and highway junction; it is an important historical and commercial and industrial center of the country. The city has domestic

manufacture of carpets and leather goods, as well as enterprises of the food industry.

Kairouan was founded in A.D. 670; in the early eighth century it became the residence of the Umayyad vicegerents in Maghreb. In the eighth century it was twice the center of the rebellious Kharijites. From 800 to 909 it was the capital of the Aghlabite dynasty (this was the city's zenith). After the capital was moved to Mahdia by the Fatimids, the political significance of Kairouan began to decrease. It long retained its role as Tunisia's religious, theological, and scientific center. In the 11th century, invading Bedouin devastated the city; it was restored by the Hafsids in the 13th century. In 1881, in spite of stubborn resistance, Kairouan was occupied by French colonizers; since 1956 it has been a part of independent Tunisia. It is a pilgrimage site for Maghreb Muslims.

One of the largest monuments of Moresque architecture—the Great Mosque (Sidi Okba; the foundation was laid in 670, and it was rebuilt in 836; additions were made and restoration carried out in 863, the 13th century, the 14th century, the 17th century, and later), with a many-columned hall, a courtyard surrounded by arcades, and a minaret—is located in Kairouan, as is the Mosque of the Three Doors (866). The city has a museum of Islamic art.

REFERENCE
Sebag, P. *Le Grande mosque de Kairouan.* Paris, 1963.   [11–547–1]

KAIROV, IVAN ANDREEVICH. Born Dec. 14 (26), 1893, in Riazan'. Soviet educator and prominent figure in Soviet public education. Doctor of pedagogical sciences. Member (from 1944) and president (1946–67) of the Academy of Pedagogical Sciences of the RSFSR. Hero of Socialist Labor (1963). Member of the CPSU since 1917.

Kairov graduated from the natural sciences division of the department of physics and mathematics of Moscow University in 1917. From 1925 to 1929 he was head of the agricultural education department in the Central Administration for Professional Education of the RSFSR People's Commissariat for Education. From 1930 to 1934 he was deputy director of the Scientific Reaserch Institute for Agricultural Cadres. From 1929 to 1948 he headed various pedagogical subdepartments at higher educational institutions in Moscow, including Moscow State University. From 1942 to 1950 he was editor in chief of the journal *Sovetskaia pedagogika* (Soviet Pedagogy). From 1949 to 1956 he was minister of education of the RSFSR. Under his direction and with his help pedagogical textbooks have been compiled for pedagogical institutes and universities. At the Twentieth Party Congress he was elected a member of the Central Auditing Commission of the CPSU. At the Nineteenth and Twenty-second Congresses he was elected a candidate member of the Central Committee of the CPSU. He was a deputy to the third through sixth convocations of the Supreme Soviet of the USSR. He has been awarded three Orders of Lenin and various medals.   [11–534–1]

KAISER, GEORG. Born Nov. 25, 1878, in Magdeburg; died June 4, 1945, in Ascona, Switzerland. German dramatist. Well-known representative of German expressionism.

Kaiser's protest against the bourgeois world bore an abstract, individualistic character. In 1911 he published *The Jewish Widow,* a comedy on a Biblical theme, and in 1914, the historical drama *The Burghers of Calais.* World War I (1914–18) and the revolutionary events of 1918 in Germany sharply intensified Kaiser's critical attitude toward the capitalist system, as can be seen in the dramas *Gas* (parts I and II, 1918–20; Russian translation, 1922) and *The Coral* (1918; Russian translation, 1923). Along with the amusing adventure comedy *Cinema Romance* (*Kolportage;* 1924; Russian translation, 1925) and such mystical, romantic dramas as *Twice Oliver* (1926) and *Two Neckties* (1930), Kaiser wrote the antimilitarist plays *Leather Heads* (1928) and *Mississippi* (1930). After the Nazis came to power, Kaiser's plays were banned. In 1938 he emigrated to the Netherlands, and then he moved to Switzerland. In 1940, while he was in Switzerland, Kaiser wrote the dramas *Klawitter* and *The English Wireless,* which portrayed the horrors of Nazi terror, and the antimilitarist play *The Soldier Tanaka.* The comedy *Napoleon in New Orleans* (1941), which is about an adventurer pretending to be the French emperor, makes fun of Hitler. Kaiser's late antimilitarist dramas are based on ancient Greek myths. In 1948 the trilogy *Twice Amphitryon, Pygmalion,* and *Bellerophon* was published. Kaiser was also the author of the novels *It's Enough* (1932) and *Villa Aurea* (1940; translated into English as *Vera*).

WORKS

In Russian translation:
Dramy. [With an introduction by A. V. Lunacharskii.] Moscow-Petrograd, 1923.

REFERENCES
Paulsen, W. *G. Kaiser.* Tübingen, 1960.
Kändler, K. *Drama und Klassenkampf.* Berlin-Weimar, 1970.

V. N. TOKMAKOV [11–537–8]

KAISERSLAUTERN, a city in the Federal Republic of Germany; located in the *Land* of Rhineland-Palatinate, on the Lauter River (Rhine Basin). Population, 90,800 (1970). Kaiserslautern is a transportation junction. Its industries include machine-tool construction, the manufacture of sewing machines and bicycles, textiles, and food-processing (including brewing). A pedagogical academy is situated in the city. Kaiserslautern was founded in 882 as a royal residence. [11–538–3]

KAIŠIADORIS, a city (since 1946), the administrative center of Kaišiadoris Raion, Lithuanian SSR. The city is a junction of railroad lines to Vilnius, Kaunas, and Šiauliai and is located 69 km northwest of Vilnius. A glue factory and a creamery are in Kaišiadoris; nearby is the Lithuanian Veterinary Research Institute. [11–550–2]

KAITAGS (self-designation, Khaidaklan), an ethnic group that is related in language and main features of culture and way of life to the Darghins, with whom they have almost merged. The Kaitags live in the southeastern part of the Dagestan ASSR and speak the Kaitag dialect of Darghin. They were first mentioned in historical literature in the ninth century A.D. In the Middle Ages they formed a large feudal domain known as the Kaitag Utsmiate. [11–548–4]

KAITARMA, a custom among the peoples of Central Asia which represented a vestige of the clan system. According to the custom, a newly married woman was detained by her parents or other relatives until the payment by the husband of the *kalym* (bride-price). In the USSR, the criminal codes of most of the Union republics have established criminal responsibility for this custom, since they regard the *kaitarma* as preventing a woman from entering into a marriage. [11–549–1]

KAITS (Spark), the first legal Bolshevik paper in the Armenian language. Published in Tbilisi from Apr. 1 (14) 1906, to Aug. 6 (19), 1906. In all, 47 issues were published. The newspaper was edited by S. G. Shaumian, S. S. Spandarian, and S. I. Kas'ian. Supporting the Bolshevik tactical line, the newspaper called for the overthrow of tsarism and the establishment of a democratic system; it dealt with the labor movement in Armenia and in Russia and with the response of the Oriental peoples to the first Russian revolution (1905–07). It printed news about the activities of party organizations and acquainted the reader with economic and political developments in the life of the country. Both party activists and rank-and-file workers contributed to *Kaits.* The newspaper was closed down by the tsarist authorities.

REFERENCE
Russkaia periodicheskaia pechat' (1895–okt. 1917): Spravochnik. Moscow, 1957. [11–550–1]

KAITUKOV, GEORGII KHARITONOVICH. Born Oct. 29 (Nov. 11), 1911, in the village of Khod, Northern Ossetia. Soviet Ossetian poet. Member of the CPSU since 1940.

The son of a poor mountaineer, Kaitukov graduated from the Northern Caucasus Pedagogical Institute in 1932. He took part in the Great Patriotic War of 1941–45. His work first appeared

in print in 1927. Among his published books of poetry are *Toward the Struggle* (1931), *My Songs* (1940), *In the Days of the War* (1944), *Verses and Poems* (1948), *The Weapons of Peace* (1951), *Selected Verse* (1956), *Spring Songs* (1958), *Thank You, Men!* (1959), *Continuation of Life* (1967; winner of the K. Khetagurov Republic Prize), and *Who Am I?* (1968). Kaitukov's poetry is civic-minded, polemical, and acutely contemporary. Kaitukov translated A. S. Pushkin's *Eugene Onegin* into Ossetian. He has been awarded three orders and various medals.

REFERENCE
Lukashenko, M., and Z. Sagutnov. "Georgii Kaitukov." In *Ocherk istorii osetinskoi sovetskoi literatury.* Ordzhonikidze, 1967. [11–549–3]

KAIUMOV, MALIK KAIUMOVICH. Born Apr. 22, 1912, in Tashkent. Soviet cameraman and director of documentary films. People's Artist of the USSR (1967). Became a member of the CPSU in 1960.

Kaiumov began his career in the Uzbek film industry in 1931 as an actor and later became a cameraman. During the Great Patriotic War he was a cameraman with film groups on the front. He began directing in the 1950's and made a number of films dealing with socialist construction in Uzbekistan both before and after the war, with Uzbekistan monuments, and with the relations between the Soviet Middle Asian republics and foreign countries. His films include *The Mighty Stream* (1940), *Soviet Tadzhikistan* (1946), *Socialist Uzbekistan* (1950), *The Dawn of the New India* (1956), *Five Hands of Mankind* (1958), *Vietnam —My Country* (1960), *Registan* (1965), *Tashkent, the Earthquake* (1968), and *Children of Tashkent* and *Samarkand After 2,500 Years* (both 1969). Kaiumov was awarded the Khamza State Prize of the Uzbek SSR in 1965. He has also been awarded seven orders, as well as medals.

REFERENCE
Khasanov, V. *Malik Kaiumov.* Tashkent, 1970. [11–1670–2]

KAJAVA, VILJO. Born Sept. 22, 1909, in Helsinki. Finnish poet. Son of a tailor.

Kajava studied at the University of Helsinki and began his literary career in 1935. His verse collections include *The Builders* (1935), *Farewell, Migratory Bird* (1938), *The Harsh Earth* (1941), *Winged Hands* (1949), *Each of Us* (1954), *Unchanging* (1955), and *Into the Blue of the Sky* (1959). The poems from the collection *Ten Cardinal Points* (1961) deal with the struggle of the African people against the colonial yoke. Many of Kajava's verses and prose works have social themes. In the novel *Do You Still Remember Paulin?* (1943) and the collections of short stories *The Lonely Women* (1950), *The Green Map* (1951), and *The Bird Seller* (1957), Kajava attacks bourgeois society from the standpoint of Christian humanism.

WORKS
Tampereen runot. Helsinki, 1966.
Käsityöläisen unet. Helsinki, 1968.

REFERENCE
Maailman kirjat ja kirjailijat. Edited by T. Anhava. Helsinki, 1957. [11–1671–2]

KAKABADZE, DAVID NESTOROVICH. Born Aug. 8 (20), 1889, in the village of Kukhi, in present-day Tsulukidze Raion, Georgian SSR; died May 10, 1952, in Tbilisi. Soviet painter.

Kakabadze studied in St. Petersburg from 1910 to 1915 under L. E. Dmitriev-Kavkazskii. He lived in France from 1919 to 1927; from 1928 to 1948 he taught in the Tbilisi Academy of Arts, becoming a professor in 1934. Kakabadze's works, noted for their ornamentation, are characterized by harmonious combinations of clearly delineated color planes, severity, and precision of design. His works include *Self-Portrait With Pomegranates* (1913); *Imeretia Still Life* (1918) and *Rion Hydroelectric Power Plant* (1934), both in the Art Museum of the Georgian SSR, Tbilisi; and the series *Svanetiia* (pencil and gouache, 1939). Kakabadze also designed theatrical sets and costumes.

REFERENCE
Alibegashvili, G. *D. Kakabadze.* Tbilisi, 1958.   [11–550–3]

KAKABADZE, POLIKARP MALKHAZOVICH. Born Feb. 23 (Mar. 7), 1895, in the village of Kukhi, present-day Tsulukidze Raion; died Oct. 17, 1972, in Tbilisi. Soviet Georgian playwright.

Kakabadze's works were first published in 1919. His play *At the Crossroads* was presented on the Georgian stage of Baku in 1918. He wrote the lyrical drama *Three Maidens* and the plays *Before Dawn* and *Prisoners of Lisbon* (produced in 1925). His most important comedies are *Kvarkvare Tutaberi* (produced in 1928), *Marriage in the Kolkhoz* (1937), and *Kakhaber's Sword* (1956). The situations of his best comedies are genuine and lively, and the characters are aesthetically convincing. Kakabadze is a master of dialogue, bringing vitality to speech on stage. His historical dramas (such as *Vakhtang I* and *Bagrat VII*) occupy an important place in the Georgian theater.

WORKS
[Kakabaze, P.] *Piesebi.* Tbilisi, 1952.
Rch'euli t'khzulebani. Tbilisi, 1954.
Dramatuli t'khzulebani. Tbilisi, 1959.
Mep'e Vakhtang Pirveli-Gorgasali. Tbilisi, 1967.
In Russian translation:
Izbr. dramaticheskie proizvedeniia. Tbilisi, 1958 and 1964.
      [11–551–1]

KAKAIDY, an urban-type settlement in Dzhar-Kurgan Raion, Surkhandar'ia Oblast, Uzbek SSR. Located on the left bank of the Surkhandar'ia, 18 km northeast of the Dzhar-Kurgan railroad station on the Termez-Dushanbe line. Oil is extracted nearby.   [11–551–3]

KAKHAROV, ABDULAKHAD. Born Apr. 4 (17), 1913, in Kanibadam, in the present-day Tadzhik SSR. Soviet statesman and party figure. Became a member of the CPSU in 1939. The son of an artisan.

Kakharov graduated from Leninabad Pedagogical Institute in 1954 as an extension student. He was engaged in Komsomol, trade union, soviet, and party work in the Tadzhik SSR from 1933 to 1947. He was secretary of the Leninabad Oblast committee of the Communist Party of Tadzhikistan from 1947 to 1954 and was chairman of the executive committee of the Leninabad Oblast soviet of working people's deputies in 1954–55. Kakharov served as deputy chairman of the Council of Ministers and chairman of the State Planning Commission of the Tadzhik SSR from 1956 to 1961. He was chairman of the Council of Ministers of the Tadzhik SSR from 1961 to 1973, simultaneously serving as the republic's minister of foreign affairs. He was elected a candidate member of the Central Committee of th CPSU at the Twenty-second through Twenty-fourth Congresses of the party and was a deputy to the fifth through eighth convocations of the Supreme Soviet of the USSR. Kakharov has been awarded two Orders of Lenin, five other orders, and medals.   [11–1629–3]

KA-KHEM, a river, better known as the Malyi Enisei, in the southeastern part of the Tuva ASSR and the northern part of the Mongolian People's Republic.   [11–1630–1]

KAKHET (Kakhetian), a mountain range in the southern part of the Greater Caucasus, in the Georgian SSR. The range is a watershed of the Iori and Alazani rivers. Length, approximately 120 km; maximum elevation, 2,506 m. The Kakhet Range is formed mainly of sandstone, marl, and schist. The slopes are covered with broad-leaved forests and shrubbery, and mountain meadows are found at elevations of 2,000 m. There are vineyards on the lower slopes.   [11–1630–7]

KAKHETIA, a historical region of Georgia, on the upper courses of the Iori and Alazani rivers, which are tributaries of the Kura. Until the eighth century, Kakhetia was part of Kartli; it became an independent feudal principality in the second half of the eighth century. David the Builder occupied Kakhetia in 1104, with the support of local *aznauri* (noblemen), and made it part of the unified Georgian state. Kakhetia became an independent kingdom in the second half of the 15th century and from the 16th to 18th centuries waged a continual struggle for independence against Iran and Turkey. In 1762, Kartli and Kakhetia were united into one kingdom, which was then annexed by Russia in 1801.

REFERENCE
Istoriia Gruzii, vol. 1. Tbilisi, 1962.   [11–1630–2]

KAKHETIAN REBELLION OF 1659, an uprising of the Georgian people against Iranian rule. The rebellion was provoked by the plan of the rulers of Iran to settle the Kakhetia plain with Turkmenian nomadic tribes, threatening the annihilation of the Georgian population living there. The uprising was led by B. Cholokashvili, the Aragvi *eristavi* (feudal ruler) Zaal, and Zaal's brother Elizbar, who were killed in battle. Tradition has also preserved the names of the popular heroes Z. Gaprindauli, N. Khoshurauli, and Gogolauri (who was from the ethnographic group known as the P'shavy). The inhabitants of Kakhetia, together with the mountain population of the country, cleared their land of Iranian troops and forced the rulers of Iran to abandon their plan.

REFERENCE
Istoriia Gruzii, vol. 1. Tbilisi, 1962.   [11–1630–5]

KAKHI, a city (a settlement until 1967), the administrative center of Kakhi Raion, Azerbaijan SSR. Located at the foot of the southern slopes of the Greater Caucasus on the Kurmukhchai River, a tributary of the Alazani. The city is 125 km northwest of the Evlakh railroad junction. Population, 6,200 (1970). A fruit cannery and a creamery and cheese dairy are located in the city.   [11–1631–1]

KAKHKHAR, ABDULLA. Born Sept. 4 (17), 1907, in Kokand; died May 24, 1968, in Moscow. Soviet Uzbek writer. Became a member of the CPSU in 1952.

Kakhkhar graduated from the Oriental department of the Middle Asian State University in 1934. He was first published in 1924 as a topical satirist and *feuilletonist.* He later began to work in the short story genre and did much for the development of this genre in Soviet Uzbek literature, creating such works as *Thief, The Blind See Again,* and *Pomegranate.* Kakhkhar's stories described both the present and the recent past of the Uzbek people (the collections *The World Becomes Younger,* 1933, and *Stories,* 1935). The novel *Mirage* (1937) exposes the bourgeois nationalists. The novellas *Hero From Dardak* (1942) and *The Gold Star* (1946) were written about events of the Great Patriotic War of 1941–45. The novel *Lights of Koshchinar* (1951–52) is dedicated to the theme of collectivization; the novella *The Little Bird* (1958; Russian translation, 1959) deals with the postwar life of an Uzbek *kishlak* (hamlet), and the novella *Love* (1968, published in 1969), with the life of youth. Kakhkhar wrote an autobiographical novella, *Tales of the Past* (1965; Russian translation, 1970), and the comedies *In a New Land, Silk Siuzane* (1950; State Prize of the USSR, 1952), and *Aching Teeth* (1954). He translated L. N. Tolstoy's *War and Peace* and works by such writers as A. S. Pushkin, A. P. Chekhov, N. V. Gogol, and M. Gorky into Uzbek. He served as chairman of the presidium of the Writers' Union of Uzbekistan from 1954 to 1956. He was awarded three orders, as well as a number of medals. Kakhkhar is buried in Tashkent.

WORKS
[Qähhär, Äbdullä.] *Äsärlär,* vols. 1–6. Tashkent, 1967–71.
Muhäbbät. Tashkent, 1969.
In Russian translation:
Izbrannye proizvedeniia. Moscow, 1959.
REFERENCES
Borolina, I. V. *Abdulla Kakhkhar: Ocherk tvorchestva.* Tashkent, 1957.
Istoriia uzbekskoi sovetskoi literatury. Moscow, 1967.
Äbdusämätov, Kh. *Äbdullä Qähhar.* Tashkent, 1960.
      V. ABDULLAEV and B. VALIKHODZHAEV   [11–1632–3]

KAKHOVKA, a city (since 1938) in Kherson Oblast, Ukrainian SSR, on the left shore of the Kakhovka Reservoir, 10 km from the Kakhovka station on the Snigirevka-Fedorovka railroad line. Population 35,000 (1971). Kakhovka was founded in 1783 on the basis of a small settlement. It was a major landing stage on the Dnieper River in the former Tauride Province until 1917.

During the Civil War of 1918–20, the offensive by Wrangel's troops was halted near Kakhovka in August and October 1920. The Traktorodetal' Works, which makes tractor components, was built in Kakhovka as part of the prewar five-year plans. During the Great Patriotic War (1941–45), Kakhovka suffered greatly under the fascist German troops, who occupied it in early September 1941. An underground party group led by K. I. Turos operated in the city during the occupation. The Soviet Army liberated Kakhovka on Nov. 2, 1943. The city was completely rebuilt in the postwar period. The city has a repair plant, as well as factories producing reinforced-concrete articles and electric-welding equipment. There is also a museum of the history of the city.   [11–1631–2]

KAKHOVKA BASE OF OPERATIONS, a fortified region on the left bank of the Dnieper, near Bol'shaia Kakhovka (now the city of Kakhovka), during the Civil War of 1918–20.

The base of operations was formed on Aug. 7, 1920, as a result of the offensive of the Right-bank Group of troops of the Southwestern Front under the command of R. P. Eideman. It created a threat to the rear and the communications lines of Wrangel's troops in Northern Taurida and the Crimea and contained their actions, preventing them from developing an offensive toward the north. The base was maintained until mid-October, under the direction of the military engineer D. M. Karbyshev. A deeply echeloned defense of three zones was organized. The advance edge of the main defense zone ran along the Ekaterinovka-Sofievka-Liubimovka line and then south of the *khutor* (privately owned homestead) of Sukhina, extending to the Dnieper. The defense zone consisted of two or three lines of trenches with communication trenches and barbed-wire barriers; mine fields were laid on the major axes. The first line of defense consisted of individual trenches and barbed-wire barriers and was about 40 km long. The base of operations was from 12 to 15 km deep and had an area of 216 sq km. A zone of bridgeheads was set up directly in front of Kakhovka. The base had artillery positions and observation points and four river crossings in the rear.

The repeated attempts of Wrangel's troops in August and September to liquidate the Kakhovka base of operations with the support of tanks, artillery, and air power were repulsed by Soviet troops (15th, 52nd, and Latvian divisions), who displayed exceptional heroism in combat. Relying on the Kakhovka base of operations, in October 1920, Soviet troops struck their main blow at Wrangel's White Guard troops in Northern Taurida.

REFERENCES
Buznik, P. "Kakhovskii platsdarm i ego inzhenernaia podgotovka." *Voenno-inzhenernyi zhurnal,* 1948, no. 2.
Sergeev, P. "Oborona Kakhovskogo platsdarma 51-i diviziei (14 oktiabria 1920 g.)." *Voenno-istoricheskii zhurnal,* 1939, no. 3.
Il'in-Mitkevich, A. "Kakhovskii ukreplennyi platsdarm." *Tekhnika i vooruzhenie,* 1939, no. 12.   [11–1631–4]

KAKHOVKA RESERVOIR, a reservoir formed by the dam of the Kakhovka Hydro-engineering Complex on the Dnieper River, located in the Kherson, Dnepropetrovsk, and Zaporozh'e oblasts of the Ukrainian SSR.

The reservoir was filled from 1955 to 1958. Area, 2,155 sq km; volume, 18.2 cu km; length, 230 km; maximum width, 25 km; average depth, 8.4 m; and maximum depth, 36 m. The reservoir's level varies within limits of 3 m; it regulates water flow over seasons and to some extent over periods of several years. The North Crimean Canal originates at the reservoir and carries water to the farms, fields, and cities of the Crimea. As a result of the construction of the Kakhovka Reservoir, a deepwater route has been formed on the lower section of the Dnieper. The reservoir has fishing (bream, carp, and pike-perch). Located along the shores of the reservoir are the cities of Zaporozh'e,

Nikopol', Novaia Kakhovka, Kakhovka, Berislav, and Kamenka-Dneprovskaia.   [11–1632–1]

KAKHOVSKII, PETR GRIGOR'EVICH. Born 1797; died July 13 (25), 1826. Aristocratic revolutionary Decembrist. One of the most active participants in the uprising of Dec. 14, 1825.

Kakhovskii was from the *dvorianstvo* (nobility or gentry) of Smolensk Province. He was a retired first lieutenant. In early 1825 he was accepted into the Northern Society of the Decembrists in St. Petersburg by K. F. Ryleev. Kakhovskii supported the introduction of the republican system into Russia. He insisted on the extermination of the entire tsarist family. On the day of the uprising, Kakhovskii brought out the Marine Guards and was one of the first to arrive on Senate Square, where he mortally wounded the governor-general of St. Petersbrug, M. A. Miloradovich, and the commander of the Grenadier Life Guards Regiment, Colonel N. K. Stiurler. After his arrest, Kakhovskii wrote several letters to Nicholas I and the investigators containing a critical analysis of conditions in Russia. Kakhovskii was executed in Peter and Paul Fortress together with P. I. Pestel', S. I. Murav'ev-Apostol, M. P. Bestuzhev-Riumin, and Ryleev.

REFERENCES
Vosstanie dekabristov: Materialy i dokumenty, vol. 1. Moscow, 1925.
Nechkina, M. V. *Dvizhenie dekabristov,* vols. 1–2. Moscow, 1955.
Podgornyi, I. *P. G. Kakhovskii.* Leningrad, 1965.   [11–1631–3]

KAKINADA (Cocanada), city and port in India, located on the Bay of Bengal in the Godavari River delta in Andhra Pradesh. Population, 164,200 (1971). Kakinada is linked with the sea by a system of canals in the delta. Cotton, rice, flour, tobacco, and steel ingots are exported. In the city and its environs there is metallurgy, salt production, and small ship building.   [11–552–4]

KAKOGAWA, a city in Japan in the southwest part of the island of Honshu, prefecture of Hyogo. Population, 127,000 (1970). Machine building (including a transportation-machine building plant), metallurgy, textiles (wool fabrics), and food flavoring are the major industries.   [11–552–5]

KAKTYNŠ, ADOLF. Born July 14 (26), 1885, in Jaunjelgava; died July 25, 1965, in California. Latvian singer (baritone).

Kaktynš was among the leading Latvian operatic artists between 1913 and 1944. He performed as a dramatic actor in the early 1900's in Riga theaters. After 1910 he sang in concerts, and after 1912, in operas. Kaktynš toured to Monte Carlo, Paris, Munich, and Petrograd. He combined an outstanding gift for drama with stage presence and a voice of rare beauty and strength. Among his parts were Lāčplēsis in Jānis Medinš' *Fire and Night* and the title roles in Verdi's *Rigoletto,* Mussorgsky's *Boris Godunov,* and A. Rubinstein's *Demon.*

IA. IA. VITOLIN'   [11–555–1]

KAKURIN, NIKOLAI EVGEN'EVICH. Born Sept. 4 (16), 1883, in Orel; died July 29, 1936. Soviet military leader and historian. Became a member of the CPSU in 1921. The son of an officer.

Kakurin graduated from the Mikhail Artillery College in 1904 and the Academy of the General Staff in 1910. He fought in World War I, reaching the rank of colonel. In late 1918 he volunteered to serve with the forces of the Western Ukrainian People's Republic. After the republic fell in mid-1919, these troops joined Petliura's forces and in February 1920 went over to the side of the Red Army. During the Soviet-Polish War of 1920, Kakurin was chief of staff of a division, acting commander of the Fourth Army, commander of the Third Army, and assistant commander of the Western Front. In 1921, as chief of staff of the Tambov group of forces, he took part in crushing the Antonov Revolt. The same year he began teaching, and in 1922 he led the forces of the Bukhara-Fergana region in the struggle against the Basmachi bands. He then returned to teaching at the Military Academy (later renamed the M. V. Frunze Military Academy) and was head of the division of history of the Civil War for the Headquarters of the Workers' and Peasants' Red

Army (RKKA). He wrote a number of major works on the history of the Civil War and on strategy, tactics, and troop education and training. He was one of the initiators and authors of the three-volume work on the war published in 1928–30. He was awarded the Order of the Red Banner and the Bukhara Order of the Red Star First Class.

WORKS

Strategiia proletarskogo gosudarstva (Etiud). [No place] 1921.
Sovremennaia taktika, 3rd ed. Moscow, 1927.
Vstrechnyi boi. Moscow, 1927.
Kak srazhalas' revoliutsiia, vols. 1–2. Moscow, 1925–26.
Russko-pol'skaia kampaniia 1918–1920. Moscow, 1922.
Strategicheskii ocherk grazhdanskoi voiny. Moscow-Leningrad, 1926.
Vosstanie chekhoslovakov i bor'ba s Kolchakom. Moscow, 1928.
Bor'ba za Petrograd v 1919. Moscow-Leningrad, 1928.
Voina s belopoliakami. Moscow-Leningrad, 1930.   [11–556–2]

KALA, an urban-type settlement in the Azerbaijan SSR, part of the Azizbekov Raion of the city of Baku. It has oil-industry equipment, electrical repair, and machine overhaul plants.
                                                            [11–556–4]

KALAA BENI-HAMMAD, an ancient city in northern Algeria. Founded in 1007, it served as the capital of the Hammadids until 1090. It is now in ruins. There are remains of the city walls, a signal tower, a mosque with minaret, and an extensive 11th-century palace complex. Included in the palace complex is the Dar al-Bahr ensemble with its pool and rich decor (painting on stucco, marble, majolica).

REFERENCE

Beylié, L. de. *La Kalaa des Béni-Hammad, une capitale berbère de l'Afrique du Nord au XI siècle.* Paris, 1909.   [11–557–2]

KALACH, a city, the administrative center of Kalach Raion, Voronezh Oblast, RSFSR. Located in the Kalach Upland at the confluence of the Tolucheevka and Podgornaia rivers (Don Basin). Population, 19,000 (1971). Kalach is the terminus of the 94-km railroad branch from the Talovaia station of the Georgiu-Dezh–Povorino line. Food industry (including a sugar plant, a flour-milling combine, a meat and poultry combine, and a foodstuffs complex) is located there, as are building-materials and mechanical plants and an agricultural mechanization technicum. Kalach was founded in the early 18th century and became a city in 1945.   [11–570–2]

KALACHINSK, a city in Omsk Oblast, RSFSR, on the left bank of the Om' River (a tributary of the Irtysh). Kalachinsk has a railroad station 88 km east of Omsk. Population, 21,000 (1970). A plant manufacturing spare parts for agricultural machinery and tractor trailers is there, as are a weaving mill, food enterprises (including a creamery and a meat combine), and a building-materials combine. Kalachinsk was founded in 1830 as a village and became a city in 1952.   [11–570–4]

KALACHINSKII, MIKHAS' IVANOVICH (Mikhail Ivanovich Kalachinskii). Born Dec. 30, 1916 (Jan. 12, 1917), in the urban-type settlement of Krupki, in present-day Minsk Oblast. Soviet Byelorussian poet. Member of the CPSU since 1942.

The son of a peasant, Kalachinskii took part in the Soviet-Finnish War of 1939–40 and the Great Patriotic War of 1941–45. He was first published in 1932. He is the author of the narrative poems for children *Kostia the Chekist* (1938) and *The Package* (1940). His published collections of verses and narrative poems include *The Sun in the Blue Sky* (1949), *Facing Life* (1951; Russian translation, 1962), *The Great March* (1952), *The Small Station in the Forest* (1955), *The Reaping Season* (1956), *Pines and Dunes* (1960), *A Cluster of Rowanberries* (1964), *Forest Tales* (1967), and *Belts* (1968). Since 1960 he has been the editor in chief of the journal *Belarus'.* He does many translations from Russian, Ukrainian, and other languages. Kalachinskii has been awarded four orders and a number of medals.

WORKS

Vybranyia tvory, vols. 1–2. Minsk, 1971.
In Russian translation:
Iz chistykh rodnikov. Leningrad, 1955.

REFERENCE

Pis'menniki Savetskai Belarusi: Karotki biiabibliiagrafichny davednik. Minsk, 1970.   [11–570–5]

KALACH-NA-DONU, a city, the center of Kalachevski Raion, Volgograd Oblast, RSFSR. A port on the left bank of the Tsimliansk Reservoir, 9 km above the entrance to the V. I. Lenin Volga-Don Ship Canal. The terminus (Don station) of a 30-km railroad branch from the Volgograd-Likhaia line. Population, 21,000 (1970). Kalach-na-Donu arose in 1716, based on a cossack *sloboda* (tax-exempt settlement), and became a city in 1951.

Kalach-na-Donu's industries include ship repair, motor-vehicle repair, and fish processing; a creamery; a lumber mill; and a meat combine.

Fierce combat took place in August 1942 around Kalach-na-Donu during the battle of Stalingrad of 1942–43. On Aug. 26, 1942, the city was occupied by fascist German troops. During the counterattack of Soviet forces the city was liberated on Nov. 23, 1942, after intense fighting. Subsequently troops from the Southwestern and Stalingrad fronts joined forces southeast of Kalach-na-Donu (near the settlement of Sovetskii) to complete the encirclement of the fascist German troops at Stalingrad.

REFERENCE

Zaitsev, M. I. *Kalach-na-Donu (Istoricheskii ocherk).* [Stalingrad] 1960.   [11–570–6]

KALACHOV, NIKOLAI VASIL'EVICH. Born May 26 (June 7), 1819; died Oct. 25 (Nov. 6), 1885. Russian historian, jurist, archivist, and archaeographist (student of old texts and manuscripts). Academician of the St. Petersburg Academy of Sciences (1893).

Kalachov was a proponent of the legalist school of historical science. He worked on the St. Petersburg Archaeographic Commission and was a professor in the subdepartment of the history of Russian law at Moscow University from 1848 to 1852. In the preparation of the reforms of Feb. 19, 1861, freeing the serfs, he was a member of the drafting commission, and he was a member-editor on the commission drafting the 1864 reform of the judiciary. From 1865 to 1885 he was in charge of the Moscow archives of the Ministry of Justice.

In 1852 and 1853, Kalachov undertook an archaeographical expedition and published the documents that he had gathered in *The Archive of Historical-Legal Information Relating to Russia* and *The Archive of Historical and Practical Information Relating to Russia.* He founded the monthly journal *Iuridicheskii Vestnik* (Legal Herald), which he edited from 1860 to 1864 and from 1867 to 1870. He was the editor and compiler of a number of other collections of documents, including *Documents Relating to the Legal Life of Ancient Russia* (vols. 1–3, 1857–84), *Supplements to Historical Documents* (vols. 7, 8 and 9, 1859–75), *Census Books of the Russian State* (vol. 1, books 1–2, 1872–77), and *Reports and Verdicts of the Government Senate in the Reign of Peter the Great* (vols. 1–2, books 1–3, 1882–83).

Kalachov wrote a number of works on the theory and practice of archival work. Under his editorship, the *Guide to the Documents and Papers Preserved in the Moscow Archives of the Ministry of Justice* began publication in 1869. He was one of the founders of the St. Petersburg Archaeological Institute in 1877. He sought to establish a network of central and local archives; he was much concerned about the preservation of documents and tried to make these documents widely available to researchers.   M. N. SHOBUKHOV [11–571–1]

KALACH UPLAND, hills in the south of the Eastern European Plain, within the Voronezh, Volgograd, and Rostov oblasts, located on the left bank of the Don between the Bitiug and Khoper rivers. Elevations range up to 240 m. The Kalach Upland is composed of Upper Cretaceous (chalk, marl) and Paleogene (clays, sands, sandstones) deposits, covered with glacial deposits and loess-like cover loams. The upland has numerous valleys, ravines, and gulches. The main rivers are left tributaries of the Don, including the Osered', Tolucheevka, and Peskovatka. Soils are ordinary and southern chernozems. Oak groves have been preserved (including the Shipov Forest). The steppes are cultivated; crops include wheat, rye, millet, and sunflowers. [11–571–2]

KALADZE, KARLO RAZHDENOVICH. Born Mar. 16 (29), 1904, in Kutaisi. Soviet Georgian poet and playwright; member of the CPSU since 1939.

Kaladze's first book of poems was published in 1926. He created poetic panoramas of the new Georgia ("Challenge of the East," 1926; "Dar'ial," 1926; and "Song of the Horseman," 1927). Cycles of poems such as *Dawns in Khertvis* reflect the construction of socialism in the 1930's. The narrative poem *Uchardioni* (1933) is dedicated to the collectivization of Georgian agriculture. Heroic themes of the Great Patriotic War (1941–45) are the basis of the cycle of poems *Meetings on the Battlefield* (1942).

A prominent theme in Kaladze's poetry is the friendship of peoples ("The Muscovites," "Songs on the Shores of the Dnieper," and "We Want Peace"). He is the author of the plays *The Way It Was* (1929), *The House on the Bank of the Kura* (1931), *Khatidzhe* (1933), and *One Night's Comedy* (produced in 1945), which have played a significant role in the growth of Georgian drama and theater. Kaladze has been awarded three orders, as well as medals.

WORKS

[Kaladze, K.] *Nat'argmni lek'sebi da poemebi.* Tbilisi, 1961.
Rch'euli lek'sebi da poemebi, vols. 1 2. Tbilisi, 1968.
In Russian translation:
Stikhi, pesni, ballady. Moscow, 1957.
Stikhotvoreniia. Moscow, 1963.
Molodost' Gruzii: Stikhi i poemy. Tbilisi, 1968.
Stikhotvoreniia i poemy. Tbilisi, 1970.

REFERENCES

Gol'tsev, V. "Karlo Kaladze." In his book *Literaturno-kriticheskie stat'i.* Tbilisi, 1957.
Margvelashvili, G. *Karlo Kaladze.* Tbilisi, 1958.
Chilaia, S. *Meoc'e saukunis k'art'uli mcerlobi*, part 3. Tbilisi, 1962.
Radiani, Sh. *T'anamedroveni*, book 2. Tbilisi, 1968.
Karlo Kaladze, bibliograp'iuli saziebeli. Tbilisi, 1967.
Gverdcit'eli, G. *Literaturuli portretebi, eskizebi, cerilebi.* Tbilisi, 1968.
A. M. MIRIANASHVILI [11–557–5]

KALAHARI DESERT, a depression in south-central Africa, coinciding with the Kalahari syneclise of the African platform; located in the territory of Angola, Zambia, Namibia, Botswana, Southern Rhodesia, and the Republic of South Africa.

The Kalahari Desert is bordered on the east and west by steplike plateaus and horst-block ridges; on the north, by the Congo-Zambezi divide; and on the south, by the Orange River. From north to south the Kalahari is about 2,000 km long; its width, east to west, is more than 1,200 km. Elevation, 900–1,000 m; area, about 630,000 sq km. The plains of the Kalahari are covered with sands, which form gently sloping dunes. There are many salt bottoms (pans or vlei) in the dry riverbeds and sinkholes. The climate is tropical (subequatorial north of the Zambezi). Rain falls in the summer. The amount of precipitation and the length of the wet season diminish moving from the northeast and north (1,000 mm, seven months) toward the southwest and south (150 mm, sporadic precipitation, often in the form of thunderstorms). Mean summer temperatures are 24°–26°C; winter temperatures are 12°–18°C; frosts occur to the south of the tropical zone.

The Kalahari is a region with poorly developed internal drainage; only in the north and south is it cut by rivers (the Zambezi and the Orange). The largest internal drainage system is the Okavango River, which feeds into the Okavango Swamp, from which an irregular flow proceeds to the Makarikari salt pans and, very rarely, to the Zambezi. The northernmost, and wettest, part of the Kalahari, which is crossed by tributaries of the Zambezi, is covered by thin forest (leafless in the dry season) growing on reddish chestnut laterized soils. In the valleys of the Okavango and the Zambezi there are parklike savannas with acacia,

spurges, and baobab trees growing on red-brown soils. There are tropical swamps in the flood plains and delta of the Okavango. There are desolate tree-brush savannas south of 20°S lat., on the gently arching Bakalahari uplift. In the southwest and south there are semideserts and deserts, with dunes up to 100 m high that are held in place by succulent brush and subshrubs. The fauna of the Kalahari belongs to the South African subregion of the Ethiopian zoogeographical region and is kept primarily in the Etosha Game Reserve in Namibia and in the Kalahari Gemsbok National Park in the Republic of South Africa.

The population of the Kalahari is made up mostly of Bushmen (population density, less than one person per sq km), whose primary occupations are hunting and gathering. In the southern part of the Kalahari (in the Republic of South Africa) there is commercial livestock raising, and irrigation farming is carried on in certain centers.

REFERENCE

Wellington, J. H. *Southern Africa: A Geographical Study*, vols. 1–2. Cambridge, 1955. L. A. MIKHAILOVA [11–569–2]

KALAHARI GEMSBOK NATIONAL PARK, national park in the Republic of South Africa. It is located in the Kalahari Desert, in the northern part of Cape of Good Hope Province. Founded in 1931. Area, about 900,000 hectares (1970). The typical landscape is barchans; vegetation consists mostly of thorny shrubs. Antelopes inhabiting the park include the gemsbok (*Oryx gazella*), springbok, common eland, and red hartebeest. Artificial watering places have been built to preserve the animals. There are two tourist camps in the park, at Twee Rivieren and Mata Mata. [11–570–1]

KALAIDOVICH, KONSTANTIN FEDOROVICH. Born May 1792 in Elets; died Apr. 19 (May 1), 1832, in Moscow. Russian archaeographer and historian.

Kalaidovich graduated from Moscow University in 1810, at which time he joined the circle of Count N. P. Rumiantsev, the first great center of archaeography in Russia. He took an active part in the work of the Moscow Society of History and Russian Antiquities and the Commission for the Printing of Government Documents and Treaties. In 1817–18 he participated with P. M. Stroev in the archaeographical expedition that discovered written remains of extreme importance for the historical sciences, including *Writings of Sviatoslav* (1073) and the works of Kirill Turovskii. Kalaidovich published *Russian Memorabilia* (vol. 1, 1815), *Old Russian Verses* collected by Kirsha Danilov (1818), the *Laws . . .* of Ivan III and Ivan IV (1819), and *Monuments of Russian Literature of the XII Century* (1821). His scholarly works were devoted to the description of manuscripts as well as to auxiliary historical disciplines. Kalaidovich played a large role in developing the scholarly publication of source materials.

REFERENCE

Sofinov, P. G. *Iz istorii russkoi dorevoliutsionnoi arkheografii.* Moscow, 1957. (Bibliography.) [11–559–3]

KALAI-MIR, an ancient, multilevel site of a fortified town in the Nasir Khisrav settlement (ancient Kobadian) in the Tadzhik SSR, on the lower course of the Kafirnigan River. The site was excavated in 1950–51. Remains of Bactrian structures and objects of material culture of the middle of the first millennium B.C. through the first centuries A.D. were discovered. As a result of the investigations at Kalai-Mir and the nearby site of Kei-Kobad-shakh, M. M. D'iakonov worked out the first stratigraphic table of the remains of northern Bactria. Five successive historical-cultural stages (Kobadian I–V) were distinguished, dating from the sixth–fourth century B.C. through the third–fourth century A.D.

REFERENCE

Materialy i issledovaniia po arkheologii SSSR, no. 37. Moscow-Leningrad, 1953. (Articles by M. M. D'iakonov and N. N. Zabelina). [11–559–1]

KALAI-MOR, an urban-type settlement in the Takhta-Bazar Raion, Mary Oblast, Turkmen SSR, on the Kushka River (a

tributary of the Murgab). Kalai-Mor is a railroad station on the Mary-Kushka line. A sovkhoz raising karakul sheep is there.
[11–559–2]

KALAKAN (Kalagan), a river in the north of Chita Oblast, RSFSR; right tributary of the Vitim. Length, 314 km; basin area, 10,600 sq km. The river flows near the southern foot of the Iankan range. It is fed primarily by rain and snow. Average annual water flow at the mouth is 74.2 cu m per sec. The Kalakan freezes over in mid-October and thaws in mid-May. It has a large left tributary, the Tundak. The Kalakan is used to float logs.
[11–559–4]

KALAKHANA, a village near the city of Shemakha in the Azerbaijan SSR. A 17th-century memorial complex has been preserved in Kalakhana. It consists of eight stone mausoleums, octahedral and covered with pyramidal marquees. Each mausoleum is set in the center of a little courtyard, enclosed by walls with a portal. On one of the mausoleums, the date of construction and name of the builder are indicated (1663–64, Abdul Azim).
[11–569–1]

KALAKUTSKII, NIKOLAI VENIAMINOVICH. Born Feb. 9 (21), 1831, in Bel'sk District, Smolensk Province; died Jan. 17 (29), 1889, in St. Petersburg. Russian scientist in metallurgy and artillery production, a major general of artillery (1884).

Kalakutskii graduated from a special military school in 1849 and served in the army until 1861. Between 1861 and 1870 he was artillery acceptance officer at the Prince Mikhail Steel Cannon Factory in Zlatoust. Between 1871 and 1884 he was an engineer at the Obukhov Plant in St. Petersburg and in 1884 became chief engineer (with the title of *glavnyi tekhnik,* chief technician) at the plant. In 1867, Kalakutskii was the first to explain fully how the forging process influences the properties of forged pieces and to explain the causes of metallurgical defects in steel. Together with A. S. Lavrov he discovered and explained the phenomenon of segregation in steel (1866). From 1870 to 1878 he conducted research to select steel for rifle barrels; his experiments measuring the pressure of powder gases in the rifle barrels and studying the effect of a number of ballistic factors on the pressure were especially important. In his well-known works on residual (internal) stresses in steel and cast iron, Kalakutskii was the first to explain the mechanism of these stresses; he developed a methodology for quantitative analysis of them in gun barrels and in the bodies of shells.

WORKS
Issledovanie vnutrennykh napriazhenii v chugune i stali, 2nd ed. St. Petersburg, 1888.
REFERENCE
Cherniak, A. Ia., and D. M. Nakhimov. *Russkii uchenyi metalloved N. V. Kalakutskii.* Moscow, 1951.
[11–560–1]

KALAMAI, a city and port in Greece, in the southern part of the Peloponnesus, on the shore of the Gulf of Messini in the Ionian Sea. It is the administrative center of Messinia Prefecture. Population, 39,300 (1971). There are textile (mostly silk) and food industries, as well as fishing.
[11–562–1]

KALAMAZOO, a city in the northern United States, in the state of Michigan. Population, 85,600 (1970; 201,600 with suburbs). Kalamazoo is a railroad junction. Industry employs 30,000 people, chiefly in metalworking, paper, chemicals, and pharmaceuticals.
[11–560–4]

KALAMBO FALLS, the site of a Paleolithic settlement in Zambia, near Lake Tanganyika. Excavations in 1953 by J. D. Clark of Great Britain uncovered seven cultural layers from the Acheulean era to the present. Items found in the lower three layers include hand axes, pebble hammers, flake tools, sticks used for digging, and fragments of planed wood and bark, possibly from baskets. Tree trunks and branches laid crosswise, which probably formed dwelling platforms, have been discovered as well as a crude arc made of stone, which was apparently the foundation for a wind screen. Piles of production wastes permit

the supposition that a workshop for the manufacture of flint implements existed at Kalambo Falls during the Lower Paleolithic. The radiocarbon method dates the lower layers of the Kalambo Falls site from 57,000 to 57,600 years ago.

REFERENCE
Clark, J. D. *The Prehistory of Southern Africa.* London, 1959.
[11–561–2]

KALAMBO FALLS, a waterfall in East Africa on the Zambia-Tanzania border, located on the Kalambo River, which flows into Lake Tanganyika. Height of the falls, 427 m. The waterfall is a tourist attraction.
[11–561–1]

KALAMITA, a medieval fortress in the Crimea. It was situated on a cliff at the mouth of the Chernaia River, near Sevastopol'. Excavations in 1950 showed that Kalamita was founded in the fifth–sixth centuries to defend the approaches to Chersonesus. The walls were made of large blocks. In the eighth–ninth centuries, a monastery complex was built; cave churches in the precipice (a basilica and baptistry, for example) have been preserved, as well as numerous living quarters (cells), arranged in several tiers. At the beginning of the 15th century, the sovereigns of the Crimean feudal principality of Theodoro built a new fortress to replace the early medieval stronghold that had been destroyed. The new fortress defended the principality's port against the Genoese colony of Cembalo (modern Balaklava). In 1475, Kalamita was taken by the Turks and named Inkerman. After the 1774 Treaty of Kuchuk Kainarji, the fortress lost its significance and fell into ruin.

REFERENCES
Bert'e-Delagard, A. P. "Ostatki drevnikh sooruzhenii v okrestnostiakh Sevastopolia i peshchernye goroda Kryma." In the collection *Zap. Odesskogo obshchestva istorii i drevnostei,* vol. 14. Odessa, 1886.
Veimarn, Ei. V. "Arkheolohichni roboty v raioni Inkermana." *Arkheolohichni pam'iatky URSR,* 1963, vol. 13.
A. L. IAKOBSON [11–562–4]

KALAMITSKII GULF, a gulf in the Black Sea, extending 13 km into the west coast of the Crimean Peninsula. Width at the entrance, 41 km; depth, approximately 30 m. The Al'ma and Bulganak rivers flow into the gulf. The shores are low-lying and sandy. Running along the edge of the gulf and separated from it by sandbars are several salt lakes, including Sasyk (Evpatoriia), Saki, and Chaika; these lakes are used for medical therapy. Evpatoriia Bay cuts into the northern shore.
[11–563–1]

KALANCHAK, an urban-type settlement, administrative center of Kalanchak Raion, Kherson Oblast, Ukrainian SSR, near the Karkinitskii Gulf of the Black Sea, 25 km from the Kalanchak station on the Kherson-Sevastopol' line. The settlement has a creamery and a brick and tile factory. The North Crimean Canal is nearby.
[11–566–2]

KALANDARISHVILI, NESTOR ALEKSANDROVICH (party pseudonyms, Nestor, Dedushka [Granddad]). Born June 26 (July 8), 1876 (1874, according to other data), in the village of Shemokmedi, in present-day Makharadze Raion, Georgian SSR; died Mar. 6, 1922, near Yakutsk. One of the leaders of the partisan movement in Eastern Siberia during the Civil War of 1918–20.

Kalandarishvili studied at Tbilisi Teachers' Seminary. He joined the Socialist Revolutionary Party in 1903 and was involved in the 1905–06 peasant uprising in Guria (in Western Georgia). Arrested in 1907, he was confined in Siberia until February 1917. In 1917 he joined the anarcho-communist group and in 1921 became a member of the Communist Party. He helped establish Soviet power in Irkutsk. In 1918, on instructions from the underground Irkutsk province committee of the RCP (Bolshevik), he formed a partisan detachment that conducted operations in Irkutsk Province against Kolchak's forces and later fought Ataman Semionov in Transbaikalia. In late 1921 he became commander of the troops in the Yakutsk region and in the Severnyi Krai. In January 1922 he went out with a unit of

300 men on an operation against a White Guard band. They were ambushed, and he was fatally wounded. He was awarded the Order of the Red Banner.

REFERENCES
Solodiankin, A. G. *Kommunisty Irkutska v bor'be s kolchakovshchinoi.* Irkutsk, 1960. [11–564–2]

KALANGUI, an urban-type settlement in Oloviannaia Raion, Chita Oblast, RSFSR, on the Turga River (Amur basin), 45 km northeast of the Khadabulak railroad station on the Karymskaia-Zabaikal'sk line. Fluorite is mined there. [11–564–1]

KALANTAR, LEVAN ALEKSANDROVICH. Born Jan. 4 (16), 1891, in Tbilisi; died Oct. 29, 1959, in Yerevan; Soviet Armenian director and theatrical figure. People's Artist of the Armenian SSR (1954); member of the CPSU (1942).

Kalantar began his stage career in 1916 as an actor and director in Tbilisi after graduating from the University of St. Petersburg. In 1921 he organized the S. Shaumian Armenian Theater in Tbilisi. He was one of the founders of the G. Sundukian Armenian Theater in Yerevan, where he was also chief director until 1928. Between 1931 and 1935 he organized and served as chief director of the M. Gorky Workers' Theater in Yerevan. Between 1937 and 1943 and between 1957 and 1959 he was chief director of the Yerevan Russian Drama Theater. During the same period he also staged operas. Among his best works are *Uncle Bagdasar* by Paronian (1927), *The Lower Depths* by Gorky (1929), *The Inspector-General* by Gogol (1930), *The Forest* by Ostrovskii (1934), *Lusabatsin* by Stepanian (1938), *Khachatur Abovian* by Muradian (1955), *Evil Spirit* by Shirvanzade (1959), and Shakespeare's *Merchant of Venice* (1940) and *Othello* (1956). Kalantar's innovative direction helped to raise the quality of stage art and establish the principles of socialist realism in the Armenian theater. Beginning in 1944 he taught at the Theater Arts Institute in Yerevan; he was made a professor there in 1946. He was the author of the book *The Paths of Art,* published in 1963. Kalantar was the recipient of two orders and various medals.

REFERENCE
Akhumian, T. *Literaturnye stat'i i vospominaniia.* Yerevan, 1966. [11–566–1]

KALAR (called the China River in its upper reaches), a river in the north of Chita Oblast, RSFSR. A right tributary of the Vitim. Length, 511 km; basin area, 17,400 sq km. It originates in the Udokan Range, cuts through the Kalar Range, and flows between the Kalar Range in the north and the Iankan Range in the south. The Kalar River has many rapids. It is fed primarily by rain. Freezing over in mid-October, it thaws in mid-May. [11–567–1]

KALAR, a mountain range in the Stanovoi upland, in northern Transbaikalia, within Chita and Amur oblasts, RSFSR. Length, approximately 350 km; maximum elevation, 2,482 m. It is composed of granite and metamorphized rocks. Flat crests predominate in the west and alpine peaks in the east. Near the peaks, bare landscapes predominate; the slopes are characterized by sparse forest and, below 1,100–1,400 m, by mountain leafy taiga. [11–567–3]

KALARASH, a city (since 1940), the administrative center of Kalarash Raion, Moldavian SSR. Kalarash has a railroad station on the Kishinev-Ungeny line 50 km from Kishinev. Population, 13,900 (1970). A wine and cognac combine, a canning factory, a creamery, and a clothing industry are there, as is a teachers school. [11–567–2]

KALASHNIKOV, MIKHAIL TIMOFEEVICH. Born Nov. 10, 1919, in the town of Kur'ia, in present-day Altai Krai. Soviet small arms designer, doctor of technical sciences (1971). Hero of Socialist Labor (1958). Became a member of the CPSU in 1953.

After World War II, Kalashnikov developed a type of small arms used as the basis for the 1947-model submachine gun called the 7.62-mm Kalashnikov Automatic (AK), which was adopted by the Soviet Army. The 7.62-mm caliber for small arms was standardized on the basis of this weapon. The 7.62-mm modernized submachine gun (AKM), the 7.62-mm light machine gun (RPK), the 7.62-mm Kalashnikov machine gun (PK or, on a stand, PKS), and later the 7.62-mm tank machine gun (PKT) were adopted. Kalashnikov was a deputy to the fourth, seventh, and eighth convocations of the Supreme Soviet of the USSR. In 1949 he was awarded the State Prize of the USSR. He has been awarded two Orders of Lenin, two other orders, and medals.

WORKS
Bolotin, D. N. *Sovetskoe strelkovoe oruzhie za 50 let.* Leningrad, 1967. [11–572–1]

KALASHNIKOV, VASILII IVANOVICH. Born Oct. 30 (Nov. 11), 1849, in Uglich; died Feb. 13 (26), 1908, in Nizhny Novgorod. Russian inventor, mechanical and heat engineer.

In 1860, Kalashnikov finished three years at the Uglich district school. In 1865 he went to work as a draftsman at a machine plant in Rybinsk, then in 1872 began working at factories (primarily in shipbuilding) in Nizhny Novgorod (now Gorky) as a designer and chief mechanical engineer. Kalashnikov designed original models of steam power plants for ships, originated the use of compound steam engines for river vessels, and also invented several devices, such as a force pump for spraying fuel oil, steam superheaters, and air-blowing machines. In 1886, Kalashnikov founded the journal *Nizhegorodskii vestnik parokhodstva i promyshlennosti* (Nizhny Novgorod Herald of Steam Navigation and Industry). In 1897, Kalashnikov was elected chairman of the Nizhny Novgorod division of the Russian Technical Society. At the All-Russian Industrial Exhibition in Moscow in 1882, he was awarded medals for his compact steam machine for ships and for his steam boiler. The writers V. G. Korolenko and M. Gorky praised Kalashnikov's work highly.

WORKS
Izbr. trudy. Moscow-Leningrad, 1952.
REFERENCES
Danilevskii, V. V. "Zhizn' i deiatel'nost' V. I. Kalashnikova." In *Trudy po istorii tekhniki,* no. 1. Moscow, 1952.
Kalashnikov, V. V., and M. E. Shekhter. *Vydaiushchiisia russkii mekhanik-sudostroitel' V. I. Kalashnikov.* Moscow, 1950. [11–571–3]

KALASHNIKOVO, an urban-type settlement in Likhoslavl' Raion, Kalinin Oblast, RSFSR. It has a railroad station on the Moscow-Leningrad line, 64 km northwest of Kalinin. Electric light bulbs are produced here, and there is a state forestry establishment and a technicum of planning and accounting. [11–572–2]

KALATA, until 1935 the name of the city now known as Kirovgrad, in Sverdlovsk Oblast, RSFSR. [11–567–4]

KALATOZOV, MIKHAIL KONSTANTINOVICH. Born Dec. 15 (28), 1903, in Tbilisi. Soviet film director. People's Artist of the USSR (1969); member of the CPSU since 1939.

Kalatozov began working in the Georgian cinema in 1923 and became a director in 1928. His films tended to emphasize space and dimension and made effective use of acute foreshortening and lighting. These features are particularly noticeable in his film *Salt of Svanetia* (1930), for which he was both director and one of the cameramen. In 1933, Kalatozov enrolled in postgraduate study at the Leningrad Academy of Art. Later he became head of the Tbilisi Film Studio. He returned to directing with his film *Courage* (1939). *Valerii Chkalov,* made in 1941, was among his most important films. The breadth of Kalatozov's artistic range and his ability to utilize diverse means of expression are apparent in his film comedy *True Friends* (1954).

The Cranes Are Flying, made in 1957, is Kalatozov's best-known film; it won both him and his cameraman, S. P. Urusevskii, worldwide recognition and a number of international prizes (including the Golden Palm at the 11th International Film Festival in Cannes). The acting of T. E. Samoilova and A. V. Batalov, the inspired montage of the crowd scenes, and the unusual mobility of the camera combine to give the film a subtle lyric beauty and a tragic force. In 1970, Kalatozov made a film based on

U. Nobile's expedition to the north pole (*The Red Tent;* a joint Soviet-Italian production). The cast of major actors from various countries and the impressive nature footage made the film an important event. Kalatozov received the State Prize of the USSR in 1951. He has been awarded three orders and various medals.

WORKS
Litso Gollivuda. [Moscow] 1949.
REFERENCE
Kremlev, G. *Mikhail Kalatozov.* Moscow, 1965.

M. KH. ZAK [11–567–5]

KALAUS, a river in Stavropol' Krai, RSFSR; a right tributary of the Vostochnyi Manych. Length, 436 km; basin area, 9,700 sq km.

The Kalaus originates in the Stavropol' uplands, fed by snow and rain. The average yearly water discharge at the village of Vozdvizhenskoe, 60 km from the mouth of the river, is 3.23 cu m per sec. The river freezes over in the first half of December and opens in mid-March. The city of Svetlograd is located on the Kalaus. The Kuban'-Kalaus irrigation system was being built as of 1973. [11–568–2]

KALBINSKII, a mountain range in the southwest Altai, in eastern Kazakhstan and Semipalatinsk oblasts, Kazakh SSR.

The Kalbinskii Range is about 400 km long. It is formed by a system of rugged, primarily low-mountain massifs that reach elevations of 1,300–1,500 m (maximum altitude, 1,608 m). Toward the west the mountains become lower and gradually turn into a hummocky topography (elevations of 450–700 m). The Kalbinskii Range is made up of Paleozoic shales, sandstones, and intrusive rocks (primarily granites). There are deposits of gold and polymetallic ores. Below elevations of 800–1,200 m, steppe vegetation predominates on mountain-chestnut and chernozem soils; higher up, one encounters occasional stands of conifers (on granites) and birch-aspen groves. There are subalpine steppe meadows on the highest peaks.

REFERENCE
Muratov, M. V., and V. I. Slavin. *Kratkii geologicheskii ocherk Kalby.* Moscow, 1953. [11–572–3]

KALCHEV, KAMEN (real name, Petr). Born July 31, 1914, in the village of Kereka, Gabrovo Okrug. Bulgarian writer. People's Worker of Culture of Bulgaria (1972). Became a member of the Bulgarian Communist Party in 1938.

Kalchev's first novella was *Wayfarer From the Mountain* (1938). The themes of his novels are the heroism of the antifascist movement (*The Living Remember,* 1950), socialist transformation in the village (*On the Border,* 1953), and the moral conflicts of contemporary life (*A Family of Weavers,* 1956–60; Russian translation, 1959). The appearance of his novel *Two in a New City* (1964; Russian translation, 1967), his novella *At the Sources of Life* (1964), and his collection *Sofia Stories* (1967) were significant events in Bulgarian literature. Kalchev wrote a fictionalized biography of G. Dimitrov, *Son of the Working Class* (1949; Russian translation, 1962). In 1962–63 he was chairman of the Union of Bulgarian Writers, and since 1966 he has been the editor in chief of the literary journal *Sentemvri.* He was awarded the Dimitrov Prize in 1950.

WORKS
In Russian translation:
Sofiiskie rasskazy. (Foreword by I. Tsvetkov.) Moscow, 1971.
"V poiskakh budushchego." *Inostrannaia literatura,* 1971, no. 5.
REFERENCE
Zarev, P. *Preobrazena literatura.* Sofia, 1969. [11–682–1]

KAL-DO PROCESS, a method of converting molten cast iron into steel without the consumption of fuel by blasting the cast iron from above with industrially pure oxygen in a rotary converter. The name "Kal-Do" came from the combination of the initial letters of the name Kalling (B. Kalling, born 1892), the Swedish metallurgist who invented the process, and the name of the city of Domnarvet (Sweden), where the first such converter (27-ton capacity) was put into operation in 1956.

The converter is installed at an angle to the horizontal plane and rotates during the process around a longitudinal axis at 1–30 rpm. The main feature of the Kal-Do process, in comparison with the usual oxygen-converter process, is the simplicity of slag formation control by means of changing the rotation frequency of the converter. The Kal-Do process yields 45–48 percent scrap iron in the metal charge as a result of the reduction in the loss of heat with the waste gases.

A disadvantage of the Kal-Do process is the low output of the converters. S. G. AFANAS'EV [11–573–6]

KALDOR, NICHOLAS. Born May 12, 1908, in Budapest. British economist.

Beginning in 1932, Kaldor was an instructor at the London School of Economics; later he taught at Cambridge University. After World War II he worked in the Economic Commission for Europe (an agency of the United Nations) and was an economic and financial adviser to a number of Asian, African, and Latin American countries. From 1966 to 1970, Kaldor served as chief adviser to the chancellor of the exchequer in the Labor government in Great Britain. Kaldor has written works on economic growth, employment, and inflation. His models for "balanced growth" are primarily technical and do not reflect the internal contradictions of the capitalist mode of production.

WORKS
Quantitative Aspects of the Full Employment Problem in Britain. [No place] 1944.
Essays in Economic Stability and Growth. London, 1960.
Essays on Value and Distribution. London–Glencoe, Ill., 1960.
Essays on Economic Policy, vols. 1–2. New York, 1965.

[11–574–1]

KALECKI, MICHAŁ. Born June 22, 1899, in Łódź; died Apr. 17, 1970, in Warsaw. Polish economist and statistician; member of the Polish Academy of Sciences (1957); recipient of an honorary doctorate from the University of Warsaw in 1964.

Kalecki studied at the Gdańsk Polytechnic Institute. From 1929 to 1935 he worked on problems of the national income of bourgeois Poland at the Research Institute of Market Conditions and Prices. In 1933, Kalecki created a mathematical economic model, the Kalecki mode, which describes the cyclical development of the capitalist economy. From 1936 he continued his studies and research first in Sweden and then in Great Britain. From 1940 he did research on problems of the military economy of Great Britain at the Oxford Institute of Statistics. From 1946 to 1954, Kalecki worked in the economic section of the UN Secretariat. After returning to Poland, Kalecki worked in planning agencies. From 1957 to 1960 he presided over the Main Commission for Long-term Planning. His postwar work was devoted to the problems of long-term planning of the rates of growth of the socialist economy and of national income. Kalecki was awarded the State Prize of the Polish People's Republic in 1966.

WORKS
Próba teorii koniunktury. Warsaw, 1933.
Prace z teorii koniunktury 1933–1937. Warsaw, 1962.
Szkice o funkcjonowaniu współczesnego kapitalizmu. Warsaw, 1962.
Z zagadnień gospodarczo-społecznych Polski Ludowej. Warsaw, 1964.
Zarys teorii wzrostu gospodarki socjalistycznej, 2nd ed. Warsaw, 1968.
Studia z zakresu koniunktury współczesnego kapitalizmu, vols. 1–4. Warsaw, 1957–60. (With A. Szeworski.)
Z zagadnień finansowania rozwoju krajów o "gospodarce mieszanej." Warsaw, 1967. (With I. Sachs.)
Selected Essays on the Dynamics of the Capitalist Economy. Cambridge, 1971.
Selected Essays on the Economic Growth of the Socialist and the Mixed Economy. Cambridge, 1972.

M. M. SELITSKAIA [11–589–1; updated]

KALEDIN, ALEKSEI MAKSIMOVICH. Born Oct. 12 (24), 1861, in the *stanitsa* (large cossack village) of Ust'-Khoperskaia, in present-day Serafimovich Raion, Volgograd Oblast; died Jan. 29 (Feb. 11) 1918, in Novocherkassk. Headed the cossack counterrevolution in the Don region in 1917–18. General of cavalry (1917). From the *dvorianstvo* (nobility or gentry).

Kaledin graduated from the Mikhail Artillery College in 1882 and from the Academy of the General Staff in 1889. During World War I, he commanded the XII Army Corps and, from May 1916 to May 1917, the Eighth Army of the Southwestern Front. On June 17 (30), 1917, at the Great Host Council he was elected ataman of the Don Cossack Host and became the head of the counterrevolutionary Don Cossack Host government. In August 1917 at the State Assembly he presented a program for suppressing the revolutionary movement. After the October Revolution he led a counterrevolutionary revolt, the Kaledin Revolt. Defeat forced Kaledin to acknowledge at a session of the Don Cossack Host government on Jan. 29 (Feb. 11), 1918, that the situation was hopeless. He relinquished his powers and on the same day shot himself. [11–576–1]

KALEDIN REVOLT (Russian, Kaledinshchina), a counterrevolutionary rebellion in the Don region from October 1917 to February 1918, initiated by the Don Cossack Host government headed by Ataman A. M. Kaledin.

Receiving a telegram on Oct. 25 (Nov. 7), 1917, from the Menshevik minister of justice N. N. Maliantovich on the armed insurrection in Petrograd and then an order from the chief of staff at General Headquarters, General N. N. Dukhonin, on the need for a struggle against Soviet power, Kaledin declared that he would "offer full support, in close alliance with the governments of the other cossack hosts," to the Provisional Government. Until its restoration, he continued, he would take into his own hands all power in the Don region. Establishing ties with the Ukrainian Central Rada and the Kuban', Terek, and Orenburg host governments, Kaledin sought to overthrow Soviet power and create a provisional counterrevolutionary government of Russia. Counterrevolutionary elements, including the Constitutional Democrat (Cadet) and monarchist leaders P. N. Miliukov, P. B. Struve, and M. V. Rodzianko, converged on the Don from all parts of Russia and began to gather around Kaledin. On November 2 (15), Generals L. G. Kornilov, M. V. Alekseev, and A. I. Denikin began to organize the Volunteer Army in Novorcherkassk. In December in Novocherkassk a governing center for the counterrevolution was created, the so-called triumvirate of Alekseev, Kornilov, and Kaledin. Imposing martial law, Kaledin moved in late November to occupy proletarian centers and eliminate the soviets. On Dec. 2 (15), after a seven-day battle, the insurgents occupied Rostov.

The governments of the United States, Great Britain, and France, seeing the Kaledin Revolt as the major national force of counterrevolution, expressed their readiness to offer financial aid and sent their representatives to Novocherkassk. "The civil war which was started by the Cadet-Kaledin counterrevolutionary revolt against the Soviet authorities, against the workers' and peasants' government, has finally brought the class struggle to a head and has destroyed every chance of settling in a formally democratic way the very acute problems with which history has confronted the peoples of Russia" (V. I. Lenin, *Poln. sobr. soch.,* 5th ed., vol. 35, p. 164). The Kaledin Revolt had developed into a serious threat to the existence of the Soviet republic. On November 25 (December 8) the Council of People's Commissars appealed to toiling cossacks to oppose the counterrevolution. Compulsory military service for cossacks was abolished and a number of privileges were granted to them. To carry on the struggle against Kaledin and the Central Rada, the Southern Revolutionary Front was established; it had its headquarters in Kharkov and was under the command of V. A. Antonov-Ovseenko. On Dec. 25, 1917 (Jan. 7, 1918), the Soviet troops began a coordinated offensive from Gorlovka (a detachment under R. F. Sivers), from Lugansk (under Iu. V. Sablin), from the direction of Millerovo (under G. K. Petrov), and from the *stanitsa* (large cossack village) of Tikhoretskaia (under A. I. Avtonomov). They were supported by uprisings among the workers and toiling Cossacks. A major role in liquidating the Kaledin Revolt was played by the Don Cossack Military Revolutionary Committee (chairman, F. G. Poltelkov; secretary, M. V. Krivoshlykov). The committee was founded at a congress of cossack veterans of World War I in the *stanitsa* of Kamen-

skaia held on Jan. 10–11, (23–24), 1918. On February 24 and 25, revolutionary troops liberated Rostov and Novocherkassk. The remnants of the counterrevolutionary cossacks, headed by Ataman P. Kh. Popov, fled into the Sal'sk steppes, and the Volunteer Army under General Kornilov retreated into the Kuban' region. In the Don region the Don Soviet Republic was formed as part of the RSFSR. Lenin regarded the annihilation of the Kaledin Revolt as the first victory over counterrevolution in the Civil War (*ibid.,* vol. 45, p. 168).

REFERENCES
Lenin, V. I. *Poln. sobr. soch.,* 5th ed., vol. 35.
Antonov-Ovseenko, V. A. *Zapiski o grazhdanskoi voine,* vol. 1. Moscow, 1924.
Oktiabr'skaia revoliutsiia na Donu: Sb. st. Rostov-on-Don, 1957.
Berz, L. I., and K. A. Khmelevskii. *Geroicheskie gody: Oktiabr'skaia revoliutsiia i grazhdanskaia voina na Donu.* Rostov-on-Don, 1964.
Polikarpov, V. D. "Kaledinshchina i ee likvidatsiia." *Voenno-istoricheskii zhurnal,* 1968, no. 3. V. D. POLIKARPOV [11–576–2]

KALEIDOSCOPE, a tube containing three longitudinally arranged reflecting plates that are mounted at an angle of 60° to one another. At one end, the tube is closed by a piece of frosted glass on which are scattered fragments of multicolored glass that are separated from the remaining tube space by a piece of clear glass; at the other end there is a cap with a round viewing hole. Upon rotation of the tube, which is held horizontally, the fragments are scattered around, forming colored patterns in the triangular central portion of the field of view bordered by the three mirrors. The reflections of the patterns in the mirror plates create a colored, triradially symmetrical design, which is repeated three more times along the edges of the field of view. The kaleidoscope was invented in 1817 by the English physicist D. Brewster; it subsequently became a child's toy.

The word "kaleidoscope" is frequently used in a figurative sense to emphasize a rapid change of events, phenomena, or persons. [11–580–2]

KALESNIK, STANISLAV VIKENT'EVICH. Born Jan. 10 (23), 1901, in St. Petersburg. Soviet glaciologist and physical geographer; academician of the Academy of Sciences of the USSR (1968; corresponding member 1953). Member of the CPSU since 1943.

Kalesnik graduated from Leningrad University in 1929. In 1950 he became head of the department of physical geography there. In 1955 he became director of the Institute of Limnology of the Academy of Sciences of the USSR. His primary works deal with theoretical questions of *Erdkunde,* landscape studies, and glaciology, as well as the geomorphology of the central Tien-Shan and the Dzungarian Alatau. He introduced new concepts and terms in glaciology and physical geography such as "hionosphere," "energy of glaciation," and "geographic structure." Since 1964 he has been president of the Geographic Society of the USSR. From 1968 to 1972 he was vice-president of the International Geographical Union. He has received honorary doctorate degrees from the University of Kraków and the University of Finland (Turku). He has been awarded two Orders of Lenin, three other orders, and medals. Glaciers in the Zailiiskii and Dzungarian Alatau and in the Polar Urals have been named for him.

WORKS
Gornye lednikovye raiony SSSR. Leningrad-Moscow, 1937.
Obshchaia gliatsiologiia. Leningrad, 1939.
Osnovy obshchego zemlevedeniia, 2nd ed. Moscow, 1955.
Kratkii kurs obshchego zemlevedeniia. Moscow, 1957.
"O klassifikatsii geograficheskikh nauk." In the collection *XIX Mezhdunarodnyi geograficheskii kongress v Stokgol'me.* Moscow, 1961.
Ocherki gliatsiologii. Moscow, 1963.
Obshchie geograficheskie zakonomernosti Zemli. Moscow, 1970.
[11–588–2]

KALEVALA, an urban-type settlement and administrative center of Kalevala Raion, Karelian ASSR.

Kalevala is situated on the left bank of Lake Srednee Kuito,

182 km west of the Kem' railroad station, with which it is linked by highway. Lumber is the major industry. [11–575–1]

KALEVALA, Karelian-Finnish national epic composed of epic songs, wedding songs, and incantations. It was compiled into a single narrative by the Finnish scholar E. Lönnrot chiefly from Karelian, Ingrian, and Finnish runes recorded from Arhippa Perttunen and other rune singers of the first half of the 19th century. The first collection, consisting of 32 runes, was published in 1835; it was followed in 1849 by a second collection of 50 runes.

The rune stories that Lönnrot used in the *Kalevala* dated as far back as the period of tribal society, and the Karelian people's epic later developed out of the old epic belonging to the Finnish Baltic tribes. Motifs of working songs and realistic descriptions of the people's everyday life and customs appeared along with fantastic and heroic themes. Enthusiasm for creative work is described with the utmost vividness in the runes. In the ideological and artistic sense the runes of the *Kalevala* are in no way inferior to the most elaborate epics of other peoples. The 1849 text of the *Kalevala* has been translated into Russian, English, German, French, Swedish, Japanese, and other languages.

REFERENCES
Kalevala: Karelo-finskii epos. [Introductory article by O. V. Kuusinen.] Moscow, 1949.
Karel'skie epicheskie pesni. [Preface, preparation of text, and commentary by V. Ia. Evseev.] Moscow-Leningrad, 1950.
Evseev, V. Ia. *Istoricheskie osnovy karelo-finskogo eposa,* books 1–2. Moscow-Leningrad, 1957–60.
Krohn, K. *Kalevalan runojen historia.* Helsinki, 1903–10.
Krohn, K. *Kalevalan kysymyksia.* Helsinki, 1918.
Setälä, E. N. *Sammon arvoitus.* Helsinki, 1932.
Kalevalan runoutta. . . . Petroskoi, 1949.
Haavio, M. *Väinämöinen.* Porvoo, 1950.
Kaukonen, V. *Vanhan Kalevalan kokoonpano,* vols. 1–2. Helsinki, 1939–45.
Kaukonen, V. *Elias Lönnrotin Kalevalan toinen painos.* Helsinki, 1956.
Kirjoittamaton kirjallisuus. Helsinki, 1963.
Ruoppila, V. *Kalevala ja kansankieli.* Helsinki, 1967.
Kalevalaseuran vuosikirja. . . . Porvoo-Helsinki, 1970.
V. IA. EVSEEV [11–575–2]

KALEVIPOEG, an Estonian national epic. From ancient times, legends about the warrior Kalevipoeg were widespread among the Estonians. F. R. Fel'man first proposed that they be collected, and F. R. Kreitsval'd compiled them. On the basis of the popular legends, he composed an entire epic, with a developed plot line and a verse meter like that of the Estonian folk song. The epic was published between 1857 and 1861 (2nd ed., 1862), along with its German translation. The *Kalevipoeg* tells of the deeds of the popular hero Kalevipoeg, leader of the ancient Estonians, and his war against the enemy forces threatening his people. The last episode deals with the invasion of the Crusaders in the early 13th century. Kalevipoeg's fate reflects through legendary and poetic motifs the historical fate of the Estonian people. The epic has played an important role in the formation of Estonian national literature and in the struggle for its recognition.

TEXTS
Kalevipoeg. Dorpat, 1857–61.
Kalevipoeg, vols. 1–2. Tallinn, 1961–63. (Scholarly edition.)
Kalevipoeg. Moscow, 1956; Tallinn, 1961.
REFERENCES
Annist, A. *"Kalevipoja" saamislugu.* Tartu, 1936.
Muistendid Kalevipojast. Tallinn, 1959.
"Kalevipoja" küsimusi, vols. 1–2. Tartu, 1957–63. [11–575–3]

KALF, WILLEM. Christened Nov. 3, 1619, in Rotterdam; died July 31, 1693, in Amsterdam. Dutch painter.

Kalf worked in France from about 1640 to 1645 and in Amsterdam after 1653. He created paintings that were modest in size and motif, but full of mood, depicting poor kitchens and backyards (for example, *The Yard of a Peasant House,* the Hermitage, Leningrad), as well as spectacular still lifes with expensive utensils and southern fruits (for example, *Breakfast,* Rijks-

museum, Amsterdam). Kalf's brilliant virtuosity as a still-life painter was revealed in the classic fineness of the composition, a subtle feeling for the uniqueness of each object, the refinement and richness of chiaroscuro and color nuances, and the skillful juxtaposition of objects differing in color and texture.

REFERENCE
Gelder, H. E. van, W. C. Heda, and A. van Beyeren. *W. Kalf.* Amsterdam [1941]. [11–681–3]

KAL'GIN, ANATOLII NIKOLAEVICH. Born Apr. 20 (May 2), 1875, in Vladikavkaz (present-day Ordzhonikidze); died Mar. 27, 1943, in Tbilisi. Soviet architect.

Kal'gin graduated from the Institute of Civil Engineering in St. Petersburg in 1900. From 1907 he lived in Georgia. He taught at the Tbilisi Academy of Arts from 1922 to 1930. A combining of modern basic structural elements with classical and traditional Georgian forms and decorative motifs is characteristic of his buildings. He created the building of the Georgian Land Bank of the Nobility (present-day Karl Marx Library of the Georgian SSR) in Tbilisi (1912–16) and the V. I. Lenin Zemo-Avchaly Hydroelectric Power Plant (1927, with K. A. Leont'ev and M. S. Machavariani). [11–686–1]

KALGOORLIE, a city in the state of Western Australia, Commonwealth of Australia. Population, 21,000 (1971; including the city of Boulder).

Kalgoorlie is a railway junction. Gold is mined there, and there are deposits of nickel ores to the south (Kambalda).
[11–573–5]

KALI, one of the names for the great goddess (Mahadeva) revered in Hinduism, the embodiment of the creative and destructive forces of nature, wife of the god Siva and his female hypostasis. Kali is honored both in the form of a goddess benevolent to people and in a terrible, frightening form. The cult of Kali is especially widespread in eastern India. [11–589–2]

KAL'IA, an urban-type settlement in Sverdlovsk Oblast, RSFSR, 19 km north of the Boksity railway station. Population, 11,000 (1970). Bauxite is mined here. [11–706–2]

KALIAEV, IVAN PLATONOVICH. Born June 24 (July 6), 1877, in Warsaw; died May 10 (23), 1905. Russian revolutionary, member of the Socialist Revolutionary Party.

Kaliaev was a student at the universities of Moscow and St. Petersburg from 1897 to 1899. He joined the St. Petersburg League of Struggle for the Liberation of the Working Class in 1898. Kaliaev became a member of the Socialist Revolutionary Party in 1903, joining its fighting organization in Geneva. In 1904 he took part in the attempted assassination of the minister of internal affairs, V. K. Plehve, in St. Petersburg. Kaliaev assassinated the governor-general of Moscow, Grand Duke Sergei Aleksandrovich, with a bomb in Moscow on Feb. 4, 1905. At his trial on Apr. 5, 1905, Kaliaev made a speech denouncing the tsarist government. He was executed at Shlissel'burg Fortress.
[11–706–6]

KALIAEV, SANDZHI KALIAEVICH. Born Jan. 2, 1905, in the village of Tsagan-Nur, in present-day Priozernyi Raion. Soviet Kalmyk writer; People's Poet of Kalmykiia (1965). Member of the CPSU since 1928.

Kaliaev is one of the founders of Soviet Kalmyk literature. His first work was published in 1924. He is the author of several collections of poetry, a cycle of poems about V. I. Lenin entitled *Only by the Precepts of Il'ich* (separate edition, 1969), and the narrative poems *Brigadier* (1935) and *Tamara* (1963), the last about a young partisan named Tamara Khakhlynova. Kaliaev is also an expert on Kalmyk folklore. He is a literary critic and a translator of the plays of Molière.

WORKS
In Russian translation:
S toboiu, Rossiia: Stikhi i poemy. Elista, 1959.
Pod neob"iatnym nebom: Poemy. Moscow, 1961.

Kogda est' liubov': Poemy. Elista, 1966.

REFERENCE

Matsakov, I. M. *Kalmytskaia sovetskaia khudozhestvennaia literatura* (20-e–30-e gg.). Elista, 1967. [11–706–7]

KALIAKRA, a cape on the coast of the Black Sea in northeastern Bulgaria near which, on July 31 (Aug. 11), 1791, occurred the naval battle that ended the Russo-Turkish War of 1787–91.

The Russian squadron (16 battleships, two frigates, and 19 auxiliary vessels), commanded by Rear Admiral F. F. Ushakov, discovered the Turkish fleet (18 battleships, 17 frigates, and 43 auxiliary vessels) lying under the protection of shore batteries near Cape Kaliakra. Using a bold tactical maneuver (breaking through between the shore and the enemy fleet), Ushakov disrupted the enemy's battle formation, cut him off from shore, and opened up with his own well-aimed guns. Kapudan Pasha Husayn, the Turkish commander, and Sayyid Ali Pasha, the commander of the Turkish advance guard, were unable to reorganize and counterattack. Having suffered serious damage, the Turkish ships retreated. The victory at Kaliakra led to the conclusion of the Jassy Peace Treaty of 1791. [11–589–5]

KALIAN, the name of a mosque and minaret in Bukhara, an outstanding masterpiece of Middle Asian architecture. Together with the Mir-Arab Madrasa (1536) the Kalian forms the central ensemble of the city—the Poi Kalian. The round minaret (1127) is covered with bands of ornamental brickwork and inscriptions. The mosque, part of which was built in the 15th century and part in 1514 on the site of a 12th-century mosque, is majestic in its dimensions (130 by 80 m); its court has four *iwans* and is surrounded by galleries with cupolas.

REFERENCE

Pugachenkova, G. A. *Samarkand, Bukhara,* 2nd ed. [Moscow, 1968.] [11–707–3]

KALIAZIN, a city and administrative center of Kaliazin Raion, Kalinin Oblast, RSFSR.

Kaliazin has a dock on the right bank of the Volga River and a railroad station on the Moscow-Sonkovo-Leningrad line. There is also a 47-km branch line from Kaliazin to Uglich. Kaliazin arose in the 12th century as a *sloboda* (tax-exempt settlement); its importance increased with the founding in the 15th century of the Kaliazin-Troitskii (Makar'evskii) Monastery on the opposite bank. The *sloboda* was declared the district city of Kaliazin in 1775.

There are felt-footwear, clothing, and shoe factories in Kaliazin, as well as a vegetable-dehydrating plant and a flax-processing plant. There is also a machine-building technicum. A museum of local lore contains architectural, ceramic, and sculptural fragments and murals from the Kaliazin-Troitskii monastery and applied art from the 18th and 19th centuries. Part of the old city was flooded with the construction of the Uglich Hydroelectric Power Plant; the monastery (a group of buildings from the 16th and 17th centuries) and certain other old structures are now in the reservoir zone. Buildings that were preserved include the bell tower of the Nikola Cathedral (1800), the group of buildings of the Voznesenskii Church, and houses dating from the 18th and 19th centuries. [11–707–1]

KALIAZIN PETITION, a classic of Russian satirical literature of the 17th century. The *Kaliazin Petition* was written in the form of a lively, graphic parody of a petition, with rhymed proverbs and sayings. It exposed the way of life of the monks of Kaliazin Monastery, located near the city of Kaliazin in present-day Kalinin Oblast.

REFERENCE

Russkaia demokraticheskaia satira XVII v. (Preparation of the texts, articles, and commentary by V. P. Adrianova-Peretts.) Moscow-Leningrad, 1954. [11–707–2]

KALIBEK, a salt lake without an outlet in Kokchetav Oblast, Kazakh SSR, in the Ishim Steppe, 100 km northeast of the city of Kokchetav. It has an area of approximately 110 sq km, a length of approximately 17 km, and a width of 7 km. The lake is fed primarily by snow. Its shores are low and gently sloping. [11–590–1]

KALIDASA. Dates of birth and death unknown. Ancient Indian poet and playwright of approximately the fifth century; Indian tradition sets Kalidasa's life in the first century B.C.

Folk legends depict Kalidasa as a shepherd who, on the strength of his talent, rose to the position of court poet. His works were closely linked with the previous development of the folklore epic and literature, but nature and the life of the people were his main source of inspiration. In the poem *Raghu-vamsha* (Dynasty of Raghu) and the chronicle of the legendary dynasty glorified in the *Ramayana,* Kalidasa paints a picture of the lives of many of the country's peoples and condemns a ruler who disregarded the interests of his subjects. The epic poem *Kumara-sambhava* (Birth of Kumara, the War God) and the lyric poem *Ritu-samhara* (Cycle of the Seasons) celebrate the triumph of simple human feelings and the all-conquering force of love.

Kalidasa's drama is evidence of the high development of ancient Indian theatrical art; it reveals a joyous world of harmony and reason, negating the boundary between the all-powerful deity and supposedly powerless man. Based on themes from the Vedas and the *Mahabharata,* Kalidasa's dramas commented on contemporary events: the scene with the fishermen and the guards in *Abhijnana-shakuntala* (Shakuntala Recognized by a Ring Token), the judgment of Agnimitra in the satirical ending of the drama *Malavikagnimitra* (Malavika and Agnimitra), and the new, completely earthly interpretation of the theme of the love of King Puruvaras for a celestial girl in *Vikramorvashiya* (Urvashi Won by Valor). Kalidasa's dramas, which affirm the value of the human personality, have been translated into many Eastern languages and almost all the European ones. They are still performed all over the world.

WORKS

In Russian translation:

"Stseny iz Sakontaly, indiiskoi dramy." (Translated and with a foreword by N. M. Karamzin.) *Moskovskii zhurnal,* 1792, part 6, books 2–3.
Sanskritskie poemy. Vologda, 1890.
Dramy. Translated by K. Bal'mont, introduction by S. F. Ol'denburg. Moscow, 1916.
"Potomki Ragkhu." *Leningrad,* 1940, nos. 15–16.
Sakuntala. Moscow, 1955.
Izbrannoe. Moscow, 1956.

REFERENCES

Kal'ianov, V. I., and V. G. Erman. *Kalidasa: Ocherk tvorchestva.* Moscow, 1958.
Pyzhova, O. V. "Ob esteticheskom ideale Kalidasy." In the collection *Iz istorii esteticheskoi mysli drevnosti i srednevekov'ia.* Moscow, 1961.
Serebriakov, I. D. *Ocherki drevneindiiskoi literatury.* Moscow, 1971.
Ivanova, N. M. *Kalidasa: Bibliogr. ukazatel'.* Moscow, 1957.
Upadhuaya Bhagwat Saram. *India in Kalidasa.* Foreword by E. Thomas. Allahabad, 1947.
Ruben, W. *Kalidasa: Die menschliche Bedeutung seiner Werke.* Berlin, 1956.

I. D. SEREBRIAKOV and V. G. ERMAN [11–595–2]

KALILA AND DIMNA, a didactic literary work in Arabic and Persian. *Kalila and Dimna* goes back to the Indian *Panchatantra,* which was translated into Pahlavi in the sixth century and called *Kalila and Dimna* (after the two jackals that appear in the first chapter).

An Arabic version was produced in the eighth century by the Persian writer ibn al-Muqaffa; subsequently, it was often put into verse. Persian versifications include a tenth-century version by Rudaki (of which only fragments remain), a version by Nasrallah Abu al-Maali in 1144, and one by Hoseyn Vaiz Kashifi in the 16th century, *The Lights of Canopus.*

In 1081, Simeon the son of Seph translated the Syriac version of *Kalila and Dimna* into Greek under the title *Stephanites kai Ichnelates* (The Crowned and the Tracker, an erroneous reading of the Arabic names Kalila and Dimna); subsequently, an Old Church Slavonic version was made from the Greek version. In the 13th century the Arabic version was translated into Spanish and Hebrew. Other translations followed: Latin (14th century), German (1470), and later French, English, and (in 1762) Russian. There are also translations into Turkish, Uzbek, Tatar, Malayan, and other Eastern languages.

Stories from *Kalila and Dimna* have repeatedly been used in other literary works.

REFERENCES
Kniga Kalilah i Dimnah. Moscow, 1889. (Translated from Arabic by M. O. Attai and M. V. Riabinina.)
Kalila i Dimna. Moscow, 1957. (Translated from Arabic by I. Iu. Krachkovskii and I. P. Kuz'min, with an introduction and commentary by I. Iu. Krachkovskii.) M. N. OSMANOV [11–603–5]

KALIM (Turkic), bride money paid originally to the kin group of a bride and later to her parents or relatives; payment for the bride by work (in lieu of money) was another form of *kalim*. The custom of paying *kalim* arose during the decay of the maternal kinship system and the replacement of matrilocal marriage by patrilocal marriage. *Kalim* was compensation paid to the bride's kin group for the loss of a female worker and of the property she took with her to her husband's kin group. The practice was common among many tribes and peoples of the world, and even today vestiges of the *kalim* are preserved among a number of peoples in the Orient. In class society a woman actually became the property of the husband upon marriage and payment of the *kalim*. At the same time, the large size of the *kalim* made it difficult for poor males to enter into marriage. In Russia, *kalim* was paid in the past among several peoples of Middle Asia, Siberia, and the Caucasus.

In the USSR, *kalim* is regarded as a survival of the past that represents a danger to society. In the criminal codes of the RSFSR, Armenian SSR, Kirghiz SSR, Tadzhik SSR, and Turkmen SSR, the payment of *kalim* is specified as a crime that infringes upon the right of a woman to freely decide the question of marriage. [11–682–2]

KALIMA (until 1968, Albertville), a city in the eastern part of the Republic of Zaïre, in Shaba Province. Population, 30,000 (1960). A trade and transportation center, it is a port on the western bank of Lake Tanganyika. It also has a railroad station. Kalima has enterprises of the light, cement, food, and pharmaceutical industries and a shipyard. There is fishing.

[11–604–1]

KALIMANTAN (Borneo), an island in the Malay Archipelago; the largest of the Greater Sunda Islands. Area, 734,000 sq km (with offshore islands, 746,500 sq km); length (from southwest to northeast), about 1,100 km. It is surrounded by the South China, Sulu, Celebes, and Java seas and the Makassar and Karimata straits. Most of Kalimantan (about 540,000 sq km), is part of Indonesia. In the northern part of the island are the states of Sarawak and Sabah, which are part of Malaysia, and the British colony of Brunei.

Natural features. The coastal areas of Kalimantan are mostly low-lying, swampy, and weakly indented, with few good harbors. The sea is shallow along the western coast of the island; there is a barrier of coral reefs in places along the eastern coast. In the northwestern part of the island is the area of the ancient pre-Mesozoic Sunda platform, and in the southern and eastern parts of the island are regions of Mesozoic and alpine plicate formations. The central part of Kalimantan is composed of block mountains with elevations of 2,000–3,000 m that radiate from the center to the outlying sections of the island. The highest point on Kalimantan is Mount Kinabalu (4,101 m), in the northern part of the island. The mountains are composed mainly of granites, gneisses, and crystalline schists. Smoothed summits and steep slopes predominate. The mountains are surrounded by a zone of hilly plains that give way to flat marshy lowlands. The mineral resources of Kalimantan include petroleum and coal, as well as ores of iron, manganese, chrome, molybdenum, and copper.

Kalimantan has an equatorial climate. The yearly average air temperature in the plains is 25°–27°C. The total annual precipitation, which is evenly distributed over the year, is 2,000–3,500 mm (up to 5,000 mm in the mountains). There is a dry season of one to three months on the eastern coast. The river network is dense, and the rivers are deep throughout the year. The Kapuas, Barito, and Mahakam rivers are navigable for distances of several hundred kilometers from their mouths. There are frequent changes of the riverbeds on the plain, and the banks of the rivers become swampy. There are sandbanks and sandbars in the mouths of the rivers.

Strongly lixiviated and podzolized lateritic soils on a thick crust of weathering are predominant. More than three-quarters of Kalimantan is covered with forests. There is mangrove vegetation along the coasts. In the plains and the foothills of the mountains there are high-trunk, multilayered humid tropical forests of palm, bamboo, screw pine, and multitrunk rubber trees. There are very luxuriant mountain forests consisting of Dipterocarpaceae, sandalwood, rubber trees, and rasamala at elevations of up to 1,500 m. The trees are often intertwined with vines and epiphytes, including abundant mosses. Evergreen oak, laurel, rhododendron, and coniferous trees (Bornean pine) are found at higher elevations. There are shrubs and meadows of various grasses on the summits of the mountains. Bushes and thickets of alang-alang and wild sugarcane predominate in the southeast as a result of the cutting of other vegetation.

The fauna of Kalimantan is extraordinarily rich and varied and includes elephants, large apes (orangutans, gibbons, and proboscis monkeys), slow loris (suborder Lemuroidea), Dermoptera (flying lemur), Chiroptera (fruit-eating flying foxes, insect-eating bats), bears, two-horned rhinoceros, and banteng. There are about 600 species of birds, including the hornbill, argus pheasant, and parrot. The insect and arthropod fauna is extraordinarily rich.

Less than 2 percent of Kalimantan is under cultivation, mainly in the valleys of the Barito and Kapuas rivers and on the northern coast. The principal items of cultivation are rice, rubber plants, and coconut palms. Copra production and fishing are also important economic activities. The population in 1969 was approximately 6.6 million, including 5 million on the Indonesian part of the island. The largest cities are Bandjermasin and Pontianak in Indonesia and Kuching in Malaysia. L. I. KURAKOVA

Historical survey. Over a period of centuries the native population of Kalimantan—the numerous Ngadju, Ot-Danom, and Klemantan tribes, which are frequently united under the name "Dayaks"—was driven back into the remote regions of the island and partially assimilated by newcomers (Malays, Javanese, and Buginese). Beginning in the 13th century, many feudal principalities that had arisen in the coastal regions of Kalimantan became dependent on various Javanese rulers. The largest principalities on Kalimantan in the 16th century were Bandjermasin and Kutei in the southeast; Sambas, Mampawa, Landak, and Sukadana in the west; and Brunei in the north.

In the 17th century the European East India companies made the first attempts to consolidate their hold on Kalimantan. However, it was not until the end of the 18th century that the Dutch East India Company succeeded in concluding an inequitable treaty with the ruler of Pontianak and placing the sultan of Bandjermasin in a position of dependence. Sarawak fell into the hands of Europeans in the early 1840's. The English adventurer James Brooke, who arrived in northern Kalimantan in 1839, was awarded the administration of Sarawak by the sultan of Brunei for his assistance in the suppression of an uprising of the local populace. Brooke soon became the independent rajah of Sarawak. Great Britain imposed an inequitable treaty upon Brunei in 1847. The Dutch colonizers began military operations in the 1850's for the subjugation of the southeastern and western regions of Kalimantan. The Dutch suppressed a strong uprising in Bandjermasin in the 1850's and 1860's and established their direct rule there. By the end of the first decade of the 20th century, the Dutch succeeded in forcing the status of "self-governing" principalities upon the remaining sultanates of southeastern and western Kalimantan, which placed them under the strict control of the Dutch colonial administration. The English expanded their possessions in northern Kalimantan, with the assistance of the British North Borneo Company, which was founded in 1881. In 1888, Great Britain established a protectorate on the territory of present-day Sabah, Brunei, and Sarawak. The borders between English and Dutch possessions on Kalimantan were defined in 1891.

Kalimantan was occupied by Japan in December 1941. After Japan's surrender in 1945, the Dutch colonizers, with the support of their protégé, Sultan Abdul Hamid of Pontianak, created a puppet "state" on Kalimantan. After the Round Table Conference of 1949, the formerly Dutch part of Kalimantan became one of the United States of Indonesia and, in 1950, part of the Republic of Indonesia. In northern Kalimantan, Great Britain redeemed the "rights" to Sarawak from the Brooke dynasty in 1946. Sarawak then became a crown colony. Sabah was also made a crown colony in 1946. Sabah and Sarawak were included as states in the Malaysian Federation in 1963. During the preparation for the creation of Malaysia, an uprising broke out in Brunei in 1962 under the slogan of the independent unification of the territory of northern Kalimantan. The uprising was brutally suppressed.

REFERENCES
Guber, A. A. *Indoneziia.* Moscow-Leningrad, 1932.
Republik Indonesia: Propinsi Kalimantan. [No place or date.]
N. A. SIMONIIA [11–604–3]

KALINČIAK, JAN. Born Aug. 10, 1822, in Horné Zaturče, a suburb of Martin; died June 16, 1871, in Martin. Slovak writer. Son of a priest.

Kalinčiak was a teacher. He began his writing career as a poet but is known chiefly as an outstanding master of Slovak romantic prose. He was associated with the romantic school of L. Štúr. In historical short stories and novellas (*Milko's Grave,* 1845–46) and the novel *The Prince of Liptov* (1852), Kalinčiak defended the ideas of the national liberation struggle. He did not always remain within the confines of romanticism. In the novella *The Election* (1860) he showed the everyday life and morals of the petty gentry in a realistic and truthful manner; a Slovak film of the same title was made from the novella in 1957.

WORKS
Spisy, vols. 1–4. Martin, 1951–52.
In Russian translation:
"Vybory." In *Slovatskie povesti i rasskazy.* Moscow, 1953.

REFERENCES
Bogdanova, I. A. "Ian Kalinchak." *Istoriia slovatskoi literatury.* Moscow, 1970.
Dějiny slovenskej literatúry. Bratislava, 1960. Pages 260–68.
[11–628–1]

KALINGA, in antiquity, a kingdom in eastern India (on the territory of modern-day Orissa). Kalinga was conquered by Asoka in approximately 260 B.C. Circa 220 B.C. it became independent once again. It reached its height of development during the rule of Kharavela (second or first century B.C.), who conducted a number of successful military campaigns and subdued even Magadha. Under Kharavela's successors, Kalinga lost its former power. In the seventh century, according to Hsuan Tsang, the territory of Kalinga became deserted and was overgrown by jungles. [11–607–2]

KALININ, ANATOLII VENIAMINOVICH. Born Aug. 9 (22), 1916, in the *stanitsa* (cossack village) of Kamenskaia (the present-day city of Kamensk-Shakhtinskii). Soviet Russian writer. Member of the CPSU since 1946.

Kalinin's novel *The Burial Mounds* was published in 1941. During the Great Patriotic War of 1941–45 he served as a correspondent at the front for *Komsomol'skaia pravda;* his novellas *In the South* (1944) and *Comrades* (1945) and his novel *The Red Banner* (1951), which grew out of the shorter works, deal with the heroism of the Soviet forces. After the war Kalinin settled on the Don, and life on the kolkhoz provided him with material for his books of essays *The Undying Roots* (1947), *At the Mean* (1954), *Moonlit Nights* (1955) and *Pomegranate Juice* (1968). His novel *Forbidden Zone* (book 1, 1962) concerns the building of the Volga-Don Canal. Scenes of the war are brought to life in Kalinin's novella *Echo of the War* (1963) and in his novel *The Harsh Field* (1958). Kalinin is also the author of the novella *The Gypsy* (parts 1–3, 1960–70; film of the same name, 1967); the novel *Bells, Ring Out!* (1967), about the problems of upbringing

in a family; and a book of essays on M. A. Sholokhov entitled *Summer in Veshensk* (1964).

Kalinin writes in the Sholokhovian tradition, his works posing the important questions of modern life. A number of Kalinin's works have been translated into foreign languages. He has been awarded three orders and various medals.

WORKS
Surovoe pole: Povesti i rasskazy. Moscow, 1960.
REFERENCES
Zlobin, S. "O pomane A. Kalinina *Surovoe pole.*" *Novyi mir,* 1959, no. 7.
Dement'ev, A. "Po povodu stat'i Stepana Zlobina." *Novyi mir,* 1959, no. 7.
Kochetov, V. "Ne tak vse prosto." *Oktiabr',* 1963, no. 11.
Survillo, V. "K voprosu o nasledstvennosti." *Novyi mir,* 1964, no. 7.
Sinel'nikov, M. "'Golos krovi' i goloslovnost' kritiki." (In reference to Survillo's article "K voprosu o nasledstvennosti.") *Literaturnaia gazeta,* 1964, Sept. 24.
Russkie sovetskie pisateli-prozaiki: Bibliograficheskii ukazatel', vol. 2. Leningrad, 1964. B. D. CHELYSHEV [11–607–3]

KALININ, GENNADII PAVLOVICH. Born Nov. 10 (23), 1916, in Baku. Soviet hydrologist. Corresponding member of the Academy of Sciences of the USSR (1970), professor (1954). Member of the CPSU since 1952.

Kalinin graduated from the Kharkov Hydrometeorological Institute in 1937. Between 1942 and 1961 he worked at the Central Forecasts Institute of the Central Hydrometeorological Services Administration of the USSR. In 1961 he went to work at the subdepartment of geography at Moscow State University, where he became head of the subdepartment of inland hydrology in 1963. The theory of the formation of river drainage developed by Kalinin has served as the basis for a number of methods of predicting and calculating this drainage; he generalized data on fluctuations of river drainage and refined methods for its calculation (genetic and probabilistic). He clarified the general rules of water exchange on the global level and elucidated the processes of formation of the world's resources of fresh water.

WORKS
Osnovy metodiki kratkosrochnykh prognozov vodnogo rezhima. Leningrad, 1952. [*Trudy Tsentr. in-ta prognozov,* issue 28 (55).]
Gidrologicheskie prognozy. Leningrad, 1960. (Coauthor.)
Problemy global'noi gidrologii. Leningrad, 1968. [11–608–1]

KALININ, KONSTANTIN ALEKSEEVICH. Born Dec. 17 (29), 1889, in Valuiki, in present-day Belgorod Oblast; died Apr. 21, 1940, in Voronezh. Soviet aviation designer. Became a member of the CPSU in 1927.

Kalinin graduated from the Odessa Military School in 1912, the Gatchina Military Aviation School in 1916, and the Kiev Polytechnic Institute in 1925. During the Civil War of 1918–20 he was a Red Army pilot. In 1926 he organized and headed an aviation design bureau in Kharkov. The K-4 and K-5 passenger aircraft, which served Soviet airlines in the 1930's, were built under his direction. In addition a number of experimental aircraft were constructed, including the seven-engine K-7 plane, one of the largest aircraft of the time. Typical of Kalinin's aircraft were the elliptical shape of the wing and the horizontal tail. Kalinin was one of the founders and first teachers of the Kharkov Aviation Institute. He was awarded the Order of the Red Banner of Labor. [11–608–2]

KALININ, MIKHAIL IVANOVICH. Born Nov. 7 (19), 1875, in the village of Verkhniaia Troitsa, in present-day Kashin Raion, Kalinin Oblast; died June 3, 1946, in Moscow. A prominent figure in the Communist Party and Soviet government. Hero of Socialist Labor (1944). Became a member of the Communist Party in 1898. The son of a peasant.

Kalinin graduated from the village school in 1889. In 1893 he began to work as an apprentice lathe operator at the Staryi Arsenal Munitions Works in St. Petersburg, and in 1896 he became a lathe operator at the Putilov Works. There he organized a Marxist study circle, which joined Lenin's League of Struggle for the Liberation of the Working Class. In July 1899,

Kalinin was arrested in the case involving the League of Struggle, and after ten months' imprisonment he was deported in April 1900 to Tbilisi, where he worked as a lathe operator in the Central Railroad Shop and joined the central group of the Tbilisi Social Democratic organization. He helped organize the strike of August 1900 and was arrested and imprisoned in the Metekhi Castle. In March 1901 he was deported to Revel (now Tallinn), where he was employed in the Vol'ta Works as a lathe operator and later in a railroad shop. In 1902 he organized a Marxist circle and an underground printing press and was an Iskra agent. In January 1903 he was arrested and confined in the Kresty Prison in St. Petersburg. In July 1903 he was once again deported to Revel, where he was arrested in early 1904 and deported to the town of Povenets in Olonets Province.

In 1905, Kalinin went illegally to St. Petersburg, where he carried out assignments from the Bolshevik center. Granted amnesty in October 1905, he came out into the open and functioned legally as the head of the Bolshevik organization at the Putilov Works; he was elected a member of the Narva raion committee of the RSDLP. He helped to organize the fighting *druzhiny* and was a member of the raion battle staff. In December 1905 he was one of the organizers of the strike by workers at the Putilov Works in solidarity with the insurrection of the Moscow workers. In 1906 he worked at a pipe factory and was elected to the St. Petersburg committee of the RSDLP. As a delegate to the Fourth Congress of the RSDLP in 1906, he supported the Leninist line. From 1908 to 1910 he worked in Moscow as a fitter at the Lubianka power plant and the Miusy streetcar station, carrying on active party work. In September 1910 he was arrested and deported in November to his home village. In 1911 and 1912, while working as a patternmaker at a cannon foundry in St. Petersburg, he was a member of the St. Petersburg committee of the RSDLP and led the party organization in the Vyborg raion.

At the Sixth (Prague) Conference of the RSDLP in 1912, Kalinin was elected a candidate member of the Central Committee of the RSDLP and placed on the Russian Bureau of the Central Committee. He participated in the founding of the newspaper *Pravda* and assisted the work of the Bolshevik faction in the Fourth State Duma. In the summer of 1912 he led a strike by the workers in the cannon foundry. From 1913 to 1915 he worked at the Aivaz plant, continuing his party activities. In January 1916 he was arrested in the case involving the Petrograd Committee of the RSDLP, and after a year of imprisonment he was sentenced to exile in Eastern Siberia but managed to go into hiding and continue his party work illegally in Petrograd. He took an active part in the February Revolution of 1917 and was a member of the first legal Petrograd Committee of the Bolsheviks and the representative of this committee on the bureau of the Central Committee of the RSDLP (Bolshevik). He was a member of the editorial staff of *Pravda*. In September 1917 he was elected councillor (*glasnyi*) of the Petrograd municipal duma and chairman of the raion board of the Lesnovskii Raion, in whose offices was held the Oct. 16, 1917, session of the Central Committee of the RSDLP(B) that adopted the resolution for armed uprising.

After the victory of the October Revolution, Kalinin was elected to the Petrograd municipal duma, which chose him to be mayor (*gorodskoi golova*). In 1918 he worked as commissar of municipal services in Petrograd. In March 1919, at the Eighth Congress of the RCP (Bolshevik), he was elected to the party's Central Committee. After the death of Ia. M. Sverdlov he was elected chairman of the All-Russian Central Executive Committee. On Mar. 30, 1919, in recommending Kalinin for this post, V. I. Lenin said: "Here we have a comrade who has been engaged in party work for nearly 20 years. He is a peasant from Tver' Province, who has close connections with peasant farming. . . . Petrograd workers have witnessed his ability to approach wide sections of the working masses" (*Poln. sobr. soch.*, 5th ed., vol. 38, p. 224). During the Civil War of 1918–20, Kalinin carried on important agitation and propaganda work among the workers, peasants, and Red Army soldiers. He was in charge of the October Revolution propaganda train, which made 12 trips through the central regions of Russia, the Ukraine, the Northern Caucasus, Siberia, and virtually all the fronts of the Civil War.

In December 1922, after the formation of the USSR, Kalinin was elected chairman of the Central Executive Committee of the USSR. After the Fourteenth Congress of the ACP (Bolshevik) in 1925 he was placed on the Politburo of the party's Central Committee. From January 1938 to March 1946 he was chairman of the Presidium of the Supreme Soviet of the USSR and after that continued to be a member of the Presidium.

Kalinin had an enormous range of experience and knew the life of the people intimately. He was instrumental in strengthening the alliance of the workers and peasants and in building the Soviet state. The "all-Union peasant elder" was the term of endearment that the Soviet working masses had for him. Kalinin wrote many works on various questions of socialist construction, communist education, and literature and art, in all of which he propounded the ideas of Marxism-Leninism. His speeches and articles devoted special attention to the tasks of developing a socialist world view among the young and of training youth in the spirit of communist morality. In 1931 the city of Tver' was renamed in honor of Kalinin, and many raions and settlements also bear his name. His awards include two Orders of Lenin and two Orders of the Red Banner, as well as many medals. He is buried on Red Square. A memorial museum for Kalinin was opened in Moscow in 1946.

WORKS

Izbr. proizv., vols. 1–3. Moscow, 1960–62.
Voprosy sovetskogo stroitel'stva: Stat'i i rechi (1919–1946). Moscow, 1958.
O molodezhi, 2nd ed. Moscow, 1940.
O kommunisticheskom vospitanii i voinskom dolge: Sb. statei i rechei. Moscow, 1958.
O vospitanii i obuchenii: Izbr. stat'i i rechi. Moscow, 1957.
O nekotorykh voprosakh agitatsii i propagandy. Moscow, 1958. (A collection.)
O profsoiuzakh: 1919–1945. [Moscow] 1958.
Ob iskusstve i literature: Stat'i, rechi, besedy. Moscow, 1957.

REFERENCES

Lenin, V. I. "O kandidature M. I. Kalinina na post predsedatelia VTsIK: Rech' na XII zasedanii VTsIK 30 marta 1919 g." *Poln. sobr. soch.*, 5th ed., vol. 38.
Zemlianskii, D. S. *M. I. Kalinin kak propagandist i agitator.* Moscow, 1960.
Tolmachev, A. *Kalinin.* [Moscow] 1963.

B. A. GAVRILOV   [11–608–3]

KALININ (until 1931, Tver'), administrative center of Kalinin Oblast, RSFSR. River port on the Volga at its confluence with the Tvertsa River. Railroad station on the Moscow-Leningrad line, 167 km northwest of Moscow. Population, 367,000 (1972; in 1939, 216,000; in 1959, 261,000). Renamed in honor of M. I. Kalinin.

Tver' took shape in the 12th century from trade and handicrafts settlements on the Volga at the mouth of the Tvertsa River, from which the city derived its name. It is first mentioned in the Laurentian Chronicle for 1208–09. At first it belonged to Novgorod, but in 1209 it became part of the Vladimir-Suzdal' Principality. From 1246 to 1485 it was the capital of the Tver' Principality. In 1327 there was a major uprising against Mongol Tatar rule. In the 14th and 15th centuries it was an important economic and cultural center of northeastern Rus', with well-developed handicraft production and commercial ties with the Baltic region, the Caucasus, the Middle East, and Middle Asia. From 1466 to 1472 the Tver' merchant Afanasii Nikitin was the first European to travel to India. In 1485, under Grand Prince Ivan III, Tver' became part of the Muscovite State. In the 18th century it played an important role as a trading center on the upper Volga. In 1775 it became the capital of Tver' Province. The textile industry began to develop in Tver' in the mid-19th century.

The first Social Democratic study circle was founded in Tver' by A. G. Kugusheva in 1894. A Social Democratic group was formed in early 1901 and became the Tver' Committee of the RSDLP in 1902. In 1905 the workers of Tver' took part in the October All-Russian Strike, established a soviet of working people's deputies, and sent a contingent of armed workers to aid the Moscow workers during the December Armed Uprising. Soviet power was established in Tver' on Oct. 28 (Nov. 10), 1917. During the Great Patriotic War (1941–45) the city was occupied by the fascist German invaders from Oct. 17 to Dec. 16, 1941, and suffered great destruction; it was completely restored in the early postwar years. Kalinin was awarded the Order of the Red Banner of Labor in 1971.

A. N. ALEKSANDROV and E. I. VEREBRIUSOVA

Kalinin is a major industrial center, producing two-fifths of the industrial output of the oblast, primarily in light industry, the chemical industry, and machine building. The major enterprises in light industry and the chemical industry include combines producing cotton textiles, synthetic fibers, worsted fabrics, and synthetic leather. Machine building is represented by plants producing railroad cars (all-metal passenger cars), excavators, diesel switch engines, and electric equipment. Kalinin also has major printing plants (the Kalinin Printing Combine and the Kalinin Children's Literature Printing Combine), building-material plants, and enterprises of the food industry.

Intensive development of Kalinin began after the fire of 1763 (1763–67; architects P. R. Nikitin, M. F. Kazakov, and A. V. Kvasov). The plan was based on a triradial design with four squares along a central artery. On the octagonal main square (formerly Fountain Square, now Lenin Square) there is a group of classical buildings: the City Council building (1770–80), the House of the Nobility (1766–70), and a school (1786). Among the other monuments of classical architecture are the Excursion Palace of Catherine II (1763–67, architect M. F. Kazakov; additions made in 1809, architect K. I. Rossi), the Church of the Ascension (1813, architect V. P. L'vov), and the Assembly House of the Nobility (1841), with a hall of columns modeled on the one in Moscow. In the Soviet period the historic design of the city has been preserved, new public buildings and residential districts have been built on its outskirts, and considerable work has gone into the provision of green areas and public services and amenities.

Kalinin has monuments to Marx (concrete, 1918), V. I. Lenin (granite and forged bronze, 1959; sculptors B. P. Barkov and P. V. Kenig, architect I. D. Mel'chakov), Afanasii Nikitin (bronze and granite, 1955; sculptor S. M. Orlov, architect G. A. Zakharov), and I. A. Krylov (bronze and granite, 1959; sculptors S. D. Shaposhnikov and D. V. Gorlov), and the Victory Obelisk (cement and bronze, 1970; sculptors I. M. Rukavishnikov and A. N. Filippova, architects N. N. Milovidov and G. E. Saevich). The city has a university, a polytechnic institute, an agricultural institute (in the settlement of Sakharovo), and a medical institute. There are ten secondary specialized schools, including railroad-car manufacturing, industrial, textile, and chemical engineering technicums. The city has a drama theater, a young people's theater, and a puppet theater, as well as a philharmonic orchestra, a museum of local lore, a gallery, the L. Chaikina Museum of Komsomol Glory, and a museum of the everyday life of Tver'.

REFERENCES

Proshloe i nastoiashchee goroda Tveri. Tver', 1917.
Kalinin: Putevoditel'. Compiled by N. I. Mazurin. Moscow, 1968.
[11–610–1]

KALININ (until 1935, Porsy), an urban-type settlement and administrative center of Kalinin Raion, Tashauz Oblast, Turkmen SSR, located 41 km northwest of the city of Tashauz and 6 km from the Lavak railway station on the Chardzhou-Kungrad line. Population, 12,800 (1972). There is a ginnery and a people's amateur theater. [11–613–1]

KALININ, UNIVERSITY OF. The university was founded in 1971 on the basis of a pedagogical institute created in 1918. In 1972 the university comprised the departments of history, philology, Romance and Germanic philology, law, economics, mathematics, physics, and chemistry and biology. It has a division preparing people for entry into the university, an evening division, and a correspondence school. It also has a graduate school, 34 subdepartments, nearly 50 study laboratories, and a scientific research center. There were 6,000 students studying at the university in the 1972–73 academic year. [11–625–3]

KALININABAD, a city in the Tadzhik SSR on the left bank of the Vakhsh River, 14 km northeast of the city of Kurgan-Tiube and 114 km southeast of Dushanbe. Population, 10,000 (1972).

Kalininabad was established in 1956 in connection with the construction of the Head Hydroelectric Power Plant. It has plants producing nitrate fertilizer, concrete, and reinforced concrete. There is also a housing-construction combine.
[11–613–3]

KALININ CHILDREN'S LITERATURE PRINTING COMBINE, a large-scale specialized enterprise in the city of Kalinin that prints children's literature and school textbooks. The combine was built in 1960–65 and in 1971 put out 35.7 million school textbooks and 86 million children's books. [11–625–2]

KALININ COTTON TEXTILE COMBINE, one of the oldest and largest textile enterprises in the USSR manufacturing cotton and staple fabrics, located in the city of Kalinin.

The Kalinin Cotton Textile Combine is an association of two spinning factories, two weaving mills, and a finishing factory. It was formed from the companies of the Tver' Textile Manufacturers' Association, founded in 1858 by S. Morozov and others. The company workers took part in the Revolution of 1905–07, the October Revolution of 1917, and socialist construction. During the Great Patriotic War of 1941–45 the combine was almost totally destroyed by the fascist German invaders. After the liberation of the city (Dec. 16, 1941) the plant was restored and modernized.

The factories of the combine are equipped with high-output equipment, such as automatic looms. The Kalinin Cotton Textile Combine was awarded the Order of Lenin in 1966.

V. PIGASIN [11–625–4]

KALININ DRAMATIC THEATER, a theater in the city of Kalinin.

E. K. Leshkovskaia, K. A. Varlamov, A. I. Iuzhin, and the Adel'geim brothers were among the performers who made appearances with touring companies in Tver' (now Kalinin) before the October Socialist Revolution. The First Tver' Theater of the RSFSR presented a performance of *The Great Communard* on Mar. 27, 1921, on the stage of the former Public Assembly Hall. Among the plays staged in the theater were *The Chancellor and the Locksmith* by Lunacharskii (1922), *Liubov' Iarovaia* by Trenev (1927), and *Terror* by Afinogenov (1930). Contemporary Soviet plays occupy the chief place in the theater's repertoire, although the theater has also presented the plays of Shakespeare, Lope de Vega, and A. N. Ostrovskii.

After the theater was rebuilt in 1934, it opened with a performance of Vishnevskii's *Optimistic Tragedy.* The performance of Pogodin's *Man With a Gun* in 1939 was a major event. Later the theater staged Pogodin's *The Kremlin Chimes* (1942) and *Third Pathétique* (1960), also devoted to Lenin.

During the Great Patriotic War of 1941–45 the Kalinin Theater presented *Russian People* by Simonov, *The Front* by Korneichuk, *The Invasion* by Leonov, and *Officer of the Fleet* by Kron. The building was destroyed during the fascist occupation and a new building was constructed in 1951.

The Kalinin Theater works with local authors, among them Vetlugin, whose plays *Vasilisa* (1943) and *The Passing Years* (1956) it has staged. In the latter a dramatic portrait of M. I. Kalinin was created for the first time. Plays in the theater's repertoire during the 1950's and 1960's included *The Days of the First Storm* by Shcheglov, *Measure for Measure* by Shakespeare, *The Story of a Real Man,* based on Polevoi's novel (all in 1955), *Goodbye, Anna,* based on the novel *On the Home Front* by Polevoi (1960), *Colleagues,* based on the novella by Aksenov (1961), and *The Ward* by Aleshin (1963).

The theater has seen performances over the years by L. V. Orlova, P. A. Konstantinov, O. M. Kholina, I. P. Lobanov, N. V. Goncharova, L. B. Borisova, E. M. Savel'ev, F. A. Droesi, and V. V. Soshal'skaia. The head director of the theater between 1942 and 1967 (with interruptions) was Honored Art Worker G. A. Georgievskii. Honored Artists of the RSFSR A. F. Godlevskii, A. M. Vol'skaia, and V. S. Rostovtsev were among the theater's troupe in 1971. The head director of the theater since 1968 has been Honored Artist of the RSFSR A. A. Vokach.   A. V. STEPANOVA [11–624–2]

KALININ GLACIATION, the penultimate Anthropogenic glaciation of the Eastern European Plain, during which glaciers reached the region of the present-day city of Kalinin (according to the charts of A. I. Moskvitin). Some investigators believe that the Kalinin glaciation was not an independent event but a stage in the Moscow glaciation.   [11–625–6]

KALININGRAD (before July 4, 1946, Königsberg; renamed in honor of M. I. Kalinin), a city and administrative center of Kaliningrad Oblast, RSFSR, situated on both banks of the Pregolia River at the point where it flows into the Vistula Lagoon of the Baltic Sea. Kaliningrad is a major hub of transport and industry, with a port that is open year round and a deep-water channel linking it with the Baltic at the port of Baltiisk. Population, 315,000 (1972; 1959, 204,000).

The city was founded in 1255. For 700 years it was a base of German feudal aggression, and later imperialist aggression, against the peoples of Poland and Russia. During the first and second world wars (1914–18 and 1939–45) it was used by the German military machine as a springboard for offensives against neighboring states.

During the Great Patriotic War of the Soviet Union (1941–45), troops of the Third Byelorussian Front, under the command of A. M. Vasilevskii, took the city (on Apr. 6–10, 1945, as part of the East Prussian Campaign of 1945). By decision of the Potsdam Conference of 1945, Königsberg and its adjacent territory (approximately one-third of what was formerly East Prussia) went to the USSR.

More than 90 percent of the city was destroyed as a result of the fierce fighting during the attack. The transportation network of the city, its water-supply and sewage systems, and its power systems were among the facilities destroyed. Soviet men and women built a new socialist city in a short time, with highly developed industry, modern municipal services, and an extensive network of cultural and educational institutions.

Fishing, the paper and cellulose industry, machine building, and metalworking are important in the city's economy. The largest enterprises in the city include railroad-car construction and ship repair and plants producing construction machinery, road-building machinery, electric welding equipment, tower cranes, spare parts for motor vehicles, and commercial machinery. Other large enterprises are a plant producing equipment for paper and woodworking enterprises, plants producing reinforced-concrete units, two paper and cellulose combines, a coke-oven gas plant, a fish cannery combine, a packaging plant, and a meat-packing combine. The Iurii Dolgorukii whaling fleet and a fishing fleet are based in Kaliningrad.

Approximately one-third of the city's territory is occupied by parks, boulevards, gardens, and reservoirs. Since 1953 the reconstruction of the city has proceeded according to a master plan. A new master plan was introduced in 1967 by a collective under the leadership of M. R. Naumov and I. G. Loginova. At the center of the city is Pobeda Square, with a monument to V. I. Lenin (1958, bronze and granite; sculptor, V. B. Topuridze). On Gvardeiiskii Prospect there is a monument to the 1,200 guardsmen who fell in the attack on Königsberg (1945–46; sculptors, J. Mikenas and B. J. Pundzius; architects, S. S. Nanush'ian and I. D. Mel'chakov). A monument of bronze and granite to M. I. Kalinin was erected in 1959 (sculptor, B. V. Edunov; architect, A. V. Guliaev). Earlier monuments that were preserved in the city include that of F. Schiller (1910; sculptor, K. Kauer) and the grave of I. Kant.

Kaliningrad has a university, a technical institute of fishing and the fishing industry, a higher naval-engineering school, the Atlantic Scientific Research Institute of Fishing and Oceanography, and eight specialized secondary educational institutions. There is a museum of local lore, a drama theater, a puppet theater, a television station, a philharmonic orchestra, and a publishing house. There are seaside climatic health resorts near the city (Svetlogorsk, Otradnoe, Zelenogradsk, Pionerskii). Kaliningrad was awarded the Order of the Red Banner of Labor in 1971.   [11–613–4]

KALININGRAD, a city in Moscow Oblast, RSFSR, a railroad station (Podlipki) on the Mytishchi-Monino branch line, 22 km northeast of Moscow. Population, 110,000 (1972).

Kaliningrad originated as a settlement in 1928 and became a city in 1938. In 1960 it was merged with the town of Kostino. It is one of the most well designed cities of the Moscow area in the provision of public services and amenities, with an abundance of greenery along with multistory residential and public buildings built according to standardized designs. The city has a mechanical-engineering technicum and a museum in a house where Lenin stayed between Jan. 17 and Mar. 1, 1922, on a sovkhoz in the village of Kostino (both the sovkhoz and the village are now considered part of the city of Kaliningrad).

[11–615–1]

KALININGRAD, UNIVERSITY OF, a university founded in 1967 in Kaliningrad, Kaliningrad Oblast, RSFSR.

As of 1972, the University of Kaliningrad had departments of physics and mathematics, history and philology, economics and law, geography, and chemistry and biology. There are preparatory, evening, and extension divisions, as well as a graduate school. There are 27 subdepartments, over 30 laboratories, and botanical gardens. The research library contains 350,000 books and journals. There was a total of 4,300 students in 1972 and more than 250 instructors, including 21 doctors of science and professors and more than 100 candidates of science and docents. *Nauchnye Trudy* (Scholarly Works) has been published by the university since 1968.   N. V. PRIKLADOV [11–619–3]

KALININGRAD OBLAST, part of the RSFSR, formed on Apr. 7, 1946. Area, 15,100 sq km. Population, 750,000 (1972). Kaliningrad Oblast borders Poland on the south and the Baltic Sea and its bays (the Kurshskii and Vistula) on the west. The oblast has 13 administrative raions, 22 cities, and five urban-type settlements. The center of the oblast is the city of Kaliningrad. Kaliningrad Oblast was awarded the Order of Lenin on April 14, 1966.

Natural features. Kaliningrad Oblast occupies part of the southern shore of the Baltic Sea, including the westernmost point of the USSR (19°38'). Low-lying, only slightly hilly relief predominates. The Baltic Ridge, with a maximum elevation of 231 m, stretches along the southeast. There is a zone of sandy beaches along the coast. Some of the northern territory of the oblast lies below sea level (polders) and is protected by dikes against flooding. There are sand dunes on the Kurshskii and Baltic spits with elevations to 60 m. The traditional name for the seacoast is the "Amber Coast," because of the presence there of the world's largest amber deposits, which provide the raw materials for an amber combine. There are also deposits of rock salt, brown coal, clay, building sand, and gravel. Prospecting for oil was undertaken in the eighth five-year plan. There are 156 deposits of industrial peat.

The climate is transitional between maritime and moderate continental, with mild winters and moderately warm summers. The average January temperature ranges from −2.6° C to −4.8° C; the average July temperature, from 15° C to 17° C. Precipitation reaches 650–700 mm per year, occurring mainly during the warm period. The growing season lasts from 155 to 180 days. Inland bodies of water occupy approximately 12 percent of the area of the oblast. The rivers are part of the Baltic Sea basin. The largest rivers are the Nemunas (with its tributary, the Sešupe) and the Pregolia (with its tributary, the Lava); the two are joined by a system of canals. Many of the rivers are controlled and regulated and are navigable. There are more than 100 lakes, the largest being the Vishtynetskoe. A total of 7 percent of the area is swamp. The soil is mainly podzolic, turf-podzolic, and acidic. Most of the land is under cultivation and requires drainage. Approximately nine-tenths of all the agricultural land is drained.

Forests occupy 15 percent of the area of the oblast (spruce, pine, oak, birch, linden, hornbeam, and alder). Meadows and pastureland make up about a third of the area of the oblast. Cultivated farmland predominates on the sites of drained swampland.

The animal world of the oblast is varied and includes the gray hare, squirrel, marten, fox, weasel, beaver, otter, mink, red deer, fallow deer, roe deer, elk, and wild boar. There are a great number and variety of birds in the oblast, across which pass the routes of many migratory species. The waters of the oblast are rich in fish. Bream, pike-perch, sparling, and eel are found in the freshwater bays, and Baltic herring, sprat, smelt, and salmon are found in the sea.

Population. Russians, mainly settlers from the central regions of the RSFSR, constitute more than 77 percent of the population; the remainder consists mainly of Byelorussians and Ukrainians. The average population density is 50 persons per sq km, including rural areas, the density of which is more than 12 persons per sq km. The rural population is most dense in Gur'ev, Nemunas, and Bagrationovsk raions. The urban population constitutes more than three-fourths of the total. Most of the rural population is concentrated in the well-designed and equipped settlements of sovkhozes and kolkhozes. The largest cities are Kaliningrad, Sovetsk, Cherniakhovsk, Baltiisk, Gusev, Svetlyi, Svetlogorsk, Pionerskii, and Zelenogradsk, all well-designed resort cities offering all public services and amenities.

Economy. Kaliningrad Oblast is characterized by a high level of industrialization combined with intensive agriculture. The principal branches of industry are machine building, paper and cellulose, and food (especially fish). The agriculture of the oblast specializes in dairy- and beef-cattle raising and pig breeding. The oblast plays a large role in the maritime commerce of the USSR, both imports and exports.

The gross output of industry in the oblast was 2.2 times higher in 1970 than it was in 1960. Power is based both upon the electrical energy that is delivered through the unified power supply system of the USSR and upon imported coal. The machine-building industry specializes in the production of hoisting and transport and road-construction machinery and in electrical-engineering production. The production of dump cars (self-unloading railroad cars with a freight-carrying capacity of up to 180 tons) is most important, along with the production of tower cranes, electric loaders, equipment for the cellulose and paper industry, remote-control systems, and searchlights. The main centers of machine building are Kaliningrad and Gusev. The cellulose and paper industry of the oblast provides more than 10 percent of the USSR's total output of cellulose and paper, including two-thirds of the paper for gravure. There are two cellulose-and-paper combines in Kaliningrad and one each in Sovetsk and Nemunas. There is a paper plant in Znamensk. More than 370,-000 tons of cellulose, 125,000 tons of paper, and 50,000 tons of cardboard are produced each year (1970).

The fishing industry occupies first place in the oblast in value of gross output (two-fifths of the total industrial output). The fishing fleet, which catches about 0.7 million tons of fish a year (1970), has more than 500 new large-tonnage seagoing ships, which have opened up to the industry the North and Norwegian seas, the equatorial Atlantic, and the South Atlantic. The Iurii Dolgorukii Whaling Fleet works off the coasts of Antarctica. The oblast accounts for more than 10 percent of the USSR's total catch of fish and sea products. The principal commercial fishes are herring, sea perch, sardine, tuna, and cod. Fish-canning combines in Kaliningrad, Mamonovo, and Svetlyi produced more than 125 million standard tins of fish in 1970. The fishing industry is closely bound up with the entire economy of the oblast (for example, with ship repair, the production of cardboard packaging, and fishing equipment), with scientific research institutions, with the port economy, and with agriculture (for which it provides fish meal). The most developed of the other branches of the food industry are butter, cheese, whole-milk products, and meat. The largest creameries are the Cherniakhovsk, Nesterov, and Ozerki plants and the Kaliningrad City Dairy. Meat production is centered in the Kaliningrad, Cherniakhovsk, and Sovetsk meat combines. Light industry and the production of construction materials are developing rapidly.

A unique branch of industry, the extraction and processing of amber, has developed in the settlement of Iantarnyi. More than 400 tons of amber are extracted annually. The amber is used for jewelry and art, more than 350 types of ornamental items, varnishes and paints, and insulating materials.

The agriculture of the oblast is characterized by a high degree of productivity. Sovkhozes account for 47 percent of the land in agricultural use and approximately 40 percent of the productive cattle. The principal branches of agriculture are dairy-cattle and beef-cattle raising, pig breeding, poultry farming, and the production of vegetables and potatoes. The area of all agricultural land comes to 840,000 hectares (plowed fields, 47 percent; hayfields, 21 percent; pasture, 32 percent). Approximately 55 percent of the sown area is used for forage crops; annual and perennial grasses are important. Cereals occupy second place in agricultural production; the summer crops are barley and oats, and the winter crops, wheat and rye. The specialization of agriculture is basically similar in all regions of the oblast, although the share of dairy and vegetable and potato production increases in suburban Kaliningrad. Fruit and berry production and orcharding are also well developed. In 1972 there were 409,000 head of cattle, 247,000 pigs, and 85,000 sheep and goats.

The ice-free port of Kaliningrad and its outer harbor, Baltiisk, are of nationwide importance, providing for a significant part of the USSR's foreign coastal trade on the Baltic Sea and the Atlantic. There is a dense and evenly distributed network of railways and highways; there are 756 km of operating railway lines and more than 3,500 km of paved highways (1970). The biggest transport junctions are Kaliningrad and Cherniakhovsk. The principal navigable rivers are the Nemunas and the Pregolia.

N. T. AGAFONOV

Cultural affairs and public health. In the 1971–72 academic year there were 138,400 students receiving instruction in 483 schools of general education of all types in Kaliningrad Oblast, 16,200 students in 13 specialized secondary schools, and 14,200 in three higher educational institutions (the university, the higher naval engineering school, and the technical institute of fishing and the fishing industry in Kaliningrad). More than 35,-000 children were enrolled in 418 preschool institutions in 1970.

As of Jan. 1, 1972, there were 367 public libraries with 6,-025,000 books and magazines, three theaters (the regional dramatic and puppet theaters in Kaliningrad and the dramatic theater in Sovetsk), a museum of local lore, 428 clubs, 608 stationary film projectors, botanical gardens (in Kaliningrad), and a number of extrascholastic children's institutions (in Kaliningrad), such as a House of Pioneers and young technicians', young naturalists', and young tourists' centers.

There are two regional newspapers: *Kaliningradskaia pravda* (since 1946) and *Kaliningradskii komsomolets* (since 1948). Regional radio and television each broadcast two programs and rebroadcast programs from Moscow. There is a television station in Kaliningrad.

As of Jan. 1, 1972, Kaliningrad Oblast had 75 hospitals with 9,600 beds (12.8 beds per thousand inhabitants). There were 2,600 working physicians (one for every 390 inhabitants). There are seaside resorts at Otradnoe, Svetlogorsk, Zelenogradsk, and Pionerskii.

REFERENCES

Kaliningradskaia oblast': Ocherki prirody. Kaliningrad, 1969.
Kaliningradskaia oblast' v tsifrakh. Kaliningrad, 1968.
Rossiiskaia federatsiia: Evropeiskii sever. Moscow, 1971. (Series *Sovetskii Soiuz.*)
Kaliningradskaia oblast' v vos'moi piatiletke. (Statistical collection.) Kaliningrad, 1972.
Vedernikov, I., and L. Zaichikova. *Geografiia Kaliningradskoi oblasti.* Kaliningrad, 1972.
[11–615–2]

KALININGRAD SEAPORT, (Kaliningrad Commercial Seaport), a major Soviet port on the southern shore of the Baltic Sea.

The geographical location of the Kaliningrad seaport favors year-round navigation. The seaport is part of the Baltic Maritime Steamship Line. Hundreds of seagoing vessels are loaded and unloaded at the docks of the port with cargoes of industrial goods, foodstuffs, grain, metals, machinery, and timber. The port is also a major base of the fishing fleet and has a maritime fishing port, at which the Iurii Dolgorukii Whaling Fleet is based.

The Kaliningrad seaport has an important role in international commercial relations. It dispatches and receives the ex-

ports and imports of the USSR and many countries of the world.
V. V. PONIATOVSKII [11–619–1]

KALININGRAD THEATER (Kaliningrad Oblast Dramatic Theater.)

The Kaliningrad Theater was founded in 1947; its first performance, Simonov's *A Lad From Our Town,* took place on November 6 of that year. The theater company was composed mainly of graduates of the A. V. Lunacharskii State Institute of Theatrical Arts, who had studied under I. M. Raevskii. In 1960 the theater moved to a new building designed by the architect P. V. Kukhtenkov. The first performance in the new building was *Unbounded Horizons* by Virta. The theater's best productions have included *Liubov' Iarovaia* by Trenev (1952), *Vassa Zheleznova* by Gorky and *Fiery Bridge* by Romashov (both 1953), *Maria Stuart* by Schiller (1954), *The Bathhouse* by Mayakovsky (1956), *The Cherry Orchard* by Chekhov (1958), *The Masquerade* by Lermontov (1959), *Even a Wise Man Stumbles* by Ostrovskii and *Richard III* by Shakespeare (both 1964), *The Seagull* by Chekhov (1966) *Mother Courage and Her Children* by Brecht and *The Barbarians* by Gorky (both 1967), and *An Optimistic Tragedy* by Vishnevskii (1970). Performances of plays devoted to V. I. Lenin have been of considerable interest, including *The Family* by Popov (1955), *The Kremlin Chimes* by Pogodin (1960), and *Snow* by Chepurin (1970). Among those who have worked at the theater at various times are the actors N. M. Andrievskaia and K. N. Ivanova-Golovko and the directors Z. Ia. Korogodskii, V. K. Danilov, and V. V. Tan. In 1971 the theater company included People's Artist of the RSFSR and Tadzhik SSR A. V. Miropol'skaia and Honored Artists of the RSFSR A. A. Potapushkina, V. P. Krasnogor, E. F. El'tsov, S. V. Klement'ev, and T. M. Kryman. The head director of the theater since 1968 has been Honored Art Worker of the Ukrainian SSR E. I. Sakharov. P. A. PONOMAREV [11–619–2]

KALININKEND, an urban-type settlement in Kazakh Raion, Azerbaijan SSR, located on the Gasansu River (a tributary of the Kura), 4 km from the Akstafa station on the Tbilisi-Baku railroad line. There is a winery in the settlement. [11–619–4]

KALININO (until 1935, Vorontsovka), an urban-type settlement, center of Kalinino Raion, Armenian SSR, located 47 km from the Tumanian railroad station on the Tbilisi-Leninakan line. Highway junction. Population, 7,000 (1970). Kalinino has a cheese-making plant and a factory for the production of enamelware. [11–620–1]

KALININO, an urban-type settlement in Krasnodar Krai, RSFSR, located 2 km from the city of Krasnodar. Population, 12,000 (1970). The people of Kalinino work at enterprises in the city of Krasnodar. [11–620–2]

KALININ OBLAST, part of the RSFSR. Formed on Jan. 29, 1935. Area, 84,100 sq km. Population, 1,705,000 (1972). The oblast is divided into 34 raions and has 22 cities and 25 urban-type settlements. The administrative center is the city of Kalinin. In 1966 the oblast was awarded the Order of Lenin.

Natural features. Kalinin Oblast is situated in the basin of the upper Volga River and at the watershed of the basins of the Baltic and Caspian seas.

The Valdai Hills, with elevations of 200–300 m and more, occupy the western part of the oblast. High morainic plains (Belyi Upland), with elevations of 250–340 m, border on the Valdai Hills in the south. The Zapadnaia Dvina Depression is located in the southwest of the oblast, with small rolling ridges alternating with frontal aprons. The eastern part of the oblast has a flatter relief. There is a belt of morainic plains in this area. Depressions (the Vyshnii Volochek, Middle Mologa, and Upper Mologa depressions) alternate with elevated ridges up to 200–250 m in elevation; (the Il'iny Hills; the Torzhok, Vyshnii Volochek, and Likhoslavl' ridges; the Bezhetsk Verkh; and the Ovinishche Upland) and the valleys of the Volga, Tvertsa, and Mologa rivers. The Upper Volga Depression (100–150 m) is located in the southeast, on both banks of the Volga, and in the lower reaches of the Tvertsa, Shosha, and Medveditsa rivers.

Kalinin Oblast has a temperate continental climate. The average January temperature ranges from -8.5° to -10.5°C; the average July temperature is 17°–18°C. Annual precipitation totals 550–750 mm. The western part of the oblast is distinguished by somewhat warmer winters and higher humidity. The growing period totals 120–133 days, and the sum of temperatures for the growing period totals 1700°–2000°C.

A major part of Kalinin Oblast lies in the basin of the Caspian Sea, with only the western and northwestern regions in the basin of the Baltic Sea. The sources and the upper reaches of the Volga River and of its tributaries the Selizharovka, T'ma, Tvertsa, Medveditsa, Kashinka, and Mologa rivers on the left and the Vazuza, Shosha, and Nerl' rivers on the right are located within the oblast. The upper course of the Zapadnaia Dvina River is in the western part of the oblast, and the Msta River is in the north. There are more than 500 lakes in the oblast, the largest being Lakes Seliger, Sterzh, Vselug, Peno, Volgo, Sig, Kaftino, and Velikoe. Lake Seliger is particularly picturesque. There are reservoirs on many of the rivers, including the Ivan'kovo, Uglich, and Rybinsk reservoirs on the Volga and the Vyshnii Volochek Reservoir on the Tsna River.

Soddy-podzolic, podzolic, and podzolic-gleyey soils predominate. The soil in the morainic deposits is mainly loamy and sandy. In the Valdai Hills and frontal aprons there is much sand and sandy loam as well as peat-podzolic-gleyey soil; some parts are marshy.

More than 3 million hectares (ha; 36 percent of the oblast's area) are covered by forests. The southwestern and northwestern regions are the most densely forested (50–70 percent of the area). Timber reserves total more than 300 million cu m. Coniferous forests (pine, spruce) make up more than half of the forests. Small-leaved trees (birch, aspen) are also widespread, and oak and linden are found in places.

Meadows, mainly of the dry-valley type, occupy approximately 2 million ha; floodplain meadows are found in the river valleys. Swamps and large peat bogs constitute approximately 9 percent of the oblast's area. The fauna of the oblast is typical of the forest zone and includes the elk, roe, brown bear, wolf, and fox. Game birds include the black grouse, capercaillie, hazel hen, willow ptarmigan, and partridge; there are also wild ducks. The oblast's lakes and rivers are rich in fish, including the whitefish, cisco, bream, pike, pike-perch, and carp.

Population. Most of the population is Russian, although Karelians and other national groups also live in the oblast. The average population density is 20.3 persons per sq km. The central and eastern regions of the oblast, where the large cities are located, are more densely settled, and the density of the rural population reaches 15–20 persons per sq km. The urban population constitutes 59.5 percent of the total population. The largest cities are Kalinin, Vyshnii Volochek, Rzhev, Kimry, Torzhok, and Bologoe.

Economy. Manufacturing is highly developed in Kalinin Oblast. The oblast's geographic position between the largest industrial centers, Moscow and Leningrad, has promoted industrialization. The fascist German occupation of the western part of the oblast from 1941 to 1943 caused great damage to the economy. Between 1940 and 1971 industrial output increased by a factor of 8 and between 1965 and 1971, by a factor of 1½. Most of the industrial production is concentrated in the central part of the oblast, in Kalinin, Vyshnii Volochek, Kimry, and Torzhok.

The power industry is based on local fuel and fuel brought in from other regions. Both peat and lignite are extracted (2.4 million tons of fuel peat and 0.7 million tons of lignite in 1971). Natural gas is supplied to the oblast through gas pipelines from the Northern Caucasus and the Komi ASSR. Coal and fuel oil are brought from the outside. Kalinin Oblast is part of the Central Power System, and there are large heat and electric power plants in Kalinin, Vyshnii Volochek, and other cities; there is also the Konakovo State Regional Power Plant.

The leading branches of industry are light industry (42.8 percent of the 1971 gross output), machine-building and metalworking (16.3 percent), food (14.6 percent), and lumber, wood products, and pulp and paper (7.2 percent). Of prime importance in the machine-building and metalworking industries is the production of railroad cars and excavators (Kalinin), agricultural machines (Bezhetsk), electrical engineering articles (Kalinin, Kashin), garage equipment (Bezhetsk), fire-extinguishing equipment (Torzhok), and instruments and lighting equipment (Likhoslavl' Rzhev). The chemical and petrochemical industries have developed during the Soviet period and produce artificial leather, rubber soles, synthetic fibers (Kalinin), tanning extracts, fiberglass, and glass-fiber-reinforced plastics. Light industry includes the following branches: cotton (Kalinin, Vyshnii Volochek), wool (Kalinin, Zavidovo), silk (Kalinin), linen (plants for the primary processing of flax fiber in flax-growing regions), leather (Ostashkov, Torzhok, Kalinin), footwear (Kimry, Torzhok, Kaliazin), and knitted goods and clothing. There are two large printing enterprises in Kalinin. Logging is conducted on a considerable scale (5.3 million cu m in 1971). The wood-products industry is highly developed, including sawmilling and the production of plywood and construction components (Vyshnii Volochek, Nelidovo, Zemtsy, Zapadnaia Dvina, Peno), furniture (Kalinin, Rzhev, Torzhok), and pulp and paper (Kuvshinovo). The production of glass (Vyshnii Volochek Raion, Spirovo) and of china and faience (Konakovo) are old branches of industry. The building-materials industry comprises the quarrying of building stones and gravel and the production of reinforced-concrete structures, brick, and lime. The food industry is connected with the processing of local agricultural raw materials, including meat, milk, potatoes, and vegetables.

Agriculture is based on flax growing and stock raising; there is also widespread cultivation of potatoes, cereals, and vegetables. Agricultural land totals 3.8 million ha, with natural forage land predominating (2.1 million ha). Arable land totals 1.65 million ha, and its proportion is significantly higher in the southern and eastern regions of the oblast. The areas of the Valdai Hills and the Upper Volga Depression are the least cultivated. There are 441 kolkhozes and 271 sovkhozes in Kalinin Oblast (1971). The sown area in 1971 totaled 1,513,000 ha. Of this, 705,000 ha were under cereals (rye, oats, wheat, and legumes), 159,000 ha under fiber flax, 128,000 ha under potatoes, and 512,000 ha under fodder crops. Cereals are cultivated throughout the oblast. Flax growing is highly developed and is concentrated in the eastern, central, and southern regions. In 1971, 585,000 quintals of flax fiber were gathered, which constituted 24 percent of the total collected in the RSFSR.

Stock raising is mainly of the meat and dairy type. In 1972 there were 956,000 head of cattle (including 462,000 cows), 421,000 pigs, and 677,000 sheep and goats.

There are approximately 1,800 km of railroad in the oblast. The most important main lines are Moscow-Leningrad, Moscow-Riga, Rybinsk-Bologoe-Pskov-Riga, and Moscow-Sonkovo-Leningrad. There is a considerable network of highways. There is navigation along the Volga River and on Lake Seliger. The main gas pipelines Serpukhov-Leningrad and Vuktyl-Torzhok pass through the oblast.

INTERNAL DIFFERENCES. The central part of Kalinin Oblast, which adjoins the Moscow-Leningrad railroad and highway, is economically the most highly developed section. The most important centers of the machine-building, chemical, textile, china and faience, and glass industries are concentrated in this area, as is the extraction of peat and the electrical power industry (Kalinin, Vyshnii Volochek, Torzhok, Konakovo, Likhoslavl', Bologoe). The agriculture in this region is mainly of the suburban type.

The eastern part of the oblast is characterized by well-developed agriculture, with flax growing and dairy stock raising occupying the leading positions. The most important industrial centers are Kimry, Bezhetsk, and Kashin.

The western part is characterized by the lumber industry and agriculture, the latter being most highly developed around Rzhev (flax growing and dairy stock raising). The principal industrial centers are Rzhev, Ostashkov, and Nelidovo. Lake Seliger, a large tourist area, is located in this region.

A. A. MINTS

Education, cultural affairs, and public health. In the 1914–15 academic year, there were 2,759 schools with 167,000 pupils, two secondary specialized schools with 330 students, and no higher educational institutions in what is now Kalinin Oblast. In the 1971–72 academic year, 283,000 pupils were studying in 2,010 general education schools of all types, 18,000 students in 49 vocational schools, 34,500 students in 40 specialized secondary schools, and 17,600 students in four higher educational institutions (a university, polytechnic institute, and medical institute in Kalinin and an agricultural institute in the settlement of Sakharovo). In 1969 there were 61,700 children enrolled in 833 preschool institutions.

As of Jan. 1, 1972, Kalinin Oblast had the following cultural institutions: 1,267 people's libraries with 13,385,000 books and magazines; the oblast dramatic theater, young people's theater, and puppet theater, all in Kalinin; the Kimry and Vyshnii Volochek dramatic theaters; the Kalinin Oblast Philarmonic Society; and the circus. Museums include the oblast museum of local lore, the museum of the everday life of Tver', the Liza Chaikina Museum of Komsomol Glory, and the picture gallery in Kalinin; the museums of local lore in Vyshnii Volochek, Kashin, Kaliazin, Kimry, Ostashkov, Rzhev, Toropets, and Bezhetsk; the M. I. Kalinin House-Museum in the village of Verkhniaia Troitsa; the A. S. Pushkin literary memorial museums in the village of Bernovo and in the city of Torzhok; and the S. D. Drozhzhin literary memorial museum in the settlement of Zavidovo. There are also 1,711 clubs and 2,344 film projectors. Extracurricular institutions include the Kalinin Palace of Pioneers, 31 Houses of Pioneers, an oblast station of young naturalists and experimenters in agriculture, and an oblast station of young technicians.

Two oblast newspapers are published: *Kalininskaia Pravda* (since 1917) and the Komsomol paper *Smena* (since 1927). The oblast radio broadcasts one radio program. Radio and television broadcasts are relayed from Moscow.

As of Jan. 1, 1972, the oblast had 214 hospitals with 20,400 beds (12 beds per 1,000 population); there were 4,200 doctors (one doctor per 410 population) working in the oblast. Kalinin Oblast is also the site of the Kashin resort and the Mitino Sanatorium for the treatment of illnesses of the nervous system. There are a number of houses of rest.

REFERENCES
Priroda i khoziaistvo Kalininskoi oblasti. Kalinin, 1960.
Tsentral'nyi raion. Moscow, 1962.
Atlas Kalininskoi oblasti. Moscow, 1964.
Kalininskaia oblast' za 50 let v tsifrakh: Statistich. sbornik. Moscow, 1967. [11–620–5]

KALININ PRINTING COMBINE, a large, specialized offset printing enterprise, located in the city of Kalinin. It was built in 1951–56. In 1971 it published 16.3 million school textbooks, 1 billion postcards, 11 million posters, and 22 million magazines. The Kalinin Printing Combine was awarded the Order of the Red Banner of Labor in 1971. [11–625–1]

KALININSK (until 1962, the settlement of Balanda), a city, center of Kalininsk Raion, Saratov Oblast, RSFSR, situated on the Balanda River (a tributary of the Medveditsa River). Terminal station (Kalininsk-Saratovskii) on a railroad branch (80 km) of the Rtishchevo-Saratov line. Population, 16,000 (1970). Kalininsk has an automobile repair enterprise and factories producing bricks, asphalt and concrete, and rubber industrial products. Enterprises of the food industry include a brewery, a poultry combine, and a milk-bottling plant. There are also sanatoriums in Kalininsk. [11–620–3]

KALININSK, an urban-type settlement in Edintsy Raion, Moldavian SSR, located 2 km from the Bratushany railroad station. Population, 5,100 (1970). Kalininsk has construction materials, sugar, and tobacco-curing plants. A cannery is under construction (1972). [11–620–4]

KALININSKII, an urban-type settlement in Voroshilovgrad Oblast, Ukrainian SSR, located 4 km from the Dolzhanskaia railroad station. Coal is mined in the vicinity. Kalininskii has a coal-cleaning plant. [11–624–1]

KALININSKOE, an urban-type settlement in Velikaia Aleksandrovka Raion, Kherson Oblast, Ukrainian SSR. Located on the Ingulets River (Dnieper basin) 7 km from the Kalinindorf railroad station on the Apostolovo-Snigirevka line. A viticultural and wine-making sovkhoz and the Kherson Cotton Combine are there. [11–625–5]

KALINKA, WALERIAN (pseudonym, Bronisław Kamieniecki). Born in 1826 in Kraków; died Dec. 15, 1886, in L'vov. Polish historian. A leading exponent of the Kraków historical school. Of petty gentry origin.

Kalinka graduated from the University of Kraków. He participated in the Kraków Uprising of 1846, emigrating to France in 1856. In the late 1860's he joined the monastic order of the Resurrectionists and settled in Galicia. Kalinka's works, notably *The Last Years of the Reign of Stanisław August* (1868) and *The Four-Year Sejm* (1880–88), are devoted primarily to the period of the partition of Poland, interpreted from a clerical and conservative standpoint.

WORKS
Dzieła, vols. 1–12. Kraków, 1891–1903. [11–626–1]

KALINKOVICHI, a city (since 1926) in Gomel' Oblast, Byelorussian SSR. Kalinkovichi is a railroad junction. Population, 26,100 (1971). Kalinkovichi has a meat-packing plant and flour-milling and fruit-canning combines, as well as a machine-overhauling plant, a furniture factory, a state poultry farm, and factories producing roofing materials, articles of reinforced concrete, and chemical products for household use. [11–626–2]

KALINNIKOV, VASILII SERGEEVICH. Born Jan. 1 (13), 1866, in the village of Voiny, in present-day Mtsensk Raion, Orel Oblast; died Dec. 29, 1900 (Jan. 11, 1901), in Yalta. Russian composer.

Kalinnikov studied at the Orel Theological Seminary. In 1892 he graduated from the Music and Drama School of the Moscow Philharmonic Society. He played in an orchestra (bassoon), taught singing in city elementary schools, and appeared as a conductor. Beginning in 1893, as a result of illness (tuberculosis), he lived mostly in the Crimea. Symphonic works, including two symphonies (Symphony No. 1, 1895, performed in 1897 in Kiev and Moscow; Symphony No. 2, 1897) and the symphonic poem *The Cedar and the Palm Tree* (1898), constitute his major creative works. Ably continuing the traditions established by P. I. Tchaikovsky and the composers known as the "Russian Five," he was a lyric composer by the nature of his talent. Symphony No. 1, his most integrated and complete work, brought him wide fame. Among his other compositions are music for A. K. Tolstoy's tragedy *Tsar Boris* (1899), piano pieces, and art songs.

WORKS
Pis'ma, dokumenty, materialy, vols. 1–2. Moscow, 1959.
REFERENCES
Pashkhalov, V. *V. S. Kalinnikov: Zhizn' i tvorchestvo.* Moscow–Leningrad, 1951.
Keldysh, Iu. *Istoriia russkoi muzyki,* part 3. Moscow, 1954. Chapter 6. [11–626–3]

KALINO, an urban-type settlement in Perm' Oblast, RSFSR, situated on the left bank of the Chusovaia River. A junction of railroad lines to Perm', Kuzino, and Chusovskaia, Kalino has an experimental plant manufacturing wall materials, a logging and timber-distribution establishment, and railroad transport enterprises. [11–626–4]

KALINOVKA, an urban-type settlement, center of Kalinovka Raion, Vinnitsa Oblast, Ukrainian SSR. A railroad junction, Kalinovka has a machine-building plant, an experimental plant for wood products, and a plant for the production of packaging items. There are also enterprises of the food industry (a distillery and others). [11–626–5]

KALINOVKA, an urban-type settlement in Vasil'kov Raion, Kiev Oblast, Ukrainian SSR. Kalinovka has a station (Vasil'kov) on the Kiev-Fastov railroad line. A plant producing reinforced-concrete construction components and joiners' articles is located in Kalinovka, as is the Kozhukhovo poultry-breeding sovkhoz. [11–626–6]

KALINOVO, an urban-type settlement in Lisichansk Raion, Voroshilovgrad Oblast, Ukrainian SSR. Located on the Lugan' River, a tributary of the Severskii Donets, 4 km from the Irmino station on the Debal'tsevo-Popasnaia railroad line. The Rossiia sovkhoz is located there. [11–626–7]

KALINOVO, an urban-type settlement in Sverdlovsk Oblast, RSFSR. Located on the western bank of Tavatui Lake, 4 km from the Murzinka station on the Sverdlovsk–Nizhnii Tagil railroad line. It is 65 km northwest of Sverdlovsk. Kalinovo has a wood-products industry and a fish hatchery. [11–627–1]

KALINOVSKAIA, VALENTINA FEDOROVNA. Born July 21, 1938, in Kiev. Soviet ballerina. People's Artist of the USSR (1968).

A graduate of the Kiev Choreographic School, Kalinovskaia has been dancing at the T. G. Shevchenko Opera and Ballet Theater since 1957. Technically perfect, her dancing is characterized by light jumps, a lyrical adagio, and a brilliant allegro. She is best suited for dramatic roles. Her best roles include Odette-Odile in Tchaikovsky's *Swan Lake,* Aegina in Khachaturian's *Spartacus,* Kitri in Minkus' *Don Quixote,* Zarema in Asaf'ev's *The Fountain of Bakhchisarai,* Mekhmene Banu in Melikov's *The Legend of Love,* and Dona Anna in Gubarenko's *The Stone Ruler.* She has been awarded the Order of the Red Banner of Labor. [11–627–2]

KALINOVSKII, KONSTANTIN BRONISLAVOVICH. Born Oct. 1 (13), 1897, in Smolensk; died July 12, 1931, in Moscow. Soviet military figure. Became a member of the CPSU in 1920. The son of an officer.

Kalinovskii volunteered for the Red Army in June 1918 and saw combat at Shenkursk in Arkhangel'sk Province. He graduated from the Higher Military Motor Vehicle and Armor School in 1919, served on an armored train in combat on the Southern Front, and commanded with distinction an armored train on the Western Front in 1920. Inspector of the Administration of Armored Units of the Caucasian Army (1921–22), Kalinovskii graduated from the Military Academy of the Workers' and Peasants' Red Army (RKKA) in 1925 and was a military advisor in China and then commander of an experimental mechanized regiment (1926–27). After being appointed inspector of the armored forces in 1929, Kalinovskii became deputy chief (and in February 1931 chief) of the Directorate of Mechanization and Motorization of the RKKA. His writings laid the foundation for the theory of the organization and combat use of Soviet armored forces. He died in a plane crash. Kalinovskii was awarded two Orders of the Red Banner.

WORKS
Tanki. Moscow, 1925.
REFERENCE
Mironov, G. "K. Kalinovskii." In *Geroi grazhdanskoi voiny.* Moscow, 1963. [11–627–3]

KALINOVSKII, KONSTANTIN SEMENOVICH (Kastus' Kalinovskii). Born Jan. 21 (Feb. 2), 1838, in Mostovliany, Grodno District; died Mar. 10 (22), 1864, in Vilnius. Revolutionary democrat, one of the leaders of the 1863–64 uprising in Lithuania and Byelorussia. The son of a noble (*shliakhtich*) who owned a small amount of land.

Kalinovskii studied law at St. Petersburg University from 1856 to 1860. During his student years, Kalinovskii and his older brother Viktor participated in student organizations of *zemliaki* (persons from the same district) and revolutionary circles, and they became close associates of S. Sierakowski, J. Dąbrowski, and W. Wróblewski. Kalinovskii's world view was shaped under the influence of the growing peasant movement and the ideas of N. G. Chernyshevskii and A. I. Herzen, as well as the best traditions of the Polish national liberation movement. Returning to his homeland in Byelorussia, Kalinovskii, together with

Wróblewski and others, organized revolutionary circles in 1861 in Grodno and Vilnius provinces. These circles became part of a united, secret Polish organization. In 1862, Kalinovskii became the head of the Committee of Movement, which directed this organization and which later was known as the Lithuanian Provincial Committee. In 1862–63, Kalinovskii directed the publication and distribution of *Muzhitskaia pravda,* the first illegal revolutionary newspaper in the Byelorussian language. The newspaper criticized the conditions of the abolition of serfdom, struggled against the tsarist illusions of the peasantry, and called on the peasants to secure "not the freedom which the tsar could wish to grant us, but the freedom which we ourselves, muzhiks, will make among ourselves." The newspaper propagated the idea of a revolutionary alliance of peoples oppressed by tsarism. Kalinovskii strongly supported the national-liberation struggle of the Polish people. His motto was, "The Polish cause is our cause, the cause of freedom."

Leading the 1863 uprising in Byelorussia, Kalinovskii came out for the broad involvement of the peasants in the struggle and for the expansion of the uprising east and north of the borders of the Severo-Zapadnyi Krai. Driven deep into the underground by the brutal government reprisals, Kalinovskii led the insurgents of Lithuania and Byelorussia until his arrest at the end of January 1864. He continued the struggle even after being sentenced to death, addressing the people in *Letters From Under the Gallows.* He was executed in Vilnius.

REFERENCE
Smirnov, A. F. *Kastus' Kalinovskii.* Minsk, 1963.

V. A. D'IAKOV [11–627–4]

KALISZ, a city in Poland, in Poznań Województwo, on the Prosna River. Population, 82,000 (1971). Kalisz is a transport junction and a center of the textile industry (silk, velvet, tulle, and knitwear). Other important branches of industry include machine building, food processing, and the manufacture of pianos and plastic goods. Kalisz has existed since the second century A.D.

REFERENCE
Dabrowski, K. *Z przeszłości Kalisza.* Warsaw, 1970. [11–636–2]

KALISZ ALLIANCE TREATY OF 1813, a treaty between Russia and Prussia on war against the French emperor Napoleon I. The treaty was signed after the expulsion of the remnants of Napoleon's army from Russia. It was signed by Field Marshal M. I. Kutuzov and the Prussian chancellor K. A. Hardenberg in Breslau on Feb. 15 (27), 1813, and at the headquarters of Alexander I in the city of Kalisz the next day. Russia and Prussia agreed to conduct joint military activities and not to conclude a separate peace or armistice. Secret points of the Kalisz Alliance Treaty stipulated the restoration of Prussia to its 1806 borders and the increase of its territory at the expense of the North German states. The Kalisz Alliance Treaty marked the beginning of the Sixth Coalition against Napoleon.

REFERENCE
Istoriia diplomatii, 2nd ed., vol. 1. Moscow, 1963. [11–637–1]

KALITA, an old Russian term for a money pouch or bag. It is mentioned in documents of the 14th century dealing with the possessions of the Muscovite princes. A *kalita* was usually made of leather, with incision, appliqué, or other decorations. The most valuable *kality* were made of Moroccan leather, decorated with gold and with embroidery depicting birds and animals. They were attached to the belt by a thong. One such *kalita,* dating from the late 15th century and uncovered during excavations in Moscow, can be seen at the Museum of the History and Reconstruction of Moscow.

Because of his wealth, the Muscovite prince Ivan Danilovich was nicknamed Kalita. [11–629–2]

KALITIN, NIKOLAI NIKOLAEVICH. Born Mar. 29, 1884, in Pavlovsk; died Aug. 21, 1949, in Leningrad. Soviet meteorologist; one of the founders of Soviet actinometry. Honored Scientist of the RSFSR (1948).

Kalitin graduated from the University of St. Petersburg in 1911. That same year he began working at the Main Physics (later Geophysical) Observatory, where he subsequently became director of the divisions of actinometry and atmospheric optics. Under his direction, a network of actinometric stations was organized in the USSR. His principal works were devoted to the study of the radiation climate of the USSR, the methodology of actinometric measurements, and problems of heliotherapy. Kalitin invented a number of actinometric and atmospheric-optical instruments.

WORKS
Aktinometriia. Leningrad-Moscow, 1938.
REFERENCES
Solov'ev, V. A. "Nikolai Nikolaevich Kalitin." *Meteorologiia i gidrologiia,* 1949, no. 3.
Sovol'ev, V. A. "Pamiati N. N. Kalitina." *Priroda,* 1950, no. 2.
[11–629–5]

KALITSKII, KAZIMIR PETROVICH. Born Mar. 4 (16), 1873, in St. Petersburg; died Dec. 28, 1941, in Leningrad. Soviet geologist and petroleum specialist. Doctor of geological and mineralogical sciences. Professor from 1941.

Kalitskii graduated from the St. Petersburg Institute of Mines in 1899. In 1901 he began working on the Geological Committee, which was later reorganized into the All-Union Geological Oil Prospecting Scientific Research Institute. He conducted numerous geological investigations in many petroleum-bearing regions of the USSR (Middle Asia, the Caucasus, the Volga Region). His primary works were devoted to the problem of the origin of petroleum and the formation of its deposits. He developed the hypothesis that petroleum originates from marine plants; he also believed that the migration of petroleum does not play a part in the formation of petroleum deposits. Kalitskii compiled one of the first textbooks on petroleum geology (1921).

WORKS
Nauchnye osnovy poiskov nefti. Moscow-Leningrad, 1944.
REFERENCES
Ezhegodnik Vserossiiskogo Paleontologicheskogo obshchestva. vol. 13. Moscow-Leningrad, 1949. Pages 129–30.
Sabbatovskii, G. K. "Znachenie trudov K. P. Kalitskogo v poznanii geologicheskikh neftianykh mestorozhdenii Turkmenii." *Tr. In-ta geologii AN Turkmenskoi SSR,* 1960, vol 3. [11–636–1]

KALITVA (also called Belaia Kalitva, Bol'shaia Kalitva), a river in Rostov Oblast, RSFSR, a left tributary of the Severskii Donets. The Kalitva measures 308 km long and drains an area of 10,600 sq km. It originates on the southern slopes of the Don Ridge and is fed primarily by snow. The largest tributaries are the Ol'khovaia, Bol'shaia, and Berezovaia rivers (on the left). The river is navigable in its lower course. The city of Belaia Kalitva is located at the confluence of the Kalitva and Severskii Donets rivers. [11–629–4]

KALIX, a river in northern Sweden. Length, from the source of the Kaitum River, 450 km; basin area, 17,900 sq km. The river originates on the slopes of Mount Kébnekaise. There are waterfalls on the river. The upper course of the Kalix passes through several lakes; the river flows into the Gulf of Bothnia. High water is in summer, and the river freezes from November to early May. It is used to float logs and to generate hydroelectric power.
[11–603–3]

KALKA (present-day Kal'chik), a tributary of the Kal'mius River which flows through the territory of the present-day Donets Oblast, Ukrainian SSR. Here on May 31, 1223, the first battle took place between Russian and Cuman troops on the one hand and the Mongol-Tatar troops of Jebe and Subutai on the other.

The Russian troops gathered in April, crossed the Dnieper near the cataracts, and smashed the Mongol-Tatar vanguard, which began a hasty retreat, intending to draw the Russians within range of the main Mongol-Tatar forces. Disagreements broke out among the Russian princes. The Galician prince Mstislav the Bold, the Volynian prince Daniil, and the Cumans proceeded to cross the Kalka while the other princes remained on the western bank. The main Mongol-Tatar forces defeated the Cuman and Galician-Volynian regiments, which fled across the Dnieper, and then besieged the camp of Mstislav of Kiev. Mstislav yielded after three days, believing the promises of the Mongols to allow him and his warriors to return home. The Mongol-Tatar forces treacherously violated their promise, and all the Russian captives were annihilated.

In 1380 a battle took place on the Kalka between the khan of the Golden Horde, Toktamish, and the military leader (*temnik*) Mamai, who were contesting for supreme power. The battle ended in the defeat of Mamai.

REFERENCES
Ocherki istorii SSSR: Period feodalizma, IX-XV vv, vol. 1. Moscow, 1953.
Pashuto, V. T. *Geroicheskaia bor'ba russkogo naroda za nezavisimost' (XIII vek)*. Moscow, 1956. [11–639–7]

KALKAMAN, an urban-type settlement in Ermak Raion, Pavlodar Oblast, Kazakh SSR. Located 75 km southwest of Pavlodar at the intersection of the Irtysh-Karaganda Canal and the railroad from Tselinograd to Pavlodar. Population, 7,000 (1970). Salt is mined nearby. [11–640–2]

KALKAN, Black Sea Turbot (*Scophthalmus maeoticus;* also, *Rhombus maeoticus*), a fish of the family Bothidae, order Pleuronectiformes (Heterosomata). Length, to 1 m; weight, to 10 kg.

There are large bony spines on the body of the *kalkan.* The fish is found in the Black and Adriatic seas and in the eastern Mediterranean. It leads a sedentary life on the bottom of the sea, feeding on fish and crabs. The fish spawn from April to June; the female deposits 1.5–12 million eggs. The larvae become asymmetrical after reaching 12 mm in length, and at a length of 3 cm the young fish move to the bottom. The *kalkan* is valuable commercially. [11–640–3]

KALKI (pseudonym of Ramasami Krushnamurthi). Born Sept. 9, 1899, in the village of Manalmedu, Tamil Nadu state; died there Jan. 5, 1954. Indian author.

Kalki was one of the pioneers of modern Tamil prose. He was descended from a Brahman family. He graduated from the National College in Tiruchchirappalli, and in 1917 he began to work in the democratic press. Kalki translated speeches and articles by M. K. Gandhi and other liberation movement leaders into Tamil, and he was subjected to repression by the English authorities. In 1925 he began to publish poetry and stories. He wrote many collections of short stories; the historical novels *The Vow of Sivahami* (1941–42) and *Beloved Son of Cauvery* (1948); and the social novels *In the Land of Selflessness* (1947), *The Beloved of a Thief* (1947), and *The Sound of the Waves* (1953; Russian translation, 1964; Literary Academy of India Prize, 1956). In his works, Kalki raised many critical issues of the national liberation movement. The journal *Kalki,* which he established in 1941, promoted unity among Tamil writers.

REFERENCES
Istoriia indiiskikh literatur. Moscow, 1964. (Translated from English.)
Chandanam, K. A. "Kalki Kirushnamurthi." *Kalki,* 1966, pp. 47–48.
Dhandayudhan, R. "Kalki—His Life and Work." *Contemporary Indian Literature,* March, 1965. V. A. MAKARENKO [11–688–4]

KALLAI, GYULA. Born June 1, 1910, in Berettyóújfalu. Politician and statesman in the Hungarian People's Republic (HPR).

Kallai joined the Hungarian Communist Party (HCP) in 1931. He played a leading role in the democratic student movement and worked on antifascist journals. He was arrested in 1939. After his release, he worked from 1939 to 1944 on the editorial board of the newspaper *Népszava,* acting on instructions of the party. He took part in the organization of the Hungarian Committee on Historically Memorable Dates (founded 1942) and in the organization of antifascist and antiwar demonstrations on Mar. 15, 1942. He was a representative of the HCP in the Executive Committee of the Hungarian National Independence Front (1944). In April 1945 he became a member of the Central Committee of the HCP, and from June to November of that year he was secretary of state of the Council of Ministers.

From September 1945 to March 1947 he was editor in chief of the newspaper *Szabad Föld.* From 1946 to 1948 he was the director of the department of culture of the Central Committee of the HCP. From 1949 to 1951 he served as the minister of foreign affairs of the HPR.

Kallai was arrested in 1951 on a false charge. After his rehabilitation (1954–55), he was the director of the Central Publishing House and the deputy minister of culture. In 1956 he became the director of the cultural department of the Central Committee of the Hungarian Workers' Party. From November 1956 to March 1975 he was a member of the Politburo of the Central Committee of the Hungarian Socialist Workers' Party (HSWP). In March 1975 he became a member of the Central Committee of the HSWP. In 1957 he was minister of education and a government minister. From 1957 to 1959 he was secretary of the Central Committee of the HSWP. From January 1960 to September 1961 he was first vice-chairman of the Revolutionary Workers' and Peasants' Government; from September 1961 to July 1965, vice-chairman of the Council of Ministers; and from July 1965 to April 1967, chairman of the Council of Ministers. From April 1967 to May 1971 he was chairman of the National Assembly of the HPR.

WORKS
Szocializmus és kultúra. Budapest, 1962.
Dvizhenie za nezavisimost' Vengrii 1936–1945. Moscow, 1968. (Translated from Hungarian.)
Szocializmus, népfront, democracia. Budapest, 1971.
[11–640–4; updated]

KALLASTE, a city in Tartu Raion, Estonian SSR, situated on the west bank of Čudskoje Lake (Lake Peipus), 51 km northeast of Tartu. [11–641–3]

KÁLLAY, MIKLÓS. Born 1887; died Jan. 14, 1967, in New York. Hungarian politician and statesman. In 1929, he was secretary of state for commerce. From 1932 to 1935 he served as minister of agriculture. From March 1942 to March 1944 he was prime minister; until July 24, 1943, he was also minister of foreign affairs.

Kállay's government continued to wage the war against the USSR begun by the government of L. Bárdossy on June 27, 1941. It increased the use of terror against the antifascist forces in the country and strove to prepare the conditions for saving the bourgeois structure in Hungary by means of a separate peace with Great Britain and the USA. It offered no resistance to the German occupation of Hungary, which began on Mar. 19, 1944. After the end of World War II, Kállay emigrated to the USA.

REFERENCES
Puskás, A. I. *Vengriia vo vtoroi mirovoi voine: Vneshniaia politika Vengrii [1938–1944].* Moscow, 1963.
Ránki, G. *Emlékiratok és valóság: Magyarország második világháborús szerepéről.* Budapest, 1964. A. I. PUSKÁS [11–641–1]

KALLIKREINS, enzymes of blood plasma and the tissues of certain organs (kidney, pancreas, salivary glands, intestinal walls) that catalyze a reaction in which the quinines bradykinin and kallidin split off from the inactive protein precursor quininogen.

Kallikreins are enzymes of the trypsin type. They have extremely narrow specificity and manifest biological activity characteristic of the quinines. A preparation of kallikreins from swine pancreas is used as a vasodilator, especially in disorders of peripheral blood circulation. [11–643–2]

KALLIMA, a genus of butterflies of the family Nymphalidae. The wingspread measures 6–8 cm. When the butterfly sits on a tree branch with folded wings, it has the shape and coloring of a dead leaf (a classic example of mimicry). The upper side of the wings is vividly colored. The genus comprises several species distributed in tropical Asia. [11–644–1]

KALLIO, KYÖSTI. Born Apr. 10, 1873, in Ylivieska; died Dec. 19, 1940, in Helsinki. Finnish state and political figure.

Kallio joined the Agrarian Party in 1906 and belonged to its right wing. In 1907 he became a deputy in the parliament and was its chairman many times (beginning in 1920). In the years 1922–24, 1925–26, 1929–30, and 1936–37, he was prime minister. From 1937 to 1940, while he was president of Finland, Kallio carried out a reactionary foreign policy favored by Finnish ruling circles.   [11–645–1]

KÁLMÁN, EMMERICH

KÁLMÁN, EMMERICH (also Imre Kálmán). Born Oct. 24, 1882, in Siófok; died Oct. 30, 1953, in Paris. Hungarian composer.

Kálmán studied at the Academy of Music in Budapest under J. Koessler. His first operetta, *Autumn Manoeuvres* (first staged in Budapest in 1908), played in many theaters in Europe and the USA. The success of the operettas *Soldier on Leave* (in its German variant entitled *A Good Pal*), *The Gypsy Premier,* and especially *The Czardas Princess (Silva)* brought Kálmán fame as an outstanding master of the "Viennese operetta." In a number of works he was not able to avoid a salon-type superficiality of plots and the banality of diverting comedy. Nevertheless, in the best of his 20 operettas (*La Bayadère, Countess Maritza, The Circus Princess*), which were marked by sharply delineated plot situations, well-developed musical dramaturgy, effective orchestration, and a combination of buffoonery with lyricism (for example, *The Violet of Montmartre,* 1930), Kálmán departed from the canons and stereotypes of Viennese operetta. One of his innovations was the use of elements of Hungarian musical folklore and a democratization of the genre: the heroes of many of his operettas are simple people (peasants, poor actors, painters, and musicians), whom he contrasts with the world of the rich bourgeoisie. In 1938, after the seizure of Austria by Nazi Germany and the banning of performances of his works, Kálmán emigrated to Switzerland. In 1940 he emigrated to the USA.

REFERENCES
Iaron, G. "Imre Kal'man—master operett." *Sovetskaia muzyka,* 1954, no. 3.
Iaron, G. "Imre Kal'man." *Muzykal'naia zhizn',* 1962, no. 20.
                                            [11–692–3]

KALMAR, a city and port in southeast Sweden, on the coast of the Baltic Sea. Kalmar is the administrative center of the county (*län*) of the same name. Population, 39,000 (1970). Machine-building and food industries are there. The city is linked by ferry with Öland Island.   [11–693–1]

KALMAR, UNION OF, an association of the kingdoms of Denmark, Norway (including Iceland), and Sweden (including Finland) in a personal union under the Danish kings, definitively shaped in 1397 in the city of Kalmar, Sweden. In the broad sense the term refers to the period 1397–1523 in Scandinavian history, when all the Scandinavian countries were at least formally in a union.

The formation of the union was in the interests of many big feudal lords of Denmark and Sweden (those who owned estates in all three kingdoms), as well as the trading cities. It was necessary for the struggle against German economic and political expansion. In the 14th century the Hanseatic League took over almost all the foreign and even part of the domestic trade of Denmark, Norway, and Sweden; German feudal lords penetrated Scandinavia; and in 1363 the German duke Albrecht (Albert) of Mecklenburg became king of Sweden and tried to gain the throne of Denmark.

The initiator of the union was Queen Margaret of Denmark. In 1380, Norway, which was economically dependent upon Denmark, joined Denmark in a personal union under the Danish queen; and in 1389, for her aid to the Swedish feudal lords in the struggle against Albrecht, Margaret was also recognized as ruler of Sweden. Nevertheless, this de facto union of the three kingdoms was unstable, since the royal power in Denmark and Sweden was elective and not hereditary. Margaret succeeded in designating as her heir in each of the three kingdoms her grandnephew, Eric of Pomerania. In 1397 in Kalmar at a congress of the feudal lords of Denmark, Sweden, and Norway, Eric was crowned king of all three kingdoms and was recognized as Margaret's coruler.

Within the framework of the Union of Kalmar, Denmark, which was economically and politically more developed, attempted to subordinate Sweden and Norway completely. The foreign policy of the union was conducted in the interests of Denmark. Danes were appointed to the highest ecclesiastical positions in Sweden and Norway, and Danish and German nobles acquired estates there. The increase in taxes caused by the wars of the Danish kings on behalf of their dynastic interests gave rise to dissatisfaction among the peasants and burghers and also part of the nobility. A general anti-Danish uprising led by Engelbrekt Engelbrektsson (1434–36) drove the Danish nobles from Sweden, although the union was not abrogated. In 1448, after the election of Karl Knutsson as the Swedish king, Sweden virtually left the union. The attempts of the Danish kings to subordinate Sweden again, culminating in the "Stockholm Bloodbath" of 1520, led to a new uprising and to the final liquidation of the tripartite union in 1523, when Gustavus I Vasa was elected king of Sweden. Norway, which was weaker than Sweden, could not maintain its independence. In 1537 it was deprived of its status as a kingdom and proclaimed a province of Denmark, a status it retained until 1814.

                          S. D. KOVALEVSKII   [11–693–3]

KALMARSUND, a sound in the Baltic Sea between Öland Island and the southeast coast of Scandinavia. Length, 130 km; width, 6 to 24 km. The currents, driven by the wind, can attain speeds of 3–4 km/hr. Kalmarsund freezes in severe winters.
                                            [11–694–1]

KALMAR WAR OF 1611–13, a war between Denmark and Sweden for domination of the Baltic Sea and for the southern part of the Scandinavian Peninsula and the northern coast of Norway (both of which belonged to Denmark). The war resulted in victory for Denmark. Danish troops, who began a siege of the Swedish city and fortress of Kalmar in the spring of 1611, captured it in August 1611, and in May 1612 they captured Älvsborg, the most important Swedish fortress and only Swedish port at that time in the Kattegat Straits. In accordance with the terms of the peace treaty concluded on Jan. 20, 1613, in Knäred, Denmark retained the rights to Älvsborg and its environs until Sweden completed payment of 1 million thalers over a six-year period. The treaty also confirmed the conditions of the Peace of Stettin of 1570, which was favorable to Denmark (this treaty had concluded the Seven Years' War of the North of 1563–70).

REFERENCE
Forsten, G. V. *Baltiiskii vopros v XVI i XVII stoletiiakh,* vol. 2. St. Petersburg, 1894.   [11–693–2]

KAL'MIUS, a river in Donetsk Oblast, Ukrainian SSR. It measures 209 km long, and drains an area of 5,070 sq km. The Kal'mius originates on the southern slopes of the Donets Ridge and empties into the Sea of Azov. The river is fed primarily by snow. The mean annual flow rate at the settlement of Primorskoe is 6.23 cu m/sec. The Kal'mius is used for irrigation and industrial water supply. The Upper Kal'mius Reservoir is located in the upper reaches; the reservoir is part of the hydraulic engineering complex of the Severskii Donets–Donbas Canal. The cities of Donetsk and Zhdanov (at the mouth) are situated on the Kal'mius.   [11–696–1]

KAL'MIUS SAKMA (*sakma* is the Tatar word for "well-worn road"), the route from the Crimean Khanate to Russia. Beginning in the south in the upper reaches of the Molochnye Vody River (now the Molochnaia River) in the basin of the Sea of Azov, the Kal'mius Sakma proceeded across the Kal'mius River and further on across the Severskii Donets River along the watershed of the Oskol and Don rivers, near the cities of Valuiki and Staryi Oskol. At the Bol'shaia Sosna River it merged with the Murava Road. In the 16th century and the first half of the 17th century the Kal'mius Sakma was one of the main routes along which the Crimean and Nogai Tatars carried out plundering raids on the southern regions of Russia.   [11–696–2]

KALMYK, the language of the Kalmyks. It is related to the Mongolian language group. It has two dialects, Torgut and Derbet. Kalmyk is spoken in the Kalmyk ASSR, Stavropol' Krai, and Astrakhan, Rostov, and Volgograd oblasts. There are approximately 126,000 Kalmyk speakers in the USSR (1970 census). Kalmyk is also spoken by about 60,000 persons in the People's Republic of China (1953–54 census).

Kalmyk phonetics is characterized by long and short vowels; vowel harmony is preserved. Kalmyk nouns are inflected for number and for ten cases. There is no category of gender. Adjectives do not agree with nouns. Verbs have categories of aspect, voice, mood, tense, person, and number. The earliest lexical borrowings into Kalmyk were Greek, Arabic, and Sanskrit, which found their way into the language through Sogdian, Uighur, and Tibetan. Modern borrowings come primarily from and through Russian. The Kalmyks used the Mongolian vertical script until the middle of the 17th century (1648), when it was replaced by the Zaya-Pandita writing system. The Russian alphabet was introduced in 1924. The writing system was based on the Roman alphabet from 1931 to 1938, when the Russian-based orthography was reintroduced.

REFERENCES

Sanzheev, G. D. *Grammatika kalmytskogo iazyka.* Moscow-Leningrad, 1940.
Badmaev, B. B. *Grammatika kalmytskogo iazyka: Morfologiia.* Elista, 1966.
Ochirov, U. U. *Grammatika kalmytskogo iazyka: Sintaksis.* Elista, 1964.
Russko-kalmytskii slovar'. Edited by I. Ilishkin. Moscow, 1964.

[11–662–1]

KALMYK AUTONOMOUS SOVIET SOCIALIST REPUBLIC (in Kalmyk, Khal'mg Avtongomi Sovetsk Sotsialistichesk Respublik), Kalmykia (Khal'mg Tangch). Part of the RSFSR. On Nov. 4, 1920, the Kalmyk Autonomous Oblast was formed; it became an autonomous soviet socialist republic on Oct. 20, 1935. It is located in the extreme southeast of the European USSR; in the southeast it borders on the Caspian Sea. Area, 75,900 sq km; population, 271,000 (1972 estimate). Located in Kalmykia are 12 raions, three cities, and five urban-type settlements. Its capital is the city of Elista.

Constitution and government. The Kalmyk ASSR is a socialist state of workers and peasants, an autonomous soviet socialist republic. Its operative constitution was adopted on June 23, 1937, by the Second Extraordinary Congress of Soviets of the Kalmyk ASSR. The highest bodies of state power are the unicameral Supreme Soviet of the Kalmyk ASSR, elected by the population for terms of four years according to the norm of one deputy per 2,000 inhabitants, and its Presidium. The Supreme Soviet forms the republic's government—the Kalmykia Council of Ministers. The Kalmyk ASSR is represented in the Council of Nationalities of the Supreme Soviet of the USSR by 11 deputies. Local bodies of state power are the municipal, raion, settlement, and village soviets of working people's deputies, elected by the population for terms of two years.

The Supreme Soviet of the Kalmyk ASSR elects for a term of five years the Supreme Court of the Kalmyk ASSR, which includes two judicial divisions (one dealing with criminal cases and the other with civil cases), as well as the Presidium of the Supreme Court. The procurator of the Kalmyk ASSR is appointed by the procurator general of the USSR for a term of five years.

Natural features. Kalmykia occupies the western part of the Caspian Lowland (the Chernye Zemli, or Black Earths, in the south and the Sarpa Lowland in the north), most of the Ergeni Highland (with elevations reaching 222 m) and the Sal'sk-Manych Ridge descending from it (with an elevation of 221 m), and the Kuma-Manych depression (with an elevation of 25 m at the drainage divide).

Mineral resources include deposits of petroleum, as well as natural gas, native salt, and various building materials.

The climate is extremely continental, with hot dry summers and winters that have little snow and are often cold. The average temperature in July ranges from 23° to 26°C; in January, from −8° to −5°C. In the south (Chernye Zemli) the winters are usually without snow, and this fact allows sheep to be kept out at pasture all winter. The aridity of the climate increases from the northwest (300–400 mm of precipitation annually) to the southeast (170–200 mm). The growing season with temperatures above 10°C lasts from 180 to 213 days.

There is little surface water. In the Caspian Lowland and the Kuma-Manych depression only shallow saline lakes are found: the Sarpa Lakes, the Sostinskie Lakes, Manych-Gudilo, and Tsagan-Khak. The streams that flow briefly during the spring through the ravines of the Ergeni form extensive estuaries in the Caspian Lowland, which partially dry up during the summers. The freshened waters of the northern Caspian Sea (which have a salinity of 2 parts per thousand) are sometimes used for water supply and for watering livestock. The low-lying, swampy coastal area of the Caspian with its undergrowth of reeds and cane makes access to the sea difficult.

Most of Kalmykia is located in a semidesert zone with a complex soil-and-vegetation cover. Widespread in the northern part are light-chestnut, loamy soils, combined with solonets soils; vegetation is represented by grassy (feather-grass–fescue), herbaceous-wormwood, and wormwood associations. The east and southeast are characterized by semidesert with wormwood-herbaceous-saltwort vegetation, growing on loamy brown soils. Predominant in the Chernye Zemli are sandy-loam brown soils with herbaceous–white-wormwood–summer-cypress grass stands, which are valuable as fodder; these are used for the winter feeding of sheep and partially for selective haying. In western Kalmykia one encounters arid steppes with herbaceous and herbaceous-forb grass stands, growing on dark chestnut soils. In the ravines of the Ergeni are groves of willow, aspen, and elm.

Mammals are represented by European hares, various rodents (the small suslik, jerboa, mole-vole), and predators (the corsac, wolf, and Siberian polecat). Common ungulates are the saiga (about 200,000 head in 1970). The muskrat has also become acclimatized. Among the birds are the steppe eagle, larks, common partridge, and bustard. The lakes and rivers are inhabited by wild carp, Caspian roach, pike, and crucian carp.

V. G. KRIUCHKOV

Population. The native population (according to the 1970 census) is made up of Kalmyks (110,000). Also living in Kalmykia are Russians (123,000), Kazakhs, Darghins, Ukrainians, Byelorussians, and Tatars. From 1959 through 1970 the population increased by 140 percent. As of 1972 the average population density was 3.6 per sq km. The most densely populated areas are the Ergeni and Stavropol' Highlands, with more than 10 persons per sq km; the Chernye Zemli have less than 1 person per sq km. As of 1972 the urban population amounted to 37 percent. The cities are Elista (54,000), Kaspiiskii, and Gorodovikovsk.

Historical survey. The territory of Kalmykia was settled as long ago as the Neolithic age. During the seventh through fifth centuries B.C. the Scythians lived here and on adjacent lands; from the fourth century B.C. to the sixth century A.D. the area was inhabited by the Alani and the Sarmatians. Around the mid-seventh century the territory of the Lower Volga became a part of the Khazar Khanate; in the mid-11th century Kalmykia was included in Polovtsian territory. During the 1240's, Kalmykia became a part of the Golden Horde; after the latter's disintegration in the 1460's it was included in the Astrakhan Khanate, which in 1556 was incorporated into Russia. The Tatar-Kipchak population, which dwelt in the area between the Volga and Don rivers, was incorporated into the Russian state.

The Kalmyks, emigrants from Central Asia who had previously lived in Dzungaria and who engaged in nomadic livestock raising, arrived in the area between the Ural, Volga, and Don rivers in the early 17th century. During the 17th century Lamaism became widespread among them. Under pressure from the feudal lords of China and Mongolia and the Kazakh khans, the Kalmyks migrated to the lower reaches of the Don and Volga, where during the late 17th century they formed the Kalmyk Khanate. In 1608–09 some Oirat feudal groups—the Derbets and Torgouts (names given to the Kalmyks in the Russian sources)—voluntarily became Russian subjects and began to migrate into Southern and Western Siberia. Other Kalmyk feudal groups became part of the Russian state in the 17th and 18th centuries. This facilitated the creation of more advanced methods of directing the economy, accustomed the Kalmyks to Russian culture, and saved them from enslavement by the backward neighboring khanates.

Kalmyks took part in the Peasant War under the leadership of S. T. Razin. In 1771, because of harassment by the tsarist administration, most of the Kalmyks yielded to the persuasions of the Kalmyk khans and migrated to China. About 13,000 of the remaining Kalmyk families were transferred to the Astrakhan Province administration. In October 1771 the Kalmyk Khanate ceased to exist. Kalmyks took part in the Peasant War led by E. I. Pugachev. During the late 18th century the tsarist government resettled some of the Kalmyks along the Ural, Terek, and Kuma rivers. In the late 18th century a small number of Kalmyks who were living in the Don area were enrolled in the cossack estate of the Oblast of the Don Cossack Host. Kalmyks fought in the ranks of the Russian Army during the Patriotic War of 1812 and in other Russian wars of the 19th century. After the early 19th century the colonization of the Kalmyk steppes was accelerated. The best lands were given to large-scale livestock raisers by the tsarist government.

In 1861 the Greater Derbet *Ulus* (feudal state formation) was transferred from Astrakhan Province to Stavropol' Province. This administrative and territorial division of the Kalmyk people retarded the process of its national consolidation. The tsarist government's establishment in 1806 of the so-called ten-*verst* zone (10.7 km), which moved the border of the Kalymk nomadic area back to a distance of 30–40 km from the Volga River and the Caspian Sea, deprived the Kalmyks of the best pasture lands, as well as of trades connected with these waterways. In 1803 there were 2.5 million head of livestock in Kalmykia; in 1863, slightly more than 1 million; and in 1896, 453,000. Many of the impoverished Kalmyks left for work in the fishing and salt industries and moved to adjacent Russian settlements.

The 1892 Law on the Abolition of Compulsory Relations between Separate Estates of the Kalmyk People, which established redemption purchase, liberated the Kalmyks from feudal dependency and created some of the conditions for the development of capitalist relations. The Russian capital that penetrated into Kalmykia was, for the most part, of a usurious, commercial nature. Class stratification intensified among the masses of nomads. In the early 20th century more than 50 percent of the livestock was concentrated on the farms of the feudal nobility, the large-scale livestock raisers, and the kulaks, all of which constituted 6 percent of the total number of farms. At this same time 75 percent of Kalmyk farms were at the poverty level. The big livestock owners in fact also controlled the land; they began to use hired labor, and rent relations came into being. Nevertheless, until 1917 powerful vestiges of the feudal-patriarchal system remained.

Under the influence of the revolutionary movement in Russia the working people of Kalmykia embarked upon the path of struggle against the colonial yoke and feudal-capitalist exploitation. In 1903 an "uprising" flared up among the Kalmyk youth who were enrolled at educational institutions in Astrakhan; it was noted by the newspaper *Iskra* (May 15, 1903, no. 40). Between 1905 and 1909 outbreaks occurred in the Khosheut, Greater Derbet, and other *uluses,* but they all were suppressed. In 1907 the national-democratic union Khal'mg Tangchin Tug, which was created by progressive teachers, came into existence, but it was banned by the authorities in 1908. During World War I the tsarist government mobilized the Kalmyks for work at the front. This caused new disturbances. After the February Revolution of 1917 the Kalmyk feudal-kulak upper class supported the bourgeois Provisional Government. On July 1 (14), 1917, by a resolution of the Provisional Government, the Steppe Region of the Kalmyk People was formed. In October 1917 the feudal nobility and the nationalists attempted to draw the Kalmyk working people into the camp of the counterrevolutionary forces in southeastern Russia.

On Jan. 25 (Feb. 7), 1918, Soviet power was established in Astrakhan, which was then the administrative center of Kalmykia. From February through March soviets arose throughout Kalmykia. A Kalmyk section of the Astrakhan provincial executive committee was created. On July 1–3, 1918, the First Kalmyk Congress of Soviets was held; it formed a Kalmyk executive committee (with the status of a district). In 1918 the first Communist cells in Kalmykia were organized. In 1919 most of Kalmykia was captured by the White Guard troops of General A. I. Denikin. On July 22, 1919, the Soviet government published a call, signed by V. I. Lenin, to the Kalmyk people to fight against the White Guards. On July 24, 1919, the Council of People's Commissars of the RSFSR issued a decree on the land system, and on October 15 another decree on the preservation and restoration of livestock raising in Kalmykia. Measures taken by the Soviet authorities consolidated the Kalymk working people and activated their struggle against the counterrevolution. Two Kalmyk cavalry regiments ware formed, as well as *ulus* mounted *sotnias* (detachments of 100 men); these units took part in battles against the White Guards. O. I. Gorodovikov, one of the most famous commanders in the Civil War, was a Kalmyk. At the beginning of 1920, Kalmykia was liberated from the White Guards. The First All-Kalmyk Congress of Soviets, held in the settlement of Chilgir on July 2–9, expressed the aspiration of the Kalmyk people for national soviet autonomy. On Nov. 4, 1920, by a decree of the All-Russian Central Executive Committee and the Council of People's Commissars, the Kalmyk Autonomous Oblast was created within the RSFSR; Kalmyks from other provinces of Russia were resettled within the oblast between 1922 and 1925. On Feb. 18–20, 1921, the First Kalmyk Oblast Conference of the RCP (Bolshevik) was held, and on Aug. 23, 1921, the First Kalmyk Oblast Conference of the Russian Communist Youth League (Komsomol).

During the prewar five-year plans (1929–40), with the fraternal aid of the Russian and other peoples of the USSR, the Kalmyk people made the transition from a feudal-patriarchal society to the building of socialism, bypassing capitalism. During the second five-year plan (1933–37) the collectivization of agriculture was almost completed, and the Kalmyks changed to a settled way of life (prior to 1917 about 80 percent had led a nomadic or seminomadic way of life). During these years local industry was established, and highways and airlines were created. A cultural revolution was carried out: illiteracy was almost entirely eliminated; the vestiges of the previous feudal-patriarchal way of life disappeared; national cadres of workers and intelligentsia came into being; and higher and secondary specialized educational institutions were established, along with scholarly and scientific research institutions.

On May 6, 1927, the Council of People's Commissars decreed the transfer of the administrative center of Kalmykia from Astrakhan to Elista. In October 1935 the Kalmyk Autonomous Oblast was transformed into an ASSR. In 1937 the Supreme Soviet of the Kalmyk ASSR adopted a constitution for the republic that reflected the victory of socialist relations. The Kalmyk people were consolidated into a socialist nation.

During the Great Patriotic War of 1941–45, a considerable part of Kalmykia was occupied by the German fascist aggressors by late 1942, but by January 1943 the Soviet Army had liberated the territory of the republic. Kalmyk troops fought courageously on the fronts and in partisan detachments in the steppes of Kalmykia, Byelorussia, the Ukraine, and the Briansk region. The 110th Kalmyk Detached Cavalry Division fought in the battles on the Don and for the Northern Caucasus. Approximately 8,000 persons were awarded orders and medals, and 21 had conferred upon them the title of Hero of the Soviet Union. In December 1943, in a violation of socialist legality, the Kalmyks were uprooted from the republic's territory and resettled in the country's eastern regions, and the Kalmyk ASSR was abolished (Dec. 27, 1943). On Jan. 9, 1957, a decree was issued by the Presidium of the Supreme Soviet of the USSR providing for the restoration of Kalmyk autonomy: the Kalmyk Autonomous Oblast was established, and on July 29, 1958, it was transformed into the Kalmyk ASSR.

In 1959 the Kalmyk people celebrated the 350th anniversary of their incorporation into Russia. As a sign of recognition of this date, on Aug. 21, 1959, the Kalmyk ASSR was awarded the Order of Lenin for its achievements in economic and cultural construction. On Oct. 30, 1970, in connection with the 50th anniversary of the republic's autonomy, it was awarded the Order of the October Revolution; to mark the 50th anniversary of the USSR on Dec. 29, 1972, it was awarded the Order of the

Friendship of Peoples. By the beginning of 1972, 24 persons had been awarded the title of Hero of Socialist Labor.

B. S. SANDZHIEV

Economy. The principal role in the economy is played by agriculture and by the branches of industry concerned with processing the products of livestock raising and fishing.

AGRICULTURE. The chief branches of agriculture are the raising of fine-wooled sheep, as well as of livestock for meat, based primarily on the utilization of pasture resources. Of 5.3 million hectares (ha) of farmlands, 4 million ha are allotted to natural fodder lands (3.4 million ha for pasture and 0.6 million ha for haying). Plowed lands occupy 1 million ha, or about 19 percent of the farmlands. In 1971 there were 65 sovkhozes and 23 kolkhozes, which had 11,300 tractors (based on 15-hp units), 4,600 trucks, and 1,900 combines of various types. The development of agriculture is closely linked to the irrigation of the territory. In the west the Pravyi Egorlyk Irrigation System has been constructed (fed by the waters of the Kuban' River); in the east, the Olia-Caspian; in the north, the Sarpa (which receives its water from the Volga); and in the south, the Chernye Zemli system (the first stage of which receives its water from the Kuma and the Terek) and the Chograisk Reservoir.

The sown area has increased from 268,000 ha in 1940 to 901,000 ha in 1971. It is concentrated for the most part in the west (in the Ergeni region). Grain (wheat) and fodder crops are sown for the most part. The sown areas of grain crops increased from 213,000 ha in 1940 to 416,000 ha in 1971; fodder crops increased during the same period from 28,400 ha to 469,000 ha. The total harvest of all grain crops in 1971 amounted to 309,300 tons (as compared with 144,600 tons in 1940).

The meat production (in dressed weight) grew from 14,300 tons in 1940 to 39,400 tons in 1971; during the same period wool production increased from 3,700 tons to 13,600 tons. State purchases of livestock and poultry (in liveweight) amounted in 1971 to 53,100 tons (as compared with 24,900 tons in 1960).

Table 1. Head of livestock on all categories of farms (at the beginning of the year)

	1916	1941	1972
Cattle	259,000	212,900	352,200
including cows	92,000	76,000	119,100
Swine	21,000	20,300	74,000
Sheep and goats	735,000	1,046,200	2,462,700

INDUSTRY. Between 1940 and 1971 the output of all industry increased 680 percent. The principal branches of industry are the machine-building and metalworking, building-materials, wood-products, light, and food-processing industries. Machine building is represented by the Kaspiiskii Machine-building Plant. About a fifth of the industrial production personnel are engaged in branches processing agricultural raw material. In the food-processing industry, which produces 35 percent of the total industrial output, the meat, dairy, canning, fishery, and bakery branches are particularly significant. The most important enterprises are the Kaspiiskii Meat-canning Combine, the Arshan' Meat-packing Plant, the Kaspiiskii Fish Plant, the Gorodovikovsk Food Combine, the Elista Dairy Plant, and the Gorodovikovsk and Iashalta creameries. In 1971 the republic produced 8,800 tons of meat, 624 tons of butter, 59 tons of vegetable oil, and 8.9 million standard cans of food. Some 2,600 tons of fish were caught. The building-materials industry, in which about 10 percent of all industrial personnel are employed, produces bricks at the Elista Building-materials Combine and the Kaspiiskii, Gorodovikovsk, and Sarpa plants; also in operation are plants making reinforced-concrete products, a home-construction combine, and quarries for extracting filler rock. Consumer goods are produced by the Elista Garment Association (since 1963), the Elista knitted-goods and furniture factories, and local industrial enterprises.

The energy system of Kalmykia (which receives electric power from the Tsimliansk Hydroelectric Power Plant) is included within the Integrated Power Grid of the European USSR. The petroleum and gas industries have great prospects. In 1971, 352,-000 tons of petroleum and 549 million cu m of gas were extracted.

TRANSPORTATION. Southeastern Kalmykia is intersected by the Astrakhan-Kizliar railroad line. In 1969 the Divnoe-Elista railroad branch connected the capital of Kalmykia with central Ciscaucasia. Truck transport plays the main role in domestic freight haulage. The Elista-Divnoe highway has been constructed (with a length of about 100 km); now under construction are the Elista-Volgograd highway (264 km) and the Elista-Astrakhan highway (305 km).

Economic ties between Kalmykia and other republics of the USSR are being expanded. Kalmykia supplies many regions of the country with meat, wool, butter and vegetable-oil, leather, and canned goods. In turn it receives metals, machinery, industrial equipment, building materials, and other products.

ECONOMIC REGIONS. The Ergeni is a region of livestock raising and grain farming. Located in the irrigated land are orchards and sown areas of potatoes, vegetables, and fodder and grain crops. There are food-processing, building-materials, consumer-goods, and metalworking industries. Its center is Elista. The coastal belt (the delta *ilmeni*, or low areas covered by river overflow) has fishing in the Caspian. Food industries (processing fish and meat) and machine building are located there. Its center is Kaspiiskii. The Manych region engages in the cultivation of grain, vegetable-oil crops, fruit orchards, and vineyards and the raising of meat-and-dairy cattle, swine, and poultry. On the basis of its agricultural raw materials there is a food industry (oil-pressing, wine-making). Its center is Gorodovikovsk. The central and southern part is a region of seasonal (primarily winter) pastures that are important for the entire Soviet Union; during the winters the fine-wooled sheep from the Lower Volga region and the Northern Caucasus and some from Transcaucasia are herded here.

Standard of living. The standard of living of the people has been rising steadily. The volume of retail trade increased 10.8-fold from 1940 to 1971 (in comparable prices). Between 1966 and 1971 housing with a total area of 747,000 sq m was built and occupied; of this, 577,000 sq m was constructed with funds from state and cooperative organizations and housing cooperatives. Social security and pension insurance have also increased.

V. G. KRIUCHKOV

Public health. Prior to the Great October Socialist Revolution there were practically no public health services in Kalmykia. Infectious diseases were widespread, and the population's death rate, especially that of children, was extremely high. In 1913 there was a total of 53 hospital beds and five working physicians. By Jan. 1, 1972, there were 86 hospitals with 3,400 beds (12.7 beds per thousand population), 101 polyclinics and out-patient stations, 28 women's consultation points, and 47 nurseries with 1,700 places. There are 600 physicians in Kalmykia (one physician per 451 inhabitants) and more than 2,000 secondary medical personnel, who are trained at a medical school in Elista. In the settlement of Lola, 35 km from Elista, there is a climatic-koumiss treatment station, where a sanatorium is located for patients with tuberculosis (it is open from April through December).

G. F. TSERKOVNYI

Education and cultural affairs. During the academic year 1914–15, Kalmykia had 78 general education schools with about 4,000 pupils; there were no secondary specialized or higher educational institutions. During the 1971–72 academic year 279 general education schools of all types had an enrollment of 69,-000 pupils, five specialized secondary educational institutions had 5,700 pupils, and Kalmyk University (in Elista) had 3,200 students. In 1971 more than 8,500 children were being educated at 113 preschool institutions.

As of Jan. 1, 1972, 154 public libraries were in operation (with 1,359,000 copies of books and journals), along with the Kalmyk Republic Museum of Local Lore in Elista, 194 club-type institutions, 336 permanent motion-picture theaters, 12 Houses of Pioneers, a station for young naturalists, and nine children's sports schools.

Scientific institutions. All the scientific institutions of Kalmykia were established during the the Soviet period. As of 1972, these included the Research Institute of Language, Literature, and History attached to the republic's Council of Ministers (founded in 1941), the Kalmyk Research Institute on Livestock Raising for Meat under the RSFSR Ministry of Agriculture (founded in 1967), the Kalmyk Experimental Forestry Station under the All-Union Research Institute for the Improvement of Agriculture and Forestry (founded in 1950), and the Kalmyk Experimental Land Improvement Station (founded in 1963).

N. SH. TASHNINOV

Press, radio, and television. In 1971, 87 books and pamphlets were published, with a total of 431,000 copies; nine magazines were issued with an annual circulation of 23,000; and 15 newspapers appeared, with an annual circulation of 71,791,000. Republic newspapers are *Khal'mg unn* (Kalmyk Pravda, since 1920) in Kalmyk and *Sovetskaia Kalmykiia* (since 1920) and *Komsomolets Kalmykii* (since 1929) in Russian; also published is an anthology of literature and the arts in Kalmyk and Russian entitled *Teegin gerl* (Light in the Steppes; since 1957).

The republic's radio and television broadcasts are carried in Kalmyk and Russian on one radio and one television program; broadcasts are also relayed from Moscow. There is a television broadcasting center in Elista.

Literature. Kalmyk written literature originated on the basis of a rich national folklore. Stories and legends, sayings and proverbs, songs, *iorels* (good wishes), *magtals* (panegyrics), *kharals* (incantations), tales, and the apex of all folk creativity—the epic *Dzhangar* (15th century)—constitute a substantial contribution to the treasury of world culture.

Prior to the creation in 1648 by Zaia Pandit (1599–1662) of a Kalmyk writing system ("clear writing"), Kalmyks employed the common Mongolian alphabet and shared a common literature with the Mongols (for example, *The Secret History of the Mongols,* 13th century). The creation of a writing system had a beneficial influence on the emergence of a national literature, resulting in the appearance of such works as *The Light of the Moon* (17th century), *A Story About the Derben-Oirats* (1739) by Gaban Sharab, and *Journey to Tibet* (1897), among others. During the 19th century wide renown was enjoyed by the freedom-proclaiming verses of Onchkhan Dzhirgal, which were directed against foreign invaders and native oppressors. Especially popular was the narrative poem by Boovan Badma (1880–1917) entitled *The Pleasure of Rumor* (1916), which exposed the vices of the Lamaist church.

The Great October Revolution unchained the people's creative forces and opened a wide scope for the emergence and formation of Kalmyk Soviet literature. Its founders were Kh. Kanukov (1883–1933) and N. Mandzhiev (1905–36). In the mid-1920's many young people entered the field of literature, including S. Kaliaev (born 1905), A. Suseev (born 1905), and Kh. Sian-Belgin (born 1909). At this time the foremost place was occupied by poetry devoted to the heroism of the revolution, the Civil War and the joys of victory, the first buds of the new life, and the unbreakable friendship among fraternal peoples.

The great revolutionary changes, along with the breakup of an age-old order, made it necessary to create a literary prose. A picture of the great transformation is drawn in the first short stories by N. Mandzhiev, "The Little Master of a Large Home" (1928) and "The Adventures of Red Mandzhik" (1933), and in the chronicle-novel *The Son of Mudresh* (1925) and the novellas *Aranzal* (1932) and *In the Steppes* (1935) by A. Amur-Sanan (1888–1939).

The late 1920's and early 1930's in Kalmykia were characterized by the further growth of literature. New names began to appear in this field: B. Basangov (1911–44), G. Davan (1913–37), Ts. Ledzhinov (1910–42), and K. Erendzhenov (born 1912). The poets strove to convey events realistically, and they created the first spiritually and emotionally rich portrayals of their contemporaries; such are the heroes of the narrative poems *The Brigadier* (1934) by Kaliaev and *The Fighting Orphan* (1935) by Sian-Belgin and of the poetry collection *Heart of Steel* (1929) by Suseev. The prose writers Mandzhiev in his *Story of a Kolkhoz* (1936), Basangov in *The Truth of Bygone Days* (1930) and *Bulgun* (1934), and Erendzhenov in *Shepherd's Song* (1932) successfully interpreted the people's historic past and depicted collectivization. During the 1930's and 1940's many new writers entered the field of literature: L. Indzhiev (born 1913), M. Narmaev (born 1915), E. Kekteev (1918–65), B. Dordzhiev (1918–

69), B. Dzhimbinov (born 1914), B. Erdniev (born 1906), D. Kugul'tinov (born 1922), I. Matsakov (born 1907), P. Dzhidleev (1913–40), and the *dzhaigarchi* (storytellers) B. Mukebenov (1878–1944) and D. Shavaliev (1884–1959). In drama the most important plays were Basangov's *The Country of Bumba* (1940), *An Incident Worthy of Amazement, The Tardy Rich Man* (1941), and *Song About Mother.* A. Balakaev (born 1928) and B. Erdniev, among others, also wrote significant plays.

Lofty civic feeling and profound patriotism were to be noted in the literature of the wartime years. The shorter forms—poems, short stories, sketches, and publicistic pieces—acquired a special significance.

The 1950's in Kalmyk literature were characterized by a heightening of interest in moral and ethical problems, as well as in the heroism of labor. The ranks of the writers were considerably enlarged by B. Sangadzhieva (born 1921), M. Khoninov (born 1919), A. Badmaev (born 1924), A. Dzhimbiev (born 1924), and T. Bembeev (born 1930), among others. The theme of the war continued to attract the attention of Kalmyk writers: the lyric and narrative poems of Kaliaev, Kulgul'tinov, Sian-Belgin, Suseev, Khoninov, and Kekteev; the novels *Lotus* by Bembeev (1965) and *Bad Weather, There in the Distance* by Badmaev (1964); and the novellas *Stalingrad* by Narmaev (1958), *When It Is Hard for a Person* by Dzimbiev (1968), and *Green Love* by Balakaev (1968).

During the 1960's many new novels appeared—a testimony to the development of the large epic-narrative form and to the maturity of Kalmyk literature: Badmaev's *Rivers Flow From Their Sources* (1969), Dordzhiev's *The True Path* (parts 1–2, 1963–64), Indzhiev's *Ol'da's Daughter* (1963), Erenzhenov's *Guard the Fire* (books 1–2, 1963–65), Narmaev's *Manych River* (1963), and Balakaev's *Stars Over Elista* (book 1, 1963). The title of People's Poet has been awarded to Kaliaev, Suseev, Sian-Belgin, and Kugul'tinov.

Notable successes have been achieved in Kalmyk children's literature, satire, and humorous literature. Criticism and literary scholarship have developed (I. Matsakov; A. Kichikov, born 1921; M. Dzhimgirov, born 1927; S. Kenzeev, born 1913; Ts. Korsunkiev, born 1919).

The Writers' Union publishes the anthology *Teegin gerl* (since 1957) in Kalmyk and Russian. Works by Kalmyk writers are translated into Russian and the languages of other peoples of the USSR.

T. O. BEMBEEV

Architecture and art. The Kalmyk nomadic or seminomadic livestock raisers during the 17th–19th centuries usually had dwellings (*ger*) that could be assembled and taken apart, with lattice frames covered by heavy felt. With the spread of Lamaism, *khurul* monasteries were built—complexes of buildings that were initially made of felt and wood, but of brick and stone after the late 18th century. The monasteries contained temples, chapels, cells, and workshops. The main temple usually had a high, central space crowned by a tower; it was richly ornamented with carving, painting, bronze sculpture, and religious figures. During the Soviet period the capital of Kalmykia, Elista, and the cities of Kaspiiskii and Gorodovikovsk, as well as Komsomol'skii and other settlements, have been laid out with modern, well-designed apartment houses and public buildings for cultural, everyday, and administrative uses (for example, the House of Soviets in Elista, 1930's; architect, I. A. Golosov). The architects M. B. Piurveev, V. M. Telegin, and N. S. Baraev have also been working in the republic.

Folk decorative art is varied in its forms. The wooden parts of dwellings, furniture, and utensils were decorated with carving and painting that created the impression of three-dimensionality. Stamping was used to imprint patterns (floral motifs, solar signs, horn motifs) on leather flasks (*bortkha*) and footwear. Embroidery and appliqué were used in making articles of felt and ceremonial women's costumes and caps (gold and silver threads were blended with colored wool, braid, and sometimes beads). Predominant in the embroidery are floral motifs (stems, leaves, rosettes, and the tulip, which became a symbol of Kalmykia's flourishing). Also widespread is the unique pattern known as the *zeeg,* consisting of a series of little arches (schematically depicting the *ger*), encircled by polychrome bands, sometimes with a rosette in the center. Silver articles, such as pendants to braids, rings, earrings, and belts, were ornamented with embossed, engraved, chased, and pierced patterns.

The art of the 18th and 19th centuries is represented by the painting of religious figures and block-printing of books and religious figures, which relied on the Tibetan-Mongolian tradition. The graphic artist F. I. Kalmyk and the painter A. E. Egorov worked beyond the borders of Kalmykia during the 18th and 19th centuries, but it was only in the Soviet period that art began to be developed intensively. During the 1930's the painters I. S. Nuskhaev, L. E. Ochirov and P. I. Emchigirova, and the theater designer D. V. Sychev came to the fore. During the 1960's the painters G. O. Rokchinskii and K. M. Ol'daev (who paint portraits and pictures on historical and everyday themes), the graphic artist B. F. Danil'chenko, and the sculptors N. A. Sandzhiev, V. S. Vas'kin, and N. Ia. Eledzhiev became well known.

Music. Prior to the October Revolution the art of Kalmyk music existed solely in the oral folk tradition. The folk song was monophonic and was performed in a special style of vocalization in a guttural sound by the folksingers—the *duuchi* and *dzhangarchi* (epic reciters). The drawn-out songs—the *ut dun*—are characterized by improvisation; their sound range frequently exceeds an octave, and the performers add vowel sounds and syllables, thereby extending the melodic line. The short songs—*akhr dun*—are simpler, usually in couplet form and with a marked rhythm. They are closely related to the joke songs and dance songs, the *keldg bildzh dun* ("spoken songs"), which are similar to *chastushki* (form of Russian folk poetry) and are performed to the accompaniment of the domra or Saratov accordion. The modal system of Kalmyk songs is diatonic, but preserves individual pentatonic turns. Men's dances have lively, quick tempos; women's dances have more lyrical and flowing melodies.

After the October Revolution amateur choral and dance groups and domra orchestras were formed. Choral performances utilizing two and three voices began to appear. A new stage in the development of a national art of the musical theater was the presentation *Ulan sar* (Red Moon; staged in 1931 in Saratov), with a chorus, a dance group, and symphonic, wind, domra, and *khural* orchestras. The year 1934 saw the publication of a collection of folk songs, transcribed by M. L. Trituz; subsequently arrangements of Kalmyk folk songs were made (D. S. Vasil'ev-Buglai, Z. L. Kompaneets).

The composers V. A. Gaigerova, A. E. Spadavekkia, M. O. Grachev, B. B. Iampilov, Zh. A. Batuev, and P. Chonkushev have written works on the basis of Kalmyk musical folklore. Among the leading figures in Kalmyk music are Honored Artist of the RSFSR V. Gariaeva, Honored Artists of the Kalmyk ASSR V. Il'tsaranova and A. Mukaeva, the conductor S. G. Dordzhin, the singer Honored Artist of the Kalmyk ASSR U. B. Lidzhieva, and the domrists B. Erdniev and B. Ochaev. The drama theater orchestra has played a prominent role in the development of a national musical art.

As of 1972 performing groups in the Kalmyk ASSR included the Tulip Kalmyk Song and Dance Ensemble (1937) and, associated with this ensemble, an orchestra of folk instruments (1970), the Kalmyk Philharmonia (1939), and a republic division of the Choral Society (1967). Musical education is provided by the School of Music in Elista (1960), 18 children's music schools, and three children's choral schools.   M. L. TRITUZ [11–648–2]

Theater. Prior to the October Revolution, Kalmyks had no theatrical art. In 1926 a Kalmyk drama school was established in Astrakhan; it was reorganized in 1930 as an arts technicum with acting, music, and choreographic divisions. In 1936 graduates of the school and technicum became members of the Kalmyk National Theater Studio. The directors V. A. Gol'dfel'd and L. N. Aleksandrov, among others, took part in the formation of the Kalmyk theater. Among the productions of the 1930's and 1940's were *The Fighting Orphan* by Kh. Sian-Belgin, *The Insurrection* by D. M. Furmanov (both in 1936), *Chuche* and *The Tardy Rich Man* by B. Basangov (both in 1937), Molière's *The Doctor in Spite of Himself* and Pushkin's *The Gypsies* (both in 1937), K. A. Trenev's *Furious Love* (1938), B. Erdniev's *Siakhlia* (1939), and A. Suseev's *In Search of Happiness* (1940).

In 1941 the Theater Studio troupe was merged with graduates of the Kalmyk Studio of the State Institute of Theatrical Arts. In 1942 the theater was closed, but it reopened in 1958 in Elista (Kalmyk and Russian troupes work there). In 1963 the theater was renamed for the writer B. Basangov. Among the theater's productions between the late 1950's and early 1970's were *Sophia's Song* by R. Khubetsovaia and G. Khugaev (1959), *Typhoon* by Ts'ao Yu (1960), *The Obelisk* by G. Mamlin (1966), *On the Night of the Lunar Eclipse* (1966) and *The Country of Aigul'* (1970) by M. Karim, *An Incident Worthy of Amazement* (1959), *The Country of Bumba* (1967), and *Song About Mother* (1969) by B. Basangov, *In the Name of the Revolution* by M. F. Shatrov (1968), and *The Snowstorm* by B. Sangadzhieva and *Lenin's Call* by S. Kaliaev (both in 1970). In 1963 the theater's troupe was merged with a group of graduates from the Kalmyk Studio of the Leningrad Institute of Theater, Music, and Cinematography.

As of 1972 those active in the theatrical arts included Honored Artist of the RSFSR and the Kalmyk ASSR M. Ts. Erendzhenov; Honored Artists of the RSFSR B. B. Balbakova and E. G. Mandzhiev; Honored Workers in the Arts of the Kalmyk ASSR L. N. Aleksandrov and D. V. Sychev; and Honored Artists of the Kalmyk ASSR N. P. Badenova, Iu. U. Il'ianov, U. B. Lidzhieva, B. B. Memeeva, U. D. Narkaeva, E. B. Rusakova, A. M. Sasykov, U. K. Susukov, I. A. Ulanov, and S. B. Iashkulov.

REFERENCES

Rossiiskaia Federatsiia: Evropeiskii Iugo-Vostok, Povolzh'e, Severnyi Kavkaz. Moscow, 1968. (In the series *Sovetskii Soiuz.*)
Iakinf (Bichurin). *Istoricheskoe obozrenie oiratov ili kalmykov s XV stoletiia do nastoiashchego vremeni.* St. Petersburg, 1834.
Ocherki istorii Kalmytskoi ASSR [vols. 1–2]. Moscow, 1967–70.
Gorodovikov, B. B. *Ordenonosnaia Kalmykiia.* Elista, 1970.
50 let pod znamenem Oktiabria: Sb. st. Elista, 1967.
Kalmytskaia ASSR za 50 let Sovetskoi vlasti. Elista, 1967.
Kozin, S. A. *Dzhangariada.* Moscow-Leningrad, 1940.
Kalmytskii epos "Dzhangar": Sb. statei. Rostov-on-Don, 1940.
Dzhimbinov, B. O. "Kalmytskaia literatura i fol'klor." In *Sovetskaia Kalmykiia.* Moscow, 1960.
Kalmytskaia khudozhestvennaia literatura na pod"eme. Elista, 1962.
Khal'mg poezin antolog. Elista, 1962.
O Dzhangare: Sb. materialov. Elista, 1963.
Matsanov, I. M. *Kalmytskaia sovetskaia khudozhestvennaia literatura (20–30 gody).* Elista, 1967.
Matsanov, I. M. *Sovremennaia kalmytskaia proza.* Elista, 1970.
Poety Kalmykii. [Foreword by B. Dzhimbinov and S. Lipkin.] Moscow, 1970.
Piurveev, V. D. *Kalmytskaia dramaturgiia.* Elista, 1970.
Dzhimgirov, M. E. *Pisateli Sovetskoi Kalmykii.* Elista, 1966.
Dzhangar: Kalmytskii narodnyi epos. Elista, 1971.
Troshin, I. I. *Ocherki izobrazitel'nogo iskusstva Kalmykii.* Volgograd, 1970. (Research Institute of Language, Literature, and History.)
Kovalev, I. G. *Kalmytskii narodnyi ornament.* [Elista, 1970.]
Sychev, D. V. *Kalmytskoe narodnoe iskusstvo:* [Album. Elista, 1970.]
Trituz, M. L. *Muzykal'naia kul'tura Kalmytskoi ASSR.* Moscow, 1965.
[11–648–2]

KALMYK CATTLE, a breed of beef cattle. Kalmyk cattle were developed by prolonged improvement of cattle brought by nomadic Kalmyk tribes from Western Mongolia about 350 years ago. The breed is noted for its strong constitution and good proportions. The body is of medium length, the chest broad and deep, the withers broad, the spine straight and broad, the rump broad, the legs strong and thin. The color is red of various shades, sometimes with white markings, mottled-red, more rarely rust-colored and mottled-brown. The weight of bulls is 600–800 kg, of cows 420–450 kg. The cattle are not particular about fodder and living conditions; they use winter pastures well, fatten rapidly in the spring and autumn, and maintain their weight well during summer droughts and long winterings. They are distinguished by their ability to fatten rapidly at a young age. By the age of 1½ young bulls left for breeding weigh 450–550 kg, steers 380–420 kg. Fattened steers 16–18 months old yield a carcass with a weight of 190–220 kg. The dressed weight is 57–60 percent. The meat has excellent flavor. Milk yield of the cows is 650–1,000 kg per year. The butterfat content of the milk is 4.2–4.4 percent. Bullocks are used as work animals. The Kalmyk breed is raised in the Kalmyk ASSR, Stavropol' Krai, and Rostov, Astrakhan, Aktiubinsk, and Dzhambul oblasts.

REFERENCES

Skotovodstvo: Krupnyi rogatyi skot, vol. 1. Moscow, 1961.
Narmaev, M. B. *Kalmytskii skot i ego sovershenstvovanie.* Elista, 1963.

[11–661–1]

KALMYKOV, BETAL EDYKOVICH. Born Oct. 24 (Nov. 5), 1893, in the village of Atazhukino, now Kuba, in Baksan Raion, Kabarda-Balkar ASSR; died Feb. 27, 1940. One of the organizers and leaders of the struggle of the mountain peoples (*gortsy*) for Soviet power in the Northern Caucasus. Soviet statesman and party figure. Became a member of the Communist Party in 1918. The son of a poor peasant.

Kalmykov began work at the age of 14 as a shepherd; then he became a worker. From 1912 on he carried out revolutionary work among the mountain peoples. He helped organize and lead the democratic revolutionary league of mountain poor called Karakhalk (The Poor). Kalmykov was persecuted by the tsarist authorities. In 1918 he was a delegate to all five congresses of the peoples of Terek Oblast and a member of the Terek people's soviet; he led the work of the first congress of Nal'chik Okrug, which proclaimed Soviet power in Kabarda and Balkaria in March 1918. He became a member of the Council of People's Commissars and emergency commissar of Kabarda-Balkaria and then was commissar for nationalities. Kalmykov was involved in the Civil War in the Northern Caucasus; he was one of the organizers of the guerrilla movement and commanded a regiment and a division in the Red Army. In 1919 he was a member of the mountain section of the Caucasian Krai committee of the RCP (Bolshevik). After the rout of the White Guard forces in March 1920, Kalmykov became the chairman of the revolutionary committee of Kabarda and Balkaria. Between 1920 and 1930 he was the chairman of the executive committee of the Kabarda-Balkar Oblast. From 1930 to 1938 he was first secretary of the Kabarda-Balkar Oblast committee of the ACP (Bolshevik). Kalmykov was elected a member of the All-Russian Central Executive Committee of the RSFSR and of the Central Executive Committee of the USSR. He was a deputy to the first convocation of the Supreme Soviet of the USSR and a delegate to the Eleventh through Seventeenth Congresses of the party. Kalmykov was awarded the Order of Lenin and the Order of the Red Banner.

REFERENCE

B. E. Kalmykov—vydaiushchiisia obshchestvennyi i gosudarstvennyi deiatel' Kabardino-Balkarii: Sb. statei i vospominanii. Nal'chik, 1960.

[11–647–1]

KALMYKOV, VALERII DMITRIEVICH. Born Aug. 28, 1908, in Rostov-on-Don; died Mar. 22, 1974. Soviet statesman and economic figure; Hero of Socialist Labor (1961). Became a member of the CPSU in 1942. The son of a clerical worker.

Kalmykov began work in 1924 as an electrician. While working, he completed studies at the Rostov Industrial Technicum in 1929 and at the Moscow Institute of Power Engineering in 1934. From 1929 to 1933, Kalmykov worked at the Moskabel' Factory as a foreman and shop superintendent. Between 1935 and 1949 he held the positions of design engineer, chief designer, and director of a research institute. After 1949 he was engaged in economic and state management. From 1954 to 1957, Kalmykov was minister of the radio-engineering industry of the USSR. From 1957 to 1965 he was chairman of the State Committee on Radioelectronics of the Council of Ministers of the USSR, a ministerial post. After March 1965 he was minister of the radioelectronics industry of the USSR. At the Twentieth Congress of the CPSU in 1956, Kalmykov was elected a candidate member of the party's Central Committee. He was elected a member of the Central Committee at the Twenty-second (1961), Twenty-third (1966), and Twenty-fourth (1971) Congresses of the party. Kalmykov was a deputy to the fifth through eighth convocations of the Supreme Soviet of the USSR. He received the State Prize of the USSR in 1948 and 1952. He was awarded seven Orders of Lenin, the Order of the October Revolution, and medals.

[11–647–2]

KALMYKOVA, ALEKSANDRA MIKHAILOVNA. Born Dec. 26, 1849 (Jan, 7, 1850), in Ekaterinoslav (now Dnepropetrovsk); died Apr. 1, 1926, in Leningrad. Progressive Russian public figure.

After completing training in a *Gymnasium,* Kalmykova received a diploma as a schoolteacher. In the 1880's she participated in the organization and operation in Kharkov and St. Petersburg of Sunday schools to eliminate illiteracy among adolescents. She took part in the Narodnik (Populist) movement and was connected with the Liberation of Labor group; later she had ties with activists in the St. Petersburg Union of Struggle for the Emancipation of the Working Class. Kalmykova was on the editorial boards of the "legal Marxist" magazines *Novoe slovo* and *Nachalo.* From 1889 to 1902 she maintained a storehouse of popular literature in St. Petersburg that served as a meeting place for Social Democrats; she supported Lenin's *Iskra* and *Zaria* with donations. In 1902, Kalmykova was exiled abroad. She gave financial assistance to Bolsheviks. According to N. K. Krupskaia, Lenin had absolute trust in Kalmykova. After the October Revolution in 1917 she worked in public education and at the K. D. Ushinskii Pedagogical Institute in Leningrad.

REFERENCE

Krupskaia, N. K. *Vospominaniia o Lenine.* Moscow, 1968. Pages 19–20.

[11–648–1]

KALMYKS (self-designation, Khal'mg), people living mainly in the Kalmyk ASSR, as well as in Astrakhan, Volgograd, and Rostov oblasts and Stavropol' Krai, RSFSR. Total Kalmyk population in the USSR, 137,000 (1970 census). Their language is Kalmyk. Lamaism, the former religion of the Kalmyks, has virtually disappeared in the Soviet period.

The Oirats, the ancestors of the Kalmyks, who inhabited Central Asia during the first and early second millennia A.D., were members of the large Tung-Hu, Hsiang-pi, Juan-Juan, and Khitan political alliances; later, in the 13th and 14th centuries, they were part of the feudal military empire of Genghis Khan and his successors. In the late 14th century the Oirats were an independent political force known as the *derben ord* (the tribes of the "four allies": the Dörbet, Khoshut, Torgut, and Choros). The state created by them represented a confederation of ethnically complex feudal formations, like the appanage principalities of other peoples. A migration of the Oirats into Russia, to the lower course of the Volga and the Caspian Sea region, took place in the late 16th century and the first third of the 17th century. The Kalmyk people, the nucleus of which were the Oirats, developed during the migration to their present homeland and settlement there. Turkic, Russian, and some other ethnic elements also played a part in their formation, although their relative significance in the formation of the Kalmyks was comparatively small.

Soviet power was established in Kalmykia in 1918; the Kalmyk Autonomous Oblast was created in 1920 and made into the Kalmyk ASSR in 1935. In late 1943 a violation of socialist law occurred, resulting in the resettlement of the Kalmyks to the eastern regions of the country. The Decree of the Presidium of the Supreme Soviet of the USSR on the Restoration of Kalmyk Autonomy (the Kalmyk Autonomous Oblast, which became the Kalmyk ASSR in 1958) was promulgated on Jan. 9, 1957. Almost all of the Kalmyks returned to their homeland.

The basic economy of most Kalmyks in the past consisted of nomadic and seminomadic livestock raising (cattle, sheep, horses, and camels); certain groups of Kalmyks engaged in fishing. In the 1830's the Kalmyks in Ergeni began to till the soil. All of the Kalmyks began to take up a settled way of life under Soviet power during the prewar five-year plans of 1929–40. Modern cities and villages sprang up. The modern Soviet way of life and new traditions and customs were accepted. Farming was transformed into mechanized kolkhoz and sovkhoz production. Large-scale industry is being developed in the republic. Cadres of the national working class and intelligentsia were formed.

REFERENCES

Narody Evropeiskoi chasti SSSR, vol. 2. Moscow, 1964.
Ocherki istorii Kalmytskoi ASSR, vols. 1–2. Moscow, 1967–70.
Erdniev, U. E. *Kalmyki (konets XIX–nachalo XX vv.): Istoriko-etnografi-cheskie ocherki.* Elista, 1970.
Nominkhanov, D. Ts.-D. *Ocherki istorii kul'tury kalmytskogo naroda.* Elista, 1969.
Zasedaniia Verkhovnogo Soveta SSSR chetvertogo sozyva: Shestaia sessiia (5–12 fevralia 1957). Moscow, 1957. (Stenographic record.)
G. G. Stratanovich and Iu. I. Zhuravlev [11–646–2]

KALMYK UNIVERSITY, founded in 1970 in Elista from the Kalmyk Pedagogical Institute, which was established in 1964. As of 1972 the university included departments of physics and mathematics, biology, history and philology, agriculture, and general technology; 19 subdepartments; 41 training and scientific laboratories; a scientific research section; and a library with 250,000 volumes. In 1972 the university's enrollment was 3,200 (in its daytime, evening, and correspondence divisions), and there were about 200 instructors, including approximately 100 with scholarly degrees and titles. [11–661–2]

KALNBERZIN, IAN EDUARDOVICH (Jan Kalnberziņš). Born Sept. 5 (17), 1893, in the *volost* (small rural district) of Katlakalns, now Riga Raion. Soviet statesman and party leader. Hero of Socialist Labor (1963). Became a member of the CPSU in 1917. The son of a worker.

In 1908, while working as an anchor-master on the docks at the port of Riga, Kalnberzin joined the revolutionary movement. In 1919 he took part in the struggle for Soviet power in Latvia. After the fall of Soviet power there, Kalnberzin left for Soviet Russia with a detachment of armed workers. He was a volunteer in the Red Army and participated in the Civil War of 1918–20. He studied at the Marchlewski Communist University of the West (1923–25 and 1928–29). From 1925 to 1928 he carried on underground party work in Latvia. In 1928 he returned to Moscow. From 1931 to 1933 he studied at the Institute of the Red Professoriat.

From 1936 to 1939, Kalnberzin directed underground party work in Riga. In 1939 he was arrested but was freed in 1940 after the overthrow of the fascist regime. From 1940 to 1959 he was first secretary of the Central Committee of the Communist Party (Bolshevik) of Latvia. He became a candidate member of the Central Committee of the ACP (Bolshevik) in 1941, and at the Nineteenth through Twenty-third Congresses of the party he was elected a member of the Central Committee of the CPSU. From 1957 to 1961 he was a candidate member of the Presidium of the Central Committee of the CPSU. In 1959 he became chairman of the Presidium of the Supreme Soviet of the Latvian SSR, and in 1960 he became vice-chairman of the Presidium of the Supreme Soviet of the USSR. He was a deputy to the first through seventh convocations of the Supreme Soviet of the USSR. Since May 1970 he has been living on a pension. Kalnberzin was awarded seven Orders of Lenin, the Order of the October Revolution, the Order of the Patriotic War First Class, and medals. [11–662–2]

KALNCIEMS, an urban-type settlement in Jelgava Raion, Latvian SSR, situated on the Lielupe River, 17 km north of the Jelgava railway junction. Population, 3,000 (1970). Kalnciems has a building-materials combine (bricks, slag wool, heat-insulating panels, glass-fiber reinforced plastic). [11–664–2]

KALNIN', ALFRED IANOVICH (also Alfrēds Kalniņš). Born Aug. 11 (23), 1879, in Cēsis; died Dec. 23, 1951, in Riga. Soviet composer and public figure; People's Artist of the Latvian SSR (1945).

Kalnin' studied at the St. Petersburg Conservatory (1897–1901). He began his career as a composer in the first decade of the 20th century and also worked as an organist and choral conductor. In 1925–26 he was one of the directors of the Latvian National Opera, and from 1927 to 1933 he lived in the USA. From 1944 to 1948 he was rector of the Lavian Conservatory (in 1947 he became a professor). He composed the first Latvian opera, *Banuta* (staged in 1920; revised version, 1941). In 1943 he composed a ballet entitled *Staburags* (*Staburadze* in its second version, 1957; State Prize of the Latvian SSR, 1958), which contained elements of Latvian musical folklore.

Kalnin' was a master of the Latvian solo and choral ballad, cantata, song, and arrangements of Latvian songs. Many of Kalnin's songs were based on texts by the poet J. Rainis. He also enriched various forms of Latvian instrumental-symphonic, piano, and organ music. Kalnin's music is characterized by national themes, melodic richness, and imagery.

REFERENCES

Vitoliņš, J. *Alfrēds Kalniņš.* Riga, 1968.
Klotiņš, A. *Alfrēda Kalniņa Klaviermūzika.* Riga, 1970. [11–663–2]

KALNIN', ARVID IANOVICH (also Arvids Kalniņš). Born Aug. 6 (18), 1894, in Bebru, present-day Stučka Raion. Soviet specialist in xylology and lumber technology; academician of the Academy of Sciences of the Latvian SSR (1946) and Honored Scientist of the Latvian SSR (1945).

After graduating from the Riga Polytechnic Institute in 1916, Kalnin' was a teacher and scientist. His main work was on problems of xylology, the chemical modification of wood, and the lumber industry. In 1925 he was the first to show that chemicals could be used to stimulate the formation and separation of soft resin when tapping conifers. In the late 1950's he substantiated the possibility of making economical the complete use of all wood by-products and significantly refining the wood of soft deciduous species. In 1946 he became director of the Institute of Lumber Industry Problems and, in 1963, director of the Institute of Wood Chemistry of the Academy of Sciences of the Latvian SSR. He was awarded the State Prize of the USSR in 1951 and the State Prize of the Latvian SSR in 1957. He has also been awarded two Orders of Lenin, three other orders, and various medals.

WORKS

Mežu tehnologija. Riga, 1925.
Technical Properties of Latvian Coniferous Timber (Pinus silvestus *L.,* Picea excelsa *Lk. and* Larix europea *DC) With Relation to Conditions of Growth.* Riga, 1938.
"Neispol'zovannye vozmozhnosti khimicheskoi pererabotki drevesiny." *Vestnik AN SSSR,* 1956, no. 4.
"Voprosy kompleksnogo khimicheskogo ispol'zovaniia lesosyr'evykh resursov v rabotakh latviiskikh uchenykh." In *Lesnoe khoziaistvo i promyshlennoe potreblenie drevesiny v SSSR: Doklady k VI Mirovomu lesnomu kongressu.* Moscow, 1966.

REFERENCE

Akademik A. I. Kalnin'sh: Bibliografiia. Riga, 1964.
Ia. V. Peive [11–663–3]

KALNIN, OSKAR IUR'EVICH (also Oskar Kalniņš; party pseudonym, Ugis). Born Mar. 29 (Apr. 10), 1895, in Ogre, present-day Latvian SSR; died Nov. 20, 1920, in the village of Kryshichi, Byelorussian SSR. Hero of the Civil War of 1918–20. Member of the Communist Party from 1911.

Kalnin took part in the revolutionary movement in Russia and Latvia. In 1915 he was drafted into the army. He studied at the Saratov Ensigns' School. In 1916 he was arrested for revolutionary propaganda, but he escaped from prison. In 1917 he became one of the leaders of the Red Guards in Moscow and participated in the October armed uprising. Kalnin was a member of the Rogozhsko-Simonovskii soviet and the Military Revolutionary Committee and a militia chief. Beginning in June 1918 he was military commissar of the Rogozhsko-Simonovskii District of Moscow. From June 1918 to July 1919 he was a member of the Revolutionary Military Council of the First Army of the Eastern Front, and from July 1919 he was a member of the Revolutionary Military Council of the Soviet Latvian Army. From September 1919 he was commissar of the 11th Rifle Division, and in 1920 he was attached to the chief of staff of the Western Front. From July 1920 he was a brigade commander in the 48th Rifle Division. He died while fighting heroically against the band of Bulak-Balakhovich. Kalnin was awarded two Orders of the Red Banner. [11–663–1]

KAL'NING, OTTO IVANOVICH (also O. I. Kalninš). Born Feb. 13 (25), 1856, in Ogre, present-day Latvian SSR; died Mar. 25 (Apr. 6), 1891, in Tartu. Russian veterinary physician.

After graduating from the Dorpat (Tartu) Veterinary Institute (1877), Kal'ning served in the Russian Army until the end of his life (in 1877–78 he participated in the liberation of Bulgaria); from 1878 to 1886, when he was in Bulgaria with other Russian veterinary physicians, he founded veterinary science in Bulgaria. In 1891 he obtained mallein from a glanders culture. He died after contracting glanders.   [11–696–3]

KÁLNOKY, GUSTAV. Born Dec. 29, 1832, in Lettowitz; died Feb. 13, 1898, in Prödlitz. Austro-Hungarian statesman and diplomat. From 1871 to 1874 he was the Austro-Hungarian representative at the Vatican. In 1874 he became envoy to Denmark; in 1880, ambassador to Russia. From 1881 to 1895, Kálnoky was minister of foreign affairs. He facilitated the establishment of the Triple Alliance of 1882. Kálnoky's policy was characterized by plans to establish Austro-Hungarian hegemony in the Balkans with the aid of Germany, after weakening Russia's position there.   [11–696–4]

KALNROZE, VALDIS (pseudonym of V. Rozenberg). Born Jan. 5 (17), 1894, in Kuldiga. Soviet landscape painter. Honored Artist of the Latvian SSR (1963).

Kalnroze studied in Riga at the Latvian Academy of Arts (1927–32) under V. Purvītis. His landscapes (primarily of the rivers and the Baltic seacoast of Latvia) convey spatial depth and are characterized by a distinctive, decorative painting technique; they contain large areas of silvery gray colors. Among Kalnroze's paintings are *Daugava* (1935), *Autumn Landscape* (1942), *Sea* (1956), and *In a River Cove* (1957)—all located in the Art Museum of the Latvian SSR in Riga. He also painted *Cloudy Day* (1962, Directorate of the Art Museums and Exhibitions of the Latvian SSR) and *Landscape With River* (1966).

REFERENCE
Straume, I. *Valdis Kalnroze*. Riga, 1969. (In Latvian and Russian.)
                    [11–664–1]

KALNYN', EDUARD FRIDRIKHOVICH. Born Oct. 12 (25), 1904, in Riga. Soviet painter. People's Artist of the USSR (1975). Member of the Academy of Arts of the USSR (1970).

Kalnyn' studied under V. Purvītis at the Latvian Academy of Arts in Riga from 1923 to 1932. He became an instructor at the Academy of Arts of the Latvian SSR in 1945; receiving a professorship there in 1955. Kalnyn's art played a large role in the development of Latvian genre painting. His landscapes and genre scenes are characterized by large-scale compositions and large, rhythmic planes of color. They are primarily devoted to the difficult work of fishermen and the magnificent beauty of the elements of the sea. Kalnyn's works include *The Raftsmen* (1935), *New Sails* (1945), *The Seventh Baltic Regatta* (1952), *Latvian Fishermen in the Atlantic* (1957), and *In the Distance* (1967)—all except the last painting are in the Museum of Art of the Latvian SSR in Riga.

REFERENCE
Eduards Kalninš (album). Riga, 1959. (In Latvian and Russian.)
                    [11–664–3]

KAL'O, RIKHARD IANOVICH. Born July 2 (15), 1914, in St. Petersburg. Soviet graphic artist. Honored Art Worker of the Estonian SSR (1964).

Kal'o studied at the Pallas School of Art in Tartu (1936–40) under A. Laigo and taught at the Tartu Art Institute (1944–48). He works mainly in the technical media of pen-and-ink drawing, wood engraving, and line engraving. Kal'o's prints (*The Liberation of the Prisoners*, colored wood engraving, 1940; *The Refugees*, wood engraving, 1942; *The Potato Harvest*, line engraving, 1947; *The Chess Players*, line engraving, 1957; and *Lunch Break*, wood engraving, 1960), book illustrations (for example, for Shakespeare's *Collected Works*, wood engraving, 1958–71), and numerous bookplates are marked by a lively narrative quality, vivid characterizations, and varied compositional solutions.

REFERENCE
Richard Kaljo teoste näitus (catalog). Tallinn, 1964.   [11–696–5]

KALOIAN (also Ivan Kaloian). Year of birth unknown; died 1207. Tsar of the Second Bulgarian Kingdom (from 1197).

Kaloian waged a successful struggle against Byzantium, as a result of which all of northern Bulgaria, the Morava region, and most of Macedonia were liberated. In 1204, because of his recognition of the ecclesiastical supremacy of the Roman curia, he was crowned by Pope Innocent III as "Tsar of the Bulgars and the Vlachs." Relying on the support of the cities and the Bogomils, Kaloian conducted a policy that strengthened royal power. On Apr. 14, 1205, he led Bulgarian troops in a battle against the Crusaders at Adrianople; he was victorious and captured new territories. Kaloian was murdered by boyar conspirators while his troops were besieging Solun (Salonika).

REFERENCE
Kazhdan, A., and G. Litavrin. *Ocherki istorii Vizantii i iuzhnykh slavian*. Moscow, 1958.   [11–675–2]

KALOMIRIS, MANOLIS. Born Dec. 14 (26), 1883, in Smyrna; died Apr. 3, 1962, in Athens. Greek composer. Member of the Athenian Academy of Sciences (1945).

Kalomiris studied in Athens and Constantinople, and during 1901–06 he completed his advanced studies at the Vienna Conservatory. From 1906 to 1910 he taught at the Kharkov School of Music (his first major work, Greek Suite for orchestra, was composed in Russia). In 1911, Kalomiris began teaching at the Hellenic Conservatory in Athens (he was director during 1919–26). In 1926 he founded the National Conservatory in Athens and was its director until the end of his life. From 1935 to 1957 he was chairman of the Union of Greek Composers. Kalomiris was one of the founders of the modern Greek school of music; his opera *The Master Builder* (1915) formed the basis for Greek operatic art. Kalomiris composed operas, symphonic works, chamber instrumental pieces, and songs. His music is permeated with Greek folk melodies.

Kalomiris also published music criticism, a textbook on music theory, and his autobiography (1946).

REFERENCE
Manolis Kalomiris. Athens, 1932.   [11–665–3]

KALONG (*Pteropus vampyrus*), a mammal of the order Chiroptera. The largest representative of this order, it measures up to 40 cm long and has a wingspread up to 1.4 m. It is distributed on the Malacca peninsula, on the Greater and Lesser Sunda Islands, and in the Philippines. The kalong lives in forests and always flies in large groups. It eats fruits and sometimes causes damage to fruit orchards.   [11–666–1]

KALOS LIMEN (literally "beautiful harbor"), an ancient Greek city in the region north of the Black Sea, founded at the end of the fourth century B.C. Its ruins are situated 1.5 km northwest of the village of Chernomorskoe in Crimean Oblast, Ukrainian SSR. Research and excavations were conducted in 1837–38, 1929, 1934, 1948, 1950, and 1959. Defensive walls with towers have been discovered as well as the remains of houses; amphorae (from Chersonesus, Sinope, Heraclea, and Rhodes); black-figure, red-figure, and modeled pottery; millstones; grain mortars; and terra-cotta figurines. The city's destruction dates from the second century B.C. and is connected with Diophantos' wars against the Scythians. In the upper layers of the site of the city, remains of the material culture of the first through third centuries A.D. and of medieval times have been discovered.

REFERENCES
Nalivkina, M. A. "Kerkinitida i Kalos-Limen." In the collection *Antichnyi gorod*. Moscow, 1963.
Shcheglov, A. N. "Issledovaniia sel'skoi okrugi Kalos-Limena." *Sovetskaia arkheologiia*, 1967, no. 3.   [11–674–3]

KALOUSEK, JOSEF. Born Apr. 2, 1838, in Vamberk; died Nov. 22, 1915, in Prague. Czech positivist historian. Member of the Czech Academy of Sciences (1890).

From 1882 to 1908, Kalousek was a professor at Charles University. He wrote a number of monographs on Czech history (primarily medieval) and state law. From 1887 to 1913 he was editor of the *Czech Archives*, a collection of documents in which he published extremely rich factual material on the history of the Czech peasantry from the 14th through the 19th century.

WORKS
Čseké státní pravo, 2nd ed. Prague, 1892.
Obrana knížete Václava Svátého, 2nd ed. Prague, 1901.
Vyklad k historické mapé Čech, 2nd ed. Prague, 1894.
Listiny a zapisy bělské o věcech městských a sedlských 1345–1708.. Prague, 1889.   [11–675–1]

KALTAN, a city in Kemerovo Oblast, RSFSR; located on the Kondoma River. Railroad station on the Novokuznetsk-Tashtagol line, 12 km south of Osinniki. Population, 28,000 (1970).

Kaltan came into being in 1946 in connection with the construction of the Southern Kuzbass State Regional Power Plant (put into operation in 1951), and in 1959 the settlement became a city. There is coal mining (for the state regional power plant), as well as a plant for making auxiliary boiler equipment and pipelines. The city has an evening power engineering technicum.
[11–675–3]

KALUGA, a city and center of Kaluga Oblast, RSFSR. Situated on the left, elevated bank of the Oka River. It has a landing and a railroad station on the Moscow–Kiev line, 188 km southwest of Moscow. Population, 224,000 (1972; compared with 89,000 in 1939).

Kaluga is first mentioned in 1371 in the charter of the Lithuanian prince Olgerd. It originated as a frontier fortress on the southwestern borders of the Muscovite state. In the 15th century Kaluga became part of the principality of Moscow. (During the period 1505–18 it was an independent appanage principality.) In 1607, Kaluga was the center of a peasant uprising led by I. I. Bolotnikov. Kaluga became a part of Moscow Province in 1708; in 1777 it was made the center of the Kaluga *namestnichestvo* (vicegerency); and in 1796 it became the capital of Kaluga Province. From the 17th through the 19th century it played an important role as a trade center. Soviet power was established on Nov. 28 (Dec. 11), 1917. K. E. Tsiolkovskii lived in Kaluga for most of his life and is buried there. In October 1941, Kaluga was occupied by the fascist German aggressors but was liberated on Dec. 30, 1941. During the postwar years the city and its industry were restored and rebuilt. Kaluga was awarded the Order of the Red Banner of Labor in 1971.

Kaluga is a major industrial center; it produces about two-fifths of the oblast's industrial output. The most important industries are machine building, instrument making, chemicals, wood products, food industry, light industry, and the production of building materials. Among Kaluga's machine-building and instrument-making enterprises are transportation-machine-building, machine-building, electrical-machinery, and electrical-engineering plants; plants manufacturing turbines, telegraph equipment, radio tubes, and electrical equipment for motor vehicles; and the Kalugopribor Plant. Wood-products enterprises include the Gigant Match and Furniture Combine, a plywood plant, and the Akkord Industrial Association, which manufactures pianos and accordions. Enterprises of the food industry and light industry are represented by a synthetic perfume agents combine, a flour milling combine, a meat-packing plant, a dairy, the Kaluzhanka Garment Industrial Association, and a footwear factory. The principal building-materials plants produce glass, silicate bricks, and precast reinforced concrete.

Among the architectural landmarks are the Korobovs' stone house (1697, built according to a standard design for wooden mansions consisting of two frames) and a number of stone houses from the 18th century with tripartite plans. Churches include the Pokrov Church on the Moat (1687), the Georgii za Verkhom Church (1700–01), the Spas Preobrazheniia Church (1709–17), and the Znamenie Church (1720–31). Another architectural landmark is the stone bridge (1777–78, architect P. R. Nikitin). Based on general plans of 1778 and 1785, buildings in the classical style were erected in Kaluga, including offices (1780–85,

architect P. R. Nikitin), Troitskii Cathedral (1786–1819, architect I. D. Iasnygin), the Gostinyi Dvor (1785–88, enlarged in 1811–21 by I. D. Iasnygin), the Zolotarevs' and Kologrivova's house (now a museum of local lore, 1805–08), the house of the Meshkovs (now the State Bank, early 19th century), and the Assembly of the Nobility (1848–50, architect P. I. Gusev). A unique quality is imparted to the city by single-story, wooden, three-window houses with projecting cornices and carved window and door lintels and posts in the Empire style. In accordance with the plan of 1949–55, the city's territory was extended to the north. The ensemble of the Teatral'nyi Square was created (1958), and various buildings were erected, including the K. E. Tsiolkovskii Museum of the History of Cosmonautics (1967, architects B. G. Barkhin and others), the Kaluga Hotel (1969), and the Philharmonic Society Concert Hall (1971). Monuments were erected to V. I. Lenin (marble and bronze, 1925, sculptor V. V. Kozlov) and K. E. Tsiolkovskii (bronze, granite, and steel, 1958, sculptor A. P. Faidysh, architects M. O. Barshch and A. N. Kolchin).

Kaluga has a pedagogical institute, a branch of the N. E. Bauman Moscow Higher Technical School, and 12 secondary specialized educational institutions. The city also has a drama theater (founded in the 18th century), a museum of local lore, an art museum, and the K. E. Tsiolkovskii Museum of the History of Cosmonautics with its branch, the Museum Home of K. E. Tsiolkovskii.

REFERENCES
Migunov, A. I. *Kaluga: Istoriko-geograficheskii ocherk*. Kaluga, 1957.
Nikolaev, E. S. *Po kaluzhskoi zemle*, 2nd ed. Moscow, 1970.
Kaluga: Putevoditel'. Tula, 1971.
Fekhner, M. V. *Kaluga*. Moscow, 1971.
                A. A. SUDARIKOVA and K. V. PASHKANG   [11–675–4]

KALUGA (*Huso dauricus*), a fish of the genus *Huso* of the family Acipenseridae. It measures up to 5.6 m long and weighs up to 1 ton; it has a large, crescent-shaped mouth. The kaluga is distributed in the Amur River basin. It reaches sexual maturity in its 17th–20th year. Spawning occurs from the end of May through June. The young feed on bottom invertebrates; the adults are carnivorous (specifically, they eat chum and pink salmon). The fish winters in the bed of the Amur River. The kaluga is a valuable commercial fish.   [11–677–1]

KALUGA OBLAST, part of the RSFSR. Established July 5, 1944. Area, 29,900 sq km. Population, 988,000 (1972). The oblast is divided into 23 raions and has 17 cities and 14 urban-type settlements. The city of Kaluga is its center. Kaluga Oblast was awarded the Order of Lenin on July 25, 1967.

Natural features. The topography of Kaluga Oblast is hilly and ridgy, and in places there are flat plains dissected by numerous river valleys, ravines, and hollows. The northwestern and northern parts of the oblast have morainic plains, the southwestern part has outwash plains, and the central and eastern parts are characterized by erosional plains. The maximum elevation is 270–280 m.

The climate is characterized by moderately warm and moist summers and moderately cold winters with a constant snow cover. The average July temperature is 17.5°–18.5°C, and the average January temperature is between −9° and −10.3°C. The average annual precipitation is 550–650 mm, with the amount decreasing to the southeast. About 70 percent of the precipitation falls from April through October. The growing season lasts from 177 to 184 days.

Most of the oblast's rivers belong to the Volga River basin, and only the western part of the oblast is traversed by rivers of the Dnieper basin, the Bolva and the Snopot'. The largest rivers are the Oka with its tributaries—the Zhizdra, Ugra, and Protva—and the Bolva, a tributary of the Desna. All the rivers are characterized by meandering channels, slow-moving currents, high-water periods in the spring, and low-water periods in the summer. The lakes are located, for the most part, in the floodplains of the Oka and Zhizdra rivers.

Soddy medium-podzolized soils predominate. In the north there are medium-loamy soils, and the southwest has sandy-loam and sandy soils. In the central and eastern raions of the oblast, light gray forest medium-loamy soils are widespread. There are also soddy and soddy-calcareous soils and typical podzolic soils.

Most of the oblast is located in the subzone of coniferous and broad-leaved forests; the central and eastern part are in a subzone of broad-leaved forests. Birch, aspen, pine, and spruce predominate. More than 40 percent of the oblast is covered by forests, with the greatest concentration occurring in the northeast.

Foxes, wolves, hares, and elk are found in the forests. Among the birds there are black grouse, capercaillie, and hazel grouse; waterfowl include ducks and geese. Among animals hunted commercially are white hares, gray hares, squirrels, and moles.

Population. Kaluga Oblast is inhabited mainly by Russians. The average population density is 33 persons per sq km, and the average density of the rural population varies from 8–10 persons per sq km to 25 per sq km and more. The northeastern raions are the most densely populated. The urban population totals 54 percent (as compared with about 20 percent in 1939). The most important cities are Kaluga, Kirov, and Liudinovo. At the beginning of the 1950's the city of Obninsk, which is a major scientific center, came into being.

Economy. The volume of industrial output increased by a factor of 12.8 from 1940 to 1971. Industrial production is based on the machine-building, metalworking, wood-products, paper and pulp, consumer, and food-processing industries.

Among the branches of industry, machine building and metalworking hold first place (more than a third of the total industrial output). Machine-building enterprises are located in Kaluga (plants manufacturing transportation machinery, turbines, electrical machinery, electrical engineering equipment), Liudinovo (diesel locomotive manufacturing plant), and Kozel'sk and Dugna (machinery plants). There are iron foundries in Duminichi, Kirov, and Liudinovo. During the years of Soviet power, major enterprises of the wood-products industry were built or redesigned, including the Gigant Match and Furniture Combine in Kaluga, a paper and pulp combine in Kondrovo, the Troitskaia and Polotniano-Zavodskaia paper mills, furniture factories (in Maloiaroslavets and Medyn'), plywood plants, and a match factory (in Balabanovo).

The chemical industry has also been developed. There is a plastic products factory (Sukhinichi), a plant for household chemicals (Tarusa), and a plant that manufactures films and pipes from plastic materials, (Duminichi).

The building-materials industry is represented by brickyards (Kaluga, Maloiaroslavets, Balabanovo, and Sukhinichi), a ceramic structural components factory (Kirov), glass plants (Kaluga, Kozel'sk, and Elenskii), and plants that make reinforced-concrete products (Kaluga and Kurovskoi). There are numerous enterprises in the field of consumer industry. They include a footwear factory in Kaluga with a workshop in Kondrovo; clothing factories in Kaluga, Kirov, Sukhinichi, Maloiaroslavets, Liudinovo, and other locations; a knitted-goods factory in Borovsk; and textile mills in Borovsk, Ermolino, and Belousovo. Among food-processing enterprises are dairy, starch, and vegetable-concentrate plants (Sukhinichi, Detchino, and Mosal'sk) and a synthetic perfume agents combine (Kaluga).

Located in Obninsk is the USSR's first atomic electric power plant for experimental and industrial purposes, which was put into operation in 1954.

Agriculture specializes in dairy livestock raising and pig breeding as well as growing potatoes, vegetables, and some flax. Arable lands occupy about two-fifths of the oblast's agricultural land, and pastures and hayfields, approximately one-fifth. In 1971 the entire sown area amounted to 921,200 hectares (ha). This included 392,700 ha under grain crops (wheat, barley, rye, oats, and buckwheat), 13,800 ha under long-fiber flax, 96,100 ha under potatoes and other vegetables, and 417,700 ha under feed crops. The principal part of the sown area is situated in the central part of the oblast. In 1972 the oblast's livestock consisted of 548,000 cattle, 279,000 sheep and goats, and 290,000 pigs.

The oblast has 868 km of railroads, more than one-third of which have been electrified. There is a dense network of roads for motor vehicles and bus transportation between the cities.

There is navigation along the Oka River. Kaluga has an airport.
K. V. PASHKANG

Education, cultural affairs, and public health. During the 1971–72 academic year there were 187,500 pupils enrolled in 1,227 general education schools of all types and 18,600 students in 24 specialized secondary educational institutions. There were also 6,100 students enrolled in the K. E. Tsiolkovskii Pedagogical Institute and branches of Moscow higher educational institutions. In 1969 some 29,500 children were being educated at 307 preschool institutions.

As of Jan. 1, 1972, the oblast had 638 public libraries (with 7,186,000 books and journals); the A. V. Lunacharskii Dramatic Theater in Kaluga; museums, including the oblast museum of local lore in Kaluga (with its branches—the Museum of the Patriotic War of 1812 in the village of Tarutino and museums of local lore in Obninsk and Kozel'sk); the oblast art museum; the K. E. Tsiolkovskii State Museum of the History of Cosmonautics (with its branch—the Museum Home of K. E. Tsiolkovskii); the Maloiaroslavets Museum of Military History of the Patriotic War of 1812; and the Tarusa Picture Gallery. The oblast also had 955 clubs, 1,047 stationary motion picture projectors, and extracurricular institutions such as the Pioneer Palace and the young naturalists' station in Kaluga.

Two oblast newspapers are published—*Znamia* (since 1917) and *Molodoi leninets* (since 1920). Oblast radio broadcasts on one radio channel. Radio and television broadcasts are also relayed from Moscow.

As of Jan. 1, 1972, Kaluga Oblast had 112 medical treatment and disease prevention institutions with 11,500 beds (that is 11.6 beds per 1,000 inhabitants). There were 2,300 physicians (one per 436 inhabitants). The Vorob'evo Sanatorium, where diseases of the circulatory organs are treated, is located near Maloiaroslavets.

REFERENCES
Kaluzhskaia oblast' za 50 let: Statisticheskii sbornik. Kaluga, 1967.
Tsentral'nyi raion. Moscow, 1962.
Nikolaev, E. V. *Po Kaluzhskoi zemle,* 2nd ed. Leningrad, 1970.
Po prostoram Kaluzhskogo kraia: Sb. st., 2nd ed. Kaluga, 1964.
[11–678–1]

KALUSH, a city (since 1939) and center of Kalush Raion, Ivano-Frankovsk Oblast, Ukrainian SSR. It has a railroad station on the Ivano-Frankovsk–Stryi line. Population, 47,400 (1972). Among its enterprises are a chemical and metallurgical combine, food-processing combines, a plant producing reinforced concrete items and structural elements, a plant producing equipment for municipal services, a machinery and repair plant, the Nefteburmashremont Plant, an assembly and components storage plant, a cheese dairy, a brewery, and a garment and haberdashery factory. Kalush is also the site of a chemical and technological technicum. [11–681–2]

KALVARIJA, a city in Kapsukas Raion, Lithuanian SSR, on the Šešupe River (a tributary of the Nemunas), on the highway from Kaunas to Suwałki (Poland), 4 km from the Kalvarija railroad station (on a branch of the Kaunas-Kaliningrad line). Kalvarija has a wool-spinning factory, a plant producing wall materials, and a food industry technicum. The city was founded in 1791. [11–572–4]

KAMA, the Hindu deity of love, usually identified as the son of Vishnu and Lakshmi. He is depicted as a young man aiming flower arrows at the hearts of human beings. His bow is a stalk of sugarcane; his bowstring is made of bees. The image of Kama often appears in Indian fiction. [11–708–2]

KAMA (until 1966, Butysh), an urban-type settlement in Kambarka Raion, Udmurt ASSR. Kama has a port (Kambarka) on the left bank of the Kama River, 9 km from the city of Kambarka, and a railroad station on the Kazan-Sverdlovsk line. [11–709–1]

KAMA (from the Udmurt *kam,* "river," "current"), a river in the European part of the USSR, a left tributary of the Volga. It measures 1,805 km long and drains an area of 507,000 sq km. The river originates in the central part of the Upper Kama Upland and flows primarily between the uplands of the High Trans-Volga Region along a broad valley that narrows in places. In its upper course the river is fluctuating and meanders across its ancient floodplain. Below its confluence with the Vishera the Kama has abundant water. The Kama Reservoir begins at the mouth of the Urolka River (996 km from the mouth of the Kama) and, directly below, is found the Votkinsk Reservoir. In its lower course the Kama flows through a broad (up to 15 km wide) valley and measures 450–1,200 m wide; then the river branches. Below the mouth of the Viatka River the Kama flows into the Kama Bay of the Kuibyshev Reservoir (whose backwater sometimes reaches the mouth of the Belaia River). The main left-bank tributaries are the Iuzhnaia Kel'tma, the Vishera with the Kolva, the Chusovaia with the Sylva, the Belaia with the Ufa, the Ik, and the Zai rivers. The main right-bank tributaries are the Kosa, the Obva, and the Viatka rivers.

The Kama is fed mainly by snow and also by ground waters and rain. More than 60 percent of the annual flow occurs during the spring flooding (March–June). The water level varies as much as 8 m in the upper course and 7 m in the lower course. The mean flow rate at the Kama Hydroelectric Power Plant is 1,630 cu m/sec; at the Votkinsk Plant about 1,750 cu m/sec; and at the mouth about 3,500 cu m/sec. The maximum flow rate is about 27,500 cu m/sec. Freezing is accompanied by abundant channel ice and ice floes for 10–20 days. The river is icebound from the beginning of November in the upper course and the end of November in the lower course to April. Spring ice floes last from two or three days to 10–15 days. The creation of reservoirs has improved conditions for navigation. The Kama is navigable up to the settlement of Kerchevskii (966 km), the site of the largest sorting and bundling plant, and at high water is navigable for another 600 km. The navigable depths of the lower Kama are maintained by dredging. When the Lower Kama Hydroelectric Power Plant is completed and the reservoir is filled, the lower Kama will also become deep. The main ports and landings are Solikamsk, Berezniki, Levshino, Perm', Krasnokamsk, Chaikovskii, Sarapul, Kambarka, Naberezhnye Chelny, and Chistopol'. From Perm' there is regular passenger service to Moscow, Gorky, Astrakhan, and Ufa. The picturesque banks of the Kama attract a large number of tourists.

REFERENCES
Davydov, L. K. *Gidrografiia SSSR*, vol. 2. Leningrad, 1955.
Kama, Volga, Don. Putevoditel'. Perm', 1967.
Golovko, V. K. *Zavtrashnii den' Kamy*. Perm', 1969.
Vendrov, S. L. *Problemy preobrazovaniia rechnykh sistem*. Leningrad, 1970.
K. G. TIKHOTSKII [11–708–3]

KAMA HYDROELECTRIC SYSTEM, a series of hydroelectric power plants on the Kama River; part of the Verkhniaia Kama, Kama, Votkinsk, and Nizhniaia Kama integrated hydroengineering complexes.

The Kama Hydroengineering Complex, located near the city of Perm', was the first part of the system built (1949–57). It consists of a powerhouse, earth dams, and a two-channel navigation lock. The world's first powerhouse of the spillway type, containing 24 hydroelectric power units, was built there. The installed capacity of the hydroelectric power plant is 504 megawatts (MW). The combination of the powerhouse with the spillway made possible a reduction in the length of the concrete works by 190 m. Another feature of the project is a six-chamber lock that makes possible simultaneous handling of several vessels and log rafts.

The Votkinsk Complex (1955–63), located near the city of Chaikovskii, Perm' Oblast, includes a powerhouse with ten hydroelectric power units, earth and concrete spillway dams, and a two-channel single-lift navigation lock. The installed capacity of the Votkinsk Hydroelectric Power Plant is 1,000 MW.

The Nizhniaia Kama Complex is under construction (1972) above the mouth of the Viatka River. It is to include a modern powerhouse, an earth dam, and a two-channel single-lift lock. The planned capacity of the plant is 1,248 MW.

Also in the planning stage is the construction of the Verkhniaia Kama Power Plant, which will involve shifting a portion of the drainage of the Pechora and Vychegda rivers into the Kama and Volga. The planned capacity of the hydroelectric power plant is approximately 600 MW.

The total output of the multistage Kama system will reach more than 8 billion kW-hr in an average year in terms of water levels. The creation of reservoirs will significantly improve navigation on the Kama and its tributaries and will provide a dependable water supply for industry and towns in the adjacent regions.

G. M. VAINSHTEIN [11–845–5]

KAMAISHI, a city and port of Japan, in the northeastern part of the island of Honshu, in Iwate prefecture. Population, 73,000 (1970). The port of Kamaishi occupies first place in the freight turnover of the economic region of Tohoku. It is the center of the country's principal iron-ore basin (approximately one-half of Japan's iron ore), which is located 15 km west of the city of Kamaishi. There is a large metallurgical enterprise in the city as well as knitted-goods and fish-canning enterprises. Kamaishi is the fishing center of northern Honshu. [11–709–4]

KAMAKURA, a city in Japan on the island of Honshu, in Kanagawa prefecture, on Sagami Bay. Population, 139,000 (1970). Kamakura is a city of great historical interest. It was founded on the site of the ancient Japanese capital of the period of the first shogunate ("the Kamakura era"). Articles of fine and applied art (luxury items and souvenirs) are produced in the city. There is a museum of fine arts and a huge bronze statue of Buddha dating from 1252. The site of Buddhist pilgrimages, Kamakura is also a tourist center and a seaside health resort.

The climate is humid and subtropical, characterized by monsoons. Winters are very mild, with average January temperatures of 3°C. Summers are hot, with average August temperatures of 26°C. Annual precipitation totals 1,600 mm. The principal therapeutic remedies are heliotherapy, aerotherapy, and sea bathing (from June to the middle of October). Patients with functional disorders of the nervous system and diseases of the respiratory organs and patients suffering from anemia, overfatigue, and other complaints are treated in Kamakura. There are sanatoriums, hydrotherapy and physiotherapy clinics, various sports facilities, hotels, boardinghouses, and comfortable sandy beaches. [11–709–5]

KAMAL, GALIASKAR (pseudonym of Galiaskar Kamaletdinov). Born Dec. 25, 1878 (Jan. 6, 1879), in Kazan; died there June 8, 1933. Soviet Tatar writer and public figure. Son of a handicraftsman.

In 1901, Kamal published the newspaper *Tärakkïy* (Progress) and organized the Mägarif (Enlightenment) Publishing House. In 1906 he began working on the newspaper *Azad* (Freedom) and later *Azad khalïk* (Free People), in which articles were published propagandizing the ideas of Marxism. He was the editor and publisher of the satirical journal *Yäshen* (Lightning, 1908–09) and worked on the newspaper *Yulduz* (Star, 1907–17). His works were first published in 1900. Kamal's most important works—the drama *The Unfortunate Youth* (1907, second version) and the comedies *Because of a Gift* (1908), *The Mistress* (1911), *Our City's Secrets* (1911), and *Bankrupt* (1912; Russian translation 1944)—sharply castigated the vices of bourgeois society. After the October Revolution he wrote satirical poems and collaborated on the newspapers *Ësh* (Labor) and *Kïzïl bayrak* (Red Banner). Kamal translated N. V. Gogol's *The Inspector-General*, A. N. Ostrovskii's *Thunderstorm*, and M. Gorky's *The Lower Depths* into Tatar.

WORKS
[Kamal, Galiäsgar.] *Äsärlär*, vols. 1–2. With an introduction by M. Gaynullin. Kazan, 1950–51.
REFERENCES
Gainullin, M. *Tatarskaia literatura i publitsistika nachala XX veka*. Kazan, 1966.
Khalit, G. *Tatar Ädähiyätïnda realizm mäs'äläläre*. Kazan, 1948.
Kamal, Ä. *Khalïk dramaturgï G. Kamal*. Kazan', 1950.
Khismätullin, Kh. *Galiäsgar Kamal*. Kazan', 1969. [11–710–1]

KAMAL, SHARIF (pseudonym of Sharif Baigil'diev). Born Feb. 16 (28), 1884, in the village of Pishlia, present-day Mordovian ASSR; died Dec. 22, 1942, in Kazan. Soviet Tatar writer and dramatist; Honored Art Worker of the Tatar ASSR (1940). Became a member of the CPSU in 1919. Son of a minister. He was an unskilled worker and miner. In St. Petersburg (1905), he was a contributor to the newspaper *Nur* (Ray), in which his articles and poems were published. His first collection of poems, *Voice,* appeared in 1906.

Kamal realistically showed the life of seasonal workers, fishermen, and miners in his short stories of 1909–12 ("Awakening," "In Search of Happiness," and "In a Strange Land"), as well as in his novella *Seagulls* (1915). His comedy *Khadzhi Efendi Is Getting Married* (1915) became a Tatar classic. Kamal was also the author of the realistic novels *At Dawn* (1927) and *When the Beautiful Is Born* (1937, Russian translation 1957). In his dramatic works *Fire* (1928), *Mountains* (1932), and *In the Fog* (1934), Kamal described the construction of socialism in the city and the countryside. He was awarded the Order of Lenin.

WORKS
[Kamal, Shärif.] *Äsärlär,* vols. 1–4. Kazan, 1951–56.
REFERENCES
Khismatullin, Kh. "Sharif Kamal." In *Istoriia tatarskoi sovetskoi literatury.* Moscow, 1965.
Gainullin, M. *Tatarskaia literatura i publitsistika nachala XX veka.* Kazan, 1966.
Nig"mätullin, Ä. *Shärif Kamal.* Kazan, 1964.

M. KH. GAINULLIN [11–710–2]

KAMALOV, FOMA GEORGIEVICH. Born 1890 in Tbilisi; died August 1918. Participant in the revolutionary movement in the Transcaucasus. Member of the Communist Party from 1911.

Kamalov studied at the Tbilisi Commercial School. In 1910 he began studying in the medical department of the University of Kiev. In 1913 he began conducting party work in Tbilisi and was twice arrested and imprisoned in Metekhi Castle in 1914. He continued party work in Kharkov and Saratov; in 1917 he resumed this work in Tbilisi. He was exiled to Vladikavkaz (now Ordzhonikidze) by the Menshevik government of Georgia in February 1918. Kamalov became chairman of the Vladikavkaz Soviet in April 1918 and participated in the creation of the Red Guard and in the struggle against the counterrevolution of the mountain regions. In August 1918 he was arrested by G. F. Bicherakhov's White Guard band, which had raided Vladikavkaz, and was shot after being brutally tortured. [11–711–1]

KAMANIN, NIKOLAI PETROVICH. Born Oct. 5 (18), 1908, in Melenki, in present-day Vladimir Oblast. Soviet military figure, colonel general of aviation (1967), Hero of the Soviet Union (Apr. 20, 1934). Became a member of the CPSU in 1932. The son of a shoemaker.

Kamanin graduated from the Leningrad Military-Theoretical Flight School in 1928 and then volunteered for the Red Army. In April 1934 he was a pilot in the rescue of the expedition on the steamship *Cheliuskin,* which was sinking in the Arctic Ocean. In 1938 he graduated from the Higher Air Force Academy and took command of an aviation brigade. He fought in the Soviet-Finnish War of 1939–40. During the Great Patriotic War (1941–45), he became commander in May 1942 of the V Assault Aviation Corps, which was active in the liberation of the Ukraine, Poland, Rumania, Hungary, and Czechoslovakia. In 1950 he graduated from the Academy of the General Staff. Between 1966 and 1972 he worked at the main headquarters of the air force; he was in charge of training cosmonauts. He retired in 1972. He has been awarded three Orders of Lenin, the Order of the Red Banner, two Orders of Suvorov Second Class, the Order of Kutuzov Second Class, the Order of the Red Star, several foreign orders, and medals.

WORKS
Letchiki i kosmonavty. Moscow, 1972.
REFERENCES
Nagornyi, A. I., and V. Travkin. *Zemli Vladimirskoi bogatyri.* Yaroslavl, 1967. Pages 163–67, 408.

Rebrov, M. "Parol' ego zhizni." In *Boitsy leninskoi gvardii.* Moscow, 1967. [11–711–2]

KAMA PULP AND PAPER COMBINE, a major enterprise of the Soviet pulp and paper industry; produces sulfite pulp, school notebooks, feed yeasts, ethyl alcohol, and book, offset, and writing paper. It is located in the city of Krasnokamsk, Perm' Oblast. It began operation in 1936 and has undergone reconstruction and expansion. The raw materials for the combine come from the Kama River basin. During the log-rafting season, the combine receives up to 1.5 million cu m of fir and spruce wood. The pulp plant that is part of the combine is equipped with large boilers for cooking the pulp, as well as with modern bleaching units. The wood-pulp mill produces white wood pulp. The paper mills of the combine have eight high-speed paper machines operating at speeds up to 450 m/min, with a trimmed paper width of 4.2 m. In 1970 the combine produced 274,000 tons of paper, exceeding its output in 1940 by a factor of more than 3.

V. I. BROVTSEV [11–846–1]

KAMA RESERVOIR (also Perm' Reservoir), a reservoir formed in 1954–56 by the dam of the Kama Hydroengineering Complex near the city of Perm'. Area, 1,915 sq km; volume, 12.2 cu km; length, 272 km (along the channel of the Kama River); maximum width, up to 30 km; average depth, 6.3 m; maximum, 30 m. The level of the reservoir varies within limits of 7 m. Bays 50 to 140 km long and up to 10–15 km wide have formed along all the main tributaries of the Kama, including the Chusovaia (with the Sylva), Obva, In'va, Kos'va, Iaiva, Kondas, and Chermoz. The Kama Reservoir was built for purposes of power engineering and water transportation and water supply, and it also provides seasonal regulation of drainage. There is fishing for bream, pike, pike perch, perch, and roach. The cities of Perm', Dobrianka, Chermoz, Berezniki, Usol'e, and Solikamsk are located on the shores of the Kama Reservoir.

REFERENCE
Dubrovin, L. I., Iu. M. Matarzin, and I. A. Pecherkin. *Kamskoe vodokhranilishche.* Perm', 1959. [11–846–2]

KAMARHATI, a city in India, in the state of West Bengal, on the Hooghly River. Kamarhati is an industrial suburb of the Calcutta conurbation. The city's industries include jute and cotton milling. Its manufactures include rubber, cement, and leather products, as well as pottery. [11–712–4]

KAMAROVSKII, LEONID ALEKSEEVICH (L. A. Komarovskii). Born 1846 in Kazan, died 1912. Russian jurist, corresponding member of the St. Petersburg Academy of Sciences (1910), professor at Moscow University.

Kamarovskii strove to base international law on the principles of natural law and the requirements of "justice"; he reviewed the questions of the restriction of the "right of war," disarmament, and peaceful means of settling international disputes. In matters of domestic policy he held reactionary views and was a member of the Octobrist Party. He became a member of the Institute of International Law, based in Brussels, in 1875 and a member of the international court of arbitration in The Hague in 1909.

WORKS
Nachalo nevmeshatel'stva. Moscow, 1874.
O mezhdunarodnom sude. Moscow 1881. (Doctoral dissertation.)
Osnovnye voprosy nauki mezhdunarodnogo prava, nos. 1–2. Moscow, 1892–95.
Voina ili mir? Odessa, 1895.
Uspekhi idei mira. Moscow, 1898. [11–712–3]

KAMASINTSY (Kamasins; self-designation; Kalmazhi), a tribe of Saian Samoyeds (population approximately 500), which lived in the 17th century along the Kan and Mana rivers (the southern part of present-day Krasnoiarsk Krai). In the 18th and 19th centuries they were divided into two groups: the Taiga Kamasintsy, who engaged in hunting, reindeer breeding, and fishing (as they did in the 17th century), and the Steppe Kamasintsy known as the Kashintsy in the 17th century, who engaged in stock raising, horse breeding, farming, and hunting. The Steppe

Kamasintsy spoke the Turkic Kachininskii language. All of the Kamasintsy had merged with the Russian peasant population by the early 20th century. [11–712–5]

KAMA TRUCK PLANT (KamAZ), a major enterprise of the Soviet automotive industry; a complex of plants to produce trucks that is under construction in the city of Naberezhnye Chelny, Tatar ASSR. Construction began in 1970. The plant is intended to produce 150,000 vehicles and 250,000 engines per year. There are plans to produce 13 models of trucks and three models of diesel engines. The complex will include foundry, forging, frame-stamping, diesel, truck, and repair-tool plants, as well as the production of special and multihead machine tools and automatic lines for the plant's requirements. Along with the Volga Automobile Works, KamAZ will occupy a leading place in the Soviet automotive industry in terms of the level of technology, engineering, mechanization, and automation. An automated production control system will be introduced. Engineering and laboratory centers are being organized to conduct various types of research, they will be equipped with the most modern facilities. The first stage of the plant will be put into operation in 1976. In addition to the plants of the complex, a new city is being built for more than 300,000 inhabitants.

B. T. KLEPATSKII [11–845–4]

KAMBAN, GUĐMUNDUR JÓNSON. Born June 8, 1888, in Álftanes, Iceland; died May 5, 1945, in Copenhagen. Icelandic author, writing mostly in Danish. In 1931–33 he was director of the Royal Theater in Copenhagen.

Kamban's first plays, including *Hadda Padda* (1914), center on a love intrigue. In the play *Marble* (1918) and the novel *Ragnar Finnsson* (1922; Russian translation, *Without Principles,* 1927), Kamban critically analyzed bourgeois legal procedure. He sharply criticized bourgeois society in the plays *We Murderers* (1920), *Arab Tents* (1921), and *Ambassador From Jupiter* (1927). The historical novels *Skálholt* (vols. 1–4, 1930–35) and *I See a Wondrous Land* (1936), written in the style of the heroic sagas, describe events from the history of Icelandic people.

REFERENCES
Andresson, K. E. *Sovremennaia islandskaia literatura, 1918–1948.* Moscow, 1957.
Einarsson, S. *A History of Icelandic Literature.* New York, 1957.
[11–714–1]

KAMBARKA, a city; administrative center of Kambarka Raion, Udmurt ASSR. The city is located on the Kambarka River (a tributary of the Kama). The port of Kambarka is in the settlement of Kama, 9 km from the city. Railroad station on the Kazan-Sverdlovsk line, 126 km southeast of Izhevsk. Kambarka has a metalworking plant and a machine-building plant producing diesel locomotives. There is also a machine-building technical school. Kambarka sprang up as a settlement in the second half of the 18th century, and became a city in 1945.
[11–715–2]

KAMBERI (also Kambari, Kambali, Kamberawa, Ewadi, or Yauri), a people living in Nigeria, between the Kaduna and Niger rivers, east of the city of Busa. The Kamberi are related to the Duka, Dakakari, and Kamuku peoples. The population of the Kamberi proper is approximately 150,000 (1970, estimate). Their language is related to the Eastern Bantoid languages. Most of the Kamberi profess Islam. Their chief occupation is farming (corn and sorghum); livestock raising and fishing are also well developed.

REFERENCE
Ismagilova, R. *Narody Nigerii.* Moscow, 1963. [11–715–1]

KAMBUJA, a feudal Khmer state that flourished from the ninth to the 13th century. Its capital was Yasodharapura, now part of the ruins of Angkor. Kambuja included present-day Cambodia and part of Laos, Thailand, Vietnam, and Burma. It is known in historical writings as Angkor Cambodia. The emergence of Kambuja completed the unification of the area inhabited by the Khmer and by the related Mon, the site of the ancient Khmer

empire of Funan (first to sixth centuries) and of the later Khmer states of Land Chenla and Water Chenla (seventh and eighth centuries). Between the ninth and the 12th centuries the feudal empire of Kambuja included territory inhabited by the Khmer and regions settled by the Cham, Mon, and other ethnic groups. The founder of the royal dynasty of Kambuja was Jayavarman II, who reigned from about 802 to 850.

During this period state ownership of land was extended, largely in the form of land ownership by state temples, and great power was concentrated in the hands of a deified monarch. An extensive irrigation system was constructed in the central regions of Kambuja, north of Lake Tonle Sap. Here majestic temples were erected in the 12th and 13th centuries (Angkor Wat, Angkor Thom), forming the world famous architectural complex of Angkor. In the 12th and early 13th centuries, particularly under Suryavarman II (1113–50) and Jayavarman VII, Kambuja fought many wars of conquest and attained its greatest expansion. In the 13th century royal power began to weaken, and class struggle, manifested in peasant uprisings, intensified. The empire lost the non-Khmer areas and disintegrated in the late 13th century. The name Kambuja long remained the official name of the Khmer state. D. V. DEOPIK [11–737–1]

KAMCHADALY, the name used in the 18th century for the Itel'mensy, the native population of Kamchatka. The name Kamchadaly later came to be used for the descendants of the Itel'my, Koriaks, and Chuvantsy on the Okhotsk coast, Kamchatka, and the Chukchi Peninsula who had merged with the Russians and also the descendants of 18th- and 19th-century Russian settlers. The Kamchadaly speak Russian, characterized by Siberian and local features. The chief occupations are fishing, fur trapping, vegetable gardening, and dairy livestock raising.
[11–850–1]

KAMCHATKA, a peninsula in northeastern Asia, in the USSR. To the west lies the Sea of Okhotsk; to the east, the Pacific Ocean and the Bering Sea. Length, 1,200 km (from north-northeast to south-southwest); width, up to 450 km; area, 370,000 sq km. It is linked to the mainland by a narrow isthmus, the Parapol'skii Dol (up to 100 km wide). The eastern shore of the peninsula is strongly indented and forms large gulfs (Kronotsk, Kamchatka, Ozernoi, Karaga, and Korfa) and bays (Avacha, Karaga, and Ossora). Rocky peninsulas jut far into the sea (Shipunskii, Kronotsk, Kamchatka, Ozernoi). The western shore is weakly indented.

The western part of Kamchatka is occupied by the Western Kamchatka Lowland, which gives way to a sloping plain in the east and north. The Sredinnyi Range, with elevations up to 3,621 m, is situated in the axial part of the peninsula, north of the Plotnikovaia River; the Ichinskaia Sopka volcano in the range has a leveled-out lava plateau in the center and an alpine landscape in the south and north. The Central Kamchatka Lowland east of the Sredinnyi Range, has low ridges that sometimes rise to 100–200 m above sea level; the lowland is narrowest in the south (5–10 km) and gradually widens toward the north, attaining a width of 80 km. The Kamchatka River and its left tributary, the Elovka River, flow through the lowlands in the north, and the Bystraia River flows in the south. The volcanoes of the Kluichevskaia group, which rise on the lowlands, include Kliuchevskaia Sopka (4,750 m), one of the world's tallest active volcanoes. The active Shiveluch volcano (3,283 m) is north of the group. The lowland is bounded in the east by steep ridges, the Vostochnyi Range, which is in fact an entire system of ranges: the Ganal'skii (elevations to 2,277 m), Valaginskii (to 1,794 m), Tumrok (to 2,485 m), and Kumroch (to 2,346 m). Between Cape Lopatka and the Kamchatka gulf lies the Eastern Volcanic Plateau (elevations of 600–1,000 m), with extinct and active volcanoes, including the Kronotsk (3,528 m), Koriak (3,456 m), Avacha (2,741 m), and Mutnovskaia (2,323 m). There are more than 160 volcanoes on Kamchatka, 28 of which are active.

Kamchatka is a plicate structure formed during the Alpine fold era. It has widespread Paleozoic, Mesozoic, and Cenozoic geosynclinal rock complexes. The Paleozoic rock emerge in the nuclei of the anticlinorium of the Sredinnyi and Vostochnyi ranges and are metamorphic schists and phyllites. The most frequent rocks are volcanogenic and sandy shale deposits of the Cretaceous and Paleocene periods, as well as Quaternary basalts and andesites (less frequently rhyolites and their oceanic and continental sedimentary analogues). Intrusive rocks include small hypabyssal bodies of granitoid and hyperbasic rock in the east. The main characteristic of the tectonic structure is the presence of genetically different structures of two strikes: the northeastern strike, which is associated with the development of the Kuril-Kamchatka volcanic arc, and the northwestern, which corresponds to the strikes of the major structures of the Okhotsk region. The first system is characterized by the development of overthrust folding; the second, by steeply sloping dislocations.

The minerals of the peninsula include various types of coal (from brown to coking, hard coal, anthracites), associated with Paleocene deposits; gold, silver, mercury, and complex metallic ores; native sulfur; and various building materials. Kamchatka has many carbon-dioxide and nitrogen mineral waters and thermal waters, with a temperature of up to 100°C (geysers, boiling lakes, and mud volcanoes), located mainly in the Vostochnyi Range.

Kamchatka has a maritime monsoon climate, more severe in the west than in the east. In the south the climate is maritime, in the central and northern parts it is moderate continental. The average February temperature is −15°C in the west, −11°C in the east, and −16°C in the central part; the corresponding August temperatures are 12°, 12.5°, and 16°C. Annual precipitation is 600 to 1,100 mm. There are modern glaciers in the highest part of the mountains. The total area of glaciation is 866 sq km; glaciation is encountered at the summits of the Sredinny Range and on the slopes of the active Shiveluch and Kliuchevskaia Sopka volcanoes. The largest rivers of the peninsula are the Kamchatka, Avacha, and Ozernaia in the east and the Bol'shaia, Icha, and Tigil' in the west. Kamchatka has many lakes, some of which form in craters (Khangar) and in volcanic calderas (Kronotskoe and Kuril'skoe).

The soil structure of Kamchatka is dominated by soddy podzolic soils that are rich in humus and mineral nutrients. In the Central Kamchatka lowlands spruce and broad-leaved forests and, less frequently, deciduous forests grow on these soils. The ridges, foothills, and lower parts of the mountain slopes have soddy meadow soils under high-grass birch groves of Erman's or common birch. Soddy peat soils are well developed in the lowlands of western Kamchatka. All types of soils have various impurities of volcanic ash. The chernozem-like meadow and alluvial soils encountered in the valley of the Kamchatka River are the most fertile. The northern, low-lying part of Kamchatka (Parapol'skii Dol) is a mossy treeless tundra. There is also a narrow belt of tundra in low-lying areas of the western shore.

The remaining regions of Kamchatka have extremely rich vegetation. The central part of the peninsula is covered with coniferous forests of Dahurian larch and Yeddo spruce. The river floodplains are covered with poplar, willow, and alder forests, as well as meadows. Siberian fir grows on the eastern shore, near the mouth of the Semiachik river. There are many park-type forests of large sparsely growing Erman's birch and, to a lesser extent, white birch; the depressions are covered with high-grass vegetation (queen of the meadows and small-reed). Higher up on the mountain slopes, the birch groves give way to dense, impassable groves of Japanese stone pine and dwarf alder, and above about 1,000 m, to alpine meadows and mountain tundras.

The fauna of Kamchatka is poor in terms of the number of species and is insular. Among the industrially important fur-bearing animals of the peninsula are the sable, fox, bear, wolf, wolverine, otter, ermine, blue hare, arctic fox, and squirrel. The muskrat and mink are becoming industrially important. Bighorn sheep and reindeer are found in the mountains up to 1,000 m, and the Kamchatka marmot (or Mongolian bobak) and Kamchatka suslik in the mountain tundras. The western coastal waters are inhabited mainly by seals (sea hare and ringed seal) and sea lions. The sea otter has been preserved on Cape Lopatka. With the coming of spring the peninsula is visited by ducks, geese, swans, various species of seagulls, murres, cormorants, woodcocks, and guillemots. The main wealth of inland waters in the sea is migratory fishes of the family Salmonidae (the humpback, Siberian, blueback, silver, and king salmon); there are also

herring, cod, and navaga. Large Kamchatka crabs are caught off the western shore of Kamchatka. The Kronotsk Preserve, with a valley of geysers and a relict grove of Siberian fir, is on Kamchatka.

The first description of Kamchatka was presented in 1701 by the Siberian cossack V. Atlasov, who made several raiding campaigns on the peninsula in 1697–99. Between 1737 and 1741, S. P. Krasheninnikov made a thorough study of Kamchatka and presented the results of his observations in *Description of the Land of Kamchatka* (1756).

REFERENCES
Komarov, V. L. "Botanicheskii ocherk Kamchatki." In *Kamchatskii sb.,* vol. 1. Moscow-Leningrad, 1940.
Zanina, A. A. *Dal'nevostochnye raiony: Kamchatka i Sakhalin.* Leningrad, 1958. (*Klimat SSSR,* fasc. 6.)
Liubimova, E. L. *Kamchatka.* Moscow, 1961.
Liverovskii, Iu. A., and I. I. Karmanov. "Pochvy." In *Dal'nii Vostok.* Moscow, 1961.
Geologiia SSSR. Vol. 31: *Kamchatka, Kuril'skie i Komandorskie ostrova.* Moscow, 1964.
Parmuzin, Iu. P. *Severo-Vostok i Kamchatka.* Moscow, 1967.
Sever Dal'nego Vostoka. Moscow, 1970
Kashintsev, B. *Kamchatska segodnia i zavtra.* Petropavlovsk-Kamchatskii, 1970.
    S. L. KUSHEV and V. I. TIKHONOV (geological structure)
[11–850–2]

KAMCHATKA (in its upper course, the Ozernaia Kamchatka), a river in Kamchatka Oblast, RSFSR. Length, 758 km, basin area, 55,900 sq km. In its upper course it is a mountain river, with many sandbars and rapids; it then flows through the Central Kamchatka Lowlands, meanders a great deal, and in places breaks up into branches. Bending around the Kliuchevskaia Sopka massif in the north, the Kamchatka turns east, crosses the Kumroch Range in its lower course, and empties into the Kamchatka Gulf of the Pacific Ocean. The mouth of the river, which is blocked by an offshore bank, is about 0.5 m deep. The Kamchatka is fed by various sources, with ground water (35 percent) predominant. The groundwater is replenished by a considerable amount of precipitation that seeps through the water-permeable volcanic rock. Snow accounts for 34 percent; glaciers 28 percent; rain, 3 percent of the water supply. High water is from May to September, and low water is from October to April. The average water discharge is 965 cu m per sec at Nizhnekamchatsk, 35 km from the river's mouth. The river freezes in November and the ice breaks in April or May; in places, where hot springs come to the surface, it never freezes. The Kamchatka is used for flotation of timber and is navigable up to 486 km from its mouth. It is a spawning ground for salmon. The port of Ust'-Kamchatsk is situated at the mouth of the river.   [11–852–1]

KAMCHATKA CURRENT, a cold current in the northeastern Pacific Ocean. It begins in the Bering Sea and moves southward along the shores of the Kamchatka Peninsula, where it becomes the Kuril Current. The current is more than 300 km wide and flows at a speed of up to 2 km/hr. The temperature in February measures below 1°C; August, up to 10°C. Salinity is less than 32.5 parts per thousand.   [11–857–3]

KAMCHATKA GULF, an inlet of the Pacific Ocean, off the eastern shore of the Kamchatka Peninsula. It cuts 74 km inland and measures approximately 148 km wide and and up to 2,000 m deep. Tides are irregular diurnal, measuring up to 2 m. The banks are low-lying. The port of Ust'-Kamchatsk is situated on the gulf.   [11–856–2]

KAMCHATKA OBLAST, part of the RSFSR. Formed Oct. 20, 1932, as a part of Khabarovsk Krai; became an independent oblast of the RSFSR in 1956. Kamchatka Oblast includes the Koriak National Okrug. Area 472,300 sq km; population, 311,-000 (1972).

Kamchatka Oblast includes the Kamchatka peninsula and the adjoining part of the mainland, as well as the Komandorskie and Karaga islands. To the west is the Sea of Okhotsk; to the east, the Bering Sea and the Pacific Ocean. The oblast has 11 raions, one city, and 14 urban-type settlements. The administrative center is the city of Petropavlovsk-Kamchatskii.

Natural features. See KAMCHATKA (peninsula), in vol. 11, and KORIAK NATIONAL OKRUG, in vol. 12.

Population. Russians constitute most of the population (more than 80 percent); Ukrainians, 7 percent; and native nationalities (Koriak, Itel'men, Even, Aleut, and Chukchi), more than 3.5 percent. The average population density is 0.7 per sq km. The highest population density is found in some areas of the southwestern and southeastern coast of the peninsula and in the valley of the Kamchatka River. The urban population is 78 percent. All urban-type settlements were created in the Soviet period.

Economy. Industry accounts for more than 90 percent of the total gross production. The gross industrial product of Kamchatka Oblast increased by a factor of 2.7 from 1960 to 1971 and by a factor of 1.8 from 1965 to 1971.

In the years of Soviet power, Kamchatka Oblast has become one of the most important fishing regions of the USSR. The fishing industry accounts for 69 percent of the oblast's total gross industrial product; if the branches directly connected with the fishing industry, such as ship repair and the production of wooden crates, are included, the figure is about 77 percent (1971). The major commercial catches are salmon herring, plaice, bass, cod, mackerel, halibut, hake, and sablefish.

Kamchatka Oblast produces up to 10 percent of the fish catch and about 4 percent of the canned fish of the USSR. Until 1957, 60 percent of the fish were caught directly in the coastal waters and in the mouth of the spawning rivers. Since 1958 active fishing on the high seas has taken a leading role, reaching a share of 95 percent of the total. The fish catch was 7.8 million centners in 1971. New fishing regions have been developed in the eastern half of the Bering Sea and in the Pacific Ocean. The output of fish is almost entirely in the form of refrigerated, frozen, or lightly salted and canned fish. The main fish-canning combines are Petropavlovsk, Oktiabr', Ozernoi, Kirov, Ust'-Kamchatskii, and Oliutorskii.

Hunting for fur, as well as caged fur farming, is important in the oblast's economy. The oblast supplies furs of the fur seal, sable, silver fox, and mink. Crabs are caught along the western shore of the oblast.

The timber industry plays a considerable role. Its enterprises are situated in the basin of the Kamchatka River, where larch and spruce trees grow; it covers 10 percent of the forest areas and its reserves are 170 million cu m. The total reserves are 1 billion cu m. In 1971 enterprises of the timber industry produced up to 549,000 cu m of commercial lumber for shipment out of the oblast; the Ust'-Kamchatsk and Kliuchi wood-products combines produce sawmill materials, semifinished products for construction, and crates and barrels for the fishing industry.

The electric power output of the oblast increased by a factor of 3.5 from 1960 to 1971. The oblast has a variety of fuel and power resources: coal, hydroelectric power, and subterranean hot springs. Thermal springs are of special importance; the USSR's first experimental industrial geothermal electric power plant has been built on the Pauzhetskii thermal springs. A central heating plant has been built in Petropavlovsk-Kamchatskii.

Kamchatka Oblast produces up to 1.3 million construction bricks and 100,000 cu m of prestressed reinforced-concrete structural members and items per year (1971).

Agriculture consists of two branches: reindeer raising in the Koriak National Okrug and animal husbandry and vegetable farming in the southern part of Kamchatka Oblast. The oblast has 31 sovkhozes, 12 fishing kolkhozes, and 11 subsidiary farms of industrial enterprises (1971). Agricultural fields amount to 173,000 hectares (ha), of which 35,000 are plowed and, 75,000 are hayfields, and 61,000 are pastures. The total sown area of all agricultural crops is 32,000 ha (1971), 80 percent of which is planted with fodder crops; the remaining area is planted with potatoes and vegetables. Drained lands (6,900 ha) are planted mainly with vegetables and fodder crops. Animal husbandry is mainly of the dairy type. As of Jan. 1, 1972, the herd of livestock consisted of 27,100 head of cattle (45 percent of which were cows), 25,700 pigs, and 619,900 fowl. The chief regions of agricultural production are in the valleys of the Avacha, Kamchatka, and Bol'shaia rivers. The plains and mountain tundras,

covering 34 million ha, are used as pastures for reindeer. As of Jan. 1, 1972, the oblast had 162,000 reindeer, 90 percent of which were in the Koriak National Okrug. A large hothouse-nursery combine has been built on the basis of the Sredniaia Paratunka thermal springs. All foreign economic links and most of the domestic links are by sea. The main ports are Petropavlovskii and Ust'-Kamchatskii. Air transportation plays a great role in passenger traffic. Motor roads connect Petropavlovsk-Kamchatskii with settlements in Elizovo Raion (Nachiki and Paratunka) and with the valley of the Kamchatka River (the village of Mil'kovo). The Kamchatka River is navigable, with the river port of Ust'-Kamchatsk.

Eastern Kamchatka is the chief region of the fishing industry. Its center is Petropavlovsk-Kamchatskii; the settlement of Elizovo is a center of agricultural production. Western Kamchatka is an old fishing region with fish-processing and fish-canning enterprises (the Ozernoi, Oktiabr', and Kirov combines). Central Kamchatka is a region of lumber procurement (Kozyrevsk and Atlasov), wood products (Kliuchi and Ust'-Kamchatsk), and agriculture (Mil'kovo). The Komandorskie Islands are a region of trapping of fur seal and the raising of silver fox. The Koriak National Okrug is a region of the fishing industry, reindeer breeding, and the fur industry.

B. F. SHAPALIN

Educational institutions and scientific and cultural institutions; public health. In the 1914–15 academic year the territory of Kamchatka Oblast had 20 general-educational schools, with 404 students, and no secondary specialized or higher schools. In the 1971–72 academic year the oblast had 138 daytime general-educational schools, with 48,800 students; evening and correspondence schools, with 4,600 students; 12 vocational and technical schools, with 3,100 students; and six secondary specialized schools, with 5,400 students. The pedagogical institute in Petropavlovsk-Kamchatskii had 1,700 students. In 1972 the oblast had 195 preschool institutions, with 22,400 children.

Kamchatka Oblast is the site of the Institute of Volcanology of the Far East Center of the Academy of Sciences of the USSR, divisions of the Pacific Ocean Institute of Fishing and Oceanology, and the Institute of Hunting and Fur Farming.

As of Jan. 1, 1972, the oblast had 156 people's libraries, with 1,550,000 books and magazines, an oblast drama theater, and an oblast museum of local lore in Petropavlovsk-Kamchatskii; 154 club institutions; and 225 motion-picture projection units. Extracurricular institutions are represented by six Houses of Pioneers, oblast young technicians' and young naturalists' stations, excursion and tourist facilities, and four sports schools.

The oblast newspapers are *Kamchatskaia Pravda* (Kamchatka Pravda; since 1918) and *Kamchatskii komsomolets* (Kamchatka Komsomol Member; since 1924). The oblast radio and television broadcasts on two radio channels and one television channel and relays programs from Moscow. The television center is located in Petropavlovsk-Kamchatskii.

As of Jan. 1, 1972, Kamchatka Oblast had 75 hospital institutions, with 4,200 beds (13.6 beds per thousand) 1,400 doctors (one doctor for 227 people); and two balneological resorts, Paratunka and Nachiki, with hot mineral springs.

REFERENCES
Narodnoe khoziaistvo Kamchatskoi oblasti: Stat. sb. Petropavlovsk-Kamchatskii, 1971.
Rossiiskaia Federatsiia: Dal'nii Vostok. Moscow, 1971. (*Sovetskii Soiuz* series.) [11–852–2]

KAMCHATKA SEA, a name for the Sea of Okhotsk found mostly on 18th-century geographic maps. [11–857–2]

KAMCHIIA, a river in Bulgaria. The Kamchiia measures 245 km long and drains an area of approximately 5,400 sq km. It is formed from the confluence of the Goliama-Kamchiia and Luda-Kamchiia rivers, which originate in the eastern spurs of the Stara Planina (Balkan Mountains). In the upper and middle courses it is a mountain-type river. In the lower course it flows along a broad marsh-ridden valley within the Longoz (Longosa) coastal plain, and empties into the Black Sea. There is high water in the winter and spring and low water in the summer and fall. The mean annual flow rate at the mouth is approximately 23 cu m per sec, with a maximum of up to 500 cu m per sec.

[11–857–4]

KAMELIK, a river in Saratov Oblast, RSFSR, left tributary of the Bol'shoi Irgiz (in the Volga River basin). The Kamelik is 222 km long and drains an area of 9,070 sq km. It originates in the Obshchii Syrt and flows through a hilly lowland. The river is fed primarily by snow. It dries up in the summer and freezes in the winter. The mean annual flow rate 21 km from the mouth is 10.1 cu m per sec.

[11–738–6]

KAMENETS, an urban-type settlement, center of Kamenets Raion, Brest Oblast, Byelorussian SSR. Situated on the Lesna River, a tributary of the Bug, 28 km from the Zhabinka railroad station on the Baranovichi-Brest line. Population, 5,100 (1972). There is a plant for drying vegetables and a butter and cheese plant in the city. Kamenets also has a branch of the Brest Oblast Museum of Local Lore (in the "Belaia Vezha" tower, an architectural monument of the 13th century). The Białowieza (Belovezha) Forest Nature Museum is located in the village of Kameniuki, 23 km from Kamenets.

[11–740–1]

KAMENETSKII, an urban-type settlement in Tula Oblast, RSFSR, located 5 km from the Uzlovaia railroad junction. Coal is mined near Kamenetskii in the Moscow Area Coal Basin.

[11–740–2]

KAMENETS-PODOL'SKII, a city in Khmel'nitskii Oblast, Ukrainian SSR, on the lower course of the Smotrich River (a left tributary of the Dnestr). Railroad station on the Kiev-Chernovtsy line; highway junction. Population, 64,900 (1972; 36,500 in 1939).

Kamenets-Podol'skii arose at the end of the 11th century and beginning of the 12th. At first, it was part of Kievan Rus', but in the 13th century and the first half of the 14th it was part of the Galician-Volynian Principality. In the second half of the 14th century the city was seized by Lithuania, and in 1430, by Poland. It became the administrative center of Podol'e Voevodstvo (territory under a military governor) in 1463 and was transformed into a fortress. The city was an important artisan and trade center in the Middle Ages. It was seized by Turkey in 1672 but was returned to Poland in accordance with the Peace of Karlowitz (1698–99). The city became part of Russia on Mar. 27 (Apr. 7), 1793.

Kamenets-Podol'skii was part of the *namestnichestvo* (vicegerency) of Iziaslav from 1793 to 1795, the administrative center of the *namestnichestvo* of Podol'e from 1795 to 1797, and the administrative center of Podol'e Province from 1797 to 1917. Soviet power was proclaimed on Nov. 1 (14), 1917. In the period 1918–20, the city was repeatedly seized by Austro-Hungarian troops, by the followers of Petliura, and by Polish White forces. It was liberated once and for all by the Red Army on Nov. 16, 1920. As a result of the socialist transformations accomplished during the years of the prewar five-year plans, Kamenets-Podol'skii has become an industrial, cultural, and scientific center. From July 10, 1941, to Mar. 26, 1944, the city was occupied by fascist German troops, who inflicted heavy damage. Kamenets-Podol'skii was completely restored after the war. Its economy, science, and culture were further developed in the 1950's and 1960's.

Enterprises of the city's industries include an instrument-making plant, a plant producing motor vehicle subassemblies, a building-materials combine, and plants for the production of cables, electrical appliances (Elektropribor), metals, agricultural machines, cold asphalt-concrete, reinforced-concrete structures, and roofing materials. There is also a poultry combine, a meat combine, a sugar factory, and a cannery. A large cement plant is under construction (1972). There are also cotton and clothing factories.

Educational institutions include pedagogical and agricultural institutes, the general technological department of the Khmel'nitskii Technological Institute of Consumer Services; industrial, construction, and agricultural technicums; a technicum of the food industry; and medical and cultural-educational schools.

There is a botanical garden. The city's parks almost completely encircle the canyon of the Smotrich River.

Structures that have been preserved in the old, medieval section of the city include the castle known as the Turkish Fortress (now the Historical Museum; 14th–16th centuries, rebuilt in the 17th and 18th centuries), the Church of Peter and Paul (16th century), a Gothic Roman Catholic Church (16th century) with a Turkish minaret (1672–92), and the town hall (16th century). Two stone bridges connect the old and new sections of the city. Large housing projects are under construction in the new section. The Railroad Terminal Square has been laid out. The wooden Krestovozdvizhenskaia Church (18th century) is located in Karvasary, a suburb.

REFERENCES
Iurchenko, P. G. "Kam'ianets'-Podil'skyi zamok." In the collection *Arkhitekturni pam'iatnyky.* Kiev, 1950.
Kam'ianets'-Podil'skyi. Putivnyk. L'vov, 1970. [11–740–3]

KAMENEV, LEV L'VOVICH. Born in 1833, in Ryl'sk, Kursk Province; died Jan. 14 (26), 1886, in Savvinskaia Sloboda, Moscow Province. Russian landscape painter.

Kamenev lived in Astrakhan until 1854, at which time he moved to Moscow. From 1854 to 1858 he studied under K. I. Rabus and A. K. Savrasov at the Moscow School of Painting, Sculpture, and Architecture. From 1862 to 1865 he lived and studied in Munich, Düsseldorf, and Switzerland. Kamenev was a founding member of the Society of Traveling Art Exhibitions (*peredvizhniki*). His work played an important role in the development of 19th-century Russian national realist landscape painting. His paintings include *Near Porech'e Village* (1869, Russian Museum, Leningrad), *Spring* (1866, Tret'iakov Gallery), *Fog: Red Pond in Moscow in the Autumn* (1871, Tret'iakov Gallery), and *Landscape* (1872, Tret'iakov Gallery).

REFERENCE
Bespalova, L. A. *L. L. Kamenev: 1833–1886.* Moscow, 1954.
[11–739–1]

KAMENEV, SERGEI SERGEEVICH. Born Apr. 4 (16), 1881, in Kiev; died Aug. 25, 1936, in Moscow. Soviet military leader, army commander first class (1935). Member of the CPSU from 1930.

The son of a military engineer, Kamenev graduated from the Alexander Military School in 1900 and from the Academy of the General Staff in 1907. In World War I he held staff positions, was chief of the operations division of the First Army, and was appointed commander of an infantry regiment with the rank of colonel in early 1917. After the October Revolution he was elected chief of staff of the XV Corps and then of the Third Army. He volunteered for the Red Army in early 1918 and was military leader of the Nevel' sector of the Western Barrage and commander of the 17th Infantry Division; he was appointed assistant military leader of the Western Barrage in August 1918. From September 1918 to July 1919, Kamenev brilliantly commanded the troops of the Eastern Front during the offensive of the front's troops in 1918 and early 1919 and then during the defense and offensive against Kochak's troops in 1919.

Kamenev was commander in chief of the armed forces of the republic from July 1919 until April 1924. Carrying out the directives of V. I. Lenin and of the Central Committee of the party, he directed the actions of the Red Army on routing the White Guard and interventionist troops. Appointed inspector of the RKKA (Workers' and Peasants' Red Army) in April 1924, Kamenev served as chief of the Staff of the RKKA from March 1925, chief inspector of the RKKA from November 1925, and chief of the Main Directorate of the RKKA from August 1926. A member of the Revolutionary Military Council of the USSR from April 1924 to May 1927, Kamenev was deputy people's commissar of military and naval affairs and deputy chairman of the Revolutionary Military Council of the USSR from May 1927 to June 1934. He was chief of the administration of the National Air Defense Forces from June 1934 and simultaneously, from November 1934, a member of the Military Council of the People's Commissariat of Defense of the USSR. He was a member of the All-Russian Central Executive Committee.

Kamenev was awarded the Gold Combat Weapon with the decoration of the Order of the Red Banner, the Honorary Revolutionary Firearm with the decoration of the Order of the Red Banner, Orders of the Red Banner of the RSFSR, the Red Banner of the Khorezm SSR, and the Red Crescent First Class of the Bukhara People's Soviet Republic. He is buried in Red Square near the Kremlin Wall.

WORKS

Zapiski o grazhdanskoi voine i voennom stroitel'stve. Moscow, 1963.

REFERENCES

Polkovodtsy grazhdanskoi voiny. Moscow, 1960.
Stebakova, L. "Glavkom Respubliki S. S. Kamenev." *Voenno-istoricheskii zhurnal,* 1971, no. 4. [11–739–2]

KAMENKA, a city (since 1956), center of Kamenka Raion, Cherkassy Oblast, Ukrainian SSR, located on the Tiasmin River (a tributary of the Dnieper). Railroad station on the Cherkassy-Znamenka line. Population, 14,600 (1972). Kamenka has a machine-building plant, a sugar plant, a distillery, a butter factory, and a building-materials plant. The literary-memorial museum of A. S. Pushkin and P. I. Tchaikovsky, who had made visits to Kamenka, is in the Green House. V. L. Davydov's estate, where the members of the Southern Society of the Decembrists used to meet in the 1820's, has been preserved in Kamenka.

[11–742–4]

KAMENKA, an urban-type settlement, center of Kamenka Raion, Moldavian SSR. Located on the left bank of the Dnestr River, 36 km from the Popeliukhi railroad station on the Zhmerinka-Razdel'naia line. Population, 12,500 (1972). Kamenka has a vegetable and fruit cannery, a bread-baking factory, and a butter factory. It also has a museum of history and local lore and a fruit and vegetable sovkhoz-technicum. [11–743–1]

KAMENKA, an urban-type settlement in Dal'negorsk (Tetiukhe) Raion, Primor'e Krai, RSFSR. Situated on the shore of the Sea of Japan, it has a fish combine. There is also fur farming (mink). [11–743–2]

KAMENKA, an urban-type settlement in Mezen' Raion, Arkhangel'sk Oblast, RSFSR. It is a port on the left bank of the Mezen' River, 38 km from the White Sea and 280 km northeast of Arkhangel'sk. The Mezen' Sawmill is located in the settlement. [11–742–5]

KAMENKA, an urban-type settlement in Vichuga Raion, Ivanovo Oblast, RSFSR. It is located on the Sunzha River, 2 km from the river's confluence with the Volga, and 25 km northwest of the Vichuga railroad station on the Ivanovo-Kineshma line. The Krasnyi Oktiabr' Textile Finishing Factory is located in Kamenka. [11–742–7]

KAMENKA, an urban-type settlement in Ostrogozhsk Raion, Voronezh Oblast, RSFSR. Railroad station (Evdakovo) on the Georgiu-Dezh–Millerovo line. There is a combine for the production of oils and fats, a butter and cheese plant, and an industrial combine in the settlement. [11–742–6]

KAMENKA, a city (until 1951, a settlement), center of Kamenka Raion, Penza Oblast, RSFSR, located on the Atmis River (of the Oka River basin). Railroad station (Belinskaia) 80 km west of Penza. Population, 30,000 (1970). Kamenka has plants for the production of farm machinery, building components, carbonic acid, groats, and seeds, a brickyard, a butter factory, a brewery, and a meat combine. It also has a machine-building evening technicum. [11–742–3]

KAMENKA, a river in Krasnoiarsk Krai, RSFSR, a right tributary of the Angara. It measures 313 km long and drains an area of 11,400 sq km. The river is meandering, and there are rapids. Its tributaries are the Uderei River on the right and the Kozhima River on the left. The Kamenka River is fed by snow and rain. It is used for floating timber. [11–742–2]

KAMENKA-BUGSKAIA (until 1944, Kamenka-Strumilovskaia), a city, center of Kamenka-Bugskaia Raion, L'vov Oblast, Ukrainian SSR. Located on the Bug River. Railroad station on the L'vov-Lutsk line. Kamenka-Bugskaia has a parquet-wood combine, a flax-processing mill, a cheese-making plant, and a clothing and haberdashery factory. There is also a historical and revolutionary museum in Kamenka-Bugskaia. [11–743–3]

KAMENKA-DNEPROVSKAIA, a city; administrative center of Kamenka-Dneprovskii Raion, Zaporozh'e Oblast, Ukrainian SSR, 8 km from Nikopol'. Landing on the shore of the Kakhovka Reservoir. Population, 16,900 (1972). The city has a butter and cheese processing plant and a cannery. Fish farming is another important economic activity. A museum of local lore is located in Kamenka-Dneprovskaia. [11–743–4]

KAMENKA GORODISHCHE, the site of a fortified settlement of the end of the fifth century to the third century B.C. It has an area of about 12 sq km and is situated near the city of Kamenka-Dneprovskaia and the village of Bol'shaia Znamenka in Zaporozh'e Oblast, Ukrainian SSR. It was excavated by D. Ia. Serdiukov in 1899–1900 and B. N. Grakov in 1938–41 and 1944–50.

On the side facing the steppe the settlement was protected by an earthen bank and a ditch and on the north and west, by precipices above the Dnieper River, the Konka River, and the Belozerska Liman. In the southwest corner there was an acropolis, where the Scythian nobility lived. The population was primarily engaged in the production of bronze and iron implements, weaving, pottery-making, farming, and stock raising. The artisans lived in pit houses and dwellings of logs set in the ground; the nobility lived in stone houses. The settlement was a large artisan and trade center and had close ties with the Greek colonies north of the Black Sea and with the local population of Scythia. At the end of the third century B.C. the settlement was abandoned (with the exception of the acropolis, which continued to be inhabited until the third century A.D.).

REFERENCE

Grakov, B. N. "Kamenskoe gorodishche na Dnepre." In *Materialy i issledovaniia po arkheologii SSSR,* no. 36. Moscow, 1954.
A. I. MELIUKOVA [11–791–3]

KAMEN'-KASHIRSKII, a city (since 1939); administrative center of Kamen'-Kashirskii Raion, Volyn' Oblast, Ukrainian SSR, on the Tsir River (a tributary of the Pripiat'). It is the terminus of the railroad branch line from the Kovel' station (on the Rovno-Brest line). The city has a wood products plant and a creamery. Kamen'-Kashirskii has been known since the 12th century. [11–793–1]

KAMENNAIA MOGILA (literally "stone grave"), a sandstone monadnock near the village of Terpen'e, in Melitopol' Raion, Zaporozh'e Oblast, Ukrainian SSR. Hundreds of carved figures of animals (bulls, horses, deer, antelope, predators), occasionally of people and of human footprints, and numerous geometric figures and symbols have been preserved on the ceilings of the ancient overhangs and caves and beneath stone slabs. Traces of a red pigment have been preserved in some places. In the opinion of some scholars, the pictures of Kamennaia Mogila date from the period between the end of the Paleolithic and the beginning of the Iron Age; according to other scholars, they are from a period not earlier than the Neolithic.

REFERENCES

Bader, O. N. "Drevnie izobrazheniia na potolkakh grotov v Priazov'e." In the collection *Materialy i issledovaniia po arkheologii SSSR,* no. 2. Moscow, 1941.
Formozov, A. P. *Ocherki po pervobytnomu iskusstvu.* Moscow, 1969.
Rudyns'kyi, M. Ia. *Kam'iana Mohyla.* Kiev, 1961. [11–744–2]

KAMEN'-NA-OBI, a city in Altai Krai, RSFSR. It is a landing on the left bank of the Ob' River and a railroad station on the Barnaul-Omsk line, 208 km northwest of Barnaul. Population, 36,000 (1970). The city has a plant producing metal goods, as well as weaving and garment factories, a cheese-processing combine, a creamery, a liqueur and vodka plant, a furniture factory, and a brickyard. There is also an agricultural technicum, medical and pedagogical schools, and a museum of local lore.

[11–793–2]

KAMENNOE, an urban-type settlement in Voroshilovgrad Oblast, Ukrainian SSR, 2 km from the Shchetovo station on the Debal'tsevo-Likhaia railroad line. Coal is mined there.

[11–746–2]

KAMENNOGORSK (until 1948, Antrea), a city in Vyborg Raion, Leningrad Oblast, RSFSR. Located on the Karelian Isthmus, on the left bank of the Vuoksa River (Lake Ladoga basin), 169 km northwest of Leningrad. Kamennogorsk is a station on the Vyborg-Petrozavodsk railroad line and is the starting point of a 26-km branch to Svetogorsk. There is a paper factory and a combine producing nonmetallic materials such as sand and gravel in the city. Granite is quarried near Kamennogorsk.

[11–746–1]

KAMENNOMOSTSKII, an urban-type settlement in Maikop Raion, Adygei Autonomous Oblast, Krasnodar Krai, RSFSR. Located on the Belaia River, a tributary of the Kuban' River, in the foothills of the Greater Caucasus. Kamennomostskii has a railroad station (Khadzhokh), the terminus of a 64-km line connecting with the Armavir-Tuapse line. There are timber procurement establishments, a timber combine, and factories producing construction materials and souvenirs made of gypsum stone in the settlement. A fruit-growing sovkhoz is also located in Kamennomostskii. The settlement is a tourist center and a starting point for trips to the Caucasian Preserve and to the mountains of the Western Caucasus.

[11–747–2]

KAMENNYI BROD, an urban-type settlement in Baranov Raion, Zhitomir Oblast, Ukrainian SSR, 30 km from the Kurnoe station on the Zhitomir–Novograd-Volynskii railroad line. Kamennyi Brod has a pottery factory and a quarry for rubble stone.

[11–769–2]

KAMENOLOMNI, an urban-type settlement, the administrative center of Oktiabr'skii Raion, Rostov Oblast, RSFSR. Located on Grushevka River, in the Don River basin. Kamenolomni has a railroad station 70 km northeast of Rostov-on-Don. Population, 12,000 (1970). There are railroad transport enterprises in the city. Kamenolomni arose in the 1860's with the construction of the Voronezh–Rostov-on-Don railroad.

[11–789–2]

KAMENOV, EVGENI GANCHEV. Born Dec. 29, 1908, in Sofia. Bulgarian statesman and public figure; economist; academician of the Bulgarian Academy of Sciences (1960); Honored Scientist (1969). Member of the Bulgarian Communist Party since 1931.

Kamenov fought in the antifascist resistance movement and was detained in concentration camps in 1941 and 1944. Deputy minister of foreign affairs from 1948 to 1951, he directed the Institute of Economics of the Bulgarian Academy of Sciences from 1951 to 1954. He was in the diplomatic service from 1954 to 1960 and became secretary of the Division of Philosophy, Economics, and Law of the Bulgarian Academy of Sciences in 1960. Kamenov is the author of works on problems of socialist economics and of economic relations with capitalist countries.

WORKS
Piroda i obshchestvo. Sofia, 1939
Geografskoto polozhenie i prirodnite osobenosti na Bulgariia, ot razeni v stopanskoto i razvitie. Sofia, 1944.
Ikonomikata na narodnite demokratsii. Sofia, 1949.
Ikonomicheskata pomoshch na Suvetskiia suiuz—reshavashch faktor za izgrazhdaneto na sotsializma v Bulgariia. Sofia, 1955.
Ikonomicheskite otnosheniia mezhdu sotsialisticheskite i kapitalisticheskite strani: Obektivni predpostavki i kharakterni cherti. Sofia, 1960.

[11–789–1]

KAMENSK, an urban-type settlement in Kabansk Raion, Buriat ASSR. Located at the foot of the Khamar-Daban Range, 2 km from the Timliui railroad station on the Trans-Siberian Railroad and 105 km northwest of Ulan-Ude. The Timliui cement works and an asbestos-cement products plant are located in the settlement. There is an evening industrial technicum in Kamensk.

[11–789–3]

KAMENSKII, FEDOR FEDOROVICH. Born Aug. 21 (Sept. 2), 1836, in Lesnoe, a suburb of St. Petersburg; died Aug. 26, 1913, in Clearwater, Fla., USA. Russian sculptor.

From 1852 to 1860, Kamenskii studied under I. P. Vitali and N. S. Pimenov at the St. Petersburg Academy of Arts. From 1863 to 1869 he studied in Italy on a fellowship. He lived in Florence between 1870 and 1873. Kamenskii became a resident of the United States in 1873. His works (primarily small-scale sculpture), which were devoted to subjects from daily life, were often marked by sentimentalism. Kamenskii sought to overcome the abstract quality of academic sculpture. His marble sculptures include *The Boy Sculptor* (1866) and *The First Step* (1872)—both are in the Russian Museum in Leningrad. Kamenskii also sculptured portraits.

REFERENCE
Samoilov, A. N. "F. F. Kamenskii, 1836–1913." In *Russkoe Iskusstvo. Ocherki o zhizni i tvorchestve khudozhnikov: Seredina deviatnadtsatogo veka.* Moscow, 1958. [11–791–1]

KAMENSKII, GRIGORII NIKOLAEVICH. Born Jan. 6 (18), 1892, in the village of Klekotki, in present-day Skopin Raion, Riazan Oblast; died July 17, 1959, in Moscow. Soviet hydrogeologist. Corresponding member of the Academy of Sciences of the USSR (1953).

Kamenskii graduated from the land reclamation engineering division of the Moscow Agricultural Institute in 1916. In 1933 he became a professor at the Moscow Institute of Geological Research. His principal works dealt with regional and theoretical hydrogeology (filtration properties of rocks and problems of the regime, dynamics, zonality, and formation of groundwater). He devised a number of instruments for determining the filtration factor, including a field instrument that was named the Kamenskii tube (1932). He was awarded two orders and various medals.

WORKS
Rezhim podzemnykh vod. Moscow-Leningrad, 1938. (Co-author.)
Osnovy dinamiki podzemnykh vod, 2nd ed. Moscow, 1943.
Poiski i razvedka podzemnykh vod. Moscow-Leningrad, 1947.
Gidrogeologicheskie issledovaniia i razvedka istochnikov vodosnabzheniia. Moscow-Leningrad, 1947.
Gidrogeologiia SSSR. Moscow, 1959. (Co-author.) [11–790–2]

KAMENSKII, VALENTIN ALEKSANDROVICH. Born Sept. 16 (29), 1907, in Tula. Soviet architect; People's Architect of the USSR (1970). Member of the CPSU since 1941.

Kamenskii graduated from the Leningrad Institute of Industrial Construction Engineers in 1931. From 1951 to 1971 he was chief architect for Leningrad. He is one of the authors of the draft for a general plan of development for Leningrad for 1960–80 and was director of projects for the planning and construction of Prospekt Stachek (1951–55) and Komsomol Square (1956), as well as the entry square of the Avtovo area (1954), and the Dachnoe area (beginning in 1960). He collaborated on the design of the Oktiabr' motion-picture and concert hall (1967) and the experimental residential district on Vasil'evskii Island (1967). He has been an instructor at the Leningrad Institute of Industrial Construction Engineers (1931–39) and the Leningrad Civil Engineering Institute (since 1941; professor since 1959). He has been awarded the Order of Lenin, the Order of the Badge of Honor, and medals.

WORKS
Leningrad segodnia i zavtra. Leningrad, 1962.

REFERENCE
V. A. Kamenskii. Introduction by I. I. Fomin. Leningrad, 1967.

[11–789–4]

KAMENSKII, VASILII VASIL'EVICH. Born Apr. 5 (17), 1884, near Perm'; died Nov. 11, 1961, in Moscow. Russian and Soviet poet; one of the first Russian pilots (1910–11).

Kamenskii was the son of a gold mine supervisor. First published in 1904, he was a futurist and a close associate of V. V. Mayakovsky. Kamenskii's "free and easy novel," *Sten'ka Razin,* with its romantic love of freedom, appeared in 1915. His early poems were marked by a futurist outlook and by verbal experimentation. The characteristic tone of his lyrics was a carefree rapture with existence and a spontaneously joyful view of life. Kamenskii's principal creative works were the three poems on leaders of peasant uprisings: *Sten'ka Razin* (1912–20), *Emel'ian Pugachev* (1931), and *Ivan Bolotnikov* (1934). He gave his heroes the traits of the *bogatyrs* (hero in Russian folklore) and of the courageous people sung about in the *byliny* (epic folk songs). Kamenskii was awarded two orders and various medals.

WORKS
Poemy. [Preface by N. Stepanov.] Moscow, 1961.
Stikhotvoreniia i poemy. Introductory article, preparation of the text, and commentary by N. L. Stepanov. Moscow-Leningrad, 1966.
Stikhi. Perm', 1967.
Put' entuziasta: Avtobiograficheskaia povest'. Perm', 1968.

[11–790–1]

KAMENSKOE PLATO, a climatic and koumiss-treatment health resort in the Kazakh SSR. It is located 10 km from Alma-Ata, in the foothills of the Zailiiskii Alatau, at an elevation of 1,250 m. Summers are warm, with average July temperatures of 20°C, and winters are clear, dry, and moderately mild, with average January temperatures of −4°C. The total annual precipitation is approximately 780 mm. Therapeutic remedies include heliotherapy, air treatments, and koumiss treatments. There are sanatoriums for patients with active forms of pulmonary tuberculosis. [11–792–1]

KAMENSK-SHAKHTINSKII, a city in Rostov Oblast, RSFSR. Landing on the Severskii Donets River. Railroad station (Kamenskaia) on the Millerovo–Rostov-on-Don line. Population, 71,000 (1972; 43,000 in 1939).

Kamensk-Shakhtinskii has combines for the production of synthetic fibers and building materials and a meat-packing plant. Other industrial enterprises include a machine-building plant (mining equipment), a plant for the manufacture of glass vessels, a brickyard, and a food-products plant. The Kamenskaia Heat and Power Plant is located in the city. Kamensk-Shakhtinskii also has an evening chemical and mechanical technicum and a pedagogical school. The city arose in 1686 as a cossack settlement. It became the cossack *stanitsa* (large village) of Kamenskaia in 1817 and the city of Kamensk-Shakhtinskii in 1927.

REFERENCE
Shumov, V. *Kamensk na Dontse Severskom.* Rostov-on-Don, 1967.

[11–792–3]

KAMENSK-URAL'SKII, a city in Sverdlovsk Oblast, RSFSR, located at the confluence of the Kamenka River and the Iset' River (of the Ob' River basin). Railroad junction of lines to Sverdlovsk, Kurgan, Serov, and Cheliabinsk. Population, 173,-000 (1972; 51,000 in 1939).

Kamensk-Uralskii arose at the end of the 17th century as a settlement attached to a cast-iron smelting works and foundry, which was put into operation in 1701. The settlement became a city in 1935. During the years of Soviet power, ferrous and nonferrous metallurgy, machine-building, metalworking, and building-materials enterprises, as well as enterprises of the food industry and light industry, have been established in the city. These include the Ural'skii Aluminum Plant, the Sinarskii Pipe Works, Stroimontazhkonstruktsiia Plant (producing equipment for nonferrous metallurgy enterprises), an electromechanical plant, a plant producing commercial equipment, an automobile repair plant, and a clothing factory. The Krasnogorskii Heat and Power Plant is located in the city. Educational institutions include the general technical department of the Urals Polytechnic Institute, an aluminum technicum, and a medical school. There is a dramatic theater and a museum of local lore in the city.

[11–792–2]

KAMER-FUR'ERSKII ZHURNAL, a collection of daily records kept at the court of the Russian tsars and emperors by courtiers, called *Kamer fur'ery,* from 1734. It was initiated in 1695 by Peter I, who began keeping a diary entitled *Zhurnal ili podennaia zapiska* (Journal, or Daily Notes) depicting the course of military operations in the Azov Campaigns (1695–96) and the Northern War (1700–21). After Peter I, the *Kamer-Fur'erskii Zhurnal* was kept containing for the most part descriptions of court ceremonies and the daily life of the imperial family. The last entries date from February 1917 and describe the revolutionary movement among the troops quartered at Tsarskoe Selo. The collections covering the period from 1695 to 1817 have been published; those of the subsequent period are preserved in the Central State Archive in Leningrad (archive 516).

REFERENCE
Kamer-fur'erskii tseremonial'nyi zhurnal, 1695–1817. St. Petersburg–Petrograd, 1853–1916.

[11–820–1]

KAMER-IUNKER (from German, *Kammerjunker*), the lowest court title in tsarist Russia.

[11–820–2]

KAMERLINGH ONNES, HEIKE. Born Sept. 21, 1853, in Groningen; died Feb. 21, 1926, in Leiden. Dutch physicist and chemist. Doctor of philosophical sciences (1879). Professor at the University of Leiden from 1882 to 1924.

In an effort to obtain liquid helium, Kamerlingh Onnes organized a specially equipped cryogenic laboratory at the University of Leiden, which became a world center for low-temperature physics and was subsequently named after him. Here he first achieved temperatures close to absolute zero and in 1908 obtained liquid helium. Kamerlingh Onnes studied the physical properties of various substances at low temperatures, especially those of mercury, lead, and tin. While investigating the electrical resistance of mercury in 1911, he observed that the resistance disappeared at a temperature of 4.1°K. This phenomenon was called superconductivity. He also worked on thermodynamics, magneto-optics, and radioactivity. Kamerlingh Onnes was awarded a Nobel Prize in 1913.

WORKS
"On the Changes of the Electrical Resistance of Pure Metals at Very Low Temperatures. V. The Disappearance of the Resistance of Mercury." *Communication From the Physical Laboratory at the University of Leiden.* 1911, no. 122, p. 13.
REFERENCE
Keesom, W. *Gelii.* Moscow, 1949. (Translated from English.) (Contains a bibliography of Kamerlingh Onnes' works.) [11–797–1]

KAMERNYI TEATR, a drama theater in Moscow (incorporated into the network of academic theaters by a resolution of the People's Commissariat for Education on Nov. 20, 1920). It opened in 1914 with a performance of Kalidasa's *Sakuntala.*

A. Ia. Tairov was the theater's founder and director; he staged its most important productions. He conceived of the Kamernyi Teatr's artistic program as a counterpoise to the stage naturalism and to the "theater of convention" of the early part of the century. The theater developed primarily as a theater of tragedy, but gravitated toward polar genres ("today—mystery, tomorrow—harlequinade") and became a theater of synthesis. Tairov expounded the idea that stagecraft has an independent value of its own; he trained actors for skilled performance in all theatrical genres and forms. He stressed the importance of pantomime, initially as an independent form and later as an element of the dramatic performance.

Many of the theater's productions were experimental and not all were successful; they occasionally aroused heated controversy. Seeking a place for itself in the system of Soviet realistic theater, the Kamernyi published manifestos defining its artistic style; in its terms "structural realism" was the complex artistic structure of stage works and "winged realism" was the need to crystallize the generalized insights of art. The theater became well known, particularly after its tours abroad in 1923, 1925, and 1930.

A. G. Koonen was the theater's leading actress. The production of *Optimistic Tragedy* by Vs. Vishnevskii (1933, with Koonen as the Commissar) was a universally recognized innovative peak in the staging of revolutionary heroism in the Soviet Union.

The most important productions of the Kamernyi Teatr included *Famira-Kifared* by Annenskii (1916); *Adrienne Lecouvreur* by Scribe and Legouvé (1919); *Phèdre* by Racine (1922); *Giroflé-Girofla* by Lecocq (1922); O'Neill's *The Hairy Ape* (1926), *Desire Under the Elms* (1926), and *All God's Chillun Got Wings* (1929); *The Three-Penny Opera* by Brecht and Weill (1930); *Madam Bovary,* based on the novel by Flaubert (1940); *While the Heart Still Beats* by Paustovskii (1943); *The Seagull* by Chekhov (1944); *Guilty Though Guiltless* by Ostrovskii (1944); and *The Old Man* by Gorky (1946). In 1950 the theater was closed. Some members of the company joined the newly organized A. S. Pushkin Moscow Drama Theater.

REFERENCES
Lunacharskii, A. V. *O teatre i dramaturgii,* vol. 1. Moscow, 1958.
Markov, P. *Noveishie teatral'nye techeniia.* Moscow, 1924.
Politicheskie otkliki zapadnoi pressy na gastroli Moskovskogo Gosudarstvennogo Kamernogo teatra. Moscow, 1924.
Derzhavin, K. *Kniga o Kamernom teatre.* Leningrad, 1934.
Tairov, A. *Zapiski rezhissera: Stat'i, Besedy, Rechi, Pis'ma.* Moscow, 1970.
Golovashenko, Iu. *Rezhisserskoe iskusstvo Tairova.* Moscow, 1970.

IU. A. GOLOVASHENKO [11–800–3]

KAMES, hills and ridges in areas of former Anthropogenic continental glaciation.

Kames are found singly and in groups, primarily in the northwest European USSR (Karelia, the Baltic region, and Leningrad Oblast). Their elevations range between 2–5 and 20–30 m. They are composed of sands containing galls and interlayers of clay with inclusions of balls and ball accumulations. Enveloping stratification that roughly repeats the contour of the cross section of the kame is characteristic. On top the kames are often overlapped with loams and, frequently, with boulders. The origin of kames is not completely understood. According to one of the most common hypotheses, kames appeared as a result of the accumulative action of streams that circulated at the surface of, within, and at the base of large blocks of dead ice during the period of glacier degradation. [11–857–5]

KAMESHKOVO, a city (until 1951, a settlement); center of Kameshkovo Raion, Vladimir Oblast, RSFSR. Railroad station on the Moscow-Gorky line, 43 km northeast of Vladimir. Kameshkovo has a weaving and textile factory, a timber combine, and a dairy plant, as well as a night textile technicum. [11–821–1]

KAMIEŃSKI, HENRYK (pseudonym, Philaret Prawdowski). Born Feb. 24, 1813, in Warsaw; died Jan. 14, 1866, in Algiers. Polish revolutionary, philosopher, and economist. The son of a general.

Kamieński fought in the Polish uprising of 1830–31. In the 1840's he was an ideologist of the Polish National Liberation Democratic Movement: he proclaimed the inseparability of antifeudal reforms from the national liberation struggle through a partisan war and called for the complete liberation of the peasantry from the oppression of the *szlachta* (Polish gentry) and the allotment of land to the peasants.

Kamieński's world view combined concern for the problems of German classical philosophy, primarily Hegelian, with the ideas of the French Utopian socialists, especially the Saint-Simonians. For Kamieński man was an absolute, a rational intellectual being whose work is embodied in social products and in actions. His major work, *The Philosophy of the Material Economy of Human Society* (vols. 1–2, 1843–45), presents a philosophical analysis of the political economy of his time.

Kamieński was arrested in 1845 and exiled to Viatka; he moved to Switzerland in 1852. In the 1850's his views evolved toward liberalism. A. I. Herzen praised Kamieński's views on Russian-Polish relations as expressed in *Russia and Europe: Poland* (1857).

WORKS
Pamietniki i wizerunki. Wrocław, 1951.
In Russian translation:
In the book *Izbr. proizvedeniia pol'skikh myslitelei,* vol. 2. Moscow, 1956.
REFERENCES
Istoriia filosofii, vol. 2. Moscow, 1957. Pages 438–39.
Przemski, L. *Henryk Kamieński,* 2nd ed. Warsaw, 1950.

KAMIEŃSKI, MACIEJ. Born Oct. 13, 1734, in Sopron, Hungary; died Jan. 25, 1821, in Warsaw. Polish composer. Slovak by birth.

Kamieński served in court chapels in Sopron and Vienna. From 1760 he lived in Warsaw, where he taught voice. He became famous as the composer of *Misery Contented* (staged 1778), the first Polish opera based on the the life of the people (libretto in Polish and utilizing Polish musical folklore). He wrote eight operas in all, of which six were staged, including *Zośka* and *Virtuous Simplicity* (both written in 1779). Among his other compositions are two vaudevilles (1780, 1788), a dramatic cantata, masses and other religious works, and polonaises. Despite the influence of French vaudevilles, the *Singspiel,* and the Italian *opera seria* on Kamieński's operas, they have a distinct Slavic character, especially in the lyrical episodes. [11–793–3]

KAMIKAZE (Japanese, literally "wind of the gods"), a suicide pilot in the Japanese armed forces in World War II used to fight enemy surface ships in a single-action airplane. In addition to conventional aircraft flown by kamikaze, in 1945 the Japanese air force had more than 5,000 single-action airplanes called Baka that carried explosive charges of up to 1 ton in their front end. The airplane, which had a small jet engine and a limited range of action, was directed by the kamikaze to the target, dived, and crashed into it. More than 2,500 suicide pilots died in combat in the Pacific Ocean in 1944 and 1945. [11–822–1]

KAMIL, MUSTAFA. Born Aug. 14, 1874, in Cairo; died there Feb. 10, 1908. Figure of the Egyptian national liberation movement. Publicist and orator.

Kamil was a lawyer by education. In 1900 he founded the newspaper *Al-Liwa* (The Banner). Kamil opposed the British occupation of Egypt. He demanded internal autonomy for Egypt within the framework of the Ottoman Empire and counted on the Turkish government's assistance in the struggle against Great Britain. Kamil created the Watan Party in 1907 and was its first chairman.

REFERENCES
Krachkovskii, I. Iu. "Mustafa Kamil i Zhiul'etta Adan." *Izbrannye sochineniia,* vol. 3. Moscow-Leningrad, 1956.
Al-Rafii Abd al-Rahman. *Mustafa Kamil....* Cairo, 1950. (In Arabic.).
Rashad Ahmad. *Mustafa Kamil . . . .* Cairo, 1958. (In Arabic.) [11–822–3]

KAMINALJUYÚ, a major cultic center of the ancient Maya in the highlands of Guatemala (near present-day Guatemala City), which flourished between the second and ninth centuries. Kaminaljuyú contains the remains of pyramids, stelae with inscriptions, tombs, and burial vaults. Excavations have unearthed figured and painted pottery and articles made of stone, bone, and shells.

REFERENCE
Kinzhalov, R. V. *Iskusstvo drevnikh maiia.* [Leningrad, 1968.] [11–823–1]

KAMIŃSKI, KAZIMIERZ. Born May 1, 1865, in Warsaw; died there Sept. 10, 1928. Polish actor and director. Son of a theater usher.

After making his debut in Warsaw in 1884, Kamiński acted in provincial theaters in Poland and Russia until 1891. From 1893 to 1901 he performed in Kraków and from 1901 to 1904 in L'vov. Subsequently, he appeared in various Warsaw theaters, including Rozmaitości (1918), Teatr Polski (1923), and Teatr Narodowy (1925), where he was also a director. A representative of realism in the Polish theater, Kamiński had a style marked by an ironic pungency. His roles included Stańczyk in Wyspiański's *The Wedding* and the Baron in Gorky's *Lower Depths*.

REFERENCE
Dąbrowski, S., and R. Gorski. *Kazimierz Kamiński.* Warsaw, 1956.
[11–824–2]

KAMINSKII, ANTON ANTONOVICH. Born Nov. 5 (17), 1862, in Sebezh District, now Pskov Oblast; died Aug. 5, 1936, in Leningrad. Soviet climatologist.

Kaminskii graduated from the University of St. Petersburg in 1888. That same year he began working in the Main Physics Observatory, where he directed the work of the department for the network of meteorological stations until 1918 and headed the division of climatology from 1922 to 1932. He participated in the organization and the work of the State Institute of Hydrology (1919–29) and the Central Hydrometeorological Bureau of the Central Administration of Marine Transportation (1922). Kaminskii was the organizer and first head of the climatology subdepartment (from 1932) at Leningrad State University. His principal works were devoted to air humidity, air pressure, the transfer of water vapor, and dry winds. He devoted a series of works to a climatological description of individual regions of the USSR and to problems of medical, agricultural, forestry, and marine meteorology, as well as to hydrology.

WORKS
Godovoi khod i graficheskoe raspredelenie vlazhnosti vozdukha na prostranstve Rossiiskoi imperii po nabliudeniiam 1871–1890 gg. St. Petersburg, 1894.
Klimat i pogoda v ravninnoi mestnosti: Klimat Voronezhskoi gubernii, part 1. Leningrad-Moscow, 1925.

REFERENCE
Nezdiurov, D. F. *A. A. Kaminskii—vydiaushchiisia meteorolog-klimatolog.* Leningrad, 1953.
[11–823–2]

KAMINSKII, GRIGORII NAUMOVICH. Born Oct. 20 (Nov. 1), 1895; died Feb. 10, 1938. Soviet statesman and party figure; one of the organizers of Soviet health care. Joined the Communist Party in 1913.

The son of a blacksmith, Kaminskii was born in Ekaterinoslav (present-day Dnepropetrovsk). He studied in the department of medicine of Moscow University and took an active part in the student revolutionary movement. In 1917 he became a member of the Moscow oblast bureau of the RSDLP(B) and secretary of the Tula committee of the party. From 1918 to 1920 he was the chairman of the Tula provincial committee of the RSDLP(B) and of the provincial executive committee and a member of the Revolutionary Military Council of the Second Army. In 1920 he became secretary of the Central Committee of the CP(B) of Azerbaijan and chairman of the Baku soviet of working people's and Red Army deputies. From 1922 to 1929 he was chairman of the Central Committee of the trade unions of Vserabotzemles (All-Russian Production Union of Farm and Forestry Workers), deputy chairman of the board of the Union of Agricultural Cooperatives, and chairman of the collective farm center. He became secretary of the Moscow city committee of the ACP(B) in 1930 and, in 1932, chairman of the Moscow oblast executive committee. He was people's commissar for health care of the RSFSR and chief public health inspector of the USSR from 1934 to 1936 and people's commissar for health care of the USSR in 1936–37.

Government decisions on the training of doctors and secondary medical personnel, the fight against malaria, the medical industry, the work of the All-Union Institute of Experimental Medicine, and the advancement of medical science were developed and adopted on Kaminskii's initiative. He was a delegate to the Sixth, Eighth, Eleventh, Thirteenth, and Seventeenth Congresses of the party. He was elected candidate member of the Central Committee of the ACP(B) at the Fourteenth and Seventeenth Congresses. He was also a member of the All-Union Central Executive Committee and the Central Executive Committee of the USSR.

REFERENCES
Grigorii Kaminskii: Sbornik vospominanii. Tula, 1965.
Lozhechko, A. B. *Grigorii Kaminskii.* Moscow, 1966.
Leonov, I. T. *G. N. Kaminskii.* Moscow, 1967.
M. A. KARLOV [11–823–3]

KAMINSKII, an urban-type settlement in Rodniki Raion, Ivanovo Oblast, RSFSR. The settlement is located on the Teza River, a tributary of the Kliaz'ma, 3 km from the Skorynino railroad station on the Ivanovo-Kineshma line. Kaminskii has a textile mill.
[11–824–1]

KAMKOV, BORIS DAVIDOVICH (pseudonym of B. D. Kats). Born June 3, 1885, in the village of Kobyl'nia, in present-day Floreshti Raion, Moldavian SSR; died in 1938. One of the leaders of the left Socialist Revolutionaries (Left SR's).

Kamkov lived in exile in France and Sweden during World War I and took an internationalist position on the war. He returned to Russia after the February Revolution of 1917 and was elected to the Petrograd committee of the SR's; he opposed the war and came out for the transfer of power to the soviets. Kamkov was elected to the All-Russian Central Executive Committee at the Second All-Russian Congress of Soviets. At the First Congress of the Party of Left SR's, held in Petrograd Nov. 19–28 (Dec. 2–11), 1917, Kamkov was elected to the Central Committee of the party. In late February 1918 he came out against the Brest peace with Germany and for an end to the alliance of the Left SR's with the Bolsheviks. He was one of the initiators and organizers of the Left SR revolt in Moscow on July 6–7, 1918. Kamkov led underground groups of his party that continued the struggle against Soviet power. He was sentenced by a military tribunal to three years imprisonment for anti-Soviet activity. In his last years he worked as a statistician in Voronezh.
[11–824–3]

KAMLANIE (from *kham, kam,* the name for shamans in a number of Turkic languages in southern Siberia), a term in the Russian language that refers to the special ritual activities of the shaman during which he appears to communicate with the spirits. Among most of the Siberian peoples, the *kamlanie* ritual was as follows: The shaman, who wore a special costume, beat on a tambourine and performed a frenzied dance; he gradually brought himself to a state of ecstasy and showed symptoms of hallucination. It appeared that he was speaking with the spirits and influencing them. The *kamlanie* ritual was performed to heal the sick. It was also performed during fortune-telling.

REFERENCE
Tokarev, S. A. *Rannie formy religii i ikh razvitie.* Moscow, 1964.
[11–825–1]

KAMLEIA, a pullover knee-length outer garment for men made of reindeer hides, sometimes decorated with beads on the front, sleeves, and hem, which in the past was worn by the Dolgan. The Russians also used the term *kamleia* (or *kamleika*) to refer to the waterproof work clothing equipped with a hood worn by the Aleuts (sewn from the intestines of sea animals). [11–825–2]

KAMMARI, MIKHAIL DAVIDOVICH. Born Feb. 17 (Mar. 1), 1898; died Sept. 21, 1965, in Moscow. Soviet philosopher. Corresponding Member of the Academy of Sciences of the USSR (1953). Joined the CPSU in 1919.

Kammari graduated from the Institute of the Red Professoriat of Philosophy and Natural Science in 1931. Beginning in 1929 he taught philosophy in higher educational institutions. Kammari was editor in chief of the journal *Voprosy filosofii* (Questions of Philosophy) from 1954 to 1959. He became senior research fellow at the Institute of Philosophy of the Academy of Sciences of the USSR in 1945. Kammari's principal works were on historical materialism (national relations and the role of the popular masses and the individual in history).

WORKS

O sovetskom sotsialisticheskom obshchestve. Moscow, 1948. (Coauthor.)
Istoricheskii materializm. Moscow, 1954. (Coauthor.)
Narod—tvorets istorii. Riga, 1954.
Chto takoe bazis i nadstroika obshchestva. Moscow, 1957.
Rol' narodnykh mass i lichnosti v istorii. Moscow, 1957. (Coauthor.)

[11–825–3]

KAMMERER, PAUL. Born Aug. 17, 1880, in Vienna; died there Sept. 23, 1926. Austrian zoologist.

Kammerer graduated from the University of Vienna in 1904 and taught a course there in experimental morphology. From 1902 to 1923 he was a member of the staff of the Institute of Experimental Biology (of the Austrian Academy of Sciences), which he helped organize. He attempted to demonstrate experimentally the inheritance of acquired traits and to prove Lamarckism. However, his failure to observe the strict requirements of such experiments evoked criticism of many of his works by other researchers. Because of his pacifist, atheistic, and antiracist views, Kammerer was persecuted by the chauvinist-minded German scientists. He committed suicide after an accusation that he falsified the results of his experiments.

WORKS

Neuvererbung oder Vererbung erworbener Eigenschaften. Stuttgart, 1925.
In Russian translation:
Obshchaia biologiia. Moscow-Leningrad, 1925.
Pol, razmnozhenie i plodovitost': Biologiia vosproizvedeniia. Leningrad, 1927.
Zagadka nasledstvennosti: Osnovy obshchei teorii nasledstvennosti. Leningrad, 1927.

REFERENCES

Gaisinovich, A. E. "U istokov sovetskoi genetiki: I. Bor'ba s lamarkizmom (1922–1927)." *Genetika,* 1968, no. 6.
Bliakher, L. Ia. *Problema nasledovaniia priobretennykh priznakov.* Moscow, 1971. Chapter 12.   A. E. GAISINOVICH   [11–825–4]

KAMNO, a site of a fortified settlement located 8 km northwest of Pskov. In the eighth to tenth centuries Kamno was a fortified artisan settlement, in which the working of iron and copper was developed. Excavations (in 1948–49 and 1951–52) have revealed foundry workshops, bloomeries and altars connected with them, crucibles, foundry ladles, small molds for the casting of small ornaments, and small stone slabs with designs. In the 12th century, when Pskov flourished, the fortified Kamno settlement went into a decline, but a graveyard of the same name existed until the 16th century.

REFERENCE

Tarakanova, S. A. "Pskovskie gorodishcha." In the collection *Kratkie soobshcheniia Instituta istorii material'noi kul'tury,* fasc. 62. Moscow, 1956.   [11–831–3]

KAMO (party pseudonym of Simon Arshakovich Ter-Petrosian). Born May 15 (27), 1882, in Gori; died July 14, 1922, in Tbilisi. Professional revolutionary. Became a member of the Communist Party in 1901. The son of a trader.

Kamo began to distribute illegal literature in Tbilisi, Baku, Batumi, Kutaisi, Gori, and other cities in 1901 and organized underground printing shops. Arrested in November 1903, he escaped from prison in September 1904. He took part in organizing armed workers' *druzhiny* (detachments) in 1905. During the armed clashes between the workers and troops in Tbilisi in December 1905, Kamo led a detachment of worker-fighters and was wounded five times in an encounter with the cossacks. He was arrested and imprisoned in the Metekhi Castle. Tortured, he managed to escape. He came to St. Petersburg in March 1906, where he met V. I. Lenin for the first time. On Lenin's instructions, Kamo went abroad to arrange for the purchase and transport of arms into Russia. He organized a series of expropriations of money from tsarist agencies from 1905 to 1907, in order to secure funds for the party. Arrested by German police in Berlin in November 1907, he avoided being tried and handed over to

the tsarist government by feigning insanity. He was delivered to the Russian police at the end of 1909, imprisoned in the Metekhi Castle, and tried by a military court. He escaped from the prison hospital on Aug. 15, 1911, and went to Paris. On Lenin's instructions, Kamo arranged for the transport of party literature into Russia. Returning to Russia in 1912, he was arrested and sentenced to death. The sentence was commuted by a 1913 amnesty to 20 years at hard labor, which he served in the Kharkov convict prison. He was freed in March 1917.

In December 1917, on the instructions of S. G. Shaumian, Kamo carried a letter from Baku to V. I. Lenin in Petrograd. On Jan. 8, 1918, he returned to Tbilisi with letters from Lenin and the decree of the Council of People's Commissars of the RSFSR appointing Shaumian temporary extraordinary commissar of the Caucasus. In the summer of 1919, Lenin instructed Kamo to organize a guerrilla detachment for action in the enemy's rear and wrote to the Revolutionary Military Council of the Republic that he knew Kamo "to be a man of absolutely exceptional dedication, courage, and energy . . ." (*Poln. sobr. soch.,* 5th ed., vol. 51, p. 42). Kamo organized a guerrilla detachment in 1919 that operated near Kursk and Orel and then in the rear of the troops of General Denikin on the Southern Front. Kamo used a fishing boat to deliver weapons and money from Astrakhan to Baku for the underground party organization and the guerrillas of the Northern Caucasus. In January 1920 he was arrested by the Menshevik government in Tbilisi and was exiled. He helped prepare the armed uprising in April 1920 in Baku to transfer power to the Soviets. Kamo came to Moscow in May 1920 and studied at the Military Academy. He worked in the Ministry of Foreign Trade in 1921. In early 1922 he started work in the People's Commissariat of Finance of Georgia. Later that year he was hit by a motor vehicle and killed.

REFERENCES

Gorky, M. "Kamo." *Sobr. soch.,* vol. 17. Moscow, 1952.
Bibineishvili, V. E. *Kamo.* Moscow, 1934.
Arutiunian, A. *Kamo.* Yerevan, 1957.
Shaumian, L. *Kamo.* [Moscow, 1959.]   L. S. SHAUMIAN   [11–832–1]

KAMO (until 1959, Nor-Baiazet), a city in the Armenian SSR. Situated on the Gavaraget River, 8 km from where the river empties into Lake Sevan, on the Sevan-Martuni-Sevan highway, 39 km from the Sevan railroad station and 90 km northeast of Yerevan. Population, 20,000 (1970). Kamo has a plant for the production of cables, an instrument-making plant, an auto-repair plant, a fish farm, and the Sevan Mineral Water Plant. Cheese is also produced. There are also knitted-goods, clothing, furniture, carpet-weaving, and footwear factories in the city. Kamo has an industrial technicum and a zoological-veterinary sovkhoz-technicum, as well as a museum of local lore and a dramatic theater. The city was renamed in honor of Kamo, the Armenian revolutionary and Bolshevik.   [11–833–3]

KAMO (also Levaia Kamo or Katalanga), a river in the Evenki National Okrug, Krasnoiarsk Krai, RSFSR, a left tributary of the Podkamennaia Tunguska River. The Kamo measures 339 km long and drains an area of 14,500 sq km. It flows in a deep valley and meanders in its lower course. The river is fed primarily by snow. There is high water in the spring and low water in the winter, and there are flash floods in the summer and fall. The main tributary is the Tokhomo (on the left).

[11–833–2]

KAMO CHOMEI. Born 1153; died 1216. Japanese writer.

Kamo Chomei lived at a time when the power of the Japanese aristocracy was crumbling under the assaults of military feudal families. An aristocrat by birth, he was a court poet; he later took monastic vows. He became famous after writing the book of essays *Notes From a Ten-foot-square Hut* (1212), which is permeated by Buddhist ideas about the fragility of the world and is considered a model of prose in the classic Japanese style of *zuihitsu.* His poems are included in imperial anthologies. He was also the author of *Nameless Notes* (1210–12), which contained comments on poets, poetry, and prosody.

WORKS
In Russian translation:
"Zapiski iz kel'i." Translated by N. I. Konrad. In N. I. Konrad, *Iaponskaia literatura v obraztsakh i ocherkakh.* Leningrad, 1927.

[11–833–1]

KAMOV, NIKOLAI IL'ICH. Born Sept. 1 (14), 1902, in Irkutsk; died Nov. 24, 1973, in Moscow. Soviet helicopter designer; Doctor of Technical Sciences (1962), Hero of Socialist Labor (1972). Became a member of the Communist Party in 1943.

Kamov graduated from the Tomsk Technological Institute in 1923. In 1929 he created the first Soviet helicopter (an autogiro), the Kaskr-1 Krasnyi Iuzhener (with the engineer N. K. Skrzhinskii). From 1931 to 1935 the A-7 combat autogiro was designed under his supervision (a squadron of autogiros participated in the Great Patriotic War, 1941–45). In 1960 he became the chief designer in the Helicopter Design Office. The coaxial helicopters built under Kamov's direction include the Ka-8 Irkutianin (1945–48), the Ka-10 (1949–53), the Ka-15 (1950–56), the Ka-18 (1955–60), the twin-turbine Ka-25 (1958–68), the twin-engine Ka-26 (1964–67), and the twin-turbine experimental rotary-wing Ka-22 (1953–64). He was awarded two Orders of Lenin, two other orders, and medals.

[11–833–4; updated]

KAMOZIN, PAVEL MIKHAILOVICH. Born July 3 (16), 1917, in Bezhitsa. Twice Hero of the Soviet Union (May 1, 1943, and July 1, 1944); captain (1944). Member of the CPSU since 1943.

Kamozin's father was a worker; Kamozin himself was a locksmith before joining the Soviet Army in 1938. That year he graduated from the Borisoglebsk Military Aviation School. During the Great Patriotic War of 1941–45 he fought on the Southern, Transcaucasian, and Northern Caucasian fronts as flight commander, deputy commander, and commander of a squadron of a fighter aviation regiment. Kamozin shot down 35 enemy aircraft in individual combat and 13 in group combat. In the reserves since 1946, Kamozin has been awarded the Order of Lenin, two Orders of the Red Banner, the Order of Alexander Nevsky, the Order of the Patriotic War First Class, and various medals.

[11–834–1]

KAMPALA, the capital of Uganda. Located in central Africa, near the northern shore of Lake Victoria, at an elevation of up to 1,300 m. The city has an equatorial climate characterized by monsoons. The average January temperature is about 22°C; the average July temperature is 20°C. Total annual precipitation is more than 1,500 mm (at Entebbe). Area, 22 sq km; population, 80,000 (1970; including suburbs, 332,000). The city is administered by the government of Uganda. There is also an elected city council.

A railroad connects Kampala with the port of Mombasa, Kenya, on the Indian Ocean. A branch railroad line connects Kampala with Port Bell on Lake Victoria. Kampala is a highway junction, and there is an airport in Entebbe, 35 km to the south. Kampala is the main economic center of the country, with textile, flour, butter, and brewery enterprises. Other important economic activities include the processing of coffee, cotton, tea, hides, and leather and the production of cigarettes and cement.

Educational institutions in Kampala include Makerere University (since 1970, the National University of Uganda), a medical school, a teachers' college, the Scientific Society of Uganda, the Regional Institute of East Africa (social research), and scientific research institutions in agriculture, medicine, and chemistry. The university library contains more than 125,000 volumes. Cultural facilities include the Museum of Uganda (with a unique collection of African musical instruments and the Center for Archaeological Research), the National Theater (its building was constructed in 1959), the Limited Theater traveling troupe (organized in 1968), and the Heartbeat of Africa song and dance ensemble (created in 1964).

[11–835–1]

KAMPAR, a city in western Malaysia, in Perak State, on the Malacca Peninsula. Population, 26,600 (1970). There is a railroad station. Industry includes primary processing of rubber,

rice, and tobacco; there is also a sawmill and production of wicker items and jewelry.

[11–840–2]

KAMPEN, a city in the Netherlands, in Overijssel Province, on the IJssel River. Population, 29,000 (1970). Kampen is linked by a navigable canal with the Zuider Zee (IJsselmeer). Timber is shipped from the city. Industry includes metal-working and the manufacture of concrete items, as well as tobacco and food enterprises. Kampen has architectural monuments dating from the 14th–17th centuries (city gates, churches, a town hall).

[11–841–2]

KAMPINOS (Kampinoski Park Narodowy), a scenic park (since 1959) in Poland. Area, 22,353 hectares (1970). It is located on the left bank of the Vistula and adjoins Warsaw to the northwest. The ancient Vistula valley has sand dunes (covered mainly by pine forest) and marshes. Elk, roe deer, and boar inhabit the park, and the common crane, black stork, short-toed eagle, and common heron nest there. The park has ten preserves (1,890 hectares) and a museum.

[11–843–1]

KAMPOT, a city and shallow-water port in southern Cambodia, on the Gulf of Siam; administrative center of Kampot Province. Population, 12,700 (1962). It is a transportation junction and is connected by a highway with the new port of Kompong Som. The city has a silk factory and food and sawmill enterprises. Kampot is the center of an important region producing black Cambodian pepper. Phosphates are extracted in the area.

[11–844–1]

KAMSKOE UST'E (formerly the village of Bogorodskoe), an urban-type settlement; administrative center of Kamskoe-Ust'e Raion, Tatar ASSR. Landing on the Kuibyshev Reservoir, opposite the mouth of the Kama River, 71 km east of the Karatun station on the Kazan'-Ul'ianovsk railroad line, 117 km south of Kazan. Gypsum is extracted near Kamskoe-Ust'e.

[11–846–3]

KAMUNTA, a high-mountain settlement on the left bank of the Komidon River, in Digora Raion, Severnaia Osetiia ASSR. It has been known since the end of the 19th century from the numerous archaeological finds discovered in the surrounding burial grounds. Some objects date from the Koban culture of the late Bronze Age. The most richly represented are objects of the medieval culture of the Alani of the sixth to eleventh centuries A.D. found in the catacomb burials of the clan nobility undergoing feudalization: gold ornaments and coins (fifth- to ninth-century Byzantine, sixth-century Sassanid, and eighth-century Abbasid silver dirhems).

REFERENCE
Kuznetsov, V. A. "Alanskie plemena Severnogo Kavkaza." In the collection *Materialy i issledovaniia po arkheologii SSR,* no. 106. Moscow, 1962.

[11–847–2]

KAMYL', an Adygeian wind instrument; a type of end-blown flute made from a reed or metal pipe, with three side holes. It is almost 700 mm long. Its scale is diatonic, pitched in fourths (overblowing produces octaves and higher).

[11–858–1]

KAMYSHANY, an urban-type settlement in Kherson Oblast, Ukrainian SSR, 9 km from the city of Kherson. Most of its inhabitants work in Kherson.

[11–858–4]

KAMYSHEVAKHA, an urban-type settlement in Lisichansk Raion, Voroshilovgrad Oblast, Ukrainian SSR. A junction of the Kharkov-Voroshilovgrad and Popasnaia–Krasnyi Liman railroad lines, Kamyshevakha has enterprises for the servicing of railroad transport, as well as a cinder-block plant and a vegetable and dairy sovkhoz.

[11–858–5]

KAMYSHEVAKHA, an urban-type settlement in Orekhov Raion, Zaporozh'e Oblast, Ukrainian SSR, on the Konka River (a tributary of the Dnieper). Railroad station (Fisaki) on the Zaporozh'e-Pologi line. Kamyshevakha has a wood-products combine and a mixed-feed plant. A plant for the production of reinforced-concrete structures is under construction (1972). There is also a stone quarry in the settlement. [11–859–1]

KAMYSHIN, a city in Volgograd Oblast, RSFSR. Situated on the right shore of the Volgograd Reservoir, at the mouth of the Kamyshinka River. Port and important transshipment point (primarily bread, salt, and petroleum). Terminal station on the Balashov-Kamyshin railroad line. Population, 101,000 (1972; 24,000, in 1939).

The city was founded in 1667 as the village of Kamyshinka on the left bank of the Kamyshinka River. In 1710 the inhabitants were moved to the right bank, where there was a fortress. This settlement was named the city of Dmitrievskii. In 1780 the city was renamed Kamyshin and made the administrative center of a district of the *namestnichestvo* (vicegerency) of Saratov; in 1797 it was made the administrative center of a district of Saratov Province. In the 19th century Kamyshin was a merchant city with sawmills and flour mills and was famed for its trade in watermelons.

Kamyshin has a cotton combine, a factory for the production of cranes, a machine-building plant (equipment for stock-breeding farms), a varnish and paint factory, and plants for the assembly of metalworking instruments and the manufacture of glass vessels. There are also food industry enterprises (a vegetable cannery, a butter and cheese combine, and a meat-packing plant) and plants producing building materials. Educational institutions include an evening textile technicum, a technicum for the mechanization of agriculture, and medical and music schools. Kamyshin also has a museum of local lore and a dramatic theater. Melon growing (watermelons) is widespread outside the city. [11–859–3]

KAMYSHLOV, a city in Sverdlovsk Oblast, RSFSR. Situated on the Pyshma River (of the Ob' River basin). Railroad station on the Sverdlovsk-Tiumen' line, 143 km east of Sverdlovsk. Population, 31,000 (1970).

Kamyshlov has enterprises for the servicing of railroad transport, as well as plants for the manufacture of insulators and building materials, a metalworking plant, leather and clothing factories, a flour mill, and a poultry combine. The city also has a medical school and a pedagogical school. Kamyshlov grew out of a *sloboda* (tax-exempt settlement), which was founded in 1668. The *sloboda* was renamed in 1781 and made the administrative center of a district of the *namestnichestvo* (vicegerency) of Perm'. In 1796 it was made the administrative center of a district of Perm' Province. [11–859–5]

KAMYSHOVAIA BUKHTA, an urban-type settlement in Crimean Oblast, Ukrainian SSR, on the Black Sea, 15 km from Sevastopol'. Population, 11,300 (1971). There is fishing. The settlement has a fish-canning combine, a ship-repair plant, and a plant producing reinforced-concrete structural members. [11–860–1]

KAMYSHOVYI RANGE, the main dividing range of the Western Sakhalin Mountains on Sakhalin Island. Length, 400 km; elevations, 500–1,000 m; maximum elevation, 1,325 m (Mount Vozvrashchenie). The continuation of the Kamyshovyi Range to the south of the Poiasok Isthmus (220 km long) is called the Iuzhno-Kamyshovyi Range. The range is composed of coal-bearing shale-sandstone rock, predominantly of the Cretaceous period, crushed into folds. On the slopes is a spruce-fir taiga with dense thickets of Kuril bamboo. The Iuzhno-Sakhalinsk-Kholmsk railroad line has been built across the Iuzhno-Kamyshovyi Range. [11–861–1]

KAMYSH-SAMAR LAKES, a group of lakes in Ural'sk Oblast, Kazakh SSR. The lakes are located in the northeastern part of the Caspian Depression, in the lower courses of the Bol'shoi Uzen' and Malyi Uzen' rivers. Total area, about 6 sq km. Some of the lakes are up to 6 km long and 2.5 m deep. Some are of the running-water type. Their water is sweetish (Lakes Gushche-Kulak, Tushche-Kulak, and Staritskoe), brackish (Lakes Raim and Sarai), or bitter brackish (Lakes Sarykulak and Aksor). The

fresher lakes abound in vegetation and fish (pike-perch, perch, and pike). [11–861–2]

KAMYSH-ZARIA, an urban-type settlement in Kuibyshev Raion, Zaporozh'e Oblast, Ukrainian SSR. Kamysh-Zaria is a railroad junction and services railroad transport. [11–859–2]

KAMYSLYBAS (also Kamyshlybash), a salt lake in Kzyl-Orda Oblast, Kazakh SSR. Area, 176 sq km. The lake is located in the northern part of the Syr Darya River delta (it is connected to the Syr Darya's main branch by a channel). During high water and when the level of the Syr Darya rises as a result of obstructions and ice jams, its water runs into Kamyslybas. The lake's area and salinity vary greatly. Common carp, bream, and Caspian roach are caught in the lake. [11–858–2]

KAN, SERGEI BORISOVICH. Born July 17 (29), 1896, in Terioki (present-day Zelenogorsk); died Mar. 7, 1960, in Moscow. Soviet historian, specialist in modern history; he became a professor and a doctor of historical sciences in 1940.

Kan was a teacher from 1924 to 1959—in the department of history of Moscow State University from 1934 to 1937 and in 1946–47, at the V. I. Lenin Pedagogical Institute from 1938 to 1941 and from 1943 to 1946, at the V. P. Potemkin Pedagogical Institute from 1955 to 1959, and at the Higher Diplomatic School from 1946 to 1949. Kan was a senior research associate at the Institute of History of the Academy of Sciences of the USSR from 1944 to 1952. He was involved in many collective works, including *The Revolution of 1848–1849* (vols. 1–2, 1952), *The Paris Commune of 1871* (vol. 1, 1961), *The History of Diplomacy* (vol. 1, 1959), and *Modern History* (vol. 1, 1963). In his book on the Silesian weavers' uprising, Kan analyzed the manufacturing stage of capitalism in Germany, based upon the example of the linen industry. He also investigated the history and historiography of the Revolution of 1848–49 in Germany.

WORKS
Dva vosstaniia silezskikh tkachei 1793–1844. Moscow-Leningrad, 1948.
Revoliutsiia 1848 g. v Avstrii i Germanii. Moscow, 1948.
Nemetskaia istoriografiia revoliutsii 1848–1849 gg. v Germanii. Moscow, 1962.
Istoriia sotsialisticheskikh idei (do vozniknoveniia marksizma). (Course of lectures), 2nd ed. Moscow, 1967. [11–863–3]

KAN, a river in Krasnoiarsk Krai, RSFSR; a right tributary of the Enisei. Length, 629 km; basin area, 36,900 sq km.

The Kan begins on the northern slopes of the Vostochnyi Saian (Kanskoe Belogor'e). As far as the mouth of the Tikhii (Quiet) Kan, the river is known as the Dikii (Wild) Kan. In its headwaters, the river flows in a narrow valley, which broadens in the middle course, where the river crosses the Kan Forest-steppe; lower down, in crossing the southern spurs of the Enisei Ridge, the river has stretches of rapids (Bol'shoi, Kosoi). The river is fed by snow and rain. The average annual flow of the river at the village of Podporog is 276 cu m per sec. The tributaries are the Agul on the right and the Rybnaia on the left. Some stretches of the river are navigable. Once clear of the mountains, the river is used to float logs. The town of Kansk is located on the river, and the eastern part of the Kansk-Achinsk Coal Basin is located in the Kan Basin. [11–864–1]

KANAGAWA, a prefecture in Japan, in the southeastern part of the island of Honshu. Area, 2,400 sq km; population, 5,472,000 (1970), of which 90 percent was urban. The administrative center is the city of Yokohama.

Kanagawa is part of Japan's largest industrial region, Kanto. Kanagawa Prefecture accounts for more than 10 percent of Japan's total industrial production (in terms of value). The main branches of industry include machine building, (particularly transportation—ships and motor vehicles; approximately 22 percent of Kanagawa's industrial output) and electrical engineering (21 percent), as well as chemistry (18 percent), metallurgy (12 percent), and the food industry (10 percent). The cities of Yokohama, Tsurumi, and Kawasaki are the main industrial centers. Agriculture includes the cultivation of rice, wheat, and tobacco. Tangerines, vegetables, and flowers are grown, and beef and dairy cattle and poultry are raised. There is fishing off the coast of the Miura Peninsula. The area also has tourism.

[11–866–1]

KAN'AMI, one of the oldest schools of actors in the Japanese *no* theater. Two members are particularly well known.

Kiyotsugu Kan'ami. Born in 1333; died in 1384. The founder of the school. Kiyotsugu Kan'ami founded the Kanzeza Theater in the city of Iga; in his productions he combined theatrical elements of the 10th–11th-century *sarugaku,* of the 11th–16th-century *dengaku,* and the early-14th-century *kuse-mai,* creating a new type of performance—the *no* theater. He was also an actor and teacher and theorist of theatrical art.

Zeami (Seami) Motokiyo Kan'ami. Born in 1363; died in 1443. The son of Kiyotsugu Kan'ami. After his father's death Zeami directed the Kanzeza Theater. Unlike his father he sought to please the tastes of the aristocracy (the emperor often attended his stage productions). Zeami Kan'ami was an outstanding actor and wrote more than 100 plays for the *no* theater, distinguished by exceptional refinement. He composed more than 20 treatises on the art of *no.*

REFERENCES
Nogami, Toyoitiro. *Kan'ami Kiyotsugu.* Tokyo, 1949.
Kobayasi, Shizuo. *Zeami.* Tokyo, 1943.
Geinojiten (Dictionary of Theatrical Art). Tokyo, 1962.

L. D. GRISHELEVA [11–1012–5]

KANAMYCIN (Kantrex, Resistomycin), an antibiotic of the amino glycoside group.

Kanamycin was first obtained from the actinomycete *Streptomyces kanamyceticus* in 1957. It is soluble in water, thermostable, and polybasic. Kanamycin is effective against most gram-negative and gram-positive bacteria and mycobacteria. It is ineffective against yeasts, fungi, enterococci, and bacteroids. Kanamycin sulfate solution is administered intramuscularly in the treatment of tuberculosis. Although kanamycin has a low level of toxicity, in large doses it produces side effects on the kidneys and acoustic nerves.

[11–936–2]

KANARESE (self-designation, Kannadiga), a people in southern India; the major part of the population of the state of Mysore.

There are 22 million Kanarese (1970 estimate). They speak Kannada, a Dravidian language. Most of the Kanarese are Hindus, although there are also some Jains, Christians, and Muslims (the last only in the cities). The chief occupations of the Kanarese are farming (rice, millet, cotton, sugarcane), livestock raising (oxen, buffaloes, small cattle), handicrafts (pottery, wood carving), industrial labor, and work on coffee and other plantations.

REFERENCE
Narody Iuzhnoi Azii. Moscow, 1963. Pages 627–43. [11–976–2]

KANARIS, KONSTANTINOS. Born circa 1790 on the island of Psara; died Sept. 14, 1877, in Athens. Greek statesman and naval commander. Participant in the Greek War of Independence of 1821–29.

Kanaris was elected to the National Assembly in 1826. In 1843–44 and 1854 he was minister of the Greek Navy. In 1864–65 and 1877, Kanaris headed the Greek government. He was a leader of the pro-constitution group. [11–938–1]

KANASH (until 1920, Shikhrany), a city in the Chuvash ASSR. Located 84 km south of Cheboksary on the Tsivil'sk-Ul'ianovsk highway. Railroad lines link Kanash to Cheboksary, Kazan, Arzamas, and Ruzaevka. Population, 43,500 (1972). Kanash is an important industrial center of the Chuvash Republic, the site of a large railroad-car repair plant, a motor-vehicle overhauling factory, and factories producing electric loading machinery, cutting tools, motor-vehicle spare parts, polymer materials, and construction materials. Clothing, felting, and furniture factories as well as food industry establishments (a meat combine, a creamery, and a bakery) are also located in Kanash. There is a

financial technicum, a night technicum for railroad transport, a pedagogical school, and a medical school in the city, as well as a museum of local lore. Kanash arose in the 1890's as a railroad station and became a city in 1925.

[11–951–1]

KANÁSZDUDA (also *kanásztülök*), wind instrument of Hungarian herdsmen; it is an ox horn with a whittled wooden mouthpiece and no holes. The instrument is used mainly for rhythmic signals, as well as for improvised melodies based on the natural (overtone) scale.

[11–939–2]

KANATCHIKOV, SEMEN IVANOVICH. Born Apr. 13, 1879, in the village of Gusevo, Moscow Province; died Oct. 19, 1940. Soviet party figure. Became a member of the Communist Party in 1898. The son of a peasant.

In 1895, Kanatchikov began to work in Moscow factories and became involved in the work of the St. Petersburg League of Struggle for the Liberation of the Working Class. He was persecuted by the authorities. Kanatchikov conducted party work in Saratov from 1900 to 1902 and was a member of the committee of the RSDLP. He became a member of the Moscow party committee in 1905 and then a member of the St. Petersburg party committee. Kanatchikov worked in Ekaterinburg (Sverdlovsk) and Nizhnii Tagil in 1906 and was a delegate to the Fourth (Unification) Congress of the RSDLP in the same year. He was again a member of the Moscow party committee in 1907. Kanatchikov worked in the St. Petersburg trade union movement from 1908 to 1910 and was in prison and in exile in Irkutsk Province from 1910 to 1916. In 1917 he was a member of the Novonikolaevsk (Novosibirsk) and Tomsk committees of the RSDLP (Bolshevik) and a member of the Novonikolaevsk soviet.

In 1918, Kanatchikov was chairman of the Tomsk military revolutionary staff and deputy chairman of the provincial executive committee and then became a member of the Perm' provincial executive committee and head of the provincial department of public education. In Moscow in 1919 he was a member of the board of the People's Commissariat of Internal Affairs, a member of the lesser Council of People's Commissars, and one of the organizers of the Ia. M. Sverdlov Communist University. In 1920 he became a member of the Siberian Revolutionary Committee, head of the Siberian department of public education, and chairman of the regional committee of the RCP(Bolshevik) of the Tatar ASSR. Kanatchikov became rector of the Communist University in Petrograd in 1921. He became head of the department of the press of the Central Committee of the RCP(B) in 1924 and head of a department of Istpart (Commission on Party History) of the Central Committee of the ACP (Bolshevik) in 1925–26. Kanatchikov was the correspondent of the Telegraph Agency of the Soviet Union (TASS) in Czechoslovakia from 1926 to 1928. He embarked upon literary work in 1928: he was editor of the journal *Krasnaia Nov'* (Red Virgin Soil), and editor in chief of *Literaturnaia gazeta* (Literary Newspaper). He was a delegate to the Fourteenth Congress of the ACP(B) in 1925.

REFERENCE
Oni borolis' za vlast' Sovetov. Novosibirsk, 1970. Pages 86–93.

[11–950–1]

KANAZAWA, a city in Japan, in the western part of the island of Honshu. Administrative center of Ishikawa Prefecture. Population, 361,400 (1970). The city is the center of the Hokuriku economic region. It is an industrial center with well-developed textile industry (natural and artificial silk, cotton fabric) and food and condiment industry, textile and agricultural machine building, and a bicycle factory; there is also production of porcelain and faience (the high-quality Kutani porcelain) and lacquerware (Wazima), as well as fishing nets. In the city is a state preserve, Kenrokuen Park. [11–916–1]

KANCHALAN, a river in the Chukchi National Okrug, Magadan Oblast, RSFSR. Length, 426 km; basin area, 20,600 sq km. It originates from several sources (the largest of which is the Iuzhnyi Tadleoan) at Mount Tumannaia and flows through the Anadyr' Lowland in a broad valley and into the Kanchalan estuary of the Anadyr' Gulf. The major tributaries are the Tnekveem and the Impeneikuiym, from the right. The Kanchalan is fed by snow and rain. It freezes in mid-October, breaking up in early June. The river is navigable for 50 km above its mouth.

[11–1012–2]

KANCHENJUNGA, a mountain in the Himalayas. Maximum elevation, 8,585 m. The mountain is composed of gneisses, granites, and schists. It has jagged peaks and steep slopes. Large valley glaciers, such as Zemu (approximately 30 km long) and Kanchenjunga, are located on the mountain. [11–1012–3]

KANCHIPURAM, a city in southern India, on the Palar River, in Tamil Nadu State. Population, 110,500 (1971). Kanchipuram's well-known cottage industries include the manufacturing of cotton and silk fabrics. Saris, the Indian national costumes for women, are made there. Kanchipuram is a Hindu religious center. It is one of the oldest cities in India. Among its numerous architectural monuments are the temples of Kailasanath (700–725), Vaikunthaperumal (begun in 725), and Ekambareshwara (begun in 1509). It is also the site of tombs.

[11–1012–4]

KANDAHAR, a city in southern Afghanistan, in the foothills of the spurs of the Western Hindu Kush, on the important Kabul-Kandahar-Herat transportation route. Administrative center of Kandahar Province. Population, 130,200 (1970). The city is the center of one of the main fruit-growing oases of the country, producing pomegranates, apricots, almonds, and grapes. Kandahar is a commercial center of extensive livestock-raising regions in the south and west of the country; there is trading in carpets, astrakhan, hides, and leather. The city has a wool-weaving factory and a fruit cannery, as well as a historical and ethnographic museum.

The founding of Kandahar is attributed to Alexander the Great. It became an important city in the 12th and 13th centuries. In the 13th century it was controlled successively by Genghis Khan and the rulers of the Kurt dynasty. At the end of the 14th century, the city was subjugated by Timur and then by his successors. In the 16th and 17th centuries, as an important commercial and strategic point, Kandahar was the object of a struggle between the Safavids and the Great Moguls. The city came under the authority of the Safavids in the mid-17th century. The populace of Kandahar and its region rose up against the Safavids in 1709, leading to the formation of the Ghilzai principality, with its administrative center in Kandahar. The city was attacked and destroyed by Nadir Shah Afshar in 1738, and a city named Nadirabad was built nearby. The city was built up anew by Ahmad Shah Durrani, named Ahmad Shah (present-day Kandahar), and made the capital of the Durrani State until 1773–74, when the capital was moved to Kabul. Ahmad Shah's mausoleum, which dates from the 18th century, remains intact. The city was the administrative center of the Kandahar principality from 1818 to 1855. Dost Muhammad seized Kandahar in 1855 and made it part of the Afghan state. [11–954–3]

KANDALAKSHA, a city in Murmansk Oblast, RSFSR. A port on the White Sea, located where the Niva River flows into Kandalaksha Bay. Kandalaksha is a station on the Murmansk-Leningrad railroad line 277 km south of Murmansk. Population, 43,000 (1970). Kandalaksha has aluminum, mechanical, motor-vehicle overhauling, and fish-canning plants, as well as a timber combine, railroad transport enterprises, and a hydroelectric power plant. Kandalaksha has been known since the 11th century and became a city in 1938.

REFERENCE
Kuz'min, G. G., and E. F. Razin. *Kandalaksha.* Murmansk, 1968. (Bibliography, pp. 202–05.) [11–955–1]

KANDALAKSHA BAY, a bay of the White Sea between the Kandalaksha and Karelian coasts. Length, 185 km; width, at the entrance, 67 km. It is divided into two regions: Kandalukha, the western, shallow part (maximum depth, 40 m); and Kandalaksha Bay proper, the eastern, deep part (including the greatest depths of the White Sea, up to 330 m). The coasts are rocky, strongly dissected, and edged by many small islands, reefs (*ludy*), and sandbars. The Niva and Kovda rivers empty into it. In summer the surface temperature of the water reaches 18.5°C.; in winter it ranges from −1° to 1.5°C. Between mid-November and May the greater part of the bay is frozen over. In winter the salinity is from 27–29 parts per thousand (‰); in summer, from 0‰ to 20–25 ‰ . The tide occurs twice daily, reaching 2.2 m. Currents are unstable, ranging from 20 to 30 cm/sec. The bay's herring, cod, and ringed seal provide the base for a maritime industry. Kandalaksha, Kovda, and Umba are the main ports on the bay, and the Kandalaksha Preserve is situated on its islands and coast. [11–955–3]

KANDALAKSHA COAST, a name for the northern shore of Kandalaksha Bay, on the White Sea. In its western part (from Kandalaksha to Cape Turii) the coast is high and rocky, with many offshore islands and reefs; east of the cape it is low and weakly dissected. It is covered with coniferous forests (pine, fir).

[11–955–2]

KANDALAKSHA PRESERVE, located on the islands and small areas of the continental coast of Kandalaksha Bay of the White Sea, as well as the Murmansk coast of the Barents Sea (the Sem' Ostrovov Archipelago, with the adjacent areas of the continent and Ainov Islands).

The Kandalaksha Preserve was formed in 1951 by combining two preserves, Kandalaksha and Sem' Ostrovov, which had been created in 1932 and 1938, respectively, to protect the nesting areas of seabirds, particularly the eider. The area of the Kandalaksha Preserve was about 29,000 hectares (ha) in 1970. There are famous rookeries on the steep and rocky shores of Kharlov and Kuvshin Islands, where murres, kittiwakes, razorbills, and black guillemots nest. On all the protected islands of the White and Barents seas there are numerous eiders and various gulls. On the islands of the Barents Sea alone, the number of eider nests increased from 500 in 1939 to 7,200 in 1970. On many islands of the Barents Sea there are the largest puffin colonies in the USSR, as well as the breeding grounds of the rare hooded seal. The islands of the Kandalaksha Preserve, including Olenii, Riazhkov, Anisimov, Lodeinyi, Medvezh'i, Lomnishnye, Vachev, Velikii, and Kem'ludskii, are covered with pine and spruce forest and, less frequently, with birch and aspen. The underbrush includes alder, ash, willow, and juniper. Elk, fox, marten, blue hare, squirrel, capercaillie, and hazel hen are common on Velikii Island (7,000 ha) and on coastal areas of the White Sea; lynx, brown bear, wolverine, and other taiga dwellers are also found. The islands of the Barents Sea are covered with tundra.

REFERENCE
Zapovedniki Sovetskogo Soiuza. Edited by A. G. Bannikov. Moscow, 1969. L. K. SHAPOSHNIKOV [11–955–4]

KANDALOV, INNOKENTII IVANOVICH. Born Jan. 21 (Feb. 2), 1891, in Eniseisk, died Sept. 30, 1962, in Moscow. Soviet hydraulic engineer. Doctor of Technical Sciences (1962) and Honored Worker in Science and Technology of the Uzbek SSR.

Kandalov graduated from the Petrograd Polytechnic Institute in 1917. From 1919 to 1927 he was deputy work superintendent for the construction of the Volkhov Hydroelectric Power Plant, and from 1927 to 1933 he was chief of hydraulic engineering work for the right bank of the Dnieper Hydropower Construction Project. Between 1933 and 1949 he was head engineer of the Chirchik and Svir' hydropower projects, as well as of the reconstruction work on the Dnieper Hydroelectric Power Plant. In 1949 he began teaching at the Moscow Institute of Power Engineering, becoming a professor in 1952. In 1959 he became head of a subdepartment at the Moscow V. V. Kuibyshev Construction Engineering Institute. His principal works were devoted to the problems of the organization of hydraulic power construction. A recipient of the State Prize of the USSR (1954), Kandalov was awarded three Orders of Lenin, a number of other orders and various medals.

WORKS
Organizatsiia stroitel'stva gidroelektrostantsii. Moscow-Leningrad, 1960.
REFERENCES
"K 70-letiiu so dnia rozhdeniia I. I. Kandalova." *Gidrotekhnicheskoe
    stroitel'stvo,* 1961, no 2.
"I. I. Kandalov" (obituary). *Ibid.,* 1962, no 12.   [11–956–1]

KANDAVA, a city in Tukums Raion, Latvian SSR. Located on
the Abava River, a tributary of the Venta, 7 km from the Kandava station on the Riga-Ventspils railroad line and 95 km west
of Riga. There is a dairy and a sovkhoz-technicum for the
mechanization of agriculture.   [11–954–2]

KANDEEVKA (KANDIEVKA) UPRISING OF 1861, a revolt
by the peasants of Chembar and Kerensk districts of Penza
Province and of Morshansk and Kirsanov districts of Tambov
Province, in response to the peasant reform of 1861.

The Kandeevka uprising began on Apr. 1, 1861, with the
refusal of the peasants of the villages of Chernogai and Studenki,
in Chembar District, to work for the *pomeshchiki* (landlords).
On April 2, in the same district, the peasants of the village of
Vysokii declared that the true content of the Statutes of Feb. 19,
1861, was being concealed from them, and that they had supposedly transferred all the land of the *pomeshchiki* to the peasants wihout redemption payments, banished the steward, and
removed the officials of the *votchina* (patrimonial estate) administration, replacing them with new officials elected from
among the peasants. The unrest gripped 26 settlements and villages in the beginning of April. On April 10, armed with scythes
and homemade pikes, the peasants of the village of Chernogai
forced a company of soldiers to retreat. The village of Kandeevka (in other sources, Kandievka, Kandevka) in Kerensk
District became the center of the Kandeevka uprising. The
retired soldiers Gavrila Strel'tsov, Anton Tikhonov, and Andrei
Elizarov and the peasant Leontii Egortsev led the Kandeevka
uprising. On April 18, soldiers fired on a crowd of 10,000 in
Kandeevka, and 19 peasants were killed. A tsarist court convicted 174 participants; 114 of them were sentenced to hard
labor and deportation to Siberia. The antiserfdom mood of the
peasants was manifested in the Kandeevka uprising and in the
Bezdna uprising of 1861.

REFERENCES
Krest'ianskoe dvizhenie v 1861 g. posle otmeny krepostnogo prava, parts
    1–2. Moscow-Leningrad, 1949.
Shvarev, V. A. *Kandievskoe vosstanie.* Penza, 1955.
Zaionchkovskii, P. A. *Otmena krepostnogo prava v Rossii,* 3rd ed. Moscow, 1968.   IA. M. SHORR   [11–956–4]

KANDELAKI, NIKOLAI PORFIR'EVICH. Born Oct. 5 (17),
1889, in the village of Kulashi, in present-day Samtredia Raion;
died Aug. 24, 1970, in Sukhumi. Soviet sculptor. People's Artist
of the Georgian SSR (1957).

Kandelaki studied under A. T. Matveev at the Leningrad
Academy of Art, graduating in 1926. In that year he became an
instructor at the Tbilisi Academy of Art, where he became a
professor in 1944. He is the creator of portraits with emphatically strong-willed, energetic characters (the artist L. Gudiashvili, stone, 1935; People's Artist of the USSR A. Khorava,
bronze, 1948; academician N. Muskhelishvili, bronze, 1954—all
in the Museum of Art of the Georgian SSR, Tbilisi); as well as
statues (Monument to F. Makharadze, bronze, 1958, in the town
of Makharadze). He was awarded the Order of the Red Banner
of Labor and medals.

REFERENCE
Kvaskhvadze, Sh. *Nikoloz Kandelaki.* Moscow, 1961.   [11–958–2]

KANDELAKI, VLADIMIR ARKAD'EVICH. Born Mar. 16
(29), 1908, in Tbilisi. Soviet Russian singer (bass-baritone) and
director; People's Artist of the USSR (1971). Member of the
CPSU since 1952.

Kandelaki graduated from the Tbilisi Conservatory in 1928
and from the State Institute of Theatrical Art (Moscow) in 1933.
Since 1929 he has been a soloist at the V. I. Nemirovich-Danchenko Music Theater (since 1941 called the K. S. Stanislavsky

and V. I. Nemirovich-Danchenko Moscow Music Theater);
from 1954 to 1964 , he was also chief director and actor for the
Moscow Musical Comedy Theater.

Performing both comic and dramatic roles, Kandelaki has
created expressive stage portraits, including Stefan in *The Gypsy
Baron* by Offenbach, Ollendorf in *The Poor Student* by Millöcker, Sultanbek in *Arshin mal alan* by Gadzhibekov, Salieri in
Mozart and Salieri by Rimsky-Korsakov, Taras in *The Family
of Taras* by Kabalevskii (State Prize of the USSR, 1952), and
Magara in *Virineia* by Slonimskii. He has worked as a director
since 1943 and has appeared in films.   [11–958–1]

KANDEV, LAMBI STANCHEV. Born 1879 in Svishtov; died
Apr. 19, 1925, in Sofia. Figure of the Bulgarian youth and workers' movements. Became a member of the Bulgarian Workers'
Social Democratic Party in 1900.

Kandev graduated from the Lom Teachers' College in 1895
and was a teacher until 1911. He began to contribute to various
periodical publications in 1902 and was editor of the newspaper
Uchitelska iskra from 1911 to 1919. Kandev was the secretary-treasurer of the Teachers' Social Democratic Organization from
1912 to 1919 and then was active in the Bulgarian Teachers'
Communist Organization and in the Union of Workers in Education. He was elected secretary of the Young Social Democratic
Workers' League in 1912, which became the Bulgarian Communist League of Youth in 1928. Kandev was killed in Sofia during
the April uprising of 1925.

In his articles, most of which were devoted to questions of
education, Kandev criticized the idealistic basis and the religious
and chauvinist tendency of the bourgeois system of education.
Considerable discussion was devoted to the organization and
leadership of educational work, the conditions of teachers, the
problems of professional and polytechnical education, and the
education of working youth. Kandev translated the book *Popular
Education and Democracy,* by N. K. Krupskaia (1922), from
Russian into Bulgarian.

WORKS
*Izbrani pedagogicheski proizvedeniia: Podrebda i vstupitelna studiia ot B.
    Ganov.* [Sofia, 1958.]   [11–956–3]

KANDIBA, BORIS NIKOLAEVICH. Born 1865; died July 28,
1929, in Moscow. Soviet hydraulic engineer.

In 1891, Kandiba graduated from the St. Petersburg Institute
of Railway Engineers, where he became a professor in 1903.
From 1891 to 1894 he took part in enlarging the Libava port.
Beginning in 1898 he headed the work on reconstructing ports,
including the ports of Arkhangel'sk, St. Petersburg, Mariupol',
Nikolaevsk, and Tuapse. From 1901 to 1929 he directed the
subdepartments of waterways, ports, and hydraulic engineering
structures at the higher educational institutions of St. Petersburg
(Leningrad) and Odessa. Kandiba participated in the design and
construction of a number of large hydraulic power complexes,
namely the Volkhov system, the Svir' System, and the Dnieper
System. He was also a consultant on the Volga-Don Canal and
other hydraulic engineering construction projects. His principal
works were concerned with the construction of ports, the hydrology of rivers, and river control.

REFERENCES
Rodevich, V. M. "B. N. Kandiba" (obituary). *Izv. Gos. gidrologicheskogo
    in-ta,* 1929, no. 25.
Sabaneev, A., and M. Malyshev. "Pamiati B. N. Kandiba." *Elektrichestvo,* 1929, nos. 21–22.   [11–959–3]

KANDIL'-KITAIKA, a variety of late winter apples, produced
by I. V. Michurinyi by crossing the Kitaika, or Chinese apple,
with the cultivated variety Kandil'-Sinap. The apples are medium-sized (120–170 g), elongated, and conic. They are yellowish
green with a slight bloom. The pulp is greenish, thick, juicy, and
tender, with a sweet vinous taste. These apples are eaten fresh
and are also used for making jam. They are harvested in late
September and are stored until April or May. The tree is of
average height. Each tree yields at least 50 kg of fruit. This
variety grows in the Ukrainian SSR, Kazakh SSR, and Kirghiz
SSR.   [11–963–1]

KANDIL'-SINAP, an early winter Crimean variety of the apple *Malus pumila,* bred by amateur growers. The apples are large (200–400 g), elongated, and conic. They are light yellow with a carmine-pink bloom. The pulp is snow-white, thick, juicy, and sweet. The fruit can be used in fresh form. It can be stored until January. The tree is tall and has a narrow pyramidal crown. Each tree yields 400–600 kg of fruit. The Kandil'-Sinap grows in the Ukrainian SSR, Moldavian SSR, and Kazakh SSR, as well as in the southern part of the RSFSR and in some republics in Middle Asia. [11–963–2]

KANDINSKII, VIKTOR KHRISANFOVICH. Born Apr. 6 (18), 1849, in Nerchinsk Raion, in what is now Chita Oblast; died Aug. 3 (15), 1899, in St. Petersburg. Russian psychiatrist.

Kandinskii graduated from the medical faculty of Moscow University in 1872. From 1882 until his death he served as senior staff physician in the St. Nicholas Mental Hospital in St. Petersburg (now the Second Mental Hospital). Kandinskii was the first to provide the classic definition of pseudohallucinations as a special symptom of mental illness (1885). His studies laid the foundation for the theory of the "syndrome of mental automatism." He was the first in Russian medicine to substantiate the concept of psychopathies, and he pointed out several symptoms of schizophrenia. He was also the first in Russia to propose a classification of mental illnesses and to advocate the use of occupational therapy in the treatment of psychoses. He worked on some problems in forensic psychiatry, defining the criteria of lack of criminal capacity and describing the symptoms of exceptional states. Kandinskii also wrote several philosophical works.

WORKS
Obshcheponiatnye psikhologicheskie etiudy. Moscow, 1881.
O psevdogalliutsinatsiiakh. Moscow, 1952.
K voprosu o nevmeniaemosti. Moscow, 1890.
REFERENCES
Snezhnevskii, A. V. "V. Kh. Kandinskii." In V. Kh. Kandinskii, *O psevdogalliutsinatsiiakh.* Moscow, 1952. [11–964–1]

KANDINSKY, WASSILY (Vasilii Vasil'evich Kandinskii). Born Dec. 4 (16), 1866, in Moscow; died Dec. 13, 1944, in Neuilly-sur-Seine, near Paris. Russian painter; one of the founders of abstract art.

In 1897 and 1898, Kandinsky studied at the Asbé School in Munich. In 1900 he was a student under F. Stück at the Munich Academy of Arts. Kandinsky lived in Berlin in 1907. He subsequently settled in Munich, where he and F. Marc founded the Blaue Reiter (Blue Rider) group in 1911. As early as 1910, the self-sufficient play of color and line gradually began to replace figurative representations in Kandinsky's paintings. This stylistic development can be observed in the paintings *Ladies in Crinoline* (1909, Tret'iakov Gallery), *Improvisation No. 7* (1910, Tret'iakov Gallery), *Vagueness* (1917, Tret'iakov Gallery), and *Composition No. 10* (1939, National Museum of Modern Art, Paris).

In his attempt to affirm the principles of "pure" painting, Kandinsky proclaimed the creative process of an artist to be a certain "self-expression and self-development of the spirit." Thus, "pure" painting reflected the individualistic and subjectivistic tendencies of the culture of 20th-century bourgeois society.

Kandinsky returned to Russia in 1914. He was among the organizers of the Museum of Pictorial Culture in Petrograd and of Inkhuk (Institute of Artistic Culture) in Moscow. In 1921 he returned to Germany, where he became a professor at the Bauhaus in 1922. He settled in Paris in 1933.

WORKS
V. V. Kandinskii (tekst Khudozhnika). Moscow, 1918.
Über das Geistige in der Kunst. Munich, 1912. (Excerpts in Russian appear in the book *Trudy Vserossiiskogo s"ezda khudozhnikov v Petrograde: Dekabr' 1911–ianvar' 1912,* vol. 1 [Petrograd, 1914], pp. 47–76.)
Punkt and Linie zu Fläche: Beitrag zur Analyse der malerischen Elemente. Munich, 1926.
REFERENCES
Reingardt, L. "Abstraktsionizm." In *Modernizm: Analiz i kritika osnovnykh napravlenii.* Moscow, 1969. Pages 101–11.

Grohmann, W. *Wassily Kandinsky: Life and Work.* New York, 1958.
B. S. TURCHIN [11–963–4]

KANDÓ, KÁLMÁN. Born July 10, 1869, in Pest; died Jan. 13, 1931, in Budapest. Hungarian electrical engineer; corresponding member of the Hungarian Academy of Sciences (1927).

Kandó graduated from the Technical University of Budapest in 1892. While taking an active part in the electrification of Italian railroads, he introduced the three-phase system of electric traction (1902–15). He invented the group driving gear for electric locomotives known as the Kandó triangle (1905). In 1917 he developed a synchronous phase converter, and in 1923 he constructed a new type of electric locomotive with three-phase induction motors connected to a Kandó phase converter, which derives its power from single-phase contact mains. Part of the Hungarian railroad from Budapest to Hegyeshalom (160 km) was electrified in 1934 using his system.

REFERENCE
Gohér, M. "Kandó Kálmán emlékezete." *Elektrotechnika,* 1969, no. 9. [11–964–3]

KANDRY, an urban-type settlement in the Bashkir ASSR. It has a railroad station 30 km east of the city of Tuimazy and is a center for petroleum prospecting. Near Kandry a rest center has been established at Lake Kandrykul'. [11–964–4]

KANDY (in Sinhalese, Maha Nuwara; literally, "great city"), a city in Sri Lanka; administrative center of Central Province. Population, 76,000 (1970). Railroad station. More than a third of the country's tea estates are concentrated in the region. A division of Ceylon University that was formerly located in Colombo is in Kandy. A palace dating from the 13th century is among the architectural monuments. The well-known Peradeniya Botanical Gardens, which were founded in 1821, are located 5 km southwest of the city. Kandy was the capital of the last Sinhalese kingdom (15th century–1815), which was dismantled by the British colonists. [11–959–2]

KANEM-BORNU EMPIRE, a medieval state in central Sudan.
The Kanem-Bornu Empire came into being in approximately the ninth century; its center was orginally located in the Kanem region northeast of Lake Chad. In the 11th century, Islam came into the area. The Kanem state was at its peak in the early 13th century, when it subdued a number of neighboring territories. In the 14th century, the center of the state was moved to Bornu, west of Lake Chad. Peasant communalists who paid rent to local feudal lords made up the bulk of the population. The use of slaves brought to the area was also a fairly widespread practice. The Bornu state maintained active trade links with North Africa and the cities and states of the Hausa peoples. The heyday of Bornu occurred during the government of the *mai* (emperor) Idris Alooma, who ruled from 1580 to 1617. In the early 20th century, the Kanem-Bornu territory was divided between Great Britain, Germany, and France; most of it was included in British possessions (in 1910 it became part of Nigeria's Northern State).

REFERENCES
Urvoy, J. *Histoire de l'Empire du Bornou.* Paris, 1949.
Cohen, R. "The Dynamics of Feudalism in Bornu." *Boston University Papers on Africa,* 1966, vol. 2. [11–967–4]

KANEV, a city; center of Kanev Raion, Cherkassy Oblast, Ukrainian SSR, 45 km from the Tagancha railroad station. Landing on the right bank of the Dnieper River. Population, 18,800 (1971). The city has a sawmill and electromechanical, concrete, and asphalt plants, as well as a plant producing domestic articles. There are enterprises of the food industry (a creamery and a brewery) and a water and timber reclamation station. The Kanev Hydroelectric Power Plant (Ukrgidroproekt; chief engineer G. S. Burtsev) was put into operation in 1972 on the Dnieper River near Kanev. A cultural and educational school and the A. P. Gaidar Museum and Library are also in the city.

Kanev has been known since the 12th century. The city's monuments include the Church of Iurii (1144), the T. G. Shevchenko memorial gravesite (on Tarasova Gora, in bronze and granite, 1939; sculptor M. G. Manizer, architect E. A. Levinson), the T. G. Shevchenko Memorial Museum (1938, architects V. G. Krichevskii and P. F. Kostyrko), and the Tarasova Gora Hotel (1961). Construction of the residential settlement for the Kanev Hydroelectric Power Plant and modernization of the center of Kanev were completed in 1969.

REFERENCE
Kilesso, S. K. *Kaniv.* Kiev, 1969. [11–965–2]

KANEV RESERVOIR, the reservoir formed in 1972 by the dam of the Kanev Hydroelectric Power Plant on the Dnieper River, in Kiev and Cherkassy oblasts of the Ukrainian SSR. Area, 675 sq km; volume, 2.6 cu km; length, 162 km; maximum width, about 5 km; and average depth, 4.4 m. The level of the Kanev Reservoir fluctuates within 0.5 m. The reservoir controls flow on a daily and monthly basis and was created to develop water transport, the power industry, and irrigation.
[11–966–1]

KANEVSKII, AMINADAV MOISEEVICH. Born Mar. 17 (29), 1898, in Elizavetgrad, present-day Kirovograd, Ukrainian SSR. Soviet graphic artist. People's Artist of the USSR (1973); corresponding member of the Academy of Sciences of the USSR (1962).

From 1924 to 1930, Kanevskii studied under P. Ia. Pavlinov, N. N. Kupreianov, V. A. Favorskii, and D. S. Moor at Vkhutemas-Vkhutein (State Higher Arts and Technical Studios-Higher Art and Technical Institute). His illustrations for children's books are distinguished by their lively humor and comic exaggeration of situations and images. Kanevskii illustrated A. L. Barto and P. N. Barto's *The Crybaby* (india ink, pen, and watercolor; first version published in 1934), K I. Chukovskii's *Moidodyr* (india ink, pen, and watercolor; 1950), Saltykov-Shchedrin's *The Pompadours and the Lady Pompadours* (india ink and pen, published in 1935) and *Abroad* (india ink and pen, published in 1939), and V. V. Mayakovsky's collection *Satirical Poems* (india ink, pen, and watercolor; published in 1964). He also illustrated several works by N. V. Gogol. His works also include caricatures, drawings, and posters. Kanevskii's caricatures have appeared in the journal *Krokodil* (Crocodile) since 1936. He has been awarded the Order of the Red Banner of Labor and various medals.

REFERENCE
Khalaminskii, Iu. *A. M. Kanevskii.* Moscow, 1961. [11–965–3]

KAN FOREST-STEPPE, a forest-steppe in the middle course of the Kan River, Krasnoiarsk Krai, RSFSR. On the northwest the Kan Forest-steppe is bounded by the Enisei Ridge, on the south by the Vostochnyi Saian Mountains, and on the northeast by the Middle Siberian Plateau. The forest-steppe occupies a tectonic depression composed primarily of sandstones and clays from the Middle and Upper Paleozoic eras and carboniferous deposits from the Jurassic period. The surface is a hilly and sloped plain with widespread loess-like loams. Elevations range from 300 m in the northeast to 470 m in the south; the climate is distinctly continental and arid—the average January temperature is from −18° to −20°C, the average July temperature more than 18°C. Yearly precipitation is 340–370 mm, with more than half falling in summer. Chernozem and turf-podzol soils predominate. The forests for the most part are birch groves along the slopes with northern exposure, with a mixture of pine and larch on the watersheds. A significant part of the forest-steppe is cultivated. Within the Kan Forest-steppe is the eastern part of the Kansk-Achinsk Coal Fields. [11–989–5]

KANGALASSY, an urban-type settlement in Yakut ASSR. The city is a landing on the left bank of the Lena River, 45 km north of Yakutsk. Brown coal is mined. [11–953–1]

KANG GAM CHANG. Born 948; died 1031. Korean general and organizer of the struggle against the Khitan invaders in the 11th century.

In 1010, when the Khitan captured the capital of Koryo, Kaesong, Kang Gam Chang was able to unite the nation despite

capitulatory sentiments in the court circles; under his direction the national forces expelled the aggressors. In late 1018, with the renewed Khitan invasion, Kang Gam Chang prepared the Korean troops for defense in advance, and in a decisive battle near the city of Kusong he crushed the enemy; out of 100,000 Khitan troops only a few thousand survived. [11–953–2]

KANGGYE, a city in the northern part of the Democratic Republic of Korea, on the Tongno River. Administrative center of the province of Chagang. Population, 130,000 (1962). The city is a transportation junction. Its industries include sawmilling, woodworking, and machine building. There are deposits of graphite, coal, copper, and other minerals in the vicinity. A hydroelectric power plant is located in Kanggye. [11–953–3]

K'ANGHSI (IIsüan Yeh). Born May 4, 1654; died Dec. 20, 1722, in Peking. Emperor of the Manchu Ch'ing dynasty in China (from 1662). The conquest of China by the Manchus was concluded during K'anghsi's rule. He cruelly suppressed the numerous popular revolts and terrorized participants in the anti-Manchu movements, including the patriotically motivated Chinese intelligentsia; he began what was known as literary inquisition ("prisons of writing").

K'anghsi implemented an aggressive policy with respect to the neighboring nationalities and countries. In 1691 he seized the Khalkha Mongol lands and began the conquest of the Oirat Khanate. K'anghsi consolidated the power of the Manuchurian and Chinese feudal lords in Tibet and led military campaigns against Russian settlements on the Amur River. The Nerchinsk Treaty was concluded with Russia in 1689. [11–989–3]

KANGHWA, TREATY OF, a treaty concluded between Japan and Korea on Feb. 26, 1876, on the island of Kanghwa (Korea).

The Treaty of Kanghwa opened the Korean port of Pusan to Japanese trade and, after 20 months, the ports of Wonsan and Inchon as well. Japan sent an envoy to Korea who in fact intervened in the country's government. Japanese subjects were granted extraterritorial rights in Korea (articles 4–10). In 1878 the Amendments to the Treaty of Kanghwa were signed, freeing the wares of Japanese merchants from customs duties and allowing the circulation of Japanese banknotes on the Korean monetary market. The Treaty of Kanghwa was the first in a series of inequitable treaties forced upon Korea by imperialist powers.

REFERENCE
"Dogovor, zakliuchennyi mezhdu Koreei i Iaponiei. . . . " In *Opisanie Korei.* Moscow, 1960. Pages 485–89. [11–1009–4]

KANGHWA MAN, a bay of the Yellow Sea on the western coast of South Korea.

The Kanghwa Man cuts deep inland for 85 km. It is 122 km wide. Its depth reaches 54 m. The banks are extremely jagged, and there are many islands, rocks, and shoals in the bay. The tides are semidiurnal and reach 10 m. The port of Inchon (Chemulpo) is located on the bay. [11–1009–3]

KANGIUI (Kangyuy), Kangha (Kangkha), or Kangdiz, a state formation in ancient Middle Asia. The core of the Kangiui population consisted of nomads who probably lived near the Syr Darya, which was called the River of the Kang as late as the Middle Ages. The period of formation of the Kangiui state is unknown, although it certainly was already in existence in the second century B.C.

In the south the Kangiui state included the present-day Tashkent Oasis and some of the lands between the Amu Darya and the Syr Darya. In the first century B.C., Kangiui also gained control of Khwarazm and several other domains. By that time it was a large state that had united a number of settled agricultural regions and nomad territories. Since it had a large army (up to 120,000 men), Kangiui took an active part in the struggle of the peoples of Fergana and Eastern Turkestan against China. Between the first and third centuries A.D., Kangiui lost Khwarazm and the Tashkent Oasis, which became part of the Kushan Kingdom, but it did retain its independence and even conquered several domains in the northern Aral and southern Ural regions.

Kangiui is not mentioned in sources later than the fourth century.

REFERENCE

Bichurin, N. Ia. *Sobranie svedenii o narodakh, obitavshikh v Srednei Azii v drevnie vremena,* vol. 2. Moscow-Leningrad, 1950.   [11–953–5]

KANGLY, a Turkic tribal alliance that first appeared in the 11th and 12th centuries in the steppes of the Aral region (north of Khorezm as far as the Volga) through the merger of the indigenous Ghuz-Pecheneg population with the Polovtsy, who had migrated from the Irtysh region in the 11th century.

The chief occupations of the Kangly were nomadic livestock raising and crafts. The Kangly played an important role in the states of medieval Middle Asia (particularly that of the Khwarazm-shah dynasty). The Kangly who had migrated eastward to the Lake Issyk-Kul' region were routed by the Mongols in the 13th century. Those that had remained in Khorezm were incorporated into the peoples then forming in Middle Asia (the Uzbeks, Kazakhs, Karakalpaks) and the Bashkirs.

REFERENCES

Istoriia Uzbekskoi SSR, 2nd ed., vol. 1, books 1–2. Tashkent, 1955–56.
Istoriia Kazakhskoi SSR, vol. 1. Alma-Ata, 1957.   [11–953–4]

KANGTING (Tatsienlu), a city on the Tatu River in China, in Szechwan Province. Altitude, more than 2,500 m above sea level.

Kangting is a commercial and transport center on the Szechwan-Tibetan highway. Transport vehicles and agricultural machinery are produced, wool is washed for market, and asbestos and mica are processed. There is also a cottage industry in silver and iron items.   [11–963–3]

KANGYU CULTURE, an archaeological culture of ancient Khwarazm dating from the fourth century B.C. to the first century A.D. and belonging to the period of developed slave-owning. Irrigation farming was the basis of the economy. Pottery-making reached a high degree of development. Vessels were distinguished by a diversity and perfection of form and were either coated with red engobe or painted. Many terra-cotta statuettes have been discovered. A decline in the quality of pottery between the end of the second century B.C. and the first century A.D. (associated with the cultural influence of the Sakian steppe tribes on the periphery of Khwarazm) makes it possible to delineate the period known as late Kangyu. Kangyu construction technique was typified by the use of unfired bricks and vaulted spans. Written remains based on the Aramaic alphabet have been discovered. The Kangyu religion was similar to the cults of Avesta. Typical remains include the Koi-Krylgan-Kala and Dzhanbas-Kala.

REFERENCES

Tolstov, S. P. *Po drevnim del'tam Oksa i Iaksarta.* Moscow, 1962.
Vorob'eva, M. G. "Keramika Khorezma antichnogo perioda." In *Tr. Khorezmskoi arkheologo-etnograficheskoi ekspeditsii,* vol. 4. Moscow, 1959.
"Koi-Krylgan-Kala—pamiatnik kul'tury drevnego Khorezma IV v. do n.e.–IV v. n.e." In *Tr. Khorezmskoi arkheologo-etnograficheskoi ekspeditsii,* vol. 5. Moscow, 1967.   IU. A. RAPOPORT   [11–954–1]

K'ANG YU-WEI. Born Mar. 19, 1858, in Nanhai District, Kuangtung Province; died Mar. 31, 1927, in Ch'ingtao. Chinese scholar; leader of the Chinese Reform Movement of the late 19th century.

K'ang Yu-wei came from a *shenshih* family. In 1887 he wrote *Ta t'ung shu* (Book on the Great Commonwealth), which expounded his utopian socialist theory and criticized not only contemporary Chinese feudal society, but also the bourgeois order of the Western world. K'ang Yu-wei advocated the abolition of private property and the creation of a society based on universal equality. In the spring of 1895 he became head of an organized bourgeois-landowner reform movement in China. He wrote a memorandum to the emperor expressing a plan of reforms that outlined the country's industrial, commercial, and cultural development.

He founded the Ch'ianghsiuohuo Reform Club (Society for National Strengthening) in August 1895 and the Paokuohuo Reform Party (Society to Preserve the Nation) in April 1898. During the period of One Hundred Days of Reform (June 11–Sept. 21, 1898), K'ang Yu-wei and his followers promulgated approximately 60 reform measures in the name of Emperor Kuangsü.

After the defeat of the Reform Party, K'ang Yu-wei left the country. Abroad, he headed the constitutional-monarchist organization Paohuanghuo (Save the Emperor Association) and opposed the revolutionary movement headed by Sun Yat-sen.

S. L. TIKHVINSKII   [11–1013–3]

KANIBADAM, a city in Leninabad Oblast, Tadzhik SSR, in the western part of the Fergana Valley, on the Bol'shoi Fergana Canal, 6 km from the Kanibadam station on the Tashkent-Khavast-Kokand railroad line, 79 km east of Leninabad. Highway junction. Population, 27,600 (1971).

Industry includes a canning and preserves combine (fruit, vegetables, and dried fruit), cotton-ginning and oil-extraction plants, the Avtozapchast' Plant (producing parts and complex components for motor vehicles and equipment for the cotton-ginning industry), and the Tadzhiksel'mash Plant (agricultural machinery). There are also spinning and garment and textile factories. Kanibadam has an engineering technicum and a teachers college, as well as the Lakhuti Music and Drama Theater. The city is mentioned in historical records from 1463, and according to some sources it existed as early as the ninth or tenth century.   [11–969–2]

KANIMEKH, an urban-type settlment and center of Kanimekh Raion, Bukhara Oblast, Uzbek SSR, 136 km northeast of the city of Bukhara. It is the center of an agricultural region (livestock-raising sovkhozes).   [11–970–2]

KANIN, ALEKSANDR IGNAT'EVICH. Born Nov. 24 (Dec. 6), 1877, in Saratov; died Nov. 3, 1953, in Riazan'. Soviet director and actor. Honored Artist of the RSFSR (1926). Became a member of the CPSU in 1950.

Kanin was a student in V. I. Nemirovich-Danchenko's class at the Moscow Art Theater. Upon graduation in 1904, he joined V. E. Meyerhold's company in Tbilisi. In 1905 and 1906 he worked in Moscow in the Studio on Povarskaia Street (under the direction of Meyerhold and K. S. Stanislavsky). Kanin subsequently worked in the provinces (Voronezh, Rostov-on-Don, Kazan, and Irkutsk). In the Soviet era he headed theaters in several cities, including Ashkhabad, Voronezh, and Kursk (1934–41). In 1948 he became the principal director of the Riazan' Theater. Kanin earned a place in theatrical history for his outstanding stagings of M. Gorky's plays. He staged nearly all of Gorky's plays and often portrayed the main roles. His best productions included *Vassa Zheleznova* (1910, Taganrog; 1935, Kursk) and *Egor Bulychov and Others* (1933, Voronezh; 1946, Buriat Theater, Ulan-Ude). In 1951, Kanin was awarded the State Prize of the USSR for his production of the play *Smug Citizens* and his portrayal of Bessemenov in the Riazan' Theater. As a director-teacher, he sought to bring out the artistic individuality of the actor and to create well thought-out stage sets. He taught at drama schools that he organized in Saratov, Kiev, Samara, Penza, Voronezh, and Kursk.

REFERENCE

Khodorkovskaia, L., and A. Klinchin. *Put' rezhissera: A. I. Kanin, 1877–1953.* Moscow, 1962.   [11–970–3]

KANIN NOS, the northwestern cape of Kanin Peninsula in the northern European USSR. The slopes, which are precipitous, reach altitudes between 15 and 20 m.   [11–970–4]

KANIN PENINSULA, a peninsula in the northern European part of the USSR, in Arkhangel'sk Oblast, RSFSR. The peninsula separates the northern part of the White Sea from the shallow Cheshskaia Guba of the Barents Sea; it has an area of about 10,500 sq km. In the extensive northern part is a plateaulike mountain ridge, Kanin Kamen', composed of crystalline schists, with elevations up to 242 m. To the northwest the peninsula ends in the rocky cape Kanin Nos; to the southeast, in the Mikul'kin Cape. The rest of the peninsula is monotonous, flat, low-lying and marsh-ridden tundra plain, composed of washed-up glacial and marine deposits with individual moraine hills 70–80 m high. There is fishing and trapping of aquatic animals off the coast.

[11–970–5]

KANISHKA. King of the Kushan Empire from A.D. 78 to A.D. 123 (dates vary) who conquered nearly all of northern India.

Kanishka transferred the political center of the state to Purushapura (present-day Peshawar, Pakistan). A process of Indianization of the Kushan conquerors began during Kanishka's reign; he himself is known to have been a Buddhist. Kanishka's rule coincided with the flowering of economic and cultural life in northern India and Central Asia; in addition, trade with China and the Roman Empire (the Great Silk Route and sea trade) grew to great proportions.

[11–971–4]

KANITEL' (from French *cannetille*), in Russian, a fine thread (usually gold or silver) used in embroidery. The word has taken on the figurative meaning of a protracted transaction involving lengthy delays and considerable effort. The expression *tianut' kanitel'* means to perform monotonous and unnecessary actions.

[11–971–1]

KANKAEV, BAKHTIAR (also, Bakhtiiar Kanykaev). Dates of birth and death unknown. "Chief colonel" of E. I. Pugachev; elder of a *volost* (small rural district) in Kazan Province.

In December 1773, Kankaev organized an uprising in eastern Tataria. In June 1774, on Pugachev's orders, he formed detachments to replenish the main insurgent army. His energetic actions created a situation favorable to the advance of Pugachev's troops along the Kama River and the seizure of Kazan. Following the defeat of Pugachev's troops at Kazan (July 12–15, 1974) and his march with the remnants of his army to the right bank of the Volga, Kankaev fell back to the area of his earlier activity, the right bank of the Kama, where he continued the struggle until the end of July 1774. Kankaev suffered a defeat at the hands of tsarist troops in a battle at Rybnaia Sloboda and fled. His subsequent fate is unknown.

[11–971–6]

KANKAN, a city in the republic of Guinea on the Milo River (Niger Basin). Population, 29,100 (1964).

Kankan is linked by railroad with Conakry. It is also a highway junction. Rice, meat, cattle, and rubber are traded and pottery is manufactured in the city.

[11–972–1]

KANKLES, a Lithuanian plucked stringed instrument. It is akin to the Latvian *kokle,* Estonian *kannel,* Karelo-Finnish *kantele,* and Russian wing-shaped ("ringing") gusli. It is 800–900 mm long. The old *kankles* had four to five strings; subsequently the number of strings increased to 25. The instrument is tuned diatonically. In the Soviet era a complete family of *kankles* (soprano, bass, and contrabass) has been created.

[11–972–3]

KANKRIN, EGOR FRANTSEVICH. Born Nov. 16 (27), 1774, in Hanau, Germany; died Sept. 9 (21), 1845, in Pavlovsk, in present-day Leningrad Oblast. Russian statesman, count (from 1829).

Born in Germany of German parents, Kankrin entered Russian service in 1797 and was minister of finance from 1823 to 1844. He advocated maintenance of serfdom and defended the interests of the *pomeshchiki* (landlords). Kankrin deliberately held back the development of industry because he saw in the working class a threat to the existing system. He stopped credit to industry almost entirely and prevented the establishment of private banks. Kankrin's reform of the merchant guilds in 1824 hindered the emergence of the capitalist elements from among the trading peasants and the town dwellers. But he also retained protectionist tariffs, which were in the interests of factory owners using serf labor and in the interests of the industrial bourgeoisie. Kankrin freed the state budget of deficits by a strict reduction of expenditures on the economy, by promoting the franchise sale of liquor, and by improving reporting and accountability in the

state finance department. From 1839 to 1843 he carried out a currency reform. He opposed the construction of railroads. Kankrin wrote on economics, his most important work being *The Economy of Human Societies and the State of Finance,* and on military and other subjects, mainly in German.

REFERENCES
Istoriia russkoi ekonomicheskoi mysli, vol. 1, part 2. Moscow, 1958.
Borovoi, S. Ia. "K istorii promyshlennoi politiki Rossii v 20–50-kh gg. XIX v." In the collection *Istoricheskie zapiski,* vol. 69. [Moscow] 1961.
Ryndziunskii, P. G. *Gorodskoe grazhdanstvo doreformennoi Rossii.* Moscow, 1958. Pages 107–28. S. IA. BOROVOI [11–972–4]

KANKRIN REFORM, a currency reform carried out in Russia from 1839 to 1843. It is named for E. F. Kankrin, the minister of finance who conceived and implemented it.

Before the Kankrin reform Russia used paper money. Military expenditures, in particular during the wars with Napoleon, were financed with paper money. As a result the value of the *assignaty* dropped sharply. The need to strengthen state credit and to normalize economic life forced the government to undertake the reform. In 1839 the currency was based on the silver ruble and a mandatory exchange rate for the *assignaty* was established: 3 rubles 50 kopeks of *assignaty* were set equal to one silver ruble. In 1843 the *assignaty* were gradually withdrawn from circulation and exchanged for treasury notes (*kreditnye bilety*) according to a mandatory rate; the treasury notes were freely exchanged for silver. The Kankrin reform temporarily strengthened Russia's finances but was aimed at preserving serfdom.

REFERENCE
Druian, A. D. *Ocherki po istorii denezhnogo obrashcheniia Rossii v XIX v.* [Moscow] 1941. Pages 5–34. [11–972–5]

KANKUSKII, an urban-type settlement in Aldan Raion, Yakut ASSR, 572 km north of the Bol'shoi Never railroad station. Mica is extracted at the Timpton mine. [11–973–3]

KANNA, ION (also Ivan Ivanovich Kanna). Born Jan. 15 (28), 1902, in the village of Goiany, present-day Dubossary Raion. Soviet Moldavian writer; member of the CPSU since 1941.

Kanna's first works were published in 1926–27. Before 1941 he published several collections of short stories and essays about the Civil War of 1918–20, collectivization in the left-bank regions of Moldavia, and new village life. His best postwar works were included in the collections *On the Banks of the Dnestr* (1946), *Collected Short Stories* (1948), and *Short Stories* (1951). Kanna creates vivid portraits of the village people. In the novella *Mother* (1947) and the novel *Morning on the Dnestr* (1951), Kanna depicts the hard lot of the peasants under the tsarist regime.

Kanna was a deputy to the second and third convocations of the Supreme Soviet of the Moldavian SSR. He has been awarded the Order of Lenin and the Order of the Red Banner of Labor.

WORKS
Kuvyntul drag. Kishinev, 1961.
Diminiatsa pe Nistru, 3rd ed. Kishinev, 1968.
In Russian translation:
Izbrannoe. Kishinev, 1956.
Rasskazy. Kishinev, 1959.
REFERENCES
Koroban, V. *Ion Kanna.* Kishinev, 1953.
Shpak, I. *Skriitorii Moldovei Sovetiche: Indiche biobibliografik.* Kishinev, 1969. [11–974–1]

KANNABIKH, IURII VLADIMIROVICH. Born Sept. 23 (Oct. 5), 1872, in St. Petersburg, died Feb. 3, 1939, in Moscow. Soviet psychiatrist. Honored Scientist of the RSFSR (1937).

Kannabikh graduated from the division of natural history of Moscow University in 1896 and from the department of medicine there in 1899, then took his specialization in E. Kraepelin's clinic. He became a professor of psychiatry at the University of Turkestan (Tashkent) in 1920. In 1921 he began working in various higher educational institutions and scientific-research organizations in Moscow. He became chairman of the subdepartment of psychiatry at the Third Moscow Medical Institute in 1936. Kannabikh's studies on cyclothymia, borderline states, and psychoneuroses are widely known. He also did research in psychotherapy. Kannabikh wrote a major work on the history of psychiatry.

WORKS
Istoriia psikhiatrii. [Moscow] 1929.
REFERENCE
Ozeretskovskii, D. S. "Yu. V. Kannabikh (K 15-letiiu so dnia smerti)." *Zhurnal nevropatologii i psikhiatrii,* 1954, vol. 54, issue 5.
[11–975–2]

KANNADA, the language of the Kanarese people; a Dravidian language, spoken in the state of Mysore in India by approximately 2 million people (1967).

The Kannada language is divided historically into Ancient Kannada (to the mid-13th century), Medieval, or Old Kannada (from the second half of the 13th century to the mid-19th century), and Modern Kannada (since the late 19th century). Modern literary Kannada is somewhat different from the spoken language. The grammatical structure of Kannada is typically agglutinative, with suffixal word-formation and form-derivation. Fixed verbal combinations with a verbal adverb as the main word are common. Word order in the sentence is fixed, the predicate usually occurring at the end. There are lexical borrowings from Hindi, Marathi, and Sanskrit. Kannada uses one of the varieties of a south Indian script that can be traced to the Brahmi writing system. The oldest inscriptions in Kannada date from the fifth, sixth, and seventh centuries A.D.; the writing system in its present form appeared in the 14th century.

REFERENCES
Andronov, M. S. *Iazyk kannada.* Moscow, 1962.
Kittel, F. *A Grammar of the Kannada Language in English.* Mangalore, 1903.
Kittel, F. *A Kannada-English Dictionary.* Mangalore, 1894.
[11–975–3]

KANNADA LITERATURE, the literature of the Kanarese people; one of the national literatures of India.

The oldest monument of Kannada literature is *The Way of the Poet King* (A.D. 825), a treatise on poetics attributed to the poet and scholar Nripatunga. The formation of Kannada literature is associated with the tenth-century Jain poets Pampa, Ponna, and Ranna, who wrote works on themes from the *Mahabharata* and the *Ramayana* and used Sanskrit literature as their model. The 12th century saw the beginnings of a process of literary democratization that culminated in the rejection of Sanskritisms and a turn to the use of the spoken language (in the works of Nayasena and Basava). The genres of the *campu* (a combination of prose and poetry) and the *ragale* (a lyrical epic poem) became popular. The songs and hymns (*padas*) of Purandaradasa and Kanakadasa, poets of the antifeudal *Haridasa* ("slaves of the god Vishnu") movement, were popular in the 15th and 16th centuries. *Yakshagana,* folk drama based on themes from epic legends, became widespread in the 18th century. In the mid-19th century press and publicism emerged in the language and modern genres and forms developed. Translations of novels appeared, followed by the first original novels in Kannada, which were imbued with the ideas of renewal (Shivarama Karantha, A. N. Krishnaraya, Ta Ra Su). Gorur and V. M. Joshi wrote in the genre of the short story. V. K. Gokak, D. R. Bendre, and D. S. Karki are regarded as the leading modern poets. National patriotic themes are predominant in narrative poetry, and themes of love and philosophy are popular in lyric poetry. Modern drama is also developing (Bendre, Sriranga).

REFERENCES
Mariyappa Bhatta, N. *Sankshipta kannada sahitya charitre.* Mysore, 1960.
Mugali, R. *Kannada sahityada itihasa.* New Delhi, 1963.
Nayak, H. M. *Kannada Literature—A Decade.* Mysore, 1967.
M. A. DASHKO [11–976–1]

KANNEL, an Estonian stringed plucked musical instrument related to the Karelo-Finnish *kantele,* the Latvian *kokle,* the Lithuanian *kankles,* and the Russian wing-shaped ("ringing") gusli.
[11–176–3]

KANO, a city in northern Nigeria, the administrative center of Kano State. Population, 351,200 (1970). Kano has a railroad station and is a highway junction; it has an international airport and is a major center of trade for peanuts, cotton, goatskins, and hides. Manufacturers of peanut oil, canned meat, soap, leather footwear, tannin, and cement are there, as well as a textile factory. Prior to the 19th century Kano was the capital of the city-state of Kano of the Hausa nation.
[11–981–1]

KANO, a school of Japanese painting, dating from the second half of the 15th century. It was named after its founders, Kano Masanobu and Kano Motonobu. Early Kano paintings, from the second half of the 15th century to the second half of the 16th, were primarily landscapes and depictions of "flowers and birds" on scrolls, screens, and folding doors. Based on the traditions of the *yamato-e* school and monochromatic painting, they are characterized by the combination of a stylized and decorative composition with emphatically lifelike details (for example, birds and tree branches). Kano painting was at the peak of its development during the late 16th and mid-17th centuries. At this time, individual details became somewhat stylized and were totally subordinated to the ornamental and decorative arrangement of the composition; this is seen in the paintings of Kano Eitoku, Kano Sanraku, and Kano Tanyu. The works of Kano artists of the late 17th to the 20th century, such as Kano Yasunobu, Kano Tsunenobu, and Taikan Yokoyama, were masterfully executed. However, sometimes these paintings are essentially repetitions of old motifs and are cold and lifeless.

REFERENCE
Brodskii, V. E. *Iaponskoe klassicheskoe iskusstvo.* Moscow, 1969.
[11–981–2]

KANONNIKOV, INNOKENTII IVANOVICH. Born May 16 (28), 1854, in Irkutsk; died March 2 (15), 1902, in Kazan. Russian chemist. He taught at the University of Kazan after his graduation (1875); he became a professor there in 1886.

In 1884, Kanonnikov demonstrated that the specific refraction of a solution is equal to the sum of the specific refractions of the solute and the solvent. He established the cyclic structure of certain terpenes, the existence of a double bond in maleic acid, and the bicyclic structure of the camphor molecule. He also discovered the relationship between the angle of rotation of the plane of polarization and the minumum angle of deflection of a refracted beam. In 1860 he showed that the specific rotation for a mixture of substances is the mean of the values for the specific rotation of the constituents.

REFERENCE
Sorokin, V. I. "Pamiati Innokentiia Ivanovicha Kanonnikova." *Zhurnal Russkogo fiziko-khimicheskogo ob-va, chast' khimicheskaia,* 1902, vol. 34, sec. 1, issue 5, pp. 450–57. [11–986–2]

KANPUR, a city in northern India in the state of Uttar Pradesh, situated on the right bank of the Ganges. Population, 1.3 million (1971).

Kanpur's location in the central part of the Ganges valley has helped to transform it into an important transportation hub and northern India's largest center of industrial factories and plants. The city's major industries are textiles (mainly cotton, but also wool) and leather footwear. Machine building (railroad cars), the chemical industry (a chemical fertilizer plant was built in 1968 that produces mainly urea), and metalworking are being developed in the city. There is an industry in food and condiments, there are a number of repair shops, and handmade brushes are produced in homes for market sale. There has been a university in Kanpur since 1966. [11–988–1]

KANSAI (Kinki), a major economic region of Japan, in the southern part of the island of Honshu.

Kansai comprises six prefectures: Osaka, Kyoto, and Hyogo (constituting the subregion of western Kansai) and Shiga, Nara, and Wakayama (constituting the subregion of eastern Kansai). The island of Awaji in the Seto Sea (Inland Sea) also belongs to Kansai. Area, 27,200 sq km; population, 17.4 million (1970). Almost 72 percent of the population of Kansai lives in the 48 cities of the region (1967). Of the working population, 7.6 million in 1965, 34 percent are engaged in manufacturing, 10.5 percent in agriculture, 13 percent in services, 20.5 percent in trade, and 7.4 percent in construction.

The geographic position of the region in the central part of the archipelago of Japanese islands, the well-developed transportation network, and convenient sea routes have all contributed to Kansai's economic development. More than half of the region consists of a maritime strip. Kansai is second in Japan in terms of the general production level after the economic region of Kanto. According to national income figures (1965), manufacturing, is the most important sector, producing 35 percent of the income, followed by trade (18 percent), construction (8 percent), and agriculture (3 percent). Most fuel, raw materials, and semiprocessed goods have to be imported. Within Kansai, copper is mined at Ikuno, Hyogo Prefecture; tin, at the Akenobe mines; lead and zinc, in Wakayama Prefecture; and manganese ore, in the prefectures of Osaka, Shiga, and Kyoto.

The leading manufacturing sectors are textiles (30 percent of total Japanese production), ferrous metals (36 percent), machinery (29 percent), electrical machinery (25 percent), and chemicals (22 percent).

The Kansai region, Osaka in particular, has long been known for its textiles, especially for its cotton fabrics. Cotton fabrics and articles from natural silk are made in the cities of Osaka, Kyoto, and Wakayama. There is large-scale military production, including naval shipbuilding. Kansai has highly developed glass, ceramic, printing, and food-processing industries. Metallurgy and machine building are basically concentrated in the Osaka-Kobe region. Kansai combines modern factory and plant production with a dispersed handicrafts industry.

Agricultural production plays a limited role in the economy of Kansai. The region has to import agricultural produce from outside. However, the maritime part of the region, the lowland of Kinki, is one of the main rice-producing regions of the country; with a yield of 1.2 million tons, it constitutes 8 percent of the total land area under rice cultivation in Japan. After the harvest, rice fields are planted a second time with barley and wheat. There are tea plantations, citrus farms (mandarin oranges in Wakayama Prefecture), and vineyards (Osaka Prefecture). Animal husbandry has secondary importance, but poultry breeding has been developed. The railroad system is electrified. Osaka and Kobe are the region's seaports.

N. A. SMIRNOV   [11–988–3]

KANSAI, an urban-type settlement in Leninabad Oblast, Tadzhik SSR. Located on the slopes of the Karamazor Range, 49 km north of the Leninabad railroad station on the Khavast-Kokand line. Population, 5,000 (1970). Lead and zinc ores are mined there.   [11–989–1]

KANSAN UUTISET (People's News), a daily newspaper; organ of the Communist Party of Finland and the Democratic Union of the Finnish People. The newspaper was founded in 1957 and is published in Helsinki. Circulation, 43,800 (1974).
    [11–989–2; updated]

KANSAS, a state in the central part of the USA. Area, 213,100 sq km; population, 2.2 million (1970), of which 66 percent is urban. The administrative center is Topeka, and Wichita and Kansas City are its most important cities. Its surface is an undulating plain, sloping gently from the foothills of the Rocky Mountains (altitude, 1,231 m) to the valley of the Missouri River. In the central part of the state are the Smoky Hills and Blue Hills (maximum altitude, 862 m). The climate is moderately continental, with the mean monthly temperatures ranging from −3°C to 26°C. Annual precipitation is 550–950 mm. In the summer there are frequent droughts. The Kansas and Arkansas rivers have little flow for most of the year.

Kansas is one of the most important agricultural states of the USA; it is first in the harvest of wheat and second in sorghum and is fourth in the number of cattle. Its most important crop is winter wheat. Nearly two-thirds of the commodity output of agriculture is provided by livestock, with meat production predominating. As of 1970 there were 6.0 million head of cattle (including 224,000 dairy cows) and 1.6 million pigs. Farms occupy 20.4 million hectares, 95 percent of the state's territory, of which 400,000 hectares are irrigated. Large mechanized farms producing grain and meat provide the bulk of the output. The number of farms diminished from 120,000 in 1954 to 87,000 in 1969.

In 1969, 12,000 workers were employed in the extraction industry and 146,000 in processing. Oil (nearly 12 million tons), natural gas, and helium (of which Kansas is the leading US producer) are the most important raw materials. In value of output, processing is increasingly overtaking agriculture. The most important products are those of the food industry (canned meat, flour, concentrated fodder). The aviation (Wichita), automobile assembly (Kansas City), oil refining, chemical, and agricultural machine industries are developed.   V. M. GOKHMAN

Prior to its occupation by Europeans, the territory of Kansas was inhabited by Indian tribes. Europeans visited the area for the first time in 1541. In 1803 it became a possession of the USA, which purchased it from France as part of the vast territories of Louisiana. In 1854 it was given the status of a territory of the USA; adoption of the Kansas-Nebraska Act of 1854 led to civil war in Kansas between the supporters and opponents of slavery. It has been one of the states of the USA since 1861.
    [11–967–7]

KANSAS CITY, a city in the central part of the USA, in the state of Missouri. Located on the Missouri River where the Kansas River flows into it. Population, 507,000 (1970). The city and Kansas City, Kansas (population, 168,000), on the opposite bank of the Kansas River, form a single urban agglomeration with a population of 1.3 million (1970). It is a major commercial and transportation hub, located in the center of an important agricultural region (meat-cattle breeding, wheat, corn). The work force numbers 511,000 (1969), of whom 26 percent are in industry, 40 percent in commerce and services, and 6.5 percent in finance. The canned-meat, flour-grinding, and metalworking industries are the most important. Steel smelting, production of agricultural and road-building machinery, motor-vehicle assembly, and oil refining are carried on there. Kansas City has chemical, soap, wood-products, printing, and radio-electronics industries, as well as agricultural elevators and stockyards. A university is located there. The city was founded in the 19th century.   [11–969–1]

KANSAS-NEBRASKA ACT OF 1854, an act that granted to the white population of Kansas and Nebraska (new territories incorporated into the USA) the right to decide the question of allowing or forbidding slavery on their territory. Adopted by the US Congress, it in effect abolished the prearranged border between the free and slaveholding states (36°30′ N lat.) established by the Missouri Compromise of 1820. In the actual historical situation of the middle of the 19th century this solution met the demands of the slaveholders alone, who were striving to spread slavery throughout the entire USA. Its adoption provoked an armed struggle in Kansas between the advocates and opponents of slavery (1854–56).   [11–968–1]

KANSAS RIVER, a river in the USA, a right tributary of the Missouri. The Kansas River is formed by the confluence of the Smoky Hill and Republican rivers, which originate on the foothill plateaus of the Rocky Mountains. Length, 500 km (approximately 1,000 km including the Smoky Hill River); basin area, 158,800 sq km (including extensive undrained regions). The Kansas flows through the High Plains and Central Plains plateaus. High water occurs in spring, with low water in summer; high floods caused by rain occur throughout the year. The average annual flow is 184 cu m per sec, with a maximum of 14,000 cu m per sec and a minimum of 4.5 cu m per sec. The river is used for irrigation. The cities of Topeka and Kansas City are on the Kansas River.   [11–967–6]

KANSK, a city in Krasnoiarsk Krai, RSFSR. Located in the southeastern part of the krai in the territory of the Kan Forest-steppe on the Kan River (a tributary of the Enisei). Kansk has a railroad station (Kansk-Eniseiskii) 247 km east of Krasnoiarsk, and it is a highway junction. Population, 94,000 (1972; 42,000 in 1939). Cotton-textile, wood-products, and building-materials combines, machine-building and metalworking enterprises, a biochemical plant, and mill and meat combines, a liqueur and vodka distillery, a brewery, and other food enterprises are there. Teachers' and medical schools, a polytechnicum, and technological, library, and evening textile technicums are located in Kansk; it also has a drama theater and a museum of local lore. The city was founded in 1626 as a fort, which was moved in 1640 to the site of present-day Kansk. When Enisei Province was established in 1822, Kansk became a city.   [11–989–4]

KANSK-ACHINSK COAL BASIN, a basin located in the southern part of Krasnoiarsk Krai, in Kemerovo and Irkutsk oblasts, RSFSR.

The Kansk-Achinsk Coal Basin extends along the Siberian railroad from the Itat station in the west to the Taishet station in the east, a distance of approximately 700 km; it ranges in width from 50 to 250 km. The area of the exposed part of the basin is approximately 45,000 sq km. The Enisei divides the Kansk-Achinsk Coal Basin into two parts: the western, formerly called the Chulym-Enisei basin, and the eastern, formerly the Kansk basin. Geological coal reserves total 601 billion tons (to a depth of 600 m, according to calculations in 1968), including 140 billion tons suitable for open-pit mining.

The coal-bearing potential of the area was first noticed in the late 19th and early 20th century during geological studies along the route of the Siberian railroad, which was then under construction. Coal mining in the basin was begun in 1904 at the Irshinskoe deposit; comprehensive development of the basin was begun in 1939. Principal deposits include Berezovskoe, Barandatskoe, Itatskoe, Bogotol'skoe, Nzarovskoe, Irsha-Borodinskoe, Abanskoe, and Saiano-Partizanskoe. The coal-bearing series of the Kansk-Achinsk coal basin is composed of continental Jurassic deposits representing an alternation of sandstone, conglomerate, gritstone, siltstone, argillites, and coal beds. The predominant part is a typical platform basin with horizontal stratification approximately 200–400 m thick of weakly lithified rocks. In the southeast the thickness of the coal-bearing stratum increases to 700–800 m; it is composed of denser rocks and has folded stratification. In certain places the Jurassic is overlapped unconformably by nonproductive deposits of the Cretaceous, Paleogene, and Neocene periods. The coal-bearing capacity of extractive importance is confined to two different deposition time cycles—the Lower Jurassic and the Middle Jurassic. The basin has up to 20 working coal beds with an overall thickness of 120 m. The Moshchnyi bed, the most important bed in terms of extraction, lies in the upper horizon of the Middle Jurassic deposits and varies in thickness from a few dozen meters to 80 m.

The coals are composed of humus, with infrequently occurring interlayers of sapropelic-humic coal. According to the degree of carbonification, they are brown coals (B1 and B2), with the exception of the Saiano-Partizanskoe deposit, which has hard coals (G grades); at this deposit the thickness of the beds is 1–1.5 m and the conditions of bedding are complex. The brown coals have a moisture content of 21–44 percent, an ash content of 7–14 percent, a sulfur content of 0.2–0.8 percent, and a volatile-matter yield of 46–49 percent; combustion heat of the working fuel is 11.7–15.7 megajoules (MJ) per kg (2,800–3,750 kilocalories [kcal] per kg) and that of the combustible mass is 27.2–28.2 MJ/kg (6,500–6,750 kcal/kg). These coals disintegrate in air and become fines after 12–14 days. The hard coals have a moisture content of 5.6 percent, an ash content of 10 percent, a sulfur content of 1.2 percent, and a volatile-matter yield of 48 percent; combustion heat of working fuel is 26.1 MJ/kg (6,220 kcal/kg) and that of the combustible mass is 33.6

MJ/kg (8,030 kcal/kg). The basin coals are also used as raw materials for the chemical industry. The shallow location of the coal beds and the great thickness of the Moshchnyi primary bed over extensive areas permit exploitation of the deposits by the open-pit mining method. In 1970, 18 million tons of coal were extracted. The explored Berezovskoe deposit, which has large coal reserves, is very promising. In addition to coals, the basin area has deposits of nonmetallic minerals, chiefly building materials.

REFERENCE
Geologiia mestorozhdenii uglia i goriuchikh slantsev SSSR, vol. 8. Moscow, 1964.   A. K. MATVEEV [11–990–1]

KANSKOE BELOGOR'E, a mountain range in the western part of the main watershed range of the Vostochnyi Saian Mountains (Krasnoiarsk Krai, RSFSR). The Kanskoe Belogor'e is situated between the Manskoe Belogor'e to the west and the Agul'skie Belki to the east, forming a watershed for the rivers of the Kan and Kizir basins. Length, approximately 110 km; elevations, 1,800–2,000 m (the highest point is Mount Piramida, 2,256 m). The mountains are predominantly of medium height with flat smooth peaks and are composed chiefly of crystalline schists, marble, and granites. The northern slopes are broken up by a dense network of well-developed, frequently broad river valleys. On the slopes everywhere are dense dark coniferous taiga, and the highest peaks have lichen-covered rocky tundra.   [11–991–1]

KANT, HERMANN. Born June 14, 1926, in Hamburg. German writer and publicist (German Democratic Republic).

Kant's first collection of short stories was *A Bit of the South Sea* (1962). His novels *The Auditorium* (1965; Russian translation, 1968) and *Impressum* (1972; Russian translation, 1974) were devoted to the problems of personality development in a socialist society. Kant was awarded the Heinrich Heine Prize in 1962 and the H. Mann Prize in 1967.

WORKS
In Stockholm. Berlin, 1971. (In collaboration with L. Reher.)
In Russian translation:
"V soiuze s narodom." *Voprosy literatury,* 1969, no. 10.
REFERENCES
Knipovich, E. "'Aktovyi zal' G. Kanta." *Inostrannaia literatura,* 1966, no. 12.
Chetverikova, N. "Prosto o slozhnom." *Pod"em,* 1969, no. 1.
Auer, A. "Eine einfache Sache: Zu dem Roman 'Die Aula' von H. Kant (1965)." In *Standorte-Erkundungen.* Halle an der Saale, 1967.
    [11–992–1]

KANT, IMMANUEL. Born Apr. 22, 1724, in Königsberg (now Kaliningrad); died there Feb. 12, 1804. German philosopher and scholar; founder of German classical philosophy.

Kant lived his whole life in Königsberg, where he graduated from the university in 1745. He was a docent there from 1755 to 1770 and a professor from 1770 to 1796. Two periods are distinguished in Kant's philosophical development: a precritical period that lasted until 1770 and a critical period. In his precritical period Kant admitted the possibility of speculative knowledge of things as they are in themselves (or of "metaphysics," in the language of the age). In his critical period he rejected the capacity for such knowledge on the basis of preliminary research into the forms of cognition and the sources and limits of our cognitive capabilities.

During his precritical period Kant wrote his *General Natural History and Theory of the Heavens* (1755), in which he elaborated a "nebular" cosmological hypothesis on the formation of the planetary system from an original nebula, that is, from a huge cloud of diffuse matter. In the estimation of F. Engels, this theory "was the greatest advance made by astronomy since Copernicus. For the first time the conception that nature had no history in time began to be shaken" (K. Marx and F. Engels, *Soch.,* 2nd ed., vol. 20, p. 56). At this time Kant also proposed the existence of a "great system of galaxies" outside our galaxy; he demonstrated the slowdown in the Earth's daily rotation on its axis as a result of tidal friction; and he also developed the idea of the relativity of movement and rest. In biology Kant presented the idea of a genealogical classification of the animal world. In his research on anthropology, he advanced the notion of the natural development of the human races. Along with his works in the natural sciences, Kant wrote a number of philosophical works during his precritical period. Under the influence of the empiricism and skepticism of the English philosopher D. Hume, he distinguished real and logical foundations and mocked the infatuation of some of his contemporaries with "spirit visions."

Kant's dissertation *The Forms and Principles of the Sensible and the Intelligible Worlds* (1770) marked the beginning of his transition to the views of his critical period, the chief works of which were the *Critique of Pure Reason* (1781), *Critique of Practical Reason* (1788), and *Critique of Judgment* (1790). Fundamental to all three *Critiques* was Kant's theory of appearances and things as they are—of "things-in-themselves." According to Kant, our cognition begins when things-in-themselves affect our external sense organs and produce our perception. This premise in his theories would make Kant a materialist. But his theories on the forms and limits of cognition showed Kant to be an idealist and agnostic. He affirmed that neither the data of sense perception nor the concepts and judgments of our understanding could give us any theoretical knowledge of things-in-themselves. These things cannot be known. To be sure, empirical knowledge of things can become broader and more profound without limit, but this does not bring us one iota closer to cognition of things-in-themselves.

Kant introduced a distinction between ordinary, or general, logic, which investigates the forms of thought and abstracts from questions of subject matter, and transcendental logic, which investigates in the forms of thinking that which imparts to knowledge an a priori, universal, and necessary character. Kant formulated his fundamental question—the sources and limits of knowledge—as the question of the possibility of a priori synthetic judgments (that is, judgments producing new knowledge) in each of the three chief forms of knowledge: mathematics, theoretical natural science, and metaphysics (speculative knowledge of the truly real). Kant attempts to resolve these three questions, posed in his *Critique of Pure Reason,* by investigating the three basic capacities of cognition: sensibility, understanding, and reason.

The foundation of mathematics lies in the perception of space and time, whose forms cease in Kant's thinking to be forms of existence of the things themselves and become only a priori forms of sensibility. The basis of these perceptions lies in "pure" forms of space and time, that is, forms independent of and preceding experience (a priori). This assures the universality and necessity of mathematical truths.

In theoretical natural science the possibility of a priori synthetic judgments is conditioned by 12 categories of understanding that, as "pure" concepts, are a priori: for example, unity, plurality, totality, reality, and negation. But for genuine knowledge to arise, there must be a joining or synthesis of sense perception with the categories of understanding. The highest condition of such a synthesis is the unity of our consciousness. In Kant's opinion, to the extent that universal and necessary laws of experience belong not to nature itself but only to understanding, which imposes them on nature, natural science constructs its own subject-matter as far as its logical form is concerned.

Kant reduces the question of the possibility of synthetic judgments in "metaphysics" to an investigation of reason, which gives birth to "ideas"—concepts of the absolute totality or unity of conditioned phenomena (such concepts as the soul, the world, and god). Kant concluded that all three speculative sciences of traditional philosophy treating these ideas ("rational psychology," "rational cosmology," and "rational theology") are only pseudosciences. Realizing that his critique tended to limit the competence of reason, Kant proposed that where cognition lost, faith gained. Since god cannot be found in experience and does not belong to the world of phenomena, his existence can neither be proved nor disproved. Religion thus becomes an object of faith and not of science or of theoretical philosophy. According to Kant, it is not only possible but necessary to believe in god, because without this faith one cannot reconcile the demands of moral conscience with the indisputable facts of evil ruling in human life.

The Kantian critique of rational cosmology played a great role in the development of philosophy. According to Kant, the claims of rational cosmology necessarily lead to the appearance of antinomies in reason, contradictory but equally provable answers to the questions of rational cosmology: the world is finite and has no limits; there are indivisible particles (atoms) and there are no indivisible particles; all processes are causally conditioned and there are processes (actions) that are accomplished freely. Thus, reason is by nature antinomic and dialectic. However, according to Kant this dialectic of cosmological statements remains only subjective. It does not express the contradictions of the things themselves and does not violate the logical prohibition on contradictions. According to Kant, all the contradictions of the cosmological "dialectic" fall away when the false assumption at their base falls away: that the world as an absolute totality can be the object of theoretical cognition by reason.

Kant constructed his ethics on the basis of his critique of theoretical reason. His initial assumption showed the influence of the French philosopher J.-J. Rousseau: the conviction that every individual is an end in himself and should in no way be seen as the means for carrying out any task whatever, even one for the general good. Kant declared the fundamental law of ethics to be the internal directive or "categorical imperative" requiring that one be guided by the purely formal rule: to act always according to a maxim that could become a universal law; or, in another formulation, to act in such a way that you always behave toward humanity—in both your own person and the person of others—as an end and not only as a means.

In aesthetics Kant reduced the beautiful to "disinterested" pleasure that does not depend on whether the object portrayed in the work of art exists or does not exist but that is conditioned only by its form. However, Kant could not consistently maintain his formalism: despite the formal character of the categorical imperative, in his ethics he advanced the principle of the value as an end in himself of every man; and despite the formalism of his conception of the beautiful, in his aesthetics he declared the highest form of art to be poetry, since it ascends to the portrayal of the ideal.

Kant's ideas on the role of antagonisms in the historical process of the life of society were progressive. According to Kant, the attainment of the greatest goal of humanity, universal legal civil status, was possible only through the action of forces that seem to be the source only of struggle and enmity. Along with this, a state of perpetual peace among all states was to be attained. Kant considered the means for establishing and preserving peace to be the development of international trade and contacts, with their mutual advantages for various states.

Although Kant's theories contained abundant contradictions, they exerted an enormous influence on the later development of scientific and philosophical thought. By his theories on the antinomies of reason, Kant played an outstanding role in the development of dialectics. Philosophers of the most diverse tendencies have both criticized Kant and tried to develop his ideas. Neo-Kantianism, which arose in the 1860's, tried to elaborate a system of idealism on the basis of Kant's ideas. The dual character of Kant's philosophy, which allowed it to be criticized both from the right and from the left, was noted by the classical writers of Marxism-Leninism, who highly valued its positive aspects while criticizing its subjective idealist and agnostic tendencies (see V. I. Lenin, *Poln. sobr. soch.,* 5th ed., vol. 18, pp. 202–14). Karl Marx considered that in terms of its social content Kant's philosophy was a German theory of the French bourgeois revolution (see K. Marx and F. Engels, *Soch.,* 2nd ed., vol. 3, p. 184).

WORKS

Gesammelte Schriften, vols. 1–23. Berlin, 1910–55.
Briefe. Göttingen, 1970.
In Russian translation:
Soch., vols. 1–6. Moscow, 1963–66.

REFERENCES

Marks, K., and F. Engels. *Nemetskaia ideologiia. Soch.,* 2nd ed., vol. 3.
Engels, F. *Anti-Dühring. Ibid.,* vol. 20.

Lenin, V. I. *Poln. sobr. soch.,* 5th ed., vol. 18. (See index of names.)
Deborin, A. M. "Dialektika u Kanta." In *Arkhiv K. Marksa i F. Engel'sa,* book 1. Moscow, 1924.
Asmus, V. F. *Dialektika Kanta,* 2nd ed. Moscow, 1930.
Asmus, V. F. *Filosofiia I. Kanta.* Moscow, 1957.
Karapetian, A. *Kriticheskii analiz filosofii Kanta.* Yerevan, 1958.
Galanza, P. N. *Uchenie I. Kanta o gosudarstve i prave.* Moscow, 1960.
Shashkevich, P. D. *Teoriia poznaniia I. Kanta.* Moscow, 1960.
Popov, S. I. *Kant i kantianstvo.* Moscow, 1961.
Paul'sen, F. *Kant, ego zhizn' i uchenie,* 2nd ed. St. Petersburg, 1905.
Fischer, K. *Istoriia novoi filosofii,* vols. 4–5. St. Petersburg, 1906–10.
Renouvier, C. B. *Critique de la doctrine de Kant.* Paris, 1906.
Caird, E. *The Critical Philosophy of I. Kant,* 2nd ed., vols. 1–2. London, 1909.
Cohen, H. *Kants Begründung der Ethik,* 2nd ed. Berlin, 1910.
Cohen, H. *Kants Theorie der Erfahrung,* 4th ed. Berlin, 1925.
Simmel, G. *Kant,* 5th ed. Munich, 1921.
Cassirer, E. *Kants Leben und Lehre.* Berlin, 1921.
Reininger, R. *Kant: Seine Anhanger und seine Gegner.* Munich, 1923.
Vorlander, K. *I. Kant,* vols. 1–2. Leipzig, 1924.
Riehl, A. *Der philosophische Kritizismus,* vols. 1–3. Leipzig, 1924–26.
Wundt, M. *Kant als Metaphysiker.* Stuttgart, 1924.
Rickert, H. *Kant als Philosoph der modernen Kultur.* Tübingen, 1924.
Adickes, E. *Kant als Naturforscher,* vols. 1–2. Berlin, 1924–25.
Heidegger, M. *Kant und das Problem der Metaphysik.* Bonn, 1929.
Vleeschauwer, H. J. de. *L'Evolution de la pensée Kantienne.* Paris, 1939.
Ritzel, W. *Studien zum Wandel der Kant-Auffassungen.* Meinsenheim/-Glan, 1952.
Kroner, R. *Von Kant bis Hegel,* vols. 1–2. Tübingen, 1961.
Bohatec, J. *Die Religionsphilosophie Kants.* Hildesheim, 1966.
Heimsoeth, H. *Transzendentale Dialektik,* vols. 1–4. Berlin, 1966–71.
Martin, G. *Immanuel Kant,* 4th ed. Berlin, 1969.
Kant-Studien, vols. 1–61. 1896–1970.
Commentaries and dictionaries to Kant's works
Eisler, R. *Kant-Lexikon.* Hildesheim, 1961.
Vaihinger, H. *Kommentar zu I. Kants Kritik der reinen Vernunft,* 2nd ed., vols. 1–2. Stuttgart, 1922.
Cohen, H. *Kommentar zu I. Kants Kritik der reinen Vernunft,* 4th ed. Leipzig, 1925.
Ratke, H. *Systematisches Handlexikon zu Kants Kritik der reinen Vernunft,* 2nd ed. Hamburg, 1965. V. F. ASMUS [11–992–2]

KANT, an urban-type settlement, administrative center of Kant Raion, Kirghiz SSR. Situated in the Chu Valley. Kant has a railroad station 20 km east of the city of Frunze. Population, 22,500 (1971). A cement and slate combine and sugar and over-haul-machinery plants are there. [11–997–2]

KANT (from Latin *cantus,* "singing"), a type of many-voiced song dealing with everyday events prevalent in Russia, the Ukraine, and Byelorussia in the 17th and 18th centuries. Initially *kanty* were based on religious texts and thus were confined to monasteries and clerical circles.

The poetic style of the *kant* is derived from literature and not from the folk song. In the 17th century texts by S. Polotskii, E. Slavinetskii, D. Rostovskii, and other representatives of syl-labic poetry, were set to music to create *kanty.* The texts and melodies existed in many variants; they were recorded in manu-script collections that were widely disseminated. The musical style of the *kant* is characterized by three-voice exposition with parallel movement of the upper voices and a common-time strophic form. They were performed a cappella by an ensemble of singers or a chorus. Their intonational structure represents a fusion of elements of the *znamennyi* chant, Russian and Ukrainian folk songs, and Polish melodic systems.

Kanty with patriotic, domestic, and romantic-lyrical themes appeared in the 18th century; salutatory and panegyrical *kanty* with fanfare-like melodic phrases, the grand rhythms of the polonaise, and exultant roulades were typical of the Petrine era. The *kant* became the favorite form of music of the urban strata of the population. The lyrical *kanty* incorporated elements from popular dance forms, primarily the minuet. While texts by V. K. Trediakovskii, M. V. Lomonosov, and A. P. Sumarokov are known, the authors and composers of most *kanty* remain anony-mous.

REFERENCES
Findeizen, N. F. *Ocherki po istorii muzyki v Rossii,* vols. 1–2. Moscow-Leningrad, 1928–29.
Livanova, T. N. *Russkaia muzykal'naia kul'tura XVIII veka . . . ,* vol. 1. Moscow, 1952.
Pozdneev, A. V. "Rukopisnye pesenniki XVII–XVIII vekov." *Uch. zapiski Moskovskogo zaochnogo ped. in-ta,* 1958, vol. 1.
Keldysh, Iu. V. *Russkaia muzyka XVIII veka.* Moscow, 1965.
Keldysh, Iu. V. "Ob istoricheskikh korniakh kanta." In the collection *Musica antiqua Europae Orientalis,* vol. 2. Bydgoszcz, 1969.
IU. V. KELDYSH [11–996–2]

KANTEGIR, a mountain range in the central part of the Zapad-nyi Saian (Krasnoiarsk Krai, RSFSR), situated between the Eni-sei River and its left tributary, the Kantegir. Length, about 90 km, with elevations of 1,800–2,000 m (the greatest elevation is 2,485 m). It is composed of crystalline schists and granites. The slopes are dissected by deep erosional valleys. Landscapes of dark coniferous mountain taiga predominate. A mountain in the upper reaches of the Kantegir River is also sometimes called Kantegir. [11–999–3]

KANTELE, a Karelian-Finnish plucked stringed instrument. It is related to the Estonian *kannel,* the Latvian *kokle,* the Lithuanian *kankles,* and the Russian wing-shaped ("ringing") *gusli.* [11–999–4]

KANTEMIR, ANTIOKH DMITRIEVICH. Born Sept. 10 (21), 1708, in Constantinople; died Mar. 31 (Apr. 11), 1744, in Paris. Russian satiric poet and diplomat. Son of D. K. Kan-temir, a Moldavian hospodar. Broadly educated, he had com-plete mastery of several languages; he studied the exact sciences and humanities and history of Russian culture.

Kantemir began his literary activity in 1725 with translations. His political epigrams and original satires (1729–31) boldly de-fended the reforms of Peter I. He became ambassador to Great Britain in 1732 and served as ambassador to France in 1738–44. While abroad he continued to write satires and translated Horace and Anacreon, attempting in vain to have his works printed in St. Petersburg. A supporter of the theory of natural law, he spread the ideas of the Enlightenment and sharply criti-cized the church and clergy.

In 1730, Kantemir translated into Russian *The Discourse On the Plurality of Worlds,* a treatise by the physicist B. Fontenelle. In 1742 he wrote a commentary to the treatise, much of which went into the letters *On Nature and Man,* which represented the first attempt at creating Russian philosophical terminology and materialistic explanations of important philosophical concep-tions. He introduced such words as *ideia* (idea), *deputat* (deputy), *materiia* (matter), and *priroda* (nature) into Russian speech. In 1756 the Holy Synod confiscated his translation of the treatise. Upon reading V. K. Trediakovskii's *New and Brief Method for the Composition of Russian Verses* (1735), Kantemir propounded a defense of syllabic versification.

Kantemir's works and translations, as well as his ties with such figures as Montesquieu and Voltaire, strained his relations with the tsarist government in the early 1740's. However, his prestige in European capitals, his deep knowledge of interna-tional relations, and his skill in the complex situation of the War for the Austrian Succession (1740–48) forced the Russian gov-ernment to tolerate his services in responsible diplomatic posts. His communiqués and diplomatic correspondence contain a seri-ous analysis of the domestic affairs and foreign policies of Euro-pean states. A large part of them have not been published and are preserved in Soviet archives. Kantemir is one of the founders of Russian classicism and the new satirical poetry.

WORKS
Sochineniia, pis'ma i izbr. perevody, vols. 1–2. St. Petersburg, 1867–68.
[Pis'ma.] In the book *Materialy dlia biografii Kantemira.* Compiled by L. N. Maikov. St. Petersburg, 1903.
Sobr. stikhotvorenii. (Introduction by F. Ia. Priima.) Leningrad, 1956.
REFERENCES
Timofeev, L. I. "Kantemir i razvitie sillabicheskogo stikha." In his book *Ocherki teorii i istorii russkogo stikha.* Moscow, 1958.

Blagoi, D. D. *Istoriia russkoi literatury XVIII v,* 4th ed. Moscow, 1960.
Plekhanov, G. V. " 'Uchenaia druzhina' i samoderzhavie," part 3 (A. D. Kantemir). *Soch.,* vol. 21. Moscow-Leningrad, 1925.
Plekhanov, G. V. "Obshchesvennaia mysl' v iziashchnoi literature." *Ibid.*
Istoriia filosofii v SSSR, vol. 1. Moscow, 1968. Pages 293–98.

E. E. IUROVSKAIA and I. Z. SERMAN   [11–999–5]

KANTEMIR, DMITRII KONSTANTINOVICH. Born Oct. 26, 1673, in Moldavia; died Aug. 21 (Sept. 1), 1723, at the Dmitrovka *pomest'e* (estate) in Kharkov Province. Scholar and political figure of Moldavia and Russia. Studied at the Constantinople Greco-Latin Academy. Son of the Moldavian hospodar Konstantin Kantemir, he himself became hospodar in 1710.

Kantemir in 1711 concluded a secret treaty of alliance with Peter I against Turkey and for Moldavia's merger with Russia. Following Peter's unsuccessful Prut campaign of 1711, Kantemir and 4,000 Moldavians fled to Russia. Here Kantemir became an adviser to the tsar on eastern questions; he received the title of prince and *pomest'ia* (estates) in the Ukraine. In 1714 he was elected a member of the Berlin Academy of Sciences, and he participated in the Persian campaign of 1722–23.

Almost all of Kantemir's works were written in Russia and they were greatly influenced by the Petrine reforms. He wrote several historical studies (*A Historical, Geographical, and Political Description of Moldavia, Chronicle of the Antiquity of the Roman-Moldavian-Walachians, and History of the Rise and Fall of the Ottoman Empire*) and philosophical works (*Metaphysics, Hieroglyphic History, and The Supreme Court, or the Dispute of the Wise Man With the Universe, or the Soul's Lawsuit Against the Body*). Patriotism, coupled with a belief that Russia could play a progressive role in the Balkans and that Moldavia would prosper, pervades all his historical works.

REFERENCES
Istoriia Moldavskoi SSR, 2nd ed., vol. 1. Kishinev, 1965. Pages 360–62.
Ermuratskii, V. N. *Obshchestvenno-politicheskie vzgliady D. Kantemira.* Kishinev, 1956.
Istoriia filosofii v SSSR, vol. 1. Moscow, 1968. Pages 452–60.

[11–1000–1]

KANTEMIROV, a family of Soviet Ossetian circus artists; trick horsemen.

Alibek Tuzarovich Kantemirov (born May 16, 1882; People's Artist of the RSFSR since 1966) was a jockey in equestrian competitions from 1902 to 1907. In 1907 he began performing in the circus as a solo horseman. In 1924 he created the Ali-Bek Caucasian Trick Horsemen group. Kantemirov added new devices to the art of circus trick riding. The group's repertoire includes equestrian games, elements of competition, and complicated stunts. The group includes Alibek Tuzarovich's sons Khasanbek (born Dec. 14, 1924; People's Artist of the Severnaia Osetiia ASSR [1960], member of the CPSU since 1945), Irbek (born June 2, 1928; Honored Artist of the RSFSR [1960], member of the CPSU since 1956), and Mukhtarbek (born Feb. 18, 1934; Honored Artist of the Severnaia Osetiia ASSR [1960]). Alibek Tuzarovich has trained a number of riders, including the famous trick horseman M. N. Tuganov. Artists from the Kantemirov group have frequently toured abroad. Alibek Tuzarovich Kantemirov has been awarded the Order of Lenin, two other orders, and a medal.   [11–1001–1]

KANTHAL, an iron-based heat-resistant alloy containing approximately 22 percent chromium, 5 percent aluminium, and 0.5 percent cobalt. A number of varieties of kanthal, whose different performance characteristics depend mainly on the special features of their production processes, are manufactured in Sweden. The alloys are characterized by high electric resistivity (up to 1.45 megohm-meters) and heat resistance (up to 1375°C). The melting point of kanthal is approximately 1510°C. Kanthal is used in wire or strip form primarily for the manufacture of heating elements for electric furnaces. It is similar to the chromal-type OKh23Iu5A and OKh27Iu5A alloys manufactured in the USSR.   [11–998–5]

KANTOKUEN, special maneuvers of the Kwantung Army, the conventional name of the strategic plan of Japan's attack on the USSR in the Great Patriotic War (1941–45).

After fascist Germany's attack on the USSR on June 22, 1941, an imperial conference of Japanese military and political leaders, held on July 2, 1941, sanctioned practical steps toward preparing a war against the USSR. The Japanese militarists expected that the defeat of the Red Army on the Soviet-German front would create favorable conditions for opening a second front against the USSR in the Far East and for blitzkrieg operations. In accordance with the Kantokuen plan, which was drawn up by the imperial headquarters and the staff of the Kwantung Army, 500,000 men were secretly mobilized in July 1941, and 300,000 of them were sent to Manchuria to reinforce the Kwantung Army. The Kwantung Army as redeployed after these measures comprised three front administrations, five field armies, and the Kwantung Defense Army, totaling 700,000 men. The Kwantung Army also had large units of the armies of Manchukuo and of Inner Mongolia at its disposal.

According to the Kantokuen plan, troops of the Eastern and Northern fronts were to open the offensive from the region of Pogranichnaia toward Voroshilov and from the region of Heiho (Sakhalian) toward Blagoveshchensk and Kuibyshevka-Vostochnaia. In the first phase they were to occupy Voroshilov, Vladivostok, Blagoveshchensk, Imam, and Kuibyshevka-Vostochnaia; in the second phase, Khabarovsk, Birobidzhan, Birokan, and the Rukhlovo region; then, if events developed favorably, they were to occupy northern Sakhalin. Nikolaevsk-na-Amure, Komsomol'sk, Sovetskaia Gavan', and Petrovavlovsk-Kamchatskii. The plan provided for cooperation between the ground troops and the navy in landing amphibious forces on Kamchatka and northern Sakhalin and for a naval blockade of Vladivostok. In case the Eastern and Northern fronts were to be successful, the Western Front was to open an offensive on Chita and capture the whole territory up to Lake Baikal.

The Japanese command originally planned to open military operations on Aug. 19, 1941. The stationing of a large Japanese army grouping in Manchuria and the danger that Japan would carry out the Kantokuen plan forced the USSR to keep large forces in the Far East. The heroic resistance of the Soviet armed forces in the summer and fall of 1941, their victory in the battle of Moscow (December 1941—April 1942), and the collapse of the strategic plan of the fascist German command forced the Japanese imperialists at first to postpone the implementation of the Kantokuen plan and then, after further victories of the Red Army, abandon it altogether.

REFERENCES
Final, 2nd ed. Moscow, 1969.
Hayashi, Saburo. *Iaponskaia armiia v voennykh deistviiakh na Tikhom okeane.* Moscow, 1964. (Translated from English.)

N. V. ERONIN   [11–1003–2]

KANTONIST SCHOOLS, educational institutions in Russia for *kantonisty* (sons of active soldiers) that appeared in the early 19th century. The *kantonisty* attended the schools from the age of seven (ten after 1824) to 15; most students then enlisted in the army for 20 years, and the rest continued their studies until they were 18 and graduated as noncommissioned officers. Special *kantonist* schools appeared in the 1830's to train noncommissioned officers for various branches of the army.

The Decree of 1758 required all soldiers' children to receive instruction. But despite their numerical growth, the schools actually were able to educate only an insignificant number of *kantonisty*: in 1842, of 223,000 *kantonisty,* only 37,500 were enrolled in the schools, and in 1856 approximately one-tenth of the 372,-000 eligible children were enrolled.

The fundamental goal of the *kantonist* schools was to train well-educated soldiers "loyal to the throne." The curriculum was very limited (reading, writing, counting, and scripture), and the routine was extremely harsh, dominated by military regimentation. A. A. Arakcheev admitted that the boys wasted away "like candles" with one out of five sickening and one out of ten dying.

As the military settlements were liquidated the *kantonist*

schools were either disbanded or transformed into military schools.

REFERENCES
Mel'nitskoi, N. *Sbornik svedenii o voenno-uchebnykh zavedeniiakh v Rossii,* vols. 1–4. St. Petersburg, 1857–60.
Lalaev, M. *Istoricheskii ocherk voenno-uchebnykh zavedenii (1700–1800),* parts 1–2. St. Petersburg, 1880.
Nikitin, V. N. *Mnogostradal'nye: Ocherki proshlogo.* St. Petersburg, 1895.   [11–1005–1]

KANTOROVICH, LEONID VITAL'EVICH. Born Jan. 6 (19), 1912, in St. Petersburg. Soviet mathematician and economist. Academician of the Academy of Sciences of the USSR (1964; corresponding member, 1958).

In 1930, Kantorovich graduated from Leningrad University, where he was an instructor from 1932 to 1934 and a professor from 1934 to 1960. From 1958 to 1971 he worked at the Siberian Division of the Academy of Sciences of the USSR; since 1971 he has been working at the Institute for the Management of the National Economy of the State Committee on Science and Technology of the Council of Ministers of the USSR. His first scientific results dealt with the theory of projective sets. In functional analysis he introduced and studied the class of semi-ordered spaces (*K*-spaces). He applied functional analysis to computational mathematics for the first time. He also developed a general theory of approximation methods and constructed efficient methods for solving operator equations (including the method of steepest descent and Newton's method for such equations). In 1939–40 he laid the foundations for linear programming—theories and methods of solution for maxima and minima problems with constraints. He established the importance of objectively determined estimates, which arise in the analysis of optimal economic models. These investigations have made it possible to create a theory of optimal planning and control of the national economy and to work out problems of socialist economics: price setting, the theory of rents, and the efficiency of capital investment.

Kantorovich is an honorary doctor of many foreign universities, and a member of the Budapest and Boston academies. A recipient of the State Prize of the USSR (1949) and the Lenin Prize (1965), he has been awarded the Order of Lenin, three other orders, and various medals.

WORKS
Matematicheskie metody organizatsii i planirovaniia proizvodstva. Leningrad, 1939.
Funktsional'nyi analiz v poluuporiadochennykh prostranstvakh. Moscow-Leningrad, 1950. (Co-author.)
Ekonomicheskii raschet nailuchshego ispol'zovaniia resursov. Moscow, 1959.
Funktsional'nyi analiz v normirovannykh prostranstvakh. Moscow, 1959. (With G. P. Akilov.)
Priblizhennye metody vysshego analiza, 5th ed. Moscow-Leningrad, 1962. (With V. I. Krylov.)

REFERENCE
"Leonid Vital'evich Kantorovich." *Uspekhi matematicheskikh nauk,* 1962, vol. 17, issue 4; 1972, issue 3.
                                        I. V. ROMANOVSKII   [11–1007–2]

KANT'S HYPOTHESIS, in astronomy, the hypothesis of the formation of the planetary system out of diffuse matter that fills all the space of this system and is in uniform rotational motion around a central condensation—the sun. It was set forth in I. Kant's *General History of Nature and the Theory of the Heavens* (1755), in which he raised the question about the natural origin of all celestial bodies ("Give me matter, and I will show you how the world must form from it") and provided a cosmogonical explanation of the regularities of planetary motion. Generally speaking, Kant's hypothesis presents a true picture of the development of a rotating dust cloud. (In the hypothesis there is reference to "particles," since in Kant's time the existence of atoms and molecules of gases and their distinction from dust particles was not known.)

The mathematical basis for the cosmogonical picture presented by Kant was supplied only in the middle of the 20th century, when the role of the transformation of mechanical energy into heat energy during collisions of solid particles was understood.   B. IU. LEVIN   [11–997–3]

KANUN, a plucked stringed musical instrument. Its use is widespread in the Middle East. In the USSR the *kanun* is played in Armenia. Its flat body measures 800–900 mm, and it has 24 strings. The *kanun* is tuned diatonically. The sound is produced with a plectrum worn on the finger. The plectrum resembles a thimble.   [11–984–1]

KANURI (also known as the Beriberi), a people in northeastern Nigeria, the southeastern part of the Republic of the Niger, and along the eastern shore of Lake Chad (Republic of Chad). Their population, together with the closely related Tubu, Kanembu, and Zaghawa peoples, totals approximately 3 million (1970, estimate). The Kanuri language belongs to the Kanuri-Tubu group. Most Kanuri are Muslims (Islam spread among them in the 11th century); vestiges of the old tribal cults are also preserved. In about the ninth century, the Kanuri created a state union, Kanem-Bornu. The Kanuri engage in farming and cattle raising. A characteristic of the Kanuri is their interweaving of feudal relations and growing capitalist relations.

REFERENCE
Meek, C. K. *The Northern Tribes of Nigeria,* vols. 1–2. London, 1925.
                                        R. N. ISMAGILOVA   [11–1008–5]

KANURI-TUBU (also Kanuri-Teda, Kanuri), a group of languages spoken in northeastern Nigeria and the republics of Niger and Chad. The number of speakers does not exceed 3 million (1970, estimate), most of whom (2.7 million) are Kanuri. Typologically, the Kanuri-Tubu languages are synthetic (partly inflectional). Kanuri-Tubu has five tones, which have grammatical and semantic meaning. The morphology is distinguished by a well-developed system of verbal inflection and by a regular and irregular conjugation system, which has an abundant variety of word-form derivations. The word order is subject-object-predicate.

REFERENCES
Lukas, J. *A Study of the Kanuri Language: Grammar and Vocabulary.* London, 1937.
Lukas, J. *Die Sprache der Tubu in der Zentralen Sahara.* Berlin, 1953.
Tucker, A. N., and M. A. Bryan. *The Non-Bantu Languages of North-Eastern Africa.* London, 1956.
Greenberg, J. H. "The Languages of Africa." *International Journal of American Linguistics,* 1963, vol. 29, no. 1.
                                        N. V. OKHOTINA   [11–1009–1]

KAOKO VELD, a plateau in Namibia (southern Africa), between the Cunene and Ugab rivers. Average elevation, 1,300–1,800 m.

The Kaoko Veld descends in stages in the west toward the Namib Desert and in the east, toward the Kalahari. The Kaoko Veld is composed of Proterozoic and Lower Paleozoic sedimentary rock, in the south overlaid by lavas of the Karroo System. Very rugged flat-topped massifs predominate. The climate is tropical and semidesert. Xerophytic turf-grasses are the dominant vegetation, and there is brush in the valleys.   [11–1014–4]

KAOLACK, a city in western Senegal. Population, 96,300 (1970). Kaolack is a port on the Saloum River (peanut export), a railway station on the Dakar-Bamako line, and a highway junction. Peanut oil is manufactured in the city.   [11–1014–5]

KAOLIN (from Kao-ling, the name of the area in China, in Kiangsi Province, where it was first found), a rock consisting basically of the mineral kaolinite, commonly with admixtures of quartz granules, feldspar, micas, and, in small quantities, other mineral impurities.

Kaolins are formed through the weathering of various magmatic, feldspathic rocks (primarily low-ferriferous granites; more rarely, argillaceous sediments or arkoses called primary kaolins). They are also formed through the rewashing of these rocks, the kaolins then being redeposited in sedimentary (chiefly sandy) strata (secondary kaolins, or kaolin clays). In primary kaolins the structure of the mother rock is usually clearly visible.

Kaolin deposits are encountered rather frequently. The rock is mined in England (Cornwall), the German Democratic Republic (near Dresden), Czechoslovakia (around Karlovy Vary), and the USA (Georgia). In the USSR, kaolin is mined in the Ukrainian SSR, the Urals, and the Kazakh SSR.

Primary and secondary kaolins are used in an unprocessed form for manufacturing refractory materials. However, in the majority of cases, it is enriched at plants usually located not far from the deposits. According to industrial requirements, the enriched kaolin should contain no more than 0.3–1.0 percent iron oxide and titanium oxide (depending upon the grade) and should be free of sand and other impurities, particularly of those that are soluble in water and weak acids. A number of types of production require powdered kaolin of a high degree of whiteness. The most important user of kaolin is the paper industry, which consumes around 40–50 percent of the total output; the kaolin is used to chalk the paper surface and as a filler. In many grades of paper, kaolin makes up as much as 30–40 percent of the total bulk of the paper and, to a significant degree, determines the paper's quality. In ceramics, kaolin is used in porcelain and earthenware (5–10 percent of the total kaolin output), of which it is a basic component. Around 20 percent of the kaolin mined is used in the rubber industry. In addition, kaolin is used in perfumery, medicine (called "china clay"), and the chemical industry (for making aluminum sulfate).

REFERENCE
Kurs mestorozhdenii nemetallicheskikh poleznykh iskopaemykh. Edited by P. M. Tatarinov. Moscow, 1969.   V. P. PETROV   [11–1014–6]

KAOLINITE, a clay mineral from the group of hydrous aluminum silicates. Its chemical composition is $Al_4[Si_4O_{10}]$ $(OH)_8$, and it contains 39.5 percent Al_2O_3, 46.5 percent SiO_2, and 14 percent H_2O. Kaolinite forms earthen masses, in which, with high magnification under an electron microscope, small hexagonal crystals can be detected. It crystallizes in the monoclinic system. The mineral's crystal structure is based on infinite sheets of $Si—O_4$ tetrahedrons, which have three common oxygens and are linked in pairs through the free apexes of the crystal lattice by the aluminum and hydroxyl. These sheets are interconnected by weak bonds and this determines the perfect cleavage of kaolinite as well as the possibility of the differing positioning of one layer on the other. This, in turn, leads to a certain change in the symmetry of the entire crystal structure. Kaolinite has a hardness of 1 on the mineralogical scale and a density of 2,540–2,600 kg/m^3. It is greasy to the touch. In heating to 500°–600° C, it loses water, and at 1,000°–1,200° C, it decomposes, liberating heat and forming initially sillimanite and then mullite. This reaction constitutes the basis of ceramic production.

A component of many clays, kaolinite is formed during weathering and hydrothermal alteration of feldspathic rock.

V. P. PETROV   [11–1015–2]

KAOLINIZATION, rock alteration leading to the formation of kaolin by the transformation of various minerals containing alumina, and, above all, of feldspars and mica. Kaolinization is most strongly manifested in the formation of a kaolin weathering mantle as a result of weathering in granites, syenites, and other feldspathic rock, evidently under humid, subtropical conditions. In this process a finely flaked, alumina-rich mica is initially formed from the feldspar. This mica is called sericite, and subsequently it becomes hydrated and is converted into hydromica and kaolinite. Remnants of hydromica are often present among the kaolinites that have formed as a result of kaolinization. Kaolinization processes are also manifested when there is perisurface hydrothermal alteration of rock in areas of volcanic activity.

Intensive processes of rock kaolinization and the formation of weathering mantles occurred during the Carboniferous, Jurassic, Paleogene, and Neocene periods, which were characterized by abundant vegetation and a relatively humid and warm climate. Modern kaolinization is most characteristic in the humid tropics.   [11–1015–1]

KAPCHAGAI, a city in Alma-Ata Oblast, Kazakh SSR. Situated 80 km north of Alma-Alta on the shore of the Kapchagai Reservoir on the Ili River, where the river is crossed by the railroad line to Alma-Ata. The city arose in connection with the construction of the Kapchagai Hydroelectric Power Plant. Industry includes a fish-processing factory and ship-repair workshops.   [11–1098–3]

KAPCHAGAI RESERVOIR, a reservoir on the Ili River in the Alma-Ata and Taldy-Kurgan oblasts of Kazakh SSR. It began to be filled in 1970. Area 1,850 sq km; volume, 28.14 cu km; length, 180 km; maximum width, 22 km; average depth, 15.2 m; maximum depth, 45 m. Its water level varies over a range of 4 m; the reservoir is used for the long-term regulation of water flow. Its water is used for production of electric energy and irrigation. The reservoir is also a recreation site for the inhabitants of Alma-Ata and other cities of southern Kazakhstan. The city of Kapchagai is located on its shore.   [11–1098–4]

KAPCHINSKII, ANATOLII KONSTANTINOVICH. Born June 6, 1912, in Saratov; died 1942. One of the first Masters of Sport of the USSR (1935), engineer. Became a member of the CPSU in 1941.

Kapchinskii was a champion and record holder of the USSR in speed ice skating (1936–40). During the Great Patriotic War of 1941–45, he fought in the partisan detachment of Hero of the Soviet Union D. N. Medvedev. He was killed behind enemy lines. Kapchinskii was awarded the Order of the Patriotic War First class, as well as medals. Since 1946 there have been annual Kapchinskii speed skating competitions in the USSR.

[11–1098–5]

KAPELIUSHNIKOV, MATVEI ALKUMOVICH. Born Sept. 1 (13), 1886, in Abastumani, in present-day Adigeni Raion, Georgian SSR; died July 5, 1959, in Moscow. Soviet petroleum scientist; corresponding member of the Academy of Sciences of the USSR (1939).

Kapeliushnikov graduated from the Tomsk Technological Insitute in 1914. In 1922 he invented (in collaboration with S. M. Volokh and N. A. Kornev) the well-hole motor, a turbodrill for drilling wells. This invention marked the beginning of turbine drilling. The first Soviet cracking plant, which played an important role in the study and development of the cracking and reforming processes, was designed by Kapeliushnikov and V. G. Shukhov and built in Baku in 1931. Kapeliushnikov developed a number of devices and mechanisms for facilitating and mechanizing well-drilling operations. High-pressure gas injection in order to increase oil-production capacity was proposed by Kapeliushnikov and V. M. Fokeev in 1949. Kapeliushnikov was awarded two Orders of Lenin, four other orders, and medals.

REFERENCE
Lisichkin, S. M. *Vydaiushchiesia deiateli otechestvennoi neftianoi nauki i tekhniki.* Moscow, 1967.   [11–1018–5]

KAPELLDIENER (archaic), a worker in a theater or concert hall who checked tickets, showed members of the audience to their seats, and maintained order.   [11–1018–2]

KAPEL'MEISTER, originally in the 16th–18th centuries, the leader of a choral or instrumental choir; in the 19th century, a theatrical, choral, or symphonic conductor. Now the director of a symphony orchestra is called *direzher* (conductor); of a military band, *voennyi direzher* (military conductor); and of a choir, *khorovoi direzher* (choral conductor) or *khormeister.*

[11–1018–3]

KAPFENBERG, a city in Austria in the province of Styria, in the valley of the Mürz River, in the Alps. Population, 26,300 (1970). There is production of steel, wire, chemicals, paper, and cardboard.   [11–1098–2]

KAPIEV, EFFENDI MANSUROVICH. Born Feb. 28 (Mar. 13), 1909, in the village of Kumukh, present-day Lakskii Raion,

Dagestan ASSR; died Jan. 27, 1944, in Piatigorsk. Soviet Dagestani writer.

Kapiev was of Lak nationality but wrote in Russian. He translated the poems of Suleiman Stal'skii and Caucasian tribal songs into Russian. His collections of examples of mountaineers' epic and lyric poetry *Songs of the Mountaineers* (1939) and *Stone Carving* (1940) were published in Moscow.The cycle of short stories *The Poet* (1940, published in 1944), which was unified by the central generalized image of the folk poet Suleiman, was widely known. *The Poet* has been translated into many languages of peoples of the USSR and into foreign languages. Kapiev was also the author of *Sketches From the Front* (1942–43, published in 1944) and *Notebooks* (*Dagestan Notebook*, 1934–40, and *Diary of the Front*, 1941–44). Kapiev's works are permeated by Soviet patriotism, belief in the friendship of peoples, and a keen feeling for modern life.

WORKS

Izbrannoe [with an introduction by N. Tikhonov]. Moscow, 1959.
Izbrannoe [notes by N. V. Kapieva, introduction by I. Kramov]. Moscow, 1966.

REFERENCES

Ocherki dagestanskoi sovetskoi literatury. Makhachkala,1957.
Sultanov, K. *Poety Dagestana.* Makhachkala, 1959.
Kramov, I. *Effendi Kapiev.* Moscow, 1964.
Kapieva, N. V. *Zhizn', prozhitaia nabelo: O tvorchestve Effendi Kapieva.* Moscow, 1969.   [11–1021–1]

KAPISCHE (from Old Slavonic *kap'*, "representation" or "idol"), a cultic structure, built by Eastern and Baltic Slavs before the Christian era. The *kapishche* is mentioned in Metropolitan Hilarion's *Discourse on Law and Grace* (11th century) and other sources. One of the most ancient *kapishche* was uncovered during excavations at Peryn', near Novgorod.

REFERENCE

Dintses, L. A. "Dokhristianskie khramy Rusi v svete pamiatnikov narodnogo iskusstva." *Sovetskaia etnografiia*, 1947, no. 2.
                                                              [11–1067–1]

KAPITAL, DAS, the most important work by K. Marx, in which, applying the dialectical materialist interpretation of the historical process to the analysis of capitalist socioeconomic formation, he discovered the economic law of development of bourgeois society and demonstrated the inevitability of the downfall of capitalism and the victory of communism. V. I. Lenin characterized *Das Kapital* as "the greatest work on political economy" (*Poln. sobr. soch.*, 5th ed., vol. 2, p. 11). At the same time, *Das Kapital* is an outstanding philosophical and historical study. "If Marx did not leave behind us 'Logic' (with a capital letter *L*)," wrote Lenin, "he did leave the logic of *Das Kapital.* . . . in *Das Kapital*, Marx applied to one science logic, dialectics, and the theory of knowledge . . . of materialism" (*ibid.*, vol. 29, p. 301). Lenin noted that the work provided the "history of capitalism and the analysis of the concepts summing it up" (*ibid.*). As F. Engels and Lenin stressed, *Das Kapital* is Marx' main work in which scientific communism is expounded (see Marx and Engels, *Soch.*, 2nd ed., vol. 19, p. 109, and Lenin, *Poln. sobr. soch.*, 5th ed., vol. 1, p. 187). "As long as capitalists and workers have existed in the world," wrote Engels, "no single book that could have had such importance for workers has appeared" (Marx and Engels, *Soch.*, 2nd ed., vol. 16, p. 240).

Marx devoted 40 years of his life—from 1843 to 1883—to the writing of *Das Kapital*. In their works of the 1840's (*A Contribution to the Critique of Political Economy, Economic and Philosophical Manuscripts of 1844, The German Ideology, The Poverty of Philosophy, Wage Labor and Capital, and The Communist Manifesto*), Marx and Engels formulated the basic propositions of the materialist interpretation of history and the theory of scientific communism that grew out of it. Thus, the indispensable methodological premises of the Marxist economic doctrine were created—the doctrine which is "the most profound, comprehensive, and detailed confirmation and application of Marx' theory" (Lenin, *Poln. sobr. soch.*, 5th ed., vol. 26, p. 60).

The bases of the theory of surplus value, which Lenin characterized as the "cornerstone" of Marx' economic doctrine (*ibid.*, vol. 23, p. 45), were set forth by Marx during the 1850's, as he was working on the manuscript "A Critique of Political Economy" (1857–58), the initial version of *Das Kapital*. Marx revealed the mechanism of capitalist exploitation and showed that the capitalists' appropriation of surplus value created by the working class takes place in complete accord with the internal laws of the capitalist mode of production—primarily the law of value. Marx reached the conclusion that the liberation of the working class from exploitation could not be achieved within the framework of capitalism. In this manuscript of 1857–58, the major propositions of the theory of scientific communism, that which concerns the ripening of the material preconditions of communism within the womb of bourgeois society, was developed to a considerable degree. Finally, Marx concluded that capitalism, in comparison to any preceding socioeconomic structure, had a deeper internal capacity to develop productive forces. In the Introduction to the manuscript "A Critique of Political Economy," Marx characterized the scientific method of the ascent from the abstract to the concrete as the method of political economy. The ascent from the abstract to the concrete is the common method of building scientific theory. Many methodological principles of "systems analysis," which later spread as a result of the generalization of the achievements of natural science, were provided by Marx in *Das Kapital*. The first installment of *A Contribution to the Critique of Political Economy*, which contained the theory of value and the theory of money, was published in 1859. In the preface to this work, Marx gave the classic formulation of the materialist interpretation of history.

Marx conducted his economic investigations during the 1850's within the framework of the "six-book plan" that he worked out from 1857 to 1859 (*On Capital, Landed Property, Wage Labor, The State, Foreign Trade,* and *The World Market*). Subsequently, Marx elaborated the most important part of this program in the four volumes of *Das Kapital;* this part formed the content of the section "Capital in General" the first section of the book *On Capital.* (The other sections of this book are "Competition of Capital," "Credit," and "Joint-Stock Capital.")

Marx essentially completed the theory of surplus value in the 1860's, in the process of working on the manuscript of *A Contribution to the Critique of Political Economy*, the second draft of *Das Kapital*.

Marx rewrote the first three volumes of *Das Kapital* (1863–65; the third draft of *Das Kapital*). A major part of this manuscript is the only draft of the third volume of *Das Kapital*. It was on the basis of this draft that Engels, using Marx's later interpolations and additions, published the third volume in 1894. In addition, of the manuscripts of 1863–65, the first of eight drafts of the second volume remained intact, as did Chapter 6, which Marx wrote as the concluding chapter of the first volume; this chapter summed up the analysis of the process of the production of capital and served as a transition to the second volume. (It was published in the *Archive of Marx and Engels*, vol. 2 [7], Moscow, 1933.) The antagonistic contradictions of the capitalist mode of production are analyzed by Marx in their concrete manifestation on the surface of capitalist society in the manuscript of the third volume of *Das Kapital*. Profit is the goal of capitalist production and the fundamental stimulus to its development. But at the same time, this goal limits the development of the productive forces of bourgeois society. The increase in the organic composition of capital results in a tendency for the rate of profit to decline. In developing production, the capitalists strive to compensate for the falling rate of profit by increasing the total amount of profit. This leads to the further increase in the organic composition of capital and to a still greater decline in the rate of profit. This process results in a level of socialization of production for which the framework of capitalist society becomes ever more confining. "The real barrier of capitalist production is capital itself . . . . The means—unconditional development of the productive forces of society—comes continually into conflict with the limited purpose, the self-expansion of the existing capital" (Marx, *op. cit.*, vol. 25, part 1, p. 274).

Having explained that the entire capitalist class exploits the entire working class, in Volume 3, Marx substantiates the necessity for unity of the working class in its struggle against the

"Masonic brotherhood" of capitalists, and he clarifies the influence that the tendency of profit rates to fall has on the workers' situation. The substantiation of the need for surplus labor in communist society also occupies an important place in the work of Marx.

In 1866, Marx began immediate preparations for the publication of the first volume of *Das Kapital*, which appeared in September 1867. In it, on the basis of previous research, Marx examined the process of capitalist production, beginning with the analysis of the commodity as the elementary cell-form of capitalism and the analysis of the twofold character of the labor that creates a commodity.

Capitalist commodity production, the direct result of the development of simple commodity production, is qualitatively different from it in that labor power is turned into a commodity. The analysis of the situation of the working class in capitalist society provided in Volume 1 of *Das Kapital* is based on the all-around analysis of the value of the commodity of labor power; in particular, Marx demonstrated that the rate of surplus value is a mathematically precise expression of the level of exploitation of the worker. "But capital has one single life impulse —the tendency to create value and surplus value, to make its constant factor, the means of production, absorb the greatest possible amount of surplus labor" (*ibid.*, vol. 23, p. 244). Capitalists achieve this goal by two means: the producion of absolute surplus value and the production of relative surplus value. The increase in absolute surplus value collides with the working class's opposition to increasing the working day. Relative surplus value is the result of technical progress, the increase of labor productivity in capitalist society, and the ensuing decrease in the period necessary to reproduce the worker's labor-power, a working day given as a constant magnitude.

Marx examined three stages in the increase of labor productivity and the development of relative surplus value: simple cooperation, the division of labor and the manufactory, and the development of machinery and large-scale industry. At the same time, the stages reflect the process of the socialization of labor occurring under the antagonistic conditions of private capitalist appropriation.

In the first volume of *Das Kapital*, Marx traced the history of the economic struggle of the working class, explained the role of factory legislation in this struggle, analyzed the capitalist application of machinery, and examined in depth the category of wages in its two forms. (The question of the use of machinery under capitalism was examined in detail for the first time by Marx in the second draft of *Das Kapital*.) Analyzing the tendency toward an increase in the organic composition of capital, Marx formulated the general law of capitalist accumulation while he explained at the same time the countervailing tendencies that modify the effect of this law. He formulated the historical tendency of capitalist accumulation thus: "The monopoly of capital becomes a fetter upon the mode of production which has sprung up and flourished along with and under it. Centralization of the means of production and socialization of labor at least reach a point where they become incompatible with their capitalist integument. Thus integument is burst asunder. The knell of capitalist private property sounds. The expropriators are expropriated" (*ibid.*, p. 772–73).

In the years that followed the appearance of Volume 1, Marx continued to work intensively on the manuscripts of the second and third volumes. (In particular, he produced seven manuscripts related to the second volume during the 1870's.) Furthermore, he prepared for publication the second German edition of the first volume (1872) and edited the translation of the first volume into French. (It was published in separate installments between 1872 and 1875.) Marx did not manage to prepare the second and third volumes of *Das Kapital* for publication.

After Marx' death, Engels did a great deal of work to prepare the second and third volumes for publication. He prepared the second volume on the basis of Marx' manuscripts of the 1870's, and it appeared in 1885. Marx had formulated, on the basis of the examination of the processes of capital circulation and social reproduction (simple and extended), the law of the realization of the social product in capitalist society. As he had demonstrated, the normal functioning of these laws presupposes the proportional distribution of the social product among the branches of production. But under capitalism, the conditions of realization "change into so many conditions of abnormal movement, into so many possibilities of crises, since a balance is itself an accident owing to the spontaneous nature of this production" (*ibid.*, vol. 24, p. 563).

In 1894, Engels published the third volume of *Das Kapital* on the basis of Marx' manuscript of 1863–65. Studying capitalist relations in the form in which they emerge on the surface of bourgeois society (commodity-trade and money-trade capital, loan capital, credit, and land rent), Marx noted the further intensification of capitalist contradictions and evidence of the historically transient nature of capitalism.

Das Kapital not only contains the solution of the paramount theoretical problems of Marxist political economy but also poses new problems requiring further elaboration. Thus, in the third volume of *Das Kapital*, Marx calls attention to the fact that the real movement of market prices is related to the doctrine of competition, which falls outside the framework of *Das Kapital* (*ibid.*, vol. 25, part 2, p. 324). Characterizing the analysis of credit and the money market in the third volume, Engels noted that it contained "much that is new and still more that is unresolved concerning this question; consequently, along with new solutions, there are new problems" (*ibid.*, vol. 38, p. 108).

The supplements to the third volume, which Engels wrote in 1895, were aimed primarily at eliminating difficulties in understanding the problems of the third volume and secondarily at analyzing new phenomena that had been established in the economy of capitalism. Studying the development of capitalism, Engels was able during the last years of his life to note such new phenomena in the capitalist economy as the rapid development of joint-stock companies and of trusts and the growing role of the stock exchange and the banks in the development of industry, the export of capital, and the division of colonies—the phenomena that signal the transition to monopoly capitalism, or imperialism. The Leninist theory of imperialism was the direct continuation and development of Marx' economic theory.

In 1883 and 1890, Engels published the third and fourth German editions of the first volume of *Das Kapital* and edited the translation of this volume into English. (The English edition appeared in 1886.) Engels also published a second German edition of the second volume of *Das Kapital* (1893). Lenin wrote of the second and third volumes: "Indeed these two volumes of *Das Kapital* are the work of two men: Marx and Engels. . . . Engels erected a majestic monument to the genius who had been his friend, a monument on which, without intending it, he indelibly carved his own name" (*Poln. sobr. soch.*, 5th ed., vol. 2, p. 12). In his letters of 1883–95, Engels repeatedly mentioned his intention to prepare for publication, in the form of a fourth, concluding volume of *Das Kapital*, the manuscript of the *Theories of Surplus Value* from the second draft of *Das Kapital*. However, his death prevented him from doing this. The *Theories of Surplus Value* was first published in the years 1905–10 by K. Kautsky, who made arbitrary changes and substantial abridgments of the text. The first genuinely scientific edition of the *Theories* . . . was made by the Institute of Marxism-Leninism of the Central Committee of the CPSU in the years 1954–61 and made up a fourth volume of *Das Kapital*.

Das Kapital comprises four volumes in the second edition of the *Works* of K. Marx and F. Engels: volumes 23–25 (parts 1–2) and volume 26 (parts 1–3). The 46th (supplementary) volume of *Works* includes the first draft of *Das Kapital*. Only the study of *Das Kapital*, along with its drafts, provides a complete notion of the economic legacy of Marx and makes it possible to enter into his creative laboratory and to trace all sides of the process of the creation of Marx's economic doctrines.

Das Kapital was published in nine languages while Marx and Engels were alive. The first translation of the three volumes of *Das Kapital* was the translation into Russian. (The volumes were published in 1872, 1885, and 1896 respectively.) By mid-1972, *Das Kapital* had been published in 40 languages outside the USSR. In the USSR, it has been published in 22 languages of the peoples of the USSR, with total editions of 6,701,000 copies.

If bourgeois science of the 19th century made every attempt possible to hush up *Das Kapital*, the 20th century has been marked by countless attempts of "Marxologists" of all sorts to refute Marx' economic doctrine or to distort its revolutionary content. According to the "Marxologists," *Das Kapital* has "become obsolete." Some bourgeois or revisionist theoreticians, who do not deny the importance of *Das Kapital* in gaining an understanding of modern capitalism, attempt to separate Marx the researcher from Marx the revolutionary. However, the revolutionary conclusions of Marx' economic theory are inseparable from the theory itself. The course of the historical development of humanity completely confirms the worldwide historical role of the proletariat as the creator of communist society, a role discovered by Marx and Engels and scientifically substantiated in *Das Kapital*. The importance of *Das Kapital* for the practice of the international workers' movement under contemporary conditions continues to grow.

REFERENCES
Marx, K., and F. Engels. *Soch.*, 2nd ed., vol. 16, pp. 211–23, 231–323; vol. 20, p. 150–326; vol. 23, p. 5–40; vol. 24, p. 3–28; vol. 25, part 1, p. 3–26; vol. 26, part 1, p. *v–xxvi*; vol. 46, part 1, p. *v–xxiv*.
Marx, K., and F. Engels. *O "Kapitale."* (Letter.) Moscow, 1968.
Lenin, V. I. *Poln. sobr. soch.*, 5th ed., vol. 1, p. 129–40; vol. 23, pp. 1–4, 40–48; vol. 26, pp. 43–93; vol. 29, pp. 131, 162, 301, 318.
Leont'ev, L. A. *O predvaritel'nom variante "Kapitala" Marksa.* Moscow-Leningrad, 1946.
Leont'ev, L. A. *Problemy ravenstva v "Kapitale" K. Marksa.* Moscow, 1960.
Leont'ev, L. A. *"Kapital" K. Marksa i sovremennaia epokha.* Moscow, 1968.
Leont'ev, L. A. *Engel's i ekonomicheskoe uchenie marksizma.* Moscow, 1965.
Rozenberg, D. I. *Ocherki razvitiia ekonomicheskogo ucheniia Marksa i Engel'sa v sorokovye gody XIX veka.* Moscow, 1954.
Rozenberg, D. I. *Kommentarii k I–III tomam "Kapitala" K. Marksa.* Moscow, 1961.
Il'enkov, E. V. *Dialektika abstraktnogo i konkretnogo v "Kapitale" Marksa.* [Moscow] 1960.
Malysh, A. I. *Formirovanie marksistskoi politicheskoi ekonomii.* Moscow, 1966.
"Kapital" K. Marksa i politicheskaia ekonomiia sotsializma. Edited by L. I. Abalkin. Moscow, 1967.
Malyi, I. G. *Voprosy statistiki v "Kapitale" Karla Marksa.* Moscow, 1967.
Uroeva, A. V. *Kniga, zhivushchaia v vekakh.* Moscow, 1967.
"Kapital" K. Marksa i problemy sovremennogo kapitalizma. Edited by N. A. Tsagolov and V. A. Kirov. Moscow, 1968.
"Kapital" Marksa: Filosofiia i sovremennost'. Moscow, 1968.
Metod "Kapitala" i voprosy politicheskoi ekonomii sotsializma. Edited by N. A. Tsagolov. Moscow, 1968.
Ocherki istorii ideinoi bor'by vokrug "Kapitala" K. Marksa, 1867–1967. Moscow, 1968.
Lapin, N. I. *Molodoi Marks.* Moscow, 1968.
Pevzner, Ia. *Metodologiia "Kapitala" K. Marksa i sovremennyi kapitalizm.* Moscow, 1969.
Vygodskii, V. S. *K Istorii sozdaniia "Kapitala."* Moscow, 1970.
Tuchscheerer, W. *Bevor "Das Kapital" entstand.* Berlin, 1968.

V. S. Vygodskii   [11–1030–1]

KAPITONOV, IVAN VASIL'EVICH. Born Feb. 10 (23), 1915, in the village of Serovskoe, in present-day Sasovo Raion, Riazan Oblast. Soviet state and party figure. Hero of Socialist Labor (1975). Member of the CPSU since 1939.

The son of a peasant, Kapitonov graduated from the Moscow Institute of Municipal Construction Engineering in 1938 and served as a senior engineer and section chief in construction. Kapitonov has held party and Soviet posts since 1941: he was at first secretary of a primary party organization and then secretary of the Krasnaia Presna City-Raion party committee. He was elected chairman of the raion executive committee of the Krasnaia Presna City-Raion of Moscow in 1947 and appointed chief of a department of the Moscow city committee of the ACP (Bolshevik) in 1948. After holding the post of secretary and second secretary of the Moscow oblast party committee in 1951–52, Kapitonov was elected first secretary of the Moscow city committee of the CPSU in 1952, first secretary of the Moscow oblast committee of the CPSU in 1954, and first secretary of the Ivanovo oblast committee of the CPSU in 1959 (to 1964). In

1964, Kapitonov became chief of a department of the Central Committee of the CPSU and in 1965, secretary of the CC. A delegate to the Nineteenth through Twenty-fourth Party Congresses, he was elected member of the CC CPSU at the Nineteenth, Twentieth, Twenty-second, Twenty-third, and Twenty-fourth Congresses. Kapitonov was a member of the Bureau on the RSFSR of the CC CPSU from 1964 to 1966, a deputy to the third through Ninth convocations of the Supreme Soviet of the USSR, and a member of the Presidium of the Supreme Soviet of the USSR from 1954 to 1962. He was awarded three Orders of Lenin, three other orders, and medals.   [11–1062–5]

KAPITONOV, VIKTOR ARSEN'EVICH. Born Oct. 25, 1933, in Kalinin. Soviet athlete; Honored Master of Sport (1958) and Honored Coach of the USSR (1970). Officer in the Soviet Army. Member of the CPSU since 1969.

Kapitonov was the first Soviet athlete to become an Olympic champion in bicycling (1960, Rome, road racing). He was a seven-time champion of the USSR (in 1956–64, in the marathon road race) and winner of the world bicycle race (as a team member) in 1958 and 1961–62. Kapitonov has been awarded the Order of Lenin, the Order of the Badge of Honor, and medals.   [11–1062–4]

KAPITSA, ANDREI PETROVICH. Born July 9, 1931, in Cambridge, England. Soviet geographer and geomorphologist. Corresponding member of the Academy of Sciences of the USSR (1970). Son of P. L. Kapitsa. Member of the CPSU since 1962. Chairman of the Presidium of the Far Eastern Scientific Center of the Academy of Sciences of the USSR (since 1970); member of the Presidium of the Academy of Sciences of the USSR (since 1971). Director of the Pacific Institute of Geography of the Far Eastern Scientific Center of the Academy of Sciences of the USSR.

Kapitsa worked at the department of geography of Moscow State University from his graduation there in 1953 until 1970. He became a professor in 1966 and was dean of the department from 1966 to 1970. Kapitsa participated in four Soviet Antarctic expeditions and in the trans-Antarctic crossings from Mirny Station to Pionerskaia (1956), Mirnyi to the south pole (1959–60), and from Vostok Station through the Pole of Inaccessibility to Molodezhnaia Station (1963–64). In 1967–69 he led the Soviet Complex Geophysical Expedition of the Academy of Sciences of the USSR to East Africa. His major works have dealt with the dynamics and morphology of the Eastern Antarctic ice cap. Kapitsa was awarded the State Prize of the USSR in 1971 for his participation in the creation of the *Atlas of Antarctica*; he also received the Order of the Red Banner of Labor.

WORKS
Dinamika i morfologiia lednikovogo pokrova tsentral'nogo sektora Vostochnoi Antarktidy. Leningrad, 1961. (*Tr. Sovetskoi Antarkticheskoi ekspeditsii*, vol. 19.)
Podlednyi rel'ef Antarktiki. Moscow, 1968.   [11–1064–2]

KAPITSA, PETR LEONIDOVICH. Born June 26 (July 8), 1894, in Kronstadt. Soviet physicist; academician (1939; corresponding member from 1929) and member of the Presidium of the Academy of Sciences of the USSR (since 1957). Hero of Socialist Labor (1945). Son of a military engineer.

Kapitsa worked at the Petrograd Polytechnic Institute after his graduation (1918). In 1921 he was sent on a scientific trip to Great Britain, where he conducted research under the supervision of E. Rutherford. From 1924 to 1932 he was deputy director of the Cavendish Laboratory and, from 1930 to 1934, director of the Mond Laboratory in Cambridge. From 1935 to 1946 and since 1955 he has been director of the Institute of Physical Problems of the Academy of Sciences of the USSR, which he founded. He has been a professor at the Moscow Physicotechnical Institute since 1947. In 1920, working with N. N. Semenov, he proposed a method for determining the magnetic moments of atoms in an atomic beam. In 1923 he was the first to place a cloud chamber in a strong magnetic field and to observe the tracks of alpha particles.

In 1924, Kapitsa proposed the pulse method of generating superstrong magnetic fields and developed a device in which fields of up to 320 kilogauss were produced. In 1928 he observed the linear dependence of the electric resistance of a number of metals on the field intensity in strong magnetic fields (Kapitsa's law). In 1934 he developed a device for liquefying helium by the adiabatic method, in which a piston-driven gas-expansion machine operated with a gaseous lubricant. In 1939 he presented a new method of liquefying air by using a low-pressure cycle accomplished in a high-efficiency expansion turbine (State Prize of the USSR, 1941), which is used widely to produce gaseous and liquid oxygen in large quantities.

In 1938, Kapitsa discovered the superfluidity of liquid helium (State prize of the USSR, 1943) and showed that on transfer of heat from a solid (such as the walls of a vessel) to liquid helium, a temperature jump (Kapitsa's temperature jump) occurs at the interface. In 1947 he conducted studies of wave and thermal processes in moving thin layers of fluid and developed the quantitative theory of the interaction of sea waves with the wind. In 1955 he presented a hydrodynamic theory of lubricated rolling and suggested the idea that ball lightning is by nature a stationary superhigh-frequency discharge in the atmosphere. In 1950–55 he developed new types of superhigh-frequency generators, the planotron and the nigotron, with a power of up to 300 kilowatts in the continuous mode, and observed that during high-frequency discharge in dense gases a stable plasma column in which the electron temperature is assumed to be 10^5–10^6 °K is formed. This work, published in 1969, opened up a new direction for research in controlled thermonuclear fusion.

Since 1955, Kapitsa has been editor in chief of *Zhurnal eksperimental'noi i teoreticheskoi fiziki* (Journal of Experimental and Theoretical Physics). He is a member of the Soviet National Committee of the Pugwash Conference. He is a member of the London Royal Society (1929), The National Academy of Sciences of the United States (1946), the Danish Royal Academy of Sciences (1946), the Swedish Royal Academy of Sciences (1966), the Polish Academy of Sciences (1963), and many other foreign academies and scientific societies. Kapitsa has received five orders of Lenin, the Order of the Red Banner of Labor, and medals.

WORKS

Elektronika bol'shikh moshchnostei. Moscow, 1962.
Zhizn' dlia nauki. Moscow, 1965.
Teoriia, eksperiment, praktika. Moscow, 1966.
Fizicheskie zadachi. Moscow, 1972.
Collected Papers, vols. 1–3. Oxford, 1964–67.

REFERENCES

" Akademik Petr Leonidovich Kapitsa (k 60-letiiu so dnia rozhdeniia)." *Zhurnal eksperimental'noi i teoreticheskoi fiziki,* 1954, vol. 27, fasc. 3.
Alekseevskii, N. E. "Petr Leonidovich Kapitsa (k 70-letiiu so dnia rozhdeniia)." *Uspekhi fizicheskikh nauk,* 1964, vol. 83, fasc. 4. (Contains a bibliography of Kapitsa's works.) P. E. RUBININ [11–1065–1]

KAPITSA'S LAW, an empirical law that established the dependence of the electric resistance of polycrystalline metal objects in strong magnetic fields on the magnetic field intensity. According to Kapitsa's law, the electric resistance of polycrystalline samples of metals in a strong magnetic field increases proportionally to the magnetic field intensity. The law was discovered by P. L. Kapitsa in 1928 in pulsed magnetic fields with an intensity of up to 350,000 oersteds. Kapitsa's law has been established most clearly for copper, gold, and silver.

[11–1066–1]

KAPITSA'S TEMPERATURE JUMP, a phenomenon in superfluid liquid helium, discovered by P. L. Kapitsa in 1941, that consists in the fact that upon transfer of heat from a solid to liquid helium a temperature difference arises at the interface. Kapitsa's temperature jump was subsequently found to be a common physical phenomenon at low temperatures: it arises at the interface of any mediums when there is a thermal flux from one medium to the other.

The temperature jump is

$$\Delta T = RQ = \frac{A}{T^3} \cdot Q$$

where Q is the thermal flux density and T is the temperature, and the factor A depends on the elasticity of the substances in contact.

Experiments have established that at the interface between lead and superfluid helium at temperature $T = 1.3°K$ and stationary thermal flux density $Q = 10$ watts per sq m (W/m²), the temperature jump is $\Delta T = 0.011°K$. Thus $R = 1.1 \times 10^{-3}$ m² · deg/W, and the coefficient $A = 2.4 \times 10^{-3}$ m² · deg⁴/W. For other metals, under the same conditions and when the surface is treated in an identical manner, the coefficient R has values close to this.

In the scientific literature the quantity R, as well as the phenomenon discovered by Kapitsa, is often called the thermal resistance of the interface or the interface thermal resistance.

It has been demonstrated theoretically (by I. M. Khalatnikov in 1952) that at low temperatures the heat exchange between a fluid and solid is due to the emission and absorption of sound quanta (phonons) at the interface of the mediums. Because of the great difference in the acoustic resistances of solids and liquids (a factor of several thousand), the coefficient of transmission of sound from one medium to the other is negligibly small: the phonons of the hotter solid are reflected almost totally from the interface. As a result, a finite temperature difference—Kapitsa's temperature jump—arises between the solid and the liquid. The jump is the main obstacle to the cooling of bodies to extremely low temperatures.

REFERENCES

Kapitsa, P. L. "Issledovanie mekhanizma teploperedachi v gelii II." *Zhurnal eksperimental'noi i teoreticheskoi fiziki,* 1941, vol. 11, fasc. 1, p. 1.
Khalatnikov, I. M. "Teploobmen mezhdu tverdym telom i geliem II." *Ibid.,* 1952, vol. 22, fasc. 6, p. 687. K. N. ZINOV'EVA [11–1066–2]

KAPLAN, VIKTOR. Born Nov. 27, 1876, in Mürzzuschlag; died Aug. 23, 1934, in Unterach. Austrian engineer and hydraulic-turbine designer.

In 1900, Kaplan began working in a German higher technical school in Brno; he became a professor there in 1913. Using models in the school's laboratory, he investigated the operation of the hydraulic turbine. Through his attempts to increase their speed, Kaplan became one of the first persons to undertake the design (in 1912) of an axial-flow reactive turbine with rotary blades, for which he obtained a patent in 1920.

REFERENCE

Klishevich, G. "Viktor Kaplan." *Gidrotekhnicheskoe stroitel'stvo,* 1935, no. 8. [11–1068–1]

KAPLANIAN, RACH'IA NIKITOVICH. Born Nov. 14, 1923, in the village of Giargiar, Armenian SSR. Soviet director, actor, and theatrical worker; People's Artist of the USSR (1971). Member of the CPSU since 1947.

Kaplanian graduated from the Yerevan Theatrical School in 1940. He worked as an actor during 1937–50, and during 1953–56 and 1959–62 he was chief director of the Yerevan Young People's Theater. Kaplanian worked as director of the G. Sundukian Armenian Theater (1956–59) and as chief director of the A. A. Spendiarov Armenian Opera and Ballet Theater (1962–65).

In 1968, Kaplanian founded and became chief director of the Yerevan Drama Theater, based on the Theater Studio of the Armenian Theatrical Society, which he had also created. His best productions were Schiller's *Cabal and Love* (1955), Iagdzhian's *Night Miracle* (at the Young People's Theater, 1960), Araksmanian's *Sixty Years and Three Hours* (at the Sundukian Theater, 1964), Armenian's *Khachatur Abovian* (at the Spendiarov Theater), Stock's *Divine Comedy* (1968), *Anush* (based on the work by Tumanian; 1968), Otian's *Love and Laughter* (at the Yerevan Drama Theater, 1970), and Dangulov's *Confession* (at the Malyi Theater, 1970). Kaplanian is the author of several plays. He became chairman of the Armenian Theatrical Society in Yerevan in 1966.

REFERENCE
Rizaev, S. *Hrachya Ghap'lanian.* Yerevan, 1969. [11–1068–2]

KAPLER, ALEKSEI IAKOVLEVICH. Born Sept. 28 (Oct. 11), 1904, in Kiev. Soviet screenwriter. Honored Art Worker of the RSFSR (1969).

Kapler became an actor in 1919, and in 1920, with S. I. Iutkevich and G. M. Kozintsev, he founded the Harlequin Theater in Kiev. He began working in motion pictures in 1926; he acted in several films (*The Overcoat,* for example). In 1929–30 he directed cultural films (movies that popularized various branches of science and technology) based on his own screenplays.

Kapler's first screenplays for feature films were *The Three Comrades* (1935, with T. S. Zlatogorova) and *The Miners* (1937). Two films based on Kapler's screenplays—*Lenin in October* (1937) and *Lenin in 1918* (1939, with T. S. Zlatogorova)—became widely known and began the trend of representing V. I. Lenin in films (the role of Lenin was performed by B. V. Shchukin). His scripts devoted to the Great October Socialist Revolution, the Civil War, and the Great Patriotic War include *She Defends the Fatherland* (1943); *Kotovskii* (1943); *The First Joys* (1956) and *The Extraordinary Summer* (1957), both based on the novels by K. A. Fedin; and *Two Lives* (1962).

Kapler was also the screenwriter of *Behind the Department Store Window* (1956), *The Striped Voyage* (1961, with V. Konetskii), *The Amphibian Man* (1962, based the novel by A. P. Beliaev), *I Accept the Battle* (1966), and the television movie *Faith, Hope and Charity* (1972). He taught at the All-Union State Institute of Cinematography. Kapler was awarded the State Prize of the USSR (1941), the Order of Lenin, the Order of the Badge of Honor, and other medals.

WORKS
"Kukhnia kharakterov." In the collection *Kak my rabotaem nad kinostsenariem.* Moscow, 1936.
Kinopovesti. Moscow, 1962.
Gody, stsenarii, fil'my. Moscow, 1966.
REFERENCE
Iurenev, R. *Aleksei Kapler.* Moscow, 1940. [11–1068–3]

KAPLUN, SERGEI IL'ICH. Born Apr. 27 (May 5), 1897, in the city of Starokonstantinov; died Oct. 22, 1943. Soviet hygienist. Member of the CPSU (1917).

Kaplun graduated from the medical department of Moscow University in 1917. Between 1918 and 1927 he directed work in the People's Commissariats of Labor of the RSFSR and USSR, with which he developed the first rules and standards for sanitary safety in labor in the history of the USSR. In 1925 (jointly with V. A. Levitskii) he organized the State Labor Protection Institute, of which he was director from 1927 to 1932. In 1924 he was appointed professor and head of the subdepartment of occupational hygiene at the Second Moscow Medical Institute (the first such subdepartment in the USSR). In 1926 he became head of the subdepartment of occupational hygiene at the First Moscow Medical Institute.

Kaplun was the first in the USSR to organize scientific and practical activities in the field of labor sanitation. Under his leadership, rules and directives were established to regulate the provision of compensation for unhealthy working conditions; sections of the Labor Legislation Code dealing with labor sanitation were worked out; and specialized bodies were set up for sanitary, technical, and legal labor inspection. Kaplun was the first industrial-sanitation inspector for the People's Commissariat of Public Health of the USSR. He had a great influence on the future of the field in the USSR. He was the founder (in 1923) and editor of the journal *Gigiena truda* (Occupational Hygiene). In 1943 Kaplun volunteered to serve on the front, where he was killed. He was posthumously awarded the Order of the Patriotic War, Second Class.

WORKS
Sanitarnaia statistika truda. Moscow-Leningrad, 1924.
Osnovy obshchei gigieny truda, parts 1–2. Moscow-Leningrad, 1925–26.
Teoriia i praktika okhrany truda, 3rd ed., parts 1–2. [Moscow] 1926–27.
Obshchaia gigiena truda. Moscow-Leningrad, 1940.
REFERENCE
"S. I. Kaplun." *Gigiena i sanitariia,* 1967, no. 11.
G. A. NIKITIN [11–1069–2]

KAPLUNOVSKII, VLADIMIR PAVLOVICH. Born July 15 (28), 1906, in Kharkov; died Feb. 14, 1969, in Moscow. Soviet artist and motion picture director; Honored Artist Worker of the RSFSR (1968).

Kaplunovskii graduated from the Kiev Institute of Art (theater and film department) in 1928. His first films were *Transbalt* (1930) and *Dress Rehearsal* (1931); Kaplunovskii's most important work as a set and costume designer were *The Lonely White Sail* (1937), *The Tractor Drivers* (1939), *Iakov Sverdlov* (1940), *The Dream* (1943), *Two Soldiers* (1943), *Spring* (1947, with K. N. Iefimov), *Glinka* (1947), *The Fall of Berlin* (1950), *Business People* (1963), and *Kidnapping Caucasian Style* (1967). In the 1950's he began directing films, most notably *The Mexican* (1956, based on the work by J. London), *The Captain's Daughter* (1958, based on the Pushkin novella), and *Liubushka* (1961). He received the State Prize of the USSR (1947, 1950) and the Order of the Badge of Honor.

REFERENCE
Batrakova, S. "Khudozhnik v kino." In the collection *Mosfil'm,* vol. 2. Moscow, 1961. G. A. MIASNIKOV [11–1069–3]

KAPNIST, VASILII VASIL'EVICH. Born Feb. 12 (23), 1758 (according to other data, 1757), in the village of Velikaia Obukhovka, in present-day Mirgorod Raion, Poltava Oblast; died Oct. 28 (Nov. 9), 1823, in the village of Kibintsy, in present-day Mirgorod Raion, Poltava Oblast. Russian writer.

Kapnist was a son of a rich Ukrainian landowner. From 1770 to 1775 he served in the Guards in St. Petersburg. There he joined the circle of poets who gathered around G. R. Derzhavin. From 1783, Kapnist lived in Obukhovka. He began publishing his works in the magazine *Sankt-Peterburgskii vestnik.* His *Satire I* (1780), written in verse, brought him fame. The writer's moderate ideals of enlightenment were reflected in it. Many of Kapnist's poems depict the everyday life of the Ukraine of his time and its natural scenery ("Obukhovka" and "In Memory of the Smooth-leaved Elm," for example). *The Ode on Slavery* (1783, published in 1806) contained a strong protest against the enslavement of the Ukrainian peasants. His most important work is a comedy in verse, *The Chicane* (1793–98), a sharp satire on the bureaucracy and the court, which was banned after the first few performances (1798). This play was on the theater repertoire until the 1840's (the contemporary production was prepared in 1970). Kapnist's preromantic poetry (odes, elegies, anacreontic verses) played an appreciable role in the development of literature in the period preceding Pushkin.

WORKS
Sobr. soch., vols. 1–2. Moscow-Leningrad, 1960.
REFERENCES
Berkov, P. N. *V. V. Kapnist.* Leningrad-Moscow, 1950.
Matsai, A. I. *"Iabeda" V. V. Kapnista.* [Kiev] 1958.
XVIII vek: Sb., vol. 4. Moscow-Leningrad, 1959. Pages 257–312.
[11–1070–2]

KAPOK, the fibers from the fruits of the ceiba plant (*Ceiba pentandra*), or silk-cotton tree, of the family Bambacaceae. The plant is native to tropical America; it is cultivated in the tropics, particularly in Asia. These white or brownish fibers have a length of 10–35 mm and a thickness of 0.02–0.04 mm. They are soft and form on the inner side of the husks not on the seeds. The fibers are nonwettable and do not become matted. In water, kapok is several times more durable than cork. After they are separated from the seeds and fruit parts, the fibers are dried, sorted, and compressed into bales. Kapok is used as a filling for life buoys, life jackets, furniture, mattresses, and pillows. It is also used as sound and heat insulation. [11–1072–2]

KAPOSVÁR, a city in southwestern Hungary, south of Lake Balaton; administrative center of the *megye* (district) of Somogy. Population, 54,000 (1970). Kaposvár is a transportation junction. There is light industry (cotton-spinning and clothing factories) and food industry (flour, sugar, meat-packing and dairy, and cheese-making), as well as production of electrical-engineering items (transformers, cable, and so on) and apparatus, parquet, and cement. [11–1074–1]

KAPOVA CAVE (also Kapovaia Cave and Shul'gan-Tash), one of the largest caves in the Southern Urals, on the right bank of the Belaia River, in the Bashkir ASSR. The cave was formed in the limestones and dolomites of Devonian age. The corridors and grottos are located on two levels and total more than 2 km long.

The zoologist A. V. Riumin discovered Paleolithic paintings in Kapova Cave in 1959. The paintings were studied by O. N. Bader between 1960 and 1974. There are drawings of mammoths, horses, and rhinoceroses on the second level of the cave, 300 m down from the entrance. The figures measure 44 to 112 cm long. The representations are silhouettes completely filled in with red pigment or undelineated contours. The presence of the mammoth and rhinoceros in the paintings makes it possible to date those of the second level to the Upper Paleolithic (probably, the time of the early Magdalenian). Red geometric representations have been discovered in the rear halls of the first level; these representations are in the form of ladders, huts (?), triangles, diagonal lines, and anthropomorphic figures. They also probably date from the Paleolithic. There are similar drawings on the second level of the cave.

REFERENCE
Bader, O. N. *Kapovaia peshchera: Paleoliticheskaia zhivopis'.* Moscow, 1965. O. N. BADER [11–1071–1]

KAPP, ARTUR IOSIFOVICH. Born Feb. 16 (28), 1878, in Suure-Jaani, in present-day Viljandi Raion, Estonian SSR; died there Jan. 14, 1952. Soviet composer; Honored Art Worker of the Estonian SSR (1945); a founder of professional Estonian music.

Kapp graduated from the St. Petersburg Conservatory, where he studied organ (1898) with L. F. Gomilius and composition (1900) with Rimsky-Korsakov. During 1920–24 he was conductor of the Estonia Theater in Tallinn. In 1920 he also began teaching, he was a professor at the Tallinn Conservatory during 1925–43. He composed symphonic works, concertos, instrumental ensembles, organ pieces, choruses, and songs. The Estonian composers E. Aav, E. A. Kapp, and G. G. Ernesaks were among his students. Kapp received the State Prize of the USSR in 1950. [11–1074–2]

KAPP, EUGEN. Born May 13 (26), 1908, in Astrakhan. Soviet composer and public figure; People's Artist of the USSR (1956). Member of the CPSU since 1947.

Kapp studied piano under P. Ramul and A. Lemba during 1928–31 and composition under his father, A. I. Kapp, after 1926 at the Tallinn Conservatory. He became an assistant in the music theory course at the conservatory in 1935, a lecturer in 1944 (professor in 1947), and the director in 1952 (until 1965). He was chairman of the Composers' Union of the Estonian SSR during 1944–66.

Kapp contributed to the establishment and development of a national music culture. He composed the first Soviet Estonian opera, *Fire of Vengeance* (1945); the first ballet, *Kalevipoeg* (Son of Kalev; 1947), based on themes from epic folk literature; and the first Estonian children's opera, *Winter Fairy Tale* (1958). His other compositions include the opera *Freedom Singer* (1950), the ballet *The Gold Spinners* (1956), symphonies, choral and chamber works, and piano pieces.

Kapp was a deputy to the fourth and fifth convocations of the Supreme Soviet of the USSR. During 1951–61 he was a member of the Central Committee of the Communist Party of Estonia. He received the State Prize of the USSR in 1946, 1949, and 1952. He was awarded the Order of Lenin, three other orders, and medals.

REFERENCES
Poliakovskii, G. *Eugen Kapp.* Moscow-Leningrad, 1951.
Kõrvits, H. *Eugen Kapp.* Moscow, 1959. [11–1074–3]

KAPPEL', VLADIMIR OSKAROVICH. Born Apr. 16 (28), 1883; died Jan. 25, 1920, in the village of Nizhneozernaia, near Nizhneudinsk. White Guard lieutenant general (1919), descendant of a noble family of Kovno Province.

Kappel' graduated from the Nicholas Cavalry School in 1903 and from the Academy of the General Staff in 1913 and fought in World War I. In the Civil War of 1918–20 he was at first commander of the troops of Komuch (Committee of Members of the Constituent Assembly), which operated on the right bank of the Volga near Syzran', Simbirsk, and Kazan from June to August 1918; he then commanded the Volga Corps of Kolchak's army, which was defeated by the Red Army in May–June 1919. From June to October the corps commanded by Kappel' operated in the region of Cheliabinsk and on the Tobol River. During the retreat of the White Guards toward Omsk, Kappel' headed the so-called Moscow group of troops. In November 1919, he became commander of the Third Army, and in December 1919 Kolchak appointed him commander in chief of the Eastern Front. Kappel' died during the retreat of the White Guards from Irkutsk. The remnants of Kolchak's troops in Transbaikalia and in the Far East called themselves *kappelevtsy* ("Kappelovites"). [11–1075–2]

KAPPEL, WARS OF, two wars fought in 1529 and 1531 in Switzerland between the Protestant cantons, primarily Zürich, and the Catholic cantons of Schwyz, Uri, Unterwaldern, Zug, and Luzern. The wars of Kappel reflected the bitter social and political struggle in Switzerland during the Reformation. H. Zwingli, the leader of the Swiss Reformation, died in the second war of Kappel, in which the forces of Zürich were crushed near the town of Kappel on October 11. According to the peace concluded in November 1531 the league of Protestant cantons was disbanded and Catholicism was restored in some of them.

REFERENCE
Sprüngli, B. *Beschreibung der Kappelerkriege.* Edited by L. Weisz. Zürich, 1932. [11–1075–3]

KAPP PUTSCH OF 1920, an unsuccessful counterrevolutionary coup d'etat in Germany.

The Kapp putsch was organized by German monarchists, Junkers, the most reactionary circles of banking and industrial capital, and militarists; the big landowner W. Kapp and the generals E. Ludendorff and W. von Lüttwitz were among its leaders. The conspirators, who relied on the Free Corps and on some segments of the Reichswehr, aimed at overthrowing the coalition government headed by the Social Democrats, crushing the bourgeois democratic republic, and establishing an open military dictatorship. On March 10, Lüttwitz moved units of the Free Corps on Berlin and presented an ultimatum to the government demanding the dissolution of the national assembly and the election of a new president and refusing to reduce the size of the Reichswehr as provided for by the Treaty of Versailles of 1919. The government did not deal resolutely with the rebels. On March 13 the putschists occupied Berlin and formed their own government headed by Kapp. President F. Ebert and the government abandoned the capital and moved to Stuttgart. The working class, large sections of the middle classes, and the pro-republican bourgeois circles came out in defense of the republic. A general strike that involved 12 million people broke out in the country. Communists and left-wing members of the Social Democratic Party and of the Independent Social Democratic Party as well as nonaffiliated workers actively opposed the putschists. Through the unity of action of the toiling masses the Kapp putsch was liquidated in five days; Kapp fled to Sweden on March 17. The revolutionary struggle had its greatest scope in the Ruhr. The Red Army, which was created under the leadership of the Communist Party and left-wing members of the Independent Social Democratic Party, cleansed the Ruhr of the putschists. Upon returning to the capital, the president and the government, who feared the armed people more than they feared the putschists, crushed the revolutionary movement with the help of the militarists. The Kapp putsch and the events accompanying it greatly weakened the authority of the opportunistic leaders of the Social Democratic Party and of the Independent Social Democratic Party and accelerated the leftward movement of the German working class.

REFERENCES
Lenin, V. I. *Poln. sobr. soch.*, 5th ed., vol. 41, p. 78.
Pankevich, F. I. *Kappovskii putch v Germanii.* Moscow, 1972.
Arbeiter Klasse siegt über Kapp und Lüttwitz, vols. 1–2. Berlin, 1971.
Könnemann, E., and H. J. Krusch. *Aktionseinheit contra Kapp-Putsch.* Berlin, 1972. D. S. DAVIDOVICH [11–1076–1]

KAPSUKAS (until 1955, Marijampolė), a city and administrative center of Kapsukas Raion, Lithuanian SSR, on the Šešupe River (a tributary of the Nemunas). Railroad station on the Kaunas-Kaliningrad line, 60 km southwest of Kaunas. Population, 30,000 (1971). Equipment is manufactured for packing food products and automobile parts. The city has a cannery, sugar refinery, creamery, textile mill, and factory for the production of furniture. Prefabricated reinforced-concrete structures are also manufactured. Kapsukas is the site of a sovkhoz technicum, a pedagogical school, and a school of culture. A museum of local lore and a branch of the Kaunas Drama Theater are also there. Kapsukas was first established in the 18th century. Its name was changed in honor of V. S. Mickevicius-Kapsukas, a leader in Lithuania's revolutionary workers' movement.

[11–1083–3]

KAPTEREV, PETR FEDOROVICH. Born July 7 (19), 1849, in the village of Klenovo, in present-day Podol'sk Raion, Moscow Oblast; died Sept. 7, 1922, in Voronezh. Russian educator and psychologist.

Kapterev graduated from the Moscow Divinity School in 1872. He taught education and psychology in high schools and higher educational institutions in St. Petersburg, and he was an active member of the St. Petersburg Committee for Literacy and various pedagogical societies. He was one of the organizers of the first Congress on Family Upbringing and the first All-Russian Congress on Educational Psychology (1906). Kapterev demanded the creation of a single school system accessible to all levels of the population. He believed the first step in this direction to be the conversion of the elementary school to a six-year program with courses equivalent to the courses given in city schools. After the revolution he worked in the city of Ostrogozhsk, Voronezh Oblast, and became a professor of education at the University of Voronezh.

Kapterev wrote works on the theory and history of education, including *The New Russian Pedagogy: Its Main Ideas, Trends, and Proponents* (1897) and *A History of Russian Pedagogy* (1910). His principal contribution was the attempt to create a psychologically sound didactics. In *Essays on Didactics* (1885) and *The Process of Education* (1905) he worked out such problems of education as the goal and tasks of instruction, the choice of subjects of a course and their distribution, and the methods of teaching.

Kapterev's *Tasks and Principles of Family Upbringing* (1898; 2nd ed., 1913), *On the Nature of Children* (1899), *On Children's Games* (1898), and *Encyclopedia of Family Upbringing and Instruction,* of which he became editor in 1898, made valuable contributions to the development of the science of family upbringing.

Kapterev was a prominent representative of empirical psychology in Russia. He wrote a number of works on child psychology and educational psychology, which, he believed, consist of three elements: general psychological data, developmental psychology, and a theory of emotional types (*Educational Psychology,* 1877). In elaborating his theory of the types of emotional life (*From the History of the Psyche: Essays on the History of the Mind,* 1890), Kapterev reexamined and developed the typological concepts of P. F. Lesgaft, A. S. Virenius, and T. Ribot.

REFERENCES
Kuz'min, P. M. "K voprosu o pedagogicheskikh ideiakh P. F. Kaptereva." *Sovetskaia pedagogika*, 1940, nos. 4–5.
Korolev, F. F. *Ocherki po istorii sovetskoi shkoly i pedagogiki, 1917–1920.* Moscow, 1956. Pages 476–78.

Tkachenko, V. G. "Pytanyia psikholohii v pratsiakh P. F. Kaptereva." In *Narysy z istorii vitchyznianoi psykholohii kintsia XIX i pochatku XX stolittia.* (Collection of articles edited by G. S. Kostiuk.) Kiev, 1959. [11–1087–5]

KAPTEYN, JACOBUS CORNELIUS. Born Jan. 19, 1851, in Barneveld; died June 18, 1922, in Amsterdam. Dutch astronomer; specialist in stellar astronomy.

Kapteyn received the doctor of philosophy degree in 1875 from the University of Utrecht.

From 1875 to 1878 he worked at the University of Leiden. He also worked at the University of Groningen, where he became a professor in 1878. From 1896 to 1900, Kapteyn published a survey catalog of 454,875 stars of the southern sky, compiled on the basis of a large amount of photographic material. In 1906 he worked out a plan for investigating the stellar sky by means of studying 206 selected areas evenly distributed throughout the sky. In 1904 he proposed a theory according to which the motions of the stars with respect to each other (the peculiar motions of stars) are not random but prefer two opposite directions in space (a theory that has not been confirmed). He worked out a number of methods for statistically studying the Milky Way Galaxy.

REFERENCE
Hertzsprung, M. H. *J. C. Kapteyn, zijn leven en werken.* Groningen, 1928. [11–1087–3]

KAPUAS, a river in the western part of the island of Kalimantan, Indonesia.

The Kapuas is 1,040 km long and has a basin area of 97,000 sq km. It originates in the Kapuas Mountains and flows for 165 km in the mountains; further downstream, it flows primarily through a marshy plain and forms a delta, emptying finally into the South China Sea. The Kapuas is full of water throughout the year, but especially in April and November (the months of maximum precipitation, when extensive areas are covered with flood waters). The Kapuas River is the chief route into the inner regions of Kalimantan. Ships with a draft up to 2 m can sail as far as Putussibau (902 km); ships with a 3-m draft can reach Sintang (465 km). The large port of Pontianak is located in the delta. There is fishing and timber rafting on the river.

[11–1088–2]

KAPUR, RAJ. Born Dec. 14, 1924, in Peshawar. Indian actor, motion-picture director, and producer.

Kapur was both actor and artist in the theater of his father, Prithviraj Kapur. In the 1940's he became a screen actor. In 1947 he founded Raj Kapur films (Bombay) and directed his first film the following year. Kapur's popularity came with *The Tramp* (1951), *Master 420* (1955), *Under the Cover of Night* (1957), and *I Am a Clown* (1970), all characterized by elements of protest against caste prejudices and social injustice. Kapur is an original lyricocomic actor and dancer with great charm and musicality.

REFERENCE
Sokol'skaia, A. L. "Raj Kapur." In *Aktery zarubezhnogo kino.* Moscow-Leningrad, 1965. Pages 88–94. [11–1089–1]

KAPUSTIN, MIKHAIL NIKOLAEVICH. Born Jan. 11, 1828, in Ekaterinoslav Province; died Nov. 11, 1899, in St. Petersburg. Russian jurist, an expert on civil and international law and on the history of the state and law.

From 1852 to 1870, Kapustin was a professor at Moscow University, and from 1870 to 1883 he was director of the Demidov Lyceum in Yaroslavl. In 1883 he became the superintendent of the Dorpat (Tartu) school district and in 1891 of the St. Petersburg school district. Kapustin was the first in Russia to write systematic handbooks on international law. In 1898 he was a member of the arbitration tribunal in the dispute between France and the Netherlands over Guiana. Kapustin attached a great importance to the historical method in jurisprudence, but many of his works were dogmatic in nature and were written in the spirit of legal positivism.

WORKS

Obozrenie predmetov mezhdunarodnogo prava. Moscow, 1856.
Istoriia prava i obshchestva v Zapadnoi Evrope. Moscow, 1866.
Istoriia prava, vol. 1. Yaroslavl, 1872.
Mezhdunarodnoe pravo. Yaroslavl, 1873.
Institutsii rimskogo prava. Moscow, 1881. [11–1092–1]

KAPUSTINSKII, ANATOLII FEDOROVICH. Born Dec. 16 (29), 1906, in Zhitomir; died Aug. 26, 1960, in Moscow. Soviet physical chemist. Corresponding member of the Academy of Sciences of the USSR (1939).

Kapustinskii was a professor at the universities of Gorky (1934–37), Kazan (1941–43), and Moscow (1945–49), the Moscow Steel Institute (1937–4!), and the Moscow Institute of Chemical Engineering (1943–60). His main works deal with the physical chemistry of metallurgical processes and the determination of the heat of formation of inorganic compounds. Kapustinskii proposed an equation for lattice energy, developed a thermal method for determining ionic radii, experimentally established the isotope effect for crystal-lattice energy, and proposed a theory of the thermal capacity and entropy of ions in solution. Kapustinskii was awarded the Order of the Red Banner of Labor and several medals.

WORKS

Fizicheskaia khimiia metallurgicheskikh protsessov, vol. 1. Moscow-Leningrad, 1933.
Termodinamika khimicheskikh reaktsii i ee primenenie v metallurgii i neorganicheskoi tekhnologii, 2nd ed. Moscow-Leningrad, 1935.
Khimicheskie ravnovesiia v neorganicheskikh sistemakh. Moscow-Leningrad, 1936.
Ocherki po istorii neorganicheskoi i fizicheskoi khimii v Rossii. Moscow, 1949.

REFERENCE

"A. F. Kapustinskii." Moscow, 1958. *(Materialy k biobibliografii uchenykh SSSR: Seriia khimicheskikh nauk,* issue 26.) [11–1092–3]

KAPUSTIN YAR, an urban-type settlement in Vladimirovka Raion, Astrakhan Oblast, RSFSR. Kapustin Yar is situated on the left bank of the Akhtuba River (a branch of the Volga), 3 km from the Kapustin Yar railroad station on the Volgograd-Astrakhan line. Population, 10,000 (1970). [11–1092–2]

KAPUSTNIK, a comic humorous performance. In prerevolutionary Russia *kapustniki* were organized by the actors for a small circle of invited guests, usually during Lent. (The name originated from *kapusta,* or cabbage, a traditional lenten meal.)

The first *kapustniki* were organized in Moscow as private performances of parodies and jokes by the Society of Art and Literature in 1888–91. Later such evenings were held at the Moscow Art Theater (MKhT), where, in 1910, admission was first charged (the receipts went for the support of the theater's needy actors). The main organizer and permanent master of ceremonies of the MKhT *kapustniki* was N. F. Baliev. Letuchaia Mysh' (The Bat), the best prerevolutionary miniature theater, based on the MKhT performances, was founded in 1908.

Soviet *kapustnik* evenings are organized in literary-theatrical circles, primarily on anniversaries and holidays. *Kapustniki* are popular as amateur performances focusing on local current events. [11–1095–1]

KAPUTDZHUKH (also Kapydzhik), the highest point of the Zangezur Range, on the border of the Nakhichevan' ASSR and the Armenian SSR. Elevation, 3,904 m. Permafrost and glaciers cover the peak. [11–1096–1]

KAPUTIKIAN, SIL'VA BARUNAKOVNA (also Sirvard Barunakovna Kaputikian). Born Jan, 5, 1919, in Yerevan. Soviet Armenian poet. Honored Cultural Worker of the Armenian SSR (1970). Member of the CPSU since 1945.

Kaputikian graduated from the department of philology of the University of Yerevan in 1941. Her work was first published in 1933. Her first book of verses, *In These Days,* appeared in 1945. She has written the collections *Verses* (1947, Russian translation), *On the Banks of the Zanga* (1947), *My Kith and Kin* (1951; Russian translation, 1951; State Prize of the USSR, 1952), *Bon*

Voyage (Russian translation, 1954), *A Frank Talk* (1955), and *Thoughts at Midpoint* (1960; Russian translation, 1962). Kaputikian's deeply emotional poetry deals with the joy of a people who have been reborn, the new life of Soviet Armenia, the problems of relating art to reality, and the emotional and intellectual world of contemporary man. Kaputikian has been awarded the Order of the Red Banner of Labor.

WORKS

[Kaputikyan, S.] *Bari ert'.* Yerevan, 1957.
K'aravannere derh k'aylum en. Yerevan, 1964.
Yot'kayaranner (Banasteghts.). Yerevan, 1966.
Im eje. Yerevan, 1968.
Depi khork'e lerhan. Yerevan, 1972.
In Russian translation:
Moia stranitsa. [Introductory article by Iu. Surovtsev.] Moscow, 1970.
Karavany eshche v puti. Yerevan, 1970.

REFERENCES

Istoriia armianskoi sovetskoi literatury. Moscow, 1966.
Manukyan, S. "Silva Kaputikian." *Sovetakan grakanut'yun,* 1959, no. 8. AR. GRIGORIAN. [11–1096–2]

KARA, a river running chiefly along the border between Arkhangel'sk and Tiumen' oblasts, RSFSR.

The Kara is 257 km long and drains a basin area of 13,400 sq km. It arises on the slopes of the northern end of the Polar Urals and flows into Baidarata Bay (the Kara Sea), fed chiefly by melting snow and rain. It freezes over in October and thaws in June. The Kara is navigable in its lower reaches. [11–1099–1]

KARABAGI, USTA GAMBAR. Born in the 1830's, in the city of Shusha, present-day Nagorno-Karabakh Autonomous Oblast; died there in 1905. Azerbaijani ornamental painter.

Karabagi created colorful ornamental paintings with floral and animal motifs in the palace of the Sheki khans in Skehi (Azerbaijan SSR) and in the houses of Rustamov and Mekhmandarov in Shusha. His works were executed in egg tempera.

REFERENCE

Miklashevskaia, N. M. "Stennye rospisi Azerbaidzhana 18–19 vekov." In *Iskusstvo Azerbaidzhana,* [vol.] 4. Baku, 1954. Pages 52–83. [11–1099–3]

KARABAGLIAR, a settlement, 40 km northwest of Nakhichevan. It is the site of a partially preserved complex of medieval structures. There is a brick mausoleum (first half of the 14th century) and a pair of minarets (12th century). Portions of the portals connecting the minarets have also been preserved. The mausoleum is in the shape of a tower. Its exterior walls are semicylindrical and are faced with decorative turquoise bricks. The four portals are adorned with polychromatic majolica.

REFERENCES

Bretanitskii, L. S. [et al.]. "Arkhitekturnyi kompleks v selenii Karabagliar." In the collection *Arkhitektura Azerbaidzhana: Epokha Nizami.* Moscow-Baku, 1947.
Bretanitskii, L. *Zodchestvo Azerbaidzhana XII–XV vv. i ego mesto v arkhitekture Perednego Vostoka.* Moscow, 1966. Pages 170–76. [11–1099–4]

KARABAIR HORSE, a saddle and pack horse of local breed produced in Uzbekistan by crossing the ancient Middle Asian Argamak breed with Mongolian, Turkmen, and Arabian breeds.

The Karabair horse is medium-sized and rather awkwardly built. The coat is gray, bay, or chestnut (rarely, black). Three types are found in the breed: a thickset type, approaching the proportions of the draft horse; a saddle horse; and a saddle and pack animal. Horses of the first type are bred chiefly in the valleys of regions of irrigated agriculture; the latter two types are bred in the mountainous regions of Uzbekistan and Tadzhikistan. The Karabair is adapted to herd life. It can be saddled, loaded with packs, or hitched as a draft animal. Its fastest time for 1 km over smooth terrain is 1 min 14 sec; for 1,600 m, 1 min 53 sec; and for 2,400 m, 2 min 52 sec. The Karabair approaches the heavy draft horse in carrying capacity. The breed is raised in the Uzbek SSR, the Tadzhik SSR, and the Karakalpak ASSR, and development of the breed is carried on at the Dzhizak Stud Farm in the Uzbek SSR.

REFERENCES
Shchekin, V. A., and V. S. Vikhrev. *Karabair.* Tashkent, 1947.
Kniga o loshadi, vol. 1. Edited by S. M. Budennyi. Moscow, 1952.
V. A. SHCHEKIN [11–1100–1]

KARABAKH, a mountain range in the Lesser Caucasus, in Nagorno-Karabakh Autonomous Oblast, Azerbaijan SSR. The Karabakh Range extends from the Terter River to the valley of the Araks, rising to an altitude of 2,725 m at Mount Beiuk-Kirs. It is made up primarily of sedimentary and volcanic rock. Oak forests cover its slopes. It is separated from the Karabakh Upland by the Akera River, which flows along the range's southwestern slope. [11–1101–1]

KARABAKH HORSE, a mountain saddle horse of very ancient origin, raised between the Araks and Kura rivers in the Nagorno-Karabakh region.

In the course of breeding, the Karabakh horse has incorporated traits of ancient Iranian, Turkmen, and, later, Arabian horses. In turn, it has itself been used in breeding certain saddle horses of southern Russia and several countries of Western Europe, such as Poland and France. The Karabakh horse is medium-sized, with a height at the withers of 138–140 cm. It is well proportioned and sinewy. Its coat is chestnut, brown, dun, bay, or gray and lemon yellow with a golden or silvery cast. There are two types: a solid, massive, short-legged breed and a breed with longer legs and a lighter body. Karabakh horses are used chiefly as saddle horses. They have the endurance for long journeys and can reach a pace of 10 km/hr, in the mountains. Their record speed on a smooth 1,600 m-track is 2 min 9 sec (1955). The Karabakh horse has been used to improve the local breeds of Transcaucasia. Breeding is conducted on the Agdam Stud Farm in the Azerbaijan SSR.

REFERENCE
Kniga o loshadi, vol. 1. Edited by S. M. Budennyi. Moscow, 1952.
G. G. KHITENKOV [11–1100–5]

KARABAKH KHANATE, a feudal state of the 18th century and early 19th century located between the Araks and Kura rivers in Azerbaijan. Founded in 1747 by Panakh Alikhan (late 1740's–1759), the khanate periodically extended its influence over the khanates of Giandzha, Yerevan, Nakhichevan', and Ardebil. The main occupations of the people were farming, stock raising, and fruit-growing. The craftsmen were renowned for their carpets and leather goods. Ibrahim Khalil-khan (1759–1806) appealed to Russia for protection in 1783 and 1797–99 under threat of imminent seizure of the Karabakh Khanate by Iran and Turkey. In 1805 a treaty was signed ceding the Khanate to Russia. In 1822 the khan administration was abolished and replaced by a Russian military administration.

REFERENCE
Dzhavanshir, A. *O politicheskom sushchestvovanii Karabakhskogo khanstva (s 1747 po 1805 g.).* Baku, 1961. [11–1101–3]

KARABAKH UPLAND, a volcanic lava plateau in Transcaucasia (in the Azerbaijan and Armenian SSR's) between the Zangezur and Karabakh mountain ranges.

The Karabakh Upland reaches a maximum altitude of 3,616 m at Mount Dalidag. The cones of extinct volcanoes rise above the surface of the plateau, reaching 3,581 m at Mount Kyzylbogaz. Detritus, known as *chingily,* is characteristic. Much of the plateau is covered with subalpine meadow. There is livestock ranching in the area. [11–1101–2]

KARA-BALTY, an urban-type settlement in Kalinin Raion, Kirghiz SSR, on the Dzhambul-Rybach'e highway. It is located on the Karabalty River (Chu basin), at the foot of the northern slope of the Kirghiz Range. Railroad station, 60 km west of Frunze. Population, 11,000 (1970). There is a sugar refinery and a food-processing technicum. A plant for the processing of essential oils is located near Kara-Balty. [11–1100–2]

KARABANOVO, a city in Vladimir Oblast, RSFSR. Railroad station, 9 km south of the city of Aleksandrov. Population, 19,000 (1970). There is a cotton combine. An evening textile technicum is located there. Karabanovo was first established in 1846 in connection with the construction of a dye factory. It became a city in 1938. [11–1100–3]

KARABAS, an urban-type settlement in Karaganda Oblast, Kazakh SSR. Railroad station, 34 km south of Karaganda. Population, 9,000 (1970). It has a combine for the production of prefabricated building materials and a plant for the production of reinforced-concrete structures. Karabas is the site of a stone quarry. [11–1100–4]

KARABASH, a city in Cheliabinsk Oblast, RSFSR. It is the terminus (Pirit) of a branch of the Sverdlovsk-Cheliabinsk railroad line. Population, 20,000 (1970). In 1910 a copper smeltery was built there as part of a mining and metallurgical combine (for the extraction of copper and the production of blister copper and zinc concentrates). The blister copper that it produces is now sent to a plant for the processing of electrolytic copper in Kyshtym. Karabash was first established at the beginning of the 18th century. It became a city in 1933.

REFERENCES
Akhmin, L. N. *Karabash.* Cheliabinsk, 1968. [11–1101–4]

KARABASH, an urban-type settlement in Bugul'ma Raion, Tatar ASSR. It is located on the Zai River (tributary of the Kama), on a highway, 27 km northwest of the Bugul'ma railroad station (on the Ul'ianovsk-Ufa line). Petroleum is extracted. Karabash is the site of a plant for the production of asphalt.
[11–1101–5]

KARABEKAUL, an urban-type settlement and center of Karabekaul Raion, Chardzhou Oblast, Turkmen SSR. It is situated on the left bank of the Amu Darya River, 90 km above the city of Chardzhou. It is the site of a people's amateur theater.
[11–1102–1]

KARABI-IAILA, the most extensive limestone massif in the main range of the Crimean Mountains (situated in its central part).

The Karabi-Iaila reaches an altitude of 1,254 m. The northern slope is gentle, but the southern slope is precipitous. Its plateaulike top is bare of forests; at lower altitudes the vegetation is of a steppe-meadow variety. Cirques, cones, and other formations typical of karst are abundant, as are caverns and natural mines.
[11–1102–5]

KARABIL', the hilly uplands in the foothills of the Paropamisus Mountains, between the Murgab and Amu Darya rivers in southern Turkmen SSR.

The Karabil' reaches an altitude of 980 m. The hills are composed of alluvial and proluvial fine-grained, loesslike Neocene and early Anthropogenic sandstones. The terrain slopes from the south to the north and is covered with ephemeral desert and semidesert and ephemeral subtropical steppe. [11–1102–2]

KARA-BOGAZ-GOL (Turkic *kara,* "black"; *bogaz,* "throat" or "passage"; and *gol,* "lake"), a shallow gulf on the eastern shore of the Caspian Sea, in the Turkmen SSR. It is separated on the west from the Caspian by the Kara-Bogaz sandspit, which is cut by the Kara-Bogaz strait (200 m to 1 km wide and about 11 km long). The gulf has an area of 12,000 sq km and a maximum depth of 3.5 m.

The water level of Kara-Bogaz-Gol is 4.5 m lower than the level of the Caspian Sea, which results in a constant flow of water into it from the Caspian at a rate of up to 1 m/sec. (In some parts of the strait the rate of flow is as high as 3 m/sec.) This difference in the levels has led to a deepening of the strait and its transformation into a kind of "marine river," with a waterfall about 4 m high on the strait's lower course and a rapidly growing delta at its mouth. Owing to the high rate of evaporation from the surface of the gulf, its water is extremely saline (280–305 parts per thousand) and turns into brine. Mirabilite is extracted from mineral solutions contained in buried salt beds on the gulf. Bekdash, which is located on the sea side of the Kara-Bogaz sandspit, is a center for the extraction and processing of sulfate. The gulf draws 10–12 cu km of water from the Caspian yearly; in relation to this, a project was worked out in 1972 for the construction of a dam across the strait to regulate the flow into the gulf.

REFERENCES
Charyev, B. Ch. *Kara-Bogaz-Gol.* Ashkhabad, 1950.
Dzens-Litovskii, A. I. *Kara-Bogaz-Gol.* Leningrad, 1967.

O. K. LEONT'EV [11–1102–6]

KARABUDAKHKENT BURIAL GROUNDS, earthen burial grounds of different periods, with the dead buried in a flexed position, found in the vicinity of the village of Karabudakhkent (Lenin Raion, Dagestan ASSR). They were investigated by K. F. Smirnov in 1950–51. The oldest one, left by the local stock raisers, dates from the early Bronze Age (first half of the second millennium B.C.). The articles found in the burials included clay vessels and copper tools and ornaments. Several burials of the early Iron Age (about the middle of the first millennium B.C.) were uncovered nearby. Two more burial grounds (dating from the turn of the Common Era) have been left by the indigenous inhabitants, possibly the Udins. Vestiges of ancient local traditions have been traced in their culture, as well as the influence of the Sarmatians and particularly of the population of Caucasian Albania.

REFERENCES
Munchaev, R. M., and K. F. Smirnov. "Arkheologicheskie pamiatniki bliz sela Karabudakhkent (Dagestanskaia ASSR)." In the collection *Materialy i issledovaniia po arkheologii SSSR,* no. 68. Moscow-Leningrad, 1958.
Smirnov, K. F. "Gruntovye mogil'niki albano-sarmatskogo vremeni u seleniia Karabudakhkent". In the collection *Materialy po arkheologii Dagestana,* vol. 2. Makhachkala, 1961.

K. F. SMIRNOV [11–1103–1]

KARABÜK, a city in northern Turkey, in Zonguldak vilayet. Located on the Ankara-Zonguldak railroad line. Population, 65,000 (1970). It is the site of a metallurgical complex.

[11–1104–1]

KARABULAK, an urban-type settlement and center of Taldy-Kurgan Raion, Taldy-Kurgan Oblast, Kazakh SSR. It is situated in the foothills of the Dzungarian Alatau. The settlement has a railroad station 17 km southeast of the city of Taldy-Kurgan. Population, 21,000 (1970). Industry includes a sugar-refining combine and a flour-milling and mixed feed combine as well as a brick yard. [11–1103–2]

KARABULAK, an urban-type settlement in Sunzha Raion, Chechen-Ingush ASSR. It is situated on the Sunzha River and has a railroad station on the Groznyi-Beslan line. Industry includes plants producing dry reagents, asphalt concrete, and gasoline. [11–1103–3]

KARA BURAN KOL, a lake in western China, on the eastern part of the Kashgar Plain, at an altitude of 831 m. It has an area of 88 sq km (as much as 250 sq km including periodically flooded marshes and reeds). The Cherchen River flows into the lake, and so does the Tarim River in years abundant in water. At such times the lake overflows and its water flows eastward into Miran Kol, a neighboring lake. Most of the lake is between 1 and 2 m deep, but near the mouth of the Cherchen it is up to 10 m deep. The lake's water is fresh in the north but salty in the south, its mineral content varying widely. [11–1103–4]

KARABURNU, a late-ripening table variety of grapes. It is also known as the Aleppo, Datie-de-Beirut, and Aphiz-Ali grape. It originated in Turkey. The Karaburnu grape is cultivated in Bulgaria, Turkey, Italy, and the USSR. It is grown in the Moldavian SSR, the Ukrainian SSR, and the Kirghiz SSR. There are long-range plans for the cultivation of this grape in Transcaucasia and

the Kazakh SSR, as well as in certain regions of the RSFSR. The fruit is large (27 mm long; 20 mm wide), oblong, greenish white, and golden. Its thick, crunchy, sugary pulp has a pleasant taste. In Turkey and Syria it is used in fresh, dried (raisins), and pickled form. It can be used in compotes and jam.

[11–1103–5]

KARACHAEVSK (Mikoian-Shakhar until 1944, Klukhori from 1944 to 1957), a city (since 1929) in the Karachai-Cherkess Autonomous Oblast (part of Stavropol' Krai, RSFSR). It is located on the Kuban' River (at its confluence with the Teberda River), at an elevation of 900 m, on the Sukhumi Military Road, 45 km south of the Dzheguta railroad station (terminus of the branch from the Armavir–Mineral'nye Vody line), 60 km southwest of Cherkessk. Population, 15,000 (1970). Industries include a tool plant, food industry, and the manufacturing of building materials. Karachaevsk is the site of a pedagogical insitute.

REFERENCE
Laipanov, S. Z. *Karachaevsk.* Cherkessk, 1968. [11–1190–1]

KARACHAI-BALKAR, the language of the Karachais and Balkars, who live mainly in the Karachai-Cherkess Autonomous Oblast and the Kabarda-Balkar ASSR. It is spoken by approximately 110,900 Karachais and approximately 58,300 Balkars (1970 census). It belongs to the Kipchak group of Turkic languages. Its main dialects are Karachai-Baksan-Chegem (the *ch* [*č*] dialect) and Malkar (the *ts* [*c*] dialect).

Karachai-Balkar is characterized by the loss of initial *y* in certain words (*akhshi,* "good," instead of *yakhshi*), first and second person singular affixes and genitive case affixes without a final consonant (*-ma/-me* rather than *-man/-men, -sa/-se* rather than *-san/-sen,* and *-nï/-ni* rather than *-nïn/-nin*), traces of a vigesimal system in the numerals, and lexical borrowings from Adyg and Ossetian (Ossetic). The Karachai-Balkar literary language is based on the Karachai-Baksan-Chegem dialect. The Karachai-Balkar writing system, which is based on the Russian alphabet, was created in 1936.

REFERENCES
Borovkov, A. K. "Ocherki karachaevo-balkarshoi grammatiki." In the collection *Iazyki Severnogo Kavkaza i Dagestana,* vol. 1. Moscow, 1935.
Akbaev, Sh. Kh. *Fonetika dialektov karachaevo-balkarskogo iazyka.* Cherkessk, 1963.
Khabichev, M. A. "Karachaevo-balkarskii iazyk." In *Iazyki narodov SSSR,* vol. 2. Moscow, 1966.
Russko-karachaevo-balkarskii slovar'. Moscow, 1965.
Qarachay-malqar tilni grammatikasi. Nal'chik, 1966. (Includes bibliography.) [11–1181–2]

KARACHAI-CHERKESS AUTONOMOUS OBLAST (Karachai-Cherkessia), part of Stavropol' Krai, RSFSR. Established on Jan. 12, 1922, it has an area of 14,100 sq km and a population of 352,000 (1972). It comprises seven raions, three cities, and eight urban-type settlements. Cherkessk is the oblast's center.

Natural features. The oblast is situated on the northern slope of the Greater Caucasus, west and north of El'brus, and extends from the summit of the Glavnyi, or Vodorazdel'nyi, Range in the south to the foothills of the Caucasus in the north. The highest peaks of the Glavnyi Range are Pshish (3,790 m), Dombai-Ul'gen (4,046 m), and Gvandra (3,984 m). To the north lies the Bokovoi Range, in which is found the highest point in the oblast, El'brus (5,642 m; along the border with the Kabarda-Balkar ASSR). The main passes are Klukhori and Marukha. The northern part of the region is occupied by cuesta ridges, of which the highest is the Skalistyi Range (Mount Bermamyt, 2,643 m). In the extreme north elevations are less than 500 m.

The climate changes with altitude zones. In January and February the average temperature ranges from −5°C in the north (in the foothills) to −10°C or lower in the south (at high altitudes); in July and August temperatures range from 21°C in the north to 8°C or lower in the south. The frost-free season ranges from 182 days in the north to 75–50 days or less in the south. Annual precipitation ranges from 550 mm (less than 500 mm in the basin of the upper reaches of the Kuban') to 2,500 mm or more. There is contemporay glaciation on El'brus and on the summits and crest of the Glavnyi Range. The main rivers—the Kuban' and its tributaries, the Teberda, the Bol'shoi Zelenchuk and Malyi Zelenchuk, the Urup, and the Bol'shaia Laba—have mixed feeding, including glacial water; high-water occurs in spring and summer. The rivers are used for hydroelectric power and irrigation.

In the north the soil is chernozem. Toward the south, as elevation increases, the chernozems give way to mountain-forest brown soil and mountain-meadow soil. The steppe vegetation of the foothills is replaced by forest steppe with meadow steppe and meadows along the crests of the cuesta ridges. In the mountains further south the steppe gives way to broadleaf forests (beech, white beech, and oak), and in the upper reaches of river valleys the steppe gives way to coniferous forests (pine, spruce, and fir) and subalpine and alpine meadows. The area covered by forests totals 344,000 hectares. The forests and high-mountain areas are inhabited by brown bears, lynx, wildcats, stone and pine marten, wild boars, red and roe deer, chamois, and turs. Birds include snow cocks and black grouse; squirrels and raccoons have become acclimatized. Alpine flora and fauna are preserved and studied at the Teberda Preserve and part of the Caucasus Preserve (in the western part of the oblast).

Population. The oblast is inhabited by Karachai (28.2 percent, 1970 census), Cherkess (9 percent), Russians (47.1 percent), Abazas (6.6 percent), Nogai (3.2 percent), Ukrainians, Ossets, and Greeks. Population density averages 25 per sq km (1972). The northern portion of the oblast is the most densely settled (in Adyge-Khabl' Raion, up to 54 per sq km), and the southern region is the least populated (in Karachaevsk Raion, seven per sq km). About 119,000 persons, or 34 percent of the population, are urban dwellers. Cherkessk (73,000 inhabitants in 1972), Karachaevsk, and Teberda are the principal cities.

Historical survey. The ancestors of the Karachai and Cherkess peoples have inhabited the territory of present-day Karachai-Cherkess Autonomous Oblast from time immemorial, as is shown by archaeological finds at the Stone Age sites of Kardonik, Ovechka, and Iavora. Relics dating from the fifth to the 13th century (Rim-gora, Adiiukhskoe Gorodishche) attest to the disintegration of the primitive communal system and to the emergence of feudal relations. In the 9th and 10th centuries the area was part of the early feudal state of Alania, which maintained political and economic ties with Byzantium, the Khazars, and the Georgians. By the tenth century the formation of the Adyg-Cherkess nationality had been completed, and in the 13th and 14th centuries the Karachai people evolved. The inhabitants engaged in livestock raising and farming. Between the 14th and 16th centuries the Abazas migrated to the area from Abkhazia, followed in the 17th century by the Nogai, who came from the Azov and Volga regions. The region suffered incursions by the Crimean-Turkish feudal lords from the 15th to the 18th century. The mountain people sought protection against these raids through an alliance with the Russian state. Missions were sent to Moscow in 1552, 1555, and 1557, resulting in a political alliance with Russia. In 1790 the Russian army, aided by bands of mountaineers, routed the Turkish corps of Batal Pasha near present-day Cherkessk.

Karachai-Cherkessia was incorporated into Russia in the first half of the 19th century, and the region's inclusion in the mainstream of Russia's development broke the isolation of the natural economy and led to the disintegration of the commune. At the same time, the oppression of the toiling masses increased: the peasants were deprived of the best land; the mountaineers were subjected to requisitions and fines; privileges were enjoyed solely by the local feudal lords; and Russian civil servants staffed the administrative apparatus and courts. Cossack *stanitsy* (villages) were founded in Karachai-Cherkessia between 1858 and 1861. Along with the *auly* (mountain villages) of Karachai and Cherkessia, the *stanitsy* became part of Batalpashinsk District, and later, of the Kuban' Region. Serfdom was abolished in 1868. In the postreform period, mines, quarries, and small enterprises of the food industry were opened. Despite the colonial policy of the tsarist government, ties between the workers who had migrated from Russia and the indigenous people expanded and were strengthened, exerting a positive influence on the economy, life,

and culture of the peoples of Karachai and Cherkessia. The working people were drawn into the revolutionary struggle of the Russian working class and peasantry. During the Revolution of 1905–07 a Social Democratic circle was organized in the *stanitsa* of Batalpashinskaia, and there were peasant uprisings in Dzheguta, Khurzuk, Teberda, and other *auly*.

Soviets of workers' and soldiers' deputies, as well as organs of the bourgeois Provisional Government, called citizens' committees, arose after the February Revolution of 1917. The October Revolution of 1917 liberated the peoples of Karachai and Cherkessia from social and national oppression. In February 1918, the working people established Soviet power, and the Executive Committee of the Soviets of Batalpashinskaia District was formed. The region was controlled by White Guards from the fall of 1918 through March 1920, when Soviet power was reestablished as a result of the victory of the Red Army in the Northern Caucasus. Revolutionary committees and a district committee of the RCP (Bolshevik) were formed. The decrees of the Soviet government were carried out, and the land confiscated from the landlords was distributed among the toiling peasantry. The Karachai-Cherkess Autonomous Oblast was established by a resolution of the All-Russian Central Executive Committee on Jan. 12, 1922. In 1926, Karachai-Cherkessia was divided into the Karachai Autonomous Oblast and the Cherkess National Okrug, which became an autonomous oblast in 1928.

In the course of the prewar five-year plans (1929–40), the region's economic and cultural backwardness was overcome, local industry was created, and agriculture was collectivized; collectivization was completed in Cherkessia in 1934, and in Karachai in 1938. Land-use regulations led to the migration of peasants from the mountains and the foundation of new *auly*. A cultural revolution took place: the Karachai and Cherkess acquired alphabets for their native languages, and mountain women became equal members of society. A national working class and intelligentsia developed.

During the Great Patriotic War (1941–45) the peoples of Karachai and Cherkessia fought at the front and took part in the partisan struggle in the Caucasus, Byelorussia, and the Ukraine. About 15,000 persons were awarded orders and medals and 14 received the title Hero of the Soviet Union. In 1942 battles with the fascist German aggressors were fought in Karachai and Cherkessia, and the oblast was occupied from August 1942 to January 1943. In late 1943 and early 1944, the Leninist national policy was violated; the Karachai Autonomous Oblast was abolished and the Karachai resettled in various parts of Kazakhstan and Middle Asia. On Jan. 9, 1957, the united Karachai-Cherkess Autonomous Oblast was established. In 1957, Karachai-Cherkessia was awarded the Order of Lenin for its achievements in socialist construction. Its economic and cultural development has been promoted by the continuous unselfish aid of the peoples of the entire Soviet Union. In 1971 there were 16 Heroes of Socialist Labor in the oblast, and 14,914 workers had been awarded orders and medals of the USSR. The oblast received the Order of Friendship of Peoples on Dec. 29, 1972, in honor of the 50th anniversary of the USSR.   V. P. NEVSKAIA

Economy. Karachai-Cherkessia is an industrial and agricultural region. Between 1922 and 1940, the gross industrial output increased 55 times over and between 1940 and 1971, 18 times over. The leading branches of industry are chemicals and petrochemicals (31.6 percent of the gross industrial output in 1971), food processing (19.7 percent), and light industry (9 percent). Machine-building and metalworking (including electrical engineering), building-materials, wood-products, coal, and ore-mining industries are developing. Power is obtained primarily from hydroelectric power plants on the Kuban' River, linked by high-voltage electrical transmission lines to the united power grid of the Northern Caucasus economic region. In 1971, 884,000,000 kW-hr of electric power were produced, as compared with 4,200,000 kW-hr in 1940. Karachai-Cherkessia is rich in minerals. Coal (194,000 tons in 1971), lead, zinc, copper, minium, limestone, andesite, granite, and marble are extracted.

Industry is found primarily in Cherkessk (65 percent of the gross output). The largest enterprises are plants producing industrial rubber articles, low-voltage equipment, refrigeration machinery, chemicals, and reinforced-concrete structural components; furniture, footwear, and clothing factories; and a meat-packing combine and dairy. The Erken-Shakhar Sugar Refinery, one of the largest in the country, is located in Adyge-Khabl' Raion. In Zelenchuk Raion there is a furniture combine, the Elektroizolit Plant in the *stanitsa* of Kardonikskaia, and a creamery. Urup Raion has the Kurdzhinovo Sawmill and a logging and timber distribution establishment, and Malokarachaievsk Raion has the Pervomaiskii Creamery. In Karachaevsk there are plants producing instruments and reinforced-concrete structural components. Between 1966 and 1970, 13 large-scale enterprises were put into operation, including the Urup mine of the copper ore-dressing combine.

There are 12 kolkhozes and 28 sovkhozes in the oblast (as of early 1972). Agricultural land constitutes about 50 percent of the total area, or 698,300 hectares (ha), of which 26.5 percent was arable land, 24.6 percent hayfields, and 48.1 percent pasture (1971 data). Livestock raising accounts for 60 percent of the gross output, and crop cultivation, 40 percent (1971). The total area under cultivation is 203,000 ha (1971). The chief crops are cereals (64,800 ha), predominantly wheat and corn (about 70 percent). Industrial crops, covering 19,000 ha, are also important, with sunflowers accounting for 38 percent of the planted area and sugar beets for 61 percent. Karachai-Cherkessia provides about half of all the potatoes grown in Stavropol' Krai; truck farming is developing. There are 83,600 ha under feed crops, including silage corn, green fodder, and annual and perennial grasses. Winter wheat, corn, sunflowers, and sugar beets are cultivated chiefly in the northern part of the oblast, and potatoes are grown everywhere. The water of the Kuban' and other rivers, brought in by the Kuban'-Kalaus Irrigation and Water Supply System, is used for irrigation. There are more than 8,000 ha of irrigated land.

Livestock is raised for meat and dairy products, and fine-wool and medium-wool sheep are raised. In 1971 there were 248,000 head of cattle (94,000 cows), 661,000 sheep and goats, and 48,000 hogs; in 1940 livestock numbered 198,000 head of cattle (71,000 cows), 450,000 sheep and goats, and 31,000 hogs. There is some horse breeding, and poultry raising and beekeeping are well developed. A resort and tourist industry is growing at Teberda, Dombai, and Arkhyz.

The Nevinnomyssk-Dzheguta railroad line passes through the oblast for a distance of 50 km. There are 3,783 km (1971) of roads, of which 1,922 km are paved. The Sukhumi Military Road crosses Karachai-Cherkessia. Air routes link the oblast with a number of cities of the Northern Caucasus.

Regional variations. In the northern part of the oblast, leading industries include chemicals, machine building and metal working, light industry, and food processing. In agriculture the chief crops are cereals, and there is sheep herding, cattle raising, dairying, and poultry farming. The main industries in the southern part are mining, woodworking, and food processing. Livestock raising is important, including cattle raising, dairy farming, sheep herding, hog breeding, and beekeeping; the principal crops are cereals.   I. KH. BAIRAMUKOV

Public health. As of Jan. 1, 1972, there were 41 hospitals with 3,200 beds (8.9 beds per 1,000 inhabitants), and 561 doctors (one per 628 inhabitants). The mountain health resort of Teberda and the climatic therapy area of Arkhyz are located in the oblast. There are sanatoriums and houses of rest. Donbaiskaia Poliana, a well-known training center for mountain touring and climbing in the USSR, is located along the upper reaches of the Teberda River. A popular tourist route passes through the valley of the Kuban' to its confluence with the Teberda, on to the Klukhori Pass (where the Severnyi Priiut tourist center is located), and then along the valley of the Kodori River to Sukhumi. Over 60 tourist and mountaineering routes branch out from the Kuban' Valley; Teberda is the starting point for most mountain touring and climbing routes. The Dombai-Ul'gen wall, with an elevation of about 1,500 m, is widely known among mountaineers. There are mountaineering camps and tourist centers.

Education and cultural affairs. Prior to the October Revolution of 1917, there were 47 schools, primarily elementary, with 2,700 pupils in Karachai-Cherkessia. There were no higher educational institutions. In 1971, 9,300 children were enrolled in 106 preschool institutions. In the 1971–72 school year, there were

84,800 pupils in 209 general-education schools of all types, 5,800 students in six special secondary schools, and 2,600 students in five vocational and technical schools. Higher education is provided by a pedagogical institute (2,100 students) in Karachaevsk and by the general technical department of the Stavropol' Polytechnic Institute in Cherkessk.

The oblast has research institutes of economics, history, language, and literature; an experimental agricultural station; and an astrophysical observatory of the Academy of Sciences of the USSR. As of Jan. 1, 1972, there were 178 public libraries with about 1,500,000 copies of books and journals, 204 clubs, and 199 film projectors. Cherkessk has a museum of local lore, a drama theater, and a palace of pioneers and schoolchildren.

Press and radio. Oblast newspapers include *Leninni bairagy* (Lenin's Banner), published in the Karachai-Balkar language since 1924; *Lenin nur* (Leninist Ray), published in Kabarda-Cherkess since 1924; *Lenin ioly* (Leninist Path), published in Nogai since 1938; *Leninskoe znamia* (Leninist Banner), published in Russian since 1918; and *Kommunizm alashara* (The Light of Communism), published in Abaza since 1938. The oblast radio broadcasts over one station in Karachai-Balkar, Kabarda-Cherkess, Abaza, Nogai, and Russian; broadcasts from Moscow are transmitted.

Literature. The literature of the four indigenous peoples of Karachai-Cherkessia—the Karachai, Cherkess, Abazas, and Nogai—developed in the Soviet period. Prior to the October Revolution, these peoples had no written languages. In the 19th and early 20th century attempts were made to create written languages and to write school textbooks in the native languages. Prominent members in this movement were Islam Teberdichi (I. Akbaev) among the Karachai, Shora Nogmov (1801–44) and Umar Bersei among the Adygeian peoples, and Umar Mikerov and Tatlustan Tabulov among the Abazas. The most important works of oral folklore were the *Narty Epic,* found among the Cherkess, Karachai, and Abazas, and the epic poems of the Nogai.

In the 1920's, with the creation of written languages, the first poems, essays, and short stories appeared. They portrayed the hard life of the working people before the revolution and the protest of the popular masses against exploitation, celebrated the proletarian revolution, and expressed the people's love for the Communist Party and its leader, V. I. Lenin. The literature of this period drew its inspiration from the rich heritage of folklore and from Russian classical and Soviet literature. The most important Karachai literary works were those of the poet A. Urtenov (1907–55), the author of *New Songs* (1927), *Sparks of Freedom* (1929), and *Verses and Poems* (1934); the poet I. Karaketov (1900–42), who wrote *New Poems* (1924) and *Revolutionary Songs* (1931); and the poet D. Baikulov (1902–42). Other noteworthy works included the collection of poems *Zuli* (1929) by the Abaza writer T. Tabulov (1879–1956) and the play *Fatimat* (1932) by the Nogai writer Kh. Bulatukov (1907–37). Prose fiction emerged in the 1930's, represented by the works of several Cherkess writers. Kh. Abukov (1900–37), who wrote the novel *On the Banks of the Zelenchuk* (1930, with V. Chernyshov); M. Dyshekov (1902–37), the author of the novel *The Glow* (1934); and I. Amirokov (born 1909), whose collection of novellas *The Young Brigade Leader* appeared in 1935. Also significant was the novel *The Black Trunk* (1935–36) by the Karachai writer Kh. Appaev (1904–38). National folklore was compiled and published by T. Tabulov and the Nogai writer A.-Kh. Dzhanibekov (1879–1955).

The struggle of the Soviet people against German fascism was depicted in the novella of the Nogai writer F. Abdulzhalilov (born 1913) entitled *Family of the Strong* (1950) and in several narrative poems, notably *The Road of the Bold* by the Cherkess poet Kh. Gashokov (born 1913) and *Zalikhat* (1959) by the Karachai poet Kh. Bairamukova (born 1917).

The literature of Karachai-Cherkessia has been developed intensively in the postwar era. Writers are striving to create a chronicle of the life of the people. Among the novels that have been published are *Rapid Current* (1959) and *Fine Is the Collective's Field* (1966) by F. Abdulzhalilov; *Azamat* by I. Tabulov (1917–59); *The Mountains Awaken* (1962) and *Father's Son* (1970) by Kh. Zhirov (born 1912); the trilogy *Amanat* (1959–63) by O. Khubiev (born 1918); *The Karchi Family* (1962) and *Cholpan* (1970) by Kh. Bairamukova; *Kazma* (vols. 1–2, 1962–65) by Ts. Tsekov; and *Bekbolat* (1970) by S. Kapaev (born 1927). Prominent poets include Kh. Bairamukova (*Spring Noon,* 1966; *Smoke of the Hearth,* 1968), O. Khubiev (*The Oath,* 1963), Kh. Gashokov, and A. Khanfenov (*Humaneness,* 1963).

L. A. BEKIZOVA

Architecture and art. The earliest relics of the art of Karachai-Cherkessia are bronze decorations and ceramics with relief and carved designs found in burial mounds of the third and second millennia B.C. and metal articles and ceramics dating from the 11th to the fifth century B.C. Surviving monuments of the Alani culture include tombs and underground crypts; the ruins of fortified towns, notably the site of Nizhne-Arkhyzskoe on the Bol'shoi Zelenchuk River (tenth to 12th centuries); and Christian cruciform-domed churches in the Byzantine style of the tenth and 11th centuries, such as Mount Shoana, near the Kosta Khetagurov settlement, and the Sentinskii Church near the settlement of Nizhniaia Teberda, in which are found remains of frescoes. In the upper Kuban' Region, the remains of dolmenlike above-ground crypts of the eighth to the 12th century (on some of which are reliefs depicting feasts, dances, and the hunt) and stone statues of warriors (tenth to 12th centuries) have been discovered. The 18th- and 19th-century indigenous dwellings of the Karachai were frame structures with heavy gabled earthen roofs; the Cherkess built houses of clay-coated wattle with reed or straw gabled roofs.

Cities and new settlements appeared in Karachai-Cherkessia in the Soviet period; a general plan has been developed for Cherkessk (1956), and many schools, hospitals, cultural institutions, and modern apartment houses have been built, often with glass-enclosed verandas and with tiled or iron roofs. The fine arts have developed, represented by the graphic artists Ia. G. Kritskii and A. M. Grechkin and by the painters I. G. Akov and M. Kh. Chomaev.

Folk art, gold embroidery, wood carving, and mat weaving with chee swamp grass were well developed in the folk art of the Karachai and Cherkess. In Soviet times the Karachai have excelled in the making of richly decorated felts, and jewelry-making is widely practiced among the Cherkess.

REFERENCES
Ocherki istorii Karachaevo-Cherkesii, vols. 1–2. Stavropol'-Cherkessk, 1967–1972.
Alekseeva, E. P. *O chem rasskazyvaiut arkheologicheskie pamiatniki Karachaevo-Cherkesii.* Cherkessk, 1960.
Alekseeva, E. P. *Karachaevtsy i balkartsy—drevnii narod Kavkaza.* Cherkessk, 1963.
Alekseeva, E. P. "Material'naia kul'tura cherkesov v srednie veka." In *Trudy Karachaevo-Cherkesskogo NII istorii, iazyka i literatury,* issue 4 (history series). [Karachaevsk] 1964. Pages 146–252.
Alekseeva, E. P. *Drevniaia i srednevekovaia istoriia Karachaevo-Cherkesii.* Moscow, 1971.
Nevskaia, V. P. *Karachai v poreformennyi period.* [Stavropol'] 1964.
Fiziko-geograficheskoe raionirovanie SSSR. Moscow, 1968.
Atlas Stavropol'skogo kraia. Moscow, 1968.
Buraev, R. A. *Ekonomiko-geograficheskii ocherk Karachaevo-Cherkesii.* Cherkessk, 1961.
Po leninskomu puti. Cherkessk, 1963.
Napso, D. A. *Pod znamenem internatsionalizma.* Mineral'nye Vody, 1967.
Karaeva, A. I. *Ocherk istorii karachaevskoi literatury.* Moscow, 1966.
Bekizova, L. *Cherkesskaia sovetskaia literatura.* Cherkessk, 1964.
Bekizova, L. *Slovo o nogaiskoi literature.* Cherkessk, 1971.
Tugov, V. B. *Ocherki istorii abazinskoi literatury.* Cherkessk, 1970.
[11–1181–3]

KARACHAIS (self-designation, Karachaily), a people related to the Balkars living in the Karachai-Cherkess Autonomous Oblast. Population, 113,000 (1970 census).

The Karachais speak Karachai-Balkar. The nationality was formed in the 13th and 14th centuries from local mountain tribes, who had lived there since the Bronze Age, and also from Alani, Bulgars, and Kipchaks. Their traditions may be traced in Karachai culture right up to the 20th century. The basic occupation in the past was migratory animal husbandry; settled farming

and trades were secondary. Feudal and patriarchal social ties were preserved among the Karachais until the middle of the 19th century. The inclusion of the Karachais in the general economy of Russia in the 19th century facilitated the development of capitalist relations. The October Revolution freed the Karachais from social and national oppression.

The Karachai-Cherkess Autonomous Oblast was formed in January 1922. Under Soviet power, large-scale mechanized agriculture was created, various branches of industry have developed, and a national working class and intelligentsia were formed. A written language was created, and a national literature developed. Violations of socialist legality led in late 1943 and early 1944 to the resettlement of Karachais in various districts of Middle Asia and Kazakhstan. A decree of the Presidium of the Supreme Soviet of the USSR dated Jan. 9, 1957, restored the national autonomy of the Karachai people and created the Karachai-Cherkess Autonomous Oblast, and almost all the Karachais returned to their native area.

REFERENCES
Ocherki istorii Karachaevo-Cherkesii, vol. 1. Stavropol', 1967.
Alekseeva, E. P. *Karachaevtsy i balkartsy—drevnii narod Kavkaza.* Cherkessk, 1963.
Narody Kavkaza, vol. 1. Moscow, 1960.
Zasedaniia Verkhovnogo Soveta SSSR chetvertogo sozyva: Shestaia sessiia (5–12 fevralia 1957): Stenograficheskii otchet. Moscow, 1957. Pages 577–78, 743–44.
E. N. STUDENETSKAIA [11–1190–2]

KARACHALA, an urban-type settlement in Sal'iansk Raion, Azerbaijan SSR. Situated on the left bank of the Kura River, 15 km south of the Ali-Bairamly station on the Baku-Nakhichevan' railroad line. There is a cotton sovkhoz in Karachala.
[11–1191–1]

KARACHEV, a city and center of Karachev Raion, Briansk Oblast, RSFSR; situated on the Snezhet' River (a tributary of the Desna). It has a railroad station on the Briansk-Orel line, 44 km southeast of Briansk. Population, 16,000 (1970).

The first mention of Karachev in sources dates to the middle of the 12th century. In 1246, after the Tatar invasion, it became the main city of a special appanage founded by Mstislav, the son of Prince Mikhail of Chernigov. At the end of the 15th century, Karachev was granted by Grand Prince Alexander of Lithuania to Prince Simeon Ioannovich of Mozhaisk, who later swore allegiance to Ivan III, grand prince of Moscow; the city served as a Russian outpost against invasions from the Crimea. During the period of Polish-Lithuanian intervention at the beginning of the 17th century, Karachev was destroyed by the Poles. In 1708 it became part of Kiev Province, and in 1732 it was part of Sevsk *provintsiia* in Belgorod Province. From 1778 it was the center of a district in the viceroyalty of Orel, and from 1796 it was the center of a district in Orel Province. Industry in Karachev includes an experimental mechanical plant, an auto spare parts plant, a garment factory, hemp-processing factories, and food industry.

REFERENCE:
Peredel'skii, L. D. *Karachev: Istoriko-ekonomicheskii ocherk.* Tula, 1969.
[11–1191–2]

KARACHI, a city in Pakistan. Located in the delta of the Indus River, 100 km north of where the river flows into the Arabian Sea.

Karachi is the administrative center of Sind Province. The transformation of Karachi into the main political and economic center of the country after the formation of Pakistan (1947) led to the rapid growth of the population, mainly because of the influx of immigrants. From 1947 to 1955, the population increased from 350,000 to 1.5 million; in 1971, the population of Karachi, including the suburbs, reached 4.2 million. Karachi is the largest city of the country. It is a transport junction of international significance: it has a large airport and its seaport is accessible to oceangoing vessels (yearly freight turnover exceeds 9 million tons). The great part of Pakistan's foreign trade is carried out through this seaport.

Approximately one-half of the industrial production of Pakistan is concentrated in Karachi and its suburbs: cotton, food (sugar), tobacco, leather, paper, cement, glass, chemical, and pharmaceutical industries; metalworking and machine-building enterprises (including motor-vehicle assembly factories, railroad workshops, and shipyards); electrotechnical plants; and petroleum refineries. A large metallurgical plant is being constructed near Karachi with the help of the USSR. There are salt evaporation ponds on the seacoast near Karachi. The boards of central banks and insurance and commercial corporations, as well as the stock exchange, are located in Karachi. Many educational institutions, including a university, research institutes, and the National Museum of Pakistan are also there. F. A. TRINICH

The city of Karachi was founded in the 18th century on the site of a Baluchi fishermen's settlement. In 1843, Karachi was captured by the British colonialists and became the administrative center of Sind Province. In the second half of the 19th century Karachi became a British naval base. From 1947 to 1959, Karachi was the capital of Pakistan.

The business center of Karachi, located on the main streets Bunder Road and McLeod Road, has buildings dating mostly from the 19th and 20th centuries, including the Supreme Court (early 20th century, neoclassical style), the Intercontinental Hotel (1962, architects W. B. Tabler and Z. Pathan), and the State Bank (designed in 1954, constructed in 1961). Northwest from Bunder Road up to the Lyari River is the Old City, with narrow streets and one- or two-story houses. Beyond the Lyari is the Sind industrial region. The city has a university (founded in 1951, architect M. Ecoshard) and an art center (1960).

REFERENCE
Pithawalli, M. B. *An Introduction to Karachi.* Karachi, 1950.

[11–1191–3]

KARACHI, a pelotherapy health resort in Novosibirsk Oblast, RSFSR. Located in the northern part of the Barabinsk Lowland, 394 km from Novosibirsk. The summers are warm (the average temperature in July is 19°C), and winters are cold (the average temperature in January is −19°C). Annual precipitation is 270 mm. The therapeutic agents include mud with a high content of hydrogen sulfide and chloride-sulfate sodium-magnesium saline water from Lake Karachi. The mineral water has the formula

$$M_{2.3} \frac{Cl51(HCO_3 + CO_3)45}{(Na + K)\,98\,Ca1} \; T30.0°C \; pH8.2$$

and is used for drinking as part of the treatment. Persons suffering from gynecological diseases and illnesses affecting the supportive and locomotor system, the peripheral nervous system, and the digestive organs are treated. Karachi has a sanatorium, a polyclinic, and a bathhouse with mineral and mud baths.

[11–1192–1]

KARADAG (Turkic, "black mountain"), a mountain massif in the Crimea, on the Black Sea coast. It rises to an altitude of 577 m. The Karadag is the remains of a volcanic cluster of the Lower Jurassic period and is composed of lava and tuff (ranging from basalt to liparite). It consists of a number of ranges and peaks with original forms of weathering. The settlement of Planerskoe (formerly Koktebel') is situated at the foot of the mountains on the east, and the Krymskoe Primor'e health resort is on the west. The Karadag Division of the Institute of the Biology of the Southern Seas of the Academy of Sciences of the Ukrainian SSR is also located there. Nearby are the vineyards of the Koktebel' sovkhoz. The area is important for tourism. [11–1120–5]

KARADAM, an ancient Azerbaijani dwelling, with a wooden roof in the form of a stepped arch. In Armenia such a structure was called a *glkhatun;* in Georgia, a *darbazi.* The *karadam* was common primarily in the Lesser Caucasus, including Nagornyi Karabakh. In some regions these dwellings are still in existence.

REFERENCE
Il'ina, M. *Drevneishie tipy zhilishch Zakavkaz'ia.* [Moscow] 1946.

[11–1121–1]

KARDAR'IA, a river in the Kirghiz SSR and the Uzbek SSR; a left headstream of the Syr Darya River. It is formed by the confluence of the Karakul'dzha and Tar rivers, which rise on the slopes of the Fergana and Alai ranges. Length, 180 km. Basin area, 30,100 sq km.

The Karadar'ia is fed by snow and glaciers. The average discharge at the point where the river leaves the mountains (140 km from its mouth) is 121 cu m per sec, with the greatest discharge occurring in June and the lowest in the winter. Its major tributaries are the Kurshab from the left and the Iassy, Kugart, and Karaunkiur from the right. Its water is used heavily for irrigation in the Fergana Valley, where the Kuigan-Iar Dam has been built on the river and where the Kardar'ia is intersected by the Bol'shoi Fergana Canal. As of 1973, the Andizhan Reservoir was being constructed on the river. The city of Uzgen is located on the Karadar'ia. [11–1121–2]

KARADZHA, STEFAN TODOROV. Born May 1840 or 1842 in the village of Ichme, Iambol Okrug, Bulgaria; died July 1868. Participant in the national liberation struggle of the Bulgarian people against the Ottoman yoke. The son of a peasant.

Karadzha emigrated to Serbia in 1861 and joined the First Bulgarian Legion there in 1862. After the legion was dissolved in September 1862, Karadzha continued the struggle against the Turks. In July 1868, a unit of 125 men led by Karadzha and Khadzhi Dimitr was defeated in battle against superior Turkish forces between the cities of Svishtov and Ruse at the mouth of the Yantra River. Karadzha was seriously wounded and taken prisoner. He was executed by the Turks in the city of Ruse.

[11–1121–4]

KARADŽIĆ, VUK STEFANOVIĆ. Born Oct. 26, 1787, in Tržić; died Jan. 26, 1864, in Vienna. Serbian philologist, historian, and folklorist; figure in the Serbian national renaissance.

The son of a peasant, Karadžić participated in the First Serbian Uprising of 1804–13. He carried out a reform of the Serbian literary language on the basis of the vernacular; he composed a grammar and a dictionary of Serbian. Karadžić's efforts ended in the 1850 agreement between Serbs and Croats on a single literary language and common principles of spelling. After walking and riding through many regions of Serbia, the Voivodina, Montenegro, and Dalmatia, Karadžić collected and published very valuable historical and ethnographic materials. He also published a large number of works from the Serbian oral tradition of lore (his collections *Serbian Folk Tales,* 1821, and *Serbian Folk Songs,* vols. 1–4, 1823–33). He played an important role in the establishment of romanticism in Serbian literature. Karadžić's work was highly esteemed by J. Grimm, J. W. Goethe, and A. Mickiewicz and by the Russian writers and scholars N. M. Karamzin, A. Kh. Vostokov, and I. I. Sreznevskii. He was a corresponding member of the St. Petersburg Academy of Sciences (1851).

WORKS
[*Spisi,* vols. 1–3]. Novi Sad, 1960.
Etnografski spisi—O Crnoj Gori. Belgrade, 1969.
Istorijski spisi. Belgrade, 1969.

REFERENCES
Kulakovskii, P. A. *V. Karadzhich, ego deiatel'nost' i znachenie v serbskoi literature.* Moscow, 1882.
Popović, M. *V. Karadžić.* Belgrade, 1964.
Arhivska građa o Vuku Karadžiću, 1813–1864. Belgrade, 1970.

[11–1122–1]

KARAERI, an urban-type settlement in Khanlar Raion, Azerbaijan SSR, 4 km from the Alabashly railroad station on the Tbilisi-Baku line. A sovkhoz specializing in viniculture and a winery are located in Karaeri. [11–1124–1]

KARAEV, KARA ABUL'FAZ OGLY. Born Feb. 5, 1918, in Baku. Soviet composer and public figure; People's Artist of the USSR (1959); member of the Academy of Sciences of the Azerbaijan SSR (1959). Member of the CPSU since 1949. Member of the CC of the CP of Azerbaijan since 1960.

Karaev graduated from the Moscow Conservatory, where he studied composition with D. D. Shostakovich, in 1946. He was artistic director of the Azerbaijan Philharmonic Orchestra and director of the music section of the Institute of Azerbaijani Art.

The music of Karaev, an innovative artist, is imbued with a lofty spiritualism and philosophical content. Its main theme is struggle for beauty in the life of man. Karaev develops the best traditions of world and national art and seeks new expressive means. His ballets stand among the great achievements of Soviet music—*The Seven Beauties,* based on motifs from Nizami (staged in 1952, Baku) and *The Path of Thunder* (staged 1958 in the S. M. Kirov Leningrad Theater of Opera and Ballet; awarded the Lenin Prize in 1967).

Karaev is the composer of three symphonies (the Third, 1965, is most noted) and a concerto for violin (1967). His other symphonic works include suites from the ballets *The Seven Beauties* and *The Path of Thunder,* the symphonic poem *Leili and Medzhnun* (1947; State Prize of the USSR, 1948), the Albanian Rhapsody (1952), and the symphonic sketches Don Quixote (1960). Karaev also composed the opera *Motherland* (*Veten;* with Dzh. Gadzhiev, 1945; State Prize of the USSR, 1946), art songs, a string quartet (1947), pieces for violin and piano, and music for dramatic productions (more than 20), including Shakespeare's *Antony and Cleopatra* (awarded the M. F. Akhundov Prize, 1965), and motion pictures (more than 20).

Karaev began teaching in 1946; in 1957 he became a professor at the Azerbaijan Conservatory (director, 1949–52). His students included R. Gadzhiev, A. Babaev, and A. Melikov. He became head of the Composers' Union of the Azerbaijan SSR in 1953 and secretary of the Composers' Union of the USSR in 1962. He was a deputy to the fifth through eighth convocations of the Supreme Soviet of the USSR. Karaev was awarded the Order of Lenin, the Order of the October Revolution, and the Order of the Red Banner of Labor.

REFERENCES
Karagicheva, L. *Kara Karaev.* Moscow, 1968.
Kara Karaev: Bibliografiia. Baku, 1969.   E. ABASOVA   [11–1123–3]

KARAGAILINSKII, an urban-type settlement in Kemerovo Oblast, RSFSR. Located 18 km north of the Kiselevsk railroad station. Coal is mined in the area, and Karagailinskii has a concrete plant.   [11–1111–1]

KARAGAILY, an urban-type settlement in Karkaralinsk Raion, Karaganda Oblast, Kazakh SSR. Terminus of a branch of the Kokchetav-Karaganda railroad, 250 km southeast of Karaganda. Population, 5,000 (1970). Karagaily is the site of a combine for dressing complex ores, an asphalt plant, and a dairy.   [11–1111–2]

KARAGANDA, a city and center of Karaganda Oblast, Kazakh SSR; located in the Kazakh Hills. Railroad station on the Petropavlovsk-Chu line. Karaganda has a population of 541,000 (1972; as compared with 154,000 in 1939) and is the second largest city in Kazakhstan (after Alma-Ata).

Karaganda was founded on the site of a miners' settlement that had formed in the center of the Karaganda Coal Basin. In 1932, Karaganda became a city and in 1936, the oblast center. The main branch of industry is coal mining. The city has machine-building plants that produce mining equipment, sanitary engineering equipment, and metal structural elements. Enterprises of such industries as light industry, food industry, and building materials are also located in the city. Karaganda consists of several developed areas that are separated by considerable distances (for example, the Old City dating to the second half of the 19th century, the New City, Maikuduk, Bol'shaia Mikhailovka, and Fedorovka). The center of modern Karaganda is the New City (the master plan of 1934–35, architects A. I. Kuznetsov and A. N. Kornoukhov; a new master plan was approved in 1971). The New City haš a large recreation park and is located on both banks of the Bol'shaia Bukpa River. The main thoroughfares are Sovetskii Prospect, Lenin Prospect, Nurken Abdirov Prospect, and Peace Boulevard. The streets are lined with large public buildings and residential houses, including the

House of Soviets (1938, architect A. M. Genin); a traumatological hospital (1948) and the Miners' Palace of Culture (1952), both by the architect I. I. Brenner; the post office and telegraph office (1953, architect A. K. Belavina); the Sports Palace (1957), and the building of the oblast party committee (1958), both by the architect A. M. Meksel'; the oblast drama theater (1962); the Palace of Pioneers (1967); and the Turist Hotel (1972). The city also has a university; polytechnical, medical, and cooperative institutes; an institute for teachers of physical education; a branch of the Alma-Ata Institute of National Economy; mining, industrial pedagogical, trade and cookery, and evening power construction technicums; a technicum for physical culture and sports; and schools of medicine, music, and culture and education. Karaganda is also the site of two drama theaters (Russian and Kazakh), a museum of local lore, and botanical gardens.

REFERENCES
Konobritskaia, E. M. *Novye goroda Tsentral'nogo Kazakhstana.* Alma-Ata, 1950.
Barag, T. Ia. *Karaganda.* Moscow, 1950.
[Grigor'ev, V.] *Karaganda.* Alma-Ata, 1968.   [11–1111–4]

KARAGANDA, UNIVERSITY OF, founded in 1972. It grew out of a pedagogical institute that opened in 1952. In 1972 the university had departments of philology, history, economics, law, mathematics, physics, chemistry, and biology; preparatory, evening, and correspondence divisions; a graduate school; 37 subdepartments; 40 laboratories; and an agrobiological station. During the 1972–73 academic year, more than 5,000 students were enrolled at the university.   [11–1118–1]

KARAGANDA COAL BASIN, one of the major hard coal basins of the USSR, the third most important source of coal after the Donets and Kuznetsk basins. It is located in Karaganda Oblast, Kazakh SSR. The area of the basin is 3,600 sq km, with a length (from west to east) of 120 km and a width of 30–50 km. The Karaganda Coal Basin is situated in the Kazakh Melkosopochnik.

Coal was discovered in the Karaganda Basin in the middle of the 19th century. At that time primitive coal mining was started to supply the nearby Spasskii Zavod copper smelting plant. The first operational and exploratory shaft mines were sunk in 1930–31. Geological prospecting in the basin developed extensively during the Great Patriotic War (1941–45) and in the postwar period. By 1954, a complete geological and industrial evaluation of the basin had been made. At the base of a thick (up to 4,500 m) coal-bearing series of Carboniferous age lie the Terekty strata of the Lower Visean, which are represented by green and bluish gray clay shales, tuffites, and limestones. The coal-bearing series is composed of alternating layers of sandstones, siltstones, argillites, coals, and, more rarely, conglomerates, limestones, and tuffs and is divided into suites (see Table 1). Lower and Middle Jurassic coal-bearing deposits with a total thickness of up to 600 m and represented by conglomerates, sandstones, argillites, and coals lie with great disconformity on the denuded surface of Carboniferous coal-bearing series. The Lower and Middle Jurassic coal-bearing deposits are overlain by an Upper Jurassic variegated conglomerate-sandstone-siltstone suite. Paleogene and Neocene deposits are represented by red and green clays and sands. Anthropogene deposits consist of loams, sands, and shingles.

Table 1. Suites in the Karaganda Coal Basin

	Age	Thickness (m)	Number of workable seams	Total thickness of coal seams (m)
Shakhan	C_2–C_3?	400	—	—
Tentek	C_2^m	600	10	13
Dolinskoe	C_2^B	700	13	21
Nadkaraganda	C_1^n	600	12	1
Karaganada	$C_1^{V_{2-3}}$	750	17	37
Ashliarik	$C_1^{V_{1-2}}$	500	12	16
Ak-Kuduk	$C_1^{V_1}$	800	—	—

The Karaganda Coal Basin is of the geosynclinal type and forms an asymmetric synclinorium stretching in a latitudinal direction. The northern limb is gentle (10°–30°), while the southern is steep (up to inverted). There are numerous faults, both longitudinal and transverse in relation to the general direction of the folds. The formation of the basin's geological structure is linked mainly with Hercynian folding. An important role in the creation of the present structure was played by Kimmerian movements, which were expressed in major latitudinal thrusts (reverse faults) of Paleozoic rock onto the Jurassic deposits along the southern edge of the basin.

The presence of coal is mostly related to the sediments of the Carboniferous system.

The thickness of workable seams ranges from 0.7 to 2.5 m, with individual seams reaching 7–8 m. Their structure is very complex. The coals are humic and hard. Approximately one-third of the coking coals are easily concentrated. The remainder, as a consequence of high ash content and difficulty of concentration, are power coals. The coals of the Ashliarik and Tentek suites have a high ash content (20–45 percent), while those of the Karanganda (8–25 percent) and Dolinskoe (4–15 percent) suites have a lower ash content. The coals are low-sulfur (sulfur content rarely exceeds 1 percent). Phosphorus content is 0.01–0.1 percent. The working moisture content is 3–6 percent; the combustion heat of the combustible mass is 29.3–35.6 megajoules per kg (7,000–8,500 kilocalories per kg), and the combustion heat of the working fuel is 20.9–25.1 megajoules per kg (5,000–6,000 kilocalories per kg). In terms of the degree of metamorphism (taking the volatile matter yield and caking capacity into account), the coals of the basin are classified in the following ranks: gas, fat, fat coking, coking, coking 2, and lean caking coals.

The presence of coal in the Jurassic deposits is related to lacustrine sediments that formed under continental conditions. The established Dubovka and Mikhailovka suites contain more than 15 lenticular coal seams ranging in thickness from 1m to 5m (rarely more than 20m). The brown coals (B-3 group) have an ash content of 15–22 percent, a sulfur content of 0.01–1.2, and a volatile matter yield of 42–52 percent of the combustible mass. The working moisture content is 9–19 percent; the tar yield is 9–13 percent; the combustion heat of the combustible mass is 26.0–29.7 megajoules per kg (6,200–7,100 kilocalories per kg), and the combustion heat of the working fuel averages 15.2 megajoules per kg (3,620 kilocalories per kg). The Jurassic coals of the Mikhailovskoe deposit are strip mined. The Kumyskudukskoe deposit is being prepared for working by the open-pit method.

The hard coals are being worked intensively by shaft mines. The total geological coal reserves down to a depth of 1,800 m have been estimated at 51.3 billion tons; the commercial reserves as of Jan. 1, 1970, were 7.8 billion tons. In 1971 production reached 39.8 million tons. The consumers of the coking coals are the metallurgical plants of Kazakhstan and the Southern Urals, while the power coals are used by railroad transport, power plants, and industrial enterprises.

In addition to coals, the Karaganda Coal Basin has significant reserves of high-quality underground water, refractory clays, building stone, gypsum, sands, limestones, and marls.

The Karaganda Coal Basin is a major industrial region. Aside from the oblast center of Karaganda, new towns, including Saran', Abai, and Shakhtinsk, have grown up in the basin. Mining machine building, metallurgy (Temirtau), chemistry, power engineering, and other industrial sectors are also developing.

REFERENCE

Kushev, G. L. *Karagandinskii uglenosnyi bassein* [2nd ed.]. Alma-Ata, 1963.   G. L. KUSHEV and A. K. MATVEEV   [11–1117–1]

KARAGANDA METALLURGICAL COMBINE, one of the major metallurgical enterprises in the USSR. It is located in the city of Temirtau, Karaganda Oblast, Kazakh SSR. The combine was formed in 1970 on the basis of the Karaganda Metallurgical Plant. It also includes the Kazakh Metallurgical Plant, the Atasu and Iuzhnyi-Topar ore administrations, and the Alekseevka dolomite quarry. Coking coals from the Karaganda Coal Basin serve as fuel for the combine. The combine produces cast iron, steel, sheet and sectional rolled products, coke, and coke by-products.

The Kazakh Metallurgical Plant was put into operation during the Great Patriotic War of 1941–45. The first open-hearth furnace began operating in 1944, and the first rolling mill in 1946. The Karaganda Plant went into service in 1960. In 1972 the combine consisted of a blast furnace plant with three furnaces, steel casting production (two open-hearth shops and an oxygen converter shop with three converters having a capacity of 250 tons each), rolling mills and coke by-product production, mines and quarries, and a sintering plant. In 1971 the combine produced 2,528,000 tons of cast iron, 3,116,000 tons of steel, and 2,670,000 tons of rolled products.

IU. O. RAEV and P. A. SHIRIAEV   [11–1116–1]

KARAGANDA OBLAST, part of the Kazakh SSR. It was formed on Mar. 10, 1932. Area, 85,400 sq km. Population, 1,223,000 (1974). The oblast has eight administrative raions, six cities, and 16 urban-type settlements. The center is the city of Karaganda. Karaganda Oblast was awarded the Order of Lenin on Oct. 16, 1958.

Natural features. The oblast is located in the northeastern part of central Kazakhstan. Most of it is occupied by the Kazakh hilly region (elevation, 300–1,000 m), from which rise outlier massifs—Kent (elevation, to 1,469 m), the Karkaralinsk Mountains (elevation, to 1,403 m), Karasoran (elevation, to 1,369 m), and Khankashty (elevation, to 1,220 m).

The climate is sharply continental and extremely arid. Summers are very hot and dry (the average July temperature is 22°C in the plains and 18°C in the mountains; the absolute maximum is 43°C), with dust storms and sharp fluctuations in diurnal temperatures. Winters are cold and long, with little snow, strong winds, and snowstorms (the average January temperature is −15°C in the northeast and −17°C in the west; the absolute minimum is −52°C). Annual precipitation totals 250–350 mm in the north, with more than 400 mm in mountainous localities. The growing season lasts 160–180 days.

The major river is the Nura. All the rivers (with the exception of the headwaters of the Ishim in the far north) belong to the landlocked basins of various small lakes. The rivers have little water; in the summer they become very shallow, break up into reaches, and become salty or dry up completely. Water pipelines, reservoirs (the major ones are the Samarkand and Sherubai-Nura), and the Irtysh-Karaganda Canal (495 km long) have been built to supply the industrial centers and agricultural regions with water. There are numerous lakes, most of which are saline (Karasor, for example); many of them are full of water only in the spring. Fresh underground water is also widely used for water supply.

The major part of the oblast has gramineous-wormwood steppes on dark chestnut and chestnut soils. This is the main region of unirrigated farming and virgin-land plowing. In the extreme southwest there is fescue and wormwood vegetation on light chestnut soils. The elevated parts of the uplands have steppes with islands of trees (pine, birch, aspen, and willow) on very rocky chestnut and mountain chernozem soils. In the virgin lands there are numerous rodents (susliks, jerboas, gerbils) and carnivores (wolf and corsac fox). Along the banks of rivers and lakes there are waterfowl.

Population. Karganda Oblast is inhabited by Kazakhs, Russians, Ukrainians, Tatars, Byelorussians, Koreans, Germans, Mordovians, Chuvashes, Bashkirs, Moldavians, and other nationalities. The urban settlements and farmsteads of the new grain sovkhozes are particularly multinational. The average population density is 14.3 persons per sq km. A total of 85.4 percent of the population is urban. Most of the rural population lives in the northern raions. Virtually all the cities of the oblast were founded during the years of Soviet power in connection with mining, the processing of minerals, and railroad construction.

Economy. Large-scale industry, consisting primarily of the extraction and processing of mineral raw materials, predominates. There is also grain farming and livestock raising. Power production is based upon local coal. The largest thermal power plants are in the cities of Abai, Karaganda, and Temirtau. The main branch of industry is coal; the Karaganda Coal Basin supplies fuel not only to enterprises of the Kazakh SSR and the Middle Asian republics but also to ferrous metallurgy in the Urals; in 1973 output was 43.3 million tons. Ferrous metallurgy to a significant degree is based on ore brought in from Kustanai and Dzhezkazgan oblasts. Among the other industries are high metal import machine building (including for the coal industry), the production of building materials (cement, brick, and lime), chemicals, light industry (garments, knitwear, and footwear), and food industry (for example, meat, butter and cheese, various dairy products, flour milling, and confectionery items). The industrial enterprises, most of which are located in and near Karaganda, include the Karaganda Metallurgical Combine, a synthetic rubber plant, and a foundry and machinery works—all in Temirtau—as well as coal industry in the cities of Saran', Abai, and Shakhtinsk. Among the other industrial centers are Aktas (a cement plant) and the urban-type settlements of Osakarovka (a furniture plant), Iuzhnyi (building materials quarrying), and Kushoky (coal mining).

Among the agricultural lands (7.9 million hectares [ha]), pastures (5.4 million ha) predominate. Winter pastures prevail in the southwest and northeast and semideserts and summer pastures in the elevated parts of the hilly region. There are only 1.8 million ha of plowed land. In the years 1954–58, large areas of virgin and fallow lands were developed and grain sovkhozes established in the northern part of the oblast (89 sovkhozes in 1974). In the steppes of the north agriculture combines unirrigated grain cultivation with meat and dairy livestock raising, hog raising, poultry raising, and fine-fleeced sheep raising. Suburban-type agriculture (dairy livestock and vegetables) prevails near the industrial centers. The planted area totals 1,664,500 ha (1973), including almost 70 percent under cereals (1,126,500 ha), with spring wheat being the main cereal. Also raised are barley, millet, and feed crops (516,500 ha), including corn for green feed and perennial grasses. Industrial crops (2,200 ha) include sunflowers, corn flax, and mustard. Potatoes are planted on 14,200 ha and vegetables on 4,100 ha. Sheep and goats (806,200 head as of Jan. 1, 1974) predominate among the livestock. Cattle (353,100 head), horses (52,300), hogs (71,300), camels (1,800), and poultry are also raised.

The length of the railroads totals 581 km (1973). The basic main lines are Tselinograd-Karaganda-Mointy-Chu, with spurs to Temirtau and Karagaily. The major motor roads are Karaganda-Temirtau, Karaganda-Tselinograd, and Karaganda-Karkaralinsk.

O. R. NAZAREVSKII

Education, cultural affairs, and public health. During the 1914–15 academic year, Karaganda Oblast had 79 schools with 4,085 students and no institutions of higher learning. During the 1971–72 academic year there were 351,600 students in 849 general educational schools of all types, 25,700 students in 55 vocational-technical schools, and 23,500 students in 24 secondary specialized schools. A total of 27,300 students were studying at the following institutions: the university; the polytechnical, medical, and co-op trade institutes; the institute for teachers of physical education (all in Karaganda); and at the plant-based higher technical institutes of the Karaganda Metallurgical Combine (in Temirtau). In 1971 there were 86,300 children in 674 preschool institutions.

As of Jan. 1, 1972, the oblast had 730 public libraries (7,651,000 books and journals), an oblast museum of local lore, the Stanislavsky Russian Oblast Dramatic Theater, and the Seifullin Kazakh Oblast Dramatic Theater (in Karaganda). There were 466 club institutions, 355 motion-picture projection units, and various extracurricular institutions such as the Palace of Pioneers, 22 Houses of Pioneers, two stations for young naturalists, six stations for young technicians, a children's railroad, and a hiking station.

The oblast has two newspapers—the Kazakh-language *Ortalyk Kazakhstan* (Central Kazakhstan, published since 1931) and *Industrial'naia Karaganda* (since 1932). Oblast radio and television broadcast one radio program (in Russian and Kazakh) and two television programs (in Kazakh, Russian, and German). Broadcasts are also relayed from Alma-Ata and Moscow. There are television broadcasting stations that produce their own programs in Karaganda, Dzhezkazgan, and Balkhash.

As of Jan. 1, 1972, the oblast had 191 hospital institutions with 22,100 beds (13.7 beds per 1,000 inhabitants) and 4,900 physicians (1 physician per 325 inhabitants).

REFERENCES

Konobritskaia, E. M. *Karagandinskaia oblast' (Ekonomiko-geograficheskaia kharakteristika).* Alam-Ata, 1954.
Narodnoe khoziaistvo Karagandinskoi oblasti: Stat. sbornik. Karaganda, 1967.
Industrial'noe serdtse Kazakhstana (Ekonomiko-geograficheskaia kharakteristika prirody, naseleniia i khoziaistva Karagandinskoi oblasti). Alma-Ata, 1968.
Narodnoe khoziaistvo Kazakhstana v 1968 g.: Stat. sbornik. Alma-Ata, 1970.
Kazakhstan. Moscow, 1969. (The series *Prirodnye usloviia i estestvennye resursy SSSR.*)
Atlas Karagandinskoi oblasti. Moscow, 1969.
Kazakhstan. Moscow, 1970. (The series *Sovetskii Soiuz.*)

[11–1112–1; updated]

KARAGANOV, ALEKSANDR VASIL'EVICH. Born Aug. 24 (Sept. 6), 1915, in the village of Martynovo, in present-day Ustiuzhna Raion, Vologda Oblast. Soviet literary and cinema scholar and critic; doctor of the arts (1969); professor (1970). Member of the CPSU since 1956.

Karaganov graduated from the Moscow Institute of the History of Philosophy and Literature (1939). He began his literary activity in 1931 as a journalist. During 1945–48 he was editor in chief of the magazine *Soviet Literature* (in English). In 1958 he became editor in chief of the Iskusstvo Publishing House and was its director during 1960–64. In 1965 he became secretary of the Cinematographers' Union of the USSR.

Karaganov has been publishing articles on problems of literature, the cinema, and the theater since 1945. He is the author of *Chernyshevskii and Dobroliubov on Realism* (1955), *Characters and Circumstances* (1959), *The Life of a Dramatist: The Creative Path of Aleksandr Afinogenov (1964), The Lights of Smol'ny* (1966), *Cinematographic Meetings* (1969), and *Born of the Revolution: Soviet Film Yesterday and Today* (1970). Karaganov is a teacher (since 1964 at the Academy of Social Sciences under the auspices of the Central Committee of the CPSU). He was awarded the order of the Red Banner of Labor and medals.

[11–1119–2]

KARAGEORGE (Karadjordje Petrović). Born Nov. 14, 1768, in the village of Viševac, Šumadija region; died July 25, 1817, in Radovanje, near Smederevo. Leader of the First Serbian Uprising (1804–13) against the Ottoman yoke.

Karageorge was the son of poor peasants. During the Austro-Turkish War of 1788–90 he headed a Serbian volunteer detachment that fought on the side of Austria. At a gathering of insurgents in February 1804, he was proposed as leader of the uprising. He proved to be a talented military commander and won a number of victories over the Turks. In the area of domestic policy, he fought the influential voivodas, who opposed the centralization of power. In 1808 the State Council and, in 1811, the *skupština* (assembly) of the insurgents acknowledged Karageorge as the supreme Serbian leader. His position was confirmed again in 1811 at a gathering of the insurgents.

Karageorge was the founder of the Karageorgevich (Karadjordjević) dynasty (1808). His foreign policy was directed toward seeking Russian help. After the uprising was put down, he fled to Austria, where he was interned. In 1814 he went to Russia and lived in Bessarabia. He secretly arrived in Serbia in 1817 and was killed on orders from Miloš Obrenović.

REFERENCES

Nenadović, K. *Život i dela velikoga Djordja Petrovića Kara-Djordja,* vol. 1. Vienna, 1883.
Jovanović, S. *Kara-Djordje i njegove vojvode.* Belgrade, 1938.

V. V. ZELENIN [11–1119–7]

KARAGEORGEVICH (Karadjordjević), in the 19th century, a princely dynasty (from 1903 to 1918, the royal dynasty) in Serbia; later the dynasty in the Kingdom of Serbs, Croats, and

Slovenes (1918–29) and in Yugoslavia (1929–45, de facto until 1941).

The founder of the Karageorgevich dynasty was Karageorge (Karadjordje Petrović), who ruled from 1808 to 1813. The members of the dynasty were Alexander (prince from 1842 to 1858), Peter I (king from 1903 to 1921), Alexander I (king from 1921 to 1934), and Peter II (king beginning in 1934). Peter II fled abroad in April 1941, after the occupation of Yugoslavia by fascist troops. On Nov. 29, 1943, the second session of the Antifascist National Liberation Council of Yugoslavia forbade Peter II to return to the country. The abolition of the monarchy was announced in the Constituent Assembly on Nov. 29, 1945.

[11–1119–6]

KARAGIE (Batyr), the deepest land basin in the USSR, reaching a depth of 132 m below sea level. It is located on the Mangyshlak plateau, on the eastern shore of the Caspian Sea. Length, 85 km; width, from 10 to 25 km. The bottom is covered with solonchaks.

[11–1120–1]

KARAGIN GULF, a gulf of the Bering Sea, extending 117 km into the eastern coast of Kamchatka. It reaches depths of 30–60 m. Karagan Island is located in the central part of the gulf. The island is separated from the mainland by Litke Strait, which measures between 21 and 72 km wide. The shores are rocky and steep. Many rivers flow into the gulf. The tides are mixed; they vary as much as 2.4 m. The surface waters are frozen between December and June.

[11–1120–2]

KARAGIN ISLAND, an island in the Karagin Gulf, of the Bering Sea, off the eastern coast of Kamchatka. Area, approximately 2,000 sq km; maximum altitude, 912 m. Its western shore is low; the eastern shore is rocky and precipitous. The island is covered with tundra vegetation. Forests of Japanese stone pine are widespread.

[11–1120–3]

KARAGODEUASHKH, a burial mound, the richest of all the known remains of the Sind-Maeotae (Meotae) population of the Kuban' region in the fourth–third century B.C. Located near Krymskaia Stanitsa (large cossack village) in Krasnodar Krai, it was excavated by E. D. Felitsin in 1888. The burial mound contained two stone funeral chambers with dromi. The skeleton of a man was discovered in the main chamber along with gold plaques that were part of his headgear and a gold torque around the neck. Next to him lay weapons decorated with gold, and bronze and silver vessels. The second chamber was empty, but several skeletons of horses with remains of a burial chariot were found in its dromos, as well as the burial of a young woman in rich ritual attire of gold and silver and the remains of a funerary feast. Karagodeuaskhh resembles the royal Scythian barrows in the lower Dnieper region.

REFERENCE
Lappo-Danilevskii, A., and V. Mal'mberg. *Drevnosti iuzhnoi Rossii: Kurgan Karagodeuashkh*. St. Petersburg, 1894. (*Materialy po arkheologii Rossii*, no. 13.)

[11–1120–4]

KARAGÖZ (Turkish; literally, black-eyed). **(1)** A character of the Turkish shadow theater, an embodiment of folk humor and native wit.

(2) A puppet theater in Turkey, whose name derives from the chief protagonist of the plays—Karagöz. Arising in the 16th century, the theater's cast of characters included Karagöz's partner Khadzhi-Vada, the townspeople, the Anatolian peasants, and the roguish dervish. Sometimes the Karagöz plays reflected the discontent of the masses with the government and the existing system.

REFERENCES
Martinovich, N. *Turetskii teatr Karagöz.* St. Petersburg, 1910.
Enver Benhan Sapolyo. *Karagözün tarihi.* Istanbul, 1935.

[11–1119–5]

KARAI (on its upper course the Mokryi Karai), a river in Saratov Oblast, RSFSR, a right tributary of the Khoper (Don basin). Length, 139 km; basin area, 2,680 sq km. It flows over the Oka-Don Plain through a broad valley and is fed chiefly by melting snow. The average annual rate of flow 16 km from the mouth is 6.3 cu m per sec. Its waters are used for irrigation.

[11–1125–4]

KARAIN, a Paleolithic cave near the city of Antalya in Turkey. It was discovered in 1946 and, over the course of several years, was excavated by K. Kökten. Karain contains several cultural layers in which stone implements of the Acheulean, Mousterian, and Aurignacian periods of the Paleolithic have been discovered. Two teeth of fossil man have been found in the Mousterian layer and the layer located between the Mousterian and Aurignacian. One of them belongs to Neanderthal man.

REFERENCES
Liubin, V. P. "Paleolit Turtsii i problema rannego rasscleniia chelovechestva." In the collection *Sovetskaia arkheologiia,* vol. 27. Moscow, 1957.
Kökten, I. Killiç. "Ein allgemeiner Überblick über die prähistorischen Forschungen in Karain-Höhle bei Antalya." *Türk Tarih Kurumu Belleten,* 1955, vol. 19, no. 75.

[11–1125–1]

KARAISKAKES, GEORGIOS. Born circa 1780 in Agrapha; died May 4, 1827, near Piraeus. Greek military leader.

At the start of the Greek War of Independence (1821–29), Karaiskakes commanded a detachment in western Greece. Later he led a detachment operating in the rear of the Turkish Army. In 1826 he was commander in chief of troops from mainland Greece that liberated a significant part of Central Greece in December of that year. He was killed in battle during the liberation of the Acropolis.

REFERENCE
Photiades, D. *Karaiskakes.* Athens, 1962.

11–1125–2]

KARAITE, the language of the Karaites, who live in cities of the Crimean Oblast and several other oblasts of the Ukrainian SSR, in Trakai Raion of the Lithuanian SSR, and in Poland. Karaite belongs to the Kipchak group of Turkic languages. It has three dialects: northern (Trakai), southern (Galich), and Crimean. Karaite syntax has been influenced by the Slavic languages (for example, postposition of the genitive case of the attributive, agreement of the attributive and the qualified member in number and case, and relatively free word order). Since 1840, Karaite has used the Hebrew, Latin, and Slavic orthographies for transcribing religious texts, secular literature, and folklore.

REFERENCES
Musaev, K. M. *Grammatika karaimskogo iazyka: Fonetika i morfologiia.* Moscow, 1964.
Musaev, K. M. "Karaimskii iazyk." In *Iazyki narodov SSSR,* vol. 2. Moscow, 1966.
Pritsak, O. "Das Karaimische." In *Philologiae Turcicae Fundamenta,* vol. 1. Wiesbaden, 1959.

[11–1124 5]

KARAITES, a small nationality living in the cities of the Crimean Oblast and several other oblasts of the Ukrainian SSR, in Trakai Raion of the Lithuanian SSR, and in Poland. Their language belongs to the Kipchak group of the Turkic languages. At the present time, the Karaites in the USSR speak mainly Russian, and their way of life and activities are not unlike those of the neighboring peoples. Religious Karaites belong to the Karaite sect, whose only holy book is the Old Testament.

The Karaites are considered to be the descendants of Turkic tribes in the Khazar Kaganate. After the defeat of the kaganate by Kievan princes in the tenth century, the Karaites remained in the Crimea. In the late 14th century some of the Karaites were resettled in Lithuania and the western regions of the Ukraine as prisoners of the Grand Duchy of Lithuania. The Karaites have preserved a rich folklore, which reflects their historical ties with the Khazars.

REFERENCE
Narody Evropeiskoi chasti SSSR, vol. 2. Moscow, 1964. [11–1124–6]

KARAJAN, HERBERT VON. Born Apr. 5, 1908, in Salzburg. Austrian conductor.

Karajan pursued his musical training at the Mozarteum in Salzburg. He was conductor of the opera in Ulm (1927–34) and Aachen (1934–41) and then of the Berlin State Chorus (1941–44). Since the war, Karajan has come to be a leading figure in the musical life of Western Europe. In 1947 he became conductor of the Vienna Gesellschaft der Musikfreunde and has participated in festivals in Salzburg, Vienna, Bayreuth, Berlin, and Munich. He has toured with the Vienna Symphony and the London Philharmonia and has appeared as conductor and director in many European opera theaters. After N. Furtwängler's death in 1954, he became head of the Berlin Philharmonic Orchestra (West Berlin); at the same time, he was musical director of the Vienna State Opera (1956–64) and the Salzburg Festival (1957–60). In 1962, 1964, and 1969, he appeared in the USSR.

Karajan's conducting is characterized by fidelity to the composer's score, irreproachable sense of musical form, and keen intellectual perception of the work.

REFERENCES

Rubin, M. "Tri portreta." *Sovetskaia muzyka,* 1962, no. 4.
Sabinina, M. "Na kontsertakh Gerberta Karaiana." *Muzykal'naia zhizn',* 1969, no. 16.
Herzfeld, F. *Herbert von Karajan,* 2nd ed. Berlin, 1962.
Haeusserman, E. *H. von Karajan: Biographie.* [Gütersloh, 1968.]

E. IA. RATSER [11–1193–1]

KARA-KALA, an urban-type settlement and the center of Kara-Kala Raion, Krasnovodsk Oblast (since Dec. 27, 1973), Turkmen SSR. Situated in the foothills of the Kopetdag on the Sumbar River (a tributary of the Atrek), 91 km south of the Kizyl-Arvat railroad station on the Krasnovodsk-Mary line, with which it is linked by highway. Population, 5,700 (1972). The Turkmen Experimental Station of the All-Union Horticultural Research Institute and a state fruit nursery are located there. A sovkhoz specializing in subtropical crops is nearby. Kara-Kala has a people's amateur theater. [11–1126–2]

KARA-KALPAK, the language of the Kara-Kalpaks, the main population of the Kara-Kalpak ASSR; Kara-Kalpaks also live in Khorezm and Fergana oblasts of the Uzbek SSR, Tashauz Oblast of the Turkmen SSR, the Kazakh SSR, and Afghanistan. Kara-Kalpak is spoken by 228,000 persons (1970 census). It belongs to the Kipchak group of Turkic languages. The principal dialects are northeastern and southwestern.

Kara-Kalpak is grouped with Nogai and Kazakh because of the characteristic replacement of Common Turkic *č* and *š* by Kara-Kalpak *sh* and *s*, respectively (Kara-Kalpak *kash-*, "to run away," instead of Common Turkic *kač-*, and *bas*, "head," instead of *baš*). The Kara-Kalpak literary language formed after the Great October Socialist Revoltion. The Kara-Kalpak writing system was based on the Arabic alphabet until 1928, on the Roman alphabet from 1928 to 1940, and on the Russian alphabet since 1940.

REFERENCES

Malov, S. E. *Zametki o karakalpakskom iazyke.* Nukus, 1966.
Baskakov, N. A. *Karakalpakskii iazyk,* vol. 1–2. Moscow-Leningrad, 1951–52.
Ubaydullaev, K. *Häzirgi zaman qaraqalpaq tili: Fonetika.* Nukus, 1965.
Berdimuratov, Ye. *Häzirgi zaman qaraqalpaq tilining leksikologiyäsï.* Nukus, 1968.
Karakalpaksko-russkii slovar'. Edited by N. A. Baskakov. Moscow, 1958.
Russko-karakalpakskii slovar'. Edited by N. A. Baskakov. Moscow, 1967.
Menges, K. *Qaraqalpaq Grammar.* Vol. 1: *Phonology.* New York, 1947.
[11–1139–2]

KARA-KALPAK AUTONOMOUS SOVIET SOCIALIST REPUBLIC (Karakalpakstan Avtomiyälï Sovet Sotsialistik Respüblikasï), Kara-Kalpakia (Kara-Kalpakstan). Formed Mar. 20, 1932. Part of the Uzbek SSR since Dec. 5, 1936. Located in the northwest of the Uzbek SSR. Area, 165,600 sq km (37 pecent of Uzbekistan's area). Population, 744,000 (1972;

about 6 percent of the Uzbek SSR's total population). The Kara-Kalpak ASSR has 12 administrative raions, eight cities, and nine urban-type settlements. The capital is the city of Nukus.

Constitution and government. The Kara-Kalpak ASSR is a socialist, workers' and peasants' state, an autonomous soviet socialist republic. The constitution now in force was adopted on Mar. 23, 1937, by the Third Extraordinary Congress of Soviets of the Kara-Kalpak ASSR. The highest organs of state power are the unicameral Supreme Soviet of the Kara-Kalpak ASSR, elected by the people for four-year terms on the basis of one deputy per 3,000 population, and its Presidium. The Supreme Soviet forms the government of the republic—the Council of Ministers of the Kara-Kalpak ASSR. The Kara-Kalpak ASSR is represented by 11 deputies in the Soviet of Nationalities of the Supreme Soviet of the USSR. The local organs of state power are the soviets of working peoples' deputies of the cities, raions, settlements, *kishlaks* (hamlets), and *auls* (villages), elected by the people for two-year terms.

The Supreme Soviet of the Kara-Kalpak ASSR elects the republic's Supreme Court, which consists of two judicial divisions (one for criminal and one for civil cases), and the Supreme Court's presidium for five-year terms. The procurator of the Kara-Kalpak ASSR is appointed by the procurator general of the USSR for a five-year term.

Natural features. Kara-Kalpakia occupies the northwestern portion of the Kyzylkum Desert, the southeastern part of the Ustiurt (Ust-Urt) plateau, and the Amu Darya Delta. The southern part of the Aral Sea is located in Kara-Kalpakia. The northwestern part of the Kyzylkum is a vast, flat plain (elevations of 75–100 m), inclined toward the Aral Sea and covered primarily by tracts of ridged sands and barchans. There are isolated mountain massifs (the largest is Sultanuizdag in the southeast with elevations to 473 m). There are many channels, small lakes, *tugai* (gallery forest) and reed thickets, and swampy areas in the Amu Darya Delta. The right-bank section of the delta has more irrigated land and irrigation canals. The Ustiurt plateau, located in the west (elevations to 292 m, Karabaur), has a number of depressions, the largest of which—Barsakel'mes and Assake-Audan—are at elevations of 29–101 m. The plateau breaks off in steep scarps toward the Aral Sea and the Amu Darya Delta. The northern edge of the Sarykamysh Depression is located to the southeast of the Ustiurt plateau.

There are deposits of common salt, Glauber salt, mineral building materials, and minerals.

The climate is sharply continental and is characterized by dry, hot summers and comparatively cold, snowless winters. Average January temperatures are −4.9°C in the south and −7.6°C in the north. Average July temperatures are 28.2°C in the south and 26°C in the north. Annual precipitation totals about 110 mm, falling primarily in the winter-spring period. The frostless period (194–214 days) is adequate for the cultivation of cotton.

The Amu Darya (lower course), Kara-Kalpakia's only river, splits up into branches 100 km from its mouth, forming a vast delta. The river's waters are used for irrigation; there are embankments. During high water, the Amu Darya frequently changes its channel, washing away its banks. In the spring, when there is ice blockage, the river floods large areas. Its flow into the Aral Sea has decreased because its waters are used for irrigation in the upper and middle courses.

In the valley and delta of the Amu Darya, the soils are Sierozem-meadow. There are primitive sandy sierozems in the Kyzylkum Desert and grayish brown soils, *takyrs* (compact clayey areas), and solonchaks on the Ustiurt plateau. The sandy expanses of the Kyzylkum are covered by sparse grassy-scrubby desert vegetation (sedges, xerophyllic grasses, wormwoods, ephemerals, *Calligonum, cherkez* [*Salsola paletzkiana*]); arborescent vegetation includes saxaul. The Amu Darya Delta is rich in *tugai* vegetation (Euphrates poplar, Russian olive, tamarisk, cane).

The desert is inhabited by reptiles (lizards and snakes), rodents (susliks, gerbils, jerboas), large mammals (Persian gazelles, wolves, foxes), birds (Pander's ground jays [saxaul jays], golden eagles, bustards, larks), and arachnids (scorpions, solpugids). The fauna of the *tugais* is richer and includes such birds as pheasants, ducks, geese, cormorants, and sandpipers and such mammals as jackals, jungle cats, wolves, foxes, cape hares, and wild boars. The muskrat has been acclimatized. The game fish inhabiting the Amu Darya and Aral Sea include the ship sturgeon, common carp, bream, and catfish. The rare shovelnose sturgeon (*Scaphirhynchus*) still survives in the Amu Darya.

Population. The Kara-Kalpaks are the indigenous population (218,000; data here and below are that of the 1970 census). Other nationalities include the Uzbeks (213,000), Kazakh (186,000), Turkmen (38,000), Russians (25,000), Koreans (9,000), Tatars (8,000), and Ukrainians (2,000). The population totaled 331,000 in 1926, 476,000 in 1939, 510,000 in 1959, and 744,000 in 1972. The average density is 4.5 persons per sq km (1972). In agricultural regions the density varies between 26 and more than 90 persons per sq km; in the desert regions it decreases to 0.5 per sq km. Between 1926 and 1972 the urban population increased from 5 percent to 36 percent. The cities are Nukus (81,000, 1972), Khodzheili (38,000), Biruni (22,000), Takhiatash (22,-000), Turtkul' (20,000), Chimbai (20,000), Kungrad (13,000), and Muinak (10,000).

Historical survey. Kara-Kalpakia was first settled in the Neolithic period (end of the fourth millennium to the beginning of the second millennium B.C.). Irrigated farming arose at the end of the second millennium B.C. The most ancient written remains of Uzbekistan (fourth century B.C.) have been found during excavations of the Koi-Krylgan-Kala cultic structure. The palace of Toprak-Kala (third century or early fourth century A.D.) is an outstanding example of the late classical period. The ethnogenesis of the Kara-Kalpaks is connected with the tribes that settled the delta and steppes regions of the Syr Darya River and the Aral Sea.

During the 17th century to the mid-18th, most of the Kara-Kalpaks occupied the area surrounding the middle and lower Syr Darya. They led a seminomadic way of life and engaged in stock raising, farming, and fishing. Power was held by the feudal clan nobility and Muslim religious leaders. The Kara-Kalpaks were dependent on the Kazakh khans of the Little Hoard. In 1742 the constant attacks of the neighboring tribes caused the Kara-Kalpaks to send ambassadors to Orenburg and St. Petersburg to request Russian citizenship. The Russian government complied with the request. This prompted the Kazakh khan Abulkhair to attack the Kara-Kalpaks in 1743. As a result, most of the Kara-Kalpaks had moved from the Syr Darya to the western channel of its delta, the Zhana Darya, by the middle of the 18th century. In the late 18th century, the Khiva khans began actions to conquer the Kara-Kalpaks, which in 1811 culminated in the subjugation of the Kara-Kalpaks and their resettlement to the Amu Darya Delta. Within a brief period of time, the Kara-Kalpaks created several new farming regions in the Khiva Khanate. The oppression of the Kara-Kalpaks by the local and Khiva nobility resulted in major uprisings against the khans in 1855–56 and 1858–59. These were harshly suppressed. The insurgents strove to rid themselves of the Khiva yoke and unite with Russia. This was prevented, however, by the Kara-Kalpak feudal lords, who collaborated with the Khiva government to preserve their privileges.

After the campaign of the tsarist forces against Khiva in 1873 and the conclusion of an agreement with the Khiva khan establishing Russia's protectorate, the territory of the Kara-Kalpaks on the right bank of the Amu Darya was united with Russia. The Amu Darya Division was formed, which in 1887 became part of the Syr Darya Region of the Turkestan Governor-Generalship. The few Kara-Kalpaks living on the left bank remained part of the Khiva Khanate. The incorporation of right-bank Kara-Kalpakia into Russia was objectively progressive: the establishment of direct ties between the peoples of Kara-Kalpakia and Russia and the entry of Kara-Kalpakia into the general stream of capitalist development promoted the growth of commodity cotton cultivation and the establishment of the first industrial enterprises. The first national groups of workers appeared at the beginning of the 20th century. Combined Russian and native general education schools were opened. Internecine feudal warfare and the continuous raids suffered by the population ceased. At the same time, the inclusion of Kara-Kalpakia in the Russian Empire brought increased oppression of the toiling masses: they were robbed both by the local *bais* (wealthy stock raisers, mer-

chants, or landowners) and religious leaders and by the tsarist administration. The population of the vassal Khiva Khanate was still more deprived of rights than that of colonial Turkestan. The farms of poor peasants and hired laborers accounted for about 70 percent of all peasant farms in prerevolutionary Kara-Kalpakia. Agricultural techniques and irrigation remained primitive. There were only a few cotton mills of a semicottage nature. Colonial oppression intensified in the early 20th century, particularly during World War 1 (1914–18). Uprisings against the autocracy erupted in Middle Asia under the influence of the revolutionary struggle of the proletariat of Russia. The Kara-Kalpaks participated in the revolutionary actions of 1905–07 and in the Middle Asian Uprising of 1916. The main seats of rebellion in Amu Darya Division were the city of Chimbai and Sarybii Volost' (small rural district), Shurakhan District. After the February Revolution of 1917, soviets were established in Petroaleksandrovsk (Turtkul'), Shurakhan, and Chimbai. The Mensheviks and Socialist Revolutionaries, who predominated in the soviets, supported the bourgeois Provisional Government. The first Bolshevik organizations arose in Petroaleksandrovsk in the second half of October 1917.

After the victory of the October Revolution in Central Russia and Turkestan, Soviet power was established in right-bank Kara-Kalpakia in the first half of December 1917. In April 1918 it became part of the Turkestan ASSR. During the Civil War (1918–20), the Kara-Kalpak workers fought against the *basmachi* (participants of counterrevolutionary bands in Middle Asia). The *basmach* bands of Junaid Khan attempted to capture the city of Petroaleksandrovsk in November and December 1918, but the city withstood the 11-day siege. Shabbaz and Nukus were also under attack by the *basmachi*. In September 1919 a revolutionary committee (chaired by the Communist N. A. Shaidakov) was established in Petroaleksandrovsk by a resolution of the Revolutionary Military Council of the Turkestan republic. It became the center of the revolutionary forces of Kara-Kalpakia. A counterrevolutionary rebellion erupted in Chimbai in August 1919. Its leaders—Ural cossack kulaks, local feudal lords, and Muslim religious leaders—received support from ataman A. I. Dutov and Junaid Khan. The rebels took Chimbai, Muinak, and Nukus. In February 1920 the rebellion was suppressed. In April 1920 the Khorezm People's Soviet Republic (1920–24), which included left-bank Kara-Kalpakia, was formed on the site of the former Khiva Khanate. In December 1920, Amu Darya Division became Amu Darya Oblast of the Turkestan ASSR. On June 25, 1921, the oblast party organization of Kara-Kalpakia was formed at the First Oblast Party Conference.

On Oct. 14, 1924, the second session of the All-Russian Central Executive Committee adopted a resolution under which the part of the Turkestan ASSR with a predominantly Kara-Kalpak population was separated out as the Kara-Kalpak Autonomous Oblast in the course of the national-state demarcation of Soviet Republics of Middle Asia. The Kara-Kalpak districts of the Khorezm Republic were also included in the autonomous oblast. The establishment of the Kara-Kalpak Autonomous Oblast was proclaimed and legislatively formalized by the First Constituent Congress of Soviets (in the city of Turtkul', Feb. 12–19, 1925). Kara-Kalpakia became part of the Kazakh ASSR and on July 20, 1930, part of the RSFSR. On Mar. 20, 1932, the autonomous oblast was transformed into the Kara-Kalpak ASSR, which became part of the Uzbek SSR in 1936.

The Kara-Kalpaks achieved the transition to socialism, bypassing the capitalist stage of development, with the aid of all the peoples of the USSR during the period of socialist construction. A local cotton-ginning industry and socialist agriculture were established. In the course of collectivization, the power of the *bais* and kulaks was destroyed. Irrigated farming was transformed. The harvest of cotton, the republic's main agricultural crop, increased considerably. The cultural revolution was carried out. Illiteracy was eliminated (before the Great October Socialist Revolution, 0.2 percent of the total population of Kara-Kalpakia was literate), the clan and feudal vestiges previously existing in Kara-Kalpakia virtually disappeared, national cadres of the working class and intelligentsia emerged, and higher educational institutions, research insititutions, libraries, clubs, and the like were established.

During the Great Patriotic War (1941–45), thousands of Kara-Kalpak workers were awarded orders and medals for patriotism displayed at the front and in the rear; 14 people were awarded the title of Hero of the Soviet Union.

The economy of Kara-Kalpakia developed and strengthened further during the postwar years. The Kara-Kalpak people consolidated into a socialist nation. On Dec. 25, 1959, Kara-Kalpakia was awarded the Order of Lenin for its successful development of cotton cultivation. It was awarded the Order of Friendship of Peoples on Dec. 29, 1972, in commemoration of the 50th anniversary of the Union of Soviet Socialist Republics.

S. K. KAMALOV

Economy. Under Soviet power, Kara-Kalpakia has been transformed into a republic with a developed socialist economy.

INDUSTRY. The branches of industry connected with the processing of agricultural raw materials, the production of building materials, and metalworking are the most highly developed. The gross industrial output in 1971 was 4.8 times greater than in 1940. Table 1 lists the output of some industrial products.

Table 1. Output of some industrial products

	1940	1950	1971
Electric power, kW-hr . . .	3,600,000	10,500,000	1,053,000,000
Building bricks	12,000,000	8,000,000	90,000,000
Cotton fiber, tons	34,500	41,000	114,000
Vegetable oil, tons	30	6,900	22,600
Canned goods, standard cans	20,000	10,600,000	12,800,000

The leading branch of industry is cotton ginning (seven plants). Directly connected with this branch is the seed oil extracting industry (three plants), which processes cotton seeds. The fishing industry is important on a nation-wide scale (the Muinak Fish-canning Combine); the 1971 catch totaled 7,600 tons. The building-materials industry is represented by plants for the production of bricks, reinforced-concrete structures, and limestone and a house-building combine. Metalworking enterprises conduct repairs of motor vehicles, ships, and agricultural, highway, and building equipment. There are enterprises producing clothing, footwear, furniture, macaroni, flour, and meat and dairy products. Most of the industrial enterprises are located in the cities of Nukus, Khodzheili, Takhiatash, Muinak, and Chimbai. The Takhiatash State Regional Power Plant (252,000 kW) supplies Kara-Kalpakia as well as Khorezm Oblast of the Uzbek SSR and Tashauz Oblast of the Turkmen SSR with electric power. In late 1969, Kara-Kalpakia was linked up with the Unified Power System of Middle Asia.

AGRICULTURE. In 1971, Kara-Kalpakia had 62 sovkhozes and 45 kolkhozes. There were more than 20,500 tractors (in 15-hp units), more than 2,000 cotton pickers, 2,800 motor vehicles, and more than 1,000 excavating machines. Agricultural land totals 2,662,000 hectares (ha; 1971), of which 209,200 ha are arable and 2,443,700 ha are occupied by hayfields and pastures (see Table 2). Farming is conducted only on irrigated land. During the years of socialist construction, the old irrigation systems have been basically reconstructed and large new irrigation canals built, including the Lenin, Kyzketken, and Pakhtaarna canals. Construction of the Takhiatash and Tiuiamuiun (with hydro-electric power plants) dams is under way on the Amu Darya (1973). These dams will facilitate the further development of new lands, as well as improve the water intake conditions of the irrigation canals of the lower Amu Darya.

Table 2. Cultivated crops, hectares

	1913	1940	1950	1971
Total sown area . . .	109,500	154,600	159,000	214,800
Cereal crops	78,900	47,800	30,900	28,700
including rice	4,100	10,900	8,100	26,100
Cotton	11,800	60,900	83,600	131,000
Potatoes, vegetables, and melon crops .	1,900	5,700	3,000	6,800
Fodder crops	13,700	38,800	38,500	48,200

The principal agricultural crop is cotton. Kara-Kalpakia accounts for 7.1 percent of Uzbekistan's total harvest of raw cotton. The main cereal crop is rice. Alfalfa is an important field crop and is cultivated for seeds and as a valuable fodder. Kara-Kalpakia is the USSR's leading producer of seed alfalfa. The gross harvest in 1971 totaled 321,000 tons of raw cotton, 67,000 tons of rice, and 27,000 tons of melons. Kara-Kalpakia is known for the famous Khorezm melons. Fruit and berry plantings total 4,500 ha.

Stock raising is based on the vast desert pastures and the rich *tugai* vegetation in the Amu Darya Delta. Sheep, particularly karakuls (6 percent of all livestock of the Uzbek SSR); cattle, particularly beef cattle (see Table 3); horses; and camels are raised. Sericulture (653 tons of cocoons in 1971) and fur farming (muskrat, mink) are developed.

In 1971 the output of livestock produce totaled 13,000 tons of meat (dressed weight; 6,800 in 1955), 91,300 tons of milk (37,-900), 1,682, tons of wool (685), and 41,800,000 eggs (14,400,-000).

The 1971 state purchases totaled 321,000 tons of raw cotton (139,000 in 1950); 57,400 tons of grain (6,500), including 56,400 tons of rice (4,100); 15,300 tons of vegetables (300); 17,400 tons of melons (200); 10,400 tons of cattle and poultry (3,500); 19,300 tons of milk (5,100); 13,700,000 eggs (962,000); 1,546 tons of wool (315 tons); and 653 tons of cocoons (302).

TRANSPORTATION. The Chardzhov-Kungrad railroad, which was constructed in the 1950's and linked Kara-Kalpakia to the railroad system of Middle Asia, has been extended through Beineu to Makat and has become the second railroad outlet from Middle Asia to the European part of the country. There is navigation on the Amu Darya and the Aral Sea. Paved highways total 1,172 km (Jan. 1, 1972). The Bukhara-Muinak highway has been built. Air transport is developed. Sections of the Bukhara-Urals and Middle Asia–Central USSR gas pipelines pass through Kara-Kalpakia.

Kara-Kalpakia is a supplier of cotton fiber, rice, canned fish, silk cocoons, karakul, muskrat pelts, and wool. Coal, petroleum products, machinery, lumber, and mineral fertilizers are brought in from other parts of the USSR.

Table 3. Livestock (number of head at beginning of year)

	1941	1951	1972
Cattle	170,900	145,300	272,100
including cows	61,800	44,800	105,700
Sheep and goats	293,500	351,000	461,600

INTERNAL DIFFERENCES. The southern part specializes in cotton growing and sericulture. Karakuls and camels are raised in the Kyzylkum. Industry comprises cotton ginning and vegetable-oil extraction. In the north, cotton and rice cultivation and stock raising are developing rapidly. In the coastal strip there is fish breeding, fur farming, stock raising, and horse breeding in herds. Industry comprises cotton ginning, fishing, seed oil extraction, and metalworking.

The standard of living is steadily rising with the republic's increasing national income. The retail trade turnover totaled 280.8 million rubles in 1971 (122.8 million rubles in 1960). In 1971 state and cooperative enterprises and organizations and home-building cooperatives constructed residences with a total area of 134,100 sq m; kolkhozes, members of kolkhozes, and the rural intelligentsia were responsible for 139,300 sq m; and industrial and office workers, at their own expense and with the aid of state credit, built 172,700 sq m. The social insurance and pension funds of the population are growing. K. N. BEDRINTSEV

Public health. In 1913 there were two hospitals with 21 beds and three paramedical stations; three doctors and three paramedics primarily serviced military units. By 1972 there were 96 hospitals with 7,600 beds (10 beds per 1,000 population), 138 outpatient clinics and polyclinics, 67 women's and children's consultation offices, and 351 rural paramedical stations. There were 1,200 doctors (one doctor per 607 population) and about 5,000 intermediate medical personnel. Malaria has been almost completely eliminated as a result of various antimalarial measures. There are four sanatoriums for patients with active forms of pulmonary tuberculosis. There is also a house of rest on the Aral Sea in the city of Muinak.

Public education and cultural affairs. In the 1914–15 academic year there were four general education schools with 200 pupils in Kara-Kalpakia; before the October Revolution there were no higher educational institutions or special secondary schools. In the 1971–72 academic year more than 200,000 pupils were enrolled in 729 general education schools. There were about 10,000 students in 16 special secondary schools and more than 5,000 students in the Kara-Kalpak State Pedagogical Institute in Nukus. In 1971, 15,000 children were being educated in preschool institutions. On Jan. 1, 1972, there were 405 public libraries (about 2 million copies of books and journals), 236 clubs, and 279 film projectors. There are two museums—the Museum of History and Local Lore and the Museum of Arts of the Kara-Kalpak SSR in Nukus.

Scientific institutions. There are a number of scientific institutions in the republic, including the Kara-Kalpak Branch of the Academy of Sciences of the Uzbek SSR (founded in 1959), with the N. Davkaraev Institute of History, Language, and Literature and the Combined Institute of Natural Sciences with its Botanical Gardens; the Kara-Kalpak Institute of Agriculture; and branches of Uzbek institutes (skin and venereology, pedagogical science, and rice); and a base of the Uzbek Scientific Research Institute of Stock Raising.

In 1972 more than 600 scientific workers, including ten doctors and more than 230 candidates of sciences, were working in the scientific research institutions and the pedagogical institute. The corresponding members of the Academy of Sciences of the Uzbek SSR M. K. Nurmukhamedov (literature), Ia. M. Dosumov (history), and I. T. Sagitove (literature), among others, work in Kara-Kalpakia.   S. K. KAMALOV

Press, radio, and television. In 1971, 133 books and pamphlets with circulations totaling 925,000 copies were published; 16 editions of newspapers (excluding factory papers) with single editions totaling 187,000 copies were published. The republic newspapers are *Sovet Karakalpakstany* (Soviet Kara-Kalpakia, since 1924), *Zhas leninshi* (Young Leninist, since 1931), and *Zhetkinshek* (Young Generation, since 1932) in the Kara-Kalpak language and *Sovetskaia Karakalpakiia* (since 1919) in Russian. Four journals with single-edition circulations of 27,000 copies are published, including *Emuder'ia* (Amu Darya, since 1932), a literary and sociopolitical journal in Kara-Kalpak.

The republic's radio and television broadcast in Kara-Kalpak, Uzbek, Turkmen, and Russian on two radio and television programs; broadcasts from Moscow and Tashkent are relayed. There is a television center in Nukus.

Literature. Since literacy among the Kara-Kalpaks was a privilege of the few before the October Revolution, literary creativity was essentially oral in nature. In terms of genre characteristics, folklore is clearly separated into lyric and epic works. The first category includes numerous types of songs—lyrical songs and songs of ritual and everyday life. Sung incantations (*badik*) are the oldest type. The epic genres include fairy tales, legends, songs of heroes, and *dastany* (epics). The most popular was the heroic epic, versions of which approximately date to the 16th century. The epic *Forty Maidens* is widely known. It reflects, in a fictional reinterpretation, historical events of the 17th and 18th centuries, but it also embodies archaic elements.

The written, prerevolutionary literature of the Kara-Kalpaks used the Arabic alphabet. The 18th-century poet Zhien Zhyrau was well-known. In his verses and in the historical narrative poem *The Ruined People,* he depicted the life of the Kara-Kalpaks during a period when, pressed by the raids of outside tribes, they were forced to migrate to Zhana Darya. The poets Kunodzha (1799–1880), Azhiniiaz (1824–78), Berdakh (1827–1900), and Omar Otesh (1828–1902) also depicted the hard life of the Kara-Kalpaks. In their poetics, these poets followed the traditions of folklore and Oriental classical literature. The plots of the narrative poems *Bozatau* by Azhiniiaz and *Ernazar bii* and *Aidos bii* by Berdakh were based on actual historical events that took place in the 19th century. In its plot, Berdakh's narrative poem *The Petty Tyrant Tsar* closely resembled a folk fairy tale, but it was socially topical, addressed to contemporary times.

Democratic points of view were maintained by poets living later, such as Omar (1879–1922), Kulmurat (1838–1927), and Sydyk Shair (1857–1917).

The founders of Soviet literature in Kara-Kalpakia were A. Musaev (1880–1936), S. Mazhitov (1869–1938), A. Dabylov (1898–1970), and S. Nurumbetov (1900–71).

Dramaturgy and prose fiction arose at the end of the 1920's. Writers reflected characteristic features of the day; they searched for ways of merging folk poetry with the experience of Kara-Kalpak and multinational Soviet poetry. The first prose and dramatic works of Mazhitov appeared, as did the the plays of A. Utepov (1904–34), the short stories and plays of N. Davkaraev (1905–53) and A. Begimov (1907–58), and the novellas of M. Daribaev (1909–42), A. Shamuratov (1912–53), and Dzh. Aimurzaev (born 1910). The novels *The Fisherman's Daughter* (1958) by A. Begimov, *On the Banks of the Amu Darya* (1958) by Dzh. Aimurzaev, and *In the Arms of the Aral* (1958) by U. Aizhanov (1919–60) were written in the 1950's.

During the 1960's, the body of prose was enlarged by the works of K. Sultanov (born 1924), Kh. Seitov (born 1917), U. Khodzhaniiazov (born 1926), and T. Kaipbergenov (born 1929). Kaipbergenov's trilogy *Daughter of a Kara-Kalpak* (books 1–2, 1963–65) depicts the life of a Kara-Kalpak woman against the background of the historical events of the first half of the 20th century. An unfortunate girl traverses a painful path through life. Only in Soviet times does she find happiness and her place in the new society as a citizen enjoying full and equal rights. The author organically links the fate of the heroine with that of the people.

Poets of the republic include Kh. Turumbetov (1926–68), B. Kaipnazarov (born 1916), I. Iusupov (born 1929), and T. Zhumamuratov (born 1915).

Literary criticism has emerged in Kara-Kalpakia during Soviet times. The pioneers in this field are N. Davkaraev, K. Aimbetov (born 1908), and I. Sagitov (born 1908). Other specialists include M. Nurmukhamedov (born 1928), S. Akhmetov (born 1929), and G. Esemuratov (born 1930). A division of the Writers' Union of the Uzbek SSR, located in Nukus, carries on organizational and creative work among the writers of Kara-Kalpakia.   K. KAMALOV

Architecture and art. The most ancient artistic remains date from the fourth century B.C. (small sculptures and pottery from excavations in Kavat-Kala). Remains of numerous irrigation structures (large dams, reservoirs, and *khauzy* [ponds]) and of houses and estates (for example, the Orunbai-Kala estate) have survived from the period of Kara-Kalpak settlement in the Zhana Darya River basin (the second half of the 18th century). The native Kara-Kalpak dwelling was the yurt (for the nomads) and the pisé house or clay and reed hut (in northern regions) with an attached yurt (for the settled people). Remains of Hellenistic Khwarazm are located in Kara-Kalpakia: Toprak-Kala, Giaur-Kala, and others. Cities (Nukus, Biruni, and others) and a number of urban-type settlements have arisen during Soviet times. Farmsteads are being replaced by rural settlements and cities with regular layouts, an organized downtown area, and standard construction. Traditional dwellings are also being preserved. Gardens and parks occupy a prominent place in urban and rural construction.

Woodcarving (the doors of yurts) with cloth and ivory inlays, leather stamping, carpet making, weaving, and embroidery have been practiced by the peoples of Kara-Kalpakia since ancient times. Rugs, felts, carpet braids (*akkur*), and broad fringes (*zhanbau*), with designs in soft tones of brown, pink, pale green, and yellow on a white background, have been extensively used to insulate and decorate the yurt. Twentieth-century articles are characterized by the combination of red and yellow with brown, green, and dark blue. Kara-Kalpak jewelers combine silver, sometimes gilded, with cornelian, coral, and turquoise to decorate women's clothing, men's belts, and harnesses for horses. Strict geometric and floral designs, the main motif of which is the *muiiz* (ram's horn), are characteristic of Kara-Kalpak art.

Easel painting, drawing, and small-scale sculpture have been developing since the 1930's. The sculptors Dzh. Kuttymuratov and D. Tureniiazov; the painters Zh. Bekanov, B. Serekeev, F. Iu. Madgazin, I. V. Savitskii, and A. Kurbanbaev; the graphic artists K. Berdimuratov and K. Nashimov; and the stage designers B. D. Kamenev and K. Saipov, among others, are presently working. 　　　　　L. A. SHARAFUTDINOVA

Music. The music of Kara-Kalpakia has an ancient history. Before the October Revolution it was represented by oral folk works. The music culture was maintained and preserved by folk singers (*bakhsy*), who performed lyrical songs and epics to the accompaniment of the *dutar;* storytellers (*zhyrau*), who performed heroic epics to the accompaniment of the *kobuz;* and instrumentalists (*sazende* and *kissakhany*), who composed songs and instrumental pieces. These included Garipniiaz, Eshchbai, Akymbet, Musa, Suieu, Shernazar, Arzy, Zhuman, Eshchan, and Orynbai. The songs of the Kara-Kalpaks vary in genre and theme. Folk songs are basically diatonic; glissando, grace notes, and other embellishments are used extensively in melodies.

The most popular musical instruments are the *dutar,* a two-stringed plucked instrument; the *kobuz* and *gyrzhak,* bowed instruments; the *balaman* (a reed pipe) and the *nai* and *surnai* (flute family), wooden wind instruments; and the *dep* (tambourine), a percussion instrument. The *shynkobuz,* made from a small piece of iron, is used by women.

Professional musical culture has been developing in Kara-Kalpakia since the October Revolution. Compositions for symphony orchestra (the symphonic poems *Kara-Kalpakia* and *Kyrk kyz* by A. Khalimov, the symphonic poem *Buzatau* and the symphonic suite *Youth* by A. Sultanov, *Kara-Kalpak Rhapsody* by F. Nazarov, the suite on Kara-Kalpak themes *Nigarim, Teke Nalysh,* and *Adynnan* by A. F. Kozlovski), choral works (*Kara-Kalpakstan* by Zh. Shamuratov and M. Nasimov, *My Homeland* by A. Sultanov, and *Peace* by A. Khalimov), and music for theatrical productions began appearing in the late 1940's. Songwriters include Zh. Shamuratov, A. Sultanov, K. Turdykulov, N. Makhamatdinov, K. Abdullaev, and M. Zhiemuratov. Notations of Kara-Kalpak folk songs have been published by A. Khalimov (1959) and V. Shafrannikov (1959).

Great contributions to the development of the national musical culture have been made by People's Artist of the USSR A. Shamuratov; People's Artists of the Uzbek SSR G. Shirazieva, R. Seitov, S. Mambetova, and A. Atamuratova; and Honored Artists of the Kara-Kalpak ASSR I. Rafikova and G. Tleumuratov.

The republic's music institutions include K. S. Stanislavsky Theater of Music and Drama (1930), the Berdakh Philharmonic Society (1946), the folk instruments orchestra (1968), the Kara-Kalpak division of the Composers' Union of the Uzbek SSR (1967), the music and choreographic school (founded 1960) in Nukus, and six music schools. The music division of the section for art studies of the Kara-Kalpak branch of the Academy of Sciences of the Uzbek SSR (1959) is engaged in collecting and studying Kara-Kalpak folk music.

Theater. Dramatic and theatrical elements were contained in the rituals and games of the Kara-Kalpak people, in folk epics, in the performing art of the folk masters (*bakhsy* and *zhyrau*), and in the art of the professional wits (the best known in the second half of the 19th century and the early 20th were Omirbek-lakky, Kampakal-kempir, Daulet-lakky, and Tynym-kyz). The *maskarapaz* art (art of masquers), borrowed from the Khwarazm Uzbeks, spread from the second half of the 19th century. The formation and development of a professional Kara-Kalpak theater began after the October Revolution and closely proceeded with the cultures of other peoples of the USSR, particularly the Uzbek and Russian cultures. Numerous amateur groups were organized in Petroaleksandrovsk, Kungrad, Khodzheili, Chimbai, Shurakhan, and elsewhere beginning in late 1917. In 1925 the first Kara-Kalpak troupe Tang Nury (Dawn) was established at the Turtkul' Pedagogical Technicum on the initiative of the educator Z. F. Kasymov. The first works of national dramaturgy appeared in the 1920's—*The Girl Who Finds an Equal* by A. Utepov, *Saieke batyr* by K. Avezov, *Ernazar—The Camel's—Eye* by S. Mazhitov. In 1928, a new theater group, also known as Tang Nury, arose on the basis of the troupe directed by Z. F. Kasymov. It was organized by the playwright A. Utepov, one of the founders of Kara-Kalpak theater and dramaturgy and author of many plays (he was also an actor and director and managed theater troupes in various parts of Kara-

Kalpakia). On the basis of this group, the Kara-Kalpak Theater of Music and Drama was created in Turtkul' in 1930 (it was transferred to Nukus in 1942); in 1939 the name of K. S. Stanislavsky was conferred upon it. In 1939, the theater troupe was strengthened by the graduates of the Kara-Kalpak studio of the State Institute of Theatrical Arts, students of O. I. Pyzhova and B. V. Bibikov. Studio plays entered the repertoire, including A. N. Ostrovskii's *Poverty Is No Crime,* Molière's *Les Fourberies de Scapin,* and V. V. Vishnevskii's *The First Cavalry Army.* Productions of the 1940's–50's included *Alpamys* by N. Davkaraev; *Maisara's Prank* by Kh. Khamza; *Love Can Neither Be Bought nor Sold* by S. Khodzhaniiazov; *Garib-Ashik* by A. Begimov and T. Allanazarov; *Ailgul' and Abat, Lieutenant Elmuratov,* and *Raushan* by Dzh. Aimurzaev; *Russian People* by K. M. Simonov; *Stolen Happiness* by I. Ia. Franko; and *Tartuffe* by Molière. The character of V. I. Lenin first appeared on the stage of the Kara-Kalpak Theater in 1967 in I. F. Popov's *Family.* Other productions of the 1960's and early 1970's included *The Source of Life* by Dzh. Aimurzaev, *Daughter of Kara-Kalpakia* by G. Abdulov and T. Baiandiev, *Taluas* by S. Khodzhaniiazov, *Lodestar* by K. Iashen, and *Othello* by Shakespeare. Working in the republic (1972) are People's Artist of the USSR A. Shamuratova; People's Artists of the Uzbek SSR and the Kara-Kalpak ASSR Iu. Mamutov, S. Avezova, O. Davletova, Z. Zaripov, R. Seitov, and G. Sherazieva; People's Artists of the Kara-Kalpak ASSR R. Adikova, S. Allamuratova, T. Akhmetova, Kh. Saparov, O. Umitkulov, S. Utepbergenov, and Sh. Utemuratov; Honored Art Worker of the Kara-Kalpak ASSR K. Saipov; and Honored Artists of the Kara-Kalpak ASSR N. Ansatbaeva, D. Ranov, and S. Paluanov.

　　　　　T. B. BAIANDIEV

REFERENCES
Ocherki istorii Karakalpakskoi ASSR, vols. 1–2. Tashkent, 1964.
Narody Srednei Azii i Kazakhstana, vol. 1. Moscow, 1962.
Tolstov, S. P. *Po drevnim del'tam Oksa i Iaksarta.* Moscow, 1962.
Kamalov, S. K. *Karakalpaki v XVIII–XIX vv. (K istorii vzaimootnoshenii s Rossiei i sredneaziatskimi khanstvami.)* Tashkent, 1968.
Bor'ba trudiashchikhsia Karakalpakii protiv sotsial'nogo i kolonial'nogo gneta (1873–fevr. 1917). Tashkent, 1971.
Karakalpakiia v period pobedy sotsializma i kommunisticheskogo stroitel'stva. Tashkent, 1969.
Tsapenko, N., and T. Tadzhimov. *Karakalpakskaia ASSR (Kratkii spravochnik).* Tashkent, 1960.
"Uzbekistan." Moscow, 1967. (The series *Sovetskii Soiuz.*)
Narodnoe khoziaistvo Karakalpakskoi ASSR. Nukus, 1967. (Statistical collection.)
Ekonomicheskoe preobrazovanie Karakalpakii za gody Sovetskoi vlasti. Nukus, 1969.
Zaripov, Kh., and Zh. Medetullaev. *Üstirtting häzirgi jaghdatï khëm keleshegi.* Nukus, 1969.
Rzaev, K. R., and Zh. M. Medetullaev. *Resursy sel'skogo khoziaistva Karakalpakii.* Nukus, 1972.
Davkaraev, N. *Ocherki po istorii dorevoliutsionnoi karakalpakskoi literatury.* Tashkent, 1959.
Nurmukhamedov, M. *Kratkii ocherk istorii karakalpaksoi sovetskoi literatury.* Tashkent, 1959.
Nurmukhamedov. M. *Karakalpakskaia sovetskaia proza.* Tashkent, 1968.
Antologiia karakalpakskoi poezii. Tashkent, 1968.
Qäräqälpäq savet ädebiyäti tariykhïnïn acherkleri. Tashkent-Samarkand, 1968.
Zhdanko, T. A. "Narodnoe ornamental'noe iskusstvo karakalpakov." In the book *Trudy khorezmskoi ekspeditsii,* vol. 3. Moscow, 1958.
Savitskii, I. V. *Rez'ba po derevu karakalpakov.* Tashkent, 1965.
Allamuratov, A. *Karakalpakstan iskusstvosïnïn tariykhïnan.* Nukus, 1968.
Allanazarov, T. *Karakalpakskii sovetskii teatr.* Tashkent, 1966.
Baiandiev, T. *Karakalpakskii teatr im. K. S. Stanislavskogo.* Tashkent, 1970. 　　　　　[11–1127–1]

KARA-KALPAKS (Kara-Kalpaks, Qaraqalpaqs), a people; the principal population of the Kara-Kalpak ASSR. The total number of Kara-Kalpaks in the USSR is 236,000 (1970, census). Of these, 218,000 live in the Kara-Kalpak ASSR, and the remainder are in the Fergana and Khorezm oblasts of the Uzbek SSR, in the Turkmen SSR, and in small groups in the Kazakh SSR.

Several thousand Kara-Kalpaks live in Afghanistan. They speak the Kara-Kalpak language, and those who profess a religion are Muslims.

The presence of two racial layers has been established in the Kara-Kalpak anthropological type: the Caucasoid race, connected with the local steppe population from the Bronze Age and classical times, and the Mongoloid race, connected with the steppe tribes who arrived later. Some of the Kara-Kalpaks' most ancient forefathers were the Saka-Massagetae tribes, who lived in the seventh to the second century B.C. on the southern shores of the Aral Sea. From the end of the second century A.D. to the fourth century A.D., the Huns swept into the Aral steppes from the east and partially merged with the native tribes; then in the sixth to the eighth century, the Turks did the same. By this time, the early medieval peoples of the Aral region, the Pechenegs (Petcheneg) and the Oghuz, had arisen; in their midst, the formation of the Kara-Kalpaks begain in the eighth century to the tenth. In the early tenth century, some of the Pechenegs migrated westward to the southern Russian steppes; the tribes that settled in Kievan Rus' were called *chernye klobuki* (black hoods) in the Russian chronicles (from the Turkic *karakalpak,* "black cap"). The eastern Pechenegs, who had remained between the Volga and the Ural rivers, gradually merged with and took the language of the Kipchaks, who had arrived from the basin of the Irtysh River. There is evidence in the sources of the tribe of the Kara-Borkli—an ethnological appellation identical to the name Kara-Kalpak—that it was part of the Kipchak tribal union. In the 14th to the 15th century, the Kara-Kalpaks' relations with the Nogai exerted a substantial influence on their ethnogenesis.

In the late 16th century, the Kara-Kalpaks already figured in Middle Asian sources under their modern name. They led a semisettled way of life, combining irrigated agriculture with stock breeding (particularly cattle) and fishing. In the 19th and early 20th century, their social structure was feudal with significant survivals of patriarchal relations and some elements of capitalistic relations. The tribal and clan structure and remnants of patrimonial relationships in economic, community, and family life were preserved. Centuries-old links with the peoples of Eastern Europe, the Cisurals, and Middle Asia can be traced in the culture of the Kara-Kalpaks. With the rise of the Soviet system, the Kara-Kalpaks adopted the path of noncapitalistic development, created their own state system, and formed themselves into a socialist nation.

REFERENCES

Narody Srednei Azii i Kazakhstana, vol. 1. Moscow, 1962. (With bibliography.)
Tolstov, S. P. "K voprosu o proiskhozhdenii karakalpakskogo naroda." In *Kratkie soobshcheniia Instituta etnografii AN SSSR,* issue 2. Moscow-Leningrad, 1947.
Zhdanko, T. A. *Ocherki istoricheskoi etnografii karakalpakov: Rodoplemennaia struktura i rasselenie v XIX–nachale XX vv.* Moscow and Leningrad, 1950.
Tolstova, L. S. *Karakalpaki za predelami Khorezmskogo oazisa v XIX–nachale XX v.* Nukus-Tashkent, 1963.
Ocherki istorii Karakalpakskoi ASSR, vol. 1. Tashkent, 1964.
Nurmukhamedov, M. K., T. A. Zhdanko, and S. K. Kamalov. *Karakalpaki: Kratkii ocherk istorii s drevneishikh vremen do nashikh dnei.* Tashkent, 1971.   T. A. ZHDANKO [11–1126–4]

KARA-KALPAK STEPPE (Iaz"iavan Steppe), the central part of the Fergana Valley in Andizhan Oblast, Uzbek SSR. The surface is composed of loam, clay, sand, and coarse gravel. The steppe has many solonchaks and swampy expanses. There are areas of takyrs (clayey tracts amid sand) and hummocky sands. The characteristic plants are saltworts, *Halocnemum, Aeluropus litoralis* (Gouan) *Parl* (on solonchaks), wormwood, ephemerals, poplar, and tamarisk (on sands). The steppe is used chiefly for pasture.   [11–1139–1]

KARAKEEV, KURMAN-GALI. Born Nov. 7, 1913, in the village of Kurmenty, present-day Tiup Raion, Issyk-Kul' Oblast, Kirghiz SSR. Soviet historian. Academician (1960) and president (from 1960) of the Academy of Sciences of the Kirghiz SSR.

Corresponding member of the Academy of Sciences of the USSR (1968). Member of the CPSU from 1938.

Karakeev, the son of peasants, graduated from the Higher Party School (1946) and the Academy of Social Sciences (1959) under the Central Committee of the CPSU. From 1939 to 1959 he was the secretary of the Tien-Shan and Issyk-Kul' oblast commitees of the party, an editor of the republic newspaper *Kyzyl Kyrgystan* (Red Kirghizia), the head of the propaganda and agitation section of the Central Committee of the Communist Party of Kirghizia, and the secretary (from 1947) of the party's Central Committee. His primary fields of research were cultural construction, the history of the CPSU, and the history of the USSR. Karakeev translated the classic Marxist-Leninist works into Kirghiz; he also edited other translations of these works. He was the coauthor and editor of several publications, including *Studies of the Communist Party of Kirghizia* (1966), *History of the Kirghiz SSR* (3rd ed., 1967), *History of the Communists Organizations of Middle Asia* (1967), and the fundamental work *The Victory of Soviet Power in Middle Asia and Kazakhstan* (1967).

Karakeev was a deputy to the sixth, seventh, and eighth convocations of the Supreme Soviet of the USSR. He was also a delegate to the Twenty-second (1961) and Twenty-third (1966) Congresses of the CPSU. Karakeev has been awarded the Order of Lenin, four other orders, and various medals.
                                                          [11–1144–1]

KARAKHAN, LEV MIKHAILOVICH (pseudonym of L. M. Karakhanian). Born Jan. 20 (Feb. 1), 1889, in Tbilisi; died Sept. 20, 1937. Soviet statesman and diplomat. The son of a lawyer.

Karakhan graduated from a *Realschule.* He became a member of the RSDLP in 1904. In 1905, Karakhan moved to Harbin, where he was arrested in 1910, his first arrest. From 1910 to 1915 he was a student at the school of law of Petrograd University. From 1912 on, he was involved in the labor union movement; and beginning in 1913 he was one of the *mezhraiontsy* (interfaction group of the Social Democrats). In 1915 he was arrested and exiled to Tomsk, where he passed examinations at the University of Tomsk. Karakhan carried on active work in underground Social Democratic organizations. On Apr. 2, 1917, he returned to Petrograd. In June 1917, at the first session of the Soviets of Workers' and Soldiers' Deputies, Karakhan was elected to the soviets' All-Russian Central Executive Committee. In August he was elected a member of the Presidium and secretary of the Petrograd Soviet of Workers' and Soldiers' Deputies. At the Sixth Congress of the RSDLP (Bolshevik), Karakhan and the *mezhraiontsy* were accepted into the Bolshevik Party. During the October Revolution of 1917 he was a member of the Petrograd Military Revolutionary Committee. From November 1917 to early 1918, Karakhan was the secretary to the Soviet delegation at the negotiations leading to the Brest-Litovsk Treaty of 1918. From March 1918 to 1920 he was deputy people's commissar for foreign affairs. In 1921 he was plenipotentiary in Poland, and from September 1923 to August 1926 he served as plenipotentiary in China. From 1927 to 1934, Karakhan was deputy people's commissar for foreign affairs. Then, until May 3, 1937, he was ambassador to Turkey. He was a member of the Central Executive Committee of the USSR.

REFERENCE

Kapitsa, M. S. "L. Karakhan (1889–1937)." In *Vidnye sovetskie kommunisty—uchastniki kitaiskoi revoliutsii.* Moscow, 1970.
                                                          [11–1179–3]

KARAKHANIDS (Ilek-khans), a Muslim Turkic dynasty of the Karakhanid state in Middle Asia from 927 to 1212. Named after the first khan, Abdulkarim Satuk Karakhan (died 955 or 956).

The family descended from the Iagma tribe and bore the title of *bogra-khan.* At the head of the Karakhanids stood the *tamgachkhan,* or khan of khans. The most powerful representatives of the Karakhanids were Nasr (late tenth century), Ibrahim (1046/47–1068), and Arslan (1102–30). The last Karakhanid, Klych-Arslan ibn Klych, was killed in 1212 by the shah of Khorezm, Muhammad.   [11–1180–2]

KARAKHANID STATE, an early feudal state which formed in the 990's in eastern Turkestan, Semirech'e, and southern Cis–Tien-Shan.

The Karakhanid state was formed from a number of Turkic tribes, including the Karluks, Chigils, and Iagma. The dynasty of the Karakhanids came from the Iagma. Islam spread among these tribes at about the middle of the tenth century. The campaign of conquest of the Turks toward Transoxiana led to the rapid fall of the Samanid state. In 992 the head of the Karakhanid state, *bogra-khan* Harun, seized Bukhara. Between 996 and 999 his successor Nasr I took possession of all of Transoxiana. The Karakhanid state was divided into appanages ruled by members of the Karakhanid line, the *ilek-khans;* central authority was weak. The capitals of the state were Kashgar, then Balasagun, Uzgen, and finally Kashgar again. The *iqta* was the chief form of feudal landowning. During the 1060's and 1070's, the state began to clash with the Seljuks. Weakened by decentralization and internal feuding, the state came under Seljuk domination, especially during the reign of the Seljuk sultan Sanjar (1118–57). Incursions by the Karakitai in the 1130's and early 1140's left the Karakhanid state under their rule. In 1212 the state was liquidated by the shah of Khorezm, Muhammad.

The culture of the Karakhanid state produced such literary works as the *Kudatkubilik* of Yusuf of Balasagun and the *Divan of Turkish Dialects* of Mahmud of Kashgar. In the field of architecture and the decorative arts, the portal mausoleums of Uzgen with their ornamental elegance are noteworthy.

REFERENCES
Istoriia Uzbekskoi SSR, vol. 1. Tashkent, 1967.
Valitova, A. A. "K voprosu o klassovoi prirode Karakhanidskogo gosudarstva." *Trudy Kirgizskogo filiala AN SSSR,* vol.1, no. 1. 1943.

A. G. PODOL'SKII [11–1180–1]

KARAKITAI (also Karakhitans—Black Kitai, or Black Khitans), the name given by medieval authors to the Khitans, a people of the Mongol group who arrived in Middle Asia after the defeat of their empire (whose tributary from the early 11th century was the Chinese kingdom) in 1125 by the Jurjen (Jurchen) tribes, and a large group of Khitans (16,000 families) who had settled there earlier. Between the mid-12th and early 13th centuries all of the Karakitai over the age of 18 served in the army of the *gurkhans* from the Khitan family of Ye-lü Ta-shih, who created the Karakitai State. The Karakitai raised livestock in the valleys of the Chu and Talasa rivers. Feudal relations, with vestiges of the patriarchal tribal system, prevailed among the Karakitai, although women had considerable rights. The Karakitai were Buddhists, although they made sacrifices to the sky, the earth, and their ancestors. The Karakitai subsequently merged with neighboring Turkic peoples, which is evidenced in the names of tribes and families (kin groups) among the Kirghiz, Kazakhs, and Kara-Kalpaks. [11–1145–1]

KARAKITAI (Karakhitan), a feudal state in Middle and Central Asia (c. 1140–1213), with its capital at Khusyordo (Balasaghun) on the Chu River.

Karakitai (Black Cathay) was founded by Ye-lü Ta-shih, a member of the family that ruled over the empire of the Khitans, one of the Mongol peoples. In 1124, Ye-lü took the title *gurkhan* (chief of a federation of tribes). After the Jurjens (Jurchens) destroyed the Khitan empire in 1125, he fled with a group of his followers to the north. After conquering all of Turkestan with the help of the Khitans who had settled there earlier, he became emperor in 1141. The *gurkhans* coined their own money in the Khitan fashion but otherwise exerted little influence on the economic and internal life of the region. Their activity was limited to the collection of taxes and tribute from their vassals (Balkh, Khwarazm, Kao-Ch'ang). Twice Karakitai was ruled by women. The state stretched from the Amu Darya and Lake Balkhash to the Kunlun Mountains and the uplands of the Pei Mountains. The fall of Karakitai is linked to the seizure of eastern Turkestan by the Mongols and the arrival of the Naimans, who had fled from the Mongols. The Naimans imprisoned the *gurkhan* in 1211. In 1218 they themselves were subjugated by Genghis Khan.

REFERENCES
Bartol'd, V. V. "Ocherk istorii Semirech'ia." *Soch.,* vol. 2, part 1. Moscow, 1963.
Kozhemiako, P. N. *Rannesrednevekovye goroda i poseleniia Chuiskoi doliny.* Frunze, 1959.
Istoriia Kirgizii, vol. 1. Frunze, 1963. [11–1144–3]

KARAKOIN, or Dabusuntuz, a salt lake in southern Karaganda Oblast, Kazakh SSR. Situated on the edge of the Betpak-Dala Desert. Area, approximately 72.5 sq km. Lake Karakoin is landlocked and has a fan-shaped shoreline. Its bays and the small lakes that have separated from it contain curative muds.
[11–1145–4]

KARAKOL, during 1869–89 and 1921–39, the name of the city of Przheval'sk in the Kirghiz SSR. [11–1146–1]

KARAKORAM (Karakorum), a mountain system in Central Asia. The Karakoram are located between the Kunluns in the north and the Transhimalayas in the south. Length, around 500 km; together with their eastern continuation, the Changchenmo and Pangong ranges, which become the Plateau of Tibet, their length is over 800 km. Width, from 150 to 250 km. The Karakoram consist of several parallel ranges and spurs of the ranges, including the Saltoro and the Sasir ranges. The central portion of the Karakoram is a monolithic crest. The Karakoram are one of the highest mountain systems in the world. The average elevation is around 6,000 m; the highest point in the system, Mt. Chogori [Godwin Austen] (8,611 m), is second in height only to Chomolungma [Mt. Everest]. Many passes in the Karakoram lie at altitudes of 4,600–5,800 m.

The topography is mountainous and alpine with rocky crests and steep slopes. The southern slope is long and the northern is short. There is considerable talus; stone-trains are found in the intramontane depressions occupied by the valleys of the Shaiok, Karakash, and other rivers. The cross valleys usually are narrow, deep, and steep-walled gorges. G. D. BESSARABOV

The territory of the Karakoram Mountains belongs to the region of alpine folding, occupying an intermediate position between the structure of the Pamirs and Himalayas. In tectonic terms, the Karakoram are a major anticlinorium with a northwestern strike. Its axial zone was formed by gneiss, crystalline schist, and marble intruded by granodiorite and granite of alpine age; the northeastern zone was formed by argillaceous and carbonaceous rock of the Upper Paleozoic and Mesozoic periods, broken through by individual granitoid bodies. The southwestern zone was formed by weakly metamorphized igneous-sedimentary formations. The structures of the northeastern zone have been tilted sharply toward the north; those of the southwest, toward the south. The systems of major fracture disturbances are the boundaries of the zones. These tectonic zones of various origins were brought together in a single system as a result of intensive uplifts of the Neocene and Anthropogenic times. In the Karakoram are known ore deposits of beryllium and molybdenum (related to the granites), gold (alluvial placers), sulfur (small postmagmatic deposits), precious stones related to the pegmatites, and mineral springs. I. V. ARKHIPOV

The climate is predominantly semidesert and sharply continental. The moisture conditions of the southern slope are influenced by the monsoon of the Indian Ocean; the northern slope is characterized by exceptional aridity. At the foot of the slopes, total precipitation is around 100 mm; over 5,000 m it exceeds 500 mm per year. Precipitation in the mountainous zone (with a summer maximum) always falls in the form of snow. Much of the Karakoram is characterized by below-freezing average annual air temperatures. Other characteristic features of the climate include intensive solar radiation, large daily fluctuations of the air temperature, and significant evaporation.

The glaciated area is 17,800 sq km. Here lie the largest glaciers of the temperate latitudes, including Siachen, which is 75 km long; Baltoro, 62 km; Rimo, 45 km; and Taldybulak, 30 km. Glaciation has developed more heavily on the southern, wetter slope. The snowline on the southern slope of the Karakoram is around 4,700 m, and the glaciers descend to 2,900 m; on the northern slope, the snowline is around 5,900 m, and the glaciers extend to 3,500–3,600 m. Traces of ancient glaciation can be found at 2,600–2,900 m and higher.

The Karakoram are the divide of the Indus and Tarim river basins. The thaw waters of the seasonal and perpetual snow and glaciers are the basic source of water for the rivers. Groundwater accumulates in the talus and contributes to a more even drainage during the year. Thick ice bodies form in the winter. The rivers receive little drainage as they flow through the middle and lower slopes of the range. Landlocked lakes and salt swamps are sometimes encountered in the central parts of the intermontane depressions.

The significant contrasts in the wetness of the northern and southern slopes and the fluctuations of altitude within the Karakoram have caused a great diversity of landscapes; this distribution is subordinate to the patterns of altitude zonality. On the northern slopes, up to 2,400–2,800 m, there are desert landscapes with a sparse vegetation cover of Russian thistle (*Salsola kali*), *Reaumuria,* and *Ephedra.* Extensive areas are completely devoid of vegetation. Only around the sources of the Raskemdar'ia River and its tributaries (the Tarim basin) does one encounter thickets of brush (chiefly barberry) and poplar. Up to an elevation of 3,100 m there are desert-steppe landscapes with sparse thickets of winterfat combined with grasses (sheep's fescue and feathergrass). Up to 3,500 m mountain steppe predominates, and the wettest areas and those best protected from wind have meadow steppes with *Cobresia.* Above this are winterfat and wormwood-winterfat alpine deserts combined with solonchak meadows. On the southern slope in the river valleys up to 3,000–3,500 m are forests of pine and Deodar cedar, as well as willow and poplar along the watercourses. Mountain steppes with elements of alpine meadows are encountered higher up.

The most characteristic fauna is the wild yak, the Tibetan antelope (*Pantholops hodgsoni*), and the addax (*Addax nasomaculata*); in the southern foothills, wild asses are also encountered. Carnivores include the snow leopard. Rodents are numerous (the Chinese striped hamster and others). The characteristic birds are the sand grouse, the Tibetan snowcock, the partridge, the ibis-bill, the snow pigeon, and the red finch (*Pyrrhospiza punicea*).

Areas along the banks of rivers and lakes are often used as pastures. In places farming has developed along the southern slopes. Up to 4,000 m, barley, peas, and alfalfa are grown, and on the lower slopes there are grapes and apricots.

REFERENCES
Puliarkin, V. A. *Kashmir.* Moscow, 1956.
Fiziko-geograficheskoe raionirovanie Kitaia. Moscow, 1957.
Sinitsyn, V. M. *Tsentral'naia Aziia.* Moscow, 1959.
Fizicheskaia geografiia Kitaia. Moscow, 1964.

G. D. BESSARABOV [11–1146–2]

KARAKORUM (Mongolian, Khara-Khorin), capital of the ancient Mongolian empire. Founded by Genghis Khan in 1220, the city existed until the 16th century. Its ruins are located on the upper Orkhon River. Information about Karakorum is contained in Chinese chronicles and the notes of the 13th-century European travelers Giovanni de Piano Carpini, Marco Polo, and Guillaume Rubruquis. The Russian scholar N. M. Iadrintsev investigated the ruins of Karakorum in the late 19th century. By analyzing historical sources, A. M. Pozdneev confirmed the city's location at the Buddhist monastery of Erdeni Dzuu (built in 1585 in the southern part of Karakorum). In 1948–49 a joint Soviet-Mongolian expedition, under the direction of S. V. Kiselev, conducted excavations at Karakorum. The remains of the palace of Ugedei, which was built on a granite foundation, were discovered in the southwestern part of the city. The remains of a Buddhist shrine with wall paintings, dating from the late 12th century or early 13th century, were discovered. The trade and artisan quarters and other objects were investigated in the central part of the city. Plowed fields irrigated by canals were located to the east of the city.

REFERENCES
Atlas drevnostei Mongolii, fasc. 1. St. Petersburg, 1899.
Pozdneev, A. *Mongoliia i mongoly,* vols. 1–2. St. Petersburg, 1896–98.
Iadrintsev, N. M. "Puteshestvie na verkhov'ia Orkhona k razvalinam Karakoruma." *Izvestiia russkogo geograficheskogo obshchestva,* 1890, vol. 26, issue 4.
Drevnemongol'skie goroda. Moscow, 1965.

L. A. EVTIUKHOVA [11–1148–1]

KARA-KOYUNLU (Turkic, "Black Sheep"; from the black sheep on their banner), a group of nomadic Oghuz Turk tribes led by the Baharlu tribe, which originally settled south of Lake Van; it is also the name of the state they created. While supporting the Ottoman Turks and the Jelairids, the tribes of the Kara-Koyunlu fought against Timur (Tamerlane) and his ally, the Ak-Koyunlu. After the death of Timur in 1405, Kara Yusuf, the leader of the Kara-Koyunlu, helped the Jelairids defeat Timur's son, Miranshah; later, however, Kara Yusuf routed the Jelairids, took possession of Azerbaijan, Iraq, and Armenia, and founded the Kara-Koyunlu state (1410). The rulers of this state, Kara Yusuf (1410–20) and Iskandar (1420–36), waged war against the Timurids and the shahs of Shirvan. In 1435, the Timurid sultan Shahrukh and the Shah of Shirvan crushed the army of Iskandar. Jahanshah, who was raised to the throne in 1436, was forced to recognize his vassalage to the Timurids, but in 1447, after Shahrukh's death, he declared his independence. Between 1453 and 1457, the Kara-Koyunlu conquered western Iran. In 1467, Jahanshah's army was routed by Uzun Hasan of the Ak-Koyunlu (ruled from 1453 to 1478). In 1468 the territory of the Kara-Koyunlu state was made part of the Ak-Koyunlu state.

I. P. PETRUSHEVSKII [11–1148–3]

KARAKOZOV, DMITRII VLADIMIROVICH. Born Oct. 23 (Nov. 4), 1840, in the village of Zhmakino, Serdobskii District, Saratov Province, present-day Penza Oblast; died Sept. 3 (15), 1866, in St. Petersburg. Participant in the Russian revolutionary movement, member of a secret revolutionary society in Moscow.

Karakozov, whose family belonged to the lower *dvorianstvo* (nobility), studied at the University of Kazan (from 1861) and Moscow University (from 1864). In early 1866 he became a member of the revolutionary Ishutin Circle, which had been founded by his first cousin N. A. Ishutin in Moscow in 1863. Karakozov arrived in St. Petersburg in the spring of 1866 with the intention of assassinating the tsar. He distributed handwritten copies of his proclamation "To Our Worker Friends," summoning the people to revolution. On Apr. 4, 1866, Karakozov shot at Emperor Alexander II at the gates of the Summer Garden. Sentenced to death by the Supreme Criminal Court, he was hanged at Smolensk Field in St. Petersburg.

E. S. VILENSKAIA [11–1145–1]

KARA-KUL', an urban-type settlement in Osh Oblast, Kirghiz SSR. Situated near the confluence of the Naryn and Karasu rivers on the Frunze-Osh highway, 78 km from the Tash-Kumyr railroad station, the terminus of a branch line from Uchkurgan. Population, 14,600 (1972). Kara-Kul' arose in 1962 with the construction of the Toktogul Hydroelectric Power Station. Branches of the Frunze Polytechnic Institute and Construction Technicum are located in Kara-Kul'. [11–1150–2]

KARAKUL (from Karakul', an oasis on the Zeravshan River, Uzbek SSR), pelts taken from lambs of the Karakul breed on the first to third day after birth. Karakul sheep have unique wool: it is thick, resilient, silky, and glossy and forms compact curls of various shapes and sizes (cylindrical, bean-shaped). The most valuable pelts have cylindrical curls, growing concentrically parallel or in straight lines. The cylinder and the bean curls are most often located on the sacrum and the back; other areas of the pelt are covered with less valuable curls (narrow manes) or defective (rings, half-rings, pea-shapes, and spirals) and deformed ones. Lambs with long cylindrical curls have even, glossy, and silky hair and a thin compact flesh side, which makes the pelts light and tough; they are the highest quality karakul.

Karakul lambs are predominantly black in color (an average of 80 percent); there are also gray lambs (12–15 percent) in several shades from light gray to dark gray and colored ones—*sur,* brown, white, pink, and mottled. The gray karakuls with blue and silver tones are most valued, and silver and gold (Bukhara *sur*) and bronze, platinum, and amber (Surkhan-Dar'in *sur*) are the most popular colored pelts. New natural shades of karakul are being developed.

The pelts are preserved by rubbing the flesh side of the hides with table salt, by keeping them in salt for seven to ten days (dry-salt preservation), and by drying. Dry-salted skins are then fermented by chemical and microbiological treatment with special mixtures of liquid barley-flour dough with salt and leavening from lactic-acid bacteria; they are then dressed and dyed. The only pelts that are dyed are the black and sometimes brown pelts with uneven shading.

There are All-Union State Standards for karakul. Black karakul has the largest number of varieties. The four groups—jacket, flat, ribbed, and Caucasian—have two grades each. Pelts are no smaller than 500 sq cm, and the large ones can exceed 1,100 sq cm. The most valuable karakul is in the jacket group: jacket grade 1, *kirpuk*, and heavy jacket, used for jackets and coats. The other groups are used to manufacture collars, hats, and other fur products.

Its beauty, toughness, and lightness keep karakul in great demand in the USSR and abroad; it is an object of international commerce. The principal suppliers of the world market are the USSR, Afghanistan, and southwestern Africa. The major trade centers are Leningrad, London, and Leipzig. Annual world production of karakul is approximately 10 million pelts.

REFERENCES
Karakul'skie smushki. Moscow-Leningrad, 1932.
Ivanov, M. F., and V. M. Iudin. *Al'bom karakul'skikh smushkov.* Moscow, 1933.
Kantsepol'skii, A. S. *Al'bom karakulia i smushki.* Moscow, 1962.
Kuznetsov, B. A. *Karakul' i smushka.* Moscow, 1955.
Karakulevo-smushkovoe syr'e. Moscow, 1966. (Collection of standards.)
N. S. GIGINEISHVILI [11–1149–2]

KARAKUL' (Turkic, "black lake"), a landlocked lake in the northern part of the Pamirs, in the Tadzhik SSR. Area, 380 sq km; length, approximately 33 km. It is situated in a basin at an altitude of 3,914 m, surrounded by high mountains. Lake Karakul' is divided into two parts, joined by two narrow channels. The western half reaches a depth of 236 m, and the eastern, 22.5 m. The saline water permits visibility to a depth of 9 m. It is covered with ice from late November through April. Summer temperature of the water is about 12°C. The most important rivers flowing into the lake include the Karadzhilga, Karaart, and Muzkol. [11–1150–1]

KARAKUL BREED, a breed of broad-tailed, coarse-wooled sheep used for lambskins. It is the leading breed in the USSR for lambskins.

The majority of researchers consider the Karakul breed a very ancient one and believe that it was developed by the peoples of Middle Asia through prolonged selection of local sheep. In the majority of Karakul sheep the head is semi-hook-nosed; the body is deep; and the tail has a large fatty deposit and ends in a thin S-shaped appendage. Most of the rams have horns; the ewes are hornless. Rams weigh 55–65 kg; ewes, 45–50 kg. The lambs are black (in 80 percent of the sheep), gray, brown, and agouti (*sur*). As they get older, black sheep turn gray; only the color of the head and legs remains the same. The fleece of newborn lambs consists mainly of cylindrical and bean-shaped curls that form a beautiful pattern. As the hair grows, the curls disappear and a coarse wool forms.

The principal product of Karakul sheep is lambskins. Karakul lambskins are in great demand in the USSR and are also exported. The wool of adult sheep is characterized by good fulling capacity and is used in making coarse woolen fabrics and carpets. The wool yield (from two shearings) is 3.5–3.8 kg for rams and 2.0–2.2 kg for ewes. Ewes freed of caring for lambs (because the lambs have been killed for their skins) are used for milk production (25–30 kg per lactation).

Breeding work with the Karakul sheep is aimed at improving the quality of the karakul and increasing the kinds of karakul. The Karakul breed is also used to improve the quality of lamb-skins of other breeds. Karakuls are raised in Iran, Afghanistan, southwestern Africa, and a few other countries. In the USSR they are raised mainly in the Middle Asian republics, Kazakhstan, and some regions of the Ukrainian SSR and the Moldavian SSR.

REFERENCES
Iudin, V. M. *Opyt plemennoi raboty s karakul'skimi ovtsami v plemkhoze "Kara-Kum" (1936–1943 gg.).* Samarkand, 1943.
Baikov, M. I. *Karakul'skaia poroda ovets.* Moscow, 1953.
Gigineishvili, N. S. *Serye karakul'skie ovtsy.* Moscow, 1954.
Ivanov, M. F. *Poln. sobr. soch.,* vol. 3. Moscow, 1964.
I. IA. AVER'IANOV [11–1150–3]

KARAKUL BREEDING, INSTITUTE OF (full name, All-Union Scientific Research Institute of Karakul Breeding), organized in 1935 in Samarkand on the basis of the Katta-Kurgan Experimental Karakul Breeding Center. In 1971 the institute had departments of breeding and genetics; selection and pure-breeding; Astrakhan lamb breeding, merchandising, and the technology of karakul raw materials; pasturing; technology of feeding and keeping; feed production; accounting and organization of agricultural production; and scientific and technical information. It has laboratories of the biology of reproduction, biochemical genetics, morphogenetics and histochemistry, and selection and seed production of pasture plants and experimental workshops. There are branches in Bukhara and Kashkadar'ia Oblast, a base at Turt-Kul, and an experimental farm, the Karnab State Pedigreed Karakul Sheep Plant, in Narpai Raion, Samarkand Oblast. The institute has regular and correspondence graduate work. It has published *Trudy* (Proceedings) since 1940.
I. N. D'IACHKOV [11–1149–1]

KARAKUM (Turkmenskie Karakumyi; in Turkmen, Qara Qum, "black sand"), a sandy desert in the south of Soviet Middle Asia occupying much of the Turkmen SSR. On the north and northeast the desert is bounded by the Sarykamysh Depression and the Amu Darya River valley, on the southeast by the Kara-bil' and Badkhyz uplands, on the south by the piedmont plain of the Kopetdag, and on the west by the old riverbed called the Zapadnyi Uzboi. Area, around 350,000 sq km.

The Karakum consists of the northern, elevated Transunguz Karakum, the southern Lowland or central Karakum, and the southeastern Karakum. In its topography the Karakum Desert is a hilly, strongly dissected plain with a general slope from east to west. The Karakum Desert was basically formed by sandy deposits of the ancient course of the Amu Darya, which flowed across this territory into the Caspian Sea. In the south the Karakum is composed of sediments of the Murgab and Tedzhen rivers; their ancient and modern deltas extend through this area. The Karakum is characterized by compacted areas known as takyrs, which have been formed from the clay deposits of ancient rivers and from alluvial floods, and by the solonchak basins known as *shory*. Around 5 percent of the Karakum is occupied by loose barchan sands virtually devoid of vegetation. They form large areas around the takyrs (*alkany*), narrow strips along the crests of ridges, and uneven sandy areas around oases. The basic area of the Karakum is semiovergrown sands with a broken-up, predominantly alveolate-ridgy and hummocky zoning. In the west the ridges extend to the southwest along the course of the winds; in the center they extend to the south, and in the east they extend to the southeast. In places there are asymmetrical barchan and semiovergrown chains that are perpendicular to the winds. In the southeastern and central Karakum, which are composed of the ancient alluvium of the Amu Darya, Murgab, and Tedzhen, the height of the sand ridges is from 3–5 to 30 m and the distance between them is 150–200 m. In the Transunguz Karakum, which is basically composed of clay-sand deposits of the Miocene and Pliocene paleo–Amu Darya, the ridges are up to 40–60 m high with an average distance of 0.5 km between them. Along the boundary of the Lowland and Transunguz Karakum runs the Unguz, a chain of isolated solonchak basins of various levels. In the west some of these were flooded by Pliocene seas, and others at times were filled with sandy debris of the paleo–Amu Darya.

The Transunguz Karakum is an Epihercynian platform with a Mesocenozoic mantle made up of a series of branching anticlinal structures, downwarped in the north (the Khorezm Depression in the lower courses of the Amu Darya) and subsiding along the flexure of the Unguz to the south. The topography has not retained its previous alluvial features and as a whole has been formed by neotectonics and aeolian processes.

The Lowland Karakum is a foredeep-type formation with an Epipaleozoic cover up to 12 km thick. The overlying Anthropogenic river deposits have basically maintained the topographic features of the delta fans of the Murgab and Tedzhen and of the plain of the paleo–Amu Darya, which extends transversely to the deltas. The thickness of the Anthropogenic alluvium varies from 500 m in the southeastern Karakum to 5,000 m and more in the west. The Amu Darya left the Lowland Karakum at the end of the Anthropogenic period (approximately 20,000–30,000 years ago). When the Khvalys' Sea (around 15,000–20,000 years ago) formed a vast bay in the Lowland Karakum with a level of +50 m absolute elevation, its waters were salty, since the Amu Darya was diverted into the Khorezm Depression. Here it formed a lake from which it began to flow initially to the north (the Akchadar'ia Channel) and later to the west into the Sarykamysh Depression. Having filled it, the Amu Darya in the fifth to the second millennia B.C. again began to flow into the Caspian, having formed the Zapadnyi Uzboi River.

The climate of the Karakum is sharply continental, with a very hot, cloudless, and protracted summer, a mild spring with rains, a warm dry autumn, and a winter that is frosty but with frequent thaws. The mean January temperature in the north is around −5°C and, in the south, about 3°C; the mean July temperatures are 28° and 34°C, respectively. There are very high daily temperature variations (up to 50°C for the air and up to 80°C for the soil). Precipitation is from 60 to 150 mm per year (more in the south). Up to 70 percent of the precipitation falls from November to April. The growing season is 200–270 days. The Amu Darya flows along the northeastern edge of the Karakum; the Tedzhen and Murgab run out in the sands without reaching a lake or sea. The Karakum is rich in groundwater, which lies at varying depths: from 3–6 m near the Amu Darya (the basic source of all the Karakum underground water) to 300 m on the Karabil' Uplands. The groundwater is recovered by wells. In those areas where river waters seep through to it, the groundwater is slightly saline, but in the central portions of the Karakum it is highly mineralized.

The Karakum soils on the overgrown sands are of the gray-brown type and are shallow; in the depressions are solonchaks and takyrs. In the spring, the entire territory of the Karakum, with the exception of the barchan sands, is covered with a green carpet of ephemerals and ephemeroids that die out in late April and early May. Typical is sand sedge (*ilak,* the basic feed for sheep) and brush, including the black and white saxauls, *kandym* [*Calligonium*], sand acacia, ephedra, and *Astragalus.* Those barchan sands that are overgrown are characterized by *Aristida* grass, sand acacia, one or two species of *Calligonium,* and the arboreal saltwort, or *cherkez* [*Salsola richteri*]. The typical animals are the Persian gazelle, the corsac, the wolf, the sand cat, and the steppe cat; rodents are particularly numerous. Of the birds, there are the saxaul jay, numerous larks, the desert raven, and sparrows. The characteristic reptiles are snakes (including the carpet viper, *Taphrometoron lineolatum,* the sand snake, and the cobra), lizards (the agama, geckos, and the monitor, which can be up to 1.5 m long), and the Horsfield's terrapin. Tarantulas and scorpions are common. Much of the desert is used as year-round pasture for sheep and camels. Minerals include sulfur, oil, and gas.

Human habitation is concentrated predominantly in the oases formed by the Amu Darya, Tedzhen, and Murgab rivers and by the small rivers flowing off the northern slopes of the Kopetdag. During the years of Soviet power, large livestock sovkhozes have been created in the Karakum, more than 6,000 wells have been reconstructed or dug, dirt roads have been built, the Chardzhou-Kungrad railroad has been constructed along the northeastern edge of the desert, and motor transport has come into wide use. Air connections have also been developed. In the southern part of the Karakum, the Karakum Canal has been built, contribut-ing to both irrigation and navigation. The Middle Asia–Center Gas Pipeline passes across the Karakum.

The development prospects of the Karakum are linked with a rapid growth in the exploitation of the very rich oil and gas deposits and with the further development of mechanized irrigation and cotton growing, particularly in the zone of the Karakum Canal; a further rise in livestock raising is also envisioned. Extensive work is being done on reforestation, on stabilization of the drifting sands, and on plant improvement of the pastures. In the southeastern Karakum lies the world's oldest center for the study of sand, the Repetek Sand Research Station of the Academy of Sciences of the Turkmen SSR.

REFERENCES

Fedorovich, B. A. *Lik pustyni,* 3rd ed. Moscow, 1954.
Ocherki prirody Kara-Kumov. Moscow, 1955.
Babaev, A. G. *Pustynia Karakumy.* Ashkhabad, 1963.
Sovetskii Turkmenistan. Ashkhabad, 1968.
Turkmenistan. Moscow, 1969. (Part of the series *Sovetskii Soiuz.*)

B. A. FEDOROVICH   [11–1153–1]

KARAKUM CANAL (full name, V. I. Lenin Karakum Canal), a canal in the Turkmen SSR, supplying water from the Amu Darya to the southern part of the republic and the nearly waterless basins of the Murgab, Tedzhen, and a number of small rivers that flow off the Kopetdag.

The first stage of the canal, from the Amu Darya to the Murgab, some 400 km long, went into service in 1959. The first 40 km runs through the widened channel of the Bosaga-Kerki Canal; for 70 km the canal crosses the chain of Kelifskii Uzboi depressions, which have been turned into a series of lakes. The Karakum Canal then crosses the southeastern Karakum. Finally the water of the Karakum Canal is brought by a pressure duct up the Murgab to Turkmen-Kala.

The second stage, from the Murgab to the Tedzhen, is some 140 km long and was built in 1960. Here the Khauz-Khan Reservoir was built with a capacity of 650 million cu m (an increase up to 875 million cu m is envisaged).

The third stage, from the Tedzhen to Geok-Tepe, some 300 km long, runs along the foothills of the Kopetdag (in 1962 it reached Ashkhabad and, in 1967, Geok-Tepe). This stage terminates in the 190 million cu m Kopetdag Reservoir, which is under construction (1973). At Ashkhabad, two reservoirs have been created, with a capacity of 48 million cu m and 6 million cu m. The general development plans for the Karakum Canal envision further lengthening, with a branch from Kazandzhik to the Kizyl-Atrek Canal, for irrigating the desert land in southwestern Turkmenia, and to the Nebit-Dag Canal, for supplying water to the oil-field zone of western Turkmenia.

The Karakum Canal is equipped with a headwork (capacity, over 300 cu m per sec) with a navigable lock, a number of escape and retaining structures, and outlets into the distribution network and reservoirs.

In the area of the canal, a drainage network is being built to eliminate the negative effect on soil fertility of a rise in the groundwater level caused by the delivery of large additional amounts of water.

As a result of completing the Karakum Canal, the water resources of the zone and the delivery of water to the irrigation systems have been significantly increased. The canal meets the water needs of the cities, industry, and agriculture in the zone. The irrigated area in the zone of the Karakum Canal has increased from 170,000 hectares (ha) to 300,000 ha; water has been supplied to 5 million ha of outlying pastures. Fishing has developed on the Karakum Canal (catfish, carp, rudd, barbel, silver carp, and grass carp). The canal is navigable for 450 km. The Directives on the Five-year Plan for the Development of the National Economy in 1971–75, put forth by the Twenty-fourth Congress of the CPSU, call for the completion of land development in the zone of the third construction stage of the Karakum Canal and the continuation of construction on this canal.

REFERENCES

Mirkin, S. L. *Vodnye melioratsii v SSSR i puti ikh razvitiia.* Moscow, 1960.

Grinberg, L. M. *Karakumskii kanal.* Ashkhabad, 1963.
Amanov, Kh., and A. Batyrov. "Karakumskii kanal—torzhestvo leninskikh idei orosheniia." *Gidrotekhnika i melioratsiia,* no. 6, 1969.
                                          S. L. MIRKIN   [11–1152–1]

KARAKURT (*Lactrodectus tredecimguttatus*), a poisonous spider. The males and sexually immature females are predominantly black with white-bordered red spots on the abdomen.
Maximum length, 2 cm. The karakurt is found in North Africa,
Southwest Asia, and Southern Europe. In the USSR it inhabits
the southern Ukraine, the deserts and piedmonts of Middle Asia,
and the steppe belt from Moldavia to the Enisei.

   Feeding primarily on insects, the karakurt does not bite animals or humans unless it is provoked. The bites of the female are
highly poisonous. They cause an acute local reaction (gangrene)
and, at times, severe poisoning resulting in death. Initially, the
victim experiences sharp pain around the area of the bite. The
pain gradually spreads throughout the entire body. The victim
becomes restless and breaks out in a cold sweat. Other symptoms
are cyanosis of the skin, chills, difficulty in breathing, paresis,
and coma.

   Treatment includes the subcutaneous or intravenous administering of karakurt antitoxin (30–70 ml), as well as the intravenous infusion of painkillers (novocaine, promedol, and
camphor), heart medicines (strophanthin), and 10 ml of a 10
percent solution of magnesium sulfate.

   It is recommended that sheep graze in pastures where karakurts might be encountered. They are least sensitive to the bite.
After the sheep trample the spiders, camels, horses, and cattle
can graze in the pasture.   E. N. PAVLOVSKII   [11–1155–2]

KARALAEV, SAIAKBAI. Born in 1894, in the village of Uch-
Koi-Su, present-day Issyk-Kul' Oblast; died May 7, 1971, in
Frunze. Soviet Kirghiz storyteller. People's Artist of the Kirghiz
SSR.

   Karalaev memorized more than half a million lines from ancient folk tales and legends, including the epic *Manas.* He dictated a complete version of *Manas.*

REFERENCES
Abramzon, S. M. *Ocherk kul'tury kirgizskogo naroda.* Frunze, 1946.
Zhirmunskii, V. M. "Sredneaziatskie narodnye skaziteli." *Izvestiia
   Vsesoiuznogo geograficheskogo obshchestva,* 1947, no. 4.
Auezov, M. O. "Skaziteli eposa." In *Mysli raznykh let.* Alma-Ata, 1959.
                                                         [11–1156–1]

KARALIICHEV, ANGEL. Born Aug. 21, 1902, in Strazhitsa,
near Turnovo. Bulgarian writer. Honored Cultural Worker of
Bulgaria (1963).

   Karaliichev's first collection of short stories, *Rye* (1925), portrayed the heroes of the antifascist September Uprising of 1923.
He emerged during the 1930's as a master of the realistic short
story (he published many collections) and as an author of children's books. Although the works of those years smoothed over
social contradictions, they expressed his love for the common
people, for Bulgaria's natural beauty, and for its heritage.

   After the establishment of the people's democratic system
(1944), Karaliichev turned to new themes: images of the contemporary peasants. Social motifs intensified in his work—for example, the collection *The Cornfields of the Falcon* (1946), *The
People's Defender* (1949), and *The Anvil or the Hammer* (1954).
He is the author of many books for children (*The Valiant Bul-
garians,* 1959). Karaliichev received the Dimitrov Prize in 1966.

WORKS
Izbrani proizvedeniia, vols. 1–3. Sofia, 1962–63.
In Russian translation:
Izbr. proizv. Sofia, 1957.
Vesna. Moscow, 1961.
REFERENCE
Sheptunov, I. "A. Karaliichev." In *Suchasni bolgars'ki pys'mennyky.*
   Kiev, 1962.   [11–1156–2]

KARAMAN, a city in southern Turkey, in Konya Vilayet on the
Konya-Adana railroad line. Population, 35,000 (1970). Industry
includes a textile factory and flour mills. The city is the commercial center for an agricultural region producing grains and wool.
                                                         [11–1156–4]

KARAMI, RASHID ABD AL'HAMID. Born 1921 in Tripoli,
Lebanon. Lebanese statesman.

   Karami was educated as a lawyer. He graduated from the
University of Cairo in 1947. From 1948 to 1951, he practiced
law. In 1951 he was elected to parliament from the city of
Tripoli. Between 1951 and 1955 he occupied various ministerial
posts. He was prime minister in 1955–56 and then from September 1958 to October 1970 (with interruptions). On May 28, 1975,
he was again appointed prime minister. Karami supports the
strengthening of the national independence and sovereignty of
Lebanon.   [11–1156–6]

KARAMIAN, ARTASHES IVANOVICH. Born Mar. 2 (15), in
1908, in Kafan, in present-day Armenian SSR. Soviet neuro-
physiologist; corresponding member of the Academy of Sciences
of the USSR (1970) and the Academy of Sciences of the Armenian SSR (1963). Member of the CPSU since 1940.

   Karamian graduated from the Yerevan Medical Institute in
1935, a student of L. A. Orbeli. He worked in the Institute of
Physiology of the Academy of Sciences of the USSR from 1945
to 1950 and in the Institute of Experimental Medicine of the
Academy of Medical Sciences of the USSR from 1950 to 1959.
He has been with the I. M. Sechenov Institute of Evolutionary
Physiology and Biochemistry of the Academy of Sciences of the
USSR since 1959. His main works deal with the evolution of
cerebellar and cerebral functions in the phylogenetic vertebrate
series (cyclostomes, fishes, amphibians, reptiles, and mammals)
and with the comparative pathology of the central nervous system and the tropic-adaptive role of the autonomic nervous
system in regulating the functions of the higher divisions of
the brain. Karamian has been awarded the I. P. Pavlov Prize of
the Academy of Sciences of the USSR (1957), the Order of the
Patriotic War Second Class, and various medals.

WORKS
Evoliutsiia funktsii mozzhechka i bol'shikh polusharii golovnogo mozga.
   Leningrad, 1956.
Metodologicheskie osnovy evoliutsionnoi neirofiziologii. Leningrad, 1969.
Funktsional'naia evoliutsiia mozga pozvonochnykh. Leningrad, 1970.
                                                         [11–1161–4]

KARAMIAN, ERAZM ALEKSANDROVICH (real surname,
Melik-Karamian). Born Mar. 2 (15), 1912, in Paris. Soviet motion-picture director; People's Artist of the Armenian SSR
(1966). Member of the CPSU since 1945.

   Karamian graduated from the School of Drama in Kharkov
in 1935. He began working in Armenian cinema in 1936. In
1947–54 he directed newsreels and in 1954 began making feature
films. His most important works (with S. A. Kevorkov) are *The
Path of Thunder* (1956), *Known Personally* (1958), *Mission Extraordinary* (1965), and *Explosion Past Midnight* (1966). He also
directed *The Ghosts Leave the Summits* (1955), *Nasreddin in
Khodzhent, or the Charmed Prince* (1960, with A. I. Bek-
Nazarov), and *The Twelve Fellow-Travelers* (1962). He took part
in writing the screenplays for several of his films. Karamian was
awarded the State Prize of the Armenian SSR (1967), two orders, and also medals.

REFERENCES
Maksimov, M. D. *Lichno izvesten.* Moscow, 1958.
Rizaev, S. *Armianskaia khudozhestvennaia kinematografiia.* Yerevan,
   1963.   [11–1162–1]

KARAMURAN (Dawan), a pass in the Arkatag (Przheval'skii)
mountain range in western China, at an altitude of 5,578 m. It
is on the route linking the Charchan oasis of the Kashgar Plain
with the inner regions of Tibet.   [11–1161–1]

KARA-MURZA, GEORGII SERGEEVICH. Born May 10
(23), 1906, in Moscow; died Aug. 22, 1945. Soviet historian and
sinologue. Became a member of the CPSU in 1939.

   Kara-Murza became a teacher in 1932. He was a professor at
the Moscow Institute of Oriental Studies from 1935 to 1938;

from 1939 to 1941 he was a professor at Moscow State University and a senior researcher at the Institute of History of the Academy of Sciences of the USSR. Kara-Murza fought in the Great Patriotic War and was killed at the front. His major works dealt with the history of China and included the *The T'aip'ings* (1941; 3rd ed., 1957), "On the Problem of the Class Nature of Sun Yat-senism" (*Problemy Kitaia,* 1931, nos. 6–7), and chapters on the history of China in the college textbook *Modern History of the Colonial and Dependent Countries* (vol. 1, 1940).

[11–1161–2]

KARAMYSH, a river in Saratov Oblast, RSFSR, with its upper course in Volgograd Oblast; a left tributary of the Medveditsa (the Don Basin). Length, 147 km; basin area, 3,380 sq km. The Karamysh originates in and flows through the Volga Upland and is fed primarily by melting snow. Its waters are used for irrigation.

[11–1161–3]

KARAMZIN, NIKOLAI MIKHAILOVICH. Born Dec. 1 (12), 1766, in the village of Mikhailovka, in present-day Buzuluk Raion, Orenburg Oblast; died May 22 (June 3), 1826, in St. Petersburg. Russian writer, publicist, and historian. Son of a landowner in Simbirsk Province.

Karamzin received his education at home and then at a boarding school in Moscow (until 1783); he also attended lectures at Moscow University. He came into contact with Freemasons through N. I. Novikov's circle. Karamzin's interest in the philosophy of the Enlightenment and the works of English and German sentimentalists helped form his philosophy and literary views. He published numerous translations, as well as his original tale *Eugene and Julia* (1789), in Novikov's journal *Detskoe chtenie dlia serdtsa i razuma* (Children's Reading for Heart and Mind). Karamzin broke with the Masons in 1789. He traveled throughout Western Europe and upon his return to Russia published *Moskovskii zhurnal* (Moscow Journal; 1791-92), in which he printed his own works as well: the main part of *Letters of a Russian Traveler;* the short novels *Liodor, Poor Liza,* and *Natalia, the Boyar's Daughter;* and the verses "Poetry" and "To Grace." The journal also published Karamzin's critical essays and reviews on literature and theater and helped propagate the aesthetic principles of sentimentalism.

Karamzin was intensely involved with the Great French Revolution. He was disenchanted with the Jacobin dictatorship of 1793–94, but later reacted positively on the whole to bourgeois law and order, which was preserved and consolidated under Napoleon I. After an almost complete silence imposed during the reign of Pavel I, Karamzin resumed his work as a publicist and used his journal *Vestnik Evropy* (The Messenger of Europe) as the platform for a program of moderate conservatism. His historical novella, *Marfa Posadnitsa, or The Conquest of Novgorod* (1803), was published in his journal and affirmed the inevitable victory of autocracy over the free city.

Karamzin was the acknowledged leader of Russian sentimentalism, and his literary activity played an enormous part in deepening Russian literature's interest in the individual, perfected the literary means used in depicting man's inner life, and contributed to the development of the Russian literary language. Karamzin's early prose influenced the work of V. A. Zhukovskii, K. N. Batiushkov, and the young Pushkin.

From the mid-1790's, Karamzin's interest focused on historical problems. He abandoned literature and worked chiefly on his *History of the Russian State* (vols. 1–8, 1816–17; vol. 9, 1821; vols. 10–11, 1824; vol. 12, 1829; reprinted repeatedly), which became not only an important historical work but also an outstanding Russian prose work and served as the principal source for Pushkin's *Boris Godunov* and Russian historical drama of the 1830's.   I. Z. SERMAN

Karamzin's historical views stemmed from the rationalistic conception of political development: the history of mankind is the history of worldwide progress, at the heart of which lies the struggle between reason and delusion and enlightenment and ignorance. According to Karamzin, great men play a decisive role in history, and he endeavored in every way possible to show the ideological and moral motivations behind the actions of historical figures. For him psychological analysis was the princi-

pal device to explain historical events. To Karamzin history was a science that exhorted people to social activity. He defended the inviolability of the autocracy and the necessity of preserving serfdom. He condemned the uprising of the Decembrists and approved of their punishment. His *A Note on Ancient and Modern Russia* (1811) sharply criticized M. M. Speranskii's program of government reforms.

Karamzin was an advocate of the Norman theory in explaining the origins of the Russian state. His division of Russian history into periods corresponded closely to that of V. N. Tatishchev and M. M. Shcherbatov. All three identified the history of the country with the history of the state, and the history of the state with that of the aristocracy. Karamzin, however, introduced much that was new, both in terms of understanding the course of Russian history and in his evaluation of specific historical events.

Unlike Tatishchev and Shcherbatov, who saw the appanage system as a regression and the result of inept politics on the part of the great princes who divided the state among their sons, Karamzin saw it as a feudal system "in conformity with the conditions and spirit of the time" and common to all Western European countries. He viewed the formation of a single state under Ivan III as a process analogous to and simultaneous with the formation of large centralized states in Western Europe.

Karamzin was not satisfied with a purely rationalistic explanation of historical events and in a number of cases used what is known as the pragmatic view of history and the comparative historical method, thus putting himself on a level with the most advanced historical methods of that time. He was the first to use a vast number of historical documents, including the Trinity, Laurentian, and Hypatian chronicles, the Dvina Statutes, the Sudebniki (Muscovy Law Codes), and accounts by foreigners. Karamzin gave excerpts from these documents in his extensive notes to the *History,* which long remained a unique archive. However, in the text Karamzin frequently deviated from his sources or showed a preference for a less accurate source in order to satisfy his political aims and monarchistic conceptions or to enliven or embroider the events.

Karamzin's *History* promoted the growth of interest in Russian history among various sectors of Russian society. It heralded a new stage in the development of Russian noble historiography. Karamzin's view of history was officially endorsed and supported by the government, and the Slavophiles considered Karamzin their spiritual father. The representatives of the progressive camp (the Decembrists, V. G. Belinskii, and N. G. Chernyshevskii) reacted negatively to Karamzin's *History.* It also was received critically by members of the newly formed school of Russian bourgeois historiography (M. T. Kachenovskii, N. A. Polevoi, and S. M. Soloviev).   I. A. KUDRIAVTSEV

WORKS
Soch., vols. 1–9, 3rd ed. Moscow, 1820.
Izbr. soch., vols. 1–2. Introduction by P. N. Berkov and G. P. Makogonenko. Moscow, 1964.
Poln. sobr. stikhotvorenii. Introduction, editing, and notes by Iu. M. Lotman. Moscow-Leningrad, 1966.

REFERENCES
Pogodin, M. P. *N. M. Karamzin po ego sochineniiam, pis'mam i otzyvam sovremennikov,* parts 1–2. Moscow, 1866.
Bestuzhev-Riumin, K. *Biografii i kharakteristiki.* St. Petersburg, 1882.
Gukovskii, G. A. "Karamzin." *Istoriia russkoi literatury,* vol. 5. Moscow-Leningrad, 1941.
Rubinshtein, N. L. *Russkaia istoriografiia.* Moscow, 1941.
Ocherki istorii istoricheskoi nauki v SSSR, vol. 1. Moscow, 1955.
Istoriografiia istorii SSSR s drevneishikh vremen do Velikoi Oktiabr'skoi sotsialisticheskoi revoliutsii. Moscow, 1961.
Kupreianova, E. N. "Russkii roman pervoi chetverti XIX v.: Ot sentimental'noi povesti k romanu." In *Istoriia russkogo romana,* vol. 1. Moscow-Leningrad, 1962.
Vatsuro, V. "Podvig chestnogo cheloveka." *Prometei,* vol. 5. Moscow, 1968.
Kisliagina, L. G. "K voprosu o razvitii sotsial'no-politicheskikh vzgliadov N. M. Karamzina v 90-x godakh XVIII stoletiia." *Vestnik MGU,* series 12: *Istoriia,* 1968, no. 5.
Kulakova, L. I. "Esteticheskie vzgliady Karamzina." In her book *Ocherki istorii russkoi esteticheskoi mysli XVIII v.* Leningrad, 1968.

Derzhavin i Karamzin v literaturnom dvizhenii XVIII–nachala XIX vv. Leningrad, 1969. (Collection.)
Istoriia russkoi literatury XIX v.: Bibliograficheskii ukazatel'. Moscow-Leningrad, 1962.   [11–1158–1]

KARANDASH (pseudonym of Mikhail Nikolaevich Rumiantsev). Born Nov. 27 (Dec. 10), 1901, in St. Petersburg. Soviet circus artist; clown. People's Artist of the USSR (1969).

Karandash graduated from a technicum of circus art in 1930 and made his debut as a floor clown. Initially he appeared as a Charlie Chaplin type, but in 1934–35, while working in the Leningrad Circus, he created a new character, adopting the pseudonym of the French caricature artist Caran d'Ache. His character is an adult who retains the spontaneity and *joie de vivre* of the child; this helps to create comic situations and to lend credence to the stunts performed by the artist. He continually appears during the acts of acrobats, gymnasts, jugglers, and animal trainers. In 1946, Karandash began heading clown troupes. His students and partners included Iu. V. Nikulin and M. I. Shuidin. He has appeared in motion pictures (*Karandash on the Ice*) and has toured abroad on a number of occasions.

WORKS
Na arene sovetskogo tsirka. Moscow, 1954.

REFERENCE
Nikulin, L. *Karandash.* Moscow, 1951.

IU. A. DMITRIEV   [11–1162–2]

KARANDEEV, KONSTANTIN BORISOVICH. Born July 5 (18), 1907, in the village of Napol'noe, present-day Muravlianka Raion, Riazan' Oblast; died Sept. 21, 1969, in L'vov. Soviet scientist in electrical measurements and automatic control; corresponding member of the Academy of Sciences of the USSR (1958), Honored Scientist and Engineer of the Ukrainian SSR (1954).

Karandeev graduated from the Leningrad Polytechnic Institute in 1930. Beginning in 1936 he taught in a number of educational institutions. He was one of the organizers of the Siberian Branch of the Academy of Sciences of the USSR. From 1958 to 1967 he was the director of the branch's Institute of Automation and Electrometry.

Karandeev was the founder of the scientific school in the theory of measurements and data measuring systems. He was awarded the Order of Lenin and medals.

WORKS
Metody elektricheskikh izmerenii. Moscow-Leningrad, 1952.
Mostovye metody izmerenii. Kiev, 1953.
Poluprovodnikovye vypriamiteli v izmeritel'noi tekhnike. Kiev, 1954.
Spetsial'nye metody elektricheskikh izmerenii. Moscow-Leningrad, 1963.
[11–1163–2]

KARANOVO, a hill in southern Bulgaria, where the remains of ancient settlements have been found; its stratigraphy serves as the foundation for the periodization of the Neolithic and Aeneolithic periods in Bulgaria. Excavations were conducted at Karanovo by V. Mikov and G. Georgiev in 1936 and between 1947 and 1957. There are seven primary cultural levels (five according to V. Mikov) in a bed with an overall thickness of 13.5 m. The lowest level contained remains of an early Neolithic culture dating from the sixth–fifth millennium B.C.: pottery with white paintings on a red background, sickles made of horn with flint insets, grain mortars, and remains of large rectangular dwellings with stoves (Karanovo I). The third level yielded remains of the late Neolithic Veselinovo culture (middle of the fifth millennium B.C.). Black and gray glazed pottery and four-legged vessels are typical of this level. The fifth level (Maritsa culture, beginning of the fourth millennium B.C.) had gray pottery with incised ornamentation filled in with white paste. The sixth level belongs to the Bulgarian variation of the Gumelniţa culture (middle of the fourth millennium B.C.). Among the discoveries in this level are houses with stoves, grain reserves, and pottery decorated with graffiti. The seventh level pertains to the early Bronze Age (third millennium B.C.). Typical remains of this level are houses with apses and black and brown pottery decorated with cord impressions.

REFERENCES
Mikov, V. "Kul'tura neolita, eneolita i bronzy v Bolgarii." *Sovetskaia arkheologiia,* 1958, no. 1.
Georgiev, G. J. "Kulturgruppen der Jungstein-und der Kupferzeit in der Ebene von Thrazien (Südbulgarien)." *L'Europe à la fin de l'âge de la pierre.* Prague, 1961.   V. S. TITOV   [11–1164–1]

KARA PENAL COLONY, a penal colony for political prisoners in tsarist Russia on the Kara River (Baikal region); part of the Nerchinsk Penal Colony.

The colony was created in 1838. Criminal convicts and, after 1873, political convicts as well were sent to the Kara to work in the goldfields. There were seven prisons on the Kara; one of these, built in 1881, was for political convicts. Through the Kara Penal Colony passed 211 to 217 political prisoners, 32 of them women. Most of them were Narodniks (Populists) sentenced at the trials of the 1870's and 1880's, including I. N. Myshkin, E. K. Breshko-Breshkovskaia, E. N. Koval'skaia, N. A. Ishutin, P. A. Alekseev, and P. I. Voinaral'skii. Of these, 25 prisoners were sentenced to penal servitude with indefinite terms; 22, to 20 years. The situation of the political prisoners sharply deteriorated in 1882 after an unsuccessful escape attempt by eight convicts led by Myshkin. The prisoners responded to the repressions with lengthy hunger strikes. New waves of disturbances broke out in 1888 at the Kara Penal Colony because of the humiliation of political prisoners (particularly E. N. Koval'skaia). Mass suicides at Kara took place during the disturbances; this so-called Kara tragedy led to the closing of the Kara Penal Colony in 1890. The political prisoners were transferred to Akatui, where they were lodged together with criminal convicts and shared their working conditions, food, and regime of punishments.

REFERENCES
Kara i drugie tiur'my Nerchinskoi katorgi. Moscow, 1927.
Gernet, M. I. *Istoriia tsarskoi tiur'my,* vol. 3. Moscow, 1961.
IA. M. SHORR   [11–1265–2]

KARAS, VJEKOSLAV. Born May 19, 1821, in Karlovac; died there July 5, 1858. Croatian painter, founder of secular realist art in Croatia.

Karas began his artistic studies in Karlovac. He subsequently entered the Florentine Academy of Arts. From 1841 to 1847 he studied under J. F. Overbeck in Rome. His paintings executed in Italy were devoted to mythological subjects; his drawings dealt with folk types. Karas returned to Karlovac in 1848, where he was a successful portraitist. His paintings, which reflect the influence of the Biedermeier style, are distinguished by keen observation, thorough modeling of forms, and subtle contemplative imagery. Among his works are *Roman Girl With a Lute* (1845–47) and the portraits of A. Krešić and M. Krešić (1852–56)—all are in the Gallery of Modern Arts of the Yugoslav Academy in Zagreb.

REFERENCE
Bulat-Simić, A. *Vjekoslav Karas.* Zagreb, 1958.   [11–1170–1]

KARAS, an elliptically shaped clay pitcher used in Armenia for fermenting, storing, and carrying wine. In Georgia small pitchers of this type are called *churi,* and large pitchers, *kvevri.*
[11–1170–2]

KARA SEA, a marginal sea of the Arctic Ocean; located between the coast of the West Siberian Lowland and the islands of Novaia Zemlia, Franz Josef Land, and Severnaia Zemlia. It has an area of approximately 880,000 sq km. The average depth is 127 m, the maximum depth 620 m, and the water volume 112,-000 cu km. The sea's greatest length, from the southwest to the northeast, is about 1,500 km. The greatest width is 800 km in the northern part. The principal inlets (Baidarata and Ob' bays and the Enisei, Piasina, and Taimyr inlets) cut into the low, and in places gently sloping, coast of the mainland. The largest rivers flowing into the sea are the Enisei, Ob', Piasina, and Kara, which gives the sea its name. They have an annual discharge of approximately 1,300 cu km, 80 percent of which occurs in the summer. The Kara Sea has numerous islands (total area of approximately

10,000 sq km). They are concentrated mainly in the northeastern part and include the Minin Islands and the Nordenshel'd Archipelago (more than 70 islands). In the central part of the Kara Sea are the Arkticheskii Institut Islands, the Izvestiia TsIK Islands, the Sergei Kirov Islands, Vize Island, Ushakov Island, Shmidt Island, and Uedinenie Island. There are many low-lying, sandy islands (Belyi, for example).

The Kara Sea is located on the continental shelf; thus, approximately 40 percent of it is less than 50 m deep and only 2 percent is more than 500 m deep. The shelf is cut in the north by two wide, deepwater troughs— St. Anne's Trough, which lies along the eastern shore of Franz Josef Land and is up to 620 m deep, and the Voronin Trough, which lies along the western shore of Severnaia Zemlia and is up to 450 m deep. Between the troughs is the underwater Central Kara Rise (less than 50 m deep) from which Vize and Ushakov islands protrude. The Novaia Zemlia Trough (200–418 m deep) stretches along the eastern shore of Novaia Zemlia.

The water area of the Kara Sea has had transgressions numerous times and assumed its present shape as the result of the retreat of Pleistocene glaciation. Traces of this glaciation are found under a thin layer of sediments—brown, gray, and light blue silts in troughs and deepwater hollows and sandy silts on underwater heights and in shallow areas. Rocky soils are found in the northeastern part of the sea. Sand predominates on shoals and near the coast of the mainland.

The climate is a severe arctic one. The polar night lasts for three to four months of the year, and the polar day lasts two to three months. The air temperature remains below 0°C for nine to ten months in the northern part of the sea and for seven to eight months in the south. The average temperature in January is from −20° to −28°C; the minimum temperature is −46°C. The average temperature in July is from 6° to −1°C; the maximum temperature is 16°C. The number of days in July during which the temperature drops below freezing ranges from six in the south to 20 in the north. Gale winds and snowstorms are common in the winter and snow squalls and fogs in the summer. The sea is covered with ice for most of the year, with ice first forming in September in the north and in October in the south. During the winter, fast ice forms near the coast and between the islands, and beyond that there is floe ice. As summer approaches the fast ice breaks up, and the ice in the southern and northern parts of the sea forms stable masses. In years when conditions for navigation are unfavorable, ice floes cover almost the entire sea during the summer; in other years there are large ice-free expanses.

The water masses are extremely cold and stratified. Most of the water has a temperature that is below −1.5°C; only in the troughs do warm Atlantic waters enter from the Arctic Basin. At depths of 150–200 m their temperature is up to 2.5°C. In the winter the temperature of the layer of water under the ice is from −1.5° to −1.7°C. In the summer the temperature of the surface water between the ice floes is only slightly higher; in regions that have become ice-free the temperature reaches 6°C in the southwestern part of the sea and 2°C in the northern. The upper layer of water is very fresh as a result of river inflow and summer thawing. In one year the river waters could form a freshwater layer 160 cm thick, the greatest of any sea in the world. (In the world ocean the average thickness of this layer is only 10 cm.) Salinity of the water near the mouths of the Ob' and Enisei is 10–12 parts per thousand (‰), near Zhelanie Cape it rises to 30‰, and near Franz Josef Land it reaches 33‰. In the southwestern part of the sea the salinity of surface waters ranges from 20 to 25‰, increasing toward the southern straits to 30–31‰.

The currents move in two slow counterclockwise rotations in the southwestern and northeastern parts of the sea. Tides are primarily semidiurnal, with an average height of 0.5–0.8 m. Owing to the wind the water level in the inlets may vary by as much as 2 m.

The Kara Sea is rich in invertebrates and semi-anadromous fish (arctic cisco, muksun, nelma, arctic char, navaga, and flounder). Marine mammals inhabiting the Kara Sea include the ringed seal, walrus, bearded seal, and beluga. There are many birds on the islands (primarily guillemots, razorbills, and little auks), where they form colonies. Land animals that visit the islands are the polar bear and the polar fox.

The Kara Sea is part of the Northern Sea Route. The chief port is Dikson. Seagoing vessels also travel up the Enisei to the cities of Igarka and Dudinka. The principal items shipped are timber, building materials, furs, and foodstuffs. With the discovery of major deposits of petroleum and natural gas in the Ob'-Enisei region, the Kara Sea routes have become much more important.

REFERENCES
Vize, V. Iu. *Moria Sovetskoi Arktiki* [3rd ed.]. Moscow-Leningrad, 1948.
Sovetskaia Arktika: Moria i ostrova Severnogo Ledovitogo okeana. Moscow, 1970.   E. G. NIKIFOROV and A. O. SHPAIKHER [11–1367–4]

KARASLAVOV, GEORGI. Born Jan. 12, 1904, in the village of Debyr, Plovdiv District. Bulgarian writer and public figure. Academician of the Bulgarian Academy of Sciences (1961). Member of the Bulgarian Communist Party since 1924. People's Cultural Worker (1963).

Karaslavov began publishing his works in 1919, contributing to the antifascist and proletarian press. His first collections of short stories—*The Homeless Children* (1926), *The Reed-Pipe Cries* (1927), and *At One's Post* (1932)—and the novella *Village Correspondent* (1933) introduced the reader to Bulgarian rural life, filled with social struggle. His novels *The Thorn Apple* (1938; Russian translation, 1958) and *The Daughter-in-law* (1942) contained realistic pictures of the life of the Bulgarian countryside during the years of monarchal-fascist reaction. His cycle of novels *Ordinary People* (books 1–4, 1951–66) presents an epic picture of the life of the Bulgarian people from the time of World War I to the mid-1920's.

Karaslavov is also the author of plays, novellas, and novels for young people; essays in literary criticism; and biographical essays on Bulgarian writers (the collection *Intimates and Acquaintances: Reflections and Reminiscences,* 1968). He received the Dimitrov Prize (1950 and 1959).

WORKS
Izbrani suchineniia, vols. 1–10. Sofia, 1956–58.
In Russian translation:
Snokha. Moscow, 1961.
Tango, Foma nevernyi. Ottsovskii grekh. Moscow, 1964.
Izbrannoe. Moscow, 1969.

REFERENCES
Kravtsov, N. I. "G. Karaslavov." In *Ocherki istorii bolgarskoi literatury XIX–XX vv.* Moscow, 1959.
Konstantinov, G., and E. Konstantinova. *Kniga za Georgi Karaslavov.* Sofia, 1971.
Aleksandrov, V. *Georgi Karaslavov.* Moscow, 1964.
                                        V. I. ZLYDNEV [11–1171–1]

KARASOR, a bitter salt lake in northeast Karaganda Oblast, Kazakh SSR.

Lake Karasor covers an area of about 154 sq km and reaches a depth of 5 m. It is situated in a broad basin. The lake bottom is miry and smells of hydrogen sulfide. The shores are low, gently sloping, and composed of clay. The water of the lake is drawn chiefly from melting snow. The lake is fed by several small rivers, which dry up in the summer. Lake Karasor freezes over in November and thaws in late April and early May. Salt is extracted from its waters.   [11–1171–2]

KARA-SU, a city (settlement until 1960) and the administrative center of Kara-Su Raion, Osh Oblast, Kirghiz SSR. Situated in the Osh–Kara-Su oasis on the Frunze-Osh highway. Railroad station on the Andizhan-Dzhalal-Abad line; a 22-km branch line connects it with Osh. Population, 16,100 (1970). Kara-Su is the site of a cotton gin, an oil-extraction plant, auto repair plants, and a milling combine.   [11–1171–4]

KARA SU (Western Euphrates) a river in eastern Turkey, the northern extension of the Euphrates River. Length, 470 km; basin area, about 22,000 sq km. It flows mainly through deep gorges, its valley widening only at the cities of Erzurum and

Erzincan. The water is in flood in the spring and very low in the summer. The river is used to float logs. [11–1171–3]

KARASUBAZAR, the former name (until 1944) of the city of Belogorsk in the Crimean Oblast, Ukrainian SSR. [11–1171–5]

KARASUK, a city (until 1954, a settlement) and center of Karasuk Raion, Novosibirsk Oblast, RSFSR. It is located on the Karasuk River in the Kulunda Plain. Karasuk is a junction for railroad lines to Barnaul, Omsk, Kulunda, and Tatarsk. Population, 23,000 (1970). It is the site of a meat-packing plant, a flour mill, and plants for the production of canned dairy goods and dried vegetables. Karasuk has a pedagogical school. There is fishing on the lakes near Karasuk. A fish-processing plant is located in the area. [11–1171–7]

KARASUK, a river in Novosibirsk Oblast, RSFSR. Length, 531 km; basin area, 11,300 sq km. The river rises and flows in a broad valley along the southern part of the Western Siberian Plain, disappearing among lakes without outlets. At high water it is connected to the Burla River by the Chuman River near the village of Karasuk-Kazakh. The city of Karasuk is situated on the Karasuk River. [11–1171–6]

KARASUK CULTURE, an archaeological culture of the late Bronze Age (end of the second millennium to the beginning of the first millennium B.C.), widespread mainly in the mountains of southern Siberia, in Kazakhstan, and along the upper Ob'. The culture is represented by the remains of settlements and burial mounds (more than 100 graves in each). The burials are in stone chests under a low mound with small quadrangular enclosures made of small upright stone slabs. The tribes of the Karasuk culture engaged in stock raising. They also extracted copper ore (bronze articles were decorated with geometric designs and sculptured representations of animals), made clay vessels and woolen fabrics, and had a knowledge of farming. The tribes were associated with the ancient populations of northern China, Mongolia, the Cisbaikal and Transbaikal regions, western Siberia, and Middle Asia.

REFERENCES
Kiselev, S. V. *Drevniaia istoriia Iuzhnoi Sibiri,* 2nd ed. Moscow, 1951.
Istoriia Sibiri s drevneishikh vremen do nashikh dnei, vol. 1. Leningrad, 1968.
Novgorodova, E. A. *Tsentral'naia Aziia i Karasukskaia problema.* Moscow, 1970. [11–1172–1]

KARATAEV, MUKHAMEDZHAN KOZHASPAEVICH. Born Dec. 27, 1910, in Kzyl-Orda Oblast; Soviet literary critic; academician of the Academy of Sciences of the Kazakh SSR (1975). Became a member of the CPSU in 1956.
Karataev's literary career began in 1933. His articles of literary criticism analyzed the work of Abai Kunanbaev, S. Seifullin, and M. Auezov. His main works are *Born of October* (1958), *Il'ias Dzhansugurov* (1959), the collection of articles *Kazakh Literature* (1960), *Saken Seifullin* (1964), *The Development of Socialist Realism in Kazakh Prose* (1965), and *From the Dombra to the Book* (1969). He wrote (with K. N. Altaiskii) a novel about the working class, *Whistle in the Steppe* (1960). He became editor in chief of the *Kazakh Soviet Encyclopedia* in 1968. He was awarded three orders and several medals.

REFERENCE
Lomidze, G. I. *V poiskakh novogo.* Moscow, 1963. [11–1172–3]

KARATAL, a river in Taldy-Kurgan Oblast, Kazakh SSR. In its upper course, until its junction with the Ushtarak River, it is known as the Nurtaiozek. Length, 390 km; basin area, about 19,100 sq km. It rises on the slopes of the Dzhungarian Alatau and flows into Lake Balkhash. In its upper sections, it is a mountain river, and in its middle and lower reaches it cuts across the Semirech'e plain. Its water is drawn chiefly from melting glaciers and snow. The river freezes over in December and thaws in March. It is used for irrigation. The cities of Taldy-Kurgan and Ushtobe are located along its course. [11–1173–2]

KARATAU, a city (until 1963, the settlement of Chulaktau), in Dzhambul Oblast, Kazakh SSR, in the Karatau Mountains. Railroad station, 90 km northwest of Dzhambul. Population, 27,000 (1970). The city is the center of the Karatau Phosphorite-bearing Basin. It is the site of a combine for the quarrying and processing of phosphorite. A general technology department of the Kazakh Polytechnical Institute and a mining-construction technicum are also located there. [11–1173–7]

KARATAU, an urban-type settlement in Kara-Kalpak ASSR, Uzbek SSR. It is a landing on the right bank of the Amu Darya River, 108 km southeast of the Khodzheili railroad station on the Chardzhou-Kungrad line. Its industries include the production of building materials. [11–1173–8]

KARATAU, a mountain range, a northwest spur of the Tien-Shan in the southern part of the Kazakh SSR. Length, about 420 km; maximum altitude, 2,176 m (Mount Bessaz). The range is composed of shale, sandstone, and a considerable amount of limestone and dolomite, in which karst formations are well developed. The mountains have flattened tops and steep slopes and are covered with steppe vegetation and mountain xerophytes. There are important deposits of phosphorite and complex ores at Mirgalimsai, Kentau, Achisai, and elsewhere. [11–1173–6]

KARATAU, a mountain range on the western slope of the southern Urals, on the border between the Bashkir ASSR and Cheliabinsk Oblast, RSFSR. Length, about 75 km; maximum altitude, 691 m. The mountains are composed chiefly of limestone, sandstone, and clay shales. Their slopes are covered with coniferous and mixed forests of spruce, fir, and linden. [11–1173–5]

KARATAU (Mangystau), mountains on the Mangyshlak Peninsula in Gur'ev Oblast, Kazakh SSR. Length, 130 km; maximum altitude, 556 m. The mountains are broken up by deep ravines and gullies. The range is made up of sandstone, limestone, marl, clay, and sand. The predominant vegetation is wormwood and saltwort, along with some low shrubs. The valleys and ravines are used for pasture. There are deposits of iron and copper ore and coal. [11–1173–4]

KARATAU PHOSPHORITE-BEARING BASIN, one of the largest such basins in the world, located in Dzhambul and Chimkent oblasts, Kazakh SSR; a 25-km-wide belt stretching more than 120 km along the northeastern slopes of the Karatau Mountains.
Phosphorite, or phosphate rock, was first exploited in the Karatau Basin during the Great Patriotic War of 1941–45. The rock is found associated with Lower Cambrian Chulaktau series. The total thickness of the productive horizon reaches 60 m; the phosphorite seams within may be as much as 30-35 m across. In the best monomineral or carbonate ores the P_2O_5 content may be as high as 25–30 percent. The ore bed is broken up by several longitudinal and transverse cracks into about 45 independent sectors that are considered individual deposits.
The Karatau Basin's total ore reserve comes to 1.6 billion tons. Three deposits were being worked in 1970, the Aksai and the Zhanatas by the open pit method and the Chulaktau (which is today a suburb of Karatau), by an underground system of layered drifts.
There is a chemical-mining combine in the city of Karatau that produces phosphorite meal and flotation concentrate with a P_2O_5 content higher than 28 percent and market ore with more than 23 percent P_2O_5. The negative feature of the ores is their high magnesium oxide content. The city of Dzhambul has a superphosphate plant and a double-superphosphate plant. The 1971–75 Five-Year Plan for the Development of the National Economy of the USSR envisions a significant increase in the extraction capacities of the Karatau Phosphorite-Bearing Basin and the completion of construction on the Chimkent phosphorus plant and the Dzhambul double-superphosphate plant.

REFERENCE
Fosfority Karatau. Moscow, 1969. V. P. PETROV [11–1173–9]

KARATE, a Japanese system of self-defense without weapons, using blows of the arms (edge of the hand, fist, elbow) and legs against the most vulnerable parts of the human body (for example, the solar plexus, carotid artery, liver, or nerve ganglia). It is also a form of combative sport. Its origins lie in means of self-defense without weapons known by various Asian peoples even in ancient times.

The modern system of karate was created at the beginning of the 20th century by the selection and modernization of the techniques of jujitsu. The founder of this modern system is considered to have been G. Funakoshi (1869–1957) of Japan. Since then, it has become widespread in the countries of Asia and Latin America and in the United States, France, Spain, and elsewhere. In the middle of this century, it was recognized as a separate variety of combative sport. In 1968, an international karate federation was formed; in 1972, it included about 40 separate national federations. The first international karate championship was held in 1970 and the first all-European championship in 1971. In matches, the combatants only indicate the use of this or that technique without carrying it out fully, so as not to injure each other. They are dressed in the traditional garb of judo fighters and fight on *tatami* mats. Competitors are not divided into separate weight categories. Karate is not widely studied in the Soviet Union.

D. I. GULEVICH and B. P. KARIAKIN [11–1178–1]

KARATEGINSKII RANGE, the southern spur of the Gissar Range in the Tadzhik SSR.

The Karateginskii Range runs along the left bank of the Kafirnigan (Sorbo) River for about 80 km, rising to an altitude of 3,950 m. The range is composed chiefly of granites. The slopes are covered with couch-grass steppe, scrub, and meadow.

[11–1174–1]

KARATEPE (Turkic, "black hill"). (1) A hill in southern Turkmenia, located 4 km south of the Artyk railroad station, where the habitations of settled farmers dating from the Aeneolithic (fifth to third millennia B.C.) have been discovered. The area measures approximately 15 hectares. Excavations were carried out in 1952 and between 1955 and 1963. Pottery with monochrome paintings, figurines of standing women, and copper tools were found in the lower layers. The middle layers contained two-color painted pottery and multichambered mud-brick houses. There are parallels between the stratigraphy at Karatepe and that at Anau and Namazgatepe. Several multichambered houses, which were the living quarters of extended-family communities, were unearthed in the upper layer, which dates from the end of the fourth or the beginning of the third millennium B.C. Among the objects found in these houses were vessels with geometric patterns and drawings of people, animals, and birds; terra-cotta statuettes of male and female deities; stone seal-amulets; and copper implements. The materials at Karatepe indicate the connection between the Aeneolithic in southern Turkmenia and similar remains in Iran, Afghanistan, and India.

REFERENCE
Masson, V. M. "Kara-depe u Artyka." *Tr. Iuzhno-Turkmenistanskoi arkheologicheskoi kompleksnoi ekspeditsii,* vol. 10. Ashkhabad, 1960.

(2) A hill near the Ceyhan River, 22 km southeast of the city of Kadirli, Turkey, where the ruins of a city dating from the ninth to seventh centuries B.C. have been unearthed (excavations have been under way since 1947).

Two gates and part of a palace have been found in the citadel. The gates are decorated with stone reliefs depicting scenes of rituals, hunting, a sea battle, and musicians. The reliefs are characteristic of late Hittite art. A hieroglyphic inscription in the Hittite and Canaanite languages found at Karatepe and dating from the eighth century B.C. allows the supposition that Karatepe was part of the state of the Danunians, which subjugated the Hittite settlements of southeast Asia Minor at the start of the first millennium B.C.

REFERENCES
Mellink, M. J. "Karatepe." *Bibliotheca orientalis,* vol. 7, no. 5.
Bossert, H. T. "Die phönizisch-hethitischen Bilinquen vom Karatepe." *Oriens,* 1948, vol. 1, no. 2. V. M. MASSON [11–1174–3]

KARATON, an urban-type settlement in Embinskii Raion, Gur'ev Oblast, Kazakh SSR, located 86 km southwest of the Kul'sary railroad station on the Makat-Uzen' line, 180 km southeast of Gur'ev. Oil drilling is done there. [11–1175–2]

KARA TRAGEDY, a mass suicide of political prisoners in Russia at the Kara Penal Colony in 1889.

The political prisoners of this colony constantly opposed the arbitrariness of the prison administration. On Aug. 11, 1888, the prisoner E. N. Koval'skaia was transferred to the Chita prison for refusing to stand before the governor-general of the Amur Region, A. N. Korf. Her transfer was accompanied by a show of disrespect for her person. Learning of this, her peers M. P. Kovalevskaia, M. V. Kaliuzhnaia, and N. S. Smirnitskaia demanded that the officer responsible for the humiliation, prison commandant Masiukov, be discharged. When this was not done, they responded with lengthy hunger strikes in August 1888 and May and September 1889. But the administration refused to make concessions. Disturbances in the prison continued. For an attempt to slap Masiukov in the face, the prisoner N. K. Sigida was flogged on Nov. 7, 1889. The same night, as a protest, Sigida, Kovalevskaia, Kaliuzhnaia, and Smirnitskaia poisoned themselves; 14 men in the men's political prison took poison on November 12 (two of these, I. V. Kaliuzhnyi and S. N. Bobokhov, died). The Kara tragedy forced the tsarist government to close the Kara Penal Colony in 1890.

REFERENCE
Gernet, M. N. *Istoriia tsarskoi tiur'my,* vol. 3 (1870–1900). Moscow, 1961. Pages 323–30. [11–1266–1]

KARATSIUPA, NIKITA FEDOROVICH. Born Apr. 12 (25), 1911, in the village of Alekseevka, in present-day Kuibyshev Raion, Dnepropetrovsk Oblast. Colonel; Hero of the Soviet Union (Jun. 21, 1965). Became a member of the CPSU in 1939.

The son of a peasant, Karatsiupa entered the frontier service in 1932. In 1933 he completed the school for junior staff officers handling service dogs; and in 1937 he graduated from the Central School for Staff Officers Handling Service Dogs in the Border Guard. Between 1933 and 1937, he was a trainer and instructor with service dogs at frontier posts. After 1939 he held various posts in the headquarters of border detachments and frontier military districts. From 1957 to 1961 he served in the headquarters of the border guard of the USSR. In 1961 he entered the reserves.

A skillful tracker, Karatsiupa participated in 120 military encounters with smugglers and diversionary forces; he apprehended 467 persons violating the state frontiers. Karatsiupa has been awarded the Order of Lenin, two Orders of the Red Banner, the Order of the Red Star, and a number of medals.

[11–1181–1]

KARATYGIN, VIACHESLAV GAVRILOVICH. Born Sept. 5 (17), 1875, in Pavlovsk; died Oct. 23, 1925, in Leningrad. Soviet music critic and composer.

Karatygin graduated from the natural sciences section of the department of physics and mathematics at the University of St. Petersburg in 1898 and worked as a chemist in a pyroxylin plant until 1907. He published several works on agricultural subjects. He studied the theory of music and composition with N. A. Sokolov. In 1906 he began writing music criticism. In 1919, Karatygin became a professor and full member of the Institute of Art History in Petrograd and was an active participant in the development of Soviet musical culture in the first few years after the October Revolution.

Karatygin was an outstanding representative of Russian music criticism of the early 20th century and a champion of the new musical currents of the time (the work of Scriabin, Prokofiev, Debussy, and Ravel). He wrote works on Mussorgsky, Balakirev, and Rimsky-Korsakov. However, Karatygin's views were aesthetically limited in some ways, which resulted in his lack of understanding of some prominent elements in Russian music (especially the work of Tchaikovsky and Rachmaninoff). Karatygin was one of the organizers of the Evenings of Modern Music.

WORKS
Zhizn', deiatel'nost': Stat'i i materialy [vol. 1]. Leningrad, 1927.
Izbr' stat'i. Introduction by Iu. A. Kremlev. Moscow-Leningrad, 1965.
IU. V. KELDYSH [11–1175–3]

KARATYGIN, a family of Russian actors.

Andrei Vasil'evich Karatygin. Born July 4 (15), 1774, in St. Petersburg; died there Dec. 26, 1831 (Jan. 7, 1832).

A. V. Karatygin graduated from St. Petersburg Theatrical School in 1794, where he had studied under I. A. Dmitrevskii. In 1791 he made his stage debut at the Bolshoi Theater in St. Petersburg in the role of Hector in Regnard's *The Player.* He initially played the roles of young libertines; after 1810 he portrayed "noble fathers." In 1819, Karatygin became the director of a St. Petersburg dramatic company. He retired from the stage in 1822. From 1794 until his death, he maintained a diary, the *Theater Journal,* in which he kept a daily record of all the events of the St. Petersburg stage. The diary is at the Institute of Russian Literature—the Pushkin House—in Leningrad. P. N. Arapov used the diary as a source for his *Annals of the Russian Theater* (1861).

Vasilii Andreevich Karatygin. Born Feb. 26 (Mar. 10), 1802, in St. Petersburg; died there Mar. 13 (25), 1853. Son of A. V. Karatygin.

V. A. Karatygin was a student at the Cadet School of Mining and served in the department of foreign trade. He studied acting under A. A. Shakhovskoi and P. A. Katenin. The latter was a prominent advocate and theorist of classical tragedy. In 1820, Karatygin made his debut at the St. Petersburg Bolshoi Theater in the title role of V. A. Ozerov's tragedy *Fingal.* Although Karatygin had been on close terms with the progressive circles of the youth of the *dvorianstvo* (nobility), which included A. S. Pushkin, A. S. Griboedov, K. F. Ryleev, and W. K. Küchelbecker, he allied himself with the conservative camp after the suppression of the Decembrist uprising.

In the early years of his career, Karatygin appeared primarily in classical tragedies. By the 1820's the characteristic features of his acting were established: lofty heroic emotionality, a grand manner, rhetorical speaking, graphic gestures, and statuesque poses. Karatygin performed the title roles in Ozerov's *Dmitrii Donskoi* and in Corneille's *Le Cid,* and the role of Hippolytus in Racine's *Phèdre.* He enjoyed great success in romantic plays and in melodramas that had been translated into Russian. Karatygin was the principal tragedian of the Aleksandrinskii Theater in St. Petersburg from its opening in 1832. He played leading roles in pseudopatriotic plays, portraying Pozharskii and Liapunov in Kukol'nik's *The Hand of the Almighty Saved the Fatherland* and *Prince Mikhailo Vasil'evich Skopin-Shuiskii* and Igolkin in Polevoi's *Igolkin, Merchant of Novgorod.* Basing his interpretations on classical aesthetics, Karatygin stressed what he believed to be the one primary characteristic of the hero—Othello's jealousy and Hamlet's desire to seize the throne (Shakespeare's *Othello* and *Hamlet,* 1836 and 1837, respectively).

Karatygin's temporary engagements in Moscow in 1833 and 1835 prompted lively discussion. The critics V. G. Belinskii and N. I. Nadezhdin (P. Shch.) took a negative view of Karatygin's ostentatious acting, contrasting it with the turbulent work of P. S. Mochalov, a favorite of popular audiences. "Watching his acting," Belinskii wrote in the article "And My Opinion About the Acting of Mr. Karatygin," "you are continually surprised, but never moved, never stirred" (*Poln. sobr. soch.,* vol. 1, 1953, p. 187).

Karatygin was influenced by Belinskii's articles, as well as by the general development of realism and his own trips to Moscow and joint appearances with many masters of the realist school. His performances acquired features of naturalism and psychological depth. "His acting is becoming less and less affected and closer to nature," noted Belinskii in an article devoted to Karatygin's performance (1839) of the leading role in Schenk's drama *Belizar* (*ibid.,* vol. 3, 1953, p. 323). Belinskii valued highly Karatygin's complex psychological development of the character of the senile, cowardly, cruel Louis XI in Auffenberg's *The Enchanted House* in 1836. Karatygin carefully tailored each role. His preparation for a role included studying numerous literary sources and pictorial materials. His career had a positive influence on the development of acting.

Karatygin was the first to perform the roles of Chatskii in Griboedov's *Woe From Wit* (1831), Don Juan and the Baron in Pushkin's *The Stone Guest* (1847) and *The Covetous Knight* (1852), and Arbenin in Lermontov's *Masquerade* (individual scenes, 1852). He translated and reworked more than 40 plays for performance on the Russian stage, including Dumas *père's Kean, or Disorder and Genius* and Shakespeare's *King Lear* and *Coriolanus.*

Alexandra Mikhailovna Karatygina (née Kolosova). Born Feb. 4 (16), 1802, in St. Petersburg; died there Mar. 7 (19), 1880. Wife of V. A. Karatygin.

A. M. Karatygina, a student of A. A. Shakhovskoi and P. A. Katenin, made her stage debut in St. Petersburg in 1818. Her repertoire was classical (Moina in Ozerov's *Fingal* and Camille in Corneille's *Horace*). She achieved her greatest success in romantic dramas, melodramas, and salon comedies. Karatygina played the title role in Schiller's *Maria Stuart,* Madame de Léry in Musset's *Woman's Wit Is Better Than All Thought* (*Un Caprice*), and the title role in Polevoi's *Elena Glinskaia.*

Petr Andreevich Karatygin. Born June 29 (July 11), 1805, in St. Petersburg; died there Sept. 24 (Oct. 6), 1879. Son of A. V. Karatygin.

P. A. Karatygin graduated from the St. Petersburg Theatrical School in 1821. He performed at the Aleksandrinskii Theater all his life. He portrayed roles primarily in comedies and vaudevilles. Best known as a vaudeville writer, he created more than 40 works (*Vaudeville Sketches,* 1937). The best of these vaudevilles include *The House on the Petersburg Side* (1838), *The First Circle Box for the Last Performance of Taglioni* (1838), *The Bakery, or the St. Petersburg German* (1843), *The Civil Service Uniform* (1845), and *Uncle With Three Legs* (1853). They were successful because of their timely subjects, lively dialogue, and entertaining satirical songs. The limitations of Karatygin's views were revealed in the vaudeville *The Natural School* (1847), in which the realistic and democratic orientations of Russian literature were ridiculed. He was the author of *Notes* (vols. 1–2, 1929–30; latest edition, 1970), which reflected the events of theatrical life during his times.

Alexandra Dmitrievna Karatygina (née Perlova). Born in 1777; died in 1859. Wife of A. V. Karatygin, mother of Vasilii and Petr Karatygin. A. D. Karatygina was a stage actress in St. Petersburg.

REFERENCES
Lebedev, V. A. " 'Zhurnal Teatral'nyi' artista Andreia Karatygina." In the collection *O teatre,* [vol.] 2. Leningrad, 1927.
Karpinskaia, E., and E. Finkel'shtein. "O Karatygine." *Teatr,* 1941, no. 5.
Rodina, T. "Russkie romanticheskie aktery: P. Mochalov, V. Karatygin." In *Teatral'nyi al'manakh,* book 8. Moscow, 1948. Pages 163–91. (Collection of articles and materials.)
Al'tshuller, A. Ia. *Teatr proslavlennykh masterov: Ocherki istorii Aleksandrinskoi stseny.* Leningrad, 1968. Pages 31–34, 42–45, 58–67.
Koroleva, N. "P. A. Karatygin i ego 'Zapiski.' " In P. Karatygin, *Zapiski.* Leningrad, 1970.   A. IA. AL'TSHULLER [11–1176–1]

KARAUGOM, a valley glacier on the northern slope of the Glavnyi Range of the Greater Caucasus, northwest of Mount Uilpata (4,638 m). The total length of the glacier is 14 km; a tongue of ice 7.5 km long descends to an elevation of 1,820 m. One of the sources of the Urukh River, a tributary of the Terek, draws its water from Karaugom.   [11–1178–2]

KARAUNKIUR (also Tentiaksai), a river in Osh Oblast, Kirghiz SSR; right tributary of the Karadar'ia River (left component of the Syr Darya). Length, 126 km; basin area, 4,130 sq km. It rises in spurs of the Fergana Range; in its lower reaches it flows through the Fergana Valley, where its waters are used for irrigation. The river is fed chiefly by melting snow. The average annual discharge at the *kishlak* (village) of Charvak (78 km from its mouth) is 29.6 cu m per sec.   [11–1179–2]

KARAVAEV, GEORGII ARKAD'EVICH. Born Mar. 21 (Apr. 3), 1913, in Leningrad. Soviet statesman. Became a member of the CPSU in 1940. The son of a worker.

Karavaev graduated from the Leningrad Institute of Water Transport Engineering in 1935. Beginning in 1936, he held a succession of management posts in engineering and technical areas: work superintendent, deputy chief engineer, chief engineer, chief of a construction project, chief of a special construction and assembly section, and director of a trust. From 1951 to 1954, Karavaev headed the Glaviugstroi Trust and was deputy minister for the construction of machine-building enterprises of the USSR; he also was the chief of the Construction Directorate for the Palace of Culture and Science in Warsaw, Poland. Between 1954 and 1959, he was first deputy minister for the construction of enterprises in the metallurgical and chemical industries of the USSR, as well as assistant chairman of the Sverdlovsk council of the national economy. From 1959 to 1961, Karavaev was an executive in the State Committee on Construction Affairs of the Council of Ministers of the USSR. Between 1962 and 1963, he was chairman of the board of the All-Union Bank for Financing Capital Investments, a post of ministerial rank in the USSR. From 1963 to 1967, Karavaev was first deputy chairman of the State Committee on Construction Affairs of the Council of Ministers of the USSR, also a ministerial post. In February 1967, Karavaev became minister of construction of the USSR. At the Twenty-fourth Congress of the party, he was elected a candidate member of the Central Committee of the CPSU. He was a deputy to the seventh and eighth convocations of the Supreme Soviet of the USSR. He received the State Prize of the USSR in 1950. Karavaev has been awarded two Orders of Lenin, the Order of the October Revolution, four other orders, and a number of medals.   [11–1106–1]

KARAVAEV, NIKOLAI MIKHAILOVICH. Born May 26 (June 7), 1890, in the *khutor* (farmstead) of Novonikolaevskii, present-day Volgograd Oblast. Soviet scientist in fuel chemisty and technology; corresponding member of the Academy of Sciences of the USSR (1946). Graduated from the Moscow Higher Technical School (1920); taught there until 1930 and then at other institutes in Moscow. From 1939 to 1951 he worked at the Institute of Fossil Fuels of the Academy of Sciences of the USSR.

Karavaev's main works deal with the study of Siberian coal (the Kuzbass and other basins) for purposes of industrial classification and the search for a method to ensure its efficient use in the national economy. His subsequent scientific research included the geochemistry and classification of fossil fuel. Karavaev was awarded the Order of the Red Banner of Labor, as well as medals.

WORKS
"Svoistva i kachestvo uglei SSSR." *Tr. XVII sessii Mezhdunarodnogo geologicheskogo kongressa . . .*, vol. 1. Moscow, 1939.
Mashiny i apparaty koksokhimicheskogo proizvodstva, vol. 1. Moscow, 1955. (With others.)   [11–1106–2]

KARAVAEVA, ANNA ALEKSANDROVNA. Born Dec. 15 (27), 1893, in Perm'. Soviet Russian writer. Daughter of an office worker. Became a member of the CPSU in 1926.

Karavaeva graduated from the Bestuzhev Higher Women's Courses in 1916. She was editor in chief of the journal *Molodaia gvardiia* (1931–38) and a correspondent for the newspaper *Pravda* (1941–43). Her first works were published in 1922. The main theme of her early period was the struggle for a new life in the rural areas before collectivization—the novella *The Household* (1926) and the novel *The Timber Mill* (1928), which concern the beneficial effect of socialist construction on the life of the peasantry.

At the center of her later works are the problems of the moral training of the young person. These works were devoted to the prerevolutionary democratic intelligentsia, the Komsomol members of the Civil War era, and the workers of the present: *Stories of Knowledge* (1934), the novel *Lena From Crane Grove* (1938), the collection of short stories *The First Generation* (1959), and the novel *Facets of Life* (1963). The heroic labor of Soviet people

on the homefront during the Great Patriotic War (1941–45) is the theme of the trilogy *Homeland* (the novels *Fires*, 1943, *Running Start*, 1948, and *Native Home*, 1950; State Prize of the USSR, 1951). She is the author of *Starry Capital: Notes and Reminiscences of a Contemporary* (1968).

Karavaeva was a delegate to the International Congress of Writers in Defense of Culture (1935) and to other congresses. She met with outstanding contemporary figures, whom she described in her memoirs—A. Serafimovich, N. Ostrovskii, A. Fadeev, and M. Zalka. She was awarded the Order of Lenin, five other orders, and various medals.

WORKS
Sobr. soch., vols. 1–5. Moscow, 1957–58.
Izbr. proizv., vols. 1–2. Moscow, 1967.
Svet vcherashnii: Vospominaniia. Moscow, 1964.
Dvor: Povesti i rasskazy. Moscow, 1969.

REFERENCES
Skorino, L. "Anna Karavaeva." In her book *Sem' portretov.* Moscow, 1956.
Stesina, S. "Vsegda v stroiu." *Molodaia gvardiia*, 1968, no. 12, pp. 174–77.
Lisina, G. "Ideino-khudozhestvennoe svoeobrazie proizvedenii A. Karavaevoi 30-kh godov." *Uch. zap. Riazanskogo ped. in-ta*, 1971, issue 72.
Russkie sovetskie pisateli-prozaiki: Biobibliograficheskii ukazatel', vol. 2. Leningrad, 1964.   V. A. KALASHNIKOV [11–1106–3]

KARAVAEVO, an urban-type settlement in Kostroma Raion, Kostroma Oblast, RSFSR. It is situated on the left bank of the Volga, 8 km from Kostroma. There is a dairy plant. A training and experimental farm of the Kostroma Agricultural Institute, formerly the Karavaevo Stock-breeding Sovkhoz, where the Kostroma breed of cattle was developed, is also located there.   [11–1107–1]

KARAVELOV, LIUBEN. Born about 1834, in Koprivshtitsa; died Jan. 21, 1879, in Ruse. Bulgarian writer and public figure. Studied at the Plovdiv Greek *Gymnasium* (1850–53).

In his travels with his father, Karavelov learned about the life of the people under the Ottoman yoke. He became interested in the customs of the people and in folklore. From 1857 to 1866 he lived in Moscow and audited courses at Moscow University. He was influenced by Slavophilism, but the decisive factor for him was the ideas of the Russian revolutionary democrats and his reading of the works of N. V. Gogol, N. A. Nekrasov, T. G. Shevchenko, I. S. Turgenev, and Marko Vovchok. He began publishing in Russian (the novella *Hetman of the Bulgarian Brigands*, 1860; *Monuments of the Life of the Bulgarian Common People*, vol. 1, 1861; and the collection of short stories and novellas *Pages From the Book of Suffering of the Bulgarian Tribe*, 1868). Karavelov lived in Serbia after 1867. He became involved with the radical democratic circles connected with the Omladina. His critical articles in the press provoked the dissatisfaction of the authorities. He moved to Novi Sad.

Karavelov was imprisoned in 1868 on a false charge of complicity in the murder of the Serbian prince Mihailo Obrenović. He was released early in 1869. He wrote articles on realism, as well as novellas and short stories, for the Serbian press. In 1869 he moved to Bucharest and began collaborating with the Bulgarian revolutionary democrats V. Levski and, later, Kh. Botev. He published (in Bulgarian) the newspapers *Freedom* (1869–72) and *Independence* (1873–74). In the fall of 1869 he became a member of the Bulgarian Revolutionary Central Committee in Bucharest. He was the author of the committee's program, and in 1872 he was elected chairman. Having no faith in the reforms promised by the Turkish government, Karavelov called for revolutionary struggle in his pointed social and political journalism, literary criticism, and works of fiction.

After 1873, stunned by the Turkish authorities' execution of Levski, Karavelov gradually withdrew from the revolutionary movement. In 1865 he began publication of the journal *Knowledge*, which was oriented toward a program of enlightenment. During the Russo-Turkish War of 1877–78 he was a translator at the General Headquarters of the Russian Army. The fiction works of Karavelov, who became one of the founders of Bulgarian critical realism, were characterized by their organic links to the antifeudal national liberation struggle, the creation of the image of the positive fighting hero, the creative perception of folk poetry, and the combination of revolutionary-romantic motifs with realism. He also defended the principles of realism in his own works of literary criticism, which initiated the development of Bulgarian materialist aesthetics.

WORKS

Izbrani proizvedeniia, vols. 1–3. Sofia, 1954–56.
In Russian translation:
Povesti i rasskazy, 2nd ed. Moscow, 1954.

REFERENCES

Sheptunov, I. M. "Liuben Karavelov." In *Ocherki istorii bolgarskoi literatury XIX–XX vv.* Moscow, 1959.
Vorob'ev, L. V. *Filosofskie i sotsiologicheskie vozzreniia L. Karavelova.* Moscow, 1962.
Dimitrov, M. *Liuben Karavelov.* Sofia, 1959.
Sharova, K. *Liuben Karavelov i bulgarskoto osvoboditelno dvizhenie 1860–1867.* Sofia, 1970.
Konev, I. *Beletristut Karavelov.* Sofia, 1970.

I. M. SHEPTUNOV [11–1109–3]

KARAVELOV, PETKO STOICHEV. Born in 1843 or 1845 in Koprivnica; died Jan. 24, 1903, in Sofia. Bulgarian statesman and political figure. Brother of L. Karavelov.

While a student in the department of history and philology of Moscow University, he was associated with the Narodniks (Populists). After the liberation of Bulgaria from the Ottoman yoke (1878), he was elected to the Constituent Assembly. He was one of the leaders of the left wing of the Liberal Party. In February 1879 he was deputy chairman, and in October chairman, of the National Assembly. He was minister of finance from March to November 1880 and served as prime minister from November 1880 to April 1881. After a coup d'etat (in April 1881), he emigrated to Eastern Rumelia, where he published the newspaper *Independence* (to 1883), opposing the dictatorship of Alexander of Battenberg and supporting the restoration of the Turnovo Constitution of 1879. In 1883 he returned to Sofia. He was prime minister from June 1884 to August 1886. After the overthrow of Battenberg, he was one of the regents of Bulgaria (August-September 1886). During the period of the Stambulov regime (1887–94) he defended bourgeois democratic liberties. He was prime minister from February to December 1901.

WORKS

[Collection of articles], 2nd ed. Sofia, 1946.

REFERENCES

Peev, P. *Petko Karavelov.* Sofia, 1946.
Kozhukharov, K. *Petko Karavelov.* . . . [Sofia, 1968.]

M. A. BIRMAN [11–1110–1]

KARAWANKEN (German; Slovene, Karavanke), a mountain range in the eastern Alps, in Austria and Yugoslavia. It extends from west to east for about 100 km and rises to an elevation of 2,558 m. The mountains are composed primarily of limestone and dolomite. The crest of the range is deeply dissected, with steep slopes, trough valleys, and karst. The slopes are covered with broad-leaved forests (oak and beech) and coniferous forests (spruce, fir, and pine). Above 1,700–1,800 m there is scrub vegetation and alpine meadows. The Klagenfurt (Austria)–Ljubljana (Yugoslavia) railroad line passes through the Karawanken.

[11–1108–3]

KARAY, REFİK HALİD. Born in 1888, in Istanbul. Turkish writer and journalist; publisher of satirical newspapers and magazines. Publicist, satirist, and humorist.

In his short stories Karay exposed the cruelty, ignorance, and banality that reign in the provincial towns of Turkey. Some of Karay's works have noticeable anti-imperialist tendencies. He is the author of the novels *Watch Out, Don't Be Deceived, Don't Believe, Avoid Temptation* (1915) and *A Handful of Nonsense* (1939), and the collections of short stories *A Swallow of Water* (1939), *Exile* (1941), *A Plea to God* (1944), *The Key* (1947), and *This Is Our Life* (1950).

REFERENCES

Al'kaeva, L. O. *Ocherki po istorii turetskoi literatury.* Moscow, 1959. Pages 47–52.
Banarlı, N. S. *Resimli türk edebiyatı tarihi.* Istanbul, 1949.
Murat, Uraz. *Şair ve ediplerin hayatı.* Istanbul, 1961. [11–1125–3]

KARAZHAL, a city (until 1963, a settlement) in Dzhezkazgan Oblast, Kazakh SSR, the terminal station on a 66-km branch of the Zharyk-Dzhezkazgan railroad line. Population, 18,000 (1970). Karazhal grew up in connection with the mining of iron ore in the area. [11–1124–2]

KARAZIN, VASILII NAZAROVICH. Born Jan. 30 (Feb. 10), 1773, in the village of Kruchik, in present-day Bogodukhov Raion, Kharkov Oblast; died Nov. 4 (16), 1842, in Nikolaev. Russian and Ukrainian liberal gentry enlightener, public figure, and scholar; founder of Kharkov University. A member of the *dvorianstvo* (nobility or gentry).

Karazin was influenced by the ideas of the Great French Revolution and was at one time close to A. N. Radishchev. Karazin's social and political views were contradictory. In a letter to Alexander I in 1801, Karazin proposed that the autocracy be limited by "inviolable laws," that the lot of the enserfed peasants be eased, that courts be open to the public, that public education be developed, and that industry and trade be encouraged. Karazin's projects contained decisive criticism of many of the negative aspects of the existing autocratic structure. Karazin was persecuted: in 1820 he was incarcerated for half a year in the Shlissel'burg Fortress and was subsequently placed under police surveillance and deprived of the right to live in St. Petersburg or Moscow. With time, Karazin moved away from his progressive views and stressed his devotion to the monarchical form of government. He considered the abolition of serfdom to be inconceivable. Among the positive contributions of Karazin were his work on rationalizing agriculture and forestry and his founding of the Philotechnical Society (1811–18).

WORKS

Sochineniia, pis'ma i bumagi. Kharkov, 1910.

REFERENCES

Svetlov, L. B. "Rukopisnoe nasledie A. N. Radishcheva." *Novyi mir,* 1956, no. 6.
Sliusarskii, A. G. *V. N. Karazin, ego nauchnaia i obshchestvennaia deiatel'nost'.* Kharkov, 1955.
V. N. Karazin: 1773–1842, Bibliografiia. Kharkov. 1953.

L. B. SVETLOV [11–1124–3]

KARBUNA TREASURE, a complex of objects of the early stage of the Tripol'e culture found at the site of a Tripol'e settlement near the village of Karbuna in present-day Novye Aneny Raion, Moldavian SSR. It is the only discovery of such a treasure in Eastern Europe. Numerous items were found in a clay vessel, covered by another vessel, including copper axes, lamellar and spiral bracelets, beads, and anthropomorphic figurines; axes and beads made of colored marble and stone; an amulet made from a human tooth; a bone female figurine; and beads and decorative plates made of seashells. The ritual significance of some of the objects permits the supposition that the owner of the treasure was a tribal chief and priest.

REFERENCE

Sergeev, G. P. "Rannetripol'skii klad u sela Karbuna." *Sovetskaia arkheologiia,* 1963, no. 1. E. A. RIKMAN [11–1214–1]

KARBYSHEV, DMITRII MIKHAILOVICH. Born Oct. 14 (26), 1880, in Omsk; died Feb. 18, 1945, in Austria, in the Mauthausen death camp. Soviet military commander; lieutenant general in the Engineer Corps (1940); professor, doctor of military sciences (1941). Hero of the Soviet Union (Aug. 16, 1946). Member of the CPSU from 1940.

The son of a military official, Karbyshev graduated from the Nikolai School of Engineering in 1900 and from the Nikolaevskaia Engineering Academy in 1911. He took part in the Russo-Japanese War of 1904–05. After 1911, he oversaw the construction of forts at the Brest Fortress. During World War I, Karbyshev served on the staff of the chief of the engineer troops of the Eleventh and Eighth armies, reaching the rank of lieutenant colonel. After December 1917 he was an engineer with a detachment of the Red Guard in Mogilev-Podol'sk. During the Civil War of 1918–20, he led the engineering side of operations that crushed the troops of Kolchak and Wrangel.

From 1921 to 1923, Karbyshev held responsible positions in the headquarters of the armed forces of the Ukraine and Crimea and of the Ukrainian military district. From 1923 to 1926 he was chairman of the Engineering Committee of the Chief Military Engineering Administration of the Red Army. After 1926 he worked as a teacher at the Frunze Military Academy, and after 1936 he taught at the Military Academy of the General Staff.

Karbyshev wrote many scientific works, including *Engineering Preparations for the Borders of the USSR* (book 1, 1924), *Demolition and Obstacles* (1931, with I. Kiselev and I. Maslov), and *Securing Infantry Units During Military Actions by Engineering* (parts 1–2, 1939–40). Karbyshev elaborated the principles for a theory of protecting operations by engineering and of the military application of an engineering corps.

At the outset of the Great Patriotic War (1941–45), Karbyshev was on the Western Byelorussian front. On Aug. 8, 1941, he suffered heavy shell shock and was taken prisoner. He led antifascist agitation among prisoners in the death camps of Zamosc and Maidanek (Lublin). He was brutally tortured by the fascists. Karbyshev was posthumously awarded the Order of Lenin. Before the war he received the Orders of the Red Banner, the Order of the Red Star, and a medal for 20 years' service in the Red Army. Monuments have been erected to Karbyshev in Mauthausen, Omsk, and Tallinn.

WORKS
Izbr. nauchnye trudy. Moscow, 1962.
REFERENCE
Soldat, geroi, uchenyi. Moscow, 1961.

A. I. IVOLGIN and V. A. PURIN [11–1214–3]

KARCAG, a city in eastern Hungary, in the *megye* (district) of Szolnok. Population, 24,600 (1970). There is extraction of natural gas, as well as food-processing industry (flour mills and rice-polishing), a glassworks, and a brickyard. Most of the populace is engaged in agriculture. [11–1459–2]

KARDASHEV, NIKOLAI NIKOLAEVICH. Born Oct. 27, 1873, in Moscow; died early in 1920 in Omsk. Revolutionary. Became a member of the Communist Party in 1897. The son of a sales clerk. He studied at the department of physics and mathematics of Moscow University.

In 1897, Kardashev was arrested in connection with the affair of the Moscow Workers' Union and exiled to Voronezh, where he joined a Social Democratic group. He was one of the founders of the Northern Union of the RSDLP and managed a printing press, the shipment of illegal literature, and the system of secret addresses. During the Revolution of 1905–07, he was a deputy of the Voronezh soviet, and during the strike of June 1914 in Baku, he was chairman of the strike committee. He was repeatedly subjected to government repression. Active in the February and October revolutions of 1917, he was chairman of the Voronezh province committee of the party. After the establishment of Soviet power, he was commissar of labor, chairman of the Voronezh provincial soviet for the economy, and chairman of the provincial executive committee of the soviet. He was a delegate to the Seventh (April) Conference of the RSDLP (Bolshevik) and to the Sixth and Eighth Congresses of the party.

REFERENCE
Polievktov, B. "Partii syn." In *Gvardeitsy revoliutsii.* Voronezh, 1967.
[11–1224–2]

KARDHITSA, a city in Greece, in Thessaly; administrative center of the *nome* (prefecture) of Kardhitsa. Population, 25,700 (1971). It is a commercial center for trade in grain, vegetables, tobacco, cotton, and dairy products. [11–1236–1]

KARDIS, TREATY OF (1661), a treaty concluded between Russia and Sweden on June 21 (July 1) in the village of Kardis, near Derpt (Tartu); it ended the Russo-Swedish War of 1656–58 with an "everlasting peace."

The Swedish delegation was headed by Bengt Horn; the Russian, by Prince I. S. Prozorovskii. Russian military defeats from 1659 to 1662 in the Russian-Polish War of 1654–67 and the conclusion of the Peace of Oliva of 1660 between Poland and Sweden created conditions unfavorable for Russia. Tsar Aleksei Mikhailovich rejected A. L. Ordin-Nashchokin's proposal to abandon claims to the Ukraine in order to conclude peace with Poland and thus have the means to continue war against Sweden over Livonia. As it was unable to continue to fight simultaneously against both Sweden and Poland, the Russian government was forced to conclude the Kardis Treaty and to return to Sweden the Estonian and Livonian cities ceded to Russia in the Valiesar Truce of 1658. The border specified in the Peace of Stolbovo of 1617 was restored. The Kardis Treaty made possible the continuation of the Russian war effort against Poland for the Ukraine and Byelorussia because Sweden was obliged not to assist Poland. [11–1234–2]

KARDOVSKII, DMITRII NIKOLAEVICH. Born Aug. 24 (Sept. 5), 1866, in the village of Osurovo, present-day Pereslavl'-Zalesskii, Yaroslavl Oblast; died Feb. 9, 1943, in Pereslavl'-Zalesskii. Soviet artist. Honored Art Worker of the RSFSR (1929).

From 1892 to 1896 and from 1900 to 1902, Kardovskii studied under P. P. Chistiakov and I. E. Repin at the St. Petersburg Academy of Arts. From 1896 to 1900 he was a student at the A. Asbé school in Munich. He received a professorship at the St. Petersburg Academy of Arts in 1907; he became a full member of the academy in 1911.

Kardovskii, who worked in a realist style, was a skilled draftsman and a master book illustrator. He illustrated Chekhov's *Kashtanka* (charcoal and india ink, 1903), Griboedov's *Woe From Wit* (india ink, watercolor, and gouache; 1907–12), Nekrasov's *To the Russian Women* (india ink, watercolor, and gouache; 1922), Gogol's *The Inspector-General* (watercolor, 1922; black lead pencil, 1933), and A. N. Tolstoy's *Peter I* (india ink, 1932). Kardovskii was also a stage artist; he was the artist for the stagings of A. N. Ostrovskii's *The Forest* (1921) and *Poverty Is No Crime* (1924) at the Malyi Theater in Moscow. His paintings, watercolors, and drawings were devoted to the era of Peter I, Pushkin's times, and the Decembrists (*On the Senate Square,* watercolor, 1927, State Historical Museum, Moscow).

Kardovskii, who was an outstanding instructor, taught at the St. Petersburg Academy of Arts (1903–18), the Moscow Vkhutemas-Vkhutein (State Higher Arts and Technical Studios–Higher Art and Technical Institute, 1920–30), and the All-Russian Academy of Arts in Leningrad (1933–34). Kardovskii also taught with K. P. Chemko at their own studio in Moscow from 1922 to 1930. Among his students were the Soviet painters V. P. Efanov, D. A. Shmarinov, and P. P. Ben'kov.

WORKS
Ob iskusstve: Vospominaniia, stat'i, pis'ma. Moscow, 1960.
REFERENCE
Podobedova, O. *Dmitrii Nikolaevich Kardovskii.* [Moscow] 1957.
[11–1236–3]

KAREEV, NIKOLAI IVANOVICH. Born Nov. 24 (Dec. 6), 1850, in Moscow; died Feb. 18, 1931, in Leningrad. Russian historian. Professor from 1879 to 1884, first at the University of Warsaw and later at St. Petersburg University. Corresponding member of the Russian Academy from 1910. Honorary member of the Academy of Sciences of the USSR from 1929. Graduated in 1873 from Moscow University, where he studied the history of the Great French Revolution under V. I. Ger'e.

In his youth Kareev was influenced by N. G. Chernyshevskii, N. A. Dobroliubov, and particularly D. I. Pisarev; later, he was influenced by P. L. Lavrov and N. K. Mikhailovskii, ideologists of Narodnichestvo (Populism). He became acquainted with Marx' *Das Kapital* in the 1870's. In his approach, he was a typical eclectic idealist, a positivist of a liberal orientation. Politically he belonged to the ranks of liberals of the postreform generation—constitutionalists and advocates of social reforms. He wrote his best book during the 1870's: *The Peasants and the*

Peasant Question in France in the Last Quarter of the XVIIIth Century (1879). In 1881 his *Studies in the History of the French Peasants From Earliest Times to 1789* was published. Because of Kareev, Russian scholarship was at the fore in the concrete study of the peasant question on the eve of and during the Great French Revolution. He showed the onerous feudal oppression to which the French peasantry was subjected, an oppression that was intensifying around the time of the revolution. Thus he refuted A. de Tocqueville's thesis that prior to the revolution feudal relations were already gradually disappearing in France and that the peasants had in the main become free landed proprietors. Marx called Kareev's work of 1879 "first-rate" (see K. Marx and F. Engels, *Soch.,* 2nd ed., vol. 34, p. 286), and Engels called it the "best work on the peasants" (*ibid.,* vol. 37, p. 125).

In his dissertation *Basic Questions of the Philosophy of History* (3 vols., 1883–90) and in other historical-philosophical and sociological works, Kareev contrasted history with sociology, in effect denying the genuinely scientific nature of history. Adopting a standpoint of extreme subjectivism, Kareev, like Mikhailovskii, proclaimed the content of the philosophy of history to be the "ideal world of norms, the world of the proper, the world of the true and the just, to which actual history will be compared." In the 1890's, he used the same subjective idealist position to combat Marxism, identifying it with "economic materialism."

Moderate as his liberalism was, Kareev was dismissed from St. Petersburg University in 1899 in connection with student disturbances there. He returned only in 1906. During the Revolution of 1905–07, he joined the Constitutional Democrats (Cadets) and was elected a member of the first State Duma. In Kareev's textbook *The History of Western Europe in Modern Times* (7 vols., 1892–1917), which is eclectic but valuable for its wealth of factual material, socioeconomic processes are accorded an important place. Between 1911 and 1915, Kareev began working on a history of the revolutionary sections of Paris. In 1924–25 he published the three-volume work *Historians of the French Revolution.* This was the first composite survey—not only in Russian but anywhere in historical literature—of the historiography of the Great French Revolution.

WORKS

Ocherk istorii reformatsionnogo dvizheniia i katolicheskoi reaktsii v Pol'she. Moscow, 1886.
Neizdannye dokumenty po istorii parizhskikh sektsii 1790–1795 gg. St. Petersburg, 1912.
Neizdannye protokoly Parizhskikh sektsii 9 termidora II goda. St. Petersburg, 1914.
Iz dalekogo i blizkogo proshlogo (collection). Petrograd-Moscow, 1923. (This and the following book contain a more complete listing of Kareev's works.)
Istoriki Frantsuzskoi revoliutsii, vol. 3. Leningrad, 1925.

REFERENCES

Ocherki istorii istoricheskoi nauki v SSSR, vols. 2–3. Moscow, 1960–63.
Veber, B. C. "Pervoe russkoe issledovanii frantsuzskoi burzhuaznoi revoliutsii XVIII v." In the collection *Iz istorii sotsial'no-politicheskikh idei.* Moscow, 1955.
Frolova, I. I. "Znachenie issledovanii N. I. Kareeva dlia razrabotki istorii frantsuzskogo krest'ianstva v epokhe feodalizma." In the collection *Srednie veka,* issue 7, 1955.   V. G. VEBER   [11–1239–1]

KARELI, an urban-type settlement and administrative center of Kareli Raion, Georgian SSR. It is situated on the right bank of the Kura River. Railroad station, 94 km southwest of Tbilisi. Population, 7,000 (1970). It is the site of a winery. There is also an electrical engineering technicum.   [11–1240–1]

KARELIAN, the language of the Karelians, related to the Balto-Finnic subgroup of the Finno-Ugric languages. It is spoken by 92,000 persons in the USSR (1970 census). Karelian is divided into three dialects: Karelian, Livonian (or Olonets), and Lude. The Karelian dialect is close to Finnish.

The main features of Karelian are the presence in the phonemic inventory of the voiced *b, d, g,* and *z,* the fricatives *š* and *ž* and the affricate *č* (*tš*), and the presence of vowel harmony, opposition between short and long vowels, and consonant

graduation. The morphological system is agglutinative, and derivation is accomplished by means of suffixes. The oldest text in Karelian dates from the 13th century. The Finnish Karelian epic *Kalevala* was published by E. Lönnrot in 1835 (32 runes) and in 1849 (50 runes). The Karelians began using the Russian and Finnish writing systems in the mid-20th century.

REFERENCE

Makarov, G. N. "Karel'skii iazyk." In *Iazyki narodov SSSR,* vol. 3. Moscow, 1966. Pages 61–80.   [11–1259–1]

KARELIAN AUTONOMOUS SOVIET SOCIALIST REPUBLIC (Karelia), a part of the RSFSR. The Karelian Workers' Commune, an autonomous oblast association, was formed on June 8, 1920, becoming the Karelian ASSR on July 25, 1923. The republic is bounded by the White Sea on the east, by Lakes Ladoga and Onega on the south, and by Finland on the west. Area, 172,400 sq km. Population, 715,000 (1972). Karelia has 15 raions, 12 cities, and 40 urban-type settlements. The capital is Petrozavodsk.

Constitution and government. The Karelian ASSR is a socialist workers' and peasants' state and an autonomous Soviet socialist republic. The present constitution was adopted by the Eleventh Extraordinary All-Karelian Congress of Soviets on June 17, 1937. The highest organs of state power are the unicameral Supreme Soviet of the Karelian ASSR, elected for a four-year term on the basis of one deputy for every 5,000 inhabitants, and the Presidium of the Supreme Soviet. The Supreme Soviet forms the Council of Ministers of Karelia, the government of the republic. The Karelian ASSR is represented by 11 deputies in the Soviet of Nationalities of the Supreme Soviet of the USSR. Local government bodies are the city, raion, settlement, and village soviets of workers' deputies, elected by the people for two-year terms.

The Supreme Soviet of Karelia elects for a five-year term the Supreme Court of the republic, comprising two divisions, one for criminal and one for civil cases, and the Presidium of the Supreme Court. The procurator of the Karelian ASSR is appointed by the procurator general of the USSR for a five-year term.

Natural features. The republic is situated in the northwestern European USSR, in the eastern part of the Baltic Shield. Its surface forms a hilly plain with strong traces of glacial activity, including moraine ridges, eskers, kames, and lacustrine basins. The highest areas are in the west and northwest, the Mansel'kia Range with elevations of up to 578 m and the West Karelian Hills with elevations of up to 417 m. The main depressions, the Pribelomorskaia, Olonets, and Vodla, are found in the regions adjoining the sea and the lakes. The coastline of the White Sea (the Pomor'e and Karelian coasts) has many inlets and bays. The chief mineral resources include various types of building stone (granite, diabase, quartzite, dolomite, and marble) and pegmatites. There are also deposits of iron ore (ferruginous quartzite at the Kostomukshskii deposit and titanomagnetites at the Pudozhgorskii deposits) and mica.

The climate combines continental and maritime features, with long, comparatively mild winters, cool summers, a high relative humidity, and a small temperature range. The average temperature in July, the warmest month, ranges from 14° to 16°C; during the coldest month, February, it ranges from −9° to −13°C. Annual precipitation averages 600 mm in the southwest and 400–500 mm in the north, with most occurring during the warm season. There is a growing season of as many as 125 days in the south and 70 days in the north. Karelia is a region of lakes, rivers, and swamps. The rivers, belonging to the basins of the White and Baltic seas, are relatively short but have large water discharge and many rapids and waterfalls. Of the largest rivers, the Kem', Vyg, and Keret' empty into the White Sea, and the Vodla, Suna, and Shuia flow into Lake Onega. Rivers are used for hydroelectric power and for floating timber; only the lower reaches of certain rivers are navigable. Lakes occupy 18 percent of the area; the greatest number lie in the north. The largest lakes, besides Ladoga and Onega, are Vygozero, Topozero, Piaozero, and Segozero. The lakes are often connected by rivers.

The main soil types are podzolic, podzolic-bog, and bog. Forests cover about half of Karelia's total area. Available timber reserves total more than 600 million cu m, of which 58 percent are pine, 38 percent spruce, and 4 percent leafy varieties (Karelian birch, alder, and asp). A substantial portion of the forests require land reclamation. Swamps, covering about 18 percent of the total area, contain more than 4 billion tons of peat. Animal life is represented by the blue hare, European beaver, muskrat (acclimatized), brown bear, caribou, and elk. Both marine and fresh-water fish are commercially important, including navaga, herring, cod, flounder, Atlantic and other kinds of salmon, trout, and many common varieties. The Greenland seal is also commercially valuable. The Kivach Preserve is located in Karelia.

Population. The indigenous people of the region are the Karelians, numbering 84,000 persons in 1970. Other nationalities include (1970 census) Russians (486,000), Byelorussians (66,000), Ukrainians (27,000), Finns (22,000), and Veps (6,000). In 1913 the population was 223,000; in 1926, 261,000; in 1939, 469,000; and in 1959, 651,000. Average population density is 4.1 per sq km (1972). The southern raions are most densely settled. The proportion of the population living in cities increased from 13 percent in 1913 to 71 percent in 1972. The major cities are Petrozavodsk, Sortavala, Kem', and several that arose during the Soviet period—Kondopoga, Medvezh'egorsk, Belomorsk, and Segezha.

Historical survey. The oldest traces of human habitation on the territory of present-day Karelia date from about the sixth millennium B.C. Rock drawings indicate that the main occupations during the third and second millennia B.C. were fishing and hunting. About 500 B.C. the inhabitants began to produce iron implements and engage in livestock raising and farming. By the end of the first millennium A.D. the Karelian Isthmus and the northern Ladoga region were settled by Karelians. Veps inhabited the area between Lakes Ladoga and Onega, and further to the north lived the Lapps. At the beginning of the second millennium A.D. some Karelians moved toward the shores of the Gulf of Bothnia and the White Sea. At the same time, Slavs entered the northern and eastern Onega region and the coastal area of the White Sea, contributing to the development of farming, saltmaking, and fishing. Between the ninth and the early 12th centuries, Karelia was part of Kievan Rus', and from the 12th century, with the disintegration of Kievan Rus', it was subject to Novgorod. The transition from primitive communal relations to feudal relations occurred between the 12th and 15th centuries. The Karelian nationality also emerged at this time. The tribal, and from the 12th and 13th centuries, administrative center of Karelia was the town of Korela (Priozersk).

In the 13th century the Swedes captured part of Karelia and built the fortress of Vyborg (1293). The Karelians living around Vyborg and on the island of Saimaa were cut off from the main part of Karelia, which along with the Novgorod lands became part of the Russian state in 1478. Nearly all the peasants in Karelia became state peasants; some were attached to monasteries. The incursions of the Swedish aggressors intensified in the late 16th century and the early 17th. By the Treaty of Stolbovo (1617), Russia was forced to relinquish the Karelian Isthmus to Sweden, which resulted in the flight of many Karelians to the Russian state. Olonets became the administrative and commercial center of Karelia. Ironworking developed among the peasantry, whose products were sold at the Tikhvin market. During the Northern War (1700–21), the Olonets metallurgical works supplied the Russian Army and Navy with cannons. The Karelian Isthmus was returned to Russia by the Treaty of Nystadt (1721). In the 18th century much of Karelia became part of St. Petersburg Province and later of Novgorod Province. Olonets Province, formed in 1784 (capital, Petrozavodsk), was abolished in 1796 and reestablished in 1801. The rest of Karelia was incorporated into Vyborg and Arkhangel'sk provinces. During the 18th century, the antifeudal struggle of the peasants became particularly evident in the Kizhi Uprising (1769–71).

Capitalist relations developed in Karelia from the second half of the 18th century. More hired labor was used in private water-powered sawmills, and migratory labor and commerce increased. After the abolition of serfdom in 1861, sawmills using steam engines were built. The number of industrial and seasonal workers increased, and lumbering and the floating of timber

down rivers expanded. Steam navigation was introduced on Lake Onega and the White Sea. On the whole, however, Karelia remained one of the backward national borderlands of Russia. Of the 215,000 persons living in Karelia (1897 census), industrial workers by the early 20th century totaled about 3,000. During the Revolution of 1905–07 the strike movement spread to the workers of Petrozavodsk and the sawmills of the White Sea region. In the spring of 1906 a Social Democratic group arose in Petrozavodsk, and in 1907 the Committee of the RSDLP was formed. The Murmansk Railroad was built across Karelia in 1914–16. Karelia's economic and cultural ties with Petrograd and other Russian cities were strengthened. After the February Revolution (1917), in addition to organs of the Provisional Government, soviets were also organized in Karelia. On June 22 (July 5) the Olonets provincial soviet of workers', peasants', and soldiers' deputies was formed.

Soviet power was established in Karelia between November 1917 and April 1918. In November, the soviets in Soroka, Sumposad, Engozero, and Popov Island assumed power. On Jan. 4 (17), 1918, Soviet power triumphed in Petrozavodsk and later that month in Olonets, Pudozh, and Povenets; in March Soviet rule was established in Kem'. Northern Karelia was captured by interventionists in the spring and summer of 1918; White Finns occupied several border districts, and Anglo-Franco-American forces held the Pomor'e. Early in 1919 the interventionists undertook an offensive to support General Iudenich in his campaign against Petrograd. In battles at Olonets (May), Petrozavodsk and Vidlitsa (June), Lizhma (September), and other points, Red Army units, sailors of the Onega flotilla, and workers' detachments defeated the aggressors, driving them out of southern Karelia in the fall of 1919. In February and March 1920 the Red Army liberated all of Karelia.

On June 8, 1920, the All-Russian Central Executive Committee adopted a decree forming an autonomous oblast, the Karelian Workers' Commune, out of the parts of Olonets and Arkhangel'sk provinces that were inhabited by Karelians. The first All-Karelian Congress of Soviets was held in February 1921. On April 26 the Council of Peoples' Commissars, under the chairmanship of V. I. Lenin, adopted a resolution outlining the direction of economic development in the Karelian Workers' Commune and granting it aid. The Karelian oblast committee of the RCP (Bolshevik) was formed in September 1921. The rebuilding of the economy was interrupted in late 1921 by the White Finn intervention. After the expulsion of the interventionists, the Karelian Workers' Commune was renamed the Karelian ASSR by the July 25, 1923, resolution of the All-Russian Central Executive Committee.

The reconstruction of the economy was essentially completed by late 1925. The prewar five-year plans promoted the industrialization of Karelia, aided both by the neighboring oblasts of the RSFSR and by other Union republics. Lumbering increased, and sawmills were modernized. New industries developed, including paper and pulp, furniture, and mining. Paper and pulp combines were built in Kondopoga (1929) and Segezha (1938). The mining of pegmatite and mica began on the White Sea coast. The White Sea–Baltic Canal was put into operation in 1933. By the end of the Second Five-year Plan, collectivization was almost completed. In June 1937 the Eleventh Congress of Soviets of Karelia adopted the republic's constitution, which consolidated in law the achievements of socialism. A cultural revolution occurred. National cadres emerged in all branches of the economy, a Karelian intelligentsia evolved, and national literature and art flourished. After the Soviet-Finnish War (1939–40), the Karelian ASSR was reorganized as the Karelian-Finnish SSR on Mar. 31, 1940.

Much of Karelia was occupied by fascist German and White Finn forces during the Great Patriotic War (1941–45). More than 100,000 inhabitants of Karelia fought in the ranks of the Soviet Army and in partisan detachments. The troops of the Karelian Front took the offensive on June 21, 1944, liberating Petrozavodsk on June 28. By the end of July, Soviet troops had reached the border between the USSR and Finland. Thousands of Karelians received government awards for their heroism at the front and self-sacrificing labor in the rear; 26 persons were awarded the title Hero of the Soviet Union. The war inflicted great losses on Karelia's economy and culture. About 200 enterprises, schools, and clubs were destroyed. By 1950, the economy had been reconstructed and was developing at a rapid rate. Between 1943 and 1972, 33 persons were awarded the title Hero of Socialist Labor, and between 1957 and 1972 alone, 6,528 persons were awarded orders and medals of the USSR.

On June 16, 1956, the Karelian-Finnish SSR was renamed the Karelian ASSR. In 1965, Karelia received the Order of Lenin for its achievements in economic and cultural development, and in 1970, in honor of the 50th anniversary of the republic, it was awarded the Order of the October Revolution. On Dec. 29, 1972, the Order of Friendship of Peoples was bestowed on Karelia in commemoration of the 50th anniversary of the USSR.

IA. A. BALAGUROV and V. I. MASHEZERSKII

Economy. Karelia is a rapidly developing industrial and agricultural autonomous republic, with more than 250 industrial enterprises. In 1971 the gross output of large-scale industry was 66 times greater than in 1913, and the total industrial output in 1971 was 261 times that of 1920. The leading branches of industry are lumbering (20 percent of the gross industrial output in 1971), woodworking (15 percent), paper and pulp milling (18 percent), machine building and metalworking (14 percent), building materials production (7 percent), fishing (5 percent), and electric energy production (2 percent). Data on the output of the major industrial products is given in Table 1.

The hydroelectric power plants built during the Soviet period on the Suna, Vyg, Kem', and other rivers provide most of Karelia's energy. The total capacity of electric power plants increased 921 times over between 1913 and 1971, and electric energy production increased 1,712 times over during that period. Hydroelectric power plants produce 77 percent of the energy.

Karelia accounts for about 5 percent of the lumber exported by the Soviet Union. Mechanized logging and timber distribution establishments have been built, mainly in the forests of southern Karelia. The center of the lumbering industry is shifting to the western and northern regions. Under the Ninth Five-year Plan (1971–75), much attention was devoted to the all-around utilization of timber. The wood-products industry includes sawmilling and the production of building components, furniture, skis, plywood, and wood-fiber board (at Petrozavodsk, Belomorsk, Medvezh'egorsk, Letnerechenskii, Segezha, and Lakhdenpokh'ia). The paper and pulp industry is well developed, with combines at Kondopoga and Segezha. The Karelian ASSR produces 11 percent of the Soviet Union's pulp, about 16 percent of its paper, and 49 percent of its paper bags. The metalworking, machine-building, and metallurgical industries are expanding. The metallurgical plant in Viartsilia produces various articles from metal shipped to Karelia from other regions. The Onega Tractor Plant in Petrozavodsk, which has been completely renovated, specializes in the production of tractors for timber hauling. There are shipyards (Pindushi and Petrozavodsk) and several ship repair and motor-vehicle repair enterprises. The Tiazhbummash, a large plant producing paper-making machines, is located in Petrozavodsk; its first assembly line was put into operation in 1964. The Nadvoitsy Aluminum Plant, using alumina shipped from Leningrad Oblast, has been in operation since 1954. The extraction of building material is best developed in the Onega area. Pegmatite is mined near Chupa and Pitkiaranta, and mica-muscovite, in Loukhi Raion. Fishing, an important branch of the food industry, is carried out primarily in the White Sea and North Atlantic. Commercial fish breeding is developing.

AGRICULTURE. The main branches of agriculture are dairy farming, the production of potatoes and other vegetables, poultry breeding, and fur farming. Agricultural land occupies less than 1.5 percent of Karelia's total area, and more than three-fifths of this land is used for hayfields and pasture. In 1972 there were 56 sovkhozes in Karelia (livestock raising for meat and milk, poultry breeding, and fur farming) and 11 fishing kolkhozes. About two-thirds of the sown area is reclaimed land. Crop cultivation is oriented mainly toward the production of feed for livestock. Feed crops occupy 84 percent of the republic's sown land, and about 15 percent of the cultivated area is sown to potatoes and other vegetables, chiefly cabbage. There are small plantings of cereals, primarily rye, oats, and barley.

In 1972 livestock numbered 86,000 cattle, 52,000 pigs, and 67,000 sheep and goats. Animal products in 1972 included 13,900 tons of meat (dressed weight), compared to 5,500 tons in 1940, and 132,600 tons of milk, as against 45,700 tons in 1940.

Karelia has 20 fur-farming sovkhozes, producing about one-sixth of all furs (mink and blue fox) supplied by sovkhozes in the RSFSR.

TRANSPORTATION. In 1971 there were more than 2,000 km of railroads (700 in 1923). The Petrozavodsk-Suoiarvi, Suoiarvi-Iushkozero, Loukhi-Sofporog, and Belomorsk-Obozerskaia lines have been built during the Soviet period. There is navigation on Lakes Ladoga and Onega and the White Sea–Baltic Canal. There are 28,000 km of timber-floating routes. Petrozavodsk is linked by air routes with Leningrad, Arkhangel'sk, Moscow, and remote areas of the republic.

REGIONAL VARIATIONS. More than 70 percent of the population lives in southern Karelia, which is also the main industrial and agricultural region, accounting for half the industrial output, three-fourths of the farmland and livestock, and 90 percent of the crops. The most important industrial centers are Petrozavodsk, producing one-fourth of Karelia's industrial output, Kondopoga, Sortavala, Suoiarvi, and Medvezh'egorsk. About one-sixth of the population inhabits central Karelia, which accounts for about 30 percent of the industrial output. The main industrial centers here are Segezha, Belomorsk, and Nadvoitsy. Northern Karelia has one-tenth of the population, and its chief industries are forestry and the extraction of mica. Developmental plans include the working of the Kostomukshskii deposits of ferruginous quartzite. There is also reindeer breeding and fur farming. The industrial centers of northern Karelia are Kem', Keret', and Chupa.   D. M. PINKHENSON

STANDARD OF LIVING. The material well-being and cultural level of the population have risen sharply as a result of achievements in economic development. Nearly two-thirds of the republic's budget is allocated for social and cultural programs. In 1971 the turnover in retail goods was about five times greater than in 1940. State and cooperative enterprises and organizations, kolkhozes, and private individuals made available 270,000 sq m of living space in 1971. The population's social security and pension funds have increased.

Public health. In 1920 there were 19 hospitals with 730 beds, ten outpatient clinics, and 82 feldsher and midwife stations, served by 31 doctors and 174 intermediate medical personnel. Public health services have developed substantially in the Soviet period. As of Jan. 1, 1972, the republic had 116 hospitals with

Table 1. Output of major industrial products

	1940	1950	1960	1971
Electric power (kW-hr)	178,000,000	347,000,000	1,130,000,000	2,569,000,000
Export of commercial lumber (compact cu m)	6,100,000	5,100,000	15,000,000	15,200,000
Sawn timber (cu m)	1,000,000	800,000	2,700,000	3,100,000
Plywood (cu m)	3,700	6,400	23,100	31,100
Pulp (tons)	35,000	88,000	224,000	533,000
Paper (tons)	48,000	121,000	256,000	708,000
Cardboard (tons)	—	13,100	18,700	34,600
Catch of fish and marine animals (tons)	8,000	11,300	39,000	72,000
Canned goods (standard containers)	118,000	860,000	4,093,000	10,073,000

10,200 beds (14.3 per 1,000 inhabitants), 142 outpatient facilities and polyclinics, 74 women's consultations (gynecological outpatient clinics), and 211 nurseries with facilities for nearly 10,000 children. Medical care is provided by 2,100 doctors (one for every 345 inhabitants) and more than 8,000 intermediate medical personnel. Doctors are trained at the medical department of the University of Petrozavodsk. There are health resorts at Medvezh'ia Gora, Martsial'nye Vody, and Sortavala. The republic has sanatoriums and houses of rest.

Tourism. Karelia's natural beauty and historical sites have made it a major tourist center. Especially interesting are Kondopoga, the site of the 18th-century Uspenskaia Church, Kem' with its 18th-century Uspenskii Cathedral, and the Kizhi Museum Site. Cruises have been organized on Lake Ladoga and the White Sea–Baltic Canal, and boating is popular on the numerous lakes and rivers. In 1971 there were five tourist centers and 40 hunting and fishing lodges. In 1972 the republic was visited by more than 300,000 tourists, including more than 2,500 from 25 foreign countries.

Education and cultural affairs. Prior to the October Revolution the area of the present-day republic had 444 schools, predominantly elementary, with 16,000 students. There were no higher educational institutions. In the 1971–72 academic year, there were 142,500 students in 560 general schools of all types, 16,500 students in 17 special secondary schools, and 10,600 students in 26 vocational and technical schools. Karelia's two higher educational institutions—the University of Petrozavodsk and the pedagogical institute—and the Petrozavodsk branch of the Rimsky-Korsakov Leningrad State Conservatory had a total enrollment of 9,700 students. In 1971, 42,700 children attended 582 preschool institutions.

On Jan. 1, 1972, there were 524 public libraries, with 7,300,000 copies of books and journals, and 502 clubs. Museums include the Karelian State Museum of Local Lore in Petrozavodsk and its branches (the Martsial'nye Vody and White Sea Petroglyphs Museums), the Olonets Raion Museum of Local Lore, the Kizhi Museum Site of History and Architecture, the Museum of Fine Arts of the Karelian ASSR in Petrozavodsk, and the museum of regional lore in Medvezh'egorsk. The republic has four theaters, a state symphony orchestra, and 646 film projectors. Extracurricular institutions include a palace of Pioneers and schoolchildren, 17 houses of Pioneers, a children's park, two stations for young technicians, a station for young naturalists, and a children's excursion and tourist center.

SCIENTIFIC INSTITUTIONS. The republic has 17 scientific institutions (1972 data), including the Karelian Branch of the Academy of Sciences of the USSR (comprising four institutes and two divisions), the Institute of Forestry, the Northern Scientific Research Institute of Fisheries, and the Karelgrazhdanproekt. The scientific and production association Tselliulozmash was established in Petrozavodsk, combining the scientific research institute for pulp-making machinery with the Tiazhbummash plant. More than 1,400 scientific workers, including 37 doctors of sciences and more than 430 candidates of sciences, are employed in higher educational institutions and scientific research institutes. Among the Honored Scientists of the RSFSR working in Karelia are corresponding member of the Academy of Sciences of the USSR N. I. P'iavchenko, doctor of historical science Ia. A. Balagurov, doctor of philological science E. S. Karkhu, and doctor of biological science A. S. Lutta. Honored Scientists of the Karelian ASSR include doctor of philological science V. Ia. Evseev and doctor of geographical science G. S. Biske.

Press, radio, and television. In 1971, 137 books and pamphlets were published in editions totaling 4,213,000 copies. Excluding local and kolkhoz newspapers, 18 newspapers were published in Finnish and Russian with a total circulation of 128,000 copies (total annual circulation, 21,328,000 copies). The republic newspapers are *Neuvosto-Karjala* (Soviet Karelia), published in Finnish since 1920; *Leninskaia pravda*, published in Russian since 1918; and *Komsomolets*, published in Russian since 1920. Nine periodicals with a total circulation of 33,000 are issued, including two journals devoted to literature and the arts and to social and political affairs—*Punalippu* (Red Banner), published in Finnish since 1940, and the Russian-language *Sever* (North), also published since 1940.

The republic's radio and television systems broadcast in Finnish and Russian over two radio stations and two television channels; broadcasts from Moscow are relayed. The television station is in Petrozavodsk.

Literature. Written literature emerged in the republic after the October Revolution and has developed in two languages, Finnish and Russian. It is thus based on common ideological principles and on a distinctive blending of the oral poetic traditions of the rune singers and narrators of folk tales. The epic of the Karelian and Finnish peoples, the *Kalevala,* is famous throughout the world. The primary influences in the development of Karelia's literature were socialist reality and classical Russian and Soviet literature. As Karelian literature developed, ties between writers of different nationalities were established and strengthened, giving it a distinctive character. Karelia's literature is not a mechanical combination of several national literatures but rather an organic union of those literatures, engendered by socialist conditions.

The literature of the Karelian ASSR began to develop at the time of the first revolutionary transformations in the region. The first literary associations were created under the auspices of the newspapers *Olonetskaia kommuna* and *Punainen Karjala* (Red Karelia). These organizations merged to form the Karelia Association of Proletarian Writers with Russian (1926), Finnish (1927), and Karelian (1927) sections. The first journals were published: the Russian-language *Krasnyi klich* (1922) and *Udarnik slova* (1931) and the Finnish-language *Punakantele* (Red Kantele, 1928). Not only Russian and Karelian writers contributed to the creation of the Soviet literature of Karelia, but also Finnish proletarian writers who had emigrated from Finland and the USA. The work of J. E. Virtanen (1889–1939), whom Gorky called a truly proletarian poet, was especially significant in this period.

The Union of Writers of the Karelian ASSR was established in 1934. A new hero began to emerge in Karelian literature in the 1930's. Portrayed in a social and historical context, he is an active fighter, an individual who transforms the world. The method of socialist realism developed, and the ideological and artistic ties between Karelian and the multinational Soviet literature were strengthened. Karelian literature depicted socialist reality and interpreted the past. The two-volume work by H. Tihlä (1872–1944) *The Page Turns* (1934–36) and the novel by E. Parras (1884–1939) *The People of Jymyvaara* (1933) recount the peasantry's road to revolution.

The transformation of the region during the prewar five-year plans was the theme of the lyric poetry of L. Helo (pseudonym of T. Huttari, 1907–53) and the essays and short stories of S. Norin (1909–42). The novelist O. Johansson (1892–1939) and the playwright R. Rusko (pseudonym of R. Nyström, 1898–1939) worked in the historical-revolutionary genre, and V. Chekhov (born 1901) wrote historical works. Journals were published in Russian (*Nachalo,* 1934–35), Karelian (*Karelia,* 1937–40), and Finnish (*Rintama* [The Front], 1932–37). The Russian-language journal *Na rubezhe* (now *Sever*) and the Finnish-language journal *Punalippu* (Red Banner), both founded in 1940, played an important role in the development of literature in Karelia and in strengthening its ties with Finnish literature. During the Great Patriotic War (1941–45) a number of writers served in the Soviet Army and in partisan detachments near the front, producing books about the war and publicistic works. F. Isakov (1918–41) and I. Kutasov (1910–41) fell in battle for the homeland.

Among the writers who entered Karelian literature in the postwar period were the Finnish writers U. Vikström (born 1910) and T. Summanen (born 1931), the Russian writers F. Trofimov (born 1910), A. Linevskii (born 1902), and D. Gusarov (born 1924), and the Karelian writers A. Timonen (born 1915), P. Perttu (born 1918), N. Laine (born 1920), Ia. Rugoev (born 1918), and N. Jaakkola (1905–67). Lyric poetry was enriched by V. Morozov (1932–59), V. Ervasti (1913–47), G. Kikinov (1923–64), Salli Lund (born 1902), A. Titov (born 1913), A. Ivanov (born 1909), M. Sysoikov (born 1920), M. Tarasov (born 1930), and B. Shmidt (B. Kuznetsov, born 1913).

In large epic works in particular, there was a marked tendency toward the multifaceted portrayal of Soviet men and women and toward a psychological deepening of the contemporary hero's character. Timonen's novel *By Native Paths* (1958), Gusarov's novel *The Worth of a Human Being* (1963), and Trofimov's novellas *Above Us, Our Stars* (1962) and *Fair Land* (1969) portray the people as they move toward communism. Outstanding contributions to the historical-revolutionary genre include the tetralogy *Watershed* (books 1–4, 1949–66) by Iakkola, the trilogy *Belomor'e* (books 1–3, 1952–65) by Linevskii, the novel *Suomi Under Fire* (1968) by Vikstrem, the novel *We Are Karelians* (1969) by Timonen, the play *In the Ring of Fire* (1958) by P. Boriskov (born 1924), and the narrative poem *Tale of the Karelians* (1949–59) by Rugoev.

Several new voices are being heard, notably those of the poets O. Mishin (born 1935) and Iu. Linnik (born 1944) and the prose writers A. Stepanov (born 1920) and V. Solov'ev (born 1923). A prominent writer of children's literature is Iu. Nikonova (born 1902).

The Second Congress of Soviet Writers of the Karelian ASSR was held in 1954, the third in 1958, the fourth in 1963, and the fifth in 1967. The 100th anniversary of the *Kalevala* was commemorated in 1949. Folklore study, literary criticism, and translating are developing.   M. V. PAKHOMOVA

Architecture and art. Rock drawings of the Neolithic and Bronze Age have survived on the shores of the White Sea (Besovy Sledki, Zalavruga) and Lake Onega (Besov Nos, Peri Nos). The chipped out representations of animals (mainly elk) and hunting, fishing, combat, and ritual scenes, although primitive, are highly dynamic and expressive. Fragments of pottery with "pit-comb" designs, elk heads carved from antlers (Olenii Ostrov burial ground on Lake Onega), and schematic male and female figurines also date from the Neolithic. Archaeological finds of the first millennium A.D. attest to links with Scandinavia and the ancient Slavs. From the beginning of the second millennium A.D. Karelia's artistic culture was closely interwoven with that of Russia.

Icon painting was practiced in Karelia from the 14th and 15th centuries. At that time it was an archaic branch of Novgorodian art, as shown by the 14th-century icon *Apostle Peter* (Russian Museum, Leningrad). By the 16th century local features had begun to appear in icon painting, such as the use of more primitive techniques and a greater simplicity of pictorial vocabulary (crudely worked panels, poorly prepared *levkas* [used in priming], and the use of impasto). Color became richer and more intense, drawing was generalized, and composition lost superfluous detail. Subject matter and spiritual significance predominated over decoration, as exemplified in the 15th-century icon *SS. Peter and Paul* (Museum of Fine Arts of the Karelian ASSR, Petrozavodsk). Favorite themes were St. Nicholas, the fiery ascent of the Prophet Elijah, and the miracle of SS. Florus and Laurus (for example, the 16th-century icon *Fiery Ascent of the Prophet Elijah*, Museum of Fine Arts of the Karelian ASSR, Petrozavodsk). Icon painting continued to develop down through the 18th century, losing its artistic qualities only in the 19th century.

The abundance of forests resulted in the extensive development of wood architecture, many of whose monuments are masterpieces of Russian national architecture. In Karelia, as in other parts of the Russian North, *klet'* churches, consisting of rectangular frames with gable roofs, were built (Church of St. Lazarus at the Muromsk monastery, late 14th century), as were *shater* (tent-roofed) churches, for example the church in the village of Chelmuzhi (1605), the church on the island of Lychnyi (1620), the churches in the villages of Lindozero (1634) and Kosmozero (1720), and the Uspenskaia Church in Kondopoga (1774). The second half of the 17th century saw the appearance of the "cube" church, a square frame covered by a modified barrel-vault roof crowned with bulbous domes, examples of which may be found in the village of Virma (1759) and in the Il'inskii churchyard in Vodlozero (1798). Another style that emerged in the 17th century was the picturesque multicupola church, represented by the 22-dome Preobrazhenskaia Church (1714) and the nine-dome Pokrovskaia Church (1764) in the Kizhi churchyard.

The predominant type of dwelling was the frame *brus* structure (living and service quarters in an elongated rectangular building under a gable roof) or the *koshel'* structure (all quarters grouped within a square frame building with a roof of two sloping surfaces of unequal length). The buildings of northern Karelia were distinguished by their severe simplicity and sparse decoration. In southern and southwestern Karelia churches and houses had a more festive appearance. With the development of industry and the growth of cities in the 18th century, stone construction began. An interesting example is the Kruglaia Square (now Lenin Square) ensemble in Petrozavodsk, which consisted initially of eight separate buildings in the classical style (1775, architect E. S. Nazarov). The ensemble was subsequently rebuilt (1787–89 and 1839) to form two large semicircular buildings with wings, distinguished by clarity of composition and noble simplicity of form.

Large-scale construction began during the Soviet era. The republic's capital, Petrozavodsk, was transformed; old cities, such as Olonets, Kem', and Serdobol' (Sortavala), were rebuilt; and new cities (Medvezh'egorsk, Belomorsk, and Segezha) arose. Large residential sections and major public buildings were erected. During the 1940's and 1950's elements of the architectural orders were employed in a number of Petrozavodsk buildings (the House of Communications, 1950, architect A. K. Andreev; the Russian Dramatic Theater of the Karelian ASSR, 1953–55, architect S. G. Brodskii, sculptor S. T. Konenkov; and the Public Library, 1959, architect K. Ia. Gutin) and in the houses of culture in Segezha and Kondopoga. Other designs drew upon the decorative motifs of wood folk architecture, for example, the summer movie theater in Petrozavodsk built in 1949 by the architect M. G. Starchenko. During the 1960's and 1970's large industrial and public buildings were erected using the designs of the Karelgrazhdanproekt Institute. These designs reflect the architects' striving for simplicity and clarity of form (Vygostrov Hydroelectric Power Plant, 1961, chief engineer G. I. Konenkov; Finnish Dramatic Theater in Petrozavodsk, renovated in 1965, architect S. G. Brodskii). The Karelian Division of the Union of Architects of the USSR was established in 1943 (22 members in 1972).

In the secular art that emerged in the 20th century the work of V. N. Popov, who was affiliated with the *peredvizhniki* (the "wanderers," a progressive art movement), occupied a special place. He headed an art school (1919–21) and a fine arts studio (opened in 1936) under the auspices of the House of Folk Art in Petrozavodsk. The works of painters of the 1930's, notably V. N. Popov, D. S. Ershov, and A. I. Katseblin, portrayed the transformation of the region and the dawn of a new life. The Union of Artists of the republic, established in 1940, had 30 members in 1972. In the paintings of the 1950's, 1960's and 1970's, there was a predominance of landscapes, frequently with genre motifs (S. Kh. Iuntunen, V. M. Avdysheva, and B. N. Pomortsev), of portraits (G. A. Stronk, F. E. Nieminen, and E. K. Pekhova), and of still lifes (L. F. Lankinen and V. M. Avdysheva).

Graphic art has been developing rapidly since the 1950's. The drawings, linocuts, and etchings of A. F. Kozlov are devoted to children's themes; the changing face of the region is captured in the etchings of Z. E. L'vovich and S. I. Griazev and in the linocuts of V. P. Tervinskii; and the poetry and beauty of nature are revealed in the color and black and white linocuts of A. I. Avdyshev and M. A. Ignat'eva. Portrait and genre sculpture have been developing in the 1960's and 1970's (L. F. Lankinen, G. F. Lankinen, V. V. Afanas'ev, and E. A. Akulov).

Decorative folk art is represented by notched and openwork woodcarving with simple designs (herringbone, diamond, rosette). Such carving adorns churches, houses, furniture, and vessels. Decorative painting is used, along with carving, to decorate buildings and everyday objects. Embroidery is widespread.

Music. In prerevolutionary Karelia, musical art existed exclusively within the folk tradition. Karelian, Finnish, Veps, and Pomor'e songs are marked by distinctive national features. The rich and varied Karelian folk songs developed through extensive contacts with neighboring peoples. One of the oldest types of folk song was the rune, a Karelian-Finnish epic song. The earliest runes had a range of a fifth or a fourth and consisted of two diatonic melodies repeated at intervals (the basic meters were 3/4 and 5/4). Runes were usually sung solo or as a dialogue between two singers, sometimes with accompaniment on the *kantele*, the national plucked instrument. Other folk instruments were the *jouhikko* and *virsikannel*, both bowed instruments, and a birch-bark shepherd's horn. The most famous 19th-century rune singers were A. Perttunen and his son Miihkali, A. Malinen, and V. Kieleväinen. Russian *byliny* (epic poems) and tales were composed and recited by T. G. Riabinin, I. T. Riabinin, and V. Shchegolenok. Karelian folk melodies may be found in the works of several Russian composers, including M. I. Glinka, M. P. Mussorgsky, and A. S. Arenskii.

After the October Revolution collections of folk songs and folk-song adaptations were published, and the first professional musical works were composed (K. E. Rautio, L. K. Iousinen, and L. Ia. Teplitskii). G. R. Sinisalo wrote the first Karelian symphony, *Heroes of the Forest* (1948), and the first national ballet, *Sampo* (staged in 1959). R. S. Pergament composed the first national comic opera, *Kumokha* (concert performance in 1949; revised version staged in 1959), the symphonic poem *Aino* (1937), and the oratorio *Happiness Found* (1952). He also introduced the folk *kantele* into the classical instrumental ensemble. Other significant works of Karelian national music include the symphony-cantata *Kanteletar* and the suite *Symphonic Runes* by E. Patlaenko and the oratorio *Songs of the Pomor'e* by A. Leman. The work of the musicologist G. I. Lapchinskii greatly assisted the development of the study of music history in Karelia.

Important in the musical life of Karelia is the Musical Theater of the Karelian ASSR, founded in 1955, whose company includes People's Artist of the RSFSR S. I. Gubina and People's Artists of the Karelian ASSR Z. N. Estrin and Iu. M. Sidorov and whose conductor is I. E. Sherman. There are also the Karelian Radio and Television Symphony Orchestra (founded in 1933), the Kantele State Song and Dance Company of the Karelian ASSR (founded in 1936), a philharmonic society (founded in 1939), a branch of the Leningrad Conservatory (founded in 1967), a music college (founded in 1938), and 17 music schools. The Union of Composers of the Karelian ASSR was founded in 1937.

Theater. Prior to the October Socialist Revolution, Karelia had no national theater and Russian companies appeared annually in Petrozavodsk. Between 1918 and 1920 the Russian National Drama Theater headed by N. V. Petrov gave performances in Petrozavodsk. The Theater of Russian Drama, founded in 1929, became the Musical-Dramatic Theater in 1955; in 1970 it was renamed the Russian Dramatic Theater of the Karelian ASSR.

The national Finnish Dramatic Theater, the first in the history of Karelia, was established in 1932. Its company includes graduates of the Karelian division of the Leningrad Art Studio and amateur actors. The theater stages Finnish, Russian, and West European classics, plays by Soviet authors, and works by progressive foreign playwrights. Its repertoire has included *The Break* by B. A. Lavrenev (1932), *Liubov' Iarovaia* by K. A. Trenev (1935), *The Shoemakers From Nummi* by A. Kiva (1937), *My Friend* by N. F. Pogodin (1940), *Egor Bulychov and the Others* by M. Gorky (1940), *On the Timber-floating River* by T. Pakkala (1946), *Women of Niskavuori* by H. Wuolijoki (1948), *South Wind,* based on the work by E. Grin (1949), *The Backwoods Awaken* by T. Lankinen and N. Jaakkola (1956), *Indian Summer* by M. Lassila (1964), *Power and Glory* by K. Čapek (1966), *Mother Courage* by B. Brecht (1966), *Fourth Vertebra* by M. Larni (1967), *The Wild Captain* by J. Smuul (1968), *The House of Bernarda Alba* by F. García Lorca (1969), *Do You Accept Me, Karelian Land?* by A. Timonen (1969), and *Under the North Star,* based on the work by V. Linna (1971).

Plays staged by the Russian Dramatic Theater include *Maiden Lake* (1939) and *The Treasure of Sampo* (1940) by D. A. Shcheglov, *The Kremlin Chimes* by N. F. Pogodin (1941), *Russians* by K. M. Simonov (1942), *Chamber* by S. I. Aleshin (1962), *Mashen'ka* by A. N. Afinogenov (1964), *The Last Ones* by M. Gorky (1968), *The Gale* by V. N. Bill'-Belotserkovskii (1968), and *Mariia* by A. D. Salynskii (1970).

In 1959 the theaters of Karelia took part in the Festival of Karelian Art and Literature in Moscow.

Outstanding actors and directors who have worked in the republic at various times include Ia. N. Charov, G. A. Belov, P. P. Gaideburov, R. Niustrem, G. S. Ol'shvanger, A. V. Pergament, P. N. Chaplygin, A. I. Shibueva, and M. V. Sulimov. Among important theatrical figures (1972) are People's Artist of

the USSR E. S. Tomberg; People's Artists of the RSFSR D. K. Karpova, T. I. Lankinen, T. I. Rompainen, and Iu. A. Khumppi; Honored Art Workers of the RSFSR V. E. Suni and S. A. Tuorila, and People's Artists of the Karelian ASSR V. D. Tomashevskaia, V. A. Finogeeva, and B. I. Khotianov. The Puppet Theater, founded in 1935, is located in Petrozavodsk.

REFERENCES:
Ocherki istorii Karelii, vols. 1–2. Petrozavodsk, 1957–64.
Bubrikh, D. V. *Proiskhozhdenie karel'skogo naroda.* Petrozavodsk, 1947.
Materialy po istorii Karelii XII–XVI vv. Petrozavodsk, 1941.
Kareliia v XVII v.: Sb. dokumentov. Petrozavodsk, 1948.
Balagurov, Ia. A. *Fabrichno-zavodskie rabochie dorevoliutsionnoi Karelii* [1861–1917]. Petrozavodsk, 1968.
Bor'ba za ustanovlenie i uprochenie Sovetskoi vlasti v Karelii: Sb. dokumentov i materialov. Petrozavodsk, 1957.
Kareliia v period grazhdanskoi voiny i inostrannoi interventsii 1918–1920 gg.: Sb. dokumentov i materialov. Petrozavodsk, 1964.
Mashezerskii, V. I. *Ustanovlenie Sovetskoi vlasti v Karelii (1917-1918).* Petrozavodsk, 1957.
Kudzhiev, V. M. *Karel'skaia Trudovaia Kommuna.* Petrozavodsk, 1970.
50 let Sovetskoi Karelii: Sb. Petrozavodsk, 1970.
Karel'skaia ASSR. Moscow, 1956.
Severo-Zapad RSFSR. Moscow, 1964.
Karel'skaia ASSR za 50 let: Stat. sb. Petrozavodsk, 1967.
Iiudin, I. M., and I. E. Krivchenok. *Karel'skaia ASSR, 50 let: Tsifry i fakty.* Petrozavodsk, 1970.
Valentik, I. Ia. *Semiletka Karelii v deistvii: Tsifry i fakty.* Petrozavodsk, 1963.
Rossiiskaia Federatsiia: Evropeiskii Sever. Moscow, 1971. (Series *Sovetskii Soiuz.*)
Ocherk istorii sovetskoi literatury Karelii. Petrozavodsk, 1969.
Karel'skaia literatura: Sbornik kriticheskikh statei. Petrozavodsk, 1959.
Letopis' literaturnoi zhizni Karelii (1917–1961). Petrozavodsk, 1963.
Letopis' literaturnoi zhizni Karelii (1962–1966). Petrozavodsk, 1968.
Pisateli Karelii. Petrozavodsk, 1970.
Agapov, V. "Vyshivki Zaonezh'ia." *Na rubezhe,* Petrozavodsk, 1948, no. 1.
Opolovnikov, A. V. *Pamiatniki dereviannogo zodchestva Karelo-Finskoi SSR.* Moscow, 1955.
Plotnikov, V. *Izobrazitel'noe iskusstvo Sovetskoi Karelii.* Leningrad, 1961.
Zhivopis' drevnei Karelii [album]. Petrozavodsk, 1966.
Savvateev, Iu. A. *Risunki na skalakh.* Petrozavodsk, 1967.
Gurina, N. N. *Mir glazami drevnego khudozhnika Karelii.* Leningrad, 1967.
Gudkov, V. P. "Muzyka karel'skikh pastukhov." In the collection *Nachalo,* book 2, 1934.
Gudkov, V. P. "Karel'skoe kantele." *Narodnoe tvorchestvo,* 1937, no. 8.
Pesni narodov Karelo-Finskoi SSR. Compiled by V. P. Gudkov and N. N. Levi. Petrozavodsk, 1941.
Riauzov, S. N. "Muzykal'naia kul'tura Karel'skoi ASSR." In *Muzykal'naia kul'tura avtonomnykh respublik RSFSR.* [Moscow] 1957.
Gavrilov, M., and G. Sinisalo. "Kantele." *Sovetskaia muzyka,* 1952, no. 9.
Gippius, E., and Z. Eval'd. "Karel'skaia narodnaia pesnia." *Ibid.,* 1940, no. 9.
Karel'skie narodnye pesni: Sb. Compiled and with an introductory article by L. M. Kershner. Moscow, 1962.
Russkie narodnye pesni Pomor'ia. Collected by S. N. Kondrat'eva. Moscow, 1966.
Lapchinskii, G. I. *Muzykal'naia kul'tura Karelii.* Leningrad, 1968.
Lapchinskii, G. I. *Muzyka Sovetskoi Karelii.* Petrozavodsk, 1970.
Gosudarstvennyi Karelo-Finskii dramaticheskii teatr. [Tallinn] 1956.
Kolosenok, S., and I. Leont'ev. "Za polveka." *Na rubezhe,* Petrozavodsk, 1958, no. 1.
Smirnov, P. Ia. *Vospominaniia o teatre: Iz istorii petrozavodskogo teatra.* Petrozavodsk, 1960.   [11–1241–2]

KARELIAN BIRCH, a distinctive type of verrucous birch, characterized by thickenings on the trunk and by the marble-like pattern and texture of the wood. The wood is light yellow with dark brown markings. The Karelian birch is distributed eastward from the Karelian forests to the Urals. It is also found in Latvia, Byelorussia, and Scandinavia. The wood is valuable for the manufacture of furniture and woodenware. It is also used in the interior decoration of buildings.

REFERENCES

Sokolov, N. O. *Karel'skaia bereza.* Petrozavodsk, 1950.
Liubavskaia, A. Ia. *Selektsiia i razvedenie karel'skoi berezy.* Moscow, 1966. [11–1257–1]

KARELIAN BRANCH OF THE ACADEMY OF SCIENCES OF THE USSR, a branch of the Academy of Sciences, established at Petrozavodsk in 1945; originally it was called the Karelo-Finnish Scientific Research Base of the Academy of Sciences of the USSR and then, from 1949 to 1956, was the Karelo-Finnish Branch of the Academy of Sciences of the USSR.

As of 1972, the Karelian Branch consisted of geology, forestry, biology, language, literature, and history research institutes and water problems and economics departments. Its major activities include detecting mineral resources and working out rational means for their exploitation, comprehensively studying the forests of the Karelian ASSR and Murmansk Oblast and the means of increasing their productivity, physically and chemically analyzing wood and its by-products, and studying the biological resources of Karelia. The branch is also concerned with theoretical approaches to draining and reclaiming marshy areas and wetlands and with long-range planning of the development of the productive forces of the Karelian ASSR. Furthermore, it is involved in the study of the history, archaeology, and ethnography of Karelia; the history and present state of Karelian and Finnish literature and folk art; the Veps, Karelian, Finnish, and Lapp languages; and contemporary problems of the construction of communism. N. I. P'IAVCHENKO [11–1258–3]

KARELIAN COAST, a name for the northern part of the western shore of the White Sea from the mouth of the Kem' River to the upper reaches of the Kandalaksha Gulf. The northern section is higher and more broken up than the southern. The coast is covered with pine forests, and there are many marshes. [11–1258–1]

KARELIAN CULTURE, an archaeological culture of hunters and fishermen inhabiting what is now the Karelian ASSR at the end of the third millennium to the end of the first millennium B.C. (in the Neolithic period, the Bronze Age, and the early Iron Age). In the Neolithic the culture was characterized by crude implements made of shale and quartz, local thick-walled pottery of the "Sperrings" type (named after the small Finnish village near which the pottery was first found), and pit-comb pottery of the Volga-Oka type. In the second and first millennia B.C. the working of stone implements improved, and thin-walled pottery with an admixture of asbestos in the clay became prevalent. The production of copper and copper articles was known in the area from the middle of the second millennium B.C. and iron, from the fourth or third century B.C. It is conjectured that the creators of the Karelian culture were tribes that were formed as result of the merging of the local population (probably, forefathers of the Lapps) with proto-Finno-Ugric peoples who penetrated into the area in the sixth to third millennium B.C. from the south and southwest.

REFERENCE

Pankrushev, G. A. *Plemena Karelii v epokhu neolita i rannego metalla.* Moscow-Leningrad, 1964. G. A. PANKRUSHEV [11–1257–2]

KARELIAN FOLDING, the tectonic processes (fold region, mountain formation, granite formation, and regional metamorphism) that concluded the accumulation of the geosynclinal beds of the Lower and Middle Proterozoic of the eastern part of the Baltic Shield. The Karelian folding is divided into two epochs (phases), the early Karelian (c. 2 billion to 1.9 billion years ago) and the late Karelian (c. 1.75–1.65 billion years ago). An analogue of the Karelian folding was the Svecofennian folding in western Finland. In the early Karelian epoch a partial stabilization of the largest part of the Baltic Shield took place; it became completely stabilized in the late Karelian. [11–1257–3]

KARELIAN ISTHMUS, an isthmus between the Gulf of Finland of the Baltic Sea and Lake Ladoga in Leningrad Oblast, RSFSR.

The Karelian Isthmus borders the Neva Lowland on the south. On the north the isthmus is formed mainly of granites and gneisses; in the center and south it is composed of glacial and glacial-lake deposits (sand and pebbles, loams, clays). It is characterized by jagged relief with predominating altitudes of about 50 m. In its southern portion the topography is of a hilly moraine type, with eskers, kames, and moraine plateaus (the Lembolovskaia Upland, altitude, to 173 m). The isthmus is crossed by the Vuoksi River, which is abundant in water, and there are numerous glacial lakes. Evergreen forests predominate, with spruce in the north and groves of pine in the south. The cities of Vyborg, Priozersk, and Vsevolzhsk are located on the isthmus, and there are numerous resorts and settlements of summer homes on the shore (Sestroretsk, Zelenogorsk, Repino), part of the Leningrad Resort District. There is a developed tourist industry.

The Karelian Isthmus was part of Rus' from the ninth century onward. It was seized by Sweden at the beginning of the 17th century. The isthmus was returned to Russia by the Treaty of Nystadt of 1721. Between 1918 and 1940, a large part of the isthmus belonged to Finland, and between 1927 and 1939, with the help of Western European powers, a strongly fortified line (the Mannerheim Line) was constructed. After the Russo-Finnish War of 1939–40 the isthmus was returned to the USSR (by the peace treaty of Mar. 12, 1940). During the Great Patriotic War of 1941–45 the isthmus was occupied (in July 1941) by German and Finnish forces. As a result of the Vyborg Operation of 1944 the isthmus was liberated by the Soviet Army and, in accordance with the armistice of Sept. 19, 1944, it once more became part of the USSR.

Many places on the Karelian Isthmus have historical importance, such as the Russian fortresses of Korela, Tiversk (13th century), and Orekhov (14th century) and the Swedish fortress of Vyborg (14th–18th centuries). The Russian artist I. E. Repin lived in the settlement of Kuokkala (now Repino) from 1902 to 1930. V. I. Lenin lived on the isthmus several times between 1906 and 1917; there are house-museums of Lenin in Vyborg and Il'ichev, as well as the monument-museums Sarai (the Shed) in the settlement of Razliv and Shalash (the Hut) in Sestroretskii Razliv. There are memorial complexes at the sites of some of the fierce battles of the Great Patriotic War, such as the Lembolovskaia Upland, Vsevolzhsk, and Vyborg (Lembolovskaia Stronghold, Rumbolovskaia Mountain). There are memorial columns along the main transport highway that linked Leningrad with the interior of the country (the "Road of Life"), and a sculpture composition entitled *The Broken Ring* has been erected on the shore of Lake Ladoga. [11–1258–2]

KARELIAN LABOR COMMUNE, an autonomous regional unit of the RSFSR, formed by a decree of the All-Russian Central Executive Committee on July 8, 1920, from the Karelian population of Olonets and Arkhangel'sk provinces. On the basis of a decree of the All-Russian Central Executive Committee of July 23, 1923, the Karelian Labor Commune was reorganized as the Karelian ASSR. [11–1257–4]

KARELIANS (self-designation, Karjalaiset), a people living mainly in the Karelian ASSR, as well as in certain parts of the RSFSR, including Kalinin (the "Tver," or "Upper Volga," Karelians, who migrated from the Lake Ladoga area in the 16th and 17th centuries), Novgorod, Leningrad, and Yaroslavl oblasts. The total number of Karelians in the USSR is 146,000 (1970 census), of whom 84,000 live in the Karelian ASSR. Some Karelians also live in Finland.

Karelians speak the Karelian language; a considerable number also speak Russian and some speak Finnish as well. Those who profess a religion are Orthodox. The original stage of the Karelians' ethnogenesis has not yet been definitively ascertained. By the ninth century A.D. the Korela tribes (the forebears of the Karelians) had settled on the northwestern shore of Lake Ladoga. In the 11th and 12th centuries they took over the western part of what is now the territory of the Karelian ASSR; later they began to advance north toward the White Sea and east to the area between Lakes Ladoga and Onega, where they merged with part of the native Veps (Ves'). The neighboring Russian population, with whom the Karelians were closely associated, had an important influence on the formation of the culture of the Karelians. The first mention of the Karelians in a Russian chronicle dates from 1143. The consolidation of the Karelians between the 12th and 15th centuries occurred within the Russian state. The principal occupation of the Karelians for ages has been farming; livestock raising, lumbering, fishing, and hunting have been of secondary importance. Among the trades, smithcraft has been particularly developed.

After the October Socialist Revolution the Karelians received national autonomy: the Karelian Labor Commune was formed in June 1920 and reorganized in 1923 as the Karelian ASSR.

Large-scale industry has been created in the republic during the years of socialist construction, and national workers' and engineering and technical cadres have been developed. The main trend in agriculture has been a high level of mechanization in dairy farming. Fishing and fur farming have been developed extensively. Great progress has been achieved in science, literature, and art (including popular applied art).

REFERENCES
Ocherki istorii Karelii, vols. 1–2. Petrozavodsk, 1957–64.
Taroeva, R. F. *Material'naia kul'tura karel (Karel'skaia ASSR)*. Moscow–Leningrad, 1965.
Bubrikh, D. V. *Proiskhozhdenie karel'skogo naroda*. Petrozavodsk, 1947.
Istoriia, arkheologiia, etnografiia Karelii: Bibliogrofich. ukazatel' sovetskoi literatury za 1917-1965 gg. Petrozavodsk, 1967.
R. F. TAROEVA [11–1241–1]

KARELIN, ANDREI OSIPOVICH. Born July 4 (16), 1837, in the village of Selezni, in present-day Tambov Raion, Tambov Oblast; died July 31 (Aug. 13), 1906, in Nizhny Novgorod (now Gorky). Russian photographer.

Karelin graduated from the St. Petersburg Academy of Arts in 1864. While working as a photo retoucher, he developed a keen interest in photography. He opened a photography studio in Kostroma and later in Nizhny Novgorod. Karelin considered photography as a new medium of the pictorial arts. His genre compositions reflected the tendencies of the *peredvizhniki* painters (the "wanderers," a progressive art movement). Karelin made many innovative contributions to the art of photography (setup and lighting effects). Through a study of optics, he advanced photographic technique. Karelin received a number of awards at Russian and European photography exhibitions.

[11–1240–2]

KARELIN, GRIGORII SILYCH. Born January 1801 in St. Petersburg Province; died Dec. 17 (29), 1872, in the city of Gur'ev. Russian explorer and naturalist.

Karelin graduated from a cadet school in St. Petersburg in 1817 and was exiled to Orenburg in 1822 for writing an epigram on Arakcheev. From 1827 to 1829 he traveled through the western part of Kazakhstan and mapped the location of the former Bukei Horde. Leading an expedition for the exploration of the northeastern part of the Caspian Sea in 1832, he mapped this part of the sea. Four years later he headed an expedition for the exploration of the eastern and southeastern shores of the Caspian Sea. Karelin and his companions mapped the gulfs of the eastern shore, including parts of the Kara-Bogaz-Gol; they gave the first description of the gulf. From 1840 to 1842, Karelin and the geographer and cartographer I. P. Kirilov explored Semirech'e and the upper course of the Irtysh and its tributaries and collected abundant materials on the flora.

WORKS
"Puteshestviia po Kaspiiskomu moriu." *Zap. Russkogo geograficheskogo ob-va*, 1883, vol. 10.
REFERENCE
Pavlov, N. V. *Naturalisty i puteshestvenniki Grigorii Silych Karelin (1801–1872) i ego vospitannik i drug Ivan Petrovich Kirilov (1821–1842)*, 2nd ed. Moscow, 1948. [11–1240–4]

KARELIN, VLADIMIR ALEKSANDROVICH. Born 1891; died 1938. One of the organizers of the left Socialist Revolutionaries (Left SR's) and a member of the party's Central Committee.

At the Second All-Russian Congress of Soviets, Karelin was elected to the Presidium of the All-Russian Central Executive Committee from the Left SR's. In December 1917 he became people's commissar for state properties in the Council of People's Commissars of the RSFSR. He was a member of the collegium of the People's Commissariat of Justice and a member of the second through fourth convocations of the All-Russian Central Executive Committee. Karelin was part of the Soviet delegation at the peace negotiations in Brest-Litovsk. In March 1918, as a result of his opposition to the signing of the Brest treaty, he resigned from the Council of People's Commissars. He was one of the organizers of the Left SR revolt in July 1918. After the rebellion was suppressed, he went into hiding. In November 1918, he was tried *in absentia* and sentenced by a Soviet court to three years in prison. In February 1919 he was arrested and then released. Karelin then fled abroad and engaged in anti-Soviet activity. [11–1240–3]

KAREN, a people living in southeastern Burma (approximately 2.4 million persons; 1970 estimate) and western Thailand (more than 100,000).

Significant vestiges of tribal division have been retained among the Karen; the principal groups are the Sgaw, the Pwo, and the Bghai. The dialects and customs of the groups differ sharply from one another. The Karen language is a member of the Tibeto-Burman branch of the Sino-Tibetan family. Buddhism, Christianity (in particular, Baptists), and ancient animistic beliefs are widespread among the Karen. The Karen have an autonomous national state (Kawthule State) in the Union of Burma, but the majority live outside its boundaries (in the Irrawaddy Delta). The chief occupation of the Karen is farming (rice, beans, cotton, tobacco, fruits, and vegetables).

REFERENCES
Narody Iugo-Vostochnoi Azii. Moscow, 1966. Pages 350–53.
Birmanskii soiuz. Moscow, 1958. (Collection.)
Marshall, H. I. *The Karens of Burma*. London, 1945. [11–1259–5]

KARENGA, a river in Chita Oblast, RSFSR, right tributary of the Vitim River (Lena Basin). Length, 366 km; basin area, 10,100 sq km. It rises in the Iablonovyi Range and flows through an intermontane basin. It is fed primarily by rain. The average flow rate is 16.5 cu m per sec, 180 km from its mouth. It is at flood stage from May to September, with sharp variations in water level. The river freezes over at the end of November and thaws in mid-April. [11–1259–3]

KARGALA, an urban-type settlement in Orenburg Raion, Orenburg Oblast, RSFSR. Railroad station, 20 km from Orenburg. In the region there are deposits of condensed natural gas that are being exploited. In 1973 the construction of gas-processing plants was undertaken. [11–1217–4]

KARGALA TREASURE, a burial of a woman (dating between the second century B.C. and the second century A.D.), possibly a female shaman, with a rich inventory. The burial was discovered in 1939 during earthworks in a gorge of the Kargala River near the city of Alma-Ata. About 300 gold objects were found, including rings, an earring, and small badges with relief designs. The most interesting item is a diadem in the form of a rectangular, openwork panel with a portrayal of a hunting scene; people and animals, including a fantastic dragon and winged horses, are set against a background of floral designs. The design of the headwear on the human figures, some of the depictions of animals, and the distinctive features of the jewelry-making technique testify to the local origin of the Kargala treasure's articles.

REFERENCES
Bernshtam, A. N. "Zolotaia diadema iz shamanskogo pogrebeniia na r. Karagalinke." In the collection *Kratkie soobshcheniia o dokladakh i polevykh issledovaniiakh Instituta istorii material'noi kul'tury*, [issue] 5. Moscow-Leningrad, 1940.
Bernshtam, A. N. *Proshloe raiona Alma-Ata*. Alma-Ata, 1948.
[11–1217–5]

KARGAPOL'E, an urban-type settlement and administrative center of Kargapol'e Raion, Kurgan Oblast, RSFSR. It is located on the Miass River (Ob' Basin), 17 km northeast of the Kargapol'e railroad station on the Kurgan-Sverdlovsk line and 111 km northwest of Kurgan. Kargapol'e has a machinery repair plant, a brickyard, and a creamery.   [11–1218–2]

KARGAPOLOV, MIKHAIL IVANOVICH. Born Nov. 9, 1928, in the village of Rusakova, Kurgan Oblast. Soviet mathematician. Corresponding member of the Academy of Sciences of the USSR (1966). Member of the CPSU since 1965.

Kargapolov graduated from the Urals University (Sverdlovsk) in 1951 and since 1964 has been a professor at the University of Novosibirsk. His principal works, which pertain to algebra, are primarily devoted to the study of the properties of infinite discrete groups, including generalized solvable and orderable groups, as well as to the study of algorithmic problems. He has been awarded the Order of the Red Banner of Labor and various medals.

REFERENCE
Matematika v SSSR, 1958–1967, vol. 2. Moscow, 1969. (Contains a bibliography.)   [11–1218–1]

KARGASOK, an urban-type settlement and administrative center of Kargasok Raion, Tomsk Oblast, RSFSR. It is a port on the left bank of the Ob' River, 535 km northwest of Tomsk. It is the site of a logging and timber procurement establishment, a fish-processing plant, and a creamery. It also has a meat and dairy sovkhoz and a livestock-fattening sovkhoz. There are petroleum and natural gas deposits and timber industries in the region.   [11–1218–3]

KARGAT, a city (until 1965, a settlement), and administrative center of Kargat Raion, Novosibirsk Oblast, RSFSR, on the Kargat River. Railroad station on the Barabinsk-Novosibirsk line. There is a dairy for the production of butter and cheese and a meat-packing plant.   [11–1219–1]

KARGAT, a river in Novosibirsk Oblast, RSFSR, right tributary of the Chulym River (Lake Chany basin). Length from the source of Kargatenok River, 387 km; basin area, approximately 7,200 sq km. It flows through the Barabinsk Lowlands and is fed primarily by melted snow. Its average annual rate of flow is 8.54 cu m per sec at the village of Nizhnii Kargat, 36 km from its mouth. The river freezes over in November and thaws in the second half of April. The city of Kargat is located along its course.   [11–1218–4]

KARGER, MIKHAIL KONSTANTINOVICH. Born May 17 (30), 1903, in Kazan. Soviet archaeologist and art historian; specialist in Slavic and Russian archaeology and the history of ancient Russian culture and art. Doctor of Historical Sciences (1959).

Karger graduated from the University of Petrograd in 1923. In 1949 he became a professor at Leningrad University and in 1964, director of the Leningrad division of the Institute of Archaeology of the Academy of Sciences of the USSR. He directed archaeological and restoration work in Novgorod, Kiev, Pereiaslav-Khmel'nitskii, Galich, Vladimir-Volynskii, Polotsk, Turov, Iziaslavl', and other cities. He was awarded the State Prize of the USSR in 1952 and the Order of Lenin.

WORKS
Drevnii Kiev, vols. 1–2. Moscow-Leningrad, 1958–61.
Novgorod Velikii. Moscow-Leningrad, 1961.
Zodchestvo drevnego Smolenska (XII–XIII vv.). Leningrad, 1964.
REFERENCE
Vagner, G. K., and A. N. Kirpichnikov. "K 60-letiiu M. K. Kargera." *Sovetskaia arkheologiia,* 1963, no. 4.   [11–1219–2]

KARGIN, VALENTIN ALEKSEEVICH. Born Jan. 10 (23), 1907, in Ekaterinoslav, present-day Dnepropetrovsk; died Oct. 21, 1969, in Moscow. Soviet chemist; academician of the Academy of Sciences of the USSR (1953; corresponding member, 1946). Hero of Socialist Labor (1966).

Kargin graduated from Moscow University in 1930. He worked at the L. Ia. Karpov Institute of Physical Chemistry from 1930 to 1956, and at Moscow State University from 1956 until his death in 1969. Kargin was one of the founders of the Soviet school of polymer physical chemistry. His main works were devoted to the investigation of the formation mechanism of colloidal systems and, in particular, to the physical chemistry of macromolecular compounds. Kargin demonstrated that polymer solutions are thermodynamically reversible systems. He studied the laws governing the mechanical and thermomechanical properties of polymers and the link between the physicochemical properties of polymer materials and their structure on the molecular and supermolecular levels; this research led to the discovery of efficient methods for carrying out structurochemical and physical modifications of plastics, rubbers, and chemical fibers. Kargin investigated the role of the structural properties of the reaction medium during the formation of macromolecules. In 1956 he founded the first university subdepartment of macromolecular compounds in the USSR at Moscow State University. Kargin was editor in chief of the journal *Vysokomolekuliarnye soedineniia* (Macromolecular Compounds; 1959–69). His works have found wide application in industry. Kargin was awarded the Lenin Prize (1962), the State Prize of the USSR (1943, 1947, 1950, 1969), three Orders of Lenin, two other orders, and several medals.

WORKS
Kratkie ocherki po fiziko-khimii polimerov, 2nd ed. Moscow, 1967. (Jointly with G. L. Slonimskii.)
REFERENCE
Valentin Alekseevich Kargin. Moscow, 1960. (*AN SSSR: Materialy k biobibliografii uchenykh SSSR: Ser. khimicheskikh nauk,* issue 29.)   [11–1219–3]

KARGOPOL', a city, the center of Kargopol' Raion, Arkhangel'sk Oblast, RSFSR; situated on the left bank of the Onega River, 5 km from its source at Lake Lacha and 89 km west of the Niandoma station on the Vologda-Arkhangel'sk railway line.

Kargopol' developed in the 14th century. During the 15th and 16th centuries it was an important commercial settlement connected with the salt trade. In 1608, I. I. Bolotnikov was sent to Kargopol', where he was blinded and drowned in the Onega. In 1612, Kargopol' resisted a Polish siege. After 1801 it became a district city of Olonets Province. The city has a creamery, a brewery, a linen-processing plant, and a plant producing asphalt concrete. Kargopol's chief architectural monuments include the Khristorozhdestvenskii Cathedral (1562), the Blagoveshchenie Church (1682–92), the Church of St. Vladimir (1653), the Rozhdestvo Bogoroditsy Church (1653), and the Church of St. John the Baptist (1751), all cubic stone churches with four-slope roofs and "patterned-style" facades. Kargopol' has a teachers college and a museum of local lore.

REFERENCES
Gemp, K. P. *Kargopol'.* Arkhangel'sk, 1968.
Bartenev, I., and B. Federov. *Arkhitekturnye pamiatniki russkogo Severa.* Leningrad-Moscow, 1968. Pages 103–15.   [11–1219–4]

KARGOPOL' CULTURE, an archaeological culture of tribes of hunters and fishermen inhabiting the region around Lakes Lacha, Vozhe, and Kenozero and part of Lake Beloe, in the present-day Vologda and Arkhangel'sk oblasts, RSFSR. The culture is named after the place of the principal finds in Kargopol' Raion, Arkhangel'sk Oblast, RSFSR.

The most ancient remains date from the end of the Mesolithic period and are characterized by crude flint implements, bone arrowheads, and other articles. Pottery with ornamentation consisting of large pits appeared in the fourth millennium B.C.; this was replaced by pottery decorated with "pit-comb" impressions. The flint tools of this period acquired a Neolithic look, and stone figurines of animals and clay representations of man appeared. At the end of the second millennium B.C., smooth and grid-faced pottery predominated and flint almost ceased to be used.

REFERENCE
Foss, M. E. "Drevneishaia istoriia severa Evropeiskoi chasti SSSR." *Materialy i issledovaniia po arkheologii SSSR,* no. 29. Moscow, 1952.
[11–1220–1]

KARI ABDULLAH. Born in 1871, in Kabul; died there Apr. 29, 1943. Afghan educator, philologist, and poet. Received a religious education.

Kari Abdullah was the author of textbooks and books of literary research in which modern methods of literary analysis were used for the first time in Afghanistan. He became famous as a master of the qasida and ghazal, updating the traditional styles with modern social subject matter. He composed a qasida on A. S. Pushkin in 1937. A number of Kari Abdullah's works are devoted to the history of Islam and to Sufism, rhetoric, stylistics, and the theory of poetry. The honorary title of Malek al-Shoara (King of Poets) was conferred on him.

WORKS
Kulliyat-i Kari. Kabul, 1334 A.H. (A.D. 1955).
REFERENCE
Gerasimova, A., and G. Girs. *Literatura Afganistana.* Moscow, 1963.
[11–1260–3]

KARI-IAKUBOV, MUKHITDIN. Born May 1, 1896, in Fergana; died Feb. 2, 1957, in Tashkent. Soviet Uzbek opera singer (baritone) and theatrical figure. People's Artist of the Uzbek SSR (1936).

Kari-Iakubov, along with Kh. Khamza, participated in the work of the Dramatic Troupe of Muslim Youth in 1918. He performed Uzbek folk songs at the International Exposition of Decorative Art and Industry in Paris in 1925. In 1926 he organized a concert and ethnographic ensemble out of which the Uzbek Musical Theater was formed. From 1928 to 1932 he served as artistic director of the theater. In 1936, Kari-Iakubov became the artistic director of the Uzbek Philharmonic Society and a soloist in the Uzbek Theater of Opera and Ballet in Tashkent. Among the roles he performed were Khosrov in Mushel' and Uspenskii's *Farkhad and Shirin,* Naufal' in Glière and Sadykov's *Leili and Medzhnun,* and Ulugbek in A. F. Kozlovskii's *Ulugbek.* He also appeared on stage as a singer of folk songs.

REFERENCE
Glikman, I. "Aktery uzbekskogo opernogo teatra." In the collection *Puti razvitiia uzbekskoi muzyki.* Leningrad-Moscow, 1946.
K. AKHMEDOVA [11–1280–1]

KARIKÁS, FRIGYES. Born Nov. 4, 1892, in the village of Borossebes; died Mar. 5, 1938, in Moscow. Hungarian writer; became a member of the CPSU in 1917.

During World War I, Karikás was in the Austro-Hungarian Army. In 1914 he was taken prisoner by the Russians. During the October Socialist Revolution he took part in the street fighting in Moscow. In 1918 he returned to Hungary, where he was political commissar in the 39th Brigade fighting for the Hungarian Soviet Republic; after it was defeated, he lived abroad. In the early 1930's, he returned to his homeland but was arrested and spent several years in prison. After this he emigrated to the USSR.

Karikás won literary renown with his stories about the Hungarian Red Army soldiers who defended Soviet Hungary from interventionists—the collection *Various People* (1932; Russian translation, from the Hungarian manuscript, *The 39th Brigade,* 1927; retranslated as *Ianosh Korbei* in 1959).

WORKS
In Russian translation:
Usy: Rasskazy. Moscow, 1970.
[11–1270–1]

KARIM, FATYKH. Born Dec. 27, 1908 (Jan. 9, 1909), in the village of Aet, in present-day Bizhbuliak Raion, Bashkir ASSR; died Feb. 19, 1945, in the settlement of Pobeda, Kaliningrad Oblast. Soviet Tatar poet.

Karim fought in the Great Patriotic War (1941–45) and died at the front. His works were first published in 1928; his first collection of verses, *Beginning Song,* was published in 1931. His most important works are *The Seventh Furnace* (1932) and *Roar-*

ing Dawn (1933), which reflect the process of the industrialization of the country and the collectivization of agriculture. Karim is the author of a number of works written at the front (the collections *Love and Hate,* 1943, and *Melody and Power,* 1944, and the novella *Notes of a Scout,* 1944). He was awarded two orders and several medals.

WORKS
Äsärlär (Z. Mäjitov keresh süze belän), vols. 1–3. Kazan, 1957.
Saylanma äsärlär. Kazan, 1969.
In Russian translation:
Izbrannye stikhi i poemy. Kazan, 1957.
REFERENCE
Giniiatullina, A. *Pisateli Sovetskogo Tatarstana: Biobibliograficheskii spravochnik.* Kazan, 1970.
M. GAINULLIN [11–1271–1]

KARIM, KHANIF (pseudonym of Khanif Karimovich Karimov). Born July 25 (Aug. 7), 1910, in the village of Verkhnie Kigi, in present-day Kiginskii Raion, Bashkir ASSR. Soviet Bashkir poet. Member of the CPSU since 1932; fought in the Great Patriotic War of 1941–45.

Karim graduated from the department of literature of the Bashkir Pedagogic Institute in Ufa, and published his first collection of verses, *Song of the Sentry,* in 1934. In the narrative poems *The Girl* (1935) and *The Mountain Village* (1940), Karim depicted the transition of the peasants to a new life. The collections *Verses* (1942), *There Is No Death for Love* (1943), and *Paths of War* expressed the thoughts and strivings of the Soviet liberation fighter. Intimacy and lyricism characterized many of Karim's postwar verses (the collections *Morning Thoughts,* 1964, and *In the Land of Youth,* 1967). He has also written prose (the collections of stories *Forest Path,* 1965; Russian translation, 1969). He has translated into Bashkir the verses of A. S. Pushkin, M. Iu. Lermontov, T. G. Shevchenko, and V. V. Mayakovsky. Karim was awarded the Order of the Red Star and various medals.

WORKS
Haylanma äthärdhär. Ufa, 1960.
In Russian translation:
Izbrannoe. Introductory article by G. Ramazanov. Ufa, 1957.
Izbr. proizv. Ufa, 1970.
S. G. SAFUANOV [11–1271–2]

KARIM, MUSTAI (pseudonym of Mustafa Safich Karimov). Born Oct. 20, 1919, in the village of Kliashevo, in present-day Chishmy Raion, Bashkir ASSR. Soviet Bashkir poet; People's Poet of the Bashkir ASSR (1963). Member of the CPSU since 1944.

Karim graduated from the department of language and literature of the Bashkir Pedagogic Institute in 1940. He fought in the Great Patriotic War (1941–45) and began publishing his works in 1935. His first verse collections were *The Detachment Set Off* (1938, with V. Nafikov) and *Vernal Voices* (1941). The heroism and tragedy of the Great Patriotic War found expression in the narrative poems *December Song* (1942), *Ul'masbai* (1942–44), and *Black Waters* (1961) and in many lyric verses. His postwar poems reflect the work and life of the Bashkir people ("Girls of Our Kolkhoz," 1948, and "Sabantui," 1953).

Karim's contemporary poetry is characterized by a deepening of sociophilosophical themes (*The Rivers Converse,* 1961, and *When the Cranes Came,* 1964). He is also a playwright: *The Wedding Continues* (1947), *The Kidnapped Girl* (1959), *On the Night of a Lunar Eclipse* (1964; K. S. Stanislavsky State Prize of the RSFSR, 1967), and *The Land of Aigul'* (1969). Karim has written novellas for children and has translated into Bashkir the works of T. G. Shevchenko and others. His works have been translated into many languages.

Karim served as chairman of the board of the Writers' Union of Bashkiria (1951–62) and as secretary of the board of the Writers' Union of the RSFSR (since 1962). A deputy to the Supreme Soviet of the RSFSR at its fourth and fifth convocations, he became vice-chairman of the Presidium of the Supreme Soviet of the RSFSR in 1963. He was awarded the Salavat Iulaev State Prize of the Bashkir ASSR (1967), the Order of Lenin, five other orders, and several medals.

WORKS

Kütärelgän qoyashka qarap. Ufa, 1960.
Haylanma äthärdhär, vols. 1–2. Ufa, 1966.
Äthärdhär, 5th ed., vols. 1–4. Ufa, 1971–72—.
In Russian translation:
Izbr. proizv., vols. 1–2. Ufa, 1969.
Godam vo sled. Moscow, 1971.
"Salavat. Dramaticheskaia poema." *Druzhba narodov,* 1973, no. 1.

REFERENCE

Khrenkov, Dm. *Mustai Karim.* Moscow, 1969.

G. B. Khusainov   [11–1270–2]

KARIMATA, a strait between the islands of Borneo (Kalimantan) and Belitung in Indonesia, linking the South China and Java
seas. At its narrowest point, it is approximately 210 km wide. It
reaches a depth of 36 m. Coral reefs and many small islands are
located in the strait.   [11–1272–1]

KARINIAN, ARTASHES BALASIEVICH (pseudonym of
A. B. Gabrielian). Born Oct. 30 (Nov. 11), 1886, in Baku. Soviet
critic and literary scholar. Academician of the Academy of
Sciences of the Armenian SSR (1956). Became a member of the
CPSU in 1907.

Upon graduation from the University of St. Petersburg in
1910, Karinian worked as a revolutionary propagandist in Baku.
In 1918 he was the people's commissar of justice for the Baku
Council of People's Commissars. From 1924 to 1928 he was the
chairman of the Central Executive Committee of Armenia. In
1929 and 1930, Karinian served as the deputy people's commissar of education of the Armenian SSR.

Karinian began his literary work in 1906. His articles were
published in the Bolshevik newspapers *Kaits* (The Spark), *Bakin-
skii rabochii* (Baku Worker), *Put' pravdy* (The Path of Truth),
and *Pravda.* He is the author of the books *Faces and Events*
(1928), *The Significance of Russian Literature for Soviet Armenian Literature* (1948), *Mikael Nalbandian and the Progressive Russians of the 1860's* (1949), *Anton Chekhov* (1954), and
Critical and Literary Articles (1962). He also wrote monographs,
including *Essays on the History of Armenian Periodicals* (vols.
1–2, 1956–60). Karinian has been awarded the Order of Lenin,
the Order of the Red Banner of Labor, and several medals.

WORKS

Karinyan, A. *Grakan ardzagank'ner.* Yerevan, 1955.
Hovhannes t'umanyan (husher ev hodvacner). Yerevan, 1971.
In Russian translation:
"Na fronte kul'tury v dni Bakinskoi Kommuny 1918 g. (Vospominaniia,
Fakty)." *Izv. AN AzSSR: Seriia istoriia, filosofii i prava,* 1966, no. 3.

REFERENCE

"Golos kritika." *Druzhba narodov,* 1956, no. 5.

L. G. Mkrtchian   [11–1273–4]

KARINSKII, MIKHAIL IVANOVICH. Born Nov. 4 (16),
1840, in Moscow; died July 20 (Aug. 2), 1917. Russian logician
and philosopher.

Karinskii graduated from the Moscow Theological Academy
in 1862. From 1869 to 1894, he taught philosophy at the St.
Petersburg Theological Academy and at other educational institutions. His first works were devoted to the history of philosophy
(*A Critical Survey of the Most Recent Period in German Philosophy,* 1873). The basic field of his activity was epistemology and
logic. His approach became ever closer to materialism—for example, his article "Appearance and Reality" in the journal *Orthodox Review,* 1878, vol. 1, and *Differences of Opinion in the
School of the New Empiricism on the Question of Self-evident
Truths,* 1914. In the field of logic, Karinskii proposed an original
classification for mental conclusions (*The Collected Works of
Russian Logicians of the 19th Century,* 1956). He wrote a number of works on the history of ancient philosophy.

REFERENCES

Radlov, E. L. *Uchenaia deiatel'nost' prof. M. I. Karinskogo* vols. [1]–2.
St. Petersburg, 1895.
Mirtov, D. "M. I. Karinskii i ego filosofskie vozzreniia." *Mysl' i slovo,*
vol. 2. Moscow, 1918–21.

Kondakov, N. I. "Vydaiushchiesia proizvedeniia russkoi logicheskoi
nauki 19 v." *Izbr. trudy russkikh logikov 19 v.* Moscow, 1956.

A. M. Plotnikov   [11–1272–2]

KARINSKII, NIKOLAI MIKHAILOVICH. Born Mar. 22
(Apr. 3), 1873, in Viatka, the present-day city of Kirov; died
Dec. 14, 1935, in Moscow. Soviet Slavicist and dialectologist;
corresponding member of the Academy of Sciences of the USSR
(1921). Son of the philosopher M. I. Karinskii.

Karinskii graduated from the University of St. Petersburg in
1896 and became a professor there in 1903. Beginning in 1911
he taught as a professor at the Women's Pedagogical Institute,
the Institute of History and Philology (1913–17), the Viatka
Pedagogical Institute (1919–23), the Second Moscow State University (1924–30), and the V. I. Lenin Moscow State Pedagogical Institute (1930–35). In 1931 he became head of the
Dialectographical Commission of the Institute of Language and
Thought of the Academy of Sciences of the USSR. Karinskii's
scientific works deal with the history of Russian and Old Bulgarian, Russian dialectology, Slavic paleography, and related
disciplines.

WORKS

Iazyk Pskova i ego oblasti v XV v. St. Petersburg, 1909.
Ocherki iz istorii pskovskoi pis'mennosti i iazyka, issues 1–2. Petrograd,
1916–17.
Obraztsy glagolitsy. St. Petersburg, 1908. (With 25 photographs.)
Obraztsy pis'ma drevneishego perioda istorii russkoi knigi. Leningrad,
1925. (With 68 photographs.)
Ocherki iazyka russkikh krest'ian. Moscow-Leningrad, 1936.

[11–1272–3]

KARINTHY, FRIGYES. Born June 24, 1887, in Budapest; died
Aug. 29, 1938, in Siófok. Hungarian writer.

Karinthy began his literary career in 1907 as a contributor to
the progressive journal *Nyugat.* His novella *Excuse Me, Teacher*
(1916; Russian translation, 1962) was written in the realistic
tradition. In 1918 he published a collection of antiwar articles
entitled *Christ or Barabbas.*

In his dramas (*Tomorrow Morning,* 1921) and novels (*Capillaria,* 1921, and *Journey Around One's Own Skull,* 1937), Karinthy used the grotesque and fantastic and exposed the flaws of
bourgeois society. He was also the author of parodies (*That's
How You Write,* 1912), topical satires, and poems. He translated
the works of Swift, Heine, and Mark Twain into Hungarian.

WORKS

Kötéltánc. Budapest, 1958.
Az iró becsülete. Budapest, 1962.
Válogatott mlivei. Budapest, 1962.

REFERENCES

Klaniczai, T., J. Szauder, and M. Szabolcsi. *Kratkaia istoriia vengerskoi
literatury XI–XX v.* Budapest, 1962. Pages 231–32.
Szalay, K. *Karinthy Frigyes.* Budapest, 1961.

V. S. Baikov   [11–1272–4]

KARINTORF, an urban-type settlement in Kirov Oblast,
RSFSR, located 13 km east of the city of Kirovo-Chepetsk.
Karintorf's main industry is peat cutting.   [11–1273–3]

KARITSKII, KONSTANTIN DIONISIEVICH. Born Sept. 13
(26), 1913, in the settlement of Zheltaia Reka, the present-day
city of Zheltye Vody, Dnepropetrovsk Oblast. One of the organizers of the partisan movement in Leningrad Oblast during the
Great Patriotic War of 1941–45; a colonel. Hero of the Soviet
Union (Apr. 2, 1944). Member of the CPSU since 1932.

Karitskii served with the border troops between 1932 and
1940. When the Great Patriotic War began he became commander of the 55th Fighter Battalion. From December 1941
through March 1944, he led a partisan detachment and the Fifth
Partisan Brigade at the enemy's rear in Leningrad Oblast. In the
course of combat operations his brigade killed more than 2,000
German soldiers and officers, disabled 15 tanks and armored
vehicles, 18 locomotives, and 160 boxcars and flatcars, and blew
up 29 bridges. During the Leningrad-Novgorod offensive of
1944, his brigade captured important sections of the Nikolaevo-
Gorodets and Utorgosh-Nikolaevo highways and held them un-

til Soviet troops arrived. Since the war, Karitskii has worked in state security agencies and, subsequently, as deputy director of the Museum of the Defense of Leningrad. He has been awarded the Order of Lenin, the Order of the Red Banner, two Orders of the Patriotic War First Class, and various medals.

[11–1279–1]

KARJALAINEN, AHTI. Born Feb. 10, 1923, in the town of Hirvensalmi. Finnish statesman and politician; son of a land-owner.

Karjalainen graduated from the faculty of political science of the University of Helsinki in 1946 and received a degree of doctor of political science in 1959. In 1946 he joined the Agrarian Union (called the Center Party since 1965) and was its information secretary from 1947 to 1950. Karjalainen was finance minister from 1957 to 1958, trade and industry minister from 1959 to 1961, and foreign minister from 1961 to 1962. From 1964 to 1970 and since September 1972, he has been minister of foreign affairs and deputy prime minister. He was prime minister in 1962–63 and 1970–71. He has been a representative of the Center Party in Parliament since 1966. Karjalainen is a supporter of Finland's peace-oriented foreign policy, the "Paasikivi-Kekkonen line." [11–1465–1]

KARJALANSELKÄ, an upland ridge in eastern Finland, located between Lake Oulu to the northwest and Pyhäselkä to the southeast. Length, about 200 km; elevations, to 355 m. The ridge is composed of ancient crystalline rock covered with moraine deposits. There are extensive taiga forests with numerous swamps and lakes. The area has lumber industry. [11–1465–2]

KARKARALINSK, a city and administrative center of Karkaralinsk Raion, Karaganda Oblast, Kazakh SSR, at the foot of the Karkaralinsk Mountains, 23 km northwest of the Karagaily railroad station. It is situated on a highway, 224 km southeast of Karaganda. Population, 9,000 (1970). It is the center of an agricultural region. There is a veterinary technicum. Karkaralinsk was first established in 1824 as a cossack settlement.

[11–1280–3]

KARKARALINSK MOUNTAINS, a mountain massif in the eastern Kazakh Hills. It reaches an altitude of 1,565 m at Mount Aksoran, which is the highest point in Central Kazakhstan. The mountains are composed of granite, porphyrite, quartzite, and other minerals. The slopes are deeply furrowed by valleys and ravines, and there are many lakes. Stands of pine forest, with feather grass and mixed grass steppe vegetation, cover the slopes. There are deposits of polymetallic ores. [11–1280–4]

KARKARALINSK SETTLEMENTS, remains of settlements of the late Bronze Age (beginning of the first millennium B.C.), near the city of Karkaralinsk, Kazakh SSR. The site was explored in the 1950's by an expedition of the Academy of Sciences of the Kazakh SSR under the leadership of A. Kh. Margulan. Excavations have unearthed rectangular semi-subterranean dwellings (of post construction, skeletal construction, or timber-frame construction) with centrally located hearths. Stone mattocks, pestles, spinning distaffs, and mortars were also found. The principal occupation of the inhabitants was apparently stock raising—cattle, smaller horned stock, and horses. Also developed, however, were the working of metal (judging from finds of ore, slag, and casting forms) and pottery-making (flat-bottomed pots with wide bodies, decorated with affixed cylindrical forms and various geometric designs). The Karkaralinsk settlements belong to the Alekseevka type of the late Andronovo culture; the Alekseevka type served as the foundation for the formation of the early Saki culture.

REFERENCE
Drevniaia kul'tura Tsentral'nogo Kazakhstana. Alma-Ata, 1966.
E. E. KUZ'MINA [11–1280–5]

KARKAVITSAS, ANDREAS (also, A. Karkavitzas). Born in 1866 in Lekhaina; died Oct. 24, 1922, in Amarousion, near Athens. Greek writer.

In Karkavitsas' short stories (first published, 1885; reissued in a collection, 1892) and novellas (for example, *Ligeri,* 1890), he idealized rural life and expressed an interest in folklore. In the novella *The Beggar* (1896; separate edition, 1897), he provided a relentlessly truthful portrayal of poverty and ignorance in the Greek countryside. A master of the modern Greek literary language, Karkavitsas made a significant contribution to the formation of realistic modern Greek prose at the turn of the 20th century.

REFERENCE
Mirambel, A. *La Littérature grecque moderne.* Paris, 1953.
[11–1280–2]

KARKHANEH, large workshops producing weapons, cloth, and clothing in Persia and Azerbaijan in the Middle Ages and the modern period.

In the *karkhaneh* of the 13th century, which belonged personally to the sovereign or to his relatives, mainly slave labor was used. In the early 14th century, under Ghazan Khan (ruled from 1295 to 1304), the workers in the *karkhaneh* received some economic independence. In the Safavid state, particularly in the 17th and early 18th centuries, free artisans paid by the government worked in the *karkhaneh.* Under the Safavids, there were state *karkhaneh* and *karkhaneh* attached to the courts of local rulers. The role of the *karkhaneh* later declined and their number decreased. In the 19th century the term came to be used for the first factories in Persia. [11–1458–2]

KARKINITSKII, a bay of the Black Sea between the northwest coast of the Crimean Peninsula and the continent. It extends 118.5 km inland. In the western part it reaches a depth of 36 m; and in the eastern, approximately 10 m. In severe winters the surface freezes over. The ports of Skadovsk and Khorly are situated on its shores. [11–1284–1]

KARLA LIBKNEKHTA IMENI (formerly Peny), an urban-type settlement in L'gov Raion, Kursk Oblast, RSFSR, on the left bank of the Seim River (tributary of the Desna). There is a railroad station (Blokhino) on the Kursk-L'gov line. Population, 10,000 (1970). It is the site of a machine-building plant and a sugar refinery. [11–1296–2]

KARLGREN, BERNHARD. Born Oct. 5, 1889, in Jonkoping. Swedish sinologue, member of the Swedish Academy of Sciences (1934) and of academies and scholarly societies of a number of countries.

Karlgren is the author of many studies on the history, philology, and art of ancient China. He employed linguistic methods to demonstrate the authenticity of the ancient Chinese literary monuments *Tso Chuan* and *Chou Li.* He has also done scholarly translations, with commentaries, of the ancient Chinese books *Shih Ching* and *Shu Ching.*

WORKS
"Legends and Cults in Ancient China." *Bulletin of the Museum of Far Eastern Antiquities,* 1946, no. 18.
"The Books of Odes." *Bulletin of the Museum of Far Eastern Antiquities,* 1944, nos. 16–17.
"The Book of Documents." *Bulletin of the Museum of Far Eastern Antiquities,* 1950, no. 22. [11–1296–5]

KARLIEV, ALTY. Born Jan. 6, 1909, in Babadaikhan 2, in present-day Tedzhen Raion, Turkmen SSR. Soviet Turkmen actor and director. People's Artist of the USSR (1955). Member of the CPSU since 1948.

Karliev graduated from the Turkmen Drama Studio (Ashkhabad) in 1929 and from the directors' department of the Baku Theatrical Technicum in 1931. He worked as an actor from 1931 to 1941 and was the principal stage director of the Turkmen Drama Theater in Ashkhabad from 1953 to 1956. Among his best roles have been Iarovoi in Trenev's *Liubov' Iarovaia,* Khlestakov in Gogol's *The Inspector-General,* and Truffaldino in Goldoni's *Servant of Two Masters.* He has also directed plays, such as Kaushutov's *Dzhuma* (1954) and *The Inspector-General* (1955). From 1941 to 1953 he was the principal stage director, and from 1960 to 1963 director and principal stage director, of the Makhtumkuli Turkmen Theater of Opera and Ballet in Ashkhabad. He has staged such operas as Shaposhnikov and Mukhatov's *Zokhre and Takhir* (1941) and Shaposhnikov and Ovezov's *Shasenem and Garib* (1955). He has been in films since 1937; his roles include Nuri in *Dursun* (State Prize of the USSR, 1941), Kerim in *The Distant Bride* (1948; State Prize of the USSR, 1949), Aaly in *Saltanat* (1955), and Bairam in *A Family's Honor* (1956). Karliev has worked as a film director and served as director of the Turkmenfilm movie studio from 1956 to 1960. He is the author of several plays and opera librettos. He was a deputy to the third and fifth convocations of the Supreme Soviet of the Turkmen SSR. He received the Makhtumkuli State Prize of the Turkmen SSR in 1966. Karliev has been awarded the Order of Lenin, two other orders, and medals.

REFERENCES
Mämiliev, A. *SSSR-its khalk artisti Altï Garliev.* Ashkhabad [1960].
Aktery sovetskogo kino, fasc. 2. Moscow, 1966.   [11–1297–2]

KARL MARX (A BRIEF BIOGRAPHICAL SKETCH WITH AN EXPOSITION OF MARXISM), an article written by V. I. Lenin in 1914 for the *Granat Encyclopedia.* Lenin worked on the article in Poronin (Galicia) in the spring and in Bern (Switzerland) in the fall. It was completed in November 1914. In a letter to the editors of Granat Publishing House dated Nov. 4 (17), 1914, Lenin wrote: "I have sent you today by registered post the article on Marx and Marxism for the dictionary. It is not for me to judge how far I have succeeded in solving the difficult problem of squeezing the exposition into a framework of about 75,000 letters and spaces. I will observe that I had to compress the literature very intensively . . . , and I had to select the essence of various tendencies (of course, with the majority for Marx). It was difficult to make up my mind to renounce many quotations from Marx . . . Readers of the dictionary should have available all the most important statements by Marx, otherwise the purpose of the dictionary would not be achieved. That is how it seemed to me" (*Poln. sobr. soch.,* 5th ed., vol. 49, p. 31).

The article "Karl Marx" was printed in incomplete form in 1915 in Volume 28 of the seventh edition of the encyclopedia over the signature of V. Il'in. Because of the conditions of censorship, the editors of the encyclopedia deleted two sections from the article: "Socialism" and "Tactics of the Class Struggle of the Proletariat"; they also made a number of changes in the text. In 1918 the article was published by Priboi Publishing House as a separate pamphlet based on the text of the encyclopedia but without the bibliographical appendix. Lenin wrote a short preface for this edition. The first complete text of the article based on the manuscript was published in 1925 in a collection of Lenin's works, *Marx, Engels, Marxism.* The outline for the article "Karl Marx" created by Lenin during March-July 1914 was published in 1959. In Lenin's *Poln. sobr. soch.* (5th ed.), all the materials indicated above were included in Volume 26 (pp. 43–93, 358–61).

After a brief biographical sketch of the main stages of the life and work of K. Marx as a scholar and revolutionary, Lenin expounded Marx' doctrine, which was a continuation and completion of classical German philosophy, classical English political economy, and French socialism (*ibid.,* p. 50). In particular, he noted the remarkable consistency and integrity of Marx' views, "whose totality constitutes modern materialism and modern scientific socialism, as the theory and program of the working-class movement in all the civilized countries of the world" (*ibid.,* pp. 50–51). Thus, Lenin considered it necessary "to present a brief outline of his world-conception in general, prior to giving an exposition of the principal content of Marxism, namely, Marx' economic doctrine" (*ibid.,* p. 51).

Lenin demonstrates that Marx' philosophical materialism not only is opposed to the various forms of idealism, but also differs fundamentally from pre-Marxist materialism, which was for the most part mechanistic, which did not consistently adhere to the ideas of development, and which did not comprehend the significance of the practical revolutionary activity of people. Marx and Engels perceived Hegelian dialectics as "the most comprehensive and profound doctrine of development, and the richest in

content" (*ibid.,* p. 53), and they consistently extended materialism to the sphere of social phenomena. This made it possible to search out the roots of social phenomena in the degree of development of material production and to investigate, with the precision of the natural sciences, the social conditions of life of various classes of society and the process of emergence, development, and decline of social and economic structures. Further on, Lenin gives an account of the most important features of the theory of classes and class struggle, and he reveals the place of this theory in the general system of Marx' views.

Noting that "Marx' economic doctrine is the most profound, comprehensive, and detailed confirmation and application of his theory" (*ibid.,* p. 60), Lenin characterized in detail the analysis of the productive relations of bourgeois society which Marx laid out in *Das Kapital* and singled out the most important features of this doctrine: the analysis of the commodity and of money, and the theories of surplus value, accumulation of capital and crises of overproduction, social reproduction, and ground rent. Having examined the main features of Marx' economic doctrine, Lenin concluded that "Marx deduces the inevitability of the transformation of capitalist into socialist society wholly and exclusively from the economic law of the development of contemporary society" (*ibid.,* p. 73).

A separate section of Lenin's article is devoted to Marx' views on the theory of class struggle. Marx exposed as one of the many shortcomings of old-style materialism its inability to understand the conditions and significance of revolutionary activity. Throughout his life, along with working out scientific theory, Marx devoted great attention to questions of tactics in the class struggle of the proletariat. "Marx justly considered that, without *this* aspect, materialism is incomplete, one-sided, and lifeless" (*ibid.,* p. 77). The consideration of the objectively inevitable dialectics of human history, the program and tactics of economic struggle and of the trade-union movement, the tactics of political struggle for the proletariat, the correlation of the legal and illegal forms of that struggle, the support of the revolutionary initiatives of the masses—these, according to Lenin, are the basic questions of proletarian tactics worked out by Marx.

Lenin's article concludes with a special section that gives an extensive bibliography on Marx and Marxism. Describing Marx' work, as well as the literature about him and about Marxism, Lenin noted the need to study the works of F. Engels in order to evaluate Marx' views correctly. "It is impossible to understand Marxism," he wrote, "and to propound it fully without taking into account *all* the works of Engels" (*ibid.,* p. 93).

V. S. VYGODSKII [11–1292–1]

KARL MARX PEAK, a mountain peak in the southwest Pamirs; the highest point in the Shakhdar'ia Range, Tadzhik SSR. It rises to an elevation of 6,726 m and has a glacier that covers an area of 120 sq km. The first ascent of the peak was made by a team of Soviet climbers in 1946.   [11–1296–3]

KARL-MARX-STADT, an administrative district in the German Democratic Republic (GDR), the country's largest in population and the second most important in industry. Area, 6,000 sq km. Population, 2,047,900 (1970; 82 percent urban) Administrative center, Karl-Marx-Stadt.

Karl-Marx-Stadt District is situated in the southern part of the GDR, covering the northern slopes of the Erzgebirge (Ore Mountains, which reach an altitude of 1,213 m at Mount Fichtelberg) and the Vogtland Plateau (altitude, between 200 and 400 m). The climate is temperate. Annual precipitation ranges from 650 mm in the foothills to 1,000 mm or more in the mountains. Mixed forest covers the mountain slopes; land on the plateau is largely cultivated.

During the GDR's period of socialist development the traditional textile industry, which accounts for more than half of the total national textile production, was supplemented by the growth of machine building and the production of transport machinery (16 percent of the national output). Industry, including construction and the crafts, employed 62.7 percent of the work force in 1970; agriculture accounted for only 6.6 percent. The basic products of the machine-building industry include textile machinery and metalworking machine tools (in the city of Karl-Marx-Stadt), equipment for light industry and food processing and automobiles (Zwickau, Karl-Marx-Stadt, Hainichen, Werdau), motorcycles (Zschopau), bicycles (Karl-Marx-Stadt), and electrical-engineering and electronic equipment. The cellulose and paper industry and woodworking industries make use of the forests which cover 30 percent of the district's area. Almost all of the coal mining in the GDR (1.5 to 2 million tons annually) is concentrated in the Zwickau-Oelsnitz basin. Lead, zinc, tungsten, tin, nickel, and bismuth ores are mined in the Ore Mountains, nickel is processed at a plant in Sankt Egidien, and lead and zinc, in Freiberg. The most important cities and industrial centers of the district include Karl-Marx-Stadt, Zwickau, Plauen, and Freiberg, all located in the foothills. Notable among the crafts of the district is the production of musical instruments, centered at Klingenthal. The agriculture of the district is of the intensive type. Dairy farming is predominant. Rye, oats, potatoes and feeds are also important. There are health resorts (Bad Elster and Bad Brambach) and tourism in the Ore Mountains.   [11–1304–2]

KARL-MARX-STADT (until 1953, Chemnitz), a city in the German Democratic Republic on the Chemnitz River, the administrative center of Karl-Marx-Stadt District. Population, 299,300 (1970).

Karl-Marx-Stadt is an important railroad and highway junction. It also has an airport. The city first began to take shape in the 12th century on a trade route through the Erzgebirge (Ore Mountains). Its economic growth was linked with the growth of the textile industry as early as the 14th century. This specialization in textiles later gave rise to the production of textile machinery for which the city became world famous. Other industry today includes machine-tool and automobile manufacturing and the production of motors, bicycles, electrical equipment for automobiles, electronic computers, electrical instruments, chemicals (dyes and other substances for use in the textile industry), clothing, sporting goods, and furniture. The major industrial districts of Karl-Marx-Stadt are located in the city's south (Alt Chemnitz) and west (Zigmarschönau). Most of the textile enterprises are located in satellite cities, such as Limbach-Oberfrohna, Burgstädt, Grüna, Hartmannsdorf, and Hohenstein-Ernstthal, much of their production then being sent to Karl-Marx-Stadt for finishing. A machine-building institute and a higher technical school are also located in the city.

Buildings of historical interest, some original and some restored since World War II, include the Red Tower (12th century), Jakobikirche (14th–15th century), Liebfrauenkirche (15th century), Schlosskirche (15th–16th century), the Late Gothic Rathaus (end of the 15th century; rebuilt in 1911), baroque homes of the 18th century, and the former Schocken department store (1929–30; architect, E. Mendelssohn). In recent years a broad program of industrial, residential, and social construction has been carried on. A design for the construction of a city center, drafted by the architect L. Hahn, is being implemented. On the central square a monument to Karl Marx of bronze and granite, designed by the Soviet sculptor L. E. Kerbel', was unveiled in 1971.   [11–1305–1]

KARLO-LIBKNEKHTOVSK, a city (since 1965) in Donetsk Oblast, Ukrainian SSR, 18 km from Artemovsk and 2 km from the Dekonskaia railroad station. Population, 14,600 (1971). Salt is mined there. It is the site of a building-materials combine and a plant for the production of fired refractory material.
                                              [11–1308–1]

KARLO-MARKSOVO, an urban-type settlement in Donetsk Oblast, Ukrainian SSR. Railroad station (Enakievo) on the Debal'tsevo-Krinichnaia line. Population, 15,000 (1972). Coal is mined there.   [11–1308–2]

KARLOVAC, a city in Yugoslavia, in the Socialist Republic of Croatia, on the Kupa River (a tributary of the Sava). Population, 47,500 (1971). It is a major transportation junction. Industry includes the Jugoturbina Electrical-engineering Plant and leather, ceramics, wood-products, and tobacco enterprises.

Nearby, in the city of Duga Resa, there is a large textile combine.
                                              [11–1306–3]

KARLOVKA, a city (until 1957, an urban-type settlement); administrative center of Karlovka Raion, Poltava Oblast, Ukrainian SSR, on the Orchik River (Dnieper Basin). Railroad station. Population, 17,100 (1971). Industry includes a machine-building plant, a sugar refinery, a distillery, and a furniture factory. The city was founded in the 1740's.   [11–1307–3]

KARLOVO (from 1953 to 1962, Levskigrad), a city in southern Bulgaria, in the Karlovo Basin between the Stara Planina (Balkan Mountains) and the Sredna Gora Range in Plovdiv District. Population, 23,000 (1970). It is the center of a region of cultivation and processing of essential-oil crops (production of roses and lavender oils and mint). Other industry includes machine-building (Bulgar light caterpillar tractors), the production of cotton and silk cloth, and food processing. A balneological health resort is located in Karlovo, and tourism is well developed. Karlovo is the birthplace of the Bulgarian revolutionary V. Levski.   [11–1307–4]

KARLOVY VARY (named for the Czech king Karl I and *vary*, "hot springs"), Karlsbad, a city in Czechoslovakia, in the West Czech region of the Czech Socialist Republic, located in a valley (altitude, 380 m) at the point of intersection of the Ohře River with the Teplá. Population, 45,000 (1970).

The porcelain industry is developed in the suburbs of Karlovy Vary. The city itself is the site of an international film festival, which has been held every two years since 1950. Karlovy Vary, 120 km west of Prague, is chiefly famous as a balneological health resort, whose waters are used both for bathing and (more important) for drinking. The resort was founded sometime between 1347 and 1358. The climate is moderately moist. The summers are warm, with an average July temperature of 17.3°C, the winters are very mild with an average January temperature of −2°C. The area receives about 620 mm of precipitation annually. The curative agents at the resort are supplied by 12 carbonated hot springs (sodium sulfate hydrocarbonate), the water temperature varying from 41.2° to 72.2°C. The waters are used for bathing, sprinkling, inhalation, enemas, drinking, and bottling. Treatments with peat and mud are also given. The chemical makeup of the water of the largest spring, the Vřídlo (Sprudel) geyser, is as follows:

$$CO_2 0.4H_2SiO_3 \quad 0.09M_{6.4} \frac{HCO_3 42SO_4 36}{Na84}$$

$$T\ 72.2°C \quad pH\ 7.1$$

It is from this spring that Karlovy Vary salt is extracted. Persons suffering from disorders of the liver, biliary and gastrointestinal tracts, metabolism, and urinary system are treated. Sanatoriums and boardinghouses are available for visitors.

REFERENCE
Borisov, A. D. *Vazhneishie kurorty sotsialisticheskikh stran Evropy.* Moscow, 1967.   L. G. GOL'DFAIL' [11–1306–4]

KARLOVY VARY UPLAND, an upland in western Czechoslovakia, averaging from 500–700 m in altitude and reaching 983 m at Mount Lesný.

The Karlovy Vary Upland is composed of granites and gneisses in the north and chiefly of amphibolites and mica shales in the south. Its gently hilly terrain drops off steeply on the northwest into the valley of the Ohře River, which separates the upland from the Erzgebirge (Ore Mountains). Spruce forests predominate, with occasional stands of beech, fir, and pine. On the western edge of the region there are numerous mineral springs, which have stimulated the development of health resorts, including Karlovy Vary, Františkovy-Lázně, and Mariánské-Lázně.   [11–1306–1]

KARŁOWICZ, MIECZYSŁAW. Born Dec. 11, 1876, in Wiszniewo, Lithuania; died Feb. 8, 1909, in Zakopane, Poland. Polish composer and conductor. Son of Jan Karłowicz, a scholar in

Slavic ethnology and connoisseur of music, who performed in both Russia and Poland as a cellist.

Karłowicz studied in Warsaw under S. Barcewicz and Z. Noskowski (1890–95), in Berlin (1895–1900), and in Leipzig (1906), where he studied conducting under A. Nikisch. From 1902 he headed the stringed orchestra of the Musical Society in Warsaw, and in 1906 he joined the "Young Poland" group. Karłowicz composed the first Polish symphony (*Renascence*), seven symphonic poems, a violin concerto, and other orchestral and chamber works, all characterized by a particular expressiveness of lyrical and dramatic elements (influenced by F. Chopin and P. I. Tchaikovsky and, later, by R. Strauss). Karłowicz published a large collection of previously unpublished material on Chopin (1904, Warsaw and Paris). He also worked as a music writer and critic, producing articles on Chopin, Russian and foreign composers, and early Polish violinists.

REFERENCES
Belza, I. *Mechislav Karlovich.* Moscow-Leningrad, 1951.
Karasin'skaia, I. "Ian i Mechislav Karlovichi i ikh rol' v razvitii russko-pol'skikh sviazei." In the collection *Russko-pol'skie muzykal'nye sviazi.* Moscow, 1963.
Chybinski, A. *Mieczysław Karłowicz.* Kraków, 1949.

I. F. BELZA   [11–1307–2]

KARLOWITZ CONGRESS OF 1698–99, an international congress that convened in October 1698 in the small village of Karlowitz in Slavonia to conclude peace between the states constituting the Holy League (Austria, Venice, Poland, and Russia) and the Ottoman Empire (Turkey).

The Karlowitz Congress was preceded by a number of Turkish military defeats in wars against the countries of the coalition, including the catastrophic rout of Turkish troops in 1683 outside Vienna. Because of the serious contradictions between the members of the Holy League (in particular the league's opposition to any strengthening of the position of Russia in the Black Sea region), a number of separate treaties were signed by the allies with Turkey: by Poland on Jan. 16, 1699, and by Austria and Venice on January 26. Russia concluded only a two-year armistice, signed on January 24; in 1700 it was superseded by the Constantinople Treaty. Poland received Podol'e and part of the Right-bank Ukraine still in Turkish hands. Austria received much of the territory of Hungary, as well as Transylvania, Croatia, and nearly all of Slavonia. Venice received the Morea, the islands of the Aegean Sea, and fortresses in Dalmatia. According to the terms of the armistice, Russia kept Azov.

The Karlowitz Congress gave juridical form to the new disposition of forces in Central and Eastern Europe after the Turkish defeats and the halting of the Ottoman movement westward.

PUBLICATION
Noradounghian, G. *Recueil d'actes internationaux de l'Empire Ottoman . . .*, vol. 1. Paris, 1897.   G. A. KLEINMAN   [11–1306–5]

KARLSBAD SALT, a salt obtained by evaporating the spring waters at the resort of Karlovy Vary (Czechoslovakia).

Karlsbad salt is used as a laxative and cholagogue. Artificial Karlsbad salt contains 44 parts sodium sulfate, 36 parts sodium hydrocarbonate, 18 parts sodium chloride, and two parts potassium sulfate. Dissolving 6 g artificial Karlsbad salt in a liter of water forms a solution that corresponds in salt concentrations to the water of the springs at Karlovy Vary.   [11–1306–2]

KARLSEN, GENRIKH GEORGIEVICH. Born Apr. 25 (May 7), 1894, in Moscow. Soviet scientist in engineering structures, doctor of technical sciences (1938), Honored Worker in Science and Technology of the RSFSR (1965). Member of the CPSU since 1960.

Karlsen graduated from the Moscow Higher Technical School in 1922. He has been a professor since 1932 at a number of higher educational institutions and at the V. V. Kuibyshev Academy of Military Engineering. He is the founder of a scientific research laboratory for wooden structures at the State Institute of Construction (1928; now the Central Scientific Research Institute of Engineering Structures). He is the author of the first standards in the USSR for the design of wooden structures (1929). He has

carried out studies on glued wooden structures. His principal works have dealt with problems of the effective use of wood in construction and the theoretical calculation and design of wooden structures. Karlsen has been awarded the State Prize of the USSR (1951), the Order of Lenin, four other orders, and several medals.

WORKS
Kurs dereviannykh konstruktsii, vols. 1–2. Moscow-Leningrad, 1942–43. (Coauthor.)
Industrial'nye dereviannye konstruktsii. Moscow, 1967. (Coauthor.)
[11–1309–1]

KARLSKOGA, a city in central Sweden, in the county of Örebro, on Lake Möckel. Population, 39,000 (1970). The most important industries in the city are metallurgy, machine building, chemicals, drugs, and timber. The Bofors military-industrial company's main industrial center is located there.   [11–1312–3]

KARLSKRONA, a city and port in southern Sweden, on the coast of the Baltic Sea, mainly on the islands in the mouth of the Lyckeby River. Administrative center of the county of Blekinge. Population, 37,000 (1970). Karlskrona is a center of shipbuilding and electrical engineering (telephones and telephone equipment). Porcelain and glazed tile are produced in the city, and it is a base for the fishing industry fleet.   [11–1312–2]

KARLSRUHE, a city in Baden-Württemberg, in the Federal Republic of Germany (FRG), near the Rhine, with which it is linked by canal. Population, 259,100 (1970).

Karlsruhe is a major transport hub and river port, with five harbors. Its freight turnover came to 10.7 million tons in 1970. The city is also the fuel-distribution center for the southwestern part of the FRG, receiving oil by ship and by pipeline from Marseille. The city's major industry includes oil refining (which produced 14.8 million tons of petroleum products in 1968), the construction of transport and electrical-engineering machinery, metalworking, chemicals manufacture, printing, and food processing. At Leopoldshafen, 10 km north of Karlsruhe, there is an atomic research center. A university, a state academy of fine arts, the Baden State Museum (with collections of antiquities), and an art museum (Kunsthalle) are also located in the city. Karlsruhe was founded in 1715 by Margrave Karl Wilhelm of Baden, and during the 18th and 19th centuries it was expanded according to a strict geometric plan (radial-annular). From the palace, built in a baroque style by the architects L. P. de la Guêpière and A. F. von Kesslau (1752–82), tree-lined walks fan out to the north and the streets of the city fan out to the south. During the first third of the 19th century the architect F. Weinbrenner filled the city with buildings in the classical style. New Karlsruhe, to the south, has buildings of the 19th and 20th centuries. The settlement of Dammerstock, designed by the architect W. Gropius in 1927–28, is located not far from Karlsruhe.

REFERENCE
Meny, H. *Unser Karlsruhe.* Karlsruhe, 1965.   [11–1309–2]

KARLSTAD, a city and port in Sweden, on the northern shore of Vänern, at the mouth of the Klar River. Karlstad is the administrative center of the county of Värmland. Population, 54,000 (1970). The city's principal industries are machine building (aircraft and turbine construction; paper-making machines), light industry, and the food industry. Karlstad is the terminal point of a timber-flotation route. There is a large timber industry combine near Karlstad, on Hammar Island. Timber, cellulose, paper, and machines are exported from Karlstad. There is a university branch in the city.   [11–1312–4]

KARLSTAD, TREATY OF (1905), a treaty signed between Sweden and Norway on October 26 after negotiations that lasted from Aug. 31 to Sept. 23, 1905, in Karlstad, Sweden.

The treaty gave legal form to the dissolution of the Swedish-Norwegian union of 1814–1905 instituted by Norway on June 7, 1905, and defined the integrity of Norwegian territory, created a neutral frontier zone, set conditions for tariff-free transit of goods through Norwegian territory to and from Sweden, and confirmed the rights of nomadic migration of Swedish Lapps on Norwegian territory. Although the treaty was initialed on September 23, the official signing took place only after it was approved by the parliaments of both countries: the Norwegian Storting gave its consent on Oct. 9, 1905; the Swedish Riksdag, on Oct. 13, 1905.

REFERENCE
Recueil international des traités du XX siècle. Compiled by E. Descamps and L. Renault. Paris [1906]. Pages 348–49.

A. S. KAN   [11–1312–5]

KARLSTEIN (in Czech, Karlštejn, Karlův Týn), a castle in Czechoslovakia on the Berounka River, 28 km southwest of Prague; a Gothic architectural monument.

Karlstein Castle was built to house the treasures of Charles IV. Designed by the architects Matthias of Arras and Petr Parléř, it was constructed on a high cliff (72 m) between 1348 and 1357. Restoration was carried out from 1888 to 1897, changing the original appearance of the castle. The picturesque, impressively laid out structural complex at Karlstein includes a medieval fortified dungeon, the Church of Our Lady (wall paintings dating from the 14th century), the Chapel of St. Catherine (stained glass windows dating from the 14th century), and the Chapel of the Holy Cross. Striking "portraits" of saints and prophets were painted in the Chapel of the Holy Cross circa 1357–67 by Master Theodorik and others. The Karlstein Castle houses a museum of its history and of medieval art.

REFERENCE
Dvořáková, V., and D. Menclová. *Karlštejn.* Prague, 1965.

[11–1311–4]

KARLUKS, a Turkic tribe consisting of three clans; it rose to eminence in the eighth century after the disintegration of the Turkic Kaganate. The tribe engaged in nomadic stock raising and hunting; gradually it shifted to settled farming. The Karluks inhabited the part of Semirech'e along the caravan route from Middle Asia to China. Between 757 and 766 they occupied the entire territory of the state of the Turgesi. The rulers of the Karluks made the city of Suab on the Chu River their capital. They ruled there from 766 to 940. Then the capital was transferred to the city of Koilyk in the valley of the Ili River. In 861 the Karluks captured Kashgar. In the tenth century they became part of the Karakhanid state; from this time, early feudal relations began to develop among the Karluks. In 960 the Karluks adopted Islam.

REFERENCES
Grum-Grzhimailo, G. E. *Zapadnaia Mongoliia i Uriankhaiskii krai,* vol. 2. Leningrad, 1926.
Bartol'd, V. V. "Ocherk istorii Semirech'ia." *Soch.,* vol. 2, part 1. Moscow, 1963.

[11–1311–1]

KARLYGAN, a mountain range of the Zapadnyi Saian, in Krasnoiarsk Krai, RSFSR; it forms the watershed of the Bol'shoi and Malyi Abakan rivers. Length, about 100 km; elevations, 2,500–2,700 m in the south and 1,200–1,500 m in the north. The range is composed of metamorphic schist and granite and is dissected by deep, narrow river valleys. Dark coniferous fir, cedar, and spruce taiga predominates on the slopes. Above 1,800–2,000 m there are mountain tundras, rock streams, and (in the south) rocky peaks.

[11–1312–1]

KARM, KAAREL IUKHANOVICH (pseudonym of Kaarel Länts). Born Oct. 5 (18), 1906, in Narva. Soviet Estonian actor. People's Artist of the USSR (1956).

From 1925 to 1949, Karm was an actor in the Estonia Theater. He joined the V. Kingissepp Estonian Theater of Drama in Tallinn in 1949. Among his best parts in the classical repertoire have been Hamlet, Othello, and Antony in Shakespeare's *Hamlet, Othello,* and *Antony and Cleopatra,* respectively; Mephistopheles in Goethe's *Faust;* Arbenin in Lermontov's *Masquerade;* Protasov in L. N. Tolstoy's *The Living Corpse;* Juhani in Kivi's *Seven Brothers;* and Jan in Kitzberg's *Whirlwinds.* Among the parts he has played in Estonian dramas are Ralf in *Life in the Citadel* and Allan in *The Jackals,* both by Jakobson; Kustas Lokk in *Conscience* and Mart Tuisk in *Prodigal Son,* both by Rannet; Jõnn in Schmuul's *Wild Captain;* and Clever Ants in Tammsaare's *New Satan From Põrgupõhja.* In plays by other Soviet writers, he has performed as Borovskii in Lavrenev's *To Those At Sea!* and as Stryzhen' in Korneichuk's *The Destruction of the Squadron.* Karm is a master of character portrayal. He has a forceful stage presence and good stage delivery. He has also appeared in movies. Karm received the State Prize of the Estonian SSR in 1949 and 1959.

REFERENCE
[Levin, S.] *Kaarel Karm.* Tallinn, 1966.   [11–1313–2]

KARMA, one of the central concepts of Indian philosophy, supplementing the doctrine of reincarnation.

The concept of karma already existed when the Vedas were being written and subsequently was incorporated into nearly all the Indian religious and philosophical systems; it is an essential part of Hinduism, Buddhism, and Jainism. In a broad sense, karma is the total sum of the actions performed by any living creature and the consequences of these actions, which together determine the character of the creature's new birth, that is, his later existence. In the narrow sense, karma generally refers to the influence of the accomplished actions on the character of the creature's present and subsequent existence. In both cases, karma appears as an invisible force: the general principle of its operation is held to be clear but its internal mechanism remains perfectly concealed. Karma not only determines the favorable or unfavorable conditions of existence (health or illness, wealth or poverty, happiness or unhappiness) and the sex, length of life, and social status of the individual but also the ultimate progress or regression in relation to the main goal of man: freedom from the ties of "profane" existence and subordination to the law of cause and effect. Karma differs from the concept of fate in its ethical coloring, since the determination of present and future existence has the character of retribution or recompense for accomplished acts and is not under the influence of inevitable divine or cosmic forces.

REFERENCES
Radhakrishnan, S. *Indiiskaia filosofiia,* vol. 1. Moscow, 1956. (Translated from English.)
Rutter, O. *The Scales of Karma.* London, 1940.
Humphreys, S. *Karma and Rebirth.* London, 1943.

V. P. LUCHINA   [11–1313–3]

KARMADON, a balneological health resort in the Severnaia Osetiia ASSR, 35 km southwest of Ordzhonikidze, at an elevation of 1,500 m (Nizhnii Karmadon) and 2,300 m (Verkhnii Karmadon). The warmest month is August (average temperature, 16.9°C); the coldest is January (−4.4°C). Annual precipitation is about 500 mm. The cures used at the resort are provided by about 80 hot (35°–58°C) and cold (18°C) mineral springs, whose waters are used for bathing and drinking and are also bottled. The formula of the water in Spring No. 9 at Verkhnii Karmadon is

$$CO_2 1.06 \ As0.0018 \ H_2SiO_3 0.083 \ M_{8.6}$$

$$\frac{Cl85 \ HCO_3 12}{(Na + K)81 \ Ca15} \ T \ 58°C \ pH \ 6.3$$

and the chemical makeup of the water in Cleft No. 6a at Nizhnii Karmadon is

$$M_{3.8} \ \frac{Cl91 \ HCO_3 9}{(Na + K)90 \ Ca8} \ T \ 41°C \ pH \ 7.6$$

A sanatorium for persons suffering from disorders of the organs of digestion and locomotion and of the nervous system is located in Karmadon.   [11–1314–1]

KARMALIUK, PAVEL PETROVICH. Born Dec. 24, 1907 (Jan. 6, 1908), in the village of Osovtsy, in present-day Korostyshev Raion, Zhitomir Oblast. Soviet Ukrainian singer (baritone). People's Artist of the USSR (1960). Member of the CPSU since 1950.

Karmaliuk graduated from the Kiev Conservatory in 1941. He became a soloist at the L'vov Theater of Opera and Ballet in 1944. Since 1950 he has taught a course in singing at the L'vov Conservatory, becoming a professor in 1970. Among his best parts have been Griaznoi in Rimsky-Korsakov's *The Tsar's Bride,* Onegin in Tchaikovsky's *Eugene Onegin,* the Demon in Rubinstein's *Demon,* Prince Igor in Borodin's *Prince Igor,* Rigoletto and Germont in Verdi's *Rigoletto* and *La Traviata,* respectively, and Bogdan in Dan'kevich's *Bogdan Khmel'nitskii.* He also performs in concerts. Karmaliuk has been awarded the Order of the Badge of Honor and a number of medals.

REFERENCE
Suslovs'kyi, O. M. *Myttsi L'vova.* L'vov, 1959.   [11–1314–2]

KARMALIUK, USTIM IAKIMOVICH (also, Ustim Iakimovich Karmeliuk). Born Feb. 27 (Mar. 10), 1787; died Oct. 10 (22), 1835. Leader of a peasant movement against serfdom in Podolia Province in the Right-bank Ukraine.

Karmaliuk was born in Podolia, the son of a serf. For repeated "insubordination," Karmaliuk was sent away by his master in 1812 as an army conscript. He escaped, however, and in early 1813 he organized a rebel detachment of serfs. He called upon the peasants to refuse to perform corvée and to deal mercilessly with their oppressors. The rebels plundered the serf-owners' estates, taking the property and money and distributing it among the serfs. The high point was reached between 1832 and 1835, when at least 20,000 serfs were involved in the struggle, in addition to a number of urban poor and runaway soldiers. Among Karmaliuk's comrades-in-arms, D. Khron, I. Chernomorets, and A. Slovinskii especially distinguished themselves. Several times Karmaliuk fell into the hands of the tsarist authorities and was sent to prison or exiled to Siberia, but after successful escapes he returned each time to his native land and renewed the struggle. The peasant movement spread over an extensive territory and played a large role in weakening the system of serfdom. Karmaliuk was treacherously murdered in the village of Karichintsy-Shliakhovy. The Ukrainian people have composed many folk songs, legends, and tales about Karmaliuk. Ukrainian written literature and painting have also paid him tribute.

REFERENCES
Kanivets, V. V. *Karmaliuk.* Moscow, 1965.
Lavrov, P. A. "U. Ia. Karmaliuk (Iz istorii krest'ianskogo dvizheniia v Podol'skoi gubernii v 20–30 gg. XIX v.)" In the collection *Trudy istoricheskogo fakul'teta Kievskogo gosudarstvennogo un-ta,* vol. 1. Kiev, 1939.
Gurzhii, I. *Ustim Karmaliuk.* Kiev, 1955.
Ustim Karmaliuk: Zbirnik dokumentiv. Kiev, 1948.
Narod pro Karmaliuka: Zbirnik fol'klornikh tvoriv. Kiev, 1961.
                                    I. A. GURZHII [11–1314–3]

KÁRMÁN, THEODORE VON. Born May 11, 1881, in Budapest; died May 7, 1963, in Aachen. Scientist in mechanics.

Kármán studied at the Royal Technical University of Budapest from 1898 to 1902 and later at the University of Göttingen. He became a professor and director of the Aeronautics Institute of the University of Aachen in 1913. From 1930 to 1949 he was the director of the Guggenheim Aeronautics Laboratory at the California Institute of Technology. Kármán's works dealt with aircraft design, applied mathematics, the strength of materials, the theory of elasticity and plasticity, structural mechanics, aerodynamics, hydrodynamics, and thermodynamics. As a scientific leader he participated in the construction of many technical devices: aircraft, helicopters, rockets, and suspension bridges, as well as the first supersonic wind tunnels and ballistic installations. Kármán was a member of the Royal Society of London and other academies of science and scientific societies.

WORKS
Collected Works, vols. 1–4. London. 1956.
The Wind and Beyond: An Autobiography. Boston, 1967.
                                                [11–1315–1]

KARMATHIANS, adherents of one of the two branches (subsects) of the Muslim Shiite sect of the Ismailis.

The Karmathian subsect arose in the ninth century in southern Mesopotamia. Most of its followers were peasants, nomadic Bedouin, and craftsmen. Toward the end of the ninth century, the Karmathians led a series of antifeudal rebellions against the Abbasids (the largest such rebellions occurred in southern Mesopotamia around 890–906; in Bahrain in 894–99; and in Syria in 900–02). Their social ideal was the restoration of communal landholding and general equality (which, incidentally, did not apply to slaves, who were to become the property not of individuals but of the entire community). The Karmathian religious and philosophical views were identical to those of the Ismailis.

About 899, the Karmathians conquered Bahrain and established their state at al-Ahsa (eastern Arabia); the state survived to the end of the eleventh century. Free farmers and craftsmen, who did not pay taxes, were predominant in the state, which owned 30,000 slaves. The latter worked in the fields and in gardens, repaired mills, and so on. Attacks by the Karmathians, who were implacable foes of Sunnism, on Sunnite territories (in 930, for example, on Mecca) were accompanied by pillage, massacre, and the enslavement of peaceful populations. Such practices were repellent to the masses, who shared the Karmathians' social ideals but not their religious beliefs. The suppression of Karmathian rebellions, the savage persecution of the Karmathians by the Ghaznavids, and internal unrest weakened the sect, which for all practical purposes ceased to exist by the late 11th or the early 12th century.

REFERENCES
Beliaev, E. A. *Musul'manskoe sektantstvo.* Moscow, 1957.
Bertel's, A. E. *Nasir-i Khosrov i ismailizm.* Moscow, 1959.
Petrushevskii, I. P. *Islam v Irane VII–XV vv.* Leningrad, 1966. Chapter 11 (contains detailed bibliography).
                          I. P. PETRUSHEVSKII [11–1316–3]

KARMEN, ROMAN LAZAREVICH. Born Nov. 16 (29), 1906, in Odessa. Soviet cameraman, film director, journalist, and scriptwriter. People's Artist of the USSR (1966). Member of the CPSU since 1939.

Karmen graduated from the camera operation department of the State Institute of Cinematography in 1931. He proved himself an adept film reporter during the National Revolutionary War in Spain (1936–39). From the film that he and B. K. Makaseev took, 22 installments of the film chronicle *On the Events in Spain* were created, as well as the documentary film *Spain* (1939) and the poetic film *Granada, Granada, My Granada* (1968, by Karmen and K. M. Simonov). At the end of the 1930's Karmen began his work as a director with the films *A Day in a New World* (with M. Ia. Slutskii, 1940), *The Sedov Men* (1940), and *In China* (1941). During the Great Patriotic War (1941–45), Karmen headed film groups at the front and helped shoot the films *Defeat of the German Armies Near Moscow* (1942), *Leningrad in Combat* (1942), and *Berlin* (1945). In 1946 he made the film *Judgment of the Nations,* which dealt with the Nuremberg trials. He later made the film *The Great Patriotic War* (1965) based on materials from the newsreels.

Karmen directed the films *Story of the Caspian Oil Workers* (1953) and *Conquerors of the Sea* (1959), both of which won the Lenin Prize in 1960. He made the first Soviet wide-screen film, *Far and Wide My Country Stretches* (1958), as well as the films *Vietnam* (1955), *Awakening of India* (1956), *Island in Flames* (1961), *Comrade Berlin* (1969), and *Continent in Flames* (1972). He teaches at the All-Union State Institute of Cinematography, where he has been a professor since 1970. Karmen received the State Prize of the USSR in 1942, 1947, and 1952 and has been awarded five orders and various medals.

WORKS
No pasaran! Moscow, 1972.
REFERENCE
Kolesnikova, N., G. Senchakova, and T. Slepneva. *Roman Karmen.* Moscow, 1959.   L. A. PARFENOV [11–1318–1]

KARMIR-BLUR (also Karmirblur), a hill on the left bank of the Razdan River, on the western outskirts of the city of Yerevan. In 1936 an Urartian cuneiform inscription with the name of King Rusa (Rusas), son of Argistis II (seventh century B.C.), was found on Karmir-Blur. Systematic excavations were conducted from 1939 through 1971, which unearthed a citadel on the hill and the remains of the city of Teishebaini around its base. Extensive material about the economy and culture of the ancient state of Urartu was obtained. The citadel was destroyed at the beginning of the sixth century B.C. by local tribes, who were attempting to throw off the Urartian yoke, and by the Scythians, with whom these tribes allied themselves. [11–1319–2]

KARNAI, ALI MAGOMETOVICH. Born Jan. 6 (19), 1904, in the village of Bol'shie Shady, in present-day Mishkino Raion, Bashkir ASSR; died June 16, 1943. Soviet Bashkir writer. Member of the CPSU from 1940. Fought in the Great Patriotic War of 1941–45 and died at the front.

Karnai's works were first published in 1924. In 1928 he published the collection of stories *Turning Point.* He depicted, on a broad, epic background, the transition of the peasantry to collectivization (the novella *Fires on the Steppe,* 1932), the birth of the petroleum industry in the Bashkir republic (the sketch "Ishimbai," 1935), and the struggle of the working people for Soviet power (the novella *We Shall Return,* 1940). He also wrote for children (the collection *The Lark,* 1936; Russian translation, 1970). He translated the works of A. S. Pushkin, N. V. Gogol, and other writers.

WORKS
Haylanma äthärdhär. [Introductory article by F. Khösäyenov.] Ufa, 1956.
In Russian translation:
Fontan. Ufa, 1935.
My vernemsia. [Introductory article by S. Safuanov.] Ufa, 1968.
REFERENCE
Safuanov, S. *Ali Karnai.* Ufa, 1960.　　S. G. SAFUANOV　[11–1320–2]

KARNAK (in ancient Egyptian, Ipet-isut), a complex of temples dating from the 20th century B.C. to the end of the first millennium B.C. It is named after an Arabic village and is located on the site of ancient Thebes. Karnak was the principal state sanctuary during the period of the New Kingdom in Egypt (the 16th to 11th centuries B.C.). Intended to glorify the power of the pharaohs, Karnak is distinguished by the complex layout of the huge architectural masses and the magnificent decoration of the buildings. The temple of the god Amon-Re (16th to 12th centuries B.C.; completed in the Hellenistic and Roman periods) is characteristic of the New Kingdom type of sanctuary, with its large and small halls and courts alternating along the longitudinal axis. Chapels and small temples built at different times are located in these halls and courts. The most striking feature of the temple of Karnak is the great pillared hall, or hypostyle, whose walls and columns were covered with painted reliefs. Each great building period ended with the construction of a wall around the temple and two tower-pylons on the facade, against which were set obelisks and statues. Near the temple of Amon-Re are the temples of the god Khonsu (12th century B.C.), the goddess Mut (16th–15th centuries B.C.), and others. An avenue of sphinxes led from the Nile to the sanctuary. Among Karnak's architects were Ineni, Hapuseneb, Puemre, Sennenmut, and Menkheperresenb (16th–15th century B.C.); Amenhotep, son of Hapu, and Amenhotep the Younger (15th century B.C.); and Maja, Iwpa, Hatjaj, and Parennefer (14th–13th centuries B.C.).

REFERENCE
Mat'e, M. *Iskusstvo Novogo tsarstva XVI–XV veka.* Leningrad, 1947. (*Istoriia iskusstva Drevnego Vostoka,* vol. 1, fasc. 3.) Pages 27–46, 48–82.　　[11–1321–1]

KARNAUKHOV, MIKHAIL MIKHAILOVICH. Born Mar. 2 (14), 1892, in Orenburg; died Dec. 22, 1955, in Leningrad. Soviet metallurgist; Academician of the Academy of Sciences of the USSR (1953; corresponding member 1939).

Karnaukhov graduated from the Petrograd Polytechnic Institute in 1914. He began his engineering career at the Alapaevsk Metallurgical Plant. In 1920 he became an instructor—and, in 1927, a professor—of ferrous metallurgy at the Leningrad Polytechnic Institute. In 1953 he became head of the Leningrad

Laboratory of the Institute of Metallurgy of the Academy of Sciences of the USSR.

Karnaukhov's principal works have been devoted to the study of the physicochemical bases of the open-hearth, Bessemer, and Thomas steel production processes and to the crystallization of steel ingots. He participated in the design of a number of metallurgical enterprises. Many of Karnaukhov's ideas were the basis of process flow diagrams for the production of steel that are being used successfully in Soviet plants. He was awarded the State Prize of the USSR (1943), two Orders of Lenin, two other orders, and medals.

WORKS
Metallurgiia stali, 2nd ed., parts 1–3. Leningrad-Moscow-Sverdlovsk, 1933–34.
REFERENCES
Vestnik AN SSSR, 1954, no. 4, p. 77.
"Mikhail Mikhailovich Karnaukhov" (obituary). *Stal',* 1956, no. 3.
　　　　　　　　　　　　　　S. I. VENETSKII　[11–1324–2]

KARNAUKHOVKA, an urban-type settlement in Dnepropetrovsk Oblast, Ukrainian SSR, on the Dnieper River, 4 km from the Sukhachevka railroad station. The Stroidetal' Plant is located in Karnaukhovka. [11–1324–3]

KARNY, ALFONS. Born Nov. 10, 1901, in Białystok. Polish sculptor-portraitist.

Karny studied under T. Breyer at the School of Fine Arts in Warsaw (1925–30). In his busts he accurately renders the distinctive physical appearance and personality of his models. His works are also characterized by a feeling of plastic expressiveness and by the use of the decorative qualities of his materials (granite, bronze, or clay). His works include portraits of M. Kotarbinski (1933), E. Godlewski (1935), L. Solski (1944), and E. Hemingway (1963)—in the National Museum (Warsaw) and other collections.

REFERENCE
Tananaeva, L. "Skul'pturnyi portret Al'fonsa Karny." *Tvorchestvo,* 1964, no. 12.　　[11–1331–1]

KAROGS (Banner), a monthly literary and sociopolitical journal; the organ of the Writers' Union of the Latvian SSR. It was first published in Riga in September 1940. During the Great Patriotic War of 1941–45, *Karogs* was issued in Moscow as a yearly anthology of Latvian literature. The journal's editors have included A. Upīts (1940–46), I. Muižnieks (1946–48), A. Balodis (1948–63), K. Kraulin' (1964–67), and A. Veian (since 1967). Latvian literature and translations of the literature of the other peoples of the USSR are published in *Karogs.* In 1972 the circulation was 22,000–23,000 copies. [11–1331–3]

KÁROLYI, MIHÁLY. Born Mar. 4, 1875, in Budapest; died Mar. 18, 1955, in Paris. Count; Hungarian political figure.

Károlyi was a deputy in Parliament from 1906 to 1918. In October 1918 he became head of the National Council, made up of representatives of the Party of Independence and 1848, the Bourgeois Radical Party, and the Social Democratic Party of Hungary. On Oct. 31, 1918, after the victory of the bourgeois-democratic revolution, Károlyi became the head of the government formed by representatives of the parties of the National Council. He was the president of the Hungarian republic from January to March 1919. He emigrated from Hungary after the proclamation of the Hungarian Soviet Republic in 1919. While living abroad, Károlyi opposed the fascist regime of M. Horthy (1920–44) and took an active part in the antifascist and antiwar movement. He headed the Movement for a Democratic Hungary in Great Britain in 1943. Károlyi returned to Hungary in 1946 and was Hungarian ambassador in Paris from 1947 to 1949. He retired in 1949 and died in Paris in 1955. Károlyi's remains were moved to Budapest in 1962. [11–1332–2]

KARONIN, S. (pseudonym of Nikolai Elpidiforovich Petropavlovskii). Born Oct. 5 (17), 1853, in the village of Voznesenskaia, in present-day Orenburg Oblast; died May 12 (24), 1892, in Saratov. Russian writer.

Karonin was educated in a theological seminary and in the 1870's participated in the movement of "going to the people," which resulted in police repressions. His first work to appear in print was the short story "Voiceless" (1879). His early writing (1879–87) dealt primarily with the problems of the countryside; later (1888–92) he wrote about the fate of the populist intelligentsia. Karonin did not idealize life in the village commune and recognized the lack of perspective in the illusions of the liberal populists, but he believed in the moral strength of the people and the soundness of the democratic ideals of the progressive intelligentsia. In one of his best tales, "From the Bottom to the Top" (1886), he portrayed the move of a young peasant from the village to the city and his transformation into a conscious proletarian as a positive phenomenon.

WORKS

Rasskazy, vols. 1–3. Moscow, 1890–91.
Soch. Introduction by A. G. Tseitlin. Moscow-Leningrad, 1932.
Soch., vols. 1–2. Introduction by G. P. Berdnikov. Moscow, 1958.

REFERENCES

Plekhanov, G. V. "Nashi belletristy-narodniki (S. Karonin)." In his book *Literatura i estetika,* vol. 2. Moscow, 1958.
Gorky, M. "N. E. Karonin-Petropavlovskii." *Sobr. soch.,* vol. 10. Moscow, 1951.
Fokht, U. R. "S. Karonin." *Semidesiatniki.* Moscow, 1935.
Egolin, A. M. "Karonin." In *Istoriia russkoi literatury,* vol. 9, part 1. Moscow-Leningrad, 1956.
Spasibenko, A. "N. E. Petropavlovskii-Karonin." *Pisateli-narodniki.* Moscow, 1968.   G. M. MIRONOV [11–1338–1]

KAROTAMM, NIKOLAI GEORGIEVICH. Born Oct. 10 (23), 1901, in Pärnu; died Sept. 26, 1969, in Moscow. Soviet statesman and party figure, one of the leaders of the partisan movement in Estonia during the Great Patriotic War of 1941–45. Doctor of economics (1964). Became a member of the CPSU in 1928. The son of a peasant carpenter.

Karotamm went to the USSR in 1925 and studied in the Leningrad branch of the J. Marchlewski Communist University of the National Minorities of the West (KUNMZ). In 1928 he was engaged in illegal party work in Tallinn. Karotamm returned to the USSR in 1929, graduated from KUNMZ in 1931, and remained in graduate school there while working at the same time on the Estonian-language journal *Klassovaia bor'ba* (Class Struggle). He began teaching in Moscow in 1933 and was then an editor in the Publishing House of Foreign Workers. In 1940, after the restoration of Soviet power in Estonia, Karotamm was managing editor of the newspaper *Kommunist,* first secretary of the Tartu district committee of the Communist Party of Estonia, and second secretary of the Central Committee of the party. Karotamm directed the Estonian staff of the partisan movement from its inception on Nov. 3, 1942. He became first secretary of the Central Committee of the Communist Party of Estonia in September 1944. In 1950, Karotamm studied in Moscow at the Academy of Social Sciences attached to the Central Committee of the CPSU. He began to work at the Institute of Economics of the Academy of Sciences of the USSR in 1951. Karotamm was awarded the Order of Lenin, the Order of the Patriotic War First Class, and medals.   [11–1340–2]

KARPACHEV, SERGEI VASIL'EVICH. Born Feb. 24 (Mar. 9), 1906, in Kostroma. Soviet inorganic chemist; specialist in electrochemistry. Corresponding member of the Academy of Sciences of the USSR (1970). Member of the CPSU since 1944. Graduated from the Urals Polytechnic Institute (1930). Member of the Presidium of the Urals Scientific Center of the Academy of Sciences of the USSR (from 1971) and director of the Sverdlovsk Electrochemical Institute.

Karpachev's main works deal with the electrochemical kinetics of processes occurring in molten and solid electrolytes. He studied the nature of metal solutions in salt melts, and determined the zero points of various metals in the liquid state. Karpachev was awarded the State Prize of the USSR (1950 and 1951), the Order of Lenin, four other orders, and several medals.

REFERENCE

Smirnov, M. V., and S. F. Pal'guev. "S. V. Karpachev (k 60-letiiu so dnia rozhdeniia)." *Elektrokhimiia,* 1966, vol. 2, fasc. 5.   [11–1349–1]

KARPECHENKO, GEORGII DMITRIEVICH. Born Apr. 21 (May 3), 1899, in the town of Vel'sk, in present-day Arkhangel'sk Oblast; died Sept. 15, 1942. Soviet cytogeneticist and professor (1938).

Karpechenko graduated from the Moscow Agricultural Academy in 1922. From 1925 to 1941 he was the head of the genetics laboratory at the All-Union Institute of Plant Raising. From 1932 to 1941 he headed the subdepartment of plant genetics at Leningrad State University. Karpechenko was one of N. I. Vavilov's closest associates. His principal works were devoted to the distant hybridization of plants. Having obtained a fertile intergeneric radish-cabbage hybrid (*Raphanobrassica*), he proved experimentally the possibility of overcoming sterility in distant hybrids by doubling the number of chromosomes. Karpechenko worked out the foundations of the theory of distant plant hybridization, giving particular attention to morphogenetic significance. He also introduced a classification of distant hybrids based on the genetic closeness of the parent plants. Karpechenko was the author of works on experimental polyploidy.

WORKS

Izbr. trudy. Moscow, 1971.

REFERENCE

Lutkov, A. N., and D. V. Lebedev. "Zhizn' i deiatel'nost' G. D. Karpechenko." In G. D. Karpechenko, *Izbr. trudy.* Moscow, 1971. (Bibliography.)   D. V. LEBEDEV [11–1352–1]

KARPENKO-KARYI, IVAN KARPOVICH (pseudonym of I. K. Tobilevich). Born Sept. 17 (29), 1845, in the village of Arsen'evka, in present-day Kirovograd Oblast; died Sept. 2 (15), 1907, in Berlin. Ukrainian dramatist, actor, and theatrical figure; one of the founders of realistic people's theater in the Ukraine.

Karpenko-Karyi was the son of an estate overseer. For more than 20 years he served as a clerk. Beginning in 1863 he took part in amateur plays; later (beginning in 1883) he performed in the companies of M. P. Staritskii, M. L. Kropivnitskii, and M. K. Sadovskii (his brother). He was a member of illegal societies and was fired from his job in 1883 as politically unreliable; from 1884 to 1887 he was a political exile in Novocherkassk. After his return to Kiev, he and P. K. Saksaganskii organized a company (in 1890) called the Association of Russo-Ukrainian Artists. Karpenko-Karyi played roles in performances of his own works, such as Puzyr' in *The Master,* Ivan in *The Ill-Fated One,* Shmigel'skii in *Savva Chalyi,* and Tereshka Surma in *Vanity.* He also performed in plays of T. G. Shevchenko, M. P. Staritskii, and I. P. Kotliarevskii.

Karpenko-Karyi's world view was formed by the nature of the society of the 1860's and 1870's and was influenced by T. G. Shevchenko and the Russian revolutionary democrats. He first appeared in print in the middle of the 1870's as a drama critic. His first story, *The Recruit* (1883), describes the difficult life of the peasants. The plays of Karpenko-Karyi constitute the classical heritage of Ukrainian dramatic literature. He wrote the dramas *The Barge Hauler* (1883; published in 1895), *The Woman Farm Laborer* (1885; published in 1887), and *The Ill-Fated One* (1886) as well as the tragedy *Savva Chalyi* (1899). His satirical social comedies *Martyn Borulia* (1886; published in 1891), *The Master* (1900; published in 1902), and *Vanity* (1903; published in 1905) are the summit of critical realism in prerevolutionary Ukrainian dramatic literature. They reflect the aggravation of the class contradictions within Ukrainian society of the second half of the 19th century and the growth of the rural bourgeoisie. Karpenko-Karyi created a gallery of characters exposing the deep social conflicts of his time. His dramatic works are distinguished by a profound knowledge of life, a wealth of dramatic situations, the dynamic nature of the action, and colorful language. Film versions have been made of some of Karpenko-Karyi's works (*The Woman Farm Laborer, Martyn Borulia, One-Hundred Thousand, Vanity*). He was buried on the Nadezhda farmstead, near the village of Kardashovo, Kirovograd Oblast.

WORKS

Tvory, vols. 1–6. Kharkov-Kiev, 1929–31.
Tvory, vols. 1–3. Kiev, 1960–61.

REFERENCES

Ryl's'kyi, M. "Hordist' ukrains'koi dramaturhii." In the collection *Nasha krovna sprava.* Kiev, 1959.
Stetsenko, L. *I. Karpenko-Karyi (I. K. Tobilevych): Zhyttia i tvorcha diial'nist'.* Kiev, 1957.
Istoriia ukrains'koi literatury, vol. 1. Kiev, 1959.
Skrypnyk, I. *Ivan Karpenko-Karyi (Ivan Karpovych Tobilevych): Literaturnyi portret.* Kiev, 1960.   V. I. MAZNOI   [11–1350–3]

KARPINSK, a city in Sverdlovsk Oblast, RSFSR; located on the Tur'ia River (Ob' basin). It is the terminus of a 50-km railroad branch from the city of Serov. Population, 38,000 (1970). Brown coal is extracted in Karpinsk by strip mining. Local industries include the manufacture and repair of mining equipment, the construction of electrical machinery, a cotton-spinning factory, and food processing. Karpinsk is the site of a technicum specializing in machine building. The city was formed in 1941 from the settlements of Bogoslovskii and Ugol'nye Kopi and named in honor of Academician A. P. Karpinskii.   [11–1352–2]

KARPIŃSKI, FRANCISZEK. Born Oct. 4, 1741, in Hołoskowo, in present-day Ivano-Frankovsk Oblast, Ukrainian SSR; died Sept. 16, 1825, in Chorowszczyzna. Polish poet and dramatist. Son of an impoverished nobleman.

Karpiński was the founder of Polish sentimentalism, as exemplified in *Diversions in Verse and Prose* (vols. 1–7, 1780–87). In his idylls (*sielanki*), love lyrics, elegies, and religious songs conventional images are combined with realistic pictures of nature and truthful descriptions of human feelings. Karpiński also wrote *Memoirs* (1844), the tragedy *Judith* (1790), and the comedy *Rent* (1789).

WORKS

Wiersze wybrane. Warsaw, 1966.

REFERENCE

Górski, K. *M. F. Karpiński.* Kraków, 1913.   [11–1355–3]

KARPINSKII, ALEKSANDR PETROVICH. Born Dec. 26, 1846 (Jan. 7, 1847), in the settlement of Tur'inskie Rudniki, present-day city of Krasnotur'insk, Sverdlovsk Oblast; died July 15, 1936, in Moscow. Russian and Soviet geologist and public figure. Son of a mining engineer. Graduated from the Mining Institute in St. Petersburg (1866). In 1869 he became a junior scientific assistant at the institute; from 1877 to 1896 he was a professor. He took an active part in the organization of the Geological Committee (1882), in which he initially was the senior geologist. From 1885 to 1903 he was its director and, from 1903 to 1929, honorary director.

In 1886, Karpinskii was made junior scientific assistant at the St. Petersburg Academy of Sciences; in 1889, academician extraordinary; and in 1896, regular academician. In 1916 he began to perform the duties of vice-president of the Academy of Sciences, and on May 15, 1917, he became its first elected president. Under his leadership the work of the Academy of Sciences was reorganized. Karpinskii played a major role in organizing the study of the nation's productive forces.

Karpinskii's scientific activities were distinguished by their diversity. He compiled summary geological maps of the Urals and the European part of the USSR. His works on tectonics, paleogeography, and paleontology are particularly well known. He was the first to reveal the basic features of the tectonic structure of the Russian Platform, pointing out (in 1880) the presence of a crystalline folded base and sedimentary mantle in its structure and distinguishing (in 1883) a zone of dislocated sedimentary rock in the south of Russia. Later (1887 and 1894), using the method of tectonic analysis with paleogeographic constructs that he had developed, Karpinskii showed that the strike of the structures created by the oscillatory movements of the earth's crust within the Russian Platform in the early Paleozoic age was parallel to the Baltic Shield and, later, to the system of ranges of the Greater Caucasus or the Urals. Only after Karpinskii's works did the phenomena of transgressions and regressions acquire a true scientific explanation in geology.

Karpinskii's monograph *On the Remains of the Edestides and Their New Genus, Helicoprion* was published in 1899; his monograph *On the Trochiliscs,* in 1906. In this thorough research, Karpinskii proved that the trochiliscs and other forms close to them were not animals (foraminifers or coelenterates), as earlier researchers had thought, but rather the calcified sporophidiums of higher thallophyte plants (charophytes).

Karpinskii was one of the first in Russia (1869) to use the microscope in studying rock. At the eighth session of the International Geological Congress in Paris in 1900, he presented a paper on the principles of classification and nomenclature of rock, pointing out that in the classification of igneous rocks, their mineralogical composition and structure should be of primary significance. Karpinskii's research in geology and petrography was closely tied to practical geology. His general geological works, in particular his geological and paleogeographic maps, were the basis for extensive practical forecasts in prospecting for minerals. Karpinskii was awarded the Konstantin Medal of the Russian Geographic Society (1892) and the Cuvier Prize of the French Academy of Sciences (1922) for his works. In 1946 the Academy of Sciences of the USSR established the Karpinskii Prize and Gold Medal, awarded for outstanding work in the area of geology.

Karpinskii was a permanent representative of Russian geological science at international geological congresses (beginning with the second session of the congress in Bologna in 1881). He participated in the compilation of the geological map of Europe and the standardization of the graphic legends in geology. He was chairman of the Organizing Committee and president of the seventh session of the International Geological Congress (St. Petersburg, 1897). From 1899 through 1936 he was president of the Mineralogical Society. Karpinskii performed a great deal of scientific and organizational work on various commissions. A city in Sverdlovsk Oblast (RSFSR), a volcano on Paramushir Island (Kuril Islands), a mountain in the Northern Urals, and the Geological Museum of the Academy of Sciences of the USSR in Leningrad have been named after Karpinskii. He was buried in Red Square beside the Kremlin wall.

WORKS

Sobr. soch., vols. 1–4. Moscow-Leningrad, 1939–49.

REFERENCES

Lichkov, B. L. *Karpinskii i sovremennost'.* Moscow-Leningrad, 1946.
Aleksandr Petrovich Karpinskii: Bibliografícheskii ukazatel' trudov. Moscow-Leningrad, 1947.
Beliankin, D. S. "Petrograficheskie issledovaniia A. P. Karpinskogo i ego napravlenie v petrografii." In *Ocherki po istorii geologicheskikh znanii,* fasc. 1. Moscow, 1953.
Borisiak, A. A. "Aleksandr Petrovich Karpinskii." In *Liudi russkoi nauki* [book 2]. Moscow, 1962.   [11–1353–1]

KARPINSKII, VIACHESLAV ALEKSEEVICH. Born Jan. 16, 1880, in Penza; died Mar. 20, 1965, in Moscow. Figure in the revolutionary movement in Russia, publicist, doctor of economics. Hero of Socialist Labor (1962). Became a member of the Communist Party in 1898. The son of a government official.

Karpinskii was expelled from the University of Kharkov for revolutionary activity. He helped organize the Union of Struggle for the Emancipation of the Working Class in Kharkov in late 1902. Persecuted by the authorities, he emigrated in 1904 to Geneva. Under V. I. Lenin's direction, he worked for the newspapers *Vpered* and *Proletarii* and contributed to *Pravda.* In World War I (1914–18) he set up the publication of the newspaper *Sotsial-demokrat* and carried out a number of Lenin's assignments. Returning to Russia in 1917, Karpinskii worked for the newspaper *Derevenskaia pravda* and directed the agitation and instruction department of the All-Russian Central Executive Committee. During the Civil War of 1918–20, Karpinskii edited the newspaper *Krasnaia zvezda,* which was published on the propaganda steamship of the same name; he became the editor of the newspaper *Bednota* in 1918. A member of the editorial board of *Pravda* and of the editorial boards of several newspapers and magazines from 1918 to 1927, Karpinskii in 1936–37 worked in the apparatus of the Central Committee of the ACP (Bolshevik). After 1937 he was engaged in scholarly and literary propaganda work.

Karpinskii was a delegate to the Eighth, Sixteenth, and Twenty-second Congresses of the party and was elected a member of the All-Russian Central Executive Committee. Lenin wrote more than 100 letters to Karpinskii. Karpinskii was the author of books, pamphlets, and articles on Lenin and on the history of the Communist Party and the Soviet state. He was awarded three Orders of Lenin. [11–1354–1]

KARPINSKII, a peak in the Northern Urals, in the Is-sledovatel'skii Range, on the border between the Komi ASSR and Tiumen' Oblast of the RSFSR. Elevation, 1,878 m. The mountain is composed of quartzites and crystalline schists. Mountain tundra predominates on the peak, and there is sparse coniferous forest in the foothills. The mountain was named in honor of the Soviet geologist A. P. Karpinskii. [11–1355–2]

KARPINSKII, an active volcano in the southern part of the island of Paramushir (in the Kuril Islands). It consists of two gently sloping cones up to 1,345 m high, composed of andesites and andesite-basalts. There are two craters; the fumaroles emit hot gases and fountains of liquid sulfur. The activity of the volcano intensified in 1952. The slopes are broken by ancient glacial cirques, the most extensive of which was erroneously thought to be a caldera. The volcano was named in honor of the Soviet geologist A. P. Karpinskii. [11–1355–1]

KARPINSKITE (named after Academician A. P. Karpinskii), a compound silicate mineral. The chemical composition conforms closely to the formula $Na_2(Be,Zn,Mg)Al_2[Si_6O_{16}(OH)_2]$. It crystallizes in the trigonal system, forming radiating aggregates of acicular crystals. White in color, it has a hardness of 2.0 on the mineralogical scale and a density of 2,545 kg/m^3. It was first found in the small cavities of albite and natrolite in the natrolite-albite pegmatites of the Lovozero Massif in the Khibiny Mountains (Kola Peninsula). The mineral was discovered and described by L. L. Shilin in 1956. [11–1352–3]

KARPOV, ALEKSANDR TERENT'EVICH. Born Oct. 4 (17), 1917, in the village of Felenevo, in present-day Peremyshl' Raion, Kaluga Oblast; died Oct. 29, 1944. Twice Hero of the Soviet Union (Sept. 28, 1943, and Aug. 22, 1944), major. Became a member of the CPSU in 1942. The son of a peasant.

Karpov graduated from a vocational training school in Kaluga in 1935 and worked as a metalworker and studied at an aviation club until 1939. He joined the Soviet Army in 1939 and graduated from the Miasnikov Military Aviation School in Kacha in 1940. From 1941, Karpov fought in air battles on the Leningrad front and rose from pilot to flight commander, deputy commander, and finally commander of a squadron of the 27th Guards Fighter Aviation Regiment. He made 456 combat flights and fought in 97 air battles; he shot down 28 enemy aircraft personally and eight more in group combat. He died while on a combat mission. Karpov was awarded the Order of Lenin, three Orders of the Red Banner, the Order of Alexander Nevsky, and medals. [11–1356–1]

KARPOV, FEDOR IVANOVICH. Date of birth unknown; died before 1545. Russian political figure and writer of the first half of the 16th century; a pupil of Maxim the Greek.

Karpov played a leading role in directing the foreign policy of the Russian government in the 1530's and 1540's. He was an *okol'nichii* (a noble ranking below the boyars). Karpov was a widely educated man, knowing Latin and being familiar with classical literature and philosophy. The best known of his few remaining works are his letters to Metropolitan Daniil, Maxim the Greek, and others; these epistles are distinguished by picturesque and stylistically refined language and by bold thought. By fighting for a strong and "just" autocracy, Karpov expressed the interests of the *dvorianstvo* (service nobility). I. S. Peresvetov later developed the views that Karpov championed.

REFERENCE
Zimin, A. A. "Obshchestvenno-politicheskie vzgliady F. Karpova." In the collection *Tr. otdela drevnerusskoi literatury* [vol.] 12. Moscow-Leningrad, 1956. [11–1357–1]

KARPOV, LEV IAKOVLEVICH. Born Apr. 18 (30), 1879, in Kiev; died Jan. 6, 1921, in Moscow. Figure of the revolutionary movement in Russia, one of the organizers of the Soviet chemical industry. Became a member of the Communist Party in 1897. The son of a sales clerk.

Karpov graduated from the Moscow Higher Technical School in 1910 and trained as a chemist. He joined the Moscow Union of Struggle for the Emancipation of the Working Class in 1898, moved to Voronezh in 1900, and was one of the organizers and leaders of the Northern Workers' Union. He was assigned by the Central Committee of the RSDLP to organize and lead the Eastern Bureau of the Central Committee (Samara) in 1903, and in 1904 he headed the Southern Bureau of the Central Committee (Kiev) and participated in founding an underground printing press in Poltava. In July 1904 he was co-opted into the Central Committee of the RSDLP. He was one of the organizers of the newspaper *Vpered* in late 1904. Karpov participated in the December armed uprising of 1905 in Moscow and was the secretary of the Moscow Committee of the RSDLP from August 1906 to May 1907. He was repeatedly arrested by the authorities.

From 1911 to 1915, Karpov organized the production of rosin and turpentine in Russia and set up the first domestic production of chloroform and liquid chlorine. He became director of the Bondiuzhskii chemical plant in 1915 and in February 1918 became chief of the department of the chemical industry and a member of the presidium of the Supreme Council on the National Economy (VSNKH). In 1918, Karpov helped found the Central Chemical Laboratory of the VSNKH in Moscow, now the L. Ia. Karpov Physical Chemistry Institute. He is buried on Red Square at the Kremlin Wall.

REFERENCES
Pisarzhevskii, O. *Stranitsy zhizni bol'shevika-uchenogo.* Moscow, 1960.
Svetom leninskikh idei, 2nd ed. Moscow, 1969. [11–1356–3]

KARPOV, VLADIMIR BORISOVICH. Born Feb. 13 (26), 1912, in the city of Khvalynsk, in present-day Saratov Oblast. Soviet Byelorussian writer.

Karpov took part in the partisan movement in Byelorussia. He is the author of the collections of literary criticism *On the Path to Maturity* (1952) and *Winged Takeoff* (1966), the novella *Without a Neutral Zone* (1950), and the novels *Year After Year* (1957), *Spring Showers* (1961), and *The Nemiga's Bloody Banks* (1962). The exploits of the Byelorussian partisans and the life of the working class are the main themes of Karpov's works. He has been awarded the Order of the Red Star and several medals.

REFERENCE
Pis'menniki Savetskai Belarusi: Karotki biiabibliiahrafichny davednik. Minsk, 1970. [11–1356–2]

KARPOVICH, PETR VLADIMIROVICH. Born Oct. 3 (15), 1874; died Mar. 31 (Apr. 13), 1917. Socialist Revolutionary (SR) terrorist.

Karpovich studied at Moscow University (1895–96) and at the University of Iur'ev (1898–99); he was expelled for his participation in the student movement. In 1899 he went abroad and entered the University of Berlin. Tsarist repressions of revolutionary students prompted Karpovich to return to St. Petersburg. There, on Feb. 14, 1901, as a symbol of protest, he mortally wounded the minister of education, N. P. Bogolepov. Karpovich was imprisoned in the Schlissel'burg Fortress and condemned to 20 years of penal servitude. He was transferred in 1906 to the prison at Akatui and later to Algachi. In 1907, after being released for deportation, he escaped abroad and joined the Fighting Organization of the SR's, becoming one of E. F. Azef's assistants. In 1908, Karpovich helped organize the unsuccessful attempt on Nicholas II's life. After Azef was denounced as a provocateur, Karpovich left the SR's. In 1917, returning to Russia, he perished in the North Sea when his steamship was sunk by a German submarine. [11–1357–2]

KARPOVKA RESERVOIR, a reservoir formed in 1952 on the Karpovka River in Volgograd Oblast, RSFSR. It is the largest reservoir on the V. I. Lenin Volga-Don Ship Canal. Area, 42 sq km; volume, 0.16 cubic km; length, 15 km; maximum width, 3.2 km; average depth, 4 m. Its level fluctuates within a range of 1 m. With the aid of pumping stations, the Karpovka Reservoir regulates flow on a seasonal basis. Created for transportation purposes, the reservoir is also used for irrigation and water supply. Bream, pike-perch, common carp, zope (*Abramis ballerus*), and pike are fished commercially. [11–1357–3]

KARPUNINSKII, a urban-type settlement in Verkhotur'e Raion, Sverdlovsk Oblast, RSFSR; located 76 km east of the city of Verkhotur'e. It has a railroad station on the Serov-Alapaevsk line. Logging is done in Karpuninskii. It is also the site of a prefabricated-housing plant. [11–1359–5]

KARPUSHIKHA, an urban-type settlement in Sverdlovsk Oblast, RSFSR; located on the Tagil River (Ob' basin), 19 km northwest of the city of Kirovgrad (the Ezhevaia railroad station). Copper ore is mined in the area. [11–1360–1]

KARRANAY, a wind instrument, a brass horn with a straight (less frequently, curved) tube and a large bell. Total length, 3 m. The sound is powerful and deep; and the scale is natural. The *karranay* was formerly used in Middle Asia and Iran as a military (signal) instrument. It was subsequently used during ceremonial processions of khans and military leaders. The *karranay* was among the instruments in ensembles of strolling musicians. It is used in the Tadzhik SSR and the Uzbek SSR as a ceremonial instrument at parades, demonstrations, and mass fetes. This instrument is also found in a number of Oriental countries. [11–1320–3]

KARREN (lapies), furrows (from several cm to 1–2 m and more in depth) characteristic for areas where denuded karst has developed. The karren lie in parallel rows or as branching labyrinths and are usually separated by narrow sharp-pointed crests. Karren occur as a result of the leaching of the surface of limestones and other soluble rock by rain, thawing snow, and more rarely sea and river water. Frequently the karren develop along cracks (crack karren). On steep rocky surfaces the karren are not related to cracks (fluted or wall karren). Often the karren occupy large areas, forming karren fields (*karrenfeld*). [11–1364–1]

KARRER, PAUL. Born Apr. 21, 1889, in Moscow. Swiss organic chemist and biochemist. Graduated from the University of Zürich in 1911. From 1912 to 1918 he conducted pharmaco-chemical research in Frankfurt am Main with P. Ehrlich on complex metal salts and produced the silver-arsphenamine complex. He has been a professor at the University of Zürich since 1918 and director of the Institute of Chemistry in Zürich since 1919.

Karrer established the structure and conducted the synthesis of a number of biologically active natural compounds (carbohydrates, alkaloids, lecithins, anthocyanides, many carotenoids, and vitamins A, B_2, E, K, and B_1 and their coenzymatic forms). He and the English scientist W. Haworth shared a Nobel Prize in 1937.

WORKS
Einführung in die Chemie der polymeren Kohlenhydrate. Leipzig, 1925.
Lehrbuch der organischen Chemie, 13th ed. Stuttgart, 1959.
Carotinoide. Basel, 1948. (With E. Jucker.)
In Russian translation:
Kurs organicheskoi khimii. Leningrad, 1960. [11–1362–1]

KARROO (Hottentot *karusa,* "dry" or "sterile"), the general name for the semidesert plateaus and intermontane depressions in South Africa; they lie to the south of the Orange River and have a subtropical climate.

The Upper Karroo is a plateau 1,000–1,300 m high between the Orange River in the north and the Great Escarpment in the south. It is composed of horizontal sandstones and shales (the continental formation of the karroo dates to the Upper Paleozoic

and Mesozoic ages) broken by numerous dolerite intrusions. Precipitation (250–400 mm per year) falls irregularly, usually in torrents. The karroo is broken by the wadi beds of the tributaries of the Orange River, which after the rains become flooded. Sparse brush vegetation has survived, as well as solitary trees, chiefly in the valleys and saucer-like depressions.

The Great Karroo is an erosion depression between the Great Escarpment and the Kaap (Cape) Mountains; it extends 400 km from west to east, with an average width of 130 km and average elevations of 450–750 m. It is composed of sandstones of the Karroo suite. The climate is semidesert and desert, with 125–400 mm of precipitation a year. The vegetation cover is sparse, particularly in the west.

The Little Karroo is a very wide (about 64 km) longitudinal depression in the Kaap Mountains, between the Zwartberg Range in the north and the Lange Bergen in the south; it stretches 320 km from west to east. Precipitation is 250 mm a year, supporting sparse brush and grasses.

L. A. MIKHAILOVA [11–1363–3]

KARRYEV, AGA KARRYEVICH. Born Apr. 4 (17), 1908, in the *aul* (village) of Kipchak, in present-day Ashkhabad Raion, Turkmen SSR. Soviet historian. Corresponding member of the Academy of Sciences of the Turkmen SSR (1951). Member of the CPSU since 1932. The son of a teacher.

Karryev graduated from the Ashkhabad Pedagogical Institute in 1939. From 1956 to 1959 he served as the director of the Institute of History, Archaeology, and Ethnography of the Academy of Sciences of the Turkmen SSR. Karryev has been head of the subdepartment of the history of the USSR at the M. Gorky Turkmen University since 1960. He has served as the director of the Institute of History of the Academy of Sciences of the Turkmen SSR since 1968. Karryev has written basic works on the history of 18th- and 19th-century Turkmenia, including *The Historical Roots of the Friendship Between the Russian and Turkmen Peoples* (1950), *The Annexation of Turkmenistan to Russia and the Progressive Significance of the Annexation* (1956), and *Leninist Friendship Between Peoples* (1969, with Iu. E. Permiak). He is also one of the authors of *The History of Soviet Turkmenistan* (parts 1–2, 1970). Karryev has been awarded two orders as well as various medals.

[11–1364–3]

KARRYEV, BAIMUKHAMED ATALIEVICH. Born Dec. 22, 1914, in the village of Geokcha, in present-day Ashkhabad Oblast, Turkmen SSR. Soviet literary scholar. Academician of the Academy of Sciences of the Turkmen SSR (1965). Member of the CPSU since 1949.

Karryev has been a professor in the subdepartment of Turkmen literature at the M. Gorky Turkmen University since 1969. His doctoral dissertation was entitled *Makhtumkuli and His Patriotism* (1943). Karryev is the author of the book *Zelili and His Times* (1943), and has also written pamphlets, articles devoted to Turkmen literature, and textbooks for Turkmen schools. He takes part in the publication of texts of Turkmen classical literature and folklore. Karryev has been awarded the Order of the Red Banner of Labor as well as medals.

WORKS
Epicheskie skazaniia o Ker-ogly u tiurkoiazychnykh narodov. Moscow, 1968. [11–1365–1]

KARS, a city in northeastern Turkey near the Soviet-Turkish frontier. It is the administrative center of Kars Vilayet. Population, 54,000 (1970). Kars has a railroad station and an airfield. It is a center for milch-cow and sheep breeding. The city has creameries and dairy plants that produce pasteurized and powdered milk. Carpets and rough cloth are manufactured.

Kars is an ancient city. In the tenth and 11th centuries it was the center of the Armenian Kingdom of Kars. In the 16th century it was seized by Turkey, which turned it into a base for the spread of its empire to Transcaucasia. During the Russo-Turkish wars of the 19th century, Kars, as a Turkish stronghold, was one of the main objectives of military operations in the Caucasian theater. In 1807, Russian troops unsuccessfully assaulted the city, and in 1828 they took it by storm. In 1855 the Turkish garrison repelled the attacks of the Russian forces but were forced by hunger to capitulate after a five-month siege. In November 1877, Russian troops took Kars by a quick assault; the Treaty of San Stefano (1878) transferred it to Russia. Turkish troops occupied Kars in May 1918 after Russia's withdrawal from World War I. After Turkey's defeat in the war, however, Armenian Dashnak brigades occupied the city. According to the Treaty of Kars (1921), the city became part of Turkey.

[11–1365–2]

KARS, TREATY OF (1921), a treaty between the Armenian, Azerbaijan, and Georgian soviet socialist republics on the one hand and Turkey on the other. The treaty was concluded in the city of Kars on October 13, with the participation of the RSFSR. The treaty conference was convened on September 26 in fulfillment of the Treaty of Moscow of March 16, 1921, between the RSFSR and Turkey. The period of validity of the treaty was not stipulated. The Treaty of Kars extended the basic provisions of the Moscow treaty to the Transcaucasian soviet republics and added a number of articles: crossing of the border by inhabitants of the frontier zone was to be eased, the inhabitants were conceded the right to make use of pastures located on the other side of the border (arts. 7, 8), and a commission was to be created for the establishment of trade relations and the regulation of economic, financial, and other questions (art. 18). The instruments of ratification were exchanged in Yerevan on Sept. 11, 1922.

PUBLICATIONS
Dokumenty vneshnei politiki SSSR, vol. 4. Moscow, 1960.
Istoriia vneshnei politiki SSSR, part 1. Moscow, 1966.

V. A. EMETS [11–1370–2]

KARSAKPAI, an urban-type settlement in Dzhezdy Raion, Dzhezkazgan Oblast, Kazakh SSR; located 90 km west of the Dzhezkazgan railroad station. Population, 6,000 (1970). Karsakpai is the site of a copper-smelting plant that uses the ore of the Dzhezkazgan deposits.

[11–1367–1]

KARSAVA (formerly Korsovka), a city in Ludza Raion, Latvian SSR. It has a railroad station on the Pskov-Daugavpils line and is a highway junction. Industry includes metalworking. The Malnava sovkhoz-technicum is located 1.5 km from the city.

[11–1365–3]

KARSAVIN, LEV PLATONOVICH. Born Dec. 1 (13), 1882, in St. Petersburg; died July 12, 1952, in Abez', Komi ASSR. Russian religious philosopher and medieval historian. Student of I. M. Grevs and brother of T. P. Karsavina.

Karsavin received his training in history at the University of St. Petersburg. In 1912 he was appointed a professor at the St. Petersburg Institute of History and Philology, and in 1916 he began teaching at the University of St. Petersburg. He was exiled abroad in 1922. In 1928 he was appointed a professor at the University of Kaunas, and between 1940 and 1946 he taught at the University of Vilnius.

Under the influence of early Christian teachings (patristic writings and Origen) and 19th-century Russian religious philosophy, particularly that of V. S. Solov'ev, Karsavin sought to create a unified and systematic Christian world view. He interpreted Solov'ev's category of *vseedinstvo* ("total-unity") as a dynamic principle of development, of "growth of being," and consequently as a fundamental category of the historical process: any existing thing does not so much "exist" as "become" and thus appears as one of the manifestations of total-unity. Interpreted in this manner, historicism becomes a universal principle in Karsavin's metaphysical system, rendering it in certain respects similar to Hegel's dialectical process. Other aspects of Karsavin's system, his epistemology, ethics, and doctrine of personality, rest on this philosophy of history. His early works are based on extensive material taken from historical sources and deal with the history of medieval religious trends and spiritual life in the Middle Ages.

WORKS
Ocherki religioznoi zhizni v Italii XII–XIII vv. St. Petersburg, 1912.
Osnovy srednevekovoi religioznosti . . . . St. Petersburg, 1915.
Kul'tura srednikh vekov. St. Petersburg-Moscow, 1914.
Katolichestvo. St. Petersburg, 1918.
Vvedenie v istoriiu. St. Petersburg, 1920.
Vostok, zapad i russkaia ideia. St. Petersburg, 1922.
D. Bruno. Berlin, 1923.
Filosofiia istorii. Berlin, 1923.
O nachalakh. Berlin, 1925.
Perí archón: Ideen zur christlichen Metaphysik. Memel, 1928.
O lichnosti. Kaunas, 1929.   S. S. KHORUZHII [11–1365–4]

KARSAVINA, TAMARA PLATONOVNA. Born Feb. 25 (Mar. 9), 1885, in St. Petersburg. Russian ballerina. Sister of L. P. Karsavin.

Tamara Karsavina graduated from P. A. Gerdt's class at the St. Petersburg Theatrical School in 1902. That same year she became a dancer at the Mariinskii Theater (St. Petersburg), where she was prima ballerina from 1912 to 1918. She was M. Fokine's partner and the principal performer in the ballets he staged. Her roles in these ballets included the title role in Shcherbachev's *Eunice,* Madeleine in N. N. Cherepnin's *Pavillon d'Armide,* and Columbine in *Le Carnival* to music by Schumann. She danced the leading roles in ballets by P. I. Tchaikovsky, A. K. Glazunov, A. Adam, and L. Minkus.

Karsavina's refined artistry reflected the influence of impressionism on the Russian academic school of dance. Her dancing was characterized by subtle changes of lyrical moods and an accentuated plasticity. Her subtle stylizations in the commedia dell'arte ballets brought her praise (Columbine in Drigo's *Harlequinade*). Karsavina danced in the Russian Seasons Abroad between 1909 and 1929 and with Diaghilev's Ballets Russes. She was the first to perform the leading roles in Fokine's stagings of Stravinsky's *The Firebird* and *Petrouchka,* Rimsky-Korsakov's *Scheherazade,* and Ravel's *Daphnis and Chloe.* She also danced with V. Nijinsky.

Karsavina left Russia in 1918 and in 1930 appeared with the Ballet Rambert. From 1930 to 1955 she was vice president of the Royal Academy of Dance in London. She is the author of a book on choreography.

WORKS
Theatre Street. London [1930].
Ballet Technique. New York [1968].

REFERENCES
Svetlov, V. "T. P. Karsavina." *Russkii balet.* St. Petersburg, 1913, pp. 13–16.
Benois, A. *Reminiscences of the Russian Ballet.* London, 1941.
Lifar, S. *Les Trois Grâces du XX siècle.* Paris, 1957.
Sokolova, L. *Dancing for Diaghilev.* London, 1960.

V. M. KRASOVSKAIA [11–1366–1]

KARSHI, a city in Kashkadar'ia Oblast, Uzbek SSR. It is situated in the center of the Karshi Oasis, on the Kashkadar'ia River, at a junction of highways and railroads leading to Kagan, Dushanbe, Kitab, and Samarkand. Population, 79,000 (1972; 23,000 in 1939).

The industry of Karshi is represented by cotton-ginning, oil-extraction and dairy plants, a brewery, mechanical and motor repair plants, meat-packing and milling combines, a garment factory, and enterprises producing building materials and railroad stock. Napless two-sided Farsi carpets (*palas*) are made in the city. Karshi is a center for the development of the Karshi Steppe.

The cultural institutions of Karshi include a pedagogical institute; a polytechnicum; agricultural, cooperative, and cultural technicums; a medical college; teachers and preschool teachers colleges; and a music and drama theater. Karshi took shape in the first half of the 14th century on the ancient caravan route from Samarkand and Bukhara to Afghanistan, India, and other countries; it became a city in 1926.

REFERENCE
Goroda Uzbekistana. Tashkent, 1965.   [11–1459–6]

KARSHI STEPPE, a rolling plain in the Uzbek SSR. It slopes from an elevation of 500 m to 200 m from east to west, from the hilly foothills of the Zeravshan and Gissar ranges to the Sundukli sands. Part of the Karshi Steppe is irrigated by the Kashkadar'ia River. The Karshi Main Canal is under construction (1972). The climate is arid, with annual precipitation of 200–400 mm. The Karshi Steppe is covered with desert wormwood, thistle, and ephemeral vegetation. Large areas of the steppe are planted with grain crops and cotton. The city of Karshi is located on the eastern part of the plain, in the southern foothills of the Kungurtau elevation. The five-year plan for the development of the national economy of the USSR for 1971–75 provides for continuing work on the development of a large new cotton-growing region on the Karshi Steppe.   [11–1460–1]

KARSKIE VOROTA, a strait in the Arctic Ocean between the islands of Vaigach and Novaia Zemlia; it joins the Barents and Kara seas. The strait is 33 km long, approximately 45 km wide, and up to 119 m deep. Its shores are high and rocky. The strait is covered with ice for most of the year.   [11–1367–2]

KARSKII, EVFIMII FEDOROVICH. Born Dec. 20, 1860 (Jan. 1, 1861), in the village of Lasha, in present-day Grodno Raion, Grodno Oblast; died Apr. 29, 1931, in Leningrad. Soviet scholar in Slavic philology. Academician of the St. Petersburg Academy of Sciences (1916).

Karskii served as a professor at the universities of Warsaw (from 1894) and St. Petersburg (from 1917). From 1905 through 1917 he edited *Russkii filologicheskii vestnik* (Russian Philological Journal), and beginning in 1920, *Izvestiia otdeleniia russkogo iazyka i slovesnosti Akademii nauk* (Proceedings of the Division of Russian Language and Literature of the Academy of Sciences). Karskii's main research was devoted to the Byelorussian language (its history and modern dialects), Byelorussian literature (folk poetry, Old Byelorussian written language, and modern literature; the work *Byelorussians,* vols. 1–3, 1903–22), and Byelorussian paleography (*Slavic Cyrillic Paleography,* 1928). He published many ancient literary texts accompanied by paleographic and linguistic analyses, including Undol'skii's Documents, the Laurentian Chronicle, and Russkaia Pravda.

WORKS
O iazyke tak nazyvaemykh litovskikh letopisei. Warsaw, 1894.
Zapadnorusskie perevody Psaltyri v XV–XVII vekakh. Warsaw, 1896.
Russkaia dialektologiia. Leningrad, 1924.
Ocherk nauchnoi razrabotki russkogo iazyka v predelakh SSSR. Leningrad, 1926.
Nabliudeniia v oblasti sintaksisa Lavrent'evskogo spiska letopisi. Leningrad [1929].
Belorusy: Iazyk belorusskogo naroda, fasc. 1–3. Moscow, 1955–56.
Trudy po belorusskomu i drugim slavianskim iazykam. Moscow, 1962.
                V. I. BORKOVSKII [11–1367–3]

KARS KINGDOM, an Armenian feudal state in the Lake Van region with its capital at the city of Kars (963–1064). It separated from the Shirak Kingdom of the Armenian Bagratids after the proclamation in 961 of the city of Ani as the capital of the Bagratid state. However, the kings of Kars of the Bagratuni dynasty were vassals of the Ani Bagratids. Under Musheg (ruled from 963 to 984), the Kars Kingdom served as an advanced outpost of the Ani Kingdom in its struggle with Byzantium. The Kars Kingdom attained its greatest power during the reign of Abbas (984–1029). After the Seljuk Turks' incursion into Transcaucasia (1064–65), King Gagik (ruled from 1029 to 1065) ceded his kingdom to Byzantium, which used the territory in the struggle against the Seljuk Turks.

REFERENCE
Eremian, S. T. "Prisoedinenie severo-zapadnykh oblastei Armenii k Vizantii v XI veke." *Vestnik obshchestvennykh nauk AN Armianskoi SSR,* 1971, no. 3.   [11–1371–1]

KARST (Kras), a limestone plateau in northwestern Yugoslavia (the western extremity is in Italy) north of the Istrian Peninsula. Maximum elevation, 643 m. There is a general development of karst forms of relief (sinks, funnel-like hollows, polje basins, sinkholes, and caves). Surface drainage is almost completely absent, and vegetation is sparse and grassy. Wine growing is carried on where the soils in the hollows are fertile. The world-famous Postojna Cave is located on the plateau. There is an institute for the study of caves in the city of Postojna.
                [11–1374–1]

KARST (German *Karst,* from the name of the Karst plateau, or Kras, in Yugoslavia), phenomena in rock that is soluble in natural water and the process by which these phenomena are formed.

Karst is characterized by a complex of surface and underground forms and by the unique circulation and regime of underground water as well as a unique river network and lakes. It develops in calcareous and noncalcareous rock. Of the exposed and buried karstic rocks on the continents, up to 40 million sq km are calcareous rock, about 7 million sq km are gypsums and anhydrites, and up to 4 million sq km are rock salt. Calcareous rock dissolves in the presence of free carbon dioxide ($CaCO_3 + H_2O + CO_2 \rightleftarrows Ca^{++} + 2HCO_3^-$) or mineral or organic acids. Sulfate rock and rock salt can dissolve in water without the accompanying reactions. Karst develops under the combined influence of surface and underground water. The dissolving of the rock is frequently accompanied by mechanical water erosion. The conditions for erosion can be created by the solution of the contacts of the grains of the rock, freeing them from one another and facilitating water erosion.

The surface of karst terrain is characterized by small furrows, or karren, and closed depressions in the form of potholes, sinks, basins, poljes, natural wells and mines, and blind (closed off at the lower end) valleys and ravines. Particularly typical are the sinks—conical, basin- or dish-shaped, or irregular pits—with a diameter of 1–200 m and a depth of 0.5–50 m. On the bottom of the sinks and other depressions water-absorbing openings, or ponors, are found. The basins and sinks can be full of water at some times and dry up at others (periodically disappearing lakes). Basins with areas up to several hundreds of square kilometers, steep sides, flat bottoms, and disappearing streams and rivers are known as poljes.

In karst massifs various underground passageways, cavities, and caves form, frequently along fissures. The world's longest caves are more than 100 km (for example, the Flint Ridge cave system in Kentucky in the United States or the Hölloch cave in the Alps in Switzerland). Deep karst wells and natural shafts or chasms form passageways between surface and underground karst forms. The deepest caverns in the world are Pierre St. Martin, which is 1,110 m deep (France-Spain), and Berger, which is 1,122 m deep (Isère, France). In the USSR the Nazarovskaia Cavern in the vicinity of Sochi in the Western Caucasus is about 500 m deep.

The complex of surface and underground karst forms is most fully expressed when the surface of the soluble rock is exposed; this is known as denuded karst. But the soluble rock can be covered over by a layer of soil and sod (then the exposed karren are absent); this is termed turf-covered karst. Mantled karst occurs when the surface is covered by insoluble loose sediments. (The surface is characterized by sinks and similar depressions that have developed owing to the washing of loose covering formations into the fissures and cavities of the karstic series.) Armored karst occurs when the surface is covered by insoluble rocky formations. (The only characteristic surface forms are sinkholes.) The soluble rock can be altogether buried beneath the nonkarstic series, in which case the karst forms are not expressed on the surface; this is termed buried karst. Unique karst landscapes are observed in tropical countries, frequently with characteristic outliers of limestone (cone karst and tower karst, for example). Karst processes in permafrost areas also occur in a unique manner.

Karst terrain has few surface watercourses. The rivers and streams frequently disappear into underground cavities and, having traveled a portion of their length in these caverns, again emerge on the surface in the form of large springs (vauclusian springs), mainly along the edges of the karst areas. The circulation of underground water is most intense in areas adjacent to valleys and in zones of tectonic disturbances, where karst develops more strongly. Under platform plain conditions, the interior parts (cores) of the divides are usually less karsted than the areas adjacent to the valleys.

Pseudokarst phenomena are externally similar to karst phenomena, and they occur in ice and permafrost (thermokarst) and in fragmental and porous soils ("clastokarst," "clay karst," "loess karst," mechanical suffosion, and subsidences). A major role in the development of pseudokarst is played by physical processes such as the thawing of ice or the mechanical effect of running water. Processes related to the leaching of salts from loose soils or to the solution of the lime and gypsum cement of sandstones and conglomerates constitute the karst-suffosion (sapping) processes. In these rocks the water dissolves only the inclusions or the cement; the basic rock mass (the clay particles, sand, or shingle) is removed by the mechanical action of running water.

Karst complicates industrial, housing, and transport construction as well as the erection of hydroelectric power plants and reservoirs. (Instances of water filtering out of reservoirs and even the destruction of dams by karst phenomena are known.) The underground cavities and fissures reduce the strength of the ground, thereby making it necessary to carry out special investigations in constructing buildings, roads, and the like. In areas where karst is only slightly developed, housing of five stories can be built if the foundations are reinforced and reinforced-concrete belts are laid.

Karst frequently impedes the mining of minerals, but sometimes its draining properties are utilized. At the same time, certain minerals fill the karst cavities, forming deposits of lead, zinc and iron ores, bauxites, phosphorites, oil and fuel gases, and gold and diamond placers.

In the USSR well-developed karst areas exist in many regions on the East European Plain, in the Crimea, the Urals and the Cisurals, on the forward ranges of the Greater Caucasus, in Middle Asia (the Ustiurt plateau and the Karatau, Alai, Zeravshan, and the Petr Pervyi ranges), areas in the Kazakh Melkosopochnik (low hills), the mountains of Southern Siberia, the Angara region, and the Far East. Abroad, karst has developed particularly extensively in Yugoslavia, which is considered to be the country of classic karst. It is also found in many other states of Western Europe, various regions of the United States, the West Indies (Cuba, Puerto Rico, and Jamaica), China (particularly in the Kwangsi Chuang Autonomous Region and Yunnan Province), on the Indochina peninsula, and elsewhere.

REFERENCES
Gvozdetskii, N. A. *Karst*, 2nd ed. Moscow, 1954.
Maksimovich, G. A. *Osnovy karstovedeniia*, vols. 1–2. Perm', 1963–69.
Sokolov, D. S. *Osnovnye usloviia razvitiia karsta.* Moscow, 1962.
Karst i ego narodnokhoziaistvennoe znachenie: Sb. st. Moscow, 1964.
Tipy karsta v SSSR: [Sb. st.]. Moscow, 1965.
N. A. GVOZDETSKII [11–1371–2]

KARSTOLOGY, a branch of knowledge devoted to karst phenomena. Karstology studies current and ancient phenomena and processes that are inherent in rocks that are soluble in natural water as well as the formation, development, extent, and practical importance of karst phenomena. [11–1374–3]

KARSUN, an urban-type settlement and center of Karsun Raion, Ul'ianovsk Oblast, RSFSR. Located on the Barysh River, a tributary of the Sura, 22 km northwest of the Veshkaima station (on the Ul'ianovsk-Inza railroad line). A hosiery factory and a creamery are located in Karsun. There is also a medical school in the settlement. [11–1374–4]

KART, a low-powered racing vehicle with a two-cycle engine. Karts are characterized by the absence of a body, flexible suspension of the front and rear wheels, and a differential gear. The chassis of a kart is a tubular frame that supports the metal floor. The soft-back seat prevents shifting of the driver during turns. The wheels, with pneumatic tires, are mounted on ball bearings. The steering gear is similar to automobile steering gear, with a circular steering wheel. The wheel brakes may be of the hydraulic drum or disk type. The motor is located next to the rear axle. Safety requires the mounting of guards to protect the driver from burns from the hot parts of the motor and the isolation of the chain transmission for the rear-wheel drive.

Five classes are permitted for kart competition in the USSR. The largest classes are Class A, with piston displacements of up to 100 cm^3, and Class B, with piston displacements of up to 125 cm^3 (gearboxes are not installed on karts of these classes).

The dimensions of a kart are as follows: wheelbase (the distance between the axles), 1,010–1,220 mm; track, not less than two-thirds of the wheelbase; maximum length, 1,820 mm; maximum wheel diameter, 350 mm. The maximum speed of karts on straightaways is 150 km/hr. A. A. SABININ [11–1374–5]

KARTALIN RANGE, a mountain range on the southern slopes of the Greater Caucasus, in the Georgian SSR. [11–1376–2]

KARTALY, a city (until 1944, a settlement) in Cheliabinsk Oblast, RSFSR, located on the Kartaly-Aiat River (in the Tobol basin), 150 km east of Magnitogorsk. Population, 43,000 (1970).

Kartaly is a railway junction of lines to Magnitogorsk, Cheliabinsk, Orsk, and Tselinograd. There are railway transport enterprises and factories producing construction materials, spare parts for agricultural machines, and carpets. [11–1376–3]

KARTING, a form of racing using karts, which are miniature motor vehicles without suspensions.

Karting race courses are distinguished by complex configurations with a large number of right and left turns of differing (primarily small) radii; the length, in accordance with the requirements of the International Automobile Federation (FIA), ranges from 400 to 1,200 m, the width is from 6 to 10 m, and the length of the straightaway does not exceed 100 m. Karting has become very widespread in the USSR, especially as a sport for youth (the first races were held in 1961 in Ventspils, Latvian SSR). Annual national championships are conducted for adults (classes with engine capacities of 125 and 175 cu cm) and youths (50 and 125 cu cm classes). Karting is included in the programs of technical military Spartakiads. Every year a world championship is held for Class A (up to 100 cu cm, without transmissions, and with vehicle weights, including the driver, of no less than 120 kg). [11–1389–3]

KARTINI, RADEN ADJENG. Born Apr. 21, 1879, in the village of Mayong, Central Java; died Sept. 17, 1904, in the city of Rembang. Indonesian reformer.

Kartini was the daughter of the regent of Japara in Java. Fluent in Dutch, she studied the literature of this language, including several works by Dutch socialists. She spoke out against old feudal customs and strove for the emancipation of women. Kartini considered education to be the primary means by which women could be emancipated and the Indonesian people could progress. She protested the oppression of the Indonesians by the Dutch colonizers. Although she promoted the adoption of the progressive European culture, she also stressed the need for Indonesians to value their own cultural heritage. Kartini was a forerunner of the organized national liberation movement, whose membership was greatly influenced by her ideas.

REFERENCE
Belen'kii, A. B. *Kartini—doch' Indonezii.* Moscow, 1966.
[11–1389–4]

KARTLI, a historical region of eastern Georgia. In classical and Byzantine sources it is referred to as Iberia. Under the hegemony of Kartli, the eastern Georgian state, with its center at Mtskheta, was formed during the fourth and third centuries B.C. Feudal relations began to develop in Kartli in the fourth century A.D. This development was facilitated by the conversion to Christianity circa 337. In the late tenth century, Kartli became the nucleus of the single Georgian state. After its fall in the second half of the 15th century, the region was partitioned into the independent Kartli Kingdom. In 1762 it joined with Kakhetia to form a united state, which was subsequently annexed to Russia in 1801. [11–1390–2]

KARTLI, a mountain range on the southern slopes of the Greater Caucasus in the Georgian SSR, between the Pshavskaia Aragvi and Iori rivers. Length, greater than 100 km; maximum elevation (in the north), 3,000 m. It is composed primarily of sandstones, marls, and shales. Beech and oak forests cover the slopes; meadows cover the northern and central heights. [11–1390–3]

KARTLIANS, the Georgians living in the historical region of Eastern Georgia known as Kartli (mainly in the basin and tributaries of the Kura River). They speak the Kartlian dialect of Georgian. In the past the Kartlians were distinguished by several local characteristics of culture and everyday life. [11–1390–5]

KARTLI KINGDOM, a feudal state in Eastern Georgia, which emerged in the second half of the 15th century as a result of the disintegration of the united Georgian Kingdom. Its capital was Tbilisi. The kingdom was in existence until 1762, at which time it united with Kakhetia to form a single Kartli-Kakhetian state under King Erekle II. Kartli Kingdom had a barter economy. It was divided into separate semi-independent units, or *satavados.* The late 17th and early 18th centuries were a period of economic and cultural progress. In the 16th, 17th, and 18th centuries, Kartli waged a continuous struggle against Iranian and Turkish aggression. Georgian statesmen, including Luarsab I, Simon, Georgii Saakadze, Rostom, Vakhtang VI, and Erekle II, fought for the preservation of the country's independence. In 1723 the Kartli Kingdom was conquered by the Turks; in 1735, by the Iranians. In 1744 the kingdom liberated itself from its foreign subjugators. In 1801 the Kartli-Kakhetian Kingdom was annexed to Russia.

REFERENCE
Istoriia Gruzii, vol. 1. Tbilisi, 1962. [11–1390–4]

KARTLIS TSKHOVREBA (The Life of Kartli), a collection of Georgian chronicles, compiled in the 12th century and supplemented until the 19th century. It is divided into the *Ancient Kartlis Tskhovreba* and the *New Kartlis Tskhovreba.* The former covers Georgian history up to the 14th century; and the latter, from the 14th to the 18th century. Several manuscripts of the *Ancient Kartlis Tskhovreba* from the 15th, 16th, and 17th centuries have been preserved. In the 18th century, King Vakhtang VI created a commission of "learned men" under the supervision of Beri Egnatashvili that compiled a history of Georgia from the 14th to the 18th century. A number of other 17th- and 18th-century historical writings dealing with events of the 15th-18th centuries were appended to the collection.

The *Kartlis Tskhovreba* deals primarily with Georgian political history. Much of its contents has been confirmed by the writings of Greek and Latin authors; by the accounts of Armenian, Arab, and Persian historians; and by archaeological and epigraphical monuments. The *Kartlis Tskhovreba* contains information concerning the histories of Armenia, Caucasian Albania, and the peoples of the Northern Caucasus. As early as the 12th century, it was translated into Armenian.

REFERENCES
"Kartlis Tskhovreba." In G. A. Melikishvili, *K istorii drevnei Gruzii,* Tbilisi, 1959, pp. 28–47.
Ocherki istorii istoricheskoi nauki v SSSR, vol. 1. Moscow, 1955. Pages 143–44. M. D. LORDKIPANIDZE [11–1390–6]

KARTODIKROMO, MARCO (pseudonym, Mas Marco Sumantri). Born 1878, in Tjepu, eastern Java; died 1928 or 1932, in Boven-Digul, West Irian. Indonesian writer and journalist;

one of the founders of modern Indonesian literature. Became a member of the first popular nationalist organization, Sarekat Islam, in 1913 and of the Communist Party of Indonesia in 1920.

In 1919, Kartodikromo headed the progressive Union of Indonesian Journalists and published journals in Indonesian and Javanese. He was repeatedly persecuted; after the defeat of the popular uprising in 1926–27 he was exiled to West Irian. His works were written in "Low Malay," a language readily understood by the people. His naturalistic novel *The Violent One* (1914) portrays the morals of the aristocratic, "golden" youth who have come under the corrupting influence of Western civilization. The novel *The Student Hidjo* (1919) is imbued with the desire to awaken a sense of national worth in the Indonesian people. In his novel *A Feeling of Freedom* (1924) and his many short stories, Kartodikromo defended the interests of the Indonesian proletariat and peasantry who had been ravaged by capitalists.

REFERENCES
Sikorskii, V. V. *Indoneziiskaia literatura.* Moscow, 1965. Pages 59–73.
Sikorskii, V. V. "Vliianie marksistskikh idei na tvorchestvo indoneziiskikh pisatelei 10–20-x godov XX veka." *Narody Azii i Afriki,* 1970, no. 5.
Bakri Siregar. *Sedjarah sastera Indonesia modern,* part 1. Djakarta, 1964.
Soe Hok Jie. "Pahlawan jang dilupakan Mas Marco Kartodikromo." *Indonesia,* 1965, no. 2. V. V. SIKORSKII [11–1424–2]

KARTOFEL' I OVOSHCHI (Potatoes and Vegetables), the monthly scientific production journal of the Ministry of Agriculture of the USSR, founded in 1956 under the title *Kartofel'* (Potatoes). It was renamed in 1960. The journal is intended for researchers, agronomists, brigade leaders, field-team leaders, and workers at sovkhozes and kolkhozes. The journal is also read by amateur gardeners. *Kartofel' i ovoshchi* presents the scientific achievements and the experiments of advanced enterprises in potato, vegetable, and melon growing. Circulation, 66,000 (1972). [11–1442–1]

KARTS, a group of eastern Georgian tribes under whose hegemony an early class state (Kartli) was formed in Eastern Georgia in the fourth to third centuries B.C.; the state also included other Georgian tribes. [11–1445–2]

KARTSEVSKII, SERGEI OSIPOVICH. Born Aug. 28, 1884, in Tobol'sk; died Nov. 7, 1955, in Geneva. Russian linguist.

Kartsevskii spent a great part of his life in Switzerland and was one of the founders of the Geneva school of linguistics. He graduated from the University of Geneva, where he had been a student of F. de Saussure. Beginning in 1920 he taught at the University of Strasbourg and later at the universities of Prague and Geneva. His principal works deal with linguistic theory and include a descriptive grammar of Russian (*A Refresher Course in Russian,* 1928).

WORKS
"Ob asimmetrichnom dualizme lingvisticheskogo znaka." In V. A. Zvegintsev, *Istoriia iazykoznaniia XIX-XX vv. v ocherkakh i izvlecheniiakh,* part 2. Moscow, 1965.
Système du verbe russe. Prague, 1927.
"Introduction à l'étude de l'interjection." *Cahiers F. de Saussure,* 1941, no. 1.
"Sur la parataxe et la syntaxe en russe." *Cahiers F. de Saussure,* 1948, no. 7.
REFERENCES
Pospelov, N. S. "O lingvisticheskom nasledstve S. Kartsevskogo." *Voprosy iazykoznaniia,* 1957, no. 4.
Cahiers F. de Saussure, 1956, no. 14. [11–1459–4]

KARTSGANAG, an Ossetian percussion instrument. The *kartsganag* is a type of rattle, with 3–9 rectangular plates fastened loosely with a thong. When shaken the plates hit against each other, emitting a nonresonant clicking sound. [11–1459–3]

KARTULI (old name, *lekuri*), a Georgian paired folk dance. It is also known as the *lezginka.* The dance developed in Kartaliniia and Kakhetiia. The music is in 6/8 time. The dance is accompanied by an instrumental ensemble, made up of a *dudka,* a *zurna,* and a *doli.* The *kartuli* is danced in Paliashvili's operas *Daisi* and *Abesalom and Eteri.*   [11-1444-4]

KARTVELI. (1) The self-designation of the Georgians. The term was derived from the Karts—an eastern Georgian tribe. The Karts, together with the Mingrelo-Laz (Chans) and Svans, were the basis for the formation of the Georgian people.

(2) The collective name of the Kartvelian tribes of ancient Georgia.   [11-1378-2]

KARTVELIAN LANGUAGES (South Caucasian or Iberian languages), the southern group of Caucasian languages. Kartvelian languages are spoken in the Georgian SSR, in part of the Azerbaijan SSR, and also in Turkey and Iran. In the USSR there are more than 3 million speakers of Kartvelian languages (1970 census). The Kartvelian languages include the Old Georgian literary language (records from the fifth century) and the unwritten Mingrelian, Chan, and Svan languages (the closely related Mingrelian and Chan languages are joined in the Zan subgroup and are often regarded as a single Zan or Mingrelo-Chan language).

Kartvelian sound systems usually have five to seven simple vowel phonemes and 25 to 28 consonant phonemes. Stress is weakly expressed dynamic. Kartvelian morphology is characterized by well-developed declension and conjugation. Synthesism and verbal prefixation occur within the generally agglutinative morphology. There are traces in the verb of an ancient system of vocalic alternation (ablaut). The noun is marked for the categories of number (singular and plural) and case (six to nine). Declension is monotypic (diverging only in Svan). There is a system of postpositions. Transitive and intransitive and static and dynamic verbs are distinguished. The principal categories of the verb are person (the conjugation is of the multipersonal type with denotation of both subject and object), version, voice (primarily by prefixation), number, tense, and mood (by suffixation). There are 11 to 15 modal-temporal forms in the Kartvelian languages.

Types of syntactic relation include government, coordination, parataxis, and agreement. There are three basic sentence types: nominative, ergative (with transitive verbs in most tenses), and dative (with verbs of perception). The order of sentence elements is free, although the verb tends to occur at the end of a sentence. Native words and derivatives from them constitute the basic vocabulary. Word derivation is prefixal, suffixal, and—most frequently—prefixal-suffixal; compounding occurs. There are many imitative words. Borrowings have entered Kartvelian languages from Arabic, Persian, and the Turkic languages.

REFERENCES
Tsagareli, A. A. *Sravnitel'nyi obzor morfologii iberiiskoi gruppy kavkazskikh iazykov,* 2nd ed. Tbilisi, 1957.
Klimov, G. A. *Sklonenie v kartvel'skikh iazykakh v sravnitel'no-istoricheskom aspekte.* Moscow, 1962.
Klimov, G. A. *Etimologicheskii slovar' kartvel'skikh iazykov.* Moscow, 1964.
Bopp, F. *Die kaukasischen Glieder des indoeuropäischen Sprachstamms.* Berlin, 1847.
Deeters, G. *Das kharthwelische Verbum.* Leipzig, 1930.
Schmidt, K.-H. *Studien zur Rekonstruktion des Lautstandes der südkaukasischen Grundsprache.* Wiesbaden, 1962.
Ch'ik'obava, A. *Chanur-megrul-k'art'uli shedarebit'i lek'sikoni.* Tbilisi, 1938.
Ch'ik'obava, A. *Saxelis p'uzis uzvelesi agebuleba k'art'velur enebshi.* Tbilisi, 1942.
Gamqrelize, T'. *Sibilantt'a shesatqvisobani da k'art'velur enat'a uzvelesi struk'turis zogi sakit'xi.* Tbilisi, 1959.
Zhgenti, S. *K'art'velur enat'a shedarebit'i p'onetika.* Volume 1: *Marc'vlis agebulebis problema.* Tbilisi, 1960.
Rogava, G. *K'art'velur enat'a istoriuli p'onetikis sakit'xebi,* vol. 1. Tbilisi, 1962.
Martirosovi, A. *Nac'valsaxeli k'art'velur enebshi.* Tbilisi, 1964.
Gamqrelize, T'., and G. Machavariani. *Sonantt'a sistema da ablauti k'art'velur enebshi.* Tbilisi, 1965.
Machavariani, G. *Saert'o-k'art'veluri konsonanturi sistema.* Tbilisi, 1965.
   G. A. KLIMOV   [11-1378-3]

KARTVELISHVILI, LAVRENTII IOSIFOVICH (party pseudonym, Lavrent'ev). Born Apr. 16 (28), 1890; died Aug. 22, 1938. Soviet statesman and party figure. Became a member of the Communist Party in 1910. The son of a peasant.

Kartvelishvili was born in the village of Ianeti, in the present-day Georgian SSR. He first became active in the revolutionary movement in 1905. Kartvelishvili studied at the Kiev Commercial Institute from 1911 to 1914. He conducted party work in Saratov in 1915–16 and was chairman of the Kiev municipal district committee of the RSDLP (Bolshevik) in 1917–18. Kartvelishvili became a member of the Central Committee of the Communist Party (Bolshevik) of the Ukraine in July 1918. He was a member of the Odessa Oblast and municipal committees of the CP(B) of the Ukraine and a member of the Odessa revolutionary committee from late 1918 to August 1919. Kartvelishvili was a member of the Revolutionary Military Council of the southern group of the Twelfth Army in 1919 and head of the organization section of the Odessa Oblast committee and editor of the newspaper *Kommunist* in 1920. From 1921 to 1923 he was secretary of the Kiev Provincial committee of the CP(B) of the Ukraine, and from 1923 to 1928 he was secretary of the Central Committee of the CP(B) of Georgia, second secretary of the Transcaucasus Krai committee of the party, and then chairman of the Council of People's Commissars of Georgia.

In 1929 and 1930, Kartvelishvili was chief of the political directorate of the Ukrainian Military District, then becoming second secretary of the Central Committee of the CP(B) of the Ukraine. From 1931 to 1933 he was secretary of the Transcaucasus Krai committee and then secretary of the Western Siberian Krai committee of the ACP (Bolshevik) and a member of the Military Council of the Special Far Eastern Army. Kartvelishvili was secretary of the Crimean Oblast committee of the ACP(B) from January to July 1937. He was a delegate to the Tenth and Eleventh and to the Thirteenth through Seventeenth Congresses of the party. He was elected a candidate member of the Central Committee at the Sixteenth Congress.   [11-1378-1]

KARUN, a river in Iran, a left tributary of the river Shatt al-Arab. Length, 820 km (according to other data, 850 km); basin area, 60,000 sq km. It rises on the slopes of the Zard Kuh massif (Zagros Mountains). In its upper and middle course it flows through canyons and crosses intermontane basins; in its lower course it flows through the Mesopotamian Lowland. The river is characterized by spring high water caused by meltwaters; there are summer flash floods, and low water is in fall and winter. The average water discharge in the lower course is 770 cu m per sec. Part of the discharge in the upper course is channeled through tunnels to irrigate the Isfahan oasis; in the lower course it is used to irrigate the Mesopotamian Lowland. The Karun is navigable up to the city of Ahvaz, where there are rapids, and above that until the city of Shushtar.   [11-1452-1]

KARVAŠ, PETER. Born Apr. 25, 1920, in Banská Bystrica. Slovak writer and playwright. Participated in the Slovak national uprising of 1944.

Karvaš studied at Charles University in Prague and the University of Bratislava. His works were first published in 1938. The drama trilogy *The Meteor* (1945; Russian translation, 1958), *The Bastion* (1948), and *Return to Life* (1949), as well as other works, such as the dramas *Midnight Mass* (1959; Russian translation, 1960) and *Antigone and Others* (1961), novels, and short stories, are devoted to the theme of the antifascist struggle of the Slovak people. The moral and aesthetic problems of socialist society are the center of his second trilogy—*People From Our Street* (1951; Russian translation, 1960), *A Heart Full of Joy* (1954), and *Patient 113* (1955; Russian translation, 1957)—and the play *The Sore* (1963). Karvaš also writes dramatic and philosophical pamphlets, satires, stories, and humorous sketches.

WORKS
Toto pokolenie, 2nd ed. Bratislava, 1955.
Pokolenie v útoku, 2nd ed. Bratislava, 1956.

Kniha úl'avy. Bratislava, 1970.
In Russian translation:
Chert ne dremlet: Ocherki. Fel'etony. Moscow, 1957.
Sotrudnik zagrustil. Moscow, 1960. [11–1217–1]

KARVINÁ, a city in Czechoslovakia, in the Czech Socialist Republic; located in the region of Northern Moravia. Population, 77,100 (1970). It is a major center for coal mining in the Ostrava-Karviná coal basin. Industry includes the production of coke and metalworking. There is also a steam power plant. [11–1217–3]

KARYMSKAIA SOPKA, an active volcano in the Vostochnyi Range of the Kamchatka Peninsula (USSR). It is a regular truncated cone (elevation, about 1,500 m) with a crater that gives off hot gases. The volcano is located in the caldera of an ancient parent volcano (the caldera is up to 5 km in diameter). The young cone is composed of andesite-dacite lavas and ashes. Some 22 eruptions are known to have occurred since 1852. Lake Karymskoe is located in the caldera of a neighboring ancient volcano. [11–1460–4]

KARYMSKOE, an urban-type settlement and center of Karymskoe Raion, Chita Oblast, RSFSR; located on the Ingoda River (in the Amur basin). It has a railroad station on the Trans-Siberian Railway, 100 km southeast of Chita. A line to Zabaikal'sk branches off from the Tarskaia station near Karymskoe. Population, 13,000 (1970). Karymskoe has railroad transportation enterprises, a plant producing reinforced concrete items, a plant producing electrical machinery, a brickyard, and a creamery. [11–1461–1]

KARYOGAMY, the fusion of the nuclei of gametes into the nucleus of a zygote.

Karyogamy is the essence of fertilization, in which the paired nature of the homologous chromosomes carrying genetic information from the maternal and paternal gametes is restored. Karyogamy may occur immediately after the gametes fuse (for example, in the sea urchin) or, more often, somewhat later, in the metaphase of the first division. In some animals (for example, the water flea), algae, and fungi, the nuclei of the male and female draw together to form a dikaryon. [11–1274–2]

KARYOGRAM, the graphic representation of a karyotype, used in the quantitative characterization of each chromosome.

One type of karyogram is an idiogram, a rough sketch of the chromosomes arranged in rows according to length. Another type is a graph for which the coordinates are (1) lengths of the given chromosome (or a part thereof) or of the entire karyotype (for example, the relative length of the chromosomes) and (2) the so-called centromere index, that is, the ratio of the length of the short arm to that of the entire chromosome. The arrangement of each point on the karyogram reflects the distribution of the chromosomes in the karyotype. The main purpose of karyogram analysis is to detect heterogeneity in externally similar chromosomes of a given group. [11–1274–3]

KARYOLOGY, the branch of cytology that studies the structure and functions both of the cell nucleus as a whole and of its substructures (chromosomes, nucleolus, nuclear membrane), using optical and electron microscopy, cytochemistry, and isotopic indicators (mainly autoradiography).

Karyology developed at the turn of the 20th century after the cell nucleus had been found to play the major part in heredity. The main achievements of the science include the establishment of the microscopic and submicroscopic structure and behavior of the nuclear elements, both during interphase and during the various forms of nuclear division (amitosis, mitosis, meiosis, endomitosis) and the determination of the structure and mechanisms of chromosomal reproduction (reduplication). The science of cytogenetics grew out of the studies of genetics and karyology. In close contact with cytogenetics, developmental biology, and molecular biology, karyology studies the regular mechanisms of the transformations and function of the chromosomes and the individual parts thereof during the development

and differentiation of cellular systems. A current concern of karyology is the structure of chromosomes and chromosomal subunits (however, finding a method of constructing elementary chromosomal strands from nucleic acids and proteins is a concern of molecular biology).

The word "karyology" is sometimes taken to mean just one of the science's traditional fields of study: the investigation of chromosomal sets (karyotypes). Comparisons of the karyotypes of the different cells of an organism and of organisms of a single species have revealed that the karyotype is constant within a given species. The theory of evolution, together with karyosystematics (karyotaxonomy), makes use of this principle to establish the degree of kinship between closely related species, to define twin species, and to isolate new species. Human karyology has been developing rapidly since the 1950's and helping to reveal the chromosomal nature of a number of hereditary diseases and developmental anomalies in man. The international journal *Caryologia* (issued by the University of Florence since 1948) publishes articles on karyology, cytology, cytosystematics, and cytogenetics. In the USSR and abroad the findings of karyology are also published in many journals of cytology and genetics.

REFERENCES
Rukovodstvo po tsitologii, vols. 1–2. Moscow-Leningrad, 1965–66.
Raikov, I. B. *Kariologiia prosteishikh.* Leningrad, 1967.
Iu. F. Bogdanov [11–1275–3]

KARYOLYSIS, dissolution of the nucleus of a cell; the last stage of necrobiosis (following karyopyknosis and karyorrhexis) before the death of a cell. In the karyolytic nucleus the ability to be stained is lost, since the nucleic acids break down into phosphoric acid and purine bases, which do not take up basic dyes. [11–1275–2]

KARYOPLASM, karyolymph, nuclear sap, the protoplasm of a cell nucleus, separated from the surrounding cytoplasm by the nuclear membrane, or karyomembrane. [11–1276–2]

KARYOPYKNOSIS, shrinkage of a cell nucleus; one of the stages of necrobiosis preceding karyorrhexis and karyolysis.

The karyopyknotic nucleus shrinks because of a loss of water. It stains more intensively with basic dyes than does the nucleus of a normally functioning cell, since the nucleic acid, which is responsible for such staining, splits off from the nucleoproteins in the nucleus. [11–1276–1]

KARYORRHEXIS, the breakdown of a cell nucleus into parts; one of the intermediate stages of necrobiosis (after karyopyknosis and before karyolysis) that precedes the death of a cell. The nuclear membrane is destroyed and the nucleic acids show up as separate clumps in the cytoplasm. [11–1276–3]

KARYOSYSTEMATICS, karyotaxonomy, a branch of systematics that studies the structure of the cell nucleus in the various groups of organisms (taxa) in order to determine the extent of their phylogenetic kinship and to use the results to construct the natural system of a given group of organisms.

Karyosystematics developed at the point of junction between the sciences of systematics, cytology (of which karyology is a branch), and genetics. The concern of karyosystematics is usually only the structure and evolution of the karyotype; however, all characteristics of the nuclear apparatus (alternation of diploid and haploid phases, comparison of types of nuclei) are used in the classification of a number of groups of protozoans. Not only the number but also the morphology of chromosomes, the amount of DNA in the nucleus and the nucleotide composition of the DNA have taxonomic significance. In karyosystematics the chromosomes are usually studied in the metaphase of mitosis (less commonly, of meiosis, this being important in determining the causes of sterility in interspecific first-generation hybrids). Russian and Soviet scientists, such as S. G. and M. S. Navashin, G. A. Levitskii, L. N. Delone, I. I. Sokolov, B. L. Astaurov, and A. A. Prokof'eva-Bel'govskaia, have made a substantial contribution to the field.

Plant karyosystematics has been developing rapidly since the beginning of the 20th century. E. Strasburger and L. Guignard were the first to determine chromosome numbers in plants (1882). The German cytologist H. Tischler described chromosome sets in 400 plant species (1915). The concern of plant karyosystematics is usually limited to the determination of chromosome numbers because of the exceptional part played by polyploidy in plant evolution. Flowering plants have been studied in the greatest detail: by 1967, the chromosome numbers of more than 35,000 species (about 15 percent of all species of flowering plants) had been described.

Animal karyosystematics has developed more slowly, but the use of modern research techniques (tissue culture, autoradiography) has resulted in considerable progress in the 1960's and 1970's. Precise data have been obtained on the morphology of individual chromosomes, and the heterochromatin and euchromatin portions of externally similar chromosomes have been distinguished. Polyploidy occurs less widely in bisexual animals, but the karyotype is characterized by greater variety than in plants. In animals, less specialized species and genera (evolutionarily earlier) have a larger number of chromosomes, with a predominance of single-armed chromosomes in the karyotype; specialized species and genera (evolutionarily later) have fewer chromosomes, and of these, the two-armed type is predominant. A diploid karyotype is considered the original form for plants, and the polyploid karyotype is derivative. The trends of evolution of the karyotype make it possible to assess the probability of karyotype transformation in a given direction and to determine the routes of dispersal of species.

Karyosystematics is of value in detecting twin species. For example, in the black rat (*Rattus rattus*), it has been found that there are in fact twin species within what was previously considered a single species: a 38-chromosome species from Europe and Southwest Asia, brought by Europeans into America and Australia, and a 42-chromosome species from Southeast Asia. Karyosystematics has shown that all breeds of domestic sheep are descended from the mouflon and that domestic horses do come from the tarpan, although not, as once was thought, from Przhevalski's horse. The methods of karyosystematics are particularly useful in the case of taxa lying between the species level and the subfamily-family level. However, karyosystematics is of little help in differentiating intraspecific and higher taxa.

Karyosystematics has practical applications in breeding. Study of the karyotypes of the species to be bred should precede attempts at remote hybridization.

REFERENCES
Levitskii, G. A. "Morfologiia khromosom i poniatie 'kariotipa' v sistematike." *Tr. po prikladnoi botanike, genetike i selektsii,*" 1931, vol. 27, issue 1.
Vorontsov, N. N. "Znachenie izucheniia khromosomnykh naborov dlia sistematiki mlekopitaiushchikh." *Biull. Moskovskogo ob-va ispytatelei prirody: Otd. biologicheskii,*" 1958, vol. 63, No. 2.
Makino, S. *An Atlas of the Chromosome Numbers in Animals.* Ames, Iowa, 1951.
Darlington, C. D., and A. P. Wylie. *Chromosome Atlas of Flowering Plants.* London, 1955.
Hsu, T. Ch., and K. Benirschke. *An Atlas of Mammalian Chromosomes,* vols. 1–6. Berlin–Heidelberg–New York, 1967–71.
Stebbins, L. *Chromosomal Evolution in Higher Plants.* London, 1971.
N. N. VORONTSOV [11–1276–4]

KARYOTYPE, chromosome set, the aggregate features of the chromosomes (number, size, shape, details of microscopic structure) in the cells of an organism of a given species.

The concept of the karyotype was introduced by the Soviet geneticist G. A. Levitskii in 1924. The karyotype is one of the most important genetic characteristics of a species, since every species has a particular karyotype that is different from that of related species (karyosystematics, a new branch of systematics, is based on this phenomenon). The fixed nature of the karyotype in the cells of a given organism is ensured by mitosis and, within a given species, by meiosis. The karyotype of an organism may change if the gametes are altered by mutation. The karyotype of individual cells sometimes differs from the species karyotype because of chromosomal or genomic somatic mutations. The karyotype of diploid cells consists of two haploid sets (genomes) from each parent; each chromosome of such a set has a homologue from the other set. The karyotype of males may differ from that of females in the shape (sometimes also in number) of the sex chromosomes, in which case they are described separately.

The chromosomes in a karyotype are studied during the metaphase stage of mitosis. The description of a karyotype must be accompanied by a microphotograph or sketch. In systematizing karyotypes, the pairs of homologous chromosomes are arranged (for example) in order of decreasing length, beginning with the longest pair. The pairs of sex chromosomes are put at the end of the series. Pairs of chromosomes of equal length are identified by the position of the centromere (primary constriction), which divides the chromosome into two arms, by the position of the nucleolar organizer (secondary constriction), and by the shape of the satellite. The karyotypes of several thousand species of plants (wild and cultivated) and animals and man have been studied.

REFERENCES
Rukovodstvo po tsitologii, vol. 2. Edited by A. S. Troshin. Moscow-Leningrad, 1966.
Lobashev, M. E. *Genetika,* 2nd ed. Leningrad, 1967.
IU. F. BOGDANOV [11–1277–2]

KAS, a river in Krasnoiarsk Krai, RSFSR; a left-bank tributary of the Enisei (before merging with the Malyi Kas, called the Bol'shoi Kas). Length, 464 km; basin area, 11,200 sq km.

The Kas flows along the eastern edge of the Western Siberian Plain. It is fed by a mixture of sources, with a predominance of snow. The average water discharge 197 km from its mouth is 53 cu m per sec. The high-water period extends from May through June. The Kas freezes over at the beginning of November and thaws out in mid-May. Together with its left-bank tributary, the Malyi Kas, it was part of the Ob'-Enisei waterway, which connected the Kas with the Ket' River. [11–1466–2]

KASACK, HERMANN. Born July 24, 1896, in Potsdam; died Jan. 10, 1966, in Stuttgart. West German writer.

Kasack was a philosopher by education. The early expressionistic lyricism of his work, exemplified by the play *Tragic Mission* (1917; published in 1920) and the collection of verse *Man* (1918), was later replaced by speculative poetry, strict in form and full of mysticism. The latter is found in the collections *Eternal Truth* (1943) and *Watermark* (1964). His novels *The City Beyond the River* (1947) and *The Big Net* (1952) were close in style to those of Kafka. Kasack's novellas *The Cloth Machine* (1949) and *The Forgeries* (1953) were strongly antifascist and dealt with the theme of the degradation of man in capitalist society, although their social criticism was blunted by the influence of existentialism. Kasack's other work included a collection of essays entitled *Mosaic* (1956). In 1949 he was awarded the Fontane Prize.

WORKS
Das unbekannte Ziel, Ausgewählte Proben und Arbeiten. Frankfurt-am-Main, 1963.
In Russian translation:
"Mekhanicheskii dvoinik." *Sovetskaia kul'tura,* Nov. 3, 1960.
REFERENCE
Bader, I. M. *Die Maske in H. Kasacks erzählender Dichtung.* Berlin, 1965.
G. V. KHOVRINA [11–389–6]

KASAI (called the Kwa near its mouth), a river in Central Africa, flowing through Angola and the Republic of Zaïre; the largest left-bank tributary of the Congo River. Length, about 2,000 km. Basin area, 880,200 sq km.

The Kasai rises on the Lunda plateau and descends from its northern slopes to the Congo valley, forming rapids and waterfalls. In several places in the lower course it becomes as wide as a lake (up to 5–6 km wide). The main tributaries are the Lulua, Sankuru, and Fimi-Lukenie from the right and the Kwango from the left. The river is fed mainly by rain, but subsurface water is also important. The water level rises from September or October to April and is lowest in August. The discharge in the lower course is 5,000–20,000 cu m per sec, with an average annual discharge of about 10,000 cu m per sec. The Kasai is navigable for 790 km from its mouth. It is a most important water transportation artery of the Congo basin. There is fishing on the river. The Kasai basin is a major region of diamond mining. Three hydroelectric power plants with a combined capacity of 9.8 megawatts operate in the diamond-mining regions. [11–1468–2]

KASAKH (also Aparanchai), a river in the Armenian SSR, a left tributary of the Sevdzhur (Araks basin). Length, 89 km; basin area, 1,480 sq km. It rises on the northern slope of Mount Aragats and flows primarily through its eastern foothills. The river is used extensively for irrigation. The Aparan Reservoir is located in the upper reaches of the Kasakh, and the city of Ashtarak is situated on the river. [11–1473–2]

KASAN, a city (prior to 1972, a *kishlak*, or hamlet), the center of the Kasan Raion, Kashkadar'ia Oblast, Uzbek SSR. Located on the river bank of the Kashkadar'ia River, on the Karshi-Bukhara highway, 4 km from the Kasan railroad station (on the Kagan-Termez line) and 30 km northwest of Karshi. Population, 24,000 (1972). Kasan has two cotton mills, a porcelain factory, a brickworks, a brewery, and a vegetable-oil extraction plant. [11–1469–2]

KASANSAI, an urban-type settlement in Chust Raion, Namangan Oblast, Uzbek SSR. Kasansai is situated on the Kasansai River (a tributary of the Syr Darya), 28 km northwest of the city of Namangan, with which it is linked by highway. Population, 14,200 (1970). Kasansai has a vegetable and dairy sovkhoz and a silk-weaving mill. [11–1470–2]

KASANSAI (in its upper course, the Chalkidysai), a river located in the Kirghiz SSR and the Uzbek SSR, a right tributary of the Syr Darya River. Its length is 127 km; its basin area is 1,780 sq km. The river rises on the southern slope of the Chatkal Range. It flows at first through a narrow mountain valley; in its lower course it enters the Fergana Valley. The average annual discharge at the *kishlak* (hamlet) of Baimak (52 km from the river's mouth) is 11.6 cu m per sec. Below Baimak water is diverted for irrigation. Located on the Kasansai River is the Orto-Tokoi Reservoir. [11–1470–1]

KASATKIN, IVAN MIKHAILOVICH. Born Mar. 30 (Apr. 11), 1880; died May 13, 1938. Soviet Russian writer.

Kasatkin was born to a poor peasant family in the village of Baranovitsy, in present-day Kologriv Raion, Kostroma Oblast. He was first published in 1907. His first book of short stories was *A Forest Story* (1916). During the 1920's and 1930's, Kasatkin was the editor of the journals *Krasnaia niva* (Red Cornfield) and *Zemlia sovetskaia* (Soviet Land). The life of the Russian peasantry was the main theme of his short stories.

WORKS
Sobr. soch., vols. 1–3. [Preface by I. Kubikov.] Moscow, 1928–29.
Izbrannye rasskazy. [Preface by V. Ivanov.] Moscow, 1957.
Derevenskie rasskazy. [Introduction by Vl. Lidin.] Moscow, 1967.

REFERENCE
Istoriia russkoi literatury kontsa XIX–nach. XX v.: Bibliograficheskii ukazatel'. Moscow-Leningrad, 1963. [11–1472–4]

KASATKIN, NIKOLAI ALEKSEEVICH. Born Dec. 13 (25), 1859, in Moscow; died there Dec. 17, 1930. Russian painter. People's Artist of the Republic (1923).

Kasatkin studied at the Moscow School of Painting, Sculpture, and Architecture (1873–83) under V. G. Perov and later taught there (1894–1917). His pupils included B. V. Ioganson and V. V. Meshkov. He was a full member of the St. Petersburg Academy of Arts (1903). He joined the *peredvizhiki* ("wanderers"—a progressive art movement) in 1891 and the Association of Artists of Revolutionary Russia (AKhRR) in 1922.

In his early period (late 1880's and early 1890's), Kasatkin executed genre pictures typical of the late *peredvizhnik* style: *Female Rivals* (1890, Tret'iakov Gallery) and *Slander* (1893, Russian Museum, Leningrad). In the 1890's, after trips to the

Donbas (1894 and 1895), Kasatkin created his most significant works; he was one of the first Russian artists to address himself to the theme of the daily life and labor of the proletariat.

In his studies and pictures with their simple yet expressive composition and an earthy gray palette, Kasatkin embodied the bright characters of the Russian workers with fervent sympathy; he truthfully rendered not only the exhausting labor and poverty of the proletariat but also the rising spirit of protest and struggle in the workers (*The Woman Miner*, 1894, and *Coal Miners: The Shift*, 1895; both in the Tret'iakov Gallery). He also created a number of works devoted to the Revolution of 1905–07: *The Fighting Worker* (1905) and *The Attack on the Factory by the Women Workers* (1906), both in the Museum of the Revolution of the USSR, Moscow.

In the Soviet period, Kasatkin worked on pictures with a historical-revolutionary theme; he aspired to create the image of the new Soviet man, as in *To Her Studies: A Young Pioneer With Her Books* (1926) and *The Rural Correspondent* (1927), both in the Museum of the Revolution of the USSR.

REFERENCES
N. A. Kasatkin (1859–1930): Katalog vystavki. Moscow, 1953.
Sitnik, K. A. *N. A. Kasatkin.* Moscow, 1955.
V. M. PETIUSHENKO [11–1472–5]

KASATKIN, VIKTOR IVANOVICH. Born Sept. 16 (28), 1831, in Moscow; died Dec. 16 (28), 1867, in Geneva. Russian revolutionary and man of letters. Son of a merchant.

Kasatkin published and contributed to the journal *Bibliograficheskie zapiski* (1858–62). In 1859 he became a correspondent of the Free Russian Printing House in London. He was a member of Moscow revolutionary circles and of the Land and Liberty group of the 1860's. From June 1862 he was one of the leaders of the Land and Liberty Printing House in Bern (1862–63) and organized the smuggling of revolutionary publications into Russia. Kasatkin was a defendant *in absentia* at the Trial of the Thirty-Two (1862–65) and was sentenced to exile from Russia.

REFERENCES
Herzen, A. I. *Sobr. soch. v 30 tt.* Moscow, 1954–66. (See index.)
Eidel'man, N. Ia. *Tainye korrespondenty "Poliarnoi zvezdy."* Moscow, 1966. [11–1472–3]

KASATONOV, VLADIMIR AFANAS'EVICH. Born July 8 (21), 1910, in Peterhof, now Petrodvorets, Leningrad Oblast. Soviet military commander, admiral of the fleet (1965), Hero of the Soviet Union (Nov. 25, 1966). Member of the CPSU since 1939.

The son of a worker, Kasatonov joined the navy in 1927. He graduated from the M. V. Frunze Naval School in 1931, from the course preparing commanders at the S. M. Kirov Submarine Training Center in 1932, and from the Naval Academy in 1941. After serving as deputy commander and commander of a submarine from 1933 to 1938 and as commander of a submarine division of the Pacific Fleet from 1938 to 1940, Kasatonov worked on the Chief Naval Staff from 1941 to 1945 and held staff positions in the Baltic Fleet and on the General Staff from 1945 to 1949. He has held the posts of first deputy commander and chief of staff of the Pacific Fleet (from 1949), commander of the Red Banner Baltic Fleet (from 1954), commander of the Black Sea Fleet (from 1955), commander of the Northern Fleet (from 1962), and first deputy commander in chief of the Navy (from June 1964). He was elected a deputy of the fifth through eighth convocations of the Supreme Soviet of the USSR and has been awarded three Orders of Lenin, the Order of the Red Banner, the Order of the Patriotic War First Class, the Order of Nakhimov Second Class, two Orders of the Red Banner of Labor, two Orders of the Red Star, and medals. [11–1473–1]

KASH, a river in western China; right tributary of the Ili. Length, about 350 km; basin area, more than 10,000 sq km. The river's sources are located in the Iren-Khabyrga massif (Eastern Tien-Shan); for the most part, it flows through the longitudinal valley between the Borohoro and Avral-Ula ranges, in places through inaccessible gorges. The Kash is fed by snows and glaciers; highwater is during the summer. The average water discharge in the lower reaches is 127 m³/sec, with a maximum of more than 700 m³/sec. The river is used for irrigation.

[11–1648–4]

KASHAN, a city in the central part of Iran, in the *ostan* (province) of Tehran. Population, 62,000 (1971). Railroad station.

Kashan was the largest artistic center of medieval Iran. It is known for the production of lustrine pottery, carpets, and fabrics. Architectural monuments of the 11th through 17th centuries include the Meydan Mosque (1224, rebuilt in 1463), the Zeyn al-Din Minaret (1073), and the mausoleum of Imam-zadeh Habib ibn Musa (1269–72), with the tomb of Shah Abbas I (1629).

[11–1649–3]

KASHAN (also Kash), a river in Mary Oblast, Turkmen SSR, and in Afghanistan; left tributary of the Murghab. Length, 252 km; basin area, about 7,000 sq km. Rises in the Paropamisus Mountains (the Safed Koh Range) and flows mainly to the north. It is fed by a mixture of sources, with snow predominating. The principal flow is in the spring, with a maximum in March. The average discharge 4 km from the river's mouth is 1.4 cu m per sec. Water from the Kashan is widely used for irrigation. The river is usually dry from June to October.

[11–1649–2]

KASHCHENKO, NIKOLAI FEOFANOVICH. Born Apr. 25 (May 7), 1855, on the Veselyi farmstead, in present-day Zaporozh'e Oblast; died Mar. 29, 1935, in Kiev. Soviet biologist; academician of the Academy of Sciences of the Ukrainian SSR (1919).

Kashchenko graduated from the University of Kharkov in 1880. In 1888 he became a professor and, in 1895, rector of the University of Tomsk. In 1912 he became a professor at the Kiev Polytechnical Institute. Between 1913 and 1935 he was the director of the acclimatization garden of the Academy of Sciences of the Ukrainian SSR in Kiev. He was also the organizer and director of the zoological museum of the Academy of Sciences of the Ukrainian SSR (1919–26). His principal works dealt with embryology (he showed that mesenchyme forms not only from mesoderm but also from ectoderm, that is, ectomesenchyme) and human pathological embryology. Kashchenko also did research on Siberian fauna (particularly mammalian) and on the acclimatization of fruit and other plants under the conditions of Siberia and the Ukraine.

REFERENCE
Izvestiia AN SSSR: Seriia biologicheskaia, 1951, no. 4. (Dedicated to Kashchenko; includes a list of his works.) [11–1668–2]

KASHCHENKO, PETR PETROVICH. Born Dec. 28, 1858 (Jan. 9, 1859), in Eisk, in present-day first Krasnodar Krai; died Feb. 19, 1920, in Moscow. Russian psychiatrist and public figure.

In 1881, Kashchenko was expelled from Moscow University for revolutionary activity and exiled from the city. In 1885 he graduated from the medical department of the University of Kazan. From 1889 to 1904 he was director of the psychiatric hospital of the Nizhny Novgorod *zemstvo* (district assembly) in Liakhovo colony. As director of the Moscow Psychiatric Hospital from 1904 to 1906 and the St. Petersburg Psychiatric Hospital from 1907 to 1917 (they both now bear his name), Kashchenko transformed both into model medical institutions. In 1905 he participated in revolutionary events in Moscow. He was the organizer and chairman of the first Russian Central Statistical Bureau for the Registration of Psychiatric Patients. In May 1917, Kashchenko became head of the neuropsychiatric section of the Council of Medical Boards, and from 1918 to 1920 he directed the neuropsychiatric care subdivision of the People's Commissariat of Public Health of the RSFSR. Kashchenko developed the principles of organization for the treatment of the mentally ill in Russia and advanced a number of progressive ideas (the need for outpatient care, the organization of patronage, the no-restraint system, occupational therapy).

WORKS
Statisticheskii ocherk polozheniia dushevnobol'nykh v Nizhegorodskoi gubernii. Nizhny Novgorod, 1895.
Blizhaishie zadachi v dele popecheniia o dushevnobol'nykh v Rossii. Moscow [1911].
Istoricheskii ocherk postroiki . . . bol'nitsy dlia dushevnobol'nykh S.-Peterburgskogo gubernskogo zemstva. St. Petersburg, 1912.
REFERENCES
Iudin, T. *Ocherki istorii psikhiatrii.* Moscow, 1951.
Andreev, A. L. "P. P. Kashchenko i ego rol' v otechestvennoi psikhiatrii." *Zhurnal nevropatologii i psikhiatrii im. S. S. Korsakova,* 1959, vol. 59, issue 3. M. I. ARUIN [11–1669–1]

KASHCHENKO, VSEVOLOD PETROVICH. Born Mar. 21 (Apr. 2), 1870; died Nov. 30, 1943. Soviet defectologist; one of the first organizers of higher defectological education and scientific research in defectology in the USSR.

Kashchenko was admitted to the medical department of Moscow University in 1891, but in 1894 he was expelled for his involvement in student revolutionary circles and exiled from Moscow. He graduated from the medical department of the University of Kiev in 1897. Deprived of his right to hold state and public positions because of political "unreliability," in 1908 he opened a private school-sanatorium, one of the first institutions for abnormal children in Moscow. In 1918 the Home for the Study of Children was organized, an expansion of the former school; soon thereafter the home was converted to the Medical-Pedagogical Experimental Station. From 1920 through 1924, Kashchenko was a professor and rector of the Pedagogical Institute for the Problems of Abnormal Children in Moscow. During the last years of his life, Kashchenko was concerned with the problems of logopedics.

Kashchenko attempted to reduce or overcome developmental deficiencies in abnormal children through medical and pedagogical means. He based the processes of education and upbringing on methods that would contribute to the child's maximum activity and independence and on the instillment of a desire to rectify the shortcomings in their behavior. He stressed that it is not the amount of knowledge that is important for abnormal children, but rather the quality of that knowledge, its vitality, and its role in developing the cognitive capacities of the student.

WORKS
Defektivnye deti i shkola. Edited by V. P. Kashchenko. Moscow, 1912. (Collection of articles.)
Vospitanie-obuchenie trudnykh detei. Moscow, 1913. (Jointly with S. Kriukov.)
Putem tvorchestva. A collection edited by V. P. Kashchenko. Moscow, 1922.
REFERENCES
Azbukin, D. I. "Obshchestvenno-pedagogicheskaia deiatel'nost' V. P. Kashchenko do i posle Velikoi Oktiabr'skoi sotsialisticheskoi revoliutsii." *Uch. zap. Moskovskogo gos. ped. in-ta im. V. I. Lenina,* 1947, vol. 49, pp. 101–109.
Zamskii, Kh. S. "Vrachebno-pedagogicheskaia deiatel'nost' professora V. P. Kashchenko i ee rol' v razvitii vspomogatel'noi shkoly SSSR." *Uch. zap. MGPI im. V. I. Lenina, Defektologicheskii fak-t,* 1959, vol. 131, issue 7. [11–1668–1]

KASHEVAROV, ALEKSANDR FILIPPOVICH. Born Dec. 28, 1809, on Kodiak Island; died Sept. 25 (Oct. 7), 1870. Russian naval officer, captain of the first rank, and hydrographer. Explorer of northwestern America.

Kashevarov graduated from the Kronstadt Pilots' School in 1828 and served in the Russian American Company from 1831 to 1843. In 1838 he led a hydrographic expedition that explored the eastern coast of the Chukchi Sea from Kotzebue Sound to a point 50 km east of Point Barrow; he was the first to describe the section of coastline from 156° to 166°W longitude. From 1845 to 1850 and from 1857 to 1862 he worked in the Hydrographic Department of the Ministry of the Navy and compiled the *Atlas of the Eastern Ocean,* which described the Sea of Okhotsk and the Bering Sea (1862). From 1850 to 1856, Kashevarov was head of the port of Aian on the Sea of Okhotsk.

REFERENCE

Zagoskin, L. *Puteshestviia i issledovaniia v Russkoi Amerike v 1842–1844 gg.* Moscow, 1956. [11–1650–6]

KASHEVAROVA-RUDNEVA, VARVARA ALEKSAN-DROVNA. Born in 1842 in Vitebsk; died Apr. 29 (May 11), 1899, in Staraia Russa. Russian scientist; the first woman in Russia to receive the title of physician and the degree of doctor of medicine.

Kashevarova-Rudneva graduated from the Midwife's Institute of the St. Petersburg Foundling Home in 1862. Subsequently she took courses on the diagnosis and treatment of syphilis at Kalinkin Hospital in St. Petersburg. In 1863 she obtained permission from the minister of war to enroll in the Medical and Surgical Academy, from which she graduated in 1868 with the diploma of "distinguished physician" and a gold medal. In 1876 she defended her doctoral dissertation (*Materials Toward a Pathological Anatomy of the Vagina*), in which vaginal sarcomas were described for the first time. She began working in the clinic of S. P. Botkin. Despite her academic degree, Kashevarova-Rudneva was not permitted to participate in scientific and pedagogical activities. She had a medical practice in St. Petersburg, Zheleznovodsk, and Voronezh Province. Kashevarova-Rudneva was also the author of fiction (including the autobiographical novella *Pioneer*, 1886).

WORKS

"K ucheniiu o pliatsentarnykh polipakh." *Zhurnal dlia normal'noi i patologicheskoi gistologii i klinicheskoi meditsiny,* September-October, 1873.
Gigiena zhenskogo organizma vo vsekh fazisakh zhizni, 2d ed. St. Petersburg, 1892.

REFERENCES

Dionesov, S. M. *V. A. Kashevarova-Rudneva—pervaia russkaia zhenshchina–doktor meditsiny.* Moscow, 1965.
Zabludovskaia, E. D. *V. A. Kashevarova-Rudneva.* Moscow, 1965.

M. I. Aruin [11–1651–1]

KASHGAR, a city in western China, in the Sinkiang-Uighur Autonomous Region, located on the Kashgar River in the center of a large oasis in the southern foothills of the Tien-Shan. Population, 90,800 (1953). The city consists of two parts—Shifu and Shule. Kashgar was a transport center on an ancient trade route. It is now an important economic center, with agricultural machine-building and textile, flour-milling, and ceramics enterprises. The handicrafts industry is also well developed. A hydroelectric power plant is located in the city. [11–1650–2]

KASHGAR (Kyzylsu), a river in western China and in the USSR, with its upper course in the Tadzhik and Kirghiz Soviet Socialist Republics. The Kashgar is 765 km long (including 685 km in China) and drains an area (together with the Gezdar'ia River) of 90,800 sq km. It rises in the slopes of the Alai and Trans-Alai ranges and has a mountain character in its upper course. The lower Kashgar flows through the Kashgar Plain, watering a large oasis of over 2,500 sq km. The average discharge in the lower course is 77 cu m per sec, with a maximum of approximately 500 cu m per sec. There are summer floods with considerable sediment discharge. The Kashgar previously flowed into the Yarkand but now is lost in the sands of Tograkkum. The city of Kashgar is located on it. [11–1650–1]

KASHGAR MOUNTAINS (Kungur Muztagh), a mountain range in China, the western terminus of the Kunlun Mountains, located between the Gezdar'ia and Tashkurgan rivers. The range is approximately 100 km long; its highest peaks are Mount Kungur (7,579 m) and Muztagata (7,555 m). Elevations of 5,000–6,000 m predominate. The range is formed primarily of gneisses, granites, and quartzites. It has sharp ridges, rocky steep slopes, and deep gorges. The area of glaciation is more than 600 sq km. In the north are mountain steppes; in the south and east, semideserts and deserts; and in the river valleys, *tugai* vegetation (bottomland complex with forests, bushes, and meadows). [11–1650–4]

KASHGAR PLAIN (Tarim Basin), a plain in Western China, bounded by the Tieu-Shan and the Pamir, Kunlun, and Pei mountains. Its length from west to east is about 1,200 km, and its width is as much as 500 km. The elevation ranges from 1,500 m in the west to 780 m in the east, near Lake Lob Nor.

Most of the Kashgar Plain is occupied by the sandy Takla-Makan Desert. Located in the foothills of the mountains are gently sloping talus trains, formed by pebble beds and sand-clay deposits. In the depressions of the terrain there are extensive solonchaks. In the west there are low, isolated ridges, formed by sedimentary rocks. The climate is moderate (warm, sharply continental, and desert). The summers are hot (with an average temperature in July of 25° or 26°C); winters are brief, with temperatures as low as −20°C but without snow. Precipitation amounts to less than 100 mm annually, with the maximum during the summer. There are mountain rivers; when they emerge onto the Kashgar Plain, they frequently dry up or are diverted for irrigation. The largest rivers are the Tarim, Khotan, Kashgar, Aksu, and Konchedar'ia. The Tarim and Konchedar'ia in their lower courses frequently change their river beds, thus causing shifts in the position of Lake Lob Nor. Most of the Kashgar Plain is covered by desert vegetation growing on sierozem soils. In the river valleys there is tugai vegetation (bottomland complex with forests, bushes, and meadows); in the oases on the piedmont plains there is agriculture and the cultivation of orchards. There are oases in the west and northwest (at the cities of Kashgar, Aksu, and Yarkand). In a more limited sense the name "Kashgar Plain" denotes the delta region of the left tributaries of the Yarkand River.

M. P. Petrov [11–1650–3]

KASHGARS (Kashgarlyks), a name designating the Uighurs who live in the Kashgar oasis (Sinkiang Province, China). During the 19th and early 20th centuries in Central Asia the term "Kashgars" was also used to designate those Uighurs who had migrated from the Kashgar oasis to Fergana Valley in the 19th century. [11–1650–5]

KASHI, JAMSHID IBN MASUD AL-. Year of birth unknown; died circa 1436–37. Mathematician and astronomer.

Al-Kashi worked from about 1420 to 1430 at the Samarkand Observatory of Ulug Beg. In his work *Key of Arithmetic* (1427) he set forth techniques for extracting roots based on the application of the binomial formula to integral powers. He also introduced decimal fractions into use and described their rules of operation. Al-Kashi proposed a method for the approximate solution of third-degree equations. In his *Treatise on the Circle* (c. 1427) he computed a value for the number π accurate to 17 decimal places. [11–1653–1]

KASHIN, DANIIL NIKITICH. Born 1770; died December 1841 in Moscow. Russian composer, painist, violinist, conductor, teacher, and compiler of folk songs.

A serf of G. I. Bibikov, Kashin was first trained in Bibikov's orchestra; he later studied with the Italian composer G. Sarti, who was working in Russia at the time. Kashin was freed in 1799. He was the first Russian musician to perform many times in Moscow and St. Petersburg, both as a pianist and as a conductor. Between 1833 and 1834 he published three collections of *Russian Folk Songs* for voice and piano. His musical arrangements were close to the music of art songs. He composed the operas *Natal'ia, the Boyar's Daughter* (1880) and *Olga the Beautiful* (1809), instrumental and vocal works, choral works, and songs. During the Patriotic War of 1812 he wrote a number of popular patriotic songs, such as *Song to the Don Warriors* and *The Defenders of the Town of Peter.* He published *Zhurnal otechestvennoi muzyki* (The Journal of Music of the Fatherland), a journal of music notes. In 1840 he organized the Music Class in Moscow. [11–1653–4]

KASHIN, a city in Kalinin Oblast, RSFSR. It is situated on the Kashinka River, a tributary of the Volga, and has a railroad station on the Kaliazin-Sonkovo line, 204 km from Moscow. Population, 18,000 (1970).

Kashin is first mentioned in the chronicles in 1238. About 1300 it became the patrimony of Prince Dmitrii Borisovich, a descendant of the princes of Rostov. The city was annexed by the Principality of Tver' in 1382, and as part of that principality it was annexed by the Principality of Moscow in 1486. In 1708, Kashin became part of Ingermanland Province and in 1719, of St. Petersburg Province. In 1775 it was the center of the Tver' *namestnichestvo* (vicegerency) and in 1796 of Tver' Province.

Kashin has a flax-processing plant, a dairy, a factory manufacturing felt boots and clothing, a meat-packing combine, and a plant producing electrical equipment. A veterinary technicum, a medical school, and a museum of local lore are located here. Architectural monuments include the St. Dmitrii Monastery (Troitsa Church, 1682), the Klobukov Monastery (Pokrovskaia Church and cells of the 17th–18th centuries), and the Sretenskii Monastery; the wooden Church of SS. Joachim and Anne (17th–19th centuries); the Vkhodoierusalimskaia Church and the Church of SS. Peter and Paul of the late 18th century; and the Voskresenskii Cathedral (completed in 1817). Since the late 18th century, Kashin has been built according to a planned layout. Other noteworthy buildings are the Assembly House (18th century), government offices and market arcades (early 19th century), and residential buildings of the 19th century.

Kashin is a balneological and mud-bath resort. It has peat mud and, for drinking, sulfate-chloride mineral water of the magnesium-calcium sodium type (from a depth of 117 m, well no. 12) with a chemical composition:

$$M_{2.8} \frac{SO_4 82 \; Cl17}{Mg39 \; Ca30 \; (Na + K) \; 30} \; T \; 7°C \; pH \; 7.6$$

Chloride-sulfate magnesium-sodium waters (from a depth of 302–384 m, well no. 14) and chloride sodium-calcium waters (from a depth of 614–640 m, well no. 22) are used for baths. Illnesses treated include muscular and bone diseases, disorders of the digestive organs, gynecological conditions, and diseases of the peripheral nervous system. Among the city's health facilities are a sanatorium, a water and mud-bath hospital, and a polyclinic.   [11–1654–1]

KASHIRA, a city in Moscow Oblast, RSFSR, situated on the high right bank of the Oka River. There is a landing on the river. Kashira is a station on the Moscow-Donbas trunk line, 109 km south of Moscow. Population, 39,000 (1970).

Kashira was founded in the 14th century. It was registered as part of Moscow Province in 1708 and remained so until 1777, when it became the district city of Tula *namestnichestvo* (viceroyalty); it became the district city of Tula Province in 1796. There is a *gorodishche* (site of a fortified town) dating from the Iron Age in Kashira. The Kashira State Regional Electric Power Plant is located in the city. Plants producing metal structures, furniture, and hosiery, as well as a shipyard and the Isentrolit Plant, are located in the city. There is also an evening power engineering technicum and an experimental combine producing cardboard and paper products.

REFERENCE
Prusakov, A. P. *Gorod Kashira*. [Moscow] 1947.   [11–1655–1]

KASHIRA GORODISHCHE, one of the most ancient (seventh–fourth centuries B.C.) sites of a fortified town of the D'iakovo culture. Located in the city of Kashira, Moscow Oblast, on the right bank of the Oka River, it was investigated by V. A. Gorodtsov in 1925–26. The town had been reinforced by an earthen bank, a moat, and an oak stockade. Approximately 22 round semisubterranean dwellings were discovered with centrally located stone hearths. Also found were articles made of clay (vessels, a distaff), bone (arrows, harpoons), iron (knives, sickles), and bronze (ornaments), as well as beads that had been brought from the south. The population of ancient Kashira consisted of a clan-type, patriarchal community. The principal occupation was stock raising; the secondary occupations were hunting and fishing. Hoe farming was not important.

REFERENCE
Gorodtsov, V. A. "Starshee Kashirskoe gorodishche (rezul'taty arkheologicheskikh issledovanii v 1925–1926 gg.)." *Izvestiia Gosudarstvennoi Akademii istorii material'noi kul'tury*, 1933, issue 85.
[11–1656–1]

KASHIRA STATE REGIONAL ELECTRIC POWER PLANT (full name, G. M. Krzhizhanovskii Kashira State Regional Electric Power Plant), one of the first Soviet regional steam power plants to be built in accordance with the plan of GOELRO (State Commission for the Electrification of Russia). It is located in Kashira, Moscow Oblast, and is a part of the Mosenergo system. The construction of the plant, to which V. I. Lenin attached great importance, was begun in April 1919.

The first plant, with two turbine units of 6 megawatts (MW) each, was put into service in 1922. Subsequently the plant was repeatedly enlarged. By 1932 its capacity of 186 MW made it the largest steam power plant in the USSR. After the addition of a number of units, including three having a power of 300 MW each in 1967–68, the rated capacity of the plant reached 1,166 MW. Provision has been made for the installation of another three units of 300 MW each.

The plant operates on two types of fuel: the 300-MW power units use coal from the Donbas and seasonal surpluses of natural gas; the other units use coal from the Moscow Area Coal Basin. The plant was awarded the Order of Lenin (1939) and the Order of the Red Banner of Labor (1945).   [11–1655–4]

KASHIRIN, NIKOLAI DMITRIEVICH. Born Feb. 4 (16), 1888; died June 14, 1938. Soviet military commander, army commander second class (1935). Member of the CPSU from 1918.

Kashirin was born in the city of Verkhneural'sk, the son of a cossack teacher who subsequently became the ataman of a *stanitsa* (large cossack village). He graduated from the Orenburg Junker School in 1909, served in the cavalry units of the Orenburg Cossack Host, fought in World War I, and was awarded six orders and rose to the rank of *pod"esaul* (a cossack rank equivalent to staff captain). Elected chairman of a cossack regiment committee in 1917, Kashirin formed a cossack volunteer detachment in Verkhneural'sk in 1918 and fought against Dutov's armies. On July 16, 1918, he was elected chief commander of the Urals Partisan Army, which operated behind the lines of the Whites in the southern Urals; after he was wounded, he became assistant to the chief commander V. K. Bliukher. Assistant chief and chief of the 4th Urals Division (later the 30th Rifle Division) from September 1918, Kashirin was appointed in 1919 commandant of the Orenburg Fortified Area and chief of the 49th Fortress Division of the Turkestan Front and in 1920 commander of the III Cavalry Corps on the Southern Front and commander of the Aleksandrovsk Troop Group to fight the Makhno movement.

From 1923 to 1925 Kashirin was commander of the XIV Rifle Corps, an officer on the staff of the Red Army for especially important assignments, and commander of the I Cavalry Corps of the Red Cossacks. Assistant commander of several military districts from 1925 to 1931, Kashirin was commander of the troops of the Northern Caucasus Military District from 1931 to 1937 and a member of the Military Council of the People's Commissariat of Defense of the USSR from 1934. Kashirin was awarded two Orders of the Red Banner and the Honorary Revolutionary Weapon. In 1960 a monument to Kashirin was erected in Verkhneural'sk.   [11–1655–2]

KASHIWA, a city in Japan, on Honshu Island, in Chiba Prefecture. Population, 150,600 (1970). The city has enterprises of the food-processing (beer; meat and dairy products), textile (woolen fabrics), and machine-building industries.   [11–1474–3]

KASHKADAR'IA (at its source, the Shin'gasoi; in its lower course, the Maimanakdar'ia), a river in the Uzbek SSR. Length, 378 km; basin area, 8,780 sq km.

The Kashkadar'ia rises in the western spurs of the Zeravshan and Gissar mountains. Below the village of Duab it flows in a broad valley and receives from the left a number of tributaries, many of which have a greater rate of stream flow than the Kashkadar'ia itself. The principal tributaries are the Aksu, Tankhazdar'ia, Iakkabagdar'ia (Kyzyldar'ia), and the Guzardar'ia. The river is fed by snow and rain. Its high-water period occurs in spring; during the summer the river has little water. The average discharge as it issues from the mountains (266 km from the mouth) is 24.9 cu m per sec. Its waters are used extensively for irrigation, and beyond the Karshi Oasis the river bed gradually disappears. The Kashkadar'ia is fed by the waters of the Zeravshan by means of the Eskiankhor Canal. Located on the Kashkadar'ia is the Chim Kurgan Reservoir, and on the Guzardar'ia is the Pachkamarskoe Reservoir.   [11–1660–1]

KASHKADAR'IA OBLAST, a part of the Uzbek SSR. Formed on Feb. 7, 1964. Located in southern Uzbekistan. Area, 28,400 sq km; population, 857,000 (1972). The oblast is divided into ten raions and has three cities and four urban-type settlements. Its center is the city of Karshi. Kashkadar'ia Oblast was awarded the Order of Lenin on Sept. 14, 1967.

Natural features. Kashkadar'ia Oblast is situated in the basin of the Kashkadar'ia river and on the western edge of the Pamir-Alai mountain system. Most of the oblast consists of a plain: the Karshi Steppe in the northwest, the Nishan Steppe in the south, and the sands of the Sundukli in the southwest. On the northeast and the southeast the steppe is bounded by the spurs of the Zeravshan and Gissar mountains. The climate is sharply continental and desert. The winters are warm with an average temperature in January on the plain varying from −0.2° to 0.8°C. The summers are hot, dry, and long, with an average temperature in July of 31.5°C. Such a temperature cycle is favorable for cultivating fine-fibered varieties of cotton. However, during the spring and autumn there are occasional frosts; during the summer there are hot dry winds (the *garmsil'*). Precipitation falls mostly during the spring and winter; the amount on the plain varies from 200 to 250 mm; in the mountains and foothills it reaches as much as 500 mm per year. The principal river is the Kashkadar'ia with its many tributaries, which flow down from the mountains; the largest of these are the Aksu, Iakkabagdar'ia (Kyzyldar'ia), and Guzardar'ia. These rivers are fed by snow and have their high-water periods in the spring and early summer. To use the river water for irrigation more fully, reservoirs have been constructed: the Chim Kurgan on the Kashkadar'ia, the Kamashi on the Iakkabagdar'ia, and the Pachkamarskoe on the Guzardar'ia. Stretching from the Kashkadar'ia and most of its tributaries are irrigation canals, which form oases for irrigated agriculture: the Kitab-Shakhrisabz, the Guzar-Kamashi, and the largest—the Karshi.

In southern Kashkadar'ia Oblast there is a predominance of sandy expanses (the sands of the Sundukli), as well as many takyrs; in the north are clay plains and solonchaks. The Kashkadar'ia valley has light and typical sierozems, solonchaks, and meadow and other soils. Altitudinal zonality may be observed in the mountains: typical sierozems, dark sierozems, brown soils, and mountain-meadow soils. The desert section is poor in vegetation (mostly ephemeral plants and wormwood). There is *tugai* vegetation (a bottomland complex with forests, bushes, and meadows) in the valleys of the Kashkadar'ia and its tributaries. The mountains are covered with scrub brush and woody vegetation; within the forests there is a predominance of savin. The lower mountain slopes are used for pastures. In the mountains live argali, roe deer, and various predators—the brown bear, wolf, jackal, and fox. Birds are represented by the rock partridge and steppe eagle. The desert is inhabited by rodents, Persian gazelles, and foxes, as well as reptiles and arachnids.

Population. Most of the oblast's population is Uzbek (85 percent, according to the 1970 census); also living in the oblast are Tadzhiks, Russians, Tatars, and Turkmens. The average population density is 30.2 persons per sq km (1972). The most densely populated areas are the Kitab-Shakhrisabz and Karshi oases; the least are the high-mountain and desert-steppe regions. The urban population increased from 41,000 in 1939 to 144,000 by 1972. Cities include Karshi, Shakhrisabz, and Kasan.

Economy. From a backward province of the Bukhara Emirate, Kashkadar'ia Oblast has become during the Soviet period a region with a well-developed socialist economy. In in-

dustry, created during the five-year plans, the most developed branches are building materials, light industry, food processing, and natural gas. In agriculture cotton growing and the raising of Karakul sheep are most significant.

The total industrial output in 1971 had increased ninefold in comparison with 1940. Industry is represented, for the most part, by building-materials enterprises, with plants producing reinforced-concrete structural components, bricks, and limestone; there is extraction of nonmetallic materials like sand and gravel. A combine producing materials for wall construction is being built. The oblast also has a food-processing industry (flour-milling and baked goods combines, vegetable-oil extraction and canning plants, a winery, meat combines, and a dairy combine), and light industry (cotton mills, garment factories, and other enterprises). Ancient artistic crafts have been developed, such as the making of *tiubeteikas* (embroidered skullcaps) and *siuzane* (embroidered squares of cotton). The most important industrial enterprises are concentrated in Karshi and Shakhrisabz. During the 1960's the natural gas and petroleum industries of the Mubarek group of deposits went into operation; they were connected with the main gas pipeline running through Tashkent to Frunze and Alma-Ata. The oblast has been made a part of the unified energy system of Middle Asia.

Productive land totals 2.4 million hectares (ha), of which 1.9 million ha are occupied by pastures and 0.5 million ha by arable lands (1971). In 1971 there were 72 kolkhozes and 42 sovkhozes. The area of irrigated lands amounts to 176,900 ha. Projects are being carried out to irrigate the Karshi Steppe. Most of the arable lands are occupied by grain crops on dry and occasionally irrigated lands in the foothills. In 1971 there were 284,000 ha (about two-thirds of all sown areas) under grain crops (for the most part, wheat and barley) and 110,000 ha (340 percent more than in 1940) under cotton. Some 252,000 tons of raw cotton were produced (5.6 percent of the republic's total harvest). The average yield of cotton is 22.9 quintals per ha. Vegetable and melon crops occupy 9,000 ha.

The pastures of the Karshi Steppe and the foothills of the Gissar Mountains serve as the base for the development of livestock raising, including that of Karakul sheep. As of Jan. 1, 1972, the oblast had 260,000 cattle (including 104,000 cows), 1,267,000 sheep and goats, 25,000 swine, and 14,000 horses. The raising of Karakul sheep has been developed in the desert regions. In the foothills there is a predominance of fat-rumped sheep and goats. Cattle are widespread throughout all the oblast's raions. Horses, mostly of the Karabair breed, are raised. Kashkadar'ia Oblast provides about 6 percent of the cocoon harvest in Uzbekistan (1,252 tons in 1971).

The total length of railroads is 344 km (1971). The Kagan-Karshi-Dushanbe railroad line cuts through the oblast in its western part. There is a branch line from Karshi to the settlement of Oktiabr'skii. In 1970 the Samarkand-Karshi railroad line (with a length of 142 km) went into operation. There are 1,804 km of paved highways (1971). The eastern part of the oblast is intersected by the Greater Uzbek Route from Tashkent to Termez (150 km of which are within Kashkadar'ia Oblast).

K. N. BEDRINTSEV

Education, cultural affairs, and public health. Prior to the October Revolution there was not a single educational institution in Kashkadar'ia Oblast. During the 1971–72 academic year there were 259,000 pupils enrolled at 786 general-education schools, 9,300 students at 11 specialized educational institutions, and 6,600 students at the Karshi State Pedagogical Institute. In 1972 some 16,500 children were enrolled in 168 preschool institutions.

In the oblast as of Jan. 1, 1972, there were 445 public libraries (with 1,833,000 copies of books and journals), 250 clubs, and 317 film-projection units.

The oblast newspaper *Kashkadare khakikati* (Kashkadar'ia Pravda) has been published since 1925 in Uzbek, and *Kashkadar'inskaia pravda* has appeared in Russian since 1943. The oblast radio carries broadcasts in Uzbek and Russian on one program, and broadcasts are relayed from Tashkent and Moscow.

As of Jan. 1, 1972, there were 95 hospital institutions, with 7,800 beds (9.1 beds per 1,000 inhabitants); 1,100 physicians

were working in the oblast (one physician per 747 inhabitants).
[11–1656–3]

KASHKAROV, DANIIL NIKOLAEVICH.
Born Mar. 30 (Apr. 11), 1878, in Riazan'; died Nov. 26, 1941, at Khvoinaia Station, Novgorod Oblast. Soviet zoologist and ecologist; doctor of biological sciences (1934). Member of the CPSU (1941).

Kashkarov graduated from the natural sciences division and medical department of Moscow University in 1903 and 1908, respectively, a student of M. A. Menzbir. From 1919 to 1933 he was head of the subdepartment of vertebrate zoology at the Middle Asian University in Tashkent and, from 1934 to 1941, at Leningrad State University. Kashkarov did research on the terrestrial vertebrates of Middle Asia and promoted an ecological approach to the study of animals (including domestic breeds). He was the author of the first compendiums in the USSR of animal ecology.

WORKS
Kurs biologii pozvonochnykh. Moscow-Leningrad, 1929.
Kholodnaia pustynia Tsentral'nogo Tian'-Shania. Leningrad, 1937. (Coauthor.)
"Ekologiia domashnikh zhivotnykh." In *Pamiati M. A. Menzbira.* Moscow-Leningrad, 1937.
Kurs zoologii pozvonochnykh zhivotnykh, 2nd ed. Moscow-Leningrad, 1940. (With V. V. Stanchinskii.)
Osnovy ekologii zhivotnykh, 2nd ed. Leningrad, 1944.

REFERENCE
Terent'ev, P. V. "Pamiati D. N. Kashkarova." *Priroda,* 1948, no. 5.
[11–1660–3]

KASHKIN, IVAN ALEKSANDROVICH.
Born June 24 (July 6), 1899, in Moscow; died there Nov. 26, 1963. Soviet Russian translator and critic.

Kashkin graduated from the Second Moscow State University in 1924 and taught at higher educational institutions in Moscow. He developed the principles of the creative reproduction of the style and individual manner of the author being translated and trained a considerable group of translators from English. He translated on a high philological level—for example, Chaucer's *Canterbury Tales,* which he translated with O. Rumer in 1946. Kashkin propagated the best achievements of contemporary English and American poetry (R. Frost, C. Sandburg) and prose (E. Hemingway, E. Caldwell, and J. Wain) and wrote historical-literary research works on J. Conrad, R. L. Stevenson, W. Faulkner, and E. Hemingway.

WORKS
"Kheminguei." In the collection *Prometei: Istoriko-biograficheskii al'manakh,* vol. 1. Moscow, 1966.
Ernest Kheminguei. Moscow, 1966.
Dlia chitatelia-sovremennika. Moscow, 1968.

REFERENCE
"Khudozhnik, pedagog, uchenyi." In *Masterstvo perevoda, 1963.* Moscow, 1964.
[11–1660–4]

KASHKIN, NIKOLAI DMITRIEVICH.
Born Nov. 27 (Dec. 9), 1839, in Voronezh; died Mar. 15, 1920, in Kazan. Russian music critic and teacher.

As a child Kashkin gave piano recitals. After he settled in Moscow in 1860, he studied piano and music theory under A. I. Diubiuk. In 1863 he began teaching at the Music Classes of the Russian Musical Society and between 1866 and 1906 taught piano, theory, and music history at the Moscow Conservatory. He became a professor in 1875. In 1918 he moved to Kazan.

Kashkin, an eminent representative of Russian music and critical thought, defended the principles of realistic music. His articles (published in periodicals over a period of almost 40 years) helped establish a Russian national music culture. Kashkin was also a proponent of Tchaikovsky's work. He was a talented memoirist and published his reminiscences of many Russian music figures. His other books include a history of the Moscow Conservatory and a textbook of music theory.

REFERENCE
Iakovlev, V. *N. D. Kashkin.* Moscow-Leningrad, 1950. [11–1661–1]

KASHKIN, NIKOLAI SERGEEVICH.
Born May 2 (14), 1829, in Kaluga; died there Nov. 29 (Dec. 12), 1914. Russian social and political figure. Member of the Petrashevskii circle.

Kashkin was a nobleman and the son of a Decembrist. He graduated from the Alexander Lycée in 1847 and served in the ministry of foreign affairs. The Petrashevskii circle (which included A. V. Khanykov, A. I. Evropeus, and D. D. Akhsharumov), whose members studied the works of utopian socialist authors, began to meet in Kashkin's home in October 1848. Kashkin was arrested in April 1849, deprived of all his rights and his possessions, and brought to trial. In 1849 in the Petrashevskii trial Kashkin was exiled to the Caucasian corps as a rank-and-file soldier. He was promoted to officer's rank in 1855. Kashkin was a member of the liberal opposition in the Kaluga provincial committee during the period of preparation for the peasant reform of 1861. He was a member of the Kaluga district court from 1870 to 1908.

REFERENCES
Delo petrashevtsev, vol. 3. Moscow-Leningrad, 1951.
Semevskii, V. I. "Petrashevtsy: Kruzhok Kashkina." *Golos minuvshego,* 1916, nos. 2–4.
[11–1661–2]

KASHLYK
(Sibir'), the capital of the Tatar Siberian Khanate (beginning in the late 15th century).

Kashlyk was located on the right bank of the Irtysh at its confluence with the Sibirka River (17 km above Tobol'sk). The city was first mentioned (as Sibir') in the literature of the early 14th century. In the 16th century the population of Kashlyk engaged in trading, crafts, fishing, farming, and cattle raising. In the fall of 1582, Kashlyk was captured by the troops of Ermak and abandoned by its residents.

REFERENCE
Istoriia Sibiri s drevneishikh vremem do nashikh dnei, vols. 1–2. Leningrad, 1968.
[11–1661–3]

KASHMIR,
a historical region in Asia, at the juncture of the Himalayas and Tibet. In ancient times and during the Middle Ages the area of Kashmir was part of various states that existed on the territory of Hindustan. In 1586, Kashmir became a part of the Mogul Empire. In 1756 it was captured by the Afghans; in 1819, by the Sikhs. Conquered during the First Anglo-Sikh War (1845–46) by the British colonizers, Kashmir was transferred by them in 1846 to the rajah of the principality of Jammu for compensation of 7.5 million rupees. The rajah was recognized as maharajah of the principality of Jammu and Kashmir. Feudal exploitation, along with national and religious discrimination, led to several uprisings by the Kashmiris, the most important of which occurred in 1931–33 and 1946.

After the formation in August 1947 of the two sovereign states of India and Pakistan, both of them attempted to annex Kashmir. On Oct. 22, 1947, an invasion of Kashmir was begun by armed Pathan tribes from Pakistan; the maharajah turned to India for aid and declared Kashmir's desire to be included in the Indian Federation. His request for aid was granted, and a charter of annexation of Kashmir by India was signed on Oct. 27, 1947. On Jan. 1, 1948, India addressed a complaint against Pakistan to the UN Security Council, accusing the former of aggression in Kashmir. On Jan. 15, 1948, Pakistan lodged a complaint against India with the Security Council. A mediation commission of five countries was created by the Security Council. By Jan. 1, 1949, military operations in Kashmir had ceased, and on July 27 a cease-fire line was established. The western and northwestern parts of Kashmir came under the control of Pakistan, and the remaining (greater) part was left to India.

The Delhi Agreement between the maharajah of Kashmir and India, according to which Kashmir became a part of India with the status of a state (Jammu and Kashmir), was signed in July 1952. On Nov. 17, 1956, the Constituent Assembly of Kashmir adopted a constitution for Kashmir, the third article of which declares that Kashmir "is and remains a component part of the Indian Federation." Proceeding from this point, the government of India considers the question of Kashmir's inclusion in the country of India to be finally resolved. The government of Pakistan insisted on a referendum in Jammu and Kashmir on the question of the annexation of the territory by India or Pakistan.

Several discussions of the Kashmir question in the UN and Indian-Pakistani bilateral negotiations on Kashmir in 1955, 1960, 1962, and 1963 were fruitless. The armed conflict that began in September 1965 between India and Pakistan was halted through the efforts of peace-loving countries, above all the USSR. At a meeting of the leaders of India and Pakistan held in Tashkent on Jan. 4–10, 1966 (in which the chairman of the Council of Ministers of the USSR took part), a declaration was signed that opened up prospects for the normalization of relations between India and Pakistan.

In December 1971 an armed conflict again took place between India and Pakistan in the course of which the cease-fire line in Kashmir was violated in several areas. At a conference of the leaders of India and Pakistan on June 30–July 3, 1972, in Simla, an agreement was signed according to which both sides promised to resolve by peaceful means the disputed questions existing between them. At the Indian-Pakistani negotiations of August 1972 in Delhi the two sides established a new control line in Kashmir to replace the previous cease-fire line. The demarcation of the line was completed by representatives of the military commands of both countries in December 1972.   [11–1661–4]

KASHMIR, VALE OF, an intermontane valley between the Greater Himalayas and the Pir Panjal ranges. Length, about 200 km; width, more than 60 km. Its floor is about 1,600 m above sea level. There are many lakes in the valley, including the large Lake Wular. The navigable Jhelum River flows through the Vale of Kashmir. The average January temperature is −1°C; the average July temperature is 22°–23°C. Total annual precipitation is about 1,000 mm. There are broad-leaved forests of oak, maple, and ash in the valley and coniferous forests on the slopes. The valley is densely populated. Rice is grown, and there are fruit orchards. There are climatic health resorts, and tourism is well developed. The city of Srinagar is located in the Vale of Kashmir.
[11–1663–2]

KASHMIRI, the language of the Kashmiris, one of the 14 official languages of India. It belongs to the Dard group of Indo-Iranian languages and is spoken by the inhabitants of the Vale of Kashmir. It has the dialects of Kashmiri proper, Kishtwari, Pogul, Siraji, and Rambani (the last three are transitional between Kashmiri and the Pahari and Punjabi dialects).

Kashmiri is spoken by approximately 2.5 million persons (1970, estimate). It has a distinction between long and short vowels. The complex consonant system contains aspirated, retroflex, palatalized, and labialized series. The morphology is characterized by a four-case system, masculine and feminine gender, and a definite-indefinite noun category. Aspectual and temporal oppositions occur in the verb system. Pronominal enclitics are used to indicate the person of the subject and object with verb forms. The syntax is characterized by an ergative construction. The modern writing system is based on Arabic script.

REFERENCES
Edel'man, D. I. *Dardskie iazyki.* Moscow, 1965.
Zakhar'in, B. A., and D. I. Edel'man. *Iazyk kashmiri.* Moscow, 1971.
Grierson, G. A. *A Manual of the Kashmīrī Language,* vols. 1–2. Oxford, 1911.
Grierson, G. A. *A Dictionary of the Kashmīrī Language,* vols. 1–4. Calcutta, 1915–32.
Grierson, G. A. *Linguistic Survey of India,* vol. 8, part 2. Calcutta, 1919.
Kachru, B. B. *A Reference Grammar of Kashmiri.* Urbana, Ill., 1968.
D. I. EDEL'MAN   [11–1663–1]

KASHMIRI LITERATURE. For centuries the principal language of Kashmir's literature and culture was Sanskrit. Literary figures who lived in Kashmir from the seventh through the 12th century include the writers Kshemendra, Somadeva, and Kalhana; the philosophers Somananda, Utpala Charya, and Bhaskara; and the authors of well-known works on poetry—Bhamaha, Anandavardhana, and Abhinavagupta. Adaptations

in Kashmiri of stories drawn from the Vedas and Puranas, such as *The Tale of the Victory Over the Demon Bana* (15th century) by Bhattavatara and *The Radiance of Siva* (16th–17th centuries) by Shitikantha, began to appear in the 13th century. The creative work of the folk poet Lalla Devi and, to some extent, that of Sheikh Nuruddin, was characterized by a blend of Hindu and Sufi mysticism and a criticism of orthodox religion.

From the 16th through the 18th century there was intensive development of poetry written in Persian: Sheikh Yakub Zarfi (1522–94) and Hodja Habibullah (1555–1617). In poetry written in Kashmiri the genre of the love song (*lal-gita*), which had been borrowed from folklore, became widespread: Haba Khatun (16th century) and Arnimal (18th century). The Hindu poets of the 18th and 19th centuries Prakash Ram, Paramananda, and Krishna Razdan revived the tradition of poetic adaptations of ancient Indian legends; the Muslim poets used traditional Persian and Tadzhik subjects and genre forms: Mahmud Gami, Makbul Shah Kralawari, Rasul Mir, Abdul Wahab Pare, Hazrat Hussain, and Halil Gah.

Ideas of the Enlightenment began to become widespread in Kashmir in the late 19th century, and a modern literature took shape: the satirical poems of Kiralavari and the poetry of Ghulam Ahmad Mahjur (1885–1952) were permeated with antifeudal moods. Abdul Ahad Azad (1902–48) opposed religious fanaticism. The theme of labor and the life of the common people resounds in the poetry of Roshan, Premi, Rahi, and Kamil. The traditions of Sivaite lyricism were continued by Zinda Kaul. New genre forms and varieties of verse penetrated into poetry.

The first prose works in Kashmiri appeared during the 1950's: Akhtar Mohiuddin, Umesh, Kaul, Kamil, D. Nadim (born 1916), Roshan, Bansi, Nirodo, and Shankar Raina. The literature of the Dogri people began to emerge in the late 1940's: the poets Dinubhan, Pant, K. Madhukar, and Padma Sachdev, and the prose writers Bhagvan Prasad Sathe, Ramnath Shastri, and Narendar Khajuria. Some contemporary writers in Kashmir also write in Urdu and Hindi.

REFERENCE
Pushp, P. N. "Kashmiri Literature." In *Contemporary Indian Literature.* New Delhi [1957].
B. A. ZAKHAR'IN and I. S. RABINOVICH   [11–1663–3]

KASHMIRIS, a people, the principal population of the state of Jammu and Kashmir in India. The Kashmiris live mainly in the Vale of Kashmir, along the Jhelum River. They number about 2.5 million (1970, estimate); their language is Kashmiri. The influence of Urdu, Hindi, and Punjabi is strong in the cities. More than 90 percent of the Kashmiris are Muslims; the rest are Hindus.

The Kashmiris have a diversified agricultural economy: they cultivate grains (rice, maize, and wheat), vegetables and melons (muskmelon, watermelon, and squash), and fruits (apricots and mulberries); they engage in beekeeping, silkworm breeding, and, in the mountains, pastoral livestock raising (goats and sheep). Handicrafts are highly developed: the production of fine woolen fabrics (cashmere) and cashmere shawls made of goat down, painted lacquerware made of wood and papier-mâché, and artistic woodcarving and metalworking. A small number of Kashmiris are employed in industry.

REFERENCES
Narody Iuzhnoi Azii. Moscow, 1963.
Puliarkin, V. A. *Kashmir.* Moscow, 1956.
Singh, S. H. *Kashmir and Its Future.* Delhi, 1955.   [11–1664–1]

KASHTAN, WILLIAM. Born 1909, in Montreal. Activist in the Canadian and international workers' movement.

Kashtan is the son of a worker. He has participated in the Canadian communist movement since 1927. He held various posts in the organizations of the Communist Party of Canada (CPC) in the provinces of Quebec and Ontario from 1938 to 1946. Kashtan was secretary of the national committee of the CPC for work in the trade unions and for organizational questions from 1946 to 1964. He has been general secretary of the CPC since January 1965.   [11–1664–4]

KASHUBS (self-designation, Kashebi), descendants of the ancient Pomors who live on the shores of the Baltic Sea in the northeastern regions of Poland. They speak the Kashubian dialect of Polish. In the early 14th century the lands of the Kashubs were seized by the Knights of the Teutonic Order. Eastern Pomor'e was reunited with Poland by the Treaty of Torun in 1466. Prussia gained control of the Kashubian lands in the first and second partitions of Poland (1772, 1793). They were returned to Poland by the Treaty of Versailles in 1919. The Kashubs have preserved their own culture despite long forced Germanization.

REFERENCES
Lavrovskii, P. "Etnograficheskii ocherk kashubov." *Filologicheskie zapiski,* Voronezh, 1873, issues 4–5.
Bukowski, A. *Regionalizm kaszubski,* Poznan, 1950.   [11–1667–4]

KAS'IAN, SARKIS IVANOVICH (pseudonym of Sarkis Oganesovich Ter-Kasparian). Born Jan. 16 (28), 1876; died December 1937. Soviet state and party activist; publicist. Member of the Communist Party from 1905.

Born to a petit bourgeois family in Shusha, Kas'ian studied at the Leipzig Commercial Institute and in the department of philosophy at Berlin University (1900–04); he became a candidate in both commercial and philosophical sciences. During the Revolution of 1905–07 he was a founder of the Armenian Bolshevik press. From 1912 to 1914 he ran the Tiflis party organization. From 1917 to 1920 he served on the Caucasian Regional Party Committee; he became a member of the Tiflis bureau of the committee in 1918 and edited Armenian Bolshevik newspapers in 1917–18. In January 1920 he was one of the organizers and leaders of the first conference of the Armenian Bolshevik Party. In 1919–20 he served as chairman of the Armenian Committee (Armenkom) of the RCP (Bolshevik).

In November 1920 he became a member of the Central Committee of the Armenian CP (Bolshevik) and chairman of the Armenian Revolutionary Committee, which by a declaration written by Kas'ian proclaimed the overthrow of the Dashnak government and the establishment of Soviet power in Armenia on Nov. 29, 1920. In a telegram of Dec. 2, 1920, addressed to Kas'ian, V. I. Lenin saluted Soviet Armenia (*Poln. sobr. soch.,* 5th ed., vol. 42, p. 54).

Kas'ian served (1924–27) as rector of the Transcaucasian Communist University of the Twenty-six Commissars, chairman of the Soviet of Nationalities, and member of the Presidium of the Central Executive Committee (CEC) of the Transcaucasian SFSR. He was also chairman of the CEC of the Armenian SSR. Kas'ian was also elected to the All-Union CEC and was a delegate to the Third Congress of the Comintern in 1921 and the Sixteenth Congress of the RCP (Bolshevik) in 1930.

WORKS
Kasyan, S. *Entir erker.* Yerevan, 1967.
REFERENCE
Karapetyan, H. N. *Mec payk'ari mardik,* book 1. Yerevan, 1963.
                        A. N. KARAPETIAN [11–1526–2]

KAS'IANOV, ALEKSANDR ALEKSANDROVICH. Born Aug. 17 (29), 1891, in the village of Bolobonovo, now in Pil'na Raion, Gorky Oblast. Soviet composer and teacher. People's Artist of the USSR (1971).

Kas'ianov graduated from the Petrograd Conservatory in 1917. In 1918 he moved to Nizhny Novgorod (now Gorky). From 1924 to 1949 he headed the music section of the drama theater and worked in the Radio Center (1930 to 1941). In 1951 he began teaching theoretical subjects at the Gorky Conservatory, becoming a professor in 1957. A master of choral writing, he has made extensive use of the intonation of Volga song folklore. Kas'ianov has composed five operas, including *Stepan Razin* (1939; second version, 1953, Gorky), *Foma Gordeev* (1946; second version, 1966, Gorky), and *Ermak* (1957, Gorky), as well as cantatas, orchestral works, instrumental pieces, works for piano, choral works, and songs. His romances are among the important contributions to Soviet chamber and vocal music. Kas'ianov has been awarded the Order of Lenin, the Order of the Red Banner of Labor, and various medals.

REFERENCES
Poluektova, N. N., and V. A. Kollar. "Muzykanty-nizhegorodtsy." *Liudi russkogo iskusstva.* Gorky, 1960. Pages 301–07.
Eliseev, I. "Rytsar' kuchkistskikh traditsii." *Sovetskaia muzyka,* 1971, no. 11.
Eliseev, I. *A. A. Kas'ianov.* Moscow, 1973.
Kollar, V. "Stareishii gor'kovskii kompozitor." *Muzykal'naia zhizn',* 1971, no. 16.

KASIIAN, VASILII IL'ICH. Born Jan. 1, 1896, in the village of Mikulintsy, in present-day Sniatyn Raion, Ivano-Frankovsk Oblast, Ukrainian SSR. Soviet graphic artist. People's Artist of the USSR; member of the Academy of Arts of the USSR (1947). Became a member of the CPSU in 1946.

From 1920 to 1926, Kasiian studied under M. Švabinský at the Prague Academy of Arts. He became a Soviet citizen in 1923 and settled in the Ukrainian SSR in 1927. Kasiian's work includes etchings, such as *The Strike* (wood engraving, 1926) and the series *Dneprostroi* (line engraving, 1932–34) and *V. I. Lenin and the Ukraine* (etching, 1947). From 1941 to 1945 he designed posters. Kasiian also executed drawings and illustrations devoted to classic Ukrainian and Russian literature. His work is distinguished by expressiveness and lofty romantic images.

Since 1927, Kasiian has been a professor at a number of higher educational art institutes, including the Kiev Institute of Art. From 1962 to 1968 he served as the chairman of the governing board of the Artists' Union of the Ukrainian SSR. Kasiian was awarded the T. G. Shevchenko State Prize of the Ukrainian SSR in 1964 and the State Prize of the Ukrainian SSR in 1971 for his work on the six-volume *History of Ukrainian Art* (Kiev, 1966–70). He was also awarded the Order of Lenin, three other orders, and various medals.

WORKS
Ukrains'ka radians'ka hrafika. Kiev, 1959.
Oforty Tarasa Shevchenka. Kiev, 1961.
Pro mystetstvo. Kiev, 1971.
REFERENCES
Vasilii Il'ich Kasiian. Moscow, 1957.
Vasyl' Kasiian: Kataloh iuvileioi vystavky. Kiev, 1966.   [11–1477–1]

KASIM AL-ANVAR. Born in Sarab (now in Iran), eastern Azerbaijan (date of birth unknown); died 1434. Azerbaijani poet.

Kasim al-Anvar wrote in Persian and Azerbaijani. He lived in Herat at the court of Shahrukh Mirza, who, suspecting him of preparing a secret plot, banished him to Samarkand in 1426. Kasim al-Anvar celebrated exalted love in his lyric poetry; in the narrative poem *Friend of the Enlightened Ones* he preached pantheism, condemned self-seeking and egoism, and extolled moral purity. His lyrical narrative poem *Degrees of the Enlightened Ones* and divans have also been preserved. Kasim al-Anvar's work was influenced by Nasimi and Rumi.

WORKS
Kolliyat-e Gasem-e Anvar. Edited and with an introduction by S. Nafisi. Teheran, 1337 A.H. (A.D. 1958).
REFERENCE
Mükhtäsär Azärbayjan ädäbiyyatï tarikhi, vol. 1. Baku, 1943.
                                              [11–1475–2]

KASIM KHAN. Year of birth unknown; died circa 1469. The first khan ("tsar") of the Kasimov Kingdom. Son of Khan Ulu Muhammad of the Golden Horde and brother of Khan Mahmudek of Kazan, who was feuding with Muscovy.

In 1446, Kasim Khan entered the service of Vasilii II Vasil'evich Temnyi, grand prince of Muscovy, and supported him against Prince Dmitrii Shemiaka in 1449 and 1450. In 1449, Kasim Khan defeated the troops of Khan Said Ahmad of the Golden Horde on the Pakhra River. Around 1450–56, Vasilii II gave Gorodets-Meshcherskii to Kasim Khan as an appanage. In 1467, Kasim Khan undertook an unsuccessful campaign against Kazan.   [11–1476–3]

KASIMOV, a city in Riazan' Oblast, RSFSR; landing on the Oka River. It is situated 164 km northeast of Riazan' and 5 km from the Kasimov railroad station (the terminal point of a branch of the Riazan'-Ruzaevka line). Population, 33,000 (1970).

The city was founded as Gorodets-Meshcherskii in 1152 by Iurii Dolgorukii. In 1471 the Muscovite grand prince Vasilii II Temnyi gave the city to the Tatar khan Kasim, who had fled from the Golden Horde to enter the Russian service. It was at this time that the city was renamed Kasimov. From the mid-15th century to 1681, it was the capital of the Kasimov Kingdom. Monuments from that period have been preserved, including a minaret (1470) and the mausoleums of Shah-Ali-Khan (1555) and Avgan-Muhammad-Sultan (1647). Among the most interesting 18th-century monuments are the Bogoiavlenie Church (1700), the St. Nicholas Church (1701), and the Troitskaia Church (1753–65). In 1780 the city was rebuilt according to a regular plan. The new buildings included a market arcade (1830's), the Voznesenskii Cathedral (1854–64), and a number of residential buildings executed in the classical style.

Industries in Kasimov include the processing of sheepskin and fur and the manufacturing of nets and refrigeration equipment. There is a shipyard. The city has an industrial technicum, a medical school, and a pedagogical school. It is also the site of a museum of local lore.

REFERENCES
Shishkin, N. I. *Istoriia goroda Kasimova s drevneishikh vremen,* 2nd ed. Riazan', 1891.
Mikhailovskii, E. V., and I. V. Il'enko. *Riazan', Kasimov.* [Moscow, 1969.]   [11–1476–1]

KASIMOV KINGDOM, an appanage principality created by Muscovite princes for Tatar khans who had entered their service.

The Kasimov Kingdom occupied an area along the Oka River (the northeastern part of present-day Riazan' Oblast), inhabited by Meshchers, Mordovians, and partly by Tatars. It was granted for the first time by Vasilii II Temnyi to the Kazan tsarevich Kasim Khan (in about 1450–56); Gorodets-Meshcherskii, the main city of the region, was renamed Kasimov after Kasim Khan. The "tsars" or "tsareviches" of the Kasimov Kingdom were appointed at the discretion of the Muscovite government from among members of the Tatar aristocracy who had chosen to become Russian subjects. Some of them played a prominent role in the political life of the Russian state, especially during the struggle with the Kazan Khanate. After Russia annexed Kazan in 1552, the importance of the Kasimov Kingdom declined. The administration of the Kasimov Kingdom was from then on virtually in the hands of Muscovite *voevodas* (military governors), and the "tsars" and "tsareviches" became ordinary landowners in the service of the Russian state. In 1681, with the death of Fatami Sultan, the last ruler of Kasimov, the Kasimov Kingdom ceased to exist even formally.

REFERENCES
Vel'iaminov-Zernov, V. V. *Issledovanie o Kasimskikh tsariakh i tsarevichakh,* parts 1–4. St. Petersburg, 1863–87.
Shishkin, N. I. *Istoriia goroda Kasimova s drevneishikh vremen,* 2nd ed. Riazan', 1891.
Tikhomirov, M. N. *Rossiia XVI stoletii.* Moscow, 1962. Pages 42–46.   [11–1476–2]

KASIMZADE, ENVER ALI OGLY. Born Jan. 30 (Feb. 12), 1912, in Sal'iany, in present-day Azerbaijan SSR; died Mar. 12, 1969, in Baku. Soviet architect and professor. Corresponding member of the Academy of Sciences of the Azerbaijan SSR (1967). Honored Builder of the Azerbaijan SSR. Became a member of the CPSU in 1941.

In 1936, Kasimzade graduated from the Azerbaijan Polytechnic Institute in Baku. From 1962 to 1968 he was the rector of the institute. His works in Baku include the Azneft'proekt building (Azerbaijan Petroleum Project; 1957) and the Ulduz subway station (1967). He also produced designs for standard multistory apartment buildings in Baku. Kasimzade was awarded four orders and various medals.

WORKS
Problemy razvitiia azerbaidzhanskoi sovetskoi arkhitektury na sovremennom etape. Baku, 1967.   [11–1475–3]

KASKELEN, a city (since 1963) and center of Kaskelen Raion, Alma-Ata Oblast, Kazakh SSR, located on a highway in the foothills of the Zailiiskii Alatau Range, 27 km west of Alma-Ata. Population, 24,000 (1970).

Kaskelen is the center of a suburban vegetable and dairying region. It has a vegetable-canning plant and plants producing building materials, clothing, and haberdashery. There is also a cultural and educational facility.   [11–1481–2]

KASLI, a city (until 1942, a settlement) in Cheliabinsk Oblast, RSFSR, located on Lake Bol'shoe Kasli, 25 km from the Mauk railroad station (on the Sverdlovsk-Cheliabinsk line) and 138 km northwest of Cheliabinsk. Population, 21,000 (as of 1970).

During the mid-18th century a metallurgical plant was founded in Kasli that became famous for its artistic cast-iron work. The city also has machine-building and fish-processing plants and a garment factory.   [11–1481–3]

KASLI CASTINGS, artistic cast-iron items (sculpture, garden tables, grillwork) produced at the iron foundry in the city of Kasli.

The traditions for which Kasli castings are known (graphic precision of outline, a combination of meticulously finished details and flat surfaces with a vigorous play of highlights) developed during the 19th century in the sculpture cast from models by P. K. Klodt, E. A. Lansere, R. R. Bakh, M. D. Kanaev, and local masters, such as V. F. Torokin. During the Soviet period, sculpture has been executed from models by N. V. Tomskii, M. G. Manizer, and the local masters P. S. Anikin, A. S. Gilev, and A. V. Chirkin.

REFERENCE
Razina, T. M., I. M. Suslov, E. N. Khokhlova, and N. S. Gorelikov. *Russkii khudozhestvennyi metall.* Moscow, 1958. Pages 93–112.   [11–1482–1]

KAŠPÁREK, a character in Czech puppet theater, the principal comic hero in folk puppet shows (usually a marionette). Until Kašpárek made his appearance around 1820 the character was called Pimperle (Petrushka). The character of Kašpárek is extremely popular in Czechoslovakia; he is a good-natured, cheerful Czech peasant, a joker and a jester. Kašpárek played an important role in political satire during Czechoslovakia's struggle against Austrian dominion.

REFERENCE
Malik, J. *Chekhoslovatskii kukol'nyi teatr.* Prague, 1948.   [11–1664–2]

KASPAROV, VLADISLAV MINASOVICH (pseudonym of V. M. Kaspar'iants). Born Jan. 20 (Feb. 1), 1884, in Khankendy, now Stepanakert; died Sept. 6 (19), 1917, in Davos, Switzerland. Participant in the Transcaucasian and Russian revolutionary movements; became a Bolshevik in 1903.

Kasparov studied at the law school of the University of St. Petersburg and at the Higher Commercial School in Berlin. From 1907 to 1912 he was a member of the Baku, St. Petersburg, and Rostov committees of the RSDLP; he emigrated in 1913. From 1914 to 1917 he lived in Bern and Davos and corresponded with V. I. Lenin (see *Poln. sobr. soch.,* 5th ed., vols. 48 and 49); on his assignment, Kasparov corresponded clandestinely on behalf of the Central Committee of the RSDLP with Bolshevik organizations in Russia. In February 1915, at the Bern conference of Bolshevik cells abroad, he was elected a member of the Committee of Foreign Organization (KZO) of the RSDLP; he was a member of the distribution committee and was treasurer of the KZO. In 1913–14 he worked on the staff of *Pravda.* Lenin praised Kasparov's work highly (*ibid.,* vol. 54, p. 83).

REFERENCES
Garmbdzhanian, G. B. *Kasparov, V. M.—vidnyi deiatel' Kommunisticheskoi partii.* Yerevan, 1965.

Karapetian, A. N. *Mec payk'ari mardik,* book 2. Yerevan, 1967.
A. N. KARAPETIAN [11–1483–5]

KASPERLE (Kasperl), a character in Austrian and German puppet theater.

The stage character of Kasperle first appeared in the late 18th century in Austria and, later, in Germany. Kasperle is a comic character. At times puppet shows featuring him have risen to the level of pointed lampoon. Kasperle appears in both marionette and puppet shows. In the 20th century the hand-puppet theater has become known as Kasperle theater.

REFERENCE
Megnin, Ch. *Histoire des marionnettes en Europe depuis l'antiquité jusqu'à nos jours,* 2nd ed. Paris, 1862. [11–1664–3]

KASPI, a city (until 1959, a settlement) and center of Kaspi Raion, Georgian SSR, located on the left bank of the Kura River at its confluence with the Lekhura. Population, 12,000 (1970).

Kaspi is a railroad station on the Tbilisi-Samtredia line, 48 km southwest of Tbilisi. The city has a building-materials industry (production of cement, slate) and plants producing electrical equipment (Elektroapparat), fruit and berry wines, and canned goods. Kaspi also has an industrial technicum and a museum of local lore. [11–1484–1]

KASPIISK (until 1947, the settlement of Dvigatel'stroi), a city in Dagestan ASSR, located on the shore of the Caspian Sea, 18 km southeast of the city of Makhachkala. Population, 43,000 (1972).

Kaspiisk has a plant producing precision machinery, a brickyard, and a heat and electric power plant. A department of the Dagestan Polytechnic Institute is also located there. [11–1484–3]

KASPIISKII (until 1944, Lagan'), a city (since 1963) and center of Kaspiiskii Raion, Kalmyk ASSR, located 9 km from the Caspian Sea and 40 km east of the Ulan-Kholl railroad station (on the Astrakhan'-Kizliar line), with which it is connected by highway.

Kaspiiskii has a meat-packing combine, fish-processing and machine-building plants, a brickyard, and a garment factory. It also has a sovkhoz raising fur-bearing animals. [11–1485–1]

KASPLIA, a river in Smolensk Oblast, RSFSR, and Vitebsk Oblast, Byelorussian SSR; a left tributary of the Zapadnaia Dvina. Length, 136 km; basin area, 5,410 sq km.

The Kasplia River originates in Lake Kasplia in the Vitebsk Upland. It is fed by a mixture of sources (predominantly snow). The average annual water discharge at the village of Lepino (13 km from the river's mouth) is 39.6 cu m per sec. The city of Demidov is located on the Kasplia. [11–1492–1]

KASPROWICZ, JAN. Born Dec. 12, 1860, in the village of Szymborz, near Inowrocław; died Aug. 1, 1926, in Poronin, near Zakopane. Polish poet.

The son of a poor peasant, Kasprowicz sympathized with the socialist movement in his youth. In the late 1880's and early 1890's he wrote realistic poetry depicting the poverty of the peasants, as in the collections *Poetry* (1889) and *From a Peasant's Field* (1891) and in the drama *The End of the World* (1891). Kasprowicz sought the solution to social conflicts in the moral transformation of man, the theme of the poem *Christ* (1890) and other works. In the second half of the 1890's Kasprowicz's poetry became more symbolic, and his vision of a dying world was imbued with a sense of Promethean rebellion against god, for example, the cycles *To a Dying World* and *Salve Regina* (1902; later included in the collection *Hymns,* 1921). After 1905, Kasprowicz's world view became religious and mystical, as reflected in the collections *The Book of the Poor* (1916) and *My World* (1926).

WORKS
Dzieła wybrane, vols. 1–4. Kraków, 1958.
In Russian translation:
Pol'skaia poeziia XIX–XX vv, vol. 2. Moscow, 1963.

REFERENCES
Bogomolova, N. Ia. "Ian Kasprovich." In *Istoriia pol'skoi literatury,* vol. 2. Moscow, 1969.
Loth, R. *Młodość J. Kasprowicza.* Poznań, 1962.
J. Kasprowicz. Introduction, selection of materials, and annotation by R. Loth. Warsaw, 1964.
Lipski, J. J. *Twórczość J. Kasprowicza w latach 1878–1891.* Warsaw, 1967.
Wspomnienia o J. Kasprowiczu. Warsaw, 1967. (Bibliography on pages 422–39.)
V. A. KHOREV [11–1492–2]

KASPRZAK, MARCIN. Born Nov. 2, 1860, in Czołow, Śrem District; died Sept. 8, 1905, in Warsaw. Active in the Polish workers' movement. Son of a farm laborer.

Kasprzak joined an underground socialist organization in Berlin in 1885. He returned to Poland that same year, established contact with the Polish revolutionary party Proletariat I, and was arrested at the end of the year. In April 1887 he escaped from prison in Poznań to Switzerland, whence he returned illegally to Warsaw in late 1887. Kasprzak was one of the founders and leaders of the party Proletariat II.

In 1891 he emigrated to London and worked at the press of *Przedświt,* the organ of the Polish socialists. He advocated the unity of the Polish and Russian revolutionary movements. In 1893 he was falsely accused by Polish social nationalists of collaboration with the tsarist Okhranka (secret police). In the same year he was arrested while crossing the border of the Kingdom of Poland.

Upon release from prison in 1896 he worked in the Polish Socialist Party in the part of Poland under Prussian rule. In 1904 he returned to the Kingdom of Poland and joined the Social Democracy of the Kingdom of Poland and of Lithuania. On Apr. 27, 1904, during a police attack on the secret Social Democratic printing press in Warsaw, Kasprzak attempted armed resistance. He was sentenced to death by the tsarist military tribunal and executed.

REFERENCE
Marcin Kasprzak, jego zycie i walka w świetle publikacji SDKPiL. Warsaw, 1954. P. N. OL'SHANSKII [11–1493–1]

KASSA, in Russian a word associated with various credit institutions, such as savings banks (*sberegatel'nye kassy*), funds for mutual assistance (*kassy vzaimopomoshchi*), and insurance funds (*strakhovye kassy*). [11–1494–2]

KASSÁK, LAJOS. Born Mar. 21, 1887, in Ershekuivar; died July 22, 1967, in Budapest. Hungarian author.

Kassák's verse in the early 1900's was influenced by W. Whitman, and it expressed faith in the historical role of the working class (*The Workmen,* 1915). During World War I, Kassák led the Hungarian vanguardists, and in 1919 he emigrated to Vienna, where he remained until 1927. Although he diverged from communism in his views on revolution and literature, Kassák truthfully described the workers' life (for example, in his novel *Angyalföld,* 1929). He also described his own difficult adolescence in his autobiographical novel *The Life of One Man* (1927–35). His lyrics are imbued with the spirit of democracy and humanism. They include his verse collections *The Paupers' Roses* (1949), *My Wealth, My Arsenal* (1963), and *The Oak Leaves* (1964). Kassák was awarded the Kossuth State Prize in 1965.

REFERENCES
Gusev, Iu. P. "Svoeobrazie formy v poezii Laiosha Kashshaka." In the collection *Khudozhestvennaia forma v literaturakh sotsialisticheskikh stran.* Moscow, 1969.
Bori, I., and E. Körner. *Kassák irodalma és festészete.* Budapest, 1967. [11–1667–5]

KASSALA, a city in northeastern Sudan in the Gash valley, on the Khartoum-Asmara (Ethiopia) highway. Administrative center of the province of Kassala. Population, 49,000 (1964).

Kassala is a railroad station and the commercial center of an agricultural region (cotton, hides, gum arabic, fruit, dried onions). [11–1495–3]

KASSANDRA, a peninsula in northeastern Greece, the southwestern tip of the Chalcidice Peninsula. Length (northwest to southeast), more than 50 km; width, from 1 to 14 km.

The Kassandra Peninsula is formed of ancient crystalline rocks. Its surface is a hilly plain (elevation, to 350 m). The peninsula is covered by groves of Aleppo pine with an undergrowth of evergreen and deciduous shrubbery. There are olive plantations, orchards, and vineyards. [11–1469–3]

KASSANDRA, a gulf of the Aegean Sea off the southern coast of the Chalcidice Peninsula (Greece), located between the hilly peninsulas of Sithonia and Kassandra. Length, 50 km; width, from 9 to 24 km; depth, to 274 m. High tide is semidiurnal and less than 0.5 m. [11–1469–4]

KASSARSKOE GORGE, a rocky gorge of the Ardon River in the Northern Caucasus, located between the settlements of Buron (in the estuary of the Tseia River) and Zaramag, where the river cuts through the granite and gneiss belt of the axial zone of the Greater Caucasus. The Ossetian Military Road passes along the Kassarskoe Gorge. [11–1495–7]

KASSEL, a city in the Federal Republic of Germany, in Hessen Land, on the Fulda River. Population, 213,500 (1970). A transportation center and a river port, the city is the center of a brown coal basin. Major industries include the production of locomotives, automobiles, railroad cars (Henschelwerke), electrical machinery, optical instruments, and textiles. Kassel is the site of an industrial academy, a higher school of architecture, and an art gallery. The medieval Old Town (tenth century) is bounded on the south by the Lower New Town (13th century) and on the northwest by Freiheit (14th century) and the Upper New Town (17th century), with planned layouts. Palace and park complexes from the 17th and 18th centuries include the Karlsaue, Wilhelmshöhe, and Wilhelmstal. [11–1498–4]

KASSEM, ABDUL KARIM. Born 1914 in Baghdad; died there Feb. 9, 1963. Iraqi statesman.

Kassem, the son of a petit bourgeois, received a military education. He became a brigadier general in 1955. He led the military coup d'etat that inaugurated the Iraqi Revolution of 1958. From 1958 to 1963, Kassem was the prime minister, minister of defense, and commander in chief of Iraq. Initially, his government carried out several progressive reforms. However, in late 1959, Kassem began to suppress the forces of democracy. During the coup d'etat of 1963, he was executed. [11–1474–1]

KASSERINE, a city in Western Tunisia, the administrative center of the province of Kasserine. Population, 9,800 (1966). The city is a highway and railroad junction. It has a paper-and-pulp mill (using esparto grass as raw material). Located within the region of Kasserine there are deposits of petroleum and phosphorites. [11–1499–1]

KASSIL', LEV ABRAMOVICH. Born June 27 (July 10), 1905, in the *sloboda* (tax-exempt settlement) of Pokrovskaia, the present-day city of Engels; died June 21, 1970, in Moscow. Soviet Russian writer; corresponding member of the Academy of Pedagogical Sciences of the USSR (1965).

Kassil' was the son of a physician. He studied at the department of physics and mathematics of Moscow University. His first works were published in 1925. His work is imbued with a profound understanding of the child's perception of the world and is directed mainly at young readers: The novels and novellas *The Conduit* (1930) and *Shvambraniia* (1933) are about the revolutionary events of 1917; *The Goalie of the Republic* (1938), about Soviet athletes; *My Dear Little Boys* (1944) and *The Street of the Younger Son* (1949, jointly with M. Polianovskii; State Prize of the USSR, 1950; film of the same name, 1962), about the life of Soviet children during the war; *The Great Opposition* (books 1–2, 1941–47) and *Early Rise* (1953), about artists. *Cheremysh, the Hero's Brother* (1938), *The Gladiator's Cup* (1961), and *Be Ready, Your Highness!* (1964) deal with acute ethical problems. Kassil' also wrote publicistic books for children, such as *Your Defenders* (1942) and *About a Very Good Life* (1959).

The works of Kassil' are marked by lyricism, humor, and expressive and precise language. His books have been translated into many foreign languages and into the languages of the peoples of the USSR. He has been awarded four orders and various medals.

WORKS
Sobr. soch., vols. 1–5. Moscow, 1965–66.
Tri strany, kotorykh net na karte. Moscow, 1970.
Avtobiografiia. In *Sovetskie pisateli: Avtobiografii,* vol. 1. Moscow, 1959.
REFERENCES
Nikolaev, V. *Dorogami mechty i poiska.* Moscow, 1965.
Baruzdin, S. "Dobryi talant." *Literaturnaia gazeta,* July 1, 1970.

V. A. KALASHNIKOV [11–1504–1]

KASSIN, NIKOLAI GRIGOR'EVICH. Born Dec 1 (13), 1885, in the village of Gnusino, Viatka Province, now Kirov Oblast; died Oct. 28, 1949, in Alma-Ata. Soviet geologist. Honored scientist of the Kazakh SSR (1943); member of the Kazakh Academy of Sciences (1946).

Kassin enrolled in the St. Petersburg Institute of Mines in 1904. He was arrested for his involvement in revolutionary activities in 1907 and was exiled from St. Petersburg in 1908. He graduated from the institute only in 1913. Early in his career he was involved with hydrogeological research in northeast Kazakhstan and in Gur'ev Oblast (1912–16) and with a geological study of Kirov Oblast (1918–24). His monograph on the geology of the Viatka (107th) sheet of the geological map of the European USSR was awarded the Przheval'skii Gold Medal in 1930. Kassin's principal works were devoted to the study of the geological structure of Kazakhstan and the tapping of its diverse raw material resources and to the development of geological science in the Kazakh SSR. The 20th volume of *Geology of the USSR,* devoted to eastern Kazakhstan, and *Materials on the Paleogeography of the Kazakh SSR* were prepared under his direction. For these works he received the State Prize of the USSR (1946). Kassin was awarded two Orders of Lenin, the Order of the Patriotic War First Class, and a medal.

REFERENCES
Borovikov, L. I. "Pamiati vydaiushchegosia geologa N. G. Kassina." *Zapiski Vsesoiuznogo mineralogicheskogo ob'va; vtoraia seriia,* 1953, part 82, issue 3.
Medoev, G. Ts., and R. A. Borukaev. "Nikolai Grigor'evich Kassin." *Izv. AN Kazakhskoi SSR; seriia geologicheskaia,* 1951, issue 13.
Osnovnye idei N. G. Kassina v geologii Kazakhstana. Alma-Ata, 1960.
[11–1504–2]

KASSIRSKII, IOSIF ABRAMOVICH. Born Apr. 4 (16), 1898, in Fergana; died Feb. 21, 1971, in Moscow. Soviet internist and hematologist; academician of the Academy of Medical Sciences of the USSR (1963), Honored Scientist of the Uzbek SSR (1960).

Kassirskii graduated in 1921 from the medical department of the University of Saratov. He became a professor at the Central Institute for the Advanced Training of Physicians. His research focused mainly on hematology, tropical diseases, rheumatology, and cardiology. It was his theory that active autobiological stimulants play a part in remissions of leukemia and in the morphodynamics of blood diseases. He suggested that kala-azar be diagnosed by means of sternal puncture, for which he designed a special needle (Kassirskii's needle). He was the first in the USSR to take punctures of the lymph nodes and viscera for cytological diagnosis. He was the first in the world to propose and carry out intrasternal blood transfusions, a procedure of great value in the treatment of injuries, burns, and cachexia. He promoted the active planned rehospitalization of rheumatic patients. Kassirskii was vice-president of the International Society of Hematology (1961–63) and an honorary member of the Polish and Hungarian medical societies and the Swiss Society of Hematology. He was awarded two Orders of Lenin, two other orders, and various medals.

WORKS
Klinika i terapiia maliarii. Moscow, 1948.

Problemy i uchenye. Moscow, 1949.
Ocherki ratsional'noi khimioterapii. Moscow, 1951.
Lektsii o revmatizme. Moscow, 1956.
Bolezni zharkikh stran, 2nd ed. Moscow, 1964. (Jointly with N. N. Plotnikov.)
Klinicheskaia gematologiia, 4th ed. Moscow, 1970. (Jointly with G. A. Alekseev.)
O vrachevanii. Moscow, 1970.

REFERENCES
"I. A. Kassirskii (K 70-letiiu so dnia rozhdeniia)." *Klinicheskaia meditsina,* 1968, no. 4.
"Professor Joseph A. Kassirsky." *Blood,* 1969, vol. 33, no. 3.

G. A. ALEKSEEV   [11–1507–1]

KASSITE, the language of the Kassites, spoken in the second and first millennia B.C. in western Iran, in the territory of present-day Luristan. About 100 Kassite roots and several grammatical suffixes (apparently agglutinative) have been established based on analysis of Kassite proper names and names for the coats of horses found in Akkadian sources. The relationship between Kassite and Elamite, which was postulated by the German scholars G. Hüsing and F. Delitzsch, has not yet received sufficient confirmation.

REFERENCES
Balkan, K. *Kassitenstudien.* Vol. 1: *Die Sprache der Kassiten.* New Haven, 1954.
Delitzsch, F. *Die Sprache der Kossäer.* Leipzig, 1884.
Hüsing, G. *Die Sprache Elams.* Breslau, 1908.   [11–1508–1]

KASSITES (also Kossaioi; Akkadian, Kashshi), ancient mountain tribes that lived in the Zagros Mountains (western Iran), in what is now Luristan, during the second and first millennia B.C. The problem of their ethnic affiliation remains unresolved. The Kassites first invaded Babylonia in the middle of the 18th century B.C. and by the 16th century B.C. had conquered the entire country (the Kassite Dynasty ruled from 1518 to 1204 B.C.). The Kassite Period in the history of Babylonia has not been studied extensively. Letters and official documents dating primarily from the end of this period have been preserved. The most well-known architectural remain is the temple of King Kara-Indash in Erech (Uruk), dating from the 15th century B.C. The Kassites of western Iran were mentioned for the last time in 324 B.C. (during the time of Alexander the Great).

REFERENCES
D'iakonov, I. M. *Istoriia Midii.* Moscow-Leningrad, 1956.
Balkan, K. *Kassitenstudien,* vol. 1. New Haven, 1954.
Brinkman, J. A. *A Political History of Post-Kassite Babylonia.* Rome, 1968. (*Analecta orientalia,* vol. 43.)   [11–1508–2]

KASSNER, RUDOLF. Born Sept. 11, 1873, in Velké Pavlovice, Moravia; died Apr. 1, 1959, in Sierre, Switzerland. Austrian writer and idealist philosopher.

Kassner studied philosophy and history in Vienna and Berlin. Between 1897 and 1913 he traveled through Europe, North Africa, India, and Russia. After that he lived mainly in Vienna (in 1938 the Nazis prohibited the publication of his works), moving to Switzerland in 1946. He was a friend of R. M. Rilke and influenced his work.

Kassner's world view derived from the panaesthetic outlook of German romanticism and was in many ways similar to the ideas and conceptions of the irrationalist *Lebensphilosophie.* He advanced the principles of a universal "physiognomy"—an intuitive interpretation of forms of life and of culture apart from any system of scientific foundation. Kassner held that in the modern world physiognomy had supplanted traditional metaphysics and that the unity of the world, as perceived through physiognomy, was revealed through diverse symbolic juxtapositions and comparisons. Kassner translated into German works from classical and European literatures, including works by A. S. Pushkin, N. V. Gogol, and L. N. Tolstoy.

WORKS
Sämtliche Werke, vols. 1—. Düsseldorf-Cologne, 1969—.
REFERENCE
Schmidt, M. *Autobiographie und Physiognomik.* Munich, 1970. (Dissertation.)   IU. N. POPOV   [11–1483–1]

KASSO, LEV ARISTIDOVICH. Born June 8 (20), 1865, in Paris; died Nov. 26 (Dec. 9) 1914, in St. Petersburg. Russian minister of education from 1911 to 1914.

Kasso, a nobleman by birth from the province of Bessarabia, was a wealthy landowner. He was educated abroad, in Paris, Heidelberg, and Berlin. A lawyer by profession, he wrote books on civil law. In 1892, Kasso became a lecturer at the University of Derpat (Tartu). In 1895 he became professor at the University of Kharkov; and in 1899, at Moscow University. From 1908 to 1910 he was the director of an imperial lyceum. Kasso was appointed the chief administrator of the Ministry of Education in September 1910 and the minister of education in February 1911. While holding the latter post, he followed an extremely reactionary policy. He ruthlessly suppressed the student movement, prohibited student unions and meetings, fired progressive professors, blocked the opening of new universities, and intensified after-school surveillance of students. In 1912 he expelled all the women students from the Higher Medical Courses in St. Petersburg.

Kasso's pogrom-like policy led to protests by wide circles of the public and was denounced by the Bolshevik deputies to the Fourth Imperial Duma. V. I. Lenin characterized Kasso's department as "a ministry of police espionage, a ministry that derides youth and jeers at the people's thirst for knowledge" (*Poln sobr. soch.,* 5th ed., vol. 23, p. 135).   [11–1509–1]

KASTAL'SKII, ALEKSANDR DMITRIEVICH. Born Nov. 16(28), 1856, in Moscow; died there Dec. 17, 1926. Soviet composer, active in choral art; music folklorist.

Kastal'skii graduated in 1893 from the Moscow Conservatory, where he studied under Tchaikovsky, S. I. Taneev, and N. A. Gubert. He began teaching in 1887 and in 1910 became director at the Moscow Synod School, which was reorganized in 1918 into the Moscow People's Choral Academy. From 1918 he was active in multifaceted educational work in the music divisions of the People's Commissariat for Education, the Proletarian Cultural and Educational Organization, the Political Education Committee, and the Military Commissariat of Moscow. In 1922, Kastal'skii became a professor at the Moscow Conservatory, where his students included the composers D. S. Vasil'ev-Buglai and A. A. Davidenko.

Kastal'skii played a leading role in the development of Russian choral music, and in the early 1920's was one of the first composers to write revolutionary songs for the masses and large-scale choral works about Soviet life—for example, *V. I. Lenin* (*At the Tomb*), 1924, for reader, chorus, and symphony orchestra. He wrote choral arrangements of folk songs and did research on Russian folk art.

REFERENCE
Stat'i, vospominaniia, materialy. [Compiled by D. V. Zhitomirskii.] Moscow, 1960. (Bibliography.)   [11–1512–1]

KASTEEV, ABYLKHAN. Born Jan. 1 (14), 1904, in the village of Chizhin, Panfilov Raion, Taldy-Kurgan Oblast, Kazakh SSR. Soviet painter and watercolorist. People's Artist of the Kazakh SSR (1944). Became a member of the CPSU in 1949.

Kasteev studied under N. G. Khludov from 1929 to 1931. His genre compositions deal with both prerevolutionary and Soviet life in Kazakhstan, for example, the series *The Old and New Life* (begun in the 1930's). Kasteev has also done portraits (*Amangel'dy Imanov,* 1950) and landscapes (the series *On the Kazakhstan Land,* watercolor, 1955–65). His other paintings include *Turksib* (watercolor, 1932) and *The Karatau Concentrator* (1967). All of the above-mentioned works, except the last, are in the T. G. Shevchenko Kazakh Art Gallery in Alma-Ata. Kasteev has been awarded three orders and various medals.

REFERENCES
Mikul'skaia, E. G. *Abylkhan Kasteev. . . .* Alma-Ata, 1956.

A. Kasteev, *Katalog iubileinoi vystavki.* Alma-Ata, 1964. [11–1514–1]

KASTLER, ALFRED. Born May 3, 1902, in Guebwiller. French physicist. Member of the Paris Academy of Sciences (1964).

In 1924, Kastler graduated from the Ecole Normale Supérieure in Paris. In 1941 he became a professor there. Beginning in 1945 he was a professor at the Sorbonne. In 1958 he became director of the Atomic Clock Laboratory and in 1968, director of research at the National Center of Scientific Research. Between 1930 and 1950, Kastler studied fluorescence and combination scattering in gases and crystals. In 1950, working with J. Brossel, he observed the phenomenon of magnetic resonance in the radio frequency band by using the optical pumping method that he had discovered and worked out in detail. Kastler was awarded a Nobel Prize in 1966.

WORKS
Orientierung von Atomkernen durch optisches Pumpen. Mosbach, 1961.
In Russian translation:
"Opticheskie metody izucheniia nizkochastotnykh rezonansov (Nobelevskaia lektsiia po fizike 1966)." *Uspekhi fizicheskikh nauk,* 1967, vol. 93, issue 1, p. 5. [11–1517–3]

KASTORNOE, an urban-type settlement and center of Kastornoe Raion, Kursk Oblast, RSFSR, located on the Olym River in the Don basin.

Kastornoe is a railroad junction for lines to Moscow, Kursk, Voronezh, and the Donbas. During the Civil War of 1918–20 and the Great Patriotic War of 1941–45 there were major battles in the Kastornoe area in connection with the Voronezh-Kastornoe Operation of 1919 and the Voronezh-Kastornoe Operation of 1943. [11–1517–7]

KASTORSKII, VLADIMIR IVANOVICH. Born Mar. 2 (14), 1871, in the village of Bol'shie Soli, present-day Nekrasovskoe, Iaroslavl' Oblast; died July 2, 1948, in Leningrad. Soviet Russian basso. Honored Art Worker of the RSFSR (1939).

As a child, Kastorskii sang in a church choir. Later, he studied under the direction of his cousin, A. Kastorskii. He took lessons from the Italian singer and voice teacher A. Cotogni. In 1894 he made his operatic debut, and beginning in 1898, he was a soloist at the Mariinskii Theater (currently, the Leningrad Academic Theater of Opera and Ballet). Among his roles were Ruslan and Susanin in Glinka's *Ruslan and Liudmila* and *Ivan Susanin* and the Miller in Dargomyzhskii's *The Mermaid.* Kastorskii was one of the best performers of Wagnerian roles; he sang Wotan in *Der Ring des Nibelungen,* Hagen in *Götterdämmerung,* and King Marke in *Tristan und Isolde.* In 1907 and 1908 he participated in the Russian Seasons Abroad. In 1907 he organized a vocal quartet to promote Russian folk songs, with which he toured in Russia and abroad (Paris, London). Kastorskii sang on the operatic stage for approximately 45 years and appeared on radio and in concerts until his death.

REFERENCE
Stark, E. *Peterburgskaia opera i ee mastera.* Leningrad-Moscow, 1940. [11–1518–1]

KASUGAI, a city in Japan, located on the island of Honshu, in the prefecture of Aichi. Population, 162,000 (1970). The city has a pulp-and-paper combine, as well as electrical engineering enterprises. [11–1525–1]

KASUM-ISMAILOV, a city (prior to 1966, a settlement), the center of the Kasum-Ismailov Raion, Azerbaijan SSR. It is located 7 km from the Geran' railroad station on the Baku-Tbilisi Line. Its population was 4,900 in 1972. The city has a hatchery and poultry-raising center. In 1973 a winery was under construction. The city was named in honor of the Bolshevik revolutionary Kasum Ismailov. [11–1525–2]

KASUMOV, MIR BASHIR FATTAKH OGLY. Born 1879 in the village of Dashbulag, Tavriz Vilayet, southern Azerbaijan; died Apr. 23, 1949, in Baku. Soviet state and party figure. Member of the Communist Party from 1905.

The son of a poor peasant, Kasumov joined the revolutionary movement in 1898. He began working in factories in Balakhany (Baku) in 1905 and took part in the Revolution of 1905–07 as a member of the combat detachment of the Baku Bolshevik organization. In 1917–18 he worked for the party in Baku and in Lenkoran' District. After the temporary fall of the Soviet government in Baku in 1918–20 he was active in the underground. He was elected a member of the Party Central Committee at the First Congress of the Communist Party (Bolshevik) of Azerbaijan in February 1920. He helped organize the uprising against the Musavat government in April 1920 and became a member of the Baku Revolutionary Committee on April 29.

Kasumov was vice-chairman of the Azerbaijan Central Executive Committee from 1921 to 1924 and again from 1931 to 1935 and chairman of that body from 1937 to 1938. He served as people's commissar of social security in Azerbaijan from 1935 to 1937. From 1938 until his death he was chairman of the Presidium of the Supreme Soviet of the Azerbaijan SSR and vice-chairman of the Presidium of the Supreme Soviet of the USSR. A deputy to the first and second convocations of the Supreme Soviet of the USSR, Kasumov was awarded two Orders of Lenin and two other orders.

REFERENCE
Stel'nik, B. Ia. *Mir Bashir Kasumov.* Baku, 1960. [11–1525–3]

KASUR, a city in Pakistan, located in the province of Punjab. Population, 74,500 (1961). It is a railroad junction and a center of wool trade. The city also has tanning, cotton, and vegetable-oil extraction industries. [11–1525–4]

KASYMOV, MUKHAMMEDZHAN. Born May 9, 1907, in the *kishlak* (hamlet) of Rishtan, in present-day Altyaryk Raion, Fergana Oblast, Uzbek SSR; died July 5, 1971, in Dushanbe. Soviet Tadzhik actor, People's Artist of the USSR (1941). Member of the CPSU (1948).

Kasymov studied at the Kokand Pedagogical Technicum and the Tashkent Cooperative Technicum and took part in amateur theatrical performances. In 1931 he joined the company of the Lakhuti Tadzhik Theater in Dushanbe; by the early 1940's he had become its leading actor. His best roles included Rakhimbek in *The Men With the Red Sticks* by Ulug-zoda, Allan in *A Family's Honor* by Mukhtarov, Salikh-bai in *The Landowner and the Farmhand* by Khamza, the Town Governor in *The Inspector-General* by Gogol, and the title roles in Shakespeare's *Othello* and *King Lear.* Kasymov had enormous stage presence, and his art was characterized by emotional expressiveness and sharp character outline. He worked also as a director and appeared in films. Kasymov was awarded two Orders of Lenin, two other orders, and medals.

REFERENCE
Nurdzhanov, N. *Mukhammedzhan Kasymov.* Moscow, 1955 [11–1526–1]

KATABASIS. (1) In Orthodox church services, a special kind of monastic tropariow during which the hirmos (beginning canticle) is sung both at the beginning and the end of the canon ode; the two choirs descend from the balcony to the center of the church to sing the katabasis.

(2) In the figurative sense, confusion or chaos. [11–1527–3]

KATAEV, IVAN IVANOVICH. Born May 14 (27), 1902, in Moscow; died May 2, 1939. Soviet Russian writer. Member of the CPSU from 1919.

Kataev's first works were published in 1921. He was active in the literary group Pereval. His works depicting the collectivization and industrialization of the country and the upbringing of the new man include the novellas *The Heart* (1928), *Milk* (1930), and *The Encounter* (1934) and the collections of essays *Movement* (1932) and *The Man on the Mountain* (1934).

WORKS
Izbrannoe. Povesti i rasskazy. Ocherki. [Introductory article by V. Goffenshefer.] Moscow, 1957.

Pod chistymi zvezdami. Povesti. Rasskazy. Ocherki. [Foreword by E. Starikova.] Moscow, 1969.

REFERENCES
Vospominaniia ob Ivane Kataeve. [Collection compiled by M. K. Terent'eva-Kataeva.] Moscow, 1970.
Russkie sovetskie pisateli-prozaiki. Biobibliograficheskii ukazatel', vol. 2. Leningrad, 1964.   [11–1529–1]

KATAEV, SEMEN ISIDOROVICH. Born Jan. 27 (Feb. 9), 1904, in the *posad* (suburb) of Elionka, in what is now Starodub Raion, Briansk Oblast. Soviet television scientist, Doctor of Technical Sciences (1951), professor (1952), Honored Scientist and Engineer of the RSFSR (1968). Member of the CPSU since 1964.

Kataev graduated from the N. E. Bauman Moscow Higher Technical School in 1929. He developed the first high-vacuum receiving television tube in the USSR (1931–32) and invented a cathode-ray transmitting tube having charge storage—the prototype of the modern iconoscope (1931). He proposed and was the first to produce under laboratory conditions a system for transmitting a high-definition television picture on a narrow-band channel—the slow-scan television, or transmission with a frame of prolonged duration (1934–38). He developed a method (1965–70) of transmitting the sound portion of television programs within the frequency band of the video signal. He studied the problems of converting television standards (1964–70). He has been awarded the Order of the Red Banner of Labor and medals.

WORKS
Elektronno-luchevye televizionnye trubki. Moscow, 1936.
Osnovy televideniia. Moscow, 1940. (Editor.)
Generatory impul'sov televizionnoi razvertki. Moscow-Leningrad, 1951.
                                                       [11–1530–1]

KATAEV, VALENTIN PETROVICH. Born Jan. 16 (28), 1897, in Odessa. Russian and Soviet Russian writer. Member of the CPSU since 1958.

Kataev is the son of a teacher and the brother of the writer E. P. Petrov. His first works were published in 1910. Between 1915 and 1917 he served as a soldier at the front. During the Great October Socialist Revolution and the Civil War of 1918–20 he fought in battles against troops of Denikin's White Guard and worked for IugROSTA (the southern division of the Russian Telegraph Agency). The short stories he wrote during that period, including "In the Besieged City" (published in 1922) and "Notes On the Civil War" (published in 1924), already showed clearly the two main trends of his work: heroic ardor and satire. Beginning in 1923, Kataev worked for the newspaper *Gudok,* the magazine *Krokodil,* and other publications. Kataev's satire in the 1920's was directed against petit-bourgeois philis, tinism, as illustrated by the novella *The Embezzlers* (1926; play of the same name, 1928) and the comedy *Squaring the Circle* (1928). Heroic, revolutionary, and patriotic themes became dominant in Kataev's work in the 1930's. This is seen in the novel *Time, Forward!* (1932) and the novellas *I Am the Son of the Working People* (1937) and *Son of the Regiment* (1945; State Prize of the USSR, 1946; film of the same name, 1946).

In 1936, Kataev published the work that brought him world fame, the novella *Lonely White Sail* (film of the same name, 1937), the first part of the tetralogy *The Waves of the Black Sea.* The second part of the tetralogy is *A Small Farm in the Steppe* (1956); the third part, *Winter Wind* (1960–61); and the fourth part, *For the Power of the Soviets* (film of the same name, 1956; another name for the fourth part is *The Catacombs:* first version, 1948; second version, 1951). The tetralogy affirms the succession of revolutionary traditions. Kataev is the author of the publicistic novella *The Small Iron Door in the Wall* (1964), dedicated to V. I. Lenin, and the lyrical, philosophical memoir-novellas *The Holy Well* (1967), *The Grass of Oblivion* (1967), and *The Little Cube* (1969).

Kataev was editor in chief of the magazine *Iunost'* from 1955 to 1961. His works have been translated again and again into foreign languages and into the languages of the peoples of the USSR. Kataev has been awarded two Orders of Lenin, two other orders, and various medals.

WORKS
Sobr. soch., vols. 1–5. (Introductory article by L. Skorino.) Moscow, 1956–57.
Sobr. soch., vols. 1–9. Moscow, 1968–72.
Raznoe. Literaturnye zametki. Portrety. Fel'etony. Retsenzii. Ocherki. Fragmenty. Moscow, 1970.
"Razbitaia zhizn', ili Volshebnyi rog Oberona." *Novyi mir,* 1972, nos. 7–8.
"Avtobiografiia." In *Sovetskie pisateli: Avtobiografii,* vol. 1. Moscow, 1959.

REFERENCES
Sidel'nikova, T. *Valentin Kataev.* Moscow, 1957.
Skorino, L. *Pisatel' i ego vremia: Zhizn' i tvorchestvo V. P. Kataeva.* Moscow, 1965.
Nagibin, Iu. "Vverkh po krutizne: K 75-letiiu so dnia rozhdeniia Valentina Kataeva." *Moskva,* 1972, no. 1
Russkie sovetskie pisateli-prozaiki. Biobibliograficheskii ukazatel', vol. 2. Leningrad, 1964.   V. A. KALASHNIKOV   [11–1528–4]

KATAISK, a city and center of Kataisk Raion, Kurgan Oblast, RSFSR, located on the Iset' River in the Irtysh basin.

Kataisk is a railroad station on the Sverdlovsk-Kurgan line, 214 km northwest of Kurgan. It has plants manufacturing pumping equipment, reinforced-concrete products, dry milk, and bricks. A teacher-training school is located in the city. Kataisk was founded in the mid-17th century and became a city in 1944.   [11–1530–2]

KATAMORPHOSIS, a direction of evolution characterized by the transition of a given group of organisms to simpler relations with the environment and resulting in general underdevelopment and simplification of structure.

The term "katamorphosis" was coined by the Soviet biologist I. I. Shmal'gauzen in 1939. Katamorphosis is usually associated with despecialization (loss of specific adaptations) and transition to a nonmotile or "hidden" mode of life (in cases, "little houses"). Examples of groups that underwent katamorphosis include the rotifers, bryozoans, aphids, coccids, tunicates, and underwater flowering plants. A special case of katamorphosis is hypomorphosis, that is, general underdevelopment of an organism (for example, permanent neoteny in *Proteus anguinus* and the axolotl). The word "catagenesis" is often used instead of katamorphosis.

REFERENCES
Shmal'gauzen, I. I. *Puti i zakonomernosti evoliutsionnogo protsessa.* Moscow-Leningrad, 1939.
Takhtadzhian, A. L. *Sistema i filogeniia tsvetkovykh rastenii.* Moscow-Leningrad, 1966.   [11–1553–1]

KATANGLI, an urban-type settlement in Nogliki Raion, Sakhalin Oblast, RSFSR. It lies in the northeastern part of Sakhalin Island, 7 km from the coast of the Sea of Okhotsk. There is a railroad station, and petroleum is extracted.   [11–1553–3]

KATANOV, NIKOLAI FEDOROVICH. Born May 6 (18), 1862, in the *ulus* (village) of Turakhov, present-day Askiz Raion, Khakass Autonomous Oblast; died Mar. 10, 1922, in Kazan. Khakass linguist and ethnographer; authority on Turkic languages and peoples.

Katanov graduated from the Oriental faculty of the University of St. Petersburg in 1888 and was appointed a professor at the University of Kazan in 1893. From 1889 to 1892, on commission from the St. Petersburg Academy of Sciences, he traveled through the southern regions of eastern Siberia, Uriankhai-Krai, and northwestern China. Katanov's principal works are *An Essay on the Study of the Uriankhai Language* (1903) and two volumes of materials on the languages, ethnography, and folklore of the Khakass, Tuvinians, and Karagasy entitled *Dialects of the Uriankhai, Abakan Tatars, and Karagasy* (published in *Examples of the Folk Literature of the Turkic Tribes* by V. V. Radlov, part 9, 1907). These studies are of considerable scholarly importance as a compilation of factual material.

REFERENCE
Ivanov, S. N. *N. F. Katanov (1862–1922): Ocherk zhizni i deiatel'nosti.* Moscow-Leningrad, 1962. (With bibliography.) [11–1554–1]

KATAV-IVANOVSK, a city in Cheliabinsk Oblast, RSFSR, located on the Katav River in the Ufa basin. Population, 20,000 (1970).

Katav-Ivanovsk is the terminal station of a 36-km branch of the Ufa-Cheliabinsk railroad line. It has a cement plant, a casting works, and a lumber industry. A mechanical technicum is located in the city. Katav-Ivanovsk was founded in the mid-18th century and became a city in 1939. [11–1527–4]

KATAYAMA, SEN. Born Dec. 3, 1859, in the village of Hadegi, Mimasaka Province, now part of the settlement of Iuge, Kumicho District, Okayama Prefecture; died Nov. 5, 1933, in Moscow. Prominent figure in the Japanese and international workers' movement.

The son of a peasant, Katayama began working as a typesetter in Tokyo in 1881. In 1884 he went to the USA, where he worked while completing his studies. After graduating from Yale University in 1895, he returned to Japan in 1896 and took an active part in organizing the socialist and workers' movement. Katayama helped found the Society for Assisting the Organization of Trade Unions; the Steelworkers' Union, the first Japanese trade union (1897); and the Society for the Study of Socialism (1898). In 1901 he helped organize the Japanese Social Democratic Party, which was immediately disbanded by the government, and in 1903–04 he contributed frequently to the newspaper *Heimin Shimbun.*

Elected a member of the bureau of the Executive Committee of the Second International *in absentia* in 1900, Katayama attended the Amsterdam Congress of the Second International in 1904, where he strongly opposed the Russo-Japanese War. In 1911, Katayama was arrested for organizing a strike of the Tokyo streetcar workers and spent nine months in prison. In 1914 police repression forced him to emigrate to the USA, where he joined the American socialist movement and organized the first Communist groups among Japanese workers in the USA (1918). In 1920 he translated Lenin's book *State and Revolution* into Japanese.

To escape persecution by the police, Katayama went to Mexico in 1921 and later to Soviet Russia. Elected a member of the Executive Committee of the Comintern in 1922, Katayama later became a member of the Presidium of the Executive Committee and was instrumental in founding the Communist Party of Japan (CPJ) in 1922. Consistently opposing deviations within the CPJ, he worked to strengthen the party ideologically and organizationally and to broaden its ties with the working people. Katayama attended the anti-imperialist congresses in Brussels in 1927 and in Frankfurt-am-Main in 1929, as well as the antiwar congress in Amsterdam in 1932. He is buried on Red Square near the Kremlin Wall.

WORKS
Stat'i i memuary (K stoletiiu so dnia rozhdeniia). Moscow, 1959.
Vospominaniia. Moscow, 1964. (Translated from Japanese.)
A. N. ROMANOV [11–1564–3]

KATEB, YACINE. Born Aug. 6, 1929, in Constantine. Algerian writer. Son of a lawyer.

Kateb was one of the first Algerian writers to employ the French language as a means for creating an Algerian national literature, for example, the lyric cycle *Conversation With Myself* (1946) and the narrative poem *Nedjma* (1948). In the drama *The Corpse in the Ring* (1954–55), the novel *Nedjma* (1956), and the lyric work *Dance in the Light of a Bonfire* (1961; Russian translation, 1962) he employs symbolism of magic and tribal myths. Combining folklore and realism, Kateb ridicules feudalism in the comedy *The Powder of Reason* (1959) and colonialism in the comedy *The Lute and the Suitcase* (1963). Kateb's recurrent themes, the awakening of the individual and the revolutionary activity of the Algerian people, merge in the symbolic character of Nedjma (the tragedy *The Savage Woman,* 1962). His predilection for surrealism, however, sometimes prevents him from fully developing these themes, as in the novel *Starry Firing Field* (1966). Kateb was awarded the Amrouche Prize in 1963.

WORKS
L'Homme aux sandales de caoutchouc. Paris, 1970.
REFERENCE
Dejeux, J. "Bibliographie de la littérature algérienne d'expression française," 1962–1967. *Cahiers algériens de littérature comparée,* 1967, no. 2. V. P. BALASHOV [11–1565–1]

KATENIN, PAVEL ALEKSANDROVICH. Born Dec. 11 (22), 1792, in the village of Shaevo, Kostroma Province; died there May 23 (June 4), 1853. Russian writer and theatrical figure.

Katenin served in the Patriotic War of 1812. One of the leaders of the Military Society, a secret Decembrist organization, he was dismissed from service in 1820 for political reasons. He spent many years living in the countryside. He began publishing before the Patriotic War of 1812 and was a leading figure of one of the branches of Decembrist romanticism. He was the author of the ballad *Ol'ga* (1816), a work vastly different in artistic principles from V. A. Zhukovskii's poetry and one that gave rise to polemics. The ballad's focus on Russian everyday life and the extensive use of forms from popular speech brought him close to A. S. Shishkov, yet at the same time the ballad reflected the Decembrist idea of the folk nature of literature. Katenin was also a playwright, translator, and drama teacher (V. A. Karatygin was one of his students).

WORKS
Izbr. proiz. [Introductory article by G. V. Ermakova-Bitner.] Moscow-Leningrad, 1965.
REFERENCE
Istoriia russkoi literatury XIX v. Bibliograficheskii ukazatel'. Moscow-Leningrad, 1962. IU. M. LOTMAN [11–1570–2]

KATERINI, a city in Greece, in Macedonia; the administrative center of the Pieria Nome, near the Gulf of Salonika in the Aegean Sea. Population, 14,000 (1971). Katerini is the center of an agricultural region. Agricultural raw materials and wood are processed in the city. [11–1572–1]

KATERINOPOL', an urban-type settlement and the center of Katerinopol' Raion, Cherkassy Oblast, Ukrainian SSR, on the Gniloi Tikich River in the Iuzhnyi Bug basin, 7 km from the Zvenigorodka railroad station. The settlement has an industrial combine. [11–1572–2]

KATHAK, one of the schools of classical Indian dance. Since ancient times, kathak has been cultivated in the Hindu temples of Rajasthan and Hindustan (in the territory of the modern state of Uttar Pradesh), and it was one of the obligatory elements of religious ceremonies. Kathaks (narrators) would relate various stories (kathas) from the life of Vishnu and Krishna, accompanying them with dances. After the conquest of India by Muslim dynasties, the art of kathak fell into decay; however, in the 17th century it was revived at the courts of the rajahs in Rajasthan and the Nawabs of Oudh. The dance is taking on a secular character, and new technical devices are appearing.

Contemporary kathak consists of *nritta,* which contains complex rhythmical movements and postures, and *nritya,* which includes song and pantomime. Everyday and lyrical scenes and the portrayal of beasts and animals serve as subjects for the pantomime. In the 1930's, the Indian dancer Menaka (Leila Sokhey) did performances in the kathak style, such as Deva Vijaya Nritya (dance of the god of victory), Menaka Lasyam (dances of Menaka), and Malavika and Agnimitra. In the early 1970's, kathak performances were done by the well-known Indian dancers and choreographers Narendra Sharma and Birju Maharaj.

REFERENCE
Ambrose, Kay. *Classical Dances and Costumes of India.* London [1951].
M. P. BABKINA [11–1602–1]

KATHAKALI (Malayalam, literally "the telling of a story"), a traditional kind of performance in the popular theater of South India, including dance, pantomime, vocal and instrumental music, and elements of circus acrobatics. The origins of Kathakali date from early antiquity, although the final form was established in the 17th century.

The basic theatrical principle of Kathakali is differentiation of the visual and the musical aspects of the show. The actor does a dance and a pantomime, and the dialogues and monologues of the characters are performed by the singers and chorus, accompanied by an orchestra. The canonical positions of the dancer's fingers and hands, which are used to convey feelings and concepts, are the basis of the actor's means of expression (the Mudra and Hasta). Subjects for Kathakali plays are drawn from the epic poems *Mahabharata* and *Ramayana* and various legends and narratives. The first plays for Kathakali are attributed to the poet Thampuranom and the maharajah T. K. Turunal, and since the first half of the 19th century, works by S. Tirunal and I. Thampa have also been used. Kathakali performances are given under the open sky on a low platform. The costumes and makeup are strictly fixed and symbolic. The characters are divided into three groups: Satvik, the noble heroes, gods, and kings; Rajasik, those representing various vices; and Tamasik, demons and spirits personifying the forces of evil.

By the early 20th century, the art of Kathakali had fallen into decline. In 1930 the Indian poet and public figure Vallathol founded the Kerala Mandalam School, initiating the revival of Kathakali. In independent India, Kathakali has become part of the national culture of the Indian people. Among the Kathakali actors are Kunju Kurup, Chandu Panikkar, Gopi Nath, G. Panikkar, and Krishnan Kutty. M. P. BABKINA [11–1602–2]

KATHEDER-SOCIALISM (German, *Kathedersozialismus;* from *Katheder,* "academic chair" [department]), a school of bourgeois socialism.

The movement originated in Germany during the 1860's and 1870's as a reaction of representatives of official German bourgeois scholarship (mostly in political economy) to the growth of social conciousness in the working class. In 1872 they joined together in the League of Social Policy for the purpose of combating Marxism and lecturing from their university podiums on the necessity of state intervention in economic and social relations, allegedly in order to introduce "socialism" from above. The ideological sources of Katheder-socialism lie in the concept of "social monarchy" advanced by L. von Stein of Germany. Katheder-socialism was "the natural and inevitable expression of the theoretical cowardice and political perplexity of the bourgeoisie there" (V. I. Lenin, *Poln. sobr. soch.,* 5th ed., vol. 2, p. 479). The Katheder-socialists (G. Schmoller, L. Brentano, A. Wagner, H. Herkner, and A. Schäffle) argued in defense of the state capitalism that had been implanted in Germany. They characterized the Prussian-Junker state as a "people's state" and the officials and the monarchical authority as "the only neutral elements in the class struggle," capable of ensuring improvement of the workers' conditions and a "just distribution of capital." They also demonstrated the possibility of a social solution to the workers' question by means of police regulation of labor, revival of the customs of the medieval guilds, and so forth.

The Katheder-Socialist interpretation of a number of the theses of Marxist political economy in the spirit of bourgeois liberalism laid the ground for revisionism in the German Social Democratic movement. K. Marx and F. Engels were critical of Katheder-socialism and of opportunists who embraced it. V. I. Lenin revealed the connections linking Katheder-socialism, "legal Marxism" in Russia, and international revisionism. At the turn of the 20th century the influence of Katheder-socialism declined considerably. Some of its ideas were later adopted by the ideologists of reformism and political reaction. In 1948 the League of Social Policy was reestablished in the Federal Republic of Germany. (Since 1956 it has been known as the Society of Economic and Social Sciences.)

REFERENCES
Marx, K. "Zamechaniia na knigu A. Vagnera . . . ." In K. Marx and F. Engels, *Soch.,* 2nd ed., vol. 19.
Engels, F. "Brentano contra Marks." *Ibid.,* vol. 22.
Lenin, V. I. "Agrarnyi vopros i 'kritiki Marksa.' " *Poln. sobr. soch.,* 5th ed., vol. 5.
Lenin, V. I. "Protiv boikota." *Ibid.,* vol. 16.
Lenin, V. I. "Anketa ob organizatsiiakh krupnogo kapitala," *Ibid.,* vol. 21.
Völkerling, F. *Der deutsche Katheder-Sozialismus.* Berlin, 1959.
E. G. PANFILOV [11–1569–3]

KATHIAWAR PENINSULA, a peninsula in western India between the gulfs of Khambhat and Kutch in the Arabian Sea. In the north, the peninsula adjoins the Rann of Kutch. The peninsula has an area of more than 40,000 sq km. In the center of the Kathiawar Peninsula are plateau-like elevations and mountains (up to 1,117 m in elevation), composed predominantly of basalts and gneisses. Along the borders there is a zone of alluvial lowlands (up to 100 km wide). Precipitation is about 500 mm annually (maximum in the summer). There are savannas, sparse forests, and thorn scrub. In the south of the Kathiawar Peninsula the Asiatic lion is found (the only place in Asia). The cities of Jamnagar, Rajkot, and Bhaunagar are located on the Kathiawar Peninsula. [11–1602–3]

KATIPUNAN, a secret patriotic anti-Spanish organization in the Philippines from 1892 to 1897. It was founded and led by A. Bonifacio, E. Jacinto, and other members of the revolutionary democratic wing of the Liga Filipina, a patriotic revolutionary organization formed in 1892. After the Liga Filipina disbanded in 1893, Katipunan became a broad-based organization, with a membership of about 100,000 in 1896 (according to some estimates, 400,000). The Katipunan's program proclaimed the equality of all men and called for the defense of the oppressed and for mutual assistance and self-sacrifice in the interest of the homeland.

The Katipunan abandoned the ineffectual reformist tactics of the Liga Filipina and began to prepare for the armed overthrow of Spanish rule. In August 1896 an uprising broke out on Bonifacio's appeal. The Supreme Council of the Katipunan not only directed the military operations but became the national organ of revolutionary power, with its provincial sections assuming the functions of local government in the wake of the victories of the popular forces. Led by E. Aguinaldo, the bourgeois and landowning elements that had joined the uprising opposed the Katipunan in favor of a "republican government" in order to eliminate radical plebeian elements from the leadership of the revolution. In March 1897, the Republic of the Philippines was proclaimed by the rebels, and Aguinaldo was elected its president. In an attempt to dominate the movement, the Aguinaldo group succeeded in dissolving the Katipunan. Bonifacio was falsely accused of conspiracy and executed on May 10, 1897. The revolutionaries who had led the Katipunan began to play a subordinate role in the government of the republic and were unable to prevent Aguinaldo's capitulation to the colonialists (the Biac-na-Bató Pact of 1897).

REFERENCES
Guber, A. A. *Filippinskaia respublika 1898 goda i amerikanskii imperializm,* 2nd ed. Moscow, 1961.
Agoncillo, T. A. *The Revolt of the Masses: The Story of Bonifacio and the Katipunan.* Quezon City, 1956. G. I. LEVINSON [11–1576–3]

KATIUSHA, the unofficial name during the Great Patriotic War (1941–45) for barrel-less field rocket artillery systems.

In 1921, N. I. Tikhomirov and V. A. Artem'ev of the Gas Dynamics Laboratory started work on rocket projectiles to be propelled by smokeless powder. Between 1929 and 1933 a group of scientists of the laboratory, directed by B. S Petropavlovskii and including G. E. Langemak, E. S. Petrov, and I. T. Kleimenov, developed and officially tested rockets of different calibers —the prototypes of the Katiusha rocket—and multishot aviation launchers and single-shot ground launchers. The final work on the rocket was carried out at the Rocket Institute under the direction of Langemak and with the participation of Artem'ev,

Kleimenov, Iu. A. Pobedonostsev, and L. E. Shvarts. The air force adopted the rocket in 1937–38, installing the RS–82 on the I–15, I–16, and I–153 fighter planes and later on the Il–2 attack planes; the RS–132 projectiles, which were developed later, were installed on SB bombers and Il–2 assault planes. In 1939 the air force used them effectively in battles against the Japanese invaders on the Khalkhin-Gol River.

In 1938–41, I. I. Gvai, V. N. Galkovskii, A. P. Pavlenko, and A. S. Popov of the Rocket Institute developed a multishot launcher mounted on a truck. The M–13 rocket and the BM–13 launcher were adopted by the artillery on the eve of the Great Patriotic War. The first salvo from a Katiusha at the fascist German troops was fired on July 14, 1941, near Orsha by Captain I. A. Flerov's battery. The Katiusha played a major role in combat. In the course of the war many versions of rockets and launchers were developed, such as the BM13–SN, the BM8–48, and the BM31–12. Between July 1941 and December 1944 Soviet industry produced more than 10,000 Katiusha truck-launchers and more than 12 million rockets of all calibers.

REFERENCES
Petrovich, G. [et al.] "Kak sozdavalas' reaktivnaia artilleriia." *Voenno-istorich. zhurnal,* 1970, no. 6.
Pobedonostsev, Iu. A., and K. M. Kuznetsov. *Pervye starty.* Moscow, 1972.   [11–1603–3]

KATKOV, MIKHAIL NIKIFOROVICH. Born Nov. 1 (13), 1818, in Moscow; died July 20 (Aug.1), 1887, in the village of Znamenskoe, in present-day Lenin Raion, Moscow Oblast. Russian journalist and publicist.

The son of a minor civil servant, Katkov graduated from Moscow University in 1838 and attended lectures at the University of Berlin in 1840 and 1841. In the 1830's he was a member of the N. V. Stankevich circle and was close to V. G. Belinskii, A. I. Herzen, and M. A. Bakunin. He worked on *Moskovskii nabliudatel'* in 1838 and 1839 and on *Otechestvennye zapiski* from 1839 to 1841. In the early 1840's, Katkov broke his old literary connections. Although in the 1840's and 1850's Katkov had been a liberal and admired the British political system, by the early 1860's he had become a stark reactionary. Editor of the newspaper *Moskovskie vedomosti* from 1850 to 1855 and from 1863 to 1887 and publisher of the journal *Russkii vestnik* from 1856 to 1887, Katkov became one of the most influential publicists. In 1863, after the uprising in Poland, he joined the camp of the reactionary nobility, championing nationalism and chauvinism and heaping slander upon the democratic movement and progressive literature. A. I. Herzen, N. G. Chernyshevskii, and M. E. Saltykov-Shchedrin fought against Katkov, who was the behind-the-scenes instigator of the reactionary policies of Alexander III's government.

REFERENCES
Lenin, V. I. "Kar'era." *Poln. sobr. soch.,* 5th ed., vol. 22.
Herzen, A. I. *Soch.,* vols. 17, 18, 19. (See name index, vol. 20, pp. 413–17.)
Chernyshevskii, N. G. *Polemicheskie krasoty,* part 1. *Poln. sobr. soch.,* vol. 7. Moscow, 1950.
Feoktistov, E. M. *Za kulisami politiki i literatury.* Leningrad, 1929.
Zaionchkovskii, P. A. *Rossiiskoe samoderzhavie v kontse XIX stoletiia (politicheskaia reaktsiia 80-kh–nachala 90-kh godov).* Moscow, 1970. Pages 66–74.
Istoriia russkoi literatury XIX veka: Bibliograficheskii ukazatel'. Moscow-Leningrad, 1962.   B. I. Esin [11–1576–4]

KATLA, an active volcano in southern Iceland, with an elevation of 970 m, covered by the southeastern part of the Mýrdalsjökull Glacier. The volcano's eruptions under the ice have caused intensive melting of the ice and the flooding of adjacent regions. Since the tenth century, 14 major eruptions have been recorded, the most recent occurring in 1918, 1934, and 1955.   [11–1577–1]

KATMAI, an active volcano in Alaska, in the northern Aleutian Range; elevation, 2,047 m.

One of Katmai's most violent eruptions occurred on June 6, 1912, and a caldera with a lake with a diameter of 1.5 km and a depth of approximately 1,200 m was formed at the site of the crater. The lower slopes of Katmai are covered with coniferous forests. The upper slopes are covered with mountain tundra. There are glaciers on the northeast slope.   [11–1577–2]

KATMANDU (or Kathmandu), the capital of Nepal, as well as the country's economic and cultural center. It is situated along the Bagmatti River, in an intramontane depression of the Himalayas, at an altitude of 1,360 m. It has a monsoon mountain tropical climate. The average July temperature is 24.5°C and the average January temperature 18.3°C, the annual precipitation is about 1,400 mm, and the humidity is 70–80 percent. Katmandu is subject to earthquakes, which greatly damaged the city in 1833 and 1934. The population is 240,000 (1971, with suburbs).

The founding of Katmandu, which was called Kantipur until the 16th century, is attributed to the eighth-century Nepalese ruler Gunakamadeva, who transferred the capital of his state from Lalitpur to Kantipur. The city retained its importance as the political center of the Valley of Nepal during the reign of the early Malla dynasty, from the 13th to the 15th century. After the disintegration of the early Malla state, Katmandu was the center of an appanage principality bearing the same name from 1482 to 1769. Since 1769, from the time the Prithvi Narayan reestablished a centralized Nepalese state, Katmandu has been the capital of Nepal.

Katmandu is an important transportation center, with three major highways branching out from it: the Tribhuvan Rajpath, going south to India; the Prithvi Rajpath, going west to the city of Pokhara; and the Arniko Rajmarg, going north to Kodari. Tribhuvan Airport provides air communication with other cities in Nepal and with India, Bangladesh, Burma, and Thailand. The city and its suburbs are the site of numerous handicraft workshops that produce various articles of art and jewelry. There are also individual enterprises, producing leather and shoes, textiles, and ceramics, as well as a brick and tile plant and machine-repair enterprises.

The Tundi Khel square is located in the center of Katmandu, and the royal Narayanhiti Durbar palace (neoclassic; early 20th century) is near it. The New Road to the west of the square is the busiest street in the city. Old quarters with narrow alleys are built up with two- or three-story houses in the national style. Modern hotels, a post office, a department store, and other buildings rise over the old structures. The architectural monuments of Katmandu are represented by the wooden Kath Mandir pagoda (Kastamandap; 1596), the Hanuman Dhoka complex of palaces and temples (15th to 18th centuries), the Singha Durbar palace (neoclassic; early 20th century), the Bhim Sen tower (1834), and the Monument to the Fighters of the Revolution of 1951. Near Katmandu are the Bodhnath stupa and the Svayambhunath architectural and sculptural complex with Buddhist stone reliefs of the sixth to eighth centuries. (Both structures were built in the third century B.C. and rebuilt in the eighth and ninth centuries.) Also found nearby is the Pashupatinath complex of Hindu temples (construction begun in the 13th century).

The cultural institutions of Katmandu include Tribhuvan University with Trichandra College and the National College of Nepal, which are affiliated with it; Sanskrit College; the Royal Academy of Nepal; the National, Central, and other libraries; and the National Museum of Nepal.   [11–1577–3]

KATO, GENICHI. Born 1890 in Okayama Prefecture. Japanese physiologist.

Kato graduated from Kyoto University in 1916. In 1919 he became a professor at Keio University in Tokyo. He was the founder of Japanese physiology and one of the pioneers of nerve and muscle microphysiology. He developed a method for preparing and stimulating single isolated muscle and nerve fibers through which he could examine the basic laws of excitation. Kato showed that the stimulating effect of electric current and chemical agents in medullated nerve fibers is carried out through the nodes of Ranvier, contributing thereby to the discovery of saltatory impulse conduction in medullated fibers.

WORKS
The Microphysiology of Nerve. Tokyo, 1934.   [11–1578–1]

KATO KIYOMASA. Born 1562; died 1611. Japanese general.

Kato Kiyomasa served his relative Hideyoshi Toyotomi, the second of the three feudal rulers of Japan in the late 16th century. He distinguished himself in several battles during the wars of unification fought by Hideyoshi Toyotomi. Kato commanded the vanguard troops during the Japanese campaign in Korea in 1592–93 and fought in battles near Ulsan during the second campaign in 1597–98. Both campaigns ended in the defeat of the Japanese. In the battle of Sekigahara in 1600, Kato fought on the side of Ieyasu Tokugawa, the third feudal unifier of Japan, but he later gave his support to Hideyori, the son of Hideyoshi Toyotomi.   [11–1578–2]

KATORGA I SSYLKA (Hard Labor and Exile), a journal devoted to the history of the revolution and the organ of the All-Union Society of Former Political Prisoners and Exiles. In all there were 116 issues, published in Moscow between 1921 and 1935. The journal had sections dealing with the history of the revolutionary movement in Russia and with hard labor, prison, exile, and emigration, as well as obituaries, bibliographies, and news items. The journal published scholarly articles, memoirs, and archival materials. Among its contributors were B. Kun, D. Z. Manuil'skii, A. M. Kollontai, Em. Iaroslavskii, and other prominent members of the Bolshevik party and the international communist movement, and the historians Iu. V. Got'e, N. M. Druzhinin, B. P. Koz'min, M. V. Nechkina, A. E. Presniakov, and E. V. Tarle. The journal was edited by V. D. Vilenskii (Sibiriakov) from 1923 to 1927, by F. Ia. Kon between 1927 and 1929, and by I. A. Teodorovich from 1929 to 1935.

REFERENCE
Kantor, R. M. *"Katorga i ssylka" za desiat' let (1921–30): Sistematiches-ki-predmetnyi ukazatel'.* Moscow, 1931.   [11–1595–1]

KATOWICE, a city in southern Poland, administrative center of Katowice Województwo. Population, 302,000 (1970).

Katowice is the most important city in the Upper Silesian conurbation. It is a railroad junction and an important industrial center, with 83,000 people employed in industry. The city's industry includes coal mining (Upper Silesian Coal Basin), ferrous and nonferrous metallurgy (including the production of zinc, lead, and rolled nonferrous metals), machine building (mining, hoisting and transport machines, and electrical equipment), the chemical industry (including superphosphates), porcelain production, food processing, and printing. The city has a university, founded in 1968, a higher school of economics, and an academy of the arts.

The city is mentioned in sources with the name of Katowice for the first time in 1598. Under Prussian rule beginning in 1742, it received German town rights in 1865 and was subjected to intense Germanization. Between 1919 and 1921, Katowice was a center of armed actions of the Polish population of Upper Silesia for national and social liberation. On Jan. 20, 1922, the League of Nations adopted a resolution returning the city to Poland. In 1923, Katowice became the most important center of a general strike of Silesian miners that had been organized by the united-front Committee of 21, which was elected by representatives of 46 of the mines and plants of Upper Silesia. The city was occupied by fascist German troops in September 1939 and liberated by troops of the First Ukrainian Front on Jan. 28, 1945.

The district of Śródmieście, the historical nucleus of Katowice, has a central square, the Rynek, and a gridlike street plan. Katowice has been growing rapidly since 1945. A new city center and public and residential buildings have been constructed since 1958. The new structures include the Zenit department store (1962), the Kosmos motion picture theater (1959–65), a sports hall (1960's), and multistory houses in the districts of Koszutka and Marchlewski. A monument to the Silesian insurgents has been erected on Armia Radziecka Street (stone, 1960's; sculptor, G. Zemla; architect, W. Zabłocki). Another monument to the Silesian rebels has been erected not far from the city (stone, 1949–52; sculptor, K. Dunikowski).

REFERENCE
Katowice, miasto nasze. Katowice, 1960.   [11–1579–1]

KATOWICE WOJEWÓDZTWO, an administrative unit in southern Poland. Area, 9,600 sq km. Population, 3,730,000 (1971; 77 percent urban). Administrative center, the city of Katowice.

Katowice Województwo is an industrial region, containing the greater part of the Upper Silesian Coal Basin. Of the 850,000 people employed in industry, three-fifths live in the Upper Silesian conurbation. Katowice Województwo produces about one-fifth of Poland's gross industrial output (1971), about one-half of the steel and coke, about four-fifths of the zinc, almost nine-tenths of the coal, more than three-fourths of the iron ore (mines near Czestochowa), about one-half of the lead and zinc ores, and one-sixth of the electric power. The major industry is machine building (190,000 employed), especially large-scale metalworking and electrical macine building; an automobile industry is being developed. Other industries include building materials, chemicals, food, and textiles.

Forests cover 31 percent of the area of Katowice Województwo; agricultural land, 55 percent (41 percent plowland). The main crops are potatoes, rye, and vegetables. Cattle raising is also important (both meat and dairy). As of 1971 there were 264,000 head of cattle (including 158,000 cows), 355,000 pigs, 197,000 sheep, and 35,000 horses.   Iu. V. ILINICH

REFERENCE
Katowickie: Rozwój województwa w Polsce Ludowej. [Warsaw, 1970.]   [11–1579–2]

KATSIEV, KHABU KHADZHIKURMANOVICH (pseudonym, Khabib). Born May 13, 1916, in the *aul* (village) of Gundelen, present-day Baksan Raion, Kabarda-Balkar ASSR. Soviet Balkar writer. Member of the CPSU since 1939.

Katsiev graduated from the Higher Party School. He is the author of lyrical poems (the collection *Heartfelt Joy,* 1936) and stories (*Stars of the Earth,* 1940), depicting the struggle of the working people of the mountains to achieve Soviet power and to build a new life. In his collection of humorous and satirical short stories *What's New* (1961), Katsiev effectively employs elements of the grotesque and popular speech. He has also written the collection of novellas and stories *Muhammad* (1964) and the novel *Tamata* (1971).

WORKS
In Russian translation:
V gornom aule. Nal'chik, 1966.
Nasmeshnik Omar. Moscow, 1969.   K. S. OTAROV   [11–1633–2]

KATSINA, a city in northern Nigeria, in the North-Central State. Population, 90,500 (1963). Katsina is a highway junction and an important commercial and handicraft center. Chief trading commodities include peanuts, cotton, leather, and hides. Until the 19th century the city was the capital of Katsina, the city-state of the Hausa people.   [11–1633–3]

KATSMAN, EVGENII ALEKSANDROVICH. Born June 26 (July 8), 1890, in Kharkov. Soviet painter and graphic artist. People's Artist of the RSFSR (1969). Corresponding member of the Academy of Arts of the USSR (1947). Became a member of the CPSU in 1949.

From 1909 to 1916, Katsman studied at the Moscow School of Painting, Sculpture, and Architecture under K. A. Korovin and S. V. Maliutin. He was one of the founders of the Association of Artists of Revolutionary Russia (AKhRR). Katsman is primarily a portraitist. Through the thorough modeling of forms, he accurately renders the external appearance of his subject. He has created portraits of K. E. Voroshilov (pastel, 1933, Central Museum of the Armed Forces of the USSR, Moscow), B. A. Lavrenev (pastel, red chalk, and pencil; 1947, Tret'iakov Gallery), and Nina Zolotova (pastel, 1958–60, Tret'iakov Gallery). Katsman has also executed a number of genre compositions, for example, *The Lacemakers of Kaliazin* (1928) and *A Story About a Real Man* (1949). Both works, which are in the

Tret'iakov Gallery, were executed in pastel, red chalk, and pencil.

REFERENCE
[Gransberg, A.] *E. A. Katsman.* Moscow-Leningrad, 1950.
[11–1633–4]

KATSONES, LAMBROS. Born in 1752 in Levadhia, central Greece; died in 1805. Participant in the Greek national liberation movement.

Katsones fought as a volunteer (1770–74) in the Russo-Turkish War of 1768–74. After the war he served as an officer in the Greek infantry regiment in Russia. During the Russo-Turkish War of 1787–91 he commanded a volunteer Greek flotilla organized in 1788 in Trieste. In 1790 he attained the rank of colonel in the Russian Army. The victories of Katsones' flotilla caused a resurgence of the liberation movement in Greece against the Turkish yoke. Katsones led the movement. In 1792 he was defeated in a battle against the Turkish fleet supported by French ships and returned to Russia, where he commanded the Balaklava Greek battalion.
[11–1634–1]

KATSUMATA, SEIICHI. Born Feb. 11, 1908, in Shizuoka Prefecture. Figure in the Japanese Social Democratic movement.

Katsumata graduated from the department of economics of the University of Kyoto in 1931 and then served in a number of governmental institutions. He has been a member of the Socialist Party of Japan (SPJ) since 1947. As a candidate of the SPJ, he has been repeatedly elected to the Diet. After the split of the SPJ in 1951 into the Left SPJ and the Right SPJ, Katsumata played a prominent role in the Left SPJ. At the Unification Congress in 1955, he was elected a member of the central executive committee of the SPJ, in which he occupied a number of leading positions from 1955 to 1967. He was chairman of the central executive committee of the SPJ in 1967–68 and has been a party advisor since 1968.
[11–1635–1]

KATSURA, TARO. Born Nov. 28, 1847, in Yamaguchi Prefecture; died Oct. 10, 1913, in Tokyo. Japanese statesman and general.

Katsura was a descendant of the samurai of the principality of Choshu. He was army minister from 1898 to 1900 and prime minister from 1901 to 1905, from 1908 to 1911, and in 1912 and 1913. Katsura was one of the initiators of the Anglo-Japanese alliance. With the assistance of Great Britain and the USA, Katsura's government unleashed a war against Russia in 1904–05.
[11–1635–2]

KATTAKURGAN, a city in Samarkand Oblast, Uzbek SSR. It is situated in the Zeravshan Valley and has a railroad station on the Tashkent-Kagan line, 76 km northwest of Samarkand, with which it is linked by a highway. Population, 44,000 (1970). Chief industries include an oil and fat combine, the Khlopkomash plant, a cotton-ginning plant, a brickyard, a dairy, meat-packing and flour-milling combines, and a steam power plant. The city has the Uzbek Drama Theater, an evening industrial technicum, and medical and pedagogical schools. The site of present-day Kattakurgan has been settled since the late 17th century. Nearby is the Kattakurgan Reservoir, also known as the Uzbek Sea.

REFERENCE
Bekmuradov, I. *Kattakurgan.* Tashkent, 1968.
[11–1597–4]

KATTEGAT, a strait between the eastern coast of the Jutland Peninsula and the southwestern part of the Scandinavian Peninsula, connecting the Baltic Sea (through the Danish Straits) with the North Sea (through the Skaggerrak). It is about 200 km long, and its width ranges from 60 km in the north to 122 km in the south. The depth varies from 10 to 30 m, and in the northern part it is more than 50 m. In the middle of the Kattegat are the islands of Anholt and Laesö. The strait has two currents: a less saline surface current flowing northward and a more saline deep current flowing southward. During the winter the Kattegat freezes over along the coastal areas. The fish catch includes herring, flounder, and mackerel. The chief port is Göteborg (Sweden).
[11–1598–5]

KATUAR, GEORGII L'VOVICH. Born Apr. 15 (27), 1861, in Moscow; died there May 21, 1926. Russian composer and music theoretician. Born into a Russianized French family.

Katuar graduated from the mathematics department at Moscow University in 1884. He studied composition for a time under N. A. Rimsky-Korsakov and A. K. Liadov in St. Petersburg. He is the composer of the Symphony in C minor (1899), the symphonic piece *Mtsyri* (The Novice; 1899, based on the M. Iu. Lermontov poem), a piano concerto (1909), quintets, quartets, trios, and sonatas for violin and piano. Katuar's early compositions are stylistically close to the classics of Russian music, particularly to Tchaikovsky. Modernist traits are apparent in his later works, chiefly the chamber instrumental pieces. Katuar wrote the *Theoretical Course in Harmony* (parts 1–2, 1924–25) and *Musical Form* (parts 1–2, 1934–36). In 1917 he became a professor at the Moscow Conservatory, where he taught composition. Among his pupils were the composers and music critics V. A. Vlasov, S. V. Evseev, D. B. Kabalevskii, L. A. Mazel', L. A. Polovinkin, and V. G. Fere.

REFERENCES
Beliaev, V. *G. L. Katuar.* Moscow, 1926.
Fere, V. G. "G. L. Katuar." In *Vydaiushchiesia deiateli teoretiko-kompozitorskogo fakul'teta Moskovskoi konservatorii.* Moscow, 1966.
[11–1599–1]

KATUKOV, MIKHAIL EFIMOVICH. Born Sept. 4 (17), 1900, in the village of Bol'shoe Uvarovo, in what is now Ozery Raion, Moscow Oblast. Soviet military commander, marshal of the armored forces (1959), twice Hero of the Soviet Union (Sept. 23, 1944, and Apr. 6, 1945). Member of the CPSU from 1932.

The son of a peasant, Katukov joined the Soviet Army in 1919 and served in the Civil War as a private. He graduated from infantry courses for commanders in 1922, from the Higher Infantry School of the Soviet Army (Vystrel) in 1927, from the Advanced Academic Training School for Officers attached to the Military Academy for the Motorization and Mechanization of the Red Army in 1935, and from the Advanced Academic Training School of the Military Academy of the General Staff in 1951. From 1938 to 1941 he was commander of an armored brigade and later of an armored division. In the Great Patriotic War (1941–45), Katukov commanded the 20th Armored Division, the Fourth (later First Guards) Armored Brigade, the I Armored and III Mechanized Corps, and from January 1943 until the end of the war, the First Guards Armored Army. Katukov fought in the battles near Moscow and the battle of Kursk, in the liberation of Right-bank and Western Ukraine and of Poland, and in the Vistula-Oder and Berlin operations.

After the war Katukov was commander of the armored and mechanized troops of the Group of Soviet Forces in Germany and, after 1955, inspector of the Chief Inspectorate of the Ministry of Defense and deputy chief of the Chief Administration of Combat Training of Ground Troops. He has held high positions in the Ministry of Defense since 1963. Katukov has been awarded four Orders of Lenin, three Orders of the Red Banner, two Orders of Suvorov First Class, Orders of Kutuzov First and Second Class, the Order of Bogdan Khmel'nitskii First Class, the Order of the Red Star, eight foreign orders, and medals.
[11–1599–2]

KATULIN, ALEKSEI ZAKHAROVICH. Born Feb. 6 (19), 1906, in Moscow. Soviet athlete, coach, and teacher. Honored Master of Sports (1936), Honored Coach of the USSR (1956), and Honored Cultural Worker (1972). Became a member of the CPSU in 1931.

From 1933 to 1935, Katulin was the USSR champion in Greco-Roman wrestling. From 1937 to 1939 and from 1958 to 1972 he was the head of the department of wrestling at the State Central Institute for Physical Education. In 1947, Katulin became the chairman of the Wrestling Federation of the USSR. From 1956 to 1970 he served as the vice-president of the International Amateur Wrestling Federation (FILA); he has been an honorary vice-president of FILA since 1970. Katulin is the recipient of three orders and various medals.

WORKS
Bor'ba klassicheskaia i vol'naia. Moscow, 1952. (In collaboration with N. M. Galkovskii and N. G. Chionov.)
Klassicheskaia bor'ba. Edited by A. Z. Katulin. Moscow, 1962.
Sportivnaia bor'ba. Edited by N. M. Galkovskii and A. Z. Katulin. Moscow, 1968.   [11–1600–1]

KATUL'SKAIA, ELENA KLIMENT'EVNA. Born May 21 (June 2), 1888, in Odessa; died Nov. 19, 1966, in Moscow. Soviet Russian singer (lyric coloratura soprano) and teacher. People's Artist of the USSR (1965).

Katul'skaia studied singing under I. P. Prianishnikov and graduated in 1909 from the St. Petersburg Conservatory (N. A. Iretskaia's class). She made her debut that same year on the stage of the Mariinskii Theater. Between 1913 and 1946, Katul'skaia sang with the troupe of the Bolshoi Theater of the USSR. An outstanding representative of Soviet vocal art, she possessed an exceptional musical talent, subtle taste, a sense of style, and extraordinary stage artistry.

Katul'skaia sang the lead roles for lyric and coloratura soprano, including Antonida and Liudmila in *Ivan Susanin* and *Ruslan and Liudmila* by Glinka, Martha and the Snow Maiden in *The Tsar's Bride* and *The Snow Maiden* by Rimsky-Korsakov, and Violetta and Gilda in *La Traviata* and *Rigoletto* by Verdi. She gave concerts frequently; her repertoire of chamber music included more than 700 works. Katul'skaia became a professor at the Moscow Conservatory in 1950; her students included T. A. Milashkina and A. D. Maslennikov. She wrote articles on vocal art. Katul'skaia was awarded the State Prize of the USSR (1950), three orders, and various medals.

REFERENCE
Grosheva, K. *Katul'skaia.* Moscow, 1957.   [11–1600–3]

KATUN' (also, the Katun' Belki), a range of the Central Altai Mountains in the Gorno-Altai AO. The range forms the divide of the Katun', Argut, and Berel' rivers. Length, approximately 150 km; maximum elevation, 4,506 m (Mount Belukha). It is composed of schists and granites. In the central regions, alpine peaks predominate; 386 glaciers descend their slopes. The total area of glaciation is 279 sq km. On the slopes with elevations up to 2,000–2,200 m, there are larch and cedar forests. At higher elevations, there are alpine meadows, bare rocks, and taluses.   [11–1601–3]

KATUN', a river in the Altai Mountains, Altai Krai, RSFSR. It joins the Biia River, 19 km southwest of the town of Biisk, forming the Ob' River. Length, 688 km; basin area, 60,900 sq km. The river's source is the Katun' Glacier on the southern slope of Mount Belukha. In its middle course it flows through a broad valley and divides into branches. In its lower course it flows in a comparatively narrow valley, with width up to 4 km. Approximately 70 km from the mouth, the river flows through a plain. It is fed by glaciers and snow. The mean annual flow rate at the population center of Srostki (53 km from the mouth) is 626 cu m per sec. The upper Katun' freezes in December; the lower, in late November. The ice breaks up in the first half of April. Tributaries are the Argut and Chuia rivers on the right, and the Koksa and Sema rivers on the left. Timber is floated on the river. The Chuia highway stretches for a significant distance through the Katun' valley.   [11–1601–4]

KATUN', a glacier descending the southern slopes of Mount Belukha in the Katun' Range in the Altai. Length, approximately 8.5 km; area, approximately 8.5 sq km. The terminus of the glacier lies at an elevation of about 1,970 m (over the last 50 years, the glacier has retreated 700 m). The Katun' River takes its source from the glacier.   [11–1601–2]

KATUNKI, an urban-type settlement in Chkalovsk Raion, Gorky Oblast, RSFSR. It is located on the right bank of the Volga River (at the Gorky Reservoir), 50 km south of the Zavolzh'e railroad station. There is a shop for the production of machinery and a branch of a drawn-thread embroidery workshop.   [11–1601–1]

KATUSHEV, KONSTANTIN FEDOROVICH. Born Oct. 1, 1927, in the village of Bol'shoe Boldino, Gorky Oblast. Soviet statesman and party leader. Member of the CPSU since 1952.

The son of an office worker, Katushev graduated from the A. A. Zhdanov Polytechnic Institute in 1951. Since 1951 he has worked successively as designer, senior designer, head designer, and deputy chief designer of the Gorky Automotive Plant. He has been active in party work in Gorky since 1957. From 1963 to 1965 he served as first secretary of the Gorky Municipal Committee of the CPSU, becoming first secretary of the Gorky Oblast Committee of the CPSU in 1965.

Since April 1968, Katushev has been a secretary of the Central Committee of the CPSU. He was a delegate to the Twenty-second, Twenty-third, and Twenty-fourth Party Congresses, and at the Twenty-third and Twenty-fourth Congresses he was elected a member of the Central Committee of the CPSU. Katushev also served as a deputy to the seventh, eighth, and ninth convocations of the Supreme Soviet of the USSR. He has been awarded the Order of Lenin.   [11–1601–5]

KATUSHKI (Russian word meaning "coils"), gastropods of the family Planorbidae of the subclass Pulmonata. Most of them are small in size (diameter of the shell measures 2–15 mm). Only one species—*Planorbarius corneus*—is large, measuring up to 30 mm. The shell is coiled in one plane. The lung serves as its respiratory organ, but a *katushka* needs less atmospheric air than other Pulmonata because it has a supplementary organ of aquatic respiration (an adaptive gill). *Katushki* were formerly all classed in the single genus *Planorbis*, but they are now divided into many genera. (In the USSR alone there are up to eight genera.) They are widely distributed.   [11–1601–6]

KATYREV-ROSTOVSKII, IVAN MIKHAILOVICH. Year of birth unknown; died 1640. Prince; Russian political figure and writer of the 17th century.

Katyrev-Rostovskii entered government service under Boris Godunov. In 1608 he was relegated to Siberia as *voevoda* (military governor) of Tobol'sk but was recalled in 1613. He was a close follower of the Romanovs and took part in the election of his brother-in-law Mikhail Fedorovich to the throne in 1613. Subsequently, Katyrev-Rostovskii held high administrative and military offices, including those of grand *voevoda* of the first host, head of the Vladimir High Court (1630–32), and first *voevoda* in Moscow, Tula, and Novgorod. Katyrev-Rostovskii is considered to be the author of *The Tales of This Book From Bygone Years: On the Origin of the Reigning City of Moscow* . . . (published 1891), in which he recounts events from the reign of Ivan the Terrible to the election of Mikhail Fedorovich. Some scholars, however, believe that Katyrev-Rostovskii merely edited the book, adding some material and his own poems.

REFERENCES
Platonov, S. F. *Drevnerusskie skazaniia i povesti o smutnom vremeni XVII v. kak istoricheskii istochnik,* 2nd ed. St. Petersburg, 1913.
Cherepnin, L. V. *Russkaia istoriografiia do XIX v.: Kurs lektsii.* Moscow, 1957. Pages 110–11, 114–16.
Gudzii, N. K. "K voprosu o sostave *Letopisnoi knigi,* pripisyvaemoi kniaziu I. M. Katyrevu-Rostovskomu." In the collection *Tr. Otdela drevnerusskoi literatury,* vol. 14. Moscow-Leningrad, 1958. Pages 290–97.   V. I. KORETSKII   [11–1603–1]

KATZ, BERNARD. Born Mar. 24, 1911, in Leipzig. English physiologist; member of the Royal Society of London since 1952 and its vice-president since 1965.

Katz graduated from the University of Leipzig in 1934. In 1935 he moved to England and taught at University College in London (1935–39 and 1946–50). Since 1952 he has been a professor and head of the biophysics department there. Katz's principal works have been on neuromuscular physiology and biophysics, mainly studying the mechanism of generation of bioelectric potentials, synaptic transmission from cell to cell, and the physicochemical properties of cell membranes. Katz won the

Nobel Prize in 1970 (jointly with J. Axelrod and U. von Euler).

WORKS

Nerv, myshtsa, sinaps. Moscow, 1968. (Translated from English.)
[11–1633–1]

KAUCHUK I REZINA (Raw and Cured Rubber), a scientific and technical journal; organ of the Ministry of the Oil-refining and Petrochemical Industry of the USSR and the D. I. Mendeleev All-Union Chemical Society. The journal has been published monthly since 1927 in Moscow. Until 1936 it was published under the title *Zhurnal rezinovoi promyshlennosti* (Journal of the Rubber Industry); since 1937 it has come out under its present title (it was not published from 1942 to 1956).

The journal is concerned with problems of the production of synthetic rubber, tires, cured-rubber and asbestos technical products, household rubber goods, carbon black, reclaimed rubber, and recapping of tires. It publishes the results of research on the properties of various materials and articles, as well as the processes of their treatment and use; discusses research and testing methodology, the problems of production methods, and the theory and calculation, as well as the practice, of designing rubber products; publishes articles on the economics of the various sectors of production and propagandizes the advanced experiments of enterprises; presents data on the achievements of foreign science and technology; and gives critiques and bibliographic reviews. Circulation in 1974 was about 6,000.
[11–1617–3]

KAUDZĪT, REINIS REINISOVIČ AND MATIS REINISOVIČ. Latvian writers. Reinis Reinisovič (pseudonym, Vidzemnieks) was born Apr. 30 (May 12), 1839, in Vecpiebalga Volost, present-day Cēsis Raion, and died there Aug. 21, 1920. His brother Matis (pseudonym, Kalninieks) was born Aug. 6 (18), 1848, in Vecpiebalga Volost and died there Nov. 8, 1926.

The Kaudzītis brothers became elementary school teachers in Vecpiebalga in 1868. In his struggle against the policies of the Baltic German landowners and pastors in public education during the 1880's, Reinis Kaudzīt emerged as a leading Latvian publicist. The brothers' most important work is the novel *The Time of the Land Surveyors* (1879). As the first major Latvian realist literary work, the novel was of great importance for the development of realism in Latvian literature. Effectively using ethnographic material, the Kaudzītis brothers vividly portrayed the coming of capitalism in the countryside in the 1870's and created a wide range of satirical characters.

WORKS

Brāļu Kaudzīšu raksti, vols. 1–6. Riga, 1939–41.
Mērnieku laiki. Riga, 1964.
In Russian translation:
Vremena zemlemerov. Riga, 1962.

REFERENCES

Istoriia latyshskoi literatury, vol. 1. Riga, 1971.
Latviešu literatūras vēsture, vol. 2. Riga, 1963.
Čakars, O. *Brāļu Kaudzīšu "Mērnieku laiki"—pirmais reālistiskais romāns latviešu literatūrā.* Riga, 1968.
I. V. KIRSHENTALE [11–1604–2]

KAUFFMANN, ANGELICA. Born Oct. 30, 1741, in Cur, Switzerland; died Nov. 5, 1807, in Rome. German painter and graphic artist. Representative of classicism.

Kauffmann lived in Italy from 1742 to 1757 and in London from 1766 to 1781. She returned to Italy in 1782 and lived there until her death. Kauffmann painted portraits (portrait of J. W. von Goethe, 1787, Goethe National Museum, Weimar) and sentimental scenes based on mythological, religious, historical, and literary themes (*The Farewell of Abelard and Heloise,* Hermitage, Leningrad).

REFERENCE

Smidt-Dörrenberg, I. *Angelika Kauffmann.* [Vienna] 1968.

KAUFMAN, ALEKSANDR ARKAD'EVICH. Born Mar. 12, 1864, in Berlin; died 1919. Russian economist and statistician. An organizer and leader of the Constitutional Democrats (Cadets).

Kaufman graduated from St. Petersburg University in 1885. From 1887 to 1906 he served in the Ministry of Agriculture and State Properties. He assembled extensive material on the economy of peasant farms in Siberia. Although V. I. Lenin utilized certain statistical works by Kaufman, he nevertheless sharply criticized his exhortations for class peace between peasants and landlords (*Poln. sobr. soch.,* 5th ed., vol. 16, pp. 224, 226, 227). After the October Socialist Revolution, Kaufman worked in central statistical institutions.

WORKS

Krest'ianskaia obshchina v Sibiri. St. Petersburg, 1897.
Pereselenie i kolonizatsiia. St. Petersburg, 1905.
Formy khoziaistva v ikh istoricheskom razvitii. Moscow, 1910.
Statistika: Ee priemy i ee znachenie dlia obshchestvennykh nauk. [Moscow, 1911.]
Agrarnyi vopros v Rossii. Moscow, 1918. [11–1616–1]

KAUFMAN, ILLARION IGNAT'EVICH. Born July 5, 1848, in Odessa; died 1916. Russian economist.

Kaufman graduated from the University of Kharkov in 1869 and was a professor at St. Petersburg University from 1893 to 1916. A specialist in the field of monetary circulation, credit, and finances, he wrote on the history of Russian finance. In 1872, Kaufman published one of the first reviews of K. Marx's *Das Kapital* in the journal *Vestnik Evropy* (Messenger of Europe), no. 5. It was, in the words of V. I. Lenin, remarkable for its correct exposition of the essence of Marx's materialistic-dialectic method (*Poln. sobr. soch.,* 5th ed., vol. 26, p. 92). Kaufman noted in his review that Marx had studied the principles of the rise, development, and decline of capitalism. However, because of the limited nature of his bourgeois world view, Kaufman could not comprehend or adopt the idea of the historical revolutionary role of the proletariat.

WORKS

Istoriia bankovogo dela v Velikobritanii i Irlandii. St. Petersburg, 1877.
Serebrianyi rubl' v Rossii ot ego vozniknoveniia do kontsa XIX v. St. Petersburg, 1910. [11–1616–3]

KAUFMAN, KONSTANTIN PETROVICH. Born Feb. 19 (Mar. 2), 1818; died May 4 (16), 1882, in Tashkent. Russian general of the engineers (1874), adjutant-general (1864).

Kaufman graduated from the Central Engineering College in 1839 and served in the Caucasus. During the Crimean War, while carrying out the duties of chief of the campaign staff, he concluded with the British general Williams the conditions for surrendering Kars to Russian troops. After 1867, Kaufman was in command of the forces in the Turkestan Military District and was the governor-general of Turkestan. He directed the military operations against the Emirate of Bukhara (1868) and the Khanate of Khiva (1873) and the suppression of the Kokand Uprising (1874–76). [11–1617–1]

KAUFMAN, NIKOLAI NIKOLAEVICH. Born Feb. 8 (20), 1834, in Moscow; died there Dec. 15 (27), 1870. Russian botanist.

Kaufman graduated from Moscow University in 1856 and then he became a lecturer (1861), director of the botanical garden (1865), and professor (1866) at the university. He was the author of *Moscow Flora* (1866), one of the first original floral compilations in Russian. It greatly influenced the development of classification and geography of plants in Russia. Kaufman developed the doctrine of metamorphosis in plant morphology.

REFERENCE

Shcherbakova, A. A. "N. N. Kaufman—morfolog rastenii i florist." *Tr. In-ta istorii estestvoznaniia i tekhniki AN SSSR,* 1959, vol. 23, fasc. 4, pp. 289–323. (Bibliography.) [11–1617–2]

KAUNAS (formerly Kovno), a city in the Lithuanian SSR, with a port on the Nemunas River at its confluence with the Neris (Viliya) River; the main section of the city is located on the right bank of the Nemunas. The Kaunas Reservoir has been constructed near the city. Kaunas is a major industrial center of the republic and is a junction of railroads and highways leading to Vilnius, Kaliningrad, Klaipėda, Riga, and elsewhere.

Kaunas is the second largest city of the Lithuanian SSR, with 322,000 inhabitants in 1972 (152,000 in 1939).

Kaunas was first mentioned in written sources in the early 11th century. During the struggle of the Lithuanian people against the Teutonic Knights (14th and early 15th centuries), Kaunas Fortress was of great strategic significance and was repeatedly destroyed and laid waste by the invaders (1362, 1385, 1391, and 1400). Beginning in the 15th century trades and commerce developed. According to the Union of Lublin (1569), Kaunas became part of the Rzecz Pospolita (the Polish-Lithuanian state); in 1795 it became part of Russia. In 1812 the city was occupied and destroyed by Napoleon's army. In 1830–31 and in 1863–64, Kaunas was one of the centers of liberation revolts in Poland and Lithuania. After 1843 it was the capital of Kovno Province.

In the second half of the 19th century industrial enterprises developed in Kaunas (there were around 45 by 1902). By the early 20th century Kaunas had become a center of the revolutionary workers' movement. In 1902, Kaunas workers held a May Day demonstration. A general strike and a protest meeting were held in connection with the events of Jan. 9, 1905. The Kaunas workers also participated in the All-Russian political strike in October 1905. In August 1915, during World War I, Kaunas was occupied by German troops. As a result of the general political strike of Dec. 17, 1918, a soviet of workers' deputies was established in Kaunas on December 21. The German occupiers and the local bourgeoisie overthrew Soviet power in Lithuania, and on Jan. 10, 1919, the soviet in Kaunas was disbanded. In October 1920 the White Poles seized Vilnius, and Kaunas became the capital of bourgeois Lithuania.

Between 1920 and 1940, Kaunas was a center of the revolutionary movement. In the city there were underground printing presses, plenums of the Central Committee of the Lithuanian Communist Party were held, and the workers and soldiers repeatedly protested the counterrevolutionary bourgeois dictatorship. There the People's Diet of Lithuania on July 21, 1940, proclaimed Soviet power in Lithuania and the establishment of the Lithuanian SSR, which on Aug. 3, 1940, became part of the USSR. From June 24, 1941, through Aug. 1, 1944, Kaunas was occupied by fascist German troops, who caused enormous damage to the city. The Ninth Fort of Kaunas Fortress (built in 1887) was turned into a death camp. After the war the 60 percent of the city's industry that had been destroyed by the German occupiers was rebuilt and greatly surpassed the prewar production level.

In the postwar years more than 30 large industrial enterprises have been built, and new industrial sectors have been created, including chemicals, radio engineering, and machine-tool and instrument manufacturing. The Kaunas Hydroelectric Power Plant was built (1956–59; P. L. Ryzhik, architect, and N. D. Khrenov, engineer). Old enterprises were completely reconstructed and enlarged. The basic sectors are machine building, metalworking, and the light and food industries. Machine-building and metalworking enterprises produce machine tools, electric motors, radiators and boilers for central heating, enamelware, and farm machinery parts. Light industry is represented by the Kauno-audiniai Silk-weaving Mill, by the P. Zibertas Silk Combine, by woolen, knitwear, and garment mills, and by a rubber footwear factory. In 1965 a synthetic fiber plant was built. The largest food industry enterprises are meat, dairy, and nonalcoholic beverages combines. There are furniture and wood-products combines, as well as the J. Janonis Factory, which produces high-grade papers. Kaunas is one of the ancient centers of artistic trades (the production of knitted woolen articles and objects made of embossed leather, wood, and stone, as well as artistic ceramics).

Among the architectural masterpieces of the Old City in the northern, oldest section of Kaunas are a castle (13th–17th centuries), the Vytautas Church (founded in 1400), the Peter and Paul Cathedral (15th century; with 17th-century additions), and the Perkūno House (15th–16th centuries); all are in the Gothic style. There is also the former Massalski Palace (in the Renaissance style, early 17th century); the Camaldolese Monastery in Pažaislis (1664–1712; L. Fredo and K. and P. Putini, architects), the Church of the Jesuits (1666–1725), all in the baroque style; and the town hall (1542; rebuilt in the 18th century).

In 1847 and in 1871 general plans of the city were developed. To the east of the Old City a new part of Kaunas was built on a regular plan, with a pseudo-Byzantine cathedral where services were conducted for the garrison (now the Gallery of Stained Glass and Sculpture; built in 1890–95 by the architect K. Kh. Limarenko). Between 1920 and 1940, Kaunas developed immensely: a bank in the neoclassical style (1924–29; architect, M. Songaila), a veterinary academy (1930–31; architect, J. Jasiukaitis), a central post office (1931–32; architect, F. Vizbaras), historical and art museums (1931–36; architect, V. Dubeneckis), the M. K. Chiurlionis Gallery (1969; architect, F. Vitas), and a savings bank (now the Municipal Executive Committee Building; built in 1936–39 by A. Lukošaitis and other architects).

In the Soviet period Kaunas has been developed according to general plans (1952, by the architect K. Bučas; 1970, by the architect P. Janulis). The J. Janonis Square has been reconstructed (1970), with a monument to V. I. Lenin (bronze, 1970; N. Petrulis, sculptor). Also constructed were residential areas (on the Street of the 25th Anniversary of Soviet Lithuania, Baršauskas Street, and elsewhere), a railroad station (1949–53; P. A. Ashastin, architect), the Promproekt Building (1963–65; A. Sprindys and V. Stauskas, architects); the Tulpė Cafe (1960–61; A. Mikėnas and V. Dičius, architects), the Tartu Cafe (1962; V. Vaivada and A. Zeidotas, architects), and the Trys Mergelės Cafe (1967; A. and T. Jakučiunas, architects). There are also the monuments to F. E. Dzerzhinskii (bronze and concrete, 1947; sculptor, S. D. Merkurov) and to S. Neris (bronze and granite, 1955; sculptor, B. Bučas). The city has four institutions of higher learning (polytechnical, medical, and physical education institutes and a veterinary academy), 12 specialized secondary schools, museums, and musical, dramatic, and puppet theaters.

REFERENCES

Gulbinskienė, A., V. Černeckis, and P. Kežinaitis. *Kaunas.* Vilnius, 1962.
Litva. Moscow, 1967. (In the series *Sovetskii Soiuz.*)
Bičiūnas, V. *Kaunas, 1030–1930.* Kaunas-Marijampolė, 1930.
Abramauskas, S., V. Černeckis, and A. Gulbinskienė. *Kaunas.* [Vilnius] 1968.   [11–1606–2]

KAUNAS ART MUSEUM (full name, M. K. Čiurlionis Kaunas Art Museum). Founded in 1921 and opened in 1925. The building was constructed between 1931 and 1936 (V. Dubeneckis, architect). The collections include examples of Lithuanian fine and decorative arts of the 17th–20th centuries, Lithuanian folk art of the 19th and 20th centuries (an extremely rich collection of wood sculpture), Western European art of the 16th–20th centuries, Oriental art, and Russian art of the 19th and 20th centuries. The M. K. Čiurlionis Gallery (1969; F. Vitas, architect) includes virtually all of the artist's main works.   [11–1609–2]

KAUNAS MEDICAL INSTITUTE, an institute for training physicians (including those with advanced preparation in biophysics, mathematics, and biometry), dentists, and pharmacists.

In 1950 the medical department of the University of Kaunas (1922) became the independent Kaunas Medical Institute. In 1972 the institute included medical, dental, and pharmaceutical departments; a graduate school; 39 theoretical and clinical subdepartments; the Institute of Cardiovascular Physiology and Pathology; and museums of anatomy and pathological anatomy. Its library contains more than 600,000 volumes. In the 1972–73 school year, about 3,000 students were taught in the institute by more than 350 teachers and scientists, including one academician of the USSR Academy of Sciences and Lithuanian Academy of Sciences, one corresponding member of the USSR Academy of Sciences, 33 professors and doctors of science, and more than 200 docents and candidates of science. The Kaunas Medical Institute is authorized to accept candidate's and doctoral dissertations for defense. Since 1970 it has been an international center of the World Health Organization for the study of the epidemiology of ischemic diseases of the heart. It publishes collections of scientific studies. The institute has trained about 5,500 specialists since it was founded.

Z. I. Januškevičus [11–1608–1]

KAUNAS POLYTECHNICAL INSTITUTE, founded in 1950 as a result of the reorganization of the University of Kaunas. In 1972 the Kaunas Polytechnical Institute included departments of automation, engineering economics, light industry, machine building, mechanics, radio electronics, electrical engineering, chemical technology, construction and sanitation engineering, as well as evening, correspondence and preparatory divisions; there are also evening departments in Klaipėda, Šiauliai and Panevėžys. It has a graduate school, 68 subdepartments, and four special-problem laboratories and 18 laboratories in various special fields. The library has holdings of around 1.4 million volumes. In the 1972–73 academic year the institute had 15,000 students, with 1,000 instructors, including 23 professors and doctors of science, and 415 docents and candidates of sciences. The institute has been authorized to accept doctoral and candidate dissertations for defense. The Kaunas Polytechnical Institute has published *Trudy* since 1949.

Since its foundation the institute has trained around 22,000 engineers. The Vilnius branch of the Kaunas Polytechnical Institute was reorganized in 1969 as the Vilnius Construction Engineering Institute. M. A. Martinaitis [11–1609–1]

KAUNAS RESERVOIR, a reservoir formed by the dam of the Kaunas Hydroelectric Power Plant on the Nemunas (Neman) River in the Lithuanian SSR. The reservoir was filled in 1959–60. It has an area of 64 sq km, a volume of 0.46 cu km, a length of 83 km, a maximum width of 5 km, and an average depth of 7 m, with a maximum of 21 m. The reservoir's level fluctuates within a range of 4 m; it provides seasonal regulation of the drainage. With the creation of the Kaunas Reservoir, flooding in the city of Kaunas was reduced and navigation was improved. There is fishing (bream, carp, and pike-perch). On the shores of the Kaunas Reservoir are located the cities of Kaunas and Prienai and the resort city of Birštonas, as well as recreational areas for the residents of Kaunas. [11–1609–3]

KAUNCHI CULTURE, an archaeological culture widespread along the middle course of the Syr Darya and along its tributaries (Angren, Chirchik, Keles) from the first century B.C. to the early eighth century A.D. It is named after the ancient town site of Kaunchi-Tepe, which was first investigated in 1934–37 by G. V. Grigor'ev.

The Kaunchi culture is characterized by settlements located near water sources and surrounded by mounded burial grounds (catacombs with a long dromos, crypts, burial vaults). Well balanced modeled pottery was typical: *khums* (large vessels for storing water and food), pots, pitchers, and cups with handles topped with an image of a ram's head. In the late third century and early fourth century the image of the ram's head on certain ceramic objects was replaced by an image of a bull's head. Weapons also began to appear in the burials during this period. The people of the Kaunchi culture engaged in nonirrigated farming (barley, millet, wheat, rice, cotton, melons, and fruits) and pastoral livestock breeding (chiefly cattle). The Kaunchi culture exerted a considerable influence on the cultures of many regions in Middle Asia.

REFERENCES
Grigor'ev, G. V. *Kaunchi-Tepe (raskopki 1935 g.).* Tashkent, 1940.
Drevnosti Chardary. Alma-Ata, 1968.
Levina, L. M. *Keramika nizhnei i srednei Syrdar'i v 1 tys. n. e.* Moscow, 1971. (*Trudy Khorezmskoi arkheologo-etnograficheskoi ekspeditsii,* vol. 17). L. M. Levina [11–1610–3]

KAUNDA, KENNETH DAVID. Born Apr. 28, 1924, in Lubwa, Northern Province (Zambia). Statesman and political figure of the Republic of Zambia.

By profession a teacher, Kaunda became one of the leaders of the African National Congress (ANC), the first African political party of Northern Rhodesia, in 1949. He was secretary-general of the ANC from 1953 to 1958. In 1958 he left the party with

a group of radical members of the ANC and in early 1959 founded the Zambia African National Congress. The party was outlawed the same year, and Kaunda was arrested. Upon his release in 1960, Kaunda became president of the United National Independence Party, which has been the governing party of Zambia since 1964. He formed the first government of Northern Rhodesia in January 1964. On Oct. 24, 1964, Kaunda became president, head of the government, and defense minister of the Republic of Zambia.

WORKS
Zambia Shall Be Free. London [et al., 1962]. [11–1609–4]

KAUNDY, a depression on the Mangyshlak Peninsula, on the eastern coast of the Caspian Sea. Length, about 50 km; width, up to 17 km. The bottom, which lies 57 m below sea level, is covered with solonchaks. [11–1610–1]

KAUNITZ, COUNT WENZEL ANTON (from 1764, Prince Wenzel Anton von Kaunitz-Rietberg). Born Feb. 2, 1711, in Vienna; died June 27, 1794, in Vienna. Austrian statesman and diplomat.

Kaunitz was minister to Turin from 1742 to 1744, ambassador to Paris from 1750 to 1753, and chancellor of state from 1753 to 1792. Under Maria Theresa, who reigned from 1740 to 1780, Kaunitz directed all Austrian policy. He viewed it as his main task to fight against Prussia, whose power was on the rise. Toward this end he strove for rapprochement with France, Austria's old rival. He brought about the conclusion of an Austrio-French alliance in 1756, facilitating the formation of an anti-Prussian coalition during the Seven Years' War (1756–63). He also promoted rapprochement between Austria and Russia. Kaunitz was an advocate of enlightened absolutism and bureaucratic centralization and supported a degree of modernization of the feudal-absolutist system through reforms from above. Kaunitz's influence on Austrian policy declined markedly during the reign of Emperor Joseph II (1780–90).

REFERENCE
Küntzel, G. *Fürst Kaunitz-Rietberg als Staatsmann.* Frankfurt-am-Main, 1923. [11–1610–2]

KAUSHANY, a city (since 1965); center of Kaushany Raion, Moldavian SSR, 22 km south of the city of Bendery and 5 km from the Kaushany railroad station. The city is located in the broad valley of the Botna River. Population, 13,000 (1970). There is a cannery and sovkhoz-plant in the city. The Uspenie Church, with paintings from the 18th century that are the work of local craftsmen, is a monument of early 18th-century architecture. [11–1624–1]

KAUSHUTOV, ATA. Born July 15, 1903, in the village of Bezmein, now the city of Bezmein, Ashkhabad Raion; died Nov. 15, 1953, in Ashkhabad. Soviet Turkmen writer.

Kaushutov was one of the founders of Turkmen prose and dramaturgy. He was first published in 1925. He studied at the Communist University of the Working Peoples of the East in Moscow. He began his literary activity as a poet and playwright. His drama *Dzhuma* (1939) and the novellas *The Last Master Sergeant* (1951) and *Turkmen Steeds* (1951) represented important contributions to Soviet Turkmen literature. In the novel *Mekhri and Vepa* (1946) he wrote about events of the Great Patriotic War of 1941–45. His novel *At the Foot of the Kopet Dagh* (1947–49) deals with the struggle between the new and the old in a Turkmen *aul* (village). Kaushutov was awarded the Order of the Red Banner of Labor and various medals.

WORKS
Ëserler, vols. 1–3. Ashkhabad, 1956–57.
In Russian translation:
Vnuk Mergena: Roman. Ashkhabad, 1965.
Poslednii starshina: Rasskazy. Moscow, 1966.
REFERENCES
Aborskii, A. *Ata Kaushutov.* Ashkhabad, 1965.
Durdïev, T. *Ata Govshudovïng romani.* Ashkhabad, 1962.
[11–1624–2]

KAUTILYA. Years of birth and death unknown. Ancient Hindu statesman of the fourth century B.C.

Historical tradition has assigned an important role to Kautilya in the overthrow of the Nanda dynasty in Magadha and the accession of Chandragupta Maurya to the throne; Kautilya became the latter's principal adviser. He is also considered to be the author of the political treatise *Arthasastra,* in which an ideal state with a ramified police system and strong royal power is described. The treatise states that any means can be used to strengthen this power. [11–1612–3]

KAUTSKY, BENEDIKT. Born Nov. 1, 1894, in Stuttgart; died Apr. 1, 1960, in Vienna. One of the leaders and ideologists of the German Social Democratic movement. The son of Karl Kautsky.

In 1919, Benedikt Kautsky was secretary of state for foreign affairs, and in 1921, he was secretary of the chamber of employees. From 1920, he occupied responsible posts in the Social Democratic Party of Austria. After the seizure of Austria by the Nazis he was arrested, and he spent the years 1938–45 in concentration camps. In 1951 he became a leader of the school of economics of the chamber of employees in Graz. In maintaining the concepts of right-wing Social Democracy concerning the transformation of capitalism, Kautsky asserted that "socialism no longer needs to carry out the expropriation of the capitalists, because this task has been taken on by the managers." Kautsky was the principal author of the reformist program of the Social Democratic Party of Austria (1958). [11–1614–1]

KAUTSKY, KARL. Born Oct. 16, 1854, in Prague; died Oct. 17, 1938, in Amsterdam. One of the leaders and theoreticians of the German Social Democratic movement and the Second International; an ideologist of centrism. At first a Marxist, but later became a renegade.

In 1874, while he was a student at the University of Vienna, Kautsky joined the socialist movement, and during this period he was close to Lassalleanism. At the end of the 1870's, and especially after he became acquainted with K. Marx and F. Engels in 1881, he began to shift to Marxist positions. At that time Marx and Engels already noted in Kautsky such negative traits as pedantry and a penchant for scholastic argumentation. From 1883 to 1917, Kautsky was the editor of *Die Neue Zeit,* the theoretical journal of the German Social Democratic movement. During 1885–88 he lived in London, where he associated with Engels. In 1890 he moved to Germany. During the 1880's and 1890's he wrote a number of works and articles that propagated Marxist ideas, such as *The Economic Doctrine of Karl Marx* (1887; Russian translation, 1956), *Thomas More and His Utopia* (1888; Russian translation, 1905), *Commentaries on the Erfurt Program (1892;* Russian translation, 1956) and *Precursors of Modern Socialism* (vols. 1–2, 1895; Russian translation, vols. 1–2, 1924–25). Kautsky's *The Agrarian Question* (1899; Russian translation, 1900) was favorably appraised by V. I. Lenin. However, even at that period Kautsky was making opportunistic errors. After E. Bernstein's display of revisionism, Kautsky joined in the struggle against him, but only after prolonged vacillation. Kautsky's book *Bernstein and the Social Democratic Program* (1899; Russian translation, 1906) in general played a positive role in the fight against revisionism, but it avoided the question of Bernstein's revision of the Marxist doctrine of the state and the dictatorship of the proletariat. After the Second Congress of the RSDLP (1903), Kautsky supported the Mensheviks.

Early in the 20th century Kautsky published a number of works that were written, despite individual deviations, in the spirit of revolutionary Marxism: for example, the article "The Slavs and Revolution," printed in 1902 in Lenin's newspaper *Iskra,* the pamphlets *Driving Forces and Prospects of the Russian Revolution* (1906–07; Russian translation, 1907, edited and with a foreword by V. I. Lenin), and *The Road to Power* (1909; Russian translation, 1959).

During the years preceding World War I, Kautsky departed even further from the revolutionary workers' movement, following a line of reconciliation with the revisionists, supporting the liquidators in the Russian Social Democratic movement, denying the party spirit of Marxist philosophy, and so forth. In supporting anti-Marxist theories of violence, such as Social Darwinism, Kautsky attempted to demonstrate the compatibility of scientific socialism with non-Marxist philosophical systems. Kautsky became the ideologist of centrism, which combined a verbal acknowledgment of Marxism with an adaptation to opportunistic elements. With the beginning of the war Kautsky made a final break with revolutionary Marxism and justified the alliance with the overt social chauvinists.

Kautsky's denial of the connection between the rule of monopolies and the predatory policy of the imperialist states, as well as his attempt to reduce imperialism to a variant policy of modern capitalism, as Lenin pointed out (*Poln. sobr. soch.,* 5th ed., vol. 27, pp. 387, 409–20), led to his obscuring the radical contradictions characteristic of the monopoly stage of the development of capitalism. Just as apologetic and reformist was Kautsky's theory of ultraimperialism, which falsely predicted the onset of a new phase constituting the peaceful development of capitalism and the elimination of its contradictions. Kautsky sowed pacifist illusions and in essence denied the inevitability of proletarian revolution. Kautsky was hostile in his attitude toward the October Socialist Revolution; he opposed the establishment of the dictatorship of the proletariat and defended bourgeois democracy. Kautsky's desertion of Marxism was exposed by Lenin in his work entitled *The Proletarian Revolution and the Renegade Kautsky (ibid.,* vol. 37, pp. 235–338).

In 1917, Kautsky took part in the establishment of the Independent Social Democratic Party of Germany. During the period of the November Revolution of 1918 he actually supported the counterrevolutionary policy of the Scheidemann group and opposed the establishment of friendly relations with Soviet Russia. While he took charge of a commission on socialization, Kautsky in fact pursued the line of preserving the capitalist structure in Germany. In 1922 he heralded the merger of the right wing of the "Independents" with the Social Democratic Party. He opposed the establishment of a unified workers' front in the struggle against fascism. In 1924, Kautsky moved to Vienna. After the seizure of Austria by Nazi Germany (March 1938) he moved to Prague and later to Amsterdam.

Contemporary right-wing socialist leaders use the opportunist and revisionist views of Kautsky to substantiate their reformist policies.

WORKS
In Russian translation:
Sobr. soch., vols. 1–4, 10, 12. Moscow-Petrograd, 1923–30.
Sotsial'nyi perevorot. St. Petersburg, 1905.
Krest'iane i revoliutsiia v Rossii. St. Petersburg, 1905.
Vozniknovenie braka i sem'i, 3rd ed. Petrograd, 1923.
Natsionalizm i internatsionalizm. Petrograd, 1918.
Proiskhozhdenie khristiantsva, 5th ed. Moscow-Leningrad, 1930.

REFERENCES
Marx, K., and F. Engels. *Soch.,* 2nd ed., vol. 35, pp. 146, 178–80, 375; vol. 36, pp. 287, 297; vol. 38, p. 133.
Lenin, V. I. "Retsenziia [na knigu K. Kautskogo 'Agrarnyi vopros']." *Poln. sobr. soch.,* 5th ed., vol. 4.
Lenin, V. I. "Retsenziia [na knigu K. Kautskogo 'Bernshtein i s.-d. programma']. *Ibid.*
Lenin, V. I. "Predislovie k russkomu izdaniu broshiury K. Kautskogo 'Net bol'she sotsialdemokratii!'" *Ibid.,* vol. 12.
Lenin, V. I. "Predislovie k russkomu perevodu broshiury K. Kautskogo 'Dvizhushchie sily i perspektivy russkoi revoliutsii.'" *Ibid.,* vol. 14.
Lenin, V. I. "Opportunizm i krakh II Internatsionala." *Ibid.,* vol. 27.
Lenin, V. I. "O 'programme mira.'" *Ibid.*
Lenin, V. I. "Imperializm i raskol sotsializma." *Ibid.,* vol. 30.
Lenin, V. I. "Patsifizm burzhuaznyi i patsifizm sotsialisticheskii." *Ibid.*
Lenin, V. I. "Gosudarstvo i revoliutsiia," chap. 6. *Ibid.,* vol. 33.
Lenin, V. I. "Proletarskaia revoliutsiia i renegat Kautskii." *Ibid.,* vol. 37.
Lenin, V. I. "O 'demokratii' i diktature." *Ibid.*
Lenin, V. I. "Tretii Internatsional i ego mesto v istorii." *Ibid.,* vol. 38.
Istoriia Vtorogo Internatsionala, vols. 1–2. Moscow, 1965–66.
B. G. TARTAKOVSKII [11–1614–2]

KAUTSKY, MINNA. Born June 11, 1837, in Graz; died Dec. 20, 1912, in Berlin. German writer.

Kautsky was the daughter of a theatrical artist and was an actress until 1862. She was the mother of Karl Kautsky. She wrote works based on the lives of the urban poor and the prole-tariat. K. Marx made favorable mention of her novel *Stefan of Grillenhof* (vols. 1–2, 1879). In a letter to Minna Kautsky, F. Engels wrote a generally positive appraisal of her novel *The Old and the New* (1884), but criticized her simplified conception of tendentiousness in artistic work.

WORKS
Victoria. Zurich, 1889.
Im Vaterhaus. [Zurich] 1904.
Die Lehre von St. Bonifaz. [Berlin] 1909.
Der Pariser Garten und anderes. Berlin, 1913.

REFERENCES
Marx, K., and F. Engels. *Ob iskusstve*, vol. 1. Moscow, 1967. Pages 3–6, 538–39.
Fridlender, G. M. *K. Marks i F. Engel's i voprosy literatury.* Moscow, 1962. Pages 244–50.   [11–1613–1]

KAUTSKYISM, one of the currents of opportunism within the Social Democratic movement; it acknowledged revolutionary Marxism only in words. Kautskyism took shape during the historical conditions of World War I and was linked with the name of one of the leaders of the Second International, K. Kautsky. The latter put forth the opportunistic slogan of "civil peace," which required an abstention from the class struggle during the war and denied the necessity of preparing for the socialist revolution. The advocates of Kautskyism (O. Bauer in Austria; R. MacDonald in Great Britain; A. Thomas in France; and L. Martov, L. Trotsky, and others in Russia) were considered by V. I. Lenin to be "the most dangerous opponents of internationalism" (*Poln. sobr. soch.,* 5th ed., vol. 49, p. 72).

In economic theory Kautskyism de-emphasized capitalism's antagonistic contradictions and viewed imperialism as only one particular policy of the industrially developed states, directed at annexing the agrarian countries. The Kautskyists treated politics as separate from economics and ignored the influence of monopolies on the bourgeois state. Such an explanation of the economic essence of imperialism was invoked to conceal the deepening contradictions, the growth of parasitism, and the decay of capitalism. The anti-Marxist theory of "ultraimperialism," advanced by Kautsky and developed by the Kautskyists, ignored the objective laws of the development of capitalism.

The Kautskyists have propagated illusions concerning the supposed transformation of capitalism into some kind of new society lacking the evils that are inherent in it by asserting that capitalism has entered a new phase of its development marked by a curtailment of the competitive struggle, by the growth of monopolies, and by the elimination of conflicts between capitalist countries; that ultraimperialism will replace the struggle between national states with the dominance of internationally unified capital; and that international monopolies are a weapon for peace. The evolution of Kautskyism in right-wing Social Democratic parties has led its leaders in West Germany, Austria, and some Scandinavian countries to a final break with Marxism and to positions of overt anticommunism. The concepts of Kautskyism are directed at a defense of capitalism and a rejection of the class struggle and of socialist revolution.

REFERENCES
Lenin, V. I. "Proletarskaia revoliutsiia i renegat Kautskii." *Poln. sobr. soch.,* 5th ed., vol. 37.
Lenin, V. I. "Retsenziia Karl Kautsky, 'Die Agrarfrage.' " *Ibid.,* vol. 4.
Lenin, V. I. "Opportunizm i krakh II Internatsionala." *Ibid.,* vol. 27.
Lenin, V. I. "Gosudarstvo i revoliutsiia." *Ibid.,* vol. 33.
Novye iavleniia v sovremennoi burzhuaznoi politekonomii, vols. 1–2. Moscow, 1962–63. (Translated from German.)   G. S. ELIN [11–1613–2]

KAVA (also, kavakava, *Piper methysticum*), a shrub of the family Piperaceae (pepper). It grows on the Polynesian Islands and New Guinea. The local population uses the stems, leaves, and rhyzomes of the plant to make a stimulating and highly intoxicating beverage.   [11–302–4]

KAVADH I. Date of birth unknown; died 531. Ruler of the state of the Sassanids from 488 to 496 and from 499 to 531.

In order to weaken the political power of the nobility and priesthood, Kavadh allied himself with the Mazdakites and carried through some measures corresponding to their objectives. About 496, Kavadh was overthrown by the nobility, whereupon he fled to the Ephthalites. With their help he returned to the throne in 499 and continued his policies against the nobility. He conducted a successful war against Byzantium (502 to 505 or 506) and repelled an invasion of the northern Huns. During his reign, a number of cities were founded, the network of canals was broadened, and reforms were begun that were later continued during the reign of his son Khosrau I. Toward the end of his reign, Kavadh broke with the Mazdakites, and with the help of his third son, Khosrau (Kavadh's eldest son was educated by the Mazdakites), organized a massacre of the Mazdakite followers (in 528–529 or 524).   [11–302–3]

KAVAJA, a city in Albania, near Durrës, the country's main port on the Adriatic Sea. Population, about 20,000 (1969). The city has metalworking, glass-making, and food-processing enterprises.   [11–315–3]

KAVAL (Bulgarian *kaval,* Rumanian *caval*), a wind instrument played in Bulgaria, Rumania, Moldavia, and Yugoslavia. It is an end-blown flute (without a mouthpiece), with a long wooden tube and 6–8 fingerholes; at the lower end of the tube there are 3 or 4 additional holes for tuning and resonance. Its scale is diatonic. The *kaval* measures from 500 mm to more than 700 mm long.   [11–303–2]

KAVALERGARDY (from French *cavalier,* "horseman," and *garde,* "guard"), a special cavalry unit in the Russian guards from the 18th to the early 20th century; they were used as bodyguards and as honor guards at coronations and other celebrations.

The Kavalergardy were formed for the first time in 1724 at the coronation of Catherine I from officers of the guard and numbered 71 men. Later, from 1725 to 1731, and again from 1762 to 1796, the Kavalergardy formed the Kavalergardy Corps, numbering from 70 to 80 men. In 1797 the corps was increased to three squadrons but was soon deactivated. In 1799 the Kavalergardy were restored as the guards of the Grand Master of the Order of St. John of Jerusalem, a title assumed by Pavel I. Until 1800 the unit was recruited only from noble officers. In 1800 the Kavalergardy were transformed into a guards cavalry regiment composed of three squadrons, which were increased to five in 1804 and to six in 1813. The Kavalergardy fought in the war with France of 1805–07, in the Patriotic War of 1812, in the foreign campaigns of the Russian Army of 1813–14, in the suppression of the Polish uprising of 1830–31 and of the Hungarian revolution of 1848–49, and in World War I.

REFERENCE
Panchulidzev, S. A. *Istoriia kavalergardov,* vols. 1–4. St. Petersburg, 1899–1912.   [11–303–5]

KAVALEROVO, an urban-type settlement, the administrative center of Kavalerovo Raion, Primor'e Krai, RSFSR. Kavalerova is situated in the upper course of the Zerkal'naia River (which flows into the Sea of Japan), 163 km east of the Varfolomeevka railroad station, with which it is linked by highway. Population, 16,000 (1970). The Khrustal'nyi Mining and Processing Combine for the extraction and dressing of tin ore is located in Kavalerovo. Other industry includes auto repair, the manufacture of reinforced-concrete structures, and sawmilling.   [11–312–1]

KAVALLA (Kabala; ancient name, Neapolis), a city and port in Greece, in northeastern Macedonia, on the shores of the Gulf of Kavalla in the Aegean Sea; it has a large harbor. Kavalla is the administrative center of Kavalla Nome; population, 46,100 (1971). Kavalla is one of the principal centers of the country's tobacco industry; well-known varieties of Macedonian tobacco are processed and exported. It also has chemical and food industries.   [11–303–3]

KAVARSKAS, a city (village until 1956) in Anikščai Raion, Lithuanian SSR. Kavarskas is situated on the Šventoji River (a tributary of the Neris), 15 km southwest of the Anikščai station on the Švenčionėliai-Panevėžys railroad line; it is 104 km northwest of Vilnius. [11–314–3]

KAVAT-KALA, the remains of a feudal, rural settlement of Khwarazm, located 30 km northeast of the city of Biruni in the Kara-Kalpak ASSR. Kavat-Kala existed in the 12th century and the beginning of the 13th. It was probably destroyed as a result of a Mongol invasion. The settlement consisted of the prince's residence, four castles of his vassals, and more than 90 peasant farmsteads. A peasant farmstead was unearthed during excavations in 1937, 1940, and 1956, as well as a columned hall decorated with woodcarving in the ruler's castle.

REFERENCES
Tolstov, S. P. *Drevnii Khorezm.* Moscow, 1948.
Vakturskaia, N. N., and O. A. Vishnevskaia. "Pamiatniki Khorezma epokhi velikikh khorezmshakhov (XII–nachalo XIII v.)." In the collection *Materialy khorezmskoi ekspeditsii,* fasc. 1. Moscow, 1959.
[11–315–2]

KAVELIN, KONSTANTIN DMITRIEVICH. Born Nov. 4 (16), 1818, in St. Petersburg; died May 3 (15), 1885, in St. Petersburg. Russian historian, lawyer, sociologist. Bourgeois liberal publicist. Member of the *dvorianstvo* (nobility or gentry).

Kavelin graduated from the law department of Moscow University in 1839. He was a professor at the University of St. Petersburg from 1857 to 1861. Close to T. N. Granovskii and A. I. Herzen, Kavelin was a Westernizer during the 1840's. In 1855 he composed and distributed copies of his *Notes* proposing the state-aided emancipation of the peasants with land in return for a redemption fee paid to the landlords. The *Notes* were published by A. I. Herzen in *Voices From Russia* (1857, book 3) and N. G. Chernyshevskii in *Sovremennik* (1858, book 4). As a result, Kavelin was dismissed from his position as lecturer in history and law to the heir to the throne.

During the preparation and implementation of the peasant reforms of 1861, Kavelin supported the government's undertakings from a liberal standpoint. However, by the end of 1861, Kavelin's moderate liberalism became transformed into outright opposition to revolutionary democratic forces. In his pamphlet *The Nobility and the Emancipation of the Peasants* (1862), Kavelin opposed the idea of a constitution and defended strong autocratic power. Beginning in the late 1850's he moved closer to the point of view of the Slavophiles. In 1866 he presented the profoundly conservative notes *On Nihilism and the Essential Measures to Be Taken Against It* to the tsar. From the 1860's through the 1880's he opposed the materialist approach in questions of psychology and ethics.

The historical views of Kavelin, who, along with B. N. Chicherin, became a founder of the "state school," were formulated most clearly in *A Look at the Legal Life of Old Russia* (1847), *A Brief Look at Russian History* (1887), and *Thoughts and Notes on Russian History* (1866). Kavelin developed the notion of the crucial role of the state in the life of the people. According to Kavelin the state was the highest form of social life in the history of Russia. In his works, Kavelin characteristically dealt with the general questions of history through the prism of legal relations, an approach that tended to give his analyses (which took a publicistic form) a highly political nature.

WORKS
Sobr. soch., vols. 1–4. St. Petersburg, 1897–1900.
REFERENCES
Lenin, V. I. *Poln. sobr. soch.,* 5th ed. (See reference volume, part 2, p. 404.)
Rozental', V. N. "Ideinye tsentry liberal'nogo dvizheniia v Rossii nakanune revoliutsionnoi situatsii." In the collection *Revoliutsionnaia situatsiia v Rossii v 1859–1861 gg.* (vol. 3). Moscow, 1963.
Rozental', V. N. "Pervoe otkrytoe vystuplenie russkikh liberalov v 1855–1856 gg." *Istoriia SSSR,* 1958, no. 2.

Ocherki istorii istoricheskoi nauki v SSSR, vol. 2. Moscow, 1960.
I. V. POROKH [11–315–5]

KAVERIN, VENIAMIN ALEKSANDROVICH. Born Apr. 6 (19), 1902, in Pskov. Soviet Russian writer.

Kaverin graduated from the Institute of Oriental Languages (1923) and the Department of History and Philology at Leningrad State University (1924). His first short story was published in 1922, and during the early 1920's he was a member of the Serapion Brothers literary group. His works, written in a variety of genres and styles, deal with people who embody the creativity of the Soviet intelligentsia. Kaverin most often selects as his heroes scholars and men of letters whose sense of being is intrinsically bound up with their work and the defense of their principles. His narratives of their life and struggle are invariably built along complex and intense plot lines—for example, the novels *The Fulfillment of Desire* (books 1–2, 1934–36), *Two Captains* (books 1–2, 1938–44; State Prize of the USSR, 1946; 42 editions in 25 years), and *The Open Book* (1949–56). The novellas *Seven Improper Couples* and *The Slanting Rain* (1962) attempted to show the consciousness on the part of Soviet people of their rights, their obligations to their Motherland, and a feeling of mutual trust. In the 1960's, Kaverin published a book of essays and memoirs, *Greetings, Brother, Writing Is Very Hard* (1965); a new edition of his book on O. I. Senkovskii, *Baron Brambeus* (1966); and the novellas *The Double Portrait* (1966) and *The School Play* (1968). His novel *In Front of the Mirror* and his literary reminiscences *In the Old House* were both published in 1971. Kaverin's books have been translated into many foreign languages and languages of the peoples of the USSR. He was awarded three orders and several medals.

WORKS
Sochineniia, vols. 1–3. Leningrad, 1930.
Sobr. soch., vols. 1–6. Moscow, 1963–66.
"Avtobiografiia." In *Sovetskie pisateli: Avtobiografii,* vol. 1. Moscow, 1959.
REFERENCES
Smirnova, V. "Dva kapitana meniaiut kurs." *Znamia,* 1945, no. 8.
Maslin, N. "Veniamin Kaverin." *Novyi mir,* 1948, no. 4.
Kostelianets, B. "Zhivoe edinstvo." *Zvezda,* 1954, no. 11.
Gor, G. "Pisatel' i nauka." *Russkaia literatura,* 1962, no. 3.
Gei, N. "O tsennostiakh mnimykh i podlinnykh." *Literaturnaia gazeta,* Aug. 18, 1971.
Russkie sovetskie pisateli-prozaiki: Biobibliograficheskii ukazatel', vol. 2. Leningrad, 1964.
G. N. MUNBLIT [11–318–1]

KAVKAZSKII RABOCHII (Caucasian Worker), a Bolshevik daily newspaper, the organ of the Caucasian-Regional and Tiflis Committees of the RSDLP (Bolshevik).

The *Kavkazskii rabochii* was published in Tbilisi from Mar. 11 (24), 1917, to Feb. 8, 1918. Its circulation was 6,000. Among those who took part in the editorial work were P. A. Dzhaparidze, M. G. Tskhakaia, S. G. Shaumian, and S. I. Kavtaradze. The *Kavkazskii rabochii* promoted Leninist ideas, fought for the implementation of the resolutions of the Seventh (April) All-Russian Conference and the Sixth Congress of the RSDLP (Bolshevik), and conducted a resolute struggle for the establishment of Soviet power and against the Transcaucasian counterrevolutionary government, the Mensheviks, and the Socialist Revolutionaries. In February 1918 the printing press of the newspaper was destroyed by order of the Transcaucasian counterrevolutionary government, and the newspaper ceased publication.
[11–356–1]

KAVKAZSKII RABOCHII LISTOK (Caucasian Workers' Leaflet), the first Bolshevik daily newspaper in the Caucasus, the organ of the Caucasian Union Committee of the RSDLP. The *Kavkazskii rabochii listok* was published in Russian in Tbilisi from Nov. 20 (Dec. 3) to Dec. 14 (27), 1905. It was headed by J. V. Stalin and S. G. Shaumian. There were 17 issues, and the circulation of the newspaper reached 15,000–17,000. A number of Lenin's articles were reprinted in the paper. The *Kavkazskii rabochii listok* dealt with problems of Marxist-Leninist theory and the practical tasks of revolutionary struggle and party-building, and it played a major role in strengthening the Bolshevik organizations. The newspaper was hounded by the authorities, and issues number 1, 2, 7, 8, 11–14, 16, and 17 were confiscated. Starting with issue number 15 the newspaper was banned, but issues number 16 and 17 came out under the title *Elizavetpol'skii vestnik.*   [11–356–2]

KAVRAISKII, VLADIMIR VLADIMIROVICH. Born Apr. 10 (22), 1884, in the village of Zherebiatnikovo in Simbirsk Province; died Feb. 26, 1954, in Leningrad. Soviet geodesist, cartographer, and astronomer.

Kavraiskii graduated from the University of Kharkov in 1916. In 1921 he began work at the Naval Academy, where in 1935 he became a professor and in 1944 a rear admiral of the engineers. He generalized the lines-of-position method for determining the position of a ship at sea and evaluating the precision of such a determination. He worked out a method, now named after him, for combined determination of time and latitude based on corresponding elevations of stars. His main works are on mathematical cartography. He invented several optical instruments, including the Kavraiskii tiltmeter and the Kavraiskii direction finder. He was awarded the State Prize of the USSR in 1952, the Order of Lenin, three other orders, and medals.

WORKS
Izbr. trudy, vols. 1–2. Leningrad, 1956–60.   [11–359–2]

KAVRAISKII METHOD, a method for the combined determination of the geographic latitude φ of a place and the time correction u (or the longitude λ) by astronomical observation.

The method was worked out during 1924–36 by V. V. Kavraiskii for the high latitudes (from $+60°$ to $+80°$). It is based on observing at least two pairs of stars at equal elevations; in other words, it is a generalization of the Tsinger and Pevtsov methods. The azimuths of the stars in the pair should differ by about 180°, and the difference between the average azimuths of the two pairs (half-sums of the azimuths of the stars of the pair) should be about 90°. During observation the moments when stars pass the horizontal lines of the grid in the sight tube of a general-purpose instrument or zenith telescope are noted by stopwatch, and readings for the end of the level tube bubble are recorded to keep track of small changes in elevation of the position of the tube. Observations of n pairs of stars produce n equations, which are solved by the method of least squares and give φ and u.

REFERENCES
Kavraiskii, V. V. *Sovmestnoe opredelenie vremeni i shiroty po sootvetstvuiushchim vysotam zvezd.* Leningrad-Moscow, 1936.
Venttsel', M. K. *Polevaia astronomiia,* part 2. Moscow, 1940.
                                         A. T. DUL'TSEV [11–359–3]

KAVTARADZE, SERGEI IVANOVICH. Born Aug. 15, 1885, in the village of Zovreti, in present-day Zestafoni Raion; died Oct. 17, 1971, in Tbilisi. Active participant in the Russian revolutionary movement; Soviet statesman. Member of the Communist Party (1903).

Kavtaradze came from a family of the nobility. He graduated in 1915 from the law department of the University of St. Petersburg, having engaged in party work in Kutaisi, Batumi, Tbilisi, Baku, and St. Petersburg. Between 1904 and 1906 he was a member of the Imeretia-Mingrelia Committee of the RSDLP and was persecuted by the government. Between 1912 and 1914 he was a contributor to *Pravda.* After the February Revolution in 1917 he became a member of the Caucasian Regional Committee of the RSDLP and editor of its newspaper, *Kavkazskii rabochii.* He was a delegate to the Sixth Congress of the RSDLP (Bolshevik). He became chairman of the Executive Committee of the Vladikavkaz Soviet in 1918. Beginning in 1919 he engaged in party work in Menshevik Georgia, where he was arrested several times. He worked as a representative of the RSFSR to the Menshevik government up until the establishment of Soviet power in Georgia in February 1921. Until May 1921 he was chairman of the Batumi and Adzhar revolutionary committees; he then became deputy chairman of the Revolutionary Committee of Georgia and people's commissar of justice. In 1922–23 he was chairman of the Council of People's Commissars of the Georgian SSR. In 1923–24 he was an advisor with the Soviet

Embassy in Ankara. From 1924 to 1928 he was first deputy procurator of the Supreme Court of the USSR. In 1927 he was expelled from the party for participation in the Trotskyist opposition. He was reinstated in 1940. In 1941 he began to work in the Ministry of Foreign Affairs of the USSR and became the country's deputy minister of foreign affairs. Kavtaradze took part in the Yalta, Potsdam (1945), and other international conferences. From 1945 to 1952 he was the USSR ambassador to Rumania. In 1961 he was a delegate to the Twenty-second Congress of the CPSU. Kavtaradze was awarded three Orders of Lenin, 2 other orders, and various medals.   [11–360–1]

KAWA (ancient name, Gem-aten), a city located between the third and fourth cataracts of the Nile, on its right bank (in the province of Dongola, Sudan). Probably founded during the Middle Kingdom (20th century B.C.), it was rebuilt by the pharaoh Amenhotep III and his successor Amenhotep IV (Ikhnaton) in the 15th century B.C. In 1930–31 and 1935–36 an expedition from Oxford University (Great Britain) discovered temples built by Ikhnaton and the kings of Kush (the "Great" Temple of Taharqa) in Kawa. Inscriptions were found containing information about the politics and events of the reigns of some kings of Napata (Taharqa, Amanketeierike).

REFERENCE
Laming Macadam, M. F. *The Temples of Kawa,* vols. 1–2. Oxford, 1949–55.   [11–301–3]

KAWABATA, YASUNARI. Born June 11, 1899, in Osaka; died Apr. 16, 1972, in Zushi. Japanese writer; member of the Japanese Academy of Art (1953). Son of a doctor.

Kawabata graduated from the department of Japanese philology of the University of Tokyo in 1924. During the early 1920's he became part of the modernistic group of neosensualists. His first important work, *The Izu Dancer* (1926), is a lyrical story about youth. Several of Kawabata's works (for example, the short story "Crystal Fantasia") were written under the influence of J. Joyce; however, the core of his artistic thought is based on the aesthetics of Zen, which rejects the rational view of the world and stresses that which is natural and artless. The originality of Kawabata's artistic style is particularly evident in his lyric novella *Snow Country* (1937), which consists of a series of short stories joined only by their poetic associations. The tea ceremony, an ancient custom raised to the level of a unique art, forms the basis of Kawabata's novella *Thousand Cranes* (1951), for which he received the prize of the Japanese Academy of Art. His novels *The Sound of the Mountain* (1953) and *The Old Capital* (1961) are characterized by their inner lyricism. In 1968, Kawabata was awarded the Nobel Prize; his books have been translated into many languages.

WORKS
Kawabata Yasunari zenshu, vols. 1–12. Tokyo, 1960.
In Russian translation:
In the collection *Iaponskaia novella.* Moscow, 1961.
Tysiachekrylyi zhuravl'. Moscow, 1971.
REFERENCES
Grigor'eva, I. "Chitaia Kavabata Iasunari." *Inostrannaia literatura,* 1971, no. 8.
Saegusa Iasutaka. *Kawabata Yasunari.* Tokyo, 1961.
                                              K. REKHO [11–301–4]

KAWAGOE, a city in Japan, on the island of Honshu, in Saitama Prefecture, northwest of Tokyo. Population, 171,000 (1970). It is a railroad junction and an important commercial and industrial center. Its economy is oriented primarily toward serving the needs of the capital, Tokyo. Industry includes furniture, textiles (cotton and synthetic fabrics), and food and condiments. There is also an aviation plant. Hothouse agriculture is well developed in the surrounding region.   [11–302–1]

KAWAGUCHI, a city and port in Japan, on the island of Honshu, in Saitama Prefecture; a northwestern suburb of Tokyo. Population, 306,000 (1970). There is foundry industry, transportation machine building, production of machine tools, construction of motor vehicles and engines, and electrical engineering industry (heavy electric machine building and production of household appliances). Chemicals, textiles, and food and condiments are also produced. [11–302–2]

KAWAKAMI, JOTARO. Born Jan. 3, 1889, in Tokyo; died Dec. 3, 1965, in Tokyo. Member of Japan's Social Democratic movement.

Kawakami graduated from the University of Tokyo in 1915. In 1919 he became a professor at Kansai University in Kobe, a lecturer in a workers' school, and a lawyer. In the 1920's he began to participate in the Social Democratic movement. He was elected to the Diet (1928–30 and 1936–42). In late 1945 he was an advisor to the Socialist Party of Japan (SPJ). Beginning in 1951, Kawakami was again a member of the Diet. From 1952 to 1955, when the Socialist Party split into right and left wings, he was chairman of the Right SPJ. From 1961 to 1965, Kawakami served as chairman of the SPJ. In June 1960 he was wounded by a terrorist associated with reactionary circles. [11–302–5]

KAWAKIBI, ABD AL-RAHMAN AL-. Born 1849; died 1903. Syrian Arab enlightener, writer, and publicist.

Persecuted in his homeland, Kawakibi emigrated to Egypt. He traveled through India and Africa. In his book *The Nature of Despotism and the Struggle Against Enslavement,* Kawakibi opposed despotism, defended the poor and the unfortunate, and called on the Arabs to struggle for national independence. His book *Mother of Cities* sets forth the utopian idea of a pan-Islamic congress in Mecca that would unite all Muslims.

REFERENCES
Krachkovskii, I. Iu. *Izbr. soch.,* vol. 3. Moscow-Leningrad, 1956.
Levin, Z. I. *"Priroda despotizma"—sotsial'no-politicheskii traktat Abd ar-Rakhmana al'-Kavakibi. (K istorii arabskoi obshchestvennoi mysli).* Moscow, 1955. [11–303–1]

KAWALEROWICZ, JERZY. Born Jan. 19, 1922, in Gvozdets, Ukraine. Polish film director.

Kawalerowicz graduated from the Film Institute in 1946 and from the Academy of Fine Arts in Kraków in 1948. His first film, *The Commune* (1952, with K. Sumerski), dealt with socialist agrarian reforms in Poland. Among his most important films are the historical and revolutionary film *Cellulose* (1954; Soviet version, *Road to Life*), based on J. Newerly's novel *Memories of a Cellulose Factory,* and its sequel *Under the Phrygian Star* (1954); *Mother Joan of the Angels* (1961; based on J. Iwaszkiewicz's play of the same title), a philosophical film about individual freedom and an attack on dogmatism and intolerance; and *The Pharaoh* (1965), based on B. Prus' novel. Kawalerowicz's films have received prizes at international film festivals in Karlový Vary and Cannes. Between 1955 and 1968 he was the artistic director of the artists' association Kadr (Frame), and since 1966 he has served as chairman of the Polish Union of Cinematographers. He was awarded the State Prize of the Polish People's Republic in 1950 and 1955.

REFERENCE
Sobolev, R. *Ezhi Kavalerovich: Fil'my, stil', metod.* Moscow, 1965.
M. M. CHERNENKO [11–311–1]

KAWASAKI, a city on the island of Honshu in Japan, in Kanagawa Prefecture. Population, 973,500 (1970). Kawasaki is situated on a plain between Tokyo and Yokohama. Together with these cities and other cities on the western shore of Tokyo Bay, it forms the core of the Kwanto industrial region. It is the chief center for the building and repair of ships in Japan. Also important are machine building (electronics, telecommunications equipment, and vacuum instruments) and both ferrous and nonferrous metallurgy. There is a petrochemical combine and two ethylene plants, each producing 300,000 tons yearly. Other industries include automobile manufacturing (buses and trucks), the construction of heavy power machinery (turbines) and equipment for nuclear power plants, and the production of cement and refractory materials. There are also several food-processing and other light industrial enterprises. A steam power plant with a capacity of 875 megawatts is located there. [11–314–4]

KAWASAKI (Japanese), a wooden motor-and-sail vessel for coastal fishing and sea hunting. Widely used in the Far East, chiefly in Japan and Korea. The *kawasaki* has a highly raised bow, a broad flat stern, a deck sloping outward, and a shallow draft. *Kawasakis* may be 10–15 m in length; their freight capacity is approximately 10 tons. [11–314–5]

KAWI (Sanskrit for "poet"), the ancient Javanese literary language formed in the second half of the first millennium A.D. when Indian cultural influence was established in Indonesia; also, the Kawi script. Numerous inscriptions on stones and metal plates dating from the late eighth and early ninth century, fictional works on subjects from the *Ramayana* and *Mahabharata,* and historical chronicles have been preserved. Although the Kawi vocabulary is predominantly of Sanskrit and Pali origin, its grammatical structure is purely Javanese. In the 14th century Kawi was supplanted by the language known as Middle Javanese, although Kawi continued to be used as the language of law and religion until Islam became firmly established in Java (15th to early 16th century). Kawi still partly fulfills these functions on the island of Bali.

REFERENCES
Teselkin, A. S. *Drevneiavanskii iazyk (kavi).* Moscow, 1963.
Uhlenbeck, E. M. *A Critical Survey of Studies on the Languages of Java and Madura.* Bibliographical Series, no. 7. The Hague, 1964. [11–320–2]

KAYA, SEIJI. Born Dec. 21, 1898, in Kanagawa Prefecture. Japanese physicist.

Kaya graduated from Tohoku University in Sendai (1923). He is a doctor of physicomathematical sciences (1929). He was a professor at the University of Hokkaido from 1931 to 1943 and the Technological Institute in Tokyo from 1941 to 1948. Kaya became a professor at the University of Tokyo in 1943 and was rector there from 1958 to 1960. He has been vice-president of the Japanese Science Council since 1954. Kaya's main works have been devoted to the magnetic properties of ferromagnetic crystals. He became a foreign member of the Academy of Sciences of the USSR in 1958. [11–1670–6]

KAYAHS, a people in Burma, living mainly in Kayah National Autonomous State and Mong Pai District of Shan National Autonomous State. Total population, about 100,000 (1967, estimate). The Kayah language belongs to the Kayah-Karen group of Tibetan-Burman languages. The anthropological type is Southern Mongoloid. Most of the Kayahs are Buddhists (southern branch); approximately 20 percent are Christians; however, considerable vestiges of ancient cult worship (tree leaves, etc.) are still preserved. The chief occupation is farming; some of the Kayahs (those known as the Lake Kayahs) engage in logging with the use of elephants.

REFERENCE
Narody Iugo-Vostochnoi Azii. Moscow, 1966. [11–1670–7]

KAYAK, a small work boat that was widely used for hunting and fishing among many peoples of the arctic; it is still used by some Canadian and Greenland Eskimo. The latticelike framework is made of wood or bone and is covered with the skins of sea animals. An opening is left in the top part, which is fastened around the waist of the paddler by means of a thong. It is propelled by two small oars (paddles) or a single double-bladed paddle. The kayak is almost unsinkable and is well suited for travel on the sea. [11–1671–4]

KAYAKUM, a Korean many-stringed plucked musical instrument. The body is flat and elongated, with two round openings at one end. The number of strings varies. The kayakum is played solo or in combination with the cross flute, the *chettae.* Ensembles of female kayakum players are very popular. [11–1671–3]

KAYES, a city in western Mali; administrative center of Kayes Region. Population, 29,900 (1969). Highway and railroad junction; port on the left bank of the Senegal River. The city is the commercial center for the agricultural region (millet, sorghum, peanuts, and livestock). There are railroad repair shops and, in the vicinity of Kayes, a hydroelectric power plant.

[11–389–2]

KAYIBANDA, GRÉGOIRE. Born May 1, 1924, in the commune of Musambira, Gitarama Province. Rwandan political figure and statesman.

Kayibanda was educated in Catholic seminaries in the cities of Kabgaye and Nyakibanda. In the second half of the 1950's he was editor in chief of the newspaper *Kinyamateka,* which was founded by a group from the intelligentsia advocating Rwanda's independence. In 1959 he was one of the chief organizers of the party known as PARMEHUTU (Hutu Emancipation Movement; since 1960 it has been called the Republican Democratic Movement). From July 1962 to July 1973 he was president of the Republic of Rwanda. Kayibanda was deposed on July 5, 1973, after a coup d'etat.

[11–538–4; updated]

KAYSERI, a city in central Turkey; administrative center of Kayseri Vilayet. Population, 168,000 (1970). Railroad station and highway junction; it is a very important industrial and trade center. The city has the largest cotton-textile combine in Turkey (constructed in 1934–35 with economic and technical aid from the USSR). The city has flour-milling, sugar, meat and dairy, and wood-products industries, as well as an aircraft assembly factory. Kayseri is one of the country's main rug-weaving centers.

[11–548–3]

KAZ, an urban-type settlement in Kemerovo Oblast, RSFSR. It is located in Gornaia Shoriia, 4 km from the Tenesh railroad station on the Novokuznetsk-Tashtagol line. Iron ore is mined there.

[11–389–4]

KAZACH'IA LOPAN', an urban-type settlement in Dergachev Raion, Kharkov Oblast, Ukrainian SSR. It is a railroad station on the Kharkov-Belgorod line. Kazach'ia Lopan' has a seed-producing sovkhoz and a milk-processing plant.

[11–518–3]

KAZACHOK, a folk dance (for example, the Ukrainian, Kuban', and Terek *kazachoks*) written in 2/4 time, the most popular of which is the Ukrainian *kazachok*—a lively, gay improvised dance performed in pairs. The Polish lutist and composer S. Dusiecki (early 17th century) is credited with the first musical adaptation of the *kazachok.* Its melody first appeared in Russian manuscripts of the second half of the 18th century. The *kazachok* began appearing in French ballets and was particularly popular in the 1820's, after Russian troops were stationed in Paris. In the early 19th century it was performed in Russia as a ballroom dance. In 1864 A. S. Dargomyzhskii composed *The Little Russian Kazachok* for symphony orchestra.

[11–518–1]

KAZAKEVICH, EMMANUIL GENRIKHOVICH. Born Feb. 11 (24), 1913, in Kremenchug; died Sept. 22, 1962, in Moscow. Soviet Russian writer. Member of the CPSU from 1944.

Kazakevich's first works to appear in print were verses, songs, and narrative poems written in Yiddish in the mid-1930's. During the Great Patriotic War (1941–45) he served in the army in capacities ranging from soldier to assistant head of army intelligence. The war provided him with the basic theme of his prose; his novella *The Star* (1947; State Prize of the USSR, 1948), which dealt with the heroism of the Soviet reconnaissance officers, showed his originality as a writer and the psychological scope and lyricism of his narrative style. The problems of duty, guilt, and freedom of will are resolved in the novella *Two in the Steppe* (1948). His novels *Spring on the Oder* (1949; State Prize of the USSR, 1950) and *The House on the Square* (1956) focus on the last period of the war and the work of Soviet authorities in Germany in the early days of peace. Kazakevich displays an inventive use of plot and a diversity of stylistic idiom, which enables him to reenact mass scenes. His story "In the Light of Day" (1961) is imbued with a sense of the value of human life.

Kazakevich's books are characterized by imagery that sustains the theme and the spiritual kinship between the heroes, whose characteristic trait is the endeavor to find meaning in their actions and in those of their comrades and whose civic and military bravery go hand in hand. His novella *The Blue Notebook* (1961) depicts Lenin living in Razliv. Many of Kazakevich's works have been adapted for the screen, and his books have been translated into both foreign languages and the national languages of the USSR. He was awarded four orders and several medals.

WORKS
Sobr. soch., vols. 1–2. Moscow, 1963.
REFERENCES
Kardin, V. "Pravo na doverie." *Oktiabr',* 1956, no. 6.
Kardin, V. "Dostoinstvo literatury." In his book *Vernost' vremeni.* Moscow, 1962.
Tvardovskii, A. "Pamiati druga." *Literaturnaia gazeta,* Sept. 27, 1962.
Survillo, V. "Mysl' khudozhnika. (O povestiakh Em. Kazakevicha.)" *Novyi mir,* 1966, no. 1.
Bocharov, A. *Emmanuil Kazakevich.* Moscow, 1967.
Russkie sovetskie pisateli-prozaiki. Biobibliograficheskii ukazatel', vol. 2. Leningrad, 1964.   V. KARDIN [11–390–3]

KAZAKH, a city (since 1909) and administrative center of Kazakh Raion, Azerbaijan SSR. Located on the Akstafa River, a tributary of the Kura, 9 km southwest of the Akstafa railroad station on the Tbilisi-Baku line. Population, 13,000 (1970). A highway junction and center for the manufacture of high-pile carpets, Kazakh has a carpet factory. It also has an agricultural technicum and a medical school. Cultural institutions include a museum of the Azerbaijani poet M. Vagif and a people's amateur theater.

[11–417–4]

KAZAKH, the language of the Kazakhs, the native population of the Kazakh SSR. The number of Kazakh speakers in the USSR is 5,193,000 (1970, census). Kazakh is also spoken by Kazakhs living in the People's Republic of China (509,000; 1953, census), the Mongolian People's Republic (43,000; 1963, estimate), and Afghanistan (3,000; 1962, estimate). Kazakh belongs to the Kipchak group of the Turkic languages.

Modern Kazakh has three dialects: northeastern, southern, and western. However, the dialectal differences are not great. The modern Kazakh literary language is based on the northeastern dialect. The principal features of Kazakh are the correspondence of Kazakh *š* to Common Turkic *č* (*qaš* instead of *qač,* "to run away"), the correspondence of Kazakh *s* to Common Turkic *š* (*qïs* instead of *qïš,* "winter"), the correspondence of Kazakh initial *ž* to initial *y* and *dž* in other Turkic languages (*žol* instead of *yol* or *džol,* "road"), and the presence of a present-future participle with the suffix *-atïn (-etin, -ytïn,* or *-ytin*).

The Kazakh literary language took shape in the second half of the 19th century as a result of the activities of the Kazakh enlighteners Abai Kunanbaev and Ibrai Altynsarin. Kazakh was first written in the Arabic alphabet and later in the Latin alphabet; a Russian-based alphabet was adopted in 1940.

REFERENCES
Melioranskii, P. M. *Kratkaia grammatika kazak-kirgizskogo iazyka,* parts 1–2. St. Petersburg, 1894–97.
Balakaev, M. B. *Sovremennyi kazakhskii iazyk: Sintaksis slovosochetaniia i prostogo predlozheniia.* Alma-Ata, 1959.
Begaliev, G. *Kratkii kazakhsko-russkii slovar'.* Alma-Ata, 1959.
Sovremennyi kazakhskii iazyk. Edited by M. B. Balakaev, N. A. Baskakov, and S. K. Kenesbaev. Alma-Ata, 1962.
Russko-kazakhskii slovar'. Edited by N. Sauranbaev. Moscow, 1954.
A. T. KAIDAROV [11–510–3]

KAZAKH AGRICULTURAL INSTITUTE, founded in 1930 in Alma-Ata. The institute has (1972 data) departments of agronomy, soil science and agronomical chemistry, fruit and vegetable growing and viticulture, plant protection, agricultural economics and organization, forestry, agricultural mechanization and electrification, and the organization and technology of machinery repair, as well as a department for the advanced training of agricultural managers and specialists. There is also a graduate school, 50 subdepartments, a teaching and experimental farm of 21,200 hectares, teaching and production workshops, a research laboratory, a nursery, and a library with 262,000 holdings. The institute has been granted the right to accept doctoral and candidates' dissertations for defense. Since 1948 it has been publishing *Trudy,* and it has trained 15,000 specialists since its foundation. In 1971 it was awarded the Order of the Red Banner of Labor. KH. A. ARYSTANBEKOV [11–508–3]

KAZAKH ARKHAR-MERINO, a breed of fine-wooled sheep raised for meat and wool, developed in the Kazakh SSR between 1934 and 1950. This is the only breed of sheep that has been produced by interspecies hybridization. New Caucasian Merino ewes were fertilized with semen from a slaughtered wild Arkhar (Pamir argali). The first-generation male crossbreeds were crossed with Precoce and Rambouillet ewes, and the third-generation crossbreeds were interbred. Kazakh Arkhar-Merinos are large, hardy, strongly built, and well proportioned. They are well adapted to mountain conditions, grazing in high-altitude pastures and moving easily over rugged terrain. Rams weigh 90–115 kg, and ewes 55–65 kg. The wool clip from rams is 7–8 kg, and from ewes 3.2–3.5 kg. The wool is mostly of the 64th grade and 7–10 cm long. The yield of pure wool is 50–55 percent. The productivity rate is 110–120 lambs per 100 ewes bred. Kazakh Arkhar-Merinos are used for crossbreeding with coarse-wooled sheep. They are raised in the Alma-Ata, Vostochnyi Kazakhstan, and Pavlodar oblasts.

REFERENCES
Butarin, N. S. "Kazakhskii arkharomerinos." *Porody sel'skokhoziaistvennykh zhivotnykh, vyvedennye v Kazakhstane.* Alma-Ata, 1960.
Isenzhulov, A. I., A. I. Zhanderkin, and O. A. Prokazin. "Kazakhskii arkharomerinos i vozmozhnosti dal'neishego sovershenstvovaniia porody." *Trudy Instituta eksperimental'noi biologii Akademii Nauk KazSSR.* 1965, vol. 2. [11–506–1]

KAZAKH ART GALLERY (full name, T. G. Shevchenko Kazakh Art Gallery). Founded in 1935, the gallery is located in Alma-Ata. Its fine arts collection and decorative-applied arts collection include 10,000 Kazakh, prerevolutionary and Soviet Russian, Western European, and oriental works.

The Kazakh section includes works by A. M. Cherkasskii, A. Kasteev, M. S. Lizogub, Kh. Khodzhilov, A. Ismailov, N.-B. Nurmukhammedov, M. S. Kenbaev, Kh. I. Naurzbaev, K. T. Tel'zhanov, S. A. Mambeev, and E. M. Sidorkin. The Russian section contains the works of D. G. Levitskii, V. A. Tropinin, K. P. Briullov, A. K. Savrasov, I. E. Repin, A. S. Golubkina, B. M. Kustodiev, V. E. Borisov-Musatov, Z. E. Serebriakova, and K. S. Petrov-Vodkin. The Soviet section comprises the works of K. F. Iuon, P. P. Konchalovskii, M. S. Sar'ian, S. D. Lebedeva, P. D. Korin, A. A. Plastov, A. A. Deineka, Ia. D. Romas, U. Tansykbaev, E. F. Belashova, G. A. Aitiev, T. N. Iablonskaia, P. F. Nikonov, and A. G. Pologova. The Western European section includes the works of J. B. C. Corot, N. V. Diaz de la Peña, and C. F. Daubigny. The applied arts section of works from China, India, and Japan includes 20th-century works.

REFERENCES
Kazakhskaia khudozhestvennaia galereia im. T. G. Shevchenko. Katalog. Issues 1–6, Alma-Ata, 1961–72; issue 7, Moscow, 1971.
Plakhotnaia L., and I. Kuchis. *Kazakhskaia gosudarstvennaia khudozhestvennaia galereia im T. G. Shevchenko.* [Album, text by I. Kuchis.] Moscow, 1966. L. G. PLAKHOTNAIA [11–505–2]

KAZAKH DRAMA THEATER (full name, M. O. Auezov Academic Kazakh Drama Theater), organized in 1925 in Kzyl-Orda and opened on Jan. 13, 1926. It was transferred to Alma-Ata in 1928.

The company initially consisted of leading amateur actors of the folk theater, notably S. Kozhamkulov, K. Kuanyshpaev, E. Umurzakov, K. U. Badyrov, and Zh. Shanin. It later included actors who had been trained in the company or in drama schools in Alma-Ata and Tashkent and graduates of the Kazakh studios of the State Institute of Theatrical Arts (1938 and 1954).

The theater was first headed by Zh. Shanin, and its most successful productions were those portraying life in the old *aul* (village), such as Auezov's *Enlik and Kebek, Rival Wives,* and *Karakoz,* all performed in 1926; Seifullin's *Red Falcons* (1926); and Shanin's *Arkalyk-batyr* (1927). Later plays dealt with the

collectivization and industrialization of the country, notably Shanin's *The Mine* (1930) and Mailin's *The Front* (1931).

From 1932 to 1935 and again from 1937 to 1939 the theater was managed by the director M. G. Nasonov. During this time various works by Russian dramatists were staged, notably Gogol's *The Inspector-General* (1936), Trenev's *Liubov' Yarovaia* (1937), and Pogodin's *My Friend* (1939), as well as works by national playwrights, such as Auezov's *Night Thunder* (1935) and Musrepov's *Amangel'dy* (1937) and *Kozy-Korpesh and Baian-Slu* (1940). During the Great Patriotic War (1941–45) the theater performed, among other works, Auezov's and Abishev's patriotic play *The Guard of Honor* (1942), Musrepov's *Akhan-Sere and Aktokty* (1942), and Shakespeare's *The Taming of the Shrew* (1943).

In the late 1940's and the 1950's plays depicting life in the republic were staged with great success, including *Friendship and Love* (1947) and *Envy* (1955) by Abishev, *Yesterday and Today* by Khusainov (1956), *Bloom, O Steppe! (One Tree Does Not Make a Forest)* by Tazhibaev (1952, 1958), and *Abai,* based on the novel by Auezov (1949; State Prize of the USSR, 1952). Performances of Russian and West European classics, such as Ostrovskii's *Talents and Admirers* (1949) and *Storm* (1950) and Molière's *The Miser* (1952), helped the company master the realistic method.

During the 1950's and 1960's the theater turned to historical themes, staging *Chokan Valikhanov* by Mukanov (1956) and *Maira* by Tazhibaev (1957, 1969), and its repertoire also included many works by young playwrights, notably *Wolf Cub in a Cap Trap* (1959) and *In a Foreign Land* (1968) by Mukhamedzhanov and *Saule* (1961) and *Snowstorm* (1966) by Akhtanov. Plays by dramatists from other republics are regularly staged, such as *The Maternal Field,* based on Aitmatov's work (1964), and *Little Shoes* by Faizi (1972).

In 1937 the theater was named the Academic Kazakh Drama Theater, and in 1946 it was awarded the Order of the Red Banner of Labor. In 1961 it was renamed the M. O. Auezov Academic Kazakh Drama Theater. The company includes (as of 1972) People's Artists of the USSR Kh. Bukeeva and S. Maikanova and People's Artists of the Kazakh SSR K. U. Badyrov, Sh. Dzhandarbekova, A. Dzholumbetov, S. Kozhamkulov, K. Karmysov, Sh. Musin, I. Nogaibaev, B. Rimova, M. Surtubaev, S. Tel'garaev, E. Umurzakov, and Z. Sharipova. The theater's chief director is People's Artist of the Kazakh SSR A. Mambetov.

REFERENCE
L'vov, N. I. *Kazakhskii akademicheskii teatr dramy.* Alma-Ata, 1957. [11–509–1]

KAZAKHFIL'M, the Soviet Kazakh motion picture studio, producing feature films, documentaries, and newsreels. The Alma-Ata Feature Film Studio was organized in 1941. With the evacuation of Mosfil'm and Lenfil'm to Alma-Ata in 1942, the studio was reorganized as the Central United Motion Picture Studio, which existed until 1944. That year, after Mosfil'm and Lenfil'm were relocated, the Alma-Ata feature film studio merged with the Alma-Ata newsreel studio (founded in 1934) to form the Alma-Ata Studio of Feature Films, Documentaries, and Newsreels. In 1960 the studio was renamed Kazakhfil'm. [11–511–3]

KAZAKH FINE-WOOLED SHEEP, a breed of sheep raised for meat and wool. The breed was developed between 1931 and 1946 at the experimental center of the Kazakh Scientific Research Institute of Animal Husbandry by crossing Kazakh Fat-tailed ewes with Precoce rams. Crossbreeds of the first and second generations with uniform fine and semifine wool were interbred. Kazakh Fine-wooled sheep are large, with strong constitutions. The ewes are hornless, and the rams may or may not have horns. The wool is uniform, of the Merino type, and no coarser than grade 60; it is 7–8 cm long (sometimes growing to 13 cm) and curly. Wool clip from rams is 7–9 kg, although as much as 14 kg have been obtained from the better ones; ewes produce 4–4.5 kg, with the better ones giving up to 8 kg. The yield of pure wool is about 50 percent.

Kazakh Fine-wooled rams have an average weight of 90–100 kg, and the largest may weigh up to 140 kg. Ewes weigh 60–65 kg, with the largest attaining 100 kg. The fertility rate is 130–140 lambs per 100 ewes bred. They are early maturing animals and fatten well. In 18 months young rams attain 70 percent of their adult weight, and young ewes 85 percent. Slaughter yield is 53–57 percent. Kazakh Fine-wooled sheep are adapted to year-round range conditions and to winter grazing. In the regions of Kazakhstan where transhumance is practiced these sheep are used to improve other strains.

REFERENCES
Bal'mont, V.A. *Kazakhskie tonkorunnye ovtsy.* Alma-Ata, 1948.
Bal'mont, V.A. "O metodakh sovershenstvovaniia ovets kazakhskoi tonkorunnoi porody." *Ovtsevodstvo,* 1966, no. 2. [11–505–1]

KAZAKH HORSE, a native steppe horse bred in the Kazakh SSR and adjacent regions. Kazakh horses were developed long ago by crossing native horses with Mongolian, Middle Asian, and European breeds raised together in herds. The Kazakh horse is found over an extensive area with diverse natural conditions and is represented by several strains: the Western Kazakhstan, Central Kazakhstan, Adaev, Southern Kazakhstan, Semirech'e, Naiman, and Southern Altai. They are generally small, rugged horses with coats of different colors. They measure 131–138 cm at the withers and have a transverse body length of 140–144 cm; the girth is 156–164 cm, and the circumference of the cannon bone, 16–18 cm. The weight ranges from 320 to 360 kg. Mares produce 8–9 liters of milk daily. The Kazakh horse is used as a saddle, pack, and work horse and for milk and meat. The most valuable animals are the heavyset, sturdy Dzhabe horses of the Western Kazakhstan strain, bred at the Mugodzhary Horse Farm in the Aktiubinsk Oblast and at several sovkhozes and kolkhozes in the Karaganda and other oblasts of the Kazakh SSR.   I. N. CHASHKIN [11–421–1]

KAZAKH MELKOSOPOCHNIK (also Saryarka), a level upland region with low-mountain massifs and ranges, located in the central and eastern parts of the Kazakh SSR.

It stretches from west to east for about 1,200 km, with a width of about 900 km in the west and some 400 km in the east. The western part of the region has elevations (absolute altitude) ranging from 300 to 500 m and a great deal of even terrain. Here are two low-mountain massifs, Ulutau (1,133 m) in the west and the Kokchetav Upland (Mount Siniukha, 947 m) in the north. The eastern part of the Kazakh Melkosopochnik is characterized by greater elevations (averaging from 500 to 1,000 m) and a more dissected terrain. In the center of the eastern part rise the Karkaralinsk Mountains, in which is found the Aksoran Massif (1,565 m), the highest in the Kazakh Melkosopochnik. Further to the east is the Chingiztau Range (1,077 m). The low-mountain massifs, whose relative height does not exceed 500–600 m, are surrounded by a *melkosopochnik,* an elevated gently rolling plain; here in series or scattered are found numerous hills and low ridges composed of bedrock with relative heights ranging from 10–50 m to 100 m.

Geologically, the Kazakh Melkosopochnik is a part of the Ural-Mongolian geosynclinal zone. It is composed of highly dislocated metamorphic shales, quartzites, sandstones, and limestones of the Paleozoic overlaid in places by Mesozoic and Cenozoic deposits. As much as 60 percent of the area is occupied by intrusive rocks (granites, diorites, porphyrites) and extrusive rocks. Of great importance in the formation of the structures were the Caledonian and Hercynian stages of tectogenesis, which differ sharply in their overall structural plan. The Caledonian system of folds has a north-east strike, whereas the Hercynian has a north-west strike. The Caledonian structures are widespread in the western part of the region, and those of the Hercynian predominate in the east. In the late Paleozoic and early Mesozoic the entire region was fractured by faults. The end of the Carboniferous saw the onset of a continental period, which has lasted until the present. As a result of erosion and denudation, the high mountainous region formed by Hercynian orogeny was worn down and gradually acquired its present appearance. The *melkosopochnik* was formed by small tectonic uplifts of

deformation and the repeated dissection of the ancient peneplain. The low-mountain massifs are the result of the most recent local uplifts of greater amplitude.

The climate is continental, becoming arid toward the south. The mean temperature in January ranges from −14° to −18°C, and in July from 20° to 24°C. During winter frosts the temperature may fall to −40°C, and in summer daytime temperatures may rise to 35°C and higher in the south. Annual precipitation totals 200–300 mm (up to 370 mm in the northern mountain massifs). In winter the snow cover is not deep, and in summer there are frequent droughts. The divide of the Irtysh basin and the subsurface drainage region of Middle Asia pass through the Kazakh Melkosopochnik. The largest rivers are the Ishim (Irtysh basin), Nura, and Sarysu; their rate of flow is very uneven. The rivers are fed mostly by spring snowmelt and partly by groundwater. In the spring there is high water, but during the summer the rivers become shallow. The spring discharge of the Nura River constitutes 88 percent of its annual flow, whereas the summer discharge is only 3 percent. In winter the rivers are frozen, the small ones freezing to the bottom. None of the rivers are navigable. There are many lakes, of which the largest is the shallow Tengiz Salt Lake.

The northern part of the Kazakh Melkosopochnik lies in the steppe zone. It is covered with mixed fescue and feather-grass vegetation growing on southern chernozems, which are partially tilled. The central part belongs to the dry-steppe zone, with fescue and feather-grass vegetation growing on dark chestnut soils (also partially tilled) and chestnut soils. The southern and eastern parts of the Kazakh Melkosopochnik are in the semidesert zone, where there is a combination of steppe (turfy-gramineous) and desert (*polyn'* [*Artemisia*] and halophytic) vegetation and where light chestnut soil predominates. The southeastern part, near Lake Balkhash, lies in the desert zone. The virgin lands of the Kazakh Melkosopochnik are used for pasture.

REFERENCES
Svarichevskaia, Z. A. *Geomorfologiia Kazakhstana i Srednei Azii.* Leningrad, 1965.
Kazakhstan. Moscow, 1969. (*Prirodnye usloviia i estestvennye resursy SSSR.*)
Gvozdetskii, N. A., and V. A. Nikolaev. *Kazakhstan.* Moscow, 1971.
                                    N. A. GVOZDETSKII [11–506–2]

KAZAKH PEDAGOGICAL INSTITUTE (full name, Abai Kazakh Pedagogical Institute). The institute was founded in Alma-Ata in 1928 with three separate divisions: physics and mathematics, natural sciences, and linguistics and literature. In 1930 it became an independent institution of higher learning. In 1935 the name of Abai Kunanbaev was conferred upon the institute.

The school comprises (1972) the departments of physics, mathematics, natural geography, philology, history, and graphic arts. It has a division for preparing people for the entrance examinations, a correspondence school, and a graduate school. The institute also has 33 subdepartments, 15 study laboratories, and an agronomic and biological station. The institute's library has approximately 500,000 holdings.

During the 1971–72 academic year there were more than 7,000 students at the Kazakh Pedagogical Institute and approximately 400 instructors, including six academicians and corresponding members of the Academy of Sciences of the USSR and of the Academy of Sciences of the Kazakh SSR, 14 professors and doctors of sciences, and 161 docents and candidates of sciences. The institute has the right to accept doctoral and candidate dissertations for defense. The institute has been publishing *Uchenye zapiski* since 1940 and interuniversity collections since 1968. Over the years, the institute has trained about 25,000 specialists.   S. E. TOLYBEKOV [11–508–1]

KAZAKH POLYTECHNIC INSTITUTE (full name, V. I. Lenin Kazakh Polytechnic Institute). The institute was founded in 1960 in Alma-Ata on the basis of the Kazakh Mining and Metallurgical Institute, founded in 1934.

The institute has (1972) the departments of mining, metallurgy, geological survey, construction engineering, engineering economics, petroleum, architecture, automation and computer technology, energetics, and geophysics and a general technical department. The institute has a correspondence school; a branch in the city of Rudnyi; general technical departments in the cities of Leninogorsk, Ust'-Kamenogorsk, and Karatau; and a graduate school. It also has 85 subdepartments, six branch laboratories, and three laboratories dealing with fundamental problems. Its library has 706,000 holdings.

During the 1971–72 academic year there were 13,500 students at the institute and more than 900 instructors, including eight academicians and corresponding members of the Academy of Sciences of the Kazakh SSR, 29 doctors of sciences and professors, and more than 300 candidates of sciences and docents. The Kazakh Polytechnic Institute has the right to accept doctoral and candidate dissertations for defense. The institute has been publishing *Sbornik nauchnykh trudov* since 1938. In 1970 the name of V. I. Lenin was conferred upon the institute. Over the years, the school has trained 13,800 specialists.

A. K. OMAROV [11–508–2]

KAZAKH RAILROAD, formed in 1958 out of the Turkestan-Siberian and the Karaganda railroads and sections of the former Tashkent, Orenburg, and Southern Urals railroads.

The railroad's administrative office is in Alma-Ata. The railroad runs through the Kazakh SSR and through parts of the RSFSR and the Kirghiz SSR. It connects with the Middle Asian Railroad (at Chengel'dy station), the Western Siberian Railroad (at Lokot', Kulunda, and Kzyltu stations), the Volga Region Railroad (at Ozinki and Aksaraiskaia stations), and the Southern Urals Railroad (at Zolotaia Sopka, Petropavlovsk, Tobol, Nikel'-Tau, and Iletsk stations). It is the country's longest railroad: in 1971, 13,250 km of track were in use, representing about 9 percent of the USSR's total rail network, and the total length of the main tracks was 15,084 km.

The Iletsk-Chengel'dy trunk line (from Orenburg to Tashkent) was the first section to be put into operation (1905–06), linking European Russia with Middle Asia and with the southern and western regions of Kazakhstan. In 1915 the Zolotaia Sopka (from Troitsk)–Kustanai lines were built; in 1916, the Arys'-Burnoe line; and in 1917, the Lokot' (from Aleisk)–Semipalatinsk line. More than 80 percent of the lines have been built during the Soviet period. Between 1922 and 1924 the Burnoe-Dzhambul and Dzhambul-Frunze lines were put into operation. In 1931 two of the USSR's most important trunk lines were built in order to develop the Karaganda Coal Basin: the Turkestan-Siberian (Turksib) line connecting Siberia and the Far East with Middle Asia and Kazakhstan and the Kurort Borovoe–Tselinograd (formerly Akmolinsk)–Karaganda line. In 1939–40, the Karaganda-Balkhash, Lokot'–Leninogorsk, and Zharyk-Dzhezkazgan lines were built to reach the copper and polymetallic-ore deposits at Balkhash, Leninogorsk, and Dzhezkazgan.

During the Great Patriotic War (1941–45) several new lines were put into operation: the Kandagach-Gur'ev line, establishing a route from the Southern Urals to the Caspian Sea and the petroleum deposits of Kazakhstan; the Kant–Bystrovka and Koksu–Tekeli lines; the very important Tselinograd (Akmolinsk)–Kartaly trunk line, linking the Karaganda Coal Basin with the industrial regions of the Urals; and the Nikel'tau (from Orsk)-Kandagach line, connecting the Southern Urals with Gur'ev and Middle Asia. In 1953 the Tselinograd-Pavlodar, Mointy-Chu, and Zashchita-Zyrianovsk lines went into operation. Among lines built between 1960 and 1971 are the Novouritskoe-Peski-Tselinnye, Peski-Tselinnye–Volodarskoe, Pavlodar-Kulunda, Esil'-Arkalyk, Tobol-Dzhetygara, Aktogai-Druzhba, Karaganda-Karagaily, Ermentau-Aisary, Tobol-Lisakovsk, Makat-Mangyshlak, Mangyshlak-Uzen'-Karatau-Zhanatas, and Dubovskaia-Uglerudnaia-Balkhash-Saiak.

The Kazakh Railroad serves regions in which are found coal mines, of ores and building materials, enterprises of ferrous and nonferrous metallurgy, and machine-building, chemical, consumer, and food-processing industries, as well as some of the country's major agricultural regions. In freight turnover, the railroad occupies second place in the country's rail network, with about 230 billion ton-km in 1971. Coal, ore, grain, and building materials account for most of the outgoing freight. Among incoming and transit shipments, coal, petroleum products, lumber, machinery, and equipment predominate, as well as freight of the consumer and the food-processing industries. Outgoing shipments constitute about 28 percent of the total freight; incoming shipments, about 21 percent; local shipments, 23 percent; and transit shipments, 28 percent. The volume of the railroad's passenger transport was about 14 billion passenger-km in 1971, or about 5 percent of the transport of the USSR's total rail network. In 1971 the Kazakh Railroad was awarded the Order of Lenin.

G. S. RAIKHER [11–420–1]

KAZAKHS (self-designation, Kazakh, Kazak), a nation and the indigenous population of the Kazakh SSR. Until 1925 and sometimes even later, the Kazakhs were erroneously referred to in literature and documents as the Kirghiz-Kazaks or simply as the Kirghiz, the name of a neighboring people. There are 5,299,000 Kazakhs in the USSR (1970), of which 4,234,000 live in the Kazakh SSR. Some Kazakhs also live in the Uzbek SSR, the Turkmen SSR, the Kirghiz SSR, the Tadzhik SSR, and some oblasts of the RSFSR. Outside the Soviet Union, Kazakhs live in the Chinese People's Republic, the Mongolian People's Republic, and Afghanistan. They speak the Kazakh language, and those who profess a religion are Sunni Muslims. In the past shamanism and ancestor worship were widely practiced.

The Kazakhs have a complex ethnic history. The ancient roots of their material culture and physicoanthropological type may be archaeologically traced to the Bronze Age tribes who inhabited the territory of present-day Kazakhstan. Among the Kazakhs' ancestors were the Sacae tribes, who dwelt in Kazakhstan and Middle Asia. In the third and second centuries B.C., the Usun tribal confederation arose in southern Kazakhstan, and tribes belonging to the K'ang-yüeh tribal union inhabited the southwest. In the first centuries A.D. the Alani, who also influenced the Kazakhs' ethnogenesis, lived west of the Aral Sea. In the sixth and seventh centuries the tribes dwelling in the southeastern part of Kazakhstan were subject to the West Turkic Kaganate. At the same time tribes from the east, such as the Turgäsh and Karluks, were settling in Kazakhstan. Later, several short-lived political unions of the early feudal type arose in various parts of Kazakhstan, including the Turgäsh (eighth century) and Karluk (eighth to the tenth century) kaganates, the Oguz confederation (ninth to the 11th century) and the confederation of the Kimaks and the Kipchaks (eighth to the 11th century). The latter occupied a large steppe region of modern Kazakhstan, called Dasht-i-Kipchak. The rise of the Karakhanid State (tenth to the 12th century) assisted the ethnic consolidation of local tribes. At the beginning of the 12th century, Kazakhstan was invaded by the Karakitai, or Khitans, who were subsequently absorbed into the native Turkic-speaking population.

At the beginning of the 13th century, remnants of the Naiman and Kerait (or Kerai) tribes fled to Kazakhstan from Mongolia and the Altai after being routed by Genghis Khan's armies. The subsequent Mongol conquest of Middle Asia and Kazakhstan resulted in a large-scale mingling, disintegration, and consolidation of different tribes. The Nogai Horde and Uzbek Khanate, which in the mid-15th century arose out of the ruins of the eastern part of the Golden Horde, comprised various Turkic-speaking tribes, including the Kipchaks, Argyns, Karluks, Kanglis, and Naimans, as well as some Mongol tribes that had been assimilated by the native Turkic population. In the mid-15th century some of these tribes began migrating to Mogulistan as a consequence of internecine feudal wars and dynastic struggle in the Uzbek Khanate; they returned to the western regions in the 1470's.

The feudal lords who led the Kazakh tribes created the Kazakh Khanate in the late 15th and early 16th century, and with its establishment the development of the Kazakh nationality was completed. Ethnically, the term "Kazakh" began to be applied in the 1520's and 1530's to all the steppe peoples who had inhabited the Uzbek Khanate and regions to the east. In the mid-16th century the ethnic composition of the Kazakhs was enlarged by tribes that had migrated to the area from beyond the Ural River after the disintegration of the Nogai Horde and from Siberia and the eastern part of Semirech'e.

Historically, the Kazakh nationality was composed of three groups of tribes, called *zhuz* (hordes), each of which was united by the common interests of the nomadic economy and territorially isolated from the others. The Greater Horde, or Uly Zhuz, in Semirech'e comprised the Dulat, Albani, Suan, Kangly, Jalair, Sirgeli, Shanshkyly, and Sary-Uisin tribes. The Middle Horde, also known as Orta Zhuz, located in the steppe regions of central Kazakhstan and in the Syr-Darya, Ishim, and Tobol river valleys, included the Argyn, Naiman, Kipchak, Kerait, and Kongrat tribes. In Western Kazakhstan the Little Horde, or Kishi Zhuz, consisted of the tribal confederations Alim-Uly, Bai-Uly (Adai, Alchyn, Zhappas clans), and the Zheti-Ru (Zhagal-Baily, Kerderi tribes). In the early 19th century the Inner, or Bukei, Horde separated from the Little Horde and withdrew beyond the Ural River.

Until the annexation of the Kazakh lands to Russia (completed in the 1860's), the Kazakhs were essentially pastoral nomads. Only in a few areas in centuries past did they work irrigated fields. From the late 18th century, agricultural development was stimulated by Russian settlers. In the second half of the 19th century, farming grew as the Kazakhs gradually began to adopt a settled way of life. Domestic industries, fishing, and hunting were also important. Russian influences profoundly affected the development of the modern culture of the Kazakhs.

Fundamental changes in the Kazakhs' economy and culture occurred after the October Revolution, when in the course of building socialism the Kazakh socialist nation was formed. Kazakhstan was transformed into a region with advanced industry and a highly developed and diversified agriculture. The Kazakhs' culture and way of life changed—nomads adopted a settled way of life, illiteracy was wiped out, and national cadres of the working class and intelligentsia emerged.

REFERENCES

Narody Srednei Azii i Kazakhstana, vol. 2. Moscow, 1963.
Istoriia Kazakhskoi SSR, vols. 1–2. Alma-Ata, 1957–59.
Istoriia Kazakhskoi SSR, 3rd ed., vol. 2. Alma-Ata, 1967.
Valikhanov, Ch. Ch. *Sobr. soch.,* vols. 1–5. Alma-Ata, 1961–72.
Vostrov, V. V., and M. S. Mukanov. *Rodoplemennoi sostav i rasselenie kazakhov (Konets XIX—nachalo XX vv.).* Alma-Ata, 1968.
Kul'tura i byt kazakhskogo kolkhozhogo aula. Alma-Ata, 1967.
Trudy Instituta istorii, arkheologii i etnografii AN Kazakhskoi SSR, vols. 3, 6, 16, 18. Alma-Ata, 1959–63.
Vostrov, V. V., and Kh. A. Kauanova. *Material'naia kul'tura kazakhskogo naroda na sovremennom etape.* Alma-Ata, 1972.

S. M. ABRAMZON [11–417–6]

KAZAKH SOVIET SOCIALIST REPUBLIC (Kazak Sovettik Sotsialistik Respublikasy), Kazakhstan (Kazakstan).

General information

The Kazakh SSR was originally formed as the Kirghiz ASSR, part of the RSFSR, on Aug. 26, 1920; on Dec. 5, 1936, the autonomous Soviet socialist republic became the Kazakh Union Republic. It is located in the southwestern Asian part of the USSR. It borders on the RSFSR to the north, the Turkmen, Uzbek, and Kirghiz SSR's to the south, China to the east, and the Caspian Sea to the west. Kazakhstan is the second largest Union republic in area (after the RSFSR) and the third largest in population (after the RSFSR and the Ukraine). Area, 2,717,300 sq km; population, 13,928,000 (as of Jan. 1, 1974). Capital, Alma-Ata.

The republic is divided into 19 oblasts and 210 raions and has 82 cities and 177 urban-type settlements (see Table 1).

[section updated]

Constitution and government

Kazakhstan is a socialist state of workers and peasants, a Union Soviet socialist republic of the USSR. The present constitution was ratified by the Extraordinary Tenth Congress of Soviets of the Kazakh SSR on Mar. 26, 1937. The supreme body of state power is the unicameral Supreme Soviet of the Kazakh SSR, which is elected for four years on the basis of one deputy for every 27,000 inhabitants. Between sessions of the Supreme Soviet, the supreme body of state power is the Presidium of the Supreme Soviet of the Kazakh SSR. The Supreme Soviet appoints the government of the republic—the Council of Ministers —and legislates for the Kazakh SSR. The local bodies of government in the oblasts, raions, cities, and *auls* (villages) are the respective soviets of working people's deputies, which are elected

Table 1. Administrative-territorial division of the Kazakh Soviet Socialist Republic (as of Jan. 1, 1974)

Oblast	Area (sq km)	Population	Number of cities	Number of urban-type settlements	Center
Aktiubinsk	298,700	592,000	7	3	Aktiubinsk
Alma-Ata	104,700	1,604,000	5	6	Alma-Ata
Chimkent	116,300	1,416,000	8	7	Chimkent
Dzhambul	144,600	870,000	4	12	Dzhambul
Dzhezkazgan	313,400	441,000	4	19	Dzhezkazgan
Gur'ev	112,000	362,000	1	14	Gur'ev
Karaganda	85,400	1,223,000	6	16	Karaganda
Kokchetav	78,100	598,000	4	6	Kokchetav
Kustanai	114,500	921,000	4	12	Kustanai
Kzyl-Orda	228,100	529,000	3	7	Kzyl-Orda
Mangyshlak	166,600	218,000	3	11	Shevchenko
Pavlodar	127,500	750,000	4	11	Pavlodar
Semipalatinsk	179,600	744,000	3	9	Semipalatinsk
Severnyi Kazakhstan	44,300	551,000	4	1	Petropavlovsk
Taldy-Kurgan	118,500	655,000	5	10	Taldy-Kurgan
Tselinograd	124,600	797,000	5	13	Tselinograd
Turgai	111,900	249,000	3	1	Arkalyk
Ural'sk	151,200	547,000	3	4	Ural'sk
Vostochnyi Kazakhstan	97,300	861,000	6	15	Ust'-Kamenogorsk

by the people for two-year terms. The Kazakh SSR is represented by 32 deputies in the Soviet of Nationalities of the Supreme Soviet of the USSR.

The highest judicial body of Kazakhstan is the Supreme Court of the republic, which is elected by the republic's Supreme Soviet for a term of five years. It operates in the form of two judicial divisions—one for civil and one for criminal cases—and a plenum. The Presidium of the Supreme Court is also formed. The procurator of the Kazakh SSR is appointed by the procurator general of the USSR for a five-year term.

Natural features

Kazakhstan stretches from the lower course of the Volga in the west to the Altai in the east and from the Western Siberian Lowland in the north to the Tien-Shan in the south. The Khan Tengri massif, with elevations to 7,000 m, rises in the southeast. A feature of Kazakhstan is its interior continental position in Eurasia.

Terrain. The terrain of Kazakhstan is extremely diverse. There are high mountains covered with glaciers, a hilly middle-altitude mountain area and plateau-like elevations, and vast plains and depressions. The northwestern part of the republic is occupied by the southern outskirts of the Obshchii Syrt and the Cis-Uralic Plateau (elevations to 354 m). South of these lies the vast, flat Caspian Depression, whose absolute elevation varies from the level of the Caspian Sea (−28 m) to 50 m above sea level. The Mangyshlak Peninsula is located in the southwest. The north is a solonchak depression; the center is occupied by the Karatau Range (elevations to 556 m), and in the south there are deep internally drained depressions whose bottoms lie below sea level: Karagie, −132 m, the deepest basin in the USSR; Karynzharyk, −70 m; and Kaundy, −54 m. East of Mangyshlak is the Ustiurt desert plateau (elevations to 340 m), which is surrounded by steep precipices, or scarps. In its low-lying northern portion there are solonchaks and large tracts of sand (Sam, Asmantai-Matai, and Karatulei). In the northeast, the Caspian Depression is bounded by the southern spurs of the Urals and the Mugodzhar Mountains (elevations to 657 m). The Turgai Plateau (elevations of 200–400 m) is northeast of the Mugodzhar Mountains. In the south it gives way to the Turan Depression, which is occupied by the Kyzylkum (elevations from 53 to 332 m). The large sand tracts of the Bol'shie and Malye Barsuki and the Aral Karakum are north of the Aral Sea.

Only the southern outskirts of the Western Siberian Lowland lie within the republic. The central portion is occupied by the Kazakh *melkosopochnik* (area of gently sloping low hills), or Saryarka, the remains of an ancient destroyed mountain area, within which there are isolated mountain massifs—Kyzylrai (1,565 m), Karkaraly (1,366 m), and Ulutau (1,133 m). To the south the Kazakh *melkosopochnik* gives way to an extremely arid desert, Betpak-Dala (elevations 250–550 m). To the south of Betpak-Dala, a great expanse is occupied by the large Muiunkum tract of sand desert (elevations to 66 m). The vast Semirech'e region is east of Betpak-Dala (elevations to 800 m); it is named after seven rivers that empty into Lake Balkhash from the south. Much of the Semirech'e is occupied by the Balkhash basin, with the large Sary-Ishikotrau sand tract; in the southwest, the basin is connected to the Ili basin, and in the east, to the Sasykkol'-Alakol' basin. The majority of the basins are filled by lakes.

The southern chains of the Altai (the southern and Rudnyi Altai), with elevations to 4,506 m (Mount Belukha), are located in the east and southeast, as are the ranges of Saur (elevations to 3,805 m), Tarbagatai (2,992 m), the Dzungarian Alatau (4,463 m), and the Northern and Western Tien-Shan: Ketmen' (to 3,-368 m), the Chu Ili Mountains (1,520 m), the Zailiiskii Alatau (4,973 m), part of the Kungei-Alatau (4,213 m), the Kirghiz Range (3,817 m), the Talasskii Alatau (4,488 m), the Ugam Range (4,229 m), and the Karatau (2,176 m).

S. A. ABDRAKHMANOV

Geological structure and mineral resources. In the west, most of the Caspian synclise of the Eastern European Platform lies in Kazakhstan; the Phanerozoic layers reach a thickness of 16–18 km. A thick saliferous series of the Upper and possibly Middle Paleozoic (4–6 km and more) occurs in the middle part

of the cross section of the syneclise; it includes veins of rock salt, potassium salt, and borates. Salt forms the nucleus of more than 350 domes. Workable oil and oil and gas deposits, confined to Permian-Triassic, Jurassic, Cretaceous, and Paleocene deposits, are associated with the salt-dome structures. Lower Cretaceous sedimentation contains deposits of phosphorites. Thick Mesozoic and Cenozoic sedimentary layers, which in some places are oil- and gas-bearing and overlap Paleozoic outcroppings and troughs, lie within the Ustiurt; the ancient foundation, composed of Paleozoic rock, underlies the outcroppings and troughs at great depths.

The Mugodzhar Mountains are composed of intricately constructed Precambrian and Paleozoic folded metamorphized magmatic and sedimentary strata permeated by intrusions of granitoids and basic and hyperbasic rock. Copper pyrite deposits have been discovered in the Silurian greenstone stratum. East and south of the Mugodzhars, a Paleozoic foundation is prevalent throughout Kazakhstan. In the Turgai downwarp, it occurs at depths ranging from several dozen meters to 1,000 m. Deposits of magnetic iron ores are found in the foundation of the Turgai downwarp (Sokolov, Sarbai, and Kachar). The Cretaceous, Paleocene, and Neocene deposits that lie almost horizontally on the Paleozoic foundation include bog iron ore (the Aiat and Lisakovsk deposits, Kustanai Oblast), brown coals (the Obagan basin), and bauxites (the Amangel'dy group of deposits).

The foundation of the Chu Depression is encountered at depths of 500–2,000 m and is overlapped by Middle and Upper Paleozoic sedimentary strata with large deposits of copper sandstones of Dzhezkazgan and a thick saliferous series, as well as by Mesozoic-Cenozoic continental rock. In the northern Kyzylkum and the region adjoining the Aral Sea, the foundation is overlapped by a series of Paleozoic and Mesozoic-Cenozoic strata 1,000–4,000 m thick. In Mangyshlak the lower layers of the sheath (Permian-Triassic), which are more than 10 km thick, form a system of compressed west-north folds. Large veins of oil and natural gas (Zhetybai, Uzen', and others) are attributed to the Mesozoic rocks in these folds. Deposits of brown coal are also associated with the Mesozoic-Cenozoic deposits there.

The folded Paleozoic structure appears on the surface in the mountains of the Altai, Tarbagatai, and Dzungarian Alatau, the northern chains of the Tien-Shan, and the Karatau, as well as in central Kazakhstan. Rock complexes of diverse composition attain thicknesses of dozens of kilometers. The most ancient rocks have been metamorphized into gneisses and schists. The upper portions of the cross section are composed of weakly altered rocks.

Among pre-Paleozoic and Paleozoic formations there are complexes influenced by folding of the Caledonian and Hercynian eras that pertain to manifestations of the main tectonic movements. Caledonides form a vast ancient mass covering all the northwestern and western parts of central Kazakhstan, as well as the northern Tien-Shan. Hercynian rock makes up the Mugodzhars, the foundation of the western part of the Turgai downwarp, the southern part of the Kyzylkum, the Balkhash area, and the mountains of the Dzungarian Alatau, Tarbagatai, Altai, and Chingiz. Volcanic beds and granites of late Paleozoic origin, as well as belts of hyperbasic rocks in places, are prevalent in a number of areas (the Mugodzhars, the Balkhash area, the northern Tien-Shan, the Rudnyi Altai, and the Kalba). Paleozoic and more ancient strata form fold bows that bulge toward the southwest. They are meridional in trend in the Mugodzhars and in the western part of central Kazakhstan; in the Tien-Shan and Dzungarian Alatau, as well as the eastern part of central Kazakhstan and the Altai, they are latitudinal and northwesterly. The most recent tectonic movements and the earthquakes accompanying them are strongly manifested in many mountain areas of Kazakhstan.

Many large deposits of metallic and nonmetallic minerals are attributed to the folded Paleozoic foundation of Kazakhstan, among which the copper and complex-ore deposits of the Rudnyi Altai, central Kazakhstan, the Dzungarian Alatau, and Karatau are prominent. The deposits of rare metals of Kalba and central Kazakhstan are associated with Paleozoic granitoids. Gold ore deposits are concentrated in northern Kazakhstan (Kokchetav and Tselinograd oblasts) and eastern Kazakhstan (western Kalba). A considerable quantity of gold is contained in the gold–pyrite–complex-ore deposits of the Rudnyi Altai, Chingiz, and Maikain. Iron-manganese and iron ores have been prospected in the Atasui iron-manganese basin (central Kazakhstan) and the Karsakpai (Ulutau) iron ore basin. Depressions of the Paleozoic foundation are occupied by deposits of the Karaganda and Ekibastuz coal and Maikuba brown coal basins. Deposits of ores of chromites (the Donskoe deposits), nickel, cobalt, copper, gold, and asbestos are prevalent in the volcanic and ultrabasic rock of the Mugodzhar fold complex. Carbonaceous-siliceous shales of the Cambrian period are contained in blanket deposits of the Karatau phosphorite and vanadium basins.

Kazakhstan is one of the richest regions of the USSR in resources and diversity of minerals. Most of its deposits were discovered during the Soviet period. The republic is a leader in the USSR in prospected reserves of chromite ores, copper, lead, zinc, silver, tungsten, phosphorites, barite, molybdenum, cadmium, bismuth, asbestos, and pyrophyllite.

A. A. BOGDANOV and T. GAPUOV

Climate. Kazakhstan's remoteness from oceans, its vastness, and its mountainous features result in a sharply continental climate with very marked zonality. Solar radiation is considerable because of the southern location and low degree of cloudiness. The sun shines 2,000 hours a year in the north to 3,000 hours in the south. Overall radiation increases from 100 kilocalories per sq cm (kcal/cm^2) in the north to 140 kcal/cm^2 in the south. In the north the winter is cold and long; in the central region, moderately cold; in the south, basically moderately mild and brief; and in the extreme south, mild. The average January temperature rises from $-18°C$ in the north to $-3°C$ in the extreme southern portion of the flat country. In winter, frosts down to $-45°C$ in the north and central regions and sometimes down to $-35°C$ in the south occur as a result of the penetration of cold continental arctic air masses from the north and northwest. On the plains the summer is long and dry; in the north, it is warm; in the center, very warm; and in the south, hot. The average July temperature increases from 19°C in the north to 28°–30°C in the south. In the mountains, summers are brief and moderate; winters are comparatively warm. There is little precipitation anywhere. Average annual precipitation in the forest-steppe is 300–400 mm, in the steppe it decreases to 250 mm, in the Kazakh *melkosopochnik* it rises to 300–400 mm, and in the semidesert and desert it drops to 200–100 mm. Precipitation is particularly low (less than 100 mm per year) in the area adjoining Lake Balkhash, the southwestern part of the Kyzylkum adjoining the Aral Sea, and the southern Ustiurt. In the foothills and mountains, annual precipitation is 400–1,600 mm. In the north and center, most of the rain comes during the summer months; in the south, in early spring. Strong winds are characteristic of almost all of Kazakhstan. In winter, southwesterly winds predominate in the north and northeasterly winds in the south; in summer, northerly winds prevail everywhere. The growing season lasts 190–200 days in the north and 230–290 days in the south.

Glaciation. There are more than 2,700 glaciers; their area is about 2,000 sq km, and the total mass of ice and névé is about 60 billion cu m. Valley glaciers account for about one-fifth of the total number but more than one-half of the total area. The main areas of glaciation are the Dzungarian Alatau, the ranges of the Tien-Shan, and the Berel' glaciation node in the Altai.

Rivers and lakes. The diversity of the terrain and climate results in uneven distribution of surface water. There are very few rivers in the deserts; in the north and the high-altitude regions there are many. There are about 85,000 rivers and temporary runoffs, of which 90 percent are less than 10 km long; there are only 228 rivers longer than 100 km. The well-moistened eastern and southern high-mountain regions, from which the largest rivers flow, have a very dense river network (0.2–0.4 km per sq km; in northern Kazakhstan, the index is 0.03–0.05 km per sq km, and in the desert zone it is still lower). Many of the rivers belong to the internal inland basins of the Caspian and Aral seas and Lakes Balkhash, Tengiz, Shalkar, and Karasor; only the Irtysh, Ishim, and Tobol rivers are part of the Ob' basin. The large rivers of the Caspian basin are the Ural and Emba; of the Aral basin, the Syr Darya. The Ili, Karatal, Aksu, and Lepsy

rivers empty into Lake Balkhash from the south; the Aiaguz, Bakanas, and Tokrau, from the north. In addition to small temporary runoffs, Lake Tengiz receives one of the major rivers of Kazakhstan, the Nura. The basins of small rivers—the Irgiz, Turgai, Sarysu, Chu, and others—form independent closed drainage regions. Snow-fed plains rivers with spring high water predominate. Many dry up in summer, partially breaking up into reaches. In the south and east there are many mountain rivers fed by glaciers and snow; high water for them is in the spring and summer. Mountain rivers have the greatest water capacity and play an important role in the economy. More than 160 billion kilowatt-hours of electric power can be produced from them annually. Surface runoff in Kazakhstan is 112 cu km a year. In the south, rivers are used for irrigation, and trunk canals branch off from many of them. The Irtysh-Karaganda canal, built to supply water for the industries of central Kazakhstan, begins at the Irtysh. The Kzyl-Orda dam, Chardar'ia Reservoir, and Kazalinsk Hydroengineering Complex on the Syr Darya, the Bukhtarma Reservoir on the Irtysh, the Kapchagai Reservoir on the Ili, the Karatomar Reservoir on the Tobol, and the Sergeevka Reservoir on the Ishim have been built to regulate discharge and to use the water for irrigation and inundation. The Irtysh, Ili, Ural, and Syr Darya (from its mouth to Kazalinsk) are navigable.

There are more than 48,000 lakes in Kazakhstan, with an area of 45,000 sq km; 94 percent of them have areas of up to 1 sq km. They are mainly floodplain and delta lakes. There are 21 lakes with areas greater than 100 sq km, including Balkhash, Zaisan (part of the Bukhtarma Reservoir), Alakol', Tengiz, Seletyteniz, Sasykkol', Kushmurun, Markakol', and Ul'ken-Karoi. The northern and northeastern Caspian Sea and the northern Aral Sea lie in Kazakhstan. There are also more than 4,000 ponds and reservoirs. Most of the lakes are undrained. Their levels fluctuate sharply over the seasons and from year to year, and their outlines and dimensions change periodically. Many of them dry up or become salinas in dry years. Lakes are most commonly found in northern Kazakhstan, where there are many enclosed depressions. In the steppe zone and mountains and along the valleys of the large rivers, freshwater lakes predominate; in the semidesert and desert zones and in intermontane basins, saltwater lakes are prevalent. Various salts are extracted from many lakes, and more than 30 have medicinal mud and natural brine.

In many regions there are large supplies of fresh and slightly saline groundwaters, which are used in part by industrial and agricultural enterprises. The groundwater resources of Kazakhstan are estimated at 7,000 cu km. There are many mineral springs.

Soils. The soil cover of Kazakhstan is marked by clearly expressed geographical and altitudinal zonality. A narrow band of chernozems lies in the north, up to 52° N lat. It is divided into leached chernozems, which are a small portion of the forest-steppe zone in Severnyi Kazakhstan Oblast; ordinary chernozems of the moderately dry steppe, which constitute 4.6 percent of the total area of the soils of Kazakhstan; and southern chernozems of the arid steppe, which account for 4.9 percent. Chestnut soils are found south of the chernozems, between 52° and 48° N lat. They are subdivided into dark chestnut soils of the moderately dry steppe (10.5 percent), typical chestnuts of the dry steppe (9.6 percent), and light chestnut soils of the semidesert (14.2 percent). The chernozems and dark chestnut soils have been plowed up. South of 48° N lat., brown and brownish gray desert soils are prevalent; they alternate with large tracts of sandy desert soils and takyr-like soils. Brown soils of the northern desert subzone (21.6 percent) and gray-brown soils confined to the middle and southern desert subzones (22 percent) stand out in this area. In the mountains of the Western and Northern Tien-Shan, the gray-brown soils give way to sierozems and light chestnut soils of the plain and foothill subzone. Higher in the mountains of the Western Tien-Shan, there is a zone of mountain brown soils, and in the mountains of the Northern Tien-Shan, Saur, Tarbagatai, and western Altai there is a zone of mountain dark chestnut soils, chestnut soils, and mountain chernozems. In the mountains of the Northern Tien-Shan, a belt of leached mountain chernozems, mountain gray-forest soils, and mountain dark-forest soils follows the preceding belt; in the western Altai, a belt of mountain-meadow chernozem-like and gray forest soils follows it. Still higher, a band of mountain-meadow subalpine and alpine soils is found in all mountain regions. Mountain soils make up 12.6 percent of Kazakhstan.

Flora. The flora of Kazakhstan is very diverse. The plains areas of Kazakhstan are divided into three main zones—steppe, semidesert, and desert—according to the nature of vegetation.

In the steppe zone (the northern part), mixed-grass vegetation prevails (feathergrasses, sheep fescue, hair-grass, oat-grass, purple-stem cat's-tail, wild rye, wormwood, and, in the floodplains of rivers, brome and couch-grass meadows). In the extreme northern part of the steppe zone are small dispersed birch groves with aspen mixed in. Pine forests survive on river banks, primarily along the Irtysh and Tobol and the granitic tracts of the Kazakh *melkosopochnik.* Fescue and feather-grass vegetation characterizes the dry steppe.

In the semidesert zone, wormwood-herbaceous vegetation (white and black wormwood, *tyrsik* [*Stipa sareptana*], and fescue) is dominant.

The desert zone (sand, clay, and gravel) occupies the greatest area. The vegetative cover of clay and gravel deserts has drought-resistant undergrowth and shrubs and various saltworts and wormwoods in combination with grasses (prostrate summer cypress, *sarsazan* [*Halocnemum*], *biiurgun* [*Anabasis salsa*], *boialych* [*Salsola arbuscula*], *kokpek* [*Atriplex cana*], glasswort, white and black wormwood, milk vetches, camel-thorn, winterfat, and tamarisk). Sand wormwood, sand sedge, Siberian wheatgrass, *Calligonum,* sand acacia, and white saxaul are widespread in sand deserts. There are tracts of black saxaul in the Kyzylkum and Sary-Ishikotrau sand deserts. Tugai forests (olive, turanga poplar, willow, tamarisk, and salt tree) are found in the valleys of large rivers in the desert zone; reeds grow around lakes and along rivers. The deserts of Kazakhstan serve as winter and, to some extent, year-round pastures. Ephemerals and ephemeraloids (little sedge, bulbous meadow grass, mottled poppy, and tulip) are very typical of foothill plains and foothills. The foothills of the mountain ranges are covered with steppe vegetation. At higher elevations, shrubs (briar, honeysuckle, and barberry) and sparse aspen and birch forests are encountered; in addition, wild apple trees, apricot trees, and hawthorn are found in the Zailiiskii Alatau. In the middle mountain belt there are typical coniferous forests. In the Altai, these forests have a Siberian habit, consisting of Siberian larch, spruce, Siberian stone pine, fir, and cedar, with a dense shrub underbrush. The Shrenk spruce, at times interspersed with Siberian fir, is prevalent in the Dzungarian Alatau. Farther south, in the Tien-Shan, the fir disappears and the Schrenk spruce remains. Above the forest belt there are subalpine and alpine meadows formed by *Kobresia capilliformis,* sedges, lady's mantle, meadow grass, and other mixed grasses; they are good summer pastures. There are juniper groves—Turkestan juniper—in higher sections of the Tien-Shan ranges. Forests cover about 10 million hectares (ha), or 3 percent of Kazakhstan, with the main tracts concentrated in the Altai, Dzungarian Alatau, and eastern Tien-Shan. Most of the forests are valuable for water and soil protection and for improving air quality; saxaul is used for fuel and securing desert sands.

Fauna. Among the contemporary fauna of Kazakhstan are 155 species of mammals, 480 species of birds, 49 species of reptiles, 11 species of amphibians, about 150 species of fish, and many invertebrates. Rodents are the most common mammals: the suslik and hamster in the steppes, yellow suslik in the deserts, water rat around bodies of water in northern Kazakhstan, and field mice, jerboas, marmots, and hares in all areas. The saiga and goitered gazelle inhabit the desert and semidesert; Caspian deer, musk deer, mountain goat, and Pamir argali are found in the mountains of the Altai and Tien-Shan; and boars and roe live on the plains and in the mountains. Among the predators are the wolf, fox, badger, weasel, and Siberian polecat. In the forests of the Altai and Tien-Shan are brown bear, snow leopard, lynx, wolverine, Siberian weasel, and squirrel. The muskrat has been acclimatized in the lower reaches of the Ili, Karatal, and other rivers. Waterfowl nesting in Kazakhstan include the gray-lag goose, sheldrake, mallard, gadwall, white-headed duck, and ruddy sheldrake; flamingo (on Lake Tengiz); and bittern and gray and white herons (in the reeds). Cormo-

rants, pelicans, and cranes are encountered; in the steppes there are bustards, little bustards, sociable plovers, curlews, larks, eagles, harriers, and kestrels. In the plains section there are many tortoises and lizards, including the genus *Phrynocephalus* and agamids, and also snakes. The lakes and rivers are rich in fish. Seals inhabit the Caspian Sea, and giant sturgeon, sturgeon, Caspian sturgeon, *Acipenser nudiventris, Stenodus leucichthys,* herring, *Clupeonella,* pike perch, bream, Caspian roach, and gray mullet are bred. In addition, the Aral Sea barbel, chub, *Clupea harengus membras,* and carp inhabit the Aral Sea. In rivers and lakes there are pike, perch, and crucian carp. In mountain lakes and rivers there are sea trout, grayling, and nelma.

Preserves. Kazakhstan has the Alma-Ata, Aksu-Dzhabagli, and Barsakel'mes preserves, as well as the Naurzum Preserve, for the protection and study of the natural complex of the most southerly pine forest in Kazakhstan (in the steppe zone), and the Kurgal'dzhin Preserve, for the protection of an untouched portion of the steppe landscape and the protection and study of the fauna of Lakes Kurgal'dzhin and Tengiz, where flamingo nest.

Natural regions. On the plains of Kazakhstan—including the tracts of *melkosopochnik* and insular low mountains—which occupy about 90 percent of its territory, natural zonality is distinct, from the forest steppe zone in the north to the desert in the south.

In Kazakhstan, the East European Plain includes the trans-Volga elevated watershed, the eastern part of the Caspian Depression, and the Cis-Uralic Plateau. The Urals include the Southern Urals, Mugodzhars, and Trans-Ural Plateau. The Western Siberian Lowland occupies the southern forest-steppe and steppe section. The Turan Depression includes the desert regions of Mangyshlak, Ustiurt, the Turgai Plateau, the Aral region, the Kyzylkum, Betpak-Dala, Muiunkum, and the Balkhash-Alakol' Basin. The Kazakh *melkosopochnik* is located in central Kazakhstan. In the southeast and east are the mountains and intermontane hollows of the Western and Southern Altai, Saur, Tarbagatai, Dzungarian Alatau, Northern and Western Tien-Shan, and their spurs, where various types of vertical landscape zonality dominate, from southern Siberian landscapes in the north to steppe and desert landscapes in the south.

S. A. ABDRAKHMANOV

REFERENCES
"Kazakhstan." Moscow, 1969. (*Prirodnye usloviia i estestvennye resursy SSSR.*)
Gvozdetskii, N. A., and V. A. Nikolaev. *Kazakhstan: Ocherk prirody.* Moscow, 1971.
Bespalov, V. F. *Geologicheskoe stroenie Kazakhskoi SSR.* Alma-Ata, 1971.
Geologiia SSSR, vol. 20: *Vostochnyi Kazakhstan,* part 1, Moscow-Leningrad, 1941; vol. 21: *Zapadnyi Kazakhstan,* part 1, books 1–2, Moscow-Leningrad, 1970.
Esenov, Sh. E., D. S. Kunaev, and S. M. Mukhamedzhanov. *Nedra Kazakhstana.* Alma-Ata, 1968.
Klimat Kazakhstana. Leningrad, 1959.
Kalachev, N. S., and L. D. Lavrent'eva. *Vodoenergeticheskii kadastr rek Kazakhskoi SSR.* Alma-Ata, 1965.
Pochvy Kazakhskoi SSR, fasc. 1–13. Alma-Ata, 1960–70.
Pavlov, N. V. *Rastitel'noe syr'e Kazakhstana.* Moscow-Leningrad, 1947.
Sobolev, L. N. *Kormovye resursy Kazakhstana.* Moscow, 1960.
Gudochkin, M. V., and P. S. Chaban. *Lesa Kazakhstana.* Alma-Ata, 1958.
Afanas'ev, A. V. *Zoogeografiia Kazakhstana.* Alma-Ata, 1960.

Population

The native population is composed of Kazakhs (4,234,000, according to the 1970 census). Substantial numbers of Russians (5,522,000) and Ukrainians (933,000) live in the republic, primarily in the virgin lands of northern Kazakhstan and the cities; there are Tatars (288,000), Uzbeks (216,000), Byelorussians (198,000), and Uighurs (121,000) living in the valleys of the upper Ili River, as well as Koreans (82,000, primarily in Alma-Ata and Kzyl-Orda oblasts) and Dungans of Middle Asia (17,000).

As of 1972 the population of Kazakhstan had increased by 2.4 times since 1913 (see Table 2). The growth has come from natural increase and the large influx from other republics in conjunction with the rapid development of industry and the exploitation of virgin and unused lands. Kazakhstan is ahead of many other Union republics in natural population increase (17.8 per thousand in 1971; the average for the USSR was 9.6).

Table 2. Population

	Population (in millions)			Percentage of total	
	Total	Urban	Rural	Urban	Rural
1913 (end-of-year estimate)	5.597	.541	5.056	9.7	90.3
1926 (census of Dec. 17)	6.025	.519	5.506	8.6	91.4
1940 (estimate as of Jan. 1)	6.148	1.833	4.315	29.8	70.2
1959 (census of Jan. 15) .	9.295	4.067	5.228	43.8	56.2
1970 (census of Jan. 15) .	13.009	6.538	6.471	50.3	49.7
1972 (estimate as of Jan. 1)	13.470	6.942	6.528	52.0	48.0

The population distribution is extremely uneven. Average density is 5 per sq km. The southern foothill zone, where the density sometimes reaches more than 100 per sq km in the oases of irrigated farming, is the most thickly settled. The density is also comparatively high in the north in the chernozem forest-steppe and steppe agricultural zone (20 and more per sq km) and a number of industrial centers and regions. At the same time, vast expanses of desert and semidesert are still very sparsely settled. The average density in western, central, and southern Kazakhstan is 1.4–1.8 per sq km.

In 1971, 4,837,000 people were employed in the economy of Kazakhstan (5.3 times more than in 1940), of which 1,075,000 worked in industry, 555,000 in construction, 983,000 in agriculture, and 566,000 in transportation and communications. Women make up 47 percent of the industrial and office workers.

The proportions of urban and rural population have changed as a result of socialist industrialization. Under Soviet power, more than 200 new urban settlements have been created. Before the October Revolution, there was no city in Kazakhstan with a population of 50,000 or more; in 1972, there were 25, of which 16 had a population of more than 100,000 and two of these—Alma-Ata and Karaganda—had more than 500,000 residents (776,000 and 541,000, respectively). New large industrial centers include Karaganda, Temirtau (179,000), Balkhash (78,000), and Dzhezkazgan (68,000) in central Kazakhstan; Shevchenko (75,000) on the Mangyshlak Peninsula; Rudnyi (101,000), Ermak, Arkalyk, and Ekibastuz in northern Kazakhstan; and Karatau, Kentau, and Tekeli in southern Kazakhstan. The population also increased in the older cities: Alma-Ata, Chimkent (265,000), Semipalatinsk (251,000), Ust'-Kamenogorsk (241,000), Pavlodar (208,000), Dzhambul (205,000), and Aktiubinsk (159,000).

Historical survey

Primitive communal system (from earliest times to the sixth century). Primitive man settled 300,000 years ago in what is now Kazakhstan, during the early Stone Age. Lower Paleolithic campsites with crudely made stone implements have been discovered in the caves of the Karatau Mountains and in areas of the northern Cis-Balkhash. Flint scrapers and other articles found in the village of Kanai in eastern Kazakhstan attest to the settlement of primitive man during the Middle Paleolithic era. Evidence of primitive man can be traced continuously beginning with the Upper Paleolithic. During the Neolithic period, man began to use bows and make pottery and microlithic implements of various types. Pastoral livestock raising and hoe farming began in the fourth and third millennia B.C. (the Aeneolithic era). Remains of the Bronze Age culture (mid-second to early first milennium B.C.), which are very widespread, are represented primarily by relics of the Andronovo culture. The Andronovo tribes engaged in pastoral livestock raising, hoe farming, hunting, and fishing and were skilled in the production of bronze weapons and tools. The shift to copper and bronze work implements and the development of livestock raising and agriculture brought major social changes: the maternal clan was replaced by

the paternal clan, and the rudiments of patriarchal family property appeared.

In the late stages of the Bronze Age, livestock-raising tribes began to separate; by the middle of the first millennium B.C., most tribes in the steppes shifted to nomadic livestock raising, which determined the specific characteristics of socioeconomic development in Kazakhstan for many centuries. Herodotus and other ancients called the tribes of this era the Asiatic Scythians. In Achaemenid cuneiform texts they are called by the collective name of Sacae. The Iranian-speaking Sacae tribes engaged in nomadic livestock raising and irrigated farming; they used iron and had commercial and cultural ties with neighboring tribes. Chiefs headed their tribal union. The tribal associations of the successors to the culture of the Sacae became established in the third and second centuries B.C. They were the tribal associations of the Usun, who occupied the territory of Semirech'e (from the Chu River to the Tien-Shan and from Lake Balkhash to Lake Issyk-Kul'), the tribes belonging to the Kangiui (Kangkha) state, who settled in regions of the Karatau and the middle course of the Syr Darya, and the tribes of Alani, who migrated nomadically from the western shores of the Aral to the northern shores of the Caspian. These tribes engaged primarily in nomadic livestock raising; crafts, including iron metallurgy, and, to some extent, farming, were developed. They had economic, political, and cultural ties with China, Transoxiana, and the Volga Region. Caravans passed through the lands of the Usun over the "Silk Route." The Usun union was headed by the grand *kunmi* (bey), whose power had become hereditary. One *kunmi,* Tsilimi (first century B.C.), established a system under which "no one would dare graze his cattle on his [Tsilimi's] pastures." The usurpation of communal lands accelerated the disintegration of the primitive communal system and the formation of feudal class relations. The intensifying internecine struggle of the aristocracy for the power of the grand *kunmi* and the invasion by the Altai Turks led to the disintegration of the Usun association.

Development of feudal relations and formation of early feudal states (sixth to mid-15th centuries). The peoples of Kazakhstan bypassed the slaveholding stage of development. The primitive communal system was gradually replaced by patriarchal-feudal relations, which developed more intensively in the south and more slowly in the steppe regions. The first early feudal state, the Turkic Kaganate, took shape in the mid-sixth century A.D. In the early eighth century, the Turgesh state formed in the area between the Ili and Chu rivers, and in 766 the Karluk state formed. In the Turgesh Kaganate and, later, the Karluk Kaganate (766–940), feudal relations developed more intensively. Cities arose and became centers for crafts and trade—for example, Taraz (present-day Dzhambul). The cities' economic ties with the surrounding nomadic tribes expanded, and money appeared (local coins were minted by the Turgesh).

Islam took hold in southern Kazakhstan from the eighth to tenth centuries. From the ninth through 11th centuries, western and southwestern Kazakhstan were part of the early feudal Oguz state. Caravans passed through Oguz territory to Transoxiana, Iran, China, the Caucasus, and the Volga Region. The Oguz Kaganate maintained ties with Rus'. Between the eighth and 11th centuries the northeastern and central areas of Kazakhstan were settled by the Turkic Kimak and Kipchak tribes. Eastern authors called this vast region Dasht-i-Kipchak (the Kipchak steppe). Feudal relations developed slowly there. The main occupation of the Kimak and Kipchak was livestock raising.

In the first half of the tenth century, Semirech'e was invaded by the Turkic Iagma tribe from eastern Turkestan. The Karakhanid feudal state was based on the Karluk Kaganate, which disintegrated under the blows of the Iagma. In the late tenth century and first half of the 11th, the Karakhanids created a strong feudal state, including Kashgaria, Semirech'e, and Transoxiana. In order to rule the conquered regions, the khan (*tamgach-khan*) appointed viceroys (*il-khans*). A feudal appanage system was established: the khans granted their vassals the right to collect taxes from the population of given regions. Métayage, a new form of feudal exploitation, appeared, and in nomadic regions the institution of commendation emerged.

The consolidation of feudal relations was aided by the further spread of Islam. In the second half of the 11th century, in the context of an internecine struggle among feudal groups, wars began against the Seljuks, who had seized Transoxiana. The collapse of the Karakhanid state was completed by the invasion of Semirech'e during the 1130's by the Khitans (Karakitais), who established the Karakitai state in Middle and Central Asia. Feudal wars in the Semirech'e brought a decline in trade, crafts, and urban culture. In the mid-12th century, Khwarazm split off from the weakened Karakitai state, but the Karakitais retained power in Semirech'e until the invasion of the Mongol Tatars.

Numerous architectural remains testify to the comparatively high level of economic and cultural development in Kazakhstan in the tenth to twelfth centuries (the mausoleums of Babadzhi-Khatun, tenth to 11th century, and Aisha-Bibi, 11th–12th century). In the river basins, which were the centers of irrigated farming, cities developed: Otrar, Sygnak, Sauran, Dzhent, and Zhankent on the Syr Darya; Taraz, Suzak, and Kumkent on the Talas; and Turtkul', Aktiube, and Kulan on the Chu. Traces of large settlements have also survived in central Kazakhstan.

From 1219 to 1221, Kazakhstan was conquered by the Mongol Tatars and divided among the sons of Ghengis Khan. The Mongol invasion undermined the productive forces of Kazakhstan and retarded the formation of the Kazakh nationality. Under Mongol Tatar rule, Kazakhstan was part of the Golden Horde; after it broke up, Kazakhstan became part of the White Horde and Mogulistan. During the late 14th and early 15th centuries, the White Horde, which had spread over an enormous area, broke up into several holdings; the largest were the Nogai Horde and the Uzbek Khanate, which included the main parts of Kazakhstan. The Nogai Horde occupied the region between the Iaik (Ural) and Volga rivers; the Uzbek Khanate occupied the area from the Aral Sea to the Iaik in the west, the Tobol in the north, and the Irtysh in the east. Ethnically, they united local Turkic-speaking tribes that had not yet formed a single nationality.

Formation of the Kazakh nationality and the Kazakh khanates (mid-15th to early 18th century). The population of the Uzbek khanate was collectively called the Uzbek Kazakhs. At that time, the terms "Uzbek" and "Kazakh" did not have a sufficiently clear ethnic meaning. Incessant internecine wars and intensified feudal oppression prompted mass migration of tribes from the Uzbek Khanate. Kazakh clans migrated nomadically to the western Semirech'e. The valleys of the Chu and Talas became the site of a mass influx from the Dasht-i-Kipchak. Semirech'e, which returned to life after the end of Mongol Tatar rule, was the center of a union of Kazakh tribes. It was here that the Kazakh khanate formed in the late 15th and early 16th centuries. By the beginning of the 16th century the protracted process of the formation of the Kazakh nationality, the main components of which were the local tribes that had been part of the early feudal states that had existed in Kazakhstan, was complete. Under Khan Kasym (ruled 1511–23) the Kazakh Khanate became strong and expanded its boundaries; the population reached 1 million. By the mid-16th century, after the breakup of the Nogai Horde and later of Mogulistan and the Siberian Khanate, the Kazakh clans that had previously belonged to these states joined the main body of their people.

The Kazakh Khanate was divided into hordes: the Great Horde (Semirech'e), the Middle Horde (central Kazakhstan), and the Little Horde (western Kazakhstan). Independent khanates formed in the hordes during the 17th century.

The leading branch of the Kazakh economy was nomadic and pastoral livestock raising. Farming was frequently primitive. Domestic trades became widespread; crafts developed slowly. Barter trade was conducted in the summer, when the livestock raisers migrated closer to the cities. Feudal relations were still entangled in numerous vestiges of the patriarchal-clan system. Among the Kazakh livestock raisers land was used as pasture. In effect, the large livestock-owning feudal lords were the owners of the pastures.

Kazakh society consisted of two main classes: the feudal lords (khans, sultans, *batyrs, bais,* and *khodzhas*) and feudally dependent peasants (*sharua*). Patriarchal slaves, or *kuls*, constituted a special stratum. Legally, the peasantry was not enserfed, but since they were dependent on the feudal lords, they paid rent in produce of various forms, in addition to the corvée. The poorest stratum of the peasantry, the *kedei,* who were not provided with draft and productive livestock, went into bondage to the *bais,* resorting to the "aid" of wealthy kinsmen. The class struggle between the feudal lords and the peasants who were dependent upon them was manifested in various forms, such as migration, cattle theft, and direct clashes. Peasants who broke away from their own *aul* communes fell into dependence on other feudal lords. Along with the diverse norms of customary law (adat), certain norms of Muslim feudal law (sharia) also operated. The Zhety-Zhargy common law code, which defined the main principles of the feudal legal order, was compiled in the early 11th century, under Khan Tauk.

Two tendencies, popular and feudal, were manifested in the development of the culture of the Kazakh people. Those who came from the people—the *akyns* (folk poets and singers) and *zhyraus* (singers and improvisers)—created a number of heroic epic works and narrative poems about social and everyday life that were transmitted orally from generation to generation (*Koblandy, Kyz-Zhibek, Er-Targyn,* and *Kozy-Korpesh and Baian-Slu*). Between the 15th and 17th centuries, written literature was largely confined to religious books. A valuable source of late 16th-century Kazakh written history is *Zhamigi-at-tavarikh* (a collection of chronicles) by Kadyrgali Kosunula. Muhammad Khaidar, the author of the historical work *Tarikh-i-Rashidi,* was an outstanding writer.

Unification with Russia; rise and development of capitalist relations (18th through second half of the 19th century). Kazakhstan experienced great difficulties in the early 18th century. The Kazakh khanates fragmented, and feudal internecine warfare was incessant. The most influential of the Kazakh khans was Abulkhair, whose power extended to the greater part of the Little Horde. In the Middle Horde were the khanates of Semeke-khan and Kushuk-khan and the independent holdings of the sultans Barak and Abulmambet. By this time the Russian state bordered on Kazakhstan. The economic and political interests of Russia prompted the Russian government to strengthen its ties with Kazakhstan and, through it, to develop trade with Middle Asia. In the 17th century the Russian cities of Iaitskii Gorodok (Ural'sk) and Gur'ev took shape in western Kazakhstan.

The Dzungarian Khanate represented a great danger to Kazakhstan in the early 18th century. The Kazakh hosts inflicted serious defeats on the troops of the Dzungarian feudal lords in 1710, 1728, and 1729, but the attacks were repeated; the era went down in the history of Kazakhstan as the "years of great disaster." As early as 1726, Khan Abulkhair requested Russian citizenship in the name of the elders of the Little Horde. In 1731 the request was granted. This was the beginning of Kazakhstan's voluntary unification with Russia. In 1735, on the request of Abulkhair, the tsarist government began construction of a fort at the mouth of the Or' River (present-day Orsk), which played an important role in strengthening Russia's influence in Kazakhstan. Between 1731 and 1740, various khans and sultans of the Middle Horde became Russian subjects. In 1741–42, Dzungarian troops again invaded the Middle and Little hordes, but the intervention of the Russian border authorities forced them to withdraw.

The voluntary acceptance of Russian citizenship by the Kazakhs of the Little Horde—and in 1740 by those of the Middle Horde—had a progressive impact on the historical fate of the Kazakh people. As early as the second half of the 18th century, social relations in Kazakhstan developed under the perceptibly growing influence of the economy of Russia. Kazakhstan's trade ties with Russia were strengthened. The construction of fortified lines and cities and the increase of the Russian population in border regions were conducive to the growth of agriculture and crafts. At the same time, the tsarist authorities carried out colonialist measures in Kazakhstan, where the tyranny of petty officials ruled. The Kazakh feudal lords continued their usurpation of land.

In the mid-18th century, the struggle among feudal groups intensified. As a result, Khan Abulkhair was killed (1748). His son, Nuraly, who became khan of the Little Horde, relied on the support of the tsarist administration and attempted without success to extend his power to a portion of the Middle Horde, as well as to Khiva. The Great Horde, much of which was under the dominion of the Dzungarians, was threatened with seizure by Manchurian feudal lords after China smashed Dzungaria (1758). The southern parts of Kazakhstan, including the city of Chimkent, were captured by the Kokand Khanate.

An important result of the unification of Kazakhstan with Russia was the increased closeness of Russian and Kazakh toilers. In particular, this was manifested in the Peasant War of 1773–75, led by E. I. Pugachev, in which Kazakhs of the Little Horde and, in part, the Middle Horde participated. An uprising of Kazakhs led by Srym Datov took place in the Little Horde between 1783 and 1797.

In the first half of the 19th century, fundamental changes took place in the economy of Kazakhstan. Trade relations became more active. Livestock products were sent to Russia, and grain and industrial goods were brought into Kazakhstan. There was a notable growth in agriculture. According to incomplete data, 5,330 farms in the Little Horde had a cultivated area of about 24,000 *desiatinas* (about 26,160 hectares). Livestock feed was stored for winter on a substantial scale. Great changes took place in the political system of the Kazakhs.

After the death of khans Bukei (1815) and Valii (1819) of the Middle Horde, the power of the khans was abolished by the tsarist government, and a new system of administration was introduced in 1822. The Statutes on the Siberian Kirghiz, developed by M. M. Speranskii, provided for the creation of eight external districts headed by district *prikazes* (departments). This led to the emergence of the cities of Aiaguz, Kokchetav, Karkaralinsk, and Atbasar on the steppe. The districts were divided into *volosts* (small rural districts) headed by *volost* managers. The administrative *aul*, headed by an elder, included 50–70 *kibitkas* (nomads' tents).

In 1824 the power of the khans was abolished in the Little Horde. The territory of the horde was divided into three parts headed by sultan managers. The territorial administration system was introduced, limiting the rights of the tribal elders. The establishment of the new system of government was carried out in the interests of tsarism and was colonialist in nature. However, despite the colonialist policy of tsarism, progressive changes took place in Kazakh society; productive forces developed and the class structure changed. The rights of the sultans, *bais*, and *batyrs* were limited and the acquisition of new *kuls* (slaves) prohibited, leading to the disappearance of patriarchal slavery.

The people of southern Kazakhstan were under the yoke of the Kokand and Khiva feudal lords, who ruined the Kazakh *auls*. Many *auls* migrated to be under the protection of the Russian forts. In 1831, 7,500 Kazakh families of the Great Horde migrated. In 1821 the peasants of the southern areas of Kazakhstan, rising up against the oppression of the Kokand beys, took Chimkent and Sairam by storm. The uprising was harshly suppressed. Certain Kazakh khans sought support from the khans of Middle Asia and opposed Russia. The most protracted feudal-monarchist movement of the 1820's to 1840's was that of Sultan Kenesara Kasymov, who strove to become the absolute feudal ruler of Kazakhstan.

In the early 19th century the Bukei Khanate arose in the area between the Urals and the Volga. In the 1820's and 1830's, land relations became more acute and class and colonial oppression increased. This provoked a mass peasant uprising (1836–37) under the leadership of I. Taimanov and M. Utemisov. The uprising was suppressed. After the death of Khan Dzhangir (1845), the tsarist government abolished the khan's power in the Bukei Khanate. The tsarist authorities established fortified lines on the Syr Darya, Irgiz, and Turgai rivers. The Raim fortification was built in 1847; Fort Kazaly, a year later. In the 1840's the frequency of predatory raids of bands from the Kokand and Khiva khanates increased. The Kazakhs addressed a request for aid to the Russian authorities. This served as the formal basis for the organization in 1853 of a campaign against the Kokand fortress of Ak-Mechet' by V. A. Perovskii, governor-general of Orenburg and Samara; the fortress was captured by tsarist troops and made into a base. In the mid-19th century, tsarism was opposed by the Syr Darya Kazakhs. After the suppression of this action, a movement began on the coast of the Aral Sea. In 1858, in the region of Aulie-Ata, Kazakhs and Kirghiz rose

up against the Kokand beys. The uprising spread rapidly to southern Kazakhstan, but it was defeated.

In 1845 the nomadic Kazakhs in the Kapal area voluntarily accepted Russian citizenship. In 1846 the part of Semirech'e up to the Ili River in which Kazakhs of the Great Horde lived became part of the Russian state. After the founding of the Vernyi fortification (now Alma-Ata) in 1854, there was an increase in the number of Russian cossacks and peasants migrating from Western Siberia to Semirech'e. The increase in Russian influence troubled the Kokand khan, who sent a force of 20,000 men against Vernyi in the fall of 1860. In October of that year, a detachment of Russian troops supported by Kazakhs routed the forces of Khudoiar-khan, the ruler of Kokand, at the Uzun-Agach natural landmark. As a result, all of Semirech'e passed to Russia.

The unification of the Kazakh lands with Russia was completed in the 1860's. The tsarist authorities carried out a reform of the administration of the region. In 1867, Semirech'e and Syr Darya regions were created in the Turkestan governor-generalship; in 1868, the Ural'sk and Turgai regions were created as part of the Orenburg governor-generalship, and Akmolinsk and Semipalatinsk regions were created in the Western Siberia governor-generalship (later the steppe governor-generalship). The regions were divided into districts, which in turn were divided into *volosts* and then into administrative *auls* (120–200 *kibitkas* each). All land was proclaimed state property. Changes were also introduced in legal procedure. The reforms of 1867–68 provoked discontent among all strata of Kazakh society: the sultans and *bais* were dissatisfied with the restriction of their rights, the elders with the breaking of their authority in the clans, and the popular masses with the further intensification of colonial oppression, increased taxes, and restrictions on land tenure. Uprisings erupted in Ural'sk and Turgai regions and Mangyshlak. The feudal leaders and Muslim clergy exploited the discontent of the masses for their own class goals. The uprisings did not spread and were suppressed.

The implementation of reforms helped draw Kazakhstan further into the system of the all-Russian economy. One of the important factors in the development of the productive forces was the migration of Russian peasants to Kazakhstan. More than 500 Russian and Ukrainian villages sprang up in the steppe regions of Kazakhstan during the 1880's and 1890's. The main occupation of the migrants was farming. The countryside settled by the migrants developed along capitalist lines. The growth of commodity production also prepared the conditions for the gradual penetration of capitalist relations into the Kazakh *auls*, and this accelerated the process of class stratification. However, patriarchal-feudal relations remained dominant. Trade and commodity-money relations grew, particularly after the construction of the Trans-Siberian Railroad (1891–1904). Transit trade routes passed through Kazakhstan. In many parts of the region, exchanges gave way to large fairs. According to the data of the 1897 census, 40,000 people were engaged in trade in Kazakhstan; in Petropavlovsk alone, 446 trade institutions were in operation (with a yearly turnover of 4 million rubles). Trade was usurious, with Russian merchants and local livestock dealers engaged in usury.

The development of cities and the increase in their population were important to the culture of the Kazakh people. The progressive culture and science of Russia influenced the activity of such Kazakh proponents of enlightenment as Chokan Valikhanov, Ibrai Altynsarin, and Abai Kunanbaev.

Period of imperialism and bourgeois-democratic revolutions in Russia (1900–17). Kazakhstan remained a colonial market and source of raw materials for Russian industry until the Great October Socialist Revolution. In the early 20th century, the penetration of Kazakhstan's economy not only by Russian capital but also by English, French, and American capital began; capitalist production was founded on this basis. Most enterprises were small. Foreign capital was invested primarily in the mining industry. Oil drilling began in Emba Region in 1911. The development of industry, the construction of the Siberian and Orenburg-Tashkent railroads (built in 1905–06), the organization of bank credit, and the increased transportation on the Irtysh stimulated the growth of commodity-capitalist farming and livestock raising and the destruction of the feudal seclusion and natural economy of the *aul.* The use of hired labor expanded on the farms of the *bais,* who were the main suppliers of the livestock sent to the Russian and foreign markets. In 1913, large-scale industry employed about 20,000 workers—refugees from the poverty of the *aul* and skilled proletarians who had come from the industrial centers of Russia. A Kazakh bourgeoisie and a national proletariat were taking shape. The capitalist structure that was developing in the late 19th and early 20th centuries and the social and cultural changes that accompanied it accelerated the formation of the Kazakh bourgeois nation; however, this process was not completed.

The first spontaneous economic strikes in Kazakhstan occurred in the 1890's. At the beginning of the 20th century, such strikes occurred more frequently and united Kazakh and Russian workers. Between 1900 and 1903, there were workers' strikes at the Spassk Copper Plant and the Ekibastuz, Karaganda, and Uspenskii mines. The first Marxists in Kazakhstan were the exiled Russian revolutionaries V. G. Kharitonov, P. M. Kashinskii, Z. V. Guseva, and P. P. Pokrovskii. The first political strike in Kazakhstan was held on May 1, 1903, on the initiative of the Marxist circle in Ural'sk. The strike movement gathered force during the revolution of 1905–07. In December 1905, under the influence of revolutionaries, the workers of the Uspenskii Copper Mine formed the Russian-Kirghiz Union; the leaders included P. N. Topornin, I. Kaskabaev, and A. Baichagirov. In 1905–07 there were peasant disturbances in Turgai, Semipalatinsk, and Ural'sk regions.

In an attempt to reduce the urgency of the agrarian problem in the interior provinces of Russia, the tsarist government began mass resettlement of Russian peasants to Kazakhstan. Between 1906 and 1912, during the Stolypin agrarian reform, more than 438,000 farms were moved to Akmolinsk, Turgai, Ural'sk, and Semipalatinsk regions. In Kazakhstan, 17.4 million *desiatinas* (about 18,966,000 ha) of land—primarily land that had already been opened up by the Kazakh population—were set aside for the migrant reserve. The migration policies of tsarism had an effect on agrarian relations in the *aul.* The *bai* leadership, supported by the tsarist administration, seized communal lands and secured them as their property. This double plundering of lands —by the tsarist authorities and the *bais*—ruined the masses of the Kazakh poor. The colonialist policy of the tsarist authorities was aimed at russification of the Kazakh people and hindering the development of its national economy and culture. During World War I the massive withdrawals of agricultural products and livestock, the increase in taxes and imposts, high prices, and the mobilization in 1916 of the Kazakh population for rearguard work provoked strikes among the workers and disturbances among the peasants. In 1916 isolated actions grew into a national liberation uprising that encompassed all of Kazakhstan. The uprising was particularly lengthy in the Turgai Region, where the insurgents were headed by the popular *batyr* Amangel'dy Imanov.

After the February Revolution of 1917, dual power was established in Kazakhstan, as in the rest of Russia. In March soviets of working people's deputies and soviets of soldiers' deputies were formed in Vernyi, Semipalatinsk, Petropavlovsk, Kustanai, Aktiubinsk, Akmolinsk, and Perovsk; in March and April 1917, most of them combined in the united soviets of working people's and soldiers' deputies. Soviets of peasants' deputies and soviets of Kirghiz (Kazakh) deputies were elected at the peasant congresses held in April and May. Initially the Mensheviks and Socialist Revolutionaries (SR's) dominated the soviets. Bodies of the bourgeois Provisional Government, such as the Turkestan Committee (April 7 [20]), regional and district committees of the Provisional Government, executive committees, and commissariats in the cities and *volosts,* formed at the same time as the soviets. Supported by the Russian bourgeoisie and the Kazakh bourgeois nationalists, these bodies continued the antipopular policies of tsarism. The Kazakh feudal *bais* and bourgeois nationalists formed the counterrevolutionary Alash party in July 1917. In August and September the Provisional Government imposed martial law in Semirech'e Region and the Bukei Steppe. By the fall of 1917 the Bolsheviks had won leadership in the Orenburg, Perovsk, and Petropavlovsk soviets. In early October the Semipalatinsk Regional Congress of Peasants' Deputies passed a resolution on the necessity of turning power over to the soviets. The first detachments of the Red Guard in Kazakhstan were organized. During September and October 1917 strikes and demonstrations were held under Bolshevik slogans in certain cities of Kazakhstan and at stations of the Orenburg-Tashkent railroad. Agrarian insurrections on the Kazakh and Russian poor took place in Temir, Kokchetav, and Petropavlovsk districts, in Semirech'e and Semipalatinsk regions, and in the Bukei Steppe.

Period of the Great October Socialist Revolution, Civil War, and military intervention (1917–20). Because of the low level of socioeconomic development in Kazakhstan, the struggle for the establishment and triumph of Soviet power proceeded amid particularly complex circumstances. In Syr Darya Region (November 1917), Akmolinsk Region (November 1917–January 1918), and the Bukei Steppe (December 1917), Soviet power was established peacefully; during January and February 1918 it was established in Turgai Region and in Semipalatinsk as a result of an armed struggle. The anti-Soviet revolt of the hetman Dutov in November 1917 in Orenburg Territory, which was supported by the Kazakh bourgeois nationalists—Alash-Orda supporters, Mensheviks, and SR's—was quickly suppressed. On Jan. 18 (31), 1918, Orenburg was liberated by detachments of Baltic sailors and Red Guards from Petrograd, the Volga Region, Middle Asia, and Kazakhstan. Led by the Bolsheviks, the toiling people of Vernyi rose up on March 2–3. Power in the region passed to the Semirech'e Military Revolutionary Committee. In Ural'sk, the Soviet took power in January 1918 but was not able to consolidate it; the counterrevolutionary "Host Government" of the Ural Cossack Host existed along with it. After the establishment of Soviet power, the old apparatus was broken and a new Soviet state apparatus created. District and region congresses of soviets were held. On the basis of the Decree on Land, large landholdings were confiscated and given to the Kazakh and Russian peasants. By the decree of May 11, 1918, of the Council of People's Commissars of the RSFSR, signed by V. I. Lenin, large industrial enterprises were nationalized. The preparation of Soviet self-government for Kazakhstan began. Two southern regions, Syr Darya and Semirech'e, became part of the Turkestan ASSR, which was created in April 1918.

In the spring and summer of 1918, most of the area was captured by the interventionists and White Guards, with whom the Kazakh bourgeois nationalists acted in concert. The gangs of the hetman Dutov, who had again captured Orenburg on July 3, cut off part of Kazakhstan and all of the Turkestan ASSR from the center of Russia. Fronts formed at Orenburg (also called the Northern Turkestan (Front), Semirech'e, and Ural'sk (the southern flank of the Eastern Front). Units of the Red Army formed in the Soviet areas (Syr Darya Region, most of Semirech'e and Turgai regions, and the Bukei Steppe). Russians, Kazakhs, and Uighurs fought in their ranks. The Communists performed selfless work (*see below:* Communist Party of Kazakhstan).

Soviet Russia offered all possible aid to the toiling people of Kazakhstan and Middle Asia. In the fall of 1918, on V. I. Lenin's instructions, a large consignment of guns and ammunition was delivered to the Orenburg front via Astrakhan, the Caspian Sea, and the Ustiurt steppes under the direction of the commissar of the Steppe Territory, A. T. Dzhangil'din. Partisan detachments, particularly that of Amangel'dy Imanov in Turgai Region, operated in the enemy's rear. On Jan. 22, 1919, as a result of a combined offensive, Soviet troops of the Eastern and Orenburg fronts freed Orenburg, and on January 24, Ural'sk was liberated. Direct ties were reestablished with the central areas of the RSFSR.

In April 1919 the White Guards seized Aktiubinsk once more, cutting off the Soviet areas of Kazakhstan from the central parts of the country for a second time. Soviet forces withdrew toward the Kandagach railroad station. In late April the White Guards besieged Ural'sk. The situation on the Semirech'e Front also became difficult. The Red Army was greatly aided by partisans. Massive popular uprisings took place under the leadership of the underground party organizations. In Kustanai District the insurgents, led by the Military Revolutionary Staff (L. I. Taran,

M. G. Letunov, and N. I. Miliaev) liberated Kustanai on April 5 and, after a forced retreat from the city, continued the struggle. In the spring of 1919 a mass uprising against the White Guards, led by the Bolsheviks, took place in the village of Mariinskoe, Akmolinsk Region. N. M. Irchenko was elected commander of the insurgent detachments. The insurrectionists were joined by the peasants of dozens of villages. It was only in May 1919 that the White Guards succeeded in suppressing the uprising. In northern Semirech'e, the inhabitants of 12 Soviet settlements surrounded by the White Guard fought from October 1918 through October 1919. Their heroic resistance came to be called the Cherkasskaia Defense. In northeastern Semirech'e, the Partisan detachments of the Red Mountain Eagles of Tarbagatai waged a struggle against the White Guards. The rout of the main White Guard forces of Admiral Kolchak by Units of the Red Army on the eastern front facilitated and hastened the liberation of the northern and eastern areas of Kazakhstan. Soviet troops of the Turkestan Front, which was formed in August 1919 (commander M. V. Frunze, member of the Military Revolutionary Council V. V. Kuibyshev), attacking from the north while the troops of the Turkestan ASSR attacked from the south, smashed Kolchak's southern army and came together on September 13. The liberation of the western areas of Kazakhstan was completed in early 1920. The Semirech'e Front was eliminated in March 1920. The remains of the White Guard forces fled to western China. The Red Army, supported by the toiling people of Kazakhstan, put down rebellions in the city of Vernyi (June) and Semipalatinsk, Ust'-Kamenogorsk, and other districts (July and August).

The formation and development of the Kazakh Soviet state is inseparably associated with V. I. Lenin. On July 10, 1919, Lenin signed a decree of the Council of People's Commissars of the RSFSR on the formation of the Revolutionary Committee for the Administration of Kirghiz Territory, the name of Kazakhstan until April 1925. S. S. Pestkovskii, A. T. Dzhangil'din, S. M. Mendeshev, and A. Aitiev were members of the Revolutionary Committee. On Aug. 26, 1920, the All-Russian Central Executive Committee and the Council of People's Commissars of the RSFSR adopted the Decree on the Formation of the Autonomous Kirghiz Soviet Socialist Republic, signed by V. I. Lenin and M. I. Kalinin, making Kazakhstan part of the RSFSR, with its capital in Orenburg. The territories of Akmolinsk, Semipalatinsk, Turgai, and Ural'sk regions and parts of the Transcaspian Region and Astrakhan and Orenburg provinces inhabited by Kazakhs became part of the republic. Guided by the Kirghiz Regional Bureau of the RCP(B), which was formed according to the resolution of the Central Committee of the RCP(B) of Apr. 30, 1920, Communists performed extensive, selfless work. The Constituent Congress of Soviets of Kazakhstan was held in Orenburg, Oct. 4–12, 1920. Central Executive Committee (chairman, S. M. Mendeshev) and the Council of People's Commissars (chairman, V. A. Radus-Zen'-kovich) of the republic were elected at the congress. Administratively, the republic was divided into Akmolinsk, Bukei (part of the former Astrakhan Province), Orenburg-Turgai (previously Turgai and Ural'sk regions and part of Orenburg Province), and Semipalatinsk provinces and Adaev Raion (part of the former Transcaspian Region). In 1921, Orenburg-Turgai Province was divided into Aktiubinsk, Kustanai, Orenburg, and Turgai provinces; Turgai Province was eliminated in the same year and made part of Kustanai Province.

Socialist construction, 1921–40. The Civil War undermined the economy of Kazakhstan. In 1920, industry, which was in any case poorly developed, provided about one-fifth of the prewar output; grain production decreased by a factor of 3, and the livestock population diminished considerably. In the *auls,* patriarchal-feudal relations were still dominant. The Communist Party and Soviet power did a great deal of work toward the rehabilitation of the economy. In 1921 the surplus-appropriation system was replaced by the tax in kind; the nomadic and seminomadic population, except for the *bais,* was exempted from taxes on meat. As a result of the land and water reform of 1921–22, more than 470,000 ha of land that had been seized from the toiling Kazakh and Kirghiz masses by the tsarist government and kulak colonizers was returned to them. With the fraternal

aid of the RSFSR, the Ukraine, and Turkestan, the consequences of the drought and famine of 1921 were overcome. A system of land tenure was established for the nomadic and seminomadic population through the decree of the All-Russian Central Executive Committee and the Council of People's Commissars of the RSFSR (April 1924). The Fourth Congress of Soviets of the republic (Jan. 5–10, 1924) discussed and adopted as a basis the draft constitution of the republic.

In 1924 and 1925, as a result of the national-state demarcation of the Soviet republics of Middle Asia, the territory of Syr Darya and Dzhetysu (formerly Semirech'e) regions settled by Kazakhs became part of the Kirghiz ASSR. The Fifth All-Kazakhstan Congress of Soviets of Kazakhstan (Apr. 15–19, 1925) restored the historically accurate name of the Kazakh people. The republic was renamed the Kazakh ASSR. The captial was moved from Orenburg to Kzyl-Orda. Orenburg Province became part of the RSFSR. Under the new administrative-territorial division, the Kazakh ASSR consisted of Akmolinsk, Aktiubinsk, Dzhetysu, Semipalatinsk, and Ural'sk provinces (the former Bukei Province was part of the republic, with the status of a district), and also Kustanai Okrug and Adaev District, which were under the direct jurisdiction of the government of the republic. From 1925 through 1930 the Kara-Kalpak Autonomous Oblast was part of the Kazakh ASSR. By 1928 the sown area and gross harvest of grains and raw cotton exceeded the 1913 level; livestock, except for hogs and horses, exceeded the 1916 level. The output of large-scale industry was 43 percent greater in 1928 than in 1913.

In the transition to socialism, the Kazakh people bypassed the capitalist stage of development. This process required the implementation of a number of specific measures aimed at strengthening Soviet power and eliminating patriarchal-feudal relations in the *aul.* The Sovietization of the Kazakh *aul*—the aggregate of measures to strengthen and make more active the work of *aul* soviets and finally rid them of the *bais,* to enlist the toiling masses in Soviet construction, and to strengthen party leadership of the activity of the soviets—was carried out from 1926 to 1929 and was of great importance. As a result of the repartition of arable land and hayfields (1926–27), poor and middle peasants received 1,250,000 ha of arable land and 1,360,000 ha of haying land that had previously been controlled by the *bais.* In 1928, 145,000 head of livestock, agricultural implements, and other property was confiscated from the major *bais* and transferred to poor and middle peasant farms. A blow had been struck against the *bai* class; the middle peasants became the central figure in the *aul.* More than 300 kolkhozes and five sovkhozes were established. The Koshchi (Plowman) union, which was established in 1920 and united large numbers of hired farm laborers, poor peasants, and some middle peasants, was strengthened.

Measures were taken to draw representatives of the native population into the state apparatus on a broader scale. In May 1929 the city of Alma-Ata became the capital of Kazakhstan. In connection with the division of the USSR into raions, provinces and districts were eliminated and division into okrugs and raions introduced in Kazakhstan in 1928. In 1929 there were 13 okrugs in Kazakhstan: Adaev, Akmolinsk, Aktiubinsk, Alma-Ata, Gur'ev, Karkaralinsk, Kzyl-Orda, Kustanai, Pavlodar, Petropavlovsk, Semipalatinsk, Syr Darya, and Ural'sk.

The crucial element in the socialist transformation of Kazakhstan, as in the rest of the country, was industrialization. In the first and second five-year plans (1928–37), 2 billion rubles of the Union budget were invested in industry. Engineers, technicians, and workers from other parts of the country were sent to construction projects and enterprises in Kazakhstan and passed on their experience to Kazakh workers. Moscow, Leningrad, and other industrial centers provided support to the industry of Kazakhstan. Miners from the Donbas worked in Karaganda, oil workers from Baku and Groznyi instructed oil workers of Emba, and machine builders from Kharkov and Sverdlovsk installed new machinery in numerous Kazakh enterprises. During the prewar five-year plans about 200 large-scale industrial enterprises, including the Chimkent Lead Plant and the Balkhash Copper Smelting Works, were built with the fraternal aid of all peoples of the USSR; the country's third coalfield was created in Karaganda; Turksib (the Turkestan-Siberia railroad) and the Karaganda-Balkhash, Rubtsovka-Ridder, Chimkent-Lenger, and Ural'sk-Iletsk railroad lines were built; and old enterprises were fundamentally reconstructed. Total industrial output in 1940 was 7.8 times greater than the 1913 level, and the output of large-scale industry was 19.5 times greater.

In 1929 the mass kolkhoz movement unfolded in Kazakhstan (in May 1930 the kolkhozes united 28.5 percent of peasant farms). Through this movement, former nomads were settled and a system of land tenure was established for them; the kulaks and *bais* were eliminated as a class. In 1937 kolkhozes made up 97.5 percent of peasant farms. In 1940 there were 41,300 tractors (in terms of standard 15-hp units) and 11,800 grain-harvesting combines operating in the republic. The planted area exceeded 6.8 million ha (4.2 million in 1913). As a result of the success of socialist construction, Kazakhstan changed from a region of nomadic livestock raising, a colonial region with few industrial centers and cultural centers, into an industrial-agrarian republic with a diversified, highly developed industry and large-scale mechanized agriculture. The working class of the USSR provided invaluable aid to Kazakhstan. More than 1,200 *dvadtsatipiatitysiachniki* (Twenty-five Thousanders) became carriers of party influence in the Kazakh *auls* and villages and organizers of collective labor in agriculture. In February 1932 the Kazakh ASSR was divided into six oblasts (okrugs were eliminated as early as 1930): Alma-Ata, Aktiubinsk, Vostochnyi Kazakhstan, Karaganda, Zapadnyi Kazakhstan (since 1962, Ural'sk), and Iuzhnyi Kazakhstan (since 1962, Chimkent).

In accordance with the 1936 Constitution of the USSR, the Kazakh ASSR was made a Union republic. The Extraordinary Tenth Congress of Soviets of Kazakhstan (March 1937) adopted the constitution of the Kazakh SSR. New oblasts formed as larger units were broken into small ones: in 1936, Kustanai and Severnyi Kazakhstan oblasts; in 1938, Gur'ev, Kzyl-Orda, and Pavlodar oblasts; and in 1939, Dzhambul, Semipalatinsk, and Akmolinsk (since 1961, Tselinograd) oblasts.

A cultural revolution was carried out in Kazakhstan; illiteracy was eliminated, previous tribal and feudal vestiges basically disappeared, skilled cadres of the national working class and people's intelligentsia emerged, and higher educational institutions, scientific and research institutions, libraries, and clubs were established. Soviet Kazakh literature and art developed. The enlistment of women in all areas of socialist construction was a great achievement of the cultural revolution. As a result of the socialist transformations, exploiting classes and the exploitation of one person by another were eliminated, and unemployment and poverty disappeared. In the Kazakh SSR, as in the rest of the country, socialism was, on the whole, built. The Kazakh people consolidated into a socialist nation under the conditions of the Soviet system.

Great Patriotic War (1941–45) and the postwar period. Kazakhstan sent hundreds of thousands of fighting men to the front during the Great Patriotic War; two-thirds of the membership of the Communist Party and Komsomol of the republic fought in the Soviet Army. The large military units formed in Kazakhstan took part in crucial battles between 1941 and 1945. The 316th (Eighth Guard) Infantry Division, commanded by I. V. Panfilov, became famous in the fighting near Moscow. The deeds of 28 heroes of the Panfilov division have been recorded for all time in the heroic history of the Soviet people. The title of Hero of the Soviet Union was awarded to 512 people from Kazakhstan, and four—the pilots T. Ia. Begel'dinov, L. I. Beda, S. D. Luganskii, and I. F. Pavlov—were twice Heroes of the Soviet Union. More than 60,000 people were awarded orders and medals for their feats of combat. More than 140 enterprises evacuated from western regions of the USSR and more than 1 million evacuated Soviet citizens were accommodated in the republic. During the war a number of large-scale enterprises and new mines and pits were put into service. The republic provided a substantial proportion of the Union's total output of copper, molybdenum, lead, and coal. Ammunition and foodstuffs flowed continuously to the army. Kazakhstan's industrial output grew considerably during the war. More than 1 billion rubles and hundreds of thousands of *poods* of grain were placed in the Defense Fund (1 *pood* = 16.38 kg). Thousands of working people of the rear guard were awarded orders and medals of the

USSR. The new oblasts of Kochetav and Taldy-Kurgan (eliminated in 1961, reestablished in 1967) were formed in 1944.

During the postwar decades the Kazakh people, along with all the other peoples of the country, took part in the completion of the construction of socialism and of communist society. With other eastern areas of the USSR, Kazakhstan aided in the rehabilitation of the industry and agriculture of oblasts and republics that had suffered from fascist German occupation. Kazakhstan provided support to 12 cities and 45 raions that had been freed from Hitler's invaders, sending specialists, industrial workers, and equipment, food, and clothing. Under conditions of mutual socialist aid of the peoples of the USSR, the toiling masses of Kazakhstan further developed the economy and culture of the republic. Kazakhstan became a huge construction site, and its rate of development accelerated. In areas that were still uninhabited, new industrial complexes took shape, new branches of industry emerged, large-scale industry and power engineering were built, and railroad, motor-vehicle, air, and water routes established. The Central Committee of the CPSU and the Council of Ministers of the USSR adopted a number of resolutions on the major problems of Kazakhstan's economy. Large-scale measures were implemented to develop agriculture, including the exploitation of virgin and unused lands. This was carried out with the aid of all the peoples of the USSR. Kazakhstan became one of the country's leading areas for grain and meat production (*see below*: Economy).

On Oct. 20, 1956, the Kazakh SSR was awarded the Order of Lenin for its success in developing virgin lands. Between 1960 and 1965, five northern oblasts (Kokchetav, Kustanai, Pavlodar, Severnyi Kazakhstan, and Tselinograd) were united in Tselinnyi Krai; Zapadryi Kazakhstan Krai (Aktiubinsk, Gur'ev, and Ural'sk oblasts) and Iuzhnyi; Kazakhstan Krai (Dzhambul, Kzyl-Orda, and Chimkent oblasts) also existed during 1962–64. Turgai Oblast was formed in 1970. In 1971 the industrial output of the Kazakh SSR was approximately 3 times greater than the output of all of tsarist Russia.

On Aug. 27, 1970, the Kazakh SSR was awarded the Order of the October Revolution for its great services in the struggle for the victory of socialist revolution, for the heroism it displayed in the fighting against the enemies of the homeland, and for its achievements in communist construction. As of Jan. 1, 1972, 1,519 people of Kazakhstan were awarded the title of Hero of Socialist Labor for their efforts in socialist and communist construction; N. Aldabergenov, I. Zhakhaev, and Zh. Kuanyshbaev were twice Heroes of Socialist Labor. On Dec. 29, 1972, the republic was awarded the Order of the Friendship of Peoples to mark the 50th anniversary of the USSR.

SOURCES
Valikhanov, Ch. Ch. *Sobr. soch. v 5 tt.*, vols. 1–4. Alma-Ata, 1961–68.
Revoliutsionnoe dvizhenie v Kazakhstane v 1905–1907 gg. (sb. dokumentov i materialov). Alma-Ata, 1955.
Pobeda Velikoi Oktiabr'skoi sotsialisticheskoi revoliutsii v Kazakhstane 1917–1918 gg.: sb. dokumentov i materialov. Alma-Ata, 1957.
Obrazovanie Kazakhskoi ASSR: Sb. dokumentov i materialov. Alma-Ata,1957.
Vosstanie 1916 g. v Srednei Azii i Kazakhstane: Sb. dokumentov. Moscow, 1960.
Kazakhsko-russkie otnosheniia v XVI–XVIII vv.: Sb. dokumentov i materialov. Alma-Ata, 1961.
Sotsialisticheskoe stroitel'stvo v Kazakhstane v vosstanovitel'nyi period (1921–1925): Sb. dokumentov i materialov. Alma-Ata, 1962.
Inostrannaia voennaia interventsiia i grazhdanskaia voina v Srednei Azii i Kazakhstane: Dokumenty i materialy, vols. 1–2. Alma-Ata, 1963–64.
Kazakhstan v period Velikoi Otechestvennoi voiny Sovetskogo Soiuza 1941–1945: Sb. dokumentov i materialov, vols. 1–2. Alma-Ata, 1964–67.

REFERENCES
Lenin, V. I. *O Srednei Azii i Kazakhstane.* Tashkent, 1960.
Istoriia Kazakhskoi SSR [2nd ed.], vols. 1–2. Alma-Ata, 1957–63.
Istoriia Kazakhskoi SSR: Epokha sotsializma. Alma-Ata, 1967.
Nusupbekov, A. N. *Ob"edinenie kazakhskikh zemel' v Kazakhskoi Sovetskoi Sotsialisticheskoi Respublike.* Alma-Ata, 1953.
Kuchkin, A. P. *Sovetizatsiia kazakhskogo aula: 1926–1929 gg.* Moscow, 1962.

Suleimenov, B. *Agrarnyi vopros v Kazakhstane poslednei treti XIX–nachala XX v. (1867–1907 gg.).* Alma-Ata, 1963.

Dakhshleiger, G. F. *Sotsial'no-ekonomicheskie preobrazovaniia v aule i v derevne Kazakhstana (1921–1929).* Alma-Ata, 1965.

Nusupbekov, A. N. *Formirovanie i razvitie sovetskogo rabochego klassa v Kazakhstane (1917–1940 gg.).* Alma-Ata, 1966.

Elagin, A. S. *Sotsialisticheskoe stroitel'stvo v Kazakhstane v gody grazhdanskoi voiny (1918–1920 gg.).* Alma-Ata, 1966.

Pobeda Sovetskoi vlasti v Srednei Azii i Kazakhstane. Tashkent, 1967.

Pokrovskii, S. N. *Razgrom inostrannykh voennykh interventov i vnutrennei kontrrevoliutsii v Kazakhstane (1918–1920).* Alma-Ata, 1967.

Tursunbaev, A. B. *Kazakhskii aul v trekh revoliutsiiakh.* Alma-Ata, 1967.

Kazakhstan v Velikoi Otechestvennoi voine: Ocherki, fasc. 1. Alma-Ata, 1968.

Beisembaev, S. B. *Lenin i Kazakhstan (1897–1924 gg.).* Alma-Ata, 1968.

Baishev, S. B. *V. I. Lenin i Sovetskii Kazakhstan,* 2nd cd. Alma-Ata, 1970.

Kenzhebaev, S. M. *Sovety v bor'be za pobedu sotsializma.* Alma-Ata, 1969.

Zimanov, S. Z. *V. I. Lenin i sovetskaia natsional'naia gosudarstvennost' v Kazakhstane.* Alma-Ata, 1970.

Pokrovskii, S. N. *Lenin i pobeda Sovetskoi vlasti v Kazakhstane.* Alma-Ata, 1970.

Kozybaev, M. K. *Kazakhstan—arsenal fronta.* Alma-Ata, 1970.

Balakaev, T. B. *Kolkhoznoe krest'ianstvo Kazakhstana v gody Velikoi Otechestvennoi voiny: 1941–1945 gg.* Alma-Ata, 1971.

A. N. NUSUPBEKOV and S. N. POKROVSKII

Communist Party of Kazakhstan

The Communist Party of Kazakhstan is a constituent part of the CPSU. The spread of Marxism and the formation of the Social Democratic movement in Kazakhstan began at the turn of the 20th century; the Social Democratic circle in Ural'sk and the Social Democratic group in Petropavlovsk were the first to appear. During the Revolution of 1905–07 in Russia, Kazakhstan had three Social Democratic organizations (in Petropavlovsk, Ural'sk, and Semipalatinsk), seven groups (in Akmolinsk, Aktiubinsk, Vernyi, Kazalinsk, Kustanai, Perovsk, and Cherniaev), and seven circles (in Atbasar, Dzharkent, Dzhusaly, Karkaralinsk, Kokchetav, Pavlodar, and Ust'-Kamenogorsk). There were more than 500 Social Democrats. The largest organizations were those of Ural'sk and Petropavlovsk (approximately 150 members each); V. V. Kuibyshev performed party work in the latter in 1907. The defeat of the Revolution of 1905–07 resulted in the crushing of Social Democratic organizations and groups. Revolutionary work was carried on in Kazakhstan by individual Social Democrats who had been able to avoid arrest and by those who had been exiled from the interior of Russia and who formed groups from time to time.

After the February Revolution of 1917, the Bolsheviks of Kazakhstan joined the organizations of the RSDLP that had merged with the Mensheviks. As a result, the liberation of toiling masses from the influence of the conciliators and the bourgeois nationalists was impeded. The Central Committee of the RSDLP(B), which had ties with 27 organizations of Kazakhstan, aided local Bolsheviks in creating independent Bolshevik groups; the leaders included A. T Dzhangil'din, P. A. Kobozev, A. V. Cherviakov, and V. F. Zinchenko. Returning front-line soldiers and Kazakhs mobilized for work on the home front played an important role in spreading Bolshevik influence. In June 1917 the Perovsk Social Democratic group became the first to adopt the platform of the Central Committee of the RSDLP(B). Beginning in September 1917 the Bolsheviks won leading positions in a number of soviets.

The final break with the Mensheviks in Kazakhstan came after the October Revolution. During November and December 1917, independent Bolshevik organizations formed in Petropavlovsk, Akmolinsk, Aulie-Ata, Ural'sk, and Ust'-Kamenogorsk; in January 1918, in Semipalatinsk; in February, in Aktiubinsk; and in March, in Vernyi. Party cells began to emerge in the villages at the end of 1917; the first cell appeared on December 1 in the settlement of Aleksandrovskii, Ural'sk Oblast. In January 1918 cells also began to appear in the *auls* of Syr Darya Region.

A single party center in Kazakhstan was lacking. The Central Committee of the party sent A. T. Dzhangil'din, P. A. Kobozev, S. M. Tsvilling, and A. A. Zvezdov there. As Bolshevik organizations began to form, the party's ranks were reinforced by representatives of the toiling Kazakhs and other eastern nationalities. The Bolsheviks led the struggle of the Kazakh people for the establishment of Soviet power; they carried out the nationalization of industrial enterprises, the confiscation of large landholdings, and the transfer of land to the poorest Kazakh and Russian peasantry.

The creation of the Communist Party of Turkestan in June 1918 was of great significance for party construction in southern Kazakhstan. The Turkestan party consisted of party organizations of Syr Darya and Semirech'e regions and parts of Turgai and Ural'sk regions. Communists directed the struggle against foreign and domestic counterrevolutionaries and led the partisan movement during the Civil War. Active party and Soviet workers who came to the fore during the establishment and consolidation of Soviet power included A. Aitiev, T. Bokin, P. Vinogradov, A. T. Dzhangil'din, A. Imanov, I. Kiselev, M. Letunov, A. Maikutov, M. Masanchi, S. Mendeshev, N. Monin, P. Paramonov, A. Rozybakiev, T. Ryskulov, P. Salov, S. Seifullin, K. Sutiushev, L. I. Taran, M. Tatimov, A. Urazbaeva, Ia. Ushanov, S. Tsarev, A. V. Cherviakov, S. Sharipov, and A. Iarmukhamedov. The strengthening of the Soviet system and party organizations of Kazakhstan was aided by the activity of Sh. Z. Eliav, M. V. Frunze, V. V. Kuibyshev, Ia. E. Rudzutak, F. I. Goloshchekin, and G. I. Bokii.

During the Civil War, the party organizations of Kazakhstan grew stronger, their authority increased, and membership grew (16,000 in 1920). On Apr. 30, 1920, the Central Committee of the RCP(B), taking into account the pressing need to unite the party organizations of Kazakhstan, established the Kirghiz (Kazakh) Regional Bureau of the RCP(B), with A. Avdeev, A. Aitiev, A. Alibekov, S. Arancheev, A. T. Dzhangil'din, M. Murzagaliev, and S. S. Pestkovskii. The first Kirghiz (Kazakh) Regional Party Conference was held in Orenburg, June 11–18, 1921. It established the ways and measures to strengthen regional party organization at the regional level and to enlist the toiling Kazakh masses in the RCP(B), and it elected a regional committee for the party. The Central Committee of the RCP(B) aided the party organizations of Kazakhstan in overcoming the difficulties resulting from the special character of their development—the great number of peasants and young Communists and their low literacy rate. Communist directed the implementation of land and water reforms, the partition of haying and plowed lands, the confiscation of the property of the major semifeudal *bais,* and other socioeconomic transformations.

The Kirghiz (Kazakh) Bureau of the Central Committee of the RCP(B) was created in April 1922. In June 1922 the Central Committee of the party sent the letter entitled "To the Communists of the Kirghiz Republic," which provided an analysis of the condition of the regional party organization, revealed the shortcomings in the implementation of the Leninist national policy, and defined tasks.

The Lenin Enrollment was of great significance in strengthening the party organization. By October 1924 about 8,000 people had been accepted into the party in Kazakhstan (with Syr Darya and Dzhetysu regions), of whom more than 6,000 were industrial workers and a substantial number were farm laborers. According to the resolution of the Central Committee of the RCP(B) of Feb. 19, 1925, the regional committee renamed the territorial committee. Communists headed the struggle of the toiling masses of Kazakhstan to rehabilitate the economy and strengthen the union of the working class and peasantry. The party organization did a great deal of work in implementing the cultural revolution. Communists exerted great efforts to give the emancipated Kazakh women access to socially useful labor and participation in the state administration. The activity of the party organization of Kazakhstan ensured the fulfillment of plans for the socialist industrialization of Kazakhstan and the formation and training of a national working class and intelligentsia. During the collectivization of agriculture and the elimination of the kulaks and *bais,* 20,500 Communists worked in rural areas, aided by experienced party workers sent from the interior of the country by the Central Committee of the ACP(B). Patriarchal-clan and feudal vestiges were elminated in the fierce struggle against the Muslim clergy and the remains of the exploiting classes. Simultaneously with the collectivization, the Communists of Kazakhstan carried out a historic task—the mass shift of the nomadic and seminomadic population to a settled way of life. The Central Committee of the ACP(B) aided the party organizations of Kazakhstan in overcoming the difficulties encountered on the path to collectivization and the transition to a settled way of life and in correcting the errors and exaggerated measures that had been taken. The resolution of the Central Committee of the ACP(B) On Agriculture and, Particularly, Livestock Raising in Kazakhstan (September 1932) played a large role. Educating the toiling people in the spirit of internationalism, the party organization of Kazakhstan struggled against national deviationists, Trotskyites, and right-wing opportunists, exposing and routing all antiparty and clan groupings in its ranks that were preventing the implementation of the Leninist national policy. By 1937 the number of Kazakh Communists had increased sixfold over 1921. On Apr. 23, 1937, in connection with the creation of the Kazakh SSR (1936), the Central Committee of the ACP(B) transformed the territorial party organization into the CP(B) of Kazakhstan. The first congress of Communists of the republic, in June 1937, completed the formation of the CP(B) of Kazakhstan.

During the years of socialist construction, a great deal of work was done in the party organization of Kazakhstan by M. Ataniiazov, I. A. Bogdanov, A. Dosov, U. Dzhandosov, T. Dzhumabaev, S. Zhanbaev, S. Eskaraev, A. I. Zavarit'ko, U. Isaev, I. Kabulov, F. Karibzhanov, I. S. Kliment'ev, D. A. Kunaev, I. Kuramysov, L. I. Mirzoian, N. Nurmakov, S. Nurpeisov, F. I. Olikov, I. Omarov, A. I. Samokhvalov, N. Syrgabekov, M. Tatimov, T. Tazhibaev, N. D. Undasynov, and Zh. Shaiakhmetov.

During the Great Patriotic War (1941–45), the CP(B) of Kazakhstan undertook an enormous amount of work to turn Kazakhstan into an arsenal for the front. Two-thirds of the Communists of Kazakhstan (82,000) went into the Soviet Army. During the war, 128,559 people joined the ranks of the CP(B) of Kazakhstan.

In the postwar years the toiling masses, led by the CP of Kazakhstan, rebuilt the economy on a peacetime footing, guaranteeing its further development. Through the resolutions of the Twentieth Congress of the CPSU (1956), the Communists of Kazakhstan waged a struggle to eliminate errors that had been made; they restored the Leninist norms of party life and socialist law. The CP of Kazakhstan directed the development of virgin and unused lands, the exploitation of mineral wealth, and the construction of large-scale industrial enterprises, railroads, and highways. Guided by the resolution of the October Plenary Session of the Central Committee of the CPSU of 1964, the party organizations of the republic eliminated the effects of voluntarism and subjectivism.

Table 3a. Membership in the Communist Party of Kazakhstan

	Members of CPSU	Candidate members of CPSU	Total members
1921 (June)	15,525	11,152	26,677
1931 (January)	24,831	32,086	60,517
1941 (January)	75,484	50,109	125,593
1951 (January)	194,714	32,954	227,668
1961 (January)	317,700	32,415	345,115
1972 (January)	568,746	26,357	595,103

Under conditions of developed socialist society, the influence of the CP of Kazakhstan has been increasing, the role of party organizations growing, and the workers' nucleus becoming stronger. In 1959 workers constituted 45.8 percent of those accepted as candidate members to the party; in 1971, 64.8 percent. The composition of the CP of Kazakhstan reflects the friendship and brotherhood of the Soviet peoples: it includes representatives of about 100 nationalities and peoples. There are more than

109,000 women in the CP of Kazakhstan, evidence of the active participation of women in labor, political, and public life.

The Thirteenth Congress of the CP of Kazakhstan (Feb. 24–26, 1971) reviewed the eighth five-year plan and outlined new measures to carry out the tasks of communist construction posed for the country by the Program of the CPSU, and it approved the draft Directives of the Twenty-fourth Congress of the CPSU on the 1971–75 five-year plan for the development of the national economy of the USSR. The congress devoted a great deal of attention to questions of intraparty and ideological work. The CP of Kazakhstan is directing the efforts of the toiling masses toward realization of the resolutions of the twenty-fourth congress of the CPSU, the completion of the ninth five-year plan for 1971–75, and the construction of the material and technical base for communist society.

Table 3b. Conferences and congresses of the Communist Party of Kazakhstan

Regional conferences	
1st	June 11–18, 1921
2nd	Feb. 19–27, 1922
3rd	Mar. 17–22, 1923
4th	May 11–16, 1924
Territorial conferences	
5th	Dec. 1–7, 1925
6th	Nov. 15–23, 1927
7th	May 30–June 6, 1930
8th	Jan. 8–16, 1934
Congresses	
1st	June 5–12, 1937
2nd	July 3–4, 1938
3rd	Mar. 10–18, 1940
4th	Feb. 25–Mar. 1, 1949
5th	Dec. 15–18, 1950
6th	Sept. 20–24, 1951
7th	Feb. 16–18, 1954
8th	Jan. 24–27, 1956
9th	Jan. 14–15, 1959
10th	Mar. 10–12, 1960
11th	Sept. 27–29, 1961
12th	Mar. 10–12, 1966
13th	Feb. 24–26, 1971

REFERENCES

Ocherki istorii Kommunisticheskoi partii Kazakhstana. Alma-Ata, 1963.
U istokov Kommunisticheskoi partii Kazakhstana. Alma-Ata, 1966.
Kommunisticheskaia partiia Kazakhstana v dokumentakh i tsifrakh: Sb. dokumentov i statisticheskikh materialov o roste i regulirovanii sostava partiinoi organizatsii. Alma-Ata, 1960.
Kunaev, D. "Leninskaia partiia i razvitie proizvoditel'nykh sil." *Kommunist,* 1972, no. 6.
Beisembaev, S. *Lenin i Kazakhstan.* Alma-Ata. 1968.
Kozybaev, M. *Kompartiia Kazakhstana v period Velikoi Otechestvennoi voiny (1941–1945 gg.).* Alma-Ata, 1964.
Tursunbaev, A. B. *Pobeda kolkhoznogo stroia v Kazakhstane.* Alma-Ata, 1957.

P. M. PAKHMURNYI

Lenin Communist Youth League (Komsomol) of Kazakhstan

The Komsomol of Kazakhstan is a constituent part of the All-Union Komsomol. The first student and youth Social Democratic organizations in Kazakhstan were formed during the Revolution of 1905–07 but were crushed. In 1917 the creation of democratic and socialist youth organizations began, but they were dominated by representatives of bourgeois-feudal and petit-bourgeois nationalist circles; the left, revolutionary-democratic wing was weak. In the course of the establishment of Soviet power, these organizations disintegrated, and their best members joined the Russian Komsomol. The youth of multinational Kazakhstan participated in the Civil War, and many of them died heroically, including the 18-year-old Communist Nastia Prokopicheva, a member of the Petropavlovsk Soviet; 16-year-old Misha Gavrilov, a member of Chapaev's force; 18-year-old Gusman Azerbaev, fighter of the First Kazakh Cavalry Regiment; and one of the organizers of the Komsomol in the city of Vernyi, Misha Stavrovskii.

The Russian Komsomol was organized in Kazakhstan in 1919–20. The Syr Darya and Semirech'e regional organizations of the Komsomol became part of the Komsomol of Turkestan, which was formed in January 1920. On June 9, 1920, the Central Committee of the Russian Komsomol created the Kirghiz (Kazakh) Bureau of the Central Committee of the Russian Komsomol. The First Congress of the Russian Komsomol of Kazakhstan (July 1921, Orenburg) completed the unification of the republic's organization, elected a regional committee, and directed the efforts of Komsomol members toward freeing the toiling youth from the influence of the upper kulak and *bai* elements and enlisting young toilers in socialist construction; serious attention was devoted to work among the youth of the *aul,* especially among young Kazakh women. Gani Muratbaev, Mirasbek Tulepov, and others did a great deal of this work in the Soviet East.

The Lenin Enrollment (1924) played a significant role in strengthening the Komsomol of Kazakhstan. The number of workers in Komsomol organizations doubled, and the number of Kazakhs increased sixfold. In 1925 the regional committee was renamed the territorial committee. The Pioneer movement took shape and developed in Kazakhstan under the leadership of the Komsomol.

Komsomol members were reliable assistants to the CP of Kazakhstan in the struggle for the socialist industrialization and the collectivization of agriculture, the implementation of a cultural revolution, and the education of youth in the spirit of Marxism-Leninism, proletarian internationalism, and friendship among peoples. During the first five-year plans, tens of thousands of Komsomol members went as volunteers to the mines of Ridder and the pits of Karaganda or to work on the Turksib railroad or in the Chimkent lead works, the Balkhash copper smelting works, the Aktiubinsk chemical combine, and the Leninogorsk complex-ore combine. With members of the Communist Party, they initiated mass socialist emulation. More than half of them worked in Komsomol shock brigades. The members of Komsomol displayed selflessness and initiative in the liquidation of patriarchal-feudal relations and in the socialist transformation of the *aul* and *kishlak,* village, and *stanitsa* (large cossack village); they were pioneers of the important measures to consolidate the new culture and life, such as cultural campaigns to eliminate illiteracy and organize Red-yurts, theaters, clubs, and other centers of culture. As they graduated from higher educational institutions, technicums, and factory apprenticeships, the Komsomol members of Kazakhstan reinforced the national cadres of the working class and working intelligentsia. There were 65,000 Komsomol members working for the elimination of illiteracy. The Komsomol organization matured and was tempered in the process of socialist construction. In 1937 it was made into the Lenin Communist Youth League of Kazakhstan.

During the Great Patriotic War (1941–45) the Lenin Komsomol of Kazakhstan sent 250,000 members, or 70 percent of its membership, to the front. Ninety-four former members were awarded the title of Hero of the Soviet Union, including Aliia Moldagulova and Manshuk Mametova, the first Heroes of the Soviet Union to come from the women of the peoples of the East. More than 200,000 boys and girls were awarded orders and medals of the USSR.

During the postwar years the Komsomol of Kazakhstan fought actively for the further development of the economy. The Komsomol played an important role in the development of the virgin and unused lands. Komsomol members of Kazakhstan are working successfully on the republic's numerous construction projects and in its industrial enterprises. Since 1956 the Komsomol of Kazakhstan has sponsored 41 all-Union and 150 republic-wide shock construction projects. In the eighth five-year plan alone, it sent more than 15,000 boys and girls to them.

The role of youth is growing in all spheres of life in Kazakhstan. Twenty percent of the resident population is in the 17–30 age group. More than one-third of the members of the Komsomol are workers representing more than 100 nationalities and peoples. The Komsomol members and youth of Kazakhstan participate actively in socialist emulation under the motto "The ninth five-year plan is the shock labor, skill, and quest of youth."

The number of young inventors and rationalizers doubled from 1967 to 1971. Since the beginning of the ninth five-year plan, almost 300,000 boys and girls have participated in exhibitions of the technical creativity of youth; they have introduced 122,000 rationalizing proposals yielding 178 million rubles to the general economy. More than 300,000 boys and girls work in the fields of Kazakhstan, and 6,000 Komsomol groups participate in the competition to achieve a high level of culture in farming and livestock raising and to increase the productivity of labor and the rational use of machinery. From 1967 to 1971 alone, more than 50,000 boys and girls on Komsomol permits became involved in livestock raising.

Table 4a. Membership in the Komsomol of Kazakhstan

1921 (January)	20,960
1930 (April)	111,946
1941 (January)	347,158
1951 (July)	394,186
1961 (January)	800,580
1972 (January)	1,336,946

The Komsomol members of Kazakhstan are performing a great deal of work in schools and higher educational institutions and devoting considerable attention to raising the general educational level of the working urban and kolkhoz youth. The Komsomol of Kazakhstan is a reliable reserve for and assistant of the CP of Kazakhstan in communist construction and the education of the rising generation. In 1971, Komsomol members constituted 56.5 percent of those accepted as candidate members to the party. For its active participation in socialist construction, the Komsomol of Kazakhstan was awarded the Order of Lenin in 1971.

Table 4b. Conferences and congresses of the Komsomol of Kazakhstan

Territorial congresses	
1st	July 7–13, 1921
2nd	July 23–30, 1922
Territorial conferences	
3rd	June 26–July 3, 1924
4th	Feb. 25–Mar. 2, 1926
5th	Apr. 8–14, 1928
6th	Nov. 12–21, 1930
7th	June 2–7, 1932
8th	Feb. 16–23, 1936
Congresses	
1st	Oct. 2–10, 1937
2nd	Feb. 12–21, 1939
3rd	Sept. 25–30, 1940
4th	June 3–5, 1948
5th	July 10–13, 1951
6th	Apr. 2–3, 1953
7th	Mar. 3–4, 1954
8th	Dec. 20–22, 1955
9th	Mar. 20–22, 1958
10th	Feb. 27–28, 1962
11th	Apr. 20–21, 1966
12th	Mar. 11–12, 1970

REFERENCES

Etapy bol'shogo puti: K 40-letiiu VLKSM. Alma-Ata, 1958.
Boevaia molodost': Vospominaniia pervykh komsomol'tsev Kazakhstana (1917–1925). Alma-Ata, 1958.
Piven', N. *Surovye gody: Iz istorii formirovaniia komsomol'skikh organizatsii Kazakhstana (1917–1921 gg.).* Alma-Ata, 1958.
Dzhanibekov, U. *Komsomol—vernyi pomoshchnik i rezerv partii.* Alma-Ata, 1964.

P. M. PAKHMURNYI

Trade unions

The trade unions of Kazakhstan are an integral part of the trade unions of the USSR. Their emergence during the Revolution of 1905–07 was closely linked to the trade union movement of the Russian proletariat. Trade union organizations were established, first at the Uspenskii Copper Mine and then among railroad workers, in the cities of Ural'sk, Semipalatinsk, and Petropavlovsk. The defeat of the Revolution of 1905–07 resulted in the crushing of the organizations.

After the October Revolution of 1917, the creation of trade union organizations began in the cities and industrial centers under the leadership of the Communist Party. They participated in the struggle for the victory of Soviet power, in the nationalization of industry, and in the rehabilitation of the Kazakhstan economy. The mass enlistment of farm laborers in trade unions was characteristic of this period. In 1919 the Trade Union of Farm and Forestry Workers of Turgai Region was established. It subsequently became the largest trade union of Kazakhstan—the Trade Union of Workers and Employees in Agriculture and Lumber Procurement, which in 1971 had 1.4 million members.

The first territorial conference, which united the uncoordinated trade union committees of Kazakhstan, was held in Orenburg in October 1921. The first congress of trade unions was held in Kzyl-Orda in May 1925 with 82,000 trade-union members who were represented by 150 delegates. During the prewar five-year plans, the trade unions fostered industrialization and collectivization, struggled to increase labor discipline and productivity and promoted a policy of austerity, and acted as organizers of socialist emulation; with their active aid the movement of shock workers and Stakhanovites was expanded and progressive methods generalized and disseminated. The trade unions did a great deal of cultural and educational work among the toiling masses. In 1932 they had more than 400,000 members.

During the Great Patriotic War the trade unions played an important role in putting the republic's economy on a war footing, in receiving and putting into service evacuated enterprises, and in making arrangements for Soviet citizens evacuated to Kazakhstan.

During the postwar years the trade unions expanded activity for the further development of the economy and the opening of virgin and unused lands. They took part in the organization of socialist emulation and improvement of the managment of production and waged a struggle for the fulfillment of production plans, an increase in labor productivity, and the improvement of working and living conditions for industrial and office workers, labor protection, and labor safety. The movement for a communist attitude toward labor involved the participation of 1.8 million people in the republic (1971); there were 30,500 communist labor brigades, 9,900 permanent production conferences, and about 8,700 communist labor schools.

There were 19 oblast trade union councils in Kazakhstan in 1972 and more than 32,000 primary organizations, with more than 4.8 million members. The trade unions of the republic control more than 2,600 clubs and houses and palaces of culture, 14,300 recreation and reading rooms, 1,600 libraries, 31,200 amateur artistic groups, 1,900 people's universities, 5,400 motion picture projection units, 13 tourist centers, 433 Pioneer camps, 363 stadiums and gymnasiums, and 27 swimming pools. In 1971 the state social security budget was 445.6 million rubles (in 1968, 352.3 million rubles).　　　　　P. A. KOVALEV

Economy

General characteristics. Until the October Revolution the economy of Kazakhstan was extremely backward, with a clearly expressed colonial character. A vast territory, very rich in natural resources, was an agricultural country with a very low level of industrial development; industry essentially consisted of small semidomestic enterprises for the initial processing of agricultural produce. The semifeudal lords and *bais* had unlimited power in the Kazakh *aul.*

Under Soviet power, Kazakhstan has become a developed industrial-agrarian republic. By 1971 its industrial output had increased by a factor of 158 in comparison with 1913. Important qualitative changes took place in the republic's economy. In the structure of the gross national product, industry and construction accounted for 63 percent; agriculture, 25 percent. The rates of industrial development of Kazakhstan are higher than for the USSR as a whole. Over the period 1961–71, the growth rate for the industrial output of the entire USSR was 245 percent, and for the Kazakh SSR it was 276 percent. During the eighth five-year plan (1966–70) the total industrial production of the republic increased by 56 percent; production of group A products increased by 55 percent and that of group B products by 59 percent. From 1961 to 1971 the amount of capital investment doubled. For the eighth five-year plan alone, 24.1 billion rubles were invested in the economy—33 percent more than in the seventh five-year plan—and fixed capital stock of industrial production increased by a factor of 1.7. The Kazakh SSR was third among the Union republics, after the RSFSR and the Ukrainian SSR, in the amount of capital investments directed toward the further development of the economy; it was first per capita.

Kazakhstan plays an important role in the further development of the agricultural production of the country. With the development of 25.5 million hectares (ha) of virgin and unused lands from 1954 to 1960, it became one of the major grain regions of the USSR. Kazakhstan's role in wheat production is particularly large. In 1971 the republic's share of the gross harvest was 12 percent, and it provided more than 19 percent of the total volume of state purchases of cereal crops in the USSR.

Kazakhstan is the largest livestock-raising base in the eastern part of the country; in number of sheep and goats (22.4 percent of the total livestock population of the USSR) and production of wool (21.9 percent of all-Union production), it is second among the Union republics, after the RSFSR; it is third, after the RSFSR and the Ukrainian SSR, in head of cattle (7.3 percent of the cattle population of the USSR) and meat production (7 percent of all-Union production).

Agricultural production is large-scale and highly—more than 99 percent—mechanized.

According to the 1971–75 five-year plan for the development of the USSR economy, Kazakhstan's industrial production is to increase by 59 percent, with development of production of the means of production playing a leading role, because of the requirements of all-Union specialization, the existence of vast resources of raw materials in the republic, and the economic efficiency of their exploitation. Electric power, nonferrous and ferrous metallurgy, the fuel industry, machine building, and light industry and the food industry are to develop further. The plan calls for 29.5 billion rubles in capital investment to be directed toward the development of the economy of Kazakhstan and the development of more than 650 new products, a considerable portion of which will be consumer goods. In agriculture the goal has been set to bring the average annual gross harvest of cereals up to 24 million tons, guarantee stable production, carry out a complex of measures to protect soils against wind erosion, and improve the structure of sown areas. Cattle and sheep raising for meat will develop at an accelerated rate, and the feed base for livestock raising will be strengthened.

Industry. There were more than 23,000 industrial enterprises and factories in Kazakhstan in 1972, more than 2,000 of which are large-scale. During the eighth five-year plan alone, more than 450 large enterprises and works were put into service and hundreds of mills and factories reconstructed and technically reequipped. Virtually all of the main branches of heavy industry have been established in the republic. In the Union-wide territorial division of labor, the Kazakh SSR is distinguished for nonferrous metallurgy (extraction and dressing of complex-metal, copper, and nickel ores, as well as bauxite; and smelting of metallic lead, zinc, copper, and other nonferrous and rare metals). The coal industry, certain branches of the chemical industry, and machine building (rolling equipment, instruments and apparatus, and forging and pressing machines) are also of all-Union significance. Great strides have been made in light industry, particularly wool and tanning, and in the food industry, especially meat, fish, salt, and butter. New branches of all-Union specialization—ferrous metallurgy (the extraction of iron ore and smelting of ferrous metals), petroleum extraction and refining, electric power, and the cotton industry—are developing (see Table 5).

In absolute volume of gross industrial output, Kazakhstan is third among the union republics after the RSFSR and the Ukrainian SSR. The branches of heavy industry are developing

Table 5. Rate of industrial growth by branch
(percent of 1960 volume)

	1965	1971
Electric power	195	384
Fuel	131	227
Ferrous metallurgy	255	429
Nonferrous metallurgy	149	236
Chemical and petrochemical industry	203	503
Machine building and metalworking	208	357
Timber, wood products, and paper and pulp industry	136	223
Building materials	174	302
Light industry	140	263
Food industry	159	233
All industry	164	384

particularly rapidly; in 1971, it accounted for about 60 percent of the industrial production of Kazakhstan (in 1920, 12 percent).

From 1961 to 1971 the gross product of industry grew by a factor of 2.8; the production of electric power increased by a factor of 3.6; ferrous metallurgy, 4.3; the chemical and petrochemical industry, 5; and machine buildng and metalworking, 3.6. The output of the major industrial products is given in Table 6.

Under Soviet power new branches of industry—machine building, petroleum refining, production of inorganic fertilizers, knitwear, and sugar—have been established; the old branches have been fundamentally reconstructed and the scale of production increased.

This growth has been accompanied by improvements in the distribution of industrial branches. New industrial centers (Arkalyk and Rudnyi) and industrial regions and junctions (Pavlodar-Ekibastuz and Mangyshlak) have been constructed near mineral deposits.

The leading branch of industry, nonferrous metallurgy, is represented by the copper, lead-zinc, and titanium-magnesium industries and by the production of rare and precious metals. In all, the production of more than 30 chemical elements has been mastered. Kazakhstan is one of the leaders in the USSR in lead, zinc, and copper production. The enterprises of the copper industry are located in Karaganda Oblast (the Balkhash and Dzhezkazgan mining and metallurgy combines, which include mines and dressing mills) and eastern Kazakhstan, where the Irtysh Copper-smelting Plant is operating in the settlement of Glubokoe. A large copper-chemical combine was under construction there in 1972 around the Nikolaevka complex-metal ore deposits. Copper smelting is expanding at the Dzhezkazgan Mining and Metallurgy Combine.

The lead and zinc industry is highly developed in the Rudnyi Altai and in southern Kazakhstan. Large-scale lead and zinc combine in Ust'-Kamenogorsk, a complex-metals combine in Leninogorsk, and mines and dressing plants have been established. The construction of the Tishinsk, Berezovka, Nikolaevka, and Orlov mines has been important in strengthening the raw-materials base for nonferrous metallurgy in the Rudnyi Altai. Lead is smelted in southern Kazakhstan at the Karatau deposits of complex-metal ore (Chimkent). A titanium and magnesium industry has been created. Aluminum production has begun around bauxite deposits of Turgai Oblast (Pavlodar). Mining of lead and zinc ores is developing in Karaganda Oblast.

Ferrous metallurgy is one of the newest branches of industry in Kazakhstan. During the Great Patriotic War the Aktiubinsk Ferroalloy Plant and the Kazakh Metallurgical Plant in Temir-tau were put into service. The Karaganda Metallurgical Plant, which has been producing finished products since 1960, was built in Temirtau after the war. Metallurgical plants in Temirtau and mining enterprises form the Karaganda Metallurgical Combine. A new ferroalloy plant has been built in the city of Ermak (Pavlodar Oblast). The iron ore industry has been developing rapidly in the Turgai Iron Ore Basin; the Sokolovskaia-Sarba Ore-dressing Combine is in operation there. The Lisakovsk Combine is under construction (the first line began operation in 1973), and the construction of the Kacharsk Ore-dressing Combine is planned. The iron ore industry of Kazakhstan will also

Table 6. Output of principal industrial products

	1913	1940	1950	1960	1971
Iron ore (tons)	—	—	—	5,800,000	18,800,000
Pig iron (tons)	—	—	—	270,000	2,500,000
Steel (tons)	—	—	130,000	300,000	3,300,000
Rolled ferrous metals (tons)	—	—	110,000	300,000	2,700,000
Coal (tons)	100,000	7,000,000	17,400,000	32,400,000	67,300,000
Petroleum, including gas condensate (tons)	120,000	700,000	1,100,000	1,600,000	16,000,000
Natural gas (cu m)	—	3,900,000	7,400,000	39,400,000	2,747,000,000
Electric power (kW-hr)	1,300,000	631,700,000	2,617,200,000	10,469,600,000	37,789,000,000
Inorganic fertilizers, in conventional units(tons)	—	—	22,300	477,000	2,822,000
Sulfuric acid, in mono-hydrate (tons)	—	49,200	58,200	551,000	1,254,000
Metal-cutting machine tools (units)	—	—	5	931	2,436
Cement (tons)	—	—	15,700	2,173,000	5,991,000
Cotton textiles (linear meters)	—	700,000	4,900,000	20,400,000	65,800,000
Wool fabrics (linear meters)	140,000	400,000	2,200,000	4,100,000	5,400,000
Leather footwear (pairs)	13,000	1,200,000	3,300,000	12,300,000	28,500,000
Meat, including first-category by-products (tons)	—	97,000	109,600	278,200	568,000
Butter (tons)	2,300	12,100	22,300	29,100	43,700
Canned goods (standard cans)	—	30,200,000	92,600,000	159,200,000	329,000,000
Granulated sugar (tons)	—	70,900	71,800	122,800	149,000
Fish and marine animals (tons)	31,800	87,100	102,200	105,300	100,800

supply raw materials to the ferrous metallurgy industry of the Southern Urals and Western Siberia.

Kazakhstan is third in the country, after the RSFSR and the Ukrainian SSR, in coal production. In 1971 the Karaganda Coal Basin provided about 60 percent of all the coal mined in the republic. The importance of the Ekibastuz deposits, where coal is mined by the opencut method, is increasing sharply; it is one of the cheapest coals in the country. The ninth five-year plan provides that more than 50 percent of the total increase of the coal industry will be supplied by the Ekibastuz deposit of power-producing coal. Small coal deposits are worked in other areas, including the Lenger deposit in southern Kazakhstan. The Mai-kuben basin of brown low-ash coals, which are used to produce power and as industrial fuel, is 80 km from Ekibastuz.

The petroleum industry is concentrated in the western part of the republic. Deposits in Emba Raion are scattered over a broad expanse in a sparsely settled semidesert region. In additon to petroleum, by-product gas is extracted. Emba low-sulfur petroleum has good industrial properties; the lubricating oils made from it are particularly valuable.

During the eighth five-year plan, the Mangyshlak Peninsula became an important petroleum-extraction region. The Zhety-bai, Uzen', Karamandybas, and Ten'ga deposits are being developed. In the ninth five-year plan more than 80 percent of the oil and 75 percent of the gas in the republic is to be extracted from the Mangyshlak deposits. Petroleum refining, which began when the Gur'ev Petroleum Refinery was put into service, is also developing. The construction of two more large refineries in Pavlodar and Chimkent and expansion of the Gur'ev refinery are planned.

The production of electric power was established in Kazakhstan during the Soviet period. Large state regional power plants have been built in Alma-Ata, Karaganda, Petropavlovsk, Dzhambul, Chimkent, Pavlodar, and other industrial centers. The Ust'-Kamenogorsk and Bukhtarma hydroelectric power plants on the Irtysh River and the Kapchagai Hydroelectric Power Plant on the Ili River are in operation. Three power units of the Ermak State Regional Electric Power Plant, which operates on cheap coal from the Ekibastuz deposit, were put into service during the eighth five-year plan, and a fourth unit was put into service in 1971. An important power center is forming in southern Kazakhstan, where the Dzhambul State Regional Electric Power Plant, with a capacity of 1.2 million kilowatts, is under construction (the first line of the plant was put into service during the eighth five-year plan; it operates on natural gas from Uzbekistan).

The machine-building industry of Kazakhstan began to develop rapidly during the Great Patriotic War, when a number of plants from the western regions of the country were evacuated to the republic. It produces forging and pressing equipment, metal-cutting machines, excavators, agricultural machines, various equipment for the coal and mining industry, and radio equipment. There is an association of plants producing mining equipment in Karaganda, a plant producing equipment for the petroleum industry in Gur'ev, heavy machine-building and electrical-engineering plants in Alma-Ata, the Kazakhsel'mash and Tselinogradsel'mash plants in Tselinograd, and plants producing transformers and excavators in Kentau. During the eighth five-year plan, the first line of a tractor plant was put into service in Pavlodar. The output of machine building grew by a factor of 1.6 over the five-year plan. Instrument-making was established (Aktiubinsk, Kokchetav, and Ust'-Kamenogorsk). The machine-building industry of Kazakhstan produces more than 2,000 types of machines, instruments, and equipment for the economy of the country and receives many kinds of machines and automatic lines from the other republics.

The chemical industry is developing around phosphorite deposits in southern Kazakhstan. A complex of enterprises producing inorganic fertilizers, elemental phosphorus, polyethylene, chromium compounds, and chemical fibers has been established. The largest are the Karatau Mining and Chemical Combine, the Chimkent Phosphoric Salts Plant, and the Dzhambul Double Superphosphate Plant. There is a polyethylene plant in Gur'ev, a synthetic-rubber plant in Temirtau, a chromium-compounds plant in Aktiubinsk, and a chemical-pharmaceutical plant in Chimkent. There are sulfuric-acid works at certain non-ferrous metallurgy plants. At the end of the ninth five-year plan, production of inorganic fertilizers had increased by a factor of 2.3 and production of chemical fibers by a factor of 1.8 in comparison with 1970.

The building-materials industry took shape under Soviet power in the central, eastern, and southern areas of Kazakhstan. It is represented by the production of lime, brick, gypsum, and cement. Artificial slate production has been organized through the cement industry. Many new types of building materials are produced, such as prefabricated reinforced concrete, slate, slag cotton, ceramet, and concrete and silica wall blocks. The production of linoleum, marble mosaic finishing tile, Ruberoid, and ceramic finishing tile is scheduled to begin during the ninth five-year plan.

Light industry is closely tied to the processing of agricultural raw materials. The main branches are tanning, footwear, sheepskin coats, wool, clothing, and knitwear. The cotton industry (Chimkent and Alma-Ata) and the furniture industry (Alma-Ata) are developing.

The food industry has a broad base for development. Meat is the main branch; the largest meat-packing plants, at Semipalatinsk, is second in capacity only to the Moscow and Leningrad plants. Butter is produced in northern and northeastern Kazakhstan. The flour-milling and groats industry is developed in large cities. Sugar refineries are located in the beet-planting regions of Dzhambul, Taldy-Kurgan, and Alma-Ata oblasts. The republic's fishing industry is well developed. Sturgeon, giant sturgeon, and *Clupeonella* are caught in the Caspian Sea; bream and barbel are caught in the Aral Sea. There is also fishing on Lakes Balkhash and Zaisan.

Agriculture. In 1971, 183.6 million ha of agricultural lands were used by enterprises and farms, including 34.5 million ha of plowed fields, 6.49 million ha of hayfields, and 141.5 million ha of pastures. The main form of agricultural enterprise is the sovkhoz, which became widespread after the massive development of virgin and unused lands. In the 1954–58 period alone, 553 new sovkhozes were established. The standards for technical equipment of farms rose sharply. Over the period of development of virgin lands (1954–60) the number of tractors and grain-harvesting combines in the sovkhozes and kolkhozes of the northern oblasts increased by a factor of almost 6, and the number of trucks increased by a factor of 6. This made possible complete mechanization of the cultivation of grain crops and the provision of an increased level of mechanization for the cultivation of other agricultural crops.

As of the end of 1971 there were 1,631 sovkhozes and 451 kolkhozes in Kazakhstan. In 1971 sovkhozes accounted for almost 82 percent of the total sown area of Kazakhstan and 81 percent of the gross harvest of cereals. In 1971 the sovkhozes accounted for 86 percent of purchases of cereals, 72 percent of purchases of cattle and fowl, 78 percent of milk purchases, and 69 percent of wool purchases.

The necessary conditions for the further development of agriculture are the consistent intensification and comprehensive mechanization and, on this basis, the increase of the general culture of production, as well as the use of science and technology. During the period 1961–71 alone, the total power of agricultural machinery increased by a factor of almost 1.6, to 35,714,000 hp. All sovkhozes and kolkhozes are completely electrified, and 70 percent of them are connected to the state power grids. In 1971 there were 525,000 tractors in agriculture (in 15-hp units), 97,000 grain-harvesting combines, and more than 103,000 trucks.

Specialization of various agricultural regions in the republic has been established. The economy of western Kazakhstan is devoted primarily to the production of cereals, meat and wool sheep raising and meat and dairy cattle raising, and the economy of southern Kazakhstan specializes in the production of karakul and in industrial crops (sugar beets and cotton), horticulture, viticulture, dairy and meat cattle raising, and rice production. In addition to the production of commercial cereals, the northern and eastern oblasts of the republic are developing meat and dairy livestock raising and swine and poultry breeding.

In 1971 farm produce accounted for 47.3 percent of gross agricultural production; livestock raising, 52.7 percent. In the all-Union division of labor, Kazakhstan is a major producer of commercial cereals, meat, and wool. The structure of sown area is shown in Table 7.

lands in Dzhambul, Alma-Ata, and Taldy-Kurgan oblasts; tobacco is grown in Alma-Ata Oblast. Other industrial crops are mustard (Ural'sk Oblast) and medicinal crops (Chimkent Oblast).

Under Soviet power plantings of potatoes, vegetables and mel-

Table 7. Sown areas
(hectares)

	1913	1940	1950	1960	1971
Grain crops	3,880,800	5,817,100	6,055,200	21,949,900	22,406,700
wheat	2,507,100	3,446,400	4,024,000	18,062,600	16,592,000
rice	25,300	28,100	29,800	13,100	90,600
millet	455,200	903,100	464,700	864,700	711,300
Industrial crops	102,800	341,300	367,500	406,700	458,200
cotton	15,000	101,800	96,900	105,600	118,500
sugar beets	—	15,400	20,300	60,000	70,400
sunflowers	18,800	164,900	157,100	134,600	102,100
Potatoes	41,500	99,700	140,600	174,200	190,400
Vegetables	12,200	22,900	28,300	46,100	53,000
Fodder crops	88,200	494,600	1,234,900	5,923,000	8,409,900
Total sown areas	4,145,700	6,808,600	7,854,300	28,542,700	31,558,400

The sown area in the republic is constantly growing. In 1971 the crop area was 7.6 times greater than in 1913 and 4.6 times greater than in 1940. Growth was particularly great from 1954 to 1956 as a result of the development of new lands. In 1971, 71.0 percent of the crop area of the republic was under cereals (including 52.6 percent under wheat), 1.5 percent was under industrial crops, 0.9 percent was under potatoes and vegetables or melons, and 26.6 percent was under feed crops. In recent years the proportion of sown area under cereals has decreased somewhat and the area under industrial and feed crops has increased.

Table 8. Gross harvest of major agricultural crops
(tons)

	1961–65[1]	1966–70[1]	1971
Cereal crops	14,525,000	20,668,000	21,085,000
wheat	11,159,000	16,077,000	15,802,000
Raw cotton	217,000	241,000	296,000
Sugar beets (industrial)	1,492,000	2,276,000	2,129,000
Potatoes	1,181,000	1,741,000	1,710,000
Vegetables	559,000	693,000	792,000

[1]Yearly average

The average annual productivity of cereals grew from 6.1 quintals per ha in 1961–65 to 8.8 quintals in 1966–70 and 9.4 quintals in 1971. One of the most important reserves for raising productivity and increasing the gross harvests of grain is the expansion and better utilization of irrigated lands, and also a redoubled struggle against losses in harvesting and processing of agricultural crops. Agricultural crops are sown on 1.25 million ha of irrigated land, of which 37 percent is under cereals. Irrigated lands are located primarily in southern Kazakhstan. Large irrigation canals and systems have been built in Kzyl-Orda, Chimkent, Dzhambul, Taldy-Kurgan, and Alma-Ata oblasts.

The main cereal region is made up of the northern virgin lands, which account for about two-thirds of all plantings of cereal crops. There are substantial plantings of cereals in the south as well as in the foothills and valleys of the Tien-Shan; grain crops are grown there on dry-farming and on irrigated lands. In 1972, Kazakhstan provided more than 17 million tons of grain, a total that was particularly significant given the difficult weather conditions in a considerable portion of the country.

Drought-resistant millet, which accounts for about 30 percent of the millet planted in the USSR, is a characteristic crop of Kazakhstan. Large areas are under millet in the northwest and northeast of the republic, which are drier and less favorable for wheat. Rice growing is developed in the valleys of the Syr Darya and Karatal. A new rice-growing region is being created in the lower reaches of the Ili River.

Among industrial crops the most important are cotton, sugar beets, sunflowers, and tobacco. Cotton is cultivated only in Chimkent Oblast. Beet growing is well developed on irrigated

ons, and feed crops have expanded substantially. Suburban farming is developing aroung Alma-Ata, Karaganda, and other large cities. The Irtysh-Karaganda canal, with its subsequent extension to Dzhezkazgan, will play a large role in the creation of a dairy and vegetable base around the cities of central Kazakhstan.

Orchards and vineyards, primarily in Alma-Ata and Chimkent oblasts occupy more than 130,000 ha. Data on the gross harvest of agricultural crops are given in Table 8.

Over the period 1966–70, average annual state purchases rose by a factor of almost 1.6 in comparison with 1961–65 for cereal crops (including wheat, which rose by a larger factor); raw cotton purchases rose by 11 percent; sugar beets, by a factor of more than 1.5; potatoes, 2.2; and vegetables, 1.4.

Publicly owned livestock raising is developing through increases in the livestock population and its productivity. Many kinds of cattle and fowl are raised in Kazakhstan (see Table 9). The leading branch of livestock raising, which providing more than 50 percent of the total livestock income, is sheep. This has been facilitated by the existence of vast areas of seasonal semidesert and desert pastures where sheep are kept on green fodder for nine to ten months a year. Before the October Revolution only simple coarse-fleeced fat-tailed sheep were raised. Under Soviet power new varieties have been bred, and a large portion of the herd consists of fine-fleeced and crossbred sheep, raised primarily in the southeastern oblasts. A new variety of high-altitude sheep, the Kazakh Arkhar-Merino, has been bred for mountainous regions. The raising of karakul is well developed in southern Kazakhstan.

Table 9. Livestock and fowl population on all categories of farms, as of January 1
(head)

	1916	1941	1961	1972
Cattle	5,040,000	3,335,000	5,543,000	7,470,000
cows	1,868,000	1,251,000	2,076,000	2,730,000
Hogs	277,000	449,000	1,773,000	2,710,000
Sheep and goats	17,926,000	7,914,000	28,516,000	32,596,000
Horses	4,311,000	885,000	1,158,000	1,266,000
Camels	—	103,000	140,000	127,000
Fowl	—	6,700,000	19,700,000	31,800,000

Cattle are raised in the agriculturally developed northern and northeastern areas, where dairy and meat cattle raising is dominant, and also in the agricultural belt of the south and east and in suburban farms around the industrial centers.

Horse breeding is developed in the mountains of eastern Kazakhstan and also in western and central Kazakhstan; camels are bred in desert and semidesert areas, primarily in the lower reaches of the Syr Darya and the rivers of the Urals, and spotted deer and Siberian stag are raised in the foothills of the Altai.

Swine are bred primarily in agricultural regions and in the suburban zones of large industrial centers.

The dynamics of state purchase of livestock products are shown in Table 10.

Table 10. Output and state purchases of main products of livestock raising on all categories of farms
(tons)

	1940	1960	1971
Output			
Meat			
liveweight	391,700	964,800	1,572,700
dressed weight	224,100	549,400	926,800
Milk	1,089,700	2,482,300	3,900,100
Eggs (million units)	307.3	861.3	2,013.1
Wool	13,400	66,200	94,100
State purchases			
Livestock and fowl			
(liveweight)	161,800	654,000	1,244,600
Milk and milk products	271,100	923,600	1,784,000
Eggs (million units)	38.5	198.2	877.1
Wool	13,800	78,900	104,700

Transportation. The railroad is the basic form of transportation. The operational length of railroads increased from 2,100 km in 1913 to 13,900 km in 1971, of which 90 percent was served by diesel traction and 10 percent by electric locomotive traction. The Petropavlovsk-Karaganda-Balkhash, Zharyk-Dzhezkazgan, Lokot'–Ust'-Kamenogorsk, Tselinograd-Kartaly, and Gur'ev-Orsk lines and the Turkestan-Siberia Trunk Line were built during the prewar five-year plans and the war years. Lines put into operation after the war include Mointy-Chu, Tselinograd-Pavlodar and a section of the South Siberian Trunk Line, Makat–Shevchenko–Novyi Uzen', Esil'-Arkalyk, Gur'ev-Astrakhan, and Kokchetav-Karasuk. The chief freights transported on the railroads are coal, grain, ore, petroleum products, timber, lumber and building materials, and inorganic fertilizers. The freight turnover of railroad transportation was 229.6 billion ton-km in 1971.

There are 110,000 km highways, of which 44,200 km are hard-surfaced. The main roads are Alma-Ata–Frunze–Chimkent–Tashkent, Alma-Ata–Taldy-Kurgan–Ust'-Kamenogorsk, Gur'ev-Ural'sk, Karaganda-Tselinograd-Kustanai-Troitsk, Tselinograd-Kokchetav-Petropavlovsk, Semipalatinsk-Pavlodar-Omsk, and the Eastern Ring (Ust'-Kamenogorsk–Kokpekty–Georgievka–Ust'-Kamenogorsk). The freight turnover of general-purpose motor-vehicle transportation reached 6.3 billion ton-km in 1971; the passenger turnover was 14 billion passenger-km.

Navigation is well developed on the Caspian and Aral seas, Lake Balkhash, the Bukhtarma Reservoir, the Irtysh, the Syr Darya, and the Ural River (from Gur'ev to Ural'sk).

Pipeline shipping has gained in importance. Oil pipelines are in operation in western Kazakhstan between the Emba oilfields and Gur'ev and Orsk and on the Mangyshlak Peninsula (Uzen'-Shevchenko); there is a main oil pipeline from Uzen' to Kuibyshev. Gas pipelines have been built in southern Kazakhstan to supply the Chimkent, Dzhambul, and Alma-Ata industrial regions with Bukhara gas. Gas pipelines from Uzbekistan to the Urals (Gazli-Cheliabinsk and Gazli-Sverdlovsk) and to the European part of the USSR (Middle Asia to the Central Zone) have been laid across Kazakhstan.

Air routes go from Alma-Ata to all oblast centers and to remote areas of the republic, as well as to Moscow, Leningrad, Sverdlovsk, Kiev, Novosibirsk, and Tashkent and the health resorts of the Crimea and Caucasus.

Kazakhstan has well-developed economic ties with all Union republics and regions of the country. The republic receives metals from the Urals; petroleum products from the Tataria and Bashkiria, Western Siberia, and the Northern Caucasus; timber and timber materials from Western and Eastern Siberia; and machines and equipment from the Central Zone of European Russia, the Baltic Region, Byelorussia, the Ukraine, and the Urals; as well as many consumer goods. In turn, Kazakhstan supplies other regions with nonferrous metals, iron, chromium, and nickel ores, inorganic fertilizers, grain, meat, wool, and hides.

Economic regions. Petrochemical and gas-chemical industrial complexes (Gur'ev Oblast) and chemical-metallurgical industrial complexes (Aktiubinsk Oblast) of Union-wide importance are concentrated in western Kazakhstan. This is the only region in Kazakhstan for petroleum extraction and refining and the gas industry; it is an important area for mining, the chemical industry, and ferrous metallurgy and the main region for fishing. Agricultural specializes are sheep raising (in the southern portion) and grain production (wheat and millet) in the northern portion of the region.

Northern Kazakhstan is the grain base of the republic and is an important livestock-raising region, specializing in dairy and meat cattle in the northern portion and sheep in the southern. The mining industry (iron ore, coal, nonferrous and rare metals, bauxite, and asbestos), ferrous metallurgy, the aluminum and chemical industries, and machine building are well developed.

Central Kazakhstan is the most important region for heavy industry, with the coal industry, ferrous and nonferrous metallurgy, chemistry, and machine building. Agriculture is represented by distant-pasture ranching and, in the northern portion, by grain production.

Southern Kazakhstan is the main region for irrigated farming, the production of rice and industrial crops, horticulture, melons, vegetables, karakul, and meat and dairy cattle. The chemical industry is developed in Dzhambul and Chimkent oblasts around the phosphorites of Karatau (the production of fertilizers); nonferrous metallurgy (mining of ore and smelting of lead), machine building, and the building-materials industry are well developed. The south is the republic's main region for light industry (wool, cotton, leather footwear, and knitwear) and the food industry (sugar, macaroni, and confections).

Eastern Kazakhstan is an important region for nonferrous metallurgy and power engineering. Instrument making, the production of mining and metallurgical equipment, and forestry are well developed. The food industry is very important (meat, butter, and seed-oil extraction). The main branch of agriculture is meat and wool sheep raising.

Standard of living. Under Soviet power the standard of living has risen sharply. By 1971 the national income of the republic had increased by a factor of 2.2 in comparison with 1960 (by 71 percent compared with 1965). From 1966 to 1971 real per capita incomes increased by a factor of 1.4, and social consumption funds by 45 percent (250 rubles in 1970 as against 173 rubles in 1965). The average monthly monetary wages of industrial and office workers are increasing steadily (127.4 rubles in 1971, 98 rubles in 1965). Expenditures from the state budget for social and cultural measures rose from 92.3 million rubles in 1940 and 743.4 million rubles in 1960 to 2,142, 800,000 rubles in 1971. From 1960 to 1971 state and cooperative enterprises and organizations, kolkhozes, and the population built and put into service 70.1 million sq m of general (actual) floor space.

In 1971 the retail merchandise turnover in the state and cooperative trade, including public catering, amounted to 7.781 billion rubles (3,468 billion rubles in 1960). From 1966 to 1971 alone, about 6,000 new stores and 3,000 cafeterias were opened. The number of savings banks increased from 1,515 in 1940 to 4,220 in 1971, and the deposits of the population grew from 14.4 million to 2.142 billion rubles.

REFERENCES

Nash Kazakhstan. Alma-Ata, 1970.
Razvitie narodnogo khoziaistva Kazakhstana za 50 let sovetskoi vlasti. Alma-Ata, 1967.
Sovetskomu Kazakhstanu—50 let. Alma-Ata, 1970.
Adamchuk, V. A., and B. Ia. Dvoskin. *Problemy razvitiia promyshlennykh uzlov SSSR (na primere Kazakhstana).* Moscow, 1968.
Kazakhstan v tsifrakh. Kratkii statisticheskii sbornik. Alma-Ata, 1971.
Kazakhstan za 50 let: Stat. sb. Alma-Ata, 1971.

Akhmedova, N. B. *Problemy razvitiia i razmeshcheniia promyshlennosti Kazakhstana.* Alma-Ata, 1971.
B. IA. DVOSKIN

Health and social welfare

Medicine and public health. There were virtually no public-health facilities and measures in prerevolutionary Kazakhstan. Difficult socioeconomic conditions and incessant epidemics led to near extinction of the population. Infant mortality was particularly high.

A large system of therapeutic and prophylactic institutions has been established under Soviet power. Plague, smallpox, and trachoma have been eliminated, and infant mortality has declined sharply. In the 1960–71 period the morbidity rate for diphtheria has decreased by a factor of 152; for tularemia, by a factor of 30; for whooping cough, by a factor of 35; for typhoid, by a factor of 4; and for brucellosis, by a factor of 5. There have been decreases in the incidence of tuberculosis (53 percent over 1961–71) and skin diseases. Helminthiases declined by a factor of 5 from 1958 to 1967. In 1971 the birthrate was 23.8 per thousand; the overall death rate, six per thousand.

With respect to medical geography, a distinction may be made among northern (steppe and forest-steppe), central (semidesert), southern (desert), northeast foothill, and southeast foothill-mountain areas of Kazakhstan. In the northern region, in areas with an abundance of fresh-water lakes, foci of nonicteric leptospirosis are encountered. In the northern, northeastern, and southeastern regions there are foci of acarid-bite encephalitis (such foci are also encountered in places in the semidesert). The incidence of opisthorchiasis is substantially higher in the northern region than elsewhere. Kala azar and tick-borne spirochetosis are endemic to the southern region. Teniarhynchoses, ascaridiasis, alveococcosis, and trichinosis are recorded in the southern and southeastern regions. Echinococcosis is recorded in areas of intensive sheep breeding. Goitrous enzootic disease is prevalent in the foothill-mountainous southeastern area. Hymenolepiasis and natural breeding grounds of Q fever are observed in all areas.

In 1971, Kazakhstan had about 2,000 functioning hospitals, with 160,900 beds (11.9 per thousand), as against 98 hospitals, with 1,800 beds (0.3 per thousand), in 1913 and 627 hospitals, with 25,400 beds (four per thousand), in 1940. Outpatient services are provided by 2,200 institutions. In 1971, 30,900 doctors, or one per 436 inhabitants, were working in Kazakhstan, as against 244 in 1913 (one per 23,000 inhabitants) and 2,700 in 1940 (one per 2,300 inhabitants); there were also more than 111,000 secondary medical personnel. In 1971 there were 203 clinics, 559 children's polyclinics and outpatient departments, 417 gynecological consultation offices, 56 maternity hospitals, 110 first-aid stations and units, 291 sanitary-epidemiologic stations, 1,300 pharmacies, and 840 pharmaceutical stations.

There are ten medical research institutions in operation in Kazakhstan (oncology and radiology, regional pathology, clinical and experimental surgery, tuberculosis, labor hygiene and occupational diseases, epidemiology, microbiology and hygiene, eye diseases, skin and venereology, motherhood and childhood, and plague-prevention). Specialists are trained at five medical institutes and 26 medical schools. An institute of advanced training has been organized. About 2,900 teaching personnel work in institutes, including 116 doctors and more than 1,000 candidates of medical science.

Health resorts in Kazakhstan are Borovoe (since 1971, Shchuchinskii), an all-Union resort; Alma-Arasan; Arasan-Kapal; Kamenskoe Plato; Muialdy; Chimgan; Ianykurgan; and Aul. There are 95 sanatoriums and 27 houses of rest in operation (1971). In 1971, 496 million rubles were allocated for public health and physical culture (24.8 million rubles in 1940).

Sports and tourism. In 1971 there were 2,906 stadiums and gymnasiums, more than 23,000 sports fields of various kinds, and 47 swimming pools. There were 2,215,000 athletes, including 714,000 women, and 2,800 masters of sport. There are 26 tourist routes, four of which are all-Union. The main tourist routes pass through the area of Lakes Sabyndykol' and Zhasybai, where there is a tourist center (northern Kazakhstan); Lake Shaitankul' in the Karkaralinsk Mountains, where the famous Gorge of Caves is located (central Kazakhstan); Lakes Rakhmanovskoe and Markakol' (eastern Kazakhstan); and, near Alma-Ata, the high-mountain Medeo skating rink and the Gorel'nik tourist center, from which a route proceeds along the banks of the Malaia Almatinka River to the Chimbulak natural landmark. A ski center is located there, at an elevation of 2,202 m, where all-Union and international competitions in alpine sports are held. Fourteen tourist centers served 139,200 tourists in 1971. There are 257 sports health camps and lodges for hunters and fishermen. Kazakhstan was visited by about 241,000 tourists in 1971 (including 8,000 from 70 foreign countries).

Veterinary services. Under Soviet power, glanders, infectious anemia of horses, plague, epidemic pneumonia of cattle, smallpox of sheep, infectious pleuropneumonia and smallpox of goats, and certain other diseases have been eliminated. Many infectious diseases of farm animals that were previously recorded everywhere are now encountered as isolated cases. As a result of natural conditions, the presence of wild ungulates, insects, and ticks and mites, foci of piroplasmosis, biohelminthiases and nematode helminthiases, and diseases that have natural breeding grounds—for example, leptospirosis, listerellosis, and rabies—have become established; planned control and preventive measures are being undertaken.

As of Jan. 1, 1972, 4,185 veterinarians and 9,048 veterinary feldshers and technicians were working in agriculture in Kazakhstan. Veterinary services are directed by the Veterinary Administration of the Ministry of Agriculture of Kazakhstan; the network of veterinary institutions covers all regions. Veterinarians are trained by the Alma-Ata and Semipalatinsk zooveterinary institutes. The leading research center for veterinary medicine is the Kazakhstan Institute of Veterinary Science (Alma-Ata).

Education and cultural institutions

Until the middle of the 19th century, Kazakhstan had only Muslim schools—*maktabs* and madrasas—where children were taught written Arabic and the dogmas of Islam. These schools trained mainly religious ministers. After unification with Russia, which was completed in the 1860's, the first secular Kazakh schools were opened. Ch. Valikhanov, I. Altynsarin, and Abai Kunanbaev, progressive exponents of the Kazakh intelligentsia, championed Russian culture and fought to spread secular education.

By the end of the 19th century, there were two instructional systems in Kazakhstan: the schools for the children of the Russian administration and the prosperous Kazakh and other non-Russian population and the religious schools. In the 1914–15 academic year there were 2,006 schools, with 105,000 pupils, only 7,900 of whom were Kazakhs. During the prerevolutionary years, literacy was 2 percent among the Kazakh population; only a handful of women were literate.

A fundamental improvement in public education in Kazakhstan came with the establishment of Soviet power. Many new schools were opened and stations for the elimination of illiteracy were organized; short-term courses produced the first detachments of teachers and champions of culture. Teaching in the native language began. A great deal of work was conducted in transferring the Kazakh written language at first into a Latinized alphabet (1928); then, in 1940, the Supreme Soviet of the Kazakh SSR adopted a law on transferring the language into a new alphabet based on Russian script. Universal elementary education was introduced in 1930; in 1931 seven-year programs were introduced in the cities, workers' settlements, and large sovkhozes. According to data of the 1939 census, literacy among persons aged 9–49 had reached 83.6 percent (90.3 percent among men and 75.8 percent among women). In the 1940–41 academic year, 1,158,000 pupils were studying in general-education schools of all types. By the 1951–52 academic year, compulsory universal seven-year education had essentially been realized. Compulsory eight-year education was introduced in 1959. The number of daytime secondary schools is growing (2,798 in 1971).

Before the October Revolution there were no preschool institutions in Kazakhstan. The first 20 kindergartens, with 610 children, were organized in 1920. With socialist reconstruction of the economy and the entry of women into socially useful activity, the system of preschool institutions continued to expand. As of Jan. 1, 1972, there were 5,319 permanent preschool institutions in operation, educating 546,000 children.

In the 1971–72 academic year there were 3,296,000 pupils in 10,101 general-education schools of all types. A system of schools for working youth had developed. Special attention is devoted to including young girls of the local nationalities in universal compulsory education and to encouraging them to continue their educations; residence facilities have been opened at many schools. During the 1971–72 academic year, 173 boarding schools were operating (62,900 pupils), and there were 2,063 boarding schools at general-education schools (137,200 children); more than 101,000 children were supported completely by the state.

The training of skilled workers began as early as the 1930's. As of Jan. 1, 1972, 379 vocational and technical schools were operating, including 370 day schools, of which 181 were municipal vocational and technical schools (88,000 students), 177 were agricultural schools (67,900 students), and 12 were technical schools (8,000 students). In 1971 the vocational and technical education system graduated 116,900 skilled workers.

Secondary specialized education has undergone extensive development. In the 1971–72 academic year, 223,400 students were studying in 198 secondary specialized schools. Before the revolution there were only seven schools (300 students) which trained teachers for the so-called Russian-Kirghiz schools. In the 1971–72 academic year, teachers for general-education schools were trained in 18 pedagogical institutes and 19 teachers colleges.

The first higher educational institution in Kazakhstan, the Abai Pedagogical Institute, was opened in 1928 in Alma-Ata. Today, specialized personnel with higher education are trained for all branches of the economy and culture at 44 higher educational institutions. The largest higher educational institutions of Kazakhstan are the S. M. Kirov Kazakh University, the Kazakh Polytechnic Institute, and the Kazakh Agricultural Institute in Alma-Ata. There were 200,500 students in higher educational institutions during the 1971–72 academic year. A university was opened in Karaganda in 1972. As of the end of 1971, 818,000 specialists with higher and secondary special education were employed in the economy of Kazakhstan.

As of Jan. 1, 1972, the republic had 7,901 public libraries (69,798,000 books and journals), the largest of which was the A. S. Pushkin State Library of the Kazakh SSR; 30 museums, including the Central State Museum of Kazakhstan, the T. G. Shevchenko Republic Art Gallery, and the M. Auezov Museum in Alma-Ata; memorial museums dedicated to T. G. Shevchenko in Fort-Shevchenko, to V. V. Kuibyshev in Kokchetav, to Abai Kunanbaev in Semipalatinsk, to F. M. Dostoevsky in Semipalatinsk, and to V. I. Chapaev in the settlement of Chapaevo; and museums of local lore in oblast centers; 7,288 club institutions (see also below: Music, Theater, and Motion pictures); and extracurricular institutions—250 Palaces and Houses of Pioneers, 39 young engineers' stations, 24 young naturalists' stations, and 301 sports schools for children and young people.

REFERENCES
Tazhibaev, T. Prosveshchenie i shkoly Kazakhstana vo vtoroi polovine XIX v. Alma-Ata, 1962.
Berzhanov, K. B. Russko-kazakhskoe sodruzhestvo v razvitii prosveshcheniia. [Alma-Ata, 1965.]
Sembaev, A. Istoriia razvitiia sovetskoi shkoly v Kazakhstane. Alma-Ata, 1962.
R. D. ESENZHOLOVA

Amateur arts. Amateur arts activity in Kazakhstan began during the Civil War (1918–20), when amateur theater circles were organized in schools, clubs, and units of the Red Army. In early 1972 there were about 44,000 amateur arts groups, including more than 9,000 choral groups, more than 6,000 musical groups, more than 5,000 dance groups, about 4,000 drama groups, and 38 circus groups; there were about 2,000 propaganda brigades. There are 226 people's amateur groups. Participants in amateur-arts activities total 792,500.

Science and scientific institutions

Natural and technical sciences. Kazakhstan was the homeland of the talented scientist al-Farabi, the founder of a progressive scientific school and the author of important works on astronomy, physics, mathematics, chemistry, medicine, and music theory. As early as the 17th century, Kazakhstan attracted the attention of Peter I, who sent a number of expeditions there to study the territory and the mineral resources of the region. The *Weltanschauung* of the first Kazakh enlighteners and scholars, Ch. Valikhanov, I. Altynsarin, and Abai Kunanbaev, formed in the second half of the 19th century under the influence of Russian culture.

The broadening of Kazakhstan's economic, political, and cultural ties with Russia aroused interest in this vast region, which had very great natural resources. From the 18th through the early 20th century the expeditions led by P. P. Semenov-Tian-Shanskii, G. N. Potanin, P. I. Rychkov, P. S. Pallas, G. S. Karelin, I. V. Mushketov, and L. S. Berg worked in Kazakhstan. With the exception of a few weather stations and experimental fields, there were no scientific institutions in prerevolutionary Kazakhstan. The Russian Geographical Society had divisions in Semipalatinsk and Vernyi.

DEVELOPMENT AFTER THE OCTOBER REVOLUTION (UNTIL 1946). The victory of the October Revolution opened up extensive opportunities for the development of science and culture in Kazakhstan. The Society for the Study of Kazakhstan, the Physico-medical Society, and the Scientific Pedagogical Society were founded. M. O. Auezov, Zh. Shanin, and the brothers N. N. and A. N. Belosliudov, students of local lore, worked in the Semipalatinsk Division of the Russian Geographical Society (1924), publishing works on the soils, fodder resources, and climate of the Semirech'e, the economy of the Altai, and the pastures of northern Kazakhstan. The Regional Plant Protection Station (1921), a public-health and bacteriology institute (1925), the Institute of Veterinary Science (1925), and a research institute for fertilizers and agricultural soil science (1926) were established.

By 1930 there were five research institutes, 24 experimental stations, and 97 hydrometeorological stations. The Institute of Livestock Raising (1933), the Vil'iams Institute of Agriculture (1934), and medical research institutes were organized later. In 1932 the Kazakhstan Base of the Academy of Sciences of the USSR was established. It undertook research in zoology, botany, and geology and trained national scientists. In 1938 the base was reorganized as the Kazakhstan Branch of the Academy of Sciences of the USSR, which was enlarged in 1939 with sections for soil science and geography and, in 1941, with the Institute of Geological Science. In 1940 there were about 100 scientific workers at the branch, including three doctors of sciences and 14 candidates of sciences.

A great deal of scientific research in Kazakhstan during the 1930's was aimed at the development of the republic's economy. A. A. Gapeev proved the great industrial value of the coals of the Karaganda Basin. M. P. Rusakov discovered the Kounradskii copper deposits. The first geological map of eastern Kazakhstan was compiled in 1939 under the direction of N. G. Kassin.

During the Great Patriotic War the scale of scientific research in Kazakhstan expanded. The intensification of work on problems pertaining to the defense and economy of Kazakhstan was aided by the most prominent Soviet scientists, among them V. L. Komarov, I. P. Bardin, A. A. Baikov, V. A. Obruchev, A. A. Skochinskii, D. N. Prianishnikov, and N. V. Tsitsin. Particular attention was devoted to the prospecting and mining of minerals, the development of the technology of dressing ores and smelting metals, the production of refractory materials and building materials, and problems of the chemical industry, irrigated agriculture and water supply, power engineering, soil science, botany, and livestock raising. A great deal of work on the natural conditions and resources of Kazakhstan was performed by the Institute of Geography of the Academy of Sciences of the USSR under the direction of Academician A. A. Grigor'ev.

The number of research institutions of the Kazakhstan Branch of the Academy of Sciences of the USSR expanded substantially. Institutes of soil science and botany (1943), power engineering and zoology (both in 1944), physiology, regional pathology, and clinical and experimental surgery (all in 1944–45), and chemical science and mining (both in 1945) were organized, and new sectors of mathematics and mechanics were established.

THE POSTWAR PERIOD. The Academy of Sciences of the Kazakh SSR, the single directing center for science in the republic, was opened in 1946. Its first president was the founder of the Kazakhstan school of geologists, K. I. Satpaev. During the immediate postwar years a leading role was played by research in geology, mining, and nonferrous metallurgy. Important work was done in the mid-1950's on the development of the virgin and unused lands of Kazakhstan, particularly the complex of geographic research work directed by Academician I. P. Gerasimov. During the 1950's and 1960's, research expanded in many new directions—nuclear physics, mathematics and mechanics, organic catalysis and electrochemistry, and high-energy physics.

Mathematics and mechanics. The main trends in mathematics and mechanics are differential and integral equations, functional analysis and the theory of functions, computer mathematics, and the mechanics of deformable solids. Research is conducted at the Institute of Mathematics and Mechanics of the Academy of Sciences of the Kazakh SSR and in departments of mathematics in higher educational institutions. Results of the greatest importance have been achieved in problems of the theory of stability, the theory of systems of calculation for differential equations, the solution of heat transfer equations, the development of the theory of rock creep, and the mathematical simulation of the origin and formation over time of folded structures in the earth's crust. Successes in mathematics and mechanics have been associated with the work of T. I. Amanov, O. A. Zhautykov, E. I. Kim, Zh. S. Erzhanov, K. P. Persidskii, A. D. Taimanov, and B. M. Urazbaev.

Physics and astronomy. The main trends in physics research are physics of the atomic nucleus and cosmic rays, applied nuclear physics, radiation physics, solid-state physics and physics of semiconductors, physics of metals, electronics, and automation. Research is conducted primarily at the Institute of Nuclear Physics, the Institute of High-energy Physics of the Academy of Sciences of the Kazakh SSR, and departments of physics in institutions of higher education. The VVR-K hot-cell reactor, a radiation chemistry unit, a cryogenic section, and the U-150-2K cyclotron have been put into service. Surface mass spectrometers and beta spectrometers with dual focusing of the electron beam have been developed.

In high-energy physics the nature of the angular and momentum distribution of particles generated by cosmic rays with an energy of more than 5×10^{11} electron volts has been studied. In solid-state physics the electron spectrum of Group II transitional metals has been studied in connection with problems of heat resistance and electrical conductivity. In metal physics anomalies of the properties of metals are studied. Attempts to produce oxygen-free copper have been successful. Great contributions to the development of physics research have been made by L. A. Vulis, V. M. Kel'man, M. I. Korsunskii, G. D. Latyshev, L. M. Nemenov, Zh. S. Takibaev, and V. V. Cherdyntsev.

The main research trends in astronomy are atmospheric optics, physics of the sun and bodies of the solar system, the physics of the interstellar medium, cosmogony, and cosmology. Work is conducted at the Institute of Astrophysics of the Academy of Sciences of the Kazakh SSR, which was founded by Academician V. G. Fesenkov. A great deal of work in astrobotany has been performed by G. A. Tikhov, a corresponding member of the Academy of Sciences of the Kazakh SSR.

Power engineering. Problems of power engineering are treated at the Kazakh Scientific Research Institute of Power Engineering (KazNIIE) and the Institute for the Mechanization and Electrification of Agriculture, in subdepartments of higher educational institutions, and in design institutes. KazNIIE has compiled general fuel, water-power, and wind-power cadastres for Kazakhstan. Work has been conducted on the optimization of the fuel-energy balance, the development of electric power and water-management systems, and the theory of regulation of river discharge during its integrated use. Preliminary planning studies of the route of the Irtysh-Karaganda canal and the Ili River have been conducted. Cyclone power engineering processes have been developed. The works of T. I. Baturov, R. Zh. Zhulaev, V. P. Zakharov, A. B. Rezniakov, Sh. Ch. Chokin, and V. V. Favorskii in power engineering in Kazakhstan are well known.

Geography. The main trends in geography are physical geography (glaciology, climatology, hydrology, limnology, and the study of floodwater erosion phenomena) and economic geography. Research is concentrated in the Geography Sector of the Academy of Sciences of the Kazakh SSR, the Kazakh Scientific Research Institute of Hydrometeorology (KazNIGMI), and the S. M. Kirov Kazakh University. A geomorphological map of the mountain regions of southeastern Kazakhstan with basic explanatory notes has been compiled, and basic data on the physical and economic geography of Kazakhstan have been summarized. The cycle and balance of the mass of glaciers have been studied, and the glaciers of high-altitude regions of Kazakhstan have been cataloged. Floodwater erosion on denuded hills and the danger of avalanches in the mountains of Kazakhstan are under study. A comprehensive picture of the climate, atmospheric circulation, and synoptic processes over Kazakhstan has been given. Comprehensive atlases of a number of regions have been published, among them Tselinnyi Krai (1964) and Karaganda Oblast (1969).

Great contributions to the development of geographical science in Kazakhstan have been made by G. A. Avsiuk, K. B. Akhmedova, N. N. Baranskii, I. P. Gerasimov, E. N. Gladysheva, M. A. Glazovskaia, A. A. Grigor'ev, K. G. Makarevich, O. R. Nazarevskii, N. N. Pal'gov, M. I. Semenova, G. A. Tokmagambetov, A. S. Uteshev, and P. A. Cherkasov.

Geology and hydrogeology. The main research trends in geology and hydrogeology are regional geology, stratigraphy, magmatism, paleontology, geophysics, geomorphology, Quaternary geology, hydrogeology, and the geology of metallic and nonmetallic minerals, coal, oil, and gas. Research is concentrated in the K. I. Satpaev Institute of Geology, the Kazakh Institute of Mineral Raw Materials, the Institute of Geology and Geophysics (in the city of Gur'ev), the Kazakh Branch of the All-Union Institute of Geophysical Prospecting, and the territorial departments of the Ministry of Geology of the Kazakh SSR.

The main results of the regional study of Kazakhstan have been reflected in small- and medium-scale geological and mineral maps. Standardized stratigraphic charts based on paleontological research and determinations of the absolute age of rocks have been developed for all regions of the republic. Comprehensive geological-metallogenic research has been conducted in the Bol'shoi Dzhezkazgan, the Rudnyi Altai, the Mugodzhars, the Karatau, and the Turgai downwarp and at many deposits of ferrous, nonferrous, precious, and rare metals, oil, coal, and other mineral raw materials. A great deal of work has been done on the comprehensive study of phosphorites, potassium borates, bauxites, vermiculite, asbestos, and by-products of mining enterprises for use in various branches of the economy. Important research has been conducted on magmatism, mineralogy, geochemistry, lithology, and the theory of ore formation.

Seismic soundings have been made along the Balkhash-Temirtau-Petropavlovsk profile, in the Dzhezkazgan-Sarysui basin, and in the Mugodzhars. Work on the perfection of geochemical and geophysical methods, the creation of new geophysical apparatus and technical means of mineral prospecting, and the introduction of research results in production is expanding. The services of geologists have been marked by the Lenin Prize on several occasions—for metallogenic and forecasting research on minerals and for the discovery of the Tishinsk deposits in the Rudnyi Altai (1963) and petroleum deposits on the Mangyshlak Peninsula (1966).

Research on hydrogeology is concentrated in the Institute of Hydrogeology and Hydrophysics of the Academy of Sciences of the Kazakh SSR, which works in cooperation with production organizations. Work has been done on the groundwaters of Kazakhstan and their hydrodynamics, chemical hydrology, regime, resources, patterns of formation, and practical use. A forecasting map of artesian basins, hydrogeological and chemical-hydrological maps of Kazakhstan, and maps of the groundwaters of pasture areas have been compiled. The total regional resources of rivers and thermal and mineral waters of Kazakhstan and the possibilities for their use have been determined. The distribution of heat and heat sources in the upper part of the earth's crust have been studied.

The development of geology in Kazakhstan is associated with I. Ia. Avrov, Zh. A. Aitaliev, U. M. Akhmedsafin, V. F. Bezrukov, A. A. Bogdanov, I. I. Bok, R. A. Borukaev, N. L. Bublichenko, Sh. E. Esenov, D. N. Kazanli, G. L. Kushev, G. Ts. Medoev, V. P. Nekhoroshev, M. P. Rusakov, K. I. Satpaev, N. S. Shatskii, G. N. Shcherba, and E. D. Shlygin.

Mining. The main trends in mining are efficient methods of opencut and underground exploitation of ore deposits, the scientific principles of mechanization and automation of underground workings, the laws of displacement of rocks and rock pressure, new methods of crushing rock, and the development of methods of improving mine atmosphere. Research is concentrated in the Institute of Mining of the Academy of Sciences of the Kazakh SSR, special higher educational institutions, VNIITsvetmet (the All-Union Scientific Research Institute of Nonferrous Metallurgy, in Ust'-Kamenogorsk), the Karaganda Scientific Research Coal Institute, and Giprouglegormash (in Karaganda). Research is aimed at increasing the miners' productivity, decreasing losses and impoverishment of ore, and improving the safety of mine workings. A system of forced block caving (Lenin Prize, 1961), new technology for underground mining of ore with self-propelled equipment, and new drills with independent bit rotation have been put into use; a number of studies on gob flushing, ventilation of mine workings, and optimization of production processes have been made. The work of O. A. Baikonurov, V. G. Bereza, A. V. Brichkin, V. V. Gurba, D. A. Kunaev, I. Z. Lysenko, N. V. Mel'nikov, A. Ch. Musin, A. S. Popov, and A. S. Saginov in mining is significant.

Chemistry. The main research trends in chemistry are the chemistry of inorganic fertilizers, macromolecular compounds, and natural physiologically active compounds; organic catalysis; methods of producing pure and ultrapure metals; petrochemistry; and the technology of processing natural salts. Research is concentrated at the institutes of chemistry of the Academy of Sciences of the Kazakh SSR, at universities, and in subdepartments of higher educational institutions. The technology of producing concentrated and composite inorganic fertilizers from the phosphorites of the Karatau has been developed. A method of polymerization of methyl metacrylate has been introduced. Electrochemical methods of studying powder catalysts are developing; in electrochemistry the fundamentals of the theory and technology of precipitating high-purity metals from solutions by means of amalgams have been established. A number of new heat-resistant, ion-exchange, and oxidation-reduction polymers and membranes have been synthesized and electrodialysis distilling units made on the basis of them. New monomers and physiologically active substances have been produced. In the various branches of chemistry, the research of I. N. Azerbaev, A. B. Bekturov, B. A. Beremzhanov, M. I. Goriaev, B. A. Zhubanov, M. T. Kozlovskii, S. R. Rafikov, D. V. Sokol'skii, and M. I. Usanovich is well known.

Metallurgy. The basic trends in metallurgy are the physicochemical bases of the production of nonferrous and rare metals, the development of processes and technological plans of production of nonferrous and rare metals, intensification of the processes of extracting nonferrous and rare metals from raw ore, and the comprehensive processing and dressing of ores of nonferrous and rare metals.

Research is conducted at the Institute of Metallurgy and Beneficiation and the Chemical and Metallurgical Institute of the Academy of Sciences of the Kazakh SSR, the V. I. Lenin Kazakh Polytechnic Institute, Kazmekhanobr, VNIITsvetmet, and the Kazakh Institute of Mineral Raw Materials. New technology for the joint extraction of elementary phosphorus and vanadium-containing intermediate material and a method of processing compounds of complex-metal raw material have been proposed. Ultrasonic methods are used to intensify the dressing of ores in extracting metal powders. Research in vacuum metallurgy is developing successfully. High-temperature refractory materials have been produced. An autoclave method of produc-

ing selenium and tellurium from electrolytic cooper sludges and the technology for smelting the complex AMS alloy, a reducing agent for steel, have been developed. New technology for processing high-silicon bauxites and a method of using natural gas and oxygen in the production of lead are being introduced. Methods are being developed for the comprehensive use of complex-metal ores, with the extraction of rare and trace elements.

Important contributions to the development of metallurgy in Kazakhstan have been made by Kh. K. Avetisian, E. A. Buketov, V. K. Gruzinov, A. M. Kunaev, V. V. Mikhailov, V. D. Ponomarev, M. A. Sokolov, V. V. Stender, and A. L. Tseft.

Soil science. The main topics of study in soil science research are soil formation in Kazakhstan, zonation, estimation of land resources and their use, classification of agrochemical and reclamation characteristics of the soils, erosion, and means of improving fertility. Research is concentrated in the Institute of Soil Science of the Academy of Sciences of the Kazakh SSR, the Kazakh Agricultural Institute, the All-Union Scientific Research Institute of Grain Farming, the V. R. Vil'iams Kazakh Institute of Agriculture, and experimental stations of the Ministry of Agriculture of the Kazakh SSR. The basic laws of the formation and spread of different soils have been determined and their composition studied; medium-scale soil maps have been compiled for all regions of the republic. Large tracts of land suitable for irrigation have been discovered on the lower course of the Syr Darya, Ili, Talas, and Chu rivers. Soil erosion maps have been compiled, and areas subject to wind erosion have been determined. A method has been proposed for reclaiming meadow-steppe solonetzes with gypsum layers close to the surface. The agrochemical characteristics of the soils most suitable for development have been determined. Great contributions to the progress of soil science in Kazakhstan have been made by A. I. Baraev, A. I. Bessonov, V. M. Borovskii, I. P. Gerasimov, P. G. Grabarov, S. P. Matusevich, A. A. Sokolov, and U. U. Uspanov.

Botany. The main trends of research in botany are the study and use of the plant resources of Kazakhstan, the biological principles of increasing the productivity of pastures and hayfields, the physiological and biochemical principles of increasing the productivity of agricultural crops, and the genetic principles of controlling heredity and mutation to create productive plant forms. Research is concentrated in the Institute of Botany of the Academy of Sciences of the Kazakh SSR, V. R. Vil'iams Kazakh Institute of Agriculture, the All-Union Scientific Research Institute of Grain Farming, the Institute of Plant Conservation, the Institute of Fruit Growing and Viticulture, and experimental stations of the Ministry of Agriculture of the Kazakh SSR.

The nine-volume *Flora of Kazakhstan* (1956–66) and the first seven volumes of *Flora of the Sporophytes of Kazakhstan* (1956–71) have been published. The biology and ecology of many fodder plants and the dynamics of their productivity have been studied; the feed balance of the desert regions of Kazakhstan has been precisely determined. The efficient cycles of mineral nourishment of many plants have been determined. A number of new interspecies and intergenus hybrids of spring wheat have been produced, and a set of wheat mutants, has been created to use as stock material for breeding. High-yield strains of corn (AN-3 and AN-4) have been produced. The Central Botanical Garden in Alma-Ata and its divisions in Karaganda, Dzhezkazgan, Leninogorsk, and Bakanas are working steadily on the introduction and acclimatization of plants and on the planting of trees in new cities and industrial centers.

Great contributions to the study of the plant resources of the republic have been made by B. A. Bykov, D. A. Zykov, N. V. Pavlov, and S. R. Shvartsman. G. Z. Biiashev, A. M. Gabbasov, T. B. Darkanbaev, L. K. Klyshev, V. P. Kuz'min, and N. L. Udol'skaia have devoted a great deal of effort to research in physiology, biology, and genetics.

Zoology. The main trends in zoology are the biological principles of development of animal life in Kazakhstan, the determination of animal resources and the scientific principles of their preservation, reproduction, and use, and the exploration of the biological principles for combating human and animal diseases, both parasitic and with natural foci, and against plant parasites. Research is concentrated in the Institute of Zoology of the

Academy of Sciences of the Kazakh SSR, the university, the Scientific Research Institute of Veterinary Science of Kazakhstan, the Middle Asian Antiplague Scientific Research Institute, the Institute of Plant Conservation, the Scientific Research Institute of Fishing in Kazakhstan, and higher educational institutions.

The geographical distribution, biology, and population of many useful species of animals and birds in Kazakhstan have been studied. Many species of game animals have been saved from extermination—for example, the saiga antelope, whose population attained commercial significance by 1972. Many economically valuable animals, such as the muskrat, have been acclimatized. A number of works concerned with certain parasites (protozoa, helminths, and arthropods) that produce human and animal diseases have been completed; the incidence of natural breeding grounds of a number of diseases of farm animals and various insect pests are being studied, and measures for controlling them are under development. Credit for the evolution of zoological science in Kazakhstan belongs to K. I. Skriabin, S. N. Boev, I. G. Galuzo, E. V. Gvozdev, I. A. Dolgushin, B. A. Dombrovskii, E. N. Pavlovskii, and A. A. Sludskii.

Experimental biology. The main trend in experimental biology is the study of the law of heredity and individual development of farm animals. Research is concentrated in the Institute of Experimental Biology of the Academy of Sciences of the Kazakh SSR, the Kazakhstan Institute of Livestock Raising, the Kazakhstan Scientific Research Institute of Veterinary Science, the Institute of Karakul Raising, and the K. Mynbaev Betpak-Dala Specialized Sheep Raising Station. Highly productive varieties of cattle and Merino sheep have been bred. The republic has become one of the country's main suppliers of karakul. A new highly productive variety of sheep, the Kazakh Arkhar-Merino, has been developed through distant interspecies hybridization. The study of heterosis in intergenus crossbreeding made possible an increase in the productivity of an experimental herd by 10–15 percent. Great contributions to the elaboration of the scientific principles of livestock raising and the breeding of new varieties of farm animals have been made by V. A. Bal'mont, N. S. Butorin, A. E. Elemanov, M. A. Ermekov, P. A. Es'kov, A. I. Zhanderkin, and F. M. Mukhamedgaliev.

Physiology. The main areas of study in physiology are circulation, respiration, and lymph formation; digestion and lactation in farm animals; and the pharmacology of certain medicinal plants of Kazakhstan. Research is concentrated in the Institute of Physiology of the Academy of Sciences of the Kazakh SSR and the subdepartments of physiology of higher educational institutions. A method of treating traumatic shock has been found. New data have been obtained on exteroceptive-interoceptive regulation of arterial and venous pressure, respiration, lymph flow, and blood deposition. The influence of certain trace elements on the activity of the digestive glands has been studied. The development of physiology in Kazakhstan has been associated with the work of N. U. Bazanova and A. P. Polosukhin.

Microbiology and virology. The main trends in microbiology and virology are the study and use of microorganisms and chemical compounds in ensilage of fodder and methods of enriching feeds with biologically valuable substances; the study of microorganisms that produce proteins, antibiotics, enzymes, and other biologically active substances for agricultural production and the food industry; the study of microbiological processes for the purpose of regulating the conversion of inorganic and organic compounds in the soil and water; and the deciphering of the molecular structure of group A viruses and development of measures for combating them. A biochemical method of accelerating the maturing of wines has been proposed and introduced. A method of bacterial leaching of copper from waste ores is being developed. The biosynthesis and breeding of producers of the antibiotic *kormogrizin* whose activity is stable are being optimized. These problems have been studied in the works of P. A. Bulanov, Kh. Zh. Zhumatov, A. N. Ilialetdinov, E. N. Mishustin, and D. L. Shamis.

Medicine. In medicine effective measures for combating malaria, brucellosis, encephalitis, tuberculosis, and trachoma have been developed. The incidence of endemic goiter has been reduced. A great deal of work is under way on occupational diseases in mining and nonferrous metallurgy. The climatic-balneological and mud-bath resorts of Kazakhstan have been studied. Thoracic and endocrine surgery, as well as neurosurgery, are developing successfully. In oncology definite strides have been made in the early diagnosis and treatment of tumors. Work is being conducted in laser therapy. Great contributions to the development of medical science have been made by I. S. Bakal, S. B. Balmukhanov, N. D. Beklemishev, M. I. Briakin, O. S. Glozman, I. K. Karakulov, S. R. Karynbaev, I. S. Koriakin, P. P. Ochkur, R. A. Satpaeva, A. N. Syzganov, G. N. Udintsev, and K. I. Chuvakov.   O. I. ALEKSEEV

Social sciences. TO THE EARLY 20TH CENTURY. Religious ideology, a combination of Islam and shamanism, was dominant in patriarchal-feudal Kazakhstan beginning in the ninth and tenth centuries. The philosophical and historical works of al-Farabi and Mahmud Kashgari, written in Arabic in the ninth to thirteenth century, make valuable observations drawn from the life of the peoples of Kazakhstan. The Mongol-Tatar invasion, which extended to Kazakhstan, halted the development of its culture. In the subsequent era, the epic works of the *akyns* (folk poets and singers) became the main source of information on the history of the Kazakhstan peoples. The exploits of the *batyrs* who defended Kazakhstan against the incursions of the conquerors were exalted in the narrative poems *Koblandy, Er-Targyn,* and *Kambar-batyr.*

During the 18th and early 19th century, great contributions to the history, geography, ethnology, and natural features of Kazakhstan were made by the Russian scholars P. S. Pallas, I. P. Fal'k, I. Georgi, I. K. Kirillov, P. I. Rychkov, A. I. Levshin, and N. Ia. Bichurin.

The unification of Kazakhstan with Russia, which was completed in the 1860's, was a crucial point in the development of social thought. The career of the first Kazakh scholar and proponent of enlightenment, Ch. Valikhanov, a writer and traveler who wrote a number of works on the history and ethnography of the Kazakhs, Kirghiz, and Uighurs, dates to that time. The Kazakh proponents of enlightenment I. Altynsarin and Abai Kunanbaev also studied the history and ethnography of Kazakhstan. They spoke out against the lack of rights and the oppression of the masses and for the elimination of Kazakhstan's backwardness, called for the development of friendship among peoples, and criticized the colonialist policies of tsarism. In substantiating their views, they relied not on religious dogma but on human reason and scientific data; they regarded knowledge as a reflection of the objective world. Problems of the socioeconomic development of Kazakh society—the conditions of nomadic livestock raising, the value of a settled way of life and farming for nomadic peoples, and the role of industry, trade, money, and education—attracted the interest of democratic Kazakh proponents of enlightenment.

In the second half of the 19th century, L. Meier, M. Krasovskii, and M. I. Veniukov studied the history of Kazakhstan, and V. V. Radlov, G. N. Potanin, A. E. Alektorov, A. N. Krasnov, and A. M. Nikol'skii dealt with its ethnology. Problems of the history and ethnology of Kazakhstan were also studied by O. Seidalin, B. Daulbaev, M. Tiaukin, and M. Babadzhanov. However, primarily historical material was collected in Kazakhstan during the prerevolutionary period. In the late 19th century, museums of history and natural science opened in Vernyi (now Alma-Ata), Semipalatinsk, and Orenburg. A. E. Alektorov and A. N. Sedel'nikov published the first bibliographies of Kazakhstan. At the turn of the 20th century, Academician V. V. Bartol'd made an important contribution to the study of the history of Kazakhstan. Archaeological investigations were begun on the territory of Kazakhstan by P. I. Lerkh and M. N. Iadrinskii.

The Revolution of 1905–07 in Russia produced an upsurge in the liberation movement. The exacerbation of social contradictions resulted in the formation of various ideological currents in Kazakh philosophical and social thought. Exponents of the religious and mystical current preached Islam (Shakarim and M.-Zh. Kopeev), although some of them (Kopeev and Aubakir) pointed out the usefulness of secular education. The interests and aspirations of the toiling masses were expressed in the work of representatives of the Kazakh democratic intelligentsia (the poet S. Toraigyrov, the satirist S. Donentaev, and the writer and pedagogue S. Kubeev). Carrying on the traditions of the enlighteners, they spoke out in opposition to the lack of rights of the masses and the tyranny of the authorities and sharply condemned the activity of the Muslim clergy.

Marxist literature spread in the early 20th century. The Bolshevik newspapers *Iskra, Zvezda,* and *Pravda* penetrated the region. In the city of Vernyi and elsewhere, illegal libraries were established that contained the classic works of Marxism-Leninism (Marx' ' *Wage Labor and Capital,* Engels' *The Development of Socialism From Utopia to Science,* and a number of works by V. I. Lenin). Local groups and organizations of the RSDLP published and distributed revolutionary leaflets.

THE SOCIAL SCIENCES IN SOVIET KAZAKHSTAN. The establishment of Soviet power initiated the national renaissance of the Kazakh people and the blossoming of its culture.

Philosophy. The prerequisites for the establishment of Marxist-Leninist philosophy and the advancement of professional philosophers were created in Kazakhstan after the October Revolution as a result of fundamental socioeconomic transformations. During the 1920's and 1930's, an ideological struggle over the question of the construction of socialism took place in Kazakhstan; the concept of the alleged innate incapacity of the Kazakhs for cultural creativity and the theory of the "common stream" were subjected to criticism, and evaluations of the social structure of prerevolutionary Kazakh society and the attitude toward the legacy of the past were reconsidered. During this period, the struggle against local nationalism and great power chauvinism was also a focus of attention. The interpretation of the patterns of the liberation movement of the Kazakh people refuted the views of the "external" relationship of the October Revolution to the history of Kazakhstan (S. Asfendiiarov and I. Iu. Kabulov). Z. A. Poriadin, A. Lekerov, and M. Tulepov wrote theoretical articles and treated questions of the development of socialism in Kazakhstan and problems of national culture from Marxist perspectives. The Kazakhstan Scientific Research Institute of Marxism-Leninism was founded in 1931 (in 1940 it was made into the Institute of Party History under the Central Committee of the Communist Party of Kazakhstan), with a philosophy sector. The translation into Kazakh of selected works of V. I. Lenin (six volumes, 1938–41) and the establishment of the department of philosophy of Kazakh State University (1949) and the Institute of Philosophy and Law of the Academy of Sciences of the Kazakh SSR (1958) were of great importance.

A major trend in the work of the philosophers of Kazakhstan is the study of the complex of questions associated with the transition to socialism, bypassing capitalism; the transformation of relationships of production; the cultural revolution; the formation of a new consciousness; and the development of language (B. A. Amantaev, N. Dzhandil'din, D. K. Kshibekov, N. Sarsenbaev, and T. S. Sarsenbaev). The laws of development of the bourgeois state under imperialism and the paths of its revolutionary transformation are being studied (L. M. Slavin). In dialectical materialism and the philosophical questions of natural science, work is being done on the problems of the theory of dialectics of the Leninist stage in the perspective of historical and logical unity (A. Kh. Kasymzhanov) and methodological problems of the individual sciences (Zh. Abdil'din, M. N. Chechin, N. A. Musabaeva, and K. Kh. Rakhmatullin). The history of social and philosophical thought in Kazakhstan is being studied (K. Beisembiev); research is being conducted on the cultural heritage of Kazakhstan, particularly al-Farabi's works; problems of overcoming vestiges of religion in national relations are analyzed in the works of M. S. Fazylov; and Muslim ideology is criticized in the works of Kh. Aknazarov and others.

A. KH. KASYMZHANOV

History. A crucial role in the formation and development of Kazakh historiography was played by the works of V. I. Lenin, his theoretical legacy, and party documents. Since there were no Marxist-educated history specialists during the first years of Soviet power in Kazakhstan, the history of Kazakhstan was initially studied by the party and state figures of the republic. The Society for the Study of Kazakhstan (the first chairman was the historian A. P. Chuloshnikov) and the Istparts (commissions on party history) of the Kazakhstan Regional Committee and prov-

ince committees of the party did a great deal for the study of the history and ethnography. Glavarkhiv (the Main Archive), which initiated the gathering, processing, and use of documentary historical material, was established in 1921.

Questions of the history of Kazakhstan were studied by scholars in Moscow, Leningrad, Tashkent, Omsk, and Orenburg (V. V. Bartol'd, A. Iu. Iakubovskii, A. K. Samoilovich, and M. E. Masson). Archaeological and ethnological expeditions of the Academy of Sciences of the USSR and of the Geographic Society were active during the 1920's, and specimens of the people's art were collected (A. A. Divaev, A. V. Zataevich, Zh. Shanin, and S. I. Rudenko). Works of Marx, Engels, and Lenin, as well as party documents, were translated into Kazakh. Erroneous concepts and views—that the social structure of the Kazakhs was classless and purely clan-based, that the triumph of the socialist revolution there was accidental and exceptional, that the extensive nomadic livestock-raising economy existed from time immemorial, and that geography had a determining influence on the history of the Kazakhs—were overcome. The first efforts were made to create generalizing works on the history of Kazakhstan, the history of the Communist Party of Kazakhstan, and the history of the national liberation movement. The training of historians expanded. Important services to science were rendered by the first Kazakh professor of history, S. D. Asfendiiarov, and by T. Ryskulov, G. Togzhanov, U. Dzhandosov, I. Kabulov, A. F. Riazanov, E. I. Fedorov, and N. T. Timofeev. Memoir literature was written by S. Seifullin.

The Kazakh Scientific Research Institute of National Culture was set up in 1934. In 1936 its sector of history and archaeology became a cell of the sector of history of the Kazakhstan Base and, in 1938, of the Kazakhstan Branch of the Academy of Sciences of the USSR. The department of history of S. M. Kirov Kazakh University was opened in 1945, and departments of history in higher educational institutions of pedagogy followed. At the same time, the Institute of History, Archaeology, and Ethnology was established under the auspices of the Academy of Sciences of the Kazakh SSR. The first generalizing work, *History of the Kazakh SSR (From Earliest Times to the Present),* was prepared and published in 1943 during the Patriotic War with the participation of A. M. Pankratova, N. M. Druzhinin, M. P. Viatkin, and S. V. Bakhrushin. Although the book had erroneous propositions concerning various problems of prerevolutionary Kazakhstan, it remained a landmark in Kazakh historiography.

During the postwar years, the problems studied by historians and their source materials expanded. Archaeological and ethnographic study of Kazakhstan proceeded according to a scheme of reconnaissance. The *History of the Kazakh SSR* was published in two volumes (2nd ed., 1949). Interest in the history of Soviet Kazakhstan grew noticeably. The socioeconomic preconditions of the October Revolution were studied; scientific substantiation was produced for the proposition that the victory of the revolution in Kazakhstan conformed with natural laws and was an integral part of the revolutionary process throughout the country and that the Kazakhs, like the toiling masses of other nationalities, participated in the struggle for Soviet power. Research was done by S. N. Pokrovskii on the history of military operations on the Kazakh fronts—(Aktiubinsk, Semirech'e, and Ural)—during the Civil War. Works were written on the formation and development of the Kazakh Soviet state system, the formation of centers of socialist industry (Turksib), and the preparation for and implementation of collectivization of agriculture in various regions of Kazakhstan. Work was done on problems of the periodization of Kazakh history. Important contributions have been made to the study of the national liberation movement, such as the movement of the Kazakhs of the Little Horde in 1783–97 under the leadership of Srym Datov (the works of M. P. Viatkin) and the uprising of 1836–37 in the Bukei Khanate headed by Isatai Taimanov and Makhambet Utemisov (the works of V. F. Shakhmatov). Ethnographers such as N. Sabitov continued to accumulate and study data on the material culture, life, and applied arts of the Kazakhs.

Beginning in the late 1940's, archaeological expeditions covered nearly all of Kazakhstan; there were excavations of the remains of the Usun and Kangly and the Western Turkic Kaganate in southern Kazakhstan and of the cultures of the Bronze Age and early nomads in eastern and central Kazakhstan (A. Kh. Margulan, A. N. Bernshtam, and S. S. Chernikov). The Khorezm archaeological-ethnological expedition of the Academy of Sciences of the USSR (S. P. Tolstov) revealed the complexes of the *gorodishcha* (sites of fortified towns) of Dzhety-Asar and Altyn-Asar. The cardinal question of the correlation and interrelation of nomadic and settled cultures was dealt with in new archaeological material.

As of the mid-1950's, the range of research in Kazakh historiography embraced all periods of history, from the Paleolithic to the present, with the problems of the history of Soviet Kazakhstan occupying the leading place. The third edition of the *History of the Kazakh SSR* (2 vols.) was published from 1957 to 1959. It introduced a great deal of new material on the fundamental problems of the history of Kazakhstan (the second volume, devoted to the era of socialism, was reprinted in 1963 and 1967). *Studies in the History of the Communist Party of Kazakhstan* (1963) was a significant contribution to Kazakh historiography. The translation into Kazakh and publication of the works of Lenin (4th ed.) was completed; many documents testifying to Lenin's concern for the Kazakh people were brought to light, and the collection *V. I. Lenin on Middle Asia and Kazakhstan* (1960) and S. Beisembaev's monograph *Lenin and Kazakhstan* (1968) were published.

The problems of socialist and communist construction in Kazakhstan and the history of the Communist Party of Kazakhstan were reflected in the works of A. N. Nusupbekov, S. N. Pokrovskii, P. M. Pakhmurnyi, A. B. Tursunbaev, M. Kozybaev, A. Akhmetov, Zh. Zhumabekov, A. Erzhanov, T. Eleuov, and A. S. Elagin. A monograph on the history of the Communist organizations of Middle Asia and Kazakhstan was written in cooperation with the scholarly institutions of other republics. The publication of documentary materials on the history of Kazakhstan expanded sharply. Collections of documents on subjects from the early 16th century to the Great Patriotic War were published.

The problem of the transition of the Kazakh people to socialism, bypassing capitalism, and the forms and methods of socialist construction in Kazakhstan have been studied by S. Baishev, D. Kshibekov, and M. Suzhikov. The formation and development of the Soviet working class in Kazakhstan—in particular, its national cadres—during the prewar period has been analyzed by A. Nusupbekov. The history of Soviet construction in the *aul* during the transition to socialism, the history of the construction of the national state, and the resolution of the national question in Kazakhstan have been investigated by S. Zimanov, A. Erenov, S. Kenzhebaev, and N. Kiikbaev. A. Kanapin, R. Suleimenov, and K. Berzhanov showed the achievements in the construction and development of the Kazakh people's culture. The study of the history of Kazakhstan during the Great Patriotic War is expanding (A. Nusupbekov, G. Abishev, M. Kozybaev, and T. Balakaev), and work is being done on the problems of the development of agriculture and of sovkhoz-kolkhoz construction during the postwar years.

The discovery and translation (with commentaries) of Eastern sources on the history of ancient and medieval Kazakhstan have expanded considerably. The study of the problem of the ethnogenesis of the Kazakh nationality is continuing. Questions concerning the unification of the Kazakh lands with Russia and the changes in the socioeconomic system of Kazakh society during the 18th and 19th centuries have been studied in monographs (E. B. Bekmakhanov, N. G. Apollova, and S. E. Tolybekov). The paths of dissemination of Russian capitalism "in breadth" and of decay of patriarchal-feudal relations in the *aul,* the history of migration, the development of the workers' and agrarian movements in the second half of the 19th and the early 20th centuries, and the history of the national liberation uprising of 1916 and the bourgeois democratic February Revolution have been elucidated (B. Suleimenov and P. G. Galuzo).

Selected works of the Kazakh enlightener I. Altynsarin and the five-volume collected works of the first Kazakh scholar, Ch. Valikhanov, have been published. A. Kh. Margulan, B. Suleimenov, T. Tazhibaev, and K. Beisembiev have published studies of the life and career of Kazakh enlighteners and

of the history of ideological currents in social thought and education in Kazakhstan. Texts of al-Farabi have been published with commentaries (A. Kasymzhanov). A complete ethnological study has been made of Kazakhstan, and the study of the culture and life of the contemporary Kazakh *aul* has developed (V. Vostrov and Kh. Argynbaev).

An archaeological map of Kazakhstan has been compiled. Archaeological finds have been made in southern and eastern Kazakhstan and in the northern Lake Balkhash area. Kazakhstan's place in the formation and spread of Bronze Age culture over the entire USSR has been determined. Excavations of settlements, *gorodishcha,* and "royal" burial mounds of the period of the early nomads and the Sacae and Usun have been completed. *The Ancient Culture of Central Kazakhstan* (1966) and books on the cities of Kazakhstan, including medieval Taraz, have been published. The Issyk Treasure, which contains about 4,000 items of the high professional art of the Sacae, is a unique find. Large permanent excavations in Otrar and the Otrar Oasis have been undertaken (A. Kh. Margulan, K. Akishev, and M. Kadyrbaev).   G. F. Dakhshleiger

Economics. Publication of the first specialized journal of political economy, which dealt with and discussed the most pressing problems of the economy, began in the mid-1920's. In the 1930's, subdepartments of political economy and branch economics were organized at higher educational institutions. The department of economics of the Kazakh University became one of the scientific centers of the republic, and from it was formed the Alma-Ata Institute of the National Economy in 1963. The Institute of the Socialist Reconstruction of Agriculture was founded in 1931 and reorganized in the 1960's as the Institute of Economics and Agricultural Organization of the Ministry of Agriculture of the Kazakh SSR. The Economics Sector of the Academy of Sciences of the Kazakh SSR became the Institute of Economics of the Academy of Sciences of the Kazakh SSR in 1952. In 1962 a research institute of economics was established under Gosplan (the State Planning Commission) of the republic. Research institutions and subdepartments of economics in higher educational institutions have participated in the compilation of economic plans for Kazakhstan and have dealt with topical regional problems of economic development.

The economists of Kazakhstan are conducting theoretical research in political economy, the history of economic thought, the economic zonation and distribution of productive forces, the economics, organization, and planning of the national economy of the republic, labor economics, the effectiveness of capital investments and new technology, profit-and-loss accounting and material incentives, finances and monetary circulation, credit, bookkeeping, and the analysis of economic activity (S. B. Baishev, T. A. Ashimbaev, R. M. Petukhov, T. Shaukenbaev, S. E. Tolybekov, T. T. Tulebaev, and M. K. Iliusizov).

Work on problems of the national economy is coordinated by the Scientific Problem Council of the Academy of Sciences of the USSR on the Economics and Distribution of Socialist Production in Kazakhstan (created in 1962), which consists of leading economics scholars and practical specialists. A branch of the Scientific Problem Council of the Academy of Sciences of the USSR on the Effectiveness of Fixed Capital Stock, Capital Investments, and New Technology was organized in 1969; a branch of the Scientific Council on the Comprehensive Study of the Scientific Foundations of Profit-and-Loss Accounting was formed in 1972. Articles on economic science are published in the journal *National Economy of Kazakhstan* (since 1926; organ of Gosplan of the Kazakh SSR) and in the *Bulletin of the Academy of Sciences of the Kazakh SSR.*

Jurisprudence. The origin of jurisprudence in Kazakhstan coincides with the opening in 1937 of the first higher educational institution of jurisprudence in the republic, the Institute of Soviet Construction in Alma-Ata. The intensive development of jurisprudence began in the 1950's. Considerable attention is devoted to the theory and history of the national Soviet state system, socialist law, and national-state construction in Kazakhstan and the Union republics of Middle Asia. The *History of the State and Law of Soviet Kazakhstan* (3 vols., 1961–65) and the monographs *V. I. Lenin and the Soviet National State System in Kazakhstan* (S. Z. Zimanov, 1970) and *Contradictions in the*

Development of the Legal Superstructure Under Socialism (M. T. Baimakhanov, 1972) have been published.

Kazakhstan is a center for the study of agrarian law. Monographs on this problem include *The Origin and Development of Socialist Legal Land Relations in the Kazakh SSR* (A. Erenov, 1963), *Theoretical Problems of the Legal Regulation of Labor Remuneration in Kolkhozes* (K. A. Shaibekov, 1968), and *The Problem of Responsibility in Kolkhoz Law* (M. S. Sakhipov, 1972). Research in law is conducted at the Institute of Philosophy and Law of the Academy of Sciences of the Kazakh SSR (established in 1958), the Kazakh Institute of Judicial Examination (established in 1957), and the department of law of the Kazakh University (the department was created in 1955 from the Alma-Ata Juridical Institute).

REFERENCES

Istoriia filosofii, vol. 2. Moscow, 1957, pp. 420–22; vol. 4, Moscow, 1959, pp. 259–63.
Ocherki po istorii filosofskoi i obshchestvenno-politicheskoi mysli narodov SSSR, vol. 2. Moscow, 1956. Pages 784–801.
Istoriia filosofii v SSSR, vols. 1–3. Moscow, 1968.
Beisembiev, K. *Iz istorii obshchestvennoi mysli Kazakhstana vtoroi poloviny XIX veka.* Alma-Ata, 1957.
Beisembiev, K. *Ideino-politicheskie techeniia v Kazakhstane kontsa XIX– nachala XX veka.* Alma-Ata, 1961.

Scientific institutions. During the Soviet period, a broad system of scientific institutions has been established in Kazakhstan. In 1972 the republic had more than 200 scientific institutions, including higher educational institutions. About 28,000 scientific workers were employed in the republic, including 109 academicians, members, and corresponding members and 483 doctors and 7,045 candidates of science (in 1940 there were 57 scientific institutions, including higher educational institutions, and more than 1,700 scientific workers).

The leading scientific center of the republic is the Academy of Sciences of the Kazakh SSR, which encompasses 26 scientific institutions. It regularly publishes *Bulletin of the Academy of Sciences of the Kazakh SSR* (in Russian and Kazakh, since 1944) and *Proceedings of the Academy of Sciences of the Kazakh SSR* (geology series, since 1944; physics and mathematics series, since 1947; chemistry series, since 1947; biology series, since 1963; and social sciences series, since 1963).

The Academy of Sciences of the Kazakh SSR is developing and strengthening its creative ties with research institutions in the USSR and abroad. Exchange of information, joint ventures, and the training of highly skilled personnel are conducted in cooperation with the academies of sciences of the republics of Middle Asia (mathematics, physics, geology, and history), the Siberian Division of the Academy of Sciences of the USSR (rock mechanics and mathematics), the Academy of Sciences of the Ukrainian SSR (chemistry and mathematics), and a number of branch institutes. Joint work is conducted with the scientists of Czechoslovakia (helminthology and organic chemistry), Poland (catalysis and high-energy physics), the German Democratic Republic (rock mechanics), and Mongolia (soil science and the chemistry of medicinal plants).

In addition to the Academy of Sciences of the Kazakh SSR, higher educational institutions and branch research institutions are conducting extensive research in the republic in nonferrous metallurgy, mining, geology, construction and building materials, power engineering, hydraulic construction, land reclamation, and agriculture.

O. I. ALEKSEEV

Press, radio, and television

Before the October Revolution of 1917 more than 1,000 Kazakh-language books were published, primarily in St. Petersburg, Kazan, Orenburg, and Semipalatinsk. The development of Kazakh book publishing was greatly influenced by the Revolution of 1905–07. In the early 20th century alone, about 400 democratic and enlightening Kazakh-language books were published. An important role in the formative process of publishing in the republics of Middle Asia was played by V. I. Lenin's letter of June 4, 1920, to Gosizdat (the State Publishing House) and VSNKh (the Supreme Council on the National Economy): "The Kirghiz comrades are asking for help in order to acquire a type foundry, a print-shop, and paper. Will you please receive them and give them every assistance" (*Poln. sobr. soch.,* 5th ed., vol. 51, p. 208). The first State Publishing House of Kazakhstan was established in November 1920, and by 1921 it had produced 20 titles with a total printing of 27,000 copies. In 1972 six republic-wide book publishing houses were operating in Kazakhstan: the Kazakhstan Publishing House (sociopolitical literature), Zhazushi (fiction), Kainar (agricultural literature), Mektep (educational and pedagogical books), and Nauka and Kazakhskaia Sovetskaia Entsiklopediia (scientific books); there were also publishing divisions of various organizations and institutions. In 1971, 2,096 books and pamphlets, with a total printing of more than 25 million copies, were issued by the publishing houses of Kazakhstan.

The progenitor of the Kazakh periodical press was the newspaper *Turkistan ualaiatynyn gazeti* (Newspaper of the Turkestan Region, 1870–82), which was published in Tashkent as a supplement to the official Russian newspaper *Turkestanskie vedomosti* (Turkestan Gazette). It was followed by *Dala ualaiatynyn gazeti* (Newspaper of the Steppe Region, 1888–1902), printed in Omsk, in which the classic works of Kazakh literature of Abai Kunanbaev were first published under the pseudonym of K. Zhamantaev. The Tatar-language Bolshevik newspaper *Oral* (The Urals) was published during the Revolution of 1905–07 from Jan. 4 through Apr. 27, 1907. The proenlightenment newspaper *Kazakhstan* was published in Urda and Ural'sk from 1911 to 1913. The first Kazakh journal, *Aikap* (1911–1915), which was founded by the Kazakh democratic and subsequently Bolshevik poet M. Seralin, had a similar orientation. The Tatar-Kazakh journal *Akmolda* (named for the poet of the late 19th century; published 1911–16) was published in Troitsk. The newspaper *Tirshilik* (Life), the organ of the youth organization Zhas Kazakh (Young Kazakh), came out from September 1917 through July 1918. Eleven newspapers were published in Kazakhstan in 1913.

The press of Soviet Kazakhstan began with the newspapers *Durystyk zholy* (Path of Truth; February 1919, Urda), *Kazakh tili* (Kazakh Word; December 1919, Semipalatinsk), and *Ushkyn* (The Spark; December 1919, Orenburg). Publication of the newspaper *Izvestiia Kirgizskogo kraia* (News of the Kirghiz Region) began on Jan. 1, 1920.

In 1971, 361 newspapers were published, including 15 republic-wide, 34 oblast, 246 raion, 10 city, 55 local, and one kolkhoz, with an annual circulation of about 842 million copies.

The republic-wide newspapers include *Sotsialistik Kazakhstan* (Socialist Kazakhstan, since 1919), *Leninshil zhas* (Leninist Youth, since 1921), *Kazakhstan mugalimi* (Kazakhstan Teacher, since 1952), *Kazakhstan pioneri* (Kazakhstan Pioneer, since 1930), *Kazakh adebieti* (Kazakh Literature, since 1934), and *Sport* (since 1959) in Kazakh and *Kazakhstanskaia pravda* (Kazakhstan Pravda, since 1920), *Leninskaia smena* (Leninist Young Generation; since 1922), *Uchitel' Kazakhstana* (Kazakhstan Teacher, since 1952), *Druzhnye rebiata* (Friendly Children, since 1933), and *Sport* (since 1959) in Russian.

Interrepublic newspapers are published for other nations and nationalities in their native languages: *Kommunizm tugi* (Banner of Communism, since 1957, with an appendix in Arabic script); *Ieni khaiat* (New Life, since 1970) and three raion newspapers in Uighur; *Lenin kichi* (Leninist Banner, since 1968) in Korean; *Freundschaft* (Friendship, since 1966) in German; and two raion newspapers in Uzbek.

In 1971, 159 journals and other periodical publications were issued, including the *Kazakhstan kommunisti* (Communist of Kazakhstan, since 1921), *Zhuldyz* (Star, since 1928), *Zhalyn* (Flame, since 1969), *Kazakhstan aielderi* (Women of Kazakhstan, since 1925), *Madeniet zhane turmys* (Culture and Life, since 1958), *Bilim zhane enbek* (Knowledge and Labor, since 1960), and *Baldyrgan* (Sprout, since 1958) in Kazakh; *Ara* (Bumblebee, since 1956) and *Kazakhstannyn auyl sharuashylygi* (Agriculture of Kazakhstan, since 1951) in Russian and Kazakh; and *Partiinaia zhizn' Kazakhstana* (Party Life of Kazakhstan, since 1930), *Narodnoe khoziaistvo Kazakhstana* (National Economy of Kazakhstan, since 1926), *Avtomobil'nyi transport Kazakhstana* (Motor Vehicle Transportation of Kazakhstan, since 1958), *Prostor* (Vista, since 1935), *Zdravookhranenie Ka-*

zakhstana (Public Health in Kazakhstan, since 1941), and *Kooperator Kazakhstana* (Cooperative Worker of Kazakhstan, since 1958) in Russian. In all, 25 journals, two agitators' periodical pamphlets, 74 issues of scholarly works and transactions, and 58 bulletins were published in 1971; the annual circulation of journals and other periodicals aside from newspapers was 45.5 million copies. The Kazakh Telegraph Agency (KazTAG) has been in operation since 1921.

The first radio broadcasts began in 1923. In 1972 the average daily volume of radio broadcasting on five republic and 17 oblast programs was 64 hours; there were 200 raion and ten city radio editorial offices. The first television broadcasts began in 1958. In 1972, 15 television studios and more than 40 relay stations were in operation; total television broadcasting throughout the republic was 192 hours per day. Republic-wide radio and television broadcast in Kazakh, Russian, Korean, Uighur, German, and Uzbek. Television broadcasts are relayed from Moscow; Alma-Ata, Dzhezkazgan, and Gur'ev receive the program "Orbit." The House of Republic Radio and Television Broadcasting and the Kazakhtelefil'm studio are located in Alma-Ata.

REFERENCES

Bekkhojin, Kh. *Qazaq baspasözïnïng damu zholdarï.* Alma-Ata, 1964.
Jirenshin, Ä. M. *Qazaq kïtaptarï tarikhïnan.* Alma-Ata, 1971.

SH. ELEUKENOV

Literature

Kazakh oral folk poetry, whose roots go far back into antiquity, is rich in songs, tales, proverbs and sayings, heroic and lyric-epic narrative poems, *aitys* (song and poetry folk singing competitions), and lyric poetry (*tolgau,* philosophical meditations, and *arnau,* dedications). The folklore includes more than 40 genres, a considerable number of which are unique to it (petitions and letters in song form). Songs are divided into pastorals, ritual and historical songs, and songs of everyday life. There is a great wealth of tales: Aldar-Kose and Zhirenshe—wits and jokers who cunningly deceived their enemies—were popular heroes of Kazakh tales. Heroic epics, particularly in the oldest narrative poems (*Koblandy, Er-Targyn, Alpamys,* and *Kambarbatyr*), sing of the exploits of the heroes (*batyrs*) who defended the independence of their people in constant battles. No less beloved were lyric-epic narrative poems (*Kozy-Korpesh, Baian-Slu,* and *Kyz-Zhibek*), whose main content was the true, self-sacrificing love of young heroes and their sometimes tragic fate.

The earliest works of oral folk poetry whose authorship may be considered to be established date from the 15th century (the *akyn* Kaztugan Suiunish-uly); from the 16th century, Asan-Kaigy, whose name became legend, Dospambet, and Shalkiiz are known. The works of Bukhar-zhyrau Kalkamanov (1693–1787; according to other sources, 1686–1799) enjoyed great popularity. He wrote poems that were sharp and politically topical for their times; however, they expressed a feudal ideology.

At the turn of the 19th century, a new stage of Kazakh culture, including literature, developed as a result of the unification of a considerable part of Kazakhstan with Russia. The *akyns* Makhambet Utemisov (1804–46), Sherniiaz Zharylgasov (1817–81), and Suiumbai Aronov (1827–96) called upon the people to struggle against their oppressors—the *bais* and tsarist satraps. The work of these *akyns* was of a democratic nature; they saw and understood the advantages of Kazakhstan's introduction to the life of Russia. Dulat Babataev (1802–71), Shortanbai Kanaev (1818–81), and Murat Monkeev (1843–1906) presented a different, clerical-conservative orientation in Kazakh culture: they criticized the existing order from the standpoint of the idealization of the patriarchal past and extolled religion (Islam).

The second half of the 19th century produced the *akyns* Birzhan Kozhagulov (1834–97) and Aset Naimanbaev (1867–1924) and the poet Sara Tastanbekova, as well as Akhan Koramsin (Akhan-Sere, 1843–1913), Zhaiau-Musa Baizhanov (1835–1929), and Dzhambul Dzhabaev (1846–1945). Their names were associated with the rapid growth of the *aitys* not only as a form of poetic competition but also as an effective means of expressing public opinion, which was directed against oppression and defended social justice.

The Kazakh enlightenment began in the mid-19th century. Its most outstanding representatives were the ethnographer and folklorist Chokan Valikhanov (1835–65); the pedagogical scholar and writer Ibrai Altynsarin (1841–89), who developed a Kazakh alphabet based on Russian script; and the poet and democrat Abai Kunanbaev (1845–1904), an innovator of poetic form and the creator of an entire school of poetry. All of these figures propagandized progressive Russian culture and called upon the Kazakh people to proceed along its path.

Written Kazakh realistic literature was inaugurated by the work of Abai. His lyrics and satire and the prose philosophical exhortation *Gakliia* reflected the life of Kazakh society in those times from the standpoint of critical realism. Abai's traditions were continued in the early 20th century by the writers and democrats Sultanmakhmut Toraigyrov (1893–1920), Sabit Donentaev (1894–1933), Spandiiar Kubeev (1878–1956), Mukhamedzhan Seralin (1872–1929), Beket Utetleuov (1874–1946), Tair Zhomartbaev (1891–1937), and Berniiaz Kuleev (1895–1923). Progressive creative forces grouped around the journal *Aikap* (published 1911–15). After the victory of the October Revolution, democratic writers took the side of Soviet power and served the construction of the new society through their literary work.

In the late 19th and early 20th centuries, the "bibliophiles'" group was also active in Kazakh literature. The bibliophiles preached religious-patriarchal views. The most prominent were Nurzhan Naushabaev (1859–1919) and Mashur-Zhusup Kopeev (1857–1931). Their activity in collecting folklore and specimens of written literature was much to their credit.

Openly nationalistic writers who crossed over to the camp of the ideological opponents of Soviet power after October (A. Baitursunov, M. Dulatov, and M. Zhumabaev) were associated with the reactionary newspaper *Kazakh* (1913).

Along with written prerevolutionary Kazakh literature, folklore also developed. The work of such folk *akyns* as Dzhambul Dzhabaev, Nurpeis Baiganin (1860–1945), Doskei Alimbaev (1855–1946), Nartai Bekezhanov (1890–1954), Omar Shipin (1879–1963), and Kenen Azerbaev (born 1884) played a large role in the cultural and social life of Kazakhstan; these *akyns* created acutely social works that were disseminated among the people. After the October Revolution, they became active builders of Soviet society.

The founders of the Soviet Kazakh literature of socialist realism were the poet and revolutionary Saken Seifullin (1894–1939), the poets Baimagambet Iztolin (1899–1921) and Il'ias Dzhansugurov (1894–1937); and the writers Bembet Mailin (1894–1939), Mukhtar Auezov (1897–1961), and Sabit Mukanov (born 1900). They were the source of all genres of contemporary Kazakh literature, vividly and uncompromisingly exposing the social structure of prerevolutionary conditions and vestiges of that structure. The hero of the new era—the man of labor who transforms the world—announced himself for the first time in their works: the narrative poem *Sovetstan* (1925) and the novella *The Excavators* (1928) by Seifullin and the novella *The Communist Woman Raushan* (1929) by Mailin.

In the mid-1920's, Kazakh literature was bolstered by fresh forces, mainly poets: Isa Baizakov (1900–46), Askar Tokmagambetov (born 1905), Kalmakan Abdukadyrov (1903–64), Tair Zharokov (1908–65), Abdil'da Tazhibaev (born 1909), Gali Ormanov (born 1907), and Dikhan Abilev (born 1907). They searched for new means of representation: contemporary themes brought to poetry a new vocabulary and new images and rhythms, although Soviet Kazakh poetry did not break away from the classical realist traditions established by the work of Abai or from the traditions represented in the best oral folk poetry.

The works of the prose writers Gabiden Mustafin (born 1902) and Gabit Musrepov (born 1902) appeared during the same period. The Kazakh Association of Proletarian Writers, which played a large role in the consolidation and ideological education of writers and in their struggle against the bourgeois nationalist ideology, was established in 1926. Publication of the literary anthology *Zhyl kusy* (The First Signs) began in 1927, and the journal *Zhana adebiet* (New Literature) began publication in 1928.

The 1930's were characterized by further expansion of the subject matter of Kazakh literature and more thorough assimilation of socialist realism. The Writers' Union of Kazakhstan was created in 1934, and the first ten-day festival of Kazakh literature and art was held in Moscow in 1936. At about that time, Kazakh literature became a mature multigenre literature, reflecting enthusiasm for the construction of socialism. Seifullin's narrative poems *Albatross* (1933) and *Sotsialistan* (1935) sing of the great Lenin and depict the liberation struggle of the people and of its new life; the hero of the novella *Fruits* (1935) is the man of free labor. Mailin's novel *Azamat Azamatych* (1934) portrays the struggle against bourgeois nationalism, the struggle for the collectivization of the Kazakh *aul*. The novel by Sattar Erubaev (1914–1937), *My Contemporaries* (published posthumously in 1939), is dedicated to the working class. The image of the contemporary figure became firmly established in the short stories of Mailin, Auezov, Musrepov, and Al'zhappar Abishev (born 1907) and in Dzhansugurov's novel *Comrades* (1933, unfinished).

One of the first novels of social history in Kazakh literature was Mukanov's *Enigmatic Banner* (new edition, *Botagoz*, 1938), about the fate of the people described against the background of the uprising of 1916, the October Revolution, and the struggle for Soviet power. A picture of the popular uprising of 1916 was also given in Auezov's drama *Night Thunder* (1934). Kazakh poetry of the 1930's reached its peak with Dzhansugurov's narrative poems *The Steppe* (1930), *The Musician* (1935), and *Kulager* (1936), whose characters were the people and folk poets. Plays on themes of folk lyric-epic narrative poems appeared (*Aiman Sholpan*, 1934, by Auezov, and *Kozy-Korpesh* and *Baian-Slu*, 1940, by Musrepov) with works on contemporary subjects, which occupied the leading place (the plays of Mailin and Tazhibaev and of Shakhmet Khusainov, 1906–72).

During the Great Patriotic War, Kazakh literature, like all Soviet literature, reflected the military exploits and feats of labor of the Soviet people. The Kazakh poetry of those years provided lofty civic and patriotic poems in both the lyric and epic genres: the lyric verses of Tokmagambetov, Zharokov, Ormanov, Abu Sarsenbaev (born 1905), Dzhuban Muldagaliev (born 1920), Khalizhan Bekkhozhin (born 1913), and Khamid Ergaliev (born 1916) were printed in newspapers, including papers of the front, and were read in the trenches. The narrative poem *Tale of the Death of a Poet* (1944) by Kasym Amanzholov (1911–55), dedicated to the deeds of the poet Abdulla Dzhumagaliev, who perished near Moscow, enjoyed great success. The lyrical-philosophical essays *I Want to Live* by Baubek Bulkishev (1916–44), who died at the front, were published in 1942. Patriotic enthusiasm also permeated the work of the folk *akyns*. Dzambul's poem "Leningraders, My Children!" became popular throughout the country.

The theme of war was reflected in the plays *In the Hour of Trial* (produced in 1941) by Auezov, *Guard of Honor* (1942) by Auezov and Abishev, and *Amangel'dy* (produced in 1936) by Khusainov. Mustafin published *Shiganak* (1945), a novel about the toilers of the rear.

During the postwar years, Kazakh literature continued to develop themes associated with the war. Among the works to appear were the novels *Soldier From Kazakhstan* (1949) by Musrepov, *Courland* (1950) by Abdizhamil Nurpeisov (born 1924), and *Stormy Days* (1957) by Takhavi Akhtanov (born 1923) and the war memoirs *Moscow Is Behind Us* (1959) of the writer and soldier Baurdzhan Momysh-ula (born 1910). Poets also continued themes of war in lyrical and narrative poems (narratives by Zharokov about Zoia Kosmodem'ianskaia and by Muldagaliev about Musa Dzhalil').

In 1956, Auezov completed the tetralogy *Path of Abai*, the first book of which was published in 1942. This work, which evoked a response in many lands, exerted considerable influence on Kazakh and other fraternal literatures. In Auezov's epic novel, national epic traditions are enriched by the artistic experience of all of Soviet literature. Major works on historical-revolutionary subjects were produced by Mukanov (*The School of Life*, 1949–53), Musrepov (*The Awakened Land*, 1953), Mustafin (*After the Storm*, 1959), Khamza Esenzhanov (born 1908; *The Iaik Is a Bright River*, 1957–60), and Nurpeisov (the trilogy *Blood and Sweat*, books 1–2, 1959–70).

Many Kazakh writers turned to contemporary themes during the postwar years. Contemporary heroes—toilers of the village, workers, members of the intelligentsia, and youth—are brought to life on the pages of the novels *Syr Darya* (1947–48) by Mukanov, *The Wide Open Spaces* (1949) by Gabdul Slanov (1911–69), *Karaganda* (1952) by Mustafin, *Temir-Tau* (2 books, 1960–62; book 2 was published under the title *Doctor Darkhanov*) by Zein Shashkin (1912–66), *The Young Generation* (published posthumously, 1962) by Auezov, *The White Stallion* (1962) by Taken Alimkulov (born 1922), *Caravan Goes Toward the Sun* (1963) by Anuar Alimzhanov (born 1930), *Horn on the Steppe* (1964, with K. Altaiskii) by Mukhamedzhan Karataev (born 1910), and *The Skirmish* (1966) by Il'ias Esenberlin (born 1915).

The development of epic forms—topical and lyrical narrative poems and the novel in verse—was particularly intense in the poetry of the postwar decades. Many narrative poems were written on historical themes, including *Maria, Daughter of Egor* (1949–54) by Bekkhozhin, *Bell in the Steppe* (1957) by Gafu Kairbekov (born 1928), *Kurmangazy* (1958) by Ergaliev, and *Estai-Khorlan* by Muzafar Alimbaev (born 1923). Narrative poems about creative labor and the rich emotional world of Soviet people were written by Tazhibaev (*Portraits*, 1957), Zharokov (*Steel Born in the Steppe*, 1954), Muldagaliev (*A Widow's Fate*, 1961), and Olzhas Suleimenov (born 1936; *Earth, Bow Down to Man!*, 1961).

Complex social, moral, and ethical conflicts were the center of attention of playwrights: Khusainov's *Spring Wind* (1952), *The Single Family* (1948) by Abishev, and *Before the Wedding* and *Friends* (both 1964) by Tazhibaev. The traditions of the historical and historical-revolutionary genres have also been developed in dramaturgy: *Chokan Valikhanov* (1954) by Mukanov, *Ibrai Altynsarin* (1953) by Musatai Akhinzhanov (born 1905), *Our Gani* (1957) by Khusainov, and *Zhaiau-Musa* (1965) by Zeitin Akishev (born 1911).

Science fiction began to develop successfully in the early 1960's: the novellas *The Seventh Wave* (1964) and *From Fire to the Atom* by Medeu Sarsekeev (born 1936), and *The Alpha of Genius* (1967) by Shokan Alimbaev (born 1941).

The traditions of children's literature were established in the mid-19th century by Altynsarin. In the Soviet period, Sapargali Begalin (born 1895), Utebai Turmanzhanov (born 1905), and Berdibek Sokpakbaev (born 1924) have been working successfully in this area.

At the Sixth Congress of Writers of Kazakhstan (1971), the main trends of contemporary Kazakh literature were recognized to be its intellectualism and the magnitude of the quest and interests, based on the growing requirements of readers and on the breadth and multifaceted nature of the problems that concern Soviet man. This idea is confirmed not only by the work of writers of the older generation but also by that of writers who came to literature in the 1960's, such as the prose writers Azil'-khan Nurshaikhov (born 1922), Magzum Sundetov (born 1936), Abish Kekil'baev (born 1939), Satimzhan Sanbaev (born 1939), Sain Muratbekov (born 1936), and Saken Zhunusov (born 1934) and the poets Kadyr Murzaliev (born 1935), Tumanbai Muldagaliev (born 1935), Sagi Zhienbaev (born 1934), Erkesh Ibragim (born 1930), Mukagali Makataev (born 1931), and Zhumeken Nazhmetdinov (born 1935).

Literary criticism made its appearance in the early 1930's with the articles of Seifullin, Dzhansugurov, Auezov, Kazhim Dzhumaliev (1907–68), Karataev, and Esmagambet Ismailov (1911–66). In the early 1970's this field was striving to be equal to the tasks posed by contemporary Kazakh literature and the development of research thought in literary criticism.

The M. O. Auezov Institute of Literature and Art of the Academy of Sciences of the Kazakh SSR consolidates scholarly forces. The works of Malik Gabdulin (1915–73), Temirgali Nurtazin (1907–73), Beisenbai Kenzhebaev (born 1904), Bel'gibai Shalabaev (born 1911), Aikyn Nurkatov (1928–65), Iskak Diusenbaev (born 1910), Serik Kirabaev (born 1927), Rakhmankul Berdybaev (born 1927), Myrzabek Duisenov (born 1928), and Tursynbek Kakishev (born 1928) are well known. Along with Kazakh scholars, Russian literary specialists and critics continue to deal with problems of the history and theory of Kazakh literature; among them are M. S. Sil'chenko (1898–1970), M. I. Fetisov (1907–60), K. L. Zelinskii (1896–70), Z. S. Kedrina (born 1904), N. S. Smirnova (born 1908), and E. V. Lizunova (born 1926). The literary journals *Zhuldyz* (Star) and *Prostor* (Vista) and the newspaper *Kazakh adebieti* (Kazakh Literature) are published.

As early as the 19th century, the Kazakh enlighteners Abai Kunanbaev and Ibrai Altynsarin translated works of A. S. Pushkin, M. Iu. Lermontov, I. A. Krylov, and L. N. Tolstoy into Kazakh. In the Soviet period the translation into Kazakh of works of other literatures of the peoples of the USSR and of world literature has achieved broad scope. The works of Kazakh writers have been translated into many languages of the peoples of the USSR and other countries. An important role in the communication of Kazakh literature with the literatures of other peoples of the USSR has been played by the translations of L. S. Sobolev, who is also the author of a number of works of literary criticism on Kazakh literature, by A. N. Pantielev, Iu. O. Dombrovskii, I. P. Shukhov, Iu. P. Kazakov, N. I. Anov, and A. I. Bragin, and by the poets K. Altaiskii, K. Vanshenkin, E. Vinokurov, A. B. Gatov, P. Kuznetsov, M. Lukonin, M. L'vov, I. Sel'vinskii, Ia. Smeliakov, D. Snegin, and M. Tarlovskii.

During the period of Soviet Kazakh literature, more than 1,000 books by writers of other peoples of the USSR and about 300 works by foreign writers have been translated into Kazakh. More than 400 books by Kazakh writers have been published in other republics of the country. The M. O. Auezov Institute of Literature and Art of the Academy of Sciences of the Kazakh SSR has a division for the study of the relation of Kazakh literature and the literatures of other peoples and countries.

The Writers' Union of Kazakhstan performs a great deal of ideological-educational and organizational-creative work. Its first congress was held in 1934, second in 1939, third in 1954, fourth in 1959, fifth in 1966, and sixth in 1971. There are sections of Russian and Uighur writers in the Writers' Union of Kazakhstan. Korean and German writers also live and work in the republic.

REFERENCES

Shalabaev, B. *Ocherki istorii kazakhskoi dorevoliutsionnoi literatury.* Alma-Ata, 1958.
Istoriia kazakhskoi literatury, vols. 1–3. Alma-Ata, 1968–71.
Ocherk istorii kazakhskoi sovetskoi literatury. Moscow, 1960.
Istoriia literatur narodov Srednei Azii i Kazakhstana. Moscow, 1960.
Karataev, M. *Kazakhskaia literatura.* Moscow, 1960.
Karataev, M. *Ot dombry do knigi.* Moscow, 1969.
Kedrina, Z. S. *Iz zhivogo istochnika (Ocherki sovetskoi kazakhskoi literatury),* 2nd ed., expanded. Alma-Ata, 1966.
Fetisov, M. I. *Zarozhdenie kazakhskoi publitsistiki.* Alma-Ata, 1961.
Lizunova, E. *Sovremennyi kazakhskii roman.* Alma-Ata, 1964.
Akhmetov, Z. A. *Kazakhskoe stikhoslozhenie.* Alma-Ata, 1964.
Sidel'nikov, V. *Bibliograficheskii ukazatel' po kazakhskomu ustnomu tvorchestvu,* fasc. 1. Alma-Ata, 1951.
Kazakhskie literaturnye sviazi: Bibliografich. ukazatel'. Alma-Ata, 1968.
Grekhovodov, N., V. Daniliuk, and P. Kosenko. *Pisateli Kazakhstana: Biograficheskii spravochnik.* Alma-Ata, 1969.
Narymbetov, A. *Kazakhskaia sovetskaia literatura: Bibliograficheskii ukazatel' po literaturovedeniiu i kritike, 1917–1940.* Alma-Ata, 1970.
Ghabdullin, M. *Qazaq khalqïnïng auïz ädebieti.* Alma-Ata, 1958.
Jümaliev, K. *Qazaq eposï men ädebiet tarikhïnïng mäselelerï.* Alma-Ata, 1958.
Kenjebaev, B. *Qazaq khalqïnïng XX ghasïr basïndaghï demokrat jazushïlarï.* Alma-Ata, 1958.
Täjïbaev, Ä. *Qazaq dramaturgiyäsïnïng damuï men kalïptasuï.* Alma-Ata, 1971.
Qazaq fol'kloristikasï. Alma-Ata, 1972.   M. KARATAEV

Architecture and art

Architecture. In the Bronze Age, the tribes that inhabited Kazakhstan left relics associated with the Andronovo culture. The settlements of that time (Atasu and Karkaralinsk in Karaganda Oblast, Alekseevka in Kustanai Oblast, and others) consisted of ten to 40 rectangular semisubterranean dwellings and domestic structures. Religious structures, such as dolmens, men-

hirs, burial enclosures made of stone slabs (the Begaza burial ground in central Kazakhstan), and burial mounds, have survived. In the period from the first millennium B.C. through the first centuries A.D., the tribes that inhabited Kazakhstan (the Sacae, Usun, and Kangly) had, in addition to the felt yurt, which is a portable dwelling, a stationary house made of pisé or mud brick in fortified settled villages (Chirikrabat, fifth to second centuries B.C., and Babyshmulla, fourth to second centuries B.C., both in Kzyl-Orda Oblast). Large barrows with mounds faced with stone and with timbered interment chambers (the Besshatyr burial ground on the Ili River, Alma-Ata Oblast), as well as burial structures made of large mud bricks (the site of the fortified settlement of Tegisken, ninth to eighth centuries B.C., Kzyl-Orda Oblast), with a number of rooms, have survived. The domed burial structure of Balanda II (fourth to second centuries B.C., Kzyl-Orda Oblast) was unique for its time.

In addition to the fortified settled villages, the Usun and Kangly also had "headquarters" cities: Chiga in Semirech'e southeast of Lake Balkhash and Bitian' on the middle course of the Syr Darya. From the sixth to eighth centuries, when Kazakhstan was part of the Turkic Kaganate, and from the eighth to tenth centuries when is was part of the Turgesh and Karluk kaganates, the cities of Isfijab (from the 11th century, Sairam, Chimkent Oblast), and Taraz (now Dzhambul) developed, and fortresses and castle-estates were constructed (the castle of the fortified settlement of Baba-Ata, on the northern slopes of the Karatau, Chimkent Oblast).

In the eighth century, with the spread of Islam, new types of buildings—mosques and madrasas—appeared and new architectural and construction methods—fired brick, vaults and domes, wall revetment of terra-cotta. *Sardabehs* (cisterns), baths, caravansaries, and mausoleums were built. Conical mausoleums of stone slabs have survived from the eighth to tenth centuries (Kozy-Korpesh and Baian-Slu on the Aiaguz River northeast of Lake Balkhash). In southern Kazakhstan during the Karakhanid state (tenth to 12th centuries), cities that developed from ancient settlements (Taraz and others) had a tripartite structure: the citadel, *shahristan* (urban sections), and *rabat* (faubourg).

In the tenth century, a type of central-plan memorial structure with a square base capped by a spherical or conical dome on arched squinches (the mausoleums of Babadzhi-khatun in the village of Golovachevka, near Dzhambul, tenth to 11th centuries, and Aisha-Bibi), began to take shape; rectangular buildings with domes and portals (the Syrly-tam mausoleum, Kzyl-Orda Oblast, 11th to 12th centuries), with a massive portal and roof, emerged later. Cities were rebuilt after the Mongol-Tatar invasion in the second half of the 13th century, and during the 14th to 16th centuries they achieved an economic and cultural upsurge (Sygnak, Taraz, and Sairam). Monumental structures—for example, the mausoleum of Alash-khan near Ulutau (Karaganda Oblast, second half of the 13th century) and the mausoleum-mosque complex of Khodzha Akhmed Iasavi in the city of Iasa (now the city of Turkestan, Chimkent Oblast; late 14th century)—were erected. The Dzungarian invasions of the 1640's to 1720's led to a decline in the culture of Kazakhstan; construction of monumental buildings, such as mausoleums and mosques, decreased, and architectural mastery was lost.

Russian military fortifications arose along the borders of Kazakhstan during the 17th and 18th centuries: Iaitskii Gorodok (Ural'sk), Gur'ev, Orenburg, Orsk, and Semipalatinsk. The economic upsurge after Kazakhstan's final unification with Russia in the 1860's spurred construction. The cities of northern and eastern Kazakhstan that grew from military fortifications generally consisted of four main parts: the fortress, the Cossack *stanitsa* (settlement), the "Tatar faubourg," and the city proper, with its rectangular system of streets.

Division into "old" and "new" parts was characteristic of the old cities of southern Kazakhstan. One-story houses, administrative and commercial buildings, and railroad stations were constructed, primarily in the eclectic spirit; mosques and madrasas were built. Traditional vaulted and domed construction was used in building mausoleums, and ornamented tiles, stone carving, and fresco painting were used for decoration. Dome-and-portal mausoleums of fired brick (Zhuzdena, first half of the 19th century, and Tort-Kara, 1840's, both in Karaganda Oblast) or central domed shell-rock mausoleums (in the area of Senek on the Mangyshlak Peninsula) were built. *Sagana-tamy*, or grave structures (rectangular, without roofs; walls decorated with carving), which were known as early as the Middle Ages, were widespread in western Kazakhstan during the late 19th and early 20th centuries. *Kulup-tasy*, or monuments in the form of carved stone columns, are frequently encountered.

In the Soviet period as early as the 1920's, simultaneous with repair and restoration work, there was construction of residential and public buildings in Kzyl-Orda, Chimkent, and other cities in which the architecture attempted to use the national traditions—iwans, courtyards, and so on. Industrialization, which expanded in the 1920's and 1930's, prompted intensive development of architecture and urban construction. Massive construction of well-equipped residential and public buildings was undertaken in the growing old cities and in the new cities —Balkhash, Karaganda, and Ridder (now Leninogorsk)—and settlements—Achisai, Lengerugol' (now the city of Lenger), and Dzhezkazgan (now a city). Cities, settlements, and plants grew up along the Turkestan-Siberia railroad. The development of the petroleum industry on the Emba River prompted new construction in Gur'ev. Buildings in the spirit of Soviet constructivism (Government House, now the university building, in Alma-Ata) were erected in the late 1920's and early 1930's.

The architecture of the mid-1930's and the 1940's was characterized by classical elements (porticoes, colonnades, and pilasters), often combined with traditional national architecture (vaulted lancet windows and other national ornamental motifs). The best structures of that time include the medical institute and the Abai Kazakh Theater of Opera and Ballet in Alma-Ata. However, the uncritical use of the legacy of the country sometimes led during the prewar years and first decade after the war to eclecticism and archaization.

After the Great Patriotic War and particularly after the second half of the 1950's, construction developed on a still larger scale. Young cities grew and their layout was improved, and new cities were created (Rudnyi, Abai, Shakhtinsk, Ermak, and Serebriansk) and old ones reconstructed. During the 1950's administrative buildings (Government House in Alma-Ata), palaces of culture, drama and motion-picture theaters, school buildings, and sports facilities were constructed in Alma-Ata and other cities. Industrial methods of construction were introduced extensively in Kazakhstan, as in other republics, beginning in the late 1950's. The construction of the late 1950's and 1960's (the Palace of Virgin Lands Workers in Tselinograd, the Hotel Kazakhstan, the Palace of Sports, and the Lenin Palace in Alma-Ata) was marked by rationality of layout, ease and clarity of architectural forms, and decorative monumental art.

Residential construction acquired vast scope during the 1960's. Vast residential sections of large-panel homes that take into consideration the natural and climatic conditions of Kazakhstan (earthquake-proof and sun-shielding structures) have been built in Alma-Ata, Karaganda, Pavlodar, Chimkent, Tselinograd, and other cities; general plans have been compiled for large cities (the general plan for Alma-Ata, 1960–63; architects, G. A. Bobovich and L. K. Vertousov) and new settlements. Construction in Alma-Ata during the late 1960's and early 1970's has been characterized by taller buildings and by innovation in the architectural forms of residential structures. The Medeo high-mountain stadium has been built near Alma-Ata (1972; architects, V. Z. Katsev, A. S. Kainarbaev, and others; engineers, M. V. Plakhotnikov and others). The development of the virgin and unused lands since 1954 inaugurated intensive contruction of rural settlements. The Architects' Union of the Kazakh SSR was founded in Alma-Ata in 1935.

M. M. MENDIKULOV

Fine and decorative-applied arts. The earliest relics of art in Kazakhstan are rock engravings of animals, which date to the Paleolithic era in the Karatau and Khantau mountains and the Neolithic era in the Dzhasybai grotto, Pavlodar Oblast, and elsewhere. Remains of the Andronovo culture—cliff totem images of animals (deer, goats, and so on), rock pictures of hunting scenes (in the Tamgaly gorge, Alma-Ata Oblast, and elsewhere), and earthenware vessels with geometric designs applied by carving, tooling, and stamping—have come down from the Bronze

Age. The art of the Sacae, which was associated with Scythian culture, was rich in pictures of real and fantastic wild animals, which was part of the "animal style"—gold plates with bas-relief pictures of deer from one of the Chilik barrows (seventh to sixth centuries B.C.) and bronze figurines of winged lionesses on the sacrificial table from the Issyk treasure (fifth to third centuries B.C.). An openwork gold Usun diadem from the Kargala treasure (second century B.C. to second century A.D.), with dynamic figures of deer, birds, winged horses, and a dragon, was also executed in the animal style.

The fine arts of Kazakhstan during the Middle Ages (seventh to 17th centuries) were represented by stone sculptures of men, women, and animals and by bronze figurines of women. Among the masterworks of decorative-applied art from this period are yurt-shaped clay vessels for storing bones (ossuaries); ceramic crockery, both unglazed—decorated with stuccoed, incised, and stamped designs—and glazed (the city of Taraz was the center) with a characteristic combination of black, brown, yellow, and red; and hide or metal articles decorated with a distinctive national design marked by large, clear patterns of scrolls grouped in rhombuses and circles.

The traditions of decorative-applied art were maintained during the 18th and 19th centuries. All items—for example, yurts and domestic articles—were decorated with the national design. An important furnishing of the yurt was the felt rug decorated with patterns—the *tekemet* (with a sunken, indistinct pattern of pale blue, golden yellow, and red), *syrmak* (mainly black and white, with a characteristic clear graphic pattern), and *tus kiiz* (decorated with appliqué work of red and black cloth, frequently combined with embroidery); woven rugs with multicolored patterns were also important. The woven rugs were both napless (*alasha*), with alternating ornamented strips, and with a nap (*tukti kilem*); the napped rugs had borders with designs that differed from the patterns of the field. Chain-stitch and satin-stitch silk or wool embroidery, gold needlework, carving (primarily bas-relief) and wood inlay with bone, tanning (stamping, inlay with contrasting hides, embroidery), and jewelry-making (stamping, engraving, inlay, filigree, niello, and large insets of carnelian) were widespread. Works of representational art reflecting the life of the Kazakh people were created in the 19th century (drawings and watercolors by the Kazakh artist Ch. Valikhanov and by T. G. Shevchenko, paintings and drawings by V. V. Vereshchagin, and so on).

In the Soviet period as early as the late 1920's and the 1930's, an entire galaxy of national painters and graphic artists worked in close cooperation with the Russian painters and graphic artists N. G. Khludov, N. I. Krutil'nikov, and V. I. Antoshchenko-Olenev. These Kazakh artists, who displayed a lively interest in the new phenomenon of Soviet reality as well as in the revolutionary past of the Kazakh people, included A. Tashbaev, Kh. Khodzhikov and K. Khodzhikov, A. Ismailov, and A. Kasteev. Their works were marked by attempts to master small-scale forms and to develop a national artistic form of expression. During the Great Patriotic War artists worked on battle and historical paintings that told of the heroism of the Soviet people and on portraits of heroes of the front and rear; they executed posters and cartoons for the "Windows of Kaz-TAG" exhibits.

The professional craftsmanship of artists began to grow in the mid-1940's and the first half of the 1950's; the narrative painting (A. Ismailov and A. Kasteev), as well as the portrait and landscape (A. M. Cherkasskii, M. S. Lizogub, and L. P. Leont'ev), developed further. At the same time, however, works marked by a tendency to make pronouncements were often created. Young artists educated in the institutes of Moscow, Leningrad, and other cities began to play a significant role in the development of Kazakh art in the late 1950's. Their work of the 1960's and early 1970's is notable for its striving to communicate the emotional state of humankind and its internal connections with the surrounding world, a state that is embodied at times in images of generalized symbolic resonance. This tendency began a quest for new means of expression. Among the prominent painters of this period are M. S. Kenbaev, K. T. Tel'zhanov, A. M. Stepanov, S. A. Mambeev, K. M. Shaiakhmetov, and S. A. Aitbaev. N. S. Gaev, R. Sakhi, Ch. B. Kenzhebaev, E. M. Sidorkin, and

I. E. Kvachko are working in graphics (illustrations, prints, and small-scale drawings), and Kh. I. Naurzbaev, B. A. Tulekov, and T. S. Dosmagambetov work in small-scale and monumental sculpture, primarily portraits. V. V. Teliakovskii, A. I. Nenashev, A. G. Galimbaeva, and G. M. Ismailova have played important roles in the development of theatrical set design. Decorative applied artists include jewelers and the wood and bone carvers O. Kenebaev, L. M. Khodzhikova, and R. S. Sarsenbin.

The Artists' Union of the Kazakh SSR was founded in Alma-Ata in 1940 (from 1933 through 1940 it was the organizing committee of the Artists' Union).   N.-B. NURMUKHAMMEDOV

REFERENCES
Basenov, T. K. *Arkhitekturnye pamiatniki v raione Sam.* Alma-Ata, 1947.
Mendikulov, M. M. *Pamiatniki arkhitektury poluostrova Mangyshlaka i Zapadnogo Ustiurta.* Alma-Ata, 1956.
Basenov, T. K. *Ornament Kazakhstana v arkhitekture.* Alma-Ata, 1957.
Margulan, A. Kh., T. K. Basenov, and M. M. Mendikulov. *Arkhitektura Kazakhstana.* Alma-Ata, 1959.
Tolstov, S. P. *Po drevnim del'tam Oksa i Iaksarta.* Moscow, 1962.
Akishev, K. A., and G. A. Kushaev. *Drevniaia kul'tura sakov i usunei doliny reki Ili.* Alma-Ata, 1963.
Izobrazitel'noe iskusstvo Kazakhstana. Editor in chief, B. G. Erzakovich. Alma-Ata, 1963.
Drevniaia kul'tura Tsentral'nogo Kazakhstana. Alma-Ata, 1966.
Mendykulov, M. M. *Obnovlennaia Sary-Arka.* Alma-Ata, 1967.
Sarykulova, G. *Grafika Kazakhstana.* Alma-Ata, 1967.
Zhivopis' Kazakhskoi SSR. [Album. Preface by N.-B. Nurmukhammedov.] Moscow [1970].
Narodnoe dekorativno-prikladnoe iskusstvo kazakhov. [Album. Introductory article by N. A. Orazbaeva.] Leningrad, 1970.
Nurmukhammedov, N.-B. *Iskusstvo Kazakhstana.* [Moscow, 1970].
Iskusstvo Kazakhskoi SSR. [Album. Compiled and with an introductory article by G. A. Sarykulova. Leningrad, 1972.]
Ejelgĭ mädeniet kuälarĭ. Alma-Ata, 1966.

Music

Before the October Revolution the music of Kazakhstan was represented solely by folk works (songs and musical pieces, or *kiui*). On the musical background of the recitative, *zhyrshi* (narrators of folk tales) performed epic poems and legends, *akyns* shaped poetic improvisations, and *ertekshi* (storytellers) recounted tales and fables. *Aitys* (competitions), which attracted large numbers of people, were widespread.

Folk music is based on seven-tone diatonic major and minor scales in which elements of the pentatonic are prominent. It is characterized by distinctive intonations, well-developed song and instrumental forms, and diverse metric and rhythmic patterns. The existing musical instruments include the two-stringed *dombra* (plucked), the two-stringed *kobyz* (bowed), the *sybyzgy* (a wind instrument like the vertical, or end-blown, flute), and the *dauylpaz* (percussion); the *syrnai* (one- or two-voiced accordions of the Kasimov and Tatar varieties) became prevalent in the late 19th century.

Of great importance for the development of music was the work of folk composer-singers, instrumentalists, and composers of the mid-19th and early 20th centuries whose *Weltanschauung* was influenced by progressive Russian culture. Among these figures were Abai Kunanbaev, a composer and the founder of modern written Kazakh poetry, and Birzhan Kozhagulov, Zhaiau-Musa Baizhanov, Dauletkerei Shigaev, Kurmangazy Sagyrbaev, Ikhlas Dukenov, Mukhit Meraliev, Baluan-Sholak Baimurzin, Akhan-Sere Koramsin, Tattimbet Kazangapov, Tlepbergenov, and Sarmalai.

After the October Revolution a national socialist music culture was born and took shape. It drew on the exceedingly rich body of folk music, the assimilation of Russian and foreign classics, and the experience of Soviet music. Public musical life became considerably more active: amateur musical theater and choral groups were formed, and a great deal of musical folklore was written down and studied. The folk-song collections of A. V. Zataevich are well known. Competitions of singers, *akyns*, and musicians received support; one of the first was held in 1919 in the city of Vernyi, now Alma-Ata. New genres of folk music

took shape, types of performance expanded, and choral singing and instrumental ensemble playing emerged. The first republic-wide gathering of folk musicians was held in 1934; the Kazakh Central Executive Committee of Kazakh Folk Instruments (after 1944, the Kurmangazy Orchestra) was organized. The Dzhambul Philharmonic Society, consisting of a Kazakh choir, an orchestra of folk instruments, a dance ensemble, and a group of folk singers, was created in 1935.

A music studio was founded in Alma-Ata in 1933, and in 1934 it was made into the Kazakh Musical Theater (after 1936, the Joint Theater of Kazakh and Russian Opera, and after 1937 the Kazakh Theater of Opera and Ballet). The singers K. Baiseitova, K. Dzhandarbekov, K. Baiseitov, and M. Erzhanov participated in performances. The first Kazakh opera, *Kyz-Zhibek* by E. G. Brusilovskii, based on the themes of the epic of the same name, was staged in 1934. It was followed by his operas *Zhalbyr* (1935) and *Er-Targyn* (Targyn the Valiant, 1937). The first national ballets were created (*see below*: Dance and ballet). The Kazakh popular song, instrumental chamber music, and symphonic and choral music developed during the 1930's and 1940's. New performance groups arose under the auspices of the radio committee: a symphony orchestra, an ensemble of Russian folk instruments, and a Kazakh choir for Soviet popular and folk songs. The organizing committee of the Composers' Union of Kazakhstan was established in 1939.

Brusilovskii's opera *Gvardiia, alga!* (Guards, Forward!), about the heroism of the Soviet people in the struggle against the fascist German invaders, was presented in 1942. An important stage was reached with the opera *Abai* by A. K. Zhubanov and L. A. Khamidi (1944), which used Abai's melodies, and Brusilovskii's third symphony, *Sary arka* (The Golden Steppe, 1944). The first conservatory in Kazakhstan opened in Alma-Ata in 1944 (since 1963, the Kurmangazy Conservatory). In 1945 a sector of art criticism was organized under the auspices of the Academy of Sciences of the Kazakh SSR.

In the postwar years Kazakh composers have chosen the path of free, creative reworking of the folk melodies, rather than the literal renderings of the past. Operas with themes grounded in contemporary reality are dominant; these include *Amangel'dy* by Brusilovskii and M. T. Tulebaev (staged in 1945; second version 1961) and *Tulegen Tokhtarov* by Zhubanov and Khamidi (staged in 1947; second version 1963). The staging in 1946 of Tulebaev's opera *Birzhan and Sara*, about the folk composer Birzhan Kozhagulov, was a great event. Brusilovskii's opera *Dudarai*, in which crowd scenes are the heart of dramatic development, was staged in 1953. The first Uighur opera was *Nazugum* by K. Kh. Kuzham'iarov (1956). Operas on contemporary subjects are *Altyn taular* (The Golden Mountains, 1960) by Kuzham'iarov and N. A. Tlendiev; the first Kazakh comic opera, *Aisulu*, by S. M. Mukhamedzhanov (1964); *Kamar-Sulu* (The Beauty Kamar, 1963) by E. R. Rakhmadiev, based on S. Toraigyrov's novel of the same name; and *Zhumbak kyz* (The Mysterious Girl, 1971) by Mukhamedzhanov. The opera *Glow of the Steppe* (1967) by A. V. Bychkov, G. I. Grizbil, and Rakhmadiev, which dealt with the struggle for Soviet power in Semirech'e, was performed on the 50th anniversary of the October Revolution.

A large number of works have been written in the symphonic genres, including *Kazakh Symphony* by V. V. Velikanov (1947); the symphonic poems *Kazakhstan* by Tulebaev (1951) and *Dzhailiauda* by K. A. Musin (1948); the first Uighur symphonic poem, *Rizvangul'*, by Kuzham'iarov (1950); the fourth, fifth, sixth (*Kurmangazy*), and seventh symphonies of Brusilovskii; the symphony *The Storm* by Mukhamedzhanov (1968, dedicated to the 100th anniversary of V. I. Lenin's birth); and the symphony *Zhiger* (Energy, 1971) by G. A. Zhubanova (1971). A number of works have been written for the Kurmangazy Kazakh Orchestra of Folk Instruments.

The cantata-oratorio has developed greatly. The first Kazakh cantata, *Soviet Kazakhstan*, was written by Brusilovskii on the 30th anniversary of the October Revolution. Works of this genre include Tulebaev's cantata *The Lights of Communism* (1951), Zhubanova's oratorios *Dawn on the Steppe* (1960) and *Lenin* (1969), and the oratorios *Voice of the Ages* by Mukhamedzhanov (1960) and *Ode to the Party* by Rakhmadiev (1970). The suites *For Peace* by B. B. Baikadamov (1953) and *Youth* by Tulebaev and the choruses *The Solitary Oak* by Zhubanova, *Evening on Balkhash* by Rakhmadiev, and *Song of the Party* by Khamidi are important choral works. The songs of Tlendiev, Sh. Kaldaiakov, A. Espaev, and S. Karimbaev enjoy great popularity.

The development of instrumental chamber music has been slower than that of other genres. String quartets include Brusilovskii's *Song of Life* and Kuzham'iarov's *In the Home Kolkhoz*, based on Uighur melodies. Works for violin and piano include Velikanov's *Improvisation in Memory of Abai*, Zhubanova's *Variations*, and Brusilovskii's suite *Bozaigyr*. An intonational connection with Soviet Russian songs is noticeable in the songs and romances of the 1950's and 1960's.

The formation and development of Soviet Kazakh music have been greatly aided by many Russian musicians: among composers, People's Artist of the Kazakh SSR E. G. Brusilovskii and Honored Art Workers of the Kazakh SSR V. V. Velikanov and S. I. Shabel'skii; among conductors, Honored Art Workers of the Kazakh SSR G. A. Stoliarov, V. I. Piradov, and L. M. Shargorodskii; and among choral directors, People's Artists of the Kazakh SSR A. V. Preobrazhenskii, B. V. Lebedev, and A. V. Molodov.

Among the promiment singers of the Kazakh SSR are People's Artists of the USSR R. M. Abdullin, R. T. Baglanova, R. U. Dzhamanova, E. B. Serkebaev, and B. A. Tulegenova and People's Artists of the Kazakh SSR M. M. Abdullin, A. Baikadamova, Sh. Beisekova, B. Dosymzhanov, Zh. Elebekov, R. Esimzhanova, K. Kenzhetaev, G. Kurmangaliev, Zh. Omarova, and A. B. Umbetbaev; among *dombra* players, People's Artists of the Kazakh SSR K. Zhantleuov and R. Omarov; among conductors, People's Artists of the Kazakh SSR G. N. Dugashev, Sh. K. Kazhgaliev, and F. Sh. Mansurov and Honored Art Worker of the Kazakh SSR T. O. Osmanov.

The musical achievements of Kazakhstan were displayed at the ten-day festivals of Kazakh art and literature in Moscow (1936 and 1958) and the Kazakh music weeks in the Tatar ASSR (1962), the Armenian SSR (1968), and the Uzbek SSR (1960 and 1971).

In 1972 the Kazakh Choir, the Kurmangazy Kazakh Orchestra of Folk Instruments, the Song and Dance Ensemble of the Kazakh SSR, the Symphony Orchestra, the Chamber Orchestra of the Kazakh Radio and Television, and the Gul'der Youth Variety Stage Ensemble were all active, as were the Kurmangazy Conservatory, music divisions of several pedagogical institutes and institutes of culture, 11 music colleges, and 156 children's music and art schools.

The Composers' Union was founded in 1939; in 1972 it had 40 members.

REFERENCES

Zataevich, A. V. *500 kazakhskikh pesen i kiuiev.* Alma-Ata, 1931.
Zataevich, A. V. *1000 pesen kazakhskogo naroda,* 2nd ed. Moscow, 1963.
Muzykal'naia kul'tura Kazakhstana: Sb. statei i materialov. [Alma-Ata] 1955.
Gizatov, B. *Kazakhskii gosudarstvennyi orkestr narodnykh instrumentov imeni Kurmangazy.* Alma-Ata, 1957.
Zhubanov, A. K. *Struny stoletii: Ocherki o zhizni i tvorcheskoi deiatel'-nosti kazakhskikh narodnykh kompozitorov.* Alma-Ata, 1958.
Zhubanov, A. K. *Solov'i stoletii.* Alma-Ata, 1967. [Translated from Kazakh.]
Kanapin, A. K., and L. I. Varshavskii. *Iskusstvo Kazakhstana.* Alma-Ata, 1958.
Kompozitory Sovetskogo Kazakhstana: Sb. statei. Alma-Ata, 1958.
Messman, Vl. *Vozrozhdenie pesni.* Alma-Ata, 1958.
Ocherki po istorii kazakhskoi sovetskoi muzyki. Alma-Ata, 1962.
Erzakovich, B. G. *Pesennaia kul'tura kazakhskogo naroda.* Alma-Ata, 1966.
Istoriia muzyki narodov SSSR, vols. 1–3. Moscow, 1970–72.
Rsaldin. J. *Ännen-operagha.* Alma-Ata, 1971.   B. G. ERZAKOVICH

Dance and ballet

The Kazakh people have long had a distinctive dance culture. Like other forms of national art, dance was part of the way of life of the nomadic cattle raisers, and all aspects of that way of life were communicated in dance images. This is confirmed by the folk dances that have survived, including work dances (the *ormek bi,* or weavers' dance), hunting dances (the *koian bi,* or

the golden eagle's hunt for the hare, and *kusbegi-dauylpaz,* or training of the hunting falcon), dance competitions (*utys bi*), comic, satirical, and humorous dances (*nasybaishi*), and dances imitating animals (*orteke,* the jumping goat; *kara zhorga* and *tepenkok,* the dance of the racehorse, or the trotter's race; and *aiu bi,* the dance of the bear). In musical folklore there were lyrical dramatized dances with singing and round dances. Festivals based on the calendar of the work year were particularly popular. Competitive dances were performed at these festivals—dances displaying agility and endurance, as well as dance games, and night round dances about campfires. Wedding rites lasted several days and were vividly dramatized presentations in pantomime and comic dances. There were religious dances, performed only by shamans to cure the sick and "drive out the evil spirit." In contrast to the Uzbeks, Tadzhiks, and other Eastern Muslim peoples, the Kazakhs had pair dances performed by boys and girls (*koian berkut*).

There were no schools for dance instruction, as there were in India, Japan, China, and other countries of the East; dancers transmitted their art from generation to generation. In the patriarchal-feudal society, each clan had its own professional masters who had the status of court jesters or belonged to the ranks of folk jester-comics, the *ku.* There were no definitive folk dance forms among the Kazakhs. Improvisation was an indispensable condition of dance folklore. The most characteristic features of dance were expressiveness of execution, abruptness of movement, mobility of the shoulders, "playing" of the joints, tension and agility of the body, and flexibility, which enables the dancers to execute complex acrobatic movements. The combination of vivid emotionality and diverse choreographic patterns was also typical, particularly in the dance competitions (*utys bi* and *sylkyma*). The dance on horseback was most specific, but it was not bareback riding. All Kazakhs knew how to ride bareback, but it was only the professionals who danced while standing in the saddle; their horses also followed the rhythm. Dance was accompanied by the *dombra* or drum. The clear and energetic rhythm of the *bi kiui* (dance melodies) regulated the rhythm and tempo of the dance.

Prejudices hindered the development of dance culture; the art of dance did not spread as widely as music. During the feudal period, dancing for the enjoyment of the people was considered a "contemptible occupation," the domain of the indigent. With the decay of the patriarchal-clan system and economic and social changes age-old customs and traditions fell into decline; ancient forms of folk dance were degraded, and by the end of the 19th century they had disappeared almost entirely.

Under the conditions of socialist society, with the development of material and intellectual culture and the creation of professional theater (the 1930's), national dance developed. Ancient Kazakh dances, interpreted by professionals, were enriched by new expressive methods and content, and they moved from the stage of the professional theater to amateur folk groups. The *aizhan kyz, kiiz basu, tepenkok, mausymzhan, saunshi zhengei, beskyz, kelinchek, mergen,* and *kokpar* became the most popular dances in folk entertainment.

In 1939, under the auspices of the Kazakh Philharmonic Society, the first folk dance company was created, with Honored Art Worker of the Kazakh SSR A. Ismailov as artistic director. The concert activity of People's Artist of the Kazakh SSR Shara Zhienkulova (director of the Ensemble of Songs and Dances of the World) and Honored Artist of the Kazakh SSR N. Tapalova (director of the Song and Dance Ensemble) was an important contribution to the development of the art of folk dance. The Song and Dance Ensemble of the Kazakh SSR was created in 1955. Its repertoire includes old Kazakh dances, and the ensemble is also working hard to create a contemporary folk dance. The leading performers include Honored Artists of the Kazakh SSR Z. Rozmukhamedova and A. Ismailov. The Young Ballet of Alma-Ata (artistic director, Honored Artist of the Kazakh SSR B. G. Aiukhanov), a classical and folk choreographic dance company, was created in 1968. Its repertoire includes the Kazakh dances *The Golden Eagle and the Fox, The Dance of the Akyns, Akku,* and *Bareback Riding* and dance scenes from E. G. Brusilovskii's opera *Kyz-Zhibek* and on epic subjects.

The first examples of stage dance appeared in the musical performance *Aiman Sholpan* (1934) and in the operas *Kyz-Zhibek* (1934), *Zhalbyr* (1935), and *Er-Targyn* (1937) by Brusilovskii. During the 1936–37 season, the Combined Kazakh and Russian Opera Theater (created in 1936; after 1937, the Kazakh Theater of Opera and Ballet) staged the ballets *Coppélia* by L. Delibes and *Swan Lake* by P. I. Tchaikovsky. The first national ballet, V. V. Velikanov's *Kalkaman and Mamyr*, was staged in 1938; I. N. Nadirov's *Koktem*, in 1940; Velikanov's *Kambar and Nazym*, in 1950; *On The Road of Friendship* (*The Dzungarian Gates*), by N. A. Tlendiev, L. B. Stepanov, and E. V. Manaev, in 1958; G. A. Zhubanova's *Akkanat* and *Hiroshima* (*Legend of the White Bird*), in 1966; the Uighur ballet *Chin-Tomur* by K. Kh. Kuzham'iarov, in 1969; and Brusilovskii's *Kozy-Korpesh* and *Baian-Slu*, in 1971. Other ballets have included *The Little Humpbacked Horse* by C. Pugni (1939), *Raymonda* by A. K. Glazunov (1940), *Laurencia* by A. A. Krein (1942), *Giselle* by A. Adam (1943), *Don Quixote* by L. Minkus (1946), *Doctor Aibolit* by I. V. Morozov (1950), *La Esmeralda* by Pugni, R. M. Glière, and S. N. Vasilenko (1953), *Shurale* by F. Z. Iarullin (1956), and *The Legend of Love* by A. D. Melikov (1963).

Among the republic's choreographers are Honored Art Workers of the Kazakh SSR D. Abirov and Z. Raibaev. The leading ballet artists include People's Artist of the Kazakh SSR S. Kusherbaev, Honored Artists of the Kazakh SSR A. Bekbosynov, D. Dzhalilov, R. Tazhieva, and S. Tulusanova.

A ballet division was opened at the music school in Alma-Ata in 1934. In 1937 it was made into the School of Choreography.

L. P. SARYNOVA

Theater

The elements of dramatic art were contained in age-old folk rituals, games, the performances of folk comics, and the song competition-dialogues of *akyns*. However, the conditions of the feudal system and the colonialist policies of the tsarist government retarded the development of Kazakh theater. Only after the Revolution of 1905–07 did the first works of national dramaturgy appear. Amateur performances in Kazakh were staged in Orenburg, Omsk, Semipalatinsk, and Tashkent.

The intensive development of the national theater began after the Great October Socialist Revolution. Semiprofessional dramatic groups were of great importance for the development of theatrical art. A. Kashaubaev, I. Baizakov, Zh. Shanin, K. Baizhanov, and Zh. Elebekov, who subsequently became prominent figures in Kazakh art, embarked upon their creative paths in one such troupe, which worked in Semipalatinsk under the name Es-aimak. The first permanent theater group formed in Orenburg in 1922 at the Kazakh Institute of Public Education. Among the actors who worked there were E. Umurzakov, S. Kozhamkulov, and K. U. Badyrov. The first Kazakh theater opened in Kzyl-Orda in 1926; in 1928 it was transferred to Alma-Ata. Masters of folk art and participants in amateur theatricals joined its troupe. Nascent national dramaturgy (the plays of M. O. Auezov, S. Seifullin, B. Mailin, and Zh. Shanin) reflected the struggle for a new life and the emancipation of women; they exposed the seamy side of life in the old *aul*. Simultaneous with the dramatic performances, concerts and evenings of folk art were organized in the newly created theater.

During the 1930's the assimilation of the Russian theater culture, combined with the development of progressive national traditions, promoted the improvement of acting skill and level of performance. The plays of N. V. Gogol, N. F. Pogodin, and K. A. Trenev were added to the theater's repertoire. The shows *Night Thunder* by Auezov (1935) and *Amangel'dy* by Musrepov (1937) were important works.

In 1932 a school for the training of dramatic actors, singers, and musicians was established in Alma-Ata. A system of raion and kolkhoz and sovkhoz theaters based on amateur groups began to develop intensively. These theaters carried on cultural and educational work in remote settlements. Oblast Kazakh and Russian drama theaters opened in many cities. After 1937 the theaters were reinforced by actors and directors who had received special training in Moscow and Leningrad. The creative work of the playwrights A. Tazhibaev, Sh. Khusainov, and

A. Abishev took shape; the life of contemporary Kazakhstan was reflected more broadly in their plays. The plays *The Inspector-General* by Gogol (1936), *Isatai and Makhambet* by M. Akinzhanov (1938), *Abai* by Auezov and L. S. Sobolev and *Kozy-Korpesh* and *Baian-Slu* by Musrepov (both 1940), and *Comrades* by Abishev and *Marabai* by M. Kaibaldin and Khusainov (both 1941) were important to the development of the national theater.

From the first days of the Great Patriotic War, plays and shows devoted to wartime themes and events were written in Kazakhstan, such as *Lightning* by Abishev (1941) and *Guard of Honor* by Auezov and Abishev (1942). The folklore-historical shows *Akhan-Sere and Aktokty* by Musrepov and *Aldar-Kose* by Khusainov (both 1942), which linked Kazakh theater to the age-old artistic culture, were prominent in the repertoires of a number of theaters.

The Theater for Children and Young People was established in Alma-Ata in 1944 (its Russian troupe has been in operation since 1945, its Kazakh troupe since 1948). Its productions have included the tales *The Golden Bat* by Akinzhanov and K. Badyrov (1948) and *Aldar-Kose* by Khusainov (1953); *Ibrai Altynsarin*, a historical play by Akinzhanov (1951); and *The Radiant Stone* (1949) and *The Naughty Child* (1954) by Khusainov, based on the lives of young people.

Plays on contemporary subjects made up the theatrical repertoire in the second half of the 1940's and the early 1950's: *The Victors* by B. F. Chirskov (1947), *Friendship and Love* (1947) and *A Single Family* (1949) by Abishev, *The Millionaire* by G. Mustafin (1950), *The Voice of America* by B. A. Lavrenev (1950), *The Guelder Rose Grove* by A. E. Korneichuk (1951), and *Bloom, Steppe!* by Tazhibaev (1952). Among the productions of Russian and foreign classics, *Talents and Admirers* (1949) and *The Thunderstorm* (1950) by A. N. Ostrovskii and *The Miser* by Molière (1952) stood out. Theaters strove to expand their range of genres and themes and sought to create rich performances.

Plays on themes of the history of Kazakhstan, such as *Chokan Valikhanov* by S. Mukanov (1956) and *Maira* by Tazhibaev (1957), were staged in the second half of the 1950's, and shows with a folklore-historical content, such as *Enlik and Kebek* by Auezov (1957) and *Akhan-Sere and Aktokty* by Musrepov (1958, under the title *The Tragedy of a Poet*) were revived. Contemporary themes were further elaborated in *One Tree Is Not a Forest* (*Bloom, Steppe!*) by Tazhibaev (1958) and *The Wolf Cub in a Cap Trap* by K. Mukhamedzhanov (1959). These productions defined a new stage of development in the national theater, associated with the quest for a deeper exposition of the characters of positive heroes and a striving to achieve a more complete reflection of the life of the people and an organic merging of the folk traditions and contemporary Soviet theater. In 1958 the M. O. Auezov Kazakh Theater and the Republic Russian Theater participated in the Ten-day Festival of Kazakh Art and Literature in Moscow.

Notable among the plays of the 1960's were *The Maternal Field* after Ch. Aitmatov (1964), *Saule* (1961) and *Snowstorm* (1966) by T. Akhtanov, *Stronger Than Death* by S. Zhunusov (1967), *Forgotten by All* by N. Khikmet (1967), *An Optimistic Tragedy* by V. V. Vishnevskii (1967), and *Lenin in 1918* by A. Ia. Kapler (1970).

In 1972, 25 theaters were in operation, including the M. O. Auezov Academic Drama Theater, the M. Iu. Lermontov Republic Russian Drama Theater, the Theater for Children and Young People, the Puppet Theater (Russian and Kazakh groups), the Uighur Theater, and the Korean Theater in Alma-Ata and Kazakh theaters in Dzhambul, Kzyl-Orda, Chimkent, Karaganda, Semipalatinsk, Gur'ev, Dzhetysai, and Arkalyk.

Kazakh theaters stage works by playwrights of the fraternal republics: *The Prodigal Son* by E. Rannet (1959), *On the Night of the Lunar Eclipse* by M. Karim (1967), *Narkes* by I. Iumagulov (1968), *The Star of Vietnam* by I. I. Kupriianov (1968), *The Mother of Her Children* by A. N. Afinogenov (both in 1971), *The Little Shoes* by D. Faizi (1972), *My Little Poplar in the Red Scarf* (1966), and *Face to Face*, after Aitmatov

(1972). Seven-day festivals of the literature and art of Uzbekistan, Tataria, Turkmenistan, the RSFSR, the Ukraine, Armenia, and Tadzhikistan have been held since 1962.

Important contributions to the development of the Kazakh drama theater have been made by People's Artists of the USSR Sh. K. Aimanov and K. Kuanyshpaev and by People's Artists of the Kazakh SSR R. Koichubaeva, M. G. Nasonov, and Zh. Shanin. Figures in the Kazakh theater (1972) include People's Artists of the USSR Kh. Bukeeva and S. Maikanova and People's Artists of the Kazakh SSR K. U. Badyrov, Sh. Dzhandarbekova, A. Dzholumbetov, N. Zhanturin, K. Karmysov, S. Kozhamkulov, A. Mambetov, I. Nogaibaev, B. Rimova, Sh. Sakiev, Z. Suleimenova, M. Surtubaev, S. Tel'garaev, E. Umurzakov, Z. Sharipova, and D. Shashkina.

REFERENCES
L'vov, N. I. *Kazakhskii akademicheskii teatr dramy.* Alma-Ata, 1957.
L'vov, N. I. *Kazakhskii teatr: Ocherk istorii.* Moscow, 1961.
Kanapin, A. K., and L. I. Varshavskii. *Iskusstvo Kazakhstana.* Alma-Ata, 1958.
Kazakhskie oblastnye teatry. Alma-Ata, 1965. [Collection of articles.]
Istoriia sovetskogo dramaticheskogo teatra, vols. 1–6. Moscow, 1966–71.
Kŭndaqbaev, B., and K. Nŭrpeyïsov. *M. Áuezov atïndaghï Qazaqtïng memlekettïq akademiyälïq, drama teatrïna 40 jïl.* Alma-Ata, 1966.
Qŭandïqov, Q. *Tŭnghïsh ŭlt teatrï.* Alma-Ata, 1969.   N. I. L'VOV

Circus. From time immemorial the folk art of Kazakhstan has included people who performed at various festivals—*baluan,* or athletes (Khadzhimukhan Munaitbasov and Baluan-Sholak), acrobatic clowns (the *akyn* Shashubai Koshkarbaev), and comic improvisers. A circus under the direction of A. I. Sosin began performing in Vernyi (now Alma-Ata) in 1919. Its repertoire also included pantomimes on revolutionary themes—"The Struggle of Labor Against Capital" and "Victims of Poverty." V. Ferroni's private circus enterprise (later the Association of Circus Artists and Wrestlers) operated in Semipalatinsk in 1923. The Studio of Music and the Variety Stage, which subsequently became a circus and variety stage studio, was established in Alma-Ata in 1965. Its graduates joined the Kazakh Circus Association, which was organized in 1970. A new circus building opened in Alma-Ata in 1972.   A. IA. SHNEER

Motion pictures

Motion pictures were first shown in Kazakhstan in 1910. Before the October Revolution there were 13 motion-picture theaters in Kazakhstan. The first filming was done in 1925, when newsreel photographers from Moscow shot the Fifth Congress of Soviets of Kazakhstan. The first documentary film about Kazakhstan, *Anniversary of the KASSR,* was made the same year. A division of the Vostok-fil'm trust, which published the periodical film journal *Poslednie novosti* (Latest News) and the essays "Alma-Ata and Its Environs," "Cooperation in the *Aul*," "On Dzhailiau," and "Kzyl-asker," was established in Alma-Ata in 1928. The film *Turksib* (1929, director V. A. Turin), about the construction of the Turkestan-Siberia railroad, was an outstanding work of Soviet documentary cinema.

During the 1920's and 1930's, feature films devoted to life in Kazakhstan were made in the country's central film studios by the directors of those studios, with the participation of Kazakh actors. The films *Mutiny* (1929), *Song of the Steppes* (1930), *Jute* (1932), *The Secret of the Karatau* (1933), and *The Enemy's Paths* (1935) helped launch national films. The film *Amangel'dy* (1939, director M. Z. Levin; E. Umurzakov played the leading role), which depicted the struggle of the Kazakh toiling people for the establishment of Soviet power, marked the birth of the Kazakh motion picture. A newsreel studio was organized in Alma-Ata in 1934; it produced the weekly film journal *Soviet Kazakhstan* and topical documentary films.

The Alma-Ata feature film studio, established in October 1941, was merged in 1942 with the evacuated Mosfil'm and Lenfil'm studios under the name Combined Central Film Studio (TsOKS). Young Kazakh cinematographers worked with prominent Soviet film figures—S. M. Eisenstein, V. I. Pudovkin, G. N. Vasil'ev and S. D. Vasil'ev, I. A. Pyr'ev, F. M. Ermler, Iu. Ia. Raizman, G. L. Roshal', and D. Vertov—which helped

to increase the number of national specialists and promoted works on the life of the Kazakh people (*The Songs of Abai,* 1946, and others).

In 1944, Mosfil'm and Lenfil'm were reevacuated, and the studio that remained in Alma-Ata was merged with the Alma-Ata Newsreel Studio; in 1960 it became the Kazakhfil'm Studio.

Among the historical and historical-revolutionary films made from the 1950's through the early 1970's were *Dzhambul* (1953, directed by E. L. Dzigan, with Sh. K. Aimanov in the role of Dzhambul); *Botagoz* (1958, directed by E. A. Aron), about the fate of a Kazakh woman who participated in the revolutionary struggle for the establishment of Soviet power in Kazakhstan; *His Time Will Come* (1958, directed by M. S. Begalin), devoted to the outstanding Kazakh public figure Chokan Valikhanov; *We Are From Semirech'e* (1959, directed by S. Khodzhikov); *Troubled Morning* (1966, directed by A. Karsakbaev); *Song of Manshuk* (1970, directed by Begalin), about the Great Patriotic War; and *The End of the Hetman* (1971, directed by Sh. K. Aimanov), about the Soviet officials of the Cheka. There were films based on folk epics, among them *Poem of Love* (1954, directed by Aimanov and K. A. Gakkel'), *Aldar-Kose* (1965, directed by Aimanov), and *Kyz-Zhibek* (1972, directed by S. Khodzhikov).

Films on contemporary themes occupy an important place; among them are *The Girl Riding Bareback* (1955, directed by P. P. Bogoliubov), *We Live Here* (1957, directed by Aimanov and M. L. Volodarskii), *Our Dear Doctor* (1958, directed by Aimanov), *If Each of Us . . .* (1962, directed by Khodzhikov), *Tale of a Mother* (1964, directed by A. Ia. Karpov), *They Call Me Kozha* (1964, directed by Karsakbaev), and *Land of the Fathers* (1966, directed by Aimanov). Documentary films include *To You, the Front* (1942), *Reflections About Good Fortune* (1956, directed by A. M. Medvedkin), *In Our City* (1957, directed by O. Abishev), *Such a Short Life* (1969, directed by Iu. Piskunov), *Irtysh-Karaganda* (1970, directed by G. Emel'ianov), *Dynasty of Miners* (1972, directed by Abishev), and *Kurmangazy* (1972, directed by S. Narymbetov and M. Uskembaeva). The actor and director Sh. K. Aimanov has played a major role in the Kazakh film industry.

Directors working in the Kazakh film industry include Sh. Beisembaev, K. Abuseitov, and Zh. Baitenov (feature films); G. Novozhilov, T. Duisebaev, A. Nugmanov, M. Dulepo, Ia. Smirnov, E. Faik, O. Zekki, I. Vereshchagin, I. Chiknoverov, A. Kulakov, and L. Mukhamedgalieva (documentaries); and A. Khaidarov (animated cartoons). Actors include N. Zhanturin, K. Kozhabekov, and A. Umurzakova. Among prominent cameramen are M. Aranyshev, A. Ashrapov, F. Absaliamov, M. Berkovich, M. Duganov, M. Dodonov, and M. Sagimbaev. The Cinematographers' Union of Kazakhstan was organized in 1958. In 1972 there were 10,700 motion-picture projection units in the republic.

REFERENCES
Siranov, K. *Kazakhskoe kinoiskusstvo.* Alma-Ata, 1958.
Kanapin, A. K., and L. I. Varshavskii. *Iskusstvo Kazakhstana.* Alma-Ata, 1958.
Siranov, K. *Kinoiskusstvo Sovetskogo Kazakhstana.* Alma-Ata, 1966.
Fedulin, A. *Kino v Kazakhstane.* Alma-Ata, 1967.
                                          K. SIRANOV [11–422–1]

KAZAKHSTAN ECONOMIC REGION, an economic region of the USSR, coinciding in area with the Kazakh SSR.
                                                        [11–511–2]

KAZAKHSTANSKAIA PRAVDA, the republic newspaper of the Kazakh SSR, published in the Russian language. Founded in 1920, it was originally published under the title *Izvestiia Kirgizskogo kraia.* Subsequently the name of the newspaper was changed several times; since 1932 it has been called *Kazakhstanskaia pravda.* It is published in Alma-Ata six times a week. In 1970 it had a circulation of 170,000.   [11–511–1]

KAZAKH THEATER OF OPERA AND BALLET (full name, Abai Academic Kazakh Theater of Opera and Ballet). Founded in 1933 in Alma-Ata as the Music Studio, it became the Music Theater in 1934. It was given its present name in 1937 and the name Abai was conferred upon it in 1945. The theater moved to new quarters in 1941. Performances are given in both Kazakh and Russian.

The establishment of a national opera repertoire was promoted by the composer E. G. Brusilovskii, the stage director Zh. Shanin, the singers and stage directors K. Baiseitov and K. Dzhandarbekov, and the singers K. Baiseitova and M. Erzhanov. The first Kazakh opera, *Kyz-zhibek,* by Brusilovskii, was performed at the theater in 1934 and in 1938, the first ballet, *Kalkaman and Mamyr,* by Velikanov. The theater's repertoire includes national Kazakh opera and ballets, classical works, and works by Soviet composers from other republics. Among the most outstanding Kazakh operas performed at the theater have been Brusilovskii's *Zhalbyr* (1935) and *Er-Targyn* (1937), Zhubanov and Khamidi's *Abai* (1944), Tulebaev's *Birzhan and Sara* (1946; State Prize of the USSR, 1949), Rakhmadiev's *Kamar-Slu* (1963), and Mukhamedzhanov's *Aislu* (1964) and *Zhumbak kyz* (1971).

The theater's most outstanding ballets include Tlendiev, Stepanov, and Manaev's *Along the Path of Friendship (The Dzhungara Gates;* 1958) and Zhubanova's *Legend of the White Bird* (*Akkanat* and *Khirosima;* 1966). In 1969 the theater staged its first Uigir ballet, *Chin-Tomur,* by Kuzham'iarov.

The Kazakh Theater was awarded the Order of Lenin in 1959. In 1972 the theater's company included the singers People's Artists of the USSR R. Abdullin, R. Dzhamanova, E. Serkebaev, and B. Tulegenova and People's Artists of the Kazakh SSR Sh. Beisekova, K. Kenzhetaev, G. Kurmangaliev, and A. Umbetaev. Its ballet soloists included People's Artist of the Kazakh SSR S. Kusherbaeva. Its principal conductor is Honored Artist of the Bashkir ASSR V. D. Rutter and its principal director, People's Artist of the Kazakh SSR B. D. Dosymzhanov.

REFERENCES

Mekishev, B., and G. Bisenova. *Kazakhskii gosudarstvennyi akademicheskii teatr opery i baleta im. Abaia.* Alma-Ata, 1954.
Messman, V. *Vozrozhdenie pesni.* Alma-Ata, 1958.

B. G. ERZAKOVICH [11–510–1]

KAZAKH UNIVERSITY (full name, S. M. Kirov Kazakh University), founded in Alma-Ata in 1934. The university has (1972 data) departments of mechanics and mathematics, physics, chemistry, biology, geography, law, history, philosophy, philology, and journalism; two departments for the advanced training of teachers in higher schools; six evening and correspondence departments; and a graduate school. Courses are conducted in Kazakh and Russian. The university also has 77 subdepartments, 12 research laboratories, a linear accelerator, and a library with 850,000 holdings.

In the 1971–72 academic year, more than 10,000 students were enrolled at the university, and there were some 1,000 instructors and research workers, including 55 professors and doctors of sciences and 370 docents and candidates of sciences. The university publishes *Uchenye zapiski* (since 1938) and has trained more than 23,000 specialists since its foundation. It was awarded the order of the Red Banner of Labor in 1971.

U. A. DZHOLDASBEKOV [11–510–2]

KAZAKH WHITE-FACED CATTLE, a breed of beef cattle developed in the kolkhozes and sovkhozes of the Kazakh SSR and the Orenburg and Volgograd oblasts by crossing native Kazakh, and, to some extent, Kalmyk cattle with Herefords; the breed was established in 1950. From the Kazakh cattle, the new White-faced breed inherited a strong constitution, and from the Hereford, early maturity and high meat yield. These cattle have a good beef conformation. The body is red, with a white head, chest, underparts, lower legs, and switch of the tail and with white markings on the withers and rump. Kazakh White-faced cattle are well adapted to seasonal changes in the level and type of feed. Depending on the rate of gain, yearlings weigh 320–350 kg; by the age of 15–16 months these calves can be slaughtered. The carcass has a moderate amount of fat and high-quality meat. Adult bulls weigh 850–1,000 kg, and cows 500–550 kg. Hybrids produced by crossing dairy breeds with the Kazakh White-faced

breed are noted for their good fleshing qualities. This breed is raised in the Kazakh SSR and the Orenburg, Volgograd, Saratov, and other oblasts of the RSFSR.

REFERENCES

Bugrimov, E. I. *Kazakhskaia belogolovaia poroda krupnogo rogatogo skota.* Moscow, 1952.
Akopian, K. *Kazakhskii belogolovyi skot na Iugo-Vostoke SSSR.* Chkalov, 1956.
Skotovodstvo: Krupnyi rogatyi skot, vol. 1. Moscow. 1961.

A. V. LANINA [11–419–1]

KAZAKIN, Russian outerwear in the 19th century and early 20th; a type of shortened caftan with hook closing and tiny gathers at the back of the waist and a short, stand-up collar. In certain districts of Russia and the Ukraine, the *kazakin* in its variants was an accessory in both men's and women's native costumes. The *kazakin* was usually made of cloth, and the collar and sleeves were sometimes trimmed with braid or galloon.

[11–390–4]

KAZAKOV, ALEKSANDR VASIL'EVICH. Born Nov. 10 (22), 1888, in Borisoglebsk; died Sept. 10, 1950, in Moscow. Soviet lithologist and geochemist. Doctor of geological and mineralogical sciences (1938).

In 1919, Kazakov was one of the directors of the first scientific center for the study of agronomical ores (now called the Scientific Research Institute of Fertilizers, Insecticides, and Fungicides). In 1925 he became deputy chairman of the Committee on Fertilizers. During the Great Patriotic War he organized the State Institute of Mining and Chemical Raw Materials. In 1944 he became head of the laboratory for the synthesis of minerals formed from sedimentary rocks at the Geological Institute of the Academy of Sciences of the USSR.

Kazakov participated in working out systems of equilibrium at low concentrations and the synthesis of minerals of sedimentary origin. His research established the physicochemical conditions for the formation of a number of sedimentary minerals, including hydroxylapatite, fluorapatite, fluorite, and siderite. He proposed a theory of the formation of phosphorites (such as chemical precipitates of seas of normal salinity), which brought him world renown. He was awarded the Order of the Red Banner of Labor and various medals.

WORKS

"Proiskhozhdenie fosforitov i geologicheskikh faktorov formirovaniia mestorozhdenii." In *Trudy nauchnogo instituta po udobreniiam i insektofungisidam,* fasc. 145. Moscow-Leningrad, 1939.
"Usloviia obrazovaniia fliuorita v osadochnykh porodakh (fliuritovaia sistema)." In *Tr. Instituta geologicheskikh nauk. Seriia geologicheskaia,* 1950, issue 114, no. 40. (With E. I. Sokolova.)

G. A. KAZAKOV [11–391–1]

KAZAKOV, ARISTARKH ANDREEVICH. Born 1878 in the village of Alekseevskoe, in present-day Tatar ASSR; died Sept. 21, 1963, in Moscow. Activist in the struggle to establish Soviet power in Middle Asia. Joined the revolutionary movement in 1906. Member of the CPSU from 1917.

Kazakov experienced political persecution. After the October Revolution of 1917 he became deputy president of the Provisional Revolutionary Committee of the Turkestan territory and people's commissar for food supplies. Kazakov was one of the organizers of the suppression of an anti-Soviet rebellion in Tashkent in January 1919. In 1919 he was president of the Provisional Revolutionary Council, and later he was president of the Central Executive Committee of the Turkestan Republic. In 1920–21 he was head of the political section on the Donbas railroad and then secretary of the Samara Province committee of the RCP (Bolshevik). Thereafter, he held supervisory administrative and economic positions and served as a member of the All-Russian Central Executive Committee. He retired with a special pension in 1956. [11–391–2]

KAZAKOV, IURII PAVLOVICH. Born Aug. 8, 1927, in Moscow. Soviet Russian writer.

Kazakov first published his works in 1952. He is the author of the collections of short stories *Man'ka* (1958), *At the Station* (1959), *Along the Road* (1961), *The Blue and the Green* (1963), *The Smell of Bread* (1965), *Arktur the Hound* (1958), *Two in December* (1966), and *Autumn in the Oak Woods* (1969). Kazakov follows the tradition of classical Russian prose stylistically and, in part, thematically. The clash between his spiritually refined heroes and the insolent petit bourgeois philistines forms the basis of many of Kazakov's stories—for example, "Going to Town" and "No Sense at All." Truth to one's goals and fulfilling one's duty in life are Kazakov's main themes in such works as the collected sketches about coast-dwellers *Northern Diary* and short stories about animals and being at one with the wise laws of nature.

REFERENCES
Nagibin, Iu. "Svoe i chuzhoe." *Druzhba narodov,* 1959, no. 7.
Solov'eva, I. "Nachalo puti." *Novyi mir,* 1959, no. 9.
Pertsovskii, V. "Osmyslenie zhizni." *Voprosy literatury,* 1964, no. 2.
Bilinkis, Ia. "A zhizn' dvizhetsia . . . [Zametki o rasskazakh Iu. Kazakova]." *Neva,* 1965, no. 6.
Ninov, A. "Iazyk rasskazov." *Druzhba narodov,* 1966, no. 4.
Gromov, E. "Khudozhnik v sovremennom mire." *Zvezda,* 1969, no. 3.
[11–395–2]

KAZAKOV, KONSTANTIN PETROVICH. Born Nov. 5 (18), 1902, in Tula. Marshal of artillery (1962). Became a member of the CPSU in 1920. The son of a worker.

Kazakov was a worker before he joined the Soviet Army in 1921. He graduated from the VTsIK Combined Military School in 1923, from the M. V. Frunze Military Academy in 1936, and from advanced academic courses of the Military Academy of the General Staff in 1948. In the Great Patriotic War (1941–45), Kazakov began as a commander of a howitzer artillery regiment; in June 1941 he became chief of operations of the artillery department of the Southwestern Front, and in April 1942 he moved to the staff of the chief of the artillery of the Red Army and in April 1943 to the staff for especially important assignments of the commander of the artillery of the Red Army. From April 1944 to May 1945 he commanded the artillery of the Second Shock Army. He participated in the liberation of the Baltic area and in battles in East Prussia and was an army artillery commander in the war with imperialist Japan.

Holding high positions after the war, Kazakov was commander of the rocket troops and of the artillery of the ground forces from 1963 to 1969 and was appointed military inspector-adviser in July 1969. Kazakov has been awarded three Orders of Lenin, the Order of the October Revolution, four Orders of the Red Banner, two Orders of Suvorov Second Class, Orders of Kutuzov First and Second Class, the Order of Bogdan Khmel'nitskii First Class, three foreign orders, and medals.

[11–392–1]

KAZAKOV, MATVEI FEDOROVICH. Born in 1738 in Moscow; died Oct. 26 (Nov. 7), 1812, in Riazan'. Russian architect; one of the founders of classicism in 18th-century Russian architecture.

From 1751 to 1760, Kazakov studied in D. V. Ukhtomskii's architectural school in Moscow. Between 1763 and 1767 he worked under P. R. Nikitin in Tver', where he took part in the drafting of a plan for the city and built the Itinerary Palace for Catherine II. From 1768 to 1774, Kazakov assisted V. I. Bazhenov in the planning of the Great Kremlin Palace in Moscow. During this time he mastered the use of classical forms and proportions; this mastery was particularly important in his later work.

Kazakov's designs demonstrate an organic combination of large-scale urban design, practical planning, and lofty architectural forms. He developed various types of residential and civic buildings, with which he organized great municipal spaces. In this way he did much to define the architectural appearance of Moscow in the late 18th and early 19th centuries. Such buildings also determined the scale and character of Moscow's later construction. Kazakov's works include the Senate building (1776–87), which now houses the Supreme Soviet and the Council of Ministers of the USSR and in which a large-diameter domed roof was first used in Russia. He also built the university building (1786–93, rebuilt by D. I. Gilardi); the Golitsyn (1796–1801) and the Pavel (1802–07) hospitals; and the manor houses of Demidov (1779–91), Gubin (1790's), and Baryshnikov (1797–1802). These buildings all display careful composition both from the street and from within. The arched gateways, the widely separated wings, and the wrought-iron open-worked fences facing the center of the street create a vista of the main building situated behind a broad courtyard. The central part of the building, characterized by domes, grand porticoes, and simple, clear design, is massive and imposing. The smooth, severe exterior walls are complemented by a few carefully designed and graphically clear details, such as cornices and window backbands, which create a calm, solemn rhythm.

Integral and modeled architectural forms predominate in Kazakov's centrally planned structures. These buildings include the Church of the Metropolitan Philip (1777–88), the Voznesenie Church (1790–93), and the Church of SS. Cosmas and Damian (1791–1803) in Moscow, as well as the mausoleum (1784–1802) in Nikolo-Pogoreloe in present-day Smolensk Oblast.

The expressiveness and ceremonial festivity of Kazakov's interiors are achieved by the introduction of a grand scale (the Hall of Columns of the House of Trade Unions, Moscow), by the use of sculpture (the Senate and university buildings), and by the use of monumental painting (the "Gilded Rooms" of the Demidov house). Kazakov remained a classicist, although he designed some structures in a pseudo-Gothic style. The basis of these structures remained classical; pre-Petrine and Gothic decorative elements were used only to adorn the facades (the Petrovskii Palace in Moscow, 1775–82; now the N. E. Zhukovskii Air Force Academy).

From 1800 to 1804, Kazakov supervised the drafting of general and "facade" plans ("bird's-eye view") of Moscow. He also completed a series of 13 architectural albums devoted to the most important buildings erected by himself and other architects in Moscow. A gifted draftsman, Kazakov mastered the technique of architectural drafting, etching, and drawing. In his graphic work he devoted a great deal of attention to the expression of the volumes of buildings. He was a master of genre drawing, which was then emerging as an art form. Kazakov's work as a graphic artist includes the drawings *Amusement Pavilions at Khodynka Field in Moscow"* (1774–75, india ink and pen) and *The Construction of Petrovskii Palace* (1778, india ink and pen)—both in the A. V. Shchusev Museum of Architecture in Moscow. He also drew views of the Kolomna Kremlin (1778, india ink and pen; now in the Russian Museum, Leningrad).

Kazakov organized an architectural school within the Department of Kremlin Construction. Among his pupils were I. V. Egotov, A. N. Bakarev, I. G. Tamanskii, M. M. Kazakov, R. R. Kazakov, and O. I. Bove.

REFERENCES
M. K. (Matvei Matveevich Kazakov). "O Matvee Fedoroviche Kazakove." *Russkii vestnik,* 1816, no. 11.
Bondarenko, I. E. *Arkhitektor Matvei Fedorovich Kazakov (1738–1813).* Moscow, 1938.
Il'in, M. A. "Fasadicheskii plan Moskvy M. F. Kazakova." In the collection *Arkhitekturnoe nasledstvo,* [fasc.] 9. Moscow-Leningrad, 1959.
Arkhitekturnye al'bomy M. F. Kazakova. (Prepared for publication and with text and commentary by E. A. Beletskaia.) Moscow, 1956.
Vlasiuk, A. I., A. I. Kaplun, and A. A. Kiparisova. *Kazakov.* Moscow, 1957.   E. A. BELETSKAIA   [11–392–2]

KAZAKOV, MIKHAIL IL'ICH. Born Sept. 26 (Oct. 9), 1901, in the village of Velikusha, in present-day Kichmengskii Gorodok Raion, Vologda Oblast. Soviet military commander, general of the army (1955). Became a member of the CPSU in 1919. The son of a peasant.

Kazakov joined the Soviet Army in 1920 and served in the Civil War as a political personnel soldier on the Southern Front. Kazakov graduated from an advanced cavalry training school for commanders in 1927, from the M. V. Frunze Military Academy in 1931, and from the Military Academy of the General Staff in 1937. He served in command and staff positions and was chief of staff of the Middle Asian Military District from 1938 to 1941. In the Great Patriotic War (1941–45), Kazakov was chief of staff of the Briansk Front (January to July 1942) and of the Voronezh Front (July 1942 to February 1943) and commander of the Sixty-ninth Army (February to March 1943). He then became assistant commander of the troops of the Reserve and Steppe fronts and deputy commander of the troops of the Briansk and Second Baltic fronts (April to December 1943), after which he commanded the Tenth Guards Army from January 1944 until the end of the war. He fought on the Don and in the battle of Kursk and participated in the liberation of the Ukraine and the Baltic.

Holding command and staff positions after the war, Kazakov was commander of the troops of the Ural Military District (1953–56), deputy commander in chief of the ground forces (1956), commander of the Southern Force Group (December 1956 to 1960), commander of the troops of the Leningrad Military District (1960–65), chief of staff of the Joint Armed Forces of the countries of the Warsaw Treaty Organization (1965–68), and military inspector-adviser (since 1968). Kazakov was a deputy to the second and to the fourth through seventh convocations of the Supreme Soviet of the USSR and a candidate member of the Central Committee of the CPSU from 1961 to 1971. He wrote *Over the Maps of Past Battles* (1965). Kazakov has been awarded two Orders of Lenin, the Order of the October Revolution, four Orders of the Red Banner, Orders of Suvorov First and Second Class, the Order of Kutuzov First Class, two Orders of the Red Star, two foreign orders, and medals.   [11–394–1]

KAZAKOV, NIKOLAI (MIKLAI) IVANOVICH. Born Jan. 15, 1918, in the village of Kutiuk-Kiner, now in Morki Raion, Mari ASSR. Soviet Mari poet. People's Poet of the Mari ASSR (1960). Member of the CPSU since 1943.

Kazakov graduated from the M. Gorky Institute of Literature in 1955. He began publishing in 1934, and his first book, *Verses,* came out in 1938. In 1950 his collection of verses *Poetry—My Beloved Friend* was published in Russian, for which he received the State Prize of the USSR (1951). Kazakov has been awarded the Order of the Red Banner of Labor and various medals.

WORKS
In Russian translation:
Izbrannye stikhi. Moscow, 1952.
Detiam. Ioshkar-Ola, 1959.
Izbrannoe. Ioshkar-Ola, 1960.
V strane moei Mariiskoi. Moscow, 1968.

REFERENCES
Kadykov, N. S. *Poeziia Miklaia Kazakova.* Ioshkar-Ola, 1960.
Ocherki istorii mariiskoi literatury, parts 1–2. Ioshkar-Ola, 1960–63.
                                                                    [11–395–1]

KAZAKOV, VASILII IVANOVICH. Born July 5 (17), 1898, in the village of Filippovo, in present-day Buturlino Raion, Gorky Oblast; died May 25, 1968, in Moscow. Marshal of artillery (1955), Hero of the Soviet Union (Apr. 6, 1945). Became a member of the CPSU in 1932. The son of a peasant.

Kazakov was a worker before he joined the army in 1916. He participated in the February Revolution of 1917 in Petrograd, joined the Soviet Army in February 1918, and served in the Civil War of 1918–20 as a battery commander. Kazakov graduated from the Second Petrograd Artillery Course (1918), an artillery school (1923), an advanced training school for commanders (1929, 1936), the M. V. Frunze Military Academy (1934), and an advanced training school for top commanders (1939). In the Great Patriotic War (1941–45), Kazakov was chief of the artillery of the Sixteenth Army (July 1941 to July 1942) and then commander of the artillery of the Briansk, Stalingrad, Don, Central, Byelorussian, and First Byelorussian fronts. He participated in the battles of Moscow, Stalingrad, and Kursk, in the liberation of Byelorussia and Poland, and in the assault on Berlin.

After the war Kazakov was the commander of the artillery of the Soviet troops in Germany and then was deputy commander, first deputy commander, and commander of the artillery of the Soviet Army and chief of the Army Air Defense Team. He was a member of the Group of Inspectors General of the Ministry of Defense of the USSR from 1965. Kazakov was awarded four Orders of Lenin, five Orders of the Red Banner, three Orders of Suvorov First Class, the Order of Kutuzov First Class, the Order of Suvorov Second Class, the Order of the Red Star, two foreign orders, and medals.   [11–391–3]

KAZAKOVA, RIMMA FEDOROVNA. Born Jan. 27, 1932, in Sevastopol'. Soviet Russian poet.

Kazakova graduated from Leningrad State University in 1954 and worked in the Far East as a lecturer at the Khabarovsk Officers' House and as an editor at a newsreel studio. She was first published in 1955. Her poetry is imbued with civic enthusiasm and the romance of the Soviet man's struggle for happiness and dignity. Her collections of verse include *Let Us Meet in the East* (1958), *Verses* (1962), *They Do Not Weep in the Taiga* (1965), *To Trust in the Snow* (1967), and *Green Firs* (1969). Kazakova is a translator of both Soviet national and foreign poets.

WORKS
Izbr. lirika. Moscow, 1964.
Piatnitsy: Kniga novykh stikhov. Moscow, 1965.
Snezhnaia baba. Moscow, 1972.

REFERENCES
Smeliakov, Ia. "Molodaia poeziia novogo vremeni." *Moskva,* 1962, no. 12.
Ovcharenko, F. "Ne kazat'sia, a byt'." *Molodaia gvardiia,* 1968, no. 11.
Mikhailov, Al. "Rytsari nemedlennogo deistviia." *Znamia,* 1970, no. 8.
    (On the poetry of V. Gordeichev and R. Kazakova.)   [11–396–1]

KAZALINSK, a city in Kazalinsk Raion, Kzyl-Orda Oblast, Kazakh SSR. It is situated 12 km south of the Kazalinsk railroad station on the Aral'sk–Kzyl-Orda line, on the right bank of the Syr Darya River. Population, 9,000 (1970). A brickyard and a fish-processing plant are located there. Kazalinsk was founded as a fort in 1853 and became a city in 1867.   [11–396–2]

KAZAN, ELIA. Born Sept. 7, 1909, in Constantinople. American film director, Greek by nationality.

Kazan graduated from the Yale University drama school and from 1932 to 1939 was an actor and director in the progressive Group Theater in New York. He made his film debut as an actor in 1940 and then as a director in 1945 with the film *A Tree Grows in Brooklyn.* In this film, as well as in *Boomerang, Gentleman's Agreement* (both 1947), and *Pinky* (1949), Kazan focused on critical social problems, such as the bad conditions of workers, corruption in the American judicial system, anti-Semitism, and racism. However, he proposed compromising solutions that worked to the advantage of reactionary circles. In his films of the 1950's, such as *A Streetcar Named Desire* (1951), *Viva Zapata* (1952), and *East of Eden* (1955), Kazan continued to focus on real problems, such as the disintegration of the human personality, social protest, and the ruin of the bourgeois family. Kazan saw the flaws of bourgeois society simply as a product of the biological nature of man. Kazan's autobiographical *America, America* (1962) was his most famous film of the 1960's. In 1972 he made the film *The Visitors,* which dealt with the moral decay, animosity, and cruelty of those who took part in America's criminal imperialist aggression in Vietnam.

V. A. UTILOV   [11–396–4]

KAZAN, a city, the capital of the Tatar ASSR, and one of the most important industrial and cultural centers of the Volga Region. Situated on the left bank of the Volga River, at its confluence with the Kazanka River, it is a major river port and a railroad station on the Moscow-Sverdlovsk line, 797 km from Moscow. Kazan is a highway junction and has an airport. Population, 904,000 (1972; 130,000 in 1897; 179,000 in 1926; 406,000 in 1939; 667,000 in 1959). The city covers an area of 285 sq km and has five districts.

History. Kazan was founded in the second half of the 13th century by Bulgars along the middle course of the Kazanka River. It was destroyed by troops of the Muscovite prince Iurii Dmitrievich in 1399 and rebuilt 30 or 40 years later on a hill that later became the site of a kremlin in which the khan's palace and mosques were located. From the 15th century Kazan was a major economic and trade center of the central Volga Region and the capital of the Kazan Khanate, which was annexed to the Russian state in 1552 as a result of the Kazan campaigns of 1545–52. The city grew rapidly from the second half of the 16th century, becoming a provincial capital in 1708. A cloth factory was built here in 1714 and a shipyard and other enterprises in 1718. The working people of Kazan actively participated in the Peasant War led by E. I. Pugachev, whose forces took the city (except the kremlin) by assault on July 12, 1774; much of the city was burned during the battle. In the 19th century large capitalist enterprises arose in Kazan, including the processing of agricultural products, metalworking, and woodworking. The University of Kazan was opened in 1804.

In the second half of the 19th century Kazan became a center of the revolutionary and democratic movement. V. I. Lenin began his revolutionary activity in Kazan in 1887 while a student in the university's law faculty. N. E. Fedoseev organized the first Marxist circles in Kazan in 1888. A Social Democratic group arose in 1897, a Social Democratic organization was founded in 1899, and the Committee of the RSDLP was formed in January 1903. During the Revolution of 1905–07 workers, under the committee's leadership, fought street battles with the police and Cossacks on Oct. 16–17, 1905, controlling the city for two days.

On Oct. 26 (Nov. 8), 1917, an armed uprising led to the establishment of Soviet power in Kazan. In late February 1918 the Tatar bourgeoisie seized the Tatar section of the city beyond the Bulak River, which was called the Transbulak Republic; the uprising was soon suppressed. On Aug. 7, 1918, Kazan was captured by White Czechs and White Guards. Terror and the restoration of bourgeois-landlord rule provoked a workers' uprising in Kazan on Sept. 3, 1918, which was suppressed by the White Guards. On Sept. 10, 1918, the Red Army liberated the city, and on May 27, 1920, Kazan became the capital of the Tatar ASSR. Under the prewar five-year plans, as a result of socialist transformations, Kazan became a major industrial, scientific, and cultural center. During the Great Patriotic War (1941–45), Kazan's industry contributed to defense, and many industrial enterprises and people evacuated from the country's western regions were relocated in the city. The postwar decades saw a further development of Kazan's economy, science, and culture.

Kazan is the birthplace of N. E. Bauman and F. I. Chaliapin, and G. R. Derzhavin, S. T. Aksakov, N. I. Lobachevskii, M. A. Balakirev, L. N. Tolstoy, A. M. Gorky, and M. Dzhalil' lived and worked here.   V. V. KUZ'MIN and IU. I. SMYKOV

Economy. New branches of industry have been established in the Soviet period, including instrument-making, photochemical, rubber, petrochemical, and synthetic rubber industries. Machine building, metalworking, and the chemical industry are the leading branches. The machine-building plants produce compressors, heat-measuring instruments, dental instruments, sanitary engineering equipment, suspension cableways, and gas ranges. Enterprises of the chemical industry include an organic-synthesis plant, the V. V. Kuibyshev Chemical Plant (motion picture film), and the M. Vakhitov Household Chemistry Plant (stearine, soap, candles, laundry detergents). Kazan is an important center of light industry; one of the largest fur combines in the country, specializing in the processing of sheepskin to resemble nutria, seal, and otter, is located here, as well as footwear and clothing factories. The well-developed food industry includes meat-packing and dairy combines, a confectionery factory, and a brewery. There are also large building-materials enterprises with plants producing reinforced-concrete structural components, silicate bricks, and large-panel housing construction materials.   P. V. ABRAMOV

Architecture. In the center of Kazan are the walls and towers of the kremlin, built in the 16th century and rebuilt in the 17th and 19th centuries. Within the kremlin are the Blagoveshchenskii Cathedral (1562; architects, Postnik Iakovlev and I. Shiriai), the Siuiumbeki Watchtower (58 m in height; late 17th to early 18th century; foundation possibly 16th century), and the former governor's palace, now the building of the Presidium of the Supreme Soviet and the Council of Ministers of the Tatar ASSR (mid-19th century; architects, K. A. Ton and V. Morgan; eclectic style). Other architectural monuments in the city include the

SS. Peter and Paul Cathedral with its six-tiered bell tower (1723–26), the Mikhliaev house (early 18th century), the Mardzhani mosque (1766; incorporating elements of Russian baroque and Tatar ornamental motifs), and the University of Kazan, built in the classical style (main building, 1825, architect P. G. Piatnitskii; library, anatomy theater, and observatory built in the 1830's by the architect M. P. Korinfskii). Architectural monuments of the Soviet period include Freedom Square, on which are found the bronze and granite monument to Lenin (1954; sculptor, P. P. Iatsyno) and the Musa Dzhalil' Theater of Opera and Ballet, a 25,000-seat stadium (1960), a river terminal (1962), a 2,400-seat circus (1967), the concert hall of the conservatory (1967), and the Tatarstan hotel (1970). Residential areas, such as the Lenin, Kirov, and Soviet districts, have expanded. A new administrative and public center is developing on the banks of the Kazanka and the Volga, linked by a new highway with the kremlin; parks and public gardens have been laid out there.
          S. S. AIDAROV

Educational and cultural institutions. In the 1971–72 academic year the city had 150 general-education schools with 132,900 students, 41 vocational and technical schools with 18,000 students, and 21 specialized secondary schools with 24,200 students. There were also ten institutions of higher learning with 56,400 students: the University of Kazan, a conservatory, and institutes of aviation, chemical engineering, civil engineering, agriculture, veterinary medicine, finance and economics, pedagogy, and medicine. In 1971 there were 302 preschool institutions with an enrollment of 43,900.

As of Jan. 1, 1972, Kazan had 180 public libraries with 4,430,000 copies of books and magazines; four museums, the State Museum of the Tatar ASSR, the Museum of Fine Arts, the V. I. Lenin Museum House, and the A. M. Gorky Literary Museum; and six theaters, the G. Kamal Tatar Academic Dramatic Theater, the Musa Dzhalil' Theater of Opera and Ballet, the V. I. Kachalov Russian Bol'shoi Dramatic Theater, the Lenin Komsomol Young People's Theater, a puppet theater, and the Tatar Traveling Dramatic Theater. Kazan also has a symphonic orchestra, a philharmonic society, a circus, a palace of sports, 36 clubs, 95 motion picture projectors, a palace of Pioneers, three houses of Pioneers, centers for young technicians, naturalists, and tourists, and seven children's sports schools.

The republic's publishing houses and radio and television, including a television center, are located in Kazan. Five republic newspapers and 11 magazines were published in Tatar and Russian in 1972. One radio station and two television channels broadcast in Tatar and Russian and transmit broadcasts from Moscow.   I. Z. MUKHUTDINOV

Public health. As of Jan. 1, 1972, Kazan had 54 hospitals with 12,700 beds (14.1 per 1,000 inhabitants), as against 900 beds in 1913, and 5,000 physicians (one per 188 inhabitants) compared with 290 physicians in 1913. Outpatient and specialized medical care is provided by 84 polyclinics and 12 dispensaries, and there are nine public health communicable diseases stations. Research work is conducted by scientific research institutes of traumatology and orthopedics, epidemiology, and microbiology and by the All-Union Scientific Research Institute of Medical Instruments. Medical personnel are trained by the S. V. Kurashov Medical Institute, the V. I. Lenin Institute for the Advanced Training of Physicians, and pharmaceutical schools. In and near the city are sanatoriums, houses of rest, and the Volga international youth camp.

REFERENCES
Bobchenko, T., A. Garzavina, and K. Sinitsyna. *Kazan: Putevoditel'.* Kazan, 1970.
Bushkanets, E. G. *Kazan: Putevoditel'.* Kazan, 1964.
Kalinin, N. F. *Kazan,* 2nd ed. [Kazan] 1955.
Kalinin, N. F. "Raskopki v Kazan'skom kremle v 1953 g." *Izv. Kazanskogo filiala AN SSSR. Ser. gumanitarnykh nauk,* 1955, issue 1.
Aidarov, S. S. *Pamiatniki arkhitektury Kazani* (collection of booklets). Kazan, 1961.   [11–410–1]

KAZAN, UNIVERSITY OF (full name, V. I. Ul'ianov-Lenin University of Kazan), one of the oldest universities in the USSR. It was founded in 1804 and comprised four faculties in the prerevolutionary period: history and philology, physics and mathematics, medicine, and law. Many scientific schools originated and developed at the university, enriching science with important discoveries.

Among prominent Russian scientists who studied and worked there were N. I. Lobachevskii (who was rector of the university from 1827 to 1846), A. M. Butlerov, the astronomer I. M. Simonov, the chemists K. K. Klaus, N. N. Zinin, V. V. Markovnikov, and A. M. Zaitsev, the astronomer M. A. Koval'skii, the biologists and medical researchers V. M. Bekhterev and P. F. Lesgaft, the Orientalists O. M. Kovalevskii and V. P. Vasil'ev, the historian A. P. Shchapov, the linguist I. A. Baudouin de Courtenay, the specialist in mechanics I. S. Gromeka, and the geologist N. I. Golovkinskii. L. N. Tolstoy and the Tatar revolutionary Kh. M. Iamashev studied at the university, and its graduates included the writers S. T. Aksakov, I. I. Lazhechnikov, P. I. Mel'nikov-Pecherskii, and I. I. Panaev, the artist V. I. Iakobi, the composer M. A. Balakirev, the first Buriat scientist D. Banzarov, and the Tatar educator K. Nasyri. The university was one of the centers of progressive social thought and revolutionary struggle in Russia. In 1887, V. I. Ul'ianov-Lenin was admitted to the law faculty, and later that year, on Dec. 4 (16), 1887, he was expelled for his part in organizing and holding a student protest rally.

In the Soviet period the university has developed into a major scientific and educational institution. A number of higher educational institutions in Kazan have evolved out of the university: schools of medicine, pedagogy, aviation, chemical engineering, agriculture, and economics and finance. The university has played an increasingly important role in the educational and cultural development of the peoples of the Volga and Ural regions. In 1925 it was renamed the V. I. Ul'ianov-Lenin University of Kazan. Among the outstanding discoveries made by scientists at the university are those of the mathematicians N. G. Chebotarev and A. Z. Petrov, the specialist in mechanics N. G. Chetaev, the biologists and medical specialists A. F. Samoilov, A. V. Vishnevskii, S. S. Zimnitskii, and N. A. Mislavskii, the linguist V. A. Bogoroditskii, the astronomer A. D. Dubiago, the chemists A. E. Arbuzov and B. A. Arbuzov, and the physicist E. K. Zavoiskii.

In 1972 the university had departments of biology and soils, geography, geology, history and philology (with a division in Tatar language and literature), mechanics and mathematics, physics, chemistry, and law. The university also has a department for the advanced training of teachers in higher educational institutions, a preparatory division, a graduate school, evening and correspondence courses, 65 subdepartments, the N. G. Chebotarev Research Institute of Mathematics and Mechanics, the A. M. Butlerov Institute of Chemistry, the V. P. Engel'gardt Astronomical Observatory, a computer center, a scientific-research section, eight special problems laboratories, the V. I. Ul'ianov-Lenin Museum, zoological, geological, and ethnographic museums, meteorological and magnetism observatories, zoological and biological stations, and a publishing house. The N. I. Lobachevskii Scientific Library contains about 4 million holdings.

In the 1971–72 academic year some 9,500 undergraduate and graduate students attended the university, and the faculty numbered 900 instructors and researchers, including 85 doctors of sciences and professors and 435 candidates of sciences and docents. The university has published *Uchenye zapiski* since 1821. A monograph was published in honor of the university's 125th anniversary (M. K. Korbut, *Kazanskii gosudarstvennyi universitet im. V. I. Ul'ianova-Lenina za 125 let,* vols. 1–2, 1930). In the Soviet period about 29,000 specialists have been trained at the university, which was awarded the Order of the Red Banner of Labor in 1955.   M. T. NUZHIN [11–406–1]

KAZAN AVIATION INSTITUTE, a school training engineers for the aviation, instrument-making, radioelectronics, and machine-building industries. It was founded in 1932 to replace the aerodynamics division of the University of Kazan.

The institute (1972 data) has departments for the study of aircraft, aircraft engines, systems of automatic aircraft control and instrumentation, radio engineering, computer and control systems, and motor-vehicle construction; evening courses in gen-

eral technology, machine building, radio engineering, and instrument-making; a graduate school; 45 subdepartments; seven laboratories for special problems and branch laboratories; and a library with 570,000 holdings.

In the 1971–72 academic year the institute had more than 10,000 students and more than 700 instructors, including 33 professors and doctors of sciences and 250 docents and candidates of sciences. The institute has the right to accept doctoral and candidates' dissertations for defense. It has been publishing *Trudy KAI* since 1933, and since its foundation it has trained over 20,000 specialists. It was awarded the Order of the Red Banner of Labor in 1957.   R. SH. NIGMATULLIN [11–403–1]

KAZAN BOL'SHOI DRAMATIC THEATER (full name, V. I. Kachalov Russian Kazan Bol'shoi Dramatic Theater), one of the oldest theaters in Russia. The first theatrical performances in Kazan were given in the 18th century, and in 1791 a public semiprofessional theater was opened. In 1803 a professional company of serf actors began performing in a specially built theater. The famous actor and playwright P. A. Plavil'shchikov greatly influenced the theater's development and largely determined the democratic orientation of its repertoire. The theater staged Fonvizin's *The Minor* in 1804 and Plavil'shchikov's *Old Bachelor* and *Ermak* in 1805.

During the 1830's and 1840's the outstanding Russian actors P. S. Mochalov and M. S. Shchepkin performed in Kazan. In 1852 a stone building was erected to house the theater, and N. K. Miloslavskii headed its first permanent company until 1858. The theater was subsequently managed by the actor and director P. M. Medvedev (1866–72, 1874–80, 1885–88) and by the entrepreneurs M. M. Borodai (1895–1900) and N. I. Sobol'shchikov-Samarin (1901–07). During this time the theater staged chiefly classical dramatic works, and its leading performers were V. N. Davydov, P. A. Strepetova, and M. G. Savina. Between 1897 and 1900 V. I. Kachalov acted in the theater.

After the October Revolution, Kazan became an important scientific and cultural center, and the Kazan Bol'shoi Dramatic theater became one of the country's leading companies. Among its best performances were Lavrenev's *The Breakup* (1927), Vs. Ivanov's *Armored Train 14–69* (1928), and Trenev's *Liubov' Iarovaia* (1932). In the 1920's and 1930's the theater numbered among its actors and directors I. N. Pevtsov, Z. M. Slavianova, I. A. Slonov, L. A. Gripich, I. A. Rostovtsev, M. I. Tsarev, M. I. Zharov, and M. F. Astangov. Between 1934 and 1962, G. D. Rigorin headed the theater; in the 1940's and 1950's its chief directors were E. A. Prostov and E. M. Beibutov, and its directors included E. G. Gakkel' and A. R. Treplev. During these years the company staged, among other plays, Chekhov's *Uncle Vanya* (1946), *The Young Guard*, based on Fadeev's novel (1947), *Road to Calvary*, based on A. N. Tolstoy's novel (1947), Stepanov and Popov's *Port Arthur* (1953), and Schiller's *Don Carlos* (1955).

The theater produced a number of plays devoted to the life of Lenin, such as *Lenin in 1918* by Kapler and Zlatogorova (1940), *Kremlin Chimes* by Pogodin (1940, 1962), *The Family* by Popov (1952), *Third Pathétique* by Pogodin (1958), *Confronting the Storm* by Ishmuratov (1963), and *Between Showers* by Shtein (1970). Works by Tatar playwrights include Isanbet's *Mullanur Vakhatov* (1950) and Ishmuratov's *Immortal Song* (1956), about the heroic deeds of Musa Dzhalil'. Among the actors appearing in the theater's most successful plays of the 1930's through the 1950's were E. E. Zhilina, N. I. Iakushenko, F. V. Grigor'ev, G. P. Ardarov, I. V. Zagorskii, L. P. Milova, D. R. Liubin, M. N. Preobrazhenskaia, A. D. Gusev, and L. S. Schmidt. The best plays of the 1960's included Mayakovsky's *Bathhouse*, Gorky's *The Zykovs*, and Bulgakov's *Flight*.

In 1948 the theater was renamed the V. I. Kachalov Russian Kazan Bol'shoi Dramatic Theater, and in 1957 it was awarded the Order of the Red Banner of Labor. As of 1972 the theater's company included People's Artist of the Uzbek SSR N. P. Alekseeva, People's Artist of the RSFSR and the Tatar ASSR V. M. Pavlova, People's Artists of the Tatar ASSR P. A. Tsvetaev and V. I. Ulik, Honored Artist of the RSFSR and Tatar ASSR E. V. Lisetskaia, and People's Artist of the Tatar ASSR, E. B. Gel'ms.

Its chief director since 1965 has been Honored Art Worker of the Tatar ASSR N. Iu. Orlov.

REFERENCE
Kruti, I. *Russkii teatr v Kazani.* Moscow, 1958.

I. G. INGVAR [11–403–2]

KAZANBULAK, an urban-type settlement in Kasum-Ismailov Raion, Azerbaijan SSR, 9 km from the Kiurok-Chai railroad station on the Tbilisi-Baku line. There is a plant producing theatrical equipment in Kazanbulak, and petroleum is extracted in the surrounding region. [11–396–5]

KAZAN CAMPAIGNS OF 1545–52, Russian military campaigns against the Kazan Khanate, which had adopted an aggressive policy toward Russia. The khanate had barred Russia from the Volga trade route and made frequent raids into Russian territory. By the mid-16th century about 100,000 Russian captives were held in Kazan.

The struggle to annex the khanate to the Russian state, begun in the late 15th century, had intensified by the 1540's. In Kazan it found support among some Tatar feudal nobles, known as the Moscow party. The campaign of 1545 was more of a military demonstration than a real assault, but it served to strengthen the position of the Moscow party and other opponents of the khan, Safa-Girei, who was banished from Kazan at the end of the year. In the spring of 1546 he was replaced by Shah-Ali, the candidate of the Muscovite grand prince, Ivan IV the Terrible. Soon, however, Safa-Girei was able to return, supported by the Crimean Tatars.

The campaigns of 1547–48 and 1549–50 were unsuccessful. The government of Ivan IV made serious preparations for a new assault, introducing a series of reforms to strengthen the army. In 1551, as a result of the diplomatic mission of P. Turgenev, the Russians gained a promise of neutrality from the Nogai Horde, an ally of Kazan. That same year the fortress of Sviazhsk was built near Kazan. In August 1551, Shah-Ali once again regained the throne, but he was unable to deal with the difficult situation and fled in February 1552. The Tatar nobility then invited Prince Iadigar of Astrakhan' to rule over the khanate.

On June 16, 1552, an army of 150,000 men and 150 guns set out from Moscow, led by Ivan IV. On news of the approach of the Crimean Army of Khan Devlet-Girei, it moved south and southeast into the region around Kashira and Kolomna. Devlet-Girei's army was defeated near Tula, and the Russian army marched on Kazan. On August 30, the siege began, in which turrets, siege weapons, and mines were used. The city's water supply was cut off by a mine explosion, and on October 2, after several breaches had been made in the walls, an all-out attack was launched. By nightfall the city was in Russian hands.

The Kazan Khanate ceased to be an independent state, and the middle Volga region was annexed to Russia. The capture of Kazan opened the way for Russian expansion into the Urals and Siberia and for the strengthening of trade relations with the Caucasus and the Orient. V. I. BUGANOV [11–401–2]

KAZAN CATHEDRAL (in Leningrad), an outstanding work of Russian classical architecture, built between 1801 and 1811 by the architect A. N. Voronikhin to house the ancient icon of Our Lady of Kazan, after which the cathedral was named. The cathedral is a cruciform domed building with an extended side facade facing Nevsky Prospect. A majestic semicircular colonnade with a six-column portico, constituting the compositional center of the building, forms an imposing square that merges with the buildings on Nevsky Prospect. The main entrance faces a small square enclosed by a large cast-iron grille.

The interior is a majestic columned hall (the nave is 69 m long and 62 m high) resembling that of a palace. The sculptural decoration was executed by I. P. Martos, I. P. Prokof'ev, V. I. Demut-Malinovskii, F. F. Shchedrin, and S. S. Pimenov. The frescoes and icons were executed by V. L. Borovikovskii, A. E. Egorov, and V. K. Shebuev. Between 1813 and 1815 trophies from the Patriotic War of 1812 were placed in the cathedral, including keys from 17 cities and eight fortresses of Europe and 105 flags and standards. M. I. Kutuzov was buried in the cathedral in 1813, and in 1837 monuments to Kutuzov and M. B. Barclay de Tolly were erected in front of the cathedral (bronze, granite; sculptor, B. I. Orlovskii; architect V. P. Stasov). On Dec. 6, 1876, the first revolutionary demonstration of students and workers in Russia took place in front of the Kazan Cathedral. In 1932 the Museum of the History of Religion and Atheism was opened there.

REFERENCE
Shurygin, Ia. I. *Kazanskii sobor.* Leningrad, 1961. [11–405–2]

KAZAN CHEMICAL-TECHNOLOGICAL INSTITUTE (full name, S. M. Kirov Kazan Chemical-Technological Institute), a school training chemical and mechanical engineers for the chemical, petroleum, and petrochemical industries and for machine building. Founded in 1919, the insitute has departments (1972 data) of polymer materials, technology, mechanical engineering, petroleum, engineering, chemical technology, compressors, and automation; evening and correspondence departments of technology, mechanical engineering, and general engineering (in Nizhnekamsk); a department for the advanced training of instructors in institutions of higher learning; a graduate school; 45 subdepartments; nine laboratories for special problems and two branch laboratories, and a library with 700,000 holdings.

In 1971–72 the institute had an enrollment of 11,000 students and a faculty of 765 instructors, including 32 professors and doctors of sciences and 350 docents and candidates of sciences. The institute has the right to accept doctoral and candidates' dissertations for defense, and it publishes collections of articles on science and methodology. Since its foundation the institute has trained more than 17,000 engineers.

P. A. KIRPICHNIKOV [11–407–1]

KAZAN CHRONICLER, a historical narrative about the Kazan Khanate from earliest times until its annexation by Russia in 1552, probably written in 1564–66. Its anonymous author had spent 20 years in Tatar captivity. In writing his history he made use of Tatar legends, written sources, and personal impressions. The work, which has survived in many copies, is a valuable source for the history of the Kazan Khanate and the Russian state prior to the mid-16th century.

PUBLICATIONS
Kazanskaia istoriia. Mosow-Leningrad, 1954.
Skazanie o tsarstve Kazanskom. Moscow, 1959. [11–405–1]

KAZAN CONSPIRACY OF 1863, an attempt to incite a soldiers' and peasants' uprising in the Volga Region in the spring of 1863, undertaken on the basis of an agreement between the leaders of the uprising in Poland and Lithuania and members of the Land and Liberty group. The advocates of immediate revolutionary action—Polish revolutionaries, the Committee of Russian Officers in Poland, and some members of the Moscow Land and Liberty group—expected to attract peasants to the uprising by using the authority of the tsarist regime. In March 1863 a false tsarist manifesto and the proclamation "The Provisional People's Government" were drawn up, calling for an immediate uprising and for the creation of local organs of revolutionary power that would transfer land to the peasants and implement other revolutionary demands.

In March 1863, M. A. Czerniak discussed with the Kazan members of the Land and Liberty organization a plan for capturing Kazan to make it the center of the uprising, but the majority of the Kazan revolutionaries did not support him. The conspiracy was carried out against the wishes of the Central and Kazan committees of the Land and Liberty organization, which considered the time inopportune for organizing an uprising. The activities of the participants of the Kazan conspiracy were halted by numerous arrests. The engineer H. W. Kieniewicz and the officers N. K. Iwanitcki, A. Mroczek, R. I. Stankiewicz, and Czerniak were executed, and members of the Kazan Land and Liberty group were subjected to repression.

REFERENCES
Koz'min, B. P. *Kazanskii zagovor 1863 g.* Moscow, 1929.

Leikina-Svirskaia, V. R. "Kazanskii zagovor 1863 g." In *Revoliutsionnaia situatsiia v Rossi v 1859–1961 gg.* Moscow, 1960.
Linkov, Ia. I. *Revoliutsionnaia bor'ba A. I. Gertsena i N. P. Ogareva i tainoe obshchestvo Zemlia i volia 1860-kh gg.* Moscow, 1964. Pages 382–90.
V. R. LEIKINA-SVIRSKAIA [11–404–1]

KAZAN DEMONSTRATION OF 1876, the first political demonstration in Russia in which politically progressive workers took part. It occurred as a result of the growing strike movement in Russia and was held in St. Petersburg on December 6 on the square in front of the Kazan Cathedral. The demonstration was organized and carried out by members of the Land and Liberty populist organization and by members of workers' circles linked with the populist group. Some 400 persons gathered on the square. G. V. Plekhanov gave an impassioned revolutionary speech, and a young worker, Ia. Potapov, raised a red flag. The demonstrators resisted the police, and 31 persons were arrested, of whom five were condemned to 10–15 years at hard labor, ten to exile in Siberia, and three workers, including Potapov, to confinement in a monastery for five years. The demonstration marked the first conscious participation of the Russian working class in the progressive social movement.

REFERENCES
Plekhanov, G. V. "Russkii rabochii v revoliutsionnom dvizhenii." *Soch.,* 3d. ed., vol. 3. Moscow-Leningrad, 1928.
Istoriko-revoliutsionnyi sbornik, vol. 2. Leningrad, 1924.
Pervaia rabochaia demonstratsiia v Rossii. Moscow-Leningrad, 1927.

[11–400–2]

KAZANDZHIK, a city (settlement until 1939), the center of Kazandzhik Raion, Krasnovodsk Oblast, Turkmen SSR, in the northwestern spurs of the Kopetdag mountain range. It is a railroad station on the Ashkhabad-Krasnovodsk line, 292 km northwest of Ashkhabad. Population, 10,000 (1970). Industry includes railroad enterprises, a brickyard, and a carpet factory. The city was founded in 1895 in connection with the construction of the railroad. [11–396–6]

KAZANE, a gorge on the Danube River, on the border of Rumania and Yugoslavia. It is 35 km long and 150 m wide at its narrowest point. The water passing through it reaches a velocity of 4 m per sec. The narrows known as the Iron Gates are part of the gorge. [11–397–3]

KAZANETS, IVAN PAVLOVICH. Born Oct. 12, 1918, in the village of Lotsmanskaia Kamenka, now within the city limits of Dnepropetrovsk, Ukrainian SSR. Soviet statesman. Member of the CPSU since 1944.

The son of a peasant, Kazanets graduated from the Dnepropetrovsk Industrial Technicum in 1937. In 1944 he graduated from the evening division of the Siberian Metallurgical Institute. Between 1937 and 1944 he worked at the Kuznetsk Metallurgical Combine as an electrician, foreman, and section chief. Between 1944 and 1952 he worked at the Enakievo Metallurgical Plant, where he held positions as the chief of a shift, the chief of the training center, the assistant secretary of the party committee of the plant, a shop superintendent, and a party organizer for the Central Committee of the CPSU. In 1952–53, Kazanets was the first secretary of the Enakievo and then of the Makeevka city committees of the Ukrainian Communist Party (UCP), Donetsk Oblast. From 1953 to 1960 he was the first secretary of the Donetsk oblast committee of the UCP; and from 1960 to 1963, second secretary of the Central Committee of the UCP. From 1963 to 1965, Kazanets was the chairman of the Council of Ministers of the Ukrainian SSR. Since October 1965 he has been the minister of the ferrous metal industry of the USSR. At the Twentieth Party Congress in 1956, Kazanets was elected a candidate member of the Central Committee of the CPSU. He was elected a full member of the Central Committee of the CPSU at the 22nd, 23rd, and 24th party Congresses, and he was a deputy to the fourth through ninth convocations of the Supreme Soviet of the USSR. He has been awarded five Orders of Lenin and a number of medals. [11–397–4]

KAZANKA, an urban-type settlement and center of Kazanka Raion, Nikolaev Oblast, Ukrainian SSR, located on the Visun' River (in the Dnieper basin), 9 km from the Kazanka station on the Nikolaev-Dolinskaia railroad line.

Kazanka has a creamery, a food-processing combine, and a museum of history and local lore. [11–398–2]

KAZANKA, a river in the Tatar ASSR; a left-bank tributary of the Volga, flowing into the Kuibyshev Reservoir.

The Kazanka is 142 km long and drains an area of about 2,600 sq km. Its waters are fed mainly by melting snow. The average annual water discharge near its mouth is about 0.88 cu m per sec. The city of Kazan is located at the point at which the Kazanka flows into the Volga. [11–398–1]

KAZAN KHANATE, a feudal state in the Middle Volga Region (1438–1552), established on the territory of what was formerly Bulgaria on the Volga as a result of the disintegration of the Golden Horde. The principal city was Kazan. The founder of the dynasty of Kazan khans was Ulu Muhammad (reigned from 1438 to 1445), who drove out the local prince. The people of the Kazan Khanate included the Kazan Tatars (descendants of the Bulgars), Mari, Chuvash, Udmurts, and some Mordvinians and Bashkirs. The principal occupation of the population was agriculture. There was also well-developed handicraft production in the cities. Trade with Rus', Siberia, and the countries of the Caucasus and the Orient also played an important role in the state's economy.

Supreme state authority in the khanate was vested in the khan, but it was directed by a council of the major feudal lords (divan). The upper stratum of the feudal nobility consisted of the *karachi,* representatives of the four leading clans (Shirin, Bargyn, Argyn, and Kypchak). Below them were the sultans and emirs, and, still lower, the *murzas, ulans,* and warriors. An important role was played by the Muslim religious leaders with their vast holdings of *waqf* lands. The bulk of the population consisted of free peasants (known as "black people") who paid the *iasak* (tribute) and other taxes to the state and feudal nobility, feudally dependent peasantry, and serfs drawn from prisoners of war and slaves. For administrative purposes, the khanate was divided into *darugas* (districts) and *uluses* (corresponding to the Turkish *vilayet*). The army consisted of the khan's guard, units of various feudal lords, and a militia comprised of the tribute-paying population.

From the very beginning of its existence, the khanate carried out a continuing series of devastating raids against the Russian lands. In the 1460's, however, the rising Russian state began an active struggle with Kazan. A campaign against Kazan and Viatka was organized in 1467–69. As a result of another Russian campaign in 1487, Ali Khan was removed from the throne of Kazan and replaced by Muhammad Emin, the candidate of Ivan III. The khanate thus found itself a vassal of Russia, a situation that continued until 1521. After the death of Muhammad Emin (1518), Shah Ali, a tsarevich of Kasimov (a Muscovite appanage held by Tatar vassals), was placed on the throne. In 1521, however, he was driven out by Sahib Girei, a brother of the Crimean khan. The Kazan Khanate then became an ally of the Crimean and Astrakhan khanates and the Nogai Horde, which were supported by Turkey. That same year, it joined the Crimeans in a devastating raid on the environs of Moscow. The Russians built the fortress of Vasil'sursk in 1523 as a defense against the Kazan Tatars. In 1524 the khanate declared itself to be a vassal of Turkey, and Safa Girei, who ruled with interruptions until 1549, was confirmed as khan.

In 1546, however, the "mountainous" (western) side of the Volga was lost to the Russians. Then, as a result of the Kazan campaigns of 1545–52 and the capture of Kazan in 1552 by Russian troops, the khanate lost its independence and the entire Middle Volga Region was annexed to the Russian state. Russian *voevodas* (military governors) were installed in Kazan and Sviiazhsk, and these, in turn, were subordinated to the Office of the Kazan Palace (Prikaz Kazanskogo Dvortsa).

REFERENCES
Kazanskaia istoriia. Moscow-Leningrad, 1954.
Istoriia Tatarskoi ASSR, vol. Kazan, 1955.

Safargaliev, M. G. *Raspad Zolotoi Ordy.* Saransk, 1960.
V. I. BUGANOV [11–1408–1]

KAZANLUK, a city in the central part of Bulgaria, in Stara Zagora District. Situated in the Kazanluk Basin, on the southern slopes of the Stara Planina (Balkan Mountains), beyond Shipka Pass. Population, 50,000 (1969). Industry includes machine building (machine tools and hydraulic equipement), textiles, food processing, and wood products. In the surrounding region are plantations where the world-famous Kazanluk rose is grown, and the city has an experimental station for the study of essential-oil crops. [11–398–3]

KAZANLUK BASIN, an intermontane tectonic basin in Bulgaria. Length, 94 km; average width, about 10 km; area, about 780 sq km; average elevation, 350 m.

The basin is bounded on the north by the slopes of the Stara Planina (Balkan Mountains) and on the south by the slopes of the Sredna Gora Range. The bottom of the valley is flat; in the east it is hilly. It is bisected by the Tundzha River, a tributary of the Maritsa. The climate is warm temperate, with January temperatures of 0° to −2°C and July temperatures of about 20°C; annual precipitation is about 600 mm. The basin has plantations of Kazanluk roses and other essential-oil crops, land sown in grains, fruit plantations, and vineyards. The G. Dimitrov Reservoir and a hydroelectric power plant are also located in the basin. [11–398–5]

KAZANLUK ROSE (*Rosa damascena f. trigintipetala*), a shrub of the family Rosaceae, with large hooked prickles on its branches. Height, up to 1.5 m. Each leaf has five to seven ovoid leaflets, which are mat on top and thinly pubescent on the veins beneath. The flowers are fragrant, double, and red or pink. The fruits are orange or red. In Bulgaria, rose oil, which is used in the production of perfume, liqueurs, and medicine, is obtained from the petals (the yield of rose oil is 0.7–1.0 kg per hectare). In the USSR the Kazanluk rose is cultivated in Georgia and on the southern Crimean coast.

REFERENCES
Leshchuk, T. Ia. *Roza aromaticheskaia.* Simferopol', 1958.
Topalov, V., and I. Irinchev. *Rozoproizvodstvoto v Bulgariia.* Plovdiv, 1967. [11–399–1]

KAZANLUK TOMB, an ancient tomb constructed beneath a mound. Located in Bulgaria, near the city of Kazanluk, it was discovered in 1944.

The Kazanluk Tomb is a round brick chamber with a short entrance passage (dromos) and a dome in the form of a truncated cone. The ceiling of the dome is covered with a multicolored mural depicting a Thracian funerary feast, executed on dry lime plastering. The mural is divided into two friezes by zones of decorative geometric design; the friezes are distinguished by the free and dynamic balance of the composition and by the organic relationship of the decorative and representational elements. The harmonic integrity of the range of colors, constructed on gradations of ochre, yellow, and dark blue tones, reflects the tranquil majesty and naturalness of the figures' movements and the mild, restrained grief that permeates the mural. The Kazanluk Tomb is an outstanding example of the Greco-Thracian art of the late fourth to the early third century B.C..

REFERENCES
Mikov, V. *Antichnaia grobnitsa bliz Kazanlyk.* Sofia, 1954. (Translated from Bulgarian.)
Vasiliev, A. *Antichnaia grobnitsa v Kazanlyke.* (Translated from Bulgarian.) Sofia, 1958. [11–398–4]

KAZANOKO, DZHABAGI. Born circa 1685; died 1750. Public and political figure of Kabarda.

According to tradition, Kazanoko's mother was a bond servant. For some time, he served as counselor to the senior prince of Kabarda—Aslanbek Kaitukin. Later, he directed the popular assemblies, at which questions were discussed about the internal life of Kabardin society and its relations with the other peoples of the Caucasus, as well as with Russia, Turkey, and Persia.

Kazanoko opposed the influence of the Crimean khans and the Turkish sultans but advocated Kabardin rapprochement with Russia. At the end of 1722 he was sent to Astrakhan', where he met with Peter I (at the time of the Persian campaign). After becoming a leader of the lower chamber of the central court (the Kheizh), Kazanoko often defended the interests of the dependent classes against the exactions of the feudal nobility.

REFERENCES
Istoriia Kabardy s drevneishikh vremen do nashikh dnei. Moscow, 1957.
Qëzënoquë Zhëbaghï. Compiled by A. T. Shortanov. Nal'chik, 1956.
[11–400–1]

KAZAN OPERATION OF 1918, an offensive carried out from September 5 to September 10 by the Fifth Army (commander P. A. Slaven, members of the Revolutionary Military Council B. D. Mikhailov and V. I. Mezhlauk) and the Arsk Group of the Second Army (group commander V. M. Azin) in cooperation with the Volga Military Flotilla against the White Czechs and units of the Socialists Revolutionary and White Guard "People's Army" during the Civil War of 1918–20.

On August 7 the Socialist Revolutionary and White Guard forces and the White Czechs had repulsed the weak and poorly organized units of the Red Army and captured Kazan, creating a serious threat to the central region of Soviet Russia. On V. I. Lenin's instructions, the best units of the Red Army and three destroyers and two floating batteries from the Baltic were sent to Kazan. On August 14 the Fifth Army was formed. Fulfilling Lenin's directive on the necessity for the immediate liberation of Kazan, the army attacked on the right bank of the Volga and drove the enemy back to the Morkvashi-Spasskoe-Burnashevo line; the Arsk Group of the Second Army was sent toward Kazan from the northeast. On August 27 the White Guard detachment of Lieutenant Colonel V. O. Kappel' tried to seize the bridge at Sviazhsk but was repulsed.

The Kazan operation, which aimed at defeating the Kazan grouping of the enemy (4,000 to 4,500 men) and capturing Kazan, was part of the general offensive of the Red Army in the Volga Region. The main attack was launched by the Fifth Army, suported by the Volga Flotilla, on both banks of the Volga, with the Arsk Group launching the secondary attack.

The strength of the Soviet troops, not counting the flotilla, was about 15,000 men and 69 guns. On September 3 a workers' uprising broke out in Kazan. Although the uprising was suppressed, it diverted the forces of the counterrevolutionaries. On September 5–6 the Fifth Army captured the key positions of Krasnaia Gorka (Iudino) and Verknhii and Nizhnii Uslon; and Azin's group captured Kinderi and Malye Klyki. Afterward action died down somewhat, whereupon Lenin intervened and ordered that Kazan be taken immediately. On September 10 the Soviet troops took the city with an attack from three sides, capturing 12 guns, two armored trains, and other equipment. The success of the Kazan operation shifted the initiative in the Volga Region to the Red Army. [11–400–3]

KAZANOVKA, an urban-type settlement in the Kimovsk Raion, Tula Oblast, RSFSR; located 4 km from the Don River and 24 km south of the Kimovsk railroad station on the Uzlovaia-Riazhsk line. Toys are manufactured in Kazanovka.
[11–399–4]

KAZAN PHYSICS AND MATHEMATICS SOCIETY, a Russian scientific society that arose in 1880 as the section of physical and mathematical sciences of the Society of Natural Scientists at the University of Kazan. The section was founded on the initiative of the astronomer M. A. Koval'skii, who became its first chairman. The section was reorganized in 1890 into the Physics and Mathematics Society. Papers on mathematics, physics, and other subjects are presented at its meetings. The society performs an important task in publicizing the ideas of N. I. Lobachevskii. A commemoration of the 100th anniversary of the date of his birth was organized in 1893. Funds collected by the society (by subscription) were used to erect a monument to Lobachevskii in 1896 and to institute the international Lobachevskii Prize in 1897 (eight competitions were held up to 1937).

REFERENCE
"Kazanskoe fiziko-matematicheskoe obshchestvo." *Uspekhi matematichskikh nauk*, 1946, vol. 2, issue 2.   [11–407–3]

KAZAN SCHOOL (in linguistics), a generally accepted but not entirely appropriate term used to designate a group of I. A. Baudouin de Courtenay's students at the University of Kazan when he was a professor there (1875–83). In addition to Baudouin himself, N. V. Krushevskii, V. A. Bogoroditskii, S. K. Bulich, and A. I. Aleksandrov are considered members of the school.

The linguists of the Kazan school leaned toward neogrammarianism: they were characterized by their differentiation of oral and written forms of speech, analysis of the interrelations between the psychological and the physiological in language, differentiation of statics and dynamics (synchrony and diachrony), clearly expressed historicism, and attention to living languages. Baudouin himself subsequently diverged from the views of the Kazan school and took a position of linguistic sociologism, becoming in this sense a predecessor of F. de Saussure and A. Meillet. The Polish linguist K. J. Appel was the closest to Baudouin during his "Kazan period." Some scholars consider the linguists of the Kazan school to be pioneers in contemporary structural linguistics (R. Jacobson).

REFERENCES
Berezin, F. M. *Ocherki po istorii iazykoznaniia v Rossii (konets XIX–nachalo XX v.).* Moscow, 1968.
Bogoroditskii, V. A. "Kazanskaia lingvisticheskaia shkola." In *Trudy Moskovskogo instituta istorii, filosofii i literatury,* vol. 5. Moscow, 1939.
Cherepanov, M. V. "Kazanskaia lingvisticheskaia shkola." *Voprosy obshchego iazykoznaniia.* Leningrad, 1967.
                                     A. A. LEONT'EV [11–401–1]

KAZANSKII, BORIS ALEKSANDROVICH. Born Apr. 13 (25), 1891, in Odessa; died Apr. 4, 1975, in Moscow. Soviet organic chemist; academician of the Academy of Sciences of the USSR (1946; corresponding member 1943). Hero of Socialist Labor (1969). Graduated from Moscow University in 1918 (as a student of N. D. Zelinskii) and became a professor there in 1935. He became the director of the Laboratory of Catalytic Synthesis of the Institute of Organic Chemistry of the Academy of Sciences of the USSR in 1936. He was the director of the institute from 1954 to 1966.

Kazanskii's research dealt with the catalytic hydrogenolysis of the cyclic hydrocarbons from C_3 to C_{15}, the discovery and study of the C_5 and C_6 dehydrocyclization of paraffins, olefins, alkylaromatic hydrocarbons and cycloalkanes (transannular dehydrocyclization) on platinum and other catalysts, and the study of the stepwise mechanism of C_6 dehydrocyclization of paraffins on oxide and metal catalysts. Other research by Kazanskii dealt with the addition of H_2 to multiple bonds in hydrocarbons on metals of Group VIII and the special feature of the behavior of H_2 depending on the nature of the metallic catalyst, and the catalytic dehydrogenation of paraffins to olefins and dienes (for the preparation of monomers for synthetic elastomers). Together with G. S. Landsberg, he developed methods for the study of individual compositions of straight-run gasoline.

Kazanskii received the State Prize of the USSR in 1949. He was awarded two Orders of Lenin, as well as three other orders and several medals.

WORKS
Kataliticheskie prevrashcheniia uglevodorodov: Sb. izbr. trudov. Moscow, 1968.
Opredelenie individual'nogo uglevodorodnogo sostava benzinov priamoi gonki kombinirovannym metodom. Moscow, 1959. (Coauthor.)

REFERENCE
Liberman, A. L. "Akademik B. A. Kazanskii." In the collection B. A. Kazanskii, *Kataliticheskie prevrashcheniia uglevodorodov.* Moscow, 1968.   [11–402–1; updated]

KAZANSKII, EVGENII SERVEEVICH. Born Jan. 21 (Feb. 2), 1896; died Sept. 26, 1937. Soviet military figure, division commander (1935). Became a member of the Communist Party in 1912. The son of a priest.

Kazankskii was born in the village of Naryshkino, in present-day Orel Oblast. A graduate of the Pavel Military School (1914), he served in World War I (1914–18) as a staff captain, joined the Red Army as a private in Vladikavkaz in July 1918, and fought in the Civil War of 1918–20, engaging in underground work in Baku in 1919 and then organizing insurgent detachments on the Black Sea coast. In January 1920, Kazanskii was appointed commander of the Black Sea Soviet Insurgent (Green) Army, which operated behind the lines of Denikin's troops. Commanding the Northern Group during the suppression of the Kronstadt mutiny of 1921, he was appointed chief of the First Petrograd Infantry School in 1921 and graduated from the military-academic courses for higher commanders in 1925. Commanding a division from 1926 to 1932, Kazanskii was chief of staff of military educational institutions and chief of the Directorate of Military Educational Institutions from 1932 to 1934, after which he was a member of the Military Council of the People's Commissariat of Defense until 1936. He was appointed corps commander in 1936. Awarded two Orders of the Red Banner, Kazanskii also was presented with honorary revolutionary arms.
                                                    [11–402–2]

KAZAN STAGE (named after the city of Kazan), one of the stages of the Upper Permian system. The name was introduced by the Russian geologist A. V. Nechaev in 1915. The Kazan stage is divided into two horizons: the lower, or Kama, horizon contains brachiopods (*Spirifer rugulatus, Productus hemisphaerium*), and the upper, or Krasnovidovo, horizon has pelecypods (*Pseudomonotis speluncaria*) and gastropods. Deposits of the Kazan stage are widespread in the eastern and northern parts of the Eastern European Platform, where they are represented by marine and lagoon-marine strata and by continental red formations (Belebei formation). Deposits of petroleum and hard coal are found in the Kazan stage. Analogues of the Kazan stage are found in the coal-bearing deposits of the Tungus formation (Eastern Siberia) and may also be identified among the Permian deposits of Western Europe (Zechstein).
                                                    [11–407–2]

KAZANTSEV, FLORENTII PIMENOVICH. Born Dec. 6 (18), 1877, in Bugul'ma, present-day Tatar ASSR; died Nov. 4, 1940, in Moscow. Soviet inventor of several automatic air brake systems for railroads.

In 1909, Kazantsev proposed an air distributor of a two-wire air brake for passenger trains. In 1925 the oil tank-car trains on the Baku-Batumi line were equipped with this brake, fitted with the Kazantsev air distributor. He also proposed an air distributor for a single-wire rigid brake, and in 1927 he proposed an air distributor for a semirigid brake (the Kazantsev brake). The engineer's brake valve that was developed in 1926 by the Moscow Brake Plant and supplied to freight locomotives in the USSR was named for Kazantsev. He was awarded the Order of the Red Banner of Labor.
                                                    [11–409–2]

KAZANTSEV, NIKOLAI DIMITRIEVICH. Born Feb. 2 (15), 1907, in the village of Obabkova, now Belozerskoe Raion, Kurgan Oblast; died Nov. 12, 1971, in Moscow. Soviet jurist; doctor of juridical sciences (1947); professor (1948). Member of the CPSU from 1944.

Kazantsev was a specialist in kolkhoz and land law. He did scholarly work and taught from 1930, and he was chairman of the subdepartment of land and kolkhoz law in the law department of Moscow State University from 1954 to 1971. In the 1960's he helped to prepare the basic acts of land legislation.

WORKS

Pravo kolkhoznoi sobstvennosti. Moscow, 1948.
Utopicheskii i nauchnyi sotsializm o pereustroistve sel'skogo khoziaistva. Moscow, 1969.
Zakonodatel'nye osnovy zemel'nogo stroia v SSSR. Moscow, 1971.

[11–409–1]

KAZANTSEV BRAKE, an automatic single-wire direct brake for railroad rolling stock with an air distributor designed by F. P. Kazantsev.

An AP series air distributor charges the reserve tank with compressed air and fills the brake cylinder and releases the air from it. The Kazantsev brake provides stepped braking and release. Prolonged braking on long downgrades does not deplete the brake—that is, if emergency braking occurs at any instant during motion, rated brake shoe pressure is produced. However, normal braking action is possible only at a certain level of charging of the brake system, to a pressure of 0.5 meganewtons per sq m (MN/m^2), or 5 kilograms-force per sq cm (kgf/cm^2). Such an air distributor was called rigid, since at higher pressures no braking occurs and at lower pressures self-braking occurs independent of the rate of pressure change, thus presenting difficulties in operation. Kazantsev also designed a semirigid air distributor (series K), which made possible normal brake operation with varying pressure in the feeder. Diaphragm sealing of pistons and the use of valves in the air distributor were design features peculiar to the Kazantsev brake.

The Kazantsev brake was first used in the USSR in 1925, replacing the Westinghouse brake in freight trains. In 1933 the Kazantsev brake was superseded by a brake with an air distributor designed by Matrosov (the Matrosov brake).

REFERENCES

Karvatskii, B. L. *Avtotormoza,* 4th ed. Moscow, 1948.
Kazarinov, V. M. *Avtotormoza,* 2nd ed. Moscow, 1963.

E. V. KLYKOV and V. G. INOZEMTSEV [11–409–3]

KAZANTZAKE, GALATEA. Born Dec. 23, 1888, in Iráklion, on Crete; died Dec. 17, 1963, in Athens. Greek writer; participant in the struggle against fascism and a member of the resistance movement. Wife of N. Kazantzakis.

Kazantzake's early works include the novella *Laugh, Clown* (1909) and the play *At Any Sacrifice* (1911). Her novel *The Women* (1933) and her collections of stories *From Eleven to One P.M.* and *Critical Minutes* criticize bourgeois family and social relations from a democratic point of view. Kazantzake's works of the 1930's—the collection of plays *The Curtain* (1959) and the collection *The Dying World and the Coming World* (1963)—reflect the ideas of socialist humanism.

WORKS

Ho kosmos pu pethainei ki ho kosmos pu erchetai. Athens, 1963.

REFERENCE

Kordatos, G. *Historia tes Neoellenikes logotechnias,* vol. 2. Athens, 1962.

DMITRIS SPATIS [11–397–1]

KAZANTZAKIS, NIKOS. Born Feb. 18, 1883, in Herakleion, Crete; died Oct. 29, 1957, in Freiburg, Federal Republic of Germany. Greek writer.

Kazantzakis studied law at the University of Athens and at the Sorbonne. His first works were the novella *The Serpent and the Lily* (1906) and the plays *The Dawn Glows* (performed in 1907) and *The Sacrifice* (1910). Between 1925 and 1929, Kazantzakis visited the USSR three times, and he hailed the October Revolution in his books *What I Saw in Russia* (1928), *Moscow Issued a Call* (in French, 1931), and *Toda Raba* (in Greek, 1934). His dramas *Nikifor Foka* (1927), *Christ* (1928), *Journeys* (1928), *Melissa* (1939), and *Julian and Buddha* from the trilogy *Prometheus* (all published after 1945), as well as his long poem *The Odyssey,* were all critical of bourgeois morality and pessimistic in tone. His novels *The Greek Passion* (Swedish ed., 1950; Greek ed., 1954; Russian translation, 1962), *The Last Temptation of Christ* (Greek ed., 1955), and *Captain Mihalis: Freedom or Death* (1953) express Kazantzakis' protest against bourgeois attitudes and religious hypocrisy. From 1947, he lived in France and the Federal Republic of Germany. In 1964, Kazantzakis'

novel *Zorba the Greek* (1946) was made into a film of the same name by M. Cacoyannis. Kazantzakis received the International Peace Prize in 1956.

WORKS

Érga. Athens, 1957–62.

REFERENCE

Brettákos, N. *Níkos Kazantzákes.* Athens, 1960.

DIMITRIS SPATIS [11–397–2]

KAZARINOVA, NINA NIKOLAEVNA. Born Oct. 27 (Nov. 9), 1907, in Perm'. Soviet Russian actress; People's Artist of the RSFSR (1957). Member of the CPSU since 1944. One of the organizers of, and an actress in, the Young People's Theater in Perm' (1926–28).

Kazarinova graduated from the Leningrad Technicum of Theatrical Arts in 1931. In 1930 she began to act with the Leningrad Young People's Theater, playing children's parts. Her heroes are impassioned youths with great dreams. Kazarinova's best roles include Sema in *The Marshal's Childhood* by Vsevolozhskii, Gavrik and Vania Solntsev in *The Lone White Sail* and *Son of the Regiment* by Kataev, Pashka in *Pashka* by Makar'ev, and Shura in *The Red Necktie* by Mikhalkov. She later played the roles of old women (Feklusha in Ostrovskii's *Thunderstorm,* for example).

REFERENCE

Brushtein, A. "Sovetskii teatr dlia detei." In *Sovetskii teatr: K tridtsatiletiiu Sovetskogo gosudarstva.* Moscow, 1947. [11–413–2]

KAZARMA (Barracks), an illegal Social Democratic newspaper published from Feb. 15, 1906, to March 1907; 13 issues of the newspaper were published, and its circulation was between 5,000 and 20,000 copies. It was printed in St. Petersburg, Moscow, and Finland. Mensheviks contributed to the first three issues, but the Bolsheviks determined its political line. *Kazarma* was the central publication of the provisional bureau of military and combat organizations of the Bolsheviks—in fact beginning with the first issue, and officially from November 1906. The editorial board of *Kazarma* included V. V. Vorovskii, M. S. Ol'minskii, V. R. Menzhinskii, V. D. Bonch-Bruevich, and Em. Iaroslavskii. *Kazarma* conducted revolutionary agitation and propaganda among the troops. Its publication was discontinued when the police smashed the military organizations of the RSDLP. In 1931 the Leningrad Institute of the History of the ACP (Bolshevik) reissued *Kazarma* as a book.

REFERENCE

Mishuris, A. L. "Bol'shevistskaia voennaia gazeta 'Kazarma.'" In *Bol'shevistskaia pechat' v dooktiabr'skii period: Sb. statei.* Moscow, 1959. [11–415–2]

KAZARNOVSKII, ISAAK ABRAMOVICH. Born Sept. 17 (29), 1890, in Nikolaev, Soviet chemist; corresponding member of the Academy of Sciences of the USSR (1939). Graduated from the University of Zürich in 1914. He has been a researcher at the L. Ia. Karpov Physicochemical Institute since 1922.

Kazarnovskii's main research was on the theory of formation and structure of metal hydrides, chlorides, and oxides. He discovered a number of new oxides, among them NaO_2 (1936) and KO_3 and NaO_3 (1949–51), elucidated their mechanism of formation, and proposed a new systematics for peroxides. He identified a new mechanism of formation of hydrogen peroxide from free hydroxyl radicals, as well as the mechanism of dissociation and oxidizing action of ozone proceeding by means of the ozonide ion O_3^- and free hydroxyl (1969).

Kazarnovskii developed industrially useful methods for the production of anhydrous aluminum chloride from clays (1935) and for the production of NaO_2 (1942), as well as a new method for the regeneration of air. He was awarded the State Prize of the USSR in 1941 and has received two orders, as well as medals. [11–416–1]

KAZARSKII, ALEKSANDR IVANOVICH. Born 1797; died June 16, 1833, in the city of Nikolaev. A hero of the Russo-Turkish War of 1828–29, naval captain first class (1831).

Kazarskii joined the navy in 1811 and was promoted to officer rank in 1814. He served in the Danube Military Flotilla and in the Black Sea Fleet and distinguished himself in 1828 during the capture of Anapa and Varna. Commander of the 18-gun brig *Merkurii* in 1829, on May 14 he accepted unequal battle with two Turkish battleships, armed with a total of 184 guns. After a four-hour battle he forced the enemy to stop the pursuit, inflicting heavy damage on the ships. For this act of bravery Kazarksii was promoted to captain second class, appointed aide-de-camp to the tsar, and awarded the Order of Saint George Fourth Class. Kazarskii commanded a frigate in 1829 and was in the retinue of Nicholas I from 1831 to 1833. In 1834 a monument was erected to him in Sevastopol' with the epitaph "Example for Future Generations." [11–417–1]

KAZATIN, a city (since 1938) and the administrative center of Kazatin Raion, Vinnitsa Oblast, Ukrainian SSR. Kazatin is an important junction of railroad lines to Kiev, Zhmerinka, Shepetovka, and Uman'. Population 27,000 (1970). Kazatin has enterprises for the maintenance of railroad transport, a poultry combine, a creamery, a bread-baking plant, a mixed-feed factory, and a clothing factory. [11–417–3]

KAZATSKOE, an urban-type settlement in Berislav Raion, Kherson Oblast, Ukrainian SSR. Situated on the Dnieper River. The Kazatskoe railroad station is on the Kakhovka-Nikolaev line. The settlement has a winery and a reinforced-concrete products plant. Kazatskoe is surrounded by vineyards. [11–511–4]

KAZBEGI, ALEKSANDR. Born Jan. 8 (20), 1848, in the village of Stepantsminda, now Kazbegi; died Dec. 10 (22), 1893, in Tbilisi. Georgian writer.

Born into the family of the administrator of Gortsy Okrug, Kazbegi conducted the affairs of his family's huge estate after his father's death. He freed the peasants from taxes but soon, rejecting the role of a feudal lord, left for the mountains. He lived the hard life of a shepherd for seven years and gained a profound knowledge of communal ways.

In 1879, Kazbegi settled in Tbilisi and worked on the paper *Droeba*, which printed his novel *Elgudzha* in 1881; the novel contains dramatic portrayals of heroic mountain peasants, fighters for honor and freedom. The novel was very successful, and the entire edition was confiscated by the police and burned. He then published his novellas *Eliso* (1882), *The Patricide* (1882), *Tsiko* (1883), *The Rejected One* (1884), *Khevisberi Gocha* (1884), and *Shepherd* (1885). All Kazbegi's works were written between 1880 and 1886. He exposed the lawless acts of tsarist officials and feudal lords and created heroic, noble, and brave peasants. Deprivation and persecution drove Kazbegi to serious mental illness, and he died alone and penniless.

Love of the motherland in Kazbegi's work is inseparable from ideals of fairness, humanity, and readiness for struggle with the oppressors of the people. Almost all Kazbegi's heroes perish in unequal battle, but his novels are permeated nonetheless with faith in the inexhaustible powers of the people.

Kazbegi depicted the captivating landscapes of the Georgian mountain country. A certain idealization of the past and of the laws of clan society are linked in his works with rejection of the stern laws of the community. A keen sense of contemporaneity and the power of authenticity in his descriptions rank Kazbegi with the great masters of 19th-century Georgian prose.

Kazbegi translated into Georgian A. S. Griboedov's *Woe From Wit*, Shakespeare's *Romeo and Juliet*, and verses by M. Iu. Lermontov.

WORKS
Qazbegi, A. *T'khzulebani*, vols. 1–4. Tbilisi, 1948–50.
T'khzulebani, 2nd ed. Tbilisi, 1962.
T'khzulebani or tomad, vols. 1–2. Introduction by G. Natroshvilis. Tbilisi, 1955.
In Russian translation:
Izbrannoe, vols. 1–2. Tbilisi, 1948–49.
Izbr. proizvedeniia, vols. 1–2. Tbilisi, 1957.

Eliso: Povesti i rasskazy. Introduction by E. Lundberg. Moscow, 1964.
REFERENCES
Baramidze, A., Sh. Radiani, and B. Zhgenti. *Istoriia gruzinskoi literatury.* Tbilisi, 1958.
Dzhibladze, G. *Romantiki i realisty v gruzinskoi literature 19 v.* Tbilisi, 1963. [11–518–4]

KAZBEGI (until 1921, Stepantsminda), an urban-type settlement, the administrative center of Kazbegi Raion, Georgian SSR. Situated at the foot of Mount Kazbek on the upper course of the Terek River; elevation 1,750 m.

Kazbegi is on the Georgian Military Road 46 km south of Ordzhonikidze. The settlement is the site of the bottling plant for Kazbegi Mineral Water (Narzan type) and of the A. Kazbegi Museum of Local Lore. Ascents to the summit of Mount Kazbek begin in Kazbegi. A cable railway runs from Kazbegi to Sameb. There is a tourist center near Kazbegi. [11–519–1]

KAZBEK (Georgian *Mkinvari*, literally, "glacial"; Ossetian *Urskhokh*, literally, "white mountain"), a peak of the Bokovoi (Side) Range of the Greater Caucasus, rising above the valley of the Terek River near the Georgian Military Road. The eastern is the main peak (altitude, 5,033 m); the western summit is 400 m lower. Kazbek is an extinct volcano 370 m tall set in a massif of lower Jurassic schist, which had yielded a series of lava flows that descended to the valley of the Terek River. Evidently Kazbek was active in Quaternary times, and now a small amount of solfatara activity is observed. The summit is covered with perpetual snow and névé, from which valley glaciers such as Suatisi, Mna, Ortsveri, Devdorakskii, and Chachskii descend along the slopes. The total area covered with ice is 135 sq km. There is a high-mountain meteorological station on the Gerget Glacier. The mountain is also a tourist resort. [11–520–1]

KAZBEK TREASURE, a complex of bronze, silver, and iron objects numbering about 200 pieces, discovered in 1877 by G. D. Filimonov on the territory of the Kazbek station of the Georgian Military Road (the modern-day settlement of Kazbegi, Georgian SSR).

The articles that have been dated include silver goblets and the figurine of a ram, executed in the style of the Achaemenid art of the sixth or fifth century B.C. Objects belonging to the late stage of the Koban culture are bronze vessels, fibulae, figurines of deer, phallic representations of man, hilts and their parts, bronze belts, and iron swords, spears, and bits. The Kazbek treasure is connected with the religious cults of the ancient tribes of the Caucasus. The principal part of the treasure is housed in the State Historical Museum in Moscow; the remainder is in the State Museum of Georgia in Tbilisi.

REFERENCES
Filimonov, G. D. "O doistoricheskoi kul'ture v Osetii." In the book *Antropologicheskaia vystavka obshchestva liubitelei estestvoznaniia, antropologii i etnografii 1879 g.*, vol. 2. Moscow, 1878–79.
Amiranashvili, Sh. Ia. *Istoriia gruzinskogo iskusstva*, vol. 1. Moscow, 1950.
Tallgren, A. M. "Caucasian Monuments: The Kazbek Treasure." *Eurasia septentionalis Antiqua*, Helsinki, 1930, no. 5.

E. I. KRUPNOV [11–520–2]

KAZ DAĞI, (Kaz), the highest point (1,767 m) of the Kaz Daği (Ida) Mountains in western Turkey. Yearly precipitation is up to 1,500 mm. The northern slopes have coniferous woods, and the southern are covered by oak shrubs. [11–521–4]

KAZEI, MARAT. Born Oct. 10, 1929, in the village of Stan'-kovo, Dzerzhinsk Raion, Minsk Oblast; died May 11, 1944, in the village of Khorometskoe, Uzda Raion, Minsk Oblast. Pioneer; member of the partisan movement in Byelorussia in the Great Patriotic War (1941–45). Hero of the Soviet Union (May 8, 1965).

Kazei joined the Twenty-fifth Anniversary of October Partisan Detachment in November 1942 and then became a reconnaissance scout on the staff of the K. K. Rokossovskii Partisan Brigade. Surrounded by fascists on a reconnaissance mission, he killed himself with a grenade. Kazei was awarded the Order of the Patriotic War First Class and the medals For Bravery and For Combat Service. A monument to Kazai was erected in Minsk in 1958 with money collected by Byelorussian Pioneers.

REFERENCE
Pionery-geroi, 3rd ed. Minsk, 1972. (Collection.) [11–522–2]

KAZEM-BEK, MIRZA MUKHAMMED ALI (Aleksandr Kasimovich Kazem-Bek). Born July 22, 1802, in Rasht, Iran; died Nov. 27, 1870, in St. Petersburg. Russian Orientalist. Corresponding member of the St. Petersburg Academy of Sciences (1835); doctor of Eastern languages (1869).

Kazam-Bek received a Muslim education at home. In 1823 he adopted Christianity. From 1826 to 1849 he was at the University of Kazan, where he taught Persian and Turkish and where he became a professor in 1836. Beginning in 1849 he was head of the subdepartment of the Persian language at the University of St. Petersburg; in 1855 he became head of the university's department of Eastern languages (first dean).

Kazem-Bek was the author of books on the history of the Caucasus, Iran, Middle Asia, and the Crimea, as well as on the history of Islam and of the Iranian and Turkic languages. He introduced many new Eastern sources into scholarship. He was the first in Russia to publish an essay on Babism and studies of the grammar of Eastern languages. A complete list of his works is given in the journal *Russkii Arkhiv,* 1894, no. 2.

REFERENCES
Grigor'ev, V. V. *Imp. Sankt-Peterburgskii universitet.* St. Petersburg, 1870.
Smirnov, N. A. *Ocherki izucheniia islama v SSSR.* Moscow, 1954.
Guseinov, G. N. *Iz istorii obshchestvennoi i filosofskoi mysli v Azerbaidzhane XIX v,* 2nd ed. Baku, 1958. Pages 117–61.
Abdullaev, M. *Kazem-Bek—uchenyi i myslitel'.* Makhachkala, 1963.
Rzaev, A. *Mirza Kazem-Bek.* Baku, 1965.
Mazitova, N. A. *Izuchenie Blizhnego i Srednego Vostoka v Kazanskom universitete 1-aia pol. XIX v).* Kazan, 1972.
G. A. KLEINMAN [11–523–1]

KAZEMI, MORTAZA MOSHFEQ. Born 1887. Persian writer.

One of the fathers of modern Persian prose, Kazemi worked for the magazine *Iran-shahr,* published in Berlin from 1924, and later edited the journal *Iran-e Javan* (Young Iran), in which he published his translations from French. His social novel *Dreadful Tehran* (part 1, *Makhuf,* was published in Tehran in 1921; part 2, entitled *Memories of the Only Night,* was published in Berlin in 1924; Russian translations, 1934–36 and 1960) reveals the negative side of life in Iranian society in the 1920's, depicting women's lack of rights. *The Faded Flower, Precious Envy* and other novels are less significant and do not deal with vital social issues.

REFERENCES
Komissarov, D. S. *Ocherki sovremennoi persidskoi prozy.* Moscow, 1960.
Kor-Ogly, Kh. *Sovremennaia persidskaia literatura.* Moscow, 1965.
[11–523–2]

KAZERUN, a city in southwest Iran, in Fars Province, on the Shiraz-Bushire highway. Population, 42,000 (1971). Kazerun is the trade center of an agricultural region (citrus fruits, date palms, wheat, barley, rice, tobacco, and livestock-raising). The city has food industries. [11–525–1]

KAZHIM, an urban-type settlement in Koigorodok Raion, Komi ASSR, situated on the Kazhim River, 4 km from the point at which it flows into the Sysola (a tributary of the Vychegda) and 245 km southeast of the city of Syktyvkar.

Kazhim has a lumbering industry and several woodworking establishments. It developed in connection with the construction of an ironworks in 1757 (closed in 1928). [11–389–3]

KAZIASKER, in the Ottoman Empire after the middle of the 14th century, an official who was the supreme judge of the army, the head of the military judicial class, and a member of the sultan's divan. As a result of the reforms of Sultan Mahmud II (1808–39), the *kaziaskers* lost their real power, but they existed

nominally as the highest religious rank until the sultanate was abolished in 1922. [11–417–2]

KAZIIAU ALI. Born Dec. 11, 1879, in Andreiaul, in present-day Khasav"iurt Raion, Dagestan ASSR; died Sept. 23, 1964, in Makhachkala. Soviet Kumyk poet; People's Poet of Dagestan (1949).

Kaziiau Ali came from a family of poor peasants. He fought in World War I (1914–18) and, during the years of the Civil War (1918–20), served in the ranks of the Red partisans. He was among the first to join a kolkhoz. He began composing verses orally and subsequently learned to read and write. His first collection of verses, *Kaziiau Ali Recites,* appeared in 1934. His later collections—for example, *The Old Man's Saber* (1944), *Selected Poems* (1959), and *I Too Am With You* (posthumous, 1969)—depict the new life in the mountains and the new people. Kaziiau Ali was awarded the Order of the Red Banner of Labor and several medals.

WORKS
Oktyabrni emishleri. Makhachkala, 1947.
Saylamlï yïrlar. Makhachkala, 1959.
Yellar va kyopyurler. Makhachkala, 1963.
In Russian translation:
Slovo starogo ashuga. Makhachkala, 1954.
["Stikhotvoreniia."] In *Poeziia narodov Dagestana,* vol. 2. Moscow, 1960.

REFERENCE
Guseinaev, A. *Istoriia dagestanskoi sovetskoi literatury,* vols. 1–2. Makhachkala, 1967. [11–527–1]

KAZI-MAGOMED, a city (since 1938) in Azerbaijan SSR, in the Kura-Araks lowland; a railroad station on the Baku-Tbilisi line, linked by a 15-km branch line with the city of Ali-Bairamly. Population, 15,000 (1970). There are railway transport enterprises in Kazi-Magomed. [11–525–3]

KAZIMIERZ DOLNY, a city in Poland, in Lublin Województwo, on the right shore of the Vistula River, 44 km from Lublin.

Kazimierz Dolny was founded in the 14th century. There are ruins of castles in the city (14th and 17th centuries) and buildings in the style of the Late Renaissance: a 14th-century church, rebuilt between 1586 and 1613; houses with richly ornamented attics and sculptured decoration, like those named "Under St. Michael" and "Under St. Christopher" (both c. 1615), and the Celej House (c. 1635); and granaries. Other sights include the baroque Church of St. Anne (late 17th century) and the Reformed church and monastery (17th century).

REFERENCE
Rutkowski, H. *Kazimierz Dolny* . . . . Warsaw, 1965. [11–525–4]

KAZIMIROVA, EKATERINA GRIGOR'EVNA. Born Dec. 8, 1921, in the village of Fedorovka, in the present-day Orgeev Raion. Soviet Moldavian actress; People's Artist of the Moldavian SSR (1960).

Kazimirova graduated from the Odessa School of Theater and began her stage career in 1939 in the A. S. Pushkin Moldavian Music and Drama Theater in Kishinev. Her best roles include Polina and Katerina in Ostrovskii's *The Profitable Place* and *The Thunderstorm,* Goneril in Shakespeare's *King Lear,* Nadia in Gorky's *Enemies,* Synziana and Safta in Aleksandri's *Synziana and Pepelia* and *Iasi at Carnival Time,* Zoia in Karadzhale's *The Lost Letter,* Nila Snizhko in Salynskii's *The Lady Drummer,* Baroness Shtral' in Lermontov's *Masquerade,* and Madame Ksidias in Slavin's *Intervention.*

Kazimirova was a deputy to the fifth convocation of the Supreme Soviet of the Moldavian SSR. She was awarded two orders and several medals. [11–526–1]

KAZIN, VASILII VASIL'EVICH. Born July 25 (Aug. 6), 1898, in Moscow. Soviet Russian poet.

Kazin was among the first to incorporate the theme of labor into Soviet lyric poetry. He was a founder of the Smithy, a literary group of proletarian writers. He first published his work in 1914. His collection of verses *Workers' May* (1922) celebrated free and joyous labor. The simplicity and concreteness of Kazin's verse ("The Mason" and "The Plane") distinguish it favorably from the cosmic and abstract qualities of other Smithy poets.

Kazin's major narrative poems are *The Fox Coat and Love* (1926), in which he denounced petit bourgeois morality; *The White Sea Poem* (1937); which depicts the new Soviet man's upbringing in labor; and *The Great Beginning* (1954), which is about the first Communist Subbotniks. Kazin was awarded two orders and various medals.

WORKS
Stikhotvoreniia i poemy. [Avtobiografiia: Slovo o sebe.] Moscow, 1957.
Stikhotvoreniia i poemy. Foreword by B. Solov'ev. Moscow, 1964.

REFERENCES
Dynnik, V. "Teplyi zvon." *Khudozhestvennaia literatura,* 1934, no. 9.
Afanas'ev, V. "Prodolzhenie puti." *Moskva,* 1961, no. 6.

[11–526–2]

KAZINCBARCIKA, a city in northeastern Hungary, in the *megye* (county) of Borsod-Abaúj-Zemplén. The city was founded in 1954, by the merger of three settlements. Population, 28,000 (1970). Kazincbarcika is one of the centers of brown-coal mining and the chemical industry. The city has a chemical combine that formerly used brown coal but now uses natural gas, delivered by the gas pipeline from Hajduszoboszló; the combine produces nitrate fertilizers, caprolactam, polyvinyl chloride, and other products based on organic synthesis. Construction materials are manufactured in Kazincbarcika, and there is a steam power plant. [11–526–4]

KAZINKA, an urban-type settlement in Lipetsk Oblast, RSFSR; a railroad station 13 km southeast of Lipetsk. Kazinka has railroad transport enterprises. [11–526–3]

KAZIRANGA, a national park in India, in Assam State. The park was founded in 1908 to prevent the extermination of the rhinoceros. The area was 52,000 hectares in 1970. On the boggy left bank of the Brahmaputra River there is high grass and sparse tree and shrub vegetation. In 1966 there were about 400 rhinoceroses, 375 wild elephants, 550 buffalo, 20 gaurs, 250 marsh deer, 300 sambars, more than 4,000 hog deer, 100 muntjacs, 30 bears, 20 tigers, and 12 leopards in Kaziranga. Elephants are used for trips in the park, which until 1968 was a preserve.

REFERENCE
Gee, E. *Dikie zhivotnye Indii.* Moscow, 1968. (Translated from English.)

[11–526–5]

KAZI ZADEH AL-RUMI. Born circa 1360 in Bursa, Turkey; died circa 1437. Mathematician and astronomer.

Kazi Zadeh worked in Samarkand in Ulug Beg's observatory. He was one of the compilers of *Zij Ulug Beg* and the author of *Treatise on the Determination of the Sine of One Degree,* which contains the derivation and solution of the equation for a chord of 2° (that is, the doubled sine of 1°).

REFERENCE
Istoriko-matematicheskie issledovaniia, 13th ed. Moscow, 1960. Pages 533–56. [11–525–2]

KAZLU-RŪDA, a city (since 1950) in Kapsukas Raion, Lithuanian SSR. Kazlu-Rūda has a station on the Kaunas-Cherniakhovsk railroad line, 36 km southwest of Kaunas. A branch line 102 km long goes from Kazlu-Rūda to the city of Alitus. There is a mechanical repair plant, a wood-products industry, and a logging and timber distribution establishment in the city. [11–527–2]

KAZ'MIN, PETR MIKHAILOVICH. Born Oct. 5 (17), 1892, in the present-day village of Tret'iaki, in Borisoglebsk Raion, Voronezh Oblast; died June 30, 1964, in Moscow. Soviet Russian folklorist; People's Artist of the USSR (1961).

Kaz'min graduated in 1915 from the literature division of the Nezhin Institute of History and Philology. That same year he defended his candidate's dissertation on Russian folklore in song. He taught in music schools in Simferopol' and Moscow

(after 1921). In 1925 he became deputy director and in 1927, art director (co-director with V. G. Zakharov from 1932) of the M. E. Piatnitskii Russian State Folk Chorus. His direction made the chorus one of the outstanding musical groups of the USSR.

Kaz'min helped promote Russian choral art. He wrote the lyrics of "By White Snow" and "Russian Beauty" and the texts for the musical-literary compositions *The Russian Wedding, Beyond the Village,* and *Young People's Gathering;* he also staged round dances and scenes from village life. Kaz'min wrote essays on folk art and compiled the collection *Remembrances of V. G. Zakharov* (1967; with V. V. Khvatov). He received the State Prize of the USSR (1952), the Order of the Red Banner of Labor, and medals.

WORKS
Stranitsy iz zhizni M. E. Piatnitskogo. Moscow, 1961.

I. M. IAMPOL'SKII [11–531–1]

KAZNACHEEV, SERGEI KONSTANTINOVICH. Born Aug. 8 (20), 1895, in Moscow; died there Sept. 11, 1956. Soviet defense lawyer.

Kaznacheev graduated from the Moscow Institute of National Economy in 1919. He became a member of the Moscow city bar in 1923. Kaznacheev acted as defense lawyer in important defense trials, such as the case of the British spies in 1927 and the case of the former officials of the Lena Goldfields concession in 1930. [11–527–5]

KAZNACHEEVSKII, an urban-type settlement in Shchekino Raion, Tula Oblast, RSFSR. It is located 3 km from the Kaznacheevka railroad station on the Tula-Orel line. There is a factory for the production of reinforced-concrete articles. [11–527–6]

KAZRETI, an urban-type settlement in Bolnisi Raion, Georgian SSR. Kazreti is located on the Mashavera River (Kura basin). It is connected by a railroad branch with the Marneuli station on the Tbilisi-Leninakan line. In 1972, an ore-dressing combine for the processing of the Madneuli deposits of polymetallic ores was under construction. [11–529–1]

KAZYM, a river in Tiumen' Oblast, RSFSR, a right tributary of the Ob'. Length, 659 km; basin area, 35,600 sq km. The Kazym flows through the northern part of the West Siberian Plain. The river valley is marsh-ridden, and the channel is winding. The Kazym River is fed mainly by snow. It freezes in early November and thaws in the second half of May. The large tributaries on the left are the Amnia and Lykhn. The river is navigable for 250 km. [11–530–3]

KAZYR, or Bolo, a river in Krasnoiarsk Krai, RSFSR (the upper course is in Irkutsk Oblast), one of the rivers forming the Tuba River (right tributary of the Enisei). Length, 388 km; basin area, 20,900 sq km. The Kazyr River originates and flows within the Vostochnyi Saian Range and its spurs. The river valley is mostly narrow and has many rapids (Verkhnii Kitatskii and Ubinskii, for example). Below the confluence of the Kizir River, the valley widens and the riverbed divides into numerous channels. The Kazyr is fed by snow and rain. The average annual flow rate at the village of Sretenka (40 km from the mouth) is 317 cu m per sec. [11–530–4]

KELAMAYI (Karamai), a city in China, in the Sinkiang Uighur Autonomous Region. It is a transport junction and the center of the important oil fields of the Dzhungarian Basin, which began to be exploited in 1955–60. Kelamayi has an oil refinery.

[11–1156–3]

KEYSERLING, HERMANN ALEXANDER. Born July 20, 1880, in Könno, present-day Valmiera Raion, Latvian SSR; died Apr. 26, 1946, in Innsbruck. German philosopher and writer.

Keyserling studied the natural sciences in various European universities between 1900 and 1910. He traveled widely and took a trip around the world in 1911 and 1912. In his best-known work, *The Travel Diary of a Philosopher* (1919), Keyserling strove to intuitively apprehend the diverse forms of culture and life of different peoples, proceeding from the idea of "self-realization in travel through the world." Keyserling's irrationalist philosophy is akin to *Lebensphilosophie* in its conception of philosophy as "wisdom," in its idea of an intuitive understanding of the world analogous to artistic creativity, and in its opposition of intellect to soul. He sought through the study of ancient philosophy, especially Eastern (ancient Indian and Chinese) wisdom, a "new synthesis of spirit and soul," a return to the integrity of being that "European man" had lost as a result of the predominance of reason. In 1920 he founded the School of Wisdom and the Society of Free Philosophy in Darmstadt. The Keyserling Society, established in Wiesbaden in 1947, has published the journal *Terra Nova* since 1963.

WORKS

Die gesammelten Werke in 6 Bd, vol. 1. Darmstadt–Baden-Baden, 1956.
Das Gefüge der Welt. Munich, 1906.
Philosophie als Kunst 2nd ed. Darmstadt, 1922.
Das Reisetagebuch eines Philosophen, 7th ed., vols. 1–2. Darmstadt, 1923.
Menschen als Sinnbilder. Darmstadt, 1926.
Kritik des Denkens. Innsbruck, 1948.   IU. N. POPOV [11–538–2]

KHAM, the southeastern outskirts of the Tibetan upland, south of the upper course of the Hwang Ho in China. High mountain ridges (the Bayan Hara Ula, Russian Geographic Society, and Woodville Rockhill ranges) divided by the deep gorges of the upper reaches of the Yangtze, Mekong, Salween, and Yalung rivers and stretching mainly from the northwest to the southeast are predominant. In the northwest there are high-mountain steppes and sedge-*Kobresia* meadows. In the south and along the slopes of the gorges are fir and spruce forests, shrub thickets (juniper, honeysuckle, hawthorn, and barberry), and rich mixed grasses. There are perpetual snows and glaciers on the summits of the ridges. In 1900, Kham was studied by the Russian explorer P. K. Kozlov.

REFERENCE
Kozlov, P. K. *Mongoliia i Kam,* 2nd ed. Moscow, 1948.
[11–708–1]

KHOND (also Kandh, Kui), a tribe of people living mainly in the forested mountainous regions of the state of Orissa in India. Numbering more than 700,000 persons (1970 estimate), the Khond speak the Kui language, which belongs to the Dravidian family. Many of the Khond are either bilingual or speak only the Oriya language. Their religion is interwoven with traditional tribal beliefs and Hinduism. The Khond are subdivided into the plains Khond, who are highly assimilated with the neighboring Oriya and engage in plow farming (they are also divided into castes), and the hill Khond, who have preserved considerable vestiges of the tribal system. The chief occupations of the latter are slash-and-burn farming, hunting, and gathering.
[11–964–5]

KING CRAB (*Paralithodes camtschatica*), an invertebrate of the family Lithodidae of the order Decapoda. Outwardly it resembles the crab, but actually it is closer to the hermit crab (family Paguridae). The cephalothoracic shell is heart-shaped and equipped with spikes. The abdomen is folded up under the cephalothorax (as in true crabs) and is covered with numerous plates placed in rows lengthwise; the females have asymmetrically placed plates. The width of the cephalothorax in large males reaches 25 cm, the legs extend to 1.5 m, and the weight reaches 7 kg. The females are smaller. The king crab lives in the Sea of Japan and the Sea of Okhotsk and in southern parts of the Bering Sea. It makes regular migrations. Particularly large numbers are found on the western shore of Kamchatka, where the most intensive exploitation is also concentrated. Only the muscles of the legs are used for food.

REFERENCES
Ivanov, A. V. *Promyslovye vodnye bespozvonochnye.* Moscow, 1955. Pages 91–112.

Zhizn' zhivotnykh, vol. 2. Moscow, 1968. Pages 527–29.   [11–857–1]

KODIAK (Kadiak), a town in the northeast part of Kodiak Island, off the shores of Alaska. Kodiak was one of the first Russian settlements in America, founded in 1784 by G. I. Shelikhov. Population, 3,800 (1970). It is the island's key fishing port, and the trade center for a cattle-raising and fur-trading region. Kodiak has fish canneries.   [11–388–4]

KODIAK (Kadiak; Eskimo, Kikhtak), an island off the southern coast of Alaska in the USA, separated from the maainland by Shelikof Strait. Area, 9,300 sq km. The shores are steep and cut by fjords. The surface is hilly (elevations, up to 1,353 m) and extensively blanketed with volcanic ash (up to 6 m thick) blown over from the Alaskan Peninsula in 1912 when Mount Katmai erupted. The climate is temperate and humid (up to 1,600 mm of precipitation annually). Vegetation is mostly tall-grass meadows. The coastal waters abound with fish (sockeye and herring). The island has fish canneries.
    Kodiak was discovered in 1763 by the Russian seafarer Stepan Glotov. Its largest inhabited area is the town of Kodiak.
[11–388–3]

KOMPONG CHAM, a city and port in Cambodia; situated on the Mekong River. Administrative center of Kompong Cham Province. Population, approximately 30,000 (1962). Rubber from surrounding plantations, timber, and fish are exported
[11–843–5]

KOMPONG SOM (also Sihanoukville), a city and port in Cambodia, on the Gulf of Siam. It is connected by railroad and highway with the capital of Phnom Penh. The port was built in the 1960's and is accessible to oceangoing ships.   [11–843–4]

KRASNORECHENSKOE, an urban-type settlement in Kremennaia Raion, Voroshilovgrad Oblast, Ukrainian SSR, on the Krasnaia River, a tributary of the Severskii Donets. It has a railroad station on the Kupiansk-Debal'tsevo line. A machine-tool plant and a brickyard are located there.   [11–250–2]

KURNOOL, city in India in the state of Andhra Pradesh, on the Tunga River. Population, 136,700 (1971). Kurnool has a railroad station, and its industries include cotton ginning, cotton textile production, and cement production. Vegetable oil is also manufactured.   [11–330–3]

KUTCH, a gulf of the Arabian Sea on the northwestern coast of India. The Gulf of Kutch extends for 165 km between the continent and the Kathiawar Peninsula. The width of the gulf at its entrance is approxmately 46 km, and its maximum depth is 38 m. The shores of the gulf are low-lying and the southern shore is bordered with coral reefs. Tides are semidiurnal, with a height of more than 3 m. The port of Okha is located on the southern side of the entrance to the gulf.   [11–1635–3]

KUTCH, RANN OF, the Greater and the Lesser, salt marshes (swamps) in western India and in Pakistan, southeast of the Indus River delta. Area, more than 20,000 sq km; total length from east to west, more than 300 km; width, 40–80 km. The Rann of Kutch is a flat, low-lying surface with a maximum elevation of 200 m, and it is covered with black silt and saline efflorescence. In places there are rises (maximum 465 m) with steep slopes and sandy hills. During the summer monsoons, the Rann of Kutch is flooded by the sea and the Banas and Luni rivers.   [11–1647–3]

KVAISI, an urban-type settlement in Dzhava Raion, Iuzhnaia Osetiia AO, Georgian SSR. It is located on the Dzhedzhora River (a tributary of the Rioni), 60 km northwest of the city of Tskhinvali, with which it is linked by highway. Lead and zinc ores are mined here (Kvaisi deposit). Kvaisi also has an ore-dressing plant.   [11–1690–2]

KVANT (Quantum), a monthly physicomathematical popular science magazine of the Academy of Sciences of the USSR and the Academy of Pedagogical Sciences of the USSR. It has been published since 1970 in Moscow. *Kvant* is designed for teachers in secondary schools and students in upper grades. Circulation, about 400,000 (1972). Since 1972 the magazine's editor in chief has been Academician I. K. Kikoin.   [11–1694–4; updated]

KVAPILOVÁ, HANNA (née Kubešová). Born Nov. 29, 1860, in Prague; died there Apr. 8, 1907. Czech actress. Daughter of a craftsman.

Kvapilová made her debut in 1886 in E. Vojan's troupe. She became an actress with the National Theater in Prague in 1888. From the beginning of her career, Kvapilová rebelled against stage routine. In 1906 she organized the Moscow Art Theater's tour in Prague. Her acting centered on the themes of active protest against social injustice and of the dream of freedom and a better life. As an actress she affirmed the art of profound feelings on the Czech stage; her work advanced the development of national drama. J. Vrchlický, J. Zeyer, A. Jirásek, and other dramatists wrote plays for her. Her roles included Ophelia and Lady Macbeth (in Shakespeare's *Hamlet* and *Macbeth*), Ismene (in Sophocles' *Antigone*), Vojnarka (in Jirásek's play of the same name), Maria Stuart (in Schiller's play of the same name), and Masha (in Chekhov's *Three Sisters*).

WORKS
Literární pozůstalost, 3rd ed. Prague, 1946.
REFERENCES
Horáček, J. *Hanna Kvapilová.* Prague, 1911.
Černý, F. *Hanna Kvapilová,* 2nd ed. Prague, 1963.

                                L. P. SOLNTSEVA [11–1805–1]

KVARELI, a city (a settlement until 1964), the administrative center of Kvareli Raion, Georgian SSR. The city is located in the valley of the Alazani River, a tributary of the Kura River, 19 km north of the Mukuzani railroad station on the Tbilisi-Telavi branch line. Population, 9,500 (1970). The city has a winery, a cognac distillery, an essential oils factory, and a brickyard, as well as vineyard sovkhozes. The I. G. Chavchavadze Museum, the K. A. Mardzhanishvili House-Museum, and a people's amateur theater are located in Kvareli.   [11–1806–1]

KVARKUSH, a mountain range in the northern Urals, in the Vishera River basin, in Perm' Oblast, RSFSR. Length, 60 km; elevation, 800–850 m; highest point, Mount Vogul'skii Kamen' (1,065 m). The mountains are formed of quartzite conglomerate, quartzite-sandstone, and crystalline schist. The slopes of the mountains are deeply indented by river valleys and are covered with a taiga forest of spruce, cedar, birch and a mixture of fir trees. The summit has mountain tundra, scattered stones, many monadnocks, and mountain meadows.   [11–1809–1]

KWAJONG POP (Law of Official Appanages), a land law in Korea, published in 1391. It restored the principle of supreme state ownership of land and with it the state's right to collect taxes on all lands. Within the framework of state ownership various forms of feudal and peasant ownership of land were provided for. The principal category of feudal land ownership consisted of official appanages (*kwajong*), the sizes of which depended upon the rank (*kwa*) of their holders. The holders of these appanages did not have the right of complete ownership, but according to the *Kwajong Pop* they collected taxes for their own benefit. The promulgation of the *Kwajong Pop* was advantageous to the middle and petty feudal lords connected with the state service, and it abolished the land privileges of the high aristocracy.   [11–1673–2]

KWAKIUTL, an Indian tribe in the province of British Columbia in Canada. Population, approximately 4,500 (1967, estimate).

The Kwakiutl are bilingual; they speak their own language, which belongs to the Wakashan language group, and English. At the time of the arrival of the Europeans in the 18th century, there were approximately 25,000 Kwakiutl. They engaged primarily in fishing; private property relations were beginning to develop, and hereditary patriarchal slavery existed among them. The Kwakiutl created a distinctive culture and art. At the present time, the Kwakiutl live on reservations; most of them work in the fishing and timber industries. They are Protestants, although some of their ancient beliefs and cults have also been preserved.

REFERENCES
Narody Ameriki, vol. 1. Moscow, 1959.
Linguistic and Cultural Affiliations of Canadian Indian Bands. Ottawa, 1967.   [11–1691–2]

KWA LANGUAGES (Guinean languages), a family of languages spoken in the eastern part of the Ivory Coast, southern Ghana, Togo, Dahomey, and the southwestern part of Nigeria. The Kwa languages are spoken by approximately 34 million people (1967). According to the classification of the American scholar J. Greenberg, they constitute a subfamily of the Niger-Kordofanian language family. He includes in the Kwa language family the Kru, Ivory Coast Lagoon, Akan, Gã, and Adangbe language groups and the Ewe, Yoruba, Nupe, Bini, Ibo, and Ijo languages.

The Kwa languages are of the isolating type. The consonant system includes coarticulated labio-velars: voiced *gb* and voiceless *kp*. In Ewe an alveolar consonant is opposed to a retroflex consonant. Tones, including tonal combinations (rising or falling), play an important role in distinguishing words. Most roots are monosyllabic. The rudiments of a noun class system, without concord, exist in the morphology of some languages (for example, Twi). In many Kwa languages, nouns have a special prefix marker (vowel or nasal) that distinguishes them from verbs (in Twi, Yoruba, Ewe, and Nupe). In the verb, grammatical functions are expressed by means of affixes, auxiliaries, reduction, and word order, and, less frequently, by changes in tone (Twi, Azande, Ewe).

REFERENCES
Hintze, U. *Bibliographie der Kwa-Sprachen und der Togo-Restvölker.* Berlin, 1959.
Greenberg, J. H. *The Languages of Africa.* Bloomington, 1963.
Westermann, D. *Languages of West Africa.* London, 1970.
                                N. V. OKHOTINA [11–1672–5]

KWANGJU, a city in South Korea, capital of the South Cholla Province. Population, 403,700 (1966). Kwangju is a transportation junction and the trade center of an agricultural region (Yonsangan plain). It also has a textile industry.
                                                [11–1694–1]

KWANGO, a river in Central Africa, in Angola and the Republic of Zaïre. The Kwango is the largest left tributary of the Kasai River in the Congo River basin. The Kwango is approximately 1,200 km long and drains an area of 263,500 sq km. The river rises in the Lunda plateau and flows north in a broad, deep valley, forming a number of rapids and waterfalls. Its main tributaries are the Wamba and Kwilu rivers on the right. The waters of the river rise in the rainy season, between September or October and April. The lowest water level occurs in August. The average annual discharge in the lower course is 2,700 cu m per sec. The river is navigable in its lower course, from its mouth to the Kingushi rapids, a distance of 307 km. It is partially navigable in its middle course, between Kingushi and the Franz Josef waterfalls, a distance of approximately 300 km. The river is used for fishing.   [11–1693–5]

KWANTO, a major economic region of Japan, situated in central Honshu Island. It includes seven prefectures: Ibaraki, Tochigi, and Gumma, which form the northern Kwanto subregion; and Saitama, Chiba, Tokyo, and Kanagawa, which form the southern Kwanto subregion. Area, 32,200 sq km; population, 29.6 million (1970), or more than one-fourth of Japan's population.

The metropolitan region of Kwanto is the most densely populated region in the country. The bulk of the population lives around Tokyo Bay. Kwanto is also the most urbanized part of Japan: in 1967 almost 73 percent of its population lived in the region's 77 cities, each of which has a population of more than 50,000. In 1965 the economically active population was 13 million, of whom 30 percent work in the manufacturing industry, 14.5 percent in agriculture, 13.7 percent in the service industries, 12.2 percent in trade, and 7 percent in construction.

Kwanto holds first place in Japan in industrial output. The manufacturing industry, which accounted for 32.5 percent of the total income in 1965, holds first place in the region's economy; followed by trade (20 percent), construction (16 percent), and agriculture (5 percent). About a third of the country's industrial employees live in Kwanto. Heavy industry is by far the most important branch of the manufacturing industry. Kwanto contains a large part of electrical machine building (59 percent of the total Japanese output) and precision machine building (58 percent), as well as oil refining (40 percent), transportation machine building (including shipbuilding), and the food and condiment, metallurgical, chemical, and leather and footwear industries. The most important branches of the food industry are fish-processing, flour milling, and brewing. Other well-developed industries of the region are textiles and clothing (the cities of Hachioji, Kiryu, Ashikaga, and Maebashi), rubber, and porcelain and pottery. Old industries such as silk weaving and spinning, which developed from crafts, are located mainly in the interior part of the region. The enterprises of new industries are located in a narrow band along the Pacific coast and Tokyo Bay.

Electric power is produced mainly by hydroelectric power plants. Steam power plants use imported fuel. Copper is mined at the Ashio deposit (Tochigi Prefecture) and the Hitachi deposit (Ibaraki Prefecture); the annual yield of pyrites is 370,000–400,000 tons (Ibaraki, Saitama, and Gumma prefectures). Kwanto imports most of its raw materials and solid and liquid fossil fuel.

Kwanto is an important agricultural region. Field husbandry is the chief branch of agriculture. Irrigated rice fields occupy 512,000 hectares, or 16 percent of Japan's rice fields, and yield a harvest of about 2 million tons; barley and wheat account for about 62 percent and 50 percent of the total Japanese harvest, respectively. Vegetables are raised. There are many mulberry orchards on the Kwanto Plain and in the western mountain valleys on dry valley lands (Saitama and Gumma prefectures). Kwanto holds first place in Japan in the harvest of cocoons (41,400 tons) and production of raw silk. Horticulture is practiced in Kwanto (tangerines are grown in Kanagawa and Chiba prefectures), and its floriculture is famous. The livestock herd consists of 414,000 head of cattle and 1,957,000 pigs (about 30 percent of the country's herd). Poultry raising is an important activity, and fishing and the maritime industry are well developed. The railroads are electrified, and the region has a dense network of commercial highways. The seaports are Tokyo, Yokohama, and the new and highly mechanized port of Kojima on the Pacific Ocean.   N. A. SMIRNOV [11–1002–2]

KWANTO, Tokyo Plain, a low-lying plain along the Pacific coast of the island of Honshu (the most extensive plain in Japan).

The Kwanto Plain is a tectonic depression filled with loose marine and fluvial silt and layers of volcanic ash; in the recent geological past part of the plain was submerged under the waters of Tokyo Bay. There are frequent earthquakes in the area, and in 1923 a catastrophic earthquake destroyed the city of Tokyo. A dense network of rivers (the navigable Tone and Sumida) and canals crosses the Kwanto Plain. The climate is wet and temperate (to 2,000 mm of precipitation per year). The plain is being intensively cultivated.   [11–1002–1]

KWANTUNG ARMY, a grouping of Japanese troops formed for aggression against China, the USSR, and the Mongolian People's Republic (MPR).

The Kwantung Army was formed in 1931 on the basis of troops stationed in the province of Kwantung (southwest tip of the Liaotung Peninsula to the Gulf of Kwantung). On Sept. 18, 1931, the Kwantung Army treacherously attacked China and by early 1932 had occupied China's northeastern province, Manchuria, where the puppet state of Manchukuo was established on Mar. 9, 1932; it became virtually a colony of the Japanese imperialists and a base of operations for the subsequent aggression.

These events were the beginning of a series of armed conflicts with neighboring states provoked by the Japanese militarists. While expanding their aggression in China, the Japanese imperialists tried at the same time to test the strength of the Soviet Far Eastern frontiers and to capture convenient staging grounds for the future invasion of the USSR and the MPR. The strength of the Kwantung Army was gradually increased, reaching eight divisions (about 200,000 men) by 1938 and 12 divisions (about 300,000 men) in 1940.

In the summer of 1938 the Kwantung Army invaded the USSR near Lake Khasan; in 1939 a still greater provocation was staged against the Soviet Union and the MPR at the Khalkin-Gol River, but the Kwantung Army was defeated in both conflicts. In 1941, when the Soviet people were locked in a bitter struggle with fascist Germany, the Kwantung Army, in accordance with the Japanese Kantokuen plan, was deployed along the Manchurian frontier and in Korea for an attack against the USSR, waiting for a convenient moment to begin combat operations, as determined by the outcome of the war on the Soviet-German front. Between 1941 and 1943 there were from 15 to 16 Japanese divisions, with a strength of about 700,000 men, in Manchuria and Korea.

At the beginning of the campaign of the Soviet armed forces in the Far East (Aug. 9, 1945), the Kwantung Army was composed of the First Front (Third and Fifth armies), the Third Front (Thirtieth and Forty-fourth armies), the 17th Front (Thirty-fourth and Fifty-ninth armies), a separate army (the Fourth), two air armies (the Second and the Fifth), and the Sungari Fleet. In addition, it had operational command over the army of Manchukuo, the troops of Inner Mongolia (of Prince Tieh), and the Suiyüan Army Group. The total strength of the Kwantung Army and the troops under its command was 37 infantry and seven cavalry divisions; 22 infantry, two tank, and two cavalry brigades (a total of 1,320,000 men); 1,155 tanks; 6,260 guns, 1,900 aircraft; and 25 vessels. The Kwantung Army also had bacteriological weapons to be used against the Soviet armed forces. After the defeat of the Kwantung Army in the Manchurian Operation of 1945, Japan lacked effective forces and capability for the continuation of the war and signed the act of unconditional surrender on Sept. 2, 1945.

REFERENCES
Final, 2d ed. Moscow, 1969.
Hayashi, Saburo. *Iaponskaia armiia v voennykh deistviiakh na Tikhom okeane.* Moscow, 1964. (Translated from English.)
        N. V. ERONIN [11–1804–2]

KWARA, a state in western Nigeria, with an area of 74,300 sq km and a population of 2.4 million (1963, census), comprising mainly the Yoruba, Igala, and Igbirra. The capital is Ilorin. The greater part of the state is located along the right bank of the Niger River. Kwara has an equatorial monsoonal climate with a rainy season lasting seven months. Precipitation ranges from 1,000 to 1,300 mm a year, and the average monthly temperature varies from 25° to 30°C. The dominant vegetation is savanna forest and savanna. In agriculture, the main subsistence crops are millet and sorghum, and small amounts of yams, rice, cotton, sugarcane, cocoa, sesame, and palm oil and kernels are produced for the market. The region has deposits of iron ore (near Lokoja), mica, coal, and talc. Industry is represented by enterprises producing sugar, cigarettes, matches, and paper and cardboard, and there are also cotton-ginning plants, vegetable-oil mills, and sawmills. Craft industries include the production of pottery.
        [11–1805–2]

LAND ROLLER, a farm implement for leveling out and compacting the soil surface layers and for breaking up and loosening soil blocks, clods, and crusts. Land rollers may be drawn by a tractor or mounted on one. The rollers are divided by type of working surfaces into flat, ring, flat-ribbed, cam, ring-toothed, and combined. The effect of the land roller on the soil depends on its weight, outside diameter, and shape of the working surface. The heavier the land roller, the more deeply it compacts the soil. The weight of some land rollers can be varied by using ballast boxes that can be attached to the roller's frame or by filling specially hollowed working parts with water.

The choice of the type of land roller depends on the nature of the work and on soil conditions. A flat, water-filled roller is used for rolling peat boggy soils after plowing or disking. The large diameter of the drums (1.25 m) allows this implement to roll over the greatly swollen cloddy peat soils. A flat, water-filled roller is also used for the rolling of plowed lands and of fields planted with winter and spring crops, as well as for the rolling of fertilizer and manure before it is plowed under. Beet plantings are rolled with flat-ribbed water-filled rollers and ring-toothed rollers. A special feature of the flat-ribbed roller is the removable ribbed sleeve; this feature allows use of the roller both in presowing and postsowing rolling. The ring-toothed rollers can be used in the form of one, two, or more sections, depending on the power of the tractor used. The working parts of the sections on the rollers are rings with rims (tapered rings) and tined rings. The rollers are effective in rolling the soil before and after sowing, and they separate the clods and blocks after plowing.

Ring-lug rollers are used for packing the lower layers, loosening the surface soil layer, leveling the surface, and breaking up crusts and blocks after plowing. The sections of the roller consist of tined disks that turn freely on an axle. Combined rollers intensively loosen the surface soil layer and pack the lower one. They are used for breaking up clods before sowing, for packing planted rows with the simultaneous loosening of the surface layer, and for breaking up crusts and harrowing. [11–1585–2]

LAND USE MAPS, maps that reflect the land resources and types of land use in the national economy. Land use maps are subdivided into land resource, land in service, and agricultural land use maps. Maps of the first group show the distribution of land by user (for example, the land use map in the *Atlas of USSR Agriculture*, 1960). Maps of the second group show the distribution of land in service (for example, the land in service maps in the atlases of Irkutsk and Kustanai oblasts). Maps of the third group reflect the use of agricultural lands (for example, the 1:1,000,000 land use map of Indonesia).

By subject matter, land use maps are divided into general, which include all kinds of lands in service, and specific, which depict such individual types of land as arable land, hay fields, and pastures.

Land use maps are published on large, medium, and small scales in more than 70 countries: for example, on scales of 1:25,000, 1:63,360, and 1:625,000 in Great Britain; of 1:25,000 in Poland; of 1:500,000 in Czechoslovakia; of 1:50,000, 1:200,-000, and 1:1,000,000 in Canada; and of 1:50,000, 1:250,000, and 1:1,000,000 in Japan.

To coordinate research on land registration, the 16th congress of the International Geographic Union appointed a commission in 1949 on land use; by 1951 the commission had worked out the key of the 1:1,000,000 world land-use survey map. Since then land use maps have been compiled on the same scale in many countries. Under the direction of the United Nations, the Geographic Institute of Agostini (Italy) prepared a world land use atlas, the first part of which was issued in 1969. In the USSR, large-scale land use maps of kolkhozes, sovkhozes, administrative regions, and oblasts are being prepared, and some of them (with a small scale) are included in regional atlases (Leningrad and Riazan' oblasts and other areas). Land use maps are compiled from topographic maps, land allocation plans, aerial photo surveys, statistical data, and results of field trips.

Land use maps are the basis for the registration and qualitative and economic evaluation (cadastres) of land resources. They show the relationship between lands in service and natural conditions, knowledge of which is essential for scientific planning of the rational use of land.

REFERENCES
Nikolaevskaia, E. M. *Karty khoziaistvennogo ispol'zovaniia zemel'*. Moscow, 1970. (*Metodicheskie ukazaniia po proektirovaniiu i sostavleniiu kompleksnykh nauchno-spravochnykh atlasov,* issue 16.)
Nikishov, M. I., Iu. V. Shumov, and N. S. Karpov. *Metodika sostavleniia obzornykh kart ispol'zovaniia zemel' SSSR.* Moscow, 1972.
M. I. NIKISHOV [11–1445–4]

LARGE WHITE BUTTERFLY (*Pieris brassicae*), a butterfly of the family Pieridae (cabbage butterflies). Wingspan, 55–60 mm. The surfaces of the fore wings are white. A black crescent-shaped border and two black spots (the females have brighter spots) mark the outer part of the hind wings. The undersides of the wings are greenish yellow. The caterpillar is 40–45 mm long, grayish green on top and yellow underneath, and covered with yellow stripes and black spots. The egg is yellow, ribbed, and turbinate. The large white butterfly is widespread in Europe, except in the extreme northeastern regions. It is also found in the Caucasus, Middle Asia, Southwest Asia, and North Africa. This butterfly mainly harms cabbage; it also damages other cruciferous plants. There are one to five generations each year. The chrysalides hibernate during the winter; the butterflies appear in the spring. The eggs are laid in groups on the underside of leaves of cruciferous plants. The larvae feed on leaves and pupate on trees, shrubs, building walls, and other places. The large white butterfly periodically reproduces in large numbers, causing damage to vegetables. Control measures include the destruction of weeds and the treatment of plants with insecticides and the Soviet-made microbiological preparation entobacterin.

[11–1092–4]

LEPISOSTEUS (gar), a genus of fish of the order Lepisosteiformes. Its three species are found in the fresh waters of North America and Cuba. Length, up to 2.5–3 m (in exceptional cases up to 6 m). Spawning occurs in the spring; the roe sticks to benthic objects. The fry have a large yolk sac. As they emerge from the eggs, the fry hang motionless, attached to benthic objects. Gars feed on other fishes; they wait in hiding for their prey. They spend the winter in the deep parts of rivers. Gars have some commercial significance. However, they cause harm to the fishing industry by tearing nets and damaging other fish. One species is known as the tropical, or Cuban, gar (*Lepisosteus tristoechus*). [11–539–5]

LIBRARY CATALOG, a list of the published works held by a library. Library catalogs serve to indicate a library's holdings, to help readers select books, and to guide reading in accordance with the ideological-political and cultural-educational aims of the library. The great range of subjects treated in published works, the diversity of the publications making up a library's holdings, and the varied needs of readers necessitate the creation of a complex system of catalogs differing in purpose and structure. The compilation of various types of catalogs is the subject of the science of cataloging. The elaboration of the theoretical and methodological questions of compiling catalogs is one of the basic tasks of library science.

According to their purpose, catalogs are divided into readers' catalogs, for general reference, and staff catalogs, which also include rarely used and obsolete works. According to the grouping of the material, there are systematic, subject, alphabetical, and numerical catalogs. Systematic catalogs group entries for published works by sections of the various branches of knowledge, following the classification system used in the library. Subject catalogs are descriptions of holdings arranged not in terms of branches of knowledge but rather according to the alphabetical order of the subjects (phenomena, concepts, or objects) of the works. The entries for published works in alphabetical catalogs are arranged in alphabetical order by the last name of the author or by title (if a description has been classified by title). Catalogs cover various types of published works, including books, periodicals, maps, musical scores, graphic arts, standards, patents, and certificates of invention. Patents and certificates of invention, in particular, are described in numerical catalogs, in which entries are arranged according to special numbers that have been assigned to the given publications.

Systematic and alphabetical catalogs are required for all Soviet libraries, as well as card indexes of newspaper and journal articles, which are normally compiled according to branch of knowledge. Subject catalogs are used in scientific and special libraries. In republic, krai, and oblast libraries, there are also local press catalogs and catalogs for the literature and various other types of materials relating to the given republic, krai, or oblast, known as local-lore catalogs.

In large libraries, besides main catalogs, giving the holdings of the entire library, catalogs of the holdings of the library's various divisions may be compiled. If a library has branches, it is often necessary to have a central catalog—a unified catalog of the holdings of the library and all its branches. Joint catalogs, which have become especially important with the broadening of libraries' functions as sources of bibliographical information and the development of interlibrary loans, describe the holdings of several independent libraries and are often compiled on the basis of territorial subdivisions or branches of knowledge. Catalogs of recommended literature for various types of libraries, such as district, rural, or children's libraries, are called model catalogs.

Catalogs may be kept in the form of card files, books, or loose-leaf notebooks with easily inserted pages. Card catalogs, which facilitate prompt changes and additions, are used most widely. Printed catalogs have the advantage of being easy to read and usable outside the library, which makes them particularly convenient as model or joint catalogs.

Z. N. Ambartsumian [11–1545–4]

LIBRARY CATALOGING

LIBRARY CATALOGING (of published works), the description, classification, and subject indexing of published works and the organization of library catalogs. In Soviet libraries cataloging has been standardized by the use of uniform rules (of which there are two versions, for large and for small libraries) for describing published works and of uniform principles of classification. Centralized cataloging has been organized in order to render cataloging more efficient, to facilitate the work of librarians, and to provide effective and prompt cataloging. Centralized cataloging is accomplished through various means, including publication of bibliographical descriptions, classification indexes, and model catalog cards in books and other publications; printed catalog cards are also issued. In the USSR (in accordance with State Standard 7.4–69), all books intended for public libraries must contain the model of an annotated catalog card. Printed catalog cards are distributed by the all-Union and republic book chambers, and the publishing house Kniga publishes the annotated cards that are prepared by the V. I. Lenin State Library of the USSR. In some republics and oblasts cards are issued by publishing houses and distributed together with the books.

E. R. Sukiasian [11–1546–1]

LOGWOOD

LOGWOOD (*Haematoxylon campechianum*), a small tree of the family Caesalpiniaceae, measuring approximately 12 m tall and 0.5 m in diameter. The leaves are pinnate, and the flowers are small and yellow. Native to tropical America, logwood is cultivated in the tropics. The heartwood is initially bright red; it subsequently turns blue, then violet-black. Logwood, which contains hematoxylin and tannins, is used for making dye. Because of its attractive color and texture, the wood is valued in the manufacture of furniture and parquetry. [11–842–3]

LONICERA CAPRIFOLIUM

LONICERA CAPRIFOLIUM, a branchy climbing shrub of the honeysuckle family, attaining a height of 4–6 m. The leaves are glabrous, vary from ovate to elliptical, and have bluish gray undersides. The lower leaves have short stems and the upper are sessile; the broad bases of the opposite leaves fuse around the branch. The flowers are reddish or yellowish and gathered at the ends of the branches in sessile whorls of three to ten flowers. The fruit is a juicy coral red berry. The species grows in forests in the Caucasus, southern Europe, and Southwest Asia. It is used in gardens and parks in making arches and arbors and in decorating walls; in the southern USSR it is grown as a hedge. It is also a medicinal plant, with diuretic and astringent properties. [11–1078–1]

LOWER CALIFORNIA

LOWER CALIFORNIA (also Baja California), a peninsula in western North America, in Mexico. It is bounded by the Gulf of California and the Pacific Ocean. Length, about 1,200 km; width, 50–250 km; area, about 144,000 sq km.

The coast of Lower California is precipitous (especially in the east); in places in the west there is a lagoon-type coast. There are numerous coastal islands and convenient harbors in the south. A chain of separate volcanic and crystalline blocks stretches along the peninsula, closer to its eastern shore. Most of them have altitudes of 500–1,500 m, with the greatest elevation being 3,078 m (La Encantada). Step-like plateaus with elevations of 1,000–1,500 m, coastal lowlands, and the short Sierra Vizcaíno range extend along the western edge. The climate is subtropical in the north and tropical in the south. In virtually all places precipitation is less than 250 mm a year. Fogs are frequent on the coast. The predominant soils are sierozems. Desert and semidesert vegetation predominates (various bushes, cacti, agaves, and yuccas); there are scattered forests in the mountains.
[11–633–2]

MAGGOTS, CABBAGE AND TURNIP

MAGGOTS, CABBAGE AND TURNIP, the common name for two species of insects of the family Muscidae: cabbage maggots (*Hylemyia brassicae*) and turnip maggots (*H. floralis*), the most dangerous pests to cabbage and other crucifers.

The cabbage maggot is 6–6.5 mm long. The male is ash gray with three stripes on his pronotum and a black lengthwise stripe on his abdomen; the female is larger than the male, with a wider abdomen. The cabbage maggot is found in Europe, Asia, and North America; in the USSR it lives almost everywhere and is most harmful in the nonchernozem zone and farther north. There are one to four generations a year. The chrysalides hibernate in puparia in the ground; the maggots come out in the spring. The eggs are laid on the root collar of plants or on the ground close to them. The larvae feed on the surface of roots or implant themselves in the roots, root collar, and lower stalks.

The turnip maggot is somewhat larger than the cabbage maggot and has yellowish wings. It is widespread in Europe and Asia; in the USSR it is found in the nonchernozem zone, primarily on peat soils, in the north, and in the Asian part. There is one generation a year. The chrysalides hibernate in puparia in the ground, and the maggots come out in late June and early July. The eggs are laid in large groups under clumps of dirt near cabbage stalks. The larvae harm the roots and stumps.

Plants harmed by the cabbage and turnip maggot do not grow tall and either reduce the harvest or die. Preventive measures include deep autumn plowing, raising the sprouts in nutrient pots with the addition of insecticides, early transplanting of healthy, strong seedlings, early spring feeding of plants with subsequent hilling up, and treating crops with insecticides.

REFERENCES
Gerasimov, B. A., and E. A. Osnitskaia. *Vrediteli i bolezni ovoshchnykh kul'tur,* 4th ed. Moscow, 1961.
Loginova, K. M. "Kapustnye mukhi." *Zashchita rastenii,* 1967, no. 6.

T. N. Bushchik [11–1095–4]

MAP COMPILATION PROCEDURES

MAP COMPILATION PROCEDURES, the operations involved in preparing the compilation and printing originals of maps. Map compilation procedures include editorial and preparatory work, compilation, and the preparation of map originals for publication (map design).

Editorial and preparatory work includes collecting, systematizing, studying, and scientifically collating cartographic source material. Depending on the purpose and nature of the map, a map montage model is made, and the scale, cartographic projection, and cartographic methods of representation and symbols are chosen. The decisions on these questions, together with the technical instructions for the method to be followed in compiling, preparing for publication, and publishing the map, are described in an editing plan, or map program. The editing plan is supplemented either by a series of graphic charts and a section with the color pattern or by the author's model. Editorial and preparatory work concludes with the computation of the cartographic projection, the construction of geographic and coordinate grids, and the entering of geodetic control points, indications of areas adjoining the map margin, the marginal representation, and the basic cartographic material.

Compilation consists in transferring the cartographic data from the source materials to a prepared base in order to make a compilation original.

The basic process in map compilation is known as cartographic generalization—the selection and simplification of the material that is to be mapped. The data are transferred from the source material to the compilation original by photoreproduction, by photo conversion, by projection through an epidiascope or optical drawing instruments, by photoelectronic conversion, or by mechanical writing methods, such as using the pantograph and perspectograph or graphic procedures (compilation by use of a grid). These methods may be combined. The topographic elements to be shown on the map are entered on the compilation original in a sequence. First, the control points and ground features serving as landmarks are entered, followed by hydrographic objects, population centers, road network, relief, vegetation, soils, and boundaries. The specialized data of thematic maps are compiled on a separate copy. Geographic names are entered immediately after depicting the items to which they refer. When nonstandard maps are being compiled, the compilation original is supplemented with a copy of the map's color pattern indicating the colors that are to be used in printing all tone elements of the map, such as the hypsometric coloring, the colors of bodies of water and vegetation, and special data.

The finished compilation original of a map sheet is edited and corrected. Since it is an author's original, its graphic qualities do not meet map printing standards and it must be prepared for publication. The publishing original is prepared either by drawing on a paper or plastic base or by scribing on specially coated plastic. An outline obtained from the compilation original is used.

The drawing is done in strict conformity with standard symbols. The drawing may be composite (all hachures entered on one copy), partially separated (one element of the map drawn on one copy and the rest on a second copy), or completely separate (individual publishing originals prepared for each hachure element). Only separate publishing originals are prepared when drawing on plastic.

The lettering is prepared by photocomposition and is usually glued directly onto the drawn originals (contour, hydrography, relief); sometimes the lettering is a separate publishing original. When map originals are being prepared for publication by scribing on plastic, separate engravings are made for each hachure element of the map. The work is done with special scribing tools. From negative engravings, diapositives are obtained onto which the typeset lettering is glued. When publication originals are being prepared either by drawing or by scribing on plastic, special masks of transparent plastic are usually made for the color pattern of the map. The work is checked visually and by preparing a line original on paper or plastic. When composite or partially separate drawings on paper are used, the process of preparing map originals for publication concludes with making separate scanning models and color (lithographic) models. The former serve as guides during retouching, and the latter are used to make the printing plates for the maps' color pattern.

In analyzing the current trends toward improving map production a number of basic directions may be identified: the development of techniques for compiling and preparing maps for publication; mechanization of photocomposition; introduction of microfilming, electrophotography, and photoluminescence; improvement of photocopying operations; automation of computing and constructing the mathematical base of the map with computers and the automatic coordinatograph; and automation of the preparation of publishing originals and the process of generalization.

REFERENCES
Garaevskaia, L. S. *Redaktirovanie melkomasshtabnykh kart i atlasov.* Moscow, 1962.
Komkov, A. M., S. A. Nikolaev, and N. I. Shilov. *Sostavlenie i redaktirovanie kart,* parts 1–2. Moscow, 1958.
Salishchev, K. A. *Sostavlenie i redaktirovanie kart,* part 1. Moscow, 1947.
Salishchev, K. A. *Osnovy kartovedeniia,* 3rd ed., vol 2. Moscow, 1962.
Solov'ev, M. D. *Matematicheskaia kartografiia.* Moscow, 1969.
A. N. LIUBKOV   [11–1429–1]

MAPPING, COMPREHENSIVE, the multifaceted depiction of natural and socioeconomic phenomena on geographic maps, taking into account their interrelationships. Three main methods are used in comprehensive mapping: (1) the preparation of a complete set of topically different but interrelated geographic maps (for example, comprehensive atlases); (2) the preparation

of a series of different topical maps according to a standard program, so that the maps supplement one another, are comparable, and, as a result, are convenient for use as a set (for example, the state geological maps of the USSR—stratigraphic, geomorphological, and mineral maps—which are often supplemented by hydrogeological maps and maps of Quaternary deposits); and (3) the compilation of comprehensive maps that show several interrelated phenomena together, each in its own indexes (for example, synoptic weather maps, which show temperature, pressure, and other meteorological elements).

Comprehensive maps are distinguished by the range of elements covered, from a comparatively limited set of phenomena or characteristics (for example, phenomena that are essential for knowledge of the structure and composition of the earth's crust or for a qualitative evaluation of farmland) to a full cartographic compendium of scientific knowledge from physical, economic, and political geography; and by territorial scope, from maps of certain key areas of a few square kilometers, which are studied in detail, to a survey of the entire planet (for example, the *Great Soviet Atlas of the World*).

The preparation of a set of interrelated maps is often one of the main tasks of comprehensive geographic research, which is organized for the thorough study of a territory in order to solve various national economic problems. Comprehensive mapping has achieved major successes in the development and compilation of geographic atlases. The letters written by V. I. Lenin in 1920–21 concerning preparation of the first Soviet geographic atlases are of great importance for the methodology of comprehensive mapping.

REFERENCE
Salishchev, K. A. *Kartografiia,* 2nd ed. Moscow, 1971.
K. A. SALISHCHEV   [11–1392–1]

MAP-PUBLISHING PROCESSES, the aggregate of production operations in publishing maps, including reproduction, retouching, photocopying, printing, and finishing work.

Black-and-white hachured, half-tone, and colored master copies made on a nondeforming base (drawing paper glued onto aluminum; plastic) are used in publishing maps. Master copies in the form of black-and-white slides on thin transparent plastics have become widespread; their use eliminates the processes of photographic reproduction. The master copies drawn on paper are photographed using special reproduction devices. The number of negatives corresponds to the number of colors to be used for the hachured elements of the map being printed. Half-tone images (washout of relief and photographic illustrations) are reproduced using autotype or contact gratings; colored master copies are reproduced by means of light filters and color-correcting optical devices. The negatives undergo technical and separation retouching: technical retouching is intended to remove all technical defects in the negative (spots, scratches, and so on), and separation retouching divides the hachured elements according to color. As a result, one element of the map that will be printed in a particular color (for example, black for contour elements, blue for elements of hydrography, and brown for relief) remains on each negative. Negatives or slides for the background elements of the map's color design (vegetation, bodies of water, and hypsometric coloring) are prepared by hand or on overlays. Separation retouching is guided by special models on which each hachured element of the map's content is defined in bright colors. Colored (lithographic) models are used for guidance in making negatives for the background elements of the map's color design. A set of slides is produced from the negatives and is used to produce plates for plane printing. The plates are made of aluminum, plastic, or bimetallic sheets. The method of positive contact photocopying is used to produce the image on the plates. The quality of photographic reproduction, retouching, and photocopying work is checked by printing a color test, which should correspond exactly to the author's original and to standards for color design. An edition of a map is printed on rotary flat offset presses.

Special cartographic grades of paper are used for printing most maps; paper reinforced with synthetic fiber, *kapron* and *lavsan* linen, and flexible plastic films is used for special-purpose maps. The final operations (the finishing process) are performed after the map edition has been printed. These operations include cutting the printer's sheets into individual maps, sorting maps by quality of printing, grouping according to tone (for multipage maps), gluing them onto cloth (school maps), stitching into sections and binding (atlases), and packing the finished products.

Modern map-publishing processes are based on the latest achievements of science and technology in electronics, electro-photography, photochemistry, and polymer chemistry. Map publishers have highly efficient printing presses, photographic reproduction and photocopying machines, sheet counters, and various types of quality-control equipment, which make possible the rapid production of high-quality maps for the country's national economy and defense.

REFERENCES
50 let sovetskoi geodezii i kartografii. Moscow, 1967. (Collection of articles.)
Itogi nauki: Kartografiia 1967–1969, issue 4. Moscow, 1970.
Edel'shtein, A. V. *Tekhnologiia izdaniia kart i atlasov.* Moscow, 1962.
A. N. LIUBKOV   [11–1425–1]

MAPS, FOREST, maps that reflect the location and the qualitative and quantitative characteristics of forests. They are divided into current, reference, and educational types. The most important type is the current map, because such maps are needed in order to manage and plan the exploitation of forests.

In the USSR, current maps are compiled when the forests are established, and they are revised every ten to 15 years. On large-scale current forest maps (1:5,000–1:50,000)—maps of forestry sections and forested areas—the sections of the forests are characterized according to the predominant species and age. Maps that show in great detail the indexes of quality and yield, density, types of trees, and ranges of the various species form a special group. The dominant species are represented by a colored background, the age of the forest is shown by the intensity of the color, and other data are shown by additional symbols. The maps of forestry sections are equivalent to forestry station maps (1:100,000–1:200,000), which show the forested area with the forestry sections divided according to the dominant species and age groups. Oblast (or krai) forest maps (1:300,000–1:1,000,000) also reflect the organization of the forested land and forestry, as well as timber enterprises. Reference forest maps on a scale of less than 1:1,000,000 reflect the forested areas of the entire country or of large regions subdivided according to the dominant species. Educational maps provide a generalized representation of forests subdivided according to species.

The first, hand-drawn forest maps were compiled in the 18th century; the first current maps, in the mid-19th century. In the USSR, current maps of all the forests in the country were compiled by 1957. A reference map for European Russia was published in 1909 (1:1,680,000), and one for Asian Russia appeared in a comprehensive atlas of Asian Russia in 1914 (1:1,260,000). Twelve reference maps of several regions have been published since 1917. Many of them are included in general geographic and comprehensive regional atlases. A forest map of the USSR (1:2,500,000) showing the location of forests according to the 17 largest forest-forming species was published in 1955.

REFERENCES
Tsvetkov, M. A. *Lesnye karty i metodika ikh sostavleniia.* Moscow-Leningrad, 1950.
Shaposhnikova, L. A. *Izobrazhenie lesa na kartakh.* Moscow, 1957.
A. F. KRUCHININ   [11–1446–1]

MAPS, INDUSTRY, maps depicting the location and development of industrial production. The various characteristics of industrial production (including development level, specialization, capacity of equipment, number of employees, volume of gross product in value or physical terms, fixed assets, production growth, and economic ties) are indicated on the industry maps for individual enterprises, populated areas, industrial centers, or territorial units (countries or regions). The industry maps are compiled based on a key method; cartograms, map-diagrams (collation maps), and area maps are also used.

In terms of content, industry maps are divided into general-industry and sectorial maps, which are divided into maps for power engineering and for mining and manufacturing industries. In turn these are divided into narrow sectorial maps for individual sectors of industrial production. Industry maps show the existing and planned location of industry and depict the characteristics essential to its further development (such as transportation, raw materials, and fuel resources). Industry maps are used in the study of the patterns of the existing location of industry, in current and long-range planning, in the day-by-day administration of the national economic sectors, and in scientific planning. Among the maps used for these purposes are scientific reference maps, planning maps, economic operational maps, variant maps, and evaluation and planning maps.

In the middle of the 19th century, industry maps (1842) and an economic statistics atlas (1851) were published for European Russia. During the years of Soviet power, many industry maps have been published, including the USSR industry maps (1927, 1929), the *Atlas of Industry of the USSR* (1929–31), and the *Atlas of Industry of the USSR at the Beginning of the Second Five-year Plan* (1934).

A large number of modern maps of industry can be found in such new Soviet and foreign atlases as the regional comprehensive atlases of the USSR and the regional planning atlases of the Federal Republic of Germany.

Industry maps are being improved by enriching their content, depicting the diverse interdependencies of the production and territorial complexes, and including technical and economic indicators (such as capital return and the level of concentration).

REFERENCES
Baranskii, N. N., and A. I. Preobrazhenskii. *Ekonomicheskaia kartografiia.* Moscow, 1962.
Kartograficheskoe obespechenie planov razvitiia narodnogo khoziaistva. Irkutsk, 1968.
Novoe v tematike, soderzhanii i metodakh sostavleniia ekonomicheskikh kart. Moscow, 1970.
Otsenochnoe kartografirovanie prirody, naseleniia i khoziaistva. Moscow, 1971.
A. Z. UMANSKII   [11–1449–1]

MAPS, INTERNATIONAL, geographic maps made in different countries according to coordinated editorial guidelines and with uniform legends.

The decision to prepare the first international map, the 1:1,000,000 general geographical map, was reached at the Fifth International Geographical Congress (Bern, 1891), but work on this map was uncoordinated in the initial stage. Uniform principles and requirements for making the map were adopted by international conferences in London (1909) and Paris (1913). Fourteen map sheets were published before 1914 (for the territory of Great Britain, Italy, France, Japan, Argentina, Chile, and the USA). The Central Bureau was set up in Southampton (Great Britain) in 1920 to coordinate the extensive work being done on the map. By the start of World War II (1939–45), 250 sheets of the map had been published; in addition, series of maps on the same scale, differing from the accepted standard in content and principles of construction, were published for a number of regions of Europe, Africa, and Latin America. During World War II international cooperation in preparation of the 1:1,000,000 international map lessened; but a series of general geographic maps on this scale, covering virtually the entire world, but with significantly different content and quality, were published for military purposes. In 1944 work began on preparation of the international World Aeronautical Chart (WAC) on a scale of 1:1,000,000.

In 1953 work on the 1:1,000,000 international map was headed by the Cartographic Bureau of UNESCO. UN international conferences on the map were held in Bonn (Federal Republic of Germany) in 1962 and in Montreal (Canada) in 1966. The conferences ratified new requirements for preparing the map, which were less rigid with regard to uniformity among sheets and envisioned the possibility of simultaneously compiling blocks of general geographic and air navigation charts on a 1:1,000,000 scale. Individual sheets of the new variation of the international map on the scale were published for the territory of Great Britain, France, the FRG, Portugal, Greece, Japan, western and eastern Africa, the island of Madagascar, the USA, Canada, and Australia.

In the USSR the first publication of a general geographical map on a scale of 1:1,000,000 was completed in 1945. It totaled 183 sheets and formed the largest single block of the 1:1,000,000 international map.

At the 1956 session of UNESCO in New York the Soviet delegation raised the question of making a uniform general geographic international map on a scale of 1:2,500,000 covering the entire land and water territory of the earth. This map is being compiled through the efforts of the USSR and the European socialist countries (Bulgaria, Hungary, the German Democratic Republic, Poland, Rumania, and Czechoslovakia). Of the 244 sheets, which cover the entire earth, 188 were published by the end of 1972. The map is being published in several variations, which makes it easier to use as the basis for various types of thematic maps.

A great deal of attention is being given to preparing thematic international maps, such as geological, geomorphological, geobotanical, land-use, and soil maps.

REFERENCES
Salishchev, K. A. "Sovremennaia tematicheskaia kartografiia i zadachi mezhdunarodnogo sotrudnichestva." *Izv. AN SSSR: Ser. geografich.*, 1968, no. 5.
Böhme, R. "Die internationale Weltkarte 1:1,000,000." *Allgemeine Vermessungs-Nachrichten*, 1971, no. 1.   IU. G. KEL'NER   [11–1447–1]

MAPS, THEMATIC, maps that show certain natural or social phenomena in relation to the basic topographic elements (the geography). There are agricultural, agroclimatic, bathymetric, botanical, climatic, demographic, economic geographic, forest, geobotanical, geochemical, geological, geomorphological, hydrological, industrial, landscape, land use, paleogeographic, soil, synoptic, tectonic, topographic, and zoological thematic maps.
[11–1451–3]

MASONRY BRIDGE, a bridge whose main load-bearing structures are made of natural stone, brick, or concrete blocks. Such a bridge is always arched, with massive supports. The main load-bearing element of a masonry bridge is the arch, over which is built the spandrel, which in turn supports the bridge roadway. The spandrel is made from a gravel or crushed stone backing held in by lateral (side) walls made of concrete masonry or stonework or in the form of an open structure of small arches resting on crosswalls.

The advantages of a masonry bridge are its architectural attractiveness and its durability. Masonry bridges are known that have been in use for more than 1,000 years. The basic shortcomings that limit the use of masonry bridges are their complexity and labor-intensiveness of construction. A variation of a masonry bridge is the concrete bridge, which has an arch made of cast concrete.
[11–786–3]

MASONRY BUILDING MATERIALS, an extensive group of building materials and articles of stonelike composition. A distinction is made between natural masonry materials, which are obtained by mechanical processing of rock (they may sometimes be produced without special processing), and artificial materials, which are produced by technological processing of a mineral raw material. Because of their good construction qualities (durability, strength, and frost resistance) and the wide distribution and unlimited reserves of natural raw materials, masonry materials are widely used in modern construction. They are the basic building materials for housing, public, and industrial construction, as well as various engineering structures.

In terms of shape, masonry materials are divided into materials consisting of irregularly shaped pieces (quarrystone or crushed rock) and dimension articles with a regular shape (blocks, slabs, and shaped articles). They are divided according to density into three groups: heavy (more than 1,800 kg/m^3), light (1,800–1,200 kg/m^3), and very light (less than 1,200 kg/m^3). Artificial masonry materials used as thermal insulation materials may have a density of about 500 kg/cu m.

The main index of masonry materials is the compressive strength, which is characterized by a grade. According to this feature, masonry materials are divided into high-strength (10–300 meganewtons per sq m [MN/m^2], or about 100–3,000 kilograms-force per sq cm [kgf/cm^2]), average (2.5–10.0 MN/m^2), and low-strength (0.4–5.0 MN/m^2). The tensile strength of masonry building materials is less than their compressive strength by a factor of 7–15; therefore, masonry materials are often reinforced with fibrous materials (asbestos, fiberglass, or organic fiber) or metal (steel reinforcement). The masonry materials used in exterior structures should have some degree of frost and water resistance. Depending on the area of use, masonry materials are also rated according to water absorption, acid resistance, and wearability.

The natural masonry materials are divided into the following basic varieties, according to the method of mechanical processing used: sand and gravel, which are produced by sifting and washing appropriate friable rock; quarrystone, which is produced mainly by mining of limestones, sandstones, and other sedimentary rock in blasting operations; crushed rock; cut stone and blocks, which are sawn from light rock (tuff and coquina) directly in the quarries using stone-cutting machines; and facing stones, slabs, and shaped articles, which are made at specialized stone-working enterprises from decorative rock (marble, granite, and limestone).

Various requirements established by the appropriate Construction Standards and Rules and GOST (All-Union State Standard) apply to natural masonry building materials (hydraulic-engineering structures, road construction, or the external or internal finishing of buildings), depending on their purpose. The most widespread natural masonry materials—sand, gravel, and crushed rock—are widely used as fillers in manufacturing concretes and mortars. Quarrystone is used mainly in laying the foundations of buildings and retaining walls. Sawn stone and blocks are used mainly as local wall materials. Facing stone, slabs, and shaped pieces with various surfaces (finishes)—for example, split, hewn, ground, and polished—are used largely for exterior and interior finishing of buildings, for flooring, and for manufacturing steps, parapets, and partitions because of their good decorative qualities and durability as well as a reduction in their cost as a result of introducing modern processing methods (diamond tools, thermal treatment, and mechanized methods of splitting).

Rock is widely used as a raw material for manufacturing various artificial masonry materials (for example, ceramics, glass, and thermal insulation materials), as well as inorganic binders (gypsum, lime, and cement). The production of these materials and articles involves processes that alter the composition, structure, and properties of the natural materials. Artificial masonry materials may be produced from clay and other ceramics, with subsequent firing (clay brick and ceramic stone); from silicate melts (stone casting, slag casting, and glass products); and from mixtures containing a binder, such as products made of concrete and mortar (for example, concrete, reinforced-concrete, and silica-concrete panels and blocks; silica brick).

The most important and most industrial artificial masonry materials are concrete and reinforced-concrete structural members and products based on mineral binders (cement and lime).

REFERENCES
Stroitel'nye normy i pravila, part 1, sec. V, chap. 8: "Materialy i izdeliia iz prirodnogo kamniia." Moscow, 1962.
Stroitel'nye materialy. Edited by M. I. Khigerovich. Moscow, 1970.
A. M. ORLOV and K. N. POPOV   [11–764–1]

MASONRY CONSTRUCTION, load-bearing and enclosing elements of buildings and structures made from stone masonry (foundations, walls, columns, partitions, arches, and vaults).

Artificial and natural stone materials are used for masonry construction, including construction brick, solid and hollow ceramic and concrete stone and blocks, stone from heavy or light rock (limestone, sandstone, tuff, and coquina), mortars, and large blocks of ordinary (heavy), silicate, and light concretes. The material for stonework is chosen according to the size and importance of the structure, the strength and thermal-insulation properties of the structural elements, and the availability of local raw materials, and also on the basis of economic considerations.

The stone material should satisfy requirements for strength, cold resistance, heat conductivity, water and air resistance, water absorption, and resistance in an aggressive medium, and it should also have a certain shape, dimensions, and finish of the outer surface. The demands made on mortars include strength, convenience in laying, and water-retention capacity.

Masonry construction is one of the oldest types of construction. In many nations a large number of outstanding architectural monuments of stonework have survived. Masonry construction is durable and resistant to fire, and local raw materials may be used; these factors have determined its extensive use in modern construction.

Among the drawbacks of masonry construction are its comparatively great weight and high thermal conductivity. The laying of piece stonework also requires significant expenditures of manual labor. In this regard the efforts of builders have been aimed at the development of effective lightened masonry construction using thermal insulation materials. The cost of masonry construction (foundations and walls) is 15–30 percent of the total cost of a building.

In contemporary construction, masonry construction (mainly brick and stone walls and foundations) is one of the widespread types of structural elements (large-panel construction predominates only in large cities). The practices of construction using stone have significantly furthered the development of the science of masonry construction. Empirical rules and insufficiently sound methods of calculation, which have not permitted full use of the load-bearing capacity of masonry construction, have been used in the design stage. The teachings on strength and the methods of calculation for masonry construction, which are based on extensive experimental and theoretical research, originated in the USSR in 1932–39 with L. I. Onishchik. A study was made of the principles of masonry work using various types of stone and mortar, as well as of the factors influencing its strength. It was established that, upon transmission of a force throughout the cross section in masonry consisting of individual alternating layers of stone and mortar, a complex stressed state arises, and individual stones (bricks) are not only compressed but are also subject to bending, tension, shear, and local compression. The reasons for this are unevenness in the stone bedding and the irregular thickness and density of the horizontal masonry joints, which reflect the thoroughness of mixing of the mortar, the degree to which it is smoothed out and compacted in laying the stone, and the conditions of hardening. Masonry laid by a skilled mason is 20–30 percent stronger than that laid by a worker of average skill. Another reason for the complex stressed state of masonry work is the different elastic and plastic properties of the mortar and stone. Significant lateral deformations arise under the influence of the vertical forces in the mortar joint, leading to the early appearance of cracks in the stone. The greatest compressive strength when using regularly shaped stone is found in masonry work of large blocks, and the least is found in rubble quarrystone and brick. The larger stones also have a greater resistance moment, which significantly increases their resistance to bending. The strength of vibration-set brick masonry under optimum vibration conditions is approximately twice the strength of hand masonry and approaches the strength of the brick because of the better compacting and filling of the mortar joint and closer contact between the mortar and the brick.

In masonry buildings, the most important elements—that is, the exterior and interior walls and the roof—are connected in a single system. Calculation of their combined spatial performance, which provides the strength of the building, makes possible the most economical design of masonry construction.

In calculating masonry construction, a distinction is made between masonry buildings with rigid and flexible structural schemes. The first group includes buildings with close placement of cross walls, in which the slabs between the floors are viewed as fixed stiffeners that create rigid ties for the walls with the effect of the cross and eccentric longitudinal loads. Such a system is used in calculating the walls and internal supports of multistory residential buildings and most public buildings. The second group consists of large-span buildings with significant distances between the cross walls. In such buildings the roofs also link the walls and the internal supports into a single system, but they cannot be viewed as fixed stiffeners; consequently, the combined deformations of the interconnected building elements are taken into account in the calculations. Most industrial buildings with load-bearing stone walls are calculated according to this system. In designing the masonry construction, the calculation of the spatial performance of the walls makes possible a substantial reduction in the calculated bending moments in the walls and of the thickness of the walls, as well as lightening of the foundations and an increase in the number of stories.

Depending on the design system of the buildings, masonry walls are divided into load-bearing walls, which receive the load from their own weight and from floors, facings, and building cranes; self-supporting walls, which bear the weight of all the floors of the building, as well as wind loads; and curtain walls, which take the load from their own weight and the wind within the limits of one floor. Masonry walls made of dimension stone and brick are divided into solid and laminar (light). The thickness of solid walls is set as a multiple of the basic brick dimensions, that is, 0.5, 1, 1.5, 2, 2.5, and 3 bricks. Material consumption, labor intensity, and the cost of erecting the walls depend on correct selection of the design and the degree to which the properties of the materials are used. The use of solid masonry construction made of heavy materials is not advisable for the exterior walls of low-rise heated buildings. In this instance, light laminar walls with thermal insulation or walls made of hollow ceramic stone, as well as stone made from light and cellular concretes, are used. A structural scheme with internal transverse load-bearing walls, which makes possible the use of exterior walls made of light, efficient materials, such as ceramics with thermal insulation, is preferable for buildings made of dimension brick or stone and having a large number of stories.

To increase its strength, masonry work is reinforced with steel or reinforced concrete (complex structural elements), as well as with casings (that is, the placement of the masonry work in reinforced-concrete or metal casings).

REFERENCES

Onishchik, L. I. *Kamennye konstruktsii promyshlennykh i grazhdanskikh zdanii.* Moscow-Leningrad, 1939.
Spravochnik proektirovshchika: Kamennye i armokamennye konstruktsii. Edited by S. A. Sementsov and V. A. Kameiko. Moscow, 1968.
Poliakov, S. V., and V. N. Falevich. *Proektirovanie kamennykh i krupnopanel'nykh konstruktsii.* Moscow, 1966.
Stroitel'nye normy i pravila, part 2, sec. C, chap. 2: "Kamennye i armokamennye konstruktsii: Normy proektirovaniia." Moscow, 1962.

V. A. KAMEIKO [11–762–1]

MASONRY DAM, a dam whose main structural elements are made from masonry materials, without binders. In the practices of modern hydroengineering construction, a distinction is made between rock-filled (filled), semifilled, and dry-set stonework. Masonry dams are usually built as fixed dams, with passage of the water through spillways on the banks or, less frequently, in the body of the dam.

The basic materials for the body of a masonry dam are rubble (from quarries), pebbles, gravel, and rocky soil. The stone for the fill and the dry masonry should have sufficient strength and resistance to weathering, the effect of frost, and destruction by filtration. The best materials for fill are igneous rock (granite, syenite, diorite, and basalt) and sedimentary rock (solid limestones and dolomites, as well as quartzites). The dimensions and shape of the stone, as well as the methods of compacting the fill, are of crucial importance, since they influence the porosity of the fill, the amount of settling in the body of the dam, and the steepness of the slopes. Virtually all types of rock are suitable for use as the base of a masonry dam; pebbles and gravel, coarse-grained sands and clays, and compact loams may also be used.

The possibility of using local materials determines the economy of masonry dams and their wide use in various geographic regions.

REFERENCE

Grishin, M. M. *Gidrotekhnicheskie sooruzheniia.* Moscow, 1968.

V. N. POSPELOV [11–744–3]

MASONRY-EARTHEN DAM, a dam in which most of the body is made from masonry materials and the antiseepage structure is made from low-permeability soil. Five main types of masonry-earthen dams are distinguished on the basis of the materials used and the methods of providing water impermeability: dams whose water-impermeable part is (1) in the form of an earthen screen; (2) built with a fill of low-permeability soil on a core of rock fill; (3) built on a layer of more permeable material; (4) in the form of a central core of clay, sandy loam, or clay concrete; and (5) built with a fill of more permeable materials.

The comparative simplicity of design and the possibility of using local building materials have made masonry-earthen dams widespread, particulary in regions remote from existing means of communication. The Nurek masonry-earthen dam in the Tadzhik SSR is 300 m high.

REFERENCES
Grishin, M. M. *Gidrotekhnicheskie sooruzheniia.* Moscow, 1968.
Moiseev, S. N. *Kamenno-zemlianye i kamenno-nabrosnye plotiny,* 2nd ed. Moscow, 1970.   [11–747–1]

MASONRY WORK, construction work performed during the erection of stonework on buildings and structures made of natural and artificial masonry materials.

Masonry work is a complex of processes that includes, in addition to the basic processes (the laying of brick or other stone in mortar, the delivery and laying out of the stone, and the smoothing of the mortar), related auxiliary processes (the erection of scaffolding and trestles and preparation of the materials at the construction site).

In ancient times, skilled masons erected stone buildings and complex engineering works (towers, arched bridges, and domes); however, the masonry work was done slowly, and the methods changed little over the centuries. Masonry work was done by hand; the master masons usually performed all the preparatory and transport jobs at the site and prepared the mortar and delivered it to the work area themselves. In building walls, cumbersome scaffolding was erected to their full height. The work was done only in the warm seasons. In the early 20th century, measures were taken in the developed countries to improve masonry work (mechanization of the delivery of materials and the preparation of mortar).

In the USSR, the technology of masonry work began to change substantially in the 1930's, a period of intensive development of construction. During the five-year plans in the Soviet Union, new principles were developed for the organization and mechanization of construction from masonry materials, and advanced, effective methods for performing masonry work, as well as efficient tools, attachments, and supplies, were introduced. The step-by-step method was widely introduced, making possible continuous performance of masonry work by combining it with the installation of prefabricated elements and other accompanying operations. The brigade method of labor organization was introduced, and the brigades were divided into teams, in which the work of the masons was clearly differentiated according to their skills. The methods for laying the mortar and stone in the structure and work procedures to be used under winter conditions, as well as the means for delivering the mortar and the stone from the producer plant to the work areas, were also improved, leading to increased labor productivity, improved quality of work, and more economical consumption of materials.

In modern construction a distinction is made among the following basic types of masonry work (stonework), depending on the materials used: brickwork on walls, columns, and other parts of buildings and structures, made with ordinary (fired) and silica brick without facing; with faced brick or ceramic stone; with hollow ceramic stones or solid or hollow slag concrete stones, which are used mainly for the walls of frame buildings or for the load-bearing walls of buildings with a limited number of floors; with sawn stone, predominantly light natural stone (tuffs and limestone); and masonry work with large concrete, reinforced-concrete, or brick blocks. Quarrystone masonry made of natural stone (hard rock) with a compressive strength of at least 40 meganewtons per sq m (MN/m^2), or 400 kilograms-force per sq cm, is used for the underground parts of buildings and structures

(foundations, the walls of cellars, and retaining walls). However, in erecting foundations and basement walls in modern large-scale construction, labor-intensive quarrystone masonry has been replaced by prefabricated reinforced-concrete and large-block elements.

The most widespread type of masonry work is the erection of solid brick masonry using individual bricks set in mortar. "Light masonry," consisting of two parallel face walls each one-half a brick thick and filled with a light concrete, loose slag, or another insulating material, is sometimes used. Such brickwork ordinarily is used for buildings not more than two stories tall. The masonry work on the walls of high-rise housing is performed simultaneously with the installation of all the prefabricated structural elements of the building, including stairways, floors, window and door units, partitions, and balconies. Ordinarily the masonry work is done with standard trestles, which provide safety and are quickly set up, disassembled, and moved to a new place using an erection crane. Suspended scaffolding, as well as building scaffolding, which is assembled from individual elements during the process of masonry work, is used for constructing the walls of industrial and other buildings more than 5 m tall. The masonry materials and mortars are also delivered by erection cranes, including the tower and jib (crawler and tire) and track types. Brick is delivered to the work areas in packets on wood and metal pallets or in packets without pallets (silica brick), and the mortar is delivered in special containers. For large volumes of work, mortar is supplied by pipe using a mortar pump.

REFERENCES
Materialy po istorii stroitel'noi tekhniki: Sb. st., fasc. 1. Moscow, 1961.
Rukovodstvo po organizatsii truda pri proizvodstve stroitel'no-montazhnykh rabot, chap. 7: "Kamennye raboty." Moscow, 1972.
                                              P. I. KOVALEVSKII [11–766–3]

METAL CARBONYLS, compounds of metals with carbon monoxide, with the general formula $Me_m(CO_n)$. Nickel carbonyl, $Ni(CO)_4$, was the first to be discovered (1890), and since then the carbonyls of several metals and nonmetals have been prepared. Metal carbonyls may be either "mononuclear" or "polynuclear," depending on the number of metal atoms in the molecule; compound metal carbonyls, such as $[Co(CO)_4]_2Zn$, also exist.

The carbonyls of nickel, iron, osmium, and ruthenium are liquids; most other carbonyls are crystalline. Metal carbonyls are diamagnetic, highly volatile, and extremely toxic. Only halide carbonyls, $Me(CO)X$, which are stable only in a carbon monoxide atmosphere, exist for copper, silver, and gold. Metal carbonyls decompose when heated above a certain temperature, releasing carbon monoxide and metal in a finely dispersed state. The physical properties of the principal metal carbonyls are presented in Table 1 (the carbonyls shown are readily soluble in organic solvents).

Table 1. Physical properties of some metal carbonyls

	Boiling point (°C)	Melting point (°C)	Density at 20°C (g/cm³)	Solubility in water
$Fe(CO)_5$	103	−20	1.455	—
$Co(CO)_4$	—	51	1.827	insoluble
$Ni(CO)_4$	43	−19	1.310	low
$Ru(CO)_5$	—	−22	—	insoluble

A common method of preparing metal carbonyls involves the reaction of carbon monoxide with metals or their salts at high temperatures and pressures. The metal carbonyls that are of the greatest commercial significance are nickel carbonyl, $Ni(CO)_4$; cobalt carbonyl, $Co(CO)_4$; and iron carbonyl, $Fe(CO)_5$. Carbonyls are used for the preparation of pure metals, which form upon their thermal dissociation. Thermal dissociation of cobalt, nickel, and chromium carbonyls is used in the application of metallic coatings, particularly on surfaces of complex shape. Cobalt and nickel carbonyls are catalysts in important chemical processes—for example, in the synthesis of carboxylic acids and their derivatives from olefins, and in the synthesis of acrylic acid from acetylene during hydroformylation:

$$CH_2 = CH_2 \xrightarrow{[Co(CO)_4]_2, H_2} CH_3CH_2CHO$$

Metal carbonyls are good antiknock compounds for motor fuels; however, the formation of oxides that are difficult to remove takes place during combustion. Certain carbonyls serve in the preparation of absolutely pure carbon monoxide.

REFERENCES
Belozerskii, N. A. *Karbonily metallov.* Moscow, 1958.
Khimiia koordinatsionnykh soedinenii. Edited by J. Bailar and D. Busch. Moscow, 1960. (Translated from English.)
Khimiia metalloorganicheskikh soedinenii. Edited by H. Zeiss. Moscow, 1964. Pages 538–604. (Translated from English.)

N. A. NESMEIANOV [11–1208–2]

MILITARY CAMPAIGN, a stage of a war during which an intermediate goal is achieved. In each military campaign a number of strategic operations and other forms of military action linked by a common concept and conducted in one or several strategic sectors or in an entire theater of war are carried out. Names such as the "summer campaign," the "winter campaign," and the "campaign of 1944" are used to designate military campaigns. Campaigns that involve military actions by armed forces in one theater are sometimes given geographic names, such as the Bohemian campaign of 1866 and the Italian campaign of 1796–97. [11–839–1]

MINERAL MAPS, maps describing the location or the conditions of formation of mineral deposits. These maps are prepared on the basis of records of mineral deposits and data obtained from geological surveying, prospecting, and exploration. The compilation of these maps often requires special metallogenetic, geochemical, hydrochemical, lithological, and paleogeographic research, as well as study of the conditions of coal accumulation and of the presence of petroleum and gas.

Depending on their purpose, mineral maps may be divided into three groups: registration maps, maps showing patterns of distribution of minerals, and prospecting maps. In terms of scale, mineral maps may be divided into small-scale maps (1:500,000 and smaller), medium-scale maps (1:200,000–1:100,000), and large-scale maps (1:50,000–1:25,000).

Registration mineral maps show the location of deposits on a general geographic or schematic geological base, with a reduced color background. If a systematic geological survey has been made, they are compiled on a full geological base. The mineral deposits are depicted by nonscale signs showing the deposit's composition, size, and genetic type or any combination of these indicators (for one mineral, for interrelated mineral groups, or for all the minerals of a given territory). These maps are often graphic appendixes to surveys of mineral resources. They are essential not only for indicating the location of mineral raw materials but also for determining the prospects for developing mining, metallurgy, and other industries, as well as transportation and agriculture.

Depending on the type of mineral, its genesis, and the methods of study, maps depicting patterns of distribution are divided into metallogenetic and geochemical maps, coal-accumulation and coal-chemical maps, maps showing the presence of gas and petroleum, maps of halogen and other formations, maps showing the ore content of weathering crusts and placer Shlikh maps, maps relating to hydrogeological research, and prospecting maps.

The metallogenetic maps show the distribution patterns of various ore-bearing areas, ore deposits, and all types of mineralization with respect to various geological factors. Sometimes metallogenetic maps are called minerogenetic maps, although this term is generally applied to maps showing the distribution not only of ores but also of non-ore deposits. Geochemical maps depict the distribution patterns of mineral deposits on the basis of the clarke (background) and increased content of chemical elements and by revealing the most characteristic chemical elements for certain areas (direct and indirect indicators) in rocks, water, and vegetation. Depending on the phase of the dispersion halos, a distinction is made between atmochemical, biochemical, hydrogeochemical, lithochemical, and other geochemical maps. Coal-accumulation maps depict the patterns of the accumulation and distribution of coal and fuel shales in coal-bearing basins, regions, and individual deposits, with respect to lithological and tectonic conditions and metamorphism. Coal-chemical maps are more specialized, providing data on the chemical and production properties of coal, for example, the yield of volatile substances, caking capacity, and ash content. Maps showing the presence of petroleum and gas give the specific features of the tectonic structure of petroleum and gas basins and regions of individual petroleum and gas deposits; they also depict oil-bearing native rock, its collector properties, and indications of hydrocarbon migration.

Mineral maps relating to hydrogeological research include water-supply maps, hydrochemical maps (indicating the chemical composition of natural waters), maps showing the distribution of mineral waters and springs (for balneological purposes), and maps of thermal and industrial waters. Prospecting maps, depicting areas in which minerals may be found, are used as guides in geological exploration.

REFERENCES
Instruktsiia po sostavleniiu i podgotovke k izdaniiu geologicheskoi karty i karty poleznykh iskopaemykh masshtaba 1:1,000,000. Moscow, 1955.
Instruktsiia po sostavleniiu i podgotovke k izdaniiu geologicheskoi karty masshtaba 1:50,000. Moscow, 1962.
Instruktsiia po sostavleniiu i podgotovke k izdaniiu geologicheskoi karty i karty poleznykh iskopaemykh masshtaba 1:200,000. Moscow, 1969.
Osnovnye printsipy sostavleniia, soderzhanie i uslovnye oboznacheniia metallogenicheskikh i prognoznykh kart rudnykh raionov. Moscow, 1964.
Metodicheskie ukazaniia po sostavleniiu kart neftegazonosnosti i uslovnye oboznacheniia k nim. Moscow, 1965.
Karta perspektiv neftegazonosnosti SSSR, masshtab 1:5,000,000. Moscow, 1969.
Atlas kart uglenakopleniia na territorii SSSR. Moscow-Leningrad, 1962.

E. T. SHATALOV [11–1448–3]

MONEY COWRIE, a marine gastropod mollusk of the family Cypraeidae (*Cypraea moneta* and, sometimes, *C. annulus*). The shell, which measures up to 3 cm tall, is shiny and white or yellowish. In live money cowries, the mantle covers most of the shell. Money cowries inhabit the tropical parts of the Indian and Pacific oceans. Their shells have been prized for their beauty and from antiquity to the early 20th century were used as a means of exchange (shell currency) among a number of peoples of Asia, Africa, and the Pacific islands; in antiquity they were used as currency in Europe as well. The money cowries were strung on strings or stored in a sack. They were obtained primarily from the Maldives, near Ceylon. In Europe and Middle Asia they were primarily used as ornaments. [11–1611–4]

MULTIPOTENTIAL STEM CELLS, cells making up the continually self-renewing tissues of both adult and developing animals. In vertebrates they are found, for example, in epithelial, hemopoietic, and bony tissues. Each tissue has characteristic multipotential stem cells, distinguished by their proliferative activity and degree of specialization. Differentiated tissue cells often have common multipotential stem cells, which can develop in different directions. For example, in mammalian hemopoietic tissue, various blood cells—erythrocytes, thrombocytes, and leukocytes—are formed from common multipotential stem cells. The perpetual presence of these stem cells in an organism ensures not only the renewal of the cell population of the corresponding tissues under normal conditions, but also the replenishing of cells when they are destroyed.

REFERENCE
Zavarzin, A. A. *Ocherki evoliutsionnoi gistologii krovi i soedinitel'noi tkani: Izbr. trudy,* vol. 4. Moscow-Leningrad, 1953. [11–716–1]

MULTISTAGE REFRIGERATION, the process of heat transfer from a lower temperature level to a higher level (that is, cooling) that is accomplished in refrigeration equipment by means of several closed refrigeration cycles operating in series.

This is the method used for deep freezing where the cooling agent in the low-temperature cycle condenses as a result of evaporation of the cooling agent in the next cooling cycle, with a higher temperature. As a rule no more than four cycles are used, because the construction of the equipment would become too complicated. The refrigeration cycles used may be the same, or they may have various thermodynamic heat transfer principles and cooling agents.

During the late 1800's the Swiss physicist R. Pictet used multistage refrigeration to liquefy air. His equipment had three refrigeration cycles. In the first high-temperature two-stage cycle the working substance was methyl chloride (CH_3Cl), in the middle cycle it was ethylene (C_2H_4), and in the third it was oxygen (O_2). The method was subsequently improved and was used to produce liquid hydrogen and helium.

Multistage refrigeration is usually used to reach temperatures as low as $-110°C$ in experimental chambers and for technological purposes in chemistry, medicine, and biology.

Multistage refrigeration with two vapor-compression cycles is most common. The cooling agent usually used in the high-temperature cycle is Freon 22 ($CHClF_2$), and in the low-temperature cycle it is Freon 13 (CF_3Cl). To produce temperatures down to $-90°C$, the low-temperature cycle has a single stage using Freon 13; for temperatures below $-90°C$, it has two stages. Heat is transferred from the low-temperature cycle to the high-temperature cycle in a heat exchanger (evaporator-condenser) as a result of condensation of the low-temperature cooling agent and boiling of the high-temperature cooling agent. The method can be improved by the use of more efficient cooling agents, better compressor designs, and more efficient heat exchangers.

L. L. GENIN [11–1480–1]

MURRES (*Uria*), a genus of birds of the suborder Alciformes, order Charadriiformes. The body is 40–48 cm long; the weight, 0.8–1.2 kg. There are two species—the common murre (*U. aalge*) and the thick-billed murre (*U. lomvia*). Murres are found in the temperate and polar seas of the northern hemisphere. Their feet are webbed. Murres move awkwardly on land, supported on the metatarsal bone and the toes. Their flight is rapid, and they swim and dive, to 10 m or more, excellently, moving under water with their wings and using their legs as rudders. They nest on sea cliffs in large colonies, appearing at the sites in April and May. One egg is laid directly on the rock. The incubation period is 35 days. Outside the reproductive period, murres keep to the open sea, feeding on small fish, crustaceans, and other marine invertebrates.

In the USSR there are large breeding colonies of murres on the western Murmansk coast, Novaia Zemlia, many Arctic islands, Chukotka, Kamchatka, the Kuril Islands, and Sakhalin. The eggs and the birds are used as food.

REFERENCE
Kozlova, E. V. *Rzhankoobraznye: Podotriad chistikovye.* (*Fauna SSSR: Ptitsy*, vol. 2., fasc. 3.) Moscow-Leningrad, 1957.
N. N. KARTASHEV [11–548–1]

MUSK DEER (*Moschus moschiferus*), an artiodactylous mammal of the family Moschidae. The body is up to 1 m long; height at the withers, up to 70 cm; weight, up to 17 kg. The hind legs are disproportionately long; hence the sacrum of a standing animal is much higher than the withers. The head is small and the ears large. There are no horns. The male has long fangs that reach below the chin when its mouth is closed and a special gland on the abdomen that secretes musk. The coloring runs from light yellowish brown to dark brown-black, usually with small, light spots. The tail is short.

The musk deer is found in Asia (the Altai, Eastern Siberia, the Far East, Eastern China, and eastern Tibet) in mountain taiga with cliffs and rock streams. It is usually solitary, though it occasionally forms small groups. It feeds on plants, predominantly tree lichens. At the beginning of winter it mates, with fights among the males over the females. Between the end of April and July the females produce one or two offspring. The musk deer is hunted in small numbers for its musk; the meat is edible but not tasty.

REFERENCE
Flerov, K. K. *Kabargi i oleni.* (*Fauna SSSR: Mlekopitaiushchie*, vol. 1, fasc. 2.) Moscow-Leningrad, 1952.   I. I. SOKOLOV [11–250–3]

MUTUAL BENEFIT FUND, in the USSR, a voluntary organization of trade union members organized to render mutual fraternal financial aid.

The mutual benefit fund is organized by the trade union committee if the given enterprise (institution or educational institution) has at least 15 trade union members who want to join. The mutual benefit fund must be registered with the higher trade union body: the trade union council or the republic (krai, oblast, raion, city) committee. The fund conducts business according to a charter and is a legal person. A standard charter for the mutual benefit fund of a trade union committee was approved by the decision of the All-Union Central Council of Trade Unions of Feb. 20, 1959. Every trade union member working in the given enterprise or institution or studying in the educational institution may join the mutual benefit fund. He must pay an entrance fee of 0.5 percent of his monthly wages or scholarship; this is also the amount of the monthly membership dues. A member who has paid his dues for 50 months is released at his request from further payments of membership dues and receives priority when applying for a loan. A member who withdraws from the mutual benefit fund is paid back all his membership dues.

The bodies of the mutual benefit fund are the general assembly (conference) of members of the fund and the board, elected at the general assembly of the mutual benefit fund by open vote for one year. In enterprises or institutions where the membership of the mutual benefit fund reaches 300 union members or more and where each workshop or department has at least 25 members of the fund, branch offices of the mutual benefit fund are established. The general assembly of the fund elects an auditing commission for a one-year term. This body makes an inspection at least twice a year, reviews the activity of the board whenever the chairman of the board, the cashier, or the accountant is replaced, makes a monthly verification of the cash on hand, and makes unannounced inspections.

By the decision of the board or the branch office of the mutual benefit fund, the fund issues long-term and short-term loans and in some cases issues free grants. The funds for these purposes are created by the entrance fees and membership dues, interest on loans, and grants from the trade union budget. Arrears on loans are recovered through certification of a judgment by a notary public office without the right of appeal or through a raion (city) people's court.   A. L. EPSHTEIN [11–1494–3]

NICKEL-CADMIUM BATTERY, an alkaline storage battery in which the active substance of the positive electrode is nickelic hydroxide (NiOOH) and that of the negative electrode is cadmium (Cd), with iron (Fe) added. The electrolyte usually used is a solution of potassium hydroxide (KOH), with an additive of lithium hydroxide (LiOH); the electromotive force is 1.3–1.0 volts.   [11–377–1]

NIGHT HERON (*Nycticorax nycticorax*), a bird of the family Ardeidae (herons and bitterns), order Ciconiiformes. The body is 60 cm long. The color of the plumage is mainly black (with a metallic sheen), whitish, and gray. The night heron is found in southern Europe, Asia, and North America as well as Africa and South America. In the USSR it inhabits the southern part of the European USSR and Middle Asia; it migrates to Africa for the winter. The night heron keeps to the banks of rivers or the shores of ponds and lakes. It is active at night. It nests in colonies, usually on trees. There are four or five greenish eggs in a clutch; both parents brood for a period of 21–22 days. Night herons feed on fish, frogs, and small invertebrate animals.

REFERENCE
Ptitsy Sovetskogo Soiuza, vol. 2. Edited by G. P. Dement'ev and N. A. Gladkov. Moscow, 1951.   [11–1690–3]

NORRA KVARKEN, a strait in the Baltic Sea, in the western part of the Vaasa Skerries. The strait, which measures 75 km wide, unites the northern (Bottenvik) and southern (Bottenhav) parts of the Gulf of Bothnia. A group of islands divides the Norra Kvarken into two straits—the eastern Kvarken and the western Kvarken. The depth of the eastern Kvarken is 6–7 m; the western Kvarken has depths up to 29 m. The currents depend on the winds and the atmospheric pressure. The strait freezes during the winter. [11–1807–1]

NUCLEAR QUADRUPOLE MOMENT, the quantity that characterizes the deviation from spherical symmetry of the electrical charge distribution in an atomic nucleus. It has the dimension of area and is usually expressed in sq cm. For spherical symmetry the nuclear quadrupole moment $Q = 0$. If a nucleus is extended along the axis of symmetry, then Q is a positive quantity, but if the nucleus is flattened along the axis, it is negative. The value of the nuclear quadrupole moment varies over a wide range. For example, the nucleus of $^{17}_{8}O$, $Q = -0.027 \times 10^{-24}$ sq cm; for the nucleus of $^{241}_{93}Am$ $Q = +14.9 \times 10^{-24}$ sq cm. Large moments are usually positive. This means that when there is a substantial deviation from spherical symmetry, the nucleus has the shape of an elongated ellipsoid of rotation. V. P. PARFENOVA [11–1680–2]

NULLIFICATION OF ELECTIONS, the voiding of voting results because of procedural violations in the campaign or in tabulation of the results. In socialist countries the main condition for the validity of the elections is the participation in the voting of at least half of all voters. If this condition is violated, the election commissions (in the USSR, the Central Election Commission), in accordance with the election regulations, fix a date for new elections (usually within two weeks). In socialist countries, by virtue of the principle of full sovereignty of the representative body as the supreme body of state power, only representative bodies can confirm the credentials of the elected deputies and only they can annul the elections of individual deputies.

In bourgeois states, the validity of the election of deputies is verified or denied by courts, as well as by the representative bodies themselves: by common law courts, in countries with the Anglo-Saxon legal system, or by special bodies—electoral or constitutional courts. For example, in Austria, Cyprus, Malta, Morocco, France, a number of African countries that were once French colonies, and, under certain conditions, the Federal Republic of Germany, the correctness of the election results is verified by constitutional supervisory bodies. In India verification is the responsibility of the Supreme Court, and in Turkey, of a superior court for elections. These bodies review the legality of elections only if the voters or the authorities of the corresponding electoral district or persons running for office submit a complaint charging a violation of election procedure. M. A. KRUTOGOLOV [11–1497–2]

OFFICE OF CONSTRUCTION, a state institution in St. Petersburg that exercised control over construction in the city and the training of builders.

The Office of Construction existed from 1706 to 1797. Founded as the Office of Urban Affairs, it was known as the Office of Construction from 1723 to 1765, the Office of Construction of Her Imperial Majesty's Homes and Gardens from 1765 to 1769, and the Bureau of Construction of Her Imperial Majesty's Homes and Gardens from 1769 to 1797. On Mar. 7, 1797, the bureau was consolidated with the Bureau of Court Supply Services. The Office of Construction comprised a "painting team" (1720–97), training in gilding, joinery, and plastering (from 1755), and the Russian School (1766–68; after 1768, the Academy), where artists received a systematic education.

The work of the Office of Construction was at various periods supervised by prominent architects, such as D. A. Trezini, Al. V. Kvasov, I. E. Starov, and Iu. M. Fel'ten. Instructors of the painting team included L. Karavak, A. M. Matveev, I. Ia. Vishniakov, and A. P. Antropov.

REFERENCE
Moleva, N., and E. Beliutin. *Zhivopisnykh del mastera: Kantseliariia ot stroenii i russkaia zhivopis' pervoi poloviny XVIII veka.* Moscow, 1965. [11–1009–6]

ONTHOPHAGUS, the largest genus of dung beetles of the family Scarabaeidae. The males usually have horns or outgrowths on the head and often on the pronotum. There are approximately 1,500 species. They are found chiefly in the tropics; there are about 60 species in the USSR. They dig little burrows and fill them with dung; the larvae develop in these burrows. *Onthophagus* are beneficial as cleaners of the environment and participants in soil formation. Some species are the intermediate hosts of a number of helminths that parasitize domestic animals. [11–665–1]

OPENCUT FIELD, the mineral deposit (or portion of it), with the overlying and enclosing barren rock that is worked as one opencut mine. The opencut field is part of the mine's land allotment, which also includes the barren rock removed from the mine and the work area and other production facilities. The upper contour of the field is the line where the sides of the mine intersect the ground surface, and the lower contour is the floor of the mine. The contouring of the opencut field consists in the establishment of the volumetric contour of the mine on geological maps and profiles; it includes the areas of the deposit that can be worked economically by the opencut method. In working horizontal and gently sloping veins, the dimensions of the opencut field in the plan view are established based on the expedient rate of advance of the mining front, the allocation of the mining equipment, and the economy of the intramine shipments. The area of large opencut fields reaches 10–40 sq km, and the volume of the rock mass reaches 2–10 billion cu m. IU. I. ANISTRATOV [11–1463–1]

OSTARIOPHYSI (also Cypriniformes), an order of bony fish, characterized by the presence of Weberian apparatus. The swim bladder is connected to the intestine. Ostariophysans are primarily found in fresh water. There are four suborders: Characinoidei, Electrophoridei (*Electrophorus electricus*), Cyprinoidei, and Siluroidei. There are five families in the suborder Cyprinoidei; three are found in the USSR—Cyprinidae, Catostomidae, and Cobitidae. There are 13 genera of the family Catostomidae; five are native to the USSR (31 species). Of the 31 families of the suborder Siluroidei, four are found in the Soviet Union: Siluridae (three species), Bagridae, Sisoridae (one species), and Amiuridae (one species). Many ostariophysans are commercially valuable. [11–1359–3]

PASS, a gap formed by the grooves of two coupled rolls through which the metal to be reduced is passed in order to give it the required shape.

A distinction is made between reducing, roughing, and finishing passes. Reducing passes serve to reduce the cross section of the initial stock without significant alteration of its shape; roughing passes are used to produce rolled metal with a cross section close to that of the finishing stage; and finishing passes are used to give the metal its final shape and dimensions. [11–591–1]

PEA TREE (*Caragana*), a genus of deciduous bushes or small trees of the family Leguminosae. The leaves are alternate or in clusters, even-pinnate, with two to ten pairs of entire leaflets. The blossoms are bisexual and grow either separately or in clusters of two to five, usually with yellow or golden yellow coloration. The pods are noticeably longer than the calyx, and their valves curl upon splitting.

There are approximately 80 species in the European part of the USSR, Middle Asia, Siberia, the Far East, Mongolia, and China. Members of *Caragana* grow in deserts, steppes, river bottoms, mountain slopes, taluses, forest borders, and thinned forests. There are 35 species in the Soviet Union. The common ones are the Siberian pea tree and the Russian pea tree (*C. frutex*), with a height of 0.5–2 m, leaves of four tightly grouped leaflets, and golden yellow blossoms. They grow in thickets in the forest and forest-steppe zones, as well as in mountainous areas.

Pea trees are raised as decorative and nectariferous plants and also are used to stabilize slopes. [11–1111–3]

PENCIL, a rod made of coal, lead, graphite, or dry pigment that is used for writing, drawing, or sketching. It is often encased in a wood or metal holder. Prototypes of the pencil included metal points, lead and silver pins that were inserted into metal holders. Used from the 12th to the 16th century, metal points produced a dark gray tone. The black chalk pencil, which was made of black clayish shale and produced a soft dull shade of black, was introduced in the 14th century. Beginning in the 16th century, graphite pencils and pencils made of charred powdered bone bound with gum were widespread. Graphite pencils provide dull strokes with a slight luster. Charred powdered bone produces mat black marks.

In 1790 the French scientist N. Conté invented the wooden pencil. At about the same time, the Czech scientist J. Hardtmuth proposed the manufacture of writing instruments made of a mixture of pulverized graphite and clay. In principle, this method forms the basis of the modern process of pencil manufacture. Mechanical, or automatic, pencils appeared in the second half of the 19th century and became particularly popular in the 20th century.

Depending on various manufacturing techniques and writing properties, there are different kinds of pencils, including black lead (graphite) pencils, colored pencils, and copying pencils. Pencils are also classified according to their use; for example, there are school, office, drafting, drawing, lettering, carpentry, and cosmetic pencils. There are also pencils used for retouching, marking, and labeling various materials. Special types of pencils include pastels and sanguine (red chalk).

In the USSR lead drawing pencils are made in several degrees of hardness, which are indicated by the letters M (soft), T (hard), and MT (medium hard). Numbers often precede the letters; the higher the number, the greater the degree of hardness or softness. Outside of the USSR the letters B and H are used instead of M and T, respectively.

The writing cores of pencils consist of a tightly pressed, uniform mixture of minute particles of different materials. Lead cores contain graphite, colloidal refractory clay (bentonite), a binder (tragacanth or pectin cement), and fats or wax. Colored leads are made of pigments, kaolin, bentonite, talc, a binder, and fats. Copying, or tracing, leads are made of water-soluble pigments (primarily methylene quinone), graphite, talc, bentonite, and a binder.

There are various types of mechanical pencils. In the split collet type, the lead is propelled by the turning of one of the pencil's components. The propel-repel-expel type has a button that forces the lead through a bored tip. Multicolored pencils have two, four, or more cores that can be alternately pushed through the holder. [11–1162–3]

PETRELS, two genera of birds of the order Procellariiformes—fork-tailed petrels (*Oceanodroma*) and storm petrels (*Hydrobates*). They are small birds (the body measures up to 20 cm). The bill is small and hooked downward. The legs are short and tetradactylous; the anterior toes are webbed.

Petrels are birds of the open sea. They feed on small invertebrates, which they catch on the wing from the surface of the water. They nest in burrows along the shores and are active near their nests at night. Fork-tailed petrels (*Oceanodrama*) are found in the Atlantic, Indian, and Pacific oceans; there are 11 species. In the USSR they are found in the Far East from the Komandorskie Islands to Vladivostok; there are three species. The storm petrels (*Hydrobates*) constitute a single species. They are found in the northeastern Atlantic Ocean and the Mediterranean Sea. They may occasionally fly to the USSR.

REFERENCE
Ptitsy Sovetskogo Soiuza, vol. 2. Edited by G. P. Dement'ev and N. A. Gladkov. Moscow, 1951. [11–1647–6]

PHALARIS, a genus of annual or perennial grasses of the family Gramineae. The inflorescence is a spicate or laciniate panicle. The spikelets are compressed laterally and monanthous; the glumes on the carina often are winged. There are approximately 40 species, found in the temperate zones of both hemispheres. The best-known species is canary grass (*Phalaris canariensis*), which thrives in the Mediterranean region. In the USSR it occasionally grows wild and is sometimes cultivated as a feed plant. The fruit of this species makes good feed (canary seed) for cage birds. Also widespread is reed canary grass (*P. arundinaceae*), which is sometimes isolated into the monotype genus *Typhoides.* Reed canary grass grows along reservoir banks, in damp meadows, and in similar places. It is used for making hay. Mottled-leaved varieties are cultivated as ornamentals.

[11–937–3]

PIGMY ANTELOPES (Neotragini), mammals of the family Bovidae of the order Artiodactyla, closely related to the gazelles. Most pigmy antelopes are small animals, some being no larger than hares, with a height at the shoulder not exceeding 25 cm. Their slender legs have either two or four hooves. The head has a short narrow snout. The horns, which usually are found only on the male, are short and straight. The coloration is various shades of reddish brown. There are five genera: *Neotragus, Ourebia* (the oribi), *Raphicerus* (the steenbok), *Madoqua* (the dik-dik), and *Oreotragus* (the klipspringer). Pigmy antelopes are distributed in sub-Saharan Africa, dwelling chiefly in forests, brush thickets, or high grasses. The klipspringer (*Oreotragus oreotragus*) and some of the dik-dik species live in mountainous terrain. The animals feed on, leaves, fruit, and grass. Pigmy antelopes have no economic significance. [11–1299–1]

PLEGADIS FALCINELLUS, a bird of the Ibis family of the order Ciconiiformes, attaining a height of 60 cm and a weight of 560–780 g. The legs, neck, and bill are long, and the plumage is chestnut brown with a metallic gloss. They are widespread in southern Europe, southern and southeastern Asia, Australia, Africa, and North and South America. In the USSR they are found in the southern part of the European USSR, in Kazakhstan, and in Middle Asia. They nest in reeds and trees, often with herons and cormorants. The clutch contains three or four eggs, and the incubation period is three weeks. The bird feeds on small invertebrates, catching its prey in shallow waters. In the USSR it is a migratory bird. A related species is *P. ridgwayi* of South America. [11–1107–2]

PLEURONECTIFORMES (Heterosomata), flatfish, an order of fishes.

The body of Pleuronectiformes is laterally compressed and, in the majority, broad and relatively short. Order Pleuronectiformes is related to order Perciformes, but members of the group are distinguished by their asymmetrical skull structure and by the location of both eyes on one side. The fins of almost all flatfish lack spiny rays. The swim bladder is absent and the body cavity is significantly shortened. The dorsal and anal fins are long, the caudal fin is usually isolated, and the ventral fins are displaced toward the throat, usually with no more than six rays. Flatfish range in length from 7 cm (*Arnoglossus kessleri*) to 4.5 m (halibut). Members of the order are predominantly marine, although some enter rivers. The adults lie on one side at the bottom of the sea. The blind side is only weakly pigmented.

There are two suborders of Pleuronectiformes. Suborder Psettodoidei (Psettoidei) consists of one family with a single genus that comprises two species. The body is up to 70 cm long. One of the species, *Psettodes erumei,* is found in the Indian Ocean and the Red Sea; the other, *P. belcheri,* lives in the coastal waters of tropical western Africa. Suborder Pleuronectoidei comprises four families: Bothidae (turbot), Pleuronectidae (flounder), Soleidae (soles), and Cynoglossidae (tonguefishes). Members of the latter two families live mainly in tropical waters. Family Pleuronectidae comprises five subfamilies, two of which live in equatorial waters and two in the waters of the southern hemisphere.

The only members of the order found in the USSR are the Pleuronectinae (the subfamily of flounder and related groups), typically bottom marine fish inhabiting coastal and moderate depths (rarely found at depths exceeding 1,000 m). Amphiboreal distribution is characteristic of a number of species. Some species enter the mouths of rivers (for example, the river flounder, the starry flounder, and the arctic flounder).

The eggs of almost all flatfish are pelagic. The larvae are structually symmetrical and have a well-developed swim bladder; they inhabit the middle depths of the water, feeding on small planktonic crustaceans. As the larvae develop, their skulls become increasingly asymmetrical, the eyes migrate to one side of the head, the swim bladder disappears, the body thickens, and the young fish move to the bottom, lying with one side of their bodies on the bottom. Flatfish can quickly change their coloration in response to the color of the background. Adult flatfish feed on benthic invertebrates; some prey on other fish.

The majority of the Pleuronectinae have tasty flesh and are of commercial value. In the USSR the group in the Far East is the most varied (25 species); there are fewer species (nine) in the Barents and White seas. In arctic seas only the arctic flounder (*Liopsetta glacialis*) is widely distributed. Along the shores of Kamchatka and in the northern part of the Sea of Japan the principal commercial flatfish are the yellowfin sole (*Limanda aspera*) and the sohachi flounder (*Cleisthenes herzensteini*); in the Barents Sea, the plaice (*Platessa platessa*), the American plaice, and the dab are commercially important. The Black Sea turbot, or *kalkan,* is caught commercially in the Black Sea. Halibuts are the most important as food.

REFERENCES

Promyslovye ryby SSR: Opisaniia ryb. [Moscow] 1949. (Text for an atlas of color illustrations of fish.)
Nikol'skii, G. V. *Chastnaia ikhtiologiia,* 3rd ed. Moscow, 1971.
Zhizn' zhivotnykh, vol. 4, part 1. Moscow, 1971.

G. V. NIKOL'SKII   [11–713–3]

PLUM POCKET, a disease of plums caused by the ascomycetous fungus *Exoascus pruni.* The fungus infects the ovaries of the flowers. Instead of fruits, long, hard, flattened, and hollow saclike formations without stones develop. Plum pocket is prevalent in Europe, Asia, and North America. In the USSR it is found in the northwestern and central regions of the RSFSR, northern Armenia, the mountainous regions of Uzbekistan, and the Far East. The plant is infected with spores of the fungus during the flowering period. The infected flowers produce diseased fruits, and sacs with spores are formed under the cuticle. When the sacs mature, the cuticle ruptures and the spores scatter. They lie dormant throughout the winter on tree crowns, in cracks in the bark, and between the bud scales. Plum varieties with a relatively late and prolonged flowering period are most severely infected. Control measures include the collection and destruction of the pockets and the application of fungicides to the trees.

[11–1317–1]

POCKET DICTIONARY OF FOREIGN WORDS THAT HAVE BECOME PART OF THE RUSSIAN LANGUAGE, a valuable source for the study of the ideology of the Petrashevtsy, a group of Russian utopian socialists.

The publication of a dictionary undertaken by officer N. S. Kirillov was used by the Petrashevtsy to spread democratic and materialist ideas and the principles of utopian socialism. Fascicle 1 was edited by V. N. Maikov in collaboration with M. V. Petrashevskii; fascicle 2 was edited by Petrashevskii (1845–46). Fascicle 2 contained subject matter of a political nature and criticized serfdom and the autocracy. In May 1846, publication was halted by the tsarist government. In subsequent years both fascicles were taken off the market and burned by the police.

REFERENCES

"Karmannyi slovar' inostrannykh slov, voshedshikh v sostav russkogo iazyka," fasc. 2. In *Filosofskie i obshchestvenno-politicheskie proizvedeniia Petrashevtsev.* Moscow, 1953.
Dobrovol'skii, L. M. *Zapreshchennaia kniga v Rossi 1825–1904.* Moscow, 1962.

[11–1315–2]

POLITICAL EDUCATION ROOMS (*kabinety politicheskogo prosveshcheniia*), facilities established in 1956 on the basis of reorganized party libraries attached to city committees, raion committees, and major primary party organizations of the CPSU.

The purpose of political education rooms is to provide theoretical and methodological support to propagandists, lecturers, and leaders of agitation groups and to individual Communists and nonparty people studying Marxist-Leninist theory. Seminars, lectures, conferences on theory and methodology, and assemblies for exchanging experiences are organized and evening question-and-answer sessions are held in the political education rooms; trips to advanced economic enterprises and to schools for propaganda skills are arranged. For those studying Marxist-Leninist theory independently, lectures or lecture series are arranged, as well as tutorials and theoretical conferences and discussions. The libraries in the political education rooms include works on society and politics, reference works, textbooks, visual aids, newspapers, and party magazines. Many of these rooms have slide or filmstrip projectors, phonographs with appropriate records, and similar materials. As of Jan. 1, 1973, there were some 6,400 political education study facilities, including 182 houses for political education (*doma politicheskogo prosveshcheniia*).

A. N. ZAKHARIKOV   [11–291–2]

POTASSIUM, K, a chemical element in group I of Mendeleev's periodic system. Atomic number, 19; atomic weight, 39.098; a silver-white, very light, soft, and low-melting metal. The element consists of two stable isotopes, ^{39}K (93.08 percent) and ^{41}K (6.91 percent), and one slightly radioactive isotope, ^{40}K (0.01 percent), with a half-life of 1.32×10^9 years.

Historical survey. Some potassium compounds (for example, potash prepared from wood ashes) have been known since antiquity. These compounds, however, were not distinguished from those of sodium. The difference between "vegetable caustic" (potash, K_2CO_3) and "mineral caustic" (soda, Na_2CO_3) was established only in the 18th century. In 1807, H. Davy electrolyzed slightly moistened solid caustic potash and caustic soda (KOH and NaOH) to obtain the corresponding metals, which he called potassium and sodium. In 1809, L. W. Gilbert proposed the names "kalium" (from the Arabic *al-kali,* "potash") and "natronium" (from the Arabic *natrun,* "natural soda"); the latter name was changed to "natrium" by J. J. Berzelius in 1811. The names "potassium" and "sodium" have been retained in Great Britain, the USA, France, and certain other countries. These names were replaced in Russia during the 1840's by "kalium" and "natrium," which had been accepted in Germany, Austria, and the Scandinavian countries.

Distribution in nature. Potassium occurs widely in nature. Its content in the lithosphere is 2.50 weight percent. Potassium, like sodium, is enriched acidic magmas from which granites and other rocks crystallize (average K content, 3.34 percent). Potassium is a constituent of feldspars and micas. Basic and ultrabasic rocks, which are rich in iron and magnesium, contain little potassium. In contrast to sodium, potassium migrates only slightly on the earth's surface. Weathering of rocks leads to partial transfer of potassium to water, but this is rapidly absorbed by organisms and clays; therefore, river waters are poor in potassium and much less potassium than sodium reaches the oceans. In the ocean, potassium is absorbed by organisms and bottom silts (it is, for example, a component of glauconite). For this reason ocean waters contain only 0.038 percent potassium (25 times less than sodium). Potassium and magnesium salts, such as carnallite ($KCl \cdot MgCl_2 \cdot 6H_2O$; Solikamsk deposit in the USSR, Stassfurt deposit in the German Democratic Republic), crystallized after the precipitation of NaCl during the later stages of the evaporation of seawater in lagunas that occurred during past geologic epochs (particularly during the Permian, about 200 million years ago). In most soils there are only small amounts of soluble potassium compounds; therefore, cultivated plants require potassium fertilizers.

The radioactive isotope ^{40}K is an important source of underground heat; this was particularly true in past epochs, when the quantities of the isotope were larger. The decay of ^{40}K leads to the formation of ^{40}Ca and ^{40}Ar, which escapes into the atmosphere. Some potassium-containing minerals do not suffer the loss of argon, so that argon content may be used for determining the absolute age of the rock (the potassium-argon method).

Physical and chemical properties. Potassium is a silver-white, very light and soft metal that may be cut with a knife without difficulty. The crystal lattice of potassium is body-centered cubic; *a* equals 5.33 Å and the atomic radius, 2.36 Å. The ionic radius of K^+ is 1.33 Å. Its density is 0.862 g per cu cm (at 20°C). Its melting point is 63.55°C; its boiling point, 760°C. Its coefficient of thermal expansion is 8.33×10^{-5} (0°–50°C). Its thermal conductivity at 21°C is 97.13 watts per $(m \cdot °K)$, or 0.232 cal per $(cm \cdot sec \cdot °C)$. Its specific heat at 20°C is 741.2 joules per $(kg \cdot °K)$, or 0.177 cal per $(g \cdot °C)$; its specific electrical resistivity at 20°C, 7.118×10^{-8} ohm·m; and its temperature coefficient of electrical resistivity, 5.8×10^{-5} (20°C). The Brinell hardness of potassium is 400 kilonewtons per sq m, or 0.04 kilograms-force per sq mm.

The outer electron-shell configuration of the potassium atom is $4s^1$, so that the valence of potassium in compounds is always 1. The sole valence electron of the potassium atom is at a greater distance from its nucleus than the corresponding valence electrons in lithium and sodium; therefore, the chemical reactivity of potassium is higher than that of the other two metals. Since potassium is rapidly oxidized in air (particularly in moist air), the metal is stored under gasoline, kerosene, or mineral oil. Potassium reacts at room temperature with the halogens. It unites with sulfur on mild heating; stronger heating is required for reaction with selenium and tellurium. When heated above 200°C in a hydrogen atomosphere, potassium forms the hydride KH, which is spontaneously combustible in air. Potassium does not react with nitrogen even when heated under pressure, but the two elements form potassium nitride K_3N and potassium azide KN_3 under the influence of an electric discharge. Heating potassium with graphite yields the carbides KC_8 (at 300°C) and KC_{16} (at 360°C). In dry air or oxygen, potassium forms the yellowish-white oxide K_2O and the orange peroxide KO_2; the known peroxides also include K_2O_2 and K_2O_3, which are prepared by the action of oxygen on potassium solutions in liquid ammonia.

Potassium reacts extremely vigorously (sometimes explosively) with water to evolve hydrogen $(2K + 2H_2O = 2KOH + H_2)$ and with aqueous acid solutions to give salts. Potassium dissolves slowly in ammonia; the resulting blue solution is a powerful reducing agent. When heated, potassium removes the oxygen in oxides and the salts of oxyacids to form K_2O and free metals or their oxides. Potassium reacts with alcohols to give alkoxides; it accelerates the polymerization of olefins and diolefins; and it forms potassium alkyls and potassium aryls in reactions with alkyl halides and aryl halides, respectively. The presence of potassium may be readily determined by the violet coloration of its flame.

Production and use. Potassium is produced industrially by using exchange reactions between metallic sodium and KOH or KCl:

$$KOH + Na = NaOH + K$$

and

$$KCl + Na = NaCl + K$$

In the first case the molten hydroxide KOH reacts with liquid sodium in countercurrent in a nickel plate column at 380°–440°C. In the second case, sodium vapor is passed through the molten salt KCl at 760°–800°C and the evolved potassium vapor is condensed. Potassium production may also be performed by heating (above 200°C) mixtures of potassium chloride with aluminum (or silicon) and lime. The production of potassium by the electrolysis of molten KOH or KCl is limited because of a low level of efficiency and safety problems.

The main use of metallic potassium is in the preparation of potassium peroxide, which is used for oxygen regeneration in submarines and other closed systems. Alloys of sodium with 40–90 percent potassium, which remain liquid at room temperature, are used as heat transfer agents in nuclear reactors, as reducing agents in titanium production, and as oxygen absorbers. Agriculture is the principal consumer of potassium salts (for use in fertilizers).

REFERENCES
"Kalii." In *Kratkaia khimicheskaia entsiklopediia*, vol. 2. Moscow, 1963.
Nekrasov, B. V. *Osnovy obshchei khimii*, vol. 3. Moscow, 1970.
Remy, G. *Kurs neorganicheskoi khimii*, vol. 1. Moscow, 1963. (Translated from German.)
                                                    S. A. POGODIN

Potassium in the organism. Potassium is one of the biogenic elements, a ubiquitous constituent of plants and animals. The daily potassium requirement for the human adult (2–3 g) is supplied by meat and vegetable products. The daily requirement for infants (30 mg per kg) is supplied completely by the mother's milk, which contains 60–70 mg percent potassium. Many marine organisms extract potassium from water. Plants derive potassium from the soil. The potassium content of animals averages 2.4 g per kg. Unlike sodium, potassium concentrates in the cells; the extracellular medium contains considerably less. Potassium is distributed unevenly within the cell.

Potassium ions participate in generating and propagating bioelectric potentials in the nerves and muscles, in regulating the contraction of heart and other muscles, in maintaining the osmotic pressure and hydration of colloids in the cells, and in activating certain enzymes. Potassium metabolism is closely associated with carbohydrate metabolism, and potassium ions affect protein synthesis. In most cases, K^+ cannot replace Na^+. K^+ is selectively concentrated by the cells. Suppression of glycolysis, respiration, and photosynthesis and impairment of the permeability of the outer cell membrane lead to a loss of potassium from cells, frequently in exchange for Na^+. Potassium is eliminated from the organism mainly with the urine. The potassium content of the blood and tissues in vertebrates is regulated by hormones of the adrenal glands (the corticosteroids).

Potassium is unevenly distributed within plants; the vegetative organs contain more potassium than do the roots and seeds. Large amounts of potassium are found in beans, beets, potatoes, tobacco leaves, and gramineous feed grains (20–30 g per kg of dry material). Potassium deficiency in the soil retards plant growth and increases the incidence of disease. The amount of potassium used in potassium fertilizers depends on the type of crop and soil.

The trace elements rubidium and cesium accompany potassium in the biosphere. Li^+ and Na^+ ions are antagonists of K^+; for this reason, an optimum K^+/Na^+ ratio in the cells, as well as in the surrounding medium, is as important as the absolute concentrations of the ions. Almost 90 percent of the natural radioactivity of organisms (gamma radiation) is caused by the presence of the natural radioisotope ^{40}K in the tissues.

REFERENCES
Kaplanskii, S. Ia. *Mineral'nyi obmen*. Moscow-Leningrad, 1938.
Vishniakov, S. I. *Obmen makroelementov u sel'skokhoziaistvennykh zhivotnykh*. Moscow, 1967.
Sutcliffe, J. F. *Pogloshchenie mineral'nykh solei rasteniiami*. Moscow, 1964. (Translated from English.)   I. A. SKUL'SKII

In medicine, the acetate CH_3COOK is used as a diuretic, mainly against edema caused by cardiac insufficiency. The chloride KCl is used in cases of potassium deficiency in the organism. Such deficiencies develop during treatment with hormonal preparations and digitalis, after great fluid losses brought about by vomiting or diarrhea, and with the administration of certain diuretics. The perchlorate $KClO_4$ inhibits thyroxine production (a hormone of the thyroid gland) and is used in cases of thyrotoxicosis. Potassium permanganate, $KMnO_4$, is used as an antiseptic.   [11–596–1]

POTASSIUM BROMIDE, KBr, a salt; colorless crystals. Density, 2.75 g/cm^3; melting point, 748°C. Solubility, 65.6 g per 100 g H_2O at 20°C; 105 g at 100°C.

Potassium bromide is obtained by the reaction of aqueous solutions of potash with iron bromide (II, III): $4K_2CO_3 + Fe_3Br_8 = 8KBr + Fe_3O_4 + 4CO_2$. Potassium bromide is used in the preparation of sensitized photographic materials and in medicine.   [11–637–3]

POTASSIUM CARBONATE, potash, K_2CO_3, a salt; colorless crystals. Density 2.3 g/cm^3; melting point, 89.4°C. Highly hygroscopic; solubility, 113.5 g per 100 g H_2O at 20°C (156 g at 100°C). The solution is alkaline.

Potash has been extracted from the ashes of wood and herbaceous plants since ancient times. It is produced commercially mainly from natural potassium salts and as a by-product of the conversion of nepheline to aluminum oxide. Potassium carbonate is used in the preparation of liquid soaps, hard and crystal glasses, dyes, and photographic materials. It is also used as a potassium fertilizer. [11–638–3]

POTASSIUM CHLORIDE, KCl, a salt; colorless crystals. Density, 1.989 g/cm^3; melting point, 768°C. Solubility, 34.7 g per 100 g H_2O at 20°C (56.6 g at 100°C).

Potassium chloride occurs in nature as sylvite. Natural sylvinite (a mixture of sylvite, KCl, and halite, NaCl) and the mineral carnallite, $KCl \cdot MgCl_2 \cdot 6H_2O$, serve as the raw material in

no known deposits of potassium salts in prerevolutionary Russia, and potassium fertilizers were not produced.

The creation of the potassium industry in the USSR began in 1929, after the discovery (in 1925) of potassium deposits in the Northern Urals (Solikamsk and Berezniki). In 1931 the country's agriculture received 210,000 tons of potassium fertilizers (in terms of K_2O); in 1940, 219,000; in 1960, 766,000; in 1965, 1,891,000; in 1967, 2,136,000; in 1968, 2,210,000; and in 1971, 2,804,000 (that is, 12.7 kg of K_2O per hectare of arable land).

Potassium fertilizers are divided into raw potassium salts, which are produced by mechanical processing (sorting, crushing, and pulverization) of natural potassium salts, and concentrated, or high-analysis, potassium fertilizers, such as potassium chloride, potassium sulfate, and 30-percent and 40-percent potassium salts (a mixture of finely ground natural kainite or sylvinite with potassium chloride), as well as potash, potassium-magnesium sulfate, potassium electrolyte, and ash. A description of the main potassium fertilizers is given in Table 1.

Table 1. Properties of main inorganic potassium fertilizers

	Chemical formula	K_2O content (percent)	Hygroscopicity	Packing
Potassium chloride	KCl	52–60	Marked	Strong
30-percent and 40-percent potassium salts	$KCl + {}_mKCl \cdot {}_nNaCl$	30–40	Slight	Marked
Potassium sulfate	K_2SO_4	45–52	Very weak	None
Sylvinite	${}_mKCl \cdot {}_nNaCl$	at least 14	Slight	Marked
Kainite	$KCl \cdot MgSO_4 \cdot 3H_2O$	8–12	Weak	Marked
Carnallite	$KCl \cdot MgCl_2 \cdot 6H_2O$	12–13	Slight	Marked
Potassium-magnesium sulfate	$K_2SO_4 \cdot MgSO_4$	24–26	Very weak	None
Potassium electrolyte	KCl and impurities	32	Marked	Marked

the preparation of potassium chloride. Potassium chloride is used as a potassium fertilizer and as a raw material for the preparation of other potassium salts and potassium hydroxide. In medicine, potassium chloride solutions are used internally or intravenously for conditions accompanied by potassium deficiency (for example, during treatment with certain preparations or after persistent vomiting) and for cases of cardiac arrhythmia. [11–639–4]

POTASSIUM FERRICYANIDE, potassium hexacyanoferriate, $K_3[Fe(CN)_6]$, a complex iron (III) compound; dark red crystals. Density, 1.86 g/cm^3.

Potassium ferricyanide is obtained by the oxidation of potassium ferrocyanide. With Fe^{2+} ions it forms a dark blue precipitate of Turnbull's blue, $Fe_3[Fe(CN)_6]_2$, which is of use in analytical chemistry. Potassium ferricyanide is also used as a reducer in photography. [11–637–4]

POTASSIUM FERROCYANIDE, potassium hexacyanoferroate, $K_4[Fe(CN)_6] \cdot 3H_2O$, a complex iron (II) compound; light yellow crystals that remain stable in air. Density, 1.85 g/cm^3.

Potassium ferrocyanide was first obtained by heating horns, hooves, and blood with K_2CO_3 and iron filings. It is used as a reagent for Fe^{3+} ions, with which it forms the blue precipitate Prussian blue, $Fe_4[Fe(CN)_6]_3$. Potassium ferrocyanide is also of use in other branches of analytical chemistry. In industry it is used in the manufacture of paints, $K_3[Fe(CN)_6]$. [11–637–5]

POTASSIUM FERTILIZERS, inorganic substances used as a source of potassium nutrition for plants; usually salts of hydrochloric, sulfuric, and carbonic acids dissolved in water—often combined with other compounds containing potassium—in a form accessible to plants.

Natural deposits of potassium salts are the primary source of potassium fertilizers. The first major deposit was discovered in Stassfurt in the 1840's. In subsequent years industry began to produce potassium chloride, potassium nitrate, and potassium sulfate. Deposits of potassium salts were discovered in France, Canada, and the United States. By 1913 world production of potassium fertilizers was 1.19 million tons (in terms of K_2O); in 1967, 14.7 million tons; and in 1970, 19 million tons. There were

Potassium fertilizers are usually used against a background of phosphorus or nitrogen and phosphorus fertilizers. The greatest gains in yield are achieved on soils that are poor in free potassium: peaty, floodplain, sandy-loam, and light loamy soddy-podzolic soils. Plants growing on gray forest loams, podzolized and leached-out chernozems, and terra rossa in the humid subtropics, where there is extensive cultivation of tea plants and citrus crops, also need potassium fertilizers. Plants that require large quantities of potassium, such as potatoes, vegetables, sugar beets, fodder root crops, tobacco, and rustic tobacco, are most responsive to it. Although flax and hemp absorb a small amount of potassium from the soil, they assimilate it poorly; therefore, their cultivation involves the application of potassium fertilizers. Under soil conditions in the nonchernozem zone of the European part of the USSR, legumes, perennial leguminous grasses, corn, winter grain crops, buckwheat, and fruit and berry plantings respond well to potassium fertilizers.

Potassium has a positive effect on the quality of products: there is an increase in the sugar content of root crops, the starch content of potatoes, the production and quality of fiber in textile crops, and the protein content in feed plants, particularly against a background of nitrogen-ammonia fertilizers. In addition, potassium fertilizers strengthen plant resistance to certain fungus diseases and increase the cold and drought resistance of winter grains, leguminous grasses, and perennial plantings.

The effectiveness of potassium fertilizers depends on their content of accompanying elements, such as sodium and chlorine. For example, in potatoes, tobacco, grapes, lupines, and other crops that are sensitive to chlorine, the quality of the harvest is usually improved merely by application of potassium nitrate or potassium carbonate. Sugar beets and certain other plants respond favorably to the sodium in raw and mixed potassium salts. Therefore, in the primary zones of sugar beet planting, sylvinite (which contains sodium in addition to potassium) produces a considerable gain in root yield and increases the sugar content much more than does pure potassium chloride. Raw potassium salts are undesirable for grapes, buckwheat, tobacco, beans, and potatoes. If these crops are fertilized with potassium chloride it is applied only during fall plowing so that there will be time for the chlorine that is not absorbed by the soil to be leached out of the tilled layer to a significant degree during the fall and early spring. The use of potassium-magnesium sulfate, potassium sulfates, potassium nitrates, and furnace ash for these crops is even better. The use of potassium fertilizers (ideally, together with phosphorus fertilizers) increases the productivity of meadows and improves hay quality.

The dosages of potassium fertilizers depend primarily on soil conditions, the physiological characteristics of the crop being fertilized, and the properties of the fertilizers. On soddy-podzolic soils the dosage of K_2O is 30–60 kilograms per hectare (kg/ha), and for hemp the dosage is increased to 120; on gray forest soils and chernozems, 30–60 and 30–45 kg/ha, respectively (for hemp, up to 90 kg/ha); on terra rossa and sierozems, 30–60 kg/ha. Potassium fertilizers are usually used as the primary fertilizer for fall or spring plowing or cultivation. Top-dressing of plants with potassium (if an insufficient quantity was applied during plowing) has become common in the cultivation of sugar beets, potatoes, corn, and certain vegetable crops. In this case it is better to use potassium fertilizers together with nitrogen and phosphorus fertilizers, applying them in the interrow spaces with plant feeders at a depth of at least 10–12 cm (calculating 20–30 kg of K_2O per hectare). Shallow placement of potassium fertilizers in the soil during top-dressing of plants does not produce favorable results. Therefore, the use of potassium for top-dressing of solidly planted crops (grains, legumes, and grasses) is not advisable. Each centner of K_2O applied in the form of potassium fertilizer provides the following average gains in yield (in centners): raw cotton, 1–2; sugar beets, 35–40; potatoes, 20–33; flax fiber, about 1.5; winter grains, 3–5; spring crops, 2–3; hay from sown grasses, 20–33; meadow hay, 8–18. The aftereffect of potassium fertilizers lasts three to four years.

REFERENCES

Pchelkin, V. U. *Pochvennyi kalii i kaliinye udobreniia.* Moscow, 1966.
Peterburgskii, A. V. *Znachenie kaliia v povyshenii urozhainosti.* Moscow, 1967.
Agronomicheskaia khimiia. Edited by V. M. Klechkovskii and A. V. Peterburgskii. Moscow, 1967.   A. V. PETERBURGSKII [11–601–1]

POTASSIUM FLUORIDE, KF, a salt; colorless transparent crystals. Deliquescent in air. Density, 2.505 g/cm³; melting point, 857°C. Solubility, 92.3 g per 100 g H_2O at 18°C.

Potassium fluoride is obtained by dissolving KOH or K_2SO_3 in hydrofluoric acid, HF. It is used in the preparation of acid-resistant cements and as a reagent in the fluorination of organic compounds. Acid-salts, or hydrofluorides, are easily fusible crystalline substances that are used as electrolytes in the preparation of elementary fluorine.   [11–639–3]

POTASSIUM HYDROXIDE, caustic potash, KOH, a strong alkali; colorless crystals. Density, 2.12 g/cm³ (25°C); melting point, 380°C.

Potassium hydroxide is readily soluble in water (97 g per 100 g H_2O at 0°C; 112 g at 20°C), liberating a considerable amount of heat. Potassium hydroxide is produced commercially in the form of an opaque solid white mass containing 90–92 percent KOH (representing a mixture of KOH and KOH·H_2O). In the air, potassium hydroxide absorbs H_2O and CO_2 and deliquesces, gradually converting to potassium carbonate K_2CO_3. Potassium hydroxide has a destructive effect on skin, paper, wool, silk, and other organic materials; it causes severe burns on human skin and is particularly dangerous to the eyes. Safety goggles and rubber gloves must be worn when working with it. Potassium hydroxide is obtained by the electrolysis of calcium chloride solutions. Potassium hydroxide is used in the manufacture of liquid soaps, as a source material in the preparation of potassium salts, in alkaline batteries, and as a laboratory reagent.
          [11–637–6]

POTASSIUM IODIDE, KI, a salt; colorless crystals. Density, 3.115 g/cm³; melting point, 686°C. Solubility, 144.5 g per 100 g H_2O at 20°C (209 g at 100°C).

Atmospheric oxygen oxidizes potassium iodide in the presence of light, precipitating iodine. Potassium iodide is obtained by the reaction of aqueous solutions of FeI_2 and K_2CO_3. Potassium iodide is used in the preparation of light-sensitive photographic materials and in medicine.   [11–638–2]

POTASSIUM-MAGNESIUM SULFATE, $K_2SO_4 \cdot MgSO_4$, potassium-magnesium sulfate fertilizer. Its gray crystals contain 24–26 percent K_2O and 11–18 percent MgO and dissolve easily in water. Potassium-magnesium sulfate fertilizer is weakly hygroscopic, does not pack, and spreads well. It is especially effective on sandy and sandy-loam soils for crops that are sensitive to chlorine (potatoes, buckwheat, legumes, fruits, and berries).
          [11–604–2]

POTASSIUM METAPHOSPHATE, KPO_3, a potassium salt of metaphosphoric acid, a white powder; a high-concentration potassium-phosphate fertilizer.

Potassium metaphosphate contains 55–60 percent P_2O_5 and 35–40 percent K_2O. It is nonhygroscopic and readily assimilated by plants (particularly those growing in acidic soils). It is most effective when applied to the soil under chlorine-sensitive crops (tobacco, tea, grapes, legumes).   [11–638–4]

POTASSIUM NITRATE, KNO_3, a salt; colorless crystals. Density, 2.11 g/cm³; melting point, 339°C. Readily soluble in water (31 g in 100 g H_2O at 20°C; 246 g at 100°C).

Mixtures of potassium nitrate and organic substances are easily flammable and burn vigorously. Potassium nitrate is prepared by reacting HNO_3 or nitrous gases with K_2CO_3 or KCl. Potassium nitrate is used as a fertilizer, in glassmaking, and in the production of gunpowder.

In agriculture, potassium nitrate containing 44 percent K_2O and 13 percent nitrogen is used as a base fertilizer (applied in the spring) and as a top-dressing for chlorine-sensitive crops (flax, potatoes, tobacco, grapes).   [11–599–2]

POTASSIUM SALTS, chemogenic sedimentary rocks formed by readily water-soluble potassium and potassium-magnesium minerals. The most important of these minerals are sylvite (KCl; 52.44 percent K), carnallite ($KCl \cdot MgCl_2 \cdot 6H_2O$; 35.8 percent K), kainite ($KMg[SO_4]Cl \cdot 3H_2O$; 14.07 percent K), polyhalite ($K_2MgCa_2[SO_4]_4 \cdot 2H_2O$; 12.97 percent K), and langbeinite ($K_2Mg_2[SO_4]_3$; 18.84 percent K). Minerals of secondary importance are leonite ($K_2Mg[SO_4]_2 \cdot 4H_2O$; 21.32 percent K), schoenite ($K_2Mg[SO_4]_2 \cdot 6H_2O$; 19.41 percent K), and syngenite ($K_2Ca[SO_4]_2 \cdot H_2O$; 23.81 percent K). The basic potassium rock types are the carnallitic, containing 45–85 percent carnallite and 18–50 percent halite, with small amounts of sylvite, anhydrite, clay minerals, and carbonates; sylvinite, containing 95–98 percent sylvite and halite, the remainder being an insoluble residue (0.5–2.0 percent in the best varieties, sometimes containing appreciable quantities of polyhalite or langbeinite and, infrequently, borates); and hard salt, containing 8–25 percent sylvite, 18–30 percent kieserite, 40–60 percent halite, and 0.5–2.0 percent carbonates, anhydrite, and clay minerals.

Potassium salts form as a result of the evaporation and cooling of the brine in potassium-containing basins, which arise in parts of the surface of halitic basins. The formation of salt deposits occurred during geologic epochs with dry, warm climates; the most favorable conditions for the accumulation of saliferous series existed during the Devonian, the Permian, and the Neocene. Concentrations of potassium salts occur in lake deposits (Eritrea) and in brine lakes (Dead Sea). Natural potassium salts are deposited as seams in rock salt or as galls, several dozens or hundreds of meters thick. Deformation of saliferous rocks with the generation of salt anticlines, brachyanticlines, and stocks, related to the flow of salt, leads to great complications of the bedding conditions of potassium-bearing deposits. This occurs maximally in salt stocks.

The K_2O content of industrially mined deposits is 12–30 percent. Large commercial deposits of potassium salts (with reserves of a billion tons or more) are encountered relatively rarely. The total reserves in the USSR amount to 166.4 billion tons (24 billion tons' worth of K_2O). The majority of the known resources are concentrated in the USSR in the Urals (Solikamsk, Perm Oblast), western Kazakhstan, the western Ukraine, and Byelorussia. Significant foreign deposits include those in the German Democratic Republic (Stassfurt), the Federal Republic of Germany (Hanover, the Harz, Hesse, Baden), the USA (the Carlsbad region in New Mexico; Lake Searles in California), Canada

(Saskatchewan), France (Alsace), and Italy (Sicily). Potassium-salt deposits are worked mainly by the underground method, using the room-and-pillar system. Potassium-salt mining by the leaching method recently began in Canada.

The principal consumer of potassium salts is agriculture. Potassium salts are also being used in electrometallurgy, medicine, photography, and pyrotechnics, in the production of glass, soap, paint, and leather, and particularly in the chemical industry, which processes the salts to produce KCl, K_2CO_3, KOH, KNO_3, K_2SO_4, and other compounds.

REFERENCES

Ivanov, A. A. "Rasprostranenie i tipy iskopaemykh mestorozhdenii kaliinykh solei." *Geologiia rudnykh mestorozhdenii,* 1959, no. 4.
Trebovaniia promyshlennosti k kachestvu mineral'nogo syr'ia, issue 22: Kashkarov, O. D., and M. P. Fiveg, *Kaliinye i magnezial'nye soli.* Moscow-Leningrad, 1963.
Yarzhemskii, Ia. Ia. *Kaliinye i kalienosnye galogennye porody.* Novosibirsk, 1967.

M. P. FIVEG [11–600–1]

POTASSIUM SULFATE, K_2SO_4, a salt; colorless crystals. Density, 2.66 g/cm^3, melting point, 1074°C. Solubility, 11.1 g per 100 g H_2O at 20°C (24.1 g at 100°C).

Potassium sulfate is a consituent of natural potassium salts, such as schoenite ($K_2SO_4 \cdot MgSO_4 \cdot 6H_2O$), from which it is also extracted. Potassium sulfate is used in the preparation of alum and potash. In agriculture, it serves as a concentrated chlorine-free potassium fertilizer, containing no less than 45–52 percent K_2O, no more than 1 percent MgO, and no more than 10 percent moisture; it is applied primarily to the soil under chlorine-sensitive crops (potatoes, tobacco, flax, grapes, citrus fruits). The presence of the sulfate ion in the fertilizer has a favorable effect on the yield of crucifers (cabbage, rutabagas, turnips) and legumes, which require a large amount of sulfur.

Heating potassium sulfate with concentrated sulfuric acid forms the acid salt potassium hydrosulfate (bisulfate): $K_2SO_4 + H_2SO_4 = 2KHSO_4$. At temperatures above its melting point (210°C), potassium hydrosulfate is converted first to potassium pyrosulfate ($2KHSO_4 = K_2S_2O_7 + H_2O$) and then to potassium sulfate and sulfuric anhydride ($K_2S_2O_7 = K_2SO_4 + SO_3$). This reaction is used for converting substances that are nearly insoluble in acids (for example, calcinated Al_2O_3, Fe_2O_3, CrO_3) into soluble sulfates. Potassium hydrosulfate is also used as a flux in metallurgy. [11–638–7]

POTASSIUM SULFIDE, K_2S, a salt; colorless crystals. Density, 1.80 g/cm^3; melting point, 471°C.

Potassium sulfide is hygroscopic and highly water-soluble. It readily oxidizes on exposure to atmospheric oxygen to potassium thiosulfate, $K_2S_2O_3$. Boiling aqueous potassium sulfide with excess sulfur forms the potassium polysulfides K_2S_2, K_2S_3, K_2S_4, K_2S_5, and K_2S_6. Potassium sulfide is obtained by the reactions:

$$KOH + H_2S = KHS + H_2O$$

$$\text{and } KHS + KOH = K_2S + H_2O$$

The fusion of potash with sulfur results in the formation of sulfurated potash, a mixture of potassium polysulfides and thiosulfates, which is used in the preparation of sulfur baths. Potassium sulfide is also used in photography. [11–639–1]

POTATO, several species of tuberous perennials of the genus *Solanum,* section Tuberarium, family Solanaceae.

There are about 200 wild and cultivated species of potato, growing primarily in South and Central America. Two closely related species are usually cultivated: the Andean potato (*S. andigenum*), which has long been grown in the territory of Colombia, Ecuador, Peru, Bolivia, and northwestern Argentina, and the Chilean potato (*S. tuberosum*), whose original range included central Chile and the neighboring islands. This species has spread widely (as an annual crop) to countries with temperate climates. The local populace of the mountainous regions of South America also cultivate *S. rybinii, S. goniocalyx, S. ajanhuiri,* and certain other species.

The plant of the Chilean potato, which grows from a tuber,

forms a bush 50–80 cm in height, usually with between three and six green or anthocyanin-containing stalks. Underground shoots, called stolons or runners, grow from the axils of embryonic leaves in the underground part of the stem. They grow to 15–20 cm (in some varieties, to 40–50 cm). As the apexes grow thicker, they give rise to new tubers (modified shoots). The eyes, each with three or four buds, are located on the surface of the tubers in pits bordered by leaf scars. The central bud usually sprouts; only when it is damaged do the other buds begin to develop. The eyes are arranged spirally and are particularly numerous near the apex of the tuber. The tuber may be round, elongated, or oval. The surface color and the pulp may be white, yellow, pinkish, red, or blue. The root system is fibrous and relatively poorly developed. The leaves are odd-pinnate dissected, with lobes of various sizes. They are downy and range in color from yellowish green to dark green. An inflorescence develops of two or three (sometimes four) furcate bostryces. The blossoms are pentamerous, with gamosepalous calyces and incompletely joined white, red-violet, or blue-violet petals. The fruit is a spherical, oval, or napiform berry with small seeds, 1,000 of which weigh 0.5–0.6 g.

Potatoes reproduce vegetatively by the tubers (for breeding purposes by the seeds). The tuber buds in the soil begin to sprout at temperatures of 5°–8° C; the optimal sprouting temperature is 15°–20° C. The optimal temperature for photosynthesis, and for stalk, leaf, and blossom development is 16°–22°C. The tubers develop most intensively at nighttime air temperatures of 10°–13°C. High temperatures (nighttime readings of about 20°C and higher) lead to the thermal degeneration of the potatoes, and the seed tubers produce plants with sharply diminished productivity. The sprouts and young plants are damaged at −2°C. The coefficient of transpiration averages 400–500. The greatest amount of water is needed by the plant during blossoming and tuber formation. Excess moisture is harmful to the potato. A great deal of nutritive substance is used in developing the foliage and tubers of the potato, especially during the period of maximum growth of the above-ground parts of the plant and at the beginning of tuber formation. A harvest of 200–250 centners per hectare removes from the soil 100–175 kg of nitrogen, 40–50 kg of phosphorus, and 140–230 kg of potassium (statistics of D. N. Prianishnikov). The best soils for potatoes are chernozems, turfy podzols, gray forest soils, and dried peats. The mechanical composition should be sandy loam or light to moderate loams.

The potato is a highly important crop with a variety of uses. On the average, its tubers contain 76.3 percent water and 23.7 percent dry matter, including 17.5 percent starch, 0.5 percent sugars, 1–2 percent proteins, and about 1 percent mineral salts. The maximum content of dry matter is 36.8 percent; the maximum starch, 29.4 percent; and the maximum protein, 4.6 percent. The potato is also a source of vitamins C, B_1, B_2, B_6, PP, and K and a source of carotenoids. More than 100 dishes can be prepared from potatoes. The food industry produces potatoes that are dried, fried (as chips), quick-frozen, flaked, and powdered. Potatoes are of great importance as a raw material for starches, syrups, and spirits. Agricultural livestock are fed the tubers, tops, processing residues, and pulp. In daylight, glycoalkaloids (for example, solanin and chaconine) form under the skin of the tubers; these substances can cause poisoning if their content surpasses 20–50 mg percent, but they partially dissolve upon boiling in water.

The potato was first cultivated (at first by using wild varieties) about 14,000 years ago by the Indians of South America. They were first introduced to Europe (Spain) in about 1565. Thereafter, the crop spread to Italy, Belgium, Germany, the Netherlands, France, and Great Britain. The Free Economic Society attributed the appearance of the potato in Russia to Peter the Great, who, at the end of the 17th century, had a sack of the tubers sent from Holland. Extensive cultivation began after the Senate issued a decree in 1765 and imported from abroad a quantity of seed potatoes for distribution about the country. The area planted to potatoes began to expand with particular speed in the 1840's. By the end of the 19th century more than 1.5 million hectares were being planted to potatoes in Russia.

Worldwide in 1970, the area planted to potatoes amounted to about 22.3 million hectares (ha): 2.7 million in Poland, 0.66 in the Federal Republic of Germany, 0.67 in the German Democratic Republic, and 0.54 million in the United States. The total tuber harvest comes to around 298 million tons, an average of 133 centners per ha: 361 centners per ha in the Netherlands, 233 in the United States, 293 in the FRG, 192 in the GDR, and 185 in Poland. In 1971 the USSR planted 7.89 million ha of potatoes; the total harvest came to 92.6 million tons, an average of 117 centners per ha (in Estonia, 178 centners per ha; in Latvia, 160; and in Byelorussia, 130). In comparison with 1913 (4.2 million ha), the area planted in potatoes has nearly doubled. The most important potato regions are in Byelorussia, the western and northern parts of the Ukraine, and the central chernozem areas of the RSFSR. Potato cultivation has been carried beyond the Arctic Circle (on the Kola Peninsula and in the valleys of the Pechora, Ob', and Kolyma rivers).

Through years of cultivation, hundreds of varieties of potatoes have developed. Most contemporary varieties have been acquired by hybridization. Selective breeding began in the USSR in 1920 at the Korenevo Potato Breeding Station, where the first Soviet varieties were developed in 1925 (the Lorkh and the Korenevskii). According to the date of maturation, potatoes are divided into early, mid-early, mid-season ripening, mid-late, and late varieties. By usage, they are classed as table, fodder, industrial, or universal. By 1972, 105 varieties had been regionalized. The most common varieties are the Priekul'skiy Early, the Lorkh, and the Berlichingen, which are grown nearly everywhere. Other important varieties are the Petrovskii, the Stolovyi 19, the Olev, the Detskosel'skii, the Kameraz, the Vol'tman, the Iubel', the Polesskii, the Parnassiia, the Loshitskii, the Sedov, and the Borodianskii.

With good soil care and proper application of fertilizer, potatoes give high yields even when grown for long periods on the same plots. In field and fodder crop rotation in nonchernozem zones, potatoes are planted on turned sod after winter crops and flax. On sandy soils, the potatoes best follow lupine. In the central chernozem districts, the Ukraine, the northern Caucasus, the Volga region, and Middle Asia, potatoes are planted after winter crops, annual grasses, and corn. In Kazakhstan and eastern Siberia, they follow grain and legume-grass mixtures. In the Urals and Far East, they are planted after grain and grain-legume mixtures. In suburban areas, potatoes are usually cultivated in vegetable rotations. The early potato is a fallow crop; it grows well on loose, weedless, deeply tilled soils. In the fall, soils planted in potatoes are plowed to a depth of 27–30 cm. Thinner soils are plowed to the bottom of the arable layer and the undersoils are loosened. Nonchernozem fields are harrowed and replowed in the spring. On flooded soils this is combined with the application of organic fertilizers. The soils are harrowed to a depth of 17–20 cm or deeply cultivated to 12–15 cm. In the forest-steppe and steppe zones the soil is loosened by cultivating twice. Organic fertilizers (manure and compost) are applied at 20–40 tons per ha in both fall and spring. Green manure is applied to sandy soils. Mineral fertilizers calculated to produce 150–200 centners of tubers per ha provide 20–60 kg per ha of nitrogen, phosphorus, and potassium if applied in combination with manure and 20–90 kg per ha if without manure. For application during sowing (in the furrows), they should provide 10–20 kg per ha of phosphorus and 15–20 kg per ha of nitrogen. Top dressings should provide 20–30 kg per ha of nitrogen and potassium.

In planting potatoes, tubers of average size are selected (50–80 g). The seed potatoes are first allowed to sprout; this speeds the appearance of the shoots by seven to ten days. They are planted when the soil at 8–10 cm reaches 6°–8°C. The early varieties are planted first on fallow fields. In Middle Asia early varieties are given winter plantings (in January and February). Potatoes are planted by potato planters. The distance between the rows may be 60, 70, or 90 cm; the distance between plants in a row may be 23, 25, 30, or 35 cm. The planting standard for seed tubers is 2.5–3.5 tons per ha, planted to a depth of 6–12 cm. The fields are harrowed twice before the shoots appear and loosened several times after they appear. In the nonchernozem zone and the northern regions of the chernozem zone, potatoes are hilled (with moist soil). Herbicides are used against weeds; 2,4-D (sodium and amino salts and ethers) and nitrophen are

most common. A potato combine or potato digger is used for harvesting. To keep a long time, the potatoes are dug after the skin has become rough. In the south they are harvested when the tops die. Early potatoes are harvested when it is most suitable for market. Between two and six days before harvesting, the tops are mowed by a special machine. After drying and sorting, the tubers are placed in storage in special warehouses.

Potatoes are attacked by various diseases. The fungal diseases include phytophthorosis, potato canker, macrosporiosis, and potato scab. The bacterial diseases include stem wilt and ring rot. The viral diseases include mosaic diseases and leaf curl. The potato and stem nematodes also cause damage. Pests include the mole cricket, the wireworm and false wireworm, the beet webworm, the cutworm, and slugs. Further damage may be caused by the Colorado beetle and, in the Far East, the 28-spotted ladybird.

REFERENCES

Lekhnovich, V. S. "K istorii kul'tury kartofelia v Rossii." In *Materialy po istorii zemledeliia v SSSR,* collection 2. Moscow-Leningrad, 1956.
Bukasov, S. M., and A. Ia. Kameraz. *Osnovy selektsii kartofelia.* Moscow-Leningrad, 1959.
Zhukova, G. S., B. A. Pisarev, and A. I. Kuznetsov. *Agrotekhnika kartofelia v osnovnykh zonakh RSFSR.* Moscow, 1964.
Kameraz, A. Ia. *Rannii kartofel'.* Leningrad, 1967.
Novoe v kartofelevodstve. Edited by N. A. Dorozhkin. Minsk, 1967.
Vereshchagin, N. I., A. I. Mal'ko, and K. A. Pshechenkov. *Kratkii spravochnik mekhanizatora-kartofelevoda.* Moscow, 1968.
Kartofel'. Edited by N. S. Batsanov. Moscow, 1970.

V. S. LEKHNOVICH, K. Z. BUDIN,
and A. IA. KAMERAZ [11–1438–2]

POTATO BACILLUS (*Bacillus mesentericus*), a spore-bearing bacterium that looks like a thin rod (0.5–0.6 microns × 3–10 microns) and often forms long threads.

The vegetative cells of the potato bacillus are motile, gram positive, and form oval spores; the cells do not swell but maintain their cylindrical form. The colonies are yellowish brown, dry, and rugose. On the surface of liquid media the potato bacillus forms a thick, creased film; it forms a thin wrinkled coating on pieces of potato. It liquifies gelatin, forms alkalis and peptone in milk, and acidifies glucose, saccharose, and maltose. It does not decompose starch. The potato bacillus is widely distributed in nature (in soil, food products). It is a pathogen for animals and man. Its spores, entering dough with the flour or yeast, are not destroyed when the bread is baked. As they grow, the soft part of the bread becomes slimy and viscous, and the bread acquires an unpleasant odor.   A. A. IMSHENETSKII [11–1443–1]

POTATO CELLAR, a building or structure for storing potatoes. Potato storage facilities are subdivided into temporary facilities, which are pits and trenches filled with potatoes and covered over with earth and straw, and permanent facilities, including underground, semiunderground, and surface buildings, rectangular in shape with one story. In addition to storage, permanent facilities also permit presale processing (sorting and sizing) of food potatoes and sprouting of seed potatoes. Storage conditions are the most stable in the underground and semiunderground facilities, but such facilities cannot be built where the water table is within 2.5–3 m of the surface. Surface potato storage facilities are used in the southern USSR and in places where the water table is close to the surface. In rural storage facilities both food and fodder potatoes are stored by spreading them on the floor or in bins; in city facilities, containers are also used. Seed potatoes are stored in bins and sprouted in boxes or on racks. Potato storage facilities hold between 250 and 3,000 tons.

The most convenient permanent storage facilities have a central corridor or driveway passage with bins and auxiliary rooms arranged along both sides. The outside walls of such facilities are usually made of brick, stone, concrete blocks, or reinforced concrete; they have an insulation layer (in areas with estimated winter temperatures of −20° C) and are banked around with dirt and planted with sod (for underground and semiunderground facilities). The inside supporting structures (columns, beams, girders, and roof slabs) are made of reinforced concrete or steel.

The roof is usually combined (that is, without a loft) and has two or three layers of roofing felt; the floor may be asphalt concrete, concrete, wood, or dirt. The entries have gates with wickets; the doors are double, heat-insulated on the outside and latticed on the inside. Loading hatches are sometimes put in the walls of underground and semiunderground facilities. The bins are made of wood or reinforced concrete.

A system of active or general forced air ventilation is installed to take off surplus heat during the winter and to cool the potatoes in the autumn and spring. With active ventilation a given quantity of air (from 50 to 200 cu m per ton per hour) at a set temperature is passed through the mound of potatoes, which causes a rapid exchange of air within the mass of potatoes and creates optimal conditions for storage. In the northern regions recirculating heating devices consisting of ventilators and electric heaters are installed to warm the air; water and steam heaters are also used to warm the storage facilities. In the southern regions air coolers are added to the ventilation system. Automatic regulator systems ensure stable storage conditions.

Conveyors, hoists, loaders, pickers, and sorting stations are used to load and unload potatoes in the facilities; and flow lines, including grading, sorting, and packing machines and machines to wash and dry the potatoes, are used when potatoes are being shipped into the commercial network. Thus the labor-intensive jobs are completely mechanized.

REFERENCES
Metlitskii, L. V., and I. L. Volkind. *Khranenie kartofelia v usloviiakh aktivnogo ventilirovaniia.* Moscow, 1966.
Zdaniia i sooruzheniia dlia khraneniia kartofelia i ovoshchei: SNiP, part 2, sec. N, ch. 10. Moscow, 1966.
Normy tekhnologicheskogo proektirovaniia zdanii i sooruzhenii dlia khraneniia kartofelia i ovoschei, NTPSKh 6–65. Moscow, 1967.
I. L. VOLKIND   [11–1436–1]

POTATO CLEANER, a machine for removing the skins from potatoes and vegetables. In the potato cleaner used at public catering enterprises and at small vegetable-processing plants, the potatoes pass through the loading hopper into the working cylinder, where a rotating disk with a wavy surface coated with silica uses friction to remove the skins from and clean the potatoes. A constant stream of water is fed through a sprayer for better mixing and washing. The skins and water are removed through the outlet tube and the cleaned potatoes are thrown out an aperture in the working cylinder by centrifugal force. The machine uses 0.8–0.9 liters of water per kilogram of potatoes; it can clean up to 400 kg of potatoes an hour. The potato cleaner may also be part of a multipurpose kitchen machine.   [11–1438–1]

POTATO DIGGER, a machine for digging up potatoes, removing the tops and dirt from the tubers, and throwing the tubers out onto the field.

USSR industry produces the elevator-type (KTN-2B), riddle-type (KVN-2M), and spinning-type (KTN-1A) potato diggers. Similar types of potato diggers are produced abroad. The elevator type has shares for digging up two rows of potatoes and three elevators (two primary rod-link types and a cascade rake) that loosen and sift the soil. The bulk matter that is caught goes to a vibration screen and excess soil and small impurities fall through the holes in it. The tubers, tops, and remaining impurities fall from the screen to the surface of the field. Then the tubers are picked up by hand. The riddle-type potato digger has a double-screen riddle instead of the rod-link elevators. The shares of this digger are secured to the front edge of the first screen and vibrate together with it. This arrangement gives better pickup on the layer of soil being dug. A screen similar to the vibration screen of the elevator-type digger is secured on the end of the second screen of the sifter. The spinning-type digger has a share that digs up one row of potatoes and a turning rotor that catches the dug-up row and throws the bulk material onto the field.

All the potato diggers are mounted implements; their working parts are driven by a takeoff shaft from the tractor engine. The productivity level of the KTN-2B is 0.30–0.45 hectare (ha) per hr; of the KVN-2M, 0.36–0.42 ha per hr; and of the KTN-1A, up to 0.4 ha per hr.   [11–1431–2]

POTATO DIGGER-WINDROWER, a machine for digging out potato tubers and putting them in windrows.

The principal working parts of the UKV-2 machine used in the USSR are trapezoidal shares for digging up two rows of potatoes, a rod-link elevator with forced shaking of the dug-up bulk matter, pneumatic rollers for breaking up clods of earth, conveyors for removing tops, and a transverse conveyor for placing the tubers in windrows. The working parts of the machine are driven by a takeoff shaft from the tractor engine.

With the several-stage method of harvesting, the potato digger-windrower digs up two rows of potatoes, removing the dirt and tops from the tubers and placing them in a windrow. During the second and third passes the machine puts the tubers on the windrow formed on the first pass. It is possible to put tubers dug from four or six rows in a common windrow. Then the windrow is picked up by a potato harvesting combine. With combine harvesting, on the frist pass of the digger-windrower the tubers are placed between two undug rows. When these rows are harvested by the combine it picks up the previously deposited windrow at the same time. The productivity of the digger-windrower is 2–4 hectares per shift.   [11–1434–2]

POTATO FARMING, INSTITUTE OF, a scientific research institute founded in 1930 on the basis of the Korenevo Potato Selection Station (in Moscow Oblast). In 1970 it had departments of physiology and biochemistry, genetics and selection, seed development and virusology, agrotechnology and fertilization, plant protection, storage, economics and organization, and technology and mechanization of potato production. Its experimental stations for potatoes are located at Elets (Lipetsk Oblast) and Ul'ianovsk (Ul'ianovsk Oblast), and it has the Zavorovo, Korenevo, and Il'inskoe experimental production farms in Moscow Oblast. The institute has graduate programs and a school for raising the qualifications of agricultural specialists. It has published its proceedings (*Trudy*) since 1964.   [11–1443–2]

POTATO GRATER, a machine for pulverizing potatoes to make starch. The grater consists of a heavy cast-iron body with a hinged cover. Inside is the basic pulverizing element, a steel drum that revolves at great speed. Replaceable toothed files made of steel are arranged on the surface of the drum (up to 210 files). A moving wooden or metallic block fits tight alongside the drum, and the potatoes are pulverized between the block and the drum. The bulk matter produced falls through holes in a screen secured on a frame beneath the drum. Currently manufactured potato graters can produce up to 100 tons in 24 hours.   [11–1434–1]

POTATO HARVESTING COMBINE, a machine for digging up potatoes, removing their tops and dirt, and collecting them in a bin, either of the combine itself or of another vehicle.

In the USSR the KKU-2 Druzhba potato combine is produced in two versions: the elevator type and the riddle type. With the elevator type a stationary share undercuts the layer of soil and the rod-link elevator loosens it and sifts the soil. In the riddle type the share vibrates with the first sieve of the riddle. Most of the soil is sifted by the elevator or fiddle screen. The bulk matter coming from the sifting elements goes to the clod breaker, whose vacuum tanks break up clods. The pulverized soil is sifted through the screens of the riddle, and the remaining material goes to the rod-link conveyor of the top-removing device. The tubers and small impurities fall between the rods of the conveyor, and the tops, with tubers that have not been broken off, and plant residue catch on the rods and, after passing through a pressing conveyor, are thrown into the field behind the combine. While the tops are being pulled between the conveyors, clearing rods cut off the remaining tubers. The tubers and impurities (clods of earth, stolons, and stones) are fed to a table by a drum conveyor and from there to a sorting conveyor where workers remove them manually and place them on the waste conveyor, which throws the stones and clods into the field. From the sorting conveyor the tubers go to the loading elevator, which feeds them into a bin with a moving bottom. When the bin is filled, the tubers go to the bed of a self-loading trailer or are loaded into a dump truck.

The potato harvesting combine can be used to harvest potatoes on sandy, sandy loam, and light loam soils that are not stony (stones obstruct the machine). The riddle-type version can also be used on stony soils if the stones are small. The productivity of the combine is 0.2–0.42 hectares per hr; its operating speed is 1.3–4.0 km/hr. It is operated by a tractor driver and four to five workers.

Potato harvesting combines are used extensively in foreign countries. Examples include the Weimar machine in the German Democratic Republic, which has various modifications for harvesting potatoes planted with 62.5–70 cm interrow spaces; the one-row and two-row potato harvesting combines used in the Federal Republic of Germany for harvesting potatoes planted with interrow spaces up to 75 cm; and the Super Duplex combine in Great Britain. The operation of these machines is similar to that of the Druzhba potato harvesting combine. [11–1435–1]

POTATO PLANTER, a machine for planting potato tubers and simultaneously applying mineral fertilizers to the soil. Tubers (either whole or cuttings) weighing 30–50, 50–80, or 80–120 grams can be planted in rows with interrow spacings of 60 and 70 cm. Ridges can be formed (ridge planting), or level-field planting can be done.

The USSR produces two-row (SRN-2) and four-row (SN-4B, SN-4B-1) planters. A six-row (SKM-6) planter has been built, as has the KSN-90 planter, which makes 90-cm interrow spacings. The working parts of the SN-4B planter are bins, cup-disc planters, shares with disc elements for covering the furrow, and fertilizer spreading devices. Each bin of the potato planter has an auger that feeds the tubers to the planter, an agitator, and shakers. The working parts of the planter are driven by a power takeoff shaft of a tractor. Productivity is 1.08–1.36 hectares (ha) per hr for the SN-4B, 1.08–1.77 ha per hr for the SN-4B-1, 1.51–2.05 ha per hr for the SKM-6, and 0.54–0.88 ha per hr for the SRN-2.

When the planter is operating, the agitator and shakers move the tubers along the slanted bottom of the bin to the feeding scoop, where they are caught by the cups of the planter and thrown into the opener. At the same time fertilizers from the fertilizer spreader enter the opener. From the opener the tubers and the fertilizer go into the furrow, which is then covered with dirt by the covering devices (twin discs for ridge planting and small harrows for level-field planting).

Two-row and four-row potato planters of various designs are common abroad. Manual placement of tubers in the pockets of the planting device is widely used. Planters with automatic placement and planting are also used. The planting devices of such planters usually take the form of moving chains of cups or a vertical disc with cup catches. [11–1432–2]

POTATO RIOTS, a mass antiserfdom movement in Russia of the *udel* peasants [those on lands belonging to the imperial family] in 1834 and the state peasants from 1840 to 1844.

The forcible measures accompanying the introduction of the sowing of potatoes provoked the disturbances; the peasants' best land was chosen for potatoes, they were subjected to severe penalties for failure to observe the directions of the authorities, and various requisitions were imposed on them. In 1834 riots flared up in the *udel* estates of Viatka and Vladimir provinces, but the movement assumed its broadest scope among the state peasants from 1840 to 1844, being simultaneously a response to the potato measures and to the reform of the state countryside carried out by P. D. Kiselev (1837–41).

More than 500,000 peasants arose in the provinces of the North, the Ural area, and the Middle and Lower Volga areas alone. They destroyed the potatoes that had been planted, beat officials, elected village elders (*starosty* and *starshiny*) who lacked proper endorsement by the authorities, and launched armed attacks on the punitive brigades. Cheremis, Chuvashes, Udmurts, Tatars, and Komi joined in the movement with the Russians. The government hurled troops into the drive to suppress the rebels. In a number of places, military executions of peasants

were carried out. Thousands of insurgents were brought to trial and were exiled to Siberia or conscripted as soldiers.

REFERENCES
Tokarev, S. V. *Krest'ianskie kartofel'nye bunty.* Kirov, 1939.
Druzhinin, N. M. *Gosudarstvennye krest'iane i reforma P. D. Kiseleva,* vol. 2. Moscow, 1958. Pages 456–524.
Krest'ianskoe dvizhenie v Rossii v 1826–1849 gg.: Sb. dok-tov. Moscow, 1961. Pages 248–55, 407–524.   V. A. FEDOROV [11–1443–3]

POTATO SORTER, a machine for separating (sorting) potato tubers into three groups; removing dirt, clods, and stones; and picking out planting material and damaged tubers. The USSR produces the RKS-10 sorter. It has a roller-type sorting surface; the smooth rollers remove dirt and plant remains from the bulk matter while the shaped rollers (arranged in pairs and forming shaped holes) separate the tubers into small (20–40 g), medium (40–80 g), and large (more than 80 g) ones. Tubers weighing less than 20 g are expelled by the rollers. There are chutes beneath to guide potatoes in each group to conveyors that pour them into containers or into the beds of trucks. The working parts of the potato sorter can be driven by an internal combustion engine, an electric motor, or a tractor's power takeoff shaft. Productivity of the sorter is 10 tons per hour. [11–1433–2]

POTATO-SORTER ASSEMBLY, a complex of machinery and equipment used for removing foreign matter from machine-harvested potatoes and separating the tubers into small (20–40 g), medium (40–80 g), and large (more than 80 g) ones. The USSR produces the KSP-15 sorter assembly. It consists of a receiving bin with a loading conveyor, a roller-type sorter, a 3.3-kW (4.5 hp) internal combustion engine for driving the working parts, and a set of portable rails with carts. Containers for the sorted tubers are mounted in the carts. The working parts of the potato sorter assembly may be driven by a tractor's power takeoff shaft or by a 2.8-kW electric motor. The productivity of the assembly is 15 tons per hour. A sorter assembly used in combination with a harvesting combine completely mechanizes the harvesting of potatoes. [11–1433–1]

POTATO WASHER, a machine for removing dirt, tops, straw, stones, and the like from potatoes.

Potato washers are used at alcohol, starch-molasses, and other enterprises that process potatoes. They are steel or concrete troughs with semicylindrical bottoms and high sides. A shaft with paddles is installed inside, and a bar grate is set at a certain height above the bottom of the trough. A constant stream of water enters the trough at the unloading end and fills it to the level of the waste gutter. The potatoes are fed into the loading end of the washer by a hydraulic conveyor or other method and are gradually pushed forward against the flow of water by the rotating paddles. As they move toward the unloading end, the dirt, heavy impurities (stones, sand), and light impurities (straw, chips) are removed. Productivity is up to 1,000 tons of potatoes every 24 hours. [11–1432–1]

PRE-ARAL KARAKUM (from Turkic *kara kum;* literally, "black sand"), a sandy desert northeast of the Aral Sea in the Kazakh SSR. Area, approximately 35,000 sq km.

The Pre-Aral Karakum is characterized topographically by basin-hummocky and barchan-hummocky undulating plains alternating with small lakes and solonchaks in fluvial depressions, derived chiefly from the overwinnowing of ancient alluvium. The climate is markedly continental; the mean January temperature ranges from −12° to −14°C; the July temperature, from 24° to 26°C (absolute maximum, 42°C; absolute minimum, −42°C). Precipitation averages between 100 and 150 mm per year. The vegetation is *erkek (Agropirum sibiricum)*–white wormwood and *erkek*–green wormwood on the slightly undulating plains and psammophilous on the hummocky and barchan-hummocky sands (calligonum, giant lyme grass, wormwoods). In the lowlands, where fresh groundwaters are nearby, there are beds of *Elaeagnus* and willow together with mesophilic grasses, such as reed. There is pastureland for small livestock, cattle, horses and camels. Water is supplied from draw wells and artesian wells.

REFERENCE
Peschanye pustyni Severnogo Priaral'ia i puti ikh osvoeniia. Alma-Ata, 1950.   [11–1155–1]

PRIMER, a thin metal or plastic cap equipped with a percussion charge (mostly mercury fulminate).

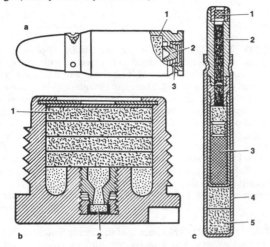

Figure 1. (a) Primer in a live cartridge: (1) powder charge, (2) anvil, (3) primer; (b) in a primer sleeve: (1) compacted powder cake, (2) primer; (c) in a blasting cap: (1) primer, (2) time fuse, (3) detonator, (4) case, (5) auxiliary detonator

The primer was invented by the Englishman J. Egg in 1818. Primers are divided into percussion (blasting) caps and detonators. The percussion cap is used in small arms cartridges and artillery ammunition (in igniters and fuses) for igniting charges. The detonating cap is designed to excite detonation and is used in blasting work and in artillery ammunition fuses, hand grenades, and mines. The primer is activated by the impact or prick of a firing pin, or by fire, and requires special precautions during handling. Primers are also used in hunting ammunition.

[11–1085–1]

PRINCELY TREASURY (*kazna kniazheskaia*). **(1)** The chancellery, archive, and depository for the valuables of the grand and appanage princes.

Ukases were written, charters compiled, current correspondence maintained, and inquiries answered at the treasury. The Princely Treasury of the Moscow grand princes was located in the Treasury Yard of the Kremlin. Prior to the organization of the Posol'skii Prikaz (Foreign Office), the treasurers in charge of the Princely Treasury played a noticeable role in ambassadorial affairs. Toward the middle of the 15th century, the Princely Treasury took on the status of a central financial department. Documents preserved in the treasury were the basis for the "tsar's archive" and for other state archives compiled in the 16th century.

(2) A term once used to designate the total property resources of the state.

REFERENCE
Leont'ev, A. K. *Obrazovanie prikaznoi sistemy upravleniia v Russkom gosudarstve.* Moscow, 1961.   [11–527–4]

PRIVATEER. (1) A privately owned ship specially armed and allowed by a government to engage in military action against enemy ships. Privateers were known from the 15th to the 18th century in various European and American states.

(2) A private individual who has received special permission from the government to engage in privateering.   [11–1019–1]

PRIVATEERING, maritime military operations by privately owned vessels with special government permits (letters of marque) to seize and destroy ships of the enemy and of neutral countries engaged in shipping for an enemy country.

Privateering was especially widespread in the Middle Ages. Initially, private persons exercised the right to seize and prey upon enemy ships without any special permit; subsequently states used privateering as a means of waging maritime war, regulating it by a definite procedure. Privateering licenses were issued by the state to its own citizens as well as to citizens of neutral countries. The privateers obligated themselves to furnish guarantees in case the state had to idemnify victims of unlawful robbery of ships belonging to neutral countries; a procedure was established to halt and search ships. A seized ship was escorted to a port belonging to the state that issued the privateering license, where a hearing on the legality of the privateer's action was held. Privateering without a license or by ships not mentioned in the given license was considered piracy.

In practice, privateering almost always turned into piracy and had an especially adverse effect on the development of trade. In the late 18th century a campaign began to prohibit privateering completely. The first legislative attempt to prohibit privateering was made in France in 1792. In the same period a number of treaties were signed among individual states containing provisions to waive the right of privateering. At the Paris Congress of 1856 a declaration was signed prohibiting privateering.

According to contemporary international law, a ship that is not a warship which engages in military actions against an enemy commercial or military ship is considered a pirate, with all ensuing consequences provided for in international conventions.   [11–1019–3]

PROBATIONARY PERIOD, a period of time stipulated in the Rules of the CPSU for those joining the party. The period is required for the prospective members "to familiarize themselves more fully with the Program and the Rules of the CPSU and to prepare to join the party as a full member. Party organizations must assist the candidate to prepare to join the CPSU and must check the personal qualities of the candidate" (*Ustav KPSS,* 1971, sec. 14).

The probationary period was introduced by the party rules adopted at the Eighth All-Russian Conference of the RCP (Bolshevik) in 1919, when the sharp increase in the number of those wishing to join the party created the need to regulate the acceptance of new members. The minimum probationary period for workers and peasants was set at two months; for others, it was six months. The Twelfth All-Russian Conference of the RCP (B) in 1922 established three different minimum probationary periods: six months for workers and Red Army men of worker or peasant origin; one year for peasants (except for Red Army men) and handicraftsmen not exploiting the labor of others; and two years for other categories (office employees). Former members of other parties had to pass through a two-year probation, regardless of their social status (class). The Fourteenth Congress of the ACP (Bolshevik) in 1925 defined the probationary period for the second category as not less than one year and for the third category as not less than two years.

The Seventeenth Congress of the ACP(B), in 1934, established a probation of one year for industrial workers with an industrial work record (experience) of not less than five years and a two-year probation for all other categories except for former members of other parties, who irrespective of their social class had to pass through a three-year probation. The Eighteenth Congress of the ACP(B), in 1939, recognizing that the victory of socialism in the USSR had led to radical changes in the class composition of the country, abolished the division into categories and established a single probationary period of one year. The congress retained the previous rules for former members of other parties.

In the extraordinary conditions of the Great Patriotic War of 1941–45, the Central Committee of the ACP(B) in December 1941 permitted the political bodies of the Red Army to accept servicemen who had distinguished themselves in battle as members of the party after a three-month probation. The Nineteenth Congress of the CPSU, in 1952, preserving the single probationary period of one year, granted primary party organizations the right to extend the probationary period for a term of not more than one year for those candidates who had valid reasons for not having demonstrated their worth in the first probation year. In 1961 the Twenty-second Congress of the CPSU did not include in the party rules the clauses on the possibility of extending probation or those on special probationary periods for former members of other political parties.

The procedure for admitting candidates for membership in the CPSU is the same as that for admitting members of the party. Candidates have the same obligations as do members of the CPSU, but they enjoy the right of a consultative vote, do not participate in voting, and are not elected to the party bodies. During their probation, candidates fulfill party assignments and become accustomed to participation in party affairs. V. I. Lenin demanded that the probation be "a serious test and not an empty formality' (*Poln. sobr. soch.*, 5th ed., vol. 45, p. 18). On the expiration of the probationary period, the primary party organization considers and decides the question of admitting the candidate to membership in the CPSU.

A. N. ZAKHARIKOV [11–961–2]

PUN, a stylistic turn of phrase or the epigram of a particular author based on the humorous use of the identical sound of words that have different meanings, of words or phrases that have similar sounds, or of different meanings of the same word or phrase. Some of the forms of puns are as follows:

(1) Juxtaposition of homonyms:

OPTIMISTENKO: *. . . U vas est' zakliuchenie?* (Are you finished?; Have you reached a finding?)

WOMAN PETITIONER: *Net, batiushka, nel'zia emu zakliuchenie davat'. . . . Mozhno, govoriat, ego na nedeliu zakliuchit', a ia chego, batiushka, kushat'-to budu?* (No, sir, he can't be confined. . . . If he's confined for a week, say, what will I eat meanwhile?)

V. V. Mayakovsky, *The Bathhouse*

[The pun is on the two meanings of the noun *zakliuchenie* and the verb *zakliuchit'*, which may mean "finding" and "to find" or "imprisonment" and "to imprison," respectively.]

(2) Sound similarity of words in a narrow context:

Na vsiakogo zaveduiushchego est' svoi zaviduiushchii. (Every director has one who envies him.)

E. Krotkii, *Unwritten Fragments*

[The similarity of the words *zaveduiushchii*, "director," and *zaviduiushchii*, "one who envies," is used.]

(3) Contrast of homophones:

Priiatno polaskat' ditia ili sobaku, no vsego neobkhodimee poloskat' rot. (It's nice to pet a child or dog, but to wet one's whistle is even more important.)

Koz'ma Prutkov, *Thoughts and Aphorisms*

[The words *polaskat'*, "to pet" or "to caress," and *poloskat'*, "to rinse" or "to wet one's whistle," have virtually identical pronunciation.]

(4) Juxtaposition of homographs:

Ia priekhal v Moskvu, plachú i pláchu. (I came to Moscow, and now I'm paying and crying.)

P. A. Viazemskii, letter to V. F. Viazemskaia, May 31, 1854

[The stress is the only means of distinguishing *plachú*, "I pay," and *pláchu*, "I cry."]

(5) Breakdown of set phrases and imparting a new meaning to them:

On nes vzdor, no nes ego v zhurnaly. (He talked nonsense but took it to the newspapers.)

E. Krotkii, *Unwritten Fragments*

[The verb *nesti* is used here first in a figurative meaning, in *nesti vzdor*, "to talk nonsense," and then in its literal meaning, "to carry," "to take."]

(6) Various meanings of the same word or phrase:

Est' p'esy nastol'ko slabye, chto ne mogut soiti so stseny. (There are plays so weak that they cannot leave the stage.)

S. J. Lec, *Unkempt Thoughts*

[The word *slabyi*, which in the context would normally mean "of low quality," is taken in its literal meaning, "weak."]

(7) Jocular etymologizing:

—*Khochesh' chaiu, Nikanor? . . .* (Want some tea, Nikanor? . . .)

—*Net, spasibo, ia uzhe otchaialsia.* (No thanks, I've already fallen into despair.)

E. Petrov, *The Jokester*

[Here a new, impossible meaning, "to have had enough tea,"

is made up for the verb *otchaiat'sia*, "to despair," based on its sound similarity to *chai*, "tea."]

The use of the pun in conveying a thought imparts to it particular expressiveness, emotional coloring, and entertaining quality, enhancing the humorous or satirical effect.

REFERENCE
Shcherbina, A. A. *Sushchnost' i iskusstvo slovesnoi ostroty (kalambura).* Kiev, 1958.

A. I. FIURSTENBERG [11–561–3]

PYGMY JERBOAS, rodents of the family Dipopidae. The body length measures up to 5.5 cm. Covered with sparse hair, the tail sometimes has a thin tuft on the end and is often greatly thickened (by fat storage). There are two genera—*Cardiocranius* (five-toed pygmy jerboas) with one species and *Salpingotus* (three-toed pygmy jerboas) with five species. Pygmy jerboas live in the deserts of Middle and Central Asia and Pakistan and, perhaps, in southern Afghanistan. In the USSR, the Satunin's pygmy jerboa (*Cardiocranius paradoxus*) is found in southern Tuva and in the vicinity of Lake Balkhash. Two species of the genus *Salpingotus* dwell in southeastern Kazakhstan and in Karakalpakia (in the Aral Region of the Karakum). The most common is the fat-tailed pygmy jerboa (*Salpingotus crassicauda*). [11–1302–2]

PYGMY SQUIRRELS, rodents of the family Sciuridae, belonging to four genera. The true pygmy squirrel (*Nannosciurus*) is represented by five (according to some sources, six) species. The length of the body measures 7.5–11.5 cm. The tail is thin and flattened, and the ears are short. The fur is soft, short, and of brownish color, with occasional black and white markings on the sides of the head. Pygmy squirrels dwell in the tropical forests of the Indo-Malay archipelago, western Africa, and South America, living in mountains to elevations of 1,650 m. They lead a semiarboreal way of life, much like chipmunks. The best-known species is the Malay pygmy squirrel, *N. exilis*.

[11–1299–2]

PYGMY WHALE (*Caperea marginata*), a mammal of the family Balaenidae. It measures up to 6.4 m long. The color of the body is black, sometimes with a white stripe on the abdomen. An extremely rare animal, the pygmy whale is found only in the temperate and cold waters of the southern hemisphere, most often near Australia and New Zealand. Its way of life has not been studied. [11–1302–5]

QAANI, HABIBOLLAH. Born 1808 in Shiraz; died 1854 in Tehran. Persian poet.

Qaani was the son of a writer. He wrote poetry in Arabic as well as Persian; approximately 22,000 of his poems have been preserved. He also wrote the prose work *Book of the Confused*. Qaani's divan includes mostly *qasidas* (odes). His panegyrics were hyperbolical. He was a member of the *baz-gasht* ("return") literary movement. Qaani had a masterly command of poetic technique; he introduced neologisms and permitted unusual word usage and violation of meter.

WORKS
Divan-e hakim-e Qaani-ye Shirazi. Edited and with a foreword by Mohammad Mahjub. Tehran, A.H. 1336 (A.D. 1957).
REFERENCES
Bertel's, E. E. "Avtobiografiia Kaani." *Doklady AN SSSR, seriia V,* 1927.
Kubičková, V. *Qaani, poète persane du XIX siècle.* Prague, 1954.

[11–244–4]

QADDAFI, MUAMMAR AL-. Born 1940, in Sirte. Libyan politician and statesman; colonel in the armed forces.

In 1965 Qaddafi graduated as a lieutenant from a military school. He then continued his training in Great Britain (1966) and achieved the rank of captain. One of the founders of the organization of "free officers," he took part in the revolutionary coup of Sept. 1, 1969, which overthrew the monarchy in Libya and established the Libyan Arab Republic (LAR). Qaddafi was named chairman of the Council of the Revolutionary Command. Since January 1970 he has also served as chairman of the National Council of Defense and commander in chief of the Libyan armed forces. From January 1970 to July 1972 he occupied the post of prime minister as well. [11–368–2]

QADI (Arabic, "judge"; in Persian and Turkish, *qazi*). In Muslim countries, a judge whose decisions are based on Islamic law (Sharia). In the Middle Ages the *qadi* was also a notary and cared for orphans or assigned them to guardians; he also saw to the execution of sentence in civil and criminal cases. In the 19th and early 20th century, with the development of the new civil courts, the *qadi's* function was limited to the deciding of questions involving family and religious law, and occasionally inheritance. In several Muslim countries (for example, Egypt, Tunisia, and Turkey) the office of *qadi* was eliminated when Sharia courts were abolished (in Turkey, in the 1930's; and in Egypt and Tunisia, in the 1950's). [11–374–5]

QAFZAH, a hill near Nazareth (Israel) on the slopes of which skeletons of ancient people were discovered in a cave (in 1933–35 and 1965–67). Two of the skeletons were in the level with Upper Paleolithic stone tools and eight were in an older level, dating from the end of the Lower Paleolithic. The latter are the more interesting. Their skulls are elongated and large with strongly developed superciliary arches, a high fornix, and a rounded occiput. The lower jaw is massive but with a developed chin. The people of Qafzah probably lived 50,000 to 60,000 years ago. The combination of a physical type resembling that of modern man and a relatively primitive culture has given rise to discussion on the place in evolution of the people of Qafzah. Some scholars consider them to be paleoanthropoids; others feel that they are ancient representatives of modern man.

REFERENCE
Poginskii, Ia. Ia. "Palestinskie i blizkie im formy gominid." In the collection *Iskopaemye gominidy i proiskhozhdenie cheloveka.* Moscow, 1966. [11–1627–1]

QAJARS. (1) A Turkic tribe in Iran, numbering about 25,000 (1970, estimate). The Qajars are concentrated in the Khazar-Jarib Valley in Mazandaran and the neighboring mountainous region in Gorgan. Some Qajars live in Tehran and certain other cities. In the late 18th century the Qajars increased in strength; from among them came the Qajar dynasty.

(2) A dynasty in Persia, which ruled from 1796 to 1925. On Oct. 31, 1925, the Fifth Majlis passed a resolution deposing the Qajar dynasty, and on December 12 it established the Pahlavi dynasty. [11–374–2]

QALAM (Arabic, from the Greek *kalamos,* "reed"), a reed pen. The *qalam* has been used for writing since ancient times. In the nations of the medieval East that used the Arabic alphabet, there were various methods of cutting, sharpening, and splitting the reed for various types of writing. In medieval Eastern treatises, a paintbrush was also called a *qalam.* [11–560–3]

QAMISHLI, AL-, a city in northern Syria, near the border with Turkey. Population, 31,100 (1967). It is a terminus of the Latakia–Aleppo–Al-Qamishli railroad line, which was under construction in 1972 with the assistance of the USSR. It is the center of an agricultural and petroleum-extraction region. The city has a steam power plant. [11–859–6]

QASHQAI, a confederation of Turkic-speaking tribes, the largest of which are the Dareshuri, Shishbuluki, Kashkuli, Amaleh, and Farsimadan, living in the Fars region of Iran. They number more than 350,000 (1970, estimate) and are Muslims. About half the Qashqai are nomads, the rest having adopted a settled way of life. The chief occupation of the nomadic Qashqai is livestock breeding; some agriculture is also practiced, and carpet weaving is well developed. The settled Qashqai are primarily farmers. Feudal relations with vestiges of the patriarchal clan system and tribal organization survive among the Qashqai. Until the mid-20th century the Qashqai tribal confederation was headed by a hereditary *ilkhani,* and the tribes and tribal subdivisions were ruled by *kalantars* and *katkhoda,* who were subject to the *ilkhani.* The Qashqai are developing into a single nationality.

REFERENCE
Narody Perednei Azii. Moscow, 1957. [11–1660–2]

QASIDA, a poetic genre in the literature of the peoples of the Middle East and Central and South Asia.

The qasida is a panegyric ode in praise of an influential person. Its formal characteristics are considerable size (from 20 to 200 bayts), a single end rhyme (*aa, ba, ca, da . . .*), and three-part composition. According to medieval canon, the qasida opens with the *nasib,* or lyrical prelude, in which the author mourns his separation from his beloved. It is followed by a description of the poet's journey to the figure being praised. The main, and last, part is the poet's tribute. Philosophical qasidas developed in the 11th and 12th centuries. The fact that the mention of an influential person is indispensible and often coupled with dates and historical events makes qasidas an important historical source. The most outstanding masters of the genre were the Arab poets Imru al-Qays (sixth century) and Abu Tammam (ninth century), the Persian-Tajik poets Unsuri and Anvari (11th century), and the Azerbaijani poet Khagani (12th century).

REFERENCES
Krachikovskii, I. Iu. "Arabskaia poeziia." *Izbr. soch.,* vol. 2. Moscow, 1956.
Bertel's, E. E. *Istoriia persidsko-tadzhikskoi literatury.* Moscow, 1960.
N. B. KONDYREVA [11–1525–5]

QASIM ALI, Qasim ibn Ali. Years of birth and death unknown. Miniaturist; student of Behzad; member of the Herat school.

Qasim worked in the late 15th and early 16th century in the court *Ketab-khaneh* (workshop for making manuscript books and book depository) of Sultan Husayn Baykara. The works of Qasim Ali—for example, the miniatures executed during the 1520's for the 1433 manuscript of *Ahsan al-qibar* by Mohammad al-Hoseyn al-Varamini, now in the Saltykov-Shchedrin Public Library, Leningrad—are marked by a genre treatment of the subject matter, an attempt at individual characterization of the figures, an abundance of color, and a virtuoso drawing technique.

REFERENCE
Persidskie miniatiury XIV–XVII vv.: [Al'bom]. With an introductory article by O. F. Akimushkin and A. A. Ivanov. Moscow, 1968. Pages 15–17, 20–22. [11–1475–1]

QASR AL-KHAYR AL-GHARBI, an Arab castle east of Homs in Syria. The castle was built in 727, and its ruins are preserved. The castle is a typical example of the architectural structures built by the Umayyads in the desert: it is square in plan, with dwelling and housekeeping quarters symmetrically located around a court and with an outer wall having a majestic entrance and towers that are semicircular in plan. Within the castle were found frescoes, stucco reliefs, and fragments of sculpture (all now in the National Museum in Damascus). Late classical traditions are combined in the decorations with an inclination for ornamentality and flatness. The decorative works are unique examples of the fine arts of the Arabic Middle Ages.

REFERENCE
Schlumberger, D. *Les Fouilles de Qasr el-Heir el-Gharbi.* [Paris, 1939.] [11–1493–2]

QASR-E SHIRIN, a city in southwestern Iran, located in the *ostan* (province) of Kermanshahan, near the border with Iraq, on the Tehran-Baghdad highway. Population, 16,000. Qasr-e Shirin is an important trade and transportation center of a petroleum-producing region. [11–1494–1]

QATAR, a state in western Asia, on the Qatar peninsula, in the eastern part of the Arabian peninsula. Qatar is washed by the Persian Gulf. It is bounded in the south by Saudi Arabia and the United Arab Emirates. It was a protectorate of Great Britain until Sept. 1, 1971. The area is 22,000 sq km. The population is 130,000 (1971). The capital is the city of Doha.

Qatar is an absolute monarchy, and the head of state is the sheikh. A temporary constitution, adopted on Apr. 2, 1970, was put into effect in July 1970.

Natural features. Most of the shores are low and flat, and some sections are sharply jagged with gulfs and framed by coral reefs. The surface, composed mainly of limestones, is a low-lying, stony, and occasionally marshy plain. The country is rich in deposits of natural gas and petroleum. Qatar has a desert climate. The annual precipitation is about 100 mm; the average January temperature is about 16°C, the average July temperature about 32°C, and the maximum temperature about 45°C. There are no permanent rivers and many dry beds. Qatar has desert vegetation, with few oases.

Population. The local Arab population numbers about 60,000 (1970 estimate); the remaining population is composed of immigrants from other Arab countries, Iran, India, and Pakistan. About 7,000 Africans also live in the country. The official language is Arabic. The majority of the local population are Wahhabi Muslims. The Muslim calendar (Hejira) and the Gregorian calendar are used.

From 1963 to 1970 the average population increase was 5.3 percent a year; this was the result of intensive immigration caused by the development of the economy, primarily in petroleum extraction. Of the 50,000 in the economically active population, agriculture accounted for 1,800 people. Most of the workers are employed in petroleum extraction (about 5,000 persons), road and building construction, and municipal services. The majority of the population is settled (in the oases, along the coast, and in the petroleum regions); an insignificant number of people are nomads. The population density is about 6 persons per sq km (1971). About 80 percent of the population lives in the region of Doha. The urban population was about 70 percent in 1970. The major cities are Doha (population about 90,000 in 1971), Dukhan, and Umm Said.

Historical survey. The Qatar peninsula was settled as early as the third or second millennium B.C. The first reference to Qatar is found in the work of the Roman writer Pliny the Elder in the first century A.D. Qatar was repeatedly conquered by the Sassanids. Incorporated into the Arab caliphate in the seventh century, Qatar was part of the state of the Karmathians after the collapse of the caliphate in the tenth century and was under the rule of the emirs of Bahrain in the 13th and 14th centuries. In the early 16th century Bahrain and Qatar were seized by the Portuguese and later by the Ottoman Turks. In the 17th century Qatar became the object of contention between Iran, Turkey, and the chiefs and rulers of various Arab tribes, of Oman, and of the Saudis. In the second half of the 18th century a small principality arose in the territory of Qatar, led by the Thani dynasty of the al-Thani tribe, which united all of Qatar in the late 19th century. The state was characterized by feudal relations, with survivals of slavery and a clan and tribal organization.

In 1868, Great Britain interfered in the strife between the rulers of Bahrain and Qatar and imposed an unequal treaty on Qatar. In 1871, Qatar was again occupied by the Ottoman Empire, and a Turkish governor (pasha) became the formal ruler of Qatar. Sheikh Kasem bin Muhammad al-Thani, who reigned from 1878 to 1913, is considered the founder of the principality of Qatar. He united the warring tribes and pursued a relatively independent policy with respect to Turkey. In 1914, Turkey renounced its rights to Qatar in favor of Great Britain. On Nov. 3, 1916, the latter imposed on Qatar a treaty establishing a British protectorate over Qatar. In 1935 the Anglo-French-American-Dutch company Petroleum Development of Qatar (changed to Qatar Petroleum Company in the 1960's) obtained concessions for prospecting and extracting petroleum in Qatar for 75 years. The extraction of petroleum began after World War II.

In the 1930's the policy of the British colonialists and the native ruling circles led to uprisings of individual tribes in the interior regions of Qatar and to protest demonstrations in big population centers. The liberation movement gained strength after World War II, culminating in demonstrations in defense of Egypt during the British, French, and Israeli aggression against Egypt in 1956. In the conditions of extreme backwardness of social and economic relations, the main forces of the national liberation movement in Qatar were the urban poor, small traders and artisans, former slaves (slavery was officially abolished only in 1952), the poorer sections of the tribes, and immigrants who had come to work in the petroleum fields. In 1960 mass popular demonstrations took place in the capital of Qatar; Emir Al ibn Abdullah ibn Kasem al-Thani, who pursued a reactionary despotic policy, was deposed and Sheikh Ahmad ibn Ali al-Thani became the ruler of Qatar; in February 1972 he was replaced by Khalifa bin Hammad al-Thani. The middle of 1963 saw a general strike of blue-collar and white-collar workers, who demanded equality of the whole population before the law, the removal of foreigners from government posts, agrarian reforms, and the democratization of the regime. The first petroleum workers' trade union was established in 1966, and political organizations arose in the 1960's, demanding the strengthening of relations with other countries of the Arab East.

In view of the growing liberation and democratic movement, the ruling elite of Qatar began implementing some reforms, such as setting up a public health and education system. Qatar came out in support of Arab solidarity, condemned the Israeli aggression against the Arab countries in 1967, and allocated funds for the aid of Palestinian Arabs. In 1968, Qatar, Bahrain, and the principalities of Trucial Oman attempted to set up the Federation of Persian Gulf Emirates.

A provisional constitution of Qatar was adopted on Apr. 2, 1970, and the first Qatari government of ten ministers, seven of them of the Thani family, was formed on May 29, 1970. On Sept. 1, 1971, Qatar was proclaimed an independent state. At the same time, it concluded a new friendship treaty with Great Britain, providing for the maintenance of "traditional relations" between Qatar and that country. In September 1971, Qatar became a member of the UN and the Arab League. Most countries have recognized Qatar; the USSR did so on Sept. 8, 1971.

L. N. KOTLOV

Press, radio, and television. The press of Qatar in 1974 was represented by the English-language weekly *Gulf News* founded in 1970 and the Arabic-language weekly *Al Uruba* founded in 1969, both published in Doha, and the Arabic-language monthly magazine *Al Doha.* Radio and television broadcasting is run by the government. The radio broadcasting service was founded in 1968, with programs in Arabic and English, and television broadcasting began in 1970. The television station is located in Doha.

Economy. Qatar is economically underdeveloped. The traditional occupation of the population is agriculture, in which feudal relations coexist with clan survivals. In the 1950's and 1960's the petroleum-extracting industry, which is controlled by foreign capital, became the main branch of the economy. The prospecting and exportation of petroleum resources have been conducted by the Anglo-French-American-Dutch company Qatar Petroleum (on land), the Anglo-Dutch company Shell of Qatar (in the shelf), and the Japanese company Qatar Oil (since 1971); a state petroleum company was established in April 1972. Petroleum extraction reached 20.5 million tons in 1971. Royalties paid by the petroleum monopolies are the source of most of the national income and of the receipts of the budget. Oil profits amounted to about 70 million pounds sterling in 1971. Crude oil is exported abroad through the Umm Said port, where it arrives along a pipeline from Dukhan. An oil refinery in Umm Said refines some of the oil for domestic consumption. Natural gas, extracted in small amounts, is used as fuel by local electric power plants (which had a capacity of 75,000 kW in 1971), desalinization installations, and a cement plant. A liquified gas plant with a capacity of 750,000 tons of gas per year and a flour milling plant are under construction (1973).

Manufacturing is insignificant, and consumer goods are produced by small handicraft enterprises. In 1969 a cement plant (100,000 tons of cement a year then, and up to 200,000 tons after the expansion) was built near Doha. An artificial fertilizer plant was built in late 1971, and a flour milling plant was under construction in 1973. Agriculture is poorly developed; the oases are sites of cultivation of date palms, millet, maize, and especially vegetables, and camel raising is the main occupation in the desert. Fishing and pearl gathering are practiced along the coast. In 1970–71 more than 500 tons of shrimps and 100 tons of fish were caught. There are no railroads. Qatar has more than 1,000 km of paved roads (1971) and 11,000 automobiles (1970). The main ports are Doha and Umm Said, and Ziqrit is a local port without mooring lines. Doha has an international airport.

Qatar exports mainly crude oil (primarily to Western Europe, by foreign companies), and small amounts of cement, pearls, dried fish, shrimps, and dates. It imports food products, primarily rice, fabrics, equipment, and machines, mainly from Great Britain, Japan, the USA, and the Federal Republic of Germany. The monetary unit is a Qatar-Dubayy riyal.

L. N. KOTLOV

Public health. There are no demographic statistics in Qatar. Infectious and parasitic diseases predominate. The population enjoys free medical care. In 1970 there were five hospital institutions with 600 hospital beds, or 4.6 beds per thousand population. Outpatient service is provided by four dispensaries in rural areas and by private practitioners in cities. There were 54 doctors, or one doctor per 2,400 population, and 190 intermediate-level medical personnel. Doctors are trained abroad and intermediate-level personnel take courses of the World Health Organization at the state hospitals. In 1970 public health expenditures constituted only about 5 percent of the state budget.

Education. Until 1952 there were no state general education schools. Children were taught elementary arithmetic, reading, and writing in mosques. The overwhelming majority of the population is illiterate. Education in the schools is sexually segregated; it has been free since 1956 and is based on English programs and textbooks. The public education system is composed of a six-year elementary school, a three-year intermediate school, and a three-year secondary school, which is divided into general education and vocational sections; there are also religious secondary schools. Three-year technical and commercial schools provide vocational and technical training. In the 1969–70 academic year there were 13,700 students in 78 elementary schools, 2,200 students in three intermediate schools, and 1,400 students in secondary general education and vocational and technical schools. In 1970 more than 400 Qatari students studied at higher schools in the Arab countries, Great Britain, and the USA.

A. A. ERSHOV

REFERENCES
Strany Aravii. Moscow, 1964.
Noveishaia istoriia arabskikh stran. Moscow, 1968.
Bodianskii, V., O. Gerasimov, and L. Medvedko. *Kniazhestva Persidskogo zaliva.* Moscow, 1970.
Al-Dabbag, M. M. *Katar-madikha va khadirukha* (Qatar—Its Past and Present). Beirut, 1961.
Qatar Progress. [Series 1] 1962.
Qatar. [Series 1] 1968.   [11–1555–2]

QATTARA DEPRESSION, a waterless depression in the north Libyan Desert in Africa, in Egypt. Area, 19,500 sq km. From the north and the west it is framed by limestone precipices with elevations as high as 100 m; near these precipices are the lowest sections of the bottom lands (133 m below sea level), occupied by salt marshes. To the east and south the bottom gradually rises; clay plains appear along with sand dunes.   [11–1598–2]

QAVAM AL-SALTANA, AHMAD. Born 1879; died 1955 in Tehran. Iranian statesman and political leader.

Qavam was a major landowner in Gilan. He was prime minister in 1921–22, 1922–23, 1942–43, and 1946–47, and from July 18 to July 21, 1952. He helped suppress the Iranian Revolution of 1905–11, the movement for national liberation in Gilan and Khorasan in the 1920's, and the democratic movement in late 1946. He was responsible for the invitations extended by Iran to American financial missions in 1922 and 1942.   [11–314–1]

QAVAMODDIN OF SHIRAZ. Date of birth unknown; died 1440. Persian architect.

Qavamoddin introduced the cupola resting on four strong intersecting arches into Persian architecture. His works include the Mosque of Gowhar Shad in Meshed (1405–18), the Mosalla ensemble (1417–38), and Mausoleum of Abdullah Ansari (1425–1428/29) near Herat, and the *madrasa* (Islamic school) in Khargird (1440).   [11–314–2]

QAYEN, mountains in the Iranian Plateau, in eastern Iran. Length, about 400 km; elevations, to 2,886 m (Mount Mirza Arbab). The mountains consist of several ranges (Kalat, Muminabad, Baqiran, Baran, and others) with a relative elevation of 800–1,000 m above the adjacent desert plains. The mountains are composed primarily of limestone and volcanic rock. The slopes are covered with sparse dry-steppe and desert vegetation.   [11–537–3]

QAZAQ ÄDEBIETĪ (Kazakh literature), a Kazakh literary newspaper, the organ of the Writers' Union of Kazakhstan. Published in Alma-Ata since 1934. The appearance of a Kazakh weekly literary newspaper was an important event in the cultural life of the Kazakh people. *Qazaq ädebietī* publishes articles on literature and art, national culture, life-style, and economics.   [11–417–5]

QAZVIN, or Kazvin, a city in northwestern Iran, near the southern foothills of the Elburz Range, in Tehran Province. Population, 92,000 (1971).

Qazvin has a railroad station and is a highway junction. It is the commercial center for an agricultural region that produces grain, grapes, and pistachios. It has vegetable-oil presses, flour mills, and textile mills and is a major rug-weaving center.

Qazvin has been known since the time of the Sassanids. In the Middle Ages trade routes from Iran to Transcaucasia passed through the city. In 1220 after bitter resistance it was captured by the Mongols and destroyed, but was later restored and became one of the cultural centers of Iran. Qazvin was at its peak in the 16th century, when it was the capital of the Safawid state (1548 to 1597–98). The city gradually lost importance in the 18th century. The Afghan conquest in 1722 led to a major anti-Afghan rebellion (December 1722–January 1723) and to the expulsion of the Afghans from Qazvin.

Two major architectural monuments have been preserved. The main hall of the Mosque of the Congregation dates from 1106–14 and the portal from the 17th century. The Haideriyeh Mosque was built in the early 12th century and is decorated with carved stucco.

REFERENCE
Hannibal, A. *Qazwin—capitale oubliée.* Tehran, 1956.   [11–520–3]

QAZVINI, HAMDALLAH MOSTOWFI. Born in Qazvin, 1281; died c. 1350. Iranian historian and geographer.

An important official under Khan Hulagu, Qazvini served the vizier Rashid al-Din as well. He wrote the *Selected History* (*Tarikh-e gozideh,* 1330), which contains a history of the Mongol *ilkhans* and the local Iranian dynasties, biographies of prominent individuals, and a description of the city of Qazvin. He is also the author of the geographical work *Delectation of the Heart* (*Nuzhat al-qulub,* 1340), an extremely important source for the economic history and geography of Iran and neighboring countries in the 13th and 14th centuries.

REFERENCES
Bartol'd, V. V. *Soch.,* vol. 3. Pages 51–54, 260–63, and elsewhere. (See index.)
Petrushevskii, I. P., "Kamdallakh Kazvini kak istochnik po sotsial'no-ekonomicheskoi istorii vostochnogo Zakavkaz'ia." *Izv. AN SSSR, Otd. obshchestvennykh nauk,* 1937, no. 4, pp. 873–920.
Storey, C. A. *Persian Literature,* part 1, fasc. 1. London, 1935. Pages 81–84.   I. P. PETRUSHEVSKII [11–521–3]

QAZVINI, MIRZA MOHAMMAD ABDULBAHHAB. Born Mar. 30, 1877, in Qazvin; died May 27, 1949, in Tehran. Iranian literary scholar and textologist.

Between 1903 and 1940, Qazvini worked in London, Paris, and Berlin on Persian and Arabic manuscripts in cooperation with noted European Orientalists and mastered European techniques of textual criticism. Characteristic of Qazvini's work is profound knowledge of language and the factual background, scrupulousness, and critical inquiry. He edited and published texts of the *Divan-e Hafez-e Shirazi* (with Q. Ghani), *Al-Mu'jam fi ma'ayiri ash'ari'l-Ajam* of Shams-e Qeys, *Lubab al-Al-bab* of Mohammad Owfi, the *Marzban-nameh* of Sad al-Din Varavini, the *Tarikh-e Jahangusha* of Joveyni, the *Chahar Maqaleh* of Nezami Aruzi, and the *Siyasat-nameh* of Nezam al-Molk. He is also the author of articles on the history of Persian literature.

WORKS AND TEXTS
In the collection *Allameh-ye Qazvini*. Tehran, 1949.
Bist maqaleh-ye Qazvini, parts 1–2. Tehran, 1953–54.   [11–521–2]

QAZVINI, ZAKARIYYA IBN MUHAMMAD, AL-. Born 1203 in Qazvin; died 1283. Arab scholar and writer.

Al-Qazvini is the author of the cosmographic work *Wonders of Creation and Remarkable Things in Existence,* which contains a description of the world in a simple and entertaining form. It is one of the few Arabic books accompanied by illustrations. The second part of the work, "Monuments of Cities and News of People," sometimes considered an independent work, devotes much space to biographies of famous people, including Persian poets.

WORKS
Zakarija Ben Muhammed Ben Muhmud el-Kazwini's Kosmographie, vols. 1–2. Edited by F. Wüstenfeld. Göttingen, 1847–48.
REFERENCES
Krachkovskii, I. Iu. *Izbr. soch.,* vol. 4. Moscow-Leningrad, 1957. Pages 358–66.
Al-Fakhuri, Kh. *Istoriia arabskoi literatury,* vol. 2. Moscow, 1961. Page 306. (Translated from Arabic.)   [11–521–1]

QSL CARD, according to the code used by radio amateur operators, a special card, usually a post card, that confirms that communication was established between radio amateur stations or that their operation was observed.

QSL cards are generally colorfully designed and illustrated. They give the call letters of the radio station and its operator and the address; the date, time, and the frequency band on which the communication (observation) was obtained; the type of operation (voice or Morse code); an evaluation of the clarity, loudness, and quality of the signals; and a brief technical description of the apparatus. The cards are filled out by the radio amateur station operators after completing a conversation or after having received a QSL card from a radio amateur observer who has heard them transmitting. The cards are forwarded by mail through radio clubs. In the Soviet Union, QSL cards are forwarded by the E. T. Krenkel' Central Radio Club of the USSR. In other countries as well, QSL cards are sent out to confirm the reception of radio broadcasting stations.

REFERENCES
Spravochnik korotkovolnovika, 3rd ed. Moscow, 1959.
Kazanskii, I. V. "Tvoi put' v efir." *Radio,* 1970, no. 8.
                                    I. V. KAZANSKII   [11–1444–2]

QUADI, a Germanic tribe that lived north of the middle course of the Danube and along the upper Elbe and Oder rivers in the first century A.D. Between 166 and 180 the Quadi took part in the war of the Marcomanni against Rome, but they were defeated and forced to recognize the supremacy of Rome. They soon regained their freedom but were again subjugated in 375. In the early fifth century some of the Quadi migrated with the Vandals to Spain where they established their own kingdom in the northwestern part of the country, which lasted until it was conquered in 585 by the Visigoths. (The Quadi in Spain are sometimes referred to as the Quado-Suevians and their kingdom as Suevia.)   [11–1680–3]

QUADRANT, in astronomy, an astronomical angle-measuring instrument that was used to measure the altitudes of celestial bodies above the horizon and the angular separations between bodies. A quadrant consisted of a quarter-circle, whose arc was divided into degrees and fractions of a degree, usually mounted in a vertical plane. A straightedge with diopters or a viewing tube usually rotated around the axis passing through the center of the circle and situated perpendicularly to its plane. Large mural quadrants were used in the past at astronomical observatories; these were fixed to stone walls of the building. Quadrants cease to be used at the end of the 17th century.   [11–1673–4]

QUADRANTIDS, a meteor shower with a radiant on the boundary between the constellations Boötes and Draco (on star maps in the early 19th century this region was designated by the constellation Qudrans Muralis). The Quadrantids have been known since 1839. They are observed annually at the end of December and in the beginning of January; on January 3–4, the earth passes through the dense central concentration of the Quadrantid meteor swarm in less than 24 hr. The Quadrantid meteor shower is one of the more active showers.   [11–1674–1]

QUADRATIC EQUATION, an equation of the form $ax^2 + bx + c = 0$, where a, b, and c are any number and are called the coefficients of the equation. A quadratic equation has two roots, which are found by the formulas

$$x_1 = \frac{-b + \sqrt{b^2 - 4ac}}{2a}$$

$$x_2 = \frac{-b - \sqrt{b^2 - 4ac}}{2a}$$

The expression $D = b^2 - 4ac$ is called the discriminant of the quadratic equation. If $D > 0$, then the roots of the quadratic equation are real and unequal; if $D < 0$, then the roots are conjugate complex numbers; if $D = 0$, then the roots are real and equal. The Vièta formulas $x_1 + x_2 = -b/a$ and $x_1 x_2 = c/a$ link the roots and coefficients of a quadratic equation. The left-hand side of a quadratic equation can be expressed in the form $a(x - x_1)(x - x_2)$. The function $y = ax^2 + bx + c$ is called a quadratic trinomial, and its graph is a parabola with the vertex at the point $M(-b/2a;\ c - b^2/4a)$ and axis of symmetry parallel to the y-axis; the direction of the branches of the parabola coincides with the sign of a. The solution of the quadratic equation was already known in geometric form to ancient mathematicians.   [11–1676–3]

QUADRATIC FORM, a second-degree form in n variables $x_1, x_2, \ldots, x_n$, that is, a polynomial of these variables, each term of which contains either the square of one of the variables or the product of two different variables. The general form of a quadratic form for $n = 2$ is

$$ax_1^2 + bx_2^2 + cx_1 x_2$$

and for $n = 3$,

$$ax_1^2 + bx_2^2 + cx_3^2 + dx_1 x_2 + ex_1 x_3 + fx_2 x_3$$

where a, b, $\ldots$, f are any number. An arbitrary quadratic form is written as

$$A(x) = \sum_{i=1}^{n} \sum_{j=1}^{n} a_{ij} x_i x_j$$

where it is assumed that $a_{ij} = a_{ji}$. Quadratic forms in two, three, and four variables are directly connected with the theory of second-order curves (in the plane) and surfaces (in space): in Cartesian coordinates the equation of a centrally symmetric second-order curve or surface has the form $A(x) = 1$, where $A(x)$ is a quadratic form. In homogeneous coordinates the left-hand side of any equation of a second-order curve or surface is a quadratic form. Upon repacement of the variables $x_1, x_2, \ldots, x_n$ by other variables $y_1, y_2, \ldots, y_n$, which are linear combinations of the old variables, a quadratic form transforms into another quadratic form. By means of an appropriate choice of new variables (nonsingular linear transformation), a quadratic form may be reduced to the form of a sum of squares of the variables, multiplied by certain numbers. Moreover, neither the number of squares (the rank of the quadratic form) nor the difference between the number of positive and the number of negative coefficients of the squares (the signature of the quadratic form) depends on the process of reducing the quadratic form to a sum of squares (the Sylvester law of inertia). The indicated reduction may even be accomplished by special (orthogonal) transformations. Such a transformation corresponds geometrically to a reduction of the second-order curve or surface to the principal axes.

If we admit complex variables, then we obtain quadratic forms of the type

$$\sum_{i=1}^{n} \sum_{j=1}^{n} a_{ij} x_i \bar{x}_j$$

where $\bar{x}_j$ is the complex conjugate of x_j. If such a quadratic form assumes only real values (this is true when $a_{ij} = a_{ji}$), then it is called Hermitian. The basic facts that are valid for real quadratic forms hold true for Hermitian forms: the possibility of reduction to a sum of squares, invariance of the rank, and the law of inertia.

REFERENCE
Mal'tsev, A. I. *Osnovy lineinoi algebry*, 3rd ed. Moscow, 1970.
[11–1674–5]

QUADRATIC RESIDUE, a concept in number theory. A number a for which the congruence $x^2 \equiv a \pmod{m}$ has a solution is called a quadratic residue modulo m; in other words, a is a quadratic residue modulo m if for a certain integer x the number $x^2 - a$ is divisible by m; if this congruence has no solution, then a is called a quadratic nonresidue. For example, if $m = 11$, then the number 3 is a quadratic residue, since the congruence $x^2 \equiv 3 \pmod{11}$ has the solutions $x = 5$ and $x = 6$, and the number 2 is a nonresidue, since there do not exist any numbers x that satisfy the congruence $x^2 \equiv 2 \pmod{11}$. Quadratic residues are a particular case of residues of degree n for $n = 2$. If m is equal to an odd prime p, then among the numbers 1, 2, . . . , $p - 1$ there are $(p - 1)/2$ quadratic residues and $(p - 1)/2$ quadratic nonresidues. The Legendre symbol (a/p) is introduced in order to study quadratic residues for a prime modulus p. It is defined as follows: if a is relatively prime to p, then we put $(a/p) = 1$ when a is a quadratic residue and $(a/p) = -1$ when a is a quadratic nonresidue. A fundamental theorem is the law of quadratic reciprocity, which states that if p and q are odd primes, then

$$\left(\frac{p}{q}\right)\left(\frac{q}{p}\right) = (-1)^{[(p-1)/2] \cdot [(q-1)/2]}$$

This relation was discovered about 1772 by L. Euler, a modern formulation was given by A. Legendre, and a complete proof was first given in 1801 by K. Gauss. A convenient generalization of the Legendre symbol is the Jacobi symbol. There are many generalizations of the law of quadratic reciprocity in the theory of algebraic numbers. The distribution of quadratic residues and of the sums of the values of the Legendre symbol has been studied by I. M. Vinogradov and other mathematicians.

REFERENCE
Vinogradov, I. M. *Osnovy teorii chisel.* Moscow, 1972.   [11–1675–3]

QUADRATURE FORMULAS, formulas for approximating definite integrals by means of the values of the integrand at a finite number of points. The most common quadrature formulas have the form

$$\int_a^b f(x)\, dx = A_1 f(x_1) + \cdots + A_n f(x_n) + R_n$$

where $x_1, x_2, \ldots, x_n$ are the nodes of the quadrature formula, $A_1, A_2 \ldots, A_n$ are its coefficients, and R_n is the remainder term. For example,

$$\int_a^b f(x)\, dx = \frac{b-a}{2}\,[f(a) + f(b)] - \frac{(b-a)^2}{12}\,f''(\xi)$$

where $a \le \xi \le b$ (trapezoidal rule). Sometimes formulas for mechanical, or numerical, quadrature are also called quadrature formulas.

REFERENCE
Krylov, V. I. *Priblizhennoe vychislenie integralov*, 2nd ed. Moscow, 1967.
[11–1678–1]

QUADRIGA, an ancient Greek and Roman two-wheeled chariot drawn by four horses, which were harnessed all abreast, and driven by a charioteer in standing position. Light-weight

quadrigae were used in horse racing, which occupied an important place in the Olympics and other public games. Descriptions of these races can be found in Homer, Virgil, and other classical authors. Large quadrigae were used by emperors and victorious military leaders in triumphal processions. Sculptured representations of quadrigae, driven by deities or allegorical figures of glory, happiness, and the like, were used to decorate ancient Greek and Roman buildings. Bas-reliefs depicting quadrigae are often found on ancient Greek and Roman medals, cameos, and intaglios. In the 18th and 19th centuries quadrigae were used to decorate the frontons of large, imposing buildings and triumphal arches in Russia and Western Europe.   11–1678–3]

QUADRILLE. (1) A dance prevalent among many peoples. As a rule, it is written in 2/4 time and consists of five or six figures, each of which has its own name and special musical accompaniment. It came to Russia from France. From the late 17th century to the late 19th, the quadrille was one of the most popular dances of the salon. It also became widespread among the common people, bearing different names; there exist Russian, Ukrainian, Byelorussian, Lithuanian, Latvian, and Estonian quadrilles.

(2) At tournaments, carousels, and the like, a group of four horsemen, usually in costume.   [11–383–1]

QUADRUPOLE, a system of charged particles whose total electric charge and electric dipole moment equal zero.

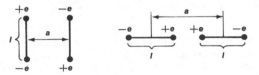

Figure 1. Examples of relative location of dipoles in a quadrupole

A quadrupole can be considered a set of two identical dipoles with the dipole moments equal in magnitude but opposite in direction and separated by a certain distance. At great distances R from the quadrupole, the field intensity of the quadrupole E decreases in inverse proportion to R to the fourth power ($E \sim 1/R^4$). The relationship between E and the charges and their location is described in the general case by a set of five independent values that together constitute the quadrupole moment of the system. The quadrupole moment also determines the energy of a quadrupole in an external electric field. In the case described by Figure 1 the absolute value of the quadrupole moment is equal to $2ela$, where e is the charge, l is the dimension of the dipoles, and a is the distance between the centers of the dipoles. A quadrupole is a second-order multipole.

REFERENCE
Landau, L. D., and E. M. Lifshits. *Teoriia polia*, 5th ed. Moscow, 1967, § 41.   G. IA. MIAKISHEV [11–1679–1]

QUADRUPOLE INTERACTION, the interaction of systems of charged particles widely separated from one another, defined by the presence in the systems of what is called a quadrupole moment. If the electric charge or the dipole moment of a system differs from zero, the quadrupole interaction can usually be neglected.

The energy of quadrupole interactions for atoms (which have no dipole moment) falls off with the distance R by $1/R^5$, while the energy of the interaction of the dipole moments induced in these atoms by their mutual polarization varies with distance by $1/R^6$. Therefore, the quadrupole interaction of atoms is predominant at large distances. The quadrupole moment of atoms can be computed by means of quantum mechanics.

Many atomic nuclei in which the electric charge distribution does not have spherical symmetry have a quadrupole moment. Quadrupole interaction plays an important role in nuclear physics when a nucleus with zero dipole moment is excited by the coulomb field of charged particles bombarding it. Nuclear quadrupole moments are determined experimentally.

G. IA. MIAKISHEV [11–1679–2]

QUAGGA (*Equus quagga*), a species of zebra.

The quagga is found in southern Africa. There are five subspecies, differentiated by color. The quagga proper (*E. quagga quagga*) was distinguished from other zebras in having less strongly developed transverse stripes on its trunk and legs. It became extinct in the wild around 1860, and the last one died in the Amsterdam Zoo in 1883. Other subspecies of quagga have transverse stripes across the entire body. Burchell's quagga (*E. quagga burchelli*) became extinct in 1910. Chapman's zebra (*E. quagga antiquorum*), Selous' zebra (*E. quagga selousi*) and Grant's zebra (*E. quagga boehmi*) are found both in natural conditions and on wildlife preserves.   [11–1673–1]

QUAKERS (originally used in an ironic sense; the Quakers call themselves The Society of Friends), the members of a religious Christian community founded in the mid-17th century in England by the craftsman G. Fox. Quakers reject the institution of the clergy and church sacraments; according to their teachings, man can enter into a direct union with god. They preach pacifism and devote themselves to good works. Persecuted by the English government and by the Anglican Church, many communities of Quakers began emigrating to North America in the 1660's. The status of English and American Quakers was legalized by the Toleration Act of 1689. In the beginning the Quaker movement drew its members from among the petite bourgeoisie, but later capitalist elements appeared among them. In the early 1970's, Quaker communities numbered about 200,000 members, found chiefly in the USA, Great Britain, and East Africa.

[11–1691–1]

QUALIFICATION. (1) The degree and kind of professional training of a worker; his knowledge, ability, and practical skill, necessary for the performance of a certain kind of work. The qualification of a worker is reflected in his tariffing (his being given a certain tariff rating depending on his qualification). The awarding of a tariff rating testifies to the worker's fitness to perform a specific range of duties.

In the USSR, the qualification of workers, as a rule, is established by a special qualification commission in accordance with the requirements of the tariff qualification manual. In addition to the rating, evidence of a worker's qualification may also be his category, or a diploma, title, or academic degree. Some positions can be occupied only if one has a diploma (for example, that of a physician or a teacher). In enterprises, institutions, and organizations in the USSR, a system is created for the teaching and improvement of professional skills among industrial and office workers.

(2) A characteristic of a certain kind of work, determined by the complexity, precision, and responsibility of the work. In the USSR, the qualification of a work is usually defined by a rating according to the tariff qualification manual. The definition of the qualification of a work is important to establish the rate of tariff and wages for workers in given positions. The qualification of engineering work and work performed by white-collar workers and others not directly involved in production is defined by the requirements established for each particular position.

(3) A characteristic of an object or a phenomenon; the attribution of it to a certain category or group, for example, qualification of a crime.   L. F. BIBIK [11–1692–3]

QUALIFICATION OF A CRIME, in criminal law, the establishing and designating in the appropriate procedural acts of the precise correspondence of the features of the act committed to the elements of the crime as provided by the criminal law. The qualification of the crime is the basis for assigning punishment and for other legal consequences of the perpetrated crime. Soviet jurisprudence considers the correct qualification of the crime an important factor in the observance of socialist legality in criminal procedure. The incorrect qualification of a crime, that is, the application of a law that does not conform to the actual circumstances of the case, misrepresents the nature of perpetrated crimes and entails the passing of an erroneous sentence. An error in the qualification of a crime constitutes a ground for reversing or modifying a sentence.   [11–1693–1]

QUALIFIED MAJORITY, an electoral majority of two-thirds, three-fourths, or the like; it differs from a simple majority, which is one vote over 50 percent. A qualified majority is usually required for adoption of the most important resolutions (for example, the introduction of amendments to constitutional laws). The Constitution of the USSR establishes that constitutional amendments by the Supreme Soviet of the USSR require a majority of not less than two-thirds of the votes in each chamber. A qualified majority is also needed for passing the verdict in a trial by jury.

[11–1693–2]

QUALIMETRY, an area of science bringing together various methods for the quantitative evaluation of product quality. The primary objectives of qualimetry are substantiation of a nomenclature for quality indexes, development of methods for determination of indexes for product quality and optimization of such indexes, optimization of standardized sizes and of parametric series of products, development of derivation principles for generalized indexes of quality, and determination of usage conditions for such indexes in standardization tasks and quality control problems. Qualimetry uses such mathematical methods as linear, nonlinear, and dynamic programming; the theory of optimal control; and the theory of mass servicing.

REFERENCE
"Standarty i kachestvo," 1970, no. 11, pp. 30–34.   [11–1692–1]

QUALITATIVE ANALYSIS, the set of chemical, physicochemical, and physical methods used to discover and identify the elements, radicals, ions, and compounds in a substance or mixture of substances under analysis.

Qualitative analysis forms one of the basic divisions of analytical chemistry. The most important features of qualitative analysis techniques are (1) specificity (selectivity), that is, the possibility of discovering an unknown element in the presence of another, and (2) sensitivity, determined by the smallest quantity of an element that can be found in a drop of solution (0.01–0.03 milliliter) by the given method; a sensitivity of 1 μg has been attained by modern techniques.

Classical qualitative analysis of inorganic substances is carried out by either the "dry" method or by the "wet" method. The dry method involves testing for flame coloration with a gas burner and the formation of colored beads (vitreous fusions) when heating the powder from the substance tested (usually a salt or metal oxide) with a small quantity of sodium tetraborate or phosphoric salt ($NaNH_4HPO_4 \cdot 4H_2O$). Wet analysis (in solutions) is effected by macro-, semimicro-, micro-, and ultra-microtechniques. In macroanalysis the quantity of analyzed substance is greater than 100 mg and the volume of solution is greater than 5 ml; in ultramicroanalysis the measurements are less than 0.1 mg and less than 0.05 ml, respectively.

Since the qualitative analysis of inorganic compounds in aqueous solutions is based on ionic reactions, it is divided into the analysis of cations and the analysis of anions. Cations are generally separated into five groups according to the solubility of their sulfur salts. Anions are most often grouped according to the different solubilities of their barium or silver salts. If the analyzed substance is found to contain ions that can be determined by selective reagents, then analysis is carried out using the fractional method.

Along with the classical chemical methods, physical and physicochemical (that is, instrumental) techniques are widely used in qualitative analysis that are based on the study of the optical, electric, magnetic, thermal, catalytic, adsorptive, and other properties of the analyzed substances. These methods have a number of advantages over the chemical techniques, since in many cases they make it possible both to eliminate the preliminary chemical separation of the analyzed sample into its component parts and to record the results of the analysis continuously and automatically. Furthermore, a considerably smaller quantity of analyzed sample is required when using physical and physicochemical methods to determine small amounts of admixtures. These methods include spectral analysis, luminescent analysis, mass spectroscopy, polarography, chromatography, activation analysis, and kinetic analysis. The qualitative analysis of organic compounds is conducted by element analysis and functional analysis and by determining the basic physicochemical properties of the analyzed substances.

V. V. Krasnoshchekov   [11–1639–3]

QUALITY, a philosophical category, expressing an object's essential determinateness, which is inseparable from its being and thanks to which it is precisely that object and no other.

Quality reflects the stable interrelationship among the constituent elements of an object. This interrelationship specifies the object and makes it possible to distinguish it from all others. It is precisely because of quality that each object exists and can be thought of as something delimited and set apart from other objects. On the other hand, quality also expresses the general factor that characterizes the entire class of objects that are of the same kind. "Two different things always have certain qualities . . . in common" (F. Engels; see K. Marx and F. Engels, *Soch.*, 2nd ed., vol. 20, p. 547). Any object constantly changes; nevertheless, it possesses a certain stability that is also expressed as a qualitative determinateness.

The category of quality was first thoroughly analyzed by Aristotle, who defined it as the "differentia of the essence" (*Metaphysics*, V 14 1020b35; Russian translation, Moscow, 1975). Aristotle noted the flux of qualities as states of things, their capacity for being transformed into their opposites. Medieval Scholasticism interpreted the so-called "hidden qualities" as eternal and unchanging "forms." The distinction between primary and secondary qualities, based on a mechanistic world view, took shape in modern philosophy.

Hegel defined quality as a logical category constituting the initial stage in the cognition of things and in the emergence of the world, as well as the immediate character of an object's being. "*Quality* is in fact a definiteness that is identical with being and is immediate to it. Something is what it is thanks to its quality, and, losing its quality, it ceases to be what it is" (*Soch.*, vol. 1, Moscow-Leningrad, 1929, p. 157).

Dialectical materialism proceeds, first of all, from the acknowledgment of the objectivity and universality of the qualitative determinateness of things. The quality of an object is revealed in the aggregate of its properties. However, an object does not consist of properties and is not a certain "cluster of properties," but rather it possesses them: "Qualities do not exist but only things with qualities, and indeed with infinitely many qualities" (F. Engels; see K. Marx and F. Engels, *Soch.*, 2nd ed., vol. 20, p. 547). What is regarded as a property is the mode of manifestation of a given aspect of an object's quality in relation to other objects with which it enters into interaction. A property of an object thus consists in its producing in another object this or that effect and in manifesting itself in its own unique mode in this action. Depending on the real and cognitive context, an object radiates, so to speak, its various aspects, its qualities. For example, a person exhibits his different qualitative facets to a physician, lawyer, writer, sociologist, anatomist, psychologist, and so forth.

The higher the level of the organization of matter, the greater is the number of qualities that it possesses. Inasmuch as each object is in infinite connections with other things, it therefore possesses an infinite number of properties. Hence all attempts to define quality as the complete aggregate of properties lead to infinity. The category of an object's quality cannot be reduced to some of its properties either. It expresses the integrated characteristic of the functional unity of an object's essential properties, of its internal and external determinateness, of its relative stability, and of its difference from other objects or its resemblance to them. Quality not only manifests itself but can change and be formed in these relations. Just as matter cannot be reduced to an aggregate of its properties, so also no object can be dissolved into its own properties: it is their bearer.

The qualitative determinateness of an object depends primarily on its structure, the nature of the relations among the elements of the whole, and on the composition of its elements. A change in quality is caused by a restructuring of the relations among the elements, by an alteration of the elements themselves, or by a transformation of both. The world consists not of finished and unchanging things but represents rather an aggregate of processes within which things are constantly coming into being, developing, and being annihilated, as well as being transformed into other things having other qualities. Inasmuch as an object, thanks to its quality, appears as this very object rather than something else, so a change in quality signifies the transformation of a given object into another one. Furthermore, qualitative changes in a thing occur each time at a different level: they may be connected with a change of that which is specific precisely for a given, unique object or for all objects of a given class. In any qualitative change there is a certain more general and, at the same time, more profound level of the object's quality that remains essentially the same: it is only a variation of its existence that changes. Thus, a qualitative change may be also connected both with the transformation of a given phenomenon into another one and with a change in the state and form of existence of essentially the same object.

The category of quality expresses a given stage in man's cognition of objective reality. In the initial stage of cognition an object of study appears before the subject primarily as a particular property or series of properties. In immediate sense perception quality appears as a certain multiplicity of properties. "First of all, impressions *flash by*, then *Something* emerges,—afterward the concepts of *quality* (the determination of the thing or the phenomenon) and *quantity* are developed. . . . The very first and most familiar to us is sensation, and *in it* there is inevitably also *quality*" (V. I. Lenin, *Poln. sobr. soch.*, 5th ed., vol. 29, p. 301). Cognition proceeds from quality to quantity and thence to their unity—measure. Any object represents a unity of quality and quantity.

REFERENCES

Marx, K. *Kapital,* vol. 1. In K. Marx and F. Engels, *Soch.,* 2nd ed., vol. 23.
Engels, F. *Anti-Dühring. Ibid.,* vol. 20.
Engels, F. *Dialektika prirody. Ibid.*
Lenin, V. I. *Filosofskie tetradi. Poln. sobr. soch.,* 5th ed., vol. 29.
Hegel, G. W. F. *Soch.,* vol. 5. Moscow 1937.
Kedrov, B. M. *O kolichestvennykh izmeneniakh v prirode.* [Moscow] 1946.

A. G. Spirkin   [11–1640–1]

QUALITY OF LABOR, the degree of complexity, intensity, and difficulty of labor.

Under capitalism the quality of labor, being another expression of the quality of labor power, is reflected spontaneously in wages. The level of wages in the labor market is influenced by the proletariat's class struggle for its own economic interests and depends on the ratio between the supply and the demand for labor power of a particular quality.

Under socialism, in accordance with the economic law of distribution on the quantity and quality of labor, labor quality is expressed in wages by means of the rate and bonus system. Increased wages for higher quality labor result because this labor creates more value in a set amount of working time than lower quality labor does.

In most of the socialist countries the basic tool for differentiating wages according to the quality of labor is the wage rate (tariff) system. All jobs performed by workers are divided according to their complexity into grades of the wage rate schedule. The schedule is given in rate and skills reference books; the schedules are worked out by summary and analytic methods and ratified in a centralized manner. With the summary method the degree of complexity of the job is determined by commissions of experts on the basis of the full set of factors that characterize the overall complexity of a job. The analytic method is more precise because it breaks the labor process down into individual work functions. As a rule the complexity of jobs analyzed according to its functions is compared by evaluating them on the basis of a point system. Rate-skill reference books are also used to distribute workers to different grades of the rate schedule according to their skills. Each grade of the wage rate schedule has a certain wage factor that is multiplied by the wage rate of the first grade to determine the rate of the particular grade. When a worker improves his skills, he is awarded a higher grade and assigned to more complex work. The wages of engineering-technical personnel and salaries of office workers are differentiated according to the complexity of their labor by means of salary schedules.

The difference in the intensity of the labor of piece-rate workers and time-rate workers is reflected in wages by differentiating wage rates (taking into account the forms and overall level of remuneration). Labor performed under difficult or unhealthy conditions is normally paid at higher rates.

To reward more intensive labor with increased earnings, piece-rate workers are paid according to fulfillment of output norms; all production workers, engineering-technical personnel, and office workers have bonus systems of various kinds. Workers receive bonuses from both the wages fund and the material incentive funds, with engineering-technical personnel and office workers receiving bonuses primarily from the enterprise's material incentive funds.   E. I. KAPUSTIN [11–1644–1]

QUALITY OF PRODUCTS, the aggregate of properties of a product determining its ability to satisfy the needs it was built to satisfy.

The Directives on the Five-year Plan for the Development of the National Economy of the USSR for 1971–75, which were put forth by the Twenty-fourth Congress of the CPSU, emphasize the need *"to raise the technical level, efficiency, and quality of all types of products.* In their qualitative and technical-economic features, newly developed products should match the leading achievements of world science and technology" (*Materialy XXIV s"ezda KPSS,* 1971, p. 247).

Under present conditions, product quality encompasses both consumer and production features of products, including design and aesthetic qualities, reliability, durability, and the level of standardization and unification of parts and units.

The characteristics that make up product quality are described by continuous or discrete magnitudes which are called indexes of product quality and which must have quantitative measures. The indexes may be absolute, relative, or specific. The values of the magnitudes depend on the conditions and methods of determining them. Indexes of product quality are determined by objective methods, including organoleptic inspection (that is, by using the sense organs), by expert evaluation, and by other means; they are considered in relation to how the products are made and used (consumed). A product quality index that describes one feature is called a single index, and one that describes two or more features is called a composite index. A relative description of product quality based on a comparison between the product quality index and a corresponding set of base indexes is called the level of product quality. Both technical and economic data are used in evaluating the level.

Product quality is of paramount importance for overall national wealth and for the specific consumers of the products because the quality determines the use value. Raising product quality is often equivalent to increasing quantity, but it usually costs less than a quantitative increase in product output.

A composite integrated index of product quality that reflects the ratio of the total use (consumption) of the product to the total costs for its making and using (consuming) can serve as the criterion of optimality for the level of product quality, that is, of its efficiency. A maximum value for the integrated index of product quality means that the benefit per ruble of expenditure is maximized, that is, that maximum societal efficiency has been achieved.

Product quality is managed—established, secured, and maintained at the necessary level—by systematic verification, that is, by checking how quality indexes meet established requirements (standards, technical specifications, and other documented normative technical parameters), and by upgrading the conditions and factors determining product quality (quality of blueprints, equipment, tools, raw and processed materials, semifinished parts, and assembly components and the skills of the producers). Economic methods, which encompass such factors as planning, incentives, and price formation, play a large part in influencing product quality.

An important element in managing product quality is planning for quality improvement, that is, establishing sound targets for turning out products with definite index values that must be reached by a given time or in an assigned period. Planning for a rise in product quality should envision maximum use of the achievements of science and technology in accord with consumer demand, the purpose and conditions of product use, and the requirements of product safety and economic efficiency. Assignments and measures to raise product quality are worked out with reference to the analysis of the quality of products being turned out and are based on the principal directions of development of national economic sectors, forecasts of technical progress, the requirements of progressive standards, and the needs of the national economy for products of a certain level of quality.

The Uniform System for Certification of the Quality of Industrial Products, which was instituted in the USSR in 1971, combines state sectorial and plant certification. All products that establish the assigned area of the ministry, association, and enterprise as well as products that are regularly produced are subject to certification. Products turned out by manufacturing enterprises are certified according to three quality categories: highest, first, and second. Products that are under development and are being turned over for series production are certified in the highest or first categories. The highest category includes products whose technical and economic indexes match or surpass the highest achievements of domestic and foreign science and technology. These products are awarded the state mark of quality in the established manner. The first category includes products whose technical and economic indexes meet the requirements of existing standards and technical specifications, whereas the second category is for products that do not meet these requirements, are out of date and subject to modernization or withdrawal from production, or are subject to standards and technical specifications that require revision in the established manner. The Uniform System is a basis for planning the volume of product output by appropriate quality categories, for ensuring a rise in quality of products, and for economically stimulating the output of products predominantly in the highest quality category.

Standards play a special role in ensuring high product quality. Establishing comprehensive standards for raw and processed materials, semifinished parts, assembly components, and finished products is an effective way to achieve a planned rise in product quality. Standards establish optimal quality indexes, parametric series of products, monitoring and testing methods, technical servicing conditions, methods of maintenance, spare part norms, and the like. Recognizing the great importance of standards in the system for controlling product quality, the Central Committee of the CPSU and the Council of Ministers of the USSR adopted in November 1970 the decree entitled Raising the Role of Standards in Improving the Quality of Output. The implementation of the decree has made it possible to strengthen the regulating and organizing influence of standards in the management of product quality.

REFERENCES
Materialy XXIV s"ezda KPSS. Moscow, 1971.
GOST 15467–70—Kachestvo produktsii: Terminy.
Ekonomicheskie problemy povysheniia kachestva promyshlennoi produktsii. Moscow, 1968.
Obshchie metodicheskie ukazaniia po planirovaniiu povysheniia kachestva promyshlennoi produktsii. Moscow, 1971.
Osnovnye polozheniia Edinoi sistemy attestatsii kachestva promyshlennoi produktsii (ESAKP). Moscow, 1971.
"Kvalimetriia (Ee soderzhanie, zadachi i metody)." *Standarty i kachestvo,* 1970, no. 11.
Zaikov, G. I., and R. G. Romanov. *Uroven' kachestva i stoimosti produktsii.* Moscow, 1970.
Tkachenko, V. V., D. M. Komarov, and Ia. B. Shor. "Kolichestvennye metody optimizatsii trebovanii standartov k kachestvu produktsii—osnova teorii standardizatsii." *Standarty i kachestvo,* 1971, no. 6.
Veniaminov, Iu. S., A. V. Glichev, and Ia. B. Shor. "Kachestvo produktsii, potrebitel'naia stoimost' i ikh pokazateli." *Standarty i kachestvo,* 1972, no. 1.

A. V. GLICHEV, IA. B. SHOR,
and IU. S. VENIAMINOV [11–1642–1]

QUANTIFIER (from the Latin *quantum,* "how much"), a logical operation that gives the quantitative character of the range of objects with which the expression obtained as a result of its application is concerned. In ordinary language, words of the type "all," "each," "some," "there exists," "there is," "any," "every," "unique," "several," "infinitely many," "a finite number," as well as all cardinal numbers, serve as conveyors of these characteristics. In formal languages in which predicate calculus is a constituent part, two kinds of quantifier turn out to be sufficient for the expression of all such characteristics: the universal quantifier ("for all x," denoted by $\forall x$, $(\forall x)$, (x), $(\mathbf{A}x)$, $\underset{x}{\cap}$, Λ, $\underset{x}{\Pi}$) and the existential quantifier ("for some x," denoted by $\exists x$, $(\exists x)$, $(\mathbf{E}x)$, $\underset{x}{\cup}$, $\underset{x}{V}$, $\underset{x}{\Sigma}$). With the aid of quantifiers it is possible to write down the four fundamental forms of judgment of traditional logic: "all A are B" is written as $\forall x [A(x) \supset B(x)]$, "no A is B" as $\forall x[A(x) \supset \sim B(x)]$, "some A are B"as $\exists x [A(x) \& B(x)]$, and "some A are not B" as $\exists x[A(x) \& \sim B(x)]$; here $A(x)$ denotes that x possesses the property A, $\supset$ is the implication sign, $\sim$ is the negation sign, and $\&$ is the conjunction sign.

The part of a formula over which the operation of any quantifier is distributed is called the scope of operation of that quantifier (it may be indicated by parentheses). The entry of any variable into the formula directly after the quantifier or within the scope of the quantifier after which the variable stands is called its bound entry. All remaining variable entries are called free. A formula containing free variable entries is dependent on them (is a function of them), but the bound entries may be "renamed"; for example, the expressions $\exists x$ $(x = ?y)$ and $\exists z(z = 2y)$ denote one and the same thing, but the same cannot be said of $\exists x(x = 2y)$ and $\exists (x)(x = 2t)$. The use of quantifiers reduces the number of free variables in logical expressions and, if the quantifier is not a "dummy" (that is, if it is related to a variable actually entering into the formula), it transforms a three-place predicate into a two-place one, a two-place one into a single-place one, and single-place one into a proposition. The use of quantifiers is codified by special "quantification postulates" (whose addition to propositional calculus essentially implies an expansion of the latter into predicate calculus)—for example, the "Bernays' postulates": the axioms $A(t) \supset \exists xA(x)$ and $\forall xA(x) \supset A(t)$ and the rules of deduction "if it has been proved that $C \supset A(x)$, then it may be considered also proved that $C \supset \forall xA(x)$" and "if it has been proved that $A(x) \supset C$, then it may be considered also proved that $\exists xA(x) \supset C$" (here x does not enter freely into C).

Other kinds of quantifiers may be reduced to the universal and existential quantifiers. For example, in place of the uniqueness quantifier $\exists !x$ ("there exists a unique x such that") it is possible to write "ordinary" quantifiers, replacing $\exists !xA(x)$ with

$$\exists xA(x) \& \forall y \forall z [A(y) \& A(z) \supset y = z]$$

Analogously, quantifiers "bound" to a single-place predicate $P(x)$—$\exists x_{P(x)}$ ("there exists an x satisfying the property P and such that") and $\forall x_{P(x)}$ ("for all x satisfying the property P it is true that")—can easily be expressed by means of the universal and existential quantifiers and the implication and conjunction operators:

$$\exists x_{P(x)}A(x) \equiv \exists x[P(x) \& A(x)]$$

and

$$\forall x_{P(x)}A(x) \equiv \forall x[P(x) \supset A(x)]$$

REFERENCES
Kleene, S. C. *Vvedenie v metamatematiku.* Moscow, 1957. Pages 72–80, 130–38. (Translated from English.)
Church, A. *Vvedenie v matematicheskuiu logiku*, vol. 1. Moscow, 1960. Pages 42–48. (Translated from English.)

IU. A. GASTEV   [11–1803–1]

QUANTILE, one of the numerical characteristics of random quantities used in mathematical statistics. If a distribution function of a random quantity X is continuous, then the quantile K_p of order p is defined as that number for which the probability of the inequality $X < K_p$ is equal to p. From the definition of quantile it follows that the probability of the inequality $K_p < X < K'_p$ is equal to $p' - p$. The quantile $K_{1/2}$ is the median of the random quantity X. The quantiles $K_{1/4}$ and $K_{3/4}$ are called

quartiles, and $K_{0.1}$, $K_{0.2}$, . . . , $K_{0.9}$ are called deciles. Knowledge of the quantiles for suitably selected values of p makes it possible to visualize the distribution function.

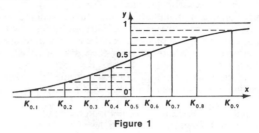

Figure 1

For example, for the normal distribution (see Figure 1)

$$\Phi(x) = \frac{1}{\sqrt{2n}} \int_{-\infty}^{x} e^{-t^2/2} \, dt$$

the graph of the function $\Phi(x)$ may be plotted by means of the deciles $K_{0.1} = -1.28$, $K_{0.2} = -0.84$, $K_{0.3} = -0.52$, $K_{0.4} = -0.25$, $K_{0.5} = 0$, $K_{0.6} = 0.25$, $K_{0.7} = 0.52$, $K_{0.8} = 0.84$, and $K_{0.9} = 1.28$. The quartiles of the normal distribution $\Phi(x)$ are $K_{1/4} = -0.67$ and $K_{3/4} = 0.67$.   [11–1694–7]

QUANTITATIVE STRESS, an emphasis on the stressed elements of a word or phrase by means of an increase in their relative duration; as a rule, the stress arises from the interaction of several components. There are no known languages in which stress would be purely quantitative; it can only be affirmed that in some languages the stress is mostly quantitative—for example, in Russian, where a stressed syllable (and especially the vowel in it) has a greater relative duration than an unstressed syllable.   [11–1695–2]

QUANTIZATION, MAGNETIC FLUX, a macroscopic quantum phenomenon whereby a magnetic flux through a superconductor ring carrying a current can only assume discrete values. The minimum value of the flux (the flux quantum) is $\Phi_0 = ch/2e \simeq 2 \times 10^{-7}$ grams force $\cdot$ cm^2, where c is the velocity of light, h is the Planck constant, and e is the charge of an electron. The magnetic flux in a superconductor may be equal only to an integral number of flux quanta. Magnetic flux quantization was theoretically predicted by F. London (1950), who obtained the value ch/e for the flux quantum. Experiments (in 1961) provided half this value for the flux quantum. This was splendid confirmation of the microscopic theory of superconductivity that had been developed by that time and according to which a superconducting current is due to the movement of pairs of electrons.   [11–1696–1]

QUANTIZATION, SECOND, a method used in quantum mechanics and quantum field theory to study systems consisting of many or an infinite number of particles (or quasiparticles). In this method the state of a quantum system is described by means of occupation numbers—quantities that characterize the average number of particles in a system in each possible state.

The method of second quantization is particularly important in quantum field theory when the number of particles in a given physical system is not constant but may change during various processes that transpire in the system. Therefore, quantum radiation theory and quantum theory of elementary particles and systems of various quasiparticles are the most important areas of application of the method of second quantization. Systems containing light quanta (photons), the number of which changes during the processes of emission, absorption, and scattering, are examined in radiation theory. In the theory of elementary particles the necessity of using the method of second quantization is connected with the possibility of mutual transformations of particles—for example, the processes of conversion of electrons and positrons into photons, and the reverse process. The method of second quantization is most effective in quantum electrodynamics—the quantum theory of electromagnetic processes, as well as in solid-state theory, which is based on the concept of quasiparti-

582 QUANTIZATION, SIGNAL

cles. The use of second quantization is less effective for describing mutual transformations of particles caused by nonelectromagnetic interactions.

In the mathematical apparatus of second quantization, the wave function of a system is taken to be a function of the occupation numbers. Here the primary role is played by "creation" and "annihilation" operators of particles. The annihilation operator is an operator under whose influence the wave function of some state of a given physical system is converted into the wave function of another state having one less particle. Similarly, the creation operator increases the number of particles in the state by 1.

The fundamental aspect of the method of second quantization does not depend on whether the particles of the system conform to Bose-Einstein statistics (for example, photons) or Fermi-Dirac statistics (electrons and positrons). The specific mathematical apparatus of the method, including the main properties of the creation and annihilation operators, differs significantly in these cases because the number of particles that may exist in a given state is in no way limited in Bose-Einstein statistics (so that the occupation numbers may assume arbitrary values), whereas in Fermi-Dirac statistics no more than one particle may be in each state (and the occupation numbers may have only the values 0 and 1).

The method of second quantization was first developed by the English physicist P. Dirac (1927) in his theory of radiation; and further work was done by the Soviet physicist V. A. Fok (1932). The term "second quantization" appeared because the method developed after "ordinary," or "first," quantization, the purpose of which was to determine the wave properties of particles. The necessity of systematic consideration of the corpuscular properties of fields as well (since particle-wave duality is inherent in all types of matter) led to the appearance of methods of second quantization. [11–1695–3]

QUANTIZATION, SIGNAL, discretization of analogue signals, the conversion of an electric signal, continuous in time and level, into a succession of discrete or discrete-analogue signals that in aggregate represent the original signal with a predetermined error. Signal quantization is used in telemechanics for data transmission, in computer engineering for analogue-to-digital conversion, and in automatic pulse systems.

In the transmission of analogue signals it is usually sufficient to transmit not the signal itself but a succession of its instantaneous values, taken from the original signal according to a particular principle. Signals can be quantized with reference to time or to level or simultaneously to both parameters. If done with reference to time, the signal is either interrupted (pulse signal) or changed abruptly (stepwise signal; see Figure 1) at equal time intervals Δt.

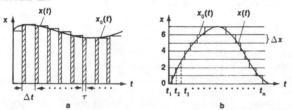

Figure 1. Signal quantization (a) by time and (b) by level; $x_0(t)$ is the original signal; $x(t)$ is the quantized signal; Δt is the quantization interval; Δx is the quantization level

For example, an analogue signal passing through the contacts of a periodically switched electric relay is converted to a succession of pulse signals. For infinitely small switching intervals (on or off), that is, for an infinitely large contact-switching frequency, an accurate representation of the original signal is obtained. If signals are quantized with reference to level, the instantaneous values of the analogue signal are replaced respectively by the nearest discrete levels, which form a discrete scale of quantization. Any value of the signal falling between levels is rounded off to the value of the nearest level. For an infinitely large number of levels, a quantized signal is converted to the initial analogue signal.

REFERENCES
Kharkevich, A. A. *Bor'ba s pomekhami*, 2nd ed. Moscow, 1965.
Marcuse, J. *Diskretizatsiia i kvantovanie*. Moscow, 1969. (Translated from French.)   M. M GEL'MAN [11–1700–1]

QUANTIZATION, SPACE, in quantum mechanics, the discreteness of the possible spatial orientations of the angular momentum of an atom (or another particle or system of particles) with respect to any arbitrarily selected axis (the z-axis).

Space quantization is manifested in that the projection M_z of the angular momentum M on this axis may only assume discrete values equal to an integer (0, 1, 2, . . .) or a half-integer (1/2, 3/2, 5/2, . . .) m multiplied by the Planck constant $\hbar$, $M_z = m\hbar$. The other two projections of angular momentum M_x and M_y remain indeterminate, since, according to the main principle of quantum mechanics, only the magnitude of the angular momentum and one of its projections can simultaneously have exact values. For the orbital angular momentum, the quantity m (m_l) can assume the values 0, ± 1, ± 2, . . . , $\pm l$, where $l = 0$, 1, 2, . . . determines the square of the momentum M_l (that is, its absolute magnitude): $M_l{}^2 = l\,(l + 1)\hbar^2$. For the total angular momentum M (orbital plus spin momentum), m (m_j) assumes values separated by unity—j to $+j$, where j determines the magnitude of the total momentum: $M^2 = j\,(j + 1)\,\hbar^2$; it may be an integer or half-integer.

If an atom is placed in an external magnetic field **H**, then a well-defined direction in space—the direction of the field (which is taken as the z-axis)—appears. In this case, space quantization leads to quantization of the projection μ_H of the magnetic moment of the atom μ on the direction of the field, since the magnetic moment is proportional to the mechanical angular momentum (hence the name of m—magnetic quantum number). This leads to splitting of the energy levels of the atom in a magnetic field, since the energy of the atom's magnetic interaction with the field, equal to $\mu_H H$, is added to its energy (*see* ZEEMAN EFFECT).   V. I. GRIGOR'EV [11–1699–1]

QUANTIZATION, SPACE-TIME, the common name for generalizations of the theory of elementary particles (quantum field theory), which are based on the hypothesis that there are finite minimum distances and time intervals. The construction of a noncontradictory theory in which all physical quantities would be finite is the immediate purpose of such generalizations.

The concepts of space and time that are used in modern physical theory are formulated most consistently in Einstein's theory of relativity. These concepts are macroscopic, that is, they rely on experience acquired in the study of macroscopic objects, large distances, and large time intervals. In the construction of a theory describing the phenomena of the microworld—quantum mechanics and quantum field theory—the classical geometric picture, which presupposes the continuity of space and time, was transferred to the new area without alteration. Experimental verification of the conclusions of quantum theory does not yet directly indicate the existence of a boundary beyond which classical geometric concepts cease to be applicable. However, the theory of elementary particles itself contains difficulties that would suggest that the geometric concepts developed on the basis of macroscopic experimentation are invalid for the infinitesimal distances and time intervals characteristic of the microworld and that the concepts of physical space and time need to be reexamined.

These theoretical difficulties are connected with the problem of divergences: calculations of certain physical quantities lead to physically meaningless, infinitely large values, or divergences. Divergences appear since, in current theory, elementary particles are considered as "points," that is, as material objects without dimension. In its simplest form, this was manifested as early as classical electromagnetic field theory (classical electrodynamics), in which there occurs a Coulomb divergence—an infinitely large value for the energy of the Coulomb field of a charged point particle [since at very small distances r from a particle ($r \to 0$) the field increases without limit].

Not only is Coulomb divergence retained in quantum field theory, but new divergences appear as well (for example, divergence for an electrical charge) that are also ultimately connected with the point nature of particles. The condition of the point nature of particles in quantum field theory appears in the form of the requirement of what is called the locality of interactions: the interaction between fields is determined by quantities that describe the fields and that are taken at the same point in space and at the same instant in time. It would seem that divergence can be easily eliminated if particles are considered not as point particles but as extended particles that are spread over some small volume. But here the theory of relativity imposes significant limitations. According to the theory the speed of any signal (that is, the rate of transfer of energy or the rate of transfer of interaction) cannot exceed the speed of light *c*. The assumption that an interaction can be transferred at velocities greater than the speed of light leads to contradiction of the traditional concepts (confirmed by all human experience) of a temporal sequence of events connected causally: it seems that an effect can precede a cause. The finite nature of the rate of propagation of an interaction cannot be coexistent with the indivisibility of particles: in principle, such powerful momentum could very rapidly be imparted to some small part of an extended particle that the particle would fly off before the signal reached the part that remained.

Thus, the requirements of the theory of relativity and causality make it necessary to consider particles as point entities. But the concept of the point nature of particles is closely connected with the nature of the geometry used in the theory and, in particular, with whether this geometry is based on the assumption that it is possible in principle to make whatever precise measurement of distances (lengths) and time intervals as may be necessary. In ordinary theory this possibility is assumed explicitly or, more often, implicitly.

In all variant geometries a major role belongs to the fundamental length *l*, which has been introduced into theory as a new universal constant (along with Planck's constant *h* and the speed of light *c*). The introduction of the fundamental length *l* corresponds to the assumption that the measurement of distances is possible in principle only with limited accuracy of the order of *l* (the measurement of time, with an accuracy of the order of *l/c*). Therefore, *l* is also called the minimum length. If particles are considered to be extended entities, then their dimensions fill the role of some minimal scale of length. Thus, the introduction of a fundamental (minimal) length in one sense conceals the extended nature of particles. This gives hope of constructing a theory free of divergences.

One of the first attempts to introduce a fundamental length was connected with the transition from the continuous coordinates *x*, *y*, *z*, and time *t* to discrete coordinates: $x \to n_1 l$, $Y \to n_2 l$, $z \to n_3 l$, and $t \to (n_4 l)/c$, where n_1, n_2, n_3, and n_4 are integers that may assume values from minus infinity to plus infinity. The replacement of continuous coordinates with discrete coordinates is somewhat reminiscent of Bohr's rules of quantization in the original theory of the atom—hence the term "space-time quantization."

If we examine large distances and time intervals, then every "elementary step" *l* or *l/c* may be considered infinitesimal. Therefore, "large-scale" geometry appears routine. However, on a "small scale" the effect of such quantization becomes significant. In particular, introduction of the minimal length *l* excludes the existence of waves with a length $\lambda < l$, that is, precisely those quanta of infinitely large frequency $\nu = c/\lambda$ and, consequently, of energies $\epsilon = h\nu$ which, as quantum field theory demonstrates, are responsible for the appearance of divergences. How the change in geometrical concepts entails important physical consequences is graphic here.

The introduction of "cellular" space (with "cells" of dimension *l*) in this manner is associated with a disruption of the isotropy of space—violation of the equivalence of all directions. This is one of the significant shortcomings of this theory.

Just as Bohr's theory (in which the quantization conditions were postulated) was replaced by quantum mechanics (in which quantization was seen as a natural consequence of the theory's fundamental propositions), more advanced variations followed the first attempts at space-time quantization. Common to all of them is the consideration of coordinates and time as operators and not as ordinary numbers (here, too, there is an analogy with

quantum mechanics, in which operators are posited to correspond to physical quantities). An important general theorem is formulated in quantum mechanics: if certain operators are not commutative (that is, if the sequence of the factors cannot be changed in multiplying such operators), then the physical quantities corresponding to these operators cannot be simultaneously determined with precision. Such, for example, are the operators of the coordinates $\hat{x}$ and the momentum $\hat{p}_x$ of a particle (operators are commonly designated by the same letters as the corresponding physical quantities but with a "cap" above them). The noncommutative nature of these operators is a mathematical reflection that the uncertainty relation

$$\Delta p_x \, \Delta x \geq \frac{h}{2\pi}$$

which shows the limits of the accuracy with which p_x and x can be determined simultaneously, obtains for the coordinates and momentum of a particle. A particle cannot have precisely defined coordinates and momentum simultaneously: the more precisely the coordinates are defined, the less precise is the momentum, and vice versa (the probabilistic description of a particle's state in quantum mechanics is associated with this).

In space-time quantization, operators that are associated with the coordinates of points in space and instants in time are considered noncommutative. The noncommutative nature of the operators $\hat{x}$ and $\hat{t}$, $\hat{x}$ and $\hat{y}$, and so on means that the precise value of the coordinate *x*, for example, at a given instant *t* cannot be determined, just as the precise value of several coordinates cannot be given simultaneously. This leads to the probabilistic description of space-time. The type of operator is chosen in such a way that the average values of the coordinates can assume only integral values that are multiples of the fundamental length *l*. The scale of error, or the uncertainty, of the coordinates is determined by the fundamental length. Some versions of the theory postulate the noncommutability of the coordinate operators and the operators that describe the field. This is equivalent to the assumption that it is impossible simultaneously to specify precisely the quantities that describe a field and the point in space to which these quantities refer (variants of this type often are called theories of nonlocalizable states).

In most known attempts at space-time quantization, postulates concerning the "microstructure" of space-time are introduced first; later the resultant space is "populated" with particles, the laws of whose motion are made to correspond with the new geometry. A number of interesting results have been obtained in this manner: certain divergences are eliminated (although new ones sometimes appear in their place) and, in some cases, the mass spectrum of elementary particles is obtained, that is, the possible masses of particles are predicted. However, radical progress has not yet been possible, although the methodological value of the work so far accomplished is indisputable. It seems likely that the difficulties that arise here attest to shortcomings in the very approach to the problem, in which the construction of new theory begins with postulates concerning "empty" space (that is, purely geometric postulates, independent of the matter populating the space).

A reexamination of geometric concepts is needed; this has been recognized almost universally. However, such a reexamination obviously should provide much greater consideration of the indivisibility of the concepts of space, time, and matter.

REFERENCES

Markov, M. A. *Giperony i K-mezony*. Moscow, 1958. Subsections 33 and 34.

Blokhintsev, D. I. *Prostranstvo i vremia v mikromire*. Moscow, 1970.

V. J. Grigor'ev [11–1696–2]

QUANTUM CHEMISTRY, a branch of theoretical chemistry that considers problems of structure and reactivity of chemical compounds as well as problems of bonding from the point of view of the concepts and methods of quantum mechanics. In principle, quantum mechanics permits calculation of the properties of atomic and molecular systems on the basis of the Schrödinger equation, Pauli exclusion principle, and universal physical constants. Various physical characteristics of the molecule (for example, energy, electric and magnetic dipole moments) may be obtained as eigenvalues of the operators of the corresponding quantities if the exact form of the wave function is known. However, it has yet proved impossible to obtain exact analytic solutions for the Schrödinger equation for systems containing two or more electrons. The use of functions with an extremely large number of variables has made it possible to obtain approximate solutions, which numerically approach the ideally exact solutions to any desired degree. Nevertheless, in spite of the use of modern electronic computers with operating speeds of hundreds of thousands, or even millions, of operations per second, such "direct" solutions of the Schrödinger equation have been achieved only for systems with several electrons, for example, for the molecules H_2 and LiH. Inasmuch as chemists are interested in systems containing tens or hundreds of electrons, simplifications become necessary. For this reason, various approximate quantum-mechanical theories have been proposed for the description of such systems. These theories have proved to be more or less satisfactory, depending on the nature of the problems under consideration: the valence bond theory, formulated in 1927 by W. Heitler and F. London in Germany and developed by J. Slater and L. Pauling in the USA; the crystal field theory, proposed by the German scientist H. Bethe in 1929 and subsequently developed by the American scientist J. Van Vleck (this theory was applied to chemical problems in the 1950's as the ligand field theory after the studies of the British scientist L. Orgel and the Danish scientists C. Jorgensen and C. Ballhausen). The molecular orbital (MO) theory appeared toward the end of the 1920's. Worked out by J. Lennard-Jones (Great Britain), R. Mulliken (USA), and F. Hund (Germany), this theory was subsequently developed by many other investigators.

These approximate theories have coexisted and even complemented each other for a long time. However, at the present time, the great successes achieved in the synthesis of molecules and in the determination of their structure and the broad development of computer technology have caused researchers to favor the MO theory. This has happened because only the MO theory has developed a universal language, which in principle is suitable for the description of any molecule with greatly varied structure and complexity. The MO theory includes the most general physical concepts of the electron structure of molecules and (which is no less important) makes use of the mathematical apparatus, which is highly suited to quantitative calculations using electronic computers.

The MO theory is based on the assumption that each electron in the molecule is located in the field of all of its atomic nuclei and remaining electrons. The atomic orbital (AO) theory, describing the electron structure of atoms, is included in the MO theory as a special case, in which the system contains only one atomic nucleus. Furthermore, the MO theory considers all chemical bonds as multicenter bonds (in accordance with the number of atomic nuclei in the molecule) and thus fully delocalized. From this point of view, every type of predominant localization of electron density in the vicinity of a certain portion of the atomic nuclei is an approximation, the validity of which must be verified in each concrete case. The ideas of W. Kossel regarding the generation of separated ions in chemical compounds (these ions being isoelectronic with the noble gases) or the views of G. Lewis (USA) concerning the two-center, two-electron chemical bonds (symbolically denoted by the valence line) are naturally included in the MO theory as certain special cases.

The MO theory is based on the one-electron approximation, in which each electron is considered as a quasi-independent particle described by its own wave function. Another frequently used approximation is the formulation of one-electron MO's from the linear combination of AO's (LCAO-MO approximation).

If the above approximations are accepted and if only the universal physical constants are used without the introduction of any experimental data (except perhaps the equilibrium internuclear distances, which are being increasingly less used at the present time), then purely theoretical calculations (ab initio calculations) can be carried out according to the scheme of the self-consistent field (SCF) method of Hartree and Fok. Such SCF-LCAO-MO calculations have now become possible even for systems containing several tens of electrons. In this case, the main difficulties arise from the need to evaluate a large number of integrals. Although such calculations are unwieldy and expensive, the results obtained, in any case, are not always satisfactory from the quantitative point of view. This arises since, in spite of various improvements in the SCF scheme (for example, introduction of the configurational interaction and other methods of taking the electron correlation into account), researchers are ultimately limited by the possibilities of the one-electron LCAO-AO approximation.

In this connection, semiempirical quantum-mechanical calculations have received extensive development. These calculations likewise go back to the Schrödinger equation, but instead of calculating an enormous number (millions) of integrals, most of them are omitted (on the basis of their small order of magnitude), whereas the remaining ones are simplified. The loss of accuracy is compensated by the corresponding calibration of parameters, which are derived experimentally. Semiempirical calculations enjoy great popularity owing to the optimum combination of simplicity and precision in solving a variety of problems.

The calculations described above cannot be compared directly with purely theoretical (nonempirical) calculations, since both types offer different possibilities and, hence, different problems. Owing to the characteristics of the parameters used in the semiempirical approach, one should not expect to obtain a wave function that would satisfactorily describe different (let alone all) one-electron properties. This constitutes the basic difference between the semiempirical calculations and the nonempirical calculations, which are capable, at least in principle, of providing a universal wave function. For this reason, the power and attractiveness of semiempirical calculations lie not in the ability to provide quantitative information as such, but in the opportunity for interpreting the results obtained in terms of physicochemical concepts. Only this type of interpretation leads to a true understanding, since without it the calculations provide merely some quantitative characteristics of phenomena, which can be determined more reliably by experiments. It is this specific feature of semiempirical calculations, which makes them invaluable and permits them to compete successfully with completely nonempirical calculations, which are increasingly realizable owing to the continuing development of computer technology.

As far as the accuracy of semiempirical quantum-mechanical calculations is concerned, it depends (as in any semiempirical approach) more on the skillful calibration of parameters than on the theoretical validity of the computation scheme. Thus, if parameters are selected from the empirical spectra of certain molecules and then used for calculation of the optical spectra of related compounds, excellent agreement is easily obtained with experiment; however, such an approach is not of general value. For this reason, the primary problem in empirical calculations is not related to the determination of parameters in general but to the use of one group of parameters (for example, those derived from optical spectra) for the calculation of other molecular characteristics (for example, thermodynamic characteristics). Only then it becomes certain that one is dealing with physically meaningful quantities, which possess general significance and are useful in conceptual thinking.

In addition to quantitative and semiquantitative calculations, modern quantum chemistry also includes a large group of results derived from qualitative considerations. It is frequently possible to obtain very convincing information concerning the structure and properties of molecules without any cumbersome calculations by using various fundamental concepts that are based mainly on the consideration of symmetry.

Considerations of symmetry play an important role in quantum chemistry, since they make it possible to check the physical meaning of the results of the approximate analysis of multielectron systems. For example, by proceeding from the point group of symmetry of a molecule, it is possible to arrive at a single-valued solution to the problem of the orbital degeneracy of the electron levels, regardless of the selection of the calculated approximation. Knowledge of the degree of orbital degeneracy is frequently sufficient for inferences concerning many important molecular properties, such as ionization potentials, magnetism, and configurational stability. The principle of conservation of orbital symmetry is the basis for the modern approach to the mechanisms of concerted reactions (Woodward-Hofmann rules). The above principle may be ultimately derived from a general topological analysis of the bonding and antibonding lobes in the molecule.

It should be kept in mind that modern chemistry deals with millions of compounds and that its scientific foundations are not monolithic. In some cases, success is achieved by using merely qualitative considerations of quantum chemistry, whereas its entire arsenal becomes inadequate in other cases. For this reason, in appraising the current state of quantum chemistry, it is always possible to cite many examples of the strength as well as the weakness of modern quantum-chemical theory. Only one thing is clear, however. If the level of quantum chemistry studies has been previously judged on the basis of the technical complexity of the computational apparatus employed, the availability of electronic computers has moved the physicochemical meaningfulness of the studies into the foreground. From the point of view of the internal interests of quantum chemistry, attempts at going beyond the boundaries of the one-electron approximation represent the most valuable studies. At the same time, the one-electron approximation still contains many unused opportunities for a variety of practical purposes in various branches of chemistry.

E. M. SHUSTOROVICH [11–1763–1]

QUANTUM CLOCK, a device for exact time measurement; its main component is the quantum frequency standard. Atoms perform the function of the "pendulum" in quantum clocks. The frequency that is emitted or absorbed by the atoms during their quantum transitions from one energy state to another controls the operation of the clock. The frequency is so stable that quantum clocks measure time more exactly than astronomic methods can. Quantum clocks are also frequently called atomic clocks.

and drive the clock's hands (or change the digits on its face) and produce exact time signals.

Most quantum clocks contain an auxiliary quartz-crystal oscillator. Because of the change in the oscillator's frequency with time (aging), the accuracy of a quartz clock based only on such an oscillator would be insufficient. In a quantum clock, the frequency of the quartz-crystal oscillator is controlled by a quantum frequency standard, which raises the accuracy of the clock to the level of the quantum standard itself. However, the introduction of periodic corrections by the operator is not always feasible. In some devices, particularly in navigation instruments, it is more efficient to increase the frequency stability of the quartz-crystal oscillator by automatic tuning of its frequency to the frequency of the quantum standard.

In one type of such a tuning mechanism (automatic phase tuning of the frequency; see Figure 1), the frequency νq of the quartz-crystal oscillator (usually about 10–20 MHz) is multiplied electronically by the required factor n and is subtracted in a mixer from the frequency of the quantum standard ν_{st}. By selecting specific values of νq and n, the difference frequency $\Delta = (\nu_{st} - n\nu_q)$ is made approximately equal to the frequency of the quartz-crystal oscillator:

The amplified signal of the difference frequency $(\nu_{st} - n\nu_q)$ is fed to one input of a phase discriminator, and the oscillations of the quartz-crystal oscillator are fed to the other input. The phase discriminator generates a potential whose magnitude and sign correspond to the difference between the difference frequency Δ and the frequency of the quartz generator ν_q. This potential is then fed into the unit that controls the frequency of the quartz-crystal oscillator and generates a shift of the oscillator frequency that compensates for the deviation of ν_q from the difference frequency Δ. Thus, any change in the frequency of the quartz-crystal oscillator causes the generation at the output of the control unit of a potential that has the corresponding magnitude and sign and shifts the frequency in the opposite direction. Therefore, a constant frequency of the quartz-crystal oscillator is automatically maintained. Consequently, its frequency stabil-

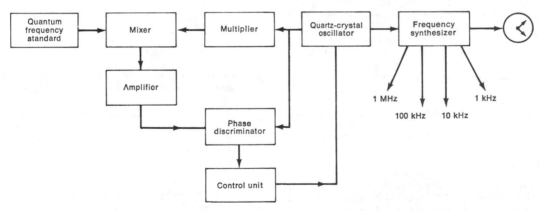

Figure 1. Block diagram of a quantum clock with automatic phase tuning of frequency

Quantum clocks are used in radio navigation systems and at astronomical observatories and research and testing laboratories, replacing the less advanced quartz clocks.

The signals from quantum frequency standards themselves cannot be used to drive the clock mechanism, since their power is negligible and their oscillation frequency is usually very high and has a noninteger value (for example, the power of an atomic hydrogen generator is 10^{-11} to 10^{-12} watts, and its frequency is 1420.406 megahertz [MHz]). This makes difficult the use of quantum frequency standards in the time service, in various navigation systems, and in laboratory practice. In such cases a set or network of standard, high-stability frequencies (1 kHz, 10 kHz, 100 kHz, 1MHz, and so on), with a high output signal power, is more convenient. For this reason, in addition to a quantum frequency standard, quantum clocks also contain special electronic devices, which form such a frequency network

ity becomes virtually equal to the frequency stability of the quantum standard. The frequency synthesizer generates a network of standard frequencies of the same accuracy from the signal of the quartz-crystal oscillator. One of these frequencies is used to run an electric clock, and the other frequencies are used for metrological and other purposes. The accuracy of operation of the best quantum clock of this type is better than 1 sec in several thousand years, given careful construction and tuning.

The first quantum clock was built in 1957. Its frequency standard was a maser based on a beam of ammonia molecules. Quantum clocks built later, which use a beam of cesium atoms as the frequency standard, do not require calibration against a standard, since the nominal value of the fundamental frequency may be determined from manipulations within the instrument itself. Disadvantages of these quantum clocks are their great weight and high sensitivity to vibration. Quantum clocks of another type—the most common—use a rubidium frequency standard with optical pumping. These clocks are lighter, more compact, and unaffected by vibration, but they require calibration, after which they maintain the established frequency value for a year, with an accuracy of the order of 10^{-11}.

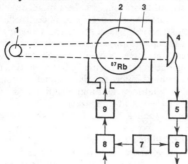

Figure 2. Schematic diagram of a rubidium frequency standard with optical pumping: (1) tube illuminating the bulb (2), which is filled with ^{87}Rb vapor; (3) cavity resonator; (4) photoelectric detector; (5) low-frequency amplifier; (6) phase discriminator; (7) low-frequency oscillator; (8) quartz-crystal oscillator; (9) frequency multiplier

The main component of a rubidium quantum clock is a special microwave spectroscope with optical pumping and optical readings that is set to the spectral line of ^{87}Rb, in the superhigh frequency band. The spectroscope contains a cavity resonator (3), within which is a bulb (2) with vapors of the isotope ^{87}Rb (Figure 2) at a pressure of about 10^{-6} mm of mercury (mm Hg). The resonator is tuned to 7835 MHz, the frequency of the spectral line of ^{87}Rb. The sensitivity of an ordinary microwave spectroscope is insufficient for locking in on the radio-frequency line of ^{87}Rb. To increase sensitivity, optical pumping of ^{87}Rb vapor and optical indication of the spectral line are used. The ^{87}Rb atoms are exposed to light whose frequency coincides with the frequency of another spectral line of ^{87}Rb lying in the optical region. The low-pressure gas discharge tube (1) illuminates the bulb containing ^{87}Rb vapor. Light that has passed through the tube strikes a photoelectric detector (for example, a photoelectric multiplier). Under the influence of the rubidium lamp (pumping), the ^{87}Rb atoms become excited—that is, they undergo a transition from the state with energy $\mathcal{E}_2$ into the state with energy $\mathcal{E}_3$ (Figure 3). If the light intensity is sufficiently high, saturation takes place (that is, the number of atoms in the states $\mathcal{E}_2$ and $\mathcal{E}_3$ becomes identical). In this case, the absorption of light by the vapor decreases (since the number of unexcited particles at level $\mathcal{E}_2$ capable of absorption of light quanta decreases) and the ^{87}Rb vapor becomes more transparent than it would be without pumping. If pumping is accompanied by irradiation of the ^{87}Rb vapor with radio waves of a frequency corresponding to the transitions of ^{87}Rb atoms between levels $\mathcal{E}_1$ and $\mathcal{E}_2$, then absorption of the radio waves will lead to the transition of ^{87}Rb atoms from level $\mathcal{E}_1$ to level $\mathcal{E}_2$ (Figure 3). Such a radio wave will inhibit the saturating action of the light wave, which will result in increased absorption of light by the ^{87}Rb vapor. Thus, by using a photoelectric detector to measure the intensity of the light that has passed through the tube with ^{87}Rb vapor, it is possible to determine exactly whether the vapor is acted upon simultaneously by light with intensity corresponding to the $\mathcal{E}_2 \rightarrow \mathcal{E}_3$ transition and by a radio wave with the frequency of the $\mathcal{E}_1 \rightarrow \mathcal{E}_2$ transition. The source of radio waves is a quartz-crystal oscillator, which excites an electromagnetic field of the resonance frequency in the resonator. If the frequency of the oscillator is varied smoothly, the intensity of the light incident on the photoelectric detector will decrease sharply when it coincides with the frequency of the spectral line of ^{87}Rb.

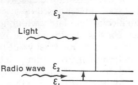

Figure 3. Energy levels of ^{87}Rb atoms used in rubidium clocks

The dependence of the intensity of the light passing through the ^{87}Rb vapor on the frequency of the radio wave is used for automatic tuning of the frequency of oscillation of the quartz-crystal oscillator depending on the frequency of the spectral line. The oscillations of the quartz-crystal oscillator are phase-modulated using an auxiliary low-frequency oscillator. Therefore, light passing through the bulb becomes intensity-modulated by the same low frequency. The more closely the frequency of the electromagnetic field coincides with the frequency of the spectral line of ^{87}Rb, the greater the modulation of light. After amplification, the electrical signal from the photoelectric detector is fed into the phase discriminator, which is also receiving the signal from the low-frequency generator. The smaller the frequency difference (detuning) between the frequency of the spectral line and the frequency of the resonator field, the greater the amplitude of the resultant output signal of the phase discriminator. The signal is fed into an element that changes the frequency of the quartz-crystal oscillator and maintains its value at a level such that it coincides with the peak of the ^{87}Rb spectral line.

The accuracy of a rubidium quantum clock is determined mainly by the width of the spectral line of ^{87}Rb. The main cause of broadening of the spectral line in gases and vapors at low pressures is the Doppler effect. To reduce its influence, a buffer gas (at a pressure of several mm Hg) is added to the bulb containing ^{87}Rb vapor. As the ^{87}Rb atoms collide with atoms of the buffer gas, they become "jammed" between them and perform rapid chaotic motions, remaining, on the average, almost in the same location and diffusing slowly through the interior of the bulb. Consequently, the spectral line assumes the shape of a narrow peak on a wide, low pedestal. The width and position of the peak depend on the composition of the buffer gas. For example, a mixture of 50 percent neon and 50 percent argon makes possible reduction of the width of the peak to about 100 Hz, in which case its position is displaced by only 0.02 Hz upon a change of 1°C in temperature or of 1 mm Hg in pressure.

The accuracy of rubidium quantum clocks is also determined by the stability of intensity of the light of the pumping lamp; therefore, automatic intensity control systems are used. It is possible to construct rubidium quantum clocks in which the optical indication system described above is replaced by a rubidium-vapor quantum generator. These quantum clocks use optical pumping of such intensity and a resonator with such a high quality factor that conditions for self-excitation are satisfied. In this case, the ^{87}Rb vapor filling the bulb in the interior of the resonator emits electromagnetic waves at a frequency of 6835 MHz. The electronic circuit of such quantum clocks also contains a quartz-crystal oscillator and a synthesizer, but in contrast to the preceding instrument, the frequency of the quartz-crystal oscillator is controlled by an automatic phase control system in which the reference frequency is the frequency of the rubidium generator.

REFERENCES

Kvantovaia elektronika, Malen'kaia entsiklopediia. Moscow, 1969. Pages 35 and 241.
Grigor'iants, V. V., M. E. Zhabotinskii, and V. F. Zolin. *Kvantovye standarty chastoty.* Moscow, 1968. Page 171.

M. E. ZHABOTINSKII [11–1785–1]

QUANTUM ELECTRODYNAMICS, the quantum theory of electromagnetic processes; the most thoroughly studied area of quantum field theory. Classical electrodynamics takes into account only the continuous properties of an electromagnetic field. However, quantum electrodynamics is based on the concept of an electromagnetic field that also has some discontinuous (discrete) properties. The carriers of such properties are field quanta, or photons. Photons have zero rest mass, energy $\mathcal{E} = h\nu$, and momentum $\mathbf{p} = (h/2\pi)\mathbf{k}$, where h is Planck's constant, ν is the frequency of the electromagnetic wave, and $\mathbf{k}$ is a wave vector of magnitude $k = 2\pi\nu/c$ (c is the speed of light), oriented in the direction of propagation of the wave. In quantum electrodynamics the interaction of electromagnetic radiation with charged particles is viewed as absorption and emission of photons by the particles.

Quantum electrodynamics quantitatively explains the effects of the interaction of radiation with matter (emission, absorption, and dispersion) and furnishes a consistent description of electromagnetic interactions among charged particles. Some of the highly important problems not explained by classical electrodynamics but successfully solved by quantum electrodynamics are the thermal radiation of bodies, X-ray scattering on free (or, more accurately, weakly bound) electrons (the Compton effect), emission and absorption of photons by atoms and more complex systems, and emission of photons during the scattering of fast electrons in external fields (bremsstrahlung). Quantum electronics describes these phenomena, as well as any other phenomena concerning the interaction of electromagnetic radiation with electrons and positrons, with a high degree of accuracy. The theory is less successful in interpreting other processes, since these processes are decisively influenced not only by electromagnetic interactions but also by interactions of other types (strong and weak interactions).

The gradual construction of quantum electrodynamics has led to a reexamination of classical concepts dealing with the motion of matter.　　　　　　V. I. GRIGOR'EV [11–1766–2]

QUANTUM ELECTRONICS, the field of physics and technology that deals with methods for the amplification and generation of electromagnetic oscillations based on the use of the effect of stimulated emission, and also with the properties of quantum mechanical amplifiers and generators and with their use. The practical interest in quantum light generators (lasers) is due primarily to the fact that, unlike other light sources, they radiate light waves having very high directivity and monochromaticity. Quantum generators of radio waves differ from other radio apparatus in that the frequency of the oscillations generated is very stable; quantum magnetic amplifiers of radio-frequency waves are distinguished by their extremely low noise level.

Physical principles. Light and radio waves are electromagnetic radiation that can be emitted in batches called quanta (or photons) by atoms, molecules, and other quantum systems that have a certain amount of excess internal energy (excited particles). The internal energy of an atom or molecule can assume only certain strictly defined discrete values, called energy levels. A reduction in internal energy indicates a transition of an atom from a higher energy level to a lower one. If the excess energy is given off as a quantum of radiation, the radiation frequency ν is determined by Bohr's condition:

$$(1) \qquad \nu = (\mathcal{E}_2 - \mathcal{E}_1)/h$$

where h is Planck's constant. Similarly, an increase in an atom's internal energy indicates its transition from a lower energy level $\mathcal{E}_1$ to a higher level $\mathcal{E}_2$. If this increase results from the absorption of a quantum of radiation, then the frequency of the absorbed radiation is determined by the same condition (1). Thus, condition (1) determines the frequency of a spectral line of absorption or radiation that is characteristic for the particular particles. The interaction of the particles with surrounding particles and fields, as well as the shortness of their lifetime at a level, causes a washing out of the energy levels. As a result, condition (1) is met not for a single fixed value of the frequency ν but rather for a range of frequencies, and the spectral lines broaden.

Excited particles are able to give up their energy in the form of quanta of radiation in two ways. They are unstable, and for each of them there is a certain probability of the spontaneous emission of a quantum of radiation (Figure 1,a). The spontaneous emissions occur randomly; therefore, the spontaneous radiation has a chaotic character. Photons are emitted by different particles at different moments, and they have different frequencies, polarizations, and directions of propagation. The intensity of spontaneous radiation is proportional to the cube of the frequency and therefore drops sharply from light waves to radio-frequency waves. All nonlaser light sources (incandescent lamps, gas-discharge lamps, and so on) radiate light as a result of events of spontaneous emission. In the radio-frequency range the noise from electronic devices and the thermal radio-frequency radiation of hot bodies have the same characteristics.

Excited particles can emit photons by passing from a higher energy level $\mathcal{E}_2$ to a lower level $\mathcal{E}_1$ not only spontaneously but also when exposed to external radiation (stimulated), if the frequency of the external radiation satisfies condition (1) (Figure 1,b). The probability of stimulated emission, which was predicted by A. Einstein in 1917, is proportional to the intensity of the stimulating radiation and can exceed the probability of the spontaneous process. Hence, the process of stimulated emission involves two quanta of radiation: the primary, or stimulating, quantum, and the secondary quantum, which is emitted by an excited atom. It is significant that the secondary quanta are indistinguishable from the primary quanta. They have exactly the same frequency, phase, and direction of propagation. This feature of stimulated emission, which is of fundamental significance for quantum electronics, was first pointed out by P. Dirac in 1927. The identical quanta form an electromagnetic wave that is an exact amplified copy of the initial radiation. As the number of events of stimulated emission per second increases, the intensity of the wave becomes greater, but its frequency, phase, polarization, and direction of propagation remain unchanged: coherent amplification of the electromagnetic radiation takes place.

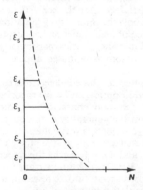

Figure 1. (a) Spontaneous emission of a photon, (b) stimulated emission, (c) resonance absorption; $\mathcal{E}_1$ and $\mathcal{E}_2$ are energy levels of the atom

For one particle the induced transitions from a higher energy level $\mathcal{E}_2$ to a lower level $\mathcal{E}_1$ (emission of a photon; Figure 1,b) and from a lower to a higher level (absorption of a photon; Figure 1,c) are equally probable. Consequently, the coherent amplification of a wave is possible only when the number of excited particles exceeds the number of unexcited particles. Under conditions of thermodynamic equilibrium there are fewer excited than unexcited particles—that is, the higher energy levels are populated by fewer particles than the lower levels, in accordance with the Boltzmann distribution for particles with respect to energy levels (Figure 2). During interaction of radiation with such a substance the radiation will be absorbed.

Figure 2. Distribution of particles with respect to energy levels $\mathcal{E}_1$, $\mathcal{E}_2$, $\mathcal{E}_3$, $\mathcal{E}_4$, and $\mathcal{E}_5$ according to Boltzmann statistics; N is the number of particles at each level

To achieve an amplifying effect, special measures must be taken so that the number of excited particles will exceed the number of unexcited particles. The state of a substance, even for only two energy levels of the particles, in which the higher level has a greater population that the lower is known as a state of population inversion. Such a substance is called active (an active medium) in quantum electronics. Stimulated emission in an active medium is used in quantum electronics for the amplification of electromagnetic waves (quantum mechanical amplifier) and for their generation (quantum generator). The feedback required for generation is accomplished by installing an active medium in a cavity resonator, in which standing electromagnetic waves can be excited. At some point in the resonator spontaneous transition of the particles in the active medium from a higher to a lower level inevitably takes place—that is, a photon is emitted spontaneously. If the resonator is tuned to the frequency of such a photon, it will not emerge from the resonator but, upon being repeatedly reflected from its walls, will generate a multitude of photons like itself, which in turn affect the active substance and produce more new events of stimulated emission of similar photons (feedback). As a result of such "multiplication" of the photons the electromagnetic energy in the resonator is built up, and a portion of the energy is passed on to the load by means of special devices (for example, a semitransparent mirror for light waves). If at a given moment the power of the stimulated emission exceeds the power caused by energy lost to heating the resonator's walls, scattering of the radiation, and so on and to the useful radiation to external space (that is, if the conditions for self-excitation are fulfilled), then undamped oscillations are developed in the resonator—generation is stimulated.

By virtue of the properties of stimulated emission, the oscillations are monochromatic. All particles of the active substance operate cophasally because of feedback. The frequency of such a generator coincides to a high degree of accuracy with the emission frequency of the excited particles, although it is also considerably affected by mistuning of the resonator frequency with respect to the emission frequency of the particles. The intensity of the oscillations is controlled by the number of excited particles per second in each cubic centimeter of active medium. If the number of such particles is Λ, then the maximum possible power P of continuous emission per cubic centimeter of the medium is

$$P = \Lambda h\nu$$

Historical survey. Although Einstein's and Dirac's theorems on induced emission were formulated in connection with optics, the development of quantum electronics began in radiophysics. Under conditions of thermodynamic equilibrium the optical (higher) energy levels are virtually unpopulated, there are very few excited particles in the substance, and they transfer spontaneously to the lower energy levels because at the low densities of light energy spontaneous transitions are more probable than induced transitions. Therefore, although the concept of monochromaticity arose in optics, in this field there were no strictly harmonic oscillations and waves (oscillations having constant amplitude, frequency, and phase). In radio physics, on the other hand, the technology for producing harmonic oscillations by means of generators with oscillatory circuits and controlled positive feedback was developed immediately after the construction of the first spark transmitters. The polychromaticity of radiation in the optical range and the absence of techniques and concepts in optics that were well developed in radio physics, particularly the concept of feedback, were the reasons why masers appeared before lasers.

Until 1950, radio physics and optics developed along different paths. Quantum theories developed in optics, and wave theories developed in radio physics. The common character of radio physics and optics that results from the generality of the quantum nature of electromagnetic wave processes was not apparent until the appearance of microwave spectroscopy—the study of the spectra of molecules, atoms, and ions lying in the super high-frequency (SHF) range (10^{10}–10^{11} Hz). An important feature of research in microwave spectroscopy (unlike research in optics) was the use of monochromatic sources of radiation, which provided enormously greater sensitivity, resolving power, and accuracy in microwave spectroscopes as compared to optical spectroscopes. No less important was the circumstance that in the radio-frequency range, unlike the optical range, the excitation levels under conditions of thermodynamic equilibrium were heavily populated and spontaneous emission was much weaker. As a result, stimulated emission directly influenced the observed value of the resonance absorption of radio-frequency waves by the substance being studied.

The reason for the population of excitation levels is the thermal motion of the particles, which at room temperature corresponds to an energy of about 4×10^{-14} erg. For visible light of wavelength $\lambda = 0.5$ microns (μ), the oscillation frequency ν is 6×10^{-14} Hz and the energy of a quantum $h\nu$ is 1×10^{-12} erg. For radio-frequency radiation of wavelength $\lambda = 0.5$ cm the oscillation frequency ν is 6×10^{10} Hz and the energy of a quantum $h\nu$ is 4×10^{-16} erg. Consequently, thermal motion can cause the excitation levels to be heavily populated at radio frequencies but not at optical frequencies.

As a result of the factors listed above, microwave spectroscopy became the basis of development of quantum electronics. In the USSR work on the microwave spectroscopy of gases was begun in the oscillation laboratory of the Institute of Physics of the Academy of Sciences of the USSR (A. M. Prokhorov), where, in addition to the solution of a number of problems of spectroscopy, research was conducted on the use of SHF spectral lines to create frequency standards.

The accuracy of a frequency standard based on measuring the position of a resonance absorption line depends on the width of the spectral line. The narrower the line, the higher the accuracy. Gases have the narrowest lines because the particles in a gas interact weakly with one another. In addition, the chaotic thermal motion of the gas particles brings about as a result of the Doppler effect the Doppler broadening of the spectral lines. An effective method of avoiding such a broadening effect is the shift from chaotic to ordered motion—for example, from gases to molecular beams. However, in this case the capability of a microwave spectroscope is severely limited by the low intensity of the resonance lines. There are few particles in the beam, and consequently the difference between the number of excited and unexcited particles is negligible. At this stage of development the idea of artificially changing the ratio between the number of excited and unexcited particles arose, making possible a substantial increase in the sensitivity of microwave spectroscopes. In addition, if a population inversion is produced in a beam, amplification of the radio-frequency waves, rather than their absorption, becomes possible. If a certain system amplifies radio-frequency radiation, it can then generate it by means of suitable feedback.

The theory of generation was well developed in radio physics. Oscillatory circuits are the basic elements in radio oscillators. In the SHF region the role of circuits is played by cavity resonators, which are particularly suitable for operation with beams of particles. Thus, it was precisely in radio physics that all the necessary elements and prerequisites for the creation of the first quantum generator were available. In the first quantum electronic device —the maser developed in 1955 simultaneously in the USSR by N. G. Basov and A. M. Prokhorov and in the USA by J. Gordon, H. Zeiger, and C. Townes—the active medium was a beam of molecules of ammonia, NH_3. The method of electrostatic spatial selection was used to produce a population inversion. The more excited molecules of NH_3, were selected from the beam, and those with lower energy were driven aside. The beam of selected molecules was passed into a cavity resonator, in which generation occurred when the conditions for self-excitation were fulfilled. The generator frequency matched that of the emission from the excited NH_3 molecules to a high degree of accuracy and was therefore extremely stable: the relative frequency stability is 10^{-11}–10^{-12}. The appearance of masers opened up new possibilities for ultraprecise clocks and accurate navigation systems. Their error is about 1 sec in 300,000 years. Hydrogen generators operating on similar principles, which were developed later, have an even greater frequency stability, about 10^{-13}.

The origin of quantum electronics in the radio-frequency region explains the emergence of the term "quantum radio physics," which is used at times instead of "quantum electronics," a term with a more general meaning that embraces the optical range.

Population inversion cannot always be achieved, particularly in solids, by selection of excited particles. In addition, if the temperature is not very high, there are virtually no excited particles at high optical levels. Therefore, as early as 1955, N. G.

Basov and A. M. Prokhorov proposed a new method of creating population inversions, in which the excited particles are produced rather than selected from the number available. In this method, which is called the three-level method, particles having an energy spectrum with three levels $\mathcal{E}_1$, $\mathcal{E}_2$, and $\mathcal{E}_3$ (Figure 3, a) are subjected to powerful auxiliary radiation (pumping), which, upon being absorbed by the particles, "pumps" them from level $\mathcal{E}_1$ to level $\mathcal{E}_3$. The pumping must be sufficiently intense so that enough particles are raised to the highest level $\mathcal{E}_3$ from the lowest to maintain virtually identical numbers of particles in each state (Figure 3,b). In this case there can then be more particles in level $\mathcal{E}_2$ than in level $\mathcal{E}_1$ (or more in level $\mathcal{E}_3$ than in level $\mathcal{E}_2$)—that is, a population inversion will occur for levels $\mathcal{E}_2$ and $\mathcal{E}_1$ (or $\mathcal{E}_3$ and $\mathcal{E}_2$). The frequency of the pumping radiation matches the resonance conditions of absorption, that is,

$$\nu_p = (\mathcal{E}_3 - \mathcal{E}_1)/h$$

The three-level method was applied as proposed by N. Bloembergen (1956, USA) to make quantum amplifiers in the radio-frequency range using paramagnetic crystals. The quantum amplifiers usually operate at the temperature of liquid helium (4.2°K), where virtually all the particles are at the lowest energy level. During pumping half of all the particles available in the crystal are transferred to a higher level $\mathcal{E}_2$ and take part in coherent amplification. Whereas the maser met the requirement for a high-stability source of monochromatic oscillations in electronics, the quantum amplifier solves the other very important problem of radio physics—the problem of drastically reducing the noise (that is, increasing the sensitivity of SHF receivers). Consequently, quantum mechanical amplifiers have come to be used in radio astronomy, radar, and global and space communications.

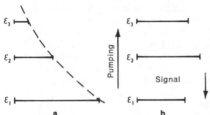

Figure 3. Three-level method: (a) populations of levels without pumping, (b) strong auxiliary radiation of the pump equalizes the populations of levels $\mathcal{E}_1$ and $\mathcal{E}_3$, creating a population inversion of level $\mathcal{E}_2$ with respect to level $\mathcal{E}_1$

The success of quantum electronics has raised the question of its progress toward the shorter wavelengths, in which the development of resonators presents the main difficulty. Closed cavities with conducting walls, whose dimensions are comparable to the wavelength, are used in the SHF region. However, in the optical range it is impossible to produce resonators of this type. An open type of resonator was proposed by A. M. Prokhorov in 1958. In the submillimeter region the resonator consists of two parallel, highly reflective metal disks between which a system of standing waves is set up. In the case of light, this resonator becomes two parallel mirrors similar to a Fabry-Perot interferometer.

The first quantum electronics achievement in the optical range was the development of the laser by T. Maiman of the USA in 1960. The working substance was a single crystal of ruby, and the three-level method was used to produce a population inversion. The reflecting mirrors of the resonator were the well-polished and silvered ends of the ruby crystal. The pump source was a flash lamp. Ruby lasers, along with neodymium-doped glass lasers, yield record-breaking energies and powers. In the free oscillation mode with powerful pumping, large ruby crystals will provide a pulse of energy of up to 1,000 joules (J) and a power of up to 10^6 watts (W). Another mode of ruby lasers is produced by switching on the resonator mirrors at the moments when a population inversion reaches its maximum value. Then all the particles accumulated in the metastable level emit at practically the same time and the generator will produce a giant radiation pulse of very short duration (10^{-8}–10^{-9} sec) and comparatively low energy (about 3 J). However, since this energy is emitted in

a very short time, the peak power of the pulse attains values of 3×10^6 to 3×10^9 W.

Very soon after the ruby laser came the development of the first gas laser (A. Javan, W. Bennett, and D. Herriott; USA, 1960) using a mixture of neon and helium atoms. It was followed by the semiconductor injection laser (R. Hall, and also W. Dumke and collaborators; USA, 1962). In gas lasers, a population inversion is achieved not by pumping with light but rather as a result of collisions of the atoms or molecules in the working gas with electrons or ions provided by an electrical discharge. Among the gas lasers the helium-neon laser and the laser using a mixture of carbon dioxide, nitrogen, and helium (the CO_2 laser) are distinguished, since they can operate in both the pulse and continuous modes. The light oscillations produced from a helium-neon laser are very stable ($\sim 10^{-13}$) and highly monochromatic ($\Delta\nu = 1$ Hz at a frequency of 10^{14} Hz). Although the efficiency of this laser is very low (0.01 percent), the high monochromaticity and directivity of its emission (which are due particularly to the homogeneity of its active medium) have made it indispensable in all types of alignment and leveling work. A powerful CO_2 laser (C. Patel, USA, 1964) generates infrared radiation ($\lambda = 10.6\mu$). Its efficiency, which reaches 30 percent, exceeds that of all existing lasers operating at room temperature. The gas dynamics laser is particularly promising because it can produce a power of several dozen kilowatts in the continuous mode. Its monochromaticity, directivity, and high power make it promising for a number of technological applications.

In semiconductor lasers a population inversion is attained mainly by injecting current carriers through a *p-n* junction into a suitable doped semiconductor. There are a number of semiconductor materials from which lasers can be made for an extensive range of wavelengths. The most common is gallium arsenide (GaAs), which at the temperature of liquid nitrogen can radiate continuously in the near infrared region at a power of up to 10 W with an efficiency of 30 percent. The power generated by injection lasers may be controlled virtually without lag by changing the injection current, suggesting their use in high-speed computers and communication systems.

Population inversions are produced in paramagnetic amplifiers and in ruby, gas, and semiconductor lasers by using completely different physical phenomena, but the common and important factor for all methods of creating a population inversion is the need to overcome the processes that tend to reestablish an equilibrium population. The processes of reestablishing a population equilibrium can be inhibited only by expending energy derived from an external source. As a rule, only a small part of the pumping energy is converted into laser emission. In the free generation mode the efficiency of a ruby laser is less than 1 percent, and for giant pulses it is even lower. However, the "loss" in the emitted energy is compensated in quantum electronics by the gain in its "quality," the monochromaticity and directivity of the radiation, which are due to the nature of stimulated emission.

Monochromaticity and high directivity make it possible to focus all the energy radiated by a laser into a spot having dimensions close to the wavelength of the radiation. In this case the electric field of a light wave attains values close to those of intra-atomic fields. When such fields interact with a substance, completely new phonemena take place.

Applications. Quantum electronics has revolutionized SHF radio physics and optics and has produced very large transformations in optics. In radio physics the development of masers denoted the appearance of radio devices that were new in principle but at the same time had properties familiar to the radio engineer. Even before the development of quantum electronics, coherent amplifiers and monochromatic generators existed in radio physics. Quantum electronics merely made a marked improvement in the sensitivity of amplifiers (by a factor of 10^3) and the stability of frequency generators (by tens of thousands of times). In optics, on the other hand, before the appearance of lasers all light sources had neither any appreciable directivity nor monochromaticity. The creation of lasers marked the appearance of light sources with completely new properties. This provided an opportunity previously unknown in optics to concentrate radiant energy both spatially and within a narrow frequency band.

Industry produces various types of lasers, which are used not only as effective research instruments but also in solving various types of practical problems. The principal advantages of the laser effect are the small area of diffusion of heat, the absence of electric charge transfer and mechanical contact, and the feasibility of operating inside vacuum flasks and in corrosive gases. One of the first applications of lasers was in measuring the distance to the moon with greater accuracy than had been possible using the radio-physics method. After a corner reflector had been set up on the moon, the distance to it was measured to an accuracy of 1.5 m. A laser radar service for the earth-to-moon distance now exists.

The use of lasers in optical communications has opened up new possibilities. The development of optical communications links, with their problems of modulation of oscillations, detection, heterodyning, and converting the frequencies of the light oscillations, made necessary the transfer into optics of methods used in radio physics and the theory of oscillations.

Nonlinear optics, which deals with nonlinear optical effects whose nature depends on the light intensity (self-focusing of light, generation of optical harmonics, induced light scattering, and self-brightening and self-darkening of light), has emerged. Methods of nonlinear optics have been used to create a new class of frequency-tunable sources of coherent radiation in the ultraviolet region. Phenomena of nonlinear optics occur only in a narrow intensity range of the laser radiation. At low intensities no nonlinear optical effects appear, but as the intensity is increased they appear and build up, but even at flux intensities of 10^{14} W/cm^2 all known substances are destroyed by a laser beam and are converted into plasma. The production and investigation of the laser plasma is one of the most interesting uses of the laser. Thermonuclear fusion initiated by laser radiation has been achieved.

Because of the high spectral and spatial concentration of electromagnetic energy lasers have come to be used extensively in microbiology, photochemistry, chemical synthesis, dissociation, and catalysis. Quantum electronics has led to the development of holography—a method of producing three-dimensional images of objects by reconstituting the structure of the light wave reflected from an object.

N. G. Basov and A. M. Prokhorov of the USSR and C. Townes of the USA received the Nobel Prize in physics in 1964 for their work on quantum electronics.

REFERENCES
Kvantovaia elektronika: Malen'kaia entsiklopediia. Moscow, 1969.
Fabrikant, V. "Klassika, kvanty i kvantovaia elektronika." *Nauka i zhizn'*, 1965, no. 10.
Prokhorov, A. M. "Kvantovaia elektronika." *Uspekhi fizicheskikh nauk*, 1965, vol. 85, fasc. 4.
Basov, N. G. "Poluprovodnikovye kvantovye generatory." *Ibid.*
Shavlov, A. "Sovremennye opticheskie kvantovye generatory." *Uspekhi fizicheskikh nauk*, 1963, vol. 81, fasc. 4.
Townes, C. "Poluchenie kogerentnogo izlucheniia s pomoshch'iu atomov i molekul." *Uspekhi fizicheskikh nauk*, 1966, vol. 88, fasc. 3.

N. V. KARLOV   [11–1767–1]

QUANTUM EVOLUTION, a form of evolution of a group of organisms that is related to abrupt transition from one adaptive zone to another.

The term "quantum evolution" was introduced by the American biologist G. G. Simpson in 1944. In this sense "quantum" is an effect that, when lower than a given threshhold, produces no reaction but, passing the threshhold, alters the equilibrium and (through the operation of harsh natural selection) leads the group either to extinction or to distinct structural modifications and the appearance of new families, orders, suborders, and so forth. Quantum evolution explains the explosive character of the evolution of many large groups of organisms that seemed to flourish suddenly. Thus, the formation of vast plains at the beginning of the Tertiary period and the appearance of herbaceous angiosperms (especially Gramineae) contributed to progressive modifications in the structure of the dental system, skull, and extremities of ungulates; this in turn led to an abrupt change in the number, diversity of form, and universal dispersion of the group.

REFERENCE
Simpson, G. G. *Tempy i formy evoliutsii.* Moscow, 1948. (Translated from English.)   A. V. IABLOKOV   [11–1766–1]

QUANTUM FIELD THEORY, the quantum theory of systems with an infinite number of degrees of freedom (physical fields). It took shape as a generalization of quantum mechanics in connection with the problem of describing the processes of production, absorption, and mutual transformations of elementary particles and later found extensive application in solid-state theory and the theory of the atomic nucleus. It is now the main theoretical method for studying quantum systems.

Particles and fields in classical and quantum theory

Duality of classical theory. In classical theory, the formation of which was basically complete by the early 20th century, the physical picture of the world consists of two elements, particles and fields. Particles are tiny bits of matter that move according to the laws of classical Newtonian mechanics. Each of them has three degrees of freedom: its position is defined by three coordinates, such as x, y, and z; if the dependence of the coordinates on time is known, exhaustive information on the particle's motion is provided.

The description of fields is much more complicated. For example, to define an electric field means to give its intensity **E** at all points in space. Thus, to describe a field it is necessary to know not three quantities, as in the case of a particle, but rather an infinitely large number of quantities at each moment; in other words, a field has an infinite number of degrees of freedom. Naturally the laws of the dynamics of an electromagnetic field, which were determined primarily as a result of the studies of M. Faraday and J. Maxwell, prove to be more complicated than the laws of mechanics. This is the main, although not the only, difference between fields and particles: particles are discrete, whereas fields are continuous; an electromagnetic field (or electromagnetic waves) may be produced and absorbed, but appearance and disappearance are alien to the particles of classical mechanics; finally, electromagnetic waves may, by superposition, amplify or damp each other or even completely suppress each other (interference of waves), which does not, of course, take place during the superposition of streams of particles.

Although particles and waves are interwoven by a complex network of interactions, each acts as the carrier of fundamentally different individual features. Distinctive features of duality are inherent in the picture of the world in classical theory. The discovery of quantum phenomena replaced this picture with another, which may be called the dual picture.

Quanta of an electromagnetic field. In 1900, M. Planck first introduced into physics the concept of a bundle, or quantum, of radiation to explain the principles of thermal radiation of bodies. The energy $\mathcal{E}$ of such a quantum is proportional to the frequency ν of the radiated electromagnetic wave: $\mathcal{E} = h\nu$, where the proportionality factor is $h = 6.62 \times 10^{-27}$ erg·sec (this came to be called Planck's constant). A. Einstein extended Planck's idea of the discreteness of radiation, assuming that it is inherent in electromagnetic radiation itself rather than being associated with some special mechanism of interaction between radiation and matter. Electromagnetic radiation "consists" of such quanta, or photons. These concepts were confirmed by experiment—the principles of the photoelectric effect and the Compton effect were explained on their basis.

Thus, characteristics of discreteness that previously were ascribed only to particles are inherent in electromagnetic radiation. Like a particle (or corpuscle), a photon has a definite energy, momentum, and spin and always exists as a unified whole. In addition to corpuscular properties, however, the photon also has wave properties that are manifested in such phenomena as diffraction and interference of light. Therefore, it could be called a wave-particle.

Wave-particle duality. The dualistic wave-particle concept of the electromagnetic field quantum—the photon—was extended by L. de Broglie to all types of matter. According to de Broglie's hypothesis, electrons, protons, and any other particles have not only corpuscular but also wave properties. This is manifested quantitatively in the de Broglie relations, which link such corpuscular quantities as the energy $\mathcal{E}$ and momentum $\mathbf{p}$ of a particle with quantities characteristic of a wave description—the wavelength λ and the frequency ν:

$$\mathcal{E} = h\nu \qquad \mathbf{p} = \mathbf{n}\frac{h}{\lambda}$$

where $\mathbf{n}$ is a unit vector indicating the direction of wave propagation.

Wave-particle duality, which was confirmed experimentally, required reexamination of the laws of motion and of the very methods of describing moving objects. Quantum mechanics (or wave mechanics) took shape. Its most important feature is the idea of giving a probabilistic description of the motion of microscopic objects. The probability amplitude, or wave function, $\psi(x, y, z, t)$, is the quantity that describes the state of a system in quantum mechanics, such as an electron moving in a given field. The square of the absolute value of the wave function, $|\psi(x, y, z, t)|^2$, defines the probability of detecting a particle at time t at a point with coordinates x, y, z. The energy and momentum, like all other corpuscular quantities, can be defined unambiguously if $\psi(x, y, z, t)$ is known. When such a probabilistic description is used, one may also speak of the "point nature" of particles. This is reflected in the localizability of an interaction, which means that an interaction between an electron and a field is determined only by the values of the field and the wave function of the electron at the same point in space and time. In classical electrodynamics, localizability means that a point charge experiences the influence of a field at the point where it is located and does not react to the field at any other points.

As the carrier of information on the corpuscular properties of a particle, the probability amplitude $\psi(x, y, z, t)$ at the same time reflects its wave properties. The equation defining $\psi(x, y, z, t)$ —the Schrödinger equation—is a wave-type equation (hence the name "wave mechanics"); the principle of superposition is valid for $\psi(x, y, z, t)$, making possible the description of interference phenomena.

Thus, the duality mentioned above is reflected in the very method of quantum-mechanical description, which eliminates the sharp boundary that divided fields and particles in classical theory. This description was dictated by the wave-particle nature of microscopic objects, and its correctness has been verified in a large number of phenomena.

Quantum field theory as an extension of quantum mechanics. Quantum mechanics brilliantly resolved the most important problem—the problem of the atom—and also provided a key to the understanding of many other puzzles of the microcosm. At the same time, however, the "oldest" of the fields, the electromagnetic field, was described in this theory by the classical Maxwell equations—that is, it was essentially considered to be a classical continuous field. Quantum mechanics makes possible description of the motion of electrons, protons, and other particles but not of their creation or annihilation—that is, it is applicable only in describing systems with a constant number of particles. The problem of the emission and absorption of electromagnetic waves by charged particles, which in quantum language corresponds to the creation or annihilation of photons, perhaps the most interesting problem in electrodynamics, is by its nature outside its competence. In a quantum-mechanical examination of the hydrogen atom, for example, a discrete set of values of the electron's energy, the angular momentum, and other physical quantities that bear on different states of the atom may be obtained, and the probability of detecting the electron at a certain distance from the nucleus may be found, but transitions of the atom from one state to another, accompanied by the emission or absorption of photons, cannot be described (at least, not consistently). Thus, quantum mechanics gives only an approximate description of the atom that is valid to the extent that radiation effects can be disregarded.

Not only photons can be produced and annihilated. One of the most striking and, as was found, most general properties of the microcosm is the universal mutual convertibility of particles. Some particles disappear and others appear in their place either "spontaneously" (at first glance) or in the process of collisions. For example, a photon can create an electron-positron pair, pi-mesons can be produced in collisions of protons and neutrons, the pi-meson decays into a muon and a neutrino, and so on. Further development of quantum theory was required to describe processes of this type. However, the new range of problems is not exhausted by the description of the mutual transformations of particles and of their production and annihilation. The more general and profound task was the "quantization" of the field—that is, the construction of a quantum theory of systems having an infinite number of degrees of freedom. The necessity of this was all the more urgent because, as noted above, the establishment of wave-particle duality revealed the wave properties of all "particles." The solution of these problems is the goal of the extension of quantum mechanics that is called quantum field theory.

To explain the transition from quantum mechanics to quantum field theory, let us use a graphic though far from complete analogy. First let us examine a single harmonic oscillator—a mass point that is oscillating like a pendulum. In the description of such a pendulum the transition from classical mechanics to quantum mechanics reveals a number of fundamentally new facts: the permissible energy values prove to be discrete, and the possibility of simultaneously determining its coordinates and momentum vanishes. However, a single pendulum (or oscillator) remains the object of study, but the quantities that described its state in classical theory are replaced, according to the general provisions of quantum mechanics, by corresponding operators.

Let us imagine that all space is filled with oscillators of this type. Instead of somehow "numbering" the oscillators, we may simply indicate the coordinates of the points at which each of them is located, thus making the transition to a field of oscillators, with an obviously infinite number of degrees of freedom. Such a field can be described by various methods. One of them consists in tracking each of the oscillators. Here quantities called local quantities—that is, quantities that are assigned to each point in space and each instant of time—take on the greatest importance, since it is these coordinates that "mark" the selected oscillator. In the transition to the quantum description these local classical quantities that describe the field are replaced by local operators. Equations that in classical theory described field dynamics are converted into equations for the corresponding operators. If the oscillators do not interact with one another or with some other field, then the overall picture of such a field of free oscillators is relatively simple, despite the infinite number of degrees of freedom; however, complications arise when interactions are present.

Another method of describing a field is based on the fact that the totality of the vibrations of oscillators may be represented as a set of waves propagating in the field under consideration. In the case of noninteracting oscillators the waves are also found to be independent; each of them is a carrier of energy and momentum and may have specific polarization. In the transition from the classical to the quantum discussion, in which the motion of each oscillator is described by probabilistic quantum laws, the waves also assume probabilistic significance. However, according to the wave-particle duality, a particle that has the same energy and momentum—and consequently, the same mass—as a wave and that has spin (the classical analogue of which is the angular momentum of a circularly polarized wave) may be compared with each such wave. Of course, this "particle" cannot be identified with any of the field oscillators taken separately—it is a result of a process encompassing an infinitely large number of oscillators and describes a certain excitation of the field. If the oscillators are not independent (if interactions are present), this is reflected in "excitation waves" or in corresponding "excitation particles," which also cease to be independent, may be scattered by each other, and may be produced and annihilated. The study of a field may thus be reduced to examination of quantized excitation waves or "particles." Moreover, when this method of description is used, no "particles" other than the "excitation particles" arise, since each particle-oscillator does not enter by itself into the overall picture of the quantized oscillatory field.

This "oscillatory model" of a field is basically illustrative in significance (although, for example, it explains rather well why the methods of quantum field theory are an effective tool of theoretical research in solid-state physics). However, it not only reflects general important features of the theory but also explains the possibility of different approaches to the problem of providing a quantum description of fields.

The former of the methods described above is closer to the Heisenberg picture (or Heisenberg's model) of a quantum field. The latter is closer to the "interaction model," which has the advantage of being more easily visualized and therefore will generally be used in the presentation that follows. Here, of course, various physical fields that do not have a mechanical nature, rather than a field of mechanical oscillators, will be considered. Thus, in examining the electromagnetic field it would be incorrect to search for any mechanical oscillations behind the electromagnetic waves: at every point in space the intensities of the electric field **E** and the magnetic field **H** fluctuate (change over time). In the Heisenberg picture for describing an electromagnetic field, the operators $\hat{\mathbf{E}}(x)$ and $\hat{\mathbf{H}}(x)$—and other operators expressed in terms of them—that appear in place of classical quantities are the objects of theoretical investigation. In the second method, the task of describing the excitations of the electromagnetic field becomes paramount. If the energy of an "excitation particle" is equal to $\mathcal{E}$ and the momentum is **p**, then the wavelength λ and frequency ν of the corresponding wave are given by formulas (1). The carrier of this parcel of energy and momentum is the quantum of the free electromagnetic field, or the photon. Thus, examination of the free electromagnetic field reduces to a discussion of photons.

Historically, quantum electromagnetic field theory began to develop first and reached a well-known degree of completeness; therefore, the chief place in this article belongs to the quantum theory of electromagnetic processes—quantum electrodynamics. However, in addition to the electromagnetic field, other types of physical fields also exist: meson fields of various types, neutrino and antineutrino fields, and nucleon and hyperon fields. If a physical field is free (that is, does not undergo any interactions, including self-stress), then it may be considered as the aggregate of noninteracting quanta of the field, which are often called simply particles of the field. When interactions are present (such as between physical fields of different types), the independence of the quanta is lost, and when the interactions begin to play a dominant role in the dynamics of the fields, the fruitfulness of introducing the quanta of these fields is also lost (at least for those stages of the processes in the fields for which the interaction cannot be disregarded). The quantum theory of such fields has been insufficiently developed and hereafter will be discussed only superficially.

Quantum field theory and relativistic theory. The description of high-energy particles should be made within the framework of relativistic theory, that is, within the framework of Einstein's special theory of relativity. In particular, this theory establishes an important relation involving the energy $\mathcal{E}$, the momentum **p**, and the mass m of a particle:

$$\mathcal{E}^2 = c^2 \mathbf{p}^2 + m^2 c^4$$

(c is a universal constant equal to the speed of light in a vacuum, $c \approx 3 \times 10^{10}$ cm/sec). It can be seen from (2) that the energy of a particle cannot be less than mc^2. Of course, the energy does not arise "from nothing." Therefore, the minimum energy necessary to form a particle of a given mass m (called the rest mass) is equal to mc^2.

If a system consisting of slow particles is examined, their energy may prove to be insufficient for the formation of new particles. In such a "nonrelativistic system" the number of particles may remain unchanged. This makes possible the use of quantum mechanics to describe the system.

All of the above applies to the production of particles that have nonzero rest mass, but for a photon, for example, the rest mass is equal to zero, so that high—relativistic—energies are not required to form it. However, here too relativity theory cannot be ignored, as is clear merely from the fact that nonrelativistic theory is applicable only at speeds much less than the speed of light c, whereas a photon always moves with speed c.

In addition to the necessity of considering the relativistic energy region, there is another reason for the importance of the theory of relativity for quantum field theory: in the physics of elementary particles, the study of which is one of the primary (and as yet unresolved) tasks of quantum field theory, the theory of relativity plays a fundamental role. This makes the development of relativistic quantum field theory particularly important.

However, even nonrelativistic quantum field theory is of considerable interest, if only because it is used successfully in solid-state physics.

Quantum electrodynamics

Quantized free field; the vacuum state of a field, or physical vacuum. Let us examine an electromagnetic field, or—in the terminology of quantum theory—a photon field. Such a field has stored energy and may release it in portions. The reduction of a field's energy by $h\nu$ signifies the disappearance of a single photon of frequency ν, or the field's transition to a state with one less photon. The end result of a sequence of such transitions is the formation of a state in which the number of photons is equal to zero, and further emission of energy by the field becomes impossible. However, from the standpoint of quantum field theory the electromagnetic field does not cease to exist but rather is only in a state of the lowest possible energy. Since there are no photons in this state, it is natural to call it the vacuum state of an electromagnetic field, or a photon vacuum. Thus, an electromagnetic field vacuum is the lowest energy state of the field.

The concept of the vacuum as one of the states of a field, which is so unusual from the standpoint of classical concepts, is physically substantiated. An electromagnetic field in a vacuum state cannot be a supplier of energy, but it does not follow from this that a vacuum cannot manifest itself in any way at all. A physical vacuum is not an "empty place" but a state with important properties manifested in real physical processes (*see below*).

Similarly, the concept of the vacuum as the lowest energy state of a particle field may be introduced for other particles as well. In the examination of interacting fields the lowest energy state of the entire system of fields is called the vacuum state.

If sufficient energy is imparted to a field in the vacuum state, excitation of the field, or the production of a particle (a quantum of the field), takes place. Thus, the production of particles may be described as a transition from an "unobservable" vacuum state to a real state. This approach makes it possible to carry over into quantum field theory the well-developed methods of quantum mechanics and to reduce a change in the number of particles in this field to the quantum transitions of the particles from certain states to others.

The mutual transformations of particles and the production of some particles and annihilation of others may be described quantitatively by using the method of "second quantization," proposed in 1927 by P. Dirac and further developed in the work of V. A. Fok (1932).

Second quantization. The transition from classical mechanics to quantum mechanics is called simply quantization or, less often, primary quantization. As stated above, such quantization does not provide any possibility of describing a change in the number of particles in a system. The main feature of the method of second quantization is the introduction of operators that describe the production and annihilation of particles. Let us explain the action of these operators by using as a simple example (or model) a theory in which identical particles in the same state are examined (for example, all photons are considered to have identical frequency, direction of propagation, and polarization). Since the number of particles in the state may be arbitrary, this case corresponds to Bose particles or bosons, which obey Bose-Einstein statistics.

In quantum theory the state of a system of particles is described by the wave function or state vector. To describe a state with N particles, let us introduce the state vector ψ_N; the square of the absolute value of ψ_N, $|\psi_N|^2$, which gives the probability of detecting N particles, obviously becomes 1 if N is known with certainty. This means that a state vector with any fixed N is normalized to 1. Let us now introduce an operator of particle annihilation, a^-, and an operator of particle production, a^+. By definition a^- transforms a state with N particles into a state with $N - 1$ particles, that is,

(3) $$a^- \psi_N = \psi_{N-1} \cdot \sqrt{N}$$

Similarly, the operator of particle production, a^+, transforms the state ψ_N into a state with $N+1$ particles:

(4) $$a^+ \psi_N = \psi_{N+1} \cdot \sqrt{N+1}$$

The factors $\sqrt{N}$ in (3) and $\sqrt{N+1}$ in (4) are introduced just to satisfy the normalization condition $|\psi_N|^2 = 1$. In particular, when $N = 0$, $a^+ \psi_0 = \psi_1$, where ψ_0 is the state vector that characterizes the vacuum; that is, a single-particle state is produced as a result of the production of one particle from the "vacuum." However, $a^- \psi_0 = 0$, since annihilation of a particle is impossible in a state in which no particles exist; this equation may be considered a definition of a vacuum. The vacuum state ψ_0 has particular significance in quantum field theory, since any state can be derived from it by using a^+ operators. Indeed, in the case under examination (when the state of the entire system is determined only by the number of particles),

(5)
$$\psi_1 = a^+ \psi_0$$
$$\psi_2 = a^+ \psi_1 \frac{1}{\sqrt{2}} = a^+ a^+ \psi_0 \cdot \frac{1}{\sqrt{2}}$$
$$\psi_N = \underbrace{a^+ a^+ \cdots a^+}_{N} \psi_0 \cdot \frac{1}{\sqrt{1 \cdot 2 \cdot 3 \cdot \ldots \cdot N}}$$

It can be easily demonstrated that the order of action of the operators a^- and a^+ is not immaterial. Indeed, $a^-(a^+ \psi_0) = a^- \psi_1 = \psi_0$, and $a^+(a^- \psi_0) = 0$. Therefore, $(a^- a^+ - a^+ a^-)\psi_0 = \psi_0$, or

(6) $$a^- a^+ - a^+ a^- = 1$$

that is, the operators a^+ and a^- are noncommutative. Relations such as (6) that establish a connection between the action of two operators taken in different order are called transposition relations or commutation relations for these operators, and expressions of the type $\hat{A}\hat{B} - \hat{B}\hat{A} \equiv [\hat{A}, \hat{B}]$ are said to be commutators of the operators $\hat{A}$ and $\hat{B}$.

If it is taken into account that particles may exist in different states, then the state of the particle to which the operators refer must also be indicated in writing the production and annihilation operators. In quantum theory the states are given by a set of quantum numbers that define the energy, spin, and other physical quantities; for simplicity the whole set of quantum numbers will be designated by a single index n: thus, a^+_n designates the production operator for a particle in a state with a set of quantum numbers n. The average numbers of particles in the states corresponding to various n are called the occupation numbers of the states.

Let us examine the expression $a^-_n a^+_m \psi_0$. First ψ_0 is acted on by the operator "closest" to it, a^+_m; this corresponds to the production of a particle in state m. If $n = m$, the subsequent action of the operator a^-_n leads again to ψ_0, that is, $a^-_n a^+_n \psi_0 = \psi_0$. If $n \neq m$, then $a^-_n a^+_m \psi_0 = 0$, since the annihilation of particles that do not exist is impossible (the operator a^-_n describes the annihilation of particles in states n that do not occur when a^+_m acts on ψ_0). With the different states of particles taken into consideration, the commutation relations for the creation and annihilation operators have the following form:

(7)
$$a^-_n a^+_m - a^+_m a^-_n = \begin{cases} 0 \text{ when } n \neq m \\ 1 \text{ when } n = m \end{cases}$$
$$a^-_n a^-_m - a^-_m a^-_n = 0$$
$$a^+_n a^+_m - a^+_m a^+_n = 0$$

However, fields exist for which the relation between the product of the production and annihilation operators taken in different order has the following form: the minus sign in (7) is replaced by a plus sign (this is called the replacement of commutators by anticommutators),

(8)
$$a^-_n a^+_m + a^+_m a^-_n = \begin{cases} 0 \text{ when } n \neq m \\ 1 \text{ when } n = m \end{cases}$$
$$a^-_n a^-_m + a^-_m a^-_n = 0 \qquad a^+_n a^+_m + a^+_m a^+_n = 0$$

These relations also apply to the class of commutation relations, although they do not have the form of (6). Operators that conform to relations (8) must be introduced for fields whose quanta have half-integral spin (that is, they are fermions) and as a result conform to the Pauli exclusion principle, according to which the existence of two or more particles in identical states (in states with identical sets of all quantum numbers) is impossible in a system of such particles (such as electrons). Indeed, by constructing the vector of a state containing two particles (a two-particle state), $a^+_n a^+_m \psi_0$, it is not difficult to prove, taking (8) into consideration, that when $n = m$ the vector is equal to itself with the opposite sign; but this is possible only for a quantity that is identically equal to zero. Thus, if the production and annihilation operators of particles satisfy the commutation relations (8), then states with two or more particles that have identical quantum numbers are automatically excluded. Such particles obey Fermi-Dirac statistics. However, for fields whose quanta have integral spin, the production and annihilation operators of particles satisfy relations (7); here states with an arbitrary number of particles having identical quantum numbers are possible.

The existence of two types of commutation relations is of fundamental importance, since it defines two possible types of statistics. The necessity of introducing noncommutative operators to describe systems having a variable number of particles is a typical feature of second quantization.

Let us note that "primary quantization" may also be considered as a transition from classical mechanics, in which the coordinates q and momentums p are ordinary numbers (that is, of course, $qp = pq$), to a theory in which q and p are replaced by noncommutative operators: $q \rightarrow \hat{q}$, $p \rightarrow \hat{p}$, $\hat{q}\hat{p} \neq \hat{p}\hat{q}$. Here the transition from classical field theory to quantum field theory (as in electrodynamics, for example) is carried out by a similar method, but the role of the coordinates (and momentums) must be played by quantities that describe the field's distribution throughout all space and at all instants of time. Thus, in classical electrodynamics a field is defined by the values of the intensity of the electric field $\mathbf{E}$ and the magnetic field $\mathbf{H}$ (as functions of the coordinates and time). When the transition to quantum theory is made, $\mathbf{E}$ and $\mathbf{H}$ become operators that do not commute with the operator of the number of photons in the field.

It has been proved in quantum mechanics that if two operators do not commute, the physical quantities corresponding to them cannot simultaneously have exact values. Hence it follows that no state of an electromagnetic field exists in which both the field intensity and the number of photons would be exactly defined. If the number of photons is known precisely by virtue of physical conditions, then the field intensities must be completely indeterminate (capable of assuming any values). However, if these intensities are known precisely, then the number of photons is indeterminate. Thus, the impossibility of simultaneously making the field intensities and the number of photons equal to zero is the physical reason why the vacuum state is not simply the absence of a field but retains important physical properties.

Field methods in the quantum theory of many particles. The mathematical methods of quantum field theory, as noted above, are used to describe systems that consist of a large number of particles: in solid-state physics, the physics of the atomic nucleus, and so on. The lowest energy states filled by a system (that is, at temperature $T \rightarrow 0$), for example, play the role of vacuum states in a solid. If energy is imparted to a system (for example, by increasing its temperature), it moves into an excited state. At low energies the process of excitation of a system may be considered to be the formation of certain elementary excitations—a process similar to the production of particles in quantum field theory. Certain elementary excitations in a solid behave like particles—they have a definite energy, momentum, and spin. They are called quasiparticles. The evolution of a system may be represented as the collision, scattering, annihilation, and production of quasiparticles. This opens the way for extensive use of the methods of quantum field theory. The theory of superconductivity is one of the most graphic examples of the fruitfulness of the methods of quantum field theory in the study of solids.

Quanta as carriers of interaction. In classical electrodynamics the interaction between charges (and currents) is accomplished through a field: the charge gives rise to a field, and the field acts on other charges. In quantum theory the interaction of a field and a charge takes on the form of the emission and absorption of field quanta (photons) by the charge. In quantum field theory an interaction between charges, such as two electrons, is a result of their exchange of photons: each of the electrons emits a photon (quanta transferring the interaction of the electromagnetic field), which is then absorbed by the other electron. This also is valid for other physical fields: in quantum field theory, interaction is a result of the exchange of field quanta.

However, this graphic picture of interaction has an aspect that requires additional analysis. Until the interaction begins, each of the particles is free, and a free particle can neither emit nor absorb quanta. Indeed, let us examine a free stationary particle (if a particle moves uniformly we may always transform to an inertial frame of reference, in which it is at rest). Such a particle has no stored kinetic or potential energy, so that radiation is energetically impossible. Somewhat more complicated arguments demonstrate that a free particle is also incapable of absorbing quanta. However, if these considerations are valid, then the seemingly inevitable conclusion is that the appearance of interactions in quantum field theory is impossible.

To resolve this paradox it is necessary to bear in mind that particles are quantum entities and that for them the uncertainty relations are effective. These relations relate the uncertainty of a particle's coordinates (Δx) and its momentum (Δp):

$$\Delta x \Delta p \geq \hbar/2 \tag{9}$$

(where $\hbar = h/2\pi$). There is also a second relation—for the uncertainty of the energy $\Delta \mathcal{E}$ and the characteristic time Δt of a given physical process (that is, the time over which the process takes place):

$$\Delta \mathcal{E} \Delta t \sim \hbar \tag{10}$$

If the interaction between particles is considered to take place by the exchange of field quanta (this field often is called an intermediate field), then the duration of the exchange act is naturally taken to be Δt. The question of the possibility of emission of a photon by a free particle vanishes: according to (10), the particle's energy is not precisely defined; when a quantum energy spread $\Delta \mathcal{E}$ is present, the laws of conservation of energy and momentum no longer impede either emission or absorption of the quanta transferring the interaction, provided they have approximately the energy $\Delta \mathcal{E}$ and exist for a time interval $\Delta t \sim \hbar/\Delta \mathcal{E}$.

The preceding arguments not only eliminate the paradox indicated above but also make it possible to draw important physical conclusions. Let us examine the interaction of particles in atomic nuclei. Nuclei consist of nucleons—protons and neutrons. Experiment has established that the interaction is imperceptible outside the boundaries of the nucleus, that is, at distances greater than approximately 10^{-13} cm, although the interaction is known to be great within the nucleus. It can therefore be accepted that the radius of action of nuclear forces is of the order of $L \sim 10^{-13}$ cm. Consequently, it is precisely this path that is traversed by quanta carrying the interaction between nucleons in atomic nuclei. The time spent by quanta en route, even if they are assumed to move at the greatest possible speed (the speed of light, c), cannot be less than $\Delta t \approx L/c$. According to the above discussion, the quantum energy spread $\Delta \mathcal{E}$ of interacting nucleons proves to be $\Delta \mathcal{E} \sim \hbar/\Delta t \approx \hbar c/L$. The energy of a quantum—the carrier of interaction—should also lie within this spread. The energy of every particle of mass m consists of its rest energy, equal to mc^2, and its kinetic energy, which increases with the particle's momentum. When the motion of particles is not too fast, the kinetic energy is small in comparison with mc^2, so that we may say $\Delta \mathcal{E} \approx mc^2$. Then it follows from the preceding formula that a quantum that carries interactions in the nucleus should have a mass of the order of $m \approx \hbar/Lc$. If we insert in this formula the numerical values of the quantities, the mass of a quantum of the nuclear field is found to be approximately 200–300 times greater than the mass of the electron.

In 1935 this semiqualitative examination led the Japanese theoretical physicist H. Yukawa to predict a new particle: experiment later confirmed the existence of this particle, called the pi-meson. This brilliant result significantly strengthened faith in the correctness of quantum concepts of interaction as the exchange of quanta of the intermediate field, a faith that is largely retained to the present time, although so far it has been impossible to construct a quantitative meson theory of nuclear forces.

If we consider two particles so heavy that they can be regarded as classical material particles, the interaction between them arising as a result of the exchange of quanta of mass m leads to the appearance of a potential energy of interaction of the particles, equal to

$$U = g^2 \frac{e^{(-mc/\hbar) \cdot r}}{r} \tag{11}$$

where r is the distance between the particles and g is the coupling constant of the particles with the field of the quanta transferring the interaction (or, in other words, the charge corresponding to the given type of interaction).

If we apply this formula to a case in which the quanta of the electromagnetic field—photons, whose rest mass $m = 0$—are the carriers of the interaction, and if we take into account that the electric charge e should be used instead of g, we obtain the well-known energy of Coulomb interaction of two particles: $U_{\mathrm{el}} = e^2/r$.

Graphic method of describing processes. Although typically quantum objects are considered in quantum field theory, graphic representations of the processes of the interaction and conversion of particles may be given. Diagrams of this type were first introduced by the American physicist R. Feynman and bear his name. Feynman diagrams are outwardly similar to the representation of the paths of all particles participating in an interaction, if they were classical (although here no classical description whatever is involved). To represent every free particle, a line (which, of course, is only a graphic symbol of the particle's propagation) is introduced: for example, a photon is represented by a wavy line, an electron by a solid line. Arrows that arbitrarily designate the "direction of propagation" of a particle are occasionally placed on the lines. Examples of such diagrams are given below.

A diagram corresponding to the scattering of a photon on an electron is presented in Figure 1: in the initial state there is one electron and one photon; at point (1) they collide and the photon is absorbed by the electron; a new, final photon appears (is emitted by the electron) at point (2). This is one of the simplest diagrams of the Compton effect.

Figure 1

The diagram in Figure 2 illustrates the exchange of a photon between two electrons: one electron at point (1) emits a photon, which then is absorbed at point (2) by the second electron. As indicated above, an exchange of this type indicates that an interaction is present; thus, this diagram represents an elementary event of electromagnetic interaction between two electrons. More complicated diagrams corresponding to such an interaction should take into account the possible exchange of several photons; one of these is shown in Figure 3.

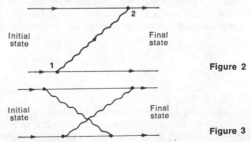

Figure 2

Figure 3

In these examples a common property of diagrams that describe an interaction between electrons and photons is manifested: all diagrams are composed of extremely simple elements, or vertices, one of which (Figure 4) represents emission, and the other (Figure 5) represents absorption of a photon by an electron. Each of these processes separately is prohibited by the laws of conservation of energy and momentum. However, if such a vertex is a component of some more complicated diagram, as was the case in the examples considered above, then the quantum uncertainty of the energy, which results from the fact that in the intermediate stage a certain particle exists for a short time Δt, lifts the energy prohibition.

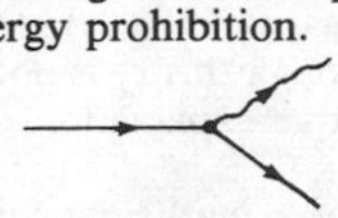

Figure 4 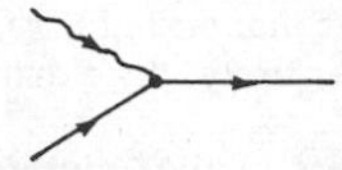   Figure 5

Particles that are produced and then absorbed at intermediate stages of the process are called virtual particles (in contrast to real particles, which exist for a rather long period). In Figure 1 a virtual electron arises at point (1) and disappears at point (2), in Figure 2 it is a virtual photon, and so on. Interaction is often said to be transferred by virtual particles. It may be assumed on a somewhat tentative basis that a particle is virtual if the quantum uncertainty of its energy $\Delta\mathcal{E}$ is of the order of the average value of the particle's energy $\bar{\mathcal{E}}$, and it may be called a real particle if $\Delta\mathcal{E} \ll \bar{\mathcal{E}}$ (for relatively slow-moving particles with nonzero rest mass m this condition reduces to the inequality $\Delta\mathcal{E} \ll mc^2$).

Feynman diagrams not only give a visual representation of processes but also make possible calculation of the probabilities of the processes by means of certain mathematical rules. Without dwelling on these rules in detail, let us note that an elementary interaction that leads to the conversion of particles (that is, to the annihilation of some particles and the production of others) occurs at every vertex. Therefore, each vertex contributes to the probability amplitude of the process, and this contribution is proportional to the interaction constant of the particles (or fields) whose lines meet at the vertex. In all of the diagrams presented above, this constant is the electric charge e. The more vertices the diagram of a process contains, the higher the power to which the charge enters the corresponding expression for the probability amplitude of the process. For example, the probability amplitude corresponding to the first and second diagrams, with two vertices, is the square of the charge ($\sim e^2$), and the third diagram, which contains four vertices, leads to an amplitude proportional to the fourth power of the charge ($\sim e^4$). Moreover, at every vertex it is necessary to take into account the conservation laws (with the exception of the law of conservation of energy, whose applicability is limited by the quantum uncertainty relation for energy and time): the law of conservation of momentum (the interaction corresponding to each peak may take place at any point in space—that is, the uncertainty of the coordinate is $\Delta x = \infty$—and consequently the momentum is precisely defined) and the law of conservation of electric charge; factors that depend on the particles' spin must also be introduced.

Only the simplest types of diagrams for certain processes were considered above. These diagrams do not exhaust the possibilities. Each of the very simple diagrams may be supplemented by an infinite number of increasingly complex diagrams that include an ever greater number of vertices. For example, the "lowest" diagram of the Compton effect presented in Figure 1 may be complicated by arbitrary selection of pairs of points on the electron lines and by joining these pairs with a wavy photon line (Figure 6), since the number of intermediate (virtual) photon lines is unlimited.

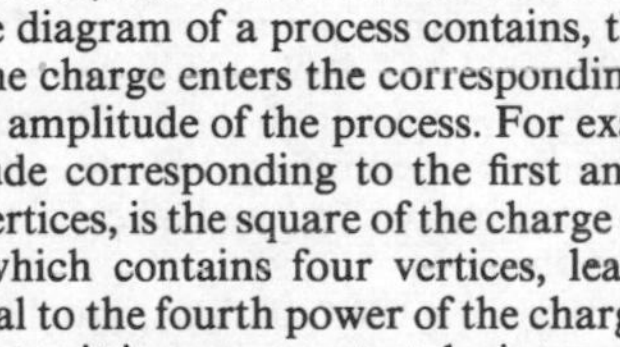

Figure 6

Interaction of a particle with the vacuum electromagnetic field; atomic radiation. In the diagrams of the interaction of two electrons presented above (Figures 2 and 3), each photon is produced by one electron and absorbed by the other. However, another process is also possible (Figure 7): the photon emitted by an electron at point (1) is absorbed after a certain interval by the same electron at point (2). Since the exchange of quanta gives rise to an interaction, such a diagram also is one of the simplest interaction diagrams, but it is a diagram only of the electron's interaction with itself or with its own field, which is the same

thing. This process may also be called the electron's interaction with a field of virtual photons or with a photon vacuum (the latter term is determined by the fact that here there are no real photons). Thus, the electron's own electromagnetic (electrostatic) field is generated by the emission and absorption of photons by the same electron. Such interactions between an electron and a vacuum give rise to experimentally observable effects, attesting to the reality of the vacuum. The most significant of these effects is the radiation of photons by atoms. According to quantum mechanics, electrons in atoms occupy certain quantum energy levels, and the radiation of a photon takes place during the transition of an electron from one (the higher) level to another level that has less energy. However, quantum mechanics leaves open the question of why such transitions, which are accompanied by so-called spontaneous ("self-produced") radiation, take place; moreover, each level here appears to be completely stable. According to quantum field theory, the interaction of the atom with the photon vacuum is the physical reason for the instability of excited levels and spontaneous quantum transitions. Figuratively speaking, interaction with the photon vacuum vibrates or rocks an atomic electron, since upon emission and absorption of every virtual photon the electron experiences a thrust or recoil; otherwise the electron would move stably in its orbit (for the sake of clarity, the semiclassical image is used). One such thrust forces the electron to "fall" into a more stable, or lower-energy, orbit; here energy is released and is used to excite the electromagnetic field—that is, to form a real photon.

Figure 7

The fact that the interaction of electrons with a photon vacuum accounts for the very possibility of transitions in atoms (and in other photon-radiating systems)—and hence for radiation—is the most far-reaching and significant effect in quantum electrodynamics. However, there also are other, much weaker "vacuum effects" that are very important in principle; some of them will be discussed later (*see below:* Perturbation method in quantum field theory).

Electron-positron vacuum. In 1928 the English physicist P. Dirac deduced the relativistic quantum equation of electron motion and from this equation predicted (1931) that the electron should have a "double"—an antiparticle differing from the electron in the sign of its electric charge. Such a particle, called the positron, was soon detected experimentally. A positron cannot be produced alone—this is precluded, for example, by the law of conservation of electric charge. Electrons and positrons may appear and disappear (be annihilated) only in pairs. A rather large quantity of energy (no less than twice the rest energy of the electron) is necessary for the production of an electron-positron pair. Such energy may be transferred, for example, by a "hard," or high-energy, photon (a gamma-ray quantum) that strikes a charged particle. However, production of a pair may also occur virtually. In that case the pair that is formed is annihilated after having existed for some very brief time Δt. The quantum energy spread $\Delta\mathcal{E} \sim \hbar/\Delta t$, if Δt is very small, makes this process permissible in terms of energy.

The process of production and annihilation of a virtual electron-positron pair is depicted graphically in Figure 8: the photon disappears at point (1), giving rise to a pair that is then annihilated at point (2), as a result of which a photon is formed once again. (The positron is represented by the same kind of solid line as the electron, on which line the arrow is, by convention, directed oppositely—that is, "backward" in time.)

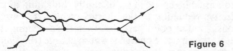

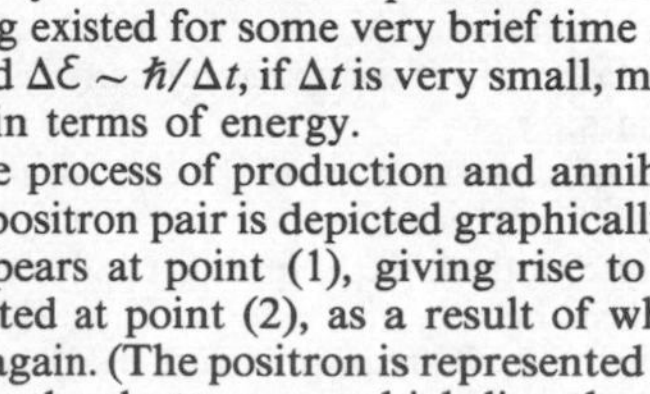

Figure 8

The fact that electrons and positrons cannot appear and disappear separately but rather are produced and annihilated only in pairs indicates the genuine physical unity of the electron-positron field. Electron and positron fields appear to be isolated only until processes that involve a change in the number of electrons and positrons are considered.

Not only electrons have antiparticles. It has been established that every particle, except for so-called truly neutral particles such as the photon and the neutral pi-meson, has an antiparticle. Processes similar to the virtual production and annihilation of electron-positron pairs exist for any particle-antiparticle pair.

Perturbation method in quantum field theory

The mathematical and physical particle; field mass; renormalization of mass. The following method, which actually has already been used above, is frequently used to describe interacting fields. The quanta of free fields (particles) are considered first. This is the zero-order approximation, in which interaction is disregarded altogether. Then the interaction is brought into consideration—the particles cease to be independent, and the possibility of their scattering, production, and annihilation as a result of interaction appears. A successive increase in the number of interaction-induced processes that are taken into account is achieved mathematically by using the perturbation method. In view of the prominent role played by this method in theory, let us discuss its physical meaning in greater detail. The procedure of successive refinement of the contribution from interactions is actually used in classical electrodynamics as well. Let us explain this by using as an example the electron and the electromagnetic field that it generates. In theory the electron is the carrier of a certain mass m_0. However, since it gives rise to an electromagnetic field with energy $\mathcal{E}_{el}$, and consequently (according to the relativistic relation $\mathcal{E} = mc^2$) mass $\mathcal{E}_{el}/c^2$, then on accelerating an electron it is also necessary to overcome the inertia of its electromagnetic field (in the simplest case, a Coulomb field).

Thus, in bringing into consideration the interaction between the electron and the electromagnetic field, the "field" part of the mass $m_{field} = \mathcal{E}_{el}/c^2$ must be added to the "nonfield," or "bare" mass m_0. Calculation of the field mass for a point particle (and the "bare" particles considered in the zero-order approximation must be considered point particles) leads to a physically meaningless result: m_{field} proves to be infinitely large. Indeed, the energy of the Coulomb field of a particle that has charge e and dimension a is equal to $\mathcal{E}_{Coulomb} = ke^2/a$ (k is a factor of the order of 1, whose numerical value depends on the charge distribution); as $a \rightarrow 0$ (point particle), $\mathcal{E}_{Coulomb} \rightarrow \infty$.

The infinite value (divergence) of field mass (although in somewhat altered, "weakened" form) is retained even in the transition from classical theory to quantum theory. Moreover, divergences of other types also appear. Analysis of the difficulties encountered here led to the emergence of the idea of renormalization. The division into field and nonfield mass arises (as can be seen from the preceding) because of the method of examination adopted: first a free "bare" particle is introduced, and then interaction is "switched on." In experiments, of course, there is neither "bare" mass nor field mass, and only the total mass of the particle is manifest. In theory it is very significant that these masses also enter as a sum and not as separate quantities. Combination of field and nonfield mass and the use for total mass of a value derived experimentally rather than theoretically is called the renormalization of mass.

The traditional means of constructing a theory within the framework of the method of perturbation theory is as follows: first, a theory of free (noninteracting) particles is formulated, and then the interaction between them is introduced. Thus, the theory of free electrons (or of the electron-positron field) is constructed first, and then the interaction of these "mathematical," or "bare," electrons with the electromagnetic field is considered. However, the "physical" electrons that actually exist in nature, in contrast to "mathematical" electrons, always interact with photons (although only with virtual photons), and this interaction may be "canceled out" only in theory. An important part of the idea of renormalization is the indication of the necessity of constructing a theory in which not the mathematical but rather the physical particles play a role.

It is interesting that to some extent nature provides the possibility of seeing the difference between a particle with "switched

on" and then "switched off" electromagnetic interaction. For example, three pi-mesons are known: with a positive electric charge (π^+), a negative charge (π^-) and a zero charge (π^0). They are different charge states of the same particle. Charged mesons (π^+ and π^-) have a greater mass than the neutral meson (π^0); obviously, an addition caused by the field (electromagnetic) mass is manifested here, although theory is not yet able to provide an entirely clear quantitative explanation of this phenomenon.

The process of the "clothing" of a mathematical particle—that is, its conversion into a physical particle—appears more complex in quantum field theory than in classical electrodynamics, where everything reduces to the "attachment" of a Coulomb "tail" to the particle. In quantum theory a physical particle differs from a mathematical particle by its "coat," which is much more complex in structure: it is formed by "clouds" of virtual quanta that are produced and then absorbed by the particle. They may be quanta of any of the fields with which the particle is interacting (such as an electromagnetic, electron-positron, or meson field). The "coat" is not something fixed; the quanta forming it are created and absorbed continuously. The "coat" pulsates—that is, the particle carrying it spends part of its time in the "clothed" state and part in the "bare" state. The part of its time that is spent in each state is determined by the degree of intensity of the interactions. For example, the meson interactions of nucleons are more than 100 times more intense than their electromagnetic interactions; one may assume that the meson "clothing" of a proton is more than 100 times "denser" than the electromagnetic. This may explain why the quantum theory of electromagnetic processes agrees brilliantly with experiment, even when vacuum effects are far from completely taken into consideration, whereas meson theory has achieved no such success. In quantum electrodynamics we may limit ourselves to consideration of processes with a small number of virtual photons and virtual electron-positron pairs, corresponding to consideration of a small number of "lower order" corrections according to the method of perturbation theory; in meson theory this does not lead to success, generating difficulties that will be examined in the next section (*see below:* Difficulties and problems in quantum field theory).

All the reasoning concerning the "coat" of particles presented above is, strictly speaking, semi-intuitive and cannot yet be translated into the language of exact theory. However, it may be useful if only because it helps to clarify the distinction between mathematical and physical particles and to understand that the description of the latter is not at all a simple task.

Polarization of a vacuum; renormalization of charge. The electric, and above all the Coulomb, field of a charged particle affects the distribution of virtual electron-positron pairs (and of pairs of any other charged particles and antiparticles). A real electron attracts virtual positrons and repels virtual electrons. This should lead to phenomena resembling the polarization of a medium into which a charged particle is introduced. Once again the perturbation theory is applicable for describing such phenomena.

The polarization of an electron-positron vacuum (use of the term suggested by the analogy cited above is accepted) is a purely quantum effect that derives from quantum field theory. The polarization leads to surrounding of the electron by a dense layer of positrons from virtual pairs, so that the effective charge of the electron must be changed significantly. Shielding of the charge, or effective reduction of the charge, results. If "bare" particles are considered as point particles, then the screening is complete —that is, the effective charge is a zero charge (the "zero charge" problem). The idea of renormalization of charge is used to overcome this difficulty. Here the arguments cited during the discussion of mass renormalization are repeated almost verbatim. Let us call "bare" a charge that would be held by a particle if the interaction with the electron-positron vacuum disappeared (we will speak only of such a particle, although, of course, the influence of virtual pairs of other fields must also be taken into account). The existence of such interaction leads to the appearance of a "correction" of the charge. Physicists are unable to calculate this correction correctly, just as they cannot determine a "bare" charge. However, since these two parts of a charge do not act alone either in experiment or in theory, the difficulty can be avoided by inserting in place of the total charge a quantity taken directly from experiment. This procedure is called renormalization of charge. Renormalization of charge and mass does not solve the problems that arise in the theory of point particles but rather only isolates these problems at some stage of theory and—extremely importantly—provides the possibility of isolating finite observable parts from infinite values for certain quantities that characterize physical particles.

Some observable "vacuum" effects. The possibility of observing the influence of a "vacuum" on particles exists. The "coat" of physical particles is found to depend on the external fields acting on the particle. In other words, field additions to a particle's energy depend on its state. The total field energy, as stated above, is infinitely large in the theory of point particles, but a finite part that changes as a function of the state of the particle and therefore can be detected experimentally can be isolated from this infinitely large quantity.

LAMB SHIFT. In the hydrogen atom (and some other light atoms) there are two states, $2S_{1/2}$ and $2P_{1/2}$, whose energies—according to quantum mechanics—should coincide. At the same time, the pattern of the motion of electrons in these states is different. Figuratively speaking, an S-electron (an electron in the S-state) spends most of its time near the nucleus, and a P-electron is located, on the average, at a greater distance from the nucleus. Therefore, on the average, an S-electron is in a stronger field than a P-electron. This leads to differences in the additional energy caused by the interaction with the photon vacuum for the P-electron and the S-electron; this may be clarified graphically. As stated above, interaction with the vacuum jolts the electron. Instead of moving in some stable orbit, such as a circular orbit, of radius r (we shall once again use this classical picture), the electron begins to be deflected at random away from this orbit. When the deflection in each direction is Δr the energy changes in different ways. Indeed, the Coulomb energy of an electron in a nuclear field changes according to the law $\mathcal{E}_{potential} \sim 1/r$; as r increases by Δr the energy changes by the amount

$$\Delta\mathcal{E} \sim \frac{1}{r+\Delta r} - \frac{1}{r} \approx -\frac{\Delta r}{r(r+\Delta r)}$$

and as r decreases by Δr, the energy changes by the amount

$$\Delta\mathcal{E}' \sim \frac{\Delta r}{r(r-\Delta r)}$$

that is, the absolute value of $\Delta\mathcal{E}'$ is greater than that of $\Delta\mathcal{E}$. As a result, the "vacuum jitter" of the electron changes the value of its potential energy. The change is particularly noticeable where the potential energy itself is great and changes rapidly with a change in r—that is, close to the nucleus. Thus, the vacuum additions to energy, called radiation corrections, should be greater for S-electrons than for P-electrons, and their energy levels, which otherwise would coincide, should split. The extent of the splitting, called the Lamb shift (it was first explained theoretically by H. Bethe and observed experimentally in 1947 by the American physicists W. Lamb and R. Retherford), is, according to quantum field theory, equal to the following (if expressed in units of frequency ν): 1057.77 MHz for hydrogen, 1058.9 MHz for deuterium, and 14,046.3 MHz for helium (conversion to energy units, ergs, is carried out according to the formula $\mathcal{E} = h\nu$, where ν is expressed in hertz). These values are in such good agreement with experimental data that further improvement of experimental accuracy would lead to the detection of effects caused by so-called strong interactions rather than electromagnetic interactions.

ANOMALOUS MAGNETIC MOMENT. No less remarkable is the accuracy with which the anomalous magnetic moment of the electron, which also shows "vacuum" (radiation) influences on this particle, is calculated. It follows from Dirac's quantum theory of the electron that the electron should have magnetic moment

$$\mu_0 = \frac{e_0 \hbar}{2m_0 c}$$

However, this applies to the "bare" electron. The process of "clothing" it changes the magnetic moment. In bringing the interaction between the electron and the vacuum into the discussion, it is necessary first of all to replace the charge (e_0) and mass (m_0) of an idealized mathematical particle with the physical values of these quantities:

$$m_0 \longrightarrow m_{phys.} \qquad e_0 \longrightarrow e_{phys.}$$

However, this does not exhaust the observed effects. The magnetic moment is a quantity that conditions the interaction between a stationary particle and an external magnetic field. It is natural to interpret the corrections that appear in the expression for the energy of the interaction as a result of the appearance of "vacuum" additions to the magnetic moment. These additions, first studied theoretically by J. Schwinger, give the so-called anomalous magnetic moment. The anomalous magnetic moment of the electron has been calculated and measured with high precision, as shown by the following data:

$$\mu_{theor.} = \mu_{normal} + \mu_{anom.}$$

(13)
$$= \mu_0 + \left(\frac{\alpha}{2\pi} - 0.328 \frac{\alpha^2}{2\pi^2}\right)\mu_0$$

$$= 1.0011596\mu_0$$

where α is the fine structure constant, equal to

(14) $\alpha = \dfrac{e^2}{\hbar c} \approx \dfrac{1}{137}$ $\left(\text{more accurately, } \alpha = \dfrac{1}{137.0388}\right)$

(15) $\mu_{exper.} = (1.0011609 \pm 0.0000024)\mu_0$

Here again the striking coincidence of the measured magnetic moment of the electron and the value obtained on the basis of quantum field theory is observed.

SCATTERING OF LIGHT BY LIGHT. There are other effects described by quantum field theory. We shall limit ourselves to examining one more effect predicted by quantum field theory. The principle of superposition is known to be valid for electromagnetic waves: upon superposition, electromagnetic waves do not have any effect on each other. This principle of the superposition of waves without mutual distortions passes from classical theory into quantum theory, where it assumes the form of the assertion that there is no interaction between photons. However, this situation changes if the effects caused by the electron-positron vacuum are taken into account.

The diagram presented in Figure 9 corresponds to the following process: In the initial state there are two photons; one of them disappears at point (1), creating a virtual electron-positron pair; and the second photon is absorbed by one of the particles of the pair (in this diagram, by the positron) at point (2). Then final photons appear: one of them is produced at point (3) by the virtual electron, and the other arises as a result of the annihilation of the pair at point (4). This diagram (and an infinite number of other, more complicated diagrams) shows that interaction between photons must appear as a result of virtual electron-positron pairs, that is, the principle of superposition must be violated. Violations should be manifested in such processes as the scattering of light by light (however, this effect is so slight that it has not yet been observed experimentally). The process of scattering of photons in an external electrostatic field, which has a somewhat higher probability, as yet lies outside experimental capabilities, but the successes of quantum electromagnetics have been so great that there can be no doubt as to the adequacy of these predictions.

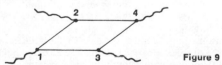

Figure 9

In addition to these effects, "higher" corrections that are calculated on the basis of the perturbation method (radiation corrections) appear in the process of the scattering of charged particles and in some other phenomena.

Difficulties and problems in quantum field theory

A success requiring explanation. The advances of quantum electrodynamics discussed above are impressive but not fully explicable. These advances are associated with the analysis of only the simplest, lowest Feynman diagrams, which take into account only a small number of virtual particles or, in mathematical language, low-order approximations of perturbation theory. In considering higher approximations, an infinite number of increasingly complex diagrams of higher orders that include an ever greater number of internal lines, each of which corresponds to a virtual particle, could be added to each diagram. It is true that an increasingly large number of vertices will be found in such complicated diagrams, and each vertex introduces into the expression for the probability amplitude of the process a factor e, or more accurately, $e/\sqrt{\hbar c}$. Since the internal lines have two ends (two vertices), the addition of each internal line changes the amplitude by a factor of approximately $e^2/\hbar c \approx 1/137$. If the amplitude is written as the sum of terms with ascending powers of the quantity $\alpha = e^2/\hbar c$ (the construction of this sum, or series, corresponds mathematically to an application of the method of perturbation theory), then a Feynman diagram with an increasingly large number of internal lines will correspond to each successive term. Therefore, every term of the series should be approximately two orders of magnitude (100 times) smaller than the previous one. Higher diagrams would indeed seem to provide a negligible contribution and can be discarded. However, more careful examination shows that, since the number of such discarded diagrams is infinitely large, assessment of their contribution is neither simple nor obvious. The task is complicated still further, since α acts in combination with a factor proportional to the logarithm of the energy, so that at high energies the perturbation method proves to be ineffective.

Although this problem may not seem very pressing in quantum electrodynamics, since here theory brilliantly describes experiment, it is quite a different matter in the theories of other fields.

Problem of strong interactions. The theory of strong interactions began to develop by analogy with quantum electrodynamics, but the role of carriers of interaction was ascribed, as indicated above, to pi-mesons—particles that have a rest mass approximately 200 times greater than the rest mass of the electron. However, a circumstance that fundamentally distinguishes electrodynamics from meson dynamics was revealed here: the interaction constant g—that is, the quantity that plays the role of the charge in strong interactions—is relatively large, and in meson dynamics the quantity $g^2/\hbar c > 1$ appears instead of $e^2/\hbar c \approx 1/137 \ll 1$. Therefore, the arguments that in electrodynamics to some extent justify the discarding of higher diagrams (that is, the use of lower approximations of perturbation theory) lose their force in meson dynamics. It is not surprising that, in the case of strongly interacting particles, consideration of only lower diagrams does not give agreement with experimental results. In other words, the perturbation method is inapplicable here for calculation of the probability amplitude.

A peculiar situation has taken shape in quantum field theory: equations for interacting fields were written many years ago, and in principle a method has been found to single out that which corresponds to physical particles, but at the same time theoreticians do not know how to solve the equations exactly. Approximate methods, above all the method of perturbation theory, are not always suitable. However, without knowing the exact solution to the equations of quantum field theory, it is difficult to assess with confidence the validity of these equations and, hence, the physical concepts on which they are based.

The difficulties in solving the equations of quantum field theory do not give rise only to "technical" problems. The method of solution largely determines the physical images with which theory operates. For example, what are the "mathematical" particles and the procedure for "clothing" them that were discussed above? All these concepts were dictated by perturbation theory: in the zero-order approximation the interaction is not taken into account at all (hence the term "bare" particles), and in subsequent approximations interaction is taken into account by introducing one, two, or more virtual particles; thus arises the picture

of the gradual "envelopment" of a particle by a cloud of virtual quanta. However, in nature there are no "mathematical" particles: all particles are "physical," and they are the ones that theory must describe. Although precisely this task is set in renormalization theory, specific calculations force a return to perturbation theory (let us note that in electrodynamics the fundamental possibility of carrying out renormalizations in any approximation is proved).

Problem of renormalizability; analysis of theoretical difficulties. Before the appearance of the idea of renormalization, quantum field theory could not be considered as a self-consistent concept, since meaningless, infinitely large values (divergences) appeared for some physical quantities and there was no understanding of what should be done with them. The idea of renormalization not only explained the observed effects but at the same time imparted to the entire theory features of logical completeness, eliminating the divergences.

Figuratively speaking, a method was proposed for taking into account changes in the "coat" of physical particles, depending on external conditions, and of quantitatively studying related effects. At the same time the "clothing" of the particle itself drops out of consideration. The particle is considered as a whole in its external manifestations—that is, in its interaction with other particles.

The renormalization program can by no means always be carried out successfully (that is, the renormalization of a finite number of quantities eliminating divergences). In some cases the consideration of diagrams of increasingly high order leads to the appearance of divergences of new types—then the theory is said to be nonrenormalizable. The first versions of the theory of weak interactions are examples of such a theory. Entities whose internal structure is manifested in their interactions may be encountered in nonrenormalizable theories.

Thus the perturbation method, in which the concept of free fields is used as the starting point and then the increasingly complex picture of interactions is examined, proves to be effective in quantum electrodynamics, since in this theory results that agree well with experiment can be obtained by means of renormalizations. However, even in this theory the problem of divergences cannot be considered to have been solved (the divergences are merely isolated, rather than eliminated). In other theories the situation is still more intricate. For example, in the theory of strong interactions the perturbation method ceases to be applicable. Thus, there are indisputable fundamental difficulties in quantum field theory that have not yet been solved.

There are several trends in explaining the reasons for the appearance of difficulties. According to one viewpoint, all complications are due to an incorrect method of solving the equations of quantum field theory. Indeed, the perturbation method has obvious shortcomings; moreover, it gives rise, for example, to the problem of renormalizations. If Heisenberg's picture is used to describe fields, the necessity of introducing "mathematical" particles and of examining their subsequent "clothing" can be avoided. Here the only particles that figure in theory are "physical." However, in order to introduce such particles it is necessary to assume that all interactions begin at some—although perhaps very remote—instant and then cease in the future, which also may be very distant. This concept is actually close to what occurs in an experiment, where an interaction begins when some particles strike other target particles and the products formed on collision fly so far apart after some period of time that interaction between them ceases. However, the possibility of asymptotic consideration of free fields (that is, at the instants $t = -\infty$ and $t = +\infty$)—and, consequently, of particles—does not remove all difficulties, since entirely effective methods of solving the equations for Heisenberg operators have not yet been found. Thus, according to this point of view, the reason for the difficulties lies precisely in the inability to solve the equations of quantum field theory with sufficient accuracy.

Also widespread is the opinion that, after ridding itself of all shortcomings of the perturbation method, theory will not attain the desired perfection—that is, the difficulties are not mathematical but physical in nature. It is pointed out, for example, that the consideration of a limited number of types of interacting fields is incorrect, since all fields are interconnected. Possibly the consistent consideration of all fields in their interaction (including the gravitational field) will lead to a correct and noncontradictory description of phenomena.

Reexamination of the concepts of interaction is also typical of the nonlocal quantum field theories that proceed from the assumption that the interaction among fields is "blurred," that is, is not determined only by the values of the fields at a single point in space and at identical moments in time. The requirements of the theory of relativity impose extremely rigid limitations on the possible types of "blurring," leading in particular to the emergence of the problem of causal description in nonlocal theories.

In another trend, the reason for the complications is that modern theory tries to give an excessively detailed description of phenomena in the microcosm. Just as such classical concepts as the trajectory of a particle and the tracking of its coordinates at all subsequent moments in time lose meaning after the transition from classical mechanics to quantum mechanics, it is impossible (and wrong) to try to describe in accepted concepts a detailed picture of the evolution of a field over time—it is possible only to raise the question of the probability of transition from the initial states of the field, when interaction has not yet begun, to the final states, when it is already ended. The task is to find laws that define the probabilities of such transitions (let us note that such a program actually goes beyond the framework of traditional quantum field theory). Here the operator (called the S-matrix) that establishes the relation between the state vector $\psi(-\infty)$, in the infinite past ($t = -\infty$), and the vector $\psi(+\infty)$, which refers to the infinite future ($t = +\infty$), $\psi(+\infty) = S\psi(-\infty)$, takes on the greatest importance. The problem is to find laws that would determine the S-matrix but not based on a detailed description of the evolution of the system at all intermediate times between $t = -\infty$ and $t = +\infty$. Studies based on an examination of the dependence of the S-matrix on the charge and leading to new types of solutions to problems of quantum field theory may, for example, attest to the possibilities that open up here.

Finally, we must not fail to mention another widely held opinion, which states that to eliminate theoretical flaws a radical step is needed—that is, a fundamentally new idea, as a result of which a new universal constant, such as a fundamental (elementary) length, is introduced. Repeated attempts at reexamining the concepts of space and time and attempts that use the concept of such a fundamental length have already been made.

Analysis of the reasons leading to the appearance of difficulties in theory is of great importance, but new ways of developing theory play no less a role. Some of them are examined below.

Some new methods in quantum field theory

The "axiomatic approach" is one important example of a new approach to the study of quantum fields. Careful analysis of the assumptions that make up the mathematical and physical foundations of theory and the isolation of the most "reliable" assumptions are typical of this approach. Among the postulates (axioms) are relativistic invariance (that is, satisfaction of the requirements of the theory of relativity); the condition of causality, or of the localizability of interaction, which leads to the requirement for commutativity of field operators referring to different points in space and to moments in time that exclude the possibility of exchanging signals at a speed exceeding the speed of light (the exclusion of signals traveling faster than the speed of light corresponds to the requirement that cause always precede effect in time); and the condition of the so-called spectral character, which means the requirement that the energy of all permissible states of a physical system (the energy spectrum) be positive if the energy of the vacuum state is taken as zero. The question of the possibility of producing experimentally verifiable predictions pertaining to interacting fields on the basis of the adopted axioms is very important. The understanding of whether a self-consistent theory of such fields can be constructed on this basis is no less important.

One of the reasons for interest in the axiomatic approach is that it should indicate effects that are accessible to experimental study and that stem from current concepts of space and time and thus should make possible direct verification of these concepts.

For example, experiments in which a violation of the axiom of localizability is detected would serve as proof of the necessity of revising the physical picture of space-time at extremely short distances.

The CIT theorem is a very important example of what can be derived from the fundamental postulates of quantum field theory. From the condition of localizability and relativistic invariance it follows that a theory must be invariant with respect to three simultaneously performed operations: spatial inversion I (the replacement of the coordinates $\mathbf{r}$ by $-\mathbf{r}$), time inversion T (replacement of the time t by $-t$), and charge conjugation C (the replacement of particles by antiparticles); more graphically, the CIT theorem is formulated as an assertion of the invariance of theory with respect to the replacement of the incident particles by the emerging antiparticles in any process. The nontrivial nature of the CIT theorem is apparent if only from the fact that, for example, in weak interactions there is no invariance only with respect to spatial inversion and/or charge conjugation.

There is yet another peculiarity of the axiomatic approach: the careful studies conducted within its framework make possible detection of the initial assumptions in traditional quantum field theory that require logical and mathematical refinement.

The intensive development of the technology of charged-particle accelerators and the resulting unprecedented increase in the flow of experimental information on elementary particles have had an appreciable effect on the direction of theoretical inquiries. Particular attention is directed to a quantity that has a direct physical meaning—the scattering amplitude (the square of its modulus defines the probability of a process). For every process a diagram resembling a Feynman diagram but with a fundamentally different meaning may be correlated with the scattering amplitude. Let us examine, for example, the diagram depicted in Figure 10. It is similar to a graph of the vertex part (see Figures 4 and 5)—and is called a vertex diagram—but it is not a graphic representation of an approximate solution (obtained by means of perturbation theory) to some equation; the graph simply records a process in which the particles A, B, and C take part. If the mass m_A of a particle A is greater than the sum of the masses $m_B + m_C$ of particles B and C, the diagram describes the real decay $A \rightarrow B + C$. If decay is prohibited in terms of energy, at least one of the lines in the diagram refers to a virtual particle. The circle in Figure 10 means that the vertex is physical—that is, it corresponds directly to what occurs in experiment. If the lines A and B refer to real nucleons (such as protons) and line C stands for a virtual photon, then the vertex part depends only on a single variable. The requirements of the theory of relativity force the selection of the quantity $p_C^2 = \mathcal{E}_C^2/c^2 - \mathbf{p}_C^2$ as such a variable, since only this combination of the energy $\mathcal{E}_C$ and the momentum $\mathbf{p}_C$ of the particle does not change upon transition from one inertial reference system to another; the quantity p_C is called the four-dimensional momentum of the particle C. For a real particle $p_C^2 = mc^2$, and the particle is said to be on a mass surface. Virtual particles lie "outside the mass surface"; this is due to the presence of a noticeable quantum energy spread or a quantum mass spread, which is equivalent.

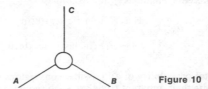

Figure 10

The dependence of the scattering amplitude on $p_C{}^2$ describes the experimentally observed distribution of electric charge, magnetic moment, and all higher electric and magnetic multipole moments of the proton (the electromagnetic form factor of the proton). Within the framework of the methods that were discussed above and are typical of quantum electrodynamics, such a form factor should, in principle, be sought by analyzing the proton's "coat"; as noted above, effective methods for such an analysis do not exist. An important feature of the new approach is the use of experimental data to fill gaps in the theory.

Let us cite yet another important example of "generalized" diagrams—the "four-tail" diagram (Figure 11). It represents either the decay of one particle into three ($A \rightarrow B + C + D$), if the process is allowed in terms of energy, or transitions of the type in which two particles yield two particles, in particular if the particles are identical at the start and end of the process (elastic scattering of the particles). Let us examine this latter process and, for the sake of simplicity, assume that all the particles have identical mass and zero spin. Then, if all four lines refer to real particles, the scattering amplitude proves to be dependent only on two invariant variables. The following variables are usually used: $s = (p_A + p_B)^2$, which is equal to the square of the energy of the colliding particles in the center-of-momentum system (that is, in a reference system in which the total momentum of particles A and B is equal to zero), and $t = (p_A + p_C)^2$, which defines the momentum transfer upon scattering.

The diagrams presented in Figures 10 and 11 do not, of course, exhaust all possibilities. However, they play a significant role and often are used as "units" for the construction of more complicated diagrams that describe processes involving a larger number of particles (more than four).

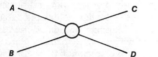

Figure 11

The apparatus of the theory of analytic functions is used in studying the scattering amplitude f. Here s and t, on which the scattering amplitude $f(s,t)$ depends, are considered to be complex variables. This approach is justified by the fact that the behavior of analytic functions is determined largely by the type and position of the singularities of the function. One of the most important types of singularity is the pole of the function $f(z)$ at some point z_0, which corresponds to the value of the function f at this point approaching infinity as $1/(z - z_0)$. The poles in the scattering amplitude can be given a descriptive interpretation. For example, if a pole of the type $1/(s - m^2c^4)$ appears in the scattering amplitude that describes the process $A + B \rightarrow C + D$, this means that the process is taking place through an intermediate (virtual) particle Q, $A + B \rightarrow Q \rightarrow C + D$, and the mass of the intermediate particle is $m_Q = m$. A pole of the type $1/(t - m^2c^4)$ corresponds to the diagram presented in Figure 12; m is the mass of the intermediate (virtual) particle on the diagram. The peculiarities of other types also may be interpreted physically as a reflection of certain important processes that are manifested at intermediate stages of scattering. If all these singularities are found, then we may try, on the basis of the general theorems of the theory of analytic functions, fully to recover the form of the scattering amplitude for all values of s and t and in particular for the real values of these quantities that are of direct interest to physicists. The fundamental principles of relativistic quantum mechanics mentioned above, as well as a number of others, are used to find the singularities. An important role is played by the condition of unitarity, which means that if a process may take place in several ways (if it may take place through different "channels"), for example,

$$A + B \rightarrow \begin{array}{l} A + B \text{ (elastic scattering)} \\ \left.\begin{array}{l} C + D \\ E + F \\ \cdots\cdots \end{array}\right\} \text{ (inelastic scattering)} \end{array}$$

then the total probability of all possible conversions is equal to unity. Despite their apparent triviality, such requirements as the unitarity and positive nature of the energies of physical particles place very strict limitations on scattering amplitudes.

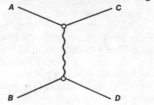

Figure 12

The requirements of symmetry, in particular the fact that particles can be divided into groups, within each of which the masses increase in direct proportion to the spins, also play a very important role in constructing the scattering amplitude for various processes. Finally, it is necessary to take into account the laws of conservation that are important for each of the specific processes under consideration (such as the laws of conservation of electric charge, baryon charge, and lepton charge).

Quantum field theory also makes successful use of some methods that first appeared in classical electrodynamics. One of them is the method that shows the relation between the frequency-dependent real and imaginary parts of the dielectric constant of a dielectric. Since the dependence of the index of refraction of a dielectric on the frequency of the light is called dispersion (and the index of refraction is defined by the dielectric constant), this connection is called the dispersion relation. It was found that even without making any specific assumptions about the structure of the dielectric it is possible on the basis of the requirement of causality, which here assumes the form of the requirement that the polarization of a dielectric at any moment be determined only by the intensities of the electric fields at the same or at previous moments (but not at subsequent moments), to obtain an expression for the imaginary part of the dielectric constant, which determines the absorption of the electromagnetic wave, if its real part is known throughout the entire infinite range of frequencies (and vice versa). Dispersion relations make it possible to draw conclusions that can be verified by direct experiment, for example, the conclusion that dispersion is normal in regions of transparency (that is, at frequencies corresponding to low absorption): the index of refraction increases with frequency. In addition, information on the asymptotic behavior of the real and imaginary parts of the dielectric permeability (at very high frequencies) can be obtained from dispersion relations.

Since the classical problem of dispersion, or the scattering of electromagnetic waves in matter, is solved within the framework of the dispersion approach without using any specific models of the structure of matter, it is natural to expect that this approach also will prove productive in an examination of other problems of scattering, and particularly in quantum field theory. Here we may also separate the real and imaginary parts of scattering amplitude (the latter of which reflects the contribution of inelastic processes during which new particles appear in the final state) and to establish relations between them. The imaginary part of the scattering amplitude takes into account all possible processes (including elastic processes). The optical theorem asserts that the imaginary part of the forward scattering amplitude is proportional to the total probability of scattering.

The dispersion approach, which found a reliable mathematical basis and development in the works of N. N. Bogoliubov and his school, has made possible the derivation of a number of interesting results. Among them are the determination of precise values of the interaction constants for pi-mesons with protons and neutrons (nucleons), and also the interaction constants for kaons, nucleons, and λ-hyperons. Predictions with respect to the asymptotic behavior of scattering amplitudes are also of considerable interest.

However, the program for the complete construction of the amplitudes of processes within the framework of the dispersion approach has not yet found a final solution. Obviously, in addition to the general principles discussed above, the theory should rely on some more specific assumptions that play the role of dynamic principles. Sometimes such new dynamics assumes the form of an indication of the rules according to which the singularities of amplitudes should be determined; finding these rules requires careful use of experimental data. However, such "indirect" consideration of dynamics is not the only possible approach.

We cannot help but comment on the revival of interest in theories in which the laws of dynamics once again assume the traditional form of equations that describe a detailed space-time picture of processes. Important studies of the systematics of elementary particles and the establishment of new symmetry properties have been the impetus for this interest. It is natural to seek dynamic laws behind the principles observed here. The very interesting, although preliminary, results of attempts to coordinate field dynamics with the symmetry properties of elementary particles apparently are leading to the necessity of examining nonlinear, or self-stressing, fields. In one sense this trend is close to a unified quantum field theory, in which attempts are made to consider matter as a whole as a unified fundamental field (or as several basic types of fundamental fields) and individual particles as different manifestations (states) of the field.

An assessment of all current attempts to solve the problems that are arising in quantum field theory would be premature. However, the very fact that such attempts are so numerous attests to the gravity of the problems and to the efforts that are being made to answer the main question of physics—the question of the structure of matter.

REFERENCES

Landau, L. D., and E. M. Lifshits. *Teoriia polia.* Moscow, 1967. (*Teoreticheskaia fizika,* vol. 2.)
Schweber, S. *Vvedenie v reliativistskuiu kvantovuiu teoriiu.* Moscow, 1963. (Translated from English.)
Bogoliubov, N. N., and D. V. Shirkov. *Vvedenie v teoriiu kvantovannykh polei.* Moscow, 1957.
Salam, A. "Fundamental'naia teoriia materii (rezul'taty i metody)." *Uspekhi fizicheskikh nauk,* 1969, vol. 99, fasc. 4, pp. 571–611.
Akhiezer, A. I., and V. B. Berestetskii. *Kvantovaia elektrodinamika,* 3rd ed. Moscow, 1969.
Ziman, J. *Sovremennaia kvantovaia teoriia.* Moscow, 1971. (Translated from English.)
Bogoliubov, N. N., I. T. Todorov, and A. A. Logunov. *Osnovy aksiomaticheskogo podkhoda v kvantovoi teorii polia.* Moscow, 1969.
Eden, R. *Soudareniia elementarnykh chastits pri vysokikh energiiakh.* Moscow, 1970. (Translated from English.)

V. I. GRIGOR'EV [11–1733–3]

QUANTUM FLUID, a fluid whose properties are determined by quantum effects. An example is liquid helium at a temperature close to absolute zero. Quantum effects begin to be manifested in a fluid at very low temperatures, when the de Broglie wavelength for particles of the fluid, calculated on the basis of their energy of thermal motion, becomes comparable to the distance between them. For liquid helium this condition is satisfied at a temperature of 3°–2°K.

According to the concepts of classical mechanics, the kinetic energy of particles of any body should decrease with temperature. At a sufficiently low temperature the particles in a system of interacting particles will display small oscillations about the positions that correspond to the minimum potential energy of the entire body. At absolute zero the oscillations should cease and the particles should begin to occupy strictly defined positions—that is, any body should become a crystal. Therefore, the very existence of fluids near absolute zero is associated with quantum effects.

The principle that the more precisely the position of a particle is fixed, the greater the spread of values for its velocity, is valid in quantum mechanics. Consequently, even at absolute zero particles cannot occupy strictly defined positions, and their kinetic energy does not become zero. So-called zero-point vibrations remain. The weaker the force of interaction among the particles and the smaller their mass, the greater will be the amplitude of the vibrations. If the amplitude of zero-point vibrations is comparable to the mean distance between particles of the body, then such a body can remain fluid down to absolute zero.

Of all substances only two isotopes of helium (^{4}He and ^{3}He) have sufficiently low mass and weak interaction among atoms at atmospheric pressure to remain fluid close to absolute zero and thus make possible the study of the specifics of a quantum fluid. Electrons in metals also have the properties of a quantum fluid.

Quantum fluids are divided into Bose fluids and Fermi fluids, depending on the difference in the properties of their particles and according to the Bose-Einstein and Fermi-Dirac statistics used to describe them. Only one Bose fluid is known—liquid ^{4}He, whose atoms have a spin (intrinsic angular momentum) of zero. Atoms of the rarer isotope ^{3}He and electrons in a metal have half-integral spin (1/2) and form Fermi fluids.

Liquid ^{4}He was the first quantum fluid to be studied comprehensively. The theoretical concepts developed to explain the basic effects in liquid helium were the basis for the general theory of quantum fluids. At 2.171°K and saturation vapor pressure, ^{4}He undergoes a second-order phase transition to the new state, He II, with specific quantum properties. The very presence of the transition point is connected with the appearance of a Bose condensate—that is, with the transition of a finite fraction of the atoms in a state having a momentum strictly equal to zero. This new state is characterized by superfluidity, which is the flow of He II without any friction through narrow capillaries and slits. Superfluidity was discovered by P. L. Kapitsa (1938) and explained by L. D. Landau (1941).

According to quantum mechanics, any system of interacting particles may exist only in certain quantum states that are characteristic of the entire system as a whole. Here the energy of the entire system may vary only in certain portions—quanta. Like an atom in which energy changes by the emission or absorption of a light quantum, in a quantum fluid a change in energy takes place by emission or absorption of elementary excitations characterized by a certain momentum p; energy $\epsilon(p)$, which depends on the momentum; and spin. These elementary excitations apply to the entire fluid as a whole rather than to the individual particles and are called quasiparticles because of their properties (such as the presence of momentum and spin). Sonic excitations in He II—phonons with energy $\epsilon = \hbar cp$, where $\hbar$ is Planck's constant divided by 2π and c is the speed of sound—are examples of quasiparticles. As long as the number of quasiparticles is small, corresponding to low temperatures, their interaction is slight, and it may be assumed that they form an ideal gas of quasiparticles. Consideration of the properties of quantum fluids on the basis of these concepts proves to be simpler, in one sense, than the study of the properties of ordinary fluids at high temperatures, when the number of excitations is great and their properties are not analogous to the properties of an ideal gas.

If a quantum fluid flows with a certain velocity v through a narrow pipe or slit, its deceleration caused by friction consists in the formation of quasiparticles with a momentum opposite the velocity of the current. As a result of deceleration, the energy of the quantum fluid should decline, but not smoothly, in particular portions. For the formation of quasiparticles with the required energy, the velocity of the flow must be no less than $v_c = \min [\epsilon(p)/p]$; this velocity is called the critical velocity. Quantum fluids in which $v_c \neq 0$ will be superfluid since at velocities less than v_c new quasiparticles are not formed and consequently the fluid is not retarded. The energy spectrum $\epsilon(p)$ of quasiparticles in He II, which was predicted by Landau's theory and confirmed by experiment, satisfies this requirement.

The impossibility of formation of new quasiparticles in He II at a flow with $v < v_c$ leads to unique two-fluid hydrodynamics. The aggregate of the quasiparticles present in He II is scattered and retarded by the walls of the vessel and constitutes the normal, viscous part of the fluid, and the remainder is superfluid. The appearance of vortices with quantized circulation of the velocity of the superfluid component under certain conditions (such as rotation of the vessel) is characteristic of a superfluid. In He II the propagation of several types of sound is possible: the first of these corresponds to ordinary adiabatic fluctuations of density, and the second corresponds to fluctuations of the density of quasiparticles and, consequently, of temperature. Liquid ^{3}He becomes superfluid at temperatures below 2.68 × 10^{-3}°K and a pressure of 33.87 atmospheres.

The presence of a gas consisting of quasiparticles is equally characteristic of both Bose and Fermi fluids. In a Fermi fluid some of the quasiparticles have half-integral spin and conform to Fermi-Dirac statistics. These are single-particle excitations. In addition, quasiparticles with integral spin that conform to Bose-Einstein statistics also exist in a Fermi fluid. The most interesting of these is the "zero sound," which was predicted theoretically and was discovered in liquid ^{3}He. Fermi fluids are divided into normal and superfluid, depending on the properties of the quasiparticle spectrum.

Electrons in nonsuperconducting metals in which the energy of single-particle excitations may be as small as desired when the value of the pulse is finite, leading to $v_c = 0$, are classified as normal Fermi fluids. The theory of normal Fermi fluids was developed by L. D. Landau (1956–58).

Electrons in superconducting metals and liquid ^{3}He are superfluid Fermi fluids. The theory of superfluid electron Fermi fluids was developed by J. Bardeen, L. Cooper, and J. Schrieffer (1957) and by N. N. Bogoliubov (1957). According to this theory, attraction predominates among the electrons in superconductors, leading to the formation of bound pairs with momentums that are opposite but equal in absolute magnitude and with a total moment equal to zero. Finite energy must be expended for the occurrence of any single-particle excitation—the breakup of a bound pair. This leads, in contrast to normal Fermi fluids, to $v_c \neq 0$, that is, to superfluidity of the electron fluid (superconductivity of the metal). A deep-seated analogy exists between superconductivity and superfluidity. As in ^{4}He, a second-order phase transition associated with the appearance of the Bose condensate of electron pairs occurs in superconducting metals. Under certain conditions vortices with a quantized magnetic flux, which are the analogue of vortices in He II, appear in second-order superconductors in a magnetic field.

In addition to the quantum fluids listed above, mixtures of ^{3}He and ^{4}He, which form a continuous transition from a Fermi fluid to a Bose fluid as the ratio of the components is gradually changed, are classified as quantum fluids. According to theoretical concepts, at exceedingly high pressures and sufficiently low temperatures all substances enter the quantum-fluid state. This may occur, for example, in some stars.

REFERENCES

Landau, L. D., and E. M. Lifshits. *Statisticheskaia fizika,* 2nd ed. Moscow, 1964.
Abrikosov, A. A., and I. M. Khalatnikov. "Teoriia fermizhidkosti." *Uspekhi fizicheskikh nauk,* 1958, vol. 66, fasc. 2, p. 177.
Fizika nizkikh temperatur. Moscow, 1959. (Translated from English.)
Pines, D., and P. Nozières. *Teoriia kvantovykh zhidkostei.* Moscow, 1967. (Translated from English.)

S. V. IORDANSKII [11–1701–1; updated]

QUANTUM FREQUENCY STANDARDS, devices in which the quantum transitions of particles (such as atoms, molecules, and ions) from one energy state to another are used for precise measurement of the frequency of oscillations or to generate oscillations with extremely stable frequency. Quantum frequency standards make possible measurement of the frequency of oscillations and, consequently, of their period (duration) with much higher accuracy than is possible with other frequency standards. This led to their introduction in metrology.

Quantum frequency standards are the basis for national frequency and time standards and secondary frequency standards, which are close to the national standard with respect to their degree of accuracy and metrological capabilities but must be calibrated with respect to it. Quantum frequency standards are used as laboratory frequency standards that have a broad range of output frequencies and are equipped with a device that compares the measured frequency with the standard frequency, as well as reference frequencies, which make possible observation of a selected spectral line without introducing any significant distortion, and comparison (with high accuracy) of a measured frequency with a frequency defined by a spectral line. The quality of quantum frequency standards is characterized by their stability—their ability to hold a selected frequency for a long period.

Quantum laws impose extremely rigid limitations on the state of atoms. Under the action of an external electromagnetic field of a certain frequency, atoms may either be excited, in which case they jump from a state of lower energy $\mathcal{E}_1$ to a state of higher energy $\mathcal{E}_2$, absorbing in the process a portion (quantum) of the energy of the electromagnetic field equal to

$$h\nu = \mathcal{E}_2 - \mathcal{E}_1$$

or they may move to a state of lower energy, radiating electromagnetic waves of the same frequency.

Quantum frequency standards are commonly divided into two classes. In active standards the quantum transitions of atoms and molecules lead directly to the radiation of electromagnetic waves whose frequency serves as a standard or reference frequency. Such instruments are also called quantum generators. In passive standards the measured frequency of the oscillations of an exter-

nal generator is compared with the frequency of the oscillations that correspond to a certain quantum transition of the selected atoms—that is, with the frequency of the spectral line. Passive quantum frequency standards using beams of cesium atoms (cesium frequency standards) were the first to achieve technical perfection and to become generally available. In 1967 by international agreement the duration of the second was defined as 9,192,631,770.0 periods of oscillations corresponding to a certain energy transition of atoms of the only stable isotope of cesium, ^{133}Cs. The zero after the decimal point means that this number is not subject to further change. A contour of the spectral line of ^{133}Cs that corresponds to the transition between the two selected energy levels $\mathcal{E}_1$ and $\mathcal{E}_2$ may be observed in the cesium frequency standard. The frequency that corresponds to the peak of this line is fixed, and frequencies being measured are compared with it by means of special devices.

An atom-beam tube in which a high vacuum is maintained is the main part of a quantum frequency standard using a beam of cesium atoms. At one end of the tube is the source of the beam of atoms, a cavity in which a certain quantity of liquid cesium is placed (Figure 1). The cavity is connected with the rest of the tube by a narrow channel or a set of parallel channels. The source is maintained at a temperature of about 100°C, when the cesium is in the liquid state (the melting point of cesium is 29.5°C) but its vapor pressure is still low, and the cesium atoms emitted from the source rather seldom pass through the channels without colliding with each other. As a result of this a slightly divergent beam of cesium atoms is formed in the tube.

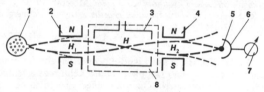

Figure 1. Diagram of an atom-beam tube: (1) source of cesium beam, (2) and (4) deflecting magnets that generate the nonuniform magnetic fields H_1 and H_2, (3) cavity resonator (in the permanent and uniform magnetic field H) in which electromagnetic waves are excited, (5) incandescent tungsten filament, (6) cesium-ion collector, (7) measuring device, (8) domain of the permanent uniform magnetic field H (bounded by broken line)

At the other end of the tube is an extremely sensitive receiver (detector) of cesium atoms, which is capable of recording negligible changes in the intensity of the atom beam. The detector consists of an incandescent tungsten filament (5) and a collector (6), between which is placed a voltage source (the positive pole is attached to the wire, the negative pole to the collector). As soon as a cesium atom touches the incandescent filament, it gives off its outer electron (the ionization energy of cesium is equal to 3.27 electron volts [eV], and the electron work function for tungsten is 4.5 eV). The cesium ion is attracted to the collector. If a sufficiently large number of cesium atoms strike the incandescent tungsten, an electric current is generated in the circuit between the collector and the tungsten filament. The intensity of the cesium beam striking the detector may be estimated by measuring this current.

In passing from the source to the detector, the beam of cesium atoms passes between the pole shoes of two strong magnets. The nonuniform magnetic field H_1 of the first magnet splits the beam of cesium atoms into several beams in which atoms of various energies (at various energy levels) travel. The second magnet (the field H_2) focuses on the detector only atoms that belong to one pair of energy levels $\mathcal{E}_1$ and $\mathcal{E}_2$, deflecting all others.

In the gap between the magnets the atoms pass through the cavity resonator (3)—a cavity with conducting walls—in which electromagnetic oscillations of a certain frequency are excited by means of a stable quartz generator. If a cesium atom with energy $\mathcal{E}_1$ moves to the energy state $\mathcal{E}_2$ under the influence of these oscillations, the field of the second magnet rejects it from the detector, since for an atom that had moved to the state $\mathcal{E}_2$ the field of the second magnet no longer will be a focusing field and the atom will bypass the detector. Thus, the current through the detector will prove to be less by a quantity proportional to the number of atoms that make energy transitions under the influence of the electromagnetic resonator. The transitions of cesium atoms from the state $\mathcal{E}_2$ to the state $\mathcal{E}_1$ will be fixed in the same manner.

The number of atoms making an induced transition per unit time under the influence of an electromagnetic field is at a maximum if the frequency of the electromagnetic field acting on the atom coincides precisely with the resonance frequency ν_0 $=(\mathcal{E}_2-\mathcal{E}_1)/h$. As the noncoincidence or detuning of these frequencies increases, the number of such atoms decreases. Therefore, by smoothly changing the field frequency near ν_0 and plotting the frequency ν along the horizontal axis and the change in the detector current along the vertical, we obtain the contour of the spectral line that corresponds to the $\mathcal{E}_1 \rightarrow \mathcal{E}_2$ transition and, conversely, $\mathcal{E}_2 \rightarrow \mathcal{E}_1$ (Figure 2,a).

The frequency ν_0, which corresponds to the peak of the spectral line, is also a reference point on the frequency scale, and the oscillation period corresponding to it is accepted as 1/9,192,-631.0 sec.

The accuracy of determination of the frequency corresponding to the peak of the spectral line is usually several percent or, at best, fractions of a percent of the width of the line. The narrower the spectral line, the higher the accuracy; thus explaining the desirability of eliminating or at least weakening all factors that lead to broadening of the spectral lines used.

In cesium standards the broadening of the spectral line (Figure 2,a) is determined by the time of interaction between the atoms and the electromagnetic field of the resonator: the shorter this time, the broader the line. The time of interaction coincides with the duration of the atom's passage through the resonator. It is proportional to the length of the resonator and inversely proportional to the speed of the atoms. However, the resonator cannot be made very long, because the dispersion of the atom beam would increase. A substantial reduction in the speed of the atoms by lowering the temperature is also impossible, since the intensity of the beam decreases in the process. Increasing the dimensions of the resonator is made more difficult since the resonator must lie within a magnetic field H of extremely uniform magnitude and direction. This condition is necessary because the energy transitions used in cesium atoms are due to the change in the orientation of the magnetic moment of the nucleus of the cesium atom with respect to the magnetic moment of its electron shell. Transitions of this type cannot be observed outside a magnetic field, and the frequency corresponding to such transitions depends, although only slightly, on the intensity of the field. It is difficult to create such a field in a large volume.

A narrow spectral line is produced by using a horseshoe-shaped resonator (Figure 3), in which the beam passes through the aperture near its ends and only there interacts with the high-frequency electromagnetic field. Therefore, uniformity and stability of the magnetic field H are required only in these two

small regions. Before the second entry into the resonator the atoms "retain" the result of their first interaction with the field. In the case of a horseshoe-shaped resonator the spectral line takes on a more intricate shape (Figure 2,b) that reflects both the passage time through the electromagnetic field within the resonator (a broad pedestal) and the total passage time between the two ends of the resonator (a narrow central peak). It is the narrow central peak that serves to fix the frequency.

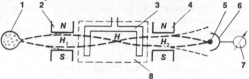

Figure 3. Diagram of an atom-beam tube with horseshoe-shaped resonator (symbols are the same as in Figure 1)

In quantum frequency standards with a beam of cesium atoms the error in the value of the frequency ν_0 occurs only in the 13th digit for one-of-a-kind devices (frequency standards) and in the 12th digit for series-manufactured high-precision devices (secondary standards).

In addition to an atom-beam tube and a quartz-crystal oscillator, quantum frequency standards using a beam of cesium atoms also incorporate special radio circuits that make possible highly accurate comparison of the measured frequency of external generators with the frequency defined by the quantum frequency standards. In addition, the cesium standard is usually supplemented with devices that generate a set of "integral" standard frequencies whose stability is equal to the stability of the standard. These systems sometimes also generate precise time signals. In such cases the quantum frequency standard is converted into a quantum clock.

One-of-a-kind laboratory quantum frequency standards that operate with beams of cesium atoms and are part of the national frequency and time standards make possible reproduction of the duration of a second—and consequently of the entire complex of measurements of frequency and time—with a relative error of less than 10^{-11}. In practice this relative error does not exceed 10^{-12}, but by international agreement extended observations are necessary to fix this value. A significant advantage of quantum frequency standards using beams of cesium atoms is that industrial designs make possible reproduction of the nominal value of a frequency (or time) with an error of 10^{-11}, that is, they are not inferior to the standard with respect to accuracy. Even small instruments of this type, which are suitable for use under ordinary laboratory conditions and in mobile facilities, operate with an error not greater than 10^{-10}, and some models have an error of 10^{-11}.

The hydrogen quantum generator (Figure 4) is the most important active quantum frequency standard. In a hydrogen generator a beam of hydrogen atoms is emitted from the source (1), where the hydrogen molecules are split into atoms at low pressure and under the influence of an electric discharge. The dimensions of the channels through which the atoms emerge from the source into the vacuum chamber are smaller than the distance traveled by the hydrogen atoms between collisions. Under this

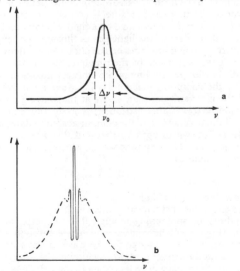

Figure 2. Shape of spectral line in cesium frequency standards: (a) with an ordinary resonator, (b) with a horseshoe-shaped resonator; (ν) resonance frequency, ($\Delta\nu$) width of spectral line

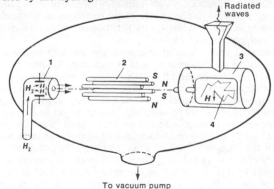

Figure 4. Design of hydrogen quantum generator: (1) atom-beam source, (2) sorting system (multipole magnet), (3) resonator, (4) accumulator bulb

condition the hydrogen atoms are emitted from the source in the form of a narrow beam, which passes between the pole shoes of the multipole magnet (2). The action of the field generated by the magnet is such that it focuses atoms in the excited state near the axis of the beam and scatters atoms in the ground (unexcited) state.

The excited atoms pass through a small aperture into the quartz bulb (4) inside the cavity resonator (3), which is tuned to a frequency corresponding to the transition of hydrogen atoms from the excited state to the ground state. Under the influence of the electromagnetic field, the hydrogen atoms radiate as they pass into the ground state. The photons radiated by the hydrogen atoms during a comparatively long period of time, which is determined by the quality factor of the resonator, remain within it, giving rise again to stimulated emission of the identical photons by the hydrogen atoms that enter later. Thus, the resonator creates the feedback necessary for self-excitation of the generator. However, the intensity of the beam of hydrogen atoms that can be attained is still insufficient to provide self-excitation of such a generator if an ordinary cavity resonator is used. Therefore, a quartz bulb (4) whose walls are coated on the inside with a thin layer of polyfluoroethylene resin (Teflon) is placed inside the resonator. The excited hydrogen atoms may strike the Teflon film more than 10,000 times without losing their excess energy. As a result, a large number of excited hydrogen atoms is collected in the bulb and the average time spent by each of them in the resonator increases to approximately 1 sec, which is sufficient for realization of the conditions of self-excitation and for the hydrogen quantum generator to begin to operate, radiating electromagnetic waves with an exceedingly stable frequency.

The bulb, which is made smaller than the generated wavelength, plays another extremely important role. The chaotic movement of the hydrogen atoms within the bulb should lead to broadening of the spectral line as a result of the Doppler effect. However, if the motion of the atoms is confined by a volume whose dimensions are less than the wavelength, the spectral line assumes the form of a narrow peak that rises above a broad, low pedestal. As a result, the width of the spectral line is only 1 hertz (Hz) in a hydrogen generator emitting radiation of wavelength $\lambda = 21$ cm.

The extreme narrowness of the spectral line ensures the low error of the frequency of a hydrogen generator, which lies within the 13th digit. The error is due to the interaction of the hydrogen atoms with the Teflon coating of the bulb. The value of this frequency, measured by means of a quantum frequency standard using a beam of cesium atoms (see above), is equal to 1,420,-405,751.7860 $\pm$ 0.0046 Hz. The power of a hydrogen generator is extremely low ($\sim 10^{-12}$ watts). Therefore, quantum frequency standards based on a hydrogen generator incorporate, in addition to circuits that compare and form the standard frequency grid, an extremely sensitive pickup.

Both types of quantum frequency standards operate in the superhigh-frequency (SHF) band. There are a number of other atoms and molecules whose spectral lines make it possible to devise active and passive quantum frequency standards in the radio band. However, they have not yet found practical application. Only rubidium quantum frequency standards, based on the method of optical pumping, are used extensively as a secondary frequency standard in laboratory practice and in navigation systems and quantum clocks.

Lasers, in which special measures are taken to stabilize the frequency of radiation, are optical quantum frequency standards. In the optical band the Doppler broadening of the spectral lines is very great, and, because of the short length of light waves, it is impossible to suppress it in the same way as in a hydrogen generator. Nor has there been any success as yet in developing an efficient laser using beams of atoms or molecules. Since several relatively narrow resonance lines of an optical resonator fall within the Doppler width of a spectral line, the generating frequency of the overwhelming majority of lasers is determined not so much by the frequency of the spectral line used as by the dimensions of the optical resonator, which define its resonance frequencies. But these frequencies do not remain constant; they change under the influence of changes in temperature and pressure, vibrations, aging, and so on. The lowest relative error of frequency in an optical quantum frequency standard ($\sim 10^{-13}$) has been achieved by using a helium-neon laser that generates at 3.39 microns (μ).

Optical quantum frequency standards are not yet connected (in a metrological sense) with radio-band quantum frequency standards, and consequently they are not connected with the unit of frequency (the hertz) or the unit of time (the second). Direct measurement of a frequency (comparison with the standard) is possible only in the longwave region of the infrared band (3.39 μ and longer).

REFERENCES
Kvantovaia elektronika: Malen'kaia entsiklopediia. Moscow, 1969. Page 35.
Grigor'iants, V. V., M. E. Zhabotinskii, and V. F. Zolin. *Kvantovye standarty chastoty.* Moscow, 1968. Pages 164 and 194.
Basov, N. G., and E. M. Belenov. "Sverkhuzkie spektral'nye linii i kvantovye standarty chastoty." *Priroda,* 1972, no. 12.

M. E. ZHABOTINSKII [11–1778–1; updated]

QUANTUM GENERATOR, a generator of electromagnetic waves that uses the phenomenon of stimulated emission. Quantum generators in the superhigh-frequency (SHF) region, like quantum mechanical amplifiers in that region, are often called masers. The first such devices in the SHF range were made in 1955 simultaneously in the USSR by N. G. Basov and A. M. Prokhorov and in the USA by C. Townes. A beam of ammonia molecules was used as the active medium, and consequently the devices where called molecular generators. Subsequently a quantum SHF generator was designed using a beam of hydrogen atoms. An important feature of such masers was the great stability of the generated frequency—up to 10^{-13}—as a result of which they are used as quantum frequency standards.

Optical quantum generators, or lasers, were developed in 1960. They operate over a broad wavelength range, from the ultraviolet to the submillimeter regions of the spectrum, in both pulse and continuous modes. There are lasers using crystals and glasses, gases, fluids, and semiconductors. Unlike other light sources, lasers emit highly coherent monochromatic light waves having all their energy concentrated within a very narrow solid angle.
[11–1791–1]

QUANTUM GYROSCOPE, an instrument that is used to detect the rotation of a body and determine its angular velocity and is based on the gyroscopic properties of electrons, atomic nuclei, or photons.

Laser (optical) gyroscope. The sensing element of an optical gyroscope consists of a ring laser, which generates two light waves that propagate in opposite directions along a common light channel in the form of narrow, monochromatic beams. The resonator of the ring laser (Figure 1) consists of three or more mirrors (1), (2), and (3), mounted on a rigid support and forming a closed system. Part of the light passes through the semitransparent mirror (3) and impinges on the photoelectric detector (5). The wavelength generated by the ring laser (within the limits of the width of the spectral line of the working medium) is determined by the condition that a traveling wave must, in passing around the resonator contour, arrive at the starting point with its original phase. If the instrument is fixed, this condition is satisfied if the perimeter P of the contour accommodates a whole multiple n of the wavelength λ_0, that is, if $P = n\lambda_0$. In this case, the laser generates two opposing waves, whose frequency is identical and is equal to

$$\nu_0 = c/\lambda_0 = cn/P$$

where c is the speed of light.

However, if the instrument rotates with angular velocity Ω about a direction subtending an angle θ to the perpendicular to its plane (Figure 2), the contour will rotate through a certain angle during the time required for the wave to travel around it. Depending on the direction of propagation of the wave, the path traversed by the wave will be less or more than P. Consequently, the frequencies of waves traveling in opposite directions become unequal. These frequencies ν_- and ν_+ may be shown to be

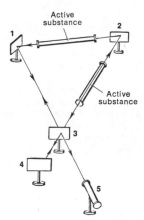

Figure 1. Diagram of a laser gyroscope: (1), (2), and (4) opaque mirrors; (3) semitransparent mirror; (5) photoelectric detector

independent of the contour shape and are related to the rotation frequency Ω of the instrument by the equation

$$\nu_\pm = \nu_0 \pm 2(\nu_0/c)([S\Omega \cos\theta]/P)$$

where S is the area surrounded by the resonator contour. In this case the photoelectric detector, which is sensitive to light intensity, records the beats with a difference frequency

$$\Delta\nu = \nu_+ - \nu_- = kF \cos\theta$$

where $F = \Omega/2\pi$ and $k = 8\pi(S/[\lambda_0 P])$. For example, for a square helium-neon quantum gyroscope with sides 25 cm long, $\lambda_0 = 6 \times 10^{-5}$ cm, leading to $k = 2.5 \times 10^6$. In this case, the rotation of the earth, which occurs with angular velocity $\Omega = 15$ deg/hr at latitude $\theta = 60°$, must lead to a beat frequency $\Delta\nu = 15$ Hz. If the axis of the quantum gyroscope is aimed at the sun, the latitude θ of the location of the quantum gyroscope may be calculated from the beat frequency with an accuracy of up to a fraction of a degree, assuming that the earth's angular velocity of rotation Ω is known.

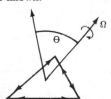

Figure 2

Integration of the angular velocity of a rotating body with respect to time (which may be performed automatically) makes possible determination of the angle of rotation as a function of time. The sensitivity limit of the quantum gyroscope is theoretically determined by the spontaneous radiation of the atoms of the active medium of the laser. If an angle of rotation of 1 deg/hr corresponds to the beat frequency $\Delta\nu = 1$ Hz, then the limiting accuracy of the quantum gyroscope is equal to 10^{-3} deg/hr. This limit has not been attained by any means in existing quantum gyroscopes.

Nuclear and electron gyroscopes. Nuclear quantum gyroscopes use materials that have nuclear paramagnetism (water, organic liquids, gaseous helium, and mercury vapor). Atoms or molecules of such materials in the ground (unexcited) state have angular momentums caused only by the nuclear spin moments (the electron spin moments are compensated in these materials, because all electrons are paired). The magnetic moments of the nuclei are related to their spins. If the nuclear magnetic moments are oriented—for example, by means of an external magnetic field—and the orienting field is subsequently switched off, in the absence of other magnetic fields (for example, the earth's magnetic field) the resulting total magnetic moment **M** will preserve its orientation in space for some time regardless of the change in orientation of the sensor. Such a static quantum gyroscope makes possible determination of the change in the position of a body connected to the sensor of the gyroscope.

Since the magnitude of the moment **M** will gradually decrease as a result of relaxation, materials with longer relaxation times are selected for quantum gyroscopes—for example, certain or-

ganic liquids, for which the relaxation time τ is several minutes, liquid ^{3}He (about 1 hr), or a solution of liquid ^{3}He in ^{4}He (about 1 yr).

In a quantum gyroscope operating in the nuclear induction mode, rotation of the sensor, which contains nuclei with oriented magnetic moments, with angular velocity Ω is equivalent to the action of a magnetic field of intensity $H = \Omega/\gamma_{nuc}$ on the nuclei, where γ_{nuc} is the gyromagnetic ratio for the nuclei. Precession of the magnetic moments of the nuclei about the direction of the field **H** leads to the appearance of a variable electromotive force in the coil L, encompassing the working substance of the quantum gyroscope (Figure 3). Determination of the frequency of rotation Ω of the body connected with the quantum gyroscope's sensor reduces to measurement of the frequency of the electric signal, which is proportional to Ω.

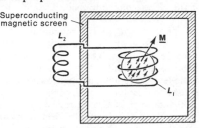

Figure 3. Diagram of a nuclear positional gyroscope: (**M**) total magnetic moment of the substance, (L_1) and (L_2) induction coils

In the dynamic nuclear gyroscope, the total nuclear magnetic moment **M** precesses about the constant magnetic field **H**, which is rigidly connected to the device. Rotation of the sensor together with the field **H** with angular velocity Ω leads to a change in the precession frequency of the magnetic moment **M** that is approximately equal to the projection of the vector Ω on **H**. This change is recorded in the form of an electric signal. To attain high sensitivity and accuracy, such devices require high stability and uniformity of the magnetic field **H**. For example, for detection of the change in the precession frequency caused by the diurnal rotation of the earth, it is necessary that $\Delta H/H < 10^{-9}$. The device is screened from the action of external magnetic fields by superconductors. For example, if the deflection of the sensor is due to the diurnal rotation of the earth, then the residual field in the screen should not exceed 3×10^{-9} oersted.

Electron quantum gyroscopes are analogous to the nuclear quantum gyroscopes, but materials are used in them that contain unpaired electrons in their atoms or molecules (for example, stable free radicals, or alkali metal atoms). Although the relaxation times of the electron spins are small, the use of such gyroscopes is promising, since the gyromagnetic ratio γ_{el} for electrons is several hundred times larger than for nuclei, and hence the precession frequency is greater, which is important for many applications.

Although quantum gyroscopes (particularly the optical types) are undergoing continuous improvement, their accuracy and sensitivity are still lower than in the best mechanical gyroscopes. However, quantum gyroscopes have a number of advantages over mechanical gyroscopes: they do not contain moving parts (they are inertialess), do not require arrestment, have a high degree of reliability and stability, may be started quickly, can withstand considerable acceleration, and are capable of operating at low temperatures. Some types of quantum gyroscopes are already being used not only as highly sensitive indicators of rotation, navigators, and gyrometers but also as gyrocompasses, surveying compasses, and sextants.

REFERENCES
Privalov, V. E., and S. A. Fridrikhov. "Kol'tsevoi gazovyi lazer." *Uspekhi fizicheskikh nauk*, 1969, vol. 97, issue 3, p. 377.
Pomerantsev, N. M., and G. V. Skrotskii. "Fizicheskie osnovy kvantovoi giroskopii." *Uspekhi fizicheskikh nauk.* 1970, vol. 100, issue 3, p. 361.
G. V. SKROTSKII [11–1791–2]

QUANTUM MAGNETOMETER, an instrument for measuring the intensity of magnetic fields, by utilizing quantum phenomena.

Quantum magnetometers are used primarily to measure the intensity of weak magnetic fields, particularly the earth's magnetic field and its anomalies, both on the surface and at great altitudes, corresponding to the orbits of ballistic missiles and artificial earth satellites, and also to measure magnetic fields of planets of the solar system and in outer space. They are also used in prospecting for minerals, for magnetic core sampling, and in searching for sunken vessels.

In a magnetic field, the energy levels of particles that have magnetic moments are split into several substates. The energy difference $\Delta \mathcal{E}$ among such substates depends on the intensity H of the magnetic field and in many cases is proportional to it. Particles may pass from one magnetic substate to another, absorbing or emitting a portion (quantum) of electromagnetic energy equal to $\hbar\omega$, where $\hbar$ is Planck's constant and ω is the frequency of the electromagnetic field. The frequency ω is exactly equal to the frequency of precession of the magnetic moment around the direction of the magnetic field—that is, $\omega = \gamma H$, where γ is the gyromagnetic ratio. The frequency ω is in the radio-frequency range. The intensity H of the magnetic field can be determined by finding the frequency ω—for example, according to the resonance absorption of radio waves by matter. Since the proportionality constant for the relationship between the frequency ω and the field H is expressed by atomic constants, which are characterized by extremely high stability and reproducibility, the sensitivity of such quantum magnetometers is very high. The most advanced quantum magnetometers of this type have a sensitivity of up to 10^{-8} oersted, or 10^{-3} gamma (1 gamma = 10^{-5} oersted).

Proton magnetometers. An ampul with a diamagnetic liquid is the sensor in proton magnetometers. The molecules of the liquid (for example, water or benzene) contain hydrogen atoms. The magnetic moments of the molecules are determined solely by the magnetic moments of the nuclei of the hydrogen atoms—that is, by protons (the electron magnetic moments in such liquids are compensated). The ampul is placed in a coil L, through which a current is passed for several seconds, creating an auxiliary magnetic field H_0 in the coil; the intensity of this field is several hundred oersteds (Figure 1). As a result of the action of the field H_0 the magnetic moments of the protons become oriented and the liquid acquires a total magnetic moment M. After the current is switched off, the magnetic moments of the protons begin to precess around the direction of the magnetic field H being measured, at a frequency $\omega = \gamma_p H$, where $\gamma_p = (2.67513 \pm 0.00002) \times 10^4$ gauss^{-1} sec^{-1}. The precession of the total magnetic moment M causes the appearance in the coil C of an alternating electromotive force with a frequency equal to the precession frequency ω. In the earth's magnetic field, $H_e \sim 0.6$ oersted and $\omega = 2.55$ kilohertz (kHz). Precession is gradually attenuated because of the process of relaxation, which is brought about by the weak interaction between the protons and atoms of paramagnetic additives dissolved in the working fluid. For pure water the relaxation time is about 3 sec. For a second measurement of the field the cycle is repeated. The cyclic nature of the sensor's operation can be eliminated by the use of a two-sensor system, with alternating operation of the sensors.

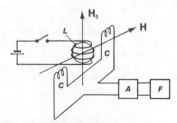

Figure 1. Diagram of a proton magnetometer: (L) coil generating an auxiliary magnetizing field H_0, (C) coil in which an electromotive force arises because of precession of nuclear moments around the magnetic field H being measured, (A) signal amplifier, (F) frequency meter, calibrated in oersteds

Electron magnetometer. The electron quantum magnetometer is analogous to the proton type. It uses the precession in a magnetic field of the unpaired electrons of paramagnetic atoms,

the frequency of which is hundreds of times greater than the precession frequency of protons. The precession frequency for electrons in a field $H \sim 1$ oersted is 2.8 MHz. A change of 1 gamma in the field causes a change of 28 Hz in the precession frequency, which is 660 times greater than for proton magnetometers.

To produce a sufficiently great electromotive force, methods of dynamic polarization of nuclei are used. The magnetic moments of the protons are oriented as a result of their interaction with the electron moments of paramagnetic ions (a paramagnetic salt dissolved in water). In this way the magnetization of nuclei can be increased by a factor of several hundred. The use of a substance containing the radicals of potassium nitrosodisulfate makes possible an additional increase in magnetization by a factor of about 40.

Optical magnetometer (magnetometer with optical pumping; Figure 2). In an optical magnetometer, a glass bulb is used as the sensor. The bulb is filled with vapors of an alkali metal, such as rubidium, whose atoms are paramagnetic, since they contain one unpaired electron.

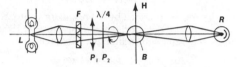

Figure 2. Diagram of an optical quantum magnetometer: (L) light source, (F) light filter, (P₁) polaroid, (P₂) plate (λ/4) generating a phase difference of 90° in order to produce circularly polarized light, (B) bulb filled with vapor of an alkali metal, (R) photoreceiver, (H) field being measured

When circularly polarized light whose frequency is equal to the frequency of the optical quantum transition between the ground state of the atom and one of its excited states is passed through the bulb, which is placed in the field H being measured, resonance scattering of light occurs. As this takes place, the angular momentum of the quanta of scattered light is transferred to the atoms, which thus become "optically oriented" and collect on one of the magnetic substates of the ground state. If an alternating magnetic field whose frequency is equal to the frequency of quantum transition between the magnetic substates of the ground state is generated inside the sensor bulb, the atom population of the magnetic substates is equalized, and atoms lose the acquired preferred orientation of magnetic moments and return to their original state. As this takes place, metal vapors filling the bulb again begin strongly to absorb and disperse the light. The intensity of the magnetic field H in which the sensor bulb is located may be determined by measuring the frequency ω of the alternating field.

Optical quantum magnetometers are particularly convenient for measurements of weak fields (less than 1 oersted). The sensitivity attainable with instruments of this type is 10^{-6} to 10^{-7} oersted, which makes possible the measurement of very weak fields, particularly in outer space.

Superconductor magnetometers. Superconductor magnetometers are based on the quantization of a magnetic flux trapped within a superconducting ring. The magnitude of the trapped flux is a multiple of a quantum of magnetic flux, $\Phi_0 = 2 \times 10^{-7}$ oersted $\cdot$ cm^2. The total current flowing through the parallel connection of two Josephson contacts (a superconducting ring divided along its diameter by a very thin layer of insulation) as a result of the addition of currents flowing through each branch (Figure 3) changes proportional to cos $e\, \Phi/\hbar$, where Φ is the magnetic flux contained within the ring and e is the charge of an electron. The current attains a maximum whenever $\Phi = n\, \Phi_0$ (n is an integer). By observing the changes in the current passing through the double Josephson contact it is possible to measure the magnetic flux Φ and, since the cross-sectional area of the contact is known, to determine the intensity of the field. If the area of two contacts is equal to 1 sq mm, the current maximums are separated by an interval of 2 gammas. An interval one-tenth as large may be recorded by this method. In this case the sensitivity of the method is 0.2 gamma. In the example discussed here the strongest field that could be measured would be about 20 gammas.

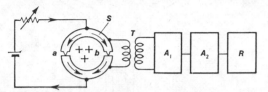

Figure 3. Diagram of a superconducting magnetometer: (S) superconducting ring with two Josephson contacts (a and b), (T) matching transformer, (A₁) narrow-band amplifier with a detector, (A₂) DC amplifier, (R) chart recorder. The magnetic flux through the ring (perpendicular to the plane of the figure and directed downward) is indicated by the crosses. Changes in the flux cause the appearance of a periodic electromotive force at the input of the amplifier (A₁).

Quantum magnetometers are not sensitive to vibration; their readings do not depend on the orientation of the instrument relative to the field H being measured and depend only weakly on changes in temperature, pressure, and humidity.

REFERENCES

Pomerantsev, N. M., V. M. Ryzhkov, and G. V. Skrotskii. *Fizicheskie osnovy kvantovoi magnitometrii.* Moscow, 1972.

Abragam, A. *Iadernyi magnetizm.* Moscow, 1963. (Translated from English.)   G. V. SKROTSKII [11–1794–1; updated]

QUANTUM MECHANICAL AMPLIFIER, a device for amplifying electromagnetic waves by stimulated emission of excited atoms, molecules, or ions. The amplifying effect is associated with a change in the energy of intra-atomic (bound) electrons, whose motion is described by quantum mechanics. Consequently, unlike thermionic amplifiers, for example, which use streams of free electrons whose motion is described by classical mechanics, these amplifiers have come to be called quantum mechanical amplifiers.

Since, in addition to the stimulated quantum transitions of excited atoms into a lower energy state, spontaneous transitions that cause the emission of waves with random amplitude, phase, and polarization are also possible, such transitions are added to the amplified wave in the form of noise. Spontaneous emission is the only source of noise in a quantum amplifier, and it is fundamentally nonremovable. Its power is very small in the radio frequency range but increases sharply in the optical range. Therefore, radio-frequency quantum mechanical amplifiers (masers) are characterized by an exceptionally low noise level (they have no noise caused by the irregularity of the electron stream that is unavoidable in electron tubes; in addition, masers operate at temperatures close to absolute zero, and the noise associated with the the thermal motion of electrons in the amplifier circuits is very small). The sensitivity of a maser—that is, its ability to amplify very weak signals—is excellent because of the extremely low noise level. Masers are used as the input stages in high-sensitivity radio receiving equipment for the wavelength range from 4 mm to 50 cm. They substantially increase the range of operation of communications links with space stations and on-planet radar and radio telescopes.

Quantum mechanical amplifiers in the optical range are used extensively as power amplifiers for laser emission. In their principle of operation and design they are highly similar to lasers.

The induced transition of an atom from a state with energy $\mathcal{E}_2$ to a state with lower energy $\mathcal{E}_1$, which is accompanied by the emission of a quantum of electromagnetic energy $\mathcal{E}_2 - \mathcal{E}_1 = \hbar\nu$ (ν is the frequency of the incident and emitted waves, and $\hbar$ is Planck's constant), leads to amplification of the oscillations. The amplification produced by one atom is very small, but if an oscillation of frequency ν propagates in a substance containing a large number of identical excited atoms at level $\mathcal{E}_2$, the amplification can become fairly high. On the other hand, the atoms at the lower level $\mathcal{E}_1$ as a result of stimulated absorption attenuate the wave. In consequence the substance will attenuate or amplify the wave depending on whether more of its atoms are unexcited or excited or, as is said, which of the energy levels has the greater atom population.

If a substance is in a state of thermodynamic equilibrium, the distribution of particles with respect to energy levels is controlled by its temperature, and the lower energy level is more populated than the higher energy level (Figure 1). Such a substance always absorbs electromagnetic waves. The substance begins to amplify —it becomes active—only when the equilibrium is disturbed and there are more excited than unexcited atoms (that is, when a population inversion exists). The greater the excess of atoms at the higher level over those at the lower level (that is, the larger the inverse population difference $\Delta N_i = N_2 - N_1$), the greater the amplifying effect.

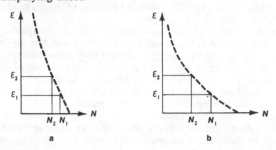

Figure 1. Particle distribution over energy levels in a state of thermodynamic equilibrium: (a) at temperature T_1, (b) at temperature $T_2 < T_1$; N is the population of the energy levels

However, the inverted state of a substance cannot exist without limit. After an external influence ceases, an equilibrium distribution of the population levels (Figure 1) is again established after a certain period of time because of thermal motion of the particles and the interaction among them. This process (relaxation), which is also present while the external disturbance is acting, tends to reestablish thermal equilibrium in the substance. Therefore, an external action should be strong enough to bring the substance into a state of population inversion and should be repeated.

Various methods exist for creating an active medium. The most satisfactory method for a quantum mechanical amplifier is the method based on the use of three energy levels as proposed by N. G. Basov and A. M. Prokhorov. The particles (atoms, molecules, or ions), which have an energy spectrum containing three levels $\mathcal{E}_1$, $\mathcal{E}_2$, and $\mathcal{E}_3$ (Figure 2), are subjected to the action of strong electromagnetic radiation (pumping). The frequency ν of this radiation corresponds to the frequency of transition between the bottom level $\mathcal{E}_1$ and the top level $\mathcal{E}_3$ ($h\nu = \mathcal{E}_3 - \mathcal{E}_1$). The pumping intensity should be great enough so that the $\mathcal{E}_1 \rightarrow \mathcal{E}_3$ transition occurs much more frequently than the reverse relaxation transitions. In this case the populations in levels $\mathcal{E}_1$ and $\mathcal{E}_3$ are equalized. Moreover, for one pair of levels $\mathcal{E}_1$ and $\mathcal{E}_2$ or $\mathcal{E}_2$ and $\mathcal{E}_3$, a population inversion will take place; it occurs for the pair of levels having the slowest relaxation time and the smallest energy difference.

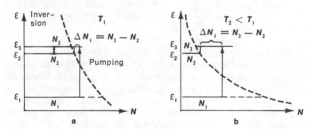

Figure 2. Formation of a population inversion for the energy levels $\mathcal{E}_2$ and $\mathcal{E}_3$ in a system having three levels $\mathcal{E}_1$, $\mathcal{E}_2$, and $\mathcal{E}_3$ under the influence of pumping: (a) when the temperature of the substance is T_1, (b) when the temperature of the substance is $T_2 < T_1$. The dotted curves show the particle distribution over energy levels for thermodynamic equilibrium.

As the temperature T decreases, both the equilibrium population difference $\Delta N = N_1 - N_2$ (Figure 1) and the inverse population difference ΔN_i (Figure 2) increase. In addition, a reduction in temperature greatly retards relaxation and thereby reduces the pumping power required. Consequently, a population inversion sufficient to create efficient masers may be produced by cooling a substance down to the boiling point of helium (4.2°K). Amplifiers exist that operate at temperatures of 77°K (the boiling point of nitrogen) and even 190°K, but they are less efficient.

The most suitable materials for masers are diamagnetic crystals with a small addition of paramagnetic ions. Ruby (Al_2O_3 with an addition of Cr^{3+} chromium ions), rutile (TiO_2 with an addition of Cr^{3+} and Fe^{3+} ions), and emerald [$Be_3Al_2(SiO_3)_6$ with an additive of chromic oxide, Cr_2O_3] are usually used. Crystals with a volume of several cu cm, grown from very pure materials with a carefully measured additive of the paramagnetic ions, are essential for masers.

In the absence of external magnetic fields, the magnetic moments of the ions are oriented randomly. In a constant magnetic field the magnetic moment can assume only certain definite angles with respect to the magnetic field **H**, and the energy of the ions is different in these positions (the Zeeman effect). A number of energy levels (magnetic sublevels) are created; the distances between them are a function of the strength H of the constant magnetic field. The number of magnetic sublevels is determined by the spin of the ion (Figure 3). The energy difference between them, given ordinary magnetic fields, corresponds to the radio frequency range and can be easily varied by altering the magnetic field. Such a substance is capable of amplifying radio waves of the desired frequency.

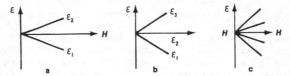

Figure 3. The energy levels of a paramagnetic ion in an external magnetic field H are split into several magnetic sublevels, the number of which depends on the value of the spin S of the ion: (a) $S = 1/2$, (b) $S = 1$, (c) $S = 3/2$

A fundamental characteristic of every amplifier of electrical oscillations is its amplification factor, or gain, K, which indicates by what factor the oscillation amplitude at the output is greater than the amplitude at the input. The longer the path that a wave travels in an active substance, the higher the gain of the amplifier. In a ruby crystal a wave that is propagating over a distance equal to its wavelength λ has a negligible increase in its amplitude. Thus, single crystals of large size, which are grown only with great difficulty, are required to produce sufficient gain. To achieve a gain of 10, crystals—and therefore magnets—several meters long would be required. Such an amplifier would be very cumbersome and costly.

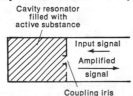

Figure 4. Cavity resonator with an active substance

Gain may be increased by passing the wave repeatedly through the active substance. For this purpose the active substance is placed in a cavity resonator (a cavity bounded by metal walls). A wave from an antenna, entering the resonator through a hole in its wall (the coupling iris), is reflected repeatedly and interacts with the active substance (Figure 4) for a long period. The amplification will be efficient if the phase of the wave reflected from the wall coincides each time with the phase of the incident wave. This condition is met for certain resonator dimensions—that is, the resonator, like the substance itself, must be tuned to the frequency of the wave being amplified. Upon each reflection from the wall with the iris, a portion of the electromagnetic energy is radiated outward as an amplified signal. The input and output of the resonator are isolated by means of a circulator (Figure 5). This is known as the reflector type of quantum mechanical amplifier.

To produce optimum characteristics, the proper size of the coupling iris of a quantum mechanical amplifier must be se-

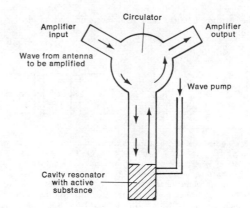

Figure 5. Schematic diagram of a reflector quantum mechanical amplifier with a single resonator

lected, since in addition to the required gain, the amplifier must have the necessary passband, which determines its ability to amplify signals that are varying rapidly over time. The more rapidly the signal varies, the wider is the frequency band it occupies. If the amplifier's passband $\Delta\nu$ is narrower than the frequency band occupied by the signal, the rapid variations of the signal are smoothed out in the amplifier.

Thus, the introduction of a resonator into the design of an amplifier increases its gain but reduces its passband by the same factor; this substantially diminishes the amplifier's useful range. Single-resonator quantum mechanical amplifiers have not gained wide acceptance because high gain and a broad passband cannot be provided simultaneously. However, a broad passband may be preserved with high gain by using several resonators. There are two types of such multiresonator masers, the reflector amplifier with a circulator (Figure 6) and the transmission amplifier (Figure 7). In transmission quantum mechanical amplifiers the wave propagates along a series of resonators filled with an active substance. Where the passband is considerable, the gain in each resonator is small, but the overall gain of the whole series can be rather large. The resonators of such an amplifier are connected to one another by ferrite isolators. When subjected to a constant magnetic field the ferrites acquire the property of passing a wave that is propagating in one direction but of absorbing a wave coming from the opposite direction. The principal disadvantage of multiresonator amplifiers is the complexity of tuning the amplifier's frequency, because when the magnetic field H changes, the natural frequency of a large number of resonators must be changed simultaneously, which is difficult technically.

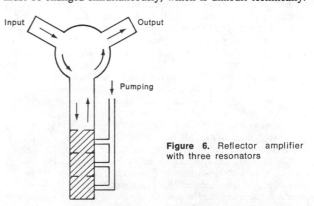

Figure 6. Reflector amplifier with three resonators

The time of interaction between a wave and a substance can be increased by using delay systems in place of a system of resonators. The propagation velocity along such a structure is much lower than in a wave guide or in free space. The gain is correspondingly increased when the wave passes through a unit length of the crystal. It is important to note that the delay structures have broad bands, which makes possible retuning of the frequency of a maser by altering only the magnetic field. The passband of such amplifiers, as well as multiresonator masers, depends on the width of the spectral line. Quantum mechanical amplifiers with a delay structure are called traveling-wave amplifiers. Ferrites, which pass a wave propagating along the delay structure in the desired direction and absorb the reflected waves coming from the opposite direction, are also used in them.

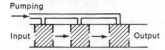

Figure 7. Diagram of a transmission quantum mechanical amplifier with three resonators

The noise of an amplifier may be measured conveniently by comparing it with the power of the thermal radiation from a blackbody. The spectrum of thermal radiation includes the optical and the radio-frequency ranges. Thus, the noise can be expressed through the absolute temperature. The minimum noise temperature of an amplifier, which is due to spontaneous emission at $\lambda = 3$ cm, is $0.5°K$. For most active substances used in quantum mechanical amplifiers the noise lies between $1°$ and $5°K$. In real amplifiers, the much higher power of thermal radiations from the feeder radio-frequency wave guides and other structural parts is added to these insignificant noises. The noise radiated by a wave guide can be described by the quantity βT, where β is the absorption coefficient of the wave and T is the wave guide's absolute temperature. To reduce noise, as many of the input parts as possible must be cooled; however, it is impossible to cool the entire input channel down to the temperature of liquid helium. Consequently, it has not been possible to reduce the noise of a quantum mechanical amplifier from an antenna below $15°–30°K$, which is approximately 100 times less than the noise level of the best amplifiers available before the advent of the quantum mechanical amplifier.

Quantum mechanical amplifiers are cooled by liquid helium in cryostats. The difficulties associated with the liquefaction, transportation, and decanting of liquid helium from transport containers into cryostats restrict the field of application of masers and complicate and raise the cost of using them. Small refrigeration machines with a closed coolant cycle have been developed. The weight of such a machine designed to cool a maser down to $40°K$ is 10–20 kg. A machine designed to reach $4°K$ weighs more than 200 kg and uses several kilowatts of power.

REFERENCES

Karlov, N. V., and A. A. Manenkov. *Kvantovye usiliteli.* Moscow, 1966.
Siegman, A. *Mazery.* Moscow, 1966. (Translated from English.)
Kvantovaia elektronika: Malen'kaia entsiklopediia. Moscow, 1969.
Shteinshleiger, V. B., G. S. Misezhnikov, and P. S. Lifanov. *Kvantovye usiliteli SVCh (mazery).* Moscow, 1971.

A. V. FRANTSESSON [11–1797–1]

QUANTUM MECHANICS (wave mechanics), a theory that establishes the laws of motion of microparticles (elementary particles, atoms, molecules, atomic nuclei) and their systems (for example, crystals) and a method of describing their motions; it also establishes the relation between quantities characterizing particles and systems and the physical quantities directly measured in macroscopic experiments.

The laws of quantum mechanics form the foundation of the study of the structure of matter. They have made it possible to determine the structure of atoms, to establish the nature of the chemical bond, to explain the periodic table of the elements, to understand the structure of atomic nuclei, and to study the properties of elementary particles. Insofar as the properties of macroscopic bodies are determined by the motion and interaction of the particles of which they consist, the laws of quantum mechanics underlie an understanding of most macroscopic phenomena. Quantum mechanics has made it possible, for example, to explain the temperature dependence and calculate the magnitude of the specific heat of gases and solids and to determine the structure and understand many properties of solids (metals, dielectrics, semiconductors). Only on the basis of quantum mechanics has it been possible to explain consistently such phenomena as ferromagnetism, superfluidity, and superconductivity; to understand the nature of such astrophysical objects as white dwarfs and neutron stars; and to determine the mechanism

of thermonuclear reactions in the sun and stars. There are also phenomena (such as the Josephson effect) in which the laws of quantum mechanics are directly manifested in the behavior of macroscopic objects.

A number of the most important technical achievements of the 20th century have been effectively based on specific laws of quantum mechanics. For example, quantum-mechanical laws underlie the operation of nuclear reactors and make thermonuclear reactions possible under terrestrial conditions; they are manifested in a number of phenomena in metals and semiconductors used in modern technology. The quantum-mechanical theory of radiation constitutes the foundation of such a rapidly developing branch of physics as quantum electronics. The laws of quantum mechanics are used in the search for and development of new materials (especially magnetic, semiconductor, and superconducting materials). Thus, quantum mechanics is becoming largely an "engineering" science a knowledge of which is necessary not only for research physicists but also for engineers.

Place among other sciences of motion. Early in the 20th century it became evident that the classical mechanics of I. Newton had a limited range of application and required generalization. First, it is inapplicable at high rates of motion of bodies—at velocities comparable to the velocity of light. Here it was replaced by relativistic mechanics, constructed on the basis of A. Einstein's special theory of relativity. Relativistic mechanics includes Newtonian (nonrelativistic) mechanics as a particular case. Hereafter, the term "classical mechanics" will include Newtonian and relativistic mechanics.

The description of particles by specifying their positions in space (their coordinates) and their velocities and the dependence of these quantities on time is characteristic of classical mechanics as a whole. The motion of particles along well-defined trajectories corresponds to such a description. However, experiment has shown that this description is not always valid, especially for particles of very small mass (microparticles). This fact constitutes a second limitation on the applicability of Newtonian mechanics. A more general description of motion is given by quantum mechanics, which includes classical mechanics as a particular case. Quantum mechanics, like classical mechanics, is divided into nonrelativistic mechanics, which is valid in the case of low velocities, and relativistic mechanics, which satisfies the requirements of the special theory of relativity. The foundations of nonrelativistic quantum mechanics are presented in this article. (However, some general propositions apply to quantum mechanics as a whole.) Nonrelativistic quantum mechanics, like Newtonian mechanics for its range of applicability, is a fully complete and logically self-consistent theory that in principle is capable of giving, within its own sphere of competence, a quantitative solution to any physics problem. Relativistic quantum mechanics is not so complete and self-consistent. Whereas in the nonrelativistic domain it may be assumed that motion is determined by forces that act (instantaneously) at a distance, this is not true in the relativistic domain. Insofar as, according to the theory of relativity, interaction is transmitted (propagated) with finite velocity, there must exist a physical agent that transmits the interaction; the field is such an agent. The difficulties of relativistic theory are the difficulties of field theory, which are encountered by both relativistic classical mechanics and relativistic quantum mechanics. The problems of relativistic quantum mechanics connected with quantum field theory will not be considered in this article.

Criteria of applicability of classical mechanics. The relationship between Newtonian and relativistic mechanics is determined by the existence of a fundamental quantity, the maximum rate of signal propagation, which is equal to the velocity of light c ($c \approx 3 \times 10^{10}$ cm/sec). If the velocity of a body v is much less than that of light (that is, $v/c \ll 1$, so that c may be considered to be infinitely large), then Newtonian mechanics is applicable.

The relationship between classical mechanics and quantum mechanics is less graphic in character. It is determined by the existence of another universal constant—Planck's constant h. The constant h (also called the quantum of action) has the dimensions of action (energy multiplied by time) and is equal to $h = 6.62 \times 10^{-27}$ erg·sec. (The quantity $\hbar = h/2\pi =$

1.0545919 $\times$ 10^{-27} erg·sec—Dirac constant—is used more often in theory; it is also called the Planck constant.) The criterion of applicability of classical mechanics formally consists in the following: classical mechanics is applicable if under the conditions of a given problem the physical quantities with the dimension of action are much greater than $\hbar$ (so that $\hbar$ may be considered very small). This criterion will be explained in greater detail during the exposition of the physical principles of quantum mechanics.

History. Two groups of phenomena (seemingly unrelated) attesting to the inapplicability of conventional classical Newtonian mechanics and classical electromagnetic field theory (classical electrodynamics) to processes of the interaction of light with matter and to processes occurring within the atom were discovered in the early 20th century. The first group of phenomena was connected with the experimental establishment of the dual nature of light (the duality of light); the second was connected with the impossibility of explaining, on the basis of classical concepts, the stable existence of the atom and the spectral regularities discovered during the study of the emission of light by atoms. The establishment of a relationship between these groups of phenomena and the attempts to explain them on the basis of a new theory ultimately led to the discovery of the laws of quantum mechanics.

Quantum concepts (in particular, the quantum constant h) were first introduced into physics by M. Planck's work (1900) on the theory of thermal radiation. The then-current theory of thermal radiation, constructed on the basis of classical electrodynamics and statistical physics, led to the meaningless result that thermal (thermodynamic) equilibrium between radiation and matter cannot be attained, since sooner or later all energy must go over into radiation. On the basis of an extraordinarily bold hypothesis, Planck resolved the contradiction and obtained results that agreed remarkably with experiment. In contrast to the classical theory of radiation, which considers the emission of electromagnetic waves as a continuous process, Planck assumed that light is emitted in definite bundles of energy—quanta. The magnitude of such a quantum of energy depends on the frequency of the light ν and is equal to $\mathcal{E} = h\nu$.

Two interconnected lines of development that culminated in the final formulation of quantum mechanics in its two forms by 1927 can be traced from this work by Planck. The first begins with Einstein's work (1905) in which the theory of the photoelectric effect—the phenomenon of the light-induced emission of electrons from matter—was given. In developing Planck's idea, Einstein assumed that not only is light emitted and absorbed in discrete bundles—quanta of radiation—but light is also propagated in such quanta, that is, discreteness is inherent in light itself; light itself consists of separate bundles—quanta of light, which were later called photons. The energy $\mathcal{E}$ of a photon is related to the wave's oscillation frequency ν by Planck's formula $\mathcal{E} = h\nu$. On the basis of this hypothesis, Einstein explained the regularities of the photoelectric effect, which contradicted the classical theory of light (which is based on classical electrodynamics).

Further proof of the corpuscular nature of light was obtained in 1922 by A. Compton, who experimentally proved that the scattering of light by free electrons takes place according to the laws of elastic collisions between two particles—a photon and an electron. The kinematics of such a collision is determined by the laws of conservation of energy and momentum, and, in addition to the energy $\mathcal{E} = h\nu$, the momentum $p = h/\lambda = h\nu/c$, where λ is the length of the light wave, must be ascribed to the photon. The energy and momentum of a photon are related by the formula $\mathcal{E} = cp$, which is valid in relativistic mechanics for a particle with zero mass.

Thus, it was proved experimentally that in addition to known wave properties (which are manifested, for example, in the diffraction of light), light also has corpuscular properties: it consists, as it were, of particles—photons. The duality of light and its complex wave-particle nature are manifested herein. The duality is already present in the formula $\mathcal{E} = h\nu$, which does not make it possible to choose either of the two concepts: in the left part of the equality the energy $\mathcal{E}$ applies to a particle, but in the right part, the frequency ν is a characteristic of a wave. A formal

logical contradiction arose: to explain certain phenomena it was necessary to assume that light has a wave nature, but to explain other phenomena, it must have a corpuscular nature. The resolution of this contradiction essentially led to the development of the physical foundations of quantum mechanics.

In 1924, L. de Broglie, seeking an explanation for the conditions postulated in 1913 by N. Bohr for the quantization of atomic orbits (*see below*), advanced the hypothesis that wave-particle duality is universal. According to de Broglie, to every particle, regardless of its nature, there should correspond a wave whose length λ is related to the momentum of the particle p by the formula

$$(1) \qquad \lambda = \frac{h}{p}$$

According to this hypothesis, not only photons but all "ordinary particles" (such as electrons and protons) as well have wave properties that should, in particular, be manifested in the phenomenon of diffraction. In 1927, C. Davisson and L. Germer first observed the diffraction of electrons. Later, wave properties were also observed for other particles, and the validity of de Broglie's formula was confirmed experimentally. In 1926, E. Schrödinger proposed an equation to describe the behavior of such "waves" in external force fields. Wave mechanics thus arose. Schrödinger's wave equation is the fundamental equation of nonrelativistic quantum mechanics. In 1928, P. Dirac formulated a relativistic equation describing the motion of an electron in an external force field; Dirac's equation has become one of the basic equations of relativistic quantum mechanics.

The second line of development begins with Einstein's work (1907) on the theory of the specific heat of solids (which is also a generalization of Planck's hypothesis). Electromagnetic radiation consisting of a set of electromagnetic waves of different frequencies is dynamically equivalent to some set of oscillators. The emission or absorption of the waves is equivalent to the excitation or damping of the corresponding oscillators. The fact that emission and absorption of electromagnetic radiation by matter take place in quanta of energy $h\nu$ may be expressed in the following manner: an electromagnetic field oscillator cannot have arbitrary energy and can have only certain energy values —discrete energy levels, the distance between which is equal to $h\nu$. Einstein generalized this idea of the quantization of the energy of an electromagnetic field oscillator to an oscillator of arbitrary nature. Inasmuch as the thermal motion of solids reduces to the vibrations of atoms, a solid is dynamically equivalent to a set of oscillators. The energy of such oscillators is also quantized, that is, the difference between adjacent energy levels (the energies that the oscillator may have) must be equal to $h\nu$, where ν is the vibration frequency of the atoms. Einstein's theory, refined by P. Debye, M. Born, and T. von Kármán, played a prominent role in the development of solid-state theory.

In 1913, Bohr applied the idea of the quantization of energy to the theory of atomic structure, a planetary model of which followed from the results of E. Rutherford's experiments (1911). According to this model, a positively charged nucleus, in which virtually the entire mass of the atom is concentrated, is located at the center of the atom; negatively charged electrons revolve about the nucleus in orbits. Examination of such motion on the basis of classical concepts led to the paradoxical result of the impossibility of the stable existence of atoms: according to classical electrodynamics, the electron cannot move in a stationary orbit since a revolving electric charge must radiate electromagnetic waves and consequently lose energy; the radius of its orbit must decrease and in a period of the order of 10^{-8} sec the electron should fall into the nucleus. This meant that the laws of classical physics were inapplicable to the motion of electrons in the atom, since atoms exist and are extremely stable.

To explain the stability of atoms, Bohr assumed that of all the orbits allowed by Newtonian mechanics for the electron's motion in the electric field of the atomic nucleus, only those that satisfy certain conditions of quantization are actually realized. In other words, discrete energy levels exist in the atom (as in an oscillator). These levels conform to a definite principle derived by Bohr on the basis of a combination of the laws of Newtonian mechanics and quantization conditions requiring that the integral of the action over the classical orbit be an integral multiple of Planck's constant $\hbar$. Bohr postulated that an electron in a specific energy level (that is, while undergoing the orbital motion allowed by the quantization conditions) does not radiate light waves. Radiation occurs only when an electron moves from one orbit to another, that is, from an energy level $\mathcal{E}_i$ to one with lower energy $\mathcal{E}_k$; here a quantum of light is produced with an energy equal to the difference in the energy levels between which the transition is accomplished:

$$(2) \qquad h\nu = \mathcal{E}_i - \mathcal{E}_k$$

Thus arises a line spectrum—the principal distinctive feature of atomic spectra. Bohr obtained the correct formula for the frequencies of the spectral lines of the hydrogen atom (and hydrogen-like atoms); this formula encompassed the aggregate of previously discovered empirical formulas.

The existence of energy levels in atoms was confirmed by the Franck-Hertz experiments (1913–14). It was established that electrons bombarding a gas lose, on collision with atoms, only definite amounts of energy equal to differences between energy levels of the atoms.

Thus, using the quantum constant h, which reflects the duality of light, Bohr demonstrated that this quantity also determines the motion of electrons in the atom (and that the laws of this motion differ significantly from the laws of classical mechanics). This fact was later explained on the basis of the universality of the wave-particle duality contained in de Broglie's hypothesis.

The success of Bohr's theory, like the previous advances in quantum theory, was achieved at the expense of disrupting the logical integrity of the theory: on the one hand, Newtonian mechanics was used, and on the other, artificial quantization rules alien to it and contradictory to classical electrodynamics were brought in. Moreover, Bohr's theory proved unable to explain the motion of electrons in complex atoms (and even in the helium atom), the origin of molecular bonds, and other phenomena. Nor could Bohr's "semiclassical" theory answer the question of how an electron moves during a transition from one energy level to another. Further intensive work on the problems of atomic theory led to the conviction that it was impossible to construct logically an orderly theory while retaining the classical picture of the electron's orbital motion. When it was recognized that the motion of electrons in the atom cannot be described in terms (or concepts) of classical mechanics (like motion along a specific trajectory), it was proposed that the problem of the motion of an electron between levels was incompatible with the nature of the laws governing the behavior of electrons in the atom and that a new theory that would incorporate only quantities applying to the initial and final stationary states of the atom was needed. In 1925, W. Heisenberg succeeded in constructing such a formal scheme, in which certain abstract algebraic quantities—matrices—figured instead of electron coordinates and velocities; the relation between the matrices and observable quantities (energy levels and the intensities of quantum transitions) was given by simple self-consistent rules. Heisenberg's work was developed by M. Born and P. Jordan. Thus arose matrix mechanics. Soon after the appearance of the Schrödinger equation, the mathematical equivalence of wave mechanics (based on the Schrödinger equation) and matrix mechanics was demonstrated. In 1926, Born gave a probabilistic interpretation of de Broglie waves (see below).

Dirac's works of this period played a major role in the development of quantum mechanics. Final formulation of quantum mechanics as a consistent physical theory with clear foundations and an orderly mathematical apparatus took place after the appearance of Heisenberg's work (1927) in which the uncertainty relation was formulated. This is a most important relation which sheds light on the physical significance of the equations of quantum mechanics, on the connection with classical mechanics, and on other fundamental questions and qualitative results of quantum mechanics. This work was continued and generalized in the works of Bohr and Heisenberg.

A detailed analysis of atomic spectra led to the concept (first introduced by G. Uhlenbeck and S. Goudsmit and developed by W. Pauli) that in addition to charge and mass yet another intrinsic characteristic (quantum number)—spin—should be ascribed to the electron. The exclusion principle (the Pauli exclusion principle, see below), discovered by Pauli in 1925 and of fundamental importance in atomic, molecular, nuclear, and solid-state theory, played an important role.

Within a short time, quantum mechanics was applied successfully to a broad range of phenomena. Theories of atomic spectra, molecular structure, the chemical bond, D. I. Mendeleev's periodic system, conductivity of metals, and ferromagnetism were devised. These and many other phenomena became, at least qualitatively, comprehensible. Subsequent fundamental development of quantum theory was connected primarily with relativistic quantum mechanics. Nonrelativistic quantum mechanics developed primarily along the lines of encompassing diverse specific problems of the physics of atoms, molecules, solids (metals and semiconductors), plasmas, and the like, while at the same time improving the mathematical apparatus and elaborating the quantitative methods of solving various problems.

Probabilities and waves. Insofar as the laws of quantum mechanics cannot be visualized to the same degree as the laws of classical mechanics, it is useful to trace the development of the ideas forming the foundation of quantum mechanics and only then to formulate its basic propositions. The facts on the basis of which the theory is constructed are not, of course, unique, inasmuch as quantum mechanics describes an extremely broad range of phenomena, and each of these is capable of providing material for its substantiation. We shall proceed from the requirements of simplicity and in close conformity with history.

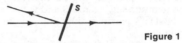

Figure 1

Let us consider a very simple experiment in light propagation (Figure 1). A transparent plate S is placed in the path of a beam of light. Some of the light passes through the plate and some is reflected. It is known that light consists of "particles"—photons. What happens to a single photon on impact with the plate? If we set up an experiment (for example, with a beam of light of extremely low intensity) in which the fate of every photon can be traced, then we may satisfy ourselves that on encountering the plate the photon is not split into two photons; its individuality as a particle is retained (otherwise the light would change its frequency, or its color). It turns out that some photons pass through the plate and some are reflected from it. Why? Perhaps there are two different types of photons? Let us set up a control experiment: we place a similar plate in the path of the transmitted light that should contain just one of the two "types" of photons. However, the same picture will be observed: some of the photons will pass through the second plate and some will be reflected. Consequently, under identical conditions identical particles may behave differently. This means that a photon's behavior on encountering a plate cannot be predicted unambiguously. Determinism does not exist in the sense in which it is construed in classical mechanics during the motion of photons. This conclusion is one of the starting points for resolving the contradiction between the corpuscular and wave properties of particles and constructing a theory of quantum-mechanical phenomena.

The problem of the reflection of light from a transparent plate does not present any difficulty for wave theory: on the basis of the properties of the plate, wave optics unambiguously predicts a correlation between the intensities of the transmitted light and the reflected light. From the corpuscular standpoint, the intensity of the light is proportional to the number of photons. Let N be the total number of photons and N_1 and N_2, the number of transmitted and the number of reflected photons ($N_1 + N_2 = N$). Wave optics defines the ratio N_1/N_2, but naturally nothing can be said of the behavior of a single photon. The reflection of a photon from the plate or its passage through it are random events: some photons pass through the plate and some are reflected from it, but when the number of photons is large the ratio N_1/N_2 is in agreement with the prediction of wave optics. In quantitative terms, the regularities that are manifested in random events can be described by means of the concept of probability. A photon can pass through a plate with a probability

w_1 and be reflected from it with a probability w_2. When the total number of photons is N, an average of $w_1 N$ particles will pass through the plate and $w_2 N$ particles will be reflected. If N is very large, then the average (expected) values of the number of particles coincide precisely with the actual values (although fluctuations exist and classical optics cannot take them into consideration). All optical relations can be translated from the language of intensities into the language of probabilities, and then they will apply to the behavior of a single photon. The probability that one of two alternative (mutually exclusive) events—transmission or reflection—will occur is equal to $w_1 + w_2 = 1$. This is the addition law of probabilities, which corresponds to the summation of intensities. The probability of passage through two identical plates is equal to $w_1{}^2$, and the probability of passage through the first and reflection from the second is $w_1 w_2$ (this corresponds to the fact that at the second plate the light that passed through the first plate is divided into transmitted and reflected light in the same proportion as at the first plate). This is the multiplication law of probabilities (which is valid for independent events).

This experiment is not unique to light. Similar experiments with a beam of electrons of other microparticles also demonstrate the unpredictability of the behavior of an individual particle. However, not only direct experiments indicate that in the most general case a probabilistic description of the behavior of microparticles should be used. It is theoretically impossible to imagine that some microparticles can be described probabilistically and others, classically: the interaction of "classical" particles with "quantum" particles would inevitably lead to the introduction of quantum uncertainties and would also make the behavior of "classical" particles unpredictable in the sense of classical determinism.

The prediction of the probabilities of various processes is a possible formulation of the task of quantum mechanics; this contrasts with the task of classical mechanics, which in principle consists in the prediction of completely certain events alone. Of course, a probabilistic description is also permissible in classical mechanics. To obtain a reliable prediction, classical mechanics requires absolutely precise assignment of the initial conditions, that is, of the positions and velocities of all particles forming the system. If the initial conditions are given not precisely but with some degree of uncertainty, the predictions will contain uncertainty, that is, will be to some extent probabilistic in character. Classical statistical physics, which operates with certain averaged quantities, may serve as an example. Therefore, the disparity between the systems of thought of quantum and classical mechanics would not be as great if probabilities were indeed the basic concepts of quantum mechanics. In order to clarify the radical distinction between quantum mechanics and classical mechanics, let us somewhat complicate the light reflection experiment examined above.

Figure 2

Let a reflected beam of light (or microparticles) be rotated by means of a mirror Z and be incident upon the same region A (for example, the same photon detector) as the transmitted beam (Figure 2). It would be natural to expect that in this case the measured intensity is equal to the sum of the intensities of the transmitted and reflected beams. However, it is common knowledge that this is not the case: the intensity may change as a function of the location of the mirror and detector over a broad range and in some cases (when the intensities of the transmitted and reflected light are equal) may vanish (the beams seemingly cancel each other). This is the phenomenon of light interference. What can be said of the behavior of a single photon in an interference experiment? The probability of its incidence on a given detector is changed significantly in contrast to the first experiment and will not be equal to the sum of the probabilities of the photon's entry into the detector by the first and second paths. Consequently, these two paths are not alternative (otherwise the probabilities would be summed). Hence it follows that the exist-

ence of two paths of arrival for the photon from the source to the detector significantly affects the probability distribution, and therefore we cannot say by which path the photon has passed from the source to the detector. We must assume that it could arrive simultaneously by two different paths.

The radical nature of the concepts that arise here must be emphasized. Indeed, it is impossible to conceive of a particle's simultaneous motion in two paths. Nor does quantum mechanics formulate such a problem. It merely predicts the results of experiments with beams of particles. Let us emphasize that in this case no hypotheses are advanced, but only an interpretation of the wave experiment from the standpoint of corpuscular concepts is given. (Let us recall that we are dealing not only with light but also with any beam of particles, such as electrons.) The result obtained signifies the impossibility of a classical description of the motion of particles in trajectories, and the nonvisualization of a quantum description.

Nonetheless, let us attempt to determine which path the particle followed by setting detectors in its possible paths. Naturally, the particle will be recorded at one site rather than at all possible sites at once. However, as soon as the measurement singles out a specific trajectory of the particle, the interference picture disappears. The probability distribution changes. Both (all) possible trajectories are needed for interference to arise. Thus, the recording of the article's trajectory changes the conditions in such a way that the two paths are alternative, and as a result the summation of intensities, which would have been obtained in the case of a "classical" particle moving in definite trajectories, is obtained.

An accurate description of the experimental conditions under which a given phenomenon is observed is very important for quantum phenomena. In particular, the conditions also include the measuring instruments. In classical physics it is assumed that, in principle, the role of a measuring instrument can be reduced solely to recording the motion and that the state of the system does not change during measurement. In quantum physics this assumption is invalid: in addition to other factors, the measuring instrument itself participates in the formation of the phenomenon studied in the experiment, and this role must be taken into account. The role of measuring instruments in quantum phenomena was comprehensively analyzed by Bohr and Heisenberg and is closely connected with the uncertainty principle, which will be examined below.

Paying heed to the role of measurements does not mean that in quantum mechanics physical phenomena such as the properties of particles per se are not studied without reference to the instruments. For example, the problems of atomic energy levels, of the scattering of microparticles on collision with each other, and of interference phenomena, all of which are solved by quantum mechanics, are problems of the properties and behavior of particles. The role of the instrument moves to the foreground when specific questions are raised, some of which, as has been found, are meaningless (such as the problem in an interference experiment concerning which trajectory an electron moves along since there is either no trajectory or no interference).

Let us return to the interference experiment. Thus far only a negative assertion has been made: a particle does not move along a specific path, and the probabilities are not summed. A constructive assumption for describing such a situation may be drawn once again from wave optics. In optics, every wave is characterized not only by intensity but also by phase (the intensity is proportional to the square of the amplitude). Both of these two real quantities—the amplitude A and the phase ϕ—are commonly combined into one complex number, which is called the complex amplitude: $\psi = A e^{i\phi}$. Then, the intensity is equal to $I = |\psi|^2 = \psi^* \psi = A^2$, where ψ^* is a function that is the complex conjugate of ψ. Since the intensity is measured directly, the phase is in no way manifested for a single wave. In the experiment involving the transmission and reflection of light, this is precisely the situation: there are two waves ψ_1 and ψ_2, but one of them exists only on the right and the other only on the left (see Figure 1); the intensities of these waves are $I_1 = A_1{}^2$ and $I_2 = A_2{}^2$, and the phases are not manifested (therefore we were able to deal only with the intensities). In the interference experiment the situation has changed: the wave ψ_2 has been directed by means of the mirror to the region where wave ψ_1 is located (see Figure 2). The wave field in the region of existence of the two waves is determined in optics by means of the principle of superposition: the waves are superimposed on one another with due consideration of their phases. The sum wave ψ has a complex amplitude equal to the sum of the complex amplitudes of the two waves:

$$(3) \qquad \psi = \psi_1 + \psi_2 = A_1 e^{i\phi_1} + A_2 e^{i\phi_2}$$

The intensity of the sum wave depends on the phase difference $\phi_1 - \phi_2$ (which is proportional to the difference in the path length of the beams of light along the two trajectories):

$$(4) \qquad \begin{aligned} |\psi|^2 &= |A_1 e^{i\phi_1} + A_2 e^{i\phi_2}|^2 \\ &= A_1^2 + A_2^2 + 2A_1 A_2 \cos(\phi_1 - \phi_2) \end{aligned}$$

In particular, when $A_1 = A_2$ and $\cos(\phi_1 - \phi_2) = -1$, then $|\psi|^2 = 0$.

In this example, the simplest case of the addition of amplitudes was considered. In the more general case, the amplitudes may change in magnitude and phase because of a change in conditions (for example, the properties of the mirror), so that the sum wave will have the form

$$\psi = c_1 \psi_1 + c_2 \psi_2$$

where c_1 and c_2 are complex numbers:

$$c_1 = |c_1| e^{i\alpha_1} \qquad c_2 = |c_2| e^{i\alpha_2}$$

Here, the fundamental essence of the phenomenon does not change, nor does the character of the phenomenon depend on the total intensity. If ψ is increased by a factor of C, then the intensity will increase by a factor of $|C|^2$, that is, $|C|^2$ will be a common factor in the formula for the distribution of intensities. The number C may be considered complex as well as real, and the physical results do not contain the phase of the number C —it is arbitrary.

Transference of the principle of superposition to quantum mechanics is necessary in order to interpret wave phenomena from the corpuscular point of view. Since quantum mechanics deals with probabilities rather than intensities, a probability amplitude $\psi = Ae^{i\phi}$ must be introduced with the assumption (by analogy with optical waves) that the probability is $w = |C\psi|^2 = |C|^2 \psi^* \psi$. Here C is a number, called the normalization factor, which should be selected such that the total probability for the detection of a particle at all possible points is equal to 1, that is, $\Sigma_i w_i = 1$. The factor C is defined only by its modulus; its phase is arbitrary. The normalization factor is important only for determining the absolute probability; relative probabilities are determined by the probability amplitudes in an arbitrary normalization. In quantum mechanics the probability amplitude is also called the wave function.

Probability amplitudes (like optical amplitudes) satisfy the principle of superposition: if ψ_1 and ψ_2 are the probability amplitudes of a particle's passage along the first and second paths, respectively, then the probability amplitude for the case in which both paths are realized should be $\psi = \psi_1 + \psi_2$. Hence the phrase "the particle traveled along both paths" acquires wave meaning, and the probability $w = |\psi_1 + \psi_2|^2$ displays interference properties.

The difference in the meaning contained in the principle of superposition in optics (and other wave processes) and in quantum mechanics should be emphasized. The addition (superposition) of ordinary waves is not at variance with visual representations, since each of the waves represents a possible type of oscillation, and the superposition corresponds to the addition of these oscillations at each point. At the same time, quantum-mechanical probability amplitudes describe alternative motions (which are mutually exclusive from the classical standpoint; for example, the waves ψ_1 and ψ_2 correspond to particles entering the detector by two different paths). From the classical point of view, the superposition of these motions is totally incomprehensible. The difficulty of visualizing the quantum-mechanical principle of superposition is manifested herein. The probabilistic interpretation makes it possible to avoid the formal logical contradiction of the quantum-mechanical principle of superposition

(the possibility that a particle may travel simultaneously along two paths). Arranging an experiment to determine the path of a particle (*see above*) leads to a situation in which the particle will travel the first path with a probability $|\psi_1|^2$ and the second path with a probability $|\psi_2|^2$. The resulting distribution of the particles on the screen will be determined by the probability $|\psi_1|^2 + |\psi_2|^2$, that is, the interference will disappear.

Thus, examination of the interference experiment leads to the following conclusion. The probability amplitude, or wave function, of a physical system is the quantity that describes its state in quantum mechanics. The main feature of this quantum-mechanical description is the assumption that the principle of the superposition of states is valid.

The principle of superposition is a fundamental principle of quantum mechanics. In its general form it asserts that if under given conditions different quantum states of a particle (or system of particles) to which the wave functions $\psi_1, \psi_2, \ldots, \psi_i, \ldots$ correspond are possible, then there also exists a state described by the wave function

$$\psi = \sum_i c_i \psi_i$$

where c_i are arbitrary complex numbers. If the ψ_i describe the different possible states, then $|c_i|^2$ defines the probability that the system is in a state that has the wave function ψ_i, and

$$\sum_i |c_i|^2 = 1$$

De Broglie waves and the uncertainty relation. One of the principal tasks of quantum mechanics is to find the wave function that corresponds to a given state of the system being studied. Let us examine the solution to this problem by using the very simple but important case of a free-moving particle. According to de Broglie, a wave having the wavelength $\lambda = h/p$ is associated with a free particle having momentum p. This means that the wave function of a free particle, $\psi(x)$—the de Broglie wave—should be a function of the coordinate x such that when x changes by λ, the wave function ψ reverts to its previous value. The function $e^{i2\pi x/\lambda}$ has this property. If we introduce the quantity $k = 2\pi/\lambda$, called the wave number, then the de Broglie relation assumes the form $p = (h/2\pi)k = \hbar k$. Thus, if a particle has a definite momentum p, its state is described by the wave function

$$(5) \qquad \psi = Ce^{ikx} = Ce^{ipx/\hbar}$$

where C is a constant complex number. This wave function has a remarkable property: the square of its modulus $|\psi|^2$ does not depend on x, that is, the probability of finding the particle described by such a wave function is the same for any point in space. In other words, a particle with a precisely defined momentum is totally nonlocalized. Of course, this is an idealization—totally nonlocalized particles do not exist. But a wave with a precisely defined wavelength, and consequently with a precisely defined momentum of the particle, is an idealization to the same extent. Therefore, it is more accurate to state this in a different manner: the better defined a particle's momentum, the less defined its position (coordinates). Herein lies the uncertainty principle that is specific to quantum mechanics. In order to obtain a quantitative expression of this principle—the uncertainty relation— let us examine a state that represents the superposition of some or, more accurately, of an infinitely large number of de Broglie waves having nearly the same wave number, that is, lying in a small interval Δk. The wave function $\psi(x)$ (called a wave packet), which is obtained as a result of superposition, has the following character: near some fixed value x_0 all amplitudes are summed, but at a distance from x_0 ($|x - x_0| \gg \lambda$) they will cancel each other out because of the large diversity in phases. It turns out that such a wave function is actually concentrated in a region Δx wide, which is inversely proportional to the interval Δk, that is, $\Delta x \approx 1/\Delta k$, or $\Delta x \Delta p \approx \hbar$ (where $\Delta p = \hbar \Delta k$ is the uncertainty in the particle's momentum). This relation is the Heisenberg uncertainty relation.

Any function $\psi(x)$ can be represented mathematically as the superposition of simple periodic waves—this is the well-known Fourier transformation on the basis of whose properties the uncertainty relation between Δx and Δk can be found in a rigorous mathematical manner. The precise relation has the form of the inequality $\Delta x \Delta k \geq 1/2$, or

$$(6) \qquad \Delta p \Delta x \geq \hbar/2$$

where the uncertainties Δp and Δx are understood to be the dispersions, that is, the mean square deviations of the momentum and coordinate from their average values. The physical interpretation of relation (6) is that (in contrast to classical mechanics) there exists no state in which the coordinate and momentum of the particle simultaneously have precise values. The extent of the uncertainties of these quantities is given by Planck's constant h, and herein lies the important meaning of this universal constant. If uncertainties connected by the Heisenberg relation can be considered small in a given problem and can be neglected, the motion of the particle will be described by the laws of classical mechanics (as motion along a definite trajectory).

The uncertainty principle is a fundamental principle of quantum mechanics, and it defines the physical content and structure of the mathematical apparatus of quantum mechanics. Moreover, it plays a major heuristic role, since many results of quantum mechanics can be derived and understood on the basis of a combination of the laws of classical mechanics and the uncertainty relation. The problem of the stability of the atom, which was discussed above, is an important example. Let us examine this problem for the hydrogen atom. Let the electron move with a velocity v in a circular orbit of radius r around the nucleus (a proton). According to Coulomb's law, the forces attracting the electron to the nucleus is equal to e^2/r^2, where e is the absolute value of the electron's charge, and the centripetal acceleration is equal to v^2/r. According to Newton's second law, $mv^2/r = e^2/r^2$, where m is the mass of the electron. From here it follows that the radius of the orbit $r = e^2/mv^2$ may be made arbitrarily small if the velocity v is made sufficiently large. But in quantum mechanics the uncertainty relation must be fulfilled. If we assume the uncertainty of the electron's position is within the limits of the radius of its orbit r and the uncertainty of its velocity within the limits of v, that is, the momentum within the limits $\Delta p = mv$, then the uncertainty relation will assume the form $mvr \geq \hbar$. By using the relationship between v and r, as defined by Newton's law, we obtain $v \leq e^2/\hbar$ and $r \geq \hbar^2/me^2$. Consequently, it is impossible for the electron to move in an orbit with a radius less than $r_0 = \hbar^2/me^2 \approx 0.5 \times 10^{-8}$ cm, and the electron cannot fall into the nucleus—the atom is stable. The quantity r_0 is the radius of the hydrogen atom (the "Bohr radius"). The greatest possible binding energy of the atom $\mathcal{E}_0$ (equal to the total energy of the electron in the atom, that is, the sum of the kinetic energy $mv^2/2$ and the potential energy $-e^2/r_0$, which gives $\mathcal{E}_0$, $= -e^2/2r_0 \approx -13.6$ electron volts), which determines its minimum energy—the energy of the ground state—corresponds to this radius.

Thus, quantum-mechanical concepts first provided the possibility of theoretically estimating the dimensions of the atom (by expressing its radius in terms of the universal constant $\hbar$, m, and e). The "smallness" of atomic dimensions proves to be related to the "smallness" of the constant $\hbar$.

It is noteworthy that modern concepts of atoms that have well-defined stable states prove to be closer to the concepts of ancient atomists than the planetary model of the atom, which is based on the laws of classical mechanics and allows the electron to be located at any distance from the nucleus.

A rigorous solution to the problem of the electron's motion in the hydrogen atom is obtained from the quantum-mechanical equation of motion—the Schrödinger equation (*see below*); solution of the Schrödinger equation gives the wave function ψ, which describes the state of an electron located in the region of attraction of the nucleus. But even without knowing the explicit form of ψ we may assert that this wave function represents a superposition of de Broglie waves that corresponds to the elec-

tron's localization in a region having the dimension $\geq r_0$ and to the momentum range $\Delta p \sim \hbar/r_0$.

The uncertainty relation also makes it possible to understand the stability of molecules and to estimate their dimensions and minimal energy. In addition, it explains the existence of a substance (helium) which, at normal pressure, is not converted into the solid state at any temperature and provides qualitative models of the structure and size of the nucleus.

The existence of energy levels is a characteristic quantum phenomenon inherent in all physical systems and does not stem directly from the uncertainty relation. It will be shown below that the discreteness of the energy levels of a bound system can be explained on the basis of the Schrödinger equation; let us observe only that the possible discrete energy values (energy levels) $\mathcal{E}_n > \mathcal{E}_0$ correspond to excited states of a quantum-mechanical system.

Stationary Schrödinger equation. De Broglie waves describe the state of a particle only in the case of free motion. If a field of forces with a potential energy v (also called the potential) that depends on the coordinates of a particle acts on the particle, then the wave function of the particle ψ is given by a differential equation obtained by the following generalization of the de Broglie hypothesis. For the case in which the motion of a particle with a given energy $\mathcal{E}$ takes place in one dimension (along the x-axis), an equation satisfied by the de Broglie wave (5) may be written in the form

$$(*) \qquad \frac{d^2\psi}{dx^2} + \frac{p^2}{\hbar^2}\psi = 0$$

where $p = \sqrt{2m\mathcal{E}}$ is the momentum of a free-moving particle of mass m. If a particle with an energy $\mathcal{E}$ moves in a potential field $V(x)$ that is independent of time, the square of its momentum (which is defined by the law of conservation of energy) is equal to $p^2 = 2m[\mathcal{E} - V(x)]$. Therefore, the equation

$$(7) \qquad \frac{d^2\psi}{dx^2} + \frac{2m[\mathcal{E} - V(x)]}{\hbar^2}\psi = 0$$

is the simplest generalization of equation (*). This is called the stationary (time-independent) Schrödinger equation and is one of the basic equations of quantum mechanics. The solution of this equation depends on the type of forces, that is, on the form of the potential $V(x)$. Let us examine several typical cases.

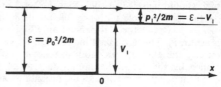

Figure 3

(1) $V = $ constant, $\mathcal{E} > V$. The solution is the de Broglie wave $\psi = Ce^{ikx}$, where $\hbar^2 k^2/2m = p^2/2m = \mathcal{E} - V$ is the kinetic energy of the particle.

(2) A potential wall:

$$V = 0 \qquad \text{when} \qquad x < 0$$
$$V = V_1 > 0 \qquad \text{when} \qquad x > 0$$

If the total energy of the particle is greater than the height of the wall, that is, $\mathcal{E} > V_1$, and if the particle moves from left to right (Figure 3), then the solution to equation (7) in the region $x < 0$ has the form of two de Broglie waves—the incident wave and the reflected wave:

$$\psi = C_0 e^{ik_0 x} + C_0' e^{-ik_0 x}$$

where

$$\hbar^2 k_0^2/2m = p_0^2/2m = \mathcal{E}$$

(a wave with a wave number $k = -k_0$ corresponds to motion from right to left with the same momentum p_0); when $x > 0$, the solution has the form of a traveling de Broglie wave:

$$\psi = C_1 e^{ik_1 x}$$

where

$$\hbar^2 k_1^2/2m = p_1^2/2m = \mathcal{E} - V_1$$

The ratios $|C_1/C_0|^2$ and $|C'_0/C_0|^2$ give the probabilities of the particle passing over the wall and being reflected from it. The existence of the reflection is a uniquely quantum-mechanical (wave) phenomenon (analogous to the partial reflection of a light wave from the interface between two transparent media): a "classical" particle passes above the barrier, and only its momentum is reduced to the value of $p_1 = \sqrt{2m(\mathcal{E} - V_1)}$.

If the energy of the particle is less than the height of the wall, $\mathcal{E} < V$ (Figure 4,a), then the kinetic energy of the particle $\mathcal{E} - V$ in the domain $x > 0$ is negative. In classical mechanics this is impossible, and the particle does not reach this region of space —it is reflected from the potential wall. Wave motion is of a different character. A negative value of k^2 ($p^2/2m = \hbar^2k^2/2m < 0$) means that k is a purely imaginary quantity, $k = i\kappa$, where κ is real. Therefore, the wave e^{ikx} is converted into $e^{-\kappa k}$, that is, the oscillatory mode is replaced by a damped mode ($\kappa > 0$); otherwise as x increases a physically meaningless, unlimited increase of the wave would result. This phenomenon is well known in the theory of oscillations. The qualitative behavior of the wave function $\psi(x)$, or more accurately of its real part, is represented beneath the energy diagram in Figure 4,a (and Figure 4,b).

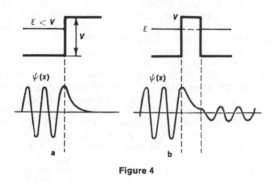

Figure 4

(3) Two regions containing no forces are separated by a rectangular potential barrier V, and the particle moves toward the barrier from the left with an energy $\mathcal{E} < V$ (Figure 4,b). According to classical mechanics, the particle will be reflected from the barrier; according to quantum mechanics, the wave function is not equal to zero even within the barrier and to the right once again will have the form of a de Broglie wave with the same momentum (that is, with the same frequency but, of course, with a smaller amplitude). Consequently, the particle can pass through the barrier. The smaller the width and height of the barrier (the smaller the difference $V - \mathcal{E}$), the greater the coefficient (or probability) of transmission. This typically quantum-mechanical effect, called the tunnel effect, is of great importance in the practical applications of quantum mechanics. It explains, for example, the phenomenon of alpha decay—the emission of α-particles (helium nuclei) from radioactive nuclei. In thermonuclear reactions, which occur at temperatures of tens and hundreds of millions of degrees, most of the reacting nuclei overcome electrostatic (Coulomb) repulsion and approach each other to distances of the order of the range of nuclear forces as a result of tunneling (subbarrier) transitions. The possibility of tunneling transitions also explains spontaneous electron emission—the phenomenon of the emission of electrons from a metal in an electric field—contact phenomena in metals and semiconductors, and many other phenomena.

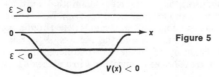

Figure 5

Energy levels. Let us examine the behavior of a particle in the field of an arbitrary potential well (Figure 5). Let the potential be nonzero in some finite region with $V < 0$ (attractive force). Here, both the classical and quantum motions are highly dependent on whether the total energy $\mathcal{E}$ of the particle is positive or negative. When $\mathcal{E} > 0$, a "classical" particle passes over and moves away from the well. The quantum-mechanical motion differs from the classical motion in that partial reflection of the wave from the well occurs in the former; also, the possible energy levels are in no way limited—the particle's energy has a continuous spectrum. When $\mathcal{E} < 0$, the particle proves to be "locked" within the well. In classical mechanics this limitation in the extent of the motion is absolute and possible for any values $\mathcal{E} < 0$. In quantum mechanics the situation changes significantly. The wave function must be attenuated in both directions from the well, that is, it assumes the form $e^{-\kappa|x|}$. However, a solution that satisfies this condition does not exist at all values of $\mathcal{E}$ but only at certain discrete values. The number of such discrete values of $\mathcal{E}_n$ may be finite or infinite but is always denumerable, that is, can be counted, and always has a least value $\mathcal{E}_0$ (which lies above the bottom of the potential well); the number n of a solution is called the quantum number. In this case it is said that the energy of the system has a discrete spectrum. The discreteness of the permissible energy values of a system (or of the corresponding frequencies $\omega = \mathcal{E}_n/\hbar$, where $\omega = 2\pi\nu$ is the angular frequency) is a typical wave phenomenon. Analogues to it can be observed in classical physics, where wave motion takes place in a bounded region. Thus, the oscillation frequencies of a string or the frequencies of electromagnetic waves in a cavity resonator are discrete and are determined by the dimensions and properties of the boundaries of the region in which the oscillations take place. Indeed, the Schrödinger equation is mathematically similar to the corresponding equations for a vibrating string or resonator.

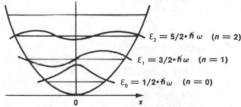

Figure 6

Let us illustrate a discrete energy spectrum by using a quantum oscillator as an example. The distance of the particle from the state of equilibrium is plotted along the x-axis in Figure 6. The curve (a parabola) represents the potential energy of the particle. In this case, the particle is "locked" within the well at all energies, and therefore the energy spectrum is discrete. The horizontal straight lines represent the particle's energy levels. The energy of the lowest level is $\mathcal{E}_0 = \hbar\omega/2$; this is the lowest energy level compatible with the uncertainty relation: if the particle were located at the bottom of the well ($\mathcal{E} = 0$), this would signify precise equilibrium, for which both $x = 0$ and $p = 0$, which is impossible according to the uncertainty principle. Subsequent, higher energy levels of the oscillator lie at equal distances at intervals of $\hbar\omega$; the formula for the energy of the nth level is:

$$(8) \qquad \mathcal{E}_n = \hbar\omega\left(n + \frac{1}{2}\right)$$

The conventional representation of the wave function of a given state is presented in Figure 6 about each horizontal line. It is characteristic that the number of nodes of the wave function (that is, the number of passages through 0) is equal to the quantum number n of the energy level. On the other side of the well (beyond the point of intersection of the level and the potential curve), the wave function attenuates rapidly in accordance with the foregoing reasons.

In the general case, every quantum-mechanical system is characterized by its own energy spectrum. Depending on the type of potential (or more accurately, on the nature of the interaction in the system), the energy spectrum may be discrete (as in an oscillator), continuous (as in a free particle, its kinetic energy may have any positive value), or partially discrete and partially continuous (for example, the levels of an atom are discrete at excitation energies less than the ionization energy but are continuous at higher energies).

Especially important is the case occurring in atoms, molecules, nuclei, and other systems when the lowest energy level corresponding to the ground state of the system lies in the region of the discrete spectrum, and consequently the ground state is separated from the first excited state by an energy gap. As a result, the internal structure of the system is not manifested until an energy exchange during interactions with other systems exceeds a certain value—the width of the energy gap. Therefore, when there is limited energy exchange, a complex system (such as a nucleus or atom) behaves like a structureless particle (a material particle). This is of fundamental importance for understanding, for example, thermal motion. Thus, at energies of thermal motion lower than the excitation energy of the atomic levels, the electrons of atoms cannot participate in the exchange of energy and do not contribute to heat capacity.

Time-dependent Schrödinger equation. Thus far we have examined only the possible quantum states of a system and have not discussed the evolution of the system with time (its dynamics), which is determined by the dependence of the wave function on time. A full solution of the problems of quantum mechanics should give the wave function ψ as a function of the coordinates and of the time t. For one-dimensional motion it is defined by

$$(9) \qquad i\hbar \frac{\partial \psi}{\partial t} = -\frac{\hbar^2}{2m}\frac{\partial^2 \psi}{\partial x^2} + V\psi$$

which is the equation of motion in quantum mechanics. This equation is called the time-dependent Schrödinger equation. It also is valid for the case when the potential energy is time-dependent: $V = V(x, t)$.

The functions

$$(10) \qquad \psi(x, t) = \psi(x)e^{-i\mathcal{E}t/h} = \psi(x)e^{-i\omega t}$$

are partial solutions to equation (9). Here $\mathcal{E}$ is the particle's energy and $\psi(x)$ satisfies the stationary Schrödinger equation (7); for free motion, $\psi(x)$ is a de Broglie wave e^{ikx}.

The wave functions (10) have an important property, namely, that the corresponding probability distributions are time-independent, since $|\psi(x, t)|^2 = |\psi(x)|^2$. Therefore, the states described by such wave functions are called stationary; they play a special role in applications of quantum mechanics.

The general solution to the time-dependent Schrödinger equation is a superposition of stationary states. In this general (nonstationary) case, when the probabilities change significantly with time, the energy $\mathcal{E}$ does not have a specific value. Thus, if

$$\psi(x, t) = C_1 e^{i(k_1 x - \omega_1 t)} + C_2 e^{i(k_2 x - \omega_2 t)}$$

then $\mathcal{E} = \hbar\omega_1$ with a probability $|C_1|^2$ and $\mathcal{E} = \hbar\omega_2$ with a probability $|C_2|^2$. For energy and time there exists the uncertainty relation

$$(11) \qquad \Delta\mathcal{E}\,\Delta t \sim \hbar$$

where $\Delta\mathcal{E}$ is the energy dispersion and Δt, the time interval over which the energy can be measured.

Three-dimensional motion. Thus far we have examined, for the sake of simplicity, one-dimensional motion. Generalization to the motion of a particle in three dimensions does not contain fundamentally new elements. In this case, the wave function depends on the three coordinates x, y, and z (and time): $\psi = \psi(x, y, z, t)$ and the de Broglie wave has the form

$$(12) \qquad \psi = \exp\left[\frac{i}{\hbar}(p_x x + p_y y + p_z z - \mathcal{E}t)\right]$$

where p_x, p_y, and p_z are the three projections of the momentum on the coordinate axes and $\mathcal{E} = (p_x^2 + p_y^2 + p_z^2)/2m$. Correspondingly, there are three uncertainty relations:

$$(13) \quad \Delta p_x\,\Delta x \geq \frac{\hbar}{2} \qquad \Delta p_y\,\Delta y \geq \frac{\hbar}{2} \qquad \Delta p_z\,\Delta z \geq \frac{\hbar}{2}$$

The time-dependent Schrödinger equation has the form

$$(14) \qquad i\hbar \frac{\partial \psi}{\partial t} = -\frac{\hbar^2}{2m}\left(\frac{\partial^2 \psi}{\partial x^2} + \frac{\partial^2 \psi}{\partial y^2} + \frac{\partial^2 \psi}{\partial z^2}\right) + V\psi$$

This equation commonly is written in the symbolic form

$$(14a) \qquad i\hbar \frac{\partial \psi}{\partial t} = \hat{H}\psi'$$

where

$$\hat{H} = -\frac{\hbar}{2m}\left(\frac{\partial^2}{\partial x^2} + \frac{\partial^2}{\partial y^2} + \frac{\partial^2}{\partial z^2}\right) + V$$

is a differential operator called the Hamiltonian operator, or the Hamiltonian.

The stationary solution to equation (14) is

$$(15) \qquad \psi = \psi_0 e^{-i\mathcal{E}t/h}$$

where ψ_0 is the solution to the Schrödinger equation for stationary states:

$$(16) \quad -\frac{\hbar^2}{2m}\left(\frac{\partial^2 \psi_0}{\partial x^2} + \frac{\partial^2 \psi_0}{\partial y^2} + \frac{\partial^2 \psi_0}{\partial z^2}\right) + V\psi_0 = \mathcal{E}\psi_0$$

or

$$(16a) \qquad \hat{H}\psi_0 = \mathcal{E}\psi_0$$

In the case of three-dimensional motion, the energy spectrum may also be continuous and discrete. The case in which several different states have identical energy is also possible; such states are said to be degenerate. In the case of a continuous spectrum, a particle moves to an infinitely great distance from the center of forces. But in contrast to one-dimensional motion (for which there are only two possibilities, transmission or reflection), during three-dimensional motion a particle can move away from the center at an arbitrary angle to the direction of the original motion, that is, it may be scattered. The wave function of the particle now is a superposition not of two but of an infinite number of de Broglie waves propagated in all possible directions. It is convenient to describe the scattered particles in spherical coordinates, that is, to define their position by their distance r from the center (by the radius) and by two angles—the latitude θ and the azimuth ϕ. At large distances r from the center of forces, the corresponding wave function has the form

$$(17) \qquad \psi \sim e^{ikz} + \frac{f(\theta, \phi)}{r}e^{ikr}$$

The first term, which is proportional to a de Broglie wave propagating along the z–axis describes the incident particles, while the second, which is proportional to a "radial de Broglie wave," describes the scattered particles. The function $f(\theta, \phi)$ is called the scattering amplitude; it defines the "differential scattering cross section" $d\sigma$, which characterizes the probability of scattering at given angles:

$$(18) \qquad d\sigma = |f(\theta, \phi)|^2 d\Omega$$

where $d\Omega$ is the solid angle element into which the scattering takes place.

A discrete energy spectrum arises, as in the case of one-dimensional motion, when a particle is located within a potential well. The energy levels are specified, in contrast to one-dimensional motion, by three, not one, quantum numbers. The problem of motion in a field of central attractive forces is of the greatest importance. In this case, it is also convenient to use spherical coordinates.

Angular momentum. The angular part of motion (rotation) is given in quantum mechanics as in classical mechanics by assigning an angular momentum, which is conserved during motion in a field of central forces. In contrast to classical mechanics, the angular momentum in quantum mechanics has a discrete spectrum, that is, can assume only certain values. This can be demonstrated by using as an example azimuthal motion—rotation around a fixed axis (we shall use the z-axis). In this case, the wave function has the form of an "angular de Broglie wave" $e^{im\phi}$, where ϕ is the azimuth and the number m is related to the angular momentum M_z in the same manner as the wave number k is related to the linear momentum p in a plane de Broglie wave, that is, $m = M_z/\hbar$. Since the angles ϕ and $\phi + 2\pi$ describe the same position, when ϕ changes by 2π the wave function should return to its former value. Thus it follows that m can assume only integral values: $m = 0, \pm 1, \pm 2, \ldots$, that is, the angular momentum must equal

$$(19) \qquad M_z = m\hbar = 0, \pm\hbar, \pm 2\hbar, \ldots$$

Rotation about the z-axis is only a part of the angular motion (it is the projection of the motion on the xy plane), and M_z is not the total angular momentum but only its component along the z-axis. In order to know the total angular momentum, it is necessary to determine its other two components. However, in quantum mechanics all three components of the angular momentum cannot be given simultaneously with precision. Indeed, a component of angular momentum contains the product of a component of linear momentum and the corresponding radius (the coordinate perpendicular to the linear momentum), and all the components of linear momentum and all the radii cannot, according to the uncertainty relations (13), simultaneously have precise values. It turns out that in addition to the projection M_z of the angular momentum on the z-axis (defined by m), the total angular momentum M, defined by the integer l, can be accurately given simultaneously:

$$(20) \qquad M^2 = \hbar^2 l(l + 1), \qquad l = 0, 1, 2, \ldots$$

Thus, angular motion gives two quantum numbers—l and m. The number l is called the orbital quantum number, and the value of the particle's energy can depend on it (as it depends in classical mechanics on the size of the orbit). The number m is called the magnetic quantum number and, for a given l, can assume the values $m = 0, \pm 1, \pm 2, \ldots, \pm l$, for a total of $2l + 1$ values. The energy does not depend on m, since the value of m itself depends on the selection of the z-axis, and the field has spherical symmetry. Therefore, a level with the quantum number l has a $(2l + 1)$-fold degeneracy. The energy of the level begins to depend on m only when the spherical symmetry is broken, for example when the system is placed in a magnetic field (the Zeeman effect).

For a given momentum, the radial motion is similar to one-dimensional motion with the difference that the rotation induces centrifugal forces. They are taken into account by introducing (in addition to the ordinary potential) a centrifugal potential, which has the form $M^2/2mr^2$ as in classical mechanics (here m is the mass of the particle). The square of the angular momentum M^2 must be replaced by the quantity $\hbar^2 l(l + 1)$. The solution to the Schrödinger equation for the radial part of an atom's wave function gives its energy levels and introduces a third quantum number—the radial quantum number n_r or the principal quantum number n, which are related by the equation $n = n_r + l + 1$, where $n_r = 0, 1, 2, \ldots$ and $n = 1, 2, 3, \ldots$. In particular, for the motion of an electron in the Coulomb field of a nucleus with charge Ze (a hydrogen-like atom), the energy levels are defined by the formula

$$(21) \qquad \mathcal{E}_n = -\frac{Z^2 e^4 m}{2\hbar^2} \cdot \frac{1}{n}$$

that is, the energy depends only on the principal quantum number n. For manyelectron atoms, in which every electron moves not only in the field of the nucleus but also in the field of the other electrons, the energy levels also depend on l.

The radial and angular distributions of the electron density (that is, the probability density or charge density) around the nucleus are given in Figure 3 in the article ATOM (see Volume 3, Figure 3, of the Russian-language edition, p. 392). It can be seen that assigning the angular momentum (that is, the numbers l and m) fully determines the angular distribution. In particular, when $l = 0$ ($M^2 = 0$), the distribution of electron density is spherically symmetrical. Thus, the quantum motion for small l is entirely different from the classical motion. Thus, a spherically symmetrical state with a mean radius $r \neq 0$ corresponds to some extent to classical motion in a circular orbit (or in a set of circular orbits inclined at different angles), that is, to motion with nonzero angular momentum (in classical mechanics, zero angular momentum corresponds to a zero radius, and here the radius $r \neq 0$). This difference between quantum-mechanical and

classical motion is a consequence of the uncertainty relation and can be interpreted on this basis. For large quantum numbers (for example, when $l \gg 1$, $n_r \gg 1$), the de Broglie wavelength becomes much less than the distances L that are characteristic of a given system's motion:

$$(22) \qquad \lambda = \frac{2\pi\hbar}{p} \ll L$$

In this case the quantum-mechanical laws of motion approximate the classical laws of motion for certain trajectories, just as under similar conditions the laws of wave optics become the laws of geometric optics (which describes the propagation of light by means of rays). Equation (22), the condition for a short de Broglie wavelength, signifies that $pL \gg \hbar$, where pL is equal in order of magnitude to the classical action for the system. Under these conditions, the quantum of action $\hbar$ may be considered to be a very small quantity, that is, the conversion of quantum-mechanical laws into classical laws is formally accomplished as $\hbar \longrightarrow 0$. At this limit, all specific quantum-mechanical phenomena disappear, for example the probability of the tunnel effect is zero.

Spin. In quantum mechanics a particle (both a complex particle such as a nucleus and an elementary particle such as an electron) can have an intrinsic angular momentum, which is called the particle's spin. This means that a quantum number (s) analogous to the orbital quantum number l can be assigned to the particle. The square of the intrinsic angular momentum has the magnitude $\hbar^2 s(s + 1)$, and the component of the angular momentum in a given direction may assume $2s + 1$ values from $-\hbar s$ to $+\hbar s$ at an interval of $\hbar$. Thus, the state of the particle is $(2s + 1)$-fold degenerate. Therefore, the de Broglie wave of a particle having spin is analogous to a polarized wave: for a given frequency and wavelength it has $2s + 1$ polarizations. The number of such polarizations can be any integer, that is, the spin quantum number s may be either an integer (0, 1, 2, ...) or a half-integer (1/2, 3/2, 5/2, ...). The spin of the electron, the proton, and the neutron is equal to 1/2 (in units of $\hbar$). The spin of nuclei consisting of an even number of nucleons (protons and neutrons) is an integer or zero, while the spin of nuclei consisting of an odd number of nucleons is a half-integer. It should be noted that for the photon the relation between the number of polarizations and the spin (which is equal to 1) is different: the photon has no rest mass, and (as relativistic quantum mechanics shows) for such particles the number of polarizations is equal to 2 (and not to $2s + 1 = 3$).

Many-particle systems; identical particles. The quantum-mechanical equation of motion for a system of N particles is obtained by appropriate generalization of the Schrödinger equation for a single particle. It contains a potential energy that depends on the coordinates of all N particles and includes both the effect of an external field on them and the interaction between the particles themselves. The wave function is also a function of the coordinates of all particles. It may be considered as a wave in $3N$-dimensional space; consequently, the visual analogy with wave propagation in ordinary space is lost. But this now is unimportant inasmuch as the meaning of the wave function as a probability amplitude is known.

If quantum-mechanical systems consist of identical particles, then a unique phenomenon that has no analogy in classical mechanics is observed for them. In classical mechanics the case of identical particles also has a certain peculiarity. For example, let two identical "classical" particles collide (the first moving from the left, the second from the right) and let them fly apart after the collision in different directions (for example, the first can fly upward, the second downward). It is of no consequence to the result of the collision which particle went upward, for example, since the particles are identical; in practice it is necessary to consider both possibilities (Figure 7,a and 7,b). However, in classical mechanics these two processes can be distinguished in principle, since the trajectories of the particles can be traced during the collision. In quantum mechanics there are no trajectories in the strict sense of the word, and both particles pass through the region of collision with some uncertainty, with "diffuse trajectories" (Figure 7,c). In the process of collision the diffuse regions overlap and it is impossible, even in principle, to distinguish these two cases of scattering. Consequently, identical particles become totally indistinguishable. It is meaningless to speak of two different cases of scattering, as there is just one—one particle went upward, the other downward; the particles have no individuality.

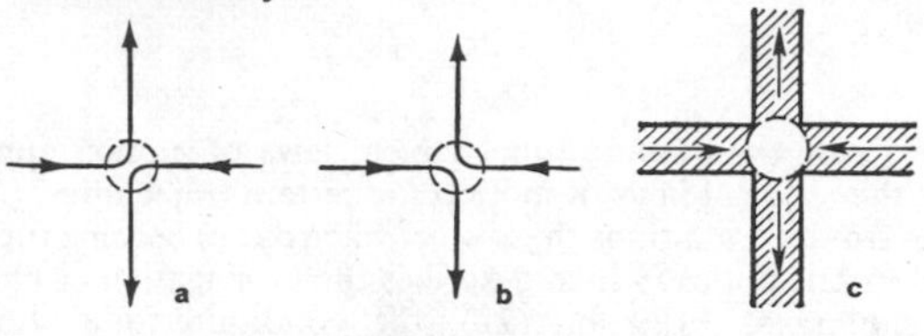

Figure 7

This quantum-mechanical principle of the indistinguishability of identical particles may be formulated mathematically in the language of wave functions. The probability of detection of two particles at given points in space is determined by the square of the modulus of the wave function, which depends on the coordinates of both particles, $|\psi(1, 2)|^2$, where 1 and 2 stand for the set of coordinates (including spin) of the first and second particles, respectively. The identity of the particles requires that when particles 1 and 2 are interchanged, the probabilities remain the same, that is,

(23) $$|\psi(1, 2)|^2 = |\psi(2, 1)|^2$$

Hence, it follows that there may be two cases:

(24a) $$\psi(1, 2) = \psi(2, 1)$$

(24b) $$\psi(1, 2) = -\psi(2, 1)$$

If, when the particles are interchanged the wave function does not change sign, then it is called a symmetrical function [case (24a)], and if it changes sign, it is antisymmetrical [case (24b)]. Since all interactions of identical particles are symmetrical with respect to the variables 1 and 2, the properties of the symmetry or antisymmetry of a wave function are conserved in time.

In a system consisting of an arbitrary number of identical particles, symmetry or antisymmetry with respect to the interchange of any pair of particles should exist. Therefore, the property of symmetry or antisymmetry is a characteristic feature of this type of particle. Correspondingly, all particles are divided into two classes: particles with symmetrical wave functions, called bosons, and particles with antisymmetric functions, called fermions. There is a relation between the value of the spin of particles and the symmetry of their wave functions: particles with integral spin are bosons, and particles with half-integral spin are fermions (for the relation between spin and statistics, *see below*). This rule originally was established empirically and later was proved theoretically by Pauli (it is one of the basic theorems of relativistic quantum mechanics). In particular, electrons, protons, and neutrons are fermions, while photons, pi-mesons, and K-mesons are bosons. Complex particles consisting of fermions are fermions if they consist of an odd number of particles and are bosons if they consist of an even number of particles; atomic nuclei, for example, have these properties.

The symmetry properties of the wave function essentially determine the statistical properties of a system. For example, let noninteracting identical particles exist under identical external conditions (for example, in an external field). The state of such a system can be given by assigning occupation numbers—the numbers of particles in each given (individual) state, that is, particles with the same set of quantum numbers. But if identical particles have the same quantum numbers, their wave function is symmetrical with respect to the interchange of particles. Hence, it follows that two identical fermions belonging to one system cannot be in the same state, since for fermions the wave function must be antisymmetrical. This property is called the Pauli exclusion principle. Thus, the occupation numbers for fermions can assume only the values 0 or 1. Since electrons are fermions, the Pauli principle significantly affects the behavior of electrons in atoms, metals, and elsewhere. For bosons (which have a symmetrical wave function) the occupation numbers can assume arbitrary integral values. Therefore, with consideration for the quantum-mechanical properties of identical particles,

there exist two types of particle statistics: Fermi-Dirac statistics for fermions and Bose-Einstein statistics for bosons. An electron gas in a metal is an example of a system consisting of fermions (a Fermi system), while a photon gas (that is, equilibrated electromagnetic radiation) and liquid ^{4}He are examples of Bose systems.

The Pauli principle is definitive for an understanding of the structure of Mendeleev's periodic table of the elements. In a complex atom there may exist at each energy level a number of electrons equal to the degree of degeneracy of this level (equal to the number of different states with an identical energy). The degree of degeneracy depends on the orbital quantum number and on the spin of the electron; it is equal to

$$(2l + 1)(2s + 1) = 2(2l + 1)$$

Thus arises the concept of the electron shells of the atom, which correspond to the periods in Mendeleev's table of the elements (*see* ATOM).

Exchange interaction; the molecule. A molecule is a system of nuclei and electrons between which electrical (Coulomb) forces (of attraction and repulsion) act. Since nuclei are much heavier than electrons, the electrons move much more rapidly and form a certain distribution of negative charge, in the field of which are located the nuclei. In classical mechanics and electrostatics it is proved that a system of this type does not have stable equilibrium. Therefore, even if the stability of atoms is assumed (an assumption that cannot, as indicated above, be explained on the basis of the laws of classical physics), it is impossible to explain the stability of molecules without specifically quantum-mechanical principles. The existence of molecules consisting of identical atoms, that is, with a covalent chemical bond (such as the simplest molecule—H_2), is especially incomprehensible from the standpoint of classical concepts. It has been shown that the property of the antisymmetry of the electron wave function so changes the character of the interaction of electrons located on different nuclei that the occurrence of such a bond becomes possible.

Let us examine as an example the hydrogen molecule H_2, which consists of two protons and two electrons. The wave function of this system is a product of two functions, one of which depends only on the coordinates and the other, only on the spin variables of the two electrons. If the total spin of the two electrons is equal to zero (the spins antiparallel), the spin function is antisymmetrical with respect to the interchange of the spin variables of the electrons. Consequently, in order for the total wave function to be antisymmetrical in accordance with the Pauli principle, the coordinate function must be symmetrical with respect to the interchange of the coordinates of both electrons. This means that the coordinate part of the wave function has the form

(25) $$\psi \sim [\psi_a(1)\psi_b(2) + \psi_b(1)\psi_a(2)]$$

where $\psi_a(i)$ and $\psi_b(i)$ are the wave functions of the ith electron ($i = 1, 2$) at the nuclei a and b, respectively.

The Coulomb interaction is proportional to the density of the electric charge $\rho = e|\psi|^2 = e\psi^*\psi$. If the symmetrical properties of the coordinate wave function (25) are taken into account, in addition to the density of the ordinary type

$$e|\psi_a(1)|^2|\psi_b(2)|^2 \qquad e|\psi_b(1)|^2|\psi_a(2)|^2$$

which correspond to the motion of single electrons about different nuclei, a density of the following type appears:

$$e\psi_a^*(1)\psi_b(1)\psi_b^*(2)\psi_a(2)$$
$$e\psi_b^*(1)\psi_a(1)\psi_a^*(2)\psi_b(2)$$

This is called the exchange density, since it appears to arise from an exchange of the electrons between the two atoms. It is this exchange density, which leads to an increase in the density of the negative charge between the two positively charged nuclei, that ensures the stability of the molecule in the case of a covalent chemical bond.

It is obvious that when the total spin of the two electrons is equal to 1, the coordinate part of the wave function is antisymmetrical, that is, a minus sign precedes the second term in (25), and the exchange density has a negative sign. This means that the exchange density will lower the density of the negative electric charge between the nuclei, that is, will lead to additional repulsion of the nuclei.

Thus, the symmetry of the wave function leads to "additional" exchange interaction. The dependence of the exchange interaction on the spins of the electrons is characteristic. The spins do not participate directly in the interaction; electrical forces that depend only on the distance between charges are the source of the interaction. But, depending on the orientation of the spins, a wave function that is antisymmetrical with respect to the complete interchange of the two electrons (together with their spins) may be symmetrical or antisymmetrical with respect to the exchange of the positions of the electrons (their coordinates) alone. The sign of the exchange density, and correspondingly the effective attraction or repulsion of the particles as a result of the exchange interaction, depends on the type of symmetry of the coordinate part of the wave function. Thus, although not participating directly in the dynamics of the interaction, the spins of the electrons actually determine the chemical bond by virtue of the specific quantum-mechanical properties of the identical particles.

Exchange interaction plays a significant role in many phenomena. For example, it explains ferromagnetism: as a result of exchange interaction the spin moments and consequently the magnetic moments of the atoms of a ferromagnetic are aligned parallel to each other. Numerous phenomena in condensed phases (such as liquids or solids) are closely related to the statistics of the particles forming them and to exchange interaction. The wave function antisymmetry for fermions leads to the fact that when the density is high, fermions effectively repel each other (even if no forces act between them). At the same time, attractive forces arise, as it were, between bosons that are described by symmetrical wave functions: the more bosons in some state, the greater the probability that other bosons in the system will pass into this state. (For example, such effects underlie the phenomena of superfluidity and superconductivity and the operating principle of quantum generators and quantum amplifiers.)

Mathematical scheme of quantum mechanics. Nonrelativistic quantum mechanics can be constructed on the basis of a few formal principles. The mathematical apparatus of quantum mechanics is logically faultless and elegant. Its precise rules establish the relation between the elements of the mathematical scheme and physical quantities.

The quantum state is the first basic concept of quantum mechanics. The selection of the mathematical apparatus of quantum mechanics is dictated by the physical principle of superposition of quantum states, which stems from the wave properties of particles. According to this principle, the superposition of any possible state of a system with arbitrary (complex) coefficients is also a possible state of the system.

The objects for which the concepts of addition and multiplication by a complex number are defined are called vectors. Thus, the principle of superposition requires that the state of a system be described by some vector—the state vector (with which the concept of the probability amplitude, or wave function, is closely connected), which is an element of the linear "state space." This makes it possible to use the mathematical apparatus developed for linear (vector) spaces. The state vector is designated as $|\psi\rangle$ after P. Dirac.

Apart from addition and multiplication by a complex number, the vector $|\psi\rangle$ may undergo two other operations. First, it can be projected onto another vector, that is, the scalar product of $|\psi\rangle$ and any other state vector $|\psi'\rangle$ may be formed; this is designated as $\langle\psi'|\psi\rangle$ and is a complex number, such that

$$(26) \qquad \langle\psi'|\psi\rangle = \langle\psi|\psi'\rangle^*$$

The scalar product of the vector $|\psi\rangle$ and itself, $\langle\psi\psi\rangle$, is a positive number; it defines the length (magnitude) of the vector. It is convenient to select the length of a state vector equal to 1; its common phase factor is arbitrary. Different states differ from each other in the direction of the state vector in the state space.

Second, we may examine the operation of the transition from the vector $|\psi\rangle$ to another vector $|\psi'\rangle$ (or may carry out the transformation $|\psi\rangle \rightarrow |\psi'\rangle$). This operation may be written symbolically as the result of the operation on the vector $|\psi\rangle$ of some linear operator $\hat{L}$:

$$(27) \qquad \hat{L}|\psi\rangle = |\psi'\rangle$$

Here, the vector $|\psi'\rangle$ may differ from $|\psi\rangle$ in "length" and "direction." Linear operators are of special importance in quantum mechanics by virtue of the principle of superposition of states; as a result of the action of a linear operator on the superposition of the arbitrary vectors $|\psi_1\rangle$ and $|\psi_2\rangle$, superposition of the transformed vectors is obtained:

$$(28)\ \hat{L}(c_1|\psi_1\rangle + c_2|\psi_2\rangle) = c_1\hat{L}|\psi_1\rangle + c_2\hat{L}|\psi_2\rangle$$
$$= c_1|\psi_1'\rangle + c_2|\psi_2'\rangle$$

The vectors $|\psi\rangle \equiv |\psi_\lambda\rangle$, for which $|\psi'\rangle$ coincides in direction with $|\psi\rangle$, that is,

$$(29) \qquad \hat{L}|\psi_\lambda\rangle = \lambda|\psi_\lambda\rangle$$

play an important role for the operator $\hat{L}$. The vectors $|\psi_\lambda\rangle$ are called the eigenvectors of operator $\hat{L}$, and the numbers λ are called its eigenvalues. The eigenvectors $|\psi_\lambda\rangle$ are commonly designated simply as $|\lambda\rangle$, that is, $|\psi_\lambda\rangle \equiv |\lambda\rangle$. The eigenvalues λ form a discrete series of numbers (then it is said that the operator $\hat{L}$ has a discrete spectrum), a continuous set (a continuous spectrum), or a partially discrete, partially continuous spectrum.

Linear Hermitian operators constitute a class of operators that is very important for quantum mechanics. The eigenvalues λ of the Hermitian operator $\hat{L}$ are real. The eigenvectors of a Hermitian operator that belong to different eigenvalues are orthogonal to one another, that is,

$$(30) \qquad \langle\lambda\langle\lambda|\lambda'\rangle = 0$$

Using these vectors, it is possible to construct an orthogonal basis ("Cartesian coordinate axes") in the state space. It is convenient to normalize these basis vectors to 1, $\langle\lambda|\lambda\rangle = 1$. An arbitrary vector $|\psi\rangle$ may be resolved with respect to this basis:

$$(31) \qquad |\psi\rangle = \sum_\lambda c_\lambda|\lambda\rangle, \qquad c_\lambda = \langle\lambda|\psi\rangle$$

Here,

$$(32) \qquad \sum_\lambda |c_\lambda|^2 = \langle\psi|\psi\rangle$$

which is equivalent to the Pythagorean theorem; if $|\psi\rangle$ is normalized for 1, then

$$(33) \qquad \sum_\lambda |c_\lambda|^2 = 1$$

The existence for every physical quantity of some isolated states of the system in which this quantity assumes a certain definite (unique) value is of fundamental importance for the construction of the mathematical apparatus of quantum mechanics. This property is essentially the definition of a measurable (physical) quantity, and the states in which the physical quantity has a defined value are called the eigenstates of this quantity.

According to the principle of superposition, any state of a system can be represented in the form of a superposition of the eigenstates of some physical quantity. The possibility of such representation is mathematically analogous to the possibility of expansion of an arbitrary vector in the eigenvectors of a linear Hermitian operator. In accordance with this, in quantum mechanics a linear Hermitian operator $\hat{L}$ is placed in correspondence to every physical quantity or observable L (such as a coordinate, momentum, angular momentum, or energy). The eigenvalue λ of the operator $\hat{L}$ is interpreted as the possible values of the physical quantity L that are manifested during measurements. If the state vector $|\psi\rangle$ is an eigenvector of the operator $\hat{L}$, then the physical quantity L has a definite value. Otherwise, L assumes different values of λ with a probability $|c_\lambda|^2$, where c_λ is the coefficient of expansion of $|\psi\rangle$ with respect to $|\lambda\rangle$:

(34)
$$|\psi\rangle = \sum_\lambda c_\lambda |\lambda\rangle$$

The coefficient $c_\lambda = \langle \lambda|\psi\rangle$ in the expansion of $|\psi\rangle$ in the basis $|\lambda\rangle$ is also called the wave function in the λ-representation. In particular, the wave function $\psi(x)$ is the coefficient of expansion of $|\psi\rangle$ with respect to the eigenvectors of the coordinate operator $\hat{x}, \psi(x) = \langle x|\psi\rangle$.

The average value $\overline{L}$ of the observed L in a given state is determined by the coefficient c_λ according to the general relation between the probability and the average value:

$$\overline{L} = \sum_\lambda |c_\lambda|^2 \lambda = \sum_\lambda |\langle \lambda|\psi\rangle|^2 \lambda$$

The value of $\overline{L}$ can be found directly through the operator $\hat{L}$ and the state vector $|\psi\rangle$ (without determining the coefficients c_λ) from the formula

(35)
$$\overline{L} = \langle \psi|\hat{L}|\psi\rangle$$

The form of the linear Hermitian operators corresponding to such physical quantities as momentum, angular momentum, and energy is determined, on the basis of the general principles for defining these quantities and the correspondence principle, which requires that in the limit $\hbar \to 0$ the physical quantities under consideration must assume "classical" values. At the same time, into quantum mechanics are introduced certain linear Hermitian operators (for example, operators corresponding to the transformation of the state vectors on reflection of the coordinate axes or interchange of identical particles), to which correspond measurable physical quantities that have no classical analogues (such as parity).

The algebraic operations of addition and multiplication can be performed with the operators. But in contrast to ordinary numbers (which in quantum mechanics are called c-numbers), operators are "numbers" (q-numbers) for which the multiplication operation is noncommutative. If $\hat{L}$ and $\hat{M}$ are two operators, then in the general case their action on an arbitrary vector $|\psi\rangle$ in a different order produces a different vector: $\hat{L}\hat{M}|\psi\rangle \neq \hat{M}\hat{L}|\psi\rangle$, that is, $\hat{L}\hat{M} \neq \hat{M}\hat{L}$. The quantity $\hat{L}\hat{M} - \hat{M}\hat{L}$ is designated as $[\hat{L}, \hat{M}]$ and is called a commutator. Only if the two operators can be transposed, that is, $[\hat{L}, \hat{M}] = 0$, can they have common eigenvectors, and consequently only then can the observable L and M simultaneously have defined (precise) values for λ and μ. In other cases these quantities do not have simultaneously defined values, and then they are connected by the uncertainty relation. It can be shown that if $[\hat{L}, \hat{M}] = c$, then $\Delta L \Delta M \geq |c|/2$, where ΔL and ΔM are the mean square deviations from the average values of the corresponding quantities.

A mathematical formulation in which the formal transition from classical mechanics to quantum mechanics is carried out by replacing c-numbers with corresponding q-numbers is possible. The equations of motion are also retained, but now they are for operators. The basic commutative relations can be found from this formal analogy between quantum mechanics and classical mechanics. Thus, for the coordinate and momentum, $[\hat{x}, \hat{p}] = i\hbar$. This leads to the Heisenberg uncertainty relation $\Delta p \Delta x \geq \hbar/2$. In particular, the explicit form of the momentum operator can be obtained from commutation relations in a coordinate (x-) representation. Then the wave function is $\lambda(x)$, and the momentum operator is the differential operator

$$\hat{p}_x = -i\hbar \frac{\partial}{\partial x} \qquad \hat{p}_x \psi = -i\hbar \frac{\partial \psi}{\partial x}$$

It can be shown that the spectrum of its eigenvalues is continuous and that the probability amplitude $\langle x|p\rangle$ is a de Broglie wave ($|p\rangle$ is the eigenvector of the momentum operator $\hat{p}$). If the energy of a system is given as a function of the coordinates and momentums of the particles $H(p, x)$, then knowledge of the commutator $[\hat{x}, \hat{p}]$ is sufficient to find $[\hat{H}, \hat{p}]$ and $[\hat{H}, \hat{x}]$, as well as the energy levels as eigenvalues of the operator of total energy $\hat{H}$.

From the definition of the angular momentum $M_z = xp_y - yp_x, \ldots$ it can be found that $[\hat{M}_x, \hat{M}_y] = i\hbar \hat{M}_z$. These commutative relations are also valid when the spins of the particles are taken into consideration. They prove sufficient to determine the eigenvalue of the square of the total angular momentum, $M^2 = \hbar^2 j(j + 1)$, where the quantum number j is an integer or half-integer, and its components $M_z = m\hbar$, for $m = -j, -j + 1, \ldots, +j$.

The equations of motion of a quantum-mechanical system can be written in two forms: in the form of an equation for the state vector

(36)
$$i\hbar \frac{\partial}{\partial t} |\psi\rangle = \hat{H}|\psi\rangle$$

—Schrödinger's form of the equation of motion—and in the form of an equation for the operators (q-numbers)

(37)
$$\frac{d\hat{L}}{dt} = \frac{i}{\hbar} [\hat{H}, \hat{L}]$$

—Heisenberg's form of the equations of motion, which is closest to classical mechanics. In particular, it follows from Heisenberg's form that the average values of physical quantities change according to the laws of classical mechanics; this proposition is called the Ehrenfest theorem.

The presence of two components that are totally different in nature is characteristic of the logical structure of quantum mechanics. The state vector (the wave function) is uniquely defined at any moment in time if it is defined at the initial moment. In this respect the theory is totally deterministic. But the state vector is not an observable quantity. Only statistical (probabilistic) predictions can be made concerning quantities that are observable on the basis of knowledge of $|\psi\rangle$. The results of individual measurement of a quantum entity are, strictly speaking, unpredictable in the general case. Attempts have been made to revive the idea of total determinism in the classical sense by introducing the assumption that the quantum-mechanical description is incomplete. For example, the hypothesis has been advanced that quantum entities have additional degrees of freedom—"latent parameters"—consideration of which would make the behavior of a system totally deterministic in the sense of classical mechanics; uncertainty arises only because these latent parameters are unknown and are not taken into account. However, J. von Neumann proved the theorem that it is impossible to give a nonstatistical interpretation of quantum mechanics while retaining its principal assumption on the correspondence between observables (physical quantities) and operators.

REFERENCES

Classical works

Heisenberg, W. *Fizicheskie printsipy kvantovoi teorii.* Leningrad-Moscow, 1932.

Dirac, P. *Printsipy kvantovoi mekhaniki.* Moscow, 1960. (Translated from English.)

Pauli, W. *Obshchie printsipy volnovoi mekhaniki.* Moscow-Leningrad, 1947. (Translated from German.)

Neumann, J. von. *Matematicheskie osnovy kvantovoi mekhaniki.* Moscow, 1964. (Translated from German.)

Textbooks

Landau, L. D., and E. M. Lifshits. *Kvantovaia mekhanika,* 2nd ed. Moscow, 1963. (*Teoreticheskaia fizika,* vol. 3.)

Blokhintsev, D. I. *Osnovy kvantovoi mekhaniki,* 4th ed. Moscow, 1963.

Davydov, A. S. *Kvantovaia mekhanika.* Moscow, 1963.

Sokolov, A. A., Iu. M. Loskutov and I. M. Ternov. *Kvantovaia mekhanika.* Moscow, 1962.

Bohm, D. *Kvantovaia teoriia.* Moscow, 1961. (Translated from English.)

Feynman, R., et al. *Feinmanovskie lektsii po fizike,* fascs. 8 and 9. Moscow, 1966–67. (Translated from English.)

Schiff, L. *Kvantovaia mekhanika,* 2nd ed. Moscow, 1959. (Translated from English.)

Fermi, E. *Kvantovaia mekhanika.* Moscow, 1965. (Translated from English.)

Popular books

Born, M. *Atomnaia fizika,* 3rd ed. Moscow, 1970. (Translated from English.)

Peierls, R. E. *Zakony prirody,* 2nd ed. Moscow, 1962. (Translated from English.)
V. B. BERESTETSKII [11–1704–1]

QUANTUM NUMBERS, integers (0,1,2, . . .) or half-integers (1/2, 3/2, 5/2, . . .) that define the possible discrete values of the physical quantities characterizing quantum systems (atomic nucleus, atom, molecule) and individual elementary particles. The use of quantum numbers in quantum mechanics reflects features of the discreteness of processes occurring in the microworld, and is closely connected with the existence of the quantum of action, or the Planck constant $\hbar$. Quantum numbers were first introduced in physics to describe the empirically determined regularities of atomic spectra, but the meaning of quantum numbers and the associated discreteness of certain quantities characterizing the dynamics of microparticles were revealed only by quantum mechanics.

A set of quantum numbers that thoroughly defines the state of a quantum system is said to be complete. The aggregate of the states that satisfy all possible values of the quantum numbers of a complete set forms the complete system of states. The state of an electron in the atom is determined by four quantum numbers corresponding to the four degrees of freedom of the electron (three degrees of freedom are connected with the three coordinates that define the electron's spatial position, and the fourth, internal, degree of freedom is connected with its spin). For the hydrogen atom and hydrogen-like atoms these quantum numbers forming a complete set are given below.

(1) The principal quantum number $n = 1, 2, 3, \ldots$ defines the energy levels of the electron.

(2) The azimuthal (or orbital) quantum number $l = 0, 1, 2, \ldots, n - 1$ gives the spectrum of the possible values of the square of the orbital angular momentum of an electron: $M^2{}_l = \hbar^2 l(l + 1)$.

(3) The magnetic quantum number m_l characterizes the possible values of a projection M_{lz} of the orbital angular momentum M_l on some arbitrarily selected direction (taken as the z-axis): $M_{lz} = \hbar m_l$. This number may assume integer values in the interval from $-l$ to $+l$ (for a total of $2l + 1$ values).

(4) The magnetic spin quantum number, or simply the spin quantum number, m_s characterizes the possible values of a projection of the electron's spin and may assume two values: $m_s = \pm 1/2$.

Definition of a state of an electron using the quantum numbers n, l, m_l, and m_s does not take into account the so-called fine structure of energy levels—the splitting of levels with a given n (when $n \geq 2$) as a result of the spin's influence on the orbital motion of the electron. When this interaction is taken into account, the quantum numbers j and m_j are used to characterize the state of the electron instead of m_l and m_s.

(5) The quantum number j of the total angular momentum M of an electron (the orbital moment + the spin moment) determines the possible values of the square of the total momentum: $M^2 = \hbar^2 j(j + 1)$ and, for a given l, may assume two values: $j = l \pm 1/2$.

(6) The magnetic quantum number m_j of the total angular momentum determines the possible values of the projection of the total angular momentum on the z-axis, $M_z = \hbar m_j$; it may assume $2j + 1$ values: $m_j = -j, -j + 1, \ldots, +j$.

The same quantum numbers approximately describe the states of individual electrons in complex (multielectron) atoms as well as the state of the individual nucleons—protons and neutrons—in atomic nuclei. In this case, n represents the successive (in order of increasing energy) energy levels with a given l. The state of a multielectron atom as a whole is defined by the following quantum numbers: (1) the quantum number of the total orbital angular momentum of an atom L, which is defined by the motion of all electrons, $L = 0, 1, 2, \ldots$; (2) the quantum number of the total angular momentum of the atom J, which may assume all values differing by units of 1 from $J = |L - S|$ to $J = L + S$, where S is the the total spin of the atom (in $\hbar$ units); and (3) the magnetic quantum number m_j, which defines the possible values of a projection of the atom's total angular momentum on the z-axis, $M_z = m_j \hbar$, and which assumes $2J + 1$ values.

Still another quantum number—the parity of the state P—is used to characterize the state of the atom and of the quantum system in general. It assumes the values $+1$ or -1 depending on whether the wave function defining the state of the system retains its sign on inversion of the coordinates $\mathbf{r}$ with respect to the origin of coordinates (that is, when $\mathbf{r} \rightarrow -\mathbf{r}$ is replaced) or changes its sign. The parity P is equal to $(-1)^l$ for the hydrogen atom and $(-1)^L$ for multielectron atoms.

Quantum numbers also have proved convenient for formulating the selection rules that determine the possible types of quantum transitions.

A number of other quantum numbers are introduced in the physics of elementary particles and nuclear physics. The quantum numbers of elementary particles are internal characteristics of the particles that define their interactions and the regularities of mutual transformations. In addition to the spin s, which may be an integer or half-integer (in $\hbar$ units), the following includes quantum numbers of elementary particles: (1) the electric charge Q, which in all known elementary particles is equal either to 0 or to a positive or negative integer (in units of the elementary electric charge e); (2) the baryon charge B, which is equal to 0 or 1 (for antiparticles, 0 or -1); (3) lepton charges, or lepton numbers—the electric number L_e and the muons L_μ—which are equal to 0 or $+1$ (for antiparticles, 0 or -1); (4) the isotopic spin T, which is an integer or half-integer; (5) the strangeness S or the hypercharge Y (which is related to S by the equation $Y = S + B$)—all known elementary particles (or antiparticles) have $S = 0$ or $\pm 1, \pm 2, \pm 3$; and (6) the intrinsic parity Π, a quantum number that characterizes the properties of the symmetry of elementary particles with respect to inversion of the coordinates and may be equal to $+1$ (such particles are called particles of even parity) or -1 (particles of odd parity). These quantum numbers also are applied to systems consisting of several elementary particles and, in particular, to atomic nuclei. Here, the total values of the electric, baryon, and lepton charges and of the strangeness of a system of particles are equal to the algebraic sum of the corresponding quantum numbers of the individual particles; the total spin and isotopic spin are obtained on the basis of the quantum rules for the addition of angular momentums; and the intrinsic parities of the particles are multiplied.

Physical quantities defining the motion of a quantum mechanical particle (or system) that are conserved in the process of motion but that do not necessarily belong to the discrete spectrum of possible values are often said to be quantum numbers in the broad sense. For example, the energy of a free-moving electron (which has a continuous spectrum of values) may be considered as one of its quantum numbers.

D. V. GAL'TSOV [11–1789–1]

QUANTUM TRANSITIONS, discontinuous transitions of a quantum system (an atom, a molecule, an atomic nucleus, a solid) from one state to another. The most important are quantum transitions between stationary states that correspond to different energies of the quantum system—the quantum transitions of a system from one energy level to another. During a transition from a higher energy level $\mathcal{E}_k$ to a lower level $\mathcal{E}_i$, the system releases the energy $\mathcal{E}_k - \mathcal{E}_i$ and during the reverse transition, absorbs it (see Figure 1).

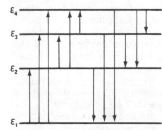

Figure 1. Part of the levels of a quantum system: $\mathcal{E}_1$ is the principal level (level with the lowest possible energy) and $\mathcal{E}_2$, $\mathcal{E}_3$, and $\mathcal{E}_4$ are the excited levels. The arrows indicate transitions involving the absorption (directed up) and release (directed down) of energy.

Quantum transitions may be radiative or nonradiative. In radiative transitions the system emits (the transition $\mathcal{E}_k \rightarrow \mathcal{E}_i$) or absorbs (the transition $\mathcal{E}_i \rightarrow \mathcal{E}_k$) a quantum of electromagnetic radiation—the photon—of energy $h\nu$ (ν is the frequency of radiation and $\hbar$ is the Planck constant), which satisfies the fundamental relation

$$(1) \qquad \mathcal{E}_k - \mathcal{E}_i = h\nu$$

(which is the law of conservation of energy for such a transition). Depending on the energy difference between the states of the system in which the quantum transitions take place, photons of radio-frequency, infrared, visible, ultraviolet, and gamma radiation and X-radiation are emitted or absorbed. The aggregate of radiative quantum transitions from lower energy levels to higher ones forms the absorption spectrum of a given quantum system, while the aggregate of the reverse transitions forms its emission spectrum.

In nonradiative quantum transitions, the system acquires or releases energy on interaction with other systems. For example, on colliding with each other and with electrons, the atoms or molecules of a gas may gain energy (be excited) or lose it.

The transition probability, which defines how often a given quantum transition occurs, is the most important characteristic of any quantum transition. It is measured by the number of transitions of a given type in the quantum system under consideration per unit time (1 sec). Therefore, it may assume any values from 0 to ∞ (in contrast to the probability of a single event, which cannot exceed 1). Transition probabilities are calculated by the methods of quantum mechanics.

Quantum transitions in atoms and molecules will be examined below.

Radiative transitions. Radiative quantum transitions may be spontaneous, independent of external influences on the quantum system (the spontaneous emission of a photon), or stimulated, induced by the action of external electromagnetic radiation of a resonance [satisfying relation (1)] frequency ν (absorption and stimulated emission of photons). Insofar as spontaneous emission is possible, a quantum system remains at an excited energy level $\mathcal{E}_k$ for some finite time, and then jumps to some lower level. The mean time period τ_k that the system remains at the excited level $\mathcal{E}_k$ is called the lifetime of the energy level. The smaller the τ_k, the greater the probability of the system's transition to a state of lower energy. The quantity $A_k = 1/\tau_k$, which defines the average number of photons emitted by a single particle (an atom or molecule) per second (τ_k is expressed in seconds) is called the probability of spontaneous emission from the level $\mathcal{E}_k$. For the simplest case of spontaneous transition from the first excited level $\mathcal{E}_2$ to the ground level $\mathcal{E}_1$, the quantity $A_2 = 1/\tau_2$ defines the probability of this transition; it may be designated A_{21}. Quantum transitions to various lower levels are possible from excited higher levels (see Figure 1). The total number A_k of photons emitted on the average by one particle with an energy $\mathcal{E}_k$ per second is equal to the total number A_{ki} of photons emitted upon the individual transitions:

$$(2) \qquad A_k = \sum_{i=1}^{i=k-1} A_{ki}$$

that is, the total probability A_k of spontaneous emission from the level $\mathcal{E}_k$ is equal to the sum of the probabilities A_{ki} of the individual spontaneous transitions $\mathcal{E}_k \longrightarrow \mathcal{E}_i$; the quantity A_{ki} is called Einstein's coefficient of spontaneous emission upon such a transition. For the hydrogen atom, $A_{ki} \simeq (10^7 - 10^8) \sec^{-1}$.

For induced quantum transitions the number of transitions is proportional to the radiation density ρ_ν of the frequency $\nu = (\mathcal{E}_k - \mathcal{E}_i)/h$, that is, to the energy of photons of frequency ν per 1 cm^3. The probabilities of absorption and stimulated emission are characterized by Einstein's coefficients B_{ik} and B_{ki}, respectively, which are equal to the number of photons absorbed and stimulated to emission on the average by one particle per second at a radiation density equal to 1. The products $B_{ik}\rho_\nu$ and $B_{ki}\rho_\nu$ define the probabilities of stimulated absorption and emission on exposure to external electromagnetic radiation of density ρ_ν, and, like A_{ki}, are expressed in sec^{-1}.

The coefficients A_{ki}, B_{ik}, and B_{ki} are interconnected by the following relations, which were first derived by Einstein and have been rigorously substantiated in quantum electrodynamics:

$$(3) \qquad g_k B_{ki} = g_i B_{ik}$$

$$(4) \qquad A_{ki} = \frac{8\pi h \nu^3}{c^3} \frac{g_i}{g_k} \qquad B_{ik} = \frac{8\pi h \nu^3}{c^3} B_{ki}$$

where $g_i(g_k)$ is the degeneration multiplicity of the level $\mathcal{E}_i(\mathcal{E}_k)$, that is, the number of different states of the system that have the same energy $\mathcal{E}_i$ (or $\mathcal{E}_k$), and c is the velocity of light. For transitions between nondegenerate levels ($g_i = g_k = 1$), $B_{ki} = B_{ik}$, that is, the probabilities of induced quantum transitions—direct and reverse—are identical. If one of the Einstein

coefficients is known, then the others can be determined from relations (3) and (4).

The probabilities of radiative transitions are different for different transitions and depend on the properties of the energy levels $\mathcal{E}_i$ and $\mathcal{E}_k$ between which the transition takes place. The more strongly the electric and magnetic properties of the quantum system that are characterized by its electric and magnetic moments change upon transition, the greater the probabilities of given quantum transitions. The possibility of radiative quantum transitions between the energy levels $\mathcal{E}_i$ and $\mathcal{E}_k$ with assigned characteristics is defined by the selection rules. (For greater detail, *see* RADIATION, ELECTROMAGNETIC.)

Nonradiative transitions. Nonradiative quantum transitions are also characterized by the probabilities of the corresponding transitions C_{ki} and C_{ik}—the average number of processes of release and acquisition of energy $\mathcal{E}_k - \mathcal{E}_i$ per 1 sec, calculated for one particle with an energy $\mathcal{E}_k$ (for the energy release process) or an energy $\mathcal{E}_i$ (for the energy acquisition process). If both radiative and nonradiative quantum transitions are possible, then the total transition probability is equal to the sum of the transition probabilities of both types.

It is essential to take into account nonradiative quantum transitions when the transition probability is of the same order or greater than the corresponding quantum transition involving radiation. For example, if spontaneous radiative transition to the ground level $\mathcal{E}_1$ from the first excited state $\mathcal{E}_2$ is possible with a probability A_{21} and nonradiative transition to the same level is possible with a probability C_{21}, then the total transition probability will be equal to $A_{21} + C_{21}$; the energy level lifetime is equal to $\tau'_2 = 1/(A_{21} + C_{21})$ instead of $\tau_2 = 1/A_2$ in the absence of a nonradiative transition. Thus, the energy level lifetime decreases because of nonradiative quantum transitions. When $C_{21} \gg A_{21}$, the time τ_2' is very small in comparison with τ_2, and the majority of particles will lose their excitation energy $\mathcal{E}_2 - \mathcal{E}_1$ in nonradiative processes—the quenching of spontaneous emissions will take place.   M. IA. EL'IASHEVICH [11—1776—1]

QUARANTINE, a system of measures taken both to prevent the spread of infectious diseases from an epidemic focus and to eliminate the focus itself.

Quarantine was first introduced in Italy in the 14th century in the form of a 40-day detention (hence the name) in port of ships arriving from places affected with plague; later it was used to control other infectious diseases as well. The first international attempts at quarantine measures to control the spread of plague, cholera, yellow fever, and smallpox (called quarantine diseases) were undertaken in the 19th century. The first international conference to work out these measures was held in Paris in 1851. Present-day quarantine measures are regulated by international health rules adopted by the fourth session of the World Health Organization in 1951 (revised in 1956 and 1957). The Rules for the Sanitation and Protection of the Territory of the USSR Against the Importation and Spread of Quarantine and Other Infectious Diseases, issued by the Ministry of Health of the USSR in 1967, regulate the measures taken to control the spread of the quarantine diseases: plague, cholera, smallpox, yellow fever, malaria, anthrax, brucellosis, foot-and-mouth disease, glanders, melioidosis, psittacosis, and rabies.

Two types of quarantine measures are used to protect the USSR: (1) administrative (prohibiting individuals refusing to meet the requirements of the medical border service from entering or leaving the USSR; banning the receipt of packages from countries affected with certain quarantine diseases; temporary closure of the borders) and (2) medical (examination by health officers and physicians of passengers crossing the frontiers of the USSR; isolation of sick persons; observation of individuals who have come in contact with sick persons).

Homes, multiple-dwelling units, ships, military units, trains carrying livestock or produce, population centers, and entire regions may be placed under quarantine. In addition to the measures already mentioned, to prevent infectious diseases from spreading within the country quarantine involves banning the admission to school and other children's institutions of carriers of infection and persons coming in contact with infected patients, detecting and isolating patients and bacilli carriers, and such sanitary measures as fumigation, disinfection, and immunization.   I. I. ELKIN

The use of quarantine in veterinary medicine is helpful in preventing the spread of infectious diseases among animals. It is imposed upon the appearance of diseases that tend to spread beyond the primary focus, namely: foot-and-mouth disease and anthrax in animals; plague, epidemic pneumonia, and emphysematous carbuncle in cattle; glanders, epizootic lymphangitis, infectious anemia, equine encephalomyelitis, and contagious pleuropneumonia in horses; swine plague and erysipelas; sheep pox; infectious pleuropneumonia in goats; fowl plague, Newcastle's disease, pasteurellosis, smallpox, mycoplasmosis, and viral hepatitis in poultry; rubella in carp; branchiomycosis, furunculosis, infectious anemia, and myxosomosis in salmon, and discocotylosis in trout. The list of diseases for which quarantine is imposed is determined by the Veterinary Regulations of the USSR. Changes in and additions to this list are introduced by the Ministry of Agriculture of the USSR and are reflected in respective instructions. Depending on the extent to which a disease has spread, individual barnyards, herds, apiaries, ponds, farms, and sections thereof may be placed under quarantine. Quarantine is imposed and lifted by decision of the executive committees of raion or municipal soviets of working people's deputies upon the presentation of the chief veterinarian. Responsibility for the observance of quarantine rests with the directors of the individual farm or enterprise. Preventive quarantine is used to monitor the health of animals while being transported from other farms (including farms abroad).

REFERENCES

Gromashevskii, L. V. *Obshchaia epidemiologiia,* 4th ed. Moscow, 1965.
Kompantsev, N. F., and A. V. Pavlov. *Organizatsiia raboty po profilaktike karantinnykh zabolevanii.* Kiev, 1968. (Bibliography.)

[11–1164–3]

QUARANTINE DISEASES, convention diseases, infectious diseases that come under the action of the International Quarantine or international health conventions.

The quarantine diseases include plague, cholera, yellow fever, and smallpox (in 1970, the 23rd Assembly of the World Health Organization removed typhus and relapsing fever from the list).

[11–1169–1]

QUARANTINE OF PLANTS, the group of measures taken by the state to prevent the introduction and spread of the pests, diseases, and weeds presenting the greatest danger to farm crops.

The quarantine of plants is aimed at protecting the plant resources of the nation. Each year plant pests and diseases destroy 20–25 percent of the potential world harvest of food crops (equaling $50 billion, according to the average price level on the world market). According to the calculations (1969) of the All-Union Scientific Research Institute for Plant Protection, the value of the farm products that could be obtained on the kolkhozes and sovkhozes of the USSR by eliminating the probable annual crop losses caused by pests, diseases, and weeds would come to around 10 billion rubles.

The first law on the quarantine of plants appeared in France in 1660 in response to epiphytotics of stem rust. From 1870 through 1915, quarantine laws were passed by a majority of the nations with developed agricultural production that were involved in the exchange of plant materials (Germany, France, Australia, Austria, the United States, Mexico). By the 1970's, more than 100 nations had established quarantine regulations and had set up institutions for supervising their execution. In Russia, the first quarantine law for plants was issued in 1873. In 1931 the USSR created a quarantine service that exercises general leadership over quarantine measures through the State Quarantine Inspectorate of the Central Administration for Plant Protection (under the Ministry of Agriculture of the USSR), along with republic and oblast quarantine inspectorates that are subordinate to it. In the same year, the first list of quarantine diseases and pests was established. In 1935 a list of quarantine weeds was established as well. These lists are periodically revised as the various types of harmful organisms are studied (area of distribution, biology, ecology) and the quarantine state of foreign countries reviewed. (The list approved in 1967 contained the quarantine pests listed in Table 1, the diseases listed in Table 2, and the weeds listed in Table 3.)

Table 1. Quarantine pests

Common name	Latin name
Not reported in the USSR	
Scale insects and mealybugs	
Citrus scale	Unaspis citri
Eastern citrus scale	Unaspis japonensis
Citrus mealybug	Pseudococcus citriculus
Fig scale	Ceroplastes rusci
Beetles	
White-fringed weevil	Pantomorus leucoloma
Khapra beetle	Trogoderma granarium
Southern cowpea weevil	Callosobruchus chinensis
Cowpea weevil	Callosobruchus maculatus
Broad-nosed grain weevil	Caulophilus latinasus
Japanese beetle	Popillia japonica
Butterflies and moths	
Potato moth	Phthorimaea operculella
Pink bollworm	Pectinophora gossypiella
Flies	
Mandarin fruit fly	Tetradacus citri
Mediterranean fruit fly	Ceratitis capitata
Apple maggot	Rhagoletis pomonella
Limited distribution in the USSR	
Plant lice and aphids	
Grape phylloxera (vine louse)	Viteus vitifoliae
Whiteflies	
Common citrus whitefly	Dialeurodes citri
Scale insects and mealybugs	
Cottony-cushion scale	Icerya purchasi
San Jose scale	Quadraspidiotus perniciosus
White peach scale	Pseudaulacaspis pentagona
Citrophilus mealybug	Pseudococcus gahani
Comstock mealybug	Pseudococcus comstocki
Japanese wax scale	Ceroplastes japonicus
Japanese peony scale	Pseudaonidia paeoniae
Japanese bacillary scale	Leucaspis japonica
Beetles	
Apple borer	Agrilus mali
Colorado potato beetle	Leptinotarsa decemlineata
Butterflies and moths	
Fall webworm	Hyphantria cunea
Oriental fruit moth	Grapholitha molesta
Hemp tortrix[1]	Grapholitha delineana
Hollyhock seed moth	Pectinophora malvella
Peach moth	Carposina sasakii
Citrus moth[1]	Phylocnistis citrella

[1]Quarantine measures applied to produce imported from abroad

The duties of the quarantine service include the inspection of plants, seeds, planting stock, grain products, fruits, and vegeta-

Table 2. Quarantine plant diseases

Disease	Causative agent
Not reported in the USSR	
Cotton anthracnose	Colletotrichum gossypii
Ascochyta blight of chrysanthemum	Ascochyta chrysanthemi
Bacterial wilt of corn	Bacterium stenarti
Bacterial citrus cancer	Xanthomonas citri
White rust of chrysanthemum	Puccinia horiana
Viral diseases of citrus (tristeza, quick decline, yellow dragon)	Virus sp. sp.
India wheat bunt	Neovossia indica
Fire blight	Erwinia amylovora
Silver leaf of beets	Corynebacterium betae
Texas root rot	Ozonium omnivorum
Limited distribution in the USSR	
Flax pasmo	Septoria linicola
Root knot of potatoes	Heterodera rostochiensis
Potato wart	Synchytrium endobioticum
Plum pox	Prunus virus 7

Table 3. Quarantine weeds

Common name	Latin name	Biological type
	Not reported in the USSR	
Coastal ragweed	Ambrosia maritima	Annual
Poverty weed	Iva axillaris	Soboliferous perennial
Trompillo (white horse nettle)	Solanum elaeagnifolium	Soboliferous perennial
Cut-leaved nightshade	Solanum triflorum	Annual
California sunflower	Helianthus californicus	Perennial
Blueweed	Helianthus ciliaris	Perennial
Prairie sunflower	Helianthus petiolaris	Annual
Stiff sunflower	Helianthus scaberrimus	Annual
Helianthus, all other weed species	Helianthus spp.	Perennials and annuals
Striga, all species	Striga spp.	Root semiparasites
	Limited distribution in the USSR	
Western ragweed	Ambrosia psilostachya	Soboliferous perennial
Common ragweed	Ambrosia artemisiifolia	Annual
Great ragweed	Ambrosia trifida	Annual
Mountain bluet	Acropotilon repens	Soboliferous perennial
Horse nettle	Solanum carolinense	Soboliferous perennial
Buffalo bur (prickly nightshade)	Solanum rostratum	Annual
Common sunflower	Helianthus lenticularis	Annual
Dodders, all species	Cuscuta spp.	Stem parasites
Sandbur grass	Cenchrus tribuloides	Annual

bles in order to uncover the presence of dangerous pests, the pathogens of plant diseases, and quarantine weeds in large commercial lots and packages, in the parcels, hand luggage, and baggage of passengers arriving from other states, and in the vehicles, warehouses, and enterprises where imported products subject to quarantine are stored and processed. Internal quarantine regulates the shipping of plant materials within the country; external quarantine protects the state against foreign pests, diseases, and weeds.

The plant quarantine service of the USSR operates in cooperation with the equivalent service in other states. In 1956 the USSR joined the international Rome Convention on Plant Quarantine and Protection. In 1957 it joined the European and Mediterranean Organization for Plant Protection. In 1960 it ratified the Cooperative Agreement Plant Quarantine and Protection, concluded between the member states of the Council for Mutual Economic Assistance. In addition, bilateral agreements have been established with 11 neighboring states stipulating reciprocal obligations for combating dangerous plant pests, diseases, and weeds.

REFERENCES
Karantin rastenii v SSSR. Edited by A. L. Efimov and N. S. Shcherbinovskii. Moscow, 1937.
Dvadtsatiletnie itogi karantinnoi ekspertizy importnykh rastitel'nykh materialov (1931–1951). Moscow-Leningrad, 1952.
Ustav gosudarstvennoi sluzhby po karantinu rastenii v SSSR. Moscow, 1962.
Vrediteli, bolezni i sorniaki, obnaruzhennye v importnykh rastitel'nykh gruzakh: Vsesoiuznaia svodka s 1937 po 1959 g. Moscow, 1964.
Spravochnik po karantinnym i drugim opasnym vrediteliam, bolezniam i sornym rasteniiam, 2nd ed. Moscow, 1970.

A. D. SOKOLOV, N. N. SHUTOVA,
and L. P. KUZ'MINA [11–1166–1]

QUARENGHI, GIACOMO. Born Sept. 20 or 21, 1744, in Valle Imagna, near Bergamo, Italy; died Feb. 18 (Mar. 2), 1817, in St. Petersburg. Architect; representative of Russian classicism of the late 18th century and the early 19th. Italian by birth.

In 1761, Quarenghi began studying painting in Rome under A. R. Mengs and S. Pozzi; later he turned to classical architecture and the work of Palladio. In 1780 he began working in Russia, where his first important project was the English Palace in Peterhof, now Petrodvorets (1781–94; entirely destroyed by the fascist Germans in 1942), a classically simple, imposing building with powerful Corinthian colonnades.

Quarenghi's main works include the Academy of Sciences (1783–89), the Currency Bank (1783–90), the Hermitage Theater (1783–87), the Obukhovskaia Hospital (1782–87, rebuilt), the Ekaterininskii Institute (1804–07), the Cavalry Guards Manège (1804–07), and the Smol'nyi Institute (1806–08)—all in Lenin-

grad. They are characterized by clarity of design, simplicity and precision of composition, and majestic modeled forms, achieved by placing imposing colonnades before smooth wall surfaces. Among the country palaces Quarenghi designed are the Alexander Palace (1792–96) at Tsarskoe Selo (now Pushkin), the center of whose main facade is emphasized by a ceremonial courtyard spatially linked with a park by an open majestic colonnade. He was a skillful builder who saw to it that his designs were carefully executed.

Quarenghi's numerous drawings meticulously depict old Russian architectural monuments, buildings by contemporary architects, and genre scenes, notably the *Teremnoi Palace in the Kremlin, Mikhailovskii Castle,* and *Kolomenskoe* (all india ink and watercolor, the Hermitage, Leningrad); *Skating on the Neva* (india ink and watercolor, Pushkin Museum of Fine Arts, Moscow); and *Panorama of the Kremlin* (watercolor and india ink, A. V. Shchusev Architecture Museum, Moscow). Quarenghi published engraved albums of his designs for the Hermitage Theater and the Currency Bank (1787 and 1791) and the first volume of his collected designs (1810).

REFERENCES
Taleporovskii, V. N. *Kvarengi.* Leningrad-Moscow, 1954.
Grimm, G. G. *Kvarengi.* Leningrad, 1962.
Arkhitekturnye proekty i risunki D. Kvarengi iz muzeev i khranilishch SSSR. Leningrad, 1967. [11–1806–2]

QUARKS, hypothetical particles of which, it is believed, all the known elementary particles participating in strong interactions (hadrons) consist.

The hypothesis of the existence of quarks was advanced independently in 1964 by the American physicist M. Gell-Mann and the Austrian physicist G. Zweig to explain the regular patterns that had been established for hadrons. The name "quark" has no precise translation; it is of literary origin, borrowed by Gell-Mann from J. Joyce's novel *Finnegans Wake,* where it meant something undefined and mystical. The name was apparently selected because of a number of unusual properties distinguishing quarks from all known elementary particles (such as fractional electric charge).

It was the discovery of a large number of hadrons and the successful systemization thereof that led to the assumption of the existence of quarks. It was established that hadrons could be grouped into several families of particles of related basic characteristics (identical baryon charges and spins, internal parities, similar masses). For example, eight particles—the proton (p), the neutron (n), and the hyperons Λ^0, Σ^+, Σ^0, Σ^-, Ξ^-, and Ξ^0—can be grouped in one family of baryons (an octet) with a spin of 1/2 and positive parity. Such families of particles are called supermultiplets. The number of particles in each super-multiplet, as well as the main properties of these particles, can be explained if it is assumed that hadrons are composite particles —that they consist of three types of fundamental particles, or p-, n-, and λ-quarks (as well as of the antiparticles $\bar{p}$, $\bar{n}$, and $\bar{\lambda}$). The characteristics indicated in Table 1, including fractional baryon and electric charges, must in that case be ascribed to quarks (see Table 1).

Table 1. Characteristics of quarks and antiquarks

	Particle	Electric charge Q	Baryon charge B	Spin J	Strange-ness S
Quarks	p	+2/3	1/3	1/2	0
	n	−1/3	1/3	1/2	0
	λ	−1/3	1/3	1/2	−1
Antiquarks	$\bar{p}$	−2/3	−1/3	1/2	0
	$\bar{n}$	+1/3	−1/3	1/2	0
	$\bar{\lambda}$	+1/3	−1/3	1/2	+1

According to the above hypothesis, baryons consist of three quarks. For example, a proton ($Q = 1$, $B = 1$) consists of two p-quarks and one n-quark; a neutron ($Q = 0$, $B = 1$) consists of two n-quarks and one p-quark; Σ^+ ($Q = 1$, $B = 1$) consists of two p-quarks and one λ-quark; and Ω^- ($Q = -1$, $B = 1$) consists of three λ-quarks. Antibaryons consist of three antiquarks, and mesons consist of one quark and one antiquark (for example, π^+ consists of one p and one $\bar{n}$ and K^0 consists of one λ and one n). Strange particles must necessarily include λ-quarks, the carriers of strangeness.

Quarks have been sought in cosmic rays and high-energy accelerators and by physicochemical methods in the environment, but all attempts have proved unsuccessful. It cannot be assumed, however, that the results of these experiments conclusively refute the hypothesis that quarks exist. The experiments merely establish the limits of the magnitude of the possible mass of quarks and the probability that quarks are produced in the processes of strong interactions. For example, in experiments at the 70-giga-electron-volt (GeV) Serpukhovo proton accelerator, in which quarks would have been produced during collisions of protons with the nucleons (protons and neutrons) of the target if their mass did not exceed approximately 5 proton masses (in energy units, approximately 5 GeV), not a single particle with a charge of $-1/3$ or $-2/3$ was recorded. This means that the mass of quarks, if they in fact exist, must be greater than 5 GeV, or that the probability of quark production, if quark mass is less than 5 GeV, must be at least 10^{10} times less than the probability of the production of π-mesons, of which more than 10^{10} were recorded during the experiment. The search for quarks in the environment has shown that if quarks do exist, then their concentration in matter cannot exceed 10^{-18}–10^{-20} of the number of nucleons (according to some data, this limit may be even less, or 10^{-24}–10^{-30}).

In addition to the hypothesis that fundamental particles with fractional charges exist, the existence of fundamental particles with integral charges (sometimes called whole-charge quarks) has also been suggested. To explain the regular patterns of hadron systematics it is necessary to assume that there are several supermultiplets of fundamental particles with whole charges (for example, three families of three particles each). Attempts to detect such particles experimentally have also failed to yield positive results.

REFERENCES
Kokkedee, J. Teoriia kvarkov. Moscow, 1971. (Translated from English.)
Fizika vysokikh energii i teoriia elementarynykh chastits. Kiev, 1967.
L. G. LANDSBERG [11–1808–1]

QUARRY, an open-cut operation for mining coal, ores, and nonmetallic materials. In the coal industry the quarry is called a pit, and in ore mining it is sometimes referred to as a mine. The word "quarry" is also used for the excavations created by open-cut operations.

In a quarry the work includes excavating, transporting, and unloading minerals, overburden, and covering and enclosing deposits. The aim of the mining is to fulfill the plan quotas for extracting minerals and to create mineral reserves ready for excavation. A notable feature of a quarry is the continually changing work area. Modern quarries are highly mechanized, with machines and equipment for breaking down, removing, transporting, and storing any rock. The basic production units of small quarries, which mine nonmetallic building materials, are the mining shop (section) and the mineral processing shop. In the large coal and ore open-cut mines, the units include territorial sections or specialized shops (for example, drilling, blasting, cutting-loading, and transport). In addition, the quarry or open-cut mine includes auxiliary and subsidiary shops and sections. In ore mining the open-cut mine itself is frequently a shop of the mining-concentrating or metallurgical combine (such as the Noril'sk Mining-Metallurgical Combine and the Krivoi Rog mining-concentrating combines).

A complex of mine excavations is involved in working the rock in benches. The rock cutting within the benches is carried out in sequential strips—that is, passes of the excavators along the faces of the benches. The upper benches are done before the lower. In working horizontal deposits, the depth of the quarry or mine is fixed, and the advance of the benches leads to an increase in the size of the quarry, with the overburden usually being returned to the dug-out area. Mining work in sloping or steeply tilted deposits necessitates the deepening of the quarry or mine and the creation (cutting) of new benches by digging cross section trenches. In this case the working of the above-lying benches must advance more rapidly. Sloping major trenches are made for providing transport between the surface and the faces in the mine. Planning the construction of the quarry or mine includes providing for the stripping and cutting of benches along the deposit, with the benches in the capping overburden being worked more rapidly than the benches below, and the construction of access transport arteries as well as production buildings and housing.

The depth of individual quarries and mines in the USSR (1970) reaches several hundred meters (for example, the Korkino Mine of 300 m), and the planned depth of a number of mines is 500–700 m. The productivity of the large quarries and mines in the USSR is tens of millions of tons of ore per year (for example, the open-cut mine of the southern mining-concentrating combine, or IuGOK, and the northern mining-concentrating combine, or SevGOK, in Krivoi Rog). In 1972 coal and ore mines were being designed to produce 40–50 million tons annually for the mineral and over 100 million tons for the overburden.

REFERENCES
Mel'nikov, N. V. Spravochnik inzhenera i tekhnika po otkrytym gornym rabotam, 4th ed. Moscow, 1961.
Rzhevskii, V. V. Tekhnologiia, mekhanizatsiia i avtomatizatsiia protsessov otkrytykh gornykh razrabotok. Moscow, 1966.
Rzhevskii, V. V. Tekhnologiia i kompleksnaia mekhanizatsiia otkrytykh gornykh rabot. Moscow, 1968.
Kuleshov, N. A., and Iu. I. Anistratov. Tekhnologiia otkrytykh gornykh rabot. Moscow, 1968. Iu. I. ANISTRATOV [11–1461–2]

QUARRY TRANSPORT, the moving of quarry loads, one of the main production processes in opencut mining. The basic quarry load is rock (mineral-bearing or barren rock), the starting point is the mining face, and the end point is the unloading area (the dumps for barren rock or below-grade ores and the receiving hoppers of loading stations; the crushing, enriching, sintering, or briquette mills; and the temporary or permanent storage areas for the mineral.)

Special features of quarry transport are the great volume of the shipments (for example, loads ranging from several tens of thousands to tens of millions of tons are moved up to 15–20 km in the quarries per year); the one-directional movement of loads, always from the faces to the receiving areas; the great inclines on the route; and the movability of the rock loading areas and the barren rock receiving points.

Quarry transport is the connecting link in all the production processes involved in working rock in a quarry; it is responsible for about half of the total labor and cost expenditures in mining the minerals.

All types of quarry transport can be divided into two groups: periodically operating transport, including rail and motor movers, skip loaders, and cable cranes; and continuous-action transport, including conveyors, overhead cableways, pipelines (hydraulic and pneumatic), gravity-fed transport (ore chutes and passes), dump transport bridges (trestles), transloaders, and swing chutes. As a consequence of the changing conditions both in the deep and hillside quarries, wide use is made of combinations of different types of transport (for example, motor and rail or motor and conveyor/skip). In this instance, the use of each type of transport for the applications best suited to it provides the highest technical and economic efficiency (for example, motor transport in the face area, skip transport in delivery of the rock from the lower levels, and rail in the last stage of the travel). Aside from the designated means of transport, the rock can be moved in the quarries by stoping-transporting machines (scrapers, loaders, and bulldozers) and stoping machines (high-productivity dragline excavators and mechanical shovels). The most promising means of quarry transport is conveyors, which are used predominantly in working soft rock and which provide continuous mining and full automation of the transporting processes.

Motor-vehicle quarry transport is being improved by increasing the load capacity, reducing the tare weight, improving maneuverability and speed, and improving efficiency (by using an electric drive, gas turbine engines, and storage batteries and fuel cells for power and light alloys and plastics to reduce weight). Rail quarry transport is being improved by increasing the weight of the loads, developing greater climbing ability, and improving braking (the introduction of high DC and AC voltages, diesel electric and turbine engines, and electromagnetic and other types of brakes). Conveyor quarry transport is being adapted for the transporting of hard rock, the conveyor's angle of incline and the flexibility of the conveyor lines are being increased, and conveyor speed and belt strength are being raised (by using high-test belts and steel, plastic, and other plates; by improving the shock-absorbing devices and transloading points; and using a supporting air cushion).

REFERENCES
Rzhevskii, V. V. *Tekhnologiia, mekhanizatsiia i avtomatizatsiia protsessov otkrytykh gornykh razrabotok.* Moscow, 1966.
Spivakovskii, A. O., M. G. Potapov, and A. V. Andreev. *Transportnye mashiny i kompleksy otkrytykh gornykh razrabotok,* 2nd ed. Moscow, 1968.
Vasil'ev, M. V. *Sovremennyi kar'ernyi transport.* Moscow, 1969.
Andreev, A. V., and E. E. Shesko. *Transportnye mashiny i kompleksy dlia otkrytoi dobychi poleznykh iskopaemykh.* Moscow, 1970.
Vasil'ev, M. V., and V. L. Iakovlev. *Nauchnye osnovy proektirovaniia kar'ernogo transporta.* Moscow, 1972.
M. V. VASIL'EV and IU. I. ANISTRATOV [11–1463–2]

QUARTERMASTER (quartermaster sergeant—Russian, *kaptenarmus*; from French *capitaine d'armes*), the official in a company (battery, squadron) responsible for registration and custody of weapons and stores in the company depot. In Russia, the post of quartermaster was created in 1716 and retained until 1917; in the Soviet Army the post existed from 1918 until the 1950's. [11–1087–4]

QUASARS, or quasi-stellar radio sources, celestial objects that resemble stars in optical appearance and gaseous nebulas in the character of their spectra; quasars also exhibit significant red shifts (exceeding the largest known red shifts of galaxies by up to a factor of 6). The last property determines the important role of quasars in astrophysics and cosmology.

The discovery of quasars was the result of increased precision in the determination of the coordinates of extragalactic sources of radio emission, which has led to a great increase in the number of radio sources identified with celestial objects seen optically. The first identification of a radio source with a starlike object was made in 1960. In 1963, when the American astronomer M. Schmidt identified the spectral lines of these objects, which had shifted owing to the effect of the red shift, they were isolated as a special class of cosmic objects—quasars. Thus, quasars with strong radio emission were discovered first; however, quasars with weak radio emission were also subsequently discovered (about 98.8 percent of all quasars accessible to observation). This numerous variety of quasar are called radio-quiet quasars, quasar-galaxies ("quasags"), interlopers, and sometimes, blue starlike objects. The total number of quasars accessible to observation is about 10^5; of these about 1,000 have so far been identified with optical objects, but using spectral criteria only approximately 200 have been established as reliably belonging to quasars.

Intense ultraviolet radiation and broad bright lines are revealed in the spectra of quasars. These are characteristic for hot gaseous nebulas (temperatures around 30,000°C) but are significantly shifted toward the red end of the spectrum. At red shifts exceeding 1.7, the $L\alpha 1216$ Å resonance line of hydrogen even becomes visible on photographs of quasar spectra. From time to time, narrow dark lines, caused by the absorption of light in the intergalactic gas surrounding the quasars, are observed in the spectra of quasars. On photographs, quasars look like stars, and thus their angular diameter is less than 1″. Only the nearest quasars reveal optical features: an elliptical form of starlike image and gas ejections. Quasars are distinguished on photographs from normal stars by their intense ultraviolet radiation, which is characterized by a blue color index, and from white dwarfs, by excessive infrared radiation, even if the quasars do not exhibit radio emission.

Variations in the brightness of many quasars are, evidently, one of the fundamental properties of quasars (the shortest variation has a period $\tau \approx 1$ hr, the maximum changes in brightness are by a factor of 25). Since the size of an object of variable brightness cannot exceed $c\tau$ (c is the velocity of light), the size of quasars cannot be more than 4×10^{12} m (less than the diameter of the orbit of Uranus). Only with the motion of the matter with a velocity close to that of light can this size be larger. In contrast to continuous radiation, variations in the intensity of the spectral lines are rare.

As radio sources, quasars are similar to radio galaxies. Quasars are often observed with two extended radio sources, not necessarily identical in intensity, which are located at significant distances in different directions from the optical object. The mechanism of radio emission in these and other quasars is synchrotron radiation. In addition, compact radio sources are observed in quasars, which give rise to variations in radio emission at centimeter wavelengths; these sources are expanding clouds of relativistic particles existing for several years. The mechanism of their radio emission is linked, evidently, with plasma oscillations.

Little has been learned about the nature of quasars. Depending on the interpretation of the nature of the red shift in the spectra of quasars, three hypotheses are under consideration (as of the early 1970's). The most plausible is the cosmological hypothesis, according to which the large red shifts indicate that quasars are located at enormous distances (up to 10 gigaparsecs) and are taking part in the expansion of the metagalaxy. Determinations of the distances to quasars (according to their red shifts) as well as estimates of their masses and luminosities are based on this assumption. In the cosmological hypothesis, quasars, according to their absolute magnitudes (-27) and masses (about 10^{38} kg, that is, 10^8 solar masses), are actually superstars. The physical nature of a quasar in this case is connected with the gravitational collapse of a mass of gas, which is stopped by magnetic turbulence or the rotation of the quasar.

The large output of energy in all forms of electromagnetic radiation, according to this hypothesis, limits the active stage of a quasar to 10^4 years. In the power of their radio emission (∞ 10^{45} W), quasars are comparable to radio galaxies. It is supposed that quasars are supermassive stars with radii on the order of 10^{12} m, whose plasma continuously and by means of great explosions ejects streams of particles of different energies. At a radius of about 10^{16} m, the quasars are surrounded by clouds of ionized gas, which produce the bright lines in the spectra of quasars, and at distances on the order of 10^{19} m are located clouds of relativistic particles, trapped in weak magnetic fields—the radio-emitting clouds of the quasars.

The nearest quasars are located at more than 200 megaparsecs. Their relative scarcity and the short duration of their existence corroborates the assumption that quasars constitute a stage in the evolution of large cosmic masses, for example, galactic nuclei. Thus, there exists a nonaccidental similarity between quasars and N-galaxies, Seyfert galaxies, and blue compact galaxies in the character of their spectra, variations of brightness, and radio emission. The nearest quasars, whose structures have been observed on photographs, have proved to be N-galaxies, on the basis of which they have been grouped into one class of compact, very bright objects. The nature of the object BL Lacertae (and several more) is puzzling. In its brightness variations, radio emission, color index, and optical structure it appears to be a typical quasar; yet at the same time it has no lines in its spectrum.

According to another hypothesis, quasars with velocities close to the velocity of light are flying out as a result of an explosion (which occurred several million years ago in the center of the galaxy) of matter with a mass of about 10^{40} kg and the subsequent ejection of this matter. According to this hypothesis, the masses of quasars are about 10^{31} kg (5 solar masses), and the distances to them range from 60 to 600 kiloparsecs. However, the physical processes that would generate the energy necessary for the explosion (10^{58} J) are not known.

The third hypothesis assumes that quasars are compact gaseous objects with sizes of 10^{16}–10^{17} m and masses of 10^{42}–10^{43} kg, in whose spectra the lines have a large red shift of a gravitational nature.

REFERENCE
Burbidge, G., and M. Burbidge. *Kvazary.* Moscow, 1969. (Translated from English.)   Iu. P. Pskovskii [11–1680–4]

QUASI-ELASTIC FORCE, a force F directed toward a center O whose magnitude is proportional to the distance r from the center O to the point where the force is applied; numerically $F = cr$, where c is a constant.

A body under the influence of a quasi-elastic force has a potential energy P equal to $1/2\ cr^2$. The name "quasi-elastic force" is derived from the analogous property of forces produced by small deformations of elastic bodies (elastic forces). For a material point under the influence of a quasi-elastic force the center O is a position of stable equilibrium. A point removed from this position will exhibit linear harmonic oscillations or describe an ellipse (in particular, a circle) about the point O.

[11–1685–2]

QUASIMODO, SALVATORE. Born Aug. 20, 1901, in Syracuse; died June 14, 1968, in Naples. Italian poet.

In the 1930's, Quasimodo wrote in the style of the "hermetic" school, which was characterized by motifs of grief and loneliness —the collections *Waters and Land* (1930), *Sunken Oboe* (1932), *Erato and Apollion* (1936), and *Poems* (1938). During the antifascist resistance he began to concern himself with social reality (the collection *Day After Day,* 1947). Quasimodo's postwar poetry deals with civic and patriotic themes—for example, *Life Is Not a Dream* (1949), and *The False and True Green* (1954)—and expresses faith in the people, whom the poet addresses directly (the collection *The Incomparable Earth,* 1958). Quasimodo was a member of the World Peace Council (1950) and received the Nobel Prize in 1959.

WORKS
Tutte le poesie. Verona, 1961.
In Russian translation:
Moia strana—Italiia. Edited by K. Zelinskii. [Introductory article by A. Surkov.] Moscow, 1961. (Translated from Italian.)
["Stikhi."] In *Ital'ianskaia lirika: XX vek.* Moscow, 1968.

REFERENCES
Tedesco, N. S. *Quasimodo e la condizione poetica del nostro tempo.* Palermo [1959]. (Contains bibliography.)
Pento, B. *Lettura di Quasimodo.* Milan [1966].
Mazzamuto, P. *Salvatore Quasimodo.* [Palermo, 1967.]
Quasimodo e la critica. Edited by G. Finzi. [Milan, 1969.]
R. I. Khlodovskii [11–1682–5]

QUASI OPTICS, a branch of physics concerned with the propagation of electromagnetic waves with a wavelength $\lambda <$ 1–2 mm (the shortwave part of the millimetric radio wave band —submillimetric waves and the adjacent optical band) under conditions in which the wave propagation conforms to the laws of geometric optics but in which diffraction phenomena also play a substantial role. A result of these studies is the development of quasi-optical devices—open resonators and quasi-optical lines —in which waves of this band may be excited and propagated.

Cavity resonators and wave guides with dimensions on the order of the wavelength λ, which are widely used for centimetric waves, are unsuited in practice for radio waves shorter than 1–2 mm. Ohmic losses at these wavelengths are so great that the wave is almost entirely attenuated in wave guides at distances of $\sim$ 10–20 cm from the source, and the quality factor of the resonator is low. Open resonators and open transmission channels (refracting and reflecting quasi-optical lines) have therefore been developed.

The simplest open resonator consists of two parallel mirrors placed opposite each other. A beam of light is reflected successively from each of the mirrors and returns to the opposite mirror. The width of the beam is much greater than the wavelength, but since the distance between the mirrors is much greater than the width of the beam, the diffraction divergence of the beam proves to be significant. This phenomenon, along with diffraction at the edges of the mirrors, leads both to nonuniformity of the field distribution in the cross section of the beam and to the occurrence of radiation energy losses. Curved mirrors (in particular, a confocal resonator), which focus the beams, are used to reduce losses (and increase the quality factor of the resonator).

Open resonators, although large in comparison with the wavelength λ, have a quite widely spaced (discrete) spectrum of natural frequences. Therefore, they have proved to be a very convenient resonant system for lasers and for all equipment using electromagnetic waves of the optical and submillimetric bands.

In quasi-optical lines the beam (whose width $\gg \lambda$) passes in sequence through a number of long-focus lenses or slightly curved mirrors (correctors). The correctors focus the beam, compensating for its diffraction expansion upon propagation between them. Such lines may also be used in optical communications systems. Radio wave guides that are wide in comparison with the wavelength λ and that use mirrors, lenses, and prisms may also be used for submillimetric and millimetric waves.

REFERENCES
Tekhnika submillimetrovykh voln. Edited by R. A. Valitov. Moscow, 1969.
Kvazioptika. Moscow, 1966. Edited by B. Z. Katsenelenbaum and V. V. Shevchenko. (Translated from English and German.)
Vainshtein, L. A. *Otkrytye rezonatory i otkrytye volnovody.* Moscow, 1966.
Katsenelenbaum, B. Z. *Vysokochastotnaia elektrodinamika.* Moscow, 1966.   B. Z. Katsenelenbaum [11–1683–1]

QUASIPARTICLES, one of the fundamental concepts of the theory of the condensed state of matter and particularly of solid-state theory. The theoretical description and explanation of the properties of condensed media (solids and liquids) based on the properties of the particles (atoms and molecules) constituting them present great difficulties, first because the number of particles is very great (about 10^{22} particles per cu cm) and second because they interact strongly with one another. Because of the interaction of the particles, the total energy of such a system— which determines many of its properties—is not the sum of the energies of the individual particles, as is the case in an ideal gas. The particles of a condensed medium obey the laws of quantum mechanics; therefore, the properties of an aggregate of particles constituting a solid or liquid can be understood only on the basis of quantum concepts. The development of the quantum theory of condensed media led to the creation of special concepts in physics, particularly the concept of quasiparticles—elementary excitations of the aggregate of interacting particles. The concept of quasiparticles has provided particularly fruitful results in the theory of crystals and liquid helium.

Properties. It was found that the energy $\mathcal{E}$ of a crystal or liquid helium may be approximately regarded as consisting of two parts: the energy of the ground (unexcited) state $\mathcal{E}_0$ (the lowest energy, corresponding to the state of the system at absolute zero), and the total energy $\mathcal{E}_\lambda$ of elementary (irreducible) motions or excitations:

$$\mathcal{E} = \mathcal{E}_0 + \sum_\lambda \mathcal{E}_\lambda \cdot n_\lambda$$

The index λ characterizes the type of elementary excitation, and n_λ is an integer that indicates the number of elementary excitations of type λ.

Thus, it has proved possible to write the energy of the excited state of a crystal (or of helium) in the same manner as the energy of an ideal gas, in the form of an energy sum. However, in the case of a gas the energies of its particles (atoms and molecules) add, whereas in the case of a crystal the energies of the elementary excitations of an entire set of atoms add (hence the term "quasiparticles"). In the case of a gas consisting of free particles, the index λ denotes the momentum $\mathbf{p}$ of the particle, $\mathcal{E}_\lambda$ denotes its energy ($\mathcal{E}_\lambda = \mathbf{p}^2/2m$, where m is the mass of the particle), and n denotes the number of particles that have momentum $\mathbf{p}$. The velocity is $\mathbf{v} = \mathbf{p}/m$.

An elementary excitation in a crystal is also characterized by the vector $\mathbf{p}$, whose properties are similar to momentum; it is called quasimomentum. The energy $\mathcal{E}_\lambda$ of an elementary excitation depends on the quasimomentum, but the relationship $\mathcal{E}_\lambda(\mathbf{p})$ is not as simple as in the case of a free particle. The velocity of propagation of an elementary excitation also depends on the quasimomentum and the form of the function $\mathcal{E}_\lambda(\mathbf{p})$. In the case of quasiparticles the index λ includes a designation of the type of elementary excitation, since elementary excitations that differ in nature are possible in a condensed medium (an analogue is a gas containing particles of different types).

The introduction of the term "quasiparticles" for elementary excitations resulted not only from the external similarity in the description of the energy of the excited state of a crystal or liquid helium and an ideal gas but also from the deep-seated analogy between the properties of a free (quantum-mechanical) particle and the elementary excitation of a set of interacting particles, which is based on the particle-wave duality. The state of a free particle in quantum mechanics is described by a monochromatic wave of frequency $\omega = \mathcal{E}/\hbar$ and wavelength $\lambda = 2\pi\hbar/\mathbf{p}$ (where $\mathcal{E}$ and $\mathbf{p}$ are the energy and momentum of the free particle, and $\hbar$ is Planck's constant). In a crystal the excitation of one particle (such as absorption of a photon by one of the atoms), which leads to excitation of neighboring particles because of the interaction (bond) between the atoms, does not remain localized but is passed on to its neighbors and propagates a wave of excitation. This corresponds to a quasiparticle with a quasimomentum $\mathbf{p} = \hbar\mathbf{k}$ and an energy $\mathcal{E} = \hbar\omega(\mathbf{k})$, where $\mathbf{k}$ is the wave vector and the wavelength is $\lambda = 2\pi/\mathbf{k}$.

The dependence of frequency on the wave vector $\mathbf{k}$ makes it possible to determine the dependence of the energy of quasiparticles on quasimomentum. This relation, $\mathcal{E}_\lambda = \mathcal{E}_{(p)}$, called the dispersion law, is the main dynamic characteristic of a quasiparticle and, in particular, defines its velocity ($\mathbf{v} = \partial\mathcal{E}/\partial\mathbf{p}$). A knowledge of the dispersion law of quasiparticles makes it possible to study the motion of quasiparticles in external fields. A quasiparticle, in contrast to an ordinary particle, is not characterized by a specific mass. However, in emphasizing the similarity between a quasiparticle and a particle it is sometimes convenient to introduce a quantity that has the dimension of mass. It is called the effective mass, m^* (as a rule the effective mass depends on the quasimomentum and on the form of the dispersion law).

All of the above makes it possible to regard an excited condensed medium as a gas consisting of quasiparticles. The similarity between a gas consisting of particles and a gas consisting of quasiparticles is also manifested in the fact that since the concepts and methods of the kinetic theory of gases may be used to describe the properties of a gas of quasiparticles. In particular, one may speak of collisions of quasiparticles (in which the specific laws of conservation of energy and quasimomentum are valid), the mean free time, and the mean free path. The Boltzmann kinetic equation may be used to describe a gas of quasiparticles.

One of the important distinguishing properties of a gas of quasiparticles (in comparison with a gas consisting of ordinary particles) is that quasiparticles may appear and disappear, that is, their number is not conserved. The number of quasiparticles depends on the temperature. For $T = 0°\text{K}$ no quasiparticles are present. The energy spectrum (the set of energy levels) may be determined for a gas of quasiparticles as for a quantum system, and it may be considered as the energy spectrum of a crystal or liquid helium. The diversity of the types of quasiparticles is great, since their nature depends on the atomic structure of the medium and the interaction among particles. Several types of quasiparticles may exist in a single medium.

Like ordinary particles, quasiparticles may have an intrinsic mechanical moment, or spin. Quasiparticles may be divided into bosons and fermions, depending on the magnitude of the spin (expressed as an integer or half-integer times $\hbar$). Bosons are produced and disappear one by one, but fermions are produced and disappear in pairs.

For fermion quasiparticles the distribution over the energy levels is determined by the Fermi distribution function; for boson quasiparticles, by the Bose distribution function. Fermi and Bose "branches" may be distinguished in the energy spectrum of a crystal (or liquid helium), which is the set of energy spectra of all possible types of quasiparticles. In some cases a quasiparticle gas may behave like a gas, obeying Boltzmann statistics (for example, a gas of conduction electrons and holes in a nondegenerate semiconductor; *see below*).

The theoretical explanation of the observed macroscopic properties of crystals or liquid helium, which is based on the concept of quasiparticles, requires knowledge of the dispersion law of the quasiparticles and also of the probability of collisions of quasiparticles with each other and with crystal defects. The numerical values of these characteristics can be obtained only by means of computers. In addition, the semi-empirical approach has developed significantly: the quantitative characteristics of quasiparticles are determined by comparing theory with experiment and are then used to calculate the characteristics of the crystals (or liquid helium).

To determine the characteristics of quasiparticles, the scattering of neutrons, the scattering and absorption of light, ferromagnetic and antiferromagnetic resonance, and ferroacoustic resonance are used, and the properties of metals and semiconductors in strong magnetic fields, particularly cyclotron resonance and galvanomagnetic phenomena, are studied.

The concept of quasiparticles is applicable only at comparatively low temperatures (near the ground state), when the properties of a quasiparticle gas are close to those of an ideal gas. As the number of quasiparticles increases, the probability of collisions grows, the mean free time of quasiparticles decreases, and, in accordance with the uncertainty relation, the uncertainty of the energy of the quasiparticles increases. The very concept of quasiparticles loses its meaning. Therefore it is clear that not all motions of atomic particles in condensed media can be described in terms of quasiparticles. For example, quasiparticles are unsuitable for describing self-diffusion (the random wandering of atoms through a crystal).

However, even at low temperatures not all possible motions in a condensed medium can be described by means of quasiparticles. Although all atoms of a body generally take part in an elementary excitation, the excitation is microscopic: the energy and momentum of each quasiparticle are of atomic scale, and every quasiparticle moves independently of the others. The atoms and electrons in a condensed medium may take part in a motion of a totally different nature, a motion that is essentially macroscopic (hydrodynamic motion), but the medium does not lose its quantum properties. Examples of such motions are superfluid motion in helium II and the electric current in superconductors. The distinguishing feature here is the strict coordination (coherence) of the motion of the individual particles.

The concept of quasiparticles has found application not only in solid-state theory and in the theory of liquid helium but also in other fields of physics, such as the theory of the atomic nucleus, plasma theory, and astrophysics.

Phonons. In a crystal, the atoms perform small oscillations that propagate through the crystal in wave form. At low temperatures, longwave acoustic oscillations—ordinary sound waves, which have the lowest energy—play the primary role. The quasiparticles corresponding to the waves of atomic displacements are called phonons. Phonons are bosons; the number of phonons at low temperatures T increases in proportion to T^3. This fact, which is connected with the linear dependence of the energy of a phonon $\mathcal{E}_{ph}$ on its quasimomentum $\mathbf{p}$ when the quasimomentum is sufficiently small ($\mathcal{E}_{ph} = sp$, where s is the speed of sound), explains why the specific heat of nonmetallic crystals is proportional to T^3 at low temperatures.

Phonons in superfluid helium. The ground state of helium resembles an extremely degenerate Bose gas. As in any fluid, sound waves (waves of density fluctuation) may propagate in helium. Sound waves are the only type of microscopic motion possible in helium near the ground state. Since in a sound wave the frequency ω is proportional to the wave vector k, $\omega = sk$, the corresponding phonons have the dispersion law $\mathcal{E} = sp$. As the momentum increases, the curve $\mathcal{E} = \mathcal{E}(p)$ deviates from linear behavior. Helium phonons also obey Bose statistics. The concept of the energy spectrum of helium as a phonon spectrum not only describes its thermodynamic properties, such as the dependence of the specific heat of helium on temperature, but also explains the phenomenon of superconductivity.

Magnons. In ferromagnetics and antiferromagnetics the spins of the atoms are strictly ordered at $T = 0°K$. The state of excitation of a magnetic system is associated with the deviation of the spin from the "correct" position. This deviation is not localized on a specific atom but rather is transmitted from atom to atom. The elementary excitation of a magnetic system assumes the form of a wave of spin-axis rotations (a spin wave), and the quasiparticle corresponding to it is called a magnon. Magnons are bosons. The energy of a magnon has a square-law dependence on the quasimomentum (in the case of low quasimomenta). This is reflected in the thermal and magnetic properties of ferromagnets and antiferromagnets (for example, at low temperatures the deviation of the magnetic moment of a ferromagnet from saturation varies as $T^{3/2}$). The high-frequency properties of ferromagnets and antiferromagnets are described in terms of magnon "creation."

Frenkel exciton. A Frenkel exciton is an elementary excitation of the electron system of an individual atom or molecule that propagates through the crystal in the form of a wave. Excitons usually have high energy (on an atomic scale), of the order of several electron volts. Therefore, the contribution of excitons to the thermal properties of solids is small. Excitons manifest themselves in the optical properties of crystals. The average number of excitons is usually very low; therefore, they may be described by classical Boltzmann statistics.

Conduction electrons and holes. In solid dielectrics and semiconductors elementary excitations caused by processes analogous to the ionization of an atom coexist with excitons. As a result of such "ionization" two independently propagating quasiparticles arise: a conduction electron and a hole (a deficiency of an electron in an atom). A hole behaves as a positively charged particle, although its motion is an electron charge exchange wave rather than the motion of a positive ion. Conduction electrons and holes are fermions. They are the carriers of electric current in a solid. Semiconductors whose "ionization" energy is low always have an appreciable number of conduction electrons and holes. The conductivity of semiconductors decreases with temperature, since the number of electrons and holes decreases as the temperature drops.

An electron and a hole, since they are attracted to each other, may form a Mott exciton (quasiatom), which is manifested in the optical spectra of crystals as hydrogen-like absorption lines.

Polarons. The interaction of an electron with lattice vibrations leads to polarization of the lattice near the electron. The interaction of the electron and the crystal lattice is sometimes so strong that the motion of the electrons through the crystal is accompanied by a polarization wave. The corresponding quasiparticle is called a polaron.

Conduction electrons in metals. The conduction electrons of a metal, which interact with each other and with the ionic field of a crystal lattice, are equivalent to a quasiparticle gas with a complicated dispersion law. The charge of each quasiparticle is equal to the charge of a free electron, and the spin is equal to 1/2. Their dynamic properties, which are due to the dispersion law, differ significantly from the properties of ordinary free electrons. Conduction electrons are fermions. In quasimomentum space at $T = 0°K$ they fill a region bounded by a Fermi surface. The excitation of conduction electrons signifies the appearance of a pair: an electron "above" the Fermi surface and a vacant site (hole) "below" the surface. An electron gas is strongly degenerate not only at low temperatures but also at room temperature. This determines the temperature dependence of most of the characteristics of a metal (in particular, the linear dependence of specific heat on temperature when $T \to 0°$).

REFERENCES
Landau, L. D., and E. M. Lifshits. *Statisticheskaia fizika,* 2nd ed. Moscow, 1964.
Ziman, J. *Printsipy teorii tverdogo tela.* Moscow, 1966. (Translated from English.)
Lifshits, I. M. "Kvazichastitsy v sovremennoi fizike." In the collection *V glub' atoma.* Moscow, 1964.
Reif, F. "Sverkhtekuchest' i 'Kvazichastitsy.'" In the collection *Kvantovaia makrofizika.* Moscow, 1967. (Translated from English.)

M. I. KAGANOV [11–1685–3]

QUASI-STATIC PROCESS, equilibrium process, the infinitely slow transition of a thermodynamic system from one equilibrium state to another, in which the physical state of the system at any given moment differs infinitesimally from the equilibrium state.

Equilibrium in a system in a quasi-static process is established many times more rapidly than change in the physical parameters of the system. Any quasi-static process is reversible. Quasi-static processes play an important role in thermodynamics, since thermodynamic cycles including only quasi-static processes yield maximum work values. The term "quasi-static process" was proposed in 1909 by C. Caratheodory. [11–1684–1]

QUASI-STATIONARY CURRENT, an alternating current that varies relatively slowly and whose instantaneous values obey the laws of direct currents with reasonable precision (direct proportionality between current and voltage—Ohm's law, Kirchhoff's law).

Like direct current, a quasi-stationary current has the same current strength in all sections of a nonbranching circuit. However, when making calculations (in contrast to direct-current circuit calculations) it is necessary to take into account the electromotive force induced when the current varies. The inductance, capacitance, and resistance of the branches in a circuit with a quasi-stationary current can be treated as lumped parameters.

Certain conditions must be met for a given alternating current to be regarded as a quasi-stationary current. In the case of sinusoidal alternating current, this means that the geometric dimensions of the electric circuit must be small in comparison to the wavelength of the current under consideration. Commercial-frequency currents can generally be treated as quasi-stationary (a frequency of 50 hertz corresponds to a wavelength of ~6,000 km). The currents in long-distance power-transmission lines, where the above condition is not satisfied, are an exception. [11–1685–1]

QUASI-STATIONARY PROCESS, a process in a limited system that spreads within the system so quickly that in the time required for it to expand to the limits of the system its state does not have time to change.

In examining a quasi-stationary process it is possible therefore to disregard the time required for it to spread through the system. For example, if a variable external electromotive force is at work in some section of a closed electric circuit but the time required for the electro-magnetic field to spread to the remotest points of the circuit is so short that the amplitude of the electromotive force does not have a chance to change appreciably, then the changes in voltages and currents in the circuit may be considered a quasi-stationary process. The variable electric and magnetic fields generated by the electric charges (whose distribution and velocities change with time) moving in the circuit prove to be the same at each instant as for stationary electric and magnetic fields (the fields of stationary charges and currents), whose distribution and velocities (which do not change in time) coincide with those of the charges present in the system at the instant under consideration.

However, in the case of nonstationary currents, eddy fields induced by changes in the magnetic fields arise in addition to the electric fields of the charges. The effect of these fields can be taken into account by introducing the induced electromotive force (in addition to the electromotive force of nonelectromagnetic origin from the sources). The introduction of the induced electromotive force does not violate the main feature of stationary currents—the equality of current intensities in all sections of a nonbranching circuit. For this reason, Kirchhoff's laws are valid for electric circuits satisfying the conditions of the quasi-stationary (quasi-stationary currents).

The conditions defining quasi-stationary processes can be formulated most simply for the case of periodic processes. Processes may be considered quasi-stationary if the propagation time between the points of the system under consideration that are most remote from each other is short in comparison to the duration of the process or if the distance between these points is small in comparison to the corresponding wavelength (which amounts to the same thing).

The concept of quasi-stationary processes may also be applied to other systems (for example, mechanical and thermodynamic). If, for example, one end of an elastic rod is acted on by a variable external force directed along the rod, and if the process is quasi-stationary, that is, if the magnitude of the force does not have time to change during the period required for a longitudinal elastic wave to spread from one end of the rod to the other, then the accelerations of all points in the rod at each instant are determined by the value of the force at the same instant. The process of thermal conductivity may be considered quasi-stationary if equalization of the temperature in the heat-conducting rod takes place much more rapidly than does the change in external conditions—the temperatures T_1 and T_2 of the ends of the rod.
[11–1684–2]

QUATRAIN, an individual stanza of four lines. The rhyming pattern in a quatrain is abab (alternating rhyme), aabb (plain rhyme), or abba (enclosing rhyme). Persian poetry and its imitations use the form aaba, and less frequently, aaaa.

The quatrain is used for inscriptions, epitaphs, epigrams, and apothegms. The four-line stanzas of sonnets are also called quatrains. The following poem by F. I. Tiutchev is an example of a quatrain as an independent verse:

> *Nam ne dano preduagadat'*
> *Kak slovo nashe otzovetsia—*
> *I nam sochuvstvie daetsia,*
> *kak nam daetsia blagodat' . . . .*

> We are not given to foresee
> What reaction our words will cause—
> So we are given sympathy
> As if we were given divine grace. . . .

[11–1596–2]

QUATREFAGES DE BRÉAU, JEAN LOUIS ARMAND DE. Born Feb. 10, 1810, in Berthezène; died Jan. 12, 1892, in Paris. French zoologist, embryologist, and anthropologist. Member of the Paris Academy of Sciences (1852).

Quatrefages was professor of zoology at the universities of Toulouse and Paris. From 1855 he was head of the chair of anthropology and ethnology at the Museum of Natural History in Paris. The author of monographs on diseases of the silkworm (1858) and the natural history of annalid worms (1865), he also published (together with the anthropologist E. T. Hamy) an album of human races. His extensive researches served as the basis for concepts of the evolution of the organic world, although he was an opponent of Darwin's doctrine of evolution. Quatre-

fages placed man in a separate "kingdom" and denied man's genetic kinship with the animal world.

WORKS
Histoire naturelle des annelés marins et d'eau douce: Annelides et géphyriens, vols. 1–2. Paris, 1865.
Crania ethnica: Les crânes des races humaines . . . , vols. 1–2 and an atlas. Paris, 1882. (With E. T. Hamy.)
L'Espèce humaine, 8th ed. Paris, 1886.
In Russian translation:
Metamorfozy cheloveka i zhivotnykh. Moscow, 1864. [11–1596–4]

QUATREMÈRE, ÉTIENNE MARC. Born July 12, 1782, in Paris; died there Sept. 18, 1857. French Oriental scholar.

In 1815, Quatremère became a member of the Academy of Inscriptions and a professor of Greek literature at the University of Rouen. In 1819 he became a professor of Semitic languages at the Collège de France and later a professor of Persian at the School of Living Oriental Languages. Quatremère is best known for his critical editions of the works of Ibn Khaldun, Rashid ad-Din, and Maqrizi; he also wrote a number of works on history, historical geography, and Eastern literature, particularly the literature of Egypt. [11–1596–3]

QUOTATION MARKS, paired punctuation marks used in a text to set off direct speech, citations, and titles, as well as words and expressions used in an ironic sense or in an unusual meaning. Quotation marks are represented graphically in two forms: guillemets, or French quotation marks (« »), and double commas, or German quotation marks („ "). In addition to these forms, single quotation marks (' ') are sometimes used to denote the translation of a foreign word—for example, German *Tisch,* 'table.' [11–361–1]

REED BOARD, an insulating material of panels pressed from reed stalks and fastened together with galvanized steel wire.

The reed board used in the USSR is 2,400–2,800 mm long, 500–1,150 mm wide, and 50–100 mm thick. The volumetric weight is 175–400 kg per cu m; the limit of strength when flexed is 18–50 meganewtons per sq m; the coefficient of thermal conductivity is 0.04–0.07 watts per (m · degrees Kelvin); and the moisture content does not exceed 18 percent. Reed board is used primarily in farm construction for insulating enclosures and filling the framework walls of low housing and production buildings. [11–859–4]

REGULAR ARMY SYSTEM, a system used in the armed forces to maintain minimum cadres in peacetime while allowing the rapid buildup of army units to war strength during mobilizations by calling up trained reserve contingents. The system exists in all modern states. Under the regular army system the soldiers and most of the sergeants (noncommissioned officers) are in active military service for the term established by law, after which they are placed in reserve and remain liable for military service until they reach some maximum age. The regular army system may use a territorial, extraterritorial, or mixed principle to build up the forces by drafted contingents.

The regular army system was introduced in Prussia in 1814, and in the middle of the 19th century it was gradually adopted by other countries, including Russia, France, Austria-Hungary, Italy, and Japan. On the basis of this system millions of men were drafted in World War I and World War II.

The Red Army was originally composed of volunteers. From the summer of 1918 the regular army system was used to build up a regular Red Army on a mass scale. The decree entitled The Organization of Territorial Troop Units and the Military Training of the Toiling Masses was issued in 1923, and the armed forces were placed on the territorial regular army system in 1924–25. This policy made it possible to meet defense needs at a time when the country's budget was limited. In combination with the territorial-militia system the necessary number of divisions with an administrative apparatus could be maintained as a nucleus for the rapid deployment of troops without withdrawing more than a minimum of the work force from industry and agriculture. In the 1930's, with the threat of an impending military attack on the USSR, the territorial regular system of the armed forces no longer satisfied the needs of state defense. Between 1935 and 1938 the territorial regular army system was replaced by the unified regular army system of the Soviet armed forces, which was provided for by the Law on Universal Military Service of Sept. 1, 1939, and confirmed by the Law on Universal Military Service of Oct. 12, 1967.

V. V. GRADOSEL'SKII [11–383–5]

RELIEF MAPS, maps that show the relief of the earth's surface or of the ocean floor. The most common and important relief maps are hypsometric, bathymetric, and geomorphological maps. Besides these there are morphometric maps, which directly show the amount (intensity) and depth of dissection of the terrain as well as the steepness of the slopes. The average width of the elementary drainage basin is usually taken as the index of the amount of dissection of the terrain. The depth of dissection is determined by the average relative elevation of water divides above the level of rivers and lakes.

Less common types are morphographic maps, which show external relief in three dimensions, and physiographic maps, on which relief is indicated by perspective designations in the areas of certain types of terrain. Physiographic maps have been developed most extensively in the United States.

IU. G. KEL'NER [11–1450–2]

REMOTE CONTROL CHANNEL, a combination of devices used to transmit remote control, telemetry, and remote signal information between distant transmitting and receiving points. The remote control channel is a variety of communication channel; it consists of an information source (transducer), a coding device, a transmitter, a communication link, a receiver, and a decoding device. It is usually designed on the multichannel principle; that is, it is made up of several channels. Information is transmitted over such a channel only after preliminary processing, encoding, and modulation, especially when there is interference. The information is recovered at the receiving end by decoding or demodulation. The coded (modulated) information in the form of discrete or continuous signals is transmitted over radio channels, wire lines, or relay links.

An example of a remote control channel is the system, with signals transmitted by radio, for artificial earth satellites and unmanned lunar stations.

REFERENCES
Vasil'ev, R. R., and G. A. Shastova. *Peredacha telemekhanicheskoi informatsii.* Moscow-Leningrad, 1960.
Velichkin, A. I. *Teoriia diskretnoi peredachi nepreryvnykh soobshchenii.* Moscow, 1970.
M. M. GEL'MAN [11–929–3]

RETROFLEX CONSONANTS, front consonants in the formation of which the tip of the tongue is raised and curved upward while the anterior part of the dorsum is bent inward (for example, in the Russian *r* and *sh*). [11–556–1]

RHYNCHITES BACCHUS, a beetle of the family Curculionidae (weevils), a pest of seed and amygdalaceous fruit crops. The golden-scarlet body is 4.5–6.5 mm long, has a violet-green metallic sheen, and is covered with brown hairs; there are longitudinal punctate grooves on the elytra.

This beetle is found in central and southern Europe and Asia. In the USSR it does great damage to plums, apricots, and apples in Krasnodar Krai, Rostov Oblast, Moldavia, and the forest-steppe and steppe of the Ukraine. It develops over a period of one to two years. The beetles damage buds, leaves, flower buds and flowers, and fruits and foster the spread of fungi of the genus *Monilia*—the causative agents of fruit rot. The larvae feed on tissue affected with brown fruit rot and burrow in the flesh of fruits, which gradually shrivel up and mummify. Control measures consist in treating crops with insecticides, shaking down the beetles onto screens (on orchards near farms), gathering and removing windfall, and controlling fruit rot. [11–414–1]

RING-TAILED LEMUR (*Lemur catta*), a lemuroid. The body is approximately 40 cm long; the tail, approximately 55 cm. The top of the body and head are gray; the underparts are whitish.

There are 15–16 black rings on the tail. The male has a scent gland on its shoulder and a second one on its forearm, next to a double horny spur and a bundle of tactile hairs (vibrissae). The ring-tailed lemur lives in open areas in the southwestern part of the island of Madagascar; it is a good rock-climber. It is diurnal. Ring-tailed lemurs are found in groups of five to 20 individuals. They feed on figs, plantains, and other fruits. They are easily tamed and bear young in captivity.

REFERENCE
Zhizn' zhivotnykh, vol. 6. Moscow, 1971. [11–1597–2]

ROAD ROLLER (compactor), a machine for compacting earth, road foundations, and road surfaces by rolling. Road rollers are used in road, railroad, industrial, mining, hydraulic-engineering, and airfield construction.

Road rollers can be either self-propelled or drawn; in their operating principle they can be static or vibrating. The working parts of a road roller are rigid steel drums. The surfaces of the drums can be flat or with a grid or cams (lugs). The rigid drums in certain designs have been replaced by pneumatic tires. Tractor-drawn rollers with flat drums (static and vibration action), cams, and balloon-tired rollers are used to compact earth and road foundations. The self-propelled rollers with flat drums (two-drum or three-drum, static or vibration action) and with balloon tires are used chiefly for compacting road surfaces. The efficiency of compacting depends on the specific pressure on the surface; the weight of the roller is increased by using ballast (reinforced-concrete blocks or containers with sand). The weight of a road roller is from 5 to 50 tons, and it operates at a speed of 2–8 km/hr.

IU. A. BROMBERG [11–1585–1]

ROCK PICKER, a mounted or pulled machine for picking up rocks in clearing farmlands, building roads and hydroengineering projects, and doing other jobs.

In the USSR rock pickers are produced to pull up, pull up and load, collect and haul, or just haul rocks. For pulling-up work, there are rock pullers that can remove rocks with a weight of up to 10 tons when shoved by a tractor or when equipped with a double-arm lever. For pulling up stones and loading them into transportation vehicles, puller-loaders are used; these can pull up stones weighing up to 10 tons and load stones with a weight of up to 3 tons into transport up to 2 m high. Small and medium-size stones (with diameters from 12 to 65 cm and weights of 20–300 kg) are picked up from the ground with the comb of a UKP-0.6 machine, which drops them into the hopper of a machine. After the hopper is full, the machine is transported to the unloading area. The productivity of the rock picker is 2–3 cu m of stones per hour. Stones weighing up to 250 kg can be picked up and removed from the field with the UKS-0.7 rock picker, which has a serrated bucket with a clam-shell clamp. The productivity of the rock picker is 0.8–1.0 cu m per hr. Small stones (with diameters of 5–30 cm) are picked up by a continuous-action machine with a device for removing the stones from the soil and a separator for sifting the soil. A self-unloading sled or a dump trailer with a capacity of up to 6 tons is used for hauling the stones from the field. [11–831–1]

ROCK SALT, halite, table salt. (1) The mineral halite, or, in terms of chemical composition, sodium chloride, NaCl (39.34 percent Na and 60.66 percent Cl). Rock salt crystallizes in a cubic system. In nature it is ordinarily encountered in granular crystalline aggregates of varying size. In pure form it is colorless and semitransparent, but more often it is found with admixtures of clay, organic matter, and iron oxide, which tint the halite gray, brown, red, or pink. The hardness on the mineralogical scale is 2; the density is 2.173 kg per cu m. Rock salt is easily soluble in water. There is significant absorption of heat when it is dissolved. Halite that is dissolved or melted (at 772°C) is characterized by high electrical conductivity. It possesses antiseptic properties, protecting saturated organic tissues against putrefactive decomposition.

(2) A sedimentary rock composed almost exclusively or predominantly of halite (in pure varieties, 99 percent or more). The impurity, when present, is usually clay or, less often, fine

sandy material, which is either finely dispersed through the rock or in the form of intercalations, seams, or galls. In the clay intercalations or along the periphery of the halite grains (occasionally inside) there are carbonates, anhydrite, authigenic quartz, clay minerals, and, less often, potassium minerals.

A considerable amount of the sodium chloride found in nature has been dissolved in the water of the seas and oceans. Most rock salt, like other salts that have been dissolved in water, was formed through exogenic processes in the basins of arid zones with a negative water balance. Rock salt is produced in small quantities through volcanic activity, in solonchaks, and as a weathering product of chlorine-containing minerals. Rock salt occurs in sedimentary rock in the form of thick seams that extend for dozens of sq km. It also forms cores of domelike structures (salt-dome tectonics) and intercalations, galls, pockets, and impregnations. Mineral deposits of rock salt are encountered in deposits of almost all geological periods. The greatest quantity of salt-bearing rock is concentrated in deposits of the Lower Cambrian, the Middle and Upper Devonian, the Permian, and the Myocene.

Recent salt deposits (native salt; Lakes Baskunchak and El'ton), associated with Permian salt stocks, are of great industrial interest in the USSR. The largest deposits are located in the Byelorussian SSR (Starobin and Davydovka), the Ukrainian SSR (Solotvin, Romny, Slaviansk and Artemovsk), the Urals (Solikamsk and Shumkovo), the Caspian depression and the adjacent Bashkir and Orenburg-Aktiubinsk salt basins, and Middle Asia. Abroad, rock salt is found in Poland, the German Democratic Republic, the Federal Republic of Germany, Switzerland, Italy, Great Britain, the United States, Canada, and India.

Rock salt deposits are worked by the underground method (with the chamber system) and by leaching. The rock salt, which is pumped out of the deposits through pipes as brine, is evaporated in special vacuum devices (vacuum salt). A considerable amount of the salt (native salt) in the USSR is also obtained by evaporation from salt lakes and salt springs. Rock salt is widely used in the national economy. Purified, it is a very important food product and preservative; it is also used in refrigeration. The chemical industry uses rock salt to produce compounds of sodium or chlorine (ammonium chloride, soda ash, gaseous chlorine, hydrochloric acid, ammonium hydroxide, calcium chloride). Rock salt is used in the aniline dye, paint and varnish, wood chemical, nitrogen, textile, pharmaceutical, metallurgical, leather, petroleum, and plastics industries. Large semi-transparent crystals of rock salt are used in optical instruments.

REFERENCES
Ivanov, A. A., and Iu. F. Levitskii. *Geologiia galogennykh otlozhenii (formatsii) SSSR.* Moscow, 1960.
Valiashko, M. G. *Geokhimicheskie zakonomernosti formirovaniia mestorozhdenii kaliinykh solei.* Moscow, 1962.
Ivanov, A. A., and M. L. Voronova. *Galogennye formatsii.* Moscow, 1972.   A. B. Pavlovskii [11–745–1]

ROCK SPARROW (*Petronia petronia*), a bird of the family Ploceidae of the order Passeriformes, similar in size and plumage to the female house sparrow. Its distinctive features are white spots on the tail feathers and a yellow spot on the throat. It is widespread in southern Europe, Asia, and North Africa. In the USSR rock sparrows are found in the Caucasus, the lower Volga region, Kazakhstan, Middle Asia, and southern Siberia. It inhabits mountains, ravines, steppes, or rocky hills and may sometimes be found near settlements. It nests on cliffs, among piles of rocks, and similar places. The clutch contains four to six speckled eggs. The rock sparrow feeds on seeds and insects, migrating from mountains to valleys in the winter.

[11–786–1]

ROCK STREAMS, accumulations of detrital rock that move slowly along the ravines of mountain slopes, primarily by gravity. They are most characteristic of areas with severe continental climates. Rock streams begin from rock placers that cover flat mountain peaks. They sometimes stretch for several kilometers along the floors of valleys and depressions.   [11–768–1]

ROCK THRUSHES, two related genera of songbirds (*Monticola* and *Orocetes*) of the family Turdidae. They are somewhat smaller than starlings. In the male plumage red or chestnut brown colors are combined with blue-gray and light blue; the females and young are brownish. There are ten species, found throughout Africa, southern Europe, and Asia. In the USSR there are three species, of which *Monticola saxatilis* may be found in Moldavia, the southern Ukraine, including the Crimea, the Caucasus, and Middle Asia. It inhabits unforested cliff areas, building its nest among rocks (the clutch has four to six eggs). It feeds on insects, sometimes berries. The species *M. solitarius* is found in the Caucasus, Middle Asia, and the southern Primor'e. The species *Orocetes gularis* inhabits the forests of southeastern Transbaikalia, the Amur, and Primor'e. It nests on the ground and in tree hollows with the clutch containing five to eight eggs.   [11–761–3]

ROLLING OF A SHIP, rocking of a floating vessel caused by waves or other external forces.

The three types of rolling are normal rolling (inclination from port to starboard), pitching (inclination from bow to stern), and heaving (translational displacement in the vertical direction). Simultaneous pitching and heaving in the same or opposite direction as the waves is called fore-and-aft rolling; simultaneous rolling and heaving with lateral choppiness is called transverse rolling. All types of rolling usually occur simultaneously. Rolling is characterized by amplitude, period (frequency), and phase shift of the oscillations relative to the external force. Resonance may be observed during rolling.

Rolling causes a reduction in the velocity of the ship, negatively affects the human organism (seasickness), and adversely affects the working of machinery and instruments and the utilization of military equipment. During intense rolling, the ship may capsize because of external loads not dangerous in the absence of rolling. Moderation in rolling is one of the most important features of the seaworthiness of a ship. The longer the period and the smaller the amplitude of rolling, the better the seaworthiness. Ship stabilizers are installed to control rolling. The fundamentals of the general theory of rolling were developed by Academician A. N. Krylov.

REFERENCES
Semenov–Tian-Shanskii, V. V., S. N. Blagoveshchenskii, and A. N. Kholodilin. *Kachka korablia.* Leningrad, 1969.
Borodai, I. K., and Iu. A. Netsvetaev. *Kachka sudov na morskom volnenii.* [Leningrad, 1969.]   L. N. Streliaev [11–1646–3]

ROLL PASS DESIGNING (pass designing, sizing), a set of methods for determining the dimensions, shape, number, and type of arrangement of rolling mill passes. Roll pass designing also includes the calculation of pressing forces and their distribution on the roll passes. Only section iron is rolled between the shaped rolls. Sheets and wide strips are pressed between rollers with a smooth cylindrical or barrel-shaped surface. Several passes are made for each section; a square or round billet acquires a specified form on each successive passage. The roll passes are designed to avoid excessive stresses in the metal being rolled, since such stresses could lead to the formation of cracks and other flaws.   [11–593–2]

ROOT-MEAN-SQUARE DEVIATION. The root-mean-square (rms) deviation of the quantities $x_1, x_2, \ldots, x_n$ from a is the square root of the expression

$$\frac{(x_1 - a)^2 + (x_2 - a)^2 + \cdots + (x_n - a)^2}{n}$$

The rms deviation has its least value when $a = \bar{x}$, where $\bar{x}$ is the arithmetic mean of the quantities $x_1, x_2, \ldots, x_n$:

$$\bar{x} = \frac{x_1 + x_2 + \cdots + x_n}{n}$$

In this case the rms deviation may serve as a measure of the dispersion of the system of quantities $x_1, x_2, \ldots, x_n$. The more general concept of weighted rms deviation

$$\sqrt{[p_1(x_1 - a)^2 + \cdots + p_n(x_n - a)^2]/(p_1 + \cdots + p_n)}$$

is also used; $p_1, \ldots, p_n$ in this case are called the weights corresponding to the quantities $x_1, \ldots, x_n$. The weighted rms deviation attains its least value when a is equal to the weighted mean:

$$(p_1x_1 + \cdots + p_nx_n)/(p_1 + \cdots + p_n)$$

In probability theory the weighted rms deviation σ_x of a random variable X (from its mathematical expectation) is the square root of the variance $\sqrt{D(X)}$, and is called the standard deviation of X.

The standard deviation is used as a measure of the quality of statistical estimates and in this case is called the standard error.
[11–1675–1]

ROPEWALKER, a circus performer who demonstrates the art of balancing on a rope secured between two points of support.

Ropewalkers have been known since antiquity (Rome, China, Persia). In the Middle Ages the art spread to Middle Asia, the Caucasus, the European countries, and, later, South America. The Russian ropewalker F. F. Molodtsov, who performed during the second half of the 19th century, was known for outstanding feats (for example, crossing the Neva and the Thames on a tightrope). At the end of the 19th century the hemp rope, used originally, was replaced with a steel wire, making it possible for several artists to perform on the rope at the same time. The best known Soviet ropewalkers are the Svirins and the Tarasovs (1920's–50's), the Khibins (1940's–50's), the Volzhanskii family (1950's–70's), the Uzbek Tashkenbaev family (1940's–70's), and the Dagestan Tsovkra group (1930's–70's).   [11–949–1]

ROSIN (or colophony), a brittle, vitreous substance varying in color from light yellow to dark red; one of the resinous substances found in pine trees and obtained in the form of residue following distillation of the volatile part from these substances. Rosin has a density of 1.07–1.085 g/cm^3 and a softening point of 52°–70°C. A poor conductor of heat and electricity, it dissolves readily in ether and alcohol but is insoluble in water. It is composed of resin acids (80–95 percent) of the general formula $C_{19}H_{29}COOH$ and of neutral unsaponifiable substances (5–12 percent).

Rosin is classified according to the type of raw material and to the method of preparation as follows: gum rosin (obtained by distillation of turpentine oil from refined turpentine), wood rosin (obtained by extraction of wood chips from tarred pine stumps using organic solvents, primarily gasoline), and tall oil rosin (obtained by fractional distillation of crude tall oil, a product of sulfate soap refining). Rosin and its derivatives are used in sizing paper and cardboard; as emulsifiers in the manufacture of synthetic rubbers, elastics, plastics, artificial leathers, linoleums, soap, varnishes, paints, and electrical insulating mastics and compounds; and as a flux in the tinning and soldering of metals.

REFERENCES
Vasechkin, V. S. *Tekhnologiia ekstraktivnykh veshchestv dereva.* Moscow-Leningrad, 1953.
Komshilov, N. F. *Kanifol', ee sostav i stroenie smolianykh kislot.* Moscow, 1965.   P. P. POLIAKOV [11–971–3]

ROTARY CASTING MACHINE, a device for pouring liquified metal into molds.

The rotary casting machine was proposed in 1897 by the American metallurgist A. Walker. It is widely used in nonferrous metallurgy for casting nickel and copper anodes, commercial lead and zinc ingots, and wirebars (bars made of electrochemically purified copper, used mainly for the production of wire).

The working section of the rotary casting machine consists of a round turntable with supports upon which the molds are set. The molds are arranged radially in the rotary casting machines used for the production of anodes and ingots; in machines producing wirebars the arrangement may be either radial or tangential. The tangential arrangement makes continuous copper casting possible, ensuring ingots of higher quality. The metal is poured into the molds with a casting ladle. When the turntable

rotates, the melt enters a water-cooled zone to be cooled. In anode rotary casting machines, the hardened anodes are removed from the turntable by a special device (stripper) and sent to a water tank for final cooling, while the empty molds are sprayed with milk of lime (in order to prevent the copper from sticking) and are readied again for pouring. Rotary casting machines for wirebars operate similarly to those designed for anode production, differing only in that the ingots are removed by tipping over the molds into a water-filled sump. The wirebars proceed from the sump to a discharge conveyer. Machines for casting lead and zinc are equipped with an ingot-stamping mechanism, stackers, and a device for removing the oxide film from the surface of the zinc melt.

In the USSR the output of rotary casting machines is as high as 50 tons of ingots per hour. In a number of zinc plants the machines are equipped with an automatic device for laying the zinc ingots in stacks and binding them.
                    K. S. D'IAKONOV [11–1453–4]

ROTARY FURNACE, an industrial furnace through which the items being heated are transported on a rotating disk sole.

Rotary furnaces are used in mass production to heat small metal billets before forging. The rotary furnace is similar in design to the ring furnace and differs only in the shape of the rotating sole and the working space. Articles are loaded and discharged through a single window, usually by hand. The outer diameter of the rotary furnace is up to 5 m. The output is up to 5 tons per hour. The furnace is heated by gas or liquid-fuel burners at the furnace wall.
                    [11–1453–3]

RUBBER, NATURAL, caoutchouc, crude rubber, a polymer of plant origin, the vulcanization of which produces processed rubber.

Natural rubber is one of the elastomers, a group of macromolecular compounds that possess the capacity for considerable reversible deformation at room temperatures and lower. Natural rubber is contained primarily in the milky sap, or latex, of rubber-bearing plants, individual inclusions also being found in the cells of the bark and leaves. Natural rubber is obtained primarily from the latex of the Para rubber tree (*Hevea brasiliensis*), which is grown on plantations in tropical countries. Malaysia is the largest producer of natural rubber (more than 40 percent of world production).

The name "caoutchouc" derives from *cauchu*, which the inhabitants of Brazil applied to the product obtained from the Para rubber tree, which grows naturally on the banks of the Amazon River (from *cau*, "tree," and *uchu*, "to leak" or "to cry"). The history of natural rubber is usually taken as beginning in 1738, when the French researcher C. de la Condamine presented to the Academy of Sciences in Paris specimens of caoutchouc, articles made from it, and a description of the methods used in South America to obtain it. The industrial use of natural rubber became possible after the discovery of the process of vulcanization (C. Goodyear in the United States in 1839 and T. Hancock in Great Britain in 1843). Basic data on the structure of natural rubber were obtained beginning in the 1870's by G. Bouchardat, H. Staudinger, and the German scientist C. Harries. Extensive research on the vulcanization of natural rubber was carried out by B. V. Byzov, B. A. Dogadkin, I. I. Ostromyslenskii, and the American scientist E. H. Farmer. The Soviet scientists A. P. Aleksandrov, V. A. Kargin, and P. P. Kobeko and the American researchers E. Guth, L. R. G. Treloar, and F. T. Wall have investigated the physical properties of natural rubber and developed a theory of its elasticity.

The latex is extracted by tapping the bark of the tree. The natural rubber is isolated by coagulation with formic, oxalic, or acetic acid. The loose mass (coagulum) that forms is washed with water and rolled on a mill, producing sheets that are then dried and usually smoked in special chambers. Smoking makes the natural rubber resistant to oxidation and microorganisms.

According to the International Standard for Quality and Packing (1969), natural rubber is divided into eight international types, including 35 international grades. The basic types of natural rubber are ribbed smoked sheet (a product of light amber color) and pale crepe (a product of light creamy color; special bleaching agents, such as sodium bisulfite, are added to the latex before isolation and the rubber is not smoked). The quality of natural rubber of international types and grades is judged both by external examination and by comparison with a standard. There is also a system of classification for technical standards that regulates the content of impurities in the rubber. Along with general-purpose natural rubber, special types of rubber are also produced (for example, with improved technical or mechanical properties, prepared in a powderlike form).

Extensive experimental work and research is being carried out with the object both of improving the quality of natural rubber and of raising the productivity of rubber-bearing plants.

The principal component of natural rubber is the rubber hydrocarbon (91–96 percent), a polyisoprene with the general formula $(C_5H_8)_n$. Natural rubber also contains 2.2–3.8 percent proteins and amino acids; 1.5–4.0 percent acetone-soluble substances (acetone extracts: oleic acid, stearic acid, linoleic acid, carotene); compounds of metals of variable valence, such as copper (to 0.0008 percent), manganese (to 0.001 percent), iron (to 0.01 percent); and sand and certain impurities. Natural rubber is one of the stereoregular polymers; 98–100 percent of the isoprene monomers in its macromolecule are joined in the cis = 1, 4 configuration:

The molecular weight of natural rubber is between 1.4 million and 2.6 million, and the content of double bonds in the macromolecule comes to 95–98.5 percent of the theoretical value. The density is 0.91–0.92 g per cu cm; the refractive index, 1.5191; the glass transition temperature, from $-70°$ to $-72°C$; the specific heat, 1.880 kilojoules per (kg · °K)[0.449 calories per (g°C)]; the thermal conductivity, 0.14 watts per (m · °K) [0.12 kilocalories per (m · hour · °C)]; the dielectric constant at a frequency of 1 kilohertz, 2.37–2.45; and the specific electric conductivity, $25.7 \cdot 10^{-18}$ ohm^{-1} · cm^{-1}.

Rubber is unaffected by water but easily soluble in benzene, toluene, xylene, gasoline, carbon tetrachloride, chloroform, carbon disulfide, and cyclohexane. It is amorphous at temperatures above 10°C. Prolonged storage at lower temperatures or stretching at room temperatures cause its partial crystallization. Among the valuable properties of natural rubber is its high cohesive strength; to a large extent it is this property that has made natural rubber irreplaceable in the production of certain tire parts. A production drawback of natural rubber, related to its high molecular weight, is the necessity of mastication before introducing the ingredients of the rubber stock.

Sulfur is the most widely used vulcanizing agent for natural rubber. Vulcanization accelerators include 2-mercaptobenzothiazole (Kaptaks), its sulfenamide derivatives (for example, Santokiur), dibenzthiazyl disulfide (Al'taks), and tetramethylthiuram disulfide (thiram). Radiation vulcanization of natural rubber and vulcanization with organic peroxides or alkylphenol-formaldehyde resins are also possible.

Crystallization of natural rubber causes the high degree of strength in stretching vulcanized rubbers based on this process. Introducing active fillers hardly alters the strength of processed rubbers, but certain other mechanical properties rise substantially (see Table 1). Processed rubbers made from natural rubber are characterized by a high degree of elasticity, durability, and frost resistance, by high dynamic properties, and by a low level of resistance to solvents and oils and lower heat resistance and weather resistance than in certain synthetic rubbers.

Tire production is the principal consumer of natural rubber, which is also used in producing industrial articles (conveyer belts, transmission belts, shock absorbers, and seals), electric insulating materials, consumer goods, and rubber cements. A certain amount of natural rubber is also used in the form of latex. The volume of production of natural rubber came to about 3 million tons in 1971. Owing to the development of stereoregular synthetic rubbers and a wide assortment of special-purpose synthetic rubbers, the demand for natural rubber in certain industrial sectors is declining.

Table 1. Properties of processed natural rubbers

Indicator	Unfilled rubber	Rubber filled with channel black
Modulus at 500-percent elongation (meganewtons per sq m [kgf per sq cm])	1.5–4.5 (15–45)	12–22 (120–220)
Tensile strength (meganewtons per sq m [kgf per sq cm]) . . .	28–34 (280–340)	30–34 (300–340)
Aspect ratio (percent)	700–900	600–800
Tearing strength (kilonewtons per m [kgf per cm])	40–50	120–170
TM-2 (Shore) hardness	30–40	50–75

REFERENCES
Byzov, B. V. *Prirodnyi kauchuk.* Leningrad, 1932.
Dogadkin, B. A. *Khimiia elastomerov.* Moscow, 1972.
Spravochnik rezinshchika: Materialy rezinovogo proizvodstva. Moscow, 1971. Page 21.   [11–1617–4]

RUBBER, SYNTHETIC, synthetic polymers that, like natural rubber, can be converted to vulcanized rubber.

All synthetic rubbers are usually classified as general-purpose or special-purpose (see Table 1). General-purpose rubbers are used in the production of articles in which the basic property of vulcanized rubbers—that is, high elasticity at ordinary temperatures—is desirable (for example, tires, conveyer belts, and footwear). Special-purpose rubbers are used in producing articles that should be resistant to the action of solvents, oils, oxygen, ozone, heat, and frost—that is, able to retain high-elastic properties over a broad range of temperatures. The classification of synthetic rubbers according to use is to a degree arbitrary, since many rubbers possess a range of properties that make them suitable as both general-purpose and special-purpose material. On the other hand, special demands are sometimes placed on certain general-purpose articles, such as in the production of frost-resistant tires and oil-resistant and gasoline-resistant rubber footwear. Polymers called thermoelastic plastics have been developed that combine the properties of elastomers and thermoplastic polymers and that therefore can be processed into rubber articles while bypassing the vulcanization stage. The special groups of synthetic rubber include aqueous dispersions of rubber (latexes), liquid rubbers (oligomers, which harden with the formation of rubberlike materials), and filled rubbers (mixtures of synthetic rubbers with fillers and plasticizers and produced in the manufacture of synthetic rubbers).

The most widely used methods of producing synthetic rubbers are emulsion and stereospecific polymerization. Polymerization makes it possible to regulate the molecular weight of the rubbers. In processing the synthetic rubbers polymerization makes it possible to do without the energy-intensive stage of mastication. The production processes (in the majority of instances these are continuous) also include the stages of separating the rubber from the dispersions or solutions (for example, by coagulation or sedimentation), removing the residues of catalysts, emulsifiers, and other impurities from the rubber, drying, briquetting, and packaging. The most important monomers in the synthesis of rubbers—butadiene, isoprene, and styrene—are obtained primarily from casinghead-gas by-products and cracking gases. For example, butadiene can be obtained by the catalytic dehydrogenation of n-butane. In addition to these monomers, acrylonitrile, fluoroolefins, and certain silicone compounds can also be used.

The successful solution to the problem of the industrial synthesis of rubber is among the most important scientific and technical achievements of the 20th century. Rubber was synthesized for the first time in the world on a large industrial scale in the USSR in 1932, using a method developed by S. V. Lebedev—that is, the polymerization with metallic sodium of 1,3-butadiene obtained from ethyl alcohol to produce SKB sodium-butadiene rubber. The industrial production of butadiene-styrene rubbers was organized in Germany in 1938, and the large-scale production of synthetic rubbers was started in the United States in 1942. By 1972 more than 20 countries were producing synthetic rubbers. The USSR holds one of the leading places in terms of the production volume of synthetic rubbers.

World production of synthetic rubbers is growing rapidly. Whereas in 1950 synthetic rubbers constituted about 22 percent of the total production volume of all rubber in the capitalist

Kirpichnikov, P. A., L. A. Averko-Antonovich, and Iu. A. Averko-Antonovich. *Khimiia i tekhnologiia sinteticheskogo kauchuka.* Leningrad, 1970.
Dogadkin, B. A. *Khimiia elastomerov.* Moscow, 1972.
Spravochnik rezinshchika: Materialy rezinovogo proizvodstva. Moscow, 1971.
[11–1620–2]

Table 1. Major industrial synthetic rubbers

Name of rubbers and their Soviet abbreviations	Chemical composition	Special properties
General-purpose rubbers		
Butadiene, SKD	*Cis*-1,4-polybutadiene	—
Styrene-butadiene (α-methyl-styrene), SKS (SKMS)	Copolymers of butadiene and styrene (α-methylstyrene)	—
Isoprene, SKI	*Cis*-1,4-polyisoprene	—
Ethylene-propylene, SKEP	Copolymers of ethylene and propylene	Resistance to oxidation, chemicals, weather
SKEPT	Copolymers of ethylene, propylene, and third comonomer	Resistance to oxidation, chemicals, weather
Butyle rubber, BK	Copolymers of isobutylene and small quantities of isoprene	Impermeability to gases, weather resistance
Chloroprene (Nairit)	Polychloroprene	Satisfactory oil resistance and gasoline resistance
Special-purpose rubbers		
Butadiene nitrile, SKN	Copolymers of butadiene and acrylonitrile	Oil resistance, gasoline resistance
Polysulfide (Thiokol)	Polysulfides	Oil resistance, gasoline resistance
Silicone, SKT	Polyorganic siloxanes	Heat and frost resistance, high electric-isolating properties, physiological inertness
Fluorine-containing rubbers, SKF	Copolymers fluoro-olefins	Heat, oil, weather, and fire resistance, resistance to attack by aggressive media
Urethane, SKU	Polyurethanes	Great strength in stretching and wear
Chlorosulfonated polyethylene, KhSPE	Polyethylene containing chlorosulfonated groups	Weather resistance, heat resistance, durability

countries, in 1960 the figure was approximately 48 percent, and by 1973 it had risen to approximately 63 percent (that is, about 5.9 million tons of synthetic rubber and about 3.5 million tons of natural rubber). The intensive growth in the output of synthetic rubbers is explained by the significantly lower prime cost of production of the most widely used general-purpose rubbers (in particular, butadiene-styrene) in comparison to the prime cost of production of natural rubber, as well as by the impossibility of using natural rubber in certain special-purpose articles, such as heat, oil, and gasoline resistant items. The development of butadiene and isoprene stereoregular synthetic rubbers has also led to a relative decline in the demand for natural rubber, since the former are competitive with natural rubber in the production of certain tires (for example, for passenger cars).

There are around 50,000 listed processed-rubber products manufactured from synthetic rubbers. The largest consumer of synthetic rubbers is the tire industry, which accounts for more than 50 percent of the total volume of synthetic rubbers consumed. Technical progress in various areas of industry has confronted the synthetic rubber industry with the task of developing rubbers that will combine high heat resistance, resistance to ionizing radiation, and oil and gasoline resistance. This problem in particular can be solved by synthesizing rubbers from monomers that contain inorganic elements, such as boron, phosphorus, nitrogen, fluorine, and silicon.

REFERENCES

Whitby, G. S. [ed.]. *Sinteticheskii kauchuk.* Moscow-Leningrad, 1957. (Translated from English.)
Litvin, O. B. *Osnovy tekhnologii sinteza kauchukov.* Moscow, 1972.
Zhurnal Vsesoiuznogo khimicheskogo ob-va im. D. I. Mendeleeva, 1968, vol. 13, no. 1. (Issue devoted to the rubber industry.)

RUBBER-BEARING PLANTS, plants that form and contain natural rubber in certain of their parts.

Depending on the tissues in which the rubber accumulates, rubber-bearing plants are divided into latex plants (the rubber contained in a milky sap, or latex), parenchymal (in the parenchyma of the axial organs, the stems and roots), and chlorenchymal (in the green tissues of young shoots and leaves). Latex trees are of commercial importance, since they both store rubber in comparatively large quantities and surrender it easily. The most important of these plants is the Para rubber tree (*Hevea brasiliensis*), which provides 95 percent of the world's natural rubber. The remaining 5 percent is obtained from other tropical latex trees of the genera *Sapium* and *Manihot* (family Euphorbiaceae), *Ficus* and *Castilloa* (family Moraceae), and *Landolphia* (family Apocynaceae). The herbaceous latex-bearing plants of the family Compositae—the tau saghyz (*Scorzonera tau-saghyz*), the kok-saghyz (*Taraxacum kok-saghyz*), and the krym-saghyz (*T. gymnanthum*)—which grow in the temperate zone (including that of the USSR), contain small amounts of rubber in the roots. They are not cultivated, however, being commercially unimportant. The parenchymal rubber-bearing plants include the Mexican guayule (family Compositae). Chlorenchymal rubber-bearing plants (for example, a number of species of genera *Senecio* and *Centaurea*) are not used industrially.

REFERENCES

Il'in, M. M., and P. A. Iakimov. "Kauchukonosy i guttaperchenosy SSSR." In *Rastitel'noe syr'e SSSR,* vol. 1. Moscow-Leningrad, 1950. Pages 61–142.
Zhukovskii, P. M. *Kul'turnye rasteniia i ikh sorodichi,* 2nd ed. Leningrad, 1964.
Siniagin, I. I. *Tropicheskoe zemledelie.* Moscow, 1968.

Franke, G. *Nutzpflanzen der Tropen und Subtropen,* vol. 1. Leipzig, 1967.   V. N. VEKHOV [11–1623–2]

SAN JOSE SCALE (*Quadraspidiotus perniciosus*), an insect of the scale family of the order Homoptera; a quarantine pest.

The adult of the San Jose scale is covered with a bark-colored scutellum. In females the scutellum is round and about 2 mm in diameter; the body is round and lemon yellow in color and has no eyes, antennae, legs, or wings. In males the scutellum is about 1 mm long and 0.6 mm wide; the body is light orange and has one pair of wings, three pairs of legs, and developed eyes and antennae. The San Jose scale is found on all continents. It was first found in the USSR in 1932; its focuses occur in the southern European part of the country, the Caucasus, Middle Asia, and the Far East. It damages more than 200 species of fruit trees, ornamental varieties, and leafy trees. The larvae winter under the scutella on the bark of tree trunks and branches. They turn into females and males in the spring. The female produces 100–300 larvae, or wanderers, which emerge from under the scutellum and adhere to the rough surfaces of the bark, where they remain motionless. There are from one to four generations a year. In sucking the sap from bark, leaves, and fruits, the San Jose scale creates spots and cracks in the bark, kills the bark, and causes the leaves to fall. Severely damaged trees die. Control measures include the use of decontaminated planting stock, the removal of dead bark from trunks and branches, the removal of dry twigs, the thinning of crowns, the destruction of root shoots and severely infested trees, the use of entomophages (ichneumon flies), and the treatment of plants with insecticides.

REFERENCE
Popova, A. I. *Kaliforniiskaia shchitovka.* Moscow-Leningrad, 1962.
                                                   T. I. BICHINA [11–630–3]

SAXIFRAGA, a genus of plants of the family Saxifragaceae. The plants are perennial, sometimes annual, herbs. The leaves are usually in rosettes. The flowers are in corymbs or panicles; they are rarely solitary. There are approximately 350 species in the temperate and cold belts of the northern hemisphere and in the Andes. In the USSR there are approximately 80 species, distributed primarily in the arctic and in the mountains of the Caucasus (the alpine belt). Many species grow in the crevices of rocks. The most common species are *Saxifraga hirculus, S. punctata, S. nivalis,* and *S. oppositifolia.* Many species are grown as ornamentals in gardens; some are cultivated indoors in hanging baskets (for example, *S. sarmentosa*).   [11–826–1]

SAXIFRAGACEAE, a family of dicotyledonous plants. They are herbs, generally with simple leaves, usually exstipulate. The flowers are solitary or, more often, in clusters; they are regular or, less frequently, irregular. The flowers are almost always bisexual. There are usually five sepals, five to ten petals (sometimes they are absent), and five to ten stamens (rarely three). The ovary is superior, half-inferior, or inferior; the fruit is a capsule. There are approximately 35 genera (600 species), growing primarily in the cold and temperate belts of the northern hemisphere, often in the mountains. In the USSR there are five genera (more than 100 species). Formerly, plants of the families Hydrangeaceae and Grossulariaceae, as well as some other groups of plants, were included in the family Saxifragaceae. They are now generally considered to be separate families. The tannin-containing plants of the genus *Bergenia* have commercial value. Species of the genera *Astilbe, Saxifraga, Chrysosplenium, Heuchera,* and *Rodgersia* are used as ornamentals.

REFERENCES
Flora SSSR, vol. 9. Moscow-Leningrad, 1939.
Takhtadzhian, A. L. *Sistema i filogeniia tsvetkovykh rastenii.* Moscow-Leningrad, 1966.   [11–826–2]

SCIATICA, ischialgia, lumbosacral radiculitis, a disease of the roots of the lumbosacral section of the spinal cord and, mainly, of the sciatic nerve (nervus ischiadicus).

The causes of sciatica are the same as those of radiculitides. Because of the great length of the sciatic nerve and its close connection with many surrounding formations, such as the or-gans of the lesser pelvis (the uterus and its appendages, the urinary bladder, the rectum, the membranes of the spinal cord, the spinal column), diseases of the sciatic nerve occur with great frequency. They occur both as primary, with the influence of some injurious factor (chilling, infection) directly on the nerve, and as associated with involvement of the nerve with diseases of the surrounding organs. Examination reveals characteristic pain points, tension symptoms (the extremities in a position in which the nerve is taut and there is acute pain, such as in the forced adduction of a raised leg or bending of the head toward the chest in a recumbent position with the legs straightened), loss of sensitivity in certain areas of the skin (according to the type of nerve root), and autonomic and trophic disturbances.

In the acute stage of sciatica, treatment involves rest (lying on a hard bed), ultraviolet irradiation of the painful area, diadynamic currents, analgesics, and novocain blocks; later, ionization with novocain and potassium iodide, diathermy, ultrahigh-frequency therapy, massage, therapeutic exercise, and vitamins B_1 and B_{12} are prescribed. Surgery is recommended in severe, protracted cases of sciatica that are the result of affection of the intervertebral disks or a dislocated disk.

REFERENCES
Guber-Grits, D. S. *Zabolevaniia poiasnichno-kresttsovogo otdela perifericheskoi nervnoi sistemy.* Moscow, 1960.
Shamburov, D. A. *Ishias,* 2nd ed. Moscow, 1954.
Shustin, V. A. *Diskogennyi poiasnichno-kresttsovyi radikulit: Klinika, diagnostika, lechenie.* Leningrad, 1966.   V. A. KARLOV [11–169–4]

SEA OTTER (*Enhydra lutris*), Kamchatka beaver, a predaceous mammal of the family Mustelidae.

The cylindrical body of the sea otter is up to 1.5 m long and weighs up to 40 kg. The limbs, especially the forelegs, are short; the hind limbs look like flippers. The head is rounded with long vibrissae covering the nostrils and ears. The flat tail is about 35 cm long. The body is covered with thick, silky fur of a dark brown, sometimes almost black, color.

The sea otter was once widely distributed in the northern Pacific and along the coast of America from Alaska to California. It has now been almost wiped out by commercial hunting. In the USSR in 1920 there were a very few individuals left on Mednyi Island (Komandorskie Islands) and on the southern tip of Kamchatka (Lopatka Cape); despite conservation measures, the number grew only slowly. After 1945 the number of sea otters began to increase rapidly, and by 1970 there were approximately 1,000 on the Komandorskie and Kuril islands and the southern tip of Kamchatka. In America the number has also been increasing. The sea otter lives in the coastal zone of the ocean, near shores that have a large number of rocks above and below the water upon which the animals can rest. They move with difficulty on dry land, but in the water they are very agile, swimming and diving with ease. In the water they rest and eat their prey while lying on their backs. Their basic foods include sea urchins, mollusks, crabs, and fish. The sea otter is diurnal. Mating and the birth of offspring occur in various seasons. The gestation period is eight or nine months; usually one pup is born (rarely, two). The sea otter is a valuable fur animal; the fur is attractive, warm, and durable. In the USSR the commercial hunting of the animal is prohibited.

REFERENCES
Kalan. (Collection of articles.) Moscow, 1947.
Barabash-Nikiforov, I. I. *Kalan: Morskaia vydra.* Leningrad, 1968.
Mlekopitaiushchie Sovetskogo Soiuza, vol. 2, part 1. Moscow, 1967.
                                                   I. I. SOKOLOV [11–563–2]

SEPIA, a genus of cephalopod mollusks of the order Decapoda. The body is elongated (up to 25 cm) and flattened, and there are fins on the sides. The arms are equipped with suckers; the two longest arms are wider at the ends and serve to capture prey. The shell is internal, located under a mantle on the back. The secretion of the large ink gland (an outgrowth of the rectum) is a means of defense. The cuttlefish of this genus can expel it into the water as an "ink bomb," similar in shape to the animal itself, thus confusing and disorienting the enemy. Upon contact with the enemy, the bomb bursts, forming a "smoke screen." The

Sepia are bottom dwellers, and their body color harmonizes with the substratum. They crawl along the bottom with the help of their arms and swim slowly with their fins. They can also swim rapidly by expelling a jet of water from the mantle. The *Sepia* inhabit coastal waters (to a depth of 200 m) of tropical and warm seas. Their flesh is edible. The secretion of the ink gland (sepia) is used in painting as a very durable dark-brown color.

I. M. LIKHAREV [11–1143–1]

SEVAN TROUT (also Gokcha trout; *Salmo ischchan*), a fish of the salmon family (Salmonidae). It is found only in the basin of Lake Sevan. It comprises five races that are distinguished by differences in time and place of spawning and rate of growth: the winter bakhtak and the bodzhak are lake fishes, the alabalakh is a river fish, and the summer bakhtak and the gegarkuni are diadromous fishes.

The Sevan trout is the largest trout found in the USSR: the bakhtak and the gegarkuni reach a length of 90 cm (they weigh up to 16 kg), and the bodzhak and alabalakh may measure up to 35 cm. It feeds chiefly on amphipods. The Sevan trout is the principal commercial fish in Lake Sevan. Fish 4–6 years old (28–33 cm long and weighing 340–560 g) predominate in catches. It is used as a food in fresh, frozen, and smoked form. Conditions of reproduction for this trout have deteriorated owing to the declining level of Lake Sevan. The breeding of Sevan trout in fish hatcheries plays a significant role in its reproduction. Sevan trout acclimatizes well in large lakes that have pure water. Gegarkuni has been introduced into Lake Issyk-Kul', where it has successfully adapted, having developed a special form.

[11–175–1]

SEWERAGE, the set of engineered structures, equipment, and sanitation measures that provide for the collection and removal of polluted waste waters beyond the limits of population centers and industrial enterprises, along with the treatment and decontamination of the waters before use or release into bodies of water.

A distinction is made between interior and exterior sewerage. The interior system is used to receive effluents at their point of formation and deliver them from a building to the exterior sewerage network. The elements of the interior system include a building's sanitary equipment, drain pipes, standpipes, and drainage outlets. The exterior system, which is designed to transport the effluents beyond the limits of population centers and industrial enterprises, consists of main pipelines (gravity-fed and pressurized), pumping stations, and sewage treatment facilities.

The sewerage system provides for the combined or separate drainage and removal of three categories of waste water: household, industrial, and rain. Both systems have been widely used in urban planning. In the combined system (see Figure 1) all three categories of waste water are removed through a common network of pipes and canals beyond the limits of the population center. In the separate system (see Figure 2), rainwater and sufficiently clean industrial waters are removed through one network of pipes and conduits and household and polluted industrial wastes are removed through another (by one or more sewer networks). The separate sewerage system may be comprehensive or partial.

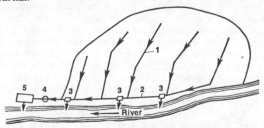

Figure 1. Combined sewerage system: (1) sewage conduits, (2) sewage mains, (3) storm sewers, (4) pumping station, (5) treatment facilities with discharge outlet

A technically and economically sound design for an accepted sewerage system that takes account of local conditions and development prospects of the sewerage project (city, settlement,

industrial, or residential area) is called a sewer plan. Every sewer plan may be implemented by a variety of technical procedures, in regard to the routing and depth of placement of networks and sewers, the number of pumping stations, the number and location of treatment facilities, the necessary degree of treatment, and the sequence of construction.

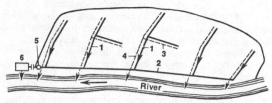

Figure 2. Separate sewerage system: (1) and (2) household network, (3) and (4) rainwater network, (5) pumping station, (6) treatment facilities

Depending on the nature of the terrain, the entire area of a population center to be provided with sewerage is conventionally divided into sewerage basins, that is, areas bounded by watersheds. In each basin the waste waters are collected in one or more sewers through the underground pipes of the street network. The waste waters move through these sewers by force of gravity. When the main is especially deep the network is divided into several districts with normal pipeline depth. The waste waters are sent from these district networks to a district pumping station, from which they are delivered through a pressurized pipeline to higher, gravity-fed mains. Pumping stations are also built for delivering sewage waters directly to the treatment facilities, from which the purified waters are released through outfall sewers into bodies of water. (See Figure 3 for an example of the general design and main facilities of a modern sewerage system in a population center.)

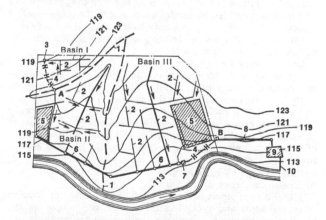

Figure 3. General plan and basic sewerage facilities of a population center: (1) boundaries of sewerage basins, (2) street network and sewage conduits, (3) district pumping station, (4) pressurized water-lines, (5) industrial enterprises, (6) sewage main, (7) main pumping station, (8) out-of-town main, (9) treatment facilities, (10) outfall sewer; (113–123) contour lines marking elevations; (A) and (B) points at which pressure lines enter gravitation network

Waste water has been removed from population centers by pipe since antiquity. Excavations in Egypt have uncovered sewage canals built 2,500 years B.C., and similar structures are known to have existed even earlier in India. The Cloaca Maxima was built in Rome in the sixth century B.C. and is still partially in use today. However, these structures required enormous expenditures of labor and materials and were provided only for palaces, temples, and the public baths. During the feudal age, and particularly during the period of capitalist development that followed, the increasing density of population led to a deterioration in urban sanitation. The growing frequency of epidemics made it essential to build water pipes and, later, sewerage systems as well. This development was also dictated by the development of industry and an increase in the volume of industrial waste waters.

Intensive construction of sewerage systems in Europe did not begin until the 19th century. In Russia, the first underground canals for removing polluted water were built in the 11th–14th centuries (Novgorod and the Moscow Kremlin), but it was not until the early 19th century (in St. Petersburg and Moscow) that they were built on a significant scale. In prerevolutionary Russia the 18 largest cities had sewage disposal systems.

In the USSR, simultaneous with the growth of cities and settlements, public services and amenities have been provided, including the construction of centralized water and sewerage systems. Standard designs have been developed and are in use for a large number of sewage disposal works. These designs significantly reduce the expenditure of labor and the building time of the systems. Industrial construction methods are widely used (in particular, the use of heading in laying sewers and of prefabricated elements for sewage disposal installations). By 1980, the Soviet Union plans to add more than 270,000 km to the existing sewer networks and to increase the capacity of sewage treatment facilities to 90 million cu m per day. The volume of industrial waste waters treated daily will reach 120 million cu m.

REFERENCE
Kanalizatsiia. Edited by A. I. Zhukov. Moscow, 1969.
S. V. IAKOVLEV and IU. M. LASKOV [11–931–4]

SEWER NETWORK, the aggregate of underground pipelines and sewers receiving and draining waste waters away from population centers and industrial enterprises and toward the appropriate treatment facilities; the principal element of a sewerage system.

An urban sewer network consists of pipe networks draining city blocks, buildings and groups of buildings, and streets, sewage mains, and pressure lines. The lines of the sewer network running within individual buildings are connected to the network of that group or block of buildings through special drainage outlets. Pumping stations are built to pump the sewage water to treatment facilities. Manholes are provided for inspection and repairs. Industrial enterprises may have several sewer networks for removing effluents of different composition (for example, strong acid and strong base).

Depending on topography, ground conditions, composition of the effluents, and sequence of construction, networks may be perpendicular, transverse, parallel, zonal, or radial. Whenever possible, sewer networks are designed to use a gravity-fed system to transport household and industrial effluents. The hydraulic calculations necessary in designing a sewer network consist in determining the diameter of the pipes and their load and the rate of flow of the effluents. The network should be deep enough (depending on the depth of soil freeze) to protect the pipes against damage by surface transport. This comes to about 2 m for the middle zone of the USSR.

The choice of pipelaying material depends on the composition of the effluents and groundwaters and on the purpose of the pipeline. A gravity-fed sewer network is made from ceramic, asbestos-cement, concrete, and reinforced-concrete pipe; the large-diameter mains are made from reinforced-concrete pipe or prefabricated sections of reinforced concrete. Metal, asbestos cement, and reinforced-concrete pipes are used for pressure lines. Pipes can also be made from synthetic materials. Careful fitting of the joints in laying the pipe helps ensure watertightness and long life.
IU. M. LASKOV [11–931–1]

SILICON-CARBIDE REFRACTORIES, articles produced from silicon carbide (carborundum) and additives, containing between 20–35 and 70–98 percent SiC.

Silicon-carbide refractories are classified, according to the method of bonding the silicon-carbide granules, as siliceous (formed in the oxidation of carbide), nitride (Si_3N_4), oxynitride (Si_2ON_2), and aluminosilicate, as well as recrystallized and self-bonded. The products are formed on presses (or by other methods) from powdered mixtures containing silicon carbide and subsequently fired at 1300°–1550°C (certain types at 2000°–2200°C).

Silicon-carbide refractories exhibit high thermal conductivity: 7–17 watts per (m·°K) at 800°C. As a result, they show good

thermal stability. They are also resistant to deformation at elevated temperatures. At 1300°–1500°C in an oxidizing medium they undergo gradual oxidation, particularly in the presence of an excess of oxygen and of water vapor. Silicon-carbide refractories are used in recuperators, retort furnaces, nonferrous-metallurgy plant units, shelves of tunnel wagons (in firing porcelain and ceramics), and boilers.

REFERENCE
Kainarskii, I. S., and E. V. Degtiareva. *Karborundovye ogneupory.* Kharkov, 1963.
A. K. KARKLIT [11–1197–2]

SIZE GRADER, an agricultural machine for separating crop seeds, fruits (apples, citrus fruit), grape stalks, potatoes, and so on by size. In the USSR size graders are produced for grading corn, sugar beet seeds, fruits, and grape stalks.

The primary working elements of the grader for separating corn and sugar beet seeds are screen mills fitted with screens with round or longitudinal holes of various sizes. The screens with round holes grade seeds by width, and those with longitudinal holes grade them by thickness into several groups. By using screens with the appropriate-sized holes, the machines can be used to grade sunflower seeds, castor beans, soybeans, kidney beans, peas, and other crops.

Size graders for sorting and grading round fruits by size or weight consist of a feeder to empty the boxes of ungraded fruits, a sorting roller conveyer along which sorting workers manually pick out nonstandard fruits, grading sections or devices, and storage trays. Band conveyers with holes of different sizes cut in the band are used in size graders for grading fruits by size. Size graders that divide fruits by weight use a grading device in the form of a conveyer with cups, into which a cellular conveyer places the fruit one at a time, and scales for weighing the cups containing the fruit. The graded fruits are carried to storage trays from which they are packed or poured into boxes.

Size graders for trimming grape stalks by length and grading them by diameter have two cutting devices, two grading rulers, and two trays set on opposite walls of the machine. In addition, the machine has compartments for picking out stalks with identical diameters; the diameter limits of the graded stalks are within 7–12 mm.

Potatoes are graded by potato-sorter assemblies and potato sorters.
[11–594–1]

SKATING RINK, a section of level ice surface designed for skating and sledding. There are two basic types: rinks intended for sports use and for general public use. Sports rinks are used for lessons, speed skating and sledding matches, figure skating, and ice hockey. General-purpose rinks are places for recreation, games, and fun. There are three types of rinks in terms of ice preparation: natural (which are constructed on natural bodies of water during winter), poured-on (arranged on a natural or artificial base, most frequently in sports arenas, stadiums, or asphalt-paved areas), and artificial (created with the aid of special refrigerating installations).

Sports skating rinks are popular primarily in countries with long winters, particularly the Scandinavian countries, the USSR, the Netherlands, Canada, and the USA. In 1971 there were approximately 18,000 skating rinks in the USSR, including close to 70 artificial ones. During the 1950's and 1960's artificial sports skating rinks were constructed in many of the major cities of Europe, Canada, and the USA. The most famous ones for speed skating are in Grenoble (France), Inzell (FRG), Göteborg (Sweden), Deventer (Netherlands), Berlin (GDR), Budapest (Hungary), and Sverdlovsk (USSR); and for ice hockey and figure skating, in Moscow (at the Lenin Central Stadium), Leningrad (the Iubileinyi), Kiev, and Minsk (USSR), Prague (the Czechoslovak SSR), Stockholm (Sweden), Zurich (Switzerland), Montreal and Toronto (Canada), and Sapporo (Japan). The most popular high-mountain skating rinks are located in Davos (Switzerland), Cortina d'Ampezzo (Italy), Inzell (FRG), and Medeo (USSR).
A. P. GALLI and V. V. LYSENKO [11–1584–1]

SKILLED LABOR, labor requiring specialized preparatory training of the worker, as well as the experiences, ability, and knowledge necessary to fulfill specific kinds of work. Unlike unskilled (simple) labor, skilled labor is complex: one hour of skilled labor is equivalent to several hours of simple labor. In accordance with this, skilled labor is paid at a higher rate than unskilled. [11–1693–4]

SÖDRA KVARKEN, a strait between the Åland Islands and the Scandinavian Peninsula, joining the Gulf of Bothnia and the Baltic Sea. Width, approximately 40 km; maximum depth, 244 m. The current is usually southern. The strait is frozen in severe winters; in milder, less cold winters it is covered with ice floes. [11–1807–2]

SOUTH AFRICA SUBREGION, a subregion in the Ethiopian zoogeographical land region. To the northeast, it borders on the East Africa subregion. The boundary between these two subregions is not fixed, and the fauna is very similar (however, the fauna is richer in the East Africa subregion). Therefore, some zoogeographers do not distinguish between the two areas. The South Africa subregion occupies desert and semidesert lands.

A number of faunal species in the subregion, mainly invertebrates, are relicts (for example, invertebrates of the class Onychophora). Vertebrate fauna is relatively scarce, since species from forested equatorial Africa (for example, anthropoid apes, otter shrews, wild chevrotains, scaly-tailed squirrels, and some ungulates) have hardly penetrated this subregion; some are found in the extreme northern section. Golden moles, tarsiers, and aardvarks are among the characteristic and partially endemic mammals of the South Africa subregion. The blue duiker, Burchell's zebra, some viverrids (for example, the suricate), and the brown hyena are among the animals that dwell in the subregion. The bird fauna is fairly rich, but there are few endemic genera (approximately 5 percent of the total number of genera); the subfamily Promeropinae is endemic. There are many species of sand grouse and bustard. Several families of birds, including Pittidae and Scopidae, that are characteristic of the Ethiopian region are absent in this subregion.

The topography, flora, and fauna of the South Africa subregion have greatly changed as a result of human activities. A number of faunal species have been destroyed, and some have been driven northward (elephants, rhinoceroses, zebras, giraffes, lions, ostriches, and various species of antelopes). Some species are preserved only in zoos.

REFERENCES
Geptner, V. G. *Obshchaia zoogeografiia.* Moscow-Leningrad, 1936.
Darlington, P. *Zoogeografiia.* Moscow, 1966. (Translated from English.)
V. G. GEPTNER [11–1081–3]

SPERM WHALE (*Physeter catodon*), an aquatic mammal of the suborder Odontoceti.

The length of the male sperm whale reaches 20 m; it may weigh as much as 70 tons. The females are as long as 15 m and weigh up to 30 tons. The head is very large (as much as one-third the length of the body), massive, and blunt in the front. The left nostril opens at the end of the snout in the left corner of the head; the right nostril ends blindly. In the frontal part of the head there is a saccular enlargement of the right nasal passage—the air sac, an adaptation to prolonged stays under water. An enormous fatty cushion of spermaceti (to 6 m) lies in the bed formed by the maxillary bones and determines the shape and size of the head. The mouth is located below this area, a considerable distance back from the tip of the snout. There are 18–30 pairs of teeth on the long and narrow lower jaw. Upper teeth are absent. The flippers are broad and blunt; the dorsal fin takes the form of an elongated hump. The skin on the sides of the body and back is usually wrinkled. The color of the whale varies from brown to dark chestnut. The males are found in all oceans and open seas except in the arctic; the females, only in the warm zone between 40° S lat. and 40° N lat.

The sperm whale feeds on cephalopods and deepwater fish, descending as far as 1.2 km. It can stay under water as long as 1.5 hours, facilitated by the high myoglobin content of the muscles and the decreased sensitivity of the respiratory center to the accumulation of carbon dioxide in the blood. The sperm whale is polygamous, 10–20 females being escorted by a single male. Sexual maturity is attained at five years. The life span may be as much as 50 years. The sperm whale is a most important object of commerce, yielding 9–10 tons of fat, as much as 6 tons of spermaceti, and ambergris. The sperm whale population is decreasing (no more than 300,000 remain).

REFERENCES
Tomilin, A. G. *Kitoobraznye.* Moscow, 1957 (*Zveri SSSR i prilezhashchikh stran,* vol. 9).
Tomilin, A. G. *Kitoobraznye fauny morei SSSR.* Moscow, 1962.
Zhizn' zhivotnykh, vol. 6. Moscow, 1971.
Berzin, A. A. *Kashalot.* Moscow, 1971. (Bibliography.)
Iablokov, A. V., V. M. Bel'kovich, and V. I. Borisov. *Kity i del'finy.* Moscow, 1972. A. G. TOMILIN [11–1649–1]

SPINY DOGFISH (*Acanthias acanthias*), a fish of the suborder Selachoidei. Body length, up to 2 m; weight, up to 15 kg. The spiny dogfish is distributed in the Pacific and Atlantic oceans. In the USSR it is found in the Barents and Black seas, as well as in the seas of the Far East. The fish has commercial value. [11–1596–1]

SPOT TEST ANALYSIS, a method of microchemical, qualitative, or semiquantitative analysis in which both the solution to be analyzed and the reagents are used in amounts of several drops.

The detection of certain ions makes use of characteristic color reactions, which are carried out on filter paper, watch glasses, drop plates, or microcrucibles. Spot test analysis uses reagents of great sensitivity and selectivity, making it possible to detect the given ions in the presence of other components in the solution to be analyzed. Semiquantitative analysis (spot test colorimetry) is performed by comparing the intensity of coloration of spots obtained on filter paper with the color of a standard. The spot test has the advantages of speed, simplicity of equipment, and a high degree of sensitivity (detection limit of ions, 0.1–0.01 microgram). The method is widely used to identify materials and control their purity, for ore and mineral and biochemical analyses, and for many other purposes. Spot test analysis is particularly convenient under field conditions for the quick analysis of industrial samples.

REFERENCE
Tananaev, N. A. *Kapel'nyi metod,* 6th ed. Moscow-Leningrad, 1954. [11–1018–4]

SPRING TRAP, a device for capturing large or small fur-bearing animals (bears, lynxes, wolverines, wolves, foxes, arctic foxes, martens, sables, ermines, squirrels, Siberian weasels) and farm pests (such as susliks and hamsters). The spring trap has been used since ancient times. Some spring traps have metal jaws that snap shut on the leg of the animal or hold it by the body (steel-jaw trap). There are also spring traps without jaws, the most widely known being the mole trap. [11–1067–2]

SQUARE HEBREW, an offshoot of Western Semitic writing that can be traced to Aramaic (third century B.C.), which had taken its basic shape by the second and first centuries B.C.

Square Hebrew is found in Aramaic and ancient Hebrew inscriptions and in literature in ancient and modern Hebrew, Yiddish, and Ladino (a Spanish-Hebrew language of the Mediterranean). Cursive varieties include the Ashkenazic (Eastern Europe), the Sephardic (Mediterranean), and the Rashic (a rabbinic script used in Italy for religious texts). The alphabet was at first purely consonantal. Several vowel-mark systems, using diacritics, were created between the sixth and eighth centuries A.D.; the principal system in use today is the Tiberian Masoretic.

REFERENCE
Diringer, D. *Alfavit.* Moscow, 1963. Pages 311–19. (Translated from English.) [11–1676–2]

SQUARING THE CIRCLE, the problem of finding a square equal in area to a given circle. To square a circle is to construct a square whose area is equal to that of the circle or to compute the area of the circle with given accuracy.

The attempt was made initially to exactly square the circle with compass and straightedge. The mathematicians of antiquity knew a number of cases when, with the help of these instruments, a curvilinear figure could be transformed into a rectilinear figure of the same area (for example, the lune of Hippocrates). Attempts to square the circle, which continued for thousands of years, were invariably unsuccessful. In 1775 the Paris Academy of Sciences, and later other academies as well, refused to consider work devoted to squaring the circle. Only in the 19th century was a scientific basis given for this refusal: the insolubility of the problem of squaring the circle with compass and straightedge was rigorously established.

If the radius of a circle is equal to r, then the side of the square of the same area is equal to $x = r\sqrt{\pi}$. Thus, the problem reduces to that of graphic multiplication of a given segment (r) by a given number ($\sqrt{\pi}$). However, the graphic multiplication of a segment by a number can be accomplished with compass and straightedge only if the number involved is the root of an algebraic equation with integral coefficients, which is solvable by square roots. Thus, the problem of squaring the circle is equivalent to the problem of determining the arithmetical nature of the number π.

At the end of the 18th century, the irrationality of the number π was established by the German mathematician J. Lambert and the French mathematician A. Legendre. In 1882 the German mathematician F. Lindeman proved that the number π (and that also means $\sqrt{\pi}$) is transcendental, that is, does not satisfy any algebraic equation with integral coefficients. Lindeman's theorem put an end to attempts to solve the problem of squaring the circle using a compass and straightedge. The problem of squaring the circle becomes solvable if the means of construction are broadened. It was already known to Greek geometers that squaring the circle could be accomplished using transcendental curves; the first solution of the problem of squaring the circle was accomplished by Dinostratus (fourth century B.C.) with the help of a special curve—the quadratrix. On the problem of finding an approximate value for the number π, see the article PI.

REFERENCES

O kvadrature kruga (Arkhimed, Giuigens, Lambert, Legendre). S prilozheniem istorii voprosa, 3rd ed. Moscow-Leningrad, 1936. (Translated from German.)
Struik, D. J. *Kratkii ocherk istorii matematiki,* 2nd ed. Moscow, 1969. (Translated from German.)   [11–1677–3]

STATE-SUPPORTED STUDENT (Russian, *kazennokoshtnyi student,* from the Polish *koszt,* "maintenance" or "cost"), a university student in Russia who was fully maintained at the state's expense, as distinct from one who paid his own way. State-supported students lived in dormitories under the supervision of inspectors. Upon graduating from the university they were obliged to serve for at least six years in the Ministry of Education; medical doctors served in the military. The institution of state-supported students endured until the 1860's. It was abolished at the University of St. Petersburg in 1850, and direct state maintenance was replaced by stipends at all other universities in 1859.   [11–524–1]

STEPHEN I, SAINT (István I). Born circa 970; died Aug. 15, 1038. Prince (from 997), first king of Hungary (from 1000 or 1001).

Stephen I was from the Árpád dynasty. During his rule the formation of Hungary into an early feudal state was completed. He abolished the tribal division of the country and introduced the crown comitats, territorial divisions headed by *iszpanak* (counts) that were used for administrative purposes. Under his leadership the attack of German feudal lords on Hungary in 1030 was repulsed. He brought about the Christianization of Hungary (in 1083 he was canonized by the Catholic Church).
[11–174–2]

STONE AGE, a cultural-historical period in the development of man during which the principal tools and weapons were primarily fashioned from stone and there was no working of metal. Wood and bone were also used. In the late stage of the

Stone Age the working of clay, from which vessels were made, became widespread. The Stone Age was superseded by the Bronze Age after a transitional period known as the Aeneolithic. The Stone Age coincides with the greater part of the epoch of the primitive communal system and encompasses the time beginning with man's emergence from the animal state (about 1.8 million years ago) and ending with the widespread use of the first metals (about 8,000 years ago in the ancient East and about 6,000–7,000 years ago in Europe).

The Stone Age is divided into the Old Stone Age, or Paleolithic, and the New Stone Age, or Neolithic. The Paleolithic is the epoch of the existence of fossil man and belongs to the far-removed time when the earth's climate, flora, and fauna differed greatly from those of modern times. Paleolithic man used nothing but chipped-stone tools and had no knowledge of polished-stone tools or clay pottery. He hunted and gathered his food (plants, mollusks). Fishing was beginning to emerge, and farming and stock raising were unknown. Neolithic man already lived in modern climatic conditions, surrounded by contemporary flora and fauna. Along with chipped-stone tools, there were polished and perforated stone tools and clay pottery in this period. Neolithic man began to engage in primitive farming using the hoe and to breed domestic animals, in addition to hunting, gathering, and fishing. The transitional period between the Paleolithic and the Neolithic is called the Mesolithic.

The Paleolithic is divided into the Lower Paleolithic (Early Paleolithic; between 1.8 million and 35,000 years ago) and the Upper Paleolithic (Late Paleolithic; between 35,000 and 10,000 years ago). The Lower Paleolithic is divided into the following archaeological epochs (cultures): Pre-Chellean (*see* PEBBLE CULTURE), Chellean (Abbevillian), Acheulean, and Mousterian. Many archaeologists place the Mousterian epoch (100,000 to 35,000 years ago) in a special period called the Middle Paleolithic.

The most ancient pre-Chellean stone tools were pebbles flaked on one end and chips broken from such pebbles. The type tools of the Chellean and Acheulean consist of *coups de poing* (hand axes), pieces of stone flaked on both sides and rounded on one end and pointed on the other; crude chopping implements (chopper-chopping tools) with less regular outlines than the *coups de poing;* and rectangular ax-like implements (cleavers) and massive chips broken from the cores (nuclei). The makers of the pre-Chellean and Acheulean tools belonged to the type Archanthropinae (*Pithecanthropus, Sinanthropus,* and the Heidelberg man) and possibly to an even more primitive type (*Homo habilis, Prezinjanthropus*). Warm climatic conditions prevailed, and man lived to the south of 50° N lat. (a large part of Africa, southern Europe, and southern Asia).

In the Mousterian epoch the stone chips became more refined because they were flaked from specially prepared disc-shaped or tortoise-shaped cores (the Levallois flake technique). The chips were fashioned into various types of sidescrapers, triangular points, knives, perforators, small hand axes, and so on. The use of bone (small anvils, retouchers, and points) became common as did the use of fire. The onset of colder weather forced man to settle more frequently in caves and to expand his territories. Burials testify to the emergence of primitive religious beliefs. The people of the Mousterian belonged to the type Paleoanthropinae (Neanderthal man). In Europe they generally lived under the severe climatic conditions of the beginning of the Würm glaciation and were contemporaries of the mammoths, woolly rhinoceros, and cave bears. Local differences in cultures, which are identified by the tools they made, have been established for the Lower Paleolithic.

During the Upper Paleolithic the human being of the modern physical type developed (*Neoanthropus, Homo sapiens*—the Cro-Magnon man, the Grimaldi man, and others). Upper Paleolithic man settled far more widely than Neanderthal man, moving into Siberia, America, and Australia.

Upper Paleolithic man typically used prismatic cores from which he broke off elongated flakes to make general end scrapers, points, gravers (burins), awls, and adzes. Articles made of bones of mammoth, antlers, and tusks appeared, such as awls, eyed needles, small shovels, picks, and so on. Man began to assume a settled way of life. Along with cave dwellings, permanent dwellings—pit houses and houses built directly on the ground—became widespread. There were large communal dwellings with several hearths as well as small dwellings (Gagarino, Kostenki, Pushkari, Buret', Mal'ta, Dolní Věstonice, Pensevan). In their construction man used the skulls, large bones, and tusks of mammoths, the antlers of reindeer, wood, and animal hides. Dwellings often formed entire communities. Hunting reached a higher level of development. Representational art appeared, often characterized by striking realism: sculptured images of animals and nude women made of mammoth tusks, stone, and sometimes of clay (Kostenki I, the Avdeevo site, Gagarino, Dolní Věstonice, Willendorf, Brassempouy); images of animals and fish engraved on bone and rock; engraved and painted symbolic geometric designs, such as zigzags, rhombuses, meanders, and wavy lines (Mezin campsite, Předmosti); and engraved and painted (monochrome and polychrome) symbols and representations of animals and sometimes of people on the walls and ceilings of caves (Altamira, Lascaux). Paleolithic art was apparently partially connected with female cults of the epoch of the matriarchal clan and with hunting magic and totemism. There were various types of burials with the body in contracted position or in sitting position, sometimes colored with pigment; various articles were buried with the dead.

There were several large cultural regions as well as a variety of smaller cultures in the Upper Paleolithic: the Périgordian, Aurignacian, Solutrean, and La Madeleine, among other cultures, in Western Europe and the Szelebian and other cultures in Central Europe.

The transition from the Upper Paleolithic to the Mesolithic coincided with the final receding of glaciation and the general establishment of the modern climate. Radiocarbon dating dates the European Mesolithic at 10,000–7,000 years ago; in northern Europe the Mesolithic continued until 6,000–5,000 years ago. The Mesolithic in the Near East was 12,000–9,000 years ago. The Mesolithic cultures include the Azilian culture, the Tardenoisian culture, the Maglemosian culture, the Ertebølle culture, and the Hoa Binh culture. The Mesolithic is characterized by the use of microliths—miniature stone implements of geometric shape (trapezoids, crescents, and triangles) set in wooden and bone mountings—as well as such flaked chopping tools as axes, adzes, and picks. The bow and arrow became common. The dog, which may have been domesticated already in the Upper Paleolithic, was widely used during the Mesolithic.

The most important characteristic of the Neolithic was the transition from the use of nature's finished products (obtained by hunting, fishing, and gathering) to the production of the vitally necessary products, although the direct use of natural products continued to be important in man's economic activity. Man began to cultivate crops, and stock raising appeared. Some researchers call the decisive changes that occurred in the economy with the transition to stock raising and farming the "Neolithic revolution." The defining elements of Neolithic culture were clay vessels (pottery) modeled by hand without a potter's wheel; stone axes, hammers, adzes, chisels, and hoes (during their production the rocks were sawed, polished, and bored); flint daggers, knives, arrowheads, lance tips, and sickles, which were made by the method of pressure flaking; microlithic and chopping tools, which had already appeared during the Mesolithic; and various kinds of articles made of bone and antler (fish hooks, harpoons, hoe tips, chisels) and wood (hollowed-out canoes, oars, skis, sleighs, and various kinds of handles). Flint workshops spread; at the end of the Neolithic there were even mines to extract flint and, in connection with this, intertribal exchange of raw material. Primitive weaving and spinning appeared. Typical of Neolithic art were various types of impressed and drawn ornamentation on pottery; clay, bone, and stone figurines of people and animals; and painted, engraved, and hollowed-out cave art (petroglyphs). The burial ritual became more complex, and burial structures were constructed. The unevenness of cultural development and the unique features in various local areas became more pronounced during the Neolithic. There were a large number of differing Neolithic cultures. The tribes of different countries went through the Neolithic stage at different times. Many of the Neolithic remains in Europe and Asia date between the sixth and third millennia B.C.

Neolithic culture developed most rapidly in the countries of the Near East, where the earliest farming and domestic livestock breeding began. The bearers of the Natufian culture of Palestine, dating from the Mesolithic (ninth–eighth millennium B.C.), gathered wild-growing cereals extensively and possibly attempted to cultivate them. Along with microliths, sickles with flint blades and stone mortars are also encountered here. In the ninth–eighth millennium B.C. primitive farming and livestock raising also began developing in northern Iraq. The settled farming communities of Jericho in Jordan, Jarmo in northern Iraq, and Çatal Huyük in southern Turkey date from the seventh–sixth millennium B.C. They are characterized by the appearance of sanctuaries and fortifications, often of considerable size. More developed Neolithic farming cultures were widespread in Iraq and Iran in the sixth–fifth millennium B.C.; they had pisé buildings, decorated pottery, and female statuettes. In the fifth–fourth millennium B.C. farming tribes of the developed Neolithic inhabited Egypt.

The development of Neolithic culture in Europe progressed on a local basis but under the strong influence of the cultures of the Mediterranean and Near East, from where the most important cultivated crops and some species of domestic animals penetrated into Europe. England and France in the Neolithic period and in the early Bronze Age were inhabited by farming and stock-raising tribes, who constructed megalithic structures from huge blocks of stone. Pile dwellings were common in Switzerland and adjacent areas (where they are known as lake dwellings) during the Neolithic period and the early Bronze Age; their inhabitants primarily engaged in stock raising and farming as well as in fishing and hunting. During the Neolithic the Danubian farming cultures in Central Europe took shape characterized by pottery with meander decorations. Tribes of Neolithic hunters and fishermen lived in northern Scandinavia at the same time and up to the second millennium B.C.

USSR. The oldest authentic remains of the Stone Age are from Acheulean times and date from the epoch preceding the Riss (Dnieper) glaciation. They have been found in the Caucasus, in the vicinity of the Sea of Azov, in the Dnestr Region, in Middle Asia, and in Kazakhstan. Finds have included chips, *coups de poing,* and choppers (crude cutting tools). Remains of Acheulean hunting encampments have been unearthed in the Kudaro, Tsonskaia, and Azykh caves in the Caucasus. Mousterian sites have been found further north. Burial sites of Neanderthal man have been found in the Kiik-Koba Grotto in the Crimea and in the Teshik-Tash Grotto in Uzbekistan, and a Neanthropic burial site has been found in the Starosel'e Grotto in the Crimea. Remains of a permanent Mousterian dwelling have been found in the Molodova I site on the Dnestr River.

Upper Paleolithic settling in the USSR was even more widespread. Successive stages have been traced in the development of the Upper Paleolithic in different parts of the USSR and also of the Upper Paleolithic cultures, for example, the Kostenki-Sungir', Kostenki-Avdeevo, Mezin, and other cultures on the Russian Plain and the Mal'ta, Afontovo, and other cultures in Siberia. Numerous multilevel Upper Paleolithic settlements have been excavated on the Dnestr (Babin, Voronovitsa, Molodova V). Another region known for the many Upper Paleolithic settlements with remains of various types of dwellings and examples of art is the basin of the Desna and Sudost' rivers (Mezin, Pushkari, Eliseevichi, Iudinovo). A third such region is the villages of Kostenki and Borshevo on the Don River, where more than 20 Upper Paleolithic sites have been found, including a number of multilevel ones, with remains of dwellings, numerous works of art, and four burials. The Sungir' site on the Kliaz'ma River, where several burials have been unearthed, stands by itself. The Medvezh'ia Cave and the Byzovaia site on the Pechora River (Komi ASSR) are among the northernmost Paleolithic remains in the world. The Kapova Cave in the southern Urals contains drawings of mammoths on the walls. The caves of Georgia and Azerbaijan help trace the development, one that differed from that on the Russian Plain, of Upper Paleolithic cultures through a number of stages—from remains of the early Upper Paleolithic, characterized by significant numbers of Mousterian triangular points, to remains of the end of the Upper Paleolithic, characterized by numerous microliths. The Samarkand site is an important Upper Paleolithic settlement in Middle Asia. In Siberia, a large number of Upper Paleolithic sites are known on the Enisei River (Afontova Gora, Kokorevo), in the basin of the Angara and Belaia rivers (Mal'ta, Buret'), in Transbaikalia, and in the Altai Mountains. Upper Paleolithic remains have also been found in the Lena and Aldan river basins and on Kamchatka.

The Neolithic is represented by numerous cultures. Some of them belong to ancient farming tribes and some, to primitive fishermen and hunters. The remains of the Bug and other cultures of the Right-bank Ukraine and of Moldavia (fifth–third millennia B.C.), the settlements of Transcaucasia (Shulaveri, Odishi, Kistrik), and the settlements of the Dzheitun type in southern Turkmenia, which resemble the settlements of Neolithic farmers in Iran, all belong to the farming Neolithic. Neolithic hunting and fishing cultures also existed in the fifth–third millennia B.C. in the south—in the vicinity of the Sea of Azov, in the northern Caucasus, and in Middle Asia (Kel'teminar culture). But they were particularly widespread during the fourth–second millennia B.C. in the north, in the forest zone from the Baltic Sea to the Pacific Ocean. Many Neolithic hunting and fishing cultures, most of which were characterized by particular types of pottery decorated with ornament of pit-and-comb impressions and prick-and-comb impressions are represented along the shores of Lakes Ladoga and Onega and the White Sea (in some places cave drawings and petroglyphs related to these cultures are also encountered), on the upper Volga, and between the Volga and Oka rivers. In the Kama Region, the forest-steppe Ukraine, and Western and Eastern Siberia, pottery decorated with comb impressions and prick-and-comb impressions were common. Other types of Neolithic pottery were represented in the Primor'e and on the island of Sakhalin.

History of the study of the Stone Age. In the first century B.C., Lucretius surmised that the age of the use of metals had been preceded by a time when stones served as weapons. In 1836 the Danish archaeologist C. J. Thomsen identified three cultural-historical epochs (the Stone Age, the Bronze Age, and the Iron Age) from archaeological data. The existence of Paleolithic fossil man was proved in the 1840's–1850's by the French archaeologist Boucher de Perthes in the course of his struggle against reactionary religious scholarship. In the 1860's the British scientist J. Lubbock divided the Stone Age into the Paleolithic and Neolithic, and the French archaeologist G. de Mortillet wrote comprehensive works on the Stone Age and developed a more detailed periodization (the Chellean, Mousterian, and other epochs). The Mesolithic kitchen middens in Denmark, Neolithic lake dwellings in Switzerland, and numerous Paleolithic and Neolithic caves and sites in Europe and Asia were investigated in the second half of the 19th century. At the end of the 19th and the beginning of the 20th century Paleolithic drawings were discovered in the caves of southern France and northern Spain.

In the second half of the 19th century the study of the Stone Age was closely connected with Darwinian ideas and with progressive, although historically limited, evolutionism. In the first half of the 20th century bourgeois investigators of the Stone Age (prehistoric archaeology, prehistory, and paleoethnology) considerably refined the methods of archaeological work; accumulated numerous new factual material that did not fit within the framework of old, simplified schemes; and revealed the diversity of Stone Age cultures and the complexity of their development. At the same time, antihistorical doctrines related to the theory of cultural cycles, to the theory of migrations, and sometimes directly to reactionary racism became widespread. Progressive bourgeois scholars and scientists who sought to trace the development of primitive man and man's economy as a regular process opposed these reactionary conceptions.

Among the major achievements of foreign researchers in the first half of the 20th century are the publication of a number of general manuals, reference books, and encyclopedias on the Stone Age in Europe, Asia, Africa, and America (the French scientists and scholars J. Dechelette and R. Vaufrey, the German M. Ebert, the British J. D. Clark, V. G. Childe, H. M. Wormington) and the elimination of vast gaps on archaeological maps. Another major achievement has been the discovery and investigation of numerous Stone Age remains in the countries of Europe (the Czech scientists and scholars K. Absolon, B. Klima, F. Prošek, and J. Neustupny; the Hungarian L. Vértes; the Rumanian C. Nicolăescu-Propşor; the Yugoslavs S. Brodar and A. Benac; the Poles L. Sawicki and S. Krukowski; the German A. Rust; the Spaniard L. Pericot-García), in Africa (the British scientist L. Leakey, the French scientist C. Arambourg), in the Middle East (the British scholars D. Garrod, J. Mellaart, and K. Kenyon; the Americans R. Braidwood and R. Solecki), in India (H. D. Sankalia, B. B. Lal), in China (Chia Lan-p'o, P'ei Wen-chung), in Southeast Asia (the French scholar H. Mansuy, the Dutchman H. van Heekeren), and in America (A. Kroeber, R. Reiney).

Excavation techniques have been improved significantly, the publication of archaeological documents has increased, and the comprehensive investigation of ancient settlements by archaeologists, geologists, paleozoologists, and paleobotanists has become common. The radiocarbon method of dating and the statistical method of studying stone tools have become widely used, and generalized works devoted to the art of the Stone Age have been compiled (the Frenchmen H. Breuil and A. Leroi-Gourhan, the Italian P. Graziosi).

In Russia a number of Paleolithic and Neolithic sites were studied in the 1870's–1890's by A. S. Uvarov, I. S. Poliakov, K. S. Merezhkovskii, V. B. Antonovich, and V. V. Khvoika. The first two decades of the 20th century were marked by generalizing work on the Stone Age. In addition, excavations of Paleolithic and Neolithic settlements were carried out on a highly sophisticated level for the time (enlisting the support of geologists and zoologists) by V. A. Gorodtsov, A. A. Spitsyn, F. K. Volkov, and P. P. Efimenko.

After the October Socialist Revolution, research on the Stone Age became extensive in the USSR. In 1917 there were 12 known Paleolithic sites in the country; in the early 1970's there were more than 1,000. For the first time, Paleolithic remains were discovered in Byelorussia (K. M. Polikarpovich); Armenia, Azerbaijan, and Georgia (G. K. Nioradze, S. N. Zamiatnin, M. Z. Panichkina, M. M. Guseinov, L. N. Solov'ev); Middle Asia (A. P. Okladnikov, D. N. Lev, V. A. Ranov, Kh. A. Alpysbaev); and the Urals (M. V. Talitskii). Numerous new Paleolithic remains were discovered and investigated in the Crimea, on the Russian Plain, and in Siberia (P. P. Efimenko, M. V. Voevodskii, G. A. Bonch-Osmolovskii, M. Ia. Rudinskii, G. P. Sosnovskii, A. P. Okladnikov, M. M. Gerasimov, S. N. Bibikov, A. P. Chernysh, A. N. Rogachev, O. N. Bader, A. A. Formozov, I. G. Shovkoplias, P. I. Boriskovskii), as well as in Georgia (N. Z. Berdzenishvili, A. N. Kalandadze, D. M. Tushabramishvili, V. P. Liubin). The northernmost Paleolithic remains in the world were discovered on the Pechora and Lena rivers, in the Aldan River basin, and on Kamchatka (V. A. Kanivets, N. N. Dikov).

Methods for excavating Paleolithic settlements were developed, which made it possible to establish the existence of settled life and permanent dwellings in the Paleolithic. Methods were developed for restoring the functions of primitive tools from traces of their use (S. A. Semenov). The historical changes that occurred in the Paleolithic were described: the development of the primitive herd and the matriarchal clan system. Upper Paleolithic and Mesolithic cultures and their interrelations were established. Numerous remains of Paleolithic art were found and generalizing works devoted to them were compiled (S. N. Zamiatnin, Z. A. Abramova). Generalizing works were compiled on the chronology, periodization, and historical description of the Neolithic remains of numerous regions, the identification of Neolithic cultures and their interrelations, and the development of Neolithic technology (V. A. Gorodtsov, B. S. Zhukov, M. V. Voevodskii, A. Ia. Briusov, M. E. Foss, A. P. Okladnikov, V. N. Chernetsov, N. N. Gurina, O. N. Bader, D. A. Krainov, V. N. Danilenko, D. Ia. Telegin, V. M. Masson). Neolithic artistic remains, the cave drawings of the northwestern USSR, the Azov Region, and Siberia, were studied (V. I. Ravdonikas, M. Ia. Rudinskii).

Soviet investigators of the Stone Age have done a great deal of work on exposing the antihistorical conceptions of reactionary bourgeois scientists and scholars and on describing and interpreting Paleolithic and Neolithic remains. Armed with the methodology of dialectical and historical materialism, they have criticized the attempts of many bourgeois investigators (especially in France) to include the study of the Stone Age among the natural sciences and to consider the development of Stone Age cultures as a biological process, as well as their attempts to devise a special science of "paleoethnology" for studying the Stone Age. This field would supposedly occupy an intermediate position between biology and the social sciences. At the same time, Soviet investigators oppose the empiricism of those bourgeois archaeologists who reduce the tasks of studying the Paleolithic and Neolithic remains to nothing more than a careful description of them and the analysis of objects and their groups while ignoring the natural relationship between material culture and social relationships and their consistent, regular development.

For Soviet investigators, Stone Age remains are not an end in themselves but rather a source for studying the early stages of the history of the primitive communal system. They are especially implacable in their opposition to bourgeois idealistic and racist theories, which are widespread among Stone Age specialists in the United States, Great Britain, and other capitalist countries. These theories erroneously interpret, and sometimes falsify, archaeological data on the Stone Age to confirm allegations that there is a division between chosen and nonchosen peoples, that some particular countries and peoples are inevitably backward, and that wars and conquests have a beneficial effect in human history. Soviet investigators of the Stone Age have demonstrated that the early stages of world history and the history of primitive culture were a process in which all peoples, large and small, participated and to which they all contributed.

REFERENCES
Engels, F. *Proiskhozhdenie sem'i, chastnoi sobstvennosti i gosudarstva.* Moscow, 1965.
Engels, F. *Rol' truda v protsesse prevrashcheniia obez'iany v cheloveka.* Moscow, 1969.
Abramova, Z. A. *Paleoliticheskoe iskusstvo na territorii SSSR.* Moscow-Leningrad, 1962.
Alimen, H. *Doistoricheskaia Afrika.* Moscow, 1960. (Translated from French.)
Beregovaia, N. A. *Paleoliticheskie mestonakhozhdeniia SSSR.* Moscow-Leningrad, 1960.
Bonch-Osmolovskii, G. A. *Paleolit Kryma,* Issues 1–3. Moscow-Leningrad, 1940–54.
Boriskovskii, P. I. *Paleolit Ukrainy.* Moscow-Leningrad, 1953.
Boriskovskii, P. I. *Drevnii kamennyi vek Iuzhnoi i Iugo-Vostochnoi Azii.* Leningrad, 1971.
Briusov, A. Ia. *Ocherki po istorii plemen Evropeiskoi chasti SSSR v neoliticheskuiu epokhu.* Moscow, 1952.
Gurina, N. N. *Drevniaia istoriia severo-zapada Evropeiskoi chasti SSSR.* Moscow-Leningrad, 1961.
Danilenko, V. N. *Neolit Ukrainy.* Kiev, 1969.
Efimenko, P. P. *Pervobytnoe obshchestvo,* 3rd ed. Kiev, 1953.
Zamiatnin, S. N. *Ocherki po paleolitu.* Moscow-Leningrad, 1961.
Clark, J. G. D. *Doistoricheskaia Evropa.* Moscow, 1953. (Translated from English.)
Masson, V. M. *Sredniaia Aziia i Drevnii Vostok.* Moscow-Leningrad, 1964.
Okladnikov, A. P. *Neolit i bronzovyi vek Pribaikal'ia,* parts 1–2. Moscow-Leningrad, 1950.
Okladnikov, A. P. *Dalekoe proshloe Primor'ia.* Vladivostok, 1959.
Okladnikov, A. P. *Utro iskusstva.* Leningrad, 1967.
Panichkina, M. Z. *Paleolit Armenii.* Leningrad, 1950.
Ranov, V. A. *Kamennyi vek Tadzhikistana,* issue 1. Dushanbe, 1965.
Semenov, S. A. *Razvitie tekhniki v kamennom veke.* Leningrad, 1968.
Titov, V. S. *Neolit Gretsii.* Moscow, 1969.
Formozov, A. A. *Etnokul'turnye oblasti na territorii Evropeiskoi chasti SSSR v kamennom veke.* Moscow, 1959.
Formozov, A. A. *Ocherki po pervobytnomu iskusstvu.* Moscow, 1969. (MIA, no. 165).
Foss, M. E. *Drevneishaia istoriia severa Evropeiskoi chasti SSSR.* Moscow, 1952.
Childe, V. G. *U istokov evropeiskoi tsivilizatsii.* Moscow, 1952. (Translated from English.)
Bordes, F. *Le Paléolithique dans le monde.* Paris, 1968.
Breuil, H. *Quatre cents siècles d'art pariétal.* Montignac, 1952.
Clark, J. D. *The Prehistory of Africa.* London, 1970.
Clark, J. G. *World Prehistory,* 2nd ed. Cambridge, 1969.
L'Europe à la fin de l'âge de la pierre. Prague, 1961.
Graziosi, P. *Palaeolithic Art.* London, 1960.
Leroi-Gourhan, A. *Préhistoire de l'art occidental.* Paris, 1965.
La Préhistoire. Paris, 1966.
La Préhistoire. Problèmes et tendances. Paris, 1968.
Man the Hunter. Chicago, 1968.
Müller-Karpe, H. *Handbuch der Vorgeschichte,* vols. 1–2. Munich, 1966–68.
Oakley, K. P. *Frameworks for Dating Fossil Man,* 3rd ed. London, 1969.

P. I. BORISKOVSKII [11–769–3]

STONE BORERS, marine animals and plants that destroy rocks, coral, and mollusk shells. Stone borers include some species of marine algae, sponges, bristle worms, barnacles and isopod crustaceans, bivalves and gastropods, and sea urchins. Most stone borers make passages in rock mechanically (crustaceans, bivalves of the genus *Pholas,* sea urchins), but some destroy rock by chemical means, secreting an acid substance (blue-green algae, worms, and, of the bivalves, the "sea dates" of the genus *Lithophagus*). Stone borers use the passageways they have made as hiding places from enemies, as a place in which to keep wet during ebb tides, and as a refuge from breakers. Rocks that have been largely damaged by stone borers are eventually completely destroyed by the action of waves. In subtropical and tropical seas stone borers do much damage to concrete structures.

[11–830–1]

STONE CASTING, a process for obtaining products made primarily from basalt (sometimes from diabase and other rocks) by remelting them at temperatures of 1350–1450°C. Cast stone is used for the manufacture of such articles as pipes, acid-resistant equipment, electrical insulators, blocks for pavements and facing plates, and artistic sculptured articles. [11–746–4]

STONE CELLS, or sclereids, plant cells with considerably thickened, stratified, lignified, sometimes suberized or cutinized walls frequently saturated with calcium salts or silica and pierced by pore canaliculi. Mature stone cells have no live contents.

Stone cells solidify tissues. The commonest are short stone cells, or brachysclereids, which are arranged in groups, or concretions, in fruit pith (pear, quince, chokeberry), rhizomes (peony, anemone), roots (horseradish), and phloem (oak, beech); less commonly, they form solid layers in the pericarp of nuts and acorns and cherry and plum pits. Elongated stone cells, or macrosclereids, usually form a solid layer in the seed coat (bean). Solitary stone cells, or idioblasts, are usually star-shaped (asterosclereids) and found in fir bark, yellow water lily stems, and petioles; others extend from the top to bottom pellicle of a leaf, thereby making it tougher (tea, camellia).

O. N. CHISTIAKOVA [11–742–1]

STONECUTTING MACHINES, machines for cutting piece stone from rock masses.

Stonecutting machines mine wall stone, large wall blocks, and block stock (in quarries and more rarely in mines); these are cut into facing slab and other architectural and structural articles. Stonecutting machines have a rigid self-propelled frame that in most models moves along tracks. Mounted on the frame are the drives for rotating the cutting tools and for moving the machine. The cutting tools of stonecutting machines are circular saws, ring cutters, and chain and rod cutters equipped with hard-alloy teeth. Stonecutting machines are differentiated by use (for quarriers and undermines), type of product obtained (wall stone and large blocks), cutting depth (short cut up to 0.42 m and long cut up to 3 m), and the extent of combination of the operations. There are single-operation units, units that are an aggregate of single-operation machines unified by a common drive and control, and universal stonecutting machines that perform three operations (cross, horizontal, and butt cutting).

Rope saws are a separate category of machine: these are designed for sawing out large blocks of hard limestone and marble. Specifications of the stonecutting machines widely used in the USSR can be found in Table 1.

Table 1. Stonecutting machines produced in the USSR

Machine type	Maximum strength of stone in compression (meganewtons/sq m [kilograms-force/sq cm])	Type of cutting tool	Cutting depth (m)	Rated power (kilowatts)	Weight (tons)	Productivity for bulk rock (cu m/year)[1]
Quarries: machines producing wall stone						
SM-89A	10 (100)	Circular saw	0.42	35.3	10.1	42,000–14,200
SM-89AU	25 (250)	Same	0.42	52	14	45,500–23,600
SM-824	3.5 (35)	Same	2.9	127	42	109,000–68,000
KM-4M	5 (50)	Same	2.31	16.8	2.8	15,000–4,000
Quarries: machines producing large blocks						
SM-580A	40 (400)	Ring cutter	0.86–1.04	51.5	16.2	34,600–15,000
SM-580M	40 (400)	Same	0.86–1.04	47.5	16.6	38,400–16,400
SM-177A[2]	40 (400)	Same	0.86–1.04	21.7	9.4	13,600–6,000
Mines						
KMAZ-188	5 (50)	Chain cutter	2.85	10.5	1.4	6,500–4,900
KMG-2	10 (100)	Circular saw	2.35	16.8	2.3	7,900–2,900

[1] The higher productivity applies to the lower stone strength and vice versa. [2] Also used for cutting marble blocks with a compression strength up to 0.12 giganewtons per sq m (1,200 kilograms-force per sq cm)

The stone is cut out of the rock mass by three cuts made in sequence: cross, horizontal, and vertical (butt). The last of these separates the stone from the solid bed. In a majority of stonecutting machines, the second and third operations are performed simultaneously with the longitudinal movement of the machine along the cut.

The development of stonecutting machines has included the creation of designs incorporating maximum rationalization of operations, improvement of cutting tools, mechanization of the removal of wastes and removal and stacking of products, standardization of basic assemblies and parts, and automation of control. The mechanized production of sawn wall stone (such as limestone and tuffs) has developed rapidly in the USSR. Production, which was 1 million cu m in 1940 and 2.5 million cu m in 1950, had climbed to 13.16 million cu m by 1971.

REFERENCES
Gal'perin, M. I., and V. D. Abezgauz. *Mashiny dlia rezaniia kamnia,* 2nd ed. Moscow, 1964.
Rodin, B. M. *Kar'ery pil'nogo kamnia.* Kiev, 1964.

B. M. RODIN [11–827–1]

STONE FISH (in Russian, *kamennye ryby*), stone images of fish (45 to 10 cm or less) widespread in Eastern Siberia (primarily along the western shores of Lake Baikal and in the Angara River valley) during the Neolithic period. The small, realistically fashioned stone fish had holes and were evidently used as lures for ice fishing. Large and fanciful fish figures were associated with magical fishing rituals.

REFERENCES
Okladnikov, A. P. "Kammenye ryby." In the collection *Sovetskaia arkheologiia,* vol. 1. Moscow, 1936.
Okladnikov, A. P. "K voprosu o naznachenii neoliticheskikh kammenykh ryb iz Sibiri." In the book *Materialy i issledovaniia po arkheologii SSSR,* no. 2. Moscow-Leningrad, 1941. [11–768–2]

STONE-HILL-GRAVES, burial structures distributed in the Estonian SSR and the northern part of the Latvian SSR. Between the first and the fifth centuries they were rectangular enclosures made of large boulders, oriented from north to south along the long axis. Later, from the sixth to 13th century, they were structureless masses of stone and earth. The interments were group burials, with inhumation practiced in the first and second centuries and cremation predominating in later periods. The stone-hill-graves were used for burying family communes or the larger kin group; burials with ten or more enclosures attached to one another are known. The articles found include iron weapons, tools, and bronze ornaments. The stone-hill-graves were left by the ancestors of the Livo-Estonian tribes.

REFERENCES
Moora, Kh. A. "Arkheologicheskie pamiatniki I–IV vv. v Pribaltike." In the collection *Kratkie soobshcheniia instituta istoriia material'noi kul'tury,* issue 53. Moscow, 1954.
Shmidel'khel'm, M. Kh. *Arkheologicheskie pamiatniki perioda razlozheniia rodovogo stroia na severo-vostoke Estonii (V v. do n. e. – V v. n. e.).* Tallinn, 1955. [11–766–1]

STONE IMAGE (in Russian, *kamennye baby*), the name for carved stone sculptures (1 to 4 m high), which in ancient times were set up on high points in the steppe regions from the Dnestr River in the west to the Altai and Mongolia in the east.

The stone images of the Black Sea coastal areas date from different periods, from the Scythian (fifth–fourth century B.C.) to the late nomadic (13–14th century A.D.). Menhir-type carved stone sculptures, which date from the Bronze Age, are known in Siberia. The stone images were apparently associated with ancestor worship.

REFERENCES
Griaznov, M., and E. Shneider. "Drevnie izvaianiia Minusinskikh stepei." In *Materialy po etnografii,* vol. 4, fasc. 2. Leningrad, 1929.
Elagina, N. G. "Skifskie antropomorfnye stely Nikolaevskogo muzeia." *Sovetskaia arkheologiia,* 1959, no. 2, pp. 187–96. [11–761–2]

STONE POLYGONS (stone wreaths), a type of permafrost microrelief consisting of a system of polygons or rings composed of aleurite surrounded by coarsely fragmented material. They occur as a result of combinations of polygonal fracturing, swelling, and permafrost sorting of soils within the active layer in lithologically heterogeneous rocks. [11–765–1]

STONEWARE CLAY, a material for ceramic articles, similar to porcelain but opaque. It has a dense consistency, almost without pores, and is usually gray or brown. Articles made of stoneware clay are usually coated with a transparent crystalline or mat glaze and are often decorated with a fine design in relief. In China stoneware clay appeared before the invention of porcelain; in Europe stoneware clay has been known since the 15th century. After the 1880's, stoneware clay again began to be used in the production of dishes imitating the styles of the 15th to the 18th centuries. In the 20th century it is used mainly for decorative purposes. [11–744–1]

STONEWORKING, the process of giving natural stone a required shape and external finishing (surface). Stoneworking includes the production of architectural elements (such as columns, cornices, and balusters) and facing (including slabs and blocks) from limestone, marble, and granite and other rock widely found in nature and suitable for dressing.

Stoneworking consists of three basic operations: sawing the stone into blocks, roughing out the slabs (blocks) for size, and giving the stone the required shape and finish of the face surface. The raw material for stonework is large blocks (at least 0.45 cu m in volume) cut out of a rock bed in a quarry (more rarely a mine). The stone blocks are cut on sawing rigs. The slabs or blocks are cut for size on shaping machines that are equipped with one or several diamond wheels. The finishing of the face surface of the stone can be done by two methods: by shearing or by grinding. In the first instance, the surface produced is somewhat rough ("rough cut") or relatively smooth (picked and batted finishes). The shearing is done with tools with hard-alloy teeth. Through grinding (abrasive working), the stone acquires a smooth surface; if needed it can be given a mirror sheen. The sheen is produced with a polishing powder (usually chromium, lead, or iron oxide) with a felt wheel. A recently proposed finishing method suggests using hard polishers on a polymer base to obtain higher productivity and better quality.

The large stoneworking enterprises of the USSR are equipped with conveyer grinding and polishing machines that simultaneously shape, grind, and polish. A highly productive grinding and polishing machine with numerical control automatically determines the trajectory of the tool's movement and its pressure on the stone; the machine can process marble (up to 15,000 sq m per year) and granite (around 5,000 sq m per year). The stoneworking machines are set in a processing line, and the material to be worked passes through all operations in sequence. Annual productivity of the line is around 80,000 sq m for marble and around 25,000 sq m for granite.

The working of stone such as rhodonite, nephrite, jasper, and amber for mosaics and small articles is carried out on small-sized machines equipped with a diamond tool. The stone is cut into tiles using small diamond wheels 200–320 mm in diameter. The mosaic work from this type of stone produced in the USSR on a wide scale is done using thin (not more than 4–5 mm) tiles glued with durable glues on a marble or metal base.

At the end of the 1960's, the USSR developed the thermojet method for fracturing stone. The method is used both in working and in mining hard rock; its underlying principle is the effect produced by a high-temperature gas jet (obtained by burning kerosene in oxygen or gasoline in a jet of compressed air) when hitting the surface of the stone at supersonic speed. Under the effect of the jet, thermomechanical stresses are created that cause the cleavage fracture of the surface layer.

A special type of stoneworking is the faceting of precious stones for jewelry work (*see* GEM CUTTING).

REFERENCES
Orlov, A. M. *Obrabotka prirodnogo dekorativnogo kamnia.* Moscow, 1956.
Rusakov, K. I., and Iu. I. Sychev. *Mashiny dlia dobychi i obrabotki kamnia.* Moscow, 1966.
Orlov, A. M., and Iu. I. Shychev. *Sovremennye stanki dlia obrabotki oblitsovochnogo kamnia i tekhnologicheskie skhemy* [a review]. Moscow, 1968.
Sychev, Iu. I., and V. N. Seliuanov. *Konveiernaia obrabotka oblitsovochnogo kamnia.* Moscow, 1970.   A. M. ORLOV   [11–826–3]

SUBMARINE CANYONS, steep-sloped, often **U**-shaped and branching valley-like landforms that cut deeply (up to 1–2 km) into the submarine edges of continents. The submarine canyons usually begin on the shelf at a depth of several scores or hundreds of meters and terminate at the base of the continental slope or within the continental rise at a depth of 2–4 km. Outcroppings of bedrock are encountered in the sides of the submarine canyons; in the lower portion of the canyons lie debris fans that at times reach enormous sizes (with radii on the order of 300–350 km). Some submarine canyons are related to river valleys; in these instances they are the submarine continuations of these valleys (including those of the Congo, Indus, Ganges, and Amazon). In many instances, lee currents have probably been involved in the formation of the submarine canyons, but their origin is basically tectonic. Submarine canyons are widely found on ocean floors throughout the world. Along the shores of the USSR, large submarine canyons are encountered in the Black Sea, the seas bordering the Far East, and the Arctic Ocean.
[11–1013–2]

TANGENT LINE, the limit of a secant. The tangent is defined as follows: Let M be a point on the curve L (Figure 1). Select a second point M' on L and draw the line MM'. Let us consider M to be stationary, and let the point M' approach M along the curve L. If, as M' approaches M, the line MM' approaches a single definite line MT, then MT is called the tangent to the curve L at the point M. Not all continuous curves have a tangent, since the line MM' may not approach a limit or may approach two different limits when M' approaches M from different sides of M (Figure 2).

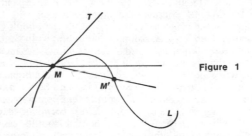

Figure 1

The curves encountered in elementary geometry have a well-defined tangent at all points, except at certain "singular" points. If a plane curve is defined in rectangular coordinates by the equation $y = f(x)$ and $f(x)$ is differentiable at the point x_0, then the slope of the tangent at the point M with abscissa x_0 is equal to the derivative $f'(x_0)$ at the point x_0. The equation of the tangent at this point has the form

$$y - f(x_0) = f'(x_0)(x - x_0)$$

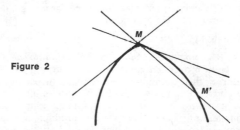

Figure 2

Any line that passes through a point M on a surface S and that lies in the tangent plane to S at the point M is called a tangent line to a surface S at a point M.   [11–1470–3]

TANGENT PLANE. The tangent plane to a surface S at a point M is the plane that passes through the point M and that is characterized by the property that the distance from this plane to the variable point M' on the surface S is infinitesimal in comparison with the distance MM' as M' approaches M. If a surface S has the equation $z = f(x, y)$, then the equation of the tangent plane at the point (x_0, y_0, z_0), where $z_0 = f(x_0, y_0)$, has the form

$$z - z_0 = A(x - x_0) + B(y - y_0)$$

if and only if the function $f(x, y)$ has a total differential at the point (x_0, y_0). In this case, A and B are the values of the partial derivatives $\partial f/\partial x$ and $\partial f/\partial y$ at the point (x_0, y_0) (*see* DIFFERENTIAL CALCULUS).   [11–1470–4]

TEUTHOIDEA (squids), a suborder of cephalopods of the order Decapoda.

The dimensions of Teuthoidea are usually between 0.25 and 0.5 m, but certain species comprise the largest known invertebrates (squids of the genus *Architeuthis* attain a length of 18 m, including tentacles). The body is elongated and tapered toward the rear (torpedo-shaped), allowing great speed in both water and air (squids can jump out of the water to a height of 7 m). There are two large fins at the posterior end of the body. The head is clearly delineated. The eyes are large. There are ten "arms," two of them used for catching and capable both of extending greatly when capturing prey and of contracting when swimming; they are usually equipped with suckers and hooks. The shell is rudimentary; it has the appearance of a thin, narrow, horny plate and is completely hidden under the mantle. The coloration of Teuthoidea varies; some deepwater forms are as transparent as glass and are equipped with luminescent organs. There are approximately 300 species, inhabiting the oceans and seas from the surface to the greatest depths. They are especially numerous in tropical waters. There are about 30 species in the USSR. They are fairly common in the northern arctic and common in the Okhotsk, Bering, and Japan seas.

Members of the suborder generally live in the middle depths of the water. They prey on fish and invertebrates. In turn, they serve as food for larger fish, birds, and sea animals; giant sperm whales feed mainly on the largest squids (*Moroteuthis, Architeuthis*). Squids deposit their eggs on floating objects. Squid meat, canned, as well as fresh, has excellent taste and high nutritional value, so that it is a valuable food product. The commercial squid of the Sea of Japan (*Ommastrephes sloanei pacificus*) migrates to spawn, swimming for five or six months from its pasturing sites in the north to the subequatorial waters where it reproduces (a distance of 2,000–3,000 km). In the USSR, squid is caught commercially in the Far East.

REFERENCES
Rukovodstvo po zoologii, vol. 2. Moscow, 1940.
Ivanov, A. V. *Promyslovye vodnye bespozvonochnye.* Moscow, 1955.
Akimushkin, I. I. *Golovonogie molliuski morei SSSR.* Moscow, 1963.
Zhizn' zhivotnykh, vol 2. Moscow, 1968.

I. M. LIKHAREV   [11–694–2]

TILL, a specially equipped place designed for receipt, payment, and safe storage of cash and other valuables.   [11–1494–2]

TILTER (Russian *kantovatel';* from Polish *kantować,* German *kanten,* "to turn over"), a mechanism for turning over (tilting) objects during their manufacture, transport, or packing. Tilters are used in forging and pressing shops, foundries, and other types of shops, as well as at warehouses for loading and unloading operations and at places where various products are packed.

The simplest chain tilter, which is used in forge shops, is suspended from the hook of an overhead-travel hoisting crane. An electric motor with a worm reducer, mounted on a rectangular frame, has an output shaft with a sprocket that drives a closed chain loop. A forging is attached to the chain and turns when the chain is moved. These tilters have load lifting capacities of up to 200 tons. More complex tilters known as manipulators (suspended and ground types) are widely used in forging and rolling shops. Suspension-type manipulators are mounted on a monorail trolley that moves along the shop on a rail located beneath the ceiling. The ground-type manipulator is a traveling bridge along which a yoke with pincer-type holding devices moves in a horizontal direction. The yoke can rotate around its own axis and can move vertically. These tilters have lifting capacities ranging from 0.75 to 75 tons.

Tilters consisting of two roller conveyers inclined at an angle, each of which can be turned to a horizontal position, are used for tilting rolls made of sheet steel. Such tilters as crank-guide swivel heads, lever mechanisms, and turning carriages are used during the welding of complex frames, beams, tanks, and the like. Tilters in the form of pushers and pull-out devices, which turn boxes moving on a conveyer by 90°, are used in machines for packing finished products into containers, boxes, liners, and so on. The use of tilters with vacuum-type holding devices will make possible the handling of sheet-type, flat-type, and other types of components (for instance, in printing, light industry, and the food industry).   V. S. KIREEV   [11–1003–1]

TORMENTIL (*Potentilla erecta*), a perennial plant of the family Rosaceae. It grows in damp fields and brushwood in the European USSR, the Caucasus, and Western Siberia. Its rhizome is rich in tannins. The tormentil is used medically as an astringent and bactericidal agent. As a medicine, it is administered externally and internally in the form of a decoction. The tormentil yields a dye.

REFERENCE
Atlas lekarstvenykh rastenii SSSR. Moscow, 1962.   [11–573–2]

TO THE YOUNGER GENERATION, a revolutionary proclamation distributed in Russia in September 1861. It was written by N. V. Shelgunov with the aid of M. L. Mikhailov. The proclamation was printed at the Free Russian Press in London and delivered illegally to St. Petersburg. It set forth such demands as replacement of the autocracy by an elected and limited regime, the nationalization of the land and its transfer to the *obshchinas* (peasant communes), the elimination of the police, the abolition of corporal punishment, equality before the law, public trial, and freedom of speech. The proclamation exposed the serfdom-oriented character of the peasant reforms of 1861 and called on the youth to conduct propaganda among the peasants and in the army in order to prepare a revolution. Reflecting one of the orientations of Russian utopian socialism, it contained various Narodnik (Populist) ideas, including the uniqueness of Russia's economic development and the potential of the peasant commune as a cell of the future social system.

REFERENCE
Shelgunov, N. V., L. P. Shelgunova, and M. L. Mikhailov. *Vospominaniia,* vol. 1. Moscow, 1967.   [11–243–1]

TREASURY. (1) A depository of money, valuables, and other material wealth of khans, tsars, grand dukes and appanage princes, and monasteries.

(2) In centralized states, the aggregate of financial resources of the state. Through the treasury, the state is legally the holder of certain property rights and interests. Socialist countries have no need for this concept of a treasury.   [11–527–3]

TREASURY, in capitalist countries a special government body in charge of the cash fulfillment of the state budget. The treasury organizes the collection of such state revenues as taxes, fees, customs duties, and the proceeds from sale of state bonds; it also allocates funds to cover budget expenditures. In many instances the treasury issues paper money.

In the USA the Department of the Treasury is the ministry of finance; in France the treasury is set up as the treasury office of the Ministry of Finance, and in Great Britain it is an independent agency. In most capitalist countries, the state makes the central banks of issue responsible for the cash fulfillment of the budget. The "bank system" reduces state expenses for maintaining the treasury administration and facilitates state control over the resources of the budget.

In Russia the treasury was established after 1863 when the department of the state treasury was created within the Ministry of Finance. The treasury exercised control over the local bodies known as financial boards. All revenues collected by the treasury system were registered in one account at the state bank.

There is no treasury in the USSR. Cash fulfillment of the state budget is accomplished by the Gosbank (State Bank) of the USSR.   A. B. EIDEL'NANT   [11–528–3]

TREASURY ISSUE, the introduction of paper money into circulation by the treasury or other state financial body.

Under capitalism, treasury issue is inflationary in nature. A bourgeois state resorts to treasury issue during crises, particularly in times of war if the current revenues (mainly taxes) of the state budget are insufficient to cover government expenditures. The treasury issue is one of the concealed ways of robbing the toiling masses and mobilizing additional resources. Before the general crisis of capitalism, when bank notes could still be exchanged for gold, a treasury issue by its economic nature and consequences greatly differed from a bank note issue, which was connected with the broadening of credit operations and the growth of commodity circulation. Since the world economic crisis of 1929–33, when the exchange of bank notes for gold was abolished and bank note issues were used to cover budget deficits, a treasury issue is not any different from a bank note issue.

In socialist countries, a treasury issue is effected in a planned manner on the same credit basis as the issue of bank notes, according to the requirements of economic circulation for paper money of the smaller denominations. In the USSR paper money is issued by the Gosbank (State Bank) of the USSR.

A. B. EIDEL'NANT [11–528–1]

TREASURY NOTES, money not exchangeable for gold and issued by the treasury, as well as short-term treasury obligations in circulation. Before World War I, treasury notes greatly differed from bank notes, which were put out by the banks of issue to credit commodity circulation and which were exchangeable for gold. During and for some time after World War I, budget deficits were often covered by treasury notes, as well as by bank notes (which ceased to be exchangeable for gold). During World War II, military expenditures were financed by short-term treasury obligations, such as the "occupation marks" issued by fascist Germany that circulated in countries temporarily occupied by Germany.

In the USSR, treasury notes are used to replace bank notes and to pay small bills. Treasury notes circulate in the country on an equal basis with bank notes. Treasury notes are issued by the Gosbank (State Bank) of the USSR according to its emission plan in denominations of one, three, and five rubles. By law, treasury notes are backed by the national property of the USSR, and their acceptance at their nominal value is mandatory throughout the entire country for all types of payments.

A. B. EIDEL'NANT [11–528–2]

TRENCH DIGGER, a machine for digging drainage ditches and irrigation channels, trenches, ditches along roads, and so on. There are trench diggers with moving parts (rotor or cutter) and nonmoving parts (plow or moldboard), as well as trench diggers with combined elements (for example, with a moldboard and rotor or with a rotor, auger, and multiscoop unit).

Cutters or rotors are mounted on a tractor, trailer, or self-propelled chassis. Trench diggers with one or two cutters are used for making drainage ditches 0.5–2 m deep in swampy-peat soils. The cutters turn at up to 30 m per sec; such a velocity is necessary to create a cutting force, break up vegetation and peat, and throw the dug-up earth up to 20 m away. Rotor trench diggers are used to make irrigation ditches up to 2 m deep in dense soils. The rotors turn at speeds up to 8 m per sec. The earth is thrown a short distance and is often used to form dikes. Depending on the type of earth and the cross section of the ditch, cutter and rotor trench diggers require one or several passes to complete the channel. The productivity of cutter and rotor trench diggers varies between 80 and 800 cu m per hr.

Plow (trailer or mounted) and moldboard trench diggers make channels using the tractive force of the tractor. The working element of plow trench diggers is a double-moldboard plow which, moved by one or several tractors, makes a channel 0.4–1.2 m deep in one pass and can move up to 1,800 cu m per hr. The working element of the moldboard trench digger is two symmetrical grader-type moldboards that work the soil by layers, shaping the bottom and walls of the channel with a productivity up to 1,500 cu m per hr.

Trench diggers with combined working elements make a channel up to 3 m deep in one pass and grade the bottom and walls. Each of the working elements works a specific part of the channel. These trench diggers are also used for making cunettes along railroads and for other earthmoving work. All elements of the channel are finished in one pass. The productivity of the combined trench digger depends on the working elements used and on the number of passes. One of the basic characteristics of trench diggers is the small pressure per unit of area on the ground (for heavy-duty trench diggers the average value should not be more than 9 meganewtons per sq m [0.9 kilogram-force per sq cm], an especially important feature for working on very moist, soft, and loose ground.

Trench diggers are used extensively in the national economy for working peat deposits, building drainage and irrigation channels, and performing other earth-moving jobs.

REFERENCES
Mashiny dlia stroitel'stva i soderzhaniia osushitel'nykh kanalov. Moscow, 1969.
Riabov, G. A., I. I. Mer, and G. T. Prudnikov. *Meliorativnye i stroitel'nye mashiny.* Moscow, 1968. S. A. SOLOMONOV [11–865–4]

TUNING FORK, a source of sound, consisting of a metal rod that is bent and fixed in the center. The ends of the rod can vibrate freely. During the tuning of musical instruments, the tuning fork serves as the standard pitch of a tone; it is also used to give the pitch in singing. Forks that produce the tone A' (A of the first octave) are usually used. Singers and choral conductors also use forks producing the tone C". There are chromatic tuning forks, with prongs that have movable little weights. Depending on the position of these weights, the prongs vibrate at different frequencies.

The tuning fork was invented by the English musician J. Shore in 1711. At that time the standard frequency of vibrations for the tone A' was 419.9 hertz (Hz). In the late 18th century the composer and conductor G. Sarti, who was working in St. Petersburg, introduced the "St. Petersburg tuning fork," with an A' = 436 Hz. In 1858 the Paris Academy of Sciences proposed a standard pitch tuning fork with A' = 435 Hz. In 1885 at an international conference in Vienna this frequency was adopted as the international standard pitch for the tone A'; the frequency was called the standard musical pitch. Since Jan. 1, 1936, an all-Union standard pitch of A' = 440 Hz has been in effect in the USSR.

REFERENCE
Muzykal'naia akustika. Edited by N. A. Garbuzov. Moscow-Leningrad, 1940. [11–802–1]

UMBILICAL TOWER, a launch position or launch system aggregate at a space center: a metal tower for delivering electrical, fuel, drainage, and pneumatic connecting lines to the rocket and for servicing the rocket. The umbilical tower is mounted on the launch system or alongside it and has detachable connecting lines between the rocket and the surface utility lines. The towers have elevators and swinging platforms; they are sometimes up to 100 m tall, and the length of a side of the rectangular base may be up to 20 m. [11–284–1]

VEGETABLE MARROW, a bush variety of the hard-shelled pumpkin (*Cucurbita pepo*). They are annual monoecious plants with erect, slightly branching shoots, which usually are not long-running. The flowers are unisexual, solitary, and yellow. The fruit is a pepo, which is generally cylindrical; more rarely, it is slightly bent. Vegetable marrow is frost-tender and needs fertile soil. It is relatively drought resistant; however, when irrigated, its yield is increased significantly. The fruits ripen early; the growth from sprouts to mature plants takes between 40 and 50 days. Young fruits are used in the preparation of various dishes; they are also a foodstuff used in the canning industry (squash paste). The fruits contain on the average 4.9 percent dry matter, including 2.55 percent sugar, 0.55 percent proteins, and 0.13 percent fats. The young fruits are also used for fodder. Vegetable marrow is used year-round as green fodder. One hundred kilograms of the fruit contain 5.5 fodder units and 0.7 kg of digestible protein.

Varieties of vegetable marrow that have been cultivated in the USSR include Greek 100 (Middle Asia), Gribovskii 37 (RSFSR, Ukrainian SSR, Byelorussian SSR, and the Baltic republics), Sauté 38 and Kul'dzhin (Moldavian SSR), and Odessa 52 (Ukrainian SSR, Moldavian SSR, and Tadzhik SSR). In the south, vegetable marrow is cultivated by planting seeds in the soil. In the central part of the European USSR and in more northerly regions the plants are cultivated by transplanting. After the spring frosts the seedlings are transplanted at the age of 20–25 days.

In the south the area of planting is 1.4 × 0.7 m; in the central region, 0.8 × 0.8 m. The fruits are harvested every seven to ten days, when they have a soft skin and incompletely formed seeds. The fruits used for fodder are gathered less frequently, and, as a result, they are larger. However, they must be harvested before the shell becomes hard. The yield of vegetable marrows reaches 200–300 centners/hectare. In order to obtain an early harvest, vegetable marrow is raised in hotbeds.

REFERENCE
Markov, V. M. *Ovoshchevodstvo.* Moscow, 1966.

A. M. SEMENKO   [11–272–2]

VERTICAL LATHE, a metal-cutting lathe designed for large articles with relatively small length *l* in comparison to diameter *D* ($l/D < 1$ for light and medium lathes, $l/D < 0.5$ for heavy lathes).

The vertical lathe makes it convenient to mount, align, and fasten the items to be worked. For this reason it has replaced the facing lathe, which was used previously. The distinguishing feature of the vertical turning lathe is the vertical position of the spindle. A chuck is located on the top of the spindle; the piece to be worked is fastened to the chuck, using radially displaced cams. It is the item itself that goes through the principal rotary motion on the vertical lathe; the cutting tool, fixed on a support, has a translatory feed motion. The strain on the spindle is partially relieved because the weight of the item and the cutting forces are absorbed by the circularly directing chucks.

There are open-sided and double-sided (portal) vertical lathes. Open-sided vertical lathes usually have both vertical and lateral supports; two-sided lathes have two vertical and either one or two lateral supports. A rotating turret is often placed on one of the vertical supports. The vertical lathe is usually driven by several electric motors (many, in the case of the heavy lathe), which, during operation, transmit the motion to the chuck spindle and supports (working and idling or accelerated) and serve to attach the crosshead and brake engagement.

The vertical lathe is used to machine and bore cylindrical, conical, and contoured surfaces and to trim face ends. Lathes with a turret can also drill, counterbore, and ream. Engraving, slotting, milling, and polishing are possible with special attachments. It is possible on a vertical lathe to work with a number of cutting tools simultaneously, with each tool fastened to a separate support. This increases efficiency significantly.

The rigidity of construction of the vertical lathe makes it possible to work on particularly large items with a high degree of precision. For example, pieces weighing as much as 500 tons and more, with diameters to 30 m (parts of powerful hydraulic turbines, turbogenerators, atomic reactors, and proton synchrotrons), may be worked on heavy two-sided models.

D. L. YUDIN   [11–1454–3]

VERTICAL SCANNING, sequential (line by line) discrete scanning of a television image in a vertical direction. A vertical scanning generator with a deflecting system moves the electronic beam from top to bottom linearly over time (direct stroke) on the screen of the kinescope or photosensitive (target) electrode of the pick-up tube and then returns rapidly to the initial position (back stroke). The duration of the back stroke is nearly 8 percent of the scan period. The vertical sweep frequency (frame frequency) is equal to the rated frequency of the commercial mains (50 or 60 cycles per sec).   [11–383–3]

VERTICAL SCANNING GENERATOR, an electronic device for vertical image scanning. Vertical scanning generators are used in television cameras and receivers for cophasal and synchronous deflection of the electron beams in camera tubes and kinescopes. In television, electromagnetic deflection of the electron beam is usually used for vertical scanning. It is created by an electric current flowing in the deflection coils; the current varies linearly according to a sawtooth law. Current of this type is produced by a vertical scanning generator, the main parts of which are a self-excited oscillator of short-duration square pulses with a repetition frequency of 50–60 hertz, a circuit or stage for the formation of the control (sawtooth) voltage, and a scanning output stage.

A blocking oscillator (less often, a multivibrator), to which the frame synchronizing pulses contained in a composite picture are fed, is most frequently used as the square-pulse oscillator. The control voltage is formed in an electron-tube stage or a transistor with a discharging circuit. Scanning output stages with a transformer output, to which the vertical deflection coils are connected, are the most common. The control voltage is fed to such an output stage in the form of a parabolic pulse.

N. G. DERIUGIN   [11–384–1]

VIBURNUM, a genus of mainly deciduous shrubs or small trees of the family Caprifoliaceae. The leaves are opposite; they are either entire or lobed. The flowers, which are white or pink, are gathered into an umbel, corymb, or panicle. The marginal flowers are sterile and often larger than the rest. The fruit is a drupe, which is used for food. The bark contains tannins, resin, and several acids. The wood is used in the manufacture of small articles. There are approximately 120–200 species in Europe, Asia, North Africa, and North, Central, and South America. In the USSR there are eight species. The most important of these is the European cranberrybush (*Viburnum opulus*), which is found in the forests of European USSR, the Caucasus, Western Siberia, and Middle Asia. It is cultivated as an ornamental throughout the European USSR, where it is known as *bul'-denezh.* The bark of the trunk and branches yield a liquid extract, which is gathered in the early spring and dried. It is used medically as a hemostatic (mainly in uterine hemorrhages). The species *V. orientalis,* which has fruiting marginal blossoms, grows in the Caucasus. The species *V. burejaeticum* and *V. sargentii* are found in the Far East. The wayfaring tree also belongs to the genus *Viburnum.*   T. G. LEONOVA   [11–607–1]

VULPES VULPES CARAGAN (Russian *karaganka*), a subspecies of the common (red) fox. It is found in the steppes and semideserts of Kazakhstan and is smaller than the Middle Russian foxes. Its winter coat is yellowish gray or sandy yellow. The pelt is comparatively coarse, short, and less valuable than that of the northern fox.   [11–1119–1]

WARBLER, the name of several genera of small songbirds of the family Sylviidae. These genera include *Acrocephalus, Locustella, Phragmaticola, Cettia,* and *Horeites.* The plumage above is brownish and monochromatic or striped; the underside is lighter in color. Males and females are colored alike.

Warblers are found throughout Europe, Asia, and Africa. In the USSR there are approximately 20 species, distributed in all zones except the tundra. Many species dwell in shrub thickets or in waterside reeds; some species live in forests or gardens. Warblers are migratory birds. Their nests are usually open; however, sometimes they have roofs. The nests are built in shrubs and reeds or, less often, on the ground. The clutch contains between four and six eggs. Warblers feed on insects, spiders, and small mollusks.   [11–860–2]

WELL LOGGING, geophysical testing of wells, used to study geologic cross sections and to detect minerals. The term "well logging," which was first used in mining, does not completely correspond to the idea described. In addition to "logging," the terms "geophysical well-testing methods," "field geophysics," and "drilling geophysics" are also used in the scientific and technical literature.

The first geophysical well tests—temperature measurements—were performed by D. V. Golubiatnikov in 1908 at the Baku oil fields. Electrical well logging by the apparent-resistivity method was proposed in 1926 by the Schlumberger brothers (France). The high effectiveness of electrical well logging has brought about its rapid adoption by the petroleum industry and provided impetus for the development of other well-testing methods. In the Soviet Union, major contributions to the theory, methods, and technology of well logging were made by L. M. Al'pin, M. I. Bal'zamov, G. V. Gorshkov, V. N. Dakhnov, A. I. Zaborovskii, A. A. Korzhev, S. G. Komarov, B. Pontekorvo, A. S. Semenov, M. M. Sokolov, V. A. Fok, and V. A. Shpak. Important research in logging theory and methods has also been done in the USA (G. Archie, H. Guyod, J. Dewan, H. Doll, M. Martin, W. Russell, and J. Wyllie).

Geophysical well testing is done by electrical, magnetic, radioactivity (nuclear), thermal, and acoustic (ultrasonic) methods. During the performance of these tests, certain measurements that depend on a single property or on a combination of physical properties of the rock through which a well is driven are made along the well bore by means of geophysical sensors lowered into the well on a cable. The signals from the sensor are transmitted to the surface and recorded in analog form (diagrams) or in digital form by ground equipment installed in a vehicle.

Resistivity, diffusion-adsorption, and artificially induced electrochemical activity of rock are studied using methods of electrical well logging. The apparent-resistivity method, including the microprobe method, the shielded-ground resistance method (side logging), and the induction method are based on the study of electrical resistivity. The difference in the diffusion-adsorption activity of rock is used in the spontaneous polarization method, but the ability of rock to become polarized under the effect of electric current is used in the induced-polarization method. The magnetic method is used to measure the magnetic susceptibility of rock. Radioactivity (nuclear) logging methods are based on well measurements of the natural or artificially induced radioactive radiation of rock. In the latter case the neutron, gamma-gamma, induced-activity, and radioactive-isotope methods are used. The nuclear-magnetic logging method consists in observation of the change in the electromotive force that occurs in rock after it has been subjected to a polarizing magnetic field. Thermal methods are used for the study of temperature in wells. The acoustic (ultrasonic) method is based on the study of the velocity and attenuation of elastic waves in rock. Gas and luminescent bituminologic logging are geochemical well-testing methods. Methods based on the study of the mechanical properties (drillability) of rock during the drilling process (mechanical logging) are also sometimes used.

The task of geophysical well logging includes correlation (comparison) of well cross sections, determination of the lithology and depth of occurrence of the rocks through which the well passes, determination and evaluation of mineral reserves (petroleum, gas, water, coal, ores, and building materials), and monitoring of the development of oil and gas fields. Logging is the principal geologic method of documentation of deep well sections.

REFERENCES
Komarov, S. G. *Geofizicheskie metody issledovaniia skvazhin.* Moscow, 1963.
Pomerants, L. I., and V. T. Chukin. *Promyslovo-geofizicheskaia apparatura i oborudovanie.* Moscow, 1966.
Dakhnov, V. N. *Interpretatsiia rezul'tatov geofizicheskikh issledovanii razrezov skvazhin.* Moscow, 1972.   V. M. DOBRYNIN [11–1338–3]

WELL-LOGGING UNIT, a mobile automatic installation for conducting geophysical tests in wells (well logging). It consists of borehole instruments and probes, which are sensors of geophysical parameters; surface equipment, which makes possible analog or digital recording of the readings of the borehole instruments and probes; special logging cable, by means of which the borehole devices are connected to the surface equipment; and winches for hoisting and lowering operations in the borehole.

An automatic well-logging unit is usually mounted on one or two vehicles; in the latter case the surface measuring equipment is installed in the laboratory vehicle, and the winch, cable, and borehole devices are installed in a separate, self-propelled hoisting vehicle. Serial well-logging units perform all types of geophysical operations in wells up to 7,000 m deep, recording as many as four or five different parameters in a single lowering and hoisting operation. Portable well-logging units are used for testing wells that are located in inaccessible areas.

V. M. DOBRYNIN [11–1340–1]

WHEATEAR, any bird of the genus *Oenanthe,* family Turdidae (thrushes). Its size is that of a sparrow to that of a starling. It has a thin beak that is broad at the base and strong, long legs.

Wheatears are found in Europe, Asia, Africa, and North America. They inhabit open places in plains or mountains. They move along the ground by hopping. Their nests are built in ravines, rock streams, crevices in cliffs, buildings, and old rodent burrows. Wheatears are insectivorous migratory birds. A clutch contains four to eight light blue eggs. In the USSR there are seven species. The common wheatear (*O. oenanthe*) is found almost everywhere throughout the country. The desert wheatear (*O. deserti*), black-eared wheatear (*O. hispanica*), Isabelline wheatear (*O. isabellina*), Indian pied wheatear (*O. picata*), (*O. finschii*), and red-rumped wheatear (*O. xanthoprymna*) are found in the southern part of the European USSR (including the Caucasus), Kazakhstan, Middle Asia, and Southern Siberia.

A. S. MAL'CHEVSKII [11–743–5]

WIRE ROD, hot-rolled wire having a round section with a diameter between 5 and 10 mm. Wire rod is produced on special wire-rod mills or combination wire-rod–section mills and wound into coils by coiling machines. Most wire rod goes into the production of cold-drawn wire up to 0.01 mm in diameter. Springs and reinforced-concrete fittings are also made from steel wire rod. [11–1553–7]

WORLD CAPITALIST ECONOMY, the aggregate of international economic intercommunications and interrelations of the countries of the nonsocialist world. It includes both advanced capitalist states and economically backward countries. Underlying the system is the dominance of private property in the means of production and bourgeois relations of distribution and exchange. The determining role in the world capitalist economy is that of the production relations arising on the basis of the capitalist mode of production; these relations are mediated in the system through the relationship of the international exchange of goods, financial means, and various kinds of commercial services.

The process of the formation of the world capitalist economy unfolds in two basic directions: the line of capitalist development in depth, that is, through the growth of capitalist production in individual capitalist countries; and the development of capitalism in breadth, chiefly through the spread of the colonial and semicolonial rule of a few capitalist countries to an increasing number of countries and territories. The material wealth expropriated by the bourgeoisie from the dependent countries served as the basis for the process of primitive accumulation of capital in the parent countries.

The long process of formation of the world capitalist economy began in the 16th century and was concluded by the beginning of the 20th century. The merging of industrial capital with banking capital and the establishment of the complete domination of finance capital in the world economy and politics resulted in the ultimate transformation of the world capitalist economy under imperialism into an antagonistic combination of two main groups of countries: the industrially developed capitalist states and the vast number of agrarian, raw-material colonial and dependent countries. By this time, the internal contradictions within the group of industrially developed countries had also intensified sharply; these contradictions were manifested in the struggle for commodity and capital markets. Studying the laws of development of the world economy of the early 20th century,

V. I. Lenin exposed the dual monopoly that had become established: first, the monopoly of finance capital in the developed capitalist countries, and second, the monopoly of these few countries over the rest of the world. At a given stage of the development of the world capitalist economy, the concentration of production and of international exchange in the hands of the monopolies became the material basis for the colonial rule of the imperialist powers. The export of capital became one of the most essential features of the world capitalist economy. The combination of precapitalist forms of production with imperialist forms and methods of exploitation deepened the contradictions of the system and resulted in a further increase in the unevenness of development of the system's various parts, of different countries and regions. This resulted in a crisis for the economic system, a crisis that was an integral part of the general crisis of capitalism.

The beginning of the crisis of the world capitalist economy, its first stage, is characterized by a substantial contraction of the sphere of imperialist dominance of the world economy and by a noticeable weakening of its colonial foundations. The victory of the Great October Socialist Revolution signified (1) the undermining of an important economic basis of imperialism—the territorial division of the world; (2) a sharply narrowed sphere of interimperialist struggle for the economic partition and repartition of the world; and (3) as a result, decreased possibilities of using the export of capital as an all-round means of imperialist expansion on an international scale. The crisis of the colonial system began under the influence of the Great October Socialist Revolution. Within the narrowed framework of the world capitalist economy, the imperialist struggle to partition monopoly spheres of influence continued to grow, although the possibilities for such a struggle were already limited. In its expansionist policies, the finance capital of these powers came into conflict with the need to deal with the relation of forces in the world arena and its changes, which were not to the advantage of finance capital. From 1929 to 1933 the economy of world capitalism was shaken to its foundation by the greatest cyclical crisis of overproduction in its history.

World War II marked the onset of the second stage of the crisis of the world capitalist economy. After the war, a number of new countries of Europe and Asia embarked on the path of socialism, and the process of the formation of the world socialist economic system began. During the first postwar years, the restoration and further development of the international economic ties of capitalism, which had been sharply disrupted by the war, also proceeded; relatively rapid, although unstable and uneven, growth in the productive forces of capitalism was also evident. By the mid-1950's, the volume of industrial production within the limits of the world capitalist economy (considerably diminished after the war) was more than twice as great as the level of the prewar years; the physical volume of the international goods turnover had grown by nearly two-thirds. But within the framework of the world capitalist economy, narrowed by socialism, imperialism found itself no longer able to determine completely the direction of development of world economics and politics as it had previously, or to rule the destinies of the peoples of many countries of the Third World. After the war, a number of colonies achieved national independence. Their rates of economic growth also accelerated.

The third stage in the crisis of the world capitalist economy, which began to take shape in about the mid-1950's, proceeded under the condition of the rapid growth of the world socialist economy, the further increase in the unevenness of development of capitalism, and the completion of the disintegration of the greatest colonial empires. The determining factor in the further deepening of the crisis of the world capitalist economy was the rapidly growing might of world socialism. At the same time, a noticeable growth of productive forces was evident in the capitalist world. Between 1955 and 1970, the magnitude of industrial production of the nonsocialist world increased 2.2 times, with an increase of approximately 2.16 times in the developed capitalist countries and nearly 3 times in the developing countries. But such growth in production did not, on the whole, lead to a strengthening of the position of imperialism in the world capitalist economy. Interimperialist contradictions further intensified as a result of the change in the relation of forces between the

monopolies of the various countries. The basic antagonism of the capitalist mode of production became steadily aggravated, and on this basis all social antagonisms within the advanced capitalist countries deepened. The expansion of the struggle for true independence of the emancipated countries, the growing might of world socialism, and world socialism's all-out support of the national liberation movement in the Third World caused the virtual breakdown of the colonial system of imperialism.

All of the aforementioned interconnected processes predetermined the consistent advance of the development of the crisis of the world capitalist economy and a progressive weakening of the hegemony of the finance capital of imperialist powers within the system. Tendencies reflecting the undermining of the monopoly position of imperialism and international economic relations as a result of the rapid growth of economic and technical cooperation among the socialist and developing countries began to acquire particular significance. As a result, imperialism's ability to use commercial-economic blockades effectively against former colonies and semicolonies is decreasing substantially. Under the new conditions, the colonial policies of the imperialist powers aim at keeping the emancipated countries in an unequal position in the international capitalist division of labor. Even under the conditions of the disintegration of the colonial system of imperialism, the vast gap between the levels of economic development of the two main groups of countries remains a feature of the greatest importance in the structure of the world capitalist economy. Less than one-sixth of the aggregate gross product of the world capitalist economy is produced in the Third World, although more than two-thirds of the population of the nonsocialist countries is concentrated there.

Fundamental changes in the economy of world capitalism have been occurring in a crucial branch of material production —industry, a branch characterized by a sharp increase in the unevenness of the rate of development of individual leading branches under the influence of scientific and technical progress. The following long-term tendencies in the structure of industry have come to light: (1) the noticeable decline, on the whole, of the extractive branches; (2) the comparatively slow growth rates of light industry and the corresponding drop in its relative role; (3) a sharp increase in the role of most branches of heavy industry, whose share in the total volume of industrial production of the world capitalist economy reached 57 percent in the early 1970's, whereas it had been about 40 percent at the end of the 1930's; and (4) the growing importance of the energy industry, whose share has correspondingly increased from 4 to 8 percent.

The growth in the role of heavy industry has been particularly marked in the course of the modern scientific and technical revolution, which embraces primarily the most monopolized sectors of the world capitalist economy. The comparatively rapid growth of these sectors predetermines the nature and characteristics of the expansion of the international capitalist division of labor, as well as a noticeable enhancement of the relative role of the industrially developed countries. The overall increase in the physical volume of the goods turnover on the world capitalist market was 2.9 times from 1955 to 1970, and the share of these countries in this turnover increased from 75 to 81 percent. In the economy of the Third World, processes that in turn are beginning to influence the structure of the international division of labor have also taken shape. These processes are bound up primarily with the appreciable acceleration of the growth rates of industry in the countries of the agrarian, raw-material periphery of the world capitalist economy. Consequently, the volume of their industrial production as a whole increased 3.2 times from 1955 to 1970. It was, fundamentally, precisely in the sphere of industrial production, that the disintegration of the colonial system began to influence the structure of the international capitalist division of labor.

In the context of the deepening of the crisis of the world capitalist economy, characteristic changes in agriculture, the other major sphere of material production, have also been taking place. The scope of these changes has been considerably smaller than in industry, a reflection of one of the most general and profound contradictions of the capitalist mode of production— that between industry and agriculture. The total volume of agricultural production within the contemporary nonsocialist world increased by 45 percent between 1955 and 1970; in 1970 it was slightly more than double the average level of 1934–38. When population growth is taken into account, the growth of per capita agricultural output was insignificant. In the early 1970's, agricultural production averaged 18–20 percent higher than in the early 1950's, with the increase coming primarily from the developed capitalist countries.

Advances in the sphere of material production to an important degree predetermined the characteristics of development of the international division of labor under contemporary capitalism. The disproportionate growth of the main branches of industry and agriculture led to a still greater imbalance in the development of various orientations in international goods turnover, on the whole and also within individual groups of countries. Competition and the struggle for markets and spheres of capital investment continue to grow among the imperialist states and among the monopolies and their allies. Measures with respect to the economic partition of the world capitalist economy become increasingly state-monopolistic in nature. At the same time, the tendency toward imperialist integration is gathering force. This is a tendency that accelerates the breakup of interstate economic partitions and increases the degree of socialization of production. But along with this, the objectively progressive process of the economic rapprochement of nations develops, as previously, in extremely distorted forms. Competing commercial-economic blocs are created—blocs that are alliances of the financial oligarchy for joint onslaughts against the position of the toiling people and for the economic subjugation and exploitation of the developing countries. The further deepening of the irreconcilable antagonisms of the world capitalist economic system is reflected in the growing disorganization of its currency and financial system. The crisis of this structure has turned into one of the most important currents of the general crisis of the capitalist world— increasing inflation, uneven balances of payments, and the expansion of currency restrictions.

State-monopoly capitalism uses every means to strengthen the capitalist world economy: the functions of the state are expanded to cover the primary areas of economic life of capitalist society, and the role of programming and regulating the world capitalist economy is enhanced.

The tasks of the socioeconomic progress of humanity and of the accelerated growth of its productive forces in the contemporary era demand with ever-increasing urgency the liquidation of the world system of economic exploitation of some countries by others and the creation of a genuinely equitable international division of labor—an all-embracing system of world economic relations that would respond to the vital interests of human society.

REFERENCES

Marx, K. *Kapital,* vols. 1–3. In K. Marx and F. Engels, *Soch.,* 2nd ed., vols. 23–26.
Lenin, V. I. "K kharakteristike ekonomicheskogo romantizma." *Poln. sobr. soch.,* 5th ed., vol. 2.
Lenin, V. I. "Imperializm, kak vysshaia stadiia kapitalizma." *Ibid.,* vol. 27.
Materialy XXIII s"ezda KPSS. Moscow, 1966.
Materialy XXIV s"ezda KPSS. Moscow, 1971.
Mezhdunarodnoe soveshchanie kommunisticheskikh i rabochikh partii: Dokumenty i materialy. Moscow, 1969.
Manukian, A. A. *Problemy poslevoennogo razvitiia ekonomiki kapitalisticheskikh stran.* Moscow, 1966.
Rymalov, V. V. *Raspad kolonial'noi sistemy i mirovoe kapitalisticheskoe khoziaistvo.* Moscow, 1966.
Bunkina, M. K. *Tsentry mirovogo imperializma: itogi razvitiia i rasstanovka sil.* Moscow, 1970.
Politicheskaia ekonomiia sovremennogo monopolisticheskogo kapitalizma, vol. 2. Moscow, 1970. V. V. RYMALOV [11–1050–1]

YEATS, JACK BUTLER. Born 1871 in Sligo; died Mar. 28, 1957, in Dublin. Irish painter. Founder and leader of the Irish national school of painting in the 20th century.

Yeats was the son of the portraitist John B. Yeats (1839–1922) and brother of the poet W. B. Yeats. He studied in Dublin and at the Westminster Art School in London. His creative work is imbued with humanism and love for his country and its national life, nature, and history. Romantic liveliness, impetuosity, and breadth are inherent in his manner of painting (*After the Races,* Tate Gallery, London; and *The Magician* and *The Old Slave Woman,* Municipal Gallery of Modern Art, Dublin).

REFERENCE

Pyle, H. *Jack B. Yeats: A Bibliography.* London, 1970. [11–217–6]

YEATS, WILLIAM BUTLER. Born June 13, 1865, in Sandymount near Dublin; died Jan. 28, 1939, in Roquebrune, France; in 1948 his remains were brought back to Sligo, Ireland; Irish poet and playwright.

Yeats grew up among the aristocracy and studied at the universities of Dublin and Oxford. During the 1890's he was the moving force behind the Irish Renaissance movement. From 1922 to 1928 he was a member of the Irish senate and from 1904 to 1938 he was one of the directors of the Abbey Theater and helped create the Irish Literary Theater. His interest in mythology and folklore influenced some of his works, such as *The Wanderings of Oisin* (1889) and *The Celtic Twilight* (1893). Irish national myth and the notion of eternal beauty in the Rose cycle (1893) and the collection *The Wind Among the Reeds* (1889) were the sources of the poetic symbols in Yeats' early poetry. The ideas behind the national liberation movement served as the inspirational source of his patriotic play *Cathleen ni Houlihan* (1902). His collection of verse entitled *Responsibilities* (1916) marked a turn toward confessional and civic poetry. History and its real heroes became a living part of Yeats' works (his poems "September 1913," "Sixteen Dead Men," and "The Rose"), and the Dublin uprising of 1916 and the execution of the patriots provided the theme of his poem "Easter 1916." In his search for a new form for his poetic drama, Yeats turned to the Japanese No theater in the early 20th century and wrote plays in which masks were to be worn (*At the Hawk's Well,* 1916; and *The Only Jealousy of Emer,* 1919). Man's courage and readiness for self-sacrifice was contrasted with the power of magic in these plays.

Yeats' spiritual crisis, precipitated by his disenchantment with the results of the struggle for national liberation that had strengthened bourgeois rule in Ireland, was reflected in his collections *The Tower* (1928) and *The Winding Stair* (1933). In the 1930's his symbolism acquired ironic and satirical overtones, and his *Last Poems and Plays* (1940) and *The Death of Cuchulain* (1939) combine a pessimistic world view with satire directed against modern society. Yeats translated Jonathan Swift's epitaph and wrote a play about him entitled *The Words Upon the Window Pane* (1931). In the poem "The Municipal Gallery Revisited" (1939), Yeats summed up all his work, the chief principle of which he felt was his link with his native land. He won the Nobel Prize in 1923.

WORKS

Autobiographies. London, 1956.
The Variorum Edition of the Poems. New York, 1957.
Essays and Introductions. London, 1961.
The Variorum Edition of the Plays. New York, 1966.
Uncollected Prose, vol. 1. London, 1970.
In Russian translation:
In *Antologiia novoi angliiskoi poezii.* Introduction by M. Gutner. Leningrad, 1937.

REFERENCES

Eremina, I. K. "Ranniaia dramaturgiia U. B. Eitsa." *Uch. zap. Moskovskogo obl. ped. in-ta,* 1967, vol. 175, issue 10.
Home, J. *W. B. Yeats: 1865–1939,* 2nd ed. London, 1962.
Ellmann, R. *The Identity of Yeats,* 2nd ed. New York, 1964.
Zwerdling, A. *Yeats and the Heroic Ideal.* New York, 1965. (Bibliography, pp. 183–90.)
Nathan, L. E. *The Tragic Drama of William Butler Yeats.* New York– London, 1965.
Ure, P. *Towards a Mythology.* New York [1968].
Jeffares, A. N. *The Circus Animals: Essays on W. B. Yeats.* [London, 1970.]
Cross, K. G., and R. T. Dunlop. *A Bibliography of Yeats Criticism: 1887–1965.* [London, 1971.] A. P. SARUKHANIAN [11–217–7]

YEKUN, WALI-AL-DIN. Born 1873 in Istanbul; died 1921 in Helwan. Egyptian Arab publicist and poet.

Yekun was the son of a Turkish pasha. In his articles and essays, he described the terrors of the regime of Abdul-Hamid II and criticized the results of the Young Turk Revolution of 1908. He also dealt with questions concerning the development of Arabic culture. Yekun wrote numerous poems, which were published in a divan in 1924. He was also the author of an unfinished novel, *Dikram and Raif,* which dealt with Turkish revolutionary youth. Yekun's style was characterized by the combination of emotionality and ardent loftiness with caustic satire.

WORKS

al-Malum wa al-Majhhul, vols. 1–2. Cairo, 1909–10.
al-Sahaif al-Sud. Cairo, 1910.
al-Tajarib. Alexandria, 1913.
In Russian translation:
In *Arabskaia proza.* Moscow, 1956.

REFERENCES

Krachkovskii, I. Iu. *Izbr. soch.,* vol. 3. Moscow-Leningrad, 1956. (See index.)
Dolinina, A. A. *Ocherki istorii arabskoi literatury novogo vremeni: Egipet i Siriia.* Moscow, 1968.
Brockelmann, K. *Geschichte der arabischen Literatur,* supplementary vol. 3. Leiden, 1942. Pages 49–56.   [11–187–5]

YELLOWKNIFE, a city in northern Canada; capital of the Northwest Territories. Population, 5,900 (1971). It is located on the Great Slave Lake, 410 km south of the arctic circle. It is the center of a gold-mining region (there are three mines, the largest of which yields about 6 tons of gold per year).   [11–188–1]

YELLOWSTONE, a river in the northwestern USA; right tributary of the Missouri. Length, about 1,600 km; basin area, 182,300 sq km. It rises in the Rocky Mountains. In its upper reaches there are canyons up to 360 m deep, as well as waterfalls; in the middle and lower course it is a calm plains river. It is fed by snow and rain; there is spring and summer flooding. The average water discharge is 365 m³/sec. The upper course of the river passes through Yellowstone National Park. In the state of Montana it is widely used for irrigation.   [11–188–2]

YELLOWSTONE NATIONAL PARK, located in the northwestern USA in Wyoming, Montana, and Idaho. Founded in 1872, it is the oldest national park in the country. Area, about 9,000 sq km (1970). It is located in the Rocky Mountains on a volcanic plateau at an elevation of 2,200–2,500 m.

In geological structure the plateau of Yellowstone National Park is a subsidence that dates from the Paleocene and is filled with later volcanic and glacial deposits. Points of interest include more than 3,000 geysers (the highest stream of the Excelsior geyser is up to 90 m) and hot springs and many mud volcanoes and lakes. Other interesting sights are the Grand Canyon of the Yellowstone, 360 m deep and 20 km long; waterfalls up to 94 m high; and petrified trees buried under volcanic ash. There is also coniferous forest (a number of species of pine, fir, and spruce, with some alder, birch, and aspen). The park is inhabited by bison, American black bear, deer, grizzly, elk, pronghorn, bighorn sheep, and coyotes and trumpeter swan, bald eagle, and white pelican (about 200 species of birds). The principal tourist season is June through August.   [11–188–3]

YEMEN, the southwestern and southern Arabian Peninsula. The Arabic name of Yemen (al-Yaman, literally "the right side") probably goes back to antiquity, when to the inhabitants of northern Arabia it meant the country located to the right-hand side (when one stands facing the sunrise), while Syria was called al-Sham, "the left side."

In ancient times Yemen included almost all of the Arabian Peninsula from the Gulf of Aqaba in the west to the lower course of the Euphrates in the east. Ancient geographers called this territory Arabia Felix (Fortunate Arabia); they evidently associated the legendary riches of "the land of fragrances," located in the extreme southwest of Arabia, with the second meaning of the word *yaman,* "fortunate." The inhabitants of ancient South Arabia itself gave the name Yemen (more precisely, Yamanat) to the region along the banks of the Hadhramawt, where there

were evidently plantations of tropical trees giving myrrh. After the appearance of Islam in the seventh century and the rise of the Muslim religious center in Mecca, the northern border of Yemen came to be considered as extending from the Red Sea to the Persian Gulf, south of Mecca.

In the late second and early first millennium B.C. a unique South Arabian civilization took shape in Yemen. This period saw the rise of the states of Hadhramawt, Qataban, Saba (Sheba), and later, Main (the Minaean state). Highly developed irrigation permitted the formation of oases, which became the basis of economic life. The most important source of prosperity for these states was the trade in myrrh, frankincense, and other fragrant resins that were in demand in the markets of Egypt, Southwest Asia, Greece, and Rome.

The main trade route connecting South Arabia with other countries (the "road of fragrances") passed through the Arabian Peninsula. Intermediate trade was entirely in the hands of the inhabitants of north Yemen (Main) and a trading colony, Gerra, on the shore of the Persian Gulf. Main and Saba (Sheba) were also centers of agriculture and livestock raising.

Around the middle of the first millennium B.C. the state of Saba, through which the "road of fragrances" passed, acquired the greatest political power; all the other states in Yemen came under its sway. Trying to free themselves from this dependency, Qataban and Hadhramawt searched for a maritime trade route to export myrrh and frankincense and to import crafted goods. The route was found: from the southern harbors of Hadhramawt across the Persian Gulf to the mouth of the Euphrates. Later, as a result of colonizing the East African shores of the Red Sea, Qataban attained a monopoly over the incense trade. In the early second century B.C., Egypt began to occupy an increasingly important place in the sea trade of Qataban (and from the first century B.C., in the trade of the Himyarite kingdom, which arose at the end of the second century B.C. in the southwestern part of the peninsula). Beginning with the first century B.C., all of the sea trade of South Arabia with the West passed through Qataban. Until the first century B.C. the harbors of South Arabia were stopover points for goods from India.

In the early fourth century A.D. all of Yemen was united under the Himyarite kingdom. Between the fourth and sixth centuries, the beginnings of feudalism appeared: village communes fell under the sway of an aristocracy whose power had grown significantly. During this time Judaism and Christianity spread throughout Yemen.

In the early sixth century Yemen was conquered by the Ethiopians; at the end of the century it was conquered by the Sassanids. In the late sixth and early seventh century there were a great number of small principalities. In 629–30 they were made part of the Arabian Caliphate. The feudal system and Arab Muslim culture became firmly established, and Islam gradually became the dominant religion.

The independent states of the Ziyadids (capital, Zabid) and the Yafurids (capital, Sanaa) arose in the ninth century. In the tenth century, part of Yemen came under the power of a Shiite sect, the Zaidis. The subsequent history of the Yemeni states is filled with internecine wars and frequent changes of dynasties. From time to time states arose that were nominally subject to Egypt. In the second half of the 12th century Yemen was subjugated by Turan-Shah (brother of the Egyptian sultan, Salah al-Din), but even during this period it was governed by an independent branch of the Ayyubid dynasty. By the early 16th century the Zaidi imams held a commanding position in the northern and central mountainous regions.

The Ottoman Turks invaded Yemen in the early 16th century. However, they succeeded in conquering the country completely only after many years of war. In the early 17th century an anti-Ottoman uprising flared up, ending with Turkish troops being driven out of most of Yemen and with the establishment in 1633 of an independent state (imamate) headed by the Zaidi imams. A brief period of comparative calm ensued, and the economy and culture developed. Direct ties with some European countries, to which Yemeni mocha coffee was sent, were established. However, the imamate remained a backward feudal country, torn by internecine feudal struggles.

Small independent feudal principalities developed in the southern regions of Yemen. By the early 19th century the imams enjoyed real power only in the environs of Sanaa; they could withstand neither the attacks of the Wahhabites nor the later invasion by the troops of the Egyptian pasha, Muhammad Ali, and acknowledged themselves vassals of the Egyptian pasha.

Egyptian power over Yemen lasted until 1840. In 1839, Great Britain seized the city of Aden and turned it into a military base. Extending its control over the remaining territory of south Yemen during the rest of the 19th and the early 20th century, Britain imposed on the sheikhs, sultans, emirs, and other rulers of principalities and tribal federations in the vicinity of Aden treaties "of friendship" and later the status of protectorates. British expansion met with stubborn resistance from the masses. Only by relying on local princes (emirs, sheikhs, and so forth), who received annual British subsidies, did Great Britain maintain control over the interior regions of the country, and its influence was not secure.

By the early 1870's the power of the Turkish sultan was restored in north Yemen, and Yemen was declared a Turkish *vilayet* (province), although there was no stable administration in the country. In 1873, Turkey was forced to acknowledge British control of Aden. Between 1903 and 1905, Anglo-Turkish protocols were signed on the borders of British possessions. (These agreements were affirmed and supplemented by the Anglo-Turkish Convention of 1914.) After World War I the question of boundaries was the cause of conflicts between Great Britain and the Kingdom of Yemen.

In the late 19th and early 20th century uprisings against Ottoman rule frequently flared up in various areas of north Yemen. In 1904 they grew into a general insurrection, led by Imam Yahya. After a stubborn and bloody struggle the Turkish government was forced in 1911 to conclude a treaty with Yahya under which the sultan recognized the autonomous status of the Zaydi districts of Yemen, where secular power was transferred to Imam Yahya. During World War I, Yahya maintained a vassal relationship to the Ottoman Empire but did not engage in any military action.

After the war Yahya declared Yemen independent and himself king. He subjugated all the mountain districts, but his possessions were surrounded by hostile states. The Idrisids, princes of the Asir region and allies of Britain, seized the Tihama, and there were continual clashes with British troops at the borders of the Aden protectorates. The struggle to unify the country, headed by Yahya, took on the nature of an anti-imperialist movement and united the mass of the population, who had suffered from internal wars, imperialist expansion, and the destruction of traditional economic ties. In 1926, Yahya succeeded in liberating al-Hudayda and the remaining territory of the Tihama, achieving ascendancy over his rivals within the country, and uniting the country under his authority.

Yahya's attempts to subjugate the southern regions of the Arabian Peninsula and the contested regions of the north were without success. In 1934 an Anglo-Yemeni agreement was concluded under which Britain acknowledged the independence of the Kingdom of Yemen but retained its Aden protectorates. That same year, after a war with Saudi Arabia that ended in failure for Yemen, Yahya relinquished his claims to the contested border regions.

Striving to preserve the existing feudal-theocratic system and at the same time to guard the country from imperialist penetration, Yahya pursued an isolationist policy. Foreigners were permitted into the country only under exceptional circumstances. However, in the interests of strengthening the country's defenses and acquiring necessary goods, trade relations were maintained with a number of European countries, especially Italy. Great importance was attached to the establishment of trade relations with the USSR: the first Soviet-Yemeni treaty on friendship and trade was concluded in 1928 (renewed in 1955). Beginning in the 1930's, Yahya's conservative internal policies began to call forth a growing mood of opposition. There arose a number of political organizations demanding reforms. These organizations were crushed.

In World War II the Kingdom of Yemen managed to maintain neutrality despite pressure from Italy, which attempted to establish military bases in its territory. In 1943, Yahya broke off diplomatic relations with Italy; Italian and German nationals who were then in the country were interned. During the war famine and epidemics broke out in the Kingdom of Yemen, which was deprived of supplies from abroad.

The feudal-theocratic regime, absence of democratic freedoms, and acute worsening of the economic situation forced a substantial part of the population to leave the country. Large colonies of Yemenis, numbering about 1 million persons in all, arose in Saudi Arabia, Ethiopia, Kenya, the Sudan, Pakistan, and the principalities of the Persian Gulf. Among the Yemeni émigrés, an opposition movement developed, led by the Yemen Liberal Party, which was founded in exile in 1944. In 1948 the opposition organized a plot against Yahya, headed by Abdullah al-Wazir, a high official from a large landowning family. On Feb. 17, 1948, Yahya was killed, and al-Wazir declared himself imam and king. However, Yahya's son Ahmad, with the help of the northern tribes, managed to remove al-Wazir and assume the throne in March 1948.

The oppression of monarchy, the continuation of the feudal system and even remnants of slavery, the unlimited authority of the imam, who was also the country's biggest landholder, the savage exploitation of the people by the aristocracy (the *saids*) —all this deepened the general dissatisfaction. In the 1950's progressive officers in the Yemeni army formed the Free Officers group, whose aim was to overthrow the royalist regime. A favorable moment for this was the death of Imam Ahmad on Sept. 19, 1962. On Sept. 26, 1962, an antiroyalist revolution occurred in north Yemen. Army units connected with the Free Officers seized the government buildings and radio station in Sanaa, and the Yemen Arab Republic was proclaimed.

The liberation struggle of the peoples of Southern Yemen against the British colonial government intensified in modern times under the influence of the successes of the liberation movement in north Yemen. Tribal insurrections erupted throughout the area in 1918. The British imperialists' "pacification" of Southern Yemen was a lengthy process, lasting until the end of the 1920's in the western districts and until World War II in the eastern districts.

In 1937, Aden was proclaimed a crown colony, and the territories having the status of British protectorates were divided into the Eastern and Western protectorates of Aden. Feudal and even prefeudal social structures were preserved untouched in Hadhramawt and the principalities of the Western Protectorate.

In the 1930's various political and social organizations sprang up in Southern Yemen (such as the Club of Arab Reforms, the Club of Arab Literature, and the Hadhramawt Movement People's Club), which carried on the fight against foreign dominance, but their influence extended only to the cities. The rebellions against the British colonialists by various tribes were of a spontaneous, disorganized nature.

After World War II the largest oil refinery in the Arab East was built in the city of Aden, which had become an important trade center, The raising of cotton, intended for the British market, was begun. As a result a relatively numerous industrial and agricultural working class came into existence.

In February 1959, Great Britain, in order to strengthen its control of Aden and the Aden protectorates, established the Federation of Arab Emirates of the South (which became the Federation of South Arabia in April 1962). By 1963 the principalities of the Western Protectorate, the colony of Aden, and Wahidi, a small principality of the Western Protectorate, had been added to the federation. Relations between the federation and Britain were regulated by a treaty "of friendship" (1959), which guaranteed the dominance of British interests. A military base and the headquarters of the British forces in the Middle East were located in Aden.

The popular masses protested strongly against the establishment of the federation and later agitated for its liquidation and for the genuine independence of Yemen. The struggle against the colonialists and their feudal allies took on a particularly wide scope after the fall of the royalist regime in north Yemen and the proclamation of the Yemen Arab Republic.

All the patriotic organizations of Aden contributed to the struggle for independence: the Aden Trades Union Congress, the

People's Socialist Party, the People's Democratic Union (all founded in 1956), and the Front for the Liberation of Occupied South Yemen (founded in 1965). The National Liberation Front of Occupied South Yemen, formed in 1963, was especially important. Under its leadership, on Oct. 14, 1963, an armed struggle began against the British colonialists, federation rulers, and local princelings (sultans, emirs, and sheikhs). After the liberation forces established control over most of the territory and paralyzed the government of the federation, the government of Great Britain was forced to recognize the independence of Southern Yemen and to evacuate its troops from Aden on Nov. 30, 1967. On that same day, the independent People's Republic of South Yemen was proclaimed (the People's Democratic Republic of Yemen since Nov. 30, 1970).

REFERENCES

Lundin, A. G. "K vozniknoveniiu gosudarstvennoi organizatsii v Iuzhnoi Aravii." In *Palestinskii sbornik*, issue 17, 1967.
Lundin, A. G. "Iuzhnaia Araviia v VI v." In *Palestinskii sbornik*, issue 8, 1961.
Lundin, A. G. *Gosudarstvo mukarribov Saba' (sabeiskii eponimat)*. Moscow, 1971.
Bauer, G. M. "'Mukarrib' i 'Tsar' (K voprosu o gosudarstvennom stroe drevnei Saby)." *Vestnik drevnei istorii*, 1964, no. 2.
Grohmann, A. *Arabien*. Munich, 1963.
Phillips, W. *Qataban and Sheba*. London, 1955.
Ryckmans, J. *L'Institution monarchique en Arabie Méridionale*. Louvain, 1951.
Ryckmans, J. *La Chronologie des rois de Saba et du Raydan*. Istanbul, 1964.
Wissmann, H. *Zur Geschichte und Landeskunde von Alt-Südarabien*. Vienna [et al.]. 1964.   G. M. BAUER and L. N. KOTLOV [11–189–1]

YEMEN, PEOPLE'S DEMOCRATIC REPUBLIC OF (Jumhuriya al-Yaman al-Dimuqratiya al-Shaabiya), PDRY, a state in Asia in the southern Arabian Peninsula, including the islands of Socotra, Perim, Kamaran, and several smaller ones. The PDRY is bordered on the northwest by the Yemen Arab Republic, on the north by Saudi Arabia, and on the east by Oman. Its southern coast is washed by the Arabian Sea and the Gulf of Aden. Area, 287,700 sq km (according to the UN *Demographic Yearbook* for 1969); population, 1.47 million (1971). The capital is Aden. The country is divided administratively into six provinces (*muhafaz*).

Constitution and government. The People's Democratic Republic of Yemen is a republic. The present constitution went into effect on Nov. 30, 1970. Since June 1969 the functions of head of state have been performed by the Presidential Council, whose members, a chairman and not more than six others, are elected by the People's Supreme Assembly.

The highest body of state power is the People's Supreme Assembly, elected by the people to a three-year term. It defines the general principles of domestic and foreign policy, adopts laws and resolutions on all of the more important matters, and appoints a permanent committee (consisting of a chairman, three other members, and a secretary). The voting franchise is granted to all citizens who have reached the age of 18. The members of the highest executive body—the government (Council of Ministers), headed by its chairman—are chosen by the People's Supreme Assembly. The formation of local bodies of state power, elected people's councils, is envisaged.

The Supreme Court heads the judicial system. L. IA. DADIANI

Natural features. The western and central regions are dominated by mountains reaching 2,508 m (Mount Adaran), which are composed chiefly of volcanic rock and limestone of the Eocene. To the north, the mountains gradually descend to the Rab al-Khali. Stratified uplands reaching 1,000 m in elevation dominate in the east. Almost everywhere along the coast the mountains end in a sharp drop to the coastal plain, which is up to 50 km wide and broken in places by rises and extinct volcanoes. The shores are mostly low, with bluffs in some places. The islands are volcanic (Perim) or coral (Kamaran) in origin.

Mineral resources have been little surveyed. There are deposits of marble, limestone, and salt, and oil prospecting is being conducted.

The climate is tropical and dry. Temperatures on the coast vary from 25°C in January to 32°C in June; it is cooler in the mountains. Aden has about 40 mm of precipitation a year. The mountains experience the effects of a southwesterly monsoon and receive up to 700 mm of precipitation a year in some places (the maximum in summer). The rivers are dry for most of the year. The most important rivers are the Masila (Hadhramawt) and the Huwayra. Soils are chiefly red-brown mountain soils and desert soils, at times saline. Savanna with acacia, cinnamon, and, occasionally, trees is found in the mountains. The coastal oases have date and coconut palms. Wildlife is characteristically represented by the baboon, hyrax, Arabian gazelle, leopard, and hyena. L. I. SPRYGINA

Population. Arabs constitute about 90 percent of the total population. Some Somalis and immigrants from India and Pakistan (Gujaratis, Punjabis, Hindustanis) live in the cities. The Arabs retain tribal relations, which are gradually being eroded; the main tribal groupings are the Quayti, Kathiri, Wahidi, Awlaqi, Fadhli, Amiri, and Yafa. The official language is Arabic, and the official religion is Islam. Both the Gregorian and Muslim (Hijra) calendars are used.

Between 1963 and 1970 the average annual population growth was 2.7 percent. The economically active population numbered 325,000 in 1970. Most of the population is sedentary, but there are seminomads in the mountains and nomads in the northeast. Wage earners constitute 60 percent of the economically active population; most are concentrated in the city of Aden.

The average population density is 4 persons per sq km. The most populous areas are the coastal strip near Aden, the mountains in the northwest, and the broad valleys where wadis descend from the Abyan and Tibban mountains. In 1970, 29 percent of the population was urban. The largest cities (1970) are Aden and its suburbs (250,000 population), al-Mukalla, Sayun, and Tarim.

Historical survey. An independent state was established in Southern Yemen in November 1967 as a result of the armed struggle of the people of Southern Yemen against the British colonialists. The independent People's Republic of Southern Yemen was proclaimed on Nov. 30, 1967; on Nov. 30, 1970, the state was renamed the People's Democratic Republic of Yemen (PDRY). Since the republic was proclaimed, the National Front for the Liberation of Occupied South Yemen (known as the National Front, or NF, after December 1967) became the ruling organization. The fourth congress of the NF (in early 1968) laid down the fundamental goals of the domestic and foreign policy of the PDRY. A series of urgent measures for the country's socioeconomic reconstruction were planned (an agrarian reform law and other reforms were to be passed). However, the moderate nationalist wing of the NF, supported by conservative officers, was in control of the government and temporarily held back the implementation of the planned reforms.

On June 22, 1969, the leadership of the NF expelled the representatives of the moderate wing from the party and from the government. The collective Presidential Council was formed, headed by Salim Rubayyi Ali. The leader of the left wing of the NF, Abdul Fattah Ismail, was chosen to be secretary-general of the party. On Aug. 2, 1971, Ali Nasir Muhammad became prime minister of the PDRY. The fifth congress of the NF (in March 1972) adopted a program and party rules. The congress's decisions emphasized that the PDRY rejected a capitalist path of development and planned to implement socialist transformations, closely cooperating with socialist countries. Between 1969 and 1972 new laws were issued directed at the creation of a national economy, and measures aimed at realizing progressive socioeconomic transformations were implemented. On Nov. 30, 1970, the third anniversary of the PDRY, the constitution of the republic was ratified. The decisions of the sixth congress of the NF (March 1975) confirmed and further developed the fundamental program tenets of the documents adopted by the fifth NF congress. In foreign policy, the government of the PDRY announced an anti-imperialist course, called for the final elimination of colonialism, condemned racial discrimination and apartheid, and called for the development of friendly relations with progressive Arab nations and with the USSR and other socialist countries. On Dec. 3, 1967, the Soviet Union and the

PDRY established diplomatic relations and on Feb. 7, 1969, signed an agreement on trade and economic and technical cooperation.

As a result of intrigues of imperialist and other foreign and domestic reactionary forces discontented with the progressive transformations in the country, relations between the PDRY and the Yemen Arab Republic (YAR) became strained after 1970. However, relations were soon normalized. On Oct. 28, 1972, the PDRY and YAR reached an agreement on conditions preliminary to forming a unified Yemeni state in the future.

L. N. KOTLOV and IU. I. REPIN

Political parties, trade unions, and other social organizations. The National Front (Al-Jabha al-Qawmiya), or NF, founded in 1963 (known as the National Front for the Liberation of Occupied South Yemen until December 1967), is the ruling political organization in the country.

The General Confederation of Workers of the PDRY, founded in 1968 from a merger between the Aden Trades Union Congress and the Hadhramawt Federation of Trade Unions has been affiliated with the World Federation of Trade Unions since 1969. It has about 30,000 members.

Other social organizations include the Women's Union, founded in 1968; the National Student Union; the Al-Salafi Yemeni Democratic Youth Organization, founded in 1961; the Committee for Peace, founded in 1970; and the Society for Friendship With Socialist Countries, founded in 1970.

Economic geography. The PDRY is an agrarian country. Until independence the economy was based on reexport operations and on servicing the British naval base, the port of Aden, foreign tourists, and sailors. The service sphere provided about 60 percent of the national income. Only one-third of the GNP came from industry, agriculture, and fishing. The economy was characterized by feudal and semifeudal relationships in the protectorates and capitalist relationships in the colony of Aden.

After winning independence, the government started on the road of socioeconomic transformations. Agrarian reform laws were passed in 1968 and 1970 according to which all the lands belonging to former sultans, sheikhs, and ministers were to be expropriated without compensation; the maximum landholding was established at 25 *faddans* (about 10 hectares) of irrigated or 50 *faddans* of *bogara* (dry-farm) land; and landless and small landholding peasants received plots of three to five *faddans* of irrigated or six to ten *faddans* of *bogara* land. By 1972, 26,800 hectares (ha) of land had been distributed among 19,800 landless peasant families. Special attention is given to the organization of agricultural cooperatives.

A state sector is being created: the PDRY has nationalized (with compensation from late 1969 to early 1970) foreign banks (mostly British), insurance firms, trading companies, companies servicing the port of Aden, a few industrial enterprises (the most important being two cotton processing plants, a ship-repair yard, and a cottonseed-oil factory), salt mining, foreign trade operations, and some facilities that had belonged to foreign companies. In industry, the state sector accounts for 9.1 percent.

The main goal of current economic policy is to develop industries that serve the domestic needs of the population. A three-year plan of economic development is being implemented (1971–72—1973–74). The PDRY is strengthening its economic and technical cooperation with the USSR, Bulgaria, East Germany, and other socialist countries and is expanding its economic ties with other Arab states and with international organizations. The socialist and Arab countries account for four-fifths of foreign economic aid to the PDRY. At the same time, foreign, chiefly British, monopoly capital still plays a considerable role in the economy. Foreign capital controls petroleum refining and several other operations, including ship bunkering and plane refueling.

Agriculture is the most important branch of the economy, employing more than two-thirds of the population. Agriculture accounted for 24 percent of the national income in 1968. Only 1.8 percent of the country is suitable for agriculture, and less than 1 percent is cultivated. The lack of water for irrigation, salinity of the soil, and a low level of mechanization have hindered the development of agriculture. New lands are being brought under cultivation and irrigation with the help of the

USSR, the People's Republic of China, the Socialist Republic of Rumania, and the UN. In 1971 two dams built with the assistance of the USSR were put into operation, which made it possible to irrigate another 6,700 ha.

The main branch of agriculture is raising crops, with 50 percent of sown lands under cereal grains and 25 percent under industrial crops. Long-fibered cotton is grown for export on irrigated lands and occupies 60 percent of the land used for industrial crops (14,000 ha and 6,000 tons of cotton fiber in 1971); in 1970 cotton production accounted for one-fifth of the value of all agricultural production. The second largest export crop is coffee (810 tons in 1970).

Other crops are raised for domestic consumption: millet and sorghum occupy 40,000 ha (80 percent of the land under grain crops) and yielded 75,000 tons in 1971; wheat (8,000 ha; 13,000 tons), barley, sesame (25 percent of the area under industrial crops), and tobacco (11 percent) are also grown.

The production of vegetables (tomatoes and lettuce) and fruits (bananas, peaches, and papayas) exceeds the country's needs, but the poorly developed transportation network interferes with selling the surplus. The date plam and coconut palm are also grown.

Animal husbandry plays an important role, but a scarcity of fodder hinders an increase in numbers and productivity of livestock. In 1970–71 there were 92,000 cattle, 215,000 sheep, 870,000 goats, 40,000 camels, and 28,000 donkeys. Fishing for tuna, herring, and other fish, a traditional sector, is well established. The catch in 1971 was 115,000 tons. Most of it is consumed domestically, but some dried fish is exported to several countries in South and Southeast Asia.

Industry accounted for 18 percent of the national income in 1968. About 90 percent of the gross industrial production comes from the oil-refining industry, 4.7 percent from light industry, 2.5 percent from the electrical power industry, 1.6 percent from food processing, and 0.6 percent from building-materials production. Small enterprises prevail. Most enterprises are concentrated in and around Aden. The largest is the oil refinery in Aden (with an approximate capacity of 6.8 million tons a year), which uses imported petroleum and belongs to British Petroleum; 80 percent of its output is exported to Great Britain, Japan, the countries of southern Africa, Australia, and the Republic of Somalia. In 1969 production was 3.6 million tons of fuel oil, 1 million tons of diesel fuel, 283,000 tons of gasoline, and 276,000 tons of kerosene. Light industry is represented by two cotton mills (in Abyan and Lahij) and two small garment factories. The food-processing industry includes enterprises making dairy products, soft drinks, vegetable oil, baked goods, and candy. There are also enterprises for the production of aluminum utensils, floor tiles, cement blocks, matches, lacquers, and dyes. There is a ship-repair yard. Salt-mining production was 63,000 tons in 1969.

The chief means of transportation is automotive. There were 480 km of highways in 1971, of which about 200 km were paved. The main seaport is Aden, through which pass almost all the country's exports and imports. The port's operations became reduced when the Suez Canal was closed as a consequence of Israeli aggression in 1967. In 1971 the airline company Yemda was formed; the state owns 51 percent of the capital.

In 1970 the exports of the PDRY totaled 60.7 million dinars, and imports, 83.8 million dinars. The percentage breakdown of the value of PDRY exports in 1970 was petroleum products, 74.2 percent; fuel for ships, 6.6 percent; raw cotton, 3 percent; and leather and hides, 2 percent. The remainder was in textiles, coffee, tobacco, fish, and salt. The main imports are food (rice, wheat flour, sugar, tea, and so on), 16.8 percent; crude oil, 39.5 percent; clothing and textiles, 7.6 percent; and machinery and equipment. The PDRY's main socialist trading partners are the USSR, the People's Republic of China, Czechoslovakia, and the People's Democratic Republic of Korea; capitalist trading partners are Great Britain, Japan, and the countries of the Indian Ocean basin. The monetary unit is the PDRY dinar. According to the exchange rate of the State Bank of the USSR for January 1973, 1 dinar = 2 rubles 16 kopecks.   A. V. VAL'KOVA

Armed forces. The armed forces include ground troops, an air force, and a navy. The supreme commander in chief is the chairman of the Presidential Council. The minister of defense (a civilian) exercises overall supervision over the defense forces, and the deputy defense minister exercises immediate supervision. The army is manned principally on the basis of universal military obligation. Armed forces in 1971 totaled 11,000 men. In addition, there are internal security troops and police forces, numbering about 10,000. Ground forces number more than 10,000 and consist of infantry brigades, detached battalions, and signal corps, engineers, and other specialized units. The air force (about 300 men) consists of three squadrons. The navy (about 150 men) has several patrol vessels. Armaments are foreign-made.

Health and social welfare. According to incomplete data, in 1968 the birth rate was 23.5 per thousand, and the death rate, 6.0 per thousand. The infant mortality rate was 79.9 per thousand live births in 1966. Intestinal infections, geohelminthoses, tuberculosis, trachoma, and venereal diseases are found throughout the country. In the hilly coastal plain are nidi of dengue, pappatachi fever, phagedenic tropical ulcer, and Maduromycosis; nidi of malaria, smallpox, and dracontiasis are also found. Malaria and schistosomiases are found in the foothills and medium-altitude hills. Cases of leprosy, leishmanioses, and wuchereriasis are recorded.

In 1970 the PDRY had 27 hospitals with 4,600 beds, or about 0.8 bed per 1,000 people. Medical services were provided by 16 polyclinic divisions, 90 health centers, five dispensaries, and two mobile clinics. In 1970 there were 222 doctors (1 per 25,800 inhabitants), 24 dentists, 23 pharmacists, and about 1,000 intermediate medical personnel. Doctors are educated abroad; intermediate medical personnel are trained in special courses of study.   R. L. KUZNETSOV and I. B. PANINA

Education and cultural affairs. The public education system includes free state-controlled four-year primary schools, three-year intermediate schools, and three-year secondary schools. On all levels, instruction is sexually segregated. About 10 percent of all schools are for females. In the 1967–68 academic year there were more than 50,000 students in primary and intermediate schools and about 17,000 students in secondary schools. Secondary technical education is given by the Technical School in Aden. Teacher training is given in separate courses for men and women.

In 1970 the first higher education institution was opened in Aden: the Higher College, consisting of a faculty of natural science and a faculty of philology. In the 1970–71 academic year there were 50 students (including nine women) in the faculty of natural science and 50 students (including 22 women) in the faculty of philology.

The largest library is administered by the Aden Municipality and has more than 30,000 volumes in English, Arabic, and Urdu. In Aden there are two archaeological museums. In 1970 a decision was adopted to found the Museum of the Revolution in Aden.   L. V. VAL'KOVA

Press, radio, and television. In 1975 one daily newspaper, several weekly newspapers and magazines, and a number of bulletins of various organizations and departments (with a total circulation of 5,000–6,000 copies) were being published. Most publications are in Arabic. The media of information and propaganda are controlled by the National Front. The main publications are *Arbaatashir Uktubr,* a daily newspaper; *Al-Thawri,* a weekly newspaper published since 1967; *Al-Thaqafat al-Jadida,* a monthly public affairs magazine published by the Ministry of Culture.

The Aden News Agency was established in 1970. Since 1954, Arabic-language radio broadcasts have been made from Aden and al-Mukalla. Television broadcasts began in 1964 (in Aden).

Architecture and art. Art on the territory of the PDRY has been insufficiently studied. Ruins are preserved of Tamna, the capital of the Qataban kingdom (ninth to first centuries B.C.): part of a stone mountain fortification; remnants of large buildings with wall inscriptions; and tomb stelae of a necropolis, holding square plates depicting the faces of the deceased, carved schematically in relief. The ruins of a palace and temples have been found on the territory of ancient Shabwa (the Himyarite kingdom). In the lower course of the Wadi Hadhramawt lie the ruins of the city of Husn al-Ur, which include a small square temple beside which was found a relief carving of grapevine.

Remains have been found of small cities from the fifth century B.C. through the first century A.D., with structures of mud-brick and stone, the remains of rectangular-planned dwellings, evidently with towers, and other buildings, including temples. Tombs and reservoirs carved into the cliffs are known (the Tawil system of reservoirs in Aden).

There are numerous cliff paintings (scratched in rock and colored with ochre) depicting goats, camels, and horsemen and interspersed with inscriptions, which date from the late first millennium B.C.

Bronze wall reliefs (including "Eros Mounted on a Lion") and statues in the Hellenistic style from Tamna have come down to us from the first century B.C. In various parts of the country, ornaments and small art objects of bronze and gold have been found: figurines of a warrior, horse, bull, and camel. The features of local representational art can be seen in an alabaster female head from Tamna, very similar to a stone sculpture from Marib. Ceramic dishes, cups, and bowls are decorated with simple motifs of waves, stripes, and zigzags.

The cities of the PDRY, which are not numerous, give an idea of what medieval architecture was like, since they have basically retained their traditional look. The "tower" type of dwelling predominates in the deep interior of the country. In the city of Shibam there are mud-brick tower-houses six or seven stories high, with an internal stairway winding around a central mud-brick column, latticed window shutters, colored windowpanes, and carvings on the exterior doors and window frames. The houses stand close together, forming an impenetrable wall on the outside, which can be entered only by a single gate leading into the city. In the city of Tarim the facades of the tall houses are covered with multicolored wall paintings. In the center of Sayun, a town distinguished by its spacious layout and built of low dwellings, stands the former palace of the emir (a cubical turreted structure), gardens, and cemeteries with domed mausoleums of saints.

On the mountain slopes above Aden, a system of fortifications erected in the mid-19th century (parts of which go back to the 16th and 17th centuries) has been preserved. Religious architecture is represented by mosques with flat or dome-roofed galleries surrounding a courtyard; cylindrical minarets tapering toward the top, with bands of crenellated mud-brick ornamentation; and *qubab,* square-planned saints' mausoleums, a high ovoid cupola, and an openwork parapet surrounding the walls.

The capital of the PDRY, Aden, has a contemporary look in its administrative buildings, schools, and hospitals; the residential part of the city, Maala, has four- and five-story buildings with latticed loggias.   V. L. VORONINA

REFERENCES
Noveishaia istoriia arabskikh stran. Moscow, 1968. Pages 271–357.
Val'kova, L. V. *Angliiskaia kolonial'naia politika v Adene i Adenskikh protektoratakh.* Moscow, 1968.
Shvakov, A. V. *Probuzhdenie Aravii.* Moscow, 1969.
Sanger, R. H. *The Arabian Peninsula.* Ithaca, 1954.
Trevaskis, K. *Shades of Amber: A South Arabian Episode.* London, 1968.
Krachkovskaia, V. A. "Zhilishche v Khadramaute." *Sovetskaia etnografiia,* 1947, no. 2.
Ingrams, W. H. "House Building in the Hadhramaut." *The Geographical Journal,* 1935, vol. 85, no. 4.
Caton-Thompson, G. *The Tombs and Moon Temple of Hureidha (Hahdhramaut).* Oxford-London, 1944.
Phillips, W. *Qataban and Sheba.* New York, 1955.
Lankester, Harding G. *Archaeology in the Aden Protectorates.* London, 1964.   [11–204–1]

YEMEN ARAB REPUBLIC (Al-Jumhuriya al-Arabiya al-Yamaniya), YAR, a state in Asia, in the southwestern Arabian Peninsula. The republic borders Saudi Arabia to the north and east and the People's Democratic Republc of Yemen to the south and faces the Red Sea on the west. Area, 195,000 sq km; population, 5.9 million (1971). The capital is Sana. The country is divided administratively into seven districts (*liwas*).

Constitution and government. The YAR is a republic. The present constitution became effective on Dec. 28, 1970. The head of state is the chairman of the Republican Council, who is elected by the council from among its members.

The Republican Council (the "presidency") is responsible for the formulation of state policy and the direction of its implementation. The council consists of three to five members elected for a term of five years by the Consultative Assembly. The chairman of the council is also commander in chief of the armed forces. He appoints the chairman of the government (the Council of Ministers), subject to the approval of the Republican Council. He also has the right to conclude international agreements, which become effective after they are approved by the Republican Council and the government (the Council of Ministers) and are ratified by the Consultative Assembly.

The highest legislative body, the Consultative Assembly, also regulates the bodies of executive power. The Consultative Assembly consists of 159 members who, as a rule, are elected by the people to a four-year term. However, up to 20 percent of the Consultative Assembly can be appointed by the Republican Council. The right to vote is enjoyed by male citizens who have reached the age of 18. The assembly is considered a continuously operating body and is called upon to give recommendations to the government (the Council of Ministers), to approve the budget prepared by the government, and to report on the budget's implementation. The highest executive body is the government (the Council of Ministers), which is headed by its chairman.

The highest constitutional court is elected by the Consultative Assembly, which recommends to the Republican Council candidates chosen from among the most highly qualified experts on the Sharia. L. IA. DADIANI

Natural features. About two-thirds of the YAR is extremely rugged mountain country (the Jabal), consisting of high plateaus (reaching 2,000–3,000 m) cut by deep valleys; it breaks off to the west and south into a multiterraced heavily eroded escarpment. There are many extinct volcanoes. The highest peak is Mount al-Nabi Shaib (3,600 m). In the eastern YAR (the Sharqa), the plateau descends by sharply marked escarpments to the desert of Rab al-Khali. The Tihama lowland extends along the Red Sea in the west in a 50- or 60-km strip. Near the foothills of the Jabal and in its central part, the Tihama lowland is cultivated and heavily populated; along the coast it is a sand and solonchak desert. The Red Sea coast has few inlets and is bordered in some places by coral reefs.

Salt is mined (in the region of al-Salif), as well as alabaster and such semiprecious stones as agate, onyx, chalcedony, and jasper.

The climate is tropical and, throughout most of the country, dry, with precipitation primarily in the summer. In the Tihama, the average temperature in January is about 20°C, temperatures in June average more than 30°C, and maximum precipitation is 100 mm a year. It is cooler in the Jabal. In the city of Sana, located at an elevation of about 2,400 m, temperatures in January average about 14°C and in June (the warmest month), 21°C; there are frosts from December through February. In certain places precipitation exceeds 1,000 mm as a result of a summer monsoon from the Indian Ocean. Permanent small streams are found only in the mountainous regions.

Soils are red-brown, and there are some solonchaks. Most of the mountain terrain is devoid of vegetation, except for an occasional sparse cover of cactus and thorny brush. On the high plateaus are dry steppes. Deciduous and evergreen bushes and trees grow in the deep valleys. The Sharqa and the coastal part of Tihama have desert and semidesert vegetation. The date-palm grows in the oases. Typical fauna includes the gazelle, the wild ass (onager), and predators: the hyena, wolf, fox, wildcat, and leopard. The hamadril monkey is common in the south.

Population. The overwhelming majority of the people are Arabs. Ethiopians, Somalis, Turks, and other nationalities also live in the country. The inhabitants of the coastal strip have noticeable negroid features as a result of long intermingling with different African peoples. The Arabs retain tribal relations. The largest tribes and tribal unions are the Hashad, Baqil, Zaraniq, Quhra, and Anis. The official language is Arabic. Most of the people are Muslims, who belong to various sects, including Zaydis, Shafiites, Hanifites, and Ismailites. Most of the country's Muslims are Zaydis. The Muslim calendar (Hijra) and the Gregorian calendar are used.

The economically active population numbers 1.65 million (1970), with 73 percent employed in agriculture. Most are peasants (*fellahin*). About three-fourths of the population is concentrated in the Jabal, where the population density in the most fertile regions is about 80 per sq km. In the Sharqa region population density is less than one per sq km, predominantly nomads. Six percent of the people are urban (1970). The most important cities are Sana (population, 120,800), al-Hudayda, and Taizz.

Historical survey. The Yemen Arab Republic was proclaimed on Sept. 26, 1962, after an antiroyalist revolution. A decisive role in overthrowing the monarchy was played by the progressive army officers, as well as by representatives of the middle-class merchants, the intelligentsia, and the Yemenis in exile. The revolution of September 26 received the support of broad segments of the population.

In its domestic policy the republican government of Yemen proclaimed the goals of achieving social justice and abolishing the feudal-theocratic system. In 1962 a decree was issued abolishing slavery and the hostage system [tribal leaders were required to send a son as hostage to the central government], which had survived in the country since ancient times. Immediately after September 26 the lands of the royal family and of active royalists who had resisted the republican regime were confiscated. A number of measures were taken to establish national industry. The YAR Federation of Trade Unions was founded in 1963.

In foreign policy the government announced its intention to establish friendly relations with all countries respecting its sovereignty and independence; to struggle against imperialism and neocolonialism; and to uphold the principles of nonalignment, noninterference in the internal affairs of other states, and mutual respect for sovereignty and territorial integrity. On Mar. 21, 1964, the USSR and the YAR signed a treaty of friendship, as well as an agreement on economic and technological cooperation. (Diplomatic relations with the USSR have existed since the late 1920's.)

The overthrow of the monarchy and the first measures taken by the republican government brought forth resistance from domestic reactionary forces who, with the support of the imperialists and Saudi Arabia, unleashed a civil war. Egyptian troops, which entered Yemen in October 1962, were instrumental in quelling reactionary rebels.

Taking advantage of the 1967 withdrawal of Egyptian troops from the YAR, the royalist forces, late that year and in early 1968, launched an attack on Sana by mercenary detachments, who blockaded the city. However, thanks to the friendly support of the USSR, other socialist countries, and most Arab states, the attempts to capture Sana and liquidate the republican regime ended in total failure. After an agreement was reached between the YAR and Saudi Arabia in the spring of 1970, the civil war was ended. The royalists recognized the republican regime and were allowed to participate in the work of the governing bodies of the state.

Beginning in 1970, because of intrigues by imperialists and the Arab reactionary forces, relations between the YAR and the People's Democratic Republic of Yemen (PDRY) became increasingly strained. However, the conflict was resolved on Oct. 28, 1972, during negotiations between the YAR and the PDRY. An agreement was also reached by both countries regarding their intent to create a unified Yemeni state.

L. N. KOTLOV and R. SH. TURDIEV

Economic geography. Yemen is an agrarian, economically backward country, with an agricultural system dominated by precapitalist relationships. The national capital is invested chiefly in commerce; early forms of capitalist association ("family firms") have developed. Most land is the property of wealthy landowners and the clergy. After the overthrow of the monarchy in 1962 the country started on the road to overcoming economic backwardness.

AGRICULTURE. Agriculture is the main branch of the economy. Land cultivation techniques are extremely backward: plowing is by wooden plows with iron plowshares, and draft power is supplied by zebus, camels, and donkeys. Crops are sown and harvested by hand.

The chief agricultural regions are the Jabal, where *bogara* (dry-farming) cultivation on terraced slopes and plateaus predominates, and the Tihama, with irrigated cultivation. Two harvests a year are gathered in the Jabal, and three in the Tihama. The main export crop is coffee (3,600 tons in 1970), most of it grown in the Jabal. The date palm is cultivated in the Tihama (60,000 tons of dates in 1970). There are vineyards and orchards of figs, apricots, mangoes, and pomegranates. Industrial and aromatic crops are also grown, including indigo, sesame, ginger, cotton, and tobacco. Kat, a narcotic plant grown in the Jabal, brings in great profits. The local food crops are durra (chiefly in the Tihama), grains (barley, wheat, corn), legumes, and vegetables.

Livestock raising is developed in the Sharqa region and in parts of the Tihama and the Jabal. The 1970–71 livestock population included 12.4 million sheep, 1.4 million zebus and other cattle, and 600,000 camels. Horses and donkeys are also raised. There is beekeeping in the Jabal and fishing (a catch of 3,000–5,000 tons a year) and pearl fishing along the Red Sea coast.

INDUSTRY. Underground resources have been little surveyed. Salt is mined along the seacoast, and rock salt in the mountains. There is also mining of iron ore and semiprecious stones (agate, onyx, chalcedony). An Algerian-Yemeni company has been formed to prospect for oil and other extractive resources. Copper has been discovered (near Taizz), as well as limestone, magnesium ore, phosphorites, and coal.

Processing industry is dominated by small-scale handcrafted production of cloth, footwear, jewelry, pottery, and daggers. Coffee beans are processed and packed for export. There is a textile factory and an arms factory in Sana and cotton mills in Sana, al-Hudayda, and Zabid. Electric power plants have a capacity of 30,000 kilowatts.

The Soviet Union has greatly assisted the development of the economy. It has helped build a seaport in al-Hudayda (1961), the Taizz–al-Hudayda highway (1969; about 200 km long), a shop producing metallic containers for petroleum products, and other projects. In 1971 a cigarette factory was built in Sana and a candy factory in Taizz. Construction of a cement factory began in 1973.

TRANSPORTATION. There are no railroads in Yemen. The country is linked internally by automobile roads and caravan routes. The main highways are Taizz–al-Hudayda, Sana–al-Hudayda, and Sana-Taizz-Mocha. There are about 1,000 km of auto roads. The main seaport is al-Hudayda (handling 312,000 tons in 1967). The ports of Mocha and al-Salif handle low-tonnage ships. Foreign-trade cargo is carried on foreign ships. There are airports in Sana, Taizz, and al-Hudayda.

FOREIGN TRADE. The main exports are coffee (51.3 percent of the value of exports in 1970), kat (26.3 percent), salt (9.5 percent), and hides (7.6 percent); dried fish, raisins, and grapes are also exported. Imports include food products (54.5 percent), manufactured goods (14.9 percent), machinery and equipment (4.8 percent), and petrochemical products. Trade is developing with the USSR (22.5 percent of trade in 1970) and other socialist countries. The YAR's main trading partner is the PDRY (38 percent of trade volume in 1970). The YAR also trades with Japan (9 percent), the USA, and West Germany.

The monetary unit is the Yemeni riyal. The exchange rate of the State Bank of the USSR in January 1973 was 100 riyals = 15 rubles 30 kopecks.   N. A. DLIN

Armed forces. The armed forces include ground troops, an air force, a navy, internal security forces, and police. The supreme commander in chief is the chairman of the Republican Council. His deputy exercises direct control of the army. The army is manned both by conscripts (universal military obligation) and volunteers. The armed forces personnel numbered about 24,000 men in 1971. Ground forces (about 20,000 men) include infantry and paratroop brigades; detached tank, artillery, and antiaircraft battalions, and service units. The air force has about 500 men and 15 war planes. The navy has about 500 men and a squadron of torpedo boats. Internal security forces and police number about 3,000 men. Arms are of foreign manufacture.

Medicine and public health. The YAR does not keep demographic data. Infectious disease is the predominant health haz-

ard and the leading cause of death. Tuberculosis and malaria are found throughout the country, as are dysentery, Maduromycosis, geohelminthoses, and trachoma. Dengue, pappatachi fever, and miliaria rubra (known locally as *harara*) are endemic in the coastal desert of the Tihama. Amebiasis, schistosomiases, and Aden ulcer are endemic to the Tihama and the foothills and low hills of the Jabal. In mid-mountain Jabal, there is amebiasis, syphilis, and kidney-stone disease, with 56 percent of the people (primarily males) suffering from schistosomiases. Filariatoses are found in the central mountains and parts of the foothills. Wuchereriasis is found near Sana and Taizz. In the southern mid-mountain region cases of leprosy are frequent. Mass afflictions of bejel, kidney and genital schistosomiases, and Aden ulcer are characteristic of the eastern districts (the Sharqa). Throughout the country children suffer from protein deficiency and rickets, and women from osteomalacia and hypovitaminoses. An unusual narcotic addiction, katophagia (chewing leaves of the kat tree), exists among the population.

In 1964 the cities of al-Hudayda and Sana had 2,100 hospital beds (or 0.4 bed per 1,000 people). In 1966 there were 82 doctors (one for every 62,600 people). Medical personnel are trained abroad. In 1967 the USSR built in Sana and donated to Yemen a hospital with 100 beds and a clinic handling 100 people per day.   I. IA. KUDOIAROVA and I. B. PANINA

Education. Before the 1962 revolution the YAR had 688 primary schools (with a six-year course of study in the city and a four-year course in the villages), attended by 38,700 pupils; 16 Muslim schools (with a 12-year course of study), attended by 1,800 students; one four-year secondary school in the capital, with 228 students; and four two-year secondary schools in the large cities, attended by 468 students. In 1962 about 90 percent of the population was illiterate. In the first days of the revolution the republican government established a new system of education. A law was passed providing for free education at all levels of study, and standard programs of study were introduced.

The present educational system is composed of secular six-year primary schools, three-year intermediate schools, vocational and general three-year secondary schools, and religious educational institutions. Instruction is sexually segregated. Children enter primary schools at the age of six. In 1969–70, 744 primary schools had 65,500 pupils; 20 intermediate schools had about 3,000 students. The secondary schools have both humanities and technical divisions; in 1969–70 four secondary schools had 939 students.

In 1967, with the help of the USSR, three general education schools were built. Centers for the elimination of illiteracy have been opened, with 24 operative in 1966 (of which three were for women). After the revolution, two schools for agriculture, three for industrial training, and three for teacher training (for primary-school teachers) were established. Specialists requiring higher education are trained abroad.   E. K. GOLUBOVSKAIA

Press and radio. As of 1975 the most important periodical publications were *Al-Thawra,* a semiofficial daily newspaper founded in 1963 and published in Sana, and *Al-Jumhuriya,* a semiofficial daily, founded in 1963 and published in Taizz; both are in Arabic. There is an official news agency, Saba, founded in 1970. Centralized radio broadcasting began in 1963; there are stations in Sana, Taizz, and al-Hudayda, which broadcast in Arabic.

Literature. Medieval Yemeni literature developed within the general stream of Arabic literature and was represented mainly by poetry on religious themes. An exception, important in its time, was the long narrative poem *Himyarite Qasida* by Nashwan al-Himyari (died 1117), which contains valuable historical information. In this period the poetical *Diwan* of al-Hamadani and the long narrative poems of Ash Hamadan were also written.

The growth of the anti-imperialist struggle helped bring about a renewal of Yemeni literature. Poets of the 1950's and 1960's, such as Yahya bin Muhammand al-Aryani and Abd al-Karim Mazhar, wrote traditional *qasidas* (odes). Realistic trends are represented by writers of the younger generation grouped around the literary journal *Al-Mustaqbal* (The Future), such as Ahmad al-Fayth, Shawqi Abdullah, and Jafar Abdu.

N. K. KOTSAREV

Architecture and art. The remains of ancient cities, Marib, Qarnaw (Main), and others, dating back to the second millennium B.C., have been discovered in the YAR. These cities usually had a square plan and were surrounded by turretted walls 10–12 m high. The remains of irrigation systems have been found (the Marib dam, seventh century B.C.). Examples of ancient stone temples, decorated with reliefs, statues, and sometimes wall paintings, include the oval-planned Awwam temple near Marib (eighth century B.C.) and the square-planned Rasf temple near Qarnaw (between 550 and 450 B.C.). Stone and bronze sculptures (including figures of people and animals and votive statuettes), glyptics, and ceramics have been found.

The city of Sana has been known since the first century B.C. There, according to the description of Arabian writers, stood the Ghumdan, a 20-story castle.

As Islam spread, mosques were built, first of the "court" type (al-Jami al-Kabir in Sana, 670's; additions of the eighth, tenth, and 12th centuries) and later in the form of one or several domed halls (the al-Sharifiya Mosque in Taizz, 13th century; the al-Bakiliya Mosque in Sana, 17th century). Minarets rise near the mosques and are usually tiered, round or polygonal (set on a square base), and capped by a little dome.

Dwellings are of various types. The characteristic dwellings in Sana are strong three- to seven-story stone and brick buildings with white frames around doorways and square, round, or arched windows and with bandings between the stories. Dwellings in Taizz are characteristically three- or four-story buildings without external decoration; those in al-Hudayda are stucco, with balconies with openwork. Village dwellings in the interior of the country are tall mud-brick or stone buildings, often with an enclosing wall and sometimes inaccessible turrets and with animal quarters on the ground floor and living quarters on the upper floors. Rural dwellings in the coastal areas are wood-frame huts covered with reeds or grass.

Industrial and irrigation structures are being built in modern Yemen. Alongside the old sections of the cities new sections are growing, with modern buildings that nonetheless preserve elements of the traditional architecture (structures in Sana, Taizz, and the port of al-Hudayda).

The ancient folk arts are still practiced: inlaying on wood and metal, the making of jewelry (silver filigreed pendants with stones, rings, bracelets) and of curving *jambiya* daggers decorated with silver and cornelian, embroidery of traditional clothing with silk, wool and metallic thread in geometrical designs, and carpet weaving (pileless woolen rugs with bright stripes of red, green, and yellow).

REFERENCES
Ankarin, G. *Po Iemenu.* Leningrad, 1931.
Strany Aravii: Spravochnik. Moscow, 1964.
Kotlov, L. N. *Iemenskaia Arabskaia Respublika.* Moscow, 1971.
Golubovskaia, E. *Iemen.* Moscow, 1965.
Golubovskaia, E. *Revoliutsiia 1962 g. v Iemene.* Moscow, 1971.
Lutskii, V. B. *Novaia istoriia arabskikh stran.* Moscow, 1966. Pages 319–22 (also see index).
Sharaf al-Din. *Yaman abr al-tarikh.* (History of Yemen.) Cairo, 1964.
Ingrams, H. *The Yemen.* [London, 1963.]
El-Attar, M. S. *Le Sous-développement économique et social du Yemen: perspectives de la révolution yemenite.* Algiers, 1964.
Krachkovskii, I. Iu. *Izbr. soch.,* vols. 2–4. Moscow-Leningrad, 1956–57.
Al-Fakhuri, H. *Istoriia arabskoi literatury,* vol. 1. Moscow, 1960. (Translated from Arabic.)
Gibb, H. A. *Arabskaia literatura.* Moscow, 1960. (Translated from English.)
Sovremennaia arabskaia literatura: Sb. stat'ei. Moscow, 1960. (Translated from Arabic.)
Krachkovskaia, V. A. "Istoricheskoe znachenie pamiatnikov iuzhnoarabskoi arkhitektury." In the anthology *Sovetskoe vostokovedenie,* vol. 4. Moscow-Leningrad, 1947.
Bowen, B., and F. P. Albright. *Archaeological Discoveries in South Arabia,* vols. 1–2. Baltimore, 1952–58.   [11–194–1]

YEN BAI UPRISING (1930), an anti-French uprising of Vietnamese soldiers of the French colonial army in the city of Yen Bai in North Vietnam in 1930, prepared and led by the Vietnam National Party. On the night of February 9 two mutinous units of soldiers of the Yen Bai garrison seized the barracks, the railroad station, and several administrative buildings of the city. From then until February 15 isolated incidents involving soldiers and the petite bourgeoisie of the city and the countryside occurred in Phu Tho, Hai Duong, and Thai Binh provinces. The colonialists quickly suppressed the uprising, because the Vietnam National Party had little contact with the people and because the uprising was poorly organized. Many participants in the uprising were executed, including Nguyen Thai Hoc, the leader of the Vietnam National Party, or sentenced to hard labor.

REFERENCE
Mkhitarian, S. A. *Rabochii klass i natsional'no-osvoboditel'noe dvizhenie vo V'etname (1885–1930).* Moscow, 1967. Pages 252–58.   [11–214–1]

YEOMEN (yeomanry), English peasantry of the 14th to 18th centuries who carried on the independent cultivation of lands that were their traditional hereditary possessions.

The term "yeoman" is a fairly ambiguous one. Originally the core of the yeomanry consisted of the peasant freeholders on medieval manors. However, with the breakdown of the manorial system, the majority of former serfs, whose de facto position came to resemble closely that of the freeholders, swelled the ranks of the yeomen. With the continuing development of commodity-monetary relations, however, the unity of the yeomanry as a group began to erode, tending toward a polarization into a well-to-do upper stratum and a mass of rural poor. Nonetheless, the yeomanry continued to represent the basic mass of English peasantry until the middle of the 17th century. During the English bourgeois revolution of the 17th century, they and the plebeian elements in the cities played a decisive role in the liquidation of the feudal absolutist regime, although they themselves were deprived of the fruits of victory. The further development of capitalist relations in the century after the revolution led to the almost total disappearance of the group from the historical arena.   M. A. BARG [11–225–2]

YERKES OBSERVATORY, a scientific institution of the University of Chicago (USA). It was organized in 1892–97, 22 km from Chicago. Its instruments include a 102–cm (40-in.) refractor (the largest in the world, constructed by A. G. Clark and paid for by C. Yerkes), a 30–cm (12-in.) double refractor, a four-camera astrograph (largest objectives, 25 and 16 cm) with a 13–cm (5-in.) visual refractor, 102–cm (40-in.) and 60-cm (24-in.) reflectors, a Schmidt camera, and a 15–cm (6-in.) comet-finder. Work is conducted at the observatory on solar research, the determination of stellar parallaxes and radial velocities, the study of double stars, stellar polarization, stellar photometry, and the photographing of stars and planets. Yerkes Observatory issues *Publications* (since 1900).   [11–216–3]

YEZD, a city in Iran, administrative center of the chief gubernatorial region of Yezd. Population, 98,000 (1971). Railroad station and highway junction. Yezd has textile and food and condiments industries and produces silk, carpets, and other handicraft items.   [11–187–4]

YODEL, a type of folk song practiced by the mountain population of the Alps in Austria, Switzerland, and Southern Bavaria, with a vocalization as the refrain. This unique type of refrain is characterized by the frequent and rapid passing from a low chest voice to a falsetto. Split common chords are vocalized at wide intervals. In the low register the singer vocalizes the vowels *a* and *o*; in the high register, *e* and *i.*

REFERENCE
Tobler, A. *Kühreihen oder Kühreigen, Jodel und Jodellied in Appenzell.* Zürich, 1891.   [11–221–4]

YOGA (Sanskrit, literally "joining," "union," "concentration," or "effort"; the term is found in texts going back to oral traditions of the ninth and eighth centuries B.C.).

(1) In the broadest sense, a doctrine and method of controlling the human mind and psychophysiology with the aim of achiev-

ing higher psychic states. In this sense, yoga is an indispensable part of all the philosophical and religious systems of ancient and medieval India, and it is regarded by these systems as an extremely important means of realizing ethical and religious ideals, of which the highest is the complete liberation of man from the bonds of material existence. The basic ideas of yoga are the parallelism between the microcosm of man's psychophysiology and the cosmic body of the universe, signifying that all man's conscious strivings for self-reconstruction find their correspondence in the play of cosmic forces; the gradualness with which man masters the practice of self-change; the possibility of controlling biological bodies and inanimate objects by the mind; and the potential existence and possible development in any living being of a special yogic force, capable of fundamentally altering the natural order of things.

The basic concepts and actions of yoga are the subordination of body functions, or *yama* (control of respiration, temperature, digestion, the heart, circulation, and so on); settling the body into particular fixed postures, or asana; meditation upon a fixed (real or mental) object, *bhavana;* a state of trance characterized by a sharp change in mental and emotional condition, dhyana; and a state of psychic equilibrium and concentration, in which the mind acquires the characteristics of a homeostatic system (nonreversibility of psychic processes), known as samadhi. The ideas and concepts of yoga served as the basis for the development of a particular system of anatomical and physiological concepts about the circulation of life energy in the organism (*kundalini-shakti*) and its concentration in the functionally important centers of the body (chakra). Yoga became especially highly developed by the Tantrist sects and schools of Hinduism and by Mahayana Buddhism.

(2) One of the six orthodox systems of Indian idealist philosophy, as summarily expounded in the *Yoga-sutra* of Patanjali (some time between the second century B.C. and the second century A.D.). Its basic idea is that the individual (purusha) can achieve spiritual liberation by stopping the flow of mental activity and bringing into equilibrium the basic tendencies of individual existence: sattva (serenity), rajas (activity), and tamas (inertia). In the yoga of Patanjali, eight stages of psychic concentration are distinguished, beginning with *yama* and ending with samadhi. Yogic exertions result in attaining the state of *mahasamadhi,* that is, a merging of the contemplator, the object contemplated, and the process of contemplation. *Mahasamadhi* is considered to be a state of absolute freedom.

(3) Yoga understood as a form of consistent meditation (in the Vedanta), rather than as psychophysiological exercises (hathayoga). This form of yoga, raja-yoga, gives an intellectual interpretation to all yogic practices, explaining them as special reflex procedures for establishing the practicing individual's identity with absolute reality.

In modern times, there have developed within yoga certain tendencies of classical Hinduist yoga, of which the most prominent representatives are Vivekananda, with his idea of integral yoga (the end of the 19th century), and Yogananda (the 1940's and 1950's). A specifically Buddhist yoga became especially developed in Tibet and Japan. The practice of yogic psychophysiological techniques to sustain the viability of the human organism under conditions of extreme scarcity of food and of anomalous rates of the functioning of the nervous, endocrine, and respiratory systems is being studied by contemporary clinical medicine, experimental psychology, and physiology.

REFERENCES
Ramacharaka. *Hatha Yoga.* St. Petersburg, 1912.
Vivekananda, S. *Filosofiia Ioga.* Sosnitsa, 1911.
Radhakrishnan, S. *Indiiskaia filosofiia,* vol. 2, pp. 296–330. Moscow, 1957. (Translated from English.)
Aurobindo. *The Synthesis of Yoga.* New Jersey, 1950.
Coster, G. *Yoga and Western Psychology.* Oxford, 1949.
Dasgupta, S. *Yoga As Philosophy and Religion.* London, 1924.
Eliade, M. *Patanjali et le Yoga.* Paris, 1962.
    D. B. ZIL'BERMAN and A. M. PIATIGORSKII [11–219–3]

YOGACARINS (also, Vijnanavadins), the followers of the second major religious and philosophical school of Mahayana Buddhism. (The other, equally important, school is Madhyamika

Buddhism.) The basic ideas of Yogacara doctrines arose in the third century A.D. The leading representatives of the Yogacarins are considered to be Asanga (fourth century A.D.), whose chief works are *Yogacharyabhumi, Mahayana Samgraha,* and *Abhidharmasamuchaya;* and Vasubandhu (fifth century A.D.), whose chief works are *Vyakhyayukti, Vimshika,* and *Tramshika.* The school reached its height in the sixth to eighth centuries A.D., when Sthiramati and Dharmapala wrote commentaries on the works of Asanga and Vasubandhu, and when the greatest Buddhist logicians, Dignaga and Dharmakirti, were active. The works of both of the latter have been preserved chiefly in Tibetan, Mongolian, and to a lesser extent, Chinese translations.

Concretizing the general Buddhist principle of the psychic existence of the personality as the sole reality and thing of value, the Yogacarins developed the idea of the supreme importance of pure consciousness (*vijnana*), freed from any content. Being in this state of consciousness, which is the aim of human strivings, is called bodhi (literally, "illumination") or nirvana. The Yogacarins cultivated yoga in particular as the means to achieve it. At the same time, the school of Yogacarins also widely held the concept of *alaya vijnana* ("treasury of consciousness," literally, "storehouse consciousness"), a unique form of omnisciousness or absolute consciousness having the nature of the Buddha and serving as a kind of overall basis for each empirical, individual consciousness.

The Yogacarins made a large contribution to the development of non-Aristotelian logic by creating an independent branch of this logic—Buddhist logic, with a completely original elaboration of the problems of dichotomic classification of categories, the construction of syllogistic figures, and so on.

REFERENCES
Shcherbatskoi, F. I. *Teoriia poznaniia i logika po ucheniiu pozdneishikh buddistov,* parts 1 to 2. St. Petersburg, 1903–09.
Radhakrishnan, S. *Indiiskaia filosofiia,* vol. 1, pp. 534–51. Moscow, 1956. (Translated from English.)
Stcherbatsky, T. *Buddhist Logic,* vols. 1–2. Leningrad, 1930–32.
Wolff, E. *Zur Lehre vom Bewusstsein* (*Vijnanavada*) *bei den späteren Buddhisten.* Heidelberg, 1930. (Dissertation.)
Takukasu, J. *The Essentials of Buddhist Philosophy.* Honolulu, 1947.
    V. P. LUCHINA [11–221–1]

YOKKAICHI, a city and port in Japan, on Ise Bay in Mie Prefecture in the south of the island of Honshu. Population, 229,300 (1970). It is one of the leading Japanese centers of oil refining and the petrochemical industry. There is a huge ethylene combine with an annual output of about 300,000 tons. Other industries are cotton cloth, porcelain and ceramics, and glass products. Nonferrous metallurgy (a copper smelting plant) and electric machine construction are also important. There is a steam power plant with a capacity of 660,000 kilowatts. The city is also a seaside health resort.   [11–223–1]

YOKOHAMA, a major economic center and port in Japan, the administrative center of Kanagawa Prefecture. It is located on Honshu Island on the coast of Tokyo Bay 30 km southwest of Tokyo. Yokohama and the capital form the Keihin agglomeration. The area of the city is 413 sq km. Population, 2,238,300 (1970).

Yokohama is an important international transportation center and one of the biggest trade and passenger ports in the Far East. The total length of the piers is 14 km, of which the biggest are Shinko, Osanbashi, and Mizuho. Yokohama is the second largest Japanese port in freight turnover (over 120 million tons in 1972) and an industrial center in the Kanto industrial region. The most developed industries are shipbuilding and other types of machine building (primarily the production of rolling stock and of electrical energy equipment), ferrous metallurgy, and petrochemistry. Other branches of industry include atomic energy, with an atomic electric power plant under construction; military plants, including aircraft construction; light industry and food industry, including cotton, silk-winding, weaving, and sewing factories; and glass and ceramics.

The main offices and branches of the biggest Japanese banks, monopoly concerns, and commercial firms are located in the city. Yokohama was founded in 1858 as an amalgamation and expansion of the two small settlements of Kanagawa and Yokohama. In the 1870's, Yokohama became a major port of Japan, accounting for 70 percent of the country's foreign trade. In 1923 a great part of the city was destroyed by the earthquake and a fire, and in 1945 it was heavily damaged by raids of the United States Air Force. [11–223–3]

YOKOSUKA, a city and port in Japan, on the Miura Peninsula on the island of Honshu. Located 16 km south of Yokohama in Kanagawa Prefecture. Population, 347,600 (1970). There are wharfs for shipbuilding and ship repair, dry docks, and a naval arsenal. A gun-making plant and underground oil reservoirs are located there, as is a steam power plant with a capacity of 1.2 million kilowatts. The city is the base of the whaling fleet. Yokosuka has an aviation research center, naval schools, and a maritime museum. It is also the site of the chief Japanese naval base. [11–223–2]

YOM, a river in Thailand, one of the tributaries of the Chao-Phraya River (also called Mae Nam or Mae Nam Chao Phraya). It originates in north Thailand on the Phi Pan plateau and flows across the Mae Nam Lowlands. Length, about 500 km. Flow is heaviest in the summer and follows a monsoon pattern. The river is used for timber rafting and irrigation. [11–225–1]

YONAGO, a city in Japan, in west Honshu Island, in Tottori Prefecture. Population, 109,000 (1970). Railroad junction; port for shallow draft vessels on the Nakanoumi lagoon. Its industries include agricultural machine building, shipbuilding, metallurgy, and other branches of metalworking. Yonago is also the site of food-flavoring and textile (based on the local production of raw silk) industries. There are sulfur mines. [11–225–4]

YONEZAWA, a city in Japan, on the northern part of Honshu Island, in Yamagata Prefecture. Population, 92,800 (1970). It is a center of the silk industry. There are also furniture, food-flavoring, and paper industries. Yonezawa is the site of an aviation factory. Nearby, in Onogawa, there are hot mineral springs. [11–226–5]

YONGAMP'O, city and port in the Korean People's Democratic Republic, in the province of Pyongan-pukdo, at the mouth of the Amnok-kang (Yalu) River, which runs along the border. It is one of the principal centers for the fishing industry on the northern coast of Korea on the Yellow Sea. Industrial goods produced in the city of Sinuiju are exported from Yongamp'o. [11–226–1]

YONKERS, a city on the Atlantic coast of the United States in the state of New York. Yonkers is a northern residential suburb of New York City and is located on the left bank of the Hudson River. Population, 205,000 (1970). There are 15,000 people engaged in industry, predominantly light industry (ready-made dresses, hats, rugs, and knitted goods). Yonkers also has a sugar refinery and a pharmaceutical factory. [11–227–1]

YONNE, a department in central France, along the middle and lower course of the Yonne River. Yonne was formed out of parts of historic Champagne and Orléanais. Area, 7,500 sq km; population, 290,000 (1971). The administrative center is Auxerre. Grain crops and grapes are grown there, and wine is made. The region raises cattle, sheep, and swine. Industries include timber processing, machine construction, electrical engineering, and garment-making. [11–227–3]

YONNE, a river in France, a left tributary of the Seine. Length, 295 km; basin area, 10,900 sq km. It rises in the Morvan Mountains and flows through the Paris Basin. The river is fed by snow and rain, with floods occurring during the cold season. After a heavy downpour, the water level fluctuates as much as 2–3 m. The average water flow at the mouth is 105 cu m per sec, with a maximum discharge of 1,000–1,300 cu m per sec. The Yonne is navigable and has locks for 108 km from the mouth; it is linked by canals with the Loire and rivers of the Rhône basin. A hydroelectric power plant is on the Yonne. [11–227–2]

YORCK VON WARTENBURG, LUDWIG. Born Sept. 26, 1759, in Potsdam; died Oct. 4, 1830, in Klein-Öls. Count, Prussian field marshal (from 1814).

During Napoleon's Russian invasion in 1812, Yorck commanded a Prussian auxiliary corps near the Baltic. On Dec. 13, 1812, against the will of the Prussian king, Frederick William III, he signed the Convention of Tauroggen with representatives of the Russian Army; according to the convention his corps suspended operations against the Russians. In the 1813 campaign, Yorck commanded a corps.

REFERENCE
Droysen, J. G. *Das Leben des Feldmarschalls Grafen Jorck von Wartenburg,* 11th ed., vols. 1–2. Leipzig, 1913. [11–231–2]

YORGAN TEPE (also Yorghan Tepe), a hill in northern Mesopotamia (13 km southwest of the city of Kirkuk, Iraq) with the remains of an ancient settlement. Yorgan Tepe contains levels from the Aeneolithic period (the second half of the fourth millennium B.C.). Next follow the remains of a Sumero-Akkadian settlement (the city of Gasur), in which a considerable number of tablets were found (from the second half of the third millennium B.C.) containing information on commercial transactions, inventories of handicraft articles, and so forth. Scholars have studied the acropolis of the Hurrian city of Nuzi (also Nuzu; first half of the second millennium B.C.) with its palace (more than 100 rooms, some decorated with wall paintings) and temple. The city was surrounded by a wall, beyond which were situated the houses of the suburbs. The inhabitants engaged in farming and stock raising. Copper implements and several thousand tablets from official and private archives have been found. The city was destroyed by the Assyrians in the middle of the second millennium B.C.

REFERENCES
Iankovskaia, N. B. "Khurritskaia Arrapkha." *Vestnik drevnei istorii,* 1957, no. 1.
Starr, R. F. "Nuzi. Report of the Excavations of Yorgan-Tepa Near Kirkuk." *Iraq,* vols. 1–2. Cambridge, 1937–39. [11–228–2]

YORK, a city and port in Great Britain in the county of Yorkshire, on the Ouse River. Population, 104,500 (1971). York is an important transportation junction. It has food (especially chocolates), glass, and printing industries. Railroad workshops are also located in the city.

York originally was a Roman fortress. It was founded circa A.D. 71 on the site of a Briton settlement. It was the capital of the Anglo-Saxon (from the sixth century) and Danish (ninth century) kingdoms. In 735, York became the seat of the archbishop of York. During the English Bourgeois Revolution of the 17th century, it was the temporary residence of Charles I (1642–44). In 1644 it was seized by the Parliamentarians.

York is the site of Roman and medieval fortifications, 15th- and 16th-century houses, and a Gothic cathedral (1070–1470). The Yorkshire Museum (archaeology) and the City of York Art Gallery are located there.

REFERENCE
Knight, C. B. *A History of the City of York.* York-London, 1944. [11–230–3]

YORK, a city in the eastern USA, in Pennsylvania. Population, 50,000 (1970; including the suburbs, 320,000). There were 60,000 people engaged in industry in York in 1969. The city is a large center for various branches of machine building and metalworking. Products include turbines, air conditioners, refrigerators, safes, agricultural equipment, and bearings. Upright and grand pianos are also manufactured. There are tobacco and textile industries in the city. York was founded in 1735. [11–231–1]

YORK, a cape on Cape York Peninsula, the northernmost point of the Australian mainland (10°41′ S lat. and 142°32′ E long.). [11–230–2]

YORK, HOUSE OF, a dynasty of British kings (1461–85), a branch of the Plantagenets. It traces its origin to the fifth son of Edward III, Edmund, the duke of York. The first representative of the House of York on the British throne was Edward IV, who deposed Henry VI (a scion of another branch of the Plantagenets, the Lancasters) during the Wars of the Roses. His son, young Edward V, was deposed in 1483 by his uncle Richard III and was murdered in the Tower of London. After the defeat of Richard III in the battle with Henry Tudor at Bosworth (1485), the throne passed to the Tudors, remote kin of the Lancasters.

[11–232–1]

YORK-ANTWERP RULES (York-Antwerp Rules of General Average, Y.A.R.), a collection of navigational rules generally accepted in international commerce that regulate the allocation between shipowners and cargo owners of losses incurred by either of them as a result of expenses and sacrifices intentionally made during transport to save the ship and cargo from any common danger; the losses are allocated in proportion to the value of the ship and cargo.

The York-Antwerp Rules were drawn up in 1864 in the city of York (Great Britain) by an international conference of representatives of the chambers of commerce, shipowners and cargo owners, and insurance companies of a number of countries engaged in maritime commerce; in 1877 a conference in Antwerp made substantial amendments in the rules.

The present version of the York-Antwerp Rules, which was adopted at the conference of the International Maritime Committee in Amsterdam in 1950, is in wide use. Although the rules have neither the power of law nor of an international agreement, their application in each single case being based on agreement between the shipowner and the cargo owner, the majority of the standard forms of freight charters and bills of lading, including those used by Soviet shipping, provide for use of the rules.

The York-Antwerp Rules are subdivided into "lettered" rules (from A to G) and "numbered" rules (from I to XXII). The numbered rules cover specific incidents of general average (the allocation of losses from jettisoning part of the cargo to save the ship and the remaining cargo, from extinguishing fires on board, and the like), as well as determination of the amount of certain kinds of losses and the value of the salvaged property. The lettered rules contain the definition of the general average (rule A) and a number of other general provisions.

The York-Antwerp Rules significantly influenced the legislation concerning general average in many states; with some sharpening of definitions and some changes, they are reproduced in the Maritime Code of the USSR.

[11–231–3]

YORKSHIRE, a county (up to 1975) in Great Britain, located between the eastern spurs of the Pennines and the North Sea. Area, 15,700 sq km; population, 5 million (1971). Yorkshire consisted of three ridings, West Riding, East Riding, and North Riding, the first two of which belong to the new official Yorkshire and Humberside economic region and the third to the North Yorkshire economic region.

Most of the industry is concentrated in West Riding, where the northern section of the country's largest coal field (the Yorkshire field) is located. The industrial centers are the Leeds-Bradford conurbation, with machine building, including machine-tool construction, and 70 percent of Great Britain's wool industry, and the cities of Sheffield and Rotherham, with high-grade steel production, machine building, and cutlery manufacture. North Riding has a ferrous metal industry in the Tyneside urban area and a large chemical industry in Billingham and Wilton. In East Riding is the Frodingham iron-ore deposit and a ferrous metal industry (in Scunthorpe). Ports serving all of Yorkshire, including Hull, Grimsby, and Immingham, are located on the Humber estuary. In the eastern part of the county, various types of agriculture predominate; in the west, in the foothills of the Pennines, sheep are raised; and, around the cities, agriculture serving city markets is developed.

N. M. POL'SKAIA [11–232–2]

YORUBA, a people living in western and southwestern Nigeria (10 to 12 million persons in 1972, according to rough estimates); Dahomey (more than 200,000 persons), where they are called the Nago or Anago; and Togo, where a small number lives.

The ethnic Yoruba groups include the Oyo, Ife, Ijesha, and Egba. They all consider themselves a single people and have a single culture. They speak the Yoruba language, which has a number of dialects. The Yoruba language has its own literature; newspapers are published in the language, and it is used for instruction in the schools. Islam and Christianity coexist among the Yoruba, along with a polytheism with a well-developed pantheon of gods. States existed among the Yoruba long before the arrival of Europeans in West Africa (in the 15th century). The Yoruba were the creators of remarkable bronze and terra-cotta sculptures that flourished from the 12th to the 14th century and that were possibly associated with the more ancient Nok culture (end of the first millennium B.C.). The Yoruba art of bronze-casting was taken up by the Benin peoples. The chief occupation of the Yoruba is farming (yams, cacao). Among the Yoruba, developing capitalist relations are closely intertwined with strong survivals of earlier social structures.

REFERENCES
Ismagilova, R. N. *Narody Nigerii.* Moscow, 1963.
Forde, D. *The Yoruba-speaking Peoples of Southwestern Nigeria.* London, 1951.
Johnson, S. *The History of the Yorubas: From the Earliest Times to the Beginning of the British Protectorate.* London, 1921.

R. N. ISMAGILOVA [11–232–3]

YORUBA, the language of the Yoruba people. Yoruba is related to the Kwa subgroup of the Guinean language group. Yoruba is spoken mainly in the western and southwestern regions of Nigeria, in some areas of Dahomey, and in the eastern regions of Togo. The number of Yoruba speakers is approximately 10 to 12 million (1972, estimate). Yoruba is divided into a number of dialects. It has seven pure and seven nasal vowels. Elision and vowel harmony are common. Monosyllabic and dissyllabic words predominate. High, low, and mid tones are clearly distinguished, although there are also sliding tones (rising and falling). The tones have semantic significance (for example, *fó*, "to break"; *fò*, "to wash"; *fo*, "to speak"). Yoruba is an isolating language. Grammatical gender and nominal declensions are absent. The verb is not marked for person, number, and voice. Syntactic relations are expressed by rigid word order and auxiliary words. The Yoruba writing system is based on the Roman alphabet.

REFERENCES
Iakovleva, V. K. *Iazyk ioruba.* Moscow, 1963.
Gaye, J. A., and W. S. Beecroft. *Yoruba Grammar,* 3rd ed. London, 1951.
Abraham, R. C. *Dictionary of Modern Yoruba.* London 1958.

[11–233–1]

YORUBA KINGDOMS, city-states founded in the 12th to 14th century in western Sudan and inhabited by the Yoruba people. The best known were the city of Ife, the cultural and religious center of the country of Yoruba; and the city of Oyo, which from the 15th century gradually began to unite the majority of the Yoruba kingdoms under its domination. In the second half of the 18th century, Oyo's political influence spread west to the Gold Coast and east to the Niger River. The social system in the Yoruba kingdoms was characterized by the predominance of communal relations, along with the sharply expressed social and economic inequality of the ordinary commune members and the ruling clique. Household slaves and the slave trade played a large role in the economic and social life of the kingdoms. At the beginning of the 19th century, Oyo disintegrated into many small, independent city-states that warred with each other. In the middle of the 19th century, the gradual seizure of the Yoruba kingdoms by Great Britain began. In 1906 the captured territories were included in the structure of the British colony and protectorate of Southern Nigeria.

REFERENCE
Kochakova, N. B. *Goroda-gosudarstva iorubov.* Moscow, 1968.
N. B. KOCHAKOVA [11-233-2]

YOSEMITE FALL, a cascade of waterfalls on Yosemite Creek, in Yosemite National Park in the state of California, USA. The total drop of the cascades is 727 m; the longest single drop (430 m) is that of the Upper Yosemite. The cascade is most full in spring and early summer, when the mountain snows are melting.
[11-234-3]

YOSEMITE NATIONAL PARK, a park located in the Sierra Nevada in California. It was the first protected scenic region of the USA (1864) and became a national park in 1890. Its area in 1970 was 304,000 hectares. The park includes the scenic valley of the Merced River, with cascades of waterfalls, coniferous forests, and three groves of giant sequoias with specimens that are thousands of years old. The mammalian fauna (78 species, including the American black bear and the mule deer) and avian fauna (200 species) are varied. More than 1.7 million tourists visited the park in 1966.
[11-234-4]

YOSEMITE VALLEY, the valley of the Merced River, on the western slope of the Sierra Nevada in the state of California, USA. Yosemite Valley is within the bounds of Yosemite National Park. Length, approximately 11 km; width, 800–1,600 m; depth, to 1,500 m. Its steep slopes are composed of granite, polished by glacial activity. There are dense coniferous forests and many waterfalls, including Yosemite Fall and Ribbon Fall.
[11-234-2]

YOSHINO, a river on the island of Shikoku in Japan. Length, 236 km. It arises in the central part of the island, on the southern slopes of the Ishizuchi, and flows primarily through the mountains until it enters Kii Strait, where it forms a delta. The river's flow follows a monsoon pattern. Its waters are used to drive a hydroelectric power station and, on its lower stretches, for irrigation. The Yoshino is navigable by boats with a shallow draft to a point 70 km from its mouth. The city of Tokushima is located along its course.
[11-234-5]

YOSU, a city in South Korea, on the shore of the Korean Strait, in Cholla-Namdo Province. Population, 102,000 (1966). Yosu is a center for the fishing industry. Other industry includes the processing of rice and the production of rubber items. There is also a shipyard. Rice, raw silk, and fish are exported.
[11-235-1]

YOZGAT, a city in central Turkey; the administrative center of Yozgat Vilayet. Population, 27,800 (1970). Highway junction. A factory producing explosives, a brewery, and several mills are located in Yozgat. Lead and manganese ore are extracted in the vicinity of the city.
[11-222-3]

YTTRIUM, Y, a chemical element in Group III of the Mendeleev periodic system. Atomic number, 39; atomic weight, 88.9059. One stable isotope, ^{89}Y, exists in nature.

Yttrium, scandium, lanthanum, and lanthanides make up the rare earths, a group of elements that are very similar in chemical properties, occurrence in nature, and history of discovery.

Yttrium is a light metal, with a density of 4.472 g/cm^3. The isotope ^{89}Y has a small capture cross section for thermal neutrons ($1.38 \times 10^{-28}m^2$, or 1.38 barns), so that the element can be used as a construction material in nuclear engineering. The high durability of relatively light yttrium-aluminum alloys makes them highly suitable for aircraft construction. Yttrium ferrites can be prepared from yttrium oxide, Y_2O_3 (of very high purity); these ferrites are used in radio electronics, hearing aids, and computer memory cells.
[11-147-3]

ZEISS OPTICAL WORKS (Carl Zeiss), the center of instrument manufacturing in the German Democratic Republic, a major enterprise for precision mechanics and optics. It is located in Jena. Instruments and instrument systems are produced there for scientific investigations and production needs, in particular for inspection and analysis in chemistry, metallurgy, agriculture, medicine, and astronomy. Most of the output is exported, a considerable part going to the Soviet Union. The factory grew up from the workshop founded in 1846 by the German master machinist Carl Zeiss. In 1920 the workers in the Zeiss factory joined workers in many other enterprises in Germany in support of the slogan: "Hands off Soviet Russia." After World War II the Zeiss Optical Works was nationalized. Between 1949 and 1972 the output of the enterprise increased by over ten times. In 1972, 20,000 people were working there. It has been awarded the Order of the Banner of Labor (1956). F. MIULLER [11-1295-3]